BUSINESS LAW AND
THE REGULATORY ENVIRONMENT

CONCEPTS AND CASES

BUSINESS LAW AND
THE REGULATORY ENVIRONMENT

CONCEPTS AND CASES

Eighth Edition

Michael B. Metzger, J.D.

Jane P. Mallor, J.D.

A. James Barnes, J.D.

Thomas Bowers, J.D.

Michael J. Phillips, J.D., L.L.M., S.J.D.

all of
Indiana University

IRWIN

HOMEWOOD, IL 60430
BOSTON, MA 02116

© RICHARD D. IRWIN, INC., 1946, 1951, 1955, 1959, 1963, 1966, 1970, 1974, 1978, 1982, 1986, 1989, and 1992

Sponsoring editor: *Craig Beytien*
Developmental editor: *Karen Eichorst*
Project editor: *Susan Trentacosti*
Production manager: *Bette K. Ittersagen*
Designer: *Matt Doherty*
Compositor: *Weimer Typesetting Co., Inc.*
Typeface: *10/12 Times Roman*
Printer: *Von Hoffmann Press, Inc.*

Library of Congress Cataloging-in-Publication Data

Business law and the regulatory environment : concepts and cases /
  Michael B. Metzger . . . [et al.].—8th ed.
       p.   cm.
  Includes bibliographical references and indexes.
  ISBN 0-256-08700-8
  1. Commercial law—United States—Cases.   2. Commercial law-
-United States.   I. Metzger, Michael B.
  KF888.B8   1991
  346.73'07—dc20
  [347.3067]   91–15076

Printed in the United States of America

1 2 3 4 5 6 7 8 9 0 VH 8 7 6 5 4 3 2 1

This is the fifteenth edition (and the eighth UCC edition) of a text that first appeared in 1935. Throughout its life, this text has been a leader in the fields of business law and the legal environment of business. The reasons for the book's long-standing success, we feel, are twofold. The first is its lucid and comprehensive treatment of the many subjects that concern businesspeople and that form the heart of the traditional business law curriculum. The second is its responsiveness both to changes in the law and to changed views about that curriculum. In each of these ways, the present edition continues the tradition set by its predecessors.

IMPORTANT CHANGES IN THIS EDITION

The Ethical Dimension

Perhaps the most important recent development in business education is its increased concern with business ethics and corporate social responsibility. In our view, business law and legal environment faculty have an important role to play in this area. To help them in that endeavor, this edition of the text aggressively incorporates ethical issues within its contents. It does so in two ways.

First, the previous edition's ethics/social responsibility/corporate control chapter has been extensively reworked and has been moved to the front of the book. The most important change to the chapter is the addition of a section dealing explicitly with ethical theory. Second, each text chapter except the corporate social responsibility chapter contains several "Ethical and Public Policy Concerns." These concerns, which generally take the form of questions, are placed toward the end of each chapter. They develop certain ethical and policy impli-

cations of the legal materials in the chapter. Their aim is to stimulate student interest in the policies underlying those legal rules, in possible ethical objections to such policies, in the tangible consequences of such rules or policies, and in practical ethical dilemmas not resolved by the chapter's legal discussion. On occasion, these concerns emphasize themes developed in the corporate social responsibility chapter. Suggested answers can be found in our Instructor's Manual.

New Pedagogy

Previous users of this text immediately will notice a significant increase in our use of figures, charts, Concept Reviews, and other visual aids. We made greater inclusion of such aids one of our top priorities for this edition.

Substantive Changes

In our view, one of the essential attributes of an outstanding business law text is its ability to keep readers apprised of the latest developments in an ever-changing legal landscape. We feel that our text long has excelled in this respect, and that the present edition continues that tradition. For example:

☐ Our previous chapter on court structure, jurisdiction, and civil procedure contains a greatly expanded discussion of alternative dispute resolution (ADR). To reflect ADR's growing importance, the chapter has been retitled "The Resolution of Private Disputes."

☐ As noted earlier, the corporate social responsibility chapter has been reorganized and now contains a section devoted to ethical theory.

☐ The copyright law discussion in the chapter on intellectual property, competitive torts, and unfair competition includes the relevant changes made by the Berne Convention Implementation Act of 1988. Similarly, the chapter's treatment of trademark law reflects the Trademark Law Revision Act of 1988. The chapter also includes an expanded treatment of section 43(a) of the Lanham Act that reflects its recent amendment.

☐ The contracts chapter on reality of consent contains an expanded discussion of the duty to disclose in fraud and misrepresentation law, and expanded coverage of the law of mistake.

☐ The contracts chapter on performance and remedies contains an expanded discussion of equitable remedies and also includes a new section on restitution.

☐ The product liability chapter continues to note the impact of state legislation in this area, especially tort reform legislation.

☐ The chapter on real property now contains an overview of insurance law concepts applicable to property.

☐ The text now devotes a separate chapter to landlord-tenant law.

☐ The real estate chapter and the landlord-tenant chapter also incorporate the recent amendments to the Fair Housing Act.

☐ The chapter on estates and trusts now contains a new explanation of will terminology. It also contains a new section entitled "Planning for Disability," which comprises a discussion of planning devices such as living wills, durable powers of attorney, and durable powers of attorney for health care. Finally, the Supreme Court's recent "right to die" decision in *Cruzan v. Missouri Department of Health* now is a text case in this chapter.

☐ The material on reorganizations in the bankruptcy chapter has been expanded.

☐ The material on checks in the final commercial paper chapter has been expanded. The chapter also includes new material on the recently implemented Expedited Funds Availability Act.

☐ The first partnership chapter has a new section on choosing a form of business.

☐ The chapter on the management of corporations contains an expanded discussion of tender offer defenses. The chapter also includes examples of recent statutes that expand the powers and the protections of corporate directors.

☐ The FTC/consumer protection chapter includes the changes made to the Truth in Lending Act by the recent Fair Credit and Charge Card Disclosure Act. The chapter also includes expanded coverage of the FTC's power to regulate unfair methods of competition.

☐ The two antitrust chapters incorporate the changes made by the Antitrust Amendments Act of 1990.

☐ The employment law chapter contains a complete discussion of the new Americans with Disabilities Act. The chapter's discussion of employee privacy has been expanded as well. The chapter also takes into account the most important changes in employment discrimination law wrought by several recent Supreme Court decisions. In the process, it is attentive to the possibility of future congressional action in this area.

☐ The text's chapter on environmental law has been expanded. For example, it now includes material on the Clean Air Amendments of 1990.

☐ Due to the ever-increasing globalization of American business, the chapter on the legal environment for international business has been reorganized and significantly expanded. The chapter now reflects recent changes in Eastern Europe and the EEC. It also adds a section on international dispute resolution. Many more examples have been included.

☐ The computer law chapter now contains discussions of important new trends in computer crime legislation and copyright protection for computer software.

Also, the opening chapter on the nature of law contains a new section on the functions of law. In addition, the chapter's Appendix on the reading and briefing of cases now includes a sample case brief.

CONTINUING FEATURES OF NOTE

This edition naturally continues the basic features that have made its predecessors so successful. These include:

Comprehensive Coverage

As the preceding discussion might suggest, we pride ourselves on our thorough and up-to-date coverage of business law. We think that this text excels both in number of topics addressed and in the detail it provides within each topic. This naturally is true of the basic business law subjects that comprise the core of the text. But it is also true of the regulatory and other areas that sometimes have been said to constitute the "legal environment" curriculum.

Style and Presentation

We like to think—and users and reviewers have confirmed—that this text is written in a direct, lucid, and organized, yet relatively relaxed and conversational, style. For this reason, when using the text we often have been able to cover certain topics by assigning them as reading without lecturing on them. As always, we continue to employ italics and boldface to emphasize key points and terms, and to make liberal use of examples. Moreover, this edition makes greater use of numbered lists and paragraphs to state elements of a legal claim or applications of legal concepts. Also aiding students' comprehension of difficult subjects is our increased use of the charts, figures, and Concept Reviews mentioned earlier. Finally, we continue to place a summary at the end of each chapter to aid student retention of chapter material.

Case Selection and Presentation

We have made great efforts to unearth cases that clearly illustrate important points made in the text. Whenever possible, we also have tried to select cases that are of interest to students and are fun to teach. Our collective in-class teaching experience with the cases contained in recent editions has helped us determine which of those cases best meet these criteria, and has influenced our decisions on retention and replacement. Except where older decisions are landmarks or best illustrate particular concepts, we have selected recent cases.

This text's cases are edited so as to maximize student comprehension. In this edition, we have made a greater effort to place the cases nearer to the textual points they illustrate, and to provide textual lead-ins to them.

AACSB Curricular Standards

This text also is well suited to advance the relevant AACSB curricular standards pertaining to business law, the legal environment, and allied areas. The well-known traditional AACSB standard states that the business curriculum should include "a background of the economic and legal environment as it pertains to profit and/or non-profit organizations, along with ethical considerations and social and political influences as they affect such organizations." The AACSB's new April, 1991 standard says that both undergraduate and MBA curricula should include coverage of: ethical and global issues; the influence of political, social, legal and regulatory, environmental, and technological issues; and the impact of demographic diversity on organizations.

Along with its obvious attention to legal issues, this text reflects the new standard in various other ways as well. Its enhanced emphasis on ethical concerns and its expanded coverage of international legal matters have already been mentioned. As was also noted, the book provides detailed coverage of the regulatory matters—including environmental law—that usually are central to legal environment courses. In addition, several of its chapters enhance students' understanding of the influence of political and social issues on business and the law. For example, the chapters on the introduction to contracts, product liability, and employment law discuss how the tremendous changes in those areas from the 19th century to the present day reflect the equally great changes in American society over that period. And the treatment of sociological jurisprudence in the chapter on the nature of law sets a context for these discussions. As for technological issues, our chapter on computer law deals specifically with the legal issues surrounding this particular technology. Finally, although we doubt whether business law or any other subject in the business curriculum does much to examine "demographic diversity," our employment law chapter's discussion of employment discrimination certainly is pertinent here.

SUPPLEMENTS PACKAGE

Instructor's Manual   We have prepared the lengthy Instructor's Manual for this text. Each chapter in the manual contains outlined suggestions for structuring presentation of the corresponding text chapter material, provides additional material and examples not mentioned in the text, discusses each text case and provides points for its discussion with students, and answers the problem cases. Each text manual chapter also contains suggested answers to the chapter's ethical and public policy concerns.

Periodic Updates   As with past editions of this text, adopters of this edition will receive periodic updates detailing major changes within affected chapters. In all likelihood, there will be two such updates over the period covered by this edition.

Student Workbook   Prepared by Arlen W. Langvardt of Indiana University, the workbook gives students practice in reviewing concepts presented in the text. The workbook contains true-false, multiple choice, and short essay questions.

Test Bank   The test bank, prepared by Thomas Bowers, Arlen W. Langvardt, and Frona M. Powell of Indiana University, contains true-false, multiple choice, and short essay questions. For this edition, we have expanded the number of true-false and multiple choice questions.

Computest 3   A computerized version of the test bank is available; it allows instructors to generate random tests and add their own questions.

Acknowledgments

We would like to extend our recognition and thanks to various people who have assisted in preparation of this edition. Most important here are the able and industrious external reviewers who provided innumerable suggestions for improving the previous edition:

Wayne Anderson   *Southwest Missouri State University*
Frank Chong   *Southeast Missouri State University*
William Elliott   *Saginaw Valley State University*
Michael Engber   *Ball State University*
Gene Marsh   *The University of Alabama*
James Morgan   *California State University, Chico*
Gregory Naples   *Marquette University*
Rick Orsinger   *College of DuPage*
Dennis Pappas   *Columbus State Community College*
Robert Peace   *North Carolina State University*
Carol Rasnic   *Virginia Commonwealth University*
Linda Samuels   *George Mason University*
Daphne Sipes   *University of Texas at San Antonio*

We would like to extend a special recognition and thanks to Sarah Jane Hughes, Visiting Professor of Law at Catholic University Law School, for her contributions to the chapter on checks and documents of title, and to Pam Solie for her technical assistance.

Also in line for thanks are Craig Beytien, Karen Eichorst, Susan Trentacosti, and Jerry Saykes of Richard D. Irwin, Inc. Finally, we wish to extend our appreciation to the faculty and students who have made unsolicited suggestions for improving previous editions.

Michael B. Metzger
Jane P. Mallor
A. James Barnes
Thomas Bowers
Michael J. Phillips

CONTENTS IN BRIEF

CONTENTS

CHAPTER 42
MANAGEMENT OF CORPORATIONS   947

FOUNDATIONS OF AMERICAN LAW

CHAPTER 1

THE NATURE OF LAW

INTRODUCTION

Today, businesspeople confront the law at every turn. For example, business firms continually utilize the law of property, the law of contract, the law of agency, and many other basic bodies of law. Indeed, business could hardly function without them. In addition to facilitating business activity, the legal system actively restricts it as well. Today, government regulates almost all aspects of a business's operations—for example, advertising, product safety, the treatment of employees, the issuance of securities, and behavior toward competitors.

Thus, businesspeople constantly use, rely on, react to, plan around—and sometimes violate—innumerable legal rules or laws. For this reason, business managers must have a general knowledge of the legal system and the most important legal rules affecting their firms. This text discusses many of these rules, often in some detail. But your ability to use and apply the legal rules affecting business is incomplete without an understanding of law's general nature, its functions, and the techniques judges use when interpreting legal rules. This understanding could go some way toward reducing business complaints about the law and lawyers.

To help provide such an understanding, this chapter examines law's nature from four different angles. First, it lists, describes, and classifies the various kinds of rules that are regarded as law in the United States. This discussion, however, only partly conveys the nature of *law* in general. Thus, the second section of this chapter discusses a subject known as *jurisprudence* or legal philosophy. One traditional concern of jurisprudence has been to establish a general definition of law, and each of the competing definitions we examine highlights an important facet of law's many-sided nature.

In a shift from the theoretical to the pragmatic, the third section of this chapter examines some of the *functions* law serves—what it *does*. After this, the chapter concludes by discussing *legal reasoning,* the set of techniques judges use when interpreting and applying legal rules. This discussion, we hope, will help dispel the common misconception that the law consists of clear and precise commands that judges merely look up and then mechanically apply.

TYPES AND CLASSIFICATIONS OF LAW

This section describes the various kinds of rules that are commonly regarded as law in the American legal system today. As you will see, most of these different types of law are made by different political bodies. The section concludes by briefly examining three ways in which each of the types of law might be classified.

3

The Types of Law

Constitutions   **Constitutions**, which exist at the state and federal levels, have two general functions.[1] First, they establish the structure of government for the political unit they control (a state or the federal government). This involves stating the branches and subdivisions of the government and the powers given and denied to each. Through its **separation of powers**, for example, the U.S. Constitution establishes a Congress and gives it power to legislate or *make* law in certain areas, provides for a chief executive (the president) whose function is to execute or *enforce* the laws, and enables the creation of a federal judiciary to *interpret* the laws. The U.S. Constitution also structures the relationship between the federal government and the states. In the process, it respects the principle of **federalism** by recognizing the states' power to make law in certain areas.

The second function performed by constitutions is to prevent all units of government within their domain from taking certain actions or passing certain laws. They do so mainly by prohibiting governmental action that restricts certain *individual rights.* The Bill of Rights to the U.S. Constitution is an example. In the *Rochin* case presented later in this chapter, the Supreme Court applied one of the U.S. Constitution's individual rights provisions to a state. By doing so, the Court exercised the power of *judicial review:* the courts' ability to declare the actions of other branches of government unconstitutional.

Statutes   **Statutes** are laws created by Congress or a state legislature. They are stated in an authoritative form in statute books or codes. As you will see later in this chapter, however, their interpretation and application are often difficult.

Throughout this text, you will encounter state statutes that originally were drafted as **uniform acts.** Uniform acts are basically model statutes dealing with business, commercial, or other matters. The aim of such acts is to produce uniformity among the states on the subjects they address. Examples include the Uniform Commercial Code (which deals with a wide range of commercial law subjects), the Uniform Partnership Act, the Revised Uniform Limited Partnership Act, and the Revised Model Business Corporation Act. By themselves, uniform acts are not law because they are not drafted by recognized political authorities. They only become law when, or to the extent that, they are enacted by a legislature.

Common Law   The **common law** (also called judge-made law or case law) is that law made and applied by judges as they decide cases not governed by statutes or other types of law. In theory, common law exists at the state level only. The common law originated in medieval England after the Norman conquest in 1066 and has been continually evolving ever since. It developed from the decisions of judges in settling actual disputes. Over time, judges began to follow the decisions of other judges in similar cases. This practice became formalized in the doctrine of *stare decisis* (let the decision stand). As you will see later in the chapter, *stare decisis* has allowed the common law to evolve to meet changing social conditions. For this reason, the common law rules in force today often differ considerably from the common law rules of earlier times.

The common law was brought to America with the first English settlers and was used by courts during the colonial period.[2] It continued to be applied after the Revolution and the adoption of the Constitution, and is still employed in many cases today. For example, the rules of tort, contract, and agency discussed in this text are mainly common law rules. However, the states have codified (enacted into statute) some parts of the common law, particularly in the criminal area. Also, many states have passed statutes superseding judge-made law in certain situations. As discussed in the Introduction to Contracts chapter, for example, the states have established special rules for contract cases involving the sale of goods by enacting Article 2 of the Uniform Commercial Code.

In the torts, contracts, and agency chapters of this text, you often see references to the *Restatement* rule on a particular subject. The *Restatements* are collections of common law (and occasionally statutory) rules covering various areas of the law. Because they are promulgated by the American Law Institute rather than by courts, the *Restatements* are not law by themselves, and do not bind the courts. However, state courts often find *Restatement* rules persuasive and adopt them as common law rules within their states. Usually, these *Restatement* rules are

---

[1] More detail on how the U.S. Constitution performs these functions can be found in the Business and the Constitution chapter.

[2] However, Louisiana adopted the Code Napoléon, which was based on Roman law, and even today the law of Louisiana differs somewhat from the law of other states. For example, Louisiana has not adopted a portion of the Uniform Commercial Code.

the rules actually followed by a majority of the states. Occasionally, however, the *Restatements* stimulate changes in the common law by stating new rules that the courts decide to follow.[3]

Equity   The body of law called **equity** has traditionally tried to do discretionary "rough justice" in situations where common law rules would produce unfair results. American equity law originated in medieval England. At that time, the existing common law rules were quite technical and rigid and the remedies available in common law courts were too few. This meant that some deserving parties could not obtain adequate relief in the common law courts. As a result, the chancellor, the king's most powerful executive officer, began to hear cases that the common law courts could not resolve satisfactorily.

Eventually, separate equity courts emerged to handle the cases heard by the chancellor. These courts assumed control of a case only when there was no adequate remedy in a regular common law court. In equity courts, procedures were more flexible than in the common law courts and rigid rules of law were de-emphasized in favor of general moral maxims. Equity courts also provided several unique remedies not available in the common law courts (which generally awarded only money damages or the recovery of property). Perhaps the most important of these *equitable remedies* is the **injunction,** a court order forbidding a party to do some act or commanding him to perform some act. Others include the contract remedies of **specific performance** (whereby a party is ordered to perform according to the terms of her contract), **reformation** (in which the court rewrites the contract's terms to reflect the parties' real intentions), and **rescission** (a cancellation of a contract in which the parties often are returned to their precontractual position).

Like the common law, equity principles and practices were brought to the American colonies by the English settlers. They continued to be used after the Revolution and the adoption of the Constitution. Over time, however, the once-sharp line between law and equity has become blurred. Most states have abolished separate equity courts, now allowing one court to handle both legal and equitable claims. Also, equitable principles have tended to merge with common law rules, and some modern common law and statutory doctrines have equitable roots. An example is the doctrine of unconscionability discussed in the chapter on illegality of contracts. Finally, courts now may combine an award of money damages with an equitable remedy in certain cases.

Administrative Regulations and Decisions   Throughout most of the 20th century, the *administrative agencies* established by Congress and the state legislatures and discussed in the Administrative Agencies chapter have grown steadily in number and size. Today, their power, importance, and influence over business activity are considerable. A major reason for the rise of administrative agencies was the myriad of social and economic problems created by the industrialization of the United States beginning late in the 19th century. Because legislatures generally lacked the time and expertise to deal with these problems on a continuing basis, the creation of specialized, expert agencies was almost inevitable.

Administrative agencies can make law because of a *delegation* (or handing over) of power from the legislature. Agencies normally are created by a statute that specifies the areas in which the agency can make law and the scope of its power in each area. Often, this statutory grant of power is worded so broadly that the legislature has, in effect, merely pointed to a problem and given the agency wide-ranging powers to deal with it. For this reason, and because legislative supervision of agencies is sometimes perfunctory, agencies are often relatively immune from popular control.

The two kinds of law made by administrative agencies are **administrative regulations** (or administrative rules) and **agency decisions.** Like statutes, administrative regulations are stated in a precise form in one authoritative source. However, administrative regulations differ from statutes because the body enacting them is an agency, not the legislature. In addition, some agencies have an internal court structure that enables them to hear cases arising under the statutes and regulations they enforce. The resulting agency decisions are another kind of law. As noted in the next chapter, agency decisions may be appealed to regular state or federal courts. Practically speaking, however, the agency's decision is often final.

Treaties   According to the U.S. Constitution, **treaties** made by the president with foreign governments and approved by two thirds of the U.S. Senate are "the supreme

---

[3] An example is section 402A of the *Restatement (Second) of Torts,* which is discussed in the Product Liability chapter.

Law of the Land." As noted later, treaties can cause state (and occasionally federal) laws to become invalid.

Ordinances   State governments have subordinate units that exercise certain functions. Some of these units, such as school districts, have limited powers. Other units, such as counties, municipalities, and townships, exercise a number of governmental functions. The enactments of municipalities are called **ordinances;** zoning ordinances are an example. The enactments of other political subdivisions may also be referred to as ordinances.

Executive Orders   In theory, the president is a chief executive who enforces the laws but has no lawmaking powers. The same is usually true of state governors. However, these officials sometimes have the power to issue laws called **executive orders.** This power usually results from a legislative delegation. Because such delegations of legislative power are often imprecise and general, the executive's power to make law is sometimes quite broad.

Priority Rules   Occasionally, different types of law conflict. Thus, rules for determining which type takes priority are necessary. The most important such rule is the principle of *federal supremacy,* which makes the U.S. Constitution, federal laws enacted pursuant to it, and treaties "the supreme Law of the Land." This means that federal law defeats conflicting state law. Also, a state constitution defeats all other state laws inconsistent with it; the same is true for the U.S. Constitution and inconsistent federal laws. When a treaty conflicts with a federal statute over a purely domestic matter, the measure that is latest in time usually prevails. Also, state statutes and any laws derived from them by delegation defeat inconsistent common law rules. Within either the state or the federal domain, finally, statutes take priority over other laws that depend on a delegation of power from the legislature for their validity. Within a particular state, for example, statutes defeat inconsistent administrative regulations, and both defeat inconsistent common law rules.

CONCEPT REVIEW

THE TYPES OF POSITIVE LAW COMPARED

	Who Enacts?	State and/or Federal?	Stated in One Authoritative Form?	Remarks
Constitutions	U.S. Constitution originally ratified by states; complex amendment process. States may vary.	Both	Yes, but see the Business and the Constitution chapter on constitutional decisionmaking	Defeat other forms of positive law within sphere (federal or state)
Statutes	Legislatures	Both	Yes, but see this chapter's discussion of statutory interpretation	Defeat other forms of positive law within sphere (federal or state) except constitutions
Common Law	Courts	In theory, state only	No. See this chapter's discussion of legal reasoning	Law of tort, contract, and agency mainly common law
Equity	Formerly equity courts; now usually courts in general	In theory, state only. But equitable principles pervade federal law as well.	No	Traditional separation of law and equity now virtually gone
Administrative Regulations	Administrative agencies	Both	Yes	See the Administrative Agencies chapter

	Who Enacts?	State and/or Federal?	Stated in One Authoritative Form?	Remarks
Administrative Decisions	Administrative agencies	Both	No	See the Administrative Agencies chapter
Treaties	President plus two thirds of Senate	Federal	Yes	Defeat inconsistent state law
Ordinances	Usually local government bodies	State (mainly local)	Yes	
Executive Orders	Chief executives	Both	Yes	Usually based on delegation from legislature

Classifications of Law

Cutting across the different *types* of law just described are three common *classifications* of law. These classifications involve distinctions between: (1) criminal law and civil law, (2) substantive law and procedural law, and (3) public law and private law. One type of law might be classified in each of these ways. For example, a state statute might be criminal, substantive, and public; or civil, procedural, and public.

Criminal and Civil Law   **Criminal law** is the law applied when the government acts in a prosecutorial role by proceeding against someone for the commission of a crime. **Civil law** is the law applied when one party sues another party because the other failed to meet some legal duty owed to the first party. Civil lawsuits usually involve private parties, but the government may be a party to a civil suit (as for instance where a city sues, or is sued by, a construction contractor). Criminal penalties (e.g., imprisonment or fines) differ from civil remedies (e.g., money damages or equitable relief). Also, violations of the criminal law often are said to be wrongs against society as a whole, while violations of the civil law frequently are viewed as injuring only specific private parties.

   Although most of the legal rules discussed in this text are civil law rules, the Crimes chapter deals specifically with the criminal law and various criminal provisions are discussed in other chapters. When considering such provisions, be aware that the same behavior can violate both the civil law and the criminal law. For instance, a party whose careless driving causes injury to another may face both a criminal prosecution by the state and a civil suit for damages by the injured party.

Substantive Law and Procedural Law   **Substantive law** sets out the rights and duties of people as they act in society. **Procedural law** controls the behavior of governmental bodies (mainly courts) as they establish and enforce rules of substantive law. A statute making murder a crime, for example, is a rule of substantive law. But the rules describing the proper conduct of a criminal trial are procedural in nature. This text is mainly concerned with substantive law. The Resolution of Private Disputes chapter and the Crimes chapter, however, examine some of the procedural rules governing civil and criminal cases, respectively. Various procedural rules also appear in other chapters.

Public and Private Law   **Public law** is concerned with the powers of government, and with the relations between government and private parties. Examples include constitutional law, administrative law, and criminal law. **Private law** establishes a framework of legal rules that enable private parties to set the rights and duties they owe each other. Examples include the rules of contract, property, and agency.

JURISPRUDENCE

Introduction

The various types of law discussed in the previous section are sometimes referred to as **positive law.** Positive law can be defined as the rules that have been laid down (or posited) by a recognized political authority. Knowing the types of positive law is essential to understanding the American legal system and the business law topics discussed in this text. But defining *law* by listing these

FIGURE 1   A Brief Sketch of the Jurisprudential Schools

	Definition of Law	Relation between Law and Morality	Practical Tendency
Legal Positivism	Command of a recognized political authority	Separate questions: "law is law, just or not"	Valid positive law should be enforced and obeyed, just or not
Natural Law	All commands of recognized political authorities that are not unjust	"Unjust law is not law"	Unjust positive laws should not be enforced and obeyed
American Legal Realism	What public decisionmakers actually do	Unclear	"Law in action" often more important than "law in the books"
Sociological Jurisprudence	Process of social ordering in accordance with dominant social values and interests	Although moral values influence positive law, no way to say whether this is right or wrong	Law inevitably does (and should?) follow dominant social values and interests

different kinds of positive law is much like defining the word *automobile* by describing all the types of vehicles going by that name. To define law properly, we need a general description that captures its essence.

One concern of the field known as **jurisprudence** or legal philosophy is to arrive at an abstract philosophical definition of law. Over time, different schools of jurisprudence have emerged, each with its own distinctive conception of law. The differences among these schools are not merely an academic matter. As Figure 1 shows, their conceptions of law often affect their approach toward real-life political and legal disputes. Whether the participants in these disputes know it or not, their positions often reflect jurisprudential assumptions.

Legal Positivism

One feature common to all types of positive law is their enactment by a recognized political authority—a legislature, a court, an administrative agency, and so forth. This common feature underlies the definition of law adopted by the school of jurisprudence called **legal positivism.** Legal positivists generally define law as the command of a recognized political authority. To the British political philosopher Thomas Hobbes, for instance, "Law properly, is the word of him, that by right hath command over others."

Legal positivism's idea that law is basically a *command* affects its view of the relationship between law and morality. The commands made by recognized political authorities obviously can be good, bad, or indifferent in moral terms. But as Figure 2 indicates, to positivists such commands are valid law irrespective of

their goodness or badness. For positivists, in other words, legal validity and moral validity are different questions. Sometimes this view is expressed by the slogan: "Law is law, just or not." For this reason, some (but not all) positivists say that every validly enacted positive law should be enforced and obeyed, whether just or not. People who argue that you should obey some law you think is unjust simply because "it's the law" are speaking as legal positivists sometimes do.

Natural Law

At first glance, legal positivism's "law is law, just or not" approach may strike you as perfect common sense. But it presents a problem, for it may mean that *any* positive law (no matter how unjust) is valid law and should be enforced and obeyed so long as some recognized political authority (no matter how wicked) enacted it. Here, the school of jurisprudence known as **natural law** takes issue with legal positivism by rejecting the positivist separation of law and morality.

The basic idea behind most systems of natural law is that some higher law or set of absolute moral rules binds all human beings in all times and places. The Roman statesman Marcus Cicero described natural law as "the highest reason, implanted in nature, which commands what ought to be done and forbids the opposite." Because this higher law determines what is ultimately good and ultimately bad, it is a criterion for evaluating positive law. To Saint Thomas Aquinas, for example, "every human law has just so much of the nature of law, as it is derived from the law of nature." As a practical matter, therefore, natural law thinkers tend to define law in the

FIGURE 2   The Positivist and Natural Law Definitions of Law

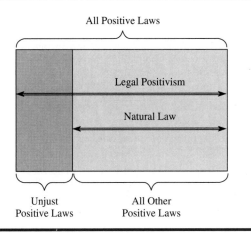

If few people openly advocate natural law these days, why should it concern you? For one thing, it is difficult to ignore the perennial moral questions natural law addresses. As the chapter on Business Ethics, Corporate Social Responsibility, and the Control and Governance of Corporations suggests, these are questions *you* may have to confront at some point in your life. In addition, beliefs and positions resembling natural law remain fairly common. The rights-based theories discussed in the business ethics chapter are a possible example. Also, people who criticize certain nations because their legal systems deny human rights are thinking and acting much like advocates of natural law have traditionally thought and acted. Finally, moral ideas resembling natural law influence judges from time to time. Keep this in mind as you read the *Rochin* case at the end of this section.

fashion suggested by Figure 2: as those commands of recognized political authorities that do not offend the higher law by being unjust.

Unjust positive laws, on the other hand, simply are not law. As Cicero put it: "What of the many deadly, the many pestilential statutes which are imposed on peoples? These no more deserve to be called laws than the rules a band of robbers might pass in their assembly." This view sometimes is expressed by the slogan: "An unjust law is not law." Because unjust positive laws are not truly law, natural law thinkers conclude that they should not be enforced or obeyed.

Despite a recent revival of interest in ethical matters, relatively few 20th-century British or American legal philosophers have openly advocated natural law. This is partly due to the many skeptical attacks on natural law's central idea: the existence of a higher law binding all people in all times and places. For example, skeptics—some of them legal positivists—note that different people and societies often have conflicting moral views. Moreover, they continue, different *systems of natural law* occasionally emphasize different values. To paper over these problems, the skeptics continue, natural law thinkers often phrase their higher law in broad, empty platitudes that mean what listeners want them to mean and that are consistent with most systems of positive law. In response to all this, natural law thinkers argue that most people and societies actually do agree on many core values, but that these values inevitably find different application in different times and places. No system of natural law, they add, can or should specify every detail of every society's positive law.

American Legal Realism

To some people, the preceding debate between natural law and legal positivism seems unreal. Not only is natural law pie-in-the-sky, such people might say, but sometimes positive law does not mean much either. For example, juries sometimes pay little attention to the legal rules that are supposed to guide their decisions, and prosecutors often have discretion whether or not to enforce criminal statutes. In some legal proceedings, moreover, the background, biases, and values of the judge—and not "the law"—strongly influence the result. As the joke goes, justice occasionally is nothing more than what the judge ate for breakfast.

Remarks such as these typify the school of jurisprudence known as **American legal realism.** Legal realists generally regard the positivist "law in the books" as less important than the "law in action"—the conduct of those who enforce and interpret that law. Thus, American legal realism defines law as the behavior of public officials (mainly judges) as they deal with matters before the legal system. Because the actions of such decision-makers—and not the rules in the books—really affect people's lives, the realists say, this behavior is most important and deserves to be called law.

It is doubtful whether the legal realists have ever developed a common position on the relation between law and morality or the duty to obey positive law. But they have been quick to give advice to judges. Many realists feel that the modern judge should be a kind of "social engineer" who weighs all relevant values and considers social science findings before deciding a case. Thus, such a judge would make the positive law only one factor in his or her decision. Because judges inevitably base their decisions on personal factors, the realists seem to say, they should at least do this in an honest and intelligent way. To promote this kind of decisionmaking, the realists have sometimes favored fuzzy, discretionary statutes and regulations that allow judges to decide each case according to its unique facts.[4]

Sociological Jurisprudence

The term **sociological jurisprudence** is a general label uniting a group of diverse jurisprudential approaches whose common aim is to examine law within its social context. Their overall outlook is well captured by the following quotation from Justice Oliver Wendell Holmes:

The life of the law has not been logic: it has been experience. The felt necessities of the time, the prevalent moral and political theories, intuitions of public policy, avowed or unconscious, even the prejudices which judges share with their fellow-men, have had a good deal more to do than the syllogism in determining the rules by which men should be governed. The law embodies the story of a nation's development through many centuries, and it cannot be dealt with as if it contained only the axioms and corollaries of a book of mathematics.[5]

Despite this common outlook, there is no distinctive sociological definition of law. If one were attempted, it might go as follows: "Law is a process of social ordering reflecting society's dominant interests and values."

Different Sociological Approaches By examining a few well-known examples of sociological legal thinking, we can put some flesh on the definition offered above. The "dominant interests" portion of the definition is exemplified by the writings of Roscoe Pound, an influential 20th-century American legal philosopher. Pound developed a detailed catalog of the social interests that press on government and the legal system and thus shape positive law. During his life, Pound's catalog changed along with changes in American society. An example of the definition's "dominant values" component is the *historical school* of jurisprudence identified with the 19th-century German legal philosopher Friedrich Karl von Savigny. Savigny saw law as an un-

planned, almost unconscious, reflection of the collective spirit (*Volksgeist*) of a particular society. In his view, legal change could only be explained historically, as a slow response to changing social conditions and values.

By describing how dominant social interests and values shape the law, Pound and Savigny undermine the legal positivist view that law is simply the command of some political authority. The early 20th-century Austrian legal philosopher Eugen Ehrlich went even further in rejecting positivism. He did so by distinguishing two different "processes of social ordering" contained within our definition of sociological jurisprudence. The first of these is "state law," or positive law. The second is the "living law," informal social controls such as customs, family ties, and business practices. By regarding both as law, Ehrlich blurred the line between positive law and other kinds of social ordering. In the process, he stimulated people to recognize that positive law is only one element within a spectrum of social controls.

The Implications of Sociological Jurisprudence Because its definition of law includes social values, you might think that sociological jurisprudence resembles natural law. But most sociological thinkers are only concerned with the *fact* that certain moral values influence the law, and not with the goodness or badness of those values. In the Introduction to Contracts chapter, for instance, we note that laissez-faire economic values were widely shared in 19th-century America and strongly influenced the contract law of that period. But we do not discuss whether this was right or wrong. Thus, it might seem that sociological jurisprudence fails to give practical advice to those who must enforce and obey positive law.

However, sociological jurisprudence does have at least one practical implication. This is a general tendency to urge that the law must change to meet changing social conditions and values. This resembles the familiar saying that "the law must keep up with the times." Thus, sociological thinkers sometimes observe that laws that fail to reflect changing social values often become ineffective or irrelevant, and that such laws almost inevitably are eliminated or modified in the long run. Some might hold to this view even when society's values are changing for the worse. To Holmes, for example, "[t]he first requirement of a sound body of law is, that it should correspond with the actual feelings and demands of the community, *whether right or wrong.*"[6]

---

[4] Some examples are found in Article 2 of the Uniform Commercial Code, which was principally authored by Karl Llewellyn, a prominent legal realist. See the Introduction to Contracts chapter.

[5] Holmes, *The Common Law* (1881).

[6] The italics have been added.

ROCHIN v. CALIFORNIA[7]

342 U.S. 165 (U.S. Sup. Ct. 1952)

In 1949, three Los Angeles County deputy sheriffs received information that Antonio Rochin was selling narcotics. In search of evidence, they entered Rochin's home one morning and forced open the door to his bedroom. They immediately spotted two capsules on a nightstand beside the bed on which the half-clad Rochin was sitting. After the deputies asked, "Whose stuff is this?" Rochin quickly put the capsules in his mouth. The deputies then jumped Rochin and tried to force the capsules from his mouth. When this proved unsuccessful, they handcuffed Rochin and took him to a hospital. Despite Rochin's opposition, they had a doctor insert a tube into his stomach and force an emetic (vomit-inducing) solution through the tube. This stomach pumping caused Rochin to vomit. Within the material he disgorged were two capsules containing morphine.

Rochin then was tried and convicted for possessing a morphine preparation in violation of California law. The two morphine capsules were the main evidence against him, and the trial court admitted this evidence over Rochin's objection. Even though it found the deputies' behavior illegal, the intermediate appellate court affirmed the conviction. The California Supreme Court also affirmed. Rochin then appealed to the U.S. Supreme Court. The main issue before the Court was whether the methods by which the deputies obtained the capsules violated the Due Process Clause of the U.S. Constitution's Fourteenth Amendment, which states that "No state shall . . . deprive any person of life, liberty, or property, without due process of law." *Note*: At the time this case was decided, evidence obtained through a forced stomach pumping probably was admissible in a majority of the states that had considered the question. Also, the Supreme Court did not then require that state courts exclude evidence obtained through an illegal search or seizure. The Crimes chapter discusses modern search-and-seizure law.

Frankfurter, Justice.   The requirements of the due process clause impose upon this Court an exercise of judgment upon the proceedings resulting in a conviction to ascertain whether they offend those canons of decency and fairness which express the notions of justice of English-speaking peoples even toward those charged with the most heinous offenses. These standards of justice are not authoritatively formulated anywhere as though they were specifics. Due process of law is a summarized guarantee of respect for those personal immunities so rooted in the traditions and conscience of our people as to be fundamental, or implicit in the concept of ordered liberty.

The vague contours of the due process clause do not leave judges at large. We may not draw upon our merely personal and private notions and disregard the limits that bind judges. These limits are derived from considerations that are fused in the whole nature of our judicial process. These are considerations deeply rooted in reason and in the compelling traditions of the legal profession. The due process clause places upon this Court the duty of exercising a judgment upon interests of society pushing in opposite directions. Due process of law thus conceived is not to be derided as a resort to the revival of "natural law."

Applying these general considerations to the present case, we conclude that the proceedings by which this conviction was obtained do more than offend some fastidious squeamishness or private sentimentalism about combatting crime too energetically. This is conduct that shocks the conscience. Illegally breaking into the privacy of Rochin, the struggle to open his mouth and remove what was there, the forcible extraction of his stomach's contents—this course of proceeding is

---

[7] At this point, you may want to examine this chapter's appendix on the reading and briefing of cases.

bound to offend even hardened sensibilities. They are methods too close to the rack and the screw to permit of constitutional differentiation.

Judgment reversed in favor of Rochin.

THE FUNCTIONS OF LAW

In traditional societies, people tended to view law as a body of unchanging rules that deserved obedience because they were part of the natural order of things. By now, however, most lawmakers treat law as a flexible *tool* or *instrument* for the accomplishment of chosen purposes. For example, much of the law of negotiable instruments discussed in this text's section on commercial paper is designed to stimulate commercial activity by promoting the free movement of such money substitutes as promissory notes, checks, and drafts. Throughout this text, moreover, you will see courts manipulating or changing existing legal rules to get the results they desire. One strength of this *instrumentalist* attitude is its willingness to adapt legal rules to further the social good. One weakness is the legal instability and uncertainty those adaptations often produce.

Just as individual legal rules further certain specific purposes, *law as a whole* serves many general social functions. Although many legal rules serve all these functions to some degree, certain areas of the law promote them better than others do. Among the most important of the law's innumerable functions are:

1. *Peacekeeping.* This basic function of any legal system is most clearly furthered by the criminal law rules discussed in the Crimes chapter. Also, as the chapter on The Resolution of Private Disputes suggests, one major function of the civil law rules discussed throughout the text is the resolution of private disputes.

2. *Checking government power and thereby promoting personal freedom.* Obvious examples are the constitutional restrictions on government regulation examined in the Business and the Constitution chapter.

3. *Facilitating planning and the realization of reasonable expectations.* The rules of contract law discussed in the section on Contracts help fulfill this function of law, which is obviously quite important to business.

4. *Promoting economic growth through free competition.* Of the many legal rules that perform this function, those that stand out are the antitrust laws discussed in the two later chapters on the Sherman Act, the Clayton Act, the Robinson–Patman Act, and the antitrust exemptions and immunities.

5. *Promoting social justice.* Throughout this century, government has intervened in private social and economic affairs to correct injustices and give all citizens equal access to life's basic goods. One example is the collection of employer-employee regulations treated in the Employment Law chapter.

6. *Protecting the environment.* The most important federal environmental statutes are discussed in the Environmental Regulation chapter.

Obviously, the law's various functions can conflict with one another. The familiar clash between economic growth and environmental protection is an example. And the *Rochin* case illustrates the equally familiar conflict between effective law enforcement and the preservation of personal rights. Only rarely does the law achieve a particular end without sacrificing other ends to some degree. In law, as in life, there is generally no such thing as a free lunch. Where the law's ends conflict, lawmakers can only try to strike the best possible balance among those ends. How this balance is struck can change over time. As compared with modern American law, for example, 19th-century law gave more weight to economic development and less to protection of the environment.

The preceding discussion suggests that there are limits on the law's usefulness as a device for promoting social goals. The most important reason is that the law's pursuit of one desirable end may force it to sacrifice others. In addition, as our earlier discussion of sociological jurisprudence suggested, it is doubtful whether laws that conflict with dominant social values will ever be enacted, or if enacted, will ever be enforced and obeyed.

As that discussion also revealed, the law is only one form of social ordering. Thus, lawmakers sometimes are reluctant to intrude in areas where other forms of ordering dominate. For example, although laws regulating family matters and the internal affairs of private groups are not uncommon, neither is completely subject to legal controls.

LEGAL REASONING

Introduction

Although it was criticized earlier in the chapter, legal positivism's conception of law as the command of a recognized political authority has at least one big virtue. Such commands usually are laid down in a fairly clear and organized fashion. Unlike the other schools of jurisprudence, therefore, legal positivism enables lawmakers to state legal rules with reasonable precision. For this reason, people and businesses can predict the legal consequences of their actions with some measure of certainty. Thus, although it occasionally examines law from functional and sociological perspectives, this text mainly adopts a positivist approach. It does so by stating the legal rules affecting business as a series of commands issued by recognized political authorities. In addition, it states these rules in what lawyers call "black letter" form, using precise sentences saying that certain legal consequences will occur if certain events happen.

This positivist black letter approach, however, can be misleading. It suggests definiteness, certainty, permanence, and predictability—attributes the law frequently lacks. To illustrate this, and to give you some idea how lawyers think, we now discuss the two most important kinds of legal reasoning: **case law reasoning**[8] and **statutory interpretation.** However, we first must examine legal reasoning in general.

Legal reasoning is basically deductive, or syllogistic. That is, the legal rule is the major premise, the facts are the minor premise, and the result is the product of combining the two. Suppose a state statute says that a driver operating an automobile between 55 and 70 miles per hour must pay a $50 fine (the rule or major premise) and

that Jim Smith drives his car at 65 miles per hour (the facts or minor premise). If Jim is arrested, and if the necessary facts can be proved, he will be required to pay the $50 fine. Legal reasoning often is more difficult than this example would suggest. The rules themselves may be inherently imprecise, ambiguities may appear as the rules are applied to new fact situations, and such applications may even cause the rules to change over time.

Case Law Reasoning

In cases governed by the common law, courts find the appropriate legal rules in prior cases or *precedents*. The standard for choosing and applying prior cases to decide present cases is the doctrine of *stare decisis*, which states that like cases should be decided alike.[9] That is, the present case should be decided in the same way as prior cases presenting the same basic facts and legal issues. If a court decides that the alleged precedent is not really "like" the present case and should not control the decision in that case, it *distinguishes* the prior case.[10]

Because every present case differs from the precedents in *some* respect, it is always theoretically possible to distinguish those precedents. For example, one *could* distinguish a prior case because both parties in that case had black hair, while one party in the present case has brown hair. Of course, such distinctions are usually ridiculous, because the differences they identify are insignificant in moral or social policy terms. In other words, a good distinction of a prior case should involve a widely accepted policy reason for treating the present case differently from its predecessor. Because people often disagree about moral ideas, public policies, and the degree to which they are accepted, and because all of these factors change over time, judges sometimes differ on the wisdom of distinguishing a prior case. This is a significant source of uncertainty in the common law. But it also gives the common law the flexibility to adapt to changing social conditions.

The following *MacPherson* case illustrates the common law's ability to change over time. In the series of New York cases it discusses, the **plaintiff** (the party suing) claimed that the **defendant** (the party being sued)

---

[8] The style of legal reasoning used in constitutional cases resembles that used in common law cases, but often is somewhat looser. For the way courts decide constitutional cases, see the chapter on Business and the Constitution.

[9] *Stare decisis* should be distinguished from the doctrine of *res judicata*, which says that a final judicial decision on the merits conclusively settles the rights *of the parties to the case.*

[10] Also, while they exercise the power infrequently, courts sometimes completely *overrule* their prior decisions.

had been negligent in the manufacture or inspection of some product, thus injuring the plaintiff, who later purchased or used the product.[11] In the mid-19th century, such suits often were unsuccessful due to the general rule that a seller or manufacturer could not be liable for negligence unless there was *privity of contract* between the defendant and the plaintiff. Privity of contract is the existence of a direct contractual relationship between two parties. Thus, the no-liability-outside-privity rule prevented the injured plaintiff from recovering against a seller or manufacturer who had sold the product to a dealer who in turn sold it to the plaintiff. Over time,

however, the courts began to allow injured plaintiffs to recover from sellers or manufacturers with whom they had not directly dealt. These courts were creating *exceptions* to the general rule; that is, they were distinguishing prior cases announcing the rule and creating new rules to govern the situations they distinguished. The *MacPherson* case describes the gradual enlargement of such an exception in New York. Eventually, the exception "consumed the rule" by covering so many situations that the original rule became relatively insignificant.[12]

---

[11] Negligence is discussed in the Negligence and Strict Liability chapter.

[12] The present status of the old no-liability-outside-privity rule in sale of goods cases is discussed in the Product Liability chapter. Today, it has relatively little impact in negligence cases of this kind. Also, as the introduction to that chapter suggests, sociological jurisprudence helps explain the rule's erosion.

MACPHERSON v. BUICK MOTOR CO.
111 N.E. 1050 (N.Y. Ct. App. 1916)

One wheel of an automobile manufactured by the Buick Motor Company was made of defective wood. Buick could have discovered the wheel's defective condition had it made a reasonable inspection after purchasing the wheel from another manufacturer. Buick sold the car to a retail dealer, who then sold it to MacPherson. While driving the car, MacPherson was injured when the wheel collapsed and he was thrown from the vehicle. He sued Buick in a New York trial court for its negligent failure to inspect the wheel. Buick's main defense was that it had not dealt directly with MacPherson and thus owed no duty to him. Following trial and appellate court judgments in MacPherson's favor, Buick appealed to the New York Court of Appeals, the state's highest court.

Cardozo, Justice.   The foundations of this branch of the law were laid in *Thomas v. Winchester* (1852). A poison was falsely labeled. The sale was made to a druggist, who sold to a customer. The customer recovered damages from the seller who affixed the label. The defendant's negligence, it was said, put human life in imminent danger. A poison, falsely labeled, is likely to injure anyone who gets it. Because the danger is to be foreseen, there is a duty to avoid the injury. *Thomas v. Winchester* became quickly a landmark of the law. In the application of its principle there may, at times, have been uncertainty or even error. There has never been doubt or disavowal of the principle itself.

The chief cases are well known. *Loop v. Litchfield* (1870) was the case of a defect in a small balance wheel used on a circular saw. The manufacturer pointed out the defect to the buyer. The risk can hardly have been an imminent one, for the wheel lasted five years before it broke. In the meanwhile the buyer had made a lease of the machinery. It was held that the manufacturer was not answerable to the lessee. *Loop v. Litchfield* was followed by *Losee v. Clute* (1873), the case of the explosion of a steam boiler. That decision must be confined to its special facts. It was put upon the ground that the risk of injury was too remote. The buyer had not only accepted the boiler, but had tested it. The manufacturer knew that his own test was not the final one. The finality of the test has a bearing on the measure of diligence owing to persons other than the purchaser.

These early cases suggest a narrow construction of the rule. Later cases evince a more liberal spirit. In *Devlin v. Smith* (1882), the defendant contractor built a scaffold for a painter. The painter's workmen were injured. The contractor was held liable. He knew that the scaffold, if improperly constructed, was a most dangerous trap. He knew that it was to be used by the workmen. Building it for their use, he owed them a duty to build it with care. From *Devlin v. Smith* we turn to *Statler v. Ray Manufacturing Co.* (1909). The defendant manufactured a large coffee urn. It was installed in a restaurant. The urn exploded and injured the plaintiff. We held that the manufacturer was liable. We said that the urn was of such a character that it was liable to become a source of great danger if not carefully and properly constructed.

It may be that *Devlin v. Smith* and *Statler v. Ray Manufacturing Co.* have extended the rule of *Thomas v. Winchester*. If so, this court is committed to the extension. The defendant argues that things imminently dangerous to human life are poisons, explosives, deadly weapons—things whose normal function is to injure or destroy. But whatever the rule in *Thomas v. Winchester* may once have been, it no longer has that restricted meaning. A scaffold is not inherently a destructive instrument. No one thinks of [a coffee urn] as an implement whose normal function is destruction.

We hold, then, that the principle of *Thomas v. Winchester* is not limited to things which are implements of destruction. If the nature of a thing is such that it is reasonably certain to place life and limb in peril when negligently made, it is a thing of danger. If to the element of danger there is added knowledge that the thing will be used by persons other than the purchaser, then, irrespective of contract, the manufacturer is under a duty to make it carefully.

The nature of an automobile gives warning of probable danger if its construction is defective. This automobile was designed to go 50 miles an hour. Unless its wheels were sound and strong, injury was almost certain. The defendant knew the danger. It knew that the car would be used by persons other than the buyer, a dealer in cars. The dealer was indeed the one person of whom it might be said with some certainty that by him the car would not be used. Yet the defendant would have us say that he was the one person it was under a legal duty to protect. The law does not lead us to so inconsequent a conclusion. Precedents drawn from the age of travel by stagecoach do not fit the conditions of travel today. The principle that the danger must be imminent does not change, but the things subject to the principle do change. They are whatever the needs of life in a developing civilization require them to be.

Judgment for MacPherson affirmed.

Statutory Interpretation

Because statutes are written in one authoritative form, their interpretation might seem easier than case law reasoning. However, this is not so. One reason for the difficulties courts face when interpreting statutes is the natural ambiguity of language. This is especially true where statutory words that appear to be clear are applied to situations the legislature did not foresee. Also, legislators may deliberately use ambiguous language when they are unwilling or unable to deal specifically with each situation that the statute was enacted to regulate. In such situations, the legislature consciously employs vague language expecting that the courts will fill in the details on a case-by-case basis. Other reasons for deliberate ambiguity include the need for legislative compromise and legislators' desire to avoid taking controversial positions.

Due to problems like these, courts need and use various techniques of statutory interpretation. As you will see shortly, different techniques can dictate different results in a particular case. Moreover, judges sometimes employ the techniques in an instrumentalist or result-oriented fashion, emphasizing the technique that will produce the result they want and downplaying the

FIGURE 3   The Steps in a Statute's Passage and the Techniques of Statutory Interpretation

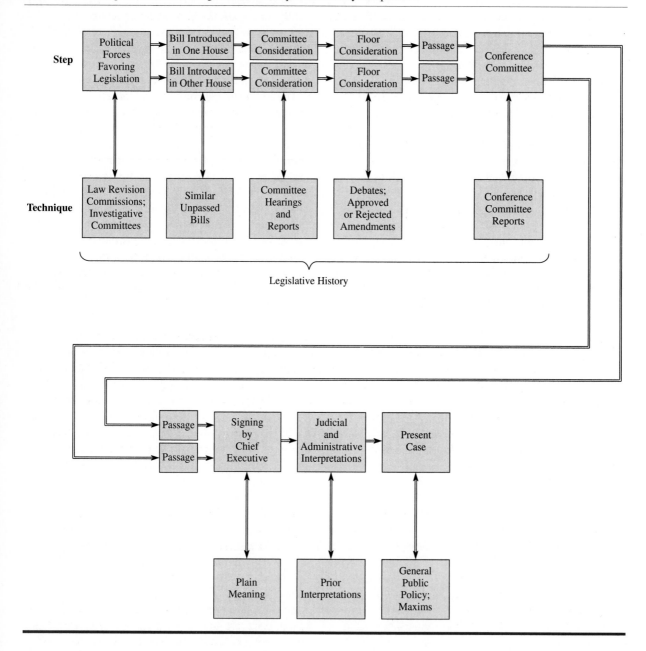

others. For this reason, it is difficult to state which technique should control when different techniques yield different results. Although there are some "rules" on this subject, courts often ignore them.

Figure 3 relates the most common techniques of statutory interpretation to the various steps in the passage of a statute. Of course, some of these techniques may be irrelevant to a particular statute. To further illustrate these techniques, the following discussion occasionally uses a hypothetical air pollution statute requiring emission controls for "automobiles, trucks, buses, and other motorized passenger or cargo vehicles."

Plain Meaning   Courts always begin their interpretation of a statute with its actual language. Where the statute's words have a clear, common, accepted meaning, some courts employ the *plain meaning rule*. This rule states that in such cases the court should simply apply the statute according to the plain, accepted meaning of its words, and should not concern itself with anything else.

Legislative History   Some courts refuse to follow a statute's plain meaning when its *legislative history* suggests a different result. And almost all courts resort to legislative history when the statute's language is ambiguous. A statute's legislative history includes the following sources: the reports of investigative committees or law revision commissions that led to the legislation, the hearings of the legislative committee(s) originally considering the legislation, any reports issued by such a committee, legislative debates, the report of a conference committee reconciling two houses' conflicting versions of the law, amendments or defeated amendments to the legislation, other bills not passed by the legislature but proposing similar legislation, and discrepancies between a bill passed by one house and the final version of the statute.

Sometimes a statute's legislative history provides no information or conflicting information about its meaning, its scope, or its purposes. Also, some sources are more authoritative than others. The worth of debates, for instance, may depend on which legislator (e.g., the sponsor of the bill or an uninformed blowhard) is being quoted. Some sources are useful only in particular situations; prior unpassed bills and amendments or defeated amendments are examples. Suppose that it is unclear whether the "other motorized passenger or cargo vehicles" language in our pollution statute applies to mopeds. If the original version of the statute specifically included mopeds but this reference was removed by amendment, it is unlikely that the legislature wanted mopeds to be covered. The same might be true if six similar unpassed bills had included mopeds but the bill that was eventually passed did not, or if one house had passed a bill including mopeds but mopeds did not appear in the final version of the legislation.

Courts use legislative history in two overlapping but nonetheless distinguishable ways. They may use it to determine *legislative intent*—what the legislature thought about the meaning of specific statutory language. They may also use it to determine *legislative purpose*—the overall aim, end, or goal of the legislation. In the latter case, they then ask whether a particular interpretation of the statute is consistent with this purpose. To illustrate the difference between these two uses of legislative his-

tory, suppose that a court has to consider whether the pollution statute's "other motorized passenger or cargo vehicles" language includes battery-powered vehicles. A court seeking to determine the legislature's intent would scan the legislative history for specific references to battery-powered vehicles or other indications of what the legislature thought about their inclusion. A court making a purpose inquiry, however, would use the same history to determine the overall aims of the statute, and then would ask whether including battery-powered vehicles is consistent with those aims. Because the history probably would reveal that our statute's purpose was to reduce air pollution from internal combustion engines, the court might well conclude that battery-powered vehicles should not be covered. As suggested above, courts sometimes follow the intent or purpose revealed by a statute's legislative history even though the plain meaning is to the contrary. In the following *Weber* case, for example, the Supreme Court evidently thought that the statute's claimed purpose was more important than its apparent plain meaning.

General Public Purpose   Occasionally, courts construe statutory language in the light of various *general public purposes* that they identify. These purposes are *not* the purposes underlying the statute in question; rather, they are widely accepted general notions of public policy. In one case, for example, the U.S. Supreme Court used the general public policy against racial discrimination in education as one argument for denying tax-exempt status to a private university that discriminated on the basis of race.[13]

Prior Interpretations   Courts sometimes follow prior cases (and even administrative decisions) interpreting a statute regardless of the statute's plain meaning or its legislative history. The main argument for following these *prior interpretations* is to promote stability and certainty by preventing each successive court that considers a statute from adopting its own interpretation. Whether courts will follow a prior interpretation depends on such factors as the number of past courts adopting the interpretation, the authoritativeness of those courts, and the number of years that the interpretation has been followed. Note that in *Weber*, the Supreme Court apparently did not follow one of its own prior interpretations.

---

[13] *Bob Jones University v. United States*, 461 U.S. 574 (1983).

UNITED STEELWORKERS v. WEBER

443 U.S. 193 (U.S. Sup. Ct. 1979)

As part of its collective bargaining agreement with the United Steelworkers of America, the Kaiser Aluminum and Chemical Company established a new on-the-job craft training program at its Gramercy, Louisiana, plant. The selection of trainees for the program was based on seniority, but at least 50 percent of the new trainees had to be black until the percentage of black skilled craft workers in the plant approximated the percentage of blacks in the local labor force.

Brian Weber was a rejected white applicant who would have qualified for the program had the racial preference not existed. He sued Kaiser and the union in federal district court, arguing that the racial preference violated Title VII of the 1964 Civil Rights Act. Section 703(a) of the act states that: "It shall be an unlawful employment practice for an employer . . . to discriminate against any individual with respect to his compensation, terms, conditions, or privileges of employment, because of such individual's race, color, religion, sex, or national origin." Section 703(d) of the act had a similar provision specifically forbidding racial discrimination in admission to apprenticeship or other training programs. Weber's suit was successful, and the federal court of appeals affirmed. Kaiser and the union appealed to the U.S. Supreme Court.

Brennan, Justice.   The only question before us is whether Title VII forbids private employers and unions from voluntarily agreeing upon bona fide affirmative action plans that accord racial preferences in the manner and for the purpose provided in the Kaiser-USWA plan. That question was expressly left open in *McDonald v. Santa Fe Trail Transp. Co.* (1976), which held, in a case not involving affirmative action, that Title VII protects whites as well as blacks from racial discrimination.

Weber argues that Congress intended in Title VII to prohibit all race-conscious affirmative action plans. His argument rests upon a literal interpretation of sections 703(a) and (d) of the act. Those sections make it unlawful to discriminate because of race in the selection of apprentices for training programs. Since, the argument runs, *McDonald* settled that Title VII forbids discrimination against whites as well as blacks, and since the Kaiser-USWA plan discriminated against white employees solely because they are white, it follows that the plan violates Title VII.

Weber's argument is not without force. But it overlooks the significance of the fact that the Kaiser-USWA plan is an affirmative action plan voluntarily adopted by private parties to eliminate traditional patterns of racial segregation. It is a familiar rule, that a thing may be within the letter of the statute and yet not within the statute, because not within its spirit. Sections 703(a) and (d) must therefore be read against the background of the legislative history of Title VII and the historical context from which the act arose. Examination of these sources makes clear that an interpretation of the sections that forbade all race-conscious affirmative action would bring about an end completely at variance with the purpose of the statute and must be rejected.

Congress's primary concern in enacting the prohibition against racial discrimination in Title VII was the plight of the Negro in our economy. Before 1964, blacks were largely relegated to unskilled and semi-skilled jobs. Because of automation the number of such jobs was rapidly decreasing. As a consequence the relative position of the Negro worker was steadily worsening. Congress feared that the goal of the Civil Rights Act—the integration of blacks into the mainstream of American society—could not be achieved unless this trend were reversed. Accordingly, it was clear to Congress that the crux of the problem was to open employment opportunities for Negroes in occupations which have traditionally been closed to them, and it was to this problem that Title VII's prohibition against racial discrimination in employment was primarily addressed.

Given this legislative history, we cannot agree with Weber that Congress intended to prohibit the private sector from taking effective steps to accomplish the goal that Congress designed Title VII to achieve. It would be ironic indeed if a law triggered by a nation's concern over centuries of racial injustice and intended to improve the lot of those who had been excluded from the American dream for so long, constituted the first legislative prohibition of all voluntary, private, race-conscious efforts to abolish traditional patterns of racial segregation and hierarchy.

Judgment reversed in favor of Kaiser and the union.

Maxims   Maxims are general rules of thumb employed in statutory interpretation. There are many maxims, and courts tend to use them or ignore them at their discretion. One example of a maxim is the *ejusdem generis* rule, which says that when general words follow words of a specific, limited meaning, the general language should be limited to things of the same class as those specifically stated. Suppose that the hypothetical pollution statute quoted earlier listed 32 types of gas-powered vehicles and ended with the words "and other motorized passenger or cargo vehicles." Here, *ejusdem generis* would probably dictate that battery-powered vehicles not be included.

Limits on Courts

From the preceding discussion, you might think that anything goes when courts decide common law cases or interpret statutes. However, many factors discourage courts from adopting a completely freewheeling approach. Due to their legal training and mental makeup, judges tend to respect established precedents and the will of the legislature. Many courts issue written opinions, which expose judges to academic and professional criticism. Trial court judges may be discouraged from innovation by the fear of being overruled by a higher court. Because those higher courts contain several judges, disagreements at this level may cancel each other out, or be moderated in the search for compromise. Finally, certain political factors inhibit judges. For example, some judges are elected, and even judges with lifetime tenure can sometimes be removed.

ETHICAL AND PUBLIC POLICY CONCERNS

1. What might be considered troubling about the result in the *Rochin* case presented in this chapter? (Hint: consult any poll in which Americans identify what they regard as the country's most serious problems.) Modern ethical theory sometimes distinguishes *deontological* ethical theories from *teleological* ethical theories. In their extreme forms, deontological theories say that certain actions are right or wrong and should be pursued or avoided, *no matter what the consequences of doing so.* Teleological theories, on the other hand, generally assess the moral worth of actions *in terms of their consequences.* Which of these approaches best describes the Supreme Court's decision in *Rochin*?

2. Earlier in this chapter, we quoted Justice Holmes's statement that "[t]he first requirement of a sound body of law is, that it should correspond with the actual feelings and demands of the community, whether right or wrong." This statement can be read as asserting that the law should adapt to reflect prevailing moral views, whatever they happen to be. What is good about such an approach to the law and to lawmaking? What is bad about it?

3. Legal positivists often take the position that even morally bad laws are still law and that such laws (or some of them, at least) should still be enforced and obeyed. What *moral* arguments can you make for this position?

SUMMARY

There are at least two ways to answer the question, "What is law?" One is to list and describe all the types of rules typically regarded as law in a particular society. In the United States, these rules are: constitutions, statutes, common law, equity, administrative regulations, administrative decisions, ordinances, treaties, and executive orders. These various types of law also may be classified as: (1) criminal or civil, (2) substantive or procedural, and (3) public or private.

Another way to answer the "What is law?" question is to attempt an abstract definition of law in general. The various efforts to provide such a definition are called *schools of jurisprudence*. The most important jurisprudential schools are *legal positivism* (which defines law as the command of a recognized political authority and excludes morality from its definition), *natural law* (which regards morality as an essential component of law and often claims that bad laws are not law), *American legal realism* (which defines law as what public decisionmakers do), and *sociological jurisprudence* (a term uniting various approaches that view law in a broad social context).

Another way to look at law is to consider the *functions* it performs. Among the law's many functions are peacekeeping, promoting individual freedom by checking government power, facilitating planning, promoting economic growth, furthering social justice, and protecting the environment. These functions can obviously conflict with one another in particular cases.

This text states the most important legal rules affecting business by describing them as a series of blackletter commands. However, this approach sometimes gives the law a false appearance of certainty, precision, stability, and predictability. Examining the reasoning processes that courts use in deciding common law cases and in interpreting statutes helps dispel this misleading impression. The doctrine of *stare decisis* used in deciding common law cases seems to compel the courts to follow the rules announced in similar prior cases. However, because it allows judges to distinguish these cases and effectively create new rules of law to govern the present case, *stare decisis* actually permits flexibility and change.

Even though statutes seem to have the certainty, precision, and stability lacking in judge-made law, legislation is often ambiguous as stated or applied. The different techniques of statutory interpretation help courts to deal with such situations. When the words of the statute have a clear, accepted meaning, some courts simply follow that meaning under the *plain meaning rule*. When the statutory language is ambiguous (or perhaps even when it is plain), courts resort to *legislative history*. They may use the many legislative history sources to determine both the legislative *intent* (some legislative conclusion about the meaning of particular words) or the legislative *purpose* (the aim, end, or object of the statute). Usually, moreover, the courts are bound to follow *prior interpretations* giving statutory language a particular meaning. On occasion, finally, courts may read a statute in light of certain *general public purposes*, or may seek assistance from the many *maxims* of statutory construction.

APPENDIX
Reading and Briefing Cases

In this chapter and most other chapters of the text, you encounter cases—the judicial opinions accompanying actual court decisions. These cases are highly edited versions of their much longer originals. What follows are a few explanations and pointers to assist you in studying these cases.

1. Each case has a *case name* that includes at least some of the parties to the case. Because the order of the parties sometimes changes when a case is appealed, do not assume that the first party listed is the plaintiff (the party suing) and the second the defendant (the party being sued). Also, because some cases have many plaintiffs and/or many defendants, the parties discussed in the court's opinion sometimes differ from those found in the case name. This is true of the *Weber* case, for example.

2. Each case also has a *citation*, which includes the volume and page number of the legal reporter in which the full case can be found, as well as the year the case was decided. The *Weber* case, for instance, begins on page 193 of volume 443 of the United States Reports (the official reporter for U.S. Supreme Court decisions), and was decided in 1979. (Each of the many different legal reporters has its own abbreviation, and they are too numerous for inclusion here.) In the parenthesis accompanying the date, we also give you some information about the court that decided the case. For example: "U.S. Sup. Ct." is the United States Supreme Court, "3d Cir." is the U.S. Court of Appeals for the Third Circuit, "S.D.N.Y." is the U.S. District Court for the Southern District of New York, "Minn. Sup. Ct." is the Minnesota Supreme Court, and "Mich. Ct. App." is the Michigan Court of Appeals (a Michigan intermediate appellate court). The various kinds of courts are described in the chapter on The Resolution of Private Disputes.

3. At the beginning of each case, there is a statement of the most important facts that gave rise to the case. This *statement of facts* is an edited version of the court's original statement, and almost all the facts it contains are important.

4. Immediately after the statement of facts, we give you a summary of the case's *procedural history*. (The chapter on The Resolution of Private Disputes discusses civil procedure and the Crimes chapter discusses criminal procedure.) Basically, this history tells you how the case arrived at the court whose opinion you are reading.

5. After all this, you reach your major concern: the *body of the court's opinion*. Here, the court typically arrives at the applicable rule(s) of law, and applies them to the facts to reach a conclusion. This is where the various examples of legal reasoning discussed in the latter part of the chapter may come into play. In many cases, the court's discussion of the relevant law is elaborate. It may include a description of prior cases, an examination of legislative history, a discussion of applicable policies, and other relevant considerations. The court's application of the law to the facts usually occurs after it has arrived at the applicable legal rule(s), but also may be intertwined with its legal discussion.

6. At the very end of the case, we complete the procedural history by telling you how this court decided the case. For example, "Judgment reversed in favor of Smith" says that a lower court judgment *against* Smith was reversed on appeal, which means that Smith's appeal was successful and Smith wins.

7. Why are the cases important? Their main function is to provide concrete examples of rules stated in the text. (Frequently, in fact, the text tells you what point or points the case illustrates.) In studying law, it is all too easy to conclude that your task is finished once you have memorized a black letter rule. In real life, however, legal problems rarely present themselves as abstract questions of law; instead, they are implicit in particular situations you encounter or particular actions you take. Without some sense of a legal rule's concrete application, therefore, your knowledge of that rule is incomplete. In addition, the cases help you to understand how courts operate and think.

8. In studying this text, you may find it helpful to "brief" the cases it contains. By doing so, you can enhance your understanding of the cases themselves, the legal rules they discuss, the practical application of those rules, and the decisionmaking processes courts use. There is no one correct way to brief a case, but most good briefs contain the following elements: (1) a short, concise statement of the relevant facts, (2) the case's prior history, (3) the question(s) or issue(s) the court had to decide, (4) the answer(s) to those question(s) (how the issue(s) were resolved), (5) the reasoning the court used to justify its decision, and (6) the final result (who won and who lost and, where relevant, whether the lower court's decision was affirmed or reversed). Using the

terms "P" and "D" for the plaintiff and defendant, a brief of the *Weber* case might look like this:

United Steelworkers v. Weber (p. 18)

Facts: The Ds here were a private employer and a union that had voluntarily established a craft training program through a collective bargaining agreement. The procedures for selecting the program's trainees favored black workers over white workers by basing entry on seniority but providing that at least 50 percent of the new trainees had to be black until the black percentage in the program approximated the black percentage of the local labor force. P, a white worker who was denied access to the program, would have qualified had the racial preference not existed.

History: P sued the Ds under Title VII of the 1964 Civil Rights Act, which expressly forbids employment discrimination on the basis of race. He won in federal district court and the court of appeals affirmed. The Ds appealed to the U.S. Supreme Court.

Issue: Does this voluntary racial preference favoring blacks violate Title VII's ban on racial discrimination in employment?

Answer: No.

Reasoning: Even though Title VII's plain meaning favors P and even though there is a prior interpretation holding that Title VII forbids racial discrimination against both whites and blacks, neither point is decisive here. The reason is that holding for P would frustrate Title VII's purpose. Title VII's legislative history and its historical context make clear that its aim was to integrate blacks into the American mainstream. This was especially true in the area of employment, an area in which blacks were falling behind. Here, the Ds' preference for blacks helped further this purpose because it helped blacks get better jobs, and declaring the preference illegal would have frustrated that purpose.

Result: Court of appeals decision reversed; Ds win.

PROBLEM CASES

1. In which way do administrative regulations resemble statutes? In which way do they differ from statutes?

2. Suppose that Congress passes a federal statute that conflicts with a state constitutional provision. The state argues that the constitutional provision should prevail over the statute because constitutions are a higher, more authoritative kind of law than statutes. Is this argument correct? Why or why not?

3. Suppose that someone objects to the president's promulgation of an executive order by claiming that the U.S. Constitution only gives the president the power to *execute* the laws, not the power to make them. What concept explains the president's power to make law through executive orders? Explain its meaning.

4. State A passes a statute declaring that those who sell heroin are to receive a mandatory 30-year prison sentence. Describe this statute in terms of the three classifications of law stated in the text—criminal/civil, substantive/procedural, and public/private.

5. Nation X is a dictatorship in which one ruler has the ultimate lawmaking power. The ruler issues a statute declaring that certain religious minorities are to be exterminated. An international convocation of jurisprudential scholars meets to discuss the question, "Is Nation X's statute truly law?" What would be the typical natural law answer to this question? What would be the typical legal positivist response? Assume that all of those present at the convocation think that Nation X's statute is morally wrong.

6. Nation Y has enacted positive laws forbidding all abnormal sexual relations between consenting adults. However, the police of Nation Y rarely enforce these laws, and even when they do, prosecutors never bring charges against violators. What observation would American legal realists make about this situation? In order to determine what a believer in natural law would think about these laws, what else would you have to know?

7. Some of the states still have so-called Sunday Closing laws—statutes or ordinances forbidding the conduct of certain business on Sunday. Today, these laws often are not obeyed or enforced. What would an extreme legal positivist tend to think about the duty to enforce and obey such laws? What would a natural law exponent who strongly believes in economic freedom tend to think about this question? What about a natural law adherent who is a Christian religious traditionalist? What *observation* would almost any American legal realist make about Sunday Closing laws? Looking at these laws from a sociological perspective, finally, what social factors help explain their original passage, their relative lack of enforcement today, and their continuance "on the books" despite their lack of enforcement?

8. Although you would not know this from reading the *MacPherson* case in this chapter, two of the cases mentioned there distinguished *Thomas v. Winchester* (the case involving the falsely labeled poison) in a certain way. The courts in *Loop v. Litchfield* (the circular saw case) and *Losee v. Clute* (the steam boiler case) both held that *Thomas v. Winchester* should not apply because in *Thomas,* the thing that caused the injury—a poison—was *by its nature intended to cause harm.* In other words, these courts held that a poison should be treated differently from a circular saw that flew apart, or an exploding steam boiler. If the relevant public policy here is to allow recovery for injuries caused by highly dangerous products, does this distinction make any sense?

9. In 1885, Congress passed a statute stating that "it shall be unlawful for any . . . corporation . . . to . . . in any way assist or encourage the importation or migration of any alien or aliens, any foreigner or foreigners, into the United States . . . under contract or agreement . . . to perform labor or service of any kind in the United States." The legislative history of this statute revealed that it was passed because American businesses were contracting with foreigners to prepay their passage to the United States, in return for the immigrant's agreement to work for low wages for a fixed time period. This practice reduced the bargaining power and wages of American laborers.

The Holy Trinity Church, a corporation, contracted with E. Walpole Warren, a U.S. alien residing in England, for Warren to travel to the United States and become Holy Trinity's rector and pastor. Pursuant to the contract, Warren did so. Which technique of statutory interpretation would you use in arguing that this contract is covered by the statute? Which technique would you use if you were arguing the contrary position?

10. In 1910, the White Slave Traffic Act (usually known as the Mann Act) went into effect. The act was passed by Congress in response to an alleged white slave traffic in which gangs of certain nationalities were said to be forcing or luring American women into prostitution. One portion of the act stated that "any person who shall knowingly transport or cause to be transported . . . any woman or girl for the purpose of prostitution or debauchery, or for any other immoral purpose, . . . shall be deemed guilty of a felony." In 1913, F. Drew Caminetti was indicted for transporting a woman from Sacramento, California, to Reno, Nevada, to be his mistress. Which technique of statutory interpretation would you use in arguing that Caminetti *is* guilty under the Mann Act? Which technique would you use to argue that Caminetti should *not* be guilty under the act?

CHAPTER 2

THE RESOLUTION OF PRIVATE DISPUTES

INTRODUCTION

As we noted in the Nature of Law chapter, one way that the law performs its peacekeeping function is by resolving private disputes. The most important example is the courts' application of substantive legal rules to decide civil cases (lawsuits between private parties).[1] Because the courts play such an important role in enforcing and formulating rules of substantive law, your understanding of business law is incomplete without some knowledge about the various kinds of courts, the cases they can decide, and the procedures under which they operate in civil suits.

The United States has 52 separate court systems—a federal system, plus a system for each state and the District of Columbia. After noting some self-imposed limits on the kinds of civil suits courts handle, this chapter describes the various state and federal courts. Included in this discussion is the *jurisdiction* of these courts, their power to decide certain kinds of cases. Then the chapter examines the *procedures* courts follow in civil cases. In-

creasingly, however, private disputes are being resolved outside the formal court system. Thus, the chapter concludes by treating some of the most important methods of *alternative dispute resolution*.

SELF-IMPOSED LIMITS ON COURTS IN CIVIL CASES

At the end of the chapter on the nature of law, we listed some factors that restrict the courts' ability to make law in any fashion they might desire. Here, we consider some doctrines through which the courts *limit themselves* to civil suits involving *real disputes*. Although these doctrines have constitutional dimensions, they mainly have been formulated by the courts and thus are largely self-imposed. They might be summed up by the following proposition: *courts only decide genuine, existing "cases or controversies" between real parties with tangible opposing interests in the lawsuit.*

Thus, courts usually do not issue *advisory opinions* on abstract legal questions presented by the parties if those questions are not part of a real dispute, and do not decide *feigned controversies* concocted by the parties to get answers to such questions. In addition, courts may refuse to rule on disputes that are insufficiently *ripe* because they have not matured into a genuine controversy

---

[1] On the distinctions between civil law and criminal law, and between procedural law and substantive law, see the Nature of Law chapter. Note that the government may sometimes be a party to a civil suit.

in which the parties have real interests at stake. They also refuse to decide disputes that are *moot* because there is no longer a real controversy between the parties and a judicial decision would have no tangible consequences for those parties. Expressing many of these ideas, finally, is the doctrine of *standing to sue*, which generally requires that the party suing have some fairly direct, tangible, and substantial stake in the outcome of the suit.[2]

Despite all these doctrines, however, state and federal *declaratory judgment* statutes enable the courts to determine the parties' rights, legal status, and other legal relations even though their controversy has not advanced to the point where harm has occurred and legal relief may be necessary. These statutes enable parties to determine their legal rights and duties without taking action that could expose them to legal liability. Where one party to a contract thinks that she is not obligated to perform it, for example, she may decide to seek a declaratory judgment on the question rather than break the contract and risk a lawsuit by the other party. For the most part, though, declaratory judgment statutes are applied only when the parties' dispute is sufficiently advanced to constitute an actual case or controversy.

STATE COURTS AND THEIR JURISDICTION

Courts of Limited Jurisdiction

Minor criminal matters and civil controversies involving small amounts of money are frequently decided in *courts of limited jurisdiction* (also known as courts of inferior or special jurisdiction). Common examples include municipal courts, justice of the peace courts, and small claims courts. Courts of limited jurisdiction often handle a large volume of cases. In these courts, the procedures normally are informal, the presiding judicial officer may not be a lawyer, and the parties may argue their own cases. Also, courts of limited jurisdiction usually are not courts of record; that is, they ordinarily do not keep a transcript of the testimony and proceedings. For this reason, appeals from their decisions require a new trial (a trial *de novo*) in a court of record such as a trial court.

---

[2] Standing requirements appear in a number of different situations and are formulated in various ways. For an example, see the discussion of standing in the antitrust context in The Sherman Act chapter.

Trial Courts

Courts of limited jurisdiction perform the basic tasks involved in the resolution of any legal controversy: finding the relevant facts, identifying the appropriate rule(s) of law, and combining the facts and the law to reach a decision. State trial courts perform the same functions, but differ from inferior courts in at least three ways. First, they are not governed by the limits on civil damages awarded or criminal penalties imposed that govern courts of limited jurisdiction. Thus, cases involving significant dollar amounts or major criminal penalties generally begin at the trial court level. Second, trial courts keep detailed records of their proceedings. Third, the trial court judge almost always is a lawyer. The trial court's fact-finding function may be handled by the judge or by a jury. Determination of the applicable law is always the judge's responsibility.

States usually have one trial court for each county. It may be called a circuit, superior, district, county, or common pleas court. Trial courts often have civil and criminal divisions. They also may contain divisions or special courts set up to hear particular matters—for example, domestic relations courts, probate courts, and juvenile courts.

State Appeals Courts

In general, state appeals (or appellate) courts only decide *legal* questions. Their judges do not make factual findings and they have no juries. Thus, although appellate courts can correct legal errors made by the trial judge, they generally accept the trial court's findings of fact. Appellate courts also may hear appeals from state administrative agency decisions. Some states have only one appeals court (usually called the supreme court), while others also have an intermediate appellate court. As Figure 1 illustrates, this court sits between the trial court and the state's highest court. Appeals from decisions of the state's highest court sometimes are heard by the U.S. Supreme Court.

State Court Jurisdiction and Venue

The party who sues in a civil case (the plaintiff) cannot sue the defendant (the party being sued) in any court he chooses. For the suit to proceed, the chosen court must have **jurisdiction** over the case. Jurisdiction is a court's power to hear a case and to issue a decision binding on the parties. In order to render a binding decision in a civil case, a state court must have *both*: (1) subject-matter jurisdiction and (2) *either* in personam jurisdiction *or*

FIGURE 1   An Illustrative State Court System

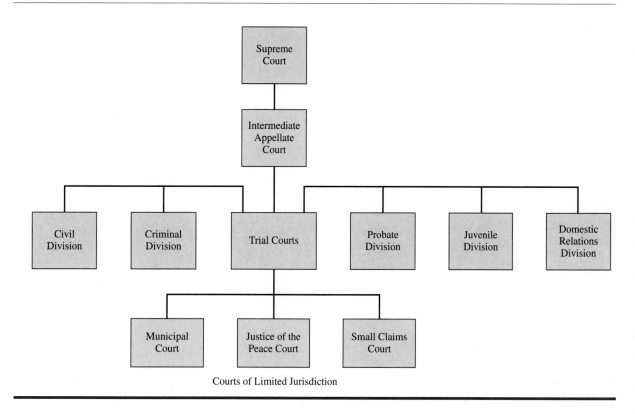

Courts of Limited Jurisdiction

in rem jurisdiction.[3] Even if the court chosen by the plaintiff has the necessary jurisdiction, it also must meet the state's **venue** requirements in order for the suit to proceed there.

Subject-Matter Jurisdiction   **Subject-matter jurisdiction** is the court's power to decide the *type* of controversy involved in the case. Criminal courts, for example, cannot hear civil matters, and a $500,000 suit for breach of contract cannot be pursued in a small claims court.

In Personam Jurisdiction   Even if a court has subject-matter jurisdiction in a civil case, it cannot decide the case if it lacks legal power over either the defendant or the property at issue in the case. The first kind of legal power, called **in personam jurisdiction,** is based on the residence, location, or activities of the defendant. A state court has in personam jurisdiction over defendants who

are citizens or residents of the state (even if situated out-of-state), those who are within the state's borders when the suit is begun by serving process against them (even if nonresidents),[4] and those who consent to the suit (for instance, by entering the state to defend against it).[5]

In addition, many states have enacted "long-arm" statutes giving their courts in personam jurisdiction over certain out-of-state defendants. Under these statutes, nonresident individuals and businesses may become subject to the state's jurisdiction through activities such as doing business within the state, contracting to supply goods or services within the state, and committing a tort (a civil wrong) within the state. As the following *Knowles* case indicates, a state's assertion of in personam jurisdiction over an out-of-state defendant is subject to federal due process standards, and some state long-arm statutes extend the state's in personam jurisdiction as far as federal due process permits.

---

[3] State *criminal* jurisdiction exists when the defendant has allegedly committed acts defined as criminal by state law and has done so within the state.

[4] Service of process is discussed later in this chapter.

[5] In some states, however, out-of-state defendants may make a *special appearance* to challenge the court's jurisdiction without consenting to that jurisdiction.

FIGURE 2   State Court Jurisdiction

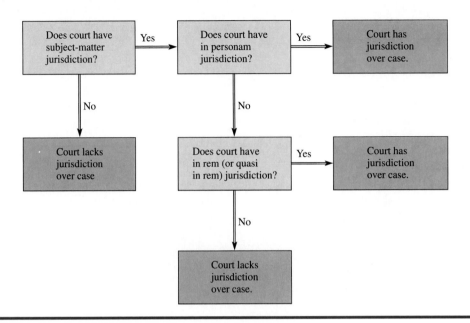

KNOWLES v. MODGLIN

553 So. 2d 563 (Ala. Sup. Ct. 1989)

Albert Knowles, an Alabama truck driver, died of natural causes in California while hauling produce from Alabama to California. After Knowles's body was discovered inside his truck, it was taken to Hems Brothers Mortuaries, where an autopsy was performed by Damon Reference Laboratories at the request of the local coroner. Both Hems and Damon did business in California. After being asked to do so by an Alabama funeral home, Hems prepared Knowles's body for shipment and arranged for it to be flown to his home town. Hems billed the Alabama funeral home for these services and for the price of a casket; it also mailed a statement to Knowles's wife.

Mrs. Knowles did not view her husband's body after its return to Alabama and before its burial, and no one positively identified the body as that of Mr. Knowles during this period. After the burial, Mrs. Knowles received an autopsy report from Damon describing a body that was different from her husband's body. As a result, she had the buried body exhumed and personally viewed it to verify that it actually was her husband's body—which it was. In her examination of the body, Mrs. Knowles found that it had been buried nude, had been packed in cotton in a "disaster pouch," was terribly discolored, and was lying in an awkward position. She described the body as looking like "a monster."

Mrs. Knowles then sued Hems and Damon in an Alabama trial court for the alleged wrongful mishandling of her husband's body. Both Damon and Hems had no contacts with Alabama other than those just described, and each moved to dismiss the claim on the basis that the court lacked in personam jurisdiction. After the court granted Damon's motion but denied Hems's motion, both Mrs. Knowles and Hems appealed to the Alabama Supreme Court.

Houston, Justice.   The issue presented is whether, consistent with the Due Process Clause of the Fourteenth Amendment to the United States Constitution, the defendants have sufficient contacts with this state to make it fair and reasonable to require them to come here to defend against the present action. Due process requires that to subject a defendant to a judgment in personam, he have certain minimum contacts with it such that the maintenance of the suit does not offend traditional notions of fair play and substantive justice. Alabama's long-arm statute has been interpreted to extend the jurisdiction of Alabama courts to the permissible limits of due process.

A relevant factor in a due process analysis is whether the defendant should have reasonably anticipated that he would be sued in the forum state. In determining [this question], it is essential that there be some act by which the defendant purposefully avails itself of the privilege of conducting activities within the forum state, thus invoking the benefits and protections of its laws. Other relevant factors include the burden placed on the defendant, the interest of the forum state in adjudicating the dispute, the plaintiff's interest in obtaining convenient and effective relief, and the interstate judicial system's interest in obtaining the most efficient resolution of the controversy.

The trial court did not err in dismissing Damon for lack of in personam jurisdiction. It does not appear that Damon ever had any contacts with Alabama, with the exception of mailing the autopsy report to Mrs. Knowles. Damon could not have reasonably anticipated that Mr. Knowles's body would make its way to Alabama, that it would not be positively identified by anyone before burial, and that, thereafter, Damon would be haled into an Alabama court to defend against a suit based on a misdescription contained in the autopsy report.

However, Hems established significant contacts with this state by agreeing to prepare and ship Mr. Knowles's body here. In addition, Hems sold Mrs. Knowles a casket, and later solicited payment by mail in Alabama. Hems purposefully availed itself of the privilege of conducting business in Alabama [and] should have reasonably anticipated being summoned to an Alabama court to answer any charges of misconduct in the handling and shipment of Mr. Knowles's body. Furthermore, given the progress in communications and transportation in recent years, we cannot say that it would be unduly burdensome for Hems to defend against the suit in an Alabama court. Considering the nature of Hems's activity, the resultant foreseeability of its being required to defend an action in Alabama, the obvious interest of the plaintiff in obtaining convenient and effective relief, and the relative lack of inconvenience that would be incurred by Hems in appearing and defending, we are convinced that it is fair and reasonable to require Hems to defend against this action in Alabama.

Trial court decision dismissing Mrs. Knowles's suit against Damon for lack of jurisdiction and finding jurisdiction over Hems affirmed.

In Rem Jurisdiction   In rem jurisdiction is based on the fact that *property* is located within the state. It gives state courts the power to determine rights in that property even if the people whose rights are affected are outside the state's in personam jurisdiction. For example, a state court's decision regarding title to land within the state is said to "bind the world."[6]

Venue   Even though a court has jurisdiction over a case, it may lack the power to decide that case because the applicable **venue** requirements have not been met. In general, a court has venue if it is a territorially fair and convenient forum in which to hear the case. Venue requirements are typically set by state statutes, which normally tell the plaintiff the county in which suit must be

---

[6] Another form of jurisdiction, *quasi in rem jurisdiction* or *attachment jurisdiction*, is also based on the location of property within the state. Unlike cases based on in rem jurisdiction, cases based on quasi in rem jurisdiction do not necessarily determine rights in the property itself. Instead, the property is regarded as an extension of the out-of-

state defendant, and this enables the court to decide legal claims unrelated to the property. For example, a plaintiff might attach the defendant's bank account in the state where the bank is located, sue the defendant on a tort or contract claim unrelated to the bank account, and recover the amount of the judgment from the account if the suit is successful.

brought. Such a statute, for instance, might say that a suit concerning land or interests in land must be brought in the county where the land is located, and that other suits must be brought in the county where the defendant resides or is doing business. In certain cases where justice so requires, the defendant may obtain a *change of venue*. This can occur when, for example, a fair trial is impossible within a particular county.

FEDERAL COURTS AND THEIR JURISDICTION

District Courts

In the federal system, lawsuits usually begin in the federal district courts, which are basically federal trial courts. Like state trial courts, the federal district courts have both fact-finding and law-finding functions. As before, fact-finding may be entrusted to either the judge or a jury, and determining the law is the judge's responsibility. Each state has at least one district court, and each district court has at least one judge.

District Court Jurisdiction and Venue   There are many bases of federal district court civil jurisdiction.[7] The two most important are **diversity jurisdiction** and **federal question jurisdiction.** Diversity jurisdiction exists when: (1) the suit is between citizens of different states, and (2) the amount in controversy exceeds $50,000. Diversity jurisdiction also exists in certain suits between citizens of a state and citizens or governments of foreign nations where the amount in controversy exceeds $50,000. Under diversity jurisdiction, a corporation generally is deemed to be a citizen of both the state where it has been incorporated and the state where it has its principal place of business.

Federal question jurisdiction exists when the case arises under the Constitution, laws, or treaties of the United States. Generally, the "arises under" requirement is met when a right created by federal law is a basic part of the plaintiff's case. There is no amount-in-controversy requirement for federal question jurisdiction.

A particular district court's diversity or federal question jurisdiction usually covers only those defendants who would be subject to the in personam jurisdiction of the state where the district court sits. Further limiting the plaintiff's choice of federal district courts are the

---

[7] Federal *criminal* jurisdiction is based on the alleged commission of acts defined as criminal by federal law.

federal system's venue requirements. The basic federal venue statute declares that: (1) where jurisdiction is based *solely* on diversity, suit may be brought only in the district where all plaintiffs or all defendants reside, or where the claim arose; and (2) where jurisdiction is not based solely on diversity, suit may be brought only in the district where all defendants reside or where the claim arose. In addition, many special federal venue provisions govern specific cases.

Concurrent Jurisdiction and Removal   The federal district courts have *exclusive jurisdiction* over some matters: for example, patent and copyright cases. This means that such cases must be heard in federal court. Often, however, they have *concurrent jurisdiction* with state courts; here, both state and federal courts have jurisdiction over the case. For example, a plaintiff may be able to assert state court in personam jurisdiction over an out-of-state defendant or may sue in a federal district court under that court's diversity jurisdiction. Also, a state court may decide a case involving a federal question if it has jurisdiction over that case. If concurrent jurisdiction is present and the plaintiff opts for a state court, the defendant may be able to *remove* the case to a federal district court. The case, of course, must be one over which the district court would have had jurisdiction if the plaintiff had sued there.

Specialized Courts

The federal court system also includes certain specialized federal courts, including the Claims Court (which hears claims against the United States), the Court of International Trade (which is concerned with tariff, customs, and other international trade matters), the Bankruptcy Courts (which operate as adjuncts of the district courts), and the Tax Court (which reviews certain IRS determinations). Usually, the decisions of these courts can be appealed to one or more of the federal courts of appeals.

Courts of Appeals

Like state intermediate appellate courts, the U.S. courts of appeals generally do not have a fact-finding function and review only the legal conclusions reached by lower federal courts. As Figure 3 illustrates, there are 13 federal courts of appeals: 11 organized territorially into circuits covering several states each, one for the District of Columbia, and the Court of Appeals for the Federal Circuit.

FIGURE 3   The Thirteen Federal Judicial Circuits

First Circuit (*Boston, Mass.*) Maine, Massachusetts, New Hampshire, Puerto Rico, Rhode Island

Second Circuit (*New York, N.Y.*) Connecticut, New York, Vermont

Third Circuit (*Philadelphia, Pa.*) Delaware, New Jersey, Pennsylvania, Virgin Islands

Fourth Circuit (*Richmond, Va.*) Maryland, North Carolina, South Carolina, Virginia, West Virginia

Fifth Circuit (*New Orleans, La.*) Louisiana, Mississippi, Texas

Sixth Circuit (*Cincinnati, Ohio*) Kentucky, Michigan, Ohio, Tennessee

Seventh Circuit (*Chicago, Ill.*) Illinois, Indiana, Wisconsin

Eighth Circuit (*St. Louis, Mo.*) Arkansas, Iowa, Minnesota, Missouri, Nebraska, North Dakota, South Dakota

Ninth Circuit (*San Francisco, Calif.*) Alaska, Arizona, California, Guam, Hawaii, Idaho, Montana, Nevada, Northern Mariana Islands, Oregon, Washington

Tenth Circuit (*Denver, Colo.*) Colorado, Kansas, New Mexico, Oklahoma, Utah, Wyoming

Eleventh Circuit (*Atlanta, Ga.*) Alabama, Florida, Georgia

District of Columbia Circuit (*Washington, D.C.*)

Federal Circuit (*Washington, D.C.*)

Except for the Court of Appeals for the Federal Circuit, the most important function of the U.S. courts of appeals is to hear appeals from decisions of the federal district courts. Appeals from a district court ordinarily are taken to the court of appeals for that district court's region. Appeals from the District Court for the Southern District of New York, for example, go to the Second Circuit Court of Appeals. The courts of appeals also hear appeals from the Tax Court and from many administrative agency and Bankruptcy Court decisions. The Court of Appeals for the Federal Circuit hears a wide variety of specialized appeals, including some patent and trademark matters, Claims Court decisions, and decisions by the Court of International Trade.

The U.S. Supreme Court

The U.S. Supreme Court is basically an appellate court, and, like all such courts, is limited to questions of law when it decides appeals. Most of the appeals considered by the Supreme Court come from the federal courts of appeals and the highest state courts.[8] Today, most appealable decisions from these courts fall within the Supreme Court's *certiorari* jurisdiction, under which the Court has discretion whether or not to hear the appeal. In fact, the Court hears only a small percentage of the appeals coming to it through its certiorari jurisdiction. In such cases, the Court is said to "grant certiorari" or "grant cert." When the Court declines to hear the appeal, it "denies certiorari" or "denies cert."

Virtually all cases coming from the federal courts of appeals are within the Court's discretionary certiorari jurisdiction. Cases appealed from the highest state courts are within the certiorari jurisdiction when: (1) the validity of any treaty or federal statute has been questioned; (2) the validity of any state statute is questioned on the basis that it is repugnant to federal law; or (3) any title, right, privilege, or immunity is claimed under federal law. As a general proposition, the Supreme Court

---

[8] There are, however, certain situations in which the Supreme Court will hear appeals directly from the federal district courts.

FIGURE 4   A Simplified Model of the State and Federal Court Systems

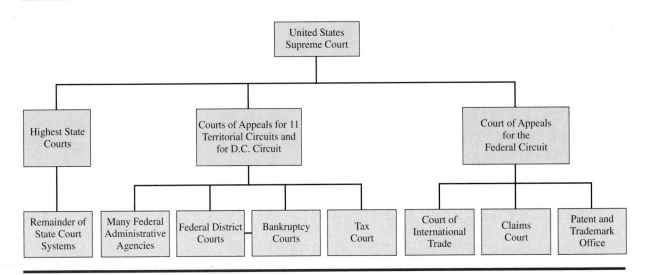

defers to the highest state courts on questions of state law, and does not hear appeals from those courts if the case involves such questions alone.

In certain fairly rare situations, finally, the U.S. Supreme Court possesses *original jurisdiction*, which means that it basically acts as a trial court. The Supreme Court has *original and exclusive* jurisdiction over all controversies between two or more states. It has *original*, but not exclusive, jurisdiction over cases involving foreign ambassadors, ministers, and like parties; controversies between the United States and a state; and cases where a state proceeds against citizens of another state or against aliens.

CIVIL PROCEDURE

Introduction

Civil procedure is the body of legal rules governing the conduct of a trial court case between private parties.[9] Much of this law is complex and technical, and it varies according to the jurisdiction[10] in question. Thus, the fol-

lowing presentation is only a general summary of the most widely accepted rules governing civil cases in state trial courts and the federal district courts. Knowledge of these basic procedural matters is useful if you or your employer become involved in a civil controversy. Such knowledge also helps you to understand the cases that appear throughout this text. Figure 5 presents the major steps through which the normal civil case proceeds and the most significant motions the parties (or *litigants*) can make at each step.

The Adversary System

In many of the stages and motions presented in Figure 5 and described below, the *adversary system* is at work. Through their attorneys, the litigants present contrary positions of fact or law before a theoretically impartial judge and possibly a jury. To win a civil case, the plaintiff must prove each element of his claim by a *preponderance of the evidence*.[11] To do this, the plaintiff must show that the greater weight of the evidence—by *credibility*, not quantity—supports the existence of each element. In other words, the plaintiff must convince the factfinder that the existence of each factual element is more probable than its nonexistence. Thus, the lawyers

---

[9] Criminal procedure is discussed in the Crimes chapter. Also, the procedures used in administrative hearings are discussed in the Administrative Agencies chapter.

[10] In the discussion that follows, the term *jurisdiction* refers to one of the 50 states, the District of Columbia, or the federal government.

[11] However, as discussed in the Crimes chapter, in a criminal case the government must prove the elements of the alleged crime *beyond a reasonable doubt*.

FIGURE 5   The Most Important Stages and Motions in Civil Litigation (Appeals Assumed)

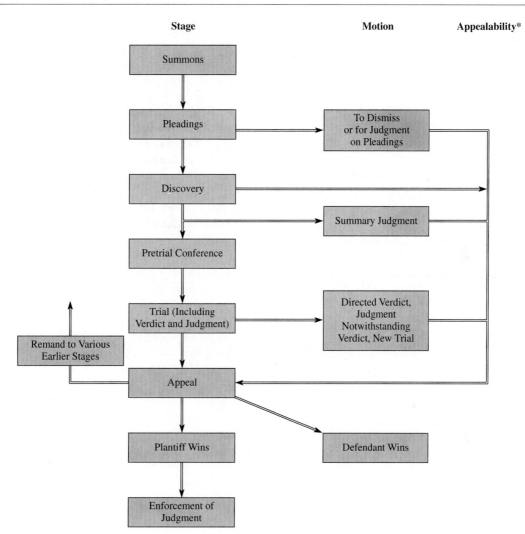

*As discussed later in the chapter, many other trial court rulings also are appealable.

for each party continually present their client's version of the facts, try to convince the judge or jury that this version is true, and attempt to rebut conflicting factual allegations by the other party. Also, the attorneys seek to persuade the judge that their interpretations of the law are correct.

The adversary system reflects the familiar American belief that truth is best discovered through the presentation of competing ideas. Supporters of the adversary system believe that allowing the litigants to make competing arguments of fact and law gives the judge and jury the best chance of making accurate determinations

because it enables both the presentation and the criticism of all relevant arguments. Critics of the adversary system contend that rather than promoting the disinterested search for truth, it encourages the parties to employ incomplete, distorted, and even false arguments if such arguments help them win the case. Defenders of the adversary system reply that it should weed out such arguments because they are attacked by the other party and because an impartial judge is present. This weeding-out process, however, may not work if one or both parties lack competent counsel. Sometimes, for example, the adversary system's competition of ideas is unequal because one litigant has superior resources and thus can obtain better representation.

Service of the Summons

The function of the **summons** is to notify the defendant that she is being sued. The summons typically names the plaintiff and states the time within which the defendant must enter an *appearance* in court (usually through her attorney). In most jurisdictions, it is accompanied by a copy of the plaintiff's complaint (which is described below).

The summons is usually delivered, or served, to the defendant by an appropriate public official after the plaintiff has filed his complaint with the court. To ensure that the defendant is properly notified of the suit, statutes, court rules, and constitutional due process guarantees set standards for proper service of the summons in particular cases. For example, personal delivery of the summons to the defendant almost always meets these standards, and many jurisdictions also permit the summons to be left at the defendant's home or place of business. Service to corporations may often be accomplished by delivery of the summons to the firm's general or managing agent. Many state long-arm statutes permit out-of-state defendants to be served by registered mail. Although inadequate service of process may sometimes defeat the plaintiff's claim, in most jurisdictions the defendant must make her objection early or it will be waived.

The Pleadings

The term **pleadings** refers to the documents that the parties file with the court when they first state their claims and defenses. The pleadings include the complaint, the answer, and (in some jurisdictions) the reply.

The Complaint   The **complaint** fully states the plaintiff's claim in separate, numbered paragraphs. It must contain sufficient facts to show that the plaintiff is entitled to some legal relief and to give the defendant reasonable notice of the nature of the plaintiff's claim. The complaint must also state the remedy requested by the plaintiff.

The Answer   Within a designated time after the complaint has been served, the defendant normally files an **answer** to the complaint. The answer responds to the plaintiff's complaint paragraph by paragraph. Usually, the answer admits the allegations of each paragraph, de-

nies them, or states that the defendant lacks the information to assess the truth or falsity of the allegations (which has much the same effect as a denial).

The answer may also include an **affirmative defense** to the claim asserted in the complaint. An affirmative defense is a rule of law enabling the defendant to win the case even if all the allegations in the plaintiff's complaint are true and, by themselves, would entitle the plaintiff to recover. For example, suppose that the plaintiff bases her suit on a contract that she alleges the defendant has breached (broken). The defendant's answer may admit or deny the existence of the contract or the assertion that the defendant breached it. In addition, the answer may present facts that, if proven, would show that the defendant has an affirmative defense because the plaintiff's fraud induced the defendant to enter the contract.

In certain circumstances, the answer may also contain a **counterclaim.** A counterclaim is a *new* claim by the defendant arising from the matters stated in the complaint. Unlike an affirmative defense, it is not merely an attack on the plaintiff's claim, but is the *defendant's* attempt to obtain legal relief. In addition to using fraud as an affirmative defense to a plaintiff's contract claim, for example, a defendant might counterclaim for damages caused by that fraud.

The Reply   In some jurisdictions, the plaintiff is allowed or required to respond to an affirmative defense or a counterclaim by making a **reply.** The reply is the plaintiff's point-by-point response (a kind of answer) to the new matters raised in the affirmative defense or counterclaim. However, many jurisdictions do not allow a reply to an affirmative defense; instead, the defendant's new allegations are automatically denied. Usually, though, a plaintiff who wishes to contest a counterclaim must reply to it.

The Functions of the Pleadings   Traditionally, the main function of the pleadings has been to define and limit the questions to be decided at later stages of the case. Only those issues raised in the pleadings have been considered part of the case; points omitted from the pleadings have been excluded from further consideration; and few, if any, amendments to the pleadings have been permitted. Also, litigants have usually been bound to allegations admitted in the pleadings; only those allegations that have not been admitted have been regarded as in dispute between them. In addition, there have been many technical pleading rules whose violation could cause a party to lose a case before a decision on the merits.

Many jurisdictions retain some of these rules. Over time, however, the main purpose behind pleading rules has shifted from defining and limiting the questions to be resolved in the case to affording the parties notice of each other's claims. Accompanying this shift have been a greater tendency to decide cases on their merits and a more relaxed attitude toward technical defects in the pleadings. Amendments to the pleadings, for example, are far more available today than they were in the past. Also, courts sometimes grant such amendments to allow issues not raised in the pleadings to be considered at trial.

Motion to Dismiss

Sometimes, it is evident from the complaint or the pleadings that the plaintiff has no case. In such situations, it is wasteful for the suit to proceed further and it is useful to have a procedural device for disposing of it. This device has various names, but it is commonly called the **motion to dismiss.** This motion is often made after the plaintiff has filed his complaint. A similar motion allowed by some jurisdictions, the **motion for judgment on the pleadings,** normally occurs after the pleadings have been completed.

The motion to dismiss may be used for several purposes—for example, attacking inadequate service of process; or, as in the earlier *Knowles* case, attacking the court's jurisdiction. The most important type of motion to dismiss, however, is the motion to dismiss for failure to state a claim upon which relief can be granted, sometimes called the **demurrer.** This motion basically says "So what?" to the factual allegations in the complaint. It asserts that the plaintiff cannot recover even if all of these allegations are true, because there is no rule of law entitling him to win on those facts. Suppose that Potter sues Davis on the theory that Davis's bad breath is a form of "olfactory pollution" entitling Potter to recover damages. Potter's complaint describes Davis's breath and the distress it causes Potter in great detail. Even if all of Potter's factual allegations are true, Davis's motion to dismiss almost certainly will succeed. Thus, Davis will win the case, for there is no rule of law allowing a civil recovery for bad breath. If the defendant's motion to dismiss fails, however, the case proceeds to the steps that follow.

Discovery

Litigants sometimes lack the factual information to prove their cases when the suit begins. To assist them in preparing their arguments and to narrow and clarify the issues to be resolved at trial, all jurisdictions permit the parties to undertake extensive **discovery** of relevant information. The most common types of discovery are **depositions** (oral examinations of a party or a party's witness by the other party's attorney), **interrogatories** (written questions directed to a party, answered in writing, and signed under oath), **requests for documents and other evidence** (including examinations of the other party's files or records), **physical and mental examinations** (which are important in personal injury cases), and **requests for admissions** (one party's written demand that the other party agree to certain statements of fact or law). The permissible limits of discovery are set by the trial judge, whose rulings are controlled by the procedural law of the jurisdiction. In an effort to make civil litigation less of a battle of wits or a sporting event and more of a disinterested search for the truth, many jurisdictions have liberalized their discovery rules to give parties freer access to all relevant facts.

The applicable state or federal law of evidence determines whether or when discovery findings are admissible trial evidence. However, almost all jurisdictions allow some discovery findings to be employed at trial for certain purposes. Depositions, for instance, may sometimes be used as "paper testimony" from dead or distant witnesses, or to attack the credibility of a witness whose trial testimony differs from statements she made at the deposition.

Summary Judgment

The court's consideration of a motion for **summary judgment** might be described as a minitrial or a trial by affidavit. The summary judgment is a device for disposing of relatively clear cases without a trial. To prevail, the party moving for a summary judgment must show that: (1) there is no genuine issue of material (legally significant) fact, and (2) he is entitled to judgment as a matter of law. A summary judgment hearing differs from the judge's decision on a demurrer because it involves factual determinations. The evidence for such determinations includes the pleadings, discovery information, and affidavits (signed and sworn statements regarding matters of fact). The moving party tries to satisfy the first element of the test by using such evidence to convince the judge that there is no genuine question about any significant fact. If the moving party's arguments are persuasive, he must still meet the second element of the test by convincing the judge that, given the established facts, the applicable law directs that he win.

Either or both parties may move for a summary judgment. If the court rules in favor of either party, that party wins the case. If no party's motion for summary judgment is granted, the case proceeds to trial. The judge may also grant a partial summary judgment, which settles some issues in the case but leaves the others to be decided at trial.

The Pretrial Conference

Depending on the jurisdiction, a **pretrial conference** may be either mandatory or called at the discretion of the trial judge. At this conference, the judge meets informally with the attorneys for both litigants. The judge may attempt to get the attorneys to *stipulate*, or agree to, the resolution of certain issues to simplify the trial. He may also encourage them to get their clients to *settle* the case by coming to an agreement that eliminates the need for a trial. Both efforts are intended to help clear the increasingly congested calendars of most civil courts. If the case is not settled, the judge enters a pretrial order including all the attorneys' stipulations and other agreements. Ordinarily, the terms of this order bind the parties throughout the remainder of the case.

The Trial

Once the case has been through discovery and has survived any pretrial motions, it is set for trial. The trial may be before a judge alone, in which case the judge makes separate findings of fact and law before issuing the court's judgment. But if the right to a jury trial exists and either party demands one, the jury handles the fact-finding function, with the resolution of legal questions still entrusted to the judge.[12] At a pretrial jury screening process known as *voir dire*, most jurisdictions: (1) allow biased potential jurors to be removed *for cause*, and (2) give the attorney for each party a certain number of *peremptory challenges* that allow him to remove potential jurors without *any* cause.

The Basic Scenario   The usual trial scenario is much the same whether the trial is before a judge alone or before both a judge and a jury. The attorneys for the plaintiff and the defendant typically make opening statements explaining what they intend to prove. After this, the plaintiff's witnesses and other evidence are introduced and these witnesses are cross-examined by the defendant's attorney. This may be followed by the plaintiff's re-direct examination of his witnesses, and perhaps by the defendant's re-cross-examination of those same witnesses. Then, using the same procedures, the defendant's evidence is presented. Throughout each side's presentation, the opposing attorney may object to the admission of certain evidence. Using the law of evidence, the judge then decides whether the challenged proof is admissible. After the plaintiff and defendant have completed their initial presentations of evidence, each is allowed to offer evidence rebutting the other's evidence. Once all of the evidence has been presented, each attorney makes a closing argument summarizing her position. In nonjury trials, the judge then makes findings of fact and law, renders judgment, and states the relief to which the plaintiff is entitled if the plaintiff is victorious.

Jury Trials   Jury trials differ in some respects from trials before the judge alone. At the end of a jury trial, the judge issues a *charge* or *instruction* to the jury. The charge sets out the rules of law applicable to the case. The judge may also summarize the evidence for the jury. Then, the jury is supposed to make the necessary factual determinations, apply the law to these, and arrive at a **verdict** on which the court's **judgment** is based.

The most common verdict is the **general verdict,** which only requires that the jury declare which party wins and the relief (if any) to be awarded. The general verdict gives the jury freedom to ignore the judge's charge and follow its own inclinations, for the jury need not state its factual findings or its application of the law to those findings. Defenders of the general verdict argue that it allows the jury to soften the law's rigors by bringing common sense and community values to bear on the case. But it also weakens the rule of law and allows juries to commit injustices. The **special verdict** is one response to this problem. Here, the jury only makes specific findings of fact, and the judge then applies the law to these findings. The decision whether to utilize a special verdict usually is within the trial judge's discretion.

Directed Verdict   The freedom that the general verdict gives the jury is a two-edged sword, and the American legal system is ambivalent about the jury. While

---

[12] The rules governing availability of a jury trial are largely beyond the scope of this text. The U.S. Constitution guarantees a jury trial in federal court suits "at common law" whose amount exceeds $20, and most of the states have similar constitutional provisions. Also, Congress and the state legislatures may allow jury trials in a variety of other cases.

granting the jury great power, the system also establishes devices for limiting that power. One of these devices, the motion for a **directed verdict,** basically takes the case away from the jury and gives a judgment to one party before the jury gets a chance to decide. The motion can be made by either party, and it usually occurs after the other (nonmoving) party has presented his evidence. The moving party basically asserts that, even when read most favorably to the other party, the evidence leads to only one result and need not be considered by the jury. Courts differ on the test governing a motion for a directed verdict: some deny the motion if there is *any* evidence favoring the nonmoving party, while others deny the motion only if there is *substantial* evidence favoring the nonmoving party. Under the former test, at least, it is difficult for the moving party to succeed.

Judgment Notwithstanding the Verdict   On occasion, the case is taken away from the jury and judgment is entered for a party even *after* the jury has reached a verdict *against* that party. The device for doing so is the motion for **judgment notwithstanding the verdict** (also known as the judgment *non obstante veredicto* or the judgment n.o.v.). Some jurisdictions require that, in order to make a motion for judgment n.o.v., the moving party have earlier made a motion for a directed verdict. In any event, the standard used to decide the motion for judgment n.o.v. usually is the same standard that the jurisdiction uses to decide the motion for a directed verdict. For this reason, and because the moving party essentially is asking the court to overturn a jury verdict, litigants may face difficulties when they move for judgment notwithstanding the verdict.

Motion for New Trial   In a wide range of situations that vary among jurisdictions, the losing party can successfully move for a new trial. Acceptable reasons for granting a new trial include errors by the judge during the trial, jury or attorney misconduct, new evidence, or an award of excessive damages to the plaintiff.

CONCEPT REVIEW

THE MAJOR CIVIL MOTIONS COMPARED

Motion	When Typically Made	By Whom Typically Made	Typical Test	Typical Effect if Successful
To Dismiss or for Judgment on the Pleadings	After complaint or pleadings	Defendant	Assuming the facts in the complaint are true, can plaintiff win as a matter of law?	Defendant wins case
For Summary Judgment	Varies; often after discovery	Either party	No genuine issue of material fact and moving party entitled to judgment as a matter of law	Moving party wins case; partial summary judgment also possible
For Directed Verdict	After other party has presented evidence at trial	Either party	Two versions. Moving party loses if: (1) *any* evidence favoring nonmoving party; or (2) *substantial* evidence favoring nonmoving party	Moving party wins case
For Judgment Notwithstanding Verdict	After adverse jury verdict	Losing party	Same test jurisdiction uses for directed verdict	Moving party wins case
For New Trial	After adverse judgment or jury verdict	Losing party	Wide range of possible grounds	New trial ordered

Appeal

As you have seen, appellate courts generally consider only alleged errors of law made by the trial court. As Figure 5 indicated earlier in the chapter, among the matters ordinarily considered "legal" and thus appealable are the trial judge's decisions on a motion to dismiss or a motion for judgment on the pleadings, the scope of discovery, a motion for summary judgment, a motion for a directed verdict, a motion for judgment notwithstanding the verdict, and a motion for a new trial. Other matters typically considered appealable include any trial court rulings on service of process, its rulings on the admission of evidence at trial, its legal findings in a nonjury trial, its instruction to the jury in a jury trial, and the damages or other relief awarded. Of course, appellate court decisions on all these matters may be considered by a higher appellate court, if one exists.

Appellate courts may, among other things, *affirm* the trial court's decision, *reverse* it, or affirm one part of the decision and reverse another part. As Figure 5 also suggested, one of three things ordinarily results from the appellate courts' disposition of the appeal: (1) the plaintiff wins the case, (2) the defendant wins the case, or (3) if the case is reversed in whole or in part, it is *remanded* (returned) to the trial court for proceedings not inconsistent with the appellate decision. Which of these results occurs generally depends on the trial court's decision, the party who appealed it, and the way the appellate courts resolved it. For example, if the plaintiff appeals a trial court decision granting the defendant's motion to dismiss and the appellate court(s) affirm that decision, the plaintiff loses. Where an appellate court reverses a trial court verdict and judgment in the defendant's favor, the plaintiff might win outright, or the case might be returned to the trial court for further proceedings not inconsistent with the appellate decision.

Enforcing a Judgment

In this text, you occasionally will see cases where someone was not sued even though he appeared to be liable to the plaintiff, and where another party was sued instead. One possible explanation is that the first party was "judgment-proof": so lacking in assets as to make a civil suit for damages impractical. In other words, a potential defendant's financial condition is an important factor affecting the plaintiff's decision whether or not to sue him. And it also affects a winning plaintiff's ability to actually recover whatever damages she has been awarded.

When the defendant fails to pay as required after losing a civil suit, the winning plaintiff must take steps to enforce the judgment. Ordinarily, the plaintiff obtains a *writ of execution* enabling the sheriff to seize designated property of the defendant and sell it at a judicial sale to satisfy the judgment. A judgment winner may also use a procedure known as *garnishment* to seize property, money, or wages of the defendant that are in the hands of a third party. If the property needed to satisfy the judgment is located in another state, the plaintiff must use the execution or garnishment procedures established by that state. Under the U.S. Constitution, the second state is required to give "full faith and credit" to the judgment of the state where the plaintiff originally sued. Where the court has awarded an equitable remedy such as an injunction, on the other hand, the defendant may be found in contempt of court and subjected to a fine or imprisonment if he fails to obey the court's order.

Class Actions

The preceding review of the stages of a civil case has proceeded as if the plaintiff and the defendant each were a single party. Actually, several plaintiffs and/or defendants can be parties to one lawsuit. Also, each jurisdiction has procedural rules stating when other parties can be *joined* to a suit that begins without them.

One special type of multiparty suit, the **class action,** allows one or more persons to sue on behalf of themselves and all others who have suffered similar harm from substantially the same wrong. Class action suits by, for example, consumers, environmentalists, women, and minorities are now common events. The usual justifications for the class action are that: (1) it allows legal wrongs causing losses to a large number of widely dispersed parties to be fully compensated, and (2) it promotes economy of judicial effort by combining many similar claims into one suit.

The requirements for a class action vary among jurisdictions. The issues addressed by class action statutes include the following: whether there are questions of law and fact common to all members of the alleged class, whether the class is small enough to allow all of its members to join the case as parties rather than use a class action, and whether the plaintiff(s) and their attorney(s) can competently represent the class without conflicts of interest or other forms of unfairness. To protect the individual class member's right to be heard, some jurisdictions have required that unnamed or absent class members be given notice of the suit if this is reasonably possible. The damages awarded in a successful class action are usually apportioned among the entire class. Establishing the total recovery and distributing it to the class, however, pose problems when the class is large, the class members' injuries are indefinite, or some members cannot be identified.

ALTERNATIVE DISPUTE RESOLUTION

Courts are not the only mechanisms for settling civil disputes. Nor are they always the best means of doing so. As the preceding discussion of civil procedure suggests, resolving private disputes through the courts can be a cumbersome, lengthy, and expensive process for litigants. With the advent of a litigious society and the increasing caseloads and delays it has produced, resolving disputes in this fashion also imposes ever-greater *social* costs. For these reasons and others to be discussed later, the various forms of **alternative dispute resolution** (ADR) have assumed increasing importance in recent years.

Some Common Forms of ADR

Not everyone agrees on how to define the term alternative dispute resolution, and new ADR devices are continually emerging. Still, the following methods of dispute resolution can be regarded as forms of ADR.

Settlement   While the settlement of a civil suit is not everyone's idea of an alternative dispute resolution mechanism, it is a very important means of avoiding protracted litigation, one that often represents a sensible compromise for the parties. Many cases settle at some stage in the civil proceedings described previously. The typical settlement agreement is a contract whereby the defendant agrees to pay the plaintiff a certain sum of money, in exchange for the plaintiff's promise to release the defendant from future liability on the claims alleged in his suit.

Arbitration   Arbitration is the submission of a dispute to a nonjudicial third party (the *arbitrator*) who is normally empowered to issue a binding decision on that dispute. Arbitration typically results from the parties' agreement to arbitrate their disputes, but sometimes it is compelled by statute. Such an agreement is usually made before the dispute arises (most often through an *arbitration clause* in a contract), but it can occur after the dispute begins. Today, arbitration is used in a wide variety of situations, including disputes arising under commercial contracts and labor contracts. The arbitrator need not be a lawyer; often, she is a professional who may be expert in the subject matter of the dispute.

Arbitration proceedings normally are less formal than court proceedings, and the arbitrator ordinarily is not required to follow the rules of evidence and procedure governing courts. Also, arbitrators have some freedom to ignore rules of substantive law that would bind a court. The arbitrator's decision, called an *award*, is filed with a court, which will enforce it if necessary. The losing party may object to the arbitrator's award, but the grounds for getting a court to overturn such an award are limited. One example is fraud or other misconduct by the arbitrator.

Court-Annexed Arbitration   This specific form of arbitration does not result from a private agreement. Rather, it is ordered by a judge after a lawsuit has been filed. In jurisdictions that allow court-annexed arbitration, the judge's decision to order it often depends on the subject matter of the dispute and the amount of money at issue. The losing party in a court-annexed arbitration still has the right to a regular trial.

Mediation   In mediation, a neutral third party called the *mediator* helps the parties reach an agreeable, cooperative resolution of their dispute by facilitating communication between them, clarifying their areas of agreement and disagreement, helping them to see each other's viewpoints, suggesting settlement options, and so forth. Unlike arbitrators, mediators cannot make a decision that binds the parties. Mediation most often occurs by agreement of the parties after a dispute has arisen. It is used in a wide variety of situations.

Med/Arb   In this hybrid of meditation and arbitration, the third party first acts as a mediator, and all issues not resolved through mediation are then subjected to binding arbitration. Here, the mediator and the arbitrator may or may not be the same person.

Other ADR Devices   Other ADR methods include: (1) the *minitrial* (an informal, abbreviated, private "trial" before a panel of independent experts and/or an executive from each party, which usually is employed after the initiation of a lawsuit and whose aim is to promote a settlement); (2) the *summary jury trial* (an abbreviated, nonpublic mock jury trial that does not bind the parties unless they so stipulate, and that aims to promote settlement by giving them an idea how they would fare before a real jury); and (3) *private panels* instituted by an industry or an organization to handle claims of certain kinds (e.g., the Better Business Bureau). Also, some formally legal processes are sometimes referred to as ADR devices; examples include small claims courts and the administrative procedures for handling matters such as claims for veterans' benefits or social security benefits.

The Pros and Cons of ADR

Taken collectively, the various forms of ADR have many advantages over litigation before a court. These advantages include:

1. *Quicker resolution of disputes.* This is due mainly to the relative informality of many ADR proceedings.

2. *Lower costs in time, money, and aggravation for the parties.* Again, these benefits flow mainly from the relative informality and speed of many ADR procedures.

3. *Reduced strains on an overloaded court system.*

4. *The possible availability of expert decision makers.* As noted earlier, for example, arbitrators may possess special expertise in the subject matter of the disputes they handle.

5. *Flexibility and consensus-building.* Some ADR methods (e.g., mediation) may help avoid the excessively adversarial climate and tendency toward either-or decisions that characterize formal litigation. Thus, they can promote consensus, compromise solutions by the parties themselves.

6. *Relative privacy.* In general, firms that settle their disputes through ADR rather than litigating them have less need to "air their dirty linen" in public.

As you might suspect, however, ADR also has a number of possible disadvantages. They include:

1. *A tendency to undermine the rule of law.* At its best, the civil law states general norms that are good in themselves, are backed by a wide social consensus, and apply to all the private disputes they cover. ADR decisions, on the other hand, are sometimes ad hoc affairs in which rules of substantive law play little role and precedent even less. Thus, the widespread use of ADR tends to undermine the *generality* and *uniformity* associated with the rule of law.

2. *A diminished role for courts in stating the norms that govern private disputes.* Arbitrators, for example, are often free to downplay the applicable rules of substantive law in making their decisions, which means that court-imposed norms may not govern such decisions. In the American system, however, courts generally are regarded as more legitimate, authoritative, and capable standard setters than private actors like arbitrators.

3. *Inaccurate or biased decisionmaking processes.* One reason for the complexity of the rules of civil procedure and evidence is that they try to give each party the utmost in procedural protection and to ensure that factual determinations are as accurate as possible. The relatively relaxed procedures and evidentiary rules—not to mention the occasional absence of lawyers—in some ADR proceedings may mean that these ends are less likely to be served under ADR.

4. *Second-class justice for the relatively powerless in their disputes with the powerful.* Sometimes, agreements to submit disputes to alternative dispute resolution are buried in complex standard-form contracts drafted by a party with superior size, knowledge, and business sophistication, and are unknowingly agreed to by less knowledgeable parties. Sometimes, too, such clauses compel ADR proceedings before decisionmakers who may be biased in favor of the stronger party.

ETHICAL AND PUBLIC POLICY CONCERNS

1. As you might expect, the preceding arguments against ADR have often come from the legal profession. Are these self-serving arguments? Who stands to lose money and influence if ADR becomes more popular? Assuming that these arguments are self-serving, is this fact alone enough to rebut them?

2. The *Knowles* case presented earlier in this chapter used a style of legal reasoning different from the simple deductive model presented in the Nature of Law chapter. This style might be called *factor-based balancing*, and you will see it again from time to time in this text. Courts using this style of reasoning typically consider several factors when deciding. They assess a particular result in light of each factor, trying to determine whether that result advances or frustrates the values embodied in each factor. Then, they try to assess the overall desirability of that result by weighing its positive and negative effects against each other and determining whether the result has a positive or negative effect on balance. Such determinations naturally vary depending on the facts of the case. In *Knowles*, the decision was easy, because almost all the factors the court considered pulled in the same direction.

What is good about this kind of legal decisionmaking? What is bad about it?

3. Recent debates in the business ethics literature have sometimes stressed the difference between *utilitarian* ethical theories and *deontological rights-based* ethical theories. Utilitarian theories generally argue that we should strive to maximize aggregate satisfaction, and they tend to approve measures that disadvantage particular individuals so long as those measures actually produce maximum *total* satisfaction. Such theories occasionally use social wealth maximization as a rough measure of satisfaction. Deontological rights-based theories generally urge that some rights are so important that they can only be overridden by certain other rights, and *not* by maximum aggregate utility.

Speaking very generally, into which category would many foes of ADR fit? Assume that these people oppose ADR because they feel that due to the looseness and sloppiness of its procedures, it inevitably causes injustices to individuals—injustices that could be avoided were normal court procedures used. Although the widespread use of such procedures costs more money than ADR, they assert, this is of no consequence because basic issues of *justice* are involved.

Speaking very generally, into which category would many proponents of ADR fit? Assume that these people stress the social and economic costs created by the court system and argue that the widespread use of ADR would free money and resources for other purposes, thus making society wealthier. This increase in wealth, they would further contend, easily outweighs the personal suffering caused by whatever injustices ADR permits.

SUMMARY

One of the most important functions performed by the American legal system is the resolution of private disputes. Courts perform this function by deciding civil lawsuits. However, certain judicially created doctrines limit the courts to the resolution of genuine controversies between real parties with tangible opposing interests.

The typical state court system contains the following courts: (1) courts of limited jurisdiction such as justice of the peace courts and municipal courts, (2) trial courts (which resolve questions of law and fact), (3) intermediate appellate courts (which handle appeals from the trial courts' rulings on questions of law), and (4) the supreme court (which handles appeals from lower courts and is the state's highest appellate court). For a state trial court to decide a case, it must have: (1) subject-matter jurisdiction (competence to handle the type of case before it), and (2) *either* in personam jurisdiction (based on the residence, location, or activities of the defendant) *or* some form of in rem jurisdiction (based on the presence of property within the state).

The most important federal courts are: (1) district courts (which resemble state trial courts), (2) courts of appeals (which resemble state intermediate appellate courts), and (3) the U.S. Supreme Court (whose main function is to handle appeals from the lower federal courts and the state supreme courts). The most important bases of district court jurisdiction are *federal question* jurisdiction (requiring an issue of federal law in the plaintiff's case) and *diversity jurisdiction* (requiring that the plaintiff and defendant be citizens of different states and that the amount in controversy exceed $50,000). There are also various specialized federal courts.

The typical procedural steps involved in a civil case before a trial court or a federal district court are: (1) the summons (whose function is to notify the defendant of the suit), (2) the complaint (which states the plaintiff's case), (3) the answer (which responds point-by-point to the complaint), (4) the reply (which "answers" an affirmative defense or a counterclaim in the answer), (5) the motions to dismiss or for judgment on the pleadings (devices for disposing of the case on the basis of the complaint or the pleadings), (6) discovery (a process of pretrial information-gathering), (7) the summary judgment (another device for disposing of the case prior to trial), (8) the pretrial conference, (9) the trial itself, (10) the directed verdict (a device for taking the case away from the jury before it decides), (11) the judgment notwithstanding the verdict (similar to a directed verdict but used after the jury has decided), (12) the motion for a new trial, (13) the trial court's verdict and judgment, (14) the possible appeal of decisions made by the trial court, and (15) the processes by which a winning plaintiff enforces his judgment. The class action, a procedural device of some importance in recent years, permits the consolidation of many similar claims into one suit, thus enabling a plaintiff to represent a larger group.

The courts are not the only means for resolving civil matters, and in recent years the various forms of alternative dispute resolution have become an increasingly important complement to the court system. These include settlement of a court case, arbitration, court-annexed arbitration, mediation, med/arb, and others. ADR processes often offer parties quicker, cheaper, and more flexible resolution of their disputes than normal judicial procedures. But they also suffer from a number of disadvantages.

PROBLEM CASES

1. Marco DeFunis was denied admission to the University of Washington Law School. He sued the law school under the Equal Protection Clause of the U.S. Constitution, alleging that the school preferred minority applicants over better qualified white applicants. While DeFunis's suit was making its way through the Washington state courts, he enrolled at another law school. By the time the case reached the U.S. Supreme Court, DeFunis was about to graduate. The Supreme Court dismissed DeFunis's appeal without deciding his equal protection claims. Why did it decide against DeFunis? Assume that DeFunis's claim included a request that he be admitted to the University of Washington Law School.

2. Peters sues Davis. At trial, Peters's lawyer attempts to introduce certain evidence to help make his case. Davis's attorney objects, and the trial judge refuses to allow the evidence to be admitted. Peters eventually loses the case at the trial court level. He appeals, his attorney arguing that the trial judge's decision not to admit the evidence was erroneous. Davis's attorney argues that the appellate court cannot consider this question, because appellate courts only review errors of *law* (not fact) at the trial court level. Is Davis's attorney correct? Why or why not?

3. Phillips sues Dilks for $500,000 in a state small claims court set up to handle cases where the amount in controversy does not exceed $5,000. The court clearly does not have jurisdiction over the case. What *kind* of jurisdiction is absent here?

4. Dial, a resident of Indiana, vandalizes a parked car in Columbus, Ohio. This action results in harm to the car, and also prevents its owner from using the car for a

period of time. In the meantime, Dial has fled to Indiana and remains there. The owner, an Ohio resident, plans to sue Dial for trespass to personal property, a tort described in the Intentional Torts chapter. He claims $5,000 in damages, and wants to sue either in an Ohio trial court or in a federal district court. Do each of these courts have jurisdiction over the case? Why or why not? Assume for purposes of this problem that: (a) subject-matter jurisdiction is present, (b) Dial has had no other contacts with the state of Ohio, and (c) Ohio has a long-arm statute with all the features described in this chapter.

5. State *two* differences between the motion to dismiss for failure to state a claim upon which relief can be granted (or demurrer) and the motion for summary judgment.

6. In a suit by Pierce against Dodge, the jury has rendered a verdict in favor of Dodge. Pierce and her attorney think that the evidence was overwhelmingly in Pierce's favor. They also have some reason to believe that the jury was bribed by someone connected with Dodge. What *two* motions can Pierce's attorney make at this point in an attempt to overturn the jury's verdict?

7. While driving to work one day, Dember runs over Pearson, causing him severe injuries. Pearson sues Dember in a state trial court. His complaint alleges that Dember's negligent driving caused his injuries. The law of the state declares that if the plaintiff's own negligence contributed to his injury, the defendant has a complete defense and the plaintiff cannot recover. Dember wants to argue that whether he was negligent or not, Pearson's own negligence helped cause his injuries and that Pearson therefore has no case. In order to be *sure* of his ability to raise this argument at trial, what should Dember's attorney do in response to Pearson's complaint?

8. What is the main difference between a motion for a directed verdict and a motion for judgment notwithstanding the verdict?

9. The state of Mississippi is planning to sue the state of Massachusetts. Mississippi's attorney general wants to sue in an appropriate federal district court. Do the federal district courts have jurisdiction over this case? If not, which federal court does have jurisdiction? You can assume that Mississippi's suit involves issues of federal law, and that the amount in controversy exceeds $50,000.

10. Jackson was born in Texas but has had absolutely no contact with that state for 20 years. Jackson's father dies, and a Texas court interprets his will so that Jackson receives none of his father's property, which is located in Texas. Assume that the court had jurisdiction to make this decision. What *kinds* of jurisdiction did it have?

11. Pike sues Dillon, alleging that his parked car was destroyed due to Dillon's negligent driving. After the pleadings and discovery have been completed, Pike's attorney concludes that the case is an obvious winner on both the facts and the law. What motion should the attorney make in an attempt to win the case without having to go to trial?

12. Does ADR really resolve disputes without any help from the courts? Give two examples of ADR processes that depend on courts for their operation or their effectiveness and state *how* they depend on the courts.

CHAPTER 3

BUSINESS AND THE CONSTITUTION

INTRODUCTION

As discussed in The Nature of Law chapter, constitutions serve two general functions. They set up the structure of government, allocating power among its various branches and subdivisions. Constitutions also prevent government from taking certain actions—in particular, actions that restrict individual rights. As the following overview of its provisions suggests, the U.S. Constitution performs both these functions.[1] *How* it performs these functions has definite political implications.

A Brief Overview of the U.S. Constitution

The U.S. Constitution embodies the principle of **separation of powers** by giving distinct powers to Congress, the president, and the federal courts.[2] Thus, Article I of the Constitution establishes a Congress composed of a Senate and a House of Representatives, gives Congress sole power to legislate at the federal level, and sets out rules for the passage of legislation. Also, Article I, section 8 states most of the specific ways Congress can

make law—its *legislative powers*. Three of these powers—Congress's commerce, tax, and spending powers—are discussed later in this chapter.

Article II of the Constitution places the *executive power* (the power to execute or enforce the laws passed by Congress) in the president. Section 2 of that article lists some other powers possessed by the president, including the powers to command the nation's armed forces and to make treaties. Article III gives the *judicial power* of the United States to the Supreme Court and the other federal courts later established by Congress. Article III also defines the scope of the federal judicial power—the kinds of cases the federal courts can decide.

In addition to establishing a separation of powers, Articles I, II, and III of the Constitution also create a system of **checks and balances** among Congress, the president, and the courts. For example, Article I, section 7 gives the president the power to veto legislation passed by Congress, and also allows Congress to override a veto by a two-thirds vote of each House. Article I, section 3 and Article II, section 4 provide that the president, the vice president, and other federal officials may be impeached by a two-thirds vote of the Senate. Article II, section 2 says that treaties made by the president must be approved by a two-thirds vote of the Senate. Article III, section 2 gives Congress some control over the Supreme Court's appellate jurisdiction.

---

[1] The full text of the U.S. Constitution is contained in Appendix A at the end of this book.

[2] The Administrative Agencies chapter discusses some separation of powers issues that pertain to administrative agencies.

The U.S. Constitution also recognizes the principle of **federalism** in the way it structures power relations between the federal government and the states. Article I, section 9 lists certain powers that Congress is not allowed to exercise. And the Tenth Amendment provides that those powers the Constitution neither gives to the federal government nor denies to the states are reserved to the states or the people.

Article VI, however, makes the Constitution, laws, and treaties of the United States supreme over state law. As you will see later in the chapter, this means that where the Constitution gives Congress the power to legislate, Article VI's principle of **federal supremacy** allows federal statutes to *preempt* inconsistent state laws. As also discussed later in this chapter, the U.S. Constitution puts specific limits on the states' law-making powers. One example is Article I, section 10's command that no state shall pass any law impairing the obligation of contracts. As noted immediately below, finally, most Bill of Rights provisions now apply to the states.

Article V sets out the procedures for amending the Constitution, procedures whose details are beyond the scope of this text. By now, the Constitution has been amended 26 times. The first 10 of these amendments comprise the Bill of Rights. Two of these rights, the First Amendment's guarantee of free speech and the Fifth Amendment's due process guarantee, receive some attention later in this chapter. Also discussed later is the Fifth Amendment's command that the government must provide just compensation when it takes private property for public use.

Although the individual rights contained in the first 10 amendments once applied to the federal government alone, most of them now apply to the states as well. As you will learn, this is due to their incorporation within the Due Process Clause of the Fourteenth Amendment, which applies to the states. Another important Fourteenth Amendment provision, its statement that the states cannot deny any person the equal protection of the laws, receives detailed attention later in this chapter.

The Evolution of the Constitution and the Role of the Supreme Court

According to the legal realists discussed in the chapter on the nature of law, understanding the law requires that one examine what public decisionmakers *actually do*. Using this approach, we discover a Constitution that differs from the written Constitution just described. For example, the actual powers of the president today far

exceed anything you would imagine merely from reading Article II. As you will see shortly, moreover, Congress's authority under the commerce, tax, and spending powers now has few internal limits. As a result, the Tenth Amendment's reservation of certain powers to the states means little today.

Many of these changes were caused by the way one public decisionmaker—the U.S. Supreme Court—has interpreted the Constitution over time. Although some people apparently regard the Constitution as an unchanging Fundamental Law, many of its provisions have a different practical meaning than they had when first enacted. Thus, constitutional law is much more *evolving* than static.

There are many reasons for the Constitution's flexibility. For one thing, it is a relatively short document some of whose key provisions are vague. Open-ended phrases like "due process of law" and "equal protection of the laws," for instance, invite diverse interpretations. Also, the history surrounding the enactment of constitutional provisions sometimes is sketchy, confused, or contradictory. Perhaps the most important reason for the Constitution's flexibility, however, is the perceived need to adapt it to changing social conditions. According to an old saying, Supreme Court decisions follow the election returns. Thus, the Court's decisions sometimes reflect the social conditions in which it operates. This may well be what the general public really wants; many of the people who believe in an unchanging Constitution, for instance, might be unhappy if they had to live under one.

In theory, constitutional change can be accomplished through the formal amendment process, but the Founders made this process fairly difficult to use and amendments to the Constitution have been relatively infrequent. For better or worse, therefore, the Supreme Court has been the Constitution's main amender. The Court has been able to assume this role because it has the final authority to determine the Constitution's meaning. Under the power of **judicial review**, the Supreme Court (and other courts) can declare the actions of other governmental bodies unconstitutional. How the Supreme Court exercises this power depends on how it chooses to read the Constitution.

Because they can declare the actions of the other branches unconstitutional under standards that are partly of their own making, the Supreme Court and other courts have political power. This is particularly true of the Supreme Court, whose nine justices often are public policymakers. For this reason, the beliefs of the justices are quite important in determining how America

FIGURE 1   Enumerated Powers and Independent Checks

	Law Does Not Conflict with Any Independent Check	**Law Conflicts with an Independent Check**
Law Is within Congress's Enumerated Powers	Law is constitutional	Law is unconstitutional
Law Is Not within Congress's Enumerated Powers	Law is unconstitutional	Law is unconstitutional

is governed. This is why their nomination and confirmation often involve so much political controversy.

But even though the Constitution is sometimes what the Supreme Court says it is, the Court's power to shape the Constitution has limits. For one thing, the Constitution's language is not completely open-ended; indeed, some of its provisions are quite clear. Also, past constitutional decisions do bind courts to some degree. Moreover, the Supreme Court is dependent on the other branches of government—and ultimately on public belief in the justices' fidelity to the rule of law—to make its decisions effective. Thus, the justices may be wary of power struggles with other, more representative, government bodies like Congress. By freely declaring the actions of these bodies unconstitutional, they run the risk of eventually provoking such conflicts.

The Structure of This Chapter

This chapter examines certain constitutional provisions that are important to business; it does not discuss constitutional law in its entirety. These provisions all help define federal and state power to regulate the economy. One of the U.S. Constitution's major concerns is to limit government power, and it does so in two general ways. First, it restricts *federal* legislative power by listing the powers that Congress can exercise and limiting Congress to these **enumerated powers.** To be constitutional, in other words, federal legislation must be based on a power specifically stated in the Constitution. Second, the U.S. Constitution limits both *state and federal* power by placing certain **independent checks** in the path of each. In effect, the independent checks declare that even if Congress has an enumerated power to act in a particular area or a state constitution authorizes a state to act in a certain way, there still are certain protected spheres into which neither can reach.

At the federal level, therefore, a law must meet two general tests in order to be constitutional. It must be based on an enumerated power of Congress, and it must

not collide with any of the independent checks. As you will see, for example, Congress has the power to regulate commerce among the states. By itself, this power might allow Congress to pass legislation declaring that certain racial minorities cannot cross state lines to buy or sell goods. But such a law, although arguably based on an enumerated power, surely would be unconstitutional. The reason is that it conflicts with an independent check: the equal protection guarantee discussed later in this chapter.

Figure 1 shows how the enumerated powers doctrine and the independent checks limit Congress's regulatory authority. By now, however, the enumerated powers doctrine has lost most of its significance and the independent checks are the main limitations on congressional power. The main reason for the decline of the enumerated powers limitation is the perceived need for greater federal regulation of the economy that began late in the 19th century.

This chapter next discusses the most important state and federal powers to regulate economic matters. Next, the chapter examines certain independent checks that apply to both the federal government and the states. After this, it considers some independent checks affecting the states alone. The chapter concludes by treating a provision—the Takings Clause of the Fifth Amendment—that both recognizes a governmental power and limits its exercise.

STATE AND FEDERAL POWER TO REGULATE

State Regulatory Power

Although state constitutions may do so, the U.S. Constitution does not specifically list the powers state legislatures can exercise. As noted above, however, the U.S. Constitution does place certain independent checks in the path of state lawmaking. It also declares that certain powers (e.g., creating currency and taxing imports) can only be exercised by Congress. In many other areas, though, Congress and the state legislatures have *concurrent powers.* Within those areas, both can make law unless Congress preempts state regulation under the Supremacy Clause. A very important state legislative power that operates concurrently with many congressional powers is called the **police power.** The police power is a broad state power to regulate for the public health, safety, morals, and welfare.

Federal Regulatory Power

Article I, section 8 of the U.S. Constitution states a number of business-related areas in which Congress can legislate. For example, it empowers Congress to coin and borrow money, regulate commerce with foreign nations, establish uniform laws regarding bankruptcies, create post offices, and regulate copyrights and patents. For our purposes, however, the most important congressional powers contained in Article I, section 8 are the powers to regulate commerce among the states, to lay and collect taxes, and to spend for the general welfare. Because they are now read so broadly, these three powers are the main constitutional bases for the extensive federal regulation of business that exists today.

The Commerce Power   Article I, section 8 states that "The Congress shall have Power . . . To regulate Commerce . . . among the several States." The original reason for giving Congress this power to regulate *interstate commerce* was to block the protectionist state restrictions on interstate trade that were common after the Revolution, and thus to nationalize economic life. This *Commerce Clause* has two major thrusts. First, as discussed later in this chapter, it is an independent check on state regulation that unduly restricts interstate commerce. Our present concern is the second aspect of the Commerce Clause: its role as a source of congressional regulatory power.

Congress's power under the Commerce Clause was of little concern for most of the 19th century. By today's standards, federal regulation of the economy was fairly infrequent and unintrusive during this period. With the wave of federal regulation that began late in the century, however, the Supreme Court became increasingly concerned with defining the limits of the commerce power. Since the late 1930s, it has abandoned almost all such limits while upholding quite extensive and intrusive federal laws regulating the economy. Today, the Commerce

Clause effectively is an all-purpose federal police power enabling Congress to regulate most activities within a state's borders (*intrastate* matters).

The literal language of the Commerce Clause simply gives Congress power to regulate *commerce* that occurs *among the states.* How, then, has the clause evolved into a broad federal power to regulate for the public health, safety, morals, and welfare, and to reach most intrastate matters while doing so? First, the Supreme Court has allowed Congress to control activities within the states by concluding that the power to regulate *interstate* commerce includes the power to reach *intrastate* activities that have some impact on commerce among the states. In the *Shreveport Rate Cases* (1914), for example, the Supreme Court upheld the Interstate Commerce Commission's regulation of railroad rates within Texas (an *intrastate* matter outside the literal language of the Commerce Clause) because these rates affected rail traffic between Texas and Louisiana (an *interstate* matter with in the clause's language). Originally, the Court limited Congress's regulatory power to intrastate activities that had a *direct* impact on interstate commerce, but this limitation has been abandoned.

The second way the Supreme Court expanded the reach of the Commerce Clause was to allow Congress to use it for noncommercial *police power* ends. In the late 19th and early 20th centuries, the Court did so by upholding federal legislation that restricted the interstate movement of disfavored people or commodities. For instance, Congress was allowed to attack sexual immorality, gambling, and food poisoning by limiting the interstate movement of prostitutes, lottery tickets, and impure food, respectively. Here, Congress was acting within the literal language of the Commerce Clause, but was using it for purposes different from its original purposes.

Eventually, these two expansions of the Commerce Clause—its extension to police matters and the affecting-commerce rationale—merged into one general doctrine. Now, Congress can regulate *intrastate police* matters that have some effect on interstate commerce. In 1964, for example, the Supreme Court upheld the application of the 1964 Civil Rights Act's "public accommodations" section to a family-owned restaurant in Birmingham, Alabama. It did so because the restaurant's racial discrimination affected interstate commerce by: (1) reducing the restaurant's business and limiting its purchases of out-of-state meat, and (2) restricting the ability of blacks to travel among the states.

As this example suggests, by now Congress can regulate intrastate activities even though they have relatively little impact on commerce among the states. In our highly interdependent society, almost all intrastate activities have *some* effect on interstate commerce. Thus, as the following *Wickard* case illustrates, few intrastate matters are outside the reach of the commerce power today.

WICKARD v. FILBURN

317 U.S. 111 (U.S. Sup. Ct. 1942)

Congress enacted the Agricultural Adjustment Act of 1938 to stabilize agricultural production and thus to give farmers reasonable minimum prices. The act empowered the secretary of agriculture to proclaim a yearly national acreage allotment for the coming wheat crop. This was apportioned among the states and their counties, and then among individual farms. Filburn was an Ohio farmer who raised a small acreage of winter wheat, some of which was sold but much of which was used on his farm. Filburn's permitted allotment for 1941 was 11.1 acres. However, he sowed and harvested 23 acres. For this, he was assessed a penalty of $117.11.

Filburn sued the secretary of agriculture (Wickard) for an injunction against enforcement of the penalty. A three-judge district court found in Filburn's favor, and the government appealed to the U.S. Supreme Court.

Jackson, Justice.   It is urged that under the Commerce Clause Congress does not possess the power it has in this instance sought to exercise. The question would merit little consideration, except that this Act extends federal regulation to production not intended in any part for commerce but wholly for consumption on the farm. Such activities are, Filburn urges, beyond the reach of congressional power under the Commerce Clause, since they are local in character, and their effects upon interstate commerce are at most "indirect."

For nearly a century, decisions of this Court dealt rarely with questions of what Congress might do under the Clause, and almost entirely with the permissibility of state activity which discriminated against or burdened interstate commerce. During this period there was perhaps little occasion for the affirmative exercise of the commerce power, and the influence of the clause on American life and law was a negative one, resulting almost wholly from its restraint upon the powers of the states. It was not until 1887, with the enactment of the Interstate Commerce Act, that the commerce power began to exert positive influence in American law and life. This was followed in 1890 by the Sherman Anti-Trust Act and, thereafter, by many others.

When it first dealt with this new legislation, the Court allowed but little scope to the power of Congress. However, other cases called forth broader interpretations of the Commerce Clause destined to supersede the earlier ones. It was soon demonstrated that the effects of many kinds of intrastate activity upon interstate commerce were such as to make them a proper subject of federal regulation. [Thus,] even if Filburn's activity be local, it may still be reached by Congress if it exerts a substantial economic effect on interstate commerce, and this irrespective of whether such effect is what might at some earlier time have been defined as "direct" or "indirect."

The effect of consumption of home-grown wheat on interstate commerce is due to the fact that it constitutes the most variable factor in the disappearance of the wheat crop. Consumption on the farm where grown appears to vary in an amount greater than 20 percent of average production. That Filburn's own contribution to the demand for wheat may be trivial by itself is not enough to remove him from the scope of federal regulation where, as here, his contribution, taken together with that of many others similarly situated, is far from trivial.

The power to regulate commerce includes the power to regulate the prices at which commodities in that commerce are dealt and practices affecting such prices. One of the primary purposes of the Act was to increase the market price of wheat, and to that end to limit the volume thereof that could affect the market. It can hardly be denied that a factor of such volume and variability as home-consumed wheat would have a substantial influence on price and market conditions. This may arise because such wheat overhangs the market and, if induced by rising prices, tends to flow into the market and check price increases. But if we assume that it is never marketed, it supplies a need of the man who grew it which would otherwise be reflected by purchases in the open market. Congress may properly have considered that wheat consumed on the farm where grown, if wholly outside the scheme of regulation, would have a substantial effect in defeating its purpose to stimulate trade therein at increased prices.

Judgment reversed in favor of Wickard.

The Taxing Power   Article I, section 8 of the Constitution also states that "The Congress shall have Power To lay and collect Taxes, Duties, Imposts and Excises." The main purpose behind this *taxing power* is to raise revenue for the federal government.[3] But the taxing power also can serve as a regulatory device. Because "the power to tax is the power to destroy," Congress can regulate by imposing a heavy tax on a disfavored activity. Although some regulatory taxes have been struck down, this has not occurred recently. Today, the reach of the taxing power, while poorly defined, is nonetheless very broad. Sometimes it is said that a regulatory tax is constitutional if its purpose could be furthered by one of Congress's *other* powers. Due to the broad scope of the commerce power, this may mean that the taxing power has few limits.

The Spending Power   If taxing power regulation uses a federal club, congressional *spending power* regulation employs a federal carrot. After stating the taxing power, Article I, section 8 gives Congress a broad ability to spend for the general welfare. By basing the receipt of federal money on the performance of certain conditions, Congress can use its spending power to advance specific regulatory ends. Conditional federal grants to the states, for instance, are common.

Over the past 50 years, congressional spending power regulation invariably has been upheld. Still, as the Supreme Court has recently announced, there are limits on

its use. First, an exercise of the spending power must serve *general* public purposes, and not particular interests. Second, when Congress conditions the receipt of federal money on certain conditions, it must do so unambiguously. Third, the condition must be reasonably related to the purpose behind the federal expenditure. For example, Congress probably cannot condition a state's receipt of federal highway money on the state's adoption of a one-house legislature. Finally, note that federal spending power regulation arguably is less intrusive than other forms of federal regulation because a state theoretically can avoid the condition by refusing federal money.

INDEPENDENT CHECKS ON THE FEDERAL GOVERNMENT AND THE STATES

Even if a regulation is within Congress's enumerated powers or a state's police power, it still is unconstitutional if it collides with one of the Constitution's *independent checks*. In examining the major independent checks affecting government regulation of the economy, we first discuss those checks that limit both the federal government and the states. The three most important such checks are familiar individual rights guarantees: freedom of speech, due process, and equal protection. Before discussing each of these guarantees, however, it is necessary to consider some preliminary matters.

Incorporation

The Fifth Amendment prevents the federal government from depriving any person "of life, liberty, or property,

---

[3] The Constitution imposes some restrictions on the types of taxes that may be used to raise revenue, but these restrictions are beyond the scope of this text.

FIGURE 2   Why Certain Individual Rights Guarantees Apply to Both the Federal Government and the States

Guarantee	Why Applicable to States	Why Applicable to Federal Government
Due Process	Text of Fourteenth Amendment	Text of Fifth Amendment
First Amendment	Incorporation within Fourteenth Amendment	Text of First Amendment
Equal Protection	Text of Fourteenth Amendment	Incorporation within Fifth Amendment

without due process of law," and the Fourteenth Amendment does the same to the states. The First Amendment, however, applies only to the federal government. And the Fourteenth Amendment merely says that no *state* shall "deny to any person . . . the equal protection of the laws." Thus, while due process clearly applies to both the federal government and the states, the First Amendment and the Equal Protection Clause seem to have a more limited reach. But the First Amendment's free speech guarantee has been included within the "liberty" protected by Fourteenth Amendment due process, and thus made applicable to the states. This is part of the process of *incorporation* by which almost all Bill of Rights provisions now apply to the states. The Fourteenth Amendment's Equal Protection Clause, on the other hand, has been made applicable to the federal government by incorporating it within the Fifth Amendment's due process guarantee. Figure 2 summarizes all these points.

Government Action

People often talk as if the Constitution protects them against all individuals or groups who try to restrict personal rights. However, most of the Constitution's individual rights provisions only protect people against the actions of *governmental* bodies, state and federal.[4] *Private* behavior that denies individual rights, while perhaps forbidden by statute, is not supposed to be a constitutional matter. This **government action** or **state action** requirement forces courts to distinguish between governmental behavior and private behavior. Making this distinction has presented immense problems.

_____

[4] However, the Thirteenth Amendment, which bans slavery and involuntary servitude throughout the United States, does not have a state action requirement. Also, some *state* constitutions have individual rights provisions that lack a state action requirement.

Before World War II, state action determinations usually were easy because only formal organs of government such as legislatures, administrative agencies, municipalities, courts, prosecutors, and state universities were deemed state actors. But after World War II, the range of activities considered to be government action increased considerably, and all sorts of traditionally private behavior was subjected to individual rights limitations. In *Marsh v. Alabama* (1946), for example, the Supreme Court treated a privately owned company town's restriction of free expression as government action under the *public function* theory because the town was like a normal municipality in most respects. Also, in *Shelley v. Kraemer* (1948), the Supreme Court held that state court enforcement of a private agreement among white homeowners not to sell their homes to blacks was unconstitutional state action under the Equal Protection Clause. Later, in *Burton v. Wilmington Parking Authority* (1961), the Court concluded that racial discrimination by a privately owned restaurant located in a state-owned and state-operated parking garage was unconstitutional state action, in part because the garage and the restaurant were intertwined in a mutually beneficial "symbiotic" relationship. Among the other factors leading courts to find state action during the 1960s and 1970s were extensive government regulation of private activity and government financial aid to a private actor.

Due mainly to the changed composition of the Supreme Court, however, the reach of state action was limited considerably in the 1970s and 1980s. Now, the Court usually treats private behavior as state action only when a regular unit of government is directly *responsible* for the challenged private behavior because it has coerced or encouraged such behavior. Also, the public function doctrine has been limited to situations where a private entity exercises powers that have *traditionally* been *exclusively* reserved to the state; private police protection is a possible example. In addition, government regulation and government funding now are relatively unimportant factors in state action determinations. The following *SFAA* case illustrates the restricted view of state action that prevails today. Despite the Supreme Court's state action cutback, however, the doctrine probably has not returned to its narrow pre–World War II definition, and much uncertainty remains in this area.

SAN FRANCISCO ARTS & ATHLETICS, INC. v. UNITED STATES OLYMPIC COMMITTEE

483 U.S. 522 (U.S. Sup. Ct. 1987)

San Francisco Arts & Athletics, Inc. (SFAA) actively promoted the "Gay Olympic Games" to be held in San Francisco during the latter part of 1982. As part of its promotional efforts, SFAA sought to sell T-shirts, buttons, bumper stickers, and other items bearing the title "Gay Olympic Games."

The United States Olympic Committee (USOC) is a federally chartered corporation. Under the Amateur Sports Act, it has broad powers to handle U.S. participation in international athletic competition and to promote amateur athletics within this country. In August of 1982, the USOC sued SFAA for its promotional activities on behalf of the Gay Olympic Games. It did so under a federal statute giving the USOC near-exclusive rights in the commercial and promotional use of the term "Olympic." A federal district court granted the USOC summary judgment and a permanent injunction against SFAA's use of the term "Olympic," and the court of appeals affirmed. One issue in the case was the SFAA's claim that the USOC had violated the equal protection component of Fifth Amendment due process because it discriminated in its enforcement of the statute. The court of appeals, however, ruled that no government action was present. SFAA appealed to the U.S. Supreme Court.

Powell, Justice.   The fundamental inquiry is whether the USOC is a governmental actor to whom the prohibitions of the Constitution apply. The USOC is a private corporation established under federal law. Congress granted the USOC a corporate charter, imposed certain requirements on the USOC, and provided for some USOC funding through exclusive use of USOC words and symbols and through direct grants.

The fact that Congress granted it a corporate charter does not render the USOC a government agent. All corporations act under charters granted by a government. They do not thereby lose their essentially private character. Even extensive regulation by the government does not transform the actions of the regulated entity into those of the government. Moreover, the intent on the part of Congress to help the USOC obtain funding does not change the analysis. The government may subsidize private entities without assuming constitutional responsibility for their actions.

The Court also has found action to be governmental action when the challenged entity performs functions that have been traditionally the exclusive prerogative of the government. Certainly the activities performed by the USOC serve a national interest. [But] the fact that a private entity serves the public does not make its acts governmental action. The Amateur Sports Act merely authorized the USOC to coordinate activities that always have been performed by private entities. Neither the conduct nor the coordination of amateur sports has been a traditional government function.

Most fundamentally, this Court has held that a government normally can be held responsible for a private decision only when it has exercised coercive power or has provided such significant encouragement, either overt or covert, that the choice must be deemed to be that of the government. The USOC's choice of how to enforce its exclusive right to use the word "Olympic" simply is not a governmental decision. There is no evidence that the federal government coerced or encouraged the USOC in the exercise of its right. At most, the federal government, by failing to supervise the USOC's use of its rights, exercised mere approval or acquiesence in the initiatives of the USOC. This is not enough to make the USOC's actions those of the government.

Because the USOC is not a governmental actor, SFAA's claim that the USOC has enforced its rights in a discriminatory manner must fail.

Court of appeals decision in favor of the USOC affirmed.

Means-Ends Tests

Throughout the remainder of this chapter, you will see tests of constitutionality that are confusing at first glance. One example is the well-established test for determining whether laws that discriminate on the basis of sex violate the Equal Protection Clause. This test says that to be constitutional, such laws must be substantially related to the achievement of an important governmental purpose. What does this language mean, and what are courts doing when they use it? The Equal Protection Clause does not contain such language. Instead, it simply states that "No State shall . . . deny to any person . . . the equal protection of the laws."

The sex discrimination test just stated is a *means-ends* test. Courts create such tests because no constitutional right is absolute; therefore, judges must weigh individual rights against the social purposes served by laws that restrict those rights. In other words, means-ends tests determine how courts strike the *balance* between individual rights and the social needs that may justify their suppression. The "ends" component of a means-ends test specifies how *significant* a social purpose must be in order to justify the restriction of a right. The "means" component states how *effectively* the challenged law must promote that purpose in order to be constitutional. In our sex discrimination test, for example, the challenged law must serve an "important" government purpose (the significance of the end) and must be "substantially" related to the achievement of that purpose (the effectiveness of the means).

Because some constitutional rights are deemed more important than others, courts use tougher tests of constitutionality in such cases and more lenient tests in other situations. Sometimes these tests are wordy, complex, and difficult. Throughout the remainder of this chapter, therefore, we sometimes simplify by employing three general kinds of means-ends tests:

1. *The rational basis test.* This is a very relaxed test of constitutionality that challenged laws usually pass with ease. A typical formulation of the rational basis test might say that government action need only have a *reasonable* relation to the achievement of a *legitimate* government purpose in order to be constitutional.

2. *Intermediate scrutiny.* This comes in many forms; the sex discrimination test we have been discussing is an example. To repeat, this test says that the challenged law must be *substantially* related to the achievement of an *important* government purpose.

3. *Full strict scrutiny.* Here, the court might say that the challenged law must be *necessary* to the fulfillment of a *compelling* government purpose. This is a rigorous test of constitutionality, and government action subjected to full strict scrutiny is almost always struck down.

Business and the First Amendment

Introduction The First Amendment says that "Congress shall make no law . . . abridging the freedom of speech." Despite its language ("*no* law"), the First Amendment has not been read as prohibiting every law that restricts speech. As Justice Oliver Wendell Holmes once remarked, the First Amendment does not protect someone who falsely shouts "Fire!" in a crowded theater. But while the First Amendment's guarantee of free speech is not absolute, government action restricting speech usually receives very strict judicial scrutiny. The justifications for this high level of protection vary, but perhaps the most important is the "marketplace" rationale. In this view, the free competition of ideas is the surest means of attaining truth and the marketplace of ideas best serves this end when restrictions on speech are kept to a minimum and all viewpoints can be considered.

This chapter does not consider most of the situations in which the First Amendment's free speech guarantee has been applied during the 20th century. Nor does it examine *corporate political speech*, which generally receives full First Amendment protection. Instead, we discuss one First Amendment issue of considerable concern to business—the government's power to regulate so-called *commercial speech*. In this area, the marketplace rationale for free speech figures prominently.

Commercial Speech   As the following *Bolger* case illustrates, the line between political speech and commercial speech is unclear. In general, though, commercial speech is expression proposing a commercial transaction; commercial advertising is the most common example. In 1942, the Supreme Court ruled that commercial speech is outside the First Amendment's protection, but the Court reversed its position during the 1970s. Now, restrictions on commercial speech receive an *intermediate* level of means-ends scrutiny that is less rigorous than the *full* strict scrutiny given laws that restrict corporate *political* speech. *Bolger* states the actual test, which is fairly complicated. However, some recent cases suggest that the Supreme Court is applying that test in a lenient fashion and is becoming more tolerant of laws restricting

commercial speech. In any event, the intermediate test stated in *Bolger* does not apply to commercial speech that is false, deceptive, or misleading, or that is related to illegal behavior. These forms of expression can be freely regulated.

The usual justification for protecting commercial speech is to promote informed consumer choice by removing barriers to the flow of commercial information. The Supreme Court's decisions striking down state restrictions on advertising by groups such as pharmacists and lawyers, restrictions that arguably promoted price-fixing within these professions, seem consistent with this marketplace rationale. However, the commercial speech doctrine could also benefit business interests if, for instance, government regulators ever decide to mount a serious attack on advertising that is not false or misleading but that attempts to manipulate consumers by appealing to irrational drives of all sorts.[5] In general, your opinion about protecting commercial speech may depend on your views about the impact of modern mass advertising and how rationally consumers respond to it.

---

[5] For a brief discussion of commercial speech challenges to the FTC's regulation of advertising, see The Federal Trade Commission Act and Consumer Protection Laws chapter. Such challenges generally have been unsuccessful.

BOLGER v. YOUNGS DRUG PRODUCTS CORPORATION

463 U.S. 60 (U.S. Sup. Ct. 1983)

Youngs Drug Products Corporation manufactured, sold, and distributed contraceptive devices (including prophylactics). It planned a marketing campaign involving the unsolicited mass mailing of advertising fliers and related materials to the general public. The mailings were to include: (1) fliers promoting a range of products obtainable in drugstores (including prophylactics); (2) fliers specifically promoting prophylactics; and (3) informational pamphlets discussing the usefulness of prophylactics in preventing venereal disease and aiding family planning. After learning of Youngs's plans, the Postal Service warned Youngs that the mailings would violate a federal statute prohibiting the mailing of unsolicited advertisements for contraceptive devices.

Youngs sued in federal district court for an injunction barring enforcement of the statute against its mailings, arguing that such enforcement would violate the First Amendment. The district court decided in Youngs's favor, and the Postal Service appealed to the U.S. Supreme Court.

Marshall, Justice.   Our decisions have recognized the commonsense distinction between speech proposing a commercial transaction and other varieties of speech. Thus, we have held that the Constitution accords less protection to commercial speech than to other constitutionally safe-guarded forms of expression. With respect to noncommercial speech, this Court has sustained content-based restrictions only in the most extraordinary circumstances. By contrast, in light of the greater potential for deception or confusion in the context of certain advertising messages, content-based restrictions on commercial speech may be permissible.

[Thus,] we must first determine the proper classification of the mailings at issue here. Most of Youngs's mailings fall within the core notion of commercial speech—speech which does no more than propose a commercial transaction. Youngs's informational pamphlets, however, cannot be characterized merely as proposals to engage in commercial transactions. The mere fact that these pamphlets are advertisements does not compel the conclusion that they are commercial speech. Similarly, the reference to a specific product does not by itself render the pamphlets commercial speech. Finally, the fact that Youngs has an economic motivation for mailing the pamphlets would clearly be insufficient by itself to turn the materials into commercial speech. The combination of all these characteristics, however, provides strong support for the conclusion that the informa-tional pamphlets are properly characterized as commercial speech. The mailings constitute com-mercial speech notwithstanding the fact that they contain discussions of important public issues such as venereal disease and family planning.

We have adopted [the following] analysis for assessing the validity of restrictions on commer-cial speech. First, we determine whether the expression is constitutionally protected. For com-mercial speech to receive such protection, it at least must concern lawful activity and not be misleading. Second, we ask whether the governmental interest is substantial. If so, we must then determine whether the regulation directly advances the government interest asserted, and whether it is not more extensive than necessary to serve that interest.[6]

The State may deal effectively with false, deceptive, or misleading sales techniques. In this case, however, the government has never claimed that Youngs's mailings fall into any of these categories. Youngs's commercial speech is therefore clearly protected by the First Amendment.

We must next determine whether the government's interest in prohibiting the mailing of unso-licited contraceptive advertisements is a substantial one. The government asserts that the statute: (1) shields recipients of mail from materials that they are likely to find offensive, and (2) aids parents' efforts to control the manner in which their children become informed about sensitive and important subjects such as birth control. The first of these interests carries little weight. At least where obscenity is not involved, we have never held that the government can shut off the flow of mailings to protect those recipients who might potentially be offended. Recipients of objectionable mailings may effectively avoid bombardment of their sensibilities simply by averting their eyes.

The second interest asserted by the government—aiding parents' efforts to discuss birth control with their children—is undoubtedly substantial. As a means of effectuating this interest, however, this statute fails to withstand scrutiny. To begin, it provides only the most limited incremental support for the interest asserted. We can reasonably assume that parents already exercise substan-tial control over the disposition of mail once it enters their mailboxes. And parents must already cope with the multitude of external stimuli that color their children's perception of sensitive subjects. Under these circumstances, a ban on unsolicited advertisements serves only to assist those parents who desire to keep their children from confronting such mailings, who are otherwise

---

[6] In *Board of Trustees of the State University of New York v. Fox*, 492 U.S. 469 (1989), the Supreme Court clarified the last part of this "means" test by holding that the challenged regulation need not be the least restrictive means of pro-moting the substantial government purpose. In other words, the regulation might still stand even if another regulation could advance the state's ends with less effect on free commercial speech. Under this standard, however, the result in *Bolger* would not change.

unable to do so, and whose children have remained relatively free from such stimuli. This marginal degree of protection is achieved by purging all mailboxes of unsolicited material that is entirely suitable for adults. A restriction of this scope is more extensive than the Constitution permits, for the government may not reduce the adult population to reading only what is fit for children. The level of discourse reaching a mailbox simply cannot be limited to that which would be suitable for a sandbox.

The justifications offered by the government are insufficient to warrant the sweeping prohibition on the mailing of unsolicited contraceptive advertisements. As applied to Youngs's mailings, the statute is unconstitutional.

Judgment for Youngs affirmed.

Due Process

Procedural Due Process   The Fifth and Fourteenth Amendments require that the federal government and the states observe **due process** when they deprive a person of life, liberty, or property. The traditional conception of due process, called **procedural due process,** establishes the procedures that government must follow when it takes life, liberty, or property. Although the requirements of procedural due process vary from situation to situation, their core idea is that people are entitled to adequate *notice* of the government action to be taken against them and to some sort of *fair trial or hearing* before that action can occur.

In order to trigger due process protections, the government must deprive a person of life, liberty, or property. Due process *liberty* includes a very broad and poorly defined range of freedoms. It even includes certain interests in personal reputation. For example, the firing of a government employee might require some kind of due process hearing if it is publicized, the fired employee's reputation is sufficiently damaged, and her future employment opportunities are restricted. The Supreme Court has said that due process *property* is not created by the Constitution, but by existing rules and understandings that stem from an independent source such as state law. These rules and understandings must give a person a *legitimate claim of entitlement* to a benefit, not merely some need, desire, or expectation for it. This definition includes almost all of the usual forms of property. It also includes the job rights of tenured public employees who can be discharged only for cause, but not the rights of untenured or probationary employees.

The following *Adams* case discusses the sort of notice required by procedural due process when government deprives a person of property.

MENNONITE BOARD OF MISSIONS v. ADAMS
462 U.S. 791 (U.S. Sup. Ct. 1983)

Alfred Jean Moore purchased some real property located in Elkhart, Indiana, from the Mennonite Board of Missions (MBM). The sale was on credit, and MBM took a mortgage on the property to secure payment of the $14,000 purchase price. Under the sales agreement, Moore was responsible for paying all property taxes. Unknown to MBM, however, she failed to do so. This eventually led Elkhart County to initiate proceedings for the sale of Moore's property in order to satisfy the tax debt.

Under Indiana law at the time in question, the only forms of notice required to be given to holders of mortgage interests (mortgagees) in property destined for a tax sale were: (1) posted notice in the county courthouse and (2) published notice once each week for three consecutive weeks. The owner of the property, on the other hand, was entitled to notice by certified mail. Elkhart County complied with all of these requirements and eventually sold Moore's property to Richard Adams. Through no fault of its own, MBM did not learn of the tax deficiency or the sale until two years after the sale occurred. By then, the statutory period within which MBM could have redeemed the property had passed and Moore still owed MBM over $8,000.

Adams later sued in an Indiana trial court to quiet title to the property that he had purchased. In opposition to Adams's motion for summary judgment, MBM argued that it had not received constitutionally adequate notice of the tax sale and of its opportunity to redeem the property following the sale. The trial court found for Adams, and a state appellate court affirmed the judgment. MBM appealed to the U.S. Supreme Court.

Marshall, Justice. In *Mullane v. Central Hanover Bank & Trust Co.* (1950), this Court recognized that prior to an action which will affect an interest in life, liberty, or property protected by the Due Process Clause of the Fourteenth Amendment, a State must provide "notice reasonably calculated, under all circumstances, to apprise interested parties of the pendency of the action and afford them an opportunity to present their objections." Invoking this elementary and fundamental requirement of due process, the Court held that published notice of an action to settle the accounts of a common trust fund was not sufficient to inform beneficiaries of the trust whose names and addresses were known. The Court explained that notice by publication was not reasonably calculated to provide actual notice of the pending proceeding and was therefore inadequate to inform those who could be notified by more effective means such as personal service or mailed notice.

This case is controlled by the analysis in *Mullane*. A mortgagee (e.g., MBM) possesses a substantial property interest that is significantly affected by a tax sale. Ultimately, the tax sale may result in the complete nullification of the mortgagee's interest, since the purchaser acquires title free of all liens and other encumbrances at the conclusion of the redemption period.

Since a mortgagee clearly has a legally protected property interest, he is entitled to notice reasonably calculated to apprise him of a pending tax sale. Unless the mortgagee is not reasonably identifiable, constructive notice alone does not satisfy the mandate of *Mullane*.

Neither notice by publication and posting, nor mailed notice to the property owner, are means such as one desirous of actually informing the mortgagee might reasonably adopt to accomplish it. Because they are designed primarily to attract prospective purchasers to the tax sale, publication and posting are unlikely to reach those who, although they have an interest in the property, do not make special efforts to keep abreast of such notices. Notice to the property owner also cannot be expected to lead to actual notice to the mortgagee. The County's use of these less reliable forms of notice is not reasonable where, as here, an inexpensive and efficient mechanism such as mail service is available.

Personal service or mailed notice is required even though sophisticated creditors have means at their disposal to discover whether property taxes have not been paid and whether tax sale proceedings are therefore likely to be initiated. A mortgage need not involve a complex commercial transaction among knowledgeable parties, and it may well be the least sophisticated creditor whose security interest is threatened by a tax sale. More importantly, a party's ability to safeguard its interests does not relieve the state of its constitutional obligation. Notice by mail or other means as certain to ensure actual notice is a minimum constitutional precondition to a proceeding which will adversely affect the liberty or property interests of *any* party, whether unlettered or well versed in commercial practice, if its name and address are reasonably ascertainable.

Judgment reversed in favor of MBM.

Substantive Due Process   A procedural due process claim does not challenge rules of *substantive law*—the rules that set standards of behavior for organized social life. Instead, it attacks the *procedures* used by government actors when they enforce substantive rules. For example, imagine that State X makes adultery a crime and allows people to be convicted of adultery without a trial. Arguments that adultery should not be a crime go to the substance of the statute, while objections to the lack of a trial are procedural in nature.

Sometimes, the Due Process Clauses have been used to attack the substance of government action. For our purposes, the most important example of this **substantive due process** occurred in the late 19th and early 20th centuries, when probusiness courts influenced by laissez-faire economic ideas struck down various kinds of social legislation as denials of due process. They did so mainly by reading freedom of contract and other economic rights into the liberty protected by the Fifth and Fourteenth Amendments and interpreting "due process of law" to require that laws denying such rights be subjected to some kind of means-ends scrutiny. The most famous example is the Supreme Court's 1905 decision in *Lochner v. New York*, where it struck down a state law setting maximum hours of work for bakery employees because the statute limited freedom of contract and did not directly advance the legitimate state goal of promoting worker health.

This "economic" form of substantive due process has been criticized as giving probusiness courts a powerful tool for striking down social and economic regulations designed to protect the powerless. After 1937, the doctrine ceased to be a significant check on government regulation of social and economic matters. Today, substantive due process attacks on such regulations trigger only the most lenient kind of rational basis review and have virtually no chance of success. In the 1970s and 1980s, however, substantive due process became increasingly important as a device for protecting *noneconomic* rights—most importantly, the ambiguously defined constitutional right of privacy. But in 1989 and 1990, the Supreme Court issued several decisions that restricted these modern applications of substantive due process.

Equal Protection

The Fourteenth Amendment and its Equal Protection Clause were added to the Constitution after the Civil War. Some scholars argue that the equal protection guarantee originally was aimed only at racial discrimination, but by the beginning of the 20th century courts applied it to governmental classifications of all sorts. The law inevitably classifies or discriminates in various ways, benefiting or burdening some groups but not others. The equal protection guarantee sets the standards such classifications must meet to be constitutional.

The Rational Basis Test   The basic equal protection standard is the *rational basis* test described earlier. This is the standard usually applied to social and economic regulations that are challenged as denying equal protection. Although formulations of the rational basis test vary, here it generally means that the government's classification must be reasonably related to the accomplishment of a legitimate public purpose. As the following *Stanglin* case indicates, this lenient test usually does not impede state and federal regulation of social and economic matters.

CITY OF DALLAS v. STANGLIN
490 U.S. 19 (U.S. Sup. Ct. 1989)

The city of Dallas, Texas, adopted an ordinance restricting admission to so-called Class E dance halls to persons between the ages of 14 and 18. However, it did not impose similar age limitations on most other establishments where teenagers might congregate—for example, skating rinks. Charles Stanglin, who in one building operated both a Class E dance hall and a roller-skating rink, sued for an injunction against enforcement of the ordinance in a Texas trial court. One of his arguments was that the ordinance denied the equal protection of the laws because its distinction between Class E dance halls and other establishments for teenagers was irrational. The Texas trial court upheld the ordinance, but a higher Texas court struck down its age restriction. The city appealed to the U.S. Supreme Court.

Rehnquist, Chief Justice.   The Dallas ordinance implicates no suspect class. The question remaining is whether the classification survives rational basis scrutiny under the Equal Protection Clause. The city has chosen to impose a rule that separates 14- to 18-year-olds from what may be the corrupting influences of older teenagers and young adults. An urban planner for the city testified: "Older kids can access drugs and alcohol, and they have more mature sexual attitudes, more liberal sexual attitudes in general. . . . And we're concerned about mixing up these individuals with youngsters [who] have not fully matured."

Stanglin claims that this restriction has no real connection with the city's stated objectives. Except for saloons and teenage dance halls, he argues, teenagers and adults in Dallas may associate with each other, including at the skating area of his rink. We think Stanglin's arguments misapprehend the nature of rational basis scrutiny, which is the most relaxed and tolerant form of judicial scrutiny under the Equal Protection Clause. If the classification has some reasonable basis, it does not offend the Constitution simply because the classification is not made with mathematical nicety or because in practice it results in some inequality. The rational basis standard is true to the principle that the Fourteenth Amendment gives the federal courts no power to impose upon the states their views of what constitutes wise economic or social policy.

In the local economic sphere, it is only the invidious discrimination, the wholly arbitrary act, which cannot stand consistently with the Fourteenth Amendment. The city could reasonably conclude that teenagers might be susceptible to corrupting influences if permitted to frequent a dance hall with older persons [and that] limiting dance hall contacts between juveniles and adults would make less likely illicit or undesirable juvenile involvement with alcohol, illegal drugs, and promiscuous sex. It is true that the city allows teenagers and adults to roller-skate together, but skating involves less physical contact than dancing. The differences between the two activities may not be striking, but differentiations need not be striking in order to survive rational basis scrutiny.

Texas court decision reversed in favor of the city.

The rational basis test is the basic equal protection standard. Some classifications, however, get tougher means-ends scrutiny. Specifically, laws that discriminate with respect to *fundamental rights* or involve *suspect classifications* now receive more rigorous review. This is a development that mainly began after World War II and greatly accelerated during the 1960s and 1970s.

Fundamental Rights   The list of rights regarded as "fundamental" for equal protection purposes is not completely clear, but it includes voting, interstate travel, and certain criminal procedure protections. Laws creating unequal enjoyment of these rights receive something resembling *full strict scrutiny*. In 1969, for instance, the Supreme Court struck down the District of Columbia's one-year residency requirement for receiving welfare benefits because that requirement unequally and impermissibly restricted the right of interstate travel.

Suspect Classifications   For various reasons, the Supreme Court has concluded that certain "suspect" bases of classification also trigger more rigorous equal protection review. As of mid-1991, these *suspect classifications* and the level of scrutiny they attract are as follows:

1. *Race and national origin.* Classifications disadvantaging racial or national minorities receive the strictest kind of strict scrutiny and are almost never constitutional. Still, the Supreme Court often has upheld so-called reverse racial discrimination—government

---

CONCEPT REVIEW

THE LEVELS OF EQUAL PROTECTION REVIEW: A ROUGH SUMMARY

Rational Basis Review	Most general social and economic regulations
	Laws discriminating against aliens under the political function exception
Intermediate Scrutiny	Sex discrimination against both men and women
	Discrimination against illegitimates
	Minority preferences enacted by Congress
Full or Nearly Full Strict Scrutiny	Discrimination regarding fundamental rights
	Most discrimination against aliens
	Most race and national origin discrimination

---

action that benefits racial minorities and disadvantages whites. In 1989, however, a majority of the Court concluded that discrimination of this kind should receive the same full strict scrutiny as discrimination *against* racial or national minorities. But in 1990, the Court held that minority preferences enacted *by Congress* should be reviewed under the *sex discrimination* test described below, which is generally regarded as a form of *intermediate scrutiny.*

2. *Alienage.* The Supreme Court has stated that classifications based on one's status as an alien also receive strict scrutiny of some kind, but it is doubtful whether this standard is as tough as the full strict scrutiny normally used in race discrimination cases. Under the "political function" exception, moreover, laws restricting aliens from employment in positions that are intimately related to democratic self-government only receive *rational basis* review. This exception has been read broadly to uphold laws excluding aliens from being state troopers, public school teachers, and probation officers.

3. *Sex.* Although sex has never formally been declared a suspect classification, for about 15 years laws discriminating on the basis of gender have been subjected to *intermediate scrutiny.* Specifically, such laws must be substantially related to the furtherance of an important governmental purpose. Under this test, measures discriminating against women have almost always been struck down. The Supreme Court has stated that classifications disadvantaging men get the same scrutiny as those disadvantaging women, but this has not pre-

vented the Court from upholding men-only draft registration and a law making statutory rape a crime for men alone.

4. *Illegitimacy.* Classifications based on one's illegitimate birth receive a form of *intermediate scrutiny* that is probably less strict than the scrutiny given gender-based classifications. Under this vague standard, the Court has struck down state laws discriminating against illegitimates in areas like recovery for wrongful death, workers' compensation benefits, social security payments, inheritance, and child support.

INDEPENDENT CHECKS APPLYING ONLY TO THE STATES

The Contract Clause

Article I, section 10 of the Constitution says: "No State shall . . . pass any . . . Law impairing the Obligation of Contracts." This *Contract Clause* applies to state laws that change the parties' performance obligations under an *existing* contract *after* that contract has been made.[7] The original purpose behind the Contract Clause was to strike down the many debtor relief statutes passed by the states after the Revolution. These statutes impaired the obligations of existing private contracts by relieving

---

[7]Also, standards similar to the Contract Clause standards described in this section apply to the federal government under the Fifth Amendment's Due Process Clause.

debtors of the obligations they owed to contract creditors. In the famous cases of *Fletcher v. Peck* (1810) and *Dartmouth College v. Woodward* (1819), however, the Contract Clause also was held to protect the obligations of *governmental* contracts and grants.

The Contract Clause probably was the most important constitutional check on state regulation of the economy in the 19th century. Beginning in the latter part of that century, though, the clause gradually became subordinate to legislation based on the states' police powers. By the mid-20th century, most observers treated the clause as a constitutional dead letter. In 1977, however, the Supreme Court gave the Contract Clause new life by announcing a fairly strict constitutional test governing situations where a state impairs *its own* contracts. Such impairments, it said, must be "reasonable and necessary to serve an important public purpose." A year later, without stating a clear constitutional standard, the Court struck down a state's alteration of *private* pension contracts.

During the 1980s, the Court seemingly returned to its earlier pattern of deference toward state regulations that impair the obligations of *private* contracts. The following *Exxon* case is an example. Where a state attempts to impair *its own* contracts, however, the fairly strict test quoted above presumably still applies.

EXXON CORPORATION v. EAGERTON

462 U.S. 176 (U.S. Sup. Ct. 1983)

For years, the Exxon Corporation paid a severance tax on the oil and gas it drilled in Alabama. Under the sales contracts that Exxon made with purchasers of its oil and gas, it was able to pass on any tax increase to the purchasers. In 1979, Alabama raised the severance tax from 4 percent to 6 percent, and forbade producers of oil and gas from passing on the increase to purchasers.

Exxon sued the Alabama commissioner of revenue in an Alabama trial court, seeking a ruling that the pass-on restriction was unconstitutional under the Contract Clause. The trial court found for Exxon, but the Alabama Supreme Court reversed. Exxon appealed to the U.S. Supreme Court.

Marshall, Justice.   By barring Exxon from passing the tax increase through to its purchasers, the pass-through prohibition nullified the purchasers' contractual obligations to reimburse Exxon for any severance taxes. While the prohibition thus affects contractual obligations, it does not follow that the prohibition constituted a "Law impairing the Obligation of Contracts" within the meaning of the Contract Clause. Although the language of the Clause is facially absolute, its prohibition must be accommodated to the inherent police power of the state to safeguard the vital interests of its people. If the law were otherwise, one would be able to obtain immunity from state regulation by making private contractual arrangements.

The Contract Clause does not deprive the states of their broad power to adopt general regulatory measures without being concerned that private contracts will be impaired, or even destroyed, as a result. Thus, a state prohibition law may be applied to contracts for the sale of beer that were valid when entered into, a law barring lotteries may be applied to lottery tickets that were valid when issued, and a workmen's compensation law may be applied to employers and employees operating under preexisting contracts of employment that made no provision for work-related injuries.

Like the laws upheld in these cases, the pass-through prohibition did not prescribe a rule limited in effect to contractual obligations or remedies, but instead imposed a generally applicable rule of conduct designed to advance a broad societal interest, protecting consumers from excessive prices. The prohibition applied to all oil and gas producers, regardless of whether they happened to be parties to sale contracts permitting them to pass tax increases through to their purchasers. The effect of the pass-through prohibition on existing contracts that did contain such a provision was incidental to its main effect of shielding consumers from the burden of the tax increase.

Judgment for the commissioner affirmed on the Contract Clause issue. Case returned to the Alabama Supreme Court for consideration of other questions.

Burden on Interstate Commerce

In addition to empowering Congress to regulate interstate commerce, the Commerce Clause also limits the states' ability to *burden* such commerce. This limitation is not expressly stated in the Constitution. Rather, it arises by implication from the Commerce Clause and reflects that clause's original purpose of blocking state protectionism and assuring free interstate trade. This *burden-on-commerce* limitation operates independently of congressional legislation under the commerce power or other federal powers. If relevant federal regulation is present, the preemption questions discussed in the next section also may arise.

Many different state laws can raise burden-on-commerce problems. For example, state regulation of transportation (e.g., limits on train or truck lengths) have been a prolific source of litigation. The same is true of state restrictions on the importation of goods or resources—for example, laws forbidding the sale of out-of-state food products unless they meet certain standards. Such restrictions sometimes benefit local economic interests. Burden-on-commerce issues also arise when states try to aid their own residents by blocking the exportation of scarce or valuable products, thus denying out-of-state buyers access to those products.

Due in part to the wide range of regulations it has had to confront, the Supreme Court has not adhered to one consistent test for determining when such regulations impermissibly burden interstate commerce. According to a recent case,[8] however, state laws are *almost always unconstitutional* under the Commerce Clause when they do one of the following:

1. *Directly regulate interstate commerce.* This can occur, for example, when state price regulations require firms to post the prices at which they will sell within the state, and to promise that they will not sell below these prices in other states. Because they affect prices in other states, such regulations directly regulate interstate commerce and usually are unconstitutional.

2. *Discriminate against interstate commerce.* This generally occurs when state laws treat local and interstate commerce unequally on their face. The following *Limbach* case below provides an example.

3. *Favor in-state economic interests over out-of-state interests.* State laws can have this effect even though they do not discriminate against interstate commerce on their face. In one case, for example, the Supreme Court considered a North Carolina statute requiring all closed containers of apples sold within the state to bear only the applicable U.S. grade or standard. Washington State, the nation's largest apple producer, had its own inspection and grading system for Washington apples, a system that generally was regarded as superior to the federal system. The Court struck down the North Carolina statute because it benefited local apple producers by forcing Washington sellers to regrade apples sold in North Carolina (thus raising their costs of doing business), and by undermining the competitive advantage provided by Washington's superior grading system.

Finally, state laws that *regulate evenhandedly and have only incidental effects on interstate commerce* are *constitutional* if they serve legitimate state interests and their local benefits exceed the burden they place on interstate commerce. There is no sharp line between such regulations and those that are almost always unconstitutional under the tests discussed above. In a 1981 Supreme Court case, a state truck-length limitation that differed from the limitations imposed by neighboring states failed to satisfy these tests. First, the Court concluded that the measure did not further the state's legitimate interest in highway safety because the trucks the state banned generally were as safe as those it allowed. Second, whatever marginal safety advantage the law provided was outweighed by the numerous problems it posed for interstate trucking companies.

---

[8] *Brown-Forman Distillers Corp. v. New York State Liquor Authority,* 476 U.S. 573 (1986).

NEW ENERGY COMPANY OF INDIANA v. LIMBACH
486 U.S. 269 (U.S. Sup. Ct. 1988)

Ethanol (ethyl alcohol) is mixed with gasoline in a 1:9 ratio to produce gasohol. Gasohol originally was conceived as a means of promoting energy independence, but lately its use has been justified on environmental grounds because ethanol substitutes for lead in enhancing fuel octane. In 1984, Ohio enacted a gasoline tax credit for each gallon of ethanol sold as a gasohol component by Ohio fuel dealers. This tax credit, however, was denied to ethanol coming from states that did not grant a similar tax credit to ethanol made in Ohio.

The New Energy Company of Indiana is an Indiana ethanol manufacturer. After Indiana repealed its tax subsidy for ethanol in 1985, New Energy's ethanol became ineligible for the Ohio tax credit. Thus, New Energy sued Joanne Limbach, Ohio's Tax Commissioner, for declaratory and injunctive relief in an Ohio trial court, arguing that the Ohio statute violated the Commerce Clause. After the Ohio trial and appellate courts upheld the measure, New Energy appealed to the U.S. Supreme Court.

Scalia, Justice.   The Commerce Clause not only grants Congress the authority to regulate commerce among the states, but also limits the power of the states to discriminate against interstate commerce. This "negative" aspect of the Commerce Clause prohibits economic protectionism—regulatory measures designed to benefit in-state economic interests by burdening out-of-state competitors. Thus, state statutes that discriminate against interstate commerce are routinely struck down, unless the discrimination is demonstrably justified by a valid factor unrelated to economic protectionism.

The Ohio provision explicitly deprives certain products of generally available beneficial tax treatment because they are made in certain other states, and thus on its face appears to violate the cardinal requirement of nondiscrimination. New Energy, in order to sell its product in Ohio, has to cut its profits by reducing its sales price sufficiently to compensate the Ohio purchaser-retailer for the foregone tax credit. The law imposes an economic disadvantage upon out-of-state sellers, and the promise to remove that [disadvantage] if reciprocity is accepted [does not] justify disparity of treatment. The threat used to induce Indiana's acceptance is, in effect, taxing a product made by its manufacturers at a rate higher than the same product made by Ohio manufacturers.

A state may validate a statute that discriminates against interstate commerce by showing that it advances a legitimate local purpose that cannot be adequately served by reasonable nondiscriminatory alternatives. Ohio advances two justifications for the clear discrimination in the present case: health and commerce. It argues that the provision encourages use of ethanol to reduce harmful exhaust emissions. But there is no reason to suppose that ethanol produced in a state that does not offer tax advantages to ethanol produced in Ohio is less healthy, and thus should have its importation into Ohio suppressed by denial of the otherwise standard tax credit. Health is not the purpose of the provision, but is merely an occasional and accidental effect of achieving what *is* its purpose, favorable tax treatment for Ohio-produced ethanol. Essentially the same reasoning also responds to Ohio's second (and related) justification for the discrimination: that the reciprocity requirement is designed to increase commerce in ethanol by encouraging other states to enact ethanol subsidies. What is encouraged is not ethanol subsidies in general, but only favorable treatment for Ohio-produced ethanol. Ohio's health and commerce justifications amount to no more than implausible speculation, which does not suffice to validate this plain discrimination against products of out-of-state manufacture.

Ohio Supreme Court decision against New Energy reversed.

Federal Preemption

The constitutional principle of **federal supremacy** dictates that where state law conflicts with valid federal law, the federal law is supreme. Where a state law conflicts with a federal statute, the state law is said to be *preempted* by the federal regulation. The central question in most federal preemption cases is Congress's intent. Thus, such cases often present questions of statutory interpretation that can be quite complex and that are decided on a case-by-case basis.[9]

Federal preemption of state law generally occurs for one or more of four reasons.

1. There is a direct conflict between the state and federal measures, so that it is impossible to follow

---

[9] See the Nature of Law chapter for a discussion of statutory interpretation.

both simultaneously. The following *McClendon* case involves such a situation.

2. The federal law specifically states that it will preempt state regulation in certain areas. Similar statements may also appear in the federal statute's legislative history, and courts may find such statements persuasive. *McClendon* involves an express statutory preemption clause.

3. The federal regulation is pervasive. The fact that Congress has "occupied the field" by regulating a subject in great breadth and/or in considerable detail suggests its intent to displace state regulation of that subject. This may be especially true where Congress has given an administrative agency broad regulatory power in a particular area.

4. The state regulation is an obstacle to fulfilling the purposes of the federal law.

INGERSOLL-RAND COMPANY v. MCCLENDON

111 S. Ct. 478 (U.S. Sup. Ct. 1990)

Perry McClendon worked as a salesman and distributor for the Ingersoll-Rand Company. In 1981, he was fired after nine years and eight months of service. The discharge supposedly was caused by a companywide reduction in force. However, McClendon believed that he was let go because Ingersoll-Rand wanted to avoid its pension fund responsibilities to him. His rights under the firm's pension plan would have vested after 10 years of service.

McClendon then sued Ingersoll-Rand in a Texas trial court. One of his claims was a common law claim for wrongful discharge. The trial court granted Ingersoll-Rand's motion for summary judgment, and an intermediate appellate court affirmed that ruling. Among each court's reasons was the doctrine of employment at will, which says that employees who are not hired for a definite time period can be terminated at any time for any reason. However, the Texas Supreme Court reversed the lower court's decision and returned the case to the trial court. It held that McClendon's claim fit within the "public policy" exception to the employment-at-will doctrine, which allows discharged employees to recover damages for certain terminations that violate public policy. Ingersoll-Rand then appealed to the U.S. Supreme Court; its argument was that McClendon's common law wrongful discharge claim had been preempted by the federal Employee Retirement Income Security Act (ERISA). McClendon did not sue under this statute.

O'Connor, Justice.   ERISA is a comprehensive statute designed to promote the interests of employees and their beneficiaries in employee benefit plans. The statute imposes participation, funding, and vesting requirements on pension plans. It also sets various uniform standards, including rules concerning reporting, disclosure, and fiduciary responsibility. As part of this regulatory system, Congress [also] included various safeguards to preclude abuse and to completely secure the rights and expectations brought into being by this landmark reform legislation. Prominent among these safeguards are [two] provisions of particular relevance to this case: ERISA's broad preemption provision, and a carefully integrated civil enforcement scheme.

We must decide whether these provisions, singly or in combination, preempt the cause of action at issue in this case. The question whether a certain state action is preempted by federal law is one of congressional intent. To discern Congress's intent, we examine the explicit statutory language and the structure and purpose of the statute. Regardless of the avenue we follow, this state law cause of action cannot be sustained.

Where, as here, Congress has expressly included a broadly worded preemption provision in a comprehensive statute, our task of discerning Congressional intent is considerably simplified. In section 514 of ERISA, Congress provided: "[T]he provisions of this subchapter and subchapter III of this chapter shall supersede any and all State laws insofar as they may now or hereafter relate to any employee benefit plan [covered by relevant ERISA provisions]." [This] preemption clause is conspicuous for its breadth. Its deliberately expansive language was designed to establish pension plan regulation as exclusively a federal concern.

Congress [also] used broad language in defining the "State law" that would be preempted. Such laws include all laws, decisions, rules, regulations, or other state action having the effect of law. [Moreover,] a law "relates to" an employee benefit plan if it has a connection with or reference to such a plan. Under this broad, common sense meaning, a state law may "relate to" a benefit plan, and thereby be preempted, even if the law is not specifically designed to affect such plans, or the effect is only indirect. Preemption is also not precluded simply because a state law is consistent with ERISA's substantive requirements.

The cause of action which the Texas Supreme Court recognized here—a claim that Ingersoll-Rand wrongfully terminated McClendon because of its desire to avoid contributing to or paying benefits under the pension fund—"relates to" an ERISA-covered plan within the meaning of section 514(a), and is therefore preempted. The Texas cause of action makes specific reference to, and indeed is premised on, the existence of a pension plan. To prevail, the plaintiff must plead, and the court must find, that an ERISA plan exists and the employer had a pension-defeating motive in terminating the employment. Because the court's inquiry must be directed to the plan, this judicially created cause of action "relates to" an ERISA plan.

[Our] conclusion is supported by our understanding of the purposes of [section 514(a)]. Section 514(a) was intended to ensure that plans and plan sponsors would be subject to a uniform body of benefit law. It is foreseeable that state courts, exercising their common law powers, might develop different standards applicable to the same employer conduct, requiring the tailoring of plans and employer conduct to the peculiarities of the law of each jurisdiction. Such an outcome is fundamentally at odds with the uniformity Congress sought to implement.

Even if there were no express preemption in this case, the Texas cause of action would be preempted because it conflicts directly with an ERISA cause of action. McClendon's claim falls within ERISA section 510, which protects plan participants from terminations motivated by an employer's desire to prevent a pension plan from vesting. Congress viewed this section as a crucial part of ERISA because without it employers would be able to circumvent the provision of promised benefits. McClendon's claim is prototypical of the kind Congress intended to cover under section 510.

The mere existence of a federal regulatory scheme, however, does not by itself imply preemption of state remedies. Accordingly, we must look for special features warranting preemption. Of particular relevance here is section 502(a)—ERISA's civil enforcement mechanism. Congress intended section 502(a) to be the exclusive remedy for rights guaranteed under ERISA, including those provided by section 510. The exclusive remedy provided by section 502(a) is precisely the kind of feature that warrants preemption in this case. The Texas cause of action purports to provide a remedy for the violation of a right expressly guaranteed by section 510 and exclusively enforced by section 502(a). When it is clear or may fairly be assumed that the activities a State purports to regulate are protected by section 510 of ERISA, state jurisdiction must yield.

Texas Supreme Court decision reversed in favor of Ingersoll-Rand, because McClendon's common law wrongful discharge claim was preempted by ERISA.

THE TAKINGS CLAUSE

The Fifth Amendment provides that "private property [shall not] be taken for public use, without just compensation." This Takings Clause has been incorporated within Fourteenth Amendment due process and thus applies to the states. Traditionally, it has most often come into play when the government formally condemns land through its power of **eminent domain,**[10] but it has many other applications as well.

The Takings Clause recognizes government's power to take private property and also limits the exercise of that power. It does so by requiring that when *property* is subjected to a governmental *taking*, that taking must be for a *public purpose* and the property owner must receive *just compensation*. We now consider these four aspects of the Takings Clause in turn. Figure 3 describes how they interact.

1. *Property.* The Takings Clause protects other property interests besides land and interests in land. Although its full scope is unclear, the clause has been held to cover takings of personal property, liens, trade secrets, and contract rights.

2. *Taking.* Due to the range of property interests it may cover, the Takings Clause potentially has a broad scope. Another reason for the clause's wide possible application is the range of government activities that may be considered takings. Of course, the government's use of formal *condemnation procedures* to acquire private property almost always is a taking. Also, as the following *Seawall* case declares, there is a taking where the government *physically occupies* private property or allows someone else to do so.

In addition, it has long been recognized that government *regulation* may so diminish the value of property or the owner's enjoyment of it as to constitute a taking. Land use regulation such as zoning is an example. Among the factors courts consider in such *regulatory taking* cases are the degree to which government deprives the owner of free possession, use, and disposition of his property; the overall economic impact of the regulation on the owner; and how much the regulation interferes with the owner's reasonable investment-backed expectations regarding the future use of the property. As the *Seawall* case demonstrates, moreover, courts sometimes apply some form of means-ends scrutiny in determining whether a taking has occurred. Although *Seawall* is an exception, this scrutiny often has been fairly relaxed.

3. *Public use.* Once a taking of property has occurred, it is unconstitutional unless it is for a public use. Here, courts now apply a relaxed version of the rational basis test, and the public use requirement is very easy to meet.

4. *Just compensation.* Even if a taking of property is for a public use, it still is unconstitutional if the property owner does not receive just compensation. Although the standards for determining just compensation vary with the circumstances, the basic test is the fair market value of the property at the time of the taking.

In the past, Takings Clause challenges to general regulatory measures usually have not succeeded. The reason is that the just compensation requirement would severely limit government's ability to regulate if many forms of regulation were considered takings. In recent years, however, there have been signs that this attitude is changing. The following *Seawall* case is an example.

---

[10] Eminent domain and the Takings Clause's application to land use problems are discussed in the Real Property and Insurance chapter.

FIGURE 3   Analyzing a Takings Clause Case

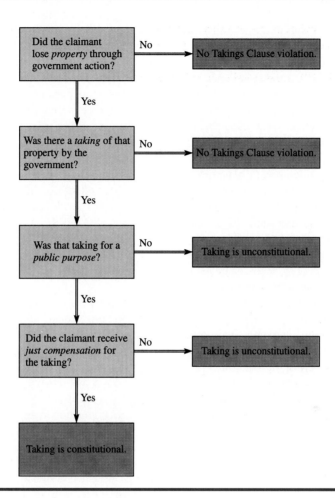

SEAWALL ASSOCIATES v. CITY OF NEW YORK

542 N.E.2d 1059 (N.Y. Ct. App. 1989)

For years, New York City had encouraged the demolition and redevelopment of single-room occupancy (SRO) housing, which it considered substandard. By the mid-1980s, however, this attitude changed because the supply of low-cost rental housing was swiftly declining and home-lessness was increasingly becoming a problem. Thus, the city enacted a number of measures to increase the supply of SRO housing, culminating with the passage of Local Law No. 9 in 1987. Among that law's provisions were: (1) a five-year moratorium on the conversion, alteration, and demolition of buildings containing SRO units; (2) a requirement that property owners with SRO units in their buildings make every such unit habitable; and (3) a requirement that SRO property owners lease every such unit to a bona fide tenant at controlled rents.

A group of real estate developers owning SRO properties challenged Local Law No. 9 as an unconstitutional taking of property without just compensation in a New York trial court. The trial court found the law unconstitutional, but an intermediate appellate court reversed that judgment. The plaintiffs appealed to New York's highest court, the New York Court of Appeals.

Hancock, Judge.   Plaintiffs contend that Local Law No. 9 has resulted in a physical occupation of their properties and is therefore a per se compensable taking. Local Law No. 9 requires the owners to rent their rooms or be subject to severe penalties; to admit persons as tenants with all the possessory and other rights that status entails; and to surrender the most basic attributes of private property, the rights of possession and exclusion. Local Law No. 9 has effected a per se physical taking because it interferes so drastically with the SRO property owners' fundamental rights to possess and to exclude. The law requires nothing less of the owners than to suffer the physical occupation of their building by third parties.

Even if Local Law No. 9 were not a physical taking, it would still be invalid as a regulatory taking. Government regulation involves the adjustment of rights for the public good. Often this adjustment curtails some potential for the use or economic exploitation of private property. There is no set formula for determining when an adjustment of rights has reached the point when justice and fairness require that compensation be paid. However, such a burden-shifting regulation will constitute a taking if: (1) it denies an owner economically viable use of his property, or (2) it does not substantially advance legitimate state interests.

As previously discussed, the coerced rental provisions deprive owners of the fundamental *right to possess* their properties. Moreover, these mandatory rental provisions—along with the prohibition against demolition, alteration, and conversion of the properties to other uses, and the requirement that uninhabitable units be refurbished—deny owners any *right to use* their properties as they see fit. The effect of the law is to strip owners—who may have purchased their properties solely to turn them into profitable investments by tearing down and replacing the existing structures with new ones—of the very right to use their properties for any such purpose. Owners are forced to devote their properties to another use which bears no relation to any economic purpose which could be reasonably contemplated by a private investor. Finally, Local Law No. 9, particularly in those provisions prohibiting redevelopment and mandating rental, impairs the ability of owners to sell their properties for any sums approaching their investments. Thus, the law must also negatively affect the owners' *right to dispose* of their properties. By any test, these restrictions deny the owners economically viable use of their properties.

Moreover, Local Law No. 9 does not substantially advance legitimate state interests. Of course, the end sought by Local Law No. 9 is of the greatest societal importance—alleviating the critical problems of homelessness. However, can it be said that imposing the [law's] burdens on the owners of SRO properties *substantially* advances the aim of alleviating the homelessness problem? The city contends that by increasing the availability of SRO units, [the law] will provide more available low-cost housing and thereby further the aim of alleviating homelessness. The city's own study, however, acknowledges that a ban on converting and destroying SRO units would do little to resolve the crisis. Indeed, the SRO units are not earmarked for the homeless or for potentially homeless low-income families, and there is no assurance that the units will be rented to members of either group. Such a tenuous connection between means and ends cannot justify singling out this group of property owners to bear the costs required by the law.

Local Law No. 9 forces property owners alone to bear public burdens which, in all fairness and justice, should be borne by the public as a whole. Because the owners are afforded no compensation, Local Law No. 9 is invalid under the Takings Clause.

Bellacosa, J., Dissenting.   In 1904, Justice Holmes wrote the quintessential dissenting opinion in *Lochner v. New York*, which presciently warned against his own court's declaring unconstitutional an act of the New York legislature attempting to limit the working hours of [bakery employees]. Eighty-five years after *Lochner*, we observe property rights, like the contract rights of that bygone era, being exalted over the legislature's assessment of social policy. We, as judges, should not inquire into the wisdom of SROs as shelter for potentially 52,000 new, displaced homeless persons—that policy choice belongs to the elected officials who enacted the law.

Appellate court decision reversed in favor of the developers.

ETHICAL AND PUBLIC POLICY CONCERNS

1. Throughout history, the main threat to individual rights of all kinds arguably has come from kings, oligarchs, dictators, and other unrepresentative rulers. Is this true of the rights discussed in this chapter? In the American system of government, who is the main threat to these rights?

2. Courts sometimes state that certain rights are fundamental and then protect those rights by imposing tough means-ends scrutiny on laws that restrict them. What fundamental ethical objection almost always applies to such actions by the courts? *Hint*: Look at the dissenting opinion in the *Seawall* case.

3. Discussions of ethical theory often distinguish between *teleological* ethical theories (which tend to judge the morality of actions by their consequences) and *deontological* theories (which say that some actions are morally obligatory regardless of their consequences). Suppose someone declares that some of the means-ends tests described in this chapter are morally wrong because certain rights are absolute and should *never* be restricted. Means-ends tests, of course, allow rights to be balanced against various social purposes, and in some cases the balancing process may require restriction of the right. Which ethical approach (teleological or deontological) does this declaration most resemble?

4. Although this chapter is mainly concerned with economic rights, one of the great generalizations about American constitutional law is that since 1937, the Supreme Court has shifted from protecting economic rights to protecting personal rights. One example of the Court's former solicitude for economic rights is the doctrine of economic substantive due process mentioned earlier in this chapter. The most important aspect of modern substantive due process, on the other hand, is the constitutional right of privacy. Today, social and economic regulations that are challenged on substantive due process grounds usually get very light means-ends review, while strict scrutiny still applies to some laws that violate privacy rights. Until recently, at least, the most important example of this strict scrutiny was the high degree of constitutional protection given the right to an abortion.

With all of the above in mind, consider the following groups of questions. Throughout, we assume for the sake of argument that it is desirable for courts to give great protection to personal rights.

a. First, consider some familiar attacks on the practice of giving personal rights greater protection than economic rights. Why are personal rights intrinsically more important than economic rights? Why, for example, is the right to an abortion more important than freedom of contract? Or consider the distinction between a right protected by the old-time substantive due process—the right to pursue a trade, occupation, or profession—and freedom of speech. To people in general, which right really matters the most in their daily lives? Finally, does the whole distinction between personal rights and economic rights make any sense? Aren't freedom of contract and the right to pursue a chosen occupation "personal" too?

b. Next, consider the possible consequences of giving greater protection to economic rights. Would this imperil social and economic regulations intended to protect the poor and the powerless? In considering this question, examine the text's discussion of the Supreme Court's 1905 *Lochner* decision and also look at the *Seawall* case. Even if such regulations would be jeopardized, is this a decisive objection to giving greater protection to economic rights?

Also, consider the following possible *positive* consequence of protecting economic rights: that it would increase economic productivity and thereby benefit both rich and poor. Many free-market economists believe that this would happen. On the other hand, even though economic rights have received little constitutional protection over the past 50 years, the U.S. economy still has grown spectacularly during that period.

c. Third, consider a common objection to giving greater protection to economic rights: that the courts are incapable of making intelligent decisions on the questions this would force them to consider. If courts ever do decide to protect economic rights more vigorously, they will have to apply tougher means-ends scrutiny to social and economic regulations. This, in turn, probably means that they will be required to make judgments on a wide range of social and economic questions. Are courts likely to do a good job if they try this? How much do most lawyers know about these matters?

On the other hand, don't courts sometimes have to consider complex questions of social policy when they apply tough scrutiny to laws that restrict *personal* rights? If so, does this mean that courts can also handle issues related to economic rights?

SUMMARY

As written, the U.S. Constitution embodies certain political principles—for example, separation of powers, checks and balances, and federalism. The Constitution as interpreted and applied by the Supreme Court, however, differs from the written Constitution.

The Constitution restricts congressional power to regulate the economy in two ways: by limiting Congress to the exercise of certain *enumerated powers* and by placing certain *independent checks* in the path of Congress when it exercises these enumerated powers. However, the U.S. Constitution does not impose an enumerated powers limitation on the state legislatures. In fact, the most important state regulatory power, the *police power*, is a broad ability to regulate for the public welfare that has few inherent limits. But the U.S. Constitution does place many independent checks on the states.

The most important business-related congressional regulatory powers are its powers to control interstate commerce, to tax, and to spend for the general welfare. By now, there are few inherent limits on the exercise of these powers when they are used to regulate social and economic matters. Today, the *commerce power* is an all-purpose federal police power with a great intrastate reach. By taxing behavior that it deems undesirable, Congress can use the *taxing power* as a regulatory tool. By conditioning the receipt of federal money on the performance of chosen conditions, it does the same with the *spending power*.

The most important business-related independent constitutional checks applying to both the federal government and the states are the *free speech, due process*, and *equal protection* guarantees. The First Amendment's free speech guarantee applies to the states through its incorporation within Fourteenth Amendment due process, and Fourteenth Amendment equal protection applies to the federal government through its incorporation within Fifth Amendment due process. These independent checks operate only where there has been *government action*.

When the government regulates *commercial speech*, the regulation is subjected to an intermediate level of review that is less rigorous than the very strict standards used in most First Amendment cases. Corporate *political* speech, however, receives full First Amendment protection.

Due process can be *procedural* (setting standards of fairness that the government must follow as it enforces its laws) or *substantive* (assessing the policy merits of laws governing social behavior). Today, however, substantive due process is of little or no consequence where government regulates economic activity.

The basic equal protection standard, and the test applied to government regulation of economic matters, is the lenient *rational basis* requirement. However, discrimination with respect to certain *fundamental rights* attracts a high level of *strict scrutiny*. The same is often, but not always, true for discrimination on the bases of race (or national origin) and alienage. Governmental classifications based on gender and illegitimacy receive some *intermediate* degree of scrutiny.

There are three important business-related independent checks that apply only to the states. The *Contract Clause* puts some limits on the states' ability to impair the obligations of existing contracts by measures passed after these contracts have come into existence. Included within the Contract Clause's definition of the term *contracts* are *governmental* contracts and grants.

In addition to serving as a source of congressional power to regulate, the Commerce Clause places an implied check on state laws that unduly *burden interstate commerce*. Over the years, the Supreme Court has not consistently followed any one set of standards when determining whether state laws are unconstitutional under the Commerce Clause.

State measures may be *preempted* by federal regulation. Determining when this occurs is basically a matter of statutory interpretation.

Finally, the Fifth Amendment's *Takings Clause* recognizes government's power to take private property and also limits that power by stating that takings of such property require just compensation and must be for a public purpose. Many forms of *property* are protected by the clause. In addition to formal condemnation procedures and physical occupations of the owners' property, various kinds of government regulation can constitute *takings*. Today, the *public purpose* test is very easy to meet. The usual *just compensation* standard is the fair market value of the property at the time of the taking.

PROBLEM CASES

1. The Kraynak brothers owned a small coal mine in Pennsylvania. They did all of the work in the mine themselves and sold all of the coal they produced, about 10,000 tons annually, to Penntech Papers Company. Penntech was located in Pennsylvania, but its products were distributed nationwide. The Kraynaks claimed that they were exempt from the provisions of the Federal Coal Mine Health and Safety Act (which was based on the Commerce Clause) because of the intrastate nature of their operation. Can the act constitutionally apply to the Kraynaks' mine?

2. In 1984, Congress passed a highway funding bill directing the secretary of transportation to withhold a percentage of the federal highway funds otherwise due to a state, if the state allowed the purchase or possession of alcoholic beverages by those less than 21 years of age. South Dakota, which by statute permitted those 19 or older to buy 3.2 beer, sued to have the statute declared unconstitutional. On what enumerated power is this federal law based? Is it a constitutional exercise of that power? If the statute is constitutional, does this mean that South Dakota cannot permit the purchase or consumption of alcoholic beverages by those under 21?

3. The Metropolitan Edison Company, a privately owned but state-regulated electrical utility, terminated Catherine Jackson's electrical service without notice or a hearing when she became delinquent in paying her electric bills. Jackson sued Metropolitan, arguing that its action violated due process. What *kind* of due process claim is Jackson making here? Assuming that Metropolitan is heavily regulated by the state, is this fact sufficient by itself to make Metropolitan's conduct state action? Can Metropolitan's conduct be state action under the "public function" theory? In answering these last two questions, you might use the *San Francisco Arts & Athletics* case as a reference.

4. The Consolidated Edison Company (Con Ed), a privately owned corporation that is a regulated public utility, placed written inserts touting nuclear power in the bills it sent to its customers. Then, the New York Public Service Commission prohibited state utilities from using bill inserts to discuss controversial public policy issues such as the desirability of nuclear power. Con Ed challenged this regulation as an unconstitutional restriction of freedom of speech under the First Amendment. Are corporations like Con Ed entitled to assert First Amendment claims? What kind of speech is at issue here? What level of scrutiny does such speech receive when laws restricting it are examined by the courts?

5. Virginia had a statute prohibiting licensed pharmacists from advertising the price of prescription drugs. The alleged purpose behind the statute was to protect the public by preventing price competition in the sale of prescription drugs, thus ensuring that the need to meet a competitor's price would not force pharmacists to dispense with full professional services in the compounding, handling, and dispensing of prescription drugs. What type of First Amendment speech is restricted by this statute? Is this speech entitled to full First Amendment protection? Did the statute survive a First Amendment challenge?

6. One provision of the federal Deficit Reduction Act of 1984 established a 15-month freeze on the fees certain physicians could charge medicare patients. A group of physicians challenged the constitutionality of this provision, alleging that it restricted freedom of contract in violation of the Fifth Amendment's Due Process Clause. What *kind* of due process attack is this? Did it succeed?

7. The Minnesota legislature passed a statute banning the sale of milk in plastic nonrefillable, nonreusable containers. However, it allowed sales of milk in other nonrefillable, nonreusable containers such as paperboard cartons. One of the justifications for this ban on plastic jugs was that it would ease the state's solid waste disposal problems because plastic jugs occupy more space in landfills than other nonreturnable milk containers. A group of dairy businesses challenged the statute, arguing that its distinction between plastic containers and other containers was unconstitutional under the Equal Protection Clause. What means-ends test or level of scrutiny applies in this case? Under that test, is easing the state's solid waste disposal problems a sufficiently important *end*? Under that test, is there a sufficiently close "fit" between the classification and that end to make the statutory *means* constitutional? In answering the last question, assume for the sake of argument that in fact there were better ways of alleviating the solid waste disposal problem than banning plastic jugs while allowing paperboard cartons.

8. Oklahoma statutes set the age for drinking 3.2 beer at 21 for men and 18 for women. The asserted purpose behind the statutes (and the sex-based classification that they established) was traffic safety. The statutes were challenged as a denial of equal protection by male residents of Oklahoma. What level of scrutiny would this measure receive if *women* had been denied the right to drink 3.2 beer until they were 21 but men had been allowed to consume it at age 18? Should this standard change because the measure discriminates against *men*? Is the male challenge to the statute likely to be successful?

9. Under a New York law, all distillers of alcoholic beverages had to file a monthly price schedule with the state's liquor authority in order to sell to wholesalers within the state, and had to adhere to the schedule for that month. Also, any distiller filing a price schedule effectively had to promise that it would not make any out-of-state sale at a price lower than the New York price for the month in question. Violations of this promise could lead to the loss of a distiller's New York license to manufacture and sell liquor. As applied to distillers

doing business outside New York, did this regulation violate the Commerce Clause?

10. The Federal Insecticide, Fungicide, and Rodenticide Act (FIFRA) requires that all covered pesticides be registered with the Environmental Protection Agency (EPA) before their sale. From 1972 through 1978, registrants under the act had broad powers to block the EPA's disclosure of their trade secrets when such secrets had to be disclosed as part of the registration process. After 1978, FIFRA was amended to give the EPA some ability to disclose such trade secrets to the public and to use trade secret data submitted by one applicant when considering later applications.

The Monsanto Company, a manufacturer of pesticides, sued to have these post-1978 FIFRA provisions declared unconstitutional under the Takings Clause. Monsanto argued that these provisions "took" its property by permitting its trade secrets to be known to competitors and by giving later registrants a free ride through the registration process when the EPA used Monsanto's data in subsequent applications. Are Monsanto's trade secrets property for Takings Clause purposes? On the taking issue, did the post-1978 provisions interfere with Monsanto's earlier reasonable expectations regarding the government's use of its trade secrets? Assuming that there was a taking of property here and that it was for a public purpose, what would the government have to do to make the taking constitutional?

CHAPTER 4

BUSINESS ETHICS, CORPORATE SOCIAL RESPONSIBILITY, AND THE CONTROL AND GOVERNANCE OF CORPORATIONS

INTRODUCTION

In recent years, business ethics has become an increasingly important part of the business curriculum. Courses and materials on this subject often present problems based on concrete dilemmas business managers may face during their careers, and might bring various ethical theories to bear on those problems. But such approaches, although valuable, fail to explore the context in which business ethics assumes significance. The current drive for more ethical business conduct is only the latest stage in a century-long struggle to control corporate misbehavior.[1] This chapter presents business ethics within the context of that struggle.

The Debate over the Large Corporation

In America, large corporations first emerged during the country's rapid industrialization toward the end of the 19th century. Ever since, such corporations have been villains to some and heroes to others. Hostility to big business was one theme in the populist movement of the late 19th century, and the control of large corporations

preoccupied the progressive movement of the early 20th century. The need to check real or perceived abuses of business power was a major force behind both the New Deal statutes of the 1930s and the wave of federal regulation that occurred during the 1960s and 1970s. Despite all this concern about abuses of corporate power, however, large corporations have been major forces behind the enormous increase in material well-being that America has experienced throughout the last century.

Over the past 25 years, those voicing dissatisfaction with the behavior of large corporations probably have overshadowed the corporation's defenders. Despite diminishing in frequency and intensity during the 1980s, the critics' litany of complaints is still very familiar. In the single-minded pursuit of profits, these critics say, corporations despoil the environment, mistreat employees, sell shoddy and dangerous products to consumers, abandon local communities without warning, distort the political processes, and abuse their power in innumerable other ways as well.

Underlying these specific criticisms are some general perceptions about modern corporations. Large corporations, it is observed, perform a great many essential national economic functions such as raw materials extraction, energy production, the provision of transportation and communications, and military production—functions that many countries entrust to government

---

[1]Of course, many of this chapter's observations apply to other business forms besides corporations.

bodies. How corporations perform these functions is critical to the nation's well-being. Despite their social importance, however, corporations are not nearly so accountable to the public as the formal organs of government. For example, they are generally not subject to constitutional checks,[2] and the public has little to say about the appointment of their officers and directors. This lack of accountability is made all the more serious, critics maintain, by the tremendous power big corporations wield in many spheres of American life. Indeed, such corporations have frequently been described as private governments.

These criticisms and perceptions have naturally generated calls for changes in the ways corporations decide and behave. Throughout the 20th century, the law has been the main device for checking corporate misdeeds. For reasons discussed later in this chapter, however, some observers have come to feel that regulation, while an important element in any corporate control scheme, is insufficient by itself. As a supplement to regulation, they urge that business should be led to adhere to a standard of ethical or socially responsible behavior higher than that imposed by existing rules of law. To promote such behavior, some corporate critics have proposed fairly sweeping changes in the internal governance of corporations. Others have argued that the business community's own internal resources should be brought to bear in the struggle to produce socially responsible corporate conduct. It is within this context that the move toward ethics instruction has arisen.

The debate about the modern corporation, however, has not been totally dominated by its critics. Arrayed against those critics are people who argue that profit maximization should be the main goal of corporations and that the only ethical norms business firms should feel bound to follow are those embodied in the law. As the economist Milton Friedman once argued, corporate management's duty is to make as much money for the shareholders as possible—within the rules of the game.[3] One justification for this position is that because "ethical" firms are unlikely to be consistent profit-maximizers, the economic efficiencies profit maximization produces would be lost if corporations were to subordinate it to other social goals. By pursuing profits, they

say, businesses ensure that scarce economic resources are allocated to the uses that society values most highly. The end result is that society as a whole benefits because its total economic welfare is maximized. For this reason, some defenders of the corporation argue that profit maximization *is* socially responsible corporate behavior. Such people are also apt to stress the ways that market forces and other private activity can curb irresponsible corporate conduct. Unlike critics of the corporation, finally, its defenders are prone to regard government regulation as all too effective in curbing corporations. Indeed, they often depict corporations as hamstrung by regulations that deter socially valuable profit-seeking without producing comparable social benefits.

Chapter Organization

This chapter has two major components. In the first part of the chapter, we examine the major arguments and counterarguments that comprise the corporate social responsibility debate. Although it does not exactly conform with the headings in this chapter, Figure 1 summarizes the most important such arguments and counterarguments. This chapter's second component assesses the strengths and weaknesses of the various means of controlling corporate misbehavior. As you will see, this portion of the chapter does not provide any neat set of answers to the questions raised by the corporate social responsibility debate. This debate has persisted for a century, and is likely to continue as long as corporations form the backbone of our economic system. The reason for the debate's persistence is the range of exceedingly complex and difficult factual issues and philosophical disagreements it presents.

The Relevance of the Debate

Enough has been said so far, we hope, to demonstrate that the debate about the large modern corporation is extremely important as a matter of general social policy. That aside, though, why should it concern *you* personally? For one thing, your life is affected directly and indirectly by the decisions of corporate managers. For example, those decisions can influence the safety of the automobile you drive, your job security and working conditions, and the quality of the environment in which you live. More importantly, the issues discussed in this chapter are likely to concern you if you become a corporate manager. In this case, *your* decisions may affect the health, physical security, livelihood, and lifestyle of em-

---

[2]This is due to the state action or government action requirement described in the Business and the Constitution chapter.

[3]*Playboy* magazine interview with Milton Friedman (1973).

FIGURE 1   The Corporate Social Responsibility Debate

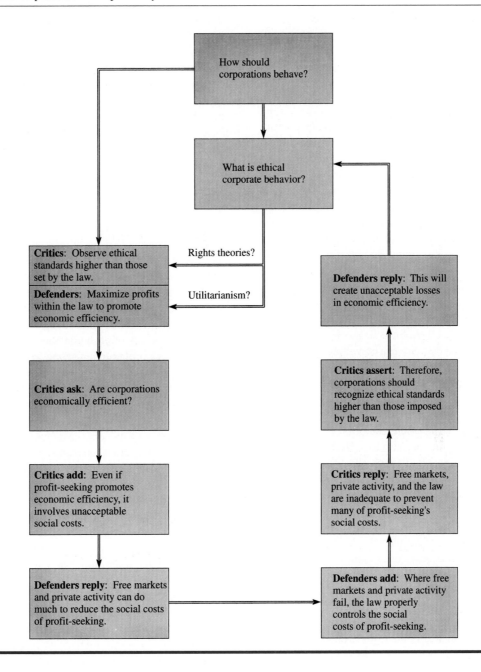

ployees, consumers, and a host of others. Thus, it is desirable that you become as informed as possible about the ethical and factual considerations affecting those decisions. In a further effort to stimulate and improve your thinking on these questions, the other chapters in this text conclude with a section discussing certain ethical and public policy concerns. Although these questions usually involve concerns specific to the chapter in which they appear, occasionally they apply ideas discussed in this chapter.

THE CASE FOR PROFIT MAXIMIZATION

The primary stated objective of business corporations is to maximize profits. Economists generally favor this objective because it results in an *efficient allocation and use of society's scarce resources*. Firms that most efficiently use resources generally can undersell their competitors and, due to the greater sales that should result, reap higher profits. As a result, they often can outbid less efficient resource users. Hence, scarce resources are allocated efficiently; that is, to the users and uses most highly valued by consumers and most capable of giving consumers a maximum return on their expenditures. If corporate managers choose to pursue goals other than profit maximization, resources will not be put to their most efficient uses and society's total wealth will be reduced by the resulting allocational inefficiencies.

To illustrate the last point, assume for the sake of argument that there is no foreign competition in the American steel industry and that all the domestic steel manufacturers spontaneously decide to observe pollution standards stricter than those now imposed by law. In addition, assume that these firms do so even though they know that their buyers may not be willing to pay more for "responsibly" produced steel. Because such socially responsible behavior costs money, the firms face a dilemma. They can try to pass on the increased costs to buyers in the form of higher prices, thus reducing the buyers' return per dollar spent and possibly their ability to purchase other goods and services. Higher prices also might cause some buyers to seek substitutes for steel, with obvious effects on the steel firms' profits. Or the firms might decide to retain existing customers by refusing to increase prices despite the higher costs they face. In this case, the firms almost certainly would have to accept lower profits. If profits fall, dividends and employee salaries might be reduced, and the firms' ability to bid for scarce resources such as iron ore also might suffer. The likely result is a flow of employees, investment funds, and resources away from the firms in question. This, in turn, may mean lower steel production and lower overall social wealth than would otherwise be the case. Thus, it seems that socially responsible corporate behavior imposes social costs.

ARE LARGE CORPORATIONS REALLY EFFICIENT?

Despite the theoretical link between profit maximization and the efficient allocation of resources, critics of the corporation and other observers long have questioned whether large corporations really do promote economic efficiency. Two views recur in their descriptions of modern business life. The first is that in their pursuit of profit, big corporations continually engage in anticompetitive behavior that produces an inefficient allocation of resources for society as a whole. The second is that some modern corporations are inefficient because they do not really *try* to maximize profits. Although these two views are conceptually distinct, both refer mainly to large, established, mature firms in oligopolistic industries.[4]

Anticompetitive Behavior

In outlining the case for profit maximization, we assumed that competitive conditions obtained within the industries and markets in question. But as Adam Smith observed over 200 years ago, "[p]eople of the same trade seldom meet together, even for merriment and diversion, but the conversation ends in a conspiracy against the public, or in some contrivance to raise prices."[5] In other words, competitors often try to thwart the market and maximize their profits by engaging in the various anticompetitive practices described in the chapters on antitrust law. To the extent that they succeed, they weaken the link between profit-seeking and allocational efficiency. A firm with monopoly power, for instance, ordinarily can maximize its sales revenues and reap monopoly profits by restricting output and raising prices. This results in an inefficient allocation of resources, because the total amount of goods or services is reduced and purchasers of those goods or services do not receive a maximum return on the dollars they spend.

Throughout this century, the main device for controlling anticompetitive corporate behavior has been antitrust regulation. The antitrust laws' effectiveness, however, has long been questioned. Section 2 of the Sherman Act generally has been successful in preventing outright monopolies. But many believe that firms in oligopolistic industries can engage in tacit price-fixing and other anticompetitive behavior without much fear of antitrust liability. This is one possible example of a theme we stress later in this chapter: the law's limits as a corporate control device.

---

[4]An oligopolistic industry is one dominated by a few large sellers.

[5]A. Smith, *The Wealth of Nations*. The first edition of this classic defense of free enterprise appeared in 1776.

Are Corporations Always Profit-Maximizers?

Economists generally view corporations as entities devoted to the rational pursuit of profit. However, sociologists, organizational psychologists, students of organizational behavior, and certain other observers of various political persuasions tend to see the corporation in a different light: as a bureaucratic organization that serves as a kind of community for its members and that pursues a variety of goals in the process. To such observers, profit maximization is only one—and perhaps not the most important—of those goals.

People who argue that corporations pursue goals other than profit maximization usually focus on large, modern, mature corporations in oligopolistic industries. They concede that smaller firms fighting for survival in competitive markets are primarily oriented toward profits. Established firms in oligopolistic industries, however, may face less severe competition, and thus may have the luxury of pursuing other aims. Such goals include the financial well-being of officers and employees, the creation of a congenial and stimulating internal environment, expansion, prestige, and innovation. Such goals are not necessarily inconsistent with profit maximization. Higher employee benefits, for instance, may increase profits by attracting better employees or increasing employee satisfaction and job performance. But sometimes the pursuit of these goals can consume resources and human energy that might otherwise be devoted to profit-seeking.

Because firms of this sort are entrenched in oligopolistic industries, the argument continues, they can and do engage in the anticompetitive activity discussed above. Like the firms just described, therefore, they do not afford consumers the maximum return on the dollars they spend. Because firms of this second kind are *internally* inefficient, moreover, they do not even maximize profits. Instead, they are said to seek only a *satisfactory* profit level: to "satisfice" (rather than maximize) profits. This generally means that such firms only try to achieve a profit level sufficient to satisfy shareholders. As a result, shareholders do not receive the returns they would receive if these firms strove to maximize profits, and the economy suffers because shareholders cannot deploy the lost returns to stimulate economic activity elsewhere.

Another argument against the claim that corporations try to maximize profits concedes the claim, but argues that the profits sought usually are only *short-term* profits. Such firms, in other words, sacrifice the future to the present and thus do not promote long-term allocational efficiency. In the interest of short-term profits, for instance, firms may forgo investments in research and production facilities that would enhance their profits and increase economic efficiency over the long haul. The reward structures that exist in many corporations are said to further this tendency. For example, salary, bonus, and promotion decisions frequently are tied to year-end profitability; and top executives often have relatively brief terms of office. Thus, the strategies that would generate long-term profits may not be in the short-term interests of managers in such firms.

Rejoinders

Defenders of the corporation, of course, are not greatly impressed by the various arguments made in this section. Although they recognize the possibility of anticompetitive behavior, they regard proper antitrust enforcement as adequate to deal with the problem. Some defenders of the corporation, in fact, contend that the antitrust laws have *frustrated* economic efficiency by imposing needless restraints on effective competitors. More often than not, they argue, size and market power are the results of superior efficiency, and the antitrust laws should not penalize the efficient. As the Sherman Act chapter relates, these Chicago School critics of traditional antitrust doctrine also urge that foreign competition and the emergence of international markets have reduced concentration levels in many industries, and that even highly concentrated industries often are competitive.

Defenders of the corporation also argue that the critics' claims ignore the facts of life in modern securities markets.[6] Due to the nature of those markets, they contend, a short-term orientation and profit satisficing are unsound strategies that ultimately create severe problems for firms that adopt them. For example, suppose that a corporation's managers make short-run decisions that detrimentally affect its long-run profitability, or try to pay only the dividends they think necessary to satisfy shareholders. In either case, the value of the corporation's shares eventually should fall below those shares' potential maximum value. This could lead some shareholders to sell their shares, which further depresses

---

[6]Some of the arguments sketched in this paragraph are based on the *efficient market hypothesis* you may encounter in your economics or finance courses. The efficient market hypothesis comes in various forms; one version states that all the relevant information about a corporate security is immediately reflected in the price of that security.

prices. In addition, a corporation with securities selling below their maximum potential value is a target for a hostile takeover. And top managers almost always lose their jobs after a hostile takeover. Hence, the counter-argument concludes, most corporations do try to maximize long-term profits and the returns they give their shareholders.

Summary and Conclusion

As you may have noticed, this section presents two wildly conflicting pictures of the American economy. To some critics of the corporation, anticompetitive practices prevail, the antitrust laws do little to prevent them, and many firms are sluggish, timid bureaucracies rather than lean-and-mean profit-making machines.[7] But to the corporation's defenders, modern business firms, while *big*, still *compete*. Because *economists* do not agree on the resolution of these differences, we do not attempt to settle them here. But the dispute is basic to the corporate social responsibility debate, for if corporations do not promote economic efficiency, their defenders' case is jeopardized.

THE SOCIAL COSTS OF PROFIT MAXIMIZATION

When critics of the corporation argue that large corporations are not profit-maximizers, they do so more to undermine the defenders' case than to extol profit-seeking. Even if it could be proven to everyone's satisfaction that corporations always compete, always try to maximize profits, and always promote economic efficiency in the process, their foes would hardly be silenced. The reason is that to modern critics of the corporation, profit maximization is the source of most of the misdeeds business commits. In this connection, they make a simple claim: allocational efficiency is not society's only (or even its most important) goal, and sometimes this goal should be subordinated to other social concerns. Just as the pursuit of corporate social responsibility forces society to make material sacrifices, the uninhibited pursuit of allocational efficiency compels it to sacrifice other values.

Critics of the idea that corporations should be concerned solely with profit maximization usually stress

that profit-seeking can harm employees, consumers, communities, the environment, and society as a whole. Obviously, for example, many products can be produced more cheaply and sold at lower prices if environmental concerns are ignored during their manufacture. Also, corporations that leave a community when they find cheaper labor, favorable tax rates, and/or low interest loans in another community may thereby enjoy increased profits, aid in the efficient allocation of scarce resources, and maximize total economic welfare. But this is small consolation to the abandoned community, which may be left with little more than an empty factory shell. Even less likely to be consoled by these results are former employees who cannot find work or schoolchildren whose schools may be underfunded due to the erosion of the community's tax base.

To all of this, defenders of the profit-maximization motive can maintain that in most cases, the allocational efficiencies achieved by profit maximization simply outweigh the social costs of that achievement. Who is right? In many cases, your answer may depend on the particular trade-off in question. For instance, if a small reduction in air pollution means big sacrifices in industrial productivity, you may have little trouble deciding that the environmental gains are not worth their material costs. But in other situations, basic moral choices may be necessary. You may have to decide, for example, whether environmental protection ultimately is more important than economic growth, or vice versa. Later in this chapter, we examine two ethical theories with conflicting criteria for making such choices and quite different ideas about how the trade-offs in question should proceed.

MARKETS AND FREE PRIVATE ACTIVITY AS CHECKS ON IRRESPONSIBLE CORPORATE BEHAVIOR

To the corporation's modern critics, the ill effects of profit maximization are compounded by the tremendous social and economic power large corporations possess and the inferior power of those who are affected by corporate decisions. For example, communities often vie for the benefits that a local business operation can bring and frequently have little power to influence corporate decisions to move to greener pastures. Also, while labor markets obviously restrict the terms employers can offer nonunionized employees, such employees generally do not engage in genuine bargaining regarding those terms. Instead, the employer's terms are offered on a take-it-or-

---

[7]However, these views once led some corporate reformers to an optimistic conclusion: that large corporations would come to behave more responsibly as the source of their misdeeds—the pressure to maximize profits—was relaxed. See the discussion of the corporate stewardship argument later in this chapter.

leave-it basis. Similarly, consumers have no direct input in determining the products corporations produce, their features, the prices at which they are sold, or the methods by which they are manufactured.

The modern corporation's defenders, however, regard such claims as exaggerated. Indeed, some would argue that, rather than being checked by corporate power, market forces and free private activity force corporations to behave in a socially responsible fashion. For this reason, they add, corporate behavior can be made more responsible without subjecting business to stifling government regulation or having managers abandon their basic profit orientation and the social benefits it creates. Manufacturers that produce and market defective products, for example, should eventually suffer as consumers move to superior alternatives. Also, consumer groups and consumer publications can publicly expose substandard and dangerous products.

What is more, defenders of profit maximization continue, in a free society with freedom of expression people can organize to make their grievances felt. In this way, free private activity can check other abuses of corporate power besides the marketing of defective and/or dangerous products. For example, letter-writing campaigns and boycotts can be organized to crack down on polluters, and consumer groups can issue press releases about their activities. Also, consumers who own stock in polluting corporations can make shareholder proposals attacking such behavior. These methods often are quite effective in getting the attention of image-conscious corporate managers.

When these various forms of private persuasion fail, defenders of the corporation might add, the failure is not necessarily due to superior corporate power. If such efforts do not attract sufficient support, this may well suggest that the complaints were not valid in the first place. Or it may indicate that those who did not join up expressly or implicitly decided that the costs of achieving success outweighed the benefits accruing from success. Who are the corporation's critics to say that these people were wrong?

However, numerous difficulties confront those who argue that free market mechanisms and private activity can influence corporate behavior in responsible directions. Some of these difficulties were described in an influential 1975 book by Christopher Stone.[8] According to Stone:

---

[8]Christopher Stone, *Where the Law Ends* 88–92 (New York: Harper & Row, 1975).

1. People who are being injured or otherwise disadvantaged by defective products may not be *aware* of the injury at the time it occurs. This is the "unknown harms" problem discussed later in this chapter. In the past, for example, many cigarette smokers did not know that smoking helps cause lung cancer. Some of the products we use today may well have harmful effects that only will be discovered in the future.

2. Even where consumers or other private parties are aware of the injury at the time it occurs, they may not know *where* to apply pressure. According to Stone, in some highly concentrated industries one competitor may sell products under several brand names. Thus, because people tend to identify products by brand name, a dissatisfied consumer who drops one of those products may well switch to a brand manufactured by the same firm.

3. Even if these first two problems are surmounted, private action may fail because consumers or other private parties are not properly situated to apply pressure on the offending corporation. For instance, suppose you are infuriated by the fact that the XYZ Corporation trades with some unsavory foreign government. If you are not a consumer of XYZ's products or a shareholder of XYZ, your options for influencing it may be limited to letter-writing campaigns, boycotts, and the like. On the other hand, what are you supposed to do if XYZ manufactures a product you vitally need, and all the other firms in its highly concentrated industry are just as offensive as XYZ?

4. Finally, even if sufficient pressure actually is applied, there is no guarantee that corporations will *respond rationally* to that pressure. Later in the chapter, we consider whether and to what extent corporations are rational actors.

How convincing are Stone's arguments? For example, how many injuries caused by defective products are "delayed manifestation" harms? How many industries contain firms that market products under several brand names? If such firms continually produce substandard products, won't they have to face competition from new entrants at some point? Also, is it really so difficult for people to obtain information about a corporation's products and activities? Once they obtain this information, what is to prevent them from notifying a corporation of their concerns or making those concerns public?

The validity of rejoinders like those just made probably varies with the circumstances. However, you should consider several things in evaluating them and in determining whether they effectively rebut Stone. First, note that these arguments concede a basic point made by critics of the corporation: In certain circumstances, some values may be more important than allocational efficiency. Also, do these arguments assume an unrealistic degree of time, energy, concern, and sophistication on the part of consumers? Do they underestimate the difficulty of competing as a new entrant in a highly concentrated industry? Do they also underestimate the difficulties involved in organizing to achieve collective purposes? Do they further underestimate the difficulty of exerting *enough* pressure to change corporate behavior? Do they underestimate corporate resistance to such activities and the power of corporations to counter them?

Finally, do the questions just posed say something about the *kinds* of corporate wrongdoing markets and free private activity are best able to check? For example, are such forces more likely to be effective in curbing the sale of defective and/or dangerous products than in stopping firms from despoiling the environment or bribing foreign governments?

THE LAW AS A CORPORATE CONTROL DEVICE

Introduction

In all likelihood, markets and free private activity are better suited for checking some forms of corporate misbehavior than others. This being the case, alternative devices for curbing irresponsible corporate behavior seem necessary. By far the most important such device, one this chapter has largely ignored until now, is the *law*.

If irresponsible corporate behavior creates sufficient public dissatisfaction, defenders of the corporation argue, that dissatisfaction will sooner or later be translated into legal action. Just as a free society permits individuals and groups to put moral and economic pressure on corporations, it also allows them to make their desires felt in the political arena. As the table of contents to this text illustrates, such efforts plainly have been successful in generating legal controls on business. Indeed, legal checks have been the main means of controlling corporate misdeeds throughout this century. And while defenders of profit maximization frequently complain that government regulation is excessive, they always recognize that corporations should obey the basic rules of the game established by the legal system. These rules, they say, state norms of behavior backed by a substantial social consensus.

The law's ability to block socially irresponsible corporate actions depends heavily on the view that corporations are *rational actors* that can be *deterred* from misbehavior by the threats the law presents. The main way the law controls behavior is through the sanctions (e.g., fines, civil damages) it imposes on those who violate its rules. For deterrence to work effectively, those the law is to control must understand when its penalties will be imposed, must fear the costs those penalties create, and must act rationally to avoid them. Even if corporations are not always profit-seekers, they still have an interest in maximizing the funds available to them for the various purposes they pursue. Thus, it seems natural that they should fear the penalties the law imposes for misbehavior, which are largely financial in nature. And if corporations are rational actors with the ability to recognize monetary threats and respond accordingly, they should be deterred from engaging in irresponsible behavior that is forbidden by law.

Unfortunately, the law's ability to control irresponsible corporate behavior, while significant, has its limits. Some of the various—and somewhat conflicting— reasons for its relative ineffectiveness are discussed below.[9] To the extent that these arguments are valid, the profit-maximizers' case against modern critics of the corporation is weakened. Some of these arguments undermine the profit-maximizers' claim that following the legal rules of the game sufficiently fulfills business's obligations to society. Others suggest that corporations are not always rational actors.

Corporate Influence on the Content of the Law

One reason the law is a less-than-ideal corporate control device is that business has a significant voice in determining the law's content. Thus, the law sometimes reflects *corporate* interests. As a result, corporations sometimes can engage in behavior that noncorporate segments of society would find unethical.

The political influence exerted by large corporations is a familiar subject. Because of their size, resources, and sophistication, they have (or can purchase) the ability to influence legislation through methods such as lobbying and contributions to business-oriented political action committees. Even if Congress or the state legisla-

---

[9]In addition, the Crimes chapter discusses some reasons why *criminal* sanctions against corporations and their directors, officers, and employees are problematic corporate control devices.

tures pass hostile regulatory legislation, moreover, corporations can sometimes blunt its impact. They may use their political influence to reduce the funding received by the agency enforcing the legislation. Over time, they may co-opt the agency by inducing it to take a pro-business view of its functions. One way this occurs is through the frequent exchange of personnel between the agency and the industry it is supposed to regulate in the public interest. And many political scientists have commented on the frequency with which an agency, the industry it regulates, and the congressional subcommittee controlling the agency form a mutually beneficial relationship that is relatively impervious to outside influence (the so-called Iron Triangle).

In evaluating such arguments, however, you should note that by now critics of the corporation have also become adept at playing the political game, and on some occasions are able to counteract corporate political power. The influence of consumer groups and environmental groups are but two examples.[10]

Conscious Lawbreaking

Even where the legal rules do not reflect business interests, corporations may consciously decide that it makes sense to violate those rules. As rational actors with a desire to maximize profits, corporations may conclude that breaking the law poses acceptable risks if the benefits gained by doing so are great, the penalties for violation are relatively light, and/or the chances of being sued or prosecuted are low. In some cases, for example, it may make sense for a firm to continue to market a defect-ridden product rather than redesign it, if competitors' products are no better and the costs of paying or settling product liability claims or of procuring product liability insurance are sufficiently low that they can be passed on to consumers in the form of higher prices. Also, as noted in the Crimes chapter, criminal fines may have little deterrent effect on corporations unless those fines are very large. Finally, the economic costs imposed by legal penalties do not always affect the careers and compensation of the responsible corporate managers.

In addition, several other factors increase the likelihood that corporations will engage in conscious or semi-conscious lawbreaking. The let's-take-the-risk mentality may be reinforced when the law is (or is perceived to be)

uncertain. Corporate or industry norms may regard a measure of illegal (or borderline) behavior as morally acceptable. This is especially likely where corporate managers regard the relevant legal rules as misguided.

The tendency toward conscious lawbreaking could be reduced, many argue, by stiffer penalties and increased enforcement efforts. But corporate political influence may prevent either from occurring. As noted above, corporations sometimes try to blunt politically popular legislation by devoting their efforts to such less visible matters as agency funding. State and federal prosecutors are usually either elected or politically appointed. And, more generally, the public is not always willing to fund increased enforcement efforts.

Another get-tough measure for reducing conscious law-breaking, increased criminal liability for key corporate decisionmakers, also may be less effective than it would appear at first glance. The realities of intracorporate life often make it difficult to pinpoint the true wrongdoers, as the discussion of this subject in the Crimes chapter makes clear. For various reasons detailed in that chapter, moreover, it is doubtful whether criminal sanctions ever will be applied with full vigor to white-collar criminals.

Unknown Harms

As Stone argued, those who rely exclusively on market forces to control corporate behavior must assume that consumers always know that they are being harmed at the time the harm occurs. Reliance on the *law* as a corporate control device involves a similar assumption: that legislators and regulators possess such knowledge. Plainly, legal action to control socially harmful corporate behavior will not be forthcoming until the need for such action is apparent. Yet it is not uncommon to discover that a product we have used with perfect confidence for years has some newly discovered harmful side effect, or that some chemical commonly used in production processes poses risks to workers, consumers, or the environment. In some cases of this kind, after-the-fact legal action may be incapable of compensating for irreparable harms that have already occurred.

Worse yet, some kinds of unknown harms may be unknown even to the corporate managers in charge of the products or production processes producing those harms. In other instances, however, corporate managers' intimate familiarity with their own products or processes may make them aware of such dangers long before they are apparent to society in general. Such

---

[10]As discussed in the Administrative Agencies chapter, such groups can influence the behavior of administrative agencies by serving as "agency shadows."

situations obviously confront corporate managers with a difficult ethical dilemma. Should they take no action until the dangers become apparent, hoping that any liability eventually imposed on their corporation will be manageable? Should they take immediate unilateral corrective action that puts their firm at a competitive disadvantage with competitors who fail to take similar corrective action? Or should they alert the public, so that the legal rules of the game are changed for all corporate players? Neither the law nor the market can effectively answer such questions.

Are Corporations Always Rational Actors?

Another argument against the law's ability to control corporations conflicts somewhat with those just presented. Instead of basing the law's ineffectiveness on the conscious, rational activities of those firms, it contends that much of their irresponsible behavior results from an *inability to respond sensibly* to legal threats. As you saw above, the law's ability to affect business behavior depends on a clear perception of the penalties for illegal actions and a rational response to the resulting risk. To the extent that corporations fail these tests of clear perception and rational response, the law's ability to control them suffers.

Proponents of the view that corporations often act irrationally could begin by noting that, as a rule, *people* are not especially perceptive and clearheaded. Everyone blocks out certain aspects of the external world, and this tendency is especially noticeable when the excluded information is troubling. Thus, for example, corporate managers planning a highly profitable venture may discount potential legal problems that would render the venture less attractive. By combining the abilities of many people, though, organizations should be able to overcome these individual deficiencies. But while this is often true, there are also certain features of organizational life that make perception and rational response *less* likely.

Social psychologists and students of organizational behavior have long been aware of a phenomenon called *risky shift*. This means that a group of people who must reach a consensus on an acceptable level of risk often decide on a level of risk *higher* than the risk they would accept as individuals. Thus, the decisions made by a team of managers may create greater legal problems than the decisions made by an isolated manager. Also relevant here is the familiar phenomenon of *groupthink*: the tendency for members of a group to internalize the group's

values and perceptions and to suppress critical thought. Thus, if our team of managers is planning a highly profitable venture to which the success of each team member is tied, each may minimize the venture's legal problems because these conflict with the group's goals.

Somewhat similar to groupthink is another familiar feature of organizational life: the tendency for bad news not to get to the top. When subordinates know that top managers are strongly committed to a particular course of action, they may not report problems for fear of provoking their superiors' disapproval. Ideally, of course, managers would want to be fully apprised of potential legal risks, but occasionally their response is to penalize the bearer of bad news instead. Also, subordinates may sometimes distort the information they present to their superiors in order to make their own performance look better than it actually is. Finally, the complex organizational structures of modern corporations sometimes diminish their capacity for rational and effective responses to external legal problems. For example, the size and complexity of organizational structures may worsen the tendency for bad news not to reach top managers. For the same reasons, it is sometimes difficult for top managers to ensure that their decisions are fully implemented at lower levels within the organization.

WHAT IS ETHICAL CORPORATE BEHAVIOR?

Introduction

If markets, free private behavior, and the law are imperfect means of controlling corporate misbehavior, what alternatives remain? One possibility is the proposition with which this chapter began: that corporations should observe a standard of ethical or socially responsible behavior higher than that imposed by law. If business could be persuaded to act in this fashion, the argument runs, corporate irresponsibility would be checked at its source. Also, the need for more stringent regulation of business would diminish.

Such suggestions, however, are incomplete unless they confront a basic question: just what *is* "ethical" or "socially responsible" corporate behavior? Recent discussions of this question reveal considerable disagreement about its resolution. Central to these discussions is the clash between deontological *rights-based* ethical theories and a moral theory known as *utilitarianism*. Although these two approaches hardly exhaust the field of ethical theory, they have implications for the corporate social responsibility debate. As you will see, there are utilitarian arguments for the positions taken by the corporation's defenders, and its critics can make good use of certain rights-based theories.[11]

Utilitarianism

Utilitarianism might be defined as the view that the moral worth of actions should be judged by *their tendency to maximize utility for a whole society.*[12] To maximize utility, we assume, is to achieve the greatest overall balance of satisfactions over dissatisfactions. Early utilitarians such as the British philosopher Jeremy Bentham generally limited these satisfactions and dissatisfactions to pleasure and pain. Believing Bentham's approach too narrowly hedonistic, later utilitarians such as John Stuart Mill broadened the notion of utility to include satisfactions such as health, knowledge, friendship, and aesthetic delights. Some modern utilitarians have gone even farther by urging that actions should be judged by their ability to promote the greatest net satisfaction of actual human preferences, whatever their nature.

Utilitarianism of this last kind, at least, generally is consistent with the view that the primary goal of corporations should be profit maximization. As you have seen, businesses that maximize profits under genuinely competitive conditions further the efficient allocation and use of scarce resources. As a result, such behavior maximizes social wealth, thus enabling the greatest possible satisfaction of individual preferences. For these reasons, social wealth maximization sometimes is regarded as a rough measure of utility maximization.

Utilitarianism has been subjected to many criticisms over time. One common objection is that utilitarianism simply is unworkable because there is no reliable method for measuring personal or societal utility, however defined. However, this might not be true if wealth maximization is an acceptable measuring rod for utility maximization. Another criticism is that so long as total utility is maximized, utilitarianism is indifferent to inequalities in its distribution among society's members. Indeed, utilitarianism is frequently attacked for its tendency to sacrifice *personal* interests to the maximiza-

tion of *collective* utility. For example, if enough Romans congregate to watch the lion devour the Christian, their collective pleasure surely will outweigh the pain of the Christian, however intense.[13] Similarly, utilitarian calculations might justify evils such as slavery, religious intolerance, infanticide, or the extermination of despised minorities—so long as total net satisfaction is maximized through such behavior.

In this connection, you should note that the law often subordinates personal rights and interests to the collective good on broadly utilitarian grounds. For example, the means-ends constitutional balancing tests discussed in the Business and the Constitution chapter exist because no constitutional right is considered absolute and some collective interests may justify suppressing rights stated in the Constitution. Despite the emergence of exceptions to the employment-at-will doctrine discussed in the Employment Law chapter, employers still enjoy considerable freedom to fire employees when it is economically efficient to do so. As the text's commercial paper chapters suggest, one reason why innocent parties with otherwise valid defenses against liability on a negotiable instrument must pay a holder in due course of that instrument is to enable commercial paper to move freely, and thus to stimulate economic activity.

Finally, some of the jurisprudential schools discussed in the chapter on the nature of law probably reflect utilitarian values. The most convincing justification for legal positivism's characteristic obey-the-law-just-or-not attitude is to promote social stability by preventing people from breaking the law every time they disagree with it. Sociological jurisprudence's tendency to say that the law should follow dominant social interests and values evidences a similar concern for stability. And social stability usually is a precondition for utility maximization.

Teleological and Deontological Theories

Because it judges acts by their ability to maximize utility, utilitarianism usually is regarded as a *teleological* theory of ethics. Teleological theories are purposive, assessing actions by their tendency to bring into being some desired state of affairs such as utility. In other words, teleological theories are *consequentialist* because they judge the moral worth of actions by their consequences. The

---

[11] However, not all utilitarians are defenders of the corporation, and not all believers in rights theories are its foes.

[12] Some utilitarians, however, argue that *average per capita utility*, and not *total utility*, should be the criterion.

[13] M. Sandel, ed., *Liberalism and Its Critics* 2 (1984).

saying that "you can't make an omelette without break-ing some eggs" expresses this consequentialist attitude.

Earlier, you saw that utilitarianism's concern with maximizing net collective satisfaction can produce con-sequences that almost anyone would regard as immoral. *Deontological* theories respond to this defect in utilitari-anism by asserting that certain actions are bad, or that certain other actions are morally obligatory, *irrespective of their consequences*. Examples of actions that are mor-ally obligatory in this sense might include telling the truth, keeping promises, or respecting the sanctity of human life. On this view, the extermination of a hated minority would be immoral even if it increases total util-ity because such behavior is simply wrong regardless of its consequences.

You have almost certainly encountered examples of deontological thinking in your life. It generally occurs where someone argues that an act should be done "no matter what" because it is absolutely right. Perhaps you have also considered such assertions extreme or even fa-natical—unless they were your own. In other words, just as utilitarianism seems to err by subordinating cer-tain values to the attainment of maximum total utility, deontology appears to fail by making those values abso-lutes and ignoring competing moral claims like utility. For example, an extreme deontologist might assert that we should *never* lie or *never* kill—no matter what the consequences of our doing so.

Responding to this difficulty by recognizing that every moral rule has its exceptions, some deontological thinkers have embraced the theory of *prima facie duties*.[14] These duties are moral rules that bind us unless they conflict with another, more compelling prima facie duty. In such cases, our *actual duty* is to obey the stronger moral rule. For example, lying might be justi-fied where this is necessary to save human life.

Rights-Based Theories

Modern rights-based theories normally are deontologi-cal theories of the second kind just described. That is, such theories usually identify certain fundamental rights, try to establish their relative importance, and as-sert that such rights should be honored unless doing so would compromise a more important right. The rights in

question may be regarded as natural and self-evident, may be derived from the choices disinterested people would make in a hypothetical presocial position, or may just express human claims that are felt to be especially important. Some examples of the natural law approach described in the Nature of Law chapter emphasize rights.

Rights also may be either *negative* or *positive*. Nega-tive rights such as freedom of expression or the right of privacy are claims that the community should not inter-fere with certain personal choices. Traditional *economic* rights such as private property and freedom of contract also are negative rights; but most modern rights theorists de-emphasize economic rights of this kind. Positive or "welfare" rights such as rights to old-age assistance or unemployment compensation are claims that the com-munity should provide people with certain goods, ser-vices, or conditions of decent living.

Although rights theorists differ in the rights they em-phasize and in the justification of those rights, they often agree on one point: *Rights-based claims override utili-tarian claims where the two conflict*. Rights, it is fre-quently said, are "trumps" that defeat arguments based on aggregate utility. Thus, some rights theorists would say that it is wrong to speak of striking a balance be-tween rights and allocational efficiency, because rights always have priority in such cases. If, for example, people are regarded as having rights to clean air or a safe workplace, no increase in aggregate utility, how-ever large, can justify the denial of those rights. However, rights *can* be trumped by *other rights*. Thus, Justice Oliver Wendell Holmes's famous statement that no one has the right to shout "Fire!" in a crowded theater would express the idea that in certain cases, the rights to life and physical safety overcome free speech rights.

Reconciliation?

By now, you may have concluded that utilitarianism and deontological rights-based theories both suffer from the same defect—overemphasizing certain values to the ex-clusion of other important moral claims—and that some means of balancing rights against utility is needed. Un-fortunately, no agreed-upon method for striking this bal-ance exists.

Both utilitarianism and rights-based theories, how-ever, try to meet this objection by incorporating each other's claims within their ethical frameworks. For in-

---

[14] The notion of prima facie duties comes from W. D. Ross, *The Right and the Good* 18–34 (1930).

stance, generations of utilitarians have argued that long-run social utility is maximized when society respects rights of both an economic and a noneconomic nature. Their basic argument, one arguably supported by history, is that a free economy in which basic civil liberties are recognized generates the most social wealth over time. Rights theorists, however, find such arguments unsatisfactory because they subordinate rights to utility maximization by making the former merely means to achievement of the latter. Where total utility can be increased by denying cherished rights, they add, these rights will not be respected by utilitarians.

For their part, most rights theories do not completely reject economic efficiency, wealth maximization, and utilitarian concerns broadly conceived. Here, everything depends on how the rights in question are defined. Thus, for example, many rights theorists might agree that highly efficient manufacturing methods that pose minor threats to worker safety are permissible because workers only have a right to *reasonably safe* working conditions. Also, some of the positive rights embraced by rights theorists seem to embody utilitarian values. Positive rights to old-age assistance or unemployment compensation, for instance, presumably increase their recipients' utility. Occasionally, rights of this kind may even help justify wealth maximization. Some rights theorists, for instance, assert that people have rights to life, basic subsistence, and some minimum level of material well-being. In conditions of economic scarcity, theorists of this kind might concede that such rights require public policies designed to promote wealth.

Finally, few rights theorists *entirely* reject economic rights such as freedom of contract and property rights—liberties central to a wealth-maximizing free enterprise economy. Occasionally, therefore, economic rights may override other rights, and total utility might be increased in the bargain. Just to confuse things further, some *defenders of the corporation* are rights theorists who give high priority to economic rights *for their own sake*, and not because they maximize utility. Such people are in a happy position: They can assert a deontological claim that arguably tends to maximize aggregate utility as well.

Despite their efforts to accommodate each other's moral concerns, however, utilitarianism and rights theory tend to pull in opposite directions on many of the issues comprising the corporate social responsibility debate. Modern defenders of the corporation, many of whom are conscious or unconscious utilitarians, tend strongly toward the view that profit maximization is the primary ethical obligation of corporations and that corporations pursuing this goal within the bounds of the law indeed do maximize wealth. Rights theorists, on the other hand, usually are among the corporation's critics. As a group, they tend to de-emphasize economic rights, to stress instead the rights of those affected by corporate activity, to assert that corporations often violate those rights, and to argue that utility maximization cannot justify such behavior.

To take a concrete example, imagine that Firm X's manufacturing processes discharge a legally permissible amount of pollutants into the atmosphere. The measures needed to eliminate such pollution would increase X's manufacturing costs and make it less efficient. A defender of the corporation who is a utilitarian probably would argue that the pollution should be permitted to continue if she could somehow conclude that net aggregate utility is maximized by such action. A critic of the corporation who is a rights theorist, on the other hand, might argue that the pollution in question is sufficiently great to violate a positive right to breathe clean air. Because rights-based claims trump claims based on aggregate utility, the critic could declare the pollution unethical even if the necessary controls would mean less efficiency and less social wealth.

WHAT IS TO BE DONE?

Introduction

No one, we presume, would argue that corporations should be free to do anything they wish in the pursuit of profit. Even the most vehement defenders of the profit motive concede that business has an obligation to obey existing legal rules. Such people would also urge that markets often penalize business misbehavior. But if some controls are necessary, which ones are most desirable? In discussing this question, we now examine the various means through which socially irresponsible corporate behavior might be checked. We present these control devices in rough order of increasing intrusiveness on a firm's freedom to behave as it wishes. Throughout our discussion, two questions recur. First, how *effective* is a particular control device likely to be in curbing the various forms of corporate irresponsibility? Second, what *costs*—especially efficiency-related costs—does each device involve?

CONCEPT REVIEW

THE CORPORATION'S CRITICS AND DEFENDERS: A ROUGH COMPARISON

	Defenders	Critics
Overall Position	Maximize profits within the law	Observe ethical standards higher than those set by law
Corporations' Ability to Promote Economic Efficiency	Generally high	Less than advertised, because some markets are uncompetitive and some firms are inefficient
Ability of Markets and Private Activity to Check Corporate Misbehavior	Much greater than generally recognized	Limited
Law's Ability to Check Corporate Misbehavior	Considerable; in fact, law sometimes intrudes needlessly	Valuable, and more regulation probably needed, but still has its limits
Tendency in Ethical Philosophy	Utilitarianism; occasionally rights theories stressing negative *economic* rights	Rights theories stressing positive rights and noneconomic negative rights
General View of Profit Maximization	Favorable, because it promotes efficiency, wealth, and utility	Mixed at best, because its effect often is to deprive people of important rights and to cause other harms

This section fails to provide a neat answer to the corporate social responsibility debate because no such answer exists. This country's inability to resolve the problems created by the rise of the large corporation and its failure to settle the debate may be inescapable features of a free market economy dominated by such corporations. Indeed, these failures may be the price we pay for the material benefits that the American economy has produced. As recent events in Communist bloc state-run command economies suggest, the problems illuminated by the debate are not the worst dilemmas a society might have to face.

Responses from within the Business Community

Here, we discuss efforts at controlling corporate irresponsibility that originate within the business community itself (including business schools). Such efforts can be regarded as responses to the critics' demand that corporations behave more ethically than they are required to behave by law. Perhaps the most important of these efforts is the growing movement toward ethics instruction in business schools and elsewhere. Also deserving atten-

tion, however, are some other, more traditional ideas for bringing the business community's internal resources to bear in attacking corporate misbehavior.

Ethics Instruction   In a sense, greater ethical awareness and a greater disposition to behave ethically on the part of business managers are *the* solutions to the problem of corporate irresponsibility. If all the important decisionmakers within corporations possessed such traits, business misbehavior should be sharply reduced and the need for other control devices should diminish appreciably. In recent years, business schools have increasingly attempted to advance this goal by injecting ethical considerations into their curricula. The same is sometimes true of executive education programs. All such efforts can be viewed as attempts to generate socially responsible corporate behavior by changing the outlook of existing and future employees and officers.

Because this chapter is intended to advance such aims, we would be among the last to deny ethics instruction's ability to generate more responsible business behavior over the long term. Due to certain practical and theoretical problems, however, it is doubtful whether such attempts to instill socially responsible corporate behavior are sufficient to the task by themselves. One set of difficulties concerns ethics education's ability to instill the chosen values and to make them stick after the educational process is completed. Instruction in business ethics is directed at people whose character—or lack thereof—has largely been formed by the time the instruction occurs. Although such instruction should increase the moral awareness of those who are already predisposed to listen, its effect on the basically self-interested, indifferent, or unethical is questionable. Even those who are positively influenced by ethics instruction, moreover, may still behave irresponsibly if their careers or their livelihoods require them to act in their employer's financial interest. For the firm itself, ethical behavior may be economically injurious unless all the firm's competitors follow suit. And for people employed by companies that retain a strong profit orientation, it is questionable whether the thoughtways acquired in a business ethics course will survive the tendency for organizations to socialize their members to accept the *group's* goals as paramount.

Even if these problems could be overcome, moreover, a more basic dilemma remains. Which ethical theory or theories should moral instruction advance? In this connection, recall once again that for some defenders of the corporation, profit maximization is socially responsible corporate behavior that can be justified on utilitarian grounds. For corporate critics, on the other hand, profit maximization is bad because it often causes cherished rights to be violated. Thus, even if all of a firm's managers are determined to behave ethically, there is no guarantee that they will agree on the content of such behavior. Worse yet, utilitarianism and deontological rights theories are not the only ethical approaches modern philosophy and American culture have to offer. Still worse, some 20th century "ethical theories" are quite skeptical about our ability to arrive at *any* genuine answers to moral questions.

Corporate or Industry Codes of Ethical Conduct

Over time, many large corporations and several industries have adopted codes of conduct to guide executive decisionmaking. For example, an industry code might define as unethical certain types of advertising or certain hiring practices. Also, some corporate codes of conduct prohibit employees from accepting gifts from suppliers of the corporation.

There are two popular views of such codes. One view sees them as genuine attempts to foster ethical behavior within a corporation or an industry. The other regards them as thinly disguised attempts to mislead the public into believing that business behaves ethically, to forestall legislation that would impose more severe constraints on business, or to limit competition under the veil of ethical standards. Even where the first view is correct, moreover, ethical codes seem subject to some of the difficulties besetting programs of ethical instruction. In addition, they do not address all possible forms of corporate misbehavior. As the previous examples suggest, they tend to emphasize the relations between competitors within a particular industry rather than corporate misbehavior that affects society generally.

The Corporate Stewardship Argument   Earlier in the chapter, we suggested that some large, entrenched corporations in oligopolistic industries may not be effective profit-maximizers. For certain observers of years past, this alleged development had great promise for promoting more responsible corporate behavior. Their argument was that once corporations become sufficiently secure to focus on other values besides profit maximization, they would be free to behave in a more ethical manner. One proponent of this position, which we call the corporate stewardship argument, contended that modern corporate managers have come to resemble a professional civil service rather than a group of entrepreneurs.[15]

Although this development is a *possible* implication of the hypothesis that corporations do not maximize profits, it is hardly a *necessary* implication of that hypothesis. As noted earlier, modern corporations may pursue such goals as maximum employee compensation, a pleasant work environment, size, and technological innovation. These goals are not exactly what critics of the corporation have in mind when they speak of ethical corporate behavior, and they can be pursued in quite irresponsible ways. Worse yet, profit satisficing corporations tend to be large, oligopolistic firms that arguably are less accountable to outside forces than smaller, profit-oriented firms. If so, the incentives for irresponsible behavior may *increase* because large, secure firms can indulge in such behavior with relative impunity. Finally, some observers have argued that there is in fact no correlation between the abandonment of profit maxi-

---

[15]A. Berle, *Power Without Property* 118 (1959).

mization and responsible corporate behavior.[16] And even if firms of this kind do have a greater propensity to behave ethically, they would still have to forge an internal consensus on what this means in theory and in practice.

Advancing Constituency Values   One variant of the corporate stewardship argument suggests that the corporations to which it applies should try to act in the best interests of all of their various constituencies. Today, it is widely recognized that the large modern corporation interacts with a number of important constituencies—for example, employees, unions, suppliers, customers, and the community in which it operates. To the extent possible, the argument runs, corporations should treat their employees fairly, bargain honestly with unions, make their products as safe as possible, be good citizens of the local community, and so forth.

If our previous criticisms of the corporate stewardship argument are valid, it is questionable whether well-entrenched corporations in oligopolistic industries will actually try to advance the interests of their constituencies. But this definition of corporate social responsibility suffers from some other problems as well. For one thing, the interests of the various relevant constituencies may conflict. For instance, consumers' interest in lower prices may conflict with employees' interest in higher wages, and perhaps with the surrounding community's interest in environmental protection. From an ethical point of view, moreover, why should a corporation's immediate constituencies be favored over the larger society? For example, firms or industries that corrupt the political processes to get unjustified tax breaks may well be helping some of their constituencies.

The Market and Other Private Forces

Where they are effective, market forces may be the best available means of producing more responsible corporate behavior, because they directly affect profits through the normal operation of a free economy. For example, firms that consistently manufacture and sell substandard or dangerous products should eventually lose business if competitors offer superior alternatives, and thus have obvious incentives to improve product

quality. However, as detailed earlier in the arguments from Stone, for market correctives to be effective: (1) those who are injured must know of the injury at the time it occurs, (2) they must know where to apply pressure, (3) they must be in a position to apply pressure, and (4) the offending corporation must respond rationally to the pressure. As we also observed earlier in the chapter, one implication of the first point is that some people will suffer irreparable harm from corporate misbehavior before the market corrects that behavior.

In addition, market forces may be ineffective in controlling corporate misbehavior that does not involve the quality of the firm's goods or services and thus does not directly affect consumers. For example, are such forces likely to have much impact on firms that despoil the environment? As discussed earlier in the chapter, however, other kinds of private activity such as boycotts and publicity campaigns may occasionally be effective in such cases. But how often? Many of Stone's objections to the efficacy of market forces apply in this context as well. In addition, some forms of real or alleged corporate irresponsibility (e.g., bribes to foreign governments) have little or no direct impact on consumers and the general public, and others (e.g., the dispersion of disease-causing substances) may affect only a few people or may take effect only years after the fact. This being the case, there may be insufficient incentives for private parties to organize. And even where existing or newly formed "public interest" groups go into action, there is no guarantee that they will prevail, especially if their corporate opponents are sufficiently powerful.

The Corporate Governance Agenda

Those who urge that corporations should observe ethical standards higher than those set by the law face an obvious practical problem. Just how is such behavior to be produced? To be sure, ethical instruction and other efforts from within the business community eventually could spur more responsible corporate conduct. But corporate critics of the 1960s and 1970s chose to produce it in a more direct fashion. They did so by making a number of proposals designed to alter the *internal structure* of corporations. By changing what corporations *are*, these critics hoped, such structural modifications might cause firms to abandon their single-minded pursuit of profits, better serve the interests of their various constituencies, and become more sensitive and responsive to the social consequences of their actions.

---

[16]E. Herman, *Corporate Control, Corporate Power* 261–64 (1981).

The Management of Corporations chapter discusses some of these proposals,[17] and our remarks supplement that discussion. Although a few such proposals have occasionally been adopted in modified form, public interest in them has diminished since the 1970s. However, they may again become popular if the political and attitudinal winds shift. Here, we discuss three such recommendations—and the problems they present—in general terms.

First, however, we must say a few words about intracorporate power relations. Corporation law gives a corporation's shareholders the power to elect directors who are empowered to manage the corporation. The directors, in turn, typically delegate this power to the corporation's officers while retaining general supervisory authority over them. This formal legal model suggests that the directors have more ultimate authority over corporate policy than management, and that such policy ultimately is set by the shareholders as they elect the directors. Yet for much of the 20th century, it has been widely agreed that management really runs the show within most large corporations, that directors tend merely to ratify managerial decisions, and that shareholders have little or no effective control over such decisions. The many reasons for this famous *separation of ownership from control* are beyond the scope of this chapter. Chief among these reasons, however, are the complexity of corporate decisionmaking and the limited time and expertise directors and shareholders can bring to bear on such matters.

Greater Shareholder Power   Some proposals for modifying internal corporate governance have advocated that shareholders be given a greater voice in shaping corporate policy. Specific recommendations along these lines include giving shareholders greater power to nominate directors and the ability to adopt resolutions binding the directors.

Of the various corporate governance proposals, granting greater power to shareholders probably has the least to recommend it. For one thing, such proposals seem less than realistic when we consider the facts of intracorporate life noted above. Of particular importance here is management's tendency to get its way on corporate policy decisions by dominating the proxy machinery through which shareholders often vote. Even if this obstacle could be surmounted, moreover, it is questionable whether greater shareholder power would produce more responsible corporate behavior. Indeed, it could lead to *greater* corporate irresponsibility. Although it is conceivable that some corporate managers do not make profit maximization their first priority, the orientation of shareholders almost always is completely pecuniary. For this reason, shareholders are unlikely to initiate or approve corporate actions avowedly hostile to profit maximization if confronted with an explicit choice. All of this is especially true, some say, of institutional investors such as pension funds and mutual funds, which own significant blocks of stock in many corporations. Such investors tend to follow the Wall Street rule, under which they either support management or sell their shares.

Even if shareholders somehow could be induced to act ethically, other difficulties with shareholder governance would remain. Effective corporate decisionmaking could be impaired as relatively uninformed shareholders issue edicts to managers. In addition, there is no guarantee that the values of "ethical" shareholders would reflect the values of society as a whole; a large number of shares are held by rather unrepresentative individuals and groups. For example, it was once estimated that fewer than 5 percent of all Americans own 60 percent of all the corporate shares held by individuals. And there is little reason to think that institutional investors can effectively represent larger social concerns. Thus, a shareholder mandate to corporate executives is very unlikely to reflect broad social interests.

Changing the Composition of the Board   Despite the general tendency for corporate management to dominate the board of directors, the formal legal powers of the board still are considerable. Recognizing this, critics of the corporation have made innumerable recommendations for changing the board's composition to make corporations more responsible. Some of the recommendations have been relatively modest: for example, creating nominating committees composed of outside directors,[18] requiring that there be more such directors and fewer insiders, and limiting the number of corporate

---

[17] Also, the History and Nature of Corporations chapter discusses a possible control device that we do not consider here—federal chartering of corporations.

[18] Outside and inside directors are discussed in the Management of Corporations chapter.

boards on which one individual can serve.[19] More extreme proposals include recommendations that constituencies of all sorts (e.g., labor, government, creditors, local communities, minorities, and environmentalists) be represented, that certain directors be assigned special areas of concern (e.g., consumer protection, environmental affairs), and that special committees of the board be assigned similar functions.

From a social responsibility perspective, the basic problem with all such proposals is that they fail to confront the main reason for management's domination of the board: the limited time, information, and expertise that directors can bring to bear when considering corporate affairs. One solution to this problem is to give outside or constituency directors a full-time staff with the power to dig for information within the corporation. Doing so, however, effectively creates another —perhaps competing—layer of management within the corporate organizational structure. Although this could curtail certain corporate misdeeds, it could also lessen a firm's ability to innovate and respond to changing developments.

Another set of problems with some of these proposals concerns the details of their implementation. Which constituencies deserve representation? How many directors should each constituency have? Within each constituency, what criteria should govern the choice of directors? For example, is it desirable or undesirable that they have business experience?

Finally, in addition to complicating the management structure, these proposals might diminish the board's own cohesiveness and thus render it incapable of coherent action. Conflicts among constituency representatives or between insiders and outsiders are not unlikely. In fact, the addition of constituency directors might simply mean the intrusion of broader social conflicts into corporate boardrooms. The board, that is, could be divided by disputes among consumers who want lower prices, workers who want higher wages and job security, environmentalists who want pollution to cease, and communities that want to preserve jobs and their tax bases. This could render the board incapable of pushing management in responsible directions. As suggested earlier, it could also check the corporation's ability to innovate and react to external stimuli.

Changes in Management Structure   As noted above, one of the great commonplaces about large 20th-century

---

[19] The chapter on the management of corporations describes some other proposals of this kind.

corporations is the separation of ownership from control: the shift of power away from shareholders and directors to the corporation's managers. Once the full implications of this shift are grasped, some corporate reformers argue, it becomes evident that the best way to produce more responsible corporate behavior is to make changes in the corporation's *management* structure. The main proponent of this view, Christopher Stone, has made a number of specific recommendations for such changes. They include the establishment of the following (each of which would probably have to be required by law): (1) certain specified offices within certain corporations (e.g., offices for environmental affairs, worker safety, and product safety); (2) requirements for holding certain corporate positions (e.g., specific educational requirements for safety engineers); (3) offices for ensuring that relevant external information (e.g., data from auto repair shops for car manufacturers or data from doctors for drug companies) is received by the corporation; and (4) internal information-flow procedures for ensuring that relevant external information gets to the proper internal corporate departments (to guarantee, for instance, that bad news gets to the top). Stone and others have also recommended that corporations be required to make certain internal findings before undertaking various activities. For example, drug companies might be required to produce a document resembling an environmental impact statement before marketing a new product.

All of these proposed requirements are procedural in the sense that they do not dictate what decisions the corporation should make. Their general aim is to ensure that corporations have the means to anticipate problems before they arise so that timely responses to them are possible. Such requirements probably would do little to deter a strongly profit-oriented corporation from taking irresponsible actions. And it is possible that the corporate personnel responsible for implementing these requirements will be influenced by a strong internal profit orientation or frozen out of the final decisionmaking process.

In cases where irresponsible corporate behavior is less the product of profit-seeking than of failed perceptions, however, such proposals could have salutary results. For example, they may be especially effective in addressing the unknown-harms problem discussed earlier. But those results would probably be obtained only at the cost of further intraorganizational complexity, with a consequent reduction in the corporation's ability to make quick responses to changing business conditions.

CONCEPT REVIEW

THE CORPORATE CONTROL DEVICES COMPARED: A TENTATIVE BOX SCORE

Device	Likely Effectiveness in Curbing Corporate Irresponsibility	Possible Costs in Efficiency and in Ineffective Corporate Decisionmaking	Remarks
Ethical Instruction	Will it take? Will it stick? Which values?	Disunity within corporation? Adverse effects on efficiency?	Effects probably long-term
Codes of Conduct	Questionable, due to limited scope	Could be anticompetitive	A sham?
Corporate Stewardship	Questionable at best	By hypothesis, firms in question are inefficient profit-satisficers	Has this really happened? Would such firms necessarily behave ethically?
Advancing Constituency Values	Interests of constituencies may conflict	Occasional adverse effects on efficiency?	Are interests of constituencies necessarily congruent with larger social good?
Market Forces and Private Action	Should vary with type of corporate misbehavior	Fairly low. Market forces tend to promote efficiency.	Subject to Stone's objections
Greater Shareholder Power	Poor, due to pecuniary orientation of shareholders	Less coherent decisionmaking?	Could this *increase* corporate irresponsibility?
Packing the Board	Likely to be minimal unless the causes of board's subservience are overcome	Could adversely affect corporate decisionmaking and efficiency	Which constituencies and interests deserve representation?
Changing the Internal Management Structure	Probably most effective for unknown harms	Could complicate corporate decisionmaking	Focus on *management* structure an advantage
The Law	Despite limits on effectiveness, has a respectable track record	Can have adverse impact on efficiency	The best of a flawed group?

The Law

Legal controls of all kinds have been the most important means of controlling corporate misbehavior throughout the 20th century. Such controls include civil suits by injured parties, administrative regulation in its many forms, and even criminal sanctions.[20] Despite the law's obvious importance as a corporate control device, however, several factors impede its effectiveness. Since most legal penalties are designed to deter corporate misbehavior by affecting profits, they assume that corporations strive to maximize those profits and behave as rational actors while doing so. As you have seen, though, there are situations where each assumption is questionable. As you have also seen, other factors retard the law's ability to check socially irresponsible corporate actions. Corporations often influence both the content and the administration of the rules that govern them, and sometimes they rationally conclude that it makes sense to violate the law. As with market checks, moreover, irreparable harm may occur before legal constraints on harm-causing activity go into operation.

---

[20] The chapter on the management of corporations discusses the criminal liability of the corporation, its directors, and its officers. The Crimes chapter discusses the usefulness of criminal sanctions in controlling corporations.

Finally, legal restraints on corporate misbehavior—especially administrative regulation—impose social costs of all sorts. These include the dollar costs of staffing and maintaining regulatory agencies, litigation expenses, and the costs of complying with regulatory edicts (which corporations may pass on to consumers). In addition, overintrusive regulation may sometimes affect profits and impede allocational efficiency to such an extent that the competitiveness of American industries suffers.

This catalog of the law's imperfections, however, reminds us of the old debate about whether a glass filled to its halfway mark is half empty or half full. Indeed, the law is probably the best—or the least bad—of the control devices discussed in this section. Of these devices, only the law and the various private controls impose real *penalties* for corporate misbehavior. Although legal norms have no special claim to moral correctness, at least they are arrived at through a fairly open political process in which competing arguments may be weighed and evaluated. Thus, they are more likely to express a social consensus than the intuitions of some "responsible" businessperson, the edicts of some "public interest" group, or the theories of some academic economist or philosopher. As a general rule, finally, the law's commands should have less adverse effect on corporations' internal functioning than many of the corporate reform proposals.

More importantly, the law has a track record as a corporate control device and this record contains a number of real accomplishments. For example, although the antitrust laws discussed in later chapters remain controversial, they have at least eliminated some of the worst anticompetitive abuses that were common before their enactment. If nothing else, similarly, the federal securities regulations examined elsewhere in this text have prevented the shady practices that, some contend, led to the stock market crash of the late 1920s. Although environmentalists often demand more regulation, virtually everyone agrees that the environmental laws treated in the chapter on environmental regulation have appreciably improved the quality of our air and water and reduced our exposure to toxic substances. Finally, the various employment regulations discussed in the Employment Law chapter—especially those forbidding employment discrimination—have worked enormous changes in the American workplace over the course of this century.

SUMMARY

Modern critics of business urge that corporations should observe standards of ethical behavior higher than those set by the law. In response, the corporation's defenders urge that business's primary moral obligation is to maximize profits within the bounds set by the law. They do so primarily because they believe that profit maximization produces economic efficiency, which in turn maximizes social wealth. Some critics of the corporation, however, question this assumption on one or both of two grounds. Some try to sever the link between profit-seeking and economic efficiency by arguing that many entrenched firms in oligopolistic industries actually are not very efficient. Such firms may engage in inefficient anticompetitive practices in order to maximize profits. In some cases, secondly, firms of this kind may not really try to maximize profits at all.

Even if modern corporations actually do promote economic efficiency, moreover, they obviously can cause much harm while doing so. In such cases, why should efficiency necessarily take priority over other relevant social values? The corporation's defenders might respond by arguing that in some of these situations, efficiency simply is the most important value. In others, they can urge that free competition and free private activity can go some way toward eliminating undesirable corporate behavior—without submitting corporations to stifling regulation or adopting the various other corporate control devices discussed in this chapter. Critics like Christopher Stone, however, respond that for many reasons, defenders of the corporation grossly overstate the ability of market forces and private action to check abuses of corporate power.

Even so, defenders of the corporation can maintain that they recognize business's moral obligation to obey the law, and that the law can control whatever irresponsible behavior markets and private activity fail to address. For many reasons, however, the law is an imperfect corporate control device. The law's ability to deter corporate misbehavior depends on the assumption that corporations are rational profit-maximizers, and this may not always be true. Even where corporations do act rationally, moreover, they sometimes may conclude that it makes sense to violate the law. In addition, the law will always be an imperfect corporate control mechanism because corporations play a significant role in shaping legal rules and in determining the processes by which they are enforced. In any event, finally, the law can only respond to dangers that are already apparent to society as a whole, and thus cannot protect those who suffer irreparable harm from unknown or unknowable dangers.

For all these reasons, the corporation's critics can maintain that they were right all along when they argued that business must recognize ethical obligations higher than those set by the law. But just what are these obligations? Under utilitarian criteria, it is arguable that the main moral obligation of business is to do just what the corporation's defenders say it should do: maximize profits and thereby promote economic efficiency. On the other hand, the rights theories expressly or impliedly favored by many corporate critics generally should impose greater ethical obligations on business. But some of these theories may pay insufficient attention to economic efficiency and the utilitarian concerns that underlie it.

With all of this in mind, which kinds of corporate controls best promote corporate social responsibility while paying due respect to the need for economic productivity? Although some of them have long-term promise, the various voluntary controls that have emerged from within the business community all have their flaws. One dilemma facing all such efforts is obvious: whose ethics should responsible corporations adopt? In addition, each of these ideas has its own particular problems. Ethics instruction, for example, may have little effect on those who are not already predisposed to accept it, and may also fail to counteract the many material incentives for irresponsible corporate behavior. Codes of ethical conduct usually address only certain forms of corporate misconduct, and in some cases may really be intended to serve the interests of the firms that adopt them. The idea that large mature corporations are in a position to behave as society's stewards is subject to a number of empirical objections. Are such corporations really free from competitive pressures? Even if they are, does this mean that they will behave responsibly? Have they in fact done so? When such corporations adopt as their goal the furtherance of constituency values, moreover, they must somehow find a way to reconcile the conflicting demands of those constituencies.

As noted above, defenders of the corporation sometimes argue that market forces and free private activity significantly curb corporate irresponsibility. But while such forces may check certain abuses over time, they hardly seem equipped to address all the ways in which corporations might misbehave.

Apparently reacting to the inadequacies of the control methods just discussed, some critics of the corporation have proposed a wide variety of measures that, in effect, seek to change what corporations *are* by changing corporate structure. These proposals include giving shareholders more control over corporate policy, incorporating members of a corporation's constituencies into its board of directors, and changing the internal management structure of corporations in various ways. All these proposals suffer from a variety of flaws. Shareholders are primarily profit-oriented, and thus are unlikely to urge responsible behavior on corporations. And the inclusion of constituency directors may simply inject broader social conflicts into corporate boardrooms, with a consequent reduction in corporate efficiency. Considerations of efficiency and workability also weaken the case for changes in internal management structure.

For all these reasons, the law may be the least bad method of checking corporations. To be sure, it has many weaknesses as a corporate control device. Because it has been the principal means of controlling business misbehavior throughout this century, however, the law at least has a track record. And that record contains a number of qualified successes.

Finally, consider whether we as a society really *want* corporations to engage in the contentious and difficult task of resolving conflicting moral claims. After all, legislatures were designed to perform this important function, and to do so in a more or less representative fashion. In cases where the law does not speak but the decisions of corporate managers pose serious ethical problems, however, those managers face an obvious dilemma. Without a moral theory that is personally compelling or that can attract broad support, such managers are left only with the ultimate guide available to all of us: individual conscience.

PROBLEMS AND PROBLEM CASES

1. This chapter's ethics discussion identified two general arguments for laissez-faire policies that maximize business freedom, one deontological and one teleological. What are they?

2. Defenders of the corporation often argue that the principal moral obligation of corporations is to maximize profits within the legal "rules of the game." But are the law's commands necessarily moral? And is there an ethical obligation to obey morally bad laws? What do the *natural law* and *legal positivist* schools of jurisprudence discussed in the chapter on the nature of law say about these questions?

3. The law's ability to control corporate misbehavior depends heavily on the assumption that corporations are rational actors that will respond sensibly to the threats the law imposes. Suppose for the sake of argument that corporations do not behave rationally, generally speaking. This would tend to undermine a position sometimes taken by defenders of the corporation: that legal threats effectively counter most kinds of irresponsible corporate behavior. But the assumption that corporations behave irrationally might undermine *another* argument typically made by the corporation's defenders. What is this argument and how would corporate irrationality weaken it?

4. The Council on Economic Priorities was founded in 1969 to enhance corporate performance as it affects society in areas such as military spending, political influence, and fair employment practices. In 1987, the Council issued a book entitled *Rating America's Corporate Conscience*, which it called the first comprehensive shopping guide for the socially conscious consumer. The book rates consumer products according to their manufacturers' performance in various categories of social responsibility, thereby allowing readers "to cast an economic vote on corporate social responsibility" when they shop. These categories include such social concerns as investment in South Africa, charitable contributions, minority and female representation on the board of directors, manufacture of weapons, and willingness to provide information on social performance. For example, it enables peanut butter consumers who wish to patronize a company with female directors to determine that they should eat a certain brand of peanut butter.

In your judgment, how effective is this book likely to be in producing more responsible corporate behavior on the part of the corporations it rates? What implications does your answer have for the effectiveness of private market activity in controlling corporations? In answering these questions, consult the arguments from Stone earlier in the chapter. Finally, do you agree with the criteria that the Council has used to assess responsible corporate behavior? Do you think that all Americans would

agree with these criteria? What fundamental problem with the notion of "responsible" or "ethical" corporate behavior do the Council's criteria suggest?

5. The ABC Corporation declares itself a socially responsible firm, and defines socially responsible behavior as behavior that maximizes the well-being of its various constituencies. Then, ABC identifies the following constituencies to which it feels responsible: its workers, consumers of its products, its shareholders, and the communities where its plants are situated. There are many possibilities, but identify three situations where the interests of two or more of these constituencies might clash. Feel free to assume whatever facts are necessary to create such conflicting interests.

6. You are president and CEO of a small, publicly held company. Your national sales manager (and best friend), Frank Wilson, started out with you 20 years before when you founded the company. His hard work, dedication, and good advice played a substantial role in your success. Now Frank, as a result of family problems and executive "burnout," has developed a drinking problem. At first you tried to ignore it, but it is clear that other employees are aware of the problem and that some important accounts have recently been lost due to Frank's growing ineffectiveness. You've tried to gently discuss the problem with Frank, but he denies he has a problem and is obviously hurt by the discussion. Your executive vice president has urged you to fire Frank saying, "We can get a young tiger in here who'll do a better job for half of what we're paying the bum." You know this to be true and you know that Frank's behavior cannot be tolerated much longer, but you also know that Frank will be devastated personally and financially if he is fired and will probably not be able to find another job. What should you do?

7. For 11 years Baxter Corporation was the exclusive distributor in a three-state area for Ramco Enterprises, a manufacturer of replacement parts for heavy industrial equipment. Although Baxter did a good job in its territory, Ramco's projections indicated that franchising four new distributors at carefully selected sites throughout Baxter's territory would increase sales of Ramco products by as much as 30 percent. Ramco also concluded that Baxter was too thinly capitalized to be able to expand its operations sufficiently to produce a similar increase in sales, and that prudence dictated not being dependent on only one distributor in such a large area. After reviewing the facts, Ramco decided to appoint the new distributors and began confidential negotiations with several candidates. Fearing the loss of sales that would result if it informed Baxter of its plans before the new distributors were ready to commence operations, Ramco decided not to inform Baxter. Ramco allowed Baxter to enter a five-year lease on new, larger warehouse facilities which it had reason to believe Baxter would not have entered had it known it would shortly be losing its exclusive distributorship. Two weeks before Ramco gave Baxter the notice of nonreappointment required by the distributorship agreement, Ramco's salesmen encouraged Baxter to place an unusually large parts order. Assuming Ramco had the legal and ethical right to appoint additional distributors, was its implementation of that decision ethical?

8. Cleanco International is informed by its legal department that the EPA has identified dioxybenzoprophilate (DBP), a byproduct produced in an essential production process at Cleanco's Bloomington, Indiana, plant, as a "probable human carcinogen." No current environmental regulation requires special treatment for DBP, so Cleanco is releasing 2,000 tons of it into the atmosphere along with similar amounts of other unregulated substances. At this point, no one in Bloomington other than a handful of Cleanco's upper management employees is even aware that Cleanco is emitting DBP. A confidentially conducted internal study indicates it would cost Cleanco at least $500,000 per year on a 10-year amortized basis to install equipment to recover the DBP and dispose of it safely. What should Cleanco do?

9. You have recently been appointed CEO of Pureco Pharmaceutical Corporation. While being briefed on company operations by your vice president for sales, you ask him about the seemingly high volume of business the company is doing in the sale of amphetamines. The vice president reluctantly admits that about 70 percent of Pureco's amphetamine sales are made to small pharmacies in Mexico. When asked why Mexican pharmacies should purchase such high quantities of amphetamines, the vice president says: "Well, I guess they buy them to resell in quantity." "You mean to drug dealers, don't you?" you respond. "Yeah, I guess so," he admits. "This means that a lot of this stuff is probably being smuggled back across the border and sold illegally, doesn't it?" you ask. "Yeah, probably," he replies, "but let me set you straight on a few things before you get too critical. First, this is a *very* profitable line of business for us, and the last thing you probably want to do as a new CEO is to take action that will negatively affect earnings. Second, we are violating no U.S. or Mexican law when we make these sales. Third, every other major U.S. pharmaceutical firm does the same thing. Fourth, if we stopped tomorrow, that would simply encourage the entry of illicit suppliers who might put *anything* in their drugs. Finally, due to the high R&D costs in this industry, losing the profits from these sales could impair our ability to develop new drugs that could do a lot of good." Should Pureco continue the Mexican sales?

10. Virginia Parker, a new MBA, has recently been hired by the First Planetary Bank. She has received an overseas assignment as assistant director of lending in the bank's office in Chauvinaria. Virginia's boss, Thomas Paine, seems friendly and professional, and appears to go out of his way to make her feel welcome in her new position. During their first joint interview with an important local client, however, Tom treats Virginia in an obviously patronizing and demeaning manner. After the interview is over, Virginia angrily demands an explanation. Tom appears genuinely surprised and says: "Gee, I'm sorry, but I thought you understood. As you know, Chauvinarians have these archaic attitudes toward women. In fact, we're taking a risk even bringing female managers out here. None of our competitors do, and we'd be committing suicide in a very lucrative market if the Chauvinarians perceived us as treating women like complete equals. Personally, I think their attitudes are nonsense, but business is business. 'When in Rome . . . ' and all that, you know."

Is Tom's position ethically justified? Assume that Tom is being honest about his reasons for treating Virginia as he did.

PART II

CRIMES AND TORTS

CHAPTER 5

CRIMES

INTRODUCTION

At first glance, a chapter on criminal law might seem out of place in a text devoted to the legal environment of business. Contracts, torts, agency, corporations, and the host of other legal topics covered in this text tend to come more readily to mind than crime. These legal subjects are traditionally viewed as being important to people in business. However, a thorough understanding of the nature of the criminal law is also an essential part of a manager's education today because people in business and their corporate employers are more likely than ever before to have some unpleasant contact with the criminal justice system.

This century has witnessed a growing tendency on the part of our legal system to use the criminal law as a major device for controlling corporate behavior. Many modern regulatory statutes provide criminal as well as civil penalties in the event of a statutory violation. Frequently, those criminal penalties apply both to individual employees and to their employers.

Those who advocate using the criminal law in this way commonly argue that the criminal law affords a level of deterrence superior to that produced by purely civil remedies such as damage awards. Corporations may be inclined to treat civil damage awards as a cost of doing business, and therefore may violate regulatory provisions when it is profitable to do so. Criminal prosecutions, on the other hand, threaten corporations with the stigma of a criminal conviction. In some cases, society may impose penalties on individual corporate employees who would not be directly affected by a civil judgment against their employer. Moreover, by alerting private individuals to the existence of a violation that can serve as the basis for a civil damage suit, criminal prosecutions may also increase the likelihood that a corporation will be forced to bear the full costs of its actions.

Whatever the merit of these arguments, the threat of criminal prosecution is an inescapable part of the legal environment of business today. Accordingly, the remainder of this chapter focuses on the nature of the criminal law in general. Then it proceeds with a discussion of many complex problems associated with the operation of the criminal law in the corporate context.

THE CRIMINAL LAW

Nature of Crime

Crimes are *public wrongs*—acts prohibited by the *state*. Criminal prosecutions are initiated by an agent of the state (the prosecutor) in the name of the state. Persons convicted of committing criminal acts are exposed to the uniquely coercive force of *criminal sanctions*—the punishment society has provided for those who violate its most important rules. This punishment may take the form of a fine, imprisonment, or, in extreme cases, execution. In addition to formal punishment, convicted criminals must bear the *stigma* associated with a criminal conviction—the social condemnation that results from being labeled a criminal offender.

Our legal system also contains a wide variety of noncriminal forms of punishment. For example, the next two chapters deal with *torts*, private wrongs punished by awards of money damages. In some cases, this punishment consists of forcing a person who commits a tort to compensate his victim for the damages resulting from the tort. In others, a court may also award punitive damages for the express purpose of punishing the wrongdoer. However, only the criminal sanction combines the threat to life or liberty with the stigma of conviction. This potent combination caused one authority to describe the criminal sanction as "the law's ultimate threat."[1]

Crimes are usually classified as felonies or misdemeanors, depending on the seriousness of the offense. A **felony** is a serious offense, such as murder, rape, or arson. Felonies generally involve serious moral culpability on the part of the offender. They are punishable by confinement to a penitentiary for a substantial period of time. A person convicted of a felony may also suffer other serious consequences, such as *disenfranchisement* (loss of voting rights) and being barred from the practice of certain professions, such as law or medicine. A **misdemeanor** is a lesser offense, such as a minor traffic violation or disorderly conduct. Misdemeanors, which often do not involve significant moral culpability, are punishable by fines or limited confinement in a city or county jail.

Whether a given act is classed as criminal is a social question. As our social values have changed over time, so have our definitions of criminal conduct. Many observers argue that criminal sanctions should be reserved for behavior involving serious moral culpability. As the rest of this chapter indicates, however, we have criminalized a wide variety of behavior that has very little moral content.

---

[1] H. Packer, *The Limits of the Criminal Sanction*, 250 (Stanford, Calif.: Stanford University Press, 1968).

Purpose of the Criminal Sanction

Much of the disagreement about the circumstances in which the criminal sanction should be employed stems from a basic disagreement about the purpose of the criminal sanction. Persons who take a *utilitarian* view of the criminal sanction believe that the *prevention* of socially undesirable behavior is the only proper purpose for applying criminal penalties. The goal of prevention includes three major components: deterrence, rehabilitation, and incapacitation.

Deterrence theory holds that the threat or imposition of punishment deters crime. Deterrence theorists focus on two types: special deterrence and general deterrence. *Special deterrence* occurs when the punishment of a convicted offender deters him from committing further criminal offenses. *General deterrence* results when the punishment of a convicted wrongdoer deters others who might otherwise have been inclined to commit a similar offense. Several factors are generally influential in determining the effectiveness of deterrence. Among these are the likelihood that the crime will be detected, that detection will be followed by prosecution, that prosecution will result in a conviction, and the severity of the punishment likely to be imposed in the event of a conviction. Put in economic terms, effective deterrence requires that the penalty imposed for an offense, discounted by the likelihood of apprehension and conviction, must equal or exceed the gains to the offender from committing the offense.

The fundamental problem with deterrence theories is that we can never say with certainty whether deterrence works because we can never know what the crime rate would be in the absence of punishment. For example, unacceptably high levels of crime and *recidivism* (repeat offenses by previously punished offenders) may be the result of the failure to impose criminal sanctions of sufficient severity and certainty, rather than evidence that criminal sanctions cannot produce deterrence. Deterrence theory has one other fundamental problem—it tends to assume that potential offenders are rational beings who consciously weigh the threat of punishment against the benefits derived from an offense. The threat of punishment, however, may not deter the commission of criminal offenses produced by irrational or unconscious drives.

Another way to prevent undesirable behavior is to *rehabilitate* convicted offenders by changing their attitudes or values so that they are not inclined to commit future offenses. Critics of rehabilitation commonly point to high rates of recidivism as evidence of the general failure of our rehabilitation efforts to date. Even if rehabilitative strategies fail, however, the incarceration of convicted offenders contributes to the goal of prevention by *incapacitating* them. While they are imprisoned, their ability to commit other criminal offenses is drastically reduced.

Prevention is not the only goal advanced for the criminal sanction. Some persons see the central focus of criminal punishment as *retribution*; that is, the infliction of deserved suffering on those who violate society's most fundamental rules. To a retributionist, punishment satisfies community and individual desires for revenge, and it vindicates and reinforces important social values. So, a retributionist is unlikely to see prevention as a sufficient reason for criminalizing behavior that is socially undesirable but morally neutral. On the other hand, when serious moral culpability is present, a retributionist would likely favor punishment even if convinced that it will not prevent future offenses.

Essentials of Crime

Before a person can be convicted of a crime, the state ordinarily must: (1) demonstrate that his alleged actions violated an existing criminal statute; (2) prove beyond a reasonable doubt that he did in fact commit the actions charged against him; and (3) prove that he had the legal capacity to form a criminal intent.

Prior Statutory Prohibition   Criminal offenses are *statutory* offenses. Only the legislature has the power to criminalize behavior. The U.S. Constitution prohibits *ex post facto* criminal laws. This means that a defendant's act must have been prohibited by statute at the time she committed it and the penalty must be the one provided for at the time of her offense.

The Constitution also limits the power of Congress and state legislatures to criminalize behavior in several other ways. They cannot criminalize behavior that is constitutionally protected. For example, as the *Johnson* case, which follows, indicates, the First Amendment to the Constitution prohibits laws that unreasonably restrict freedom of speech and expression. Similarly, in *Griswold v. Connecticut,* the Supreme Court struck down state statutes prohibiting the use of contraceptive devices and the counseling or assisting of others in the use of such devices on the ground that the statutes violated a constitutionally protected *right of privacy* implicit in the Bill of Rights.[2] This decision provided the constitutional basis for the Court's historic decision in *Roe v. Wade* that limited the states' power to criminalize abortions.[3]

---

[2] 381 U.S. 479 (U.S. Sup. Ct. 1965).
[3] 410 U.S. 113 (U.S. Sup. Ct. 1973).

TEXAS v. JOHNSON

109 S. Ct. 2533 (U.S. Sup. Ct. 1989)

Gregory Johnson was arrested and convicted for violating a Texas statute prohibiting the "desecration of a venerated object" after he burned an American flag during a protest demonstration at the Republican National Convention in Dallas in 1984. He was sentenced to a year in prison and fined $2,000. The Texas Court of Criminal Appeals reversed his conviction on First Amendment grounds, and the state appealed.

Brennan, Justice.   The First Amendment literally forbids the abridgement only of "speech," but we have long recognized that its protection does not end at the spoken or written word. While we have rejected the view that an apparently limitless variety of conduct can be labeled "speech" whenever the person engaging in the conduct intends thereby to express an idea, we have acknowledged that conduct may be sufficiently imbued with elements of communication to fall within the scope of the First and Fourteenth Amendments. The expressive, overtly political nature of Johnson's conduct was both intentional and overwhelmingly apparent.

The Government generally has a freer hand in restricting expressive conduct than it has in restricting the written or spoken word. It may not, however, proscribe particular conduct *because* it has expressive elements. Thus, although we have recognized that where "speech" and "nonspeech" elements are combined in the same course of conduct, a sufficiently important governmental interest in regulating the nonspeech element can justify incidental limitations on First Amendment freedoms, we have limited the applicability of this standard to those cases in which the governmental interest is unrelated to the suppression of free expression.

Texas claims that its interest in preventing breaches of the peace justifies Johnson's conviction. However, no disturbance of the peace actually occurred or threatened to occur because of Johnson's burning of the flag. The State's position amounts to a claim that an audience that takes serious offense at particular expression is necessarily likely to disturb the peace and that the expression may be prohibited on that basis. Our precedents do not countenance such a presumption. On the contrary, they recognize that a principal function of free speech is to invite dispute. Thus, we have not permitted the Government to assume that every expression of a provocative idea will incite a riot, but have instead required careful consideration of the factual circumstances surrounding such expression, asking whether the expression is directed to inciting or producing imminent lawless action and is likely to incite or produce such action. We conclude that the State's interest in maintaining order is not implicated on these facts.

The State also asserts an interest in preserving the flag as a symbol of nationhood and national unity. It is not the State's ends, but its means, to which we object. It cannot be gainsaid that there is a special place reserved for the flag in this Nation, and thus we do not doubt that the Government has a legitimate interest in making efforts to preserve the flag as an unalloyed symbol of our country. Forbidding criminal punishment for conduct such as Johnson's will not endanger the special role played by our flag or the feelings it inspires. Nobody can suppose that this one gesture of an unknown man will change our Nation's attitude towards its flag.

We are tempted to say, in fact, that the flag's cherished place in our community will be strengthened, not weakened, by our holding today. Our decision is a reaffirmation of the principles of freedom and inclusiveness that the flag best reflects, and of the conviction that our toleration of criticism such as Johnson's is a sign and source of our strength. The way to preserve the flag's special role is not to punish those who feel differently about these matters. It is to persuade them that they are wrong. We can imagine no more appropriate response to burning a flag than waving one's own, no better way to counter a flag-burner's message than by saluting the flag that burns, no surer means of preserving the dignity even of a flag that burned than by—as one witness here did—according its remains a respectful burial. We do not consecrate the flag by punishing its desecration, for in doing so we dilute the freedom that this cherished emblem represents.

Reversal of Johnson's conviction affirmed.

In addition to limiting the *kinds* of behavior that can be made criminal, the Constitution also limits the *manner* in which behavior may be criminalized. The Due Process Clauses of the Fifth and Fourteenth Amendments require that a criminal statute must clearly define the behavior prohibited so that an ordinary person can understand which behavior violates the statute.[4] Statutes that fail to provide such fair notice are stricken down as "void for vagueness." In addition, the Equal Protection

---

[4] The Business and the Constitution chapter discusses due process in greater detail.

Clause of the Fourteenth Amendment[5] prohibits criminal statutes that treat persons of the same class in a discriminatory fashion or that *arbitrarily* discriminate among different classes of persons.[6] As a general rule, legislatures have considerable latitude in making statutory classifications, so long as the classifications have some rational basis. "Suspect" classifications, such as those based on race, however, are subjected to much closer judicial scrutiny.

Finally, the Constitution also limits the *type of punishment* imposed on convicted offenders. The Eighth Amendment forbids the imposition of "cruel and unusual punishments" for criminal offenses. This has been interpreted as barring sentences *disproportionate* to the defendant's offense. In making a disproportionality analysis, courts consider the harshness of the penalty imposed, other sentences imposed in the same jurisdiction for similar offenses, and the sentences imposed in other jurisdictions for the same offense. The Eighth Amendment provides the constitutional basis for those cases establishing constitutional limits on the circumstances in which the death penalty may be imposed.[7]

Proof beyond a Reasonable Doubt   Our legal system has long placed significant limits on the state's power to convict a person of a crime. These limits are thought to be essential due to the serious matters at stake in a criminal case—the life and liberty of the accused. One of the most fundamental safeguards that characterize the criminal justice system is the *presumption of innocence*: defendants in criminal cases are presumed to be innocent until proven guilty. The Due Process Clause requires the state to overcome this presumption by proving every element of the offense charged against the defendant *beyond a reasonable doubt*. Requiring the state to meet that severe burden of proof is the primary way to minimize the risk of erroneous criminal convictions. It also reflects a strong belief shared by all common law juris-

dictions about the proper way laws should be enforced and justice administered.

The Defendant's Capacity   *Mens rea*, or criminal intent, is an element of most serious crimes. The *level* of fault required for a criminal violation depends on the wording of the statute in question. Some criminal statutes require proof of intentional wrongdoing, while others impose liability for *reckless* or *negligent* conduct. In the criminal context, recklessness generally means that the accused consciously disregarded a substantial risk that the harm prohibited by the statute would result from her actions. Negligence, in criminal cases, means that the accused failed to perceive a substantial risk of harm that a reasonable person would have perceived. Criminal intent may be *inferred* from the nature of an accused's behavior, because a person is normally held to have intended the natural and probable consequences of her acts. The basic idea behind requiring intent for criminal responsibility is that the criminal law generally seeks to punish *conscious* wrongdoers. Accordingly, proof that the defendant had the *capacity* to form the required criminal intent is a traditional prerequisite of criminal responsibility. The criminal law recognizes three general types of incapacity: *intoxication*, *infancy*, and *insanity*.

Voluntary intoxication, although not a complete defense to criminal liability, can sometimes diminish the degree of a defendant's liability. This is so because a highly intoxicated person may be incapable of forming the *specific* criminal intent that is an element of some crimes. For example, many first degree murder statutes require proof of *premeditation*, a conscious decision to kill. A person who kills while highly intoxicated may not be capable of premeditation and may, therefore, be convicted of only second degree murder, which generally does not require proof of premeditation. Involuntary intoxication may be a complete defense to criminal liability.

At common law, a child under the age of seven was conclusively presumed to be incapable of forming a criminal intent. Children between the ages of 7 and 14 were presumed to be incapable of doing so, and those between the ages of 14 and 21 were presumed to be capable of doing so. These presumptions about a child's capacity, however, were rebuttable by specific evidence concerning the accused's moral and intellectual development. Most states currently treat juvenile offenders below a certain statutory age (usually 16 or 17) differently from adult offenders, with special juvenile court systems and separate detention facilities. Juvenile law today

---

[5] The Business and the Constitution chapter discusses equal protection in greater detail.

[6] For an example, see *McLaughlin v. Florida*, 379 U.S. 1984 (U.S. Sup. Ct. 1964), where the Court struck down a Florida statute forbidding cohabitation between black males and white females on the ground that no valid statutory purpose justified prohibiting only interracial cohabitation.

[7] See, for example, *Thompson v. Oklahoma*, 487 U.S. 815 (U.S. Sup. Ct. 1988), where the Court held that the Eighth Amendment bars the execution of a defendant who was under 16 at the time of his offense.

tends to emphasize rehabilitation rather than capacity. Repeat offenders or offenders charged with very serious offenses may sometimes be treated as adults.

Insanity on a criminal defendant's part can affect a criminal prosecution in a number of ways. Insanity rendering a defendant incapable of assisting in the defense of his case can delay his trial until he regains his sanity. Insanity that becomes manifest after conviction, but before sentencing, can delay sentencing until sanity is regained. The Supreme Court has recently recognized that the Eighth Amendment's prohibition of cruel and unusual punishment bars the execution of a condemned prisoner who becomes insane while awaiting execution.[8] Finally, insanity at the time a criminal act was committed can serve as a complete defense to liability. This type of insanity has generated much controversy in recent years.

This controversy stems from two major sources: significant disagreement concerning the proper test for insanity in criminal cases and public dissatisfaction with the insanity defense in general. The courts have adopted a variety of tests for criminal responsibility, all of which are designed to punish conscious wrongdoers. These tests are *legal* tests, not medical tests. A defendant who was medically insane at the time of the criminal act may still be legally responsible.

The primary common law test for insanity is the *M'Naghten* rule: a criminal defendant is not responsible if, at the time of the offense, he did not know the nature and quality of his act, or, if he did know it, he did not know that his act was wrong.[9] Some states have replaced or supplemented this rule with the *irresistible impulse* rule. This rule absolves a defendant of responsibility if mental disease rendered her incapable of controlling her behavior and resisting the impulse to commit a crime. One modern insanity test adopted by a large number of jurisdictions is that proposed by the American Law Institute. This test provides that a defendant is not criminally responsible if at the time the act was committed, due to mental disease or defect, he lacked the substantial capacity to appreciate the wrongfulness of his act or to conform his conduct to the law's requirements. Public reaction to certain highly publicized cases in which insanity defenses were raised, however, has produced a noticeable tendency to return to the narrower *M'Naghten* standard. For example, the Comprehensive

---

[8] *Ford v. Wainwright*, 477 U.S. 399 (U.S. Sup. Ct. 1986).

[9] This rule is derived from *Daniel M'Naghten's Case*, 8 Eng. Reprint 718 (House of Lords 1843).

FIGURE 1   Essentials of Crime Checklist

☐ Did the accused violate an existing statute?

☐ Is the statute constitutionally valid?
Does it prohibit constitutionally protected behavior?
Does it clearly define the prohibited behavior?

☐ Did the accused have the required criminal intent?
Did he have the capacity to form the required intent?
Can the necessary level of intent be inferred from his actions?

☐ Did the state prove each element of the crime beyond a reasonable doubt?

Crime Control Act of 1984 governs the insanity standard applicable in federal criminal cases. It provides that only defendants who are incapable of understanding the nature and wrongfulness of their acts are absolved from responsibility.

Public dissatisfaction with the insanity defense has produced another noticeable trend in recent years: the creation of procedural rules that make it more difficult for defendants to successfully raise an insanity defense. Criminal defendants are presumed to be sane. Traditionally, once an accused had introduced evidence tending to prove insanity, the state had the burden of proving his sanity beyond a reasonable doubt. Today, however, many states treat insanity as an *affirmative defense* and require the defendant to bear the burden of proving insanity. The Comprehensive Crime Control Act of 1984 adopts this approach. In addition, some states have instituted a "guilty, but mentally ill" verdict as an alternative to the traditional "not guilty by reason of insanity" verdict. This new alternative verdict allows jurors to convict rather than acquit mentally ill defendants, with the assurance that they will be given treatment after conviction.

Figure 1 summarizes the essential components of criminal liability under our legal system.

CRIMINAL PROCEDURE

Criminal Prosecutions

Persons who have been arrested for allegedly committing a crime are taken to the police station and booked. *Booking* is an administrative procedure for recording the suspect's arrest and the offenses involved. In some states, temporary release on bail may be available at this stage. After booking, the police file an arrest report with the prosecutor, who decides whether to charge the suspect with an offense. After deciding to prosecute, the prosecutor has a complaint prepared identifying the accused and detailing the charges.

Most states require that arrested suspects be promptly taken before a public official (a magistrate, commissioner, or justice of the peace) for an *initial appearance*. During this appearance the magistrate informs the accused of the charges against him and the nature of his constitutional rights. In misdemeanor cases, when the accused pleads guilty at this point, the sentence may be imposed without further proceedings. If the accused pleads not guilty, the case is set for trial. In felony cases, or misdemeanor cases in which the accused pleads not guilty, the magistrate sets the amount of bail.

In many states, defendants in felony cases are protected against unjustified prosecutions by an additional procedural step, the *preliminary hearing*. The prosecutor must introduce enough evidence at this hearing to convince a magistrate that there is *probable cause* to believe that the accused committed a felony. When the magistrate is so convinced, he binds over the defendant for trial in a criminal court.

After a bindover, the formal charge against the defendant is filed with a criminal court. This is accomplished by either an *information* filed by the prosecutor or an *indictment* returned by a *grand jury*. About half of the states require that a grand jury approve the decision to prosecute a person accused of a felony. Grand juries are bodies of citizens selected in the same manner as the members of a trial (petit) jury; often they are chosen through random drawings from a list of registered voters. Grand juries were originally composed of 23 members, a majority of whose votes were necessary to sustain an indictment. Today, many states have reduced the size of the grand jury; there is significant variation in the number of votes required for an indictment. Indictment of an accused prior to a preliminary hearing normally disposes of the need for a preliminary hearing. This is because the grand jury indictment serves essentially the same function as a magistrate's probable cause determination.

The remainder of the states allow felony defendants to be charged by either indictment or information, at the prosecutor's discretion. An *information* is a formal charge signed by the prosecutor outlining the facts supporting the charges against the defendant. In states that allow felony prosecution by information, the vast majority of felony cases are prosecuted in this way. Misdemeanor cases are almost exclusively prosecuted by information in virtually all jurisdictions.

Once an information or indictment has been filed with a trial court, the defendant is *arraigned* by being brought before the court, informed of the charges, and asked to enter a plea. The defendant may plead guilty, not guilty, or nolo contendere to the charges. Although technically not an admission of guilt, nolo contendere pleas are an indication that the defendant does not contest the charges. Nolo pleas are frequently attractive to corporate defendants who believe that their chances of mounting a successful defense are poor. This is because nolo pleas would be inadmissible as evidence of guilt in later civil suits against them based on the same statutory violations.

At the arraignment, the defendant also elects whether to be tried by a judge or a jury. Persons accused of serious crimes for which incarceration for more than six months is possible have a constitutional right to be tried by a jury of their peers. The accused, however, generally has the power to waive this right.

Procedural Safeguards

In the preceding pages, you have encountered several procedural devices designed to protect persons accused of crime. The Bill of Rights, the first 10 amendments to the U.S. Constitution, contains additional provisions to safeguard the rights of criminal defendants. These procedural safeguards reflect two basic public policies. First, they are designed to protect against unjustified or erroneous criminal convictions. Second, and perhaps equally important, they reflect a conclusion about government's proper role in the administration of justice in a democratic society. Justice Oliver Wendell Holmes aptly addressed this latter point when he said, "I think it less evil that some criminals should escape than that the government should play an ignoble part." Although the specific language of the Bill of Rights applies only to the federal government, the U.S. Supreme Court has applied the most important Bill of Rights guarantees to the states by "selectively incorporating" them into the Fourteenth Amendment's Due Process Clause. Once a particular safeguard has been found to be "implicit in the concept of ordered liberty" or "fundamental to the American scheme of justice," it has been applied equally in state and federal criminal trials.

The Fourth Amendment The Fourth Amendment provides:

The right of the people to be secure in their persons, houses, papers, and effects, against unreasonable searches and seizures, shall not be violated, and no Warrants shall issue, but upon probable cause, supported by Oath or affirmation, and particularly describing the place to be searched, and the persons or things to be seized.

The basic purpose of the Fourth Amendment is to protect individuals from arbitrary and unreasonable governmental violations of their privacy rights. Both the language of the amendment and the case law it has generated reflect the difficulties inherent in finding a proper balance between government's legitimate interest in securing evidence of wrongdoing and its citizens' legitimate expectations of privacy. Citizens are not protected against all searches and seizures—only against unreasonable ones. Because the Fourth Amendment only protects reasonable individual privacy expectations, the Supreme Court has extended its protection to private dwellings and those areas immediately surrounding them (often called the *curtilage*), telephone booths, sealed containers, and first class mail. The Court has denied protection to areas or items in which it found no reasonable expectations of privacy, such as open fields, personal bank records, and voluntary conversations between criminal defendants and government informants. Even where plainly protected items or areas are concerned, not every governmental intrusion is deemed sufficiently intrusive to constitute a search or seizure within the meaning of the Fourth Amendment. Thus, the Court held that exposing an airline traveler's luggage to a narcotics detection dog in a public place was not a search in view of the minimally intrusive nature of the intrusion and the narrow scope of information revealed by such tests.[10] In the *Dow Chemical* case, which follows, the Court refused to hold that aerial photographs of an industrial complex violated the Fourth Amendment.

A similar balancing of individual and governmental interests is evident in the Court's handling of the Fourth Amendment's Warrant Clause. The idea behind the warrant requirement is to further protect individual rights by having a neutral party (a judge or a magistrate) authorize and define the scope of intrusive governmental action. Thus, as a general rule, the Court has held that searches carried out without a proper warrant are, by definition, unreasonable. Nonetheless, the Court has authorized warrantless searches of the area within the immediate control of an arrestee, of automobiles (due to their highly mobile nature), of premises police enter in hot pursuit of an armed suspect, and of contraband items in the plain view of officers who are otherwise acting lawfully. Customs searches, stop and frisk searches, inventory searches of property in an arrestee's possession, and consensual searches also have been upheld, despite the absence of a warrant. Finally, the Court has upheld warrantless administrative inspections of closely regulated businesses.[11]

The basic device employed by the Court to enforce the Fourth Amendment is the **exclusionary rule:** Evidence seized in illegal searches cannot be used in a subsequent trial against an accused whose constitutional rights have been violated.[12] Because the exclusionary rule often operates to exclude convincing evidence of crime, it has generated enormous controversy. Supporters of the rule argued that it is necessary to deter police from violating citizens' constitutional rights. Opponents of the rule argued that it would not deter police who believed they were acting lawfully. Because the exclusion of illegally seized evidence imposed no direct penalties on police officers who acted unlawfully, opponents believed the rule was a poor device for achieving deterrence. A common complaint was that "because of a policeman's error, a criminal goes free." In recent years, the Court has responded to such criticism by restricting the operation of the rule. For example, in *Nix v. Williams*, the Court held that illegally obtained evidence can be introduced at a trial if the prosecution can convince the trial court that it would inevitably have been obtained by lawful means.[13] More importantly, in *United States v. Leon*, the Court created a "good faith" exception to the exclusionary rule to allow the use of evidence seized by police officers who reasonably believed they were acting under a lawful search warrant.[14] Although the Court has not extended this exception to warrantless searches, it did expand the exception's scope to include searches made in reliance on a statute which is later declared invalid.[15]

---

[10]*United States v. Place*, 426 U.S. 696 (U.S. Sup. Ct. 1983). In this case, however, the Court also held that the warrantless detention of the defendant's luggage for 90 minutes was unlawful, given the fact that the agents in question had several hours' advance notice of the defendant's arrival.

[11] See, e.g., *New York v. Burger*, 482 U.S. 691 (U.S. Sup. Ct. 1987).

[12] The exclusionary rule was first applied to the states in *Mapp v. Ohio*, 367 U.S. 643 (U.S. Sup. Ct. 1961).

[13]467 U.S. 431 (U.S. Sup. Ct. 1984).

[14] 468 U.S. 897 (U.S. Sup. Ct. 1984).

[15]*Illinois v. Krull*, 480 U.S. 340 (U.S. Sup. Ct. 1987).

DOW CHEMICAL CO. v. UNITED STATES

476 U.S. 227 (U.S. Sup. Ct. 1986)

Dow Chemical Company operates a 2,000-acre chemical manufacturing facility at Midland, Michigan. The facility consists of numerous covered buildings, with manufacturing equipment and piping conduits between various buildings plainly visible from the air. At all times, Dow maintained elaborate security around the perimeter of the complex barring ground-level public views of these areas. It also investigated any low-level flights by aircraft over the facility. Dow did not, however, attempt to conceal all manufacturing equipment within the complex from aerial views because the cost was prohibitive.

In early 1978, enforcement officials of the Environmental Protection Agency (EPA) made an on-site inspection of two power plants in this complex with Dow's consent. When a subsequent request for a second inspection was denied, EPA did not thereafter seek an administrative search warrant. Instead, EPA employed a commercial aerial photographer, using a standard floor-mounted, precision aerial mapping camera, to take photographs of the facility from altitudes of 12,000, 3,000, and 1,200 feet. At all times the aircraft was lawfully within navigable airspace.

EPA did not inform Dow of this aerial photography. When Dow became aware of it, the company brought suit in the District Court alleging that EPA's action violated the Fourth Amendment. The District Court granted Dow's motion for summary judgment. EPA was permanently enjoined from taking aerial photographs of Dow's premises and from disseminating, releasing, or copying the photographs already taken. When the Sixth Circuit Court of Appeals reversed, Dow appealed.

Burger, Chief Justice. Dow claims that the EPA's use of aerial photography was a "search" of an area that was within an "industrial curtilage" rather than an "open field," and that it had a reasonable expectation of privacy from such photography protected by the Fourth Amendment. In making this contention, however, Dow concedes that a simple flyover with naked-eye observation, or the taking of a photograph from a nearby hillside overlooking such a facility, would give rise to no Fourth Amendment problem.

In *California v. Ciraolo*, decided today, we hold that naked-eye aerial observation from an altitude of 1,000 feet of a backyard within the curtilage of a home does not constitute a search under the Fourth Amendment. The curtilage area immediately surrounding a private house has long been given protection as a place where the occupants have a reasonable and legitimate expectation of privacy that society is prepared to accept.

As the curtilage doctrine evolved to protect much the same kind of privacy as that covering the interior of a structure, the contrasting "open fields" doctrine evolved as well. From *Hester v. United States* (1924) to *Oliver v. United States* (1984), the Court has drawn a line as to what expectations are reasonable in the open areas beyond the curtilage of a dwelling; open fields do not provide the setting for those intimate activities that the Fourth Amendment is intended to shelter from governmental interference or surveillance. In *Oliver*, we held that "an individual may not legitimately demand privacy for activities out of doors in fields, except in the area immediately surrounding the home." To fall within the open fields doctrine the area need be neither "open" nor a "field" as those terms are used in common speech.

Dow plainly has a reasonable, legitimate, and objective expectation of privacy within the interior of its covered buildings. Moreover, it could hardly be expected that Dow would erect a huge cover over a 2,000-acre tract. Dow argues that its exposed manufacturing facilities are analogous to the curtilage surrounding a home because it has taken every possible step to bar access from ground level. In *Oliver*, the Court described the curtilage of a dwelling as "the area to which extends the intimate activity associated with the sanctity of a man's home and the privacies of life." The intimate activities associated with family privacy and the home and its curtilage simply do not reach the outdoor areas of spaces between structures and buildings of a manufacturing plant.

Admittedly, Dow's enclosed plant complex does not fall precisely within the "open fields" doctrine. The area at issue here can perhaps be seen as falling somewhere between "open fields" and curtilage, but lacking some of the critical characteristics of both. Dow's inner manufacturing areas are elaborately secured to ensure they are not open or exposed to the public from the ground. Any actual physical entry by EPA into any enclosed area would raise significantly different questions, because the businessman, like the occupant of a residence, has a constitutional right to go about his business free from unreasonable official entries upon his private commercial property. The narrow issue raised by Dow's claim of search and seizure, however, concerns aerial observation of a 2,000-acre outdoor manufacturing facility *without* physical entry. The Government has greater latitude to conduct warrantless inspections of commercial property because the expectation of privacy that the owner of commercial property enjoys in such property differs significantly from the sanctity accorded an individual's home. Unlike a homeowner's interest in his dwelling, the interest of the owner of commercial property is not one in being free from any inspections. With regard to regulatory inspections, we have held that what is observable by the public is observable without a warrant, by the Government inspector as well.

Oliver recognized that in the open field context, "the public and police lawfully may survey lands from the air." Here, the EPA was not employing some unique sensory device that, for example, could penetrate the walls of buildings and record conversations in Dow's plants, offices, or laboratories, but rather a conventional, albeit precise, commercial camera commonly used in mapmaking. The Government asserts it has not yet enlarged the photographs to any significant degree, but Dow points out that simple magnification permits identification of objects such as wires as small as one-half inch diameter.

It may well be that surveillance of private property by using highly sophisticated surveillance equipment not generally available to the public, such as satellite technology, might be constitutionally proscribed absent a warrant. But the photographs here are not so revealing of intimate details as to raise constitutional concerns. The mere fact that human vision is enhanced somewhat, at least to the degree here, does not give rise to constitutional problems.

We conclude that the open areas of an industrial plant complex with numerous plant structures spread over an area of 2,000 acres are not analogous to the curtilage of a dwelling for purposes of aerial surveillance; such an industrial complex is more comparable to an open field and as such it is open to the view and observation of persons in aircraft lawfully in the public airspace immediately above or sufficiently near the area for the reach of cameras.

We hold that the taking of aerial photographs of an industrial plant complex from navigable airspace is not a search prohibited by the Fourth Amendment.

Judgment for the EPA affirmed.

The Fifth Amendment   In addition to the Due Process Clause with its guarantee of basic procedural and substantive fairness, the Fifth Amendment contains two other provisions that safeguard criminal defendants' rights. The Fifth Amendment protects against *compulsory testimonial self-incrimination* by providing that no "person . . . shall be compelled in any criminal case to be a witness against himself." This provision prevents the state from forcing a defendant to assist in his own prosecution by compelling him to make incriminating testimonial admissions. In *Miranda v. Arizona*, the Supreme Court held that the Fifth Amendment required police to warn criminal suspects of their right to remain silent before commencing any custodial interrogation of them.[16] The Court also required police to inform suspects that any statements they make may be used as evidence against them and that they have the right to the presence of an attorney, either retained or appointed. Any incriminating statements that the accused makes in the absence of a *Miranda* warning, or other evidence resulting from such statements, is inadmissible in a subsequent trial.

This right to silence has always been limited in a variety of ways. For example, the traditional limitation of the Fifth Amendment's scope to *testimonial* admissions has long been held to allow the police to compel an accused to furnish nontestimonial evidence such as fingerprints, samples of bodily fluids, and hair. In recent years, however, Supreme Court decisions have recognized further significant limitations on the right to silence. For example, for a long time an implicit part of the right to silence was a corresponding limitation on any prosecutorial trial comments about the accused's failure to speak in her own defense. The Court's recent decisions still support this limitation when an accused's silence after arrest or after receiving a *Miranda* warning is at issue.

However, the Court has allowed prosecutors to use a defendant's pretrial silence to impeach his trial testimony in some circumstances. For example, the Court has held that the Fifth Amendment is not violated when a defendant's silence (either prearrest or postarrest, but in advance of any *Miranda* warning) is used to discredit his trial testimony that he had killed his victim in self-defense.[17]

A similar tendency to narrow *Miranda's* scope is evident in *Moran v. Burbine*, one of the Court's recent controversial Fifth Amendment decisions.[18] In *Moran*, the Court disagreed with the majority of lower federal courts and state courts that had considered the issue and upheld a suspect's waiver of his *Miranda* rights despite the failure of the police to notify him that a lawyer retained for him by a third party was seeking to contact him.

While the preceding discussion of the privilege against self-incrimination has focused on the rights of criminal defendants in general, the Fifth Amendment has long had particular relevance to persons in business who are charged with crimes. Documentary evidence can be of critical importance to the government's case in many white-collar crime prosecutions. To what extent does the Fifth Amendment protect business records? In *Boyd v. United States*, the first case to consider the question, the Supreme Court held that the Fifth Amendment protected individuals against being compelled to produce their private papers.[19] In subsequent decisions, however, the Court has drastically limited the scope of this private papers protection. A number of the Court's decisions have held that the private papers privilege is a *personal* privilege that cannot be asserted by a corporation, partnership, or other "collective entity." Because such entities have no Fifth Amendment rights, the Court has held that an individual officer or member of an organization who has custody of organizational records cannot assert any personal privilege to prevent their disclosure, even if the contents of such records incriminate her personally. Finally, it has long been held that the government has the power to require business proprietors to keep certain records relevant to transactions that are appropriate subjects for government regulation. Such "required records" are not entitled to private papers protection; therefore, they may be subpoenaed and used against the recordkeeper in prosecutions for regulatory violations.

The Court's most recent business records decisions cast further doubt on the future of the private papers doctrine. Instead of focusing on whether the subpoenaed records are private in nature, the Court now focuses on whether the *act of producing* the records in response to a subpoena is sufficiently testimonial to violate the privilege against self-incrimination. In *Fisher v. United States*, the Court held that an individual subpoenaed to produce personal documents may only assert his privilege against compelled self-incrimination if the act of producing such documents would involve incriminating testimonial admissions.[20] This is likely where the individual producing the records is in effect admitting the existence of records previously unknown to the government (demonstrating that he had access to the records and, therefore, possible knowledge of any incriminating contents) or certifying the records' authenticity.

---

[16] 384 U.S. 436 (U.S. Sup. Ct. 1966).

[17] *Fletcher v. Weir*, 455 U.S. 603 (U.S. Sup. Ct. 1982); *Jenkins v. Anderson*, 447 U.S. 231 (U.S. Sup. Ct. 1980).

[18] 475 U.S. 412 (U.S. Sup. Ct. 1986).

[19] 116 U.S. 616 (U.S. Sup. Ct. 1886).

[20] 425 U.S. 391 (U.S. Sup. Ct. 1976).

More recently, in *United States v. Doe*, the Court extended the act-of-production privilege to a sole proprietor whose proprietorship records had been subpoenaed.[21] The Court, however, held that normal business records were not themselves protected by the Fifth Amendment because they were voluntarily prepared, and therefore not the product of compulsion. Some interested observers thought that this new emphasis on the testimonial and potentially incriminatory aspects of the act of producing business records meant that officers of collective entities that are targets of a government investigation might be able to assert their personal privilege against self-incrimination to avoid producing potentially incriminatory business records. Such hopes were dashed when the Court, in *Braswell v. United States*, refused to extend its holding in *Doe* to cover the sole shareholder of a corporation acting in his capacity as custodian of corporate records.[22] Because he operated his business as a corporation, the Court held that Braswell was bound by the collective-entity rule, which says that such entities have no Fifth Amendment privilege. Because he acted in a representative capacity in turning over the requested records, the government could make no evidentiary use of his act of producing the records, but could use the contents of the record against him and his corporation.

One other Fifth Amendment provision worthy of note is the **Double Jeopardy Clause.** This provision protects criminal defendants from multiple prosecutions for the same offense. It prevents an accused from being charged with more than one count of the same statutory violation for one offense, for example, being charged with two robbery violations for a one-time robbery of one individual. This clause also prevents a second prosecution for the same offense after the defendant has been acquitted or convicted of that offense, and it bars the imposition of multiple punishments for the same offense.

The Double Jeopardy Clause does not, however, preclude the possibility that a single criminal act may result in several criminal prosecutions. For example, one criminal act may produce several statutory violations, all of which may be proper subjects for prosecution. A defendant who commits a rape may also be prosecuted for battery, assault with a deadly weapon, and kidnapping if the facts of the case indicate that several statutes were violated. In addition, the Supreme Court has long used a same evidence test to determine what constitutes the same offense.[23] This means that a single criminal act with multiple victims (e.g., a robbery of a restaurant where several patrons are robbed) could result in several prosecutions because the identity of each victim would be an additional fact of proof in each case. Finally, the Double Jeopardy Clause does not protect against multiple prosecutions by *different sovereigns*. A conviction or acquittal in a federal court does not prevent a subsequent prosecution in a state court for a state offense arising out of the same event, or vice versa.

The Sixth Amendment   The Sixth Amendment contains several provisions that safeguard criminal defendants' rights. It entitles defendants in criminal cases to a speedy trial by an impartial jury, at which they may confront and cross-examine the witnesses against them. It also gives the accused in a criminal case the right "to have the assistance of counsel" in her defense. This provision has been interpreted to mean not only that the defendant has the right to employ his own attorney to represent him, but that indigent defendants charged with a crime are entitled to court-appointed counsel.[24] An accused must be informed of his *right to counsel* once he has been taken into custody.[25] Once the accused has requested the assistance of counsel, he may not be interrogated further unless he voluntarily initiates further conversations with the authorities.[26] Finally, an accused is entitled to *effective* assistance by his counsel. This means that the accused is entitled to counsel at a point in the proceedings when counsel can effectively assist him.[27] Inadequate assistance by counsel can be a proper basis for setting aside a conviction and ordering a new trial.[28]

---

[23]*Blockburger v. United States*, 284 U.S. 299 (U.S. Sup. Ct. 1932). The Court has recently qualified *Blockburger* by saying that the Double Jeopardy Clause bars any subsequent prosecution "in which the government, to establish an essential element of an offense charged in that prosecution, will prove conduct that constitutes an offense for which the defendant has already been prosecuted." *Grady v. Corbin*, 110 S. Ct. 2084 (U.S. Sup. Ct. 1990).

[24] *Gideon v. Wainwright*, 372 U.S. 335 (U.S. Sup. Ct. 1963).

[25] *Miranda v. Arizona*, 384 U.S. 436 (U.S. Sup. Ct. 1966).

[26] *Edwards v. Arizona*, 451 U.S. 477 (U.S. Sup. Ct. 1981).

[27] *Powell v. Alabama*, 287 U.S. 45 (U.S. Sup. Ct. 1932).

[28] In *Strickland v. Washington*, 446 U.S. 668 (U.S. Sup. Ct. 1984), the Court held that a defendant's conviction would not be set aside unless his attorney's performance fell below an objective standard of reasonableness and so prejudiced him as to result in the denial of a fair trial.

---

[21] 463 U.S. 605 (U.S. Sup. Ct. 1984).

[22] 487 U.S. 99 (U.S. Sup. Ct. 1988).

FIGURE 2   Major Procedural Safeguards

Fourth Amendment
   Prohibits unreasonable searches and seizures
Fifth Amendment
   Due Process Clause (federal)
       Presumption of innocence
       Prohibits vague criminal statutes
       Requires basic procedural and substantive fairness
   Right to silence
   Double Jeopardy Clause
Sixth Amendment
   Speedy trial
   Impartial jury
   Confront and cross-examine prosecution's witnesses
   Right to counsel
Eighth Amendment
   Forbids cruel and unusual punishments

Figure 2 summarizes the major procedural safeguards enjoyed by defendants under our criminal justice system.

WHITE-COLLAR CRIMES AND THE DILEMMAS OF CORPORATE CONTROL

Introduction

White-collar crime is the term broadly used to describe a wide variety of nonviolent criminal offenses committed by businesspersons and by business organizations. Although this term often includes offenses committed by corporate employees against their corporate employers, such as theft, embezzlement, or accepting a bribe, our discussions in this part of the text focus on criminal offenses committed by corporate employers and their employees against society as a whole. Each year, corporate crime costs consumers billions of dollars. It may take a variety of forms, from consumer fraud, securities fraud, and tax evasion to price-fixing, environmental pollution, and other regulatory violations. Corporate crime confronts our legal system with a variety of problems—problems we have failed to resolve satisfactorily.

Corporations form the backbone of the most successful economic system in history. They dominate the international economic scene, and they have provided us with incalculable benefits in efficiently produced goods and services. Yet these same corporations may pollute the environment, swindle their customers, produce dangerously defective products, and conspire with others to injure or destroy competition. How are we to effectively control these large organizations so important to our existence? Increasingly, we have come to rely on the criminal law as a major instrument of corporate control.

The criminal law, however, was developed with individual wrongdoers in mind. Who is at fault when a large organization causes some social harm? Corporate crime is *organizational* crime: Any given corporate action may be the product of the combined actions of many individuals acting within the corporate hierarchy. None of them may have had sufficient knowledge to possess individually the *mens rea* necessary for criminal responsibility under traditional criminal law principles. How are we to apply such criminal sanctions as imprisonment or death to a legal person like a corporation?

Evolution of Corporate Criminal Liability

The common law initially rejected the idea that corporations could be criminally responsible for the actions of their employees. Early corporations were small in size and number; they had little impact on public life. Their small size meant that it was relatively easy to pinpoint individual wrongdoers within the corporation and thereby avoid the difficult conceptual problems associated with corporate criminal liability. After all, corporations were legal entities; they lacked a "mind," and it was hard to conceive of them as having the criminal intent necessary for common law crimes. Lacking physical bodies, they were immune to imprisonment, the basic common law criminal sanction.

As corporations grew in size and power, however, and the social need to control their activities grew accordingly, the common law rules on corporate criminal liability began to change. The first cases in which criminal liability was imposed on corporations involved suits against public corporations such as municipalities—then the most common corporation—for the failure to perform such public duties as road and bridge repair. As commercial corporations grew in size and number, similar liability was imposed on them by statutes creating *public welfare offenses*, regulatory offenses requiring no proof of *mens rea*.

By the turn of this century, American courts had begun to impose criminal liability on corporations for general criminal offenses that required proof of *mens rea*. This expansion of corporate criminal liability *imputed* the criminal intent of its employees to the corporation in a fashion similar to the imposition of tort or contract liability on corporations under the doctrine of *respondeat superior.*[29]

Today, it is generally thought that a corporation can be criminally liable for almost any criminal offense if the statute in question indicates a legislative intent to hold corporations liable. This legislative intent requirement can sometimes be problematic, because many state criminal statutes are derived from common law crimes and may contain language that suggests an intent to hold only humans liable. For example, many state manslaughter statutes define the offense as "the killing of one human being by the act of another." However, where statutes are framed in more general terms, referring to "persons" for example, the courts are generally willing to apply them to corporate defendants.

Corporate Criminal Liability Today

The modern rule on corporate criminal liability is that a corporation can be held liable for criminal offenses committed by its employees *acting within the scope of their employment* and *for the benefit of the corporation.* A major current issue in corporate criminal liability concerns the classes of corporate employees whose intent can be imputed to the corporation. Some commentators have argued that a corporation should be criminally responsible only for offenses committed by high corporate officials or those linked to them by authorization or acquiescence. (Virtually all courts impose criminal liability on a corporation under such circumstances.) Such arguments are based on notions of fairness: If any group of corporate employees can fairly be said to constitute a corporation's mind, that group is its top officers and directors.

The problem with imposing corporate liability only on the basis of the actions or knowledge of top corporate officers is that such a policy often insulates the corporation from liability. Many corporate offenses may be directly traceable only to middle managers or more subordinate corporate employees. It may be impossible to demonstrate that any higher-level corporate official had sufficient knowledge to constitute *mens rea*. Recognizing this fact, the federal courts have adopted a general rule that a corporation can be criminally liable for the actions of any of its agents, whether or not any link

between such agents and higher-level corporate officials can be demonstrated.

Another significant current controversy regarding the nature of corporate criminal responsibility concerns whether courts should recognize a *due diligence* defense to corporate criminal liability. Advocates of such a defense say it is unfair to impute the intent of some employees to their corporate employer without also considering good faith corporate efforts to prevent statutory violations. They also point out that the major justification advanced for corporate criminal liability is deterrence: The hope that the threat or imposition of criminal penalties will encourage corporate efforts to comply with legal rules. Thus, they argue that recognizing a due diligence defense would encourage corporate compliance efforts, whereas imposing liability regardless of such efforts undermines deterrence by discouraging them. Most courts, however, have found these arguments unconvincing and have generally rejected the idea of a due diligence defense.

Problems with Corporate Criminal Liability Despite the legal theories that justify corporate criminal liability, the punishment of corporations still remains a highly problematic subject. Does a corporate criminal conviction stigmatize a corporation in the same way that being branded a criminal stigmatizes an individual? The idea of viewing a corporation as a criminal may be difficult for most people to embrace. Perhaps the only stigma resulting from a corporate criminal conviction is felt by corporate employees, many of whom are entirely innocent of any wrongdoing. Is it just to punish the innocent in an attempt to punish the guilty?

And what of the cash fine, the primary punishment imposed on convicted corporations? Most critics of contemporary corporate control strategies argue that the fines imposed on convicted corporations tend to be too small to provide effective deterrence. What is needed, they argue, are fines keyed in some fashion to the corporate defendant's wealth, such as a percentage of the defendant's income or total capital. Such large fines present a variety of practical and conceptual difficulties. Where market conditions permit, criminal fines are likely to be passed on to consumers as higher prices; where a pass-on is impossible, corporate shareholders are likely to absorb the loss. Fines large enough to threaten corporate solvency may cause injury to corporate employees and those economically dependent on the corporation's financial well-being. Yet most of these individuals have neither had the power to prevent the violation nor derived any benefit from it. On the other

---

[29] The Third-Party Relations of the Principal and the Agent chapter discusses *respondeat superior in* detail. For an early landmark case on this subject, see *New York Central & Hudson River R.R. v. United States*, 212 U.S. 481 (U.S. Sup. Ct. 1909).

hand, fines imposed on a corporation may place no direct burden on the managers responsible for a violation. Given the element of randomness inherent in criminal fines, legislatures may be unwilling to authorize, and courts reluctant to impose, fines that are large enough to produce deterrence.

Aside from such problems of practicality and fairness, other deficiencies make fines less-than-adequate corporate control devices. Fine strategies tend to assume that all corporations are rationally acting profit-maximizers. Fines of sufficient size, it is argued, will erode the profit drive that underlies most corporate violations. Numerous studies of actual corporate behavior, however, suggest that many corporations are neither profit-maximizers nor rational actors. Mature firms with well-established market shares may embrace goals other than profit maximization, such as technological prominence, increased market share, or higher employee salaries. In addition, the interests of the managers who make corporate decisions and establish corporate policies may not be synonymous with the long-range economic interests of their corporate employers. The fact that their employers may at some future point have to pay a sizable fine may not make much of an impression on top managers, who tend to have relatively short terms in office and are often compensated in part by large bonuses keyed to year-end profitability.

Even if corporate managers were otherwise motivated to avoid corporate violations, there are reasons to doubt whether they would always be capable of doing so. Most organization theorists acknowledge that large organizations suffer from problems of control. Many corporate wrongs result from internal bureaucratic malfunctions rather than the conscious actions of any intracorporate individual or group. Fines are as unlikely to deter such structural violations as they are to encourage internal reform efforts in response to a fine imposed after a violation has occurred.

Individual Liability for Corporate Crime

Individuals committing criminal offenses while acting in their corporate capacities have always been personally exposed to criminal liability. In fact, most European nations reject corporate criminal liability in favor of exclusive reliance on individual criminal responsibility. Certainly, individual liability has many attractive features, particularly in view of the problems connected with imposing criminal liability on corporations. Individual liability is more consistent with traditional criminal law notions about the personal nature of guilt.

Individual liability may provide better deterrence than corporate liability if it enables society to bring the threat of criminal punishment to bear against the individual corporate officers who make important corporate decisions. The possibility of personal liability may induce individuals to resist corporate pressures to violate the law and may prevent corporations from treating financial penalties merely as a cost of doing business. And to the extent that guilty individuals can be identified and punished, the ends of the criminal law may be achieved without unfairly stigmatizing innocent corporate employees or punishing innocent shareholders or consumers.

Problems with Individual Liability   Attractive as individual liability may sound, it too poses some significant problems when applied in the corporate context. Identifying responsible individuals within the corporate hierarchy is a difficult and often impossible task if we adhere to traditional notions of criminal responsibility and insist on proof of some criminal intent as a precondition of liability. The division of authority that typifies large corporations produces a diffusion of responsibility often making it difficult to assign individual responsibility. Corporate decisions are often *collective* decisions, the products of the combined actions of numerous individuals within the corporate hierarchy, none of whom may have had complete knowledge or any specific intent.

It may be particularly difficult to prove knowledge on the part of high-level executives, because bad news may not reach them or because they may consciously avoid such knowledge. It may, therefore, only be possible to demonstrate culpability on the part of middle-level managers. But juries may be unwilling to convict such individuals if they seem to be scapegoats for their unindicted superiors. Finally, some corporate crimes may be structural in the sense that they are the products of internal bureaucratic failures rather than the conscious actions of any individual or group. Even when a culpable individual can be identified, significant problems can prevent effectively applying the criminal sanction to him. The individual in question may have died, retired, or been transferred to another post outside the jurisdiction where the offense occurred. White-collar defendants are rarely imprisoned after conviction; when imprisonment does result, it is commonly in the form of a short sentence to a "country club" institution, where early parole is a high possibility. The reluctance to imprison white-collar offenders is generally attributed to the positive image that such offenders normally possess—they tend to be well-educated, well-spoken community leaders. Also, there are public doubts about the moral culpability involved in most white-collar offenses. Thus, most convicted white-collar offenders merely receive fines that are often small in comparison to their wealth and are frequently indemnified by their corporate employers.[30]

These difficulties in imposing criminal penalties on individual corporate employees have led to the creation of regulatory offenses imposing *strict* or *vicarious* liability on corporate officers. **Strict liability offenses** dispense with the requirement of proof of any criminal

intent on the part of the defendant, but ordinarily require proof that the defendant committed some wrongful act. **Vicarious liability offenses** impose criminal liability on a defendant for the acts of third parties (normally employees under the defendant's personal supervision), but may require proof of some form of *mens rea*, such as a negligent or reckless failure to supervise on the defendant's part. Frequently, a statute embodies elements of both approaches by imposing liability on a corporate executive for the acts or omissions of other corporate employees without requiring proof of criminal intent on the part of any corporate employee. The following *Park* case is probably the most famous recent example of such a prosecution.

---

[30] The Management of Corporations chapter discusses indemnification in detail.

UNITED STATES v. PARK
421 U.S. 658 (U.S. Sup. Ct. 1975)

John R. Park was the chief executive officer of Acme Markets, Inc., a national retail food chain with approximately 36,000 employees, 874 retail outlets, and 16 warehouses. Acme and Park were charged with five counts of violating the Federal Food, Drug, and Cosmetic Act by storing food shipped in interstate commerce in warehouses where it was exposed to rodent contamination.

The violations were detected during Food and Drug Administration (FDA) inspections of Acme's Baltimore warehouse. A 12-day inspection during November and December 1971 disclosed evidence of rodent infestation and unsanitary conditions at the warehouse. Among other things, mouse droppings were found on the floor of the hanging meat room and beside bales of lime Jell-O, and one bale of Jell-O contained a hole chewed by a rodent. The FDA notified Park by letter of these findings. After receiving the letter, Park conferred with Acme's vice president for legal affairs, who told him that the Baltimore division vice president "was investigating the situation immediately and would be taking corrective action." When a subsequent FDA investigation, in March 1972, disclosed continued rodent contamination at the Baltimore warehouse despite improved sanitation there, the charges were filed against Acme and Park. Acme pleaded guilty to the charges, but Park refused to do so. Park was convicted on each count and fined $50 per count.

Park appealed his conviction, arguing that the trial court's instructions to the jury were defective because they could have been interpreted as justifying a conviction based solely on his corporate position. He also argued that the trial court erred in allowing the government to introduce evidence of a 1970 FDA letter that informed him of similar problems at Acme's Philadelphia warehouse. The Fourth Circuit Court of Appeals agreed, reversing Park's conviction. The government appealed.

Burger, Chief Justice. In *United States v. Dotterweich* (1943), this Court looked to the purposes of the Act and noted that they "touch phases of the lives and health of people which, in the circumstances of modern industrialism, are largely beyond self-protection." It observed that the Act is of "a now familiar type" which "dispenses with the conventional requirement for criminal conduct—awareness of some wrongdoing. In the interest of the larger good it puts the burden of acting at hazard upon a person otherwise innocent but standing in responsible relation to a public danger."

The Court was aware of the concern that literal enforcement "might operate too harshly by sweeping within its condemnation any person however remotely entangled in the proscribed shipment." In this context, the Court concluded, the offense was committed "by all who have a responsible share in the furtherance of the transaction which the statute outlaws."

The interpretation given the Act in *Dotterweich*, as holding criminally accountable persons whose failure to exercise authority and supervisory responsibility resulted in the violation, has been confirmed in our subsequent cases. The Court has reaffirmed the proposition that the public interest in the purity of its food is so great as to warrant the imposition of the highest standard of care on distributors.

Thus *Dotterweich* and the cases which have followed reveal that in providing sanctions which reach and touch the individuals who execute the corporate mission—and this is by no means necessarily confined to a single corporate agent or employee—the Act imposes not only a positive duty to seek out and remedy violations when they occur but also, and primarily, a duty to implement measures that will insure that violations will not occur. The duty imposed by Congress on responsible corporate agents is, we emphasize, one that requires the highest standard of foresight and vigilance, but the Act, in its criminal aspect, does not require that which is objectively impossible. The theory upon which responsible corporate agents are held criminally accountable for "causing" violations of the Act permits a claim that a defendant was "powerless" to prevent or correct the violation to be raised defensively at a trial on the merits. If such a claim is made, the defendant has the burden of coming forward with evidence, but this does not alter the Government's ultimate burden of proving beyond a reasonable doubt the defendant's guilt, including his power, in light of the duty imposed by the Act, to prevent or correct the prohibited condition.

Turning to the jury charge in this case, it is arguable that isolated parts can be read as intimating that a finding of guilt could be predicated solely on Park's corporate position. Viewed as a whole, the charge did not permit the jury to find guilt solely on the basis of Park's position; rather, it fairly advised the jury that to find guilt it must find Park "had a responsible relation to the situation," and "by virtue of his position . . . had authority and responsibility" to deal with the situation.

Our conclusion that the Court of Appeals erred in its reading of the jury charge suggests as well our disagreement concerning the admissibility of evidence that Park was advised by FDA in 1970 of unsanitary conditions in Acme's Philadelphia warehouse. Park testified that he had employed a system in which he relied upon his subordinates, and that he was ultimately responsible for this system. He testified further that he had found these subordinates to be "dependable" and had "great confidence" in them. By this and other testimony Park evidently sought to persuade the jury that, as the president of a large corporation, he had no choice but to delegate duties to those in whom he reposed confidence, that he had no reason to suspect his subordinates were failing to insure compliance with the Act, and that, once violations were unearthed, acting through those subordinates he did everything possible to correct them.

This testimony clearly created the need for rebuttal evidence. That evidence was not offered to show that Park had a propensity to commit criminal acts, that the crime charged had been committed; its purpose was to demonstrate that Park was on notice that he could not rely on his system of delegation to subordinates to prevent or correct unsanitary conditions at Acme's warehouses, and that he must have been aware of the deficiencies of this system before the Baltimore violations were discovered. The evidence was therefore relevant since it served to rebut Park's defense that he had justifiably relied upon subordinates to handle sanitation matters.

Judgment of the Court of Appeals reversed; Park's conviction sustained.

Strict liability offenses have been widely criticized on a variety of grounds. First, it is often argued that *mens rea* is a basic principle in our legal system and that it is unjust to stigmatize with a criminal conviction persons who are not morally culpable. Second, the critics commonly express doubts about whether strict liability offenses produce the deterrence that their proponents seek. They may reduce the moral impact of the criminal sanction by applying it to relatively trivial offenses. And they may not result in enough convictions or severe enough penalties to produce deterrence because juries and judges are unwilling to convict or punish defendants who may not be morally culpable. Although the courts have generally upheld the constitutionality of strict liability offenses, they are generally disfavored. Most courts require a clear indication of a legislative intent to dispense with the element of *mens rea*.[31]

Third, even if prosecutors could identify and convict responsible individuals within the corporation and judges and juries imposed significant penalties on such individuals, individual liability in the absence of corporate liability would probably fail to achieve effective corporate control. If corporations were immune from criminal liability, they could benefit financially from employee law violations. Individual liability, unlike corporate fines, does not force a corporation to give up the profits flowing from a violation. Thus, corporations would have no incentive to avoid future violations and incarcerated offenders would merely be replaced by others who might eventually yield to the pressures that produced the violations in the first place. Also, corporate liability may, in some cases, encourage corporate efforts to prevent future violations. Corporate liability is uniquely appropriate when an offense has occurred but no identifiable individual is sufficiently culpable to justify an individual prosecution.

New Directions

The preceding discussion suggests that future efforts at corporate control are likely to include both corporate and individual criminal liability. It also suggests, however, that new approaches are necessary if society is to gain more effective control over corporate activities. We need new remedies reflecting both our historical experience with attempts to apply the criminal sanction in the corporate context and our knowledge of the nature of corporate behavior.

In the area of individual liability, a variety of novel criminal penalties have been suggested. For example, white-collar offenders could be deprived of their leisure time or sentenced to render public service rather than being incarcerated or fined. Some have even suggested the licensing of managers and license suspensions as a penalty for offenders. The common thread in all these approaches is an attempt to create penalties meaningful to the defendant, yet not so severe that judges and juries are unwilling to impose them with sufficient certainty to produce deterrence.

In the area of corporate liability, one of the most novel and promising recent suggestions involves more imaginative judicial use of corporate probation for convicted corporate offenders.[32] Courts could require convicted corporations to do, or hire independent consultants to do, self-studies identifying the source of a violation and proposing appropriate steps to prevent future violations. If bureaucratic failures caused the violation, the court could order a limited restructuring of the corporation's internal decision-making processes as a condition of obtaining probation or avoiding a penalty. Possible orders might include requiring the collection and monitoring of the data necessary to discover or prevent future violations and the creation of new executive positions to monitor such data. Restructuring would minimize the harm to innocent persons inherent in corporate financial penalties. It might also be a more effective way of achieving corporate rehabilitation than relying exclusively on a corporation's desire to avoid future fines as an incentive to police itself. Because restructuring would represent a new form of governmental intrusion into the private sector, it should be applied sparingly and with discretion.

IMPORTANT WHITE-COLLAR CRIMES

Regulatory Offenses

A wide range of federal and state regulatory statutes prescribe criminal as well as civil liability for violations. Several major federal regulatory offenses are discussed in detail in later chapters, including violations of the Sherman Antitrust Act, the Securities Act of 1933, the

---

[31] See, for example, *United States v. U.S. Gypsum Co.*, 425 U.S. 422 (U.S. Sup. Ct. 1978).

[32] See Note, "Structural Crime and Institutional Rehabilitation: A New Approach to Corporate Sentencing," 89 *Yale L . J.* 353 (1979).

Securities Exchange Act of 1934, the Clean Waters Act of 1972, the Resource Conservation and Recovery Act, and the Electronic Funds Transfer Act. The Food, Drug, and Cosmetic Act, at issue in the *Park* case, makes it a federal offense to mislabel or adulterate food, drugs, or cosmetic products in interstate commerce.

Fraudulent Acts

Many business crimes involve some form of *fraudulent* conduct. In most states, it is a crime to obtain money or property by fraudulent pretenses, to issue fraudulent checks, to make false credit or advertising statements, or to give short weights or measures. Various forms of fraud in bankruptcy proceedings, such as fraudulent concealment or transfer of a debtor's assets or false claims by creditors, are federal criminal offenses.[33] In addition, federal Mail Fraud and Wire Fraud acts make it a federal offense to use the mail or telephone or telegrams to accomplish a fraudulent scheme. The Travel Act of 1961 makes it a federal offense to travel or use facilities in interstate commerce to commit criminal acts.

Bribery

Offering gifts, favors, or anything of value to *public officials* to influence their official decisions to benefit private interests has long been a criminal offense under state and federal law. In 1977 Congress passed the Foreign Corrupt Practices Act, making it a federal offense to give anything of value to officials of foreign governments in an attempt to influence their official actions.[34] In addition, most states have enacted *commercial bribery* statutes making it illegal to offer kickbacks and payoffs to private individuals to secure some commercial advantage.

RICO

When Congress passed the Racketeer Influenced and Corrupt Organizations Act (RICO)[35] as part of the Organized Crime Control Act of 1970, lawmakers were primarily concerned about organized crime's increasing

---

[33] The Bankruptcy chapter discusses bankruptcy in detail.

[34] The Securities Regulation chapter discusses the Foreign Corrupt Practices Act in detail.

[35] 18 U.S.C. §§ 1961-1968 (1976).

entry into legitimate business enterprises. The broad language of the RICO statute, however, has resulted in its application in a wide variety of cases having nothing to do with organized crime. This development has made RICO one of the most controversial pieces of legislation affecting business in our legal history. Supporters of RICO argue that it has become an effective and much-needed tool for attacking a wide range of unethical business practices. Its critics assert, however, that RICO is an overbroad statute that needlessly taints business reputations. They also argue that it has operated unduly to favor plaintiffs in commercial litigation rather than serving as an aid to law enforcement. The lower federal courts have disagreed on many important points about the meaning of this controversial statute. As a result, some significant issues concerning RICO's scope await ultimate judicial or legislative resolution.

Criminal RICO   The criminal sections of the RICO statute make it a federal crime to: (1) use income derived from a "pattern of racketeering activity" to acquire an interest in an enterprise, (2) acquire or maintain an interest in an enterprise through a pattern of racketeering activity, (3) conduct or participate in the affairs of an enterprise through a pattern of racketeering activity, or (4) conspire to do any of the preceding acts. RICO is a *compound* criminal statute because it requires both the proof of a "predicate" criminal offense and a pattern of racketeering activity. *Racketeering activity* includes the commission of 1 of over 30 state or federal criminal offenses. Although most of the offenses that qualify (e.g., arson, gambling, extortion) have no relation to normal business transactions, mail and wire fraud, securities fraud, and bribery are also included. Thus, almost any business fraud may be alleged to be a racketeering activity. To show a *pattern* of such activity, the prosecution must prove the commission of two predicate offenses within a 10-year period. Most courts have interpreted the statutory term *enterprise* broadly to include partnerships and unincorporated associations as well as corporations.

Individuals found guilty of RICO violations are subject to a fine of up to $25,000 per violation and imprisonment for up to 20 years. In addition, they risk the forfeiture of any interest gained in any enterprise as a result of a violation. To prevent defendants from hiding assets that may be forfeitable upon conviction, federal prosecutors may seek pretrial orders freezing a defendant's assets. Some critics of RICO have argued that the harm that such a freeze may work on a defendant's ability to conduct its business, coupled with the threat of forfeiture of most or all of the business upon conviction, has led some business defendants to make plea bargains rather than risk all by fighting prosecutions they believe to be unjustified.

Civil RICO   The RICO statute also allows the government to seek numerous civil penalties for violations. These include *divestiture* of a defendant's interest in an enterprise, the *dissolution* or *reorganization* of the enterprise, and *injunctions* against future racketeering activities by the defendant.

The most controversial sections of RICO, however, are those allowing private individuals to recover *treble damages* (three times their actual loss) plus attorney's fees for injuries caused by a statutory violation. This highly attractive remedy has led in recent years to the frequent use of RICO by plaintiffs in commercial fraud cases. Stockbrokers, banks, insurance companies, and accounting firms have been typical targets of recent civil RICO suits. To qualify for recovery under RICO, a plaintiff must allege that the defendant has violated RICO's provisions and that, as a result, the plaintiff was "injured in his business or property."

In its decision in *Sedima, S.P.R.L. v. Imrex Co., Inc.*, the Supreme Court resolved two major issues concern-ing RICO's scope in an expansive fashion.[36] First, the Court rejected the requirement imposed by some lower federal courts that civil RICO plaintiffs must prove that the defendant had been convicted of a predicate offense. Second, the Court also rejected the idea that civil RICO plaintiffs must prove a "distinct racketeering injury" as a precondition of recovery. The Court also recognized the lower courts' concern with the breadth of the RICO statute and the fact that the majority of civil RICO suits are filed against legitimate businesses, rather than against "the archetypal, intimidating mobster." However, the Court noted that: "This defect—if defect it is— is inherent in the statute as written, and its correction must lie with Congress."

Since *Sedima,* several RICO reform proposals have been unsuccessfully introduced in Congress. As the following *Northwestern Bell* case illustrates, in the absence of Congressional action, the Court has continued to interpret RICO expansively. Most recently, in *Tafflin v. Levitt,* the Court unanimously resolved a split among the lower federal courts by ruling that civil RICO suits may be brought in state courts as well as in federal courts.[37]

---

[36] 473 U.S. 479 (U.S. Sup. Ct. 1985).

[37] 110 S. Ct. 792 (U.S. Sup. Ct. 1990).

H. J. INC. v. NORTHWESTERN BELL TELEPHONE CO.
109 S. Ct. 2893 (U.S. Sup. Ct. 1989)

Customers of Northwestern Bell Telephone Company filed a class action suit alleging violations of RICO based on allegations that between 1980 and 1986 Northwestern Bell sought to influence members of the Minnesota Public Utilities Commission (MPUC) to approve rates for Northwestern in excess of a fair and reasonable amount. They alleged that Northwestern made cash payments to commissioners, negotiated with them regarding future employment, and paid for parties and meals, for tickets to sporting events, and for airline tickets. These acts, they alleged, were in violation of the state bribery statute and state common law prohibiting bribery. The district court dismissed their civil RICO claims because the complaint failed to allege the "multiple illegal schemes" which the Eighth Circuit Court of Appeals had previously held were necessary to establish a "pattern of racketeering activity" under RICO.

Brennan, Justice.   In *Sedima, S.P.R.L. v. Imrex Co.*, we acknowledged concern in some quarters over civil RICO's use against "legitimate" businesses, as well as "mobsters and organized criminals." But we suggested that RICO's expansive uses "appear to be primarily the result of the breadth of the predicate offenses, and the failure of Congress and the courts to develop a meaningful concept of 'pattern.'" Congress has done nothing in the interim to illuminate RICO's key requirement of a pattern of racketeering activity, and developing a meaningful concept of "pattern" within the existing statutory framework has proved to be no easy task.

It is, nevertheless, a task we must undertake in order to decide this case. Our guides must be the text of the statute and its legislative history. We find no support in those sources for the proposition that predicate acts of racketeering may form a pattern only when they are a part of separate illegal schemes. Nor can we agree with those courts that have suggested that a pattern is established by proving two predicate acts, or with *amici* in this case who argue that the word "pattern" refers only to predicates that are indicative of a perpetrator involved in organized crime.

As we remarked in *Sedima*, the section of the statute headed "definitions," section 1961, does not so much define a pattern of racketeering activity as state a minimum necessary condition for the existence of such a pattern. Unlike other provisions in section 1961 that tell us what various concepts used in the Act "mean," section 1961(5) says of the phrase "pattern of racketeering activity" only that it "requires at least two acts of racketeering activity, one of which occurred after October 15, 1970 and the last of which occurred within ten years after the commission of a prior act of racketeering activity."

Section 1961(5) does indicate that Congress envisioned circumstances in which no more than two predicates would be necessary to establish a pattern. But the statement that a pattern "requires at least" two predicates implies that while two acts are necessary, they may not be sufficient. Section 1961(5) concerns only the minimum *number* of predicates necessary to establish a pattern; and it assumes that there is something to a RICO pattern *beyond* simply the number of predicate acts involved. The legislative history bears out this interpretation, for the principal sponsor of the Senate bill expressly indicated that "proof of two acts of racketeering activity, without more, does not establish a pattern." Section 1961(5) does not identify, though, these additional prerequisites for establishing the existence of a RICO pattern.

In normal usage, the word "pattern" here would be taken to require more than just a multiplicity of racketeering predicates. A "pattern" is an "arrangement or order of things or activity," 11 Oxford English Dictionary 357 (2d ed. 1989). It is not the number of predicates but the relationship that they bear to each other or to some external organizing principle that renders them "ordered" or "arranged."

RICO's legislative history reveals Congress' intent that to prove a pattern of racketeering activity a plaintiff or prosecutor must show that the racketeering predicates are related, *and* that they amount to or pose a threat of continued criminal activity. In the Organized Crime Control Act of 1970, Congress defined a pattern requirement solely in terms of the *relationship* of the defendant's criminal acts one to another: "criminal conduct forms a pattern if it embraces criminal acts that have the same or similar purposes, results, participants, victims, or methods of commission, or otherwise are interrelated by distinguishing characteristics and are not isolated events." We have no reason to suppose that Congress had in mind for RICO's pattern component any more constrained a notion of the relationships between predicates that would suffice.

RICO's legislative history tells us, however, that the relatedness of racketeering activities is not alone enough to satisfy the pattern element. It must also be shown that the predicates themselves amount to, or that they otherwise constitute a threat of, *continuing* racketeering activity. It is this aspect of RICO's pattern element that has spawned the "multiple scheme" test adopted by the Court of Appeals in this case. But although proof that a defendant has been involved in multiple criminal schemes would certainly be highly relevant to the inquiry into the continuity of the defendant's racketeering activity, it is implausible to suppose that Congress thought continuity might be shown *only* by proof of multiple schemes. We adopt a less inflexible approach that seems to us to derive from a common-sense, everyday understanding of RICO's language and Congress' gloss on it. What a plaintiff or prosecutor must prove is continuity of racketeering activity, or its threat.

A party alleging a RICO violation may demonstrate continuity over a closed period by proving a series of related predicates extending over a substantial period of time. Predicate acts extending over a few weeks or months and threatening no future criminal conduct do not satisfy this requirement: Congress was concerned in RICO with long-term criminal conduct. Often a RICO action will be brought before continuity can be established in this way. In such cases, liability depends on whether the *threat* of continuity is demonstrated.

The threat of continuity is sufficiently established where the predicates can be attributed to a defendant operating as part of a long-term association that exists for criminal purposes. Such associations include, but extend well beyond, those traditionally grouped under the phrase "organized crime." The continuity requirement is likewise satisfied where it is shown that the predicates are a regular way of conducting defendant's ongoing legitimate business, or of conducting or participating in an ongoing ligitimate RICO "enterprise."

Plaintiffs' complaint alleges that at different times over the course of at least a 6-year period the defendants gave five members of the MPUC numerous bribes, in several different forms, with the objective—in which they were allegedly successful—of causing these Commissioners to approve unfair and unreasonable rates. RICO defines bribery as a "racketeering activity," so plaintiffs have alleged multiple predicate acts. They may be able to prove that the multiple predicates alleged constitute a "pattern of racketeering activity," in that they satisfy the requirements of relationship and continuity. The acts of bribery alleged are said to be related to a common purpose, to influence Commissioners to win approval of unfairly high rates for Northwestern Bell. Furthermore, the racketeering predicates allegedly occurred over at least a 6-year period, which may be sufficient to satisfy the continuity requirement. Alternatively, a threat of continuity might be established at trial by showing that the alleged bribes were a regular way of conducting or participating in the conduct of the alleged and ongoing RICO enterprise, the MPUC. The Court of Appeals thus erred in affirming the District Court's dismissal of plaintiff's complaint for failure to plead "a pattern of racketeering activity."

Judgment reversed in favor of plaintiffs; case remanded for trial.

ETHICAL AND PUBLIC POLICY CONCERNS

1. Few issues have managed to provoke more prolonged, heated controversy than the death penalty. Many of the arguments both for and against the death penalty are, at base, ethical arguments. Identify and briefly discuss some fundamental arguments on both sides of the issue.

2. Are strict and vicarious liability ethically defensible? Who would be more likely to support such liability, a utilitarian or a rights theorist? Which form of liability would a rights theorist find more palatable?

3. Business opponents of RICO have argued that federal prosecutors have used the threat of asset forfeitures under the RICO statute to coerce business defendants to enter settlement agreements that they would not otherwise enter. Assuming these allegations are sometimes true, are such prosecutorial practices defensible?

SUMMARY

A thorough knowledge of the criminal law is an important component of a contemporary businessperson's education because in recent years the criminal sanction has been increasingly used as a major device for controlling business behavior. In major part, this trend reflects the belief that the criminal law provides a greater degree of deterrence than civil remedies.

Crimes are public wrongs, offenses against the state prosecuted by the state. The criminal sanction is the law's ultimate threat because it combines a threat to life or liberty with the stigma of a criminal conviction.

Crimes are classified as felonies or misdemeanors, depending on the seriousness of the offense involved. Conviction of a felony, a serious criminal offense, entails far more serious consequences than does conviction of a misdemeanor.

Significant social disagreement concerns the definition of criminal behavior and the underlying purpose of the criminal sanction. Utilitarians view the prevention of socially undesirable behavior as the only proper justification of criminal penalties. Retributionists see criminal punishment as the infliction of deserved suffering on those who violate fundamental social rules.

Given the powerful nature of the criminal sanction, several important restrictions operate to limit the state's power to convict a person of a crime. All crimes are statutory in the United States. Criminal responsibility requires the violation of an existing statute that does not criminalize constitutionally protected behavior and that is worded clearly enough to give an ordinary person notice of the conduct prohibited. The state must prove each element of a criminal offense beyond a reasonable doubt and within an extensive framework of procedural restraints to safeguard the rights of the accused.

The state must also prove that the defendant had the capacity to entertain the criminal intent required for all serious criminal offenses. Traditionally, the courts have recognized three kinds of incapacity: infancy, insanity, and intoxication. The common law initially refused to hold corporations responsible for criminal offenses. Over time, however, this rule changed to the point where today a corporation can be found to have committed almost any criminal offense that has been given proper statutory wording. Corporate criminal intent is normally derived by imputing the intent of corporate agents to the corporation. Significant disagreement exists, however, about whether a corporation should be criminally responsible for the actions of any of its employees or only for the actions of its higher officials. Disagreement also exists concerning whether good faith corporate efforts to avoid violations should be a defense to liability.

Individual corporate employees who commit crimes in the course of their employment are personally criminally responsible. Due to the nature of corporate decision making, however, it is often difficult to pinpoint the individuals responsible for corporate crimes. This has led to regulatory statutes imposing strict or vicarious criminal responsibility on corporate officers.

For a variety of reasons, neither corporate nor individual liability has been a very effective means of controlling corporate crime. We need to find new approaches that seek to learn from this lack of success and to employ our knowledge about the true nature of corporate behavior if society is to achieve a greater level of control.

PROBLEM CASES

1. In August of 1984, James Miller was convicted by a Florida court of sexual battery with slight force. When the offense in question was committed on April 25, 1984, the sentencing guidelines in effect in Florida would have resulted in a 3 $\frac{1}{2}$- to 4 $\frac{1}{2}$-year sentence. On May 8, 1984, the Florida Supreme Court proposed revisions to the guidelines, which were adopted by the Florida legislature and became effective July 1, 1984. When Miller was sentenced on October 2, 1984, the judge applied the revised guidelines to impose a 7-year sentence. Miller appealed on the ground that his sentence was unconstitutional. Was he correct?

2. A jury convicted Liberta of raping and sodomizing his estranged wife in violation of a New York statute. Liberta challenged his conviction on the ground that the statute was unconstitutional because it provided that only men could be guilty of rape. Upon what constitutional provision should Liberta have based his claim? Should his claim succeed?

3. Johnny Paul Penry was convicted of murder and sentenced to death after a jury rejected his insanity defense. His defense had presented evidence that due to organic brain damage he had the intelligence of a six-year-old child. Penry challenged his conviction on a number of grounds, including the argument that the Eighth Amendment forbids execution of the retarded. Was he correct?

4. Police officers who suspected Billy Greenwood of dealing drugs asked trash collectors to pick up and turn over plastic garbage bags that Greenwood left at the curb. The officers found drug-related items in the bags and used them to secure a search warrant for Greenwood's home. The search revealed narcotics and Greenwood was arrested on felony narcotics charges. A California Superior Court dismissed the charges against Greenwood on the ground that the warrantless search of his trash was in violation of the Fourth Amendment. Was the dismissal proper?

5. Doe, the target of a federal grand jury investigation, was subpoenaed to produce records of his accounts in banks in the Cayman Islands and Bermuda. He produced some records, testified that he had no other records in his possession or control, and invoked the Fifth Amendment when asked to reveal the existence or location of other records. After the U.S. branches of Doe's banks cited their nations' bank secrecy laws and refused to comply with subpoenas ordering them to produce records of his accounts, the district court, at the government's request, ordered Doe, without identifying or acknowledging the existence of any such accounts, to sign a consent directive authorizing the banks to turn over records of any and all accounts over which he had a right of withdrawal. When he refused, the court found him in contempt. Would being forced to sign the consent directive violate Doe's Fifth Amendment rights?

6. Reckmeyer was charged with running a massive drug importation and distribution scheme alleged to be a continuing criminal enterprise (CCE) in violation of the federal CCE statute. Relying on a portion of the CCE statute authorizing forfeiture to the government of property acquired as a result of drug violations, the indictment sought forfeiture of specified assets in Reckmeyer's possession. The district court entered a restraining order forbidding Reckmeyer from transferring any of the potentially forfeitable assets, but Reckmeyer nonetheless transferred $25,000 to Caplin & Drysdale, a law firm, for preindictment legal services. The firm placed the money in escrow and continued to represent Reckmeyer after he was indicted. Reckmeyer subsequently entered a plea agreement with the government in which he pled guilty to the CCE charge and agreed to forfeit all the assets listed in the indictment. A forfeiture order was entered by the district court when Reckmeyer was sentenced. Caplin & Drysdale filed a petition challenging the order, claiming an interest in $170,000 of Reckmeyer's assets for expenses incurred in conducting his defense, seeking the $25,000 held in escrow, and arguing that forfeiture of attorney's fees under the CCE statute would violate Reckmeyer's Sixth Amendment right to counsel. Was their argument correct?

7. On November 23, 1976, Warner-Lambert Company retained the investment banking firm of Morgan Stanley & Co. to assess the desirability of acquiring Deseret Pharmaceutical Company, to evaluate Deseret's stock, and to recommend an appropriate price per share for a tender offer for Deseret. On November 30, 1976, E. Jacques Courtois, Jr., an employee of Morgan Stanley's mergers and acquisitions department who had learned of Warner's plans to acquire Deseret, told Adrian Antoniu, an employee of Kuhn Loeb & Co.,

about the impending acquisition and urged him to buy Deseret stock. Antoniu in turn informed James Newman, a stockbroker, who bought 11,700 shares of Deseret for his and their accounts. Newman also advised certain of his customers to buy Deseret. All told, 143,000 shares of Deseret changed hands that day, among them 5,000 shares sold by Michael Moss for $28 per share. On the following day, December 1, 1976, the New York Stock Exchange suspended trading in Deseret pending announcement of a tender offer, which Warner publicly announced (at $38 per share) on December 7, 1976. Moss filed damage claims under the securities laws and RICO against Morgan Stanley and Newman. The federal district court dismissed his RICO claims, in part because Moss had failed to show any tie between the defendants and organized crime. Was this a proper basis for dismissal?

8. Under authority granted by Congress in the Motor Vehicle Information and Cost Savings Act, the Secretary of Transportation mandated that motor vehicle dealers give all buyers a written odometer statement disclosing the mileage registered on the odometer of the vehicle they bought and a notice if the odometer reading was known to be inadequate. The secretary also mandated that dealers retain for four years copies of all odometer statements they issue or receive and keep such records at the dealer's place of business in a systematically retrievable order. In late 1984, the Department of Justice investigated possible violations of the act by some Kentucky automobile dealers. During these investigations, a grand jury issued a subpoena to Randall Underhill, a sole proprietor automobile dealer, calling for him to appear and testify before the grand jury and to bring with him all odometer statements for motor vehicles he bought and sold between June 1, 1981, and June 1, 1982. Underhill moved to quash the subpoena insofar as it required production of the odometer statements on the ground that forcing him to produce them would violate his Fifth Amendment rights. Should he be compelled to produce the records?

9. Several individuals were charged with violating section 647(d) of the California Penal Code, which provides that any person "who loiters in or about any toilet open to the public for the purpose of engaging in or soliciting any lewd or lascivious or any unlawful act" is guilty of a misdemeanor. They argued that the statute was unconstitutionally vague. Was it?

10. In August 1981, Larry Heath hired two men to kill his wife Rebecca, who was then nine-months pregnant, for $2,000. The men kidnapped Rebecca from her home in Alabama, took her across the nearby state line into Georgia, and shot her in the head. On February 10, 1982, Heath pleaded guilty to a murder charge in Georgia in exchange for a sentence of life imprisonment, which he understood could involve his serving as few as seven years in prison. However, on May 5, 1982, an Alabama grand jury indicted Heath for the capital offense of murder during a kidnapping. He was tried, convicted, and sentenced to death. The Alabama Supreme Court rejected his appeal based on the argument that his Alabama conviction violated the Double Jeopardy Clause of the Fifth Amendment. Was the Alabama Court's decision correct?

11. In December of 1983, a grand jury indicted Automated Medical Laboratories, Inc. (AML), Richmond Plasma Corporation (RPC) (a wholly owned AML sub-

sidiary), and three former RPC managers for engaging in a conspiracy that included falsification of logbooks and records required to be maintained by businesses producing blood plasma. The falsification was designed to conceal from the Food and Drug Administration (FDA) various violations of federal regulations governing the plasmapheresis process and facilities. The evidence introduced at trial indicated that the managers and several other members of the team charged with assuring compliance with FDA regulations had actively participated in record falsification. AML was convicted and appealed on the ground that there was no evidence that any officer or director of AML knowingly or willfully participated in or authorized the unlawful practices at RPC. Was AML's conviction in the absence of such proof proper?

CHAPTER 6

INTENTIONAL TORTS

NATURE AND FUNCTION OF TORT LAW

Torts are *private (civil) wrongs* against persons or their property. The basis of tort liability is a breach of a legal duty owed to another person resulting in some legally recognizable harm to that person. The primary aim of tort law is to compensate injured persons for such harms. Thus, persons injured by the tortious act of another may file a civil suit for the *actual (compensatory) damages* that they have suffered as a result of a tort. Depending on the facts of the particular case, these damages may be for direct and immediate harms, such as physical injuries, medical expenses, and lost pay and benefits, or for harms as intangible as loss of privacy, injury to reputation, or emotional distress.

In cases where the behavior of the person committing a tort is particularly reprehensible, injured victims may also be able to recover an award of *punitive damages*. Punitive damages are not intended to compensate tort victims for their losses. Instead, they are designed to punish flagrant wrongdoers and to deter them and others from engaging in similar conduct in the future. Accordingly, they are theoretically reserved for only the most egregious forms of wrongdoing. Punitive damages have always been controversial, but they have grown more so in recent years because of the size of some punitive dam-

age awards and the perception that juries are awarding them in cases where they are not justified.

The punishment function of punitive damage awards is obviously similar to the deterrent function in criminal law. Some kinds of behavior can give rise to both criminal and tort liability. For example, a rapist may be criminally liable for rape and also liable for the torts of assault, battery, false imprisonment, and intentional infliction of mental distress. However, since tort suits are civil rather than criminal, the plaintiff's burden of proof in a tort case is the *preponderance of the evidence*, rather than the more stringent beyond-a-reasonable-doubt standard that applies to criminal cases. This means that the greater weight of the evidence introduced at the trial must support the plaintiff's position on every element of the case. Figure 1 summarizes the important differences between criminal and tort liability.

In tort law, society is engaged in a constant balancing of competing social interests. Excessive protection of some people's physical integrity, for example, may unduly impair other people's freedom of movement. Likewise, undue protection of peace of mind, privacy, and personal reputation may inordinately restrict constitutionally protected freedoms of speech and of the press. Over time, our tort law has demonstrated a tendency to protect an increasingly broad range of personal interests.

FIGURE 1 Crimes and Intentional Torts

	Crimes	**Intentional Torts**
Nature	Criminal	Civil
Elements	(1) Violation of a statute (2) Intent	(1) Harm to another person or property (2) Intent
Actors	Prosecutor versus defendant	Plaintiff (victim) versus defendant (tortfeasor)
Burden	Prosecutor must establish the defendant's guilt beyond a reasonable doubt	Plaintiff must establish the defendant's liability by a preponderance of the evidence
Punishment	Fines, imprisonment, execution	Defendant may have to pay the plaintiff compensatory and punitive damages

Some commentators have explained this tendency by saying it demonstrates the courts' growing sensitivity to the nature of life in an increasingly interdependent urban industrialized society. Whatever its origins, this and the next chapter demonstrate that, although the range of the human interests that tort law protects is expanding, the courts have remained mindful of the fact that the protection of any given interest necessarily involves a trade-off in the form of limitations placed on other competing social interests.

Torts are generally classified according to the level of fault exhibited by the wrongdoer's behavior. This chapter deals with **intentional torts:** behavior that indicates either the wrongdoer's conscious desire to cause harm to a legally protected interest or the wrongdoer's knowledge that such harm is substantially certain to result from his actions. The following chapter discusses tort liability founded on principles of *negligence* and *strict liability*, neither of which require proof of any intentional wrongdoing by a defendant.

INTERFERENCE WITH PERSONAL RIGHTS

Battery

The tort of **battery** protects a fundamental personal interest—the right to be free from harmful or offensive bodily contacts. Battery is the *intentional, harmful* or *offensive touching of another without* his *consent*. A contact is *harmful* if it produces any bodily injury. As the following *England* case illustrates, even nonharmful contacts may be considered battery if they are *offensive*, that is, calculated to offend a reasonable sense of personal dignity. Direct contact between a wrongdoer's body and the body of another is not necessary for a battery to result. For example, if Delano throws a rock at Stevens or places a harmful or offensive substance in her food, Delano has committed a battery if Stevens is hit by the rock or if she eats the food. Nor is it necessary that the wrongdoer actually intend to produce the contact if contact in fact results and the wrongdoer's intent was merely to threaten the victim with contact. So, if Delano threatens to shoot Stevens with a gun he mistakenly believes is unloaded and ends up shooting Stevens, Delano would be liable for battery.

Also, the person who suffers the harmful or offensive touching does not have to be the person whom the wrongdoer intended to injure for liability for battery to occur. Under a general intentional tort concept called the doctrine of *transferred intent*, a wrongdoer who intends to injure one person, but injures another, is nonetheless liable to the person injured, despite the absence of any specific intent to injure him. So, if Walters is hit by the rock thrown at Stevens, or if he eats Stevens's food, Delano would be liable to Walters for battery. Finally, touching anything connected with a person's body in a harmful or offensive manner can also create liability for battery. So, if Johnson snatches Martin's purse, or kicks her dog while she is walking her dog on a leash, he may be liable for battery even though he has not touched her body.

Some of the most interesting battery cases involve the nature of the *consent* that is necessary to avoid liability for battery. As a general rule, consent must be *freely* and *intelligently* given to be a defense to battery. In some cases, consent may be inferred from a person's voluntary participation in an activity. Such consent is ordinarily limited, however, to contacts that are considered a normal consequence of the activity in question. For example, Joe Frazier would be unable to win a battery suit against Muhammad Ali for injuries he suffered during their famous "Thrilla in Manila" title fight. However, the quarterback who is knifed on the 50-yard line during a game has a valid battery claim.

Assault

The tort of **assault** protects the personal interest in freedom from the *apprehension* of battery. Any *attempt* to cause a harmful or offensive contact with another, or any *offer* to cause such a contact, is an assault if it causes a *well-grounded apprehension of imminent (immediate) battery* in the mind of the person threatened with contact. Whether the threatened contact actually occurs is irrelevant.

Because assault is limited to threats of *imminent* battery, threats of *future* battery do not create liability for assault. Likewise, because assault focuses on the apprehension in the mind of the victim, the threats in question must create a reasonable apprehension of battery in the victim's mind. Therefore, threatening words, unaccompanied by any other acts or circumstances indicating an intent to carry out the threat, do not amount to an assault. Finally, the elements of assault require that the victim must actually experience an apprehension of imminent battery before liability results. Therefore, if Markham fires a rifle at Thomas from a great distance and misses him, and Thomas learns of the attempt on his life only at a later date, Markham is not liable to Thomas for the tort of assault.

ENGLAND v. S & M FOODS, INC.
511 So.2d 1313 (La. Ct. App. 1987)

Betty England worked at a Dairy Queen restaurant owned by S & M Foods in Tallulah, Louisiana. One day while she was at work, her manager, Larry Garley, became upset when several incorrectly prepared hamburgers were returned by a customer. Garley allegedly expressed his dissatisfaction by using profane language and throwing a hamburger, which hit England on the leg. England filed a battery suit against Garley and S & M and won a $1,000 judgment. Garley and S & M appealed.

Jones, Judge.   Defendants contend no battery was committed because Garley did not intend to inflict bodily harm upon England. They argue Garley was disgusted about the returned hamburgers and threw one toward the trash can and it inadvertantly splattered on her and Alcie Rash, another employee. They contend that England's embarrassment was caused as much by her overreaction to the situation as by Garley's conduct.

England said that Garley used profane language when he told her to prepare the hamburgers correctly. She said Garley, while looking straight at her, then threw the hamburger which hit her on the leg. She testified that she argued with Garley about the matter and that several patrons observed the incident, which caused her to cry and become emotionally upset.

Rash said that she did not see Garley throw the hamburger, but observed it hit the floor and splatter mayonnaise and mustard on her and England.

A battery is any intentional and unpermitted contact with the plaintiff's person or anything attached to it. In the area of intentional torts, intent means the defendant either desired to bring about the physical results of his act or believed they were substantially certain to follow from what he did. Mental distress and humiliation in connection with a battery are compensable items of damage.

The totality of the evidence provided a substantial basis for the trial judge to conclude Garley must have been substantially certain the hamburger would hit England or splatter on her when he threw it toward her. His contact with her was, therefore, intentional and unpermitted and constituted a battery.

Judgment for England affirmed.

False Imprisonment

The tort of **false imprisonment** protects the personal interest in freedom from *confinement*. False imprisonment is the intentional *confinement of another* for an *appreciable time* (a few minutes is enough) *without his consent*. Confinement may result from physical barriers to the plaintiff's freedom of movement, such as locking a person in a room with no other doors or windows, or the use of physical force or the threat to use physical force against the plaintiff. Confinement also results from the assertion of legal authority to detain the plaintiff, or the detention of the plaintiff's property, for example, a purse containing a large sum of money. Likewise, a threat to harm another, such as the plaintiff's spouse or child, can also be confinement if it prevents the plaintiff from moving.

The confinement required for false imprisonment must be *complete*. Partial confinement of another by blocking her path or by depriving her of one means of escape where several exist, such as locking one door of a building having other, unlocked doors, does not amount to false imprisonment. The fact that a means of escape exists, however, does not render a confinement partial if the plaintiff cannot reasonably be expected to know of its existence. The same is true if it involves some unreasonable risk of harm to the plaintiff, such as walking a tightrope or climbing out of a second-story window, or some affront to his sense of personal dignity (e.g., Jones steals Smith's clothes while Smith is swimming in the nude).

The personal interest in freedom from confinement protected by false imprisonment involves a mental element, knowledge of confinement, as well as a physical element, freedom of movement. Therefore, courts generally hold that the plaintiff must have *knowledge* of his confinement before liability for false imprisonment arises. Similarly, liability for false imprisonment does not arise in cases where the person has *consented* to his confinement. Such consent, however, must be freely given; consent in the face of an implied or actual threat of force or an assertion of legal authority by the confiner is not freely given. As the following *Speight* case indicates, many contemporary false imprisonment cases involve shoplifting. The common law held store owners liable for any torts committed while detaining a suspected shoplifter if subsequent investigation revealed that the detainee was innocent of any wrongdoing. In an attempt to accommodate the legitimate interests of store owners in preventing theft of their property, most states have passed statutes giving store owners a *conditional privilege* to stop persons who they reasonably believe are shoplifting. However, the owner must act in a reasonable manner and only detain the suspect for a reasonable length of time. Store owners who act within the scope of such a statute are not liable for any torts committed in the process of detaining a suspected shoplifter.

J. H. HARVEY CO. v. SPEIGHT

344 S.E.2d 701 (Ga. Ct. App. 1986)

Acting upon information that someone had just stolen several cartons of cigarettes from the store, the manager of Harvey's Supermarket stepped outside and approached Speight, who had himself walked out of the store only moments earlier. Upon being asked by the manager if he had anything that did not belong to him, Speight answered, "No, do you want to see?" He then briefly held the sides of his jacket open and let them close, at which point the manager parted the jacket with his hands to see if anything was concealed there. Simultaneously, Speight pointed to another person in the immediate vicinity and said, "I think that is the man you are looking for." The manager then left Speight to pursue this other person. Speight subsequently filed suit against Harvey's for false imprisonment and assault and battery. When a jury awarded him $2,500 in compensatory damages and $30,000 in punitive damages, Harvey's appealed.

Banke, Chief Judge.   Speight testified that the store manager had not been rude to him but stated that he did not consider the manager's conduct in looking inside his jacket as courteous. He admitted that he had invited this search and that the manager had not cursed him nor spoken loudly to him; however, he testified that he felt the manager was angry because of the look in his eyes and the fact that several people had followed the manager out of the store. At trial, Speight testified that the entire encounter had lasted about 45 seconds, whereas during an earlier deposition he had testified that the encounter lasted between 15 and 30 seconds.

According to *Prosser, Law of Torts* (4th ed.), in false imprisonment:

"[T]he imprisonment need not be for more than an appreciable length of time, and . . . it is not necessary that any damage result from it other than the confinement itself, since the tort is complete with even a brief restraint of the plaintiff's freedom. . . . It is essential, however, that the restraint be against the plaintiff's will, and if he agrees of his own free choice to surrender his freedom of motion, as by remaining in a room or accompanying the defendant voluntarily, to clear himself of suspicion or to accommodate the desires of another, rather than yielding to the constraint of a threat, then there is no imprisonment."

Speight's testimony in this case fails to establish any involuntary restraint by Harvey's store manager or employees. Although a person need not make an effort to escape or await application of open force before he can recover, there must be restraint whether by force or fear. With regard to the second count of the complaint, Speight admitted that any touching of his person had been invited by him; and such invitation is inconsistent with the torts of assault and battery. The evidence was consequently insufficient to support any recovery.

Judgment reversed in favor of Harvey's.

Defamation

The tort of *defamation* protects the individual's interest in his *reputation*. It recognizes the value that society places on reputation, not only the individual's personal dignity, but also the value that a good reputation has in the individual's business dealings with others. Defamation is ordinarily defined as the unprivileged *publication of false and defamatory statements* concerning another. A defamatory statement is one that harms the reputation of another by injuring his community's estimation of him or by deterring others from associating or dealing with him. Whether an ambiguous statement is defamatory is ordinarily decided by a jury.

Because the primary focus of defamation is to protect the *individual's* right to reputation, an essential element of defamation is that the alleged defamatory statement must be "of and concerning" the plaintiff. That is, the statement must harm the particular plaintiff's reputation. This causes several problems. First, can allegedly fictional accounts such as those found in novels and short stories amount to defamation if the fictional characters bear a substantial resemblance to real persons? Most courts that have dealt with the issue say they can, if a reasonable reader would identify the plaintiff as the subject of the story. Similarly, humorous or satirical accounts ordinarily do not amount to defamation unless a reasonable reader would believe that they purport to describe real events. Likewise, statements of personal opinion are ordinarily not the proper subjects of defamation because they are not statements of fact concerning the plaintiff, unless such statements imply the existence of undisclosed facts that are false and defamatory. Thus, the statement that "Smedley is a lousy governor" would probably not be actionable. However, the statement "I think Irving must be a thief" may be defamatory, because a jury may believe that the statement implies that its maker knows facts that justify this opinion.

What about defamatory statements concerning particular groups of persons? The courts generally hold that an individual member of a defamed group cannot recover for damage to her personal reputation unless the group is so small that the statement can reasonably be understood as referring to specific members. This is also true when the circumstances in which the statement is made are such that it is reasonable to conclude that a particular group member is being referred to. So, the statement that "all Germans are thieves," standing alone, would not provide the basis for a defamation suit by any person of German descent. However, if Schmidt, a person of German origin, is being considered for a controller's position in her employer's company and a fellow employee makes the same statement in response to a question concerning Schmidt's qualifications for the job, the statement would probably be a proper basis for a defamation suit.

Finally, the courts have placed some limits on the persons or entities that can suffer injury to reputation. For example, it is generally held that no liability attaches to defamatory statements concerning the dead. Corporations and other business entities have a limited right to reputation and can file suit for defamatory statements that harm them in conducting their business or deter others from dealing with them. As a general rule, statements about a corporation's officers, employees, or shareholders do not amount to defamation of the corporation unless such statements also reflect on the manner in which the corporation conducts its business. Statements concerning the quality of a corporation's products or the quality of its title to land or other property may be the basis of an *injurious falsehood* suit.[1]

Publication   The elements of the tort of defamation require *publication* of a defamatory statement before liability for defamation arises. This requirement can be misleading because, as a general rule, no widespread communication of a defamatory statement is required for publication. Communication of the defamatory state-

ment to *one person* other than the person defamed is ordinarily sufficient for publication. Making a defamatory statement about a person in a personal conversation with him or in a private letter sent to him does not, therefore, satisfy the publication requirement. In addition, the courts generally hold that one who repeats or republishes a defamatory statement is liable for defamation, regardless of whether he identifies the source of the statement.

Libel and Slander   The courts have divided the tort of defamation into two categories, libel and slander, depending on the medium used to communicate the defamatory statement. **Libel** refers to written or printed defamations, or to those that have a physical form, such as a defamatory picture or statue. **Slander** refers to oral defamation. The advent of radio and television initially resulted in some judicial confusion concerning the proper classification of defamatory statements communicated by these new media. Today, the great majority of courts treat broadcast defamations as libel. The distinction between libel and slander is important because the courts have traditionally held that libel, due to its more permanent nature and the seriousness that we tend to attach to the written word, is actionable without any proof of special damage (the loss of anything of monetary value) to the plaintiff. Slander, however, is generally not actionable without proof of special damage, unless the nature of the slanderous statement is so serious that it can be classified as *slander per se*. In slander per se, injury to the plaintiff's reputation is presumed. Four defamatory statements ordinarily qualify for per se treatment: allegations that the plaintiff has committed a crime involving moral turpitude or potential imprisonment, that he has a loathsome disease (usually a venereal disease or leprosy), that he is professionally incompetent or guilty of professional misconduct, or that he is guilty of serious sexual misconduct.

Defamation and the Constitution   Nowhere is the social balancing task of tort law more obvious than in cases of defamation. Overzealous protection of individual reputation could result in an infringement of our constitutionally protected freedoms of speech and of the press, and thereby inhibit the free flow of information necessary to a free society. In recent years, the Supreme Court has balanced these conflicting social interests in a series of important cases that define the amount of protection the Constitution affords to otherwise defamatory statements. Under the common law, defendants were

---

[1] The Intellectual Property, Competitive Torts, and Unfair Competition chapter discusses injurious falsehood in detail.

strictly liable (liable without fault) for defamatory statements. In *New York Times v. Sullivan*, however, the Court held that *public officials* seeking to recover for defamatory statements relating to performance of their official duties must prove *actual malice* (knowledge of falsity or reckless disregard for the truth) on the part of a media defendant to recover any damages.[2] This significant limitation on public officials' right to reputation was justified largely by the public interest in "free and unfettered debate" on important social issues.

For similar reasons, the Court subsequently extended the actual malice test to *public figures*, that is, persons in the public eye because of their celebrity status or because they have voluntarily involved themselves in matters of public controversy.[3] Then, in *Gertz v. Robert Welch, Inc.*, the Court refused to extend the actual malice test to media defamation of private citizens who involuntarily become involved in matters of public concern.[4] Instead, the Court held that to recover compensatory damages such persons must prove some degree of fault at least amounting to negligence on the part of the defendant and that to recover punitive damages they must prove actual malice. Most recent was *Dun & Bradstreet, Inc. v. Greenmoss Builders, Inc.*, a case involving a private figure plaintiff—a construction contractor—and defamatory speech about a matter of purely private concern—a false credit report.[5] The Court refused to apply the *Gertz* standard and upheld a recovery based on the common law strict liability standard.

The amount of protection the Constitution affords to otherwise defamatory statements appears to depend on two factors: whether the plaintiff is a public figure/official or private person and whether the subject matter of the speech at issue is a matter of public concern or private concern. The Court has yet to speak definitively on the standard that it will apply to cases involving defamatory statements about private matters concerning public figures and officials. Its decisions to date, however, suggest that the *Gertz* test is likely to be applied to such cases.

Defenses to Defamation   *Truth* is an absolute defense to defamation. The tort of defamation requires that a

statement serving as the basis of a defamation suit be *false* as well as defamatory.

Even where defamatory statements are false, a defense of *privilege* may serve to prevent liability in some cases. The idea of privilege recognizes the fact that, in some circumstances, other social interests may be more important than an individual's right to reputation. Privileges are either *absolute* or *conditional*. Absolute privileges shield the author of a defamatory statement regardless of her knowledge, motive, or intent. Absolutely privileged statements include those made by participants in judicial proceedings, by legislators or witnesses in the course of legislative proceedings, by certain executive officials in the course of their official duties, and by spouses in private. Conditional privileges are conditioned on their proper use. One who *abuses* a conditional privilege by making a defamatory statement with the knowledge that it is false, or in reckless disregard of the truth, loses the protection afforded by the privilege. Conditional privileges are abused when the author of a defamatory statement acts with an improper motive, such as a purpose other than protecting the interests justifying the privilege. The author can also exceed the scope of the privilege by communicating the defamation unnecessarily to third persons who do not share his interests. Conditional privileges are often recognized when the author of a defamatory statement acts to protect her own legitimate interests or those of a third person with whom she shares some interest or to whom she owes some duty.

In recent years, the courts have also begun to recognize a conditional privilege of "fair comment." This privilege protects fair and accurate media reports of defamatory matter in reports or proceedings of official action or originating from public meetings. The privilege is justified by the public's right to know what occurs in such proceedings and meetings. The conditional privilege most important to business, however, is the traditional privilege enjoyed by employers who provide prospective employers with reference letters about former employees. Despite this privilege, employers in recent years have faced a growing number of defamation claims from disgruntled former employees. As a result, many companies as a matter of policy refuse to divulge any information about former employees other than to confirm that they did work for the company at one time and the duration of their employment. However, as the following *Lewis* case indicates, even such a policy does not always shield employers from liability.

[2] 376 U.S. 254 (U.S. Sup. Ct. 1964).
[3] *Curtis Publishing Co. v. Butts*, 388 U.S. 130 (U.S. Sup. Ct. 1967).
[4] 418 U.S. 323 (U.S. Sup. Ct. 1974).
[5] 472 U.S. 749 (U.S. Sup. Ct. 1985).

LEWIS v. EQUITABLE LIFE ASSURANCE SOCIETY

389 N.W. 2d 876 (Minn. Sup. Ct. 1986)

Carole Lewis, Mary Smith, Michelle Rafferty, and Suzanne Loizeaux were employed as dental claim approvers in the St. Paul, Minnesota, office of the Equitable Life Assurance Society of the United States. In October of 1980 they were sent to assist in Equitable's Pittsburgh office. None of the women had ever traveled on company business before, and they departed for Pittsburgh without being given copies of Equitable's travel expense policies or being told that expense reports would have to be filed. Instead, they were verbally given information on Equitable's daily meal and maid tip allowances and told to keep receipts for hotel bills and airfare. In addition, each was given a $1,400 travel allowance which, having no instruction to the contrary, they spent in full.

When they returned to St. Paul, each of the women received a personal letter from management commending her on her job performance in Pittsburgh. Each was also told for the first time that she would have to submit expense reports detailing her daily expenses in Pittsburgh. This they did, but a dispute subsequently arose over the amount of allowable expenses because Equitable's written guidelines differed from the instructions they had received prior to departure. After first changing their reports with respect to maid tips, they were asked to change their reports again, the net effect of which would have been to obligate each employee to return approximately $200 to Equitable. They refused to do this, arguing that the expenses shown on their reports were honestly incurred, a claim that Equitable never disputed. Subsequently, the women were fired for "gross insubordination."

In seeking new jobs, each woman was asked by prospective employers why she had left Equitable, and each said she had been terminated. When asked in interviews to explain their terminations, each stated that she had been terminated for gross insubordination and attempted to explain the situation. Only one of the women found a new job by being forthright with a prospective employer about her termination from Equitable. The others had various difficulties finding new jobs. They filed a defamation suit against Equitable, and when a jury ruled in their favor, Equitable appealed.

Amdahl, Chief Justice.   In order for a statement to be considered defamatory, it must be communicated to someone other than the plaintiff, it must be false, and it must tend to harm the plaintiff's reputation. Generally, there is no publication where a defendant communicates a statement directly to a plaintiff, who then communicates it to a third person. Plaintiffs themselves informed prospective employers that they had been terminated for gross insubordination. They did so because prospective employers inquired why they had left their previous employment. The question raised is whether a defendant can ever be held liable for defamation when the statement in question was published to a third person only by the plaintiff.

We have not previously been presented with the question of defamation by means of "self-publication." Courts that have considered the question, however, have recognized a narrow exception to the general rule that communication of a defamatory statement to a third person by the person defamed is not actionable. These courts have recognized that if a defamed person was in some way compelled to communicate the defamatory statement to a third person, and if it was foreseeable to the defendant that the defamed person would be so compelled, then the defendant could be held liable for the defamation.

Several courts have specifically recognized this exception for compelled self-publication in the context of employment discharges. The trend of modern authority persuades us that Minnesota law should recognize the doctrine. Compelled self-publication does no more than hold the originator of the defamatory statement liable for damages caused by the statement where the originator knows, or should know, of circumstances whereby the defamed person has no reasonable means of avoiding publication of the statement or avoiding the resulting damages. In such circumstances, the damages are fairly viewed as the direct result of the originator's actions.

The St. Paul office manager admitted that it was foreseeable that plaintiffs would be asked by prospective employers to identify the reason that they were discharged. Their only choice would be to tell them "gross insubordination" or to lie. Fabrication, however, is an unacceptable alternative.

Finding that there was a publication, we next turn to the issue of truth. True statements, however disparaging, are not actionable. The company contends the relevant statement to consider when analyzing the defense of truth is the one that plaintiffs made to their prospective employers, that is, that they had been fired for gross insubordination. Plaintiffs counter that it is the truth or falsity of the underlying statement—that they engaged in gross insubordination—that is relevant.

Requiring that truth as a defense go to the underlying implication of the statement, at least where the statement involves more than a simple allegation, appears to be the better view. Here, the company's charges against plaintiffs went beyond accusations and were conclusory statements that plaintiffs had engaged in gross insubordination. The record amply supports the jury verdict that the charge of gross insubordination was false. Even though an untrue defamatory statement has been published, the originator of the statement will not be held liable if the statement is published under circumstances that make it conditionally privileged and if privilege is not abused. The doctrine of privileged communication rests upon public policy considerations. The existence of a privilege results from the court's determination that statements made in particular contexts or on certain occasions should be encouraged despite the risk that the statements might be defamatory.

In the context of employment recommendations, the law generally recognizes a qualified privilege between former and prospective employers as long as the statements are made in good faith and for a legitimate purpose. Plaintiffs argue that a self-publication case does not properly fit within the qualified privilege doctrine, but the logic of imposing liability upon a former employer in a self-publication case appears to compel recognition of a qualified privilege. A former employer in a compelled self-publication case may be held liable as if it had actually published the defamatory statement directly to prospective employers. Where an employer would be entitled to a privilege if it had actually published the statement, it makes little sense to deny the privilege where the identical communication is made to identical third parties with the only difference being the mode of publication. Finally, recognition of a qualified privilege seems to be the only effective means of addressing the concern that every time an employer states the reason for discharging an employee it will subject itself to potential liability for defamation. It is in the public interest that information regarding an employee's discharge be readily available to the discharged employee and to prospective employers, and we are concerned that, unless a significant privilege is recognized by the courts, employers will decline to inform employees of reasons for discharges.

This conclusion does not necessarily determine that the company's statements were privileged. A qualified privilege is abused and therefore lost if the plaintiff demonstrates that the defendant acted with actual malice. The jury found that the company's statements were "actuated by actual malice."

Judgment for the plaintiffs affirmed.

Invasion of Privacy

The recognition of a personal *right of privacy* is a relatively recent development in tort law. At present, four distinct behaviors provide a proper basis for an invasion of privacy suit: (1) intrusion on a person's solitude or seclusion, (2) public disclosure of private facts concerning a person, (3) publicity placing a person in a false light in the public eye, and (4) appropriation of a person's name or likeness for commercial purposes. The thread tying these different behaviors together is that they all infringe on a person's "right to be let alone."

Intrusion on Solitude

Any intentional intrusion on the solitude or seclusion of another constitutes an invasion of privacy if that intrusion would be highly offensive to a reasonable individual. The intrusion in question may be physical, such as illegal searches of a person's home or body or the opening of his mail. It may also be a nonphysical intrusion such as tapping his telephone, examining his bank account, or subjecting him to harassing telephone calls. As a general rule, no liability attaches to examining public records concerning a person, or observing or photographing him in a public place, because a person does not have a reasonable expectation of privacy in these instances.

Publicity Concerning Private Facts

Publicizing facts concerning a person's private life can be an invasion of privacy if their publicity would be highly offensive to a reasonable person. The idea is that the public has no legitimate right to know certain aspects of a person's private life. Thus, publicity concerning a person's failure to pay his debts, humiliating illnesses that he has suffered, and details concerning his sex life constitute an invasion of privacy. Truth is *not* a defense to this type of invasion of privacy, because the essence of the tort is giving unjustified publicity to purely private matters. Publicity in this context means a widespread dissemination of private details.

This variant of invasion of privacy, similiar to the tort of defamation, represents a potential source of conflict with the constitutionally protected freedoms of the press and of speech. The courts have attempted to accommodate these conflicting social interests in several ways. First, no liability ordinarily attaches to publicity concerning matters of public record or of legitimate public interest. Second, public figures and public officials have no right of privacy concerning information that is reasonably related to their public lives.

False Light

Publicity that places a person in a *false light* in the public eye can be an invasion of privacy if that false light would be highly offensive to a reasonable person. This variant of invasion of privacy may in some cases also involve defamation. As in defamation cases, truth is an absolute defense to liability. For liability for invasion of privacy to arise, however, it is not necessary that a person be defamed by the false light in which he is placed. All that is required is unreasonable and highly objectionable publicity attributing to a person characteristics that he does not possess or beliefs that he does not hold. Signing a person's name to a public telegram or letter without her consent or attributing authorship of an inferior scholarly or artistic work to her are examples of this form of invasion of privacy. Because of the overlap between this form of invasion of privacy and defamation, and the obvious First Amendment issues at stake, defendants in false light cases enjoy constitutional protection similar to that enjoyed by defamation defendants.

Appropriation of Name or Likeness

Some of the earliest invasion of privacy cases involved the appropriation of a person's name or likeness for commercial purposes without his consent. Liability for invasion of privacy can be created by using a person's name or image in an advertisement to imply his endorsement of a product or service or a nonexistent connection with the person or business placing the ad. This variant of invasion of privacy differs markedly from those previously discussed in that it recognizes the personal property right connected with a person's identity and that he has the exclusive right to its control.

The potential for conflict between this property right and the freedoms of speech and of the press has been illustrated in recent years by cases involving public figures' *right of publicity*, such as the following *Midler* case. To what extent do public persons have the right to control the use of their names, likenesses, or other matters associated with their identities? For example, should a well-known movie star have the right to prevent the writing of a book about her life or the televising of a docudrama about her? At this point, the scope of a public person's right of publicity varies greatly from state to state; considerable disagreement exists concerning such issues as its duration and inheritability.

Other Limitations

In addition to the various limitations on the right of privacy discussed earlier, two further limits are applicable to invasion of privacy actions. First, with the exception in some states of cases involving the appropriation of a person's name or likeness, the right of privacy is a purely *personal* right. This means that only living individuals whose personal privacy has been invaded can bring suit for invasion of privacy. Therefore, family members of a person exposed to publicity ordinarily cannot maintain an invasion of privacy action unless their personal privacy has also been violated. Second, corporations and other business organiza- tions generally have no personal right of privacy. They do, however, have limited rights associated with the use of their names and identities. These rights are protected by the law of unfair competition.[6]

---

[6] The Intellectual Property, Competitive Torts, and Unfair Competition chapter discusses this subject in detail.

MIDLER v. FORD MOTOR CO.

849 F.2d 460 (9th Cir. 1988)

In 1985, Ford Motor Company and its advertising agency, Young & Rubicam, Inc., ran a series of 19 television commercials in what the agency called "The Yuppie Campaign." The aim was to make an emotional connection with Yuppies, bringing back memories of their college days. Different pop songs of the 70s were sung on each commercial, and the agency tried to get the original artists to sing the songs. One of the songs selected was "Do You Want to Dance," a song from Bette Midler's 1973 album, "The Divine Miss M." The agency acquired a license from the copyright holder to use the song, but Midler refused to do the commercial.

The agency then hired a former backup singer for Midler to record the commercial, instructing her to "sound as much as possible like the Bette Midler record." After the commercial was aired, a number of people told Midler that it "sounded exactly" like her recording. Midler filed suit against Ford and Young & Rubicam. The trial judge described the defendants' conduct as that "of the average thief" who decided, "If we can't buy it, we'll take it." Nonetheless, he granted summary judgment for the defendants because he believed no legal principle prevented the imitation of Midler's voice. Midler appealed.

Noonan, Circuit Judge.   The First Amendment protects much of what the media do in the reproduction of likenesses or sounds. A primary value is freedom of speech and press. The purpose of the media's use of a person's identity is central. If the purpose is informative and cultural, the use is immune; if it serves no such function but merely exploits the individual portrayed, immunity will not be granted.

Moreover, federal copyright law preempts much of the area. Mere imitation of a recorded performance would not constitute a copyright infringement even where one performer deliber- ately sets out to simulate another's performance as exactly as possible. Midler does not seek damages for Ford's use of "Do You Want to Dance," and thus her claim is not preempted by copyright law. Copyright protects "original works of authorship fixed in any tangible medium of expression." A voice is not copyrightable. What is put forward as protectible here is more personal than any work of authorship.

In *Motschenbacher v. R.J. Reynolds Tobacco Co.* (1974) the defendants used in the television commercial for Winston cigarettes a photograph of a famous racing driver's car. The number of the car was changed and a "spoiler" was attached to the car; the car's features of white pinpoint- ing, an oval medallion, and solid red coloring were retained. The driver, Lothar Motschenbacher, was in the car but his features were not visible. Some persons, viewing the commercial, correctly inferred that the car was his and that he was in the car and was therefore endorsing the product. The defendants were held to have invaded a proprietary interest of Motschenbacher in his own identity.

Midler's case is different from Motschenbacher's. He and his car were physically used by the tobacco company's ad; he made part of his living out of giving commercial endorsements. But, as Judge Koelsch expressed it in *Motschenbacher*, California will recognize an injury from "an appropriation of the attributes of one's identity." It was irrelevant that Motschenbacher could not be identified in the ad. The ad suggested that it was he. The ad did so by emphasizing signs or symbols associated with him. In the same way the defendants here used an imitation to convey the impression that Midler was singing for them.

Why did they ask Midler to sing if her voice was not of value to them? Why did they studiously acquire the services of a sound-alike and instruct her to imitate Midler if Midler's voice was not of value to them? What they sought was an attribute of Midler's identity. Its value was what the market would have paid for Midler to have sung the commercial in person.

A voice is more distinctive and more personal than the automobile protected in *Motschenbacher*. A voice is as distinctive and personal as a face. The human voice is one of the most palpable ways identity is manifested. We are all aware that a friend is at once known by a few words on the phone. These observations hold true of singing, especially singing by a singer of renown. The singer manifests herself in the song. To impersonate her voice is to pirate her identity.

We need not and do not go so far as to hold that every imitation of a voice to advertise merchandise is actionable. We hold only that when a distinctive voice of a professional singer is widely known and is deliberately imitated in order to sell a product, the sellers have appropriated what is not theirs and have committed a tort in California.

Summary judgment against Midler reversed; case remanded for trial.

Infliction of Emotional Distress

For many years, the courts refused to allow recovery for purely emotional injuries in the absence of some other tort. Thus, victims of such torts as assault, battery, and false imprisonment could recover for the emotional injuries resulting from these torts, but the courts were unwilling to recognize an independent tort of infliction of emotional distress. The reasons for this judicial reluctance included a fear of spurious or trivial claims, concerns about the difficulty in proving purely emotional harms, and uncertainty concerning the proper boundaries of an independent tort of intentional infliction of emotional distress. Recent advances in medical knowledge concerning emotional injuries, however, have helped to overcome some of these judicial impediments. Today, most courts allow recovery for *severe* emotional distress regardless of whether the elements of any other tort are proven.

The courts are not, however, in complete agreement on the elements of this new tort. All courts require that a wrongdoer's conduct must be *outrageous* before liability for emotional distress arises. The *Restatement (Second) of Torts* speaks of conduct "so outrageous in character, and so extreme in degree as to go beyond all possible bounds of decency, and to be regarded as atrocious and utterly intolerable in a civilized community."[7] Some courts, however, still fear fictitious claims and require proof of some bodily harm resulting from the victim's emotional distress. The courts also differ in the extent to which they allow recovery for emotional distress suffered as a result of witnessing outrageous conduct directed at persons other than the plaintiff. The *Restatement (Second) of Torts* suggests that persons be allowed to recover for severe emotional distress resulting from witnessing outrageous behavior toward a member of their immediate family.[8] Where the third person is not a member of the plaintiff's immediate family, the *Restatement (Second)* restricts liability to severe emotional distress that results in some bodily harm.[9]

The tendency to expand the circumstances in which recovery for intentional infliction of emotional distress

---

[7] *Restatement (Second) of Torts* § 46, comment *d* (1965).

[8] *Restatement (Second) of Torts* § 46(2)(a) (1965).

[9] *Restatement (Second) of Torts* § 46(2)(b) (1965).

will be allowed is a matter of growing concern for business because in recent years a number of emotional distress claims have been filed by employees who have been discharged or required to take drug tests. As the *Ford* case that follows indicates, sexual harassment cases can also give rise to emotional distress claims.

FORD v. REVLON, INC.

734 P.2d 580 (Ariz. Sup. Ct. 1987)

Leta Fay Ford's supervisor in the purchasing department of Revlon, Inc., Karl Braun, made numerous sexual advances toward her. At Revlon's annual service awards picnic on May 3, 1980, Braun grabbed Ford, restrained her in a chokehold with his right arm, and ran his hand over her breasts, stomach, and crotch. Later in May, Ford began a series of meetings with various members of Revlon management to report her complaints about Braun, who continued to verbally harass her. Despite the fact that Ford spoke with numerous persons at Revlon, no action was taken until nine months after her first complaint, when a meeting was held in the personnel office. Ford submitted a handwritten complaint about Braun's actions, asked for protection from him, and said she was collapsing emotionally and physically due to Braun's actions. Braun was called in and confronted, and Ford was told that he would be closely monitored.

Three months later, Revlon's personnel director submitted a report confirming Ford's charges and recommending that Braun be censured. One month later, Revlon gave Braun a letter of censure. During the time of the harassment, Ford developed high blood pressure, a nervous tic in her left eye, chest pains, rapid breathing, and other symptoms of emotional stress. Four months after Braun's censure, Ford attempted suicide. Later, Ford filed suit against Revlon for intentional infliction of emotional distress. When a jury ruled in her favor, Revlon appealed.

Cameron, Justice. The *Restatement* states that the tort of emotional distress inflicted intentionally or recklessly is recognized as a separate and distinct basis of tort liability. There is no need to show elements of other torts such as assault and battery. A comment to section 46 states that there is liability:

> where the conduct has been so outrageous in character, and so extreme in degree, as to go beyond all possible bounds of decency, and to be regarded as atrocious, and utterly intolerable in a civilized community . . . in which . . . an average member of the community would . . . exclaim, "Outrageous!"

Intentional infliction of emotional distress is often based upon claims of sexual harassment. The failure of an employer to promptly investigate complaints of sexual harassment is significant in making a determination to impose liability on an employer for its supervisors' acts of sexual harassment.

The three required elements of intentional infliction of emotional distress are: *first*, the conduct by the defendant must be "extreme" and "outrageous"; *second*, the defendant must either intend to cause emotional distress or recklessly disregard the near certainty that such distress will result from his conduct; and *third*, severe emotional distress must indeed occur as a result of defendant's conduct.

We believe that the conduct of Revlon met these requirements. First, Revlon's conduct can be classified as extreme or outrageous. Ford did everything that could be done, both within the announced policies of Revlon and without, to bring this matter to Revlon's attention. Revlon ignored her and the situation she faced, dragging the matter out for months and leaving Ford without redress.

Second, even if Revlon did not intend to cause emotional distress, Revlon's reckless disregard of Braun's conduct made it nearly certain that such emotional distress would in fact occur. Revlon knew that Braun had subjected Ford to physical assaults, vulgar remarks, that Ford continued to feel threatened by Braun, and that Ford was emotionally distraught, all of which led to a manifestation of physical problems. Despite Ford's complaints, Braun was not confronted for nine months, and then only upon *Ford's* demand for a group meeting. Another three months elapsed before Braun was censured. Revlon not only had actual knowledge of the situation but it also failed to conduct promptly any investigation of Ford's complaint.

Third, it is obvious that emotional distress did occur. Ample evidence, both medical and otherwise, was presented describing Ford's emotional distress.

We also note that Revlon had a specific policy and several guidelines for the handling of sexual harassment claims and other employee complaints, yet Revlon recklessly disregarded these policies and guidelines. Ford was entitled to rely on the policy statements made by Revlon. Once an employer proclaims a policy, the employer may not treat the policy as illusory.

Judgment for Ford affirmed.

Misuse of Legal Proceedings

Three intentional tort theories protect persons against the harm that can result from wrongfully instituted legal proceedings. **Malicious prosecution** affords a remedy for the financial and emotional harm, and the injury to reputation, that can result when *criminal* proceedings are wrongfully brought against a person. This tort balances society's interest in efficient enforcement of the criminal law against the individual's interest in freedom from unjustified criminal prosecutions. A plaintiff seeking to recover for malicious prosecution must prove *both* that the defendant *acted maliciously*, that is, without probable cause to believe that an offense had been committed and for an improper purpose, and that the criminal proceedings were *terminated in the plaintiff's favor*. As a general rule, proof that the defendant acted in good faith on the advice of legal counsel, after fully disclosing the relevant facts, conclusively establishes probable cause. Also, proof of the plaintiff's guilt is generally held to be a complete defense to liability, and the issue of his guilt can be retried in the malicious prosecution suit, despite his acquittal in the criminal proceedings. Proof of the plaintiff's innocence, however, cannot support a malicious prosecution action if the criminal proceedings were not terminated in his favor.

The tort of **wrongful use of civil proceedings** is similar to malicious prosecution, but is designed to protect persons from wrongfully instituted *civil* suits. Its elements are very similar to those of malicious prosecution: It requires proof that the civil proceedings were initiated without probable cause and for an improper purpose and proof that the suit was terminated in favor of the person sued.

The tort of **abuse of process** imposes liability on those who initiate legal proceedings for a primary purpose other than the one for which such proceedings are designed. Abuse of process cases normally involve situations in which the legal proceedings compel the other person to take some action unrelated to the subject of the suit. For example, Rogers wishes to buy Herbert's property, but Herbert refuses to sell. To pressure him into selling, Rogers files a nuisance suit against Herbert contending that Herbert's activities on his land interfere with Rogers' use and enjoyment of his adjoining property. Rogers may be liable to Herbert for abuse of process despite the fact that he had probable cause to file the suit and regardless of whether he wins the suit.

Deceit (Fraud)

Deceit is the formal name of the tort action for damages that is available to victims of knowing misrepresentation, often called *fraud*. The elements of deceit are a false statement of material fact, knowingly made by the defendant, with the intent to induce reliance by the plaintiff, justifiable reliance by the plaintiff, and harm to the plaintiff due to his reliance. The second element, technically called *scienter*, separates deceit from other forms of misrepresentation. Scienter is present only when the maker of a statement believes it is untrue, doesn't believe it is the truth, or recklessly disregards its truth. So, neither negligent nor innocent misrepresentations can serve as the basis for a deceit action.[10] Because most deceit actions arise in a contractual setting, and because a tort action for deceit is only one of the remedies available to a victim of fraud, a fuller discussion of this topic is deferred until the Reality of Consent chapter.

INTERFERENCE WITH PROPERTY RIGHTS

Nature of Property Rights

The rights associated with the acquisition and use of property have traditionally occupied an important position in our legal system. Tortious interference with property rights is generally treated as an offense against the right to *possession*. Therefore, where the party entitled to possession is not the same as the owner of the property in question (e.g., a tenant leasing property from its owner), the party entitled to possession is ordinarily the proper person to file suit for interference with his possessory rights. If the interference also results in lasting damage to the property, however, its owner may also have a right to recover for such damage.

Trespass to Land

A person is liable for **trespass** if he (1) intentionally and unlawfully enters land in the possession of another, (2) unlawfully remains on such land after entering lawfully, such as a tenant who refuses to move at the end of a lease,

(3) unlawfully causes anything to enter such land, or (4) fails to remove anything that he has a duty to remove from such land. No actual harm to the land is required for liability for intentional trespasses, but actual harm is required for liability for reckless or negligent trespasses. In addition, a person can be liable for trespass even though the trespass resulted from his mistaken belief that his entry was legally justified. This could arise from a belief that he had a right to possess the land, had the consent of the party entitled to possession, or had some other legal right or privilege entitling him to enter.

Nuisance

Unlawful and unreasonable interferences with another person's right to the use or enjoyment of his land are called **nuisances.** Nuisance suits, unlike trespass actions, do not necessarily involve any physical invasion of a person's property. Noise, vibration, and unpleasant odors are all examples of things that could be nuisances but would not justify a trespass action. In nuisance suits, the courts attempt to balance the competing interests of landowners to use their land as they see fit. Nuisance law recognizes an unfortunate fact of life: To preserve freedom, it must be limited. Put another way, my free use of my property may destroy your enjoyment of yours. For example, should I be able to open a solid waste disposal plant next to your restaurant? The law of nuisance attempts to resolve such perplexing issues.[11] As the following *Borland* case illustrates, it is sometimes very difficult to distinguish between nuisance and trespass.

---

[10] The Legal Responsibilities of Accountants chapter discusses negligent misrepresentation as an important basis of professional liability for accountants. Innocent misrepresentations can sometimes serve as a defense to the enforcement of a contract. The Reality of Consent chapter discusses this aspect of misrepresentation in detail.

[11] The Real Property and Insurance chapter discusses nuisances in detail.

BORLAND v. SANDERS LEAD CO.
369 So. 2d 523 (Ala. Sup. Ct. 1979)

In 1968, Sanders Lead Company started an operation for recovering lead from used automobile batteries on property near 159 acres of farmland owned by J. H. and Sarah Borland. Sanders's smelter, which reduced plates from batteries, was located on the part of Sanders's land that was closest to the Borlands' property. The Borlands argued that, despite the fact that the smelter was equipped with a filter system designed to reduce lead particulate emissions, their property had been damaged by a dangerous accumulation of lead particulates and sulfoxide deposits from the smelter. They filed a trespass suit against Sanders. When the trial judge ruled in Sanders's favor, the Borlands appealed.

Jones, Justice.   In *Rushing v. Hooper-McDonald, Inc.* (1974), this Court held that a trespass need not be inflicted directly on another's realty, but may be committed by discharging foreign polluting matter at a point beyond the boundary of such realty. *Rushing* specifically held that a trespass is committed by one who knowingly discharges asphalt in such a manner that it will in due course invade a neighbor's realty and cause harm. *Rushing* further cited with approval the case of *Martin v. Reynolds Metals Co.* (Or. 1959). In *Martin*, a case remarkably similar to the present case, the plaintiffs alleged that the operation by defendants of an aluminum reduction plant caused certain fluoride compounds in the form of gases and particulates, invisible to the naked eye, to become airborne and settle on plaintiffs' property, rendering it unfit for raising livestock.

The defendants in *Martin* contended that there had not been a sufficient invasion of plaintiffs' property to constitute trespass, but at most, defendants' acts constituted a nuisance. This would have allowed the defendants to set up Oregon's two-year statute of limitations applicable to non-possessory injuries to land rather than Oregon's six-year statute for trespass to land. The *Martin* Court pointed out that trespass and nuisance are separate torts for the protection of different interests invaded—trespass protecting the possessor's interest in exclusive possession of property and nuisance protecting the interest in use and enjoyment. The Court noted, and we agree, that the same conduct on the part of a defendant may, and often does, result in the actionable invasion of both interests.

In the traditional sense, the law of nuisance applies where the invasion results in no substantial damage to the land, but where there is interference with the use and enjoyment of one's property. The classic cases of the barking dog, the neighboring bawdy house, noise, smoke, fumes, or obnoxious odors generally invoke the law of nuisance. These intrusions are not relegated to the nuisance remedy simply because of their indirect nature; rather, they do not constitute a trespass because all of the requisite elements of trespass to land are not present.

For an indirect invasion to amount to an actionable trespass, there must be an interference with plaintiff's exclusive possessory interest; that is, through the defendant's intentional conduct, and with reasonable foreseeability, some substance has entered upon the land itself, affecting its nature and character, and causing substantial actual damage to it. For example, if the smoke or polluting substance emitting from a defendant's operation causes discomfort and annoyance to the plaintiff in his use and employment of the property, then the plaintiff's remedy is for nuisance; but if, as a result of the defendant's operation, the polluting substance is deposited upon the plaintiff's property, thus interfering with his exclusive possessory interest by causing substantial damage to the property, then the plaintiff may seek his remedy in trespass.

It might appear from our holding today that every property owner in this State would have a cause of action against any neighboring industry which emitted particulate matter into the atmosphere, or even a passing motorist, whose exhaust emissions come to rest upon another's property. But we hasten to point out that there is a point where the entry is so lacking in substance that the law will refuse to recognize it, applying the maxim *de minimis non curat lex*—the law does not concern itself with trifles. In the present case, however, we are not faced with a trifling complaint. The Borlands have suffered a real and substantial invasion of a protected interest.

Judgment reversed in favor of the Borlands.

Trespass to Personal Property

Any intentional intermeddling with personal property in the possession of another is a trespass if it (1) results in harm to that property (e.g., Franks strikes Goode's dog or throws paint on his car), or (2) deprives the party entitled to possession of its use for an appreciable time (e.g., Franks hides Goode's car and Goode cannot find it for several hours).

Conversion

Conversion is the intentional exercise of dominion or control over another's property. To amount to conversion, the defendant's actions must be such a serious interference with another's right to control the property that they justify requiring the defendant to pay damages for the full value of the property. The difference between conversion and trespass to personal property is based on the *degree* of interference with another's property rights. In considering whether an interference with another's property amounts to its conversion, the courts consider such factors as the extent of the harm done to the property, the extent and duration of the interference with the other's right to control the property, and whether the defendant acted in good faith. For example, Sharp goes to Friendly Motors and asks to test-drive a new Ford Thunderbird. If Sharp either wrecks the car, causing major damage, or drives it across the United States, he is probably liable for conversion and obligated to pay Friendly Motors the reasonable value of the car. On the other hand, if Sharp is merely involved in a fender bender, or keeps the car for eight hours, he is probably only liable for trespass. Therefore, he is only obligated to pay damages to compensate Friendly for the loss in value of the car or for its loss of use of the car.

Evolving Concepts of Tort Liability

Recent developments indicate a continuing tendency to expand the scope of tort law as society recognizes an increasing range of personal interests that deserve legal protection. For example, recent cases have recognized the right of fired employees to recover against their employers for a new tort of *wrongful* or *abusive discharge.*[12] Also, some courts have allowed plaintiffs to recover punitive damages in tort suits arising out of a defendant's bad faith breach of contract,[13] and employee drug testing programs have spawned a number of claims against employers on intentional tort theories such as defamation, intentional infliction of emotional distress, and invasion of privacy.

Finally, plaintiffs in so-called toxic tort suits, mass actions seeking to recover for a variety of injuries resulting from exposure to toxic substances, are currently attempting to employ novel tort theories to support their claims. Should persons exposed to carcinogenic substances be able to recover for the emotional distress caused by the fear that they may contract cancer in the future? Should employees whose employers knowingly expose them to such substances in the workplace be allowed to sue their employers for damages in tort that would not be recoverable under their state's workers' compensation statute? All of these examples illustrate the dynamic nature of our legal system in general and of tort law in particular. Given the historical development of tort law, one can reasonably expect that as growing technical knowledge or changing social circumstances create the need to protect new personal interests, tort law will evolve to satisfy that need.

Business Torts

Figure 2 summarizes the many and varied interests protected by the intentional tort theories we have discussed in this chapter. Today, courts also recognize a variety of tort actions designed to protect various economic interests. The Intellectual Property, and Competitive Torts, and Unfair Competition chapter discusses these torts in detail.

---

[12]The Employment Law chapter discusses this subject in detail.

[13]The Performance and Remedies chapter discusses this subject in detail.

FIGURE 2   Interests Protected by Tort Law

Interest	Tort Theory
Freedom from harmful/offensive contacts	Battery
Freedom from apprehension of battery	Assault
Freedom from confinement	False imprisonment
Right to reputation	Defamation
Right of privacy	Invasion of privacy
Freedom from disagreeable emotions	Intentional infliction of emotional distress
Freedom from improper criminal proceedings	Malicious prosecution
Freedom from improper civil proceedings	Wrongful use of civil proceedings and abuse of process
Possession and enjoyment of personal property	Trespass and conversion
Possession and enjoyment of real property	Trespass and nuisance
Freedom from knowing misstatements	Deceit

ETHICAL AND PUBLIC POLICY CONCERNS

1. Tort law attempts to protect various individual interests by giving persons whose rights are violated by others the right to sue for money damages. Can monetary awards, however, ever truly compensate persons who have suffered harms such as an invasion of privacy or emotional distress? If not, how do we justify such awards?

2. Safeco Plastics Corporation owns a plant upstream from Morrison's farm. Safeco periodically discharges large amounts of water into the stream, a practice that occasionally results in the flooding of Morrison's property. Assuming that it is cheaper for Safeco to pay damages to Morrison for trespass than it is to take corrective steps to prevent the flooding, is it ethically proper for Safeco to continue to flood Morrison's land?

3. Maxwell is defamed by an article in a local newspaper as a result of careless reporting. When confronted with its error, the paper promptly apologizes and runs an article retracting the defamatory statement. Maxwell has noticed no negative effects from the article, but his lawyer advises him that he would have no trouble proving defamation by the paper and that, as a result, the paper's liability insurance company would probably be eager to settle in the event that Maxwell files suit. Should Maxwell sue?

SUMMARY

The basis of tort liability is a breach of a legal duty owed to another person resulting in a legally recognizable harm to that person. Tort law seeks to compensate injured persons by allowing them to recover money damages for any harm they have suffered. In some cases, tort law also allows injured persons to recover punitive damages in excess of their actual losses. Punitive damages are designed to punish flagrant wrongdoers and to deter them and others from engaging in similar conduct in the future. Tort law involves a constant attempt to balance conflicting social rights and duties. Over time, the law of torts has recognized an expanding number of personal interests deserving of protection. At present, tort law protects a wide variety of personal interests: the right to be free from harmful or offensive bodily contacts (battery), the right to be free from the apprehension of such contacts (assault), the right to reputation (defamation), the right to privacy (invasion of privacy), the right to be free from disagreeable emotions (intentional infliction of emotional distress), and the right to be free from improperly instituted criminal or civil proceedings (malicious prosecution, wrongful use of civil proceedings, and abuse of process).

Intentionally causing a harmful or offensive contact with another can give rise to liability for battery. Causing another to have a reasonable apprehension of an imminent battery constitutes assault. Confining another against his will for an appreciable time can create liability for false imprisonment. The publication of false and defamatory statements about another can result in liability for defamation. Defamation is divided into slander (verbal defamation) and libel (written defamation). Broadcast defamations, whether by radio or television, are normally treated as libels. To balance the individual's right to reputation against the constitutionally protected rights of freedom of speech and of the press, public officials and public figures face higher burdens of proof in defamation suits than do private persons. Also, the law recognizes several other defenses to defamation. Truth is an absolute defense to defamation, and some defamatory statements, though untrue, may be privileged.

The tort of invasion of privacy protects the individual's right to be let alone by imposing liability for four behaviors: intruding on a person's physical solitude or seclusion, publicizing private facts about a person, casting a person in a false light in the public eye, and appropriating a person's name or likeness for commercial purposes. As in the case of defamation, public officials and public figures enjoy narrower privacy rights than do private persons.

Although the courts disagree on the elements of the tort, most courts now recognize an independent tort of intentional infliction of emotional distress. The courts do agree, however, that only outrageous conduct creates liability and that the resulting emotional distress must be severe. Some courts also require some significant bodily harm to the plaintiff as a result of the emotional distress she suffered, but there is a discernible trend in favor of allowing recovery for severe emotional distress standing alone.

The tort of malicious prosecution protects against wrongful initiation of criminal proceedings. Both it and the tort of wrongful use of civil proceedings require that the proceedings in question be initiated without probable cause and that they be terminated in favor of the person wrongfully subjected to them. The tort of abuse of process imposes liability on those who employ legal proceedings for wrongful purposes. Unlike liability for either malicious prosecution or wrongful use of civil proceedings, liability for abuse of process is possible even if the defendant had probable cause to initiate legal proceedings and in spite of the fact that the proceedings were ultimately resolved against the person wrongfully subjected to them.

Tort law also protects personal rights in property. The torts of trespass and nuisance protect an individual's right to possess and enjoy the use of his land. The torts of trespass and conversion protect the individual's rights in the possession and enjoyment of her personal property. The basic distinction between trespass and conversion is that conversion deals with interferences that are serious enough to justify forcing the defendant to pay the full value of the property in question, rather than requiring him merely to pay for the loss of value or use of the property.

PROBLEM CASES

1. Barbara A. hired John G., an attorney, to represent her in a legal proceeding. When he subsequently filed suit against her for legal fees, she filed a cross-complaint against him for battery and deceit. She alleged that she had twice had sex with him and, as a result, had suffered a tubal pregnancy which necessitated surgery that rendered her sterile. She also alleged that she had sex with him despite the fact that neither party used any means of contraception because he had assured her: "I can't possibly get anyone pregnant." The trial court dismissed her claim for failure to state a cause of action. Was the dismissal proper?

2. On September 16, 1975, David Manning, Jr., was a spectator at Fenway Park in Boston for a baseball game between the Baltimore Orioles and the Boston Red Sox. Ross Grimsley was a pitcher for Baltimore. During the first three innings, Grimsley was warming up by throwing a ball from a pitcher's mound to a plate in the bull pen located near the right-field bleachers. The spectators in the bleachers continuously heckled Grimsley. On several occasions immediately following the heckling, Grimsley looked directly at the hecklers, not just into the stands. At the end of the third inning, after his catcher had left his position and was walking over to the bench, Grimsley faced the bleachers and wound up or stretched as though to pitch in the direction of the plate. Instead, the ball traveled from Grimsley's hand at more than 80 miles per hour at an angle of 90 degrees to the path from the pitcher's mound to the plate and directly toward the hecklers in the bleachers. The ball passed through the wire mesh fence in front of the bleachers and struck Manning. Manning filed a battery action against Grimsley. The trial judge directed a verdict for Grimsley. Should Manning win his appeal?

3. On April 14, 1984, during the "Saturday Night News" segment of NBC's "Saturday Night Live" program, a skit was presented as the "Fast Frank Feature." A performer was introduced to the audience as Maurice Frank, a tax consultant. The performer bore a noticeable physical resemblance to Maurice Frank, a resident of Westchester County, New York, who was engaged in business as an accountant, tax consultant, and financial planner. The performer proceeded to give "ludicrously inappropriate" tax advice, suggesting, among other things, that viewers claim houseplants as dependents and write off acne medicine under an oil depletion allowance, and guaranteeing that taxpayers who used his service would receive refunds in excess of their earnings. The real Maurice Frank filed a defamation suit against the network. Was he defamed by the skit?

4. In February of 1986, Lois Grimsley, a 46-year-old security inspector, unexpectedly gave birth in her home less than two days after doctors had told her that her stomach pains were nothing more than a urinary tract infection and a case of hemorrhoids. A reporter from a local newspaper interviewed Grimsley about the birth, and Grimsley provided details about it and posed for a picture with the child. The story appeared in the local paper the following day, was subsequently picked up by the Associated Press, and also appeared in several other newspapers. In July 1986, a synopsis of the article (including a photo of Grimsley and her son) appeared in the "Hard Times" section of *Penthouse* magazine (a section that the magazine describes as "a compendium of bizarre, idiotic, lurid, and ofttimes witless driblets of information culled from the nation's press") under the heading "Birth of a Hemorrhoid." Grimsley filed suit against *Penthouse* for defamation, invasion of privacy, and intentional infliction of mental distress. Should her suit succeed?

5. In September 1987, *The National Enquirer* ran an article reporting Henry Dempsey's harrowing escape from injury or death when he fell out of a small airplane while in flight but clung to the open boarding ladder of the plane, surviving his copilot's landing with only a few scratches. Dempsey had refused to be interviewed for the article, despite repeated attempts by an *Enquirer* reporter to gain an interview. The reporter allegedly came to his home twice, repeatedly drove past his home for three quarters of an hour after the first refusal, and followed him to a restaurant where she attempted to photograph him and again requested an interview. After the article appeared, Dempsey filed suit against the *Enquirer* for invasion of privacy and intentional infliction of emotional distress. Should Dempsey's suit succeed?

6. On February 25 and 26, 1987, ABC broadcast an investigative new report entitled "South Africa Connection" which purported to describe efforts by the Reagan administration to enlist the assistance of South Africa in aiding the Nicaraguan Contras by supplying aircraft and flight crews. In an attempt to flesh out the alleged connection, the program highlighted the participation of Southern Air Transport in the venture, and stated at one point that Southern Air was "known for its past relationship with the Central Intelligence Agency." Southern Air filed suit against the network for libel and invasion of privacy, arguing that its business had suffered as a result of the program. The network moved to dismiss the suit on the ground that a corporation cannot be defamed and possesses no right of privacy. Should the network's motion be granted?

7. Susan B. went to the Crisis Pregnancy Center for a "free pregnancy test." During an interview with a counselor she disclosed the fact that she had had an abortion at age 15 and had found it to be a traumatic experience. She told the counselor that if she were pregnant she would not consider aborting the child. She also said that she had been hospitalized for depression and that she was taking antidepressant and antianxiety medications prescribed by a psychiatrist. Susan's pregnancy test was negative, but the Center withheld this information from her. Instead, she said that they showed her a film "featuring mutilated advanced fetuses" and containing "purported personal and medical" comments on "the evil of abortion and the ineradicable harm" it does to pregnant women. After the film was shown, the counselor and another employee of the Center told Susan their personal moral views on sex and abortion, and told her that religion was the "sole means of expiation" for a woman who had undergone an abortion. They then told her she was not pregnant. Susan filed suit against the Center for intentional infliction of emotional distress, arguing that she became highly distressed as a result of the experience, necessitating emergency psychiatric care and increased dosages of her medication. Was the trial court order dismissing her suit proper?

8. The Blanks purchased a lot in the Indian Fork subdivision next to a lot owned by Gary Rawson. When Rawson built his home, he located a basketball goal and dog pen immediately next to the property separating the two lots. The Blanks complained to the subdivision developer that Rawson was violating the minimum setback restrictions applicable to the subdivision and were told that Rawson had received permission from the developer to do so. They then filed a nuisance suit against Rawson. At the trial, they alleged that the sound of the basketball hitting the backboard when Rawson's son played was offensive and that, when he missed, the ball could come into their yard. They also stated that the dog was a large one and that the pen was not cleaned regularly, with the result that offensive odors continued to reach their property despite the 10-foot privacy fence Rawson had erected between their properties shortly after their complaint against him was filed. Was the trial judge's order forcing Rawson to remove or relocate the goal and the dog pen proper?

9. Moore was receiving treatment for hairy-cell leukemia at a university hospital. After his spleen was removed as part of that treatment, the treating physician and another university employee determined that his cells were unique. Without Moore's knowledge or consent, they applied genetic engineering techniques to his cells, producing a cell line that they patented and marketed very successfully through agreements with a pharmaceutical company and a biotechnology firm. To further their research, they continued to monitor him and take tissue samples from him for almost seven years after his spleen was removed. When Moore discovered the truth, he filed a conversion suit against the university, which moved to dismiss his claim, arguing that he had no property right in his spleen and that, in any event, his cells were worthless without their subsequent modifications to them. Should Moore's suit survive their motion to dismiss?

10. Gilbert Smith owned land in Alviso, California, that he leased by oral agreement to George Interiano. Without Smith's knowledge, Interiano subleased the property to Carson Grimes, who was in the used lumber business. Grimes arranged for Cap Concrete to deliver between 60 to 70 loads of broken concrete material to the property to use as fill. When Smith learned of the presence of the concrete on his property a month later, he filed a trespass suit against Cap Concrete. The evidence at trial indicated that it would cost $6,000 to remove the concrete and that the presence of the concrete on the land seriously reduced the land's utility for other purposes. Cap argued that Grimes was the only party who could properly file a trespass suit over the concrete and that, in any event, Grimes's consent to the deliveries barred any suit by Smith. The trial court ruled in Cap's favor and Smith appealed. Should his appeal succeed?

CHAPTER 7

NEGLIGENCE AND STRICT LIABILITY

NEGLIGENCE

Origins and Elements

The Industrial Revolution that changed the face of 19th-century America created serious problems for the law of torts. Railroads, machinery, and other newly developing technologies contributed to a growing number of injuries to persons and their property. These injuries did not fit within the intentional torts framework, however, because most of them were unintended. Some injuries were simply the unavoidable consequences of life in a high-speed, technologically advanced, modern society. Holding infant industries totally responsible for all of the harms they caused could have seriously impeded the process of industrial development. To avoid such a result, new tort rules were needed. In response to these growing social pressures, the courts created the law of negligence.

Negligence focuses on conduct that falls below the legal standards that the law has established to protect members of society against unreasonable risks of harm. Negligence essentially involves an unintentional breach of a legal duty owed to another that results in some legally recognizable injury to the other's person or property. A plaintiff in a negligence suit must prove several things to recover: (1) that the defendant had a *duty* not to

injure him, (2) that the defendant *breached* that duty, and (3) that the defendant's breach of duty was the *actual* and *legal (proximate) cause* of his *injury*. To be successful, a plaintiff must also overcome any *defenses* to negligence liability that are raised by the defendant. Most of these defenses involve behavior by the plaintiff that may have originally contributed to his injury. (These elements are summarized graphically in Figure 2, which appears later in the chapter.)

Duty

The basic idea of negligence is that each member of society has a duty to conduct her affairs in a way that avoids an unreasonable risk of harm to others. The law of negligence holds each of us up to an *objective*, yet *flexible* standard of conduct: that of a "reasonable person of ordinary prudence in similar circumstances." This standard is objective because the reasonable person is a hypothetical person who is always thoughtful and cautious and never unreasonably endangers others. It is flexible because it allows consideration of all the circumstances surrounding a particular injury. For example, the law does not require the same level of caution and deliberation of a person confronted with an emergency requiring rapid decisions and action as it does of a person in circumstances allowing for calm reflection and deliberate action. Likewise, to a limited extent, the law considers the personal characteristics of the particular defendant whose conduct is being judged. For example, children are generally required to act as a reasonable person of similar age, intelligence, and experience would act under similar circumstances. Persons with physical disabilities are required to act as would a reasonable person with the same disability. Mental deficiencies, however, ordinarily do not relieve a person from the duty to conform to the reasonable person standard.

Special Duties   The question of whether a particular duty exists is entirely a question of law. Does the law recognize a duty of the defendant to protect the interests of this particular plaintiff from harm? Legal duties can originate from several sources. A *contractual relationship* between the plaintiff and the defendant can give rise to a variety of duties that might not exist otherwise. For example, most professional malpractice cases are based on claims that professionals negligently breached professional duties owed to their clients or to third persons who rely on their competent performance of professional tasks.[1]

Other *special relationships* between the parties have long been recognized as the source of special legal duties. For example, common carriers and innkeepers have long been held virtually strictly liable for damaging or losing the property of their customers. In recent years, many courts have extended this duty to include an affirmative duty to protect passengers or guests against the foreseeable wrongful acts of third persons. This has happened despite the fact that the law has long refused to recognize any general duty to aid and protect others from third-party wrongdoing unless a defendant's actions foreseeably increased the risk of such wrongdoing. Some recent decisions have imposed a similar duty on landlords to protect their tenants against the foreseeable criminal acts of others.

The relationship between the parties can also affect the *level* of duty that one person owes to another. For example, the common law has long held that the level of duty that a person in possession of land owes to other persons who enter on the land depends on whether such persons were invitees, licensees, or trespassers. **Invitees** are members of the public who are lawfully on public land, such as a park, swimming pool, or government

office; they are also customers, delivery persons, or paying boarders, who are on private premises for a purpose connected with the business interests of the possessor of the land. **Licensees** are those whose privilege to enter on the land depends entirely on the possessor's consent. Licensees include persons who are on the land solely for their own purposes such as someone soliciting money for charity, members of the possessor's household, and social guests. **Trespassers** are persons who enter or remain on another's land without any legal right or privilege to do so.

At common law, a possessor of land owed invitees a duty to exercise reasonable care to keep the premises in reasonably safe condition for their use. He also had a duty to protect invitees against dangerous conditions on the premises that he knew about, or reasonably should have discovered, and that they were unlikely to discover. He only owed licensees a duty to warn them of known dangerous conditions that they were unlikely to discover. The possessor of land owed no duty to trespassers to maintain his premises in a safe condition, and only a duty not to willfully and wantonly injure them once their presence was known. Recent years have seen a marked tendency to erode these common law distinctions. Many courts today, for example, no longer distinguish between licensees and invitees, holding that the possessor of land owes the same duties to licensees that he owes to invitees. Also, the courts have made numerous exceptions to the minimal duties that possessors of land owe to trespassers. For example, a higher level of duty is ordinarily owed to trespassers who the possessor of land knows are constantly entering the land (e.g., using a well-worn path across the land) and greater duties are ordinarily owed to protect children if the possessor of land knows that they are likely to trespass.

Finally, *statutes* can create legal duties that can be the source of a negligence action. The doctrine of **negligence per se** provides that one who violates a statute is guilty of negligent conduct if a harm that the statute was designed to prevent results to a person whom the statute was intended to protect. The defendant who has violated a statute may still seek to avoid liability by arguing that his violation was not the legal cause of the plaintiff's injury or by asserting some other general defense to liability, but the statutory violation is generally held to be conclusive evidence of breach of duty. The *Nixon* case later in this chapter is a good example of a court imposing a duty on the basis of a statute where other courts, such as the court in the following *Waters* case, have been unwilling to do so in the absence of a statute.

---

[1] The Legal Responsibilities of Accountants chapter discusses this subject in detail.

WATERS v. NEW YORK CITY HOUSING AUTHORITY

505 N.E.2d 922 (N.Y. Ct. App. 1987)

At 6:45 A.M. on July 25, 1982, Simone Waters, 16 years of age, was walking on a public street where she was accosted by a knife-wielding man who forced her to walk with him to a building around the corner. Once inside the building, which was unlocked, the man forced her to the roof and, after taking her money, sodomized her. The building was owned by the New York Housing Authority.

The evidence at the trial indicated that the front door locks on the building had been either broken or missing for at least two years before Simone was attacked, that several tenants had complained about the condition over that two-year period, and that there had been at least five criminal incidents in the building involving outsiders. The evidence also included an affidavit from an investigator employed by Waters stating that "had the door locks on this building been in proper working order, this sexual attack would in all probability not have occurred." When the trial court granted a summary judgment in favor of the Housing Authority, Waters appealed.

Titone, Judge.   It is now beyond dispute that a landlord, private or public, may have a duty to take reasonable precautionary measures to secure the premises if it has notice of a likelihood of criminal intrusions posing a threat to safety. A building owner who breaches such a duty may be held liable to an individual who is injured in a reasonably foreseeable criminal encounter that was proximately caused by the absence of adequate security. These basic principles, however, do not resolve the unusual problem presented here. Although Waters has made the necessary allegations of negligent security maintenance, notice of prior criminal intrusion, and proximately caused injury, her case differs significantly from those in which the landowner's liability for inadequate security has previously been upheld. Unlike the tenant in *Miller v. State of New York* and the business guest in *Nallan v. Helmsley-Spear, Inc.*, Waters had no connection whatsoever to the building in which her injuries ultimately occurred. Accordingly, we must look beyond *Nallan* and *Miller* to determine whether a landlord's duty should be extended to a person in Waters's position.

The question of the scope of an alleged tort-feasor's duty is, in the first instance, a legal issue for the court to resolve. In this analysis, not only logic and science, but policy play an important role. The common law of torts is, at its foundation, a means of apportioning risks and allocating the burden of loss. While moral and logical judgments are significant components of the analysis, we are also bound to consider the larger social consequences of our decisions and to tailor our notion of duty so that the legal consequences of wrongs are limited to a controllable degree.

With these principles in mind, we turn now to the question whether Waters was within the orbit of duty imposed on the owner of the building in which her injuries occurred. Initially, we note that the duty that was allegedly breached——to maintain the front door locks in working condition—exists principally to protect the safety and possessions of the tenants and visitors inside the premises. The risk to be reasonably apprehended in this instance is that of intrusion by outsiders with criminal motive who might do harm to those who have a right to feel at least minimally secure inside a dwelling place. In this case both logic and public policy weigh heavily in favor of confining the scope of defendant landowner's duty to protect against criminal acts to tenants and others who might reasonably be expected to be on the premises. An important consideration in this context is the fact that the landowner has no control over either the acts of the primary wrongdoer or the conditions on the public byways that make such acts all too commonplace. Another significant factor is the virtually limitless liability to which defendant and other landowners would be exposed if their legal obligations were extended to Waters and to all others in her position.

Finally, we note that the important public goals of minimizing crime and encouraging the maintenance of urban property would not materially be advanced by expanding the scope of landowners' duties in the manner Waters suggests. The possibility of tort liability arising from injury to tenants or others on the premises provides a strong incentive to landlords to keep locks and other security systems in good repair. Moreover, it is unlikely that the incidence of street crime would be meaningfully affected, since the urban environment includes many nooks and crannies, other than unsecured dwellings, which afford malefactors the privacy they need to commit their misdeeds. Thus, the social benefits to be gained do not warrant the extension of the landowner's duty to maintain secure premises to the millions of individuals who use the sidewalks of New York City each day and are thereby exposed to the dangers of street crime.

Judgment for the Housing Authority affirmed.

Breach

A person is guilty of breach of duty if she exposes another to an *unreasonable, foreseeable* risk of harm. Negligence consists of doing something that a reasonable person would not have done under the circumstances, or failing to do something that a reasonable person would have done under the same circumstances. If a person guards against all foreseeable risks and exercises reasonable care, but harm to others nonetheless occurs, no liability for negligence ordinarily results. For example, if Wilson is carefully driving his car within the speed limit and has a heart attack that causes him to lose control and crash into a car driven by Thomas, Wilson would ordinarily not be liable to Thomas for his injuries. As another member of the public using the highways, Wilson owed Thomas a duty to exercise reasonable care while driving. However, the accident was not the result of any breach of that duty because it was unforeseeable. If, on the other hand, Wilson's doctor had advised him that he had a heart condition that made driving dangerous, his failure to heed his doctor's warning would probably amount to a breach of duty because he was plainly exposing others to a foreseeable risk of harm by driving.

Of course, many behaviors involve some risk of harm to others, but the risk must be an *unreasonable* one before that behavior amounts to a breach of duty. In deciding the reasonableness of the risk, the courts balance the social utility of a person's conduct and the ease of avoiding or minimizing the risk against the likelihood that harm will result and the probable seriousness of that harm. As the risk of serious harm to others increases, so does the duty to take steps to avoid that harm. The following *Culli* case illustrates the steps a court follows in deciding whether a business has breached its duty to an invitee.

CULLI v. MARATHON PETROLEUM CO.
862 F. 2d 119 (7th Cir. 1988)

On Saturday, August 4, 1984, Elizabeth Culli stopped at a 24-hour self-service gas station operated by Marathon Petroleum in Mt. Vernon, Illinois. She filled her gas tank and then picked up five eight-pack cartons of soda that were featured as part of a special soda sale the station was running that day. After paying for the gas, she headed back toward her car. Before she reached her car, however, she slipped and fell on what an ambulance attendant who was called to the scene later described as a "clearish" slippery substance in a pool approximately 8 to 10 inches in width and length. Culli suffered a compound fracture of her ankle and had to use a wheelchair and walker for several months thereafter.

At the trial of her suit against Marathon, the evidence indicated that the station was typically staffed by one person, who would primarily stay inside and run the cash register, and who was also responsible for replenishing supplies of the other items sold at the station, such as milk, candy, hot food, and sandwiches. The station lot was normally swept once a day during the night shift, but the attendant on duty the evening prior to the accident could not recall whether or not he had swept that night. There was also testimony that spills in general occurred once or twice each day and that one employee had asked the station manager to hire more help because the station was understaffed, a request which he relayed to his superiors, but which went unheeded. When a jury awarded Culli $87,500, Marathon appealed.

Will, Senior District Judge.   The defendant owed the plaintiff invitee the duty of maintaining its property in a reasonably safe condition. This includes a duty to inspect and repair dangerous conditions on the property or give adequate warnings to prevent injury. To be liable, Marathon must have had actual or constructive notice of the dangerous condition. Both parties agree that Marathon did not have actual notice.

Constructive notice can be established under Illinois law under two alternative theories: (1) the dangerous condition existed for a sufficient amount of time so that it would have been discovered by the exercise of ordinary care, or (2) the dangerous condition was part of a pattern of conduct or a recurring incident.

In *Hresil v. Sears, Roebuck & Co.* (1980), plaintiff sought damages for injuries she suffered when she slipped on a "gob" of phlegm in the defendant's self-service store. At the time of her accident, there were few customers in the store and, due to the inactivity in the store at the place where she fell, the foreign substance could have been on the floor for at least 10 minutes. The court found that, as a matter of law, 10 minutes was not long enough to give Sears constructive notice of the gob, and "to charge the store with constuctive notice would place upon the store the unfair requirement of the constant patrolling of its aisles."

Because of the lack of testimony establishing how long the substance in this case was present, we do not know if it was present for a period of time which would have placed Marathon on constructive notice of it. It could have been present for a few minutes or several hours. Under the first constructive notice theory evidence establishing how long the particular substance was present is necessary.

Under the second constructive notice theory what is needed is a pattern of dangerous conditions which were not attended to within a reasonable time. There was substantial evidence presented at trial establishing that there were spills on a daily basis in the pump area and that the volume of sales on the day in question made it unreasonable for Marathon to sweep the lot only at night and operate for most of the day with only one attendant who was primarily confined to the cash register. The evidence is sufficient to support the jury's verdict that Marathon's maintenance of its property was unreasonable and proximately caused Culli's injury.

Judgment for Culli affirmed.

Causation

Even if a person breaches a duty that he owes to another person, no liability for negligence results unless the breach of duty was the *actual cause*, or the cause in fact, of injury to the other person. To determine the existence of actual cause, many courts employ a *but for* test: A defendant's conduct is the actual cause of a plaintiff's injury if that injury would not have occurred *but for* the defendant's breach of duty. In some cases, however, a person's negligent conduct may combine with the negligent conduct of another to cause a plaintiff's injury. For example, on a windy day Allen negligently starts a fire by using gasoline to start his charcoal grill. The fire started by Allen spreads and joins forces with another fire started by Baker, who was burning brush on his property but who failed to take any precautions to prevent the fire from spreading. The combined fires burn Clark's home to the ground. Clark sues both Allen and Baker for negligence. In such a case, the court would ask whether each defendant's conduct was a *substantial factor* in bringing about Clark's loss. If the evidence indicates that Clark's house would have been destroyed by either fire in the absence of the other, both Allen and Baker are liable for Clark's loss.

Proximate Cause Holding persons guilty of negligent conduct responsible for all of the harms that actually result from their negligence could, in some cases, expose them to potentially catastrophic liability. Although the law has long said that those who are guilty of intentional wrongdoing are liable for all of the direct consequences of their acts, however bizarre or unforeseeable, the courts have also recognized that a person who was merely negligent should not necessarily be responsible for every injury actually caused by her negligence. This idea of placing some legal limit on a negligent defendant's liability for the consequences of her actions is called **proximate cause.** Courts often say that a negligent defendant is liable only for the *proximate* results of her conduct. Thus, although a defendant's conduct may have been the *actual cause* of a particular plaintiff's injury, she is liable only if her conduct was also the *proximate (legal) cause* of that injury.

The courts have not, however, reached any substantial agreement on the test that should be employed for proximate cause. In reality, the proximate cause question is one of social policy. In deciding which test to adopt, a court must weigh the possibility that negligent persons can be exposed to catastrophic liability by a lenient test for proximate cause against the fact that a restrictive test inevitably prevents some innocent victims from recovering any compensation for their losses. Courts have responded in a variety of ways to this difficult choice.

Some courts have said that a negligent person is liable only for the "natural and probable consequences" of his actions. Others have limited a negligent person's liability for unforeseeable injuries by saying that he is liable only to plaintiffs who are within the "scope of the foreseeable risk." Thus, such courts hold that if the defendant could not have reasonably foreseen *some* injury to the plaintiff as a result of his actions, he is not liable to the plaintiff for any injury that in fact results from his negligence. Although this rule is often characterized as a rule of causation, in reality it is a rule limiting the defendant's *duty,* because courts adopting the rule hold that a defendant owes *no duty* to those to whom he cannot foresee any injury. On the other hand, such courts commonly hold that a defendant may be liable even for unforeseeable injuries to persons whom he has exposed to a foreseeable risk of harm.[2] The *Restatement (Second) of Torts* suggests that a defendant's negligence is not the legal cause of a plaintiff's injury if, looking back after the harm, it appears "highly extraordinary" to the court that the defendant's negligence should have brought about the plaintiff's injury.[3] In the following *Republic of France* case the defendant is able to avoid tremendous liability because the court refuses to hold the defendant responsible for unforeseeable consequences of its negligence.

---

[2] The most famous case adopting this approach is *Palsgraf v. Long Island Railroad Co.*, 12 N.E. 99 (N.Y. Ct. App. 1928).

[3] *Restatement (Second) of Torts* § 435(2) (1965).

REPUBLIC OF FRANCE v. UNITED STATES
290 F. 2d 395 (5th Cir. 1961)

On April 16, 1947, the SS *Grandchamp*, a cargo ship owned by the Republic of France and operated by the French Line, which was also 80 percent owned by the Republic of France, was loading a cargo of Fertilizer Grade Ammonium Nitrate (FGAN) at Texas City, Texas. A fire began on board the ship, apparently as a result of a cigarette or match carelessly discarded by a longshoreman in one of the ship's holds. Despite attempts to put it out, the fire spread quickly. A little over an hour after the fire was first discovered, the *Grandchamp* exploded with tremendous force.

Fire and burning debris spread throughout the waterfront, touching off accompanying fires and explosions in other ships, refineries, gasoline storage tanks, and chemical plants which were not brought under complete control for days. When the conflagration was over, 500 people had been killed and more than 3,000 had been injured.

The evidence indicated that despite the fact that ammonium nitrate was known throughout the transportation industry as an oxidizing agent and as a fire hazard, no one aboard the *Grandchamp* made any attempt to prevent smoking in the ship's holds. Numerous lawsuits were filed after the incident, many of them against the United States because the FGAN had been manufactured in army ordinance plants. After the United States was found not liable, Congress passed the Texas City Relief Act in 1955. The act left insurance underwriters to bear their own losses, but allowed those with uninsured claims to recover up to $25,000 per claim. The government paid out approximately $16 million to victims of the disaster, obtaining in return assignments of their claims for death, personal injuries, and property damage totalling approximately $70 million. The government sought to recover the full $70 million. The Republic of France and the French Line argued that they should not be liable for claims arising out of the explosion because FGAN was not known to be capable of exploding under such circumstances. When the trial court rejected their petition for limitation of liability, they appealed.

Rives, Circuit Judge.   In Texas, as elsewhere, not only proximate causal connection but also the very existence of a duty depends upon reasonable foreseeability of consequences. The test of whether a negligent act or omission is a proximate cause of an injury is whether the wrongdoer might by the exercise of ordinary care have foreseen that *some similar injury* might result from the negligence.

The United States argues with much force that the district court found that fault or negligence of the owners caused the fire and permitted it to increase in intensity, and that the fire caused the disastrous explosion. It insists that that causal connection is sufficient. The fallacy in that chain of argument is that it is only the operation of natural forces theretofore recognized as normal which one is charged with foreseeing.

The district court found it "undoubtedly true that the force and devastating effects of this explosion shocked and surprised the scientific field as well as the transportation industry." The court further found as to ammonium nitrate, which constituted approximately 95 percent of the FGAN, and which, with the benefit of hindsight, we now know to be the explosive part of the mixture:

Despite its use as a principal ingredient of high explosives, at the time of the disaster ammonium nitrate was not, and is not now, classified as an "explosive" for transportation purposes by the Interstate Commerce Commission or the Coast Guard. This is true because it was considered that to cause the detonation of ammonium nitrate, an initial shock or "booster" of considerable magnitude was required. The chances of such an initial or booster detonation being encountered in normal conditions of transportation has always been considered so remote as to be negligible.

Substantially all of the evidence is to the effect that the explosion, as distinguished from the fire, could not reasonably have been foreseen.

It would be ironic indeed if the United States were permitted to impose liability for these claims on the Republic of France and the French Line by claiming now that, unlike the officials and employees of the United States, the officials and employees of the French Government and the master of the *Grandchamp* should have known that FGAN was a dangerous explosive and that an explosion from fire should reasonably have been anticipated.

Judgment reversed in favor of the Republic of France.

Superseding Causes In some cases, an *intervening force* occurring after a defendant's negligence may play a significant role in bringing about a particular plaintiff's injury. For example, a high wind may spring up that causes a fire set by Davis to spread and damage Parker's property, or, after Davis negligently runs Parker down with his car, a thief may steal Parker's wallet while he is lying unconscious in the street. Such cases present difficult problems for the courts, which must decide when an intervening force should relieve a negligent defendant from liability. As the following *Nixon* case indicates, if the intervening force is a *foreseeable* one, either because it frequently occurs in the ordinary course of human events or because the defendant's negligence substantially increases the risk of its occurrence, it will *not* relieve the defendant from liability. So, in the first example given above, if high winds are a reasonably common occurrence in the locality in question, Davis may be liable for the damage to Parker's property even though his fire would not have spread that far under the wind conditions that existed when he started it. Likewise, in our second example, Davis may be responsible for the theft of Parker's wallet if the theft is foreseeable, given the time and location of the accident.

On the other hand, if the intervening force that contributes to the plaintiff's injury is unforeseeable, most courts hold that it is a **superseding** or **intervening cause** that absolves the defendant of any liability for negligence. For example, Dalton negligently starts a fire that causes injury to several persons. The driver of an ambulance summoned to the scene to aid the injured has been drinking on duty and, as a result, loses control of his ambulance and runs up onto a sidewalk, injuring several pedestrians. Most courts would not hold Dalton responsible for the pedestrians' injuries. One important exception to this general rule, however, concerns intervening forces that produce a harm identical to the harm risked by the defendant's negligence. For example, the owners of a concert hall fail to install the number of emergency exits required by law for the protection of patrons. A negligently operated aircraft crashes into the hall during a concert, and many patrons are burned to death in the ensuing fire because the few available exits are jammed by panicked patrons trying to escape. Most courts would probably find that the owners of the hall were liable for the patrons' deaths.

NIXON v. MR. PROPERTY MANAGEMENT

690 S.W. 2d 546 (Tex. Sup. Ct. 1985)

At about 7:00 P.M. on August 7, 1981, a young man abducted R.M.V., age 10, from the sidewalk in front of her home and dragged her across the street to a vacant apartment at the Chalmette Apartments. He raped her, put her in the closet, told her not to leave, and disappeared. The apartment in question was described by the police officer called to the scene as "empty, filthy, dirty, and full of debris." Glass was broken from its windows and the front door was off its hinges.

In the two years prior to the attack on R.M.V., Dallas police had investigated numerous crimes committed at the Chalmette Apartments complex, including 1 attempted murder, 2 robberies, 2 aggravated assaults, 16 apartment burglaries, 4 vehicle burglaries, 4 cases of theft, and 5 cases of criminal mischief. A Dallas City Ordinance established minimum standards for property owners, requiring them, among other things, to "keep the doors and windows of a vacant structure or vacant portion of a structure securely closed to prevent unauthorized entry." Gaile Nixon, R.M.V.'s mother, filed a negligence suit against Brett Davis, Chalmette's owner, and Mr. Property Management Company, Inc., the manager of the complex. When the trial court granted a summary judgment in favor of Davis and Mr. Property, Nixon appealed.

Hill, Chief Justice. In affirming the trial court's judgment, the court of appeals held that, since R.M.V. was on Mr. Property's property without its knowledge and consent, R.M.V. was a trespasser and Mr. Property's duty toward her was no greater than not to injure her willfully, wantonly, or through gross negligence. The court also held that the condition of the apartment complex was not a proximate cause of the rape because R.M.V.'s abduction and rape were not a reasonably foreseeable consequence thereof.

In this case, the question of what duty Mr. Property owed to R.M.V. is answered by the ordinance. This ordinance legislatively imposes a standard of conduct which we adopt to define the conduct of a reasonably prudent person. The unexcused violation of a statute or ordinance constitutes negligence as a matter of law if such statute or ordinance was designed to prevent injury to the class of persons to which the injured party belongs. A reasonable interpretation of this ordinance is that it was designed to deter criminal activity by reducing the conspicuous opportunities for criminal conduct. An ordinance requiring apartment owners to do their part in deterring crime is designed to prevent injury to the general public. R.M.V. falls within this class. Since the ordinance was meant to protect a larger class than invitees and licensees, and since R.M.V. committed no wrong in coming onto the property, these premise liability distinctions are irrelevant to our analysis.

Using the mandated standard for reviewing summary judgment, we conclude that a genuine issue of material fact exists as to Mr. Property's breach of duty. If the trier of fact concludes that Mr. Property violated the ordinance without a valid excuse, Mr. Property is negligent per se. This does not end our inquiry; we must still determine if there is a material fact issue on the question of proximate cause.

The two elements of proximate cause are cause in fact and foreseeability. Cause in fact denotes that the negligent act or omission was a substantial factor in bringing about the injury and without it no harm would have been incurred. Viewing the summary judgment as we must, drawing all reasonable inferences in favor of R.M.V., we conclude that a reasonable inference exists that, but for Mr. Property's failure to comply with the ordinance regarding maintenance of its apartment complex, this crime would have never taken place. There is evidence that the assailant took R.M.V. "directly to a vacant apartment," the inference being that the assailant was acutely aware of the vacant unit's existence and embarked upon his course of criminal conduct at this particular time and place knowing that this unit was an easily accessible place in which to perpetrate this assault in isolation.

Finally, we turn to the question of foreseeability. Foreseeability means that the actor, as a person of ordinary intelligence, should have anticipated the dangers that his negligent act created for others. Usually, the criminal conduct of a third party is a superseding cause relieving the negligent actor from liability. However, the tortfeasor's negligence will not be excused where the criminal conduct is a foreseeable result of such negligence. The evidence is replete with instances of prior violent crimes occurring at Chalmette Apartments. This record certainly provides evidence that further acts of violence were reasonably foreseeable. Evidence of specific previous crimes on or near the premises raises a fact issue on the foreseeability of criminal activity.

Judgment reversed in favor of Nixon; case remanded for trial.

Generally Accepted Causation Rules   Whatever test for proximate cause a court says it adopts, most courts generally agree on certain basic principles of causation. One such basic principle is that persons guilty of negligence "take their victims as they find them." This means that a negligent defendant is liable for the full extent of his victim's injuries even if those injuries are aggravated by some preexisting physical characteristic of the victim. Similarly, negligent defendants are normally held liable for diseases contracted by their victims while in a weakened state caused by their injuries. They are *jointly* liable—along with the attending physician—

for negligent medical care that their victims receive for their injuries.

Negligent defendants also are commonly held responsible for injuries sustained by persons seeking to avoid being injured by the defendant's negligence. For example, Peters swerves to avoid being hit by Denning's negligently driven car and in the process loses control of her own car and is injured. Denning is liable for Peters's injuries. Finally, it is commonly said that "danger invites rescue." This means that negligent persons are liable to those injured in attempting to rescue the victims of their negligence. One corollary of this rescue rule is that the claim of a would-be rescuer ordinarily is not defeated by contributory fault on the part of the rescuer so long as he is not reckless in making the rescue attempt.

Res Ipsa Loquitur

In some cases, negligence may be difficult to prove because the defendant has superior knowledge of the circumstances surrounding the plaintiff's injury. Thus, it may not be in the defendant's best interests to disclose those circumstances if they point to liability on his part. Consider, for example, the position of a person who goes into the hospital for an appendectomy and awakens after the operation to find that both of his legs have been amputated. Since he was anesthetized during the operation, he has no way of knowing what caused his loss. The only persons who do know are the hospital personnel who performed the operation, but the odds are that they are the ones responsible for the tragedy. The doctrine of *res ipsa loquitur* ("the thing speaks for itself") can aid such a plaintiff in proving his case. *Res ipsa* applies when (1) the defendant has *exclusive control* of the instrumentality of harm (and therefore probable knowledge of, and responsibility for, the cause of the harm), (2) the harm that occurred *would not ordinarily occur* in the absence of negligence, and (3) the plaintiff was in no way responsible for his own injury. When these elements are present, most states hold that an *inference* may arise that the defendant was negligent and that her negligence was the cause of the plaintiff's injury. Practically speaking, this may force the defendant to come forward with evidence to rebut the inference that she is responsible. If she fails to do so, a court or jury *may* choose to impose liability on her. Some courts, however, give *res ipsa* much greater effect, holding that it creates a *presumption* of negligence that requires a directed verdict for the plaintiff in the absence of proof by the defendant rebutting the presumption.

Injury

The plaintiff in a negligence case must prove not only that the defendant breached a duty owed to the plaintiff and that the breach of duty was the legal cause of her injury, but also that the resulting injury was to an interest that the law seeks to protect. Ordinarily, purely physical injuries to a person or her property present no problem in this respect, because the law has long protected such interests. Serious problems arise, however, when injuries are purely *emotional* in nature. As you learned in the Intentional Torts chapter, the law has long demonstrated a considerable reluctance to afford recovery for purely emotional harms. The courts' reluctance is due, among other things, to the danger of spurious claims and the difficulty inherent in placing a monetary value on emotional injuries. Given our great reluctance to impose liability for purely emotional harms caused by intentional wrongs, one might correctly assume that an even greater reluctance would exist when the conduct producing an emotional injury was merely negligent.

Negligent Infliction of Emotional Distress   Until fairly recently, most courts would not allow a plaintiff to recover for emotional injuries resulting from a defendant's negligent behavior in the absence of some impact or contact with the plaintiff's person. Today, many courts have abandoned the impact rule and allow recovery for foreseeable emotional injuries standing alone. A large number of such courts, however, still require, as a precondition of recovery, proof that some serious physical injury or symptoms resulted from the plaintiff's emotional distress. Nonetheless, a growing number of courts have dispensed with the injury requirement where the plaintiff has suffered serious emotional distress as a foreseeable consequence of the defendant's negligent conduct.

Third-Party Emotional Distress   In recent years, more and more negligence cases have involved claims by third persons for emotional injuries that they suffered by witnessing a negligently caused harm to another person, usually a spouse or child. For example, Mr. Porter has a heart attack after seeing Mrs. Porter run down by a car negligently driven by Denton. Is Denton liable for Mr. Porter's injury? Until fairly recently, most courts would have denied Mr. Porter any recovery on the ground that he had suffered no impact as a result of Denton's negligence. In recent years, however, many courts have abandoned the impact rule in third-party cases in favor of the "zone of danger" test. This test allows third parties who are themselves in the zone of danger created by a defendant's negligence to recover for emotional injuries resulting from the threat of harm to them, regardless of whether any impact ever occurred. Courts following this rule would, therefore, allow Mr. Porter to recover if he was close enough to his wife to be in danger of being hit by Denton's car. Some courts would insist, in addition, that Mr. Porter prove that he suffered some physical injury as a result of his emotional distress.

Today, some courts have abandoned the zone of danger requirement entirely and allow recovery for emotional injuries suffered by third parties, regardless of whether there was any threat of injury to them. However, as the following *Mazzagatti* case indicates,

most courts that have taken this step still attempt to limit recovery in a variety of ways. For example, such courts commonly require that a close personal relationship exist between the third-party plaintiff and the direct victim of the defendant's negligence and that the third party's emotional distress result from actually witnessing the injury to the direct victim. Also, they impose a requirement that the third party demonstrate some physical "injury" resulting from his emotional distress. This area of the law is undergoing rapid development, however, and some recent cases may be found dispensing with the injury requirement or allowing recovery for emotional distress suffered as a result of seeing the direct victim in an injured state shortly after the injury occurred.

MAZZAGATTI v. EVERINGHAM

516 A.2d 672 (Pa. Sup. Ct. 1986)

On August 12, 1980, 14-year-old Mumtaz Mazzagatti was struck and fatally injured by a car driven by Ricky Allen Everingham. Mazzagatti had been riding her bike in the residential area near her home. At the time of the accident her mother, Jane Mazzagatti, was at work, approximately one mile away. She received a telephone call immediately after the collision informing her that her daughter had been involved in an automobile accident. She arrived on the scene a few minutes later and saw her daughter lying in the road. She filed a negligent infliction of emotional distress suit against Everingham. In her complaint she alleged that she "became hysterical, unnerved, and emotionally shattered" at the sight of her injured daughter and that as a result of the observation, she suffered shock to her nervous system and grievous mental pain and suffering, resulting in severe depression and an acute nervous condition. She also alleged that she was tortured by flashbacks and nightmares in which she saw Mumtaz lying in the road. When the trial court granted a summary judgment in favor of Everingham, Mazzagatti appealed.

Nix, Chief Justice. In *Sinn v. Burd*, we were confronted with the issue whether a close relative who witnessed the accident, albeit outside of the zone of danger, could recover for the negligent infliction of emotional distress. We concluded that in such instances the defendant did owe a duty of care to the bystander, noting that "the scope of potential liability commonly finds theoretical expression in such concepts as duty and proximate cause." We held that the resultant harm was foreseeable and stated:

We are confident that the application of the traditional tort concept of foreseeability will reasonably circumscribe the tortfeasor's liability in such cases. Foreseeability enters into the determination of liability in determining whether the emotional injuries sustained by the plaintiff were reasonably foreseeable to the defendant.

We adopted the *Dillon v. Legg* (Cal. Sup. Ct. 1968), parameters for determining whether the infliction of emotional distress was reasonably foreseeable. We held that a cause of action is stated when the following criteria are met:

(1) Whether plaintiff was located near the scene of the accident as contrasted with one who was a distance away from it;

(2) Whether the shock resulted from a direct emotional impact upon plaintiff from the sensory and contemporaneous observance of the accident, as contrasted with learning of the accident from others after its occurrence;

(3) Whether plaintiff and the victim were closely related as contrasted with an absence of any relationship or the presence of only a distant relationship.

In *Sinn* the plaintiff-mother was present at the time of the accident and actually witnessed the injury to her child. We thus found a contemporaneous observation of the accident which proximately caused emotional distress to the mother. We limited our holding solely to those cases in which the plaintiff alleges psychic injury as a result of actually witnessing the defendant's negligent act.

When a plaintiff is a distance away from the scene of the accident and learns of the accident from others after its occurrence rather than from a contemporaneous observance, the sum total of policy considerations weigh against the conclusion that that particular plaintiff is legally entitled to protection from the harm suffered. We believe that where the close relative is not present at the scene of the accident, but instead learns of the accident from a third party, the close relative's prior knowledge of the injury to the victim serves as a buffer against the full impact of observing the accident scene. By contrast, the relative who contemporaneously observes the tortious conduct has no time span in which to brace his or her emotional system. The negligent tortfeasor inflicts upon this bystander an injury separate and apart from the injury to the victim. Hence, the critical element for establishing such liability is the contemporaneous observance of the injury to the close relative. Where, as here, the plaintiff has no contemporaneous sensory perception of the injury, the emotional distress results more from the particular emotional makeup of the plaintiff rather than from the nature of defendant's actions.

In reality this is a claim for affectional loss or solatium to recompense a surviving relative for her feelings of anguish, bereavement and grief caused by the fact of the injury to and death of the decedent. In *Sinn* we noted that the common law has traditionally denied a damage award for solatium. The feelings of anguish and bereavement suffered by Mazzagatti are not substantially different from those suffered by any parent who sees his or her dying injured child, whether it be at the scene of the accident or in the hospital room afterwards.

Judgment for Everingham affirmed.

Defenses to Negligence

The common law traditionally recognized two defenses to negligence: **contributory negligence** and **assumption of risk.** Both of these defenses are based on the idea of *contributory fault*: If a plaintiff's own behavior contributed in some way to his injury, this fact should relieve the defendant from liability. As the following paragraphs indicate, however, the contributory fault idea often produced harsh results, and recent years have witnessed a significant erosion of its impact in negligence cases.

Contributory Negligence   The doctrine of *contributory negligence* provides that plaintiffs who *fail to exercise reasonable care for their own safety* are totally

FIGURE 1   Plaintiff's Recovery under Contributory and Comparative Negligence Systems

Plaintiff's Relative Fault	Contributory Negligence	Comparative Negligence (Pure)	Comparative Negligence (Mixed)
0%	100%	100%	100%
10	0	90	90
60	0	40	0
90	0	10	0

barred from any recovery if their contributory negligence is a *substantial factor* in producing their injury. So, if Parker steps into the path of Dworkin's speeding car without first checking to see whether any cars are coming, Parker would be denied any recovery against Dworkin because of the clear causal relationship between his injury and his failure to exercise reasonable care for his own safety. On the other hand, if Parker is injured one night when his speeding car crashes into a large, unmarked hole in the street caused by a city street repair project, and the facts indicate that the accident would have occurred even if Parker had been driving at a legal speed, he is not barred from recovering damages from the city for its negligence.

In some cases, a contributorily negligent plaintiff may be able to overcome an otherwise valid contributory negligence defense by arguing that the defendant had the **last clear chance** to avoid harm. The doctrine of last clear chance focuses on who was *last* at fault *in time*. Therefore, if despite the plaintiff's contributory negligence, the harm could have been avoided if the defendant had exercised reasonable care, the defendant's *superior opportunity* to avoid the accident makes him more at fault. For example, Durban pulls into the path of Preston's speeding car without looking, causing an accident. When Preston files suit to recover for the damage, Durban argues that the fact that Preston was speeding amounts to contributory negligence. If Preston can convince the court that the accident could have been avoided if Durban had looked before pulling onto the highway, she has a good chance of overcoming Durban's contributory negligence defense.

Comparative Negligence   Contributory negligence can sometimes produce harsh results because it may operate to prevent slightly negligent persons from recovering any compensation for their losses. In reaction to this potential unfairness, a growing majority of the states have adopted **comparative negligence** systems either by statute or by judicial decision. The details of these systems vary by state, but the principle underlying them is essentially the same: Courts seek to determine the *relative fault* of the parties to a negligence action and award damages in proportion to the degree of fault determined. For a simple example, assume that Dunne negligently injures Porter and Porter suffers $10,000 in damages. A jury, however, determines that Porter was 20 percent at fault. Under a comparative negligence system, Porter could recover only $8,000 from Dunne. But what if Porter is determined to be 60 percent at fault? Here, the results vary depending on whether the state in question has adopted a *pure* or a *mixed* comparative fault system. Under a pure comparative fault system, plaintiffs are allowed to recover a portion of their damages even if they are more at fault than the defendant, so Porter could recover $4,000. Under a mixed system, plaintiffs who are as much at fault as, or, in some states, more at fault than, the defendant are denied any recovery. Such a state refuses Porter any recovery, just as though contributory negligence principles still applied. Figure 1 graphically illustrates the effects of the various ways of handling plaintiffs' contributory fault.

The full extent of the impact that comparative fault systems will have on tort law is as yet undetermined. What is clear, however, is that comparative fault is affecting other tort doctrines besides contributory negligence. For example, as the following *Roggow* case indicates, many comparative negligence states have discarded the doctrine of last clear chance. In addition, some states now apply comparative fault principles to recklessness and strict liability cases, as well as to negligence cases.

ROGGOW v. MINERAL PROCESSING CORP.

698 F. Supp. 1441 (S.D. Ind. 1988)

Charles Roggow, a long-distance truck driver out of Buffalo, New York, made a delivery of scrap aluminum to a processing plant located in Needmore, Indiana, and owned by Mineral Processing Corporation—Needmore Division (Needmore). After making delivery, Roggow was to pick up an unloaded trailer. Because Needmore's employees had failed to secure the header bar of the trailer (the part that secures the sides of the trailer to prevent damaging vibration), Roggow had to fasten the bar before leaving Needmore's plant. The bar had to be set in place at the very top of the trailer, but Needmore had no ladder available for Roggow's use. Consequently, Tracy Phillips, a Needmore employee, offered to assist Roggow by placing him in the bucket of a highloader and raising him high enough to set the bar in place.

Roggow accepted the offer and succeeded in fastening the header bar, but as Phillips was lowering him to the ground, Phillips's sleeve caught the highloader's dump lever, causing the bucket to overturn and dump Roggow approximately 9 feet onto a concrete floor. Roggow filed suit against Needmore. The jury found Roggow's damages to be $80,000, but reduced his award to $48,000 because they found him to be 40 percent at fault. Roggow filed a motion for a new trial, arguing, among other things, that the trial court erred in refusing to instruct the jury on the doctrine of last clear chance.

Endsley, U.S. Magistrate.   This matter was tried under Indiana's Comparative Fault Act (the Act). Prior to the enactment of comparative fault, Indiana followed the common law rule of contributory negligence. This antiquated "all-or-nothing" rule totally bars a plaintiff from recovering damages for injuries if he is guilty of negligence, albeit slight. During the twentieth century, common law doctrines were developed to alleviate the harsh results of contributory negligence. Last clear chance was one of those doctrines. Roggow now invites the Court to determine the applicability of this exception to contributory negligence under the Act even though the statute is silent and no Indiana court of review has yet passed on these issues.

Because no Indiana court has addressed this issue, this federal court must determine how the highest court in Indiana would decide this issue if it were presented with the question. Under the Act, assumption of risk is not available as an absolute defense for the defendant. Specifically, "assumption of risk not constituting an enforceable express consent" is a factor to be considered by the fact finder when weighing the fault attibutable to the individual actors. Similarly, by its definition in the Act, "fault" necessarily includes the factors which make up last clear chance. The Indiana legislature defined fault as "any act or omission that is negligent, willful, wanton, or reckless toward the person or property of the actor or others." Consequently, just as assumed risk is no longer available to completely excuse the negligence of the defendant, so too, this Court believes, is the doctrine of last clear chance no longer available to completely excuse the negligence of the plaintiff. This conclusion is in accord with the holdings and statutes of a majority of states which have addressed the issue. Consequently, failure to give Roggow's tendered instruction was not error in this case.

Motion for new trial denied.

FIGURE 2   Elements of Negligence

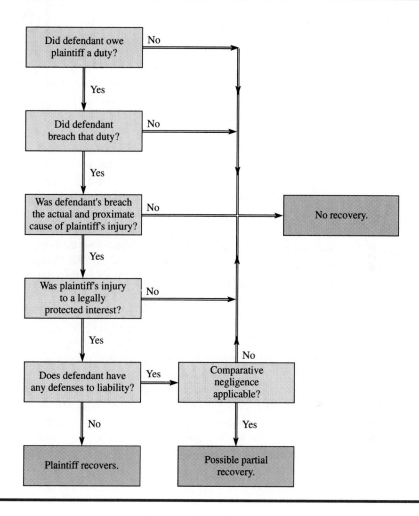

Assumption of Risk   In some cases, a plaintiff has *voluntarily* exposed herself to a *known danger* created by the defendant's negligence. Such plaintiffs are said to have *assumed the risk* of their injury and ordinarily are denied any recovery for it. The idea here is that the plaintiff *impliedly* consented to accept the risk, thereby relieving the defendant of the duty to protect her against it. For example, Stevens voluntarily goes for a ride in Markley's car, even though Markley has told her that his brakes are not working properly. Stevens has assumed the risk of injury as a result of the car's defective brakes. A person must fully understand the nature and extent of the risk, however, to be held to have assumed it. A plaintiff can also assume the risk of injury *expressly* by enter-ing a contract containing a provision purporting to relieve the defendant of a duty of care that he would otherwise owe to the plaintiff. Such contract provisions are called *exculpatory clauses*. The Illegality chapter discusses in detail exculpatory clauses and the numerous limitations that courts have imposed on their enforceability. As the *Roggow* case indicated, some states that have adopted comparative negligence systems have done away with the assumption of risk defense in negligence cases and treat all forms of contributory fault under their compara-tive negligence scheme. The following *Hull* case, how-ever, proves that assumption of risk remains a viable defense in some jurisdictions. Figure 2 graphically illus-trates all of the elements of a negligence case.

HULL v. MERCK & CO., INC.

758 F. 2d 1474 (11th Cir. 1985)

On September 4, 1980, Augusta Fiberglass Coatings (AFC) began work replacing fiberglass sewer lines at three adjacent Albany, Georgia, chemical plants operated by Merck & Co., Inc. The lines delivered waste chemicals into a 1-million-gallon neutralizing pool. Merck warned AFC that it intended to continue in operation throughout the replacement activity, and that bypass pipes and various safety equipment would be necessary to the work. AFC relayed Merck's warnings to its employees and provided them with rubber boots, pants, coats, and gloves, as well as goggles and masks.

Jim Dale Hull was AFC's supervisor on the job at Merck. Although Hull had substantial experience working with chemicals, he quit wearing any of the safety gear after a few days on the job. Hull spent four hours each day in the trench dug to expose the pipelines. He regularly breathed gases and allowed liquid to spill on his clothing and body. He noted at the time that the chemical fumes in and around the pipes were a health hazard. On September 22, 1980, Hull stuck his head inside a 20-inch connecting pipe that, due to an accidental spill in the factories, contained an 80 to 85 percent solution of toluene, rather than the 2 percent solution the pipes were supposed to carry. He became dizzy and nauseous and was given oxygen at the plant infirmary.

Within a year after completion of the Merck contract, Hull suffered bone marrow depression, followed by leukemia. Hull sued Merck for $2.5 million plus punitive damages, alleging that (1) Merck had negligently failed to disclose the nature and health dangers of the waste chemicals carried by the pipelines, (2) Merck had negligently failed to inform him adequately of the necessity for wearing protective gear during construction, (3) the intermittent discharge without warning of high-concentration spills into the pipelines resulted from the negligent operation of the factories, and (4) Merck's decision to continue plant operations and consequently the flow of waste chemicals during the pipeline replacement project amounted to negligence. After being charged by the trial judge that assumption of risk on Hull's part would bar his recovery under Georgia's comparative fault law, the jury ruled in favor of Merck. Hull appealed.

Per Curiam. Under Georgia law, a plaintiff assumes the risk when he "deliberately chooses an obviously perilous course of conduct and fully appreciates the danger involved." The plaintiff must do so voluntarily, "without restriction from his freedom of choice either by the circumstances or by coercion." Georgia typically applies assumption of risk to situations where the plaintiff races to beat a train at a crossing, drag races, or walks onto a pond covered with thin ice. Although assumption of the risk presupposes awareness of the nature and extent of the threat posed, perfect knowledge is not necessary. But Georgia law offers little guidance as to the depth of knowledge a plaintiff must possess to assume the sometimes very subtle risks posed by chemical exposure.

There was ample evidence to justify the charge in this case, especially as it pertained to Hull's allegation that Merck negligently decided to operate the factories during the replacement of the pipelines. Hull knew before he ever entered the plant grounds that Merck and AFC planned for operations to continue, with waste chemicals to be expelled via a bypass system of hoses assembled by AFC workers. Although Hull might or might not have had knowledge of any specific carcinogenic risk posed by toluene, he knew from long experience that the handling of waste chemicals warranted protective measures, and that coping with a continued flow of waste warranted an even greater degree of caution.

He also knew Merck and AFC were supplying adequate safety gear, which he used only for the first few days, but which many of his coworkers wore throughout the project without hampering their work. The gear remained available for his use at all times. He testified that while he was working he concluded the fumes were dangerous to good health. Finally, his severe exposure on September 22, 1980 forcefully brought home the risk posed by Merck's operations, yet he voluntarily remained, exposing himself for another month or more. The evidence at the trial left the jury free to conclude that Hull's leukemia was caused by post-September 22nd exposure, and Hull's remaining after that date might be construed as a knowing assumption of all four of the risks arising from Merck's alleged negligence. In any case, there was more than enough evidence to warrant the jury finding that Hull assumed the risk posed by working around a continuing flow of waste chemicals during the replacement of the pipes.

Judgment for Merck affirmed.

RECKLESSNESS

Behavior that indicates a conscious disregard for a known high risk of probable harm to others amounts to **recklessness.** In terms of the moral culpability of the defendant, recklessness lies midway between intentional wrongdoing and negligence. Recklessness involves conduct posing a foreseeable risk of harm to others, but that risk of harm must be significantly greater than the degree of risk necessary to make conduct negligent. In recklessness, as in negligence, the objective reasonable person test is applied to the defendant. Would a reasonable person, knowing all the facts at the defendant's disposal, have perceived the aggravated risk of harm to others that resulted from her conduct?

Proof of reckless behavior offers a plaintiff several significant advantages over proof of mere negligence. First, as a general rule, mere contributory negligence on the part of the plaintiff does *not* prevent recovery for recklessly caused injuries. Only proof that the plaintiff acted in reckless disregard for his own safety or assumed the risk of injury created by the defendant's recklessness operates as a defense to recklessness. For example, Roberts bets his friends that he can drive down a busy street blindfolded. In doing so, he runs down Mann. Because Roberts's conduct amounted to recklessness, the fact that Mann stepped into the path of Roberts's car without looking would *not* bar Mann's recovery. However, if Mann saw Roberts's car weaving down the road and still attempted to cross the street in front of it, or if Mann had bet Roberts's friends that he could run in front of the car without being hit, Mann *would* be denied any recovery. Also, as a general rule, courts are more willing to find that a reckless defendant's conduct was the legal cause of a plaintiff's injuries than they would be if the defendant's conduct was merely negligent. Finally, because reckless-

ness involves a higher degree of fault than negligence, a plaintiff who can prove recklessness on the defendant's part stands a good chance of recovering punitive as well as compensatory damages. Ordinarily, compensatory damages are the only damages recoverable for mere negligence.

STRICT LIABILITY

Introduction

In addition to intentional wrongdoing and negligence, the third fundamental basis of tort liability is **strict liability.** Strict liability means that defendants who participate in certain harm-producing activities may be held *strictly liable* for any harm that results to others, even though they did not intend to cause the harm and did everything in their power to prevent it. Also, defendants in strict liability cases traditionally have fewer defenses to liability than do defendants in negligence cases. This is because most courts hold that contributory negligence is *not* a defense to strict liability, although assumption of risk is a good defense. The imposition of strict liability represents a social policy decision that the risk associated with an activity should be borne by those who pursue it, rather than by wholly innocent persons who are exposed to that risk.

Such liability has been justified either by the defendant's voluntary decision to engage in a particularly risky activity or, more recently, by the defendant's superior ability to bear losses. Thus, corporations are often said to be superior to individuals as risk-bearers due to their ability to pass the costs of liability on to consumers in the form of higher prices for goods or services. The owners of trespassing livestock and the keepers of naturally dangerous wild animals were among the first classes of defendants on whom the courts imposed strict liability. Today, the two most important activities subject to judicially imposed strict liability are *abnormally dangerous (or ultrahazardous) activities* and the *manufacture or sale of defective and unreasonably dangerous products*. The Product Liability chapter discusses the product liability dimension of strict liability in detail.

Abnormally Dangerous Activities

Abnormally dangerous activities are those that *necessarily involve a risk of harm to others that cannot be eliminated by the exercise of reasonable care.* Activities that have been classed as abnormally dangerous include blasting, crop dusting, stunt flying, and, in one case, the transportation of large quantities of gasoline by truck. The following *American Cyanamid* case discusses the numerous factors that courts must consider before deciding whether a particular activity should be classified as abnormally dangerous. It also illustrates the fact that the greater the social utility attached to an activity and the greater the costs of minimizing the risk associated with that activity, the less likely a court is to label the activity as an abnormally dangerous one.

INDIANA HARBOR BELT RAILROAD CO. v. AMERICAN CYANAMID CO.
916 F. 2d 1174 (7th Cir. 1990)

On January 9, 1979, a railroad car leased by American Cyanamid Co. (American) and containing 20,000 gallons of acrylonitrile manufactured by American began leaking. At the time, the car was sitting just south of Chicago in the Blue Island yard of the Indiana Harbor Belt Railroad Co. (Indiana) awaiting switching to Conrail for delivery to its final destination. Indiana's employees were able to stop the leak, but were uncertain about how much of the car's contents had escaped. Because acrylonitrile (a chemical used in the manufacture of plastics, dyes, acrylic fibers, and pharmaceutical chemicals) is flammable, highly toxic, and possibly carcinogenic, Illinois authorities ordered homes near the yard temporarily evacuated.

Later, it was discovered that only about one quarter of the car's contents had leaked, but the Illinois Department of Environmental Protection, fearing that the soil and water had been contaminated, ordered Indiana to take decontamination measures costing $981,000. Indiana filed suit against American on negligence and strict liability theories seeking to recover its expenses. When the trial court dismissed Indiana's negligence claim but entered summary judgment for Indiana on the strict liability claim, both parties appealed.

Posner, Circuit Judge. The question whether the shipper of a hazardous chemical by rail should be strictly liable for the consequences of a spill or other accident to the shipment en route is a novel one in Illinois. The parties agree that the question is a question of law, so we owe no particular deference to the conclusion of the district court. They also agree that the Supreme Court of Illinois would treat as authoritative the provisions of the *Restatement (Second) of Torts* governing abnormally dangerous activities. The key provision is section 520, which sets forth six factors to be considered in deciding whether an activity is abnormally dangerous.

The roots of section 520 are in nineteenth-century cases. The most famous one is *Rylands v. Fletcher* (1868), but a more illuminating one in the present context is *Guille v. Swan*, 19 Johns. (N.Y.) 381 (1822). A man took off in a hot-air balloon and landed, without intending to, in a vegetable garden in New York City. A crowd that had been anxiously watching his involuntary descent trampled the vegetables in their endeavor to rescue him when he landed. The owner of the garden sued the balloonist for the resulting damage, and won. Yet the balloonist had not been careless. In the then state of ballooning it was impossible to make a pinpoint landing.

Guille was a paradigmatic case for strict liability. (a) The risk (probability) of harm was great, and (b) the harm that would ensue if the risk materialized could be, although luckily was not, great (the balloonist could have crashed into the crowd). The confluence of these two factors established the urgency of seeking to prevent such accidents. (c) Yet such accidents could not be prevented by the exercise of due care; the technology of ballooning was insufficiently developed. (d) The activity was not a matter of common usage, so there was no presumption that it was a highly valuable activity despite its unavoidable riskiness. (e) The activity was inappropriate to the place in which it took place—densely populated New York City. (f) Reinforcing (d), the value to the community of the activity of recreational ballooning did not appear to be great enough to offset its unavoidable risks.

These are, of course, the six factors in section 520. Each is a different facet of a common quest for a proper legal regime to govern accidents that negligence liability cannot adequately control. The interrelations might be more perspicuous if the six factors were reordered. One might for example start with (c), inability to eliminate the risk of an accident by the exercise of due care. The baseline common law regime of tort liability is negligence. When it is a workable regime, because the hazards of an activity can be avoided by being careful, there is no need to switch to strict liability. Sometimes, however, a particular type of accident cannot be prevented by taking care but can be avoided, or its consequences minimized, by shifting the activity to another locale, where the risk or harm of an accident will be less [(e)]. By making the actor strictly liable—by denying him in other words an excuse based on his inability to avoid accidents by being more careful—we give him an incentive, missing in negligence, to experiment with methods of preventing accidents that involve not greater exertions of care, assumed to be futile, but instead relocating, changing or reducing (perhaps to the vanishing point) the activity giving rise to the accident.

The greater the risk of an accident [(a)] and the costs of an accident if one occurs [(b)], the more we want the actor to consider the possibility of making accident-reducing activity changes; the stronger, therefore, is the case for strict liability. Finally, if an activity is extremely common [(d)], like driving an automobile, it is unlikely either that its hazards are perceived as great or that there is no technology of care available to minimize them; so the case for strict liability is weakened.

Against this background we turn to the particulars of acrylonitrile, one of a large number of chemicals that are hazardous in the sense of being flammable, toxic, or both. A table in the record contains a list of 125 hazardous materials that are shipped in highest volume on the nation's railroads. Acrylonitrile is the 53rd most hazardous on the list. Among the other materials that rank higher on the hazard scale are phosphorous (number 1), anhydrous ammonia, liquified petroleum gas, vinyl chloride, gasoline, crude petroleum, motor fuel antiknock compound, methyl and ethyl chloride, sulphuric acid, and chloroform. The plaintiff's lawyer acknowledged at argument that the logic of the district court's opinion dictated strict liability for all 52 materials that rank higher than acrylonitrile on the list, and quite possibly for the 72 that rank lower as well, since all are hazardous if spilled in quantity while being shipped by rail. Every shipper of any of the materials would therefore be strictly liable for the consequences of a spill or other accident that occurred while the material was being shipped through a metropolitan area.

No cases recognize so sweeping a liability. Several reject it, though none has facts much like those of the present case. Cases that impose strict liability for the storage of a dangerous chemical provide a potentially helpful analogy to our case, but they can be distinguished on the ground that the storer (like the transporter) has more control than the shipper. So we can get little help from precedent, and might as well apply section 520 to the acrylonitrile problem from the ground up. To begin with, we have been given no reason for believing that negligence is not perfectly adequate to remedy and deter, at reasonable cost, the accidental spillage of acrylonitrile from rail cars. Although acrylonitrile is flammable and toxic, it is not so corrosive or otherwise destructive that it will eat through or otherwise damage or weaken a tank car's valves although they are maintained with due care. No one suggests that the leak in this case was caused by the inherent properties of acrylonitrile. It was caused by carelessness—whether that of the lessor in failing to maintain or inspect the car properly, or of American in failing to maintain or inspect it, or of the railroad which had custody of the car prior to Indiana, or of Indiana itself in failing to notice the ruptured lid which caused the leak, or some combination of these possible failures of care. Accidents due to a lack of care can be prevented by taking care; and when a lack of care can be shown in court, such accidents are adequately deterred by the threat of liability for negligence.

The district judge and the plaintiff's lawyer make much of the fact that the spill occurred in a densely populated metropolitan area. But this argument overlooks the fact that the railroad network is a hub-and-spoke system and the hubs are in metropolitan areas. With most hazardous chemicals (by volume of shipment) being at least as hazardous as acrylonitrile, it is unlikely that they can be rerouted around all metropolitan areas in the country, except at prohibitive cost. Even if it were feasible to reroute them one would hardly expect shippers, as distinct from carriers, to be the firms best situated to do the rerouting. The difference between shipper and carrier points to a deep flaw in the plaintiff's case. Unlike *Guille*, here it is not the actor—that is, the transporters of acrylonitrile and other chemicals—but the manufacturers, who are sought to be held strictly liable. Is it realistic to suppose that shippers will become students of railroading in order to lay out the safest route by which to ship their goods? Anyway, rerouting is no panacea. Often it will increase the length of the journey, or compel the use of poorer track, or both. When this happens, the probability of an accident is increased, even if the consequences of an accident if one occurs are reduced; so the expected accident cost, being the product of the probability of an accident and the harm if the accident occurs, may rise. It is easy to see how the accident in this case might have been prevented at reasonable cost by greater care on the part of those who handled the tank car of acrylonitrile. It is difficult to see how it might have been prevented at reasonable cost by a change in the activity of transporting the chemical. This is therefore not an apt case for strict liability.

Judgment of trial court reversed; case remanded for trial on the issue of negligence.

Statutory Strict Liability

Strict liability is not an exclusive creation of the courts. Strict liability principles are also embodied in modern legislation. The most important examples of this phenomenon are the *Workers' Compensation Acts* passed by most states in the early decades of this century. Such statutes allow employees to recover statutorily limited amounts from their employers despite the absence of any fault on the part of the employer or the presence of contributory fault on the part of the employee. Employers participate in a compulsory liability insurance system and are expected to pass the costs of the system on to consumers, who then become the ultimate bearers of the human costs of industrial production. Other examples of statutory strict liability include the Dram Shop statutes of some states; such laws impose liability on sellers of alcoholic beverages without proof of any negligence when third parties are harmed due to a buyer's intoxication. Also included is the statutory liability without proof of fault that some states impose on the operators of aircraft for ground damage resulting from aviation accidents.

TORT REFORM

By 1990, most states had enacted some form of tort reform legislation. The primary beneficiaries of such legislation were physicians, local governments, and manufacturers. The main driving force behind the tort reform movement is the "crisis" in the liability insurance system. In recent years, the insurance system has been characterized by outright refusals of coverage, reductions in coverage, and dramatically escalating premiums when coverage remains available. The supporters of tort reform argue that the main factors underlying the insurance crisis are the trend toward strict liability for various harms and escalating damage awards. Observers often attribute this latter factor to the increased frequency with which punitive damages are awarded and to a tendency toward more frequent damage awards for noneconomic harms, such as pain and suffering, in tort cases.

Tort reform advocates also argue that large jury awards contribute to inflation because, where market conditions permit, those who initially bear the cost of liability insurance will pass such costs on to their customers in the form of higher prices. Supporters of tort reform also argue that the threat of huge jury awards impedes the development of new products and technologies.

States have enacted a variety of devices in the name of tort reform. Statutes that limit the amounts recoverable for noneconomic harms are now fairly common, as are statutes that limit the liability of social hosts or businesses for the damage caused by intoxicated persons to whom they serve alcohol. Local governments in many states now enjoy statutory limits on their liability for negligence, affording them partial relief from the negligence claims for improper maintenance of streets and traffic signals; such claims now routinely accompany many automobile accident cases. Likewise, physicians in a number of states have received some relief from spiraling liability costs by reform devices such as caps on the amount recoverable in liability suits and mandatory pretrial mediation of all claims over a prescribed threshold. Finally, statutory ceilings on punitive damage awards or rules making such damages more difficult to recover are also common reform measures.

Critics of the tort reform movement argue that the liability insurance crisis is largely the fault of the insurance industry. Some have argued that insurers have manufactured the crisis to get unjustified premium increases and to divert attention from insurer mismanagement of invested premium income. Others argue that insurers are raising premiums to offset income losses resulting from the drop in interest rates in recent years. Whatever the truth of such allegations, it is becoming increasingly common for state legislatures to couple tort reform legislation with increased regulation of insurers, something that is understandably dulling the insurance industry's enthusiasm for tort reform. For example, Florida forced a rate rollback as a price of tort reform. Other common reform devices include requiring prior approval of rate increases and placing closer restraints on insurer policy cancellation and nonrenewal practices.

The battle for tort reform is far from over, however. Tort reform opponents who lost the fight against tort reform in the legislature have continued it in the courts. Thus, tort reform statutes have been challenged by arguments that statutes capping damage awards violate state constitutional provisions guaranteeing jury trials because they limit jury discretion in setting damages, and by arguments that reform measures targeted at certain types of cases (e.g., medical malpractice cases) violate equal protection guarantees by unjustifiably discriminating against plaintiffs in such cases. Such challenges have succeeded in some states and have been rebuffed in others. Whatever the outcome of the current struggle, the tort reform debate highlights the perennial dilemma facing tort law: how to fashion a system adequately compensating the victims of civil wrongs in an economically efficient manner that does not impose undue burdens on business or society as a whole.

ETHICAL AND PUBLIC POLICY CONCERNS

1. In the *Waters* case earlier in this chapter, the New York City Housing Authority escapes liability to Simone Waters because the court found they had no duty to her. Yet the investigator who testified at the trial said that Waters would probably not have been attacked if the Housing Authority properly maintained the locks on its building. If this testimony is true and the Housing Authority contributed in this way to the attack, does it have any ethical duty to Waters even if it has no legal duty?

2. Implicit in the idea of proximate cause is the fact that a negligent defendant can be the actual cause of some plaintiffs' injuries but avoid any liability for those injuries because his negligence was not the proximate cause of such injuries. Is the doctrine of proximate cause ethically justifiable?

3. While the doctrine of proximate cause allows defendants to avoid responsibility for some consequences of their negligence, the doctrine of strict liability imposes liability on persons who participate in abnormally dangerous activities even though they exercised all possible care to avoid injuring anyone. Can such liability be ethically justified?

SUMMARY

Negligence is the unintentional breach of a duty owed to another person that results in some legally recognizable injury to that person or her property. Each member of society has a general duty to conduct himself as would a reasonable person of ordinary prudence in similar circumstances. Other sources of duty include statutes and contractual or other special relationships between the parties. Statutory violations amount to negligence per se (a presumption of negligence) if they result in the suffering of a harm that the statute was designed to prevent by a person whom the statute was designed to protect.

Breach of duty results when a defendant exposes a person to whom the duty is owed to an unreasonable, foreseeable risk of harm. To determine whether a particular risk of harm is an unreasonable one, the courts balance the social utility of the defendant's conduct and the ease of reducing or eliminating the risk against the likelihood that harm will occur and the seriousness of the probable harm.

Breach of duty standing alone, however, does not produce negligence liability. The plaintiff in a negligence suit must also prove that the defendant's breach of duty was the actual and proximate (legal) cause of his injury. To determine the existence of actual cause, courts employ a "but for" or a "substantial factor" test. The courts have employed a variety of tests for proximate cause. The *Restatement (Second) of Torts* suggests that negligent defendants should not be held responsible for highly extraordinary consequences of their negligence. In some cases, intervening forces may combine with a negligent defendant's conduct to produce a particular plaintiff's injury. Whether such intervening forces amount to an intervening or superseding cause that absolves the defendant of liability depends on several factors. The most prominent factors are the foreseeability of the intervening force, whether the defendant's act increased the risk that the intervening force would come into play, and whether the resulting harm is similar in nature to the harm risked by the defendant's conduct.

In some cases, negligence may be difficult to prove because the person or persons who are most likely to be responsible for the plaintiff's injury have superior knowledge about the causes of the injury and a strong disincentive to share that knowledge with the plaintiff if it points to their liability. The doctrine of *res ipsa loquitur* aids plaintiffs in such cases by creating an inference of negligence when the harm that occurred would not ordinarily occur in the absence of negligence and the defendant had exclusive control of the instrumentality of harm. Where *res ipsa* applies, a defendant must come forward with evidence to rebut the inference that he was negligent and that his negligence caused the plaintiff's injury, or risk being found liable by a court or jury.

In recent years, there has been a trend toward increasing the kinds of injuries for which negligent defendants may be held responsible. Fearing spurious claims and concerned about the difficulties in evaluating purely emotional injuries, the courts long refused to allow persons who had suffered negligently inflicted emotional distress to recover for their injuries in the absence of some impact or physical contact with the victim. Recently, many courts have dispensed with the impact requirement, but many still require some physical injury or symptoms as a result of the victim's emotional distress before they allow recovery. Similarly, the courts traditionally refused to allow recovery for emotional distress caused by witnessing negligently inflicted harms to third persons in the absence of some impact with the person suffering the emotional injury. Today, many courts allow third parties who were themselves within the zone of danger created by the defendant's negligence to recover for their emotional injuries. Some courts have gone even farther and dispensed with the zone of danger requirement where the person injured was a close relative of the third party suffering emotional distress and the distress was the product of the third party's witnessing of the harm to the person injured. However, many courts taking this more liberal position still insist on proof of some physical injury or symptoms resulting from the third party's emotional distress.

Even if a defendant's breach of duty was the actual and proximate cause of a plaintiff's injury, contributory fault on the plaintiff's part can operate to bar or diminish the plaintiff's right to recover. The doctrine of contributory negligence bars any recovery by plaintiffs whose failure to exercise reasonable care for their own safety was a substantial factor in producing their injury. In some cases, however, contributorily negligent plaintiffs can still recover if they can prove that the defendant had the last clear chance to avoid the harm. A growing majority of the states have reacted to the potential harshness of contributory negligence by adopting comparative negligence systems. The details of these systems vary by state, but the essential idea of comparative negligence involves weighing the relative fault of the parties and diminishing a plaintiff's recovery in proportion to his fault.

Plaintiffs who voluntarily expose themselves to a known risk of harm created by a defendant's negligence are held to have assumed the risk of injury and are barred from any recovery. After adopting comparative negligence systems, some states have dispensed with both assumption of risk and contributory negligence, treating all issues of contributory fault in negligence cases under their comparative negligence system. Some states also apply comparative fault principles in recklessness and strict liability cases.

Conduct that demonstrates a conscious disregard for a known high degree of probable harm to others constitutes recklessness. In terms of moral culpability, recklessness lies midway between negligence and intentional wrongdoing. Mere contributory negligence by the plaintiff is not a good defense to recklessness. Reckless defendants are more likely to be found legally responsible for the consequences of their actions and to be subjected to punitive damages than are defendants who were merely negligent.

In some instances, the law imposes strict liability on defendants for injuries produced by their activities, even though the defendants did not intend any harm and may have done everything possible to avoid harm. Strict liability represents a social policy decision that those who participate in certain activities must shoulder all of the risks associated with them. The two most important types of conduct that are subjected to strict liability are the manufacture or sale of defective and unreasonably dangerous products and participation in ultrahazardous or abnormally dangerous activities. We discuss the product liability dimension of strict liability later in the text. Abnormally dangerous activities are those necessarily involving a significant risk of harm to others; this risk cannot be eliminated by the exercise of reasonable care. The decision to classify a particular activity as abnormally dangerous involves judicial consideration of a wide variety of factors in addition to the risk associated with the activity. These include the social utility of the activity, the costs associated with minimizing or eliminating the risk, and whether the activity is one commonly pursued in the area in which the injury occurred. Finally, as a general rule, mere contributory negligence by a plaintiff does not prevent her recovery on a strict liability theory, but assumption of risk by the plaintiff bars recovery.

PROBLEM CASES

1. On September 5, 1984, the Citizens for Bob Olexo Campaign Committee rented three tanks of helium from James Dawes Company. The helium was to be used to fill balloons that were to be handed out to the public during the Belmont County Fair. Although the agreement with Dawes called for the Committee to return the used cylinders, they were left at the fairgrounds leaning up against a commercial building. On September 28, Philip C. Jeffers III, age 14, attended a football game at the fairgrounds, where he and some friends discovered the tanks. Despite the warning on the tanks that said "CAUTION! HIGH PRESSURE GAS. CAN CAUSE RAPID SUFFOCATION," Jeffers inhaled some helium from one of the tanks, collapsed, and died. Jeffers's father sued the Dawes Company, which moved for a summary judgment on a number of grounds, among which was the argument that it owed no duty to Jeffers. Should Dawes's motion be granted?

2. At 1:45 A.M. on September 26, 1982, Gary Knapstad seriously injured his knee when he tripped over a tipped-over "no parking" sign lying in Smith's Management Corporation's parking lot while jogging across the lot to Smith's store. The sign was normally placed in front of the store, along with several barrels, to prevent customers from parking in the fire lane. At the time of his fall, the store was open and the lot was well lit. Knapstad sued Smith's for negligence and won a $22,855 verdict. Smith's appealed, arguing that the trial court's instructions improperly suggested that Smith's would be negligent if, as an expert witness hired by Knapstad testified, the sign failed to comply with federal and state occupational safety and health statutes aimed at providing a safer work environment for employees. Was the trial court's instruction proper?

3. On September 3, 1984, Valerie Jones, a lab technician at Kelco's chemical plant in Okmulgee, Oklahoma, stole a cupful of sulphuric acid from the plant. After work, she drove to the home of her sister-in-law, Gwendolyn Henry. After a brief verbal altercation with Henry over the fact that Henry, who had been babysitting Jones's two-year-old son, had trimmed the child's hair, she threw the acid in Henry's face. Henry suffered severe and permanent injuries, and Jones was ultimately sentenced to seven years in prison for the attack. Henry filed a negligence suit against Kelco, and a jury awarded her $450,000. Kelco appealed, arguing that it owed no duty to Henry and that, in any event, Jones's act was an intervening cause that relieved it of liability. The evidence at trial indicated that Jones had been a model employee who had to have access to the chemical storage area to perform her duties. Should the jury's verdict be reversed?

4. On July 9, 1980, Erroll Dobelle was a passenger on an Amtrak passenger train that left New York City bound for Philadelphia. When the train reached Linden, New Jersey, it passed an Amtrak work train proceeding in the opposite direction on adjoining tracks. As the trains passed, a 15-foot section of unsecured steel buffer rail carried on the work train struck the passenger train, which was moving at 60 miles per hour. The 755-pound buffer rail sliced through the passenger car in which Dobelle was riding, dismembering and killing one passenger, and critically injuring 17 others. Dobelle saw the rail come through the car, feared it would strike him, and at first thought it had because he was spattered with blood. The man on his immediate left was hit, but Dobelle emerged unscathed. When he realized he was all right, he began to help rescue workers assisting the injured passengers. Dobelle suffered serious emotional and psychological problems after the accident, was fired from his position as a vice president of a multimillion dollar company, and was hospitalized on three separate occasions seeking treatment for acute depression. He filed suit against Amtrak for negligent infliction of emotional distress. Amtrak admitted negligence, but moved to dismiss Dobelle's claim. It argued that his emotional injuries were caused by witnessing the harm to the other passengers, and that since none of those injured was a close relative of Dobelle's, he was barred from recovering for those injuries. Should the trial court dismiss Dobelle's claim?

5. Higgins and some friends went to a night baseball game at Comiskey Park in Chicago. Near the end of the game, Higgins went to the men's room. On his way back to his seat, he walked down a corridor that ran past a concession stand. As he passed the stand, the door to the front of the stand (a 4-foot by 6-foot sheet of plywood attached to the top of the stand and hooked to an eyelet in the ceiling when opened) fell from its open position and struck him on the head, causing permanent head and neck injuries. None of the eyewitnesses to the incident saw anyone touch either the door or the hook securing it, or do anything that might have caused the door to fall. There was, however, testimony that, just before the door fell, the crowd in the stadium was screaming and stamping, and that one "could feel the place tremble." Higgins filed suit against the Chicago White Sox, owners of the stadium, arguing that *res ipsa loquitur* should be applied to the case. Was he right?

6. Between 1982 and 1983, Long and Adams, then residents of Cobb County, Georgia, were involved in a sexual relationship. In 1984 Long filed suit against Ad-

ams, arguing that she had negligently infected him with genital herpes. Long argued that Adams knew she was infected with the disease, but had failed to inform him of this crucial fact before having sexual relations with him. Adams moved for a summary judgment on the ground that she owed Long no duty of disclosure. The trial court agreed and granted her motion. Should the trial court's decision be reversed on appeal?

7. Jenkins, an employee of Acme Paper Stock Company, was riding on a freight elevator in Acme's plant when the elevator cable broke. As a result, the hoist motor fell on Jenkins, fatally injuring him. The hoist motor and lifting cables had been installed by Edwards Transfer Company. The evidence at trial indicated that Edwards used steel cables to mount the hoist from an I-beam that ran along the ceiling of Acme's plant, but failed to use "softeners" to protect the cables against the sharp edges of the beam. The evidence also indicated that Acme had warned employees that the elevator was only to be used for freight and was not safe for use as a personnel elevator, and that Jenkins himself had told an Edwards employee prior to the accident that the hoist was improperly secured. Jenkins's heirs filed a negligence suit against Edwards. The trial judge refused to instruct the jury on contributory negligence on the ground that Jenkins could not reasonably have foreseen that he could be injured by the falling hoist motor. Was this refusal proper?

8. On April 25, 1984, Allen Beckett, a fourth-year player on his high school baseball team, was injured when he collided with another player during outfielder practice. The accident occurred after the coach conducting the practice hit a fly ball to Beckett. Beckett called for the ball, but the wind was blowing so hard that neither the coach nor the other players heard him. The coach called for another player to catch the ball, and that player and Beckett collided head-on. Beckett's jaw was broken, and he filed suit against the school, arguing that it had failed to warn him of the danger of such collisions, failed to adequately supervise the practice, and had conducted the practice in an unreasonably dangerous manner. At one point in his testimony Beckett denied that he had ever heard of baseball players colliding and said that he had no knowledge of any accidents happening on baseball fields. Under cross-examination, however, he admitted that his coaches had repeatedly stressed communication among players to avoid accidents, that it was possible on such a windy day for his voice to have gotten lost in the wind, and that the same type of thing could have happened in a game. Was the trial court summary judgment in favor of the school proper?

9. Chris Ewing went to the Cloverleaf Bowl on his 21st birthday. In the cocktail lounge of the bowling alley, Ewing was given a free vodka collins when the bartender discovered that it was his birthday. In the next hour and a half, despite the fact that he was obviously becoming intoxicated, Ewing was served 10 straight shots of 151-proof rum and two beer chasers. He died of acute alcohol poisoning the following day. His two small sons filed suit against the Cloverleaf Bowl. The trial court granted Cloverleaf's motion for a nonsuit, finding as a matter of law that Ewing was guilty of contributory negligence and that the bartender was not reckless. Should the trial court have allowed the jury to hear the case?

10. Lee Ann Laird, age 12, was injured when her bicycle was hit by a car driven by Larry Kostman. Lee Ann was in the process of pulling into the street from a driveway, and she emerged from behind a van parked at the curb. At the trial, Kostman testified that he hit his brakes as soon as he saw the bicycle. His passenger testified that Laird "came out of nowhere," and that he didn't see her until the moment of impact. Laird testified that she saw Kostman's car turn onto the street from an intersection more than 200 feet from the point of impact, that no more than two feet of her bicycle extended into the street from behind the parked van, and that, when she tried to move the bike back to avoid the collision, the brakes locked. After the trial judge refused to instruct the jury on the doctrine of last clear chance, the jury ruled in favor of Kostman. Was the trial judge's refusal proper?

11. Kent, a state highway worker, was killed when the aluminum handle of a rake he was using came into contact with a high voltage distribution line belonging to Gulf States Utilities. Kent's father sued Gulf States, and won a $1 million jury award. Gulf States appealed, and the Louisiana Court of Appeals reversed the trial award on the ground that Kent had been contributorily negligent. Kent's father appealed to the Lousiana Supreme Court, arguing that Gulf States should be held strictly liable for his son's death. Should the jury verdict be reinstated?

CHAPTER 8

INTELLECTUAL PROPERTY, COMPETITIVE TORTS, AND UNFAIR COMPETITION

INTRODUCTION

This chapter discusses a number of legal rules that limit free competition by allowing business parties to recover for certain abuses of that freedom. It opens by considering three such abuses—patent, copyright, and trademark infringement—that together involve the law of *intellectual property.* After examining the misappropriation of *trade secrets,* the chapter then describes three *intentional torts* that limit the behavior in which competitors can engage. The chapter concludes by briefly considering an evolving provision that often is regarded as a general federal ban on unfair competition—section 43(a) of the Lanham Act. Indeed, the term *unfair competition* is sometimes used to collectively describe the rules discussed in this chapter.[1]

Most of the rules discussed in this chapter are supported by one or both of two general policies. The first is to stimulate creative and inventive endeavor and thus to benefit society. If competition is so free that individuals cannot protect the results of such endeavor, their incentive to create and innovate may be reduced. Similarly, in a system of utterly free competition where *anything* goes, creative and inventive people might fall prey to ruthless competitors. Thus, society would be denied the fruits of their endeavor. Second, most of the rules described here further ends that have little to do with stimulating creativity and innovation. By establishing certain minimum standards of ethical competitive behavior, such rules make commercial life more humane and civilized than would otherwise be the case.

PATENTS

Introduction

A patent can be regarded as an agreement between its inventor and the federal government. Under the terms of this agreement, the inventor gets an exclusive right to make, use, and sell his invention, in return for making the invention public by submitting information to the government. The temporary monopoly acquired by the patent holder, or **patentee,** encourages the creation and disclosure of inventions, because there is less incentive to create and to disclose one's creations if others can freely appropriate them. Also, the submission of information to the government enables third parties to learn about the patented invention and to develop it in ways that do not infringe the patentee's rights.

---

[1]You should note that the law regulates unfair competition in other ways besides allowing private parties to recover when they are injured by such competition. Perhaps the clearest example is section 5 of the Federal Trade Commission Act, which gives the FTC the power to attack unfair or deceptive acts or practices.

What Is Patentable?

Any of the following may be the subject matter of a patent: (1) a *process* (as described in the following *Diamond* case), (2) a *machine*, (3) a *manufacture* or product, (4) a *composition of matter* (a combination of elements possessing qualities not found in the elements taken individually, such as a new chemical compound), (5) an *improvement* of any of the above, (6) an *ornamental design* for a product, and (7) a *plant* produced by asexual reproduction. Naturally occurring things (e.g., a new wild plant) and new business methods (e.g., an innovative accounting technique) are not patentable. Also, as the *Diamond* case states, abstract ideas, scientific laws, and other mental concepts are not patentable, although their practical applications often are.

Even though an invention fits within one of the above categories, it is not patentable if it lacks novelty, is obvious, or is without utility.[2] One example of the *novelty* requirement is the doctrine of *anticipation*, which states that no patent should be issued where *before the invention's creation* it has been: (1) known or used in the United States, (2) patented in the United States or a foreign country, or (3) described in a printed publication in the United States or a foreign country. Another example is the requirement that no patent should be issued if more than one year before the *patent application* the invention was: (1) patented in the United States or a foreign country, (2) described in a printed publication in the United States or a foreign country, or (3) in public

use or on sale in the United States. In addition, there can be no patent if at the time of its occurrence the invention would have been *obvious* to a person having ordinary skill in the area. Finally, there is a general requirement that the invention possess *utility*, or usefulness, in order to be patentable.

Also, there can be no patent if the party seeking it did not create the invention in question, or if she abandoned the invention. *Creation* problems frequently arise where several people allegedly contributed to the invention. *Abandonment* can be by express statement, such as publicly devoting an invention to mankind, or by implication from conduct, such as delaying for an unreasonable length of time before making a patent application.

Obtaining a Patent

The Patent and Trademark Office of the Department of Commerce handles patent applications. The application must include a *specification* describing the invention with sufficient detail and clarity to enable any person skilled in the area to make and use it. It must also state the inventor's *claims*: the allegedly novel, nonobvious, and useful features of the invention. The Patent Office checks the application for detail and clarity of description, and determines whether the invention meets the various tests for patentability. If the application is rejected, the applicant may amend and resubmit it. Once any of the applicant's claims has been twice rejected, the applicant may appeal to the Office's Board of Patent Appeals and Interferences. Subsequent appeals to the federal courts also are possible. In the *Diamond* case, the government appealed a federal court decision in favor of the patentee.

---

[2] Plant and design patents are subject to slightly different requirements than those stated in this section.

DIAMOND v. DIEHR

450 U.S. 175 (U.S. Sup. Ct. 1981)

Diehr and Lutton attempted to obtain a patent covering a process for molding raw, uncured synthetic rubber into cured precision products. The process used a mold for shaping the uncured rubber under heat and pressure and then curing it in the mold. Previous efforts at curing and molding synthetic rubber had suffered from an inability to measure the temperature inside the molding press, and thus to determine a precise curing time. Diehr and Lutton's invention involved a process for constantly measuring the temperature inside the mold, feeding this information to a computer that constantly recalculated the curing time, and enabling the computer to signal the molding press to open at the correct instant.

The patent examiner rejected Diehr and Lutton's patent application. The Patent and Trademark Office Board of Appeals (now the Board of Patent Appeals and Interferences) agreed with the examiner, but the now-defunct Court of Customs and Patent Appeals reversed. The Patent Office appealed to the U.S. Supreme Court.

Rehnquist, Justice.   In defining the nature of a patentable process, this Court has stated:

> A process is a mode of treatment of certain materials to produce a given result. It is an act, or a series of acts, performed upon the subject matter to be transformed and reduced to a different state or thing. If new and useful, it is just as patentable as is a piece of machinery. The machinery pointed out as suitable to perform the process may or may not be new or patentable; whilst the process itself may be altogether new and produce an entirely new result.

Recently, we repeated the above definition, adding: "Transformation and reduction of an article to a different state or thing is the clue to the patentability of a process claim that does not include particular machines." That Diehr and Lutton's claims involve the transformation of an article, raw uncured synthetic rubber, into a different state or thing cannot be disputed. Industrial processes such as this have historically been eligible to receive the protection of our patent laws.

Excluded from patent protection are laws of nature, physical phenomena, and abstract ideas. Only last Term, we explained:

> A new mineral discovered in the earth or a new plant found in the wild is not patentable subject matter. Likewise, Einstein could not patent his celebrated law that $E = mc^2$; nor could Newton have patented the law of gravity. Such discoveries are manifestations of nature, free to all men and reserved exclusively to none.

Diehr and Lutton do not seek to patent a mathematical formula. Instead, they seek patent protection for a process of curing synthetic rubber. Their process employs a well-known mathematical equation, but they do not seek to preempt the use of that equation. They seek only to foreclose from others the use of that equation in conjunction with all the other steps in their process. It is now a commonplace that an *application* of a law of nature or mathematical formula to a known structure or process may be deserving of patent protection.

It may later be determined that the process is not deserving of patent protection because it fails to satisfy the statutory conditions of novelty or nonobviousness. A rejection on either of these grounds does not affect the determination that Diehr and Lutton's claims recited subject matter which was eligible for patent protection.

Judgment for Diehr and Lutton affirmed.

Ownership and Transfer of Patent Rights

One who obtains a patent generally gets exclusive rights to make, use, and sell the patented invention for a 17-year period. Design patents, however, are effective for only 14 years. The patentee can transfer title to all or part of his patent rights by *assigning* them. He may also retain title and *license* all or some of his rights.

Usually, the party who created the invention is the patent holder. What happens, however, when the creator of the invention is an employee and her employer seeks rights in her invention? If the invention was developed by an employee *hired to do inventive or creative work*, she must use the invention solely for the employer's benefit and must assign any patents she obtains to the employer. But if the employee was hired for purposes *other than invention or creation*, she owns any patent she acquires. Regardless of the purpose for which the employee was hired, finally, the *shop right* doctrine gives the employer a nonexclusive, royalty-free *license* to use the employee's invention if it was created on company time and through company facilities. In such situations, the employee still has normal patent rights against parties other than the employer.

Patent Infringement

A *direct* patent infringement occurs when a third party makes, uses, or sells a patented invention without the patentee's authorization. It is fairly easy to establish a direct infringement where the subject matter made, used, or sold is clearly within the language of a successful patent application. Courts also find direct infringement where this subject matter is substantially equivalent to the protected subject matter. Under this *doctrine of equivalents*, an infringement occurs where the third party's subject matter performs substantially the same function as the protected invention in substantially the same way to produce substantially the same result. The aim of this doctrine is to prevent third parties from capitalizing on the patentee's creativity by slightly altering the patented invention before making, using, or selling it.

Also, one who *actively induced* another's infringement of a patent is liable as an infringer if he knew and intended that the infringement occur. This can happen where, for example, a party sells an instruction manual for using a patented machine to a direct patent infringer. Finally, if one knowingly sells to a direct patent infringer a component of a patented invention or something useful in employing a patented process, the seller may be liable for *contributory infringement*. For such liability to exist, the thing sold must be a material part of the invention and must not be a staple article of commerce with some other significant use. For example, suppose that Davis directly infringes Potter's patent for a radio by selling almost-identical radios. If Thomas sells Davis sophisticated circuitry for the radios with knowledge of Davis's infringement, Thomas may be liable for contributory infringement if the circuitry is an important component of the radios and has no other significant uses. This would be true even where the circuitry itself is not patented or patentable.

Defenses   An obvious defense to a patent infringement suit is that the subject matter of the alleged infringement is neither within the literal scope of the patent nor substantially equivalent to the patented invention. Also, the alleged infringer may defend by attacking the validity of the patent. Despite their approval by the Patent and Trademark Office, many patents are declared invalid when challenged in court.

Further, in certain cases the defendant may be able to assert that the patentee has been guilty of *patent misuse*. This is behavior unjustifiably exploiting the patent monopoly. For example, the patent owner may require the purchaser of a license on his patent to buy his unpatented goods, or may tie the obtaining of a license on one of his patented inventions to the purchase of a license on another.[3] In such cases, one who refuses to accept the patentee's terms and later infringes the patent may be able to escape liability by arguing that the patent holder misused his monopoly position.

Remedies   If successful in an infringement suit, the patentee gets damages adequate to compensate for the infringement, plus court costs and interest. The damages must not be less than a reasonable royalty for the use made of the invention by the infringer. Also, the court may in its discretion award damages of up to three times those actually found to exist. Finally, injunctive relief is available to prevent violation of any right secured by the patent, and attorney's fees may be awarded in exceptional cases.

COPYRIGHTS

Introduction

By giving creative people certain exclusive rights to their intellectual endeavors, copyright law lets them prevent others from using their work in certain ways. This benefits society by giving such individuals an incentive toward innovative activity. But copyright law also attempts to balance this purpose against the equally compelling public interest in the free movement of ideas, information, and commerce. It does so mainly by limiting the intellectual products it protects, and by allowing the fair use defense described later.

Coverage

Federal copyright law protects a wide range of creative works, including books, periodicals, dramatic and musical compositions, works of art, motion pictures, sound recordings, lectures, computer programs, and architectural plans. To merit copyright protection, such works must be *fixed*: set out in any tangible medium of expression from which they can be perceived, reproduced, or communicated. They must also be *original* (the author's own work), but unlike

---

[3] Some forms of patent misuse may be antitrust violations. This text's second antitrust chapter discusses the interaction between patent law and antitrust law.

the inventions protected by patent law, they need not be novel.

Copyright protection does not extend to ideas, concepts, principles, discoveries, procedures, processes, systems, and methods of operation as such. However, it may protect the *form in which they are expressed*. The story line of a play, for instance, probably is protected, but the original idea underlying it or an abstract statement of its theme probably is not. Although there can be no copyright in facts as such, nonfiction works and compilations of fact are protectible if their creation involved originality. The *Narell* case at the end of this section discusses the protection of phrases and expressions within a copyrighted work.

Creation and Notice

A copyright comes into existence upon the creation and fixing of a protected work. For works created in 1978 and thereafter, the copyright usually lasts for *the life of the author plus 50 years*. Although a copyright owner may register the copyright with the Copyright Office of the Library of Congress, registration is not necessary for the copyright to exist. However, registration often *is* necessary before the owner can begin a suit for copyright infringement, which we discuss shortly.[4]

Copyright owners often provide *notice* of the copyright once the work is published. Federal law authorizes various forms of notice for different copyrighted works. A book, for example, might include the term *Copyright*, the year of its first publication, and the name of the copyright owner in a location likely to give reasonable notice to readers. Due to a 1988 amendment to federal copyright law, notice now is only optional, but it can be useful to copyright owners. If proper notice is present, for example, the defendant in an infringement suit usually cannot reduce the actual or statutory damages described at the end of this section by claiming that the infringement was innocent.

Ownership Rights

The owner of a copyright has the exclusive rights to: (1) reproduce the copyrighted work, (2) prepare derivative works based on it (e.g., a movie version of a novel), (3) distribute copies of the work by sale or otherwise, and

(4) perform or display the work publicly. Because these rights are exclusive, a valid copyright blocks their exercise by parties other than the owner.

Ownership of a copyright initially resides in the creator of the copyrighted work, but the copyright may be transferred to another party. Also, the original owner may individually transfer each of the listed rights, or a portion of each, without losing ownership of the remaining rights. Most transfers of copyright ownership require a writing signed by the owner or his agent. The owner also may retain ownership while licensing the copyrighted work or a portion of it.

Infringement

Anyone violating any of the copyright owner's exclusive rights may be liable for *copyright infringement*. Infringement is easily proven where direct evidence of copying exists; verbatim copying of protected material is an example. But as the *Narell* case states, infringement usually is established by showing that the defendant had *access* to the copyrighted work and that there is *substantial similarity* between that work and the allegedly infringing work. Access can be proven circumstantially—for example, by wide circulation of the copyrighted work. Determining substantial similarity necessarily involves discretionary case-by-case judgments; *Narell* provides one example.

Fair Use   The main defense to a copyright infringement suit is the doctrine of **fair use.** This defense involves the weighing of several factors whose application varies from case to case. These factors are: (1) the purpose and character of the use, (2) the nature of the copyrighted work, (3) the amount and substantiality of the portion used in relation to the copyrighted work as a whole, and (4) the effect of the use on the potential market for the copyrighted work or on its value. *Narell* discusses and applies these factors.

Remedies   The basic remedy available in a successful copyright infringement suit is an award of the owner's actual damages plus the profits received by the infringer. However, the plaintiff may elect to receive statutory damages in lieu of the basic remedy. Now, these range from $500 to $20,000 for nonwillful infringements, with a ceiling of $100,000 where the infringement was willful. Injunctive relief and awards of costs and attorney's fees are possible in certain cases. Criminal penalties for willful infringements involving the pursuit of commercial advantage also exist.

---

[4] Due to the Berne Convention Implementation Act of 1988, registration is *not* a prerequisite to suits for the infringement of copyrights in certain works whose country of origin is not the United States.

NARELL v. FREEMAN

872 F.2d 907 (9th Cir. 1989)

Irena Narell wrote a social history of the Bay area Jewish community entitled *Our City: The Jews of San Francisco*. After its publication in 1981, her book sold fewer than 5,000 copies. In 1986, Narell repurchased the copyright and the remaining inventory from the publisher.

Illusions of Love, a novel by Cynthia Freeman, was published in hardcover in 1984 and in paperback in 1986, selling approximately 1 million copies. *Illusions* told a fictional story about the heir of a large, wealthy Jewish family who had to choose between his family and a lover from a vastly different background. Freeman consulted and used *Our City* in writing *Illusions*, and portions of *Illusions* were based on historical events described in *Our City*. Also, *Illusions* contained several instances of verbatim copying from *Our City*; these totaled about 300 words. On several more occasions, Freeman also paraphrased passages from Narell's book.

Narell sued Freeman and her publishers for copyright infringement in federal district court. The court granted the defendants' motion for summary judgment and Narell appealed.

Farris, Circuit Judge.   To establish a successful copyright infringement claim, Narell must show that she owns the copyright and that Freeman copied protected elements of the work. Because in most copyright cases direct evidence of copying is not available, a plaintiff may establish copying by showing that the infringer had access to the work and that the two works are substantially similar. Narell's ownership of the copyright and Freeman's access to Narell's work are not in dispute.

The [first] question is whether Freeman's admitted takings—several instances of identical phrases and the more numerous paraphrases—were of protected material. Copyright law protects only an author's expression. Facts and ideas within a work are not protected. Freeman largely took unprotected factual information from *Our City*.

Freeman did copy a few phrases from Narell. Ordinary phrases [and] phrases and expressions conveying an idea typically expressed in a limited number of stereotyped fashions are not subject to copyright protection. Most of the phrases Freeman copied are commonly used expressions, such as describing a muddy street as a "cow path." The appropriation of expressive elements is minimal. The more numerous paraphrasings cited by Narell [also] cannot be said to take the expressive elements of her work. Instead, unprotected factual details are taken, although in some cases commonly used expressions are echoed, such as "mosquitos ravished his flesh" versus "mosquitos feasted on his flesh." Freeman's borrowings did not take a sequence of creative expression, as opposed to an ordinary phrase, and therefore were not infringing.

The arguments of the parties and the decision of the district court focused on the issues of substantial similarity and fair use. Viewed as a whole, the two works have slight resemblance to each other. *Illusions* is a romantic novel. *Our City* is a historical treatment of the Bay area Jewish community. The similarities between the two works are neither quantitatively nor qualitatively significant. Quantitatively insignificant infringement may be substantial only if the material is qualitatively important to either work. The passages at issue are a small part of Narell's book. The material taken is not qualitatively important to either book. Because of the fundamental differences between the works and the insubstantial nature of the copied passages, no reasonable reader could conclude that the works are substantially similar.

The doctrine of fair use allows [one] to use copyrighted material in a reasonable manner without the consent of the copyright owner. The copyright act sets out four factors for evaluating whether a use is a fair use.

Purpose and Character of the Use—The first factor strongly weighs against Freeman, because commercial use of copyrighted material is presumptively unfair. Freeman's use is admittedly commercial.

Nature of the Copyrighted Work—The scope of permissible fair use is greater with an informational work than a creative work. Although this factor weighs slightly in Freeman's favor, Narell's work contains enough creative expression that any use of it is not presumptively fair.

Amount and Substantiality of Portions Used—This factor essentially repeats the analysis of the substantial similarity test. This factor weighs strongly in Freeman's favor.

Effect on the Market—This is the single most important element of fair use. The publication of *Illusions* has not had, and is not likely to have, any effect on the value or marketability of *Our City*. The works are directed to fundamentally different purposes. Readers interested in Narell's book are highly unlikely to find historical romance novels an acceptable substitute.

In sum, the first factor weighs strongly in Narell's favor and the second factor slightly favors Freeman. However, the third and final factors strongly favor Freeman. Because of the predominant role of the market factor, the district court's grant of summary judgment on the fair use defense should be affirmed.

Summary judgment for Freeman affirmed.

TRADEMARKS

Introduction

The main reason trademark owners enjoy legal protection against users of their marks is to help purchasers identify favored products and services. This end would be defeated if competition were so free that anyone could use another's trademark whenever he desired. Also, sellers and manufacturers would have less incentive to innovate and to strive for quality if consumers could not identify the source of superior products or services because competitors were free to appropriate each other's trademarks. For these reasons, trademarks are protected under the federal Lanham Act.[5]

Protected Marks

The Lanham Act recognizes four kinds of marks. It defines a *trademark* as any word, name, symbol, device, or combination thereof used by a manufacturer or seller to identify its products and to distinguish them from the products of competitors. On occasion, federal trademark protection has been extended to colors, pictures, label and package designs, slogans, sounds, arrangements of numbers and/or letters (e.g., "7-Eleven"), and shapes of goods or their containers (e.g., Coca-Cola bottles). *Service marks* are similar to trademarks, but are used to identify and distinguish services.

Certification marks certify the origin, materials, quality, method of manufacture, or other aspects of goods and services. Here, the user of the mark and its owner are distinct parties. A retailer, for example, may sell products bearing the Good Housekeeping Seal of Approval. *Collective marks* are trademarks or service marks used by organizations to identify themselves as the source of goods or services. Trade union and trade association marks fall into this category. Although all of these different marks receive federal protection, the discussion in this text mainly involves trademarks and service marks, using the terms *mark* or *trademark* to refer to both.

Distinctiveness

Because their aim is to help consumers identify products and services, trademarks must be *distinctive* to merit maximum Lanham Act protection. As stated later in the *Levi Strauss* case, marks fall into four general categories of distinctiveness:

---

[5] In addition, the owner of a trademark may enjoy legal protection under common law trademark doctrines and state trademark statutes.

1. *Arbitrary or fanciful marks.* These marks are the most distinctive—and the most likely to be protected—because they do not describe or suggest the qualities of the product or service they identify. The "Exxon" trademark is an example.

2. *Suggestive marks.* These marks convey the nature of a product or service only through the exercise of imagination, thought, and perception. A "Dietene" trademark for a dietary food supplement is an example. Although not as secure as arbitrary or fanciful marks, suggestive marks still are good candidates for protection.

3. *Descriptive marks.* These marks directly describe the product or service they identify—for example, "Exquisite" wearing apparel. Descriptive marks are usually not protected unless they acquire a *secondary meaning.* This occurs when their identification with particular goods or services has become firmly established in the minds of a substantial number of buyers. Among the factors considered in secondary meaning determinations are the length of time the mark has been used, the volume of sales associated with that use, and the nature of the advertising employing the mark. When applied to a package delivery service, for instance, the term "overnight" is usually just descriptive and thus not protectible. But it may come to deserve trademark protection through long use by a single firm that advertised it extensively and made many sales while doing so.

4. *Generic marks.* Generic marks (e.g., "diamond" or "truck") simply refer to the general class of which the particular product or service is one example. Because any seller has the right to call a product or service by its common name, generic marks are quite unlikely to receive Lanham Act protection.

Federal Registration

Once the seller of a product or service uses a mark in commerce or forms a bona fide intention to do so, she may attempt to register the mark with the U.S. Patent and Trademark Office. The office reviews applications for distinctiveness. Its decision to deny or grant the application can usually be contested either by the applicant or by a party who feels that he would be injured by registration of the mark. Such challenges eventually may find their way to the federal courts.

Trademarks that are sufficiently distinctive are placed on the Principal Register of the Patent and Trademark Office. A mark's inclusion in the Principal Register gives its owner several advantages. For example, it: (1) is prima facie evidence that the registrant owns the mark, which is useful in trademark infringement suits; (2) gives nationwide constructive notice of the owner's exclusive right to use the mark as of the time the application was filed, thus eliminating the need to show that the defendant in an infringement suit had notice of the mark; and (3) makes the mark incontestable after five years, as described later.

Excluded Marks   Regardless of their distinctiveness, however, some kinds of marks are specifically denied placement on the Principal Register. Examples include marks that: (1) consist of the flags or other insignia of governments; (2) consist of the name, portrait, or signature of a living person; (3) are immoral, deceptive, or scandalous; or (4) are likely to cause confusion or deceive because they resemble a mark previously registered or used in the United States. Certain other marks are not placed on the Principal Register unless they have acquired a secondary meaning. Examples include marks that: (1) are deceptively misdescriptive (such as "Dura-Skin" plastic gloves); (2) are geographically descriptive (e.g., "Nationwide" Life Insurance); or (3) are primarily a surname (because everyone should have the right to use his own name in connection with his business).

Transfer of Rights

Due to the purposes underlying trademark law, the transfer of trademark rights is more difficult than the transfer of copyright or patent interests. The owner of a trademark may license the use of the mark, but only if the licensee is a related company through which the owner can control the nature and quality of the goods or services identified by the mark. An uncontrolled "naked license" would allow the sale of goods or services bearing the mark but lacking the qualities formerly associated with it, and could confuse purchasers. Trademark rights also may be assigned or sold, but only along with the sale of the goodwill of the business originally using the mark.

Losing Federal Trademark Protection

Due to a 1988 amendment to the Lanham Act, federal registration of a trademark now lasts for 10 years rather than the previous 20 years. Renewals for additional

10-year periods are possible. However, trademark protection may be lost before the period expires. First, a third party may undertake a successful *cancellation proceeding* before the Patent and Trademark Office. If the mark is on the Principal Register, the proceeding must occur within five years of its issuance or the mark becomes *incontestable*. This means that a challenger's permissible reasons for attacking the mark become quite limited.

A second way in which the owner may lose trademark protection is by *abandonment*. This can occur through an express statement or agreement to abandon, through the mark's losing its significance as an indication of origin, or through the owner's failure to use the mark. Abandonment of the mark is presumed if it is not used for two years. Thirdly, the owner may lose protection if the trademark acquires a *generic meaning* by coming to refer to a class of products or services rather than a particular product or service. This has happened to such once-protected marks as aspirin and cellophane, and may yet happen to Xerox copiers. Finally, *improperly licensing or assigning* trademark rights under the rules described above may also result in their loss.

Trademark Infringement

Under section 32(1) of the Lanham Act, a registered trademark is infringed when, without the registrant's consent, another party uses a substantially similar mark in connection with the advertisement or sale of goods or services, and this is likely to cause confusion, mistake, or deception regarding their origin. The *Levi Strauss* case discusses many of the factors that courts sift and weigh when determining whether the use is likely to cause confusion, mistake, or deception.[6]

Remedies   A trademark owner who wins an infringement suit can obtain an injunction against uses of the mark that are likely to cause confusion. In certain circumstances, the owner can also obtain money damages for provable injury resulting from the infringement and for profits realized by the defendant from the sale of infringing products or services.

---

[6] As the case indicates, Lanham Act section 43(a), which is discussed at the end of the chapter, also provides a remedy for trademark infringement. In fact, section 43(a)'s protection extends to *unregistered* trademarks.

LOIS SPORTSWEAR, INC. v. LEVI STRAUSS & CO.

799 F. 2d 867 (2d Cir. 1986)

Levi Strauss & Co. makes Levi Jeans. Each pair of Levi Jeans has a distinctive back pocket stitching pattern consisting of two intersecting arcs that roughly bisect both pockets. Levi Strauss has continuously used this pattern on all its jeans since 1873, and has an incontestable federal trademark in the pattern. Over the years, the pattern has become strongly identified with Levi Jeans in the minds of consumers.

Lois Sportswear, Inc. imported jeans made by a Spanish manufacturer into the United States. These jeans had a back pocket stitching pattern substantially similar to the Levi Strauss pattern. Levi Strauss sued Lois under the Lanham Act in federal district court. After Levi Strauss successfully moved for a summary judgment, Lois appealed.

Timbers, Circuit Judge.   As a threshold matter, we have found it useful to decide how much protection a trademark is to be given by determining what type of trademark is at issue. Arrayed in an ascending order which roughly reflects their eligibility to trademark status and the degree of protection accorded, the classes are: (1) generic, (2) descriptive, (3) suggestive, and (4) arbitrary or fanciful. Superimposed on this framework is the rule that registered trademarks are presumed to be distinctive and should be afforded the utmost protection. Under this framework, Levi

Strauss's pattern deserves the highest degree of protection. First, the mark is registered and incontestable. Second, the mark, being a fanciful pattern of interconnected arcs, is entitled to the most protection the Lanham Act can provide.

In either a claim of trademark infringement under [Lanham Act] section 32 or a claim of unfair competition under section 43, a prima facie case is made out by showing the use of one's trademark by another in a way that is likely to confuse consumers as to the source of the product. In deciding the issue of likelihood of confusion, [we rely] on a multifactor balancing test. The factors serve as a useful guide through a difficult quagmire.

The first factor—the strength of the mark—weighs heavily in Levi Strauss's favor. The strength of a mark [is] its tendency to identify goods as emanating from a particular source. Levi Strauss's stitching pattern is a fanciful registered trademark with a very strong secondary meaning. Virtually all jeans customers associate the pattern with Levi Strauss's products. This makes it likely that consumers will assume wrongly that Levi Strauss is somehow associated with Lois's jeans or has authorized the use of its mark.

The second factor—the degree of similarity of the marks—also weighs in favor of Levi Strauss. The two stitching patterns are essentially identical. The third factor—the proximity of the products—likewise weighs in favor of Levi Strauss. Both products are jeans. Although Lois argues that its jeans are designer jeans and are sold to a different market segment than Levi Strauss's jeans, there is evidence of an overlap of market segments. Even if the two jeans are in different segments, a consumer observing Levi Strauss's striking pattern on Lois's designer jeans might assume that Levi Strauss had chosen to enter that market segment using a subsidiary corporation.

The fourth factor—bridging the gap—does not aid Lois's case. Under this factor, if the owner of a trademark can show that it intends to enter the market of an alleged infringer, that showing helps establish a future likelihood of confusion. Levi Strauss has an interest in preserving its trademark should it ever wish to produce designer jeans with the stitching pattern.

The fifth factor—actual confusion—while not helping Levi Strauss, does not really hurt its case. Levi Strauss's only evidence of actual confusion was a consumer survey which the district court discounted due to methodological defects. Of course, actual confusion need not be shown to prevail under the Lanham Act, since actual confusion is very difficult to prove and the act only requires a likelihood of confusion. While the complete absence of actual confusion evidence may weigh in a defendant's favor, the survey evidence, even with its defects, is still somewhat probative of actual confusion.

The sixth factor—the junior user's good faith in adopting the mark—weighs in favor of Lois. The evidence indicates that Lois happened on the stitching pattern serendipitously. The seventh factor—the quality of the respective goods—also adds some weight to Lois's position. Lois's jeans are not of an inferior quality, arguably reducing Levi Strauss's interest in protecting its reputation from debasement.

The eighth and final factor—the sophistication of relevant buyers—does not favor Lois. The typical buyer of designer jeans is sophisticated with respect to jeans buying. It is a sophisticated jeans consumer who is most likely to assume that the presence of Levi Strauss's stitching pattern on Lois's jeans indicates some sort of association between the two. Presumably, it is these sophisticated buyers who pay the most attention to back pocket stitching patterns and their "meanings."

Judgment in favor of Levi Strauss affirmed.

CONCEPT REVIEW

THE THREE FORMS OF INTELLECTUAL PROPERTY COMPARED

	Patent	**Copyright**	**Trademark**
What Is Protected?	Process, machine, product, composition of matter, improvement, ornamental design, plant produced by asexual reproduction, if *novel*, *nonobvious*, and *useful*	Wide range of creative works that are *fixed* and *original*	Trademarks, service marks, certification marks, and collective marks of sufficient distinctiveness
Registration Needed?	Yes	Although copyright exists absent registration, registration often necessary for infringement suit	Necessary for infringement suit under section 32(1). Unregistered marks protected under section 43(a).
Duration	17 years (14 years for design patents)	Life of author plus 50 years	10 years, with 10-year renewals possible
Transferability	By assignment or license	By assignment or license	Limited
How Infringed	Making, using, or selling patented invention or its substantial equivalent	Violation of owner's exclusive rights to reproduce, prepare derivative works, distribute copies, perform, or display. But *fair use* defense available.	Use of mark in connection with advertisement or sale that is likely to cause confusion, mistake, or deception regarding origin

TRADE SECRETS

Introduction

By providing a civil remedy for the misappropriation of trade secrets, the law affords an alternative means of protecting creative inventions. Owners of such inventions may go public and obtain monopoly patent rights. Or they may keep the invention secret and rely on trade secrets law to protect it. Figure 1 sketches some of the advantages and disadvantages of each alternative.

However, the policies underlying the granting of patent rights and the protection of trade secrets differ. As you have seen, the general aim of patent law is to encourage the creation and disclosure of inventions by granting the patentee a temporary monopoly in the patented invention in exchange for his making the invention public. Trade secrets, however, are nonpublic by definition. Although protecting valuable trade secret information may stimulate creative activity, it also keeps the information from becoming public knowledge. Thus, the main justification for such protection is simply to preserve certain standards of commercial ethics. In general, parties who acquire another's trade secrets are only liable when they use improper means or breach some duty of confidentiality.

Definition of a Trade Secret

A trade secret can be defined as any secret formula, pattern, process, program, device, method, technique, or compilation of information that is used in its owner's business and that gives the owner an advantage over competitors who do not know it or use it.[7] Examples

---

[7] This definition comes mainly from *Restatement of Torts* section 757, comment b (1939), with some additions from *Uniform Trade Secrets Act* section 1(4) (1985). About half of the states have adopted the Uniform Trade Secrets Act (UTSA) in some form. The discussion in this text is a composite of the *Restatement's* and the UTSA's rules. One difference between the *Restatement's* and the UTSA's definitions of a trade secret is that the UTSA does not require that the secret be used in the owner's business. Thus, the UTSA's broader definition of a trade secret protects owners who have not yet put their secret information to use.

FIGURE 1   Patent and Trade Secrets Protection Compared

Factor	Patent Law	Trade Secrets Law
Range of Protected Matter?	Probably narrower than trade secrets law	Probably broader than patent law
Need to Register?	Yes	No
Burden of Maintaining Secrecy?	No	Yes
Duration	Usually 17 years	So long as secrecy maintained?
Transferability	Fairly easy	Fairly easy
Ability to Keep Knowledge Secret?	No	Yes, if secrecy really maintained
Effective Monopoly over Protected Matter?	Yes	No, because discovery/use by proper means is permissible

include chemical formulas, manufacturing processes, designs for machines, and customer lists. To be protectible, a trade secret usually must have the kind of value or originality that provides an actual or potential competitive advantage. But it need not possess the novelty required for patent protection.

The following *Mason* case lists and applies some factors courts may consider when determining whether a trade secret exists. As several of those factors suggest, a trade secret must actually be *secret*. Absolute secrecy is not required, but a substantial measure of secrecy is necessary. Thus, information that becomes public knowledge or becomes generally known in the industry cannot be a trade secret. Also, information that is reasonably discoverable by proper means may not be protected. Here, *proper means* include independent invention of the secret, observation of a publicly displayed product, the owner's advertising, published literature, product analysis, and reverse engineering (starting with a legitimately acquired product and working backward to discover how it was developed).

In addition, a firm claiming a trade secret must usually show that it took *reasonable measures to assure secrecy*. Examples of such measures include advising employees about the secrecy of the secret, limiting access to the secret on a need-to-know basis, requiring those given access to sign a nondisclosure agreement, disclosing the secret only on a confidential basis, and controlling access to an office or plant. Because the owner is only required to make such efforts as are reasonable under the circumstances, the required measure or measures vary with the facts of the case. As a general

rule, though, owners are not required to adopt extreme measures to block every ingenious form of industrial espionage.

Ownership and Transfer of Trade Secrets

Usually, the owner of a trade secret is the person who developed it or the business under whose auspices it was generated. But establishing the original ownership of a trade secret can be a problem where an employee has developed a secret in the course of her employment. In such cases, courts often find the *employer* to be the owner if: (1) the employee was hired to do creative work related to the secret, (2) the employee agreed not to divulge or use trade secrets, or (3) other employees contributed to the development of the secret. Even where the employee owns the secret, the employer still may obtain a royalty-free license to use it through the shop right doctrine discussed in the section on patents earlier in this chapter.

The actual owner of a trade secret can transfer rights in the secret to third parties. This can occur by assignment (in which case the owner loses title) or by license (in which case the owner retains title but allows the transferee certain uses of the secret).

Misappropriation of Trade Secrets

Misappropriation of a trade secret can occur in various ways, most of which involve *disclosure or use* of the secret. For example, misappropriation liability occurs when the secret is disclosed or used by one who:

1. Acquired it by *improper means*. In general, improper means are means that fall below generally accepted standards of commercial morality and reasonable conduct. These include theft, trespass, wiretapping, spying, bugging, bribery, fraud, impersonation, and eavesdropping.

2. Acquired it from a party who *is known or should be known* to have obtained it by improper means. For example, a free-lance industrial spy might obtain one firm's trade secrets by improper means and sell them to the firm's competitors. If those competitors know or have reason to know that the spy obtained the secrets by improper means, they are liable for misappropriation along with the spy.

3. *Breached a duty of confidentiality* regarding the secret. Where an employer owns a trade secret, for example, an employee generally is bound not to use or disclose it either during her employment or thereafter. The employee may, however, utilize general knowledge and skills acquired during her employment.[8]

Remedies

A plaintiff who is successful in a suit for misappropriation of a trade secret may obtain damages, which might include both the actual loss caused by the misappropriation and the defendant's unjust enrichment (where this is not duplicative). In some states, punitive damages are awarded for willful and malicious misappropriations. Also, an injunction may be issued against actual or threatened misappropriations.

---

[8] This is an application of the agent's duty of loyalty, which is discussed in this text's first agency law chapter.

MASON v. JACK DANIEL DISTILLERY
518 So. 2d 130 (Ala. Civ. App. 1987)

Tony Mason created a mixed drink that he named "Lynchburg Lemonade." The drink consisted of Jack Daniel's whiskey, Triple Sec, sweet and sour mix, and 7-Up. Mason served the drink at his restaurant and lounge, where it became very popular. Later, Winston Randle, a sales representative for Jack Daniel Distillery, drank Lynchburg Lemonade while in Mason's restaurant and lounge. Although the source of his information was not clear, he also learned the recipe for the drink at this time. Randle informed his superiors about Lynchburg Lemonade and its recipe, and about one year later Jack Daniel was developing a national promotion campaign for the drink.

Mason, who never received any compensation for this use of Lynchburg Lemonade, sued Jack Daniel and Winston for misappropriation of a trade secret. Mason won a trial court jury verdict, and the defendants appealed the trial court's refusal to grant their motion for a directed verdict.

Holmes, Judge.   The defendants contend that Mason's recipe for Lynchburg Lemonade was not a trade secret. The *Restatement* provides in pertinent part:

A trade secret may consist of any formula, pattern, device, or compilation of information which is used in one's business, and which gives him an opportunity to obtain an advantage over competitors who do not know or use it. . . .

An exact definition of a trade secret is not possible. Some factors to be considered in determining whether given information is one's trade secret are: (1) the extent to which the information is known outside of his business; (2) the extent to which it is known by employees and others involved in his business; (3) the extent of measures taken by him to guard the secrecy of his information; (4) the value of the information to him and to his competitors; (5) the amount of effort or money expended by him in developing the information; (6) the ease or difficulty with which the information could be properly acquired or duplicated by others. *Restatement of Torts* section 757, comment b (1939).

Applying these factors to this case, we find that some support and some negate the conclusion that Lynchburg Lemonade was Mason's trade secret.

Mason apparently spent little time, effort, or money in concocting the recipe for Lynchburg Lemonade. He seems to have created the beverage one evening to ease a sore throat. However, he put much effort into making the beverage an exclusive specialty of his restaurant and lounge. Mason testified that Lynchburg Lemonade comprised about a third of his total sales of alcoholic drinks. Obviously, the exclusive sale of Lynchburg Lemonade was of great value to Mason. The beverage could also have been valuable to his competitors in the area.

Mason [also] testified that he told only a few of his employees the recipe. He stated that each one was specifically instructed not to tell anyone the recipe. To prevent customers from learning the recipe, the beverage was mixed in the back of the restaurant and lounge. Mason's efforts to keep the recipe a secret were apparently successful until Randle learned the recipe. It appears that one could not order a Lynchburg Lemonade in any establishment other than that of the plaintiff. Absolute secrecy is not required for the recipe to constitute a trade secret—a substantial element of secrecy is all that is necessary.

The defendants contend that Mason's recipe was not a trade secret because it could be easily duplicated by others. The defendants' [expert] testimony characterized Lynchburg Lemonade as a member of the Collins family of drinks, of which there are dozens, if not hundreds, with essentially the same elements. At least one witness testified that he could duplicate the recipe after tasting a Lynchburg Lemonade. Certainly, this testimony is a strong factor against the conclusion that Mason's recipe was a trade secret. We do not think, however, that this evidence in and of itself could prevent such a conclusion. Rather, this evidence should be weighed and considered along with the evidence tending to show the existence of a trade secret. Courts have protected information as a trade secret despite evidence that it could easily be duplicated by others competent in the given field.

A motion for directed verdict should not be granted if there is a scintilla of evidence supporting an element essential to the plaintiff's claim. Our review of the record indicates that Mason did present a scintilla of evidence that his recipe, or formula, for Lynchburg Lemonade was a trade secret.

Trial court's refusal to grant the defendants' motion for a directed verdict affirmed.

COMMERCIAL TORTS

In addition to the intentional torts discussed in the Intentional Torts chapter, certain other intentional torts apply mainly to business or commercial activities, especially the activities of competitors. These torts may help promote innovation by protecting creative businesses against certain competitive abuses. But their main aim is simply to uphold certain minimum standards of commercial morality.

Injurious Falsehood

The tort of injurious falsehood also is known by names such as product disparagement, slander of title, and trade libel. It involves the publication of false statements that disparage another's business, property, or title to property and thus harm another's economic interests. The two most common kinds of injurious falsehood are false statements disparaging another's *property rights* in land, things, or intangibles; and false statements disparaging the *quality* of another's land, things, or intangibles. These two types of injurious falsehood cover all of the legally protected property interests that are capable of being sold. Examples include leases, mineral rights, trademarks, copyrights, and corporate stock. As the later *Atlas* case indicates, injurious falsehood also covers false statements that harm another's economic interests and cause loss even though they do not disparage property as such.

Elements and Damages   In injurious falsehood cases, the plaintiff must prove a statement of the sort just described, its falsity, and its communication to a third party. As the *Atlas* case suggests, the degree of fault required for liability is not completely clear. It is often said that the standard is malice, but formulations of this have differed widely. The *Restatement* requires either knowledge that the statement is false, or reckless disregard as to its truth or falsity.[9] There is usually no liability for false statements that are made negligently and in good faith.

A plaintiff seeking to recover for injurious falsehood must also prove that the false statement played a substantial part in causing him to suffer *special damages*, or economic loss. These special damages may include: losses resulting from the diminished value of disparaged property, the expense of measures for counteracting the false statement (e.g., advertising or litigation expenses), losses resulting from the breach of an existing contract by a third party, and the loss of prospective business. In cases involving the loss of prospective business, the plaintiff usually is required to show that some specific person(s) refused to buy because of the disparagement. But as *Atlas* states, this rule is often relaxed where these losses are difficult to prove.

The special damages that the plaintiff is required to prove are his usual remedy in injurious falsehood cases. Damages such as personal injury, emotional distress, and amounts that would have been earned by utilizing or investing the proceeds from lost business generally are not recoverable. Punitive damages and injunctive relief are sometimes obtainable. Because proof of special damages is part of the plaintiff's cause of action, these last two remedies are available only when special damages have been shown.

Injurious Falsehood and Defamation   Injurious falsehood and defamation can overlap in some cases. Statements impugning a businessperson's character or conduct probably are only defamatory. If the false statement is limited to the plaintiff's business, property, or property rights, on the other hand, his normal claim is for injurious falsehood. Both claims may be made where the injurious falsehood implies something about the plaintiff's character and affects his overall reputation. For example, suppose that the defendant falsely alleges that the plaintiff knowingly sells dangerous products to children.

Defamation law's various absolute and conditional privileges generally apply to injurious falsehood.[10] Certain additional privileges are also recognized in injurious falsehood cases. For example, a rival claimant may in good faith disparage another's property rights by asserting his own competing rights. Similarly, one may make a good faith allegation that a competitor is infringing one's patent, copyright, or trademark. Finally, a person may sometimes make unfavorable comparisons between her own property and that of a competitor. This privilege is generally limited to sales talk asserting the superiority of one's own property (e.g., "I sell the best cars in town"). It does not cover specific unfavorable statements about the competitor's property.

---

[9] *Restatement (Second) of Torts* § 623A(b) (1977).

[10] On these privileges, see the Intentional Torts chapter.

CHARLES ATLAS, LTD. v. TIME-LIFE BOOKS, INC.

570 F. Supp. 150 (S.D.N.Y. 1983)

Time-Life Books, Inc. published a book entitled *Exercising for Fitness*. The book contained a reproduction of the famous Charles Atlas advertisement depicting a 97-pound weakling who uses Atlas's Dynamic Tension body-building program to become a real man after a bully kicks sand in his face and the face of his girlfriend. The caption accompanying the reproduction told the book's readers that Atlas's program is a system of isometric exercises. On the same page of the book, the author warned readers about the extreme dangers of isometric exercises.

Charles Atlas, Ltd. sued Time-Life Books in federal district court for product disparagement (injurious falsehood). It basically alleged that the book's caption was false because Atlas's method was not isometric, and that this falsehood, coupled with the text warning about the dangers of isometric exercises, caused it to suffer economic loss. Time-Life moved to dismiss Atlas's complaint. The question before the court was whether the facts in the complaint were sufficient to state a claim upon which relief could be granted.

Goettel, District Judge.   This court cannot say as a matter of law that the alleged misstatements are not reasonably susceptible to a defamatory meaning and that no reasonable reader could conclude that the statements [concern] the plaintiff's product. When the caption is read in conjunction with the text, a reasonable reader could conclude that Atlas markets an isometric exercise program, that isometric exercises are dangerous, and that therefore Atlas's exercise program is dangerous. Whether the trier of fact will conclude that a defamatory connotation was indeed conveyed will have to await trial.

Malice is pleaded adequately. It is extremely questionable whether the plaintiff must show common law malice to state a claim for product disparagement. Rather, it appears that the plaintiff must show knowledge of the alleged false statement or reckless disregard as to the truth of the statement [citing the *Restatement*]. Atlas alleges that the allegedly false statements were known by Time-Life to be false when they were made, or were made with recklessness, malice, and intent to injure Atlas.

Finally, Atlas has pleaded special damages adequately. According to Atlas, the alleged disparagement has caused it to lose $30,323 in sales and revenues and to expend $14,000 in special advertising expenses and $16,687 in legal expenses to counteract the alleged disparagement. Special damage is the pecuniary loss resulting directly from the effect of a defendant's allegedly wrongful conduct. Among the losses deemed to constitute special damages are the expenses necessary to counteract the alleged wrongful conduct. Thus, Atlas can recover at least the special advertising expenses incurred to counteract the alleged product disparagement, and the pleading of these expenses is sufficient to support the claim at this stage of the litigation.

Loss of sales is also a proper item of special damages. However, Time-Life argues that Atlas has failed to plead this adequately because it has failed to identify lost customers. Adopting such a rule would be grossly unfair in this case. Atlas sells only through mail orders. It is, therefore, virtually impossible to identify those who did not order Atlas's product because of *Exercising for Fitness*. As Dean Prosser has noted: "[A] more liberal rule has been applied, requiring the plaintiff to be particular only where it is reasonable to expect him to do so. It is probably still the law everywhere that he must either offer the names of those who have failed to purchase or explain why it is impossible for him to do so; but where he cannot, the matter is dealt with by analogy to the proof of lost profits resulting from breach of contract."

Whether legal fees expended to prosecute a claim for product disparagement can be recovered as an item of special damages is an interesting issue. It can be argued that the expenses incurred in bringing the lawsuit are similar to other expenses necessary to counteract the alleged wrongful conduct. Be that as it may, the court need not resolve the question at this time because it has already determined that Atlas has stated a claim for product disparagement.

Time-Life's motion to dismiss denied.

Interference with Contractual Relations

In cases of intentional interference with contractual relations, one party to a contract sues the defendant because the defendant's interference with the other party's performance of the contract caused the plaintiff to lose the benefit of that performance. A defendant can interfere with the performance of a contract by causing the other party to repudiate it, or by wholly or partly preventing that party's performance. The means of interference can range from threats of violence at one extreme, to mere persuasion at the other.

Liability for interference with contractual relations occurs only where the interference affected performance of an *existing* contract. This includes contracts that are voidable, unenforceable, or subject to contract defenses. However, there is no liability for interference with void bargains, contracts that are illegal on public policy grounds, or contracts to marry. To be liable, the defendant must have *intended* to cause the breach; there usually is no liability for negligent contract interferences.

Improper Interference   Even if the plaintiff proves the threshold requirements just stated, the defendant is liable only if his behavior was *improper*. The following *Bar J Bar* case lists the factors the *Restatement* uses for determining whether performance is improper. Despite the flexible, case-by-case nature of such situations, a few generalizations about improper interference are possible.

1. Where the contract's performance was blocked by such clearly improper means as threats of physical violence, misrepresentations, defamatory statements, bribery, harassment, or bad faith civil or criminal actions, the defendant usually is liable. Liability also is likely where it can be shown that the interference was motivated *solely* by malice, spite, or a simple desire to meddle.

2. Assuming that his means or motives are legitimate, the defendant generally is not liable when he acts in the *public interest*—for example, by informing an airport that an air traffic controller is a habitual user of hallucinogenic drugs. The same is true where the defendant acts to *protect a person for whose welfare she is responsible*—for example, where a mother induces a private school to discharge a diseased student who could infect her children.

3. A contract interference resulting from the defendant's good faith effort to protect her own *existing* legal or economic interests usually does not create liability so long as appropriate means are used. For example, a landowner who leases land to a tenant probably can induce the tenant to breach a sublease to a party whose business detracts from the land's value. However, business parties generally cannot interfere with existing contract rights merely to further some *prospective* competitive advantage. For example, a seller cannot entice its competitors' customers to break existing contracts with those competitors.

4. Finally, competitors are unlikely to incur liability where, as is often still true of employment contracts, the agreement interfered with is *terminable at will*.[11] The reason is that in such cases the plaintiff only has an *expectancy* that the contract will be continued, and not a *right* to have it continued. Thus, a firm that hires away its competitors' at-will employees usually escapes liability. This factor also may help explain the result in *Bar J Bar*.

Damages   The basic measure of damages for intentional interference with contractual relations is the value of the lost contract performance. In addition, some courts award compensatory damages reasonably linked to the interference (including emotional distress and damage to reputation). In certain cases, the plaintiff may obtain an injunction prohibiting further interferences.

---

[11]The Employment Law chapter discusses terminable-at-will employment contracts.

BAR J BAR CATTLE CO. v. PACE
763 P.2d 545 (Ariz. Ct. App. 1988)

The New Mexico and Arizona Land Company (New Mexico) owned a sizable tract of land in Arizona. It leased a valuable portion of this land containing water for grazing to the Bar J Bar Cattle Company. New Mexico had the right to cancel the lease on 30 days' notice once it sold the land.

Malcolm Pace owned a ranch adjoining the Bar J Bar ranch. Even though Pace's ranch had ample water supplies, he had long tried to get Bar J Bar to sublease its leasehold interest to him. However, Bar J Bar repeatedly rebuffed him. Eventually, Pace got control of the land leased to Bar J Bar by purchasing it from New Mexico. Immediately after signing the contract of sale, New Mexico gave Bar J Bar 30 days' notice of termination.

Bar J Bar sued Pace for intentional interference with contractual relations in an Arizona trial court. The court granted Pace's motion for summary judgment, and Bar J Bar appealed.

Ares, Judge.   The elements of intentional interference with contract in Arizona are: (1) a valid contractual relationship, (2) knowledge of the relationship on the part of the interferer, (3) intentional interference inducing or causing a breach, (4) resultant damage to the party whose relationship has been disrupted, and (5) improper action on the part of the defendant. The evidence establishes four of these five elements. Pace, knowing that Bar J Bar was the lessee of the property, successfully negotiated to buy the property and thereby caused New Mexico to exercise its right to cancel the lease. The cancellation clearly damaged Bar J Bar's interests.

The somewhat amorphous [fifth] standard of liability, *improper* action, must be applied with discrimination, particularly in the context of competitive business activities. Caution is doubly required where the effect of the actor's interference is only to cause the cancellation of a terminable contract. In the case before us, two ranchers sought control of grazing land through which life-giving water flows. Under circumstances like these, courts must take care that in their desire to protect the reasonable expectations of parties to contracts, they do not impose undesirable restrictions on competition.

The [Arizona] Supreme Court [has] adopted the seven factors enumerated in *Restatement (Second) of Torts* section 767 in determining whether interfering conduct was improper. Under this standard, the court should consider: (a) the nature of the actor's conduct, (b) the actor's motive, (c) the interests of the other with which the actor's conduct interferes, (d) the interests sought to be advanced by the actor, (e) the social interests in protecting the freedom of action of the actor and the contractual interests of the other, (f) the proximity or remoteness of the actor's conduct to the interference, and (g) the relations between the parties.

Nature of Pace's Conduct. Bar J Bar had to offer evidence that Pace acted illegally or inequitably, as for example, committing fraud [or] duress or abusing economic power. There is no evidence that Pace's conduct in offering to purchase the property was improper.

Pace's Motive. Bar J Bar argues that Pace had an improper motive in that he was acting out of ill will toward Bar J Bar because it had earlier declined to sublease the property to him. We reject the argument for two reasons. First, to attribute a motive of revenge or spite on this slim footing requires utter speculation. The most that one could conclude is that Pace continued to want the property. Second, even if Pace had an improper motive, that would not necessarily make him liable. One who interferes with the contractual rights of another for a legitimate competitive reason does not become a tortfeasor simply because he may also bear ill will toward his competitor.

Interests of the Parties. Bar J Bar argues that its interest in retaining access to [the grazing water] far outweighs Pace's interest in acquiring more water because he already has ample windmills and stock tanks. To make the entire decision turn simply on the weight of one party's interest as compared to the other's would be to ignore all the other elements of the calculus. Moreover, the interests of both parties are legitimate and substantial. Bar J Bar had access to [the water] for years and wanted to keep it. Pace sought to add [the land] to his own ranch as a buffer against unwanted development and as a source of water. To attempt to weigh these interests against each other would involve the court in a risky and perhaps impossible task.

The Social Interests at Stake. The tort of unlawful interference with contract operates as a restraint on competition and freedom of contract. In this case, because it is asserted with respect to a contract to sell land, its effect would be to impose a restraint on New Mexico's right to sell its land as it chose and on Pace's right to pursue his economic interests as he viewed them.

Summary judgment for Pace affirmed.

Interference with Prospective Advantage

The rules and remedies for interference with prospective advantage parallel those for interference with contractual relations. The main difference is that the former tort covers interferences with *prospective* relations rather than existing contracts. The future relations protected against interference are mainly potential contractual relations of a business or commercial sort. Liability for interference with such relations is based on intent, and plaintiffs usually cannot sue for negligent interferences.

The "improper interference" factors weighed in interference with contract cases generally apply to interference with prospective advantage as well. One difference, however, is that interference with prospective advantage can be justified if: (1) the plaintiff and the defendant are in competition for the prospective relation with which the defendant interferes; (2) the defendant's purpose is at least partly competitive; (3) the defendant does not use such improper means as physical threats, misrepresentations, bad faith lawsuits, and so forth; and (4) the defendant's behavior does not create an unlawful restraint of trade under the antitrust laws or other regulations.[12]

Thus, a competitor can ordinarily win customers by offering lower prices, and can attract suppliers by offering higher prices. Unless this is illegal under antitrust law or other regulations, he can also refuse to deal with suppliers or buyers who also deal with his competitors. Remember, however, that such conduct often results in

liability for intentional interference with contractual relations if the defendant disrupts an *existing* contract. Here, the social interest in the security of established contract rights outweighs society's interest in free competition.

Lanham Act Section 43(a)

Section 43(a) of the Lanham Act, which was amended in 1988, has long been regarded as creating a general federal law of unfair competition. Section 43(a) is not a consumer remedy; it is normally available only to commercial parties, who are usually the defendant's competitors. The section creates civil liability for a wide range of false, misleading, confusing, or deceptive descriptions of fact made in connection with goods or services. Among section 43(a)'s many applications are the following:

1. *Common law tort suits for "palming off" or "passing off."* This tort involves false representations that are likely to induce third parties to believe that the defendant's goods or services are those of the plaintiff. Such representations include imitations of the plaintiff's trademarks, trade names, packages, labels, containers, employee uniforms, and place of business.

2. *Trade dress infringement claims.* A product's trade dress is its overall appearance and sales image. Section 43(a) prohibits a party from passing off its goods or services as those of a competitor by employing a substantially similar trade dress that is likely to confuse consumers as to the source of its products or services.

---

[12] *Restatement (Second) of Torts* § 768 (1979).

For example, a competitor that sells antifreeze in jugs that are similar in size, shape, and color to a well-known competitor's jugs may face section 43(a) liability. As this discussion suggests, trade dress cases resemble palming off cases.

3. The infringement of both *registered and unregistered* trademarks.

4. Some cases involving a form of invasion of privacy discussed in the Intentional Torts chapter: *the appropriation of another's name or likeness for commercial purposes.*

5. *Commercial advertising that misrepresents the nature of goods or services.*[13] Before its 1988 amendment, section 43(a) only covered ads involving false statements about the advertiser's *own* products or services. Now, however, it also applies to ads that misrepresent the nature or origin of a *competitor's* products and services.

This application of section 43(a) also covers ads that are likely to deceive buyers even if they are not clearly false on their face. The legislative history to the new section 43(a) suggests that it may apply to advertising containing certain deceptive *omissions* as well. To illustrate these last two points, a seller of artificial fur coats that calls one of its brands "Normink" and does not disclose the coat's true nature may be liable under section 43(a).

ETHICAL AND PUBLIC POLICY CONCERNS

1. An ethical theory known as *utilitarianism* generally urges that the test for assessing the worth of actions is their ability to produce the greatest degree of aggregate net satisfaction throughout society. Some utilitarians say that satisfaction is maximized when people are best able to realize their individual preferences. Some say that one measure of satisfaction is the creation of economic wealth.

Look at the portion of this chapter's introduction that states the two general purposes underlying the legal rules discussed in this chapter. Which of these is most clearly utilitarian? Why? Also, look at the purposes said

---

to underlie trademark law. Are these generally utilitarian? Why or why not?

2. Legal reasoning sometimes is deductive or syllogistic. In such cases, the court states a general rule as a major premise, treats the facts as a minor premise, and applies the rule to the facts to generate a result. But another style of legal reasoning called *factor-based balancing* proceeds differently. In cases of this kind, the court states various factors that are relevant to its decision and decides by weighing these factors against one another under the facts before it. Which cases in this chapter use this method in whole or in part? Based on those cases, what is good about this style of legal reasoning? Are sensible decisions possible in any other way? On the other hand, what is bad about this decision-making process? In answering the last question, consider how well this process enables business parties to predict the legal consequences of their behavior.

3. People who defend free competition might do so on either of two grounds. They might justify free competition by its ability to promote economic efficiency and to maximize wealth over time. Or they might assert that free competition involves economic liberties which are so innately valuable that they should be protected regardless of whether they maximize wealth or not. Of course, defenders of free competition might stress both justifications.

With all this in mind, look at the *Bar J Bar* case earlier in the chapter. Which rationale for free economic activity predominates there? Back up your conclusion with specific language from the court's opinion.

SUMMARY

This chapter discusses certain forms of unfair competition whose main objects are to provide incentives for innovation and to preserve certain basic standards of competitive morality. By protecting the works of creative persons against infringement, copyright law motivates such persons to express their ideas in tangible form, and thus gives society the benefit of those ideas. Similarly, patent law promotes the creation and disclosure of new devices, products, processes, and designs by blocking infringing uses of such inventions. By allowing competitors to preserve the secrecy of their innovations, trade secrets law provides an alternative means for realizing these ends. The Lanham Act's prohibitions against trademark infringement also pro-

---

[13] Deceptive advertising also may be attacked by the Federal Trade Commission under FTC Act section 5. See this text's chapter on the FTC Act and consumer protection laws.

vide incentives for innovation and superior quality by making it easier for consumers to identify products possessing those traits. Perhaps more importantly, they also promote informed consumer choice by helping prevent confusion about the origin of favored products.

Many of the same considerations underlie the various commercial torts discussed in this chapter. An environment where injurious falsehoods, interferences with established contracts, and interferences with prospective business relations run rampant is an environment where creativity, inventiveness, and superior quality probably receive less than their maximum reward. However, the most important justification for these rules is their tendency to uphold certain minimum standards of ethical business behavior.

Finally, section 43(a) of the Lanham Act has created a federal law of unfair competition with a wide potential sweep. Section 43(a)'s most important application, however, is to false or deceptive advertising.

PROBLEM CASES

1. Huey J. Rivet patented an "amphibious marsh craft" for hauling loads and laying pipeline in swamps. Rivet's model could "walk" over stumps for extended periods while carrying heavy loads. Later, Robert Wilson, who had once worked for Rivet as a welder, began marketing a similar craft. The craft sold by Wilson differed from the craft described in the specification accompanying Rivet's patent application in several respects. Overall, though, the Wilson boat performed much the same functions about as effectively as the Rivet craft, and used much the same engineering techniques and concepts to do so. Has Wilson infringed Rivet's patent?

2. Lorna Nelson, half sister of the rock star Prince, sued Prince for copyright infringement. She alleged that Prince's hit "U Got the look" infringed her copyrighted song "What's Cooking in This Book." Lorna's song, to which Prince had access, had six verses totaling 35 lines and 176 words. "U Got the look" had eight verses totaling 47 lines and 242 words. The alleged infringements concerned the following verses and words from the two songs:

a. *Lorna's Verse Two*: "I glanced up and saw you, a smile so pretty." *Prince's Verses Two and Seven*: "I woke up, I've never seen such a pretty girl."

b. *Lorna's Verse Three*: "Makeup was rolling down my face." *Prince's Verse Five*: "A whole hour just to make up your face."

c. *Lorna's Verse Six*: "What's cooking in this book, what's cooking in . . ." *Prince's Verses Four and Six*: "U sho 'nuf do be cooking in my book."

d. *Lorna's Verses One and Six*: "Take a look, Take another look." *Prince's Verses One and Seven*: "U got the look."

The main issue in the case was whether there was substantial similarity between the lyrics just quoted. Do you think that these lyrics are sufficiently similar to justify imposing liability on Prince?

3. In 1970–71, James Doran, a student at Iowa State University, helped produce a 28-minute film biography of Dan Gable, an Iowa State wrestler who eventually won a gold medal at the 1972 Olympics. Iowa State obtained a valid statutory copyright to the film. In 1972, when Doran was employed by the American Broadcasting Company, he helped arrange for ABC to use a $2\frac{1}{2}$-minute segment of the film for the network's broadcasts of the 1972 Olympics. He did so without Iowa State's knowledge or consent. Is the fact that ABC only used about 9 percent of the film sufficient by itself to give ABC a fair use defense in a copyright infringement suit by Iowa State?

4. Accuride, International, Inc. is a wholly owned subsidiary of Standard Precision, Inc., a leading producer of drawer slide mechanisms. Standard Precision and Accuride market drawer slide mechanisms under the "ACCURIDE" trademark. Is this mark arbitrary or fanciful, suggestive, descriptive, or generic?

5. Suppose that Toys "R" Us, Inc., a chain of children's toy and clothing stores, has a registered trademark in the name Toys "R" Us. Is this mark best described as suggestive or descriptive? So far as protection of the mark against use by third parties is concerned, does it matter which characterization is best? In answering the second question, assume that Toys has been doing business under the mark for at least 20 years, and that the association between its products and its mark is well established in the minds of consumers.

6. E. I. du Pont de Nemours & Co., Inc. was building a plant to develop a highly secret unpatented process for producing methanol. During the construction, some of its trade secrets were exposed to view from the air because the plant in which they were contained did not yet have a roof. These secrets were photographed from an airplane by two photographers who were hired by persons unknown to take pictures of the new construction. Did this action amount to a misappropriation of du Pont's trade secrets?

7. Frank and Frances Gardner sued Sailboat Key, Inc. to prevent it from constructing certain improvements pursuant to building permits issued by the city of Miami. Sailboat Key later sued the Gardners for injurious falsehood. It alleged that false statements contained in the Gardners' pleadings in the earlier case caused it to lose its interest in the land where the construction was to occur, because it could not obtain financing. The Gardners claimed that defamation law's absolute privilege for statements made in the course of judicial proceedings also applied to this injurious falsehood action, and thus protected them from liability. Are the Gardners correct?

8. Joanna Wells and Paula Snyder visited the Brownsville Golden Age Nursing Home in connection with their interest in placing a relative in a nursing home. Appalled at the conditions they found there, Wells and Snyder communicated their concerns to a variety of sources, including the governor of Pennsylvania, President Ronald Reagan, CBS News, and the television show "60 Minutes." Their various communications eventually caused Golden Age to lose its state operating license due to various violations of state regulations. Golden Age sued Wells and Snyder for intentional interference with its contractual relations. Did Golden Age win? Why or why not?

9. After retiring from professional football, ex-Notre Dame and Green Bay Packer star Paul Hornung began a career as a television sports announcer. From the mid-1960s until 1980 he worked as a play-by-play announcer and color commentator at both college and professional games. In 1981 or 1982, the Atlanta television station WTBS contracted with the NCAA to telecast 19 college football games during the 1982 and 1983 seasons. The contract gave the NCAA the right to approve or disapprove any announcer or color commentator used on the broadcasts. When WTBS proposed Hornung as a color analyst for the games, the NCAA rejected him. The stated reasons for Hornung's rejection were his close association with professional football, his suspension for gambling while an NFL player, and his participation in Miller Lite beer commercials. The NCAA, however, itself accepted advertising revenue from the Miller Brewing Company.

Hornung sued the NCAA for intentional interference with prospective advantage. Did he win? Why or why not?

10. A television commercial for the "Premium Pack" orange juice manufactured by Tropicana Products, Inc. showed Olympic athlete Bruce Jenner squeezing an orange while saying: "It's pure, pasteurized juice as it comes from the orange." The ad then showed Jenner pouring the fresh-squeezed juice into a Tropicana carton. In fact, pasteurization involves heating the juice to approximately 200 degrees Fahrenheit, and Premium Pack juice is heated and sometimes frozen before packaging. The Coca-Cola Company, which makes Minute Maid orange juice, sued Tropicana for false advertising. Can Coca-Cola recover against Tropicana on the theory that the ad amounts to injurious falsehood? On what other claim discussed in the text might Coca-Cola succeed in recovering against Tropicana?

CONTRACTS

CHAPTER 9

INTRODUCTION TO CONTRACTS

THE NATURE OF CONTRACTS

If a covenant be made, wherein neither of the parties perform presently, but trust one another; in the condition of mere nature, which is a condition of war of every man against every man, upon any reasonable suspicion, it is void: but if there be a common power set over them both, with right and force sufficient to compel performance, it is not void. For he that performeth first, has no assurance the other will perform after; because the bonds of words are too weak to bridle men's ambition, avarice, anger, and other passions, without the fear of some coercive power; which in the condition of mere nature, where all men are equal, and judges of the justness of their own fears, cannot possibly be supposed. And therefore he which performeth first, does but betray himself to his enemy; contrary to the right, he can never abandon, of defending his life, and means of living.

Thomas Hobbes, *Leviathan*

Definition

Scholars and courts have formulated numerous definitions of the term *contract*. The *Restatement (Second) of Contracts* defines a contract as "a promise or set of promises for the breach of which the law gives a remedy, or the performance of which the law in some way recognizes as a duty."[1] The essence of this definition for our

---

[1] *Restatement (Second) of Contracts* § 1 (1981).

purposes is that a contract is a *legally enforceable promise or set of promises*. In other words, parties to contracts are entitled to call upon the state (the "common" or "coercive" power referred to by Hobbes in the quotation above) to force those with whom they have contracted to honor their promises. However, not all of the promises that people make attain the status of contracts. We have all made and broken numerous promises without fear of being sued by those to whom our promises were made. If you promise to take a friend out to dinner, but fail to do so, you do not expect to be sued for breaching your promise. What separates such social promises from legally enforceable contracts?

Elements

Over the years, the common law courts have developed several basic tests that a promise must meet before it is treated as a contract. These tests comprise the basic elements of contract. A contract is an *agreement* (an *offer*, made and *accepted*) that is *voluntarily* created by persons with the *capacity* to contract. The objectives of the agreement must be *legal* and, in most cases, the agreement must be supported by some *consideration* (a bargained-for exchange of legal value). Finally, the law requires *written* evidence of the existence of some agreements before enforcing them. Figure 1 shows how these elements relate to deciding whether a contract

FIGURE 1 Getting to Contract

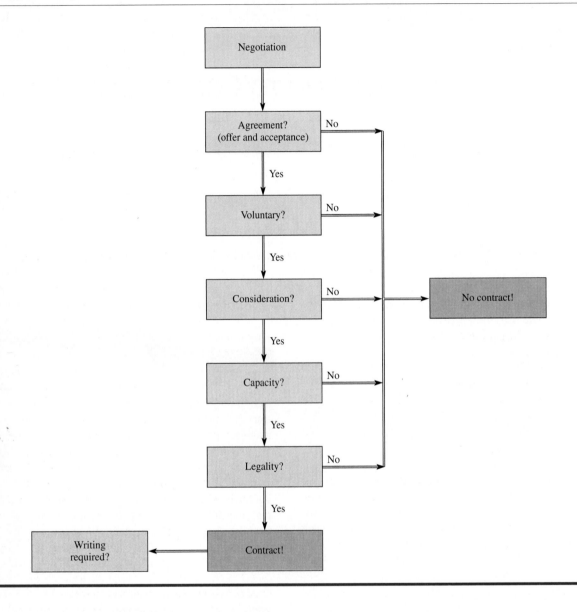

exists. The following chapters discuss each of these elements and other points necessary to enable you to distinguish contracts from unenforceable, social promises.

THE SOCIAL UTILITY OF CONTRACTS

As the introductory quotation indicates, contracts enable persons acting in their own interests to enlist the support of the law in furthering their personal objec-

tives. Contracts enable us to enter into agreements with others with the confidence that we may call on the law, and not merely the good faith of the other party, to ensure that those agreements will be honored. Within broad limits defined by contract doctrine and public policy, the contract device enables us to create the private law that governs our relations with others: the terms of the agreements we make.

Contracts facilitate the private planning that is necessary in a modern, industrialized society. Few people would invest in a business enterprise if they could not rely on the fact that the builders and suppliers of their facilities and equipment, the suppliers of the raw materials necessary to manufacture products, and the customers who agree to purchase those products will all honor their commitments. How could we make loans, sell goods on credit, or rent property unless loan agreements, conditional sales agreements, and leases were backed by the force of the law? Contract, then, is an inescapable and valuable part of the world as we know it. Like that world, its particulars tend to change over time, while its general characteristics remain largely stable.

THE EVOLUTION OF CONTRACT LAW

Classical Contract Law

The contract idea is ancient. Thousands of years ago, Egyptians and Mesopotamians recognized devices like contracts; by the 15th century, the common law courts of England had developed a variety of theories to justify enforcing certain promises. Contract law did not, however, assume major importance in our legal system until the 19th century, when numerous social factors combined to shape the common law of contract. Laissez-faire (free market) economic ideas had a profound influence on public policy thinking during this period, and the Industrial Revolution created a perceived need for private planning and certainty in commercial transactions. The typical contract situation in the early decades of the 19th century involved face-to-face transactions between parties with relatively equal bargaining power who dealt with relatively simple goods.

The contract law that emerged from this period was strongly influenced by these factors. Its central tenet was *freedom of contract*: Contracts should be enforced because they are the products of the free wills of their creators, who should, within broad limits, be free to determine the extent of their obligations. The proper role of the courts in such a system of contract was to enforce these freely made bargains, but otherwise to adopt a hands-off stance. Contractual liability should not be imposed unless the parties clearly agreed to assume it, but once an agreement had been made, liability was near absolute. The fact that the items exchanged were of unequal value was usually legally irrelevant. The freedom to make good deals carried with it the risk of making bad deals. As long as a person voluntarily entered a contract, it would generally be enforced against him, even if the result was grossly unfair. And since equal bargaining

power tended to be assumed, the courts were usually unwilling to hear defenses based on unequal bargaining power. This judicial posture allowed the courts to formulate a pure contract law consisting of precise, clear, and technical rules that were capable of general, almost mechanical, application. Such a law of contract met the needs of the marketplace by affording the predictable and consistent results necessary to facilitate private planning.

Modern Contract Law Development

As long as most contracts resembled the typical transaction envisioned by 19th-century contract law, such rules made perfect sense. If the parties dealt face to face, they were likely to know each other personally or at least to know each other's reputation for fair dealing. Face-to-face deals enabled the parties to inspect the goods in advance of the sale, and since the subject matter of most contracts was relatively simple, the odds were great that the parties had relatively equal knowledge about the items they bought and sold. If the parties also had equal bargaining power, it was probably fair to assume that they were capable of protecting themselves and negotiating an agreement that seemed fair at the time. Given the truth of these assumptions, there was arguably no good reason for judicial interference with private contracts.

America's Industrial Revolution, however, undermined many of these assumptions. Regional, and later national, markets produced longer chains of distribution. This fact, combined with more-efficient means of communication, meant that people often contracted with persons whom they did not know for goods that they had never seen. And rapidly developing technology meant that those goods were becoming increasingly complex. Thus, sellers often knew far more about their products than did the buyers with whom they dealt. Finally, the emergence of large business organizations after the Civil War produced obvious disparities of bargaining power in many contract situations. These large organizations found it more efficient to standardize their numerous transactions by employing standard form contracts, which also could be used to exploit disproportionate bargaining power by dictating the terms of their agreements. Figure 2 highlights these factors that shaped modern contract law.

The upshot of all this is that many contracts today no longer resemble the stereotypical agreements envisioned by the common law of contract. It has been estimated that over 90 percent of all contracts today are form

FIGURE 2 Factors that Shaped Modern Contract Law

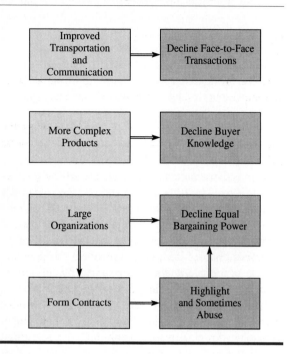

contracts.[2] How should courts respond to contracts where the terms have been dictated by one party to another party who may not have read or understood them, and who, in any event, may have lacked the power to bargain for better terms? Contract law is changing to reflect these changes in social reality. The 20th century has witnessed a dramatic increase in public intervention into private contractual relationships. Think of all the statutes governing the terms of what were once purely private contractual relationships. Legislatures commonly dictate many of the basic terms of insurance contracts. Employment contracts are governed by a host of laws concerning maximum hours worked, minimum wages paid, employer liability for on-the-job injuries, unemployment compensation, and retirement benefits. In some circumstances, product liability statutes impose liability on the manufacturers and sellers of products regardless of the terms of their sales contracts. The avowed purpose of much of this public intervention has been to protect persons who lack sufficient bargaining power to protect themselves.

Nor have the legislatures been the only source of public supervision of private agreements. Twentieth-century courts have been increasingly concerned with creating contract rules that produce just results. The result of this concern has been an increasingly hands-on posture by courts that often feel compelled to intervene in private contractual relationships to protect weaker parties. In the name of avoiding injustice, some modern contract doctrines impose contractual liability, or something quite like it, in situations where traditional contract rules would have denied liability. Similarly, other modern contract doctrines allow parties to avoid contract liability in cases where traditional common law rules would have recognized a binding agreement and imposed liability.

As contract law evolves to accommodate changing social circumstances, the basic nature of contract rules is changing. The precise, technical rules that characterized traditional common law contract are giving way to broader, imprecise standards such as good faith, injustice, reasonableness, and unconscionability. The reason for such standards is clear. If courts are increasingly called on to intervene in private contracts in the name of fairness, it is necessary to fashion rules that afford the degree of judicial discretion required to reach just decisions in the increasingly complex and varied situations where intervention is needed.

This heightened emphasis on fairness, like every other choice made by law, carries with it some cost. Imprecise, discretionary modern contract rules do not produce the same measure of certainty and predictability that their precise and abstract predecessors afforded. And because modern contract rules often impose liability in the absence of the clear consent required by traditional common law contract rules, one price of increased fairness in contract cases has been a diminished ability of private parties to control the nature and extent of their contractual obligations.

This change in the nature of contract law is far from complete, however. The idea that a contract is an agreement freely entered into by the parties still lies at the heart of contract law today, and contract cases may be found that differ very little in their spirit or ultimate resolution from their 19th-century predecessors. It is probably fair to say, however, that these are most likely to be cases where 19th-century assumptions about the nature of contracts are still largely valid. Thus, these cases involve contracts between parties with relatively equal bargaining power and relatively equal knowledge about the subject of the contract. Despite the existence of such

[2] Slawson, "Standard Form Contracts and Democratic Control of Lawmaking Power," 84 *Harv. L. Rev.* 529 (1971).

cases, it is evident that contract law is in the process of significant change. Subsequent chapters highlighting the differences between modern contract rules and their traditional common law forebears render this conclusion inescapable. Before discussing particular examples of this new thrust in contract law, however, we should familiarize ourselves with the basic contract terminology that is used throughout the text.

BASIC CONTRACT CONCEPTS AND TYPES

Bilateral and Unilateral Contracts

Contracts have traditionally been classified as **bilateral** or **unilateral,** depending on whether one or both of the parties have made a promise. In unilateral contracts, only one party makes a promise. For example, if a homeowner says to a painter, "I will pay you $1,000 if you paint my house," the homeowner has made an offer for a unilateral contract, a contract that will be created only if and when the painter paints the house. If the homeowner instead says to the painter, "If you promise to paint my house, I will promise to pay you $1,000," he has asked the painter to commit to painting the house rather than just to perform the act of painting. This offer contemplates the formation of a bilateral contract. If the painter makes the requested promise to paint the house, a bilateral contract is created at that point.

In succeeding chapters, you will learn that unilateral contracts cause some particular problems related to offer and acceptance and to mutuality of obligation. These problems have caused many commentators to argue that the unilateral-bilateral contract distinction should be abandoned. The *Restatement (Second) of Contracts* and the Uniform Commercial Code, both of which are discussed later in this chapter, do not expressly use unilateral-bilateral terminology. However, both of these important sources of modern contract principles contain provisions for dealing with typical unilateral contract problems. Despite this evidence of disfavor, the courts continue to use unilateral contract terminology, in part because it enables them to do justice in some cases by imposing contractual liability on one party without the necessity of finding a return promise of the other party. For example, many recent employment cases have used unilateral contract analyses to hold employers liable for promises relating to pension rights, bonuses or incentive pay, and profit-sharing benefits, though the employees in question did not make any clear return promise to continue their employment for any specified time or to do anything else in exchange for the employer's promise.[3]

Valid, Unenforceable, Voidable, and Void Contracts

A **valid contract** is one that meets all of the legal requirements for a binding contract. Valid contracts are, therefore, enforceable in court.

An **unenforceable contract** is one that meets the basic legal requirements for a contract but may not be enforceable due to some other legal rule. The Writing chapter discusses the statute of frauds, which requires written evidence of certain contracts. An otherwise valid oral contract that the statute of frauds requires to be in writing, for example, may be unenforceable due to the parties' failure to reduce the contract to written form. Another example of an unenforceable contract is an otherwise valid contract whose enforcement is barred by the applicable contract statute of limitations.

Voidable contracts are those in which one or more of the parties have the legal right to cancel their obligations under the contract. They are enforceable against both parties unless a party with the power to void the contract has exercised that power. The Reality of Consent chapter, for example, states that contracts induced by misrepresentation, fraud, duress, or undue influence are voidable at the election of the injured party.

Void contracts are agreements that create no legal obligations because they fail to contain one or more of the basic elements required for enforceability. A void contract is, in a sense, a contradiction in terms. It would be more accurate to say that no contract was created in such cases. The Illegality chapter, for example, mentions that a contract to commit a crime, such as an agreement for the sale of cocaine, does not create a binding legal obligation. Nonetheless, practical constraints may sometimes encourage a party to such a contract to perform his agreement rather than raise an illegality defense.

Express and Implied Contracts

In an **express contract,** the parties have directly stated the terms of their contract orally or in writing at the time the contract was formed. As the following *Cook v. Cook* case illustrates, however, the mutual agreement

---

[3] See Petit, "Modern Unilateral Contracts," 63 *B.U.L. Rev.* 551 (1983).

necessary to create a contract may also be demonstrated by the conduct of the parties. When the surrounding facts and circumstances indicate that an agreement has in fact been reached, an **implied contract** (also called a *contract implied in fact*) has been created. When you go to a doctor for treatment, for example, you do not ordinarily state the terms of your agreement in advance, although it is clear that you do, in fact, have an agreement. A court would infer a promise by your doctor to use reasonable care and skill in treating you and a return promise on your part to pay a reasonable fee for her services.

Executed and Executory Contracts

A contract is **executed** when all of the parties have fully performed their contractual duties, and it is **executory** until such duties have been fully performed.

Any contract may be described using one or more of the above terms. For example, Eurocars, Inc. orders five new Mercedes-Benz 500 SLs from Mercedes. Mercedes sends Eurocars its standard acknowledgment form accepting the order. The parties have a *valid, express, bilateral* contract that will be *executory* until Mercedes delivers the cars and Eurocars pays for them.

COOK v. COOK

691 P.2d 664 (Ariz. Sup. Ct. 1984)

Intending to marry as soon as Donald's divorce became final, Rose Elsten and Donald Cook moved to Tucson in 1969 and lived there together until 1981. Although they did not marry, Rose used Donald's last name and they represented themselves to the community as husband and wife. Both parties worked throughout most of the relationship, pooling their income in two joint accounts and acquiring a house, two cars, and a number of shares of stock, all owned as joint tenants with right of survivorship. Rose left Donald in 1981. Of their joint assets, she received only one car and a few hundred dollars; Donald retained the balance.

Rose filed suit against Donald, arguing that he had breached their agreement to share their assets equally. In her deposition she said: "[E]verything we did and purchased, whether it be a vacuum cleaner or a car, was together as husband and wife. It was just something *that we agreed on*, that is how we were going to do it." When the trial court ruled against her, she appealed.

Feldman, Justice.   The *sine qua non* of any contract is the exchange of promises. From this exchange flows the obligation of one party to another. Although it is most apparent that two parties have exchanged promises when their words express a spoken or written statement of promissory intention, mutual promises need not be express in order to create an enforceable contract. Indeed, a promise "may be inferred wholly or partly from conduct," and "there is no distinction in the effect of the promise whether it is expressed in writing, or orally, or in acts, or partly in one of these ways and partly in others." *Restatement (Second) of Contracts.*

Thus, two parties may by their course of conduct express their agreement, though no words are ever spoken. From their conduct alone the finder of fact can determine the existence of an agreement. Although isolated acts of joint participation such as cohabitation or the opening of a joint account may not suffice to create a contract, the fact finder may infer an exchange of promises, and the existence of the contract, from the entire course of conduct between the parties.

The conduct of the parties certainly demonstrates such an agreement and intent. Rose and Donald maintained two joint accounts, a checking account and a credit union savings account, in the names of "Rose and Don Cook" and held them as joint tenants with right of survivorship. Neither Rose nor Donald maintained a separate account. Both deposited portions of their paychecks into the accounts and used the funds to pay for household expenses and various assets they purchased. In addition, Rose and Donald held jointly a number of shares of Southwest Gas stock purchased with funds from the credit union account. In 1972 they purchased a house, taking the deed as husband and wife in joint tenancy with right of survivorship. Both signed the mortgage, incurring liability for the full purchase price of the house, and payments on the mortgage were made out of the joint checking account. There is ample evidence to support a finding that Rose and Donald agreed to pool their resources and share equally in certain accumulations; their course of conduct may be seen as consistently demonstrating the existence of such an agreement.

Judgment reversed in favor of Rose; case remanded for further proceedings.

QUASI-CONTRACT   *C4·*

The traditional common law insistence on the presence of all the elements required for a binding contract before contractual obligation is imposed can cause injustice in some cases. One person may have provided goods or services to another person who benefited from them but has no contractual obligation to pay for them, because no facts exist that would justify a court in implying a promise to pay for them. Such a situation can also arise in cases where the parties contemplated entering into a binding contract but some legal defense exists that prevents the enforcement of the agreement. Consider the following examples:

1. Jones paints Smith's house by mistake, thinking it belongs to Reed. Smith knows that Jones is painting his house but does not inform him of his error. There are no facts from which a court can infer that Jones and Smith have a contract, because the parties have had no prior discussions or dealings.

2. Thomas Products fraudulently induces Perkins to buy a household products franchise by grossly misstating the average revenues of its franchisees. Perkins discovers the misrepresentation after he has resold some products that he has received but before he has paid

Thomas for them. Perkins elects to rescind (cancel) the franchise contract on the basis of the fraud.

In the preceding examples, both Smith and Perkins have good defenses to contract liability; however, enabling Smith to get a free paint job and Perkins to avoid paying for the goods he resold would *unjustly enrich* them at the expense of Jones and Thomas. To deal with such cases and to prevent such unjust enrichment, the courts imply *as a matter of law* a promise by the benefited party to pay the *reasonable value* of the benefits he received. This idea is called **quasi-contract** (or contract implied in law) because it represents an obligation imposed by law to avoid injustice, not a contractual obligation created by voluntary consent. Quasi-contract liability has been imposed in situations too numerous and varied to detail. In general, however, quasi-contract liability is imposed when one party *confers a benefit* on another who *knowingly accepts it* and *retains it* under circumstances that make it *unjust* to do so without paying for it. So, if Jones painted Smith's house while Smith was away on vacation, Smith would probably not be liable for the reasonable value of the paint job because he did *not* knowingly accept it and because he has no way to return it to Jones. The following *Salamon* case highlights the centrality of the unjust enrichment idea to quasi-contract liability.

implied in law

SALAMON v. TERRA
477 N.E.2d 1029 (Mass. Sup. Ct. 1985)

In February of 1981, Walter Salamon, a builder, entered into written agreements to buy two lots owned by Albert Terra, Jr., for $9,000 each. The agreement provided that Salamon would take possession of the lots by April 15, 1981, but would not have to pay the bulk of the purchase price ($8,500 per lot) until delivery of the deeds in August 1981. Salamon intended to build a house on each lot and then sell the houses to third parties, paying off Terra with the proceeds of the house sales. Salamon partially completed the two houses, but due to adverse economic conditions was unable either to obtain financing to complete them or to find purchasers for them. Terra extended the date of performance under the purchase agreements by several months, but because Salamon was never able to pay for the lots he retained ownership of them. Salamon filed a quasi-contract suit against Terra seeking to recover the value of the partially completed houses. The trial judge ruled that Terra had been unjustly enriched in the amount of $15,000, but the Appellate Division reversed the trial court's decision. Salamon appealed.

Abrams, Justice.   A quasi-contract or a contract implied in law is an obligation created by law "for reasons of justice, without any expressions of assent and sometimes even against a clear expression of dissent . . . [C]onsiderations of equity and morality play a large part in constructing a quasi-contract. . . ." 1 A. Corbin, *Contracts* § 19 (1963). The underlying basis for awarding damages in a quasi-contract case is unjust enrichment of one party and unjust detriment to the other party. The Appellate Division stated the rule as follows: "The injustice of the enrichment or detriment in quasi-contract equates with the defeat of someone's reasonable expectations."

Generally, if a landowner has requested that a person construct a structure on his or her property, it is reasonably expected that the landowner will pay for the services and benefit conferred, even if there was no express contract for the construction or if a contract has been violated. The evidence in this case, however, does not support a conclusion that either party should reasonably have expected that Terra would pay for the value of partially completed houses or expenses incurred by Salamon in the building of partially completed houses on his property. Terra did not request or even desire that houses be built on property which he intended to use or to retain. He intended to convey the lots to Salamon in exchange for cash. The fact that Salamon built two houses on property owned by Terra was merely part of the financing arrangement. Terra had no interest in the value or expense of the houses, but was interested only in receiving the balance of the purchase price of the lots. There was no agreement that Terra would pay for unfinished (or finished) houses on his land in the event that Salamon was unable to fulfill his contractual obligations. Salamon could reasonably have expected that he would be paid for his labor, but both parties understood payment would be made by a third party purchaser of the houses. Terra could not reasonably have been expected to pay for Salamon's efforts in what appears to have been a speculative commercial transaction. Where a builder, with the permission of a seller, undertakes the construction of a house in furtherance of his own objectives (payment for lots from proceeds of sales) and at his own risk, he cannot recover his disbursements.

Judgment for Terra affirmed.

PROMISSORY ESTOPPEL

Another very important idea that 20th-century courts have developed to deal with the unfairness that would sometimes result from the strict application of traditional contract principles is the doctrine of **promissory estoppel.** In numerous situations, one person may *rely* on a promise made by another even though the promise and surrounding circumstances are not sufficient to justify the conclusion that a contract has been created, because one or more of the required elements is missing. To allow the person who made such a promise (the promisor) to argue that no contract was created would sometimes work an injustice on the person who relied on the promise (the promisee). For example, John's parents told him that they would give him the family farm when they died. Relying on this promise, John stayed at home and worked on the farm for several years. However, when John's parents died, they left the farm to his sister Martha. Should Martha and the parents' estate be allowed to defeat John's claim to the farm by arguing that the parents' promise was unenforceable because John gave no consideration for the promise? His parents did not request that John stay home and work on the farm in exchange for their promise.

In the early decades of this century, many courts began to protect the reliance of promisees like John. They said that persons who made promises that produced such reliance were *estopped*, or equitably prevented, from raising any defense they had to the enforcement of their promise. Out of such cases grew the doctrine of promissory estoppel. Section 90 of the *Restatement (Second) of Contracts* states:

A promise which the promisor should reasonably expect to induce action or forbearance on the part of the promisee or a third person and which does induce such action or forbearance is binding if injustice can be avoided only by enforcement of the promise. The remedy granted for breach may be limited as justice requires.

Thus, the elements of promissory estoppel are a *promise* that the *promisor should foresee is likely to induce reliance, reliance* on the promise by the promisee, and *injustice* as a result of that reliance.

When you consider these elements, it is obvious that promissory estoppel is fundamentally different from traditional contract principles. Contract is traditionally thought of as protecting *agreements* or bargains. Promissory estoppel, on the other hand, protects *reliance*. Early promissory estoppel cases applied the doctrine only to donative or gift promises like the one made by John's parents in the previous example. As subsequent chapters demonstrate, however, promissory estoppel is now being used by the courts to prevent offerors from revoking their offers, to enforce indefinite promises, and to enforce oral promises that would ordinarily have to be in writing. Given the basic conceptual differences between estoppel and contract, and the judicial tendency to use promissory estoppel to compensate for the absence of the traditional elements of contract, its growth as a new device for enforcing promises is one of the most important developments in modern contract law.

CONCEPT REVIEW

CONTRACT AND CONTRACTLIKE THEORIES OF RECOVERY

Theory	Key Concept	Remedy
Contract	Voluntary agreement	Enforce promise
Quasi-Contract	Unjust enrichment	Reasonable value of services
Promissory Estoppel	Foreseeable reliance	Enforce promise or recover reliance losses

---

THE UNIFORM COMMERCIAL CODE

Origins and Purposes of the Code

The Uniform Commercial Code (UCC) was created by the American Law Institute and the National Conference of Commissioners on Uniform State Laws. All of the states have adopted it except Louisiana, which has adopted only part of the Code. The drafters of the Code had several purposes in mind, the most obvious of which was to establish a uniform set of rules to govern commercial transactions, which are often conducted across state lines in today's national markets. Despite the Code's almost national adoption, however, complete uniformity has not been achieved. Many states have varied or amended the Code's language in specific instances, and some Code provisions were drafted in alternative ways, giving the states more than one version of particular Code provisions to choose from. Also, the various state courts have reached different conclusions about the meaning of particular Code sections.

In addition to promoting uniformity, the drafters of the Code sought to create a body of rules that would realistically and fairly solve the common problems occurring in everyday commercial transactions. Finally, the drafters tried to formulate rules that would promote fair dealing and higher standards in the marketplace.

Scope of the Code

The Code contains nine substantive articles, most of which are discussed in detail in Parts IV, VI, and VII of this book. The most important Code article for our present purposes is Article 2, the sales article of the Code.

Nature of Article 2

Many of the provisions of Article 2 exhibit the basic tendencies of modern contract law discussed earlier in this chapter. Accordingly, they differ from traditional contract law rules in a variety of important ways. The Code is more concerned with rewarding people's legitimate expectations than with technical rules, so it is generally more flexible than contract law. A court that applies the Code is more likely to find that the parties had a contract than is a court that applies contract law [2–204] (the numbers in brackets refer to specific Code sections). In some cases, the Code gives less weight than does contract law to technical requirements such as consideration [2–205 and 2–209].

The drafters of the Code sought to create practical rules to deal with what people actually do in today's marketplace. We live in the day of the form contract, so some of the Code's rules try to deal fairly with that fact [2–205, 2–207, 2–209(2), and 2–302]. The words *reasonable, commercially reasonable*, and *seasonably* (within a reasonable time) are found throughout the Code. This reasonableness standard is different from the hypothetical reasonable person standard in tort law. A court that tries to decide what is reasonable under the Code is more likely to be concerned with what people really do in the marketplace than with what a nonexistent reasonable person would do.

The drafters of the Code wanted to promote fair dealing and higher standards in the marketplace, so they imposed a **duty of good faith** [1–203] in the performance and enforcement of every contract under the Code. Good faith means "honesty in fact," which is required of all parties to sales contracts [1–201(19)]. In addition, merchants are required to observe "reasonable commercial standards of fair dealing" [2–103(1)(b)]. The parties cannot alter this duty of good faith by agreement [1–102(3)]. Finally, the Code expressly recognizes the concept of an **unconscionable contract,** one that is grossly unfair or one-sided, and it gives the courts broad discretionary powers to deal fairly with such contracts [2–302].[4]

The Code also recognizes that buyers tend to place more reliance on professional sellers and that professionals are generally more knowledgeable and better able to protect themselves than nonprofessionals. So, the Code distinguishes between **merchants** and nonmerchants by holding merchants to a higher standard in some cases [2–201(2), 2–205, and 2–207(2)]. The Code defines the term *merchant* [2–104(1)] on a case-by-case basis. If a person regularly deals in the kind of goods being sold, or pretends to have some special knowledge about the goods, or employed an agent in the sale who fits either of these two descriptions, that person is a merchant for the purposes of the contract in question. So, if you buy a used car from a used-car dealer, the dealer is a merchant for the purposes of your contract. But, if you buy a refrigerator from a used-car dealer, the dealer is probably not a merchant.

Application of the Code

Article 2 expressly applies only to *contracts for the sale of goods* [2–102]. The Code contains a somewhat complicated definition of *goods* [2–105], but the essence of the definition is that *goods* are tangible, movable, personal property. So, contracts for the sale of such items as motor vehicles, books, appliances, and clothing are covered by Article 2. But Article 2 does *not* apply to contracts for the sale of real estate, stocks and bonds, or other intangibles. Article 2 also does not apply to *service* contracts. This can cause confusion because, although contracts of employment or other personal services are clearly not covered by Article 2, many contracts involve elements of both goods and services. As the following *Neilson* case illustrates, the test that the courts most frequently use to determine whether Article 2 applies to such a contract is to ask which element, goods or services, *predominates* in the contract. Is the major purpose or thrust of the agreement the rendering of a service, or is it the sale of goods, with any services involved being merely incidental to that sale? This means that contracts calling for services that involve significant elements of personal skill or judgment in addition to goods probably are not governed by Article 2. Construction contracts, remodeling contracts, and auto repair contracts are all examples of mixed goods and services contracts that may be considered outside the scope of the Code.

Two other important qualifications must be made concerning the application of Code contract principles. First, the Code does not change *all* of the traditional contract rules. Where no specific Code rule exists, traditional contract law rules apply to contracts for the sale of goods. Second, and ultimately far more important, the courts have demonstrated a significant tendency to apply Code contract concepts by analogy to contracts not specifically covered by Article 2. For example, the Code concepts of good faith dealing and unconscionability have enjoyed wide application in cases that are technically outside the scope of Article 2. Thus, the Code is an

---

[4] The Illegality chapter discusses unconscionability in detail.

FIGURE 3 When the Code Applies

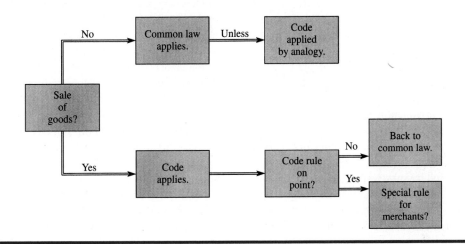

important influence in shaping the evolution of contract law in general, and if this trend toward broader application of Code principles continues, the time may come when the dichotomy between Code principles and traditional contract rules is a thing of the past. Figure 3 illustrates the rules governing the Code's application.

NEILSON BUSINESS EQUIPMENT CENTER v. MONTELEONE
524 A.2d 1172 (Del. Sup. Ct. 1987)

Dr. Italo V. Monteleone, a neurologist, entered into a lease-purchase agreement for a turnkey computer system from Neilson Business Equipment Center, Inc. The system included both hardware and software recommended by Neilson after two Neilson representatives studied Dr. Monteleone's manual billing system. When the computer was delivered in July of 1982, problems immediately developed. The system printed a separate bill for each treatment instead of one bill listing all of the doctor's services to a patient during a billing period. The bills and medical insurance forms were incompatible with Dr. Monteleone's records, and incorrect balances appeared in the accounts receivable register.

Neilson's initial attempts to modify the software, which it had acquired elsewhere and renamed the "Neilson Medical Office Management System," were unsuccessful. In August of 1982, Neilson hired a consultant to solve the problems. However, in February of 1983, before the consultant was able effectively to make the needed modifications, Dr. Monteleone notified Neilson that he was terminating the lease for cause. Dr. Monteleone later filed suit against Neilson, and the trial court awarded him $34,983.42 in damages for breaches of the implied warranties of merchantability and fitness for a particular purpose. Neilson appealed, arguing that the trial court had erred in holding that the case was governed by the UCC.

Moore, Justice. The central issue before us is whether a contract for a computer system consisting of computer hardware, software, and services constitutes "goods" under the UCC. Article Two of the UCC applies to "transactions in goods." The contract between Dr. Monteleone and

Neilson is a mixed contract for both goods and services. When a mixed contract is presented, it is necessary for a court to review the factual circumstances surrounding the negotiation, formation, and contemplated performance of the contract to determine whether the contract is predominantly or primarily a contract for the sale of goods. If so, the provisions of Article Two apply.

Neilson urges us to separate the contract into three distinct subparts—hardware, software, and services. It contends that only the hardware can be classified as "goods" under the Code, that there was nothing defective about the hardware, and thus Monteleone's claims for breaches of implied warranties fail. Neilson further argues that software is an intangible, and that intangibles do not constitute "goods" subject to the Code.

That argument is innovative, but unpersuasive. Neilson contracted to supply a turn-key computer system; that is, a system sold as a package which is ready to function immediately. The hardware and software elements are combined into a single unit—the computer system—prior to sale. The trial court's factual conclusion that the computer system is predominantly "goods" is supported by substantial evidence. Dr. Monteleone did not intend to contract separately for hardware and software. Rather, he bought a computer system to meet his information processing needs. Any consulting services rendered by Neilson were ancillary to the contract, and cannot reasonably be treated as standing separately to escape the implied warranties of the UCC.

Judgment for Dr. Monteleone affirmed.

No Force Law ~ Very Influential

RESTATEMENT (SECOND) OF CONTRACTS

Nature and Origins

In 1932, the American Law Institute published the first *Restatement of Contracts*,[5] an attempt to codify and systematize the soundest principles of contract law gleaned from thousands of often conflicting judicial decisions. As the product of a private organization, the *Restatement* did not have the force of law, but as the considered judgment of some of the leading scholars of the legal profession, it was highly influential in shaping the evolution of contract law. The *Restatement (Second) of Contracts,* issued in 1979, is an attempt to reflect the significant changes that have occurred in contract law in the years following the birth of the first *Restatement*. The tone of the *Restatement Second* differs dramatically from that of the *Restatement*, which is often characterized as a positivist attempt to formulate a system of black letter rules of contract law. The *Restatement Second*, in contrast, reflects the "shift from rules to standards" in modern contract law: the shift from precise, technical rules to broader, discretionary principles that

produce just results.[6] The *Restatement Second* plainly bears the mark of the legal realists, discussed in The Nature of Law chapter, and has been heavily influenced by the UCC. In fact, many *Restatement Second* provisions are virtually identical to their Code analogues. For example, the *Restatement Second* has explicitly embraced the Code concepts of *good faith*[7] and *unconscionability.*[8]

Impact

The *Restatement Second*, like its predecessor, does not have the force of law, and its relative newness prevents any accurate assessment of its impact on contemporary contract cases. Nonetheless, given the influential role played by the first *Restatement* and the previously mentioned tendency of the courts to employ Code principles by analogy in contract cases, it seems fair to assume that the *Restatement Second* will serve as a major inspiration for contract developments in the decades to come. For this reason, we give significant attention to the *Restatement Second* in the following chapters.

---

[5] See the Nature of Law chapter for a general discussion of the *Restatement* phenomenon.

[6] Speidel, "*Restatement Second*: Omitted Terms and Contract Method," 67 *Cornell L. Rev.* 785, 786 (1982).

[7] *Restatement (Second) of Contracts* § 205 (1981).

[8] *Restatement (Second) of Contracts* § 208 (1981).

ETHICAL AND PUBLIC POLICY CONCERNS

1. Compare and contrast the ethical values at the heart of classical contract law with those at the heart of modern contract law. If all contracts today fit the typical model assumed by classical contract law, would we necessarily feel ethically compelled to treat them differently than they were treated under classical contract law?

2. Do a brief social cost-benefit analysis of the "shift from rules to standards" that has occurred in modern contract law. Do a contrasting cost-benefit analysis of the rule-oriented approach of classical contract law.

3. The idea that contracts should be enforced because they are voluntary agreements can obviously be justified on ethical grounds. What ethical justifications, if any, can you give for departing from the notion of voluntary agreement in quasi-contract and promissory estoppel cases?

SUMMARY

Contracts are legally enforceable promises or sets of promises. To attain contract status, promises must conform to certain legal requirements prescribed by contract law. Contract law, like other bodies of law, is constantly changing in response to changing social needs and values. Modern contract law, in a quest for just results, is evolving in the direction of increased public supervision of private contracts and broad, discretionary rules. The basic essence of contract law, however, still derives from the idea that contracts are consensual, private agreements.

In their search for justice, the courts have developed doctrines that can operate to impose obligations on people in the absence of the agreement required by traditional contract law. *Quasi-contract* doctrine is used by the courts to prevent persons who have received goods or services from others from being unjustly enriched, by implying a promise to pay for those goods or services as a matter of law. *Promissory estoppel* protects persons who rely on the promises of others by preventing promisors from raising legal defenses to the enforcement of their promises. In recent years, promissory estoppel principles have been applied to an increasing range of contract problems, leading some scholars to conclude that contract is in danger of being eclipsed by promissory estoppel.

Article 2 of the Uniform Commercial Code is an important source of modern contract principles. Technically, it applies only to contracts for the sale of *goods*, and it dramatically changes some of the basic rules governing such contracts. The Code, however, has had significant influence on the rules governing other contracts because the courts often apply Code principles to such contracts by analogy.

The *Restatement (Second) of Contracts* clearly reflects the influence of the Code. Many *Restatement Second* provisions were obviously inspired by their Code counterparts. The *Restatement Second* is also similar to the Code in its tendency to employ broad discretionary standards that facilitate judicial supervision of contracts in the name of fairness. Although the *Restatement Second* does not have the force of law, the influence formerly enjoyed by the first *Restatement* and the existing tendency of many courts to employ Code principles like those adopted by the *Restatement Second* suggest that it will also be a significant source of inspiration for future contract developments.

PROBLEM CASES

1. In 1973, Baker and Ratzlaff entered a contract requiring Ratzlaff to grow 380 acres of popcorn and Baker to buy it at $4.75 per hundredweight. The contract gave Ratzlaff the right to terminate if Baker failed to pay for any of the popcorn on delivery. Early in 1974, Ratzlaff made the first two deliveries under the contract to Baker's plant. Baker's plant manager gave Ratzlaff weight tickets acknowledging receipt of the popcorn. Ratzlaff was not given payment and did not ask for it. Nor did he stop by Baker's business office, which was on a direct route between his farm and Baker's plant, to ask for payment. When Baker called to ask for further deliveries, Ratzlaff offered excuses, but did not mention payment. Ratzlaff later told Baker he was terminating due to Baker's failure to pay upon delivery, selling the remaining 1.6 million pounds of popcorn elsewhere for $8.00 per hundredweight. After hearing evidence that Baker's normal practice was to make payments at its office on the basis of copies of weight tickets sent from the plant, and that Baker would have paid promptly had Ratzlaff requested payment, the trial court ruled that Ratzlaff's termination was a breach of his duty to act in good faith. Was this ruling proper? p204 YES.

2. The Schinmanns had been growing spearmint and peppermint for oil since 1946. In 1981, they wanted to purchase Scotch mint (spearmint) roots and approached the Moores. At first, the Moores said they had none for sale, but later decided to take out and sell one field of roots. Although the Moores had been raising mint for oil since the early 1960s, this was their first sale of roots. Later, a dispute arose among the parties over the quality of the roots. The Schinmanns argued that the Moores were merchants under the UCC and, as such, they had made and breached an implied warranty of merchantability in the sale of the mint roots. Were the Moores merchants? *No. p204   FIRST SALE – ROOTS   DOES NOT APPLY*

3. Edgar C. Faris conceived the idea for a sports quiz show. He contacted television sports announcer Dick Enberg to see whether Enberg would be willing to be the show's master of ceremonies. He also offered Enberg the opportunity of becoming a coproducer and part owner of the show. Enberg met with Faris, expressed interest in his proposal, and asked for and was given a copy of the format for the show. Later, the "Sports Challenge" show appeared on television with a different producer and with Enberg as master of ceremonies. There were certain differences and similarities between the show and Faris's idea. Faris filed suit against Enberg for breach of implied contract. Did Enberg have a contract with Faris? *NO! NEVER EXPRESS AGREEMENT & MADE NO CONSIDERATION*

4. First National Bank filed suit against Jessie Ordoyne and Patricia Ordoyne Bordelon for failure to pay sums due on a VISA card account. Ordoyne argued that he did not know that the account existed until the bank called him to inquire about his failure to make payments. He then told the bank that he and Patricia were divorced, and that she must have forged his signature to the account application form. The bank argued that he was nonetheless liable on a quasi-contractual basis, although it failed to prove that he had received any of the merchandise charged to the card. Was the trial court's decision in Jessie's favor correct? *YES. p201*

5. On December 13, 1978, Benjamin Ravelo was informed that his application for a job as a police officer with the County of Hawaii had been accepted and that he would be sworn in as a police recruit on January 2, 1979. Ravelo then resigned from his job as a police officer with the Honolulu Police Department, and his wife also gave notice of termination to her employer. On December 20, 1978, Ravelo was informed by the county that he would not be hired after all. He and his wife tried to cancel their resignations, but were told it was too late to get their old jobs back. When Ravelo filed suit, the county moved to dismiss his complaint on the ground that under the applicable provisions of the civil service law Ravelo was at best a probationary employee who could be dismissed without cause at any time. The trial court agreed and dismissed Ravelo's suit. Should the dismissal be reversed on appeal? *Yes. PROMISSORY ESTOPPEL*

6. Commercial Cornice, a subcontractor, entered a contract with Camel Construction, a general contractor, to furnish labor and materials for a construction project owned by Malarkey's, Inc. Commercial completed its obligations under the contract, but only received $78,000 of the $177,773. When Commercial filed suit against Camel and Malarkey's for the remaining $99,773, Malarkey's moved to dismiss Commercial's claims against it on the ground that Commercial's only contract was with Camel. The trial court granted Malarkey's motion, despite the fact that the evidence indicated that Malarkey's had never payed Camel for the work. Was the dismissal of Commercial's claim against Malarkey's proper? *Two Contracts. Comm must collect from Camel*

7. Early in 1986, Gray Communications contacted various television tower builders concerning the manufacture and erection of a television tower. After several discussions with Kline Iron & Steel, Gray received a signed written proposal from Kline to build and install the tower for $1,485,368. The proposal said that it could be revoked or modified by Kline prior to acceptance by Gray, and it required Kline's approval after acceptance by Gray. Gray refused to sign the proposal after Kline would not lower its bid to meet a competitor's lower bid, and Kline filed suit for breach of contract. At trial, Gray argued that no contract existed, and that even if a contract existed it was unenforceable because Gray had never signed the writing the UCC requires for all contracts for $500 or more. Kline argued that the contract was not covered by the UCC because it was a services contract. The evidence at trial indicated that the service component of the agreement amounted at most to 26 percent of the total cost. Should the court apply the UCC? *Should apply*

8. Data Processing Services, Inc. (DPS), a custom computer programmer, entered into an agreement to develop computer software for an accounting system for the L. H. Smith Oil Corporation. Smith refused to pay DPS's final billing on the ground that DPS's work had been unsatisfactory. DPS filed a breach of contract suit against Smith, and Smith counterclaimed for damages *p. 204.*

resulting from DPS's alleged failure to perform satisfactorily. The trial court ruled that the UCC applied to the parties' dispute. Was the trial court's ruling correct?

NOT UNDER UCC.

9. Stephen Gall and his family became ill after drinking contaminated water supplied to their home by the McKeesport Municipal Water Authority. They filed suit against the utility, arguing, among other things, that the utility had breached the UCC implied warranty of merchantability when it sold them contaminated water. The utility moved to dismiss their complaint, arguing that since water was not "goods" the UCC did not apply. Should the Galls's complaint be dismissed? *UCC DOES N APPLY HERE*

10. Tedesco listed his property for sale with Judd Realty, signing a "listing contract" which obligated him to pay Judd an 8% commission if Judd found a "pur-

Mutual Contract

chaser" for the property. Two days before the listing agreement was due to expire, Judd's president delivered to Tedesco a signed written offer to purchase the property for the stated price, together with a $1,000 deposit check from the buyer. Tedesco then said he had changed his mind and did not want to sell. He refused to sign the agreement or pay Judd's commission. When Judd filed suit, Tedesco argued that there was no contract because the sale was not consummated and therefore the buyer found by Judd never became a "purchaser" within the meaning of the listing agreement. Was Judd entitled to a commission?

Yes! BECAUSE He FILLED HIS PART!

CHAPTER 10

THE AGREEMENT: OFFER

INTRODUCTION

The concept of mutual agreement lies at the heart of traditional contract law. Courts faced with deciding whether two or more persons entered into a contract look first for an *agreement* between the parties. Did the parties arrive at an understanding on terms that each party found acceptable, or did their negotiations falter before a true agreement was reached? But should courts seeking to answer such questions concern themselves with the *subjective* (actual) intent of the parties, or with the *objective* intent manifested by their words and deeds? Early American courts took a subjective approach to contract formation, asking whether there truly was a "meeting of the minds" between the parties. This subjective standard, however, threatened the certainty and predictability of contracts because it left every contract vulnerable to disputes about actual intent. The desire to meet the needs of the marketplace by affording predictable and consistent results in contract cases dictated a shift toward an *objective theory of contract*. By the middle of the 19th century, the objective approach to contract formation was firmly established in American law. Judge Learned Hand once described the effect of objective contract theory as follows:

A contract has, strictly speaking, nothing to do with the personal, or individual, intent of the parties. A contract is an obli-

gation attached by the mere force of law to certain acts of the parties, usually words, which ordinarily accompany and represent a known intent. If however, it were proved by twenty bishops that either party when he used the words intended something else than the usual meaning which the law imposes on them, he would still be held, unless there were mutual mistake or something else of that sort.[1]

Keep the objective theory well in mind as you read the following material on the contract formation process. You will see many examples of its operation.

WHAT IS AN OFFER?

Definition

Section 24 of the *Restatement (Second) of Contracts* defines an offer as "the manifestation of willingness to enter into a bargain, so made as to justify another person in understanding that his assent to that bargain is invited and will conclude it." In other words, when we consider all that the parties said and did, did one of the parties ever, in effect, say to the other: "This is it—if you agree to these terms, we have a contract." The question of whether an offer was ever made is a critically important

---

[1]*Hotchkiss v. National City Bank*, 200 F. 287, 293 (S.D.N.Y. 1911).

211

first step in the contract formation process. A person who makes an offer (the **offeror**) gives the person to whom she makes the offer (the **offeree**) the power to bind her to a contract by accepting the offer. If no offer was ever made, however, there was nothing to accept and no contract results.

Traditional contract law rules on contract formation are designed to assure that persons are never bound to contracts unless they clearly intend to be bound. Therefore, the basic thing that the courts require for the creation of an offer is some objective indication of a *present intent to contract* on the part of the offeror. Two of the most important things from which courts infer an intent to contract are the *definiteness* of the alleged offer and the fact that it has been *communicated to the offeree*.

Definiteness of Terms

If an alleged offer fails to state specifically what the offeror is willing to do and what he asks in return for his performance, there is a good chance that the parties are still in the process of negotiation. If Smith says to Ford, "I'd like to buy your house," and Ford responds, "You've got a deal," do we have a contract? Obviously not. Smith's statement is merely an invitation to offer or an invitation to negotiate. It does not indicate a present intent to contract on Smith's part. It merely indicates a willingness to contract in the future if the parties can reach agreement on mutually acceptable terms. However, if Smith sends Ford a detailed and specific written document stating all of the material terms and conditions on which he is willing to buy the house and Ford writes back agreeing to Smith's terms, a contract has probably been created.

Definiteness and specificity in offers are also important in contract law because the offer often contains all the terms of the parties' contract. This is so because all that offerees are allowed to do in most cases is to accept or reject the terms of the offer. Agreements that are incomplete or indefinite because they omit material terms or imprecisely state such terms pose several problems for courts applying traditional contract principles. The fact that the parties' agreement is indefinite on some important points or lacks certain significant terms that such contracts normally address may, of course, indicate that the parties never, in fact, reached agreement on the omitted or indefinite terms. Even if the parties apparently intended to create a binding contract, how can a court that takes the traditional hands-off approach justify imposing contractual liability when the parties have failed to clearly indicate their intent on a particular issue? Classical contract principles see courts as contract enforcers, not as contract makers. Therefore, as the following *Action Ads* case indicates, agreements that are too indefinite are generally unenforceable at common law.

ACTION ADS, INC. v. JUDES

671 P.2d 309 (Wyo. Sup. Ct. 1983)

On April 23, 1981, Action Ads, Inc., hired Kenneth Judes as a salesman in the Sheridan, Wyoming, area. The employment contract provided that: "Sixty days from your date of hire, Action Ads will provide a medical insurance program for you and your dependents." Judes was not very successful as a salesman for Action, earning only $580.09 in commissions during the entire tenure of his employment with the company. Action never provided the promised medical insurance, a fact Judes learned when he inquired about whether he was covered on August 27, 1981.

Judes did little or no solicitation for Action after August, and the last order he placed with Action was in October of 1981. During the period in which he was purportedly working for Action, Judes held himself out as unemployed, collecting $2,448 in employment benefits. On November 14, 1981, Judes was seriously burned in a gas explosion at a mobile home. He filed suit against Action to recover his medical expenses, arguing that Action had breached the employment contract by failing to provide insurance coverage for him. When a trial court awarded Judes $18,824.86, Action appealed.

Rose, Justice.   The determinative question on appeal is whether the agreement by Action to provide insurance coverage was sufficiently definite and certain to constitute an enforceable contract. In a suit on a contract to procure insurance, the plaintiff has the burden of proving the elements of the insurance policy with sufficient certainty to enable the court to establish damages in the event of a breach. The corollary to that principle is a well-known rule: The measure of damages for breach of a contract to obtain insurance is that amount which would have been recovered had the insurance been furnished as agreed. Judes offered no evidence as to the risks insured against, the amount of coverage, or any other details of the "insurance program" that Action Ads, Inc., was obligated to provide. There was no proof of the insurance carrier contemplated by the parties. Most important, there was no showing that the injury actually sustained by Judes would have been covered by the insurance program had Action Ads fully complied with the employment contract.

It is apparent that the pertinent contract term is not sufficiently definite and certain to permit this court to determine the extent of the promised performance. Without that information, we are unable to measure the damages to which Judes might reasonably be entitled in the event of a breach. The indefiniteness of the agreement is due to the absence of any evidence whatsoever concerning the elements of the insurance coverage that Action Ads was obligated to provide. Since Judes failed to show to what extent, if any, the promised insurance program would have compensated him for his injury, we hold that the agreement to provide insurance was too uncertain and indefinite to be enforceable.

Judgment reversed in favor of Action Ads.

Definiteness and Modern Contract Law   The traditional contract law insistence on definiteness can serve useful ends. It can prevent a person from being held to an agreement when none was reached or from being bound by a contract term to which he never assented. Often, however, it can operate to frustrate the expectations of parties who intend to contract but, for whatever reason, fail to procure an agreement that is sufficiently definite. Modern contract principles, with their increased emphasis on furthering people's justifiable expectations and their encouragement of a hands-on approach by the courts, often create contractual liability in situations where no contract would have resulted at common law. Perhaps no part of the Code better illustrates this basic difference between modern contract principles and their classical counterparts than does the basic Code section on contract formation [2–204]. Sales contracts under Article 2 can be created "in any manner sufficient to show agreement, including conduct which recognizes the existence of a contract" [2–204(1)]. So, if the parties are acting as though they have a contract by delivering or accepting goods or payment, for example, this may be enough to create a binding contract, even if it is impossible to point to a particular moment in time when the contract was created [2–204(2)].

As the following *Schmieding* case illustrates, the fact that the parties left open one or more terms of their agreement does not necessarily mean that their agreement is too indefinite to enforce. A sales contract is created if the court finds that the parties *intended* to make a contract and that their agreement is complete enough to allow the court to reach a fair settlement of their dispute ("a reasonably certain basis for giving an appropriate remedy" [2–204(3)]). The Code contains a series of gap-filling rules to enable courts to fill in the blanks on matters of price [2–305], quantity [2–306], delivery [2–307, 2–308, and 2–309(1)], and time for payment [2–310] when such terms have been left open by the parties.[2] Of course, if a term was left out because the parties were *unable* to reach agreement about it, this would indicate that the intent to contract was absent and no contract would result, even under the Code's more liberal rules. Intention is still at the heart of these modern contract rules; the difference is that courts applying Code principles seek to further the parties' *underlying* intent to contract even though the parties have failed to express their intention about specific aspects of their agreement.

---

[2] The Formation and Terms of Sales Contracts chapter discusses these Code provisions in detail.

H. C. SCHMIEDING PRODUCE CO. v. CAGLE

529 So.2d 243 (Ala. Sup. Ct. 1988)

On March 6, 1985, Alvin Cagle, a potato farmer, entered into a written agreement to buy seed potatoes from H. C. Schmieding Produce Company. The terms of the contract obligated Cagle to pay a portion of the purchase price immediately, with the balance to be paid when the crop to be raised from the seed potatoes was harvested. Cagle paid the preharvest portion of the price and proceeded to cultivate the potatoes. He failed to harvest most of the resulting crop, however, or to pay Schmieding the postharvest portion of the purchase price.

When Schmieding sued him for breach of contract, Cagle filed a counterclaim arguing that Schmieding had breached a second contract, which obligated him to purchase Cagle's crop. According to Cagle, this second contract resulted from two telephone conversations with Schmieding's employees, occurring in late February of 1985 and in May of 1985. Cagle intro-duced evidence to show that Schmieding had agreed in those conversations to pay him $5.50 per bag for approximately 10,000 bags of white potatoes and to pay him market price at harvest time for all of his red potatoes grown on 30 acres of land. Cagle also introduced a letter from Schmied-ing, dated May 26, 1985, which said: "We are looking forward to working with you on the shipment of your crop," and asked him to "give us a week notice before you are ready to ship, in order for us to prepare our sales orders." When the trial court directed a verdict for Schmieding against Cagle on the contract for seed potatoes and the jury found in favor of Cagle on the contract for the purchase of Cagle's crop, Schmieding appealed.

Houston, Justice.   A contract for the sale of potatoes to be harvested is manifestly a "transac-tion in goods," and we will therefore apply the UCC to this case. Schmieding argues that the alleged contract fails for indefiniteness due to its numerous "open terms," such as time and place of delivery and various warranties that the potatoes would meet certain specifications. In addition, Schmieding also argues that the price term for the red potatoes, i.e., "market price at time of harvest," is also too indefinite to allow enforcement of the contract.

Although Schmieding's argument might have had some merit under pre-UCC cases, this argu-ment has no chance of success under the UCC. The controlling section is 2–204(3), which provides:

Even though one or more terms are left open a contract for sale does not fail for indefiniteness if the parties have intended to make a contract and there is a reasonably certain basis for giving an appropriate remedy.

Evidence was presented at trial indicating that at least the following terms were agreed upon: 1) the type of potatoes ordered (red and white), 2) the quantity ordered (in terms of bags or acreage), 3) the price to be paid for the quantity ordered ($5.50 per bag for whites, market price at harvest for reds), and 4) the approximate delivery date (at harvest).

This evidence puts to rest any argument as to whether the parties "intended to make a con-tract"—sufficient evidence was introduced by Cagle to require that this question of fact be sub-mitted to the jury. Similarly, these terms, if in fact entered into, would also provide a "reasonably certain basis for giving an appropriate remedy." The value of this contract to either party is susceptible to reasonably certain measurement by a court and jury, and an appropriate remedy for its breach could be provided.

Accordingly, even though the contract contains several open terms in addition to those expressly noted, the contract does not fail for indefiniteness, because such open terms may be supplemented by the UCC's "gap-filler" provisions. For instance, time, place, and manner of delivery are dealt with in sections 2–307, –308, –309, and similarly, the quality of the potatoes would likely have been guaranteed under one or more of the Code's warranty provisions. Moreover, a market-based open price term (such as that chosen for the red potatoes in the instant contract) is expressly recognized by the Code as an acceptable price term in section 2–305(1)(c). The trial court did not err in submitting this claim to the jury.

Judgment in favor of Cagle affirmed.

The *Restatement (Second) of Contracts* takes an approach to the definiteness question that is quite similar to the Code approach. The terms of an alleged offer must be reasonably certain before they can form the basis of a contract.[3] Reasonable certainty merely means that those terms "provide a basis for determining the existence of a breach and for giving an appropriate remedy."[4] The basic thrust of the *Restatement Second*, however, is still to further the intent of the parties; it expressly recognizes the fact that open or uncertain terms may indicate the absence of an intent to contract.[5] Where an agreement is sufficiently definite to be a contract, but essential terms are left open, the *Restatement Second* provides that "a term which is reasonable in the circumstances is supplied by the court."[6] Similar to the Code, the *Restatement Second* specifically indicates that where the parties' conduct indicates an intent to contract, a contract may result "even though neither offer nor acceptance can be identified and even though the moment of formation cannot be determined."[7] Unlike the Code, the *Restatement Second* also indicates that "action in reliance" on an indefinite agreement may justify its full or partial enforcement.[8] This provision highlights one of the most intriguing recent developments in contract law—the use of **promissory estoppel** to enforce indefinite agreements.[9] It has long been the rule that promissory estoppel could not be used to enforce indefinite agreements because their indefiniteness meant that the court was left with no promise capable of being enforced. Sometimes people do, however, act in reliance on indefinite agreements, and to protect that reliance a few courts have deviated from the general rule. In such cases, it is common for courts to overcome the indefiniteness problem by awarding damages based on the promisee's losses due to reliance rather than by attempting to enforce the indefinite agreement.

Hoffman v. Red Owl Stores, Inc., is probably the most famous case of this type.[10] Hoffman wanted to acquire a Red Owl franchised convenience store and, in reliance on Red Owl's promises during their negotiations, sold his bakery at a loss, bought a small grocery to gain experience, moved his family, and bought an option on a proposed site for the franchised store. The negotiations fell through, and when Hoffman sued, Red Owl argued that no contract resulted, because the parties had never reached agreement on the essential terms governing their relationship. The Supreme Court of Wisconsin agreed, but nonetheless allowed Hoffman to recover his reliance losses on the basis of promissory estoppel. In doing so, the court noted that nothing in the language of section 90 of the *Restatement* required that a promise serving as the basis of promissory estoppel be "so comprehensive in scope as to meet the requirements of an offer."

Considering cases like *Hoffman* and the way in which the definiteness problem is handled by both the Code and the *Restatement Second*, it is safe to say that indefiniteness is no longer the obstacle to the creation of contractual liability that it once was.

Communication to Offeree

When an offeror communicates the terms of an offer to an offeree, he objectively indicates an intent to be bound by those terms. An uncommunicated offer, on the other hand, may be evidence that the offeror has not yet decided to enter into a binding agreement. For example,

---

[3] *Restatement (Second) of Contracts* § 33(1) (1981).

[4] *Restatement (Second) of Contracts* § 33(2) (1981).

[5] *Restatement (Second) of Contracts* § 33(3) (1981).

[6] *Restatement (Second) of Contracts* § 204 (1981).

[7] *Restatement (Second) of Contracts* § 22(2) (1981).

[8] *Restatement (Second) of Contracts* § 34(3) (1981).

[9] See the general discussion of promissory estoppel in the Introduction to Contracts chapter.

[10] 26 Wis.2d 683, 133 N.W.2d 267 (Wis. Sup. Ct. 1965).

assume that Stevens and Meyer have been negotiating over the sale of Meyer's restaurant. Reilly, Stevens's secretary, tells Meyer that Stevens has decided to offer him $150,000 for the restaurant and has drawn up a written offer to that effect. After learning the details of the offer from Reilly, Meyer telephones Stevens and says, "I accept your offer." Is Stevens now contractually obligated to buy the restaurant? No. Since Stevens did not communicate the proposal to Meyer, there was no offer for Meyer to accept.

SPECIAL OFFER PROBLEM AREAS

Advertisements

The courts have generally held that advertisements for the sale of goods at specified prices are *not* offers; instead, they are treated as invitations to offer or negotiate. The same rule is generally applied to signs, handbills, displayed goods, catalogs, price lists, and price quotations. This rule probably fairly reflects the intentions of the sellers involved, who probably only have a limited number of items to sell, and do not intend to give every person who sees their ad, sign, or catalog the power to bind them to contract. Thus, would-be buyers are, in legal effect, making *offers* to purchase the goods, which the seller is free to accept or reject. This is so because the buyer is manifesting a present intent to contract on the definite terms of the ad, sign, or catalog and there is no offer for him to accept.

In some cases, however, particular ads have been held to amount to offers. Such ads are usually highly specific about the nature and number of items offered for sale and what is requested in return. This specificity precludes the possibility that the offeror could become contractually bound to an infinite number of offerees. In addition, many of the ads treated as offers have required special performance by would-be buyers or have in some other way clearly indicated that immediate buyer action creates a binding agreement. The potential for unfairness to those who attempt to accept such ads and their fundamental difference from ordinary ads probably justify treating them as offers. So, if Monarch Motors runs this special 10th anniversary advertisement, "Our 10th customer on Saturday, March 25, 1992, will be entitled to purchase a new Rolls-Royce Silver Shadow with every available option for 10 percent under dealer cost," most courts would probably hold that this ad was an offer and that the 10th customer was entitled to purchase the car as advertised.

Rewards

Advertisements offering rewards for lost property, for information, or for the capture of criminals are generally treated as offers for unilateral contracts. To accept the offer and be entitled to the stated reward, offerees must perform the requested act—return the lost property, supply the requested information, or capture the wanted criminal. Some courts have held that only offerees who started performance with knowledge of the offer are entitled to the reward. Other courts, however, have indicated the only requirement is that the offeree know of the reward before completing performance. In reality, the result in most such cases probably reflects the court's perception of the equities of the particular case at hand.

Auctions

Sellers at auctions are generally treated as making an invitation to offer. Those who bid on offered goods are, therefore, treated as making offers that the owner of the goods may accept or reject. Acceptance occurs only when the auctioneer strikes the goods off to the highest bidder; the auctioneer may withdraw the goods at any time before acceptance. However, when an auction is advertised as being "without reserve," the seller is treated as having made an offer to sell the goods to the highest bidder and the goods cannot be withdrawn after a call for bids has been made unless no bids are made within a reasonable time.[11]

Bids

The bidding process is a fertile source of contract disputes. Advertisements for bids are generally treated as invitations to offer. Those who submit bids are treated as offerors. According to general contract principles, bidders can withdraw their bids at any time prior to acceptance by the offeree inviting the bids and the offeree is free to accept or reject any bid. The previously announced terms of the bidding may alter these rules, however. For example, if the advertisement for bids unconditionally states that the contract will be awarded to the lowest responsible bidder, this will be treated as an offer that is accepted by the lowest bidder. Only proof by the offeror that the lowest bidder is not responsible can prevent the formation of a contract. Also, under some circumstances discussed later in this chapter,

---

[11] These rules and others concerned with the sale of goods by auction are contained in section 2–328 of the UCC.

promissory estoppel may operate to prevent bidders from withdrawing their bids.

Bids for governmental contracts are generally covered by specific statutes rather than by general contract principles. Such statutes ordinarily establish the rules governing the bidding process, often require that the contract be awarded to the lowest bidder, and frequently establish special rules or penalties governing the withdrawal of bids.

WHICH TERMS ARE INCLUDED IN OFFERS?

After making a determination that an offer existed, a court must decide which terms were included in the offer so that it can determine the terms of the parties' contract. Put another way, which terms of the offer are binding on the offeree who accepts it? Should offerees, for example, be bound by fine print clauses or by clauses on the back of the contract? Originally, the courts tended to hold that offerees were bound by all the terms of the offer on the theory that every person had a duty to protect himself by reading agreements carefully before signing them.

In today's world of lengthy, complex form contracts, however, people often sign agreements that they have not fully read or do not fully understand. As the following *McAdoo* case indicates, modern courts tend to recognize this fact by saying that offerees are bound only by terms of which they had *actual* or *reasonable notice*. If the offeree actually read the term in question, or if a reasonable person should have been aware of it, it will probably become part of the parties' contract. So, a fine-print provision on the back of a theater ticket would probably not be binding on a theater patron, because a reasonable person would not expect such a ticket to contain contractual terms. However, the terms printed on a multipage airline or steamship ticket might well be considered binding on the purchaser.

This modern approach to deciding the terms of a contract gives courts an indirect, but effective, way of promoting fair dealing by refusing to enforce unfair contract terms on the ground that the offeree lacked reasonable notice of them. Disclaimers and exculpatory clauses (contract provisions that seek to relieve offerors of some legal duty that they would otherwise owe to offerees) are particularly likely to be subjected to close judicial scrutiny. Many courts insist on proof that the offeree had actual notice of such terms before they are considered a part of the contract. Also, as you will learn in greater detail in the Illegality chapter, even terms that would otherwise clearly be part of the parties' contract may be inoperative if they are unconscionable or contrary to public policy.

ST. JOHN'S EPISCOPAL HOSPITAL v. MCADOO

405 N.Y.S.2d 935 (N.Y. City Civ. Ct. 1978)

Less than an hour before his estranged wife underwent emergency surgery for an ectopic pregnancy caused by another man, Charles McAdoo was asked to sign a standard form contract prepared by St. John's Episcopal Hospital. McAdoo testified that at the time he signed the form his wife's physical appearance and declared mental state convinced him that she was near death. Further, he stated that, under such circumstances, it did not occur to him to read carefully or question the implications of the papers he was being asked to sign. The form contained a provision that read as follows:

ASSIGNMENT OF INSURANCE BENEFITS: I hereby authorize payment directly to the above named hospital of the hospital expense benefits otherwise payable to me but not to exceed the hospital's regular charges for this period of hospitalization. *I understand that I am financially responsible to the hospital for the charges not covered by my group insurance plan.*

Mrs. McAdoo survived and was discharged from St. John's eight days later. McAdoo did not visit her after the day of the operation and had not had any further contact with her when the hospital filed suit against him to collect her hospital bill.

Feldman, Judge.   The principle that signed contracts are binding cannot be lightly disregarded. To do so would endanger the orderly functioning of commerce and allow individuals to escape the consequences of their agreements because of a change in circumstance. However, it is also unrealistic to continue insisting that in a society of mass marketing it is reasonable still to expect individuals, unrepresented by counsel, to read each clause of the many standardized contracts used by the various institutions with which we all deal. In certain instances it is certainly appropriate for courts to examine the circumstances under which a contract was signed in order to determine whether 1) there was a genuine opportunity for the signer to have read the clause in dispute; or 2) if he did not read it whether a reasonable person should have expected to find such a clause in the particular instrument he was signing. Where there are negative answers to these questions, a court can then address itself to the fairness of enforcing that clause.

It is reasonable in this situation for McAdoo to have seen himself as powerless to do anything other than sign the form. A hospital emergency room is certainly not a place in which any but the strongest can be expected to exercise calm and dispassionate judgment. The law of contracts is not intended to use "superman" as its model. If the reasonable man standard is applied here, McAdoo's failure to read the document or to give it more than the most cursory attention is understandable.

It thus becomes vital that a document like the form involved here be clearly labeled and organized so that the signer is made aware of what it entails. Here, the paragraph signed by McAdoo bore a heading totally unrelated to the sentence on which St. John's now relies to argue his financial liability. McAdoo would have been entirely justified in concluding from the heading that he was agreeing only to have his union insurance pay for his wife's hospital bills. This is a far cry from agreeing to assume personal liability.

St. John's is surely no stranger to the trauma and anxiety experienced by those confronted with emergency medical crises. Armed with this knowledge it should have prepared the form so that the person being asked to sign it can readily grasp its meaning, even through a quick reading. Moreover, St. John's should not be permitted to enforce a contractual obligation entered into under such tension-laden circumstances as those McAdoo described.

Judgment for McAdoo.

TERMINATION OF OFFERS

After a court has determined the existence and content of an offer, it must determine the *duration* of the offer. Was the offer still in existence when the offeree attempted to accept it? If not, no contract was created and the offeree is treated as having made an offer that the original offeror is free to accept or reject. This is so because, by attempting to accept an offer that has terminated, the offeree has indicated a present intent to contract on the terms of the original offer though he lacks the power to bind the offeror to a contract due to the original offer's termination.

Terms of the Offer

The offeror is often said to be "the master of the offer." This means that offerors have the power to determine the terms and conditions under which they are bound to a contract. As the following *Newman* case indicates, an offeror may include terms in the offer that limit its effective life. These may be specific terms, such as "you must accept by December 5, 1989" or "this offer good for five days," or more general terms, such as "for immediate acceptance," "prompt wire acceptance," or "by return mail." General time limitation language in an offer can raise difficult problems of interpretation for courts trying to decide whether an offeree accepted before the offer terminated. Even more specific language, such as "this offer good for five days," can cause problems if the offer does not specify whether the five-day period begins when the offer is sent or when the offeree receives it. Not all courts agree on such questions, so wise offerors should be as specific as possible in stating when their offers terminate.

NEWMAN v. SCHIFF
778 F.2d 460 (8th Cir. 1985)

Irwin Schiff, a self-styled tax rebel who had made a career out of his tax protest activities, appeared live on the February 7, 1983, CBS News "Nightwatch" program. During the course of the program, which had a viewer participation format, Schiff repeated his longstanding position that "there is nothing in the Internal Revenue Code which says anyone is legally required to pay the tax." Later in the program, Schiff stated: "If anybody calls this show and cites any section of this Code that says an individual is required to file a tax return, I will pay them $100,000."

Attorney John Newman failed to see Schiff live on "Nightwatch," but saw a two-minute taped segment of the original "Nightwatch" interview several hours later on the "CBS Morning News." Certain that Schiff's statements were incorrect, Newman telephoned and wrote "CBS Morning News," attempting to accept Schiff's offer by citing Internal Revenue Code provisions requiring individuals to pay federal income tax. CBS forwarded Newman's letter to Schiff, who refused to pay on the ground that Newman had not properly accepted his offer. Newman sued Schiff for breach of contract. The trial court ruled in Schiff's favor, and Newman appealed.

Bright, Senior Circuit Judge.   It is a basic legal principle that mutual assent is necessary for the formation of a contract. A significant doctrinal struggle in the development of contract law revolved around whether it was a party's actual or apparent assent that was necessary. This was a struggle between subjective and objective theorists. The subjectivists looked to actual assent. Both parties had to actually assent to an agreement for there to be a contract. The objectivists, on the other hand, looked to apparent assent. The expression of mutual assent, and not the assent itself, was the essential element in the formation of a contract. By the end of the nineteenth century the objective approach to the mutual assent requirement had become predominant, and courts continue to use it today.

Courts determine whether the parties expressed their assent to a contract by analyzing their agreement process in terms of offer and acceptance. An offer is the "manifestation of willingness to enter into a bargain, so made as to justify another person in understanding that his assent to that bargain is invited and will conclude it." *Restatement (Second) of Contracts* § 24 (1981). Schiff's statement on "Nightwatch" that he would pay $100,000 to anyone who called the show and cited any section of the Internal Revenue Code "that says an individual is required to file a tax return" constituted a valid offer for a reward. If anyone had called the show and cited the code sections that Newman produced, a contract would have been formed and Schiff would have been obligated to pay the $100,000 reward.

Newman, however, never saw the live CBS "Nightwatch" program on which Schiff appeared and this lawsuit is not predicated on Schiff's "Nightwatch" offer. Newman saw the "CBS Morning News" rebroadcast of Schiff's "Nightwatch" appearance. This rebroadcast served not to renew or extend Schiff's offer, but rather only to inform viewers that Schiff had made an offer on "Nightwatch." An offeror is the master of his offer and it is clear that Schiff by his words, "If anybody calls this show," limited his offer in time to remain open only until the conclusion of the live "Nightwatch" broadcast. A reasonable person listening to the news rebroadcast could not conclude that the above language constituted a new offer rather than what it actually was, a news report of the offer previously made, which had already expired.

Although Newman has not "won" his lawsuit in the traditional sense of recovering a reward that he sought, he has accomplished an important goal in the public interest of unmasking the "blatant nonsense" dispensed by Schiff. For that he deserves great commendation from the public. Perhaps now CBS and other communication media who have given Schiff's mistaken views widespread publicity will give John Newman equal time in the public interest.

Judgment for Schiff affirmed.

Lapse of Time

Offers that fail to provide a specific time for acceptance are valid for a *reasonable time*. What constitutes a reasonable time depends on the circumstances surrounding the offer. How long would a reasonable person in the offeree's position believe she had to accept the offer? Offers involving things subject to rapid fluctuations in value, such as stocks, bonds, or commodities futures, have a very brief duration. The same is true for offers involving goods that may spoil, such as produce.

The nature of the parties' negotiations is another factor relevant to determining the duration of an offer. Most courts hold that when parties bargain face-to-face or over the telephone, the normal time for acceptance does not extend past the conclusion of their conversation unless the offeror indicates a contrary intention. Where negotiations are carried out by mail or telegram, the time for acceptance would ordinarily include at least the normal time for communicating the offer and a prompt response by the offeree. It is often said, for example, that a mailed offer is promptly accepted when an acceptance is mailed at any time on the day the offer was received. However, the absence of any rapid fluctuations in the value of the items offered could extend the time for acceptance. Finally, in cases where the parties have dealt with each other on a regular basis in the past, the timing of their prior transactions would be highly relevant in measuring the reasonable time for acceptance.

Revocation

As the masters of their offers, offerors can give offerees the power to bind them to contracts by making offers.

They can also terminate that power by *revoking* their offers. The general common law rule on revocations is that offerors may revoke their offers *at any time prior to acceptance*, even if they have promised to hold the offer open for a stated period of time. However, several exceptions to this general rule can prevent offerors from revoking. Figure 1 summarizes the situations when offerors cannot revoke their offers.

Options   An **option** is a separate contract in which an offeror agrees not to revoke her offer for a stated time in exchange for some valuable consideration.[12] The offeree who enters an option contract has no obligation to accept the offeror's offer; in effect, she has merely purchased the right to consider the offer for the stated time without fear that the offeror will revoke it. The traditional common law rule on options requires the actual payment of the agreed-on consideration before an option contract becomes enforceable. Therefore, if, in exchange for $100, Martin gave Berry a 30-day option to purchase his house for $150,000 and Berry never, in fact, paid the $100, no option was created and Martin could revoke his offer at any time prior to its acceptance by Berry.

Firm Offers   The Code makes a major change in the common law rules governing the revocability of offers by recognizing the concept of a **firm offer** [2–205]. A firm offer is irrevocable for the *time stated in the offer*. If no time is stated, it is irrevocable for a *reasonable time*. Regardless of the terms of the offer, the outer limit on a firm offer's irrevocability is three months. Not all offers

---

[12] The Consideration chapter discusses consideration in detail.

FIGURE 1 When Offerors Cannot Revoke

Options	Offeror has promised to hold offer open and has received consideration for that promise
Firm Offers	Merchant offeror makes written offer to sell goods, giving assurances offer will be held open
Unilateral Contract Offers	Offeree has started to perform requested act before offeror revokes
Promissory Estoppel	Offeree foreseeably and reasonably relies on offer being held open, and will suffer injustice if it is revoked

for the sale of goods qualify as firm offers, however. To be a firm offer, an offer must be made by a *merchant* in a *signed writing* that contains *assurances* that the offer will be held open and not revoked. An offer for the sale of goods that fails to satisfy these three requirements is governed by the general common law rule and revocable at any time prior to acceptance.

Indicating that an offer will be held open for a particular time can sometimes serve an offeror's interests because it may increase the likelihood of ultimate acceptance by an offeree who is given assurance that sufficient time will be available to investigate the merits of the offer. The receipt of such an offer creates obvious expectations about the duration of the offer in the minds of offerees; the Code's firm offer provision is designed to protect these expectations. In some cases, however, *offerees* are the true originators of an assurance term in an offer. When offerees have effective control of the terms of the offer by providing their customers with preprinted purchase order forms or order blanks, they may be tempted to take advantage of their merchant customers by placing an assurance term in their order forms. This would allow offerees to await market developments before deciding whether to fill the order, while their merchant customers, who may have signed the order without reading all of its terms, would be powerless to revoke. To prevent such unfairness, the Code requires that assurance terms on forms provided by offerees be *separately signed* by the offeror to effect a firm offer.

Offers for Unilateral Contracts The general rule that an offeror can revoke at any time prior to acceptance causes special problems when applied to offers for unilateral contracts. Because the offeree in a unilateral contract must fully perform the requested act to accept, the application of the general rule would allow an offeror to revoke after the offeree has begun performance but before he has had a chance to complete it. To prevent injustice to offerees who rely on such offers by beginning performance, two basic approaches are available to modern courts. Some courts have held that once the offeree has begun to perform, the offeror's power to revoke is suspended for the amount of time reasonably necessary for the offeree to complete performance. Section 45 of the *Restatement Second* takes a similar approach for offers that unequivocally require acceptance by performance by stating that once the offeree begins performance, an option contract is created. The offeror's duty to perform his side of the bargain is conditional on full performance by the offeree. This approach clearly protects the offeree, but from an offeror's standpoint it is less than desirable because the offeree has no duty to complete the requested performance.

Another approach to the unilateral contract dilemma is to hold that a bilateral contract is created once the offeree begins performance. This is essentially the position taken by section 62 of the *Restatement Second*, which states that when the offer invites acceptance either by a return promise or performance, the beginning of performance operates as an acceptance and a promise by the offeree to render complete performance. This approach protects both the offeror and the offeree, but may be contrary to the actual intent of the parties, neither of whom may wish to be bound to a contract until achieving complete performance.

Promissory Estoppel In some cases, the doctrine of promissory estoppel can operate to prevent offerors from revoking their offers prior to acceptance. Section 87(2) of the *Restatement Second* says:

An offer which the offeror should reasonably expect to induce action or forbearance of a substantial character on the part of the offeree before acceptance and which does induce such action or forbearance is binding as an option contract to the extent necessary to avoid injustice.

As the following *Warner Electric* case illustrates, promissory estoppel has often been used to prevent revocation in the bidding context.

JOHN PRICE ASSOCIATES, INC. v. WARNER ELECTRIC, INC.

723 F.2d 755 (10th Cir. 1983)

Warner Electric, an electrical subcontractor, submitted a bid to the Utah Subcontractors Bid Depository Service for the electrical subcontract on the construction of the General Services Administration (GSA) Metallurgy Research Center in Salt Lake City, Utah. Warner based its bid on specifications and bid forms supplied by the GSA. John Price Associates, a general contractor, used Warner's subcontract bid, which was the lowest submitted, in preparing its bid for the general contract.

Price was the lowest bidder and was awarded the contract for the project. A few days after Price had signed a contract with the GSA, Warner told Price that it had a problem with its subcontract bid because the bid did not include certain laboratory work described in section 11600 of the GSA plans, work which Warner had thought would be performed by the general contractor. Warner refused to sign the subcontract without a promise of additional payment for the section 11600 work. Price notified Warner by mailgram that it was accepting Warner's bid. Later that day, Warner's attorney delivered a letter to Price withdrawing Warner's bid.

Price then contacted the other subcontractors who had submitted bids asking for new bids. It ultimately hired the lowest bidder in the second round of bidding, the Foley Company, for $94,845 more than Warner's bid price. Foley, like Warner, had not initially included the section 11600 work in its original bid, but its revised bid included the increased costs attributable to that work. Price later filed a claim against the GSA for its losses due to Warner's withdrawal, arguing, as Warner had, that the specifications for the project were ambiguous. After the GSA Board of Contract Appeals denied his claim he filed suit against Warner. When the trial court ruled in Price's favor, Warner appealed.

Logan, Circuit Judge.   We agree with the trial court that the doctrine of promissory estoppel barred Warner from withdrawing its bid. That doctrine provides that a promise that the promisor should reasonably expect to induce action by the promisee and that does induce such action is binding if injustice can be avoided only by enforcement of the promise. Warner submitted a bid through the Subcontractors Bid Service with the expectation that companies bidding on the general contract would rely on its bid in making their bids. Price relied on Warner's bid, and when Price found out that it would probably get the general contract, Price notified Warner of its reliance. Price had entered into a binding contract before Warner notified it of any problems with the bid. In this situation promissory estoppel should prevent Warner from withdrawing its bid.

Ambiguity in the GSA plans and specifications should not constitute a legal defense in the instant case. The government, not Price, provided the plans and specifications. The accompanying materials directed that inquiries about them be directed to government officials. Nothing put Price on notice that something was wrong with Warner's bid. The difference between Warner's bid and those of other electrical subcontractors was insufficient to raise Price's suspicion that Warner had made a mistake in computing its bid. Before Warner discovered its error Price was bound as general contractor on the project. Under these circumstances, the trial court correctly required Warner rather than Price to bear any loss caused by the alleged ambiguity.

When Warner withdrew its bid, Price acted reasonably. Price contacted the four next lowest bidders, who were no longer bound by their original bids, and accepted the lowest bid on resubmittal. At this point the only other step Price could take to mitigate damages was to seek additional payments from the GSA because of the alleged ambiguities in the plans.

Price pursued this remedy at its own expense. The trial court properly awarded Price damages and interest.

Judgment for Price affirmed.

Effectiveness of Revocations   The question of when a revocation is effective to terminate an offer is often a critical issue in the contract formation process. For example, Davis offers to landscape Winter's property for $1,500. Two days after making the offer, Davis changes his mind and mails Winter a letter revoking the offer. The next day, Winter, who has not received Davis's letter, telephones Davis and attempts to accept. Contract? Yes. As the following *Lyon* case indicates, the general rule on this point is that revocations are effective only when they are *actually received* by the offeree. The basic idea behind this rule is that the offeree is justified in relying on the intent to contract manifested by the offeror's offer until she actually knows that the offeror has changed his mind.

This explains why many courts have also held that if the offeree receives reliable information indicating that the offeror has taken action inconsistent with an intent to enter the contract proposed by the offer, such as selling the property that was the subject of the offer to someone else, this terminates the offer. In such circumstances, the offeree would be unjustified in believing that the offer could still be accepted.

The only major exception to the general rule on effectiveness of revocations concerns offers to the general public. Because it would be impossible in most cases to reach every offeree with a revocation, it is generally held that a revocation made in the same manner as the offer is effective when published, without proof of communication to the offeree.

LYON v. ADGRAPHICS
540 A.2d 398 (Conn. Ct. App. 1988)

Edward Sherman engaged V. R. Brokers as listing agent for the sale of Adgraphics, his business. On December 5, 1985, William Lyon made a written offer to purchase the business for $75,000 and attached certain conditions to the offer. Later the same day, Sherman signed a written counteroffer offering to sell for $80,000 and rejecting two of the conditions contained in Lyon's offer. On December 7, at 11:35 A.M., Lyon signed the counteroffer before a notary public and then brought it to the office of V. R. Brokers around noon on that day. Before Lyon could hand the signed counteroffer to Robert Renault, the principal of V. R. Brokers, Renault told him that Sherman wanted to cancel his counteroffer. Lyon filed a breach of contract suit, and, when the trial court ruled in his favor, Sherman appealed.

Borden, Judge.   It is a basic principle of contract law that in order to form a binding contract there must be an offer and acceptance based on a mutual understanding of the parties. The counter offer by Sherman created a power of acceptance in Lyon. That counteroffer, however, was revocable by Sherman at any time prior to acceptance by Lyon.

The trial court's conclusion that Lyon's acceptance of the counteroffer was effective when he signed it was contrary to our law. Revocation of an offer in order to be effectual must be received by the offeree before he has exercised his power of creating a contract by acceptance of the offer. Acceptance is operative, if transmitted by means which the offeror has authorized, as soon as its transmission begins and it is put out of the offeree's possession. Lyon's act of signing the written counteroffer failed to communicate the acceptance to Sherman or his agent and failed to put the acceptance out of Lyon's possession. It was, therefore, ineffective to create a contract.

When Sherman, through his agent, informed Lyon that the counteroffer was withdrawn, Lyon's power to accept the counteroffer no longer existed. This was done before Lyon had properly accepted the counteroffer by transmitting the signed counteroffer to Renault. Accordingly, no enforceable contract between the parties was ever created.

Judgment reversed in favor of Sherman.

Rejection

An offeree may *expressly reject* an offer by indicating that he is unwilling to accept it. He may also *impliedly reject* it by making a **counteroffer,** an offer to contract on terms materially different from the terms of the offer.[13] As a general rule, either form of rejection by the offeree terminates his power to accept the offer. This is so because an offeror who receives a rejection may rely on the offeree's expressed desire not to accept the offer by making another offer to a different offeree. Therefore, if either party manifests an intent to keep the offer open despite a rejection, many courts hold that no termination has occurred. If the offeror indicates in the offer that it will continue in effect despite a rejection, there is no need to fear that he will rely on rejection terminating the offer. Likewise, if the offeree indicates that she rejects the offer at the present time but will take it under advisement in the future, there is no basis for reliance by the offeror. One further exception to the general rule that rejections terminate offers concerns offers that are the subject of an option contract. Some courts hold that a rejection does not terminate an option contract and that the offeree who rejects still has the power to accept the offer later, so long as the acceptance is effective within the option period.[14]

Effectiveness of Rejections   As a general rule, rejections, like revocations, are effective only when *actually received* by the offeror. This is because there is no possibility that the offeror can rely on a rejection by making another offer to a different offeree until she actually has notice of the rejection. Therefore, an offeree who has mailed a rejection could still change her mind and accept

if she communicates the acceptance before the offeror receives the rejection.[15]

Death or Insanity of Either Party

The death or insanity of either party to an offer automatically terminates the offer without notice. A meeting of the minds is obviously impossible when one of the parties has died or become insane.

Destruction of Subject Matter

If, prior to an acceptance of an offer, the subject matter of a proposed contract is destroyed without the knowledge or fault of either party, the offer is terminated.[16] So, if Marks offers to sell Wiggins his lakeside cottage and the cottage is destroyed by fire before Wiggins accepts, the offer was terminated on the destruction of the cottage. Subsequent acceptance by Wiggins would not create a contract.

Intervening Illegality

An offer is terminated if the performance of the contract it proposes becomes illegal before the offer is accepted. So, if a computer manufacturer has offered to sell sophisticated computer equipment to the Republic of South Africa, but two days later, before the offer has been accepted, Congress places an embargo on all sales to South Africa to protest apartheid, the offer is terminated by the embargo.[17]

---

[13] The Acceptance chapter discusses counteroffers in detail.

[14] Section 37 of the *Restatement Second* adopts this rule.

[15] The Acceptance chapter discusses this subject in detail.

[16] In some circumstances, destruction of subject matter can also serve as a legal excuse for a party's failure to perform his obligations under an existing contract. The Performance and Remedies chapter discusses this subject.

[17] In some circumstances, intervening illegality can also serve as a legal excuse for a party's failure to perform his obligations under an existing contract. The Performance and Remedies chapter discusses this subject.

CONCEPT REVIEW

WHAT TERMINATES OFFERS?

- ☐ Their own terms
- ☐ Lapse of time
- ☐ Revocation
- ☐ Rejection
- ☐ Death or insanity of offeror or offeree
- ☐ Destruction of subject matter
- ☐ Intervening illegality

ETHICAL AND PUBLIC POLICY CONCERNS

1. Classical contract theory has traditionally found strong ethical justification in the notion of voluntary consent. To parties who want out of their contracts and ask why they should be held to them, the law has often responded: "Because you agreed to them." How does this ethical justification square with the objective theory of contract, which can in some cases result in holding people to agreements that are inconsistent with their subjective intent? Is there some other ethical justification for holding people to the objective manifestations of consent, regardless of their actual or subjective intent?

2. Compare and contrast the underlying ethical justifications of the classical and modern contract positions on what terms are included in offers. Is it ethical for businesses who deal with consumers or other unsophisticated parties to "hide" contract terms under misleading headings, in small print, or on the reverse side of contracts? What about putting form contracts in complex, technical language that consumers are unlikely to understand?

3. As you learned earlier in this chapter, there are now a number of exceptions to the traditional rule that offerors can revoke at any time prior to acceptance, even if they have promised not to. Is there an ethical basis for each of these exceptions? If so, what is it?

SUMMARY

Courts seeking to determine the existence of a contract look for evidence of an agreement between the parties. The first step in this process is to determine whether an offer existed that, when accepted by the offeree, resulted in the formation of a contract. An offer is a combination of facts and circumstances that objectively indicate a present intent to contract on the part of the offeror. Traditional contract law principles require not only that an alleged offer be definite and specific but also that it be communicated to the offeree by the offeror. Modern contract principles embodied in the UCC and the *Restatement (Second) of Contracts*, however, require a significantly lesser degree of definiteness in offers, with the result that courts applying these principles are more likely to recognize the existence of a contract and, in some cases, to supply contract terms omitted or left indefinite by the parties.

Several common business situations involve questions concerning the existence of offers. Advertisements, price quotes, catalogs, signs, and so forth are generally treated as invitations to offer. As a result, in such cases, would-be buyers are normally treated as offerors, not offerees. Under some extraordinary circumstances, however, an advertisement or a price quote can amount to an offer. Offers of rewards are generally treated as offers for unilateral contracts that can only be accepted by performance of the act that the reward requests. Bids are generally treated as offers that the bidder may revoke at any time prior to acceptance and that the offeree is free to accept or reject. In some circumstances, an offeree's reliance on a bid may operate to estop the offeror from revoking it. Bidders at auctions are normally treated as making offers unless the auction is "without reserve," in which case the seller is treated as having made an offer to sell to the highest bidder; that offer cannot be revoked once bidding starts.

Modern courts hold that offerees are bound by all the terms in the offer of which they have reasonable notice. In some cases, this means that fine print terms or terms on the back of the contract are not part of the parties' contract. Disclaimers and exculpatory clauses are particularly likely to be excluded from a contract on this basis.

The duration of offers is limited. Offerees who attempt to accept terminated offers are treated as having made an offer that the original offeror is free to accept or reject. An offer may expire by its own terms or, if no terms are stated, after the passage of a reasonable time. As a general rule, offerors can revoke their offers at any time prior to acceptance. There are several limitations on this rule, however. Offerors who enter option contracts, agreeing not to revoke in exchange for some valuable consideration, cannot revoke for the option period. The Code recognizes the concept of an irrevocable firm offer, which applies to offers for the sale of goods that meet certain other qualifications. Promissory estoppel may also operate to prevent revocation in some circumstances. Finally, once an offeree attempts to accept an offer for a unilateral contract by beginning performance of the acts requested by the offer, modern courts employ a variety of theories to prevent the offeror from revoking prior to the offeree's completion of performance.

Rejection of an offer by the offeree, whether express or implied, also terminates the offer. Both revocations and rejections are effective only when actually communicated to the other party. The death or insanity of either party automatically terminates an offer. Likewise, destruction of the subject matter of an offer or the subsequent illegality of the performance called for by an offer also cause termination.

PROBLEM CASES

1. After some negotiations, Empro Manufacturing sent Ball-Co a three-page "letter of intent" to purchase Ball-Co's assets. Empro proposed a price of $2.4 million, with $650,000 to be paid on closing and a 10-year promissory note for the remainder, secured by Ball-Co's inventory and equipment. The letter provided that it was "subject to . . . a definitive Asset Purchase Agreement signed by both parties" and that the purchase was also "subject to" the satisfaction of certain other conditions, including the approval of Empro's shareholders and board. Ball-Co signed the letter of intent, but later broke off discussions after Empro refused to secure the promissory note with a security interest in the land under Ball-Co's plant. Empro filed suit against Ball-Co, arguing that by signing the letter of intent Ball-Co had contracted to sell to Empro. Was the trial court justified in dismissing Empro's suit? *[handwritten: ? NO RELIANCE NO CONSIDERATION]*

[handwritten margin: p215] *[handwritten: → DOES NOT MAKE CONTRACT]*

2. Rhen Marshall (RM) received a mailed "Christmas Comes Early at Purolator" advertising circular describing premiums available with orders for Purolator products. Premiums varied with order size. Deal 5A stated that an order for 100,000 pounds of Purolator products entitled customers to a premium of a new 1978 Buick Electra automobile and 100 EK-6 Kodak Instant cameras. The ad said: "You will be billed $500 for the package, which has a retail value of $17,450." RM ordered over 100,000 pounds of Purolator oil filters and also ordered "Deal 5A as outlined in your brochure." The circular contained no billing or discount provisions. RM's order requested a 5 percent truckload discount and "30–60–90 day billing." (In previous dealings between these parties, a "30–60–90 day billing" meant a

[handwritten at bottom: DEFINATALEY AN OFFER / IF WE ALLOW YOU TO BUY / THEN HAVE AN OFFER]

[handwritten margin: p216]

2 percent discount if paid within 30 days, a 1 percent discount if paid within 60 days, or payment in full at the end of 90 days.) Purolator rejected RM's order, and RM filed suit for breach of contract. Should RM have recovered? *[handwritten: NO CONTRACT]*

3. On August 4, 1980, Normile made a written offer to buy property owned by Miller. Miller signed and returned the offer after making several substantial changes in its terms and initialing those changes. The executed form was delivered to Normile by Byer, the real estate agent who had shown him the property. In the early afternoon of August 5, 1980, Miller accepted an offer by Segal to buy her property on terms similar to those in the modified offer she had returned to Normile. At 2:00 P.M. that day, Byer told Normile: "You snooze, you lose; the property has been sold." Shortly thereafter, Normile attempted to accept Miller's proposal. Was the trial court correct in ruling that Normile and Miller had no contract? *[handwritten: YES. BECAUSE NOTIFIED OF COUNTEROFFER.]*

[handwritten margin: p224] *[handwritten right margin: REJECTION X COUNTEROFFER]*

4. In November of 1977, Cagle went to Buckner Chevrolet to discuss the purchase of a 1978 Limited Edition Corvette (referred to as an "Indy Vette" because one or more of them was used as a pace car at Indianapolis). Cagle talked to Buckner's used car manager, who partially filled out a buyer's order form, which was then presented to Kelly, Buckner's new car sales manager. After discussing the matter, Kelly agreed to sell Cagle an Indy Vette at list price. He wrote "list price" and signed his name on the partially completed form, signing in the middle of the page, rather than in the space provided for the signature of an officer of Buckner. Cagle also signed the form and made a $500 deposit. At the time, Buckner did not have any Indy Vettes. Two were later received, but, in the interim, market demand for the cars had driven their value far above list price. Buckner refused to deliver either car to Cagle and attempted to return his deposit, arguing that the order form was too indefinite to amount to a contract. Did the parties have a contract?

[handwritten: YES. Reliance]

5. Hulsey enrolled in a First Jump Course at the Elsinore Parachute Center (EPC). He signed an "Agreement and Release of Liability," which, in bold-faced capital letters, warned of the risk of injury and death associated with sport parachuting and purported to release EPC of any liability for injury to him. During classroom instruction at EPC, the instructor advised students that students occasionally break their legs when jumping. On Hulsey's first jump, he was unable to reach the target landing area, colliding instead with electric power lines as he tried to land in a vacant lot. He broke

[Handwritten margin note top-left:] Reasonable person should have been aware of

his wrist in the accident and later filed suit against EPC. At trial, Hulsey said that he did not remember reading or signing the release. Was the trial court justified in granting EPC's motion for summary judgment? *[Handwritten:] YES!*

6. Phyllis Chaplin filed a class action suit against Consolidated Edison (Con Ed) for allegedly discriminating against epileptics in violation of the Rehabilitation Act of 1973. In August 1981, Con Ed's lawyer sent Chaplin's lawyer a settlement offer. Chaplin's lawyer replied by saying that Chaplin had "objections" to the proposed settlement. On September 16, 1981, Con Ed's lawyer replied, saying: "Any further negotiation is an impossibility; if this agreement is not satisfactory to your client in its present form, I must withdraw all offers of settlement." In a letter dated September 17, 1981 Chaplin's lawyer answered that "after careful consideration" Chaplin still had "objections" to Con Ed's offer. Later, on September 17, a federal appellate court ruled that private suits such as Chaplin's were not allowed under the Rehabilitation Act. On September 30, 1981, Chaplin's lawyer told Con Ed's lawyer Chaplin had had "a change of heart" and was accepting the settlement offer. Con Ed's lawyer replied that the settlement was no longer acceptable. Was Con Ed bound by the settlement offer? *[Handwritten:] HE REJECTED, SO THERE WAS THEN NO OFFER.*

7. In October of 1981, Christy and Andrus were involved in an automobile accident. On November 8, 1982, Aetna Casualty and Surety Company, Andrus's insurer, sent a letter to Christy and his insurer, Travelers Insurance Company, offering to settle Christy's claim against Andrus for $8,507. Neither Christy nor Travelers responded to this letter until February 4, 1984, when an attorney for Travelers sent Aetna a letter attempting to accept the settlement offer. Aetna then responded that any claim Christy had against Andrus was barred by the state's two-year statute of limitations and that Travelers' attempt to accept was not timely. Christy filed suit against Andrus and Aetna, arguing that they were bound by the settlement. At trial, Aetna introduced uncontradicted testimony that customary practice in the insurance industry was to respond to settlement offers within a few weeks. Was the trial court decision in Aetna's favor correct? *[Handwritten:] ABSOLUTLEY P220*

8. City University of New York (CUNY) solicited "firm" bids for the sale of a used IBM computer system. The highest bid was submitted by Finalco, Inc. Finalco, however, attempted to withdraw its bid because the customer to whom it intended to lease the computer had backed out of the lease deal. CUNY accepted Finalco's bid, and after Finalco refused to take delivery of the computer CUNY sued Finalco for breach of contract. At trial, Finalco argued that it had revoked its bid prior to acceptance by CUNY and that even if it lacked the power to revoke, its bid, which contained price, packaging, and delivery terms, was too indefinite to amount to an offer because it failed to include certain other terms. Was the trial court's decision in favor of CUNY correct? *[Handwritten:] NO - BECAUSE YOU CAN REVOKE BID PRIOR TO ACCEPTANCE*

9. On June 19, 1973, Berryman signed an agreement giving Kmoch, a real estate broker, a 120-day option to purchase 960 acres of Berryman's land in exchange for "$10.00 and other valuable consideration," which was never paid. Kmoch hired two agricultural consultants to produce a report that he intended to use in order to interest other investors in joining him to exercise the option. In late July 1973, Berryman telephoned Kmoch and asked to be released from the option agreement. Nothing definite was agreed to, and Berryman later sold the land to another person. In August, Kmoch decided to exercise the option and contacted the local Federal Land Bank representative to make arrangements to buy the land. After being told by the representative that Berryman had sold the property, Kmoch sent Berryman a letter attempting to exercise the option. Kmoch argued that the option was still in effect and that, in any event, Berryman was estopped from revoking it. Was Kmoch right? *[Handwritten:] NO CONSIDERATION*

10. Thomson was a tenant in a building owned by Coronet properties that Coronet decided to convert into a cooperative. The applicable state law required Coronet to offer existing tenants the right to purchase cooperative shares at a less-than-market insider price. Coronet made the required offer to Thomson, but she died before accepting. When De Kovessey, the executrix of Thomson's estate, attempted to accept Coronet's offer on behalf of the estate, Coronet refused to go through with the deal. Did De Kovessey have the power to accept? *[Handwritten:] DEATH Auto Revokes Contract*

CHAPTER 11

THE AGREEMENT: ACCEPTANCE

WHAT IS AN ACCEPTANCE?

The idea of *mutual agreement* lies at the heart of traditional contract law. Thus, after determining that one of the parties to a dispute made an *offer*, the court next seeks to determine whether the offeree *accepted* that offer. In this inquiry, the court is looking for the same *present intent to contract* on the part of the offeree that it found on the part of the offeror. The difference is that the offeree must objectively indicate a present intent to contract *on the terms of the offer* before a contract results. As the master of the offer, the offeror may specify in detail what behavior is required of the offeree to bind him to a contract. If the offeror does so, the offeree must ordinarily comply with all the terms of the offer before a contract results. These requirements for acceptance are evident in the *Restatement (Second) of Contracts* definition of an **acceptance** as "a manifestation of assent to the terms [of the offer] made by the offeree in the manner invited or required by the offer."[1]

---

[1] *Restatement (Second) of Contracts* § 50(1) (1981).

Intention to Accept: Counteroffers

The traditional contract law rule is that an acceptance must be the mirror image of the offer. As the following *Benya* case indicates, attempts by offerees to change the terms of the offer or to add new terms to it are treated as **counteroffers** because they impliedly indicate an intent by the offeree to reject the offer instead of being bound by its terms. However, if an offeree merely asks about the terms of the offer without indicating its rejection (an *inquiry regarding terms*), or accepts the offer's terms while complaining about them (a *grumbling acceptance*), no rejection is implied. Also, recent years have witnessed a judicial tendency to apply the mirror image rule in a more liberal fashion by holding that only material variances between an offer and a purported acceptance result in an implied rejection of the offer. Distinguishing among a counteroffer, an inquiry regarding terms, and a grumbling acceptance is often a difficult task. The fundamental issue, however, remains the same: Did the offeree objectively indicate a present intent to be bound by the terms of the offer?

BENYA v. STEVENS AND THOMPSON PAPER CO.
468 A.2d 929 (Vt. Sup. Ct. 1983)

On September 24, 1979, Vincent Benya's agent presented Stevens and Thompson Paper Company (S&T) with a sales agreement to purchase 5,243 acres of timber land owned by S&T for $605,366.50. S&T's lawyer made several modifications to the agreement, raising the cash to be paid at closing from $5,000 to $10,000, raising the interest rate on the mortgage S&T would hold on the property until it was fully paid for from 9 percent to 10 percent, providing for quarterly rather than annual payments on the mortgage, and changing the deed S&T was to provide from a warranty to a special warranty deed. S&T's vice president then initialed each change and signed the document, which was mailed back to Benya's agent. In early November, S&T received a new sales agreement from Benya, which differed from the two previous versions in a number of ways. S&T neither signed this agreement nor responded to it in any way. On November 7, S&T sold the property to someone else. Benya filed suit for breach of contract, and, when the trial court ruled in his favor, S&T appealed.

Billings, Chief Justice.   The trial court found that the September 24th sales agreement constituted a binding contract as both parties had signed it. The court concluded that the changes made by S&T to Benya's sales agreement were minor since the purchase price, closing date and deposit were substantially the same, and therefore did not constitute a counteroffer.

   The law relative to contract formation has long been well settled in Vermont and elsewhere. For an acceptance of an offer to be valid, it must substantially comply with the terms of the offer. An acceptance that modifies or includes new terms is not an acceptance of the original offer; it is a counteroffer by the offeree that must be accepted or rejected by the original offeror. The offeror's acceptance of the offeree's counteroffer may be accomplished either expressly or by conduct.

   On the record before us it is clear that the September 24th purchase and sales agreement was an offer from Benya to S&T that S&T never accepted. Instead, S&T significantly altered the terms of Benya's offer. These changes were not, as characterized by the trial court, minor and therefore of no effect on Benya's offer. Taken together, they constitute S&T's proposal for a new deal, or, more precisely, a counteroffer. Also clear from the record is that Benya never accepted, either expressly or otherwise, S&T's counteroffer. After Benya and his agent discussed S&T's counteroffer, the decision was made to draft a third proposal, which in turn altered the deposit and time of payment terms of S&T's counteroffer. S&T never signed or in any other way expressed its assent to this proposal. Additionally, the conduct of the parties demonstrates their understanding that agreement had not yet been reached.

Judgment reversed in favor of S&T.

The "Battle of the Forms"   Strictly applying the mirror image rule to modern commercial transactions, most of which are carried out by using preprinted form contracts, would often result in frustrating the parties' true intent. Offerors use standard order forms prepared by their lawyers, and offerees use standard acceptance or acknowledgment forms drafted by their counsel. The odds that these forms will agree in every detail are slight, as are the odds that the parties will read each other's forms in their entirety. Instead, the parties to such transactions are likely to read only crucial provisions concerning the goods ordered, the price, and the delivery

FIGURE 1   The "Battle of the Forms"—A Section 2–207 Flow Chart

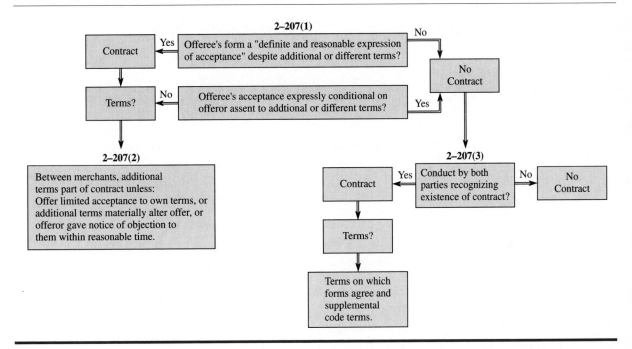

date called for, and if these terms are agreeable, believe that they have a contract. If a dispute arose before the parties started to perform, however, a court strictly applying the mirror image rule would hold that no contract resulted, due to the variance in their forms. If a dispute arose after performance had commenced, the court would probably hold that the offeror had impliedly accepted the offeree's counteroffer and was bound by its terms.

Because neither of these results is very satisfactory, the Code, in a very controversial provision often called the "Battle of the Forms" section [2–207] (see Figure 1), has changed the common law mirror image rule for contracts involving the sale of goods. As the following *Egan Machinery* case indicates, the Code provides that a definite and timely *expression of acceptance* creates a contract, even if it includes terms that are *different* from those stated in the offer or even if it states *additional* terms on points that the offer did not address [2–207(1)]. The only exception to this rule occurs when the attempted acceptance is *expressly conditional* on the offeror's agreement to the terms of the acceptance [2–207(1)].

What are the terms of a contract created in this fashion? The *additional* terms are treated as "proposals for addition to the contract." If the parties are both *merchants*, the *additional* terms become part of the contract unless: (1) the offer *expressly* limited acceptance to its own terms; (2) the new terms would *materially alter* the offer; or (3) the offeror gives *notice of objection* to the new terms within a reasonable time after receiving the acceptance [2–207(2)].

When the offeree has made his acceptance expressly conditional on the offeror's agreement to the new terms or when the offeree's response to the offer is clearly not "an expression of acceptance" (e.g., an express rejection), no contract is created under section 2–207(1). A contract will only result in such cases if the parties engage in conduct that "recognizes the existence of a contract," such as an exchange of performance. Unlike his counterpart under traditional contract principles, however, the offeror who accepts performance in the face of an express rejection or expressly conditional acceptance is not thereby bound to all of the terms contained in the offeree's response. Instead, the Code provides that the terms of a contract created by such performance are those on which the parties' writings *agree*, supplemented by appropriate gap-filling provisions from the Code [2–207(3)].

EGAN MACHINERY CO. v. MOBIL CHEMICAL CO.

660 F. Supp. 35 (D. Conn. 1986)

On April 27, 1973, in response to a request from Mobil Chemical for a bid on a two-sided precoater, Egan Machinery submitted a "quotation" describing the components of the precoater and the details of its operation. The quotation stated a price for the precoater, but did not contain conditions of sale.

On May 2, 1973, Mobil sent Egan a purchase order for the precoater. The purchase order contained the following language:

Important—this order expressly limits acceptance to terms stated herein, and any additional or different terms proposed by the seller are rejected unless expressly agreed to in writing.

Egan responded with an order acknowledgment on May 8, 1973, which provided that:

This order is accepted on the condition that our Standard Conditions of Sale, which are attached hereto and made a part hereof, are accepted by you, notwithstanding any modifying or additive conditions contained on your purchase order. Receipt of this acknowledgment by you without prompt written objection thereto shall constitute an acceptance of these terms and conditions.

One of the terms included in Egan's Standard Conditions required Mobil to indemnify Egan against any liability Egan might incur to persons injured by the precoater if the injury resulted from Mobil's failure to require its employees to follow safety procedures and/or use safety devices while operating it. When a Mobil employee who was injured while operating the precoater later won a $75,000 judgment against Egan, Egan filed suit against Mobil seeking indemnity. Mobil moved for a summary judgment on the ground that the indemnity clause was not part of its contract with Egan.

Eginton, District Judge.   In a classic UCC section 2–207 battle of the forms the warring parties use their boilerplate armies in an attempt to control the high ground by making their assent conditional on their right to set the conditions of the contract. In fashioning a peace between the combatants the court first looks to whether the exchanged forms created a contract. If a contract has been formed, the court next determines which additional or different terms control by reference to section 2–207(2).

The clause in Egan's Acknowledgment conditioning acceptance on Egan's Standard Conditions of Sale is not sufficiently explicit to declare Egan's intention to abort the contract unless it were sure of Mobil's assent to additional or different terms. Courts have required that clauses such as the one here be strictly construed. The conditional acceptance clause will convert an acceptance into a counteroffer only where the offeree clearly reveals its unwillingness to proceed with the transaction unless it is assured of the offeror's assent to additional or different terms. This Egan's clause did not do. The focus of 2–207(1) is on explicit, not implicit, statements of intent.

Egan's failure to explicitly declare its unwillingness to proceed with the contract unless its conditions were accepted compels the conclusion that a contract was formed by the exchanged forms on the consistent terms but leaves unresolved the issue of whether the indemnity provision became a term of the contract. With this established, the question narrows to whether Mobil's offer, under 2–207(2)(a), expressly limits acceptance to the terms of the offer. This it clearly did with the language "this order expressly limits acceptance to terms stated herein." As a result, the indemnity provision did not become part of the contract.

Mobil's motion for summary judgment granted.

Acceptance in Unilateral Contracts

A unilateral contract involves the exchange of a promise for an act. To accept an offer to enter such a contract, the offeree must *perform the requested act.* As you learned in the last chapter, however, courts applying modern contract rules may prevent an offeror from revoking such an offer once the offeree has begun performance. This is achieved by holding either that a bilateral contract is created by the beginning of performance or that the offeror's power to revoke is suspended for the period of time reasonably necessary for the offeree to complete performance.

Acceptance in Bilateral Contracts

A bilateral contract involves the exchange of a promise for a promise. As a general rule, to accept an offer to enter such a contract, an offeree must *make the promise requested by the offer.* This may be done in a variety of ways. For example, Wallace sends Stevens a detailed offer for the purchase of Stevens's business. Within the time period prescribed by the offer, Stevens sends Wallace a letter that says, "I accept your offer." Stevens has *expressly* accepted Wallace's offer, creating a contract on the terms of the offer. Acceptance, however, can be *implied* as well as *express.* Offerees who take action that objectively indicates agreement risk the formation of a contract. For example, offerees who act in a manner that is inconsistent with an offeror's ownership of offered property are commonly held to have accepted the offeror's terms. So, if Arnold, a farmer, leaves 10 bushels of corn with Porter, the owner of a grocery store, saying, "Look this corn over. If you want it, it's $5 a bushel," and Porter sells the corn, he has impliedly accepted Arnold's offer. But what if Porter just let the corn sit and, when Arnold returned a week later, Porter told Arnold that he did not want it? Could Porter's failure to act ever amount to an acceptance?

Silence as Acceptance   Since contract law generally requires some objective indication that an offeree intends to contract, the general rule is that an offeree's silence, without more, is *not* an acceptance. In addition, it is generally held that an offeror cannot impose on the offeree a duty to respond to the offer. So, even if Arnold had said to Porter, "If I don't hear from you in three days, I'll assume you're buying the corn," Porter's silence would still not amount to acceptance.

On the other hand, the circumstances of a case sometimes impose a duty on the offeree to reject the offer affirmatively or be bound by its terms. These are cases in which the offeree's silence objectively indicates an intent to accept. Customary trade practice or prior dealings between the parties may indicate that silence signals acceptance. So, if Arnold and Porter had dealt with each other on numerous occasions and Porter had always promptly returned items that he did not want, Porter's silent retention of the goods for a week would probably constitute an acceptance. Likewise, an offeree's silence can also operate as an acceptance if the offeree has indicated that it will. For example, Porter tells Arnold, "If you don't hear from me in three days, I accept."

Finally, it is generally held that offerees who accept an offeror's performance knowing what the offeror expects in return for his performance have impliedly accepted the offeror's terms. So, if Apex Paving Corporation offers to do the paving work on a new subdivision being developed by Majestic Homes Corporation, and Majestic fails to respond to Apex's offer but allows Apex to do the work, most courts would hold that Majestic is bound by the terms of Apex's offer.

Acceptance when a Writing Is Anticipated   Frequently, the parties to a contract intend to prepare a written draft of their agreement for both parties to sign. This is a good idea not only because the law requires written evidence of some contracts,[2] but also because it provides

---

[2] The Writing chapter discusses this subject in detail.

written evidence of the terms of the agreement if a dispute arises at a later date. If a dispute arises before such a writing has been prepared or signed, however, a question may arise concerning whether the signing of the agreement was a necessary condition to the creation of a contract. A party to the agreement who now wants out of the deal may argue that the parties did not intend to be bound until both parties signed the writing. As the following *Texaco* case indicates, a clear expression of such an intent by the parties during the negotiation process prevents the formation of a contract until both parties have signed. However, in the absence of such a clear expression of intent, the courts ask whether a reasonable person familiar with all the circumstances of the parties' negotiations would conclude that the parties intended to be bound only when a formal agreement was signed. If it appears that the parties had concluded their negotiations and reached agreement on all the essential aspects of the transaction, most courts would probably find a contract at the time agreement was reached, even though no formal agreement had been signed.

TEXACO, INC. v. PENNZOIL, CO.

729 S.W.2d 768 (Tex. Ct. App. 1987)

On December 28, 1983, in the wake of well-publicized dissension between the board of directors of Getty Oil Company and Gordon Getty, Pennzoil announced an unsolicited, public tender offer for 16 million shares of Getty Oil at $100 each. Gordon Getty was a director of Getty Oil and the owner, as trustee of the Sarah C. Getty Trust, of 40.2 percent of the 79.1 million outstanding shares of Getty Oil. Shortly thereafter, Pennzoil contacted both Gordon Getty and a representative of the J. Paul Getty Museum, which held 11.8 percent of the shares of Getty Oil, to discuss the tender offer and the possible purchase of Getty Oil.

The parties drafted and signed a Memorandum of Agreement providing that Pennzoil and the Trust (with Gordon Getty as trustee) were to become partners on a $3/7$ths to $4/7$ths basis, respectively, in owning and operating Getty Oil. The museum was to receive $110 per share for its 11.8 percent ownership, and all other outstanding public shares were to be cashed in by the company at $110 per share. The memorandum provided that it was subject to the approval of Getty Oil's board. On January 2, 1984, the board voted to reject the memorandum price as too low and made a counterproposal to Pennzoil of $110 per share plus a $10 debenture. On January 3, the board received a revised Pennzoil proposal of $110 per share plus a $3 "stub" that was to be paid after the sale of a Getty Oil subsidiary. After discussion, the board voted 15 to 1 to accept Pennzoil's proposal if the stub price was raised to $5. This counteroffer was accepted by Pennzoil later the same day. On January 4, Getty Oil and Pennzoil issued identical press releases announcing an agreement in principle on the terms of the Memorandum of Agreement. Pennzoil's lawyers began working on a formal transaction agreement describing the deal in more detail than the outline of terms contained in the Memorandum of Agreement and press release.

On January 5, the board of Texaco, which had been in contact with Getty Oil's investment banker, authorized its officers to make an offer for 100 percent of Getty Oil's stock. Texaco first contacted the Getty Museum, which, after discussion, agreed to sell its shares to Texaco. Later that evening, Gordon Getty accepted Texaco's offer of $125 per share. On January 6, the Getty Board voted to withdraw its previous counteroffer to Pennzoil and to accept Texaco's offer. Pennzoil later filed suit against Texaco for tortious interference with its contract with the Getty entities. At trial, Texaco argued, among other things, that no contract had existed between Pennzoil and the Getty entities. The jury disagreed, awarding Pennzoil $7.53 billion in actual damages and $3 billion in punitive damages. Texaco appealed.

Warren, Justice.   Texaco contends that there was insufficient evidence to support the jury's finding that at the end of the Getty Oil board meeting on January 3, the Getty entities intended to bind themselves to an agreement with Pennzoil. Pennzoil contends that the evidence showed that the parties intended to be bound to the terms in the Memorandum of Agreement plus a price term of $110 plus a $5 stub, even though the parties may have contemplated a later, more formal document to memorialize the agreement already reached.

If parties do not intend to be bound to an agreement until it is reduced to writing and signed by both parties, then there is no contract until that event occurs. If there is no understanding that a signed writing is necessary before the parties will be bound, and the parties have agreed upon all substantial terms, then an informal agreement can be binding, even though the parties contemplated evidencing their agreement in a formal document later. It is the parties' expressed intent that controls which rule of contract formation applies. Only the outward expressions of intent are considered—secret or subjective intent is immaterial to the question of whether the parties were bound.

Several factors have been articulated to help determine whether the parties intended to be bound only by a formal, signed writing: (1) whether a party expressly reserved the right to be bound only when a written agreement is signed; (2) whether there was any partial performance by one party that the party disclaiming the contract accepted; (3) whether all essential terms of the alleged contract had been agreed upon; and (4) whether the complexity or magnitude of the transaction was such that a formal, executed writing would normally be expected.

Any intent of the parties not to be bound before signing a formal document is not so clearly expressed in the press release to establish, as a matter of law, that there was no contract at that time. The press release does refer to an agreement "in principle" and states that the "transaction" is subject to execution of a definitive merger agreement. But the release as a whole is worded in indicative terms, not in subjunctive or hypothetical ones. The press release describes what shareholders *will* receive, what Pennzoil *will* contribute, that Pennzoil *will* be granted an option, etc.

We find little relevant partial performance in this case that might show that the parties believed that they were bound by a contract. However, the absence of relevant part performance in this short period of time does not compel the conclusion that no contract existed.

There was sufficient evidence for the jury to conclude that the parties had reached agreement on all essential terms of the transaction with only the mechanics and details left to be supplied by the parties' attorneys. Although there may have been many specific items relating to the transaction agreement draft that had yet to be put in final form, there is sufficient evidence to support a conclusion by the jury that the parties did not consider any of Texaco's asserted "open items" significant obstacles precluding an intent to be bound.

Although the magnitude of the transaction here was such that normally a signed writing would be expected, there was sufficient evidence to support an inference by the jury that that expectation was satisfied here initially by the Memorandum of Agreement, signed by a majority of shareholders of Getty Oil and approved by the board with a higher price, and by the transaction agreement in progress that had been intended to memorialize the agreement previously reached.

Judgment for Pennzoil affirmed.

[Note: The court's decision was contingent on a reduction in the punitive damages awarded by the jury from $3 billion to $1 billion. Texaco ultimately sought reorganization under the protection of the Bankruptcy Court and the parties finally settled the case for $3 billion.]

Acceptance of Ambiguous Offers

Although offerors have the power to specify the manner in which their offers can be accepted by requiring that the offeree make a return promise (a bilateral contract) or perform a specific act (a unilateral contract), often an offer is unclear about which form of acceptance is necessary to create a contract. In such a case, both the Code [2–206(1)(a)] and the *Restatement Second*[3] suggest that the offer may be accepted in any manner that is *reasonable* in light of the circumstances surrounding the offer. Thus, either a promise to perform or performance, if reasonable, creates a contract.

Acceptance by Shipment   The Code specifically elaborates on the rule stated in the preceding section by stating that an order requesting prompt or current shipment of goods may be accepted either by a *prompt promise to ship* or by a *prompt* or *current shipment* of the goods [2–206(1)(b)]. So, if Ampex Corporation orders 500 IBM personal computers from Marks Office Supply, to be shipped immediately, Marks could accept either by promptly promising to ship the goods or by promptly shipping them. If Marks accepts by shipping, any subsequent attempt by Ampex to revoke the order will be ineffective.

But what if Marks did not have 500 IBMs in stock and Marks knew that Ampex desperately needed the goods? Marks might be tempted to ship another brand of computers, hoping that Ampex would be forced by its circumstances to accept them because by the time they arrived it would be too late to get the correct goods elsewhere. Marks would argue that by shipping the wrong goods it had made a counteroffer because it had not performed the act requested by Ampex's order. If Ampex accepts the goods, Marks could argue that Ampex has impliedly accepted the counteroffer. If Ampex rejects the goods, Marks would arguably have no liability since it did not accept the order. The Code prevents such a result by providing that prompt shipment of either *conforming goods* (what the order asked for) or *nonconforming goods* (something else) operates as an acceptance of the order [2–206(1)(b)]. This protects buyers such as Ampex because sellers who ship the wrong goods have simultaneously *accepted* their offers and *breached* the contract by sending the wrong merchandise.

---

[3] *Restatement (Second) of Contracts* § 30(2) (1981).

But what if Marks is an honest seller merely trying to help out a customer that has placed a rush order? Must Marks expose itself to liability for breach of contract in the process? The Code prevents such a result by providing that no contract is created if the seller notifies the buyer within a reasonable time that the shipment of nonconforming goods is intended as an accommodation [2–206(1)(b)]. In this case, the shipment is merely a counteroffer that the buyer is free to accept or reject and the seller's notification gives the buyer the opportunity to seek the goods he needs elsewhere.

Who Can Accept an Offer?

As the masters of their offers, offerees have the right to determine who can bind them to a contract. So, the only person with the legal power to accept an offer and create a contract is the *original offeree*. An attempt to accept by anyone other than the offeree is treated as an offer, because the party attempting to accept is indicating a present intent to contract on the original offer's terms. For example, Price offers to sell his car to Waterhouse for $5,000. Anderson learns of the offer, calls Price, and attempts to accept. Anderson has made an offer that Price is free to accept or reject.

COMMUNICATION OF ACCEPTANCE

Necessity of Communication

To accept an offer for a *bilateral* contract, the offeree must make the *promise* requested by the offer. In the Offer chapter, you learned that an offeror must communicate the terms of his proposal to the offeree before an offer results. This is so because communication is a necessary component of the present intent to contract required for the creation of an offer. For similar reasons, it is generally held that an offeree must communicate his intent to be bound by the offer before a contract can be created. To accept an offer for a *unilateral contract*, however, the offeree must *perform the requested act*. The traditional contract law rule on this point assumes that the offeror will learn of the offeree's performance and holds that no further notice from the offeree is necessary to create a contract unless the offeror specifically requests notice.

Because this rule can sometimes cause hardship to offerors who may not, in fact, know that the offeree has commenced performance, the Code and the *Restatement*

Second have modified the traditional rule. If the offeree has reason to know that the offeror has no way of learning of his performance with reasonable promptness and certainty, the *Restatement Second* provides that the offeror may be discharged from any contractual obligation.[4] This is so unless the offeree takes reasonable steps to notify him of performance, the offeror learns of performance within a reasonable time, or the offer indicates that notification of acceptance is not required.

The Code takes a different approach by saying that, in cases where the *beginning of performance* operates as an acceptance, an offeror who is not notified of acceptance within a reasonable time may treat the offer as having lapsed before acceptance [2–206(2)]. The full meaning of this provision is unclear. It apparently does not require notice when the offeree accepts by *performing*, for example, by shipping the goods. In such a case, it is apparently assumed that the offeror will learn of performance within a reasonable time. It expressly applies

only when acceptance is accomplished by *beginning performance*. Whether loading goods on a truck for shipment is enough to constitute beginning performance, or whether the statute is intended to apply only to more specific offeree behavior, such as beginning to manufacture specially ordered goods, is not apparent from the language of the statute.

Manner of Communication

As the following *Great Western Sugar* case indicates, the offeror, as the master of the offer, has the power to specify the precise time, place, and manner in which acceptance must be communicated. If the offeror does so, and the offeree deviates from the offer's instructions in any significant way, no contract results unless the offeror indicates a willingness to be bound by the deviating acceptance. If the offer merely suggests a method or place of communication, or is silent on such matters, the offeree may accept within a reasonable time by any reasonable means of communication.

---

[4] *Restatement (Second) of Contracts* § 54 (2) (1981).

GREAT WESTERN SUGAR CO. v. LONE STAR DONUT CO.

567 F. Supp. 340 (N.D. Texas 1983)

Since 1974, Lone Star Donut Company had placed orders for its sugar requirements with Great Western Sugar Co. (GWS) through a sugar broker. In October of 1980, GWS adopted a new policy of requiring a letter agreement for each order. The first such letter was forwarded from GWS to Lone Star by the broker on October 9, 1980. It concluded with the following language:

This letter is a written confirmation of our agreement, and unless it is signed by the buyer and returned to Great Western within 15 days of the date hereof, the agreement shall be deemed breached by Buyer and automatically terminated. Please sign and return to me the enclosed counterpart of this letter signalling your acceptance of the above agreement.

Lone Star signed and returned this letter. On December 2, Lone Star again ordered sugar. GWS initially neglected to send a letter agreement, finally doing so in late January of 1981, in response to prodding by the broker. This letter concluded as follows:

This letter is a written confirmation of our agreement. Please sign and return to me the enclosed counterpart of this letter signalling your acceptance of the above agreement.

Lone Star, angered over the delay, refused to sign and subsequently refused to purchase sugar. When GWS filed suit for breach of contract, Lone Star moved for summary judgment arguing that no contract was ever created.

Fish, District Judge.   In *Southwestern Stationery & Bank Supply, Inc. v. Harris Corp.* (10th Cir. 1980), the court had before it a purchase order signed by buyer and returned to seller, specifying that the order was subject to acceptance by the seller, who was to indicate acceptance by mailing the purchaser a signed duplicate copy. Seller did not sign the purchase order. The court denied the buyer recovery against the seller. The court noted that under the Uniform Commercial Code parties retain their power to require specific methods of acceptance.

Dealing with a dispute over a tender offer, the court in *Kroeze v. Chloride Group* (1978) relied both on the common law and, by analogy, the UCC. The court emphasized a cardinal rule of contracts, that the offeror is the master of his offer. He may prescribe as many conditions, terms, or the like as he may wish, including but not limited to, the time, place and method of acceptance. The drafters of the UCC explicitly recognized this principle in section 2–206(1)(a). In *Kroeze*, the court reasoned that because the offeror had expressly and unambiguously required signing of the transmittal letter to effect acceptance of the offer, the offerees who had not signed the transmittal letters could not recover.

In the case before this court, GWS has unambiguously indicated, by the language concluding the letter agreement, the manner and medium of acceptance: the buyer was to sign and return a copy. While the 1981 letter agreement, in contrast to the 1980 letter agreement, no longer specified that the agreement would be terminated if the buyer did not sign and return the copy, the only reasonable construction of GWS's requirement that the buyer signal acceptance is that if he failed to do so, he would not be bound.

Summary judgment granted for Lone Star.

When Is Acceptance Communicated?

The question of when an acceptance has been effectively communicated is often a critically important issue in contract cases. The offeror may be trying to revoke an offer that the offeree is desperately trying to accept. A mailed or telegraphed acceptance may get lost and never be received by the offeror. The time limit for accepting the offer may be rapidly approaching. Was the offer accepted before a revocation was received or before the offer expired? Does a lost acceptance create a contract when it is dispatched, or is it totally ineffective?

When the parties are dealing face-to-face or the offeree is accepting by telephone, these problems are minimized. As soon as the offeree says, "I accept," or words to that effect, a contract is created as long as the offer is still in existence. Problems with the timing of acceptances multiply, however, when the offeree is using a means of communication that creates a time lag between the dispatching of the acceptance and its actual receipt by the offeror. Offerors have the power to minimize these problems by requiring in their offer that they must *actually receive* the acceptance for it to be effective. Offerors who do this maximize the time that they have to revoke their offers and ensure that they

will never be bound by an acceptance that they have not received.

Offerors who fail to require actual receipt of an acceptance may find to their dismay that the law has developed rules that make some acceptances effective the moment they are dispatched, regardless of whether the offeror ever receives them. These rules generally apply when the offeror has made the offer under circumstances that might reasonably lead the offeree to believe that acceptance by some means other than telephone or face-to-face communication is acceptable. They protect the offeree's reasonable belief that a binding contract was created when the acceptance was dispatched.

Authorized Means of Communication   As the following *Soldau* case illustrates, an acceptance is generally effective *when dispatched*, or delivered to the agency of communication, if the offeree accepts by the **authorized means** of communication. This is so even if the acceptance is never received by the offeror. An offeror may *expressly* authorize acceptance by a particular means of communication by saying, in effect: "You *may* accept by mail." If the offeror does so, the offeree's acceptance is effective when mailed. Any attempt by the offeror to revoke thereafter, such as by a letter of revocation mailed before the acceptance was mailed but received after it was mailed, would be ineffective.

A means of communication may also be *impliedly* authorized by the offeror. Under traditional contract principles, if the offer or circumstances do not indicate otherwise, the offeror impliedly authorizes the offeree to accept by the *same means* that the offeror used to communicate the offer. So, mailed offers impliedly invite mailed acceptances, telegraphed offers impliedly invite acceptance by telegram, and so forth. In addition, *trade usage* can impliedly authorize a given means of acceptance. Thus, if the parties are both members of a particular trade and the trade custom is to offer by mail and accept by telegram, a telegram would be the impliedly authorized means of accepting such an offer unless the offer indicates to the contrary.

In recent years, the authorized means concept has been broadened considerably by numerous cases holding that offerors who remain silent impliedly authorize acceptance by *any reasonable means*. What is reasonable depends on the circumstances in which the offer was made. These include the speed and reliability of the means used by the offeree, the nature of the transaction (e.g., does the agreement involve goods subject to rapid price fluctuations?), the existence of any trade usage governing the transaction, and the existence of prior dealings between the parties (e.g., has the offeree previously used the mail to accept telegraphed offers from the offeror?). So, under proper circumstances, a mailed response to a telegraphed offer or a telegraphed response to a mailed offer might be considered reasonable, and therefore effective on dispatch. The Code expressly adopts the reasonable means test for offers involving the sale of goods [2–206(1)(a)], and the *Restatement Second* suggests that it be used in all contract cases.[5]

---

[5] *Restatement (Second) of Contracts* §§ 30(2), 63, 65 (1981).

SOLDAU v. ORGANON, INC.
860 F.2d 355 (9th Cir. 1988)

John Soldau was fired by Organon, Inc. He received a letter from Organon offering to pay him double the normal severance pay if he would sign a release giving up all claims against the company. The letter incorporated the proposed release, which Soldau signed, dated, and deposited in a mailbox outside a post office. When he returned home, Soldau found that he had received a check from Organon in the amount of the increased severance pay. He returned to the post office and persuaded a postal employee to open the mailbox and retrieve the release. Soldau cashed Organon's check and subsequently filed an age discrimination suit against Organon. When the trial court granted a summary judgment in Organon's favor, Soldau appealed.

Per Curiam.   The district court held that "the release was deemed fully communicated to Organon, and a binding contract was formed, at the time Soldau deposited the executed release in the mailbox. The fact that he retrieved the release from the mailbox is of no consequence under California law." Soldau contends that the formation and validity of the release are governed by federal law, and would not have been effective unless and until it had been received by Organon.

We need not decide which body of law controls. Under federal as well as California law, Soldau's acceptance was effective when it was mailed. The so-called "mailbox" or "effective when mailed" rule was adopted and followed as federal common law by the Supreme Court prior to *Erie R.R. Co. v. Thompkins* (1938). We could not change the rule, and there is no reason to believe the Supreme Court would be inclined to do so. It is almost universally accepted in the common law world.

Soldau rests his case upon decisions of the Court of Claims, beginning with *Dick v. United States* (1949), rejecting mailing of the acceptance as the crucial event resulting in a contract, in favor of the receipt of the acceptance by the offeror. No other federal court has agreed. Commentators are also virtually unanimous in rejecting the Court of Claims' repudiation of the "effective when mailed" rule, pointing to the long history of the rule; its importance in creating certainty for the contracting parties; and its essential soundness, on balance, as a means of allocating the risk during the period between the making of the offer and the communication of the acceptance to the offeror.

Since Soldau's contractual obligation to release Organon in return for Organon's payment arose when Soldau deposited his acceptance in the mailbox, his subsequent withdrawal of the acceptance was ineffectual.

Judgment for Organon affirmed.

Acceptance by Nonauthorized Means   What if an offeree attempts to accept the offer by mail when the authorized means for acceptance was clearly by telegram? The traditional rule in such cases is that an acceptance by a nonauthorized means is effective only when it is *actually received* by the offeror, provided that it is received within the time that an acceptance by the authorized means would have been received. This rule seems somewhat artificial, however, because once an acceptance reaches the offeror, she has actual notice that a contract has been created and is not in any danger of acting in reliance on the impression that she is not bound by a contract by selling offered goods to a third party. At this point, the means that the offeree used to communicate acceptance would logically seem to be irrelevant because the end result from the offeror's standpoint is the same, regardless of the means used by the offeree. Why, then, should we allow the offeror to revoke prior to timely receipt of an acceptance by a nonauthorized means but deny her the power to revoke after the dispatch of an acceptance by the authorized means? The Code has accepted this reasoning by providing that in all contracts for the sale of goods an acceptance by a nonauthorized means is effective *on dispatch* if it is received within the time that an acceptance by the authorized means would normally have arrived [1–201(38)]. Section 67 of the *Restatement Second* adopts the Code rule for all contracts.

Contradictory Offeree Responses   Consider this example: White mails Case an offer to sell his house for $75,000. Case mails White a counteroffer, offering to pay $70,000 for the house. In the last chapter, you learned that Case's counteroffer would be effective to terminate White's offer only when White actually receives it. Therefore, if Case changed his mind and communicated an acceptance of the offer to White before White received his counteroffer, a contract would result. But what if Case mails an acceptance to White four hours after mailing the counteroffer? If we applied the normal rules of offer and acceptance to these facts, we might conclude that the parties had a contract because Case's acceptance by mail—the authorized means—was effective on dispatch, and was probably dispatched before White received Case's counteroffer. White, however, may receive Case's counteroffer and sell the house to a third party before he receives Case's acceptance. To prevent such an unfair result, most courts hold that when an offeree dispatches an acceptance after first dispatching a rejection, the acceptance does not create a contract unless it is received before the rejection. Therefore, if White receives the counteroffer before he receives the acceptance, no contract results. If, on the other hand, he receives the acceptance before receiving the counteroffer, a contract results.

However, what if Case mailed White an acceptance, changed his mind, and shortly thereafter mailed White a rejection? Applying normal offer and acceptance rules to these facts, we would conclude that Case's acceptance was effective on dispatch and that Case no longer had the power to reject the offer. But what if White received Case's rejection first and relied on it by selling to someone else? In such a situation, Case would be *estopped* from enforcing the contract due to White's reliance.

Stipulated Means of Communication   An offer may *stipulate* the means of communication that the offeree must use to accept by saying, in effect: "You *must* accept by mail." An acceptance by the **stipulated means** of communication is effective on dispatch, just like an acceptance by an authorized means of communi-

cation. The difference is that an acceptance by other than the stipulated means does not create a contract because it is an acceptance at variance with the terms of the offer.

CONCEPT REVIEW

WHEN ACCEPTANCE IS EFFECTIVE

Means of Communication	Traditional Contract Law	UCC and *Restatement Second*
Authorized	Dispatch (even if never received)	Dispatch (even if never received)
Nonauthorized	Receipt (if received when authorized acceptance would have been received)	Dispatch (if received when authorized acceptance would have been received)

ETHICAL AND PUBLIC POLICY CONCERNS

1. It should be apparent to you from the discussion of section 2–207 of the Code, the "Battle of the Forms" section, that the application of that section can sometimes result in a party being held to a contract term that she has not actually consented to. How can this be justified?

2. Compare the ethical standards underlying the traditional contract law approach to the seller who ships nonconforming goods with the ethical standards reflected by section 2–206(1)(b) of the Code.

3. Compare the public policy stances implicit in the different ways in which classical contract law and the UCC treat offeree attempts to accept by a nonauthorized means of communication.

SUMMARY

In determining whether an offer was accepted to create a binding contract, the courts look for behavior by an offeree that objectively indicates a present intent to contract on the terms of the offer. This behavior may be in the form of words or action by the offeree. Also, in some limited cases, silence or inaction by the offeree may signal his assent to the terms of the offer. Acceptance of offers for unilateral contracts requires that the offeree

perform the act requested by the offer. In bilateral contract cases, the offeree must make the promise requested by the offer. In some cases, the offer is unclear about whether acceptance may be accomplished by performing an act or making a promise. In such cases, both the Code and the *Restatement Second* provide that an offeree can accept either by performing or promising to perform.

Traditional contract principles require the offeree's acceptance to be the mirror image of the offer and treat acceptances that attempt to vary the terms of an offer as counteroffers. Recent years, however, have witnessed a judicial tendency to relax the strict application of this rule by treating only acceptances containing material variances as counteroffers. The Code, in its controversial "Battle of the Forms" section [2–207], expressly changes the mirror image rule by allowing acceptances stating additional or different terms to operate as acceptances. Between merchants, these new terms become part of the contract unless the offer limits acceptance to its own terms, the new terms would materially alter the offer, or the offeror objects to the new terms within a reasonable time after he has notice of them.

As a general rule, acceptances, like offers, must be communicated to the other party to the agreement before they become effective. In the case of offers for unilateral contracts, however, the traditional rule is that the offeree's performance of the act requested by the offer is all that is required for acceptance. To prevent unfairness to offerors who may assume that no acceptance has occurred because they have not, in fact, learned of the offeree's performance, the Code and the *Restatement Second* require in some cases that the offeree give notice of performance to the offeror.

As the master of the offer, the offeror can specify the exact means that the offeree must use to accept the offer. Attempts by offerees to accept in any other way do not create a contract. When the offeror fails to specify the exact means of acceptance, the offeree may accept by any reasonable means.

When the parties are dealing face-to-face or over the telephone, an acceptance is effective the instant that it is communicated to the other party. When the offeree uses some delayed means of communication, such as mail or telegram, critical timing questions can arise about when an acceptance is effective. An offeror can specify that she will be bound to a contract only after she actually receives an acceptance. In the absence of such a statement by the offeror, an acceptance is effective when dispatched by the offeree if the offeree uses the *authorized means* of communication. A means of communication may be expressly or impliedly authorized. Traditional contract law rules provide that the offeror who does not indicate a contrary intent impliedly authorizes the offeree to accept by the same means of communication used to communicate the offer. Trade usage can also operate to authorize a particular means of communication. Many contemporary courts have broadened these rules by holding that the offeror who remains silent impliedly authorizes acceptance by any reasonable means. The Code and the *Restatement Second* adopt this position.

Under traditional contract principles, an acceptance by a nonauthorized means is effective only when it is received by the offeror, and then only if it is received within the time in which a properly dispatched acceptance would have been received. The Code and the *Restatement Second* change this rule by providing that an acceptance by a nonauthorized means is effective on dispatch if it reaches the offeror within the same time in which a properly dispatched acceptance would have been received.

An offeror may also *stipulate* that the offeree must accept by a particular means of communication. Acceptances by a stipulated means, like those by an authorized means, are effective on dispatch, even if never received by the offeror. Acceptances by a nonstipulated means, however, are never effective to create a contract.

PROBLEM CASES

1. In April of 1975, Bio-Zyme Enterprises, a livestock feed manufacturer, began selling feed to Vanderhoof, a feed dealer, on open account. The monthly statements Vanderhoof received from Bio-Zyme contained the following sentence at the bottom of each statement: "Accounts not paid within 30 days will on our billing date (the 26th day of each month) be charged 1 percent each month." Whenever a finance charge was imposed, this was conspicuously noted on the statement. By April of 1976, Vanderhoof, owed Bio-Zyme over $45,000. When Bio-Zyme filed suit on the account, Vanderhoof argued that he had not agreed to pay the 1 percent finance charge. Was he right?

2. First Texas Savings Association promoted a "$5,000 Scoreboard Challenge" contest. Contestants who completed an entry form and deposited it with First Texas were eligible for a random drawing. The winner was to receive an $80 savings account with First Texas, plus four tickets to a Dallas Mavericks home basketball game chosen by First Texas. If the Mavericks held their opponent in the chosen game to 89 or fewer points, the winner was to receive an additional $5,000 money market certificate. In October of 1982, Jergins deposited a completed entry form with First Texas. On November 1, 1982, First tried to amend the contest rules by posting notice at its branches that the Mavericks would have to hold their opponent to 85 or fewer points before the contest winner would receive the $5,000. In late December, Jergins was notified that she had won the $80 savings account and tickets to the January 22, 1983, game against the Utah Jazz. The notice contained the revised contest terms. The Mavericks held the Jazz to 88 points. Was Jergins entitled to the $5,000?

3. The Stortroens, through Panio, a realtor who showed them property owned by Beneficial Finance under a multiple-listing agreement, submitted an offer of $105,000 for the property. Beneficial responded with a counteroffer delivered to the Stortroens by Panio and offering to sell for $110,000. While its counteroffer was still in effect, Beneficial received an offer through another broker for $112,000. Wishing to accept this higher offer, Beneficial had the listing broker call Panio's office at 4:30 P.M. and leave a phone message withdrawing its counteroffer. Beneficial then accepted the higher offer. Unbeknownst to Beneficial, Panio had taken the counteroffer to the Stortroens' home and they had signed it at 4:10 P.M. that same day. Beneficial refused to convey the property to the Stortroens. Assuming Panio was legally Beneficial's agent, was it contractually bound to convey to the Stortroens? *Yes Because contract was given to agent*

4. Atwood bought a new pickup truck from Best Buick. When he took it home, his wife objected to the purchase. Atwood returned the car to Best, which agreed to take the truck back as a trade-in on another vehicle. Atwood traded for a new station wagon, which he registered and insured and sought to title in his name. When he took the car home, however, his wife objected to the color of its interior. Atwood returned the car to Best, but refused to accept any of the numerous other vehicles Best made available to him. He also refused to sign an application that would allow Best to retrieve the title to the car so it could sell it to someone else. Best then told him that unless he removed the car from its premises it would charge him a $5 per day storage fee. The Atwoods later sued Best for the return of the purchase price. Best counterclaimed for the storage fee. Should the Atwoods prevail?

5. Western Tire, Inc., had a lease on a building owned by the Skredes that was due to expire on April 30, 1978. The lease gave Western the right to renew the lease for an additional five-year term if the Skredes were given written notice of Western's intent to renew at least 30 days prior to the expiration date. It also specifically provided that notice would only be effective when it was deposited in a U.S. Post Office by registered or certified mail. On February 27, Western's attorney sent the Skredes a notice of Western's intent to renew by ordinary mail, which the Skredes did not receive until after April 1, 1978. On April 5, 1978, Western's lawyer, discovering his mistake, sent a second notice by certified mail. On April 14, 1978, the Skredes told Western the lease was cancelled. Did they have the right to cancel? *Yes. Unauthorized Means & past time limit*

6. In September of 1969, Roberts, an insurance agent, sent Buske a policy that was a renewal of one Buske's father had previously held. Buske had not ordered or requested issuance of this policy, but he accepted it and paid the premium. In September of 1970, just prior to the expiration date of the policy, Roberts sent a second unsolicited renewal to Buske and attached to it a printed notice stating that if Buske did not wish to accept it he must return it or be liable for the premium. Buske did not respond either to this notice or to two subsequent bills mailed to him. When Roberts telephoned Buske in December to ask about the premium, Buske said he had purchased a policy from another company in August and would not pay for the renewal since

he had not ordered it. The policy was then returned to the insurer and canceled, resulting in a loss to Roberts for the prorated portion of the premium that he had advanced. Should the trial court's ruling for Roberts be reversed on appeal? *No. Roberts Loses the Money*

7. Foremost, a photofinisher, submitted two orders to Kodak for photofinishing equipment. The order forms were supplied by Kodak's sales representatives, specified no delivery date, and specifically stated that all orders were "subject to acceptance" by Kodak. Kodak had no further communications with Foremost, but ultimately shipped the goods Foremost had ordered. Foremost later filed a breach of contract suit against Kodak, arguing that Kodak's delivery of the goods had been untimely. Should Kodak be liable for breach of contract? *Timeliness on Kodak Part! PROMPTNESS OF SHIPMENT?*

8. On March 30, Cushing, a member of an antinuclear protest group, applied to the New Hampshire adjutant general's office for permission to hold a dance in the Portsmouth armory. On March 31, the adjutant general mailed a signed contract offer agreeing to rent the armory to the group. The agreement required Cushing to accept by signing a copy of the agreement and returning it to the adjutant general within five days after its receipt. On April 3, Cushing received the offer and signed it. At 6:30 P.M. on April 4, Cushing received a call from the adjutant general attempting to revoke the offer. Cushing told the adjutant general that he had signed the contract and placed it in the office outbox on April 3, customary office practice being to collect all mail from outboxes at the end of the day and deposit it in the U.S. mail. On April 6, the adjutant general's office received the signed contract in the mail, dated April 3 and postmarked April 5. Assuming Cushing was telling the truth, did the parties have a contract? *Yes. there is contract*

9. Krack Corporation bought steel tubing from Metal-Matic for 10 years. The parties' usual practice was for Krack to send Metal-Matic purchase orders to which Metal-Matic would respond by sending an acknowledgment form and shipping the requested tubing. Metal-Matic's form provided that its acceptance was "expressly made conditional" on Krack's assent to the acknowledgment's terms, which included a clause limiting Metal-Matic's liability for consequential damages due to breach of warranty. Krack sold a cooling unit it had made with Metal-Matic's tubing to Diamond Fruit. The tubing was defective, causing losses to Diamond's fruit. When Diamond sued Krack, Krack sought indemnity from Metal-Matic. Metal-Matic

It is part of the contract p231

argued that it was not responsible, citing the consequential damages clause in its acknowledgment. Was that clause part of the contract between Krack and Metal-Matic? *Clause was part of contract.*

10. H&W Industries, a Mississippi pipe manufacturer, mailed a purchase order for resin (which is manufactured in Louisiana) to Occidental Chemical's office in Pottstown, Pennsylvania. Occidental replied with an acceptance form that said H&W's order was accepted subject to the terms and conditions appearing on the face and reverse side of the acceptance. Later, a dispute arose between the parties and Occidental filed a breach of contract suit against H&W in a U.S. district court in Pennsylvania. H&W moved to dismiss Occidental's complaint on the ground that the court lacked jurisdiction over the case. Occidental admitted that this would normally be true, but pointed to a forum selection clause on the back of its acceptance form stating: "The parties agree that any litigation arising out of this agreement shall be brought only in the federal or state courts in the State of Pennsylvania." Is H&W bound by this clause?

P231.

They are bound and the terms apply.

CHAPTER 12

CONSIDERATION

THE IDEA OF CONSIDERATION

One of the things that separates a contract from an unenforceable social promise is that a contract requires *voluntary agreement* by two or more parties. Not all agreements, however, are enforceable contracts. At a fairly early point in the development of classical contract law, the common law courts decided not to enforce gratuitous (free) promises. Instead, only promises *supported by consideration* were enforceable in a court of law. This was consistent with the notion that the purpose of contract law was to enforce freely made *bargains*. As one 19th-century work on contract put it: "The common law . . . gives effect only to contracts that are founded on the mutual exigencies of men, and does not compel the performance of any merely gratuitous agreements."[1] A common definition of **consideration** is *legal value, bargained for and given in exchange for an act or a promise*. Thus, a promise generally cannot be enforced against the person who made it (the *promisor*) unless the person to whom the promise was made (the *promisee*) has given up something of legal value in exchange for the promise. In effect, the requirement of consideration means that a

promisee must pay the price that the promisor asked to gain the right to enforce the promisor's promise. So, if the promisor did not ask for anything in exchange for making her promise or if what the promisor asked for did not have legal value (e.g., because it was something to which she was already entitled), her promise is not enforceable against her because it is not supported by consideration. Figure 1 graphically illustrates the elements of consideration.

Consider the early case of *Thorne v. Deas*, in which the part owner of a sailing ship named the *Sea Nymph* promised his co-owners that he would insure the ship for an upcoming voyage.[2] He failed to do so, and when the ship was lost at sea, the court found that he was not liable to his co-owners for breaching his promise to insure the ship. Why? Because his promise was purely gratuitous; he had neither asked for nor received anything in exchange for making it. Therefore, it was unenforceable because it was not supported by consideration.

This early example illustrates two important aspects of the consideration requirement. First, the requirement *tended to limit the scope of a promisor's liability for his promises* by insulating him from liability for gratuitous

---

[1] T. Metcalf, *Principles of the Law of Contracts*, p. 161 (1874).

[2] 4 Johns. 84 (N.Y. 1809).

FIGURE 1 The Elements of Consideration

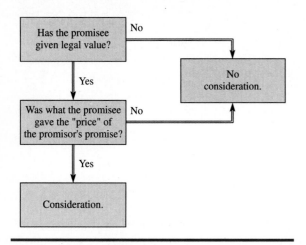

promises and by protecting him against liability for reliance on such promises. Second, the mechanical application of the requirement *often produced unfair results*. This potential for unfairness has produced considerable dissatisfaction with the consideration concept. As the rest of this chapter indicates, the relative importance of consideration in modern contract law has been somewhat eroded by numerous exceptions to the consideration requirement and by judicial applications of consideration principles designed to produce fair results.

LEGAL VALUE

Consideration can be an *act* in the case of a unilateral contract or a *promise* in the case of a bilateral contract. An act or a promise can have *legal value* in one of two ways. If, in exchange for the promisor's promise, the promisee does, or agrees to do, something he had no prior legal duty to do, that provides legal value. If, in exchange for the promisor's promise, the promisee refrains from doing, or agrees not to do, something she has a legal right to do, that also provides legal value. Note that this definition does not require that an act or a promise have *monetary* (economic) value to amount to consideration. Thus, in a famous 19th-century case, *Hamer v. Sidway*,[3] an uncle's promise to pay his nephew $5,000

---

[3] 27 N.E. 256 (N.Y. Ct. App. 1891).

if he refrained from using tobacco, drinking, swearing, and playing cards or billiards for money until his 21st birthday was held to be supported by consideration. Indeed, the nephew had refrained from doing any of these acts, even though he may have benefited from so refraining. He had a legal right to indulge in such activities, yet he had refrained from doing so at his uncle's request and in exchange for his uncle's promise. This was all that was required for consideration.

Adequacy of Consideration

The point that the legal value requirement is not concerned with actual value is further borne out by the fact that the courts generally will not concern themselves with questions regarding the *adequacy* of the consideration that the promisee gave. As the *Harrington* case on the opposite page plainly demonstrates, this means that as long as the promisee's act or promise satisfies the legal value test, the courts do not ask whether that act or promise was worth what the promisor gave, or promised to give, in return for it. This rule on adequacy of consideration reflects the laissez-faire assumptions underlying classical contract law. Freedom of contract includes the freedom to make bad bargains as well as good ones, so promisors' promises are enforceable if they got what they asked for in exchange for making their promises, even if what they asked for was not nearly so valuable in worldly terms as what they promised in return. Also, a court taking a hands-off stance concerning private contracts would be reluctant to step in and second-guess the parties by setting aside a transaction that both parties at one time considered satisfactory. Finally, the rule against considering the adequacy of consideration can promote certainty and predictability in commercial transactions by denying legal effect to what would otherwise be a possible basis for challenging the enforceability of a contract: the inequality of the exchange.

Several qualifications must be made concerning the general rule on adequacy of consideration. First, if the inadequacy of consideration is apparent *on the face of the agreement*, most courts conclude that the agreement was a disguised gift rather than an enforceable bargain. Thus, an agreement calling for an unequal exchange of money (e.g., $500 for $1,000) or identical goods (20 business law textbooks for 40 identical business law textbooks) and containing no other terms would probably be unenforceable.

Gross inadequacy of consideration may also give rise to an inference of fraud, duress, lack of capacity, or some other independent basis for setting aside a contract. However, inadequacy of consideration, standing alone, is never sufficient to prove lack of true consent or contractual capacity.

Although gross inadequacy of consideration is not, by itself, ordinarily a sufficient reason to set aside a contract, the courts may refuse to grant specific performance or other equitable remedies to persons seeking to enforce unfair bargains. Finally, some agreements recite "$1," or "$1 and other valuable consideration," or some other small amount as consideration for a promise. If no other consideration is actually exchanged, this is called *nominal consideration*. Often, such agreements are attempts to make gratuitous promises look like true bargains by reciting a nonexistent consideration. Most courts refuse to enforce such agreements unless they find that the stated consideration was truly bargained for. Similar reasoning (holding that an agreement is not a true bargain) has been employed by a few courts to strike down agreements where the alleged consideration was so inadequate that it "shocks the conscience of the court."

Adequacy and Unconscionability   The advent of the Uniform Commercial Code has given modern courts a potentially powerful tool for policing unfair agreements: the Code's broad section on unconscionable contracts [2–302].[4] In recent years, a few courts have used this section to strike down contracts involving grossly unfair

---

[4] The Illegality chapter discusses unconscionability in detail.

price provisions. These cases normally involve situations where a consumer has agreed to pay a merchant two or three times the market price for the goods. They also commonly involve other factors frequently encountered in unconscionability cases, such as complex, well-hidden, or deceptive contract terms and high-pressure sales tactics. Although such cases are still fairly rare, they may represent the seeds of a significant new direction in the evolution of contract law.

Illusory Promises

For a promise to serve as consideration in a bilateral contract, the promisee must have promised to do, or to refrain from doing, something at the promisor's request. It seems obvious, therefore, that if the promisee's promise is *illusory* because it really does not bind the promisee to do or refrain from doing anything, such a promise could not serve as consideration. Such agreements are often said to lack the *mutuality of obligation* required for an agreement to be enforceable. So, a promisee's promise to "buy all the sugar that I want" or to "paint your house if I feel like it" would not be sufficient consideration for a promisor's return promise to sell sugar or hire a painter. In neither case has the promisee given the promisor anything of legal value in exchange for the promisor's promise. The following *Harrington* case reminds us, however, that so long as the promisee has given legal value the agreement will be enforceable even though what the promisee gave is worth substantially less than what the promisor promised in return.

HARRINGTON v. HARRINGTON
365 N.W.2d 552 (N.D. Sup. Ct. 1985)

When Nancy and Gerald Harrington were divorced in 1981, they executed a property settlement agreement giving him ownership of their farm. In return, he agreed to pay her $150,000; a $10,000 down payment and 15 annual payments. He gave her two mortgages on the farm to secure the debt. Gerald paid Nancy the initial $10,000, but was able to pay her only $3,000 in subsequent payments due to financial difficulties.

Late in 1981, Gerald asked Nancy to execute satisfactions of the two mortgages so he could obtain refinancing of previous bank loans, which lenders were unwilling to provide as long as the farm was encumbered by the mortgages she held. At that time Nancy and Gerald's son, Ronn, was farming the land with Gerald. Nancy was afraid that Ronn would not inherit the farm because Gerald had remarried and his wife had become pregnant. In exchange for Gerald's promise to will the farm to Ronn, Nancy promised on December 30, 1981, to execute satisfactions of the mortgages and to release Gerald from liability on his debt to her under their original agreement.

Gerald subsequently made a will leaving his land to Ronn, but Nancy did not execute satisfactions of the mortgages. Instead, on October 3, 1983, she filed a foreclosure suit against Gerald. When the trial court found that she was bound by her December 30, 1981, promise to satisfy the mortgages and release Gerald from liability for the debt, she appealed.

Gierke, Justice.   If consideration exists, courts will generally not inquire into the adequacy of the consideration. However, it is important to distinguish the adequacy of consideration from its existence. One instance where the lack of consideration invalidates a contract is when the contract is illusory. An illusory contract may be defined as an expression cloaked in promissory terms, but which, upon closer examination, reveals that the promisor has not committed himself in any manner. In other words, an illusory promise is a promise that is not a promise.

Nancy argues that Gerald's promises contained in the December 30, 1981, agreement were illusory. The agreement subjected the devise to Ronn to the following conditions: Ronn would inherit the land subject to all its encumbrances; Ronn would be obligated to make annual payments of 25 percent of all the crops raised on the land to Gerald's widow as long as she had any farm-related debt; Gerald is permitted to convey a portion of the land for purposes of continuing the farming operation in the event "future economic exigencies" so require; and finally, Ronn was granted the first option to purchase any of the farm land sold by Gerald.

Although the agreement may not be entirely equitable for Nancy, it is not illusory and is supported by consideration—in return for Nancy's satisfaction of the mortgages and underlying debt Gerald gave up something which he was privileged to retain: the legal right to devise his farm land to one of his own choosing. The fairness of the agreement is irrelevant. Gerald's relinquishment of a legal right constituted consideration for the agreement regardless of the value of that right to Nancy.

The possibility that Ronn may inherit only a reduced and encumbered portion of the farm land does not alter the fact that Gerald relinquished a legal right which constitutes consideration. Merely because future events may affect the nature and extent of Ronn's devise does not invalidate the legal detriment suffered by Gerald.

Judgment for Gerald affirmed.

Cancellation or Termination Clauses   The fact that an agreement allows one or both of the parties to cancel or terminate their contractual obligations does not necessarily mean that the party or parties with the power to cancel have given an illusory promise. Such provisions are a common and necessary part of many business relationships. The central issue in such cases concerns whether a promise subject to cancellation or termination actually represents a binding obligation. A right to cancel or terminate at any time, for any reason, and without any notice would clearly render illusory any other promise by the party possessing such a right. However, limits on the circumstances under which cancellation may occur, such as a dealer's failure to live up to dealership obligations; or the time in which cancellation may occur, such as no cancellations for the first 90 days; or a requirement of advance notice of cancellation, such as a 30-day notice requirement, would all effectively remove a promise from the illusory category. This is so because in each case the party making such a promise has bound himself to do *something* in exchange for the other party's promise.

Of course, some parties to agreements may not want their agreements to amount to binding contracts. For example, a manufacturer selling through a system of independent retail dealers may want to retain maximum flexibility by giving itself a unilateral right to terminate a dealer at any time, for any reason, without notice. Such an "intentional no contract" strategy relies on the fact that the manufacturer's greater bargaining power may allow it to impose such terms on its dealers. This kind of business strategy is very difficult, if not impossible, to pursue today, however, given the numerous "dealer day in court" statutes that past abuses have produced and the fact that many courts have stricken down unilateral cancellation clauses as unconscionable.

Output and Requirements Contracts   Contracts in which one party to the agreement agrees to buy all of the other party's production of a particular commodity (*output* contracts) or to supply all of another party's needs for a particular commodity (*requirements* contracts) are common business transactions that serve legitimate business purposes. They can reduce a seller's selling costs and provide buyers with a secure source of supply. Nonetheless, many common law courts refused to enforce such agreements on the ground that their failure to specify the quantity of goods to be produced or purchased rendered them illusory. The courts also feared that a party to such an agreement might be tempted to exploit the other party. For example, subsequent market conditions could make it profitable for the seller in an output contract or the buyer in a requirements contract to demand that the other party buy or provide more of the particular commodity than the other party had actually intended to buy or sell. The Code legitimizes such contracts by limiting a party's demands to those quantity needs that occur in good faith and are not unreasonably disproportionate to any quantity estimate contained in the contract, or to any normal prior output or requirements if no estimate is stated [2–306(1)]. The Formation and Terms of Sales Contracts chapter discusses this subject in greater detail.

Exclusive Dealing Contracts   When a manufacturer of goods enters an agreement giving a distributor the exclusive right to sell the manufacturer's products in a particular territory, does such an agreement impose sufficient obligations on both parties to meet the legal value test? Put another way, does the distributor have any duty to sell the manufacturer's products and does the manufacturer have any duty to supply any particular number of products? Such agreements are commonly encountered in today's business world, and they can serve the legitimate interests of both parties. The Code recognizes this fact by providing that, unless the parties agree to the contrary, an exclusive dealing contract imposes a duty on the distributor to use her best efforts to sell the goods and imposes a reciprocal duty on the manufacturer to use his best efforts to supply the goods [2–306(2)].

Preexisting Duties

The legal value component of our consideration definition requires that promisees do, or promise to do, something in exchange for a promisor's promise that they had *no prior legal duty* to do. Thus, as a general rule, performing or agreeing to perform a preexisting duty is *not* consideration. This seems fair because the promisor in such a case has effectively made a gratuitous promise, since she was already entitled to the promisee's performance.

Preexisting Public Duties   Every member of society has a duty to obey the law and refrain from committing crimes or torts. Therefore, a promisee's promise not to commit such an act can never be consideration. So, Thomas's promise to pay Brown $100 a year in exchange for Brown's promise not to burn Thomas's barn would not be enforceable against Thomas. Since Brown has a preexisting duty not to burn Thomas's barn, his promise lacks legal value.

Similarly, public officials, by virtue of their offices, have a preexisting legal duty to perform their public responsibilities. For example, Smith, the owner of a liquor store, promises to pay Fawcett, a police officer whose beat includes Smith's store, $50 a week to keep an eye on the store while walking her beat. Smith's promise is unenforceable because Fawcett has agreed to do something that she already has a duty to do.

Preexisting Contractual Duties   The most important preexisting duty cases are those involving preexisting *contractual* duties. These cases generally occur when the parties to an existing contract agree to *modify* that contract. As the *Gross* case which follows indicates, the general common law rule on contract modification holds that an agreement to modify an existing contract requires some *new consideration* to be binding.

For example, Turner enters into a contract with Acme Construction Company for the construction of a new office building for $350,000. When the construction is partially completed, Acme tells Turner that due to rising labor and materials costs it will stop construction unless Turner agrees to pay an extra $50,000. Turner, having already entered into contracts to lease office space in the new building, promises to pay the extra amount. When the construction is finished, Turner refuses to pay more than $350,000. Is Turner's promise to pay the extra $50,000 enforceable against him? No. All Acme has done in exchange for Turner's promise to pay more is build the building, something that Acme had a preexisting contractual duty to do. Therefore, Acme's performance is not consideration for Turner's promise to pay more.

Although the result in the preceding example seems fair (why should Turner have to pay $400,000 for something he had a right to receive for $350,000?) and is consistent with consideration theory, the application of the preexisting duty rule to contract modifications has generated a great deal of criticism. Plainly, the rule can protect a party to a contract such as Turner from being pressured into paying more because the other party to the contract is trying to take advantage of his situation by demanding an additional amount for performance. However, mechanical application of the rule could also produce unfair results when the parties have freely agreed to a fair modification of their contract. Some critics argue that the purpose of contract modification law should be to enforce freely made modifications of existing contracts and to deny enforcement to coerced modifications. Such critics commonly suggest that general principles such as good faith and unconscionability, rather than technical consideration rules, should be used to police contract modifications.

Other observers argue that most courts in fact apply the preexisting duty rule in a manner calculated to reach fair results, because several exceptions to the rule can be used to enforce a fair modification agreement. For example, any new consideration furnished by the promisee provides sufficient consideration to support a promise to modify an existing contract. So, if Acme had promised to finish construction a week before the completion date called for in the original contract, or had promised to make some change in the original contract specifications such as to install a better grade of carpet, Acme would have done something that it had no legal duty to do in exchange for Turner's new promise. Turner's promise to pay more would then be enforceable because it would be supported by new consideration.

Many courts also enforce an agreement to modify an existing contract if the modification resulted from *unforeseen circumstances* that a party could not reasonably be expected to have foreseen, and which made that party's performance far more difficult than the parties originally anticipated. For example, if Acme had requested the extra payment because abnormal subsurface rock formations made excavation on the construction site far more costly and time consuming than could have been reasonably expected, many courts would enforce Turner's promise to pay more.

Courts can also enforce fair modification agreements by holding that the parties mutually agreed to terminate their original contract and then entered a new one. Because contracts are created by the will of the parties, they can be terminated in the same fashion. Each party agrees to release the other party from his contractual obligations in exchange for the other party's promise to do the same. Because such a mutual agreement terminates all duties owed under the original agreement, any subsequent agreement by the parties would not be subject to the preexisting duty rule. A court is likely to take this approach, however, only when it is convinced that the modification agreement was fair and free from coercion.

GROSS v. DIEHL SPECIALTIES INTERNATIONAL

776 S.W.2d 879 (Mo. Ct. App. 1989)

In 1977, Dairy Specialties, Inc. (Dairy), hired George Gross to develop nondairy products for customers allergic to milk and to serve as general manager. The employment contract was for a term of 15 years and provided for annual wages of $14,400 plus cost of living increases. It also provided that when 10 percent of Dairy's gross profits exceeded Gross's annual salary he would receive the difference between the two figures, and gave Gross a royalty of 1 percent of the selling price of all products Dairy produced using one or more of Gross's inventions or formulae. This royalty increased to 2 percent after the expiration of the agreement, at which time ownership of the inventions and formulae (which was jointly held during the term of the agreement) would revert to Gross.

In 1982, Dairy was bought from its original owner by the Diehl family. The Diehls insisted on renegotiation of Gross's contract with Dairy as a condition of the purchase. Although he was not a party to the sale and received nothing tangible from it, Gross agreed to a new contract that had the same expiration date as the first one, but that eliminated his cost of living increases, gave Dairy exclusive ownership of his inventions and formulae during and after the term of the agreement, and eliminated his right to royalties after the agreement expired. After the sale, Gross was given additional duties but no additional compensation. In 1984, after a business downturn, Gross was fired. He filed suit, arguing that his termination benefits should be calculated under his original contract. When the trial court ruled in the company's favor, he appealed.

Smith, Presiding Judge.   A modification of a contract constitutes the making of a new contract and such new contract must be supported by consideration. Where a contract has not been fully performed at the time of the new agreement, the substitution of a new provision, resulting in a modification of the obligation of *both* sides, for a provision in the old contract still unperformed is sufficient consideration for the new contract. A promise to carry out an existing contractual duty does not constitute consideration.

Under the 1982 agreement the company undertook no greater obligations than it already had. Gross on the other hand received less than he had under the original contract. His base pay was reduced back to its 1977 amount despite the provision in the 1977 contract calling for cost of living adjustments. He lost his equal ownership in his formulae during the term of the agreement and his exclusive ownership after the termination of the agreement. He lost all royalties after termination of the agreement. In exchange for nothing, the company acquired exclusive ownership of the formulae during and after the agreement, eliminated royalties after the agreement terminated, and achieved a reduction in Gross's base salary. The company did no more than promise to carry out an already existing contractual duty. There was no consideration for the 1982 agreement.

Judgment reversed in favor of Gross; case remanded for recalculation of damages.

Code Contract Modification   The drafters of the Code sought to avoid many of the problems caused by the consideration requirement by dispensing with it in two important situations: As discussed in the Offer chapter, the Code does not require consideration for firm offers [2–205]. The Code also provides that an agreement to modify a contract for the sale of goods needs *no consideration* to be binding [2–209(1)]. For example, Video World orders 500 RCA videodisc players at $150 per unit in response to an RCA promotional campaign heralding the introduction of this new home entertainment device. Initial sales figures indicate, however, that the consuming public is unimpressed with videodisc technology. Video World seeks to cancel its order, but RCA refuses to agree to cancellation. Instead, RCA seeks to mollify a valued customer by offering to reduce the price to $100 per unit. Video World agrees, but when the players arrive, RCA bills Video World for $150 per unit. Under classical contract principles, RCA's promise to reduce the price of the goods would not be enforceable because Video World has furnished no new consideration in exchange for RCA's promise. Under the Code, no new consideration is necessary and the agreement to modify the contract is enforceable.

Several things should be made clear about the operation of this Code rule. First, RCA had no duty to agree to a modification and could have insisted on payment of $150 per unit. Second, as the following *Roth Steel Products* case illustrates, modification agreements under the Code are still subject to scrutiny under the general Code principles of good faith and unconscionability, so unfair agreements or agreements that are the product of coercion are unlikely to be enforced. Finally, the Code contains two provisions to protect people from fictitious claims that an agreement has been modified. If the original agreement requires any modification to be in writing, an oral modification is unenforceable [2–209(2)]. Regardless of what the original agreement says, if the price of the goods in the modified contract is $500 or more, the modification is unenforceable unless the requirements of the Code's statute of frauds section [2–201] are satisfied [2–209(3)].[5]

---

[5] The Writing chapter discusses section 2–201 of the Code in detail.

ROTH STEEL PRODUCTS v. SHARON STEEL CORPORATION

705 F.2d 134 (6th Cir. 1983)

In November 1972, when conditions in the steel industry were highly competitive and the industry was operating at about 70 percent of its capacity, Sharon Steel Corporation agreed to sell Roth Steel Products several types of steel at prices well below Sharon's published book prices for such steel. These prices were to be effective from January 1 until December 31, 1973.

In early 1973, however, several factors changed the market for steel. Federal price controls simultaneously discouraged foreign steel imports and encouraged domestic steel producers to export a substantial portion of their production to avoid domestic price controls, sharply reducing the domestic steel supply. In addition, the steel industry experienced substantial increases in labor, raw material, and energy costs, compelling steel producers to increase prices. The increased domestic demand for steel and the attractive export market caused the entire industry to operate at full capacity; as a consequence, nearly every domestic steel producer experienced substantial delays in delivery.

On March 23, 1973, Sharon notified Roth that it was discontinuing all price discounts. Roth protested, and Sharon agreed to continue to sell at the discount price until June 30, 1973, but refused to sell thereafter unless Roth agreed to pay a modified price that was higher than that agreed to the previous November, but still lower than the book prices Sharon was charging other customers. Because Roth was unable to purchase enough steel elsewhere to meet its production requirements, it agreed to pay the increased prices. When a subsequent dispute arose between the parties over late deliveries and unfilled orders by Sharon in 1974, Roth filed a breach of contract suit against Sharon, arguing, among other things, that the 1973 modification agreement was unenforceable. When the trial court ruled in favor of Roth, Sharon appealed.

Celebrezze, Senior Circuit Judge.   The ability of a party to modify a contract which is subject to Article Two of the UCC is broader than common law, primarily because the modification needs no consideration to be binding. [UCC Sec. 2–209(1)]. A party's ability to modify an agreement is limited only by Article Two's general obligation of good faith. In determining whether a particular modification was obtained in good faith, a court must make two distinct inquiries: whether the party's conduct is consistent with "reasonable commercial standards of fair dealing in the trade," and whether the parties were in fact motivated to seek modification by an honest desire to compensate for commercial exigencies.

The first inquiry is relatively straightforward; the party asserting the modification must demonstrate that his decision to seek modification was the result of a factor, such as increased costs, which would cause an ordinary merchant to seek a modification of the contract. The second inquiry, regarding the subjective honesty of the parties, is less clearly defined. Essentially, this requires the party asserting the modification to demonstrate that he was, in fact, motivated by a legitimate commercial reason and that such a reason is not offered merely as a pretext. Moreover, the trier of fact must determine whether the means used to obtain the modification are an impermissible attempt to obtain a modification by extortion or overreaching.

The single most important consideration in determining whether the decision to seek a modification is justified is whether, because of changes in the market or other unforeseeable conditions, performance of the contract has come to involve a loss. In this case, the district court found that Sharon suffered substantial losses by performing the contract as modified. We are convinced that unforeseen economic exigencies existed which would prompt an ordinary merchant to seek a modification to avoid a loss on the contract.

The second part of the analysis, honesty in fact, is pivotal. The district court found that Sharon "threatened not to sell Roth any steel if Roth refused to pay increased prices after July 1, 1973" and, consequently, that Sharon acted wrongfully. We believe that the district court's conclusion that Sharon acted in bad faith by using coercive conduct to extract the price modification is not clearly erroneous. Therefore, we hold that Sharon's attempt to modify the November 1972 contract, in order to compensate for increased costs which made performance come to involve a loss, is ineffective because Sharon did not act in a manner consistent with Article Two's requirement of honesty in fact when it refused to perform its remaining obligations under the contract at 1972 prices.

[handwritten: IN MODIFIED CONTRACTS]

[handwritten: THE CODE STATES THAT CONSIDERATION NOT NECESSARY AS LONG AS THERE IS AGREEMENT BY THE PARTIES]

Judgment for Roth affirmed.

Debt Settlement Agreements

One special variant of the preexisting duty rule that causes considerable confusion occurs when a debtor offers to pay a creditor a sum less than the creditor is demanding, in exchange for the creditor's promise to accept the part payment as full payment of the debt. If the creditor later sues for the balance of the debt, is the creditor's promise to take less enforceable? The answer depends on the nature of the debt and on the circumstances of the debtor's payment.

Liquidated Debts A promise to discharge a **liquidated debt** for part payment of the debt *at or after* its due date is *unenforceable* for lack of consideration. Liquidated debts are both *due* and *certain*; that is, there is no bona fide dispute about either the *existence* or the *amount* of the debt. If a debtor does nothing more than pay less than an amount he clearly owes, how could that be consideration for a creditor's promise to take less? Such a debtor has actually done less than he had a preexisting legal duty to do, namely, to pay the full amount of the debt.

For example, Connor borrows $10,000 from Friendly Finance Company, payable in one year. On the day payment is due, Connor sends Friendly a check for $9,000 marked: "Payment in full for all claims Friendly Finance has against me." Friendly cashes Connor's check, thus impliedly promising to accept it as full payment by cashing it, and later sues Connor for $1,000. Friendly is entitled to the $1,000 because Connor has given no consideration to support Friendly's implied promise to accept $9,000 as full payment.

However, had Connor done something he had no preexisting duty to do in exchange for Friendly's promise to settle for part payment, he could enforce Friendly's promise and avoid paying the $1,000. For example, if Connor had paid early, before the loan contract called for payment, or in a different medium of exchange than that called for in the loan contract (such as $4,000 in cash and a car worth $5,000), he would have given consideration for Friendly's promise to accept early or different payment as full payment.

Unliquidated Debts A bona fide (good faith) dispute about either the existence or the amount of a debt makes the debt an **unliquidated debt.** For example, Computer Corner, a retailer, orders 50 personal computers and associated software packages from Computech for $75,000. After receiving the goods, Computer Corner refuses to pay Computech the full $75,000, arguing that some of the computers were defective and that some of the software it received did not conform to its order. Computer Corner sends Computech a check for $60,000 marked: "Payment in full for all goods received from Computech." A creditor in Computech's position obviously faces a real dilemma. If Computech cashes Computer Corner's check, it will be held to have impliedly promised to accept $60,000 as full payment. This promise would be enforceable against Computech if it later sought to collect the remaining $15,000, because by agreeing to settle a disputed claim, Computech has entered a binding **accord and satisfaction.** Computech's promise to accept part payment as full payment would be enforceable because Computer Corner has given consideration to support it: Computer Corner has given up its right to have a court determine the amount it owes Computech. This is something that Computer Corner had no duty to do; by giving up this right and the $60,000 in exchange for Computech's implied promise, the consideration requirement is satisfied. The result in this case is supported not only by consideration theory but also by a strong public policy in favor of encouraging parties to settle their disputes out of court. Who would bother to settle disputed claims out of court if settlement agreements were unenforceable?

Computech could refuse to accept Computer Corner's settlement offer and sue for the full $75,000, but doing so involves several risks. A court may decide that Computer Corner's arguments are valid and award Computech less than $60,000. Even if Computech is successful, it may take years to resolve the case in the courts through the expensive and time-consuming litigation process. And, there is always the chance that Computer Corner may file for bankruptcy before any judgment can be collected. Faced with such risks, Computech may feel that it has no practical alternative other than to cash Computer Corner's check.

In some states, a creditor such as Computech has a third, and much more desirable, alternative course of action to either returning the debtor's full-payment check or cashing it and entering an accord and satisfaction. Some state courts have held that the Code has changed the common law accord and satisfaction rule by allowing a creditor to accept a full-payment check "under protest" or "without prejudice" without giving up any rights to sue for the balance due under the contract [1–207]. As the following *County Fire Door* case indicates, whether section 1–207 was ever intended to have this effect is a matter of controversy, and many courts have rejected such an interpretation of the Code. However, in states where the courts have applied section 1–207 to accord and satisfaction cases, a creditor can now accept part payment under protest and still seek to collect the remainder of the debt.

COUNTY FIRE DOOR CORP. v. C. F. WOODING CO.

520 A.2d 1028 (Conn. Sup. Ct. 1987)

On November 17, 1981, C. F. Wooding Company (Wooding) ordered a number of metal doors and door frames from County Fire Door Corporation (County) for a construction project Wooding was working on. After County was allegedly late in delivering the goods to the work site, Wooding told County that it would only pay $416.88 of the $2,618.88 that County claimed was the balance due because the delays in delivery caused Wooding additional installation expenses. County denied the validity of Wooding's claim and insisted that the full amount was due.

Wooding then sent County a check for $416.88. On its face was a notation stating that it was final payment for the project, and on its reverse side the check stated: "By its endorsement, the payee accepts this check in full satisfaction of all claims against the C. F. Wooding Co. arising out of or relating to Purchase Order #3302, dated 11/17/81." County cashed the check, but only after crossing out the conditional language on the reverse side and adding the following language: "This check is accepted under protest and with full reservation of rights to collect the unpaid balance for which this check is offered in settlement."

County filed suit against Wooding for the unpaid balance, arguing that section 1–207 of the UCC prevented its cashing of Wooding's check from amounting to an accord and satisfaction. The trial court ruled in County's favor, and Wooding appealed.

Peters, Chief Justice.   When there is a good faith dispute about the existence of a debt or about the amount that is owed, the common law authorizes the debtor and the creditor to negotiate a contract of accord to settle the outstanding claim. Such a contract is often initiated by the debtor, who offers an accord by tendering a check as "payment in full" or "in full satisfaction." If the creditor knowingly cashes such a check, or otherwise exercises full dominion over it, the creditor is deemed to have assented to the offer of accord. Upon acceptance of the offer of accord, the creditor's receipt of the promised payment discharges the underlying debt and bars any further claim relating thereto.

Application of these settled principles to this case establishes that the parties entered into a valid accord and satisfaction. Wooding offered in good faith to settle an unliquidated debt by tendering, in full satisfaction, the payment of an amount less than that demanded by County. Under the common law, County could not simultaneously cash such a check and disown the condition on which it had been tendered.

The principal dispute between the parties is what meaning to ascribe to section 1–207 when it states that: "A party who with explicit reservation of rights assents to performance in a manner offered by the other party does not thereby prejudice the rights reserved. Such words as 'without prejudice,' 'under protest' or the like are sufficient." County contends that this section gave it the authority to cash Wooding's check "under protest" while reserving the right to pursue the remainder of its underlying claim against Wooding at a later time. We noted in *Kelly v. Kowalsky* (1982) that there was considerable disagreement in the cases and the scholarly commentaries about the scope of the transactions governed by section 1–207, but did not then undertake to resolve this disagreement.

It is apparent that section 1–207 contemplates a reservation of rights about some aspect of a possibly nonconforming tender of goods or services or payment in a situation where the aggrieved party may prefer not to terminate the underlying contract as a whole. Indeed, the Official Comment to section 1–207 itself explains that the section supports ongoing contractual relations by providing "machinery for the continuation of performance along the lines contemplated by the contract despite a pending dispute." It is significant, furthermore, that the text of section 1–207 recurrently refers to "performance," for "performance" is a central aspect of the sales transactions governed by article 2.

By contrast, article 3 instruments, which promise or order the payment of money, are not characteristically described as being performed by anyone. The contracts encapsulated in various forms of negotiable instruments instead envisage conduct of negotiation or transfer, indorsement or guaranty, payment or acceptance, and honor or dishonor. We conclude, therefore, that in circumstances like the present, when performance of a sales contract has come to an end, section 1–207 was not intended to empower a seller, as payee of a negotiable instrument, to alter that instrument by adding words of protest to a check tendered by a buyer on condition that it be accepted in full satisfaction of an unliquidated debt.

Our conclusion is supported by the emerging majority of cases in other jurisdictions. It is now the view of the substantial majority of courts that have addressed the issue that section 1–207 does not overrule the common law of accord and satisfaction. The majority finds support as well in much of the recent scholarly commentary. Both under prevailing common law principles, and under the Uniform Commercial Code, the parties in this case negotiated a contract of accord whose satisfaction discharged Wooding from any further monetary obligation to County. County might have avoided this result by returning Wooding's check uncashed, but could not simultaneously disregard the condition on which the check was tendered and deposit its proceeds in County's bank account.

Judgment reversed in favor of Wooding.

Composition Agreements Composition agreements are agreements between a debtor and two or more creditors who agree to accept as full payment a stated percentage of their liquidated claims against the debtor at or after the date on which those claims are payable. Composition agreements are generally enforced by the courts despite the fact that enforcement appears to be contrary to the general rule on part payment of liquidated debts. Many courts have justified enforcing composition agreements on the ground that the creditors' mutual agreement to accept less than the amount due them provides the necessary consideration. The main reason why creditors agree to compositions is that they fear that their failure to do so may force the debtor into bankruptcy proceedings, in which case they might ultimately recover a smaller percentage of their claims than that agreed to in the composition.

Forbearance to Sue

An agreement by a promisee to refrain, or forbear, from pursuing a legal claim against a promisor can be valid consideration to support a return promise—usually to pay a sum of money—by a promisor. The promisee has agreed not to file suit, something that she has a legal right to do, in exchange for the promisor's promise. The courts do not wish to sanction extortion by allowing people to threaten to file spurious claims against others in the hope that those threatened will agree to some payment to avoid the expense or embarrassment associated with defending a lawsuit. On the other hand, we have a strong public policy favoring private settlement of disputes and we do not want to require people to second-guess the courts. Therefore, it is generally said that the promisee must have a *good faith* belief in the validity of his or her claim before forbearance amounts to consideration.

BARGAINED FOR EXCHANGE

Up to this point, we have focused on the legal value component of our consideration definition. But the fact that a promisee's act or promise provides legal value is not, in itself, a sufficient basis for finding that it amounted to consideration. In addition, the promisee's act or promise must have been *bargained for* and *given in exchange* for the promisor's promise. In effect, it must be the price that the promisor asked for in exchange for making his promise. Over a hundred years ago, Oliver Wendell Holmes, one of our most renowned jurists, expressed this idea when he said, "It is the essence of a consideration that, by the terms of the agreement, it is given and accepted as the motive or inducement of the promise."[6]

Past Consideration

It is generally said that *past consideration is no consideration.* To understand the meaning of this statement, consider once again the famous case of *Hamer v. Sidway,* discussed earlier in this chapter. There, an uncle's promise to pay his nephew $5,000 for refraining from smoking, drinking, swearing, and other delightful pastimes until his 21st birthday was supported by consideration because the nephew had given legal value by refraining from participating in the prohibited activities. However, what if the uncle had said to his nephew on the eve of his 21st birthday: "Your mother tells me you've been a good lad and abstained from tobacco, hard drink, foul language, and gambling. Such goodness should be rewarded. Tomorrow, I'll give you a check for $5,000." Should the uncle's promise be enforceable against him? Clearly not, because although his nephew's behavior still passes the legal value test, in this case it was not bargained for and given in exchange for the uncle's promise. The following *Spickelmier* case is a contemporary illustration of the operation of the past consideration rule.

Moral Obligation

As a general rule, promises made to satisfy a preexisting moral obligation are unenforceable for lack of

---

[6] O. W. Holmes, *The Common Law*, p. 230 (1881).

SPICKELMIER INDUSTRIES, INC. v. PASSANDER

359 N.E.2d 563 (Ind. Ct. App. 1977)

Robert Passander was executive vice president of Spickelmier Industries. Because Spickelmier was facing financial difficulties, a committee of creditors had been formed to oversee its operations. In November of 1971, the committee projected a small profit for the year and recommended that bonuses be given to certain key employees if the profit materialized. This recommendation was adopted by Spickelmier's board of directors in late December, and Passander was promised a $1,500 bonus.

In January of 1972, however, the board's executive committee discovered that the earlier profit estimates had been overly optimistic and that insufficient funds were available to pay the bonuses. Instead of taking the board's recommendation that the bonuses not be paid, the chairman of the board negotiated a compromise whereby one half of the originally specified bonus would be paid as planned, with the balance to be paid when funds were available. Passander accepted the half bonus, and later in the month his contract with Spickelmier was renegotiated to provide for a 25 percent salary increase and guaranteed quarterly bonuses of $500.

In June of 1972, Passander quit his job, later filing suit against Spickelmier for the remaining half of his 1971 bonus. When the trial court ruled in his favor, Spickelmier appealed.

Buchanan, Presiding Judge.   Not every promise creates a legal obligation which the law will enforce. A promise must be predicated upon adequate consideration before it can command performance. The record is barren of any evidence indicating Passander furnished consideration for Spickelmier's promise. The promise of a year-end bonus was made after Passander had already performed the terms of his 1971 employment contract. It was a promise of more compensation to an employee who had already performed the agreed services.

"[A] new promise of additional compensation should not be enforceable if it is made after the first party has already rendered his promised performance. In such a case the promisor bargains for nothing and receives nothing in exchange for his promise. He has already received everything before he makes the new promise. The element of agreed exchange, or bargain, is lacking. In addition, the promisee has done nothing in reliance on the new promise, so that the action in reliance doctrine is also inapplicable."

Corbin on Contracts, section 235 (1952). So, Passander's prior service in 1971 was not in reliance on payment of a year-end bonus, and no consideration therefore existed for Spickelmier's promise. Nor did Passander make a reciprocal promise or perform any act concomitant with Spickelmier's promise. The bonus was merely a means by which Spickelmier could reward Passander's diligence during 1971. There was no evidence the bonus was intended to elicit any present response from Passander other than ordinary gratitude.

Judgment reversed in favor of Spickelmier.

consideration. The fact that a promisor or some member of the promisor's family, for example, has received some benefit from the promisee in the past (e.g., food and lodging, or emergency care) would not constitute consideration for a promisor's promise to pay for that benefit, due to the absence of the bargain element. Some courts find this result distressing and enforce such promises despite the absence of consideration. In addition, a few states have passed statutes making promises to pay for past benefits enforceable if such a promise is contained

---

CONCEPT REVIEW

CONSIDERATION

Consideration*	Not Consideration
Doing something you had no preexisting duty to do	Doing something you had a preexisting duty to do
Promising to do something you had no preexisting duty to do	Promising to do something you had a preexisting duty to do
Paying part of a liquidated debt prior to the date the debt is due	Nominal consideration (unless actually bargained for)
Paying a liquidated debt in a different medium of exchange than originally agreed to	Paying part of a liquidated debt at or after the date the debt is due
Agreeing to settle an unliquidated debt	Making an illusory promise
Agreeing not to file suit when you have a good faith belief in your claim's validity	Past consideration
*Assuming bargained for	Preexisting moral obligation

---

in a writing that clearly expresses the promisor's intent to be bound.

EXCEPTIONS TO THE CONSIDERATION REQUIREMENT

The consideration requirement is a classic example of a traditional contract law rule. It is precise, abstract, and capable of almost mechanical application. It can also, in some instances, result in significant injustice. Modern courts and legislatures have responded to this potential for injustice by carving out numerous exceptions to the requirement of consideration. Some of these exceptions (for example, the Code firm offer and contract modification rules) have already been discussed in this and preceding chapters. In the remaining portion of this chapter, we focus on several other important exceptions to the consideration requirement.

Promissory Estoppel

As discussed in the Introduction to Contracts chapter, the doctrine of **promissory estoppel** first emerged from attempts by courts around the turn of this century to reach just results in donative (gift) promise cases. Classical contract consideration principles did not recognize a promisee's reliance on a donative promise as a

sufficient basis for enforcing the promise against the promisor. Instead, donative promises were unenforceable because they were not supported by consideration. In fact, the essence of a donative promise is that it does not seek or require any bargained-for exchange. Yet people continued to act in reliance on donative promises, often to their considerable disadvantage.

Refer to the facts of *Thorne v. Deas*, discussed earlier in this chapter. The co-owners of the *Sea Nymph* clearly relied to their injury on their fellow co-owner's promise to get insurance for the ship. Some courts in the early years of this century began to protect such relying promisees by *estopping* promisors from raising the defense that their promises were not supported by consideration. In a wide variety of cases involving gratuitous agency promises (like *Thorne v. Deas*), promises of bonuses or pensions made to employees, and promises of gifts of land, courts began to use a promisee's detrimental (harmful) reliance on a donative promise as, in effect, a *substitute for* consideration.

In 1932 the first *Restatement of Contracts* legitimized these cases by expressly recognizing promissory estoppel in section 90. The elements of promissory estoppel were then essentially the same as they are today: a *promise* that the promisor should reasonably expect to induce reliance, *reliance* on the promise by the promisee, and *injustice* to the promisee as a result of that reliance. As the following *Grouse* case illustrates, promissory estoppel is now widely used as a consideration substitute, not only in donative promise cases, but also in cases involving commercial promises, those contemplating a bargained-for exchange. The construction contract bid cases discussed in the Offer chapter are another example of this expansion of promissory estoppel's reach. In fact, although promissory estoppel has expanded far beyond its initial role as a consideration substitute into other areas of contract law, it is probably fair to say that it is still most widely accepted in the consideration context.

GROUSE v. GROUP HEALTH PLAN, INC.

306 N.W.2d 114 (Minn. Sup. Ct. 1980)

John Grouse, a recently graduated pharmacist who was working as a retail pharmacist for Richter Drug, applied for a job with Group Health Plan, Inc. Grouse was interviewed at Group Health by Cyrus Elliott, Chief Pharmacist, and Donald Shoberg, General Manager. On December 4, 1975, Elliott telephoned Grouse at work and offered him a job as a pharmacist at Group Health's St. Louis Park Clinic. Grouse accepted, informing Elliott that he would give Richter two weeks' notice. That afternoon Grouse received an offer from a Veterans Administration Hospital in Virginia which he declined because of Group Health's offer. Elliott called back to confirm that Grouse had resigned.

Sometime in the next few days, Elliott mentioned to Shoberg that he had hired, or was thinking of hiring, Grouse. Shoberg told him that company hiring requirements included a favorable written reference, a background check, and approval of the general manager. Elliott contacted two faculty members at the University of Minnesota School of Pharmacy who declined to give references. He also contacted an internship employer and several pharmacies where Grouse had done relief work. Their responses were that they had not had enough exposure to Grouse's work to form a judgment about his capabilities.

Because Elliott was unable to supply a favorable reference for Grouse, Shoberg hired another person to fill the position. On December 15, 1975, Grouse called Group Health and reported that he was free to begin work. Elliott informed Grouse that someone else had been hired. Grouse had difficulty regaining full-time employment and suffered wage loss as a result. He filed suit against Group Health, and when the trial court ruled in Group Health's favor, he appealed.

Otis, Justice.   The parties focus their arguments on whether an employment contract which is terminable at will can give rise to an action for damages if anticipatorily repudiated. Group Health contends that recognition of a cause of action on these facts would result in the anomalous rule that an employee who is told not to report to work the day before he is scheduled to begin has a remedy while an employee who is discharged after the first day does not. We cannot agree since under appropriate circumstances we believe section 90 would apply even after employment has begun.

In our view the principle of contract law applicable here is promissory estoppel. On these facts no contract exists because due to the bilateral power of termination neither party is committed to performance and the promises are, therefore, illusory. The elements of promissory estoppel are stated in Restatement of Contracts section 90 (1932):

A promise which the promisor should reasonably expect to induce action or forbear . . . on the part of the promisee and which does induce such action or forbearance is binding if injustice can be avoided only by enforcement of the promise.

Group Health knew that to accept its offer Grouse would have to resign his employment at Richter. Grouse promptly gave notice to Richter and informed Group Health that he had done so when specifically asked by Elliott. Under these circumstances it would be unjust not to hold Group Health to its promise.

The conclusion we reach does not imply that an employer will be liable whenever he discharges an employee whose term of employment is at will. What we do hold is that under the facts of this case Grouse had a right to assume he would be given a good faith opportunity to perform his duties to the satisfaction of Group Health once he was on the job. He was not only denied that opportunity but resigned the position he already held in reliance on the offer which Group Health tendered him. Since, as Group Health points out, the prospective employment might have been terminated at any time, the measure of damages is not so much what he would have earned from Group Health as what he lost in quitting the job he held and in declining at least one other offer of employment elsewhere.

Judgment reversed in favor of Grouse and remanded for a new trial on the issue of damages.

Debts Barred by Statutes of Limitations

Statutes of limitations set an express statutory time limit on a person's ability to pursue any legal claim. A creditor who fails to file suit to collect a debt within the time prescribed by the appropriate statute of limitations loses the right to collect it. Many states, however, enforce a *new promise* by a debtor to pay such a debt, even though technically such promises are not supported by consideration because the creditor has given nothing in exchange for the new promise. Most states afford debtors some protection in such cases, however, by requiring that the new promise be in writing to be enforceable.

Debts Barred by Bankruptcy Discharge

Once a bankrupt debtor is granted a discharge,[7] creditors no longer have the legal right to collect discharged debts. Most states enforce a new promise by the debtor to pay (reaffirm) the debt regardless of whether the creditor has given any consideration to support it. To reduce creditor attempts to pressure debtors to reaffirm, the Bankruptcy Reform Act of 1978 made it much more difficult for debtors to reaffirm debts discharged in bankruptcy proceedings. The act requires that a reaffirmation promise be made prior to the date of the discharge, and gives the debtor the right to revoke his promise within 30

days after it becomes enforceable. This act also requires the Bankruptcy Court to counsel individual (as opposed to corporate) debtors about the legal effects of reaffirmation, and requires Bankruptcy Court approval of reaffirmations by individual debtors. In addition, a few states require reaffirmation promises to be in writing to be enforceable.

Charitable Subscriptions

Promises to make gifts for charitable or educational purposes are often enforced, despite the absence of consideration, when the institution or organization to which the promise was made has acted in reliance on the promised gift. This result is usually justified on the basis of either promissory estoppel or public policy.

ETHICAL AND PUBLIC POLICY CONCERNS

1. In this chapter you learned the general rule that the law does not enforce promises that are not supported by consideration. Are there ethical arguments that one could make to support the proposition that people should generally honor their promises to others regardless of whether they are legally required to do so? What might those arguments be? Do any of them help to explain the doctrine of promissory estoppel as an exception to the consideration requirement?

---

[7] The Bankruptcy chapter discusses bankruptcy in detail.

2. Discuss the public policy behind the rule that courts will not inquire into the adequacy of consideration. What social benefits are purchased by such a rule and at what price? Refer to the *Harrington* case earlier in the chapter: What ethical arguments can you make for and against holding Mrs. Harrington to her promise to execute satisfactions of the mortgages?

3. Discuss the ethical dimensions of offers by debtors to satisfy a liquidated debt by part payment before the due date. Are such offers ever ethical? What factors would be relevant in determining whether such an offer was ethical?

SUMMARY

As a general rule, only promises supported by consideration are enforceable as contracts. Consideration is defined as legal value, bargained for and given in exchange for an act or a promise. Legal value means that, in exchange for the promisor's promise, a promisee must have done, or agreed to do, something that he had no duty to do, or that a promisee refrained from doing, or agreed not to do, something that he had a right to do. Illusory promises—those that do not really obligate a promisee to do anything—cannot serve as consideration.

Likewise, performing or agreeing to perform an act that the promisee had a preexisting duty to perform does not amount to consideration. This is true whether the preexisting duty is public or contractual in nature. At common law, an agreement to modify an existing contract must be supported by new consideration to be enforceable. Some commentators have argued that this rule, while it properly prevents the enforcement of coerced modifications, can also prevent the enforcement of voluntary and equitable modification agreements. There are many ways, however, in which a court can enforce a fair modification agreement. Any new consideration furnished by the promisee, however slight, can support a modification agreement. Modification agreements made in the face of unforeseeable circumstances that make performance of the contract unduly burdensome are also commonly enforced by the courts. Also, a court may find that the parties mutually agreed to terminate their original agreement and their duties to each other under that agreement. In such circumstances, a subsequent agreement entered into by the parties would be supported by consideration even though one of the parties has not agreed to do anything more than he was obli-gated to do under the original contract, because the termination of the original contract relieved him of any duty to perform.

The Code simplifies the contract modification process by providing that agreements to modify contracts for the sale of goods do not need to be supported by consideration [2–209(1)]. Such agreements must meet the Code good faith requirements, however, and unconscionable modification agreements are not enforced. In some circumstances, oral modification agreements may be unenforceable under the Code [2–209(2) and (3)].

Agreements to settle debts for part payment may or may not be enforceable, depending on the nature of the debt and on the circumstances of the part payment. An agreement to settle a liquidated debt for part payment received at or after the due date of the debt is unenforceable for lack of consideration. An agreement to settle an unliquidated debt, however, creates a binding accord and satisfaction. Some state courts have interpreted section 1–207 of the Code in a way that would allow a creditor to accept a partial payment of an unliquidated debt without entering an accord and satisfaction, even though the debtor clearly intends the part payment to fully satisfy the debt. Other courts have rejected this interpretation of the Code. Also, composition agreements are ordinarily enforced on public policy grounds despite the fact that they involve the settlement of liquidated claims by part payment.

Forbearing or agreeing to forbear from asserting a legal right can amount to consideration. As a general rule, the courts do not require that a forbearing promisee have a legally valid claim, but do require that the promisee have a good faith belief in the validity of her claim.

To say that a promisee's act or promise must have legal value, however, does not mean that it must have any actual value or that its value must in any way equal the value of the promisor's promise. As a general rule, the courts do not inquire into the adequacy of consideration. However, grossly inadequate consideration may be evidence of fraud, duress, or contractual incapacity; many courts refuse to grant equitable remedies such as specific performance to promisees who have driven too hard a bargain. Grossly inadequate consideration may also support the conclusion that the agreement in question is a disguised gift rather than an enforceable bargain. Finally, a few courts have refused to enforce contracts for the sale of goods at prices far in excess of their value on the ground that such contracts are unconscionable.

In addition to having legal value, a promisee's act or promise must be bargained for if it is to serve as consideration. This means that it must be the price that the promisor asked for in exchange for making his promise. Thus, past performances by a promisee cannot serve as consideration for a present promise by a promisor, because performance rendered in advance of a promise is, by definition, unbargained for. The common law courts adhered to the rule that "past consideration is no consideration" even in cases where the promisee's prior performance could be viewed as creating a moral duty on the part of the promisor to pay for that performance. Some modern courts, however, enforce promises based on moral obligations; a few states have passed statutes making such promises enforceable if they are made in writing.

In recent years, the courts have made a number of exceptions to the requirement of consideration. The most important of these is the doctrine of promissory estoppel, which originated in cases where courts sought to protect reliance on gratuitous promises. Promises to pay debts barred by bankruptcy discharge or by the applicable statute of limitations are enforced by many courts despite the absence of consideration. Promises of charitable subscriptions are also commonly enforced when the institution or organization to which the promise was made has acted in reliance on the promised gift.

PROBLEM CASES

1. Dr. Browning entered into a contract to sell his osteopathy practice to Dr. Johnson. Browning later changed his mind, however, and asked to be released from the contract. Johnson initially refused to do so, but after Browning offered to pay him $40,000 at a specified future date in exchange for the release, Johnson released him from the sale contract. Later, Browning filed suit for a declaratory judgment that he was not bound by his promise to pay Johnson the $40,000 on the ground that his promise was not supported by consideration. Was Johnson's cancellation of the contract consideration?

2. Omni Group, Inc., signed an earnest money agreement offering Mr. and Mrs. John Clark $2,000 per acre for a piece of property the Clarks owned, which was thought to contain about 59 acres. The agreement provided that Omni's obligation was subject to receipt of a satisfactory engineer's and architect's feasibility report assessing the property's development potential. The Clarks signed the earnest money agreement, but later refused to proceed with the sale. When Omni filed suit

for breach of contract, the Clarks argued that their promise to sell was unenforceable because Omni's promise to buy was illusory due to the fact that it was conditioned on a satisfactory feasibility report. Was Omni's promise illusory?

3. In 1971, the Sederlunds signed a "royalty pool" agreement covering land they owned in Brookfield Township, Michigan. The royalty pool was a device to spread among participants the benefits of discovery of oil or gas and the risk that no oil or gas would be discovered. Under the pool agreement, landowners agreed to contribute one half of all royalties they received from oil and gas production on their property to a common pool. Later, after oil was discovered on their land, the Sederlunds moved to have the agreement set aside, arguing that they had to contribute far more to the pool than their common share of the pool allowed them to withdraw from it. Are they bound by the terms of the agreement?

4. When Mademoiselle Fashions received clothing it had ordered from Buccaneer Sportswear, it was dissatisfied with the quality and condition of several items. In response to Mademoiselle's complaint, Buccaneer gave Mademoiselle a credit for several of the items. Buccaneer later sent Mademoiselle a bill for the amount owed for the shipment, less the agreed-on credit. Mademoiselle sent back a check for $11,520, the full face amount of invoice no. 6832, one of the three it had received with the goods. The check contained the following language: "Invoices 6832–6833 and 6508, this represents any and all debt paid in full." Buccaneer cashed the check, and when Mademoiselle refused to make any further payments, Buccaneer filed suit to recover the $3,633.29 due on the remaining invoices. Mademoiselle raised the defense of accord and satisfaction. Was the trial court's decision in Buccaneer's favor correct?

5. Roland and Leslie lived together for four years and had a child together. In June of 1983, Roland filed suit to evict Leslie from his house in Duxbury, Massachusetts and to obtain custody of their child. Leslie then filed a breach of contract action against Roland arguing that she had a right to a share of the property. In September of 1983, Leslie and Roland agreed to settle both actions. She and his child were to return to live with him and he was to support them. Roland also promised to pay her legal fees from both actions. Roland and Leslie later separated again, and he refused to pay her legal fees, arguing that his promise was not supported by consideration because Massachusetts does not recognize "palimony" actions by unmarried cohabitants. Is Roland right?

6. Marna Balin, who had suffered two automobile accidents in 1972, hired Norman Kallen, an attorney, to represent her. Kallen did not do much work on the cases and urged Balin to settle for $25,000. She became dissatisfied with his representation, and in 1974 she asked Samuel Delug, another attorney, to take over the cases and get her files from Kallen. Delug wrote and called Kallen several times, but Kallen refused to forward the files or sign a Substitution of Attorney form (things he was obligated to do by the California rules of professional conduct) because he was afraid Balin would not pay him for the work he had done. Only when Delug promised to give him 40 percent of his attorney's fee did Kallen forward the files and sign the form. Delug negotiated a settlement of $810,000, and the attorney's fees amounted to $324,000. When he refused to pay Kallen 40 percent, Kallen filed suit. Is Delug's promise enforceable?

7. The Larabees owned a farm in Dearborn County, Indiana, subject to a life estate held by Mrs. Larabee's mother. In the autumn of 1971, the Larabees gave their friends, the Booths, permission to build a summer cottage on the farm. Construction began in the spring of 1972. Shortly thereafter, the Booths asked if they could build a permanent home there, and Mrs. Larabee agreed. In September of 1972, she and her husband signed an agreement promising to convey a piece of the farm to the Booths on the expiration of Mrs. Larabee's mother's life estate. The agreement specifically provided that the land was to be conveyed for "no consideration." When the house was completed and Mrs. Larabee's mother had died, however, the Larabees refused to convey the land as promised. Is their promise to convey enforceable?

8. Moyer, a subcontractor, entered into a contract with Crookham, a general contractor, to do excavation and dirt work on a project to build a railroad extension for the Little Rock Port Authority. The Port Authority's Invitation to Bid required each bidder to inspect the job site and provided that bidders whose bids were accepted would not be relieved of any contract duties due to their failure to inspect. Moyer inspected the site and then submitted a bid, which was later accepted. Shortly after he commenced work, Moyer discovered that water would not drain from the ditches he dug due to clogged culverts. This caused his ditches to collapse, necessitating extra digging. He told Crookham that he would not continue work unless he received extra pay for redigging the ditches. Crookham later refused to pay the extra amount. Crookham argued its promise to pay extra was not supported by consideration. Was Crookham right?

9. T & S Brass, a plumbing fixture manufacturer, contracted with Pic-Air, Inc., for the purchase of 52,500 faucet handles to be used by T & S in its own production. The contract provided that time was of the essence and provided that Pic-Air would bear the expense of delivery. As the time for delivery approached, Pic-Air told T & S that it would not be able to deliver on time unless T & S agreed to pay to have the handles shipped by air freight. T & S agreed to pay the air freight, but in a later lawsuit argued that it was not bound by its promise. Was T & S right?

10. Sigler lived in Mariotte's home and paid rent to her from 1949 until 1977. During this period, Sigler and Mariotte were close companions and shared food expenses. In 1976, Mariotte was hospitalized and later entered a nursing home. Anxious for Mariotte to return home, Sigler told Mariotte's son that if Mariotte were released from the nursing home, she would take care of her at no charge. Because he felt that more than one person was needed to care for Mariotte, the son hired another woman to care for her full-time after she came home for $85 a week plus room and board. Sigler assisted the woman in taking care of Mariotte, and on December 21, 1977, she demanded compensation for taking care of Mariotte. Mariotte's son then agreed to pay for her room and board. On June 15, 1979, Mariotte signed a document prepared by Sigler directing the administrator of her estate to pay Sigler $85 per week, plus room and board, from August 1, 1976, for as long as Sigler continued to live with her and care for her. The payment was to be deferred until after Mariotte's death. Was the 1979 agreement enforceable?

CHAPTER 13

REALITY OF CONSENT

INTRODUCTION

In a complex economy that depends on planning for the future, it is crucial that the law can be counted on to enforce contracts. In some situations, however, there are compelling reasons for permitting people to escape or *avoid* their contracts. An agreement obtained by force, trickery, unfair persuasion, or error is not the product of mutual and voluntary consent. A person who has made an agreement under these circumstances will be able to avoid it, because his consent was not *real*.

Five doctrines that permit people to avoid their contracts because of the absence of real consent are discussed: misrepresentation, fraud, mistake, duress, and undue influence. Two doctrines that involve similar considerations, capacity and unconscionability, will be discussed in the Capacity to Contract chapter and the Illegality chapter.

Effect of Doctrines Discussed in This Chapter

Contracts that involve the circumstances discussed in this chapter are generally considered to be **voidable.** This means that the person whose consent was not real has the power to **rescind** (cancel) the contract. Upon rescission, the person who rescinds is entitled to the return of anything he gave the other party. By the same token, he must return anything that he has received from the other party.

Necessity for Prompt and Unequivocal Rescission
A person who wants to rescind a contract on one of the grounds discussed in this chapter must act promptly and unequivocally. He must avoid any behavior that would suggest that he affirms or **ratifies** the contract. Ratification of a voidable contract means that a person who had the right to rescind has elected not to do so. The effect of ratification is that he loses the right to rescind.

A person who has grounds to rescind a contract must object promptly upon learning the facts that give him the right to rescind and must clearly express his intent to cancel the contract. He should avoid unreasonable delay in notifying the other party of his rescission, because unreasonable delay communicates that he has ratified the contract. He should also avoid any conduct that would send a "mixed message," such as continuing to accept benefits from the other party or behaving in any other way that is inconsistent with his expressed intent to rescind.

MISREPRESENTATION AND FRAUD

Nature of Misrepresentation

A *misrepresentation* is an assertion that is not in accord with the truth. When a person enters a contract because of his justifiable reliance on a misrepresentation about some important fact, the contract is voidable.

It is not necessary that the misrepresentation be intentionally deceptive. Misrepresentations can be either "innocent" (not intentionally deceptive) or "fraudulent" (made with knowledge of falsity and intent to deceive). A contract may be voidable even if the person making the misrepresentation believes in good faith that what he says is true. Either innocent misrepresentation or fraud gives the complaining party the right to rescind a contract.

Nature of Fraud

Fraud is the type of misrepresentation that is committed knowingly, with the intent to deceive. The legal term for this knowledge of falsity, which distinguishes fraud from innocent misrepresentation, is **scienter**. A misrepresentation is "knowingly" made if the defendant knew that his statement was false, if he knew that he did not have a basis for making the statement, or even if he made the statement without being confident that it was true. The intent to deceive can be inferred from the fact that the defendant knowingly made a misstatement of fact to a person who was likely to rely on it.

As is true for innocent misrepresentation, the contract remedy for fraudulent misrepresentation is rescission. The tort liability of a person who commits fraud is different from that of a person who commits innocent misrepresentation, however. A person who commits fraud may be liable for damages, possibly including punitive damages, for the tort of **deceit**.[1] As you will learn in following sections, innocent misrepresentation and fraud share a common core of elements.

Election of Remedies   In some states, a person injured by fraud cannot rescind the contract *and* sue for damages for deceit; he must elect (choose) between these remedies. In other states, however, an injured party may

pursue both rescission and damage remedies, and does not have to elect between them. Under every state's law, however, a person injured by fraud in a contract for the *sale of goods* can both rescind the contract and sue for damages. This is made clear by section 2–721 of the Uniform Commercial Code, which specifically states that no election of remedies is required in contracts for the sale of goods.

REQUIREMENTS FOR RESCISSION ON THE GROUND OF MISREPRESENTATION

The fact that one of the parties has made an untrue assertion does not in itself make the contract voidable. Courts do not want to permit people who have exercised poor business judgment or poor common sense to avoid their contractual obligations, nor do they want to grant rescission of a contract when there have been only minor and unintentional misstatements of relatively unimportant details. A drastic remedy such as rescission should be used only when a person has been seriously misled about a fact important to the contract by someone he had the right to rely on. A person seeking to rescind a contract on the ground of innocent or fraudulent misrepresentation must be able to establish each of the following elements:

1. An untrue assertion of fact was made.
2. The fact asserted was material *or* the assertion was fraudulent.
3. The complaining party entered the contract because of his reliance on the assertion.
4. The reliance of the complaining party was reasonable.

In tort actions in which the plaintiff is seeking to recover damages for deceit, the plaintiff would have to establish a *fifth* element: injury. He would have to prove that he had suffered actual economic injury because of his reliance on the fraudulent assertion. In cases in which the injured person seeks only rescission of the contract, however, proof of economic injury usually is not required.

Untrue Assertion of Fact

To have misrepresentation, one of the parties must have made an untrue assertion of fact or engaged in some conduct that is the equivalent of an untrue assertion of

---

[1] The tort of deceit is discussed in the Intentional Torts chapter.

fact. The fact asserted must be a *past or existing fact*, as distinguished from a promise or prediction about some future happening.

The **concealment** of a fact through some active conduct intended to prevent the other party from discovering the fact is considered to be the equivalent of an assertion. Like a false statement of fact, concealment can be the basis for a claim of misrepresentation or fraud. For example, if Summers is offering his house for sale and paints the ceilings to conceal the fact that the roof leaks, his active concealment constitutes an assertion of fact. Under some circumstances, **nondisclosure** also can be the equivalent of an assertion of fact. Nondisclosure differs from concealment in that concealment involves the active hiding of a fact, while nondisclosure is the failure to offer information.

Problem Area: Nondisclosure   Suppose you are a prospective home buyer who inspects a house for possible purchase. The seller of the house knows that there is a hidden but serious structural defect in the house that will cost approximately $30,000 to correct, but does not mention this to you. Neither you nor the professional inspector you hire to examine the house for defects observes any evidence of structural defects, and you contract to purchase the house based on your assumption that it is in good condition. You later learn about the existence of this defect. Do you have the right to rescind the contract? The issue raised by this problem is whether the seller's silence about the defect was misrepresentation. In other words, was his nondisclosure the equivalent of an assertion that the structural defect did not exist?

Under traditional contract law, the answer to this question probably would have been "no." Under the traditional view of nondisclosure, the circumstances under which the law required disclosure were very limited. (These are the first three circumstances described in the next section.) Mere silence on the part of a contracting party generally did not amount to misrepresentation. One reason for this treatment of nondisclosure was that, unlike concealment and outright statements of fact, which are active forms of misconduct, nondisclosure is passive. Fundamentally, though, the traditional view of nondisclosure expressed the highly individualistic philosophy that each contracting party is responsible for taking care of himself and is not his "brother's keeper."

In recent years, however, courts and legislatures have expanded the circumstances under which a person has the duty to take affirmative steps to disclose relevant information. This is consistent with modern contract law's emphasis on influencing ethical standards of conduct and achieving fair results. Some duties of disclosure have been created by statutes, such as the Truth in Lending Act[2] and the federal securities laws,[3] but courts also have been increasingly active in expanding the duty to disclose. In addition to the circumstances in which federal or state statutes would require a contracting party to disclose facts, there are four circumstances in which most courts today require disclosure.

When Nondisclosure Is the Equivalent of an Assertion of Fact   Under the circumstances listed below, the law requires individuals to disclose information material to a contract. In these situations, the person's failure to disclose a fact would be the equivalent of an assertion that the fact did not exist.

   1. *Fiduciary relationship.* If a fiduciary relationship (a relationship of trust and confidence) exists between the parties to the contract, a party who knows of an important fact that the other person does not know about would have the duty to disclose it. This makes sense, because a person who has good reason to believe that the other party is looking out for his welfare will not approach the contract with the same degree of vigilance as the person who is dealing at arm's length with a stranger. This sort of duty to disclose would not apply to ordinary contracting parties who are bargaining at arm's length.

   2. *Correcting "half-truths."* The saying that "a half-truth is a whole lie" recognizes that it is possible to create a very distorted impression in the mind of another person by revealing only part of the truth. The law has long held that when a person makes a statement about a situation, he has the duty to disclose any facts that would be necessary to correct a half-truth. For example, Carlson, a car salesman who is trying to sell a used car, knows that the previous owner of the car used it exclusively for drag racing on Sundays. If Carlson tells a customer that the previous owner of the car "drove it only on Sundays," he would have the legal duty to disclose the additional material fact that the car had been used exclusively for drag racing.

---

[2] See the Introduction to Credit and Secured Transactions chapter for a discussion of the Truth in Lending Act.

[3] These laws are discussed in the Securities Regulation chapter.

3. *Correcting statements made false by supervening events.* A person has the duty to disclose information that will be necessary to correct a previous statement that may have been true when made, but that has become false because of supervening events. For example, White, who wants to sell her house, tells a prospective purchaser truthfully that the roof of the house does not leak. Several days later, the roof leaks after a heavy storm. White has the legal duty to make the disclosure that is necessary to correct her previous statement.

4. *Good faith and fair dealing require correcting the other party's mistake about a basic assumption.* In the hypothetical case with which we began this discussion of nondisclosure—the case of the seller who failed to disclose the existence of a hidden structural defect in the house he was selling—the home buyer entered into the contract under the mistaken assumption that the house was free of structural defects. The *Restatement (Second) of Contracts* provides for a duty to disclose that would be applicable in this situation. Under section 161 of the *Restatement*, a person must disclose facts necessary to correct the other party's mistake about a basic assumption of the contract when nondisclosure amounts to a failure to act in good faith and in accordance with reasonable standards of fair dealing. Most states today apply a duty to disclose along these lines.

Note that this sort of duty to disclose has broader application than the first three circumstances described above, because it can apply even when the parties are dealing at arm's length and no partial disclosures have been made. Note also that this duty to disclose is intertwined with concepts of good faith and fair dealing. The *Restatement* does *not* say that a person who possesses information always has the obligation to educate the other party. Rather, the duty to speak arises only when failing to do so would constitute a failure to behave in a way that is in accord with prevailing concepts of good faith and reasonable standards of dealing. Nondisclosure is most likely to constitute a failure to act reasonably and in good faith when a party has access to information that is not readily available to the other party. In addition, sellers are more likely to be required to disclose information than are buyers.

Transactions involving the sale of real estate are among the most common situations in which this duty to disclose arises. Most states now hold that a seller who knows about a latent (hidden) defect that materially affects the value of the property he is selling has the obligation to speak up about this defect. *Reed v. King*, which follows, involves an interesting application of the duty to disclose in the context of a sale of real estate.

REED v. KING

193 Cal. Rptr. 130 (Cal. Ct. App. 1983)

Dorris Reed purchased a house from Robert King. Neither King nor his real estate agents told Reed that a woman and her four children had been murdered there 10 years earlier. Reed learned of the gruesome episode from a neighbor after the sale. She sued King and his real estate agents, seeking rescission of the contract and damages. The trial court dismissed Reed's complaint on the ground that it failed to state a claim. Reed appealed the dismissal.

Blease, Associate Justice.   The critical question is: does the seller have the duty to disclose here? Resolution of this question depends on the materiality of the fact of the murders.

In general, a seller of real property has a duty to disclose where the seller knows of facts *materially* affecting the value or desirability of the property which are known or accessible only to him and also knows that such facts are not known to, or within the reach of the diligent attention and observation of the buyer.

Numerous cases have found nondisclosure of physical defects and legal impediments to the use of real property are material. However, to our knowledge, no prior real estate sale case has faced an issue of nondisclosure of the kind presented here. Should this variety of ill-repute be required to be disclosed? Is this a circumstance where nondisclosure of the fact amounts to a failure to act in good faith and in accordance with reasonable standards of fair dealing?

The paramount argument against an affirmative conclusion is if such an "irrational" consideration is permitted as a basis of rescission, the stability of all conveyances will be seriously undermined. Any fact that might disquiet the enjoyment of some segment of the buying public may be seized upon by a disgruntled purchaser to void a bargain. In our view, keeping this genie in the bottle is not as difficult a task as these arguments assume.

Reed alleges the fact of the murders has a quantifiable effect on the market value of the premises. If information known or accessible only to the seller has a significant and measurable effect on market value, and the seller is aware of this effect, we see no principled basis for making the duty to disclose turn upon the character of the information. Reputation and history can have a significant effect on the value of realty. "George Washington slept here" is worth something, however physically inconsequential that consideration may be. Ill-repute or "bad will" conversely may depress the value of property.

Whether Reed will be able to prove her allegation that the decade-old multiple murder has a significant effect on market value we cannot determine. If she is able to do so by competent evidence she is entitled to a favorable ruling on the issues of materiality and duty to disclose. Her demonstration of objective tangible harm would still the concern that permitting her to go forward will open the floodgates to rescission on subjective and idiosyncratic grounds.

Judgment reversed in favor of Reed, reinstating her action.

Problem Area: Statements of Opinion   Although contract law traditionally has distinguished between assertions of *fact* and assertions of *opinion*, such a distinction is hard to maintain because an assertion of opinion *is* an assertion of fact—it is an assertion of fact about one's state of mind. Thus, if Johnson, a seller of an apartment building, tells Rice, a prospective buyer, that the electrical system is "good," Rice is entitled to conclude that Johnson is being truthful about his state of mind and that he knows no facts that are inconsistent with his statement.

There is an important distinction between a statement that communicates a person's knowledge and a statement that communicates only his uncertain belief about a fact or his personal judgment about such matters as quality or value, however. The latter sort of statement usually cannot be the basis of a misrepresentation claim because the person to whom such a statement of opinion is made is not justified in relying on it. This is especially true when the statement relates to something about which the parties have relatively equal knowledge and people's points of view are likely to differ. In such a case, each party is expected to form his own opinion. A classic example of this sort of statement of opinion is a seller's "puff" (sales talk or general praise of an item being sold), such as "This suit will look terrific on you."

Even when the statement is clearly one of opinion, there are three situations in which the statement of opinion can be the basis of a misrepresentation claim because reliance is justifiable under the circumstances.[4] These include:

1. *Relationship of trust and confidence.* A person can be justified in relying on a statement of opinion if it is reasonable to do so because of a relationship of trust and confidence between him and the speaker. For example, if Madison, the longtime financial adviser of the elderly Holden, persuades Holden to invest her money in Madison's failing business by telling her that it is a wise investment, Holden would be justified in relying on Holden's statement of opinion.

2. *Relying party is unusually susceptible.* Reliance on a statement of opinion can be justifiable when the relying party is someone who is particularly susceptible

---

[4] *Restatement (Second) of Contracts* § 169.

to the particular type of misrepresentation involved. This sort of case would be likely to involve relying parties who are vulnerable to being misled because of some obvious disadvantage such as illiteracy or lack of intelligence or experience.

3. *Reliance on person who has superior skill or judgment.* Reliance on an assertion of opinion also can be justifiable when the relying party reasonably believes that the person on whose opinion he is relying has superior skill or judgment about the subject matter of the contract. This would apply when the opinion relates to some matter about which superior training or experience is necessary to form the opinion. For example, Buyer, who knows that Salesman is an experienced auto mechanic, would be justified in relying on Salesman's statement that a particular used car is "in A-1 condition."

Materiality

If the misrepresentation was innocent, the person seeking to rescind the contract must establish that the fact asserted was **material.** A fact will be considered to be material if it is likely to play a significant role in inducing a reasonable person to enter the contract or if the person asserting the fact knows that the other person is likely to rely on the fact. For example, Rogers, who is trying to sell his car to Ferguson and knows that Ferguson idolizes professional bowlers, tells Ferguson that a professional bowler once rode in the car. Relying on that representation, Ferguson buys the car. Although the fact Rogers asserted might not be important to most people, it would be material here because Rogers knew that his representation would be likely to induce Ferguson to enter the contract.

Even if the fact asserted was not material, the contract may be rescinded if the misrepresentation was *fraudulent.* The rationale for this rule is that a person who fraudulently misrepresents a fact, even one that is not material under the standards previously discussed, should not be able to profit from his intentionally deceptive conduct.

Actual Reliance

Reliance means that a person pursues some course of action because of his faith in an assertion made to him.

For misrepresentation to exist, there must have been a causal connection between the assertion and the complaining party's decision to enter the contract. If the complaining party knew that the assertion was false or was not aware that an assertion had been made, there has been no reliance.

Justifiable Reliance

Courts also scrutinize the reasonableness of the behavior of the complaining party by requiring that his reliance be *justifiable.* A person does not act justifiably if he relies on an assertion that is obviously false or not to be taken seriously.

Problem Area: The Relying Party's Failure to Investigate the Accuracy of an Assertion One problem involving the justifiable reliance element is determining the extent to which the relying party is responsible for investigating the accuracy of the statement on which he relies. Classical contract law held that a person who did not attempt to discover readily discoverable facts generally was not justified in relying on the other party's statements about them. For example, under traditional law, a person would not be entitled to rely on the other party's assertions about facts that are a matter of public record or that could be discovered through a reasonable inspection of available documents or records.

The extent of the responsibility placed on a relying party to conduct an independent investigation has declined in modern contract law, however. For example, section 172 of the *Restatement* states that the complaining party's fault in not knowing or discovering facts before entering the contract does not make his reliance unjustifiable unless the degree of his fault was so extreme as to amount to a failure to act in good faith and in accordance with reasonable standards of fair dealing. Recognizing that the traditional rule operated to encourage misrepresentation, courts in recent years have tended to decrease the responsibility of the relying party and to place a greater degree of accountability on the person who makes the assertion. The case of *Cousineau v. Walker,* which follows, is an excellent example of this trend.

COUSINEAU v. WALKER

613 P.2d 608 (Alaska Sup. Ct. 1980)

Devin and Joan Walker owned property in Eagle River, Alaska. In 1976, they listed the property for sale with a real estate broker. They signed a multiple listing agreement, which described the property as having 580 feet of highway frontage and stated, "ENGINEER REPORT SAYS OVER 1 MILLION IN GRAVEL ON PROP." A later listing contract signed with the same broker described the property as having 580 feet of highway frontage, but listed the gravel content as "minimum 80,000 cubic yds of gravel." An appraisal prepared to determine the property's value stated that it did not take any gravel into account, but described the ground as "all good gravel base."

Wayne Cousineau, a contractor who was also in the gravel extraction business, became aware of the property when he saw the multiple listing. After visiting the property with his real estate broker and discussing gravel extraction with Mr. Walker, Cousineau offered to purchase the property. He then attempted to determine the lot's road frontage, but was unsuccessful because the property was covered with snow. He was also unsuccessful in obtaining the engineer's report allegedly showing "over 1 million in gravel." Walker admitted at trial that he had never seen a copy of the report either. Nevertheless, the parties signed and consummated a contract of sale for the purchase price of $385,000. There was no reference to the amount of highway frontage in the purchase agreement.

After the sale was completed, Cousineau began developing the property and removing gravel. Cousineau learned that the description of highway frontage contained in the real estate listing was incorrect when a neighbor threatened to sue him for removing gravel from the neighbor's adjacent lot. A subsequent survey revealed that the highway frontage was 410 feet—not 580 feet, as advertised. At about the same time, the gravel ran out after Cousineau had removed only 6,000 cubic yards.

Cousineau stopped making payments and informed the Walkers of his intention to rescind the contract. Cousineau brought an action against the Walkers, seeking the return of his money. The trial court found for the Walkers, and Cousineau appealed.

Boochever, Justice.   An innocent misrepresentation may be the basis for rescinding a contract. There is no question that the statements made by Walker and his real estate agent in the multiple listing were false.

The bulk of the Walkers' brief is devoted to the argument that Cousineau's unquestioning reliance on Walker and his real estate agent was imprudent and unreasonable. Cousineau failed to obtain and review the engineer's report. He failed to obtain a survey or examine the plat available at the recorder's office. He failed to make calculations that would have revealed the true frontage of the lot. Although the property was covered with snow, the buyer, according to Walker, had ample time to inspect it. The buyer was an experienced businessman who frequently bought and sold real estate. Discrepancies existed in the various property descriptions which should have alerted Cousineau to potential problems. In short, the Walkers urge that the doctrine of *caveat emptor* precludes recovery.

There is a split of authority regarding a buyer's duty to investigate a vendor's fraudulent statements, but the prevailing trend is toward placing a minimal duty on a buyer. The recent draft of the *Restatement of Contracts* allows rescission for an innocent material misrepresentation unless a buyer's fault was so negligent as to amount to "a failure to act in good faith and in accordance with reasonable standards of fair dealing." We conclude that a purchaser of land may rely on material representations made by the seller and is not obligated to ascertain whether such representations are truthful. A buyer of land, relying on an innocent misrepresentation, is barred from recovery only if the buyer's acts in failing to discover defects were wholly irrational, preposterous, or in bad faith.

Although Cousineau's actions may well have exhibited poor judgment for an experienced businessman, they were not so unreasonable or preposterous in view of Walker's description of the property that recovery should be denied.

Judgment reversed in favor of Cousineau.

CONCEPT REVIEW

MISREPRESENTATION AND FRAUD

	Innocent Misrepresentation	Fraud
Remedy	Rescission	Rescission *or* action for damages
Elements	1. Untrue assertion of fact Includes: a. Statement of past or existing fact b. Concealment c. Nondisclosure if: 　(1) Relationship of trust and confidence, 　(2) Half-truth, 　(3) Statement made false by supervening event, or 　(4) Good faith and fair dealing require correcting party's mistake about basic assumption d. Statement of opinion if: 　(1) Relationship of trust and confidence, 　(2) Unusually susceptible party, or 　(3) Person stating opinion has superior skill or judgment	
	2. Assertion relates to material fact	2. Assertion made with knowledge of falsity (*scienter*) and intent to deceive
	3. Actual reliance 4. Justifiable reliance	
		5. Economic loss (in action for damages)

MISTAKE

Nature of Mistake

Anyone who enters a contract does so on the basis of his understanding of the facts that are relevant to the contract. His decision about what he is willing to exchange with the other party is based on this understanding. If the parties are wrong about an important fact, the exchange that they make is likely to be quite different than what they contemplated when they entered the contract, and this difference will be due to simple error rather than to any external events such as an increase in market price. For example, Fox contracts to sell to Ward a half-carat stone, which both believe to be a tourmaline, at a price of $65. If they are wrong and the stone is actually a diamond worth at least $2,500, Fox will have suffered an unexpected loss and Ward will have reaped an unexpected gain. The contract would not have been made at a price of $65 if the parties' belief about the nature of the stone had been in accord with the facts. In such cases, the person adversely affected by the mistake can avoid the contract under the doctrine of mistake. The purpose of the doctrine of mistake is to prevent unexpected and unbargained-for losses that result when the parties are mistaken about a fact central to their contract.

What Is a Mistake?   In ordinary conversation, we may use the term "mistake" to mean an error in judgment or an unfortunate act. In contract law, however, a mistake is a *belief about a fact* that is *not in accord with the truth.*[5] The erroneous belief forming the basis of a mistake case must relate to facts as they exist at the time the contract is created. An erroneous belief or prediction about facts that might occur in the future would not qualify as a mistake.

As in misrepresentation cases, the complaining party in a mistake case enters a contract because of a belief that is at variance with the actual facts. Mistake is unlike misrepresentation, however, in that the erroneous belief is not the result of the other party's untrue statements.

The *Wilkin v. 1st Source Bank* case illustrates the concept and effect of mistake in contract law.

_____

[5] *Restatement (Second) of Contracts* § 151.

WILKIN v. 1ST SOURCE BANK
548 N.E.2d 170 (Ind. Ct. App. 1990)

Olga Mestrovic, the widow of internationally known sculptor and artist, Ivan Mestrovic, owned a large number of works of art created by her late husband. Mrs. Mestrovic died, leaving a will in which she directed that all the works of art created by her husband were to be sold and the proceeds distributed to surviving members of the Mestrovic family. Mrs. Mestrovic also owned real estate at the time of her death. 1st Source Bank, as the personal representative of Mrs. Mestrovic's estate, entered into a contract to sell this real estate to Terrence and Antoinette Wilkin. The purchase agreement provided that certain personal property on the premises would be sold to the Wilkins, too: specifically, the stove, refrigerator, dishwasher, drapes, curtains, sconces, and French doors in the attic.

After taking possession of the property, the Wilkins complained to the bank that the property was left in a cluttered condition and would require substantial cleaning effort. The trust officer of the bank offered the Wilkins two options: Either the bank would obtain a rubbish removal service to clean the property or the Wilkins could clean the property and keep any items of personal property they wanted. The Wilkins opted to clean the property themselves. At the time these arrangements were made, neither the bank nor the Wilkins suspected that any works of art remained on the premises.

During the clean-up efforts, the Wilkins found eight drawings apparently created by Ivan Mestrovic. They also found a plaster sculpture of the figure of Christ with three small children. The Wilkins claimed ownership of these works of art by virtue of their agreement with the bank. The probate court ruled that there was no agreement for the purchase of the artwork, and the Wilkins appealed.

Hoffman, Judge.   Mutual assent is a prerequisite to the creation of a contract. Where both parties share a common assumption about a vital fact upon which they based their bargain, and that assumption is false, the transaction may be avoided if because of the mistake a quite different exchange of values occurs from the exchange of values contemplated by the parties. *J. Calamari & J. Perillo, The Law of Contracts* section 9–26 (1987).

The necessity of mutual assent is illustrated in the classic case of *Sherwood v. Walker* (1887). The owners of a blooded cow indicated to the purchaser that the cow was barren. The purchaser appeared to believe that the cow was barren. Consequently, a bargain was made to sell at a price per pound at which the cow would have brought approximately $80.00. Before delivery, it was discovered that the cow was with calf and that she was, therefore, worth from $750.00 to $1,000.00. The court ruled that the transaction was voidable: "[T]he mistake . . . went to the very nature of the thing. A barren cow is substantially a different creature than a breeding one."

Like the parties in *Sherwood*, the parties in the instant case shared a common presupposition as to the existence of certain facts which proved false. The bank and the Wilkins considered the real estate which the Wilkins had purchased to be cluttered with items of personal property variously characterized as "junk," "stuff," or "trash." Neither party suspected that works of art created by Ivan Mestrovic remained on the premises.

As in *Sherwood*, one party experienced an unexpected, unbargained-for gain while the other experienced an unexpected, unbargained-for loss. Because the bank and the Wilkins did not know that the eight drawings and the plaster sculpture were included in the items of personalty that cluttered the real property, the discovery of those works of art by the Wilkins was unexpected. The resultant gain to the Wilkins and loss to the Bank were not contemplated by the parties when the bank agreed that the Wilkins could clean the premises and keep such personal property as they wished.

The following commentary on *Sherwood* is equally applicable to the case at bar:

"Here the buyer sought to retain a gain that was produced, not by a subsequent change in circumstances, nor by the favorable resolution of known uncertainties when the contract was made, but by the presence of facts quite different from those on which the parties based their bargain." *Palmer, Mistake and Unjust Enrichment* 16–17 (1962).

The probate court properly concluded that there was no agreement for the purchase, sale, or other disposition of the eight drawings and plaster sculpture.

Judgment for 1st Source Bank affirmed.

Mistakes of Law

A number of the older mistake cases state that mistake about a principle of law will not justify rescission. The rationale for this view was that everyone was presumed to know the law. More modern cases, however, have granted relief even when the mistake is an erroneous belief about some aspect of law.

Negligence and the Right to Avoid on the Ground of Mistake

Courts sometimes state that relief will not be granted when a person's mistake was caused by his own negli- gence. However, a review of mistake cases reveals that courts have often granted rescission even when the mis- taken party was somewhat negligent. Section 157 of the *Restatement (Second) of Contracts* focuses on the *de- gree* of a party's negligence in making the mistake. It states that a person's fault in failing to know or discover facts before entering the contract will not bar relief un- less his fault amounted to a failure to act in good faith.

Effect of Mistake

The mere fact that the contracting parties have made a mistake is not, standing alone, a sufficient ground for avoidance of the contract. The right to avoid a contract because of mistake depends on several factors that are discussed in following sections. One important factor that affects the right to avoid is whether the mistake was made by just one of the parties (**unilateral mistake**) or by both parties (**mutual mistake**).

Mutual Mistake

A mutual mistake exists when both parties to the contract have erroneous assumptions about the same fact. A contract can be avoided on the ground of mutual mistake if the three following elements are present:

1. Both parties made a mistake as to a basic assumption on which the contract was made.
2. The mistake has a material effect on the agreed-upon exchange.
3. The party adversely affected by the mistake does not bear the risk of the mistake.[6]

Mistake about a Basic Assumption Even if the mistake is mutual, the adversely affected party will not have the right to avoid the contract unless the mistake concerns a *basic assumption* on which the contract was based. Assumptions about the identity, existence, quality, or quantity of the subject matter of the contract are among the basic assumptions on which contracts typically are founded. It is not necessary that the parties be consciously aware of the assumption; an assumption may be so basic that they take it for granted. For example, if Peterson contracts to buy a house from Tharp, it is likely that both of them assume at the time of contracting that the house is in existence and that it is legally permissible for the house to be used as a residence.

An assumption, even if shared by both parties, would not be considered a basic assumption if it concerns a matter that bears an indirect or collateral relationship to the subject matter of the contract. For example, mistakes about matters such as a party's financial ability or market conditions usually would not give rise to avoidance of the contract.

Material Effect on Agreed-Upon Exchange A person adversely affected by a mistake will be able to avoid a contract only if the mistake has a *material effect on the agreed-upon exchange*. It is not enough for the adversely affected person to show that the exchange is something different from what he expected. He must show that the imbalance caused by the mistake is so severe that it would be unfair for the law to require him to perform the contract. He will have a better chance of establishing this element if he can show not only that the contract is *less* desirable for him because of the mistake, but also that the other party has received an unbargained for advantage.

Adversely Affected Party Does Not Bear the Risk of Mistake Even if the first two elements are present, a party adversely affected by a mistake cannot avoid the contract if he is considered to bear the risk of mistake.[7] Courts have the power to allocate the risk of a mistake to the adversely affected person whenever it is reasonable under the circumstances to do so.

One situation in which an adversely affected person would bear the risk of mistake is when he has expressly contracted to do so. For example, if Buyer contracted to accept property "as is," he may be considered to have accepted the risk that his assumption about the quality of the property may be erroneous.

The adversely affected party also bears the risk of mistake when he contracts with *conscious awareness* that he is ignorant or has limited information about a fact—in other words, he *knows that he does not know* the true state of affairs about a particular fact, but he binds himself to perform anyway. Suppose someone gives you an old, locked safe. Without trying to open it, you sell it and "all of its contents" to one of your friends for $25. When your friend succeeds in opening the safe, he finds $10,000 in cash. In this case, you would not be able to rescind the contract because, in essence, you gambled on your limited knowledge . . . and lost.

Mutual Mistakes in Drafting Writings

Sometimes, mutual mistake takes the form of erroneous *expression* of an agreement, frequently caused by a clerical error in drafting or typing a contract, deed, or other

---

[6] *Restatement (Second) of Contracts* § 152.

[7] *Restatement (Second) of Contracts* § 154.

document. In such cases, the remedy is *reformation* of the writing rather than avoidance of the contract. Reformation means modification of the written instrument to express the agreement that the parties made but failed to express correctly. Suppose Arnold agrees to sell Barber a vacant lot next to Arnold's home. The vacant lot is "Lot 3, block 1"; Arnold's home is on "Lot 2, block 1." The person typing the contract strikes the wrong key, and the contract reads, "Lot 2, block 1." Neither Arnold nor Barber notices this error when they read and sign the contract, yet clearly they did not intend to have Arnold sell the lot on which his house stands. In such a case, a court will reform the contract to conform to Arnold and Baker's true agreement.

Unilateral Mistake

A unilateral mistake exists when only one of the parties makes a mistake about a basic assumption on which he made the contract. For example, Plummer contracts to buy from Taylor 25 shares of Worthright Enterprises, Inc., believing that he is buying 25 shares of the much more valuable Worthwrite Industries. Taylor is correct in his belief about the identity of the stock he is selling; only Plummer is mistaken in his assumption about the identity of the stock.

Courts are more likely to allow avoidance of a contract when both parties are mistaken than when only one is mistaken. The reason it is more difficult to avoid a contract in cases of unilateral mistake is that, in such cases, at least one party's assumption about the facts was correct, and allowing avoidance disappoints the reasonable expectations of that nonmistaken party.

A person who wants to avoid a contract because of unilateral mistake must establish the same elements discussed earlier that a person who wants to avoid for mutual mistake must establish. That is, he must show (1) that he made a mistake as to a basic assumption on which he entered the contract, (2) that the mistake had a material effect on the agreed exchange of performance, and (3) that he does not bear the risk of mistake. *In addition* to these elements, he must prove *either one* of the following elements to be able to avoid the contract:

1. The effect of the mistake was such that it would be unconscionable to enforce the contract, or

2. The other party caused the mistake or had reason to know of the mistake.[8]

Unconscionable to Enforce the Contract   To meet this element, the mistaken party would have to show that the consequences of the mistake were such that it would be unreasonably harsh or oppressive to enforce the contract.[9] For example, Ace Electrical Company makes an error when preparing a bid that it submits to Gorge General Contracting. Without any reason to realize that a mistake has been made, Gorge accepts the bid. Ace might show that it would be unconscionable to enforce the contract by showing that not only will its profit margin not be what Ace contemplated when it made its offer, but also that it would suffer a grave loss by having to perform at the mistaken price. As you will read in the Illegality chapter, however, unconscionability is a flexible concept that depends heavily on the circumstances of an individual case. In the foregoing hypothetical, for example, it is less likely that enforcing the contract between Ace and Gorge would be unconscionable if Gorge had relied on Ace's bid, say, by preparing and submitting a bid of its own that incorporated Ace's bid.

Other Party Caused or Had Reason to Know of Mistake   Courts permit avoidance in cases of unilateral mistake if the nonmistaken party caused the mistake, knew of the mistake, or even if the mistake was so obvious that the nonmistaken party had reason to realize that a mistake had been made. This is true even if enforcing the contract would not be so harsh as to be unconscionable. For example, if the mistake in Ace's bid was so obvious that Gorge knew about it when it accepted Ace's offer, Ace could avoid the contract.

The reasoning behind this rule is that the nonmistaken person could have prevented the loss by acting in good faith and informing the person in error that he had made a mistake. It also reflects the judgment that people should not take advantage of the mistakes of others.

---

[8] *Restatement (Second) of Contracts* § 153.

[9] The concept of unconscionability is developed more fully in the Illegality chapter.

CONCEPT REVIEW

AVOIDANCE ON THE GROUND OF MISTAKE

	Mutual Mistake	**Unilateral Mistake**
Description	Both parties mistaken about same fact	One party mistaken about fact
Elements	1. Mistake about basic assumption on which contract was made. 2. Material effect on agreed exchange. 3. Person adversely affected by mistake does not bear the risk of the mistake.	
		4. Effect of mistake is such that it would be unconscionable to enforce the contract or Nonmistaken party caused mistake or had reason to know of mistake

DURESS

Nature of Duress

Duress is wrongful coercion that induces a person to enter or modify a contract. One kind of duress is physical compulsion to enter a contract. For example, Thorp overpowers Grimes, grasps his hand, and forces him to sign a contract. This kind of duress is rare, but when it occurs, a court would find that the contract was **void.** A far more common type of duress occurs when a person is induced to enter a contract by a *threat* of physical, emotional, or economic harm. In these cases, the contract is considered **voidable** at the option of the victimized person. This is the form of duress addressed in this chapter.

The elements of duress have undergone dramatic changes. Classical contract law took a very narrow view of the type of coercion that constituted duress, limiting duress to threats of imprisonment or serious physical harm. Today, however, courts take a much broader view of the types of coercion that will constitute duress. For example, modern courts recognize that threats to a person's economic interests can be duress.

Elements of Duress

To rescind a contract because of duress, one must be able to establish the following elements:

1. The contract was induced by an improper threat and
2. The victim had no reasonable alternative but to enter the contract.[10]

Improper Threat   Every contract negotiation involves the implied threat that a person will not enter the contract unless his demands are met. This is not the type of threat that is considered to be duress. The threat must be one that the law would consider *improper*. A threat to commit a crime or a tort would clearly be improper, but many actions that are not torts or crimes can be considered to be an improper way of inducing a contract.

Under some circumstances, threats to institute legal actions can be considered improper threats that will constitute duress. A threat to file either a civil or a criminal suit without a legal basis for doing so would clearly be improper. What of a threat to file a well-founded lawsuit or prosecution? Generally, if there is a good faith dispute over a matter, a person's threat to file a lawsuit to resolve that dispute is *not* considered to be improper. Otherwise, every person who settled a suit out of court could later claim duress. However, if the threat to sue is made in bad faith and for a purpose unrelated to the issues in the lawsuit, the threat can be considered improper. In one case, for example, duress was found when a husband who was in the process of divorcing his wife threatened to sue for custody of their children—something he had

---

[10] *Restatement (Second) of Contracts* § 175.

the right to do—unless the wife transferred to him stock that she owned in his company.[11] Section 176 of the *Restatement (Second) of Contracts* takes the position that a threat to institute a criminal prosecution is always impermissible pressure to enter a contract, even if the person making the threat has good reason to believe that the other person has committed a crime.

The *Restatement* also provides that it is improper for a contracting party to make a threat that would constitute a breach of the duty of good faith and fair dealing under his contract with the person who is the recipient of the threat.[12] This provision is relevant to the many duress cases that arise in the context of coerced modifications of existing contracts or settlements of existing debts.

Victim Had No Reasonable Alternative   The person complaining of duress must be able to prove that the coercive nature of the improper threat was such that he had no reasonable alternative but to enter or modify the contract. Classical contract law applied an objective standard of coercion, which required that the degree of coercion exercised had to be sufficient to overcome the will of a person of ordinary courage. The more modern standard for coercion focuses on the alternatives open to the complaining party. For example, Barry, a traveling salesman, takes his car to Cheatum Motors for repair. Barry pays Cheatum the full amount previously agreed upon for the repair, but Cheatum refuses to return Barry's car to him unless Barry agrees to pay substantially more than the contract price for the repairs. Because of his urgent need for the return of his car, Barry agrees to do this. In this case, Barry technically had the alternative of filing a legal action to recover his car. However, this would not be a *reasonable alternative* for someone

who needs the car urgently because of the time, expense, and uncertainty involved in pursuing a lawsuit. Thus, Barry could avoid his agreement to pay more money under a theory of duress.

Problem Area: Economic Duress   Today, the doctrine of duress is often applied in a business context. **Economic duress,** or **business compulsion,** are terms commonly used to describe situations in which one person induces the formation or modification of a contract by threatening another person's economic interests. A common coercive strategy is to threaten to breach the contract unless the other party agrees to modify its terms. For example, Moore, who has contracted to sell goods to Stephens, knows that Stephens needs timely delivery of the goods. Moore threatens to withhold delivery unless Stephens agrees to pay a higher price. Another common situation involving economic duress occurs when one of the parties offers a disproportionately small amount of money in settlement of a debt and refuses to pay more. Such a strategy exerts great economic pressure on a creditor who is in a desperate financial situation to accept the settlement because he cannot afford the time and expense of bringing a lawsuit.

Classical contract law did not recognize economic duress because this type of hard bargaining was considered neither improper nor coercive. After all, the victim of the sorts of economic pressure described above had at least the theoretical right to file a lawsuit to enforce his rights under the contract. Modern courts recognize that improper economic pressure can prevent a resulting contract or contract modification from being truly voluntary, and the concept of economic duress is well accepted today. Even in recent cases, however, it is not always clear how much hard bargaining is tolerated. *Rich & Whillock, Inc. v. Ashton Development, Inc.,* is a good example of hard bargaining that went too far.

---

[11] *Link v. Link,* 179 S.E.2d 697 (1971).

[12] *Restatement (Second) of Contracts* § 176.

RICH & WHILLOCK, INC. v. ASHTON DEVELOPMENT, INC.

204 Cal. Rptr. 86 (Cal. Ct. App. 1984)

Ashton Development, acting through its general contractor, Bob Britton, hired Jim Rich and Greg Whillock, subcontractors doing business as Rich & Whillock, Inc., to do grading and excavating work for $112,990 on one of Ashton's construction projects. After a month's work, Rich & Whillock encountered rock on the project site. Britton and Ashton's president agreed that the rock would have to be blasted and that this would involve extra costs since the original contract between Ashton and Rich & Whillock specified that any rock encountered would be considered an extra. Britton directed Rich & Whillock to go ahead with the blasting and bill for the extra cost. Rich & Whillock did so, submitting separate invoices for the regular contract work and the extra blasting work and receiving payment every two weeks.

After completing the work and receiving payments totalling over $190,000, Rich & Whillock submitted a final billing for an additional $72,286.45. This time Britton refused to pay, stating that he and Ashton's president had no money left to pay the final billing. Whillock told Britton that Rich & Whillock would "go broke" without this final payment because it was a new business with rented equipment and numerous subcontractors waiting to be paid. In response, Britton replied that he and Ashton would pay $50,000 or nothing, and Rich & Whillock could sue for the full amount if unsatisfied with the compromise.

The next month, Britton presented Rich with an agreement for a final compromise payment of $50,000, stating, "I have a check for you, and just take it or leave it, this is all you get. If you don't want this, you have got to sue me." Rich then signed the settlement agreement and received a $25,000 check after telling Britton the agreement was "blackmail" and he was signing it only because he had to in order to survive. Rich & Whillock later signed a release form and received a second check for $25,000. Several months afterward, however, they filed this action for breach of contract against Ashton and Bob Britton. The trial court found that the settlement agreement and release were unenforceable due to economic duress and entered judgment in favor of Rich & Whillock for the $22,286.45 balance due under the contract. Ashton and Britton appealed this judgment.

Wiener, Associate Judge. Economic duress may come into play upon the doing of a wrongful act which is sufficiently coercive to cause a reasonably prudent person faced with no reasonable alternative to succumb to the perpetrator's pressure. The assertion of a claim known to be false or a bad faith threat to breach a contract or to withhold a payment may constitute a wrongful act for purposes of the economic duress doctrine.

The underlying concern of the economic duress doctrine is the enforcement in the marketplace of certain minimal standards of business ethics. Hard bargaining, "efficient" breaches, and reasonable settlements of good faith disputes are all acceptable, even desirable, in our economic system. That system can be viewed as a game in which everybody wins, to one degree or another, so long as everyone plays by the common rules. Those rules are not limited to precepts of rationality and self-interest. They include equitable notions of fairness and propriety which preclude the wrongful exploitation of business exigencies to obtain disproportionate exchanges of value. Such exchanges make a mockery of freedom of contract and undermine the proper functioning of our economic system. The economic duress doctrine serves as a last resort to correct these aberrations when conventional alternatives and remedies are unavailing.

Here, Britton and Ashton acted in bad faith when they refused to pay Rich & Whillock's final billing and offered instead to pay a compromise amount. At the time of their bad faith breach and settlement offer, Britton, and through him, Ashton, knew Rich & Whillock was a new company overextended to creditors and subcontractors and faced with imminent bankruptcy if not paid its final billing. Whillock and Rich strenuously protested these coercive tactics, and succumbed to them only to avoid economic disaster to themselves and the adverse ripple effects of their bankruptcy on those to whom they were indebted. Under these circumstances, the trial court's finding that the agreement and release were the product of economic duress is consistent with legal principles and supported by substantial evidence.

Judgment for Rich & Whillock affirmed.

UNDUE INFLUENCE

Nature of Undue Influence

Undue influence is unfair persuasion. Like duress, undue influence involves wrongful pressure exerted on a person during the bargaining process. In undue influence, however, the pressure is exerted through *persuasion* rather than through coercion. The doctrine of undue influence was developed to give relief to persons who are unfairly persuaded to enter a contract while in a position of weakness that makes them particularly vulnerable to being preyed upon by those they trust or fear. Undue influence is not a tort, so the only remedy is rescission of the contract. A large proportion of undue influence cases arise after the death of the person who has been the subject of undue influence, when his relatives seek to set aside that person's contracts or wills.

Determining Undue Influence All contracts are based on persuasion. There is no precise dividing line between permissible persuasion and impermissible persuasion. Nevertheless, several hallmarks of undue influence cases can be identified. Undue influence cases normally involve the following elements:

1. The relationship between the parties is either one of trust and confidence or one in which the person exercising the persuasion dominates the person being persuaded, and
2. The persuasion is unfair. [13]

Relation between the Parties In normal bargaining situations, individuals who have capacity to contract are expected to be able to fend for themselves, resist the persuasion of others, and make their own choices about whether to enter a contract. In undue influence cases,

however, this normal expectation is not realistic. Undue influence cases involve people who, though they have capacity to enter a contract, are in a position of particular vulnerability in relationship to the other party to the contract. This relationship can be one of trust and confidence, in which the person being influenced justifiably believes that the other party is looking out for his interests, or at least that he would not do anything contrary to his welfare. Examples of such relationships would include parent and child, husband and wife, or lawyer and client.

The relationship also can be one in which one of the parties holds dominant psychological power that is not derived from a confidential relationship. For example, Royce, an elderly man, is dependent on his housekeeper, Smith, to care for him. Smith persuades Royce to withdraw most of his life savings from the bank and make an interest-free loan to her. If the persuasion Smith used was unfair, the transaction could be avoided because of undue influence.

Unfair Persuasion The mere existence of a close or dependent relationship between the parties that results in economic advantage to one of them is not sufficient for undue influence. It must also appear that the weaker person entered the contract because he was subjected to unfair methods of persuasion. In determining this, a court will look at all of the surrounding facts and circumstances. Was the person isolated and hurried into the contract, or did he have access to outsiders for advice and time to consider his alternatives? Was the contract he entered a reasonably fair one that he might have entered voluntarily, or was it so lopsided and unfair that one could infer that the person probably would not have entered it unless he had been unduly influenced by the other party? In *Odorizzi v. Bloomfield School District*, which follows, the court discusses the factors to be considered in determining whether the line between permissible and impermissible persuasion has been crossed.

---

[13] *Restatement (Second) of Contracts* § 177.

ODORIZZI v. BLOOMFIELD SCHOOL DISTRICT

54 Cal. Rptr. 533 (Cal. Dist. Ct. 1966)

Donald Odorizzi was an elementary school teacher employed by the Bloomfield School District. He was arrested on criminal charges of homosexual activity. After having been arrested, questioned by police, booked, and released on bail, and going 40 hours without sleep, he was visited in his home by the superintendent of the school district and the principal of his school. They told him that they were trying to help him and that they had his best interests at heart. They advised him to resign immediately, stating that there was no time to consult an attorney. They said that if he did not resign immediately, the district would dismiss him and publicize the proceedings, but that, if he resigned at once, the incident would not be publicized and would not jeopardize his chances of securing employment as a teacher elsewhere. Odorizzi gave them a written letter of resignation, which they accepted.

The criminal charges against Odorizzi were later dismissed, and he sought to resume his employment with the district. When the district refused to reinstate him, he attempted to rescind his letter of resignation on several grounds, including undue influence. (He also alleged duress, but the facts of his case did not constitute duress under California law.) His complaint was dismissed, and he appealed.

Fleming, Justice.   In essence, undue influence involves the use of excessive pressure applied by a dominant subject to a servient object. In combination, the elements of undue susceptibility in the servient person and excessive pressure by the dominating person make the latter's influence undue. Undue susceptibility may consist of weakness which need not be longlasting nor wholly incapacitating, but may be merely a lack of full vigor due to age, physical condition, emotional anguish, or a combination of such factors. In the present case, Odorizzi has pleaded that such weakness at the time he signed his resignation prevented him from freely and competently applying his judgment to the problem before him. He declares he was under severe mental and emotional strain at the time. It is possible that exhaustion and emotional turmoil may incapacitate a person from exercising his judgment.

Overpersuasion is generally accompanied by certain characteristics which tend to create a pattern. The pattern usually involves several of the following elements: (1) discussion of the transaction at an unusual or inappropriate time, (2) consummation of the transaction in an unusual place, (3) insistent demand that the business be finished at once, (4) extreme emphasis on untoward consequences of delay, (5) the use of multiple persuaders by the dominant side against a single servient party, (6) absence of third-party advisers to the servient party, (7) statements that there is no time to consult financial advisers or attorneys.

The difference between legitimate persuasion and excessive pressure rests to a considerable extent in the manner in which the parties go about their business. For example, if a day or two after Odorizzi's release on bail the superintendent of the school district had called him into his office during business hours and directed his attention to those provisions of the Education Code compelling his leave of absence and authorizing his suspension on the filing of written charges, had told him that the district contemplated filing written charges against him, had pointed out the alternative of resignation available to him, had informed him he was free to consult counsel or any adviser he wished and to consider the matter overnight and return with his decision the next day, it is extremely unlikely that any complaint about the use of excessive pressure could ever have been made against the school district. Rather, the representatives of the school board undertook to achieve their objective by overpersuasion and imposition to secure Odorizzi's signature but not his consent to his resignation through a high-pressure carrot-and-stick technique. Odorizzi has stated sufficient facts to put in issue the question whether his free will had been overborne by the district at a time when he was unable to function in a normal manner.

Judgment reversed in favor of Odorizzi.

CONCEPT REVIEW

WRONGFUL PRESSURE IN THE BARGAINING PROCESS

	Duress	Undue Influence
Nature of Pressure	Coercion	Unfair persuasion of susceptible individual
Elements	1. Contract induced by improper threat 2. Threat leaves party no reasonable alternative but to enter or modify contract	1. Relationship of trust and confidence or dominance 2. Unfair persuasion

ETHICAL AND PUBLIC POLICY CONCERNS

1. You read that modern contract law has expanded the circumstances under which a contracting party has the duty to disclose facts material to the contract. Keep in mind that the facts that he is required to disclose would almost always harm his bargaining position—otherwise he would have been only too happy to have volunteered the information. What are some ethical and public policy justifications for requiring an individual to volunteer information that is contrary to his interests?

2. Do you think the legal rules applied today regarding misrepresentation and duress encourage a higher standard of ethical dealing than did the legal rules applicable under classical contract law? Why or why not?

3. In this chapter you learned a few of the circumstances under which a contracting party owes a higher duty of conduct to someone with whom he is in a relationship of trust and confidence than he would owe to individuals with whom he stood in an arm's-length relationship. What is the justification for requiring a higher standard of ethical dealing in such relationships? Would you favor the law's imposing the same high standards of conduct in relation to the rest of the world? Why or why not?

SUMMARY

The doctrines discussed in this chapter involve situations in which people have the ability to avoid contractual obligations because their consent was either based on a distorted impression of important facts or extorted through unscrupulous means. Generally, contracts induced by misrepresentation, fraud, mistake, duress, or undue influence are voidable. To take advantage of this right to avoid a contract, the complaining party must

disaffirm the contract promptly and unequivocally. If he does not, he will be deemed to have ratified the contract, the effect of that is to surrender his right to avoid the contract.

Misrepresentation is an assertion about a fact material to a contract that is not in accordance with the truth and upon which the other party justifiably relies. Misrepresentation can be either innocent or fraudulent, depending on the knowledge and intent of the person making the misrepresentation. Fraud is misrepresentation knowingly made (*scienter*) with intent to deceive. Fraud may lead to either rescission or liability for the tort of deceit. The remedy for innocent misrepresentation is rescission.

A person seeking to prove misrepresentation must prove that there had been an untrue assertion of past or existing fact. Concealment of a material fact is the equivalent of an assertion of fact. Although traditional law normally held that a person's mere silence was not misrepresentation, modern law has created duties of disclosure in a broadening range of situations. In such a situation, nondisclosure can be the equivalent of an assertion of fact. Although statements of opinion, especially those classified as "sales talk" or "puffing," may not be considered an assertion of fact on which a person is justified in relying, modern contract law has developed a variety of situations in which reliance on a statement of opinion could permit a party to avoid a contract.

The untrue assertion must be either fraudulent or material. The person seeking a remedy for fraud or misrepresentation must have relied on the assertion, and his reliance must have been reasonable. Modern contract law has reduced the responsibility of the relying party to investigate the truth of assertions made to him. Under modern law, his fault in failing to discover the truth will not prevent rescission unless he failed to comply with the duty of good faith and with reasonable standards of commercial dealing. To recover damages for fraud, the plaintiff must be able to prove economic loss resulting from the fraud.

Mistake is an erroneous belief about some fact that exists at the time of formation of the contract. Mistake must be distinguished from ignorance, limited knowledge, or poor judgment. One who enters a contract knowing that he is ignorant or has limited knowledge about a material fact relating to the contract cannot later escape the contract by claiming mistake. However, there are circumstances under which the courts will relieve a party of a contractual obligation on the ground of mistake. In determining whether to grant relief in the form of rescission or reformation, courts distinguish between mutual mistakes and unilateral mistakes. If both parties are mistaken about a material fact (mutual mistake), courts will allow avoidance of the contract if the mistake relates to a fact that was a basic assumption on which the contract was made, the fact was material, and the person adversely affected by the mistake does not bear the risk of the mistake. If only one of the parties is mistaken (unilateral mistake), the person seeking avoidance must prove, *in addition to* the elements of mutual mistake, that the consequences of the mistake are such that it would be unconscionable to enforce the contract *or* that the other party caused or had reason to know about his mistake.

Though courts have often said that no relief will be granted where the mistake flows from a party's own negligence, in practice, they have granted rescission or reformation in cases involving some negligence on the part of mistaken parties. Mistakes in drafting documents will be corrected through the remedy of reformation.

Duress is the exertion of wrongful coercion that induces another person to enter a contract. To constitute duress, the threat must be one that the law considers improper. Threats to commit a tort or a crime, file an unfounded criminal or civil lawsuit, or breach a contract without justification are all considered to be improper and can be the basis for a claim of duress. Sometimes, threatening to do an act that one has the right to do can be considered improper if the threat is made in bad faith, for an ulterior motive. The degree of coercion must have been such that it left the wronged party no reasonable alternative but to consent to the contract. In recent decades, courts have been much more willing to recognize threats to economic interests as coercive.

Undue influence is unfair persuasion of a person by one who stands in a relationship of trust and confidence or domination with that person. If such a relationship exists between the parties and the stronger one has used his position to effect a transaction by which he benefits at the expense of the weaker one, the courts will hold the transaction voidable on the ground of undue influence.

PROBLEM CASES

1. King Chevrolet provided a 1982 Chevrolet Cavalier to one of its salesmen, Stein. During the eight months Stein drove the car, it was repaired or adjusted 10 times. There were repairs to the carburetor, choke, speedometer, door moldings, seat belt buzzer alarm, and spark plugs as well as a complete paint job. Of the 36 demonstrators Stein had driven over the years as a car salesman, this was the worst. Stein finally complained to the service department about the car and asked Lewis, King Chevrolet's sales manager, if he could have another demonstrator because his car was so unreliable. Not long afterward, Muzelak, who had purchased her previous car from Lewis, contacted Lewis about buying a new car. Lewis told her that the "right car for her" was the 1982 Chevrolet Cavalier demonstrator that Stein had used. Lewis did tell Muzelak that the car was a demonstrator, but he did not mention any of the previous repair problems with the car. (Stein later testified that Lewis told him it took someone with his sales ability to "get rid of" that car.) Muzelak bought the car. Over the course of the next eight months, Muzelak's car was in King Chevrolet's service department for repairs 13 times. Some of the problems were never corrected. The car was so unreliable that Muzelak did not drive it after the first eight months of use. Does Muzelak have grounds for an action for fraud? *YES· p266-7 NON DISC GOOD-FAITH*

2. On May 17, Cobaugh was playing in the East End Open Golf Tournament. When he arrived at the ninth tee, he found a new Chevrolet Beretta, together with signs which proclaimed: "HOLE-IN-ONE Wins this 1988 Chevrolet Beretta GT Courtesy of KLICK-LEWIS Buick Chevy Pontiac $49.00 OVER FACTORY INVOICE in Palmyra." Cobaugh aced the ninth hole and attempted to claim his prize. Klick-Lewis refused to deliver the car, however. Klick-Lewis had offered the car as a prize for a charity golf tournament sponsored by the Hershey-Palmyra Sertoma Club two days earlier and had neglected to remove the car and signs prior to Cobaugh's hole-in-one. Cobaugh sued to compel delivery of the car. Would the doctrine of mistake provide a ground for Klick-Lewis to avoid the contract? *NO! Cobaugh get the car/ Yes, unilateral mistake*

3. West Branch Land Co. owned a tract of land, which it listed for sale. The listing that was published in the local multiple-listing service listing sheet and distributed to all subscribing real estate agencies described the property as being "zoned multi for 35 townhouses" when in fact it was really zoned for only 30. Acleson, a licensed real estate broker, received a copy of the listing and, after calculating the costs per unit on the basis of 35 units, submitted an offer to purchase the property. The parties ultimately contracted for the sale of the property for $65,000. The final contract made no mention of the acreage of the land or of its zoning status. Acleson could have determined the true acreage and zoning status by checking the plat map that was available at the local city planner's office. Almost two years after the sale, Acleson learned that the property was really zoned for only 30 units. Will Acleson's failure to investigate the zoning of the land prevent him from obtaining a remedy for misrepresentation or fraud? *No, He's not responsible for checking (ACKLESON)*

4. For many years, Briggs had been Smoker's attorney. In 1970, Smoker executed a will that Briggs had prepared. The will named Briggs as attorney for the estate and provided for payment of $1,000 to Briggs as well as payment of all of Briggs's son's college and graduate educational expenses. Six years later, in November of 1976, Smoker signed documents again prepared by Briggs. In these documents, she stated that she wanted Briggs to be appointed as her guardian if she should need one, agreed to pay Briggs $10,000 for legal services and "kindnesses" that he had rendered to her in the past and might render her until her death, and executed a check to pay for those services. At the time, Smoker was a diabetic and suffered periods of blackouts when she did not know what she was doing. Shortly thereafter, she was hospitalized for insulin imbalance and Briggs had himself appointed as Smoker's guardian. When her physical condition improved, she stated that she had no memory of the documents she had signed in November and sought to rescind them on the ground of undue influence. Will she be successful? *Unfair persuasion* *YES! p280.*

5. Mullan had been a teacher at Bishop Moore School for 25 years. He had a written employment contract that covered the academic year 1986–87 and that permitted termination during that time only for good cause as described in the contract. In the fall of 1986, Mullan's principal, Massaro, told Mullan that he was being terminated because of an accusation that he had hit a student while disciplining him. When Mullan protested, Massaro told him that he (Mullan) could resign with compensation or be fired without being paid, but that

p277

either way, Mullan was "gone." Massaro presented Mullan with a typed resignation, which Mullan signed. Mullan denied hitting the student. He filed suit in which he claimed that his resignation was procured by duress. Are the elements of duress present here?

6. Boskett, a part-time coin dealer, paid $450 for a dime purportedly minted in 1916 at Denver and two additional coins of relatively small value. After carefully examining the dime, Beachcomber Coins, a retail coin dealer, bought the coin from Boskett for $500. Beachcomber then received an offer from a third party to purchase the dime for $700, subject to certification of its genuineness from the American Numismatic Society. That organization labeled the coin a counterfeit. Can Beachcomber rescind the contract with Boskett on the ground of mistake? *No! IN MISTAKE! MAYBE on MISREP*

7. Eikill and Schilling owned a tract of land, which they listed for sale. The listing agreement stated that the property was zoned M-1 (industrial). Newspaper advertisements described the property as commercial property. Gartner expressed his interest in buying the land for investment or speculation. He asked Eikill and Schilling's real estate agent how the property was zoned, and the agent responded that it was zoned M-1, industrial, which was commercial, or "better than commercial." Gartner did not ask specifically whether the property was available for development, and the real estate agent made no representation about that. In fact, a rezoning decision by the City Council some years before Eikill and Schilling bought the land had imposed a restriction allowing only one building ever to be built on the land. The one permitted building had been built years before the land in question was sold to Eikill and Schilling. Thus, while it was true that the land was zoned M-1, it could not be used for any commercial or industrial purpose because no additional structure could be built on the property. Eikill, Schilling, and Gartner were all completely unaware of this restriction. Gartner contracted to purchase the land for $40,000. He learned of the one-building restriction a year later. Gartner then sent Eikill and Schilling a letter demanding cancellation of the sale. Does he have the right to avoid the contract on the ground of mutual mistake? *YES!*

8. Robert and Wendy Pfister asked Foster & Marshall, a stock brokerage firm, to evaluate some stocks that they owned. One of these stocks was 100 shares of Tracor Computing Corporation. The stock was no longer traded on the New York Stock Exchange. The Pfisters did not know the value of the stock, but they believed it to be of little value. They were surprised when Foster & Marshall told them that the stock was trading at $49.50 under its new name, Continuum Co., Inc., so that the value of the Pfisters' stock was $4,950. They asked Foster & Marshall to recheck the figures and brought their stock certificates in for verification. Based on Foster & Marshall's reassurances that they owned 100 shares of Continuum and that these were worth $4,950, the Pfisters sold the stock to Foster & Marshall. As a result of receiving this money for the stock, the Pfisters made a commitment to build a new home, which before the sale had been a "borderline decision." A year after the transaction, Foster & Marshall discovered that the Tracor Computing stock had been exchanged for Continuum stock at a 10-to-1 ratio and that the Pfisters had owned only 10 shares of Continuum. Foster & Marshall claimed relief under the doctrine of mistake and sued the Pfisters to recover the $4,466.25 it had overpaid them. Will Foster & Marshall win? *No. Prof. Borelick of Montana*

9. Reilly, who was interested in purchasing purebred Arabian horses of the Egyptian strain, approached Forbis, who owned and operated a breeding farm. Forbis had been in the business of breeding Arabian horses for 25 years and had published several books and numerous magazine articles on Arabian horses. Reilly visited Forbis's farm to examine a broodmare called Il Shirin. Il Shirin had produced one colt previously and was at that time in foal with another. During this visit, Forbis allegedly stated that Il Shirin was very reasonably priced and that she was "a good mare to start a breeding program with." Reilly bought Il Shirin for $30,000. After the sale, Il Shirin lost the foal she was carrying and despite numerous attempts to breed her, she never conceived again. Reilly sues Forbis for rescission and damages on the ground of fraud. What result? *No Fraud! Can't Prove!*

10. Wurtz owned a hotel, which Fleishman wanted to purchase. For tax reasons, Wurtz wanted to exchange the property for real estate rather than cash. After long negotiations, they agreed that Fleishman would buy a McDonald's restaurant in New Mexico and a warehouse in Wisconsin to exchange for Wurtz's hotel. Fleishman made commitments to purchase these properties and spent substantial sums for architectural studies, title investigation, and legal fees related to the hotel. The night before the closing, Wurtz threatened to back out of the deal unless Fleishman agreed to pay him $50,000 extra. Fleishman feared bankruptcy if the deal fell through and offered Wurtz stock worth $47,000. After the closing, Fleishman refused to transfer the promised stock, however, claiming economic duress. Wurtz sued to get the stock. Will Wurtz win? *No! Wurtz will not win*

11. The Mancinis were interested in buying the Morrows' house. The first time they inspected the house, they noticed a musty odor in the basement. However, they could not see any water stains on either the floor or walls of the basement because most of the floor was covered by a large area rug. There also were eight large posters on the basement walls, and numerous large boxes of ceiling tiles were lined along the perimeter of the basement floor. They inspected the garage and found it to be in a cluttered condition. In addition, a paneled wall was obscured by pool equipment hung on the wall and access was blocked by a work bench. The next day, the Mancinis signed a contract to buy the house. They asked several times to inspect it again, but were only permitted one further inspection before the final consummation of the sale. They did not notice anything new at this inspection. After buying the house, however, the Mancinis soon discovered that the basement had had severe water damage, that it became inundated by six inches of water following a normal rainfall, and that the plywood paneling on the wall of the garage concealed a cracked and bulging wall that would have alerted the buyers to a structural defect present there. The Mancinis claim that the Morrows committed fraud. Did they? *Maybe Fraud but misrepresentation defamatory*

CHAPTER 14

CAPACITY TO CONTRACT

INTRODUCTION

One of the major justifications for enforcing a contract is that the parties *voluntarily consented* to be bound by it. It follows, then, that a person must have the *ability* to give consent before he can be legally bound to an agreement. For truly voluntary agreements to exist, this ability to give consent must involve more than the mere physical ability to say yes or shake hands or sign one's name. Rather, the person's maturity and mental ability must be such that it is fair to presume that he is capable of representing his own interests effectively. This concept is embodied in the legal term **capacity.**

Capacity means the ability to incur legal obligations and acquire legal rights. Today, the primary classes of people who are considered to lack capacity are minors (who, in legal terms, are known as *infants*), persons suffering from mental illnesses or defects, and intoxicated persons.[1] Contract law gives them the right to *avoid* (escape) contracts that they enter during incapacity. This rule provides a means of protecting people who, because of mental impairment, intoxication, or youth and inexperience, are disadvantaged in the normal give and take of the bargaining process.

---

[1] In times past, married women, convicts, and aliens were also among the classes of persons who lacked capacity to contract. These limitations on capacity have been removed by statute and court rule, however.

Usually, lack of capacity to contract comes up in court in one of two ways. In some cases, it is asserted by a plaintiff as the basis of a lawsuit for the money or other benefits that he gave the other party under their contract. In others, it arises as a defense to the enforcement of a contract when the defendant is the party who lacked capacity. The responsibility for alleging and proving incapacity is placed on the person who bases his claim or defense on his lack of capacity.

Degrees of Capacity

There are varying degrees of contractual capacity. It might be helpful to visualize capacity on a continuum like the one shown in Figure 1. The validity of a contract will depend on the degree to which the contracting parties have capacity to contract. At one end of the continuum, both parties have full capacity to contract. Provided that the other requirements of a valid contract are met, the contract will be valid. At the other end of the continuum, one or more of the parties completely lacks capacity to contract because at the time the agreement was made either (1) a court had already **adjudicated** (adjudged or decreed) him to be mentally incompetent or (2) he was so impaired that he could not even manifest assent (for example, he was comatose or unconscious). In such a case, the contract is considered to be *void*. In cases in the middle, in which one or more of the parties

287

FIGURE 1   Capacity to Contract

Full Capacity Both Parties Have Capacity	Partial Capacity One or Both Parties a Minor, Mentally Impaired, or Intoxicated	No Capacity One or Both Parties Adjudicated Incompetent or Unable to Manifest Assent
Contract Valid	Contract Voidable	Contract Void

was younger than the age of majority, mentally incapacitated (but had not yet been adjudicated incompetent at the time of contracting), or intoxicated, the parties are considered to have at least partial capacity. In these cases, the contracts are **voidable.** They may enter a contract and enforce it if they wish, but they also have the right to avoid the contract.

MINORS' CONTRACTS

Minor's Right to Disaffirm

Courts have long recognized that minors are in a vulnerable position in their dealings with adults. Courts granted minors the right to avoid contracts as a means of protecting against their own improvidence and against overreaching by adults. The exercise of this right to avoid a contract is called **disaffirmance.** The right to disaffirm is personal to the minor. That is, only the minor or a legal representative such as a guardian may disaffirm the contract. No formal act or written statement is required to make a valid disaffirmance. Any words or acts that effectively communicate the minor's desire to cancel the contract can constitute disaffirmance.

If, on the other hand, the minor wishes to enforce the contract instead of disaffirming it, the adult party must perform. You can see that the minor's right to disaffirm puts any adult contracting with a minor in an undesirable position: He is bound on the contract unless it is to the minor's advantage to disaffirm it. The right to disaffirm has the effect of discouraging adults from dealing with minors.

Exceptions to the Minor's Right to Disaffirm   Not every contract involving a minor is voidable, however. State law often creates statutory exceptions to the mi-

nor's right to disaffirm. These statutes prevent minors from disaffirming such transactions as marriage, agreements to support their children, educational loans, life and medical insurance contracts, contracts for transportation by common carriers, and certain types of contracts approved by a court (such as contracts to employ a child actor).

Period of Minority

At common law, the age of majority was 21. However, the ratification in 1971 of the 26th Amendment to the Constitution giving 18-year-olds the right to vote stimulated a trend toward reducing the age of majority. The age of majority has been lowered by 49 states. In almost all of these states, the age of majority for contracting purposes is now 18.

Emancipation

Emancipation is the termination of a parent's right to control a child and receive services and wages from him. There are no formal requirements for emancipation. It can occur by the parent's express or implied consent or by the occurrence of some events such as the marriage of the child. In most states, the mere fact that a minor is emancipated does *not* give him capacity to contract. A person younger than the legal age of majority is generally held to lack capacity to enter a contract, even if he is married and employed full-time.

Time of Disaffirmance

Contracts entered during minority that affect title to *real estate* cannot be disaffirmed until majority. This rule is apparently based on the special importance of real estate and on the need to protect a minor from improvidently

FIGURE 2   Timeline Showing Effect of Ratification

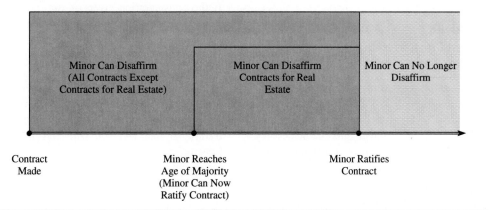

disaffirming a transaction (such as a mortgage or conveyance) involving real estate. All other contracts entered during minority may be disaffirmed as soon as the contract is formed. The minor's power to avoid his contracts does not end on the day he reaches the age of majority. It continues for a period of time after he reaches majority.

How long after reaching majority does a person retain the right to disaffirm the contracts he made while a minor? A few states have statutes that prescribe a definite time limit on the power of avoidance. In Oklahoma, for example, a person who wishes to disaffirm a contract must do so within one year after reaching majority.[2] In most states, however, there is no set limit on the time during which a person may disaffirm after reaching majority. In determining whether a person has the right to disaffirm, a major factor that courts consider is whether the adult has rendered performance under the contract or relied on the contract. If the adult has relied on the contract or has given something of value to the minor, the minor must disaffirm within a reasonable time after reaching majority. If he delays longer than a period of time that is considered to be reasonable under the circumstances, he will run the risk of **ratifying** (affirming) the contract. (The concept and consequences of ratification are discussed in the next section.) If the adult has neither performed nor relied on the contract, however, the former minor is likely to be accorded a longer period of time in which to disaffirm, sometimes even years after he has reached majority.

---

[2] Okla. Stat. Ann. tit. 15 sec. 18 (1983).

Ratification

Though a person has the right to disaffirm contracts made during minority, this right can be given up after the person reaches the age of majority. When a person who has reached majority indicates that he intends to be bound by a contract that he made while still a minor, he surrenders his right to disaffirm. This act of affirming the contract and surrendering the right to avoid the contract is known as **ratification.** Ratification makes a contract valid from its inception. Because ratification represents the former minor's election to be bound by the contract, he cannot later disaffirm. Ratification can be done effectively only after the minor reaches majority. Otherwise, it would be as voidable as the initial contract. The effect of ratification is illustrated in Figure 2.

There are no formal requirements for ratification. Any of the former minor's words or acts after reaching majority that indicate with reasonable clarity his intent to be bound by the contract are sufficient. Ratification can be *expressed* in an oral or written statement, or, as is more often the case, it can be *implied* by conduct on the part of the former minor. Naturally, ratification is clearest when the former minor has made some express statement of his intent to be bound. Predicting whether a court will determine that a contract has been ratified is a bit more difficult when the only evidence of the alleged ratification is the conduct of the minor. A former minor's acceptance or retention of benefits given by the other party for an unreasonable time after he has reached majority can constitute ratification. Also, a former minor's continued performance of his part of the contract after reaching majority has been held to imply his intent to ratify the contract.

Duty to Return Consideration upon Disaffirmance

If neither party has performed his part of the contract, the parties' relationship will simply be canceled by the disaffirmance. Since neither party has given anything to the other party, no further adjustments are necessary. But what about the situation where, as is often the case, the minor has paid money to the adult and the adult has given property to the minor?

Upon disaffirmance, each party has the duty to return to the other any consideration that the other has given. This means that the minor must return any consideration given to him by the adult that remains in his possession. However, if the minor is unable to return the consideration, most states will still permit him to disaffirm the contract.

The duty to return consideration also means that the minor has the right to recover any consideration he has given to the adult party. He even has the right to recover some property that has been transferred to third parties. One exception to the minor's right to recover property from third parties is found in section 2–403 of the Uniform Commercial Code, however. Under this section, a minor cannot recover *goods* that have been transferred to a good-faith purchaser. For example, Simpson, a minor, sells a 1980 Ford to Mort's Car Lot. Mort's then sells the car to Vane, a good-faith purchaser. If Simpson disaffirmed the contract with Mort's, he would *not* have the right to recover the Ford from Vane.

Must the Disaffirming Minor Make Restitution?: A Split of Authority

If the consideration given by the adult party has been lost, damaged, destroyed, or simply has depreciated in value, is the minor required to make restitution to the adult for the loss? The traditional rule is that the minor who cannot fully return the consideration that was given to him is *not* obligated to pay the adult for the benefits he has received or to compensate the adult for loss or depreciation of the consideration. Most states still follow this traditional rule. (As you will read in the next section, however, a minor's misrepresentation of age can, in some states, make him responsible for reimbursing the other party upon disaffirmance.) The rule that restitution is not required is designed to protect minors by discouraging adults from dealing with them. After all, if an adult knew that he might be able to demand the return of anything that he transferred to a minor, he would have little incentive to refrain from entering into contracts with minors.

The traditional rule can work harsh results for innocent adults who have dealt fairly with minors, however. It strikes many people as unprincipled that a doctrine intended to protect against unfair exploitation of one class of people can be used to unfairly exploit another class of people. As courts sometimes say, the minor's right to disaffirm was designed to be used as a "shield rather than as a sword." For these reasons, a number (although still a minority) of states have rejected the traditional rule. The courts and legislatures of these states have adopted rules that require disaffirming minors to place the adult in *status quo* (the position he was in before the creation of the contract) by reimbursing him for use or depreciation of his property. The following case, *Dodson v. Shrader*, discusses this controversy.

DODSON v. SHRADER

1989 Tenn. App. Lexis 683 (Tenn. Ct. App. 1989)

Joseph Dodson, age 16, bought a 1984 Chevrolet truck from Shrader's Auto Sales for $4,900 cash. At the time, Shrader's did not ask Dodson's age and Dodson did not disclose it. Dodson drove the truck for about eight months when he learned from an auto mechanic that there was a burned valve in the engine. He continued to drive the truck without repair for another month until the engine "blew up" and stopped operating. While parked, the truck was later struck by an unknown automobile and further damaged. Dodson disaffirmed the contract and offered to return the truck and the title to the truck, but Shrader's refused to return Dodson's money. It argued that Dodson should be responsible for paying the difference between the present value of the truck ($500) and the $4,900 purchase price.

Dodson sued to recover his money. The trial court found in his favor and Shrader's appealed.

Todd, Presiding Judge.   Shrader's [insists] that the law of Tennessee ought to be revised to require a minor to restore the consideration in full, that is, to tender the depreciated property and the amount of depreciation in order to rescind a contract, or the recovery of Dodson should be reduced by the difference between the value of the truck when delivered to him and its value when delivered to Shrader's.

Tennessee authorities recognize the general rule that the contract of a minor is voidable. But no Tennessee authority is found which would require a disaffirming minor to return more than the consideration remaining in his possession at the time of disaffirmance. The general policy of the law of infancy is stated in 43 C.J.S., Infants, section 166, pp. 448, as follows: "It is the policy of the law to protect infants against their own mistakes or improvidence, and from designs of others, and to discourage adults from contracting with an infant. A person who deals with an infant does so at his peril. . . ."

Seventeen states unequivocally deny depreciation absent misrepresentation or tort. Minnesota denies depreciation unless the contract is fair, reasonable and provident. Idaho denies use, and Utah denies depreciation by statute. Depreciation is allowed by court opinion in four states and by statute in three states. The distinct weight of authority supports the admittedly harsh rule which penalizes the adult who deals with a minor.

Reason and justice also support the view that any change in the traditional harsh rule should be accomplished by statute rather than by court decision. Aside from the traditional reluctance of the judiciary to legislate, there is the difficulty of effective date and age limitations of a change. Legislation would constitute fair notice to all makers of future contracts as to the law applicable thereto.

Admittedly, it "goes against the grain" to permit a minor who is a few days or weeks short of majority to negotiate and subsequently disaffirm a contract to the severe loss of the other contracting party. The correction of this apparent injustice by a ruling affecting all minors regardless of their tender age would countenance a greater injustice. Courts are ill equipped and have doubtful authority to determine an arbitrary age limit within which the harsh rule should be relaxed. The Legislature is far better equipped and has clear authority to make such a determination. Indeed, the Legislature has already acted to reduce the age of majority from 21 to 18. This court has therefore determined that the traditional harsh rule should not be relaxed by the courts, and that the judgment of the trial court should be affirmed.

Judgment for Dodson affirmed.

Effect of Misrepresentation of Age: No Uniform Rule

It is not unheard of for a minor occasionally to pretend to be older than he is. Many of the normal rules dealing with the minor's right to disaffirm and his duties upon disaffirmance can be affected by a minor's misrepresen- tation of his age.[3] Suppose, for example, that Jones, age 17, wants to lease a car from Acme Auto Rentals, but knows that Acme rents only to people who are at

---

[3] You might want to refer back to the Reality of Consent chapter to review the elements of misrepresentation.

least 18. Jones induces Acme to lease a car to him by showing false identification that represents his age to be 18. Acme relies on the misrepresentation. Jones wrecks the car, attempts to disaffirm the contract, and asks for the return of his money. What is the effect of Jones's misrepresentation?

The answer depends on which state's law applies, because there is no uniform rule regarding misrepresentation of age. The different approaches to the problems fall into four categories:

1. *Traditional rule: Misrepresentation has no effect.* The traditional rule, which is followed in some states, is that a minor's misrepresentation about his age does not affect his right to disaffirm and does not create any obligation to pay for benefits received. The theory behind this rule, which can create severe hardship for innocent adults who rely on minors' misrepresentations of age, is that one who lacks capacity cannot acquire it merely by claiming to be of legal age.

2. *Minor estopped from disaffirming.* Other states take the position that the minor who misrepresents his age will be *estopped* (prevented) from asserting his infancy as a defense. In other words, he will be treated as if he really were of legal age and will be prevented from disaffirming the contract.

3. *Minor liable for tort of deceit.* Some states hold the misrepresenting minor liable for damages for the tort of deceit. The amount of damages in such a case is likely to be the amount of depreciation of the relying party's property.

4. *Disaffirming minor must place adult in status quo.* Still other states condition the minor's right to disaffirm upon his placing the relying party in *status quo.* Even in a state that usually follows the majority rule that disaffirming minors need only return the consideration that remains in their possession, a minor who has misrepresented his age may be required to reimburse the relying adult for use or depreciation of his property. You will see an example of this approach and the estoppel approach in the following case, *Haydocy Pontiac, Inc. v. Lee.*

HAYDOCY PONTIAC, INC. v. LEE
250 N.E.2d 898 (Ohio Ct. App. 1969)

At a time when the age of majority in Ohio was 21, Jennifer Lee, age 20, contracted to buy a 1964 Plymouth Fury for $1,552 from Haydocy Pontiac. Lee represented herself to be 21 when entering the contract. She paid for the car by trading in another car worth $150 and financing the balance. Immediately following delivery of the car to her, Lee permitted one John Roberts to take possession of it. Roberts delivered the car to someone else, and it was never recovered. Lee failed to make payments on the car, and Haydocy Pontiac sued her to recover the car or the amount due on the contract. Lee repudiated the contract on the ground that she was a minor at the time of purchase. The trial court found in favor of Lee, and Haydocy Pontiac appealed.

Strausbaugh, Judge. At a time when we see young persons between 18 and 21 years of age demanding and assuming more responsibilities in their daily lives; when we see such persons emancipated, married, and raising families; when we see such persons charged with the responsibility for committing crimes; when we see such persons being sued in tort claims for acts of negligence; when we see such persons subject to military service; when we see such persons engaged in business and acting in almost all other respects as an adult, it seems timely to reexamine the case law pertaining to contractual rights and responsibilities of infants to see if the law as pronounced and applied by the courts should be redefined.

To allow infants to avoid a transaction without being required to restore the consideration received where the infant has used or otherwise disposed of it causes hardship on the other party. We hold that where the consideration received by the infant cannot be returned upon disaffirmance because it has been disposed of, the infant must account for the value of it, not in excess of the purchase price, where the other party is free from any fraud or bad faith and where the contract has been induced by a false representation of the age of the infant. Under this factual situation, the infant is estopped from pleading infancy as a defense where the contract has been induced by a false representation that the infant was of age.

The necessity of returning the consideration as a prerequisite to obtaining equitable relief is still clearer where the infant misrepresents age and perpetrated an actual fraud on the other party. The common law has bestowed upon the infant the privilege of disaffirming his contracts in conservation of his rights and interests. Where the infant, 20 years of age, through falsehood and deceit enters into a contract with another who enters therein in honesty and good faith and, thereafter the infant seeks to disaffirm the contract without tendering back the consideration, no right or interest of the infant exists which needs protection. The privilege given the infant thereupon becomes a weapon of injustice.

Judgment reversed in favor of Haydocy Pontiac.

Minors' Obligation to Pay Reasonable Value of Necessaries

Though the law regarding minors' contracts is designed to discourage adults from dealing with (and possibly taking advantage of) minors, it would be undesirable for the law to discourage adults from selling minors the items that they need for basic survival. For this reason, disaffirming minors are required to pay the reasonable value of items that have been furnished to them that are classified as "necessaries." A necessary is something that is essential for the minor's continued existence and general welfare that has not been provided by the minor's parents or guardian. Examples of necessaries include food, clothing, shelter, medical care, tools of the minor's trade, and basic educational or vocational training.

A minor's liability for necessaries supplied to him is **quasi-contractual.** That is, the minor is liable for the *reasonable value* of the necessaries that she actually receives. She is not liable for the entire price agreed upon if that price exceeds the actual value of the necessaries, and she is not liable for necessaries that she contracted for but did not receive. For example, Joy Jones, a minor, signs a one-year lease for an apartment in Mountain Park at a rent of $300 per month. After living in the apartment for three months, Joy breaks her lease and moves out. Because she is a minor, Joy has the right to disaffirm the lease. If shelter is a necessary in this case, however, she must pay the reasonable value of what she has actually received—three months' rent. If she can establish that the actual value of what she has received is less than $300 per month, she will be bound to pay only that lesser amount. Furthermore, she will not be obligated to pay for the remaining nine months' rent, because she has not received any benefits from the remainder of the lease.

Whether a given item is considered a necessary depends on the facts of a particular case. The minor's age, station in life, and personal circumstances are all relevant to this issue. As is emphasized in the *Webster Street Partnership* case, which follows, an item sold to a minor is not considered a necessary if the minor's parent or guardian has already supplied him with similar items. For this reason, the range of items that will be considered necessaries is broader for married minors and other emancipated minors than it is for unemancipated minors.

WEBSTER STREET PARTNERSHIP v. SHERIDAN

368 N.W.2d 439 (S. Ct. Neb. 1985)

Webster Street owns real estate in Omaha, Nebraska. On September 18, 1982, Webster Street entered into a written contract to lease an apartment to Matthew Sheridan and Pat Wilwerding for one year at a rental of $250 per month. Although Webster Street did not know this, both Sheridan and Wilwerding were younger than the age of majority (which was 19) when the lease was signed.

Sheridan and Wilwerding paid $150 as a security deposit and rent for the remainder of September and the month of October, for a total of $500. They failed to pay their November rent on time, however, and Webster Street notified them that they would be required to move out unless they paid immediately. Unable to pay rent, Sheridan and Wilwerding moved out of the apartment on November 12. Webster Street later demanded that they pay the expenses it incurred in attempting to rerent the property, rent for the months of November and December (apparently the two months it took to find a new tenant), and assorted damages and fees, amounting to $630.94. Sheridan and Wilwerding refused to pay any of the amount demanded on the ground of minority and demanded the return of their security deposit. Webster Street then filed this lawsuit. The district court found that the apartment was a necessary and that Sheridan and Wilwerding were liable for the 12 days in November in which they had actually possessed the apartment without paying rent, but that they were entitled to the return of their security deposit. Webster Street appealed from this ruling.

Krivosha, Chief Justice.   The privilege of infancy will not enable an infant to escape liability under all circumstances. For example, it is well established that an infant is liable for the value of necessaries furnished him. Just what are necessaries, however, has no exact definition. The term is flexible and varies according to the facts of each individual case. A number of factors must be considered before a court can conclude whether a particular product or service is a necessary. The articles must be useful and suitable. To be necessaries the articles must supply the infant's personal needs, either those of his body or those of his mind. However, the term "necessaries" is not confined to merely such things as are required for bare subsistence. What may be considered necessary for one infant may not be necessaries for another infant whose state is different as to rank, social position, fortune, health, or other circumstances. To enable an infant to contract for articles as necessaries, he must have been in actual need of them, and obliged to procure them for himself. They are not necessaries as to him, however necessary they may be in their nature, if he was already supplied with sufficient articles of the kind, or if he had a parent or guardian who was able and willing to supply them. The burden of proof is on the plaintiff to show that the infant was destitute of the articles and had no way of procuring them except by his own contract.

The undisputed testimony is that both tenants were living away from home, apparently with the understanding that they could return home at any time. It would appear that neither Sheridan nor Wilwerding was in need of shelter but, rather, had chosen to voluntarily leave home, with the understanding that they could return whenever they desired. One may at first blush believe that such a rule is unfair. Yet, on further consideration, the wisdom of such a rule is apparent. If landlords may not contract with minors, except at their peril, they may refuse to do so. In that event, minors who voluntarily leave home but who are free to return will be compelled to return to their parents' home—a result which is desirable. We therefore hold that the district court erred in finding that the apartment was a necessary.

Because the rental of the apartment was not a necessary, the minors had the right to avoid the contract, either during their minority or within a reasonable time after reaching their majority. Disaffirmance by an infant completely puts an end to the contract's existence both as to him and as to the adult with whom he contracted. Because the parties then stand as if no contract had ever existed, the infant can recover payments made to the adult, and the adult is entitled to the return of whatever was received by the infant.

The record shows that Wilwerding clearly disaffirmed the contract during his minority. Moreover, when Webster Street ordered the minors out for failure to pay rent and they vacated the premises, Sheridan likewise disaffirmed the contract. The record indicates that Sheridan reached majority on November 5. To suggest that a lapse of 7 days was not disaffirmance within a reasonable time would be foolish. Once disaffirmed, no contract existed between the parties and the minors were entitled to recover all of the moneys which they paid and to be relieved of any further obligation under the contract. The judgment of the district court is therefore reversed and the cause remanded with directions to vacate the judgment in favor of Webster Street and to enter a judgment in favor of Matthew Sheridan and Pat Wilwerding in the amount of $500, representing September rent in the amount of $100, October rent in the amount of $250, and the security deposit in the amount of $150.

Judgment reversed in favor of Sheridan and Wilwerding.

CAPACITY OF MENTALLY IMPAIRED PERSONS

Theory of Incapacity

Like minors, people who suffer from a mental illness or defect are at a disadvantage in their ability to protect their own interests in the bargaining process. Contract law makes their contracts either void or voidable to protect them from the results of their own impaired perceptions and judgment and from others who might take advantage of them.

Test for Mental Incapacity

Incapacity on grounds of mental illness or defect, often referred to in cases and texts as "insanity," encompasses a broad range of causes of impaired mental functioning, such as mental illness, brain damage, mental retardation, or senility. The mere fact that a person suffers from some mental illness or defect does not necessarily mean that he lacks capacity to contract, however. He could still have full capacity unless the defect or illness affects the particular transaction in question. For example, a person could have periodic psychotic episodes, yet enter a binding contract during a lucid period.

The usual test for mental incapacity is a *cognitive* one; that is, courts ask whether the person had sufficient mental capacity to understand the nature and effect of the contract. Some courts have criticized the traditional test as unscientific because it does not take into account the fact that a person suffering from a mental illness or defect might be unable to *control* his conduct. The *Restatement (Second) of Contracts* provides that a person's contracts are voidable if he is unable to *act* in a reasonable manner in relation to the transaction and the other party has reason to know of his condition.[4] Where the other party has reason to know of the condition of the mentally impaired person, the *Restatement* standard would provide protection to people who understood the transaction but, because of some mental defect or illness, were unable to exercise appropriate judgment or to control their conduct effectively.

The Effect of Incapacity Caused by Mental Impairment

The contracts of people who are suffering from a mental defect at the time of contracting are usually considered to be *voidable*. In some situations, however, severe mental or physical impairment may prevent a person from even being able to manifest consent. In such a case, no contract could be formed.

As mentioned at the beginning of this chapter, contract law makes a distinction between a contract involving a person who has been **adjudicated** (judged by a court) incompetent at the time the contract was made and a contract involving a person who was suffering from some mental impairment at the time the contract was entered but whose incompetency was not established until *after* the contract was formed. If a person is under guardianship at the time the contract is formed—that is, if a court has found a person mentally incompetent after holding a hearing on his mental competency and has appointed a guardian for him—the contract is considered **void.** On the other hand, if, *after* a contract has been formed, a court finds that the person who manifested consent lacked capacity on grounds of mental illness or defect, the contract is usually considered **voidable** at the election of the party who lacked capacity (or his guardian or personal representative).

The Right to Disaffirm

If a contract is found to be voidable on the ground of mental impairment, the person who lacked capacity at

---

[4] *Restatement (Second) of Contracts* § 15.

the time the contract was made has the right to disaffirm the contract. A person formerly incapacitated by mental impairment can ratify a contract if he regains his capacity. Thus, if he regains capacity, he must disaffirm the contract unequivocally within a reasonable time, or he will be deemed to have ratified it.

As is true of a disaffirming minor, a person disaffirming on the ground of mental impairment must return any consideration given by the other party that remains in his possession. A person under this type of mental incapacity is liable for the reasonable value of **necessaries** in the same manner as are minors. Must the incapacitated party reimburse the other party for loss, damage, or depreciation of nonnecessaries given to him? This is generally said to depend on whether the contract was basically fair and on whether the other party had reason to be aware of his impairment. If the contract is fair, bargained for in good faith, and the other party had no reasonable cause to know of the incapacity, the contract cannot be disaffirmed unless the other party is placed in *status quo*. However, if the other party had reason to know of the incapacity, the incapacitated party is allowed to disaffirm without placing the other party in *status quo*. This distinction discourages people from attempting to take advantage of mentally impaired people, but it spares those who are dealing in good faith and have no such intent.

CONTRACTS OF INTOXICATED PERSONS

Intoxication and Capacity

Intoxication (either from alcohol or the use of drugs) can deprive a person of capacity to contract. The mere fact that a party to a contract had been drinking when the contract was formed would *not* normally affect his capacity to contract, however. Intoxication is a ground for lack of capacity only when it is so extreme that the person is unable to understand the nature of the business at hand. The *Restatement (Second) of Contracts* further provides that intoxication is a ground for lack of capacity only if *the other party has reason to know* that the affected person is so intoxicated that he cannot understand or act reasonably in relation to the transaction.[5]

The rules governing the capacity of intoxicated persons are very similar to those applied to the capacity of people who are mentally impaired. The basic right to disaffirm contracts made during incapacity, the duties upon disaffirmance, and the possibility of ratification upon regaining capacity are the same for an intoxicated person as for a person under a mental impairment. In practice, however, courts traditionally have been less sympathetic with a person who was intoxicated at the time of contracting than with minors or those suffering from a mental impairment. It is rare for a person to actually escape his contractual obligations on the ground of intoxication. As the following case, *First Bank of Sinai v. Hyland*, demonstrates, a person incapacitated by intoxication at the time of contracting might nevertheless be bound to his contract if he fails to disaffirm in a timely manner.

---

[5] *Restatement (Second) of Contracts* § 16.

FIRST BANK OF SINAI v. HYLAND

399 N.W.2d 894 (S.D. S. Ct. 1987)

Randy Hyland owed money to the First State Bank of Sinai on two promissory notes that had already become due. On October 20, 1981, William Buck, acting for the bank, agreed to extend the time of payment if Randy's father, Mervin, acted as a cosigner. Mervin had executed approximately 60 promissory notes with the bank and was a good customer. A new note was prepared for Mervin's signature. Buck knew that Mervin drank, but later testified that he was unaware of any alcohol-related problems.

Mervin had been drinking heavily from late summer through the early winter of 1981. During this period, his wife and son managed the farm, and Mervin was weak, unconcerned with family and business matters, uncooperative, and uncommunicative. When he was drinking, he spent most of his time at home, in bed. He was involuntarily committed to hospitals twice during this period. He was released from his first commitment on September 19 and again committed on November 20. Between the periods of his commitments, he did transact some business himself, such as paying for farm goods and services, hauling his grain to storage elevators, and making decisions concerning when grain was to be sold.

When Randy brought this note home, Mervin was drunk and in bed. On October 20 or 21, he rose from the bed, walked into the kitchen and signed the note. Later, Randy returned to the bank with the note, which Mervin had properly signed, and added his own signature. The due date on this note was April 20, 1982.

On April 20, the note was unpaid. Buck notified Randy of the overdue note, and on May 5, Randy brought to the bank a blank check signed by Mervin with which the interest on the note was to be paid. Randy filled in the check for the amount of interest owing. No further payments were made on the note, and Randy filed for bankruptcy in June of 1982. After unsuccessfully demanding the note's payment from Mervin, the bank ultimately filed this suit against Mervin. Mervin asserted incapacity on the ground of intoxication, claiming that he had no recollection of seeing the note, discussing it with his son, or signing it. The trial court rendered judgment for Mervin, and the bank appealed.

Henderson, Justice.   Contractual obligations incurred by intoxicated persons may be voidable. Voidable contracts (contracts other than those entered into following a judicial determination of incapacity) may be rescinded by the previously disabled party. However, disaffirmance must be prompt, upon the recovery of the intoxicated party's mental abilities, and upon his notice of the agreement, if he had forgotten it. A delay in rescission which causes prejudice to the other party will extinguish the first party's right to disaffirm.

A voidable contract may also be ratified by the party who had contracted while disabled. Upon ratification, the contract becomes a fully valid legal obligation. Ratification can either be express or implied by conduct. In addition, a failure of a party to disaffirm a contract over a period of time may, by itself, ripen into a ratification, especially if rescission will result in prejudice to the other party.

Mervin received both verbal notice from Randy and written notice from the bank on or about April 27, 1982, that the note was overdue. On May 5, Mervin paid the interest owing with a check which Randy delivered to the bank. This by itself could amount to ratification through conduct. If Mervin wished to avoid the contract, he should have then exercised his right of rescission.

Mervin's failure to rescind, coupled with his apparent ratification, could have jeopardized the bank's chances of ever receiving payment on the note. As we know, Mervin unquestionably was aware of his obligation in late April 1982. If he had disaffirmed then, the bank could have actively pursued Randy and possibly collected part of the debt. By delaying his rescission and by paying the note's back interest, Mervin lulled the bank into a false sense of security that may have hurt it when on June 22, 1982, Randy filed for bankruptcy and was later fully discharged of his obligation on the note.

We conclude that Mervin's obligation on the note was voidable and his subsequent failure to disaffirm and his payment of interest then transformed the voidable contract into one that is fully binding upon him.

Judgment reversed in favor of the bank.

1. You read that the age of majority for contracting purposes is 18 in almost all states today. We all know that maturity at a given age varies greatly from individual to individual. Does it make sense for the law to *presume* that a person is sufficiently mature to be responsible for his agreements merely because he has reached the age of 18? Would public policy be better served if the maturity of contracting parties were determined on a case-by-case basis in the same way that we now determine the capacity of those who are mentally impaired or intoxicated? Why or why not?

2. In *Dodson v. Shrader*, the court held that a minor who disaffirmed a contract was not required to make restitution to the adult party for damage to the adult's property. The court stated that this rule "goes against the grain," but it opined that it is the role of the legislature rather than the court to change the rule. It stated that "[t]he correction of this apparent injustice by a ruling affecting all minors regardless of their tender age would countenance a greater injustice." Should the rule permitting minors to disaffirm without paying for use, damage, or depreciation be changed? Why or why not? Do you agree that it is not the proper role of a court to change this rule? Discuss.

3. In recent years, there has been growing public concern over alcohol and drug abuse. Through legal developments such as vigorous enforcement of drunken driving laws and the imposition of tort liability on the part of alcohol suppliers, the law encourages moderation in the use of alcohol. Yet, the law also makes it possible for a person who is so intoxicated that he does not appreciate the business at hand to escape his contractual obligations. Is this rule about the capacity of intoxicated persons out of step with sound public policy?

SUMMARY

Minors, people suffering from mental illnesses or defects, and intoxicated persons are considered to lack capacity to enter a contract because they are at an inherent disadvantage in their dealings with others. When a contracting party is so impaired that he is unable to manifest assent or where he has been adjudicated (judged by a court to be) incompetent before the time of contracting, the contract is void. Other contracts in which one or more of the parties lacks capacity because of age, mental impairment, or intoxication are considered voidable.

The age of majority in almost all states is 18. A contract formed when a party is younger than the age of majority is voidable at the option of the minor. The minor has the right to avoid his obligations under a contract by disaffirming the contract. In most states, this is true for emancipated minors, too. Contracts for the sale of real estate cannot be disaffirmed until after the former minor reaches majority. A minor may disaffirm all other types of contracts as soon as they are formed. Contracts made during minority can be disaffirmed for a period of time after the former minor has reached majority. Some states specify this period of time in statutes. Generally, however, courts distinguish between contracts in which the adult has performed or relied on the contract and those that are completely executory. In executory contracts, the former minor will be allowed a considerable period of time—possibly years—after reaching majority in which to disaffirm. When the adult has given performance or relied on the contract, however, the minor must disaffirm within a reasonable time after reaching majority. His failure to do so can be considered ratification of the contract.

Once a minor reaches majority, he can ratify a contract in any way that shows his intent to be bound by the contract. Ratification operates as a surrender of the right to avoid the contract. It can be made expressly, in specific words, or impliedly, through conduct of the former minor. When a contract has been ratified, it is treated as valid from its inception and cannot later be disaffirmed.

If the minor disaffirms, however, he must return any consideration given him by the other party that remains in his possession. The majority rule is that the disaffirming minor is entitled to the return of anything he has given the other party and that he does not have to pay the other party for loss or depreciation in value of the consideration given to him by that party. Some states have declined to follow this rule, however, and have designed other rules to promote the fair treatment of innocent adults who have dealt fairly with minors. If the disaffirming minor has purchased something from the other party that is considered to be a *necessary*, the minor must pay the reasonable value of what he has actually received.

A minor's misrepresentation of his age has different results in different states. In some states, misrepresentation of age makes no difference in the minor's rights and obligations. In others, it places an obligation on the minor to put the adult in *status quo* (the position he was in before the contract was formed), makes him liable in tort for deceit, or precludes him from asserting his minority as a claim or defense.

A contract entered into by a person who lacks capacity because of a mental illness or defect is voidable, unless the person was under guardianship at the time the contract was formed. In that case, the contract would be considered void. In determining mental capacity, courts generally ask whether the person was capable of understanding the nature and consequences of the contract. The *Restatement* and some courts permit disaffirmance if a person is unable to act reasonably because of a mental defect or illness and the other party has reason to know of his impairment. Upon disaffirmance, the incapacitated person must return any consideration that remains in his possession. He may be obligated to place the other party in *status quo* if the contract was fair and the other party had no reason to know of his mental impairment. Like the minor, the mentally incapacitated person must pay the reasonable value of necessaries that he has actually received and can, upon obtaining full mental capacity, bind himself to a contract made during incapacity by ratifying it.

Persons who are so intoxicated at the time they enter a contract that they do not understand the nature and consequences of a contract are often treated as lacking capacity to contract. The *Restatement* provides that a contract formed at a time when one of the parties was intoxicated to this extent would be voidable if the other person had reason to know that he was unable to understand the contract or act in a reasonable way in relation to it because of his intoxication. If he wants to avoid the contract, he must disaffirm it within a reasonable time after regaining sobriety, or he may be deemed to have ratified it.

Problem Cases

1. Smith, age 17, purchased a car from Bobby Floars Toyota, signing an agreement to pay the balance of the purchase price in 30 monthly installments. Ten months after he reached majority (which was 18 in that state), Smith voluntarily returned the car to Floars and stopped making payments. At this point, he had made 11 monthly payments, 10 of which were made after his 18th birthday. Floars sold the car at public auction and sued Smith for the remaining debt. Will Smith be required to pay? *YES. Because payed, Ratified contract* *p289*

2. Robertson, while a minor, contracted to borrow money from his father for a college education. His father mortgaged his home and took out loans against his life insurance policies to get some of the money he lent to Robertson, who ultimately graduated from dental school. Two years after Robertson's graduation, his father asked him to begin paying back the amount of $30,000 at $400 per month. Robertson agreed to pay $24,000 at $100 per month. He did this for three years before stopping the payments. His father sued for the balance of the debt. Could Robertson disaffirm the contract? *FATHER RELIEVED, NO because of Ratification at majority* *p289*

3. Green, age 16, contracted to buy a Camaro from Star Chevrolet. Green lived about six miles from school and one mile from his job and used the Camaro to go back and forth to school and work. When he did not have the car, he used a car pool to get to school and work. Several months later, the car became inoperable due to a blown head gasket, and Green gave notice of disaffirmance to Star Chevrolet. Star Chevrolet refused to refund the purchase price, claiming in part that the car was a necessary. Was it? *NO, could get to School, work By car Pool* *p293*

4. In 1983, George Lloyd purchased an annuity and named his daughters by a previous marriage, Jordan and Pitts, as co-beneficiaries. In June of 1985, he executed a will in which he devised property to his daughters but made no provision for his current wife, Olivia Lloyd. Mr. and Mrs. Lloyd were divorced after the execution of the will. In April of 1987, Mr. Lloyd's physician noticed that Lloyd was showing signs of mental instability and chronic dementia. In August of 1987, Mr. and Mrs. Lloyd remarried. That same month, Mrs. Lloyd obtained a change of beneficiary form and Mr. Lloyd executed the form to change the beneficiary of the annuity to Mrs. Lloyd. Mrs. Lloyd later testified that she "couldn't say" that Mr. Lloyd "knew what he was doing on the day he signed the form." His mental condition deteriorated to the point that he was adjudicated mentally incompetent in September of 1987 and a guardian was appointed for him. Is the change of beneficiary form that he executed in August of 1987 valid? *VOIDABLE* *p295*

5. Odem, a minor, contracted for medical services to be provided by Children's Hospital to her infant son. The hospital treated Odem's son, and Odem later disaffirmed the contract. The hospital sued Odem to collect the hospital bill plus the legal fees incurred by the hospital in collecting the bill. Must Odem pay for the medical services? What about the hospital's legal fees? *QUASI- MEDICAL BUT LEGAL* *p293 p296*

6. Ortolere had been a teacher for 40 years when she suffered a nervous breakdown at the age of 60 and went on a leave of absence. She was under the care of a psychiatrist, who diagnosed her illness as involutional psychosis and cerebral arteriosclerosis. Ortolere belonged to a retirement system that gave her the right to certain retirement and death benefits. While still under the care of her psychiatrist, Ortolere wrote a letter to the retirement board stating that she intended to retire and listing eight detailed questions that reflected great understanding of the retirement system and the various alternatives available. Within a few days, she changed her election of retirement benefits, selecting an option that did not make much sense in her situation. She died several months later. Her husband filed suit to disaffirm her second selection of retirement benefits on the ground of mental incapacity. Did Ortolere lack capacity because of mental impairment? *DIDN'T LACK CAPACITY*

7. Howard and Carol Scherer, a married couple, had decided to get a divorce. In December of 1976, they met with a lawyer and both signed a separation agreement that contained a property settlement and a power of attorney that was to be used to obtain a divorce in the Dominican Republic. Mr. Scherer later claimed that he had had a "considerable amount" to drink the night before signing, that the parties were drinking when the documents were signed, and that he had been taking Valium as a tranquilizer and did not realize that mixing it with alcohol caused him to feel "high and uncaring" as to his actions. In January of 1977, the divorce was obtained in the Dominican Republic. Mr. Scherer later told people that he was divorced and that he had plans to remarry. In July

Can get out of it because lack of capacity. Because they knew

of 1977, however, he filed a divorce action in Indiana against Mrs. Scherer and requested an equitable division of property. This suit claimed that the power of attorney that had enabled his wife to get the Dominican divorce was invalid because of his intoxication at the time of signing the documents. Will Mr. Scherer be bound by the documents he signed?

8. Halbman, a minor employed at a gas station managed by Lemke, agreed to buy a 1968 Oldsmobile from Lemke for $1,250. Halbman paid $1,000 in cash and took possession of the car. He agreed to pay $25 per week until the balance was paid. About five weeks later, after Halbman had paid $1,100 of the purchase price, a connecting rod in the car's engine broke. Halbman took the car to a garage to be repaired. He disaffirmed the contract and demanded the return of his money, but Lemke refused to return it. When the repair bill remained unpaid for several months, the garage removed the car's engine and transmission in satisfaction of the debt and had the rest of the car towed to the house of Halbman's father. There, the car was vandalized, making it unsalvageable. Halbman brought suit, seeking the return of the $1,110 he had paid toward the contract. Lemke argues that he should be compensated for the value of the car up to the time of disaffirmance. What will the result be under the majority rule regarding minors' duties after disaffirmance?

Can get all money back because minor and can disaffirm

CHAPTER 15

ILLEGALITY

INTRODUCTION

The public interest normally favors the enforcement of contracts. Sometimes, however, the interests that usually favor the enforcement of an agreement are subordinated to conflicting social concerns. As you read in the Reality of Consent chapter and Capacity to Contract chapter, for example, people who did not truly consent to a contract or who lacked the capacity to contract have the power to cancel their contracts. In these situations, concerns about protecting disadvantaged persons and preserving the integrity of the bargaining process outweigh the usual public interest in enforcing private agreements. Similarly, when an agreement involves an act or promise that violates some legislative or court-made rule, the public interests threatened by the agreement outweigh the interests that favor its enforcement. Such an agreement will be denied enforcement on grounds of **illegality,** even if there is voluntary consent between two parties who have capacity to contract.

Meaning of Illegality

When a court says that an agreement is illegal, it does not necessarily mean that the agreement violates a criminal law—although an agreement to commit a crime is one type of illegal agreement. Rather, an agreement is illegal either because the legislature has declared that particular type of contract to be unenforceable or void or because the agreement violates a **public policy** that has been developed by courts or that has been manifested in constitutions, statutes, administrative regulations, or other sources of law.

The term **public policy** is impossible to define precisely; generally, it is taken to mean a widely shared view about what ideas, interests, institutions, or freedoms promote public welfare. For example, in our society there are strong public policies favoring the protection of human life and health, free competition, and private property. Judges' and legislators' perceptions of desirable public policy influence the decisions they make about the resolution of cases or the enactment of statutes. Public policy may be based on a prevailing moral code, on an economic philosophy, or on the need to protect a valued social institution such as the family or the judicial system. If the enforcement of an agreement would create a threat to a public policy, a court may determine that it is illegal.

Determining whether an Agreement Is Illegal

If a statute states that a particular type of agreement is unenforceable or void, courts will apply the statute and refuse to enforce the agreement. Relatively few such statutes exist, however. More frequently, a legislature will forbid certain conduct but will not address the enforceability of contracts that involve the forbidden conduct. In such cases, courts must determine whether the importance of the public policy that underlies the statute in question and the degree of interference with that policy are sufficiently great to outweigh any interests that favor enforcement of the agreement.

In some cases, it is relatively easy to predict that an agreement will be held to be illegal. For example, an agreement to commit a serious crime is certain to be illegal. However, the many laws enacted by legislatures are of differing degrees of importance to the public welfare. The determination of illegality would not be so clear if the agreement violated a statute that was of relatively small importance to the public welfare. For example, in one Illinois case,[1] a seller of fertilizer failed to comply with an Illinois statute that required that a descriptive statement accompany the delivery of the fertilizer. The sellers prepared the statements and offered them to the buyers, but did not give them to the buyers at the time of delivery. The court enforced the contract despite the sellers' technical violation of the law because the contract was not seriously injurious to public welfare.

Similarly, the public policies developed by courts are rarely absolute; they, too, depend on a balancing of several factors. In determining whether to hold an agreement illegal, a court will consider the importance of the public policy involved and the extent to which enforcement of the agreement would interfere with that policy. They will also consider the seriousness of any wrongdoing involved in the agreement and how directly that wrongdoing was connected with the agreement.

For purposes of our discussion, illegal agreements will be classified into three main categories: (1) agreements that violate statutes, (2) agreements that violate public policy developed by courts, and (3) unconscionable agreements, which violate both statutory and judicial bans on unconscionability.

AGREEMENTS IN VIOLATION OF STATUTE

Agreements Declared Illegal by Statute

State legislatures occasionally enact statutes that declare certain types of agreements unenforceable, void, or

voidable. In a case in which a legislature has specifically stated that a particular type of contract is void, a court need only interpret and apply the statute. These statutes differ from state to state. Some are relatively uncommon. For example, Indiana's legislature recently enacted a statute declaring surrogate birth contracts to be void.[2] Others are relatively common. Three of the most frequently encountered statutes invalidating certain types of contracts are *usury statutes, Sunday laws*, and *wagering statutes*.

Usury Statutes Federal law and the law of most states set limits on the amount of interest that can be charged for a loan or forbearance (refraining from making a demand for money that is already due). **Usury means obtaining interest beyond the amount that is authorized by law for these transactions.** A contract that requires payment of a usurious interest rate would be illegal under such laws.

The statutes that define usury and set the maximum permissible limit for interest are not uniform in their prohibitions or their penalties. Some states have tended to deregulate usury. States frequently make distinctions among different types of debtors, setting limits on interest as to some debtors and providing higher limits or no limits as to others. For example, usury statutes often make distinctions between loans to individuals and loans to corporations.

When a transaction is covered by usury laws and the rate of interest charged for the use of money exceeds the statutory limit, the contract to pay that interest rate is unenforceable. The precise effect of usury differs from state to state, however. Some jurisdictions employ the traditional remedy for usury, in which the lender forfeits both principal and interest. The usual penalty for usury is forfeiture of interest earned on the transaction, either the entire interest or the excessive interest. In some states, there are also criminal penalties for usury.

Sunday Laws *Sunday laws* are statutes that prohibit the transaction of certain business and the performance of certain types of work on Sunday. Like usury laws, Sunday laws vary substantially from state to state. Under some Sunday laws, contracts and sales made on Sunday are invalidated if they are not the result of necessity or charity. Although Sunday laws used to be prevalent, many states today have either repealed their Sunday laws or no longer vigorously enforce them.

---

[1] *Amoco Oil Co. v. Toppert*, 56 Ill. App. 3d 1294 (Ill. Ct. App. 1978).

[2] Ind. Code 31-8-2-2 (1988).

Wagering Statutes All states either prohibit or regulate wagering, or gambling. There is a thin line separating wagering, which is illegal, from well-accepted, lawful transactions in which a person will profit from the happening of an uncertain event. How is illegal wagering distinguished from insurance contracts and stock and commodity transactions, for example? The hallmark of a wager is that neither party has any financial stake or interest in the uncertain event except for the stake that he has created by making the bet. The person making a wager *creates* the risk that he may lose the money or property wagered upon the happening of an uncertain event. Suppose Ames bets Baker $20 that the Cubs will win the pennant this year. Ames has no financial interest in a Cubs victory other than that which he has created through his bet. Rather, he has created the risk of losing $20 for the sole purpose of bearing that risk. If, however, people make an agreement about who shall bear an existing risk in which one of them has an actual stake or interest, that is a legal risk-shifting agreement. Property insurance contracts are classic examples of risk-shifting agreements. The owner of the property pays the insurance company a fee (premium) in return for the company's agreement to bear the risk of the uncertain event that the property will be damaged or destroyed. If, however, the person who takes out the policy had no legitimate economic interest in the insured property (called an **insurable interest** in insurance law), the agreement is an illegal wager.

Stock and commodity market transactions are good examples of speculative bargains that are legal. In both cases, the purchasers are obviously hoping that their purchases will increase in value and the sellers believe that they will not. The difference between these transactions and wagers lies in the fact that the parties to stock and commodities transactions are legally bound to the purchase agreement, even though the purchaser may never intend to take delivery of the stock or commodity. In an illegal wager—such as a bet on the performance of certain stock—no purchase or ownership is involved. Nothing is at stake except the risk that the parties have created by their bet.

Agreements that Violate the Public Policy of a Statute

As stated earlier, an agreement can be illegal even if no statute specifically states that that particular sort of agreement is illegal. Legislatures enact statutes in an effort to resolve some particular problem. If courts enforced agreements that involve the violation of a statute, they would frustrate the purpose for which the legislature passed the statute. They would also promote disobedience of the law and disrespect for the courts.

Agreements to Commit a Crime For the reasons stated above, contracts that require the violation of a criminal statute are illegal. If Grimes promises to pay Judge John Doe a bribe of $5,000 to dismiss a criminal case against Grimes, for example, the agreement is illegal. Sometimes the very formation of a certain type of contract is a crime, even if the acts agreed upon are never carried out. An example of this is an agreement to murder another person. Naturally, such agreements are considered illegal under contract law as well as under criminal law. Contracts in which a party agrees to obstruct justice by refraining from disclosing a crime or prosecuting a crime are also illegal.

Agreements that Promote Violations of Statutes Sometimes a contract of a type that is usually perfectly legal—say, a contract to sell goods—is deemed to be illegal under the circumstances of the case because it promotes or facilitates the violation of a statute. Suppose Davis sells Sims goods on credit. Sims uses the goods in some illegal manner and then refuses to pay Davis for the goods. Can Davis recover the price of the goods from Sims? The answer depends on whether Davis knew of the illegal purpose and whether she intended the sale to further that illegal purpose. Generally speaking, such agreements will be legal unless there is a direct connection between the illegal conduct and the agreement in the form of active, intentional participation in or facilitation of the illegal act. Knowledge of the other party's illegal purpose, standing alone, generally is not sufficient to render an agreement illegal. When a person is aware of the other's illegal purpose *and* actively helps to accomplish that purpose, an otherwise legal agreement—such as a sale of goods—might be labeled illegal.

The *Blossom Farm Products* case, which follows, is an example of a case in which the court found the connection between the agreement and a violation of statute sufficiently close for the public interest to be harmed by enforcement of the agreement.

BLOSSOM FARM PRODUCTS CO. v. KASSON CHEESE CO.
395 N.W.2d 619 (Wis. Ct. App. 1986)

PTX Corp. manufactured a product known as Isokappacase, which is used in the production of cheese. The label on Isokappacase says that it is "a starter medium, a bacteriophage preventative medium." Because of its high protein content, Isokappacase can also be used as a yield enhancer by adding it directly into cheese milk. When the product is used in this way, however, federal law requires that the resulting product be labeled as an imitation cheese and that it list the ingredients in the end product to reflect the characteristics of imitation cheese. Julian Podell, a salesman for Blossom, was the sole U.S. distributor for PTX's sale of Isokappacase. Over the course of three years, Blossom sold a large volume of Isokappacase to Kasson Cheese.

Kasson used Isokappacase as a yield enhancer, introducing it directly into cheese milk to enhance cheese yields from the milk, but did not label its final product as imitation cheese as required by federal standards. Had Kasson labeled its end product as an imitation cheese, it would have been able to sell the end product for only $.70 per pound rather than the $1.40 per pound it received for selling it as real cheese. Blossom was aware of the fact that Kasson's extremely large volume purchases of the product could only be accounted for by Kasson's use of Isokappacase as a yield enhancer. Podell acknowledged that once he recognized that Kasson was ordering about one hundred times more Isokappacase than would be needed if it were using the products as a starter medium, he realized that such large volume orders could only mean that Kasson was using the product as a yield enhancer. Blossom also tacitly knew that Kasson was mislabeling its product. Both Kasson and Blossom benefited economically from this volume purchase and use.

This case arose when Kasson failed to pay $138,306 for its last order of Isokappacase, and Blossom brought suit to collect the money. Kasson defended on the ground that the contract was illegal. The trial court agreed and dismissed Blossom's action. Blossom then brought this appeal.

Scott, Chief Justice.   Generally, if a promisee has substantially performed its part of the contract, enforcement of a promise is not precluded on grounds of public policy because of some improper use that the promisor intends to make of what he obtains; however, if the promisee acts for the purpose of furthering the promisor's improper use, the promisee is barred from recovering. Whether the promisee has acted for such purpose is a question of fact which may be evidenced by the promisee's doing of specific acts to facilitate the promisor's improper use and/or a course of dealing with persons engaged in improper conduct.

Even with Kasson's intended purpose of improperly labeling its end product, enforcement of Kasson's promise to pay Blossom for sale and delivery of the Isokappacase would not be precluded on grounds of public policy without knowledgeable involvement by Blossom. Testimony from several parties provides sufficient evidence of Blossom's knowledgeable involvement in Kasson's improper conduct. Based on this evidence, the trial court had sufficient evidence on which to base its finding that Blossom, aware of Kasson's use of Isokappacase and subsequent mislabeling of its end product, nonetheless continued to sell Isokappacase to Kasson in large quantities, thereby facilitating Kasson's improper conduct.

State legislation which adopted federal standards of identity enforces the public policy of accurately distinguishing imitation or analog cheese from real cheese and labeling it accordingly. Because mislabeling cheese involves conduct offensive to public policy, the trial court correctly concluded that the transaction which anticipated such improper conduct is unenforceable.

Judgment for Kasson affirmed.

Licensing Laws: Agreement to Perform an Act for which a Party Is Not Properly Licensed   Congress and the state legislatures have enacted a variety of statutes that regulate professions and businesses. A common type of regulatory statute is one that requires a person to obtain a license, permit, or registration before engaging in a certain business or profession. For example, state statutes require lawyers, physicians, dentists, teachers, and other professionals to be licensed to practice their professions. In order to obtain the required license, they must meet specified requirements such as attaining a certain educational degree and passing an examination. Real estate brokers, stockbrokers, insurance agents, sellers of liquor and tobacco, pawnbrokers, electricians, barbers, and others too numerous to mention are also often required by state statute to meet licensing requirements to perform services or sell regulated commodities to members of the public.

What is the status of an agreement in which one of the parties agrees to perform an act regulated by state law for which she is not properly licensed? Once again, the answer to this question depends on a balancing of the public interest that would be harmed by enforcement against the public and individual interests that favor enforcement. In determining whether to enforce the agreement, a court will consider the importance of the public policy that has been offended by the agreement. This will often be determined by looking at the purpose of the legislation that the unlicensed party has violated. If the statute is **regulatory**—that is, the purpose of the legislation is to protect the public against dishonest or incompetent practitioners—an agreement by an unlicensed person is generally held to be unenforceable. For example, if Spencer, a first-year law student, agrees to draft a will for Rowen for a fee of $150, Spencer could not enforce the agreement and collect a fee from Rowen for drafting the will, because she is not licensed to practice law. This result makes sense, even though it imposes a hardship on Spencer. The public interest in assuring that people on whose legal advice others rely have an appropriate educational background and proficiency in the subject matter outweighs any interest in seeing that Spencer receives what she bargained for.

On the other hand, where the licensing statute was intended primarily as a **revenue-raising measure**—as a means of collecting money rather than as a means of protecting the public—an agreement to pay a person for performing an act for which she is not licensed will generally be enforced. For example, suppose that in the above example, Spencer is a lawyer who is licensed to practice law in her state and who met all of her state's educational, testing, and character requirements but neglected to pay her annual registration fee. In this situation, there is no compelling public interest that would justify the harsh measure of refusing enforcement and possibly inflicting forfeiture on the unlicensed person.

Whether a statute is a regulatory statute or a revenue-raising statute depends on the intent of the legislature, which may not always be expressed clearly. Generally, statutes that require proof of character and skill and impose penalties for violation are considered to be regulatory in nature. Their requirements indicate that they were intended for the protection of the public. Those that impose a significant license fee and allow anyone who pays the fee to obtain a license are usually classified as revenue raising. The fact that no requirement other than the payment of the fee is imposed indicates that the purpose of the law is to raise money rather than to protect the public. Because such a statute is not designed for the protection of the public, a violation of the statute is not as threatening to the public interest as is a violation of a regulatory statute.

CONCEPT REVIEW

CONTRACTS THAT VIOLATE A LICENSING STATUTE

Type of Licensing Statute	Regulatory	Revenue Raising
Purpose of Statute	Protect the public welfare	Provide source of revenue
Typical Characteristics of Statute	Require proof of character, training, or character and impose penalties for violation	Impose fee with no or few other requirements
Status of Contracts that Violate Statute	Contracts violating statute usually illegal	Contracts violating statute still legal (validity of contract not affected by statute)

It would be misleading to imply that cases involving unlicensed parties always follow such a mechanical test. In some cases, courts may grant recovery to an unlicensed party even where a regulatory statute is violated. If the public policy promoted by the statute is relatively trivial in relation to the amount that would be forfeited by the unlicensed person and the unlicensed person is neither dishonest nor incompetent, a court may conclude that the statutory penalty for violation of the regulatory statute is sufficient to protect the public interest and that enforcement of the agreement is appropriate. Under section 181 of the *Restatement (Second) of Contracts*, an agreement to pay an unlicensed person for doing an act for which a license is required is unenforceable only if the licensing statute has a regulatory purpose *and* if the interest in enforcement of the promise is clearly outweighed by the public policy behind the statute. The *Noble* case, which follows, is a good example of the method by which courts analyze cases involving unlicensed parties.

NOBLE v. ALIS

474 N.E.2d 109 (Ind. Ct. App. 1985)

Andrew Noble and Stuart Odle signed a lease to rent an apartment in Bloomington, Indiana, from Linda Alis for one year, to begin on August 16, 1983. In August, prior to their arrival in Bloomington, Noble and Odle decided not to take possession of the apartment and attempted to find a sublessee. On August 29, they showed the apartment to prospective sublessees and noticed several defects. They contacted the City of Bloomington's Housing Code Enforcement Officer and requested that he inspect the premises for housing code violations. After the inspection, the enforcement officer informed Noble and Odle that the landlord was in violation of Bloomington Municipal Code Sec. 16.12.080(e), which states that "[i]t shall be a violation of this chapter for any owner to maintain a rental unit without an occupancy permit." The landlord had also failed to register it as a residential unit, as required by the Housing Code. Further, the enforcement officer advised Noble and Odle that, even if the house were registered, it would not pass a housing inspection. Believing that they could not legally find a sublessee and that their lease was void, Noble and Odle informed Alis on September 1 that they would no longer assume responsibility for locating a sublessee. The property was later rented to other tenants. Alis brought suit against Noble and Odle in small claims court for rent and damages she alleged that they owed. The court awarded her $1,266, and Noble and Odle appealed. Although the Housing Code does not address the enforceability of lease agreements for unregistered and permit-less property, Noble and Odle based their appeal on the argument that the lease was illegal because it violated the Housing Code.

Neal, Judge. Broadly speaking, a contract made in violation of a statute is void. Courts hesitate to brand an "illegal" bargain necessarily void; they engage in a balancing test and evaluate circumstances such as the nature of the subject matter of the contract, the strength of the public policy underlying the statute, the likelihood that a refusal to enforce the bargain or term will further the policy, and how serious or deserved would be the forfeiture suffered by the party attempting to enforce the bargain. Judicial decisions emphasize a distinction between statutes for revenue and statutes for protection of the public health, safety, and welfare. In the case of an agreement made in contravention of a statute designed for the protection of the public, it is more likely that the statute breaker will be denied the enforcement of his bargain.

In our opinion, the lease in the instant case is unenforceable. We agree with Noble and Odle's contention that the policies of protection of public health, safety, and welfare and encouragement of compliance with the housing code are advanced by the registration and occupancy permit provisions of the Municipal Code. The procedure to receive such a permit necessitates compliance with minimum housing standards: Once the unit is registered residential, a temporary occupancy permit is issued. The issuance of the temporary permit triggers an inspection by the Housing Department. After the inspection, an occupancy permit is issued; or, if the unit did not "pass" inspection, additional time is granted to make the repairs necessary to bring the unit into compliance with the code. Clearly, the policy of protecting the public from substandard housing is served by the registration-inspection-permit process: until the unit is registered, the Housing Code Enforcement Office is not aware of its existence and thus is unable to check its compliance with the housing standards set down in the code. Another important factor in our determination turns on the specific factual pattern of this case. Here, Noble and Odle never moved into the apartment and thus never benefited in any way from the lease agreement.

In conclusion, the clear purpose of the Bloomington Housing Code is to provide minimum standards for rental units to protect the health, safety, and welfare of the public. To that end, Bloomington clearly forbids landlords to rent property for the human habitation without complying with the ordinance. Any contrary decision by us would render the ordinance a nullity and permit landlords to ignore it and continue to rent substandard housing as before, taking a chance that the renters, ignorant of the ordinance, would not complain.

The decision of the trial court as to damages for rental payments is reversed, and Alis is ordered to return the $330 security deposit plus interest accrued at the statutory rate.

Judgment reversed in favor of Noble and Odle.

AGREEMENTS IN VIOLATION OF PUBLIC POLICY ARTICULATED BY COURTS

Legislative bodies manifest public policy by the laws they enact, which contain rules that lawmakers consider necessary for the public welfare. Courts, too, have broad discretion to articulate public policy and to decline to lend their powers of enforcement to an agreement that would contravene what they deem to be in the best interests of society. There is no simple rule for determining when a particular agreement is contrary to public policy. Public policy may change with the times; changing social and economic conditions may make behavior that was acceptable in an earlier time unacceptable today, or vice versa. The following are examples of agreements that are frequently considered vulnerable to attack on public policy grounds.

Agreements in Restraint of Competition

The policy against restrictions on competition is one of the oldest public policies declared by the common law. This same policy is also the basis of the federal and state antitrust statutes. The policy against restraints on competition is based on the economic judgment that the public interest is best served by free competition. Nevertheless, courts have long recognized that some contractual restrictions on competition serve legitimate business interests and should be enforced. Therefore, agreements that limit competition are scrutinized very closely by the courts to determine whether the restraint imposed is in violation of public policy.

If the *sole* purpose of an agreement is to restrain competition, it violates the public policy and is illegal. For example, if Martin and Bloom, who own competing businesses, enter an agreement whereby each agrees not to solicit or sell to the other's customers, such an agreement would be unenforceable. Where the restriction on competition was part of (*ancillary to*) an otherwise legal contract, the result may be different because the parties may have a legitimate interest to be protected by the restriction on competition.

For example, if Martin had *purchased* Bloom's business, the goodwill of the business was part of what she paid for. She has a legitimate interest in making sure that Bloom does not open a competing business soon after the sale and attract away the very customers whose goodwill she paid for. Or suppose that Martin hired Walker to work as a salesperson in her business. She wants to assure herself that she does not disclose trade secrets, confidential information, or lists of regular customers to Walker only to have Walker quit and enter a competing business.

To protect herself, the buyer or the employer in the above examples might bargain for a contractual clause that would provide that the seller or employee agrees not to engage in a particular competing activity in a specified *geographic area* for a specified *time* after the sale of the business or the termination of employment. This type of clause is called an **ancillary covenant not to compete,** or as it is more commonly known, a **non-competition clause.** They most frequently appear in *employment contracts, contracts for the sale of a business, partnership agreements*, and *small business buy-sell agreements*. In an employment contract, the non-competition clause might be the only part of the contract that the parties put in writing.

Enforceability of Non-Competition Clause Although non-competition clauses restrict competition and thereby affect the public policy favoring free competition, courts enforce them if they meet the following three criteria.

1. *Clause must serve a legitimate business purpose.* This means that the person protected by the clause must have some justifiable interest—such as an interest in protecting goodwill or trade secrets—that is to be protected by the non-competition clause. It also means that the clause must be *ancillary* to (part of) an otherwise valid contract. For example, a non-competition clause that is one term of an existing employment contract would be ancillary to that contract. By contrast, a promise not to compete would not be enforced if the employee made the promise *after* he had already resigned his job, because the promise not to compete was not ancillary to any existing contract.

2. *The restriction on competition must be reasonable in time, geographic area, and scope.* Another way of stating this is that the restrictions must not be any greater than necessary to protect a legitimate interest. It would be unreasonable for an employer or buyer of a business to restrain the other party from engaging in some activity that is not a competing activity or from doing business in a territory in which the employer or buyer does not do business, because this would not threaten his legitimate interests. Of course, what is reasonable depends on the facts of the case. In the sale of a business conducted throughout a three-state area, a restriction on the seller's engaging in the same business in those three states would probably be reasonable. If the company sold engages in business only within a 30-mile radius of the capital city of one of those states, however, the three-state restriction would be unreasonable.

3. *The non-competition clause should not impose an undue hardship.* A court will not enforce a non-competition clause if its restraints are unduly burdensome either on the public or on the party whose ability to compete would be restrained. In one recent case, for example, the court refused to enforce a non-competition clause against a gastroenterologist because of evidence that the restriction would have imposed a hardship on patients and other physicians requiring his services.[3]

Non-competition clauses in employment contracts that have the practical effect of preventing the restrained person from earning a livelihood are unlikely to be enforced as well. This is discussed further in the next section.

Non-Competition Clauses in Employment Contracts Restrictions on competition work a greater hardship on an employee than on a person who has sold a business. For this reason, courts tend to judge non-competition clauses contained in employment contracts by a stricter standard than they judge similar clauses contained in contracts for the sale of a business. In fact, there is a trend toward refusing enforcement of these clauses in employment contracts unless the employer can bring forth very good evidence that he has a protectible interest that justifies enforcement of the clause. The employer can do this by showing that he has entrusted the employee with trade secrets or confidential information, or that his goodwill with "near-permanent" customers is threatened. Absent this kind of proof, a court might conclude that the employer is just trying to avoid competition with a more efficient competitor and refuse enforcement because there is no legitimate business interest that requires protection. You will see this approach in the case of *Steamatic of Kansas City, Inc. v. Rhea*, which follows.

Furthermore, many courts refuse to enforce non-competition clauses if they restrict employees from engaging in a "common calling." A *common calling* is an occupation that does not require extensive or highly sophisticated training and which involves relatively simple, repetitive tasks. Under this common calling restriction, various courts have refused to enforce non-competition clauses against salespersons, a barber, and an auto-trim repairperson. In some states, statutes prohibit or limit the use of non-competition clauses in employment contracts.

---

[3] *Iredell Digestive Disease Clinic, P.A. v. Petrozza*, 373 S.E.2d 449 (N.C. Ct. App. 1988).

STEAMATIC OF KANSAS CITY, INC. v. RHEA

763 S.W.2d 190 (Mo. Ct. App. 1988)

Steamatic of Kansas City, Inc., specialized in cleaning and restoring property damaged by fire, smoke, water, or other elements. It employed Samuel Rhea as a marketing representative. His duties included soliciting customers, preparing cost estimates, supervising restoration work, and conducting seminars. At the time of his employment, Rhea signed a non-competition agreement prohibiting him from entering into a business in competition with Steamatic within six counties of the Kansas City area for a period of two years after the termination of his employment with Steamatic.

Late in 1987, Rhea decided to leave Steamatic. In contemplation of the move, he secretly extracted the agreement restricting his postemployment activity from the company's files and destroyed it. Steamatic learned of this and discharged Rhea. Steamatic filed suit against Rhea to enforce the non-competition agreement when it learned that he was entering a competing business. The trial court enforced the non-competition agreement and granted an injunction against Rhea. Rhea appealed.

Clark, Presiding Judge. Covenants not to compete restrain commerce and limit the freedom of an employee to pursue his trade. Enforcement of such agreements is, therefore, carefully restricted. An employer cannot extract a restrictive covenant from an employee merely to protect himself from competition but a limited time and geographical restraint may be deemed reasonable and enforceable if a legitimate protectible interest of the employer is served. An employer has a protectible and proprietary right in his "stock of customers" and their good will.

In the present case, before Steamatic may claim to enforce the agreement prohibiting Rhea from engaging in a competing business, it must appear that Steamatic has a stock of customers who regularly deal with Steamatic. A customer in this sense is one who repeatedly has business dealings with a particular tradesman or business. Unless the proponent of the restrictive covenant has a trade following, that is, a group of customers who regularly patronize the business of the particular employer, there can be no stock of customers and no protectible interest.

In this case the facts showed that disaster victims engaged Steamatic to provide restoration services only on a single occasion after the event of a fire or other casualty. The only possible repeat business which Steamatic could anticipate would be in those rare instances when a second casualty befell the same victim. No evidence was adduced to show that such had occurred in the past, or, indeed, that Steamatic enjoyed any repeat business at all. Steamatic was not shown to have had any contact with the customer before the casualty gave rise to a need for restoration services. After the services were performed, there was no repeat business. Prospects for restoration services were not contacted and solicited through any confidential or privileged source, but merely upon knowledge generally available to the public at large that a casualty had occurred. There was, therefore, no ongoing customer relationship between Steamatic and any identifiable persons or companies.

Steamatic cites *Osage Glass, Inc. v. Donovan* to support enjoining Rhea from engaging in a business in competition with Steamatic. The case is distinguishable. Osage was in the business of installing automobile windshields. Its dealings were with insurance companies, fleet operators, body shops and automobile dealerships. Donovan was the manager of the Kansas City office and, as such, he had developed substantial customer contacts. After leaving Osage and taking employment with a competitor, he was in a position, if not enjoined, to divert that business from Osage to his new employer. It was on this ground that the court decided in favor of enforcing the restrictive covenant. There were no comparable facts in the present case because Rhea was not shown to have any customer following nor, indeed, were there any identifiable customer contacts by reason of the nature of the business.

The evidence did show that Rhea was careful to maintain a good reputation for Steamatic with the [insurance] adjustors as a company which "got the job done" and satisfied the insured. The purpose was to procure a favorable recommendation for Steamatic by the adjustor if the latter's advice were sought by a disaster victim. The evidence was that the owner of the damaged property decided whether to employ Steamatic, or some other company, and it was the owner's responsibility to pay the charges even though the proceeds of an insurance claim would defray the expense in whole or in part. The insurance companies were not Steamatic customers and therefore Steamatic had no protectible interest in the good will of the adjustors.

It is apparent Rhea set about to enter employment competitive with Steamatic under the impression that he would be in violation of his agreement. His conduct in surreptitiously removing and destroying the agreements leads to this conclusion. Guilty conduct, however, is not the test by which the availability of injunctive relief is measured. The question is whether Steamatic had a protectible interest in a stock of customers. It did not and therefore Rhea's conduct in removing his papers from Steamatic's files is not relevant. The trial court erred when it enjoined Rhea from engaging in the damage restoration business.

Judgment reversed in favor of Rhea.

The Effect of Overly Broad Non-Competition Clauses The courts of different states treat unreasonably broad non-competition clauses in different ways. Some courts will strike the entire restriction if they find it to be unreasonable, and will refuse to grant the buyer or employer any protection. Others will refuse to enforce the restraint as written, but will adjust the clause and impose such restraints as would be reasonable. In case of breach of an enforceable non-competition clause, the person benefited by the clause may seek damages or an injunction (a court order preventing the promisor from violating the covenant).

Exculpatory Clauses

An **exculpatory clause** is a provision in a contract that purports to relieve one of the parties from tort liability. Exculpatory clauses are suspect on public policy grounds for two reasons. First, courts are concerned that a party who can contract away his liability for negligence will not have the incentive to use care to avoid hurting others. Second, courts are concerned that an agreement that accords one party such a powerful advantage might have been the result of the abuse of superior bargaining power rather than truly voluntary choice. Although exculpatory agreements are often said to be "disfavored" in the law, courts do not want to prevent parties who are dealing on a fair and voluntary basis from determining how the risks of their transaction shall be borne if their agreement does not threaten public health or safety.

Courts enforce exculpatory clauses in some cases and refuse to enforce them in others, depending on the circumstances of the case, the characteristics and relationship of the parties, and the language of the agreement. A few ground rules can be stated. First, an exculpatory clause cannot protect a party from liability for any wrongdoing greater than negligence. One that purports to relieve a person from liability for fraud or some other willful tort will be considered to be against public policy. In some cases, in fact, exculpatory clauses have been invalidated on this ground because of broad language stating that one of the parties was relieved of "all liability." Second, exculpatory clauses will not be effective to exclude tort liability on the part of a party who owes a duty to the public (such as an airline), because this would present an obvious threat to the public health and safety.

A third possible limitation on the enforceability of exculpatory clauses arises from the increasing array of statutes and common law rules that impose certain obligations on one party to a contract for the benefit of the other party to the contract. Workers' compensation statutes and laws requiring landlords to maintain leased property in a habitable condition are examples of such laws. Sometimes the person on whom such an obligation is placed will attempt to escape it by inserting an exculpatory or waiver provision in a contract. Such clauses are often—though not always—found to be against public policy because, if enforced, they would frustrate the very purpose of imposing the duty in question. For example, an employee's agreement to relieve her employer from workers' compensation liability is likely to be held illegal as a violation of public policy.

Even if a clause is not against public policy on any of the above three grounds, a court may still refuse to enforce it if a court finds that the clause was **unconscionable** or the product of abuse of superior bargaining power. (Unconscionability is discussed later in this chapter.) This determination depends on all of the facts of the case. Facts that tend to show that the exculpatory clause was the product of *knowing* consent will increase the likelihood that it will be enforced. For example, a clause that is written in clear language and conspicuous print is more likely to be enforced than one written in "legalese" and presented in fine print. Facts that tend to show that the exculpatory clause was the product of *voluntary* consent increase the likelihood of enforcement of the clause. For example, a clause contained in a contract for a frivolous or unnecessary activity, such as the Ironman Decathlon in *Milligan v. Big Valley Corporation*, is more likely to be enforced than is an exculpatory clause contained in a contract for a necessary activity such as medical care.

MILLIGAN v. BIG VALLEY CORPORATION

754 P.2d 1063 (Sup. Ct. Wyo. 1988)

Dean Griffin, an expert skier and certified ski instructor, entered the Ironman Decathlon held at the Grand Targhee ski resort, which was owned and operated by Big Valley Corporation. The decathlon was held for fun rather than profit. It consisted of several events, including swimming five pool laps, bowling one line, drinking a quart of beer, throwing darts, and skiing in both downhill and cross-country races. The downhill ski race was the first event in the decathlon. It was held early in the morning before the resort was opened to the public. Prior to the race, Griffin and all of the other downhill contestants were required to sign a document entitled "General Release of Claim." This provided in part:

In consideration of my being allowed to participate in IRONMAN DECATHLON at Targhee Resort, Alta, Wyoming, I irrevocably and forever hereby release and discharge any and all of the employees, agents, or servants and owners of Targhee Resort and the other sponsors of IRONMAN DECATHLON officially connected with this event of and from any and all legal claims or legal liability of any kind involving bodily injury or death sustained by me during my stay at Targhee Resort. I hereby personally assume all risks in connection with said event and I further release the aforementioned resort, its agents, and operators, for any harm which might befall me as a participant in this event, whether foreseen or unforeseen and further save and hold harmless said resort and persons from any claim by me or my family, estate, heirs or assigns.

/s/ Dean Griffin 4/13/84

About ten minutes after the race began, Griffin was found unconscious approximately three quarters of the way down the mountain. He died a few hours later. No one witnessed the incident that caused his death, but it was speculated that he lost control of his skis and hit a tree.

Elizabeth Milligan, as personal representative for Griffin's estate, filed a wrongful death action against Big Valley on behalf of Griffin's son. The trial court granted a summary judgment in favor of Big Valley on the ground that the exculpatory agreement signed by Griffin released Big Valley from all liability. Milligan appealed.

Cardine, Justice.   Exculpatory agreements releasing parties from negligence liability for damages or injury are valid and enforceable in Wyoming if they do not violate public policy. Generally, agreements absolving participants and proprietors from negligence liability during hazardous recreational activities are enforceable, subject to willful misconduct limitations.

To determine whether this type of release is valid and enforceable, we consider:

(1) Whether there exists a duty to the public;

(2) The nature of the service performed;

(3) Whether the contract was fairly entered into;

(4) Whether the intention of the parties is expressed in clear and unambiguous language.

A duty to the public exists if the nature of the business or service affects the public interest and the service performed is considered an essential service. Types of services thought to be subject to public regulation and therefore demanding a public duty or considered essential have included common carriers, hospitals and doctors, public utilities, innkeepers, public warehousemen, employers, and services involving extra-hazardous activities. Generally, a private recreational business does not qualify as a service demanding a special duty to the public, nor are its services of a special, highly necessary or essential nature. The Ironman Decathlon can best be labeled a recreational type of activity of no great public import.

The agreement in question does not involve severe disparity of bargaining power. A disparity of bargaining power will be found when a contracting party with little or no bargaining strength has no reasonable alternative to entering the contract at the mercy of the other's negligence. For example, a member of the public contracting with a public utility, common carrier, hospital, or employer often has no real choice or alternative and is, therefore, at the mercy of the other. Such is not the case here. Grand Targhee did not force Griffin to ski in the race. Skiing in the race was not a matter of practical necessity for the public, and putting on the race was not an essential service. Thus, no decisive bargaining advantage existed. No evidence suggests that Griffin was unfairly pressured into signing the agreement or that he was deprived of an opportunity to understand its implications.

Milligan argues that the release was entered into unfairly because it contained boilerplate language prepared solely by the resort and was an adhesive contract. The argument is without merit. The mere fact that a contract is on a printed form prepared by one party and offered on a "take it or leave it" basis does not automatically establish it as an adhesive contract. There must be a showing that the parties were greatly disparate in bargaining power and that there was no opportunity for negotiation for services which could not be obtained elsewhere. Here no such showing was made. Indeed, the evidence is to the contrary. The release was fairly executed and satisfies the first three criteria.

The final factor requires us to determine whether the release agreement evidences the parties' intent to release Big Valley from liability for negligent acts in clear and unambiguous language. The language could not be clearer. Examining the release in light of the purpose of the contract, it is clear that the parties intended to release the ski resort and all those involved in the Ironman Decathlon from liability. It is clear that the intent was to release Big Valley from negligence liability. The absence of the word "negligence" is not fatal to an exculpatory clause if the terms of the contract clearly show intent to extinguish liability.

We conclude that the release is not void as a matter of public policy and that Big Valley was entitled to judgment as a matter of law.

Judgment for Big Valley affirmed.

Family Relationships and Public Policy   In view of the central position of the family as a valued social institution, it is not surprising that an agreement that unreasonably tends to interfere with family relationships will be considered illegal. Examples of this type of contract include agreements whereby one of the parties agrees to divorce a spouse or agrees not to marry.

In recent years, courts have been presented with an increasing number of agreements between unmarried cohabitants that purport to agree upon the manner in which the parties' property will be shared or divided upon separation. It used to be widely held that contracts between unmarried cohabitants were against public policy because they were based on an immoral relationship. As unmarried cohabitation has become more widespread, however, the law concerning the enforceability of agreements between unmarried couples has changed. For example, in the 1976 case of *Marvin v. Marvin*, the California Supreme Court held that an agreement between an unmarried couple to pool income and share property could be enforceable.[4] Today, most courts hold that agreements between unmarried couples are not against public policy unless they are explicitly based on illegal sexual relations as the consideration for the contract or unless one or more of the parties is married to someone else.

UNCONSCIONABILITY

Development of the Doctrine of Unconscionability

Under classical contract law, courts were reluctant to inquire into the fairness of an agreement. Because the prevailing social attitudes and economic philosophy strongly favored freedom of contract, American courts took the position that so long as there had been no fraud, duress, misrepresentation, mistake, or undue influence in the bargaining process, unfairness in an agreement entered into by competent adults did not render the agreement unenforceable.

As the changing nature of our society produced many contract situations in which the bargaining positions of the parties were grossly unequal, the classical contract assumption that each party was capable of protecting himself was no longer persuasive. Legislatures responded to this problem by enacting a variety of statutory measures to protect individuals against the abuse of superior bargaining power in specific situations. Examples of such legislation include minimum wage laws and rent control ordinances. Courts became more sensitive to the fact that superior bargaining power often led to **contracts of adhesion** (contracts in which a stronger party is able to dictate unfair terms to a weaker party, leaving the weaker party no practical choice but to "adhere" to the terms). Some courts responded by borrowing a doctrine that had been developed and used for a long time in courts of equity,[5] the doctrine of **unconscionability.** Under this doctrine, courts would refuse to grant the equitable remedy of specific performance for breach of a contract if they found the contract to be oppressively unfair, or unconscionable.

One of the most far-reaching efforts to correct abuses of superior bargaining power was the enactment of section 2–302 of the Uniform Commercial Code, which gives courts the power to refuse to enforce all or part of a contract for the sale of goods or to modify such a contract if it is found to be unconscionable. By virtue of its inclusion in Article 2 of the Uniform Commercial Code, the prohibition against unconscionable terms applies to every contract for the sale of goods. The concept of unconscionability is not confined to contracts for the sale of goods, however. Section 208 of the *Restatement (Second) of Contracts*, which closely resembles the unconscionability section of the UCC, provides that courts may decline to enforce unconscionable terms or contracts. The prohibition of unconscionability has been adopted as part of the public policy of many states by courts in cases that did not involve the sale of goods, such as banking transactions and contracts for the sale or rental of real estate. It is therefore fair to state that the concept of unconscionability has become part of the general body of contract law.

Meaning of Unconscionability

Neither the UCC nor the *Restatement (Second) of Contracts* attempts to define the term unconscionability. Though the concept is impossible to define with precision, unconscionability is generally taken to mean the *absence of meaningful choice* together with *terms unreasonably advantageous* to one of the parties.

---

[4] 134 Cal. Rptr. 815 (1976).

[5] The Nature of Law chapter discusses courts of equity.

The facts of each individual case are crucial to determining whether a contract term is unconscionable. Courts will scrutinize the process by which the contract was reached to see if the agreement was reached by fair methods and whether it can fairly be said to be the product of knowing and voluntary consent.

Procedural Unconscionability   Courts and writers often refer to unfairness in the bargaining process as *procedural unconscionability.* Some facts that may point to procedural unconscionability include the use of fine print or inconspicuously placed terms; complex, legalistic language; and high-pressure sales tactics. One of the most significant facts pointing to procedural unconscionability is the lack of voluntariness as shown by a marked imbalance in the parties' bargaining positions, particularly where the weaker party is unable to negotiate more favorable terms because of economic need, lack of time, or market factors. In fact, in most contracts that have been found to be unconscionable, there has been a serious inequality of bargaining power between the parties. It is important to note, however, that the mere existence of unequal bargaining power does not make a contract unconscionable. If it did, every consumer's contract with the telephone company or the electric company would be unenforceable. Rather, in an unconscionable contract, the party with the stronger bargaining power *exploits* that power by driving a bargain containing a term or terms that are so unfair that they "shock the conscience of the court." You will see several examples of procedural unconscionability in *John Deere Leasing Company v. Blubaugh.*

JOHN DEERE LEASING COMPANY v. BLUBAUGH

636 F. Supp. 1569 (U.S. Dist. Ct., D. Kan. 1986)

Reuben Blubaugh, a farmer, leased a Model 6620 combine from John Deere Leasing (JDL). The lease, which was printed on very lightweight paper, provided that Blubaugh would pay four annual rentals of $15,991.37, beginning July 1983, and at the end of the lease term would have the option to purchase the equipment for $27,191.25. On the reverse side of the lease, printed in light colored fine print, were several terms that spelled out what JDL's remedies would be if Blubaugh failed to make a rental payment. These provisions gave JDL the right to repossess the combine, sell it, and keep the proceeds of such a sale. Even though Blubaugh was only agreeing to rent the combine rather than to buy it, these default provisions also made Blubaugh responsible for an additional amount of money that represented the difference between the "termination value" of the combine (as defined in a complicated formula on the reverse side of the lease) and any money received by JDL if it repossessed and sold the combine.

Blubaugh read and signed the front of the contract but did not read the back. His understanding was that he had entered a basic lease with an option to purchase arrangement. His potential liability under the lease was not explained to him by anyone from JDL. Blubaugh paid $30,939.16 toward the first two rental payments, then made no further payments. JDL repossessed the combine and sold it for $42,000. JDL then sued Blubaugh for an additional $12,054.63, which was the amount due under the default clauses on the reverse side of the lease. Blubaugh defended on the ground that the default clauses were unconscionable.

Kelly, District Judge.   Before turning to the discussion of the legal principles which are controlling in this case, the court makes the following observations. The terms in question herein are on the back of the lease, and are written in such fine, light print as to be nearly illegible. In fact, the print is so light that neither party was able to obtain a satisfactory photocopy. The court was required to use a magnifying glass to read the reverse side. The court found the wording to be date. Murphy entered the lease because she believed that she could acquire ownership of a television set without first establishing credit, as was stressed in McNamara's ads. At no time did McNamara inform Murphy that the terms of the lease required her to pay a total of $1,268 for the set. The retail sales price for the same set was $499.

After making $436 in payments over a period of about six months, Murphy read a newspaper article criticizing the lease plan and realized the amount that the agreement required her to pay. She stopped making payments, and McNamara sought to repossess the set, threatening to file a criminal complaint against her if she failed to return it. Murphy, claiming that the agreement was unconscionable, filed suit for an injunction barring McNamara from repossessing the TV set or filing charges against her.

Berdon, Judge.   An excessive price charged a consumer with unequal bargaining power can constitute a violation of 2–302 of the Uniform Commercial Code. In the case of *Jones v. Star Credit Corp.*, the plaintiffs, welfare recipients, purchased a home freezer unit for $900.00. The freezer had a retail value of approximately $300.00. The court held the contract was unconscionable under 2–302 of the Uniform Commercial Code and reformed the contract by excusing further payments over the $600.00 already paid by the plaintiffs. There have been similar holdings by other courts. The failure on the part of McNamara to advise Murphy of the total price she would be required to pay under the terms of the contract further compounded the unfairness of his trade practices.

In sum, an agreement for the sale of consumer goods entered into with a consumer having unequal bargaining power and which calls for an unconscionable purchase price, constitutes an unfair trade practice. By unequal bargaining power, the court means that at the time the contract was made there was such an inequality of bargaining power (for example, because of the consumer's need for credit) that the merchant could insist on the inclusion of unconscionable terms in the contract which were not justifiable on the grounds of commercial necessity. The intent of this rule is not to erase the doctrine of freedom of contract, but to make realistic the assumption of the law that the agreement has resulted from real bargaining between parties who had freedom of choice and understanding and ability to negotiate in a meaningful fashion. Viewed in that sense, freedom to contract survives but the marketers of consumer goods are brought to an awareness that the restraint of unconscionability is always hovering over their operations and that courts will employ it to balance the interests of the consumer public and those of the seller.

Injunction granted, prohibiting McNamara from repossessing the TV set, using harassing collection techniques, or filing criminal charges against Murphy, but permitting McNamara to file suit for the difference between the amount Murphy paid and the value of the set.

Procedure for Determining Unconscionability

Section 2–302 states that when a claim of unconscionability is asserted or when it appears to the court that a term may be unconscionable, the court must afford the parties the opportunity to present evidence about the setting, purpose, and effect of the contract. This apparently means that the court must hold a hearing on the issue of unconscionability. The purpose of such a hearing is to enable the court to make a determination of whether the term is unconscionable. Section 2–302 specifically states that unconscionability is a *matter of law*. That is, only the judge can decide whether a clause is unconscionable; it is not a matter for consideration by the jury.

Consequences of Unconscionability

The UCC and the *Restatement* sections on unconscionability give courts the power to manipulate a contract containing an unconscionable provision so as to reach a just result. If a court finds that a contract or a term in a contract is unconscionable, it can do one of three things: it can refuse to enforce the entire agreement; it can refuse to enforce the unconscionable provision but enforce the rest of the contract; or it can "limit the application of the unconscionable clause so as to avoid any unconscionable result." This last alternative has been taken by courts to mean that they can make adjustments in the terms of the contract.

EFFECT OF ILLEGALITY

General Rule

As a general rule, courts will refuse to give any remedy for the breach of an illegal agreement. A court will refuse to enforce an illegal agreement and will also refuse to permit a party who has fully or partially performed her part of the agreement to recover what she has parted with. This "hands-off illegal agreements" approach is reflected in the *Blossom Farm Products* case, which appeared earlier in this chapter. The reason for this rule is to serve the public interest, not to punish the parties.

In some cases, the public interest is best served by allowing some recovery to one or both of the parties. Such cases constitute exceptions to the "hands off" rule. The following discussion concerns the most common situations in which courts will grant some remedy even though they find the agreement to be illegal.

Excusable Ignorance of Facts or Legislation

Though it is often said that ignorance of the law is no excuse, courts will, under certain circumstances, permit a party to an illegal agreement who was excusably ignorant of facts or legislation that rendered the agreement illegal to recover damages for breach of the agreement. This exception is used where only *one* of the parties acted in ignorance of the illegality of the agreement and the other party was aware that the agreement was illegal. For this exception to apply, the facts or legislation of which the person claiming damages was ignorant must be of a relatively minor character—that is, it must not involve an immoral act or a serious threat to the public welfare. Finally, the person who is claiming damages cannot recover damages for anything that he does after learning of the illegality. For example, Warren enters a contract to perform in a play at Craig's theater. Warren does not know that Craig does not have the license to operate a theater as required by statute. Warren can recover the wages agreed upon in the parties' contract for work that he performed before learning of the illegality.

When *both* of the parties are ignorant of facts or legislation of a relatively minor character, courts will not permit them to enforce the agreement and receive what they had bargained for, but they will permit the parties to recover what they have parted with.

Rights of Parties Not Equally in the Wrong

The courts will often permit a party who is not equally in the wrong (in technical legal terms, not *in pari delicto*) to recover what she has parted with under an illegal agreement. One of the most common situations in which this exception is used involves the rights of "protected parties"—people who were intended to be protected by a regulatory statute—who contract with parties who are not properly licensed under that statute. Most regulatory statutes are intended to protect the public. As a general rule, if a person guilty of violating a regulatory statute enters into an agreement with another person for whose protection the statute was adopted, the agreement will be enforceable by the party whom the legislature intended to protect. For example, most states require foreign corporations—those incorporated outside the state—to get a license before doing business in the state. These statutes often specifically provide that an unlicensed corporation cannot enforce contracts that it enters into with citizens of the state. Citizens of the licensing state, however, are generally allowed to enforce their contracts with the foreign corporation.

Another common situation in which courts will grant a remedy to a party who is not equally in the wrong is one in which the less guilty party has been induced to enter the agreement by misrepresentation, fraud, duress, or undue influence.

Rescission before Performance of Illegal Act

Obviously, public policy is best served by any rule that encourages people not to commit illegal acts. People who have fully or partially performed their part of an illegal contract have little incentive to raise the question

FIGURE 1   Effect of Illegality

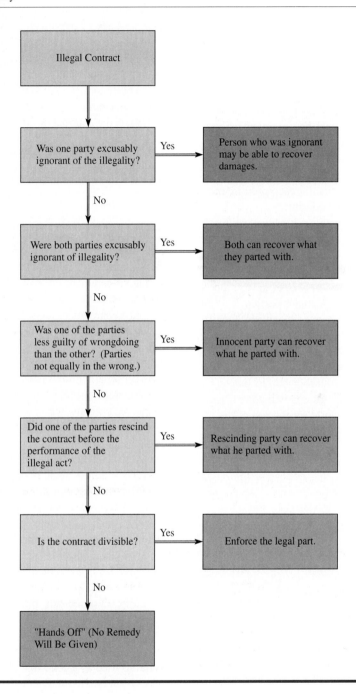

of illegality if they know that they will be unable to recover what they have given because of the courts' hands-off approach to illegal agreements. To encourage people to cancel illegal contracts, courts will allow a person who rescinds such a contract before any illegal act has been performed to recover any consideration that he has given. For example, Dixon, the owner of a restaurant, pays O'Leary, an employee of a competitor's restaurant, $1,000 to obtain some of the competitor's recipes. If Dixon has second thoughts and tells O'Leary the deal is off before receiving any recipes, he can recover the $1,000 he paid O'Leary.

Divisible Contracts

If part of an agreement is legal and part is illegal, the courts will enforce the legal part so long as it is possible to separate the two parts. A contract is said to be *divisible*—that is, the legal part can be separated from the illegal part—if the contract consists of several promises or acts by one party, each of which corresponds with an act or a promise by the other party. In other words, there must be a separate consideration for each promise or act for a contract to be considered divisible.

Where no separate consideration is exchanged for the legal and illegal parts of an agreement, the agreement is said to be *indivisible*. As a general rule, an indivisible contract that contains an illegal part will be entirely unenforceable unless it comes within one of the exceptions discussed above. However, if the major portion of a contract is legal, but the contract contains an illegal provision that does not affect the primary, legal portion, courts will often enforce the legal part of the agreement and simply decline to enforce the illegal part. For example, suppose Alberts sells his barbershop to Bates. The contract of sale provides that Alberts will not engage in barbering anywhere in the world for the rest of his life. The major portion of the contract—the sale of the business—is perfectly legal. A provision of the contract—the ancillary covenant not to compete—is overly restrictive, and thus illegal. A court would enforce the sale of the business but modify or refuse to enforce the restraint provision.

Figure 1 illustrates the effect of illegality.

ETHICAL AND PUBLIC POLICY CONCERNS

1. Was it right that the defendant in the *Blossom Farm Products* case did not have to pay its debt to the plaintiff, when the defendant was the one who used the product for an illegal purpose? What is the justification for giving a windfall to the primary wrongdoer?

2. You read that the law makes a distinction between contracts that violate regulatory statutes and contracts that violate revenue-raising statutes. What is the rationale for this distinction? Would it be better for the law simply to hold that *any* contract that violates *any* statute would be illegal? Why or why not?

3. What are some ethical justifications for the decisions that the courts reached in the *Murphy* and *Blubaugh* cases? In both cases, the contracts in question were held to be unconscionable even though the individuals who signed the contracts *could have* read them and figured out their obligations. Who should have the responsibility to make sure that the person signing a contract understands his obligations, the person who drafts and offers the contract or the person who signs it?

SUMMARY

An illegal agreement is one that involves a violation of some *public policy* (public interest recognized by a court, legislature, or other lawmaker) and threatens the public welfare to the extent that the normal interests favoring enforcement of contracts are outweighed by the need to avoid the danger to the public. Deciding whether to hold an agreement illegal requires courts to balance a number of factors. They must consider how important the public policy is and how much the agreement in question would interfere with that policy. They must also consider whether any serious wrongdoing was involved in the agreement and how directly the agreement was connected with any wrongdoing.

Sometimes, a legislature, in a statute prohibiting a certain act, will expressly provide that a contract that involves the performance of that act is void. Examples of such statutes include statutes prohibiting usury, wagering, and certain transactions on Sundays. Agreements that involve violations of statutes can also be illegal, even if the statute in question does not specifically address the enforceability of contracts that involve a violation of the statute. If the formation or performance of an agreement requires the commission of a serious crime, the agreement will be considered illegal. Similarly, an agreement that promotes the commission of a crime can be illegal.

State and local legislation also require persons who practice a variety of trades, businesses, and professions to be licensed as a condition of doing business. When a person enters into an agreement to perform a regulated act for which she is not properly licensed, the agreement would be considered illegal if the violated licensing statute was *regulatory*, that is, designed for the protection of the public. If the purpose of the licensing statute was *revenue raising*, or if the purpose of the statute is relatively unimportant compared to the forfeiture that would result from a denial of enforcement, the agreement is not illegal.

Courts have broad discretion to articulate public policies and to refuse to enforce agreements that present a serious threat to those policies. One such policy is the public policy against restrictions on competition. If the sole purpose of an agreement is to restrain competition, it is illegal. If an agreement that restrains competition is part of an otherwise legal contract, the agreement is called an *ancillary covenant not to compete* or *noncompetition clause*. Such clauses are legal so long as they serve a legitimate business purpose, the restriction is no greater than is needed to protect a valid business interest, and they present no undue hardship to the public or to the person whose freedom is restricted. Non-competition clauses in employment contracts are usually subjected to a stricter standard of scrutiny than are such clauses in contracts for the sale of a business. The employer must be able to satisfy the court that it had some protectible interest such as trade secrets, confidential information, or the goodwill of a stock of regular customers. The non-competition clause will be scrutinized to determine whether the nature of the restriction and the time and geographic area of the restriction are reasonable. If a court finds that the restriction is too broad, it may refuse to enforce it completely or it may enforce the restriction to the extent that is reasonable under the circumstances.

Exculpatory agreements (agreements to relieve a party of tort liability) are held to be illegal if the exculpated party owes a duty to the public or if such an agreement purports to excuse a person from liability for fraud or other willful torts. Such agreements are often held to be ineffective in relieving a party to a contract from a statutory or common law duty to act for the benefit of the other party to the contract. An exculpatory clause relieving a person who owes no duty to the public from negligence liability might still be found to be against public policy if the parties to the agreement were not dealing on a fair and equal bargaining basis or other facts tended to show the lack of voluntary, knowing consent. In such a situation, the exculpatory agreement might be found to be unconscionable. A variety of other public policies have been recognized by courts, such as the public policy favoring the protection of the family.

A very important development in contract law regarding the protection of public policy is the enactment of section 2–302 of the Uniform Commercial Code, which gives courts the power to refuse to enforce *uncon-*

scionable provisions in contracts. An unconscionable provision is a term that is unreasonably favorable to one of the parties and about which the other party had no meaningful choice. If a court finds, after holding a hearing at which evidence about unconscionability is presented, that a provision in a contract is unconscionable, the court can refuse to enforce the entire contract, refuse to enforce the unconscionable provision, or make adjustments in the contract so as to avoid the unconscionable result. The doctrine of unconscionability has been adopted widely as part of the common law of many states, so that it is frequently applied even in cases that do not involve the sale of goods.

When an agreement is held to be illegal, it is generally unenforceable. Furthermore, a party who has partially or fully performed his part of an illegal agreement generally will not be able to recover what he has parted with. Courts make exceptions to this rule when it is in the public interest to do so. When one of the parties to an illegal agreement was excusably ignorant of the facts or laws that made the agreement illegal, courts will permit him to enforce the agreement as to any performance rendered before he learned of the illegality, provided that the law involved is of a relatively minor character. If both parties are ignorant of a fact or law under conditions similar to those stated above, either will be able to recover for consideration given.

Another exception is that a party who is not equally in the wrong with the other party to an illegal agreement may have a remedy. A party protected by a regulatory statute may recover for breach of an agreement entered into with a person who has not complied with the provisions of the statute. A person who has been induced to enter an illegal agreement by fraud, misrepresentation, duress, or undue influence may recover any consideration he has parted with.

Another exception to the rule that courts will give no remedy to parties to an illegal agreement is that a person who withdraws from an illegal agreement by rescinding it before the illegal act has been committed will be permitted to recover any consideration given. An additional exception is that if an agreement is *divisible*, courts will enforce the legal portion and refuse enforcement to the illegal portion. If an agreement that contains an illegal portion is indivisible, courts will normally refuse enforcement to the entire agreement unless the illegal part is a relatively minor provision of the agreement that does not affect the major, legal portion.

PROBLEM CASES

1. Zientara and Kaszuba, both citizens of Indiana, were friends and coworkers. Kaszuba's wife worked in an Illinois tavern that sold Illinois Lotto tickets. Zientara requested that Kaszuba obtain an Illinois Lotto ticket for him, as he had done in the past. Kaszuba agreed and Zientara gave him an envelope containing the purchase price and the number selections for the ticket. Zientara's was a winning number combination worth $1,696,800, but Kaszuba refused to give Zientara the ticket and made an effort to collect the winnings. At the time of this case, Indiana law prohibited lotteries, the sale of lottery tickets in Indiana, and gambling. Zientara filed suit in Indiana against Kaszuba, claiming the proceeds of the ticket. Kaszuba filed a motion to dismiss on the basis that the parties had entered an illegal, and therefore unenforceable, transaction. Was the transaction illegal? *Yes ILLEGAL IN STATE & UNCERTAIN EVENT*

2. Discount Fabric House, Inc., had placed an ad in the Yellow Pages every year since 1975. Each year, it signed an advertising contract with Wisconsin Telephone Company for the Yellow Pages ad. The contract was a printed form used by all subscribers who desired to place such an ad. No subscriber could bargain for or change any terms. One of the terms of the contract was that the subscriber agreed to relieve the telephone company of liability for any negligent act. In 1978, the telephone company omitted important trade identification from Discount Fabric House's ad. Discount Fabric House sued the telephone company for business losses resulting from this omission. As a defense, the telephone company set up the exculpatory clause contained in the advertising contract. Will the exculpatory clause be enforced? *No because against public policy*

3. Stern and Whitehead entered into a surrogacy contract in New Jersey. The contract provided that in exchange for $10,000, Whitehead would become pregnant through artificial insemination using Stern's sperm, carry the child to term, bear it, and surrender her parental rights to the child so that the child could be adopted by Stern's wife. A New Jersey criminal statute prohibits paying or accepting money in connection with any placement of a child for adoption. New Jersey also has a comprehensive statutory scheme regulating the termination of parental rights. This law provides that parental rights can be terminated only in cases of voluntary, written surrender of a child to an approved agency or where there has been a showing of parental abandonment or unfitness.

Whitehead did become pregnant with Stern's child and carried it to term. After the child's birth, however, she resisted surrendering the child. Stern sued to enforce the surrogacy contract, but Whitehead asserted that it was illegal. Should the surrogacy contract be enforced? *No illegal against statute*

4. James Strickland attempted to bribe Judge Sylvania Woods to show leniency toward one of Strickland's friends who had a case pending before the judge. Judge Woods immediately reported this to the state's attorney and was asked to play along with Strickland until the actual payment of money occurred. Strickland gave $2,500 to the judge, who promptly turned it over to the state's attorney's office. Strickland was indicted for bribery, pled guilty, and was sentenced to a four-year prison term. Three months after the criminal trial, Strickland filed a motion for the return of his $2,500. Will the court order the return of his money? *P303 Agreement to commit a crime even though did not occur*

5. Baker Pacific Corp., a licensed asbestos abatement and remediation contractor, contracted with Metropolitan Life to remove asbestos from one of Metropolitan's buildings. As was required by its contract with Metropolitan, Baker Pacific made it a condition of employment for workers on this project to sign an exculpatory agreement that released Baker Pacific and Metropolitan from "any and all claims whatsoever, at common law or otherwise" with the exception of liability under worker's compensation laws and in which the workers relinquished "any and all claims of every nature" that are related to exposure to asbestos. Is this exculpatory agreement enforceable? *Yes because workers subject to perils of JOB & could get WorkersComp*

6. Ben Lee Wilson had been licensed to practice architecture in the state of Hawaii, but his license lapsed in 1971 because he failed to pay a required $15 renewal fee. A Hawaii statute provides that any person who practices architecture without having been registered and "without having a valid unexpired certificate of registration . . . shall be fined not more than $500 or imprisoned not more than one year, or both." In 1972, Wilson performed architectural and engineering services for Kealakekua Ranch, for which he billed the Ranch $33,994.36. When the Ranch failed to pay Wilson's fee, he brought this action for breach of contract. What will the result be? *P305 WILSON WILL GET FEES*

7. Ralph contracted to purchase a business, American Horse Enterprises, from Bovard. He executed promissory notes to Bovard in connection with this purchase. American Horse Enterprises was primarily in the business of manufacturing drug paraphernalia such as "roach clips" and "bongs" used to smoke marijuana. At the time of the sale of American Horse Enterprises, the manufacture of drug paraphernalia was not itself illegal, but state criminal statutes made it illegal to possess, use, and transfer marijuana. Both Ralph and Bovard knew that the products produced by American Horse Enterprises were used for illegal purposes. Ralph defaulted on the promissory notes and Bovard sued to recover on them. Ralph defends on the ground that the sale of the business was illegal. Was it? *Yes, 302 Manufact prod.*

8. Dr. Ellis, an orthopedic surgeon, entered into a contract of employment with the Elko Clinic. Among other provisions, the contract of employment contained a non-competition clause in which Dr. Ellis agreed not to practice medicine within a distance of five miles from the city limits of Elko, Nevada, for a period of two years from the termination date of his employment. During Dr. Ellis's employment, he treated patients who would otherwise have had to travel to Reno, Salt Lake City, or elsewhere to seek the services of an orthopedic surgeon. At the expiration of his employment contract, Dr. Ellis gave notice to the Clinic that he intended to establish his own office in Elko for the practice of his specialty. The Clinic sued Dr. Ellis to enforce the non-competition clause. Should the non-competition clause be enforced as written? *No undue hardship on the Doctor.*

9. Hiram Ricker & Sons contracted with the Students International Meditation Society (SIDS) to furnish lodging and food to approximately 1,000 SIDS students at a one-month teacher training course to be held on Ricker's property in Poland Springs, Maine. At the end of the month, SIDS paid $185,000 to Ricker. Alleging that SIDS owed an additional $65,780, Ricker filed suit against SIDS for breach of contract. SIDS defended on the ground that the contract was illegal because Ricker's victualer's license, which was required by state law, had expired and because Ricker did not have sanitation permits for all of its premises during the entire period of the contract. SIDS demands the return of the $185,000 it paid. What should the result be? *Should be returned $185 because against public policy*

10. Gianni Sport was a New York manufacturer and distributor of women's clothing. Gantos was a clothing retailer headquartered in Grand Rapids, Michigan. In 1980, Gantos's sales total was 20 times greater than Gianni Sport's, and in this industry, buyers were "in the driver's seat." In June of 1980, Gantos submitted to Gianni Sport a purchase order for women's holiday clothing to be delivered on October 10, 1980. The purchase order contained the following clause:

Buyer reserves the right to terminate by notice to Seller all or any part of this Purchase Order with respect to Goods that have not actually been shipped by Seller or as to Goods which are not timely delivered for any reason whatsoever.

Gianni Sport made the goods in question especially for Gantos. This holiday order comprised 20 to 22 percent of Gianni Sport's business. In late September of 1980, before the goods were shipped, Gantos canceled the order. It later agreed to accept the shipment in exchange for a 50 percent price reduction. Was the cancellation clause unconscionable? *Yes, unreasonable & advantage one side*

11. Jones signed a contract with Free Flight Sport Aviation that gave him the right to use Free Flight's recreational skydiving facilities, including an airplane that ferried skydivers to the parachute jumping site. An exculpatory clause exempting Free Flight from liability for negligence was included in the contract. About one year later, Jones was injured while riding in a Free Flight airplane that crashed shortly after takeoff. He sued Free Flight for negligence, and Free Flight asserted the exculpatory clause as a defense. Will the exculpatory clause be enforced? *Yes, because knows the risk that he is bearing*

12. Triangle Leasing, which was in the business of leasing vans, trucks, and cars in Alabama, Georgia, and North Carolina, hired McMahon as the manager of its Wilmington, North Carolina, office. As part of his employment contract, McMahon signed a non-competition agreement. The non-competition agreement restricted McMahon from soliciting or attempting to procure Triangle Leasing's customers and from attempting to make car or truck-van rentals to any Triangle Leasing customers. According to the agreement, these activities were restricted within the state of North Carolina and any other state in which Triangle Leasing did business. The agreed-upon duration of the restriction was two years after the termination of McMahon's employment. Triangle Leasing trained McMahon and gave him access to its list of regular customers in Wilmington and other confidential information relating to the Wilmington market. Although McMahon's only contact with Triangle Leasing's customers was with Wilmington customers, Triangle Leasing also maintained offices in Greensboro-High Point and Raleigh-Durham, North Carolina. McMahon decided to terminate his employment and start his own rental business in North Carolina. Is the non-competition agreement likely to be enforced as written? *Yes confidential information state to state business*

CHAPTER 16

WRITING

INTRODUCTION

Your study of contract law so far has focused on the requirements for the formation of a valid contract. You should be aware, however, that even when all the elements of a valid contract exist, the enforceability of the contract and the nature of the parties' obligations can be greatly affected by the *form* in which the contract is set out and by the *language* that is used to express the agreement. An otherwise valid contract can become unenforceable if it does not comply with the formalities required by state law. A person may be unable to offer evidence about promises and agreements made in preliminary negotiations, because the parties later adopted a written contract that did not contain those terms. And, of course, the legal effect of any contract is determined in large part by the way in which a court interprets the language it contains. This chapter discusses the ways in which the enforceability of a contract and the scope of contractual obligations can be affected by the manner in which people express their agreements.

THE STATUTE OF FRAUDS

Despite what many people believe, there is no general requirement that contracts be in writing. In most situations, oral contracts are legally enforceable, assuming that they can be proven. Still, oral contracts are less desirable than written contracts in many ways. They are more easily misunderstood or forgotten than written contracts. They are also more subject to the danger that a person might fabricate terms or fraudulently claim to have made an oral contract where none exists.

In 17th-century England, the dangers inherent in oral contracts were exacerbated by a legal rule that prohibited parties to a lawsuit from testifying in their own cases. Since the parties to an oral contract could not give testimony, the only way they could prove the existence of the contract was through the testimony of third parties. As you might expect, third parties were sometimes persuaded to offer false testimony about the existence of contracts. In an attempt to stop the widespread fraud and perjury that resulted, Parliament enacted the Statute of Frauds in 1677. It required written evidence before certain classes of contracts would be enforced. Although the possibility of fraud exists in every contract, the statute focused on contracts in which the potential for fraud was great or the consequences of fraud were especially serious.

The legislatures of American states adopted very similar statutes, also known as statutes of frauds. These statutes, which require certain kinds of contracts to be

325

evidenced by a signed writing, are exceptions to the general rule that oral contracts are enforceable.

Statutes of frauds have produced a great deal of litigation, due in part to the public's ignorance of their provisions. It is difficult to imagine an aspect of contract law that is more practical for businesspeople to know about than the circumstances under which an oral contract will not suffice.

EFFECT OF FAILURE TO COMPLY WITH THE STATUTE OF FRAUDS

The statute of frauds applies only to executory contracts. If an oral contract has been completely performed by both parties, the fact that it did not comply with the statute of frauds would *not* be a ground for rescission of the contract.

What happens if an executory contract is within the statute of frauds but has not been evidenced by the type of writing required by the statute? It is not treated as an illegal contract because the statute of frauds is more of a formal rule than a rule of substantive law. Rather, the contract that fails to comply with the statute of frauds is *unenforceable.* Although the contract will not be enforced, a person who has conferred some benefit on the other party pursuant to the contract can recover the reasonable value of his performance in an action based on *quasi-contract.*

CONTRACTS WITHIN THE STATUTE OF FRAUDS

A contract is said to be "within" the statute of frauds if the statute requires that sort of contract to be evidenced by a writing. In almost all states, the following types of contracts are within the statute of frauds:

1. Collateral contracts in which a person promises to perform the obligation of another person.
2. Contracts for the sale of an interest in real estate.
3. Bilateral contracts that cannot be performed within a year from the date of their formation.
4. Contracts for the sale of goods for a price of $500 or more.
5. Contracts in which an executor or administrator promises to be personally liable for the debt of an estate.
6. Contracts in which marriage is the consideration.

Of this list, the first four sorts of contracts have the most significance today, and our discussion will focus primarily on them.

The statutes of frauds of the various states are not uniform. Some states require written evidence of other contracts in addition to those listed above. For example, a number of states require written evidence of contracts to pay a commission for the sale of real estate. Others require written evidence of ratifications of infants' promises or promises to pay debts that have been barred by the statute of limitations or discharged by bankruptcy.

The following discussion examines in greater detail the sorts of contracts that are within most states' statute of frauds.

Collateral Contracts

A *collateral contract* is one in which one person (the *guarantor*) agrees to pay the debt or obligation that a second person (the *principal debtor*) owes to a third person (the *obligee*) if the principal debtor fails to perform. For example, Cohn, who wants to help Davis establish a business, promises First Bank that he will repay the loan that First Bank makes to Davis if Davis fails to pay it. Here, Cohn is the guarantor, Davis is the principal debtor, and First Bank is the obligee. Cohn's promise to First Bank must be in writing to be enforceable.

As you can see in Figure 1, a collateral contract involves at least three parties and at least *two* promises to perform (a promise by the principal debtor to pay the obligee and a promise by the guarantor to pay the obligee). In a collateral contract, the guarantor promises to pay *only if the principal debtor fails to do so.* The essence of the collateral contract is that the debt or obligation is owed primarily by the principal debtor and the guarantor's debt is *secondary.* Thus, not all three party transactions are collateral contracts. The contracts described below are common three-party situations that are *not* within the statute of frauds.

Not within Statute of Frauds: Three-Party Contracts that Are Original Rather than Collateral   When a person undertakes an obligation that is not conditioned on the default of another person, and the debt is his own rather than that of another person, his obligation is said to be *original* or *direct*, not collateral. For example, when Timmons calls Johnson Florist Company and says, "Send flowers to Elrod," Timmons is undertaking

FIGURE 1   Collateral Contract

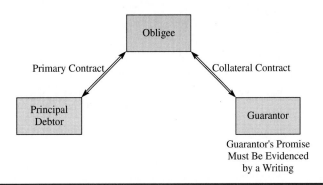

an obligation to pay his *own*—not someone else's—debt. This is not changed by the fact that Elrod is benefited by the contract between Timmons and Johnson Florist. The contract between Timmons and Johnson Florist is an original contract and would not have to be in writing.

The same result is reached when a creditor agrees to accept a contract with a new debtor in satisfaction of a debt previously owed by another debtor. Such transactions are called **novations.** In a novation, a creditor releases the original debtor and permits a new debtor to take his place. For example, Barnes owes $300 to First Bank. First Bank accepts Williamson's promise to pay Barnes's debt as satisfaction of that debt. This is a type of original contract, because Barnes has been released from liability for the debt and Williamson is now the only debtor.

Another common three-party transaction that is outside the statute of frauds occurs when two people are *jointly liable* on a debt to a third person. For example, if Brice and Evans together borrow money from First Bank to buy inventory for their joint business, they are *both* personally liable for the loan. Both of their promises are original, and no writing is required.

Exception: Main Purpose or Leading Object Rule There are some situations in which a contract that is technically collateral is treated like an original contract because the person promising to pay the debt of another does so for the primary purpose of securing some personal benefit. Under the **main purpose** or **leading object** rule, no writing is required where the guarantor makes a collateral promise for the main purpose of obtaining some personal economic advantage. When the consideration given in exchange for the collateral promise is something the guarantor seeks primarily for his own benefit rather than for the benefit of the primary debtor, the contract is outside the statute of frauds and does not have to be in writing. *Al Booth's, Inc. v. Boyd-Scarp Enterprises, Inc.,* which follows, is a good example of the operation of this exception.

AL BOOTH'S, INC. v. BOYD-SCARP ENTERPRISES, INC.

518 So. 2d 422 (Fla. Ct. App. 1988)

Boyd-Scarp Enterprises, a building contractor, was building a new home for James Rathmann. Rathmann paid Boyd-Scarp for appliances for the new home and Boyd-Scarp contracted with Al Booth's, an appliance supplier, for the purchase of the appliances. Al Booth's had heard that Boyd-Scarp was having financial problems. Before delivering the appliances to the Rathmann's new home, it contacted Rathmann and asked him to guarantee payment. Al Booth's alleges that Rathmann orally promised to pay for the appliances if Boyd-Scarp failed to pay. Al Booth's then delivered the appliances. Boyd-Scarp became insolvent and did not pay Al Booth's for the appliances. Al Booth's turned to Rathmann for payment. It later brought this action when Rathmann refused to pay for the appliances. Rathmann asserted the statute of frauds as a defense, and the trial court granted a summary judgment in favor of Rathmann on the ground that the action was barred by the statute of frauds.

Upchurch, Chief Judge. Our statute of frauds, section 725.01, Florida Statutes, provides that "no action shall be brought to charge the defendant upon any special promise to answer for the debt of another person unless the agreement or promise upon which such action shall be brought or some note or memorandum thereof shall be in writing and signed by the party to be charged." This statutory language creates a distinction between direct promises and collateral promises to pay debts. Where the alleged oral promise is a direct promise to be obligated in the first instance, it is outside the statute of frauds and enforceable.

In the present case, the evidence reflects that if in fact Rathmann made a promise, it was a promise to pay in the event Boyd-Scarp did not. Such a promise would be a promise to answer for the debt of another. However, this does not necessarily mean that the statute of frauds bars Al Booth's action. Florida case law on the point is in accord with the weight of authority in following the "leading object" rule.

The "leading object" rule recognizes that an important difference exists between cases where the promisor makes his promise for the benefit of another and where the promisor makes it for his own pecuniary benefit. One court has explained the rule as providing that a promise, though collateral, is deemed enforceable because the promisor does not need the protection against his own generous impulses afforded by the statute of frauds. If the promisor's main purpose was to advance his own interests and he received a substantial, immediate and pecuniary benefit, the promise is outside the statute of frauds.

Since there is evidence here indicating that Rathmann agreed to guarantee payment and that the promise was for his own economic benefit, the "leading object" rule applies to take the promise out of the statute of frauds. This being so, summary judgment was improperly entered for Rathmann.

Reversed and remanded in favor of Al Booth's.

Interest in Land

Any contract that creates or transfers an interest in land is within the statute of frauds. The inclusion of real estate contracts in the statute of frauds reflects the values of an earlier, agrarian society in which land was the primary basis of wealth. Our legal system historically has treated land as being more important than other forms of property. Courts have interpreted the land provision of the statute of frauds broadly to require written evidence of any transaction that will affect the ownership of an interest in land. Thus, a contract to sell or mortgage real estate must be evidenced by a writing, as must an option to purchase real estate or a contract to grant an easement or permit the mining and removal of minerals on land. A lease is also a transfer of an interest in land, but most states' statutes of frauds do not require leases to be in writing unless they are long-term leases, usually those for one year or more. On the other hand, a contract to erect a building or to insure a building would not be within the real estate provision of the statute of frauds, because such contracts do not involve the transfer of interests in land.[1]

---

[1] Note, however, that a writing might be required under state insurance statutes.

Exception: Full Performance by the Vendor   An oral contract for the sale of land that has been completely performed by the vendor (seller) is "taken out of the statute of frauds," that is, is enforceable without a writing. For example, Peterson and Lincoln enter into an oral contract for the sale of Peterson's farm at an agreed-upon price and Peterson, the vendor, delivers a deed to the farm to Lincoln. In this situation, the vendor has completely performed and most states would treat the oral contract as being enforceable.

Exception: Part Performance (Action in Reliance) by the Vendee   When the vendee (purchaser of land) does an act in clear reliance on an oral contract for the sale of land, an equitable doctrine commonly known as the "part performance doctrine" permits the vendee to enforce the contract notwithstanding the fact that it was oral. The part performance doctrine is based on both evidentiary and reliance considerations. The doctrine recognizes that a person's conduct can "speak louder than words" and can indicate the existence of a contract almost as well as a writing can. The part performance doctrine is also based on the desire to avoid the injustice that would otherwise result if the contract were repudiated after the vendee's reliance.

Under section 129 of the *Restatement (Second) of Contracts*, a contract for the transfer of an interest in land can be enforced even without a writing if the person seeking enforcement:

1. Has *reasonably relied* on the contract and on the other party's assent.
2. Has changed his position to such an extent that *enforcement of the contract is the only way to prevent injustice.*

In other words, the vendee must have done some act in reliance on the contract and the nature of the act must be

such that restitution (returning his money) would not be an adequate remedy. The part performance doctrine will not permit the vendee to collect damages for breach of contract, but it will permit him to obtain the equitable remedy of **specific performance,** a remedy whereby the court orders the breaching party to perform his contract.[2]

A vendee's reliance on an oral contract could be shown in many ways. Traditionally, many states have required that the vendee pay part or all of the purchase price and either make substantial improvements on the property or take possession of it. For example, Contreras and Miller orally enter into a contract for the sale of Contreras's land. If Miller pays Contreras a substantial part of the purchase price and either takes possession of the land or begins to make improvements on it, the contract would be enforceable without a writing under the part performance doctrine. These are not the only sorts of acts in reliance that would make an oral contract enforceable, however. Under the *Restatement* approach, if the promise to transfer land is clearly proven or is admitted by the breaching party, it is not necessary that the act of reliance include making payment, taking possession, or making improvements.[3] It still is necessary, however, that the reliance be such that restitution would not be an adequate remedy. For this reason, a vendee's payment of the purchase price, standing alone, usually is *not* sufficient for the part performance doctrine. The following *Hickey v. Green* case provides a good example of the use of the part performance doctrine.

---

[2] Specific performance is discussed in more detail in the Performance and Remedies chapter.

[3] *Restatement (Second) of Contracts* § 129, comment d.

HICKEY v. GREEN
442 N.E.2d 37 (Mass. Ct. App. 1982)

Gladys Green owns a lot (Lot S) in the Manomet section of Plymouth, Massachusetts. In July 1980, she advertised it for sale. On July 11 and 12, Thomas and Patricia Hickey discussed with Green purchasing Lot S and orally agreed to a sale for $15,000. On July 12, Green accepted the Hickeys's check for $500. Hickey had left the payee line of the deposit check blank, because of uncertainty whether Green or her brother was to receive the check. Hickey asked Green to fill in the appropriate name. Green, however, held the check, did not fill in the payee's name, and neither cashed nor endorsed it. Hickey told Green that his intention was to sell his home and build on the lot he was buying from Green. Relying on the arrangements with Green, the Hickeys advertised their house in newspapers for three days in July. They found a purchaser quickly. Within a short time, they contracted with a purchaser for the sale of their house and accepted the purchaser's deposit check. On the back of this check, above the Hickeys's signatures endorsing the check, was noted: "Deposit on purchase of property at Sachem Rd. and First St., Manomet, Ma. Sale price, $44,000."

On July 24, Green told Hickey that she no longer intended to sell her property to him and instead had decided to sell it to someone else for $16,000. Hickey offered to pay Green $16,000 for the lot, but she refused this offer. The Hickeys then filed a complaint against Green seeking specific performance. Green asserted that relief was barred by the Statute of Frauds, but the trial court granted specific performance. Green appealed.

Cutter, J.   The present rule applicable in most jurisdictions in the United States is succinctly set forth in *Restatement (Second) of Contracts* section 129 (1981). The section reads: "A contract for the transfer of an interest in land may be specifically enforced notwithstanding failure to comply with the Statute of Frauds if it is established that the party seeking enforcement, in reasonable reliance on the contract and on the continuing assent of the party against whom enforcement is sought, has so changed his position that injustice can be avoided only by specific enforcement." Two distinct elements enter into the application of the rule of this Section: first, the extent to which the evidentiary function of the statutory formalities is fulfilled by the conduct of the parties; second, the reliance of the promisee, providing a compelling basis for relief in addition to the expectations created by the promise.

The present facts reveal a simple case of a proposed purchase of a residential vacant lot, where the vendor, Green, knew that the Hickeys were planning to sell their former home (possibly to obtain funds to pay her) and build on Lot S. The Hickeys, relying on Green's oral promise, moved rapidly to make their sale without obtaining any adequate memorandum of the terms of what appears to have been intended to be a quick cash sale of Lot S. So rapid was action by the Hickeys that, by July 21, less than ten days after giving their deposit to Green, they had accepted a deposit check for the sale of their house, endorsed the check, and placed it in their bank account. Above their signatures endorsing the check was a memorandum probably sufficient to satisfy the Statute of Frauds. At the very least, the Hickeys had bound themselves in a manner which, to avoid a transfer of their own house, they might have had to engage in expensive litigation. No attorney has been shown to have been used either in the transaction between Green and the Hickeys or in that between the Hickeys and their purchaser.

There is no denial by Green of the oral contract between her and the Hickeys. This, under section 129 of the *Restatement*, is of some significance. There can be no doubt that Green made the promise on which the Hickeys so promptly relied, and also that she, nearly as promptly, but not promptly enough, repudiated it because she had a better opportunity. In equity, Green's conduct cannot be condoned. This is not a case where either party is shown to have contemplated the negotiation of a purchase and sale agreement. If a written agreement had been expected, even by only one party, or would have been natural, a different situation might have existed. It is a permissible inference from the facts that the rapid sale of the Hickeys' house was both appropriate and expected.

[At the time of the trial court's decision in this case], the principal facts bearing on the extent of the injury to the Hickeys were those based on the Hickeys's obligation to convey their house to a purchaser. Performance of that agreement had been extended. If enforcement of that agreement still will be sought, or if that agreement has been carried out, the conveyance of Lot S by Green should be required now.

Remanded to trial court for action consistent with this opinion. If the Hickeys's contract to sell their house has been performed or will be performed, the trial court is to order Green to convey Lot S. If the Hickeys will not be required to sell their house, however, Green will be ordered to reimburse the Hickeys for any deposits or expenses of advertising and litigation rather than being ordered to convey the lot.

Contracts that Cannot Be Performed within One Year

A bilateral, executory contract that cannot be performed within one year from the day on which it comes into existence is within the statute of frauds and must be evidenced by a writing. The apparent purpose of this provision is to guard against the risk of faulty or willfully inaccurate recollection of long-term contracts. Courts have tended to construe it very narrowly.

One aspect of this narrow construction is that most states hold that a contract that has been fully performed by *one* of the parties is "taken out of the statute of frauds" and is enforceable without a writing. For example, Nash enters into an oral contract to perform services for Thomas for thirteen months. If Nash has already fully performed his part of the contract, Thomas will be required to pay him the contract price.

In addition, this provision of the statute has been held to apply only when the *terms* of the contract make it impossible for the contract to be completed within one year. If the contract is for an indefinite period of time, it is not within the statute of frauds. This is true even if, in retrospect, the contract was *not* completed within a year. Thus, Weinberg's agreement to work for Wolf for an indefinite period of time would not have to be evidenced by a writing, even if Weinberg eventually works for Wolf for many years. As demonstrated by *Hodge v. Evans Financial Corporation*, which follows, the mere fact that performance is unlikely to be completed in one year does not bring the contract within the statute of frauds. In most states, a contract "for life" is not within the statute of frauds, because it is possible—since death is an uncertain event—for the contract to be performed within a year. In a few states, such as New York, contracts for life are within the statute of frauds.

HODGE v. EVANS FINANCIAL CORPORATION
823 F.2d 559 (D.C. Cir. 1987)

On two occasions in 1980, Albert Hodge met with John Tilley, president and chief operating officer of Evans Financial Corporation, to discuss Hodge's possible employment by Evans. Hodge was 54 years old at that time and was assistant counsel and assistant secretary of Mellon National Corporation and Mellon Bank of Pittsburgh. During these discussions, Tilley asked Hodge what his conditions were for accepting employment with Evans, and Hodge replied, "No. 1, the job must be permanent. Because of my age, I have a great fear about going back into the marketplace again. I want to be here until I retire." Tilley allegedly responded, "I accept that condition." Regarding his retirement plans, Hodge later testifed, "I really questioned whether I was going to go much beyond 65." Hodge subsequently accepted Evans's offer of employment as vice president and general counsel. He moved from Pittsburgh to Washington, D.C., in September 1980 and worked for Evans from that time until he was fired by Tilley on May 7, 1981.

Hodge brought a breach of contract suit against Evans. The case was tried before a jury, which rendered a verdict in favor of Hodge for $175,000. Evans appeals.

Wald, Chief Justice.   Evans argues that the oral employment agreement between Evans and Hodge is unenforceable under the statute of frauds. Because the agreement here contemplated long-term employment for a number of years, Evans argues that the statute requires it to have been in writing in order to be enforceable.

Despite its sweeping terms, the one-year provision of the statute has long been construed narrowly and literally. Under prevailing interpretation, the enforceability of a contract under the statute does not depend on the actual course of subsequent events or on the expectations of the parties. Instead, the statute applies only to those contracts whose performance could not possibly or conceivably be completed within one year. The statute of frauds is thus inapplicable if, at the time the contract is formed, any contingent event could complete the terms of the contract within one year.

Hodge argues that, under this interpretation of the statute of frauds, a permanent or lifetime employment contract does not fall within the statute because it is capable of full performance within one year if the employee were to die within the period. Hodge's view of the statute's application to lifetime or permanent employment contracts has, in fact, been accepted by an overwhelming majority of courts and commentators.

The employment contract in this case cannot reasonably be interpreted as a contract for a specified period of time. Hodge unequivocally alleged a contract for permanent employment, not a contract until he reached age sixty-five or for any other stated period of time. The fact that Hodge expected to retire at some point does not mean that his contract could not possibly be performed within one year. All employment contracts of permanent, lifetime, or indefinite duration undoubtedly contemplate retirement; such contracts certainly do not mean that employees are bound to work until the moment they drop dead. Hodge's permanent employment contract with Evans could therefore be fully performed, according to its terms, upon Hodge's retirement or upon his death. Under the conventional view the latter possibility is sufficient to take the contract out of the statute. That Hodge expected to retire before he died is completely irrelevant to this case so long as the contract was legally susceptible of performance within one year. The applicability of the statute of frauds does not depend on the expectations of the parties.

We recognize that the conventional view of the statute is somewhat "legalistic." Yet the statute of frauds itself is widely understood as a formal device that shields promise breakers from the consequences of otherwise enforceable agreements. The conventional, narrowing interpretation overwhelmingly adopted by courts and commentators is designed to mollify the often harsh and unintended consequences of the statute. Here the jury concluded, despite Evans's vigorous defense, that Hodge was promised permanent employment and that he was nonetheless fired without cause. Under the traditional, narrow view of the statute, the statute of frauds does not bar the enforcement of such jury verdicts.

Judgment for Hodge affirmed.

Computing Time   In determining whether a contract is within the one-year provision, courts begin counting time on the date on which the contract comes into existence. If, under the terms of the contract, it is possible to perform it within one year from this date, the contract does not fall within the statute of frauds and does not have to be in writing. If, however, the terms of the contract make it impossible to complete performance of the contract (without breaching it) within one year from the date on which the contract came into existence, the contract falls within the statute and must meet its requirements to be enforceable. Thus, if Hammer Co. and

McCrea agree on August 1, 1986, that McCrea will work for Hammer Co. for one year, beginning October 1, 1986, the terms of the contract dictate that it is not possible to complete performance until October 1, 1987. Because that date is more than one year from the date on which the contract came into existence, the contract falls within the statute of frauds and must be evidenced by a writing to be enforceable.

Sale of Goods for $500 or More

The original English Statute of Frauds required a writing for contracts for the sale of goods for a price of 10 pounds sterling or more. In the United States today, the writing requirement for the sale of goods is governed by section 2–201 of the Uniform Commercial Code. This section provides that contracts for the sale of goods for the price of $500 or more are not enforceable without a writing or other specified evidence that a contract was made. There are a number of alternative ways of satisfying the requirements of section 2–201. These will be explained later in this chapter.

Modifications of Existing Sales Contracts   Just as some contracts to extend the time for performance fall within the one-year provision of the statute of frauds, agreements to modify existing sales contracts can fall within the statute of frauds if the contract as modified is for a price of $500 or more.[4] Section 2–209(3) provides that the requirements of the statute of frauds must be satisfied if the contract as modified is within its provisions. For example, if Carroll and Kestler enter into a contract for the sale of goods at a price of $490, the original contract does *not* fall within the statute of frauds. However, if they later modify the contract by increasing the contract price to $510, the modification falls within the statute of frauds and must meet its requirements to be enforceable.

Promise of Executor or Administrator to Pay a Decedent's Debt Personally

When a person dies, a personal representative is appointed to administer his estate. One of the important tasks of this personal representative, who is called an executor if the person dies leaving a will or an administrator if the person dies without a will, is to pay the debts owed by the decedent. No writing is required when an executor or administrator—acting in his representative capacity—promises to pay the decedent's debts from the funds of the decedent's estate. The statute of frauds requires a writing, however, if the executor, acting in her capacity as a private individual rather than in her representative capacity, promises to pay one of the *decedent's* debts out of her own (the executor's) funds. For example, Thomas, who has been appointed executor of his Uncle Max's estate, is presented with a bill for $10,500 for medical services rendered to Uncle Max during his last illness by the family doctor, Dr. Barnes. Feeling bad that there are not adequate funds in the estate to compensate Dr. Barnes for his services, Thomas promises to pay Dr. Barnes from his own funds. Thomas's promise would have to be evidenced by a writing to be enforceable.

Contracts in which Marriage Is the Consideration

The statute of frauds also requires a writing when marriage is the consideration to support a contract. The marriage provision has been interpreted to be inapplicable to agreements that involve only mutual promises to marry. It can apply to any other contract in which one party's promise is given in exchange for marriage or the promise to marry on the part of the other party. This is true whether the promisor is one of the parties to the marriage or a third party. For example, if Hicks promises to deed his ranch to Everett in exchange for Everett's agreement to marry Hicks's son, Everett could not enforce Hicks's promise without written evidence of the promise.

Prenuptial (or **antenuptial**) agreements present a common contemporary application of the marriage provision of the statute of frauds. These are agreements between couples who contemplate marriage. They usually involve such matters as transfers of property, division of property upon divorce or death, and various lifestyle issues. Assuming that marriage or the promise to marry is the consideration supporting these agreements, they are within the statute of frauds and must be evidenced by a writing.[5]

---

[4] Modifications of sales contracts are discussed in greater detail in the Consideration chapter.

[5] Note, however, that "nonmarital" agreements between unmarried cohabitants who do not plan marriage are not within the marriage provision of the statute of frauds, even though the agreement may concern the same sorts of matters that are typically covered in a prenuptial agreement. The legality of agreements between unmarried cohabitants is discussed in the Illegality chapter.

CONCEPT REVIEW

CONTRACTS "WITHIN" THE STATUTE OF FRAUDS

Provision	Description	Exceptions (situations in which contract does not require a writing)
Marriage	Contracts, other than mutual promises to marry, where marriage is the consideration	—
Year	Bilateral contracts that, *by their terms*, cannot be performed within one year from the date on which the contract was formed	Full (complete) performance by one of the parties
Land	Contract that creates or transfers an ownership interest in real property	1. Full performance by vendor (vendor deeds property to vendees) or 2. "Part performance" doctrine: Vendee relies on oral contract, for example, by: a. Paying substantial part of purchase price and b. Taking possession or making improvements
Executor's Promise	Executor promises to pay estate's debt out of his own funds	—
Sale of Goods at Price of $500 or More (UCC 2–201)	Contracts for the sale of goods for a contract price of $500 or more; also applies to modifications of contracts for goods where price as modified is $500 or more	See alternative ways of satisfying statute of frauds under UCC
Collateral Contracts, Guaranty	Contracts where promisor promises to pay the debt of another if the primary debtor fails to pay	"Main purpose" or "leading object" exception: Guarantor makes promise primarily for her own economic benefit

MEETING THE REQUIREMENTS OF THE STATUTE OF FRAUDS

Nature of the Writing Required

The statutes of frauds of the various states are not uniform in their formal requirements. However, most states require only a *memorandum* of the parties' agreement; they do not require that the entire contract be in writing. The memorandum must provide written evidence that a contract was made, but it need not have been created with the intent that the memorandum itself would be binding. In fact, in some cases, written offers that were accepted orally have been held sufficient to satisfy the writing requirement. A memorandum may be in any form, including letters, telegrams, receipts, or any other writing indicating that the parties had a contract. The

memorandum need not be made at the same time the contract comes into being; in fact, the memorandum may be made at any time before suit is filed. If a memorandum of the parties' agreement is lost, its loss and its contents may be proven by oral testimony.

Contents of the Memorandum   Although there is a general trend away from requiring complete writings to satisfy the statute of frauds, an adequate memorandum must still contain several things. Generally, the essential terms of the contract must be indicated in the memorandum, although states differ in their requirements concerning how specifically the terms must be stated. The identity of the parties must be indicated in some way, and the subject matter of the contract must be identified with reasonable certainty. This last requirement causes particular problems in contracts for the sale of land, since many statutes require a detailed description of the property to be sold.

Contents of Memorandum under UCC   The standard for determining the sufficiency of the contents of a memorandum is more flexible in cases concerning contracts for the sale of goods. This looser standard is created by the language of UCC section 2–201, which states that the writing must be sufficient to indicate that a contract for sale has been made between the parties but a writing can be sufficient even if it omits or incorrectly states a term agreed upon. However, the memorandum is not enforceable for more than the *quantity* of goods stated in the memorandum. Thus, a writing that does not indicate the quantity of goods to be sold would not satisfy the Code's writing requirement.

Signature Requirement   The memorandum must be signed by the *party to be charged* or his authorized agent. (The *party to be charged* is the person using the statute of frauds as a defense—generally the *defendant* unless the statute of frauds is asserted as a defense to a counterclaim.) This means that it is not necessary for purposes of meeting the statute of frauds for *both* parties' signatures to appear on the document. It is, however, in the best interests of both parties for both signatures to appear on the writing; otherwise, the contract evidenced by the writing is enforceable only against the signing party. Unless the statute expressly provides that the memorandum or contract must be signed at the end, the signature may appear any place on the memorandum. Any writing, mark, initials, stamp, engraving, or other symbol placed or printed on a memorandum will suffice as a signature, as long as the party to be charged intended it to authenticate (indicate the genuineness of) the writing.

Memorandum Consisting of Several Writings   In many situations, the elements required for a memorandum are divided among several documents. For example, Wayman and Allen enter into a contract for the sale of real estate, intending to memorialize their agreement in a formal written document later. While final drafts of a written contract are being prepared, Wayman repudiates the contract. Allen has a copy of an unsigned preliminary draft of the contract that identifies the parties and contains all of the material terms of the parties' agreement, an unsigned note written by Wayman that contains the legal description of the property, and a letter signed by Wayman that refers to the contract and to the other

two documents. None of these documents, standing alone, would be sufficient to satisfy the statute of frauds. However, Allen can combine them to meet the requirements of the statute, provided that they all relate to the same agreement. This can be shown by physical attachment, as where the documents are stapled or bound together, or by references in the documents themselves that indicate that they all apply to the same transaction. In some cases, it has also been shown by the fact that the various documents were executed at the same time.

ALTERNATIVE MEANS OF SATISFYING THE STATUTE OF FRAUDS IN SALE OF GOODS CONTRACTS

As you have learned, the basic requirement of the UCC statute of frauds [2–201] is that a contract for the sale of goods for the purchase price of $500 or more must be evidenced by a written memorandum that indicates the existence of the contract, states the quantity of goods to be sold, and is signed by the party to be charged. Recognizing that the underlying purpose of the statute of frauds is to provide more evidence of the existence of a contract than the mere oral testimony of one of the parties, however, the Code also permits the statute of frauds to be satisfied by any of four other types of evidence. Under the UCC, then, a contract for the sale of goods for a purchase price of $500 or more for which there is no written memorandum signed by the party to be charged can meet the requirements of the statute of frauds in any of the ways discussed below. These different methods of satisfying the UCC statute of frauds are depicted in Figure 2.

Confirmatory Memo between Merchants

Suppose Gardner and Roth enter into a contract over the telephone for the sale of goods at a price of $5,000. Gardner then sends a memorandum to Roth confirming the deal they made orally. If Roth receives the memo and does not object to it, it would be fair to say that the parties' conduct provides some evidence that a contract exists. Under some circumstances, the UCC permits such confirmatory memoranda to satisfy the statute of frauds even though the writing is signed by the party who is seeking to enforce the contract rather than the party against whom enforcement is sought [2–201(2)]. This exception applies only when *both* of the parties to a contract are *merchants*. (As you will see in the following case, *Goldkist, Inc. v. Brownlee*, it is sometimes difficult to determine whether a seller will be deemed to be a merchant.) Furthermore, the memo must be sent within a reasonable time after the contract is made and must be sufficient to bind the person who sent it if enforcement were sought against him (that is, it must indicate that a contract was made, state a quantity, and be signed by the sender). If the party against whom enforcement is sought receives the memo, has reason to know its contents, and yet fails to give written notice of objection to the contents of the memo within 10 days after receiving it, the memo can be introduced to meet the requirements of the statute of frauds. The *Goldkist* case illustrates the satisfaction of the statute of frauds by a confirmatory memorandum.

GOLDKIST, INC. v. BROWNLEE

355 S.E.2d 773 (Ga. Ct. App. 1987)

Mark and Barney Brownlee were farmers who, as a partnership doing business as Brownlee Brothers, grew and sold crops. In addition to farming, Barney Brownlee owned a gas station. On July 22, 1983, Barney Brownlee allegedly telephoned Goldkist and, after checking on the current price of soybeans, allegedly agreed to deliver 5,000 bushels of soybeans to Goldkist between August 22 and September 22, at $6.88 per pound. Although no written agreement signed by either of the Brownlees was created, Goldkist did send the Brownlees a written memorandum dated July 22, which confirmed the agreement to sell 5,000 bushels of soybeans on the terms described above. The Brownlees received the memorandum but did not respond to it. They also did not deliver the soybeans, and Goldkist was forced to "cover" the contract (buy soybeans from another source). Goldkist then brought this action to recover its losses arising out of the necessity to cover.

The Brownlees asserted as a defense the fact that there was no writing signed by either of them as required by UCC section 2–201. The trial court agreed with the Brownlees and granted summary judgment in their favor. Goldkist appealed.

Beasley, Judge.   The [trial] court agreed with the Brownlees that the circumstances did not fit any of the exceptions provided for in UCC section 2–201. On appeal, Goldkist asserts that the Brownlees came within subsection (2), relating to dealings "between merchants." The Brownlees admit that their crops are "goods." The partnership had been operating the row crop farming business for 14 years, producing peanuts, soybeans, corn, milo, and wheat on 1,350 acres, and selling the crops.

It is also established that Barney Brownlee was familiar with the marketing procedure of "booking" crops, which sometimes occurred over the telephone between the farmer and the buyer, rather than in person, and a written contract would be signed later. He periodically called Goldkist's agent to check the price, which fluctuated. If the price met his approval, he sold soybeans. At this time the partnership still had some of its 1982 crop in storage, and the price was rising slowly. Mr. Brownlee received a written confirmation in the mail concerning a sale of soybeans and did not contact Goldkist to contest it but simply did nothing.

To allow a farmer who deals in crops of the kind at issue, or who otherwise comes within the definition of "merchant" to renege on a confirmed oral booking for the sale of crops would result in a fraud on the buyer. The farmer could abide by the booking if the price thereafter declined but reject it if the price rose; the buyer, on the other hand, would be forced to sell the crop following the booking at its peril, or wait until the farmer decides whether to honor the booking or not.

The Brownlees' narrow construction of "merchant" would, given the booking procedure used for the sale of farm products, thus guarantee to the farmers the best of both possible worlds (fulfill booking if price goes down after booking and reject it if price improves) and to the buyers the worst of both possible worlds. On the other hand, construing "merchants" as not excluding as a matter of law farmers such as the ones in this case protects them equally as well as the buyer. If the market price declines after the booking, they are assured of the higher booking price; the buyer cannot renege, as UCC section 2–201(2) would apply.

We believe this is the proper construction to give the two statutes, UCC section 2–104 [which defines "merchant"] and 2–201, as taken together they are thus further branches stemming from the centuries-old simple legal idea *pacta servanda sunt*—agreements are to be kept. So construed, they evince the legislative intent to enforce the accepted practices of the marketplace among those who frequent it.

Judgment reversed in favor of Goldkist.

Part Payment or Part Delivery

Suppose Rice and Cooper enter a contract for the sale of 1,000 units of goods at $1 each. After Rice has paid $600, Cooper refuses to deliver the goods and asserts the statute of frauds as a defense to enforcement of the contract. The Code permits part payment or part delivery to satisfy the statute of frauds, but *only for the quantity of goods that have been delivered or paid for* [2–201(3)(c)]. Thus, Cooper would be required to deliver only 600 units rather than the 1,000 units Rice alleges that he agreed to sell.

Admission in Pleadings or Court

Another situation in which the UCC statute of frauds can be satisfied without a writing occurs when the party being sued admits the existence of the oral contract in his trial testimony or in any document that he files with the court. For example, Nelson refuses to perform an oral contract he made with Smith for the sale of $2,000 worth of goods, and Smith sues him. If Nelson admits the existence of the oral contract in pleadings or in court proceedings, his admission is sufficient to meet the statute of frauds. This exception is justified by the strong evidence that such an admission provides. After all, what better evidence of a contract can there be than is provided when the party being sued admits under penalty of perjury that a contract exists? When such an admission is made, the statute of frauds is satisfied as to *the quantity of goods admitted* [2–201(3)(b)]. For exam-ple, if Nelson only admits contracting for $1,000 worth of goods, the contract is enforceable only to that extent.

Specially Manufactured Goods

Finally, an oral contract within the UCC statute of frauds can be enforced without a writing in some situations involving the sale of *specially manufactured goods*. This exception to the writing requirement will apply only if the nature of the specially manufactured goods is such that they are not suitable for sale in the ordinary course of the seller's business. Completely executory oral contracts are not enforceable under this exception. The seller must have made a substantial beginning in manufacturing the goods for the buyer, or must have made commitments for their procurement, before receiving notice that the buyer was repudiating the sale [2–201(3)(a)]. For example, Bennett Co. has an oral contract with Stevenson for the sale of $2,500 worth of calendars imprinted with Bennett Co.'s name and address. If Bennett Co. repudiates the contract *before* Stevenson has made a substantial beginning in manufacturing the calendars, the contract will be unenforceable under the statute of frauds. If, however, Bennett Co. repudiated the contract *after* Stevenson had made a substantial beginning, the oral contract would be enforceable.

The specially manufactured goods provision is based both on the evidentiary value of the seller's conduct and on the need to avoid the injustice that would otherwise result from the seller's reliance.

FIGURE 2 Satisfying the Statute of Frauds for a Contract for the Sale of Goods for a Price of $500 or More

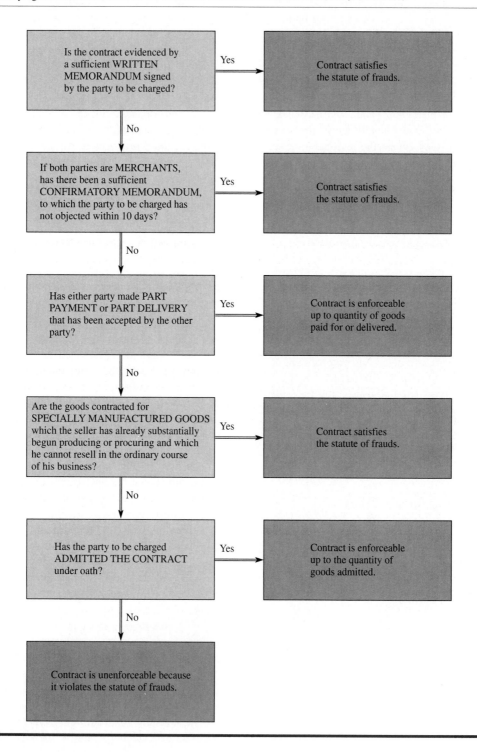

PROMISSORY ESTOPPEL AND THE STATUTE OF FRAUDS

The statute of frauds, which was created to prevent fraud and perjury, has often been criticized because it can create unjust results. One of the troubling features of the statute is that it can as easily be used to defeat a contract that was actually made as it can to defeat a fictitious agreement. As you have seen, courts and legislatures have created several exceptions to the statute of frauds that reduce the statute's potential for creating unfair results. In recent years, courts in some states have begun to use the doctrine of **promissory estoppel**[6] to allow some parties to recover under oral contracts that the statute of frauds would ordinarily render unenforceable.

Courts in these states hold that, when one of the parties would suffer serious losses because of her reliance on an oral contract, the other party is estopped from raising the statute of frauds as a defense. This position has been approved in the *Restatement (Second) of Contracts*. Section 139 of the *Restatement* provides that a promise that induces action or forbearance can be enforceable notwithstanding the statute of frauds if the reliance was foreseeable to the person making the promise and if injustice can be avoided only by enforcing the promise. The idea behind this section and the cases employing promissory estoppel is that the statute of frauds, which is designed to prevent injustice, should not be allowed to work an injustice. Section 139 and these cases also impliedly recognize the fact that the reliance required by promissory estoppel to some extent provides evidence of the existence of a contract between the parties, since it is unlikely that a person would materially rely on a nonexistent promise.

The use of promissory estoppel as a means of circumventing the statute of frauds is still controversial, however. Many courts fear that enforcing oral contracts on the basis of a party's reliance will essentially negate the statute. In cases involving the UCC statute of frauds, an additional source of concern involves the interpretation of section 2–201. Some courts have construed the provisions listing specific alternative methods of satisfying 2–201's formal requirements to be *exclusive*, precluding the creation of any further exceptions by courts.

---

[6] The doctrine of promissory estoppel is discussed in the Introduction to Contracts chapter and the Consideration chapter.

THE PAROL EVIDENCE RULE

Explanation of the Rule

In many situations, contracting parties prefer to express their agreements in writing even when they are not required to do so by the statute of frauds. Written contracts rarely come into being without some prior discussions or negotiations between the parties, however. Various promises, proposals, or representations are usually made by one or both of the parties before the execution of a written contract. What happens when one of those prior promises, proposals, or representations is not included in the terms of the written contract? For example, suppose that Jackson wants to buy Stone's house. During the course of negotiations, Stone states that he will pay for any major repairs that the house needs for the first year that Jackson owns it. The written contract that the parties ultimately sign, however, does not say anything about Stone paying for repairs, and, in fact, states that Jackson will take the house "as is." The furnace breaks down three months after the sale, and Stone refuses to pay for its repair. What is the status of Stone's promise to pay for repairs? The basic problem is one of defining the boundaries of the parties' agreement. Are all the promises made in the process of negotiation part of the contract, or do the terms of the written document that the parties signed supersede any preliminary agreements?

The **parol evidence rule** provides the answer to this question. The term *parol evidence* means written or spoken statements that are *not contained in the written contract*. The parol evidence rule provides that, when parties enter a *written contract* that they intend as a complete **integration** (a complete and final statement of their agreement), a court will not permit the use of evidence of *prior* or *contemporaneous* statements to add to, alter, or contradict the terms of the written contract. This rule is based on the presumption that when people enter into a written contract, the best evidence of their agreement is the written contract itself. It also reflects the idea that later expressions of intent are presumed to prevail over earlier expressions of intent. In the hypothetical case involving Stone and Jackson, assuming that they intended the written contract to be the final integration of their agreement, Jackson would not be able to introduce evidence of Stone's promise to pay for repairs. The effect of excluding preliminary promises or statements from consideration is, of course, to confine the parties' contract to the terms of the written agreement. The lesson to be learned from this example is that people who put their agreements in writing should make sure that all the terms of their agreement are included in the writing. The following case, *Slivinsky v. Watkins-Johnson Company*, illustrates the application of the parol evidence rule.

SLIVINSKY v. WATKINS-JOHNSON COMPANY
270 Cal. Rptr. 585 (Cal Ct. App. 1990)

In July of 1984, Sandra Slivinsky applied for a job as a materials scientist with Watkins-Johnson Company, a large aerospace manufacturer. Directly above the signature line on the application she signed was the statement: "I understand that employment by WATKINS-JOHNSON COMPANY is conditional upon . . . execution of an Employment Agreement. . . . I further understand that if I become employed by Watkins-Johnson Company, there will be no agreement, expressed or implied, between the company and me for any specific period of employment, nor for continuing or long-term employment." Over the next several months, Watkins-Johnson contacted Slivinsky's references, requested her transcripts, and set up a series of interviews. Slivinsky claims that at these interviews she was promised "long-term," "indefinite," and "permanent" employment, not dependent on business cycles, and subject to termination only for cause. Finally, Watkins-Johnson made a verbal offer of employment to Slivinsky and she accepted. On January 7, 1985, which was Slivinksky's first day at work, Slivinsky signed the employee agreement that had been referred to in her employment application. Set apart in bold type, the last paragraph of this agreement provided that there was no express or implied agreement between the parties regarding the duration of her employment and that the employment could be terminated at any time with or without cause.

As a result of the space shuttle Challenger disaster in January 1986, Watkins-Johnson experienced significant business losses and government contract cancellations. The management decided that employee cutbacks were essential to cope with the loss of business. Ultimately, 24 employees, including Slivinsky, were selected for the Reduction in Force program. Watkins-Johnson terminated her employment in June of 1986.

Slivinsky brought suit against Watkins-Johnson for breach of the employment contract, asserting that she had been terminated without cause in violation of the parties' express and implied agreement. She also claimed that the reasons given for her termination were pretextual and that she was really fired for other reasons such as her supervisor disliking her. The trial court granted Watkins-Johnson's motion for summary judgment, and Slivinsky appealed.

Cottle, Associate Justice.   Slivinsky claims that the parties' employment agreement includes factors such as oral assurances of job security and Watkins-Johnson's personnel policies and practices not to terminate employees except for good cause. Watkins-Johnson [argues] that it is limited to the parties' express written contract defining the employment as at-will.

The dispositive issue, therefore, is whether we can look beyond the four corners of the parties' written agreements to ascertain the complete agreement of the parties. The answer to that question involves application of the parol evidence rule, a rule of substantive law precluding the introduction of evidence which varies or contradicts the terms of an integrated written instrument. If the parties intended that the Application and Employment Agreement constituted an integration, *i.e.*, the final expression of their agreement with respect to grounds for termination, then those agreements may not be contradicted by evidence of any prior agreement or of a contemporaneous oral agreement. No particular form is required for an integrated agreement. When only part of the agreement is integrated, the parol evidence rule applies to that part.

Applying these standards, we conclude that the contract was integrated with respect to the grounds for termination. Slivinsky's employment application specifically conditioned employment upon execution of an employment agreement. It further provided that if Slivinsky were to become employed by Watkins-Johnson, there "will be no agreement, expressed or implied, . . . for any specific period of employment, nor for continuing or long term employment." When Slivinsky executed the Employee Agreement, she acknowledged "that there is no agreement, express or implied, between employee and the Company for any specific period of employment, nor for continuing or long-term employment. Employee and the Company each have a right to terminate employment, with or without cause." Reading these documents together, the only reasonable conclusion that can be drawn is that the parties intended that there would be no other agreement regarding termination other than that set forth in the Employee Agreement. Consequently, evidence of an implied agreement which contradicts the terms of the written agreement is not admissible. There cannot be a valid express contract and an implied contract, each embracing the same subject, but requiring different results.

Because we hold that the contract is a contract for employment terminable at will, we do not reach the issues regarding whether good cause existed for Slivinsky's termination based on Watkins-Johnson's decision to reduce its work force. Even if the reduction in force were a pretextual ground for terminating Slivinsky's employment, it would not be actionable with an at-will employment contract unless the employer's motivation for a discharge contravenes some significant public policy principle. No such public policy violation is alleged here.

Judgment for Watkins-Johnson affirmed.

Scope of the Parol Evidence Rule

The parol evidence rule is relevant only in cases in which the parties have expressed their agreement in a *written* contract. Thus, it would *not* apply to a case involving an oral contract or to a case in which writings existed that were not intended to embody the final statement of at least part of the parties' contract. The parol evidence rule has been made a part of the law of sales in the Uniform Commercial Code [2–202], so it is applicable to contracts for the sale of goods as well as to contracts governed by the common law of contracts. Furthermore, the rule excludes only evidence of statements made *prior to* or *during* the signing of the written contract. It does not apply to statements made *after* the signing of the contract. Thus, evidence of *subsequent statements* is freely admissible.

Admissible Parol Evidence

In some situations, evidence of statements made outside the written contract is admissible notwithstanding the parol evidence rule. Parol evidence is permitted in the situations discussed below either because the writing is not the best evidence of the contract or because the evidence is offered, not to contradict the terms of the writing, but to explain the writing or to challenge the underlying contractual obligation that the writing represents.

Additional Terms in Partially Integrated Contracts In many instances, parties will desire to introduce evidence of statements or agreements that would *supplement* rather than contradict the written contract. Whether they can do this depends on whether the written contract is characterized as **completely integrated** or **partially integrated.** A completely integrated contract is one that the parties intend as a *complete and exclusive* statement of their entire agreement. A partially integrated contract is one that expresses the parties' final agreement as to some but not all of the terms of their contract. When a contract is only partially integrated, the parties are permitted to use parol evidence to prove the *additional* terms of their agreement. Such evidence cannot, however, be used to contradict the written terms of the contract.

To determine whether a contract is completely or partially integrated, a court must determine the parties' intent. A court judges intent by looking at the language of the contract, the apparent completeness of the writing, and all the surrounding circumstances. It will also consider whether the contract contains a **merger clause** (also known as an **integration clause).** These clauses, which are very common in form contracts and commercial contracts, provide that the written contract is the complete integration of the parties' agreement. They are designed to prevent a party from giving testimony about prior statements or agreements and are generally effective in indicating that the writing was a complete integration. Even though a contract contains a merger clause, parol evidence could be admissible under one of the following exceptions.

Explaining Ambiguities Parol evidence can be offered to *explain an ambiguity* in the written contract. Suppose a written contract between Lowen and Matthews provides that Lowen will buy "Matthews's truck," but Matthews has two trucks. The parties could offer evidence of negotiations, statements, and other circumstances preceding the creation of the written contract to identify the truck to which the writing refers. Used in this way, parol evidence helps the court interpret the contract. It does not contradict the written contract.

Circumstances Invalidating Contract Any circumstances that would be relevant to show that a contract is not valid can be proven by parol evidence. For example, evidence that Holden pointed a gun at Dickson and said, "Sign this contract, or I'll kill you," would be admissible to show that the contract was voidable because of duress. Likewise, parol evidence would be admissible to show that a contract was illegal or was induced by fraud, misrepresentation, undue influence, or mistake.

Existence of Condition It is also permissible to use parol evidence to show that a writing was executed with the understanding that it was *not to take effect until the occurrence of a condition* (a future, uncertain event that creates a duty to perform).[7] Suppose Farnsworth signs a contract to purchase a car with the agreement that the contract is not to be effective unless and until Farnsworth gets a new job. If the written contract is silent about any conditions that must occur before it becomes effective, Farnsworth could introduce parol evidence to prove the existence of the condition. Such proof merely elaborates on, but does not contradict, the terms of the writing.

Subsequent Agreements As you read earlier, the parol evidence rule does not forbid parties to introduce proof of *subsequent agreements*. This is true even if the terms of the later agreement cancel, subtract from, or add to the obligations stated in the written contract. The idea here is that when a writing is followed by a later statement or agreement, the writing is no longer the best evidence of the agreement. You should be aware, however, that subsequent modifications of contracts may sometimes be unenforceable due to lack of consideration or failure to comply with the statute of frauds. In addition, contracts sometimes expressly provide that modifications must be written. In this situation, an oral modification would be unenforceable.

---

[7] Conditions are discussed in greater detail in the Performance and Remedies chapter.

CONCEPT REVIEW

PAROL EVIDENCE RULE

The Parol Evidence Rule	*Applies when . . .* parties create a writing intended as a final and complete integration of at least part of the parties' contract.	*Provides that . . .* evidence of statements or promises made before or during the creation of the writing cannot be used to supplement, change, or contradict the terms of the written contract.
But Parol Evidence *Can* Be Used to	1. Prove consistent, additional terms when the contract is *partially integrated.* 2. Explain an ambiguity in the written contract. 3. Prove that the contract is void, voidable, or unenforceable. 4. Prove that the contract was subject to a condition. 5. Prove that the parties subsequently modified the contract or made a new agreement.	

INTERPRETATION OF CONTRACTS

Once a court has decided what promises are included in a contract, it is faced with *interpreting* the contract to determine the *meaning* and *legal effect* of the terms used by the parties. Courts have adopted broad, basic standards of interpretation that guide them in the interpretation process.

The court will first attempt to determine the parties' *principal objective*. Every clause will then be determined in the light of this principal objective. Ordinary words will be given their usual meaning and technical words (such as those that have a special meaning in the parties' trade or business) will be given their technical meaning, unless a different meaning was clearly intended.

Guidelines grounded in common sense are also used to determine the relationship of the various terms of the contract. Specific terms that follow general terms are presumed to qualify those general terms. Suppose that a provision that states that the subject of the contract is "guaranteed for one year" is followed by a provision describing the "one-year guarantee against defects in workmanship." Here, it is fair to conclude that the more specific term qualifies the more general term and that the guarantee described in the contract is a guarantee of workmanship only, and not of parts and materials.

Sometimes, there is internal conflict in the terms of an agreement and courts must determine which term should prevail. When the parties use a form contract or some other type of contract that is partially printed and partially handwritten, the handwritten provisions will prevail. If the contract was drafted by one of the parties, any ambiguities will be resolved *against* the party who drafted the contract.

If both parties to the contract are members of a trade, profession, or community in which certain words are commonly given a particular meaning (this is called a *usage*), the courts will presume that the parties intended the meaning that the usage gives to the terms they use. For example, if the word *dozen* in the bakery business means 13 rather than 12, a contract between two bakers for the purchase of 10 dozen loaves of bread will be presumed to mean 130 loaves of bread rather than 120. Usages can also add provisions to the parties' agreement. If the court finds that a certain practice is a matter of common usage in the parties' trade, it will assume that the parties intended to include that practice in their agreement. If contracting parties are members of the same trade, business, or community but do not intend to be bound by usage, they should specifically say so in their agreement.

ETHICAL AND PUBLIC POLICY CONCERNS

1. The statute of frauds requires written evidence of *some*, but not all, contracts. Is this defensible from a public policy standpoint? Would it be preferable for the law to simply require that *all* contracts be evidenced by a writing?

2. What ethical problem was the statute of frauds designed to prevent, and what ethical problem does the statute of frauds create? Is the "cure worse than the disease"?

3. Under the law of some states, the doctrine of promissory estoppel permits the enforcement of promises that induce reliance, even when those promises do not comply with the statute of frauds. Should all states adopt this position? What effect would this have on the statute of frauds?

4. For those parties who draft and proffer standardized form contracts, the parol evidence rule can be a powerful ally because it has the effect of limiting the scope of an integrated, written contract to the terms of the writing. Although statements and promises made to a person before he signs a contract might be highly influential in persuading him to enter the contract, the parol evidence rule effectively prevents these precontract communications from being legally enforceable. Consider also that standardized form contracts are usually drafted for the benefit of and proffered by the more sophisticated and powerful party in a contract (e.g., the insurance company rather than the insured, the automobile dealer rather than the customer, the landlord rather than the tenant). Considering all of this, do you believe that the parol evidence rule promotes ethical behavior?

SUMMARY

All states have enacted statutes patterned after the English Statute of Frauds. These statutes state that certain types of contracts must be evidenced by a writing to be enforceable. Although the statutes are not uniform, generally included in the class of contracts for which a writing is required are collateral contracts; contracts for the sale of an interest in land; bilateral, executory contracts that cannot be performed within a year from the date on which the contract came into existence; and contracts for the sale of goods for a price of $500 or more. The statute of frauds applies only to executory contracts. A contract that fails to comply with the requirements of the statute of frauds is unenforceable, not void or voidable. Violation of the statute of frauds will not be a ground for invalidating a contract that has already been performed. A person who has conferred benefits pursuant to a contract that is unenforceable because of the statute of frauds can recover what he has parted with under the doctrine of *quasi-contract*.

A collateral contract is a contract in which one person promises to pay the debt or obligation of another person. A collateral contract must be distinguished from an original contract (in which a person obligates herself to perform an obligation in all events rather than merely to pay if another person fails to do so). No writing is required for an original contract unless it falls within some other provision of the statute of frauds. If a person's primary purpose in promising to pay the debt of another is to benefit himself, the *leading object* or *main purpose* exception to the statute of frauds provides that the promise does not have to be evidenced by a writing.

A contract involving the creation or transfer of ownership of any interest in land is within the statute of frauds. This includes ownership interests less than full ownership, such as easements, long-term leases, options, and mortgages. If a person has done acts in reliance on an oral contract for the sale of land, he may be able to obtain specific performance of the contract (but not damages) if the nature of his reliance is such that restitution (the return of what he parted with) would not be an adequate remedy.

Bilateral contracts that cannot be performed within a year from the date on which the contract came into existence are also within the statute of frauds. To determine whether a contract comes within the one-year provision, the amount of time between the date on which the contract came into being and the date on which the terms provide that performance will be completed must be calculated. Contracts for an indefinite period of time, even those "for life," are not within the statute of frauds of most states, because they *can* be performed within a year. In most states, complete performance by one of the parties will take the contract out of the statute of frauds and an oral contract will be enforceable.

Under UCC section 2–201, contracts for the sale of goods for a price of $500 or more are within the statute of frauds and must be evidenced by a writing or come within an exception to the writing requirement specified in the UCC. Modifications of sale of goods contracts are within the statute of frauds if the sales price of the contract as modified exceeds $500.

If a contract is within the statute of frauds and none of the exceptions to the statute of frauds is applicable, the contract must be evidenced by a memorandum indicating the existence of the contract. The memorandum does not have to *be* the contract, or even be intended by the parties as binding, but it must provide written evidence tending to prove that a contract exists. The memorandum must be signed by the party who is using the statute of frauds as a defense ("the party to be charged"). It must identify the parties and the subject matter and, to varying degrees controlled by state law, describe the important terms of the agreement. In sale of goods contracts, the UCC states that it does not matter whether the memorandum states all of the important terms, or even states some of them incorrectly, but the contract cannot be enforced for more than the quantity indicated in the memorandum.

The UCC provides for four additional ways of satisfying the statute of frauds in sale of goods contracts for $500 or more. Parties can use these ways to satisfy the statute when they do not have a writing or when they have a writing, but it is not signed by the party to be charged. First, if both parties are merchants and one of them sends a *confirmatory memorandum* signed by him, stating a quantity and indicating that a contract has been made, the memo will be sufficient to meet the statute of frauds if the other party receives it, has reason to know of its contents, and does not object in writing within 10 days. Second, an oral contract for the sale of $500 or more worth of *specially manufactured goods* is enforceable if the specially manufactured goods are of a type that cannot be resold in the ordinary course of the seller's business and if the seller has already made a substantial beginning in manufacturing the goods or has made commitments to procure the goods. Third, an oral contract for the sale of goods for a price of $500 or more can be enforced up to the quantity paid for or delivered if there has been *part payment or part delivery*. Fourth, an oral sale of goods contract for a price of $500 or more can be enforced up to the quantity admitted if the party against whom enforcement is sought *admits the existence of the contract* in court proceedings or pleadings.

In some states, the doctrine of promissory estoppel has been applied to estop a party from asserting the statute of frauds when the other party has been induced to rely materially on an oral contract and would suffer serious losses if the contract were not enforced.

The parol evidence rule provides that evidence of statements made prior to or during the signing of a written contract cannot be admitted to add to, alter, or vary the terms of the written contract. The parol evidence rule is part of the UCC as well as the common law of contracts. There are a variety of purposes for which parol evidence (evidence of statements not contained in the written contract) can be used, however. First, the parol evidence rule applies to prevent the use of evidence of prior or contemporaneous statements only. Evidence of *subsequent agreements* is admissible. Second, parol evidence can be used to add to or supplement a written contract if the contract is only *partially integrated*. Courts will look at the language and completeness of the contract and all the surrounding circumstances to tell whether the contract is completely or partially integrated. Contracts often contain *merger clauses* (also known as *integration clauses*), which specifically state that the writing is the complete statement of the parties' agreement. Third, parol evidence can be used to demonstrate *circumstances invalidating the contract,* for example, to show that the contract was unenforceable due to illegality or voidable due to duress, undue influence, mistake, fraud, or misrepresentation. Fourth, parol evidence can be used to *explain ambiguous terms* in the contract. Fifth, parol evidence is admissible to show that *the contract was not to be effective until the occurrence of a condition.*

Courts have developed guidelines to help them interpret the meaning and legal effect of language in a contract. They attempt to understand the parties' principal objective and to interpret the individual provisions of the contract so as to further that objective. Courts use specific rules to resolve situations in which ambiguity exists or there is an internal inconsistency in the terms used in the contract. Usages of a trade or industry are also helpful in determining the meaning and effect of contract terms.

PROBLEM CASES

1. Golomb allegedly orally agreed to sell to Lee for $275,000 the Ferrari once owned by King Leopold of Belgium. Golomb ultimately refused to sell the car and Lee sued him. At trial, Golomb denied ever promising to sell the car to Lee. Can Lee enforce this alleged promise? *No because must be in writing*

2. Gross was the primary creditor of Wind Surfing, a manufacturer of ski apparel. Gross, who had loaned $47,000 to Wind Surfing, also had hopes of acquiring a one-third interest in the company. Wind Surfing also owed money to White Stag, and White Stag was unwilling to fill any new orders until Wind Surfing's past due balance was paid. Gross persuaded White Stag to extend credit to Wind Surfing for the upcoming ski season by assuring it that he would give White Stag a letter of credit or his personal guaranty to secure payment of Wind Surfing's past due balance. White Stag agreed to give Wind Surfing an open line of credit for $25,000 if Gross would give his guaranty or provide a bank letter of credit. White Stag sent Gross a confirmatory letter, with which it enclosed a personal guaranty form for Gross to sign. The personal guaranty form was never signed and returned. White Stag nevertheless released Wind Surfing's order and made shipments of goods over the next months until Wind Surfing's outstanding balance was $49,637.87. Wind Surfing never paid its accounts. White Stag sued Gross to collect the debt. Is Gross's oral promise to guarantee the debt enforceable? *Yes Because Exception*

3. In 1977, Barrett and her husband moved to San Antonio to live in a house that stood on property owned by her father, Field. The parties agreed that the Barretts would live in it and pay rent for at least six months before deciding whether to buy it. The Barretts spent two or three months fixing up the house before they moved in. When they moved in, they began paying Field $100 per month rent. After several years, the Barretts orally agreed to buy the property from Field. Under the terms of this agreement, the purchase price was to be the appraised value of the property, payments were to be $100 per month, and the money that they had paid Field for rent was to be applied to the purchase price. Field and Mr. Barrett "paced off" the land that was to be sold. A survey performed later indicated that this was 2.981 acres. All of the monthly checks for $100 that the Barretts wrote to Field were labeled "rent." Field died as a result of an unsolved homicide. His residence was largely destroyed by arson. No records were found pertaining to the sale of the property to the Barretts. Is the oral contract enforceable? *Yes, Exception, part performance*

4. The Palermos <u>orally</u> ordered carpeting, padding, and tile for a sales price of more than $4,000 from Colorado Carpet, a retailer and installer of such goods. All of these items were stock items with no special dying, cutting, or other special features. Colorado Carpet ordered the carpeting from manufacturers, who filled the orders and delivered the carpeting to a Denver warehouse. Colorado Carpet also purchased and delivered tile to the Palermos, but, after a disagreement with the Palermos, Colorado Carpet removed the tile, returned half of it to the supplier for a refund, and sold the other half. It also shipped part of the carpeting back to its manufacturer for some credit and sold the rest to a local purchaser. Colorado Carpet then sued the Palermos for its lost profits, labor, and storage and shipping costs. Is its contract with the Palermos enforceable? *No contract over $500, must be in writing*

5. In June 1976, Moore went to First National Bank and requested the president of the bank to allow his sons, Rocky and Mike, to open an account in the name of Texas Continental Express, Inc. Moore promised to bring his own business to the bank and orally agreed to make good any losses that the bank might incur from receiving dishonored checks from Texas Continental. The bank then furnished regular checking account and bank draft services to Texas Continental. Several years later, Texas Continental wrote checks totaling $448,942.05 that were returned for insufficient funds. Texas Continental did not cover the checks, and the bank turned to Moore for payment. When Moore refused to pay, the bank sued him. Does Moore have a good statute of frauds defense? *Yes, Not in writing*

6. In January 1980, Mayer entered into an oral contract of employment with King Cola for a three-year term. Mayer moved from Chattanooga to St. Louis and began working. King Cola paid his moving expenses. In accordance with the parties' negotiations, Mayer awaited a written contract, but none was ever executed. The employment relationship soon began to deteriorate, and after several months King Cola's president told Mayer that he was not going to be given a contract. In May 1980, King Cola discharged Mayer. In a state that does not recognize the doctrine of promissory estoppel as an exception to the statute of frauds, will Mayer be able to enforce the contract? *No! because they don't enforce Promissory estoppel*

7. Everlener Dyer purchased a used Ford from Walt Bennett Ford for $5,895. She signed a written contract, which showed that no taxes were included in the sales price. Dyer contended, however, that the salesman who negotiated the purchase with her told her both before and after her signing of the contract that the sales tax on the automobile had been paid. The contract Dyer signed contained the following language:

The above comprises the entire agreement pertaining to this purchase and no other agreement of any kind, verbal understanding, representation, or promise whatsoever will be recognized.

It also stated:

This contract constitutes the entire agreement between the parties and no modification hereof shall be valid in any event and Buyer expressly waives the right to rely thereon, unless made in writing, signed by Seller.

PAROLE EVIDENCE RULE   *Not specific written in contract*
Later, when Dyer attempted to license the automobile, she discovered that the Arkansas sales tax had not been paid on it. She paid the sales tax and sued Bennett for breach of contract. What result? *won't win*

8. On Labor Day weekend, Grove participated in the Dickinson Elks Club's annual Labor Day Golf Tournament, which he had learned about from a poster that was placed at a golf course. Included in the poster was an offer by Charbonneau Buick-Pontiac of a 1974 automobile "to the first entry who shoots a hole-in-one on Hole No. 8." This offer was also placed on a sign on the automobile at the tournament. The Dickinson golf course at which the tournament was played had only 9 holes, but there were 18 separately located and marked tee areas, so that the course could be played as an 18-hole course by going around the 9-hole course twice. The first nine tees were marked with blue markers and tee numbers. The second nine tees were marked with red markers and tee numbers. Because of this layout of the course, the tee area marked "8" and the tee area marked "17" were both played to the eighth hole. The tee area marked "17" lay to one side of the tee area marked "8" and was approximately 60 yards farther from the hole. Grove scored a hole-in-one on hole No. 8 on the first day of the tournament while playing from the 17th tee in an 18-hole match. Grove claimed the prize, but Charbonneau refused to award it, insisting that Grove had not scored his hole-in-one on the 8th hole, as required, but had scored it on the 17th hole. Grove brought suit against Charbonneau for breach of contract. Will he win? *No. Written what suppose to do.*

9. Wilson entered into an oral contract over the telephone to sell Cargill 28,000 bushels of ordinary winter wheat at $1.48 per bushel and 6,000 bushels of higher-protein wheat at $1.63 per bushel. Both parties were merchants. Following the telephone call, Cargill's manager completed two standard grain purchase contracts, signed them as Cargill's agent, signed Wilson's name to them, and sent them to Wilson. Wilson received the contracts and made no objection to their contents or to the fact that Cargill's manager had signed Wilson's name to them. Wilson began delivering wheat, but several months later Cargill discovered that Wilson did not intend to deliver the rest of the wheat. It sued Wilson for breach of contract. Wilson asserted the statute of frauds as a defense. Will Cargill prevail? *Yes. V/L agreement*

10. Katz, by his agent, made a written offer to buy real estate from the Joiners. On October 13, Katz called Mr. Joiner to ask his intentions. Mr. Joiner replied that everything was agreeable, that they had a deal, and that he was going to execute the contract and mail it back. The Joiners signed the contract and deposited it in the mail on October 20 to be delivered to Katz. Also on October 20, however, Mr. Joiner sent a telegram to arrive before the arrival of the contract. It stated, "In reference to Earnest Money Contract for Lot 4, Block 19, CB9919 Unit 3, Rollingwood Estates, Bexar County, Texas. I have signed and returned contract but have changed my mind. Do not wish to sell property." Does this contract satisfy the requirements of the statute of frauds?

Contract for Real Estate within Statute of Frauds

11. Lovely was living in Ann Arbor, Michigan, and working at two jobs there when Dierkes offered Lovely employment with the Real Food Company in Jackson, Michigan. Dierkes promised Lovely a three-year employment contract, a salary of $400 per week, and a percentage interest in Real Food. He also promised that Lovely would not be discharged without good cause. Lovely relocated his family to Jackson in reliance on Dierkes's promise. He began performing under the agreement and requested several times that Dierkes reduce the contract to writing. Dierkes allegedly assured Lovely that a writing was forthcoming. After two months of employment, Dierkes discharged Lovely. Lovely sued Dierkes and Real Food for breach of contract. Dierkes claims that the contract is unenforceable because of the statute of frauds. Can Lovely enforce this contract?

Reliance
Specific performance
to get job & contract   P 329

CHAPTER 17

RIGHTS OF THIRD PARTIES

INTRODUCTION

In preceding chapters, we have emphasized the way in which an agreement between two or more people creates legal rights and duties *on the part of the contracting parties*. Since a contract is founded upon the consent of the contracting parties, it might seem to follow that they are the only ones who have rights and duties under the contract. Although this is generally true, there are two situations in which people who were not parties to a contract have legally enforceable rights under it: when a contract has been **assigned** (transferred) to a third party and when a contract is intended to benefit a third person **(third party beneficiary).** This chapter discusses the circumstances in which third parties have rights under a contract.

ASSIGNMENTS OF CONTRACTS

Contracts give people both rights and duties. If Murphy buys Wagner's motorcycle and promises to pay him $1,000 for it, Wagner has the *right* to receive Murphy's promised performance (the payment of the $1,000) and Murphy has the *duty* to perform the promise by paying $1,000. In most situations, contract rights can be transferred to a third person and contract duties can be delegated to a third person. The transfer of a *right* under a contract is called an **assignment.** The appointment of another person *to perform a duty* under a contract is called a **delegation.**

Nature of Assignment of Rights

A person who owes a duty to perform under a contract is called an **obligor.** The person to whom he owes the duty is called the **obligee.** For example, Samson borrows $500 from Jordan, promising to repay Jordan in six months. Samson, who owes the duty to pay the money, is the obligor, and Jordan, who has the right to receive the money, is the obligee. An assignment occurs when the obligee transfers his right to receive the obligor's performance to a third person. When there has been an assignment, the person making the assignment—the original obligee—is then called the **assignor.** The person to whom the right has been transferred is called the **assignee.**

Suppose that Jordan, the obligee in the example above, assigns his right to receive Samson's payment to Kane. Here, Jordan is the assignor and Kane is the assignee. The relationship between the three parties is represented in Figure 1. Notice that the assignment is a separate transaction; it occurs *after* the formation of the original contract.

FIGURE 1   Assignment of Rights

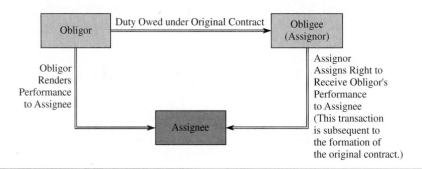

The effect of the assignment is to extinguish the assignor's right to receive performance and to transfer that right to the assignee. In the above example, Kane now owns the right to collect payment from Samson. If Samson fails to pay, Kane, as an assignee, now has the right to file suit against Samson to collect the debt.

People assign rights for a variety of reasons. A person might assign a right to a third party to satisfy a debt that he owes. For example, Jordan, the assignor in the above example, owes money to Kane, so he assigns to Kelly the right to receive the $500 that Samson owes him. A person might also sell or pledge the rights owed to him to obtain financing. In the case of a business, the money owed to a business by customers and clients is called *accounts receivable*. A business's accounts receivable are an asset to the business that can be used to raise money in several ways. For example, the business may pledge its accounts receivable as collateral for a loan. Suppose Ace Tree Trimming Co. wants to borrow money from First Bank and gives First Bank a security interest (an interest in the debtor's property that secures the debtor's performance of an obligation) in its accounts receivable.[1] If Ace defaults in its payments to First Bank, First Bank will acquire Ace's rights to collect the accounts receivable. A person might also make an assignment of a contract right as a gift. For example, Lansing owes $2,000 to Father. Father assigns the right to receive Lansing's performance to Son as a graduation gift.

Evolution of the Law Regarding Assignments   Contract rights have not always been transferable. Early common law refused to permit assignment or delegation

because debts were considered to be too personal to transfer. A debtor who failed to pay an honest debt was subject to severe penalties, including imprisonment, because such a failure to pay was viewed as the equivalent of theft. The identity of the creditor was of great importance to the debtor, since one creditor might be more lenient than another. Courts also feared that the assignment of debts would stir up unwanted litigation. In an economy that was primarily land-based, the extension of credit was of relatively small importance. As trade increased and became more complex, however, the practice of extending credit became more common. The needs of an increasingly commercial society demanded that people be able to trade freely in intangible assets such as debts. Consequently, the rules of law regarding the assignment of contracts gradually became more liberal. Today, public policy favors free assignability of contracts.

Sources of Assignment Law Today   Legal principles regarding assignment are found not only in the common law of contracts, but also in Articles 2 and 9 of the Uniform Commercial Code. Section 2–210 of Article 2 contains principles applicable to assignments of rights under a *contract for the sale of goods*. Article 9 governs security interests in accounts and other contract rights as well as the outright sale of accounts. Article 9's treatment of assignments will be discussed in more detail in the Security Interests in Personal Property chapter but some provisions of Article 9 relating to assignments will be discussed in this chapter.

Creating an Assignment

An assignment can be made in any way that is sufficient to show the assignor's intent to assign. No formal

---

[1] Security interests in accounts and other property are discussed in the Security Interests in Personal Property chapter.

language is required, and a writing is not necessary unless required by a provision of the statute of frauds or some other statute. Many states do have statutes requiring certain types of assignments to be evidenced by a writing, however. Additionally, an assignment for the purposes of security must meet Article 9's formal requirements for security interests.[2]

It is not necessary that the assignee give any consideration to the assignor in exchange for the assignment. Gratuitous assignments (those for which the assignee gives no value) are generally revocable until such time as the obligor satisfies the obligation, however. They can be revoked by the assignor's death or incapacity or by notification of revocation given by the assignor to the assignee.

Assignability of Rights

Most, but not all, contract rights are assignable. Although the free assignability of contract rights performs a valuable function in our modern credit-based economy, assignment is undesirable if it would adversely affect some important public policy or if it would materially vary the bargained-for expectations of the parties. There are several basic limitations on the assignability of contract rights.

First, an assignment will not be effective if it is *contrary to public policy*. For example, most states have enacted statutes that prohibit or regulate a wage earner's assignment of future wages. These statutes are designed to protect people against unwisely impoverishing themselves by signing away their future incomes.

Second, an assignment will not be effective if it *adversely affects the obligor in some significant way*. An assignment is ineffective if it materially changes the obligor's duty or increases the burden or risk on the obligor. Naturally, any assignment will change an obligor's duty

---

[2] These requirements are discussed in the Security Interests in Personal Property chapter.

to some extent. The obligor will have to pay money or deliver goods or render some other performance to X instead of to Y. These changes are not considered to be sufficiently material to render an assignment ineffective. Thus, a right to receive money or goods or land is generally assignable. In addition, covenants not to compete are generally considered to be assignable to buyers of businesses. For example, Jefferson sells RX Drugstore to Waldman, including in the contract of sale a covenant whereby Jefferson promises not to operate a competing drugstore within a 30-mile radius of RX for 10 years after the sale. Waldman later sells RX to Tharp. Here, Tharp could enforce the covenant not to compete against Jefferson. The reason for permitting assignment of covenants not to compete is that the purpose of such covenants is to protect an asset of the business— goodwill—for which the buyer has paid.

An assignment could be ineffective because of its variation of the obligor's duty, however, if the contract right involved a *personal relationship* or an element of *personal skill, judgment, or character*. For this reason, contracts of employment in which an employee works under the direct and personal supervision of an employer cannot be assigned to a new employer. An employer could assign a contract of employment, however, if the assignee-employer could perform the contract without adversely affecting the interests of the employee, such as would be the case when an employment relationship does not involve personal supervision by an individual employer. This point is illustrated by the following case, *Special Products Manufacturing, Inc. v. Douglass*.

A purported assignment is ineffective if it significantly increases the burden of the obligor's performance. For example, if Walker contracts to sell Dwyer all of its requirements of wheat, a purported assignment of Dwyer's rights to a corporation that has much greater requirements of wheat would probably be ineffective because it would significantly increase the burden on Walker.

SPECIAL PRODUCTS MANUFACTURING, INC. v. DOUGLASS
553 N.Y.S.2d 506 (N.Y. S. Ct., App. Div. 1990)

Thaddeus Douglass was a highly trained servicer of hardness-testing machinery who was employed by Page-Wilson Corporation. In August and April of 1983, Douglass signed two employment agreements governing the terms and conditions of his employment with Page-Wilson. The first agreement prohibited Douglass, while he was working for Page-Wilson and for one year after the termination of his employment, from using, to Page-Wilson's detriment, any of its customer lists or other intellectual property acquired from his job there. The second agreement, which applied to the same time period, prohibited Douglass from accepting employment from or serving as a consultant to any business that was in competition with Page-Wilson. In April of 1987, Canrad Corporation purchased all assets and contractual rights of Page-Wilson, including Douglass's two employment contracts. Special Products Manufacturing (Special Products), a wholly owned subsidiary of Canrad, assumed plant operations. Douglass worked for Special Products until his resignation in February of 1988.

Shortly after that, Special Products filed this lawsuit against Douglass, alleging that Douglass had affixed his name and home telephone number to the machines he serviced, so that the ensuing maintenance calls would reach him personally. It also alleged that, following his resignation, Douglass established a competing business and actively solicited Special Products's clientele. Douglass did not answer the complaint in a timely manner, and, after a long delay, the trial judge entered a default judgment in favor of Special Products. Douglass appealed this order, arguing in part that Special Products did not have the right to enforce the agreements not to compete.

Yesawich, Justice.   We perceive no merit in the contention that because Douglass entered into the agreements with Page-Wilson, they are unenforceable by Special Products. In an uncontroverted affidavit based upon personal knowledge, Special Products's vice-president of sales avows that Special Products acquired all of Page-Wilson's contract rights, including Douglass's. Douglass's consent was not required to effectuate this transfer. When the original parties to an agreement so intend, a covenant not to compete is freely assignable. Here, such intent is unmistakably evident in the first employment agreement which expressly "inure[s] to the benefit of the successors and assigns of Page-Wilson." And, while the second document contains no similar provision, neither does it specifically forbid assignment. Because executory contracts, which do not involve exceptional personal skills on the part of the assignor and which the assignee can perform without adversely affecting the rights and interests of the adverse party, are freely assignable absent a contractual, statutory or public policy prohibition, a clear and unambiguous prohibition is essential to effectively prevent assignment. Accordingly, the assignment to Special Products perpetuated the restrictive covenant provision, the very terms of which Douglass violated without justification.

Order in favor of Special Products affirmed.

Contract Clauses Prohibiting Assignment   A contract right may also be nonassignable because *the original contract expressly forbids assignment*. For example, leases often contain provisions forbidding assignment or requiring the tenant to obtain the landlord's permission for assignment.[3]

Antiassignment clauses in contracts generally are enforceable. Because of the strong public policy favoring assignability, however, such clauses are often interpreted narrowly. For example, a court might view an assignment made in violation of an antiassignment clause as a breach of contract for which damages may be recovered, but not as an invalidation of the assignment. Another tactic is to interpret a contractual ban on assignment as prohibiting only the delegation of duties.

The UCC takes this latter position. Under section 2–210(2), a contract term that forbids assignment is interpreted as forbidding only the delegation of duties. Section 2–210 also states that a right to damages for breach of a whole sales contract or a right arising out of the assignor's performance of his entire obligation may be assigned even if a provision of the original sales contract prohibited assignment. In addition, UCC section 9–318(4) invalidates contract terms that prohibit (or re-

---

[3] The assignment of leases is discussed further in the Landlord and Tenant chapter.

quire the debtor's consent to) an assignment of an account or creation of a security interest in a right to receive money that is now due or that will become due.

Nature of Assignee's Rights

When an assignment occurs, the assignee is said to "step into the shoes of his assignor." This means that the assignee acquires all of the rights that his assignor had under the contract. The assignee has the right to receive the obligor's performance, and if performance is not forthcoming, the assignee has the right to sue in his own name for breach of the obligation. By the same token, the assignee acquires no greater rights than those possessed by the assignor.

Because the assignee has no greater rights than did the assignor, the obligor may assert any defense or claim against the assignee that he could have asserted against the assignor, subject to certain time limitations discussed below. A contract that is void, voidable, or unenforceable as between the original parties does not become enforceable just because it has been assigned to a third party. For example, if Richards induces Dillman's consent to a contract by duress and subsequently assigns his rights under the contract to Keith, Dillman can assert the doctrine of duress against Keith as a ground for avoiding the contract.

Importance of Notifying the Obligor   An assignee should promptly notify the obligor of the assignment. Although notification of the obligor is not necessary for the assignment to be valid, such notice is of great practical importance. One reason notice is important is that an obligor who does not have reason to know of the assignment could render performance to the assignor and claim that his obligation had been discharged by performance. An obligor who renders performance to the assignor without notice of the assignment has no further liability under the contract. For example, McKay borrows $500 from Goodheart, promising to repay the debt by June 1. Goodheart assigns the debt to Rogers, but no one informs McKay of the assignment, and McKay pays the $500 to Goodheart, the assignor. In this case, McKay is not liable for any further payment. But if Rogers had immediately notified McKay of the assignment and, after receiving notice, McKay had mistakenly paid the debt to Goodheart, McKay would still have the legal obligation to pay $500 to Rogers. Having been given adequate notice of the assignment, he may remain liable to the assignee even if he later renders performance to the assignor.

An assignor who accepts performance from the obligor after the assignment holds any benefits that he receives as a trustee for the assignee. If the assignor fails to pay those benefits to the assignee, however, an obligor who has been notified of the assignment and renders performance to the wrong person may have to pay the same debt twice.

An obligor who receives notice of an assignment from the assignee will want to assure himself that the assignment has in fact occurred. He may ask for written evidence of the assignment or contact the assignee and ask for verification of the assignment. Under UCC section 9–318(3), a notification of assignment is ineffective unless it reasonably identifies the rights assigned. If requested by the account debtor (an obligor who owes money for goods sold or leased or services rendered), the assignee must furnish reasonable proof that the assignment has been made, and, unless he does so, the account debtor may disregard the notice and pay the assignor.

Defenses against the Assignee   An assignee's rights in an assignment are subject to the defenses that the obligor could have asserted against the assignor. Keep in mind that the assignee's rights are limited by the terms of the underlying contract between the assignor and the obligor. When defenses arise from the terms or performance of that contract, they can be asserted against the assignee even if they arise after the obligor receives notice of the assignment. For example, on June 1, Worldwide Widgets assigns to First Bank its rights under a contract with Widgetech, Inc. This contract obligates Worldwide Widgets to deliver a quantity of widgets to Widgetech by September 1, in return for which Widgetech is obligated to pay a stated purchase price. First Bank gives prompt notice of the assignment to Widgetech. Worldwide Widget fails to deliver the widgets and Widgetech refuses to pay. If First Bank brought an action against Widgetech to recover the purchase price of the widgets, Widgetech could assert Worldwide Widget's breach as a defense, even though the breach occurred after Widgetech received notice of the assignment.[4]

---

[4] Similarly, if the assignor's rights were subject to discharge because of other factors such as the nonoccurrence of a condition, impossibility, impracticability, or public policy, this can be asserted as a defense against the assignee even if the event occurs after the obligor receives notice of assignment. See *Restatement (Second) of Contracts* § 336(3). The doctrines relating to discharge from performance are explained in the Performance of Remedies chapter.

In determining what other defenses can be asserted against the assignee, the time of notification plays an important role. After notification, as we discussed earlier, payment by the obligor to the assignor will not discharge the obligor.

Counterclaims against the Assignee The obligor may also assert against the assignee certain counterclaims (claims entitling the obligor to some relief or remedy) that he could have asserted against the assignor. Unless the assignee has contracted for greater liability, he is liable on a counterclaim only to the extent of his claim against the obligor. In other words, a counterclaim by the obligor will only operate to subtract from the amount of the money to which the assignee is entitled.

A claim asserted by the obligor that arises from the original contract between assignor and obligor is known as **recoupment.** Such claims can be asserted even if they arise after notice of assignment. In the hypothetical case described earlier concerning the delivery of widgets, suppose that Worldwide Widgets had delivered widgets by September 1, but it breached a warranty by delivering widgets that were defective. When First Bank attempts to recover the purchase price of the widgets from Widgetech, Widgetech can assert Worldwide Widget's breach of warranty as a recoupment. The effect will be to reduce or negate its debt to First Bank.

An obligor is also permitted to assert against the assignee certain claims against the assignor that arose independently of the assigned contract. When an obligor asserts a counterclaim based on some obligation that arose independent of the assigned contract, this is called **set off.** An important limitation on the right of set off is that the claim must have accrued *before the obligor receives notification of the assignment.* For example, Doaks, the owner of an office building, leases space to Margolis. On April 1, Doaks makes an interest-free loan of $5,000 to Margolis, which Margolis agrees to repay in full on July 1. In an unrelated transaction on April 2, Doaks agrees to reimburse Margolis for the $200 that Margolis has spent to have a plumber repair some leaky pipes in the leased space. On June 1, Doaks assigns to Ruiz the right to receive the $5,000 from Margolis. Ruiz gives prompt notice of the assignment. If Margolis fails to pay his debt on time and Ruiz sues him to collect the $5,000, Margolis would be entitled to set off (subtract from that debt) the $200 that Doaks had agreed to pay for the plumber's bill.

Subsequent Assignments

An assignee may "reassign" a right to a third party, who would be called a **subassignee.** The subassignee then acquires the rights held by the prior assignee. He should give the obligor prompt notice of the subsequent assignment, because he takes his interest subject to the same principles discussed above regarding the claims and defenses that can be asserted against him.

Successive Assignments

Notice to the obligor may be important in one other situation. If an assignor assigns the same right to two assignees in succession, both of whom pay for the assignment, a question of priority results. An assignor who assigns the same right to different people will be held liable to the assignee who acquires no rights against the obligor, but which assignee is entitled to the obligor's performance? Which assignee will have recourse only against the assignor? There are several views on this point.

In states that follow the "American rule," the first assignee has the better right. This view is based on the rule of property law that a person cannot transfer greater rights in property that he owns. In states that follow the "English rule," however, the assignee who first gives notice of the assignment to the obligor, without knowledge of the other assignee's claim, has the better right. The *Restatement (Second) of Contracts* takes a third position. Section 342 of the *Restatement* provides that the first assignee has priority unless the subsequent assignee gives value (pays for the assignment) and, without having reason to know of the other assignee's claim, does one of the following: obtains payment of the obligation, gets a judgment against the obligor, obtains a new contract with the obligor by novation, or possesses a writing of a type customarily accepted as a symbol or evidence of the right assigned (such as a passbook for a savings account).

Assignor's Warranty Liability to Assignee

Suppose that Ross, a 16-year-old boy, contracts to buy a used car for $2,000 from Donaldson. Ross pays Donaldson $500 as a down payment and agrees to pay the balance in equal monthly installments. Donaldson assigns his right to receive the balance of the purchase price to Beckman, who pays $1,000 in cash for the assignment. When Beckman later attempts to enforce the contract, however, Ross disaffirms the contract on grounds of lack of capacity. Thus, Beckman has paid $1,000 for a worthless claim. Does Beckman have any recourse against Donaldson? When an assignor is *paid* for making an assignment, the assignor is held to have made certain *implied warranties* about the claim assigned.

The assignor impliedly warrants that the claim assigned is *valid*. This means that the obligor has capacity to contract, the contract is not illegal, the contract is not voidable for any other reason known to the assignor (such as fraud or duress), and the contract has not been discharged prior to assignment. The assignor also warrants that he has *good title* to the rights assigned and that any written instrument representing the assigned claim is *genuine*. In addition, the assignor impliedly agrees that he *will not do anything to impair the value of the assignment*. These guarantees are imposed by law unless the assignment agreement clearly indicates to the contrary. One important aspect of the assigned right that the assignor does *not* impliedly warrant, however, is that the obligor is *solvent*.

DELEGATION OF DUTIES

Nature of Delegation

A delegation of duties occurs when an obligor indicates his intent to appoint another person to perform his duties under a contract. For example, White owns a furniture store. He has numerous existing contracts to deliver furniture to customers, including a contract to deliver a sofa to Coombs. White is the *obligor* of the duty to deliver the sofa and Coombs is the *obligee*. White decides to sell his business to Rosen. As a part of the sale of the business, White assigns the rights in the existing contracts to Rosen and delegates to him the performance of those contracts, including the duty to deliver the sofa to Coombs. Here White is the *delegator*, Rosen is the *delegatee*. White is appointing Rosen to carry out his duties to the obligee, Coombs. A diagram of the delegation of a duty appears in Figure 2.

In contrast to an assignment of a *right*, which extinguishes the assignor's right and transfers it to the assignee, the delegation of a *duty* does *not* extinguish the duty owed by the delegator. This point is made clearly in *Brooks v. Hayes*. The delegator remains liable to the obligee unless the obligee agrees to substitute the delegatee's promise for that of the delegator (this is called a **novation,** and will be discussed in greater detail below). This makes sense, because, if it were possible for a person to escape his duties under a contract by merely delegating them to another, any party to a contract could avoid liability by delegating duties to an insolvent acquaintance. The significance of an effective delegation is that *performance* by the delegatee will discharge the delegating party. In addition, if the duty is a delegable one, the obligee cannot insist on performance by the delegator; he must accept the performance of the delegatee.

FIGURE 2   Delegation of Duties

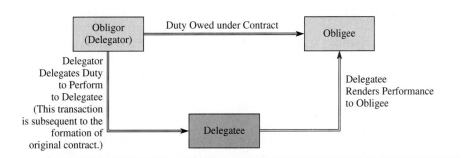

BROOKS v. HAYES

395 N.W.2d 167 (Wis. S. Ct. 1986)

In May of 1978, John and Judith Brooks contracted with Wayne Hayes, doing business as Wayne Hayes Real Estate, to construct a Windsor Home (a packaged, predesigned, and precut home) on a lot that they owned. Hayes was primarily a real estate broker, but also sold Windsor Homes. The construction contract required Hayes to "provide all necessary labor and materials and perform all work of every nature whatsoever to be done in the erection of a residence for" the Brookses. The Brookses and Hayes contemplated that Hayes would hire subcontractors to perform much of the home construction work and Hayes, who had no personal experience in construction, would not control the method of construction. During the construction, the Brookses requested that a "heatilator" be installed as an extra to increase the efficiency of the fireplace. Claude Marr, the mason hired by Hayes to do the fireplace and other masonry work, installed the heatilator.

The Brookses moved into the house in the winter of 1978. When they used the fireplace, they smelled smoke in areas of the house remote from the fireplace. Both the Brookses and Hayes hired several masons to inspect the fireplace system, but none of the masons was able to discover the cause of the problem. The Brookses used the fireplace with some frequency until November 1980, when a fire in the home caused structural damage around the fireplace and smoke damage to the house and the couple's personal property. It was discovered that Marr's negligence in installing the heatilator had caused the fire. The Brookses sued both Marr and Hayes. The case against Marr was dismissed because Marr went bankrupt. The trial court also dismissed the complaint against Hayes on the ground that Hayes was neither personally negligent nor legally responsible for the negligence of an independent contractor. Mr. and Mrs. Brooks appealed.

Abrahamson, Justice.   The Brookses contend that the contract implicitly imposed on Hayes the duty to perform with due care. Their interpretation is supported by *Colton v. Foulkes*, in which the court adopted the rule that "accompanying every contract is a common law duty to perform with care, skill, reasonable expediency, and faithfulness the thing they agreed to be done, and a negligent failure to observe any of these conditions is a tort, as well as a breach of contract."

Although Hayes assumed a contractual duty to the Brookses to perform the construction contract with skill and due care, Hayes delegated the performance of the contract to others. The question then is whether the delegation of performance of the masonry work relieved Hayes of liability for breach of contract when the mason, an independent contractor, negligently performed that part of Hayes' contractual obligation.

The Brookses assert that Hayes may not avoid responsibility to them for his failure to perform his contractual duty of due care merely by hiring an independent contractor. We agree with this assertion. The hornbook principle of contract law is that the delegation of the performance of a contract does not, unless the obligee agrees otherwise, discharge the liability of the delegating obligor to the obligee for breach of contract.

Hayes argues he is not liable for breach of contract for the mason's negligence because the Brookses knew about and acquiesced in his hiring the independent contractor. We are not persuaded by Hayes' argument. Hayes has confused delegation of the performance of an obligation with delegation of responsibility for the performance of an obligation. The rule for delegation of the performance of a contractual obligation is that the obligor may delegate a contractual duty without the obligee's consent unless the duty is "personal." The rule for delegation of responsibility is that if the obligor delegates the performance of an obligation, the obligor is not relieved of responsibility for fulfilling that obligation.

Where the obligee consents to the delegation, the consent itself does not release the obligor from liability for breach of contract. More than the obligee's consent to a delegation of performance is needed to release the obligor from liability for breach of contract. For the obligor to be released from liability, the obligee must agree to the release. If there is an agreement between the obligor, obligee, and a third party by which the third party agrees to be substituted for the obligor and the obligee assents thereto, the obligor is released from liability and the third person takes the place of the obligor. Such an agreement is known as a novation. This court cannot make such findings on the record.

We hold that Hayes could hire subcontractors to perform the construction contract but that Hayes' delegation of the performance part of the contract to an independent contractor did not itself relieve Hayes of liability to the Brookses. Although we conclude that the Brookses have a good cause of action against Hayes, this court cannot make a final determination of Hayes' liability on the record before it. There are several issues that the circuit court did not consider. For example, Hayes argues that the heatilator was not part of the construction contract and that he had no responsibility for it. We cannot decide these issues. For the reasons set forth, we hold that Hayes may be liable for the mason's negligence and that the cause must be remanded to the circuit court for a new trial.

Judgment reversed in favor of the Brookses and remanded for a new trial.

Delegable Duties

A duty that can be performed fully by a number of different persons is delegable. Not all duties are delegable, however. The grounds for finding a duty to be nondelegable resemble closely the grounds for finding a right to be nonassignable. A duty is nondelegable if delegation would violate public policy or if the original contract between the parties forbids delegation. In addition, both section 2–210(1) of the UCC and section 318(2) of the *Restatement (Second) of Contracts* take the position that a party to a contract may delegate his duty to perform to another person unless the parties have agreed to the contrary or unless the other party has a "substantial interest" in having the original obligor perform the acts required by the contract. The key factor used in determining whether the obligee has such a substantial interest is the degree to which performance is dependent on the individual traits, skill, or judgment of the person who owes the duty to perform. For example, if Jansen hires Skelton, an artist, to paint her portrait, Skelton could not effectively delegate the duty to paint the portrait to another artist. Similarly, an employee could not normally delegate her duties under an employment contract to some third person, because employment contracts are made with the understanding that the person the employer hires will perform the work. The situation in which a person hires a general contractor to perform specific work is distinguishable, however. In that situation (typified by *Brooks v. Hayes*), the person hiring the general contractor would normally understand that at least part of the work would be delegated to subcontractors.

Language Creating a Delegation

No special, formal language is necessary to create an effective delegation of duties. In fact, since parties frequently confuse the terms *assignment* and *delegation*, one of the problems frequently presented to courts is determining whether the parties intended an assignment only or both an assignment and a delegation. Unless the agreement indicates a contrary intent, courts tend to interpret assignments as *including* a delegation of the assignor's duties. Both the UCC 2–210(4) and section 328 of the *Restatement (Second) of Contracts* provide that, unless the language or the circumstances indicate to the contrary, general language of assignment such as an assignment of "the contract" or of "all my rights under the contract" is to be interpreted as creating *both* an assignment and a delegation.

Assumption of Duties by Delegatee

A delegation gives the delegatee the right to perform the duties of the delegator. The mere fact that duties have been delegated does not always place legal responsibility on the delegatee to perform. The delegatee who fails to perform will not be liable to either the delegator or the obligee unless the delegatee has *assumed* the duty by expressly or impliedly undertaking the obligation to perform. However, both section 2–210(4) of the UCC and section 328 of the *Restatement* provide that an assignee's acceptance of an assignment is to be construed as a promise by him to perform the duties under the contract, unless the language of the assignment or the circumstances indicate to the contrary. Frequently, a term of the contract between the delegator and the delegatee provides that the delegatee assumes responsibility for performance. A common example of this is the *assumption* of an existing mortgage debt by a purchaser of real estate. Suppose Morgan buys a house from Friedman, agreeing to assume the outstanding mortgage on the property held by First Bank. By this assumption, Morgan undertakes personal liability to both Friedman and First Bank. If Morgan fails to make the mortgage payments, First Bank has a cause of action against Morgan personally. An assumption does *not* release the delegator from liability, however. Rather, it creates a situation in which both the delegator and the assuming delegatee owe duties to the obligee. If the assuming delegatee fails to pay, the delegator can be held liable. Thus, in the example described above, if Morgan fails to make mortgage payments and First Bank is unable to collect the debt from Morgan, Friedman would have secondary liability. Friedman, of course, would have an action against Morgan for breach of their contract.

Discharge of Delegator by Novation

As you have seen, the mere delegation of duties—even when the delegatee assumes those duties—does not release the delegator from his legal obligation to the obligee. A delegator can, however, be discharged from performance by **novation.**

A *novation* is a particular type of substituted contract in which the obligee agrees to discharge the original obligor and to substitute a new obligor in his place. The effects of a novation are that the original obligor has no further obligation under the contract and the obligee has the right to look to the new obligor for fulfillment of the contract. A novation requires more than the obligee's

consent to having the delegatee perform the duties. In the example used above, the mere fact that First Bank accepted mortgage payments from Morgan would not create a novation. Rather, there must be some evidence that the obligee agrees to *discharge* the old obligor and substitute a new obligor. This can be inferred from language of a contract or such other factors as the obligee's conduct or the surrounding circumstances.

THIRD PARTY BENEFICIARIES

There are many situations in which the performance of a contract would constitute some benefit to a person who was not a party to the contract. Despite the fact that a nonparty may expect to derive advantage from the performance of a contract, the general rule is that no one but the parties to a contract or their assignees can enforce it. In some situations, however, parties contract for the purpose of benefiting some third person. In such cases, the benefit to the third person is an essential part of the contract, not just an incidental result of a contract that was really designed to benefit the parties. Where the parties to a contract *intended* to benefit a third party, courts will give effect to their intent and permit the third party to enforce the contract. Such third parties are called **third party beneficiaries.** Figure 3 illustrates the relationship of third party beneficiaries to the contracting parties.

Intended Beneficiaries versus Incidental Beneficiaries

For a third person (other than an assignee) to have the right to enforce a contract, she must be able to establish that the contract was made with the *intent* to benefit her. A few courts have required that *both* parties must have intended to benefit the third party. Most courts, however, have found it to be sufficient if the person to whom the promise to perform was made (the *promisee*) intended to benefit the third party. In ascertaining intent to benefit the third party, a court will look at the language used by the parties and all the surrounding circumstances. One factor that is frequently important in determining intent to benefit is whether the party making the promise to perform (the *promisor*) was to render performance directly to the third party. For example, if Allison contracts with Jones Florist to deliver flowers to Kirsch, the fact that performance was to be rendered to Kirsch would be good evidence that the parties intended to benefit

FIGURE 3   Third Party Beneficiaries

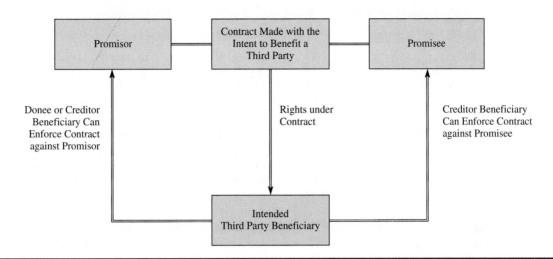

Kirsch. This factor is not conclusive, however. There are some cases in which intent to benefit a third party has been found even though performance was to be rendered to the promisee rather than to the third party. Intended beneficiaries are often classified as either *donee* or *creditor* beneficiaries. These classifications are discussed in greater detail below.

A third party who is unable to establish that the contract was made with the intent to benefit her is called an *incidental beneficiary*. A third party is classified as an incidental beneficiary when the benefit derived by that third party was merely an unintended by-product of a contract that was created for the benefit of those who were parties to it. Incidental beneficiaries acquire no rights under a contract. For example, Hutton contracts with Long Construction Company to build a valuable structure on his land. The performance of the contract would constitute a benefit to Keller, Hutton's next-door neighbor, by increasing the value of Keller's land. The contract between Hutton and Long was made for the purpose of benefiting themselves, however. Any advantage derived by Keller is purely incidental to their primary purpose. Thus, Keller could not sue and recover damages if either Hutton or Long breaches the contract.

As a general rule, members of the public are held to be incidental beneficiaries of contracts entered into by their municipalities or other governmental units in the regular course of carrying on governmental functions. A member of the public cannot recover a judgment in a suit against a promisor of such a contract, even though all taxpayers will suffer some injury from nonperformance. A different result may be reached, however, if a party contracting with a governmental unit agrees to reimburse members of the public for damages or if the party undertakes to perform some duty for individual members of the public.

Donee Beneficiaries   If the promisee's primary purpose in contracting is to make a *gift* of the agreed-upon performance to a third party, that third party is classified as a *donee beneficiary*. If the contract is breached, the donee beneficiary will have a cause of action against the promisor, but not against the promisee (donor). For example, Miller contracts with Perpetual Life Insurance Company, agreeing to pay premiums in return for which Perpetual agrees to pay $100,000 to Miller's husband when Miller dies. Miller's husband is a donee beneficiary and can bring suit and recover judgment against Perpetual if Miller dies and Perpetual does not pay. The following case, *Warren v. Monahan Beaches Jewelry Center, Inc.*, provides another example of a donee beneficiary. It also demonstrates the implications of a person's status as an intended beneficiary.

WARREN v. MONAHAN BEACHES JEWELRY CENTER, INC.

548 So. 2d 870 (Fla. Ct. App. 1989)

Jay Andreson went to Monahan Beaches Jewelry Center (Monahan) to shop for a diamond engagement ring for his fiancée, Laneya Warren. Andreson told Monahan that the ring was to be given to Warren. Andreson and a salesman discussed several aspects of the size, type, and style of the ring, and the salesman made suggestions about what would be likely to be pleasing to Warren. Shortly before Christmas, Monahan sold Andreson a ring, which Monahan represented as being a diamond ring, for $3,974.25. Andreson gave the ring to Warren for Christmas as a symbol of their engagement. Warren soon noticed a small chip in the stone under the setting. She returned the ring to Monahan shortly after the Christmas holidays, and Monahan agreed to replace the stone with one of equal or greater value at no charge to Warren. After making this agreement, Warren took the ring to another jeweler to have it appraised. There she learned for the first time that the alleged diamond that Monahan sold to Andreson was in fact nothing more than cut glass or cubic zirconia.

Warren filed suit against Monahan on several counts, including breach of contract and violation of the Florida Deceptive and Unfair Trade Practices Act. The trial court dismissed her complaint and Warren appealed.

Booth, Judge.   The law is that a person not party to a contract may sue for breach of contract where the parties' dealings clearly express the parties' intent to create a right primarily and directly benefiting a third party. In the present case, the precontract dealings between Andreson and Monahan, and the subsequent dealings between Warren and Monahan, clearly establish Warren as an intended third party beneficiary of the contract at issue. The complaint properly alleges that Monahan breached the contract when he failed to deliver a diamond ring to Andreson. The alleged breach of contract deprived Warren of the benefit of owning a diamond ring, which was the purpose of the sale. Warren has a valid cause of action for breach of contract as an intended third party beneficiary.

The trial court also erred in dismissing Warren's claim brought pursuant to [the Florida Deceptive and Unfair Trade Practices Act]. One of the purposes of Florida's Deceptive and Unfair Trade Practices Act is to protect consumers from suppliers who commit deceptive and unfair trade practices. Nothing in the statute or case law limits causes of action to the immediate purchaser. The issue of whether the intended beneficiary of a gift may be classified as a "consumer" appears to be an issue of first impression in this state. We hold that [the Act] applies and that Warren, as the beneficiary of the consumer transaction is a "consumer" in her own right and entitled to the remedies afforded.

Judgment reversed in favor of Warren and case remanded for further proceedings.

Creditor Beneficiaries   If the promisor's performance is intended to *satisfy a legal duty* that the promisee owes to a third party, the third party is a *creditor benefi-* *ciary.* The creditor beneficiary has rights against *both* the promisee (because of the original obligation) and the promisor. For example, Smith buys a car on credit from

Jones Auto Sales. Smith later sells the car to Carmichael, who agrees to pay the balance due on the car to Jones Auto Sales. (Note that Smith is *delegating* his duty to pay to Carmichael, and Carmichael is *assuming* the personal obligation to do so). In this case, Jones Auto Sales is a creditor beneficiary of the contract between Smith and Carmichael. It has rights against both Carmichael and Smith if Carmichael does not perform. *Spiklevitz v. Markmil Corporation*, which follows, presents an example of a creditor beneficiary.

SPIKLEVITZ v. MARKMIL CORPORATION
357 N.W.2d 721 (Mich. Ct. App. 1984)

In 1974, Stuart Spiklevitz loaned money to Vincent and Geraldine Heron. The Herons signed a promissory note agreeing to repay the debt by January 15, 1975. On April 1, 1980, the Herons sold their business to Markmil Corp. At that time, $3,510 of their debt to Spiklevitz remained unpaid. Markmil executed an "Assumption of Obligation," which stated that as part of the purchase price of the Herons' business, Markmil agreed to pay the list of debts written on an attached sheet of paper labeled "Exhibit A." Spiklevitz was listed as a creditor in Exhibit A for the balance owed to him.

In June of 1981, Spiklevitz sued Markmil to recover the amount remaining due on the note. Markmil moved for judgment in its favor, claiming that Spiklevitz could no longer enforce Herons' debt because the statute of limitations had elapsed on the promissory note executed by the Herons back in 1974. Markmil further denied that Spiklevitz was a third party beneficiary of the "Assumption of Obligation" contract between Markmil and the Herons. The trial court held for Markmil, and Spiklevitz appealed.

Per Curiam.   Where a person makes an agreement to pay off another's obligation, it creates a new and separate obligation; a right of action on this obligation accrues only from the date on which the new obligation becomes overdue. Markmil can prevail only if Spiklevitz was not an intended beneficiary of the contract embodied in the "Assumption of Obligation" entered into between it and the Herons.

Any person for whose benefit a promise is made by way of contract has the same right to enforce the promise that he would have had if the promise had been made directly to him as the promisee. A promise is construed to have been made for the benefit of a person whenever the promisor has undertaken to give or to do or refrain from doing something directly to or for said person.

Spiklevitz is not an atypical third party beneficiary. Instead, this is the normal creditor beneficiary type of case where the promise is to pay the promisee's own debt to his creditor, the beneficiary. Where one sells his business or other property and the buyer undertakes to pay the seller's debts, those to be paid are creditor beneficiaries and actions by them lie against the buyer on his promise. Under Michigan law, Spiklevitz was a third party beneficiary of the contract between Markmil and the Herons.

Judgment reversed in favor of Spiklevitz.

Defenses against Beneficiary

The promisor who breaches a contract that was intended to benefit a third party is subject to suit by both the promisee and the third party beneficiary. Since the rights of the third party beneficiary derive from the original contract between the promisor and the promisee, any circumstances that make that contract unenforceable or voidable can defeat the claim of the third party beneficiary. In a suit brought by the third party beneficiary against the promisor, the promisor can assert any defenses against the third party beneficiary that he could assert against the promisee (such as fraud and lack of consideration).

Vesting of Beneficiary's Rights

Another possible threat to the interests of the third party beneficiary is that the promisor and the promisee might modify or discharge their contract so as to extinguish or alter the beneficiary's rights. For example, Gates, who owes $500 to Sorenson, enters into a contract with Connor whereby Connor agrees to pay the $500 to Sorenson. What happens if, before Sorenson is paid, Connor pays the money to Gates and Gates accepts it or Connor and Gates otherwise modify the contract? Courts have held that there is a point at which the rights of the beneficiary *vest*, that is, the beneficiary's rights cannot be lost by modification or discharge. A modification or discharge that occurs after the beneficiary's rights have vested cannot be asserted as a defense to a suit brought by the beneficiary. The exact time at which the beneficiary's rights vest differs from jurisdiction to jurisdiction. Some courts have held that vesting occurs when the contract is formed, while others hold that vesting does not occur until the beneficiary learns of the contract and consents to it or does some act in reliance on the promise.

The contracting parties' ability to vary the rights of the third party beneficiary can also be affected by the terms of their agreement. A provision of the contract between the promisor and the promisee stating that the duty to the beneficiary cannot be modified would be effective to prevent modification. Likewise, a contract provision in which the parties specifically reserved the right to change beneficiaries or modify the duty to the beneficiary would be enforced. For example, provisions reserving the right to change beneficiaries are very common in insurance contracts.

ETHICAL AND PUBLIC POLICY CONCERNS

1. You learned that an assignor's rights are extinguished as soon as he assigns them. Should a delegator's duties be extinguished by his delegation of them?

2. Why does public policy favor allowing third parties to enforce contracts made for their benefit? Should incidental beneficiaries have a right to enforce contracts? Why or why not?

SUMMARY

There are two situations in which people who were not parties to a contract can claim rights under the contract. The first is where there has been an assignment of a contract right. An assignment occurs when a person (the assignor) who has a right to receive the performance of an obligor transfers that right to a third person (the assignee). An assignment extinguishes the rights of the assignor and gives the assignee the right to enforce the contract. Most contract rights can be assigned. There are, however, three limitations on assignability. First, an assignment that would materially change the obligor's duty or increase the risk or burden on the obligor will be held ineffective. Second, an assignment that would violate public policy will be held ineffective. Third, an agreement between the assignor and the obligor specifically prohibiting assignment of rights will prevent effective assignment if the agreement is held to be enforceable. Courts tend to interpret such agreements narrowly, however.

The assignee is subject to any claims or defenses arising from the assigned contract that the obligor could have asserted against the assignor. The obligor should be notified of the assignment promptly, or his rendering of performance to the assignor will be a discharge of the claim. Once the obligor has received notice of the assignment, however, the assignee's rights will not be defeated by the obligor's performance to the assignor. The assignee's rights are also subject to any claims against the assignor that arose independent of the assigned contract and that have accrued before the time of notification. This is called *set off*.

In making an assignment, the assignor impliedly warrants that he has title to the claim, that any writings on which the claim is based are genuine, that the claim is valid, and that he will not do anything to defeat or impair the value of the claim. Thus, the assignee will be able to recover damages from the assignor if the assignee's rights are defeated by a defense asserted by the obligor. The assignor is also subject to liability to the assignee if he collects the assigned claim or if he causes the assignee to lose his right to the performance by making successive assignments of the same claim. The assignor does not, however, impliedly warrant the obligor's solvency.

The appointment of another person (the delegatee) to perform the duties of the obligor (the delegator) under a contract is called a *delegation*. Duties are delegable unless the obligee has a substantial interest in having the delegator perform or supervise the performance of the contract (as where performance depends on the personal skill, discretion, or character of the delegator), or public policy would be violated by a delegation, or the parties have agreed in their contract that delegation will not be permitted. Unless the language of the contract or the surrounding circumstances indicate to the contrary, general language of assignment is held to constitute a delegation of duties as well as an assignment of rights. An effective delegation only means that performance by the delegatee will discharge the duty. It does *not* release the delegator from his duty to the obligee.

The delegatee is not under a legal duty to perform unless he has expressly or impliedly *assumed* the duty of performance. The UCC and the *Restatement* presume that a delegatee's acceptance of an assignment is to be construed as a promise by him to carry out the duties owed under the contract. If a delegatee assumes a duty, he undertakes a legal duty to both the delegator and the obligee. Assumption does not discharge the delegator. When assumption occurs, both the delegator and the delegatee are under a duty to the obligee. The delegator remains liable for the performance of the duty unless the obligee has released him by novation. A novation occurs when the obligee agrees to release the delegator in return for the delegatee's promise to perform. The obligee's mere acceptance of performance from the delegatee—even when there has been an assumption—is not sufficient to constitute a novation. Some further evidence of the obligee's intent to substitute the delegatee's duty to perform for that of the delegator is necessary for a novation.

A second situation in which a third party can claim rights under a contract occurs when the contracting parties made the contract with the intent to benefit a third person. Such third persons are called third party benefi-

ciaries. In order to claim rights as a third party beneficiary, the third party must prove that she was an *intended beneficiary*. This means that she must prove that the promisee intended to benefit her. Intended beneficiaries are generally classified as either *donee beneficiaries* or *creditor beneficiaries*. When the promisee intended to bestow the promised performance as a gift, the beneficiary is called a *donee beneficiary*. When the promisee intended the performance to satisfy a legal duty to the third party, the beneficiary is called a *creditor beneficiary*. If a person can prove that she was an intended beneficiary, either donee or creditor, she can bring suit to enforce the contract. The creditor beneficiary will also have rights against the *promisee* under the original obligation. When the benefit to a third person is merely incidental and the contracting parties formed the contract primarily for their own benefit, the third person is classified as an *incidental beneficiary*. An incidental beneficiary has no rights under a contract, and cannot sue for its nonperformance.

Although intended beneficiaries can sue to enforce a contract, they are subject to any defenses that the promisor could assert against the *promisee*. Unless the contracting parties have agreed not to modify the rights of the third party beneficiary, those rights are subject to modification or discharge by the original contracting parties if the modification or discharge occurs before the rights of the third party beneficiary have *vested*. There are several views about the time at which the rights of a third party beneficiary vest (become invulnerable to modification or discharge). The variation of the rights of a third party beneficiary can be affected by an agreement between the contracting parties forbidding modification or reserving the right to modify.

PROBLEM CASES

1. In 1976, C. W. and C. T. White executed a lease with Lewis Grocery Co. whereby the Whites agreed to build a convenience food store and parking lot and lease it to Lewis for 10 years with an option to renew. One of provisions of the lease stated that if the leased property were to be destroyed by fire, the elements, or other casualty, the Whites would repair the damages or rebuild within a reasonable time after such an occurrence. The lease was later assigned to John Ford. Only three days after the assignment to Ford, a series of tornadoes struck

terms of performance of contract
p354

the area, and the building was destroyed. Ford called the Whites requesting that they fulfill their contractual duty to rebuild, but they did not act upon these calls. Ford brought suit against the Whites because of their refusal to reconstruct the store and parking lot, and the Whites filed a motion to dismiss Ford's complaint on the ground that no contractual relationship existed between the Whites and Ford. Should the court dismiss Ford's complaint? *No. Assignee has no duty to inform, obligee*

2. Peterson was employed by Post–Newsweek as a newscaster-anchorman on station WTOP–TV (Channel 9) under a three-year employment contract that was to end June 30, 1980, and could be extended for two additional one-year terms at the option of Post–Newsweek. In June 1978, Post–Newsweek sold its operating license to the Evening News Association (Evening News), and Channel 9 was then designated as WDVM-TV. The contract of sale between Post–Newsweek and Evening News provided for the assignment of all contracts, including Peterson's employment contract. Peterson continued working for the station for more than a year after the change of ownership and received all of the compensation and benefits provided by his contract with Post–Newsweek. In early August 1979, he negotiated a new contract with a competing television station and tendered his resignation to Evening News. Evening News sued Peterson. Peterson defended on the ground that his employment contract was not assignable. Is he correct? *Not correct   Could fulfill contract or his past*

3. Milford sold a registered quarter horse, Hired Chico, to Stewart. The parties signed a written contract in which Milford reserved the right to two breedings each year on Hired Chico, "regardless to whom the horse may be sold to." Stewart later sold the horse to McKinnie, who knew of and had read the contract between Milford and Stewart. After McKinnie purchased the horse, he refused to permit Milford any of the breedings provided for in the original agreement. Was McKinnie obligated by the terms of the contract? *No obligated; public policy*

4. On April 20, Chapman-Harkey Company ordered a quantity of toys known as "hang-ups" from A. G. Bond Company, at a total cost of $13,378.56. Under the agreement between Chapman-Harkey and A. G. Bond, the hang-ups were sold on a "guaranteed-sale" basis; that is, Chapman-Harkey could return to A. G. Bond any hang-ups that it could not sell and receive a credit. On May 17, Chapman-Harkey received notice that A. G. Bond had assigned the account for this sale to Equitable Factors. In a letter dated May 19, Chapman-Harkey received written confirmation from

A. G. Bond's agent that the goods were being sold on a guaranteed-sale basis. Chapman-Harkey failed to pay for the hang-ups, and Equitable Factors brought suit against it to recover the purchase price of the goods sold. At this point, Chapman-Harkey still had in its possession $5,753.78 worth of hang-ups, which it had been unable to sell. Can the guaranteed-sale term be raised as a defense against Equitable Factors, even though the defense did not become available until after notification of the assignment? *Yes.*

5. Jones paid Sullivan, the chief of the Addison Police Department, $6,400 in exchange for Sullivan's cooperation in allowing Jones and others to bring marijuana by airplane into the Addison airport without police intervention. Instead of performing the requested service, Sullivan arrested Jones. The $6,400 was turned over to the district attorney's office and was introduced into evidence in the subsequent trial in which Jones was tried for and convicted of bribery. After his conviction, Jones assigned his alleged claim to the $6,400 to Melvyn Bruder. Based on the assignment, Bruder brought suit against the state of Texas to obtain possession of the money. Will he be successful? *p353*

Void contract

6. Friendly Mobile Manor, Inc. owned and operated a mobile home park, in which it sold mobile homes and rented mobile home sites. Friendly also had agreed to be legally responsible for indebtedness to certain banks that had financed the original purchase of several of the mobile homes on its property. In 1986, Friendly sold its real property and 30 mobile homes situated on the property to Homa. Homa assumed the debt on those homes. Later in 1986, Homa assigned all of his rights and interests in the sales contract with Friendly to P/T Ltd. During the negotiations leading up to that assignment, P/T made it perfectly clear to Homa that under no circumstances would P/T assume any liability for the debts on the mobile homes. P/T refused to sign a first draft of a contract that contained language providing that P/T would assume the mobile home debt. Finally, Homa and P/T reached and signed an agreement that did not contain any assumption language. P/T did agree to forward monthly installment checks to the banks that had financed these mobile homes from rents that came in from the tenants of those homes. In early 1987, some of the tenants who were occupying some of the financed mobile homes were evicted for nonpayment of rent. Since no rent money was coming in, P/T did not forward installment payments to the banks involved. The banks foreclosed on the mobile homes and sought payment of the remaining debt from P/T. Is P/T legally responsible for the debts?

7. Jay Beard Trucks entered into a franchise Dealer Sales and Service Agreement with General Motors (GMC). The agreement contained a provision limiting the possible future transfer of ownership of the dealership. These provisions required Beard to give notice to GMC of any proposed sale of the dealership and gave GMC the right to select each successor and replacement dealer. The contract also provided that GMC "shall not arbitrarily refuse to agree to such proposed change or sale" and that, in determining whether the proposal is acceptable to it, "GMC will take into account the qualifications, personal and business reputation, and financial standing of the proposed dealer operator and owners." Noller, the owner-operator of a Ford dealership and a Toyota dealership and one of the top 100 Ford dealers in the country, entered into negotiations to purchase Beard's dealership. The parties worked out a proposed buy-sell agreement and submitted it to GMC. GMC never contacted Noller, sent dealership transfer applications to him, obtained any documentation or additional information from him, nor made inquiries to Beard about Noller's qualifications. Without doing an investigation about these matters, GMC refused to grant the franchise to Noller, apparently because he was also a Ford dealer. As a result, the contract between Noller and Beard fell through and Beard sold the dealership to a third party. Noller brought suit against GMC, asserting that he was an intended beneficiary of the Dealer Sales and Service Agreement between GMC and Beard, wherein GMC had agreed to specifically consider the proposed dealer's qualifications, personal and business reputation, and financial standing. Was he an intended beneficiary?

8. Spartan, a general contractor, hired Sunbelt to perform the electrical work on a project known as the "Logo Shops" for the 1984 World's Fair. The World's Fair filed for bankruptcy without having fully paid its general contractors, and Spartan did not pay Sunbelt. On October 22, Sunbelt assigned its right to payment to Powerhouse. Powerhouse gave notification of the assignment on October 24. Powerhouse eventually sued Spartan to collect the debt. Spartan asserted that it was entitled to set off the damages that Sunbelt had caused Spartan by abandoning an unrelated project involving the electrical work that Sunbelt had been obligated to

perform on the Sea King Restaurant. These damages were caused when Spartan had had to pay another electrical subcontractor to complete the job that Sunbelt had abandoned. The first of these payments was made on October 8, the second on October 23, and the third on October 31. Can Spartan set these payments off against the amount it owes Powerhouse?

9. Mercantile-Safe Deposit & Trust Company frequently advised its long-time customer, Chaplin, about the planning of her estate. Merrick, Chaplin's former son-in-law, maintained a close relationship with Chaplin, and this relationship was reflected in the wills that Chaplin executed. At Chaplin's request, one of Mercantile's trust officers visited her at her home to discuss making certain changes in her will. Without first consulting with Mercantile's attorneys or other estate planning personnel about the appropriateness of these changes, the trust officer instructed Chaplin's attorney to draft a new will reflecting the changes that Chaplin requested. Merrick would have benefited under this will. The will was executed and Chaplin died in 1981. Because of a technical problem overlooked by Mercantile's trust officer, the will provision benefiting Merrick and his children was held to be ineffective and Merrick lost the bequest that he would have had otherwise. Merrick brought suit against Mercantile because of its failure to advise Chaplin properly. Does Merrick have any rights under the contract between Chaplin and Mercantile?

10. In June of 1979, Ruwet-Sibley Equipment Corporation leased a 1979 International Harvester truck to Stebbins, a proprietor of a refuse collection business. The lease was for 60 months and required Stebbins to pay $1,186.87 per month. In August of 1981, Stebbins and Greenbaum, the proprietor of another refuse collection business, met in Ruwet-Sibley's office and signed an agreement whereby Stebbins agreed to turn over the truck to Greenbaum and Greenbaum would thereafter make the payments due under the lease. Shortly after this agreement was made, however, Greenbaum defaulted and made no further payments under the lease. Greenbaum later filed for bankruptcy. In June of 1983, the truck was returned to Ruwet-Sibley in inoperable condition. Ruwet-Sibley sued Stebbins to collect the outstanding lease payments plus the cost of repairs. Stebbins asserted that his contract with Greenbaum excused him from all liability under the lease and established Greenbaum as the sole debtor. Is he correct?

CHAPTER 18

PERFORMANCE AND REMEDIES

INTRODUCTION

Contracts generally are formed before either of the parties renders any actual performance to the other. A person may be content to bargain for and receive the other person's promise at the formation stage of a contract because this permits him to plan for the future. Ultimately, however, all parties bargain for the *performance* of the promises that have been made to them.

In most contracts, each party carries out his promise and is **discharged** (released from all of his obligations under the contract) when his performance is complete. Sometimes, however, a party fails to perform or performs in an unsatisfactory manner. In such cases, courts are often called upon to determine the respective rights and duties of the parties. This frequently involves deciding such questions as whether performance was due, whether the contract was breached, to what extent it was breached, and whether performance was excused. This task is made more difficult by the fact that contracts often fail to specify the consequences of nonperformance or defective performance. In deciding questions involving the performance of contracts and remedies for breach of contract, courts draw upon a variety of legal principles that attempt to do justice, prevent forfeiture and unjust enrichment, and effectuate the parties' presumed intent.

This chapter presents an overview of the legal concepts that are used to resolve disputes arising in the performance stage of contracting. It describes how courts determine whether performance is due and what kind of performance is due, the consequences of contract breach, and the excuses for a party's failure to perform. It also includes a discussion of the remedies that are used when a court determines that a contract has been breached.

CONDITIONS

Nature of Conditions

One issue that frequently arises in the performance stage of a contract is whether a party has the duty to perform. Some duties are *unconditional* or *absolute*—that is, the duty to perform does not depend on the occurrence of any further event other than the passage of time. For example, if Root promises to pay Downing $100, Root's duty is unconditional. When a party's duty is unconditional, he has the duty to perform unless his performance is *excused*. (The various excuses for nonperformance will be discussed later in this chapter.) When a duty is unconditional, the promisor's failure to perform constitutes a *breach of contract*.

In many situations, however, a promisor's duty to perform depends on the occurrence of some event that is called a **condition.** A condition is an uncertain, future event that affects a party's duty to perform. For example, if Melman contracts to buy Lance's house on condition that First Bank approve Melman's application for a mortgage loan by January 10, Melman's duty to buy Lance's house is *conditioned* on the bank's approving his loan application by January 10. When a promisor's duty is conditional, his duty to perform is affected by the occurrence of the condition. In this case, if the condition does not occur, Melman has no duty to buy the house.

His failure to buy it because of the nonoccurrence of the condition will *not* constitute a breach of contract. Rather, he is discharged from further obligation under the contract. The case of *Gildea v. Kapenis* provides an example of the effect of nonoccurrence of a condition.

Almost any event can be a condition. Some conditions are beyond the control of either party, such as when Morehead promises to buy Pratt's business if the prime rate drops by a specified amount. Others are within the control of a party, such as when one party's performance of a duty under the contract is a condition of the other party's duty to perform.

GILDEA v. KAPENIS

402 N.W.2d 457 (Iowa Ct. App. 1987)

In October of 1984, David and Penny Gildea put their house on the market and held an open house to attract potential buyers. James Kapenis went to the open house. That evening, Kapenis met with the Gildeas' realtor, Susan Murphy, to talk about making a bid on the Gildea home. Murphy told Kapenis that First Federal Savings & Loan offered a 25-year adjustable rate mortgage with monthly payments of $343 and that the interest rate under this type of mortgage could be adjusted only once a year. Murphy prepared several purchase offers and, after some negotiation, both Kapenis and the Gildeas agreed to a contract that contained a clause stating that the contract was "subject to buyer obtaining suitable financing interest rate no greater than $12\frac{3}{4}\%$." Kapenis and Murphy then began a search for financing.

When Kapenis talked with an officer of First Federal Savings & Loan, he learned that under this mortgage his interest rate could be adjusted *twice* a year and that 2 percentage points could be added to the adjusted rate after the two-year fixed period. He was dissatisfied with this and asked that Murphy find additional forms of financing. Murphy continued to inform Kapenis about various loan programs, but Kapenis rejected them because the monthly payments were too high. Another broker located a loan program of a 15-year term at $12\frac{1}{2}\%$ interest with monthly payments of $419, but Kapenis stated that the monthly payments would be too high and not assumable and that these terms were unsatisfactory. Kapenis then informed the Gildeas that he could not find suitable financing and that he was withdrawing his offer. The Gildeas then filed a lawsuit against Kapenis. The trial court found in favor of the Gildeas, and Kapenis appealed.

Donielson, Presiding Judge.   The "subject to financing" clause, such as the one which is the subject of this appeal, has been held to constitute a condition precedent. Conditions precedent are those facts and events occurring subsequently to the making of a valid contract that must occur before there is a right to immediate performance, before there is a breach of contract duty, before the usual judicial remedies are available. A determination that a condition precedent exists does not, however, depend on the particular form of the words used, but rather depends upon the intention of the parties gathered from the language of the entire instrument. The document must be read in light of the surrounding circumstances and will be given such a practical meaning as the parties themselves have placed upon it. Doubtful language will be construed against the party which selected it.

We believe that the term "suitable financing" as used by the parties in the present case means suitable according to the ability of Kapenis to repay. The financing clause contains only a general provision that the interest rate be no greater than $12\,^3\!/_4\%$ and is silent as to the amount, the term of the note, and points. We recognize that in today's financial lending market, there are a wide variety of financial packages available. The length of the mortgage, the monthly repayments, discount points, and amortization provisions contained in a mortgage are all important factors to be considered by a buyer when applying for financing. A mortgage taken on an interest rate of 12% may not be as favorable in its terms as a mortgage taken on $12\,^3\!/_4\%$ interest. All the above noted factors are interdependent, and a provision for a ceiling cap of $12\,^3\!/_4\%$ does little to aid in a determination as to what constitutes suitable financing.

The actions of the parties and the circumstances surrounding the present agreement indicate that the sale of the Gildea property was conditioned upon Kapenis obtaining financing terms compatible with his ability to repay. At the time Kapenis made his purchase offer, he did not consider what interest rate to specify, nor was he familiar with what financing was available. Murphy, the Gildeas' realtor, suggested that he put in an interest rate in the financing clause and also suggested that the term "suitable financing" be included in the clause. At trial, Murphy testified that she had included the term "suitable financing" to enable Kapenis the opportunity to determine what he could afford. Mr. Gildea additionally admitted that the term "suitable financing" meant financing that would be acceptable to the buyer.

We therefore conclude, based upon the circumstances and events surrounding the contract between the parties, that the term "suitable financing" meant financing terms that were acceptable to Kapenis. Kapenis entered the offer to purchase with the expectation that he would be able to obtain favorable financing. It is apparent from the conduct of the parties that the condition precedent, stating that the purchase was contingent upon Kapenis's obtaining financing at an interest rate of no greater than $12\,^3\!/_4\%$, was intended to benefit Kapenis. When Kapenis was unable to obtain favorable financing, the condition precedent did not occur, and the contract therefore was no longer valid.

Reversed in favor of Kapenis.

Types of Conditions

There are two ways of classifying conditions. One way of classifying conditions focuses on the effect of the condition on the duty to perform. The other way focuses on the way in which the condition is created.

Classifications of Conditions Based on Their Effect on the Duty to Perform   As Figure 1 illustrates, conditions vary in their effects on the duty to perform.

1. *Condition precedent.* A **condition precedent** is a future, uncertain event that *creates* the duty to perform. If the condition does not occur, performance becomes due. If the condition does occur, the duty to perform

arises. In *Gildea v. Kapenis*, Kapenis's duty to purchase the house was subject to a condition precedent.

2. *Concurrent condition.* When the contract calls for the parties to perform at the same time, each person's performance is conditioned on the performance or **tender** of performance (offer of performance) by the other. Such conditions are called **concurrent conditions.** For example, if Martin promises to buy Johnson's car for $5,000, the parties' respective duties to perform are subject to a concurrent condition. Martin does not have the duty to perform unless Johnson tenders his performance, and vice versa.

3. *Condition subsequent.* A **condition subsequent** is a future, uncertain event that *discharges* the duty to

FIGURE 1   Effect of Conditions

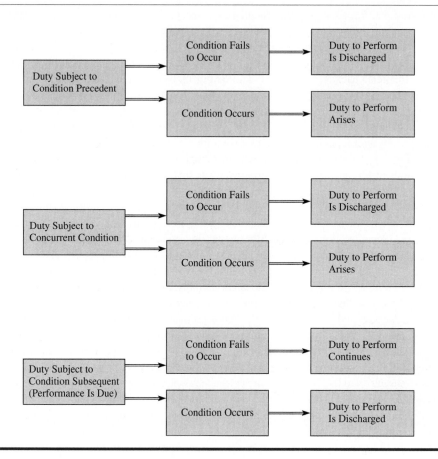

perform. When a duty is subject to a condition subsequent, the duty to perform arises, but is discharged if the future, uncertain event occurs. For example, Wilkinson and Jones agree that Wilkinson will begin paying Jones $2,000 per month but that, if XYZ Corporation dissolves, Wilkinson's obligation to pay will cease. In this case, Wilkinson's duty to pay is subject to being discharged by a condition subsequent. The major significance of the distinction between conditions precedent and conditions subsequent is that the plaintiff bears the burden of proving the occurrence of a condition precedent, while the defendant bears the burden of proving the occurrence of a condition subsequent.

Classifications of Conditions Based on the Way in which They Were Created   Another way of classifying conditions is to focus on the means by which the condition was created.

1. *Express condition.* An **express condition** is a condition that is specified in the language of the parties' contract. For example, if Grant promises to sell his regular season football tickets to Carson *on condition that* Indiana University wins the Rose Bowl, Indiana's winning the Rose Bowl is an express condition of Grant's duty to sell the tickets. The "subject to suitable financing" condition in *Gildea v. Kapenis* is another example of an express condition.

When the contract expressly provides that a party's duty is subject to a condition, courts take it very seriously. When a duty is subject to an express condition, that condition must be strictly complied with in order to give rise to the duty to perform.

2. *Implied-in-fact condition.* An **implied-in-fact condition** is one that is not specifically stated by the parties but is *implied* by the nature of the parties' promises. For example, if Summers promises to unload cargo from Knight's ship, the ship's arrival in port would be an implied-in-fact condition of Summer's duty to unload the cargo.

3. *Constructive condition.* **Constructive conditions** (also known as *implied-in-law conditions*) are conditions that are imposed by law rather than by the agreement of the parties. The law imposes constructive conditions to do justice between the parties. In contracts in which one of the parties is expected to perform before the other, the law normally infers that that performance is a constructive condition of the other party's duty to perform. For example, if Thomas promises to build a house for King, and the parties' understanding is that King will pay Thomas an agreed-upon price when the house is built, King's duty to pay is subject to the constructive condition that Thomas complete the house. Without such a constructive condition, a person who did not receive the performance promised him would still have to render his own performance.

Creation of Express Conditions

Although no particular language is required to create an express condition, the conditional nature of promises is usually indicated by such words as *provided that, subject to, on condition that, if, when, while, after*, and *as soon as*. The process of determining the meaning of conditions is not a mechanical one. Courts look at the parties' overall intent as indicated in language of the entire contract.

The following discussion explores two common types of express conditions.

Example of Express Condition: Satisfaction of Third Parties   It is common for building and construction contracts to provide that the property owner's duty to pay is conditioned on the builder's production of certificates to be issued by a specific architect or engineer. These certificates indicate the satisfaction of the architect or engineer with the builder's work. They often are issued at each stage of completion, after the architect or engineer has inspected the work done.

The standard usually used to determine whether the condition has occurred is a *good faith* standard. As a general rule, if the architect or engineer is acting honestly and has some good-faith reason for withholding a certificate, the builder cannot recover payments due. In legal terms, the condition that will create the owner's duty to pay has not occurred. The rationale for this is

that the court will not substitute its judgment for that of the architect or engineer for whose expert judgment the parties freely contracted.

If the builder can prove that the withholding of the certificate was fraudulent or done in bad faith (as a result of collusion with the owner, for example), the court may order that payment be made despite the absence of the certificate. In addition, production of the certificate may be excused by the death, insanity, or incapacitating illness of the named architect or engineer.

Example of Express Condition: Personal Satisfaction   Contracts sometimes provide that a promisee's duty to perform is conditioned on his *personal satisfaction* with the promisee's performance. For example, Moore commissions Allen to paint a portrait of Moore's wife, but the contract provides that Moore's duty to pay is conditioned on his personal satisfaction with the portrait. How will a court determine whether the condition of personal satisfaction has occurred? If the court applies a standard of actual, subjective satisfaction and Moore asserts that he is not satisfied, it would be very difficult for Allen to prove that the condition has occurred. If, on the other hand, the court applies an objective, "reasonable man" standard of satisfaction Allen stands a better chance of proving that the condition has occurred.

In determining which standard of satisfaction to apply, courts distinguish between cases in which the performance bargained for involves personal taste and comfort and cases that involve mechanical fitness or suitability for a particular purpose. If personal taste and comfort are involved, as they would be in the hypothetical case described above, a promisor who is honestly dissatisfied with the promisee's performance has the right to reject the performance without being liable to the promisee. If, however, the performance involves mechanical fitness or suitability, the court will apply a reasonable man test. If the court finds that a reasonable man would be satisfied with the performance, the condition of personal satisfaction has been met and the promisor must accept the performance and pay the contract price. For example, Kitt Manufacturing Company hires Pace to design a conveyor belt system for use in its factory, conditioning its duty to pay on its personal satisfaction with the system. A court would be likely to find that this is a contract involving mechanical fitness and suitability for which an objective test of satisfaction could be used. These standards are illustrated in Figure 2. Because the "honest satisfaction" standard involves a danger of

FIGURE 2   Duty to Perform Conditioned on "Personal Satisfaction" (A Form of Express Condition Precedent)

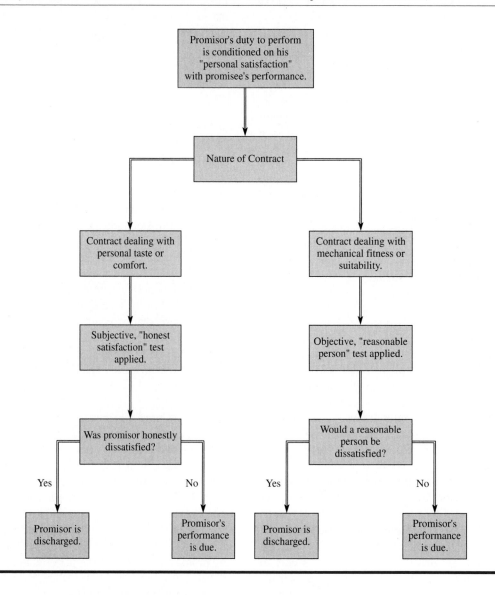

forfeiture by the performing party, courts prefer the objective test of satisfaction when objective evaluation is feasible.

Excuse of Conditions

In most situations involving conditional duties, the promisor does not have the duty to perform unless and until the condition occurs. There are, however, a variety of situations in which the occurrence of a condition will be *excused*. In such a case, the person whose duty is conditional will have to perform even though the condition has not occurred.

One ground for excusing a condition is that the occurrence of the condition has been *prevented* or *hindered* by the party who is benefited by the condition. For example, Connor hires Ingle to construct a garage on Connor's land, but when Ingle attempts to begin construction, Connor refuses to allow Ingle access to the land. In this case, Connor's duty to pay would normally be subject to a constructive condition that Ingle build the garage. However, since Connor prevented the occurence of the condition, the condition will be excused, and Ingle can sue Connor for damages for breach of contract even though the condition has not occurred.

Other grounds for excuse of a condition include **waiver** and **estoppel.** When a person whose duty is conditional voluntarily gives up his right to the occurrence of the condition (waiver), the condition will be excused. Suppose that Buchman contracts to sell his car to Fox on condition that Fox pay him $2,000 by June 14. Fox fails to pay on June 14, but, when he tenders payment on June 20, Buchman accepts and cashes the check without reservation. Buchman has thereby *waived* the condition of payment by June 14.

When a person whose duty is conditional leads the other party to rely on his noninsistence on the condition, the condition will be excused because of estoppel. For example, McDonald agrees to sell his business to Brown on condition that Brown provide a credit report and personal financial statement by July 17. On July 5, McDonald tells Brown that he can have until the end of the month to provide the necessary documents. Relying on McDonald's assurances, Brown does not provide the credit report and financial statement until July 29. In this case, McDonald would be *estopped* (precluded) from claiming that the condition did not occur.

A condition may also be excused when performance of the act that constitutes the condition becomes *impossible.* For example, if a building contract provides that the owner's duty to pay is conditioned on the production of a certificate from a named architect, the condition would be excused if the named architect died or became incapacitated before issuing the certificate.

In all of these situations, the significance of excuse of a condition is that the person whose duty otherwise would not arise until the occurrence of the condition will have the duty to perform even though the condition has not occurred.

PERFORMANCE OF CONTRACTS

When a promisor has performed his duties under a contract, he is discharged. Because his performance constitutes the occurrence of a constructive condition, the other party's duty to perform is also triggered, and the person who has performed has the right to receive the other party's performance. In determining whether a promisor is discharged by performance and whether the constructive condition of his performance has been fulfilled, courts must consider the standard of performance expected of him.

Level of Performance Expected of the Promisor

In some situations, no deviation from the promisor's promised performance is tolerated; in others, less-than-perfect performance will be sufficient to discharge the promisor and give him the right to recover under the contract.

1. *Strict performance.* A **strict performance** standard is a standard of performance that requires virtually perfect compliance with the contract terms. Remember that, when a party's duty is subject to an express condition, that condition must be strictly and completely complied with in order to give rise to a duty of performance. Thus, when a promisor's performance is an express condition of the promisee's duty to perform, that performance must *strictly* and *completely* comply with the contract in order to give rise to the other promisee's duty to perform. For example, if McMillan agrees to pay Jester $500 for painting his house "on condition that" Jester finish the job no later than June 1, 1992, a standard of strict or complete performance would be applied to Jester's performance. If Jester does not finish the job by June 1, his breach will have several consequences. First, since the condition precedent to McMillan's duty to pay has not occurred, McMillan does not have a duty to pay the contract price. Second, since it is now too late for the condition to occur, McMillan is discharged. Third, McMillan can sue Jester for breach of contract. The law's commitment to freedom of contract justifies such results in cases in which the parties have expressly bargained for strict compliance with the terms of the contract.

The strict performance standard is also applied to contractual obligations that can be performed either exactly or to a high degree of perfection. Examples of this type of obligation include promises to pay money, deliver deeds, and, generally, promises to deliver goods. A promisor who performs such promises completely and in strict compliance with the contract is entitled to receive the entire contract price. The promisor whose performance deviates from perfection is not entitled to receive the other party's performance if he does not render perfect performance within an appropriate time. He may, however, be able to recover the value of any benefits that he has conferred on the other party under a theory of quasi-contract.

2. *Substantial performance.* A **substantial performance** standard is a somewhat lower standard of performance that is applied to duties that are difficult to perform without some deviation from perfection *if* performance of those duties is *not* an express condition.

A common example of this type of obligation is a promise to erect a building. Other examples include promises to construct roads, to cultivate crops, and to render some types of personal or professional services. Substantial performance is performance that falls short of complete performance in minor respects. As you will see in *Reale v. Linder*, it does not apply when a contracting party has been deprived of a material part of the consideration he bargained for. When a substantial performance standard is applied, the promisor who has substantially performed is discharged. His substantial performance triggers the other party's duty to pay the contract price less any damages resulting from the defects in his performance. The obvious purpose behind the doctrine of substantial performance is to prevent forfeiture by a promisor who has given the injured party most of what he bargained for. Substantial performance is generally held to be inapplicable to a situation in which the breach of contract has been *willful*, however.

REALE v. LINDER
514 N.Y.S.2d 1004 (N.Y. Dist. Ct. 1987)

Thomas Linder hired Orlando Reale to build a 12 foot by 12 foot extension on his house with a raised wooden deck, sliding glass doors, and a gas-fired barbeque. Their written contract made no provision regarding obtaining a building permit or compliance with building codes, although it did contain a notation stating "plairs (sic) and permit $500 Dep." The agreed price for these improvements was $22,560.

It became evident that several features of the finished addition deviated from the state building code and the building plans that had been approved by the town. Reale had built the crawl space beneath the addition some 4 to 7 inches less than the 18 inches mandated by the state building code, which prevented inspection underneath the addition for structural defects. In addition, Reale sealed the framing of the addition, where substantial problems existed, without a prior inspection by the city building department or his own architect. Serious defects existed in the roof, and the plumbing work was not done by a licensed plumber, although it was later corrected. Improper or incomplete materials were used for the gas line for the barbeque, which caused a gas leak that had to be corrected. The steps leading down from the main dwelling to the addition are each 4 inches high rather than the 6 and 8 inches each that appear in the plan. In addition, Reale did no grade survey of the property before building, although expert witnesses testified that a grade survey was necessary to build the addition properly. The city building department initially denied a certificate of occupancy because the construction had been "closed up" and could not be inspected. It was issued only after Reale procured an architect's affadavit stating that he had inspected the location and that the work had been done in conformity with the approved plans and the state fire and building code, but this was apparently based on false information that Reale gave to the architect.

Linder made partial payment under the contract but withheld $5,855. Reale sued Linder to collect the unpaid balance. A trial was held before a judge and this is the trial court's opinion.

Mogil, Judge. The crux of Reale's argument in support of his complaint is that he substantially performed the contract. In order for a building contractor to be able to take advantage of the doctrine of substantial performance, he must not be guilty of a willful or intentional departure from the terms of his contract. This doctrine, however, permits compensation for all defects caused by the contractor's performance. Under this rule the party sued is protected as to any damages he may suffer due to the contractor's failure to strictly perform. The contractor must prove that the defects or omissions were insubstantial. This he has not done.

Although the written agreement does not expressly provide that the contract be performed in conformance with state and local fire prevention and building code regulations, it must be presumed that the parties intended that the contract be performed in accordance with state and local laws. In every home improvement contract, the contractor has an implied duty to perform the contract in accordance with fire prevention and building code requirements. The consumer homeowner relies upon the contractor's skill and expertise to perform the improvements. Reale's failure to construct the extension to code requirements renders the alterations illegal and frustrates the purpose of the contract.

The doctrine of substantial performance is an equitable one intended to prevent injustice where a contractor inadvertently caused trivial, minor, non-essential deficiencies which may be easily and inexpensively remedied. Where the defect cannot be corrected without partially reconstructing the building, the doctrine of substantial performance does not apply. It has been shown that any request for a new or currently revised certificate of occupancy will be denied unless the defect of an improper crawl space is corrected. To correct the defect, the floor of the extension must be removed, the walls braced, excavations undertaken to remove additional earth, and the concrete and floor rebuilt. These corrections are tantamount to reconstructing the addition. Reale has not therefore shown either complete or substantial performance.

Judgment entered in favor of Linder.

CONCEPT REVIEW

SUBSTANTIAL PERFORMANCE

Definition	Application	Effects	Limitation
Performance that falls short of complete performance in some minor respect, but which does not deprive the other party of a material part of the consideration for which he bargained	Applies to performance that (1) is *not* an express condition of the other party's duty to perform and (2) is difficult to do perfectly	Triggers other party's duty to perform Requires other party to pay the contract price minus any damages caused by defects in performance	Breach cannot have been willful

Good Faith Performance

One of the most significant trends in modern contract law is that courts and legislatures have created a duty to perform in good faith in an expanding range of contracts.[1] The Uniform Commercial Code specifically imposes a duty of good faith in every contract within the scope of any of the articles of the Code [1–203]. A growing number of courts have applied the duty to use good faith in transactions between lenders and their customers as well as insurance contracts, employment contracts, and contracts for the sale of real property.

This obligation to carry out a contract in good faith is usually called the **implied covenant of good faith and fair dealing.** It is a broad and flexible duty that is imposed by law rather than by the agreement of the parties. It is generally taken to mean that neither party to a contract will do anything to prevent the other from obtaining the benefits that he has the right to expect from the

---

[1] This trend is discussed in the Introduction to Contracts chapter.

parties' agreement or their contractual relationship. The law's purpose in imposing such a term in contracts is to prevent abuses of power and encourage ethical behavior.

Breach of the implied covenant of good faith gives rise to a contract remedy. In some states, it can also constitute a tort, depending on the severity of the breach. A tort action for breach of the implied covenant of good faith is more likely to be recognized in situations in which a contract involves a special relationship of dependency and trust between the parties or where the public interest is adversely affected by a contracting party's practices. Numerous cases exist, for example, in which insurance companies' bad faith refusal to settle claims or perform duties to their insured has led to large damage verdicts against the insurers. Likewise, in states in which the implied duty of good faith has been held applicable to contracts of employment, employers who discharge employees in bad faith have been held liable for damages.[2] In the emerging area of professional liability known as *lender liability*, lenders who have failed to exercise good faith in their dealings with customers have recently been subjected to tort liability for breach of the duty of good faith.

BREACH OF CONTRACT

When a person's performance is due, any failure to perform that is not excused is a breach of contract. Not all breaches of contract are of equal seriousness, however. Some are relatively minor deviations, whereas others are so extreme that they deprive the promisee of the essence of what he bargained for. The legal consequences of a given breach depend on the extent of the breach.

At a minimum, a party's breach of contract gives the nonbreaching party the right to sue and recover for any damages caused by that breach. When the breach is serious enough to be called a **material breach,** further legal consequences ensue.

Effect of Material Breach

A *material breach* occurs when the promisor's performance fails to reach the level of performance that the promisee is justified in expecting under the circumstances. In a situation in which the promisor's performance is judged by a *substantial performance* standard,

saying that he failed to give substantial performance is the same thing as saying that he materially breached the contract.

The party who is injured by a material breach has the right to withhold his own performance. He is discharged from further obligations under the contract and may cancel it. He also has the right to sue for damages for total breach of contract.

Effect of Nonmaterial Breach   By contrast, when the breach is *not* serious enough to be material, the nonbreaching party may sue for only those damages caused by the particular breach. In addition, he does not have the right to cancel the contract, although a nonmaterial breach can give him the right to suspend his performance until the breach is remedied. Once the breach is remedied, however, the nonbreaching party must go ahead and render his performance, minus any damages caused by the breach.

Determining the Materiality of the Breach   The standard for determining materiality is a flexible one that takes into account the facts of each individual case. The key question is whether the breach deprives the injured party of the benefits that he reasonably expected. For example, Norman, who is running for mayor, orders campaign literature from Prompt Press, to be delivered in September. Prompt Press's failure to deliver the literature until after the election in November deprives Norman of the essence of what he bargained for and would be considered a material breach.

In determining materiality, courts take into account the extent to which the breaching party will suffer forfeiture if the breach is held to be material. They also consider the magnitude (amount) of the breach and the willfulness or good faith exercised by the breaching party. The timing of the breach can also be important. A breach that occurs early on in the parties' relationship is more likely to be viewed as material than is one that occurs after an extended period of performance. Courts also consider the extent to which the injured party can be adequately compensated by the payment of damages.

Time for Performance   A party's failure to perform on time is a breach of contract that may be serious enough to constitute a material breach, or it may be relatively trivial under the circumstances.

At the outset, it is necessary to determine when performance is due. Some contracts specifically

---

[2] This is discussed in the Employment Law chapter.

state the time for performance, which makes it easy to determine the time for performance. In some contracts that do not specifically state the time for performance, such a time can be inferred from the circumstances surrounding the contract. In the Norman and Prompt Press hypothetical example, the circumstances surrounding the contract probably would have implied that the time for performance was some time before the election, even if the parties had not specified the time for performance. In still other contracts, no time for performance is either stated or implied. When no time for performance is stated or implied, performance must be completed within a "reasonable time," as judged by the circumstances of each case.

Consequences of Late Performance   After a court determines when performance was due, it must determine the *consequences* of late performance. In some contracts, the parties expressly state that "time is of the essence" or that timely performance is "vital." This means that each party's timely performance by a specific date is an *express condition* of the other party's duty to perform. Thus, in a contract that contains a time is of the essence provision, any delay by either party constitutes a *material* breach. You will see an example of this in *F. J. Miceli and Slonim Development Corporation v. Dierberg*, which follows. Sometimes, courts will imply such a term even when the language of the contract does not state that time is of the essence. A court would be likely to do this if late performance is of little or no value to the promisee. For example, Schrader contracts with the local newspaper to run an advertisement for Christmas trees from December 15, 1991, to December 24, 1991, but the newspaper does not run the ad until December 26, 1991. In this case, the time for performance is an essential part of the contract and the newspaper has committed a material breach.

When a contract does not contain language indicating that time is of the essence and a court determines that the time for performance is not a particularly important part of the contract, the promisee must accept late performance rendered within a reasonable time after performance was due. The promisee is then entitled to deduct or set off from the contract price any losses caused by the delay. Late performance is not a material breach in such cases unless it is *unreasonably* late.

F. J. MICELI AND SLONIM DEVELOPMENT CORPORATION v. DIERBERG

773 S.W.2d 154 (Mo. Ct. App. 1989)

Joanne and Louis Basso contracted with Mary Dierberg to purchase her property for $1,310,000. One term of the contract stated "The sale under this contract shall be closed . . . at the office of Community Title Company . . . on May 16, 1988 at 10:00 A.M. . . . . Time is of the essence of this contract." After forming this contract, the Bassos assigned their right to purchase Dierberg's property to F. J. Miceli and Slonim Development Corporation.

At 10:00 A.M. on May 16, 1988, Dierberg appeared at Community Title Company for closing. No representative of Miceli and Slonim was there, nor did anyone from Miceli and Slonim inform Dierberg that there would be any delay in the closing. At 10:20 A.M., Dierberg declared the contract null and void because the closing did not take place as agreed, and she left the title company office shortly thereafter. Dierberg had intended to use the purchase money to close another contract to purchase real estate later in the day. At about 10:30 A.M., a representantive of Miceli and Slonim appeared at Community Title Company to begin the closing procedures, but the representative did not have the funds for payment until 1:30 P.M. Dierberg refused to return to the title company to close, stating that Miceli and Slonim had breached the contract by failing to tender payment on time. She had already made alternative arrangements to finance her purchase of other real estate to meet her obligation under that contract.

Miceli and Slonim sued Dierberg for specific performance of the contract, claiming that the contract did not require closing exactly at 10:00 A.M., but rather sometime on the day of May 16. Dierberg filed a motion for summary judgment, and the trial court granted it. Miceli and Slonim appealed.

Karohl, Judge.   Parties to a contract may provide that time is of the essence. A clause specifying time is of the essence ordinarily means a specific contractual provision fixing the time of performance is to be regarded as a vital element of the contract. If a contract specifies a certain time for performance, the contract must be performed at that time, even if time is specified by the hour. Custom will not alter express agreement of the parties.

Here, the contract clearly and precisely stated closing was to occur at 10:00 A.M. on May 16, 1988. Time and date were specifically referred to in three separate sections of the contract. It was agreed time was of the essence of the contract. This provision would relate to all three times and dates. Dierberg was obligated to close under another contract to purchase real estate later the same day. She relied on receiving the proceeds of her sale at 10:00 A.M. Because closing did not occur as agreed, Dierberg was required to make other arrangements to meet her obligation. These facts lend meaning to the judgment of the trial court that "10:00 A.M." was the agreement of Bassos and Dierberg, not a mere guideline.

When there is no ambiguity in a contract, it is the duty of the court to state its clear meaning. Here, the court found there was no ambiguity in the contract and that the contract required closing at or reasonably near 10:00 A.M. We find no error in the judgment. Miceli and Slonim's failure to tender payment until 1:30 P.M. combined with its failure to inform Dierberg of the delay in closing, was a breach of contract. On undisputed facts, summary judgment was proper.

Summary judgment for Dierberg affirmed.

CONCEPT REVIEW

TIME FOR PERFORMANCE

Contract Language	Time for Performance	Consequences of Late Performance
"Time is of the essence" or similar language	The time stated in the contract	Material breach
Specific time is stated in or implied by the contract and late performance would have little or no value	The time stated in or implied by the contract	Material breach
Specific time is stated in or implied by the contract, but the time for performance is a relatively unimportant part of the contract	The time stated in or implied by the contract	Not a material breach unless performance is unreasonably late
No time for performance is stated in or implied by the contract	Within a reasonable time	Not a material breach unless performance is unreasonably late

Anticipatory Repudiation   One type of breach of contract occurs when the promisor indicates *before the time for his performance* that he is unwilling or unable to carry out the contract. This is called **anticipatory repudiation** or **anticipatory breach.** Anticipatory breach generally constitutes a material breach of contract that discharges the promisee from all further obligation under the contract.

In determining what constitutes anticipatory repudiation, courts look for some unequivocal statement or voluntary act that clearly indicates that the promisor cannot or will not perform his duties under the contract. This may take the form of an express statement by the promisor. The promisor's intent not to perform could also be implied from actions of the promisor such as selling to a third party the property that the promisor was obligated to sell to the promisee. For example, if Ross, who is obligated to convey real estate to Davis, conveys the property to some third person instead, Ross has repudiated the contract.

When anticipatory repudiation occurs, the promisee is faced with several choices. For example, Marsh and Davis enter a contract in which Davis agrees to deliver a quantity of bricks to Marsh on September 1, 1992, and Marsh agrees to pay Davis a sum of money in two installments. The agreement specifies that Marsh will pay 50 percent of the purchase price on July 15, 1992, and 50 percent of the purchase price within 30 days after delivery. On July 1, 1992, Davis writes Marsh and unequivocally states that he will not deliver the bricks. Must Marsh go ahead and send the payment that is due on July 15? Must he wait until September 1 to bring suit for total breach of contract? The answer to both questions is no.

When anticipatory repudiation occurs, the nonbreaching party is justified in withholding his own performance and suing for damages right away, without waiting for the time for performance to arrive.[3] If he can show that he was ready, willing, and able to perform his part of the contract, he can recover damages for total breach of the contract. The nonbreaching party is not obligated to do this, however. If he chooses, he may wait until the time for performance in case the other party changes his mind and decides to perform.

Recovery by a Party Who Has Committed Material Breach

A party who has materially breached the contract (that is, has not substantially performed) does not have the right to recover the contract price. If a promisor who has given some performance to the promisee cannot recover under the contract, however, the promisor will face forfeiture and the promisee will have obtained an unearned gain. There are two possible avenues for a party who has committed material breach to obtain some compensation for the performance he has conferred on the nonbreaching party.

1. *Quasi-contract.* A party who has materially breached a contract might recover the reasonable value of any benefits he has conferred on the promisee by bringing an action under quasi-contract.[4] This would enable him to obtain compensation for the value of any performance he has given that has benefited the nonbreaching party. Some courts take the position that a person in material breach should not be able to recover for benefits he has conferred, however.

2. *Partial performance of a divisible contract.* Some contracts are **divisible.** That is, each party's performance can be divided in two or more parts and each part is exchanged for some corresponding consideration from the other party. For example, if Johnson agrees to mow Peterson's lawn for $20 and clean Peterson's gutters for $50, the contract is divisible. When a promisor performs one part of the contract, but materially breaches another part, he can recover at the contract price for the part that he did perform. For example, if Johnson breached his duty to clean the gutters but fully performed his obligation to mow the lawn, he could recover at the contract price for the lawn-mowing part of the contract.

EXCUSES FOR NONPERFORMANCE

Although nonperformance of a duty that has become due will ordinarily constitute a breach of contract, there are some situations in which nonperformance is excused because of factors that arise after the formation of the contract. When this occurs, the person whose performance

---

[3] Uniform Commercial Code rules regarding anticipatory repudiation in contracts for the sale of goods are discussed in the Performance of Sales Contracts chapter.

[4] Quasi-contract is discussed in the Introduction to Contracts chapter. It involves the use of the remedy of restitution, which is discussed later in this chapter.

is made impossible or impracticable by these factors is discharged from further obligation under the contract. The following discussion concerns the most common grounds for excuse of nonperformance.

Impossibility

When performance of a contractual duty becomes impossible after the formation of the contract, the duty will be discharged on grounds of **impossibility.** This does not mean that a person can be discharged merely because he has contracted to do something that he is simply unable to do or that causes him hardship or difficulty. Impossibility in the legal sense of the word means "it cannot be done by anyone" rather than "I cannot do it." Thus, promisors who find that they have agreed to perform duties that are beyond their capabilities or that turn out to be unprofitable or burdensome generally are not excused from performance of their duties. Impossibility will provide an excuse for nonperformance, however, when some unexpected event arises *after* the formation of the contract and renders performance objectively impossible. The event that causes the impossibility need not have been entirely unforeseeable. It must, however, have been one that the parties would not have reasonably thought of as a real possibility that would affect performance.

There are a variety of situations in which a person's duty to perform may be discharged on grounds of impossibility. The three most common situations involve illness or death of the promisor, supervening illegality, and destruction of the subject matter of the contract.

Illness or Death of Promisor   Incapacitating illness or death of the promisor excuses nonperformance when the promisor has contracted to perform personal services. For example, if Pauling, a college professor who has a contract with State University to teach for an academic year, dies before the completion of the contract, her estate will not be liable for breach of contract. The promisor's death or illness does *not*, however, excuse the nonperformance of duties that can be delegated to another, such as the duty to deliver goods, pay money, or convey real estate. For example, if Odell had contracted to convey real estate to Ruskin and died before the closing date, Ruskin could enforce the contract against Odell's estate.

Supervening Illegality   If a statute or governmental regulation enacted after the creation of a contract makes performance of a party's duties illegal, the promisor is excused from performing. Statutes or regulations that merely make performance more difficult or less profitable do not, however, excuse nonperformance.

Destruction of the Subject Matter of the Contract   If something that is essential to the promisor's performance is destroyed after the formation of the contract through no fault of the promisor, the promisor is excused from performing. For example, Woolridge contracts to sell his car to Rivkin. If an explosion destroys the car after the contract has been formed but before Woolridge has made delivery, Woolridge's nonperformance will be excused. The destruction of nonessential items that the promisor intended to use in performing does not excuse nonperformance if substitutes are available, even though securing them makes performance more difficult or less profitable. Suppose that Ace Construction Company had planned to use a particular piece of machinery in fulfilling a contract to build a building for Worldwide Widgets Company. If the piece of machinery is destroyed but substitutes are available, destruction of the machinery before the contract is performed would *not* give Ace an excuse for failing to perform.

Frustration of Venture

Closely associated with impossibility is the doctrine of **frustration of venture** (also known as **commercial frustration** or **frustration of purpose**). This doctrine provides an excuse for nonperformance when events that occur after the formation of the contract would deprive the promisor of the benefit of return performance. Although courts often include frustration cases within the general terminology of impossibility, frustration can be distinguished from impossibility and impracticability by the fact that the promisor in a frustration case is not necessarily prevented from performing. Rather, in frustration cases, the promisor is excused because the return performance by the other party has become worthless to him. For example, Boyd signs a contract for a one-year membership in an Eden Exercise Salon, for which he agrees to pay $50 per month. One week after signing the contract, Boyd is involved in a serious automobile accident and suffers injuries that cause him to be bedridden for a year. In such a case, the automobile accident and Boyd's resulting injuries did not prevent him from performing his duties under the contract (paying money each month), but this unexpected event does deprive Boyd of the benefit of receiving Eden's return performance. In such a case, a court might excuse Boyd's performance on the ground of frustration of venture.

Commercial Impracticability

Section 2–615 of the Uniform Commercial Code has extended the scope of the common law doctrine of impossibility to cases in which unforeseen developments make performance by the promisor highly impracticable, unreasonably expensive, or of little value to the promisee. Rather than using a standard of impossibility, then, the Code uses the more relaxed standard of **impracticability.** Despite the less stringent standard applied, cases actually excusing nonperformance on grounds of impracticability are relatively rare. To be successful in claiming excuse based on impracticability, a promisor must be able to establish that the event that makes performance impracticable occurred without his fault and that the contract was made with the basic assumption that this event would not occur. This basically means that the event was beyond the scope of the risks that the parties contemplated at the time of contracting and that the promisor did not expressly or impliedly assume the risk that the event would occur.

Case law and official comments to section 2–615 indicate that neither increased cost nor collapse of a market for particular goods is sufficient to excuse nonperformance, because those are the types of business risks that every promisor assumes. However, drastic price increases or severe shortages of goods resulting from unforeseen circumstances such as wars and crop failures can give rise to impracticability.

If the event causing impracticability affects only a part of the seller's capacity to perform, the seller must allocate production and deliveries among customers in a "fair and reasonable" manner and must notify them of any delay or any limited allocation of the goods. You can read more about commercial impracticability in the Performance of Sales Contracts chapter.

The impracticability standard has been adopted in section 261 of the *Restatement (Second) of Contracts*, which closely resembles the provisions of section 2–615 of the UCC. States that follow the *Restatement* approach apply the impracticability standard to all types of contracts, not just those for the sale of goods. You will see an example of the use of the *Restatement* standard in the following case, *The Opera Company of Boston, Inc. v. The Wolf Trap Foundation for the Performing Arts.*

THE OPERA COMPANY OF BOSTON, INC. v. THE WOLF TRAP FOUNDATION FOR THE PERFORMING ARTS

817 F.2d 1094 (4th Cir. 1987)

Wolf Trap, an organization for the advancement of the performing arts, sponsors operas and other artistic programs at the Filene Center. The Filene Center is located in the Wolf Trap National Park, a national park owned by the United States government and operated by the National Park Service. The Center, which consists of a main stage tower, an auditorium, and an open lawn, provides both covered and uncovered seating for approximately 6,500 people. The park provides the parking space, which is separated from the Center and accessible by a number of pathways. Wolf Trap entered into a contract with the Opera Company of Boston whereby it agreed to pay the Opera Company $272,000 to perform four operas at the Filene Center on the nights of June 12, 13, 14, and 15, 1980. Among Wolf Trap's duties under the contract was the duty "to provide lighting equipment as shall be specified by the Opera Company of Boston's lighting designer."

All four performances were sold out. Both parties performed their obligations for the first three performances. On June 15, the day of the last performance, however, the weather was hot, humid, and rainy. In the early evening, there was a severe thunderstorm, which caused an electrical power outage that blacked out all electrical service in the park, its roadways, parking area, pathways, and auditorium. Representatives of the National Park Service and Wolf Trap held several conferences to decide what to do about the performance. The public utility advised that electrical service would not be resumed in the park until 11:00 P.M. or perhaps not even until the next morning. Various alternatives for supplying power were considered but none was regarded as being sufficient to resolve the problem. The Park Service was concerned about the safety of the 3,000 people who were already in the park; 3,500 more were expected before 8:00 P.M. The Park Service recommended the immediate cancellation of the performance and advised Wolf Trap that it disclaimed responsibility for the safety of the people who were to attend the performance. Wolf Trap agreed and the performance was canceled. A representative of the Opera Company was present at this meeting, but she neither took part in the decision nor voiced objection to the decision.

Since the performance was canceled, Wolf Trap did not make the final payment called for in the contract to the Opera Company. The Opera Company sued Wolf Trap to recover the balance due under the contract, and Wolf Trap defended on the ground of impossibility. The trial court rejected this defense on the ground that Wolf Trap was obligated to provide sufficient lighting and power outages were reasonably foreseeable. It entered judgment in favor of the Opera Company, and Wolf Trap appealed.

Russell, Circuit Judge.   The modern doctrine of impossibility or impracticability has been formulated in section 265 of the *Restatement (Second) of Contracts* in these words:

> Where, after a contract is made, a party's principal purpose is substantially frustrated without his fault by the occurrence of an event the non-occurrence of which was a basic assumption on which the contract was made, his remaining duties to render performance are discharged, unless the language or the circumstances indicate the contrary.

Impossibility arises as a defense to breach of contract when the circumstances causing the breach have made performance so vitally different from what was anticipated that the contract cannot reasonably be thought to govern. It is implicit in the doctrine of impossibility (and the companion rule of frustration of purpose) that certain risks are so unusual and have such severe consequences that they must have been beyond the scope of the assignment of risks inherent in the contract, that is, beyond the agreement made by the parties.

Manifestly the first fact to be established in making out this defense of impossibility or impracticability of performance is the existence of an "occurrence of an event, the non-occurrence of which was a basic assumption on which the contract was made." The occurrence must be unexpected but it does not necessarily have to have been unforeseeable. A requirement of absolute nonforeseeability as a condition to the application of the doctrine would in effect nullify the doctrine. Practically any event can be foreseen but whether the foreseeability is sufficient to render unacceptable the defense of impossibility is one of degree of the foreseeability.

The second fact to be determined in the application of the doctrine is that the frustration of performance was substantial. To satisfy this requirement the frustration must be so severe that it is not fairly to be regarded as within the risks the obligor assumed under the contract. And, finally, the defendant asserting the defense must establish that performance was impossible as that term has been defined in the refinements of the doctrine.

Applying the law to the facts of this case, we conclude that the existence of electric power was necessary for the satisfactory performance by the Opera Company on the night of June 15. The district judge, however, refused to sustain the defense because he held that if the contingency that occurred was one that could have been foreseen, reliance on the doctrine of impossibility as a defense to a breach of contract suit is absolutely barred. As we have said, this is not the modern rule. Foreseeability, as we have said, is at best one fact to be considered in resolving whether its occurrence, based on past experience, was of such reasonable likelihood that the obligor should not merely foresee the risk but, because of the degree of its likelihood, the obligor should have guarded against it or provided for non-liability against the risk.

The judgment must be vacated and the action remanded to the district court to make findings whether the possible foreseeability of the power failure in this case was of that degree of reasonable likelihood as to make improper the assertion by Wolf Trap of the defense of impossiblity of performance.

Judgment vacated and remanded in favor of Wolf Trap.

OTHER GROUNDS FOR DISCHARGE

Additional Grounds for Discharge

Earlier in this chapter, you learned about several situations in which a party's duty to perform could be discharged even though that party had not himself performed. These include the nonoccurrence of a condition precedent or concurrent condition, the occurrence of a condition subsequent, performance, material breach by the other party, and excuse from performance by impossibility, impracticability, or frustration. The following discussion deals with additional ways in which a discharge can occur.

Discharge by Mutual Agreement

Just as contracts are created by mutual agreement, they can also be discharged by *mutual agreement*. An agreement to discharge a contract must be supported by consideration to be enforceable.

Discharge by Accord and Satisfaction

An **accord** is an agreement whereby a promisee who has an existing claim agrees with the promisor that he will accept some performance different from that which was originally agreed upon. When the promisor performs the accord, that is called a **satisfaction.**[5] When accord and satisfaction occurs, the parties are discharged. For example, Root contracts with May to build a garage on May's property for $30,000. After Root has performed his part of the bargain, the parties then agree that instead of paying money, May will transfer a one-year-old

Porsche to Root instead. When this is done, both parties are discharged.

Discharge by Waiver

A party to a contract may voluntarily relinquish any right he has under a contract, including the right to receive return performance. Such a relinquishment of rights is known as a **waiver.** If one party tenders an incomplete or defective performance and the other party accepts that performance without objection, knowing that the defects will not be remedied, the party to whom performance was due will have discharged the other party from his duty of performance. For example, a real estate lease requires Long, the tenant, to pay a $5 late charge for late payments of rent. Long pays his rent late each month for five months but the landlord accepts it without objection and without assessing the late charge. In this situation, the landlord has probably waived his right to collect the late charge. The Uniform Commercial Code provides in section 1–107 that "any claim or right arising out of an alleged breach can be discharged in whole or in part without consideration by a written waiver or renunciation signed and delivered by the aggrieved party."

To avoid waiving rights, a person who has received defective performance should give the other party prompt notice that she expects complete performance and will seek damages if the defects are not corrected.

Discharge by Alteration

If the contract is represented by a *written* instrument, and one of the parties intentionally makes a material alteration in the instrument without the other's consent, the alteration acts as a discharge of the other party. If the other party consents to the alteration or does not object

---

[5] Accord and satisfaction is also discussed in the Consideration chapter.

to it when he learns of it, he is not discharged. Alteration by a third party without the knowledge or consent of the contracting parties does not affect the parties' rights.

Discharge by Statute of Limitations

Courts have long refused to grant a remedy to a person who delays bringing a lawsuit for an unreasonable time. All of the states have enacted statutes known as **statutes of limitation,** which specify the period of time in which a person can bring a lawsuit.

The time period for bringing a contract action varies from state to state, and many states prescribe time periods for cases concerning oral contracts that are different from those for cases concerning written contracts. Section 2–725 of the Uniform Commercial Code provides for a four-year statute of limitations for contracts involving the sale of goods.

The statutory period ordinarily begins to run from the date of the breach. It may be delayed if the party who has the right to sue is under some incapacity at that time (such as minority or insanity) or is beyond the jurisdiction of the state. A person who has breached a contractual duty is discharged from liability for breach if no lawsuit is brought before the statutory period elapses.

Discharge by Decree of Bankruptcy

The contractual obligations of a debtor are generally discharged by a decree of bankruptcy. Bankruptcy is discussed in a later chapter.

REMEDIES FOR BREACH OF CONTRACT

Our discussion of the performance stage of contracts so far has focused on the circumstances under which a party has the duty to perform or is excused from performing. In situations in which a person is injured by a breach of contract and is unable to obtain compensation by a settlement out of court, a further important issue remains: What remedy will a court fashion to compensate for breach of contract?

Contract law seeks to encourage people to rely on the promises made to them by others. The objective of granting a remedy in a case of breach of contract is not to punish the breaching party. Contract remedies focus on the economic loss caused by breach of contract, not on the moral obligation to perform a promise. The objective of contract remedies is simply to compensate the injured party.

Types of Contract Remedies

There are a variety of ways in which this can be done. The basic categories of contract remedies include:

1. Legal remedies (money damages).
2. Equitable remedies.
3. Restitution.

The usual remedy is an award of money damages that will compensate the injured party for his losses. This is called a **legal remedy** or **remedy at law**, because the imposition of money damages in our legal system originated in courts of law. Less frequently used but still important are **equitable remedies**, such as specific performance. Equitable remedies are those remedies that had their origins in courts of equity rather than in courts of law.[6] Today they are available at the discretion of the judge. A final possible remedy is **restitution**, which requires the defendant to pay the value of the benefits that the plaintiff has conferred on him.

Interests Protected by Contract Remedies

Remedies for breach of contract protect one or more of the following interests that a promisee may have:[7]

1. *Expectation interest.* A promisee's **expectation interest** is his interest in obtaining the objective or opportunity for gain that he bargained for and "expected." Courts attempt to protect this interest by formulating a remedy that will place the promisee in the position he would have been in if the contract had been performed as promised.

2. *Reliance interest.* A promisee's **reliance interest** is his interest in being compensated for losses that he has suffered by changing his position in reliance on the other party's promise. In some cases, such as when a promisee is unable to prove his expectation interest with reasonable certainty, the promisee may seek a remedy to compensate for the *loss suffered* as a result of relying on the promisor's promise rather than for the expectation of profit.

3. *Restitution interest.* A **restitution interest** is a party's interest in recovering the amount by which he has enriched or benefited the other. Both the reliance and restitution interests involve promisees who have changed

---

[6] The nature of equitable remedies is also discussed in the Nature of Law chapter.

[7] *Restatement (Second) of Contracts* section 344.

their position. The difference between the two is that the reliance interest involves a loss to the promisee that does not benefit the promisor, whereas the restitution interest involves a loss to the promisee that *does* constitute an unjust enrichment to the promisor. A remedy based on restitution enables a party who has performed or partially performed her contract and has benefited the other party to obtain compensation for the value of the benefits that she has conferred.

LEGAL REMEDIES (DAMAGES)

Limitations on Recovery of Damages in Contract Cases

An injured party's ability to recover damages in a contract action is limited by three principles:

1. *A party can recover damages only for those losses that he can prove with reasonable certainty.* Losses that are purely speculative are not recoverable. Thus, if Jones Publishing Company breaches a contract to publish Powell's memoirs, Powell may not be able to recover damages for lost royalties (her expectation interest), since she may be unable to establish, beyond speculation, how much money she would have earned in royalties if the book had been published. (Note, however, that Powell's reliance interest might be protected here; she could be allowed to recover provable losses incurred in reliance on the contract.)

2. *A breaching party is responsible for paying only those losses that were foreseeable to him at the time of contracting.* A loss is foreseeable if it would ordinarily be expected to result from a breach or if the breaching party had reason to know of particular circumstances that would make the loss likely. For example, if Prince Manufacturing Company renders late performance in a contract to deliver parts to Cheatum Motors without knowing that Cheatum is shut down waiting for the parts, Prince will not have to pay the business losses that result from Cheatum's having to close its operation.

3. *Plaintiffs injured by a breach of contract have the duty to **mitigate** (avoid or minimize) damages.* A party cannot recover for losses that he could have avoided without undue risk, burden, or humiliation. For example, an employee who has been wrongfully fired would be entitled to damages equal to his wages for the remainder of the employment period. The employee, however, has the duty to minimize the damages by making reasonable efforts to seek a similar job elsewhere. The *Parker v. Twentieth Century-Fox Film Corporation* case involves the question of whether an injured party carried out her duty to mitigate.

PARKER v. TWENTIETH CENTURY-FOX FILM CORPORATION

474 P.2d 689 (Cal. Sup. Ct. 1970)

Shirley MacLaine Parker entered into a contract with Twentieth Century-Fox to play the female lead in Fox's contemplated production of a movie entitled *Bloomer Girl*. The contract provided that Fox would pay Parker a minimum "guaranteed compensation" of $53,571.42 per week for 14 weeks, beginning May 23, 1966, for a total of $750,000. Fox decided not to produce the movie, and in a letter dated April 4, 1966, it notified Parker that it would not "comply with our obligations to you under" the written contract. In the same letter, with the professed purpose "to avoid any damage to you," Fox instead offered to employ Parker as the leading actress in another movie, tentatively entitled *Big Country, Big Man*. The compensation offered was identical. Unlike *Bloomer Girl*, however, which was to have been a musical production, *Big Country* was to be a dramatic "western type" movie. *Bloomer Girl* was to have been filmed in California; *Big Country* was to be produced in Australia. Certain other terms of the substitute contract varied from those of the original. Parker was given one week within which to accept. She did not, and the offer

lapsed. Parker then filed suit against Fox for recovery of the agreed-upon guaranteed compensation. The trial court held for Parker, and Fox appealed.

Burke, Justice.　The general rule is that the measure of recovery by a wrongfully discharged
employee is the amount of salary agreed upon for the period of service, less the amount which the
employer affirmatively proves the employee has earned or with reasonable effort might have
earned from other employment. However, before projected earnings from other employment
opportunities not sought or accepted by the discharged employee can be applied in mitigation, the
employer must show that the other employment was comparable, or substantially similar, to that
of which the employee has been deprived; the employee's rejection of or failure to seek other
available employment of a different or inferior kind may not be resorted to in order to mitigate
damages.

In the present case, the sole issue is whether Parker's refusal of Fox's substitute offer of "Big
Country" may be used in mitigation. Nor, if the "Big Country" offer was of employment different
or inferior when compared with the original "Bloomer Girl" employment, is there an issue as to
whether Parker acted reasonably in refusing the substitute offer.

It is clear that the trial court correctly ruled that Parker's failure to accept Fox's tendered
substitute employment could not be applied in mitigation of damages because the offer of the "Big
Country" lead was of employment both different and inferior. The mere circumstance that
"Bloomer Girl" was to be a musical review calling upon Parker's talents as a dancer as well as an
actress, and was to be produced in the City of Los Angeles, whereas "Big Country" was a straight
dramatic role in a "western type" story taking place in an opal mine in Australia, demonstrates
the difference in kind between the two employments; the female lead in a western style motion
picture can by no stretch of the imagination be considered the equivalent of or substantially
similar to the lead in a song-and-dance production.

Judgment for Parker affirmed.

Compensatory Damages

Subject to the limitations discussed above, a person who
has been injured by a breach of contract is entitled to
recover **compensatory damages.** In calculating the
compensatory remedy, a court will attempt to protect the
expectation interest of the injured party by giving him
the "benefit of his bargain" (placing him in the position
he would have been in *had the contract been performed
as promised*). To do this, the court must compensate the
injured person for the provable losses he has suffered as
well as for the provable gains that he has been prevented
from realizing by the breach of contract. Normally, compensatory damages include one or more of three possible
items: loss in value, any allowable consequential damages, and any allowable incidental damages.

1. *Loss in value.* The starting point in calculating
compensatory damages is to determine the **loss in value**
of the performance that the plaintiff had the right to expect. This is a way of measuring the expectation interest.

The calculation of the loss in value experienced by an
injured party differs according to the sort of contract involved and the circumstances of the breach. In contracts
involving nonperformance of the sale of real estate, for
example, courts normally measure loss in value by the
difference between the contract price and the market
price of the property. Thus, if Willis repudiates a contract with Renfrew whereby Renfrew was to purchase
land worth $20,000 from Willis for $10,000, Renfrew's
loss in value was $10,000. Where a seller has failed to
perform a contract for the sale of goods, courts may
measure loss in value by the difference between the contract price and the price that the buyer had to pay to
procure substitute goods.[8] In cases in which a party
breaches by rendering defective performance—say, by

---

[8] Remedies under Article 2 of the Uniform Commercial Code
are discussed in detail in the Remedies for Breach of Sales Contracts
chapter.

breaching a warranty in the sale of goods—the loss in value would be measured by the difference between the value of the goods if they had been in the condition warranted by the seller and the value of the goods in their defective condition.[9]

2. *Consequential damages.* **Consequential damages** (also called **special damages**) compensate for losses that occur as a consequence of the breach of contract. Consequential losses occur because of some special or unusual circumstances of the particular contractual relationship of the parties. For example, Apex Trucking Company buys a computer system from ABC Computers. The system fails to operate properly, and Apex is forced to pay its employees to perform the tasks manually, spending $10,000 in overtime pay. In this situation, Apex might seek to recover the $10,000 in

overtime pay in addition to the loss of value that it has experienced.

Lost profits flowing from a breach of contract can be recovered as consequential damages if they are foreseeable and can be proven with reasonable certainty. It is important to remember, however, that the recovery of consequential damages is subject to the limitations on damage recovery discussed earlier. As *Richmond Medical Supply Co., Inc. v. Clifton* indicates, foreseeability of the damages is of particular concern in cases in which consequential damages are sought.

3. *Incidental damages.* **Incidental damages** compensate for reasonable costs that the injured party incurs after the breach in an effort to avoid further loss. For example, if Smith Construction Company breaches an employment contract with Brice, Brice could recover as incidental damages those reasonable expenses he must incur in attempting to procure substitute employment, such as long-distance telephone tolls or the cost of printing new resumes.

---

[9] See the Product Liability chapter for further discussion of the damages for breach of warranty in the sale of goods.

RICHMOND MEDICAL SUPPLY CO., INC. v. CLIFTON

369 S.E.2d 407 (Va. Sup. Ct. 1988)

Richmond Medical Supply (RMS) occupied commercial space that it leased from Robert Clifton. When the lease was renewed, the parties included an addendum that required Clifton to make certain repairs, including "replacement and make in good working order the rear overhead door on or before the commencement of this lease, August 1, 1983." RMS continued in possession of the property even though Clifton failed to repair or replace the door. On November 8, 1983, thieves broke into the leased property by knocking out a wooden panel in the overhead door and removed cases, equipment, and inventory valued by RMS at $60,000, none of which was ever recovered.

RMS brought this action for breach of contract, alleging that its loss was the direct consequence of Clifton's breach of his express promise to replace the door and that the damages RMS had sustained were within the contemplation of the parties. (Under Virginia law, a tort action against Clifton would not have been successful.) Clifton moved for summary judgment, and the trial court granted summary judgment in his favor. RMS appealed.

Russell, Justice.   There are two broad categories of damages which may arise from a breach of contract. Direct damages are those which naturally or ordinarily flow from the breach; consequential damages arise from the intervention of special circumstances not ordinarily predictable. Consequential damages are compensable only if it is determined *as a matter of fact* that the special circumstances were within the contemplation of the contracting parties at the time of contracting. "Contemplation," in this context, includes both that which was actually foreseen and that which was reasonably foreseeable. Whether special circumstances were within the contemplation of the parties so as to justify the recovery of consequential damages is a question of fact for the jury. Thus, having properly determined that RMS's claimed damages were consequential in nature, the trial court erred in failing to submit the "contemplation" issue to the jury unless the recovery of any damages was barred by the doctrine of *Gulf Reston, Inc. v. Rogers*.

In *Gulf Reston*, we considered a claim that a landlord was liable in tort to a tenant for failure to protect the tenant from the criminal act of a third party. We held that the landlord had no duty to provide such protection. We were faced with the determination whether a duty was imposed by general law upon the defendant somehow to foresee and to take effective measures to guard against the danger of criminal acts by a third person. The defendant [had not] expressly assumed a duty, by contract, to take some specific action to protect the plaintiff from a danger within the contemplation of the parties at the time of contracting.

Contracting parties are entirely capable of assuming duties toward one another beyond those imposed by general law and, in fact, do so in nearly every contractual arrangement. RMS pleaded a contractual duty, a breach thereof, and damages flowing from the breach. Each of these should have been considered by the fact-finder. Accordingly we reverse the order granting summary judgment and remand the case for further proceedings consistent with this opinion.

Summary judgment reversed in favor of RMS.

Alternative Measures of Damages The foregoing discussion has focused on the most common formulation of damage remedies in contracts cases. The normal measure of compensatory damages is not appropriate in every case, however. When it is not appropriate, a court may use an alternative measure of damages. For example, where a party has suffered losses by performing or preparing to perform, he might seek damages based on his *reliance interest* instead of his expectation interest. In such a case, he would be compensated for the provable losses he suffered by relying on the other party's promise. This measure of damages is often used in cases in which a promise is enforceable under promissory estoppel.[10]

Nominal Damages

Nominal damages are very small damage awards that are given when a technical breach of contract has occurred without causing any actual or provable economic loss. The sums awarded as nominal damages typically vary from two cents to a dollar.

Liquidated Damages

The parties to a contract may expressly provide in their contract that a specific sum shall be recoverable if the contract is breached. Such provisions are called **liquidated damages** provisions. For example, Murchison rents space in a shopping mall in which she plans to operate a retail clothing store. She must make improvements in the space before opening the store, and it is very important to her to have the store opened for the Christmas shopping season. She hires Ace Construction Company to construct the improvements. The parties agree to include in the contract a liquidated damages provision stating that, if Ace is late in completing the construction, Murchison will be able to recover a specified sum for each day of delay. Such a provision is highly desirable from Murchison's point of view because, without a liquidated damages provision, she would have a difficult time in establishing the precise losses that would result from delay. Courts scrutinize these agreed-upon damages carefully, however.

If the amount specified in a liquidated damages provision is reasonable and if the nature of the contract is such that actual damages would be difficult to determine, a court will enforce the provision. When liquidated damages provisions are enforced, the amount of damages agreed upon will be the injured party's exclusive damage remedy. If the amount specified is unreasonably great in relation to the probable loss or injury, however, or if the amount of damages could be readily determined in the event of breach, the courts will declare the provision to be a *penalty* and will refuse to enforce it.

---

[10] Promissory estoppel is discussed in the Introduction to Contracts; Offer; Acceptance; and Writing chapters.

Punitive Damages

Punitive damages are damages awarded *in addition to* the compensatory remedy that are designed to punish a defendant for particularly reprehensible behavior and to deter the defendant and others from committing similar behavior in the future. The traditional rule is that punitive damages are *not* recoverable in contracts cases unless a specific statutory provision (such as some consumer protection statutes) allows them or the defendant has committed *fraud* or some other *independent tort*. A few states will permit the use of punitive damages in contracts cases in which the defendant's conduct, though not technically a tort, was malicious, oppressive, or tortious in nature.

Punitive damages have also been awarded in many of the cases involving breach of the implied covenant of good faith. In such cases, courts usually circumvent the traditional rule against awarding punitive damages in contracts cases by holding that breach of the duty of good faith is an independent tort. The availability of punitive damages in such cases operates to deter a contracting party from deliberately disregarding the other party's rights. Insurance companies have been the most frequent target for punitive damages awards in bad-faith cases, but employers and banks have also been subjected to punitive damages verdicts.

EQUITABLE REMEDIES

In exceptional cases in which money damages alone are not adequate to fully compensate for a party's injuries, a court may grant an **equitable remedy** either alone or in combination with a legal remedy. Equitable relief is subject to several limitations, however, and will be granted only when justice is served by doing so. The primary equitable remedies for breach of contract are *specific performance* and *injunction*.[11]

Specific Performance

Specific performance is an equitable remedy whereby the court orders the breaching party to perform his contractual duties as promised. For example, if Barnes breached a contract to sell a tract of land to Metzger and a court granted specific performance of the contract, the court would require Barnes to deed the land to Metzger. (Metzger, of course, must pay the purchase price.) This remedy can be advantageous to the injured party because he is not faced with the complexities of proving damages, he does not have to worry about whether he can actually collect the damages, and he gets exactly what he bargained for. However, the availability of this remedy is subject to the limitations discussed below.

The Availability of Specific Performance Specific performance, like other equitable remedies, is available only when the injured party has no adequate remedy at law—in other words, when money damages do not adequately compensate the injured party. This generally requires a showing that the subject of the contract is *unique* or at least that no substitutes are available. Even if this requirement is met, a court will withhold specific performance if the injured party has acted in bad faith, if he unreasonably delayed in asserting his rights, or if specific performance would require an excessive amount of supervision by the court.

Contracts for the sale of real estate are the most common subjects of specific performance decrees because every tract of real estate is considered to be unique. Specific performance is rarely granted for breach of a contract for the sale of goods because the injured party can usually procure substitute goods. However, there are situations involving sales of goods contracts in which specific performance is given. These cases involve goods that are unique or goods for which no substitute can be found. Examples include antiques, heirlooms, works of art, and objects of purely sentimental value.[12] Specific performance is not available for the breach of a promise to perform a personal service (such as a contract for employment, artistic performance, or consulting services). A decree requiring a person to specifically perform a personal-services contract would probably be ineffective in giving the injured party what he bargained for. It would also require a great deal of supervision by the court. In addition, an application of specific performance in such cases would amount to a form of involuntary servitude.

---

[11]Another equitable remedy, *reformation*, allows a court to reform or "rewrite" a written contract when the parties have made an error in expressing their agreement. Reformation is discussed along with the doctrine of mistake in the Reality of Consent chapter.

[12] Specific performance under section 2–716(1) of the UCC is discussed in the Remedies for Breach of Sales Contracts chapter.

Injunction

Injunction is an equitable remedy that is employed in many different contexts and is sometimes used as a remedy for breach of contract. An **injunction** is a court order requiring a person to do something (**mandatory injunction**) or ordering a person to refrain from doing something (**negative injunction**). Unlike legal remedies that apply only when the breach has already occurred, the equitable remedy of injunction can be invoked when a breach has merely been *threatened*. Injunctions are available only when the breach or threatened breach is likely to cause *irreparable injury*.

In the contract context, specific performance is a form of mandatory injunction. Negative injunctions are appropriately used in several situations, such as contract cases in which a party whose duty under the contract is forbearance threatens to breach the contract. For example, Norris sells his restaurant in Gas City, Indiana, to Ford. A term of the contract of sale provides that Norris agrees not to own, operate, or be employed in any restaurant within 30 miles of Gas City for a period of two years after the sale.[13] If Norris threatens to open a new restaurant in Gas City several months after the sale is consummated, a court could *enjoin* Norris from opening the new restaurant.

RESTITUTION

Restitution is a remedy that can be obtained either at law or in equity. Restitution applies when one party's performance or reliance has conferred a benefit on the other. A party's restitution interest is protected by compensating him for the value of benefits he has conferred on the other person.[14] This can be done through **specific restitution,** in which the defendant is required to return the exact property conferred on him by the plaintiff, or **substitionary restitution,** in which a court awards the plaintiff a sum of money that reflects the amount by which he benefited the defendant. In an action for damages based on quasi-contract, substitutionary restitution would be the remedy.

Restitution can be used in a number of circumstances. Sometimes, parties injured by breach of contract seek restitution as an alternative remedy instead of

damages that focus on their expectation interest. In other situations, a *breaching party* who has partially performed seeks restitution for the value of benefits he conferred in excess of the losses he caused. In addition, restitution often applies in cases in which a person rescinds a contract on the grounds of lack of capacity, misrepresentation, fraud, duress, undue influence, or mistake. Upon rescission, each party who has been benefited by the other's performance must compensate the other for the value of the benefit conferred.[15] Another application of restitution occurs when a party to a contract that violates the statute of frauds confers a benefit on the other party.[16] For example, Boyer gives Blake a $10,000 down payment on an oral contract for the sale of a farm. Although the contract is unenforceable (that is, Boyer could not get compensation for his expectation interest), the court would give Boyer restitution of his down payment.

ETHICAL AND PUBLIC POLICY CONCERNS

1. Is it good public policy for a party who has materially breached a contract to be able to obtain restitution for the benefits he has conferred on the nonbreaching party?

2. How does the duty of good faith and fair dealing encourage ethical dealings? Do you see any problems with such a duty?

3. You have seen that contract remedies focus solely on the economic effect of contract breaches rather than on the moral implications of such breaches or the emotional harms that might result from a breach of contract. As a result, contract remedies are much more limited than are remedies in tort cases. Is this sound public policy? Explain.

SUMMARY

A problem arising in the performance stage of contracts that is frequently presented to courts is determining when performance is due. A party's duty to perform is absolute unless it is subject to some condition. A

---

[13] Ancillary covenants not to compete, or noncompetition agreements, are discussed in detail in the Illegality chapter.

[14] Quasi-contract is discussed in detail in the Introduction to Contracts chapter.

[15] These doctrines are discussed in the Reality of Consent chapter and Capacity to Contract chapter.

[16] The statute of frauds is discussed in the Writing chapter.

condition is an uncertain event, other than the passage of time, that affects a party's duty to perform. An event that must occur before performance is due is called a *condition precedent*. An event that discharges a party from his duty to perform is called a *condition subsequent*. A condition that requires simultaneous performance of duties by the parties is called a *concurrent condition*.

Conditions may be created in several ways. They may be created by the express language of a contract (express conditions) or implied by the circumstances surrounding the contract or by the nature of the contract (implied-in-fact conditions). Although no particular language is necessary to create an express condition, such conditions are usually created by such language as "on condition that," "so long as," "subject to," and "provided that."

A type of express condition that is common in building contracts is a contractual provision stating that one party's duty to perform is conditioned on a third party's satisfaction with the promisor's performance. The third person is held to a standard of honest satisfaction. Another type of express condition exists when a contract provides that a party's duty to pay is conditioned on his personal satisfaction with the other party's performance. In such cases, the standard for determining whether the condition has occurred will depend on whether the subject of the contract involves a matter of personal taste or convenience or whether it involves mechanical suitability or use. In the former type of case, a standard of honest or good faith satisfaction is applied. In the latter type of case, an objective, reasonable man standard is used to determine whether the condition has occurred.

Sometimes, conditions are imposed by courts even when the parties' contract does not state or imply a condition. This type of condition is called a constructive condition or an implied-in-law condition. It is imposed to do justice between the parties.

Although a party whose duty is conditional normally has no obligation to perform unless a condition occurs, there are some circumstances under which the occurrence of a condition may be excused. When a condition is excused, a party whose duty is conditional will have the obligation to perform notwithstanding the nonoccurrence of the condition.

When a promisor's performance is an express condition of the promisee's duty to render return performance or when a contract is capable of perfect performance, the promisor will be held to a standard of strict compliance with the contract. However, when performance is only a constructive condition and the nature of the contract is such that the promised performance is very diffi-

cult to render perfectly, the promisor will be held to the lower standard of substantial performance. Substantial performance falls somewhat short of complete performance, but does not deprive the promisee of a material part of the consideration for which he bargained. If the promisor substantially performs his obligations, he will be entitled to receive the other party's promised performance. Any recovery that he might receive is decreased by the amount of damages that his imperfect performance has caused. If the promisor's performance is defective in some major respect, he is guilty of material breach. When material breach occurs, the promisee is entitled to withhold his own performance. If the breach is not cured, he is discharged from further obligations and entitled to sue for damages for total breach of contract.

Modern contract law places the duty on each party to a contract to perform in good faith. The implied covenant of good faith and fair dealing has been imposed in an increasing range of contracts. The UCC places a duty of good faith on each party to a contract covered by any article of the UCC. Courts have also implied the duty of good faith in many contracts outside the scope of the UCC, such as insurance contracts. Breach of the duty of good faith creates contract liability. Depending on state law and the circumstances of the breach, a breach of the duty of good faith may give rise to tort liability.

In some exceptional circumstances in which unforeseen events occur after the formation of a contract, a promisor will be excused from performing. That is, even though the promisor had the legal duty to perform, his nonperformance will not be considered a breach of contract and he will be discharged from his obligations. A major basis for excusing nonperformance is impossibility. When an event occurs after the formation of the contract that renders performance impossible to carry out, the promisor will be excused. Impossibility means that the act cannot be done, not that the promisor is personally unable to do it. The mere fact that the promisor contracted to do something that he was incapable of doing or has suffered insolvency does not render the performance impossible. Impossibility generally arises in one of three situations: incapacitating illness or death of the promisor in contracts that require the promisor to perform personal services, supervening illegality caused by the enactment of statutes or governmental regulations that make performance illegal, and destruction of subject matter essential to the performance of the contract.

The UCC adopted a somewhat lower standard for excuse based on unforeseen events. It provides that performance is excused if performance is made *commercially impracticable* by a contingency occurring after the formation of the contract, the nonoccurrence of which was a basic assumption of the contract. The *Restatement (Second) of Contracts* contains a similar provision. A basis for excuse that is closely related to impossibility and impracticability is the doctrine of commercial frustration or frustration of venture. When a promisor has contracted to obtain a specific objective, his performance can be excused if an event that occurs subsequent to the formation of the contract would cause that objective to be frustrated.

When a party is released from further duties under a contract, it is said that his duties are *discharged*. Contracts are generally discharged by performance. Duties are also discharged by the other party's material breach, nonoccurrence of a condition precedent (unless such a condition has been excused), occurrence of a condition subsequent, and impossibility or the related doctrines of impracticability or frustration. Discharge can also occur by mutual agreement, waiver, or the promisee's failure to comply with the statute of limitations.

A variety of remedies are available for compensating parties who have been injured by a breach of contract. Included among the possibilities are legal remedies (money damages), equitable remedies, and restitution. The remedies available for breach of contract seek to protect one or more distinct interests on the part of a promisee: the expectation interest, the reliance interest, and the restitution interest.

To recover damages in a contract case, the plaintiff must be able to prove his loss with reasonable certainty, and the loss must be one that was foreseeable to the breaching party at the time of contracting. When a contract has been breached, the injured party has the duty to take actions to mitigate, or decrease, the amount of damages that he might suffer. The objective in granting a remedy that protects a party's expectation interest is to place the injured party in the position in which he would have been if the contract had been performed as promised. Compensatory damages for breach of contract consist of the net value of the unfulfilled promise plus allowable consequential and incidental damages. Consequential damages are those that result from special circumstances of the injured party that are a direct result of the breach of contract. Incidental damages compensate for reasonable costs incurred by the plaintiff in attempting to avoid further loss. Courts sometimes use alternative damage remedies, such as permitting an injured party to recover money spent in reliance on the contract, when the normal measure of damages is inappropriate.

Nominal damages are damages in a very small amount that are awarded in cases in which there has been a technical breach of contract that has caused no actual loss. Sometimes, parties will include a term in their contract whereby they agree that damages in a specified sum will be due upon breach of contract. These provisions are called *liquidated damages provisions*. Courts will enforce liquidated damages provisions where the amount of damages specified is reasonable in light of the injured party's probable losses and where it would be difficult to assess the amount of damages. Where the amount of damages specified is unreasonably great in relation to probable losses or where damages would be easy to calculate, courts will refuse to enforce the liquidated damages provision on the ground that it constitutes a penalty. Punitive damages generally are not awarded in contracts cases unless the breaching party is guilty of fraud or some other independent tort (including tortious breach of the implied covenant of good faith and fair dealing). A few states will, however, impose punitive damages in contracts cases in which the breaching party has been guilty of oppressive or malicious conduct.

When damages remedies alone appear to be inadequate to fully compensate the injured party, courts will sometimes grant an equitable remedy. The two most common equitable remedies are specific performance and injunction. When specific performance is decreed, the breaching party is ordered to perform his duties under the contract. One limitation on specific performance is that it is used only when the subject of the contract is unique. Contracts for the sale of real property are the most frequent subjects of specific performance, because each tract of real property is considered to be unique. Specific performance is not given in cases concerning contracts for personal property unless the property is of a special, unique nature, such as antiques or works of art or is the type of property for which substitutes cannot be found. Specific performance is not granted in contracts for the performance of personal services. An injunction is an order to do a certain act (mandatory injunction) or to refrain from doing a certain act (negative injunction). They may be granted only when an act threatens to do irreparable harm to an injured party.

Restitution is a remedy that applies when a plaintiff has conferred a benefit on the defendant. It requires the defendant to return the benefit or to pay the plaintiff the value of the benefit. It is used in a variety of contracting situations involving a contract that has been partially performed but the remedy compensating for the party's expectation interest is either unavailable or undesirable.

PROBLEM CASES

1. Commercial Cotton maintained an essentially dormant non-interest-bearing commercial checking account at the United California Bank, with only two or three checks a month being written. The sole signatory on the account since 1972 had been Calvin, a practicing neurosurgeon who was Commercial Cotton's principal shareholder. In 1972, Calvin's wife reported to the bank the loss of a series of blank checks. She did not report the checks stolen because she thought they had only been inadvertently discarded. Four years later, one of the missing checks in the amount of $4,000 containing two unauthorized signatures was negligently paid by the bank. This showed up on Commercial Cotton's bank statement for September of 1976, but Calvin did not read the statement or discover the loss until March of 1978. He then promptly presented the faulty check to the branch manager of the bank. The bank admitted that it had erred but refused to reimburse Calvin. Even though a California Supreme Court case directly involving the bank as a defendant had held that a three-year statute of limitations applies when a bank has been negligent, the bank persisted in claiming that Calvin's claim was barred by a *one-year* statute of limitations. Commercial Cotton ultimately filed suit against the bank. Does it have a good claim for breach of the implied covenant of good faith and fair dealing? *Yes because Bank has duty to uphold the law*

2. Asphalt International chartered a tanker, the *Oswego Tarmac*, from Enterprise Shipping. The contract provided that Enterprise was obligated to maintain the vessel in good order but that it was absolved of responsibility for any loss or damage resulting from a collision and that, if the vessel should be lost, the contract would cease. While loading cargo alongside a pier, the *Oswego Tarmac* was rammed amidships by the bow of the motor vessel *Elektra* with such heavy impact that four of its tanks ruptured and heated asphalt spewed across the harbor. Expert appraisers estimated the cost of repair at not less than $1.5 million. The fair market value of the *Oswego Tarmac* prior to the collision was $750,000. Enterprise advised Asphalt International that the *Oswego Tarmac* was a complete loss. It refused Asphalt International's request to repair the vehicle. Asphalt International brought suit against Enterprise for breach of contract. Will it be successful? *No because the contract stated that this kind of loss was not covered*

3. Light contracted to build a house for the Mullers. After the job was completed, the Mullers refused to pay Light the balance they owed him under the contract, claiming that he had done some of the work in an un-

workmanlike manner. When Light sued for the money, the Mullers counterclaimed for $5,700 damages for delay under a liquidated damages clause in the contract. The clause provided that Light must pay $100 per day for every day of delay in completion of the construction. The evidence indicated that the rental value of the home was between $400 and $415 per month. Should the liquidated damages provision be enforced? *Yes but not for that amt with the stated infor. It's unreasonable*

4. The Warrens hired Denison, a building contractor, to build a house on their property. They executed a written contract in which the Warrens agreed to pay $73,400 for the construction. Denison's construction deviated somewhat from the specifications for the project. These deviations were presumably unintentional, and the cost of repairing them was $1,961.50. The finished house had a market value somewhat higher than the market value would have been without the deviations. The Warrens failed to pay the $48,400 balance due under the contract, alleging that Denison had used poor workmanship in constructing the house and that they were under no obligation to perform further duties under the contract. Are they correct? *No because substantial performance and unmaterial breach in his favor*

5. Forman made a written offer to buy real estate from Benson under terms whereby Forman would pay the purchase price over a 10-year period. Benson did not know Forman and was concerned about his creditworthiness, so Forman's real estate agent suggested a term stating that the contract was "subject to seller's approving buyer's credit report." This term was agreed to by both parties and was inserted in the contract before it was signed. Forman then gave Benson a credit report and a personal financial statement. Benson said that the report "looks real good" and that he would have his attorney review it and begin the title work on the property. Over the course of the next six weeks, however, Benson met with Forman three times. During these meetings, he attempted to negotiate for a higher purchase price and interest rate. He also requested more financial information. Finally, Benson informed Forman that he rejected Forman's credit rating. Forman brought suit to enforce the contract. Will he prevail? *Should enforce contract because gave some approval & contract condition has met*

6. Kim, a homeowner, entered into a contract with Kilianek, an experienced contractor, to add an additional room onto his home. The architectural work in designing the room was to be done by Park & Associates. One provision of the contract between Kim and Kilianek stated that "Final payment . . . shall be paid by the Owner to the Contractor when the work has been completed, the contract fully performed, and a final Certificate for Payment has been issued by the Architect."

Kim made periodic payments for a total of $14,100 toward the costs of construction. Although no final certificate for payment was issued by the architect, Kilianek demanded a final payment of $2,739. Is Kim obligated to make this payment? *NO! CONDITION PRECEDENT!*

7. In March of 1986, Bowling Green State University (BGSU) made a request for bids for carpet installation at Conklin West, a student housing facility at BGSU. This request contained a completion date of August 1, 1986. BGSU canceled this request for bids. On June 2, 1986, BGSU made another request for bids for the Conklin West project. This time, the request did not contain a completion date. Turner Brooks of Ohio, Inc. ("Turner Brooks"), submitted a bid (an offer) to perform the carpet installation on the Conklin West project. BGSU selected Turner Brooks and accepted its offer on June 20. Turner Brooks immediately placed an order for carpet to be installed at Conklin West. Customarily, the receipt of the carpet ordered occurs within six to eight weeks. In this case, Turner Brooks received the carpet five weeks after it ordered it, on July 29. Turner Brooks began the installation the very next day. During the installation, an abnormal floor surface that was not previously known to Turner Brooks caused some unforeseen labor. Turner Brooks completed the Conklin West project on or about August 22, 1986. BGSU claimed that Turner Brooks's performance was not timely and withheld more than $7,000 from the contract price as a setoff for custodial overtime purportedly incurred from Turner Brooks's alleged delay in completion. Did BGSU have the right to withhold this money? *No because no time stated and circumstances that were proud Turner completes full proyal*

8. Elmore Bean Warehouse contracted to buy pinto beans from a grower, Lawrance, at a fixed price. When the market price of beans dropped dramatically below the contract price, Elmore attempted to avoid paying the agreed price on the ground of commercial impracticability. Is this defense likely to be successful?

?, is it drastic to be unforeseeable
then good defense
if no then they are assumed to take
that risk

SALES

CHAPTER 19

FORMATION AND TERMS OF SALES CONTRACTS

INTRODUCTION

In the Contracts section you studied the common law rules that govern the creation and performance of contracts generally. Throughout much of recorded history, special rules—the law merchant—were developed to control mercantile transactions in goods. Because transactions in goods commonly involve buyers and sellers located in different states—and even different countries—a common body of law to control these transactions can greatly facilitate the smooth flow of commerce. To address this need, a Uniform Sales Act was drafted in the early 1900s and adopted by about two thirds of the states. Subsequently, the Uniform Commercial Code (UCC or Code) was prepared to simplify and modernize the rules of law governing commercial transactions.

This chapter reviews some Code rules that govern the formation of sales contracts previously discussed. It also covers some key terms in sales contracts, such as delivery terms, title, and risk of loss. Finally, it discusses the rules governing sales on trial, such as sales on approval and consignments.

Sale of Goods

The **sale of goods** is the transfer of ownership to tangible personal property in exchange for money, other goods, or the performance of services. The law of sales of goods is codified in Article 2 of the Uniform Commercial Code. While the law of sales is based on the fundamental principles of contract and personal property, it has been modified to accommodate current practices of merchants. In large measure, the Code has discarded many technical requirements of earlier law that did not serve any useful purpose in the marketplace and has replaced them with rules that assure merchants and consumers of the most just and equitable results in keeping with commercial expectations.

Article 2 of the Code applies only to *transactions in goods*. Thus, it does not cover contracts to provide services or to sell real property. However, some courts have applied the principles set out in the Code to such transactions. When a contract appears to call for the furnishing of both goods and services, a question may arise as to whether the Code applies. For example, the operator of a beauty parlor may use a commercial permanent solution intended to be used safely on humans that causes injury to a person's head. The injured person might then bring a lawsuit claiming that there was a breach of the Code's warranty of the suitability of the permanent solution. In such cases, the courts commonly see whether the sale of goods is the *predominant* part of the transaction or merely an *incidental* part; where the sale of goods predominates, the Code will normally be applied.

The *Data Processing Services, Inc. v. L. H. Smith Oil Corp.* case illustrates the type of analysis courts go through to determine whether a particular contract should be considered as one for the sale of goods governed by the Code.

DATA PROCESSING SERVICES, INC. v. L. H. SMITH OIL CORP.

1 UCC Rep.2d 29 (Ind. Ct. App. 1986)

Data Processing Services (DPS) is in the business of custom computer programming. L. H. Oil Corporation sells petroleum products. Smith and DPS entered into an oral agreement under which DPS was to develop computer software for Smith's IBM System-32 computer. Later, DPS was engaged to develop and implement a data processing system for Smith's new IBM System-34 computer. DPS was to develop an accounting system to meet Smith's specific needs.

After having paid several billings submitted by DPS, Smith refused to pay DPS's billing of $7,166.25. DPS brought suit against Smith, alleging breach of contract. The trial court held in favor of Smith and DPS appealed. One of the issues in the lawsuit was whether the Uniform Commercial Code was applicable to these agreements.

Conover, Judge.   The trial court found Smith contracted for the development and the delivery of a "program" by DPS. It determined the program was a specially manufactured good within the meaning of Section 2–501(1)(a) and (b). DPS contends the court erred when it determined the contract was for a "good," subject to the provisions of Article 2 of the UCC. DPS asserts it was supplying "services," not "goods."

Heretofore this court has not been called upon to determine whether a contract to provide computer programming is a contract for the sale and purchase of goods and thus subject to the provisions of Article 2 of the UCC, or one for the performance of services, and thus subject to common law principles. We note in passing the Second District of our court has disagreed with us concerning the proper mode of analysis when we are faced with the question of whether the UCC or the common law applies to contracts for the mixed sale of goods and services.

This district bifurcates its analysis of such transactions. That is, cases involving actual goods as defined by 2–105 will be analyzed as falling within the purview of Article 2 of the UCC, whereas, cases not falling within that definition will be analyzed in accordance with principles of common law.

Our Second District has declined to follow this approach. Instead, it determined mixed transactions should be analyzed in terms of the transaction's "dominant thrust," i.e., if the predominant thrust of the transaction is the sale of goods, all of the contract should fall within Article 2 of the UCC. If the predominant thrust of the transaction is the sale of services, common law principles apply.

In this case, however, whichever mode of analysis is used, the facts found by the trial court do not support a conclusion DPS sold goods to Smith. Thus the transaction does not fall within Article 2 of the UCC.

The transaction here is clear-cut. Unlike many of the cases reported in other jurisdictions, DPS sold no "hardware" to Smith. Instead, DPS was retained to design, develop and implement an electronic data processing system to meet Smith's specific needs. The very terminology used by the trial court and the parties here shows services, not goods, were that for which Smith contracted. DPS was to act with specific regard to Smith's need. Smith bargained for DPS's skill in developing a system to meet its specific needs. Although the end result was to be preserved by means of some physical manifestation such as magnetic tape, floppy or hard disks, etc., which would generate the recordkeeping computer functions DPS was to develop, it was DPS's knowledge, skill and ability for which Smith bargained. The sale of computer hardware or generally-available standardized software was not here involved. *Cf., RRX Industries, Inc. v. LabCon, Inc. (9th Cir. 1985)* (in a transaction in which software was apparently a prepackaged product, not specifically developed for the buyer, the sales aspect of the transaction predominated; employee training, repair services, and system upgrading were incidental to the sale of the software package and thus the transaction was a sale of goods); *Chatlos Systems, Inc. v. National Cash Register (D.N. J. 1979)* (transaction involving sale of hardware and software was a sale of goods notwithstanding the incidental services aspects of the transaction); *Triangle Underwriters, Inc. v. Honeywell, Inc. (2nd Cir. 1979)* (Triangle purchased hardware, standard programming aids of general application and custom application software specifically designed for individual needs. Predominant factor was sale of goods, services were merely incidental.)

The means by which DPS's skills and knowledge were to be transmitted to Smith's computers was incidental. The situation here is more analogous to a client seeking a lawyer's advice or a patient seeking medical treatment for a particular ailment than it is to a customer buying seed corn, soap, or cam shafts. While a tangible end product, such as floppy disks, hard disks, punch cards or magnetic tape used as a storage medium for the program may be involved incidentally in this transaction, it is the skill and knowledge of the programmer which is being purchased in the main, not the devices by which this skill and knowledge is placed into the buyer's computer. The means of transmission is not the essence of the agreement. Thus, the provisions of the UCC, including the implied warranty of merchantability and the implied warranty of fitness for a particular purpose, do not apply.

Judgment for Smith affirmed on other grounds.

Thus, the first question you should ask when faced with a contracts problem is: Is this a contract for the sale of goods? If it is not, then the principles of common law that were discussed in the Contracts section are to be applied. If the contract is one for the sale of goods, then the Code applies. This analysis is illustrated in Figure 1.

FIGURE 1   Choice of Law

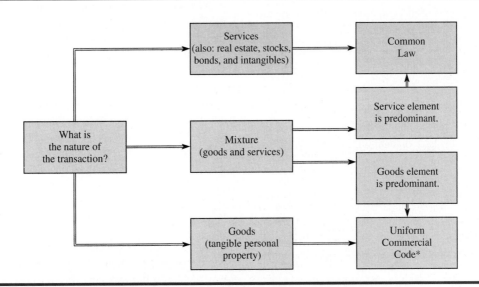

*If there is no specific Uniform Commercial Code provision governing the transaction, use the common law.

Merchants

Many of the Code's provisions apply only to **merchants** or to transactions between merchants.[1] In addition, the Code sets a higher standard of conduct for merchants because persons who regularly deal in goods are expected to be familiar with the practices of that trade and with commercial law. Ordinary consumers and nonmerchants, on the other hand, frequently have little knowledge of or experience in these matters.

Code Requirements

The Code requires that parties to sales contracts act in good faith and in a commercially reasonable manner. Further, when a contract contains an unfair or unconscionable clause, or the contract as a whole is unconscionable, the courts have the right to refuse to enforce the unconscionable clause or contract [2–302].[2] The Code's treatment of unconscionability is discussed in detail in the Illegality chapter.

A number of the Code provisions concerning the sale of goods were discussed in the chapters on contracts. The following is a list of some of the important provisions discussed earlier, together with the section of the Code and the chapters in the text where the discussion can be found.

1. *Firm offers.* Under the Code, an offer in writing by a merchant that gives assurance that the offer will be held open is not revocable for lack of consideration during the time stated, or for a reasonable time if no time is stated, up to a period of three months [2–205]. (See the chapter The Agreement: Offer.)

2. *Formation.* Under the Code, a contract for the sale of goods may be made in any manner that shows that the parties reached agreement, even though no particular moment can be pointed to as the time when the contract was made. Where the parties intended to make a contract but left one or more terms open, the contract is valid despite the lack of definiteness so long as the

court has a basis forgiving a remedy [2–204]. (See the chapter The Agreement: Offer.)

3. *Additional terms in acceptances.* The Code states that an expression of acceptance or written confirmation sent within a reasonable time operates as an acceptance even if it states terms additional to or different from those offered, unless acceptance is expressly made conditional on assent to the additional or different terms [2–207]. (See the chapter The Agreement: Acceptance.)

4. *Statute of frauds.* The **statute of frauds** in the Code applies to the sale of goods at a price of $500 or more. The Code makes special exceptions for written confirmations between merchants, part payment or part delivery, admissions in legal proceedings, and specially manufactured goods [2–201]. (See the Writing chapter.)

TERMS OF THE CONTRACT

General Terms

Within broad limits, the parties to a contract to sell goods may include any terms on which they agree. Many practices have become common in the everyday transactions of business, and under the Code, if a particular matter is not specifically covered in a contract or is unclear, common trade practices are used to fill out the terms of the contract.

The Code sets out in some detail the rights of the parties when they use certain terms, and those meanings apply unless the parties agree otherwise. For example, if a contract includes an open-price clause where the price is to be determined later, or if a contract is silent about price, the price is what would be considered *reasonable* at the time of delivery. If the price is to be fixed by either the buyer or the seller, that person must act in *good faith* in setting the price. However, if it is clear from their negotiations that the parties do not intend to be bound unless they agree on a price, and the price is not agreed on or fixed, no contract results [2–305].

Quantity Terms

In some cases, the parties may state the quantity of goods covered by their sales contract in an indefinite way. Contracts that obligate a buyer to purchase a seller's *output* of a certain item or all of the buyer's *require-*

---

[1]Under the Code, a "merchant" is defined as "a person who deals in goods of the kind or otherwise by his occupation holds himself out as having knowledge or skill peculiar to the practices or goods involved in the transaction or to whom such knowledge or skill may be attributed by his employment of an agent or broker or other intermediary who by his occupation holds himself out as having such knowledge or skill" [2–104(1)].

[2]The numbers in brackets refer to the sections of the Uniform Commercial Code.

ments of a certain item are commonly encountered. These contracts caused frequent problems under the common law because of the indefiniteness of the parties obligations. If the seller decided to double its output, did the buyer have to accept the entire amount? If the market price of the item soared much higher than the contract price, could the buyer double or triple its demands?

Output and Needs Contracts

In an "output" contract, one party is bound to sell its entire output of particular goods and the other party is bound to buy that output. In a "needs" or "requirements" contract, the quantity of goods is based on the needs of the buyer. In determining the quantity of goods to be produced or taken pursuant to an output or needs contract, the rule of *good faith* applies. Thus, no quantity can be demanded or taken that is unreasonably disproportionate to any stated estimate in the contract or to "normal" prior output or requirements if no estimate is stated [2–306(2)].

For example, Farmer contracts to supply Sam's Grocery with all of the apples it requires for sale to customers. If Sam's has sold between 500 and 700 bushels of apples a year over the past 10 years, Farmer could not be required to deliver 5,000 bushels of apples to Sam's one year because Sam had an unusual demand for them. Similarly, it would not be reasonable for Sam to say he would take only 10 bushels one year.

Exclusive Dealing Contracts

The Code takes a similar approach to *exclusive dealing contracts*. Under the common law, these contracts were sources of difficulty due to the indefinite nature of the parties' duties. Did the dealer have to make any effort to sell the manufacturer's products, and did the manufacturer have any duty to supply the dealer? The Code says that unless the parties agree to the contrary, sellers have an obligation to use their best efforts to supply the goods to the buyer and the buyers are obligated to use their best efforts to promote their sale [2–306(2)].

Time for Performance

If no time for performance is stated in the sales contract, a *reasonable time* for performance is implied. If a contract requires successive performances over an indefinite period of time, the contract is valid for a reasonable time; however, either party can terminate it at any time upon the giving of reasonable notice unless the parties have agreed otherwise as to termination [2–309]. For example, Farmer Jack agrees to sell his entire output of apples each fall to a cannery at the then current market price. If the contract does not contain a provision spelling out how and when the contract can be terminated, Farmer Jack can terminate it if he gives the cannery a reasonable time to make arrangements to acquire apples from someone else.

Delivery Terms

Standardized shipping terms that through commercial practice have come to have a specific meaning are customarily used in sales contracts. The terms **FOB (free on board)** and **FAS (free alongside ship)** are basic delivery terms. If the delivery term of the contract is FOB or FAS the place at which the goods originate, the seller is obligated to deliver to the carrier goods that *conform to the contract* and are *properly prepared for shipment* to the buyer, and the seller must make a *reasonable contract for transportation of the goods* on behalf of the buyer. Under such delivery terms, the goods are at the risk of the buyer during transit and he must pay the shipping charges. If the term is *FOB destination*, the seller must deliver the goods to the designated destination and they are at the seller's risk and expense during transit. These terms will be discussed in more detail later in this chapter.

TITLE

Passage of Title

Title to goods cannot pass from the seller to the buyer until the goods are identified to the contract [2–401(1)]. For example, if Seller agrees to sell Buyer 50 chairs and Seller has 500 chairs in his warehouse, title to 50 chairs will not pass from Seller to Buyer until the 50 chairs that Buyer has purchased are selected and identified as the chairs sold to Buyer.

The parties may agree between themselves when title to the goods will pass from the seller to the buyer. If there is no agreement, then the *general rule* is that the *title to goods passes to the buyer when the seller completes his obligations as to delivery* of the goods:

1. If the contract requires the seller to "ship" the goods to the buyer, then title passes to the buyer when the seller delivers conforming goods to the carrier.

2. If the contract requires the seller to "deliver" the goods to the buyer, title does not pass to the buyer until the goods are delivered to the buyer and tendered to him.

3. If delivery is to be made without moving the goods, then title passes at the time and place of contracting. An exception is made if title to the goods is represented by a document of title such as a warehouse receipt; then, title passes when the document of title is delivered to the buyer.

4. If the buyer rejects goods tendered to him, title reverts to the seller [2–401(4)].

Importance of Title

At common law, most of the problems relating to risks, insurable interests in goods, remedies, and similar rights and liabilities were determined on the basis of who was the technical title owner at the particular moment the right or liability arose. Under the Code, however, the rights of the seller and buyer and of third persons are determined irrespective of the technicality of who has the title, unless the provision of the Code expressly refers to title.

Determination of who has title to the goods is important in instances in which the rights of the seller's or the buyer's creditors in the goods are an issue. The *Russell v. Transamerica Insurance Co.* case, which follows, illustrates another instance in which determination of the title holder may be important: whether the seller's insurance policy covers a particular loss.

RUSSELL v. TRANSAMERICA INSURANCE CO.

322 N.W.2d 178 (Mich. Ct. App. 1982)

Russell, a full-service boat dealer and marine equipment service company, entered into an agreement to sell a 19-foot Kinsvater boat to Robert Clouser for $8,500. Pursuant to the agreement, Clouser made a down payment of $1,700, with the balance of the purchase price to be paid when he took possession of the boat. Under the agreement, Russell was to retain possession of the boat in order to transfer an engine and drive train from another boat. Upon the completion of these alterations, Clouser was to take delivery of the boat at Russell's marina.

While the boat was being tested by employees of Russell, prior to delivery to Clouser, it hit a seawall and was completely destroyed. Russell was insured by Transamerica Insurance under a policy that excluded watercraft hazards, except for damage to any watercraft under 26 feet in length not owned by Russell. Transamerica refused to honor a claim from Russell for the damage to Clouser's boat, contending that the damage was excluded because Russell owned the boat at the time of the accident. Russell then brought suit against Transamerica Insurance. The trial court ruled in favor of Transamerica Insurance, and Russell appealed.

Lambros, Judge. The trial court, granting summary judgment in favor of Transamerica, stated: The facts reflect that the boat was in possession of Russell on August 4, 1977. Robert Clouser could not have taken delivery of the boat on the day in question. Under § 2–401(2), therefore, title had not passed to Clouser. . . . Effectively speaking, the risk of loss was, on August 4, 1977, on Russell's shoulders.

Under subsection (3)(b) of § 2–401, if delivery is to be made without moving the goods and no documents of title are involved, title passes at the time of contracting if the goods are already identified at the time of contracting. We note that goods need not be in a deliverable state to be identified to the contract.

In the instant case, because the 19-foot Kinsvater boat had been identified at the time the parties contracted for sale, because no documents of title were to be delivered by the sellers, there being no Michigan requirement for documents of title for boats at that time, and because delivery of the boat was to be effected without its being moved, title passed to the buyer at the time of contracting under § 2–401(3)(b). The fact that the boat was not outfitted with all the equipment specified in the contract did not prevent its identification to the contract nor did it prevent title from passing at that time.

In addition, we find that the trial court erred in its decision in equating risk of loss with title. Under § 2–509, risk of loss passes to the buyer on his receipt of the goods or on tender of delivery by the seller. Risk of loss, then, does not necessarily follow title. In the instant case, because Russell retained possession of the boat after title passed, he bore the risk of loss. Title in the buyer, however, triggered the policy exception to the watercraft hazard exclusion regardless of where risk of loss lay.

We hold that the trial court erred in granting summary judgment in favor of Transamerica because title in the boat at the time of the accident was in one other than Russell and the boat was, thus, covered under Russell's policy.

Judgment reversed in favor of Russell.

TITLE AND THIRD PARTIES

Obtaining Good Title

A fundamental rule of property law is that a buyer cannot receive better title to goods than the seller had. If Thief steals a television set from Adler and sells it to Brown, Brown does not get good title to the set, because Thief had no title to it. Adler would have the right to recover the set from Brown. Similarly, if Brown sold the set to Carroll, Carroll could get no better title to it than Brown had. Adler would have the right to recover the set from Carroll.

Under the Code, however, there are several exceptions to the general rule that a buyer cannot get better title to goods than his seller had. The most important exceptions include the following: (1) a person who has a voidable title to goods can pass good title to a bona fide purchaser for value; (2) a person who buys goods in the regular course of a retailer's business takes free of any interests in the goods that the retailer has given to others; and (3) a person who buys goods in the ordinary course of a dealer's business takes free of any claim of a person who entrusted those goods to the dealer.

Transfers of Voidable Title

A seller who has a **voidable title** has the power to pass good title to a *good faith purchaser for value* [2–403(1)]. A seller has a voidable title to goods if he has obtained his title through fraudulent representations. For example, a person would have a voidable title if he obtained goods by impersonating another person or by paying for them with a bad check or if he obtained goods without paying the agreed purchase price when it was agreed that the transaction was to be a cash sale. Under the Code, **good faith** means "honesty in fact in the conduct or transaction concerned" [1–201(19)] and a buyer has given **value** if he has given any consideration sufficient to support a simple contract [1–201(44)].

For example, Jones goes to the ABC Appliance Store, convinces the clerk that he is really Clark, who is a good customer of ABC, and leaves with a stereo charged to Clark's account. If Jones sells the stereo to Davis, who gives Jones value for it and has no knowledge of the fraud that Jones perpetrated on ABC, Davis gets good title to the stereo. ABC cannot recover the stereo from Davis; instead, it must look for Jones, the person who deceived it. In this situation, both ABC and Davis were innocent of wrongdoing, but the law considers Davis to be the more worthy of its protection because ABC was in a better position to have prevented the wrongdoing by Jones and because Davis bought the goods in good faith and for value. The same result would be reached if Jones had given ABC a check that later bounced and then sold the stereo to Davis, who was a good faith purchaser for value. Davis would have good title to the stereo, and ABC would have to pursue its right against Jones on the bounced check.

The *R. H. Macy's New York, Inc. v. Equitable Diamond Corp.* case, which follows, illustrates the difficulty of trying to determine whether a subsequent buyer can qualify as a good faith purchaser for value and thus get good title from a seller with a voidable title.

R. H. MACY'S NEW YORK, INC. v. EQUITABLE DIAMOND CORP.

34 UCC Rep. 896 (N.Y. Civ. Ct. 1982)

Macy's, a retail department store chain, sold a 2.25-carat diamond solitaire ring to Marie Draper for $9,742.50. Draper paid for the ring with a check that was subsequently dishonored for insufficient funds. On November 18, 1981, Equitable Diamond Corporation, a diamond dealer in a building that housed numerous diamond dealers, purchased the ring from Draper for $2,500. On December 7, 1981, Equitable sold the ring for $4,000 to Ideal Cut Diamonds, another diamond dealer who occupied a counter adjoining the one occupied by Equitable. The following day, Ideal sold the ring to a customer for $4,900.

Macy's brought suit against Equitable and Ideal to recover the value of the diamond ring. Equitable and Ideal moved to have the case dismissed on the ground that Macy's had not stated a cause of action against them.

Tomkins, Judge.   Macy's argues that Equitable never acquired title to the ring since as a "thief," Ms. Draper had no title to transfer. Equitable and Ideal on the other hand counter that Draper had voidable title to the ring and that as good faith purchasers for value they acquired full title to the ring notwithstanding the defects in Ms. Draper's title [§ 2–403(1)].

Macy's contends that the exceptionally low price asked by Draper should have alerted Equitable to the defects in title. Macy's asserts that the excellent condition of the ring made it obvious to Equitable that the ring was worth much more than the price Equitable paid. As further evidence is the low price at which Equitable sold the ring within a short period of time at a substantial profit to a fellow dealer. Accordingly, Macy's urges that Equitable was not a good faith purchaser for value.

The Uniform Commercial Code provides that if passage of title is conditioned upon the performance of an act, then title is voidable and full title can be transferred to a third party if that third party was a "good faith purchaser for value" [§ 2–403(1)]. In the instant case, passage of title from Macy's to Ms. Draper was conditioned upon the payment of her check. Therefore, she had voidable title to the ring and could only transfer full title to the ring to a third party who qualified as a good faith purchaser for value under the Code.

Equitable and Ideal assert that they acted in good faith in the purchase of the ring and that they did all they were required to do under the circumstances including the filing of a notice of purchase with the Police Department and requiring Ms. Draper to represent in writing to them that the property sold was her personal property and she was the sole owner thereof. Equitable and Ideal also point out that in the diamond industry, dealers purchase diamonds for prices far below those charged to retail customers by stores such as Macy's. According to them, Macy's allegedly marks up items such as jewelry substantially over the wholesale price which the item could be obtained for in the diamond district. Mr. Friedman, principal of Equitable, stated in his affidavit that in the diamond market $2,500 for the ring in question was entirely fair and reasonable.

"Good faith" has been defined in this context as "honesty in fact and the observance of reasonable commercial standards of fair dealing." The question of whether the price at which Equitable purchased the ring was so low as to put it on notice that title to the ring may be defective is an issue to be resolved at trial and may be determinative of the good faith issue.

If a merchant chooses to take advantage of the low price at which an item is being offered for sale and purchases, when the unusually low price puts the merchant on notice of possible defective title, he does so at his peril and without the protection of the Uniform Commercial Code 2–403(1). It appears to the court that where a diamond dealer purchases a ring for $2,500, sells it to a fellow dealer for $4,000, who in turn sells the ring to another dealer for $4,900, the good faith requirements of Uniform Commercial Code 2–403(1) become an issue of fact to be resolved at trial. It cannot be said as a matter of law that honesty in fact and the observance of reasonable commercial standards of fair dealing are present.

Based upon the foregoing, the court finds that Equitable and Ideal have not established to the satisfaction of this court that Equitable acted as a good faith purchaser for value. A determination on this issue can only be made after a trial at which time the credibility of all witnesses will be judged.

The motion to dismiss denied and case set for trial.

Buyers in the Ordinary Course of Business

A person who buys goods in the ordinary course of business from a person dealing in goods of that type takes free of any security interest in the goods given by his seller to another person [9–307(1)]. A **buyer in ordinary course** is a person who in *good faith* and *without knowledge* that the sale to him is in violation of the ownership rights of a third party buys goods in the *ordinary course of business* of a *person selling goods of that kind*, other than a pawnbroker [1–201(9)].

For example, Brown Buick may borrow money from Bank in order to finance its inventory of new Buicks; in turn, Bank may take a security interest in the inventory to secure repayment of the loan. If Carter buys a new Buick from Brown Buick, he gets good title to the Buick free and clear of the Bank's security interest if he is a buyer in the ordinary course of business. The basic purpose of this exception is to protect those who innocently buy from merchants and thereby to promote confidence in such commercial transactions. The exception also reflects the fact that the bank is more interested in the proceeds from the sale than in the inventory. Security interests and the rights of buyers in the ordinary course of business are discussed in more detail in the Security Interests in Personal Property chapter.

Entrusting of Goods

A third exception to the general rule is that if goods are *entrusted* to a merchant who deals in goods of that kind, the merchant has the power to transfer all rights of the entruster to a buyer in the ordinary course of business [2–403(2)]. For example, Gail takes her watch to Jeweler, a retail jeweler, to have it repaired, and Jeweler sells the watch to Mary. Mary would acquire good title to the watch, and Gail would have to proceed against Jeweler for conversion of her watch. The purpose behind this rule is to protect commerce by giving confidence to buyers that they will get good title to the goods they buy from merchants in the ordinary course of business. However, a merchant-seller cannot pass good title to stolen goods even if the buyer is a buyer in the ordinary course of business. This is because the original owner did nothing to facilitate the transfer.

As you will see in the *Porter v. Wertz* case, which follows, not only should the owner of property be careful as to whom he entrusts the property, but also a buyer must exercise some caution to be sure he will get a good title.

PORTER v. WERTZ

416 N.Y.S.2d (N.Y. Sup. Ct. 1979) aff'd 439 N.Y.S.2d 105 (N.Y. Ct. App. 1981)

Samuel Porter, a collector of artworks, was the owner of a painting by Maurice Utrillo entitled *Chacteau de Lion-sur-Mer*. In 1972–73, he entered into a number of transactions with a Harold Von Maker, who was using the name Peter Wertz—a real person who was an acquaintance of Von Maker. Von Maker bought one painting from Porter, paying $50,000 cash and giving him a series of 10 promissory notes for $10,000 each. Von Maker also convinced Porter to let him hang the Utrillo in his home while he decided whether or not to buy it.

When payment on the first of the $10,000 notes was not made on the due date, Porter investigated and found that he was dealing, not with Peter Wertz, but with Von Maker, a man with a history of fraudulent dealings. A letter that Porter had obtained from Von Maker, which was signed with the name Peter Wertz, acknowledged receipt of the Utrillo. The letter also stated that the painting was on consignment with a client of Von Maker and that within 30 days Von Maker would either return the painting or pay Porter $30,000. However, at the time Von Maker had given this assurance to Porter, he had already disposed of the Utrillo by using the real Peter Wertz to sell it to the Richard Feigen gallery for $20,000. Wertz delivered the painting to a Ms. Drew-Bear at the Feigen gallery after being introduced to Feigen by an art associate of Von Maker.

Porter then brought an action against Peter Wertz and Richard Feigen to recover either possession of the painting or its equivalent value. Feigen claimed to have obtained good title to the painting as a buyer in the ordinary course of business.

Birns, Judge.   The provisions of statutory estoppel are found in section 2–403 of the Uniform Commercial Code. Subsection 2 provides that "any entrusting of possession of goods to a merchant who deals in goods of that kind gives him power to transfer all rights of the entruster to a buyer in the ordinary course of business." Uniform Commercial Code, section 1–201, subdivision 9, defines a "buyer in the ordinary course of business" as "a person who in good faith and without knowledge that the sale to him is in violation of the ownership rights or security interest of a third party in the goods buys in ordinary course from a person in the business of selling goods of that kind."

In order to determine whether the defense of statutory estoppel is available to Feigen, we must begin by ascertaining whether Feigen fits the definition of "buyer in the ordinary course of business" [UCC, § 1–201(9)]. Feigen does not fit that definition, for two reasons. First, Wertz, from whom Feigen bought the Utrillo, was not an art dealer—he was not "a person in the business of selling goods of that kind" [UCC, § 1–201(9)] in the transaction with Wertz. Uniform Commercial Code, § 2–103, subdivision (1)(b), defines "good faith" in the case of a merchant as "honesty in fact and the observance of reasonable commercial standards of fair dealing in the trade." Although this definition by its terms embraces the "reasonable commercial standards of fair dealing in the trade," it should not—and cannot—be interpreted to permit, countenance or condone commercial standards of sharp trade practice or indifference as to the "provenance," i.e., history of ownership or the right to possess or sell an objet d'art, such as is present in the case before us.

We note that neither Ms. Drew-Bear nor her employer Feigen made any investigation to determine the status of Wertz, i.e., whether he was an art merchant, "a person in the business of selling goods of that kind" [1–201(9)]. Had Ms. Drew-Bear done so much as call either of the telephone numbers Wertz had left, she would have learned that Wertz was employed by a delicatessen and was not an art dealer. Nor did Ms. Drew-Bear or Feigen make any effort to verify whether Wertz was the owner or authorized by the owner to sell the painting he was offering. Ms. Drew-Bear had available to her the Petrides volume on Utrillo which included *Chacteau de Lion-sur-Mer* in its catalogue of the master's works. Although this knowledge alone might not have been enough to put Feigen on notice that Wertz was not the true owner at the time of the transaction, it should have raised a doubt as to Wertz's right of possession, calling for further verification before the purchase by Feigen was consummated. Thus, it appears that statutory estoppel provided by Uniform Commercial Code, § 2–403(2), was not available as a defense to Feigen.

Judgment for Porter.

Risk of Loss

The transportation of goods from sellers to buyers can be a risky business. The carrier of the goods may lose, damage, or destroy them; floods, tornadoes, and other natural catastrophes may take their toll; thieves may steal all or part of the goods. If neither party is at fault for the loss, who should bear the risk? If the buyer has the risk when the goods are damaged or lost, the buyer is liable for the contract price. If the seller has the risk, he is liable for damages unless substitute performance can be tendered.

The common law placed the risk on the party who had technical title at the time of the loss. The Code rejects this approach and provides specific rules governing risk of loss that are designed to provide certainty and to place the risk on the party best able to protect against loss and most likely to be insured against it. Risk of loss under the Code depends on the terms of the parties' agreement, on the moment the loss occurs, and on whether one of the parties was in breach of contract when the loss occurred.

The Terms of the Agreement

The contracting parties, subject to the rule of good faith, may specify who has the risk of loss in their agreement [2–509(4)]. This they may do directly or by using certain commonly accepted shipping terms in their contract. In addition, the Code has certain general rules on risk of loss that amplify specific shipping terms and control risk of loss in cases where specific terms are not used [2–509].

Shipment Contracts

If the contract requires the seller to ship the goods by carrier but does not require their delivery to a specific destination, the risk passes to the buyer when the seller delivers the goods to the carrier [2–509(1)(a)].

The following are commonly used shipping terms that create shipment contracts:

1. *FOB (free on board) point of origin.* This term calls for the seller to deliver the goods free of expense and at the seller's risk at the place designated. For example, a contract between a seller located in Chicago and a buyer in New York calls for delivery FOB Chicago. The seller must deliver the goods at his expense and at his risk to a carrier in the place designated in the contract, namely Chicago, and arrange for their carriage. Because the shipment term in this example is FOB Chicago, the seller bears the risk and expense of delivering the goods to the carrier, but the seller is not responsible for delivering the goods to a specific destination. If the term is "FOB vessel, car, or other vehicle," the seller must load the goods on board at his own risk and expense [2–319(1)].

2. *FAS (free alongside ship).* This term is commonly used in maritime contracts and is normally accompanied by the name of a specific vessel and port, for example, "FAS (the ship) Calgary, Chicago Port Authority." The seller must deliver the goods alongside the vessel *Calgary* at the Chicago Port Authority at his own risk and expense [2–319(2)].

3. *CIF (cost, insurance, and freight).* This term means that the price of the goods includes the cost of shipping and insuring them. The seller bears this expense and the risk of loading the goods [2–320].

4. *C & F.* This term is the same as CIF, except that the seller is not obligated to insure the goods [2–320].

The *Morauer v. Deak & Co., Inc.* case, which follows, provides an example of the risk borne by a buyer in a shipment contract.

MORAUER v. DEAK & CO., INC.

26 UCC Rep. 1142 (D.C. Super. Ct. 1979)

On March 12, 1975, Raymond Morauer contracted with Deak & Co., a dealer in foreign currency, to purchase for investment purposes several bags of silver coins and a quantity of gold coins. He paid for his purchase with personal checks totaling $35,000. After his checks had cleared, he came to Deak's place of business to take delivery. Morauer had a discussion with Deak's assistant manager about the District of Columbia tax on the sale of gold. Both parties agreed that in order to avoid the tax, an admittedly legal endeavor, Deak would ship all of Morauer's gold coins to his residence in suburban Maryland. There was no District of Columbia tax on silver coins so Morauer took possession of them.

Deak placed the gold coins in two packages and, as authorized by Morauer, sent the packages to his house by registered mail, return receipt requested. Deak did not insure the packages with the U.S. Postal Service but instead, in accordance with its custom, relied on its own insurance contract with its insurer to cover any risk of loss. Only one package was received by Morauer; however, he did not open it and thus did not realize at the time that he had received only a portion of his gold coins. More than two years later, while making an inventory of his collection, Morauer discovered the problem and notified Deak. By that time, the Post Office had destroyed its records of the shipment and Deak's insurance coverage for that shipment had expired. Morauer then brought a lawsuit asking the value at their time of purchase of the gold coins that he had not received.

Smith, Judge.   The court must determine whether the risk of loss of the gold coins in question passed from the defendant Deak to Morauer upon Deak's delivery of the coins to the Post Office for shipment to Morauer. If so, then Deak is not liable to Morauer for the value of the lost shipment. If the risk of loss did not pass, however, then Deak is liable for the full value of the coins at time of purchase.

The case is governed by § 2–509(1) of the UCC, and the court must determine whether paragraph (a) or paragraph (b) of subsection (1) controls. If the contract was a so-called "shipment" contract, then the risk of loss passed to Morauer, the buyer, on Deak's delivery to the carrier, § 2–509(1)(a), provided, however, that Deak also satisfied the UCC's requirements for a valid "shipment" contract, § 2–504. If, on the other hand, the contract called for delivery at a particular destination, then the risk of loss never passed to Morauer, because the goods were never delivered, and Morauer must prevail, § 2–509(1)(b).

The fact that the parties had agreed that Deak would ship the coins to Morauer's residence in Maryland is not dispositive of this controversy. A "ship to" term in a sales contract has no significance in determining whether the agreement is a "shipment" or "destination" contract. Moreover, there is a preference in the UCC for "shipment" contracts. The drafters of the UCC state the preference and give the reasons for it in the following manner:

For the purposes of subsections (2) and (3) there is omitted from this Article the rule under prior uniform legislation that a term requiring the seller to pay the freight or cost of transportation to the buyer is equivalent to an agreement by the seller to deliver to the buyer or at an agreed destination. This omission is with the specific intention of negating the rule, for *under this Article the "shipment" contract is regarded as the normal one and the "destination" contract as the variant type. The seller is not obligated to deliver at a named destination and bear the concurrent risk of loss until arrival, unless he has specifically agreed so to deliver or the commercial understanding of the terms used by the parties contemplates such delivery.* Uniform Code Comment No. 5; § 2–503.

Here we have an order and payment by Morauer in person to Deak with receipts signed by Kirsch, Deak's agent, indicating Morauer's home address and, in one instance, including the further instruction, "c/o Mrs. Geraldine Morauer." Morauer and Kirsch discussed delivery of the coins, and Morauer decided that to avoid payment of the District of Columbia sales tax, he would have them shipped to his residence. Deak mailed the gold coins in two packages, both of which were properly addressed, stamped and deposited at the United States Post Office. Deak also included the cost of postage as part of Morauer's total bill. Therefore, we hold that Deak was authorized by the contract to ship the gold coins to Morauer by carrier, and that the risk of loss passed from Deak to Morauer on delivery of the packages of coins to the Post Office.

Although the court's finding that the parties were operating under a "shipment" contract puts the risk of loss on Morauer from the time of Deak's delivery to the authorized carrier, there remains the question whether defendant Deak met all the statutory requirements of "shipment" contracts under the applicable UCC section 2–504. That section states:

> Where the seller is required or authorized to send the goods to the buyer and the contract does not require him to deliver them at a particular destination, then unless otherwise agreed he must
>
> (a) put the goods in the possession of such a carrier and make such a contract for their transportation as may be reasonable having regard to the nature of the goods and other circumstances of the case; and
>
> (b) obtain and promptly deliver or tender in due form any document necessary to enable the buyer to obtain possession of the goods or otherwise required by the agreement or by usage of trade; and
>
> (c) promptly notify the buyer of the shipment.
>
> Failure to notify the buyer under paragraph (c) or to make a proper contract under paragraph (a) is a ground for rejection only if material delay or loss ensues.

In the case now before this court Deak followed its regular practice of insuring the shipments with its own insurance company, properly addressed each package and sent both by first-class, registered mail, with a return receipt requested. Deak therefore made all arrangements with the carrier, the United States Postal Service, as were "reasonable having regard to the nature of the goods and other circumstances of the case." § 2–504(a). Deak had no obligation under paragraph (b) of § 2–504, insofar as there were no documents necessary to enable Morauer to obtain possession of the goods, and none "otherwise required by the agreement or by usage of trade." And finally, Deak was in compliance with § 2–504(c) in that Kirsch notified Morauer of the mailing of the gold coins when Morauer went to Deak's office to take delivery personally of the silver coins he had also purchased.

Judgment in favor of Deak.

Destination Contracts

If the contract requires the seller to deliver the goods to a specific destination, the seller bears the risk and expense of delivery to that destination [2–509(1)(b)]. The following are commonly used shipping terms that create *destination* contracts:

1. *FOB destination.* An FOB term coupled with the place of destination of the goods puts the expense and risk of delivering the goods to that destination on the seller [2–319(1)(b)]. For example, a contract between a seller in Chicago and a buyer in Phoenix might call for shipment FOB Phoenix. The seller must ship the goods to Phoenix at her own expense, and she also retains the risk of delivery of the goods to Phoenix.

2. *Ex-ship.* This term does not specify a particular ship, but it places the expense and risk on the seller until the goods are unloaded from whatever ship is used [2–322].

3. *No arrival, no sale.* This term places the expense and risk during shipment on the seller. If the goods fail to arrive through no fault of the seller, the seller has no further liability to the buyer [2–324].

For example, a Chicago-based seller contracts to sell a quantity of shirts to a buyer FOB Phoenix, the buyer's place of business. The shirts are destroyed en route when the truck carrying the shirts is involved in an accident. The risk of the loss of the shirts is on the seller, and the buyer is not obligated to pay for them. The seller may have the right to recover from the trucking company, but between the seller and the buyer, the seller has the risk of loss. If the contract had called for delivery FOB the seller's manufacturing plant, then the risk of loss would have been on the buyer. The buyer would have had to pay for the shirts and then pursue any claims that he had against the trucking company.

Goods in the Possession of Third Parties

If the goods are in the possession of a bailee and are to be delivered without being moved, the risk of loss passes to the buyer upon *delivery* to him *of a negotiable document of title* for the goods; if no negotiable document of title has been used, the risk of loss passes when the bailee *indicates* to the buyer that the buyer has the *right to the possession* of the goods [2–509(2)]. For example, if Farmer sells Miller a quantity of grain currently stored at Grain Elevator, the risk of loss of the grain will shift from Farmer to Miller (1) when a negotiable warehouse receipt for the grain is delivered to Miller or (2) when Grain Elevator notifies Miller that it is holding the grain for Miller.

Risk Generally

If the transaction does not fall within the situations discussed above, the risk of loss passes to the buyer upon *receipt* of the goods if the seller is a merchant; if the seller is not a merchant, then the risk of loss passes to the buyer upon the *tender of delivery* of the goods to the buyer [2–509(3)]. If Jones bought a television set from ABC Appliance on Monday, intending to pick it up on Thursday, and the set was stolen on Wednesday, the risk of loss remained with ABC. However, if Jones had purchased the set from his next-door neighbor and could have taken delivery of the set on Monday (i.e., delivery was tendered then), the risk of loss was Jones's.

Effect of Breach on Risk of Loss

When a seller tenders goods that do not conform to the contract and the buyer has the right to reject the goods, the risk of loss remains with the seller until any defect is cured or until the buyer accepts the goods [2–510(1)]. Where the buyer rightfully revokes his acceptance of goods, the risk of loss is with the seller to the extent that any loss is not covered by the buyer's insurance [2–510(2)]. This rule gives the seller the benefit of any insurance carried by the buyer.

For example, if Adler bought a new Buick from Brown Buick that he later returned to Brown because of serious defects in it and if through no fault of Adler's the automobile was damaged while in his possession, then the risk of loss would be with Brown. However, if Adler had insurance on the automobile covering the damage to it and recovered from the insurance company, Adler would have to turn the insurance proceeds over to Brown or use them to fix the car before returning it to Brown.

When a buyer repudiates a contract for goods and those goods have already been set aside by the seller, the risk of loss stays with the buyer for a commercially reasonable time after the repudiation [2–510(3)]. Suppose Cannery contracts to buy Farmer's entire crop of peaches. Farmer picks the peaches, crates them, tenders delivery to Cannery, and stores them in his barn. Cannery then tells Farmer that it does not intend to honor the contract. Shortly thereafter, but before Farmer has a chance to find another buyer, the peaches are spoiled by a fire. If Farmer's insurance covers only part of the loss, Cannery must bear the rest of the loss.

Insurable Interest

The general practice of insuring risks is recognized and provided for under the Code. A buyer may protect his interest in goods that are the subject matter of a sales contract before he actually obtains title. The buyer obtains an insurable interest in existing goods when they are identified as the goods covered by the contract even though they are in fact nonconforming. The seller retains an insurable interest in goods so long as he has either title or a security interest in them [2–501(2)]. The importance of the seller's retention of an insurable interest in goods he has sold is illustrated in the *Russell v. Transamerica Insurance Co.* case, which apppeared earlier in this chapter.

CONCEPT REVIEW

RISK OF LOSS

The point at which the risk of loss or damage to goods identified to a contract passes to the buyer is as follows:

1. If there is an agreement between the parties, the risk of loss passes to the buyer at the time they have agreed to.

2. If the contract requires the seller to ship the goods by carrier but does not require that the seller guarantee their delivery to a specific destination (shipment contract), the risk of loss passes to the buyer when the seller has delivered the goods to the carrier and made an appropriate contract for their carriage.

3. If the contract requires the seller to guarantee delivery of the goods to a specific destination (destination contract), the risk of loss passes to the buyer when the goods are delivered at the designated destination.

4. If the goods are in the hands of a third person and are to be delivered without being moved, the risk of loss passes to the buyer when the buyer has the power to take possession of the goods; for example, when he receives a document of title.

5. In any situation other than those noted above where the seller is a merchant, the risk of loss passes to the buyer on his receipt of the goods.

6. In any situation other than those noted above where the seller is not a merchant, the risk of loss passes to the buyer on the tender of delivery to the buyer by the seller.

7. When a seller tenders goods that the buyer could lawfully reject because they do not conform to the contract description, the risk of loss stays on the seller until the defect is cured or the buyer accepts them.

8. When a buyer rightfully revokes acceptance of goods, the risk is on the buyer to the extent it is not covered by the buyer's insurance.

9. If a buyer repudiates a contract for identified, conforming goods before risk of loss has passed to the buyer, the buyer is liable for a commercially reasonable time for any loss or damage to the goods that is not covered by the buyer's insurance.

SALES ON TRIAL

A common commercial practice is for a seller of goods to entrust possession of goods to a buyer to either give the buyer an opportunity to decide whether or not to buy them or to try to resell them to a third person. The entrusting may be known as a **sale on approval,** a **sale or return** or a **consignment,** depending on the terms of the entrusting. Occasionally, the goods may be damaged, destroyed, or stolen, or the creditors of the buyer may try to claim them; on such occasions, the form of the entrusting will determine whether the buyer or the seller had the risk of loss and whether the buyer's creditors can successfully claim the goods.

Sale on Approval

In a sale on approval, the goods are delivered to the buyer with an understanding that he may use or test them for the purpose of determining whether he wishes to buy them [2–326(1)(a)]. In a sale on approval, neither the risk of loss nor title to the goods passes to the buyer until he accepts the goods. The buyer has the right to use the goods in any manner consistent with the purpose of the trial, but any unwarranted exercise of ownership over the goods is considered to be an acceptance of the goods. Similarly, if the buyer fails to notify the seller of his election to return the goods, he is considered to have accepted them [2–327]. For example, if Dealer agrees to let Hughes take a new automobile home to drive for a day to see whether she wants to buy it and Hughes takes the car on a two-week vacation trip, Hughes will be considered to have accepted the automobile because she used it in a manner beyond that contemplated by the trial and as if she were its owner. If Hughes had driven the automobile for a day, decided not to buy it, and parked it in her driveway for two weeks without telling Dealer of her intention to return it, Hughes would also be deemed to have accepted the automobile.

Once the buyer has notified the seller of his election to return the goods, the return of the goods is at the seller's expense and risk. Because the title and risk of loss of goods delivered on a sale on approval remain with the seller, goods held on approval are not subject to the claims of the buyer's creditors until the buyer accepts them [2–326].

Sale or Return

In a sale or return, goods are delivered to a buyer for resale with the understanding that the buyer has the right to return them [2–326(1)(b)]. Under a sale or return, the title and risk of loss are with the buyer. While the goods are in the buyer's possession, they are subject to the claims of his creditors [2–326 and 2–327]. For example, if Publisher delivers some paperbacks to Bookstore on the understanding that Bookstore may return any of the paperbacks that remain unsold at the end of six months, the transaction is a sale or return. If Bookstore is destroyed by a fire, the risk of loss of the paperbacks was Bookstore's and it is responsible to Publisher for the purchase price. Similarly, if Bookstore becomes insolvent and is declared a bankrupt, the paperbacks will be considered part of the bankruptcy estate. If the buyer elects to return goods held on a sale or return basis, the return is at the buyer's risk and expense.

Sale on Consignment

Sometimes, goods are delivered to a merchant on consignment. If the merchant to whom goods are consigned maintains a place of business dealing in goods of that kind under a name other than that of the person consigning the goods, then the consignor must take certain steps to protect his interest in the goods or they will be subject to the claims of the merchant's creditors. The consignor must (1) make sure that a sign indicating the consignor's interest is prominently posted at the place of business, or (2) make sure that the merchant's creditors know that he is generally in the business of selling goods owned by others, or (3) comply with the filing provisions of Article 9 of the Code—Secured Transactions.[3]

For example, Jones operates a retail music store under the name of City Music Store. Baldwin Piano Company delivers some pianos to Jones on consignment. If no notices are posted indicating Baldwin's interest in the pianos, if Jones is not generally known to be selling from a consigned inventory, and if Baldwin does not file its interest with the recording office pursuant to Article 9 of the Code, then the goods are subject to the claims of Jones's creditors. This is crucial to Baldwin because it may have intended to retain title. However, the Code treats a consignment to a person doing business under a name other than that of the consignor as a "sale or return" [2– 326(3)]. If Jones did business as the Baldwin Piano Company, Baldwin's interest would be protected from the claims of Jones's creditors without the need for Baldwin to post a sign or to file under Article 9.

The case that follows, *In Re Fisher*, illustrates the risks borne by a person who makes goods available on a sale or return or consignment basis.

---

[3] These provisions are discussed in detail in the Security Interests in Personal Property chapter.

IN RE FISHER

100 BR 351 (Bankr. S.D. Ohio 1989)

On December 12, 1984, Almiro Fur Fashion Design (Almiro) shipped two mink coats with a wholesale value of approximately $6,800 to Julius Fisher, the owner and operator of Kingston Lee Furriers; the two mink coats were returned to Almiro on December 18, 1984. On December 17, 1984, another mink coat was shipped to Fisher; it was returned to Almiro on December 19, 1984. The mink coats received by Fisher were to be sold on consignment—that is, if the coats received were sold, Fisher was to remit a portion of the sale proceeds to Almiro in payment of the coats. Unsold coats could be returned to Almiro for credit.

On March 7, 1985, Fisher filed a voluntary petition in bankruptcy under Chapter 7 of the Bankruptcy Code. One of the questions in the bankruptcy proceeding was whether the return of the mink coats (the Minks) to Almiro within the 90 days preceding the bankruptcy filing constituted an "avoidable preference" under the bankruptcy law. If it did, the Minks could be recovered from Almiro by the bankruptcy trustee for the benefit of Fisher's creditors.

Almiro claimed that the shipment of the Minks to Fisher was not for the purpose of transferring a property interest to him but rather for the sole purpose of consigning the Minks to him for inspection only. Almiro also argued that because Fisher had possession of the Minks for no more than six days, it would be inequitable to hold that the transfers of the Minks were avoidable preferences and could be recovered for the benefit of other creditors.

Cole, Bankruptcy Judge.   To establish that a transfer constitutes an avoidable preference, the threshold requirement of a transfer of an interest of the debtor in property must be met. "Transfer" is defined as "every mode direct or indirect, absolute or conditional, voluntary or involuntary, of disposing of or parting with property or with an interest in property." In returning the Minks to Almiro, Fisher obviously parted with the property in question. The dispute here centers upon whether Fisher possessed a transferable property interest in the Minks. According to Almiro, because the Minks were transferred on a consignment basis, for inspection only, Fisher never obtained a transferable property interest in the Minks.

This argument ignores Ohio law. Because the Minks were delivered to Fisher primarily for resale, and Fisher could return the Minks to Almiro for credit even though the Minks conformed to the contract, pursuant to Ohio law, this transaction would be classified as a "sale or return." Section 2–326(1)(b). Under section 2–326(2), goods held on a "sale or return" basis are subject to the claims of the buyer's creditors while in the possession unless compliance with one of provisions of section 2–236(3) is demonstrated. Absent such a showing, then, the Minks were subject to the claims of Fisher's creditors while in his possession and must be deemed to be "property" of the debtor within the meaning of the Bankruptcy Code.

Under section 2–326(3), goods held on "sale or return" are subject to the claims of the buyer's creditors while they are in the buyer's possession, unless the seller of such goods does one of the following:

(1) complies with an applicable state law providing for a consignor's interest to be evidenced by a sign;

(2) establishes that the person conducting the business is generally known by his creditors to be substantially engaged in selling the goods of others; or

(3) complies with the filing requirements of [UCC Article 9].

Almiro's failure to comply with any of the requirements of section 2–326(3) is clear as a matter of fact and law. Ohio has no applicable law providing for a consignor's interest to be evidenced by a sign. And, Almiro does not assert that Fisher was generally known by his creditors to be substantially engaged in the sale of goods of others. Finally, Almiro's failure to file financing statements with respect to the Minks is likewise undisputed. Hence, the relationship between Almiro and Fisher is not that of consignor-consignee under Ohio law. Rather the transaction was a "sale or return" within the meaning of section 2–326(1)(b) and, pursuant to section 2–326(2), the Minks were subject to the claims of Fisher's creditors while in his possession.

Judgment against Almiro for $13,205.

BULK TRANSFERS

Bulk Transfer Legislation

There is one other situation where the creditors of a party to a sales contract may claim an interest (other than an Article 9 security interest) in the goods. This is in the case of a **bulk transfer** as covered by Article 6 of the Code. A bulk transfer occurs when a person whose main business is selling goods from stock (a retailer, a wholesaler, and in some cases a manufacturer) sells a major part of the materials, supplies, merchandise, or other inventory of the business *in bulk and not in the ordinary course of business* [6–102].

The danger in such cases is that financially troubled sellers may secretly dispose of their assets, pocket the proceeds, and disappear. In order to protect such a seller's creditors from being defrauded in this manner, Article 6 is designed to give them notice of the sale and enable them to file any claims they may have against the

goods. The seller must give the buyer a sworn list of the seller's creditors and a schedule of the property to be transferred [6–104]. The buyer must keep this list available for inspection and copying by the seller's creditors for six months after the sale [6–104].

Notice to Creditors

The buyer must notify all known creditors of the sale at least 10 days before taking possession of the goods [6–105]. Failure to comply with the requirements means that the buyer holds the goods in trust for the seller's creditors. In some states (Pennsylvania, for example), an optional provision of the Code has been enacted requiring that the proceeds of the bulk transfer be paid to the seller's creditors [6–106].

The following case, *In Re Curtina International, Inc.*, provides an example of a purchaser's failure to comply with the bulk transfer law and illustrates the consequences of that noncompliance.

IN RE CURTINA INTERNATIONAL, INC.
MURDOCK v. PLYMOUTH ENTERPRISES, INC.

23 B.R. 969 (Bankr. S.D. N.Y. 1982)

Curtina International was a corporation engaged in the business of importing and distributing confectionery products, mainly varieties of wafers manufactured in Austria. From its inception in 1979, Curtina's business was not financially successful. By early 1981, Curtina was insolvent. Its largest unsecured creditor was one of its Austrian suppliers of wafers.

In February 1981, Curtina's president approached Plymouth Enterprises, a corporation engaged in the business of buying and selling closeouts (excess, old, or out-of-season inventory) from manufacturers and wholesalers at a fraction of their normal selling prices. He offered to sell Plymouth Curtina's line of wafers. In March, Plymouth agreed to purchase substantially all of Curtina's inventory of wafers at approximately $12 per case, for a total of about $66,000; the wafers usually sold for about $50 a case to retail stores. Plymouth's representative was not aware that wafers constituted Curtina's entire inventory. At no time did Plymouth ask Curtina for a list of its creditors, and Plymouth did not furnish notice of the sale to Curtina's creditors. It took Plymouth approximately nine months to resell the wafers.

Curtina was involuntarily thrown into bankruptcy in April 1981. Murdock, the trustee in bankruptcy, sought to avoid the sale of the wafers to Plymouth, contending that it was made in violation of the state bulk sales law.

Schwartzberg, Bankruptcy Judge. Under Article 6 of the New York Uniform Commercial Code, referred to as the Bulk Transfer Article, a creditor of a bulk transferor may look to § 6–104 and § 6–105 for purposes of avoiding a transfer that fails to comply with the notice requirements of the Bulk Transfer Article.

There is no question that Plymouth did not give the prescribed notice or otherwise comply with the Bulk Transfer Article. Plymouth maintains that the transaction in question was not a bulk transfer. A bulk transfer is defined under § 6–102(1) of the Uniform Commercial Code as: "Any transfer in bulk and not in the ordinary course of the transferor's business of a major part of the materials, supplies, merchandise, or other inventory (Section 9–109) of an enterprise subject to this Article."

It is undisputed that Curtina sold all of its inventory of wafers to Plymouth. Therefore, in order to avoid Curtina's sale to Plymouth, the trustee must establish that the transfer was not in the ordinary course of Curtina's business. Consideration must therefore be given to the nature of Curtina's business and the manner in which it sold its merchandise. Evidence that Curtina had similar transactions in the past, and that such transfers were common practice in the trade, would be indicative that the questioned transfer occurred in the ordinary course of Curtina's business. Thus, the New York Court of Appeals in *Sternberg v. Rubenstein* ruled that the sale of off-season shoes, the type of merchandise that was rendered "obsolete" by the passage of time, was exempt from the New York Bulk Sales Act. The New York Court of Appeals observed that the sale of obsolete inventory was an inevitable incident to the conduct of the transferor's business, provided that the sale did not constitute a discontinuance of a branch of business or a line of merchandise.

Other courts, interpreting a bulk sales provision similar to UCC § 6–102, have flatly rejected close-out sales as an excluded normal business practice. In *Jubas v. Sampsell*, a retail shoe store sold 25 percent of the number of pairs of shoes in its inventory, amounting to 15 percent in value, for one dollar per pair to another dealer, and then voluntarily filed a petition in bankruptcy. The one dollar per pair was the best offer obtainable. The trustee in bankruptcy was able to set aside the sale as violative of the California bulk sales law, despite the transferee's claim that "unloading" unmarketable shoes in that manner was a normal business practice. The court held that: "The plain meaning of the statute is that when a storekeeper disposes of a substantial part of his stock in trade in bulk, and selling in bulk sales is not the usual and ordinary way in which he conducts his business from day to day, the sale falls within the statute."

The *Jubas* case was quoted with approval in *Danning v. Daylin*, where the court noted that the transferee's good faith and the absence of fraudulent intent are no defenses to a violation of the bulk sales law. The reason for such strict liability was to discourage a merchant who owes debts from selling out his stock in trade to anyone at any price, pocketing the proceeds, and disappearing without paying his creditors.

In the instant case, Plymouth has established that a close-out sale of the confectionery goods prior to total loss of shelf life is a common practice in the industry. However, there was no evidence that Curtina ever sold any portion of its line of wafers on a close-out basis since its inception in late 1979, and up to the time when it sold off all of its inventory in March of 1981. Moreover, the transfer to Plymouth resulted in the discontinuance of Curtina's entire business; it retained no other merchandise lines nor did it remain open as a going business. Based upon the foregoing, it is held that the trustee has established, and Plymouth has failed to rebut, that Plymouth purchased Curtina's entire inventory of vanilla, raspberry, and orange wafers without complying with the notice provisions in § 6–104 and § 6–105 under Article 6 of the New York Uniform Commercial Code, referred to as the Bulk Transfer Article. Article 6 of the New York Uniform Commercial Code imposes no specific remedy for failure to comply with the bulk sales law. Under § 6–104 and § 6–105 a noncomplying transfer is "ineffective" against creditors of the transferor. The Official Comment suggests that an objecting creditor may levy on or obtain possession of the merchandise but is silent as to money damages, especially where the merchandise has been resold by the transferee.

The New York cases interpreting the bulk sales law have held that a transfer in violation of the law obligates the transferee to account to the transferor's creditors for the value of the merchandise transferred.

In the instant case, it has been found that the reasonable equivalent value of the vanilla, raspberry, and orange wafers sold in bulk by Curtina to Plymouth was $66,766.32 at the time of the sale. Accordingly, Plymouth is liable to the Curtina estate and must account for this amount. However, Plymouth has paid the full purchase price to the debtor, and the funds appear to have been deposited by the debtor in its account with the European American Bank and Curtina's schedules reveal a sum of $44,639.49 on deposit in its account with the European American Bank at the time the involuntary petition was filed. In accounting for the value of the inventory, Plymouth is entitled to a credit for that portion of the proceeds from the sale that are traceable to the funds held by the trustee in bankruptcy.

Judgment for Murdock, the trustee in bankruptcy.

Statute of Limitations

Creditors have only six months from the time the transfer took place to enforce their rights under Article 6, unless the transfer was concealed from them. In such a case, they have six months after the transfer was discovered [6–111].

Current Developments

For some time there has been general dissatisfaction with the current bulk sales law. The National Conference of Commissioners on Uniform State Laws has prepared a draft revision to UCC Article 6 (Bulk Sales) for consideration by the states; at the same time, the commissioners have voted to recommend to the states that they repeal Article 6 and do without a bulk sales law. Thus, the future for bulk sales laws is in doubt.

ETHICAL AND PUBLIC POLICY CONCERNS

1. Suppose you are the owner of a small jewelry store that sells new and antique jewelry. A customer leaves a family heirloom—an elaborate diamond ring—with you for cleaning and resetting. By mistake, a clerk in your store sells it to another customer. What would you do? If you were the buyer of the ring and had given it to your fiancée as a gift and then were informed of the circumstances, what would you do?

2. Under the pre-Code law, most issues relating to risks and insurable interests in goods were determined on the basis of who was technical title owner at the particular moment the problem of a right or liability arose. What policy considerations do you believe were in-volved in the decision by the drafters of the Code to provide for resolution of issues concerning risk of loss and insurable interest independent of who was the technical title owner?

3. In the *In Re Fisher* case, the wholesaler that made the mink coats available to the retailer for resale lost out to other creditors of the retailer when it filed for bankruptcy even though the mink coats had been returned to the wholesaler when the petition in bankruptcy was filed. Does this strike you as a reasonable result? What policy considerations underlie the Code provisions on which the court based its decision?

SUMMARY

Article 2 of the Uniform Commercial Code codifies the law of the sale of goods. Although the Uniform Commercial Code does not apply to contracts to provide services or contracts to sell real property, some courts have applied Code principles by analogy to such contracts. The Code permits parties considerable flexibility to form a contract to sell goods. It sets out the rights of the parties when certain terms are used, and it contains certain other provisions that are to be used if the parties do not specifically agree to the contrary.

Unless otherwise agreed, title passes when the seller has completed his performance. If he is to ship goods, title passes upon delivery to the carrier; if he is to deliver goods, title passes upon delivery and tender. If the goods are in the possession of a bailee and a document of title has been issued, title passes at the place and time of the making of the contract. Rejection of the goods by the buyer reverts title in the seller.

A fundamental rule of property law is that a seller cannot pass better title to goods than he has. Among the exceptions to this general rule are: (1) a person who has voidable title to goods can pass good title to a bona fide purchaser for value; (2) a buyer in the ordinary course of a retailer's business takes free of any interests in the goods that the retailer has given to others; and (3) a person who buys goods in the ordinary course of a dealer's business takes free of any claims of a person who entrusted those goods to the dealer.

The parties to the sales contract may by explicit agreement designate who shall bear the risk of loss or how the risk of loss shall be divided. The inclusion in the sales contract of delivery terms will indicate which of the parties shall bear the risk of loss during transit. If the delivery term is FOB point of origin, the risk of loss passes to the buyer when goods are delivered to the carrier and a reasonable contract for their carriage is made. If the delivery term is FOB destination, the risk of loss passes upon tender of delivery to the buyer. If goods are in the possession of a bailee and are not to be moved, the risk of loss passes to the buyer upon delivery of a negotiable document of title. If there is no negotiable document of title, the risk of loss passes when the bailee acknowledges the buyer's rights.

In a sale on approval, the goods are delivered to the buyer for use or trial and the risk of loss and title remain in the seller. The goods are not subject to claims of the buyer's creditors, and any return of the goods is at the seller's risk and expense. In a sale or return, the goods are sold to the buyer for resale but may be retained at the buyer's option. The risk of loss and title is in the buyer, and the goods are subject to the claims of the buyer's creditors. The return of the goods is at the buyer's risk and expense.

The bulk transfer law is designed to prevent commercial fraud, and anyone who buys substantially all of the materials, supplies, inventory, or equipment of a business must comply with it to make sure he will take title free of claims from the seller's creditors.

PROBLEM CASES

1. Helen Preston consulted Dr. Benjamin Thompson, a specialist in filling and preparing dentures, about obtaining a new set of dentures. She paid him $750, and after numerous appointments during which measurements were taken, she received her new dentures. She experienced some pain and had trouble eating with the lower set. Dr. Thompson made numerous adjustments to the lower set and indicated a willingness to continue working with her until the fit was satisfactory. She refused to continue, however, and filed suit against Dr. Thompson for breach of the Code's warranty of merchantability (discussed in the Product Liability chapter). Was Preston's agreement with Dr. Thompson a sale of goods under the Code?

2. Club Pro Golf Products was a distributor of golf products. It employed salesmen who called on customers to take orders for merchandise. The merchandise was sent by Club Pro directly to the purchaser and payment was made by the purchaser directly to Club Pro. A salesman for Club Pro, Carl Gude, transmitted orders for certain merchandise to Club Pro for delivery to several fictitious purchasers. Club Pro sent the merchandise to the fictitious purchasers at the fictitious addresses where it was picked up by Gude. Gude then sold the merchandise, worth approximately $19,000, directly to Simpson, a golf pro at a golf club. Gude retained the proceeds of sale for himself. Club Pro discovered the fraud and brought suit against Simpson to recover the merchandise. Club Pro alleged that Gude "stole" the merchandise from it "with intent to defraud it" and as a result had no authority to transfer title to Simpson. Did Gude have a "void" or a "voidable" title to the merchandise when he obtained it from Club Pro?

3. SST Grain Company hired William McColery to haul a quantity of soybeans from Fall City, Nebraska, to the Far-Mar-Co grain elevator in St. Joseph, Missouri. Although McColery's primary business was as a trucker, he also had a reputation in the Fall City area as a sometime "merchant" who bought and sold grain. When McColery arrived at Far-Mar-Co's elevator with SST's soybeans, he represented that they were his and received payment. He then absconded with the money. SST brought suit against Far-Mar-Co, claiming that Far-Mar-Co had converted SST's soybeans by paying McColery rather than SST. Far-Mar-Co contends that it got good title to the beans from McColery and that SST's remedy is to find McColery and go against him. Which one is correct?

4. Lane, a dealer in new and used boats, sold a new boat and trailer to Johnson. Johnson paid for the boat and trailer by a check that was later dishonored. Johnson then resold the boat and trailer to Honeycutt. Lane attempted to get the boat and trailer from Honeycutt. Can Lane recover them?

Destination Contract [handwritten]

5. In February, Hayward purchased a boat from Postma, a boat dealer, for $10,000. They agreed that the boat was to be delivered to a nearby lake in April. Prior to the time the boat was to be delivered, a fire at Postma's showroom destroyed the boat. Between Hayward and Postma, who had the risk of loss? *Postma p407* [handwritten]

6. Debs, a dress manufacturer, sold Rose Stores 288 dresses. The order was on a Rose Stores printed form that stated, "Ship via Stuarts Express." Stuarts Express picked up the dresses at Debs, and one week later wrote Debs a letter informing it that the entire shipment was lost. Since Stuarts's liability is extremely limited by the shipping contract who, between Debs and Rose, must absorb the risk of loss? *shipment contract — Buyer risk of loss p407* [handwritten]

7. Legendary Homes, a home builder, purchased various appliances from Ron Mead T.V. & Appliance, a retail merchant selling home appliances. They were intended to be installed in one of Legendary Homes's houses and were to be delivered on February 1, 1984. At 5 o'clock on that day, the appliances had not been delivered. Legendary Homes's employees closed the home and left. Sometime between 5 and 6:30, Ron Mead delivered the appliances. No one was at the home so the deliveryman put the appliances in the garage. During the night, someone stole the appliances. Legendary Homes denied it was responsible for the loss and refused to pay Ron Mead for the appliances. Ron Mead then brought suit for the purchase price. Did Legendary Homes have the risk of loss of the appliances? *No! Ron Mead if closed on time — close early* [handwritten]

8. White Motor Company, a manufacturer of trucks, delivered to Bronx Trucks an autocar truck pursuant to an order placed by Bronx Trucks. White Motor received a signed receipt from the manager of Bronx Trucks for the delivery and invoiced Bronx Trucks for the agreed purchase price. After the truck had been delivered and invoiced, it was stolen from Bronx Truck's garage. The title papers to the truck were not delivered to Bronx Truck until after the truck had been stolen. White Motor sued Bronx Truck for the purchase price of the truck, and Bronx Truck defended on the grounds that it did not have title to the truck when it was stolen and thus White Motor was still the owner of it and had the risk of loss. Is Bronx Truck responsible for paying the purchase price to White Motor? *Yes Title doesn't matter, tendered, accepts possession* [handwritten]

9. The Cedar Rapids YMCA bought a large number of cases of candy from Seaway Candy under an agreement by which any unused portion could be returned. The YMCA was to sell the candy to raise money to send boys to camp. The campaign was less than successful, and 688 cases remained unsold. They were returned to Seaway Candy by truck. When delivered to the common carrier, the candy was in good condition. When it arrived at Seaway four days later, it had melted and was completely worthless. Seaway then brought suit against the YMCA to recover the purchase price of the candy spoiled in transit. Between Seaway and the YMCA, which had the risk of loss? *YMCA p412* [handwritten]

10. Collier, a retail store operator, accepted a delivery of stereo tapes, cartridges, and equipment from B & B Sales. The invoice noted that the goods had been "sold to" Collier and stated: "Terms 30–60–90 this equipment will be picked up if not sold in 90 days." Shortly thereafter, Collier's store was burglarized and all the merchandise was stolen. B & B filed suit against Collier for the purchase price of the merchandise, claiming that the transaction was a sale and that Collier was liable to pay for the merchandise. Collier argued that the transaction was a consignment and that B & B had the risk of loss. Did Collier or B & B have the risk of loss of the merchandise?

p412 SALE OR RETURN CONTRACT Collier had the risk of Loss. [handwritten]

CHAPTER 20

PRODUCT LIABILITY

INTRODUCTION

Imagine you are a high-level manager of a firm manufacturing goods for sale to the public. In all likelihood, one of your major concerns would be your company's exposure to civil liability for defects in the products it makes and sells. In your role as manager, you would probably be concerned about changes in the law that make such liability more frequent or more severe. In other contexts, however, these same changes might strike you as a good idea. This is especially true if *you* suffer injury or other loss from defective products you purchase as a consumer. Such changes might also appeal to you if your firm wants to sue a supplier that has sold your company defective products.

Each of the situations just sketched involves the law of **product liability**. Product liability law applies to civil suits for damages resulting from the sale of defective goods.[1] As you will see, it is a complicated and ever-changing area of the law whose development has been greatly influenced by changes in social values and economic conditions. Product liability is also one of the more controversial subjects discussed in this text.

---

[1]This chapter does not discuss the various federal consumer protection laws involving the payment and credit aspects of consumer transactions. Nor does it discuss product safety regulation. On these subjects, see the Federal Trade Commission Act and Consumer Protection Laws chapter. Also, some product liability implications of the sale of computers are discussed in the Computer Law chapter.

THE EVOLUTION OF PRODUCT LIABILITY LAW

The 19th Century

In the 19th century, the rules governing suits for defective goods were very much to the seller's or manufacturer's advantage. This was the era of *caveat emptor* (let the buyer beware). In contract cases, there was usually no liability unless the seller had made an express promise to the buyer and the goods did not conform to that promise. Some courts went further, requiring that the words *warrant* or *guarantee* accompany the promise before liability would exist. In negligence suits, the maxim of "no liability without fault" was in full force, and plaintiffs frequently faced problems in proving the defendant's negligence because the necessary evidence was under the defendant's control. In both contract and negligence cases, finally, the doctrine of "no liability outside privity of contract" often prevented plaintiffs from successfully suing a party with whom they had not dealt directly.[2]

The social and economic conditions that prevailed for much of the 19th century go some way toward explaining these prodefendant rules. At that time, laissez-faire

---

[2]Privity of contract is the existence of a direct contractual relationship between two parties. The gradual demise of the no-liability-outside-privity rule in New York in the late 19th and early 20th centuries is discussed in the chapter on the Nature of Law.

values strongly influenced public policy and the law. One expression of these values was the belief that sellers and manufacturers should be contractually bound only where they deliberately assumed such liability by actually making a promise to someone with whom they had dealt directly. Another factor limiting manufacturers' liability for defective products, some say, was the desire to promote industrialization by preventing potentially crippling damage recoveries against infant industries.

Certain features of the 19th-century economy, however, made that century's prodefendant product liability rules less hard on plaintiffs than would otherwise have been the case. Chains of distribution tended to be short, so the no-liability-outside-privity defense could not always be used. Because goods tended to be simple, buyers sometimes could inspect them for defects. Before the rise of the large corporation late in the 19th century, sellers and buyers were often of relatively equal size, sophistication, and bargaining power. This permitted a certain amount of genuine sharp trading between them.

The 20th Century

Today, many of the 19th-century social and economic tendencies just discussed are conspicuous by their absence. Despite their recent revival, laissez-faire values do not exercise the influence that they did a century ago. Instead, a somewhat more protective, interdependent climate has emerged. With the development of a viable industrial economy, there has been less need to protect manufacturers from liability for defective goods. The emergence of long chains of distribution has meant that consumers often do not deal directly with the party ultimately responsible for defects in the products they buy. With the development of a corporate-based economy, consumers have been less able to bargain on equal terms with such parties in any event. The growing complexity of goods has made buyer inspections more difficult. Finally, the emergence of a full-fledged consumer society has meant that product-related losses occur more frequently and that the quality of consumer goods looms larger in the array of national concerns.

Due to all these developments, product liability law has moved from its earlier *caveat emptor* emphasis to a stance of *caveat venditor* (let the seller beware). This has been especially true since the 1960s, the decade marking the beginning of the "product liability explosion." Now, courts and legislatures intervene in private contracts for the sale of goods and impose liability regardless of fault in order to protect consumers. As a result, sellers and manufacturers of defective goods face greater liability and higher dollar damage recoveries for those defects. Underlying this shift toward *caveat venditor* is the belief that sellers, manufacturers, and their insurers are best able to bear the economic costs associated with product defects, and that such parties can often pass on these costs in the form of higher prices. Thus, the economic risk associated with defective products has been effectively spread throughout society, or socialized.

The Current "Crisis" in Product Liability Law

Modern product liability law and the socialization of risk strategy it reflects have come under increasing attack over the past 10 to 15 years. Such attacks often stress the difficulty some sellers and manufacturers have encountered in obtaining product liability insurance, and the increased costs of such insurance for almost all firms. Some observers blame insurance industry practices for most of these problems, while others trace them to the increased liability and greater damage recoveries generated by the product liability explosion.

Whatever their origin, the lessened availability and increased cost of product liability insurance sometimes have put sellers and manufacturers in a bind. Businesses unwilling or unable to secure expensive product liability insurance have run the risk of being crippled by large damage awards unless they self-insure, and the possibility of such awards makes self-insurance an expensive proposition today. Firms that decide to purchase insurance, on the other hand, face increased expenditures. In either case, the resulting costs may be difficult to completely pass on.

For all these reasons, recent years have witnessed many efforts to scale back the product liability explosion. This is one aspect of the tort reform movement discussed in the Negligence and Strict Liability chapter. However, despite the introduction of several federal reform bills, Congress has yet to make any major changes in product liability law. As a result, the state legislatures have become the major battlegrounds in the war over tort reform. Later in this chapter we occasionally note the results of such political activity.

THE PLAN OF THIS CHAPTER

Imagine that you buy a new automobile from a local car dealer. If you are a typical consumer, you might well expect that: (1) sales talk aside, the car will do what the salesperson said it would do; (2) the car also will live up to specific claims that the manufacturer and the dealer made in their advertisements; (3) the manufacturer and the dealer will perform as promised under the written warranty accompanying the car; (4) the car will be suitable for the ordinary purposes for which such cars are used (i.e., not perfect, but not a lemon either); (5) the car will be suitable for any *special* purposes that you relied on the dealer to consider when it advised you on model, engine, options, and so forth; (6) the car was properly designed and manufactured; (7) the car is free of significant defects or unusual problems about which you have not been warned; and (8) the car is free of any defects that would make it unreasonably dangerous to drive.

The first half of this chapter discusses certain *theories of product liability recovery* that help protect the expectations just described. These theories are rules of law allowing plaintiffs to recover for defective goods once they prove certain facts. Although product liability is an area where tort and contract overlap, technically some of these theories are contractual and some are tort-based. The contract theories all involve a product **warranty**: a contractual promise regarding the nature of the product sold. In warranty cases, plaintiffs claim that the product failed to live up to the seller's promise. In tort cases, on the other hand, plaintiffs usually argue that the defendant was negligent or that strict liability should apply.[3]

The second half of the chapter considers certain legal problems that are common to all the theories of recovery. For example, what kinds of damages can be obtained under each theory? When is the absence of privity still a defense for the seller or manufacturer? What happens if a seller or manufacturer includes contract language attempting to disclaim liability for defects or to limit a plaintiff's remedies? When and how does the plaintiff's carelessness, misuse of the product, or voluntary acceptance of a known product risk affect her ability to recover? The answers to these and other questions may vary from theory to theory.

EXPRESS WARRANTY

Creating an Express Warranty

An **express warranty** is based on the seller's words or on certain other voluntary behavior from which a promise can be inferred. UCC section 2–313(1) states that an express warranty can be created in any of three ways.

1. Any *affirmation of fact or promise* regarding the goods creates an express warranty that the goods will conform to that affirmation. For instance, a seller's statement that an insecticide kills certain insects creates an express warranty to that effect.

2. Any *description* of the goods creates an express warranty that the goods will conform to the description. This express warranty sometimes is difficult to distinguish from an express warranty by affirmation of fact or promise. But common examples include: (1) statements that goods are of a certain brand, type, or model (e.g., an IBM dot-matrix computer printer); (2) descriptive adjectives characterizing the product (e.g., shatterproof glass); and (3) drawings, blueprints, and technical specifications.

3. A *sample* or *model* of goods to be sold creates an express warranty that the rest of the goods will conform to the sample or model. A sample is an object drawn from an actual collection of goods to be sold, while a model is a replica offered for the buyer's inspection when the goods themselves are unavailable.

The first two kinds of express warranties can be either written or oral. Also, magic words like *warrant* or *guarantee* no longer are necessary to create an express warranty. Nor is it necessary that the seller have a specific intention to make a warranty.

Value, Opinion, and Sales Talk

Statements of *value* ("This chair would bring you $2,000 at an auction") or *opinion* ("I think that this chair is a genuine antique Louis XIV") do not create express warranties. Statements that amount to *sales talk* ("This chair is a good buy") also do not create express warranties. Of course, there is no sharp line between statements of value or opinion and sales talk, on the one hand, and express warranties, on the other. In close cases, a statement is more likely to be considered an express warranty if it is specific rather than indefinite, if it is stated in the sales contract rather than elsewhere,[4] or if it is unequivocal rather than hedged or qualified. Also, the relative knowledge possessed by the seller and the buyer can be an important factor. A car salesperson's statement about a used car, for instance, stands a greater chance of being an express warranty where

---

[3] Negligence and strict liability are discussed in the Negligence and Strict Liability chapter.

[4] Parol evidence rule problems can arise in express warranty cases. For example, a seller who used a written sale contract may argue that the rule excludes an alleged oral warranty. On the parol evidence rule, see the contracts chapter entitled Writing.

the buyer knows little about cars than where the buyer is another car dealer.

The Basis of the Bargain Problem

Under pre-Code law, there was no recovery for breach of an express warranty unless the buyer *relied* on that warranty in making the purchase. The UCC, however, only requires that the warranty be *part of the basis of the bargain*. The meaning of the Code's test is unclear. Some courts read it as saying that reliance still is necessary. Others, such as the *Ewers* court below, only require that the seller's warranty have been a *contributing factor* in the buyer's decision to purchase.

Advertisements

Statements made in advertisements, catalogs, or brochures *may* be express warranties. Such sources, however, often are filled with sales talk. Also, basis of the

bargain problems may arise where it is unclear whether or to what degree the statement really induced the buyer to make the purchase. For example, suppose that the buyer read an advertisement containing an express warranty one month before actually purchasing the product.

Multiple Express Warranties

What happens when the seller gives two or more express warranties and those warranties arguably conflict? UCC section 2–317 says that such warranties should be read as consistent with each other and as cumulative if it is reasonable to do so. If not, the intention of the parties controls. In determining that intention, courts should apply the following rules: (1) exact or technical specifications defeat a sample, a model, or general descriptive language; and (2) a sample defeats general descriptive language.

The following *Ewers* case involves a number of issues discussed in this section.

EWERS v. EISENZOPF
276 N.W.2d 802 (Wis. Sup. Ct. 1979)

Ewers, who owned a saltwater aquarium with tropical fish, purchased several seashells, a piece of coral, and a driftwood branch from the Verona Rock Shop. Just before the purchase, Ewers asked the salesclerk whether the items he bought were suitable for placement in a saltwater aquarium. The clerk replied that the items were "suitable for saltwater aquariums, if they [are] rinsed."

Ewers then made the purchase, took the items home, rinsed them for 20 minutes in a saltwater solution, and placed them in his aquarium. Within one week, 17 of Ewers's tropical fish died. The cause of death was pollution from toxic matter released into the water by the decay of once-living creatures contained in the shells and the coral. Preventing such pollution would have required a week-long cleansing process that involved soaking the shells and the coral in boiling water.

Ewers sued Eisenzopf, the owner of the shop, for breach of express warranty. The state small claims court, trial court, and circuit court found for Eisenzopf. The circuit court concluded that even if an express warranty existed, it was not breached, because the proper method for cleaning the purchased items was "little more than an extended rinsing or soaking." Ewers appealed to the Wisconsin Supreme Court.

Coffey, Justice.   Although section 2–313(2) does not require the magic words "warrant" or "guarantee" to establish an express warranty, a buyer has the burden of proving the purchase was consummated on the basis of factual representations regarding the title, character, quantity, quality, identity, or condition of the goods. No technical or particular words need be used to constitute an express warranty, yet whatever words are used must substantially mean the seller promises or undertakes to insure that certain facts are, or shall be, as he represents them. The statement by the sales clerk that the shells, coral, and branch were "suitable for salt water aquariums, if they [are] rinsed" is an affirmation of fact regarding the quality and condition of the goods sold.

The second element required to establish an express warranty is that the affirmation of fact pertaining to the goods must become a basis of the bargain. The statutory language does not require the affirmation to be the sole basis for the sale, only that it is *a factor* in the purchase. The seller's intent to establish a warranty and the buyer's reliance on the affirmation are not determinative. Certainly, the sales clerk's representations regarding the suitability of the goods induced Ewers to purchase the shells, coral, and branch, for if these items were not suitable for the fish tank, Ewers would not have consummated the transaction.

Additionally, we cannot agree with the circuit court that the curing or cleansing process to make the shells satisfactory for use is the same as the colloquial meaning of the word "rinsed." Had the seller more thoroughly described the required cleansing process of submerging the items in boiling water for a period of a week, we would be reaching a different result. But the goods did not and could not conform to the seller's affirmation of suitability for their intended use.

We hold that the seller's statements constituted an express warranty when the seller specifically stated that the merchandise would be suitable for use in the aquarium after rinsing. Therefore, the buyer is entitled to recover, as the terms of the warranty were not fulfilled. Judicial decisions must not inhibit the free flow of relevant information between the buyer and the seller. Nevertheless, a merchant must be cautious in going beyond "puffing" in making claims and representations about its product. Further, the seller must give specific directions when he claims the goods are suitable for an intended and limited use. A merchant's vague or incomplete directions will induce the purchase of merchandise, and often these directions are as misleading as when erroneous affirmations of fact are given. A merchant who knows the limitations of his product will bear no liability as long as he is truthful and accurate in his representations to the customer.

Judgment reversed in favor of Ewers.

IMPLIED WARRANTY OF MERCHANTABILITY

An **implied warranty** is a warranty created by *operation of law* rather than by the seller's express statements. Implied warranties arise once certain tests are met; whether the seller has assented to the warranty is of no concern. UCC section 2–314(1) creates the Code's **implied warranty of merchantability** by stating that "a warranty that the goods shall be merchantable is implied in a contract for their sale if the seller is a merchant with respect to goods of that kind." The implied warranty of merchantability is a clear example of government intervention into private contracts to protect an allegedly weaker party—here, one who buys goods from a merchant.

In an implied warranty of merchantability case, plaintiffs argue that the seller breached the warranty by selling goods that were not merchantable, and that this breach caused the loss of which they complain. Under section 2–314, such claims can be successful only where the seller is a *merchant with respect to goods of the kind sold.*[5] A housewife's sale of homemade preserves or a hardware store owner's sale of a used car, for example, do not trigger the implied warranty of merchantability.

The Merchantability Standard

UCC section 2–314(2) states that, to be merchantable, goods must at least: (1) pass without objection in the trade; (2) be fit for the ordinary purposes for which such goods are used; (3) be of even kind, quality, and quantity within each unit (case, package, or carton); (4) be

---

[5] The term merchant is defined in the Introduction to Contracts chapter.

adequately contained, packaged, and labeled; (5) conform to any promises or statements of fact made on the container or label; and (6) in the case of fungible goods, be of fair average quality. The most important of these requirements is that the goods must be *fit for the ordinary purposes for which such goods are used.* The goods need not be perfect to be fit for their ordinary purposes. Rather, they only must meet the reasonable expectations of the average consumer.

Application of the Standard

The tests of merchantability just stated are broad, flexible standards whose application requires courts to exercise case-by-case discretion. Tests of this kind are almost inevitable given the wide range of products sold in the United States today and the varied defects they can present. Still, a few generalizations about these tests are possible.

Where the goods fail to function properly or have harmful side effects, it is easy to conclude that they are not merchantable. A crop herbicide that fails to kill weeds or damages the crop, for example, is not fit for the ordinary purposes for which crop herbicides are used. In cases involving allergic reactions to drugs or other products, courts frequently find the defendant liable if it was reasonably foreseeable that an appreciable number of consumers would suffer the reaction. As the following *Marriott* case reveals, there is some disagreement about the applicable standard when food products are alleged to be unmerchantable because they contain harmful objects or substances. Under the *foreign-natural* test used by some courts, the defendant is liable if the object or substance is "foreign" to the product, but not if it is "natural" to that product. Increasingly, however, courts employ a test that is probably more advantageous to plaintiffs: whether the food product met the consumer's *reasonable expectations.*

YONG CHA HONG v. MARRIOTT CORPORATION
3 UCC Rep. Serv. 2d 83 (D. Md. 1987)

Yong Cha Hong purchased some take-out fried chicken from a Roy Rogers Family Restaurant owned by the Marriott Corporation. While eating a chicken wing from her order, she bit into an object that she perceived to be a worm. Claiming permanent injuries and great physical and emotional upset from this incident, Hong sued Marriott for $500,000 in federal district court under the implied warranty of merchantability. After introducing an expert's report alleging that the object in the chicken wing was not a worm, Marriott moved for summary judgment. It claimed that the case involved no disputed issues of material fact, and that there was no breach of the implied warranty of merchantability as a matter of law.

Smalkin, District Judge. It appears that the item encountered by plaintiff was probably not a worm or other parasite, although plaintiff, in her deposition, steadfastly maintains that it was a worm. If it was not a worm (i.e., if the expert analysis is correct), it was either one of the chicken's major blood vessels (the aorta) or its trachea, both of which would appear worm-like (although not meaty like a worm, but hollow). For [present] purposes, the court will assume that the item was not a worm. Precisely how the aorta or trachea wound up in this hapless chicken's wing is a fascinating, but as yet unanswered (and presently immaterial), question.

Does Maryland law provide a breach of warranty remedy for personal injury flowing from an unexpected encounter with an inedible part of the chicken's anatomy in a piece of fast food fried chicken? Marriott contends that there can be no recovery unless the offending item was a foreign object, i.e., not part of the chicken itself.

In many cases that have denied [implied] warranty recovery as a matter of law, the injurious substance was, as in this case, a natural (though inedible) part of the edible item consumed. Thus, in *Shapiro v. Hotel Statler Corp.* (1955), recovery was denied for a fish bone in "Hot Barquette of Seafood Mornay." But in all these cases the natural item was reasonably to be expected in the dish by its very nature, under the prevailing expectation of any reasonable consumer. Indeed, precisely this "reasonable expectation" test has been adopted in a number of cases. The reasonable expectation test has largely displaced the foreign-natural test adverted to by Marriott. This court is confident that Maryland would apply the reasonable expectation rule.

The court cannot conclude that the presence of a trachea or an aorta in a fast food fried chicken wing is so reasonably to be expected as to render it merchantable, as a matter of law. This is not like the situation [in a previous case] involving a one centimeter bone in a piece of fried fish. Everyone but a fool knows that tiny bones may remain in even the best filets of fish. This case is more like [another decision], where the court held that the issue was for the trier of fact, on a claim arising from a cherry pit in cherry ice cream. Thus, a question is presented that precludes the grant of summary judgment. The jury must determine whether a piece of fast food fried chicken is merchantable if it contains an inedible item of the chicken's anatomy. Of course, the jury will be instructed that the consumer's reasonable expectations form a part of the merchantability concept.

Marriott's motion for summary judgment denied.

Note: In another part of its opinion, the court also allowed the plaintiff to argue that the item was actually a worm when the case went to trial.

IMPLIED WARRANTY OF FITNESS

As stated in the following *Dempsey* case, the Code's **implied warranty of fitness for a particular purpose** is narrower and more specific than the implied warranty of merchantability. According to UCC section 2–315, the implied warranty of fitness arises where: (1) the seller has reason to know a particular purpose for which the buyer requires the goods, (2) the seller has reason to know that the buyer is relying on the seller's skill or judgment to select suitable goods, and (3) the buyer actually relies on the seller's skill or judgment in purchasing the goods. If these tests are met, there is an implied warranty that the goods will be fit for the buyer's *particular* purpose.

In many fitness warranty cases, buyers effectively put themselves in the seller's hands by making their needs known and stating that they are relying on the seller to select goods that will satisfy those needs. But sellers also can be liable where the circumstances reasonably indicate that the buyer has a particular purpose and is relying on the seller to satisfy that purpose, even though the buyer fails to make either explicit. However, buyers may have trouble recovering where they are more expert than the seller, submit specifications for the goods they wish to buy, inspect the goods, actually select them, or insist on a particular brand.

The implied warranty of fitness differs from the implied warranty of merchantability in several ways. The seller need not be a merchant for the fitness warranty to exist. Otherwise, however, the fitness warranty has a narrower scope than the implied warranty of merchantability. Section 2–315's three-part test obviously limits the range of situations in which the fitness warranty can arise. Under section 2–315, moreover, sellers only warrant that the goods will be fit for the buyer's *particular* purposes, not the *ordinary* purposes for which such goods are used. If a 400-pound man asks a department store for a hammock that will support his weight but is sold a hammock that only can support normally sized people, there is a breach of the implied warranty of fitness but no breach of the implied warranty of merchant ability. If the hammock cannot support *anyone's* weight, however, both warranties are breached.

DEMPSEY v. ROSENTHAL

468 N.Y.S.2d 441 (N.Y. Civ. Ct. 1983)

Ruby Dempsey purchased a nine-week-old pedigreed male poodle from the American Kennels Pet Stores. She named the poodle Mr. Dunphy. Dempsey later testified that before making the purchase, she told the salesperson that she wanted a dog suitable for breeding purposes. Five days after the sale, she had Mr. Dunphy examined by a veterinarian, who discovered that the poodle had one undescended testicle. This condition did not seriously affect Mr. Dunphy's fertility, but it was a genetic defect that would probably be passed on to any offspring sired. Also, a dog with this condition could not be used as a show dog.

Dempsey demanded a refund from American Kennels, but her demand was denied. She then sued in small claims court, alleging that American Kennels had breached the implied warranty of fitness.

Saxe, Judge.   UCC sections 2–314 and 2–315 make it clear that the warranty of fitness for a particular purpose is narrower, more specific, and more precise than the warranty of merchant-ability, which involves fitness for the *ordinary* purposes for which goods are used. The following are the conditions that are not required by the implied warranty of merchantability, but that must be present if a plaintiff is to recover on the basis of the implied warranty of fitness: (1) the seller must have reason to know the buyer's particular purpose, (2) the seller must have reason to know that the buyer is relying on the seller's skill or judgment to furnish appropriate goods, and (3) the buyer must, in fact, rely upon the seller's skill or judgment.

I find that the warranty of fitness for a particular purpose has been breached. Dempsey testified that she specified to the salesperson that she wanted a dog that was suitable for breeding purposes. Although this is disputed by the defendant, the credible testimony supports Dempsey's version of the event. Further, it is reasonable for the seller of a pedigreed dog to assume that the buyer intends to breed it. But it is undisputed by the experts here (for both sides) that Mr. Dunphy was as capable of siring a litter as a male dog with two viable and descended testicles. This, the defendant contends, compels a finding in its favor. I disagree. While it is true that Mr. Dunphy's fertility level may be unaffected, his stud value, because of this hereditary condition (which is likely to be passed on to future generations), is severely diminished.

Judgment for Dempsey.

NEGLIGENCE

Product liability suits based on the theory of **negligence** discussed in the Negligence and Strict Liability chapter generally allege that the seller or manufacturer breached a duty to the plaintiff by failing to eliminate a reasonably foreseeable risk of harm associated with the product. Such suits typically claim one or more of the following: (1) improper *manufacture* of the goods (including improper materials and packaging), (2) improper *inspection*, (3) a failure to provide adequate *warnings* regarding hazards or defects, and (4) defective *design*.

Improper Manufacture

Negligence suits alleging the manufacturer's improper assembly, materials, or packaging often encounter problems because the evidence needed to prove a breach of duty is under the defendant's control. However, liberal modern discovery rules and the doctrine of *res ipsa loquitur* can help plaintiffs establish a breach in such situations.[6]

Improper Inspection

Manufacturers have a general duty to inspect their products for defects that create a reasonably foreseeable risk of harm, if such an inspection would be practicable and effective. As before, *res ipsa loquitur* and modern discovery rules can help plaintiffs prove their case against the manufacturer.

The courts of most states traditionally have held that middlemen such as retailers and wholesalers have a duty to inspect the goods they sell only when they have actual knowledge or reason to know of a defect. In addition, such parties generally have no duty to inspect where this would be unduly difficult, burdensome, or time-consuming. Unless the product defect is obvious, for example, middlemen usually are not liable for failing to inspect goods sold in the manufacturer's original packages or containers.

On the other hand, sellers who prepare, install, or repair the goods they sell ordinarily have a duty to inspect those goods. Examples include restaurants, automobile dealers, and installers of household products. Usually, however, the scope of the inspection need only be consistent with the preparation, installation, or repair work performed. Thus, it is unlikely that such sellers are required to discover hidden or latent defects.

In cases where there was a duty to inspect and the inspection would have revealed a defect, further duties obviously can arise. For example, a seller or manufacturer may be required not to sell the product in its defective state, or at least to give a suitable warning.

Failure to Warn

Sellers and manufacturers have a general duty to give an appropriate warning when their products pose a reasonably foreseeable risk of harm. But in determining whether there was a duty to warn and whether the defendant's warning was adequate, courts often consider other factors in addition to the reasonable foreseeability of the risk. One such factor is the *magnitude or severity* of the likely harm. Another is the *ease or difficulty of providing an appropriate warning*. In addition, there is no duty to warn where the risk is *open and obvious*. The likely *effectiveness* of a warning is another factor courts consider.

Design Defects

Manufacturers have a general duty to design their products so as to avoid reasonably foreseeable risks of harm. Like failure-to-warn cases, however, design defect cases frequently involve other factors in addition to the reasonable foreseeability of harm. As before, one of these factors is the *magnitude or severity* of the foreseeable harm. Two others are *industry practices* at the time the product was manufactured and the *state of the art* (the state of existing scientific and technical knowledge) at that time. Yet another is the product's compliance or noncompliance with *government safety regulations*.[7]

Sometimes courts employ *risk-benefit analysis* when weighing these factors. In such analyses, three other factors—the design's *social utility*, the *effectiveness of alternative designs*, and the *cost of safer designs*—often figure prominently in the weighing process. Even where the balancing process indicates that the design was not defective, courts still may impose a duty to provide a suitable warning.

The following *Daniell* case involves both a design defect claim and a failure-to-warn claim.

---

[6] Discovery is discussed in The Resolution of Private Disputes chapter, and *res ipsa loquitur* in the Negligence and Strict Liability chapter.

[7] Some states have statutes stating that a product's compliance with state or federal product safety regulations creates a rebuttable presumption that it was not defective. Also, a few states have statutory state-of-the-art defenses.

DANIELL v. FORD MOTOR COMPANY

581 F. Supp. 728 (D.N.M. 1984)

Connie Daniell attempted to commit suicide by locking herself inside the trunk of her 1973 Ford LTD. Daniell remained in the trunk for nine days, but survived after finally being rescued. Later, Daniell sued Ford in negligence to recover for her resulting physical and psychological injuries. She contended that the LTD was defectively designed because its trunk did not have an internal release or opening mechanism. She also argued that Ford was liable for negligently failing to warn her that the trunk could not be unlocked from within. Ford moved for summary judgment.

Baldock, District Judge.   As a general principle, a design defect is actionable only where the condition of the product is unreasonably dangerous to the user or consumer. Under negligence, a manufacturer has a duty to consider only those risks of injury which are foreseeable. A risk is not foreseeable where a product is used in a manner which could not reasonably be anticipated by the manufacturer and that use is the cause of the plaintiff's injury.

The purposes of an automobile trunk are to transport, stow, and secure the spare tire, luggage, and other goods and to protect those items from the weather. The design features of a trunk make it well near impossible that an adult intentionally would enter the trunk and close the lid. The dimensions of a trunk, the height of its sill and its load floor, and the efforts to first lower the lid and then to engage its latch, are among the design features which encourage closing and latching the trunk lid while standing outside the vehicle. The court holds that the plaintiff's use of the trunk compartment as a means to attempt suicide was an unforeseeable use as a matter of law. Therefore, the manufacturer had no duty to design an internal release or opening mechanism that might have prevented this occurrence.

Nor did the manufacturer have a duty to warn the plaintiff of the danger of her conduct, given the plaintiff's unforeseeable use of the product. Another reason why the manufacturer had no duty to warn the plaintiff of the risk inherent in crawling into an automobile trunk and closing the lid is [that] such a risk is obvious. There is no duty to warn of known dangers. Moreover, the potential efficacy of any warning, given the plaintiff's use of the trunk for a deliberate suicide attempt, is questionable.

Having held that the plaintiff's conception of the manufacturer's duty is in error, the court need not reach the issues of comparative negligence or other defenses such as assumption of risk.

Ford's motion for summary judgment granted; Daniell loses.

STRICT LIABILITY

Introduction

Beginning in the early 1960s, courts seeking to compensate those injured by defective products began to impose **strict liability** (liability irrespective of fault) on sellers of such products. This movement toward strict liability received a big boost when the American Law Institute promulgated section 402A of the *Restatement (Second) of Torts* in 1965. By now, the vast majority of the states have adopted some form of strict products liability. As the following *Roysdon* case makes evident, a few states have even codified section 402A in some form.

Of the various legal developments comprising the product liability explosion, none is more important than the states' adoption of strict product liability. The main reason for strict liability's adoption is the socialization of risk strategy discussed at the beginning of this chapter. Another common justification for strict liability is that it stimulates manufacturers to design and build safer products. Strict liability also removes a barrier to recovery that has long plagued plaintiffs in negligence suits: the need to prove a breach of duty.

Section 402A's Requirements

Because it is the most common form of strict product liability, we limit our discussion of the subject to section 402A. Section 402A provides that a "seller . . . engaged in the business of selling" a particular product is liable for physical harm or property damage suffered by the ultimate user or consumer of that product, if the product was "in a defective condition unreasonably dangerous to the user or consumer or to his property." This rule applies even though "the seller has exercised all possible care in the preparation and sale of his product." Thus, section 402A states a rule of strict liability that eliminates the plaintiff's need to prove a breach of duty.

However, the liability imposed by section 402A is not absolute, for the section applies only if certain tests are met.

1. The seller must be *engaged in the business of selling the product that harmed the plaintiff.* Thus, section 402A imposes liability only on parties who resemble UCC merchants because they regularly sell the product at issue. For example, the section does not apply to a college professor's or a clothing store's sale of a used car.

2. The product must be in a *defective condition* when sold, and also must be *unreasonably dangerous* because of that condition. The usual test of a product's defective condition resembles the general test of merchantability discussed above: whether the product meets the reasonable expectations of the average consumer. The *Roysdon* case develops a similar standard.

As *Roysdon* states, an unreasonably dangerous product is one that is dangerous to an extent beyond the reasonable contemplation of the average consumer. Under this test, good whiskey is not unreasonably dangerous even though it can cause harm in certain circumstances,

but whiskey contaminated with a poisonous substance falls within section 402A. However, some courts balance the product's social utility against its danger when determining whether it is unreasonably dangerous.

Due to section 402A's unreasonably dangerous requirement, it covers a smaller range of product defects than the implied warranty of merchantability. A power mower that simply fails to operate, for instance, is not unreasonably dangerous, although it would violate the merchantability standard. Many courts, however, blur the defective condition and unreasonably dangerous requirements, and a few have done away with the latter test. Under the state statute in *Roysdon*, on the other hand, a defendant could be liable if the product was *either* defective or unreasonably dangerous.

3. Finally, defendants can avoid section 402A liability where the product was *substantially modified* by the plaintiff or another party after the sale, and the modification contributed to the plaintiff's injury or other loss.

Applications of Section 402A

Design defect and failure-to-warn suits can be brought under section 402A. Even though section 402A is a strict liability provision, the standards applied in such cases closely resemble those used in negligence cases. Thus, our previous discussion of negligence-based design defect and failure-to-warn suits generally governs section 402A as well.

Because it applies to sellers, section 402A covers retailers and other middlemen who market goods containing defects that they did not create and may not have been able to discover. As we have seen, such parties often escape negligence liability. But some courts have found them liable under section 402A's strict liability rule. Using a variety of methods, however, other states have given middlemen some protection against 402A liability.

Finally, some courts have concluded that section 402A, or strict liability in general, does *not* apply in certain nonconsumer contexts. The *Salt River* case later in the chapter, for example, states that strict liability does not govern cases in which the plaintiff and the defendant both are business entities who: (1) dealt in a commercial setting, (2) had relatively equal bargaining power, (3) bargained the specifications of the product, and (4) negotiated the risk of loss from defects in the product.

ROYSDON v. R. J. REYNOLDS TOBACCO CO.

849 F. 2d 230 (6th Cir. 1988)

Floyd Roysdon began smoking Camel cigarettes in 1946, switching to Winstons during the 1960s. Both brands are products of the R. J. Reynolds Tobacco Company. In late 1983, Roysdon's left leg had to be amputated below the knee after two surgical incisions of his foot failed to heal due to severe peripheral atherosclerotic vascular disease. Some medical evidence indicates that this condition is caused by cigarette smoking.

In 1984, Roysdon sued R. J. Reynolds for his personal injury in federal district court, alleging that the Reynolds cigarettes he smoked were defective and/or unreasonably dangerous. After limiting Roysdon's possible recovery to the period 1974–84 under Tennessee's 10-year statute of repose, the court directed a verdict for R. J. Reynolds. Roysdon appealed. (Statutes of repose are discussed later in the chapter.)

Ryan, Circuit Judge.   We must determine whether, under Tennessee law, a products liability action will lie where the product is *either* defective or unreasonably dangerous, or only when the product is *both* defective and unreasonably dangerous. Tennessee Code section 29–28–105(a) provides: "A manufacturer or seller of a product shall not be liable for any injury to person or property caused by the product unless the product is determined to be in a defective condition *or* unreasonably dangerous at the time it left the control of the manufacturer or seller" (emphasis added). Prior to the enactment of section 29–28–105, Tennessee had judicially adopted section 402A of the *Restatement (Second) of Torts*, which requires the plaintiff to prove that the product was both defective *and* unreasonably dangerous. However, clearly the Tennessee legislature intended to deviate from section 402A and allow a products liability action when the product is either defective or unreasonably dangerous.

Tennessee law defines a "defective condition" as a condition of a product that renders it unsafe for normal or anticipatable handling and consumption. Thus, consumer knowledge about the risks inherent in the use of a product is one factor to be considered when determining if a product is defective. The normal use of cigarettes is known by ordinary consumers to present grave health risks, but that is not to say that defendant's cigarettes were flawed in the sense that they were improperly manufactured or contained dangerous impurities. Because the record contains no evidence that the use of the defendant's cigarettes presents risks greater than those known to be associated with smoking, a reasonable jury could not find that the cigarettes were defective.

 A product is "unreasonably dangerous" if it is dangerous to an extent beyond that which could be contemplated by the ordinary consumer who purchases it, with the ordinary knowledge common to the community as to its characteristics. The district court took judicial notice that knowledge that cigarette smoking is harmful can be considered part of the common knowledge of the community. Remembering that this action is limited to the ten years preceding the filing of the complaint, this approach was appropriate. The extensive information regarding the risks of smoking available to the public during that time precluded the existence of a jury question as to whether cigarettes are unreasonably dangerous. Whether there was knowledge regarding Roysdon's specific medical problem is irrelevant in light of the serious nature of the other diseases known at that time to be caused by cigarette smoking.

Directed verdict for R. J. Reynolds affirmed.

CONCEPT REVIEW

COMPARING THE MAJOR PRODUCT LIABILITY THEORIES—THE BASICS

Theory	Tort or Contract	Type of Defendant	Nature of Goods Sold	Remarks
Express Warranty	Contract	Seller of goods	Not as warranted by affirmation of fact or promise, description, sample, or model	Exemption for statements of value, opinion, or sales talk
Implied Warranty of Merchantability	Contract	Merchant for goods sold	Not merchantable; usually, not fit for ordinary purposes for which such goods used	Merchantability has other aspects
Implied Warranty of Fitness	Contract	Seller of goods	Not fit for buyer's particular purposes	Seller must have reason to know of buyer's needs and buyer's reliance, and buyer must actually rely
Negligence	Tort	Manufacturer or seller of goods	"Defective" due to improper manufacture, inspection, design, or failure to give suitable warning	Limited inspection duty for middlemen
Section 402A	Tort	Seller engaged in business of selling product sold	Defective and unreasonably dangerous	Strict liability; design defect and failure-to-warn suits possible

OTHER THEORIES OF RECOVERY

Warranty of Title

In addition to the other implied warranties discussed earlier, a seller of goods normally warrants that: (1) the title he conveys is good and transfer of that title is rightful, and (2) the goods are free from any lien or security interest of which the buyer lacks knowledge. Thus, a buyer may recover damages against his seller where, for example, the seller has marketed stolen goods or goods that are subject to a third party's security interest. Also, a seller who is a merchant in goods of the kind sold normally warrants that the goods are free of any rightful patent, copyright, or trademark infringement claim of a third party.

The Magnuson-Moss Act

The portions of the federal Magnuson-Moss Warranty Act that are relevant here apply to sales of *consumer products* that cost more than *$10 per item* and that are made to a *consumer*.[8] The act defines a consumer product as tangible personal property normally used for personal, family, or household purposes. If a seller gives a *written warranty* for such a product to a *consumer*, the warranty must be designated full or limited. If the seller elects to give a full warranty, it must promise to: (1) *remedy* any defects in the product and (2) *replace*

---

[8] Other portions of the Magnuson-Moss Act are discussed later in this chapter and in the Federal Trade Commission Act and Consumer Protection Laws chapter.

the product or *refund* its purchase price if, after a reasonable number of attempts, it cannot be repaired.[9] These terms are not imposed where the seller chooses to give a limited warranty; in this case, the seller is bound to whatever promises it actually makes. Remember, however, that neither warranty applies if the seller simply declines to give a written warranty.

Misrepresentation

Section 402B of the *Restatement (Second) of Torts* allows *consumers* to recover for *personal injury* resulting from certain *misrepresentations* regarding goods they have purchased. For the consumer to recover, the misrepresentation must: (1) be made by one engaged in the business of selling goods of the kind purchased; (2) be made to the public by advertising, labels, or similar means; (3) concern a fact *material* to the goods purchased; and (4) be *actually* and *justifiably* relied on by the consumer. Suppose that the manufacturer of a laxative states in its advertising that the laxative will produce no adverse side effects if used as directed. Smith, who has been influenced by the advertisements and has no reason to doubt their accuracy, buys a bottle of the laxative from a drugstore. If after using it according to directions, Smith suffers injury to his digestive system, he will be able to recover from the manufacturer for that injury.

INDUSTRYWIDE LIABILITY

The recent development that we term *industrywide liability* is a way for plaintiffs to bypass problems of *causation* that exist where several firms within an industry have manufactured a harmful standardized product, and it is impossible for the plaintiff to prove *which* firm produced the product that injured her. In such cases, each potential defendant can argue that the plaintiff should lose because she has not shown that its product caused the harm of which she complains. The usual reasons for the plaintiff's inability to identify the manufacturer whose product caused the harm are the number of firms producing the product and the time lag between exposure to the product and the appearance of the injury. Most of the cases presenting this problem have involved DES (an antimiscarriage drug that has produced various ailments in the daughters of the women to whom it was administered) or diseases resulting from long-term exposure to asbestos.

In such cases, some courts continue to deny recovery under traditional causation rules. Using various theories whose many details are beyond the scope of this text, however, other courts have made it easier for plaintiffs to recover. Where recovery is allowed, some of these courts have *apportioned* liability among the firms that might have produced the harm-causing product. Typically, the apportionment is based on market share at some chosen time. Courts allowing such recoveries still disagree on many key points.

DAMAGES IN PRODUCT LIABILITY SUITS

At this point, we begin to consider several problems that are common to each major theory of product liability recovery, but that may be resolved differently from theory to theory.[10] The first such problem is the damages obtainable in product liability cases.

The relief sought by the plaintiff is one of the most important factors influencing his choice of theories in a product liability suit. Thus, it is important to determine which kinds of damages are awarded under each theory. The three major types of damages recoverable in product liability cases—basis of the bargain damages, consequential damages, and punitive damages—and the theories under which they can be recovered are described below. It is possible for one lawsuit to involve claims for all these sorts of damages.

Basis of the Bargain Damages   Where goods are defective, the buyer has not received full value for the purchase price. The resulting loss, usually called basis of the bargain damages or direct economic loss, is measured by the value of the goods as promised under the contract, minus the value of the goods actually received.

Where awarded: Under the UCC, basis of the bargain damages are recoverable where there was privity of

---

[9] Also, many states have enacted so-called lemon laws that may apply only to motor vehicles, or to various other consumer products as well. The versions applying to motor vehicles generally require the manufacturer to replace the vehicle or refund its purchase price once certain conditions are met. These conditions may include the following: a serious defect covered by warranty, a certain number of unsuccessful attempts at repair or a certain amount of downtime due to attempted repairs, and the manufacturer's failure to show that the defect is curable.

[10] We do not consider how these problems are resolved under the warranty of title, the Magnuson-Moss Act, or section 402B.

contract (a direct contractual relation) between the plaintiff and the defendant.[11] Thus, plaintiffs who dealt directly with the defendant can recover such damages in *express and implied warranty* cases. As you will see in the next section, however, only occasionally will a plaintiff who sues for breach of warranty and who lacks privity with the defendant obtain basis of the bargain damages. Such recoveries most often occur where an express warranty was made to a remote plaintiff through advertising, brochures, or labels. Finally, basis of the bargain damages usually are not recoverable in *negligence and strict liability* cases.

Consequential Damages   This is an umbrella term used to describe various kinds of losses that are consequences of the product defect. Consequential damages include: **personal injury**, **property damage** (damage to the plaintiff's other property), and **indirect economic loss** (e.g., lost profits or lost business reputation).

Another sort of consequential damages, often called **noneconomic loss**, includes losses attributable to pain and suffering, physical impairment, mental distress, loss of enjoyment of life, loss of companionship or consortium, inconvenience, and disfigurement. Noneconomic loss usually is regarded as part of the plaintiff's personal injury claim. In recent years, several states have limited noneconomic loss recoveries, typically by imposing a $250,000 to $500,000 cap on such recoveries.

Where awarded: In UCC *express and implied warranty* suits where privity exists between the plaintiff and the defendant, the plaintiff can recover for: (1) personal injury and property damage, if either proximately resulted from the breach of warranty; and (2) indirect economic loss, if the defendant had reason to know that this was likely. As you will see in the next section, a UCC plaintiff who lacks privity with the defendant has a fairly good chance of recovering for any personal injury or property damage she may have suffered. But recovery for indirect economic loss is rare because remote sellers usually cannot foresee such losses.

Plaintiffs in *negligence and strict liability* cases normally can recover for provable personal injury and property damage. Recoveries for foreseeable indirect economic loss sometimes are allowed.

Punitive Damages   Punitive or exemplary damages are intended to punish defendants who have acted in an especially outrageous fashion, and to deter them and others from so acting in the future. Under product liability theories where punitive damages are allowed, the standards for their recovery vary. Perhaps the most common standard is the defendant's conscious or reckless disregard for the safety of those likely to be affected by the goods. Examples of such behavior include concealment of known product hazards, knowing violation of government or industry product safety standards, failure to correct known dangerous defects, and grossly inadequate product testing or quality control procedures. Among the other standards employed by state punitive damages statutes are terms such as fraud, oppression, wantonness, and malice.

Due to their perceived frequency, size, and effect on business firms, punitive damages have been subjected to state tort reform regulation throughout the 1980s. The approaches taken by these statutes vary. Many state the standards for punitive damage recovery and the plaintiff's burden of proof (often clear and convincing evidence); some state a variety of factors courts should consider when ruling on punitive damage awards; and some establish special procedures for punitive damage determinations. Also, several states have limited the size of punitive damage recoveries, usually by restricting them to some multiple of the plaintiff's actual damages (e.g., one to three times those damages), or by putting a flat dollar cap on punitive damage awards (e.g., $250,000).

Where awarded: Due to the traditional rule that punitive damages are not available in contract cases, they are usually not awarded in *express and implied warranty* suits. In tort suits based on *negligence and strict liability*, punitive damages generally are recoverable under the standards set out above.

Figure 1 summarizes the plaintiff's chances of recovering the most important kinds of damages in contract and tort cases.

THE NO-PRIVITY DEFENSE

Introduction

Today, defective products often move through long chains of distribution before reaching the person they harm. This means that the plaintiff in a product liability suit often has not dealt directly with the party who was

---

[11] The Remedies for Breach of Sales Contracts chapter contains a general discussion of the buyer's remedies under Article 2 of the UCC.

FIGURE 1 When the Various Kinds of Damages Are Recoverable

Type of Damages	Express and Implied Warranty	Negligence and Section 402A
Basis of the Bargain	*Within privity:* Yes *Outside privity:* Occasionally	Rarely
Personal Injury and Property Damage	*Within privity:* If proximate result of breach *Outside privity:* Fairly good chance	Yes
Indirect Economic Loss	*Within privity:* If defendant has reason to know this likely *Outside privity:* Rarely	Sometimes
Punitive Damages	Rarely	Yes, in appropriate cases

ultimately responsible for his losses. Figure 2 depicts a hypothetical chain of distribution in which goods defectively produced by a manufacturer of component parts move vertically through the manufacturer of a product in which those parts are used, a wholesaler, and a retailer, ultimately reaching the buyer. Depending on the nature of the defect, its consequences may move horizontally as well, affecting members of the buyer's family, guests in his home, and even bystanders. If the buyer or one of these parties suffers some loss due to the defect in the component parts, can he successfully sue the component parts manufacturer or any other party in the vertical chain of distribution with whom he did not directly deal?

As you saw at the beginning of this chapter, such suits were unlikely to succeed under 19th-century law. This was due to the general rule that there could be no recovery for losses caused by defective goods unless there was privity of contract between the plaintiff and the defendant. In the example above, for instance, the buyer would have been required to sue his dealer. If the buyer was successful, the retailer might have sued the wholesaler, and so on up the chain. For a variety of reasons (including a middleman's limited negligence liability for failure to inspect), the party ultimately responsible for the defect often escaped liability.

Negligence and Strict Liability Cases

By now, the old no-liability-outside-privity rule has been severely eroded in tort suits. It has little, if any, effect in *strict liability* cases, where even bystanders frequently recover against remote manufacturers. In *negligence* cases, a plaintiff generally can recover against a remote defendant if the plaintiff's injury was a

FIGURE 2 A Hypothetical Chain of Distribution

reasonably foreseeable consequence of the defect. Thus, depending on the circumstances, bystanders and other distant parties might recover against a manufacturer in negligence as well.

Warranty Cases

However, the no-privity defense still retains some vitality in cases brought under the UCC. The "law" on this subject is complex and confusing. Under the Code, the privity question is formally governed by section 2–318, which comes in three alternative versions from which the states can choose. The language of section 2–318, however, sometimes is a poor guide to the courts' actual behavior in UCC privity cases.

UCC Section 2–318   Alternative A to section 2–318 declares that a seller's express or implied warranty runs to natural persons in the family or household of *his* (the seller's) buyer and to guests in his buyer's home, if they suffer personal injury and if it was reasonable to expect that they might use, consume, or be affected by the goods sold. On its face, Alternative A does little to undermine the traditional no-privity defense. In Figure 2, Alternative A would merely allow the buyer, his family, and guests in his home to sue the *retailer* for their personal injury.

Alternatives B and C go much further. Alternative B extends the seller's express or implied warranty to any natural person who has suffered personal injury, if it was reasonable to expect that this person would use, consume, or be affected by the goods sold. Alternative C is much the same, but it also extends the warranty to "any person" (not just natural persons) and to those suffering injury in general (not just personal injury). If the reasonable-to-expect test is met, these two provisions should extend the warranty to many remote parties, including bystanders.

Departures from Section 2–318   For various reasons, the literal language of section 2–318 is of questionable relevance in UCC privity cases. For one thing, some states have adopted their own provisions on the privity question and do not follow any version of section 2–318. For another, one of the comments to section 2–318 says that Alternative A should not restrict courts from extending liability farther than the section expressly permits. The courts in states adopting Alternative A often have taken this hint, allowing recoveries by plaintiffs who would not have won if Alternative A were

read literally. Finally, versions B and C are fairly open-ended as written.

For these reasons, the plaintiff's ability to recover outside privity in warranty cases varies from state to state and situation to situation. Here, we merely indicate the most important factors affecting resolution of this question. These factors are:

1. Whether it is *reasonably foreseeable* that a party like the plaintiff would be harmed by the product defect in question. This factor is suggested by section 2–318's reasonable-to-expect language.

2. The *status of the plaintiff.* This factor is suggested by the "natural person" language of Alternatives A and B. On the average, consumers and other natural persons probably fare better outside privity than corporations and other business concerns.

3. The *type of damages* the plaintiff has suffered. This factor was noted in the previous section. In general, remote plaintiffs are: (a) most likely to recover for personal injury, (b) somewhat less likely to recover for property damage, (c) occasionally able to obtain basis of the bargain damages, and (d) rarely able to recover for indirect economic loss. Recall from the previous section that a remote plaintiff is most likely to receive basis of the bargain damages where an *express warranty* was made to him through advertising, brochures, or labels.

DISCLAIMERS AND REMEDY LIMITATIONS

Introduction

A product liability **disclaimer** is a clause in the sales contract whereby the seller attempts to eliminate its liability under one or more theories of recovery. A **remedy limitation** is a sales contract clause attempting to block the recovery of certain kinds of damages. Disclaimers attack the plaintiff's *theory of recovery*; if the disclaimer is effective, no damages of any sort are recoverable under that theory. A successful remedy limitation, on the other hand, prevents the plaintiff from recovering certain *types of damages*, but does not attack the plaintiff's theory of recovery. Damages not excluded still may be recovered, because the theory is left intact.

The basic argument for enforcing disclaimers and remedy limitations is freedom of contract. Also, because goods accompanied by an effective disclaimer or remedy limitation are apt to be cheaper than other goods, enforcing such clauses gives buyers the flexibility to get a lower price by accepting a greater risk of uncompensated defects. For purchases by ordinary consumers and other unsophisticated, relatively powerless buyers, however, these arguments often are illusory. In many such situations, the disclaimer or remedy limitation is presented in a standardized, take-it-or-leave-it fashion by the seller or manufacturer. In addition, it is doubtful whether many consumers read disclaimers and remedy limitations at the time of purchase, or would comprehend them if they were read. As a result, there is usually little or no genuine bargaining over product liability disclaimers or remedy limitations in consumer situations. Instead, they are effectively dictated by a seller with superior size and organization. These observations, however, are much less valid where the buyer is a business entity with the size, power, and business sophistication to engage in genuine bargaining with sellers.

Because the realities surrounding the sale differ from situation to situation, and because some theories of recovery are more hospitable to contractual limitation than others, the law regarding product liability disclaimers and remedy limitations is complicated. We begin with a lengthy discussion of implied warranty disclaimers. Then we examine disclaimers of express warranty liability, negligence liability, and strict liability, before considering remedy limitations separately.

Implied Warranty Disclaimers

To determine the enforceability of implied warranty disclaimers, one must consider several sets of intricate legal rules.[12] Figure 3 at the end of this subsection attempts to structure the various steps in this analysis.

The Basic Tests of UCC Section 2–316(2)   UCC section 2–316(2) seemingly makes it easy for sellers to disclaim the implied warranties of merchantability and fitness for a particular purpose. The section states that to exclude or modify the implied warranty of *merchantability*, the seller must: (1) use the word merchantability, and (2) make the disclaimer conspicuous if it is in writing. To exclude or modify the implied warranty of *fitness*, the seller must: (1) use a writing, and (2) make the disclaimer conspicuous. A disclaimer is conspicuous if it is so written that a reasonable person ought to have noticed it. Capital letters, larger type, contrasting type, and contrasting colors usually satisfy this test. In close cases, courts are less likely to deem a disclaimer conspicuous if the plaintiff is a consumer rather than a party of some business sophistication.

Note that unlike the fitness warranty disclaimer, a disclaimer of the implied warranty of merchantability can be oral. Note also that while disclaimers of the latter warranty always must use the word *merchantability*, no special language is needed to disclaim the implied warranty of fitness. For example, a conspicuous written statement that "THERE ARE NO WARRANTIES WHICH EXTEND BEYOND THE DESCRIPTION ON THE FACE HEREOF" disclaims the implied warranty of fitness but not the implied warranty of merchantability.

Other Ways to Disclaim Implied Warranties: Section 2–316(3)   According to UCC section 2–316(3)(a), sellers also can disclaim either implied warranty by using such terms as *with all faults*, *as is*, and *as they stand*. Some courts have held that these terms must be conspicuous in order to be effective as disclaimers. Also, because they ordinarily refer to used goods, these terms may be ineffective as disclaimers where *new* products are sold.

UCC section 2–316(3)(b) describes two situations where the buyer's *inspection* of the goods or her *refusal to inspect* can have the same practical effect as a disclaimer. If the buyer examines the goods before the sale and fails to discover a defect that should have been reasonably apparent to her, there can be no implied warranty suit based on that defect. Also, if the seller requests that the buyer examine the goods and the buyer refuses to do so, the buyer is not allowed to base an implied warranty suit on a defect that would have been reasonably apparent had she made the inspection. The definition of a "reasonably apparent" defect varies with the buyer's expertise. Unless the defect is blatant, ordinary consumers often may have little to fear from section 2–316(3)(b).

Finally, UCC section 2–316(3)(c) declares that an implied warranty can be excluded or modified by *course of dealing* (the parties' previous conduct), *course of performance* (the parties' previous conduct under the same contract), or *usage of trade* (any practice regularly observed in the trade). For example, if it is accepted in the local cattle trade that buyers who inspect the seller's cattle and reject certain animals must accept all defects in the cattle actually purchased, such buyers cannot mount an implied warranty suit for those defects.

---

[12] Also, sellers may try to *modify* the coverage of an implied warranty, or to *limit its duration*.

Unconscionable Disclaimers   From the above discussion, you might conclude that any seller who retains a minimally competent attorney can escape implied warranty liability almost at will. In fact, though, a seller's ability to disclaim implied warranties is restricted in various ways. As the *Salt River* case later in this section recognizes, one of these restrictions is the doctrine of *unconscionability* established by UCC section 2–302 and discussed in the contracts chapter entitled Illegality.

By now, almost all courts apply section 2–302's unconscionability standards to implied warranty disclaimers even though those disclaimers satisfy UCC section 2–316(2).[13] In making the unconscionability determination, courts consider and weigh the many factors typically examined in 2–302 cases. As *Salt River* suggests, courts tend to reject unconscionability claims where business parties have contracted in a commercial context. Nonetheless, there is a growing tendency to invalidate disclaimers imposed on relatively unsophisticated small- to medium-sized businesses by corporate giants. And implied warranty disclaimers

are often declared unconscionable in personal injury suits by ordinary consumers.

The Impact of Magnuson-Moss   The Magnuson-Moss Act creates another important set of limitations on a seller's ability to disclaim implied warranties. As you saw earlier, the act says that the sale of consumer goods to a consumer by a seller giving a written warranty obligates the seller to designate the warranty full or limited if the price of the goods exceeds $10 per item. If a full warranty is given, the seller may not disclaim, modify, or limit the duration of any implied warranty. If a limited warranty is given, the seller may not disclaim or modify any implied warranty but may limit its duration to the duration of the limited warranty if this is done conspicuously and if the limitation is not unconscionable. These provisions significantly restrict a seller's ability to disclaim implied warranty liability where the seller has given a written warranty to a consumer. Presumably, however, a seller still can disclaim by refusing to give a written warranty while placing the disclaimer on some other writing.

Figure 3 summarizes the enforceability of implied warranty disclaimers.

---

[13] Unconscionability probably has little application where implied warranty liability is disclaimed under UCC section 2–316(3).

FIGURE 3   The Enforceability of Implied Warranty Disclaimers

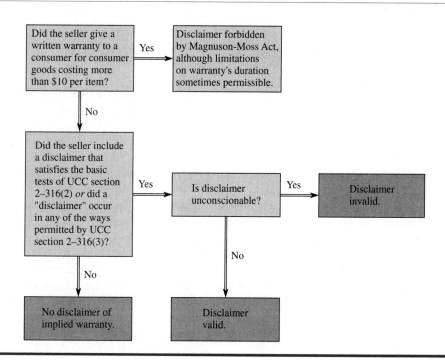

Express Warranty Disclaimers

UCC section 2–316(1) states that an express warranty and contract language seeming to disclaim it should be read consistently if possible, but that the disclaimer must give way if such a reading is unreasonable. Because it is generally unreasonable for a seller to exclude with one hand what she has freely and openly promised with the other, it is very difficult to disclaim an express warranty.

Negligence and Strict Liability Disclaimers

Disclaimers of negligence liability and strict liability are usually ineffective in cases involving ordinary consumers. As the *Salt River* case states, however, such disclaimers are enforced where business parties of relatively equal bargaining power dealt in a commercial setting and negotiated both the product's specifications and the risk of loss from defects in it (i.e., the disclaimer itself).

SALT RIVER PROJECT AGRICULTURAL IMPROVEMENT & POWER DISTRICT v. WESTINGHOUSE ELECTRIC CORPORATION

694 P. 2d 198 (Ariz. Sup. Ct. 1984)

The Salt River Agricultural Improvement and Power District, Arizona's second-largest electric utility, purchased a Local Maintenance Controller (LMC) from the Westinghouse Electric Corporation in 1973. The LMC was a device permitting manual (rather than computerized) operation of Salt River's gas turbine generators. Due to an apparent defect in the design of the LMC, the rotating blades in one of Salt River's gas turbine units were destroyed in 1974. The resulting damages were in excess of $1.9 million.

Salt River sued Westinghouse under, among other theories, section 402A and the implied warranty of fitness for a particular purpose. One issue in the case was the legal effect of certain clauses in Westinghouse's standard form acceptance (which were determined to be part of the parties' contract). These clauses included a disclaimer of the implied warranty of fitness that complied with UCC section 2–316 and another clause that the courts chose to read as a disclaimer of section 402A liability. After the trial court and the Arizona Court of Appeals held that these clauses blocked Salt River's claims and entered partial summary judgment for Westinghouse, Salt River appealed to the Arizona Supreme Court.

Feldman, Justice.   Salt River concedes the effectiveness of [the implied warranty disclaimer], but asserts that under the circumstances here [it is] unconscionable. Evidence showing that one party failed to negotiate a better deal than actually achieved does not establish that the agreement was unconscionable. Although a commercial purchaser is not doomed to failure in pressing an unconscionability claim, findings of unconscionability in a commercial setting are rare. We approve the court of appeals' resolution of the unconscionability issue as to the warranty disclaimer.

There is a difference between attempts to disclaim warranty liability and attempts to disclaim liability in tort. Some courts have held that disclaimers of tort liability are *per se* unenforceable. We do not go this far, but do acknowledge that the UCC rules for effectively disclaiming warranty obligations have no bearing on a seller's tort liability.

In a commercial setting there are often sound reasons for an enterprise to forgo warranty protections and to bargain away recourse to other means of recovery, including tort, should losses occur. For instance, a lower price for a product may be the *quid pro quo* for the buyer's assumption of risks of latent defects in the product. The cases indicate that courts are willing to give effect to contractual limitations on liability where the parties are on an equal footing. Courts take the most relaxed view when the parties are business entities. The California court of appeals has concluded that [strict liability] does not apply as between parties who: (1) deal in a commercial setting; (2) from positions of relatively equal bargaining strength; (3) bargain the specifications of the product; and (4) negotiate concerning the risk of loss from defects in it.

There is no doubt that Salt River and Westinghouse are both commercial giants and bargained for the LMC in a commercial setting. However, comparability of size among corporations does not mean that in a particular transaction a corporation has bargaining strength relatively equal to all other corporations of similar size. Much depends on the nature of the transaction, the nature of the product, the relative knowledge of the parties concerning the product, and the availability of other products to fit the needs of the purchaser. These are factual questions that need to be answered before the second factor will be satisfied. The finder of fact may conclude here that Salt River was forced to accept the LMC on Westinghouse's terms because no other device was available to enable it to save its $9,000,000 investment in turbines.

Moreover, there are factual questions concerning the bargaining for the specifications of the product, the third factor. Even though Salt River may be considered an expert in the field of electric utilities generally, its specific expertise in the manufacture of the LMC was not established. Thus, it is questionable whether Salt River bargained for the product specifications at all.

Most importantly, there is a genuine factual question whether the [disclaimer] was actually bargained for. The affidavit of Salt River's assistant general manager indicates that there was merely an exchange of standardized forms and that the language of the [disclaimer] was never discussed, much less negotiated. There is no evidence that any responsible Salt River official was aware of the disclaimer on the Westinghouse form. The law frowns upon tort disclaimers because they tend to undermine the prophylactic principles of tort law. The party asserting the effectiveness of a disclaimer must show, therefore, that the appearance of the disclaimer in any agreement, especially a standardized form, was not merely inadvertent.

The evidence here presents several issues of fact, and it was therefore error to grant summary judgment.

Court of Appeals decision approved in part and vacated in part. Case remanded for further proceedings not inconsistent with the Supreme Court's opinion.

Limitation of Remedies

In negligence and strict liability cases, the tests for the enforceability of remedy limitations are much the same as the tests stated immediately above for disclaimers. Under the UCC, however, the standards applied in remedy limitation cases differ somewhat from those applied in disclaimer cases.

Due to the expense they can create for sellers, consequential damages are the usual target of remedy limitations. UCC section 2–719(3) allows the limitation of consequential damages in express and implied warranty cases, but also states that such a limitation may be unconscionable. The section goes on to say that a limitation of consequential damages is quite likely to be unconscionable where the sale is for *consumer goods* and the plaintiff has suffered *personal injury*. Where the loss is

commercial, however, the limitation may or may not be unconscionable. Just what is meant by the term *commercial* is unclear, but presumably it at least excludes personal injury. Where the loss is deemed commercial, courts must consider the many factors relevant to unconscionability determinations on a case-by-case basis.

TIME LIMITATIONS

Due in part to recent tort reform efforts, the states now impose a variety of limitations on the time within which product liability suits must be brought.[14] Traditionally,

---

[14] Also, in express and implied warranty cases, the buyer must notify the seller of the breach within a reasonable time after the buyer discovers or should have discovered it. There is no notice requirement for negligence and strict liability suits.

the main time limits on product liability suits have been the applicable contract and tort *statutes of limitations.* The usual UCC statute of limitations for express and implied warranty claims is four years after the seller offers the defective goods to the buyer (usually, four years after the sale). In negligence and strict liability cases, the applicable tort statute of limitations frequently is shorter, but it only begins to run when the defect was or should have been discovered—often the time of the injury. As a result, the tort statute of limitations can be more advantageous to the plaintiff despite its shorter time period.

In response to the problems created by the product liability explosion, some states have enacted additional timing limitations over the last decade. Often, these limitations apply only to claims for death, personal injury, and property damage. They override the states' other time limitations where they do apply. Among these additional time limitations are:

1. *Special statutes of limitations for product liability cases involving death, personal injury, or property damage.* Usually, these are from one to three years after the time the injury or death occurred or should have been discovered.

2. *Special time limits for "delayed manifestation" injuries such as those resulting from exposure to asbestos.*

3. *Statutes of repose.* The aim of these statutes is to limit seller and manufacturer liability for goods that have been in use for extended periods. Statutes of repose usually run for a 10-to-12 year period that begins when the product is sold to the first buyer not purchasing for resale—often an ordinary consumer. In a state with a 10-year statute of repose, for example, such parties cannot recover for injuries that occur more than 10 years after they purchased the product causing the injury. This is true even when the suit is begun quickly enough to satisfy the applicable statute of limitations.

4. *Useful safe life defenses.* As their name suggests, useful safe life statutes prevent plaintiffs from suing where the harm occurs after the product's "useful safe life" has passed. The product's useful safe life is the period during which it is normally likely to perform in a safe manner. Like statutes of repose, useful safe life statutes are attempts to limit liability for products that have been in use for extended periods.

DEFENSES

Some of the topics discussed above—for example, the absence of privity or a valid disclaimer—can be considered defenses to a product liability suit. Here, however, we are concerned with product liability defenses that involve the plaintiff's behavior.

The Traditional Defenses

Traditionally, the three main defenses in a product liability suit have been the overlapping trio of product misuse, assumption of risk, and contributory negligence.[15] **Product misuse** (or abnormal use) occurs when the plaintiff uses the product in some unusual, unforeseeable way and this causes the loss for which she sues. Examples include ignoring the manufacturer's instructions, mishandling the product, and using the product for purposes for which it was not intended. But if the defendant had reason to foresee the misuse and failed to take reasonable precautions to protect against it, there is no defense. Product misuse usually is available to the defendant in warranty, negligence, and strict liability cases.

Assumption of risk is the plaintiff's voluntary consent to a known danger. It can arise any time that the plaintiff willingly exposes herself to a known product hazard—for example, by consuming obviously adulterated food. Like product misuse, assumption of risk ordinarily is a defense in warranty, negligence, and strict liability cases.

Contributory negligence is the plaintiff's failure to act with reasonable, prudent self-protectiveness. In the product liability context, perhaps the most common example is the simple failure to notice a hazardous product defect. Contributory negligence is clearly a defense in a negligence suit, but the courts have disagreed about whether or when it should be a defense in warranty and strict liability cases.

Comparative Principles

Where they are allowed and proven, the three traditional product liability defenses have completely absolved

---

[15] Contributory negligence and assumption of risk are discussed in the Negligence and Strict Liability chapter.

the defendant from liability. Dissatisfaction with the resulting all-or-nothing situation has led to the increasing use of *comparative* principles in product liability cases. In a growing number of states, courts and legislatures now refuse to let the traditional defenses completely absolve the defendant. Instead, they apportion damages on the basis of relative fault by reducing the plaintiff's recovery in proportion to his percentage share of the responsibility for the harm he has suffered. Such states, that is, typically require the factfinder to establish the plaintiff's and the defendant's percentage shares of the total fault for the injury, and then make the plaintiff's recovery equal the plaintiff's total provable damages times the defendant's percentage share of the fault. Such comparative principles may be based on an existing comparative negligence or comparative fault statute,[16] or may arise through judicial changes in common law rules.

The movement just described, however, is far from complete. Some states retain the traditional defenses and have not adopted comparative principles. Among the states that have adopted comparative principles, moreover, differences and unsettled questions remain. First, it is not always clear what kinds of fault will reduce the plaintiff's recovery. However, some state comparative negligence statutes have been read as embracing assumption of risk and product misuse, and state comparative fault statutes generally define fault broadly. Second, comparative principles may operate in either the *pure* or *mixed* fashions described in the Negligence and Strict Liability chapter. In states using the mixed version, for example, the defendant has a complete defense where the plaintiff is more at fault than the defendant. Finally, there may be some uncertainty regarding the theories of recovery and the types of damage claims to which comparative principles apply.

---

[16] Comparative negligence is discussed in the Negligence and Strict Liability chapter. Some of the newer state statutes, however, speak of comparative *fault*. Although courts and commentators often use the terms *comparative fault* and *comparative negligence* interchangeably, it is not always clear whether comparative negligence statutes embrace forms of fault other than the plaintiff's negligence.

ETHICAL AND PUBLIC POLICY CONCERNS

1. As suggested earlier in this chapter, one explanation for the prodefendant thrust of 19th-century product liability law was the courts' desire to protect infant industries by preventing them from suffering potentially crippling damage awards. If this explanation is accurate, it means that those injured by defective products and the survivors of those who were killed by such products were denied compensation so that the country might be industrialized. Is this right? Should people be sacrificed in this way? In answering this question, assume for the sake of argument that these denials of recovery actually were necessary for industrialization to proceed.

2. Suppose someone argues that strict liability is immoral because people should be forced to pay tort damages only when they are *at fault* in some way. Do you agree? In any event, why are courts (and legislatures) apparently so unimpressed with this argument?

3. Courts are much more likely to find disclaimers and remedy limitations enforceable when the plaintiff is a business firm than when the plaintiff is an ordinary consumer. What is the justification for this difference in treatment? What possible benefit of disclaimers is lost by making them unenforceable in consumer cases?

One possible way to get around the arguments against enforcing disclaimers and remedy limitations in consumer cases is to enforce them when the seller has used various kinds of "superdisclosure" to make buyers aware of the disclaimer. Possibilities include: positioning the disclaimer or limitation outside the product package, using signs to alert buyers to it, explaining it to buyers, and requiring buyers to sign separately near a conspicuous disclaimer or limitation. Try to think of some problems with superdisclosure and with allowing disclaimers and remedy limitations to be enforced on this basis.

SUMMARY

The most important theories of product liability recovery are: (1) express warranty, (2) implied warranty of merchantability, (3) implied warranty of fitness for a particular purpose, (4) negligence, and (5) strict liability. An *express warranty* is created by: (1) any affirmation of fact or promise relating to the goods, (2) any description of the goods, or (3) a sample or model of the goods.

Statements of value or opinion regarding the goods, including sales talk, do not create express warranties.

The *implied warranty of merchantability* arises when goods are sold by a merchant who deals in goods of the kind sold. The most important aspect of merchantability is that the goods must be fit for the ordinary purposes for which such goods are used. The *implied warranty of fitness* arises when the seller has reason to know any particular purpose for which the buyer requires the goods and that the buyer is relying on the seller's skill or judgment to select suitable goods, and the buyer actually relies on the seller's skill or judgment. In such cases, the seller impliedly warrants that the goods are fit for the buyer's *particular* purposes.

In the product liability context, *negligence* cases ordinarily involve claims of: (1) careless manufacture of the goods, (2) careless inspection, (3) the failure to provide suitable warnings, and (4) design defects. Under section 402A of the *Restatement (Second) of Torts,* a seller engaged in the business of selling a particular product is *strictly liable* for defects in that product if it is defective and unreasonably dangerous. The product is defective if it fails to meet the reasonable expectations of the average consumer. It is unreasonably dangerous if it is dangerous to an extent beyond that contemplated by the ordinary consumer. Design defect and failure-to-warn cases can be brought under section 402A.

The only *damages* ordinarily recoverable in negligence and 402A cases are personal injury and property damage. In express and implied warranty cases, a plaintiff who has dealt directly with the defendant may recover for basis of the bargain damages, personal injury, property damage, and indirect economic loss if certain tests are met. A plaintiff who lacks privity with the defendant usually is limited to a personal injury or property damage recovery. Punitive damages are sometimes available in negligence and 402A cases, but only rarely in cases brought under the UCC. In recent years, the states have begun to limit both punitive damage recoveries and recoveries for noneconomic losses like pain and suffering.

In negligence and 402A cases, the absence of *privity of contract* is rarely a defense. Occasionally, however, the no-privity defense may be effective in cases brought under the UCC. In warranty cases, the defense is *least* likely to work where: (1) the plaintiff's loss or injury was a foreseeable consequence of the product defect; (2) the plaintiff is an ordinary consumer; and/or (3) the case involves personal injury or property damage.

Disclaimers of liability by the seller or manufacturer rarely are effective in express warranty cases and in negligence or strict liability cases involving ordinary consumers. However, disclaimers may work in negligence and 402A cases involving fully negotiated commercial contracts between sophisticated parties with equal bargaining power. To disclaim the implied warranty of merchantability, the seller must use the word *merchantability* and must make the disclaimer conspicuous if it is written. To disclaim the implied warranty of fitness, the seller must use a writing and must make the disclaimer conspicuous. Implied warranty disclaimers also are possible where: (1) the seller uses such terms as *with all faults* and *as is*; (2) the buyer fails to discover a reasonably apparent defect after actually inspecting the goods or refusing to inspect following the seller's request to inspect; or (3) trade usage, course of dealing, or course of performance so dictate. However, otherwise-valid implied warranty disclaimers increasingly are being invalidated as unconscionable. Also, the federal Magnuson-Moss Act imposes severe limitations on a seller's ability to disclaim implied warranties in consumer cases.

In negligence and strict liability cases, *remedy limitations* are treated much like disclaimers. In express and implied warranty cases, remedy limitations are likely to be unconscionable where the sale is for consumer goods and the plaintiff suffered personal injury, and may be unconscionable in other cases as well.

The failure to sue within the time limit set by the applicable contract or tort *statute of limitations* defeats the plaintiff's product liability case. Some states have recently enacted: (1) special statutes of limitations governing claims for death, personal injury, or property damage; (2) special statutes of limitations for injuries whose manifestation is delayed; and (3) statutes of repose or useful safe life defenses whose aim is to eliminate liability on products that have been in use for extended periods.

Traditionally, defendants often had a complete *defense* where the plaintiff's injury was caused by his own contributory negligence, assumption of risk, or product misuse. But many states have begun to employ *comparative* principles in product liability cases, reducing the plaintiff's recovery in proportion to her percentage share of the responsibility for the harm she suffered.

PROBLEM CASES

1. Ike Shaw was injured when a truck used for pothole repairs by the city of Colorado Springs was backed over him. The truck's cab and chassis were manufactured by General Motors Corporation. One of Shaw's claims against GM was that the cab and chassis were not fit for this particular application. Therefore, he argued, the truck did not conform to the following promise made by GM in one of its publications: "Chevy's business is providing the right truck for your business." Assuming that the cab and chassis actually were unfit for the particular application, can Shaw recover against GM on the theory that GM breached an express warranty? *No! p921*

2. Steven Taterka purchased a 1972 Ford Mustang from a Ford dealer in January of 1972. In October of 1974, after Taterka had put 75,000 miles on the car and Ford's express warranty had expired, he discovered that the taillight assembly gaskets on his Mustang had been installed in such a way that water was permitted to enter the taillight assembly, causing rust to form. Even though the rusting problem was a recurrent one of which Ford was aware, Ford did nothing for Taterka. Is Ford liable to Taterka under the implied warranty of merchantability? *No, 423*

3. Wilson, a farmer engaged in raising squash, asked an agent of the E-Z Flo Chemical Company about preemergent herbicides for use on his crops. The agent recommended a new product, Alanap, distributed by E-Z Flo and manufactured by Uniroyal Chemical. Relying on the agent's recommendation, Wilson bought a supply of Alanap. E-Z Flo had received a manual from Uniroyal along with the Alanap; the manual stated that the product should not be applied in cold, wet weather. E-Z Flo did not alert Wilson to this warning when he bought the Alanap. Wilson applied the Alanap to his land on the last day of winter, using it on all but four rows of his crop. Except for these four rows, the crop turned out to be a total loss. Wilson sued E-Z Flo for breach of the implied warranty of fitness for a particular purpose. Will he succeed? *Yes! p425*

4. Cathy Adelman-Tremblay purchased a Nailene Nail Kit at a drug store. The kit included artificial fingernails, a nail sander file, and a tube of cyanoacrylate liquid glue (also known as Super Glue). After attaching the artificial nails to her fingernails with the glue, Adelman-Tremblay experienced pain and eventually suffered the permanent loss of all of her natural fingernails. The cause of the loss was an allergic reaction called allergic contact dermatitis.

The manufacturer of the Nailene kit had sold more than 1 million such kits, and Adelman-Tremblay's reaction was the only known adverse reaction to the glue. Also, the relevant medical literature indicated that allergic reactions to the glue were virtually impossible. Nonetheless, a few cases of allergic contact dermatitis from exposure to the glue occurred after Adelman-Tremblay suffered her reaction. Is the manufacturer liable in negligence for failing to warn users *p423* of the possibility of such an allergic reaction? Can Adelman-Tremblay recover under the implied warranty of merchantability? *NO NEGLIGENCE* *↳ All other good?*

5. Dennis Podrat underwent back surgery at the Presbyterian University Hospital. During the operation, the tip of the forceps used by the surgeon broke off and lodged within his back. The forceps allegedly was manufactured by Codman-Shurtleff, Inc. The tip was later removed, but Podrat claimed injury for which he sued Codman-Shurtleff and the hospital under section 402A. Podrat was unable to recover against Codman-Shurtleff because he could not prove that it manufactured the defective forceps. Can he recover against the hospital under section 402A? *No! Can't Recover from Hosp! p429.*

6. Curtis Hagans lost the ring finger of his left hand while operating an industrial table saw manufactured by the Oliver Machinery Company. The saw originally was equipped with a detachable blade guard assembly that would have prevented Hagans's injury had it been attached to the saw while Hagans was working. This assembly was detachable rather than permanently affixed to the saw because many common woodworking functions could not be performed with the assembly in place. Also, the saw exceeded industry safety practices and national and associational safety standards in effect at the time of its manufacture. In addition, few competing manufacturers included blade guards as standard equipment, and none offered a table saw with a permanently affixed blade guard. *if FAILED To GIVE PROPER WARNING*

Hagans sued Oliver in negligence and under section 402A, alleging that the saw was defectively designed because it did not include a permanent blade guard assembly. Did Hagans win? You can assume that injuries of the kind Hagans suffered were foreseeable consequences of manufacturing the saw without a permanent guard, and that Hagans was not careless in his operation of the saw. *IF OTHER COMPANIES offered A FIXED GUARD THEN NO! IF*

7. Joe Kysar purchased a baler built by the Vermeer Manufacturing Company after a Vermeer sales representative told him that the baler in question would produce bales weighing 3,000 pounds. In fact, the baler never produced a 3,000-pound bale. Kysar eventually sued Vermeer in a Wyoming trial court. The court found Vermeer liable under the UCC, but did not specify the exact basis of its holding. As a remedy, it ordered Vermeer to return the purchase price to Kysar, after which Kysar was to return the baler to Vermeer. Assuming that

Vermeer breached either an express warranty or the implied warranty of fitness, was this the proper measure of recovery for defective goods under the UCC? Assume for the sake of argument that Kysar suffered no consequential damages of any kind.

8. Arlyn and Rose Spindler were dairy farmers who leased a feed storage silo from Agristor Leasing. The silo was supposed to limit the oxygen reaching the feed and thus to hinder its spoilage. The Spindlers alleged that the silo was defective and that the dairy feed it contained was spoiled as a result. They further alleged that due to the spoilage of the feed, their dairy herd suffered medically and reproductively and their milk production dropped. The Spindlers sued Agristor in negligence and under section 402A for their resulting lost income. What *type* of damages are they claiming? Under the majority rule, can they recover for such damages in negligence or under section 402A? Would your answer be different if the Spindlers had sued for the damage to the *dairy feed* itself? Assume for purposes of argument that both section 402A and negligence suits are possible in this case.

9. Duane Martin, who had a small farm, placed an order for cabbage seed with the Joseph Harris Company, a large national producer and distributor of seed. Harris's order form included the following language:

NOTICE TO BUYER: Joseph Harris Company, Inc. warrants that seeds and plants it sells conform to the label descriptions as required by Federal and State seed laws. IT MAKES NO OTHER WARRANTIES, EXPRESS OR IMPLIED, OF MERCHANTABILITY, FITNESS FOR PURPOSE, OR OTHERWISE, AND IN ANY EVENT ITS LIABILITY FOR BREACH OF ANY WARRANTY OR CONTRACT WITH RESPECT TO SUCH SEEDS OR PLANTS IS LIMITED TO THE PURCHASE PRICE OF SUCH SEEDS OR PLANTS.

All of Harris's competitors used similar clauses in their contracts.

After Martin placed his order, and unknown to Martin, Harris stopped using a cabbage seed treatment that had been effective in preventing a certain cabbage fungus. Later, Martin planted the seed he had ordered from Harris, but a large portion of the resulting crop was destroyed by fungus because the seed did not contain the treatment Harris had previously used. Martin sued Harris for his losses under the implied warranty of merchantability.

Which portion of the notice quoted above is an attempted disclaimer of implied warranty liability, and which is an attempted limitation of remedies? Will the disclaimer language disclaim the implied warranty of merchantability under UCC section 2–316(2)? If Martin had sued under the implied warranty of fitness for a particular purpose, would the disclaimer language disclaim that implied warranty as well? Assuming that the disclaimer and the remedy limitation contained the correct legal boilerplate needed to make them effective, what argument could Martin still make to block their operation? What are his chances of success with this argument?

10. Moulton purchased a 1969 Ford LTD from Hull-Dobbs, a Ford dealer. His sales contracts with Ford and Hull-Dobbs contained perfectly valid disclaimers of the implied warranty of merchantability that satisfied the requirements of UCC section 2–316(2). One year later, while Moulton was driving his car along an interstate highway, the Ford suddenly veered to the right, jumped the guardrail, and fell 26 feet to the street below. The accident was caused by a defect in the car's steering mechanism, and Moulton was seriously injured. Moulton sued Ford under the implied warranty of merchantability. Ford defended on the basis of its disclaimer. Moulton argued that the disclaimer was invalid in a personal injury case under UCC section 2–719(3), which makes the exclusion of consequential damages unconscionable in a case involving consumer goods and personal injury. Did Moulton's argument succeed?

CHAPTER 21

PERFORMANCE OF SALES CONTRACTS

INTRODUCTION

In the two previous chapters, we have discussed the formation and terms of sales contracts, including those terms concerning express and implied warranties. In this chapter, the focus is on the legal rules that govern the performance of contracts. Among the topics covered are the basic obligations of the buyer and seller with respect to delivery and payment, the rights of the parties when the goods delivered do not conform to the contract, and the circumstances under which the performance of a party's contractual obligations are excused.

GENERAL RULES

The parties to a contract for the sale of goods are obligated to perform the contract according to its terms. The Uniform Commercial Code (UCC or Code) gives the parties great flexibility in deciding between themselves how a contract will be performed. The practices in the trade or business as well as any past dealings between the parties are used to supplement or explain the contract. The Code gives both the buyer and the seller certain rights, and it also sets out what is expected of them on points that they did not deal with in their contract. It should be kept in mind that the Code changes basic contract law in a number of respects.

Good Faith

The buyer and seller must act in **good faith** in the performance of a sales contract [1–203].[1] Good faith is defined to mean "honesty in fact" in performing the duties assumed in the contract or in carrying out the transaction [1–201(19)]. Thus, if the seller is required by the contract to select an assortment of goods for the buyer, the selection must be made in good faith; the seller should pick out a reasonable assortment [2–311]. It would not, for example, be good faith to include only unusual sizes or colors.

Course of Dealing

The terms in the contract between the parties are the primary means for determining the obligations of the buyer and seller. The meaning of those terms may be explained by looking at any performance that has already taken place. For example, a contract may call for periodic deliveries of goods. If a number of deliveries have been made by the buyer without objection by the seller, the way the deliveries were made shows how the parties intended them to be made. Similarly, if there were any past contracts between the parties, the way the

---

[1] The numbers in brackets refer to the sections of the Uniform Commercial Code.

parties interpreted those contracts is relevant to the interpretation of the present contract. If there is a conflict between the express terms of the contract and the past course of dealing between the parties, the express terms of the contract prevail [2–208(2)].

Usage of Trade

In many kinds of businesses there are customs and practices of the trade that are known by people in the business and that are usually assumed by parties to a contract for goods of that type. Under the Code, these trade customs and practices—known as **usage of trade**—can be used in interpreting a contract [2–202; 1–205]. If there is a conflict between the express terms of the contract and trade usage, the express terms prevail [2–208(2)].

The *Williams v. Curtin* case illustrates how a court may consider the terms of a contract, the course of dealing between the parties, and trade usage in determining the interpretation of a contract between merchants.

WILLIAMS v. CURTIN
807 F.2d 1046 (D.C. Cir. 1986)

In January 1982, Ray Williams, a resident of Georgia, orally agreed to sell the "slaw cabbage" to be grown on 30 acres of farmland in Georgia to Thomas Curtin, a resident of New York, who intended to resell the cabbage to cole slaw manufacturers. The expected yield was 600 to 800 tons of cabbage, the agreed-upon price was $136 per ton, and delivery FOB was to be made between May 1, 1982 and June 15, 1982. Large cabbages are generally preferable for making cole slaw, and Curtin orally advised Williams that he desired large cabbage; that is, 12 heads or less per 50-pound sack. This request was not, however, incorporated into the written memorandum of agreement the parties executed in late March. Earlier agreements between Williams and Curtin had called for the sale of "large cabbage." The cabbage was planted in March in a way to provide the best assurance possible that the cabbage would be large cabbage as requested by Curtin.

Curtin made an advance payment of $4,000 to Williams in January and a further payment was made when Curtin visited Williams's field on May 6. By that time, the price of cabbage had unexpectedly increased dramatically, selling at three to four times the price at which it was selling in January. When Curtin visited the field, he found that as a result of poor growing conditions, most of the cabbage was not growing to the desired size. He told Williams that he would take all of the cabbage he could get from the field and that he would be satisfied if he got 400 tons out of the field. Curtin also made an additional $6,000 advance payment to Williams.

When the cabbage was harvested in June, Williams delivered only the large cabbages to Curtin (approximately 150 tons) and sold the smaller cabbages to other buyers at a price about three times higher than the price at which he had contracted to sell cabbage to Curtin. When Curtin did not pay for the cabbage delivered, Williams filed a complaint with the U.S. Department of Agriculture pursuant to the Perishable Agricultural Commodities Act (PACA) seeking to recover the purchase price; Curtin counterclaimed, alleging that Williams had breached the contract by failing to deliver all of the cabbage required by the contract. Williams contended that in the trade in Georgia, "slaw cabbage" referred only to large cabbage with 12 cabbage heads or less per 50-pound bag. However, other witnesses said that the term *slaw cabbage* was seldom used, that in their experience it had never been used to define a specific cabbage size, and that it meant simply cabbage suitable for processing into cole slaw. The U.S.D.A. judicial officer and the district court held in favor of Curtin, and Williams appealed.

Jameson, Senior District Judge.   While the record indicates that Curtin preferred large cabbage, it is clear that the contract was not limited to large cabbage. The judicial officer and the district court found that the May 6 meeting modified the contract with respect to the volume of cabbage to be delivered. The discussions and conduct of the parties at that time are also evidence of the parties' initial intent with respect to the size of the cabbage to be delivered. *See Tymshare, Inc. v. Covell* ("The historical interpretation given to a contract by the parties is strong evidence of its meaning."). As the judicial officer noted, it was then

> obvious that much of the cabbage was not of the large size that Mr. Curtin indicated that he desired when he entered the contract with Mr. Williams in January, 1982. . . . After visiting the field with Mr. Williams, Mr. Curtin paid another $6,000 on account for delivery of cabbage under the contract. A party simply does not make payment of that nature if there is any indication that there is a question as to whether the contract terms will be met. Mr. Williams accepted the tender of payment, and eventually cashed the check. If Mr. Williams did not intend to deliver 400 tons, he should not have accepted the tender.

Williams's failure to object when he obviously knew the field would not produce enough large cabbage to deliver 400 tons is strong evidence that the contract was not limited to large cabbage.

The district court noted that the Uniform Commercial Code defines a "usage of trade" as any "practice or method of dealing having such regularity of observance in a place, vocation or trade as to justify an expectation that it will be observed with respect to the transaction in question." Section 1–205(2).

Williams contends that the district court failed to determine whether "slaw cabbage" was a usage of trade in Georgia. He argues that because the contract's focus of performance was Georgia, the district court should have looked solely to the significance of the term "slaw cabbage" as used in Georgia. Williams argues that because the planting, nurturing, cutting, sizing and bagging of the cabbage was to occur in Georgia, the court should have considered only evidence of usage of trade in Georgia. We disagree.

Williams had failed to recognize that the relevant aspect of performance is not the planting, nurturing, cutting, sizing and bagging of the cabbage. Rather the relevant aspect of performance is delivery of the cabbage. Although the cabbage was to be grown in Georgia, the contract called for delivery in the interstate market. The parties live and transact business in separate states. Both are licensed under the PACA to buy and sell perishable agricultural commodities in interstate commerce. The record indicates that Williams does business with out-of-state buyers on a regular basis. Clearly, the transaction did not involve a sub-trade market consisting of only the Georgia market. Since the transaction is an interstate transaction, it cannot fairly be expected that the parties contracted only with reference to the Georgia market. Where parties enter into an interstate transaction, they expect the terms of their agreement to be interpreted in light of the customs and usages of the particular interstate market involved. The district court properly construed the term "slaw cabbage" with reference to the interstate cole slaw processing market.

The judicial officer stated that Williams was the only witness who testified that there was such a term as "slaw cabbage" and that it means 12 heads or less per 50 pound sack. Williams presented additional witnesses before the district court. The court noted, however, that two of those witnesses were "clearly not disinterested witnesses as they both admit that they had previous dealings with Mr. Curtin and prefer not to do business with him. Weighing all the evidence, the district court found Curtin's expert witnesses more pursuasive and that Williams had failed to show that the term "slaw cabbage" was regularly used in the trade to mean 12 cabbage heads or less per 50 pound bag.*

Judgment for Curtin affirmed.

*It may also be noted that there had been a course of dealing between the parties and that the term "slaw cabbage" had never been used in any prior transaction. Rather they had used the words "large cabbage."

It has long been recognized that in actions under the Perishable Agricultural Commodities Act, the existence of a usage or custom can only be proved by numerous instances of actual practice, and not by the opinion of a witness; and that the evidence must be clear and uncontradicted.

Modification

Under the Code, consideration is not required to support a modification or rescission of a contract for the sale of goods. However, the parties may specify in their agreement that modification or rescission must be in writing, in which case a signed writing is necessary for enforcement of any modification to the contract or its rescission [2–209].

Waiver

In a contract that entails a number of instances of partial performance (such as deliveries or payments) by one party, the other party must be careful to object to any late deliveries or payments. If the other party does not object, it may be waiving its rights to cancel the contract if other deliveries or payments are late [2–208(3), 2–209(4)]. For example, a contract calls for a fish market to deliver fish to a supermarket every Thursday and for the supermarket to pay on delivery. If the fish market regularly delivers the fish on Friday and the supermarket does not object, it will be unable to cancel the contract for that reason. Similarly, if the supermarket does not pay cash but sends a check the following week, then unless the fish market objects, it will not be able to assert the late payments as grounds for later canceling the contract.

A party that has waived rights to a portion of the contract not yet performed may retract the waiver by giving reasonable notice to the other party that strict performance will be required. The retraction of the waiver is effective unless it would be unjust because of a material change of position by the other party in reliance on the waiver [2–209(5)].

Assignment

Under the Code, the duties of either the buyer or the seller may generally be delegated to someone else. If there is a strong reason for having the original party perform the duties, perhaps because the quality of the performance might differ otherwise, the duties cannot be delegated. Also, duties cannot be delegated if the parties agree in the contract that there is to be no assignment of duties. However, rights to receive performance—for example, the right to receive goods or payment—can be assigned [2–210].

DELIVERY

Basic Obligation

The basic duty of the seller is to deliver the goods called for by the contract. The basic duty of the buyer is to accept and pay for the goods if they conform to the contract [2–301]. The buyer and seller may agree that the goods are to be delivered in several lots or installments. If there is no such agreement, then a single delivery of all the goods must be made. Where delivery is to be made in lots, the seller may demand the price of each lot upon delivery unless there has been an agreement for the extension of credit [2–307].

Place of Delivery

The buyer and seller may agree on the place where the goods will be delivered. If no such agreement is made, then the goods are to be delivered at the seller's place of business. If the seller does not have a place of business, then delivery is to be made at his home. If the goods are located elsewhere than the seller's place of business or home, the place of delivery is the place where the goods are located [2–308].

Seller's Duty of Delivery

The seller's basic obligation is to tender delivery of goods that conform to the contract with the buyer. Tender of delivery means that the seller must make the goods available to the buyer. This must be done during reasonable hours and for a reasonable period of time, so that the buyer can take possession of the goods [2–503]. The contract of sale may require the seller merely to ship the goods to the buyer but not to deliver the goods to the buyer's place of business. If this is the case, the seller must put the goods into the possession of a carrier, such as a trucking company or a railroad. The seller must also make a reasonable contract with the carrier to take the goods to the buyer. Then, the seller is required to notify the buyer that the goods have been shipped [2–504]. Shipment terms were discussed in the Formation and Terms of Sales Contracts chapter. If the seller does not make a reasonable contract for delivery or notify the buyer and a material delay or loss results, the buyer has the right to reject the shipment. Suppose the goods are perishable, such as fresh produce, and the seller does not have them shipped in a refrigerated truck or railroad car. If the produce deteriorates in transit, the buyer can reject the produce on the ground that the seller did not make a reasonable contract for shipping it.

In some situations, the goods sold may be in the possession of a bailee such as a warehouse. If the goods are covered by a negotiable warehouse receipt, the seller must indorse the receipt and give it to the buyer [2–503(4)(a)]. This enables the buyer to obtain the goods from the warehouse. Such a situation exists when grain being sold is stored at a grain elevator. The law of negotiable documents of title, including warehouse receipts, is discussed in the Checks and Documents of Title chapter.

If the goods in the possession of a bailee are not covered by a negotiable warehouse receipt, then the seller must notify the bailee that the goods have been sold to the buyer and must obtain the bailee's consent to hold the goods for delivery to the buyer or release of the goods to the buyer. The risk of loss as to the goods remains with the seller until the bailee agrees to hold them for the buyer [2–503(4)(b)].

INSPECTION AND PAYMENT

Buyer's Right of Inspection

Normally, the buyer has the right to inspect the goods before he accepts or pays for them. The buyer and seller may agree on the time, place, and manner in which the inspection will be made. If no agreement is made, then the buyer may inspect the goods at any reasonable time and place and in any reasonable manner [2–513(1)].

If the shipping terms are cash on delivery (COD), then the buyer must pay for the goods before inspecting them unless they are marked "Inspection Allowed." However, if it is obvious even without inspection that the goods do not conform to the contract, the buyer may reject them without paying for them first [2–512(1)(a)]. For example, if a farmer contracted to buy a bull and the seller delivered a cow, the farmer would not have to pay for it. The fact that a buyer may have to pay for goods before inspecting them does not deprive the buyer of remedies against the seller if the goods do not conform to the contract [2–512(2)].

If the goods conform to the contract, the buyer must pay the expenses of inspection. However, if the goods are nonconforming, he may recover his inspection expenses from the seller [2–513(2)].

Payment

The buyer and seller may agree in their contract that the price of the goods is to be paid in money or in other goods, services, or real property. If all or part of the price of goods is payable in real property, then only the transfer of goods is covered by the law of sales of goods. The transfer of the real property is covered by the law of real property [2–304].

The contract may provide that the goods are sold on credit to the buyer and that the buyer has a period of time to pay for them. If there is no agreement for extending credit to the buyer, the buyer must pay for them upon delivery. The buyer can usually inspect goods before payment except where the goods are shipped COD, in which case the buyer must pay for them before inspecting them.

Unless the seller demands cash, the buyer may pay for the goods by personal check or by any other method used in the ordinary course of business. If the seller demands cash, the seller must give the buyer a reasonable amount of time to obtain it. If payment is made by check, the payment is conditional on the check being honored by the bank when it is presented for payment [2–511(3)]. If the bank refuses to pay the check, the buyer has not satisfied the duty to pay for the goods. In that case, the buyer does not have the right to retain the goods and must give them back to the seller.

ACCEPTANCE, REVOCATION, AND REJECTION

Acceptance

Acceptance of goods occurs when a buyer, after having a reasonable opportunity to inspect them, either indicates that he will take them or fails to reject them. To **reject** goods, the buyer must notify the seller of the rejection and specify the defect or nonconformity. If a buyer treats the goods as if he owns them, the buyer is considered to have accepted them [2–606].

For example, Ace Appliance delivers a new color television set to Baldwin. Baldwin has accepted the set if, after trying it and finding it to be in working order, she says nothing to Ace or tells Ace that she will keep it. Even if the set is defective, Baldwin is considered to have accepted it if she does not give Ace timely notice that she does not want to keep it because it is not in working order. If she takes the set on a vacation trip even though she knows that it does not work properly, this is also an acceptance. In the latter case, her use of the television set would be inconsistent with its rejection and the return of ownership to the seller.

If a buyer accepts any part of a **commercial unit** of goods, he is considered to have accepted the whole unit [2–606(2)]. A commercial unit is any unit of goods that is treated by commercial usage as a single whole. It can be a single article (such as a machine), a set or quantity of articles(such as a dozen, bale, gross, or carload), or any other unit treated as a single whole [2–105(6)]. Thus, if a bushel of apples is a commercial unit, then a buyer purchasing 10 bushels of apples who accepts $8\frac{1}{2}$ bushels is considered to have accepted 9 bushels.

Effect of Acceptance

Once a buyer has accepted goods, he cannot later reject them unless at the time they were accepted, the buyer had reason to believe that the nonconformity would be cured. By accepting goods, the buyer does not forfeit or waive remedies against the seller for any nonconformities in the goods. However, if the buyer wishes to hold the seller responsible, he must give the seller *timely notice* that the goods are nonconforming.

The buyer is obligated to pay for goods that are accepted. If the buyer accepts all of the goods sold, he is, of course, responsible for the full purchase price. If the buyer accepts only part of the goods, he must pay for that part at the contract rate [2–607(1)].

Revocation of Acceptance

Under certain circumstances, a buyer is permitted to **revoke** or undo the acceptance. A buyer may revoke acceptance of nonconforming goods where: (1) the non-conformity *substantially impairs* the value of the goods and (2) the buyer accepted them without knowledge of the nonconformity because of the difficulty of discovering the nonconformity, or the buyer accepted the goods because of the seller's *assurances* that the defect would be cured [2–608(1)].

The right to revoke acceptance must be exercised within a *reasonable time* after the buyer discovers or should have discovered the nonconformity. Revocation is not effective until the buyer notifies the seller of the intention to revoke acceptance. After a buyer revokes acceptance, his rights are the same as they would have been if the goods had been rejected when delivery was offered [2–608].

The right to revoke acceptance could arise, for example, where Arnold buys a new car from Dealer. While driving the car home, Arnold discovers that it has a seriously defective transmission. When she returns the car to Dealer, Dealer promises to repair it, so Arnold decides to keep the car. If the dealer does not fix the transmission after repeated efforts to fix it, Arnold could revoke her acceptance on the grounds that the nonconformity substantially impairs the value of the car, that she took delivery of the car without knowledge of the nonconformity, and that her acceptance was based on Dealer's assurances that he would fix the car. Similarly, revocation of acceptance might be involved where a serious problem with the car not discoverable by inspection shows up in the first month's use.

Revocation must be invoked prior to any *substantial change* in the goods, however, such as serious damage in an accident or wear and tear from using them for a period of time. What constitutes a "substantial impairment in value" and when there has been a "substantial change in the goods" are questions that courts frequently have to decide when an attempted revocation of acceptance results in a lawsuit. The case below of *McCullough v. Bill Swad Chrysler-Plymouth, Inc.* contains an excellent discussion of many of these issues.

MCCULLOUGH v. BILL SWAD CHRYSLER-PLYMOUTH, INC.

449 N.E.2d 1289 (Ohio Sup. Ct. 1983)

On May 23, 1978, Deborah McCullough purchased a 1978 Chrysler LeBaron from Bill Swad Chrysler-Plymouth. The automobile was covered by both a limited warranty and a vehicle service contract (extended warranty). Following delivery, McCullough advised the salesman that she had noted problems with the brakes, transmission, air conditioning, paint job, and seat panels, and the absence of rustproofing. The next day, the brakes failed and the car was returned to the dealer for the necessary repairs. When the car was returned to her, McCullough discovered that the brakes had not been properly repaired and that none of the cosmetic work had been done. The car was returned several times to the dealer to correct these problems and others that developed subsequently. On June 26, the car was again returned to the dealer, who kept it for three weeks. Many of the defects were not corrected, however, and new problems with the horn and brakes arose. While McCullough was on a shopping trip, the engine abruptly shut off and the car had to be towed to the dealer. Then, while she was on her honeymoon, the brakes again failed. The car was taken back to the dealer with a list of 32 defects that needed correction.

After repeated efforts to repair it were unsuccessful, McCullough sent a letter to the dealer calling for rescission of the purchase, requesting return of the purchase price, and offering to return the car upon receipt of shipping instructions. She received no answer and continued to drive it. McCullough then filed suit. In May 1979, the dealer refused to do any further work on the car, claiming that it was in satisfactory condition. By the time of the trial, in June 1980, it had been driven 35,000 miles, approximately 23,000 of which had been logged after McCullough mailed her notice of revocation.

Locher, Justice.   The case essentially poses but a single question: Whether McCullough, by continuing to operate the vehicle she had purchased from Swad Chrysler-Plymouth after notifying the latter of her intent to rescind the purchase agreement, waived her right to revoke her initial acceptance. After having thoroughly reviewed both the relevant facts in the present cause and the applicable law, we find that McCullough, despite her extensive use of the car following her revocation, in no way forfeited such right.

The ultimate disposition of the instant action is governed primarily by UCC § 2–608, which provides, in pertinent part:

(A) The buyer may revoke his acceptance of a lot or commercial unit whose nonconformity substantially impairs its value to him if he has accepted it: (1) on the reasonable assumption that its nonconformity would be cured and it has not been seasonably cured;

(B) Revocation of acceptance must occur within a reasonable time after the buyer discovers or should have discovered the ground for it and before any substantial change in condition of the goods which is not caused by their own defects. It is not effective until the buyer notifies the seller of it.

(C) A buyer who so revokes has the same rights and duties with regard to the goods involved as if he had rejected them.

Swad Chrysler-Plymouth essentially argues that McCullough's revocation of her initial acceptance of the automobile was ineffective as it did not comply with the mode prescribed for revocation in § 2–608. Specifically, Swad Chrysler-Plymouth asserts that McCullough's continued operation of the vehicle after advising Swad of her revocation was inconsistent with her having relinquished ownership of the car, that the value of the automobile to McCullough was not substantially impaired by its alleged nonconformities, and that the warranties furnished by Swad Chrysler-Plymouth provided the sole legal remedy for alleviating the automobile's defects. Each of these contentions must be rejected.

Although the legal question presented in Swad Chrysler-Plymouth's first objection is a novel one for the bench, other state courts which have addressed the issue have held that whether continued use of goods after notification of revocation of their acceptance vitiates such revocation is solely dependent upon whether such use was reasonable. In ascertaining whether a buyer's continued use of an item after revocation of its acceptance was reasonable, the trier of fact should pose and divine the answers to the following queries: (1) Upon being apprised of the buyer's revocation of his acceptance, what instructions, if any, did the seller tender the buyer concerning return of the now rejected goods? (2) Did the buyer's business needs or personal circumstances compel the continued use? (3) During the period of such use, did the seller persist in assuring the buyer that all nonconformities would be cured or that provisions would otherwise be made to recompense the latter for the dissatisfaction and inconvenience which the defects caused him? (4) Did the seller act in good faith? (5) Was the seller unduly prejudiced by the buyer's continued use?

It is manifest that, upon consideration of the aforementioned criteria, McCullough acted reasonably in continuing to operate her motor vehicle even after revocation of acceptance. First, the failure of the seller to advise the buyer, after the latter has revoked his acceptance of the goods, how the goods were to be returned entitles the buyer to retain possession of them. Swad, in the case at bar, did not respond to McCullough's request for instructions regarding the disposition of the vehicle. Failing to have done so, Swad can hardly be heard now to complain of McCullough's continued use of the automobile.

Second, McCullough, a young clerical secretary of limited financial resources, was scarcely in a position to return the defective automobile and obtain a second in order to meet her business and personal needs. A most unreasonable obligation would be imposed upon McCullough were she to be required, in effect, to secure a loan to purchase a second car while remaining liable for repayment of the first car loan. Additionally, Swad Chrysler-Plymouth, by attempting to repair McCullough's vehicle even after she tendered her notice of revocation, provided both express and tacit assurances that the automobile's defects were remediable, thereby inducing her to retain possession. Moreover, whether Swad Chrysler-Plymouth acted in good faith through this episode is highly problematic, especially given the fact that whenever repair of the car was undertaken, new defects often miraculously arose while previous ones frequently were uncorrected. Swad's refusal to honor the warranties before their expiration also evidences less than fair dealing.

Finally, it is apparent that Swad was not prejudiced by McCullough's continued operation of the automobile. Had Swad retaken possession of the vehicle pursuant to McCullough's notice of revocation, the automobile, which at the time had been driven only 12,000 miles, could easily have been resold. Indeed, the car was still marketable at the time of trial, as even then the odometer registered less than 35,000 miles. In any event, having failed to reassume ownership of the automobile when requested to do so, Swad alone must bear the loss for any diminution of the vehicle's resale value occurring between the two dates.

Swad maintains, however, that even if McCullough's continued operation of the automobile after revocation was reasonable, such use is "prima facie evidence" that the vehicle's nonconformities did not substantially impair its value to McCullough, thus precluding availability of the remedy of revocation. Such an inference, though, may not be drawn. As stated earlier, external conditions beyond the buyer's immediate control often mandate continued use of an item even after revocation of its acceptance. Thus, it cannot seriously be contended that McCullough, by continuing to operate the defective vehicle, intimated that its nonconformities did not substantially diminish its worth in her eyes.

We must similarly dismiss Swad's assertion that, as McCullough's complaints primarily concerned cosmetic flaws, the defects were trivial. First, the chronic steering, transmission, and brake problems which McCullough experienced in operating the vehicle could hardly be deemed inconsequential. Moreover, even purely cosmetic defects, under the proper set of circumstances, can significantly affect the buyer's valuation of the good. Whether a complained of nonconformity substantially impairs an item's worth to the buyer is a determination exclusively within the purview of the fact finder and must be based on objective evidence of the buyer's idiosyncratic tastes and needs. Any defect that shakes the buyer's faith or undermines his confidence in the reliability and integrity of the purchased item is deemed to work a substantial impairment of the item's value and to provide a basis for revocation of the underlying sales agreement.

Judgment for McCullough.

Buyer's Rights on Improper Delivery

If the goods delivered by the seller do not conform to the contract, the buyer has several options. The buyer can (1) reject all of the goods, (2) accept all of them, or (3) accept any commercial units and reject the rest [2–601]. The buyer, however, cannot accept only part of a commercial unit and reject the rest. The buyer must pay for the units accepted at the price per unit provided in the contract.

Where the contract calls for delivery of the goods in separate installments, the buyer's options are more limited. The buyer may reject an installment delivery only if the nonconformity *substantially affects the value* of that delivery and *cannot be corrected* by the seller in a timely fashion. If the nonconformity is relatively minor, the buyer must accept the installment. The seller may offer to replace the defective goods or give the buyer an allowance in the price to make up for the nonconformity [2–612].

Where the nonconformity or defect in one installment impairs the value of the whole contract, the buyer may treat it as a breach of the whole contract but must proceed carefully so as not to reinstate the remainder of the contract [2–612(3)].

Rejection

If a buyer has a basis for rejecting a delivery of goods, the buyer must act within a *reasonable time* after delivery. The buyer must also give the seller *notice* of the rejection, preferably in writing [2–602]. The buyer should be careful to state all of the defects on which he is basing the rejection, including all of the defects that a reasonable inspection would disclose. This is particularly important if these are defects that the seller might cure (remedy) and the time for delivery has not expired. In that case, the seller may notify the buyer that he intends to redeliver conforming goods.

If the buyer fails to state in connection with his rejection a particular defect that is ascertainable by reasonable inspection, he will not be permitted to use the defect to justify his rejection if the seller could have cured the defect had he been given reasonable notice of it. In a transaction taking place between merchants, the seller has, after rejection, a right to a written statement of all the defects in the goods on which the buyer bases his right to reject and the buyer may not later assert defects not listed in justification of his rejection [2–605].

In the case that follows, *Tai Wah Radio Manufactory Ltd. v. Ambassador Imports Ltd.*, the buyer kept a shipment of defective goods to use as leverage against the seller concerning a claim for damages on an earlier defective shipment. The court found that the buyer was considered to have accepted the shipment because it had not rejected it in a timely fashion.

TAI WAH RADIO MANUFACTORY LTD. v. AMBASSADOR IMPORTS LTD.
3 UCC Rep.2d 117 (S.D. N.Y. 1987)

Tai Wah Manufactory Ltd., a Hong Kong company, is a manufacturer of electronic goods. Ambassador Imports Ltd., a New York company, is an importer and wholesale distributor of various products, including electronic goods. The two companies had been doing business with each other for about five years when in February 1985 Ambassador placed an order with Tai Wah for 2,000 stereo cassette recorders, which were delivered to and accepted by Ambassador in Los Angeles on April 15. On April 4, Ambassador placed another order for cassette recorders with Tai Wah, this time for 2,040 units.

Ambassador claimed that in May it began to receive complaints from its customers about the recorders from the first shipment and several hundred units were returned to Ambassador before June 24. On May 31 and June 7, Ambassador sent telexes to Tai Wah advising it of problems with the quality of the plastic in the dial and with breakage of the cassette door, and asking that the problem be corrected for all future orders. On June 1, Tai Wah indicated that it was trying to improve the quality of the plastic and that future orders would be corrected. It also advised Ambassador that the second shipment had been sent on May 24. Despite the complaints about the quality of the recorders, Ambassador picked up the second shipment of recorders in Los Angeles on June 24. It made no effort to inspect the goods. On June 29, it notified Tai Wah that it did not want the second shipment, that it had picked it up only to hold as collateral to assure that it would be compensated for its damages on the first shipment, and that it would return the second shipment when such compensation was arranged.

Tai Wah then brought a lawsuit against Ambassador to recover the contract price of the second shipment of recorders.

Motley, District Judge. Tai Wah asserts that it is entitled to judgment as a matter of law because Ambassador did not timely reject the second shipment of recorders as required by the Uniform Commercial Code. Ambassador contends that the notice of defects in the first shipment constituted notice of defects in the second shipment.

It is undisputed that Ambassador accepted the second shipment for the sole purpose of negotiating a settlement with Tai Wah concerning money owing on the first shipment. Ambassador obviously did not intend to pay for the second shipment with the knowledge that it would reject the recorders. In addition, it knew that the recorders were allegedly defective at the time of acceptance.

Section 2–608 of the U.C.C. provides:

(1) The buyer may revoke his acceptance of a lot or commercial unit whose non-conformity substantially impairs its value to him if he has accepted it

(a) on the reasonable assumption that its non-conformity would be cured and it has not been seasonably cured; or

(b) without discovery of such non-conformity if his acceptance was reasonably induced either by the difficulty of discovery before acceptance or by the seller's assurances.

Thus, a buyer with knowledge that goods are defective when he accepts them does not lose his right to revoke the acceptance if the acceptance was based on the reasonable assumption that the nonconformity would be seasonably cured but the cure was not effected. In addition, acceptance may be revoked if the buyer, without discovering the nonconformity, was reasonably induced to accept the goods either by the difficulty of discovery before acceptance or by the seller's assurances. Neither of these exceptions is applicable to this case. When Ambassador accepted the second shipment of cassette recorders, it had knowledge of the recorder's allegedly defective nature. Ambassador did not assume Tai Wah would cure the nonconformity. Thus, Ambassador did not have the right to revoke the contract for the second shipment.

Although Ambassador may not have intended to keep the products when it took possession of the second shipment, this does not change the result. From the undisputed facts in this case, it is obvious that Ambassador was attempting to engage in a form of commercial "kidnapping" to compel Tai Wah to resolve its differences with Ambassador. Ambassador, instead of taking possession of the second shipment of recorders, should have rejected the second shipment. Tai Wah, in telexes, had advised Ambassador, prior to Ambassador's receipt of the second shipment, that the recorders had been shipped prior to Tai Wah's receipt of Ambassador's first complaints about the first shipment and prior to Tai Wah having the opportunity to make the needed corrections. Thus, Ambassador, with knowledge of the allegedly defective nature of the goods, should have rejected them. Accordingly, Tai Wah is entitled to payment for the second shipment.

However, if it is established at trial that Ambassador complained in a timely manner about the defects in the goods, Ambassador is entitled to damages for breach of warranty—the difference between the contract price of the recorders and their actual value. This would be an offset against the money Ambassador owes Tai Wah.

Partial summary judgment awarded to Tai Wah.

CONCEPT REVIEW

ACCEPTANCE, REVOCATION, AND REJECTION

Acceptance	1. Occurs when buyer, having had a reasonable opportunity to inspect goods, either (a) indicates he will take them or (b) fails to reject them.
	2. If buyer accepts any part of a commercial unit, he is considered to have accepted the whole unit.
	3. If buyer accepts goods, he cannot later reject them *unless* at the time they were accepted buyer had reason to believe that the nonconformity would be cured.
	4. Buyer is obligated to pay for goods that are accepted.
Revocation	1. Buyer may revoke acceptance of nonconforming goods where (a) the nonconformity *substantially impairs the value* of the goods and, (b) buyer accepted the goods without knowledge of the nonconformity because of the difficulty of discovering the nonconformity *or* buyer accepted because of assurances by the seller.
	2. Right to revoke must be exercised within a *reasonable* time after buyer discovers *or* should have discovered the nonconformity.
	3. Revocation must be invoked before there is any *substantial* change in the goods.
	4. Revocation is not effective until buyer notifies seller of his intent to revoke acceptance.
Rejection	1. Where the goods delivered do not conform to the contract, buyer may (a) reject all of the goods, (b) accept all of the goods, or (c) accept any commercial unit and reject the rest. Buyer must pay for goods accepted.
	2. Where the goods are to be delivered in installments, an installment delivery may be rejected *only if* the nonconformity substantially affects the value of that delivery and cannot be corrected by the seller.
	3. Buyer must act within a reasonable time after delivery.

Right to Cure

If the seller has some reason to believe that the buyer would accept nonconforming goods, then the seller can take a reasonable time to reship conforming goods. The seller has this opportunity even if the original time for delivery has expired. For example, Ace Manufacturing contracts to sell 200 red baseball hats to Sam's Sporting Goods, with delivery to be made by April 1. On March 1, Sam's receives a package from Ace containing 200 blue baseball hats and refuses to accept them. Ace can notify Sam's that it intends to cure the improper delivery by supplying 200 red hats, and it has until April 1 to deliver the red hats to Sam's. If Ace thought that Sam's would accept the blue hats because on past shipments Sam's did not object to the substitution of blue hats for red, then Ace has a reasonable time even after April 1 to deliver the red hats [2–508].

If the buyer wrongfully rejects goods, he is liable to the seller for breach of the sales contract [2–602(3)].

Buyer's Duties after Rejection

If the buyer is a merchant, then the buyer owes certain duties concerning the goods that he rejects. First, the buyer must follow any reasonable instructions that the seller gives concerning disposition of the goods.

The seller, for example, might request that the rejected goods be shipped back to the seller. If the goods are perishable or may deteriorate rapidly, then the buyer must make a reasonable effort to sell the goods. The seller must reimburse the buyer for any expenses that the buyer incurs in carrying out the seller's instructions or in trying to resell perishable goods. In reselling goods, the buyer must act reasonably and in good faith [2–603(2)].

If the rejected goods are not perishable or if the seller does not give the buyer instructions, then the buyer has several options. First, the buyer can store the goods for the seller. Second, the buyer can reship them to the seller. Third, the buyer can resell them for the seller's benefit. If the buyer resells the goods, the buyer may keep his expenses and a reasonable commission on the sale. If the buyer stores the goods, the buyer should exercise care in handling them. The buyer must also give the seller a reasonable time to remove the goods [2–604].

If the buyer is not a merchant, then his obligation after rejection is to hold the goods with reasonable care for a sufficient time to give the seller an opportunity to remove them. The buyer is not obligated to ship the goods back to the seller [2–602]. The case that follows, *Lykins Oil Company v. Fekkos*, illustrates these principles.

LYKINS OIL COMPANY v. FEKKOS

507 N.E.2d 795 (Ohio Ct. Comm. Pl. 1986)

Haralambos Fekkos purchased from Lykins Sales & Service a Yammar Model 165D, 16–horse-power diesel tractor and various implements. On Saturday, April 27, Fekkos gave Lykins a check for the agreed-on purchase price, less trade-in, of $6,596, and the items were delivered to his residence. The next day, while attempting to use the tractor for the first time, Fekkos discovered it was defective. The defects included a dead battery requiring jump starts, overheating while pulling either the mower or the tiller, missing safety shields over the muffler and the power takeoff, and a missing water pump.

On Monday, Fekkos contacted Lykins's sales representative who believed his claims to be true and agreed to have the tractor picked up from Fekkos's residence; Fekkos also stopped payment on his check. Fekkos placed the tractor with the tiller attached in his front yard as near as possible to the front door without driving it onto the landscaped area closest to the house. Fekkos left the tractor on his lawn because his driveway was broken up for renovation and his garage was inaccessible, and because the tractor would have to be jump started by Lykins's employees when they picked it up. On Tuesday, Fekkos went back to Lykins's store to purchase an Allis-Chalmers tractor and reminded Lykins's employees that the Yammar tractor had not been picked up and remained on his lawn.

On Wednesday, May 1, at 6:00 A.M., Fekkos discovered that the tractor was missing although the tiller had been unhitched and remained in the yard. Later that day, Lykins picked up the remaining implements. The theft was reported to the police. On several occasions, Fekkos was assured that Lykins's insurance would cover the stolen tractor, that it was Lykins's fault for not picking it up, and that Fekkos had nothing to worry about. However, Lykins subsequently brought suit against Fekkos to recover the purchase price of the Yammar tractor. Both Lykins and Fekkos moved for summary judgment in their favor.

Watson, Judge.   Lykins argues in support of its motion for summary judgment that section 2–602 applies to this matter. Subsections 2(a) and (b) provide that:

Subject to the provisions of the two following sections on rejected goods:
   (a) after rejection any exercise of ownership by the buyer with respect to any commercial unit is wrong-ful as against the seller; and
   (b) if the buyer has before rejection taken physical possession of goods in which he does not have a security interest under the provisions of this Article (subsection (3) of Section 2–711), he is under a duty after rejection to hold them with reasonable care at the seller's disposition for a sufficient time to permit the seller to remove them.

Lykins argues that because Fekkos was already in possession of the tractor at the time he rejected it, he had the duty to hold it for a sufficient length of time for Lykins to remove it from Fekkos's premises. Lykins asserts that Fekkos breached this duty and is liable to Lykins because the tractor was unavailable to be picked up by Lykins on May 1, the day after the purchase order was cancelled and two days after Fekkos rejected the tractor.

On the other hand, Fekkos, in support of his motion for summary judgment argues that section 2–510 controls the matter. Section 2–510(1) provides:

(1) Where a tender or delivery of goods so fails to conform to the contract so as to give a right of rejection the risk of their loss remains on the seller until cure or acceptance.

Fekkos argues that because the tractor was of no use to him as delivered, it failed to conform to the contract so as to give him the right to reject it. Thus, Fekkos asserts, under section 2–510 the risk of loss remained on the seller at the point of the tractor's theft on May 1, 1985, because no cure or acceptance had been made at that point.

Alternatively, Fekkos argues that if section 2–602 is applicable to the case, he still is entitled to summary judgment because subsequent to his rejection he held the tractor with reasonable care, forced because of the necessity of jump starting, the impassibility of his driveway and inaccessibility of his garage. Fekkos argues that it would be unreasonable to assume that he could have anticipated that someone would "go to the trouble of removing the tiller, and then push or winch a 1,200-plus pound tractor onto a truck or drag or whatever."

The court in its research of Ohio sales law discovered no Ohio case law on the precise issue presented in this case. Indeed, there is little case law nationwide on this issue. However, the court sees no reason that the two aforementioned statutes are not to be read *in pari materia* to provide the law to be applied.

As to the instant case, while it may be said that Lykins retained the risk of loss of the nonconforming tractor, the liability for loss would fall on Fekkos if the facts show that Fekkos breached his duty to hold the tractor with reasonable care for sufficient time for removal, after notification of rejection to seller.

On the facts, the court finds that the actions taken by Fekkos were reasonable under all the circumstances and that Fekkos did not breach his duty to use reasonable care to hold the tractor until Lykins would retrieve it. The court notes that there is no evidence whatsoever that any of Lykins's employees indicated their dissatisfaction with Fekkos's decision to park the tractor on his front lawn when told by Fekkos that that was where he would leave it until they came. The evidence shows to this court's satisfaction that Fekkos acted reasonably because of the inaccessibility of his garage on account of the demolition of his driveway.

Summary judgment for Fekkos.

ASSURANCE, REPUDIATION, AND EXCUSE

Assurance

The buyer or seller may become concerned that the other party may not be able to perform his contract obligations. If there is a reasonable basis for that concern, the buyer or seller can demand **assurance** from the other party that the contract will be performed. If such assurances are not given within a reasonable time not exceeding 30 days, the party is considered to have repudiated the contract [2–609].

For example, a farmer contracts to sell 1,000 bushels of apples to a canner, with delivery to be made in September. In March, the canner learns that a severe frost has damaged many of the apple blossoms in the farmer's area and that 50 percent of the crop has been lost.

The canner has the right to demand assurances in writing from the farmer that he will be able to fulfill his obligations in light of the frost. The farmer must provide those assurances within 30 days. Thus, he might advise the canner that his crop sustained only relatively light damage or that he had made commitments to sell only a small percentage of his total crop and expects to be able to fulfill his obligations. If the farmer does not provide such assurances in a timely manner, he is considered to have repudiated the contract. The canner then has certain remedies against the farmer for breach of contract. These remedies are discussed in the next chapter.

The *Creusot-Loire International, Inc. v. Coppus Engineering Corp.* case, which follows, illustrates a situation where a buyer became concerned about the seller's ability to perform and demanded assurances from the seller.

CREUSOT-LOIRE INTERNATIONAL, INC. v. COPPUS ENGINEERING CORP.

535 F. Supp. 45 (S.D. N.Y. 1983)

Creusot-Loire, a French manufacturing and engineering concern, was the project engineer to construct ammonia plants in Yugoslavia and Syria. The design process engineer for the two plants—as well as a plant being constructed in Sri Lanka—specified burners manufactured by Coppus Engineering Corporation. After the burner specifications were provided to Coppus, it sent technical and service information to Creusot-Loire. Coppus expressly warranted that the burners were capable of continuous operation using heavy fuel oil with combustion air preheated to 260 degrees Celsius. The warranty extended for one year from the start-up of the plant but not exceeding three years from the date of shipment.

In January 1979, Creusot-Loire ordered the burners for the Yugoslavia plant and paid for them; in November 1979, the burners were shipped to Yugoslavia. Due to construction delays, the plant was not to become operational until the end of 1983. In 1981, however, Creusot-Loire became aware that there had been operational difficulties with the Coppus burners at the Sri Lanka and Syria plants and that efforts to modify the burners had been futile. Creusot-Loire wrote to Coppus expressing concern that the burners purchased for the Yugoslavia plant, like those in the other plants, would prove unsatisfactory and asking for proof that the burners would meet contract specifications. When subsequent discussions failed to satisfy Creusot-Loire, it requested that Coppus take back the burners and refund the purchase price. Coppus refused. Finally, Creusot-Loire indicated that it would accept the burners only if Coppus extended its contractual guarantee to cover the delay in the start-up of the Yugoslavia plant and if Coppus posted an irrevocable letter of credit for the purchase price of the burners. When Coppus refused, Creusot-Loire brought an action for breach of contract, seeking a return of the purchase price.

Cannella, District Judge.   Turning to Coppus's claim that Creusot-Loire's request for assurance was unreasonable, the court notes that Coppus promised to do more than just deliver the burners. The contract plainly states that Coppus was obligated to provide burners which would operate under certain conditions. The present record establishes that Creusot-Loire was justified in seeking assurances that the burners were able to meet the Yugoslavian operating specifications. As the Official Comment to 2–609 recognizes, a buyer of precision parts has reasonable grounds for insecurity "if he discovers that his seller is making defective deliveries of such parts to other buyers with similar needs." Coppus's own documents indicate that the burners delivered to Sri Lanka did not conform to specifications; thus Creusot-Loire was justified in seeking assurances from Coppus.

With respect to Coppus's claim that the assurances sought by Creusot-Loire were unreasonable, the court initially observes that after being asked for technical assurances in February, Coppus did not respond until September, thereby heightening Creusot-Loire's suspicions. Further, the court finds that the assurances later sought by Creusot-Loire—an extension of contractual guarantee and the posting of a letter of credit—were not unreasonable in light of the circumstances. First, Creusot-Loire's contention that its demand for a letter of credit comported with accepted international business practice is not seriously contested. Second, the record demonstrates that Coppus's stalling and lack of candor forced Creusot-Loire to request security in the form of a letter of credit and an extension of the warranty. Third, while it understands that Coppus bargained for a contract that included a limited warranty, in view of the strategy adopted to meet Creusot-Loire's demand for assurances, the court concludes that Creusot-Loire's request to extend its warranty also was reasonable. Thus, Coppus's failure to provide any assurances, save its statement that the burners would work if installed, constitutes a repudiation of the contract.

Coppus's claim that Creusot-Loire did not timely revoke its acceptance is also without merit. What constitutes a reasonable time for Creusot-Loire to revoke its acceptance depends upon the nature, purpose and circumstances of the case. UCC 1–204(2).

While case law indicates that as a matter of law revocation within the warranty period, which occurred in this case, is timely, the evidence establishes that Creusot-Loire timely revoked its acceptance. After Creusot-Loire sought assurances in February 1981, it did not receive an answer until September. Moreover, Coppus's September response indicates that further assurances were forthcoming. Thus, it was not until November that Creusot-Loire learned that Coppus had no experience with burners operating under "Yugoslavian-like" conditions and that it was unlikely that the burners could satisfy the contract specifications. Accordingly, the court concludes that any delay in revoking acceptance occurred because Creusot-Loire reasonably relied on Coppus's assurances that the burners would work. Moreover, it is clear that after it learned that Coppus had been less than candid with its assurances, Creusot-Loire revoked its acceptance within a reasonable time. Finally, as Creusot-Loire correctly observes, Coppus has not shown that it was prejudiced by this alleged delay.

Judgment for Creusot-Loire.

Anticipatory Repudiation

Sometimes, one of the parties to a contract *repudiates* the contract by advising the other party that he does not intend to perform his obligations. When one party repudiates the contract, the other party may suspend his performance. In addition, he may either await performance for a reasonable time or use the remedies for breach of contract that are discussed in the next chapter [2–610].

Suppose the party who repudiated the contract changes his mind. Repudiation can be withdrawn by clearly indicating that the person intends to perform his obligations. The repudiating party must do this before the other party has canceled the contract or has materially changed position by, for example, buying the goods elsewhere [2–611].

Excuse

Unforeseen events may make it difficult or impossible for a person to perform his contractual obligations. The Code rules for determining when a person is excused from performing are similar to the general contract rules. General contract law uses the test of **impossibility.** In most situations, however, the Code uses the test of **commercial impracticability.**

The Code attempts to differentiate events that are unforeseeable or uncontrollable from events that were part of the risk borne by a party. If the goods required for the performance of a contract are destroyed without fault of either party prior to the time that the risk of loss passed to the buyer, the contract is voided [2–613]. Suppose Jones agrees to sell and deliver an antique table to Brown. The table is damaged when Jones's antique store is struck by lightning and catches fire. The specific table covered by the contract was damaged without fault of either party prior to the time that the risk of loss was to pass to Brown. Under the Code, Brown has the option of either canceling the contract or accepting the table with an allowance in the purchase price to compensate for the damaged condition [2–613].

If unforeseen conditions cause a delay or the inability to make delivery of the goods, and thus make performance impracticable, the seller is excused from making delivery. However, if a seller's capacity to deliver is only partially affected, the seller must allocate production in any fair and reasonable manner among his customers. The seller has the option of including any regular customer not then under contract in his allocation scheme. When the seller allocates production, he must notify the buyers [2–615]. When a buyer receives this notice, the buyer may either terminate the contract or agree to accept the allocation [2–616].

For example, United Nuclear contracts to sell certain quantities of fuel rods for nuclear power plants to a number of electric utilities. If the federal government limits the amount of uranium that United has access to, so that United is unable to fill all of its contracts, United is excused from full performance on the grounds of commercial impracticability. However, United may allocate its production of fuel rods among its customers by reducing each customer's share by a certain percentage and giving the customers notice of the allocation. Then, each utility can decide whether to cancel the contract or accept the partial allocation of fuel rods.

In the absence of compelling circumstances, courts do not readily excuse parties from their contractual obligations, particularly where it is clear that the parties anticipated a problem and sought to provide for it in the contract. The unsuccessful effort of a seller to excuse its nonperformance of a contract to supply coal because of an increase in the cost of production is illustrated by *Missouri Public Service Co. v. Peabody Coal Co.,* which follows.

MISSOURI PUBLIC SERVICE CO. v. PEABODY COAL CO.

583 S.W.2d 721 (Mo. Ct. App. 1979)

In 1967, Peabody Coal Company made an offer to supply the coal needs of one of Missouri Public Service Company's electric generating plants for 10 years at a base price of $5.40 per net ton, subject to certain price adjustments from time to time relating to the cost of labor, taxes, compliance with government regulations, and increases in transportation costs as reflected in railroad tariffs. Peabody's offer also included an inflation cost escalator based on the Department of Labor's Industrial Commodities Index. The parties signed an agreement on December 22, 1967.

Performance of the contract was profitable for Peabody for two years, but then production cost increases outpaced the price adjustment features of the contract. In 1974, Peabody requested a number of modifications in the price adjustment mechanisms. Public Service rejected this request, but did offer a $1 a ton increase in the original cost per net ton. Following further discussions between the parties, on May 6, 1975, Peabody notified Public Service by letter that all coal shipments would cease in 60 days unless the modifications it sought were immediately agreed to by Public Service. Public Service treated the letter as an anticipatory repudiation and brought suit against Peabody for specific performance.

At the trial, Peabody introduced evidence that its losses under the contract were $3.4 million. It also claimed that the Industrial Commodities Index, which prior to the execution of the contract had been an accurate measure of inflation, had ceased to be an effective measure because of the 1973 oil embargo, runaway inflation, and the enactment of new mine safety regulations. The trial court ruled in favor of Missouri Public Service, and Peabody appealed.

Swofford, Chief Judge.   Peabody's final allegation of error is that the trial court erred in refusing to relieve or excuse it from its obligations under the contract upon the basis of "commercial impracticability" under Section 2–615 (UCC), which section reads, in part:

Excuse by failure of presupposed conditions. Except so far as a seller may have assumed a greater obligation and subject to the preceding section on substituted performance:

(a) Delay in delivery or nondelivery in whole or in part by a seller who complies with paragraphs (b) and (c) is not a breach of his duty under a contract for sale if performance as agreed has been made impracticable by the occurrence of a contingency the nonoccurrence of which was a basic assumption on which the contract was made or by compliance in good faith with any applicable foreign or domestic governmental regulation or order whether or not it later proves to be invalid.

The comments accompanying this section treat it as dealing with the doctrine of "commercial impracticability," and central to this concept is that the doctrine may be applicable upon the occurrence of a supervening, unforeseen event not within the reasonable contemplation of the parties at the time the contract was made. Such occurrence must go to the heart of the contract.

Further light is shed upon the provisions of Section 2–615, in Comment No. 4 accompanying that section, which states:

4. Increased cost alone does not excuse performance unless the rise in cost is due to some unforeseen contingency which alters the essential nature of the performance. Neither is a rise or a collapse in the market in itself a justification, for that is exactly the type of business risk which business contracts made at fixed prices are intended to cover. But a severe shortage of raw materials or of supplies due to a contingency such as war, embargo, local crop failure, unforeseen shutdown of major sources of supply or the like, which either causes a marked increase in cost or altogether prevents the seller from securing supplies necessary to his performance, is within the contemplation of this section.

It should again be emphasized that in the negotiations leading to the contract now before this court an escalator clause was agreed upon to cover the contingencies of increase in Peabody's costs due to wages reflected by labor contracts; payments for unemployment, social security taxes and Workers' Compensation insurance premiums; costs of compliance with federal, state and local laws, regulations or orders; railroad tariffs; and increase in the costs of material and supplies, explosives, electric power and administrative and supervisory expense based upon the Industrial Commodities Index of the Department of Labor. There is no evidence nor, indeed, serious claim that Public Service did not abide by the letter of these provisions, and in addition, prior to suit, agreed to a further price increase of $1 per net ton, which Peabody rejected.

The facts as shown by the record lead to the conclusion that at least some of the loss resulted from the fact that for some unexplained reason the Industrial Commodities Index lagged behind the Consumer Price Index, the measuring factor first proposed by Peabody, in reflecting inflationary cost increases. That such indexes were based upon different commercial and economic factors was presumably known by both parties since each was skilled and experienced in those areas and the divergence between the indexes could not be said to be unforeseeable. Be that as it may, Peabody agreed to the use of the Industrial Commodities Index factor.

The other claim made by Peabody, alleged to bring it within the doctrine of "commercial impracticability," is the Arab oil embargo. Such a possibility was common knowledge and had been thoroughly discussed and recognized for many years by our government, media economists and business, and the fact that the embargo was imposed during the term of the contract here involved was foreseeable. Peabody failed to demonstrate that this embargo affected its ability to secure oil or petroleum products necessary to its mining production, albeit at inflated cost. In fact, as previously stated, this embargo can reasonably be said to have, at least indirectly, contributed to the marked appreciation to the value of Peabody's coal reserves by forcing the market value of that alternative source of energy upward in this country.

It is apparent that Peabody did make a bad bargain and an unprofitable one under its contract with Public Service, resulting in a loss, the cause and size of which is disputed. But this fact alone does not deal with either the "basic assumption" on which the contract was negotiated or alter the "essential nature of the performance" thereunder so as to constitute "commercial impracticability." The court below properly decreed specific performance.

Judgment for Public Service affirmed.

ETHICAL AND PUBLIC POLICY CONCERNS

1. The *Williams v. Curtin* case illustrates a problem that can readily arise in situations where supplies of the goods that are the subject of a contract are either in significantly shorter, or more plentiful, supply than when the agreement was made and/or there has been a significant change in the market price. When, if ever, is a buyer or seller ethically justified in trying to find a way out of a contractual obligation because the supply or market price conditions have so changed that he can make a better deal elsewhere? Concomitantly, are there circumstances under which the other party, acting in an ethically responsible manner, should voluntarily release the disadvantaged party from her contractual commitment?

2. Suppose that you recently purchased a new automobile. The automobile has a number of problems that the dealer is unable to completely fix after you have left it with the dealer on two occasions. Although the dealer indicates a willingness to fix the remaining problems and confidence that they can be remedied quickly and completely, you have now concluded that you would prefer to have a car made by another manufacturer. Are there any ethical considerations involved in a decision on your part to attempt to revoke your acceptance of the automobile?

3. Where a contract calls for delivery in installments, the buyer can reject an installment delivery containing nonconforming goods only where the nonconformity substantially affects the value of the delivery and cannot be corrected; where the defects are relatively minor the buyer has to keep the installment if the seller, for example, offers an allowance to make up for the nonconformity. Suppose you are a seller with some goods you know have minor defects and that you would like to get rid of. Would it be ethical for you to send them to a customer with whom you have a contract for installment deliveries of the goods, knowing that they do not conform to the contract and that the customer will have to accept them as long as you give him a price allowance?

SUMMARY

The basic rules of contract law regarding the performance of contracts apply to sales contracts. Granting options as to performance to the buyer and seller does not affect the validity of a sales contract that is otherwise valid. Each party must act in good faith and within the scope of what is commercially reasonable in exercising his options and must cooperate in a reasonable manner in the performance of the contract.

The conduct of the parties, the course of dealing, and trade usage are considered along with the contract terms in determining the parties' duties of performance. An assignment of a sales contract, unless otherwise agreed, includes the delegation of duties, and a general prohibition of the assignment of a contract bars only the delegation of duties. The assignor does not relieve himself of his liability for the performance of the contract by delegating his duties.

The basic duty of the seller is to deliver the goods called for by the contract, and the basic duty of the buyer is to accept and pay for the goods. Where the seller is to ship the goods, he must deliver conforming goods to a carrier and make a reasonable contract for their carriage. At delivery, the buyer generally has the right to inspect the goods before accepting and paying for them.

An acceptance of goods occurs when a buyer indicates to the seller, after the buyer has inspected the goods or has had an opportunity to inspect them, that he will keep the goods or when a buyer exercises acts of ownership over goods that are inconsistent with the seller's ownership. Acceptance of any part of a commercial unit is acceptance of the entire unit. The buyer must pay for accepted goods at the contract rate. If the buyer accepts nonconforming goods, he must, if he wishes to hold the seller liable, give the seller timely notice that the goods are nonconforming.

A buyer may revoke an acceptance if the nonconformity of the goods substantially impairs their value and was not discoverable or if the buyer relied on the seller's assurance of cure. Revocation of acceptance must be exercised before there is a substantial change in the goods. The buyer must act within a reasonable time and give the seller reasonable notice of his revocation.

If the contract is an installment contract, the buyer has the right to reject any nonconforming installment if the nonconformity substantially impairs the value of the installment and cannot be cured. The seller may cure the defect, but if the defect impairs the value of the whole contract, it is a breach of the whole contract.

If nonconforming goods are tendered, the buyer may reject all, accept all, or accept any commercial unit and reject the rest. Upon rejection, if the goods are in the buyer's possession or control, the buyer owes a duty to use reasonable care to protect them. He must hold the goods for a period sufficient to permit the seller to remove them; if the seller does not have a place of business or an agent in the market, the buyer must follow the seller's instructions as to disposition of the goods. If no instructions are given, the buyer must, if the goods are perishable or subject to a rapid change in value, sell them for the seller's account. If the goods are not perishable, he may store or reship them or sell them for the seller's account. The buyer is entitled to reimbursement for his expenses plus a commission. If the buyer wrongfully rejects goods, he is liable to the seller for breach of contract.

If either party to a sales contract deems himself insecure, as tested by commercial standards, he may demand assurance before proceeding with performance. If a party repudiates a sales contract, the aggrieved party may wait or he may bring an action for breach of the contract. In the event of repudiation, the usual remedies for the breach of the sales contract are available to the aggrieved party. If the party who has repudiated a sales contract wishes to withdraw his repudiation, he may do so by giving the aggrieved party notice of his withdrawal before the aggrieved party has canceled the contract or materially changed his position in reliance on the repudiation.

A party to a sales contract is excused from performance if his performance, due to no fault on his part, becomes commercially impracticable. If the impracticability is as to means of transportation or means of payment, the affected party may resort to substitute means, if available. If the impracticability causes delay or ability to perform only partially, the seller must allocate performances among his buyers. A buyer may accept his allotment or cancel the contract.

PROBLEM CASES

1. Baker was a buyer and distributor of popcorn. Ratzlaff was a farmer who grew popcorn. In 1983, Baker and Ratzlaff entered into a written contract pursuant to which Ratzlaff agreed that in 1983 he would raise 380 acres of popcorn and sell the popcorn to Baker. Baker agreed to furnish the seed popcorn and to pay $4.75 per hundred pounds of popcorn. The popcorn was to be delivered to Baker as he ordered it, and Baker was to pay for the popcorn as it was delivered. At Baker's request, the first delivery was made on February 2 of the following year and the second on February 4. On neither occasion did Ratzlaff ask Baker to pay or Baker offer to pay. During that week, Ratzlaff and Baker had several

phone conversations about further deliveries, but there was no discussion about payments. On February 11, Ratzlaff sent written notice to Baker that he was terminating the contract because Baker had not paid for the two loads of popcorn that had been delivered. In the meantime, Ratzlaff sold his remaining 1.6 million pounds of popcorn to another buyer at $8 per hundred pounds. Baker then sued Ratzlaff for breach of contract. Did Ratzlaff act in good faith in terminating the contract? *No. Ratzlaff waived rights to payment p448*

2. On October 15, Bell Brand Foods entered into one contract with Heggblade-Marguleas-Tenneco, Inc. (HMT), under which HMT was to deliver 5,000 hundredweight (cwt.) sacks of Kennebec potatoes between May 15 and July 15 of the following year at $2.60 per sack, and another contract under which HMT was to deliver 95,000 cwt. sacks of Kennebec potatoes between May 15 and July 15 at $2.35 per sack. HMT was a company that had been formed through the merger of a potato grower and a company that marketed agricultural products and had had no prior experience in marketing processing potatoes. Because processing potato contracts are executed eight or nine months before the harvest season, the custom in the processing potato industry is to treat the quantity solely as a reasonable estimate of the buyers' needs based on their customers' demands and of the growers' ability to supply based on the anticipated yield for the delivery period. As a result of a decline in demand for Bell Brand products from May through July, Bell Brand's sales for the late spring and summer decreased substantially. Consequently, Bell Brand's need for potatoes from its suppliers was severely reduced and it prorated the reduced demand among its suppliers, including HMT, as fairly as possible. By the end of the harvest season, Bell Brand was able to take only 60,105 cwt. sacks from HMT on the two contracts. HMT claimed to have sustained damages of $87,000 because it overplanted and brought a lawsuit against Bell Brand seeking damages for breach of contract. HMT contended that the quantity terms in the contracts were definite and unambiguous, and that the judge should not admit into evidence the custom of the processing potato industry that the amounts specified were only reasonable estimates. Should the evidence as to the custom in the potato industry be admitted to aid in the interpretation of the contract? *No. Since express term must prevail*

3. Harold Ledford agreed to purchase three used Mustang automobiles (a 1966 Mustang coupe, a 1965 fastback, and a 1966 convertible) from J. L. Cowan for $3,000. Ledford gave Cowan a cashier's check for $1,500 when he took possession of the coupe, with the understanding he would pay the remaining $1,500 on the delivery of the fastback and the convertible. Cowan arranged for Charles Canterberry to deliver the remaining vehicles to Ledford. Canterberry dropped the convertible off at a lot owned by Ledford and proceeded to Ledford's residence to deliver the fastback. He refused to unload it until Ledford paid him $1,500. Ledford refused to make the payment until he had an opportunity to inspect the convertible, which he suspected was not in the same condition that it had been in when he purchased it. Canterberry refused this request and returned both the fastback and the convertible to Cowan. Cowan then brought suit against Ledford to recover the balance of the purchase price. Was Ledford entitled to inspect the car before he paid the balance due on it?

4. Spada, an Oregon corporation, agreed to sell Belson, who operated a business in Chicago, two carloads of potatoes at "4.40 per sack, FOB Oregon shipping point." Spada had the potatoes put aboard the railroad cars; however, it did not have floor racks placed under the potatoes, as was customary during the winter months. As a result, there was no warm air circulating and the potatoes were frozen while in transit. Spada claims that its obligations ended with the delivery to the carrier and that the risk of loss was on Belson. What argument would you make for Belson?

5. In April, Reginald Bell contracted to sell potatoes to Red Ball Potato Company for fall delivery. The contract specified that the potatoes were to be "85 percent U.S. 1's." In Red Ball's dealings with Bell and other farmers, potatoes were delivered and paid for in truckload quantities. In the fall, Bell delivered several truckloads of potatoes. Samples of each load were taken for testing, and most of the loads were determined to be below 85 percent U.S. No 1. What options are open to Red Ball?

6. James Shelton, an experienced musician, operated the University Music Center. On Saturday, Barbara Farkas and her 22-year-old daughter, Penny, went to Shelton's store to look at violins. Penny had been studying violin in college for about nine months. They advised Shelton of the price range in which they were interested, and Penny told him that she was relying on his expertise. He selected a violin that was priced at $368.90, including the case and sales tax. Shelton claimed that the instrument had originally been priced

at $465 but that he had discounted it because Mrs. Farkas was willing to take it on an "as is" basis. Mrs. Farkas and Penny alleged that Shelton had represented that the violin was "the best" and "a perfect violin for you" and that it was of high quality. Mrs. Farkas paid for it by check. On the following Monday, Penny took the violin to her college music teacher, who immediately told her that it had poor tone and a crack in the body and that it was not the right instrument for her. Mrs. Farkas telephoned Shelton and asked for a refund. He refused, saying that she had purchased and accepted the violin on an "as is" basis. Had Farkas "accepted" the violin so that it was too late for her to "reject" it?

7. Dade purchased a new Jaguar automobile from Orange Motors. Almost immediately after delivery, Dade had problems with the car. The power steering was stiff, the air conditioner leaked and rattled, the doors did not close properly, and the steering column almost fell off. The car was in the shop for one half of the three months that Dade had it. Dade then filed a lawsuit seeking to revoke his acceptance of the car and to rescind the sales contract. Orange Motors claimed that it should only be required to repair the car. Is Orange Motors's contention correct?

8. Walters, a grower of Christmas trees, contracted to supply Traynor with "top quality trees." When the shipment arrived and was inspected, Traynor discovered that some of the trees were not top quality. Within 24 hours, Traynor notified Walters that he was rejecting the trees that were not top quality. Walters did not have a place of business or an agent in the town where Traynor was. Christmas was only a short time away. The trees were perishable and would decline in value to zero by Christmas Eve. Walters did not give Traynor any instructions, so Traynor sold the trees for Walters's account. Traynor then tried to recover from Walters the expenses he incurred in caring for and selling the trees. Did Walters act properly in rejecting the trees and reselling them for the seller?

9. Bende, a seller of military supplies internationally, agreed to sell the government of Ghana 10,000 pairs of combat boots for $158,000. Bende contracted with Kiffe Products, a seller of camping and military supplies, to provide him with 10,000 pairs of boots "leather upper, lace-up front, black, with reinforced bottom sole, Korean made, but all Korean markings removed from boots, in neutral boxes." The boots were manufactured in Korea and shipped to the United States, where they were loaded on railroad cars for shipment to the East

Coast. The train transporting the boots derailed near Omaha, Nebraska, and most of the boots were destroyed. When Bende sued Kiffe for failing to deliver the boots to it, Kiffe claimed that the derailment excused its performance under the contract. Has Kiffe stated a valid defense? *Yes. Contract voided upon Destruction since risk had not shifted*

10. Whelan ordered fuel oil from Griffith to be delivered at his farm home, which was located on a country road. The oil was to be delivered on a COD basis. Griffith made two attempts to deliver the oil, but each time no one was found at home. The morning after a heavy snow fall, the heaviest in 20 years, Griffith equipped the truck with chains and made a third attempt to deliver the oil but found on arrival that the driveway to the house was impassable due to snowdrifts approximately six feet high. When the driver drove past the house and attempted to turn around, the truck became stuck in the snow and had to be towed back to the main highway. Whelan ran out of oil and, as a result of having no fuel, his heating plant froze, causing substantial damage to it. Whelan sued Griffith to recover for the damage to the heating plant, claiming the breach of the contract to deliver the oil was the cause of the damage. Should Griffith be held liable? *No! because he made three attempts (reasonable to deliver the oil) lets assume that reasonable amt of time (reasonable hours*

CHAPTER 22

REMEDIES FOR BREACH OF SALES CONTRACTS

INTRODUCTION

Usually, both parties to a contract for the sale of goods perform the obligations that they assumed in the contract. Occasionally, however, one of the parties to a contract fails to perform his obligations. When this happens, the Uniform Commercial Code (UCC or Code) provides the injured party with a variety of remedies for breach of contract. This chapter will set forth and explain the remedies available to an injured party, as well as the Code's rules that govern buyer-seller agreements as to remedies, and the Code's statute of limitations. The objective of the Code remedies is to put the injured person in the same position that he would have been in if the contract had been performed. Under the Code, an injured party may not recover consequential or punitive damages unless such damages are specifically provided for in the Code or in another statute [1–106].[1]

Agreements as to Remedies

The buyer and seller may provide their own remedies in the contract, to be applied in the event that one of the parties fails to perform. They may also limit either the remedies that the law makes available or the damages

---

[1]The numbers in brackets refer to the sections of the Uniform Commercial Code.

that can be covered [2–719(1)]. If the parties agree on the amount of damages that will be paid to the injured party, this amount is known as **liquidated damages.** An agreement for liquidated damages is enforced if the amount is *reasonable* and if *actual* damages would be *difficult to prove* in the event of a breach of the contract. The amount is considered reasonable if it is not so large as to be a *penalty* or so small as to be *unconscionable* [2–718(1)].

For example, Carl Carpenter contracts to build and sell a display booth for $5,000 to Hank Hawker for Hawker to use at the state fair. Delivery is to be made to Hawker by September 1. If the booth is not delivered on time, Hawker will not be able to sell his wares at the fair. Carpenter and Hawker might agree that if delivery is not made by September 1, Carpenter will pay Hawker $2,750 as liquidated damages. The actual sales that Hawker might lose without a booth would be very hard to prove, so Hawker and Carpenter can provide some certainty through the liquidated damages agreement. Carpenter then knows what he will be liable for if he does not perform his obligation. Similarly, Hawker knows what he can recover if the booth is not delivered on time. The $2,750 amount is probably reasonable. If the amount were $500,000, it likely would be void as a penalty because it is way out of line with the damages that Hawker would reasonably be expected to sustain. And if the amount were too small, say $1, it might be considered unconscionable and therefore not enforceable.

If a liquidated damages clause is not enforceable because it is a penalty or unconscionable, the injured party can recover the actual damages that he suffered. The *Stock Shop v. Bozell and Jacobs* case, which follows, illustrates a situation where a court refused to enforce a purported liquidated damages clause in a contract.

STOCK SHOP, INC. v. BOZELL AND JACOBS, INC.

481 N.Y.S.2d 269 (N.Y. Sup. Ct. 1984)

Stock Shop delivered to Bozell and Jacobs, an advertising agency, 697 stock photographs to consider for possible use as part of a slide show for a client. They depicted various U.S. cities and other points of interest. The delivery memo between the parties stated: "The monetary damage for loss or damage of an original color transparency or photograph shall be determined by the value of each individual photograph. Recipient agrees, however, that the reasonable minimum value of such lost or damaged photographs or transparency shall be no less than fifteen hundred ($1,500) dollars."

Thirty-nine of the photographs that Bozell and Jacobs agreed to license were never returned. Stock Shop brought suit against Bozell and Jacobs to recover for the photographs. It moved for summary judgment, claiming that based on the liquidated damages clause, it was entitled to $1,500 per photograph.

Saxe, Judge. Bozell and Jacobs' main argument is that even if it is liable for the non-return of 39 photographs, the $1,500 per photograph liquidated damage bears no relationship to the actual or fair or reasonable value of the photographs and is therefore a penalty.

In early English legal history, parties used penal bonds to secure performance of a contract. Upon a breach, the entire amount of the bond was due immediately, regardless of the actual damages suffered. Courts sitting in equity, however, had jurisdiction to intervene and mitigate the harsh results where the breach did not cause any actual damage. American courts recognized the parties' right to set damages in advance of a breach, and distinguished valid clauses from penalties. These courts allowed recovery where the parties had attempted to reasonably estimate in advance the damages that might result from a breach.

The controlling principle of law is contained in section 2–718(1) of the Uniform Commercial Code which reads:

Damages for breach by either party may be liquidated in the agreement but only at an amount which is reasonable in the light of the anticipated or actual harm caused by the breach, the difficulties of proof of loss, and the inconvenience or nonfeasibility of otherwise obtaining an adequate remedy. A term fixing unreasonably large liquidated damages is void as a penalty.

The first sentence of subdivision (1) of section 2–718 focuses on the situation of the parties both at the time of contracting and at the time of breach. So a liquidated damages provision will be valid if reasonable with respect to either (1) the harm which the parties anticipate will result from the breach at the time of contracting or (2) the actual damages suffered by the nondefaulting party at the time of breach.

Stock Shop contends that the $1,500 per photograph liquidated damage provision is an industry wide standard or custom. Bozell and Jacobs disputes this. But the fact remains that even assuming this amount is accepted throughout the industry, section 2–718(1) requires that an examination be made to determine the reasonableness of the sum from the aspect of anticipated harm determined at the time of entry into the contract or actual harm determined at the time of breach. Stock Shop has not made a successful demonstration under either prong of this test. The $1,500 per photograph figure may bear no relationship to the actual value of a photograph which (a) may never have generated any past revenue, (b) is neither unique or novel, and (c) may be able to be duplicated by the photographer who submitted the photograph.

In terms of assessing the reasonableness of the anticipated harm, depending upon the nature and quality of the photograph, an amount required for the loss of one or more of them would, of necessity, vary. I conclude, therefore, that the liquidated damage provision is invalid because it is not reasonable with respect to the anticipated or actual harm.

Alternatively, the provision in question is indefinite, rendering it unenforceable. The $1,500 figure is a minimum value and permits Stock Shop to prove a greater value if disposed to do so. There is, therefore, no true liquidation of damages since Stock Shop is given the option to disregard the liquidated sum and sue for actual damages. Such a clause is invalid. The clause would allow Stock Shop to have its cake and eat it too. Accordingly, it is no liquidated damages clause at all.

Stock Shop's motion for summary judgment denied.

Liability for consequential damages resulting from a breach of contract (such as lost profits or damage to property) may also be limited or excluded by agreement. The limitation or exclusion is not enforced if it would be unconscionable. Any attempt to limit consequential damages for injury caused to a person by consumer goods is considered prima facie unconscionable [2–719(3)]. Suppose an automobile manufacturer makes a warranty as to the quality of an automobile that is purchased as a consumer good. It then tries to disclaim responsibility for any person injured if the car does not conform to the warranty and to limit its liability to replacing any defective parts. The disclaimer of consequential injuries in this case would be unconscionable and therefore would not be enforced. Exclusion of or limitation on consequential damages is permitted where the loss is commercial, as long as the exclusion or limitation is not unconscionable.

The *Hartzell v. Justus Co., Inc.* case, which follows, illustrates how the Code applies to a situation where circumstances cause a limited remedy agreed to by the parties to fail in its essential purpose. When this happens, the limited remedy is not enforced and the general Code remedies are available to the injured party.

HARTZELL v. JUSTUS CO., INC.
693 F.2d 770 (8th Cir. 1982)

Dr. Allan Hartzell purchased a log home construction kit manufactured by Justus Homes. Hartzell purchased the package for $38,622 from Del Carter, who was Justus Homes's dealer for the Sioux Falls area. He also hired Carter's construction company to build the house, which eventually cost about $150,000. Hartzell was dissatisfied with the house in many respects. His chief complaints were that knotholes in the walls and ceilings leaked rain profusely and that the home was not weathertight because flashings were not included in the roofing materials and because the timbers were not kiln-dried and therefore shrank. He also complained that an undersized support beam, which eventually cracked, was included in the package. This defect resulted in floor cracks and in inside doors that would not close. Hartzell claimed that the structural defects were only partially remediable and that the fair market value of the house was reduced even after all practicable repairs had been made. Hartzell brought suit against Justus Homes, alleging negligence and breach of implied and express warranties and seeking damages for loss in value and the cost of repairs. A jury awarded Hartzell a verdict of $34,794.67. Justus Homes appealed.

Arnold, Circuit Judge.   Justus Homes contends the district court failed to adequately consider a limitation-of-remedies clause contained in its contract with Hartzell. Justus Homes relies on Clause 10c of the contract, which says that Justus will repair or replace defective materials, and Clause 10d, which states that this limited repair or replacement clause is the exclusive remedy available against Justus. These agreements, Justus asserts, are valid under the Uniform Commercial Code, § 2–719(1). Section 2–719(1) states:

(1) Subject to the provisions of subsections (2) and (3) of this section and of § 2–718 on liquidation and limitation of damages,

(a) The agreement may provide for remedies in addition to or in substitution for those provided in this article and may limit or alter the measure of damages recoverable under this article, as by limiting the buyer's remedies to return of the goods and repayment of the price or to repair and replacement of nonconforming goods or parts; and

(b) Resort to a remedy as provided is optional unless the remedy is expressly agreed to be exclusive, in which case it is the sole remedy.

Subsection (1) of § 2–719 is qualified by subsection (2): "Where circumstances cause an exclusive or limited remedy to fail of its essential purpose, remedy may be had as provided in this title." The jury's verdict for Hartzell in an amount almost exactly equal to Hartzell's evidence of cost of repairs plus diminution in market value means it must have found that the structural defects were not entirely remediable. Such a finding necessarily means that the limited warranty failed of its essential purpose.

Two of our recent cases support this conclusion. In *Soo Line R.R. v. Fruehauf Corp.*, the defendant claimed, relying on a limitation-of-remedies clause similar to the one involved here, that the plaintiff's damages should be limited to the reasonable cost of repairing the railroad cars that plaintiff had bought from defendant. The jury verdict included, among other things, an award for the difference between the value of the cars as actually manufactured and what they would have been worth if they had measured up to the defendant's representations. This court affirmed the verdict for the larger amount. We held, construing the Minnesota UCC, which is identical to § 2–719 as adopted in South Dakota, that the limitation-of-remedies clause was ineffective because the remedy as thus limited failed of its essential purpose. The defendant, though called upon to make the necessary repairs, had refused to do so, and the repairs as performed by the plaintiff itself "did not fully restore the cars to totally acceptable operating conditions."

Here, Justus Homes attempted to help with the necessary repairs, which is more than Fruehauf did in the Soo Line case, but after the repairs had been completed, the house was still, according to the jury verdict, not what Justus had promised it would be. The purpose of a remedy is to give to a buyer what the seller promised him—that is, a house that did not leak. If repairs alone do not achieve that end, then to limit the buyer's remedy to repair would cause that remedy to fail of its essential purpose.

An analogous case is *Select Port, Inc. v. Babcock Swine, Inc.*, applying § 2–719 as adopted in Iowa. The defendant had promised to deliver to plaintiff certain extraordinary pigs known as Midwestern Gilts and Meatline Boars. Instead, only ordinary pigs were delivered. Plaintiff sued for breach of warranty, and defendant claimed that its damages, if any, should be limited to a return of the purchase price by an express clause to that effect in the contract. The district court held that the clause was unenforceable because it was unconscionable, see § 2–719(3), and because it failed of its essential purpose. We affirmed. "Having failed to deliver the highly-touted special pigs, defendants may not now assert a favorable clause to limit their liability."

So here, where the house sold was found by the jury to fall short of the seller's promises, and where repairs could not make it right, Justus Homes's liability cannot be limited to the cost of repairs. If the repairs had been adequate to restore the house to its promised condition, and if Dr. Hartzell had claimed additional consequential damages, for example, water damage to a rug from the leaky roof, the limitation-of-remedies clause would have been effective. But that is not this case.

The evidence in the record all demonstrates that the repair or replacement clause was a failure under the circumstances of this case. Some of the house's many problems simply could not be remedied by repair or replacement. The clause having failed of its essential purpose, that is, effective enjoyment of implied and express warranties, Dr. Hartzell was entitled, under UCC § 2–719(2), to any of the buyer's remedies provided by the Code. Among these remedies are consequential damages as provided in § 2–714 and § 2–715(2).

Judgment for Hartzell affirmed.

Statute of Limitations

The Code provides that a lawsuit for breach of a sales contract must be filed within four years after the breach occurs. The parties to a contract may shorten this period to one year, but they may not extend it for longer than four years [2–725]. Normally, a breach of warranty is considered to have occurred when the goods are delivered to the buyer. However, if the warranty covers future performance of goods (for example, a warranty on a tire for four years or 40,000 miles), then the breach occurs at the time the buyer should have discovered the defect in the product. If, for example, the buyer of the tire discovers the defect after driving 25,000 miles on the tire over a three-year period, he would have four years from that time to bring any lawsuit to remedy the breach.

In the *Wilson v. Hammer Holdings, Inc.* case, which follows, the court rejected the argument that a warranty given in connection with the sale of a painting extended to the future performance of the painting.

WILSON v. HAMMER HOLDINGS, INC.
6 UCC Rep.2d 321 (1st Cir. 1988)

In 1961, Dorothy and John Wilson purchased a painting entitled *Femme Debout* from the Hammer Galleries. They paid $11,000 for the work that was expressly guaranteed to be an original work of art by Edouard Vuillard. The purchase agreement stated that "the authenticity of this picture is guaranteed." In 1984, in preparation for selling it, the Wilsons had the picture examined by an expert. He determined that the painting was not done by the French artist Vuillard, and he refused to authenticate it.

The Wilsons returned the painting to the Hammer Galleries, and then brought a lawsuit seeking damages for breach of warranty. Hammer Galleries asserted that the claim was barred by the UCC's four-year statute of limitations. The district court held that the claim was barred by the statute of limitations, and Wilson appealed.

Coffin, Circuit Judge.   The Massachussets statute of limitations for breach of a sales contract is set out in section 2–725. That section provides that

(1) An action for breach of any contract for sale must be commenced within four years after the cause of action has accrued. . . .

(2) A cause of action accrues when the breach occurs, regardless of the aggrieved party's lack of knowledge of the breach. A breach of warranty occurs when tender of delivery is made, except that where a warranty explicitly extends to future performance of the goods and discovery must await the time of such performance, the cause of action accrues when the breach is or should have been discovered.

There is no question that the Wilsons' action was untimely under this statute if it accrued at the time they purchased the painting and received the warranty because those events occurred twenty-six years before suit was filed. The Wilsons therefore contend that this case falls within the exception to section 2–725(2), and they argue that their cause of action accrued upon their discovery in 1985 that the painting was not authentic.

The district court found the exception in section 2–725(2) to be inapplicable because Hammer's warranty made no explicit reference to future performance as required by the statute. The Wilsons do not argue that the district court erred in reading the warranty to lack an explicit promise of future performance. Rather, they argue that a warranty of authenticity *necessarily* relates to the future condition of the artwork, despite the absence of explicit language to that effect, and for that reason, they claim that the exception in section 2–725(2) should apply to them.

Section 2–725(2) refers to a warranty of "future performance," and so the Wilsons' theory depends first on extending the concept of a "performance" to a painting. They concede that paintings, unlike consumer goods like automobiles and washing machines, generally are not purchased based on how they "perform" or "function." They suggest, however, that a painting "performs" "by being what it is represented to be." In this case, they say, "Femme Debout" could "perform" only by being an authentic Vuillard.

Accepting at least for the sake of argument that a painting does "perform" by being genuine, the question then becomes whether Hammer's express warranty of authenticity not only guaranteed the present "being" of the painting as an authentic Vuillard but also extended, as required by section 2–725(2), to the future existence of a painting as a Vuillard. On this point, the Wilsons argue that because the authenticity of a painting does not change over time, Hammer's warranty necessarily guaranteed the present *and* future existence of the painting as an authentic Vuillard. Therefore, they contend, explicit words warranting future performance would be superfluous in this context.

One difficulty with this argument, however, is that it asks us to ignore the literal language of the statute requiring an *explicit* promise of future performance. The Wilsons argue essentially that because the statutory exception's requirement of an explicit prospective warranty does not make sense in the context of the sale of paintings, we should dispense with that requirement. We are reluctant, however, to waive the specific eligibility requirements established by the legislature for what, it must be remembered, is an *exception* to the general limitations rule.

Even if we were to accept the Wilsons' argument that Hammer's warranty necessarily extended to future performance of the painting, and thus met the prospective warranty requirement of section 2–725(2), we nevertheless would conclude that their action is time-barred. The statute also requires that discovery of the breach "*must* await" the time of such future performance. That is not the case here. Because of the static nature of authenticity, the Wilsons were no less capable of discovering that "Femme Debout" was a fake at the time of purchase than they were at a later time.

Our reluctance to enlarge the scope of the exception in section 2–725(2) is strengthened by the recognition that the statute of limitations for art buyers could run indefinitely. Indeed, in this case suit was filed 26 years after the purchase. Although Massachussetts legislators may choose to provide perpetual protection for consumers of artistic products, it would be presumptuous for us to assume they would. Moreover, we think it is more likely that, if Massachusetts chooses to extend protection to art buyers in the way the Wilsons suggest, the legislature would fix some endpoint to the seller's possible liability—perhaps similar to the 20-year limitations period for an action seeking the recovery of land.

Judgment in favor of Hammer Galleries affirmed.

SELLER'S REMEDIES

Remedies Available to an Injured Seller

A buyer may breach a contract in a number of ways. The most common are: (1) by wrongfully refusing to accept goods, (2) by wrongfully returning goods, (3) by failing to pay for goods when payment is due, and (4) by indicating an unwillingness to go ahead with the contract.

When a buyer breaches a contract, the seller has a number of remedies under the Code, including the right to:

- ☐ Cancel the contract [2–703(f)].
- ☐ Withhold delivery of undelivered goods [2–703(a)].
- ☐ Resell the goods covered by the contract and recover damages from the buyer [2–706].
- ☐ Recover from the buyer the profit that the seller would have made on the sale or the damages that the seller sustained [2–708].
- ☐ Recover the purchase price of goods delivered to or accepted by the buyer [2–709].

In addition, a buyer may become insolvent and thus unable to pay the seller for goods already delivered or for goods that the seller is obligated to deliver. When a seller learns of a buyer's insolvency, the seller has a number of remedies, including the right to:

- ☐ Withhold delivery of undelivered goods [2–703(a)].

- ☐ Recover goods from a buyer upon the buyer's insolvency [2–702].
- ☐ Stop delivery of goods that are in the possession of a carrier or other bailee [2–705].

Cancellation and Withholding of Delivery

When a buyer breaches a contract, the seller has the right to cancel the contract and to hold up his own performance of the contract. The seller may then set aside any goods that were intended to fill his obligations under the contract [2–704].

If the seller is in the process of manufacturing the goods, he has two choices. He may complete manufacture of the goods, or he may stop manufacturing and sell the uncompleted goods for their scrap or salvage value. In choosing between these alternatives, the seller should select the alternative that will minimize the loss [2–704(2)]. Thus, a seller would be justified in completing the manufacture of goods that could be resold readily at the contract price. However, a seller would not be justified in completing specially manufactured goods that could not be sold to anyone other than the buyer who ordered them. The purpose of this rule is to permit the seller to follow a reasonable course of action to mitigate (minimize) the damages. In *Madsen v. Murrey & Sons Co., Inc.*, which follows, the seller, who did not complete the manufacture of goods on the buyer's repudiation, but rather dismantled and largely scrapped the existing goods, was held not to have acted in a commercially reasonable manner.

MADSEN v. MURREY & SONS CO., INC.

743 P.2d 1212 (Utah Sup. Ct. 1987)

Murrey & Sons Co., Inc. (Murrey) was engaged in the business of manufacturing and selling pool tables. Erik Madsen was working on an idea to develop a pool table that, through the use of electronic devices installed in the rails of the table, would produce lighting and sound effects in a fashion similar to a pinball machine. Murrey and Madsen entered into a written contract whereby Murrey agreed to manufacture 100 of its M1 4-foot by 8-foot six-pocket coin operated pool tables with customized rails capable of incorporating the electronic lighting and sound effects desired by Madsen. Under the agreement, Madsen would design the rails and provide the drawings to Murrey who would manufacture them to Madsen's specifications. Madsen was to design, manufacture, and install the electronic components for the tables. Madsen agreed to pay $550 per table or a total of $55,000 for the 100 tables and made a $42,500 deposit on the contract.

Murrey began the manufacture of the tables while Madsen continued to work on the design of the rails and electronics. Madsen encountered significant difficulties and notified Murrey that he would be unable to take delivery of the 100 tables. Madsen then brought suit to recover the $42,500 he had paid Murrey.

Following Madsen's repudiation of the contract, Murrey dismantled the pool tables and used salvageable materials to manufacture other pool tables. A good portion of the material was simply used as firewood. Murrey made no attempt to market the 100 pool tables at a discount or at any other price in order to mitigate the damages. It claimed the salvage value of the materials it reused as $7,448. The trial court ordered Murrey to return $21,250 to Madsen and Murrey appealed.

Howe, Justice.   Murrey contends that the trial court erred in concluding that it had failed to mitigate or minimize its damages in a commercially reasonable manner by not attempting to sell the 100 pool tables on the open market. It is a well-settled rule of the law of damages that "no party suffering a loss as the result of a breach of contract is entitled to any damages which could have been avoided if the aggrieved party had acted in a reasonably diligent manner in attempting to lessen his losses as a consequence of that breach." We have held:

Where a contractual agreement has been breached by a party thereto, the aggrieved party is entitled to those damages that will put him in as good a position as he would have been had the other party performed pursuant to the agreement. A corollary to this rule is that the aggrieved party may not, either by action or inaction, aggravate the injury occasioned by the breach, but has a duty actively to mitigate his damages.

Murrey asserts that it sufficiently mitigated its damages by dismantling the pool tables and salvaging various components that could be used to manufacture other pool tables. The salvage value to Murrey was claimed to be $7,448. Murrey presented testimony that selling the tables as "seconds" would damage its reputation for quality and that the various holes, notches and routings placed in the tables to accommodate the electrical components to be installed by buyer weakened the structure of the tables so as to submit seller to potential liability if they were sold on the market.

On the other hand, Ronald Baker, who had been involved with the manufacturing and marketing of pool tables for 25 years testified on behalf of the buyer that the notches, holes and routings made in the frame to accommodate electrical wiring would not adversely affect the quality or marketability of the 100 pool tables. According to Baker, the tables could have been sold at full value or at a discounted price. In addition to this testimony, the trial court had the opportunity to view the experimental table developed by Madsen and his associates and observe the holes, notches, and routings necessary for the electrical components.

The trial court found that Murrey's action in dismantling the tables and using the materials for salvage and firewood, rather than attempting to sell or market the tables at full or discounted price, was not commercially reasonable. The court then concluded that seller had a duty to mitigate its damages and failed to do so. The finding is supported by competent evidence.

Applying the trial court's finding that the pool tables, if completed, could have been sold for at least $21,250, Murrey's damages are the difference between the market price ($21,250) and the contract price ($55,000) or $33,750. The trial court found that Murrey was not entitled to any incidental damages. Under section 2–718(2), (3), Madsen's right to restitution of advance payments on the contract ($42,500) is subject to offset to the extent that seller establishes damages ($33,750), for a total recovery of $8,750.

Judgment for Madsen affirmed, with the recovery set at $8,750.

Resale of Goods

If the seller sets aside goods intended for the contract or completes the manufacture of such goods, he is not obligated to try to resell the goods to someone else. However, he may resell them and recover damages. The seller must make any resale in good faith and in a commercially reasonable manner. If the seller does so, he is entitled to recover from the buyer as damages the difference between the resale price and the price the buyer agreed to pay in the contract [2–706].

If the seller resells, he may also recover incidental damages, but the seller must give the buyer credit for any expenses that the seller saved because of the buyer's breach of contract. Incidental damages include storage charges and sales commissions paid when the goods were resold [2–710]. Expenses saved might be the cost of packaging the goods and/or shipping them to the buyer.

If the buyer and seller have agreed as to the manner in which the resale is to be made, the courts will enforce the agreement unless it is found to be unconscionable [2–302]. If the parties have not entered into an agreement as to the resale of the goods, they may be resold at public or private sale, but in all events the resale must be made in good faith and in a commercially reasonable manner. The seller should make it clear that the goods he is selling are those related to the broken contract.

If the goods are resold at private sale, the seller must give the buyer reasonable notification of his intention to resell [2–706(3)]. If the resale is a public sale, such as an auction, the seller must give the buyer notice of the time and place of the sale unless the goods are perishable or threaten to decline in value rapidly. The sale must be made at a usual place or market for public sales if one is reasonably available; and if the goods are not within the view of those attending the sale, the notification of the sale must state the place where the goods are located and provide for reasonable inspection by prospective bidders. The seller may bid at a public sale [2–706(4)].

The purchaser at a public sale who buys in good faith takes free from any rights of the original buyer even though the seller has failed to conduct the sale in compliance with the rules set out in the Code [2–706(5)]. The seller is not accountable to the buyer for any profit that the seller makes on a resale [2–706(6)].

Recovery of the Purchase Price

In the normal performance of a contract, the seller delivers conforming goods (goods that meet the contract specifications) to the buyer. The buyer accepts the goods and pays for them. The seller is entitled to the purchase price of all goods accepted by the buyer. He is also entitled to the purchase price of all goods that conformed to the contract and were lost or damaged after the buyer assumed the risk for their loss [2–709].

For example, a contract calls for Frank, a farmer, to ship 1,000 dozen eggs to Sutton, a grocer, with shipment "FOB Frank's Farm." If the eggs are lost or damaged while on their way to Sutton, she is responsible for paying Frank for them. Risk of loss is discussed in the Formation and Terms of Sales Contracts chapter.

In one other situation, the seller may recover the purchase or contract price from the buyer. This is where the seller has made an honest effort to resell the goods and was unsuccessful or where it is apparent that any such effort to resell would be unsuccessful. This might happen where the seller manufactured goods especially for the buyer and the goods are not usable by anyone else. Assume that Sarton's Supermarket sponsors a bowling team. Sarton's orders six green-and-red bowling shirts to be embroidered with "Sarton's Supermarket" on the back and the names of the team members on the pocket. After the shirts are completed, Sarton's wrongfully refuses to accept them. The manufacturer will be able to recover the agreed purchase price if it cannot sell the shirts to someone else.

If the seller sues the buyer for the contract price of the goods, he must hold the goods for the buyer. Then, the seller must turn the goods over to the buyer if the buyer pays for them. However, if resale becomes possible before the buyer pays for the goods, the seller may resell them. Then, the seller must give the buyer credit for the proceeds of the resale [2–709(2)].

Damages for Rejection or Repudiation

When the buyer refuses to accept goods that conform to the contract or repudiates the contract, the seller does not have to resell the goods. The seller has two other ways of determining the damages that the buyer is liable for because of the breach of contract: (1) the difference between the contract price and the market price at which the goods are currently selling and (2) the "profit" that the seller lost when the buyer did not go through with the contract [2–708].

The seller may recover as damages the difference between the contract price and the market price at the time and place the goods were to be delivered to the buyer. The seller may also recover any incidental damages, but must give the buyer credit for any expenses that the seller has saved [2–708(1)]. This measure of damages is most commonly sought by a seller when the market price of the goods dropped substantially between the time the contract was made and the time the buyer repudiated the contract.

For example, on January 1, Toy Maker, Inc., contracts with the Red Balloon Toy Shop to sell the shop 100,000 hula hoops at $3.50 each, with delivery to be made in Boston on June 1. By June 1, the hula hoop fad has passed and hula hoops are selling for $1 each in Boston. If Toy Shop repudiates the contract on June 1 and refuses to accept delivery of the 100,000 hula hoops, Toy Maker is entitled to the difference between the contract price of $350,000 and the June 1 market price in Boston of $100,000. Thus, Toy Maker could recover $250,000 in damages plus any incidental expenses, but less any expenses saved by it in not having to ship the hula hoops to Toy Shop (such as packaging and transportation costs).

If getting the difference between the contract price and the market price would not put the seller in as good a financial position as the seller would have been in if the contract had been performed, the seller may choose an alternative measure of damages based on the lost profit and overhead that the seller would have made if the sale had gone through. The seller can recover this lost profit and overhead plus any incidental expenses. However, the seller must give the buyer credit for any expenses saved as a result of the buyer's breach of contract [2–708(2)].

Using the hula hoop example, assume that the direct labor and material cost to Toy Maker of making the hoops was 75 cents each. Toy Maker could recover as damages from Toy Shop the profit Toy Maker lost when Toy Shop defaulted on the contract. Toy Maker would be entitled to the difference between the contract price of $350,000 and its direct cost of $75,000. Thus, Toy Maker could recover $275,000 plus any incidental expenses and less any expenses saved.

The circumstances under which a seller is entitled to recover his "lost profit" are discussed in the *R. E. Davis Chemical Corp. v. Diasonics, Inc.* case, which follows.

R. E. DAVIS CHEMICAL CORP. v. DIASONICS, INC.

4 UCC Rep.2d 369 (7th Cir. 1987)

Diasonics was engaged in the business of manufacturing and selling medical diagnostic equipment. On February 23, 1984, R. E. Davis Chemical Corporation entered into a written contract to buy a piece of medical diagnostic equipment and placed a $300,000 deposit with Diasonics. Prior to that time Davis had entered into a contract with two individuals to establish a medical facility where the equipment was to be used. The two individuals subsequently breached their contract with Davis, and Davis, in turn, breached its contract with Diasonics by refusing to take delivery of the equipment or to pay the balance due under the agreement. Diasonics later resold the equipment to a third party for the same price at which it was to be sold to Davis.

Davis sued Diasonics to recover its $300,000 down payment under section 2–718(2). Diasonics did not deny that Davis was entitled to recover its $300,000 deposit, less $500 as provided in section 2–718(2), but contended that it was entitled to offset the "profit" it lost from the sale when Davis breached the contract. The District Court held that Diasonics was not entitled to recover its "lost profit" but rather was limited to recovering the difference between the resale price and the contract price plus any incidental damages. Diasonics appealed.

Cudahy, Circuit Judge.   Diasonics alleged that it was a "lost volume seller," and, as such, it lost the profit from one sale when Davis breached its contract. Diasonics' position was that, in order to be put in as good a position as it would have been in had Davis performed, it was entitled to recover its lost profit on its contract with Davis under section 2–708(2). Section 2–708 provides:

(1) Subject to subsection (2) and to the provisions of this Article with respect to proof of market price (Section 2–723), the measure of damages for nonacceptance or repudiation by the buyer is the difference between the market price at the time and place for tender and the unpaid contract price together with any incidental damages provided in this Article (Section 2–710), but less expenses saved in consequence of the buyer's breach.

(2) If the measure of damages provided in subsection (1) is inadequate to put the seller in as good a position as performance would have done, then the measure of damages is the profit (including reasonable overhead) which the seller would have made from full performance by the buyer, together with any incidental damages provided in this Article (Section 2–710), due allowance for costs reasonably incurred and due credit for payments or proceeds of resale.

We must first consider Diasonics' claim that the District Court erred in holding that Diasonics was limited to the measure of damages provided in Section 2–706 and could not recover lost profits as a lost volume seller under Section 2–708(2). Surprisingly, given its importance, this issue has never been addressed by an Illinois court. Courts applying the laws of other states have unanimously adopted the position that a lost volume seller can recover its lost profits under Section 2–708(2). Contrary to the result reached by the district court, we conclude that the Illinois Supreme Court would follow these other cases and would conclude that a reselling seller, such as Diasonics, is free to reject the damage formula prescribed in Section 2–706 and to choose to proceed under Section 2-708.

Concluding that Diasonics is entitled to seek damages under Section 2–708, however, does not automatically result in Diasonics being awarded its lost profit. Two different measures of damages are provided in Section 2–708. The profit measure of damages, for which Diasonics is asking, is contained in Section 2–708(2). However, one applies Section 2–708(2) only if "the measure of damages provided in subsection (1) is inadequate to put the seller in as good a position as performance would have done." Diasonics claims that Section 2–708(1) does not provide an adequate measure of damages when the seller is a lost volume seller. To understand Diasonics' argument, we need to define the concept of a lost volume seller. Those cases that have addressed this issue have defined a lost volume seller as one that has a predictable and finite number of customers and that has the capacity either to sell to all new buyers or to make the one additional sale represented by the resale after the breach.

According to a number of courts and commentators, if the seller would have made the sale represented by the resale whether or not the breach occurred, damages measured by the difference between the contract price and market price cannot put the lost volume seller in as good a position as it would have been in had the buyer performed. The breach effectively cost the seller a "profit," and the seller can only be made whole by awarding it damages in the amount of its "lost profit" under Section 2–708.

We agree with Diasonics' position that, under some circumstances, the measure of damages provided under Section 2–708(1) will not put a reselling seller in as good a position as it would have been in had the buyer performed because the breach resulted in the seller losing sales volume. However, we disagree with the definition of "lost volume seller" adopted by other courts. Courts awarding lost profits to a lost volume seller have focused on whether the seller had the capacity to supply the breached units in addition to what it actually sold. In reality, however, the relevant questions include, not only whether the seller could have produced the breached units in addition to its actual volume, but also whether it would have been profitable for the seller to produce both units. Therefore, on remand, Diasonics must establish not only that it had the capacity to produce the breached unit in addition to the unit resold, but also that it would have been profitable for it to have produced and sold both.

Judgment in favor of Davis reversed.

Seller's Remedies Where Buyer Is Insolvent

If the seller has not agreed to extend credit to the buyer for the purchase price of goods, the buyer must make payment on delivery of the goods. If the seller tenders delivery of the goods, he may withhold delivery unless the agreed payment is made. Where the seller has agreed to extend credit to the buyer for the purchase price of the goods, but discovers before delivery that the buyer is insolvent, the seller may refuse delivery unless the buyer pays cash for the goods together with the unpaid balance for all goods previously delivered under the contract [2–702(1)].

At common law, a seller had the right to rescind a sales contract induced by fraud and to recover the goods unless they had been resold to a bona fide purchaser for value. Based on this general legal principle, the Code provides that where the seller discovers that the buyer has received goods while insolvent, the seller may reclaim the goods upon demand made within 10 days after their receipt. This right granted to the seller is based on constructive deceit on the part of the buyer. Receiving goods while insolvent is equivalent to a false representation of solvency. To protect his rights, all the seller is required to do is to make a demand within the 10-day period; he need not actually repossess the goods.

If the buyer has misrepresented his solvency to this particular seller in writing within three months before the delivery of the goods, the 10-day limitation on the seller's right to reclaim the goods does not apply. However, the seller's right to reclaim the goods is subject to the prior rights of purchasers in the ordinary course of the buyer's business, good faith purchasers for value, creditors with a perfected lien on the buyer's inventory [2–702(2) and (3)], and a trustee in bankruptcy. The relative rights of creditors to their debtor's collateral are discussed in the Security Interests in Personal Property chapter.

The case that follows, *Conoco, Inc. v. Braniff, Inc.*, illustrates some of issues that may arise when a creditor seeks to reclaim goods from an insolvent buyer.

CONOCO, INC. v. BRANIFF, INC.

11 UCC Rep.2d 519 (Bankr. M.D. Fla. 1990)

Braniff, an airline, had an agreement with Conoco whereby Conoco supplied Braniff with its needs for Jet A aviation fuel. The fuel was sent through an interstate common carrier pipeline used by numerous suppliers, including Conoco. The pipeline contained breakout points where fuel was directed out of the pipeline and into tank farm storage facilities operated by Ogden Allied Aviation Services, Braniff's designated fueling agent, at the Dallas–Fort Worth and Kansas City airports.

The agreement called for Braniff to make advance payments for its designated fuel needs for the following week, with settlement of overages or shortages on a monthly basis. Braniff made a payment of $320,000 on September 20, 1989, for its anticipated needs through September 27 and was scheduled to make a $420,000 payment on September 27, 1989. The payment was not made on September 27, and early the next morning Braniff filed a petition in bankruptcy under Chapter 11 of the Bankruptcy Code.

On September 29, 1989, Conoco sent Braniff a "Notice of Reclamation" seeking reclamation of unpaid fuel delivered into the tank farms at the Dallas–Fort Worth airports and Kansas City during the previous 10-day period. The reclamation notice identified the fuel for which reclamation was sought by specifying 14 bills of lading representing unpaid shipments occurring from September 19 through September 27.

Corcoran, Bankruptcy Judge.   In order to establish entitlement to reclamation from a debtor under section 2–702 of the UCC and section 546 of the Bankruptcy Code, a reclaiming seller must satisfy the following four-part test:

1. The debtor was insolvent at the time the goods were delivered by the seller;
2. A written demand was made on the debtor within ten days after the goods were delivered to the debtor;
3. The goods were identifiable at the time the demand was made; and
4. The goods were in the possession and control of the debtor at the time the demand was made.

Braniff contends that the fuel at issue here was neither identifiable nor in its possession and control at the time the reclamation demand was made because of the commingling that occurred in the common carrier pipelines and at the airport tank farms. Braniff points out that the fuel was pumped through a common carrier pipeline from Conoco's refineries with petroleum products belonging to numerous other suppliers. Once the fuel was received at the Ogden Allied tank farms, it was then commingled in large tanks with fuel supplied by other suppliers and allocated to and for the use of numerous users. At Dallas–Fort Worth, the commingled fuel allocated to Braniff had been supplied solely by Conoco. At Kansas City, the fuel allocated to Braniff had been supplied by four suppliers, including Conoco.

In the case of fungible, bulk petroleum products, such as jet fuel, the "identification" and "possession and control" requirements of the Code and the UCC mandate that the reclaiming party:

trace the [fuel] from its possession into an identifiable mass and to show that the mass contains only [fuel] of like kind and grade. If the mass of [fuel into which the fuel is traced] is subject to [the debtor's] control, then it is both "identifiable" and "in the possession of the debtor."

In this case the jet fuel type A was shipped from Conoco's refineries through a common carrier pipeline where it was commingled with other jet fuel type A refined by other suppliers and sold to other users. The commingling further occurred in the airport tank farms, from which many airlines withdrew the fuel that was ultimately pumped into airplanes. Plainly, on these facts, Conoco has traced its fuel into an identifiable mass containing only fuel of like grade and quality.

Likewise Conoco has shown that the mass of fuel in the airport tank farms was subject to Braniff's control. The tank farms were owned and operated by Braniff's fueling agent. The fueling agent would then draw down from the fuel in the storage tanks the amount needed to fuel Braniff aircraft. On this record, it is clear that the fueling agent abided Braniff's instructions.

The fact that the tanks contained fuel allocated to other airlines, by itself, is irrelevant to the "identification" and "possession and control" issue. The inquiry here deals solely with the fuel in the tanks allocated to Braniff.

The fact that the fueling agent also served as fueling agent for other airlines and that other airlines controlled their allocable portion of the fuel in the tank farm storage tanks does not diminish the control Braniff exercised over its allocable portion. The point, of course, is that Braniff had the ability and authority to control the disposition of its fuel at the time the reclamation notice was received.

Conoco desires to reclaim 284,107 gallons for which it is unpaid from the ending pool of 397,735. In effect, Conoco wants the court to assume that Braniff used during the ten-day reclamation period the fuel that it had on hand before the period began, the fuel that Conoco supplied during the reclamation period for which payment was made, and the fuel provided by three other suppliers during the reclamation period. In other words, Conoco says only Conoco fuel for which payment had *not* been made was left in the tank at the end of the reclamation period and that Conoco can now claim this "identified" fuel.

Braniff, of course, contends just the opposite. Braniff would have the court assume that Braniff used during the ten-day reclamation period the Conoco fuel for which payment was *not* made so that the fuel remaining in the tank at the end of the period represents only fuel that was there before the reclamation period began, fuel supplied by Conoco for which payment was made during the reclamation period, and fuel supplied by other suppliers.

The court concludes that it is required to reject both approaches. Where, as here, there are several suppliers delivering fungible, bulk goods into a common tank, the supplier must do more than merely trace its fungible, bulk goods into the pool. The supplier must go further and show what quantity of goods was in the pool at the beginning of the relevant reclamation period. The supplier must also show when, and how much of the goods, each of the suppliers contributed to the pool during that period. Finally, the supplier must show how much of the total remained in the pool at the end of the relevant period. With that information the court can then determine the amount of each bulk shipment that was consumed by the debtor during the period. The court can also determine to which supplier the amount remaining in the tank at the end of the period should be attributed or the proportional way in which the amount remaining should be allocated among the suppliers. Implicit in the rule the court states here is a "first in, first out" theory of bulk fuel use to be used in cases such as this where fungible, bulk goods are pooled or commingled.

On the evidence presented, Conoco established its right to reclaim only the 100,002 gallons of fuel it delivered to Dallas–Fort Worth on September 26.

Judgment for Conoco.

Seller's Right to Stop Delivery

If the seller discovers that the buyer is insolvent, he has the right to stop the delivery of any goods that he has shipped to the buyer, regardless of the size of the shipment. If a buyer repudiates a sales contract or fails to make a payment due before delivery, the seller has the right to stop delivery of any large shipment of goods, such as a carload, a truckload, or a planeload [2–705].

To stop delivery, the seller must notify the carrier or other bailee in time for the bailee to prevent delivery of the goods. After receiving notice to stop delivery, the carrier or other bailee owes a duty to hold the goods and deliver them as directed by the seller. The seller is liable to the carrier or other bailee for expenses incurred or damages resulting from compliance with his order to stop delivery. If a nonnegotiable document of title has been issued for the goods, the carrier or other bailee does not have a duty to obey a stop-delivery order issued by any person other than the person who consigned the goods to him [2–705(3)].

Liquidated Damages

If the seller has justifiably withheld delivery of the goods because of the buyer's breach, the buyer is entitled to recover any money or goods he has delivered to the seller over and above the agreed amount of liquidated damages. If there is no such agreement, the seller will not be permitted to retain an amount in excess of $500 or 20 percent of the value of the total performance for which the buyer is obligated under the contract, whichever is smaller. This right of restitution is subject to the seller's right to recover damages under other provisions of the Code and to recover the amount of value of benefits received by the buyer directly or indirectly by reason of the contract [2–718].

CONCEPT REVIEW

SELLER'S REMEDIES (on breach by buyer)

Problem	Seller's Remedy

Buyer Refuses to Go Ahead with Contract and Seller Has Goods	1. Seller may cancel contract, suspend performance, and set aside goods intended to fill the contract.
	  a. If seller is in the process of manufacturing, he may complete manufacture or stop and sell for scrap, picking alternative that in his judgment at the time will minimize the seller's loss.
	  b. Seller can resell goods covered by contract and recover difference between contract price and proceeds of resale.
	  c. Seller may recover purchase price where resale is not possible
	  d. Seller may recover damages for breach based on difference between contract price and market price, or in some cases based on lost profits.

Goods Are in Buyer's Possession	1. Seller may recover purchase price. 2. Seller may reclaim goods in possession of insolvent buyer by making a demand within 10 days after their receipt. If the buyer represented solvency to the seller in writing within three months before delivery, the 10-day limitation does not apply.
Goods Are in Transit	1. Seller may stop any size shipment if buyer is involvent. 2. Seller may stop carload, truckload, planeload, or other large shipment for reasons other than buyer's insolvency.

BUYER'S REMEDIES

Buyer's Remedies in General

A seller may breach a contract in a number of ways. The most common are: (1) failing to make an agreed delivery, (2) delivering goods that do not conform to the contract, and (3) indicating that he does not intend to fulfill the obligations under the contract.

A buyer whose seller breaks the contract is given a number of alternative remedies. These include:

☐ Buying other goods (covering) and recovering damages from the seller based on any additional expense that the buyer incurs in obtaining the goods [2–712].

☐ Recovering damages based on the difference between the contract price and the current market price of the goods [2–713].

☐ Recovering damages for any nonconforming goods accepted by the buyer based on the difference in value between what the buyer got and what he should have gotten [2–714].

☐ Obtaining specific performance of the contract where the goods are unique and cannot be obtained elsewhere [2–716].

In addition, the buyer can in some cases recover consequential damages (such as lost profits) and incidental damages (such as expenses incurred in buying substitute goods).

Buyer's Right to Cover

If the seller fails or refuses to deliver the goods called for in the contract, the buyer can purchase substitute goods; this is known as **cover**. If the buyer does purchase substitute goods, the buyer can recover as damages from the seller the difference between the contract price and the cost of the substitute goods [2–712]. For example, Frank Farmer agrees to sell Ann's Cider Mill 1,000 bushels of apples at $10 a bushel. Farmer then refuses to deliver the apples. Cider Mill can purchase 1,000 bushels of similar apples, and if it has to pay $11 a bushel, it can recover the difference ($1 a bushel) between what it paid ($11) and the contract price ($10). Thus, Cider Mill could recover $1,000 from Farmer.

The buyer can also recover any incidental damages sustained, but must give the seller credit for any expenses saved. In addition, he may be able to obtain consequential damages. The buyer is not required to cover, however. If he does not cover, the other remedies under the Code are still available [2–712].

The case that follows, *Saboundjian v. Bank Audi (USA)*, illustrates that a court will not allow an aggrieved party to speculate on the market at the defaulting party's expense.

SABOUNDJIAN v. BANK AUDI (USA)

11 UCC Rep.2d 1165 (N.Y. Sup. Ct., App. Div. 1990)

Vrej Saboundjian, a customer of Bank Audi, was a sophisticated international businessman well acquainted with the foreign exchange market. In April 1986, he began to speculate in foreign currency through the bank. The foreign currency trading market, which is global, operates without a central exchange and with individual banks throughout the world setting their own rates. Thus, a foreign exchange speculator like Saboundjian, by sending orders to Far East, Middle East, and European markets, is able to participate in foreign exchange trading even after the close of business at domestic banks.

On January 7, 1987, Saboundjian was holding a short position in deutsche marks. That afternoon he asked the foreign exchange trader at Bank Audi (USA) to liquidate his short position when "deutsche marks reached 1.9360 per dollar." As was customary for the bank when an order was placed in the late afternoon or evening and the customer's price was not available in the domestic mark, Bank Audi relayed the order to a foreign bank, in this case, Investbank in the United Arab Emirates, to be executed. The bank's commission covering profit and expenses for performing the trade was added to the price requested by Saboundjian. Thus, the order placed at 3:24 P.M., EST, called for the bank to sell $2 million against deutsche marks at the rate of 1.9380 deutsche marks per dollar.

At 8 A.M. the following morning, the Bank Audi trader noticed that confirmation of the requested trade had not been received and telephoned Investbank and was advised that it had been unable to execute the requested trade. He was advised by Bank Audi (Paris) that the market had been very hectic and that the requested price had been quoted in the market only very briefly and thereafter dropped quickly.

At about 9 A.M., Saboundjian was advised that Investbank had been unable to effect the order; he was also advised of the current market price and that his order could be executed at that price if he desired. He indicated that he did not want the bank to execute at that price and that he was "bullish." At the time, he could have made a profit of approximately $4,700, somewhat less than the approximately $8,000 he would have made if his requested trade had been executed. He subsequently testified that "I thought if I wait maybe a couple of hours or one day, that I could see my price again and if I don't see the price, I said, you have to take the loss as the bank."

During the day, Saboundjian's position deteriorated to a small loss by the end of the day. He did not ask the bank to close out his position until February 6, 1987, at which time the value of the dollar in terms of deutsche marks had fallen to 1.8695. His losses on this and other unrelated trading positions exceeded $420,000. He subsequently brought an action against Bank Audi for failure to execute the January 6 trade and sought consequential damages in excess of $400,000. The bank filed a motion for partial summary judgment, seeking to limit its liability to the difference between Saboundjian's profit had the transaction been carried out as requested and the smaller profit he would have made had he acted to cover on January 8 when he learned of the failure of the January 7 trade. The trial court denied the motion and the bank appealed.

Sullivan, Judge.   Even assuming the bank is liable for failing to execute the January 7, 1987, trade, liability is limited to the difference between the price at which Saboundjian could have executed the trade at issue were it not for the failure to carry it out, and the price at which he could have executed the transaction within a reasonable time after he learned that it had not been effected earlier. Since Saboundjian had a duty to act reasonably and mitigate any damages he may have sustained, the bank cannot be liable for his entire speculation, including losses realized on unrelated transactions. Thus, when a broker rightfully fails to purchase or sell a security as directed, the customer's damages are limited to the cost of covering or replacing the security. If the customer fails to cover within a reasonable time, damages are limited to the potential cost to cover as measured from the time he learns of the broker's failure and for a reasonable time thereafter in which he must decide on his course of action. A customer may not refuse to cover a transaction previously requested and thereby speculate on the market entirely at the risk of the broker.

Article 2 of the Uniform Commercial Code is instructive on the issue of damages. Under section 2–712(1), in the event of a breach, "the buyer may 'cover' by making in good faith and without unreasonable delay any reasonable purchase or contract to purchase goods in substitution for those due from the seller." The buyer may only recover from the seller "as damages the difference between the cost of cover and the contract price together with any incidental or consequential damages." Consequential damages are restricted, however, to those "which could not reasonably be prevented by cover or otherwise." Section 2–715(2). Thus Saboundjian is not entitled to consequential damages since he was in a position to effect cover immediately after having been notified of the bank's failure to execute the January 7 order.

Saboundjian's damages are therefore limited to no more than the difference between the profit he would have earned had the subject trade been executed on January 7, 1987, or approximately $8,000 as alleged in the complaint, and the profit that Saboundjian would have earned had he directed the execution of the trade within a reasonable time after he learned that his original order had not been executed.

Judgment reversed in favor of Bank Audi.

Incidental Damages

Incidental damages include expenses that the buyer incurs in receiving, inspecting, transporting, and storing goods shipped by the seller that do not conform to those called for in the contract. Incidental damages also include any reasonable expenses or charges that the buyer has to pay in obtaining substitute goods [2–715(1)].

Consequential Damages

In certain situations, an injured buyer is able to recover consequential damages, such as the buyer's lost profits caused by the seller's breach of contract. The buyer must be able to show that the seller knew or should have known at the time the contract was made that the buyer would suffer special damages if the seller did not perform his obligations. The buyer must also show that he could not have prevented the damage by obtaining substitute goods [2–715(2)].

Suppose Knitting Mill promises to deliver 15,000 yards of a special fabric to Dorsey by September 1. Knitting Mill knows that Dorsey wants to acquire the material to make garments suitable for the Christmas season. Knitting Mill also knows that in reliance on the contract with it, Dorsey will enter into contracts with department stores to deliver the finished garments by October 1. If Knitting Mill fails to deliver the fabric or delivers the fabric after September 1, it may be liable to Dorsey for any consequential damages that she sustains if she is unable to acquire the same material elsewhere in time to fulfill her October 1 contracts.

Consequential damages can also include an injury to a person or property caused by a breach of warranty. For example, an electric saw is defectively made. Hanson purchases the saw, and while he is using it, the blade comes off and severely cuts his arm. The injury to Hanson is consequential damage resulting from a nonconforming or defective product.

Damages for Nondelivery

If the seller fails or refuses to deliver the goods called for by the contract, the buyer has the option of recovering damages for the nondelivery. Thus, instead of covering, the buyer can get the difference between the contract price of the goods and their market price at the time he learns of the seller's breach. In addition, the buyer may recover any incidental damages and consequential damages, but must give the seller credit for any expenses saved [2–713].

Suppose Biddle agreed on June 1 to sell and deliver 1,500 bushels of wheat to a grain elevator on September 1 for $7 per bushel and then refused to deliver on September 1 because the market price was then $8 per bushel. The grain elevator could recover $1,500 damages from Biddle, plus incidental damages that could not have been prevented by cover.

The *Sun Maid Raisin Growers of California v. Victor Packing Co.* case, which follows, illustrates the application of the measure of damages for nondelivery. In this case, the market price of the goods at the time of delivery was significantly higher than the contract price, and the seller, who had gambled that the price would fall, had to pay substantial damages.

SUN MAID RAISIN GROWERS OF CALIFORNIA v. VICTOR PACKING CO.

In November 1975, Victor Packing Company agreed to sell Sun Maid Raisin Growers 1,900 tons of raisins. The first 100 tons were sold at 39 cents per pound and the remainder at 40 cents per pound. No specific delivery date was agreed on. Victor indicated to Sun Maid on August 10, 1976, that it would not complete performance, being unable to deliver the last 610 tons. Sun Maid was able to purchase 200 tons at 43 cents per pound. Because of heavy rains in September 1976, the new crop of raisins suffered extensive damage and the price of raisins increased dramatically.

Sun Maid brought suit against Victor to recover damages. The trial court awarded $307,339 in damages to Sun Maid. Victor appealed, claiming that the increase in the lost profits due to the disastrous rain damage was not foreseeable.

Franson, Acting Presiding Judge. The basic measure of damages for a seller's nondelivery or repudiation is the difference between the market price and the contract price.

In addition to the difference between the market price and the contract price, the buyer can recover incidental damages such as expenses of cover and consequential damages such as lost profits to the extent that they could not have been avoided by cover. The inability to cover after a prompt and reasonable effort to do so is a prerequisite to recovery of consequential damages. If the buyer is only able to cover in part, he is entitled to the net cost of cover (the difference between the cover price and the contract price plus expenses) together with any consequential damages but less expenses saved in consequence of the seller's breach.

Under § 2–715(2)(a), consequential damages include "any loss resulting from general or particular requirements and needs of which the seller at the time of contracting had reason to know and which could not reasonably be prevented by cover or otherwise." The "reason to know" language concerning the buyer's particular requirements and needs arises from *Hadley v. Baxendale*. The Code, however, has imposed an objective rather than a subjective standard in determining whether the seller should have anticipated the buyer's needs. Thus, actual knowledge by the seller of the buyer's requirements is not required. The only requirement under § 2–715(2)(a) is that the seller reasonably should have been expected to know of the buyer's exposure to loss.

Furthermore, comment 6 to § 2–715 provides that if the seller knows that the buyer is in the business of reselling the goods, the seller is charged with knowledge that the buyer will be selling the goods in anticipation of a profit. "Absent a contractual provision against consequential damages a seller in breach will therefore always be liable for the buyer's resulting loss of profit."

Finally, a buyer's failure to take any other steps by which the loss could reasonably have been prevented bars him from recovering consequential damages. This is merely a codification of the rule that the buyer must attempt to minimize damages. In the present case, the evidence fully supports the finding that after Victor's breach of the contract on August 10, 1976, Sun Maid acted in good faith in a commercially reasonable manner and was able to cover by purchase only some 200 tons of substitute raisins at a cost of 43 cents per pound. There were no other natural Thompson seedless free tonnage raisins available for purchase in the market at or within a reasonable time after Victor's breach. Although the evidence indicates that Sun Maid actually was able to purchase an additional 410 tons of raisins after the September rainfall in its efforts to effect cover, these were badly damaged raisins which had to be reconditioned at a substantial cost to bring them up to market condition. According to Sun Maid, if the trial court had used the total cost of cover of the full 610 tons as the measure of damages rather than lost profits on resale, its damages would have totaled $377,720.

Although the trial court did not specify why it determined damages by calculating lost profits instead of the cost of cover, the court probably found that damages should be limited to the amount that would have put Sun Maid in "as good a position as if the other party had fully performed." Thus, Sun Maid was awarded the lesser of the actual cost of cover (treating the reconditioning of the 410 tons as a cost) and the loss of prospective profits.

In contending that the foreseeability requirement applies to the amount of the lost profits and not just to the fact of lost profits, Victor apparently acknowledges that it knew at the time of contracting that Sun Maid would be reselling the raisins to its customers in the domestic market. Victor has no alternative to this concession since it was an experienced packer and knew that Sun Maid marketed raisins year round in the domestic market. Furthermore, Victor must be presumed to have known that if it did not deliver the full quota of raisins provided under the contracts (1,800 tons) by the end of the crop year or before such reasonable time as thereafter might be agreed to, Sun Maid would be forced to go into the market to attempt to cover its then existing orders for sale of raisins. This is exactly what occurred.

Victor nonetheless contends it should not be liable for damages based on the extraordinarily high price of raisins in the fall of 1976 which was caused by the "disastrous" rains in September. These rains reportedly caused a 50 percent loss of the new crop which with the lack of a substantial carryover of 1975 raisins drove the market price from approximately $860 per packed weight ton to over $1,600 per packed weight ton. Victor does not assert the doctrine of impossibility or impracticability of performance as a defense [§ 2–615]. This is understandable since the nondelivery of raisins was not caused by the failure of a presupposed condition (continuance of the $860 per ton market price) but solely by Victor's failure to deliver the 610 tons of raisins during the 1975 crop year. This is where the trial court's findings of Victor's bad faith become pertinent. A reasonable inference may be drawn that from early spring Victor was gambling on the market price of raisins in deciding whether to perform its contracts with Sun Maid. If the price would fall below the contract price, Victor would buy raisins and deliver them to Sun Maid. If the market price went substantially above the contract price, Victor would sit tight. While we cannot read Victor's mind during the late spring and summer months, we can surmise that it speculated that the market price would remain below the contract price after the current crop year so that it could purchase new raisins for delivery to Sun Maid at the contract price. It threw the dice and lost. The possibility of "disastrous" rain damage to the 1976 raisin crop was clearly foreseeable to Victor. Such rains have occurred at sporadic intervals since raisins have been grown in the San Joaquin Valley. Raisin packers fully understand the great risk in contracting to sell raisins at a fixed price over a period of time extending into the next crop year. The market price may go up or down depending on consumer demand and the supply and quality of raisins. If the seller does not have sufficient inventory to fulfill his delivery obligations within the time initially required or as subsequently modified by the parties, he will have to go into the market to purchase raisins. The fact that he may be surprised by an extraordinary rise in the market price does not mean that the buyer's prospective profits on resale are unforeseeable as a matter of law.

Judgment for Sun Maid affirmed.

Damages for Defective Goods

If a buyer accepts defective goods and wants to hold the seller liable, the buyer must give the seller notice of the defect within a reasonable time after the buyer discovers the defect [2–607(3)]. Where goods are defective or not as warranted and the buyer gives the required notice, he can recover damages. The buyer is entitled to recover the difference between the value of the goods received and the value the goods would have had if they had been as warranted. He may also be entitled to incidental and consequential damages [2–714].

For example, Al's Auto Store sells Anders an automobile tire, warranting it to be four-ply construction. The tire goes flat when it is punctured by a nail, and Anders discovers that the tire is really only two-ply. If Anders gives the store prompt notice of the breach, she can keep the tire and recover from Al's the difference in value between a two-ply and a four-ply tire.

Buyer's Right to Specific Performance

Sometimes, the goods covered by a contract are unique and it is not possible for a buyer to obtain substitute goods. When this is the case, the buyer is entitled to specific performance of the contract.

Specific performance means that the buyer can require the seller to give the buyer the goods covered by the contract [2–716]. Thus, the buyer of an antique automobile such as a 1910 Ford might have a court order the seller to deliver the specified automobile to the buyer because it was one of a kind. On the other hand, the buyer of grain in a particular storage bin could not get specific performance if he could buy the same kind of grain elsewhere.

Buyer and Seller Agreements as to Remedies

As mentioned earlier in this chapter, the parties to a contract may provide remedies in addition to or as substitution for those expressly provided in the Code [2–719]. For example, the buyer's remedies may be limited by the contract to the return of the goods and the repayment of the price or to the replacement of nonconforming goods or parts. However, a court looks to see whether such a limitation was freely agreed to or whether it is unconscionable. In the latter case, the court does not enforce the limitation and the buyer has all the rights given to an injured buyer by the Code.

CONCEPT REVIEW

BUYER'S REMEDIES (on breach by seller)

Problems	Buyer's Remedy
Seller Fails to Deliver Goods or Delivers Nonconforming Goods that Buyer Rightfully Rejects or Justifiably Revokes Acceptance of	1. Buyer may cancel the contract and recover damages. 2. Buyer may "cover" by obtaining substitute goods and recover difference between contract price and cost of cover. 3. Buyer may recover damages for breach based on difference between contract price and market price.
Seller Delivers Nonconforming Goods that Are Accepted by Buyer	Buyer may recover damages based on difference between value of goods received and value of goods if they had been as warranted.
Seller Has the Goods but Refuses to Deliver Them and Buyer Wants Them	Buyer may seek specific performance if goods are unique and cannot be obtained elsewhere, or buyer may replevy goods identified to contract if buyer cannot obtain cover.

ETHICAL AND PUBLIC POLICY CONCERNS

1. In the *Wilson v. Hammer Holdings, Inc.*, case, the court held that the statute of limitations barred a claim of breach of warranty. Even if the gallery is not legally obligated to make good on its "guarantee" of authenticity, does it have any ethical responsibility to the purchaser for selling a painting that was not painted by the artist to whom it was attributed at the time of the sale?

2. Problem case 8 involves the sale of a yacht as new that previously had sunk in salt water. How would you assess the ethicacy of the representations made by the salesman to the purchaser in response to his question? In a case like this, should it be incumbent on a purchaser to ask the "right" questions in order to protect himself, or should there be an ethical obligation on the seller to voluntarily disclose material facts that may be relevant to the purchaser making an informed decision?

3. Suppose you own an automobile dealership. The manufacturer whose cars you sell produces a limited edition of a particular model, sets a sticker price of $60,000 on it, and makes only two of the cars available to you. You agree to sell one of the cars to a customer for $60,000. Before you deliver the car, another customer, who collects rare and classic cars, offers you a $30,000 per car premium over the sticker price if you will sell both cars to him. Would you accept his offer? What ethical considerations are involved in making your decision?

SUMMARY

The Code remedies for breach of contract are designed to put the injured party in the same position that he would have been in if the contract had been performed.

As a general rule, the courts will enforce an agreement of the parties relating to the damages to which the parties will be entitled, provided that the agreement is not void as an unconscionable contract or clause. A liquidated damages provision in a contract is enforceable if the amount is reasonable and the damages for the injury suffered by the injured party are not readily provable. The parties by agreement may provide for additional or supplemental damages, and they may limit or exclude consequential damages, except damages for injury to a person from consumer goods.

The statute of limitations on sales contracts is four years from the time the cause of action accrues. The parties may, by agreement, reduce the time limit to one year, but they cannot extend the time limit.

The seller is entitled to the purchase price of conforming goods delivered to and accepted by the buyer. The seller may also recover the purchase price of any conforming goods that were sent to the buyer and were lost or destroyed after the risk of loss had passed to the buyer. Also, if the goods have been identified to the contract and the buyer repudiates the sale, the seller is entitled to the purchase price of the goods that cannot, by a reasonable effort on the part of the seller, be resold for a fair price.

The seller is entitled to recover compensatory damages that were reasonably within the contemplation of the parties. The seller upon breach by the buyer is also entitled to incidental damages. If necessary to put the seller in the position he would have held had the buyer performed, the seller may be granted his lost profits, including overhead, as damages. The seller is not obligated to resell upon the buyer's refusal to accept goods, but if he does resell the goods in a commercially reasonable manner, he may recover as damages the difference between the sales price and the contract price.

Upon the buyer's insolvency, the seller may reclaim the goods if he makes the demand within 10 days after the buyer's receipt. If the buyer misrepresented his solvency in writing to the particular seller within the previous three months, the 10-day limitation does not apply. The seller may also, upon the buyer's insolvency, stop delivery of the goods by a carrier or other bailee. Delivery of large lots may be stopped upon the buyer's repudiation or failure to pay the amount due before delivery. Reasonable notice to stop delivery must be given to the carrier or other bailee.

As damages for nondelivery or repudiation on the seller's part, the buyer may recover the difference between the market price of the goods and the contract price plus incidental and, under some circumstances, consequential damages. If the buyer covers, the measure of his compensatory damages is the difference between the cost of the cover and the contract price.

In the event that goods are defective and the buyer accepts them, he can, upon giving the seller notice of the breach, recover as damages the difference between the value of the goods received and what their value would have been if they had been conforming goods, plus incidental, and under some circumstances consequential, damages.

The buyer may be entitled to the remedy of specific performance if the goods that are the subject matter of the contract are unique or cannot be obtained by cover.

PROBLEM CASES

1. Lobianco contracted with Property Protection, Inc., for the installation of a burglar alarm system. The contract provided in part:

Alarm system equipment installed by Property Protection, Inc., is guaranteed against improper function due to manufacturing defects of workmanship for a period of 12 months. The

installation of the above equipment carries a 90-day warranty. The liability of Property Protection, Inc. is limited to repair or replacement of security alarm equipment and does not include loss or damage to possessions, persons, or property.

As installed, the alarm system included a standby battery source of power in the event that the regular source of power failed. During the 90-day warranty period, burglars broke into Lobianco's house and stole $35,815 worth of jewelry. First, they destroyed the electric meter so that there was no electric source to operate the system, and then they entered the house. The batteries in the standby system were dead, and thus the standby system failed to operate. Accordingly, no outside siren was activated and a telephone call that was supposed to be triggered was not made. Lobianco brought suit, claiming damage in the amount of her stolen jewelry because of the failure of the alarm system to work properly. Did the disclaimer effectively eliminate any liability on the alarm company's part for consequential damages? Yes,

2. Parzek purchased from New England Log Homes a log home kit consisting of hand-peeled logs, window frames, and door frames. The brochure that Parzek had seen before buying the log home contained a statement that the logs were treated with a preservative "to protect the treated wood against decay, stain, termites, and other insects." Other statements indicated the maintenance-free nature of the logs, and there was a guarantee against any materials and engineering defects. The logs were delivered in May 1974 to the construction site, where they were stored in stacks covered with heavy tarpaulins. By fall of 1976, the walls were erected and the roof was on. In 1979, Parzek discovered 15 medium-sized blue metallic beetles on the interior walls of the home. He was assured by the dealer for New England Log Homes that the problem was not serious. The following April, however, Parzek observed hundreds of beetles and discovered larvae and "excavation channels" in the logs. When he contacted New England Log Homes, he was told that it did not guarantee that its logs were insect free. Parzek had the home treated by an exterminator and then brought suit against New England Log Homes. Relying on section 2–725 of the Code, New England Log Homes contended that the lawsuit was barred by the statute of limitations because it was filed more than four years after the date of delivery. Is Parzek's lawsuit barred by the statute of limitations? Guarantee oneyear

3. Bechtel ordered an alabaster-colored mink coat from Pollock Furs. The coat had to be specially made because she required an unusually large size and requested a particular styling. The coat cost $5,500, of which Bechtel paid $250. Several months later, she decided that she did not want the coat and canceled the order, even though the coat had been completed. Pollock Furs then filed suit for the balance of the purchase price. What can Bechtel argue in her defense? *The store should try to sell & mitigate damage*

4. Cohn advertised a 30-foot sailboat for sale in *The New York Times*. Fisher saw the ad, inspected the sailboat, and offered Cohn $4,650 for the boat. Cohn accepted the offer. Fisher gave Cohn a check for $2,535 as a deposit on the boat. He wrote on the check, "Deposit on aux sloop, D'arc Wind, full amount $4,650." Fisher later refused to go through with the purchase and stopped payment on the deposit check. Cohn readvertised the boat and sold it for the highest offer he received, which was $3,000. Cohn then sued Fisher for breach of contract. He asked for damages of $1,679.50. This represented the $1,650 difference between the contract price and the sale price plus $29.50 in incidental expenses in reselling the boat. Is Cohn entitled to this measure of damages? *Yes, provided that he notified Fisher of the action*

5. The Republic of Iran entered into a contract to purchase a 747 aircraft and a quantity of spare parts from Boeing. At the time Iran seized a number of American hostages, the contract was canceled. This left Boeing with one 747 airplane and a quantity of spare parts that it had stocked to fill Iran's order. Boeing then resold the 747 to another purchaser and also resold the parts. Boeing then filed a counterclaim for damages in a lawsuit filed against Boeing concerning alleged defects in a 747 previously purchased from Boeing by Iran that had crashed. In its counterclaim, Boeing sought damages based on the difference between the contract price of the 747 to Iran and the resale price. It also sought the profits it lost when Iran repudiated the agreement to purchase the spare parts. Was Boeing entitled to these measures of damages on the breach of contract by Iran? *Resold item commonly get incidental*

6. McCain Foods sold on credit and delivered a quantity of frozen french fries to Flagstaff Food Service Company. Several days later, when the potatoes had not yet been paid for, McCain discovered that Flagstaff was insolvent and had just filed a petition in bankruptcy. What would you advise McCain Foods to do? *Make a claim on French fries within 10 day period*

7. Kneale bought two chairs from Modernage Furniture that were on sale for $97.50 apiece. The regular price of the chairs was $147.57 each, or $50.07 more than the sale price. Because the store had oversold that particular chair, it failed to deliver the items to Kneale,

although she had paid the full purchase price in cash. She brought suit for breach of contract against Modernage Furniture. Modernage contended that its liability was limited to return of the purchase price. Was Modernage's liability for breach of contract limited to return of the purchase price? *No! Incidental, consequential. Could recover difference between Sale & Mkt price!*

8. Barr purchased from Crow's Nest Yacht Sales a 31-foot Tiara pleasure yacht manufactured by S-2 Yachts. He had gone to Crow's Nest knowing the style and type yacht he wanted. He was told that the retail price was $102,000 but that he could purchase the model they had for $80,000. When he asked about the reduction in price he was told that Crow's Nest had to move it because there was a change in the model and they had new ones coming in. He was assured that the yacht was new, that there was nothing wrong with it, and that it only had 20 hours on the engines. Barr installed a considerable amount of electronic equipment on the boat. When he began to use it, he experienced tremendous difficulties with equipment malfunctions. On examination by a marine expert it was determined that the yacht had earlier been sunk in salt water, resulting in significant rusting and deterioration in the engine, equipment, and fixtures. Other experts concluded that significant replacement and repair was required, that the engines would have only 25 percent of their normal expected life, and that following its sinking, the yacht would have only half of its original value. Barr then brought suit against Crow's Nest and S-2 Yachts for breach of warranty. To what measure of damages is Barr entitled to recover for breach of warranty? *Incidental, consequential. 102,000 - 2 = amt Crow's Nest - 80,000*

9. De La Hoya bought a used handgun for $140 from Slim's Gun Shop, a licensed firearms dealer. At the time neither De La Hoya nor Slim's knew that the gun had been stolen prior to the time Slim's bought it. While De La Hoya was using the gun for target shooting, he was questioned by a police officer. The officer traced the serial number of the gun, determined that it had been stolen, and arrested De La Hoya. De La Hoya had to hire an attorney to defend himself against the criminal charges. He then brought a lawsuit against Slim's Gun Shop for breach of warranty of title. He sought to recover the purchase price of the gun plus $8,001, the amount of his attorney's fees, as consequential damages. Is he entitled to recover these damages? *Recover damages from seller*

10. In 1972, Schweber contracted to purchase a certain black 1973 Rolls-Royce Corniche automobile from Rallye Motors. He made a $3,500 deposit on the car. Rallye later returned his deposit to him and told him that the car was not available. However, Schweber learned that the automobile was available to the dealer and was being sold to another customer. The dealer then offered to sell Schweber a similar car, but with a different interior design. Schweber brought a lawsuit against the dealer to prevent it from selling the Rolls-Royce Corniche to anyone else and to require that it be sold to him. Rallye Motors claimed that he could get only damages and not specific performance. Approximately 100 Rolls-Royce Corniches were being sold each year in the United States, but none of the others would have the specific features and detail of this one. Is the remedy of specific performance available to Schweber?

PROPERTY

CHAPTER 23

PERSONAL PROPERTY AND BAILMENTS

INTRODUCTION

The concept of property is crucial to the organization of society. The essential nature of a particular society is often reflected in the way it views property, including the degree to which property ownership is concentrated in the state, the extent it permits individual ownership of property, and the rules that govern such ownership. History is replete with wars and revolutions that arose out of conflicting claims to, or views concerning, property. Significant documents in our own Anglo-American legal tradition, such as the Magna Carta and the Constitution, deal explicitly with property rights.

This chapter will discuss the nature and classification of property. It will also examine the various ways that interests in personal property can be obtained and transferred, such as by production, purchase, or gift. The last half of the chapter explores the law of bailments. A bailment is involved, for example, when you check your coat in a coatroom at a restaurant or when you park your car in a public parking garage and leave your keys with the attendant.

NATURE OF PROPERTY

The word *property* is used in several distinct ways. The word sometimes is used to refers to *a thing that is capable of being owned*. It is also used to refer to *a right or interest* associated with a thing that gives the owner the ability to exercise dominion over that thing.

When we talk about ownership of property, we are talking about a *bundle of rights* that are recognized and enforced by the law. For example, ownership of a building includes the exclusive right to use, enjoy, sell, mortgage, or rent the building. If someone else tries to use the property without the owner's consent, the owner can use the courts and legal procedures to eject that person. Ownership of a patent includes the right to sell it, to license others to use it, or to produce the patented article personally.

In the United States, private ownership of property is protected by the Constitution, which provides that the government shall deprive no person of "life, liberty or property without due process of law." We recognize and encourage the rights of individuals to acquire, enjoy, and use property. These rights, however, are not unlimited. For example, a person cannot use property in an unreasonable manner to the injury of others. Also, the state has **police power** through which it can impose reasonable regulations on the use of property, tax it, and take it for public use by paying the owner compensation for it.

Property can be divided into a number of categories based on its characteristics. The same piece of property may fall into more than one class. The following discussion explores the meaning of **personal property** and the numerous ways of classifying property.

CLASSIFICATIONS OF PROPERTY

What Is Personal Property?— Personal Property versus Real Property

Personal property is defined by process of exclusion. The term *personal property* is used in contrast to *real property*. Real property is the earth's crust and all things firmly attached to it.[1] For example, land, office buildings, and houses are all considered to be real property. All other objects and rights that can be owned are personal property. Clothing, books, bank accounts, and stock in a corporation are all examples of personal property.

Real property can be turned into personal property if it is detached from the earth. Similarly, personal property can be attached to the earth and become real property. For example, marble in the ground is real property. When the marble is quarried, it becomes personal property, but if it is used in constructing a building, it becomes real property again. Perennial vegetation that does not have to be seeded every year, such as trees, shrubs, and grass, is usually treated as part of the real property on which it is growing. When trees and shrubs are severed from the land, they become personal property. Crops that must be planted each year, such as corn, oats, and potatoes, are usually treated as personal property. However, if the real property on which they are growing is sold, the new owner of the real property also becomes the owner of the crops.

When personal property is attached to, or used in conjunction with, real property in such a way as to be treated as part of the real property, it is known as a **fixture.** The law concerning fixtures is discussed in the next chapter.

Tangible versus Intangible Personal Property
Personal property can be either *tangible* or *intangible*. Tangible property has a physical existence. Cars, animals, and computers are examples. Property that has no physical existence is called intangible property. For example, rights under a patent, copyright, or trademark would be intangible property.[2]

The distinction between tangible and intangible property is important primarily for tax and estate planning purposes. Generally, tangible property is subject to tax in the state in which it is located, whereas intangible property is usually taxable in the state where its owner lives.

Public and Private Property   Property is also classified as public or private based on the ownership of the property. If the property is owned by the government or a governmental unit, it is classified as public property. If it is owned by an individual, a group of individuals, a corporation, or some other business organization, it is private property.

ACQUIRING OWNERSHIP OF PERSONAL PROPERTY

Production or Purchase

The most common ways of obtaining ownership of property are by producing it or purchasing it. A person owns the property that he makes unless the person has agreed to do the work for someone else. In that case, the employer is the owner of the product of the work. For example, a person who creates a painting, knits a sweater, or develops a computer program is the owner unless he has been hired by someone to do the painting, knit the sweater, or develop the program. Another major way of acquiring property is by purchase. The law regarding the purchase of tangible personal property (that is, sale of goods) is discussed in the Formation and Terms of Sales Contracts chapter.

---

[1]The law of real property is treated in the Real Property and Insurance chapter.

[2]These important types of intangible property are discussed in the Intellectual Property, Competitive Torts, and Unfair Competition chapter.

Possession of Unowned Property

In very early times, the most common way of obtaining ownership of personal property was simply by *taking possession* of unowned property. For example, the first person to take possession of a wild animal became its owner. Today, one can still acquire ownership of personal property by possessing it *if the property is unowned*. The two major examples of unowned property that can be acquired by possession are *wild animals* and *abandoned property*. Abandoned property will be discussed in the next section, which focuses on the rights of finders.

The first person to take possession of a wild animal property normally becomes the owner.[3] To acquire ownership of a wild animal by taking possession, a person must obtain enough control over it to deprive it of its freedom. If a person fatally wounds a wild animal, the person becomes the owner. Wild animals caught in a trap or fish caught in a net are usually considered to be the property of the person who set the trap or net. If a captured wild animal escapes and is caught by another person, that person generally becomes the owner. However, if that person knows that the animal is an escaped animal and that the prior owner is chasing it to recapture it, then he does not become the owner.

RIGHTS OF FINDERS OF LOST, MISLAID, AND ABANDONED PROPERTY

The old saying "finders keepers, losers weepers" is *not* a reliable way of predicting the legal rights of those who find personal property that originally belonged—or still belongs—to another. The rights of the finder will be determined by whether the property he finds is classified as *abandoned*, *lost*, or *mislaid*.

1. *Abandoned property.* Property is considered to be *abandoned* if the owner intentionally placed the property out of his possession with the intent to relinquish ownership of it. For example, Norris takes his TV set to the city dump and leaves it there. The finder of abandoned property who takes possession of abandoned property with intent to claim ownership becomes the owner of the property. This means he acquires better rights to the property than anyone else in the world,

including the original owner. For example, if Fox finds the TV set, puts it in his car, and takes it home, Fox becomes the owner of the TV set.

2. *Lost property.* Property is considered to be *lost* when the owner did not intend to part with possession of the property. For example, if Barber's camera fell out of her handbag while she was walking down the street, it would be considered lost property. The person who finds lost property does not acquire ownership of it, but he acquires better rights to the lost property than anyone other than the true owner. For example, suppose Lawrence finds Barber's camera in the grass where it fell. Jones then steals the camera from Lawrence's house. Under these facts, Barber is still the owner of the camera. She has the right to have it returned to her if she discovers where it is—or if Lawrence knows that it belongs to Barber. As the finder of lost property, though, Lawrence has a better right to the camera than anyone else except Barber. This means that Lawrence has the right to require Jones to return it to him if he finds out that Jones has it.

If the finder does not know who the true owner is or cannot easily find out, the finder must still return the property if the real owner shows up and asks for the property. If the finder of lost property knows who the owner is and refuses to return it, the finder is guilty of conversion and must pay the owner the fair value of the property.[4]

A finder who sells the property that he has found can only pass to the purchaser those rights that he has; he cannot pass any better title to the property than he himself has. Thus, the true owner could recover the property from the purchaser.

3. *Mislaid property.* Property is considered to be mislaid if the owner intentionally placed the property somewhere and accidentally left it there, not intending to relinquish ownership of the property. For example, Fields places her backpack on a coatrack at Campus Bookstore while shopping for textbooks. Forgetting the backpack, Fields leaves the store and goes home. The backpack would be considered to be mislaid rather than lost because Fields intentionally and voluntarily placed it on the coatrack. The consequences of property being classified as mislaid are that the finder acquires no rights to the property. Rather, the person in possession of the real property on which the personal property was mislaid has the right to hold the property for the true owner

---

[3]As wildlife is increasingly protected by law, however, some wild animals cannot be owned because it is illegal to capture them (e.g., endangered species).

[4]The tort of conversion is discussed in the Intentional Torts chapter.

and has better rights to the property than anyone other than the true owner. For example, if Stevens found Fields's backpack in Campus Bookstore, Campus Bookstore would have the right to hold the mislaid property for Fields. Stevens would acquire neither possession nor ownership of the backpack.

The rationale for this rule is that it increases the chances that the property will be returned to its real owner. A person who knowingly placed the property somewhere but forgot to pick it up might well remember later where she left the property and return for it.

Some states have a statute that allows finders of property to clear their title to the property. The statutes generally provide that the person must give public notice of the fact that the property has been found, perhaps by putting an ad in a local newspaper. All states have **statutes of limitations** that require the true owner of property to claim it or bring a legal action to recover possession of it within a certain number of years. A person who keeps possession of lost or unclaimed property for longer than that period of time will become its owner.

The following case, *Michael v. First Chicago Corporation,* presents an example of a conflict between a finder and an original owner over rights to personal property.

MICHAEL v. FIRST CHICAGO CORPORATION

487 N.E.2d 403 (Ill. Ct. App. 1986)

First National Bank of Chicago (First Chicago) sold a number of used file cabinets on an "as is" basis to Zibton, a new and secondhand office supply and furniture dealer. Zibton had bought used furniture from First Chicago before. On this and previous occasions, Zibton bought the used furniture as a group even if some pieces were damaged or locked.

In the summer of 1983, Zibton sold some of these cabinets to Charles Strayve. Strayve gave one of the cabinets, a locked one with no keys, to his friend, Richard Michael. About six weeks later, Michael was moving the file cabinet in his garage when it fell over and several of the locked drawers opened. Inside were more than 1,600 certificates of deposit (CDs), including seven that had not been canceled or stamped paid and that were worth a total of $6,687,948.85, with maturity dates ranging from October 1982 to January 1983. Six of the CDs were payable to "Bearer."

First Chicago had placed the CDs in the cabinet between March and May of 1983, when the responsibility for storing paid CDs was changed to a different unit of the bank. The CDs were moved from a vault to file cabinets at that time. Each drawer had been labeled with a card stating "Paid Negotiable CDs" and indicating the numbers of the CDs contained in the drawer. The new unit responsible for storing CDs determined that they could not use the file cabinets, so the CDs were transferred to tote boxes. First Chicago employees randomly checked to determine if the contents were gone and then transferred the file cabinets to the warehouse for sale.

Michael called the FBI, which took possession of all of the CDs. Michael and his wife then filed this declaratory judgment to determine who owned the CDs. The trial court ruled in favor of First Chicago, and the Michaels appealed.

Reinhard, Justice. The Michaels' primary argument is that they were entitled to possession of the CDs because the certificates were the subject of a sale from First Chicago. They maintain that First Chicago's actions in the handling and sale of the CDs showed an objective intent to transfer the certificates along with the used file cabinets in which the documents were stored.

Here, First Chicago was selling only used furniture to Zibton. Neither First Chicago nor Zibton suspected that CDs or any other type of valuable had been left in the file cabinet. The evidence clearly shows that the intention of the parties was for First Chicago to sell used furniture only, and Zibton was not speculating that other valuable items might be contained in the used furniture.

Where both buyer and seller were ignorant of the existence or presence of the concealed valuable, and the contract was not broad enough to indicate an intent to convey all the contents, known or unknown, the courts have generally held that as between the owner and purchaser, title to the hidden article did not pass by the sale. The evidence here is that used office furniture was being sold, and the possibility that something valuable might be in any of the used furniture had nothing to do with the sale. The fact that the sale of the used furniture was "as is" indicates the furniture was sold in its present condition, damaged or otherwise, and does not show an intent to sell the contents of the used furniture. Accordingly, the evidence does not support the Michaels' contention that the CDs as contents of the used furniture were intended by either party to the sale to be sold along with the furniture.

The Michaels' alternative contention is that the CDs are abandoned property, rather than lost or mislaid property, which the finder is entitled to keep. Mislaid property is that which is intentionally put in a certain place and later forgotten; property is lost when it is unintentionally separated from the dominion of its owner; and property is abandoned when the owner, intending to relinquish all rights to the property, leaves it free to be appropriated by any other person. A finder of property acquires no rights in mislaid property, is entitled to possession of lost property against everyone except the true owner, and is entitled to keep abandoned property.

For the purposes of this appeal, we need only determine whether the CDs are abandoned property. If otherwise, the owner is entitled to possession. Abandonment is generally defined as an intentional relinquishment of a known right. As a general rule, abandonment is not presumed and the party seeking to declare an abandonment must prove the abandoning party intended to do so.

The Michaels basically argue that the CDs were abandoned as shown by evidence that they were intentionally placed in the cabinets, they were not forgotten, and the cabinets were sold with no reservations. We disagree. It is readily apparent from the evidence that the CDs were to be transferred to other storage and some simply were overlooked and left in the file cabinets. The relinquishment of possession, under the circumstances here, without a showing of an intention to permanently give up all right to the CDs is not enough to show abandonment.

Judgment for First Chicago affirmed.

CONCEPT REVIEW

RIGHTS OF FINDERS OF PERSONAL PROPERTY

Character of Property	Description	Rights of Finder	Rights of Original Owner
Lost	Owner unintentionally parted with possession	Rights superior to everyone except the owner	Retains ownership; has the right to the return of the property
Mislaid	Owner intentionally put property in a place but unintentionally left it there	None; person in possession of real property on which mislaid property was found holds it for the owner, and has rights superior to everyone except owner	Retains ownership; has the right to the return of the property
Abandoned	Owner intentionally placed property out of his possession with intent to relinquish ownership of it	Finder who takes possession with intent to claim ownership acquires ownership of property	None

Leasing

A lease of personal property is a transfer of the right to possess and use personal property belonging to another.[5] Although the rights of one who leases personal property (a **lessee**) do not constitute ownership of personal property, leasing is mentioned here because it is becoming an increasingly important way of acquiring the use of many kinds of personal property, from automobiles to farm equipment.

In most states, Article 2 and Article 9 of the UCC are applied to personal property leases by analogy. However, rules contained in these articles sometimes are inadequate to resolve special problems presented by leasing. For this reason, a new article of the UCC dealing exclusively with leases of goods, Article 2A, was written in 1987. Article 2A has been presented to state legislatures for possible adoption, but only six states have adopted Article 2A as of the time of this writing.

Gifts

Title to personal property can be obtained by gift. A gift is a voluntary transfer of property to the **donee** (the person who receives a gift), for which the **donor** (the person who gives the gift) gets no consideration in return. To have a valid gift, the following elements are necessary:

1. The donor must intend to make a gift,
2. The donor must make delivery of the gift, and
3. The donee must accept the gift.

The most critical requirement is delivery. The person who makes the gift must actually give up possession and control of the property either to the donee or to a third person to hold it for the donee. Delivery is important because it makes clear to the donor that he is voluntarily giving up ownership without getting something in exchange. A promise to make a gift is usually not enforceable;[6] the person must actually part with the proper�221; In some cases, the delivery may be *symbolic* or *co structive.* For example, handing over the key to a stron box can be symbolic delivery of the property in strongbox.

There are two kinds of gifts: gifts *inter vivos* and g *causa mortis.* A gift **inter vivos** is a gift between t living persons. For example, when Tweedle's part give her a car for her 21st birthday, that is a gift i *vivos.* A gift **causa mortis** is a gift made in contem tion of death. For example, Uncle John, who is abou undergo a serious heart operation, gives his watch to nephew, Sam, and tells Sam that he wants him to ha if he does not survive the operation. A gift *causa mo. ..* is a *conditional* gift. A gift *causa mortis* is effective *unless any of the following occurs:*

1. The donor recovers from the peril or sickness under fear of which the gift was made, or
2. The donor revokes or withdraws the gift before he dies, or
3. The donee dies before the donor.

If one of these events takes place, ownership of the property goes back to the donor.

The elements of a valid gift, as well as the difference between an *inter vivos* gift and a gift *causa mortis,* are discussed in the *Welton v. Gallagher* case, which follows.

---

[5]A lease of personal property is a form of bailment, a "bailment for hire." Bailments are discussed later in this chapter.

[6]This idea is discussed in the Consideration chapter.

WELTON v. GALLAGHER

630 P.2d 1077 (Hawaii Ct. App. 1981)

In October 1973, Richard Welton, a businessman in his late 60s, met Florence Gallagher, a widow in her late 40s. Welton subsequently underwent several operations for cancer. After he was released from the hospital, Gallagher devoted much time and attention to him. In 1975, she helped him operate an ice cream business that he had purchased. Shortly thereafter, he moved into her house and spent considerable money fixing it up. Welton subsequently moved out to live with Gallagher's niece, Sandra Kwock, a woman in her 20s, who agreed to take care of him for the rest of his life in return for his giving her $25,000 in bearer bonds. Kwock left town with the bonds, much to Welton's dismay. In April 1976, Welton moved back in with Gallagher, gave her $20,000 in bearer bonds, and told her to place them in her safe-deposit box. Gallagher said that he told her he wanted her to have them as a gift because she was much more deserving than her niece. Later in 1976, Welton and Gallagher ended their relationship and he moved out of her house. He also demanded that she return the bonds, but she refused.

Welton filed suit against Gallagher seeking return of the bonds. The trial court held that Welton had made a completed *inter vivos* gift of the bonds. Welton appealed.

Burns, Judge.   Mr. Welton asserts that Mrs. Gallagher has failed to prove the elements of gift. For a transaction to amount to a gift, it must appear that there was a sufficient delivery of the property, an acceptance of the property, and an intention to make a gift.

Delivery is not a complex matter. As the Hawaii Supreme Court stated in *Siko v. Sequirant,* "[a] donor must divest himself of control of the gift for delivery to be complete." In other words, the donor must do acts sufficient to strip himself of dominion and control over the property. Here, Mr. Welton gave Mrs. Gallagher bearer bonds, bonds which by definition are redeemable by whosoever holds them. She testified that he told her he was giving her the bonds with no strings attached and that she should place the bonds in her own safe-deposit box, a box to which he had no rights of entry. Clearly he ceased to have any control over the bonds and can be deemed therefore to have delivered them to Mrs. Gallagher.

The matter of acceptance is likewise fairly straightforward. The exercise by the donee of dominion over the subject of the gift or an assertion of a right thereto is generally held to be evidence of acceptance; and where the gift is beneficial to the donee and imposes no burdens upon her, acceptance is presumed. Here, Mrs. Gallagher exercised dominion over the bonds by placing them in her safe-deposit box. She has always maintained they belong to her; certainly they benefit and do not burden her. Therefore, acceptance is presumed.

The final element necessary for a finding of a valid gift is donative intent. The most difficult element to establish a completed gift is the donative intent of the donor. Whether such an intent exists is addressed to the perception of the trial court. The existence or absence of intent to make a gift is an evidentiary issue to be resolved by the finder of fact. His resolution of that issue will not be overturned on appeal if his finding is supported by substantial evidence.

The trial court did base its finding of donative intent on substantial evidence: Mr. Welton was very fond of Mrs. Gallagher; he had made substantial gifts to her in the past. He was particularly grateful to her for taking him back after his misadventure with Sandra Kwock. He was an experienced businessman and was fully aware of the consequences of relinquishing all control over bearer bonds. He did not demand that the bonds be placed in a joint account or depository; he did not convey any written instructions or reservation of authority when he gave the bonds to Mrs. Gallagher. Because all the elements of a valid gift are present, we hold that there was no error in the finding of the lower court that such a gift was made.

Mr. Welton's alternative theory on this appeal is that even though a valid gift was made, it was a gift *causa mortis* and, therefore, revocable. The elements of a gift *causa mortis* are these: (1) The gift must be made in view of approaching death from some existing sickness or peril; (2) the donor must die from such sickness or peril without having revoked the gift; (3) there must be a delivery of the subject of the gift to the donee, subject, however, to revocation in the event of recovery from the pending sickness. The vital, although not the only difference between a gift *causa mortis* and one *inter vivos* is that the former may be revoked by the donor if he survives the pending sickness or peril, and does not pass an irrevocable title until the death of the donor, while a gift *inter vivos* is irrevocable and vests an immediate title. In this case, although Mr. Welton had undergone cancer surgery in 1973, there is no indication in the testimony that in April of 1976 he felt himself to be in immediate peril. Indeed his own statements regarding starting a new business and his active social life strongly indicate that he was not preeminently occupied in contemplating the transience of life and the prospect of his own imminent departure therefrom. The trial court was correct in finding that the gift was *inter vivos*.

Judgment for Gallagher affirmed.

Conditional Gifts   Sometimes, a gift is made on condition that the donee comply with certain restrictions or perform certain actions. A conditional gift is not a completed gift, and it may be revoked by the donor before the donee complies with the conditions. Gifts in contemplation of marriage, such as engagement rings, are the primary example of a conditional gift. Such gifts are generally considered to have been made on an implied condition that marriage between the donor and donee take place. If the donee breaks the engagement without legal justification or if the engagement is broken by mutual consent, the donor will be able to recover the ring or other engagement gift. However, if the engagement is unjustifiably broken by the donor, he or she is generally not entitled to recover gifts made in contemplation of marriage. These rules are not uniformly applied in all states, however. Some states have enacted legislation prescribing the rules applicable to the return of engagement presents.

Uniform Transfers to Minors   The Uniform Transfers to Minors Act, which has been adopted in one form or another in every state, provides a fairly simple and flexible method for making gifts and other transfers of property to minors.[7] As defined in this act, a minor is anyone under the age of 21. Under the act, an adult may transfer money, securities, real property, insurance policies, and other property. The specific ways of doing this vary according to the type of property transferred. In general, however, the transferor (the person who gives or otherwise transfers the property) delivers, pays, or assigns the property to, or registers the property with, a custodian who acts for the benefit of the minor "under the Uniform Transfers to Minors Act." The custodian is given fairly broad discretion to use the gift for the mi-

nor's benefit and may not use it for the custodian's personal benefit. The custodian may be the transferor himself, another adult, or a trust company, depending again on the type of property transferred. If the donor or other transferor fully complies with the Uniform Transfers to Minors Act, the transfer is considered to be irrevocable.

Will or Inheritance

Ownership of personal property can also be transferred upon the death of the former owner. The property may pass under the terms of a will if the will was validly executed. If there is no valid will, the property is transferred to the heirs of the owner according to state laws. Transfer of property at the death of the owner will be discussed in the Estates and Trusts chapter.

Confusion

Title to personal property can be obtained by **confusion.** Confusion is the intermixing of goods that belong to different owners in such a way that they cannot later be separated. For example, suppose wheat belonging to several different people is mixed in a grain elevator. If the mixing was by agreement or if it resulted from an accident without negligence on anyone's part, each person owns his proportionate share of the entire quantity of wheat. However, a different result would be reached if the wheat was wrongfully or negligently mixed. Suppose a thief steals a truckload of Grade #1 wheat worth $8.50 a bushel from a farmer. The thief dumps the wheat into his storage bin, which contains a lower-grade wheat worth $4.50 a bushel, with the result that the mixture is worth only $4.50 a bushel. The farmer has first claim against the entire mixture to recover the value of his wheat that was mixed in. The thief, or any other person whose intentional or negligent act results in confusion of goods, must bear any loss caused by the confusion.

---

[7]This statute was formerly called, and is still called in some states, the Uniform Gift to Minors Act.

Accession

Ownership of personal property can also be acquired by **accession.** Accession means increasing the value of property by adding materials or labor, or both. As a general rule, the owner of the original property becomes the owner of the improvements. This is particularly likely to be true if the improvement was done with the permission of the owner. For example, Hudson takes his automobile to a shop that replaces the engine with a larger engine and puts in a new four-speed transmission. Hudson is still the owner of the automobile as well as the owner of the parts added by the auto shop.

Problems can arise if materials are added or work is performed on personal property without the consent of the owner. If property is stolen from one person and improved by the thief, the original owner can get it back and does not have to reimburse the thief for the work done or the materials used in improving it. For example, a thief steals Rourke's used car, puts a new engine in it, replaces the tires, and repairs the muffler. Rourke is entitled to get his car back from the thief and does not have to pay him for the engine, tires, or muffler.

The result is less easy to predict, however, if property is mistakenly improved *in good faith* by someone who believes that he is the owner of the property. In such a case, a court must weigh the respective interests of two *innocent* parties: the original owner and the improver. For example, Johnson, a stonecarver, finds a block of limestone by the side of the road and, assuming that it has been abandoned, takes it home and carves it into a sculpture. In fact, the block was owned by Hayes and, having fallen off a flatbed truck during transportation, is merely lost property, which Hayes ordinarily could recover from the finder. In a case such as this, a court could decide the case in one of two ways. The first alternative would be to give the original owner (Hayes) ownership of the improved property, but to allow the person who has improved the property in good faith (Johnson) to recover the cost of the improvements. The second alternative would be to hold that the improver, Johnson, has acquired ownership of the sculpture, but that he is required to pay the original owner the value of the property as of the time he obtained it. The greater the extent to which the improvements have increased the value of the property, the more likely it is that the court will choose the second alternative and permit the improver to acquire ownership of the improved property.

BAILMENTS

Nature of Bailments

A **bailment** is the delivery of personal property by its owner or one who has the right to possess it (the **bailor**) to another person (the **bailee**) who accepts it and is under an express or implied agreement to return it to the bailor or to someone designated by the bailor. Only personal property can be the subject of bailments.

Although the legal terminology used to describe bailments might be unfamiliar to most people, everyone is familiar with transactions that constitute bailments. For example, Lincoln takes his car to a parking garage where the attendant gives Lincoln a claim check and then drives the car down the ramp to park it. Charles borrows his neighbor's lawn mower to cut his grass. Carne, who lives next door to Axe, agrees to take care of Axe's cat while Axe goes on a vacation. These are just a few of the everyday situations that involve bailments. The case of *York v. Jones*, which follows, involves a bailment that is much more unusual, but nevertheless illustrates the essential characteristics of a bailment.

YORK v. JONES
717 F. Supp. 421 (E.D. Va. 1989)

Steven York and Risa Adler-York contacted the Jones Institute for Reproductive Medicine to determine if they were viable candidates for in vitro fertilization (IVF). This process involves removing one or more oocytes or eggs from the woman's body, fertilizing those eggs in vitro (outside of the womb) with the husband's sperm, and then depositing the developing masses into the woman's uterus. The Yorks were accepted into the Jones Institute's IVF program. In May of 1987, the

Yorks signed a Cryopreservation Agreement outlining the procedure for cryopreservation or freezing of pre-zygotes and detailing the Yorks' rights in the frozen pre-zygote. The agreement explained that the cryopreservation procedure is available if more than five pre-zygotes are retrieved during the IVF treatment, so that the possibility for multiple births could be reduced while maintaining optimal chances for pregnancy. The agreement also provided in part:

We may withdraw our consent and discontinue participation at any time . . . and we understand our pre-zygotes will be stored only as long as we are active IVF patients at . . . Jones Institute. . . . We have the principal responsibility to decide the disposition of our pre-zygotes. Our frozen pre-zygotes will not be released from storage for the purposee of intrauterine transfer without the written consent of us both. In the event of divorce, we understand legal ownership of any stored pre-zygotes must be determined in a property settlement. . . . Should we for any reason no longer wish to attempt to initiate a pregnancy, we understand we may choose one of three fates for our pre-zygotes that remain in frozen storage. *Our pre-zygotes may be: 1) donated to another infertile couple. . . . 2) donated for approved research investigation 3) thawed but not allowed to undergo further development.*

The Yorks underwent IVF treatment on four occasions. Six eggs were removed from Mrs. York and fertilized with her husband's sperm, creating six embryos. Five of these embryos were transferred to Mrs. York's uterus, and the remaining embryo was cryogenically preserved in accordance with the procedures outlined in the Cryopreservation Agreement. None of the in vitro fertilization attempts resulted in pregnancy.

During the course of treatment, the Yorks moved to California. They sought to have the remaining frozen pre-zygote transferred from the Jones Institute in Norfolk, Virginia, to the Institute for Reproductive Research in Los Angeles, where the Yorks planned to attempt in vitro fertilization again. The Yorks arranged for proper transportation and handling of the pre-zygote, but the Jones Institute refused to allow such a transfer.

The Yorks brought suit against the Jones Institute and its physicians, claiming that its continued dominion and control over the pre-zygote was contrary to law and the parties' agreement. The Jones Institute filed a motion to dismiss, alleging that the Yorks' complaint did not state a claim on which relief could be granted. This is the trial court's ruling on that motion.

Clarke, Jr., United States District Judge.

The Yorks' complaint in this case raises an issue of first impression in the rapidly developing field of human reproductive technology. The Jones Institute argues that the Yorks' proprietary rights in the pre-zygote are limited to the "three fates" enumerated in the [Cryopreservation Agreement] because there is no established protocol for the inter-institutional transfer of pre-zygotes.

The court begins its analysis by noting that the Cryopreservation Agreement created a bailor-bailee relationship between the Yorks and Jones Institute. While the parties in this case expressed no intent to create a bailment, under Virginia law, no formal contract or actual meeting of the minds is necessary. Rather, all that is needed is the element of lawful possession however created, and duty to account for the thing as the property of another that creates the bailment. The essential nature of a bailment relationship imposes on the bailee, when the purpose of the bailment has terminated, an absolute obligation to return the subject matter of the bailment to the bailor. The obligation to return the property is implied from the fact of lawful possession of the personal property of another.

In the instant case, the requisite elements of a bailment relationship are present. The Jones Institute consistently refers to the pre-zygote as the "property" of the Yorks. Although the Cryopreservation Agreement constitutes a bailment contract, the Agreement is nevertheless governed by the same principles as apply to other contracts.

The Cryopreservation Agreement should be more strictly construed against the Jones Institute, the parties who drafted the Agreement. The Jones Institute has defined the extent of its possession interest as bailee of the pre-zygote by the following provision of the Agreement: "We may withdraw our consent and discontinue participation at any time . . . and . . . our pre-zygote will be stored only as long as we are active IVF patients at the [Jones Institute.]" The Jones Institute has further defined the limits of its possessory interest by recognizing the Yorks' proprietary rights in the pre-zygote. The Agreement repeatedly refers to "our pre-zygote" and further provides that the Yorks have the "principal responsibility to decide the disposition" of the pre-zygote.

The Jones Institute takes the position that the plain language of the Cryopreservation Agreement limits the Yorks' proprietary right to the pre-zygote to the "three fates" listed in the Agreement. The Court finds, however, that the applicability of the three fates is limited by the following language, "Should we for any reason no longer wish to initiate a pregnancy, we understand we may chose one of three fates for our pre-zygotes. . . ." The allegations of the Yorks' complaint and the entire thrust of this litigation suggest that the Yorks continue to desire to achieve pregnancy. The Agreement does not state that the attempt to initiate a pregnancy is restricted to procedures employed at the Jones Institute. The "three fates" are therefore inapplicable to the case at bar. For the reasons stated, the Court finds that the Yorks' complaint states a claim upon which relief can be granted.

Motion to dismiss denied in favor of the Yorks.

Elements of a Bailment

The essential elements of a bailment are as follows:

1. The bailor must own or have the right to possess the property,
2. The bailor must deliver exclusive possession of and control over the property to the bailee, and
3. The bailee must knowingly accept the property with the understanding that he owes a duty to return the property as directed by the bailor.

Creation of a Bailment

A bailment is created by an express or implied contract. Whether the elements of a bailment have been fulfilled is determined by examining all the facts and circumstances of the particular situation. For example, a patron goes into a restaurant and hangs her hat and coat on an unattended rack. It is unlikely that this created a bailment, because the restaurant owner never assumed exclusive control over the hat and coat. However, if there is a checkroom and the hat and coat are checked with the attendant, a bailment will arise. If a customer parks his car in a parking lot, keeps the keys, and can drive the car out himself whenever he wishes, a bailment has not been created. The courts treat this situation as a lease of space. Suppose he takes his car to a parking garage where an attendant gives him a claim check and then the attendant parks the car. There is a bailment of the car because the parking garage has accepted delivery and possession of the car. However, a distinction is made between the car and some packages locked in the trunk. If the parking garage was not aware of the packages, it would probably not be a bailee of them as it did not knowingly accept possession of them.

The creation of a bailment is illustrated in Figure 1.

Types of Bailments

Bailments are commonly divided into three different categories:

1. Bailments for the sole benefit of the bailor.
2. Bailments for the sole benefit of the bailee.
3. Bailments for mutual benefit.

The type of bailment involved in a case can be important in determining the liability of the bailee for loss of or damages to the property. As will be discussed later, however, some courts no longer rely on these distinctions for this purpose.

Bailments for Benefit of Bailor   A bailment for the sole benefit of the bailor is one in which the bailee renders some service but does not receive a benefit in return. For example, Brown allows his neighbor, Reston, to park her car in Brown's garage while she is on vacation and Brown does not ask for any compensation. Here, Reston, the bailor, has received a benefit from the bailee, Brown, but Brown has not received a benefit in return.

FIGURE 1 Creation of a Bailment

Bailor
(Owns or Has
Right to Possess
Property)

Express or
Implied Contract

Delivery of Exclusive
Possession of and
Control over Property

Bailee
(Knowingly Accepts
Property with the
Understanding That
He Must Return It)

Bailee Has Duty to
Return Property upon
Termination of Bailment

Bailments for Benefit of Bailee   A bailment for the sole benefit of the bailee is one in which the owner of the goods allows someone else to use them free of charge. For example, Anderson lends a lawn mower to her neighbor, Moss, so he can cut his grass.

Bailments for Mutual Benefit   If both the bailee and the bailor receive benefits from the bailment, it is a bailment for mutual benefit. For example, Sutton rents china for his daughter's wedding from E-Z Party Supplies for an agreed-on price. Sutton, the bailee, benefits by being able to use the china, while E-Z benefits from his payment of the rental charge. On some occasions, the benefit to the bailee is less tangible. For example, a customer checks a coat at an attended coatroom at a restaurant. Even if no charge is made for the service, it is likely to be treated as a bailment for mutual benefit because the restaurant is benefiting from the customer's patronage.

Special Bailments

Certain kinds of professional bailees, such as innkeepers and common carriers, are treated somewhat differently by the law and are held to a higher level of responsibility than is the ordinary bailee. The rules applicable to common carriers and innkeepers are detailed later in this chapter.

Duties of the Bailee

The bailee has two basic duties:

1. To take care of the property that has been entrusted to him.

2. To return the property at the termination of the bailment.

The following discussion examines the scope of these duties.

Duty of Bailee to Take Care of Property

The bailee is responsible for taking steps to protect the property during the time he has possession of it. If the bailee does not exercise proper care and the property is lost or damaged, the bailee is liable for negligence. The bailee would then be required to reimburse the bailor for the amount of loss or damage. If the property is lost or damaged without the fault or negligence of the bailee, however, the bailee is not liable to the bailor.

The degree of care required of the bailee traditionally has depended in large part on the type of bailment involved—that is, which party or parties are benefiting from the bailment.

1. *Bailment for the benefit of the bailor.* If the bailment is solely for the benefit of the bailor, the bailee is expected to exercise only a minimal, or slight, degree of care for the protection of the bailed property. He would be liable, then, only if he were grossly negligent in his care of the bailed property. The rationale for this is that if the bailee is doing the bailor a favor, it is not reasonable to expect him to be as careful as when he is deriving some benefit from keeping the goods.

2. *Bailment for mutual benefit.* Where the bailment is a bailment for mutual benefit, the bailee is expected to exercise ordinary or reasonable care. This degree of care requires the bailee to use the same kind of care a reasonable person would use to protect his own property in that situation. If the bailee is a professional that holds itself out as a professional bailee, such as a warehouse, it must use the degree of care that would be used by a person in that profession. This is likely to be more care than the ordinary person would use. In addition, there is usually a duty on a professional bailee to explain any loss or damage to property, that is, to show it was not negligent. If it cannot do so, it will be liable to the bailor.

3. *Bailment for the benefit of the bailee.* If the bailment is solely for the benefit of the bailee, the bailee is expected to exercise a high degree of care. A person who lends a sailboat to a neighbor would probably expect the neighbor to be even more careful with the sailboat than the owner might be, for example. In such a case, the bailee would be liable for damage to the property if he committed a relatively small degree of negligence.

A number of courts today view the type of bailment involved in a case as just one factor to be considered in determining whether the bailee should be liable for loss or damage to bailed goods. The modern trend appears to be moving in the direction of imposing a duty of reasonable care on bailees, regardless of the type of bailment. This flexible standard of care permits courts to take into account a variety of factors such as the nature and value of the property, the provisions of the parties' agreement, the payment of consideration for the bailment, and the experience of the bailee. In addition, the bailee is required to use the property only as was agreed between the parties. For example, Jones borrows Morrow's lawn mower to mow his lawn. If Jones uses the mower to cut the weeds on a trash-filled vacant lot and the mower is damaged, he would be liable because he was exceeding the agreed purpose of the bailment—to cut his lawn.

Bailee's Duty to Return the Property

One of the essential elements of a bailment is the duty of the bailee to return the property at the termination of the bailment. If the bailed property is taken from the bailee by legal process, the bailee should notify the bailor and must take whatever action is necessary to protect the bailor's interest. In most instances, the bailee must return the identical property that was bailed. A person who lends a 1985 Volkswagen Rabbit to a friend expects to have that particular car returned. In some cases, the bailor does not expect the return of the identical goods. For example, a farmer who stores 1,500 bushels of Grade #1 wheat at a local grain elevator expects to get back 1,500 bushels of Grade #1 wheat when the bailment is terminated, but not the identical wheat he deposited.

The bailee must return the goods in an undamaged condition to the bailor or to someone designated by the bailor. If the goods have been damaged, destroyed, or lost, there is a rebuttable presumption of negligence on the part of the bailee. To overcome the presumption, the bailee must come forward with evidence showing that the accident, damage, or loss resulted from some cause consistent with the exercise of the relevant level of due care on his part. The operation of the rebuttable presumption can be seen in the *Magee v. Walbro* case, which follows. If the property is lost or damaged without the fault or negligence of the bailee, however, the bailee is not liable to the bailor.

MAGEE v. WALBRO, INC.
525 N.E.2d 975 (Ill. Ct. App. 1988)

Walbro, Inc., doing business as Mysel Furs, was in the business of storing furs. It had arranged for United Parcel Service (UPS) to pick up furs from its customers and deliver them to Mysel's. In May 1982, Mysel's solicited Crella Magee's business to store her furs for the summer, and Magee agreed. Pursuant to an arrangement with Mysel's to pick up three furs from Magee, UPS delivered three empty boxes labeled with unique call numbers to Magee on May 25. Magee inserted a fur in each of the boxes, and UPS then picked up the three boxes, giving Magee's husband three tickets bearing call numbers identical to those marked on the boxes. UPS delivered the boxes to

Mysel's on May 26. A Mysel's employee signed for the boxes, but did not check to be sure that none of the boxes was empty. In July, Mysel's issued a storage receipt to Magee that showed only two furs. This storage receipt also contained a term that limited Mysel's liability for lost property to $100. Magee called Mysel's immediately and received assurances that the three furs were in storage. When Magee went to pick up her three furs in October of 1982, however, one of them—a blue fox jacket worth $3,400—was missing. Mysel's did not compensate Magee, arguing that its liability for lost articles was limited to $100. Magee then brought suit against Walbro, Mysel's, and UPS for breach of bailment and conversion. The trial court ruled for the defendants, and Magee appealed. (Magee voluntarily dismissed her case against UPS, so its liability is not involved in this appeal.)

O'Connor, Justice. Establishing a *prima facie* case of bailment raises a presumption of negligence by the defendant, which the defendant must rebut with evidence sufficient to support a finding of the nonexistence of the presumed fact. The trial court ruled that the evidence established a bailment between Magee and Walbro and Mysel's, thus raising the presumption of negligence. Walbro and Mysel produced no evidence, however, to rebut the presumption of negligence.

Based on the evidence presented, the trial court ruled that the lost jacket was delivered to Mysel Furs. Walbro and Mysel's argued that, assuming delivery of the jacket, any presumption of negligence was defeated by the procedures used in storing furs. The furs were placed in a locked, alarmed vault to which several, identifiable Mysel's employees had access. Mysel's then prepared and issued a storage receipt to the customer. Walbro presented no evidence to show that these procedures were followed for Magee's furs, and the storage receipt was not issued until six weeks after the jacket was delivered. It is reasonable to assume that the defendants' procedures and security precautions customarily resulted in the return of the customer's fur. Magee's fur was not returned; therefore, without showing more than the mere existence of safety and security measures, the defendants failed to rebut the presumption of negligence. Magee was therefore entitled to recover her damages.

Finally, the defendants asserted the defense of limitation of liability. Walbro and Mysel's argue that they effectively limited their liability to $100, citing *Schoen v. Wallace,* which upheld an agreement between a fur owner and fur storage company to limit the storage company's liability to $100. *Schoen* and [other cases] indicate, however, that the customer was aware of the limitation of liability *before* the furs were placed in storage. The *Schoen* decision was based in part on the fact that the plaintiff had dealt with the defendant before, knew of its insurance practices, [and] could have chosen another furrier had she found the limitation objectionable.

In the instant case, Magee testified that she was not told of the limitation until after the fur was lost. Defendants rely on the receipt of July 1982, which stated that liability was limited to $100. Magee should have known of the limitation after she received the receipt in July, but by that time her furs had been at Mysel's for six weeks.

The limitation does not apply in the instant case because Magee had no knowledge of the limitation before agreeing to store her furs. In *Schoen*, the court stated that it would be "unjust to permit the plaintiff to repudiate [the agreement to limit liability] because the coat was lost." In the instant case, it would be unjust to permit Mysel and Walbro to assert a limitation that was not made clear at the time that the bailment contract was made because the coat was lost. We therefore hold that the $100 limitation of liability is inapplicable in this case.

For the foregoing reasons, judgment in favor of the defendants is reversed, and this case is remanded to the trial court to enter judgment against Walbro and Mysel's and in favor of Magee in the amount of $3,400.

Reversed and remanded in favor of Magee.

Bailee's Liability for Misdelivery   The bailee is also liable to the bailor if he misdelivers the bailed property at the termination of the bailment. The property must be returned to the bailor or to someone specified by the bailor.

If a third person claims to have rights in the bailed property that are superior to the rights of the bailor and demands possession of the bailed property, the bailee is in a dilemma. If the bailee refuses to deliver the bailed property to the third-person claimant and the third-person claimant is entitled to its possession, the bailee is liable to the claimant. If the bailee delivers the bailed property to the third-party claimant and the third-party claimant is not entitled to possession, the bailee is liable to the bailor. The circumstances may be such that the conflicting claims of the bailor and the third-person claimant can be determined only by judicial decision. In some cases, the bailee may protect himself by bringing the third-party claimant into a lawsuit along with the bailor so that all the competing claims can be adjudicated by the court before the bailee releases the property, but this remedy is not always available.

Limits on Liability

Bailees may try to limit or relieve themselves of liability for the bailed property. Some examples include the storage receipt purporting to limit liability to $100 in the *Magee v. Walbro, Inc*. case, signs near checkrooms, such as "Not responsible for loss of or damage to checked property," and disclaimers on claim checks, such as "Goods left at owner's risk." The standards used to determine whether such limitations and disclaimers are enforceable are discussed in detail in the Illegality chapter.

Any attempt by the bailee to be relieved of liability for *intentional wrongful acts* is against public policy and will not be enforced. A bailee's ability to be relieved of liability for *negligence* is also limited. Courts look to see whether the disclaimer or limitation of liability was communicated to the bailor at the time of the bailment. Did the attendant point out the sign near the checkroom to the person when the coat was checked? Did the parking lot attendant call the person's attention to the disclaimer on the back of the claim check? If not, as in the *Magee* case, the court may hold that the disclaimer was not communicated to the bailor and did not become part of the bailment contract. Even if the bailor was aware of the disclaimer, it still may not be enforced on the ground that it is contrary to public policy.

If the disclaimer was offered on a take-it-or-leave-it basis and was not the subject of arm's-length bargaining, it is less likely to be enforced than if it has been negotiated and voluntarily agreed upon. A bailee may be able to limit liability to a certain amount or to relieve himself of liability for certain perils. Ideally, the bailee will give the bailor a chance to declare a higher value and to pay an additional charge to be protected up to the declared value of the goods. Common carriers, such as railroads and trucking companies, often take this approach. Courts do not look with favor on efforts by a person to be relieved of liability for negligence. For this reason, terms limiting the liability of a bailee stand a better chance of being enforced than do terms completely relieving the bailee of liability.

The bailor's knowledge of the bailee's facilities or of his method of doing business or the nature of prior dealings may give rise to an implied agreement as to the bailee's duties. The bailee may, if he wishes, assume all the risks incident to the bailment and contract to return the bailed property undamaged or to pay any damage to or loss of the property.

Right to Compensation

The express or implied contract creating the bailment controls whether the bailee has the right to receive compensation for keeping the property or must pay for having the right to use it. If the bailment is made as a favor, then the bailee is not entitled to compensation even though the bailment is for the sole benefit of the bailor. If the bailment is the rental of property, then the bailee must pay the agreed rental rate. If the bailment is for the storage or repair of property, then the bailee is entitled to the contract price for the storage or repair services. If no specific price was agreed upon, yet compensation was contemplated by the parties, then the bailee gets the reasonable value of the services provided.

In many instances, the bailee will have a **lien** (a charge against property to secure the payment of a debt) on the bailed property for the reasonable value of the services. For example, Silver takes a chair to Ace Upholstery to have it recovered. When the chair has been recovered, Ace has the right to keep it until the agreed price—or, if no price was set, the reasonable value of the work—is paid. This is an example of an **artisan's lien**, which is discussed in greater detail in the Security Interests in Personal Property chapter.

Bailor's Liability for Defects in the Bailed Property

When personal property is rented or loaned, the bailor makes an implied warranty that the property has no hidden defects that make it unsafe for use. If the bailment is for the sole benefit of the bailee, then the bailor is liable for injuries that result from defects in the bailed property only if the bailor knew about the defects and did not tell the bailee. For example, Price lends his car, which he knows has bad brakes, to Sloan. If Price does not tell Sloan about the bad brakes and if Sloan is injured in an accident because the brakes fail, Price is liable for Sloan's injuries.

If the bailment is a bailment for mutual benefit, then the bailor has a larger obligation. The bailor must use reasonable care in inspecting the property and seeing that it is safe for the purpose for which it is intended. The bailor is liable for injuries suffered by the bailee because of defects that the bailor either knew about or should have discovered by reasonable inspection. For example, Friedman's Rent-All, which rents trailers, does not inspect the trailers after they are returned. A wheel has come loose on a trailer that Friedman's rents to Hirsch. If the wheel comes off while Hirsch is using the trailer and the goods Hirsch is carrying in it are damaged, Friedman's is liable to Hirsch.

In addition, product liability doctrines that apply a higher standard of legal responsibility have been applied to bailors who are commercial lessors of personal property.[8] Express or implied warranties of quality under either Article 2 or Article 2A of the UCC may apply. Liability under these warranties does not depend on whether the bailor knew about or should have discovered the defect. The only question is whether the property's condition complied with the warranty. Some courts have also imposed strict liability on lessors-bailors of goods that cause personal injury or property damage to the lessee-bailee because they are defective and unreasonably dangerous. This liability is imposed regardless of whether the lessor was negligent.

---

[8]Product liability doctrines are discussed in the Product Liability chapter.

CONCEPT REVIEW

DUTIES OF BAILEES AND BAILORS

Type of Bailment	Duties of Bailee	Duties of Bailor
Sole Benefit of Bailee	1. Must use great care; liable for even slight negligence. 2. Must return goods to bailor or dispose of them at his direction. 3. May have duty to compensate bailor.	1. Must notify the bailee of any known defects.
Mutual Benefit	1. Must use reasonable care; liable for ordinary negligence. 2. Must return goods to bailor or dispose of them at his direction. 3. May have duty to compensate bailor.	1. Must notify bailee of all known defects and any defects that could be discovered on reasonable inspection. 2. Commercial lessors may be subject to warranties of quality and/or strict liability in tort. 3. May have duty to compensate bailee.
Sole Benefit of Bailor	1. Must use at least slight care; liable for gross negligence. 2. Must return goods to bailor or dispose of them at his direction.	1. Must notify bailee of all known defects and any hidden defects that are known or could be discovered on reasonable inspection. 2. May have duty to compensate bailee.

SPECIAL BAILMENTS

Common Carriers

Bailees that are **common carriers** are held to a higher level of responsibility than that to which bailees that are private carriers are held. Common carriers are licensed by governmental agencies to carry the property of anyone who requests the service. Airlines licensed by the Department of Transportation and trucks and buses licensed by the Interstate Commerce Commission are examples of common carriers. *Private contract carriers* carry goods only for persons selected by the carrier.

Both common carriers and private contract carriers are bailees. However, the law makes the common carrier an absolute insurer of the goods it carries. The common carrier is responsible for any loss of or damage to goods entrusted to it. The common carrier can avoid responsibility only if it can show that the loss or damage was caused by:

1. An act of God,
2. An act of a public enemy,
3. An act or order of the government,
4. An act of the person who shipped the goods, or
5. The nature of the goods themselves.

The common carrier is liable if goods entrusted to it are stolen by some unknown person but not if the goods are destroyed when a tornado hits the warehouse. If goods are damaged because the shipper improperly packages or crates them, then the carrier is not liable. Similarly, if perishable goods are not in suitable condition to be shipped and deteriorate in the course of shipment, the carrier is not liable so long as it used reasonable care in handling them.

Common carriers are usually permitted to limit their liability to a stated value unless the bailor declares a higher value for the property and pays an additional fee.

Hotelkeepers

Hotelkeepers are engaged in the business of offering food and/or lodging to transient persons. They hold themselves out to serve the public and are obligated to do so. Like the common carrier, the hotelkeeper is held to a higher standard of care than that of the ordinary bailee.

The hotelkeeper is not a bailee in the strict sense of the word. The guest does not usually surrender the ex-clusive possession of his property to the hotelkeeper. However, the hotelkeeper is treated as the virtual insurer of the guest's property. The hotelkeeper is not liable for loss of or damage to property if he can show that it was caused by:

1. An act of God,
2. An act of a public enemy,
3. An act of a governmental authority,
4. The fault of a member of the guest's party, or
5. The nature of the goods.

Most states have passed laws that limit the hotelkeeper's liability, however. Commonly, the law requires the hotel owner to post a notice advising guests that any valuables should be checked into the hotel vault. The hotelkeeper's liability is then limited, usually to a fixed amount, for valuables that are not so checked.

Safe-Deposit Boxes

If a person rents a safe-deposit box at a local bank and places some property in the box, the box and the property are in the manual possession of the bank. However, it takes both the renter's key and the key held by the bank to open the box, and in most cases the bank does not know the nature, amount, or value of the goods in the box. Although a few courts have held the rental of a safe-deposit box not to be a bailment, most courts have found that the renter of the box is a bailor and the bank is a bailee. As such, the bank is not an insurer of the contents of the box. However, it is obligated to use due care and to come forward and explain loss of or damage to the property entrusted to it.

Involuntary Bailments

Suppose a person owns a cottage on a beach. After a violent storm, a sailboat washed up on his beach. As the finder of lost or misplaced property, he may be considered the **involuntary bailee** or **constructive bailee** of the sailboat. This relationship may arise when a person finds himself in possession of property that belongs to someone else without having agreed to accept possession.

The duties of the involuntary bailee are not well defined. The bailee does not have the right to destroy the property or to use it. If the true owner shows up, the property must be returned to him. Under some circumstances, the involuntary bailee may be under an obligation to assume control of the property or to take some minimal steps to ascertain who the owner is, or both.

In the case that follows, *Capezzaro v. Winfrey,* a constructive and involuntary bailee was held liable for disposing of the bailed property because it had knowledge of an adverse claim to the property.

CAPEZZARO v. WINFREY

379 A.2d 493 (N.J. Super. Ct. 1977)

Michael Capezzaro reported to the police that he had been robbed of $7,500 at gunpoint by a woman. The following day, Henrietta Winfrey was arrested with a total of $2,480.66 in her possession. Capezzaro positively identified her as the woman who had robbed him and claimed that the money found on her was part of the money that she had taken from him. Winfrey was jailed, and the money was impounded by the police as evidence of the crime. Several months later, Winfrey was indicted for the armed robbery of Capezzaro. Approximately two years afterward, this and other indictments against Winfrey were dismissed by the prosecutor based on medical opinion that she was unable to know right from wrong at the time she allegedly committed the crimes with which she had been charged.

When the warden of the county jail notified the police officers in charge of the police department's property room that the indictment against Winfrey had been dismissed, the police officers released the $2,480.66 claimed by Capezzaro to Winfrey. Eventually, Capezzaro found out about the dismissal of the indictment and the release of the money. He then instituted a lawsuit against Winfrey and the city of Newark, claiming that the released money was his. The trial court held in his favor and the city appealed.

Per Curiam. A constructive bailment or a bailment by operation of law may be created when a person comes into possession of personal property of another, receives nothing from the owner of the property, and has no right to recover from the owner for what he does in caring for the property. Such person is ordinarily considered to be a gratuitous bailee, liable only to the bailor for bad faith or gross negligence. *Zuppa v. Hertz Corp.* states:

It is the element of lawful possession, however created, and the duty to account for the thing as the property of another, that creates the bailment, regardless of whether such possession is based upon contract in the ordinary sense or not.

Where possession has been acquired accidentally, fortuitously, through mistake or by an agreement for some other purpose since terminated, the possessor, "upon principles of justice," should keep it safely and restore or deliver it to its owner. Under such circumstances, the courts have considered the possession quasi-contracts of bailment or constructive and involuntary bailments.

Here the police seized and obtained custody of the money which was found in Winfrey's girdle during a search in her cell after her arrest on the robbery charge and after Capezzaro claimed Winfrey had stolen it from him. It is undisputed that the money was being kept by the police as evidence for use in Winfrey's prosecution. It follows, then, that the City of Newark, through its police department, was holding the money for its own benefit as well as for the benefit of its rightful owner.

Ordinarily, a person who has possession of property may be presumed by another to be the rightful owner thereof in the absence of any knowledge to the contrary. However, here the police were fully aware of Capezzaro's adverse claim, but notwithstanding such knowledge and without notice to Capezzaro turned the money over to Winfrey.

The city contends that when the indictment was dismissed, any claim by Capezzaro lost its validity and it was obligated to return the monies in question to Winfrey as bailor. We disagree. A bailee with knowledge of an adverse claim makes delivery to the bailor at his peril, and only if he is ignorant of such a claim will he be protected against a subsequent claim by the rightful owner.

The police returned the money to Winfrey after being informed by the warden of the county jail that the indictments had been dismissed. They did not contact Capezzaro before doing so, even though they were on notice of his adverse claim. The dismissal of the indictment for the reasons here present did not vitiate Capezzaro's adverse claim to the money. Inherent in the jury's verdict is a finding that the city was negligent in releasing the money without a determination of the validity of the adverse claim. This finding and the verdict are amply supported by the evidence.

Judgment for Capezzaro affirmed.

ETHICAL AND PUBLIC POLICY CONCERNS

1. Does a finder of lost or mislaid property have an ethical duty to look for the owner of the property? How effective are the legal principles that you learned in encouraging a finder to do so?

2. What part does ethical conduct play in determining whether a person acquires ownership of personal property by confusion? By accession?

3. You learned that, in formulating the degree of care that a bailee must exercise over bailed property, courts traditionally have applied standards based on the amount of relative benefit the parties derive from the bailment. Where both parties benefit, reasonable care is required; where the bailee alone benefits, great care is required; and where the bailor alone benefits, only slight care is required. Modern courts seem to be moving in the direction of applying a standard of *reasonable care* to all bailments, however. Which approach is preferable, and why?

SUMMARY

Ownership of property is the exclusive right to possess, enjoy, and dispose of objects or rights having economic value. In law, property is a bundle of legal rights to things having economic value, which rights are recognized and protected by society. Property is classified according to its various characteristics. The earth's crust and all things firmly attached to it are classified as real property. All other objects and rights subject to ownership are classified as personal property. Property that has a physical existence is classified as tangible property. Rights that have economic value but are not related to things having a physical existence are classified as intangible property. Property owned by the government or a governmental unit is classified as public property. Property owned by any person or association, even though used exclusively for public purposes, is classified as private property.

Ownership of personal property may be acquired by (1) production or purchase, (2) taking possession of unowned property, (3) finding lost property (the finder acquires rights superior to everyone except the owner), (4) gift, (5) will or inheritance, (6) confusion, and (7) accession. In addition, the right to exclusive use and possession of personal property is frequently acquired by leasing.

A person owns property produced by his own labor or by the labor of persons whom he hires to work for him. The owner of personal property may sell or barter his property to another, and the purchaser then becomes the owner of the property. The person who first reduces unowned property—wildlife or abandoned property—to possession with the intent of claiming ownership of the property acquires ownership.

A gift is the transfer of the ownership of property from the donor to the donee without any consideration being given by the donee. To have a valid gift, the donor must deliver the possession of the property to the donee or to some third person with the intent of vesting ownership in the donee.

The finder of lost property acquires ownership of the property against everyone except the original owner. When property is mislaid, however, the owner of the real property on which it is found has the right to possess the property as a bailee until the true owner is found. If a person confuses his property with that of another person, the other person may acquire ownership of the entire mass through the doctrine of confusion. If property is improved by the labor and addition of materials by another without the owner's consent, the owner of the original property becomes the owner of the property in its improved state. This is known as obtaining title by accession.

A bailment is created when an owner of personal property, the bailor, delivers the possession of the property to another, the bailee, who intends to take control of it and who is obligated to return the property to the bailor or to dispose of it as directed by the bailor. A bailment is created by an express or implied agreement.

The bailee owes a duty of due care to prevent loss of or damage to the bailed property. In determining whether or not due care has been exercised by the bailee, the nature of the bailment is of considerable importance, as is the type of property and the bailee's skill. The trend today is to apply a standard of reasonable care to all bailees. Within the limits of the legality of their contract, the parties may, by agreement, increase or decrease the scope of the bailee's liability.

When the bailment terminates, the bailee must return the bailed property to the bailor or dispose of it according to the bailor's direction. If a third person having a right of possession superior to that of the bailor demands the surrender of the property, the bailee is obligated to deliver the property to that person.

The bailee is entitled to any compensation expressly or impliedly agreed upon for services rendered in the care of the property. If the bailor rents property to the bailee, the bailor owes a duty to inspect the property to see that it is free from dangerous defects. Product liability doctrines such as implied warranty and strict liability have been applied to commercial lessors of personal property.

A common carrier is the insurer of the goods it carries against loss or damage, unless such loss or damage is caused by an act of God, an act of a public enemy, an act of the state, an act of the shipper, or the nature of the goods. A hotelkeeper is an insurer of the goods of his guests, subject to certain exceptions. Many states have statutes permitting hotelkeepers to limit their liability.

A person may become an involuntary bailee if the goods of another are placed in his possession, such as where goods are deposited on his land by storm or flood or by the acts of third persons, where he finds lost or mislaid property, or if the domestic animals of another stray onto his land. Such a bailee owes a minimum duty of care. He cannot willfully destroy the property or convert it to his own use.

PROBLEM CASES

1. Charrier was an amateur archeologist. After researching colonial maps and records, he concluded that the Trudeau Plantation near Angola, Louisiana, was the possible site of an ancient village of the Tunica Indians. Charrier obtained the permission of the caretaker of the Trudeau Plantation to survey the property with a metal detector for possible burial locations. At the time, he mistakenly believed that the caretaker was the Plantation's owner. He located and, over the next three years, excavated approximately 150 burial sites containing: beads, European ceramics, stoneware, glass bottles, iron kettles, vessels, skillets, knives, muskets, gunflints, balls, shots, crucifixes, rings, bracelets, and native pottery. Did Charrier acquire ownership of the burial goods?

[handwritten margin note: MUTAIKI DOES NOT HAVE OWNERSHIP OF GOODS, FINDER]

2. Vallejo, a customer at Martin Chevrolet Sales, requested and received permission to test-drive a 1986 Chevrolet Camaro IROC. Vallejo took the car out for a test-drive alone. While test-driving the car, Vallejo was involved in an accident and "totaled" the car, which was worth more than $13,000. Martin Chevrolet's insurer brought suit against Vallejo on a bailment theory, claiming that the car had been damaged due to Vallejo's "willful and wanton" acts. Vallejo argued that there was no bailment relationship between Martin Chevrolet and himself. Is he correct? *[handwritten: BAILMENT / MUTUAL BENEFIT]*

3. Jackson was a maid in a hotel owned by Steinberg. She found eight $100 bills under the paper lining in a dresser in a guest room. She turned the money over to Steinberg. Steinberg tried to locate the true owner by sending a letter to everyone who had occupied the room over the last three months. However, no one claimed it.

[handwritten: Yes - she is entitled]

Jackson demanded that the money be returned to her, but Steinberg refused. Was Jackson entitled to the money she found in the dresser drawer in Steinberg's hotel?

4. Taylor lived with Hattie Smith. Taylor rented a safe-deposit box at the Crown Center Bank in the name of Hattie Smith and gave her both keys to the box. Smith signed a card that authorized and directed the bank to allow Hunter Taylor to enter "my box" at any time. On several occasions, Taylor borrowed the key to the box without explanation and then returned it to Smith. Smith claimed that Taylor told her he had put money in the box, and none was put in the day the box was rented. Taylor was murdered, and at the time of the murder he had both of the keys to the box in his possession. Smith had the box opened by the bank, and $8,000 was found in it. The administrator of Taylor's estate claimed the money for the estate. Smith claimed that the money was a gift to her. Had Taylor made a valid gift of the money to Smith?

5. The Kahrs put their silver (worth about $3,800), jewelry, and a wallet containing their credit cards in bags and stored them in their attic while they were on vacation. After they returned, they retrieved the bags containing the valuables and placed them on their dining room table along with bags containing some used clothing that they had decided to donate to Goodwill. Mr. Kahr mistakenly picked up the bags containing the silver and wallet and delivered them to Goodwill along with the bags of used clothing. He told Goodwill at that time that he was donating used clothing. A Goodwill employee who was marking the items for resale found the Kahrs's wallet in a bag and, realizing it was a mistake, called the Kahrs's residence about the wallet. She did not mention the silver, though, because she had not yet found it. Even when she did find it, she did not realize that it was sterling silver. The Kahrs realized the mistake about two hours later. They called Goodwill only to find that the silver had been sold for $15 to Markland. Markland refused to return the silver, and the Kahrs brought suit. Can the Kahrs get their silver back?

6. Ochoa's Studebaker automobile was stolen. Eleven months later, the automobile somehow found its way into the hands of the U.S. government, which sold it at a "junk" auction for $85 to Rogers. At the time it was purchased by Rogers, no part of the car was intact. It had no top except a part of the frame; it had no steering wheel, tires, rims, cushions, or battery; the motor, radiator, and gears were out of the car; one wheel was gone,

as was one axle; the fenders were partly gone; and the frame was broken. It was no longer an automobile but a pile of broken and dismantled parts of what was once Ochoa's car. Having purchased these parts, Rogers used them in the construction of a delivery truck at an expense of approximately $800. When the truck was completed, he put it to use in his furniture business. Several months later, Ochoa was passing Rogers' place of business and recognized the vehicle from a mark on the hood and another on the radiator. He discovered that the serial and engine numbers matched those on the car he had owned. Ochoa demanded the vehicle from Rogers, who refused to surrender it. Ochoa brought suit to recover possession of the property. In the alternative, he asked for the value of the vehicle at the time of the suit, which he alleged to be $1,000, and for the value of the use of the car from the time Rogers purchased it from the government. Was Ochoa entitled to recover possession of his property, which Rogers had substantially improved?

7. Pond owned and operated a parking lot. Rehling parked his automobile on Pond's lot, which was near Crosley Field, and proceeded with others to a night baseball game. Rehling paid $1 to the parking lot attendant, for which he received a "claim check." Before leaving his automobile, Rehling rolled up the windows, locked the doors, and took the keys with him. When he returned after the ballgame to get his automobile, it was gone. The parking lot attendants testified that at about the third inning of the ballgame, they saw a person walk directly to Rehling's automobile, get in, back up, and drive away. There was no showing that the claim check was ever used for anything but identification in case a patron was unable to find his automobile on the lot. Is Pond liable as bailee for the loss of the automobile?

8. Dolitsky rented a safe-deposit box from Dollar Savings Bank. The safe-deposit vault of the bank was in the basement, and the vault area was walled off from all other parts of the bank. Only box renters and officers and employees of the bank were admitted to this area. To gain access to the area, a box renter had to obtain an admission slip, fill in the box number and sign the slip, have the box number and signature checked by an employee against the records of the bank, and then present the slip to a guard who admitted the renter to the vault area. On November 7, 1951, Dolitsky requested access to her box. While Dolitsky was in the booth, she was

[handwritten margin notes: LOST PROPERTY ↓ NO DON'T HAVE A DUTY TO KEEP]

looking through an advertising folder that the bank had placed there and found a $100 bill, which she turned over to the attendant. Dolitsky waited one year, and during that time the rightful owner of the $100 bill made no claim for it. Dolitsky then demanded that the bank surrender the bill to her, claiming that she was entitled to the bill as finder. The bank claimed that the bill was mislaid property and that it owed a duty to keep the bill for the rightful owner. Is this correct? *No!*

9. Pringle, the head of the drapery department at Wardrobe Cleaners, went to the Axelrods' home to inspect some dining room draperies for dry-cleaning purposes. He spent about 30 minutes looking at the drapes and inspected both the drapes and the lining. He pointed out some roach spots on the lining that could not be removed by cleaning, but this was not of concern to the Axelrods. He did not indicate to them that the fabric had deteriorated from sunburn, age, dust, or air conditioning so as to make it unsuitable for dry cleaning. He took the drapes and had them dry cleaned. When the drapes were returned, they were unfit for use. The fabric had been a gold floral design on an eggshell-white background. When returned, it was a blotchy gold. Wardrobe Cleaners stated that it was difficult to predict how imported fabrics would respond to the dry-cleaning process and that the company was not equipped to pretest the fabric to see whether it was colorfast. The Axelrods sued Wardrobe Cleaners for $1,000, the replacement value of the drapes. Was Wardrobe Cleaners liable for the damage caused to the drapes during the dry-cleaning process? *BAILMENT MUTABLE BENEFIT HAD DUTY to INFORM of REASONABLE CARE → RISK*

10. In the spring of 1973, Carter brought her fur coat to Reichlin Furriers for cleaning, glazing, and storage until the next winter season. She was given a printed form of receipt, upon the front of which an employee of Reichlin had written $100 as the valuation of the coat. There was no discussion of the value of the coat, and Carter did not realize that such a value had been written on the receipt, which she did not read at the time. A space for the customer's signature on the front of the receipt was left blank. Below this space in prominent type appeared a notice to "see reverse side for terms and conditions." The other side of the receipt stated that it was a storage contract and that by its acceptance the customer would be deemed to have agreed to its terms unless notice to the contrary were given within 10 days. Fifteen conditions were listed. One of the conditions was

as follows: "Storage charges are based upon valuation herein declared by the depositor, and amount recoverable for loss or damage to the article shall not exceed its actual value or the cost of repair or replacement with materials of like kind and quality or the depositor's valuation appearing in this receipt, whichever is less." In the fall of 1973, after Carter had paid the bill for storage and other services on the coat, Reichlin informed her that the coat was lost. At that time, the fair market value of the coat was $450. Carter sued Reichlin for loss of the coat and sought $450 damages. Reichlin claimed that its liability was limited to $100. Is this correct?

11. The Satterthwaites operated the Crystal Palace Barber and Beauty Shop. The Crystal Palace consisted of a suite of three rooms, the back room being the barber shop, the middle room being the operating area of the beauty shop, and the room facing the outside—which is visible to outsiders through a glass door—being a reception room. There was a conspicuous sign in the shop that read, "Not responsible for hats, coats, and purses." Theobald had patronized the beauty shop numerous times and knew the arrangement of the rooms. On a previous visit, she had asked Mrs. Satterthwaite if the reception room was a safe place to leave her coat and had been assured that it was safe. Nothing had been stolen from the reception room in 20 years of operation, and the hooks there were the only ones on which customers could hang their coats. There was no bell or warning device on the door that sounded when someone entered the reception room. A thief could well see into the reception room, remove a coat, and leave without being seen from the operating area of the beauty shop. On December 24, 1946, Theobald came into the beauty shop to get a permanent and sat in the reception room wearing a fur coat until it was time for her appointment. She then removed her fur coat, hung it on a hook in the reception area, and went into the operating area of the beauty shop. Neither of the Satterthwaites was aware that Theobald had worn her fur coat that day. While Theobald was getting her permanent, someone stole the coat. Theobald alleges that there was a bailment and the Satterthwaites are therefore responsible for the loss of the coat. Was there a bailment? *BARBER DID NOT TAKE POSSESSION NO BAILMENT*

12. Andrews delivered his quarter horse mare named "I'll Call Ya" to Oak Hills Ranch and its owner Stone for the purpose of boarding. Stone was in the business of brokering, stabling, and training racehorses for profit. Several months later, Andrews asked Stone if he would arrange for I'll Call Ya to be transported to a trainer in Louisiana. Consequently, when the Allen brothers, who were also in the business of boarding and training horses for profit and had previously done business with Stone, delivered two horses to Oak Hills Ranch, Stone asked them if they would haul I'll Call Ya back to their training stable in east Texas where the Louisiana trainer could pick her up. Andrews agreed to these plans even though he did not know the Allen brothers. On March 16, 1983, the Allens loaded I'll

Call Ya into their trailer and began the drive to east Texas. Shortly after leaving Oak Hills Ranch, the trailer became disengaged from the Allens' truck, rolled over, and came to rest on the side of the road. I'll Call Ya was severely cut and bruised as a result of the accident and lingered for several hours by the side of the road before she died without veterinary treatment. The fair market value of the horse before the accident was $150,000. Andrews brought suit against Stone and the Allens to recover the value of I'll Call Ya. Will he prevail?

BAILOR → BAILEE & BAILEE

CHAPTER 24

REAL PROPERTY AND INSURANCE

INTRODUCTION

Land has always occupied a position of special importance in the law. In the agrarian society of previous eras, land was the basic measure and source of wealth. In an industrialized society, land is not only a source of food, clothing, and shelter but also an instrument of commercial and industrial development. It is not surprising, then, that a complex body of law exists regarding the ownership, acquisition, and use of land. This body of law is known as the law of **real property.**

This chapter presents an overview of the law of real property. It will discuss the scope of real property, the various ownership interests in real property, the ways in which real property is transferred, and the controls that society places on an owner's use of real property. It will also present a brief overview of insurance concepts applying to property insurance.

SCOPE OF REAL PROPERTY

Real property includes not only land but also things that are firmly attached to the land or embedded in the land. Thus, buildings and other permanent structures are considered part of real property. The person who owns a tract of real property also owns the air above his property, the minerals below its surface, and any trees or other vegetation growing on the property.[1] Real property is distinguished from personal property by the fact that real property is *immovable* or attached to something immovable, while personal property is not. The distinction is important because the rules of law governing real property transactions such as sale, taxation, and inheritance are frequently different from those applied to personal property transactions.

It is possible for an item of personal property to be attached to or used in conjunction with real property in such a way that it is treated as being part of the real property. This type of personal property is called a **fixture.**

Fixtures

A **fixture** is a type of property that bridges the gap between real and personal property. When an item is found to be a fixture, it ceases to be personal property and becomes part of the real property to which it is attached. A conveyance (transfer of ownership) of the real property will also convey the fixtures on that property, even if the fixtures are not specifically mentioned.

---

[1] Ownership of air above one's property is not an unlimited interest, however. Courts have held that the flight of aircraft above one's property is not a violation of a landowner's rights, so long as it does not unduly interfere with the owner's enjoyment of his land.

It is very common for people to install items of personal property on the real property that they own or rent. A variety of disputes can arise regarding rights to such property. Suppose that Lubarsky buys a chandelier and installs it in his home. When he sells the house to Jarrett, can Lubarsky remove the chandelier, or is it part of the home that Jarrett has bought? Suppose Winston, a commercial tenant, installs showcases and tracklights in the store that he leases from Johnson. When Winston's lease expires, can he remove the showcases and the lights, or do they now belong to Johnson? If the parties' contract is silent on these matters, a court will resolve the case by referring to the law of fixtures.

Factors Determining whether an Item Is a Fixture

There is no mechanical formula for determining whether an item has become a fixture, but courts will consider the following factors:

1. *Attachment.* One of the factors that helps to determine whether an item is a fixture is the degree to which the item is **attached** or **annexed** to the real property. If the item is firmly attached to the real property and cannot be removed without damaging the property, it is likely to be considered a fixture. An item of personal property that can be removed with little or no injury to the property is less likely to be considered a fixture.

Actual physical attachment to real property is not necessary, however. A close physical connection between the item of personal property and the real property may be sufficient for a court to conclude that the item is **constructively annexed.** For example, heavy machinery or automatic garage door openers can be considered fixtures even though they are not physically attached to real property.

2. *Adaptation.* Another factor to be considered is the degree to which the use of the item is necessary or beneficial to the use of the real property. This factor is called *adaptation.* It is particularly relevant in cases in which the item is either not physically attached to the real property at all or the physical attachment is slight. When an item would be of little value except for use with a particular piece of property, it is likely to be considered a fixture even though it is unattached or could easily be removed. For example, keys and custom-sized window screens and storm windows have been held to be fixtures.

3. *Intent.* The third factor to be considered is the *intent* of the person who installed the item. Intent is judged not by what that person subjectively intended, but by what the circumstances indicate that he intended. To a great extent, intent is indicated by the first two factors, annexation and adaptation. There is a presumption that an owner of real property who improves it by attaching items of personal property intended those items to become part of the real estate. Thus, if the owner does *not* want an item to be considered a fixture, he must specifically reserve the right to keep the attached property. A seller of a house who wants to keep an antique chandelier that has been installed in the house should either replace the chandelier before the house is shown to prospective purchasers or make it clear in the contract of sale that the chandelier will be excluded from the sale.

The *Ford v. Venard* case, which follows, presents a typical example of a court's analysis of whether an item of personal property has become a fixture.

FORD v. VENARD
340 N.W.2d 270 (S. Ct. Iowa 1983)

In 1973, Norman Van Sickle moved his double wide mobile home to a plot of land owned by Luelia Jedlicka. Van Sickle had the real estate landscaped, a foundation poured, concrete blocks set, and steel girders aligned on the blocks. After removing the hitches and wheels from the mobile home, he had it set on the foundation by a crane and hooked together. Since that time, Van Sickle substantially modified his residence by welding it into a single unit, placing a roof over the entire building, and joining the exterior with siding to the point that it could not be disassembled without tearing it apart and could not be moved as one unit except by a house mover.

Van Sickle had paid Jedlicka $500 as a down payment for the purchase of the land back in 1973, but had never made any further payments. He had never been asked to pay taxes and was told by Jedlicka that she paid them. Van Sickle had been told by the bank that held a security interest on the mobile home that the house would become part of Jedlicka's real estate after it was set on a foundation. He did not consider himself the owner of the real estate; he believed the land belonged to Jedlicka.

In 1977, Henry Edsel Ford contracted with Jedlicka to buy the land. A clause of the contract between Ford and Jedlicka specified that all "attached fixtures" were included as part of the real estate included in the sale. The ownership of the mobile home was brought to a head in 1982, when William Venard, a creditor of Van Sickle's, attempted to enforce a judgment against Van Sickle by attaching the mobile home and executing against it. Ford brought this action claiming that he owns the mobile home. He requested an injunction to restrain Venard from executing against the mobile home, and the trial court granted the injunction. Venard appeals.

Harris, J.   The question is whether the mobile home was a fixture included under the terms of the land contract between Jedlicka and Ford. We think it plainly was. Under our common law rule personal property becomes a fixture when:

(1) it is actually annexed to the realty, or to something appurtenant thereto;

(2) it is put to the same use as the realty with which it is connected; and

(3) the party making the annexation intends to make a permanent accession to the freehold.

The intention of the party annexing the improvement is the "paramount factor" in determining whether the improvement is a fixture. Physical attachment of the structure to the soil or to an appurtenance thereto is not essential to make the structure a part of the realty. On the other hand, a building which cannot be removed without destruction of a substantial part of its value becomes almost unavoidably an integral part of the real estate.

Venard argues that Van Sickle's home was not physically annexed to the realty and that Van Sickle never intended for his home to be permanently attached to the freehold. Ford, on the other hand, relies on the facts that the home's tongues and wheels have been removed; it was set on a foundation and girders; it has been extensively remodeled into a single unit; and its removal would be expensive and damaging. He points out that the home was used as a homestead, which is the use for which the realty had been appropriated. He points to the bank's advice to Van Sickle that his home would become the property of Jedlicka when set on her land.

We have found buildings to be fixtures in a number of cases. We are convinced the home became attached to the land. It could not be removed from its present location except in the sense that any permanent home could be. We hold that it has become an integral part of the real estate. The trial court was right in ordering the issuance of the permanent injunction.

Affirmed in favor of Ford.

Express Agreement   If the parties have formed an express agreement that clearly states their intent about whether a particular item is to be considered a fixture, a court will generally enforce that agreement. For example, the buyer and seller of a house might agree to permit the seller to remove a fence or shrubbery that would otherwise be considered a fixture. The parties' right to dictate the classification of property is not unlimited, however. A court would not enforce an agreement that provided that a piece of land was to be treated as personal property, for example.

Tenants' Fixtures   An exception to the normal rules about fixtures is made when a *tenant* attaches personal property to leased premises for the purpose of carrying on his trade or business. Such fixtures are called **trade fixtures.** Trade fixtures remain the personal property of the tenant and can be removed at the termination of the lease. The purpose of making an exception for trade fixtures is to encourage trade and industry.

There are two limitations on the tenant's right to remove trade fixtures. First, the tenant cannot remove the fixtures if doing so would cause substantial damage to the landlord's realty. Second, the tenant must remove the fixtures by the end of the lease if the lease is for a definite period; if the lease is for an indefinite period, the tenant may be given a reasonable time after the expiration of the lease to remove the fixtures. If she does not remove the fixtures within the appropriate time, they become the property of the landlord.

Leases may contain terms that expressly address the parties' rights in any fixtures. A lease might give the tenant the right to attach items or make other improvements and to remove them later. The reverse may also be true. The lease might state that any improvements made or fixtures attached will become the property of the landlord at the termination of the lease. Courts will gen-erally enforce the parties' agreement about the owner-ship of fixtures.

Security Interests in Fixtures   Special rules apply to personal property that is subject to a lien or security interest[2] at the time it is attached to real property. For example, a person buys a dishwasher on a time-payment plan from an appliance store and has it installed in his kitchen. To protect itself, the appliance store must take a security interest in the dishwasher and perfect that inter-est by filing a financing statement in the local real estate records within a period of time specified by the Uniform Commercial Code. The appliance store would then be able to remove the dishwasher if the buyer defaulted in his payments. It could, however, be liable to third par-ties, such as prior real estate mortgagees, for any dam-age to the real estate caused by the removal of the dishwasher. The rules concerning security interests in personal property that will become fixtures are covered in the Security Interests in Personal Property chapter.

---

[2]Liens and security interests are discussed in the Security Interests in Personal Property chapter.

CONCEPT REVIEW

FIXTURES

Concept	A *fixture* is an item of personal property attached to or used in conjunction with real property in such a way that it is treated as being part of the real property.
Significance	A conveyance of the real property will also convey the fixtures on that property.
Factors Considered in Determining whether Property Is a Fixture	1. Attachment: Is the item physically attached or closely connected to the real property? 2. Adaption: How necessary or beneficial is the item to the use of the real property? 3. Intent: Did the person who installed the item manifest intent for the property to become part of the real property?
Express Agreement	Express agreements clearly stating intent about whether property is a fixture are generally enforceable.
Trade Fixtures (Tenants' Fixtures)	Definition of *trade fixture:* personal property attached to leased real property by a tenant for the purpose of carrying on his trade or business. Trade fixtures can be removed and retained by the tenant at the termination of the lease except when one or more of the following apply: 1. Removal would cause substantial damage to the landlord's real property. 2. Tenant fails to remove the fixtures by the end of the lease (or within a reasonable time, if the lease is for an indefinite period of time). 3. An express agreement between the landlord and tenant provides otherwise.

RIGHTS AND INTERESTS IN REAL PROPERTY

When we think of ownership of real property, we normally think of one person owning all of the rights in a particular piece of land. However, real property involves a *bundle of rights* capable of ownership—sometimes by different people. The discussion that follows will examine the most common forms of present, **possessory interests** (rights to exclusive possession of real property): **fee simple absolute** and **life estate.** It will also explore the various ways in which two or more people can share ownership of the same possessory interest in real property. Finally, it will examine the interests and rights that one may have in another person's real property, such as the right to use another's property or restrict the way he uses it. These include **easements, profits, licenses,** and **restrictive covenants.** Each of these rights and interests will be discussed in turn.

Estates in Land

The term **estate** is used to describe the nature of a person's ownership interests in real property. Estates in land can be classified as being either **freehold estates** or **nonfreehold estates.** Nonfreehold (or leasehold) estates are those held by persons who lease real property. They will be discussed in the next chapter, which focuses on landlord-tenant law. Freehold estates are ownership interests in real property that are of uncertain duration. The most common types of freehold estates are fee simple absolute and life estates.

Fee Simple Absolute   The **fee simple absolute** is the highest form of land ownership in the United States. What we normally think of as "full ownership" of land is the fee simple absolute. A person who owns real property in fee simple absolute has the right to possess and use the property for an unlimited period of time, subject only to governmental regulations or private restrictions. He also has the unconditional power to dispose of the property during his lifetime or upon his death. A person who owns land in fee simple absolute may grant many rights to others without giving up the ownership of his fee simple. For example, he may lease the property to a tenant or grant mineral rights, easements, or mortgages to another.

Life Estate   A **life estate** is a property interest that gives a person the right to possess and use property for a time that is measured by his lifetime or that of another person. For example, if Toffler has a life estate in Black-

acre (a hypothetical tract of land) that is measured by his life, he has the right to use Blackacre during his life. At his death, the property will revert to the person who conveyed the estate to him or it will pass to some other designated person. While a life tenant such as Toffler has the right to use the property, he has the obligation not to do acts that will result in permanent injury to the property.

Co-Ownership of Real Property

Co-ownership of real property exists when two or more persons share the same estate (the same type of ownership interest) in the same property. The co-owners do not have separate rights to any portion of the real property; each has a share in the whole property. Seven types of co-ownership are recognized in the United States.

Tenancy in Common   People who own property under a **tenancy in common** have undivided interests in the property and equal rights to possess the property. When property is transferred to two or more people without a specification about their form of co-ownership, there is a presumption that they will take the property as tenants in common. The ownership interests of the tenants in common do not have to be equal. Thus, one tenant could have a two-thirds ownership interest in the property and the other tenant could have a one-third interest.

Each tenant in common has the right to possess and use the property. However, she cannot exclude the other tenants in common from also possessing and using the property. If the property is rented or otherwise produces income, each tenant has the right to share in the income in proportion to her share of ownership. Similarly, each must pay her proportionate share of the cost of taxes and necessary repairs. Where one tenant is in sole possession of the property and receives no rents or profits from the property, she is not required to pay rent to her cotenant unless her possession is adverse to or inconsistent with her cotenant's property interests.

A tenant in common can dispose of her interest in the property during life and at death. Similarly, her interest is subject to the claims of her creditors. When one tenant dies, her share passes to her heirs or, if she has made a will, to the person or persons specified in her will. Suppose Reynolds and MacGuire own Blackacre as tenants in common. Reynolds dies, having executed a valid will in which she leaves her share to a third person, Kelly. In this situation, MacGuire and Kelly become tenants in common.

FIGURE 1   Tenancy in Common, Joint Tenancy, and Tenancy by the Entirety

	Tenancy in Common	**Joint Tenancy**	**Tenancy by the Entirety**
Equal Possession and Use?	Yes	Yes	Yes
Share Income?	Yes	Yes	Presumably
Contribution Requirement?	Generally	Generally	Generally
Free Conveyance of Interest?	Yes; transferee becomes tenant in common	Yes, but joint tenancy is severed on conveyance and reverts to tenancy in common	Both must agree; divorce severs tenancy
Effect of Death?	Interest transferable at death by will or inheritance	Right of survivorship; surviving joint tenant(s) take decedent's share	Right of survivorship; surviving spouse takes decedent's share

Tenants in common can sever the cotenancy by agreeing to divide up the property or, if they are unable to agree, by petitioning a court for **partition** of the property. The court will physically divide the property if that is feasible, so that each tenant will get her proportionate share. If physical division is not appropriate, the court will order the property sold and divide the proceeds.

Joint Tenancy   A **joint tenancy** is created when *equal* interests in real property are conveyed to two or more people by a single document that specifies that they are to own the property as joint tenants. The rights of use, possession, contribution, and partition are the same for a joint tenancy as for a tenancy in common. The distinguishing feature of a joint tenancy is that it gives the owners the **right of survivorship.** This means that upon the death of one of the joint tenants, that person's interest automatically passes to the surviving joint tenant(s). This feature makes it easy for a person to transfer property at death without making a will. For example, Bromwell buys property with his grandson, the two of them taking title to the property as joint tenants. At Bromwell's death, his interest will pass to his grandson without even going through the normal probate process.[3] By the same token, a provision in a joint tenant's will that purports to devise (transfer by will) his interest to someone other than his surviving joint tenants is ineffective.

A joint tenant may mortgage, sell, or give away his interest in the property during his lifetime. For that reason, a joint tenant's interest in property is subject to the claims of his creditors. When a joint tenant transfers his interest, the joint tenancy is *severed* and a tenancy in common is created as to the share affected by the transaction. When a joint tenant sells his interest to a third person, the third person becomes a tenant in common with the remaining joint tenant(s).

Tenancy by the Entirety   Approximately half of the states permit married couples to own real property as **tenants by the entirety.** A tenancy by the entirety is basically a type of joint tenancy with the added requirement that the owners be married. Like the joint tenancy, the tenancy by the entirety involves the right of survivorship. Neither spouse can transfer the property by will if the other is still living. Upon the death of the husband or wife, the property passes automatically to the surviving spouse.

This tenancy cannot be severed by the act of only one of the parties. Neither spouse can transfer the property unless the other one also signs the deed. Thus, a creditor of one tenant cannot claim an interest in that person's share of the property held in tenancy by the entirety. Divorce, however, will sever a tenancy by the entirety and transform it into a tenancy in common. Figure 1 compares the features of tenancy in common, joint tenancy, and tenancy by the entirety.

Community Property   A number of western and southern states recognize a system of co-ownership of property by married couples that is known as **community property.** This type of co-ownership is based on the theory that marriage is a partnership in which each spouse contributes to the property base of the family.

[3]The probate process is discussed in the Estates and Trusts chapter.

Property that is acquired during the marriage through a spouse's industry or efforts is classified as *community* property, in which each spouse has an equal interest. This is true regardless of who produced or earned the property. Since each spouse has an equal share in the community property, neither can convey the property without the other's joining in the transaction. A number of community property states permit the parties to dispose of their interests in community property at death.

Not all property owned by a married person is community property, however. Property that a spouse owned before marriage or acquired during marriage by gift or inheritance is *separate property*. Property exchanged for separate property also remains separately owned. The details of each state's community property system vary, depending on the specific provisions of that state's community property statutes.

Tenancy in Partnership   When a partnership takes title to property in the name of the partnership, its form of co-ownership is called **tenancy in partnership.** The incidents of tenancy in partnership are set out in the Uniform Partnership Act. You can read more about this form of co-ownership in the Introduction to Forms of Business and Formation of Partnerships chapter.

Condominium Ownership   Condominiums are an ancient form of co-ownership that has become very common in the United States in recent years, even in locations outside urban and resort areas. In a condominium, a purchaser takes title to her individual unit and also becomes a tenant in common with other unit owners in facilities that are shared, such as hallways, elevators, swimming pools, and parking areas. The condominium owner pays property taxes on her individual unit. She can generally mortgage or sell her individual unit without the approval of the other unit owners. She also makes a monthly payment for the maintenance of the common areas. For federal income tax purposes, she is treated in the same way as the owner of a single-family home and is allowed to deduct her property taxes and mortgage interest expenses.

Cooperative Ownership   In a cooperative, an entire building is owned by a corporation or by a group of people. A person who wants to buy a unit buys stock in the corporation and holds his apartment under a long-term lease (called a **proprietary lease**), which he can renew. Frequently, the cooperative owner must obtain the approval of the other owners to sell or sublease his unit.

INTERESTS IN REAL PROPERTY OWNED BY OTHERS

In a variety of situations, a person may hold a legally protected interest in real property that is owned by someone else. Such interests are not *possessory*, that is, they do not give their holder the right to complete dominion over the land. Rather, they give him the right to *use* another person's property or to limit the way in which the other person uses his own property. The following discussion explores the nature of these types of interests.

Easements

An **easement** is the right to make certain uses of another person's property (*affirmative easement*) or the right to prevent another person from making certain uses of his own property (*negative easement*). The right to run a sewer line across another person's property is an example of an affirmative easement. An easement that prevents a neighbor from erecting a structure on his land that would block your solar collector is an example of a negative easement.

When an easement is considered to be an **easement appurtenant,** it will pass with the land. This means that if the owner of the land benefited by an easement appurtenant sells or otherwise conveys his tract, the new owner will also get the easement. An easement appurtenant is one that is primarily designed to benefit a certain tract of land, rather than merely giving an individual a personal right. For example, Agnew and Gross are next-door neighbors. They share a common driveway that runs along the borderline of their property. Each has an easement in the part of the driveway that lies on the other's property. If Agnew sells his property to a third person, Donaldson, Donaldson will also get the easement in the part of the driveway that is on Gross's land. By the same token, Gross still has an easement in the part of the driveway that lies on Donaldson's land.

Creation of Easements

Easements can be acquired in a number of different ways:

1. *By grant.* When an owner of property expressly gives an easement in his property to another while retaining his ownership of the property, he is said to **grant** an easement. For example, Long may sell or give Madison, the owner of adjoining property, the right to use his land to reach an alley behind his land.

2. *By reservation.* When a person transfers ownership of his land but retains the right to use the transferred land for some specified purpose, he is said to **reserve** an easement in the land that was once his. For example, Swanson sells land to Jentz, reserving the mineral rights to the property and also reserving an easement to enter the land to remove the minerals.

3. *By prescription.* An **easement by prescription** is created when one person uses another person's land openly, continuously, and in a manner adverse to the owner's rights for a period of time specified by state statute. (This period of time varies from state to state.) The property owner should thus be on notice that someone else is acting as if he has certain rights to use the property. If the property owner does not take action to assert his rights during the statutory period, he may lose his right to stop the other person from making use of his property. Suppose State X provides that easements by prescription can be obtained through 15 years of prescriptive use. Daniels, who lives in State X, uses the driveway of his next-door neighbor, Solt, for 20 years. He does this openly, on a daily basis, and without Solt's permission. If Solt does not take action to stop Daniels within the 15-year period provided by statute, Daniels will have obtained an easement by prescription. This means that Daniels not only has the right to use the driveway while Solt owns the property but also that if Solt sells his property to a third person, Daniels still will

be entitled to use the driveway. This type of easement is similar to the concept of *adverse possession,* which will be discussed later in the chapter.

4. *By implication.* Sometimes, easements are *implied* by the nature of the transaction rather than created by express agreement of the parties. Such easements are called **easements by implication.** There are two types of easements by implication: *easements by prior use* and *easements by necessity.*

An **easement by prior use** is created when land is subdivided and a path, road, or other apparent and beneficial use exists at the time that part of the land is conveyed to another person. In this situation, the new owner will have an easement to continue using the path, road, or other prior use that runs across the other person's land. For example, a private road running through Greenacre from north to south links the house located on the northern portion of Greenacre to the highway that lies beyond Greenacre to the south. Durant, the owner of Greenacre, sells the northern portion of Greenacre to Cohen. Cohen would have an easement by implication to continue making use of the private road running across the portion of the land that has been retained by Durant. To prevent this type of easement from arising, the parties must specify in their contract that such an easement will not exist.

An **easement by necessity** is created when real property once held in common ownership is subdivided in such a way that the only way the new owner can gain access to his land is through passage over the land of another that was once part of the same tract. An easement by necessity is based on the *necessity* of obtaining access to property. *Attaway v. Davis,* which follows, presents a good example of the acquisition of an easement by necessity.

ATTAWAY v. DAVIS

707 S.W.2d 302 (S. Ct. Ark. 1986)

Hester Davis bought a 12-acre tract of land in 1967. The tract was landlocked, although it had some frontage on Beaver Lake, a navigable watercourse. At one time, a single owner, A. O. Clark, had owned all the land now owned by Davis, her neighbors, Albert and Sarah Attaway, and others in the area. At first, Davis got to her property by using an old trail across the Attaways' property and another tract. In 1975, however, the Attaways put in a gate to obstruct that trail. After that, Davis walked to her land. She later filed this action to acquire a right-of-way giving her access from a public road, Walnut Road, to her tract. The trial court awarded Davis a right-of-way running along the east side of the Attaways' property, and the Attaways appealed this order.

Smith, J.   Davis's right to obtain access arises from her status as a landlocked owner. [One of the Attaways'] argument is that Davis already has access to her property, because it has some frontage on Beaver Lake, a navigable watercourse. The statute does refer to access to a public road or a navigable watercourse, but this law was adopted more than a century ago, in 1871. What Davis must show is a reasonable necessity for a road, not an absolute necessity. Now that travel even for short distances is almost always by motor vehicle, it is not reasonable to require Davis and those wishing to visit her to make the trip by boat.

The Attaways insist that they have been willing since 1975 to permit Davis to reach her property by using a second trail that crosses their land. Any such use of neighboring property would be permissive and revocable. Davis is entitled to obtain a permanent right-of-way by proceeding under the statute and paying reasonable compensation.

Order for Davis affirmed.

Easements and the Statute of Frauds   Because an easement is a type of interest in land, it is within the coverage of the statute of frauds.[4] An express agreement granting or reserving an easement must be in writing and signed by the party to be charged to be enforceable. Under the statutes of most states, the grant of an easement must be executed with the same formalities as are observed in executing the grant of a fee simple interest in real property. However, easements not granted expressly, such as easements by prior use, necessity, or prescription, are enforceable even though they are not in writing.

Profits

A **profit** is a right to enter another person's land and remove some product of the land (such as timber) or some part of the land (such as gravel or minerals). For example, Jones is the holder of a profit that allows him to enter Wilson's land to drill for oil and remove such oil as he may find. Generally, profits are governed by the same rules that govern easements. In fact, profits are sometimes called **easements with a profit.**

License

A **license** is a temporary right to enter the land of another for a specific purpose. A license is generally much more informal than an easement and may be created orally or in any other manner that shows the landowner's permission for the licensee to enter the property. Licenses are considered to be personal rights that are not really interests in land. A license can be revoked at the will of the licensor unless the license is coupled with an interest, such as ownership of personal property that exists on the licensor's property, or unless the licensee has paid money or something else of value for the license or in reliance on the license. For example, Woolridge pays Arbuckle $600 for trees on Arbuckle's land, which are to be cut and hauled away. Woolridge has an irrevocable license to enter Arbuckle's land to cut and haul away the trees.

Restrictive Covenants   Within certain limitations, owners of real estate can create private and enforceable agreements that restrict the use of real property. Such private agreements are called **restrictive covenants.** For example, Daily owns two adjacent lots. He sells one to Grant with the express agreement that Grant promises not to operate on the property any business involving the sale of liquor. This commitment is included in the deed that Daily gives to Grant. Similarly, a developer sells lots in a subdivision, placing a restriction in each deed concerning the minimum size of houses that can be built on the property.

The validity and enforceability of such private restrictions on the use of real property depend on the purpose, nature, and scope of the restriction. A restraint that

---

[4]The land provision of the statute of frauds is discussed in the Writing chapter.

violates a statute or other public policy will not be enforced. For example, under the Fair Housing Act, a federal law that will be discussed later in this chapter, it is illegal for a person covered by the law to enforce a covenant that precludes the sale or rental of a dwelling to any person because of his race, color, religion, sex, handicap, familial status, or national origin.[5]

A restrictive covenant will also be unenforceable if it effectively prevents the sale or transfer of the property. This would constitute a violation of the public policy that favors free alienation (transfer) of land. Since public policy favors the unlimited use and transfer of land, ambiguous language in a restrictive covenant is construed in favor of the less restrictive interpretation. However, a restraint that is clearly expressed and that does not unduly restrict the use and transfer of the property or otherwise violate public policy will be enforced. For example, restrictions that relate to the minimum size of lots, maintenance of the area as a residential community, or the size and design of buildings are usually enforceable.

An important question that frequently arises regarding restrictive covenants is whether subsequent owners of the property are bound by the restriction even though they were not parties to the original agreement. Under certain circumstances, the covenant is said to "run with the land" so as to bind subsequent owners of the restricted land. For a covenant to run with the land, it must have been *binding* on the people who were originally parties to it and must show that the original parties *intended* the covenant to bind their successors. The covenant must also *"touch and concern"* the restricted land. This means that it must involve the use, value, or character of the land in question and not just a personal obligation of one of the original parties. In addition, a covenant will not bind a subsequent purchaser unless he had *notice* of the existence of the covenant at the time he took his interest. This notice would commonly be provided by the recording of the deed or other document containing the covenant.

Restrictive covenants can be enforced by the parties to the agreement, by persons who were intended to benefit from the covenant, and—if the covenant runs with the land—by the successors of the original parties. If the restriction is contained in a subdivision plat (recorded description of a subdivision) in the form of a general building scheme, other property owners in the subdivision may be able to enforce it.

Termination of Restrictive Covenants   Restrictive covenants can be terminated in a variety of ways. They can be voluntarily relinquished, or *waived*. They can also be terminated *by their own terms* (such as when the covenant specifies that it is to endure for a certain length of time) or by *dramatically changed circumstances*. For example, if Brown's property is subject to a restrictive covenant that restricts it to residential use, the covenant may be terminated by the fact that all of the surrounding property has come to be used for industrial purposes. When a restriction has been held invalid or has been terminated, the basic deed remains valid but is treated as if the restriction had been stricken from it.

ACQUISITION OF REAL PROPERTY

Title to real property can be obtained in a number of ways, including purchase, gift, will or inheritance, tax sale, and adverse possession. Original title to land in the United States was acquired either from the federal government or from a country that held the land prior to its acquisition by the United States. The land in the 13 original colonies had been granted by the king of England either to the colonies or to certain individuals. The land in the Northwest Territory was ceded by the states to the federal government, which in turn issued grants or patents of land. Original ownership of much of the land in Florida and the Southwest came by grants from the rulers of Spain.

Acquisition by Purchase

The right to sell real property is a basic ownership right. In fact, unreasonable restrictions on the right of an owner to sell her property are considered to be unenforceable as against public policy. Most people who own real property acquired title by buying it from someone else. Each state sets the requirements for the conveyance of real property located within that state. The various elements of selling and buying real property will be discussed later in this chapter.

Acquisition by Gift

Ownership of real property may be acquired by gift. For such a gift to be valid, the donor must deliver a properly

---

[5]24 C.F.R. section 100.80 (b) (1990).

executed deed to the property to the donee or to some third person who is to hold it for the donee. It is not necessary that the donee or the third person actually take possession of the property. The essential element of the gift is the *delivery* of the deed. Suppose West makes out a deed to the family farm and leaves it in a safe-deposit box for delivery to her son when she dies. The attempted gift will not be valid, because West did not deliver the gift during her lifetime.

Acquisition by Will or Inheritance

The owner of real property generally has the right to dispose of that property by will. The requirements for making a valid will are discussed in the Estates and Trusts chapter. If the owner of real property dies without leaving a valid will, the property will go to his heirs as determined under the laws of the state in which the real property is located.

Acquisition by Tax Sale

If the taxes assessed on real property are not paid, they become a *lien* on the property. This lien has priority over all other claims to the land. If the taxes remain unpaid for a period of time, the government can sell the land at a tax sale, and the purchaser at the tax sale acquires title to the property. However, some states have statutes that give the original owner a limited time (perhaps a year) in which to buy the property back from the tax sale purchaser for his cost plus interest.

Acquisition by Adverse Possession Each state has a statute of limitations that gives an owner of land a specific number of years in which to bring a lawsuit to regain possession of his land from someone who is trespassing on it. This period generally ranges from 5 to 20 years, depending on the state. If someone wrongfully possesses land and acts as if he were the owner, the real owner must take steps to have the person ejected from the land. If this is not done within the statutory period, the right to eject the possessor will be lost. The person who stayed in possession of the property for the statutory period will acquire title to the land by **adverse possession.**

To acquire title to land by adverse possession, a person must possess land in a manner that puts the true owner on notice that he has a cause of action against that person. The adverse possessor's possession must be:

1. Open,
2. Actual,
3. Continuous,
4. Exclusive,
5. Hostile (or adverse) to the owner's rights.

As you will read in *Chaplin v. Sanders,* the hostility element is not a matter of subjective intent. Rather, it means that the adverse possessor's possession must be inconsistent with the owner's rights. If a person is in possession of another's property under a lease, as a cotenant, or with the permission of the owner, his possession is not hostile. In some states, the person in possession of land must also pay the taxes on the land in order to gain title by adverse possession.

It is not necessary that the same person occupy the land for the statutory period. The periods of possession of several adverse possessors can be "tacked" together for purposes of calculating the period of possession if each possessor claims rights from the other. The possession must, however, be continuous for the necessary time.

CHAPLIN v. SANDERS

676 P.2d 431 (Wash. Sup. Ct. 1984) (en banc)

In 1957 or 1958, Mr. and Mrs. Hibbard decided to clear their land of woods and overgrowth and set up a trailer park. There was no obvious boundary between the Hibbards' land and the land of their neighbor to the east, so they cleared the land up to a deep drainage ditch and opened their park. Mr. Hibbard also built a road to be used for entering and leaving the park. In 1960, the Hibbards' neighbor, Mr. McMurray, had a survey conducted and discovered that the Hibbards had encroached on his land ("the eastern parcel") by approximately 20 feet. He informed the Hibbards of this. In 1962, the Hibbards sold their land ("the western parcel") to the Gilberts. The contract between these two parties specifically noted that the Hibbards' road encroached on the eastern parcel. Over the course of ensuing years, the western parcel changed hands several times until Peter and Patricia Sanders bought it in 1976. The Sanders had actual notice of the contract provision referring to McMurray's claim, but purportedly mistook which road the contract referred to. In 1978, Kent and Barbara Chaplin bought the eastern parcel without having a survey conducted.

There was little change in the use of the western parcel since its initial development by Hibbard. The road remained in continuous use in connection with the trailer park. The area between the road and the drainage ditch was also used by trailer park residents for parking, storage, garbage removal, and picnicking. Trailer personnel and tenants moved grass up to the drainage ditch and planted flowers. In the spring of 1978, the Sanders installed underground wiring and surface power poles in the area between the roadway and the drainage ditch.

The eastern parcel remained essentially undeveloped, but soon after the Chaplins bought it, they contacted an architectural consultant for the purpose of designing commercial buildings for their property. A survey conducted for this purpose discovered the Sanders's encroachments. The Chaplins then brought this action to quiet title to the road and its shoulder ("Parcel A") and the area between the road and the drainage ditch ("Parcel B"). The trial court held that the Sanders had acquired Parcel A by adverse possession, but had not acquired Parcel B because their use of it was not open and notorious. The case was appealed and the Court of Appeals found that the Sanders had not acquired *either* parcel because they had had actual notice of McMurray's ownership of the disputed area of land and therefore their possession was not hostile.

Utter, Justice.   To establish a claim of adverse possession, the possession must be (1) exclusive, (2) actual and uninterrupted, (3) open and notorious, and (4) hostile and under a claim of right made in good faith. The period throughout which these elements must concurrently exist is 10 years. Hostility, as defined by this court, does not import enmity or ill-will, but rather imports that the claimant is in possession as owner, in contradistinction to holding in recognition of or subordination to the true owner. We have traditionally treated the hostility and claim of right requirements as one and the same.

The doctrine of adverse possession was formulated at law for the purpose of assuring maximum utilization of land, encouraging the rejection of stale claims and, most important, quieting titles. Because the doctrine was formulated at law and not at equity, it was originally intended to protect both those who knowingly appropriated the land of others and those who honestly entered and held possession in full belief that the land was theirs. Thus, when the original purpose of the adverse possession doctrine is considered, it becomes apparent that the claimant's motive in possessing the land is irrelevant and no inquiry should be made into his guilt or innocence.

For these reasons, we are convinced that the dual requirement that the claimant take possession in "good faith" and not recognize another's superior interest does not serve the purpose of the adverse possession doctrine. The "hostility/claim of right" element of adverse possession requires only that the claimant treat the land as his own as against the world throughout the statutory period. The nature of his possession will be determined solely on the basis of the manner in which he treats the property. His subjective belief regarding his true interest in the land and his intent to dispossess or not dispossess another is irrelevant to this determination. Under this analysis, permission to occupy the land, given by the true title owner to the claimant or his predecessors, will still operate to negate the element of hostility. Under our holding today, what is relevant is the objective character of Hibbard's possession and that of his successors in interest.

The trial court found the character of possession [of Parcel A] to have been hostile for at least a 10-year period. We agree. The Sanders and their predecessors used and maintained the property as though it was their own for over the statutory period. This was sufficient to satisfy the element of hostility.

The Sanders also appeal from the trial court's finding that Parcel B was not possessed in an open and notorious manner. The requirement of open and notorious [use] is satisfied if the title holder has actual notice of the adverse use throughout the statutory period. We are compelled to conclude, from the evidence, that McMurray was aware of the Hibbards' use of the strip abutting the roadway. This conclusion is all the more compelling when the disparate condition of McMurray's undeveloped, overgrown property and the cleared, mowed, and maintained strip of land separating the roadway and McMurray's land is considered. In determining what acts are sufficiently open and notorious to manifest to others a claim to land, the character of the land must be considered. The necessary use and occupancy need only be of the character that a true owner would assert in view of its nature and location. Accordingly, the case is reversed and remanded with directions to quiet title to the disputed property in the Sanders.

Judgment reversed in favor of the Sanders.

TRANSFER BY SALE

Steps in a Sale

The major steps normally involved in the sale of real property are:

1. Contracting with a real estate broker to locate a buyer for the property.

2. Negotiating and signing a contract to sell the property.

3. Arranging for the financing of the purchase and the satisfaction of other requirements, such as arranging for a survey or for the acquisition of title insurance.

4. Closing the sale, at which time the sale is consummated, usually by payment of the purchase price and transfer of the deed.

5. Recording the deed.

Contracting with a Real Estate Broker

Although engaging a real estate broker is not a legal requirement for the sale of real property, it is common for a person who wants to sell his property to "list" the property with a broker. A listing contract empowers the seller's broker to act as his agent in procuring a ready, willing, and able buyer on the seller's terms and managing the details of the transfer of the property. A number of states' statutes of frauds require listing contracts to be evidenced by a writing and signed by the party to be charged.

Real estate brokers are regulated by state and some federal law. As trusted agents, real estate brokers owe **fiduciary duties** (duties of trust and confidence) to their clients. You can read more about the types of duties imposed on such agents in the Agency Relationship chapter.

Types of Listing Contracts   Matters such as the duration of the listing period, the terms on which the seller will sell, and the amount and terms of the broker's commission are specified in the listing contract. There are several different types of listing contracts.

1. *Open listing.* In an open listing contract, the broker is authorized to sell the property, but this right is *not exclusive.* This means that the seller or a third party (for example, another broker) also have the right to find a buyer for the property. Under an open listing, the broker would have the right to a commission only if he were the first one to find a ready, willing, and able buyer.

2. *Exclusive agency listing.* Under an exclusive agency listing, the broker will earn a commission if he *or any other agent* finds a buyer during the period of time specified in the contract. Thus, the broker under an exclusive agency listing would have the right to a commission if the seller had employed another broker who found a ready, willing, and able buyer. Under the exclusive agency listing, however, the seller retains the right to sell the property himself without paying a commission.

3. *Exclusive right to sell.* Under an exclusive right to sell listing, the broker will earn his commission no matter who procures the buyer. As the name suggests, he is given the exclusive right to sell the property for a specified period of time. Under this type of listing, a seller would have to pay the commission even if the seller or some third party found a buyer during the duration of the listing contract.

Contract for Sale

The principles regarding contract formation, performance, assignment, and remedies that you learned in earlier chapters are applicable to contracts for the sale of real estate. The contract provides for such matters as the purchase price, the type of deed the purchaser will get, the items of personal property that are included in the sale, and any other aspect of the transaction that is important to the parties. The contract may make the "closing" of the sale contingent on the buyer's finding financing at a specified rate of interest and the seller's procurement of a survey, title insurance, and termite insurance. Because the contract is within the statute of frauds, it must be evidenced by a writing and signed by the party to be charged to be enforceable.

Fair Housing Act

The Fair Housing Act, first enacted by Congress in 1968 and substantially revised in 1988, is designed to prevent discrimination in the housing market. Its provisions apply to real estate brokers, sellers (other than those selling their own single-family dwellings without the use of a broker), lenders, lessors, and appraisers. Originally, the Act prohibited discrimination on the basis of race, color, religion, sex, and national origin. The 1988 amendments added handicap and "familial status" to this list. The familial status category was intended to prevent discrimination in the housing market against families with children and pregnant women.[6] "Adult" or "senior citi-

zen" communities restricting residents' age are not illegal under the Fair Housing Act—even though they exclude families with children—so long as the housing meets the requirements of the Act's "housing for older persons" exemption.[7]

The Act prohibits discrimination in a wide range of activities relating to the sale or lease of housing, such as refusing to sell or rent, discriminating in the terms, conditions, or privileges of sale or rental, the provision of services and facilities involved in sale or rental, and representing that housing is not available when, in fact, it is.[8] It also prohibits discrimination in appraisals and financing of dwellings and in the provision of brokerage services.

Included in the concept of discrimination on the basis of handicap are the refusal to permit a handicapped person to make (at his own expense) reasonable modifications in the property and the refusal to make reasonable accommodations in rules, policies, practices, or services when such modifications or accommodations are necessary to afford the handicapped person full enjoyment of the property. The Act also makes it unlawful to build multifamily housing that is inaccessible to people with handicaps. The Fair Housing Act invalidates any state or municipal law that requires or permits an action that would be a discriminatory housing practice within the meaning of federal law.

A violation of the Fair Housing Act can result in a civil action brought by either the government or the aggrieved individual. The 1988 amendments give aggrieved persons the right to bring a private civil action. When such a person prevails, a court may award actual and punitive damages, injunctions, attorney's fees and costs, or any other appropriate relief.

Financing the Purchase The various arrangements for financing the purchase of real property, such as mortgages, land contracts, and deeds of trust, are discussed in the Introduction to Credit and Secured Transactions chapter.

---

[6] Familial status is defined as one or more individuals under the age of 18 who are domiciled with a parent, some other person who has custody over them, or the designee of such parent or custodial individual. It also applies to a person who is pregnant or in the process of attempting to secure custody of children under the age of 18.

[7] The Fair Housing Act defines "housing for older persons" as housing provided under any state or federal program that the Secretary of HUD finds is specifically designed and operated to assist elderly persons, housing intended for and solely occupied by persons 62 years old or older, or housing intended and operated for occupancy by at least one person 55 years old or older and that meets the requirements of federal regulations.

[8] The aspects of the Fair Housing Act that apply to rentals are discussed in the Landlord and Tenant chapter.

Deeds

Each state has statutes that set out the formalities necessary to accomplish a valid conveyance of land. As a general rule, a valid conveyance is accomplished by the execution and delivery of a **deed.** A deed is a written instrument that conveys title from one person *(the grantor)* to another person *(the grantee).* There are three basic types of deeds in general use in the United States: *quitclaim deeds, warranty deeds,* and *deeds of bargain and sale* (also called *grant deeds).* The precise rights conveyed by a deed depend on the type of deed that the parties use.

Quitclaim Deeds   A **quitclaim deed** conveys whatever title the grantor has at the time he executes the deed. It does not, however, contain any warranties of title. The grantor who executes a quitclaim deed does not claim to have good title, or in fact, any title at all. The grantee has no action against the grantor under a quitclaim deed if the title proves to be defective. Quitclaim deeds are frequently used to cure a technical defect in the chain of title to property.

Warranty Deeds   A **warranty deed,** unlike a quitclaim deed, contains covenants of warranty. In addition to conveying title to the property, the grantor who executes a warranty deed guarantees the title that she has conveyed. There are two types of warranty deeds.

1. *General warranty deed.* In a general warranty deed, the grantor warrants against (and agrees to defend against) all defects in the title and all encumbrances (such as liens and easements), even those that arose before the grantor received her title.
2. *Special warranty deed.* In a special warranty deed, the grantor warrants against (and agrees to defend against) those defects in the title or those encumbrances that arose after she acquired the property. If the property conveyed is subject to some encumbrance such as a mortgage, a long-term lease, or an easement, it is a common practice for the grantor to give a special warranty deed that contains a provision excepting those specific encumbrances from the warranty.

Deed of Bargain and Sale   In a **deed of bargain and sale,** also known as a **grant deed,** the grantor does not make covenants. The grantor uses language such as "I grant" or "I bargain and sell" or "I convey" property. In such a deed, it is implied that the grantor is at least making the representation that he owns the land and that he has not previously conveyed the property to someone else or encumbered it.

Form and Execution of Deed

Some states have enacted statutes setting out a suggested form for deeds. The statutory requirements of the different states for the execution of deeds are not uniform, but they do follow a similar pattern. As a general rule, a deed states the *name of the grantee,* contains a *recitation of consideration* and a *description of the property conveyed,* and is *signed by the grantor.* In most states, the deed must be notarized (acknowledged by the grantor before a notary public or other authorized officer) to be eligible for recording in public records.

No technical words of conveyance are necessary for a valid deed. Any language is sufficient if it indicates with reasonable certainty the intent to transfer the ownership of property. The phrases "grant, bargain, and sell" and "convey and warrant" are commonly used. Deeds contain recitations of consideration primarily for historical reasons. The consideration recited is not necessarily the purchase price of the property. Deeds often state that the consideration for the conveyance is "one dollar and other valuable consideration."

The property conveyed must be described in such a manner that it can be identified. Generally, this means that the *legal description* of the property must be used. Several methods of legal description are used in the United States. In urban areas, descriptions are usually by lot, block, and plat. In rural areas in which the land has been surveyed by the government, property is usually described by reference to the government survey. It may also be described by a metes and bounds description that specifies the boundaries of the tract of land.

Recording Deeds

The delivery of a valid deed conveys title from a grantor to a grantee. Nevertheless, in order to prevent his interest from being defeated by third parties who may claim an interest in the same property, the grantee should immediately **record** the deed. The grantee will have to pay a fee for recording the deed. When a deed is recorded, it is deposited and indexed in a systematic way in a public office, where it operates to give notice of the grantee's interest to the rest of the world.

Recording Statutes   Each state has a **recording statute** that establishes a system for the recording of all transactions that affect the ownership of real property. The statutes are not uniform in their provisions. In general, they provide for the recording of all deeds, mortgages, land contracts, and similar documents.

Types of Recording Statutes   State recording statutes also provide for priority among competing claimants to rights in real property, in case conflicting rights or interests in property should be deeded to more than one person. (Obviously, a grantor has no right to deed the same property to two different people, but, in case it should occur, these statutes provide rules to decide which of the purchasers has superior title.) These rules apply only to grantees who have given value for their deeds (primarily purchasers and lenders), and not to donees. There are three basic types of priority systems provided by state recording statutes.

1. *Race statute*. Under a "race" statute—so called because the person who wins the race to the courthouse wins the property—the first grantee who records a deed to a tract of land has superior title. For example, if Grantor deeds Blackacre to Jones on March 1 and deeds Blackacre to McBride on April 1, McBride will have superior title to Blackacre *if he records his deed before Jones does.* Race statutes are relatively uncommon today.

2. *Notice statutes*. Under a notice system of priority, a grantee who acquires his interest without notice of an unrecorded deed to any other grantee will have superior title. For example, Grantor deeds Greenacre to Wright on June 1, but Wright does not record his deed. On July 1, Bopp buys Greenacre, not knowing of Wright's competing claim, and Grantor executes and delivers a deed to Bopp. In this situation, Bopp would have superior rights to Greenacre even if Wright ultimately records his deed before Bopp does.

3. *Race-notice statutes*. The race-notice priority system combines elements of both systems discussed previously. Under race-notice statutes, the grantee who has priority is the one who both takes his interest without notice of any prior unrecorded claim *and* records first. For example, Grantor deeds Redacre to Pratt on September 1. On October 1, at which time Pratt has not yet recorded his deed, Grantor deeds Redacre to Allen. If Allen records his deed before Pratt, Allen has superior rights to Redacre.

Methods of Assuring Title

One of the things that a person must be concerned about in buying real property is whether the seller of the prop-

erty has *good title* to it. In buying property, a buyer is really buying the seller's ownership interests. Because the buyer does not want to pay a large sum of money for something that turns out to be worthless, it is important for him to obtain some assurance that the seller has good title to the property. This is commonly done in one of three ways.

1. *Title opinion*. In some locations, it is customary to have an **abstract of title** examined by an attorney. An abstract of title is a history of the passage of title of a piece of real property according to the public records. It is *not* a guarantee of good title. After examining the abstract, an attorney will render an opinion about whether the grantor has **marketable title** to the property. Marketable title is title that is free from defects or reasonable doubt about its validity. If the title is defective, the nature of the defects will be stated in the title opinion.

2. *Torrens system*. A method of title assurance that is possible in a few states is the **Torrens system** of title registration. Under this system, a person who owns land in fee simple obtains a certificate of title. When the property is sold, the grantor delivers a deed and a certificate of title to the grantee. All liens and encumbrances against the title are noted on the certificate, so that the purchaser is assured that the title is good except as to the liens and encumbrances noted on the certificate. However, some claims or encumbrances, such as adverse possession, do not appear on the records and must be discovered by making an inspection of the property. In some Torrens states, certain encumbrances, such as tax liens, short term leases, and highway rights, are valid against the purchaser even though they do not appear on the certificate.

3. *Title insurance*. The preferred and most common means of protecting title to real property is to purchase a policy of **title insurance.** Title insurance is designed to reimburse the insured for loss if the title turns out to be defective. Title insurance not only compensates for loss of the title; it also pays litigation costs if the insured must go to court to defend the title. Lenders commonly require that a separate policy of title insurance be obtained for the lender's protection. Title insurance may be obtained in combination with the other methods of assuring title that were discussed earlier.

SELLER'S RESPONSIBILITIES REGARDING THE QUALITY OF RESIDENTIAL PROPERTY

A major concern of buyers of improved real estate is that the structures on the property be in good condition. This concern is especially acute if the buyer intends to use the property for residential purposes. Traditionally, the rule of *caveat emptor* ("let the buyer beware") applied to the sale of real property unless the seller committed fraud or misrepresentation or made *express warranties* about the condition of the property. In addition, under most situations, sellers had no duty to disclose hidden defects that they knew about. The legal environment for sellers, especially for real estate professionals such as developers and builder-vendors of residential property, has changed substantially, however. The following discussion explores two important sources of liability for sellers of real property.

Implied Warranty of Habitability

Traditionally, sellers made no *implied warranties* that property sold for residential purposes was habitable or suitable for the buyer's use. The law's attitude toward the relationship of buyer and seller in the sale of residential property began to change as a result of the rapid growth of product liability law in the late 1960s. Courts began to see that the same policies that favored the creation of implied warranties in the sale of goods applied with equal force to the sale of residential real estate.[9] Like goods, housing is frequently mass-produced. As in the sale of goods, there is often a disparity of knowledge and bargaining power between the builder-vendor and the buyer of a house. Many defects in houses are of a type that evades discovery during a buyer's inspection. This creates the possibility of serious loss, since the purchase of a home is often the largest single investment that a person ever makes.

For these reasons, courts in the majority of states now hold that builders, builder-vendors (persons who build and sell houses), and developers make an **implied warranty of habitability** when they build or sell real property for residential purposes.

The implied warranty of habitability is basically a guarantee that the house is free of *latent* (that is, hidden) defects that would render it unsafe or unsuitable for human habitation. A breach of warranty will subject the defendant to liability for damages, measured by either the cost of repairs or the loss in value of the house.[10] The application of the warranty has been limited to builders,

builder-vendors, and developers. That is, an ordinary seller of a house who is not the builder or developer does not make a warranty of habitability.

One further issue that has caused a great deal of litigation is whether the warranty extends to subsequent purchasers of the house. For example, ABC Development Co. builds a house and sells it to Sharp. If Sharp later sells the house to Richey, can Richey sue ABC for breach of warranty if a serious defect renders the house uninhabitable? Although some courts have rejected the possibility of implied warranty actions brought by subsequent purchasers, the bulk of opinion today is that an implied warranty of habitability made by a builder-vendor would extend to a subsequent purchaser.

Another issue that has arisen regarding the implied warranty of habitability is whether the warranty can be *disclaimed* or *limited* in the contract of sale. Subject to the doctrine of unconscionability, concerns about public policy,[11] and doctrines of contract interpretation,[12] it appears to be at least possible to disclaim or limit the warranty by a contract provision. Courts construe such clauses very strictly against the builder-vendor, however, and often reject disclaimers that are not specific about the rights that the purchaser waives.

Duty to Disclose Hidden Defects

Under traditional contract law, a seller had no duty to *disclose* to the buyer defects in the property he was selling, even if the seller knew about the defects and there was no reasonable way for the buyer to find out about them on his own. Since the seller had no duty to volunteer information, his failure to do so could not constitute fraud or innocent misrepresentation. This rule was another expression of the prevailing notion of *caveat emptor*.

The traditional rule of nondisclosure was subject to a number of exceptions.[13] For example, a person who stood in a confidential or fiduciary relationship with the other party to the contract would have the duty to make disclosures of material defects. The typical buyer-seller relationship was considered to be an arm's-length transaction, however, and *not* a confidential or fiduciary

---

[9]See the Product Liability chapter for a discussion of the development of similar doctrines in the law of product liability.

[10]Remedies are discussed in the Performance and Remedies chapter.

[11]See the Illegality chapter for further discussion of these doctrines.

[12]The interpretation of contracts is discussed in the Writing chapter.

[13]These traditional exceptions are discussed in detail in the Reality of Consent chapter.

relationship, so there was no duty to disclose in most sales of real property.

Today, courts in many jurisdictions have substantially eroded the traditional rule regarding nondisclosure and have placed a duty on the seller to disclose any known defect that materially affects the property's value and is not reasonably observable by the buyer. His failure to make disclosure under these circumstances is the equivalent of an assertion that the defect does not exist, and that assertion may form the basis for a finding of fraud or misrepresentation.[14] *Johnson v. Davis* presents an example of the trend of expanding the duty to disclose.

---

[14]Fraud and misrepresentation are discussed in the Reality of Consent chapter.

JOHNSON v. DAVIS

480 So. 2d 625 (Fla. Sup. Ct. 1985)

In May of 1982, Morton and Edna Davis entered into a contract to buy a house from Clarence and Dana Johnson for $310,000. The house was three years old at the time. The contract required a $5,000 initial deposit payment and an additional $26,000 deposit payment within five days. After the Davises had paid the initial $5,000 deposit but before they had paid the $26,000 deposit, Mrs. Davis noticed some buckling and peeling plaster around the corner of a window frame and stains on ceilings in several rooms. Mrs. Davis inquired about this, and Mr. Johnson told her that the window had had a minor problem that had been corrected long ago and that the stains were wallpaper glue. The parties disagree about whether Mr. Johnson told Mrs. Davis at this time that there had never been any problems with the roof or ceilings. The Davises then paid the remaining $26,000 deposit and the Johnsons moved out of the house. Several days later, following a heavy rain, Mrs. Davis entered the house and discovered water gushing in from around the window frame, the ceiling of the family room, the light fixtures, the glass doors, and the stove in the kitchen. The Davises hired roofers, who reported that the roof was inherently defective and that any repairs would be temporary because the roof was "slipping." Only a new roof (at a cost of $15,000) could be watertight. The Davises then filed this action alleging breach of contract, fraud, and misrepresentation, and seeking rescission of the contract and return of their deposit payments. The trial court awarded the Davises $26,000 plus interest but permitted the Johnsons to keep the initial $5,000 deposit plus interest. Both parties appealed from this judgment, and the District Court of Appeals held that the entire deposit should have been returned to the Davises. The Johnsons appealed.

Adkins, Justice.   We agree with the district court's conclusions under a theory of fraud and find that the Johnsons' statements to the Davises regarding the condition of the roof constituted a fraudulent misrepresentation entitling the Davises to the return of the $26,000 deposit payment. The record reflects that the statement made by the Johnsons was a false representation of material fact, made with knowledge of its falsity, upon which the Davises relied to their detriment as evidenced by the $26,000 paid to the Johnsons. The fact that the false statements as to the quality of the roof were made after the signing of the purchase agreement does not excuse the seller from liability where the misrepresentations were made prior to the conveyance of the property.

In determining whether a seller of a home has a duty to disclose latent material defects to a buyer, the established tort law distinction between misfeasance and nonfeasance, action and inaction, must carefully be analyzed. The highly individualistic philosophy of the earlier common law consistently imposed liability upon the commission of affirmative acts of harm, but shrank from converting the courts into an institution for forcing men to help one another. Liability for nonfeasance has therefore been slow to receive recognition in the evolution of tort law.

In theory, the difference between misfeasance and nonfeasance is quite simple and obvious; however, in practice it is not always easy to draw the line and determine whether conduct is active or passive. That is, where failure to disclose a material fact is calculated to induce a false belief, the distinction between concealment and affirmative representations is tenuous. Both proceed from the same motives and are attended with the same consequences; both are violative of the principles of fair dealing and good faith.

Still there exists in much of our case law the old tort notion that there can be no liability for nonfeasance. The courts in some jurisdictions hold that where the parties are dealing at arm's length and the facts lie equally open to both parties, with equal opportunity of examination, mere nondisclosure does not constitute a fraudulent concealment.

These unappetizing cases are not in tune with the times and do not conform with current notions of justice, equity, and fair dealing. One should not be able to stand behind the impervious shield of caveat emptor and take advantage of another's ignorance. Our courts have taken great strides since the days when the judicial emphasis was on rigid rules and ancient precedents. Modern concepts of justice and fair dealing have given our courts the opportunity and latitude to change legal precepts in order to conform to society's needs. Thus, the tendency of the more recent cases has been to restrict rather than extend the doctrine of caveat emptor. The law appears to be working toward the ultimate conclusion that full disclosure of all material facts must be made whenever elementary fair conduct demands it.

The harness placed on the doctrine of caveat emptor in a number of other jurisdictions has resulted in the seller of a home being liable for failing to disclose material defects of which he was aware. We are of the opinion that the same philosophy regarding the sale of homes should also be the law in the state of Florida. Accordingly we hold that where the seller of a home knows of facts materially affecting the value of the property which are not readily observable and are not known to the buyer, the seller is under a duty to disclose them to the buyer. This duty is equally applicable to all forms of real property, new and used.

In the case at bar, the evidence shows that the Johnsons knew of and failed to disclose that there had been problems with the roof of the house. Mr. Johnson admitted during his testimony that the Johnsons were aware of roof problems prior to entering into the contract of sale and receiving the $5,000 deposit payment. Thus, we find that the Johnsons' fraudulent concealment also entitles the Davises to the return of the $5,000 deposit payment plus interest.

Judgment for the Davises affirmed.

LAND USE CONTROL

Introduction

While an owner of real property generally has the right to make such use of his property as he desires, society has placed a number of limitations on this right. This is one example of the principle that, to protect freedom, it is sometimes necessary to limit it. A property owner's unrestrained use of his property may destroy the value of his neighbor's property. One such limitation on the use of property is found in nuisance law, which permits public and private actions against landowners who use their property in a way that causes injury to others. Other limitations are created by zoning and subdivision ordinances, which contain specific requirements and prohibitions about the use of real property. Finally, the government, through its power of eminent domain, can deprive a person of his ownership of land. The following discussion explores in detail these controls on land use.

Nuisance Law

A person's enjoyment of his own land depends to a great extent on the uses that his neighbors make of their land. When the uses of neighboring landowners conflict, the aggrieved party frequently resorts to a court for resolution of the conflict. A person who unreasonably interferes with another person's interest in the use or enjoyment of his property is subject to an action for **nuisance.**

The term *nuisance* has no set definition. It may be conceived of as any use or activity that unreasonably interferes with the rights of others. Property uses that are inappropriate to the neighborhood (such as operating a funeral parlor in a single-family residential neighborhood), bothersome to neighbors (such as keeping a pack of barking dogs in one's backyard), dangerous to others (such as storing large quantities of gasoline in 50-gallon drums in one's garage), or immoral (such as operating a house of prostitution) can all be held to be nuisances. To amount to a nuisance, a use does not have to be illegal. The mere fact that a use is permitted under relevant zoning laws does not mean that it cannot be a nuisance. Furthermore, the fact that a use was in existence before neighboring landowners acquired their property does not mean that it cannot be a nuisance.

The test for determining whether conduct will be considered a nuisance is necessarily flexible and highly dependent on the facts of the individual case. A court will balance a number of factors, such as the social importance of the parties' respective uses, the extent and duration of the aggrieved party's loss, and the feasibility of abating (stopping) the nuisance. A plaintiff who puts his land to an unusually sensitive or "delicate" use cannot enjoin the activities of others that interfere with the delicate use.

Nuisances may be *private* or *public.* To bring a *private nuisance* action, the plaintiff must be a landowner or occupier whose enjoyment of his own land is substantially lessened because of a nuisance. The remedies for private nuisance include damages and injunctive relief. A *public nuisance* occurs when a nuisance causes harm to members of the public, who need not necessarily be injured in their use of property. For example, if a power plant creates noise and emissions that constitute a health hazard to pedestrians and workers in nearby buildings, a public nuisance may exist even though the nature of the injury is something other than the loss of enjoyment of the injured persons' property. Public nuisances involve a broader class of affected parties than do private nuisances. The action to abate the nuisance must usually be brought by the government in the name of the public. Remedies generally include criminal-type fines and injunctive relief. Private parties can sue for the abatement of a public nuisance or for damages caused by a public nuisance only when they can show that they have suffered a unique harm different from that suffered by the general public.

The following case, *Wood v. Picillo,* concerns the application of nuisance law to a property owner who maintained a hazardous waste dump.[15]

---

[15]For a detailed discussion of liability relating to hazardous waste, see the Environmental Regulation chapter.

WOOD v. PICILLO

443 A.2d 1244 (R.I. Sup. Ct. 1982)

The Picillos maintained a chemical dump site on a clearing on the their land. The site was a huge trench about 200 feet long, 15 to 30 feet wide, and 15 to 20 feet deep. A thick layer of pungent, varicolored liquid covered the trench bottom. Along the periphery of the pit lay more than 100 55-gallon drums and 5-gallon pail containers, some of which were upright and sealed, some tipped, and some partially buried. About 600 feet downhill of this site is a marshy wetland that drains into a river and several ponds. A witness testified that he saw the operator of a truck knock barrels marked "Combustible" off the truck's tailgate directly onto the earth, where the chemicals poured freely from the damaged barrels into the trench. Neighbors smelled "sickening," "heavy," and "terrible" odors that forced them to stay inside their homes. Several neighbors were made ill by the odors.

The attention of state officials was drawn to the site when an enormous explosion erupted into 50-foot flames in a trench on the Picillos' land and the fire could not be extinguished. Investigators from the state environmental management department began an investigation of the site and the state fire marshal ordered the dumping to cease, but dumping operations continued. Edward Wood and other plaintiffs brought a nuisance action against the Picillos. The trial court found that the dumping operation was a nuisance. It entered an injunction against further chemical disposal operations on the Picillo property and ordered them to finance the cleanup and removal of the toxic wastes. The Picillos appealed.

Weisberger, J.   The dump site proper might best be described in the succinct expresssion of the trial justice as "a chemical nightmare." At trial expert witnesses developed a scientific connection between the neighbors' experiences and the Picillos' operations. Laboratory analyses of samples taken from the trench, monitoring wells, and adjacent waters revealed the presence of five chemicals: toluene, xylene, chloroform, III trichloroethane, and trichloroethylene. According to the experts, the chemicals present on the Picillos' property and in the marsh, left unchecked, would eventually threaten wildlife and humans well downstream from the dump site. Expert testimony further revealed that the chemicals had traveled and would continue to travel from the dump site into the marsh at the rate of about one foot per day. From the marsh, predicted the experts, the chemicals would flow [into waters that are] inhabited by fish and used by humans for recreational and agricultural purposes.

The Picillos contend that the evidence adduced at trial was insufficient to support a finding of public and private nuisance. We find [this] to be without merit. The essential element of an actionable nuisance is that persons have suffered harm or are threatened with injuries that they ought not to have to bear. Distinguished from negligence liability, liability in nuisance is predicated upon unreasonable injury rather than upon unreasonable conduct. Thus, plaintiffs may recover in nuisance despite the otherwise nontortious nature of the conduct which creates the injury.

The Picillos have accurately stated that the injury produced by an actionable nuisance "must be real and not fanciful or imaginary." The Picillos next suggest that the injuries in the case at bar are of the insubstantial, unactionable type. It is this statement, however, rather than the purported injuries, that is fanciful. The testimony to which reference is made in this opinion clearly establishes that the Picillos' dumping operations have already caused substantial injury to their neighbors and threaten to cause incalculable damage to the general public. The Picillos' neighbors have displayed physical symptoms of exposure to toxic chemicals and have been restricted in the reasonable use of their property. Moreover, expert testimony showed that the chemical presence on the Picillos' property threatens both aquatic wildlife and human beings with possible death, cancer, and liver disease. Thus, there was ample evidence at trial to support the finding of substantial injury.

For the reasons stated, the Picillos' appeal is denied and dismissed.

Judgment for Wood affirmed.

Eminent Domain

The Fifth Amendment to the Constitution provides that private property shall not be taken for public use without just compensation. Implicit in this provision is the principle that the state has the power to take property for public use by paying "just compensation" to the owner of the property. This power, which is called the power of **eminent domain,** makes it possible for the government to acquire private property for highways, water control projects, municipal and civic centers, public housing, urban renewal, and other public uses. Governmental units can delegate their power of eminent domain to private corporations such as railroads and public utilities.

Although the eminent domain power is probably necessary to efficient government, there are several major problems inherent in its use. One of them is determining when the power can be properly exercised. When the governmental unit itself uses the property taken, as would be the case in property acquired for the use of a municipal building or a public highway, the exercise of the power is proper. The exercise of the power is not so clearly justified, however, when the government acquires the property and resells it to a private developer. Although such acquisitions may be more vulnerable to challenge, recent cases have applied a very lenient standard in determining what constitutes a public use[16]

Another problem with regard to the eminent domain power is determining what is meant by *just compensation.* A property owner is entitled to receive the "fair market value" of his property, but some people believe that this measure of compensation falls short of reimbursing the owner for what he has lost, since it does not cover the lost goodwill of a business or the emotional attachment a person may have to his home.

A third problem is determining when a "taking" has occurred. The answer to this is easy when the government institutes a legal action to condemn property. In some cases, however, the government causes or permits the physical invasion of a landowner's property without having instituted formal condemnation proceedings. For example, a government engaging in building a dam floods Johnson's land. In such cases, courts have recognized the right of property owners to institute an action for compensation against the governmental unit that has taken their land. These cases are called **inverse condemnation** cases. In an inverse condemnation case, the property owner says, in effect, "You have taken my land, now pay for it."

Zoning and Subdivision Laws

State legislatures commonly delegate to cities and other political subdivisions the *police power* to impose reasonable regulations designed to promote the public health, safety, and morals and the general welfare of the community. **Zoning ordinances,** which regulate the use

of real property, are created in the exercise of this police power. Normally, zoning ordinances divide a city or town into a number of districts and specify or limit the use to which property in those districts can be put. They also prescribe and restrict the improvements that are built on the land.

Zoning ordinances restrict the use of property in a number of ways. One common type of restriction is a *control of uses* on the land, such as restriction of an area to single-family or high-density residential uses or commercial, light industry, or heavy industry uses. Another type of restriction is *control of height and bulk,* which prescribe the height of buildings; the setback from front, side, and rear lot lines; and the portion of a lot that can be covered by a building. *Control of population density* is another common type of restriction. Such restrictions specify the amount of living space that must be provided for each person and specify the maximum number of persons who can be housed in a given area. Zoning ordinances also commonly contain *controls of aesthetics,* whereby the use of land is restricted to maintain or create a certain aesthetic character of the community. Restrictions on the architectural style of buildings, the use of billboards and other signs, and the creation of special zones for historical buildings are examples of this type of restriction.

Many local governments also have ordinances dealing with proposed subdivisions. These ordinances often require that the developer meet certain requirements as to lot size, street and sidewalk layout, and sanitary facilities. They also require that the city or town approve the proposed development. The purpose of such ordinances is to protect the prospective purchasers of property in the subdivision and the community as a whole, by ensuring that minimum standards are met by the developer.

Nonconforming Uses A zoning ordinance has prospective effect. That is, the uses and buildings that already exist at the time the ordinance is passed (*nonconforming uses*) are permitted to continue. However, the ordinance may provide for the gradual phasing out (*amortization*) of nonconforming uses and buildings that do not conform to the general zoning plan.

Relief from Zoning Ordinances A property owner who wants to initiate some use of his property that is not permitted by the existing zoning ordinance can try several avenues of relief from that ordinance. He can try to have the zoning law **amended** on the ground that the proposed amendments are in accordance with the

---

[16] This and other issues relating to eminent domain are discussed further in the Business and the Constitution chapter.

overall zoning plan. To seek an amendment is to seek a change in the law itself.

A different approach would be to seek permission to deviate from the zoning law. This is called a **variance.** A person seeking a variance would claim that the ordinance works an undue hardship on him by depriving him of opportunity to make reasonable use of his land. For example, a landowner might attempt to obtain a variance to use the property in some way that is not normally allowed or to deviate from normal setback or building size requirements.

Attempts to obtain amendments or variances often produce heated battles before the zoning authorities because they often conflict with the interests of nearby property owners who have a vested interest in maintaining the status quo.

Challenges to the Validity of the Zoning Ordinance

A disgruntled property owner might also attack the validity of the zoning ordinance. Zoning ordinances have produced a great deal of litigation in recent years, as cities and towns have used their zoning power as a means of social control. For example, a city might create special zoning requirements for adult bookstores or other uses that are considered moral threats to the community. This has given rise to challenges that such ordinances unconstitutionally restrict freedom of speech. The Supreme Court has upheld the constitutionality of a zoning ordinance that prohibited the operation of adult bookstores within 1,000 feet of specified uses such as residential areas and schools, even though the ordinance had the effect of restricting adult bookstores to a small area of the community in which no property was currently available.[17]

Another type of litigation has involved ordinances by which some municipalities have attempted to "zone out" residential facilities such as group homes for mentally retarded adults. The Supreme Court held that a zoning ordinance that required a special use permit for a group home for the mentally retarded was an unconstitutional

violation of the Equal Protection Clause of the Constitution.[18] The 1988 amendments to the Fair Housing Act, which forbid discrimination on the basis of handicap and familial status, also have been used as a basis for challenging zoning decisions that operate to zone out group homes. It appears that such a challenge can be successful when the plaintiff can show that the zoning board's actions were a mere pretext for discrimination.[19]

Many cities and towns have attempted to restrict single-family residential zones to living units of traditional families related by blood or marriage and to prevent the presence of other living groups such as groups of unrelated students, communes, or religious cults by specifically defining the term *family* in a way that excludes these groups. In the case of *Belle Terre v. Boraas*,[20] the Supreme Court upheld such an ordinance as applied to a group of unrelated students. It subsequently held, however, that an ordinance that defined "family" in such a way as to prohibit a grandmother from living with her grandsons was an unconstitutional intrusion on personal freedom regarding marriage and family life.[21] In some cases, restrictive definitions of the term *family* have been held unconstitutional under *state constitutions.* In others, such definitions have been narrowly construed by the courts.

Land Use Regulation and "Taking"   An additional type of litigation has involved zoning laws and other land use regulations that restrict the use of land in a way that makes it less profitable for development.[22] Affected property owners have challenged the application of such regulations on the ground that they constitute an unconstitutional "taking" of property without just compensation. States have broad discretion to use their police power for the public benefit, even when that means interfering to some extent with an owner's right to develop his property as he desires. While it is possible for a regulation to interfere with an owner's use of his property to such an extent that it constitutes a taking, the mere fact that the regulation deprives the owner of the highest and

[17]*City of Renton v. Playtime Theatres, Inc.,* 106 S. Ct. 925 (U.S. Sup. Ct. 1986). In a recent case, however, the Supreme Court held that a licensing scheme in a comprehensive zoning ordinance that required licensing of adult cabarets and other adult entertainment establishments was an unconstitutional violation of the First Amendment, because the ordinance did not have appropriate procedural safeguards against arbitrary denials of the licenses. (The ordinance failed to provide for a time limit within which city authorities were required to act on such a license application.) *FW/PBS, Inc. v. City of Dallas,* 110 S. Ct. 596 (U.S. Sup. Ct. 1990).

[18]*City of Cleburne v. Cleburne Living Centers,* 473 U.S. 432 (U.S. Sup. Ct. 1985).

[19]For example, see *Baxter v. City of Nashville,* 720 F. Supp. 720 (S.D. Ill. 1989), which involves a challenge by a hospice for AIDS patients to a city's denial of a special use permit.

[20]416 U.S. 1 (U.S. Sup Ct. 1974).

[21]*Moore v. City of East Cleveland,* 431 U.S. 494 (U.S. Sup. Ct. 1977).

[22]This issue is also discussed in the Business and the Constitution chapter.

most profitable use of his property does not mean that there has been a taking.

There is no set formula used to determine whether a regulation has gone "too far" and has become a taking. Courts look at all the facts of the case and weigh a variety of factors, such as the economic impact of the regu-lation, the degree to which the regulation interferes with an investor's reasonable expectations, and the character of the government's invasion. In *Nollan v. California Coastal Commission,* which follows, you will see an example of a case in which the Supreme Court found regulation to constitute a taking.

NOLLAN v. CALIFORNIA COASTAL COMMISSION

107 S. Ct. 3141 (U.S. Sup. Ct. 1987)

James and Marilyn Nollan own a beachfront lot in Ventura County, California. A quarter mile north of their property is Faria County Park, an oceanside public park with a public beach. Another public beach area, known as "the Cove," lies 1,800 feet south of their lot. A concrete seawall separates the beach portion of the Nollans' property from the rest of the lot. The historic mean high-tide line determines the lot's oceanside boundary.

The Nollans wanted to tear down a small bungalow that was on the property and build a three-bedroom house on the lot. California law required that they obtain a coastal development permit from the California Coastal Commission to do this. They submitted the permit application and were later informed that they could have the permit on condition that they allow the public an easement to pass across a portion of their property bounded by the mean high-tide line on one side and their seawall on the other. This would make it easier for the public to get to Faria County Park and the Cove. The Nollans challenged the access condition, but the Commission affirmed it. On appeal, the California Court of Appeals upheld the action of the Coastal Commission. The Nollans appealed to the United States Supreme Court, arguing that the access condition was a taking.

Scalia, Justice.   Had California simply required the Nollans to make an easement across their beachfront available to the public on a permanent basis to increase public access to the beach, rather than conditioning their permit to rebuild their house on their agreeing to do so, we would have no doubt there would have been a taking. Indeed, one of the principal uses of the eminent domain power is to assure that the government be able to require conveyance of just such interests, so long as it pays for them. We have repeatedly held that, as to property reserved by its owner for private use, the right to exclude others is one of the most essential sticks in the bundle of rights that are commonly characterized as property.

Where governmental action results in a permanent physical occupation of the property, by the government itself or by others, our cases uniformly have found a taking to the extent of the occupation, without regard to whether the action achieves an important public benefit or has only minimal economic impact on the owner. We think a "permanent physical occupation" has oc-curred, for purposes of that rule, where individuals are given a permanent and continuous right to pass to and fro, so that the real property may continuously be traversed.

Given that requiring uncompensated conveyance of the easement outright would violate the Fourteenth Amendment, the question becomes whether requiring it to be conveyed as a condition for issuing a land use permit alters the outcome. We have long recognized that land use regulation does not effect a taking if it substantially advances legitimate state interests and does not deny an owner economically viable use of his land.

The Commission argues that among these permissible purposes are protecting the public's ability to see the beach, assisting the public in overcoming the "psychological barrier" to using the beach created by a developed shorefront, and preventing congestion on the public beaches. We assume that the Commission would be able to deny the Nollans their permit outright if their new house would substantially impede these purposes, unless the denial would interfere so drastically with the Nollans' use of their property as to constitute a taking. If the Commission attached to the permit some condition that would have protected the public's ability to see the beach notwithstanding construction of the new house—for example, a height limitation, a width restriction, or a ban on fences—so long as the Commission could have exercised its police power to forbid construction of the house altogether, imposition of the condition would also be constitutional.

The evident constitutional propriety disappears, however, if the conditional substituted for the prohibition utterly fails to further the end advanced as the justification for the prohibition. The lack of nexus between the condition and the original purpose of the building restriction converts that purpose to something other than what it was. The purpose then becomes, quite simply, the obtaining of an easement to serve some valid governmental purpose, but without payment of compensation. In short, unless the permit condition serves the same governmental purpose as the development ban, the building restriction is not a valid regulation of land use but "an out-and-out plan of extortion."

It is quite impossible to understand how a requirement that people already on the public beaches be able to walk across the Nollans' property reduces any obstacles to viewing the beach created by the new house. It is also impossible to understand how it lowers any "psychological barrier" to using the public beaches, or how it helps to remedy any additional congestion on them caused by construction of the Nollans' new house. We therefore find that the Commission's imposition of the permit condition cannot be treated as an exercise of its land use power for any of these purposes. California is free to advance its "comprehensive program" if it wishes, by using its power of eminent domain for this public purpose, but if it wants an easement across the Nollans' property, it must pay for it.

Reversed in favor of the Nollans.

Another Supreme Court case, *First English Evangelical Lutheran Church of Glendale v. County of Los Angeles,*[23] dealt with the issue of remedies for regulatory taking. In this case, the Court held that when the government takes land by a land use regulation, the landowner may recover damages in an inverse condemnation action, even if the taking was temporary because the regulation was later declared invalid.

INSURANCE

One of the risks faced by a property owner is the possibility that his property might be damaged or destroyed by any number of perils beyond his control—fire, lightning, or flood, just to name a few. Although the property owner may not be able to prevent harm to his property, he can secure some protection against the resulting financial loss by contracting for insurance. The purpose of insurance contracts is to allow people to shift to another a risk of loss that they would ordinarily have to bear.

There are many different kinds of insurance, each of which protects against different types of risks. For example, you are undoubtedly familiar with life insurance, health insurance, and automobile insurance and the risks they insure against. Earlier in this chapter, we discussed another type of insurance—title insurance—which protects an owner of property against the possibility of loss caused by a faulty title. Our discussion in this part of the chapter will explore some basic concepts in insurance

---

[23]107 S. Ct. 1987 (U.S. Sup. Ct. 1987).

law. It will also present an overview of a form of property insurance that is important to property owners: **fire insurance.**

The Nature of an Insurance Contract

The insurance relationship is a contract that may involve more than two persons. The **insurer** (usually a corporation), in exchange for the payment of consideration (called a **premium**), agrees to pay for losses caused by specific events (**perils**). The **beneficiary** is the person to whom the insurance proceeds are payable. The **insured** is the person who acquires insurance on property in which she possesses an interest or, in the case of life insurance, the person whose life is being insured. In most instances, the insured will also be the *owner* of the policy (the person who can exercise the contractual rights set out in the insurance contract); however, this is not always the case.

A distinction is made between valid insurance contracts and wagering contracts. A wagering contract creates a new risk that did not previously exist and is illegal as contrary to public policy. Insurance contracts, on the other hand, transfer existing risks.

Insurable Interest

In order for an insurance contract not to be considered an illegal wagering contract, the person who purchases the policy (the owner) must have an **insurable interest** in the property being insured. To have an insurable interest, a person must have a legal or equitable interest in the property such that he has some economic interest in the property's continued existence and in the preservation of its condition. Another way of putting this is that a person has an insurable interest if he will suffer a financial loss from the destruction of the insured property. If no insurable interest is present, the policy is void.

Those who have an insurable interest in property must have that interest at the time the loss occurs. This means that in addition to the legal owner of the insured property, any other person who has an interest in the insured property when the loss occurs has the required insurable interest. Thus, both the buyer and the seller of property, lessees, secured creditors (mortgagees or lienholders), and those holding other interests in the insured property all have the required insurable interest.

The extent of a person's insurable interest in property is limited to the value of his or her interest in the property. For example, Fidelity Savings & Loan extends Williams a $65,000 loan on her home and retains a mortgage interest in the house as security. In order to protect this investment, it obtains a $65,000 insurance policy on the property. Several years later, the house is completely destroyed by fire. At the time of the fire, the balance due on the loan is $43,000. Accordingly, $43,000 is all that Fidelity can recover under the insurance policy. That amount is the full extent of its insurable interest.

The concept of insurable interest is illustrated in the *Crowell v. Delafield Farmers Mutual Fire Insurance Company,* which follows.

CROWELL v. DELAFIELD FARMERS MUTUAL FIRE INSURANCE COMPANY

453 N.W.2d 724 (Minn. Ct. App. 1990)

Earl and Vonette Crowell own and operate a farm in Cottonwood County, Minnesota. In 1980, the Crowells took out a mortgage on the property with Farm Credit Services. They also took out a fire insurance policy with Delafield Farmers Mutual Insurance Company, which ran from October 1985 until October 1988. The Crowells failed to make their mortgage payments and Farm Credit began foreclosure proceedings. Upon foreclosure, mortgagors such as the Crowells have a right of redemption for a specified time, during which they have the right to buy back their property *after* it has been sold to another. In November of 1987, the Crowells' right of redemption ended. Under

Minnesota law, however, farmers who lose their farms to corporate lenders are given an additional opportunity to repurchase their farms under a "right of first refusal." Under this law, Farm Credit was forbidden to sell the farm to anyone else before offering it to the Crowells at a price no higher than the highest price offered by a third party. Farm Credit allowed the Crowells to remain on the farm while they tried to secure financing to buy the property under their right of first refusal.

On November 27, 1987, the farmhouse was substantially destroyed by fire. The Crowells filed a claim for the loss with Delafield. Delafield paid the claim on the Crowells' personal effects inside the house, but denied the claim on the structure itself. It claimed that since the Crowells' period of redemption had expired, they no longer had an insurable interest in the farmhouse. The Crowells brought suit. The trial court granted summary judgment for the Crowells and Delafield appealed.

Kalitowski, Judge.   To be entitled to recovery for a loss, an insured must have an insurable interest in the property covered by the policy. To have an insurable interest, the party must suffer a loss of property interest that is substantial and real. A person has an insurable interest in property when the relationship between him and the property is such that he has a reasonable expectation, based upon a real or legal right, of benefit to be derived from the continued existence of the property and of loss or liability from its destruction. The Minnesota Supreme Court has stated that it is not necessary that the insured should have an absolute right of property, and that he has an insurable interest if, by the destruction of the property, he will suffer a loss, whether he has or has not any title to, lien upon, or possession of the property itself.

Farm Credit foreclosed on the Crowells' farm mortgage. The Crowells remained on and continued to operate the farm. After the redemption period, Farm Credit became the absolute owner of the property. The record indicates Farm Credit allowed the Crowells to remain on the farm after the redemption period expired because it was involved in the Crowells' effort to secure financing to enable them to exercise their statutory right of first refusal. In addition, Farm Credit did not purchase and the Crowells did not cancel fire insurance on the property.

By creating a right of first refusal, the legislature gave financially distressed farmers who had lost their farms to corporate lenders an opportunity to repurchase the farms. The legislative purpose of this right of first refusal is to encourage and protect the family farm as a basic economic unit, to insure it as the most socially desirable mode of agricultural production, and to enhance and promote the stability and well-being of rural society in Minnesota and the nuclear family.

This right of first refusal gives family farmers some additional right or interest in the property they lost to corporate lenders. Based on this legal right in the property, the Crowells had a reasonable expectation to derive a benefit from the continued existence of the farmhouse. Although the Crowells no longer had title to the farm, they were allowed to remain on the land with all parties' knowledge and intention that they would exercise their right of first refusal and regain the farm. Therefore, they expected the benefit of living in the farmhouse until they exercised that right.

It is clear the Crowells suffered a loss from the destruction of the farmhouse. Since the fire the Crowells have been unable to live in the farmhouse. This situation forces the Crowells to live several miles from their farm and commute between their home and the farm, causing additional expenses and inconvenience. The advantage of living on the farm is clearly lost.

Under the facts of this case we hold the trial court was correct in holding this right gave the Crowells an insurable interest in the farm and its structures.

Judgment for the Crowells affirmed.

FIGURE 2　Insurance Recovery for a Total Loss

Face Value of Policy	Fair Market Value at Time of Loss	Recovery	
		Valued Policy	Open Policy
$50,000	$42,000	$50,000	$42,000
50,000	65,000	50,000	50,000

FIRE INSURANCE CONTRACTS

Fire insurance, as the name suggests, insures against losses caused by accidental fire. Companies that write fire insurance commonly also insure against loss caused by other perils such as lightning, water, wind, and hail. Fire insurance contracts are **indemnity** contracts. This means that the insurer is obligated to reimburse the insured for any actual losses that the insured suffered due to damage to the insured property. The loss must occur during the period of time that the policy is in force. The amount that the insured may recover is generally limited to the extent of the loss sustained as long as it does not exceed the amount of coverage that the insured purchased.

Types of Losses Covered

Fire insurance contracts distinguish between *friendly fires,* which are those contained in a place intended for a fire, such as fires in a woodstove or fireplace, and *hostile fires,* which burn where no fire is intended to be, such as fires caused by lightning, outside sources, electrical shorts, or those that started out as a friendly fire and escaped their boundaries. Generally, fire insurance policies cover the losses caused by hostile fires and not those caused by friendly fires. The insurer will cover losses caused by negligent acts of the insured's employees, but not those resulting from intentional destruction of the insured's property.

Fire insurance policies generally cover more than direct damage caused by the fire. They also cover indirect damage caused by smoke and heat, and the damage caused by the efforts of firefighters to put out the fire. Generally, however, lost profits are not covered.

Types of Policies

Some fire insurance contracts are called **valued policies.** If property covered by a valued policy is totally

destroyed, the insured can recover the face amount of the policy regardless of the fair market value of the building. For example, Smith bought a home with a fair market value of $50,000 in 1980 and purchased a valued policy with a face value of $50,000 to insure the house against the risk of fire. In the next few years, because of deterioration in the surrounding neighborhood, the home's fair market value decreased. In 1985, when the home had a fair market value of only $42,000, it was totally destroyed by fire. Despite the reduced fair market value, Smith is entitled to $50,000 (the face value of the policy).

Most fire insurance policies are **open policies.** Open policies allow the insured to recover the fair market value of the property at the time it was destroyed, up to the limits stated in the policy. Thus, in the example presented in the previous paragraph, Smith would be entitled to only $42,000 when the home was destroyed in 1985.

Suppose instead that Smith's home had increased in value so that at the time of the fire its fair market value was $65,000. In this case, it does not matter what type of policy Smith had. Under both the valued and open policies, his recovery would be limited to the face value of the policy—$50,000.

Figure 2 illustrates the recovery under both of these types of policies.

Special Terms of a Fire Insurance Contract

The insurance contract may contain special terms relating to the insured's rights upon destruction of the property. It is common for some policies to give the insurer the option of replacing or restoring the damaged property instead of paying its fair market value.

Coinsurance Clause　Some fire insurance policies contain a coinsurance clause that can operate to limit the insured's right to recovery. The coinsurance provision

FIGURE 3   Coinsurance Clause

Fair Market Value at Time of Loss	Face Value of Policy	Amount of Insurance Required	Actual Loss	Recovery
$100,000	$60,000	$80,000	$ 40,000	$30,000
100,000	60,000	80,000	100,000	60,000

requires the insured to insure the property to a specified percentage of its fair market value in order to fully recover the value of partial losses. Generally, most policies require that the insured purchase insurance equal to at least 80 percent of the fair market value.

For example, ABC Manufacturing Company has a fire insurance policy on its warehouse with Friendly Mutual Insurance Group. The policy has an 80 percent coinsurance clause. The warehouse had a fair market value of $100,000. (Therefore ABC was required to carry at least $80,000 of insurance on the building.) However, ABC purchased a policy with a face value of only $60,000. A fire partially destroyed the building, causing $40,000 worth of damage to the structure. Because of the coinsurance clause, ABC will recover only $30,000 from Friendly. (This figure was arrived at by taking the amount of insurance carried ($60,000) divided by the amount of insurance required ($80,000) times the loss ($40,000).)

The coinsurance formula for recovery for partial losses is stated as follows:

$$\frac{\text{Amount of insurance carried}}{\text{Coinsurance percent} \times \text{Fair market value}} \times \text{Loss} = \text{Recovery}$$

Remember that the coinsurance formula only applies to "partial" losses of property. If the warehouse had been totally destroyed by the fire, ABC could have recovered $60,000 (the face value of the policy), and the formula would not have been applicable. If the formula had been used, it would have indicated that Friendly owed ABC $75,000. Yet this would have been more than the face amount of the policy. This is not possible; whether the loss is total or partial, the insured can never recover more than the face value of the policy. This example is depicted in Figure 3.

Pro Rata Clause   With the limited exception of the valued policy discussed above, the insured can never re-

cover more than the amount of the actual loss. To allow otherwise would encourage unscrupulous people to destroy their property intentionally. Accordingly, when the insured has purchased insurance policies from more than one insurer, the loss will be apportioned among the insurance companies. The amount for which any particular insurer is liable is calculated by determining the total amount of the insurer's policy in proportion to the total amount of insurance covering the property. For example, Andrews purchases two insurance policies to cover his home against the risk of fire. His policy from Farmers Mutual has a face value of $50,000 while the coverage by States Insurance is for $100,000. The home is partially destroyed by fire with the losses amounting to $30,000. As you will see in Figure 4, Farmers Mutual is responsible for $10,000, while States Insurance is liable for the remaining $20,000.

The formula for determining each insurer's liability is stated as follows:

$$\frac{\text{Amount of insurer's policy}}{\text{Total coverage by all insurers}} \times \text{Loss} = \text{Liability of insurer}$$

Thus, Farmers' liability was calculated as follows:

$$\frac{\$50,000 \text{ (Farmers' policy)}}{\$150,000 \text{ (Total of both policies)}} \times \$30,000 \text{ (Loss)} = \$10,000$$

The liability of States Insurance could be similarly calculated by substituting $100,000 (States' policy) for the $50,000 (Farmers' policy) in the numerator of the equation. This formula may be used for both partial and total losses. However, each company's liability is limited by the face value of the policy. Thus, Farmers could never be liable for more than $50,000 and States' liability is limited to a maximum of $100,000.

INSURANCE POLICIES AS CONTRACTS

The insurance relationship is basically contractual in nature. As a result, insurance policies must satisfy all of the elements required for a binding contract.

FIGURE 4   Pro Rata Insurance

Policy A	Policy B	Total Insurance (Policy A plus Policy B)	Actual Loss	Liability of Insurer A	Liability of Insurer B
$50,000	$100,000	$150,000	$30,000	$10,000	$20,000

Offer and Acceptance   The standard practice in insurance is to have the potential insured make an offer to enter an insurance contract by completing an application provided by the insurer's agent and submitting it and the premium to the insurer. The insurer may then either accept or reject this offer. What constitutes acceptance depends on the kind of insurance requested and the language of the application. It is very important to know the precise time when an acceptance occurs. Any losses suffered prior to this point must be borne by the insured, not the insurer.

In fire insurance contracts, the application may be worded so that insurance coverage begins when the insured signs the application. This can provide temporary coverage until the insurer either accepts or rejects the policy. The same result may also be achieved by the use of a **binder,** an agreement for temporary insurance pending the insurer's decision to accept or reject the risk. Acceptance in fire insurance contracts generally occurs when the insurer (or agent, if authorized to do so) indicates to the insured an intent to accept the application. Figure 5 depicts the formation of an insurance contract.

A common problem that occurs in insurance law is the effect of the insurer's delay in acting on the application. If the applicant suffers a loss after applying, but before the insured formally accepts, who must bear the loss? As a general rule, the insurer's delay does not constitute acceptance. Some states, however, have held that an insurer's retention of the premium for an unreasonable time constitutes an acceptance. Others have allowed tort suits against insurers for negligent delay in acting on an application. The theory of these cases is that insurance companies have a public duty to insure qualified applicants and that an unreasonable delay prevents applicants from obtaining insurance protection from some other source. A few states have also enacted statutes holding that insurers are bound to the insurance contract unless they have rejected the application within a specified period of time.

Misrepresentation

Applicants for insurance have a duty to reveal to insurers all the material facts about the nature of the risk so that the insurer can make an intelligent decision about whether to accept the risk. When an insured makes a statement about a material fact and that statement is not substantially correct, the insured's misrepresentation, if relied upon, has the same effect that it would in other contracts: It makes the contract voidable at the election of the insurer. This means that the insurer can avoid paying the claim. Similarly, failure to act in good faith to disclose known material facts to the insurer permits the insurer to avoid the policy.

It is important to distinguish between warranties and representations that the insured makes to induce the insurer to enter an insurance contract. Warranties are express terms in an insurance policy that are intended to operate as conditions on which the insurer's liability is based. Breach of such a condition by the insured terminates the insurer's duty to perform under the policy. Traditionally, this has been true whether or not the breach was material to the insurer's risk. In view of the potential harshness of this rule, some states have refused to allow insurers to escape liability on the ground of breach of warranty unless such breach was material.

Capacity

Generally speaking, both parties to a contract must have the capacity to contract for the agreement to be enforceable. Therefore, an insurance policy taken out by a minor would be voidable at the election of the minor. Many states, however, have made the insurance contracts of minors enforceable against them by statute.[24]

---

[24]An insurance contract taken out on the life of a minor (the insured) by an adult (the owner) is not voidable, however. It is only when the minor is the owner of the policy that this rule of capacity comes into effect.

FIGURE 5   Creation of an Insurance Contract

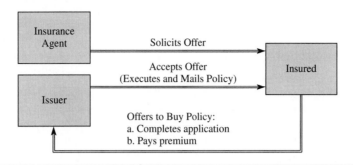

Form and Content

State law governs whether insurance contracts are within the statute of frauds and must be evidenced by a writing. Some states require specific types of insurance contracts to be in writing. Contracts for fire insurance are not usually within the statute of frauds, and thus may be either written or oral unless they come within some provision of the statute of frauds such as the "one-year" provision.[25] Even when a writing is not legally required, however, wisdom dictates that the parties reduce their agreement to written form whenever possible.

The insurance business is highly regulated. This is due partly to the importance of the interests protected by insurance and partly to the states' recognition of the difference in bargaining power that often exists between insurers and their insureds. Many states, in an attempt to remedy this imbalance, require the inclusion of certain standard clauses in insurance policies. Some states also regulate such matters as the size and style of the print used in insurance policies.

Interpreting Insurance Contracts

Modern courts realize that many people who buy insurance do not have the training to fully understand the technical language contained in many policies. As a result, such courts interpret provisions in insurance contracts as they would be understood by an average person. Any ambiguities in insurance contracts are generally interpreted against the insurer that drafted the contract.

Third Parties and Insurance Contracts   As a general rule, contracts are assignable only when the assignment will not materially alter the promisor's burden of performance. An important element of the risk in fire insurance policies is the character of the insured. Therefore, such policies are generally nonassignable. It is also common for the policy's terms to limit assignability. Those who purchase property from the insured get no interest in any policy the insured owned covering the purchased property. After a loss has occurred, however, the insured can assign the right to receive benefits under the policy, since no change in the insurer's risk is involved.

Many policies require notice to the insurer of any assignment. Failure to comply with such requirements renders an attempted assignment void.

NOTICE AND PROOF OF LOSS

A person who seeks to recover benefits under an insurance policy must notify the insurer that a loss covered by the policy has occurred and must furnish proof of loss. Fire insurance policies ordinarily require the insured to furnish a sworn statement of loss.

Time Limits

It is common for insurance policies to specify that notice and proof of loss must be given within a specified time. The policy may state that compliance with these requirements is a condition of the insured's recovery and that failure to comply terminates the insurer's obligation. Some policies, however, merely provide that failure to comply suspends the insurer's duty to pay until proper compliance is made. Some courts require the insurer to

---

[25]The usual provisions of the statute of frauds are discussed in detail in the Writing chapter.

prove it has been injured by the insured's failure to give notice before they allow the insurer to avoid liability on the ground of tardy notice.

Right of Subrogation

The insurer may be able to exercise a right of subrogation if it is required to pay for the loss of property under a fire insurance contract. Under the right of subrogation, the insurer obtains all of the insured's rights to pursue legal remedies against anyone who may have negligently or intentionally caused the fire. For example, Ellis purchased a fire insurance policy on her home from Countywide Insurance Company. The house was completely destroyed in a fire that was caused when Davidson threw a firecracker in the garage while Ellis was away at work. After Countywide pays Ellis the face amount of her policy, it may sue Davidson for that amount under its right of subrogation.

A general release of the third party from liability by the insured will release the insurer from liability to the insured. Thus, in the previous example, suppose that Davidson persuaded Ellis to sign an agreement releasing him from any liability for the fire. Because this interferes with Countywide's right of subrogation, it may not have to pay Ellis for the loss. A partial release between David-

son and Ellis will relieve Countywide of liability to Ellis to the extent of her release. (The right of subrogation is not available in life insurance contracts.)

CANCELLATION AND LAPSE

Cancellation of an insurance policy occurs when a party who has the power to terminate the policy (extinguish all rights under the policy) has exercised that power. Lapse occurs when the policy is permitted to expire by failure to renew it after its term has run, or by some default on the part of the insured.

Cancellation

Property insurance policies frequently contain clauses that terminate the insurer's liability if the insured does anything that materially increases the insurer's risk. They may also specifically list certain kinds of behavior that will cause termination. Common examples of such behavior are keeping flammable or explosive material and allowing the premises to remain vacant for a stated period of time. You will see an example of "increase of hazard" in the following case, *Good v. Continental Insurance Company.*

GOOD v. CONTINENTAL INSURANCE COMPANY
291 S.E.2d 198 (Sup. Ct. S.C. 1982)

Sims and Dorothy Good purchased a standard fire insurance policy on their home from Continental Insurance Company. The policy contained an "increased hazard" clause that held that the insurer would not be liable if the risk of fire was increased "by any means within the control or knowledge of the insured." A fire occurring on November 29, 1977, almost completely destroyed the house. While putting out the fire, firefighters discovered an illegal liquor still on the second floor concealed in a false closet under the eaves of the roof. The still, encased by bricks and mortar, consisted of a 90-gallon copper vat over an 8- to 10-inch butane gas burner. Firefighters also discovered 22 half-gallons of "moonshine" and many 55-gallon drums full or partially full of mash. A police department detective who dismantled and examined the still's burner after the fire opined that the still was in operation when the fire occurred. Good denied this, although he admitted installing the still two years earlier, some time after his insurance policy became effective. Continental refused to pay for the destruction on the grounds that the still was an increased hazard.

The Goods brought suit against Continental to recover proceeds under the policy. The trial court awarded damages to the Goods, and Continental appealed.

Harwell, Justice.   In [previous cases], this court held that coverage under an insurance policy was suspended if the increased risk was permanent and continuous even though it did not produce the loss. However, if the increased risk caused the loss, an occasional, temporary increase of risk was sufficient to void a policy.

In addition to these guidelines, to void the policy the increase of hazard must be material and substantial such that the insurer could not reasonably be presumed to have contracted to assume it. Also, according to the policy, increased hazard must be accomplished by means solely within the control and knowledge of Good after the insurance contract was effected.

The evidence leads unmistakably to the following: the distillery was permanently installed; it was regularly used at least during the holiday season; Good installed the still after the insurance policy became effective; and only he operated the still. We conclude that the only reasonable inference from the evidence is that there had been an increase of hazard, thereby voiding the policy.

The use to which the Goods put their dwelling was so foreign to the normal uses of a dwelling as to become beyond the contemplation of the insurer. Surely the insurer did not contemplate providing insurance coverage on a residence which concealed an illegal still and the fruits of its operation.

Reversed in favor of Continental.

Lapse

Insurance policies that are written for a stated period of time lapse at the expiration of the policy term. The insured's failure to pay premiums also causes a policy to lapse.

ETHICAL AND PUBLIC POLICY CONCERNS

1. You read that a person can acquire title to another person's real property by adversely possessing that property for a certain period of time. What are some justifications for this doctrine?

2. In recent years, the law has placed increasing duties on sellers of real property regarding the quality of their property, such as a seller's duty to disclose hidden defects in property and the implied warranty of habitability, which guarantees that a home purchased from a builder-vendor or developer will be fit for human habitation. Do you believe these developments are steps in the right direction? Should the law go further and impose the implied warranty of habitability on *all* sellers, and not just on builder-vendors and developers? Should it require disclosure of all defects, not just hidden ones?

3. The law requires that the person who purchases fire insurance must have an insurable interest in the property being insured. Why? Does this requirement encourage ethical conduct?

SUMMARY

Real property includes not only land but also things that are firmly attached to it or embedded under it. A fixture is an item of personal property which, because of its attachment or association with land, is regarded as real property. In determining whether articles shall be considered fixtures, courts consider the intent of the party who annexed the articles, the manner in which the articles are annexed or attached to the property, and the degree to which the articles are necessary or beneficial to the use of the property. Fixtures become part of real property and are conveyed along with a conveyance of the property to which they are attached. An exception to this rule is made in the case of fixtures attached by a tenant for the purpose of carrying on a trade or business. Trade fixtures can be removed by the tenant, provided that she does so by the time the lease expires and provided that removal does not cause substantial harm to the leased property.

There are a variety of ownership interests in real property. The basic form of ownership is fee simple absolute. Another common form of ownership is the life estate. Seven types of co-ownership of real property are recognized: (1) tenancy in common, (2) joint tenancy, (3) tenancy by the entirety, (4) community property, (5) tenancy in partnership, (6) condominiums, and (7) cooperatives.

A person can also have a right or interest in land owned by another. Such interests include easements, profits, licenses, and restrictive covenants. These interests are not possessory, meaning that they do not give the holder of the interest the right to possess another person's land. Rather, they give him the right to use the land for certain purposes or to limit the way in which the land is used by the owner.

Real property may be acquired in a number of ways. The formal requirements for the transfer of real property are determined by the statutes of the state in which it is located. The most common way of acquiring real property is by purchasing it, whereby the vendor delivers a deed to the purchaser in exchange for some consideration. Real property may also be acquired by gift. To have a valid gift, the donor must deliver to the donee or to some third person for the benefit of the donee, a deed that complies with the statutory requirements of the given state. A person may also acquire real property through adverse possession. Adverse possession requires that a person possess property openly, exclusively, continuously, and adversely for the statutory period. In addition, some states require that the adverse possessor pay taxes on the property. Real property may also be acquired at a tax sale. Under the laws of most states, the government can have property sold to collect unpaid taxes. The purchaser at the tax sale will be given a tax deed that, if valid, cuts off prior claims to the real property.

As noted earlier, the most common means of acquiring ownership of real property is by purchasing it. One of the earliest steps most people take with regard to the sale of real property is to contract with a real estate broker. There are several different types of listing contracts, and the broker's right to a commission will depend in part on which type of listing contract was agreed upon.

Parties arranging the purchase of real property will enter a contract. This contract is governed by the rules of contract law discussed in earlier chapters. Any agreement affecting an interest in land and a conveyance of real property is required to be in writing. The Fair Housing Act is a comprehensive federal law that forbids discrimination on the basis of race, color, sex, religion, national origin, handicap, or familial status in selling, leasing, financing, advertising, and appraising dwellings and in providing brokerage services.

Three forms of deeds are in general use in the United States: the quitclaim deed, the warranty deed, and the deed of bargain and sale (grant deed). In a quitclaim deed, the grantor conveys his interest in the property, whatever that interest may be. The quitclaim deed does not represent that the grantor has good title, or any title at all. In the warranty deed, on the other hand, the grantor conveys his interest and, in addition, warrants the title to be free from all defects except those stated in the deed. In the deed of bargain and sale, the grantor does not make warranties, but he does impliedly represent that he has title to the land and has not encumbered it. To be valid, a deed must comply with certain formal requirements. These requirements are not uniform, but, as a general rule, the deed must name the grantee, contain words of conveyance, describe the property, and be executed by the grantor.

Once the deed is delivered to the grantee, it should be recorded promptly. State recording statutes provide the means by which a person who has an interest in land can put the rest of the world on notice of his interest. These statutes also provide priority systems that are applied in case two or more people have conflicting rights in the same property. There are three types of recording statutes: race statutes, notice statutes, and race-notice statutes.

There are three means by which a buyer of real property can attempt to get assurance of the seller's title: have a lawyer examine an abstract of title and render a title opinion; register the property and obtain a certificate of title through the Torrens system (which is in use in some states); or purchase a title insurance policy.

In recent years, most states have imposed on builder-vendors of residential property an implied warranty of habitability, which is an implied guarantee that the property will be safe and suitable for human habitation. A number of courts have extended this warranty to subsequent purchasers of residential property. In addition, a seller today is required to disclose to a buyer any hidden defects in the property that the buyer would be unlikely to discover.

Society places a number of restraints on the ownership of real property. First, a person may not create or contribute to a nuisance on property that unreasonably interferes with another person's enjoyment of his own land. Second, legislative bodies have the police power to regulate health, safety, and welfare, which they may use to impose reasonable restrictions on the use of real property, as is done in zoning ordinances. Third, the government may acquire ownership of property for public use through the power of eminent domain. This requires that the government pay the owner just compensation for the property.

A property owner will usually purchase insurance to protect his property against a variety of perils. This insurance will permit him to shift to his insurer the risk of loss that the property owner would normally bear. In an insurance contract, the insured is the person who acquires insurance on his property. The insurer is the business that, in exchange for consideration (a premium), agrees to pay for losses caused by specific perils. To have a valid insurance contract, the insured must have an insurable interest in the property that is insured. This means that he must have some legal or equitable interest in the property so that he stands to gain economically by the continued existence and good condition of the property and he stands to lose economically by its destruction.

Fire insurance is a common sort of property insurance. Fire insurance protects losses caused by *hostile fires,* including indirect damage caused by smoke, heat, and the efforts of firefighters to extinguish the fire. Other perils may be covered as well. Fire insurance policies may be either valued, which give the insured the ability to recover the face amount of the policy, or open policies, which permit the insured to recover the fair market value of the property at the time it was destroyed, up to the limits stated in the policy. Some fire insurance policies contain a coinsurance clause, which requires the insured to insure the property to a specified percentage of its fair market value in order to fully recover the value of partial losses. Under pro rata clauses, which apply to situations in which the insured has purchased insurance policies from more than one insurer, the loss will be apportioned among the insurance companies.

Insurance contracts generally are governed by the same rules that apply to other types of contracts. The offer to enter the contract is normally made by the prospective insured, who completes an application and submits it with a premium to the insurer. The time at which the acceptance occurs depends on the language of the application and the type of insurance. As in other contracts, the insured's material misrepresentation or bad-faith failure to disclose material information has the effect of permitting the insurer to avoid the contract. State law controls whether insurance contracts need to be evidenced by a writing, but, generally, fire insurance contracts can be either oral or in writing. In interpreting insurance contracts, courts interpret provisions as they would normally be interpreted by an average person. In case of ambiguity, the court will interpret the contract against the insurer who drafted the contract.

A person who seeks to recover benefits under an insurance policy must notify the insurer that a loss covered by the policy has occurred and must furnish proof of the loss. The policy may provide that such notice and proof of loss must occur within a stated time. The insurer may be able to exercise a right of subrogation if it covers a loss; that is, it obtains all of the insured's rights to pursue legal remedies against anyone who might be responsible for the loss. Insurance contracts can end by either cancellation or lapse.

PROBLEM CASES

1. In 1971, Swafford bought three metal buildings and installed them on his ranch. The buildings included (1) a horse barn with a dirt floor middle; (2) an office, a trophy room, and a tack room; and (3) an open-air hay shed with no siding. The buildings were prefabricated at a factory and were assembled at the ranch by Swafford's agent and bolted to concrete slabs. They were never moved after their assembly and installation. In 1973, Swafford mortgaged the property to Kerman. Swafford later defaulted on the debt, and Kerman instituted foreclosure proceedings. Kerman bought the ranch at the foreclosure sale. Swafford claims that the portable buildings belong to him and that he can remove them. Do they belong to Swafford?

2. The Grant family owned property from 1938 to 1946. The property was separated from neighboring property by a fence attached to a hickory tree. In 1946, the Grants sold the property to Ford. The fence was still standing at this time. Some time prior to 1960, the fence was removed. Ford, however, continued to mow and take care of what she believed to be her property up to where the fence had been located. In 1960, the property on the other side of where the fence had been located was sold to Eckert. A survey disclosed that the true boundary line between Ford's property and Eckert's was not the line assumed by Ford and that the strip she had been mowing was in fact located on Eckert's side of the line. Applying a 20-year statute of limitations for adverse possession, had Ford acquired ownership of the disputed strip by adverse possession by 1960?

3. In 1956, the Wakes owned a tract of land, part of which they used for the operation of a farm and part of which they used as a cattle ranch. As part of the ranching operation, the Wakes drove their cattle from the ranch each spring and autumn over an access road on the farm to Butler Springs, which was also located

P523-4

on the farm. From Butler Springs, they ranged the cattle further eastward onto adjacent government land, where they used their grazing rights. In December 1956, the Wakes sold the farm portion of the land on contract to the Hesses. The contract of sale between the Wakes and the Hesses contained a clause expressly reserving an easement in the Wakes (1) to use the Butler Springs water and (2) to use the right-of-way from Butler Springs across the property to the federal reserve land. The contract described the Butler Springs area, but it did not describe the access road leading to Butler Springs from the county road. In 1963, the Hesses sold the farm to the Johnsons, and the contract between these parties referred to the easement held by the Wakes. The Wakes continued to use the access road and Butler Springs until 1964, when they sold their ranch. The sale of the ranch specifically granted the Butler Springs easement to the purchasers. The ranch then changed hands several times, but all of the owners continued to use the access road and Butler Springs. In 1978, the Nelsons bought the ranch. Shortly after the Nelsons took possession of the ranch, the Johnsons sent a letter to them "revoking permission" for the use of the access road. Later, the Johnsons placed locks on the gates across the access road. The Nelsons alleged that they had easement rights in *both* the Butler Springs area and the access road leading to it. Do they? *EASEMENT BY PRESCRIPTION (APPOINTMENT)*

4. Major developed a subdivision in which he built a number of houses and offered them for sale. The Rozells bought a house from Major. Upon the first rain, water entered under the crawl space of the house and accumulated to a depth of 17 inches in a room in which the furnace and hot water heater were located, frequently putting out the hot water heater. Major's attempts to keep the water out were unsuccessful. Water continued to accumulate in the room every time there was a rainfall of any consequence. As a result, the house was damp and had a peculiar odor and things mildewed. Do the Rozells have a cause of action against Major? *Implied Warranty HABITABILITY*

5. The Pecks owned a lawn and garden supply store. Standard Marine was the insurer of the store and its contents. The Pecks placed a fireworks display in the store, where it was subsequently set off by a young boy. A fire resulted that damaged or destroyed much of the Pecks's merchandise. Standard Marine refused to reimburse the Pecks for their loss, citing a clause in the policy that read: "The Company shall not be liable for loss occurring while the hazard is increased by any means within the control or knowledge of the insured." Is Standard Marine liable for the Pecks's loss? *p544 No increased Risk LAWN & GARDEN not typically*

6. The Parkers use part of their property for the purposes of housing, breeding, raising, and selling German shepherd dogs. As many as 25 dogs have been on the Parkers' property at one time. Many of these dogs are trained as guard dogs, protection dogs, or attack dogs. The dogs' barking and offensive odors annoyed adjacent property owners. The Parkers sometimes let some of their dogs wander around the neighborhood unsupervised, which raised concerns on the part of neighbors for the safety of their children. The defendants' property was subject to a restriction that prohibited any noxious or offensive activity and provided that no animal could be raised, bred, or kept for any purpose except household pets. Three homeowners of adjacent homes brought suit against the Parkers, seeking to enjoin them from keeping a number of dogs. The Parkers argue that the subdivision restriction does not prohibit them from keeping the dogs. Will the neighbors be able to obtain an injunction against the Parkers? If so, on what grounds?

7. In 1972, Betty DeWitt and her husband, Joseph, bought a house, taking title in Betty's name. On March 5, 1979, the DeWitts were divorced. As a part of the divorce settlement, Joseph was given possession of the house and Betty was ordered to sign the deed over to him. On January 29, 1980, Joseph died. Soon thereafter, Betty moved into the house and purchased a fire insurance policy from American Family Mutual Insurance Company with a face value of $38,500. In August of 1980, the house was completely destroyed by fire. At this time, American Family learned of her divorce and the decree ordering her to convey title to Joseph. It refused to pay on the policy, arguing that she did not have an insurable interest. Was it correct? *She has an insurable interest*

8. The opening and a considerable portion of the cavity of Marengo Cave were located on land owned by the Marengo Cave Company. From 1883, when the cave was discovered, until 1932, Marengo Cave Company and its predecessors in title exercised complete control over the entire cave, charging a fee for admission to others who wished to view it and making improvements in the cave. In 1908, Ross bought land adjoining the Marengo Cave Company land. In 1932, a survey showed that part of the cave lay under Ross's land. Marengo Cave Company claims adverse possession of the part of the cave that extends under Ross's land. Are the elements of adverse possession met here? *Yes.*

9. Glover and Santangelo are the owners of adjacent parcels of property in Oregon. Both lots are on a hillside with a view of Mt. Shasta and overlooking Lake Ewana and the downtown area of Klamath Falls. Santangelo's lot (Lot 10), which is on the downhill side of Glover's lot (Lot 9), is encumbered by a restrictive covenant that was executed at a time when Glover's house was almost completed and Lot 10 was bare. The covenant prohibits any second story from ever being erected on any building in a specified area of Lot 10. The covenant expressly stated that it was intended to run with the land and that it was executed "so that the value of Lot 9 as a 'view lot' would not be impaired by future erections on Lot 10." Santangelo began construction on his house, a substantial proportion of which lay in the portion of Lot 10 that was covered by the restrictive covenant. The house consisted of a main level and a "daylight basement." On the uphill side of the house, approximately one third of the basement was constructed above what would have been the original grade of the property. This basement had windows on the uphill side and the main floor was raised several feet off the ground. The house substantially impaired Glover's western view, but did not disturb Glover's view to the south, across another neighbor's land. As it became apparent to Glover that the house would impair his western view, he attempted to halt the construction. With full knowledge of Glover's complaint, Santangelo proceeded to complete the house. What are Glover's legal rights in this case?

10. Catherine lived with William for a number of years until his death in 1978, but they were not legally married because William was married to another woman, Arlene. Catherine and William owned their home as tenants in common. Upon William's death, Arlene inherited William's share in the home he had shared with Catherine. Catherine remained in the house, living there alone. Arlene sought possession of the property and claimed that Catherine was required to pay her rent, since Catherine was living in the house. In what form of co-ownership do Arlene and Catherine hold this property? Is Catherine legally required to pay rent to Arlene?

11. Mosher was a member of a food cooperative in which members pooled their grocery money to buy in bulk at lower unit prices. In response to a newspaper advertisement by Hudson Food Warehouse Corporation, displaying lower prices than competitive stores and advising shoppers to "check and compare," Mosher and his family drove to the food warehouse with the intention of purchasing food for the cooperative. Upon entering the store, Mosher began to write down prices, as was his custom, so that he could make comparisons for the most economical purchases. Mosher was then approached by Hudson employees who informed him that it was against store policy to write down prices and that he must either stop doing so or leave the store. Mosher refused either alternative. Did Mosher have the right to remain on Hudson's property after being asked to leave?

12. The Duchaines own real estate that they leased to Southern Massachusetts Broadcasters for the period September 1, 1975, to August 31, 1980. Southern installed a radio tower, which it used to transmit radio broadcasts. The tower is a 390-foot steel-frame structure standing on three legs and attached by iron bolts to five-foot-square cement foundations. Although the tower was capable of being removed from the property, Southern did not attempt to remove the tower or claim the right to remove it until two and one-quarter years after vacating Duchaines's property. Southern then filed suit claiming ownership of the tower. Will it prevail?

CHAPTER 25

LANDLORD AND TENANT

INTRODUCTION

In the past three decades, the law of landlord and tenant has undergone dramatic change, due in large part to the changing nature of the landlord-tenant relationship. In England and in early America, farms were the most common subjects of leases. The tenant's primary object was to lease land on which crops could be grown or cattle grazed. Accordingly, traditional landlord-tenant law viewed the lease as primarily a conveyance of land and paid relatively little attention to its contractual aspects.

In our industrialized society, however, the landlord-tenant relationship is typified by the lease of property for residential or commercial purposes. The tenant occupies only a small portion of the total property. He bargains primarily for the use of structures on the land rather than for the land itself. He is likely to have signed a form lease provided by the landlord, the terms of which he may have had little opportunity to negotiate. In areas where there is a shortage of affordable housing, a residential tenant's ability to bargain for favorable lease provisions is further hampered. Thus, tenants no longer can be presumed to be capable of negotiating to protect their own interests, because the typical landlord-tenant relationship can no longer be fairly characterized as one in which the parties have equal knowledge and bargaining power.

The law was slow to recognize the changing nature of the landlord-tenant relationship, but its view of the lease as being primarily a conveyance of property has gradually given way to a view of the lease as primarily a contract. The significance of this new view of the lease is that modern contract doctrines, such as unconscionability, constructive conditions, the duty to mitigate damages, and implied warranties, can be applied to leases. Such doctrines can operate to compensate for tenants' lack of bargaining power. In addition, state legislatures and city councils have enacted statutes and ordinances that increasingly regulate leased property and the landlord-tenant relationship.

Our discussion of the law of landlord and tenant will focus on the nature of leasehold interests, the traditional rights and duties of both landlord and tenant, and recent statutory and judicial developments that affect those rights and duties.

Nature of Leases

A **lease** is a contract whereby an owner of property, the **landlord** (also called the **lessor**), conveys to the **tenant** (also called the **lessee**) the exclusive right to possess property for a period of time. As you can see, the lease is both a contract *and* a conveyance of a property interest.

The interest conveyed to the tenant (or lessee) is called a **leasehold estate.**

Types of Leases

There are four different kinds of leases, each of which differs in the duration of the tenants' right to possess the property and in the manner in which that right terminates.

1. *Tenancy for a term (also called tenancy for years).* A **tenancy for a term,** or a tenancy for years, is a tenancy in which the landlord and tenant have agreed on a specific duration of the lease and have fixed the date on which the tenancy will terminate. For example, if Nolan, a college student, leases an apartment for the academic year ending May 30, 1992, a tenancy for a term will have been created. The tenant's right to possess the property ends on the date agreed upon without any further notice, unless the lease contains a provision that permits extension.

2. *Periodic tenancy.* A **periodic tenancy** is a tenancy that is created when the parties agree that rent will be paid in regular successive intervals until notice to terminate is given, but do not agree on a specific duration of the lease. If the tenant pays monthly, the tenancy is from month-to-month; if the tenant pays yearly, as is sometimes done in agricultural leases, the tenancy is from year-to-year. (Thus, periodic tenancies are sometimes called *tenancies from month-to-month* or *tenancies from year-to-year.*)

To terminate a periodic tenancy, either party must give advance notice to the other. The precise amount of notice required is defined by state statutes. To terminate a tenancy from month-to-month, for example, most states require that the notice be given at least one month in advance.

3. *Tenancy at will.* A **tenancy at will** is a tenancy that occurs when property is leased for an indefinite period of time and is terminable at the will of either party. Generally, tenancies at will involve situations in which the tenant does not pay rent or does not pay it in any certain intervals. For example, Nance allows his friend Rogers to live in the apartment over his garage. Although the tenancy at will is terminable by either party "at will," most states require that the landlord give advance notice to the tenant before terminating the tenancy.

4. *Tenancy at sufferance.* A **tenancy at sufferance** is a tenancy that occurs when a tenant remains in possession of the property ("holds over") after the expiration of a lease. The landlord has the option of treating the tenant as a trespasser, and bringing an action to eject him or of continuing to treat him as a tenant and collecting rent from him. Until the landlord makes his election, the tenant is a tenant at sufferance. Suppose that Bates has leased an apartment for one year from Burnham. At the end of the year, Bates holds over and does not move out. Bates is a tenant at sufferance. The landlord may eject him as a trespasser or continue treating him as a tenant. If the landlord elects the latter alternative, a new tenancy will be created. The new tenancy will be either a tenancy for a term or a periodic tenancy, depending on the facts of the case and any presumptions that are made by state law. Thus, a tenant who holds over for even a few days runs the risk of creating a new tenancy that he might not want.

CONCEPT REVIEW

TYPES OF TENANCIES

Type of Lease	Characteristics	Termination
Tenancy for a Term	Landlord and tenant agree on a specific duration of the lease and fix the date on which the tenancy will end	Ends automatically on the date agreed upon; no additional notice necessary
Periodic Tenancy	Landlord and tenant agree that tenant will pay rent at regular, successive intervals (e.g., month-to-month)	Either party may terminate by giving the amount of advance notice required by state law

Type of Lease	Characteristics	Termination
Tenancy at Will	Landlord and tenant agree that tenant may possess property for an indefinite amount of time, with no agreement to pay rent at regular, successive intervals	May be terminated "at will" by either party, but state law requires advance notice
Tenancy at Sufferance	Tenant remains in possession after the termination of one of the leaseholds described above, until landlord has brought ejectment action against tenant or collected rent from him	Landlord has choice of: 1. Treating tenant as a trespasser and bringing ejectment action against him, or 2. Accepting rent from tenant, thus creating a new leasehold

Execution of a Lease

As a transfer of an interest in land, a lease may be covered by the statute of frauds. In most states, a lease for a term of more than one year from the date it is made must be evidenced by a writing and signed by the party to be charged to be enforceable. In a few states, however, only leases for a term of more than three years have to be evidenced by a writing.

Good business practice demands that leases be carefully drafted to define clearly the parties' respective rights and obligations. The need to use care in drafting leases is especially great in the case of long-term and commercial leases. Leases normally contain provisions covering such essential matters as the uses that the tenant can make of the property, the circumstances under which the landlord has the right to enter the property, the rent to be paid, the duty to repair, any warranties regarding the quality of the property, any limitations on the parties' right to assign the lease or sublet the property, the term of the lease, and the possible extension of the term.

Permissible lease terms are often regulated by state or local law. For example, approximately 15 states have enacted the Uniform Residential Landlord and Tenant Act, which prohibits the inclusion of certain lease provisions, such as an agreement by the tenant to pay the landlord's attorney's fees in an action to enforce the lease.

RIGHTS, DUTIES, AND LIABILITIES OF THE LANDLORD

Landlord's Rights

The landlord is entitled to receive the agreed rent for the term of the lease. At the expiration of the lease, the landlord has the right to the return of the property in as good a condition as it was when leased, except for normal wear and tear and any destruction by an act of God.

Traditional Duties of a Landlord

Landlords have certain traditional obligations that are imposed by law whenever a landlord leases property. One of these obligations is the landlord's **implied warranty of possession.** This means that the tenant will have the right to possess the property for the term of the lease. Suppose Sharp rents an apartment from Oaks for a term to begin on January 2, 1992, and to end on January 1, 1993. When Sharp attempts to move in on January 2, 1992, he finds that Carlson, the previous tenant, is still in possession of the property. In this case, Oaks has breached the implied warranty of possession.

By leasing property, the landlord also makes an **implied warranty of quiet enjoyment** (or **covenant of quiet enjoyment**). This is a guarantee that the tenant's possession will not be interfered with as a result of any act or omission on the landlord's part. In the absence of an emergency that threatens the property or a provision in the lease to the contrary, the landlord may not enter the leased property during the term of the lease. If he does, he will be liable for trespass. In some cases, courts have held that the warranty of quiet enjoyment was breached by landlords' failure to stop third parties, such as trespassers or other tenants of the landlord who make excessive noise, from interfering with the tenant's enjoyment of the leased property.

Constructive Eviction The doctrine of **constructive eviction** gives relief to a tenant when property becomes unsuitable for the purposes for which it was leased because of some act or omission of the landlord, such as the breach of a covenant to repair or the breach of a covenant of quiet enjoyment.

Under this doctrine, the tenant may terminate the lease because the condition of the property has effectively evicted him. The doctrine applies both to residential and commercial property. Constructive eviction gives a tenant the right to vacate the property without obligation to pay further rent if he does so *promptly* after giving the landlord reasonable notice and opportunity to correct the problem. Because constructive eviction requires the tenant to vacate the leased premises, it is an unattractive option for tenants who cannot afford to move, such as residential tenants who live in an area where there is an acute shortage of the type of property in question.

In the *Fidelity Mutual Life Insurance Company v. Kaminsky* case, which follows, you will see a situation in which a landlord's failure to eject third parties from the property justified the tenant's claim that he had been constructively evicted.

FIDELITY MUTUAL LIFE INSURANCE COMPANY v. KAMINSKY

768 S.W.2d 818 (Tex. Ct. App. 1989)

Dr. Kaminsky is a gynecologist whose practice includes performing elective abortions. In May 1983 he executed a lease space from Fidelity for a medical office in the Red Oak Atrium Building for a two-year term, beginning June 1983. The lease included an express covenant of quiet enjoyment.

Dr. Kaminsky took possession of the property and paid rent as agreed. In June 1984, anti-abortion protestors began picketing at the building. The protests took place chiefly on Saturdays, the day when Dr. Kaminsky generally scheduled abortions. During the protests, singing and chanting demonstrators picketed in the building's parking lot and inner lobby and atrium area. They approached patients to speak to them, distributed literature, discouraged patients from entering the building, and often accused Dr. Kaminsky of killing babies. As the protests increased, the demonstrators often occupied the stairs leading to Dr. Kaminsky's office and prevented patients from entering the office by blocking the doorway. Occasionally, they succeeded in gaining access to the office waiting area.

Dr. Kaminsky complained to Fidelity and asked for help keeping the protestors away, but became increasingly frustrated by a lack of response to his requests. No security personnel were present on Saturdays to exclude protestors from the building, although the lease required Fidelity to provide security service on Saturday. In addition, Fidelity's lawyers prepared a notice to be distributed to the protestors, informing them that they risked criminal prosecution by not leaving if asked to do so, but Fidelity's agent did not distribute them. The Sheriff's office refused to ask the protestors to leave without a directive from Fidelity, but Fidelity's only response was to state that it was aware of Dr. Kaminsky's problems. In early December 1984, Dr. Kaminsky abandoned the property. He had paid his rent through November 1984.

Fidelity sued for the balance due under the lease contract. Dr. Kaminsky claimed that Fidelity constructively evicted him by breaching the covenant of quiet enjoyment. The jury found for Dr. Kaminsky, agreeing that he had been constructively evicted. Fidelity appealed.

Murphy, Justice.   A constructive eviction occurs when the tenant leaves the leased premises due to conduct by the landlord which materially interferes with the tenant's beneficial use of the property. Texas law relieves the tenant of contractual liability for any remaining rentals due under the lease if he can establish a constructive eviction by the landlord.

To prevail on his claim that Fidelity constructively evicted him and thereby relieved him of his rent obligation, Dr. Kaminsky had to show the following: 1) Fidelity intended that he no longer enjoy the premises, which intent the trier of fact could infer from the circumstances; 2) Fidelity committed a material act or omission which substantially interfered with use and enjoyment of the premises for the leased purpose; 3) Fidelity's act or omission permanently deprived Dr. Kaminsky of the use and enjoyment of the premises; and 4) Dr. Kaminsky abandoned the premises within a reasonable period of time after the act or omission.

Fidelity insists the evidence conclusively establishes that it did nothing to encourage or sponsor the protestors and that the protestors rather than Fidelity caused Dr. Kaminsky to abandon the premises. We disagree. Both action and lack of action can constitute "conduct" by the landlord which amounts to a constructive eviction. In *Steinberg v. Medical Equip. Rental Serv., Inc.,* the court upheld a jury's determination that the landlord's failure to act amounted to a constructive eviction and breach of the covenant of quiet enjoyment. Like Dr. Kaminsky, the tenant in *Steinberg* abandoned the leased premises and refused to pay additional rent after repeatedly complaining to the landlord. The *Steinberg* tenant complained that Steinberg placed trash bins near the entrance to the business and allowed trucks to park and block customers' access to the tenant's business. The tenant's repeated complaints yielded only a request "to be patient." Fidelity responded to Dr. Kaminsky's complaints in a similar manner: although it acknowledged his problems with the protestors, Fidelity effectively did nothing to prevent the problem.

This case shows ample instances of Fidelity's failure to act in the face of repeated requests for assistance despite its having covenanted Dr. Kaminsky's quiet enjoyment of the premises. These instances provided a legally sufficient basis for the jury to conclude that Dr. Kaminsky abandoned the leased premises, not because of the trespassing protestors, but because of Fidelity's lack of response to his complaints about the protestors. While it is undisputed that Fidelity did not "encourage" the demonstrators, its conduct essentially allowed them to continue to trespass.

Judgment for Dr. Kaminsky affirmed.

Landlord's Responsibility for the Quality of Leased Property

At common law, a landlord made no implied warranties about the *condition* or *quality* of leased premises. In fact, as an adjunct to the landlord's right to receive the leased property in good condition at the termination of the lease, the *tenant* had the duty to make repairs. Even in situations in which the lease contained an express warranty or an express duty to repair on the landlord's part, a tenant was not entitled to withhold rent if the landlord failed to carry out his obligations. This was because the contract principle that one party is not obligated to perform if the other party fails to perform was not considered to be applicable to leases. In recent years, however, changing concepts of the landlord-tenant relationship have resulted in dramatically increased legal responsibility on the part of landlords for the condition of property leased for residential purposes.

The Implied Warranty of Habitability The legal principle that landlords made no implied warranty about the quality of leased property was developed in an era in which tenants bargained primarily for the use of land for agricultural purposes. Any buildings that existed on the property were frequently of secondary importance. Buildings were rather simple structures, lacking modern conveniences such as plumbing and wiring. They were also more easily inspected and repaired by the tenant, who was generally more self-sufficient than the typical tenant is today. Because of the relative simplicity of the structures, the landlord and tenant were considered to have equal knowledge of the condition of the property at the time the property was leased. Thus, a rule requiring the tenant to make repairs was considered reasonable.

The position of modern residential tenants differs greatly from that of the typical agricultural tenant of an earlier era. The typical modern tenant bargains not for the use of the land itself, but rather for the use of a building on the land for dwelling purposes. The structures on land today are much more complex, frequently involving systems (such as plumbing and electrical systems) to which the tenant does not have physical access. This complexity makes it difficult for the tenant to perceive defects during inspection, and even more difficult for the tenant to make repairs, especially since the typical tenant today is far less adept at making repairs than his grandparents might have been. Likewise, placing a duty on tenants to negotiate for express warranties and duties to repair is no longer feasible, because residential leases are frequently executed on standard forms provided by landlords.

For these reasons, statutes or judicial decisions in most states now impose an **implied warranty of habitability** in the lease of property for residential purposes. According to the vast majority of cases, this warranty is applicable only to *residential* property, and not to property leased for commercial uses. The content of the implied warranty of habitability is basically the same in lease situations as it is in sales: the property must be safe and suitable for human habitation. In lease situations, however, the landlord must not only deliver a habitable dwelling at the beginning of the lease but must also *maintain* the property in a habitable condition during the term of the lease. A number of statutes and judicial decisions provide that the warranty requires that leased property comply with any applicable housing codes. From a tenant's point of view, the implied warranty of habitability is superior to constructive eviction, because a tenant does not have to vacate leased premises in order to seek a remedy for breach of warranty. The *Breezewood Management* case, which appears below, is a good example of the implied warranty of habitability.

BREEZEWOOD MANAGEMENT COMPANY v. MALTBIE

411 N.E.2d 670 (Ind. Ct. App. 1980)

On August 2, 1978, Dan Maltbie and John Burke, students at Indiana University, entered into a one-year written lease with Breezewood Management Company for the rental of an apartment in an older house in Bloomington, Indiana. The agreed rent was $235 per month. When Burke and Maltbie moved in, they discovered numerous defects: rotting porch floorboards, broken and loose windows, an inoperable front door lock, leaks in the plumbing, a back door that would not close, a missing bathroom door, inadequate water pressure, falling plaster, exposed wiring over the bathtub, and a malfunctioning toilet. Later, they discovered a leaking roof, cockroach infestation, the absence of heat and hot water, more leaks in the plumbing, and pigeons in the attic.

The City of Bloomington had a minimum housing code in effect at that time. Code enforcement officers inspected the apartment and found over 50 violations, 11 of which were "life-safety" violations, defined as conditions that might be severely "hazardous to health of the occupant." These conditions remained largely uncorrected after notice by the code officers and further complaints by Burke and Maltbie.

On May 3, 1979, Maltbie vacated the apartment, notified Breezewood, and refused to pay any further rent. Breezewood agreed to let Burke remain and pay $112.50 per month. Breezewood then filed suit against Burke and Maltbie for $610.75, which was the balance due under the written rental contract plus certain charges. Burke and Maltbie each filed counterclaims against Breezewood, claiming damages and abatement of the rent for breach of the implied warranty of habitability. At trial, Burke and Maltbie presented evidence showing that the reasonable rental value of the apartment in its defective condition was only $50 per month during colder weather and $75 per month during warmer weather. The trial court entered judgment against Breezewood on its claim and awarded Burke and Maltbie a total of $1,030 in damages on their counterclaims. Breezewood appealed.

Robertson, Presiding Judge.   Over time, many exceptions have eroded the common law doctrine of *caveat lessee.* In most circumstances, the modern tenant lacks the skill and "know-how" to inspect and repair housing to determine if it is fit for its particular purpose. In *Boston Housing Authority v. Hemingway,* the court treated the lease agreement as a contract in which the landlord promised to deliver premises suitable to the tenant's purpose in return for the tenant's promise to pay rent. In *Javins v. First National Realty Corporation,* the United States Court of Appeals for the District of Columbia found an implied warranty of habitability in the lease agreement, the minimum habitability standards being established by the Housing Regulations for the District of Columbia. The court stated that landlord tenant law should be governed by the same implied warranty of fitness which covers a sale of goods under the Uniform Commercial Code. The court said:

In the case of the modern apartment dweller, the value of the lease is that it gives him a place to live. The city dweller who seeks to lease an apartment on the third floor of a tenement has little interest in the land 30 or 40 feet below, or even in the bare right to possession within the four walls of his apartment. When American city dwellers seek shelter today, they seek a well known package of goods and services—a package which includes not merely walls and ceilings, but also adequate heat, light, and ventilation, serviceable plumbing facilities, secure windows and doors, proper sanitation, and proper maintenance.

In the case at bar, the Bloomington Housing Code was in effect at the time of the lease agreement, and, by law, was incorporated into it. Burke and Maltbie had a reasonable expectation that their basic housing needs would be met: heating, plumbing, electricity, and structural integrity of the premises. For the reasons that a housing code was in effect and the premises violated many of its provisions, we hold that Breezewood breached an implied warranty of habitability.

Judgment for Burke and Maltbie affirmed.

Remedies for Breach of the Implied Warranty of Habitability   The precise nature of the remedies for breach of the implied warranty of habitability differs from state to state. Some of the remedies a tenant may pursue include:

1. *Action for damages.* The breach of the implied warranty of habitability is a breach of an implied term in the lease contract and renders the landlord liable for damages. The damages generally are measured by the diminished value of the leasehold. The landlord's breach of the implied warranty of habitability also can be asserted as a counterclaim or a defense to nonpayment of rent if the landlord files an action to evict the tenant or sues the tenant for nonpayment of rent.

2. *Termination of lease.* In extreme cases, the landlord's breach of the implied warranty of habitability can justify the tenant in termination of the lease. The breach would have to be substantial enough to constitute a material breach on the landlord's part.

3. *Rent abatement.* State law often permits rent abatement, which is the right of the tenant to withhold part of the rent for the period in which the landlord was in breach of the implied warranty of habitability. This would permit the tenant to pay a reduced rent that reflects the *actual* value of the leasehold in its defective condition. There are different ways of computing this, and state law determines the amount by which the rent will be reduced.

4. *Repair-and-deduct.* A growing number of states have statutes that permit the tenant to have the defect repaired and deduct the cost of repairs from the rent. The repairs authorized in these statutes are usually limited to essential services such as electricity and plumbing. They also require that the tenant give notice of the defect to the landlord and give the landlord adequate opportunity to make the repairs himself.

Housing Codes   Many cities and states have enacted housing codes that impose duties on a property owner with respect to the condition of property leased to others. Typical of these provisions is Section 2304 of the District of Columbia Housing Code, which provides: "No person shall rent or offer to rent any habitation or the furnishing thereof unless such habitation and its furnishings are in a clean, safe and sanitary condition, in repair and free from rodents or vermin." Such codes also commonly call for the provision or maintenance of specified minimum space per tenant and specified minimum temperatures in the building, ceiling heights, bathroom and kitchen facilities, and heat, water, and other services. They also usually require that windows, doors, floors, and screens be kept in repair, that keys and locks meet certain specifications, that the property be painted and free of lead paint, and that the landlord issue written receipts for rent payments. A landlord's failure to conform to the housing code may result in the imposition of a fine or liability for injuries that result from disrepair. It may also result in the landlord's losing part or all of his claim to the agreed-upon rent. As you saw in the *Breezewood* case, the violation of an applicable housing code can give rise to or strengthen a tenant's claim that there has been a breach of the implied warranty of habitability. Some housing codes provide that a tenant has the right to withhold rent until the repairs have been made and that the tenant may have the right to move out.

Security Deposits   Landlords commonly require their tenants to make security deposits or advance payments of rent. Such deposits operate to protect the landlord's legal right to the reversion of the property in good condi-

tion and his right to receive rent. In recent years, many cities and states have enacted statutes or ordinances designed to prevent abuse of security deposits. Some of these laws limit the amount that a landlord can demand and may also require that the landlord place the funds in interest-bearing accounts in leases for more than a minimal amount of time. Such laws also commonly require landlords to account to tenants for such deposits within a specified period of time (30 days, for example) after the termination of the lease. The landlord's failure to comply with these laws may result in the imposition of a penalty prescribed by law.

Landlord's Tort Liability: Traditional No-Liability Rule

The traditional rule that a landlord had no legal responsibility for the condition of leased property had two effects. The first has already been discussed: the uninhabitability of the premises traditionally did not give a tenant the right to withhold rent, assert a defense to nonpayment, or terminate a lease. The second effect was that, subject to a few exceptions, a landlord was not liable in tort for injuries suffered on leased property. This rule was based on the idea that the tenant had the ability and responsibility to inspect the property for defects before leasing it. By leasing the property, the tenant was presumed to take it as it was, with any existing defects. As to any defects that might arise during the term of the lease, the landlord's immunity was justified by the fact that he had no control over the leased property, because he had surrendered it to the tenant.

Landlord's Tort Liability: Traditional Exceptions to the No-Liability Rule   Even before the current era of protenant legal developments, courts created a number of exceptions to the no-liability rule, however. In the following situations, landlords would have a duty toward the tenant (or an appropriate third party), the breach of which could constitute a tort:

1. *Duty to maintain common areas.* Landlords have a duty to use reasonable care to *maintain the common areas* (such as stairways, parking lots, and elevators) over which they retain control. If a tenant or a tenant's guest is injured by the landlord's negligent maintenance of a common area, the landlord can be held liable.

2. *Duty to disclose hidden defects.* Landlords have the duty to disclose hidden defects that they know about if the defects are not reasonably discoverable by the tenant. The landlord can be held liable if a tenant or third party suffers injury because of a hidden danger that was known to the landlord but undisclosed.

3. *Duty to use reasonable care in performing repairs.* If a landlord repairs leased property, he has the duty to *exercise reasonable care in making the repairs.* The landlord can be liable for the consequences of negligently made repairs, even if he was not obligated to make them.

4. *Duty to maintain property leased for admission to the public.* The landlord has a duty to maintain property that is leased for *admission to the public,* such as a theater.

5. *Duty to maintain furnished dwellings.* The landlord who rents a *fully furnished dwelling for a short time* impliedly warrants that the premises are safe and habitable.

Except for these circumstances, the landlord was not liable for injuries suffered by the tenant on leased property. Note that none of these exceptions would apply to what is one of the most common occasions for injury: when the tenant is injured by a defect in his own apartment and the defect is caused by the landlord's failure to repair rather than by negligently done repairs.

Landlord's Tort Liability: Current Trends   Currently, there is a strong trend toward abolishing the traditional rule of landlord tort immunity. The proliferation of housing codes and the development of the implied warranty of habitability have persuaded a sizable number of courts to impose on landlords the duty to use *reasonable care* in their maintenance of the leased property. As we have discussed, a landlord's duty to keep the property in repair may be based on an express clause in the lease, the implied warranty of habitability, or provisions of a housing code or statute. Given the duty to make repairs, the landlord can be liable if injury results from his negligent failure to carry out his duty to make repairs. As a general rule, a landlord will not be liable unless he had *notice* of the defect and a reasonable opportunity to make repairs.

The duty of care that landlords owe to their tenants has been held to include the duty to take steps to protect their tenants from unreasonable risks created by other tenants. Courts have held landlords liable for injuries to tenants that result from dangerous conditions (such as vicious animals) maintained by other tenants in circumstances in which the landlord either knew or had reason to know of the danger.

One area of possible future expansion of landlords' liability is the application of product liability principles to the lease of residential property. In *Becker v. IRM Corporation,*[1] the California Supreme Court held a landlord strictly liable for a tenant's physical injuries that were caused by a hidden defect that was present when the tenant leased the property.

Liability for the Criminal Conduct of Third Parties
One aspect of the overall trend toward increasing the legal accountability of landlords is that many courts have imposed on landlords the duty to protect tenants and others on their property from foreseeable criminal conduct. Although landlords are not insurers of the safety of persons on their property, an increasing number of courts have found them liable for injuries sustained by individuals who have been criminally attacked on the landlord's property when the attack was facilitated by the landlord's failure to comply with housing codes or failure to maintain the degree of security that would be reasonable under the circumstances. This liability has been imposed on commercial landlords (such as shopping mall owners) as well as residential landlords. Some courts have held that the implied warranty of habitability includes the obligation to provide reasonable security, but in most of the states that have imposed this type of liability, the landlord's liability is based on ordinary negligence or negligence per se.[2]

The following case, *Muniz v. Lefran Realty Corporation,* takes these principles one step further. In *Muniz,* the court held that a pedestrian injured by criminal conduct on the landlord's property stated a cause of action against the landlord when the criminal conduct causing the injury was made more likely by a tenant's known and unlawful use of the leased property.

---

[1] 213 Cal. Rptr. 213 (Cal. Sup. Ct. 1985) (in bank).
[2] The law of negligence is covered in detail in the Negligence and Strict Liability chapter.

MUNIZ v. LEFRAN REALTY CORPORATION

553 N.Y.S.2d 313 (Sup. Ct. of N.Y., App. Div. 1990)

Miguel Muniz, a nine-year-old boy, was permanently blinded when he was shot in the head while passing in front of a building owned by Lefran Realty. The bullet that struck Miguel was shot from inside the building during a robbery of the allegedly known, illegal "drug supermarket" operated by the tenant of a store on Lefran Realty's property. The illegal use of the store was well known to many people prior to the day when Miguel was shot. It had been raided by police on five occasions, but reopened with the sale of drugs and narcotics soon after each raid. The superintendent of the building stated that patrons of the store went there to buy drugs rather than clothing and that he had reported the misuse of the store to the landlord several times before the shooting. The executive director of the neighborhood association had received many complaints about the store from people in the neighborhood.

Miguel and his mother brought suit against Lefran Realty. The trial court granted a summary judgment in favor of Lefran Realty and dismissed the case. The Munizes appealed.

Rosenberger, Justice.   The [lower court] concluded that even if the landlord had knowledge of the drug operation, it "stretches foreseeability much too far" to conclude the landlord should have foreseen an attempted robbery of the drug operation. We disagree.

While the intervening criminal act of a third person will generally be deemed a superseding cause which severs the liability of the original tortfeasor, this is not the case "when the intentional or criminal intervention of a third party is reasonably foreseeable." Thus, a landlord may be held liable for the personal injury inflicted upon a tenant or guest by a criminal intruder in a common area of the building if the landlord should have anticipated a risk of harm from criminal activity to persons on the premises.

In this case, however, neither the injured infant nor his mother had any relationship with Lefran Realty; they were merely passersby. Consequently, Lefran Realty argues, the Munizes were not within the orbit of duty imposed on the owner of the building, and a landlord has no duty to the public at large, with no connection to the premises, who might be victimized by street predators.

The Munizes contend that the crime which led to the infant's injury was directly related to the illegal drug operation which was openly and notoriously conducted on Lefran Realty's premises. Lefran Realty's building was not merely a fortuitous site randomly chosen by a malefactor, but was itself the scene of an unlawful activity which is known to attract violent crime.

It is the duty of the owner of a building, abutting upon a public street, to maintain it in such a condition that it shall not become dangerous to the traveling public. We need not look to the terms of the lease to determine whether the landlord retained the power to remedy a dangerous condition arising from unlawful activity on his premises. Under Real Property Law section 231, an owner of real property who knowingly allows that property to be used or occupied for any unlawful trade, manufacture, or business is liable for any damage resulting from such unlawful use. This statute expresses the clear public policy of the state which requires that owners of real property be vigilant in preventing their property from being used for unlawful purposes. To this end, [the law] provides that whenever a lessee uses any part of a building for an unlawful trade or business, the lease shall thereupon become void, and the landlord of such lessee may enter upon the premises so let. It is to be noted that the owner of these premises was not reluctant to enlist the aid of the courts when the tenant of the premises was late in rent payments, having twice commenced summary proceedings for non-payment. The common law also imposes a duty upon landlords to control the conduct of persons on their premises when they are reasonably aware of the necessity to do so and this duty extends to the protection of persons lawfully present in public places adjacent to the landlords' premises.

These compelling reasons of public policy lead us to conclude that the intervening criminal act of another is not a superseding cause which will relieve a landlord, who knows or has reason to know of illegal activities on his premises, of liability for injuries to innocent persons not in privity with the landlord where the intervening criminal act is a reasonably foreseeable sequela of such illegal use. Public policy is furthered by requiring that property owners not permit illegal enterprises which attract violent confrontations to flourish on their premises.

The plaintiffs' allegations are legally sufficient to state a cause of action against Lefran Realty.

Order reversed and complaint reinstated in favor of the Munizes.

Fair Housing Act

As discussed in the Real Property and Insurance chapter, Congress amended the Fair Housing Act in 1988 to prohibit housing discrimination on the basis of handicap and familial status[3] in addition to race, color, sex, religion, and national origin. The Fair Housing Act prohibits discriminatory practices in the rental of dwellings,[4] among other transactions affecting housing. When based on illegal discrimination, the act makes it illegal to refuse to rent property, to discriminate in the terms, conditions, or privileges of rental, to publish any advertisement or statement that indicates any preference, limitation, or discrimination, or to represent that a dwelling is not available for rental when, in fact, it is available.

Under the 1988 amendments, it is a discriminatory practice for a landlord to refuse to permit a tenant who has a handicap to make—at his own expense—reasonable modifications in leased property, although a landlord can condition such permission on the tenant's agreement to restore the property to its previous condition at the termination of the lease, reasonable wear and tear excepted. A landlord is prohibited from refusing to make reasonable accommodations in rules, policies, practices, or services when such accommodations are necessary to afford a tenant with a handicap equal op-

portunity to use and enjoy the leased premises. It is also illegal to design or construct certain types of multi-family housing for first occupancy in a way that makes them inaccessible to persons with handicaps.

The 1988 amendments would also prohibit landlords from excluding families who have children, unless the dwelling comes under the act's "housing for older persons" exception.[5]

RIGHTS, DUTIES, AND LIABILITIES OF THE TENANT

Rights of the Tenant

The tenant has the right to *exclusive possession* and *quiet enjoyment* of the property during the term of the lease. The landlord does not have the right to enter the leased property without the tenant's consent, unless an emergency threatens the leased property or he is acting under an express provision of the lease that gives him the right to enter. The tenant may use the leased property for any lawful purpose that is reasonable and appropriate, unless the purpose for which it may be used is expressly limited in the lease. Furthermore, the tenant now has the right to receive leased residential property in a habitable condition at the beginning of the lease and the right to have it maintained in a habitable condition throughout the lease.

[3]Familial status is defined in the Real Property and Insurance chapter.

[4]The act provides an exemption for certain people who own and rent single-family houses, provided that they do not use a broker or an illegal advertisement and that they own no more than three such houses at one time. It also exempts owners who rent rooms or units in dwellings in which they themselves reside, if those dwellings house no more than four families.

[5]The "housing for older persons" exception is described in the Real Property and Insurance chapter.

FIGURE 1   Comparison of Assignment and Sublease

	Assignment	Sublease
Does the tenant transfer to the third party *all* his remaining rights under the lease?	Yes	No
Does the tenant remain liable on the lease?	Yes	Yes
Does the third party (assignee or sublessee) acquire rights and duties under the tenant's lease with the landlord?	Yes	No

Duty of the Tenant to Pay Rent

The tenant has the duty to *pay rent* in the agreed amount and at the agreed times. If more than one individual enter a lease together as cotenants, their liability under the lease is **joint and several.** This means that each of them has complete responsibility—not just partial responsibility—for performing the tenants' duties under the lease. For example, Collier and Moore rent an apartment from Lester Properties, both Collier and Moore signing a one-year lease. If Collier should move out after three months, Lester Properties can hold Moore responsible for the entire rent, not just half of it. (Naturally, Collier remains liable on the lease, too, but Lester can opt to proceed against Moore solely.)

Duty of the Tenant Not to Commit Waste

The tenant also has the duty not to commit **waste** on the property. This means that the tenant is responsible for the care and upkeep of the property and that he has the duty not to do any act that would harm the property. In the past, the fulfillment of this duty required that the tenant perform ordinary repairs. Today, the duty to make repairs has generally been shifted to the landlord by court ruling, statute, or lease provision. The tenant now has no duty to make major repairs unless the damage has been caused by his own negligence. When damage exists through no fault of the tenant, the tenant still has the duty to take steps to prevent further damage from the elements, as when a window breaks or a roof leaks.

Assignment and Subleasing

As is true of most other types of contracts, the rights and duties under a lease generally can be assigned and delegated to third parties. **Assignment** occurs when the landlord or the tenant transfers all of his remaining rights under the lease to another person. For example, a land-lord may sell an apartment building to another person and assign the leases to the buyer, who will then become the new landlord. A tenant may assign the remainder of his lease to someone else, who then acquires whatever rights the tenant had under the lease (including, of course, the right to exclusive possession of the leased premises).

Subleasing occurs when the tenant transfers to a third person some but not all of his remaining right to possess the property under the lease. The relationship of tenant to sublessee becomes that of landlord and tenant. For example, Boyer, a college student whose two-year lease on an apartment is to terminate on May 1, 1992, sublets his apartment to Chambers for the summer months of 1991. This is a sublease because Boyer has not transferred all of his remaining rights under the lease.

The significance of the distinction between an assignment and a sublease is that a sublessee does not acquire rights or duties under the lease between the landlord and tenant, whereas an assignee does. An assignee steps into the shoes of the original tenant and acquires any rights that he had under the lease.[6] For example, if the lease contained an option to renew, the assignee tenant would have the right to exercise this option if he desired to do so. The assignee is also personally liable to the landlord for the payment of rent.

In both an assignment and a sublease, the tenant remains liable to the landlord for the commitments made in the lease. If the assignee or sublessee fails to pay rent, for example, the tenant has the legal obligation to pay it. Figure 1 compares the characteristics of assignments and subleases.

---

[6]Assignment is discussed in detail in the Rights of Third Parties chapter.

Lease Provisions Limiting Assignment Leases—especially commercial leases—commonly contain limitations on assignment and subleasing. These provisions may require the landlord's consent to any assignment or sublease or may totally prohibit such a transfer of the tenant's interests. The provisions requiring the landlord's consent to assignment are upheld by the courts, although some courts place the duty on the landlord not to withhold consent unreasonably. Although total prohibitions against assignment can be enforced, too, they are disfavored in the law. Typically, they are construed narrowly and any ambiguities are resolved against the landlord.

Tenant's Liability for Injuries to Third Persons

The tenant is normally liable to persons who suffer physical injury or property damage on the part of the property over which the tenant has control, if the injuries are caused by his negligence.

TERMINATION OF THE LEASEHOLD

Normally, a leasehold is terminated by the expiration of the term. Sometimes, however, the lease terminates early because of a breach of the lease by one of the parties or because of mutual agreement.

Eviction

If a tenant breaches the lease (most commonly, by non-payment of rent), the landlord may take action to **evict** the tenant. State statutes usually provide for a relatively speedy procedure for eviction. The landlord who desires to evict a tenant must be careful to comply with any applicable state or city regulations governing evictions. Such regulations may forbid forcible entry to change locks or other self-help measures taken by the landlord. At common law, a landlord had a lien on the tenant's personal property, which entitled him to remove and hold such property as security for the rent. This lien has been abolished in many states. Where the lien still exists, it is subject to constitutional limitations that require that the tenant be given notice of the lien and an opportunity to defend and protect his belongings before they can be sold to satisfy it.

Agreement to Surrender

A lease can terminate prematurely by a mutual agreement between the landlord and tenant to **surrender** the lease, that is, return the property to the landlord prior to the end of the lease. A surrender that is valid will discharge the tenant from further liability under the lease; it is essentially a discharge by mutual agreement.

Abandonment

Abandonment occurs when the tenant unjustifiably and permanently vacates the leased premises before the end of the lease term and defaults in the payment of rent. If a tenant abandons the leased property, he is making an offer to surrender the leasehold. As shown in Figure 2, the landlord must make a decision at this point. If the landlord's conduct shows acceptance of the tenant's offer of surrender, he relieves the tenant of the obligation to pay rent for the remaining period of the lease. If the landlord does not accept the surrender, he can sue the tenant for the rent due until such time as he rerents the property, or if he cannot find a new tenant, for the rent due for the remainder of the term.

At common law, the landlord had no obligation to mitigate (decrease) the damages caused by the abandonment by attempting to rerent the leased property. In fact, taking possession of the property for the purpose of trying to rent it to someone else was a risky move for the landlord: His retaking of possession might be construed as acceptance of the surrender. Many states now place the duty on the landlord to attempt to mitigate damages by making a reasonable effort to rerent the property. These states also hold that the landlord's retaking of possession for the purpose of rerenting does not constitute a waiver of his right to pursue an action to collect unpaid rent.

ETHICAL AND PUBLIC POLICY CONCERNS

1. Suppose you own an older house that you rent to a family with three young children. A state statute forbids painting new property with lead-based paint, but it does not forbid renting older property previously painted with lead-based paint. Should you disclose the lead-based paint to your tenants? Would the current law of landlord and tenant require you to do so?

2. You read that the implied warranty of habitability guarantees that leased residential property will be fit for human habitation, and that the landlord will make such repairs as needed to keep it in this condition during the term of the lease. Should this warranty be applied to landlords who are not in the business of leasing property, but who make occasional rentals? Should it apply to obviously run-down housing leased at very low rents?

FIGURE 2   Termination of a Leasehold by Abandonment

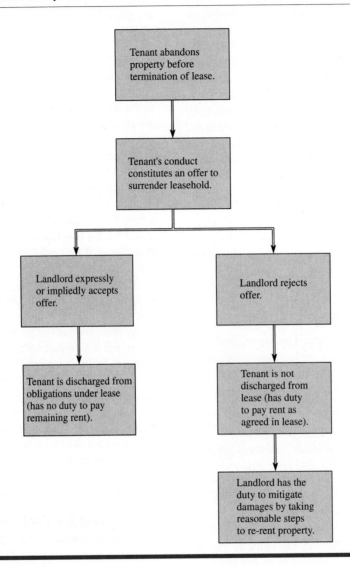

SUMMARY

The law regarding the relationship of landlord and tenant has changed dramatically in recent years. A lease is a contract whereby an owner of property conveys to a tenant the exclusive right to possess the leased property for a period of time. There are four types of tenancies or leasehold interests: tenancy for a term, periodic tenancy, tenancy at will, and tenancy at sufferance. A lease must be evidenced by a writing under the statute of frauds of most states if it is for a term of one year or more; in a few states, only leases for three years or more are within the statute of frauds. The particular rights, duties, and liabilities of landlords and tenants are determined by express provisions of the lease, common law, and statute or ordinance.

The landlord is entitled to receive the agreed rent and has the right to have the premises returned to him at the end of the lease in as good a condition as they were in when leased, except for normal wear and tear. When leasing property, the landlord makes an implied warranty that the tenant will be put in possession at the beginning of the lease and an implied warranty of quiet enjoyment, which guarantees that the landlord will not do anything to interfere with the tenant's possession during the term of the lease. If an act or omission of the landlord causes a substantial defect in leased property that renders it unsuitable for its intended purposes, the doctrine of constructive eviction gives the tenant the right to vacate the property without liability for further rent if he does so promptly after giving the landlord reasonable notice and opportunity to cure the problem.

While under traditional law the landlord did not warrant the condition of the premises, there is now a strong trend toward increasing the legal responsibility of landlords for the quality of leased residential property. The law of most states now provides that the landlord makes an implied warranty of habitability whenever he leases property for residential use. This warranty guarantees that the property will be safe and suitable for human habitation. In many states, it guarantees that the property will comply with any applicable housing code. Housing codes are prevalent now. They commonly impose duties to repair on landlords and set out various requirements concerning the condition of leased property and such rental practices as the handling of security deposits. In addition, the Fair Housing Act makes it illegal to discriminate in rentals of dwellings on the basis of race, color, sex, religion, national origin, handicap, or familial status.

Traditionally, landlords were not liable for injuries suffered by tenants or their visitors on leased property unless the case fell within a number of exceptions that had been created by courts. Now, however, there is a trend toward abolishing the tort immunity of landlords and holding them to a duty of reasonable care toward tenants and others who are lawfully on leased property. This may include liability for foreseeable criminal conduct committed by third parties, if the landlord's acts or omissions increase the risk of such conduct.

The tenant has the right to quiet possession of the leased property and the right to use it for any lawful purpose, unless the lease limits the purposes for which the property may be used. The tenant has the obligation to pay the agreed rent and to refrain from committing acts that would damage the property. Where more than one person lease property as cotenants, they are jointly and severally liable on the lease. The tenant can be liable if his negligence causes damage to leased property or damage to third persons on the leased property under his control.

Leases can generally be assigned or subleased unless some provision of the lease limits those rights. Total prohibitions of assignments are disfavored and are construed narrowly. When a tenant assigns or subleases property, he remains liable for all of his obligations under the lease, including the obligation to pay rent if the assignee or sublessee fails to pay.

Normally, a lease is terminated by the tenant's surrender of the leased premises at the end of the agreed lease term. The landlord may terminate the lease early by evicting the tenant if the tenant defaults in some obligation under the lease. If a tenant abandons the property prior to the end of the lease, he may be subject to liability for unpaid rent if the landlord does not accept his offer of surrender. Many states now place the duty on the landlord to make a reasonable effort to rerent the property in order to mitigate damages caused by a tenant's default.

PROBLEM CASES

1. Jendralski lived in a five-unit apartment complex owned by Gil and managed by Black, who lived in the complex. Black rented the apartment above Jendralski's to the O'Campos. The lease between Gil and the O'Campos permitted them to keep one caged bird. Jendralski was invited into the O'Campo apartment, where she saw hundreds of birds as well as squirrels and a monkey. The monkey attacked Jendralski, severely injuring her head and right hand. Three to four weeks before this injury, Jendralski had heard noises emanating from the apartment, including screeching, screaming, cheeping, howling, squealing, cooing, thumping, bumping, and banging. She had complained about these noises to Black, who allegedly responded, "Yes, I have to check it out." Under a modern approach to landlords' tort liability, would Jendralski stand a good chance of recovering damages from Gil?

2. Garwacki and Mastello shared a second-story apartment, which Garwacki rented from LaFraneire. Mastello invited Young to attend a dinner party at the apartment. Young went to the porch of the apartment to call down to Mastello, who was in the driveway below. As she placed her hands on the porch railing and leaned forward, the railing gave way. Young fell to the ground and was injured. The porch is accessible only from the living room of the apartment, and it is not a common area shared with other tenants. Should LaFraneire be liable for Young's injuries?

3. The Mailhots leased an apartment in Oakwood Village from the Gottdieners. They experienced no problems until new tenants moved into the apartment beneath theirs. On several occasions, the Mailhots complained to the Gottdieners of "intolerable noise" coming from the downstairs apartment, such as slamming doors, yelling and screaming children, and excessive volume from the television and radio after 10:00 P.M. The Gottdieners made some efforts to resolve the conflict, but these efforts were not successful. According to Mr. Mailhot, the downstairs neighbors then began a campaign of harassment and retaliation against them. The Mailhots again requested the help of their landlords, but a subsequent meeting proved fruitless. Although the Mailhots' lease was not due to lapse until January 31, 1980, they notified the Gottdieners that they intended to terminate their tenancy as of August 31, 1979. The Gottdieners could not find another tenant until December 1979. They then sued the Mailhots for rent for the months of September, October, and November. Will they win? *No.*

4. Kridel entered into a lease with Sommer, owner of the Pierre Apartments, to lease apartment 6-L for two years. Kridel, who was to be married in June, planned to move into the apartment in May. His parents and future parents-in-law had agreed to assume responsibility for the rent, since Kridel was a full-time student who had no funds of his own. Shortly before Kridel was to have moved in, his engagement was broken. He wrote Sommer a letter explaining his situation and stating that he could not take the apartment. Sommer did not answer the letter, and when a third person inquired about renting apartment 6-L, the person in charge told her that the apartment was already rented to Kridel. Sommer did not enter the apartment or show it to anyone until he rented apartment 6-L to someone else when there were approximately eight months left on Kridel's lease. He sued Kridel for the full rent for the period of approximately 16 months before the new tenant's lease took effect. Kridel argued that Sommer should not be able to collect rent for the first 16 months of the lease, because he did not take reasonable steps to rerent the apartment. Should Sommer be able to collect the rent? *No unless apartment shown*

5. Stephens leased a town house in a Boise apartment complex from Stearns. The town house had two separate floors connected by an internal stairway. One night, Stephens was descending the internal stairway in her town house when she slipped or fell forward at the top of the stairs. She "grabbed" in order to catch herself, but was unable to do so, and fell down the stairs. She suffered serious injury. The stairway was not equipped with a handrail, although handrails were required by a Boise ordinance. Stephens filed suit against Stearns. Will she prevail? *Yes. Liable. Because did not follow code*

6. Kessler was employed as a part-time rental agent at White Oak Park Apartments. Her duties included showing and renting apartments, receiving rent money, arranging for repairs, and the like. According to Kessler, her supervisor, Chase, instructed her to enter the apartments of tenants whose rent was overdue while the tenants were not present and to "snoop" around the apartments, looking through private papers in order to obtain information regarding their places of employment, wage or salary information, and other information that might be helpful in collecting overdue rent. Kessler did so reluctantly a few times, but felt bad about having done so and told Chase that she would not do this anymore. Kessler was ultimately discharged and alleges that she was discharged because of her refusal to carry out her supervisor's instructions about snooping into tenants' apartments. Is the type of surreptitious entry that Kessler was allegedly instructed to do illegal? *Yes. Should not have entered*

7. From 1984 to 1986, Hardy occupied an apartment at 18 Arthur Street, which she leased from Griffin. Griffin had painted the apartment, but the previous coat of paint had not been scraped off. It was described as "thick, chipped, and peeling." Hardy saw her young son, Verron, eating paint chips in the apartment, and this prompted her to have him tested for the presence of lead in his blood. She learned that Verron had abnormally high levels of lead in his blood and that this condition was due to his exposure to the lead-based paint present at 18 Arthur Street. Verron suffered severe brain damage as a result. Griffin admitted that in January 1987 he had received notice from the city about the presence of lead paint at 18 Arthur Street. On previous occasions, he had been put on notice that repairs to Hardy's unit were necessary. A state statute provides that "[t]he presence of paint which does not conform to federal standards as required in accordance with the Lead-Based Paint Poisoning Prevention Act . . . or of cracked, chipped, blistered, flaking, loose or peeling paint which constitutes a health hazard on accessible surfaces in any dwelling unit, tenement or any real property intended for human habitation shall be construed to render such dwelling unit . . . unfit for human habitation. . . ." A city ordinance imposes a duty on landlords to "make all repairs and do whatever is necessary to put and keep the premises in a fit and habitable condition." Hardy brings suit against Griffin for Verron's injuries. Is Griffin likely to be liable?

8. In October 1981, Cook entered into an oral lease to rent a residence to Melson. Melson agreed to pay $400 per month, in advance, as rent. In November of 1987, Cook sent Melson a letter advising that the rent would be increased to $525 per month, effective January 1, 1988, and asked if Melson was going to pay. On December 10, 1987, Melson replied that he would not pay the increased rent. On January 2, 1988, Melson sent Cook a check for $400 as rent for January. Cook returned the check and stated that the rent was now $525. Melson did not vacate the premises until February 1, 1988. Cook brought a suit against Melson for $525 for the unpaid rent for the month of January. Is Melson liable for the $525?

Yes

Tenant At
SUFFERANCE PROVIDED THAT E HE
LAW ALLOWS Could Collect $525

CHAPTER 26

ESTATES AND TRUSTS

INTRODUCTION

One of the basic features of the ownership of property is the right to dispose of the property during life and at death. You have already learned about the ways in which property is transferred during the owner's life. The owner's death is another major event for the transfer of property.

Most people want to be able to choose who will get their property when they die. There are a variety of ways in which a person may control the ultimate disposition of his property. He may take title to the property in a form of joint ownership that gives his co-owner a right of survivorship. He may create a trust and transfer property to it to be used for the benefit of a spouse, child, elderly parent, or other beneficiary. He may execute a will in which he directs that his real and personal property be distributed to persons named in the will.

If, however, a person makes no provision for the disposition of his property at his death, his property will be distributed to his heirs as defined by state law. This chapter focuses on the transfer of property at death and on the use of trusts for the transfer and management of property, both during life and at death.

ESTATE PLANNING

A person's **estate** is all of the property owned by that person. **Estate planning** is the popular name for the complicated process of planning for the transfer of a person's estate in later life and at death. Estate planning also concerns planning for the possibility of prolonged illness or disability. An attorney who is creating an estate plan will take an inventory of the client's assets, learn the client's objectives, and draft the instruments necessary to carry out the plan. This plan is normally guided by the desire to reduce the amount of tax liability and to provide for the orderly disposition of the estate.

WILLS

Right of Disposition by Will

The right to control the disposition of property at death has not always existed. In the English feudal system, the king owned all land. The lords and knights had only the right to use land for their lifetime. A landholder's rights in land terminated upon his death, and no rights descended to his heirs. In 1215, the king granted the nobility the right to pass their interest in the land they held to their heirs. Later, that right was extended to all property owners. In the United States, each state has enacted statutes that establish the requirements for a valid will, including the formalities that must be met to pass property by will.

Nature of a Will

A **will** is a document executed with specific legal formalities by a **testator** (person making a will) that contains his instructions about the way his property will be disposed of at his death. A will can dispose only of property belonging to the testator at the time of his death. Furthermore, wills do not control property that goes to others through other planning devices (such as life insurance policies) or by operation of law (such as by right of survivorship). For example, property held in joint tenancy or tenancy by the entirety is not controlled by a will, because the property passes automatically to the surviving cotenant by right of survivorship. In addition, life insurance proceeds are controlled by the insured's designation of beneficiaries, not by any provision of a will. (Because joint tenancy and life insurance are ways of directing the disposition of property, they are sometimes referred to as "will substitutes.")

Common Will Terminology

Some legal terms commonly used in wills include the following:

1. *Bequest.* A **bequest** (also called **legacy**) is a gift of personal property or money. For example, a will might provide for a bequest of a family heirloom to the testator's daughter. Since a will can direct only property that is owned by the testator at the time of his death, a specific bequest of property that the testator has disposed of before his death is ineffective. This is called **ademption.** For example, Samuel's will states that Warren is to receive Samuel's collection of antique guns. If the guns are destroyed before Warren's death, however, the bequest is ineffective because of ademption.

2. *Devise.* A **devise** is a gift of real property. For example, the testator might devise his family farm to his grandson.

3. *Residuary.* The **residuary** is the balance of the estate that is left after specific devises and bequests are made by the will. After providing for the disposition of specific personal and real property, a testator might provide that the residuary of his estate is to go to his spouse or be divided among his descendants.

4. *Issue.* A person's **issue** are his lineal descendants (children, grandchildren, great-grandchildren, and so forth). This category of persons includes adopted children.

5. *Per capita.* This term and the next one, *per stirpes,* are used to describe the way in which a group of persons are to share a gift. **Per capita** means that each of that group of persons will share equally. For example, Grandfather dies, leaving a will that provides that the residuary of his estate is to go to his issue or descendants *per capita.* Grandfather had two children, Mary and Bill. Mary has two children, John and James. Bill has one child, Margaret. Mary and Bill die before Grandfather (in legal terms, *predecease* him), but all three of Grandfather's grandchildren are living at the time of his death. In this case, John, James, and Margaret would each take one-third of the residuary of Grandfather's estate.

6. *Per stirpes.* When a gift is given to the testator's issue or descendants **per stirpes** (also called **by right of representation**), each surviving descendant divides the share that his or her parent would have taken if the parent had survived. In the preceding example, if Grandfather's will had stated that the residuary of his estate was to go to his issue or descendants *per stirpes,* Margaret would take one half and John and James would take one quarter each (that is, they would divide the share that would have gone to their mother). Figure 1 illustrates the difference between *per capita* and *per stirpes.*

Testamentary Capacity

The capacity to make a valid will is called **testamentary capacity.** To have testamentary capacity, a person must be *of sound mind* and *of legal age,* which is 18 in most states. A person does not have to be in perfect mental health to have testamentary capacity. Because people often delay executing wills until they are weak and in ill health, the standard for mental capacity to make a will is fairly low. To be of "sound mind," a person need only be sufficiently rational to be capable of understanding the nature and character of his property, of realizing that he is making a will, and of knowing the persons who

FIGURE 1   Comparison of Per Capita and Per Stirpes

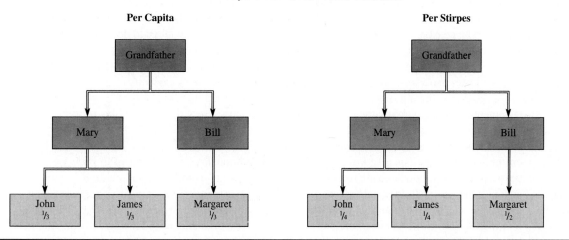

Note: Grandfather, Mary and Bill are deceased.
Mary and Bill both died before Grandfather.

would normally be the beneficiaries of his affection. A person could move in and out of periods of lucidity and still have testamentary capacity if he executed his will during a lucid period.

Lack of testamentary capacity is a common ground upon which wills are challenged by persons who were excluded from a will. Fraud and undue influence are also common grounds for challenging the validity of a will.[1] The *Prigge* case, which follows, is a good example of a will contest based on lack of testamentary capacity and undue influence.

_____

[1]Fraud and undue influence are discussed in detail in the Reality of Consent chapter.

IN THE MATTER OF ESTATE OF PRIGGE

352 N.W.2d 443 (Minn. Ct. App. 1984)

John Prigge died in 1982, survived by two sisters, Marian and Jean; one brother, Louis; and some nephews and nieces. John had never married and had been a farmer all his life. In 1980, he sold his farm and moved in with his sister Marian. While John was living with her, Marian, at John's request, prepared a handwritten document expressing his testamentary intent. John took the document to a lawyer, who prepared a will based on the contents of the document. John executed the will in 1981. In the will, John devised his entire estate to Marian and her six children in equal shares and specifically excluded Louis and Jean. John died in 1982. Louis and Jean contested the will on grounds of lack of testamentary capacity and undue influence. The trial court found that the will was valid. Louis and Jean appealed.

Nierengarten, Judge.   Louis and Jean initially contend that John did not possess the capacity to make a will. A testator will be found to have testamentary capacity if, when making the will, he understands the nature, situation, and extent of his property and the claims of others on his bounty or his remembrance, and he is able to hold these things in his mind long enough to form a rational judgment concerning them. Less mental capacity is required to make a will than to conduct regular business affairs.

It is undisputed that John was a man of average or below average intelligence who sometimes needed direction. His mother would have to balance his checkbook and take care of his bookwork. He had to be constantly reminded to do things around the house. He failed to do his tax returns in 1978 and 1979 and did not keep good track of his bills. Following the death of his mother and uncle, who helped him farm, the family operation declined in quality. These are the characteristics that Louis and Jean claim evidenced John's lack of testamentary capacity.

To rebut this, the attorney who drafted John's will testified that John was of sound mind, had testamentary capacity, knew the natural heirs of his bounty, knew the extent of his property, and was under no restraint when he made his will. The attorney also testified that John did not appear to have any doubts as to what he wanted in his will and had no difficulty arriving at the decisions on the various questions asked of him. There was additional testimony that John had, over the years, signed many documents, such as security agreements, mortgages, and contracts, without anyone's aid. In 1980, John held an auction in which he sold most of his farming equipment. The sale required execution of an auction sale agreement with the Lake City Bank. The Vice-President of the bank testified he had no doubt that John had the ability to understand the agreement. A first cousin of John testified that John mentioned to her he had made out a will and that "some of them aren't going to like it." The circumstances here are not so unusual as to disturb the trial court's findings of testamentary capacity.

Louis and Jean also argue that John was unduly influenced and susceptible to suggestion. To show undue influence, the evidence must show not only that the influence was exerted, but that it was so dominant and controlling of the testator's mind that he ceased to act of his own free volition and became a mere puppet of the wielder of that influence. Among the factors important as bearing upon undue influence are the opportunity to exercise it, active participation in the preparation of the will by the party exercising it, a confidential relationship between the person making the will and the party exercising the influence, disinheritance of those whom the decedent probably would have remembered in his will, singularity of the provisions of the will, and the exercise of influence or persuasion to induce him to make the will.

Louis and Jean's undue influence claim centers around the handwritten will drafted by John's sister, Marian, while he lived with her. That act, in itself, creates a situation where close scrutiny of possible undue influence is required. Where the beneficiary sustains confidential relations and drafts the will, or controls its drafting, a presumption of undue influence arises or an inference to that effect may be drawn.

John requested Marian to write down what he wanted in his will and to make sure the spelling of the names was correct. But it didn't end there. John then took the draft into an attorney's office where he received advice and assistance. As the attorney testified, John knew what he wanted and what he was doing. The relationship between John and his brothers and sisters negated undue influence. Whereas Marian and her husband had helped John on many occasions for at least eight years before he sold the family farm, John had an estranged relationship with Louis and Jean and had not associated with them except on a very limited basis. The record supports a finding of no undue influence.

Judgment upholding the validity of the will affirmed.

Execution of a Will

Unless a will is executed with the formalities required by state law, it is *void*. The courts are strict in interpreting statutes concerning the execution of wills. If a will is declared void, the property of the deceased person will be distributed according to the provisions of state laws that will be discussed later.

The formalities required for a valid will differ from state to state. For that reason, an individual should consult the laws of his state before making a will. If he should move to another state after having executed a will, he should consult a lawyer in his new state to determine whether a new will needs to be executed. All states require that a will be *in writing*. State law also requires that formal wills be *witnessed*, generally by two or three *disinterested* witnesses (persons who do not stand to inherit any property under the will), and that it be *signed* by the testator or by someone else at the testator's direction. Most states also require that the testator *publish* the will, that is, declare or indicate at the time of signing that the instrument is his will. Another formality required by most states is that the testator sign the will in the presence and the sight of the witnesses and that the witnesses sign in the presence and the sight of each other. As a general rule, an **attestation clause,** which states the formalities that have been followed in the execution of the will, is written following the testator's signature. These detailed formalities are designed to prevent fraud.

In some situations, a lawyer might arrange to have the execution of a will *videotaped* to provide evidence relating to the testator's capacity and the use of proper formalities. (Note that the will is executed in the normal way; the videotape merely records the execution of the will.) Some state probate codes specifically provide that videotapes of the executions of wills are admissible into evidence.

Informal Wills

Some states recognize certain types of wills that are not executed with these formalities. These are:

1. *Nuncupative wills*. A **nuncupative** will is an oral will. Such wills are recognized as valid in some states, but only under limited circumstances and to a limited extent. In a number of states, for example, nuncupative wills are valid only when made by soldiers in military service and sailors at sea, and even then they will be effective only to dispose of personal property that was in the actual possession of the person at the time the oral will was made. Other states place low dollar limits on the amount of property that can be passed by a nuncupative will.

2. *Holographic wills*. **Holographic wills** are wills that are written and signed in the testator's handwriting. They are recognized in about half of the states, even though they are not executed with the formalities usually required of valid wills. For a holographic will to be valid in the states that recognize them, it must evidence testamentary intent and must actually be *handwritten* by the testator. A typed holographic will would be invalid. Some states require that the holographic will be *entirely* handwritten, and some also require that the will be dated.

Construction of Wills

Even in carefully drafted wills, questions sometimes arise as to the meaning or legal effect of a term or provision. Disputes about the meaning of the will are even more likely to occur in wills drafted by the testator himself, such as holographic wills. To interpret a will, a court will examine the entire instrument in an attempt to determine the testator's intent. The following case, *Haag v. Stickley,* provides a good example of the methods and principles courts use to interpret wills.

HAAG v. STICKLEY

389 S.E.2d 691 (Va. 1990)

Kenneth Haag owned Front Royal Supply Company. Charles Smoot had worked for Haag as the manager of the Front Royal store for a number of years. John Stickley was the manager of the company's Winchester store but had not worked for Haag as long as Smoot had. Wayne Blye was assistant manager of the Winchester store and had worked for the company for a lesser amount of time than had Stickley. Melvin Printz was also an employee of Haag's, but was fired in 1984–85.

On January 20, 1983, Haag executed a holographic will. The will contained a specific bequest of stock to his employees who were still with Front Royal at the time of his death. It stated as follows:

In October of 1985, Haag executed a holographic codicil. This codicil provided that "In case Chs. Smoot is deceased or any other receipitent [sic] their stare [sic] will go back in the estate." Haag died in 1986. His will was admitted to probate, and his former wife, Helen, was named executor. At the time of Haag's death, he owned 689 shares of Front Royal stock, the value of which was at least $254,000. A dispute arose between Mrs. Haag, as executor, and Stickley and Blye about whether they were entitled to any shares. Mrs. Haag maintained that the will should be interpreted to give 500 shares of stock to Smoot, and none to Stickley and Blye, with the remaining 189 shares going into the residuary of the estate. Stickley and Blye filed this action asking the court to construe and interpret the will in order to determine their rights to the shares of stock. The court determined that Smoot should get the first 500 shares, and the remaining 189 shares should be divided equally between Stickley and Blye, with the odd share going to the person with longer service. Mrs. Haag appealed.

Compton, Justice. In construing a will, the testator's intention controls, unless contrary to an established rule of law. The whole will must be examined to determine the testator's intention and effect should be given to all parts of the document, as far as possible. Even though the language of the will may be obscure or uncertain, the testator's intention will prevail, if it can be ascertained.

Moreover, when the words of the will are capable of two different constructions, that should be adopted which is most consistent with the intention of the testator as ascertained by other provisions in the will; and when the intention of the testator is incorrectly expressed, the court will effectuate it by supplying the proper words.

It is true that in ascertaining the testator's intent we examine the words used in light of the circumstances surrounding the testator at the time of the will's execution. However, we cannot ignore subsequent changes to the will as we consider that intent. A will is an ambulatory instrument, not intended or allowed to take effect until the death of the maker. It may be changed during life as often as the mind and purposes of the testator change.

Against the background of the foregoing principles, we cannot say that the chancellor misinterpreted or misconstrued the testamentary documents. Insofar as the bequest of company stock is concerned, the testator's plan clearly appears from the will and from the circumstances prevailing at the time the will was drawn. The testator wished to reward company employees for their past and continued service by leaving all his stock in the company to such of those employees who were living and still working for the company at the time of his death.

Thus, he bequeathed "my shares of the stock" in the company, intending to give all the shares he owned. The quantity "500 shares" follows Smoot's name. No quantity is shown after Stickley's or Blye's names. Mrs. Haag contends the bequest is incomplete because it contains what she has labeled "blanks" or omissions. We perceive no blanks or omissions. Rather, we view the terms to state individual bequests.

Where a bequest is to several individuals, whatever may be their relationship to each other, equality is the rule, unless the testator has established a different one. Therefore, we conclude from the language and arrangement of the words that the testator intended to make a gift of all of his shares to three persons with one receiving 500 shares and the other two receiving the balance, which they divide equally, the longer in service to the company receiving the odd share.

The testator's intent is further indicated by the manner in which he made corrections on the holograph. He struck through the name of Melvin Printz, probably after Printz had been fired in 1984–85. He initialled the deletion writing "no" before "shares." This demonstrates the testator's method of deleting a beneficiary and canceling a bequest. He made other deletions in other portions of the will and codicil and initialled them also. In contrast, the names of Stickley and Blye remained in the will without being initialled but separately joined to the words "shares" by dashes or connecting lines, not blanks. The lines are undulating and not straight as a blank line usually appears. It cannot be successfully argued that these lines serve to negate the bequest to Stickley or Blye. There are at least two plausible reasons why the testator did not specify the number of shares allocated to Stickley or Blye. First, the testator was probably uncertain whether both would remain company employees until his death. Second, the testator was uncertain about the number of shares of company stock he would own when he died. For these reasons, the testator probably concluded that the exact number of shares passing to these two employees could be more accurately determined after his death.

For these reasons, we find no error in the decision of the trial court.

Judgment for Stickley and Blye affirmed.

Limitations on Disposition by Will

A person who takes property by will takes it subject to all outstanding claims against the property. For example, if real property is subject to a mortgage or other lien, the beneficiary who takes the property gets it subject to the mortgage or lien. In addition, the rights of the testator's creditors are superior to the rights of beneficiaries under his will. Thus, if the testator was insolvent (his debts exceeded his assets), persons named as beneficiaries do not receive any property by virtue of the will.

Under the laws of most states, the surviving spouse of the testator has statutory rights in property owned solely by the testator that cannot be defeated by a contrary will provision. This means that a husband cannot effectively disinherit his wife, and vice versa. Even if the will provides for the surviving spouse, he or she can elect to take the share of the decedent's estate that would be provided by state law rather than the amount specified in the will. As a general rule, a surviving spouse is given the right to use the family home for a stated period as well as a portion of the deceased spouse's estate. At common law, a widow had the right to a life estate in one third of the lands owned by her husband during their marriage. This was known as a widow's **dower right.** A similar right for a widower was known as **curtesy.** A number of states have changed the right by statute to give a surviving spouse a one-third interest in fee simple in the real and personal property owned by the deceased spouse at the time of his or her death. Naturally, a testator can leave his spouse more than this if he desires. In community property states, each spouse has a one-half interest in community property that cannot be defeated by a contrary will provision. (Note that the surviving spouse will obtain *full* ownership of any property owned by the testator and the surviving spouse as joint tenants or tenants by the entirety.)

Children of the testator who were born or adopted after the will was executed are called **pretermitted** children. There is a presumption that the testator intended to provide for such a child, unless there is evidence to the contrary. State law gives pretermitted children the right to a share of the testator's estate. For example, under the Uniform Probate Code, which is law in 15 states, a pretermitted child has the right to receive the share he would have received under the state intestacy statute unless it appears that the omission of this child was intentional, the testator gave substantially all of his estate to the child's other parent, or the testator provided for the child outside of the will.[2]

Revocation of Wills

One important feature of a will is that it is *revocable* until the moment of the testator's death. For this reason, a will confers *no present interest* in the testator's property.

A person is free to revoke a prior will and, if she wishes, to make a new will. Wills can be revoked in a variety of ways. Physical destruction and mutilation done with intent to revoke a will constitute revocation, as do other acts such as crossing out the will or creating a writing that expressly cancels the will. In addition, a will is revoked if the testator later executes a valid will that expressly revokes the earlier will. A later will that does not *expressly* revoke an earlier will operates to revoke only those portions of the earlier will that are inconsistent with the later will. In some states, a will is presumed to have been revoked if it cannot be located after the testator's death, although this presumption can be rebutted with contrary evidence.

Wills can also be revoked by operation of law without any act on the part of the testator signifying revocation. State statutes provide that certain changes in relationships operate as revocations of a will. In some states, marriage will operate to revoke a will that was made when the testator was single. Similarly, a divorce may revoke provisions in a will made during marriage that leave property to the divorced spouse. Under the laws of some states, the birth of a child after the execution of a will may operate as a partial revocation of the will.

Codicils

A **codicil** is an amendment of a will. If a person wants to change a provision of a will without making an entirely new will, she may amend the will by executing a codicil. One may *not* amend a will by merely striking out objectionable provisions and inserting new provisions. The same formalities are required for the creation of a valid codicil as for the creation of a valid will.

---

[2]*Uniform Probate Code* section 2–302.

FIGURE 2   A Living Will

DECLARATION made this 31st day of December, 1987.

I, JOHN SMITH, being at least eighteen (18) years old and of sound mind, willfully and voluntarily make known my desires that my dying shall not be artificially prolonged under the circumstances set forth below, and I declare: If at any time I have an incurable injury, disease, or illness certified in writing to be a terminal condition by my attending physician, and my attending physician has determined that my death will occur within a short period of time, the use of life-prolonging procedures would serve only to artificially prolong the dying process, I direct that such procedures be withheld or withdrawn, and that I be permitted to die naturally with only the provisions of appropriate nutrition and hydration and the administration of medication and the performance of any medical procedure necessary to provide me with comfort, care, or to alleviate pain.

In the absence of my ability to give directions regarding the use of life-prolonging procedures, it is my intention that this declaration be honored by my family and physician as the final expression of my legal right to refuse medical or surgical treatment and accept the consequence of the refusal.

I UNDERSTAND THE FULL IMPORT OF THIS DECLARATION.

Signed: _____
JOHN SMITH

PLANNING FOR DISABILITY

Living Wills

Advances in medical technology now permit a person to be kept alive by artificial means, even in many cases in which there is no hope of the person being able to function without life support. Many people are opposed to their lives being prolonged with no chance of recovery. In response to these concerns, most states have enacted legislation allowing individuals to execute **living wills.** Living wills are documents in which a person states his intention to forego certain life-prolonging medical procedures. The execution of a living will is often part of the process of planning a person's estate. The effect of a valid living will is to serve as an expression of the person's beliefs regarding life support systems.

If the attending physician is opposed to a living will, it is up to that physician to transfer the patient's care. In some states, living wills are to be given to the physician and are to be placed with the patient's medical records. Because living wills are created by statute, it is important that all terms and conditions of the statute be followed. Figure 2 shows an example of a living will, which is contained in Indiana's living will statute.[3]

The importance of living wills and durable powers of attorney (which are discussed in the next section) was underscored in the recent Supreme Court case of *Cruzan v. Director, Missouri Department of Health. Cruzan,* which follows, holds that it is constitutionally permissible for a state to refuse to permit the guardians of an incompetent person to terminate life support without clear and convincing evidence that the incompetent person would consent to such termination.

---

[3]Indiana Code 16–8–11–12.

CRUZAN v. DIRECTOR, MISSOURI DEPARTMENT OF HEALTH

110 S. Ct. 2841 (U.S. S. Ct. 1990)

On the night of January 11, 1983, 25-year-old Nancy Cruzan lost control of her car while driving down Elm Road in Jasper County, Missouri. The vehicle overturned, and Cruzan was discovered lying face down in a ditch without detectable respiratory or cardiac function. Paramedics were able to restore her breathing and heartbeat at the accident site, and she was transported to a hospital. There she was diagnosed as having sustained probable cerebral contusions compounded by significant anoxia (lack of oxygen). She remained in a coma for three weeks and then progressed to an unconscious state in which she was able to orally ingest some nutrition. To ease feeding and further her recovery, surgeons implanted a gastrostomy feeding and hydration tube. She then lay in a Missouri state hospital in what is commonly referred to as a persistent vegetative state.

After it became apparent that Cruzan had virtually no chance of regaining her mental faculties, her parents (also her legal guardians) asked hospital employees to terminate the artificial nutrition and hydration procedures, which would cause her death. The employees refused to do so without court approval. The parents then sought authorization from the state trial court for termination. Cruzan had not executed a living will, but a former roommate of Cruzan's testified that Cruzan had told her that if she were sick or injured she would not wish to continue her life unless she could live at least halfway normally. The trial court granted authorization to terminate nutrition and hydration, holding that a person in Cruzan's position had a fundamental constitutional right to refuse or direct the withdrawal of "death prolonging procedures." It also found that Cruzan's conversation with her roommate indicated that she would not want to continue with life support. The Supreme Court of Missouri reversed on the ground that no one can assume the choice regarding termination of medical treatment for an incompetent person in the absence of the formalities required under the Living Will Statute or clear and convincing evidence, which evidence it found to be lacking in this case. The U.S. Supreme Court then granted certiorari to consider whether the U.S. Constitution would require the hospital to withdraw life-sustaining treatment from Cruzan under these circumstances.

Rehnquist, Chief Justice.   Petitioners insist that the forced administration of life-sustaining medical treatment, and even of artificially-delivered food and water essential to life, would implicate a competent person's liberty interest. For purposes of this case, we assume that the United States Constitution would grant a competent person a constitutionally protected right to refuse life-saving hydration and nutrition.

Petitioners go on to assert that an incompetent person should possess the same right in this respect as is possessed by a competent person. The difficulty with petitioners' claim is that an incompetent person is not able to make an informed and voluntary choice to exercise a hypothetical right to refuse treatment or any other right. Such a "right" must be exercised for her, if at all, by some sort of surrogate. Here, Missouri has in effect recognized that under certain circumstances a surrogate may act for the patient in electing to have hydration and nutrition withdrawn in such a way as to cause death, but it has established a procedural safeguard to assure that the action of the surrogate conforms as best it may to the wishes expressed by the patient while competent. Missouri requires that evidence of the incompetent's wishes as to the withdrawal of treatment be proved by clear and convincing evidence. The question, then, is whether the United States Constitution forbids the establishment of this procedural requirement by the State. We hold that it does not. The choice between life and death is a deeply personal decision of obvious and overwhelming finality. We believe Missouri may legitimately seek to safeguard the personal element of this choice through the imposition of heightened evidentiary requirements. It cannot be disputed that the Due Process Clause protects an interest in life as well as an interest in refusing life-sustaining medical treatment. Not all incompetent patients will have loved ones available to serve as surrogate decisionmakers. And even where family members are present, there will, of course, be some unfortunate situations in which family members will not act to protect a patient. A State is entitled to guard against potential abuses in such situations. Similarly, a State is entitled to consider that a judicial proceeding to make a determination regarding an incompetent's wishes may very well not be an adversarial one, with the added guarantee of accurate factfinding that the adversary process brings with it. Finally, we think a State may properly decline to make judgments about the "quality" of life that a particular individual may enjoy, and simply assert an unqualified interest in the preservation of human life to be weighed against the constitutionally protected interests of the individual.

It is also worth noting that most, if not all, States simply forbid oral testimony entirely in determining the wishes of parties in transactions which, while important, simply do not have the consequences that a decision to terminate a person's life does. In most states, the parol evidence rule prevents the variations of the terms of a written contract by oral testimony. The statute of frauds makes unenforceable oral contracts to leave property by will, and statutes regulating the making of wills universally require that those instruments be in writing. There is no doubt that [these statutes] on occasion frustrate effectuation of the intent of a particular decedent just as Missouri's requirement of proof in this case may have frustrated the effectuation of the not-fully-expressed desires of Nancy Cruzan. But the Constitution does not require general rules to work faultlessly; no general rule can.

In sum, we conclude that a State may apply a clear and convincing evidence standard in proceedings where a guardian seeks to discontinue nutrition and hydration of a person diagnosed to be in a persistent vegetative state. The Supreme Court of Missouri held that the testimony adduced at trial did not amount to clear and convincing proof of the patient's desire to have hydration and nutrition withdrawn. We cannot say that the Supreme Court of Missouri committed constitutional error in reaching the conclusion that it did.

Judgment for the Missouri Department of Health affirmed.

Durable Power of Attorney

Another concern that people have as they plan for the future is that an accident or illness would deprive them of the ability to take care of themselves. One technique used to plan for this possibility is the execution of a document that gives another person the legal authority to act on one's behalf in the case of mental or physical incapacity. This document is called a **durable power of attorney.**

A *power of attorney* is an express statement in which one person (the **principal**) gives another person (the **attorney in fact**) the authority to do an act or series of acts on his behalf. For example, Andrews enters into a contract to sell his house to Willis, but he must be out of state on the date of the real estate closing. He gives Paulsen a power of attorney to attend the closing and execute the deed on his behalf. Ordinary powers of attorney terminate upon the principal's incapacity. By contrast, the *durable power of attorney* is not affected if the principal becomes incompetent.

A durable power of attorney permits a person to give someone else extremely broad powers to make decisions and enter transactions such as those involving real and personal property, bank accounts, and health care, and to specify that those powers will not terminate upon incapacity. The durable power of attorney is an extremely important planning device. For example, a durable power of attorney executed by an elderly parent to an adult child at a time in which the parent is competent would permit the child to take care of matters such as investments, property, bank accounts, and hospital admission. Without the durable power of attorney, the child would be forced to apply to a court for a guardianship, which is a more expensive, and often a less efficient manner in which to handle personal and business affairs.

Durable Power of Attorney for Health Care A growing number of states have enacted statutes specifically providing for **durable powers of attorney for health care** (sometimes called **health care representatives**). This is a type of durable power of attorney in which the principal specifically gives the attorney in fact the authority to make certain health care decisions for him if the principal should become incompetent. Depending on state law and the instructions given by the principal to the attorney in fact, this could include decisions such as consenting or withholding consent to surgery, admitting the principal to a nursing home, and possibly withdrawing or prolonging life support. Note that the durable power of attorney becomes relevant only in the event that the principal becomes incompetent. So long as the principal is competent, he retains the ability to make his own health care decisions. This power of attorney is also revocable at the will of the principal. The precise requirements for creation of the durable power of attorney differ from state to state, but all states require a written and signed document executed with specified formalities, such as witnessing by disinterested witnesses. Figure 3 provides an example of a durable power of attorney for health care which is contained in the District of Columbia's statute.[4]

INTESTACY

If a person dies without making a will, or if he makes a will that is declared invalid, he is said to have died **intestate.** When that occurs, his property will be distributed to the persons designated as the intestate's heirs under the appropriate state's **intestacy** or **intestate succession** statute. The intestate's real property will be distributed according to the intestacy statute of the state in which the property is located. His personal property will be distributed according to the intestacy statute of the state in which he was **domiciled** at the time of his death. A domicile is a person's permanent home. A person can have only one domicile at a time. Determina-

---

[4]D.C. Code section 21–2207 (1990).

tions of a person's domicile turn on facts that tend to show that person's intent to make a specific state his permanent home.

Characteristics of Intestacy Statutes

The provisions of intestacy statutes are not uniform. Their purpose, however, is to distribute property in a way that reflects the *presumed intent* of the deceased, that is, to distribute it to the persons most closely related to him. In general, such statutes first provide for the distribution of most or all of a person's estate to his surviving spouse, children, or grandchildren. If no such survivors exist, the statutes typically provide for the distribution of the estate to parents, siblings, or nieces and nephews. If no relatives at this level are living, the property may be distributed to surviving grandparents, uncles, aunts, or cousins. Generally, persons with the same degree of relationship to the deceased person take equal shares. If the deceased had no surviving relatives, the property **escheats** (goes) to the state.

Figure 4 depicts a typical distribution scheme of an intestacy statute.

Special Rules

Under intestacy statutes, a person must have a relationship to the deceased person through blood or marriage in order to inherit any part of his property. State law includes adopted children within the definition of "children," and treats adopted children in the same way as it treats biological children. (An adopted child would inherit from his adoptive parents, not from his biological parents.) Half brothers and half sisters are usually treated in the same way as brothers and sisters related by whole blood. An illegitimate child may inherit from his mother, but as a general rule, illegitimate children do not inherit from their fathers unless paternity has been either acknowledged or established in a legal proceeding.

A person must be alive at the time the decedent dies to claim a share of the decedent's estate. An exception may be made for pretermitted children or other descendants who are born *after* the decedent's death. If a person who is entitled to a share of the decedent's estate survives the decedent but dies before receiving his share, his share in the decedent's estate becomes part of his own estate.

Murder Disqualification Many states provide that a person who is convicted of the homicide (murder or

FIGURE 3   Example of a Durable Power of Attorney for Health Care

INFORMATION ABOUT THIS DOCUMENT:

THIS IS AN IMPORTANT LEGAL DOCUMENT. BEFORE SIGNING THIS DOCUMENT, IT IS VITAL FOR YOU TO KNOW AND UNDERSTAND THESE FACTS:

THIS DOCUMENT GIVES THE PERSON YOU NAME AS YOUR ATTORNEY IN FACT THE POWER TO MAKE HEALTH-CARE DECISIONS FOR YOU IF YOU CANNOT MAKE THE DECISIONS FOR YOURSELF.

AFTER YOU HAVE SIGNED THIS DOCUMENT, YOU HAVE THE RIGHT TO MAKE HEALTH-CARE DECISIONS FOR YOURSELF IF YOU ARE MENTALLY COMPETENT TO DO SO. IN ADDITION AFTER YOU HAVE SIGNED THIS DOCUMENT, NO TREATMENT MAY BE GIVEN TO YOU OR STOPPED OVER YOUR OBJECTION IF YOU ARE MENTALLY COMPETENT TO MAKE THAT DECISION.

YOU MAY STATE IN THIS DOCUMENT ANY TYPE OF TREATMENT THAT YOU DO NOT DESIRE AND ANY THAT YOU WANT TO MAKE SURE YOU RECEIVE.

YOU HAVE THE RIGHT TO TAKE AWAY THE AUTHORITY OF YOUR ATTORNEY IN FACT, UNLESS YOU HAVE BEEN ADJUDICATED INCOMPETENT, BY NOTIFYING YOUR ATTORNEY IN FACT OR HEALTH-CARE PROVIDER EITHER ORALLY OR IN WRITING. SHOULD YOU REVOKE THE AUTHORITY OF YOUR ATTORNEY IN FACT, IT IS ADVISABLE TO REVOKE IN WRITING AND TO PLACE COPIES OF THE REVOCATION WHEREVER THIS DOCUMENT IS LOCATED.

IF THERE IS ANYTHING IN THIS DOCUMENT THAT YOU DO NOT UNDERSTAND, YOU SHOULD ASK A SOCIAL WORKER, LAWYER, OR OTHER PERSON TO EXPLAIN IT TO YOU.

YOU SHOULD KEEP A COPY OF THIS DOCUMENT AFTER YOU HAVE SIGNED IT. GIVE A COPY TO THE PERSON YOU NAME AS YOUR ATTORNEY IN FACT. IF YOU ARE IN A HEALTH-CARE FACILITY, A COPY OF THIS DOCUMENT SHOULD BE INCLUDED IN YOUR MEDICAL RECORD.

POWER OF ATTORNEY FOR HEALTH CARE

I, John Jones, hereby appoint Carla Woods* as my attorney in fact to make health-care decisions for me if I become unable to make my own health-care decisions. This gives my attorney in fact the power to grant, refuse, or withdraw consent on my behalf for any health-care service, treatment or procedure. My attorney in fact also has the authority to talk to health-care personnel, get information and sign forms necessary to carry out these decisions.

If the person named as my attorney is not available or is unable to act as my attorney in fact, I appoint the following persons to serve in the order listed below: 1) Timothy Jones;* 2) Fred Jones.*

With this document, I intend to create a power of attorney for health care, which shall take effect if I become incapable of making my own health-care decisions and shall continue during incapacity.

My attorney in fact shall make health-care decisions as I direct below or as I make known to my attorney in fact in some other way.

(a) STATEMENT OF DIRECTIVES CONCERNING LIFE-PROLONGING CARE, TREATMENT, SERVICES, AND PROCEDURES:

(b) SPECIAL PROVISIONS AND LIMITATIONS:

BY MY SIGNATURE I INDICATE THAT I UNDERSTAND THE PURPOSE AND EFFECT OF THIS DOCUMENT.

"I sign my name to this form on _____December 20, 1991___ at ___2:00 p.m.___"

_____John Jones_____
Signature*

FIGURE 3   *(concluded)*

WITNESSES

I declare that the person who signed or acknowledged this document is personally known to me, that the person signed or acknowledged this durable power of attorney for health care in my presence, and that the person appears to be of sound mind and under no duress, fraud, or undue influence. I am not the person appointed as the attorney in fact by this document, nor am I the health-care provider of the principal or an employee of the health-care provider of the principal.

First Witness
Signature:*   *Matilda Webb*

Second Witness
Signature:*   *Howard Rabb*

(At least one of the witnesses listed above shall also sign the following declaration.)

I further declare that I am not related to the principal by blood, marriage, or adoption, and to the best of my knowledge, I am not entitled to any part of the estate of the principal under a currently existing will or by operation of law.

Signature: *Matilda Webb*

Signature: *Howard Rabb*

---

*The suggested form calls for the addresses and telephone numbers of the principal, attorney-in-fact, as well as the addresses of the witnesses.

FIGURE 4   The Distribution Scheme under a Typical Intestacy Statute

Person Dying Intestate Is Survived by	Result
1. Spouse* and child or issue of a deceased child	Spouse $\frac{1}{2}$, Child $\frac{1}{2}$
2. Spouse and parent(s) but no issue	Spouse $\frac{3}{4}$, Parent $\frac{1}{4}$
3. Spouse but no parent or issue	All of the estate to spouse
4. Issue but no spouse	Estate is divided among issue
5. Parent(s), brothers, sisters, and/or issue of deceased brothers and sisters but no spouse or issue	Estate is divided among parent(s), brothers, sisters, and issue of deceased brothers and sisters
6. Issue of brothers and sisters but no spouse, issue, parents, brothers, and sisters	Estate is divided among issue of deceased brothers and sisters
7. Grandparents, but no spouse, issue, parents, brothers, sisters, or issue of deceased brothers and sisters	All of the estate goes to grandparents
8. None of the above	Estate goes to the state

*Note, however, second and subsequent spouses who had no children by the decedent may be assigned a smaller share.

manslaughter) of another person may not inherit any of the victim's property. Similarly, a person usually cannot share in the proceeds of life insurance on the life of a person he has murdered.

Simultaneous Death   A statute known as the Uniform Simultaneous Death Act provides that where two persons who would inherit from each other (such as husband and wife) die under circumstances that make it difficult or impossible to determine who died first, each person's property is to be distributed as though he or she survived. This means, for example, that the husband's property will go to his relatives and the wife's property to her relatives.

ADMINISTRATION OF ESTATES

When a person dies, an orderly procedure is needed to collect his property, settle his debts, and distribute any remaining property to those who will inherit it under his will or by intestate succession. This process occurs under the supervision of a probate court and is known as the **administration process** or the **probate process.** Summary (simple) procedures are sometimes available when an estate is relatively small—for example, when it has assets of less than $7,500.

The Probate Estate

The probate process operates only on the decedent's property that is considered to be part of his **probate estate.** The probate estate is that property belonging to the decedent at the time of his death other than property held in joint ownership with right of survivorship, proceeds of insurance policies payable to a trust or a third party, property held in a revocable trust during the decedent's lifetime in which a third party is the beneficiary, or retirement benefits, such as pensions, payable to a third party. Assets that pass by operation of law and assets that are transferred by other devices such as trusts or life insurance policies do not pass through probate.

Note that the decedent's probate estate and his *taxable estate* for purposes of federal estate tax are two different concepts. The taxable estate includes all property owned or controlled by the decedent at the time of his death. For example, if a person purchased a $1,000,000 life insurance policy made payable to his spouse or children, the policy would be included in his taxable estate, but not in his probate estate.

Determining the Existence of a Will

The first step in the probate process is to determine whether the deceased left a will. This may require a search of the deceased person's personal papers and safe-deposit box. If a will is found, it must be *proved* to be admitted to probate. This involves the testimony of the persons who witnessed the will, if they are still alive. If the witnesses are no longer alive, the signatures of the witnesses and the testator will have to be established in some other way. In many states, a will may be proved by an affidavit (declaration under oath) sworn to and signed by the testator and the witnesses at the time the will was executed. This is called a **self-proving affidavit.** If a will is located and proved, it will be admitted to probate and govern many of the decisions that must be made in the administration of the estate.

Selecting a Personal Representative

Another early step in the administration of an estate is the selection of a **personal representative** to administer the estate. If the deceased left a will, it is likely that he designated his personal representative in the will. The personal representative under a will is also known as the **executor.** Almost anyone could serve as an executor. The testator may have chosen, for example, his spouse, a grown child, a close friend, an attorney, or the trust department of a bank.

If the decedent died intestate, or if the personal representative named in a will is unable to serve, the probate court will name a personal representative to administer the estate. In the case of an intestate estate, the personal representative is called an **administrator.** A preference is usually accorded to a surviving spouse, child, or other close relative. If no relative is available and qualified to serve, a creditor, bank, or other person may be appointed by the court.

Most states require that the personal representative *post a bond* in an amount in excess of the estimated value of the estate to ensure that her duties will be properly and faithfully performed. A person making a will often directs that his executor may serve without posting a bond, and this exemption may be accepted by the court.

Responsibilities of the Personal Representative

The personal representative has a number of important tasks in the administration of the estate. She must see that an inventory is taken of the estate's assets and that the assets are appraised. Notice must then be given to creditors or potential claimants against the estate so that they can file and prove their claims within a specified time, normally five months. As a general rule, the surviving spouse of the deceased person is entitled to be paid an allowance during the time the estate is being settled. This allowance has priority over other debts of the estate. The personal representative must see that any properly payable funeral or burial expenses are paid and that the creditors' claims are satisfied.

Both the federal and state governments impose estate or inheritance taxes on estates of a certain size. The personal representative is responsible for filing estate tax returns. The federal tax is a tax on the deceased's estate, with provisions for deducting items such as debts, expenses of administration, and charitable gifts. In addition, an amount equal to the amount left to the surviving spouse may be deducted from the gross estate before the tax is computed. State inheritance taxes are imposed on the person who receives a gift or statutory share from an estate. It is common, however, for wills to provide that the estate will pay all taxes, including inheritance taxes, so that the beneficiaries will not have to do so. The personal representative must also make provisions for filing an income tax return and for paying any income tax due for the partial year prior to the decedent's death.

When the debts, expenses, and taxes have been taken care of, the remaining assets of the estate are distributed to the decedent's heirs (if there was no will) or to the beneficiaries of the decedent's will. Special rules apply when the estate is too small to satisfy all of the bequests made in a will or when some or all of the designated beneficiaries are no longer living.

When the personal representative has completed all of these duties, the probate court will close the estate and discharge the personal representative.

TRUSTS

Nature of a Trust

A **trust** is a legal relationship in which a person who has legal title to property has the duty to hold it for the use or benefit of another person. The person benefited by a trust is considered to have **equitable title** to the property, because it is being maintained for his benefit. This means that he is the real owner even though the trustee has the legal title in his or her name. A trust can be created in a number of ways. An owner of property may *declare* that he is holding certain property in trust. For example, a mother might state that she is holding 100 shares of General Motors stock in trust for her daughter. A trust may also arise *by operation of law*. For example, when a lawyer representing a client injured in an automobile accident receives a settlement payment from an insurance company, the lawyer holds the settlement payment as trustee for the client. Most commonly, however, trusts are created through *express instruments* whereby an owner of property transfers title to the property to a trustee who is to hold, manage, and invest the property for the benefit of either the original owner or a third person. For example, Long transfers certain stock to First Trust Bank with instructions to pay the income to his daughter during her lifetime and to distribute the stock to her children after her death.

Trust Terminology

A person who creates a trust is known as a **settlor** or **trustor.** The person who holds the property for the benefit of another person is called the **trustee.** The person for whose benefit the property is held in trust is the **beneficiary.** Figure 5 illustrates the relationship between these parties. A single person may occupy more than one of these positions; however, if there is only one beneficiary, he cannot be the sole trustee. The property held in trust is called the **corpus** or **res.** A distinction is made between the property in trust, which is the principal, and the income that is produced by the principal.

A trust that is established and effective during the settlor's lifetime is known as an *inter vivos* **trust.** A trust can also be established in a person's will. Such trusts take effect only at the death of the settlor. They are called **testamentary trusts.**

Why People Create Trusts

Bennett owns a portfolio of valuable stock. She has two young children and an elderly father for whom she would like to provide. Why might it be advantageous to Bennett to transfer the stock to a trust for the benefit of the members of her family?

First, there may be income tax or estate tax advantages in doing so, depending on the type of trust she establishes and the provisions of that trust. The tax implications of a trust are very complicated. A person who is interested in setting up a trust to obtain tax advantages should seek the advice of a competent attorney experi-

FIGURE 5   A Trust

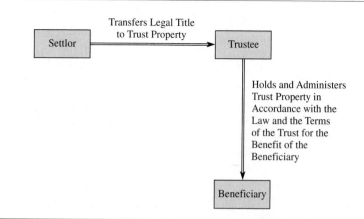

enced in estate planning. In addition, the trust property can be used for the benefit of others and may even pass to others after the settlor's death without the necessity of having a will. Many people prefer to pass their property by trust rather than by will because trusts afford more privacy: unlike a probated will, they do not become an item of public record. Trusts also afford greater opportunity for postgift management than do outright gifts and bequests. If Bennett wants her children to enjoy the income of the trust property during their young adulthood without distributing unfettered ownership of the property to them before she considers them able to manage it properly, she can accomplish this through a trust provision. A trust can prevent the property from being squandered or spent too quickly. Trusts can be set up so that a beneficiary's interest cannot be reached by his creditors in many situations. Such trusts, called **spendthrift trusts,** will be discussed later.

Placing property in trust can operate to increase the amount of property held for the beneficiaries if the trustee makes good investment decisions. Another important consideration is that a trust can be used to provide for the needs of disabled beneficiaries who are not capable of managing funds.

Creation of Express Trusts

There are five basic requirements for the creation of a valid express trust, although special and somewhat less restrictive rules govern the establishment of charitable trusts. The requirements for forming an express trust are:

1. *Capacity.* The settlor must have had the *legal capacity* to convey the property to the trust. This means that the settlor must have had the capacity needed to make a valid contract if the trust is an *inter vivos* trust or the capacity to make a will if the trust is a testamentary trust. For example, a trust would fail under this requirement if at the time the trust was created, the settlor had not attained the age required by state law for the creation of valid wills and contracts (age 18 in most states).

2. *Intent and formalities.* The settlor must *intend* to create a trust at the present time. To impose enforceable duties on the trustee, the settlor must meet certain formalities. Under the laws of most states, for example, the trustee must accept the trust by signing the trust instrument. In the case of a trust of land, the trust must be in writing so as to meet the statute of frauds. If the trust is a testamentary trust, it must satisfy the formal requirements for wills.

3. *Conveyance of specific property.* The settlor must convey *specific property* to the trust. The property conveyed must be property that the settlor has the *right to convey.*

4. *Proper purpose.* The trust must be created for a *proper purpose.* It cannot be created for a reason that is contrary to public policy, such as the commission of a crime.

5. *Identity of the beneficiaries.* The *beneficiaries* of the trust must be described clearly enough so that their identities can be ascertained. Sometimes, beneficiaries may be members of a specific class, such as "my children."

Charitable Trusts

A distinction is made between private trusts and trusts created for charitable purposes. In a private trust, property is devoted to the benefit of specific persons, whereas in a charitable trust, property is devoted to a charitable organization or to some other purposes beneficial to society. While some of the rules governing private and charitable trusts are the same, a number of these rules are different. For example, when a private trust is created, the beneficiary must be known at the time or ascertainable within a certain time (established by a legal rule known as the **rule against perpetuities**). However, a charitable trust is valid even though no definitely ascertainable beneficiary is named and even though it is to continue for an indefinite or unlimited period.

The Doctrine of Cy Pres   A doctrine known as **cy pres** is applicable to charitable trusts when property is given in trust to be applied to a particular charitable purpose that becomes impossible, impracticable, or illegal to carry out. Under the doctrine of *cy pres,* the trust will not fail if the settlor indicated a general intention to devote the property to charitable purposes. If the settlor has not specifically provided for a substitute beneficiary, the court will direct the application of the property to some charitable purpose that falls within the settlor's general charitable intention.

Totten Trusts

A **Totten trust** is a deposit of money in a bank or other financial institution in the name of the depositor *as trustee* for a named beneficiary. For example, Bliss deposits money in First Bank in trust for his daughter, Bessie. The Totten trust creates a revocable living trust. At Bliss's death, if he has not revoked this trust, the money in the account will belong to Bessie.

Powers and Duties of the Trustee

In most express trusts, the settlor names a specific person to act as trustee. If the settlor does not name a trustee, the court will appoint one. Similarly, a court will replace a trustee who resigns, is incompetent, or refuses to act.

The trust codes of most states contain provisions giving trustees broad management powers over trust property. These provisions can be limited or expanded by express provisions in the trust instrument. The trustee must use a *reasonable degree of skill, judgment, and care* in the exercise of his duties unless he holds himself out as having a greater degree of skill, in which case he will be held to a higher standard. He *may not commingle* the property he holds in trust with his own property or with that of another trust.

A trustee owes a *duty of loyalty* (fiduciary duty) to the beneficiaries. This means that he must administer the trust for the benefit of the beneficiaries and avoid any conflict between his personal interests and the interest of the trust. For example, a trustee cannot do business with a trust that he administers without express permission in the trust agreement. He must not prefer one beneficiary's interest to another's, and he must account to the beneficiaries for all transactions. Unless the trust agreement provides otherwise, the trustee must make the trust productive. He may not delegate the performance of discretionary duties (such as the duty to select investments) to another, but he may delegate the performance of ministerial duties (such as the preparation of statements of account).

A trust may give the trustee discretion as to the amount of principal or income paid to a beneficiary. In such a case, the beneficiary cannot require the trustee to exercise his discretion in the manner desired by the beneficiary.

Allocating between Principal and Income   One of the duties of the trustee is to distribute the principal and income of the trust in accordance with the terms of the trust instrument. Suppose Wheeler's will created a testamentary trust that provided that his wife was to receive the income from the trust for life and, at her death, the trust property was to be distributed to his children. During the duration of the trust, the trust earns profits, such as interest or rents, and has expenses, such as taxes or repairs. How should the trustee allocate these items as between Wheeler's surviving spouse, who is an **income beneficiary,** and his children, who are **remaindermen?**

The terms of the trust and state law bind the trustee in making this determination. As a general rule, ordinary profits received from the investment of trust property are allocated to income. For example, interest on trust property or rents earned from leasing real property held in trust would be allocated to income. Ordinary expenses such as insurance premiums, the cost of ordinary maintenance and repairs of trust property, and property taxes, would be chargeable to income. The principal of the trust includes the trust property itself and any extraordinary receipts, such as proceeds or gains derived from the sale of trust property. Extraordinary expenses— for example, the cost of long-term permanent improvements to real property or expenses relating to the sale of property—would ordinarily be charged against principal.

Spendthrift Trusts

Generally, the beneficiary of a trust may voluntarily assign his rights to the principal or income of the trust to another person. In addition, any distributions to the beneficiary are subject to the claims of his creditors. Sometimes, however, trusts contain provisions known as spendthrift clauses, which restrict the voluntary or involuntary transfer of a beneficiary's interest. Such clauses are generally enforced, and they preclude assignees or creditors from compelling a trustee to recognize their claims to the trust. The enforceability of such clauses is subject to four exceptions, however:

1. A person cannot put his own property beyond the claims of his own creditors. Thus, a spendthrift clause is not effective in a trust when the settlor makes himself a beneficiary.

2. Divorced spouses and minor children of the beneficiary can compel payment for alimony and child support.

3. Creditors of the beneficiary who have furnished necessaries can compel payment.

4. Once the trustee distributes property to a beneficiary, it can be subject to valid claims of others.

The *Tidrow v. Director, Missouri State Division of Family Service* case, which follows, presents an example of the use of spendthrift trusts.

TIDROW v. DIRECTOR, MISSOURI STATE DIVISION OF FAMILY SERVICE
688 S.W.2d 9 (Mo. Ct. App. 1985)

Bruce Tidrow, age 34, has been severely mentally retarded since birth. Bruce was cared for at home until his mother became critically ill. When Bruce's mother died, his father applied for future residential services for him, which at that time cost $1,234 per month. Mr. Tidrow was aware that funds were generally available for financial assistance of residential-type programs and that Bruce would have to be institutionalized as long as he lived. A week after making this application, Mr. Tidrow executed a will, leaving the bulk of his estate in a discretionary, spendthrift trust for the benefit of Bruce, and secondarily for the benefit of his other son, Kim, with the remainder to go to Kim outright upon Bruce's death. The assets of the trust, valued at approximately $175,000, consisted mainly of a residence and proceeds of life insurance policies.

Mr. Tidrow died in July 1981, and Bruce was placed in a residential program. Medical assistance to pay the cost of this residential care was applied for. State law prohibits assistance payments to anyone who is the owner or beneficial owner of cash or securities in the amount of $1,000 or more or any kind of property of a value in excess of $20,500. The Division of Family Services imputed the $175,000 trust assets to Bruce and denied his application on the ground that he had "resources in excess of the maximum allowed," and was thus financially unqualified for public assistance. Bruce appealed to the Circuit Court, which affirmed the decision of the Division of Family Services. Bruce appealed.

Stephan, Judge.   The trust here in question is a true spendthrift trust in that it expressly provides that no beneficiary may alienate his interest therein and that no creditor of a beneficiary may reach such interest in satisfaction of any claim against a beneficiary.

Similarly, the trust is wholly discretionary in that it authorizes but does not require the trustee to pay from interest or principal any amount the trustee deems necessary, in its discretion, to provide for Bruce's "reasonable comfort" during his life. The trustee is also authorized to pay to Bruce's younger brother, Kim, such amounts as may be warranted by his needs.

The Director concedes that if Mr. Tidrow were living, his net worth would not disqualify his adult retarded son from receiving the medical assistance benefits here in issue. From the instrument involved here, it is abundantly clear that Bruce's father intended that payments from the trust for Bruce were to supplement, rather than supplant the benefits to which Bruce would otherwise be entitled. Earl Tidrow was aware that Bruce's age and good physical health augured a long life expectancy for him, that Bruce will need custodial care for as long as he lives, and that the cost of such care was increasing. In view of such facts, it would not comport with common sense to have created a gift of total support which would be wholly dissipated in a matter of a few years. On the contrary, the repeated references in the trust to Bruce's "lifetime" as well as the provision that, upon Bruce's death, the remaining assets would be paid to Kim or his descendants argue forcefully for the conclusion that settlor's intent was that the trust would continue throughout Bruce's life and that it would be supplementary to support received from the State. A contrary conclusion would totally frustrate the settlor's intent that his other son Kim would, at least ultimately, derive benefits from the settlor's estate.

Although the trust authorizes and contemplates the bestowal of benefits upon Bruce, it does not mandate payments. Thus, at any given time, Bruce may or may not have in his possession anything received from the trust and nothing had been received at the time this application for benefits was made. The Director's determination that the total assets of the trust are presently available to Bruce is in conflict with the clear intent that the trust would last for the duration of Bruce's life and beyond.

Judgment reversed in favor of Bruce.

Termination and Modification of a Trust

Normally, a settlor cannot revoke or modify a trust unless he reserves the power to do so at the time he establishes the trust. However, a trust may be modified or terminated with the consent of the settlor and all of the beneficiaries. When the settlor is dead or otherwise unable to consent, a trust can be modified or terminated by consent of all the persons with a beneficial interest, but only when this would not frustrate a material purpose of the trust. Because trusts are under the supervisory jurisdiction of a court, the court can permit a deviation from the terms of a trust when unanticipated changes in circumstances threaten accomplishment of the settlor's purpose.

Implied and Constructive Trusts

Under exceptional circumstances in which the creation of a trust is necessary to effectuate a settlor's intent or avoid unjust enrichment, the law *implies* or imposes a trust even though no express trust exists or an express trust exists but has failed. One trust of this type is a **resulting trust,** which arises when there has been an incomplete disposition of trust property. For example, if Hess transferred property to Wickes as trustee to provide for the needs of Hess's grandfather and the grandfather died before the trust funds were exhausted, Wickes will be deemed to hold the property in a resulting trust for Hess or Hess's heirs. Similarly, if Hess had transferred the property to Wickes as trustee and the trust had failed because Hess did not meet one of the requirements of a valid trust, Wickes would not be permitted to keep the trust property as his own. A resulting trust would be implied.

A **constructive trust** is a trust created by operation of law to avoid fraud, injustice, or unjust enrichment. This type of trust imposes on the constructive trustee a duty to convey property he holds to another person on the ground that the constructive trustee would be unjustly enriched if he were allowed to retain it. For example, when a person procures the transfer of property by means of fraud or duress, he becomes a constructive trustee and is under an obligation to return the property to its original owner.

ETHICAL AND PUBLIC POLICY CONCERNS

1. What should a state legislature take into account when adopting a living will statute or a durable power of attorney for health care statute?

2. Why should the law require so much formality to create a valid will? Would it be preferable for the law to lift some of the formalities surrounding wills and allow people to make valid wills orally, by informal letters, or by videotapes or audio recordings?

3. What is the ethical basis of a constructive trust?

SUMMARY

A person may dispose of his property by will if he has testamentary capacity and executes a will in compliance with the formalities required by state statute. State statutes normally require that the will be in writing, that it be witnessed by a specified number of disinterested persons, and that it be published and signed by the testator in the presence of witnesses. A will procured by fraud or undue influence will not be accepted as a valid will. Property that passes to another by operation of law or by a contract such as a life insurance contract is not controlled by the provisions of a will. Surviving spouses have statutory rights to receive a share of the estate of their deceased spouses. A will transfers no interest in property until the death of the testator. The testator can revoke the will at any time before his death. In addition, wills can be revoked by operation of law, such as by the divorce or marriage of the testator after the will has been executed.

As part of the estate planning process, a person may want to plan for the possibility of disability. Most states permit a person to execute a living will, in which he can state his intention to forego life-prolonging medical treatment if there is no chance that he will recover from an illness or accident. A durable power of attorney permits a person to appoint another to make decisions and enter transactions on his behalf if he becomes incapacitated. Some states permit the principal to appoint a special durable power of attorney for health care to give or withhold consent to medical treatment on his behalf if he should become incompetent.

The property of a person who dies intestate (without leaving a valid will) will be distributed to the persons who are his heirs under state intestacy laws, or laws of intestate succession. Real property will descend according to the laws of the state in which the intestate had his permanent home or domicile.

Estates are administered under the supervision of a probate court. If a will exists, the testator may have named a personal representative called an executor to administer his estate. The personal representative for an intestate estate is called an administrator. If there is no will or the named executor cannot serve, the court will select a personal representative. The personal representative has a number of important duties, including the duty to prepare estate and income tax returns. The steps in the administration of an estate include taking an inventory of the assets, having them appraised, determining the creditors and the persons to whom the estate is to be distributed, paying all proper debts, taxes, and expenses, and distributing the remainder to those who are entitled to it.

A trust arises when one person who has legal rights to certain property also has the duty to hold it for the use or benefit of another person. *Inter vivos* trusts are those that are established during the lifetime of the person who created the trust (the settlor). Testamentary trusts are those that are created in a will and take effect at death. Trusts may be expressly created, or they may arise by implication or the operation of law. Totten trusts are created when the depositor opens a bank account *as a trustee* for some other person. They create revocable living trusts. If not revoked at the trustee's death, the beneficiary will receive the money in the account.

Generally, the beneficiary of a trust has the right to assign the principal or interest in his share of the trust and his rights are subject to the claims of his creditors, unless the trust is a spendthrift trust. Normally, the creator of a trust may not revoke or modify the trust unless he reserves the right to do so at the time he establishes it; however, there are some exceptions. The trustee owes a duty to use reasonable skill, judgment, and care in the exercise of his duties. He also owes the beneficiaries a duty of loyalty.

PROBLEM CASES

1. Cunningham died in 1983, leaving a writing that purported to be his will. The writing was on a preprinted will form in which the first and last part of the will were printed and the rest of the will was handwritten by Cunningham. The first paragraph reads: "In the name of God, Amen. I," which is printed, followed by the handwriting: "Thomas John Cunningham—Social Security

MAIN PART IN HANDWRITTEN

number 55–24–3083," which in turn is followed by printing: "being of sound mind, memory and understanding, do make and publish this my Last Will and Testament, in the manner following, that is to say: . . ." This is followed by the body of the will in Cunningham's handwriting, which gives instructions concerning the donation of bodily remains, specific bequests, and the distribution of the remainder of his estate. A printed clause appears after the body of the will, and immediately below this clause is a printed line upon which a testator normally signs his name, at the end of which is printed "Seal." Cunningham did not sign his name on this line; instead, the line contains the signature of a Notary Public of New Jersey, together with his notarial seal impressed over the printed word "Seal." Two people, a realtor (who was also the notary) and the realtor's secretary, witnessed the writing. Cunningham came to the realtor's office with the proposed will fully completed except for the witnesses' signatures. The writing was offered for probate as a will. Is the will valid? *CAN BE Y*

2. In January of 1980, Borsch, age 80, wrote a will dividing his property among several friends and his niece. Borsch had a close friend, Herbert, who had been his friend for 25 years. Borsch saw Herbert and his wife on a daily basis and they frequently ate meals together. Borsch consulted Herbert on all of his business and personal matters. In 1981, Borsch showed Herbert the will that he had previously written. Herbert advised Borsch that it "won't stand up for 30 seconds," and suggested seeing an attorney. In March of 1981, Herbert helped Borsch prepare an inventory of his holdings and accompanied Borsch to an attorney's office. Although Herbert did not sit in on the conferences, he gave the attorneys a small notebook containing a listing of Borsch's properties and a list of the particular percentages allotted to various individuals. In March of 1981, Borsch executed another will leaving virtually all of his property to the Herberts. In July of 1981, Herbert noticed some clerical errors in this will and took Borsch back to the attorney's office for the execution of a new will correcting these errors. Borsch died in November of 1981, leaving no surviving spouse, siblings, or children. The nearest relatives at the time of his death were his niece and nephew. The July 1981 will was offered for probate, and the niece and nephew contested the will on the ground of undue influence. Will they be successful? *No Can't prove undue influence*

3. Roy and Icie Johnson established two revocable *inter vivos* trusts in 1966. The trust provided that upon Roy and Icie's deaths, income from the trusts was to be paid in equal shares to their two sons, James and Robert, for life. Upon the death of the survivor of the sons, the trust was to be *divided equally between all of my grandchildren, per stirpes.* James had two daughters, Barbara and Elizabeth. Robert had four children, David, Rosalyn, Catherine, and Elizabeth. James and Robert disclaimed their interest in the trust in 1979, and a dispute arose about how the trust should be distributed to the grandchildren. The trustee filed an action seeking instructions on how the trusts should be distributed. What should the court hold?

4. Natalie Elson was killed in an automobile accident at the age of 27. She had lived almost all of her life in Illinois, where she pursued a strong interest in horsemanship. After graduating from college in Illinois and receiving further training in horsemanship, she decided to move to Pennsylvania to study dressage. She hoped to compete in the 1984 Olympics as a rider. She told several friends that she intended to return to Illinois after a year. Her stepmother found an unmailed letter that Natalie had written to her sister shortly before her death, stating that she had "moved to Pennsylvania!" When Natalie left for Pennsylvania, she took her horse and a carload of her belongings with her. She left some items in storage in Illinois, and she left her jewelry in a safe-deposit box in Illinois. Upon arriving in Pennsylvania, she opened new bank accounts in Delaware (she lived near the Delaware border) and also established a safe-deposit box there. She retained her Illinois driver's license. Had Natalie changed her domicile to Pennsylvania? *No!*

5. Damme died leaving a valid will, which was admitted to probate. Prior to Damme's death, he owned substantial properties, consisting mostly of land, securities, and crops in storage. A large amount of the land, which was located in five states, was held by Damme in joint tenancy with right of survivorship with his brothers, William and Theodore. In his will, Damme gave his widow a life estate in all of his property. He then distributed the remainder of his estate as follows: he gave all real and personal property he owned in Kansas and all real property other than his Texas property to William and Theodore. He then specified that "[a] like amount in value . . ." should be divided half to his brothers-in-law, Percy and Duane, and half to his five nieces. A dispute arose about whether the property that passed to William and Theodore as joint tenants with right of survivorship should be included in the calculation of "like amount in value" for purposes of determining the amount of the bequest to Percy, Duane, and the five nieces. Should the properties held in joint tenancy be included in the calculation of "like amount in value?" No !

6. Bauert and Lightfoot operated a business partnership. Each took out a policy of life insurance in the amount of $200,000 and named the other as beneficiary. The premiums on the insurance were paid from the partnership bank account. The two men orally agreed that if either of them died, the survivor would use the life insurance proceeds to pay any partnership indebtedness and would pay the remaining proceeds to the widow and heirs of the deceased partner. Bauert died. At the time, the partnership owed a debt of $48,000 to First National Bank. Lightfoot assigned the proceeds of the insurance policy to the bank to partially cover a debt of $400,000 that he personally owed to the bank. Bauert's widow then brought an action against the bank, claiming that she was entitled to the insurance proceeds that exceeded the $48,000 debt. Should the court impose a constructive trust for the benefit of Mrs. Bauert? No !

7. Hotarek's parents were divorced when he was two. For about 13 years after that, Hotarek's mother, Benson, had no contact with him, did not provide financial support to him, and did not display interest in her son. In 1986, at the age of 15, Hotarek was killed in an automobile accident. After his death, his estate settled a claim against the other driver for $20,000 and was awarded uninsured motorist's benefits in the amount of $525,000. These proceeds made up Hotarek's estate. Following Hotarek's death, Benson could not be located.

Once she was located, the probate court ordered half of Hotarek's estate distributed to her in accordance with Connecticut's intestacy statute. It provides that if a person dies intestate leaving no spouse or children, the residue of the estate shall be distributed equally to the decedent's parent or parents. Hotarek's father objected to the distribution to Benson on the ground that she had abandoned her minor child during his life and should not be entitled to share in his estate after his death. Is Benson entitled to share in her intestate son's estate? Yes

8. Weir was a lifelong bachelor. Shortly after World War II, he met Holmstead, a widow who was about his age. They were close friends until Weir died in 1971. Although they had separate apartments, they traveled together, ate their meals together, and were constant companions. In 1956, Weir executed a will that left a life estate to Holmstead and the remainder to his brother, or, if his brother was dead, to his brother's children. In 1965, Weir's brother died. In 1966, Weir executed a new will that left $10,000 each to his niece and nephew and the remainder of his estate to Holmstead. When Weir died, his niece, Margaret, challenged the 1966 will. She claimed that Weir did not have testamentary capacity and that he had been unduly influenced by Holmstead. Margaret said that Weir dressed conservatively, was occasionally forgetful, was sometimes untidy (he left his socks on the floor), and had some strange habits such as picking dust up from the floor and inspecting it. Was Weir's 1966 will invalid on the grounds of lack of capacity and undue influence? No !

CREDIT

CHAPTER 27

INTRODUCTION TO CREDIT AND SECURED TRANSACTIONS

INTRODUCTION

In the United States, a substantial portion of business transactions involves the extension of credit. The term **credit** has many meanings. In this chapter, it will be used to mean transactions in which goods are sold, services are rendered, or money is loaned in exchange for a promise to pay for them at some future date.

In some of these transactions, a creditor is willing to rely on the debtor's promise to pay at a later time; in others, the creditor wants some further assurance or security that the debtor will make good on his promise to pay. This chapter will discuss the differences between secured and unsecured credit and will detail various mechanisms that are available to the creditor who wants to obtain security. These mechanisms include obtaining liens or security interests in personal or real property, sureties, and guarantors. Security interests in real property, sureties and guarantors, and common law liens on personal property will be covered in this chapter, and the Uniform Commerical Code (UCC or Code) rules concerning security interests in personal property will be covered in the Security Interests in Personal Property chapter. The last chapter in this part deals with bankruptcy law, which may come into play when a debtor is unable to fulfill his obligation to pay his debts when they are due.

CREDIT

Unsecured Credit

Many common transactions are based on unsecured credit. For example, a person may have a charge account at a department store or a MasterCard account. If the person buys a sweater and charges it to his charge account or MasterCard account, unsecured credit has been extended to him. He has received goods in return for his promise to pay for them later. Similarly, if a person goes to a dentist to have a tooth filled and the dentist sends him a bill payable by the end of the month, services have been rendered on the basis of unsecured credit. Consumers are not the only people who use unsecured credit. Many transactions between business people utilize it. For example, a retailer buys merchandise or a manufacturer buys raw materials, promising to pay for the merchandise or materials within 30 days after receipt.

The unsecured credit transaction involves a maximum of risk to the creditor—the person who extends the credit. When goods are delivered, services are rendered, or money is loaned on unsecured credit, the creditor gives up all rights in the goods, services, or money. In return, the creditor gets a promise by the debtor to pay or to perform the promised act. If the debtor does not pay or keep the promise, the creditor's options are more limited than if he had obtained security to assure the debtor's performance. One course of action is to bring a lawsuit against the debtor and obtain a judgment. The creditor might then have the sheriff execute the judgment on any property owned by the debtor that is subject to execution. The creditor might also try to **garnish** the wages or other moneys to which the debtor is entitled. However, the debtor might be **judgment-proof;** that is, the debtor may not have any property subject to execution or may not have a steady job. Under these circumstances, execution or garnishment would be of little aid to the creditor in collecting the judgment.

A businessperson may obtain credit insurance to stabilize the credit risk of doing business on an unsecured credit basis. However, he passes the costs of the insurance to the business, or of the unsecured credit losses that the business sustains, on to the consumer. The consumer pays a higher price for goods or services purchased, or a higher interest rate on any money borrowed, from a business that has high credit losses.

Secured Credit

To minimize his credit risk, a creditor may contract for security. The creditor may require the debtor to convey to the creditor a security interest or lien on the debtor's property. Suppose a person borrows $1,000 from a credit union. The credit union might require him to put up his car as security for the loan or might ask that some other person agree to be liable if he defaults. For example, if a student who does not have a regular job goes to a bank to borrow money, the bank might ask that the student's father or mother cosign the note for the loan.

When the creditor has security for the credit he extends and the debtor defaults, the creditor can go against the security to collect the obligation. Assume that a person borrows $8,000 from a bank to buy a new car and that the bank takes a security interest (lien) on the car. If the person fails to make his monthly payments, the bank has the right to repossess the car and have it sold so that it can recover its money. Similarly, if the borrower's father cosigned for the car loan and the borrower defaults, the bank can sue the father to collect the balance due on the loan.

Development of Security

Various types of security devices have been developed as social and economic need for them arose. The rights and liabilities of the parties to a secured transaction depend on the nature of the security, that is, on whether (1) the security pledged is the promise of another person to pay if the debtor does not, or (2) a security interest in goods, intangibles, or real estate is conveyed as security for the payment of a debt or obligation.

If personal credit is pledged, the other person may guarantee the payment of the debt—that is, become a guarantor—or the other person may join the debtor in the debtor's promise to pay, in which case the other person would become surety for the debt.

The oldest and simplest security device was the pledge. To have a pledge valid against third persons with an interest in the goods, such as subsequent purchasers or creditors, it was necessary that the property used as security be delivered to the pledgee or a pledge holder. Upon default by the pledger, the pledgee had the right to sell the property and apply the proceeds to the payment of the debt.

Situations arose in which it was desirable to leave the property used as security in the possession of the debtor. To accomplish this objective, the debtor would give the creditor a bill of sale to the property, thus passing title to the creditor. The bill of sale would provide that if the debtor performed his promise, the bill of sale would become null and void, thus revesting title to the property in the debtor. A secret lien on the goods was created by this device, and the early courts held that such a transaction was a fraud on third-party claimants and void as to them. An undisclosed or secret lien is unfair to creditors who might extend credit to the debtor on the strength of property that they see in the debtor's possession but that in fact is subject to the prior claim of another creditor. Statutes were enacted providing for the recording or filing of the bill of sale, which was later designated as a chattel mortgage. These statutes were not uniform in their provisions. Most of them set up formal requirements for the execution of the chattel mortgage and also stated the effect of recording or filing on the rights of third-party claimants.

To avoid the requirements for the execution and filing of the chattel mortgage, sellers of goods would sell the goods on a "conditional sales contract" under which the seller retained title to the goods until their purchase price had been paid in full. Upon default by the buyer, the seller could (a) repossess the goods or (b) pass title and recover a judgment for the unpaid balance of the purchase price. Abuses of this security device gave rise to some regulatory statutes. About one half of the states enacted statutes that provided that the conditional sales contract was void as to third parties unless it was filed or recorded.

No satisfactory device was developed whereby inventory could be used as security. The inherent difficulty is that inventory is intended to be sold and turned into cash and the creditor is interested in protecting his interest in the cash rather than in maintaining a lien on the sold goods. Field warehousing was used under the pledge, and an after-acquired property clause in a chattel mortgage on a stock of goods held for resale partially fulfilled this need. One of the devices used was the trust receipt. This short-term marketing security arrangement had its origin in the export-import trade. It was later used extensively as a means of financing retailers of consumer goods having a high unit value.

Security Interests in Personal Property

The Security Interests in Personal Property chapter will discuss how a creditor can obtain a security interest in the personal property or fixtures of a debtor. It will also explain the rights to the debtor's property of the creditor, the debtor, and other creditors of the debtor. These security interests are covered by Article 9 of the Uniform Commercial Code, which sets out a comprehensive scheme for regulating security interests in personal property and fixtures. The Code abolishes the old formal distinctions between different types of security devices used to create security interests in personal property.

Security Interests in Real Property

Three types of contractual security devices have been developed by which real estate may be used as security: (1) the real estate mortgage, (2) the trust deed, and (3) the land contract. In addition to these contract security devices, all of the states have enacted statutes granting the right to mechanic's liens on real estate. Security interests in real property are covered later in this chapter.

SURETYSHIP AND GUARANTY

Sureties and Guarantors

As a condition of making a loan, granting credit, or employing someone (particularly as a fiduciary), a creditor may demand that the debtor, contractor, or employee provide as security for his performance the liability of a third person as surety or guarantor. The purpose of the contract of suretyship or guaranty is to provide the creditor with additional protection against loss in the event of default by the debtor, contractor, or employee.

A **surety** is a person who is *liable for the payment of another person's debt or for the performance of another person's duty*. The surety joins with the person primarily liable in promising to make the payment or to perform the duty. For example, Kathleen Kelly, who is 17 years old, buys a used car on credit from Harry's Used Cars. She signs a promissory note, agreeing to pay $75 a month on the note until the note is paid in full. Harry's has Kathleen's father cosign the note; thus, her father is a surety. Similarly, the city of Chicago hires the B&B Construction Company to build a new sewage treatment plant. The city will probably require B&B to have a surety agree to be liable for B&B's performance of its contract. There are insurance companies that, for a fee, will agree to be a surety on the contract of a company such as B&B. If the person who is primarily liable (the principal) defaults, the surety is liable to pay or perform. Upon default, the creditor may ask the surety to pay even if he has not asked the principal debtor to pay. If the surety makes good on his contract of suretyship, he is entitled to be reimbursed by the principal. While a contract of surety does not have to be in writing to be enforceable, it normally is.

A guaranty contract is similar to a suretyship contract in that the promisor agrees to answer for the obligation of another. However, a guarantor does not join the principal in making a promise; rather, a guarantor makes a separate promise and agrees to be liable upon the happening of a certain event. For example, a father tells a merchant, "I will guarantee payment of my son Richard's debt to you if he does not pay it," or "If Richard becomes bankrupt, I will guarantee payment of his debt to you." While a surety is *primarily* liable, a guarantor is *secondarily* liable and can be held to his guarantee only after the principal defaults and cannot be held to his promise or payment. Generally, a guarantor's promise must be made in writing to be enforceable under the statute of frauds.

The rights and liabilities of the surety and the guarantor are substantially the same. No distinction will be made between them in this chapter except where the distinction is of basic importance. Moreover, most commercial contracts and promissory notes today that are to be signed by multiple parties provide for the parties to be "jointly and severally" liable, thus making the surety relationship the predominate one.

Creation of Principal and Surety Relation

The relationship of principal and surety, or that of principal and guarantor, is created by contract. The basic rules of contract law apply in determining the existence and nature of the relationship as well as the rights and duties of the parties.

Defenses of a Surety

Suppose Jeffrey's father agrees to be a surety for Jeffrey on his purchase of a motorcycle. If the motorcycle was defectively made and Jeffrey refuses to make further payments on it, the dealer might try to collect the balance due from Jeffrey's father. As a surety, Jeffrey's father can use any defenses against the dealer that Jeffrey has if they go to the merits of the primary contract. Thus, if Jeffrey has a valid defense of breach of warranty against the dealer, his father can use it as a basis for not paying the dealer.

Other defenses that go to the merits include (1) lack or failure of consideration, (2) inducement of the contract by fraud or duress, and (3) breach of contract by the other party. Certain defenses of the principal cannot be used by the surety. These defenses include lack of capacity, such as minority or insanity, and bankruptcy. Thus, if Jeffrey is only 17 years old, the fact that he is a minor cannot be used by Jeffrey's father to defend against the dealer. This defense of Jeffrey's lack of capacity to contract does not go to the merits of the contract between Jeffrey and the dealer and cannot be used by Jeffrey's father.

A surety contracts to be responsible for the performance of the principal's obligation. If the principal and the creditor change that obligation by agreement, the surety is relieved of responsibility unless the surety agrees to the change. This is because the surety's obligation cannot be changed without his consent.

For example, Fredericks cosigns a note for his friend Kato, which she has given to Credit Union to secure a loan. Suppose the note was originally for $2,500 and payable in 12 months with interest at 11 percent a year. Credit Union and Kato later agree that Kato will have 24 months to repay the note but that the interest will be 13 percent per year. Unless Fredericks consents to this change, he is discharged from his responsibility as surety. The obligation he agreed to assume was altered by the changes in the repayment period and the interest rate.

The most common kind of change affecting a surety is an extension of time to perform the contract. If the creditor merely allows the principal more time without the surety's consent, this does not relieve the surety of responsibility. The surety's consent is required only where there is an actual binding agreement between the creditor and the principal as to the extension of time. In addition, the courts usually make a distinction between **accommodation sureties** and **compensated sureties.** An accommodation surety is a person who acts as a surety without compensation, such as a friend who cosigns a note as a favor. A compensated surety is a person, usually a professional such as a bonding company, who is paid for serving as a surety.

The courts are more protective of accommodation sureties than of compensated sureties. Accommodation sureties are relieved of liability unless they consent to an extension of time. Compensated sureties, on the other hand, must show that they will be harmed by an extension of time before they are relieved of responsibility because of a binding extension without their consent. A compensated surety must show that a change in the contract was both material and prejudicial to him if he is to be relieved of his obligation as surety. This principle is illustrated in the *United States v. Reliance Insurance Co.* case, which follows.

UNITED STATES v. RELIANCE INSURANCE CO. v. ARMY-NAVY '83 FOUNDATION

799 F.2d 1382 (9th Cir. 1986)

On February 18, 1983, the Army-Navy Foundation, a nonprofit organization formed to facilitate preparations for the 1983 Army-Navy game, and the U.S. Military and Naval Academies entered into a contract to play the game at the Rose Bowl in Pasadena. Traditionally, the game was played in Philadelphia. The parties drew the contract to insure that the Academies would receive approximately the same revenue from the 1983 game as they had received from the 1982 game and would not incur additional expenses as a result of the change in location.

The Foundation was entitled to "revenue generated from ticket sales and broadcast rights." The Foundation was required to pay each Academy $875,000–$550,000 from television revenues and $325,000 from ticket sales and concession proceeds. The Foundation agreed to compensate each Academy up to $100,000 for additional costs that were "in excess of those expenses actually incurred by the Army and Navy in conjunction with the 1982 Army-Navy game." Finally, the Foundation agreed to provide funds to transport cadets, midshipmen, and support personnel to Pasadena and to provide housing and meals for them while there.

The contract required the Foundation to obtain two bonds. One bond guaranteed the Foundation's obligation of $650,000 for ticket sales and concession proceeds. The Academies released this bond when they collected the money. The second bond guaranteed the Foundation's obligation to pay up to $200,000 to cover additional expenses incurred by the Academies.

An insurance broker put the Foundation in touch with Reliance Insurance Company to obtain the bonds. Because the Foundation had no assets, Reliance required 100 percent collateral. The Foundation assured Reliance that it was entitled to the television proceeds from the game and by letter dated February 18 assured Reliance that it would assign the television proceeds to it up to the face amount of the bonds. Although initially estimated to be $1,100,000, after negotiation with ABC, the television contract amounted to $1,450,000. The Foundation never made the assignment and on their face the bonds did not mention an assignment of the television proceeds.

Subsequent to the issuance of the bonds, the Academies and the Foundation executed three modifications to the contract. The first modification changed the date of the game from December 3 to November 25; this change was required by ABC. The second modification was required by the National Collegiate Athletic Association and changed the contract to direct payment of the television proceeds to the Army as the host school, rather than to the Foundation. As a result of this modification, the Foundation was entitled to only $350,000 of the television proceeds; however, it was relieved of its $1,100,000 obligation to the Academies. Finally, less than a week before the game, a third modification to the contract was executed. Because the air carriers hired to transport the cadets, midshipmen, and support personnel to Pasadena unexpectedly required payment prior to takeoff and the Foundation was unable to meet its contractual responsibility to make such payments because it had not yet received any ticket or television revenue, the Academies made the payments. In turn, the Foundation waived its rights to ticket revenue already retained by the Academies, which was payable to the Foundation, and to television revenues in excess of $1,100,000 (i.e., $350,000).

The only persons who had knowledge of both the Foundation's assurance that Reliance would receive an assignment of the television proceeds and the three subsequent modifications to the contract were the officers of the Foundation. Reliance knew nothing of the modifications to the contract and the Academies knew nothing of the agreement to assign the television proceeds to Reliance. When the Foundation failed to pay for the Academies' additional expenses, the Academies brought suit to recover on the bond provided by Reliance. The trial court held for Reliance and the Foundation appealed.

Jameson, District Judge. The primary issue is whether modifications of the bonded contract exonerate Reliance. As a general rule a surety will be discharged where a bonded contract is materially altered or changed without the surety's knowledge or consent. In addition, where, as here, a compensated surety seeks exoneration, it must show that the alteration caused prejudice or damage. Thus Reliance must demonstrate that the modifications were material and that some prejudices resulted.

The second modification had no net effect. The Foundation lost the rights to $1,100,000 in television revenues, but it was also relieved of its obligation to guarantee that amount. The third modification did not relieve the Foundation of its obligation to pay the airlines. The language of the third modification clearly indicates that the Foundation remained liable for the costs of transportation. The third modification merely shifted from the Foundation to the Academies the immediate burden of providing funds for transportation. In exchange, the Foundation relinquished its sole remaining right of any significance under the contract—the right to receive the excess television revenues.

The Academies argue that this court should view the modifications of the contract only to the extent they modify the Foundation's obligation which was the subject of the bond in question—the obligation to cover the Academies' additional expenses for the football team. Because the modifications did not affect this obligation, the Academies argue that there was no material alteration of the bonded contract. This view is much too narrow. First, courts construe a bond and its underlying contract together. Second, the bond specifically incorporated the contract. Reliance guaranteed the Foundation's obligation on the basis of the entire contract, not just a single provision. When the bond and its underlying contract are viewed together, it is clear that the modifications were both material and prejudicial.

The contract funded the otherwise assetless Foundation with ticket, concession, and television proceeds. These funds provided the Foundation with a means to satisfy its obligations. As evidenced by the Foundations's February 18 letter promising to assign television proceeds, Reliance relied on the Foundation's funding as provided in the original contract. As the District Court concluded, "The impact of the third modification on the Foundation was that it was deprived of the excess television revenues on which it depended to meet its contractual obligations, including those secured by the bond in question." Absent the provision that the Foundation would receive the television proceeds, Reliance would likely have determined the risk was too great and declined to issue the bonds. Had there been no third modification, the Foundation may have had funds available to cover its obligations. The prejudice suffered by Reliance is the increased risk resulting from the modifications. As the Court of Appeals for the District of Columbia has stated:

> A surety company is not a public utility. It may, for any or no reason conclude not to furnish its bond with respect to a particular contract. When it has committed itself with respect to one contract, amendments which convert that agreement into a significantly different one should be brought to the attention of the surety so that it may exercise its own business judgment as to whether it wishes to continue its commitment. It is not for the parties to the contract to decide among themselves that their amendments are of no interest to the surety, at least when, as here, those amendments go beyond mere matters of form.

The modifications of the contract between the Academies and the Foundation were material, at least one of which, the third, was prejudicial to the rights of Reliance as surety. Reliance had no knowledge of the modifications and did not consent to them.

Judgment for Reliance affirmed.

If the debtor's obligation to the creditor is paid or satisfied, the surety is discharged from her obligation.

Creditor's Duties to Surety

The creditor is required to disclose any material facts about the risk involved to the surety. If he does not do so, the surety is relieved of liability. For example, a bank (creditor) knows that an employee, Arthur, has been guilty of criminal conduct in the past. If the bank applies to a bonding company to obtain a bond on Arthur, the bank must disclose this information about Arthur. Similarly, suppose the bank has an employee, Alison, covered by a bond and discovers that Alison is embezzling money. If the bank agrees to give Alison another chance but does not report her actions to the bonding company, the bonding company is relieved of responsibility for further wrongful acts by Alison.

If the debtor posts security for the performance of an obligation, the creditor must not surrender the security without the consent of the surety. If the creditor does so, the surety is relieved of liability to the extent of the value surrendered.

Subrogation, Reimbursement, and Contribution

If the surety has to perform or pay the principal's obligation, then the surety acquires all of the rights that the creditor had against the principal. This is known as the surety's **right of subrogation.** The rights acquired could include the right to any collateral in the possession of the creditor, any judgment right the creditor had against the principal on the obligation, and the rights of a creditor in bankruptcy proceedings.

If the surety performs or pays the principal's obligation, she is entitled to recover her costs from the principal; this is known as the surety's **right to reimbursement.** For example, Amado cosigns a promissory note for $250 at the credit union for her friend Anders. Anders defaults on the note, and the credit union collects $250 from Amado on her suretyship obligation. Amado then not only gets the credit union's rights against Anders, but also the right to collect $250 from Anders.

Suppose several persons (Tom, Dick, and Harry) are cosureties of their friend Sam. When Sam defaults, Tom pays the whole obligation. Tom is entitled to collect one third from both Dick and Harry since he paid more than his prorated share. This is known as the cosurety's **right to contribution.** The relative shares of cosureties, as well as any limitations on their liability, are normally set out in the contract of suretyship.

LIENS ON PERSONAL PROPERTY

Common Law Liens

Under the common—or judge-made—law, artisans, innkeepers, and common carriers (such as airlines and trucking companies) were entitled to liens to secure the reasonable value of the services they performed. An artisan such as a furniture upholsterer or an auto mechanic uses his labor or materials to improve personal property that belongs to someone else. The improvement becomes part of the property and belongs to the owner of the property. Therefore, the artisan who made the improve-

ment is given a **lien** on the property until he is paid. For example, the upholsterer who recovers a sofa for a customer is entitled to a lien on the sofa.

The innkeeper and common carrier are in business to serve the public and are required by law to do so. Under the common law, the innkeeper, to secure payment for his reasonable charges for food and lodging, was allowed to claim a lien on the property that the guest brought to the hotel or inn. Similarly, the common carrier, such as a trucking company, was allowed to claim a lien on the goods carried for the reasonable charges for the service. The justification for such liens was that the innkeeper and common carrier were entitled to the protection of a lien because they were required by law to provide the service to anyone seeking it.

Statutory Liens

While common law liens are still generally recognized today, many states have incorporated this concept into statutes. Some of the state statutes have created additional liens, while others have modified the common law liens to some extent. The statutes commonly provide a procedure for foreclosing the lien. **Foreclosure** is the method by which a court authorizes the sale of the personal property subject to the lien so that the creditor can obtain the money to which he is entitled.

Carriers' liens and warehousemen's liens are provided for in Article 7, Documents of Title, of the Code. They are covered in the Checks and Documents of Title chapter.

Characteristics of Liens

The common law lien and most of the statutory liens are known as **possessory liens.** They give the artisan or other lienholder the right to keep possession of the debtor's property until the reasonable charges for services have been paid. For the lien to come into play, possession of the goods must have been entrusted to the artisan. Suppose a person takes a chair to an upholsterer to have it repaired. The upholsterer can keep possession of the chair until the person pays the reasonable value of the repair work. However, if the upholsterer comes to the person's home to make the repair, the upholsterer would not have a lien on the chair as the person did not give up possession of it.

The two essential elements of the lien are: (1) possession by the improver or the provider of services and (2) a debt created by the improvement or the provision of services concerning the goods. If the artisan or other lienholder gives up the goods voluntarily, he loses the lien. For example, if a person has a new engine put in his car and the mechanic gives the car back to him before he pays for the engine, the mechanic loses the lien on the car to secure the person's payment for the work and materials. However, if the person uses a spare set of keys to regain possession, or does so by fraud or another illegal act, the lien is not lost. Once the debt has been paid, the lien is terminated and the artisan or other lienholder no longer has the right to retain the goods. If the artisan keeps the goods after the debt has been paid, or keeps the goods without the right to a lien, he is liable for conversion or unlawful detention of goods.

Another important aspect of common law liens is that the work or service must have been performed at the request of the owner of the property. If the work or service is performed without the consent of the owner, no lien is created. This is one of the issues raised in the *Navistar Financial Corporation v. Allen's Corner Garage and Towing Service, Inc.* case that follows.

NAVISTAR FINANCIAL CORPORATION v. ALLEN'S CORNER GARAGE AND TOWING SERVICE, INC.

505 N.E.2d 1321 (Ill. App. Ct. 1987)

Wieslaw Wik was the owner of a truck tractor on which Navistar Financial Corporation held a lien to secure a purchase loan agreement. On February 21, 1986, Wik was driving his truck tractor and pulling a trailer owned by the V. Seng Teaming Company. The tractor/trailer unit overturned in a ditch. Allen's Corner Garage and Towing Service was called by the Illinois State Police. Its crew removed the cargo from the trailer and hoisted the tractor and trailer out of the ditch and onto the highway. They then took the truck, trailer, and cargo to Allen's garage for storage. The uprighting and towing of semitrailer trucks is an intricate process and involves a good deal of specialized equipment. Allen's was licensed by the Interstate Commerce Commission and the Illinois Commerce Commission as a common carrier and owned over 50 specialized trucks and trailers for such operations.

Wik defaulted on his loan agreement with Navistar and the right to possession passed to Navistar. One of its employees contacted Allen's and offered to pay the towing plus storage charges on the truck in exchange for possession of it. Allen's refused, saying it would not release the truck unless the charges for the truck, trailer, and cargo were all paid. Navistar then brought suit against Allen's to recover possession of the truck. Subsequently, V. Seng Teaming Company paid $13,000 in towing and storage charges on the trailer and cargo and took possession of them. Navistar then reiterated its willingness to pay the towing charges but refused to pay any storage charges accruing after its initial offer.

The trial court held that Allen's had a common law artisan's lien against the tractor for towing charges but not for storage fees. It held that Navistar was entitled to possession of the tractor, subject to payment of $1,162 for towing. Allen's appealed and Navistar cross-appealed the portion of the order granting Allen's a common law lien for towing.

Unverzagt, Judge. Illinois recognizes the common law possessory lien. Such liens are fundamentally consensual in nature and can be created only by agreement, by some fixed rule of law, or by usage of trade or commerce. The common law lien has no provision for forfeiture and sale, but is limited to the right to possession of the chattel until all charges are paid. The lien applies to categories of persons: (1) those who impart added value to the property and (2) common carriers who are bound by law to accept and carry the goods. In Illinois, a common carrier has a lien on goods delivered to it for carriage; the carrier is not bound to part with the goods until the charges are paid.

Allen's argues that its services fall within both categories of common law liens. It claims that its towing and cargo salvaging operations are so specialized as to qualify it as an artisan, or alternatively, that it is a common carrier. Navistar responds that Allen's is not an artisan, citing a number of cases from Illinois and from foreign jurisdictions for the principle that mere towing of a vehicle, no matter how difficult or specialized, does not give rise to a common law lien. Most of these cases are distinguishable as they involve towing of a vehicle without the owner's consent. Nonetheless, we agree with Navistar that mere towing of a vehicle from one place to another does not add anything of value to the "intrinsic value" of the vehicle towed.

We agree with Allen's, however, that it is entitled to a lien as a common carrier. As a common carrier, it is entitled to a lien for carriage charges. Navistar does not directly challenge this conclusion, but argues that Allen's towed the tractor without its consent. As an agreement is a necessary element of a common law lien, Navistar's lack of consent would defeat Allen's lien. Although police have the power to remove disabled vehicles from highways, they may not create a lien upon a vehicle without the owner's consent. John Allen testified that a representative from Seng was at the scene when he arrived and that the entire unit was under Seng's control. Allen also testified that the driver came to Allen's place of business the following day. Testifying later, Allen stated unequivocally that Allen's Corner Garage was authorized to make the tow. The court could have concluded that the representative of Seng was authorized to and did give his consent to the towing, or that the driver subsequently ratified these actions.

Having decided that Allen's was entitled to a common law lien as a common carrier, we now turn to the question of whether it may also claim a lien for storage charges. The rule has been stated that when a common carrier hauls freight and then stores it at the destination until claimed by the receiver, the carrier becomes a warehouseman and obtains a lien for storage charges. [Citations omitted.] In those cases, the commodities involved, coal and grain, required special handling and storage. The carrier in each case sustained some inconvenience or expense by storing the property until the receiver was ready to remove it.

In the present case, Allen's did not keep the truck on the lot for the benefit of Navistar, but did so only to preserve its lien right. A garage owner is not entitled to a lien for storage in a garage. Since Allen's retained and stored the truck for no reason other than to be able to insist on its lien rights, the trial court was correct in denying it a lien for storage charges.

Judgment affirmed.

Foreclosure of Lien

The right of a lienholder to possess goods does not automatically give the lienholder the right to sell the goods or to claim ownership if his charges are not paid. Commonly, there is a procedure provided by statute for selling property once it has been held for a certain period of time. The lienholder is required to give notice to the debtor and to advertise the proposed sale by posting or publishing notices. If there is no statutory procedure, the lienholder must first bring a lawsuit against the debtor. After obtaining a judgment for his charges, the lien-holder can have the sheriff seize the property and have it sold at a judicial sale.

SECURITY INTERESTS IN REAL PROPERTY

There are three basic contract devices for using real estate as security for an obligation: (1) the real estate mortgage, (2) the deed of trust, and (3) the land contract. In addition, the states have enacted statutes giving mechanics such as carpenters and plumbers, and materialmen such as lumberyards, a right to a lien on real property into which their labor or materials have been incorporated.

Historical Developments of Mortgages

A **mortgage** is a security interest in real property or a deed to real property that is given by the owner (the **mortgagor**) as security for a debt owed to the creditor (the **mortgagee**). The real estate mortgage was used as a form of security in England as early as the middle of the 12th century, but our present-day mortgage law developed from the common law mortgage of the 15th century. The common law mortgage was a deed that conveyed the land to the mortgagee, with the title to the land to return to the mortgagor upon payment of the debt secured by the mortgage. The mortgagee was given possession of the land during the term of the mortgage. If the mortgagor defaulted on the debt, the mortgagee's title to the land became absolute. The land was forfeited as a penalty, but the forfeiture did not discharge the debt. In addition to keeping the land, the mortgagee could sue on the debt, recover a judgment, and seek to collect the debt.

The early equity courts did not favor the imposition of penalties and would relieve mortgagors from such forfeitures, provided that the mortgagor's default was minor and was due to causes beyond his control. Gradually, the courts became more lenient in permitting redemptions and allowed the mortgagor to **redeem** (reclaim his property) if he tendered performance without unreasonable delay. Finally, the courts of equity recognized the mortgagor's right to redeem as an absolute right that would continue until the mortgagee asked the court of equity to decree that the mortgagor's right to redeem be foreclosed and cut off. Our present law regarding the foreclosure of mortgages developed from this practice.

Today, the mortgage is generally viewed as a lien on land rather than a conveyance of title to the land. There are still some states where the mortgagor goes through the process of giving the mortgagee some sort of legal title to the property. Even in these states, however, the mortgagee's title is minimal and the real ownership of the property remains in the mortgagor.

Form, Execution, and Recording

Because the real estate mortgage conveys an interest in real property, it must be executed with the same formality as a deed. Unless it is executed with the required formalities, it will not be eligible for recording in the local land records. Recordation of the mortgage does not affect its validity as between the mortgagor and the mortgagee. However, if it is not recorded, it will not be effective against subsequent purchasers of the property or creditors, including other mortgagees, who have no notice of the earlier mortgage. It is important to the mortgagee that the mortgage be recorded so that the world will be on notice of the mortgagee's interest in the property. See Figure 1 for an example of a mortgage.

Rights and Liabilities

The owner (mortgagor) of property subject to a mortgage can sell the interest in the property without the consent of the mortgagee. However, the sale does not affect the mortgagee's interest in the property or the mortgagee's claim against the mortgagor. In some cases, the mortgage may provide that if the property is sold, then any remaining balance becomes immediately due and payable. This is known as a "due on sale" clause.

Suppose Eric Smith owns a lot on a lake. He wants to build a cottage on the land, so he borrows $35,000 from First National Bank. He signs a note for $35,000 and gives the bank a $35,000 mortgage on the land and cottage as security for his repayment of the loan. Several years later, Smith sells his land and cottage to Melinda Mason. The mortgage he gave First National might make the unpaid balance due on the mortgage payable on sale. If it does not, Smith can sell the property with the mortgage on it. If Mason defaults on making the mortgage payments, the bank can foreclose on the mortgage. If at the foreclosure sale the property does not bring enough money to cover the costs, interest, and balance due on the mortgage, First National is entitled to a deficiency judgment against Smith. However, some courts are reluctant to give deficiency judgments where real property is used as security for a debt. If on foreclosure the property sells for more than the debt, Mason is entitled to the surplus.

A purchaser of mortgaged property may buy it **subject to** the mortgage or may **assume** the mortgage. If she buys subject to the mortgage and there is a default and foreclosure, the purchaser is not personally liable for any deficiency. The property is liable for the mortgage debt and can be sold to satisfy it in case of default; in addition, the original mortgagor remains liable for its payment. If the buyer assumes the mortgage, then she becomes personally liable for the debt and for any deficiency on default and foreclosure.

FIGURE 1   A Mortgage

MORTGAGE

THIS INDENTURE, made this 18th day of October, A.D. 1992, BETWEEN Raymond A. Dole and Deborah H. Dole, hereinafter called the Mortgagor, and First Federal Savings and Loan Association, hereinafter called the Mortgagee,

WITNESSETH, That the said Mortgagor, for and in consideration of the sum of One Dollar, to us in hand paid by the said Mortgagee, the receipt whereof is hereby acknowledged, have granted, bargained, and sold to the said Mortgagee, its heirs and assigns forever, the following described land situate, lying and being in the County of Genesee, State of Michigan, to wit:

All that certain plot, piece, or parcel of land located in the County of Genesee, State of Michigan and known and described as Lot number Thirty-nine (39) in William D. Green's subdivision of part of Lot numbered Twenty-two (22) in Square numbered Twelve Hundred Nineteen (1219), as per plot recorded in the Office of the Surveyor for the County of Genesee in Liber 30 at folio 32, together with the buildings and improvements thereon, and the said Mortgagor do hereby fully warrant the title to said land, and will defend the same against the lawful claims of all persons whomsoever.

PROVIDED ALWAYS, That if said Mortgagor, their heirs, legal representatives, or assigns shall pay unto the said Mortgagee, its legal representatives or assigns, a certain promissory note dated the 18th day of October, A.D. 1992, for the sum of Thirty-eight Thousand Dollars ($38,000.00), payable in monthly installments of Three Hundred Fifteen Dollars ($315.00) with interest at ten percent (10%) beginning on November 18, 1992, and signed by Raymond A. Dole and Deborah H. Dole and shall perform, comply with, and abide by this mortgage, and shall pay all taxes which may accrue on said land and all costs and expenses said Mortgagee may be put to in collecting said promissory note by foreclosure of this mortgage or otherwise, including a reasonable attorney's fee, then this mortgage and the estate hereby created shall cease and be null and void.

IN WITNESS WHEREOF, the said Mortgagor hereunto set their hands and seals the day and year first above written. Signed, sealed, and delivered in presence of us:

John R. Bacon) *Raymond A. Dole*

James A. Brown) *Deborah H. Dole*

ACKNOWLEDGEMENT OF MORTGAGE
State of Michigan   )
County of Genesee) s s

I, an officer authorized to take acknowledgments according to the laws of the State of Michigan, duly qualified and acting, HEREBY CERTIFY that Raymond A. Dole and Deborah H. Dole to me personally known, this day personally appeared and acknowledged before me that they executed the foregoing Mortgage, and I further certify that I know the said persons making said acknowledgment to be the individuals described in and who executed the said Mortgage.
Susan B. Clark
Notary Public

Susan B. Clark

Susan B. Clark
Notary Public

The creditor (mortgagee) may assign his interest in the mortgaged property. To do this, the mortgagee must assign the mortgage as well as the debt for which the mortgage is security. In most jurisdictions, the negotiation of the note carries with it the right to the security and the holder of the note is entitled to the benefits of the mortgage.

Foreclosure

Foreclosure is the process by which any rights of the mortgagor or the current property owner are cut off. Foreclosure proceedings are regulated by statute in the state in which the property is located. In many states, two or more alternative methods of foreclosure are available to the mortgagee or his assignee. The methods in common use today are (1) strict foreclosure, (2) action and sale, and (3) power of sale.

A small number of states permit what is called **strict foreclosure**. The creditor keeps the property in satisfaction of the debt, and the owner's rights are cut off. This means that the creditor has no right to a deficiency and the debtor has no right to any surplus. Strict foreclosure is normally limited to situations where the amount of the debt exceeds the value of the property.

Foreclosure by **action and sale** is permitted in all states, and it is the only method of foreclosure permitted in some states. Although the state statutes are not uniform, they are alike in their basic requirements. In a foreclosure by action and sale, suit is brought in a court having jurisdiction. Any party having a property interest that would be cut off by the foreclosure must be made a defendant, and if any such party has a defense, he must enter his appearance and set up his defense. After the case is tried, a judgment is entered and a sale of the property ordered. The proceeds of the sale are applied to the payment of the mortgage debt, and any surplus is paid over to the mortgagor. If there is a deficiency, a deficiency judgment is, as a general rule, entered against the mortgagor and such other persons as are liable on the debt. Deficiency judgments are generally not permitted where the property sold is the residence of the debtor.

The right to foreclose under a **power of sale** must be expressly conferred on the mortgagee by the terms of the mortgage. If the procedure for the exercise of the power is set out in the mortgage, that procedure must be followed. Several states have enacted statutes that set out the procedure to be followed in the exercise of a power of sale. No court action is required. As a general rule, notice of the default and sale must be given to the mort-

gagor. After the statutory period, the sale may be held. The sale must be advertised, and it must be at auction. The sale must be conducted fairly, and an effort must be made to sell the property at the highest price obtainable. The proceeds of the sale are applied to the payment of costs, interest, and the principal of the debt. Any surplus must be paid to the mortgagor. If there is a deficiency and the mortgagee wishes to recover a judgment for the deficiency, he must bring suit on the debt.

Right of Redemption

At common law and under existing statutes, the mortgagor or an assignee of the mortgagor has what is called an **equity of redemption** in the mortgaged real estate. This means that he has the absolute right to discharge the mortgage when due and to have title to the mortgaged property restored free and clear of the mortgage debt. Under the statutes of all states, the mortgagor or any party having an interest in the mortgaged property that will be cut off by the foreclosure may redeem the property after default and before the mortgagee forecloses the mortgage. In several states, the mortgagor or any other party in interest is given by statute what is known as a redemption period (usually six months or one year, beginning either after the foreclosure proceedings are started or after a foreclosure sale of the mortgaged property has been made) in which to pay the mortgaged debt, costs, and interest and to redeem the property.

As a general rule, if a party in interest wishes to redeem, he must, if the redemption period runs after the foreclosure sale, pay to the purchaser at the foreclosure sale the amount that the purchaser has paid plus interest up to the time of redemption. If the redemption period runs before the sale, the party in interest must pay the amount of the debt plus the costs and interest. The person who wishes to redeem from a mortgage foreclosure sale must redeem the entire mortgage interest; he cannot redeem a partial interest by paying a proportionate amount of the debt or by paying a proportionate amount of the price bid at the foreclosure sale.

Deed of Trust

States typically use either the mortgage or the **deed of trust** as the primary mechanism for holding a security interest in real property. There are three parties to a deed of trust: (1) the owner of the property who borrows the money (the debtor), (2) the trustee who holds legal title to the property put up as security, and (3) the lender who is the beneficiary of the trust. The trustee serves as a fiduciary for both the creditor and the debtor. The purpose of the deed of trust is to make it easy for the security to be liquidated. However, most states treat the deed of trust like a mortgage in giving the borrower a relatively long period of time to redeem the property, thereby defeating this rationale for the arrangement.

In a deed of trust transaction, the borrower deeds to the trustee the property that is to be put up as security. See Figure 2 for an example of a deed of trust. The trust agreement usually gives the trustee the right to foreclose or sell the property if the debtor fails to make a required payment on the debt. Normally, the trustee does not sell the property until the lender notifies him that the borrower is in default and demands that the property be sold. The trustee must notify the debtor that he is in default and that the land will be sold. The trustee advertises the property for sale. After the statutory period, the trustee will sell the property at a public or private sale. The proceeds are applied to the costs of the foreclosure, interest, and debt. If there is a surplus, it is paid to the borrower. If there is a deficiency, the lender has to sue the borrower on the debt and recover a judgment.

Land Contracts

The **land contract** is a device for securing the balance due the seller on the purchase price of real estate. Essentially it is an installment contract for the purchase of

---

FIGURE 2   A Deed of Trust

DEED OF TRUST

THIS DEED made this 14th day of August, 1992, by and between Harold R. Holmes, grantor, party of the first part, and Frederick B. Cannon, trustee, party of the second part, and Sarah A Miles, party of the third part,

WITNESSETH:

The party of the first part does hereby grant unto the party of the second part, the following described property located in the District of Columbia and known as Lot number One Hundred Fourteen (114) in James B. Nicholson's subdivision in Square numbered Twelve Hundred Forty-seven (1247), formerly Square numbered Seventy-seven (77), "Georgetown," as per plat recorded in the Office of the Surveyor for the District of Columbia in Liber Georgetown 2 at folio 34, in trust, however, to secure the balance only of the purchase price of the above described premises, evidenced by the following described obligation:

Promissory note executed by the party of the first part, payable to the party of the third part and dated August 14, 1992, in the principal sum of Sixty-four Thousand Dollars ($64,000.00) bearing interest at the rate of ten percent (10%) per annum until paid. Said principal and interest are payable in monthly installments of Seven Hundred Thirty-five Dollars ($735.00) on the 14th day of each and every month beginning September 14, 1992, and continuing every month thereafter, with the unpaid balance of said principal and interest due and payable in full on August 14, 2002.

IN WITNESS WHEREOF, the party of the first part has set his hand and seal this the day and year first above written.

Harold R. Holmes

(SEAL)

Acknowledgment
This Deed of Trust accepted this 14th day of August, 1992.

Frederick B. Cannon

Trustee

land. The buyer agrees to pay the purchase price over a period of time. The seller agrees to convey title to the property to the buyer when the full price is paid. Usually, the buyer takes possession of the property, pays the taxes, insures the property, and assumes the other obligations of an owner. However, the seller keeps legal title and does not turn over the deed until the purchase price is paid.

If the buyer defaults, the seller usually has the right to declare a forfeiture and take over possession of the property. The buyer's rights to the property are cut off at that point. Most states give the buyer on a land contract a limited period of time to redeem his interest. Moreover, some states require the seller to go through a foreclosure proceeding. Generally, the procedure for declaring a forfeiture and recovering property sold on a land contract is simpler and less time-consuming than foreclosure of a mortgage. In most states, the procedure in case of default is set out by statute. If the buyer, after default, voluntarily surrenders possession to the seller, no court procedure is necessary; the seller's title will become absolute, and the buyer's equity will be cut off.

Purchases of farm property are commonly financed through the use of land contracts. See Figure 3 for an example of a land contract. As an interest in real estate, a land contract should be in writing and recorded in the local land records so as to protect the interests of both parties.

As can be seen in the following case, *Looney v. Farmers Home Administration*, some courts have invoked the equitable doctrine against forfeitures and have required that the seller on a land contract must foreclose on the property in order to avoid injustice to a defaulting buyer.

LOONEY v. FARMERS HOME ADMINISTRATION

794 F.2d 310 (7th Cir. 1986)

On October 7, 1976, Lowry and Helen McCord entered into a land contract to purchase a 260-acre farm from John and Esther Looney for $250,000. The contract specified that this was to be amortized over a 20-year period at an annual interest rate of 7 percent. The McCords were to make annual payments of $23,280 on November 15 of each year until the purchase price and all accrued interest was paid. They also agreed to pay real estate taxes, insurance, and maintenance costs for the property.

Four years later, the McCords received an economic emergency loan of $183,000 from the Farmers Home Administration (FmHA). They signed a promissory note for the amount of the loan with interest at 11 percent and, as security, also granted the FmHA a second mortgage on the land subject to the land sales contract.

The McCords subsequently defaulted on their obligations to the Looneys. At the time of the default, the McCords had paid $123,280 to the Looneys but still owed $249,360.12 on the contract price. At the time, the property was worth $455,000. The Looneys brought suit against the McCords and the FmHA seeking to eject the McCords from the property and forfeiture of the contract. The FmHA objected to the proposed forfeiture and argued that the court should order foreclosure proceedings.

The district court denied the FmHA's motion for foreclosure. It held that the traditional presumption under Indiana law did not apply because the McCords had made only minimal payments on the contract and had not paid their fall taxes or insurance installments. Because $249,360.12 was still owed on an initial base price of $250,000, the court found the McCords's equity to be $639.88, only .26 percent of the principal. The court therefore found forfeiture appropriate, awarded the FmHA $639.88 and extinguished the FmHA's mortgage. The FmHA appealed.

Cudahy, Circuit Judge.   Under Indiana law a conditional land sales contract is considered in the nature of a secured transaction, "the provisions of which are subject to all proper and just remedies at law and in equity." *Skendzel v. Marshall*. Recognizing the common law maxim that "equity abhors forfeitures," the *Skendzel* court concluded that "judicial foreclosure of a land sales contract is in consonance with the notions of equity developed in American jurisprudence." Foreclosure generally protects the rights of all parties to a contract. Upon judicial sale the proceeds are first applied to the balance of the contract principal and interest owed the seller. Then, any junior lienholders take their share. Any surplus goes to the buyer.

Skendzel recognized, however, two instances where forfeiture was the appropriate remedy:

In the case of an abandoning, absconding vendee, forfeiture is a logical and equitable remedy. Forfeiture would also be appropriate where the vendee has paid a minimal amount on the contract at the time of default and seeks to retain possession while the vendor is paying taxes, insurance, and other upkeep in order to preserve the premises.

The district court did not rely on the first *Skendzel* exception in finding forfeiture appropriate. No evidence in the record supports such a finding.

If forfeiture is justified, then, it is only because the second *Skendzel* exception is met. This requires that the vendee have paid only a minimum amount on the contract at the time of default. In this case, the district court concluded that "this is patently a situation contemplated by the court in *Skendzel* in which forfeiture is the logical and equitable remedy." However, the buyers in *Skendzel* had in fact paid more than a minimum amount on the contract and the court cited no examples of what would "patently" constitute a "minimum amount." Rather, later Indiana cases have interpreted *Skendzel* as requiring a case by case analysis that examines the totality of circumstances surrounding the contract and its performance.

Here, while $123,280 was paid to the Looneys, the court considered all but $639.88 to be interest rather than a part of the contract price. The court equated contract price with what was paid to reduce principal. But nothing in Indiana law compels the district court's construction of payments on the contract. On the contrary, several Indiana courts have considered and given weight to both payments to reduce principal and those to reduce interest in determining whether a buyer falls within the second *Skendzel* exception.

Even where no principal is paid, a buyer's stake in the property may be sufficient to justify foreclosure. Here, two uncontested affidavits indicate the property to be worth over $200,000 more than the McCords owe the Looneys. With the evidence of appreciation, the court was incorrect to conclusively value the McCords' equity at only $639.88.

When the second *Skendzel* exception has been invoked it frequently has been because the vendee is contributing to a decline in the value of the security. There is no allegation or evidence of waste in this case. Even the Looneys admit that the buyers "had paid substantial monies pursuant to the terms of the contracts." The Looneys received $123,280 and the McCords paid the necessary real estate taxes, insurance premiums and upkeep expenses for over six years. The Looneys make no showing that foreclosure would not satisfy their interest and the court below made no such determination. While foreclosure would appear to satisfy all parties' needs, forfeiture leaves the FmHA with a $639.88 recovery on a $183,800 loan. In view of the "totality of circumstances" this result seems inequitable.

Judgment reversed in favor of Farmers Home Administration.

FIGURE 3 A Land Contract

LAND CONTRACT

THIS AGREEMENT, made this 15th day of September, A.D. 1992, between Sarah A. Collins, a single woman, hereinafter designed "Vendor," and Robert H. Bowen, a single man, hereinafter designated "Vendee," in the manner following: The Vendor hereby agrees to sell and the Vendee agrees to buy all that certain piece or parcel of land being in the Township of Fenton, County of Genesee and State of Michigan, and more particularly described as follows:

Part of the Northeast ¼ of the Northwest ¼ of Section 20, Township 5 North, Range 5 East, described as follows: Beginning at a point on the North line of said Section 20, which is West along said North line, 797.72 feet from the North ¼ corner of said Section 20; thence continuing West along said North line, 522.72 feet; thence South 0 degrees, 18 minutes, 12 seconds East along the West ⅛ line of said Section, 1000.0 feet; thence East parallel to the North line of said Section, 522.72 feet; thence North 0 degrees, 18 minutes, 12 seconds West parallel to said West ⅛ line 1000.0 feet to the point of beginning, containing 12.0 acres of land, more or less, and known as 1135 Long Lake Road.

Subject to all easements, laws, ordinances, reservations, applying to this property.

For the sum of Sixty-four Thousand Nine Hundred Dollars ($64,900.00), payable as follows: Ten Thousand Dollars ($10,000.00), cash in hand, receipt of which is hereby acknowledged before the signing of this contract and the balance payable as follows: Three Hundred Dollars ($300.00) or more payable on the 1st day of November, 1992, and a like amount on the 1st day of each and every month thereafter until the full sum of both interest and principal has been paid in full. Interest at the rate of ten percent (10%) per annum, starting October 1, 1992, shall be deducted from each and every monthly payment and the balance applied on the principal. The entire balance, both principal and interest, to be paid in full on or before 5 years from date of closing. It is understood and agreed that the above monthly payment includes taxes and insurance that may become due and payable subsequent to the date of this contract; said amounts to be paid by Vendor and added to the principal balance.

Vendee also agrees to pay all taxes and assessments extraordinary as well as ordinary that may be levied thereon, including taxes for the year 1992, and also deferred payments on special assessments that shall become due and payable after the date thereof to be prorated to date.

The Vendee agrees to keep the buildings upon or to be placed upon the premises insured against damage by fire and wind, in such company and amount as is approved by the Vendor, for the benefit of all parties in interest; such policies shall be delivered to and held by the Vendor.

And Vendee agrees to keep the buildings and other improvements on the premises in good repair. In case the Vendee shall fail to pay taxes, effect insurance, or make necessary repairs, the Vendor may do any or all of these things and the amount paid therefore by the Vendor shall be deemed a part of the principal sum under this contract and become payable immediately with interest at the rate of ten percent (10%) per annum until paid.

The Vendor on receiving payment in full of the principal and interest, and of all other sums chargeable under the contract, agrees, at his own proper cost and expense, to execute and deliver to the Vendee, or to his assigns, upon surrender of this contract, a good and sufficient conveyance in fee simple of the above described premises, free and clear of all liens and encumbrances, except such as may have accrued thereon subsequent to the date of this contract by or through the acts or negligences of others than the Vendor, and at the option of the Vendor furnish the Vendee an abstract of title or a policy of title insurance in an amount equal to the purchase price under this contract. The Vendor hereby reserves the right to mortgage said premises at any time in an amount not in excess of the amount then due on this contract, and the Vendee agrees that the said mortgage shall be a first lien on the premises.

It is mutually agreed that the Vendee shall have possession of said premises from and after October 1, 1992.

If the Vendee shall fail to comply with the terms of this contract, the Vendor may take possession of the property and all the improvements on it and treat the Vendee as a tenant holding over without permission and remove him therefrom and retain any money paid hereon as stipulated damages for nonperformance of this contract. It is hereby expressly understood and declared that time is and shall be taken as of the very essence of this contract. Notice of said forfeiture may be given by depositing the notice in post office, addressed to Vendee at his last known address.

It is agreed that the stipulations contained in this contract are to apply to and bind the heirs, executors, administrators, and assigns of the respective parties to this contract.

In witness whereof, the said parties have set their hands and seals the day and year first above written. Signed, sealed and delivered in presence of:

Harriet Greene)   *Sarah A. Collins*
                          Sarah A. Collins

Samuel A. Giggs)   *Robert H. Bowen*
                          Robert H. Bowen

CONCEPT REVIEW

SECURITY INTERESTS IN REAL PROPERTY

Type of Security Instrument	Parties	Features
Mortgage	1. Mortgagor (property owner/debtor) 2. Mortgagee (creditor)	1. Mortgagee holds a security interest (and in some states, title) in real property as security for a debt. 2. If mortgagor defaults on his obligation, mortgagee must *foreclose* on property to realize on his security interest. 3. Mortgagor has a limited time after foreclosure to *redeem* his interest.
Deed of Trust	1. Owner/debtor 2. Lender/creditor 3. Trustee	1. Trustee holds legal title to the real property put up as security. 2. If debt is satisfied, the trustee conveys property back to owner/debtor. 3. If debt is not paid as agreed, creditor notifies trustee to sell the property. 4. While intended to make foreclosure easier, most states treat it like a mortgage for purposes of foreclosure.
Land Contract	1. Buyer 2. Seller	1. Seller agrees to convey title when full price is paid. 2. Buyer usually takes possession, pays property taxes and insurance, and maintains the property. 3. If buyer defaults, seller may declare a forfeiture and retake possession (most states) after buyer has limited time to redeem; some states require foreclosure.

MECHANIC'S AND MATERIALMAN'S LIENS

Each state has a statute that permits persons who contract to furnish labor or materials to improve real estate to claim a lien on the property until they are paid. There are many differences among states as to exactly who can claim such a lien and the requirements that must be met to do so.

Rights of Subcontractors and Materialmen

A general contractor is a person who has contracted with the owner to build, remodel, or improve real property. A subcontractor is a person who has contracted with the general contractor to perform a stipulated portion of the general contract. A materialman is a person who has contracted to furnish certain materials needed to perform a designated general contract.

Two distinct systems—the New York system and the Pennsylvania system—are followed by the states in allowing mechanic's liens on real estate to subcontractors and materialmen. The New York system is based on the theory of subrogation, and the subcontractors or mate-

rialmen cannot recover more than is owed to the contractor at the time they file a lien or give notice of a lien to the owner. Under the Pennsylvania system, the subcontractors or materialmen have direct liens and are entitled to liens for the value of labor and materials furnished, irrespective of the amount due from the owner to the contractor. Under the New York system, the general contractor's failure to perform his contract or his abandonment of the work has a direct effect on the lien rights of subcontractors and materialmen, whereas under the Pennsylvania system, such breach or abandonment by the general contractor does not directly affect the lien rights of subcontractors and materialmen.

Basis for Mechanic's or Materialman's Lien

Some state statutes provide that no lien shall be claimed unless the contract for the improvement is in writing and embodies a statement of the materials to be furnished and a description of the land on which the improvement is to take place and of the work to be done. Other states permit the contract to be oral, but in no state is a licensee or volunteer entitled to a lien. No lien can be claimed unless the work is done or the materials are furnished in the performance of a contract to improve specific real property. A sale of materials without reference to the improvement of specific real property does not entitle the person furnishing the materials to a lien on real property that is, in fact, improved by the use of the materials at some time after the sale.

Unless the state statute specifically includes submaterialmen, they are not entitled to a lien. For example, if a lumber dealer contracts to furnish the lumber for the erection of a specific building and orders from a sawmill a carload of lumber that is needed to fulfill the contract, the sawmill will not be entitled to a lien on the building in which the lumber is used unless the state statute expressly provides that submaterialmen are entitled to a lien.

At times, the question has arisen as to whether materials have been furnished. Some courts have held that the materialman must prove that the material furnished was actually incorporated into the structure. Under this ruling, if material delivered on the job is diverted by the general contractor or others and not incorporated into the structure, the materialman will not be entitled to a lien. Other courts have held that the materialman is entitled to a lien if he can provide proof that the material was delivered on the job under a contract to furnish the material.

The *Overhead Door v. Sharkey* case, which follows, discusses the requirement that a person claiming a materialman's lien must show that the materials were delivered to the property under a contract with the owner to improve the property.

OVERHEAD DOOR CO. v. SHARKEY

395 N.W.2d 186 (Iowa Ct. App. 1986)

Albert Sharkey was the owner of a commercial building that was leased to Consolidated Freightways Corporation for more than 10 years before the lease was terminated by Consolidated on October 25, 1982. Consolidated's lease with Sharkey provided that Consolidated would leave the property in as good condition as received. Consolidated was responsible for damaging 10 overhead doors and contacted Dewco Building Systems to repair the damage. Dewco ordered new doors from Overhead. Overhead specially ordered the doors and paid for them on delivery from the manufacturer. On March 18, 1983, Overhead submitted its bill to Dewco. Overhead was unable to collect since Dewco had gone out of business and filed for bankruptcy. Dewco had already collected $10,397 from Consolidated and owed $6,685 to Overhead.

On May 10, 1983, Overhead filed a mechanic's lien against Sharkey's property and brought a lawsuit to enforce the lien. The trial court held for Sharkey and Overhead Door appealed.

Schlegel, Judge.   We are asked to decide if, under the facts and circumstances present here, a mechanic's lien claimant may establish his lien against the owner when the owner had imposed upon the lessee the burden of making all repairs. Iowa Code Section 572.2 (1985) provides that:

Every person who shall furnish any material or labor for, or perform any labor upon, any building or land for improvement, alteration or repair thereof, including those engaged in the construction or repair of any work of internal or external improvement, by virtue of any contract with the owner, his agent, trustee, contractor, or subcontractor shall have a lien upon such building or improvement, and land belonging to the owner on which the same is situated, to secure payment for material or labor furnished or labor performed.

The burden is upon a mechanic's lien claimant to prove either an express contract with or on behalf of the lessor, or else to prove such facts as will give rise to an implied contract with him, in order to claim a lien against the lessor's realty. When such a contract exists, the claimant must further establish that (1) the improvements will become the property of the lessor in a comparatively short time; (2) the additions or alterations were in fact substantial, permanent, and beneficial to the realty and were so contemplated by the parties to the agreement; and (3) that the rental payments reflected the increased value of the property as a result of these improvements.

We find that the trial court did not err in concluding that Overhead failed to prove there was either an express or implied contract between Sharkey and Consolidated. The relationship between them was that of lessee and lessor. The lease contained the following provision requiring the lessee to:

(e) Make no alterations or additions in or to the leased premises, except as expressly provided for herein, without the written consent of lessor, which consent should not be unreasonably withheld;

(f) Leave these premises in as good condition as received or in which they may be put by lessor, excepting reasonable wear and tear, damage arising from the negligence or default of lessor, or its agents or employees;

By replacing the damaged doors Consolidated was acting under the required terms of the lease, not as agent, trustee, contractor or subcontractor for Sharkey.

Even if Overhead Door had shown a contract for improvement existed between Sharkey and Consolidated, the evidence does not support that the factors required to satisfy the terms of Section 572.2 have been met. The repaired doors were replacements not improvements. The parties do not appear to have been contemplating substantial improvements or alterations. It is unfortunate that Overhead must bear the burden of the result of Dewco's bankruptcy. Equity, however, would not be served by substituting Sharkey for Overhead as the loss bearer.

Judgment for Sharkey affirmed.

Requirements for Obtaining Lien

The requirements for obtaining a mechanic's or material-man's lien must be complied with strictly. Although there is no uniformity in the statutes as to the requirements for obtaining a lien, the statutes generally require the filing of a notice of lien with a county official such as the register of deeds or the county clerk, which notice sets forth the amount claimed, the name of the owner, the names of the contractor and the claimant, and a description of the property. Frequently, the notice of lien must be verified by an affidavit of the claimant. In some states, a copy of the notice must be served on the owner or be posted on the property.

The notice of lien must be filed within a stipulated time. The time varies from 30 to 90 days, but the favored time is 60 days after the last work performed or after the last materials furnished. Some statutes distinguish between labor claims, materialmen's claims, and claims of general contractors as to time of filing. The lien, when filed, must be foreclosed within a specified time, which generally varies from six months to two years.

Priorities and Foreclosure

The provisions for priorities vary widely, but most of the statutes provide that a mechanic's lien has priority over all liens attaching after the first work is performed or after the first materials are furnished. This statutory provision creates a hidden lien on the property, in that a mechanic's lien, filed within the allotted period of time after completion of the work, attaches as of the time the first work is done or the first material is furnished, but no notice of lien need be filed during this period. And if no notice of lien is filed during this period, third persons would have no means of knowing of the existence of a lien. There are no priorities among lien claimants under the majority of the statutes. The procedure followed in the foreclosure of a mechanic's lien on real estate follows closely the procedure followed in a court foreclosure of a real estate mortgage. The rights acquired by the filing of a lien and the extent of the property covered by the lien are set out in some of the mechanic's lien statutes. In general, the lien attaches only to the interest that the person has in the property that has been improved at the time the notice is filed. Some statutes provide that the lien attaches to the building and to the city lot on which the building stands, or if the improvement is to farm property, the lien attaches to a specified amount of land.

Waiver of Lien

The question often arises as to the effect of an express provision in a contract for the improvement of real estate that no lien shall attach to the property for the cost of the improvement. In some states, there is a statute requiring the recording or filing of the contract and making such a provision ineffective if the statute is not complied with. In some states, courts have held that such a provision is effective against everyone; in other states, courts have held that the provision is ineffective against everyone except the contractor; and in still other states, courts have held that such a provision is ineffective as to subcontractors, materialmen, and laborers. Whether the parties to the contract have notice of the waiver of lien provision plays an important part in several states in determining their right to a lien.

It is common practice that before a person who is having improvements made to his property makes final payment, he requires the contractor to sign an affidavit that all materialmen and subcontractors have been paid and to supply him with a release of lien signed by the subcontractors and materialmen.

ETHICAL AND PUBLIC POLICY CONCERNS

1. Suppose you operate an appliance store in an inner-city neighborhood. Many of your potential customers do not have sufficient income to pay cash for goods such as television sets, VCRs, and stereo sets and they also have difficulty qualifying for credit cards or store charge accounts. You develop a "lease to buy" sales program whereby you offer those prospective customers the opportunity to lease a TV, VCR, or stereo on a weekly rental basis and after they have leased it for two years, they will be the owner of it. The total amount they would pay as rent for the item over the two years is about three times the retail cash price for the item. This element is not disclosed in your ads; rather, the focus is on the "opportunity to own" and the "low weekly payment." What ethical considerations are involved in your proposed sales program?

2. Suppose you own and operate a small loan business. A young man applies for a $1,000 loan. When you

run a credit check on him, you find that he has had difficulty holding a job and has a terrible credit record. You conclude that he is a poor credit risk and inform him that you are willing to make the requested loan only if he can find someone who has a good credit rating to cosign a promissory note with him. The next day he comes by the office with a young woman who meets your criteria for a good credit rating and who indicates she is willing to cosign the note. Do you have any ethical obligation to share with the young woman the information you have about the young man's employment and credit history?

3. Suppose you have sold a farm to a young couple on a land contract that calls for them to pay off the purchase price over a 10-year period. After the couple has paid about a third of the purchase price, a serious drought damages their crop and they miss several payments, triggering your right to declare a default and reclaim possession of the property. Are there any ethical considerations involved in your taking such an action that you are otherwise legally entitled to take? If you proceed with a forfeiture action in court, what policy considerations should the court take into account in deciding whether to grant your request?

SUMMARY

Credit is a transaction in which goods are sold and delivered, services are rendered, or money is loaned in exchange for the recipient's promise to pay at some future date. Unsecured credit is credit given on the recipient's unsupported promise to pay. Secured credit is credit supported by the grant of an interest in real or personal property or the supporting promise of a third person to whom the creditor can resort for payment if the debtor does not pay.

A surety, in the broad sense, is a person who is liable for the payment of another person's debt. Technically, the surety joins with the principal in making the promise to the promisee, whereas the guarantor makes a collateral promise, promising to perform the principal's promise upon the happening of a condition precedent. The relationship of surety is created by contract, and the general rules of contract law apply in determining the existence of a contract and the rights and liabilities of the parties. As a general rule, any defense the principal has that goes to the merits of the case is available to the surety. Also, any agreement between the principal and the creditor that alters the risks involved in the primary contract will discharge the surety unless he consents to or ratifies the agreement or unless the rights against the surety are reserved. The creditor owes a duty to use reasonable care in his dealings and not to increase unnecessarily the burden of risk assumed by a surety. If a surety pays his principal's debt, the surety is entitled to all of the rights that the creditor had against the principal. If there are cosureties and one surety pays more than his share of his principal's debt, he is entitled to contribution from his cosureties.

Artisans, innkeepers, and common carriers are entitled to common law liens for their reasonable charges. The common law lien is a possessory lien, and an artisan is not entitled to a lien unless possession of the property on which work is to be done is surrendered to him. The two essential elements of a common law lien are (1) a debt and (2) possession of the property by the creditor. Most states have enacted statutes defining the rights to liens on personal property. If the lienholder wishes to foreclose a common law lien, he must sue the debtor, obtain a judgment, have an execution issued on the judgment and levied on the goods, and have the goods sold at a sheriff's sale. In most states, a simplified foreclosure procedure has been provided for by statute.

There are three basic contract devices for using real estate as security for an obligation: (1) the real estate mortgage, (2) the deed of trust, and (3) the land contract. A mortgage is a security interest in real property or a deed that is given by the owner (the mortgagor) as security for a debt owed to the creditor (the mortgagee). Because the real estate mortgage conveys an interest in real property, it must be executed with the same formality as a deed and it should be recorded to protect the mortgagee's interest in the property. The owner of property subject to a mortgage can sell the property without the mortgagee's consent, but the sale does not affect the mortgagee's interest in the property or his claim against the mortgagor. Foreclosure is the process by which any rights of the mortgagor or the current property owner are cut off. Foreclosure proceedings are regulated by state law and vary from state to state, but usually the mortgagor is given a period of time to redeem the property.

The deed of trust is a three-party transaction that is used in lieu of a mortgage in some states. The owner of the property, who is borrowing the money, conveys the property to a trustee. If the borrower defaults, the trustee, at the request of the lender, sells the property and pays the debt from the proceeds.

Where the owner of real property sells it on a land contract, he retains title to the property until the purchase price is paid in full. If the buyer defaults, the seller usually has the right to reclaim the property.

A mechanic's or materialman's lien is a statutory lien based on the improvement of one person's real estate by the addition of another person's labor or materials. To obtain a lien, the lien claimant must comply strictly with the statutory requirements as to the form, content, and time of giving notice of lien and any other statutory requirements. As a general rule, a mechanic's or materialman's lien dates from the time the first labor or materials are furnished and has priority over all subsequent liens. A lien is foreclosed in the same manner as that followed in a court foreclosure of a real estate mortgage. Under the provisions of some statutes, the right to a mechanic's or materialman's lien may be waived by the insertion of a waiver provision in a contract for the improvement of real estate.

PROBLEM CASES

1. Bayer was the general contractor on a Massachusetts state highway contract. He hired Deschenes as a subcontractor to do certain excavation work. Deschenes was to start the job by November 24, 1988, and to complete it on or before March 1, 1989. Deschenes was required to furnish a bond of $91,000 to assure his faithful performance of the subcontract, and he purchased such a bond from Aetna Insurance Company. Deschenes began the work on December 1, 1988, and quit on June 22, 1989, after completing only about half of the work. Bayer had made numerous efforts to get Deschenes to do the work and then completed the job himself when Deschenes walked off the job. Bayer brought a lawsuit against Aetna on the bond, and Aetna claimed that it was discharged by the extension of time given to Deschenes. Should Bayer recover on the bond?

2. Rusty Jones, a used car dealer, applied to First Financial Federal Savings and Loan Association for a $50,000 line of credit to purchase an inventory of used cars. First Financial refused to make the loan to Jones alone but agreed to do so if Worth Camp, an attorney and friend of Jones, would cosign the note. Camp agreed to cosign as an accommodation maker or surety. The expectation of the parties was that the loans cosigned by Camp would be repaid from the proceeds of the car inventory. The original note for $25,000 was signed on

August 2, 1984, and renewals were executed on January 25, 1985, September 11, 1985, and March 15, 1986, and the amount was eventually increased to $50,000. In August 1985, as Camp was considering whether to sign the September renewal note, he was advised by First Financial's loan officer that the interest on the loan had not been paid. In fact, interest payments were four months delinquent. In addition, unknown to Camp, as the $50,000 credit limit was approached, First Financial began making side, or personal, loans to Jones totaling about $25,000, which were also payable out of the used car inventory. Camp knew nothing of these loans and thought that Jones's used car business was making payments only on the loans he had cosigned. Jones defaulted on the $50,000 note cosigned by Camp and First Financial brought suit against Camp on his obligation as surety on the note. Was Camp relieved of his obligation as surety by First Financial's failure to disclose material facts to him? *Yes, Anything Material, Surety then Dismissed*

3. Mr. and Mrs. Marshall went to Beneficial Finance to borrow money but were deemed by Beneficial's office manager, Ruckett, to be bad credit risks. The Marshalls stated that their friend Garren would be willing to cosign a note for them if necessary. Ruckett advised Garren not to cosign because the Marshalls were bad credit risks. This did not dissuade Garren from cosigning a note for $480, but it prompted him to ask Beneficial to take a lien or security interest in Marshall's custom-built Harley-Davidson motorcycle, then worth over $1,000. Beneficial took and perfected a security interest in the motorcycle. Marshall defaulted on the first payment. Beneficial gave notice of the default to Garren and advised him that it was looking to him for payment. Garren then discovered that Beneficial and Marshall had reached an agreement whereby Marshall would sell his motorcycle for $700; Marshall was to receive $345 immediately, which was to be applied to the loan, and he promised to pay the balance of the loan from his pocket. Marshall paid Beneficial $89.50 and left town without giving the proceeds of the sale to Beneficial. Because Beneficial was unable to get the proceeds from Marshall, it brought suit against Garren on his obligation as surety. When Beneficial released the security for the loan (the motorcycle) without Garren's consent, was Garren relieved of his obligation as surety for repayment of the loan? *Yes Relieved of Liab*

4. During May and June, John Shumate regularly parked his automobile on a vacant lot in downtown Philadelphia. At that time, no signs were posted prohibiting parking on the lot or indicating that vehicles parked

there without authorization would be towed. On July 7, Shumate again left his car on the lot. When he returned two days later, the car was gone and the lot was posted with signs warning that parking was prohibited. Shumate learned that his car had been towed away by Ruffie's Towing Service and that the car was being held by Ruffie's at its place of business. Ruffie's refused to release the car until Shumate paid a towing fee of $44.50 plus storage charges of $4 per day. Shumate refused to pay the fee, and Ruffie's kept possession of the car. Did Ruffie's have a common law possessory lien on the car?

5. On July 18, Anna Parker conveyed certain land to Benjamin Coombs and took back a mortgage to secure the payment of $16,160, which was the balance due on the purchase price. The mortgage was recorded on November 11 of that year. Several days earlier, on October 30, Coombs executed a mortgage to Mayham on that same property to secure the payment of $12,690. Mayham recorded his mortgage on October 30. Coombs defaulted on the Mayham mortgage and Mayham brought suit to foreclose on it. Parker contended that her mortgage had priority over Mayham's because Mayham knew of it at the time he received his mortgage. The state law provides that mortgages "shall take effect from the time they are recorded." Which mortgage has priority? *MAYHAM*

6. Philip and Edith Beh purchased some property from Alfred M. Gromer and his wife. Sometime earlier, the Gromers had borrowed money from City Mortgage. They had signed a note and had given City Mortgage a second deed of trust on the property. There was also a first deed of trust on the property at the time the Behs purchased it. In the contract of sale between the Behs and the Gromers, the Behs promised to "assume" the second deed of trust of approximately $5,000 at 6 percent interest. The Behs later defaulted on the first deed of trust. Foreclosure was held on the first deed of trust, but the proceeds of the sale left nothing for City Mortgage on its second deed of trust. City Mortgage then brought a lawsuit against the Behs to collect the balance due on the second deed of trust. When the Behs "assumed" the second deed of trust, did they become personally liable for it? *YES.*

7. Pope agreed to sell certain land to Pelz and retained a mortgage on the property to secure payment of the purchase price. The mortgage contained a clause providing that if Pelz defaulted, Pope had the "right to enter upon the above-described premises and sell the same at public sale" to pay the balance of the purchase price, accounting to Pelz for any surplus realized on the sale. What type of foreclosure does this provision contemplate: (1) strict foreclosure, (2) action and sale, or (3) private power of sale?

8. In October 1972, Verda Miller sold her 107-acre farm for $30,000 to Donald Kimball, who was acting on behalf of his own closely held corporation, American Wonderlands. Under the agreement, Miller retained title and Kimball was given possession pending full payment of all installments of the purchase price. The contract provided that Kimball was to pay all real estate taxes. If he did not pay them, Miller could discharge them and either add the amounts to the unpaid principal or demand immediate payment of the delinquencies plus interest. Miller also had the right to declare a forfeiture of the contract and regain possession if the terms of the agreement were not met. In 1975, Miller had to pay the real estate taxes on the property in the amount of $672.78. She demanded payment of this amount plus interest from Kimball. She also served a notice of forfeiture on him that he had 30 days to pay. Kimball paid the taxes but refused to pay interest of $10.48. Miller made continued demands on Kimball for two months, then filed notice of forfeiture with the county recorder in August 1975. She also advised Kimball of this. Was Miller justified in declaring a forfeiture and taking back possession of the land?

9. Edwin Bull was the owner of an 80-foot fishing trawler named the Bull Head that had been leased for use in dismantling a bridge over the Illinois River at Pekin, Illinois. At the termination of the lease, the Bull Head was towed upriver to Morris, Illinois, not operating on its own power. At Morris, a tugboat owned by Iowa Marine Repair Corporation was used to remove the Bull Head from the tow and to move it to the south bank of the river where it was tied up. Several months later, the Bull Head was moved across the river by Iowa Marine and moored at a place on the north bank where it maintained its fleeting operations. The Bull Head remained there for several years and greatly deteriorated. Iowa Marine sent Bull a bill for switching, fleeting, and other services. Bull refused to pay and brought suit against Iowa Marine to recover possession of the boat. In turn, Iowa Marine claimed that it had a mechanic's lien on the Bull Head and that the boat should be sold to satisfy the lien. Illinois law provides that:

any architect, contractor, subcontractor, materialman, or other person furnishing services, labor, or material for the purpose of, or in constructing, building, altering, repairing or ornamenting a boat, barge, or watercraft shall have a lien on such boat for the value of such services, labor, or material in the same manner as in this act provided for the purpose of building, altering, repairing, or ornamenting a house or other building.

Does Iowa Marine have a valid mechanic's lien on the boat for its switching, fleeting, and storage services?

10. Bowen-Rodgers Hardware Company was engaged in the business of furnishing materials for the construction of buildings. It delivered a quantity of materials to property owned by Ronald and Carol Collins. The materials were for the use of a contractor who was building a home for the Collinses as well as several other houses in the area. The hardware company was not paid for the materials by the contractor, and it sought to obtain a mechanic's lien against the Collinses' property. The Collinses claimed that even though the materials were delivered to their home, they were actually used to build other houses in the area. Was the Collinses' property subject to a mechanic's lien because payment had not been made for materials delivered to it?

CHAPTER 28

SECURITY INTERESTS IN PERSONAL PROPERTY

INTRODUCTION

In many credit transactions the creditor, in order to protect his investment, takes a security interest, or lien, in personal property belonging to the debtor. The law covering security interests in personal property is set forth in Article 9 of the Uniform Commercial Code. Article 9, entitled Secured Transactions, applies to situations that consumers and businesspeople commonly face; for example, the financing of an automobile, the purchase of a refrigerator on a time-payment plan, or the financing of business inventory.

If a creditor wants to obtain a security interest in the personal property of the debtor, he also wants to be sure that his interest is superior to the claims of other creditors. To do so, the creditor must carefully comply with Article 9. In Part IV, Sales, we pointed out that businesspersons sometimes leave out important terms in a contract or insert vague terms to be worked out later. Such looseness is a luxury that is not permitted in secured transactions. If a debtor gets into financial difficulties and cannot meet her obligations, even a minor noncompliance with Article 9 may cause the creditor to lose his preferred claim to the personal property of the debtor. A creditor who loses his secured interest is only a general creditor if the debtor is declared bankrupt. As a general creditor in bankruptcy proceedings, he may have little chance of recovering the money owed by the debtor because of the relatively low priority of such claims. The Bankruptcy chapter covers this in detail.

Article 9 has not been adopted in exactly the same form in every state. The law of each state must be examined carefully to determine the procedure for obtaining a secured interest and the rights of creditors and debtors in that state. The general concepts are the same in every state, however, and these concepts are the basis of our discussion in this chapter.

SECURITY INTERESTS UNDER THE CODE

Security Interests

Basic to a discussion of secured consumer and commercial transactions is the term **security interest**. A security interest is an interest in personal property or fixtures obtained by a creditor to secure payment or performance of an obligation [1–201(37)].[1] For example, when a person borrows money from a bank to buy a new car, the bank takes a security interest, or puts a lien, on the car

---

[1] The numbers in brackets refer to the sections of the Uniform Commercial Code.

until the loan is repaid. If the person defaults on the loan, the bank can repossess the car and have it sold to cover the unpaid balance. A security interest is a property interest in the collateral.

While one usually thinks of goods as being put up as collateral, the Code actually covers secured interests in a much broader grouping of personal property. The Code breaks down personal property into a number of different classifications that are important in determining how a creditor acquires an enforceable security interest in a particular collateral.

The Code classifications are:

1. *Instruments*. This category includes checks, notes, drafts, stocks, bonds, and other investment securities [9–105].

2. *Documents of title*. This category includes bills of lading, dock warrants, dock receipts, and warehouse receipts.

3. *Accounts*. This category includes rights to payment for goods sold or leased or for services rendered that are not evidenced by instruments or chattel paper but are carried on open account. The category includes such rights to payment whether or not they have been earned by performance [9–106].

4. *Chattel paper*. This category includes written documents that evidence both an obligation to pay money and a security interest in specific goods [9–105]. A typical example of chattel paper is what is commonly known as a conditional sales contract. This is the type of contract that a consumer might sign when she buys a large appliance, such as a refrigerator, on a time-payment plan.

5. *General intangibles*. Among the items in this catchall category are patents, copyrights, literary royalty rights, franchises, and money [9–106].

6. *Goods*. Goods are divided into several classes; the same item of collateral may fall into different classes at different times, depending on its use.

a. *Consumer goods*. These goods are used or bought for use primarily for personal, family, or household purposes. They include automobiles, furniture, and appliances.

b. *Equipment*. This includes goods used or bought for use primarily in business, including farming and professions.

c. *Farm products*. These are crops, livestock, or supplies used or produced in farming operations as long as they are still in the possession of a debtor engaged in farming.

d. *Inventory*. This includes goods held for sale or lease or for use under contracts of service as well as raw materials, work in process, and materials used or consumed in a business.

e. *Fixtures*. These are goods so affixed to real property as to be considered a part of it [9–109].

In different situations, an item such as a stove could be classified as inventory, equipment, or consumer goods. In the hands of the manufacturer or an appliance store, the stove is "inventory" goods. If it is used in a restaurant, it is "equipment." If it was purchased by a consumer for use in her home, it is "consumer goods."

Obtaining a Security Interest

The goal of a creditor is to obtain a security interest in certain personal property that will be good against (1) the debtor, (2) other creditors of the debtor, and (3) a person who might purchase the property from the debtor. In case the debtor defaults on the debt, the creditor wants to have a better right to claim the property than anyone else. Obtaining an enforceable security interest is a two-step process—attachment and perfection.

ATTACHMENT OF THE SECURITY INTEREST

Attachment

A security interest is not legally enforceable against a debtor until it is attached to one or more particular items of the debtor's property. The **attachment** of the security interest takes place in a legal sense rather than in a physical sense. There are three basic requirements for a security interest to be attached to the goods of a debtor [9–203]: First is an *agreement* in which the debtor grants the creditor a security interest in particular property (collateral) in which the debtor has an interest. Second, the debtor must have *rights in the collateral*. Third, the creditor must give *value* to the debtor. The creditor must, for example, lend money or advance goods on credit to the debtor. Unless the debtor owes a debt to the creditor, there can be no security interest. The purpose of obtaining a security interest is to secure a debt.

The Security Agreement

The agreement in which a debtor grants a creditor a security interest in the debtor's property must generally be in writing and signed by the debtor. A written agreement is required in all cases except where the creditor has possession of the collateral [9–203]. Suppose Cole borrows $50 from Fox and gives Fox her wristwatch as a security for the loan. The agreement whereby Cole put up her watch as collateral does not have to be in writing to be enforceable. Because the creditor (Fox) is in possession of the collateral, an oral agreement is sufficient.

The security agreement must reasonably describe the collateral so that it can readily be identified. For example, it should list the year, make, and serial number of an automobile. The security agreement usually spells out the terms of the arrangement between the creditor and the debtor. Also, it normally contains a promise by the debtor to pay certain amounts of money in a certain way. The agreement specifies which events, such as nonpayment by the buyer, constitute a default. In addition, it may contain provisions that the creditor feels are necessary to protect his security interest. For example, the debtor may be required to keep the collateral insured, not to move it without the creditor's consent, or to periodically report sales of secured inventory goods. See Figure 1 for an example of a security agreement.

In the case that follows, *In Re Hardage*, Sears was deemed to have obtained a valid security agreement from its debtor even though the document constituting it was missing certain critical terms.

IN RE HARDAGE
99 BR 738 (Bankr. N.D. Tex. 1989)

On June 14, 1986, Jimmy Hardage purchased a videocassette recorder for $315.36 from Sears Roebuck & Co. (Sears), and on November 8, 1987, he purchased a guitar board from Sears for $181.89. In each case he used his Sears charge card to make the purchase and signed the sales slips at the time of purchase. The sales slips contained, among other things, this information:

1. Hardage's credit account number.
2. Hardage's name.
3. The date of purchase.
4. The amount of the purchase.
5. A brief description of the goods sold.
6. An invoice number.
7. Hardage's address.
8. Hardage's signatures immediately below the legend:

    This purchase is subject to the approval of the Sears Credit Sales Department and is made under my SearsCharge Account Security Agreement for my SearsCharge Modernizing Credit Plan Security Agreement which is incorporated herein by reference. I agree that Sears retains a security interest under the Uniform Commercial Code in the merchandise purchased until fully paid.

On December 17, 1987, Hardage and his wife, Danelle, filed for relief under Chapter 7 of the Bankruptcy Code. They listed Sears as an unsecured creditor to whom they owed $1,453.07. Sears claimed that it had a security interest in the videocassette recorder and the guitar board for the amount of $402.64 (the balance remaining unpaid on the two items).

Akard, Bankruptcy Judge.   The issue before the court is: Do the sales slips denominated "credit billing copy," of Sears, Roebuck & Co. (Sears), constitute valid security agreements such that pursuant to Uniform Commercial Code (U.C.C.) Article 9 Sears has perfected security interests in the consumer goods sold?

The Texas version of the U.C.C. sets forth the formal requisite a party must follow to create an Article 9 security interest enforceable against the buyer or third parties with respect to the collateral. In pertinent part, these steps are: (1) the debtor signs a security agreement which contains a description of the collateral; (2) value has been given; and (3) the debtor has rights in the collateral. Section 9–203(a). A financing statement is not necessary to perfect a purchase money security interest in consumer goods.

The writing requirement may be simply expressed as follows; it must: (1) contain sufficient language to embody a "security agreement"; (2) include an adequate description of the collateral; and (3) be signed by the debtor. Since items 2 and 3 are not in dispute, we turn to item one, the sufficiency of the language to embody a security agreement.

Section 9–105(a)(12) states a security agreement means "an agreement which creates or provides for a security interest." Where the parties are in dispute on the issue, the court may have to resolve first, as a question of law, whether the language in the agreement objectively indicates the parties may have intended to create or provide for a security interest.

Although some courts read "may have intended" to require more, other courts rely on Comment 5 to section 9–203, which states that the writing requirement is more in the nature of satisfaction of the statute of frauds.

The U.C.C. does not require special words or any special form to show a possible security interest. Further, the courts have recognized unorthodox documents containing certain words as adequate security agreements. Even when conventional words do not appear, some courts find security agreements. Or, where one document is not sufficient to create a valid security interest, creditors may show such creation by introducing multiple executed documents. Therefore, once the agreement meets the section 9–203 writing requirement, the court may or may not ask for other evidence of whether the parties *actually* intended to create a security interest, a question of fact.

The court concludes that as a matter of law the sales slips retained a security interest in the items purchased. Clearly Sears intended for the sales slips to be a security agreement and the intention of Mr. Hardage for the sales slips to be a security agreement must be found from the fact that he signed the sales slips immediately below the language creating the security interest.

Judgment for Sears.

Future Advances

A security agreement may stipulate that it covers advances of credit to be made at some time in the future [9–204(3)]. Such later extensions of credit are known as **future advances.** Future advances would be involved where, for example, a bank grants a business a line of credit for $100,000 but initially advances only $20,000. When the business draws further against its line of credit, it has received a future advance and the bank is considered to have given additional "value" at that time. The security interest that the creditor obtained earlier also covers these later advances of money.

After-Acquired Property

A security agreement may be drafted to grant a creditor a security interest in the **after-acquired property** of the debtor. After-acquired property is property that the debtor does not currently own or have rights in but that he may acquire in the future. However, the security interest does not attach until the debtor actually obtains some rights to the new property [9–204].[2] For example, Dan's Diner borrows $25,000 from the bank and gives it a security interest in all of its present restaurant equipment as well as all of the restaurant equipment that it may "hereafter acquire." If Dan's owns only a stove at the time, then the bank has a security interest only in the stove. However, if a month later Dan's buys a refrigerator, the bank's security interest would

---

[2]The Code imposes an additional requirement as to security interests in after-acquired consumer goods. Security interests do not attach to consumer goods other than accessions unless the consumer acquires them within 10 days after the secured party gave value [9–204(2)].

FIGURE 1   A Security Agreement

Account No.

~~Mr. and Mrs.~~
~~Mrs.~~
BUYER Miss *Cheryl Cole*
ADDRESS *542 Oakdale*
CITY *Chicago, Il.*   TEL. NO. *828-0290*
DELIVER TO: *542 Oakdale*

C-1005

Date

SECURITY AGREEMENT
ACE APPLIANCE

THIS AGREEMENT, executed between Ace Appliance, as Secured Party ("Seller"), and Buyer named above, as Debtor ("Buyer"): Seller agrees to sell and Buyer agrees to purchase, subject to the terms, conditions, and agreements stated in this agreement, the goods described below (the "Collateral"), Seller reserving and Buyer granting a purchase money security interest in the Collateral to secure the payment of the balance owed (Item 7) and all other present and future obligations of Buyer to Seller.

DESCRIPTION OF COLLATERAL

Quan.	Article	Unit Price	Total		TERMS
1	Refrig	545 —	545		(1) Cash Price *104 00*
1	Stove	495 —	495		(2) Down Payment *100 00*
					Trade-in
					Unpaid Principal
					(3) Balance Owed *94 00*
					(4) Finance Charge *100 00*
					Time Balance
					(5) Owed *1040 00*
					(6) Sales Tax *40 00*
					(7) Balance Owed *1080 00*

Buyer agrees to pay Seller, without relief from valuation and appraisement laws, the balance owed (Item 7) of $ *1080 00*

~~weekly~~

in *11* successive   installments of $ *90 00* each and a final installment of $ *90 00* , commencing on

monthly

~~week~~

Jan. 1 , 19 *92* and continuing thereafter on the same day of each   until paid, together with all delinquent

month

charges, costs of repossession, collection, disposition, maintenance, and other like charges, allowed by law, and reasonable attorney's fees.

   This sale is made subject to the terms, conditions, and agreements stated above on the reverse side. Buyer represents that the correct name and address of Buyer is as stated above, and that all statements made by buyer as to financial condition and credit information are true.

   Buyer acknowledges delivery by Seller to Buyer of a copy of this agreement.

   Buyer warrants and represents that the Collateral will be kept at Buyer's address unless otherwise specified as follows:_____;

and will be used or is purchased for use primarily for: (check one) family or household purposes ☒ ; business use ☐ ; farming operations ☐ . The Collateral will not be affixed to real estate unless checked here ☐ . If the Collateral is to be affixed to real estate, a description of the real estate is as follows: _____

and the name of the record owner is _____

FIGURE 1 (*concluded*)

IN WITNESS WHEREOF, the parties have executed this agreement on this *1st* day of *Dec.* 19 *91.*
BUYER'S SIGNATURE (Ace Appliance) Seller (as Secured party) *Cheryl Cole* By *Frank Singer*
(as debtor)

TERMS, CONDITIONS, AND AGREEMENTS

1. The security interest of Seller shall extend to all replacements, proceeds (including tort claims and insurance), and accessories, and shall continue until full performance by Buyer of all conditions and obligations under this agreement.

2. Buyer shall maintain the Collateral in good repair, pay all taxes and other charges levied upon the Collateral when due, and shall defend the Collateral against any claims. Buyer shall not permit the Collateral to be removed from the place where kept without the prior written consent of Seller. Buyer shall give prompt written notice to Seller of any transfer, pledge, assignment, or any other process or action taken or pending, voluntary or involuntary, whereby a third party is to obtain or is attempting to obtain possession of or any interest in the Collateral. Seller shall have the right to inspect the Collateral at all reasonable times. At its option, but without obligation to Buyer and without relieving Buyer from any default, Seller may discharge any taxes, liens, or other encumbrances levied or placed upon the Collateral for which Buyer agrees to reimburse Seller upon demand.

3. If the Collateral is damaged or destroyed in any manner, the entire balance remaining unpaid under this agreement (the "Agreement Balance") shall immediately become due and payable and Buyer shall first apply any insurance or other receipts compensating for such loss to the Agreement Balance. Buyer shall fully insure the Collateral, for the benefit of both Seller and Buyer, against loss by fire, theft, and other casualties by comprehensive extended coverage insurance in an amount equal to the balance owed under this agreement.

4. Buyer shall pay all amounts payable when due at the store of Seller from which this sale is made or at Seller's principal office in *Gary*, Indiana, and upon default shall pay the maximum delinquent charges permitted by law. Upon prepayment of the Agreement Balance, Seller shall allow the minimum discount permitted by law.

5. Time is of the essence of this agreement. Buyer agrees that the following shall constitute an event of default under this Security Agreement: (*a*) the failure of Buyer to perform any condition or obligation contained in this agreement; (*b*) when any statement, representation, or warranty made by Buyer shall be found to have been untrue in any material respect when made; or (*c*) if Seller in good faith believes that the prospect of payment or performance is impaired. Upon a default, Seller, at its option and without notice or demand to Buyer, shall be entitled to declare the Agreement Balance immediately due and payable, take immediate possession of the Collateral and enter the premises at which the Collateral is located for such purpose or to render the Collateral unusable. Upon request, Buyer shall assemble and make the Collateral available to Seller at a place to be designated by Seller which is reasonably convenient to both parties. Upon repossession, Seller may retain or dispose of any or all of the collateral in the manner prescribed by the Indiana Uniform Commercial Code and the proceeds of any such disposition shall be first applied in the following order; (*a*) to the reasonable expenses of retaking, holding, preparing for sale, selling, and the like; (*b*) to the reasonable attorney's fees and legal expenses incurred by Seller; and (*c*) to the satisfaction of the indebtedness secured by this security interest. Buyer convenants to release and hold harmless Seller from any and all claims arising out of the repossession of the Collateral. No waiver of any default or any failure or delay to exercise any right or remedy by Seller shall operate as a waiver of any other default, or of the same default in the future or as a waiver of any right or remedy with respect to the same or any other occurrence.

6. All rights and remedies of seller specified in this agreement are cumulative and are in addition to, and shall not exclude, any rights and remedies Seller may have by law.

7. Seller shall not be liable for any damages, including special or consequential damages, for failure to deliver the Collateral or for any delay in delivery of the Collateral to Buyer.

8. Buyer agrees that Seller may carry this agreement, together with any other agreements and accounts, with Buyer in one account upon its records and unless otherwise instructed in writing by Buyer, any payment of less than all amounts then due on all agreements and accounts shall be applied to any accrued delinquent charges, costs of collection and maintenance, and to the balances owing under all agreements or accounts in such order as Seller in its discretion shall determine.

9. Buyer authorizes Seller to execute and file financing statements signed only by Seller covering the Collateral described.

10. Any notice required by this agreement shall be deemed sufficient when mailed to Seller (state Seller's address), or to Buyer at the address at which the Collateral is kept.

11. Buyer shall have the benefit of manufacturers' warranties, if any; however, Seller makes no express warranties (except a warranty of title) and no implied warranties, including any warranty of MERCHANTABILITY or FITNESS. Buyer agrees that there are no promises or agreements between the parties not contained in this agreement. Any modification or rescission of this agreement shall be ineffective unless in writing and signed by both Seller and Buyer.

12. ANY HOLDER OF THIS CONSUMER CREDIT CONTRACT IS SUBJECT TO ALL CLAIMS AND DEFENSES WHICH THE DEBTOR COULD ASSERT AGAINST THE SELLER OF GOODS OR SERVICES OBTAINED WITH THE PROCEEDS HEREOF. RECOVERY HEREUNDER BY THE DEBTOR SHALL NOT EXCEED AMOUNTS PAID BY THE DEBTOR HEREUNDER.

"attach" to the refrigerator when Dan's acquires some rights to it.

A security interest in after-acquired property may not have priority over certain other creditors if the debtor acquires his new property subject to what is known as a **purchase money security interest**. When the seller of goods retains a security interest in goods until they are paid for, or when money is loaned for the purpose of acquiring certain goods and the lender takes a security interest in those goods, the security interest is a purchase money security interest. Later in this chapter, the section entitled Priority Rules discusses the rights of the holder of a purchase money security interest versus the rights of another creditor who filed earlier on after-acquired property of the debtor.

Proceeds

The creditor is commonly interested in having his security interest cover not only the collateral described in the agreement but also the **proceeds** on the disposal of the collateral by the debtor. For example, if a bank lends money to Dealer to enable Dealer to finance its inventory of new automobiles and the bank takes a security interest in the inventory, the bank wants its interest to continue in any cash proceeds obtained by Dealer when the automobiles are sold to customers. Under the 1972 amendments to Article 9, these proceeds are automatically covered unless the security agreement specifically excludes them [9–203(3)].

Assignment

In the past, installment sales contracts and security agreements commonly included a provision that the buyer would not assert against the assignee of a sales contract any claims or defenses that the buyer had against the seller. Such clauses made it easier for a retailer to assign its installment sales contracts, or security agreements, to a financial institution such as a bank. The bank knew that it could collect from the buyer without having to worry about any claims that the buyer had against the retailer, such as for breach of warranty. The waiver clauses were usually presented to the buyer on a take-it-or-leave-it basis.

Such clauses can operate to the disadvantage of the buyer. For example, Ellen Horn agrees to buy some storm windows from Ace Home Improvement Company. She signs an installment sales contract, or security agreement, promising to pay $50 a month for 24 months and giving the company a security interest in the windows. The contract contains a waiver of defenses clause. Ace assigns the contract to First Bank and goes out of business. If the storm windows were of a poorer quality than was called for by the contract, Horn would have a claim of breach of warranty against Ace. She would not have to pay Ace the full amount if it tried to collect from her. Under these circumstances, however, Horn has to pay the full amount to the bank; then she can try to collect from Ace for breach of warranty. Here, Horn might be out of luck.

Under the Uniform Commercial Code, an express or implied waiver of defenses is generally valid and enforceable by an assignee who takes his assignment for value, in good faith, and without notice of a claim or defense [9–206(1)]. The two exceptions to this rule are (1) the waiver is not effective as to any type of defense that could be asserted against a holder in due course of a negotiable instrument; (2) the waiver is not effective if a statute or court decision establishes a different rule for buyers of consumer goods [9–206(1)].

Some states have enacted comprehensive legislation to abolish waiver of defenses clauses in consumer contracts, and other states have limited their use. The Uniform Consumer Credit Code (UCCC), which has been adopted by a number of states, gives the adopting states two alternatives regarding waiver of defenses clauses: Alternative A provides that an assignee of a consumer sales contract takes subject to all of the defenses that the buyer has against the seller arising out of the sale, regardless of whether the contract contains a waiver of defenses clause. Alternative B permits the enforcement of such clauses only by an assignee who is not related to the seller and who acquires the assignment of the contract in good faith and for value, gives the buyer notice of the assignment, and is not advised by the buyer in writing within three months that the buyer has any claims or defenses against the seller.

In addition, the Federal Trade Commission has promulgated a regulation that applies to situations in which a buyer signs a waiver of defenses clause as part of an installment sales contract. For a detailed discussion of this regulation see the Negotiation and Holder in Due Course chapter. The FTC regulation requires that a seller or financing agency insert in all consumer contracts and direct loan agreements a clause putting any holder of the contract on notice that the holder is subject to all of the claims and defenses that the buyer-debtor could assert against the seller of the goods or services covered by the contract.

PERFECTING THE SECURITY INTEREST

Perfection

While attachment of a security interest to collateral owned by the debtor gives the creditor rights vis-à-vis the debtor, a creditor is also concerned about making sure that she has a better right to the collateral than any other creditor if the debtor defaults. In addition, a creditor may be concerned about protecting her interest in the collateral if the debtor sells it to someone else. The creditor gets protection against other creditors or purchasers of the collateral by perfecting her security interest. Perfection is not effective without an attachment of the security interest [9–303].

Under the Code, there are three main ways of perfecting a security interest:

1. By filing a public notice of the security interest.
2. By the creditor taking possession of the collateral.
3. In certain transactions, by mere attachment of the security interest; this is known as automatic perfection.

Perfection by Public Filing

The most common way of perfecting a security interest is to file a **financing statement** in the appropriate public office. The financing statement serves as constructive notice to the world that the creditor claims an interest in collateral that belongs to a certain named debtor. The financing statement usually consists of a multicopy form that is available from the office of the secretary of state. (See Figure 2.) However, the security agreement can be filed as the financing statement if it contains the required information and has been signed by the debtor.

To be sufficient, the financing statement must (1) contain the names of the debtor and of the secured party, or creditor; (2) be signed by the debtor; (3) give an address of the secured party from which additional information about the security interest can be obtained; (4) give a mailing address for the debtor; and (5) contain a statement listing the collateral or a description of the collateral. If the financing statement covers goods that are to become fixtures, a description of the real estate must be included.

Each state specifies by statute where the financing statement has to be filed. In all states, a financing statement that covers fixtures must be filed in the office where a mortgage on real estate would be filed [9–401]. To obtain maximum security, the secured party acquiring a security interest in property that is a fixture or is to become a fixture should double file, that is, file the security interest as a fixture and as a nonfixture.

In regard to collateral other than fixtures, the state may require only central filing, usually in the office of the secretary of state. However, most states require the local filing of local transactions, such as transactions in which the collateral is equipment used in farming operations; farm products; accounts, contract rights, or general intangibles arising from or relating to the sale of farm products by a farmer; or consumer goods.

A financing statement is effective for a period of five years from the date of filing, and it lapses then unless a continuation statement has been filed before that time. An exception is made for real estate mortgages that are effective as fixture filings—they are effective until the mortgage is released or terminates [9–403].

A **continuation statement** may be filed within six months before the five-year expiration date. The continuation statement must be signed by the secured party, identify the original statement by file number, and state that the original statement is still effective. Successive continuation statements may be filed [9–403(3)].

When a consumer debtor completely fulfills all debts and obligations secured by a financing statement, she is entitled to a **termination statement** signed by the secured party or an assignee of record. Failure of the affected secured party to furnish a termination statement after proper demand subjects him to a fine of $100 plus damages for any loss caused to the debtor by such failure [9–404].

Possession by Secured Party as Public Notice

Public filing of a security interest is intended to put any interested members of the public on notice of the security interest. A potential creditor of the debtor, or a potential buyer of the collateral, can check the records to see whether anyone else claims an interest in the debtor's collateral. The same objective can be reached if the debtor gives up possession of the collateral to the creditor or to a third person who holds the collateral for the creditor. If a debtor does not have possession

FIGURE 2   A Financial Statement

UNIFORM COMMERCIAL CODE   **STATE OF INDIANA**   FORM UCC-1
                                            FINANCING STATEMENT

INSTRUCTIONS

1. Please type this form. Fold only along perforation for mailing.
2. Remove Secured Party and Debtor copies and send other three copies with interleaved carbon paper to the filing officer. Enclose filing fee of $1.00
   (plus $ .50 if collateral is or to become a fixture).
3. When filing is to be with more one office. Form UCC-2 may be placed over this set to avoid double typing.
4. If the space provided for any item(s) is inadequate, the item(s) may be continued on additional sheets, preferably 5"x 8" or sizes convenient to
   secured party in case of long schedules, indentures, etc. Only one sheet is required. Extra names of debtors may be continued below box "1" in
   space for description of property.
5. If the collateral is crops or goods which are or are to become fixtures, describe the goods and also the real estate with the name of the record owner
   if he is other than the debtor.
6. Persons filing a security agreement (as distinguished from a financing statement) are urged to complete this form with or without signature and send
   with security agreement.
7. If collateral is goods which are or are to become fixtures, use Form UCC-1a over this Form to avoid double typing, and enclose regular fee plus $ .50
8. The filing officer will return the third page of this Form as an acknowledgment. Secured party at a later time may use third page as a Termination
   Statement by dating and signing the termination legend on that page.

This Financing Statement is presented to Filing Officer for filing pursuant to the UCC: 3. Maturity Date (if any):

1. Debtor(s) (Last Name First) and Address(es)	2. Secured Party(ies) and Address(es)	For Filing Officer (Date, Time, Number, and Filing Office)

4. This financing statement covers the following types (or items) of property (also describe realty
where collateral is crops or fixtures):

Assignee of Secured Party

This statement is filed without the debtor's signature to perfect a security interest in collateral
(check ☐ if so)

☐ under a security agreement signed by debtor authorizing secured party to file this statement, or
☐ already subject to a security interest in another jurisdiction when it was brought into this state, or
☐ which is proceeds of the following described original collateral which was perfected:

Check ☐ if covered: ☐ Proceeds of Collateral are also covered.   ☐ Products of Collateral are also covered. No. of additional Sheets presented:

Filed with: ☐ Secretary of State   ☐ Recorder of_____County

By: _____   By: _____
      Signature(s) of Debtor(s)   Signature(s) of Secured Party(ies)

(1) Filing Officer Copy—Alphabetical   Approved by:
    FORM UCC-1—INDIANA UNIFORM COMMERCIAL CODE
                                                            Secretary of State

of collateral that he claims to own, then a potential creditor or debtor is on notice that someone else may claim an interest in it. Thus, a security interest is perfected by change of possession of collateral from the debtor to the creditor/secured party or his agent [9–302(1)(a)]. For example, Simpson borrows $50 from a pawnbroker and leaves his guitar as collateral for the loan. The pawnbroker's security interest in the guitar is perfected by virtue of her possession of the guitar.

Generally, possession by the secured party is the means for perfecting a security interest in instruments such as checks or notes and in money.[3] Possession of the collateral by the secured party is an alternative means, and often the most satisfactory means, of perfecting a security interest in chattel paper and negotiable documents of title. Possession is also a possible means for perfecting a security interest in inventory. This is sometimes done through the **field warehousing** arrangement, whereby part of the debtor's inventory is fenced off and withdrawals from it are permitted only

---

[3]Sections 9–304(4) and (5) permit a 21-day temporary perfection.

on the approval of the secured party or his on-the-scene representative.

Possession by the secured party is usually not a practical means for perfecting a security interest in equipment, farm products, or consumer goods. Of course, it is not possible at all with accounts or general intangibles.

The person to whom the collateral is delivered holds it as bailee, and he owes the duties of a bailee to the parties in interest [9–207].

The case that follows, *Reinhardt v. Nikolaisen*, illustrates the use of possession to perfect a secured interest in personal property.

REINHARDT v. NIKOLAISEN

775 S.W.2d 284 (Ct. App. Mo. 1989)

Siegfried Reinhardt was a well-known St. Louis artist and a close friend of Peter Nikolaisen, who owned and operated Nikolaisen's Sunset 44 Restaurant. Sometime between 1970 and 1972, Nikolaisen and Reinhardt agreed that Reinhardt could display and sell his artwork at Nikolaisen's restaurant. They also agreed that Reinhardt could charge his food and drink purchases at the restaurant and pay later. In addition, in December 1978, Nikolaisen loaned $3,000 to Reinhardt. Reinhardt agreed to pay the loan in full by June 30, 1979, or in monthly installments beginning on July 31, 1979. Reinhardt also orally agreed that the paintings in Nikolaisen's possession were pledged as security for the repayment of the $3,000 loan and any outstanding debt owed for food and drink.

Reinhardt died in October 1984. At the time, 45 of his paintings were on display at the restaurant. Sometime after this, the administrator of Reinhardt's estate asked Nikolaisen to sign a memorandum confirming the estate's ownership interest in the paintings, which he did. The administrator subsequently demanded that Nikolaisen return the paintings to the estate. He returned 41 of the 45, continuing to hold 4 paintings as collateral for the debt owed him. Nikolaisen claimed that the debt totaled $7,693.17, including $5,734.52 for the loan with interest and $1,958.65 for outstanding restaurant bills.

The administrator then brought a lawsuit on behalf of Reinhardt's estate against Nikolaisen to determine ownership of the paintings. The trial court held that the paintings were subject to Nikolaisen's lien and the administrator appealed.

Grimm, Presiding Judge. The estate alleges that the trial court erred in allowing Nikolaisen to testify as to the existence of a lien for the reason that the statute of frauds bars such testimony.

When considering whether a security interest is enforceable, the determinative statute is section 9–203. As the comment to this section says: "This section is in the nature of a statute of frauds."

Section 9–203(1) establishes that a security interest is not enforceable unless "(a) the collateral is in the possession of the secured party or (b) the debtor has signed a security agreement. . . ." The collateral here, Reinhardt's works, was in the possession of the secured party, Nikolaisen. Thus, the requirements of 9–203(1)(a) were met; and a writing was not required to make this security interest enforceable.

Judgment for Nikolaisen affirmed.

Perfection by Attachment

Perfection by mere attachment of the security interest, sometimes known as automatic perfection, is the only form of perfection that occurs without the giving of public notice. It occurs automatically when all the requirements of attachment are complete. This form of perfection is limited to certain classes of collateral; in addition, it may be only a temporary perfection in some situations.[4]

---

[4]Temporary perfection without filing or possession is automatically obtained for 21 days after attachment of the security interest in instruments and negotiable documents [9–304]. To get protection beyond the 21-day period, the secured party must perfect by filing or possession. During the 21-day period of temporary perfection, however, any holder in due course of commercial paper or any bona fide purchaser of a security or a negotiated document will prevail over the secured party relying on temporary perfection [9–309].

A creditor who sells goods to a consumer on credit, or who lends money to enable a consumer to buy goods, can obtain limited perfection of a security interest merely by attaching the security interest to the goods. A creditor under these circumstances has what is called a **purchase money security interest** in consumer goods. For example, an appliance store sells a television set to Margaret Morse on a conditional sales contract, or time-payment plan. The store does not have to file its purchase money security interest in the set. The security interest is considered perfected just by virtue of its attachment to the set in the hands of the consumer.

In the case that follows, *In Re Phillips*, the court rejected a creditor's claims that its security interest was perfected by attachment, holding that the goods were equipment and not consumer goods.

IN RE PHILLIPS
CREDITWAY OF AMERICA v. PHILLIPS
42 UCC Rep. 679 (Bankr. W.D. Va. 1985)

Jacob Phillips and his wife, Charlene, jointly owned the Village Variety 5&10 Store in Bluefield, Virginia. In addition, Mrs. Phillips was a computer science teacher at the Wytheville Community College. On December 1, 1984, Mrs. Phillips entered into a retail installment sales contract with Holdren's, Inc., for the purchase of a Leading Edge color computer and a Panasonic printer. The contract, which was also a security agreement, provided for a total payment of $3,175.68, with monthly payments of $132.32 to begin on March 5, 1985. On December 1, 1984, Holdren's assigned the contract to Creditway of America.

At the time of purchase, Mrs. Phillips advised Holdren's that she was purchasing the computer for professional use in her teaching assignments as well as for use in the variety store. One of the software programs purchased was a practical accounting program for business transactions. Mrs. Phillips also received a special discount price given by Holdren's to state instructors buying for their teaching use. She used the computer in the Village Variety 5&10 Store until it closed in April 1985. In June, the Phillips' filed a petition under Chapter 7 of the Bankruptcy Act. At the time, they owed $2,597.79 on the computer. No financing statement was ever filed.

Creditway filed a motion in the bankruptcy proceeding, claiming that it had a valid lien on the computer and seeking to be permitted to repossess it.

Pearson, Bankruptcy Judge.   The key factor in determining whether to grant Creditway's motion for relief is the classification of the collateral. Virginia Code Section 9–302(1)(d) provides that "a financing statement shall be filed to perfect all security interests except a purchase money security interest in consumer goods." If the computer goods are classified as consumer goods, then Creditway, as assignee of Holdren's, would not need to file a financing statement to have a perfected security interest in the collateral. However, if the computer items are classified as equipment, then, pursuant to Section 9–401(1)(c), it would be necessary for Creditway to have a dual filing to perfect its security interest.

Virginia Code Section 9–109 outlines the classification of collateral. In pertinent part it provides that

Goods are

(1) "consumer goods" if they are used or bought for use primarily for personal, family, or household purposes;

(2) "equipment" if they are used or bought for use primarily in business (including farming or a profession.

The test for the classification of goods is the owner's use of the goods. The two classes of goods are mutually exclusive. The same property cannot be in two classes at the same time and as to the same person. Thus, an item cannot, for example, be classified as both consumer goods and equipment.

The evidence before this court indicates that the computer items were purchased for use primarily in business rather than for personal, family, or household purposes. Mrs. Phillips' uncontradicted testimony is that at the time of purchase she informed the salesperson at Holdren's that the computer would be used for her teaching assignments as well as in the variety store. She received a special discount as a state instructor for purchase of the items for use in teaching. Mrs. Phillips also indicated that she purchased this computer with its memory capability to handle business transactions, and that she purchased a software package on Practical Accounting for business billing. These facts and circumstances should have provided sufficient notice of the use of the items for classification purposes such that financing statements could have been filed properly to perfect the security interest.

Courts have held without exception that the Uniform Commercial Code filing requirements are mandatory and that the filing of a financing statement in an improper place or not in all the places required is ineffective to perfect a security interest. Although the application of rules in a given case may be harsh, any other result would invite inconsistency which the Uniform Commercial Code was enacted to avoid. On the evidence presented the collateral should be found to be classified as equipment and, having not filed in all places required, Creditway holds an unperfected security interest against the debtor.

Motion of Creditway to repossess the collateral denied.

Perfection by attachment is not effective if the consumer goods are motor vehicles for which the state issues certificates of title and has only limited effectiveness if the goods are fixtures [9–302]. A later section of this chapter discusses the special rules covering these kinds of collateral.

There is also a major limitation to the perfection by attachment principle. A retailer of consumer goods who relies on attachment of a security interest to perfect it prevails over other creditors of the debtor-buyer. However, the retailer does not prevail over someone who buys the collateral from the debtor if the buyer (1) has no knowledge of the security interest; (2) gives value for the goods; and (3) buys the goods for his personal, family, or household use [9–307(2)]. The retailer does not have priority over such a **bona fide purchaser** unless it filed its security interest.

For example, an appliance store sells a television set to Arthur for $750 on a conditional sales contract, reserving a security interest in the set until Arthur has paid for it. The store does not file a financing statement, but relies on attachment for perfection. Arthur later borrows money from a credit union and gives it a security interest in the television set. When Arthur defaults on his loans and the credit union tries to claim the set, the appliance store has a better claim to the set than does the credit union. The credit union then has the rights of an unsecured creditor against Arthur.

Now, suppose Arthur sells the television set for $500 to his neighbor Andrews. Andrews is not aware that Arthur still owes money on the set to the appliance store. Andrews buys it to use in her home. If Arthur defaults on his obligation to the store, it cannot recover the television set from Andrews. To be protected against such a purchaser from its debtor, the appliance store must file a financing statement rather than relying on attachment for perfection.

One potential concern for a creditor is that the use of the collateral will change from that anticipated when the security interest was obtained. For example, in the *Phillips* case, assume that the computer was originally purchased to be used in the home and later converted to use in the business. It is important that the creditor properly perfect the security interest initially so that it will not be adversely affected by a subsequent change in use and will continue to have the benefit of its initial perfection.

Motor Vehicles

If state law requires a certificate of title for motor vehicles, then a creditor who takes a security interest in a motor vehicle must have the security interest noted on the title [9–302]. Suppose a credit union lends Carlson money to buy a new car in a state that requires certificates of title for cars. The credit union cannot rely on attachment of its security interest in the car to perfect that interest; rather, it must have its security interest noted on the certificate of title.

This requirement protects the would-be buyer of the car or another creditor who might extend credit based on Carlson's ownership of the car. By checking the certificate of title to Carlson's car, a potential buyer or creditor would learn about the credit union's security interest in the car. If no security interest is noted on the certificate of title, the buyer can buy—or the creditor can extend credit—with confidence that there are no undisclosed security interests that would be effective against him.

Fixtures

The Code also provides special rules for perfecting security interests in consumer goods that become fixtures by virtue of their attachment to or use with real property. While a creditor gets perfection merely by attachment of his security interest to a consumer good, the creditor will not prevail against other creditors who hold an interest in the real estate to which the consumer good is attached unless a financing statement is filed with the real estate records to perfect the security interest [9–401(1)(a)]. Suppose a hardware store takes a security interest in some storm windows. Because the storm windows are likely to become fixtures through their use with the homeowner's home, the hardware store cannot rely merely on attachment to protect its security interest. It should file a financing statement to protect that security interest against other creditors of the homeowner with an interest in his home.

This rule helps protect a person interested in buying the real property or a person considering lending money based on the real property. By checking the real estate records, the potential buyer or creditor would learn of the hardware store's security interest in the storm windows.

Removal of Collateral

Even where a creditor has a perfected security interest in the collateral of her debtor, she needs to be concerned about the possibility that the debtor can take the collateral from the state where the creditor has filed on it to another state where the creditor does not have her claim filed on the public record. Commonly, the security agreement between the creditor and the debtor provides where the collateral is to be kept and stipulates that it is not to be moved unless the debtor gives notice to and/or obtains the permission of the creditor. There is, however, no absolute assurance that the debtor will be faithful to such an agreement.

Under the Code, a secured creditor who has perfected his security interest generally has four months after the collateral is brought into the new state to perfect his security interest in that state. If the creditor does not reperfect within the four months, his security interest becomes unperfected and he could lose the collateral to a person who purchases it, or takes an interest in it, after it has been removed [9–103(1)]. If the creditor has not perfected his security interest by the time the collateral is removed, or within the time period that the creditor has to perfect his security interest in the former location of the collateral, then his interest is unperfected and he does not obtain the advantage of the four-month grace period.

CONCEPT REVIEW

OBTAINING AN ENFORCEABLE SECURITY INTEREST

Step	Purpose	Necessary Action
Attachment of Security Interest	To secure a debt. The debtor gives the creditor rights in the debtor's property to secure the debt owed by the creditor to the debtor.	1. Agreement by the debtor giving the creditor a security interest in specific property (collateral) in which the debtor has a legal interest. This can include after-acquired property and proceeds of the collateral. 2. The debtor must have a legal interest in the collateral. 3. The creditor must give something of value to the debtor (e.g., money or goods). Future advances are value when actually given to the debtor.
Perfection	To obtain protection against other creditors of the debtor and against purchasers of the collateral from the debtor.	1. *Public filing.* Filing a financing statement with the appropriate state or local office to put the world on notice that the creditor claims an interest in specific collateral belonging to the debtor; or in the case of a motor vehicle, noting the security interest on the certificate of title; or 2. *Possession by creditor.* The creditor may take possession of the collateral, thus putting other creditors and potential purchasers on notice that the creditor has an interest in the collateral (this is not practical for all kinds of collateral); or 3. *Perfection by attachment.* Limited perfection merely by attachment of the security interest is obtained where (a) a creditor sells consumer goods to a consumer on credit or (b) a creditor loans money to a consumer to enable him to buy consumer goods.

The Code rules that govern the removal of collateral covered by a state certificate of title—such as an automobile—are more complicated. If an automobile covered by a certificate of title on which a security interest is noted is moved to another state, the perfected security interest is perfected for four months in the new state, or until the automobile is registered in the new state. If the original state did not require that security interests be noted on the title, and if a new title is used in the second state without notation of the security interest, then under certain circumstances a buyer of the automobile can take free of the original security interest. To qualify, the buyer must not be in the business of buying and selling automobiles and must (1) give value, (2) take delivery after issuance of the new title, and (3) buy without notice of the security interest [9–103(2)].[5]

---

[5]Other rules are set out in the Code for accounts, general intangibles, chattel paper, and mobile goods removed to other states [9–103(3) and (4)].

PRIORITY RULES

Importance of Determining Priority

Because several creditors may claim a security interest in the same collateral of a debtor, the Code establishes a set of rules for determining which of the conflicting security interests has priority. Determining which creditor has priority, or the best claim, takes on particular importance in bankruptcy situations, where unless a creditor has a preferred secured interest in collateral that fully protects the obligation owed to him, the creditor may realize nothing or only a few cents on every dollar owed to him.

General Priority Rules

The basic rule established by the Code is that when more than one security interest in the same collateral has been filed or otherwise perfected, the first security interest to be filed or perfected has priority over any that are filed or perfected later. If only one security interest has been perfected, for example, by filing, then that security interest has priority. However, if none of the conflicting security interests has been perfected, then the first security interest to be attached to the collateral has priority [9–312(5)].

Thus, if Bank A filed a financing statement covering a retailer's inventory on February 1, 1992, and Bank B filed a financing statement covering that same inventory on March 1, 1992, Bank A would have priority over Bank B even though Bank B might have made its loan and attached its security interest to the inventory before Bank A did so. However, if Bank A neglected to perfect its security interest by filing and Bank B did perfect, then Bank B, as the holder of the only perfected security interest in the inventory, would prevail.

If both of the creditors neglected to perfect their security interest, then the first security interest that attached would have priority. For example, if Bank Y has a security agreement covering a dealer's equipment on June 1, 1992, and advances money to the dealer on that date, whereas Bank Z does not obtain a security agreement covering that equipment or advance money to the dealer until July 1, 1992, then Bank Y would have priority over Bank Z. In connection with the last situation, unperfected secured creditors do not enjoy a preferred position in bankruptcy proceedings, thus giving additional impetus to the desirability of filing or otherwise perfecting a security interest.

Purchase Money Security Interests in Inventory

There are several very important exceptions to the general priority rules: First, a perfected purchase money security interest in inventory has priority over a conflicting security interest in the same inventory if the purchase money security interest is perfected at the time the debtor receives possession of the inventory and if the purchase money secured party gives notification in writing to the prior secured creditor before the debtor receives the inventory [9–312(3)].

Assume that Bank A takes and perfects a security interest in all the present and after-acquired inventory of a debtor. Then, the debtor acquires some additional inventory from a wholesaler, who retains a security interest in the inventory until the debtor pays for it and perfects this security interest. The wholesaler has a purchase money security interest in inventory goods and has priority over the prior secured creditor (Bank A) if the wholesaler has perfected the security interest by the time the collateral reaches the debtor and if the wholesaler sends notice of her purchase money security interest to Bank A before shipping the goods. Thus, to protect itself, the wholesaler must check the public records to see whether any of the debtor's creditors are claiming an interest in the debtor's inventory. When the wholesaler discovers that some are claiming an interest, it should file its own security interest and give notice to the existing creditors.

As the following *Borg-Warner Acceptance Corp.* case illustrates, the subsequent seller of inventory can obtain a priority position if it files a financing statement and notifies the prior secured party in a timely fashion.

BORG-WARNER ACCEPTANCE CORP. v. TASCOSA NATIONAL BANK

784 S.W.2d 129 (Tex. Ct. App. 1990)

On March 1, 1982, the Tascosa National Bank of Amarillo (Bank) extended a loan to T & L Ventures, Inc. d/b/a The Video Connection (T & L) in the amount of $30,006. A financing statement was obtained and filed with the secretary of state on March 4, 1982. The Bank's financing statement described the collateral as:

Video software and hardware, computer games hardware and software, all inventory, furniture, fixtures of above located at Amarillo, Potter County, Texas.

From time to time, the indebtedness was renewed and extended and additional funds were provided T & L, with the last note dated April 18, 1986, in the principal amount of $153,613.84. All indebtedness was evidenced by notes and secured by the same collateral.

On March 7, 1982, Borg-Warner Acceptance Corporation (Borg-Warner) entered into an Inventory Security Agreement pursuant to which T & L granted to Borg-Warner a security interest in its inventory purchased with the proceeds of loans made by Borg-Warner. Borg-Warner perfected its security interest as a purchase money security interest (PMSI) under section 9–312(3) by: (1) filing on March 11, 1982, a financing statement describing the collateral with the secretary of state's office; and (2) notifying the Bank of Borg-Warner's interest in T & L's inventory.

Following the perfection of Borg-Warner's PMSI, Borg-Warner commenced financing the acquisition of inventory by T & L and continued such financing through May 22, 1986. Pursuant to a "floor-planning arrangement," Borg-Warner purchased from vendors and paid directly to vendors the invoice purchase price of inventory acquired by T & L for resale. Indebtedness to Borg-Warner was not incurred for any purpose other than the purchase of inventory.

T & L defaulted on its indebtedness. On May 11, 1986, the Bank repossessed T & L's inventory, removed it from T & L's premises, and placed it in a warehouse. Borg-Warner demanded that the Bank deliver the inventory to it on the grounds it had a superior claim to it. The Bank refused and Borg-Warner brought suit against the Bank. The trial court granted summary judgment in favor of the Bank, and Borg-Warner appealed.

Dodson, Judge. The determinative issue on Borg-Warner's appeal is the priority of liens question. If Borg-Warner's security interest qualifies as a PMSI under section 9–312(3), Borg-Warner prevails. However, if Borg-Warner's security interest does not so qualify, then the Bank prevails under the "first to file rule." Section 9–312(5)(1).

The Uniform Commercial Code defines two types of PMSI's, that claimed by sellers and that claimed by financing agencies:

A security interest is a "purchase money security interest" to the extent that it is
    (1) taken or retained by the seller of the collateral to secure all or part of its price; or
    (2) taken by a person who by making advances or incurring an obligation gives value to enable the debtor to acquire rights in or the use of collateral if such value is so used.

Section 9–107.

We reiterate, the general rule of priority among conflicting security interests in the same collateral where both interests are perfected by filing, is that the secured party who first files a financing statement prevails. Section 9–312(5)(1). However, section 9–312(3) states a special rule for a PMSI in inventory. That subsection reads in full as follows:

(3) A *perfected purchase money security interest in inventory has priority over a conflicting security interest in the same inventory* and also has priority in identifiable cash proceeds received on or before the delivery of the inventory to a buyer if
    (1) the purchase money security interest is perfected at the time the *debtor* receives possession of the inventory; and
    (2) except where excused by section 9–319 (oil and gas production), the *purchase money secured party gives notification in writing to the holder of the conflicting security interest if the holder had filed a financing statement covering the same types of inventory (i) before the date of the filing made by the purchase money secured party, or (ii) before the beginning of the 21 day period where the purchase money security interest is temporarily perfected without filing or possession (Subsection (e) of Section 9–304);* and
    (3) *the holder of the conflicting security interest receives any required notification within five years before* the debtor receives possession of the inventory; and
    (4) *the notification states that the person giving the notice has or expects to acquire a purchase money security interest in inventory of the debtor, describing such inventory by item or type.* (emphasis added)

Section 9–312(3).

Under the above provisions, Borg-Warner's security interest is a PMSI to the extent that it is taken by Borg-Warner who by incurring an obligation gave value to enable T & L to acquire rights in or the use of collateral if such value was in fact used.

In determining the priority between Borg-Warner and the Bank, we note that the legislature has provided that a PMSI in inventory such as Borg-Warner's has priority over a conflicting security interest in the same inventory if: (1) the PMSI was perfected at the time T & L received possession of the inventory; (2) Borg-Warner gave notice in writing to the Bank who had filed a financing statement covering the same type of inventory before the date of the filing by Borg-Warner; (3) the Bank received any required notification within five years before T & L received possession of the inventory; and (4) the notification stated that Borg-Warner expected to acquire a PMSI in the inventory of T & L, describing such inventory by item or type. Section 9–312(3).

Our earlier explication of the undisputed facts reveal that Borg-Warner complied with the statutory code requirements.

Judgment reversed in favor of Borg-Warner.

Purchase Money Security Interests in Noninventory Collateral

The second exception to the general priority rule is that a purchase money security interest in collateral other than inventory has priority over a conflicting security interest in the same collateral if the purchase money security interest is perfected at the time the debtor receives the collateral or within 10 days afterward [9–312(4)].

Assume that Bank B takes and perfects a security interest in all the present and after-acquired equipment belonging to a debtor. Then, a supplier sells some equipment to the debtor, reserving a security interest in the equipment until it is paid for. If the supplier perfects the purchase money security interest by filing at the time the debtor obtains the collateral or within 10 days thereafter, it has priority over Bank B. This is because its purchase money security interest in non-inventory collateral prevails over a prior perfected security interest if the purchase money security interest is perfected at the time the debtor takes possession or within 10 days afterward.

The preference given to purchase money security interests, provided that their holders comply with the statutory procedure in a timely manner, serves several ends. First, it prevents a single creditor from closing off all other sources of credit to a particular debtor and thus possibly preventing the debtor from obtaining additional inventory or equipment needed to maintain his business. Second, the preference makes it possible for a supplier to have first claim on inventory or equipment until it is paid for, at which time it

may become subject to the after-acquired property clause of another creditor's security agreement. By requiring that the first perfected creditor be given notice of a purchase money security interest at the time the new inventory comes into the debtor's inventory, the Code serves to alert the first creditor to the fact that some of the inventory on which it may be relying for security is subject to a prior secured interest until it is paid for.

Buyers in the Ordinary Course of Business

A third exception to the general priority rule is that a **buyer in the ordinary course of business** (other than a person buying farm products from a person engaged in farming operations) takes free from a security interest created by his seller even though the security interest is perfected and even though the buyer knows of its existence [9–307(1)]. For example, a bank loans money to a dealership to finance that dealership's inventory of new automobiles and takes a security interest in the inventory, which it perfects by filing. Then, the dealership sells an automobile out of inventory to a customer. The customer takes the automobile free of the bank's security interest even though the dealership may be in default on its loan agreement. As long as the customer is a buyer in the ordinary course of business, she is protected. The reasons for this rule are that a bank really expects to be paid from the proceeds of the dealership's automobile sales and that the rule is necessary to the smooth conduct of commerce. Customers would be very reluctant to buy goods if they could not be sure they were getting clear title to them from the merchants from whom they buy.

In the following case, *DBC Capital Fund, Inc. v. Snodgrass*, a buyer of an automobile from a dealer obtained title free of a security interest previously given by the dealer to his creditor.

DBC CAPITAL FUND, INC. v. SNODGRASS

On February 19, 1988, DBC Capital Fund, Inc. (DBC) entered into an agreement with the owner of Devers Auto Sales whereby DBC obtained a security interest in the automobile inventory maintained by Devers. This security interest was perfected by filing with the secretary of state on February 25, 1988.

On March 24, 1989, Cheryl Snodgrass purchased a 1984 Oldsmobile from Devers for $5,000 in cash. This automobile was taken from the inventory covered by DBC's security interest, although Snodgrass was not made aware of the financing agreement between Devers and DBC. When Snodgrass took possession of the Oldsmobile, Devers told her that the automobile's certificate of title would be mailed to her. In the meantime, she was issued a temporary registration.

On April 28, 1989, Snodgrass was informed by letter that DBC had physical possession of the certificate of title for the Oldsmobile and that DBC considered itself to have a valid lien on the automobile. In a later telephone conversation, DBC's attorney informed Snodgrass that DBC would not release the certificate of title to the 1984 Oldsmobile until Snodgrass paid DBC $4,200.

On April 25, 1989, the temporary registration issued to Snodgrass by Devers expired. Because Snodgrass was not in possession of the certificate of title for the Oldsmobile, she was unable to obtain proper licensing for the vehicle and, therefore, could not use the automobile. In an effort to obtain the certificate of title, Snodgrass then filed suit against DBC. The trial court entered judgment in her favor on June 28, 1989, awarding her $1,920 in triple damages and $1,748.45 in attorney's fees. DBC appealed.

Ratliff, Judge.   DBC first contends that the trial court erred in determining that Snodgrass was a buyer in the ordinary course of business, and that, therefore, the trial court failed to recognize that, as a holder of a valid secured interest, DBC was entitled to possession of the certificate of title to the 1984 Oldsmobile. We disagree.

At the hearing the parties stipulated to the fact that DBC had a valid security interest in the 1984 Oldsmobile. The main issue litigated at trial was whether Snodgrass was in a legal position which would make her claim to the automobile superior to that of DBC. Under the relevant provision of the Uniform Commercial Code (U.C.C.) the interest of a "buyer in the ordinary course of business" is superior to that of a holder of valid secured interest. Section 9–307(1).

DBC claims that Snodgrass cannot be considered a buyer in the ordinary course of business "because she failed to require delivery of the title at the time of purchase." According to DBC Snodgrass was charged with knowledge of Indiana Code sections 9-1-2-2(a) and 9-1-2-3(b) which made it unlawful for Devers to fail to deliver a certificate of title at the time of purchase. Because Devers failed to deliver the certificate of title at the time of sale, Snodgrass knew or should have known that the sale of the 1984 Oldsmobile was in violation of the ownership rights of a third party. DBC concludes that because Snodgrass was not a buyer in the ordinary course of business, Snodgrass cannot defeat DBC's valid security interest.

It is true that if there are grounds for suspecting that a security interest is being imperiled by a mode of dealing, a transaction cannot be considered in the ordinary course of business. However, we conclude that DBC has failed to prove that the mode of dealing in the present case was grounds for such a suspicion. DBC's analysis is flawed in that it rests on the supposition that sections 9-1-2-2(a) and 9-1-2-3(b) were enacted to protect the interests of secured creditors. Such simply is not the case. The plain purpose for enacting these statutes was to impede the trade in stolen vehicles. As stated by Judge Posner of the United States Court of Appeals, "as the statute is intended to protect purchasers . . . rather than lenders, there would be a considerable paradox in interpreting the statute to defeat the purchaser's interest." Therefore, we reject DBC's contention that these statutes create a duty on behalf of a purchaser to demand delivery of the certificate of title to an automobile at the time of sale.

Absent such a duty, nothing in the evidence suggests that Snodgrass' purchase of the 1984 Oldsmobile was outside the ordinary course of business. Therefore, under the provisions of section 9–307(1), as a buyer in the ordinary course of business, Snodgrass took free of the security interest held by DBC.

Judgment in favor of Snodgrass.

Artisan's and Mechanic's Liens

The Code also provides that certain liens arising by operation of law (such as an artisan's lien) have priority over a perfected security interest in the collateral [9–310]. For example, Marshall takes her automobile, on which a credit union has a perfected security interest, to Frank's Garage to have it repaired. Under common or statutory law, Frank's may have a lien on the car to secure payment for the repair work; such a lien permits Frank's to keep the car until it receives payment. If Marshall defaults on her loan to the credit union, refuses to pay Frank's for the repair work, and the car is sold to satisfy the liens, Frank's is entitled to its share of the proceeds before the credit union gets anything.

Fixtures

A separate set of problems arise when the collateral is goods that become fixtures by being so related to particular real estate that an interest in them arises under real estate law. Determining the priorities among a secured party with an interest in the fixtures, subsequent purchasers of the real estate, and those persons who have a secured interest—such as a mortgage—on the real property can involve both real estate law and the Code. However, the Code does set out rules for determining when the holder of a perfected security interest in fixtures has priority over an encumbrancer or owner of the real estate. Some of the Code priority rules are as follows:

First, the holder of the secured interest in a fixture has priority if: (1) his interest is a purchase money security interest obtained prior to the time the goods become fixtures; (2) the security interest is perfected by "fixture filing"; that is, by filing in the recording office where a mortgage on the real estate would be filed prior to, or within 10 days of, the time when the goods become fixtures [9–313(4)(a)]; and (3) the debtor has a recorded interest in the real estate or is in possession of it.

For example, Restaurant Supply sells Arnie's Diner a new gas stove on a conditional sales contract, reserving a security interest until the stove is paid for. The stove is to be installed in a restaurant for which Arnold Schwab has a 10-year lease. Restaurant Supply can assure that its security interest in the stove has priority over any claims to it by the owner of the restaurant and anyone holding a mortgage on it. To do this, Restaurant Supply must (1) enter into a security agreement with Schwab before the stove is delivered to him; and (2) perfect its security interest by fixture filing before the stove is hooked up by a plumber or within 10 days of that time.

Second, the secured party whose interest in fixtures is perfected has priority where: (1) the fixtures are removable factory or office machines or readily removable replacements of domestic appliances that are consumer goods; and (2) the security interest was perfected before the goods became fixtures [9–313(4)(c)]. For example, Harriet Hurd's dishwasher breaks down and she contracts with The Appliance Store to buy a new one on a time-payment plan. The mortgage on Hurd's house provides that it covers the real property along with all kitchen appliances, or their replacements. The Appliance Store's security interest in the dishwasher has priority over the interest of the holder of the mortgage if The Appliance Store perfects its security interest before the new dishwasher is installed in Hurd's home. Perfection in consumer goods can, of course, be obtained merely by attaching the security interest through the signing of a valid security agreement.

Once a secured party has filed his security interest as a fixture filing, he has priority over purchasers or encumbrancers whose interests are filed after that of the secured party [9–313(4)(b) and (d)].

Where the secured party has priority over all owners and encumbrancers of the real estate, he generally has the right on default to remove the collateral from the real estate. However, he must make reimbursement for the cost of any physical injury caused to the property by the removal [9–313(8)].

CONCEPT REVIEW

PRIORITY RULES

Parties	Rule
Buyer of Collateral from Debtor versus Creditor with a Security Interest in the Collateral	1. A *buyer in ordinary course of business* (other than a person buying farm products from a person engaged in farming operations) takes *free* of a security interest created by his seller even though the security interest is *perfected* and even though the buyer knows of its existence. 2. A *bona fide purchaser* of collateral that is *consumer goods* from a debtor has priority over a creditor who holds a purchase money security interest in the collateral but did not file its security interest if the buyer (a) has no knowledge of the security interest, (b) gives value for the goods, and (c) buys them for her own personal, family, or household use. 3. Otherwise, buyers take subject to perfected security interests but free of unperfected security interests.

Secured Creditor versus Other Creditors	1. As to collateral *other than fixtures*, the general rule is that when more than one security interest in the same collateral has been filed (or otherwise perfected), the first security interest to be perfected has priority over other security interests.
	2. Exceptions to this general rule are:
	  a. *Inventory.* A perfected purchase money security interest in inventory has priority over a conflicting security interest in the same inventory *if* the purchase money security interest is perfected at the time the debtor receives possession of the inventory *and* if the purchase money secured party gives notification in writing to the prior secured creditor *before* the debtor receives the inventory.
	  b. *Noninventory collateral.* A purchase money security interest in noninventory collateral prevails over a prior perfected security interest *if* the purchase money security interest is perfected at the time the debtor takes possession or within 10 days afterward.
	  c. *Liens by operation of law.* Liens that arise by operation of law—such as artisan's liens—have priority over even perfected security interests in collateral.
	3. If none of the conflicting security interests has been perfected, then the *first* security interest to be *attached* to the collateral has priority.

Secured Creditor versus Other Persons with an Interest in Real Property on which Fixture Is Located	1. As to collateral that will become a *fixture:*
	  a. A creditor with a secured interest in a fixture has priority if (1) the interest is a purchase money security interest that was obtained prior to the time the goods became fixtures; (2) the security interest was perfected by fixture filing prior to, or within 10 days of the time when the goods became fixtures; and (3) the debtor has a recorded interest in the real estate or is in possession of it.
	  b. A creditor with a perfected secured interest in fixtures will have priority where: (1) the fixtures are removable factory or office machines or readily removable replacements of domestic appliances that are consumer goods; and (2) the security interest is perfected *prior* to the time the goods become fixtures.

DEFAULT AND FORECLOSURE

Default

Usually, the creditor and debtor state in their agreement which events constitute a default by the buyer. The Code does not define what constitutes default. Defining default is left to the parties' agreement, subject to the Code requirement that the parties act in good faith in doing so. If the debtor defaults, the secured creditor has several options:

1. Forget the collateral, and sue the debtor on his note or promise to pay.
2. Repossess the collateral, and use strict foreclosure—in some cases—to keep the collateral in satisfaction of the remaining debt.
3. Repossess and foreclose on the collateral, and then, depending on the circumstances, either sue for any deficiency or return the surplus to the debtor.

Right to Possession

The agreement between the creditor and the debtor may authorize the creditor to repossess the collateral in case of default. If the debtor does default, the creditor is entitled under the Code to possession of the collateral. If the creditor can obtain possession peaceably, he may do so. If the collateral is in the possession of the debtor and cannot be obtained without disturbing the peace, then the creditor must take court action to repossess the collateral [9–503]. See the following *Wade v. Ford Motor Credit Co.* case for a discussion of what constitutes repossession without breach of the peace.

If the collateral is intangible, such as accounts, chattel paper, instruments, or documents, and performance has been rendered to the debtor, the secured party may give notice and have payments made or performance rendered to him [9–502].

WADE v. FORD MOTOR CREDIT CO.

668 P.2d 183 (Kan. Ct. App. 1983)

In August 1979, Norma Wade purchased a Ford Thunderbird automobile and gave Ford Motor Credit a security interest in it to secure her payment of the $7,000 balance of the purchase price. When Wade fell behind on her monthly payments, Ford engaged the Kansas Recovery Bureau to repossess the car.

On February 10, 1980, an employee of the Recovery Bureau located the car in Wade's driveway, unlocked the door, got in, and started it. He then noticed a discrepancy between the serial number of the car and the number listed in his papers. He shut off the engine, got out, and locked the car. When Wade appeared at the door to her house, he advised her that he had been sent by Ford to repossess the car but would not do so until he had straightened out the serial number. She said that she had been making payments, that he was not going to take the car, and that she had a gun, which she would use. He suggested that Wade contact Ford to straighten out the problem. She called Ford and advised its representative that if she caught anybody on her property again trying to take her car, she would use her gun to "leave him laying right where I saw him."

Wade made several more payments, but Ford again contracted to have the car repossessed. At 2 A.M. on March 5, 1980, the employee of the Kansas Recovery Bureau successfully took the car from Wade's driveway. She said that she heard a car burning rubber, looked out of her window, and saw that her car was missing. There was no confrontation between Wade and the employee since he had safely left the area before she discovered that the car had been taken.

Wade then brought a lawsuit against Ford claiming that the car had been wrongfully repossessed. She sought actual and punitive damages, plus attorney's fees. Ford filed a counterclaim for the deficiency of $2,953.44 remaining after the car had been sold at public auction. The trial court found that Ford had breached the peace in repossessing the car and was liable to Wade for damages. It also found for Ford on its counterclaim. Ford appealed.

Swinehart, Justice.   Ford contends that the trial court erred in finding that Ford breached the peace on March 10, 1980, when its agent repossessed Wade's car. The issue presented can be stated as follows: Does the repossession of a car, when there is no contact or confrontation between the repossessor and the debtor at the time and place of repossession, constitute a breach of the peace when there has been a prior threat of deadly violence if repossession is attempted? This particular set of facts has not been addressed by the courts before.

The trial court found that Ford had breached the peace in repossessing Wade's car. In its findings and conclusions made at the conclusion of the trial, the trial court emphasized Wade's lack of consent to the repossession and stated: "It's this court's view that the Legislature, when it permitted self-help repossession, it was meant to cover amicable situations where there was no dispute as there apparently was in this particular case." It appears that the trial court put a great deal of emphasis on Wade's lack of consent and the great potential for violence involved in the second repossession attempt. Section 9–503 provides in part: "Unless otherwise agreed a secured party has on default the right to take possession of the collateral. In taking possession a secured party may proceed without judicial process if this can be done without breach of the peace or may proceed by action."

The statutes do not define the term *breach of the peace*. The courts are left with that job. We find it is clear from a survey of the cases dealing with self-help repossession that the consent of the debtors to the repossession is not required. Section 9–112 even presupposes the lack of consent: "Upon default by a consumer, unless the consumer *voluntarily surrenders* possession." (Emphasis supplied.) The trial court's emphasis on the lack of consent by Wade in the present case and its view that "the Legislature, when it permitted self-help repossession, meant to cover amicable situations where there was no dispute" are not founded in case law. Repossession, without the consent of the debtor, absent more, does not constitute a breach of the peace by the creditor.

The trial court also emphasized the potential for violence brought on by Wade's threats made during the first repossession attempt. A breach of the peace may be caused by an act likely to produce violence. The facts presented in this case do not, however, rise to that level. A period of one month elapsed between the repossession attempts. During that period, Wade and Ford were in communication and two payments were made. We find the potential for violence was substantially reduced by the passage of time. Moreover, the actual repossession was such that in all likelihood no confrontation would materialize. In fact, Wade was totally unaware of the repossession until after the agent had successfully left the premises with the car. We therefore find that as a matter of law there was no breach of the peace in the repossession of Wade's car.

Judgment reversed in favor of Ford.

Sale of the Collateral

The secured party may dispose of the collateral by sale or lease or in any manner calculated to produce the greatest benefit to all parties concerned. However, the method of disposal must be *commercially reasonable* [9–504]. Notice of the time and place of a public sale must be given to the debtor, as must notice of a private sale. If the creditor decides to sell the collateral at a public sale such as an auction, then the creditor must give the debtor notice of the time and place of the public sale. Similarly, if the creditor proposes to make a private sale of the collateral, notice must be given to the debtor. This gives the debtor a chance to object or to otherwise protect his interests [9–504].

Until the collateral is actually disposed of by the creditor, the buyer has the right to **redeem** it. This means that the buyer can pay off the debt and recover the collateral from the creditor [9–506].

Consumer Goods

If the creditor has a security interest in consumer goods and the debtor has paid 60 percent or more of the purchase price or debt (and has not agreed in writing to a strict foreclosure), the creditor must sell the repossessed collateral. If less than 60 percent of the purchase price or debt related to consumer goods has been paid, and as to any other security interest, the creditor may propose to the debtor that the seller keep the collateral in satisfaction of the debt. The consumer-debtor has 21 days to object in writing. If the consumer objects, the creditor must sell the collateral. Otherwise, the creditor may keep the collateral in satisfaction of the debt [9–505].

Distribution of Proceeds

The Code sets out the order in which any proceeds are to be distributed after the sale of collateral by the creditor. First, any expenses of repossessing, storing, and selling the collateral, including reasonable attorney's fees, are paid. Second, the proceeds are used to satisfy the debt. Third, any junior liens are paid. Finally, if any proceeds remain, the debtor is entitled to them. If the proceeds are not sufficient to satisfy the debt, then the creditor is usually entitled to a **deficiency judgment.** This means that the debtor remains personally liable for any debt remaining after the sale of the collateral [9–504].

For example, suppose a loan company lends Christy $5,000 to purchase a car and takes a security interest. After making several payments and reducing the debt to $4,800, Christy defaults. The loan company pays $50 to have the car repossessed and then has it sold at an auction, where it brings $4,500, thus incurring a sales commission of 10 percent ($450) and attorney's fees of $150. The repossession charges, sales commission, and attorney's fees, totaling $650, are paid first from the $4,500 proceeds. The remaining $3,850 is applied to the $4,800 debt, leaving a balance due of $950. Christy remains liable to the loan company for the $950.

Liability of Creditor

A creditor who holds a security interest in collateral must be careful to comply with the provisions of Article 9 of the Code. A creditor acting improperly in repossessing collateral or in its foreclosure and sale is liable to the parties injured. Thus, a creditor can be liable to a debtor if she acts improperly in repossessing or selling collateral [9–507].

Constitutional Requirements in Regard to Repossession

In 1972, in *Fuentes v. Shevin*, the U.S. Supreme Court held that state repossession statutes that authorize summary seizure of goods and chattels by state agents such as a sheriff, on an application by some private person who claims he is lawfully entitled to the property and posts a bond, are unconstitutional.[6] This is because these statutes deny the current possessor of the property an opportunity to be heard in court before the property is taken from him. The Court did not accept the argument that because the possessors of the property in question had signed conditional sales contracts authorizing the sellers to take back or repossess the property on default, they had waived their rights to a hearing. This decision raised some speculation that the provisions of the Code permitting secured parties to repossess collateral, in some cases without even judicial process, might be constitutionally defective.

Then, in 1974, in *Mitchell v. W. T. Grant*, the Supreme Court limited the *Fuentes* holding to a requirement that where only property rights are involved, there must be some opportunity for a judicial hearing prior to any final determination of the rights of the parties claiming an interest in the property in question.[7] This decision permits property to be seized by state officials, following the filing of an application and the posting of a bond, so long as the person from whom the property is seized has a later opportunity in court to assert his rights to the property.

The repossession provisions of the Code have been attacked in court as lacking in due process. However, the courts to date have upheld the Code repossession provisions as they relate to private repossession without judicial process.[8] Where judicial process is used, the procedures must conform to the standards laid down in *Fuentes* and *Mitchell*.

---

[6]407 U.S. 67 (1972).

[7]407 U.S. 600 (1974).

[8]See, for example, *Gibbs v. Titelman*, 502 F.2d 1107 (3d Cir. 1974), and cases cited therein.

ETHICAL AND PUBLIC POLICY CONCERNS

1. In the *Wade* case earlier in this chapter, a car was repossessed by driving it away from the debtor's residence at 2 A.M. In Problem Case 10 of this chapter, an automobile was repossessed by forcing it off the road and then forcing the driver to drive it to the dealer/creditor. Are the techniques used in these two cases ethical?

2. Should creditors be able to obtain deficiency judgments against consumers who default on their obligations in connection with the time-purchase of consumer goods and where the proceeds on resale are not sufficient to satisfy the balance due? Or should the creditor have to look solely to the collateral for his security?

3. Suppose that you own an appliance business in a working-class neighborhood that makes most of its sales on credit. What considerations would you take into account in determining whether and when to foreclose or repossess items on which customers have fallen behind in making their payments? Should you be swayed by the personal circumstances of your debtor or look only to protecting your financial interests? For example, would you consider the value of the item to the debtor—such as whether it is a necessity for her life, such as a refrigerator, or a luxury? Would you consider the reason the person had fallen behind—that is, whether she had been ill or had recently lost her job?

SUMMARY

A security interest is an interest in personal property or fixtures that secures payment or performance of an obligation. The Uniform Commercial Code sets out rules for obtaining secured interests in instruments, documents of title, accounts, contract rights, chattel paper, general intangibles, and goods. Goods may be consumer goods, equipment, inventory, farm products, or fixtures. To obtain the maximum protection for his security interest, the creditor must attach and perfect that interest.

A security interest is not enforceable until it has been attached to the collateral. To effect this attachment, there must be an agreement between the debtor and the secured party that the security interest attach, that value must be given to the debtor, and that the debtor must have rights in the collateral. A security agreement may cover future advances to be made by the creditor to the debtor. A security agreement may also create a security interest in proceeds of the collateral and in after acquired property of the debtor.

To protect his security interest against other creditors of the debtor and purchasers of the collateral, the secured party must perfect his security interest. Under the Code, there are three means of perfection: public filing of a financing statement; taking possession of the collateral; and, in some limited cases, mere attachment of the security interest. A financing statement is filed at either the secretary of state's office or the local recorder's office, depending on the collateral that it secures. If no maturity date is stated, the filing is good for five years. It may be extended for additional five-year periods by filing continuation statements. A debtor who has fulfilled his obligations is entitled to a termination statement, which removes the financing statement from the records.

The Code sets out a series of rules for determining the priority of conflicting claims of secured creditors to the same collateral. Where more than one security interest has been perfected, the first security interest to be perfected has priority over any security interests that are perfected later or any that are unperfected. If none of the security interests have been perfected, then the first security interest to attach has priority. However, special rules provide that creditors who have purchase money security interests can prevail over prior secured creditors if they file. In addition, a buyer in the ordinary course of business takes free of a security interest created by his seller even though the security interest is perfected and the buyer knows about it.

A secured party holding a security interest in goods that may become fixtures must take special steps so that her claim is shown on the real estate records.

Within stated limitations, the parties may agree about the rights of the secured party if the debtor defaults. Unless otherwise agreed, the secured party has the right to possess the collateral. If it is bulky or hard to remove, he may render it useless and sell it where it is located. He may sell the collateral at public or private sale, and he may buy the collateral, but he must act in good faith and the sale must be commercially reasonable. The proceeds of the sale are distributed as follows: expenses; reasonable attorney's fees; satisfaction of indebtedness; junior creditors, if any; and the balance to the debtor. Unless otherwise agreed, the seller is entitled to a deficiency judgment if the proceeds are not sufficient to cover the debt. If the security interest is in consumer goods, the secured party must sell if 60 percent of the debt has been paid. If less than 60 percent has been paid, the secured party may, upon appropriate notice, keep the collateral and cancel the debt.

PROBLEM CASES

1. Symons, a full-time insurance salesman, bought a set of drums and cymbals from Grinnel Brothers. A security agreement was executed between them but was never filed. Symons purchased the drums to supplement his income by playing with a band. He had done this before, and his income from his two jobs was about equal. He also played several other instruments. Symons became bankrupt, and the trustee tried to acquire the drums and cymbals as part of his bankruptcy estate. Grinnel's claimed that the drums and cymbals were consumer goods and thus it had a perfected security interest merely by attachment of the security interest. Were the drums and cymbals consumer goods? *Not Had to be perfected within 10 days*

2. On December 13, 1982, Joseph Modafferi borrowed $10,000 from Peg-Leg Productions in exchange for a promissory note payable on demand with interest at 10 percent per annum. The note was silent as to the existence of any collateral to secure payment. On January 14, 1983, Peg-Leg Productions filed a financing statement signed by Modafferi. The financing statement stated that it covered "all office equipment, furniture and accounts payable." In December 1983, Modafferi filed a voluntary petition in bankruptcy. At the time he still owed the $10,000 to Peg-Leg Productions. Peg-Leg claimed that it had a perfected security claim for the $10,000 by virtue of the promissory note and the subsequent filing of a financing statement. Did Peg-Leg Productions have a perfected secured interest in Modafferi's office equipment, furniture, and accounts payable? *Yes*

3. Robert and Billie Brown operated a paint and gift store. They borrowed $36,628.31 from the First National Bank of Dewey and gave the bank a security interest in "all goods, wares, merchandise, gifts, inventory, fixtures, and accounts receivable owned or thereafter acquired and used in the business." The security agreement also covered "all additions, accessions, and substitutions" to or for collateral and required the Browns to insure the collateral for the benefit of the bank. The bank perfected its security interest. The Browns obtained fire insurance but did not name the bank as a loss payee. The Browns's business was destroyed by fire, and the Browns received a $25,000 check from the insurance company for the loss of inventory. The bank then filed suit to obtain the check. Shortly thereafter, the Browns were adjudicated bankrupt. Does the bank have a perfected security interest in the insurance check? *Yes!*

4. Nicolosi bought a diamond ring on credit from a Rike-Kumler store as an engagement present for his fiancée. He signed a purchase money security agreement giving Rike-Kumler a security interest in the ring until it was paid for. Rike-Kumler did not file a financing statement covering its security interest. Nicolosi filed for bankruptcy. The bankruptcy trustee claimed that the ring was part of the bankruptcy estate because Rike-Kumler did not perfect its security interest. Rike-Kumler claimed that it had a perfected security interest in the ring. Did Rike-Kumler have to file a financing statement to perfect its security interest in the ring? *No! Purchase Money Security Intrest*

5. On October 28, 1983, Steve Gresham, doing business as Midway Cycle Sales, entered into a Wholesale Financing Agreement with ITT Commercial Finance Corporation. The agreement was to finance the purchase of new motorcycles from Suzuki Motor Corporation. ITT filed a financing statement with the Indiana secretary of state on December 16, 1983. The description of the collateral in which ITT asserted a security interest included "all inventory . . . replacements and proceeds." On January 9, 1984, Union Bank filed a financing statement with the Indiana secretary of state claiming it was engaged in "floor planning of new motorcycles" for Midway Cycle Sales. In August 1984, ITT began paying Suzuki invoices for Gresham. In July 1985, ITT sent a letter to Union Bank notifying it that it expected to acquire purchase money security interests in the inventory of Stephan Gresham d/b/a Midway Cycle Sales. In early 1986, Union Bank began loaning money to Gresham under its floor planning agreement with him. Actually, Gresham was "double floor planning"—that is, he was taking invoices for motorcycles that had been paid for by ITT to the Union Bank and claiming that he had paid for the motorcycles, but had decided to floor plan them. When Union Bank advanced money to him, he used the money to make payments on the loans to ITT. He made no payments to Union Bank and did not pay off all of his loan to ITT. Midway Cycle Sales went bankrupt when Union Bank repossessed 22 new Suzuki motorcycles. ITT brought suit against Union Bank, claiming it had paid for the motorcycles and had a perfected security interest in the motorcycles that had priority over Union Bank's security interest in them. Did ITT's security interest have priority over Union Bank's security interest?

Yes Purchase Money Security had to take property   pb34p3

6. On November 18, Firestone & Company made a loan to Edmund Carroll, doing business as Kozy Kitchen. To secure the loan, a security agreement was executed, which listed the items of property included, and concluded as follows: "together with all property and articles now, and which may hereafter be, used or mixed with, added or attached to, and/or substituted for any of the described property." A financing statement that included all the items listed in the security agreement was filed with the town clerk on November 18, and with the secretary of state on November 22. On November 25, National Cash Register Company delivered a cash register to Carroll on a conditional sales contract. National Cash Register filed a financing statement on the cash register with the town clerk on December 20, and with the secretary of state on December 21. Carroll defaulted in his payments to both Firestone and National Cash Register. Firestone repossessed all of Carroll's fixtures and equipment covered by its security agreement, including the cash register, and then sold the cash register. National Cash Register claimed that it was the title owner of the cash register and brought suit against Firestone for conversion. Did Firestone or National Cash Register have the better right to the cash register? *NCR has right to cash register* *p639*

7. Grimes *NOT INVENTORY* purchased a new Dodge car from Hornish, a franchised Dodge dealer. The sale was made in the ordinary course of Hornish's business. Grimes paid Hornish the purchase price of the car at the time of the sale. Hornish had borrowed money from Sterling Acceptance and had given it a perfected security interest in its inventory, including the car Grimes bought. Hornish defaulted on its loan to Sterling and Sterling then tried to recover the Dodge from Grimes. Was the car Grimes bought from Hornish still subject to Sterling Acceptance's security interest? *No*

8. On April 10, Benson purchased a new Ford Thunderbird automobile. She traded in her old automobile and financed the balance of $4,325 through the Magnavox Employees Credit Union, which took a security interest in the Thunderbird. In July, the Thunderbird sustained major damage in two accidents. It was taken to ACM Garage for repairs that took seven months to make and resulted in charges of $2,139.54. Benson was un-able to pay the charges, and ACM claimed a garageman's lien. Does Magnavox Credit Union's lien or ACM's lien have priority? *ACM's*

9. Kahn applied for a home improvement loan to construct an in-ground swimming pool. Union National Bank approved the loan, and construction began on Kahn's land. State Bank held a valid mortgage on this land. After the pool was completed, Union National gave Kahn the money with which he paid the contractor. Union National then perfected its interest by filing. State Bank later attempted to foreclose on its mortgage. Union National claimed the value of the pool. Is Union National entitled to recover the value of the pool?

10. C. W. Rutherford purchased a Cadillac from Big Three Motors. Rutherford fell behind in his payments to the dealer on the car. One day, while his wife, Christine, was driving the Cadillac on an interstate highway, two Big Three Motors employees driving a truck forced her off the road and blocked her direct access back to the highway. One of the employees then got into the car with Christine and rode with her to the Big Three Motors dealership. Christine locked the car, took the keys, and went into the office. When she left later, she discovered that someone had taken the Cadillac from where she had parked it. An employee of Big Three Motors told her that the car had been put "in storage" because C. W. Rutherford owed payments. She then took a taxi home. The Rutherfords then brought suit against Big Three Motors, seeking punitive damages for wrongful repossession. Do they have a valid claim? *Yes!*

11. Gibson, a collector of rare old Indian jewelry, took two of his pieces to Hagberg, a pawnbroker. The two pieces, a silver belt and a silver necklace, were worth $500 each. Hagberg loaned only $45 on the belt and $50 on the necklace. Gibson defaulted on both loans, and immediately and without notice, the necklace was sold for $240. A short time later, the belt was sold for $80. At the time of their sale, Gibson owed interest on the loans of $22. Gibson sued Hagberg to recover damages for improperly disposing of the collateral. Is Gibson entitled to damages because of Hagberg's actions in disposing of the collateral? *Yes! Because no notice was given to the debtor*

CHAPTER 29

BANKRUPTCY

INTRODUCTION

When an individual, a partnership, or a corporation is unable to pay its debts to creditors, problems can arise. Some creditors may demand security for past debts or start court actions on their claims in an effort to protect themselves. Such actions may adversely affect other creditors by depriving them of their fair share of the debtor's assets. Also, quick depletion of the debtor's assets may effectively prevent the debtor who needs additional time to pay off his debts from having an opportunity to do so.

At the same time, creditors need to be protected against the actions a debtor in financial difficulty might be tempted to take to their detriment. For example, the debtor might run off with his remaining assets or might use them to pay certain favored creditors, leaving nothing for the other creditors. Finally, a means is needed by which a debtor can get a fresh start financially and not continue to be saddled with debts beyond his ability to pay. This chapter focuses on the body of law and procedure that has developed to deal with the competing interests when a debtor is unable to pay his debts in a timely manner.

The Bankruptcy Act

The Bankruptcy Act is a federal law that provides an organized procedure under the supervision of a federal court for dealing with insolvent debtors. Debtors are considered insolvent if they are unable or fail to pay their debts as they become due. The power of Congress to enact bankruptcy legislation is provided in the Constitution. Through the years, there have been many amendments to the Bankruptcy Act. Congress completely revised the act in 1978 and then passed significant amendments to it in 1984. In 1986, Congress added provisions dealing with family farms.

The Bankruptcy Act has several major purposes. One is to assure that the debtor's property is fairly distributed to the creditors and that some creditors do not obtain unfair advantage over the others. At the same time, the act protects all of the creditors against actions by the debtor that would unreasonably diminish the debtor's assets to which they are entitled. The act also provides the honest debtor with a measure of protection against the demands for payment by his creditors. Under some circumstances, the debtor is given additional time to pay the creditors, freeing him of those pressures creditors might otherwise exert. If the debtor makes a full and honest accounting of his assets and liabilities and deals fairly with his creditors, the debtor may have most—if not all—of the debts discharged so as to have a fresh start.

At one time, bankruptcy carried a strong stigma for the debtors who became involved in it. Today, this is less true. It is still desirable that a person conduct her financial affairs in a responsible manner. However, there is a greater understanding that such events as accidents, natural disasters, illness, divorce, and severe economic dislocations are often beyond the ability of individuals to control and may lead to financial difficulty and bankruptcy.

Bankruptcy Proceedings

The Bankruptcy Act covers a number of bankruptcy proceedings. In this chapter, our focus will be on:

1. Straight bankruptcy (liquidations).
2. Reorganizations.
3. Family farms.
4. Consumer debt adjustments.

The Bankruptcy Act also contains provisions regarding municipal bankruptcies, which are not covered in this chapter.

Liquidations

A liquidation proceeding, traditionally called **straight bankruptcy,** is brought under Chapter 7 of the Bankruptcy Act. The debtor must disclose all of the property he owns and surrender this bankruptcy estate to the **bankruptcy trustee.** The trustee separates out certain property that the debtor is permitted to keep and then administers, liquidates, and distributes the remainder of the bankrupt debtor's estate. There is a mechanism for determining the relative rights of the creditors, for recovering any preferential payments made to creditors, and for disallowing any preferential liens obtained by creditors. If the bankrupt person has been honest in his business transactions and in the bankruptcy proceedings, he is usually given a **discharge** (relieved) of his debts.

Reorganizations

Chapter 11 of the Bankruptcy Act provides a proceeding whereby a debtor engaged in business can work out a plan to solve its financial problems under the supervision of a federal court. A reorganization plan is essentially a contract between a debtor and its creditors. The proceeding is intended for debtors, particularly businesses, whose financial problems may be solvable if they are given some time and guidance and if they are relieved of some pressure from creditors.

Family Farms

Historically, farmers have been accorded special attention in the Bankruptcy Code. Chapter 12 of the Bankruptcy Act provides a special proceeding whereby a debtor involved in a family farming operation can develop a plan to work out his financial difficulties. Generally, the debtor remains in possession of the farm and continues to operate it while the plan is developed and implemented.

Consumer Debt Adjustments

Under Chapter 13 of the Bankruptcy Act, individuals with regular incomes who are in financial difficulty can develop plans under court supervision to satisfy their creditors. Chapter 13 permits compositions (reductions) of debts and/or extensions of time to pay debts out of the debtor's future earnings.

The Bankruptcy Courts

Bankruptcy cases and proceedings are filed in federal district courts. The district courts have the authority to refer the cases and proceedings to bankruptcy judges, who are considered to be units of the district court. If a dispute falls within what is known as a **core proceeding,** the bankruptcy judge can hear and determine the controversy. Core proceedings include a broad list of matters related to the administration of a bankruptcy estate. However, if a dispute is not a core proceeding, but rather involves a state law claim, then the bankruptcy judge can only hear the case and prepare draft findings and conclusions for review by the district court judge.

Certain proceedings affecting interstate commerce have to be heard by the district court judge if any party requests that this be done. Moreover, even the district courts are precluded from deciding certain state law claims that could not normally be brought in federal court, even if those claims are related to the bankruptcy matter. Bankruptcy judges are appointed by the president for terms of 14 years.

CHAPTER 7: LIQUIDATION PROCEEDINGS

Petitions

All bankruptcy proceedings, including liquidation proceedings, are begun by the filing of a petition. The petition may be either a **voluntary petition** filed by the debtor or an **involuntary petition** filed by a creditor or creditors of the debtor. A voluntary petition in bankruptcy may be filed by an individual, a partnership, or a corporation. However, municipal, railroad, insurance, and banking corporations and savings or building and loan associations are not permitted to file for straight bankruptcy proceedings. A person filing a voluntary petition need not be insolvent that is, her debts need not be greater than her assets. However, the person must be able to allege that she has debts. The primary purpose for filing a voluntary petition is to obtain a discharge from some or all of the debts.

Involuntary Petitions

An involuntary petition is a petition filed by creditors of a debtor. By filing it, they seek to have the debtor declared bankrupt and his assets distributed to the creditors. Involuntary petitions may be filed against many debtors. However, involuntary petitions in straight bankruptcy cannot be filed against (1) farmers; (2) ranchers; (3) nonprofit organizations; (4) municipal, railroad, insurance, and banking corporations; (5) credit unions; and (6) savings or building and loan associations. If a debtor has 12 or more creditors, an involuntary petition to declare him bankrupt must be signed by at least 3 creditors. If there are fewer than 12 creditors, then an involuntary petition can be filed by a single creditor. The creditor or creditors must have valid claims against the debtor exceeding the value of any security they hold by $5,000 or more. To be forced into involuntary bankruptcy, the debtor must be unable to pay his debts as they become due—or have had a custodian for his property appointed within the previous four months.

If an involuntary petition is filed against a debtor engaged in business, the debtor may be permitted to continue to operate the business. However, the court may appoint an **interim trustee** if this is necessary to preserve the bankruptcy estate or to prevent loss of the estate. A creditor who suspects that a debtor may dismantle her business or dispose of its assets at less than fair value may apply to the court for protection.

Automatic Stay Provisions

The filing of a bankruptcy petition operates as an **automatic stay,** holding in abeyance various forms of creditor action against a debtor or her property. These actions include: (1) beginning or continuing judicial proceedings against the debtor; (2) actions to obtain possession of the debtor's property; (3) actions to create, perfect, or enforce a lien against the debtor's property; and (4) setoff of indebtedness owed to the debtor before commencement of the bankruptcy proceeding. A court may give a creditor relief from the stay if the creditor can show that the stay does not give her "adequate protection" and jeopardizes her interest in certain property. The relief to the creditor might take the form of periodic cash payments or the granting of a replacement lien or an additional lien on property.

The case that follows, *In Re Ionosphere Clubs, Inc.,* is an example of creditors trying to proceed independent of a bankruptcy court and having their efforts blocked.

IN RE IONOSPHERE CLUBS, INC.

111 B.R. 423 (Bankr. S.D. N.Y. 1990)

On March 4, 1989, the International Association of Machinists and Aerospace Workers, AFL–CIO (IAM) initiated a strike against Eastern Air Lines, Inc. Thereafter, both the Airline Pilots Association (ALPA) and the Transport Workers Union of America (TWU) initiated a sympathy strike. As a result, on March 9, 1989, Eastern and its affiliate, Ionosphere Clubs, Inc., each filed a voluntary petition for relief under Chapter 11. Since the bankruptcy filing, Eastern and Ionosphere continued to operate their businesses as debtors in possession.

During the strike, Eastern hired new pilots as permanent replacements for the striking pilots. On November 22, 1989, the ALPA notified Eastern that the sympathy strike had been concluded and that the approximately 2,000 striking pilots were willing to return to work. Eastern was not willing to displace the replacement pilots to make room for the returning strikers.

In February 1990, Morteson Rolleston and 17 formerly striking pilots filed a class action lawsuit in federal district court in Atlanta, claiming, among other things, that Eastern had failed to fund its pilot pension plan and to pay interest on certain pension benefits that had already been paid. The lawsuit sought to freeze the assets of Eastern until amounts allegedly due to certain benefit plans were paid. Eastern sought an injunction from the bankruptcy court enjoining the Rolleston lawsuit as a violation of the automatic stay provisions of the Bankruptcy Act.

Lifland, Chief Judge.   Section 362(a)(3) of the Code provides in pertinent part as follows:

(a) . . . a petition filed under . . . this title . . . operates as a stay, applicable to all entities, of—

(1) the commencement or continuation . . . of a judicial, administrative or other proceeding against the debtor that was or could have been commenced before the commencement of the case under this title, or to recover a claim against the debtor that arose before the commencement of the case under this title;

* * * * *

(3) an act to obtain possession of the property of the estate or of property from the estate or to exercise control over property of the estate;

* * * * *

(6) any act to collect, assess or recover a claim against the debtor that arose before the commencement of the case under this title.

It is beyond dispute that the Rolleston Plaintiffs seek to exercise control of at least $281 million of the cash assets of Eastern's estate by seeking to secure a court order "freezing" Eastern's assets and directing Eastern to pay this amount to the pilot pension plans. Additionally, the Rolleston Plaintiffs appear to request a temporary restraining order that would prohibit distributions under a reorganization plan, because "if the assets are distributed to creditors, it will be impossible for Plaintiffs to recover those assets." This direct attempt to secure preferred status for a discrete group of creditors runs directly counter to the distribution and oversight scheme established by the Code.

The Rolleston Plaintiffs also allege that the funds they seek to recover from Eastern on behalf of the pension plans "are not Eastern's assets but . . . are assets of the [Rolleston] Plaintiffs." It would appear that the Rolleston Plaintiffs are merely asserting unliquidated, contingent pre-petition claims against the Eastern estate and have no specific interest (other than the interest that all of Eastern's creditors have in property of the estate) in the property which they are attempting to gain control over.

Any attempt to "freeze" Eastern's assets and obtain an order requiring Eastern to transfer cash from its estate to the pilot pension plans is a direct and blatant attempt to assert control over the assets of the estate for the benefit of the Rolleston Plaintiffs. Such a distribution will reduce the amount to be paid to creditors and have an adverse effect on the feasibility of any plan of reorganization. Additionally, the Rolleston lawsuit interferes with this court's jurisdiction over essential core matters in the Eastern case, including claims issues and confirmation of a plan of reorganization.

Judgment in favor of Eastern enjoining the Rolleston lawsuit.

Order of Relief

Once a bankruptcy petition has been filed, the first step is a court determination that relief should be ordered. If a voluntary petition is filed by the debtor, or if the debtor does not contest an involuntary petition, this step is automatic. If the debtor contests an involuntary petition, then a trial is held on the question of whether the court should order relief. The court orders relief only (1) if the debtor is generally not paying his debts as they become due, or (2) if within four months of the filing of the petition a custodian was appointed or took possession of the debtor's property. The court also appoints an interim trustee pending election of a trustee by the creditors.

Meeting of Creditors and Election of Trustee

The bankrupt person is required to file a list of his assets, liabilities, and creditors and a statement of his financial affairs. Then, the court calls a meeting of the creditors. The creditors may elect a creditors' committee and a trustee who, if approved by the judge, takes over administration of the bankrupt's estate. The trustee represents the creditors in handling the estate. At the meeting, the creditors have a chance to ask the debtor questions about his assets, liabilities, and financial difficulties. These questions commonly focus on whether the debtor has concealed or improperly disposed of assets. See Figure 1.

Duties of the Trustee

The trustee takes possession of the debtor's property and has it appraised. The debtor must also turn over her records to the trustee. For a time, the trustee may operate the debtor's business. The trustee sets aside the items of property that a debtor is permitted to keep under state exemption statutes or federal law.

The trustee examines the claims filed by various creditors and objects to those that are improper in any way. The trustee separates the unsecured property from the secured and otherwise exempt property. He also sells the bankrupt's nonexempt property as soon as possible, consistent with the best interest of the creditors.

The trustee is required to keep an accurate account of all the property and money he receives and to promptly deposit moneys into the estate's accounts. At the final meeting of the creditors, the trustee presents a detailed statement of the administration of the bankruptcy estate.

Exemptions

Even in a liquidation proceeding, the bankrupt is generally not required to give up all of his property; he is permitted to **exempt** certain items of property. Under the new Bankruptcy Act, the debtor may choose to keep certain items or property either exempted by state law, or exempt under federal law—unless state law specifically forbids use of the federal exemptions. However, any such property concealed or fraudulently transferred by the debtor may not be retained.

The debtor must elect to use *either* the set of exemptions provided by the state or the set provided by the federal bankruptcy law; she may not pick and choose between them. A husband and wife involved in bankruptcy proceedings must both elect either the federal or the state exemptions; where they cannot agree, the federal exemptions are deemed elected.

The **exemptions** permit the bankrupt person to retain a minimum amount of the assets considered necessary to life and to his ability to continue to earn a living. They are part of the fresh start philosophy that is one of the purposes of the Bankruptcy Act. The general effect of the federal exemptions is to make a minimum exemption available to debtors in all states. States that wish to be more generous to debtors can provide more liberal exemptions.

The specific items that are exempt under state statutes vary from state to state. Some states provide fairly liberal exemptions and are considered "debtors' havens." Items that are commonly made exempt from sale to pay debts owed creditors include the family Bible, tools or books of the trade, life insurance policies; health aids, such as wheelchairs and hearing aids; personal and household goods, and jewelry, furniture, and motor vehicles worth up to a certain amount.

Eleven categories of property are exempt under the federal exemptions, which the debtor may elect in lieu of the state exemptions. The federal exemptions include:

1. The debtor's interest (not to exceed $7,500 in value) in real or personal property that the debtor or a dependent of the debtor uses as a residence.

2. The debtor's interest (not to exceed $1,200 in value) in one motor vehicle.

3. The debtor's interest (not to exceed $200 in value for any particular item) up to a total of $4,000 in household furnishings, household goods, wearing apparel, appliances, books, animals, crops, or musical instruments that are held primarily for

FIGURE 1 Order and Notice of Chapter 7 Bankruptcy Filing

Order and Notice of Chapter 7 Bankruptcy Filing

B16A United States Bankruptcy Court for the District of Maryland	ORDER AND NOTICE OF CHAPTER 7 BANKRUPTCY FILING, MEETING OF CREDITORS, AND FIXING OF DATES (Individual or Joint Debtor No Asset Case)

A. GENERAL INFORMATION		

Name of Debtor John B. Jones D/B/A THE BATH SHOP	Address of Debtor 195 MAIN STREET ANNAPOLIS MD, 21401	

	Date Filed 01/24/92	Case Number 90–60300–SD	Soc. Sec. Nos./Tax ID Nos. 050–30–4701

Addressee: WICKER PRODUCTS, INC. 2000 SMITH PIKE ALMA, MI 48030	Address of the Clerk of the Bankruptcy Court United States Bankruptcy Court 101 W. Lombard Street Baltimore, Maryland 21201
Name and Address of Attorney for Debtor MARC A. BURNS 215 WATER STREET, BALTIMORE MD 21202	Name and Address of Trustee BRUCE A. SMITH 136 S. CHARLES STREET, BALTIMORE MD 21201

B. DATE, TIME AND LOCATION OF MEETING OF CREDITORS

February 28, 1992, 09:15 A.M., U.S. Trustee, Fallon Federal Bldg., Rm. G–13, 31 Hopkins Plaza, Baltimore, MD 21201

C. DISCHARGE OF DEBTS

Deadline to File a Complaint Objecting to the Discharge of the Debtor or Dischargeability of a Debt: April 30, 1992

D. BANKRUPTCY INFORMATION

THERE APPEAR TO BE NO ASSETS AT THIS TIME FROM WHICH PAYMENT MAY BE MADE TO CREDITORS. DO NOT FILE A PROOF OF CLAIM UNTIL YOU RECEIVE NOTICE TO DO SO.

FILING OF A BANKRUPTCY CASE. A bankruptcy petition has been filed in this court for the person or persons named above as the debtor, and an order for relief has been entered. You will not receive notice of all documents filed in this case. All documents which are filed with the court, including lists of the debtor's property and debts, are available for inspection at the office of the clerk of the bankruptcy court.

CREDITORS MAY NOT TAKE CERTAIN ACTIONS. Anyone to whom the debtor owes money or property is a creditor. Under the bankruptcy law, the debtor is granted certain protection against creditors. Common examples of prohibited actions are contacting the debtor to demand repayment, taking action against the debtor to collect money owed to creditors or to take property of the debtor, except as specifically permitted by the bankruptcy law, and starting or continuing foreclosure actions, repossessions, or wage deductions. If unauthorized actions are taken by a creditor against a debtor, the court may punish that creditor. A creditor who is considering taking action against the debtor or the property of the debtor should review 11 U.S.C. § 362 and may wish to seek legal advice. The staff of the clerk's office is not permitted to give legal advice to anyone.

MEETING OF CREDITORS. The debtor (both husband and wife in a joint case) shall appear at the meeting of creditors at the date and place set forth above in box 'B' for the purpose of being examined under oath. ATTENDANCE BY CREDITORS AT THE MEETING IS WELCOMED, BUT NOT REQUIRED. At the meeting the creditors may elect a trustee as permitted by law, elect a committee of creditors, examine the debtor, and transact such other business as may properly come before the meeting. The meeting may be continued or adjourned from time to time without further written notice to the creditors.

LIQUIDATION OF THE DEBTOR'S PROPERTY. A trustee has been appointed in this case to collect the debtor's property, if any, and turn it into money. At this time, however, it appears from the schedules of the debtor that there are no assets from which any dividend can be paid to creditors. If at a later date it appears that there are assets from which a dividend may be paid, creditors will be notified and given an opportunity to file claims.

EXEMPT PROPERTY. Under state and federal law, the debtor is permitted to keep certain money or property as exempt. If a creditor believes that an exemption of money or property is not authorized by law, the creditor may file an objection. Any objection must be filed no later than 30 days after the conclusion of the meeting of creditors.

DISCHARGE OF DEBTS. The debtor is seeking a discharge of debts. A discharge means that certain debts are made unenforceable. Creditors whose claims against the debtor are discharged may never take action to collect the discharged debts. If a creditor believes the debtor should not receive a discharge under 11 U.S.C. § 727 or a specific debt should not be discharged under 11 U.S.C. § 523(c) for some valid reason specified in the bankruptcy law, the creditor must take action to challenge the discharge. The deadline for challenging a discharge is set forth above in box 'C.' Creditors considering taking such action may wish to seek legal advice.

DO NOT FILE A PROOF OF CLAIM UNLESS YOU RECEIVE A COURT NOTICE TO DO SO

For the Court:	
January 31, 1992 Date	Michael Kostishak Clerk of the Bankruptcy Court

the personal, family, or household use of the debtor or a dependent of the debtor.

4. The debtor's aggregate interest (not to exceed $500 in value) in jewelry held primarily for the personal, family, or household use of the debtor or a dependent of the debtor.

5. $400 in value of any other property of the debtor's choosing, plus up to $3,750 of any unused homestead exemption.

6. The debtor's aggregate interest (not to exceed $750 in value) in any implements, professional books, or tools of the trade.

7. Life insurance contracts.

8. Interest up to $4,000 in specified kinds of dividends or interest in certain kinds of life insurance policies.

9. Professionally prescribed health aids.

10. Social security, disability, alimony, and other benefits reasonably necessary for the support of the debtor or his dependents.

11. The debtor's right to receive certain insurance and liability payments.

The term *value* means "fair market value as of the date of the filing of the petition." In determining the debtor's interest in property, the amount of any liens against the property must be deducted.

Avoidance of Liens

The debtor is also permitted to **void** certain liens against exempt properties that impair her exemptions. Liens that can be voided on this basis are judicial liens or nonpossessory, nonpurchase money security interests in: (1) household furnishings, household goods, wearing apparel, appliances, books, animals, crops, musical instruments, or jewelry that are held primarily for the personal, family, or household use of the debtor or a dependent of the debtor; (2) implements, professional books, or tools of the trade of the debtor or a dependent of the debtor; and (3) professionally prescribed health aids for the debtor or a dependent of the debtor. Debtors are also permitted to **redeem** exempt personal property from secured creditors by paying them the value of the collateral. Then, the creditor is an unsecured creditor as to any remaining debt owed by the debtor.

The case that follows, *In Re Moore*, illustrates the considerations a court might take into account in determining whether liens on particular items can be avoided.

IN RE MOORE

110 B.R. 53 (Bankr. N.D. Ala. 1988)[1]

In September 1987, Joseph and Justine Moore filed a voluntary Chapter 7 petition. In the petition, the Moores claimed as exempt all of their household goods and furnishings as well as certain guns. Listed as a secured creditor was ITT Financial Services (ITT), which held a nonpurchase money security interest in household goods. In July 1987, the Moores had refinanced a loan with ITT. As security for the loan, ITT insisted on, and was granted, a security interest in the Moores's personal property, which consisted of household furnishings, appliances, and musical instruments.

On November 30, 1987, the Moores filed a motion to avoid ITT's security interest in the household goods they were claiming as exempt. Bankruptcy Code section 522(f)(2) authorizes avoidance of nonpossessory, nonpurchase money security interests in "household goods." ITT objected to the motion on the grounds it sought avoidance of liens as to items of property that did not qualify as household goods. Specifically, ITT objected to the avoidance of its lien as to a .243 caliber rifle, a .308 caliber rifle, a 12-gauge shotgun, a Stihl chainsaw, a Kodak movie camera, a Kodak movie projector, and a 10-speed bicycle. ITT did not object to the motion as it affected its

---

[1] Printed as Appendix to In Re Gonshorowski, 110 B.R. 51 (Bankr. N.D. Ala. 1990).

lien on: (1) a television set, (2) stereo equipment, (3) musical instruments, (4) home workshop tools, and (5) garden equipment.

Wright, Chief Judge.   While numerous courts have addressed the question of what constitutes "household goods" under the Bankruptcy Act, there appears to be little uniformity in the manner in which the question has been answered. Some courts have decreed that section 522(f)(2)(A) should be construed strictly while other courts have adopted a more liberal view of the scope of lien avoidance.

Individuals who favor defining household in the narrowest of terms have relied heavily on guidelines published by the Federal Trade Commission (FTC). The FTC defines household goods as "clothing, furniture, appliances, one radio and one television, linens, china, crockery, kitchenware, and personal effects (including wedding rings) of the consumer and his or her dependents, provided that the following are not included within the scope of the term 'household goods': (1) works of art; (2) electronic entertainment equipment (except one television and one radio); (3) items acquired as antiques; and (4) jewelry (except wedding rings)."

Judges have however generally refused to adopt the FTC definition. As stated in the case of *In Re Boyer*, "it does not follow that if an item does not fall within the FTC definition of household goods, that it is not household goods for purpose of lien avoidance under the Bankruptcy Code." The FTC's definition, after all, was not promulgated simply for use in a bankruptcy context, but reflects a cost-benefit analysis of credit practice involving all consumer debtors. In *Boyer*, the court went on to hold that "household goods include more than those items that are indispensable to the bare existence of a debtor and his family. Items which, while not being luxuries, are convenient or useful to a reasonable existence must also be included."

The theme running throughout most of the cases which favor a broader definition of household goods is the belief that Congress intended to allow debtors to begin again without requiring them to give up each and every item of property they owned.

In order for debtors to have any meaningful chance at a fresh start bankruptcy courts must be willing to show some flexibility in deciding questions which arise under section 522(f)(2)(A). Thus this Court declines to adopt the FTC definition and instead adopts a rebuttable presumption that items used by debtors or their dependents in or around their residence are household goods. Since the presumption is a rebuttable one, the Court also adopts the following list of factors which it will consider in a case in which a lien avoidance question arises.

1. Whether the item in question is included within those items defined as household goods under the FTC definition;
2. The number of other like or similar items owned by the debtor;
3. The ages, sex and number of the debtor's dependents;
4. The standard of living to which the debtor and his family have become accustomed viewed in light of his annual income;
5. The standard of living of members of the debtor's neighborhood;
6. The use to which the item is put (i.e. recreational, personal or business);
7. Whether the item is one for which a certificate of title is issued;
8. Whether the items are luxury goods.

In applying the above cited factors to this case, the Court is of the opinion that the Moores's motion to avoid ITT's lien on the .243 caliber rifle, the .308 caliber, and the 12-gauge shotgun is due to be denied. The Court is presented with a more difficult decision as it relates to the Kodak movie camera, the Kodak projector, the Stihl chainsaw, and the 10-speed bicycle. While the camera, projector and bike are undisputedly recreational vehicles, the Court is not prepared to hold that recreational items are automatically excluded from being treated as household goods. Surely, there can be recreation in the home. The appropriate test is whether the items are (1) used in or around the debtor's home, (2) whether the goods are luxury goods, (3) whether the items are used for personal enjoyment as opposed to being used for the production of income, and (4) whether ownership of the goods would be considered outrageous in light of the community's standard of living. Based on these considerations, the Court is of the opinion that the Kodak camera, the Kodak projector, and the bike should be classified as household goods under the facts of this case. In addition, the Court holds that the Stihl chainsaw is an item of machinery used for the purpose of maintenance or upkeep of the homeplace and as such should be treated as a household good.

Judgment for ITT denying the motion as to avoidance of its lien on the guns, but otherwise granting the Moores's motion.

Preferential Payments

A major purpose of the Bankruptcy Act is to assure equal treatment for the creditors of an insolvent debtor. The act also prevents an insolvent debtor from distributing her assets to a few favored creditors to the detriment of the other creditors.

The trustee has the right to recover for the benefit of the bankruptcy estate all **preferential payments** in excess of $600 made by the bankrupt person.[2] A preferential payment is a payment made by an insolvent debtor within 90 days of the filing of the bankruptcy petition. Such a payment enables that creditor to obtain a greater percentage of a preexisting debt than other similar creditors of the debtor. It is irrelevant whether the creditor knew that the debtor was insolvent.

For example, Fredericks has $1,000 in cash and no other assets. He owes $650 to his friend Roberts, $1,500 to a credit union, and $2,000 to a finance company. If Fredericks pays $650 to Roberts and then files for bankruptcy, he has made a preferential payment to Roberts. Roberts has had his debt paid in full, whereas only $350 is left to satisfy the $3,500 owed to the credit union and finance company. They stand to recover only 10 cents on each dollar that Fredericks owes them. The trustee has the right to get the $650 back from Roberts.

If the favored creditor is an insider—a relative of an individual debtor or an officer, director, or related party of a company—then a preferential payment made up to one year prior to the filing of the petition can be recovered.

Preferential Liens

Preferential liens are treated in a similar manner. A creditor might try to obtain an advantage over other creditors by obtaining a lien on the debtor's property to secure an existing debt. The creditor might seek to get the debtor's consent to a lien or to obtain a lien by legal process. Such liens are considered *preferential* and are invalid if they are obtained on property of an insolvent debtor within 90 days of the filing of a bankruptcy petition and if their purpose is to secure a preexisting debt. A preferential lien obtained by an insider within one year of the bankruptcy can be avoided.

The provisions of the Bankruptcy Act that negate preferential payments and liens do not prevent a debtor from engaging in current business transactions. For example, George Grocer is insolvent. He is permitted to purchase and pay for new inventory, such as produce or meat, without the payment being considered preferential. His assets have not been reduced. He has simply traded money for goods to be sold in his business. Similarly, he could buy a new display counter and give the seller a security interest in the counter until he has paid for it. This is not a preferential lien. The seller of the counter has not gained an unfair advantage over other creditors, and Grocer's assets have not been reduced by the transaction. The unfair advantage comes where an existing creditor tries to take a lien or obtain a payment of more than his share of the debtor's assets. Then, the creditor has obtained a preference over other creditors, which is disallowed.

The act also permits payments of accounts in the ordinary course of business. Such payments are not considered preferential.

---

[2]In the case of an individual debtor whose debts are primarily consumer debts, the trustee is not entitled to avoid preferences unless the aggregate value of the property is $600 or more.

Fraudulent Transfers

If a debtor transfers property or incurs an obligation with *intent to hinder, delay, or defraud creditors*, the transfer is *voidable* by the trustee. Transfers of property for *less than reasonable value* are similarly voidable. Suppose Kasper is in financial difficulty. She "sells" her $5,000 car to her mother for $100 so that her creditors cannot claim it. Kasper did not receive fair consideration for this transfer. The transfer could be declared void by a trustee if it was made within a year before the filing of a bankruptcy petition against Kasper. The provisions of law concerning **fraudulent transfers** are designed to prevent a debtor from concealing or disposing of his property in fraud of creditors. Such transfers may also subject the debtor to criminal penalties and prevent discharge of the debtor's unpaid liabilities.

The *In Re Beckman* case, which follows, illustrates the attempt of some debtors in anticipation of bankruptcy to put some of their assets beyond the reach of their creditors and the response of the trustee who was able to avoid the transfers as fraudulent.

IN RE BECKMAN

104 B.R. 866 (Bankr. S.D. Ohio 1989)

In September 1985, Richard and Nancy Beckman believed they collectively owned assets in excess of $3 million and had a joint net worth in excess of $1.5 million. However, after consulting an attorney and having their assets appraised, it became apparent during October of 1985 that they had a negative net worth, that they were insolvent, and that bankruptcy was inevitable.

In December, the Beckmans each signed applications to Bankers National Life Insurance Company to purchase $100,000 worth of additional life insurance. At the time, Richard Beckman already had $300,000 in term life insurance, $100,000 in accidental life insurance, $10,000 in whole life, and $14,000 in credit life insurance. On January 11, 1986, Richard Beckman delivered $15,000 in cash to Bankers Life as the initial premium on the two policies ($10,000 on his policy and $5,000 on her policy). The source of the funds was fees earned in his dentistry practice during the preceding October through December. The beneficiaries on all of the insurance policies (except the credit life policy) were either the Beckmans or their children.

On January 9, 1986, the Beckmans signed a Chapter 7 bankruptcy petition, and it was filed on January 14, 1986. The trustee sought to avoid the purchase of insurance from Bankers Life as a fraud on creditors.

Cole, Bankruptcy Judge.   The Beckmans argue that it was perfectly proper and, hence, not fraudulent, to convert non-exempt cash to exempt property—the life insurance policies—on the eve of bankruptcy. Further, according to the Beckmans, the insurance purchase was made merely to "provide for each other and their children in the event that one or both of them died." For these reasons, the Beckmans submit that because the insurance purchase was not fraudulent under either federal or state law, the transfer of $15,000 is not avoidable.

The Trustee maintains the insurance purchase was undertaken with actual intent to hinder, delay and defraud the creditors of the estate, thereby rendering the transaction avoidable pursuant to Bankruptcy Code section 548(a)(1). This section states:

(a) The trustee may avoid any transfer of an interest of the debtor in property or any obligation incurred by the debtor that was made or incurred on or within one year before the date of the filing of the petition, if the debtor voluntarily or involuntarily

(1) made such transfer or incurred such obligation with actual intent to hinder, delay or defraud any entity to which the debtor was or became, on or after the date that such transfer was made or such obligation was incurred, indebted;

The issue for decision is whether the Beckmans's eve-of-bankruptcy conversion of non-exempt cash into exempt life insurance policies constitutes fraudulent conduct or merely prudent pre-bankruptcy planning.

Considerable debate in the case law has been engendered by pre-bankruptcy engineering—i.e., the practice of converting non-exempt property into exempt property in contemplation of filing a bankruptcy case. The general rule which has emerged from the decisional law is that mere conversion of property from non-exempt to exempt status on the eve of bankruptcy does not establish fraud. However, if extrinsic evidence of intent to defraud creditors is adduced, courts have: (1) disallowed the debtor's exemption claim and (2) held that the pre-bankruptcy transactions constitute avoidable fraudulent transfers.

Hence, the Court must determine here whether the Trustee has shown the existence of extrinsic evidence of fraud. Among the circumstances which courts focus upon in determining a debtor's intent in purchasing exempt life insurance on the eve of bankruptcy are the following:

1. Whether there was fair consideration paid for the life insurance policy;
2. Whether the debtor was solvent or insolvent as a result of the transfer or whether he was insolvent at the time of the transfer;
3. The amount of the policy;
4. Whether the debtor intended, in good faith, to provide by moderate premiums some protection to those to whom he had a duty to support;
5. The length of time between the purchase of a life insurance policy and the filing of the bankruptcy;
6. The amount of non-exempt property which the debtor had after purchasing the life insurance policy; and
7. The debtor's failure to produce available evidence and to testify with significant preciseness as to the pertinent details of his activities shortly before filing the bankruptcy petition.

Utilizing the foregoing factors as a guide, the Court concludes that in carrying out the insurance purchase the Beckmans intended to defraud their creditors. The factors delineated in paragraphs (2), (5) and (6) of the above list are clearly present. Debtors converted all of their remaining non-exempt property (p6) two days before their bankruptcy petition was filed (p5) and while they were admittedly insolvent (p2).

The amount of insurance purchased by the Beckmans (p3) likewise evinces a fraudulent purpose on their part. Notwithstanding the substantial amount of life insurance they had, the Beckmans consummated the purchase of additional insurance a mere three days prior to their bankruptcy filing. The Beckmans maintain the additional coverage was necessary for the protection of their family. But, having considered the record as a whole, the Court concludes that this testimony is not credible. To purchase an additional $200,000 in life insurance on the eve of bankruptcy and pre-pay the premiums thereon so that the cash surrender value of the the policies would be obtainable by the Beckmans upon the termination of their bankruptcy proceeding goes far beyond "providing in good faith by moderate premiums some protection to those to whom they had a duty to support."

Perhaps the most telling indicator of the Beckmans fraudulent intent is their attempted concealment or, at best, obfuscation of the insurance purchase in their bankruptcy schedule and the accompanying schedules.

Judgment in favor of Trustee avoiding the insurance purchase as made in fraud of creditors.

Claims

If creditors wish to participate in the estate of a bankrupt debtor, they must file a **proof of claim** in the estate within a certain time—usually six months—after the first meeting of creditors. Only unsecured creditors are required to file proofs of claims. However, a secured creditor whose secured claim exceeds the value of the collateral is an unsecured creditor to the extent of the deficiency. That creditor must file a proof of claim to support the recovery of the deficiency.

Allowable Claims

The fact that a proof of claim is filed does not assure that a creditor can participate in the distribution of the assets of the bankruptcy estate. The claim must also be allowed. If the trustee has a valid defense to the claim, he can use the defense to disallow or reduce it. For example, if the claim is based on goods sold to the debtor and the seller breached a warranty, the trustee can assert the breach as a defense. All of the defenses available to the bankrupt person are available to the trustee.

Secured Claims

The trustee must also determine whether a creditor has a lien or secured interest to secure an allowable claim. If the debtor's property is subject to a secured claim of a creditor, that creditor has first claim to it. The property is available to satisfy claims of other creditors only to the extent that its value exceeds the amount of the debt secured.

Priority Claims

The Bankruptcy Act declares certain claims to have **priority** over other claims. The six classes of priority claims are:

1. Expenses and fees incurred in administering the bankruptcy estate.

2. Unsecured claims in involuntary cases that arise in the ordinary course of the debtor's business after the filing of the petition but before the appointment of a trustee or the order of relief.

3. Unsecured claims of up to $2,000 per individual for employees' wages earned within 90 days before the petition was filed.

4. Contributions to employee benefit plans up to $2,000 per person (moreover, the claim for wages plus pension contribution is limited to $2,000 per person).

5. Claims of up to $900 each by individuals for deposits made on goods or services for personal use that were not delivered or provided.

6. Certain taxes owed to governmental units.

Distribution of the Debtor's Estate

The priority claims are paid *after* secured creditors realize on their collateral but *before* other unsecured creditors are paid. Payments are made to the six priority classes, in order, to the extent there are funds available. Each class must be paid in full before the next class is entitled to receive anything. To the extent there are insufficient funds to satisfy all the creditors within a class, each class member receives a pro rata share of his claim.

Unsecured creditors include: (1) those creditors who had not taken any collateral to secure the debt owed to them; (2) secured creditors to the extent their debt was not satisfied by the collateral they held; and (3) priority claimholders to the extent their claims exceed the limits set for priority claims.

Unsecured creditors, to the extent any funds are available for them, share in proportion to their claims. Unsecured creditors frequently receive little or nothing on their claims. Secured claims, trustee's fees, and other priority claims often consume a large part of the bankruptcy estate.

Special rules are set out in the Bankruptcy Act for distribution of the property of a bankrupt stockbroker or commodities broker.

CONCEPT REVIEW

DISTRIBUTION OF A DEBTOR'S ESTATE (Chapter 7)

Secured creditors proceed directly against the collateral. If debt is fully satisfied, they have no further interest; if debt is only partially satisfied, they are treated as general creditors for the balance.

↓

Debtor's Estate Is Liquidated and Distributed

↓

Priority Creditors (six classes)

1. Costs and expenses of administration.
2. If involuntary proceeding, expenses incurred in the ordinary course of business after petition filed but before appointment of trustee.
3. Claims for wages, salaries, and commissions earned within 90 days of petition; limited to $2,000 per person.
4. Contributions to employee benefit plans arising out of services performed within 180 days of petition; limit of $2,000 (including claims for wages, salaries, and commissions) per person.
5. Claims of individuals, up to $900 per person, for deposits made on consumer goods or services that were not received.
6. Government claims for certain taxes.

Distribution is made to the six classes of priority claims in order. Each class must be fully paid before the next class receives anything. If funds available are not sufficient to satisfy everyone in a class, then each member of the class receives same proportion of claim.

↓

General Creditors

1. General unsecured creditors.
2. Secured creditors for the portion of their debt that was not satisfied by collateral.
3. Priority creditors for amounts beyond priority limits.

If funds remaining are not sufficient to satisfy all general creditors, then they each receive the same proportion of their claims.

↓

Debtor

Debtor receives any remaining funds.

DISCHARGE IN BANKRUPTCY

Discharge

A bankrupt person who has not been guilty of certain dishonest acts and has fulfilled his duties as a bankrupt is entitled to a **discharge in bankruptcy.** A discharge relieves the bankrupt person of further responsibility for dischargeable debts and gives him a fresh start. A corporation is not eligible for a discharge in bankruptcy. A bankrupt person may file a written waiver of his right to a discharge. An individual may not be granted a discharge if she obtained one within the previous six years.

Objections to Discharge

After the bankrupt has paid all of the required fees, the court gives creditors and others a chance to file objections to the discharge of the bankrupt. Objections may be filed by the trustee, a creditor, or the U.S. attorney. If objections are filed, the court holds a hearing to listen to them. At the hearing, the court must determine whether the bankrupt person has committed any act that is a bar to discharge. If the bankrupt has not committed such an act, the court grants the discharge. If the bankrupt has committed an act that is a bar to discharge, the discharge is denied. The discharge is also denied if the bankrupt fails to appear at the hearing on objections or if he refused earlier to submit to the questioning of the creditors.

Acts that Bar Discharge

Discharges in bankruptcy are intended for honest debtors. Therefore, these acts bar a debtor from being discharged: (1) the unjustified falsifying, concealing, or destroying of records; (2) making false statements, presenting false claims, or withholding recorded information relating to the debtor's property or financial affairs; (3) transferring, removing, or concealing property in order to hinder, delay, or defraud creditors; (4) failing to account satisfactorily for any loss or deficiency of assets; and (5) failing to obey court orders or to answer questions approved by the court.

Nondischargeable Debts

Certain debts are not affected by the discharge of a bankrupt debtor. The Bankruptcy Act provides that a discharge in bankruptcy releases a debtor from all provable debts except those that:

1. Are due as a tax or fine to the United States or any state or local unit of government.
2. Result from liabilities for obtaining money by false pretenses or false representations.
3. Are due for willful or malicious injury to a person or his property.
4. Are due for alimony or child support.
5. Were created by the debtor's larceny or embezzlement or by the debtor's fraud while acting in a fiduciary capacity.
6. Are certain kinds of educational loans that became due within five years prior to the filing of the petition.
7. Were not scheduled in time for proof and allowance because the creditor holding the debt did not have notification of the proceeding even though the debtor was aware that he owed money to that creditor.

The case that follows, *In Re Hott*, involves a denial of discharge of a debt on the grounds that the debtor obtained a loan using a materially false financial statement.

IN RE HOTT

99 B.R. 664 (Bankr. W.D. Pa. 1989)

David Hott was a college graduate with a degree in business administration who was employed as an insurance agent. He and his wife graduated from college in 1986. At the time he graduated, Hott had outstanding student loans of $14,500 for which he was given a grace period before he had to repay them.

Hott became unemployed. Bills began to accumulate and a number of outstanding bills were near the credit limits on his accounts. About that time, he received a promotional brochure by mail from Signal Consumer Discount Company, offering the opportunity to borrow several thousand dollars. The Hotts decided that it appeared to be an attractive vehicle for them to use to consolidate their debts. Hott went to the Signal office and filled out a credit application. He did not list the student loan as a current debt. He later claimed that someone in the office told him he didn't have to list it if he owned an automobile, but there was significant doubt about this claim. Had he listed it, he would not have met the debt/income ratio required by Signal and it would not have made the loan. As it was, Signal agreed to make the loan on the condition that Hott pay off a car debt in order to reduce his debt/income ratio and Hott agreed to do so. On March 30, 1987, Signal loaned the Hotts $3,458.01.

On June 24, 1988, the Hotts filed for bankruptcy. Signal objected to the discharge of the balance remaining on its loan on the grounds it had been obtained through the use of a materially false financial statement.

Markovitz, Bankruptcy Judge.   Section 523(a)(2)(B) a discharge under section 72 . . . does not discharge an individual debtor from any debt—

(2) for money . . . to the extent obtained by—
(B) use of a statement in writing—
(i) that is materially false;
(ii) respecting the debtor's financial condition;
(iii) on which the creditor to whom the debtor is liable for such money . . . reasonably relied; and
(iv) that the debtor caused to be made with intent to deceive. . . .

The parties agree that Hott did in fact obtain money as a result of his submission to Signal of a written statement of his financial condition. It appears that Hott does not contest Signal's reliance on the statement and it is clear that Signal's loss was proximately caused by Hott's financial statement. It is not clear if Hott concedes that the omission of the student loan caused the statement to be materially false. The major contested issue is whether Hott intentionally deceived Signal as to his true financial status in order to obtain the funds.

Material falsity has been defined as "an important or substantial untruth." It includes any omission, concealment or understatement of the Hotts' material liabilities. By omitting his single largest debt, a debt which by itself is as great as the remainder of his debt in combination, Hott created a material falsity in his financial statement.

Hott asserts that he fully intended to list his student loan debt on the application. He claims that said debt was in fact listed on the payment schedule his wife had prepared for him to take to Signal's office. That paper has admittedly long since been destroyed. Hott claims to have discussed the placement of the student loan with one of Signal's employees. Hott provided a physical description of the alleged employee. Signal's manager advised that the office had only three employees including himself. None of the three people even vaguely matched Hott's description.

Hott claims that the employee told him not to worry about the debt, so he did not. Given the size of the student loan in relation to the reminder of his debt, Hott's attitude certainly qualified as indifference and/or reckless disregard for accuracy.

We additionally reiterate Hott's education and qualifications in relation to his claim of innocence. Hott has a Bachelor's Degree in Business. He admits to having a knowledge of the concept called debt/income ratio and its purpose. Hott would easily have been able to determine that inclusion of his student loan on his application would cause his debt/income ratio to skyrocket. Hott asserts that he never stopped to perform any of the calculations. Hott may not assume the position of an ostrich with his head in the sand and ignore facts which were readily available.

This court finds that Hott's position lacks credibility and that Signal's witness was fully credible. We find at the very least Hott recklessly omitted the existence of his student loan when completing the credit application submitted for Signal's approval. Therefore, the debt must be found to be nondischargeable.

Judgment in favor of Signal.

The 1984 amendments established several additional grounds for nondischargeability relating to debts incurred in contemplation of bankruptcy. Congress was concerned about debtors who ran up large expenditures on credit cards shortly before filing for bankruptcy relief. Cash advances in excess of $1,000 obtained by use of a credit card and a revolving line of credit at a credit union obtained within 20 days of filing a bankruptcy petition are presumed to be nondischargeable. Similarly, a debtor's purchase of more than $500 in *luxury goods or services* on credit from a single creditor within 40 days of filing a petition is presumed to be nondischargeable.

There is also an exception from dischargeability for debts reflected in a judgment arising out of a debtor's operation of a motor vehicle while legally intoxicated.

All of these nondischargeable debts are provable debts. The creditor who owns these claims can participate in the distribution of the bankrupt's estate. However, the creditor has an additional advantage: His right to recover the unpaid balance is not cut off by the bankrupt's discharge. All other provable debts are dischargeable; that is, the right to recover them is cut off by the bankrupt's discharge.

Reaffirmation Agreements

Sometimes, creditors put pressure on debtors to reaffirm, or to agree to pay, debts that have been discharged in bankruptcy. When the 1978 amendments to the Bankruptcy Act were under consideration, some individuals urged Congress to prohibit such agreements. They argued that reaffirmation agreements were inconsistent with the fresh start philosophy of the Bankruptcy Act.

Congress did not agree to a total prohibition; instead, it set up a rather elaborate procedure for a creditor to go through to get a debt reaffirmed. Essentially, the creditor must do so before the discharge is granted, and the court must approve the reaffirmation. The debtor has 60 days after he agrees to a reaffirmation to rescind it. Court approval is not required for the reaffirmation of loans secured by real estate.

A debtor may voluntarily pay any dischargeable obligation without entering into a reaffirmation agreement.

Dismissal for Substantial Abuse

As it considered the 1984 amendments to the Bankruptcy Act, Congress was concerned that too many individuals with an ability to pay their debts over time pursuant to a Chapter 13 plan were filing petitions to obtain Chapter 7 discharges of liability. The consumer finance industry urged Congress to preclude Chapter 7 petitions where a debtor had the prospect of future disposable income to satisfy more than 50 percent of his prepetition unsecured debts. Although Congress rejected this approach, it did authorize Bankruptcy Courts to dismiss cases that they determined were a **substantial abuse** of the bankruptcy process. This provision appears to cover situations where a debtor has acted in bad faith or where she has the present or future ability to pay a significant portion of her current debts.

The case that follows, *In Re Newsom*, illustrates a situation where the court found the filing of a Chapter 7 petition by debtors with the ability to eventually pay off much of the unsecured debt they had accumulated to be a "substantial abuse" of the bankruptcy process.

IN RE NEWSOM

69 B.R. 801 (Bankr. D. N.D. 1987)

John and Christine Newsom were noncommissioned officers in the U.S. Air Force who each earned $1,408 net a month. In October 1986, they filed a voluntary petition in bankruptcy under Chapter 7. At the time, they had three secured debts totaling $21,956, $21,820 of which stemmed from the purchase of a 1986 Ford Bronco and a 1985 Pontiac Trans Am. They proposed to surrender the Bronco and a secured television set to the trustee, leaving $10,000 owing on the Pontiac as the only secured debt. Their unsecured debts totaled $20,911: $6,611 from bank card use, $12,764 from retail credit, and $1,350 from credit union loans. Of the unsecured debt, $11,563 was incurred in 1986.

The Newsoms filed an income and expense schedule showing that their monthly expenses totaled $2,232, including $100 per month for recreation and $150 for cigarettes and "walk around money." This left a surplus of $276 per month. The Bankruptcy Court, on its own motion, issued an order to the Newsoms to show why their petition should not be dismissed pursuant to the substantial abuse provision of the Bankruptcy Code.

Hill, Bankruptcy Judge.   Section 707(b) of the Bankruptcy Code, providing for the dismissal of Chapter 7 cases, provides as follows:

(b) After notice and a hearing, the court on its own motion or on a motion by the United States Trustee but not at the request or suggestion of any party in interest, may dismiss a case filed by an individual debtor under this chapter whose debts are primarily consumer debts if it finds that the granting of relief would be a substantial abuse of the provisions of this chapter. There shall be a presumption in favor of granting the relief requested by the debtor.

This section was enacted as part of the consumer credit amendments to the Bankruptcy Act in 1984 as a means of combating what Congress viewed as an abuse of Chapter 7 by consumer debtors who had the ability to pay.

From the developing case law, this court has adopted the following as criteria against which the facts of a particular case ought to be judged in determining whether substantial abuse exists sufficient to mandate dismissal under section 707(b):

1. Whether the debtors have a likelihood of sufficient future income to fund a Chapter 13 plan which would pay a substantial portion of the secured claims;

2. Whether the debtors' petition was filed as a consequence of illness, disability, unemployment or some other calamity;

3. Whether the schedules suggest the debtors incurred cash advances and consumer purchases in an excess of their ability to repay them;

4. Whether the debtors' proposed family budget is excessive or extravagant;

5. Whether the debtors' statement of income and expenses is misrepresentative of their true financial condition.

The Newsoms' unsecured obligations are comprised exclusively of consumer debt. Their schedule of unsecured debt is highly suggestive of individuals who, already aware of their financial limitations and already faced with financial difficulties, went ahead and rang up at least $11,500 of consumer debt in 1986—an amount equal to thirty percent of their combined annual net income and which was incurred when they already had unsecured obligations of over $9,000. Even worse, they apparently purchased a second vehicle during this time period. Such action can only be regarded by the court as a completely irresponsible use of credit for non-essential items.

The Newsoms' proposed family budget seems extravagant insofar as they profess to need $250 for entertainment and recreation, including $150 for cigarettes and "walk around money." The court finds this aspect of the budget as unacceptable. It appears that the Newsoms are making no effort to tighten their belts or maintain a conservative life style. With a combined annual net income of nearly $34,000 and no dependents, the Newsoms are far better off than many and ought to be able to live quite comfortably while at the same time making an effort to pay back at least a portion of their unsecured creditors.

The ability to pay back a substantial portion of unsecured debt does not require an ability to pay back one hundred percent. All that is required is that the payback be significant and that there be a likelihood of sufficient future income to maintain such a payback. In the present case, assuming future income and expenses remain stable, the Newsoms would at a minimum, be able to contribute $276 per month or $3,312 per year toward a repayment plan. Over a three-year period, they would have contributed $9,936 resulting in a repayment of forty-seven percent of their unsecured claims. Contributions over a five-year period would result in an eighty-percent payback. None of these figures can be regarded as insignificant as far as creditors are concerned and strongly suggest that a meaningful payback could be accomplished. An even greater payback could be accomplished by honing the Newsoms' entertainment budget to a more realistic level. At any rate, this court believes that the Newsoms have the financial means at hand and will continue to have the means to fund a Chapter 13 plan which would retire a substantial portion of the unsecured claims.

Newsoms' petition for Chapter 7 relief dismissed.

CHAPTER 11: REORGANIZATIONS

Reorganization Proceeding

Sometimes, creditors benefit more from the continuation of a bankrupt debtor's business than from the liquidation of the debtor's property. Chapter 11 of the Bankruptcy Act provides a proceeding whereby, under the supervision of the Bankruptcy Court, the debtor's financial affairs can be reorganized rather than liquidated. Chapter 11 proceedings are available to individuals and to virtually all business enterprises, including individual proprietorships, partnerships, and corporations (except banks, savings and loan associations, insurance companies, commodities brokers, and stockbrokers).

Petitions for reorganization proceedings can be filed voluntarily by the debtor or involuntarily by its creditors. Once a petition for a reorganization proceeding is filed and relief is ordered, the court usually appoints (1) a committee of creditors holding unsecured claims, (2) a committee of equity security holders (shareholders), and (3) a trustee. The trustee may be given the responsibility for running the debtor's business. He is also usually responsible for developing a plan for handling the various claims of creditors and the various interests of persons such as shareholders.

The reorganization plan is essentially a contract between a debtor and its creditors. This contract may involve recapitalizing a debtor corporation and/or giving creditors some equity, or shares, in the corporation in exchange for part or all of the debt owed to them. The plan must (1) divide the creditors into classes; (2) set forth how each creditor will be satisfied; (3) state which claims, or classes of claims, are impaired or adversely affected by the plan; and (4) provide the same treatment to each creditor in a particular class, unless the creditors in that class consent to different treatment.

The plan is then submitted to the creditors for approval. Approval generally requires that creditors holding two thirds in amount and one half in number of each class of claims impaired by the plan must accept it. Once approved, the plan goes before the court for confirmation. If the plan is confirmed, the debtor is responsible for carrying it out.

The case that follows, *Official Committee of Equity Security Holders v. Mabey,* shows that until a plan is confirmed, the bankruptcy court has no authority to distribute a portion of the bankruptcy assets to a portion of the unsecured creditors.

OFFICIAL COMMITTEE OF EQUITY SECURITY HOLDERS v. MABEY

832 F.2d 299 (4th Cir. 1987)

The A. H. Robins Company is a publicly held company that filed a voluntary petition for relief under Chapter 11 of the Bankruptcy Code. Robins sought refuge in Chapter 11 because of a multitude of civil actions filed against it by women who alleged they were injured by use of the Dalkon Shield intrauterine device that it manufactured and sold as a birth control device. Approximately 325,000 notices of claim against Robins were received by the Bankruptcy Court.

In 1985, the court appointed the Official Committee of Equity Security Holders to represent the interest of Robins's public shareholders. In April 1987, Robins filed a proposed plan of reorganization but no action was taken on the proposed plan because of a merger proposal submitted by Rorer Group, Inc. Under this plan, Dalkon Shield claimants would be compensated out of a $1.75 billion fund, all other creditors would be paid in full, and Robins's stockholders would receive stock of the merged corporation. However, at the time of other critical activity in the bankruptcy proceeding, no revised plan incorporating the merger proposal had been filed or approved.

Earlier, in August of 1986, the court had appointed Ralph Mabey as an examiner to evaluate and suggest proposed elements of a plan of reorganization. On Mabey's suggestion, a proposed order was put before the district court supervising the proceeding that would require Robins to establish a $15 million emergency treatment fund "for the purpose of assisting in providing tubal reconstructive surgery or in-vitro fertilization to eligible Dalkon Shield claimants." The purpose of the emergency fund was to assist those claimants who asserted that they had become infertile as a consequence of their use of the product. A program was proposed for administering the fund and for making the medical decisions required.

On May 21, 1987, the district court ordered that the emergency treatment fund be created, and the action was challenged by the committee representing the equity security holders.

Chapman, Circuit Judge.   The May 21, 1987, order of the district court approving the Emergency Treatment Fund makes no mention of its authority to establish such a fund prior to the allowance of the claims of the women who would benefit from the fund, and prior to the confirmation of a plan of reorganization of Robins. In its order denying the Equity Committee's Motion for a Stay Pending Appeal of the May 21 order, the district court relied on the "expansive equity power" of the court to justify its action.

While one may understand and sympathize with the district court's concern for the Dalkon Shield claimants who may desire reconstructive surgery or in-vitro fertilization, the creation of the Emergency Treatment Fund at this stage of the Chapter 11 bankruptcy proceedings violates the clear language and intent of the Bankruptcy Code, and such action may not be justified as an exercise of the court's equitable powers.

The Bankruptcy Code does not permit a distribution to unsecured creditors in a Chapter 11 proceeding except under and pursuant to a plan of reorganization that has been properly presented and approved. Sections 1122–1129 of the Bankruptcy Code set forth the required contents of the reorganization plan, the classification of claims, the requirements of disclosure of the contents of the plan, the method for accepting the plan, the hearing required on confirmation of the plan, and the requirements for confirmation. The clear language of these statutes does not authorize the payment in part or full, or the advance of monies to or for the benefit of unsecured claimants prior to the approval of the plan of reorganization. The creation of the Emergency Treatment Fund has no authority to support it in the Bankruptcy Code and violates the clear policy of Chapter 11 reorganizations by allowing piecemeal pre-confirmation payments to certain unsecured creditors. Such action also violates Bankruptcy Rule 3021 which allows distribution to creditors only after the allowance of claims and the confirmation of a plan.

Judgment reversed in favor of Official Committee of Equity Security Holders.

Use of Chapter 11

During the 1980s, attempts by a number of corporations to seek refuge in Chapter 11 as a means of escaping problems they were facing received considerable public attention. Some of the most visible cases involved efforts to obtain some protection against massive product liability claims and judgments for damages for breach of contract, and to escape from collective bargaining agreements. Thus, for example, Johns-Manville Corporation filed under Chapter 11 because of the claims against it arising out of its production and sale of asbestos years earlier, while A. H. Robins Company, as illustrated in the preceding case, was concerned about a surfeit of claims arising out of its sale of the Dalkon Shield, an intrauterine birth control device. And, in 1987, Texaco, Inc., faced with a $10.3 billion judgment in favor of Pennzoil in a breach of contract action, filed a petition for reorganizational relief under Chapter 11. Companies such as LTV and Allegheny Industries sought changes in retirement and pension plans, and other companies such as Eastern Airlines sought refuge in Chapter 11 while embroiled in labor disputes.

As the 1990s begin, a number of companies that were the subject of highly leveraged buyouts (LBOs) financed with so-called junk bonds, including a number of retailers, have resorted to Chapter 11 to seek restructuring and relief from their creditors. Similarly, companies such as Pan Am that were hurt by the economic slowdown and the increase in fuel prices filed Chapter 11 petitions.

Collective Bargaining Agreements

Collective bargaining contracts pose special problems. Prior to the 1984 amendments, there was concern that some companies would use Chapter 11 reorganizations as a vehicle to avoid executed collective bargaining agreements. The concern was heightened by the Supreme Court's 1984 decision in *NLRB v. Bildisco and Bildisco*. In that case, the Supreme Court held that a reorganizing debtor did not have to engage in collective bargaining before modifying or rejecting portions of a collective bargaining agreement and that such unilateral alterations by a debtor did not violate the National Labor Relations Act.

Congress then acted to try to prevent the misuse of bankruptcy proceedings for collective bargaining purposes. The act's 1984 amendments adopt a rigorous multistep process that must be complied with in determining whether a labor contract can be rejected or modified as part of a reorganization. Among other things that must be done before a debtor or trustee can seek to avoid a collective bargaining agreement are the submission of a proposal to the employees' representative that details the "necessary" modifications to the collective bargaining agreement and assures that "all creditors, the debtor and all affected parties are fairly treated." Then, before the bankruptcy court can authorize a rejection of the original collective bargaining agreement, it must review the proposal and find that (1) the employees' representative refused to accept it without good cause, and (2) the balance of equities clearly favors the rejection of the original collective bargaining agreement.

The case, *In Re Royal Composing Room, Inc.*, shows the scrutiny that the court gives the action of a debtor seeking to avoid a collective bargaining agreement.

IN RE ROYAL COMPOSING ROOM, INC.

78 B.R. 671 (S.D. N.Y. 1987)

Royal Composing Room, Inc., is an advertising typography company, and one of the last unionized shops in an industry that was subjected to considerable stress as computer technology replaced the linotype machine. Royal was a party to a collective bargaining agreement with Typographical Union No. 6. Royal was a profitable company until 1982, when its gross revenues declined by $2 million; over the next four years, it sustained operating losses. Confronted with these difficulties, in 1983 Royal began to cut expenses by sharply cutting the compensation of its principal executives, freezing the salaries of salesmen and middle management foremen, eliminating company automobiles, and moving to a smaller location to save rent. At the start of 1986, Royal lost its largest customer, Doyle Dane Bernbach, Inc., and sought to convince the union, which theretofore had not made any sacrifices or concessions, to forgo a 3 percent wage increase agreed to earlier. When the union refused, Royal filed a petition for reorganization under Chapter 11 and sought to reject its collective bargaining agreement.

Under section 1113(b) of the Bankruptcy Code, before it could reject the collective bargaining agreement, Royal was required to make a proposal to the union "which provides for those necessary modifications in the employees' benefits and protections that are necessary to permit the reorganization of the debtor and assures that all creditors, the debtor and all of the affected parties are treated fairly and equally." Royal held a meeting with officals of the union and offered a proposal that included a reduction of benefits, changes in work rules, the elimination of the scheduled wage increase, and the elimination of the union's right to arbitration as the way to change the contract. The union rejected the proposal and did not negotiate. After a trial before the bankruptcy judge, Royal's motion to reject the existing collective bargaining contract was granted. The union then appealed to the District Court.

Keenan, District Judge.   Local 6 raises two arguments on appeal: (1) the Bankruptcy Court did not apply the proper definition of "necessary" under section 1113, and (2) Royal's proposal did not treat all affected parties fairly and equitably. Both positions are unavailing.

The Second Circuit has indicated that the term "necessary" contained in section 1113 does not mean "essential" or "bare minimum." It has ruled that "the necessary requirement places on the debtor the burden of proving that its proposal is made in good faith, and that it contains necessary, but not absolutely minimal, changes that will enable the debtor to complete the reorganization process successfully."

Applying the standard of necessity endorsed by the Second Circuit, Bankruptcy Judge Abram found that Royal had, "established that it had in good faith attempted to negotiate for necessary changes but had been unsuccessful because of the union's unwillingness to engage in serious discussions." The record supports this finding. Local 6 was unresponsive and dilatory in the face of management's financial condition and resulting proposal. Likewise, Judge Abram was correct in her analysis of Royal's proposal. She found that Royal had cut nonunion management and executive salaries, eliminated trade association memberships, and even reused old doorknobs. During this time, union labor costs were the only expenses not cut.

The correctness of Judge Abram's legal conclusion is bolstered by the Second Circuit's statement in Carey Transportation that courts "must consider whether rejection of a collective bargaining agreement would increase the likelihood of successful reorganization." This court cannot envision Royal being able to successfully reorganize absent at least enforcement of its proposal under section 1113. Rejection clearly increases the likelihood of successful reorganization.

Local 6 further asserts that Royal did not satisfy the statutory requirement that under the proposal "all creditors, the debtor and all affected parties are treated fairly and equitably." Judge Abram correctly found that Royal "had spread the burden of financial sacrifice." As noted earlier, Royal cut costs in many ways, including a decrease in executive compensation, the rescinding of raises and freezing of salaries of salesmen and middle level management, the elimination of company cars, and the moving of its premises to smaller quarters. The union's wages were neither frozen nor cut. The Second Circuit observed that a debtor need not show that managers and nonunion employees have their benefits cut to the degree union benefits are cut. In this case, the union's benefits were the last to be cut, and it certainly was not the only constituency in Royal to feel the financial pinch. Royal's proposal satisfied the statute's requirement of fairness and equity.

Judgment of the Bankruptcy Court rejecting the collective bargaining agreement affirmed.

CHAPTER 12: FAMILY FARMS

Relief for Family Farmers

Historically, farmers have been accorded special treatment in the Bankruptcy Code. In the 1978 act, as in earlier versions, small farmers were exempted from involuntary proceedings. Thus, a small farmer who filed a voluntary Chapter 11 or 13 petition could not have the proceeding converted into a Chapter 7 liquidation over his objection so long as he complied with the act's requirements in a timely fashion. Additional protection was also accorded through the provision allowing states to opt out of the federal exemption scheme and to provide their own exemptions. A number of states used this flexibility to provide generous exemptions for farmers so they would be able to keep their tools and implements.

Despite these provisions, the serious stress on the agricultural sector in the mid-1980s led Congress in 1986 to further amend the Bankruptcy Act by adding a new Chapter 12 targeted to the financial problems of the family farm. During the 1970s and 1980s, farmland prices appreciated and many farmers borrowed heavily to expand their productive capacity, creating a large debt load in the agricultural sector. When land values subsequently dropped and excess production in the world kept farm product prices low, many farmers faced extreme financial difficulty.

Chapter 12 is modeled after Chapter 13, which is discussed next. It is available only for family farmers with regular income. To qualify, a farmer and spouse must have not less than 80 percent of their total noncontingent, liquidated debts arising out of their farming operations. The aggregate debt must be less than $1.5 million and at least 50 percent of an individual's or couple's income during the year preceding the filing of the petition must have come from the farming operation. A corporation or partnership can also qualify, provided that more than 50 percent of the stock or equity is held by one family or its relatives and they conduct the farming operation. Again, 80 percent of the debt must arise from the farming operation; the aggregate debt ceiling is $1.5 million.

The debtor is usually permitted to remain in possession to operate the farm. Although the debtor in possession has many of the rights of a Chapter 11 trustee, a trustee is appointed under Chapter 12 and the debtor is subject to his supervision. The trustee is permitted to sell unnecessary assets, including farmland and equipment, without the consent of secured creditors and before a plan is approved. However, the secured creditor's interest attaches to the proceeds of the sale.

The debtor is required to file a plan within 90 days of the filing of the Chapter 12 petition—although the bankruptcy court has the discretion to extend the time. A hearing is held on the proposed plan, and it can be confirmed over the objection of creditors. The debtor may release to any secured party the collateral that secures the claim to obtain confirmation without the acceptance by that creditor.

Unsecured creditors are required to receive at least liquidation value under the Chapter 12 plan. If an unsecured creditor or the trustee objects to the plan, the court may still confirm the plan despite the objection so long as it calls for full payment of the unsecured creditor's claim or it provides that the debtor's disposable income for the duration of the plan is applied to making payments on it. A debtor who fulfills his plan, or is excused from full performance because of subsequent hardship, is entitled to a discharge.

CHAPTER 13: CONSUMER DEBT ADJUSTMENTS

Relief for Individuals

Chapter 13 of the Bankruptcy Act, entitled Adjustments of Debts for Individuals, gives individuals who do not want to be declared bankrupt an opportunity to pay their debts in installments under the protection of a federal court. Under Chapter 13, the debtor has this opportunity free of such problems as garnishments and attachments of her property by creditors. Only individuals with regular incomes (including sole proprietors of businesses) who owe individually (or with their spouse) liquidated, unsecured debts of less than $100,000 and secured debts of less than $350,000 are eligible to file under Chapter 13. Under the pre-1978 Bankruptcy Act, Chapter 13 proceedings were known as "wage earner plans." The 1978 amendments expanded the coverage of these proceedings.

Procedure

Chapter 13 proceedings are initiated only by the voluntary petition of a debtor filed in the Bankruptcy Court. Creditors of the debtor may not file an involuntary petition for a Chapter 13 proceeding. The debtor in the petition states that he is insolvent or unable to pay his debts as they mature and that he desires to effect a composition or an extension, or both, out of future earnings or income. A **composition of debts** is an arrangement whereby the amount the person owes is reduced, whereas an **extension** provides the person a longer period of time in which to pay his debts. Commonly, the debtor files at the same time a list of his creditors as well as a list of his assets, liabilities, and executory contracts.

Following the filing of the petition, the court calls a meeting of creditors, at which time proofs of claims are received and allowed or disallowed. The debtor is examined, and she submits a plan of payment. The plan is submitted to the secured creditors for acceptance. If they accept the plan and if the court is satisfied that the plan is proposed in good faith, meets the legal requirements, and is in the interest of the creditors, the court approves the plan. The court then appoints a trustee to carry out the plan. The plan must provide for payments over three years or less, unless the court approves a longer period of up to five years.

No plan may be approved if the trustee or an unsecured creditor objects, unless the plan provides for the objecting creditor to be paid the present value of what he is owed or provides for the debtor to commit all of his projected disposable income for a three-year period to pay his creditors.

Under the 1984 amendments, a Chapter 13 debtor must begin making the installment payments proposed in her plan within 30 days after the plan is filed. The interim payments must continue to be made until the plan is confirmed or denied. If the plan is denied, the money, less any administrative expenses, is returned to the debtor by the trustee. The interim payments give the trustee an opportunity to observe the debtor's performance and thus to be in a better position to make a recommendation about whether the plan should be approved.

Once approved, a plan may be subsequently modified on petition of a debtor or a creditor where there is a material change in the debtor's circumstances.

Suppose Curtis Brown has a monthly take-home pay of $1,000 and a few assets. He owes $1,500 to the credit union, borrowed for the purchase of furniture; he is supposed to repay the credit union $75 per month. He owes $1,800 to the finance company on the purchase of a used car; he is supposed to repay the company $90 a month. He has also run up charges of $1,200 on a MasterCard account, primarily for emergency repairs to his car; he must pay $60 per month to MasterCard. His rent is $350 per month, and food and other living expenses run him another $425 per month. Curtis was laid off from his job for a month and fell behind on his payments to his creditors. He then filed a Chapter 13 petition. In his plan, he might, for example, offer to repay the credit union $50 a month, the finance company $60 a month, and MasterCard $40 a month—with the payments spread over three years rather than the shorter time for which they are currently scheduled.

The *In Re Doersam* case, which follows, illustrates the scrutiny a bankruptcy judge may give a proposed plan.

IN RE DOERSAM

849 F.2d 237 (6th Cir. 1988)

Winifred Doersam was the borrower on three student loans made to her by First Federal Savings and Loan and guaranteed by the state of Ohio Student Loan Commission (OSLC) totaling $10,000 to finance her graduate education at the University of Dayton. Doersam also signed as the cosigner for a $5,000 student loan for her daughter, also made by First Federal and guaranteed by OSLC. With the use of the loans, she was able to obtain a position as a systems analyst with NCR Corporation, which required her to obtain a master's degree in order to retain her position at an annual salary of $24,000.

Approximately six weeks before her graduation, and before the first payment on her student loans was due, Doersam filed a petition and plan under Chapter 13. In her plan, she proposed to pay $375 a month to her unsecured creditors over a 36-month period. Doersam's total unsecured debt was $18,418, 81 percent of which was comprised of the outstanding student loans. Her schedules provided for payment of rent of $300 per month and food of $400 per month. Her listed dependents included her 23-year-old daughter and her 1-year-old grandaughter. At the time, her daughter was employed in the Ohio Work Program, a program designed to help welfare recipients, for which she was paid a small salary.

The OLSC objected to the plan proposed by Doersam on the grounds that it was filed in bad faith.

Keith, Circuit Judge.   The bankruptcy court chose not to deal with the question of bad faith, but did find that there was no hardship situation which prevented Doersam from satisfying the student loan debt. On appeal, the district court held that Doersam's plan was filed in bad faith.

In evaluating good faith in specific situations, we find helpful, as did the district court, the factors enumerated in *In Re Kitchens:*

1. The amount of debtor's income from all sources;
2. The living expenses of the debtor and his dependents;
3. The amount of attorney's fees;
4. The probable or expected duration of the debtor's Chapter 13 plan;
5. The motivations of the debtor and his sincerity in seeking relief under the provisions of Chapter 13;
6. The debtor's degree of effort;
7. The debtor's ability to earn and the likelihood of fluctuation in his earnings;
8. Special circumstances such as inordinate medical expenses;
9. The frequency with which the debtor has sought relief under the Bankruptcy Act;
10. The circumstances under which the debtor has contracted his debts and his demonstrated bona fides, or lack of same, in dealing with his creditors; and
11. The burden which the plan's administration would place on the trustee.

The fact that all or part of the debt consists of educational loans presents special problems. Ordinarily, such loans are not dischargeable under Chapter 7. The mere fact a debtor attempts to discharge a debt that would be nondischargeable under Chapter 7 is not sufficient in itself to warrant a finding that the plan was not proposed in good faith. However, whether the debt would be nondischargeable under Chapter 7 is a factor which is relevant to the determination of good faith. Moreover, the debt which the debtor seeks to discharge is also germane to the question of good faith. Here, the repayment structure of educational loans is of particular relevance.

Unlike most commercial loans which are granted only upon a showing of creditworthiness and ability to make repayments, most student loans, on the other hand, are granted only upon a debtor establishing need. Unlike most loans, guaranteed student loans do not require a borrower to commence repayment until the borrower has completed his or her education. It is therefore most questionable when a debtor accepts a student loan and then, prior to maturity, attempts to extinguish the debt in bankruptcy without ever making an attempt to repay it. It stretches credulity to say that the debtor has made an honest effort to pay these debts as required by 11 U.S.C. Section 1325(a)(3).

Based on the foregoing considerations, the district court correctly found that Doersam's plan had not been proposed in good faith. The bulk of Doersam's unsecured indebtedness consists of student loans which would not have been dischargeable under Chapter 7. Doersam made absolutely no effort to repay these loans despite their long-term character, and despite the fact that they were instrumental in her securing a position paying approximately $24,000 per year. Indeed, her student loans had not yet become due at the time she submitted her plan. Moreover, as both the bankruptcy court and the district court noted, the listing of a working daughter and a minor grandchild for whom Doersam is not legally responsible, and the budgeting of $400.00 per month for food based on those questionable listings, are further grounds for finding that the plan was not filed in good faith.

Judgment of district court affirmed.

Discharge

When the debtor has completed his performance of the plan, the court issues an order that discharges him from the debts covered by the plan. The debtor may also be discharged even though he did not complete his payments within the three years if the court is satisfied that the failure is due to circumstances for which the debtor cannot justly be held accountable. An active Chapter 13 proceeding stays, or holds in abeyance, any straight bankruptcy proceedings and any actions by creditors to collect consumer debts. However, if the Chapter 13 proceeding is dismissed (for example, because the debtor fails to file an acceptable plan or defaults on an accepted plan), straight bankruptcy proceedings may begin.

Advantages of Chapter 13

A debtor may choose to file under Chapter 13 to avoid the stigma of bankruptcy or to retain more of his property than is exempt from bankruptcy under state law. Chapter 13 can provide some financial discipline to a debtor as well as an opportunity to get his financial affairs back in good shape. It also gives him relief from the pressures of individual creditors so long as he makes the payments called for by the plan. The debtor's creditors may benefit by recovering a greater percentage of the debt owed to them than would be obtainable in straight bankruptcy.

CONCEPT REVIEW

COMPARISON OF MAJOR FORMS OF BANKRUPTCY PROCEEDINGS

Purpose	Chapter 7 Liquidation	Chapter 11 Reorganization	Chapter 12 Adjustments of Debts	Chapter 13 Adjustments of Debts
Eligible Debtors	Individuals, partnerships, and corporations *except* municipal corporations, railroads, insurance companies, banks, and savings and loan associations. Farmers and ranchers are eligible only if they petition voluntarily.	Generally same as Chapter 7 *except* a railroad may be a debtor, and a stockbroker and commodity broker may *not* be a debtor under Chapter 11.	Family farmer with regular income, at least 50 percent of which comes from farming, and less than $1.5 million in debts, at least 80 percent of which is farm related.	Individual with regular income with liquidated unsecured debts less than $100,000 and secured debts of less than $350,000.
Initiation of Proceeding	Petition by debtor (voluntary). Petition by creditors (involuntary).	Petition by debtor (voluntary). Petition by creditors (involuntary).	Petition by debtor.	Petition by debtor.

Purpose	Chapter 7 Liquidation	Chapter 11 Reorganization	Chapter 12 Adjustments of Debts	Chapter 13 Adjustments of Debts
Basic Procedure	1. Appointment of trustee. 2. Debtor retains exempt property. 3. Nonexempt property is sold and proceeds distributed based on priority of claims. 4. Dischargeable debts are terminated.	1. Appointment of trustee and committees of creditors and equity security holders. 2. Debtor submits reorganization plan. 3. If plan is approved and implemented, debts are discharged.	1. Trustee is appointed but debtor usually remains in possession of farm. 2. Debtor submits a plan in which unsecured creditors must receive at least liquidation value. 3. If plan is approved and fullfilled, debtor is entitled to a discharge.	1. Debtor indicates in petition that he is seeking a composition of debts or an extension. 2. If plan is approved after submitted to creditors, then trustee is appointed. 3. If plan is approved and fulfilled, debts covered by plan are discharged.
Advantages	After liquidation and distribution of assets, most or all of debts may be discharged and debtor gets a fresh start.	Debtor remains in business and debts are liquidated through implementation of approved reorganization plan.	Debtor generally remains in possession and has opportunity to work out of financial difficulty over period of time (usually three years) through implementation of approved plan.	Debtor has opportunity to work out of financial difficulty over period of time (usually three years) through implementation of approved plan.

ETHICAL AND PUBLIC POLICY CONCERNS

1. If a person receives a discharge of debts in bankruptcy, should the person feel an ethical obligation to reaffirm or to repay the debts that were discharged?

2. Is it ethical for a person facing the prospect of seeking relief under the bankruptcy laws to try to convert nonexempt property into exempt property on the eve of the filing of his petition? Does the relative economic condition of the debtor have any bearing on your response to this question?

3. As you have learned in this chapter, during the past decade corporations have filed petitions under Chapter 11 in order to deal with a variety of problems, including the threat of massive product liability claims and the desire of the company to get out of labor contracts. Is it ethical for a company to use Chapter 11 to try to get out of, or to modify, labor contracts or pension agreements that it now deems unfavorable to its interests? Is it ethical for a company to seek the shelter of Chapter 11 when faced with claims for product liability? Is the decision of the appeals court in *Official Committee of Equity Security Holders v. Mabey* to disallow the proposed emergency treatment fund good public policy?

4. As was discussed in this chapter, the federal bankruptcy law makes special provision for small farmers and some states are particularly generous in the exemptions they make available to farmers. Is this special treatment of farmers justifiable as sound and fair public policy?

SUMMARY

The Bankruptcy Act is a federal law providing an organized procedure for dealing with insolvent debtors under the supervision of a federal court. The act protects the rights of both creditors and debtors and also gives the debtor an opportunity to have most, if not all, of his debts discharged so that he will have a fresh start.

A liquidation proceeding under Chapter 7 can be initiated either by a voluntary petition of the debtor or by an involuntary petition filed by his creditors. After a determination that a debtor is entitled to relief, a meeting of creditors is held and a trustee in bankruptcy is elected or appointed. The trustee takes possession of all the assets of the bankrupt, collects all claims, sets aside the bankrupt's exemptions, liquidates the assets, and distributes the proceeds among the creditors.

A creditor wishing to participate in the bankrupt's estate must usually file a proof of claim in the estate within six months of the first meeting of creditors. Certain debts are given priority by the provisions of the Bankruptcy Act. Any payment made to a creditor by an insolvent debtor within three months of the filing of a bankruptcy petition, which enables the creditor to realize a greater percentage of his claim than is realized by other creditors of the same class, is a preferential payment. It may be recovered for the bankruptcy estate by the trustee. A preferential lien given by an insolvent debtor to secure a preexisting debt within three months of the filing of a bankruptcy petition is voidable by the trustee. Any transfer made or obligation incurred without consideration within one year before the filing of a bankruptcy petition is void as to creditors.

A bankrupt is granted a discharge unless she has been guilty of certain dishonest acts or has failed to fulfill her duties as a bankrupt. Corporations are not eligible to have their debts discharged, and an individual may not be granted a discharge if she has had one in the past six years. The grounds for denying a bankrupt's discharge are set out in the Bankruptcy Act. Certain kinds of debts are not dischargeable.

Under Chapter 11, business debtors can enter into reorganization proceedings under the supervision of the Bankruptcy Court to reorganize their financial affairs. A plan, which is essentially a contract between the debtor and the creditors, sets out how the various claims of the creditors will be met over a period of time.

Chapter 12, which was added to the Bankruptcy Code in 1986, makes a special provision for family farmers to work out their financial difficulties over a period of time under the protection of the court.

Plans for individual debtors under Chapter 13 give them voluntary opportunities to effect a composition or an extension of their debts under the protection of a court and free of certain action by their creditors.

PROBLEM CASES

1. Lois Perry filed a voluntary petition pursuant to Chapter 7 of the Bankruptcy Act. Among the items of personal clothing that Perry listed as exempt from her creditors was a mink coat with a value of approximately $2,500. The trustee objected to the claimed exemption, contending that the mink coat was not necessary clothing. The state of Virginia provides an exemption in bankruptcy for "all necessary wearing apparel of the debtor and his family." While limits were placed on the value of certain other kinds of property that could be retained under the exemption (such as a clothes dryer not to exceed $150 in value), no such limitation was specified as to wearing apparel. Should the mink coat be exempt? *Yes if its only winter coat!*

2. On June 29, 1979, Gary Johnson filed a Chapter 13 bankruptcy petition. Acting on the advice of his lawyer shortly before filing the petition, Johnson sold an interest in real estate and used the proceeds to buy a life insurance policy with a face value of $31,460 and a cash value of $12,118. His wife was named as the beneficiary. Johnson claimed that the policy was exempt under South Dakota law, which provides for an exemption of up to $20,000 for the proceeds of a life insurance policy payable directly to the insured, his surviving spouse, or his family. A creditor objected to the exemption but made no showing of fraudulent intent on Johnson's part. Should the exemption be allowed? *Yes as long as state law*

3. On October 19, 1976, Wallace Tuttle, an attorney, and Peninsula Roofing entered into a retainer agreement for the performance of legal services at a stipulated hourly rate. In 1978 and 1979, Peninsula became delinquent in its payments for attorney's fees. The delinquencies reflected overall corporate financial problems that resulted in the permanent closing of Peninsula on July 25, 1979. On August 6, 1979, Peninsula received a check for $3,250 representing an account receivable due it. Peninsula turned the check over to Tuttle, who deposited it to his trust account, credited $1,946.96 against the past-due account, and created a trust fund from which payments for current services and disbursements would be made. On October 18, 1979, an involuntary petition was filed against Peninsula. The bankruptcy trustee sought to require Tuttle to return the $3,250 to him as a preferential payment. Should Tuttle be required to return the money he received? *Yes Preferential Treatment*

4. On September 17, 1979, a jury rendered its verdict in favor of Chrysler Credit Corporation in the amount of $86,704 against Joseph Newman. Several days later, he assigned promissory notes due to him from the New Rochelle Manufacturing Corporation to his father-in-law, Andrew Charla. The notes were worth $93,337 at the time, but his father-in-law paid him only $54,500. On September 28, 1979, Newman formed a corporation known as J.E.S. Equities, Inc. Newman's children were the sole officers and stockholders. On November 15, Newman transferred $40,000 in cash to the corporation in return for a promissory note from it. The note called for no payment of principal or interest until November 1982, at which time the note was to be paid off with interest at 7 percent over a period of nearly 37 years at the rate of $100 per month. On November 24, an involuntary petition in bankruptcy under Chapter 7 was filed against Newman. The trustee in bankruptcy then brought an action to recover the transfers of assets to Charla and J.E.S. Equities. Should the conveyances made by Newman to Andrew Charla and J.E.S. Equities, Inc., be avoided as fraudulent transfers? *Yes on Both*

5. Augustine Calvo was the president and one-third owner of a Florida corporation that did business as Marine Mart. It was in the business of selling new and used boats, motors, and other products associated with recreational boating. Marine Mart borrowed money from Bombardier Credit in order to finance its inventory of boats. The security agreement between Marine Mart and Bombardier was personally guaranteed by Calvo. At the time, Calvo supplied a personal financial statement in which he listed $8,500 in promissory notes receivable and a 52-foot sailboat valued at $75,000 to $85,000 as part of assets of $291,800 and a net worth of $107,506. Marine Mart defaulted on its agreement with Bombardier and it sought to hold Calvo liable for $170,000 pursuant to his personal guarantee. Calvo then filed a petition for relief under Chapter 7. In his schedule of assets and liabilities, Calvo included his 52-foot sailboat, the same boat he had earlier included in his personal financial statement, and claimed it as part of his exemptions. In his bankruptcy filing, he swore under oath that it had little or no value. A boat appraiser valued it at $4,500 and established that it was in essentially the same condition as it had been in when Calvo had valued it at $75,000–85,000. It also turned out that he did not have $8,500 in promissory notes receivable but had based his earlier assertion on loans made 10 years earlier for which he had no written promise of repayment. Bombardier objected to the discharge in bankruptcy of Calvo's obligation to it on the grounds that Calvo had submitted a materially false statement to it with intent to deceive it and that it had relied on the statement. Should the court grant a discharge of Calvo's debt to Bombardier? *No!.*

6. Paul George Conrad filed a voluntary petition in bankruptcy in October 1979, listing $37,354 in liabilities and $25 in assets. Conrad's obligations consisted of a loan executed in connection with a business venture, the Double Dip Ice Cream Company;

signature loans; revolving credit card accounts; and a student loan of $4,125.79 owed to the U.S. Department of Health, Education, and Welfare. Conrad had used the GI Bill of Rights to study at five different colleges and had also obtained three federally guaranteed long-term, low-interest student loans. After receiving his bachelor's degree, he had been employed as a teacher. He was terminated as a full-time teacher in April 1979; since that time, he had been on call as a substitute teacher, for which he was paid $33 each day he taught. He had not sought other full-time employment. He lived at home with his 75-year-old mother. He did not have a car of his own and used his mother's van. Several months after filing for bankruptcy, Conrad obtained a $5,000 loan, with his mother as a guarantor on the note. He used the proceeds only to make the monthly payments on the note. Section 523(a) of the Bankruptcy Code provides that a bankruptcy discharge will not extend:

(8) to a governmental unit, or a nonprofit institution of higher education, for an educational loan, unless . . . (B) excepting such debt from discharge under this paragraph will impose an undue hardship on the debtor.

Conrad sought to have his educational loan discharged and based his claim of hardship on two asserted facts: (1) that he had to support and provide for his elderly mother and (2) that he was unable to obtain employment because of his physical appearance (described by the court as "corpulent"). Is Conrad's student loan dischargeable in bankruptcy? *No! → Does not impose undue*

7. On December 19, 1986, Brian Scholz was involved in an automobile collision with a person insured by The Travelers Insurance Company. At the time, Scholz was cited for, and plead no contest to, a criminal charge of driving under the influence of alcohol arising out of the accident. Travelers paid its insured $4,303.68 and was subrogated to the rights of its insured against Scholz. Subsequently, Travelers filed a civil action against Scholz to recover the amount it had paid, and a default judgment was entered against Scholz. Eleven months later, Scholz sought relief from the bankruptcy court by filing a voluntary petition under Chapter 7. One of the questions in the bankruptcy proceeding was whether the debt owing to Travelers was nondischargeable. Is the debt dischargeable? *No!*

8. Bryant filed a Chapter 7 petition on January 7, 1984. On March 8, she filed an application to reaffirm an indebtedness owed to General Motors Acceptance Corporation (GMAC) on her 1980 Cadillac automobile. Bryant was not married, and she supported two teenage daughters. She was not currently employed, and she collected $771 a month in unemployment benefits and $150 a month in rental income from her mother. Her monthly house payments were $259. The present value of the Cadillac was $9,175; she owed $7,956.37 on it, and her monthly payments were $345.93. Bryant indicated that she wanted to keep the vehicle because it was reliable. GMAC admitted that Bryant had been, and continued to be, current in her payments. GMAC said that the car was in no danger of being repossessed but that, absent reaffirmation, it might decide to repossess it. Should the court grant Bryant's application to reaffirm her indebtedness to GMAC?

9. Roy Satterwhite filed a Chapter 13 petition. In his petition, Satterwhite listed his monthly take-home pay as $1,458 and his monthly expenses as $2,072.24, leaving a negative balance of $614.24. He claimed that all of his assets were exempt. He listed no secured debts and five unsecured debts totaling over $16,450. The largest of these debts was for a judgment against Satterwhite in the amount of $15,749.30 plus interest that stemmed from an action for assault brought against him by A. R. Regan. Under his Chapter 13 plan, Satterwhite pro- posed to make a one-time payment of $1 to each creditor. Approval of the plan would have resulted in a payout to unsecured creditors of substantially less than 1 percent on their claims, which was more than they would have received under a liquidation distribution. The bankruptcy trustee objected to confirmation of the plan. Should the court approve the Chapter 13 plan that provides only for a $1 payment to each creditor?

10. On December 8, 1981, Thomas Thompson filed a petition under Chapter 13 to pay his debts through a wage earner plan. After the notice to creditors, Ford Motor Credit Company, a secured creditor to which Thompson was indebted for payments on a 1980 Ford, filed a proof of claim and rejected the plan. The plan was confirmed over Ford's objections. It provided for payments to Ford of $22.90 a week, equivalent to the same rate and adding up to the same total as in the original sales contract, and enjoined Ford from foreclosing on the automobile. In 1982, Thompson was injured at work and able to work only part time. He then fell behind in his payments to Ford, even though he was regularly submitting his disability checks to the trustee. Ford then filed a petition to reclaim the car, alleging that Thompson had failed to make the payments due on the car. Should Ford be permitted to have the plan disregarded so that it can foreclose its security interest on the car?

COMMERCIAL PAPER

CHAPTER 30

NEGOTIABLE INSTRUMENTS

INTRODUCTION

As commerce and trade developed, people moved beyond exclusive reliance on barter to the use of money and then to the use, as well, of substitutes for money. The term *commercial paper* encompasses such substitutes in common usage today as checks, promissory notes, and certificates of deposit.

History discloses that every civilization that engaged to an appreciable extent in commerce used some form of commercial paper. Probably the oldest commercial paper used in the carrying on of trade is the promissory note. Archaeologists found a promissory note made payable to bearer that dated from about 2100 B.C. The merchants of Europe used commercial paper, which under the law merchant was negotiable, in the 13th and 14th centuries. Commercial paper does not appear to have been used in England until about A.D. 1600.

This chapter and the three following chapters outline and discuss the body of law that governs commercial paper. Of particular interest are those kinds of commercial paper having the attribute of negotiability—that is, they can generally be readily transferred, and accepted, as a substitute for money. This chapter discusses the nature and benefits of negotiable instruments and then outlines the requirements an instrument must meet to qualify as a negotiable instrument. Subsequent chapters discuss transfer and negotiation of instruments, the rights and liabilities of parties to negotiable instruments, and the rules applicable to checks.

NATURE OF NEGOTIABLE INSTRUMENTS

When a person buys a television set and gives the merchant a check drawn on his checking account, that person is using a form of negotiable commercial paper. Similarly, a person who goes to a bank or a credit union to borrow money might sign a promissory note agreeing to pay the money back in 90 days. Again, a form of negotiable commercial paper is being used.

Commercial paper is basically a *contract for the payment of money.* Commonly used as a substitute for money, it can also be used as a means of extending credit. When a television set is bought by giving the merchant a check, the check is a substitute for money. If a credit union gives a borrower money now in exchange for the borrower's promise to repay it later on certain terms, the promissory note signed by the borrower is a means of extending credit as well as a substitute for money.

Uniform Commercial Code

The law of commercial paper is covered in Article 3 (Commercial Paper) and Article 4 (Bank Deposits and Collections) of the Uniform Commercial Code. Other

681

negotiable documents such as investment securities and documents of title are treated in other sections of the Code. Essentially, the Code makes no drastic changes in the basic rules governing the use of commercial paper that have been recognized for centuries, but it has adopted modern terminology and has coordinated, clarified, and simplified the law.

Commercial Paper

The two basic types of commercial paper are *promises to pay* money and *orders to pay* money. **Promissory notes** and **certificates of deposit** issued by banks are promises to pay someone money. **Drafts** and **checks** are orders to another person to pay money to a third person. A check is an order directed to a bank to pay money from a person's account to a third person.

Negotiability

Commercial paper that is **negotiable** or a **negotiable instrument** is a special kind of commercial paper. Commercial paper is negotiable, passes readily through our financial system, and is accepted in place of money. It has many advantages.

For example, Searle, the owner of a clothing store in New York, contracts with Amado, a swimsuit manufacturer in Los Angeles, for $10,000 worth of swimsuits. If negotiable instruments did not exist, Searle would have to send or carry $10,000 across the country, which would be both inconvenient and risky. If the money were stolen along the way, Searle would lose the $10,000 unless he could locate the thief. By using a check in which

Searle orders his bank to pay $10,000 from his account to Amado, or to someone designated by Amado, Searle makes the payment in a far more convenient manner. He has sent only a single piece of paper to Amado. If the check is properly prepared and sent, sending the check is less risky than sending money. Even if the check is stolen along the way, Searle's bank may not pay it to anyone but Amado or someone authorized by Amado. And because the check gives Amado the right to either collect the $10,000 or transfer the right to collect it to someone else, the check is a practical substitute for cash to Amado as well as Searle.

In this chapter and in the three following chapters, we discuss the requirements necessary for a contract to qualify as a negotiable instrument. We also explain the features that not only distinguish a negotiable instrument from a contract but also have led to the widespread use of negotiable instruments as a substitute for money.

KINDS OF COMMERCIAL PAPER

Promissory Notes

The **promissory note** is the simplest form of commercial paper; it is simply a *promise to pay money*. A promissory note is a two-party instrument in which one person (known as the **maker**) makes an unconditional promise in writing to pay another person (the **payee**), or a person specified by that person, a sum of money either on demand or at some particular time in the future.

The promissory note, shown in Figures 1 and 2, is a credit instrument; it is used in a wide variety of transac-

---

FIGURE 1   A Promissory Note

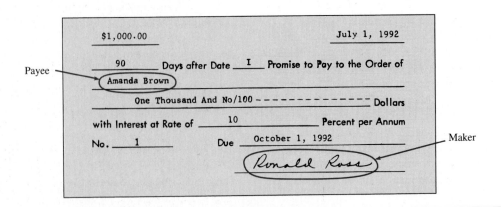

tions in which credit is extended. For example, if a person purchases an automobile on credit, the dealer probably has the person sign a promissory note for the unpaid balance of the purchase price. Similarly, if a person borrows money to purchase a house, the lender who makes the loan and takes a mortgage on the house has the person sign a promissory note for the amount due on the loan. The note probably states that it is secured by a

---

FIGURE 2   A Promissory Note (consumer loan note)

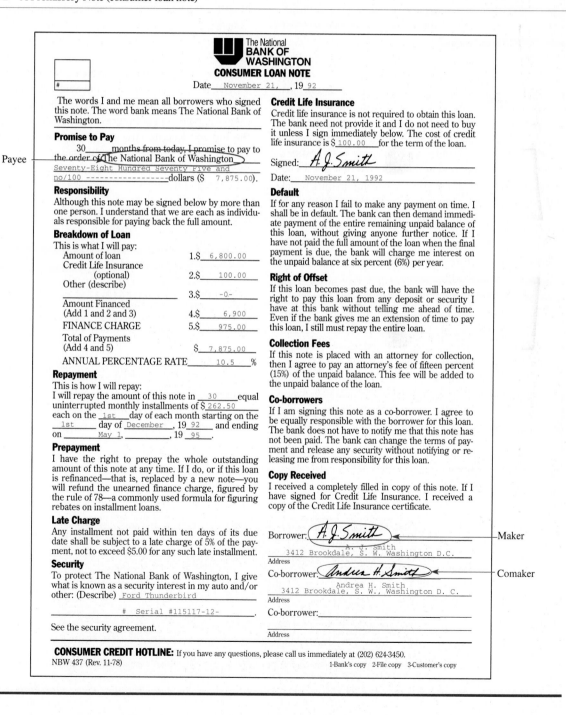

mortgage. The terms of payment on the note should correspond with the terms of the sales contract for the purchase of the car or the house.

Certificates of Deposit

The **certificate of deposit** given by a bank or a savings and loan association when a deposit of money is made is a form of commercial paper and a type of note. Similiar to the promissory note, the certificate of deposit is a *promise to pay money.* When a bank issues a certificate of deposit (CD), as shown in Figure 3, it acknowledges receipt of a specific sum of money. The bank also agrees to pay the owner of the certificate the sum of money plus a stated rate of interest at some time in the future.

Many banks no longer issue certificates of deposit in paper form. Rather, the bank maintains an electronic deposit (CD) and provides the customer with a statement indicating the amount of principal held on a CD basis and the terms of the CD, such as the maturity and interest rate. Thus in these instances, the certificate of deposit is not in negotiable instrument form.

Drafts

A **draft** is a form of commercial paper that involves an *order to pay money* rather than a promise to pay money. The most common example of a draft is a check. A draft has three parties to it: one person (known as the **drawer**) orders a second person (the **drawee**) to pay a certain sum of money to a third person (the **payee**).

Drafts other than checks are used in a variety of commercial transactions. If Brown owes Ames money, Ames may draw a draft for the amount of the debt, naming Brown as drawee and herself or her bank as payee, and send the draft to Brown's bank for presentment and collection.

In freight shipments in which the terms are "cash on delivery," it is a common practice for the seller to ship the goods to the buyer on an "order bill of lading" consigned to himself at the place of delivery. The seller then indorses the bill of lading and attaches a draft naming the buyer as drawee. He then sends the bill of lading and the draft through banking channels to the buyer's bank. The draft is presented to the bank for payment, and when payment is made, the bill of lading is delivered to the buyer. Through this commercial transaction, the buyer gets the goods and the seller gets his money.

When credit is extended, the same procedure is followed, but a time draft—a draft payable at some future time—is used. See Figure 4. In such a transaction, the buyer "accepts" the draft instead of paying it. To accept the draft, he writes his name across its face, thereby obligating himself to pay the amount of the draft when due.

Checks

A **check** is a *draft* on which the *drawee is always a bank* and that is *payable on demand.* Checks are the most widely used form of commercial paper. The issuer of a check is ordering the bank at which he maintains an account to pay a specified person, or someone designated by that person, a certain sum of money from the account. For example, Elizabeth Brown has a checking account at the National Bank of Washington. She goes to Sears Roebuck & Co. and agrees to buy a washing machine priced at $459.95. If she writes a check to pay for it, she is the drawer of the check, the National Bank of Washington is the drawee, and Sears is the payee. By

---

FIGURE 3   A Certificate of Deposit

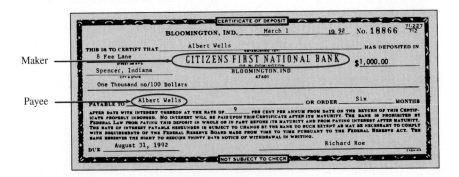

writing the check, Elizabeth is ordering her bank to pay $459.95 from her account to Sears or to Sears's order, that is, to whomever Sears asks the bank to pay the money. See Figure 5.

BENEFITS OF NEGOTIABLE INSTRUMENTS

Rights of an Assignee of a Contract

As we noted in the Rights of Third Parties chapter, which discussed the assignment of contracts, the assignee of a contract can obtain no greater rights than the assignor had at the time of the assignment. For example, Frank Farmer and Neam's Market enter into a contract providing that Farmer will sell Neam's a dozen crates of fresh eggs a week for a year and that Neam's will pay Farmer $4,000 at the end of the year. If at the end of the year Farmer assigns to Bill Sanders his rights under the contract—including the right to collect the money from Neam's—then Sanders has whatever rights Farmer had at that time. If Farmer has delivered all the eggs to Neam's as he promised, then Farmer would be entitled to $4,000 and Sanders would obtain that right from him. However, if Farmer has not delivered all the eggs that he had promised to deliver, or if the eggs he delivered were not fresh, then Neam's might have

---

FIGURE 4   A Draft

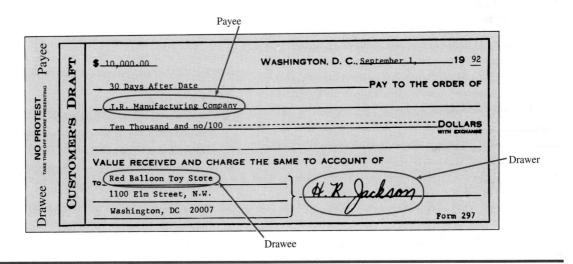

FIGURE 5   A Check

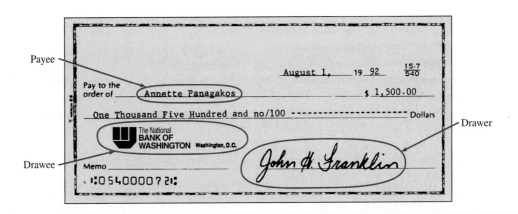

a valid defense or reason to refuse to pay the full $4,000. In that case, Sanders would have only what rights Farmer had and would also be subject to the defense Neam's has against full payment.

Taking an assignment of a contract involves assuming certain risks. The assignee (Sanders) may not be aware of the nature and extent of any defenses that the party liable on the contract (Neam's) might have against the assignor (Farmer). An assignee who does not know for sure what rights he is getting, or which risks he is assuming, may be reluctant to take an assignment of the contract.

Rights of a Holder of a Negotiable Instrument

The object of commercial paper (a contract for the payment of money) is to have it accepted readily as a substitute for money. To accept it readily, a person must be able to take it free of many of the risks assumed by the assignee of a regular contract. Under the law of negotiable instruments, this is possible if two conditions are met: (1) the contract for the payment of money must be in the proper form to qualify as a **negotiable instrument;** and (2) the person who is acquiring the instrument must qualify as a **holder in due course.** Basically, a holder in due course is a person who has good title to the instrument, paid value for it, acquired it in good faith, and had no notice of any claims or defenses against it.

The next section of this chapter discusses the proper form for a negotiable instrument. The Negotiation and Holder in Due Course chapter outlines the requirements that a person must meet to qualify as a holder in due course.

A holder in due course of a negotiable instrument takes the instrument free of all *personal defenses and claims* to the instrument except *those that concern its validity*; these are known as *real* defenses. For example, a holder in due course of a note given in payment for goods does not have to worry if the buyer is claiming that the seller breached a warranty. However, if the maker of a note wrote it under duress, such as a threat of force, or was a minor, then even a holder in due course who acquires the note is subject to the real defenses of duress or lack of capacity. The person who holds the note could not obtain the payment from the maker but would have to recover from the person from whom he got the note.

The Federal Trade Commission (FTC) has adopted a regulation that alters the holder in due course situation. This regulation is designed to allow a consumer who gives a negotiable instrument to use any defenses against payment of the instrument against even a holder in due course. Similarly, some states have enacted the Uniform Consumer Credit Code (UCCC), which produces a similar result. The Negotiation and Holder in Due Course chapter discusses the rights of a holder in due course, as well as the FTC rule.

FORMAL REQUIREMENTS FOR NEGOTIABILITY

Basic Requirements

An instrument such as a check or a note must meet certain formal requirements to be a negotiable instrument. If the instrument does *not* meet these requirements, it is *nonnegotiable*; that is, it is treated as a simple contract and not as a negotiable instrument. A primary purpose for these formal requirements is to ensure the willingness of prospective purchasers of the instrument, particularly financial institutions such as banks, to accept the instrument as a substitute for money.

For an instrument to be negotiable, it must:

1. Be in *writing*.
2. Be *signed by the maker or drawer*.
3. Contain an *unconditional promise or order to pay a sum certain in money*.
4. Be *payable on demand or at a definite time*.
5. Be *payable to order or to bearer*.
6. *Not contain any other promise, order, obligation, or power unless* it is *authorized* by the Code [3–104].[1]

Importance of Form

Whether or not an instrument is drafted so that it satisfies these formal requirements is important for only one purpose, that is, for determining whether an instrument is negotiable or nonnegotiable. Negotiability should not be confused with validity or collectibility. If an instrument is *negotiable*, the *law of negotiable instruments* in the Code controls in determining the rights and liabilities of the parties to the instrument. If an instrument is *nonnegotiable*, the *general rules of contract law control*. The purpose of determining negotiability is to ascertain whether a possessor of the instrument can become a holder in due course.

---

[1] The numbers in brackets refer to the sections of the Uniform Commercial Code.

An instrument that fills all of the formal requirements is a negotiable instrument even though it is void, voidable, unenforceable, or uncollectible. Negotiability is a matter of form and nothing else. Suppose a person gives an instrument in payment of a gambling debt in a state that has a statute declaring that any instrument or promise given in payment of a gambling debt is null and void. The instrument is a negotiable instrument if it is negotiable in form even though it is absolutely void. Also, an instrument that is negotiable in form is a negotiable instrument even though it is signed by a minor. The instrument is voidable at the option of the minor, but it is negotiable.

IN WRITING AND SIGNED

Writing

To be negotiable, an instrument must be *in writing* and must be *signed by the creator of the instrument, known as the maker or the drawer.* An instrument that is handwritten, typed, or printed is considered to be in writing [1–201(46)]. The writing does not have to be on any particular material; all that is required is that the instrument be in writing. A person could draw a negotiable instrument in pencil on a piece of wrapping paper. It would be poor business practice to do so, but the instrument would meet the statutory requirement that it be in writing.

Signed

An instrument has been *signed* if the maker or drawer has put a name or other symbol on it with *the intention of validating it* [3–401(2)]. Normally, the maker or drawer signs an instrument by writing his name on it; however, this is not required. A person or company may authorize an agent to sign instruments for it. A typed or rubber-stamped signature is sufficient if it was put on the instrument to validate it. A person who cannot write her name might make an X and have it witnessed by someone else.

UNCONDITIONAL PROMISE OR ORDER

Requirement of a Promise or Order

If an instrument is promissory in nature, such as a note or a certificate of deposit, it must contain an *uncondi-tional promise to pay* or else it cannot be negotiable. Merely acknowledging a debt is not sufficient. For example, indicating "I owe you $100," does not constitute a promise to pay. An IOU in this form is not a negotiable instrument.

If an instrument is an order to pay, such as a check or a draft, it must contain an *unconditional order.* A simple request to pay as a favor is not sufficient; however, a politely phrased demand can meet the requirement. The language "Pay to the order of" is commonly used on checks. This satisfies the requirement that the check contain an order to pay. The order is the word *pay*, not the word *order*. The word *order* has another function—that of making the instrument payable "to order or to bearer."

Promise or Order Must Be Unconditional

An instrument is not negotiable unless the promise or order is *unconditional.* For example, a note that provides, "I promise to pay to the order of Karl Adams $100 if he replaces the roof on my garage," is not negotiable because it is payable on a condition.

To be negotiable, an instrument must be written so that a person can tell from reading the instrument alone what the obligations of the parties are. If a note contains the statement, "Payment is subject to the terms of a mortgage dated November 20, 1992," it is not negotiable. To determine the rights of the parties on the note, another document—the mortgage—would have to be examined.

However, the negotiability of a note would not be affected if the note contained this statement: "This note is secured by a mortgage dated August 30, 1992." In this case, the rights and duties of the parties to the note are not affected by the mortgage. It would not be necessary to examine the mortgage document to determine the rights of the parties to the note. The parties need only examine the instrument.

The negotiability of an instrument is not affected by a statement of the consideration for which the instrument was given or by a statement of the transaction that gave rise to the instrument. For example, a negotiable instrument may contain a notation stating that it was given in payment of last month's rent or a statement that it was given in payment of the purchase price of goods. The statement does not affect the negotiability of the instrument. The effect of a notation in the lower left corner of a check following the printed word *memo* is discussed in the *Western Bank v. RaDEC Construction Co., Inc.* case, which follows.

WESTERN BANK v. RaDEC CONSTRUCTION CO., INC.

42 UCC Rep. 1340 (S.D. Sup. Ct. 1986)

RaDEC Construction Company was involved as a general contractor in the construction of a medical center in Huron, South Dakota. One of RaDEC's subcontractors on this job was Carpet Center. RaDEC became aware that Carpet Center's financial problems were making it difficult to furnish the necessary materials and labor for the medical center job. RaDEC's president, Clarence Hoesing, had a conversation with Carpet Center on December 13, 1982, in which he agreed to send a check for $8,743.52 to Carpet Center, provided that Carpet Center (1) furnish certain paid invoices for material delivered, (2) provide certain additional material, and (3) assure the installation of the material on December 14. Hoesing then made out a handwritten check to Carpet Center. In the lower left corner of the check following the printed word *memo*, Hoesing typed the phrase, "Payee must prove clear title to material." Hoesing considered the check to be conditioned on Carpet Center's performance of the three conditions. After the check was delivered on December 14, Carpet Center deposited the check in the Western Bank, which allowed it to make an immediate withdrawal of the money. Later that day, RaDEC learned that Carpet Center had not performed the three requirements and filed a stop payment order on the check.

Unable to recover the money from Carpet Center, which was insolvent, the bank brought suit against RaDEC, claiming to be a holder in due course of the check. The trial court held in favor of the bank and RaDEC appealed.

Hertzel, Justice.   The trial court held as a matter of law that the phrase typed in at the lower left hand corner of the check, "Payee must prove clear title to material," did not have the effect of making the check conditional and that the bank was a bona fide holder in due course.

Section 3–104(1) sets forth four elements necessary to constitute a negotiable instrument: (a) It must be signed by the maker; (b) contain an unconditional promise or order to pay a sum certain in money and no other promise, order, obligation or power given by the maker or drawer except as authorized by this chapter; (c) be payable on demand or at a definite time; and (d) be payable to order or to bearer.

In this case there is no dispute that elements (a), (c) and (d) have been fulfilled. RaDEC claims, however, that element (b) has not been met because the check was a "conditional instrument" and therefore subject to its defenses.

RaDEC relies heavily on our decision in *Bank of America v. Butterfield*. In that case, the draft in question stated: "Subject to approval of title, pay to the order of Vernon H. Butterfield and Laura E. Butterfield." It is important to note that the phrase "subject to approval of title," immediately precedes the standard phrase, "Pay to the order of." In affirming the trial court we said: "The promise to pay money contained in the draft in question is clearly not unconditional. The payment ordered is subject to approval of title. Consequently, it is not a negotiable instrument."

Negotiability is determined from the face of the instrument without reference to extrinsic facts. The conditional or unconditional character is to be determined by what is expressed in the instrument itself.

RaDEC claims that the check was not a negotiable instrument because of the condition written on its face. Moreover, RaDEC argues that the location of the conditional language in the place usually reserved for "memo" is of little consequence, since the language itself was sufficient to give the bank notice that RaDEC's obligation to pay was conditioned upon Carpet Center's having proved clear title to the material. The bank, on the other hand, argues that the instant factual situation can be distinguished from that of Bank of America because in that case the conditional language, i.e., "subject to approval of title," preceded the words "Pay to the order of."

We conclude that the phrase "payee must prove clear title to material" written where it was, did not make the check conditional thereby depriving the bank of its status as a holder in due course. It appears that the notation in the "memo" area of the check is nothing more than a self-serving declaration by RaDEC for its own benefit and recordkeeping and for informational purposes only. An otherwise unconditional instrument cannot be rendered conditional by such a device.

Judgment for Western Bank affirmed.

A check may contain a notation as to the account to be debited without making the check nonnegotiable. For example, a check could contain the notation, "payroll account" or "petty cash." Similarly, the account number that appears on personal checks does not make the instrument payable only out of a specific fund. On the other hand, if a check states that it is payable only out of a specific fund, the check is generally not negotiable. In this case, the check is conditioned on there being sufficient funds in the account. Thus, the check would not be unconditional and could not qualify as a negotiable instrument. This rule does not apply to instruments issued by a government or a governmental agency. It is permissible for the instruments of such bodies to contain a provision saying that the instruments are payable only out of a particular fund [3–105(1)(g)].

A conditional indorsement does not destroy the negotiability of an otherwise negotiable instrument. We discuss conditional indorsements in the Negotiation and Holder in Due Course chapter. Negotiability is determined at the time an instrument is written, and it is not affected by subsequent indorsements.

SUM CERTAIN IN MONEY

Sum Certain

The promise or order in an instrument must be to pay a sum certain in money. The sum is certain if a person can compute from the information in the instrument the amount that is required to discharge—or pay off—the instrument at any given time. The Code permits an instrument to state different rates of interest before or after default. It also allows provisions for a discount or an addition if the note is paid early or if it is paid late. The key element is that a person can compute the amount that is due on the instrument at any given time. Thus, a provision for interest at "current bank rates" would not satisfy the requirement for a "sum certain."

The following *Taylor v. Roeder* case discusses the negotiability of a note that provided for interest at "3 percent over the Chase Manhattan Prime to be adjusted monthly." The Virginia Supreme Court held that the note was not negotiable because the current interest rate could not be determined from the face of the note. A number of states, concluding that such notes are recognized by commercial practice, have now acted to make adjustable rate notes negotiable.

TAYLOR v. ROEDER

360 S.E.2d 191 (Va. Sup. Ct. 1987)

VMC Mortgage Company was a mortgage lender that in the conduct of its business borrowed money from investors, pledging as security the notes secured by deeds of trust obtained from its borrowers. Olde Towne Investment Corporation borrowed $18,000 from VMC, evidenced by a promissory note secured by a deed of trust on land. The note provided for interest at "three percent (3.00%) over Chase Manhattan Prime to be adjusted monthly."

Subsequently, Frederick Taylor entered into a contract to buy from Olde Towne the land secured by the deed of trust. After requesting the payoff figure from VMC, Taylor forwarded the money it claimed was due on the note to VMC. Taylor, however, never received the canceled note.

In the meantime, VMC had borrowed money from a pension fund for which Roeder was the trustee and had pledged the Olde Towne note as collateral. No notice was given to Olde Towne that the note had been transferred and VMC accepted payments on the note. VMC defaulted on its obligation to the pension fund for which the note was collateral and filed a petition in bankruptcy. When Roeder tried to foreclose on the property Taylor had purchased, he filed suit against Roeder to stop the foreclosure. A key question in the litigation was whether the note was negotiable. If it was, then the liability on it would have been extinguished only by paying it to the holder—Roeder. If the note was not negotiable, then the liability on the note was satisfied by paying it to VMC where there was no notice received by Olde Towne of the assignment of the right to payment to Roeder.

Russell, Justice.   The dispositive question in this case is whether a note providing for a variable rate of interest, not ascertainable from the face of the note, is a negotiable instrument. We conclude that it is not.

Section 3–104 provides, in pertinent part, that: "Any writing to be a negotiable instrument . . . must . . . contain an unconditional promise or order to pay a sum certain in money." The meaning of "sum certain" is clarified by Section 3–106. Official Comment 1, to that section, states in part:

It is sufficient [to establish negotiability] that at any time of payment the holder is able to determine the amount then payable from the instrument itself with any necessary computation. . . . The computation must be one which can be made from the instrument itself without reference to any outside source, and this section does not make negotiable a note payable with interest "at the current rate."

We conclude that the drafters of the Uniform Commercial Code adopted criteria of negotiability intended to exclude an instrument which requires reference to any source outside the instrument itself in order to ascertain the amount due, subject only to the exceptions provided for in the UCC. Roeder points out the Official Comment to Section 3–104 holds open the possibility that some new types of commercial paper may be made negotiable by statute or by judicial decision. Roeder urges us to create, by judicial decision, just such an exception in favor of variable-interest notes.

Taylor concedes that variable-interest loans have become a familiar device in the mortgage lending industry. Their popularity arose when lending institutions, committed to long-term loans at fixed rates of interest to their borrowers, were in turn required to borrow short-term funds at high rates during periods of rapid inflation. Variable rates protected lenders when rates rose and benefited borrowers when rates declined. They suffer, however, from the disadvantage that the amount required to satisfy the debt cannot be ascertained without reference to an extrinsic source—in this case the varying prime rate charged by the Chase Manhattan Bank. Although that rate may readily be ascertained from published sources, it cannot be found within the "four corners" of the note.

The UCC introduced a degree of clarity into the law of commercial transactions which permits it to be applied by laymen daily to countless transactions without resort to judicial interpretation. The relative predictability of results made possible by that clarity constitutes the overriding benefit arising from its adoption. In our view, that factor makes it imperative that when change is thought desirable, the change should be brought about by statutory amendment, not through litigation and judicial interpretation. Therefore, we decline Roeder's invitation to create an exception, by judicial interpretation, in favor of instruments providing for a variable rate of interest not ascertainable from the instrument itself.

Judgment for Taylor.

Compton, Justice, Dissenting. Instruments providing that loan interest may be adjusted over the life of the loan routinely pass with increasing frequency in this state and many others as negotiable instruments. This court should recognize this custom and usage, as the commercial market has, and hold these instruments to be negotiable.

The commercial market requires a self-contained instrument for negotiability so that a stranger to the original transaction will be fully apprised of its terms and will not be disadvantaged by terms not ascertainable from the instrument itself. For example, interest payable at the "current rate" leaves a holder subject to claims that the current rate was established by one bank rather than another and would disadvantage a stranger to the original transaction.

The rate which is stated in the note in this case, however, does not similarly disadvantage a stranger to the original agreement. Anyone coming into possession could immediately ascertain the terms of the notes: interest payable at three percent above the prime rate established by the Chase Manhattan Bank of New York City. This is a third-party objective standard which is recognized as such by the commercial market. The rate can be determined by a telephone call to the bank or from published lists obtained upon request.

Sometimes, notes contain a clause that provides for the payment of collection fees or attorney's fees in the event of a default on the note. Even though this would make the amount due on default uncertain until the collection or attorney's fees were determined, such a clause does not make the note nonnegotiable [3–106]. The amount can be determined at some time, and business practice justifies the inclusion of such a clause in the instrument.

Payable in Money

The amount specified in the instrument must be payable in *money,* which is a medium of exchange authorized or adopted by a government as part of its currency [1–201(24)]. If the person obligated to pay off an instrument can do something other than pay money, the instrument is not negotiable. For example, if a note reads, "I promise to pay to the order of Sarah Smith, at my option, $40 or five bushels of apples, John Jones," the note is not negotiable.

PAYABLE ON DEMAND OR AT A DEFINITE TIME

To be negotiable, an instrument must be payable either *on demand* or *at a specified time in the future*. This is so that the time when the instrument is payable can be determined with some certainty. An instrument that is payable on the happening of some uncertain event is not negotiable [3–109(2)]. Thus, a note payable "when my son graduates from college" is not negotiable, even though the son does graduate subsequently.

Payable on Demand

An instrument may state that it is payable on demand. If no time for payment is stated in an instrument, the instrument is considered to be payable on demand [3–108]. For example, if the maker forgets to state when a note is payable, it is payable immediately at the request of the holder of the note. A check is considered to be payable on demand. However, a postdated check is treated as a draft and is not properly payable until the day it is dated. An instrument can be negotiable even though it is undated, postdated, or antedated [3–114].

Payable at a Definite Time

An instrument is payable at a definite time if: (1) it is payable on or before a stated date, such as "on July 1, 1992," or "on or before July 1, 1992"; (2) it is payable at a fixed time after a stated date, such as "30 days after date," provided that the instrument is dated; or (3) it is payable at a fixed time "after sight," which is in effect a provision that it will be paid at a fixed time after it is presented to the drawee for acceptance.

If an instrument that is payable "30 days after date" is not dated, then it is not payable at a fixed date and it is not negotiable; however, this defect may be cured if the holder of the instrument fills in the date before he negotiates it to someone else [3–115].

Under the Code, an instrument may contain a clause permitting the time for payment to be accelerated at the option of the maker. Similarly, an instrument may contain a clause allowing an extension of time at the option of the holder or allowing a maker or acceptor to extend payment to a further definite time. Or the due date of a note might be triggered by the happening of an event, such as the filing of a petition in bankruptcy against the maker. These clauses are allowed as long as the time for payment can be determined with certainty [3–109].

PAYMENT TO ORDER OR BEARER

To be negotiable, an instrument must be *payable to order* or *to bearer*. A check that provides, "Pay to the order of Sarah Smith" or "Pay to Sarah Smith or bearer" is negotiable; however, one that provides "Pay to Sarah Smith" is not. The words *to the order of* or *to bearer* show that the drawer of the check, or the maker of a note, intends to issue a negotiable instrument. The drawer or maker is not restricting payment of the instrument to just Sarah Smith but is willing to pay someone else designated by Sarah Smith. This is the essence of negotiability.

The original payee of a check or a note can transfer the right to receive payment to someone else. By making the instrument payable "to the order of" or "to bearer," the drawer or maker is giving the payee the chance to negotiate the instrument to another person and to cut off certain defenses that the drawer or maker may have against payment of the instrument.

A check that is payable to the order of a specific person is known as **order paper.** Order paper can be negotiated or transferred only by indorsement. A check that is payable to bearer is known as **bearer paper.** A check made payable "to the order of cash" is considered to be payable to bearer and is also known as bearer paper [3–111]. Bearer paper can be negotiated or transferred without indorsement.

An instrument can be made payable to two or more payees. For example, a check could be drawn payable "to the order of John Jones and Henry Smith." Then, both Jones and Smith have to be involved in negotiating it or enforcing its payment. An instrument can also be made payable to alternative persons, for example, "to the order of Susan Clark or Betsy Brown." In this case, either Clark or Brown could negotiate it or enforce its payment.

CONCEPT REVIEW

REQUIREMENTS FOR NEGOTIABILITY

Requirement	Basic Rules
Must Be in Writing	The instrument may be handwritten, typed, or printed.
Must Be Signed by the Maker or Drawer	1. Person signing must do so with intent of validating his or her obligation. 2. Signature can be affixed in a variety of ways: for example, by word, mark, or rubber stamp. 3. Signature can be provided by an authorized agent or representative.
Must Contain a Promise or Order to Pay	1. Promise must be more than acknowledgment of a debt. 2. Order requirement is met by the word *pay.*
The Promise or Order Must Be Unconditional	1. Entire obligation must be found in the instrument itself and not in another document or documents. 2. Payment cannot be conditioned on the occurrence of an event. 3. Payment may not be limited to funds in a particular account (except government checks).

Requirement	Basic Rules
Must Call for Payment of a Sum Certain	1. Must be able to compute from the face of the instrument the amount required to pay it off. 2. May contain a clause providing for payment of collection or attorney's fees.
Must Be Payable in Money	1. Obligation must be payable in a medium of exchange authorized or adopted by a government as part of its currency. 2. Maker or drawer cannot have the option to pay in something other than money.
Must Be Payable on Demand or at a Definite Time	1. Requirement is met if instrument says it is payable on demand or if no time for payment is stated (then it is payable on demand). 2. Requirement is met if it is payable on a stated date, at a fixed time after a stated date, or a fixed time "after sight." 3. Instrument may contain an acceleration clause or a clause allowing holder to extend the payment date.
Must Be Payable to Bearer or to Order	1. Bearer requirement is met if instrument is payable "to bearer" or "to cash." 2. Order requirement is met if instrument is payable "to the order of" a specified person or persons.
May Not Contain any Other Promise, Order, Obligation, or Power unless Authorized by the Code	Certain terms such as the place of payment or a confession of judgment clause may be included without destroying negotiability.

SPECIAL TERMS

Additional Terms

Banks and other businesses sometimes use forms of commercial paper that have been drafted to meet their particular needs. These forms may include terms that do not affect the negotiability of an instrument. Thus, a note form may provide for a place of payment without affecting the instrument's negotiability. Similarly, insurance reimbursement checks frequently contain a clause on the back stating that the payee, by indorsing or cashing the check, acknowledges full payment of the claim. This clause does not affect the negotiability of the check [3–112(1)(f)].

A term authorizing the **confession of judgment** on the instrument when due does not affect the negotiability of the instrument [3–112(1)(d)]. A confession of judgment clause authorizes the creditor to go into court if the debtor defaults and, with the debtor's acquiescence, to have a judgment entered against the debtor.

However, such clauses are not permitted in some states; moreover, even where they are permitted, some courts have held that a note is rendered nonnegotiable by a clause that authorizes confession of judgment and a demand for payment *prior* to the due date of the note.

Ambiguous Terms

Occasionally, a person may write or receive a check on which the amount written in figures differs from the amount written in words. Or a note may have conflicting terms or an ambiguous term. Where a conflict or an ambiguous term exists, there are general rules of interpretation that are applied to resolve the conflict or ambiguity: Where words and figures conflict, the words control the figures, unless the words are ambiguous. Similarly, handwritten terms prevail over printed and typed terms, and typed terms prevail over printed terms [3–118]. The following *Yates v. Commercial Bank & Trust Co.* case involves a check on which there was a difference between the figures and the written words.

YATES v. COMMERCIAL BANK & TRUST CO.
36 UCC Rep. 205 (Fla. Dist. Ct. 1983)

Emmett McDonald, acting as the personal representative of the estate of Marion Cahill, wrote a check payable to himself, individually, on the estate checking account in the Commercial Bank & Trust Company. The instrument contained an obvious variance between the numbers and the written words that indicated the amount of the check. It said: "Pay to the order of Emmett E. McDonald $10075.00 Ten hundred seventy five . . . Dollars."

The bank paid the $10,075 sum stated by the numerals to McDonald, who absconded with the funds. Yates, the successor representative, sued the bank on behalf of the estate to recover the $9,000 difference between that amount and the $1,075 that was written out. The trial court dismissed the complaint, and Yates appealed.

Schwartz, Chief Judge.   It is clear that the complaint stated a cognizable claim against the bank. Section 3–118 provides: "The following rules apply to every instrument: . . . (3) Words control figures except that if the words are ambiguous figures control."

Under this provision of the UCC, it was clearly improper for the bank to have paid the larger sum stated in numbers, rather than the smaller one unambiguously stated by McDonald's words. It is, therefore, prima facie liable to the estate for the excess.

Judgment reversed in favor of Yates.

If a note provides for the payment of interest, but no interest rate is spelled out, then interest is payable at the judgment rate (the rate of interest imposed on court awards until they are paid by the losing party) at the place of payment.

ETHICAL AND PUBLIC POLICY CONCERNS

1. The *Taylor v. Roeder* case presents the policy dilemma of whether the Uniform Commercial Code should be amended to accommodate the adjustable rate note that is in common use. If you were a commissioner on uniform state laws, how would you assess the policy considerations involved in this question?

2. The Uniform Commercial Code currently provides that in the case of ambiguity or conflict between the words and figures on a negotiable instrument, the words control the figures. A number of banks argue that in an era of computers, they encode checks based on the amount stated in figures and that the Code should be changed to provide for the dominance of figures over words. What policy considerations are involved in deciding whether or not to adopt the bank's position in the Code?

SUMMARY

Commercial paper is basically a contract for the payment of money. The two types of commercial paper are promises to pay money and orders to pay money. Notes and certificates of deposit issued by banks are promises to pay people sums of money. Drafts and checks are orders to other persons to pay sums of money to third persons.

Commercial paper that is negotiable can pass readily through our financial system and be accepted in place of money. This gives it a number of advantages over a simple contract. Normally, the assignee of a contract can obtain no greater rights than his assignor had. However, a transferee of a negotiable instrument who qualifies as a holder in due course can obtain greater rights than his assignor had.

To qualify as a negotiable instrument, an instrument must (1) be in writing, (2) be signed by the maker or drawer, (3) contain an unconditional promise or order to pay a sum certain in money, (4) be payable on demand or at a definite time, (5) be payable to order or to bearer, and (6) not contain any other promise or obligation unless it is authorized by the Code. Since negotiability is merely a matter of form, an instrument that meets the formal requirements can be negotiable even though it is void, voidable, unenforceable, or uncollectible. If an instrument is negotiable, the law of negotiable instruments as set out in the Code controls in determining the rights and liabilities of the parties to the instrument. If an instrument is nonnegotiable, the general rules of contract law control.

Printed forms for commercial paper may contain certain clauses for business reasons that do not affect the negotiability of the instruments. If there are ambiguous terms in a negotiable instrument, the general rule of interpretation is that handwritten terms control typewritten and printed terms and that typewritten terms control printed terms. If there is a conflict between words and figures, the words control unless they are ambiguous, in which case the figures control.

PROBLEM CASES

1. Is the following instrument a note, a check, or a draft? Why? If it is not a check, how would you have to change it to make it a check?

To: *Arthur Adams* January 1, 1992
TEN DAYS AFTER DATE PAY TO THE ORDER OF:
    Bernie Brown
THE SUM OF: Ten and no/100 DOLLARS
SIGNED: *Carl Clark*

2. Wiley, Tate & Irby, buyers and sellers of used cars, sold several autos to Houston Auto Sales. Houston wrote out the order for payment on the outside of several envelopes. He signed them and they were drawn on his bank, Peoples Bank & Trust Co., to be paid on the demand of Wiley, Tate & Irby. Can the envelopes qualify as negotiable instruments? *No!*

3. Is the following a negotiable instrument? *No!*

IOU, A. Gay, the sum of seventeen and 5/100 dollars for value received.
    John R. Rooke

Not proper form does not contain unconditional pr

4. Holly Hill Acres, Ltd., executed a promissory note and mortgage and delivered them to Rogers and Blythe. The note contained the following stipulation:

This note with interest is secured by a mortgage on real estate, of even date herewith, made by the maker hereof in favor of the said payee, and shall be construed and enforced according to the laws of the State of Florida. *The terms of said mortgage are by this reference made a part hereof.* (Emphasis added.)

Rogers and Blythe assigned the note to Charter Bank of Gainesville to secure payment of an obligation they owed to Charter Bank. When the Holly Hill note was not paid, Charter Bank brought suit to collect the note and foreclose the mortgage. As a defense, Holly Hill asserted that fraud on the part of Rogers and Blythe induced the sale giving rise to the note and mortgage. Charter Bank contended that it was a holder in due course of a negotiable instrument and thus not subject to the defense of fraud. Was the note a negotiable instrument?

5. An instrument, otherwise in negotiable form, contained the following provision: "This note is given in payment for merchandise and is to be liquidated by payments received on account of sale of such merchandise." Is this a negotiable instrument? *No!*

6. Nation-Wide Check Corporation sold money orders to drugstores. The money orders contained the words, "Payable to," followed by a blank. Can the money order qualify as a negotiable instrument? *No!*

7. A note, otherwise negotiable in form, payable five years after date, contained the provision, "due if ranch is sold or mortgaged." Is the note negotiable? *Yes!*

8. In 1964, S. Gentilotti wrote a check for $20,000 payable to the order of his son, Edward J. Gentilotti. He postdated the check to November 4, 1984, which would be his son's 20th birthday. The father also wrote on the check that it should be paid from his estate if he died prior to November 4, 1984. The father then gave the check to Edward's mother for safekeeping. On May 31, 1972, the father died. The check was then presented for payment, but the bank refused to pay it. The mother and the son then brought a lawsuit against the executor of the father's estate to require payment. The executor claimed that the check was not a valid negotiable instrument because it had been postdated. Can a check be a negotiable instrument if it is postdated 20 years?

9. Holliday made out a promissory note to Anderson, leaving the date of payment of the note blank. Anderson filled in the words "on demand" in the blank

ON DEMAND IF SILENT

without Holliday's knowledge. Does this alter the rights or obligations of the parties? *No!*

10. Louis Canino signed the following instrument:

$27,000   March 11, 1980
LOUIS G. CANINO for value received, does promise to pay to the order of CARL MESS the sum *Two Hundred Twenty-five* .... Dollars at *Lakewood, Colorado,* said principal *on the first day of each and every month commencing on April 1, 1980,* with interest at the rate of 8 percent per annum.

                                        /s / Louis G. Canino

When Mess sued Canino for nonpayment of the note, Canino argued that the words "Two Hundred Twenty-five Dollars" should control the figures "$27,000" and that he was obligated to pay only $225. Is this a valid argument?

Yes!!

CHAPTER 31

NEGOTIATION AND HOLDER IN DUE COURSE

INTRODUCTION

The preceding chapter discussed the nature and benefits of negotiable instruments. It also outlined the requirements an instrument must meet to qualify as a negotiable instrument and be accepted as a substitute for money.

This chapter focuses on negotiation—the process by which rights to a negotiable instrument are passed from one person to another. Commonly, this involves an indorsement and delivery of the instrument. This chapter also develops the requirements that a transferee must meet to qualify as a holder in due course and thus attain special rights under negotiable instruments law. We discuss these rights, which put a holder in due course in an enhanced position compared to an assignee of a contract, in some detail.

NEGOTIATION

Nature of Negotiation

Negotiation is the transfer of an instrument in such a way that the person who receives it becomes a holder. A **holder** is a person who is in possession of an instrument that *(1) was issued to him, (2) has been indorsed to him*

or to his order, or (3) is payable to bearer [1–201(20)].[1] For example, when an employer gives an employee a paycheck payable to her order, she is the holder of the check because the check was issued to her. When she writes her name on the back of the check and cashes it at the grocery store, she has negotiated the check to the grocery store because the store is in possession of a check indorsed to it.

Formal Requirements for Negotiation

The formal requirements for negotiation are very simple. If an instrument is payable to the order of a specific payee, it is called **order paper** and it can be negotiated only by delivery of the instrument after indorsement by the payee [3–202(1)].

For example, if Rachel Stern's employer gives her a check payable "to the order of Rachel Stern," then Stern can negotiate the check by indorsing her name on the back of the check and giving it to the person to whom she wants to transfer it. The check is order paper, not merely because the word *order* appears on the check, but also because it names a specific payee, Rachel Stern.

---

[1]The numbers in brackets refer to the sections of the Uniform Commercial Code.

If an instrument is *payable to bearer or to cash*, it is called **bearer paper** and negotiating it is even simpler. A person given a check made payable "to the order of cash" can negotiate the check by giving it to the person to whom he wishes to transfer it. No indorsement is necessary to negotiate an instrument payable to bearer [3–202(1)]. However, the person who takes the instrument may ask for an indorsement for his protection. Indorsing the check signifies an agreement to be liable for its payment to that person if the drawee bank does not pay it when it is presented for payment. We discuss this liability in the next chapter.

Nature of Indorsement

An **indorsement** is made by adding the signature of the holder of the instrument to the instrument, usually on the back [3–202(2)]. The signature can be put there either by the holder or by someone who is authorized to sign on behalf of the holder. For example, a check payable to "H&H Meat Market" might be indorsed "H&H Meat Market by Jane Franklin, president" if Franklin is authorized to do this on behalf of the market.

If the back of an instrument is full of indorsements, further indorsements should be made on a paper attached firmly to the instrument. Such a paper is called an **allonge.**

Wrong or Misspelled Name

The indorser of an instrument should spell his name in the same way as it appears on the instrument. If the indorser's name is misspelled or wrong, then legally the indorsement can be made either in his name or in the name that is on the instrument. However, any person who pays the instrument or otherwise gives something of value for it may require the indorser to sign both names [3–203].

Suppose Joan Ash is issued a check payable to the order of "Joanne Ashe." She may indorse the check as either "Joan Ash" or "Joanne Ashe." However, if she takes the check to a bank to cash, the bank may require her to sign both "Joanne Ashe" and "Joan Ash."

Indorsements by a Depository Bank

When a customer deposits a check to his account with a bank and the customer forgets to indorse the check, the bank normally has the right to supply the customer's indorsement [4–205]. Instead of actually signing the

customer's name to the check as the indorsement, the bank may just stamp on it that it was deposited by the customer or credited to his account. The only time the bank does not have the right to put the customer's indorsement on a check that the customer has deposited is when the drafter of the check specifically requires the payee's signature. Insurance and government checks commonly require the payee's signature.

Transfer of Order Instrument

If an order instrument is transferred without indorsement, the instrument has not been negotiated and the transferee cannot qualify as a holder. For example, Sue Brown gives a check payable "to the order of Susan Brown" to her grocer in payment for her groceries. Unless Sue indorses the check, it has not been "negotiated" and the grocer could not qualify as a "holder" of the check.

The transferee has the right to the unqualified indorsement of the transferor. Should the transferor refuse to indorse the instrument with an unqualified indorsement, the transferee would be entitled to a court order ordering the transferor to so indorse the instrument. The negotiation takes effect only when the indorsement is made, and until that time there is no presumption that the transferee is the owner.

INDORSEMENTS

Effects of an Indorsement

There are two aspects to an indorsement. First, an indorsement is necessary to negotiate an instrument that is payable to the order of a specific payee. Thus, if a check is payable to the order of James Lee, Lee must indorse the check before it can be negotiated. The form of the indorsement that Lee uses also affects future attempts to negotiate the instrument. For example, if Lee indorses the check "Pay to Sarah Hill," Hill must indorse it before it can be negotiated further.

Second, an indorsement generally makes a person liable on the instrument. By indorsing an instrument, a person makes a contractual promise to pay the instrument if the person primarily liable on it (for example, the maker of a note) does not pay it. The next chapter, Liability of Parties, discusses the contractual liability of indorsers. This chapter discusses the effect of an indorsement on further negotiation of an instrument.

Kinds of Indorsements

The four basic indorsements are (1) special, (2) blank, (3) restrictive, and (4) qualified.

Special Indorsement A **special indorsement** contains the signature of the indorser along with words indicating to whom, or to whose order, the instrument is payable. For example, if a check drawn "Pay to the Order of Marcia Morse" is indorsed by Morse "Pay to the Order of Sam Smith, Marcia Morse" or "Pay to Sam Smith, Marcia Morse," it has been indorsed with a special indorsement. An instrument that is indorsed with a special indorsement remains or becomes order paper. It can be negotiated only with the indorsement of the person specified [3–204(1)]. In this example, Sam Smith must indorse the check before it can be negotiated to someone else. See Figure 1 for an example of a special indorsement.

Blank Indorsement If an indorser merely signs her name and does not specify to whom the instrument is payable, the instrument has been indorsed in **blank.** For example, if a check drawn "Pay to the Order of Natalie Owens" is indorsed "Natalie Owens," it has been indorsed in blank. See Figure 2 for an example of a blank indorsement. An instrument indorsed in blank is payable to the bearer; that is, the person in possession of it. This means that the check is bearer paper. As such, it can be negotiated by delivery alone and no further indorsement is necessary for negotiation [3–204(2)].

If Owens indorsed the check in blank and gave it to Karen Foley, Foley would have the right to convert the blank indorsement into a special indorsement [3–204(3)]. She could do this by writing the words "Pay to the Order of Karen Foley" above Owens's indorsement. Then, the check would have to be indorsed by Foley before it could be negotiated further.

Similarly, the payee of a bearer instrument can make the instrument an order instrument by a special indorsement. For example, Harold Fisher is the holder of a check made payable to "cash." If Fisher indorses the instrument on the back "Pay to Arlene Jones, Harold Fisher," it would be an order instrument and it would have to be indorsed by Arlene Jones before it could be negotiated further.

If a person takes a check indorsed in blank to a bank and presents it for payment or for collection, the bank normally asks the person to indorse the check. The check does not need an indorsement to be negotiated, because the check indorsed in blank can be negotiated merely by delivering it to the bank cashier. The bank asks for the indorsement because it wants to make the person liable on the check if it is not paid when the bank sends it to the drawee bank for payment. The Liability of Parties chapter discusses the liability of indorsers.

The *Walcott v. Manufacturers Hanover Trust* case, which follows, illustrates how an instrument indorsed in blank can be negotiated merely by delivery. As you read this case, consider what the payee should have done to protect his interest in the check.

FIGURE 1 A Special Indorsement

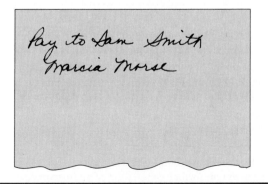

FIGURE 2 A Blank Indorsement

WALCOTT v. MANUFACTURERS HANOVER TRUST
507 N.Y.S.2d 961 (N.Y.C. Civ. Ct. 1986)

Kenneth Walcott was obligated to make monthly mortgage payments to Midatlantic Mortgage Company. He claimed that on November 1, 1985, he sent his October 19 paycheck in the amount of $359.05 along with a money order for $251.54 to Midatlantic as his November payment. He further claimed that he signed his name to the back of the check and placed his mortgage number and the Midatlantic mailing sticker on the back of the check. Then he put the checks in an envelope addressed to Midatlantic and put the envelope in a postal box.

In mid-November, he received a note that his November mortgage payment had not been received. When he inquired, he found that his check had been cashed by the Bilko Check Cashing Corporation on November 4 and deposited into the Bilko account at Manufacturers Hanover Trust. The money order was never cashed; payment was stopped on it and it was later replaced by a new money order. The check, as received by Manufacturers Hanover, contained Walcott's indorsement and the mortgage number 603052 but no sign of the sticker. Walcott claimed that an intervening thief must have stolen the check and cashed it at Bilko. He brought suit against Bilko and Manufacturers Hanover, claiming they had converted his interest in the check, which he intended to go to Midatlantic.

Harkavy, Judge.   The issue presented to this court is whether Walcott's indorsement of his paycheck was such to be a special or restrictive indorsement, thus limiting the negotiation of the instrument or did it have the effect of creating a bearer instrument.

Uniform Commercial Code Section 3–204 (1) defines a special indorsement as being one that "specifies the person to whom or to whose order it makes the instrument payable. Any instrument specially indorsed becomes payable to the order of the special indorsee and may be further negotiated only by his indorsement."

Examination of the back of the check reveals that Walcott did not specify any particular indorsee. In order for the alleged attached sticker to have served that purpose it must have also complied with Section 3–202(2): "An indorsement must be written by or on behalf of the holder and on the instrument or a paper so firmly affixed thereto as to become a part thereof." The back of the check shows no sticker attached at all. Even if it had originally been affixed thereto, as Walcott claims, it obviously became detached easily, thus failing to meet the indorsement requirements under the UCC to constitute a special indorsement.

As to the numbers written underneath Walcott's signature, they do not have the effect of restricting Walcott's indorsement. Section 3–205 is very specific as to what constitutes a restrictive indorsement. The series of numbers representing Walcott's mortgage account was insufficient to restrict negotiation of Walcott's check.

Walcott's indorsement had the effect of converting the check into a bearer instrument. The series of numbers having no restrictive effect, Walcott indorsed the check in blank, or otherwise stated, he simply signed his name. A blank indorsement under Section 3–204(2) "specifies no particular indorsee and may consist of a mere signature." Additionally, "An instrument payable to order and indorsed in blank becomes payable to bearer and may be negotiated by delivery alone . . . " Consequently, since Walcott failed to limit his blank indorsement, the check was properly negotiated to Bilko and cashed by it.

Judgment for Manufacturers Hanover Bank and Bilko Check Cashing Corporation.

FIGURE 3   A Restrictive Indorsement

> For Deposit Only to
> My Account at
> the First National
> Bank
>   Jane Frank

Restrictive Indorsement   A **restrictive** indorsement is one that specifies the purpose of the indorsement or the use to be made of the instrument. See Figure 3 for an example of a restrictive indorsement. Among the more common restrictive indorsements are:

1. Indorsements for deposit. For example, "For deposit only" or "For deposit only to my account at the First Trust Company."

2. Indorsements for collection, which are commonly put on by banks involved in the collection process. For example, "Pay to any bank, banker, or trust company" or "For collection only."

3. Indorsements indicating that the indorsement is for the benefit or use of someone other than the person to whom it is payable. For example, "Pay to Arthur Attorney in trust for Mark Minor."

4. Indorsements purporting to prohibit further negotiation. For example, "Pay to Carl Clark only."

5. Conditional indorsements, which indicate that they are effective only if a certain condition is satisfied. For example, "Pay to Bernard Builder only if he completes construction of my house by November 1, 1992."

Must be unconditional

A similar restriction by a maker or drawer would destroy the negotiability of the instrument; however, indorsers are permitted to so limit payment without affecting negotiability.

A restrictive indorsement does not prevent further negotiation of an instrument [3–206(1)]. However, the person who takes an instrument with a restrictive indorsement must pay or apply any money or other thing of value he gives for the instrument consistently with the indorsement.[2] Suppose a person takes a check payable to "Arthur Attorney in trust for Mark Minor." The money for the check should be put in Mark Minor's trust account. A person would not be justified in taking the check in exchange for a television set that he knew Attorney was acquiring for his own—rather than Minor's—use.

Similarly, suppose Clark indorses a check payable to his order "for deposit" and deposits it in a bank in which Clark has a commercial account. The bank then credits Clark's account with the amount of the check. The bank is a holder for value to the extent that it allows Clark to draw on the credit for the check because the bank has applied the value it gave for the instrument consistently with the indorsement. However, if the transferee of a restrictively indorsed instrument does not make payment in accordance with the restrictive indorsement, the transferee is liable to the indorser for any loss that results from the failure to comply with the indorsement.

In *AmSouth Bank, N.A. v. Reliable Janitorial Service, Inc.,* which follows, a depository bank was held responsible for following its customer's restrictive indorsement and required to credit the customer's account; the bank had improperly permitted the checks to be credited to another person's account.

---

[2]Except an intermediary bank, which, under § 3–206(2), is not affected by a restrictive indorsement of any person except its immediate transferor or the person presenting for payment.

AMSOUTH BANK, N.A. v. RELIABLE JANITORIAL SERVICE, INC.

548 So.2d 1365 (Ala. Sup. Ct. 1989)

Reliable Janitorial Service, Inc., maintained a bank account with AmSouth Bank. Rosa Pennington was employed by Reliable as a bookkeeper/office manager. She deposited checks made payable to Reliable but did not have authority to write checks on Reliable's account.

Beginning in January 1985, Pennington obtained counter deposit slips from AmSouth. She wrote on the deposit slips that the depositor was "Reliable Janitorial Services, Inc.," but in the space for the account number, Pennington wrote the account number for her own personal account with AmSouth. She stamped the checks that were made payable to "Reliable Janitorial Service, Inc.," with the indorsement "For Deposit Only. Reliable Carpet Cleaning, Inc." Over an 11-month period, Pennington was able to deposit 169 checks so indorsed. AmSouth credited the deposits to Pennington, not Reliable. Pennington spent all the funds that she diverted to her account. When Reliable discovered the fraud, it brought suit against AmSouth for conversion and sought to have its account credited with the improperly paid checks. The trial court granted summary judgment to Reliable, and AmSouth appealed.

Almon, Justice.   AmSouth's first issue is whether the trial court erred by granting summary judgment on Reliable's conversion claim. To examine this issue, we look to the statutes concerning restrictive indorsements and those concerning conversion. There is no dispute that Pennington stamped the checks whose funds she misdirected with the indorsement "For Deposit Only, Reliable Janitorial Service, Inc." or "For Deposit Only, Reliable Carpet Cleaning, Inc." Sections 3–205 and 3–206 address such indorsements. Section 3–205 provides:

§ 3–205. Restrictive indorsements.
  An indorsement is restrictive which either:
  (a) Is conditional; or
  (b) Purports to prohibit further transfer of the instrument; or
  (c) Includes the words "for collection," "pay any bank," or like terms signifying a purpose of deposit or collection; or
  (d) Otherwise states that it is for the benefit or use of the indorser or of another person.

Undeniably, the indorsements Pennington stamped on the checks were restrictive indorsements within the meaning of section 3–205(c).

Section 3–206 addresses the effect of such an indorsement, and pertinently, that section provides:

(3) Except for an intermediary bank, any transferee under an indorsement which is conditional or includes the words "for collection," "for deposit," "pay any bank," or like terms (subparagraphs (a) and (c) of section 3–205) *must* pay or apply any value given by him for or on the security of the instrument consistently with the indorsement. (Emphasis added.)

Thus, under the exact words of the statute, AmSouth *must* apply the value of Reliable's checks consistently with the indorsement, i.e., for deposit to Reliable's account.

Case remanded to trial court on other grounds.

Qualified Indorsement   A **qualified indorsement** is one in which the indorser disclaims or limits his liability to make the instrument good if the drawer or maker defaults on the instrument. Words such as "without recourse" are used to qualify an indorsement; they can be used with a special, a blank, or a restrictive indorsement and thus make it a qualified special, a qualified blank, or a qualified restrictive indorsement. See Figure 4 for an example of a qualified indorsement. The use of a qualified indorsement does not change the negotiable nature of the instrument. The effect is to limit the contractual liability of the indorser. The chapter on Liability of Parties discusses this contractual liability in detail.

FIGURE 4   A Qualified Indorsement

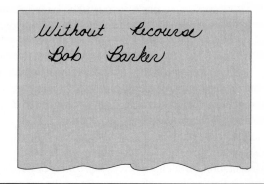

Without Recourse
Bob Barker

CONCEPT REVIEW

INDORSEMENTS

(Assume a check is payable "To The Order of Mark Smith.")

Type	Example	Consequences
Blank	Mark Smith	1. Satisfies the indorsement requirement for the negotiation of order paper. 2. The instrument becomes bearer paper and can be negotiated by delivery alone. 3. The indorser becomes contractually liable on the instrument. (See Liability of Parties chapter.)
Special	Pay to the Order of Joan Brown Mark Smith	1. Satisfies the indorsement requirement for the negotiation of order paper. 2. The instrument remains order paper and Joan Brown's indorsement is required for further negotiation. 3. The indorser becomes contractually liable on the instrument. (See Liability of Parties chapter.)
Restrictive	For deposit only to my account in First American Bank Mark Smith	1. Satisfies the indorsement requirement for the negotiation of order paper. 2. The person who pays value for the instrument is obligated to pay it consistent with the indorsement (i.e., to pay it into Mark Smith's account at First American Bank). 3. The indorser becomes contractually liable on the instrument. (See Liability of Parties chapter.)
Qualified	Mark Smith (without recourse)	1. Satisfies the indorsement requirement for negotiation of order paper. 2. Eliminates the indorser's contractual liability. (See Liability of Parties chapter.) 3. Modifies one of the transferor warranties made by the indorser. (See Liability of Parties chapter.)

Rescission of Indorsement

Negotiation is effective to transfer an instrument even if the negotiation is (1) made by a minor, a corporation exceeding its powers, or any other person without contractual capacity; (2) obtained by fraud, duress, or mistake of any kind; (3) part of an illegal transaction; or (4) made in breach of duty. A negotiation made under the preceding circumstances is subject to **rescission** before the instrument has been negotiated to a transferee who can qualify as a holder in due course [3–207]. The situation in such instances is analogous to a sale of goods where the sale has been induced by fraud or misrepresentation. In such a case, the seller may rescind the sale and recover the goods, provided that the seller acts before the goods are resold to a bona fide purchaser for value.

HOLDER IN DUE COURSE

A person who qualifies as a **holder in due course** of a negotiable instrument gets special rights. Normally, the transferee of an instrument—like the assignee of a contract—receives only those rights in the instrument that the transferor had in the instrument. But a holder in due course can obtain better rights than his transferor had. A holder in due course takes a negotiable instrument free of all **personal defenses** and claims to the instrument except for so-called **real defenses,** which go to the validity of the instrument. We develop the differences between personal and real defenses in more detail later in this chapter. The following example illustrates the advantage that a holder in due course of a negotiable instrument may have.

Carl Carpenter contracts with Helen Homeowner to build a garage for $10,500, payable on October 1, when the garage is expected to have been completed. Assume that Carpenter assigns his right to the $10,500 to First National Bank to obtain money for materials. If the bank tries to collect the money from Homeowner on October 1, but Carpenter has not finished building the garage, then Homeowner may assert the fact that the garage is not complete as a defense to paying the bank. As assignee of a simple contract, the bank has only those rights that its assignor, Carpenter, has and is subject to all of the claims and defenses that Homeowner has against Carpenter.

Now assume that instead of simply signing a contract with Homeowner, Carpenter had Homeowner give him a negotiable promissory note in the amount of $10,500 payable to the order of Carpenter on October 1. Carpenter then negotiated the note to the bank. If the bank qualifies as a holder in due course, it would be entitled to collect the $10,500 from Homeowner on October 1, even though she might have a personal defense against payment of the note in that Carpenter had not completed the work on the garage. Homeowner cannot assert that personal defense against a holder in due course. She would have to pay the note to the bank and then independently seek to recover from Carpenter for breach of their agreement. The bank's improved position is due to its status as a holder in due course of a negotiable instrument. If the instrument in question was not negotiable, or if the bank could not qualify as a holder in due course, then it would be in the same position as the assignee of a simple contract and would be subject to the personal defense.

We turn now to a discussion of the requirements that must be met for the possessor of a negotiable instrument to qualify as a holder in due course.

General Requirements

To become a holder in due course, a person who takes a negotiable instrument must be a *holder* and must take the instrument for *value*, in *good faith*, *without notice* that it is *overdue* or has been *dishonored*, and *without notice* of any *defense* against it or *claim* to it [3–302]. If a person who takes a negotiable instrument does not meet these requirements, he is not a holder in due course and is in the same position as an assignee of a contract.

Holder

To be a holder of a negotiable instrument, a person must have *possession* of an instrument that has *all of the necessary indorsements* and is *delivered* to him. For example, if Teresa Gonzales is given a check by her grandmother that is made payable "to the order of Teresa Gonzales," Teresa is a holder of the check because it is made out to her. If Teresa indorses the check "Pay to the order of Ames Grocery, Teresa Gonzales" and gives it to Ames Grocery in payment for some groceries, then Ames Grocery is the holder of the check. Ames Grocery is a holder because it is in possession of a check that is indorsed to its order and delivered to it. If Ames Grocery indorses the check "Ames Grocery" and deposits it in its account at First National Bank, the bank becomes the holder. The bank is in possession of an instrument that is indorsed in blank and has been delivered to it.

All indorsements on the instrument at the time it is payable to the order of a specified payee must be *authorized* indorsements. A *forged* indorsement is not an effective indorsement, and it prevents a person from becoming a holder. For example, the U.S. government mails to Robert Washington an income tax refund check payable to him. Tom Turner steals the check from Washington's mailbox, signs (indorses) "Robert Washington" on the back of the check, and cashes it at a shoe store. The shoe store cannot be a holder of the check, because a necessary indorsement has been forged. The check has to be indorsed by Robert Washington for there to be a valid chain of indorsements and for any subsequent possessor to be a holder. Turner's signature is not effective for this purpose, because Washington did not authorize Turner to sign Washington's name to the check.

The case which follows, *La Junta State Bank v. Travis*, illustrates that a party in possession of a check indorsed in blank is a holder of the instrument.

LA JUNTA STATE BANK v. TRAVIS

727 P.2d 48 (Colo. Sup. Ct. 1986)

On November 15, 1979, Katherine Warnock purchased a cashier's check in the amount of $53,541.93 payable to her order and drawn on the Pueblo Bank and Trust Company. At some time between November 15 and November 30, Warnock indorsed "Katherine Warnock" on the reverse side of the check, and Warnock's attorney, Jerry Quick, wrote the words "deposit only" under Warnock's indorsement. On November 30, Quick deposited the check into a trust account he maintained at the La Junta State Bank. Warnock did not maintain any type of account with La Junta State Bank. It collected the amount of the check from Pueblo Bank. Warnock died on November 10, 1981. Robert Travis, Warnock's personal representative, was unable to find a receipt in her personal papers for the sum of $53,541.93. On June 24, Travis demanded that the La Junta Bank repay that sum to Warnock's estate. At the time, no funds remained in Quick's trust account at the bank.

When the La Junta Bank refused the representative's demand, he brought suit against the bank claiming it had improperly paid the check by allowing it into any account other than one in Warnock's name. The trial court determined that Warnock had indorsed the check in blank and delivered it to Quick, that the check therefore became bearer paper upon Warnock's indorsement, and that the check was negotiable on delivery alone; it granted judgment to the bank. A divided court of appeals reversed in favor of the representative, holding that Quick's addition of the words "deposit only" below Warnock's signature created a restrictive indorsement and that because the bank failed to treat it as such, it was liable to the representative for the full amount of the check. The bank appealed.

Kirshbaum, Justice. It is undisputed that when Warnock indorsed the check in blank and delivered it to Quick, it was converted from order paper to bearer paper, negotiable by delivery alone until specially indorsed [3–204(2)]. The trial court also concluded that Quick's addition of "deposit only" below Warnock's signature did not convert Warnock's blank indorsement into a special indorsement.

Implicit in the trial court's conclusions is the assumption that Quick added the words "deposit only" to the check some time after Warnock's indorsement thereof. This implicit finding is supported by the stipulation of facts and the evidence disclosed by the record. Therefore, we also conclude that when Warnock indorsed the check in blank and delivered it to Quick, Quick became a holder of the instrument in bearer form with the right to transfer or negotiate it by delivery alone.

Warnock's representative argues that, assuming Quick was initially a holder of a check in bearer form, his act of affixing the words "deposit only" to the check deprived him of that status, destroyed the negotiability of the check, and converted Warnock's blank indorsement into a restrictive indorsement. This argument is untenable.

Quick, as holder of an instrument, was not authorized by any Code provision to conver this transferor's blank indorsement into a restrictive one (see section 3–204(3)—"The holder may convert a blank indorsement by writing over the signature of the indorser in blank any contract consistent with the character of the indorsement."). Furthermore, the representative incorrectly assumes that a blank indorsement and a restrictive indorsement create mutually exclusive methods for negotiation. As U.C.C. section 3–206 official comment 5 (1978) indicates, "indorsements 'for collection' or 'for deposit' may be either special or blank." A single indorsement, therefore, may be both in blank and restrictive. The nonrestrictive character of Warnock's indorsement was determined when she affixed her signature to the check. The fact that Quick was a holder of bearer paper does not end the inquiry into the propriety of the bank's conduct. Section 3–206(3) of Code requires a depositary bank, upon being presented with a negotiable instrument containing an indorsement which includes the words "for deposit" or like terms, to "pay or apply any value given by him for or on the security of the instrument consistently with the indorsement. . . ." This obligation affords protection to payees or indorsers who indorse items "for deposit" in the belief that such indorsement will guard against further negotiation of the instrument to a holder in due course by a finder or a thief.

In this case the bank, as a depository bank, received a check containing what appeared to be a restrictive indorsement by Katherine Warnock. The record does not reveal who actually delivered the check and deposit slip to the bank. Thus, at the moment it received the restrictively indorsed check, the bank appeared to owe a duty to Warnock to either comply with the directions of the indorsement or to inquire further concerning the transaction because of the simultaneous receipt of a deposit slip into an account other than Warnock's. However, because the check was bearer paper when Quick received it, he was free to direct its deposit in any manner he elected. Any inquiry by the bank would have revealed that, although the language inscribed on the instrument appeared to constitute a restrictive indorsement by Katherine Warnock, the words "deposit only" had been added by Quick on his own behalf; and the bank owed a duty to Quick on November 30, 1979, to honor his restrictive indorsement. Under the circumstances of the case, the bank owed no duty to Warnock and Warnock's representative is entitled to no damages.

Judgment for La Junta State Bank.

Value

To qualify as a holder in due course of an instrument, a person must give **value** for it. Value is different from simple consideration. Under the provisions of the Code, a holder takes an instrument for value if: (1) the agreed consideration has been performed—for example, if the instrument was given in exchange for a promise to deliver a refrigerator and the refrigerator has been delivered; (2) he acquires a security interest in, or a lien on, the instrument; (3) he takes the instrument in payment of, or as security for, an antecedent claim; (4) he gives a negotiable instrument for it; or (5) he makes an irrevocable commitment to a third person [3–303]. Thus, a person taking an instrument as a gift would not be able to qualify as a holder in due course.

A bank or any person who discounts an instrument in the regular course of trade has given value for it. Likewise, if a loan is made and an instrument is pledged as security for the repayment of the loan, the secured party has given value for the instrument to the extent of the amount of the loan. If Axe, who owes Bell a past-due debt, indorses and delivers to Bell, in payment of the debt or as security for its repayment, an instrument issued to Axe, Bell has given value for the instrument. If a bank allows its customer to draw against a check deposited for collection, it has given value to the extent of the credit drawn against.

The purchaser of a limited interest in an instrument can be a holder in due course only to the extent of the interest purchased [3–302(4)]. For example, Arthur Wells agrees to purchase a note payable to the order of Helda Parks. The note is for the sum of $5,000. Wells pays Parks $1,000 on the negotiation of the note to him and agrees to pay the balance of $4,000 in 10 days. Before making the $4,000 payment, Wells learns that James Dell, the maker of the note, has a valid defense to it. Wells can be a holder in due course for only $1,000.

A person who has given all of the value for an instrument that he agreed to give can be a holder in due course for the full amount of the instrument even if the amount is less than the face amount. For example, if Stu Hanks pays Linda Parish $975 for a $1,000 note, Hanks can be a holder in due course for the entire $1,000.

Good Faith

To qualify as a holder in due course of a negotiable instrument, a person must take it in **good faith,** which means that the person must obtain it honestly [1–201(19)]. If a person obtains a check by trickery or with knowledge that it has been stolen, the person has not obtained the check in good faith and cannot be a holder in due course. A person who pays too little for an instrument, perhaps because he suspects that something may be wrong with the way it was obtained, may have trouble in meeting the good faith test. The high discount itself suggests that the purchase was not in good faith. For example, because a finance company works closely with a door-to-door sales company engaging in shoddy practices, it is aware of past consumer complaints against the sales company. If the finance company buys consumers' notes from the sales company at a significant discount, it will not be able to meet the good faith test and qualify as a holder in due course of the notes.

The *Arcanum National Bank v. Hessler* case, which follows, illustrates the analysis a court goes through to ascertain whether good faith is present in a situation where the payee and a subsequent holder have had a close working relationship.

ARCANUM NATIONAL BANK v. HESSLER
69 Ohio St.2d 549 (Ohio Sup. Ct. 1982)

Kenneth Hessler was in the business of raising hogs for the John Smith Grain Company. John Smith Grain Company delivered hogs and feed to Hessler and required him to sign a promissory note payable to it to cover the cost of the hogs and feed. Without Hessler's knowledge or consent, John Smith Grain Company then sold the note to the Arcanum National Bank, which opened a commercial loan account in Hessler's name. When the hogs were sold by John Smith Grain Company, a portion of the proceeds was applied to satisfy Hessler's note held by the bank. Hessler received a flat fee and a share of the net profits on each hog sold.

On January 4, 1977, Hessler signed a promissory note for $16,800 payable to John Smith Grain Company for hogs delivered on that date. On the advice of an officer of John Smith Grain Company, Hessler also signed his wife's name, Carla Hessler, to the note, placing his initials, K. H., after her name. John Smith Grain Company, as payee, assigned the note to the Arcanum National Bank. The pigs delivered on January 4 had previously been mortgaged by John Smith Grain Company. Early in 1977, the mortgagee took the pigs from Hessler's farm because John Smith Grain Company was in serious financial difficulty. The company later went into receivership. As a result, no funds were available to pay the bank for Hessler's note.

The bank sued Kenneth and Carla Hessler to collect the face amount of the note. The Hesslers claimed that they had a defense of want of consideration and should not be liable to the bank on the note. The trial court and the court of appeals held that the bank was a holder in due course and that the defense of want of consideration could not be asserted against it. Hessler appealed.

Krupansky, Judge.   The sole issue in this case is whether the bank is a holder in due course who takes the note free from Hessler's defense of want of consideration.

Hessler contends the bank has not established holder in due course status because the bank took the instrument with notice of a defense against it. We agree.

The requirement that the purchaser take the instrument without notice of a claim or defense in order to qualify as a holder in due course is explained, under the heading of "Notice to Purchaser," at § 3–304, which provides in relevant part: "(A) The instrument is so incomplete, bears such visible evidence of forgery or alterations, or is otherwise so irregular as to call into question its validity, terms, or ownership or to create an ambiguity as to the party to pay."

Whether a transferee has taken an instrument with notice of a defense depends upon all the facts and circumstances of a particular situation and is generally a question of fact to be determined by the trier of fact.

Here the trial court, sitting as fact finder, weighed the evidence of the relationship between the bank and Hessler and reasoned: "The defect on the promissory note is that the signature of Carla Hessler was added by Kenneth Hessler and, since the Arcanum National Bank handled the Hesslers' personal finances, it should have noticed that there was a defect on the face of the instrument . . . The note also bears the initials 'K. H.,' indicating that Kenneth Hessler has signed Carla Hessler's name." Accordingly, the trial court specifically found "this 'irregularity' does call into question the validity of the note, the terms of the note, the ownership of the note or create an ambiguity as to the party who is to pay the note." Thus, the trial court, while specifically finding the bank took the note with notice of a defense, nonetheless erroneously held the bank qualified as a holder in due course.

Hessler also contends, in essence, the bank failed in its burden of proving holder in due course status because it failed to establish it took the note in good faith as required under 3–302(1)(b).

"Good faith" is defined as "honesty in fact in the conduct or transaction concerned." Under the "close connectedness" doctrine, which was established by the Supreme Court of New Jersey in *Unico v. Owen,* a transferee does not take an instrument in good faith when the transferee is so closely connected with the transferor that the transferee may be charged with knowledge of an infirmity in the underlying transaction. The rationale for the close connectedness doctrine was enunciated in *Unico* as follows:

In the field of negotiable instruments, good faith is a broad concept. The basic philosophy of the holder in due course status is to encourage free negotiability of commercial paper by removing certain anxieties of one who takes the paper as an innocent purchaser knowing no reason why the paper is not sound as its face would indicate. It would seem to follow, therefore, that the more the holder knows about the underlying transaction, and particularly the more he controls or participates or becomes involved in it, the less he fits the role of a good faith purchaser for value; the closer his relationship to the underlying agreement which is the source of the note, the less basis there is for giving him the tension-free rights considered necessary in a fast-moving, credit-extending world.

Soon after the decision in *Unico* was reached, the close connectedness doctrine was adopted by Ohio courts. *American Plan Corp. v. Woods* announced the following:

A transferee of a negotiable note does not take in "good faith" and is not a holder in due course of a note given in the sale of consumer goods where the transferee is a finance company involved with the seller of the goods, and which has a pervasive knowledge of factors relating to the terms of the sale.

According to White and Summers, noted authorities on the Uniform Commercial Code, the following five factors are indicative of a close connection between the transferee and transferor: (1) Drafting by the transferee of forms for the transferor; (2) approval or establishment or both of the transferor's procedures by the transferee (e.g., setting the interest rate, approval of a referral sales plan); (3) an independent check by the transferee on the credit of the debtor or some other direct contract between the transferee and the debtor; (4) heavy reliance by the transferor upon the transferee (e.g., transfer by the transferor of all or a substantial part of his paper to the transferee); and (5) common or connected ownership or management of the transferor and transferee.

An analysis of the above factors in relation to the facts of this case reveals an unusually close relationship between the bank (the transferee) and the John Smith Grain Company (the transferor-payee). The bank provided John Smith Grain Company with the forms used in the transaction and supplied the interest rate to be charged. At the time of the purchase of the first note, the bank ran an independent credit check on Hessler. There is evidence of a heavy reliance by John Smith Grain Company upon the bank insofar as it was customary for the grain company to transfer substantially all of its commercial paper to the bank. There was a common director of the bank and John Smith Grain Company.

The facts of this case clearly indicate such close connectedness between the bank and John Smith Grain Company as to impute knowledge by the bank of infirmities in the underlying transaction.

Judgment reversed in favor of Hessler.

Overdue and Dishonored

To qualify as a holder in due course, a person must take a negotiable instrument before it is overdue or has been dishonored. The reason for this is that obligations are generally performed when they are due. If a negotiable instrument is not paid when it is due, this is considered to put the person taking it on notice that there may be defenses to its payment.

Overdue Instruments   If a negotiable instrument due on a certain date is not paid by that date, then it is overdue at the beginning of the next day after the due date. For example, if a promissory note dated January 1 is payable "30 days after date," it is due on January 31. If it is not paid by January 31, it is overdue beginning on February 1.

If a negotiable instrument is payable on demand, a person must acquire it within a reasonable time after it was issued. A reasonable time for presenting a check for payment is presumed to be 30 days [3–304(3)(c)]. Thus, a person who acquires a check 60 days after the date it is dated is probably taking it after it is overdue.

In determining when a demand note is overdue, business practices and the facts of the particular case must be considered. In a farming community, the normal period for loans to farmers may be six months. A demand note might be outstanding for six or seven months before it is considered overdue. On the other hand, a demand note issued in an industrial city where the normal period of such loans is 30 to 60 days would be considered overdue in a much shorter period of time.

Dishonored Instruments

To be a holder in due course, a person must not only take a negotiable instrument before it is overdue but must also take it before it has been **dishonored.** A negotiable instrument has been dishonored when it has been *presented for payment* and payment has been *refused*.

For example, Susan Farley writes a check on her account at First National Bank that is payable "to the order of Sven Sorensen." Sorensen takes the check to First National Bank to cash it, but the bank refuses to pay it because Farley has insufficient funds in her account to cover it. The check has been dishonored. Sorensen then takes Farley's check to Harry's Hardware and uses it to pay for some paint. Harry's could not be a holder in due course of the check if Harry's is on notice that the check has been dishonored. It would have such notice if First National stamped the check "Payment Refused NSF" (not sufficient funds).

Similarly, suppose Carol Carson signs a 30-day note payable to Ace Appliance for $500 and gives the note to Ace as payment for a stereo set. When Ace asks Carson for payment, she refuses to pay because the stereo does not work properly. Ace then negotiates the note to First National Bank. If First National knows about Carson's refusal to pay, it cannot be a holder in due course.

Notice of Defenses

To qualify as a holder in due course, a person must also acquire a negotiable instrument without *notice* that there are any *defenses* or *adverse claims* to it. Notice of a possible defense might appear on the face of the instrument as it did in the *Arcanum National Bank* case, which appeared earlier, where a signature was accompanied by initials showing that it had been put there by someone other than the person whose name was signed. Similarly, in the *Key Bank of Southeastern New York, N.A. v. Strober Bros., Inc.* case, which follows, the notice was apparent on the face of the instrument.

KEY BANK OF SOUTHEASTERN NEW YORK, N.A. v. STROBER BROS., INC.

523 N.Y.S.2d 855 (N.Y. Sup. Ct., App. Div. 1988)

Eric Strober, the chairman of the board of Strober Bros., Inc., was approached by a business acquaintance, Sidney Pal, to make a short-term loan of $150,000 to a business venture operated by Pal. Pal indicated the loan would be collateralized by a negotiable certificate of deposit. Strober agreed to make the loan and made out a check for $150,000 drawn on the Strober Bros. account and made payable to the Tamara Trust, Pal's business venture. Pal urged the immediate delivery of the check to him and promised to deliver the negotiable certificate of deposit the next day. Strober agreed to deliver the check only on the condition that it be made nonnegotiable, that a stop order be placed on it, and that a trust agreement and the certificate of deposit be delivered by 4 o'clock the following day, at which point the stop order would be removed.

Strober struck out the words "the order of" on the check so that it read "pay to Tamara Trust" and placed a stop order on the check. Pal deposited the check in an account at the Key Bank and was allowed to draw out the funds in the account. When the check was sent to Strober's bank, payment was refused and it was returned marked "Payment Stopped." Pal never delivered a negotiable certificate of deposit.

Key Bank brought suit against Strober Bros. on the check seeking to hold Strober Bros. liable on the basis of its drawer's liability on the check. Key Bank claimed to be a holder in due course of the check who held it free of any defenses Strober Bros. might have against Pal and the Tamara Trust. The trial court granted summary judgment to Strober Bros. and Key Bank appealed.

Memorandum by the Court. The Supreme Court, Orange County, found that the check was nonnegotiable and that Key Bank was not a holder in due course. Upon determining that Strober Bros. had established its defense of a failure of a condition precedent to payment under the check, the court granted Strober Bros.'s motion for summary judgment.

We agree. The Key Bank has failed to demonstrate that it was a holder in due course of the check. The striking of the words "the order of" on the face of the check served to provide notice to the Key Bank that a claim or defense existed in favor of someone with an interest therein (see UCC section 3–304[1][a]). Therefore, Key Bank did not acquire the rights of a holder in due course under the requirements of UCC section 3–302. Since Key Bank was not a holder in due course of the instrument, it took the instrument subject to all claims and defenses against it (see UCC sections 3–305, 3–306).

Although UCC article 3 applies to non-negotiable checks such as the one at bar, it is specifically provided that there can be no holder in due course of such an instrument. Therefore, Key Bank must defend against the claims or defenses of Strober Bros.

Judgment for Strober Bros. affirmed.

Incomplete Paper   A person cannot be a holder in due course of a check or other negotiable instrument if a *material term* is blank. If a person is given a check that has been signed, but the space where the amount of the check is to be written has been left blank, then he cannot be a holder in due course of that check. The fact that a material term is blank puts the person on notice that the drawer may have a defense to its payment. To be material, the omitted term must be one that affects the legal obligations of the parties to the negotiable instrument. Material terms include the amount of the instrument and the name of the payee. If a negotiable instrument is completed after it was signed but before it is acquired, the person who acquires it can qualify as a holder in due course if he had no knowledge about any unauthorized completion.

For example, Fred Young writes a check payable to the order of Slidell's Shoes and leaves the amount blank. He gives the check to his friend Alice Termon, asks her to pick up a pair of shoes for him at Slidell's, and tells her to fill in the amount of the purchase. If Termon gives the incomplete check to Slidell, it cannot be enforced as is. If Slidell fills in the check for $79.95, the cost of the shoes, the check could be enforced as completed because the completion was authorized.

However, if Slidell watched as Termon filled the blank in as $100 (and obtained the $20.05 difference in cash), Slidell could take the check as a holder in due course as long as he had no knowledge or notice that the completion was unauthorized. In addition, if Termon filled the amount in as $100 before she got to Slidell's, Slidell could be a holder in due course and enforce the check for $100. In each case, Young, who made the unauthorized completion possible, must bear the loss until he locates Termon.

Irregular Paper   If there is something apparently wrong with a negotiable instrument, such as an obvious alteration in the amount, then it is considered to be **irregular paper.** A person who takes an irregular instrument is considered to be on notice of any possible defenses to it. For example, Kevin Carlson writes a check for "one dollar" payable to Karen Held. Held inserts the word *hundred* in the amount, changes the figure "$1" to "$100," and gives the check to a druggist in exchange for a purchase of goods. If the alterations in the amount should be obvious to the druggist, perhaps because there are erasures, different handwritings, or different inks, then the druggist cannot be a holder in due course. The druggist would have taken irregular paper and would be considered to be on notice that there might be defenses to it. These defenses include Carlson's defense that he is liable for only $1 because that is the original amount of the check.

A person is put on notice if someone of his experience and training should, in the exercise of reasonable prudence, detect the irregularity. Any noticeable alteration makes an instrument irregular on its face, but a clever alteration does not. However, an alteration that might put a bank cashier on notice might not put on notice a person unaccustomed to handling negotiable instruments.

Voidable Paper   A person cannot qualify as a holder in due course of a negotiable instrument if he is aware that the obligation of a party to it is *voidable*. Thus, if a person knows that a signature on the instrument was obtained by fraud, misrepresentation, or duress, he cannot be a holder in due course. If he knows that the instrument has already been paid, he cannot become a holder in due course. Of course, the best way for the person who is liable on an instrument to be protected after he pays it is to mark it "paid" or "canceled."

Negotiation by a Fiduciary   A person may also be considered to be on notice of defenses if he is taking a negotiable instrument from a fiduciary such as a trustee. If a negotiable instrument is payable to a person as a trustee or an attorney for someone, then any attempt by that person to negotiate it on his own behalf or for his use (or benefit) puts the person on notice that the beneficiary of the trust may have a claim [3–304(2)].

For example, a check is drawn "Pay to the order of Anthony Adams, Trustee for Mary Minor." Adams takes the check to Ace Appliance Store, indorses his name to it, and uses it to purchase a television set for himself. Ace Appliance cannot be a holder in due course, because it should know that the negotiation of the check is in violation of the fiduciary duty Adams owes to Mary Minor. Ace should know this because Adams is negotiating the check for his own benefit, not Minor's. The following *Smith v. Olympic Bank* case illustrates this principle.

SMITH v. OLYMPIC BANK
693 P.2d 92 (Wash. Sup. Ct. 1985)

Charles Alcombrack was appointed guardian for his son Chad who was the beneficiary of his grandfather's life insurance policy. The insurance company issued a check for $30,588.39 made payable to "Charles Alcombrack, Guardian of the Estate of Chad Stephen Alcombrack a Minor." The attorney for the son's estate instructed the father to take the check, along with the guardianship papers, to the bank and open up a guardianship savings and checking account. Instead, the father took the check, without the guardianship papers, to the bank and opened personal savings and checking accounts in his own name. Despite the fact that the check was payable to Alcombrack as Guardian and that he indorsed the check as Guardian, the bank allowed him to place the entire amount in his newly opened personal accounts.

The father, and later his new wife, used all but $320.60 of the trust money for their own personal benefit. After the depletion of the son's estate, J. David Smith was appointed successor guardian. He obtained a judgment against the father and then brought suit against the bank, contending that it had converted the son's interest in the check. The trial court granted judgment in favor of the bank and Smith appealed.

Dore, Justice.   Olympic Bank claims that it is a holder in due course (HIDC) and, as such, is not subject to the claims of Smith. In order to qualify as a HIDC, the bank must meet five requirements. It must be (1) a holder (2) of a negotiable instrument, (3) that took the instrument for value (4) in good faith and (5) without notice that it was overdue, dishonored, or of any defense or claim to it on the part of any person. We need not decide whether the bank met the first four conditions as we hold that the bank took the check with notice of an adverse claim to the instrument and, therefore, is not a holder in due course. Consequently, the bank is liable to the son's estate.

A purchaser has notice of an adverse claim when "he has knowledge that a fiduciary has negotiated the instrument in payment of or as security for his own debt or in any transaction for his own benefit or otherwise in breach of duty." Section 3–304(2). Thus the issue raised by this case is whether the bank had knowledge that the guardian was breaching his fiduciary duty when it allowed him to deposit a check, made payable to him in his guardianship capacity, into his personal accounts.

The bank knew it was dealing with guardianship funds. The check was payable to the father as guardian and not to him personally. The father indorsed it in his guardianship capacity. The bank received a call from the guardian's attorney inquiring about the fee charged for guardianship accounts, and a trust officer for the bank replied in a letter referring to the "Estate of Chad Alcombrack."

Reasonable commercial practices dictate that when the bank knew that the funds were deposited in a personal account instead of a guardianship account, it knew that the father was breaching his fiduciary duty. The funds lost the protection they would have received in a guardianship account. If the funds had been placed in a guardianship account, the bank would not have been permitted to accept a check drawn on the guardianship account, from the father in satisfaction of the father's unsecured personal loan in the amount of approximately $3,000. Nor could the father, or bank, have authorized his new wife to write checks against the guardianship account without court approval. A fiduciary has a duty to ensure that trust funds are protected. Here, the father breached his duty.

The policy reasons for holding a bank liable are compelling—especially in the situation presented in this case. The ward has no control of his own estate. He must rely on his guardian and on the bank for the safekeeping of his money. In order to protect the ward, the guardian and bank must be held to a high standard of care. For the guardian, this means that he must deposit guardian funds in a guardianship account. For the bank, it means that when it receives a check made payable to an individual as a guardian, it must make sure that the check is placed in a guardianship account. This will not place an undue burden on either banks or guardians and will have the beneficial effect of protecting the ward.

Judgment reversed in favor of son's guardian.

Payee as Holder in Due Course

A payee may be a holder in due course if he complies with all the requirements for a holder in due course [3–302(2)]. Ordinarily, a payee has notice or knowledge of defenses to the instrument and knows whether it is overdue or has been dishonored; consequently, he could not qualify as a holder in due course. For example, Drew draws a check on First Bank as drawee, payable to the order of Parks, but leaves the amount blank. Drew delivers the check to Axe, his agent, and instructs Axe to fill in $300 as the amount. Axe, however, fills in $500 as the amount, and Parks gives Axe $500 for the check. Axe then gives Drew $300 and absconds with the extra $200. In such a case, Parks, as payee, is a holder in due course of the check since he has taken it for value, in good faith, and without notice of defenses.

Similarly, assume that Jarvis owes Fields $200. Jarvis agrees to sell Kirk a used television set for $200 that Jarvis assures Kirk is in working condition. In fact, the set is broken. Jarvis asks Kirk to make her check for $200 payable to Fields and then delivers the check to Fields in payment of the debt. Fields, as the payee, can be a holder in due course of the check if she is not aware of the misrepresentation that Jarvis made to Kirk to obtain the check.

Shelter Provision

When an instrument is transferred, the transferee obtains those rights that the transferor had. This means that any person who can trace his title to an instrument back to a holder in due course receives the same rights of a holder in due course even if he cannot meet the requirements himself. This is known as the *shelter* provision of the Code. For example, Archer makes a note payable to Bryant. Bryant negotiates the note to Carlyle, who qualifies as a holder in due course. Carlyle then negotiates the note to Darby, who cannot qualify as a holder in due course, because she knows the note is overdue. Because Darby can trace her title back to a holder in due course (Carlyle), Darby has the rights of a holder in due course when she seeks payment of the note from Archer.

There is, however, a limitation on the shelter provision. A transferee who has himself been a party to any fraud or illegality affecting the instrument, or who as a prior holder has notice of a claim to or defense against the instrument, cannot improve his position by taking from a later holder in due course [3–201(1)]. For example, Archer, through fraudulent representations, induces Bryant to execute a negotiable note payable to Archer and then negotiates the instrument to Carlyle, who takes it as a holder in due course. If Archer thereafter takes the note for value from Carlyle, Archer cannot acquire Carlyle's rights as a holder in due course. Archer was a party to the fraud that induced the note, and the holder of an instrument cannot improve her position by negotiating the instrument and then reacquiring it.

CONCEPT REVIEW

REQUIREMENTS FOR HOLDER IN DUE COURSE STATUS

Requirement	Rule
1. Must be a *holder*.	A holder is a person who is in possession of an instrument "drawn, issued, or indorsed to him or his order or to bearer or in blank."
2. Must take for *value*.	A holder has given value: a. To the extent the agreed-on consideration has been paid or performed. b. To the extent a security interest or lien has been obtained. c. By payment of—or granting security for—an antecedent claim. d. By giving a negotiable instrument for it. e. By making an irrevocable commitment to a third person.
3. Must take in *good faith*.	Good faith means "honesty in fact."
4. Must take *without notice* that the instrument is *overdue*.	An instrument payable on a certain date is overdue at the beginning of the next day after the due date. An instrument that is payable on demand is overdue after a reasonable time after its date of issue. A reasonable time for presenting a check for payment is presumed to be 30 days.
5. Must take *without knowledge* that the instrument has been *dishonored*.	An instrument has been dishonored when it has been presented for payment and payment has been refused.
6. Must take *without knowledge* of a *claim or defense* against it.	A person who takes an instrument with a material term blank is on notice of possible claims or defenses. A person who takes irregular paper containing an obvious alteration is on notice of possible claims or defenses. A person who knows that an obligation or any part of the instrument is voidable is on notice of possible claims or defenses. A person who takes an instrument from a fiduciary is on notice of possible claims or defenses.

RIGHTS OF A HOLDER IN DUE COURSE

Importance of Being a Holder in Due Course

The Negotiable Instruments chapter showed that the advantage of negotiable instruments over other contracts is that they are accepted as substitutes for money. People are willing to accept negotiable instruments as substitutes for money because they can generally take them free of claims or defenses to payment between the original parties to the instruments. On the other hand, a person who takes an assignment of a simple contract receives only the same rights as the person had who assigned the contract.

A person who acquires a negotiable instrument must be concerned about two conditions in order to be free of claims or defenses between the original parties. First, the person who acquires the negotiable instrument must be a holder in due course. If not, he is subject to all of the claims or defenses to payment that any party to the instrument has. Second, the only claims or defenses that the holder in due course has to worry about are so-called **real defenses**—those that affect the validity of the instrument. For example, if the maker or drawer did not have legal capacity because she was a minor, the maker or drawer has a real defense. The holder in due course does not have to worry about so-called **personal defenses**.

Personal Defenses

The basic rule of negotiable instruments law is that a holder in due course of a negotiable instrument is not subject to any **personal,** or limited, **defenses** or claims that may exist between the original parties to the instrument [3–305]. Personal defenses include:

1. Lack or failure of consideration. For example, that a promissory note for $100 was given to someone without intent to make a gift and without receiving anything in return.

2. Breach of contract, including breach of warranty. For example, a check was given in payment for repairs to an automobile but the repair work was defective.

3. Fraud in the inducement of any underlying contract. For example, an art dealer sells a lithograph to Cheryl Crane, telling her that it is a Picasso, and takes Crane's check for $500 in payment. The art dealer knows that the lithograph is not a genuine Picasso but a forgery. Crane has been induced to make the purchase and give her check by the art dealer's fraudulent representation. Because of this fraud, Cheryl has a personal defense against having to honor her check to the art dealer.

4. Incapacity to the extent that state law makes the obligation voidable, as opposed to void. For example, where state law makes the contract of a person of limited mental capacity, but who has not been adjudicated incompetent, voidable, the person has a personal defense to payment.

5. Illegality that makes a contract voidable, as opposed to void. For example, where the payee of a check given for certain professional services was required to have a license from the state but did not have one.

6. Duress, to the extent it is not so severe as to make the obligation void but rather only voidable. For example, if an instrument was signed under a threat to prosecute the maker's son if it was not signed, the maker might have a personal defense.

7. Unauthorized completion or material alteration of the instrument. For example, the instrument was completed in an unauthorized manner, or a material alteration was made to it after it left the maker's or drawer's possession.

8. Nondelivery of the instrument. For example, that the person in possession of the instrument obtained it by theft or by finding it, rather than through an intentional delivery of the instrument to him.

The following example illustrates the limited extent to which a maker or drawer can use personal defenses as a reason for not paying a negotiable instrument that he signed: Trent Tucker bought a used truck from Honest Harry's, giving a 60-day promissory note for $2,750 in payment for the truck. Honest Harry's guaranteed the truck to be in good working condition, when in fact the truck had a cracked engine block. If Harry's tries to collect the $2,750 from Tucker, Tucker could claim breach of warranty as a reason for not paying Harry's the full $2,750 because Harry's is not a holder in due course. However, if Harry's negotiated the note to First National Bank and the bank was a holder in due course, the situation would be changed. If the bank tried to collect the $2,750 from Tucker, Tucker would have to pay the bank. Tucker's defense or claim of breach of warranty cannot be used as a reason for not paying a holder in due course. It is a personal defense and cannot be used against the bank, which qualifies as a holder in due course. Tucker must pay the bank the $2,750 and then pursue his breach of warranty claim against Honest Harry's.

The rule that a holder in due course takes a negotiable instrument free of any personal defenses or claims to it has been modified to some extent, particularly in relation to instruments given by consumers. We discuss these modifications in the next section of this chapter.

Real Defenses

Some claims and defenses to the payment of an instrument go to the *validity* of the instrument. These claims and defenses are known as **real,** or universal, **defenses.** They can be used as reasons against payment of a negotiable instrument to any holder, including a holder in due course (or a person who has the rights of a holder in due course) [3–305(2)]. Real defenses include:

1. Minority or infancy that under state law makes the instrument void or voidable. For example, if Mark Miller, age 17, signs a promissory note as maker, he can use his lack of capacity to contract as a defense against paying it even to a holder in due course.

2. Incapacity that under state law makes the instrument void. For example, if a person has been declared mentally incompetent by a court, then the person has a real defense if state law declares all contracts entered into by the person after the adjudication of incompetency to be void.

3. Duress that voids or nullifies the obligation of a party liable to pay the instrument. For example, if Carl

Hammond points a gun at his grandmother and forces her to execute a promissory note, the grandmother can use duress as a defense against paying it even to a holder in due course.

4. Illegality that under state law renders the obligation void. For example, in some states, checks and notes given in payment of gambling debts are void.

5. Fraud in the essence (or fraud in the factum). This occurs where a person signs a negotiable instrument without knowing or having a reasonable chance to realize that it is a negotiable instrument. For example, Amy Jones is an illiterate person who lives alone. She signs a document that is actually a promissory note, but she is told that it is a grant of permission for a television set to be left in her house on a trial basis. Jones has a real defense against payment on the note. She does not have to pay the note to even a holder in due course. Fraud in the essence is distinguished from fraud in the inducement, discussed earlier, which is only a personal defense.

6. Discharge of the party liable in bankruptcy proceedings. For example, if the maker of a promissory note had the debt discharged in a bankruptcy proceeding, she

is no longer liable on it and has a real defense against payment.

7. Forgery. For example, if a maker's signature has been put on the instrument without his authorization, the maker has a real defense against payment of the note.

8. Material alteration of a completed instrument. This is a complete defense against a nonholder in due course and a partial defense against a holder in due course. For example, a holder in due course can enforce a materially altered instrument against the maker or drawer according to its original tenor.

Real defenses can be asserted even against a holder in due course of a negotiable instrument, because it is more desirable to protect people who have *signed* negotiable instruments in these situations than it is to protect persons who have *taken* negotiable instruments in the ordinary course of business.

The case that follows, *Standard Finance Co., Ltd. v. Ellis*, illustrates the distinction between fraud in the inducement (a personal defense) and fraud in the essence (a real defense) and discusses the real defense of duress and the personal defense of failure of consideration.

STANDARD FINANCE CO., LTD. v. ELLIS
657 P.2d 1056 (Hawaii Ct. App. 1983)

On September 30, 1976, Betty Ellis and her then husband, W. G. Ellis, executed and delivered a promissory note for $2,800 payable to Standard Finance Company. Nothing was paid on the note, and on May 15, 1980, Standard Finance brought a collection action against Betty Ellis, who was divorced from W. G. The trial court awarded a judgment of $5,413.35 against Ellis. She appealed, claiming that she had defenses against payment of misrepresentation, duress, and failure of consideration.

Tanaka, Justice.   Betty Ellis indicates that "shortly before" W. G. Ellis executed the note, he gave her "constant assurance" that her "signature was a formality and that he alone was liable and that the debt would be repaid without any participation by her." Thereafter, Betty Ellis accompanied W. G. Ellis to Standard Finance's office and executed the note. Betty Ellis argues that W. G. Ellis's misrepresentation induced her to sign the note and since such misrepresentation dealt with its essential terms, her execution of the note was not a manifestation of her assent. Consequently, the note was void *ab initio* and unenforceable as to her.

The principles of law as to when misrepresentation prevents the formation of a contract and when it makes a contract voidable are set forth in *Restatement (Second) of Contracts*. Section 163 states:

§ 163. When a Misrepresentation Prevents Formation of a Contract.

If a misrepresentation as to the character or essential terms of a proposed contract induces conduct that appears to be a manifestation of assent by one who neither knows nor has reasonable opportunity to know of the character or essential terms of the proposed contract, his conduct is not effective as a manifestation of assent.

Comment a to § 163 provides in part as follows:

This Section involves an application of that principle where a misrepresentation goes to what is sometimes called the "factum" or the "execution" rather than merely the "inducement." If, because of a misrepresentation as to the character or essential terms of a proposed contract, a party does not know or have reasonable opportunity to know of its character or essential terms, then he neither knows nor has reason to know that the other party may infer from his conduct that he assents to that contract. In such a case there is no effective manifestation of assent and no contract at all.

Based on the facts in the record, we hold as a matter of law that the misrepresentation by W. G. Ellis was not a "fraud in the factum" or a "fraud in the execution" to render the note void at its inception.

A common illustration of "fraud in the factum" is that of the "maker who is tricked into signing a note in the belief that it is merely a receipt or some other document."

In the instant case, no representation was made to Betty Ellis that the note was anything other than a note. In fact, as indicated above, it is uncontradicted that Standard Finance's representative explained the "terms and conditions of the note" to Betty and W. G. Ellis prior to their execution of the note. Comment 7 to § 3–305 further states that the defense of "fraud in the factum" is that of "excusable ignorance of the contents of the writing signed" and the party claiming such fraud "must also have had no reasonable opportunity to obtain knowledge." *Page v. Krekey* and *First National Bank of Odessa v. Fazzari*, both cited by Betty Ellis, are examples in this category of "fraud in the factum." In *Page*, an intoxicated, illiterate defendant, who could not read or write, was induced to sign a guaranty on a false representation that it was an application for a license. In *Fazzari*, a defendant who was unable to read or write English was induced to sign a note upon the misrepresentation that it was a statement of wages earned.

The record in this case fails to show any fact constituting "excusable ignorance" of the contents of the paper signed or "no reasonable opportunity to obtain knowledge" on the part of Betty Ellis.

In her answers to interrogatories, Betty Ellis states that she was "forced" to sign the note under duress. "Physical beatings" and "psychological pressure" on her by Ellis for at least three years prior to signing the note constituted the duress. She argues that her execution of the note which was compelled by duress was not a manifestation of her assent. Thus, the note is void and unenforceable.

The law concerning duress resulting in void or voidable contracts is discussed in *Restatement (Second) of Contracts*. Section 174 reads:

§ 174. When Duress by Physical Compulsion Prevents Formation of a Contract.

If conduct that appears to be a manifestation of assent by a party who does not intend to engage in that conduct is physically compelled by duress, the conduct is not effective as a manifestation of assent.

Comment a to § 174 provides in part:

This Section involves an application of that principle to those relatively rare situations in which actual physical force has been used to compel a party to appear to assent to a contract. . . . The essence of this type of duress is that a party is compelled by physical force to do an act that he has no intention of doing.

We hold that as a matter of law the facts in the record do not constitute the type of duress which renders the note void under § 174. Such duress involves the use of actual physical force to compel a person to sign a document. It may include the example given in Comment 6 to § 3–305 of an "instrument signed at the point of a gun" being void.

Here, the only evidence of duress is "physical beatings" and "psychological pressure" by W. G. Ellis on Betty Ellis over a course of three years prior to her signing of the note. Without more, such evidence does not constitute duress resulting in the voiding of the note. From such evidence it cannot reasonably be inferred that the physical beatings by W. G. Ellis directly resulted in Betty Ellis signing the note in question.

Finally, Betty Ellis claims that the entire amount of the loan of $2,800 went to Ellis and she received no part of it. Thus, there was lack or failure of consideration and summary judgment was improper. We cannot agree.

Standard Finance's check for $2,800 was made payable to "W. G. Ellis and Betty Ellis." The reverse side of the check bears the indorsement of "Betty Ellis." This was sufficient evidence of consideration for the transaction involved.

However, Betty Ellis states that she "never got the money or the use of it" and "it all went to my ex-husband and this was understood by Standard Finance." This fact does not constitute lack or failure of consideration. It is fundamental that consideration received by a co-maker on a note from the payee is sufficient consideration to bind the other co-maker.

Judgment for Standard Finance affirmed.

Persons Not Holders in Due Course

As you have learned, negotiable commercial paper is basically a contract to pay money. If the holder of such paper is not a holder in due course, his rights are no greater than the rights of any promisee or assignee of a simple contract. Such a holder takes the paper subject to all valid claims on the part of any person and subject to all defenses of any party that would be available in an action on a simple contract [3–306].

CONCEPT REVIEW

DEFENSES AGAINST PAYMENT OF NEGOTIABLE INSTRUMENTS

Type of Defense	Examples
Personal (or Limited) Defense Valid against plain holders of instruments—but not against holders in due course or holders who have the rights of in due course holders through the shelter rule.	1. Lack or failure of consideration. 2. Breach of contract (including breach of warranty). 3. Fraud in the inducement. 4. Lack of capacity that makes the contract voidable (except minority). 5. Illegality that makes the contract voidable. 6. Duress that makes the contract voidable. 7. Unauthorized completion of an incomplete instrument, or material alteration of the instrument. 8. Nondelivery of the instrument.

Type of Defense	Examples
Real (or Universal) Defense Valid against all holders, including holders in due course and holders who have the rights of a holder in due course.	1. Minority that under state law makes the contract void or voidable. 2. Other lack of capacity that makes the contract void. 3. Duress that makes the contract void. 4. Illegality that makes the contract void. 5. Fraud in the essence (fraud in the factum). 6. Discharge in bankruptcy. 7. Forgery of the instrument. 8. Material alteration (partial defense).

CHANGES IN THE HOLDER IN DUE COURSE RULE

Consumer Disadvantages

The rule that a holder in due course of a negotiable instrument is not subject to personal defenses between the original parties to it makes negotiable instruments a readily accepted substitute for money. This rule can also result in serious disadvantages to consumers. Consumers sometimes buy goods or services on credit and give the seller a negotiable instrument such as a promissory note. They often do this without knowing the consequences of signing a negotiable instrument. If the goods or services are defective or not delivered, the consumer would like to withhold payment of the note until the seller corrects the problem or makes the delivery. Where the note is still held by the seller, the consumer can do this, because any defenses of breach of warranty or nonperformance are good against the seller.

However, the seller may have negotiated the note at a discount to a third party such as a bank. If the bank qualifies as a holder in due course, the consumer must pay the note in full to the bank. The consumer's personal defenses are not valid against a holder in due course. The consumer must pay the holder in due course and then try to get her money back from the seller. This may be difficult if the seller cannot be found or does not accept responsibility. The consumer would be in a much stronger position if she could just withhold payment, even against the bank, until the goods or services are delivered or the performance is corrected.

State Legislation

Some state legislatures and state courts have limited the holder in due course doctrine, particularly as it relates to consumers. In 1968, the National Conference of Commissioners on Uniform State Laws promulgated a Uniform Consumer Credit Code, and various consumer organizations have developed model consumer acts. The Uniform Consumer Credit Code, which has been adopted by a relatively small number of states, virtually eliminates negotiable paper in consumer credit sales by prohibiting the seller from taking a negotiable instrument other than a check as evidence of the obligation of the buyer. Some states now require that instruments evidencing consumer indebtedness must carry the legend "consumer paper" and must state that instruments carrying the legend are not negotiable. Other states have enacted comprehensive measures that effectively abolish the holder in due course doctrine. The law at the state level is far from uniform, and the position of a consumer who has signed a negotiable instrument varies from state to state. The trend, though, is clearly toward limiting the holder in due course doctrine as it adversely affects consumers in consumer transactions.

Federal Trade Commission Rules

The Federal Trade Commission (FTC) has promulgated a regulation designed to protect consumers against the operation of the holder in due course rule. The FTC rule applies to persons who sell to, or who finance sales to, consumers on credit and have consumers sign notes or installment sales contracts. The rule makes it an unfair trade practice for a seller, in the course of financing a consumer purchase of goods or services, to employ procedures that make the consumer's duty to pay independent of the seller's duty to fulfill his obligations.

The FTC regulation provides protection to the consumer in those situations where: (1) the buyer executes a sales contract that includes a promissory note; (2) the buyer signs an installment sales contract that includes a "waiver of defenses" clause; or (3) the seller arranges with a third-party lender for a direct loan to finance the buyer's purchase.

The FTC regulation deals with the first two situations by requiring that the following clause be included in bold type in any consumer credit contract to be signed by the consumer:

NOTICE: ANY HOLDER OF THIS CONSUMER CREDIT CONTRACT IS SUBJECT TO ALL CLAIMS AND DEFENSES WHICH THE DEBTOR COULD ASSERT AGAINST THE SELLER OF THE GOODS OR SERVICES OBTAINED PURSUANT HERETO OR WITH THE PROCEEDS HEREOF. RECOVERY HEREUNDER BY THE DEBTOR SHALL NOT EXCEED AMOUNTS PAID BY THE DEBTOR HEREUNDER.

Where the seller arranges for a direct loan to be made to finance a customer's purchase, the seller may not accept the proceeds of the loan unless the consumer credit contract between the buyer and the lender contains the following clause in bold type:

NOTICE: ANY HOLDER OF THIS CONSUMER CREDIT CONTRACT IS SUBJECT TO ALL CLAIMS AND DEFENSES WHICH THE DEBTOR COULD ASSERT AGAINST THE SELLER OF GOODS OR SERVICES OBTAINED WITH THE PROCEEDS HEREOF. RECOVERY HEREUNDER BY THE DEBTOR SHALL NOT EXCEED AMOUNTS PAID BY THE DEBTOR HEREUNDER.

The effect of the clause is to make a potential holder of the note or contract subject to all claims and defenses of the consumer. If the clause is not put in a note or contract where it is required, the consumer does not gain any rights that he would not otherwise have under state law. Thus, if the clause is omitted from the note or contract, the subsequent holder might qualify as a holder in due course. However, the FTC does have the right to seek a fine of as much as $10,000 for each violation against the seller, that is, each note or contract that fails to contain the required clause. The following *de la Fuente* case illustrates a situation where the clause required by the FTC was included in a note and served to preserve the makers' rights against a subsequent holder of the note.

The court decisions, new state laws, and the FTC regulations modifying the holder in due course doctrine are an effort to balance the societal interests (1) in protecting the consumer and (2) in assuring the availability of credit along with the marketability of commercial paper.

DE LA FUENTE v. HOME SAVINGS ASSOCIATION
38 UCC Rep. 196 (Tex. Ct. App. 1984)

Pedro and Paula de la Fuente were visited by a representative of Aluminum Industries, Inc., who was seeking to sell them aluminum siding for their home. They agreed to purchase the siding and signed a number of documents, including a retail installment contract and a promissory note for $9,138.24. The contract granted Aluminum Industries, Inc., a first lien on the de la Fuentes's residence; this was in violation of the Texas Civil Code, which prohibited such provisions. The promissory note contained a notice in bold type as required by the Federal Trade Commission. It read in part:

NOTICE: ANY HOLDER OF THIS CONSUMER CREDIT CONTRACT IS SUBJECT TO ALL CLAIMS AND DEFENSES WHICH THE DEBTOR COULD ASSERT AGAINST THE SELLER OF GOODS OR SERVICES OBTAINED PURSUANT HERETO OR WITH THE PROCEEDS THEREOF.

Aluminum Industries assigned the promissory note and first lien to Home Savings Association. Aluminum Industries subsequently went out of business. Home Savings brought suit against the de la Fuentes to collect the balance due on the note. The trial court held that Home Savings was a holder in due course and that the de la Fuentes could not assert any defenses against it that they had against Aluminum Industries. They appealed.

Kennedy, Judge.   We disagree that Home Savings was entitled to the protection of a holder in due course of a negotiable instrument because the holder in due course doctrine has been abolished in consumer credit transactions by FTC regulations, and this FTC Rule, subjecting the holder of the notice to the claims and defenses of the debtor, is in direct conflict with the doctrine of the holder in due course. The federal courts have stated, without so holding, that the effect of this FTC Rule is to abolish the holder in due course doctrine in consumer transactions.

The FTC, in its Statement of Basis and Purpose, specifically named the holder in due course doctrine as the evil addressed by its Holder in Due Course Rule. "A consumer's duty to pay for goods and services must not be separated from a seller's duty to perform as promised." The FTC intended the Rule to compel creditors to either absorb the costs of the seller misconduct or return the contracts to the sellers. The FTC "reached a determination that it constitutes an unfair and deceptive practice to use contractual boiler plate to separate a buyer's duty to pay from a seller's duty to perform." The effect of this Rule is to "give the courts the authority to examine the equities in an underlying sale, and it will prevent sellers from foreclosing judicial review of their conduct. Sellers and creditors will be responsible for seller misconduct." It was clearly the intention of the FTC Rule to have the holder of the paper bear the losses occasioned by the actions of the seller; therefore, the benefits of the holder in due course doctrine under § 3–302 are not available when the notice required by the FTC is placed on a consumer credit contract.

Judgment reversed in favor of the de la Fuentes.

ETHICAL AND PUBLIC POLICY CONCERNS

1. Suppose you have taken a promissory note from a customer in payment of some repair work you did on her house. You have some reason to believe that she is not pleased with the quality of the work you performed. Would it be ethical for you to try to sell the promissory note to a third person in order to make it more difficult for your customer to assert a claim of failure of consideration or breach of warranty against you? If you did try to sell the note, what ethical considerations are involved as to whether you should advise a prospective purchaser of the potential defenses against payment of the note even if you are not asked about them?

2. If you are in the business of buying commercial paper—such as consumer notes—from businesses such as home improvement companies, how much of an ethical obligation, if any, do you have to look into the sales practices and performance records of the companies to whom the consumers have made the notes payable? For example, would you have a concern about buying notes from a home improvement company that has a record of using high-pressure sales tactics and having shoddy workmanship?

3. Suppose you have given a check in payment of a gambling debt in a state that makes such obligations void. Are there any ethical considerations involved as to whether you should assert the real defense of illegality against payment of the check to a holder in due course?

SUMMARY

Negotiation is the transfer of an instrument in such a way that the person who receives it becomes a holder. A holder is a person who is in possession of an instrument that was issued to him, that has been indorsed to him or to his order, or that is payable to bearer. An instrument payable to a specific payee is called *order paper*; it can be negotiated by delivery after indorsement by the payee. An instrument payable to bearer or to cash is called *bearer paper*; it can be negotiated simply by delivering it to the person to whom its possessor wishes to transfer it.

The holder of an instrument makes an indorsement by signing his name on the instrument or on a paper firmly affixed to it. When an instrument is transferred, the transferee acquires all of the rights that his transferor had in the instrument. The transferee for value of an unindorsed order instrument has the right, unless otherwise agreed, to have the unqualified indorsement of his transferor.

The four basic indorsements are (1) special, (2) blank, (3) restrictive, and (4) qualified. The first three have an effect on the negotiation of the instrument; the last affects the liability of the indorser who qualifies her indorsement.

To qualify as a holder in due course, the holder must take the instrument for value, in good faith, and without notice that it is overdue or has been dishonored or of any defense against or claim to it on the part of any other person. A payee may be a holder in due course. One who purchases a limited interest in an instrument can be a holder in due course only to the extent of the interest purchased.

A holder in due course of negotiable commercial paper takes free from the personal defenses existing between the parties but takes subject to the real defenses that generally go to the validity of the instrument. These include: minority and other incapacities available as a defense to a simple contract; duress or illegality of the transaction, which renders the obligation a nullity; fraud in the essence; and discharge in bankruptcy proceedings. A holder who is not a holder in due course takes negotiable commercial paper subject to all of the defenses that would be available to a promisor on a simple contract to pay money.

The holder in due course doctrine as it relates to negotiable instruments signed by consumers has been abolished or modified by new state laws and court decisions. In addition, a regulation promulgated by the Federal Trade Commission renders the doctrine inapplicable in certain consumer credit transactions.

PROBLEM CASES

1. Stone & Webster drew three checks in the total amount of $64,755.44 payable to the order of Westinghouse Electric Corporation. An employee of Stone & Webster obtained possession of the checks, forged West-

inghouse's indorsement to them, and cashed them at the First National Bank & Trust Company, and put the proceeds to his own use. The first two checks were indorsed in typewriting, "For Deposit Only: Westinghouse Electric Corporation By: Mr. O. D. Costine, Treasury Representative," followed by the ink signature "O. D. Costine." The third check was indorsed in typewriting, "Westinghouse Electric Corporation by: [Sgd.] O. D. Costine, Treasury Representative." Were the checks negotiated to the bank?

2. Louis Agaliotis took out a policy of insurance on his son, Robert. Louis paid all of the premiums on the policy, and under the terms of the policy he was entitled to any refunds on the premiums. The insurance company sent a refund check for $1,852 to Louis. By mistake, the check was made payable to "Robert L. Agaliotis." Louis indorsed the check "Robert L. Agaliotis" and cashed it. Robert then sued Louis to get the $1,852. Was Louis entitled to sign his son's name to the check and to keep the money when he cashed it?

3. A bank cashed the checks of its customer, Dental Supply, Inc., when they were presented to the bank by an employee of Dental Supply named Wilson. The checks were indorsed in blank with a rubber stamp of Dental Supply. Wilson had been stealing the checks by taking cash rather than depositing them to Dental Supply's account. What could Dental Supply have done to avoid this situation?

4. Raye Walker was a bookkeeper for O.K. Moving & Storage Company. She opened a checking account in her name at Elgin National Bank. She then took checks that were made payable to O.K. Moving & Storage, indorsed them "For Deposit Only, O.K. Moving & Storage Co., 80 Carson Drive, N.E., Fort Walton, Florida," and deposited them in her individual account at Elgin National Bank. In a period of one year, she deposited, and Elgin Bank accepted for deposit to her account, checks totaling $19,356.01. When O.K. Moving & Storage discovered this, it sued Elgin Bank for $19,356.01 for conversion of its checks. Should Elgin Bank have permitted the checks restrictively indorsed "For Deposit Only" to a corporation's account to be deposited to an individual account?

5. Reggie Bluiett worked at the Silver Slipper Gambling Hall and Saloon. She received her weekly paycheck made out to her from the Silver Slipper. She indorsed the check in blank and left it on her dresser at home. Fred Watkins broke into Bluiett's house and stole the check. Watkins took the check to the local auto store, where he bought two tires at a cost of $71.21. He obtained the balance of the check in cash. Could the auto store qualify as a holder in due course?

6. Horton wrote a check for $20,000 to Axe who in turn indorsed it to Halbert. In return, Halbert advanced $8,000 in cash to Axe and promised to cancel a $12,000 debt owed him by Axe. The check, when presented by Halbert to the bank, was not paid due to insufficient funds. Halbert thus never regarded the debt as canceled. To what extent can Halbert be a holder in due course of the check?

7. Kamensky gave a note for $19,000 to his brother. The sum of $1,000 was payable on February 15, 1985, and a like amount was payable on the 15th day of each month for the next 19 months. On January 17, 1987, after the note was past due, Kamensky's brother indorsed it over to Srochi, who knew it was past due. Srochi brought an action on the note for payment, and Kamensky sought to interpose personal defenses. Can they be asserted against Srochi?

8. Two smooth-talking salesmen for Rich Plan of New Orleans called on Leona and George Henne at their home. They sold the Hennes a home food plan. One of the salesmen suggested that the Hennes sign a blank promissory note. The Hennes refused. The salesman then wrote in ink "$100" as the amount and "4" as the number of installments in which the note was to be paid, and the Hennes signed the note. Several days later, the Hennes received a payment book from Nationwide Acceptance. The payment book showed that a total of $843.38 was due, payable in 36 monthly installments. Rich Plan had erased the "$100" and "4" on the note and typed in the figures "$843.38" and "36." The erasures were cleverly done but were visible to the naked eye. Rich Plan then negotiated the Hennes's note to Nationwide Acceptance. The Hennes refused to pay the note. Nationwide claimed that it was a holder in due course and was entitled to receive payment. Was Nationwide Acceptance a holder in due course?

9. Factor Cab Corporation issued a series of notes payable "to the order of Donald E. Richel as attorney for Francisco Silvestry." Twenty-one of the notes were indorsed by Richel and sold to Maber, Inc. In purchasing the notes, Maber made its check payable to Richel in his individual name, without qualification or restriction, in

the amount of $5,796.24. In addition, it discharged by payment Richel's personal indebtedness to a bank in the amount of $3,903.75. Richel indorsed the notes as an individual and not in his fiduciary capacity. Can Maber be a holder in due course of the notes?

10. Panlick, the owner of an apartment building, entered into a written contract with Bucci, a paving contractor, whereby Bucci was to install asphalt paving on the parking lot of the building. When Bucci finished the job, Panlick gave Bucci a check for $6,500 and a promissory note for $7,593 with interest at 10 percent due six months from its date. When the note came due, Panlick refused to pay it. Bucci brought suit to collect the note, and Panlick claimed there had been a failure of consideration because the asphalt was defectively installed. Can Panlick assert this defense against Bucci?

11. Ralph Herrmann wrote a check for $10,000 payable to Ormsby House, a hotel-casino in Carson City, Nevada, and exchanged it for three counter checks he had written earlier that evening to acquire gaming chips. Ormsby House was unable to collect the proceeds from the check because Herrmann had insufficient funds in his account. The debt evidenced by the check was assigned to Sea Air Support, Inc., d/b/a Automated Accounts Associates, for collection. Sea Air was also unsuccessful in its attempts to collect and filed a lawsuit against Herrmann to recover on the dishonored check. Nevada law provides that all instruments drawn for the purpose of reimbursing or repaying any money knowingly lent or advanced for gaming are "utterly void, frustrate, and of none effect." Is Herrmann liable to Sea Air to make good the check?

12. Nickerson signed a promissory note marked "consumer note" to cover the cost of having his house covered with aluminum siding. The note was negotiated to a finance company, which claimed to be a holder in due course of the note. When the finance company tried to collect the note from Nickerson, he tried to defend against payment on the grounds that the aluminum siding was defective. A Massachussetts statute requires any note for the retail sale of consumer goods to be labeled "consumer note" and makes it nonnegotiable. Can Nickerson use the defense of breach of warranty against the finance company even if it is a holder in due course?

CHAPTER 32

LIABILITY OF PARTIES

INTRODUCTION

Thus far in this Commercial Paper section, the focus has been on the nature of, and requirements for, negotiable instruments as well as the rights that a party to an instrument can obtain and how to obtain them. There is another important aspect to negotiable instruments; namely, how a person becomes liable on a negotiable instrument and the nature of the liability incurred.

When a person signs a promissory note, he expects to be liable for paying the note on the day it is due. Similarly, when a person signs a check and mails it off to pay a bill, he expects that it will be paid by the drawee bank out of his checking account and that if there are not sufficient funds in his account to cover it, he will have to make it good out of other funds he has. The liability of the maker of a note and of the drawer of a check is commonly understood.

However, a person can become liable on a negotiable instrument in other ways. A person who indorses a paycheck is assuming liability on it; and a bank that cashes a check with a forged indorsement on it is liable for conversion of the check. This chapter and the following chapter discuss the liabilities of the various parties to a negotiable instrument. These two chapters also cover what happens when an instrument is not paid when it is supposed to be paid. For example, a check may not be paid if there are insufficient funds in the drawer's account or if the check has been forged. In addition, this chapter discusses the ways in which liability on an instrument can be discharged.

LIABILITY IN GENERAL

Liability may be based on the fact that a person has signed a negotiable instrument or has authorized someone else to sign it. In that case, the liability depends on the capacity in which the person has signed the instrument. Liability can also be based on (1) certain warranties that are made when an instrument is transferred or presented for payment, (2) negligence, (3) improper payment, or (4) conversion.

CONTRACTUAL LIABILITY

When a person signs a negotiable instrument, whether as maker, drawer, or indorser, or in some other capacity, he generally becomes *contractually liable* on the instrument. This contractual liability depends on the *capacity* in which the person signed the instrument. The terms of the contract of the parties to a negotiable instrument are not written out on the instrument; these terms are supplied by Article 3 of the Uniform Commercial Code, which deals with Commercial Paper. The terms of the contract are provided by law and are as much a part of the instrument as if they were written on it.

Primary and Secondary Liability

A party to a negotiable instrument may be either *primarily liable* or *secondarily liable* for payment of it. A person who is primarily liable has agreed to pay the negotiable instrument. For example, the maker of a promissory note is the person who is primarily liable on the note. A person who is secondarily liable is like a guarantor on a contract and is required to pay the negotiable instrument only if a person who is primarily liable defaults on that obligation. The Introduction to Credit and Secured Transactions chapter discusses guarantors.

Contract of a Maker

The maker of a promissory note is primarily liable for payment of it. The maker has made an unconditional promise to pay a sum certain and is responsible for making good on that promise. The *contract of the maker* is to *pay the negotiable instrument according to its terms at the time he signs it* [3–143].[1] If the material terms of the note are not complete when the maker signs it, then the maker's contract is that he will pay the note as it is completed, provided that the terms filled in are as authorized.

Contract of a Drawee

At the time a check or other draft is written, *no party is primarily liable on it.* Usually, a check is paid by the drawee bank when it is presented for payment and no

---

[1] The numbers in brackets refer to the sections of the Uniform Commercial Code.

person becomes primarily liable. However, the drawee bank may be asked by the drawer or by a holder of the check to **certify** the check. The drawee bank certifies the check by signing its name to the check and thereby accepting liability as drawee. The drawee bank debits, or takes the money out of, the drawer's account and holds the money to pay the check. If the drawee bank certifies the check, it becomes primarily, or absolutely, liable for paying the check as it reads at the time it is certified [3–413].

A drawee has no liability on a check or other draft unless it certifies or accepts the check; that is, agrees to be liable on it. However, a drawee bank that refuses to pay a check when it is presented for payment may be liable to the drawer for wrongfully refusing payment, if the drawer had sufficient funds in his checking account to cover it. The next chapter discusses this liability of a drawee bank.

Contract of a Drawer

The *drawer's contract* is that *if the check (or draft) is dishonored* and *if the drawer is given notice of the dishonor, he will pay the amount of the check (or draft) to the holder or to any indorser who takes it back* [3–413(2)]. For example, Janis draws a check on her account at First National Bank payable to the order of Collbert. If First National does not pay the check when Collbert presents it for payment, then Janis is liable to Collbert on the basis of her drawer's contractual liability.

Because a drawer's liability on a draft or check is secondary, she may *disclaim* this liability by drawing it *without recourse* [3–413(2)].

The case that follows, *First American Bank of Virginia v. Litchfield Company of South Carolina, Inc.,* illustrates circumstances under which a drawer might be held liable on its drawer's contractual liability.

FIRST AMERICAN BANK OF VIRGINIA v. LITCHFIELD COMPANY OF SOUTH CAROLINA, INC.

353 S.E.2d 143 (S.C. Ct. App. 1987)

On February 9, 1983, Litchfield Company drew a check payable to Jensen Farley Pictures, Inc., in the amount of $13,711.11, on its account with Bankers Trust of South Carolina. Litchfield sent the check to Jensen Farley, which negotiated the check on September 16 to First American Bank of Virginia with whom it had a checking account. First American gave Jensen Farley immediate credit on the check and forwarded it to Bankers Trust for payment. Unknown to First American, Litchfield had given Bankers Trust an oral stop payment order on the check. On September 19, Jensen Farley withdrew most of the balance in its First American account; it subsequently filed for bankruptcy. On September 21, Bankers Trust returned the Litchfield check to First American marked "payment stopped." First American then brought suit against Litchfield claiming that as drawer of the check, it was liable to First American, a holder in due course of the check. The trial court awarded First American Bank judgment for $9,369.37 (representing the amount it had been unable to recover from Jensen Farley), and Litchfield appealed.

Bell, Judge.   The drawer of a check engages that upon dishonor he will pay the amount of the draft to a holder in due course. Section 3–413(2). The drawer has the right to stop payment, but remains liable on the instrument to a holder in due course. Section 4–403 and comment 8; section 3–413(2). Since Litchfield has conceded First American was a holder in due course, Litchfield remains liable on the instrument unless it can establish a valid defense or set off.

Litchfield argues that its liability was discharged by First American's failure to give timely notice the check had been dishonored. This defense is unavailing for two reasons.

First, failure to give notice of dishonor discharges a drawer only to the extent he is deprived of funds maintained with the drawee bank to cover the check because the drawee bank became insolvent during the delay. Sections 3–501(2)(b) and 3–502(1)(b). A drawer is not otherwise discharged. In this case, Litchfield was not deprived of any funds in its account with Bankers Trust nor did Bankers Trust become insolvent during the delay.

Second, notice of dishonor is excused when the party to be charged has himself countermanded payment. Section 3–511(2)(b). Since Litchfield ordered payment stopped, it was not entitled to notice of dishonor.

Litchfield argues strenuously that it is unfair to apply section 3–511(2)(b) to the drawer of a check who has no means of knowing whether the check has been negotiated to a holder. This reasoning misses the mark. The maker of an outstanding negotiable instrument is presumed to know the instrument is subject to transfer to a holder in due course. The drawer is often without actual knowledge that his check has been negotiated, but that ignorance in no way diminishes the rights of a holder in due course. To hold otherwise would, as a practical matter, destroy the negotiability of a check.

Judgment for First American affirmed.

Contract of an Indorser

A person who indorses a negotiable instrument is usually secondarily liable. Unless the indorsement is qualified, the *indorser agrees* that *if the instrument is not paid when presented for payment, then the indorser will make it good to the holder or to any later indorser who had to pay it* [3–414]. The indorser can avoid this liability only by putting a qualified indorsement, such as "without recourse," on the instrument when he indorses it.

Indorsers are liable to each other in the chronological order in which they indorse, from the last indorser back to the first. For example, Mark Maker gives a promissory note to Paul Payee. Payee indorses it and negotiates it to Fred First, who indorses it and negotiates it to Shirley Second. If Maker does not pay the note when Second takes it to him for payment, then Second can require First to pay it to her. First is secondarily liable on the basis of his indorsement. First, in turn, can require Payee to pay him because Payee also became secondarily liable when he indorsed it. Then, Payee is left to try to collect the note from Maker. Second also could have skipped over First and gone directly against Payee on his indorsement. First has no liability to Payee, however, because First indorsed after Payee indorsed the note.

Contract of an Accommodation Party

An **accommodation party** is a person who signs a negotiable instrument for the purpose of lending his credit to another party to the instrument. For example, a bank might be reluctant to lend money to and take a note from Payee because of his shaky financial condition. However, the bank may be willing to lend money to Payee if he signs the note and has a relative or a friend also sign the note as an accommodation maker.

The contractual liability of an accommodation party depends on the capacity in which the party signs the instrument [3–415]. If Payee has his brother Sam sign a note as an accommodation maker, then Sam has the same contractual liability as a maker. Sam is primarily liable on the note. The bank may ask Sam to pay the note before asking Payee to pay. However, if Sam pays the note to the bank, he has the right to recover his payment from Payee—the person on whose behalf he signed.

Similarly, if a person signs a check as an accommodation indorser, his contractual liability is that of an indorser. If the accommodation indorser has to make good on that liability, he can collect in turn from the person on whose behalf he signed.

Signing an Instrument

No person is contractually liable on a negotiable instrument unless his authorized signature appears on the instrument. A **signature** can be any name, word, or mark used in place of a written signature [3–401]. A negotiable instrument can be signed either by a person or by an authorized agent. As discussed earlier, the capacity in which a person signs an instrument affects his liability on the instrument.

In determining the capacity in which a person has signed a negotiable instrument, the position of the signature is important. If a person signs a check in the lower right corner, the presumption is that he signed it as the drawer. If a person signs a promissory note in the lower right corner, the presumption is that she signed it as the maker. If the drawee named in a draft signs across the face of the instrument, it is a clear indication that he has accepted the draft; however, his signature on any part of the instrument, front or back, will be held to be an acceptance in the absence of credible evidence of an intent to sign in some other capacity. A signature on the back of an instrument is presumed to be an indorsement [3–402].

Signature by an Authorized Agent

A negotiable instrument can be signed by an authorized agent [3–403(1)]. If Sandra Smith authorized her attorney to sign checks as her agent, then she is liable on any checks properly signed by the attorney as her agent. All negotiable instruments signed by corporations have to be signed by an agent of the corporation who is authorized to sign negotiable instruments.

If an agent or a representative signs a negotiable instrument on behalf of someone else, the agent should clearly indicate that he is signing as the representative of someone else. For example, Kim Darby, the president of Swimwear, Inc., is authorized to sign negotiable instruments for the company. If Swimwear borrows money from the bank and is given a 90-day promissory note to sign, Darby should sign it either "Swimwear, Inc. by Kim Darby, President" or "Kim Darby, President, for Swimwear, Inc." Similarly, if Arthur Anderson, an attorney, is authorized to sign checks for Clara Carson, he should sign them "Clara Carson by Arthur Anderson, Agent." Otherwise, he risks being personally liable on them.

The agents or representatives who sign negotiable instruments are *personally liable* if they do not indicate that they are signing in a representative capacity and if they do not state the name of the person on whose behalf they are signing [3–403(2)]. Thus, if Kim Darby signed the promissory note merely "Kim Darby," she would be personally liable on the note. To protect herself and to ensure that the corporation is liable, Darby should sign the name of the company and her title or office as well as her signature. In the *Schwartz v. Disneyland Vista Records* case, which follows, the president of a company was held personally liable on some notes he signed for the corporation because he failed to indicate that he was signing in a representative capacity.

SCHWARTZ v. DISNEYLAND VISTA RECORDS

383 So.2d 1117 (Fla. Ct. App. 1980)

American Music Industries, Inc., and Disneyland Vista Records had ongoing business dealings during 1975 and 1976. As of May 21, 1976, American owed Disneyland over $93,000. As evidence of that indebtedness, American issued 10 promissory notes, payable to Disneyland and signed by Irv Schwartz, the president of American Music. The notes contained no reference to American Music Industries, Inc., nor was there any indication that Schwartz signed in a representative capacity.

American paid four of the notes, then defaulted on the rest. Disneyland brought suit against Schwartz to recover on the remaining six promissory notes. Schwartz claimed that the notes had been prepared by Disneyland; that they did not correctly reflect the intent of the parties, because they did not name American as the maker; and that he signed the notes individually by mistake. The trial court ruled in favor of Disneyland, and Schwartz appealed.

Downey, Judge.   Summary judgment against Schwartz was proper because his claim is controlled by § 3–403(2):

(2) An authorized representative who signs his own name to an instrument:
(a) Is personally obligated if the instrument neither names the person represented nor shows that the representative signed in a representative capacity;
(b) Except as otherwise established between the immediate parties, is personally obligated if the instrument names the person represented but does not show that the representative signed in a representative capacity.

The notes in question are payable to Disneyland and signed by Irv Schwartz. There is no indication that they are obligations of the corporation, American Music Industries, Inc., or that Irv Schwartz signed them in a representative capacity. Thus, under Section (2)(a), above, Irv Schwartz is liable on these notes as a matter of law.

The main thrust of Schwartz's defense is that he should be allowed to use parol evidence to show the parties intended the notes to be corporate obligations and that Schwartz's signing individually was a mistake. However, the evidence is not admissible to "disestablish" obligations such as the notes here involved. Paraphrased, the example used in the comment indicates the results that various signatures have upon the individual liability of an agent. If American Music Industries, Inc., is a principal and Irv Schwartz is its agent, a note might bear the following signatures affixed by the agent:

(a)   American Music Industries, Inc.;
(b)   Irv Schwartz;
(c)   American Music Industries, Inc., by Irv Schwartz, agent;
(d)   Irv Schwartz, agent;
(e)   American Music Industries, Inc., Irv Schwartz.

A signature in form (a) does not bind Irv Schwartz if authorized. A signature as in (b) personally obligates Irv Schwartz, and parol evidence is inadmissible under § 3–403(2)(a) to disestablish his obligation. The unambiguous way to make clear that Irv Schwartz is signing in his representative capacity without personal liability is to sign as in (c).

Judgment for Disneyland affirmed.

An authorized representative might sign a negotiable instrument in his own name in a way that clearly indicates he has signed in a representative capacity, but he might fail to name the person represented. In this case, *parol evidence* is admissible, between the immediate parties to the instrument, to prove that they intended the principal to be liable and not the party who signed in the representative capacity. For example, a negotiable instrument is signed "Axe, agent" and retained by the payee, who then sues Axe on the instrument. Parol evidence would be admitted in a lawsuit to prove that the payee knew that Axe was acting as agent for Parks, his principal, and that the parties intended Parks to be bound rather than Axe. If this instrument had been negotiated to a holder in due course, however, Axe would be personally liable on the instrument and would be unable to use parol evidence to disprove his liability [3–403(2)].

Some state courts, albeit a minority, have declined to hold corporate officers personally liable on corporate checks they signed without indicating they were signing in a representative capacity. Typically, these courts have found that because the checks in question were imprinted with the corporation's name, the circumstances disclosed that the individuals signed as representatives. In the following *Valley National Bank v. Cook* case, the court followed the minority rule.

If a negotiable instrument is signed in the name of an organization and the name of the organization is preceded or followed by the name and office of an authorized individual, the organization and not the officer who signed the instrument in a representative capacity is bound [3–403(3)].

VALLEY NATIONAL BANK v. COOK
36 UCC Rep. 578 (Ariz. Ct. App. 1983)

J. M. Cook, then treasurer of Arizona Auto Auction, signed three corporate checks totaling $9,795 payable to Central Motors Company, which deposited them in its corporate account at Valley National Bank. Cook did not indicate on the check that she was signing as a representative of Arizona Auto Auction. When Valley National Bank sent the checks to the drawee bank, payment was refused because a stop payment order had been put on them. Valley National Bank charged back the checks to the account of Central Motors, but it was unable to recover the money from Central Motors.

Valley National Bank then brought suit against Arizona Auto Auction and J. M. Cook. The trial court held that the bank was a holder in due course, that Arizona Auto Auction was liable to the bank, and that J. M. Cook was not personally liable on the checks. The bank appealed the portion of the decision in favor of Cook.

Corcoran, Presiding Judge.   The issue raised in this appeal is whether an individual who signs a check without indicating her representative capacity is personally liable on the obligation evidenced by the check when the check has the name of the corporate principal printed on it. We adopt the minority rule and hold that the individual is not personally liable.

The question of whether Cook signed in her individual or representative capacity is governed by § 3–403 of the Uniform Commercial Code as adopted in this state. It provides:

A. A signature may be made by an agent or other representative, and his authority to make it may be established as in other cases of representation. No particular form of appointment is necessary to establish such authority.

B. An authorized representative who signs his own name to an instrument:

1. Is personally obligated if the instrument neither names the person represented nor shows that the representative signed in a representative capacity;

2. Except as otherwise established between the immediate parties, is personally obligated if the instrument names the person represented but does not show that the representative signed in a representative capacity, or if the instrument does not name the person represented but does show that the representative signed in a representative capacity.

C. Except as otherwise established, the name of an organization preceded or followed by the name and office of an authorized individual is a signature made in a representative capacity.

The Bank argues that this section conclusively establishes Cook's personal liability on the checks. We do not agree. Admittedly, the checks fail to specifically show the office held by Cook. However, we do not find that this fact conclusively establishes liability since § 3–403(B)(2) imposes personal liability on an agent who signs his or her own name to an instrument only "if the instrument does not show that the representative signed in a representative capacity." Thus, we must look to the entire instrument for evidence of the capacity of the signer.

The checks are boldly imprinted at the top "Arizona Auto Auction, Inc.," and also "Arizona Auto Auction, Inc." is imprinted above the signature line appearing at the lower right-hand corner. Under the imprinted name of Arizona Auto Auction appears the signature of Cook without any designation of office or capacity on each of the checks before us. Cook did not indorse the checks on the back. The record does not reflect that Cook made any personal guaranty of these checks or any other corporate obligation. The Superior Court of Pennsylvania was confronted with a similar situation in *Pollin v. Mindy Mfg. Co., Inc.* There the court denied recovery by a third-party indorsee against one who affixed his signature to a payroll check directly beneath the printed corporate name without indicating his representative capacity. In *Pollin* the checks were boldly imprinted at the top with the corporate name, address, and appropriate check number. The printed name of the drawee bank appeared in the lower left-hand corner of the instrument, and the corporate name was imprinted in the lower right-hand corner. Directly beneath the corporate name were two blank lines. The officer had signed the top line without any designation of office or capacity. Pointing out that the Code imposes liability on the individual only when the instrument controverts any showing of representative capacity, the court considered the instrument in its entirety. The court in *Pollin* held that disclosure on the face of the instrument that the checks were payable from a special payroll account of the corporation over which the officer had no control as an individual negated any contention that the officer intended to make the instrument his own order to pay money to the payee.

In this case the checks clearly show the name of the corporation in two places and the money was payable from the account of Arizona Auto Auction, Inc., over which Cook as an individual had no control. Considering the instruments as a whole, we conclude under these circumstances that they sufficiently disclose that Cook signed them in a representative and not an individual capacity.

Judgment for Cook affirmed.

Unauthorized Signature

If a person's name is signed to a negotiable instrument without that person's authorization or approval, the person is not bound by the signature. For example, if Tom Thorne steals Ben Brown's checkbook and signs Brown's name to a check, Brown is not liable on the check because Thorne was not authorized to sign Brown's name. Thorne is liable on the check, however, because he did sign it, even though he did not sign it in his own name. Thorne's forgery of Brown's signature operates as Thorne's signature [3–404].

CONTRACTUAL LIABILITY IN OPERATION

To bring the contractual liability of the various parties to a negotiable instrument into play, it is generally necessary that the instrument be *presented for payment*. In addition, to hold the parties that are secondarily liable on the instrument to their contractual liability, it is generally necessary that the instrument be *presented for payment* and *dishonored*.

Presentment of a Note

The maker of a note is primarily liable to pay it when it is due. Normally, the holder takes the note to the maker at the time it is due and asks the maker to pay it. Sometimes, the maker sends the payment to the holder at the due date. The party to whom **presentment** is made may, without dishonoring the instrument, require the exhibition of the instrument, reasonable identification of the person making presentment, and evidence of his authority to make it if he is making it for another person [3–505]. If the maker pays the note, he is entitled to have the note marked "paid" or "canceled" or to have it returned so that it can be destroyed.

If the maker does not pay a note when it is presented at its due date, the note has been **dishonored** [3–507(1)]. If the note is dishonored, the holder can seek payment from any persons who indorsed the note before the holder took it. The basis for going after the indorsers is that they are secondarily liable on it. To hold the indorsers to their contractual liability, the holder must give notice of the dishonor. The notice can be either written or oral [3–508].

For example, Susan Strong borrows $100 from Jack Jones and gives him a promissory note for $100 at 9 percent annual interest payable in 90 days. Jones indorses the note "Pay to the order of Ralph Smith" and negotiates the note to Ralph Smith. At the end of the 90 days, Smith takes the note to Strong and presents it for payment. If Strong pays Smith the $100 and accrued interest, she can have Smith mark it "paid" and give it back to her. If Strong does not pay the note to Smith when he presents it for payment, then the note has been dishonored. Smith should give notice of the dishonor to Jones and advise him that he intends to hold Jones secondarily liable on his indorsement. Smith is entitled to collect payment of the note from Jones. Jones, after making the note good to Smith, can try to collect the note from Strong on the ground that she defaulted on the contract she made as maker of the note. Of course, Smith could also sue Strong on the basis of her maker's liability.

Presentment of a Check or a Draft

A check or draft should be presented to the drawee. The presentment can be either for payment or for acceptance (certification) of the check or draft. *No one is primarily liable on a check or draft*, and the *drawee is not liable on a check or draft unless it accepts (certifies) it*. An acceptance of a draft is the drawee's signed commitment to honor the draft as presented. The acceptance must be written on the draft, and it may consist of the drawee's signature alone [3–410].

A drawer who writes a check is issuing an order to the drawee to pay a certain amount out of the drawer's account to the payee (or to someone authorized by the payee). This order is not an assignment of the funds in the drawer's account [3–409]. The drawee bank does not have an obligation to the payee to pay the check unless it has certified the check. However, the drawee bank usually does have a contractual obligation to the drawer to pay any properly payable checks for which funds are available in the drawer's account.

For example, Janet Payne has $100 in a checking account at First National Bank and writes a check for $10 drawn on First National and payable to Ralph Smith. The writing of the check is the issuance of an order by Payne to First National to pay $10 from her account to Smith or to whomever Smith requests it to be paid. First National owes no obligation to Smith to pay the $10 unless it has certified the check. However, if Smith presents the check for payment and First National refuses to pay it even though there are sufficient funds in Payne's account, then First National is liable to Payne for breaching its contractual obligation to her to pay items properly payable from existing funds in her account. The Checks and Documents of Title chapter discusses the liability of a bank for wrongful dishonor of checks in more detail.

If the drawee bank does not pay or certify a check when it is properly presented for payment or acceptance (certification), the check has been **dishonored** [3–507]. The holder of the check can then proceed against either the drawer of the check or any indorsers on their secondary liability. To do so, the holder must give them **notice** of the dishonor [3–508].

Suppose Matthews draws a check for $100 on her account at a bank payable to the order of Williams. Williams indorses the check "Pay to the order of Clark, Williams" and negotiates it to Clark. When Clark takes the check to the bank, it refuses to pay the check because there are insufficient funds in Matthews's account to cover the check. The check has been presented and dishonored. Clark has two options: He can proceed against Williams on Williams's secondary liability as an indorser because by putting an unqualified indorsement on the check, Williams contracted to make the check good if it was not honored by the drawee. Or he can proceed against Matthews on Matthews's drawer's contractual liability because in drawing the check, Matthews promised to make it good to any holder if it was dishonored and he was given notice. Because Clark dealt with Williams, Clark is probably more likely to return the check to Williams for payment. Williams then has to go against Matthews on Matthews's contractual liability as drawer.

Time of Presentment

If an instrument is payable at a definite time, it should be presented for payment on the due date. In the case of a demand instrument, a reasonable time for presentment for acceptance or payment is determined by the nature of the instrument, by trade or bank usage, and by the facts of the particular case. In a farming community, for example, a reasonable time to present a promissory note that is payable on demand may be six months or within a short time after the crops are sold, because it is expected that the payment can be made from the proceeds of the crops.

A reasonable time to present a check to hold the drawer liable is presumed to be 30 days [3–503]. Delay in presentment may be excused where, for example, the party is without notice that the instrument is due, or where the delay is caused by circumstances beyond his control and he operates with reasonable diligence [3–511].

Effect of Unexcused Delay in Presentment

If presentment of a negotiable instrument is delayed beyond the time it is due, and if there is no valid excuse for the delay, then the indorsers are *discharged from liability* on the instrument. Under certain circumstances, a drawer or maker can also be discharged of liability if the bank in which the funds to pay the note or draft were deposited becomes insolvent during the delay [3–502(1)].

To be able to hold an indorser of a check liable, the check should be presented for payment within seven days after the indorser signed it. If the holder of the check waits longer than that without a valid excuse, the indorsers are relieved of their secondary liability and the holder's only recourse is against the drawer. The holder must give the indorsers timely notice of any dishonor.

WARRANTY LIABILITY

Whether or not a person signs a negotiable instrument, a person who transfers such an instrument or presents it for payment may incur liability on the basis of certain implied warranties. These warranties are (1) **transferor's warranties,** which are made by persons who *transfer* negotiable instruments; and (2) **presentment warranties,** which are made by persons who *present* negotiable instruments *for payment or acceptance (certification).*

Transferor's Warranties

A *person who transfers a negotiable instrument* to someone else and receives something of value in exchange makes five *warranties* to his transferee. The warranties are:

1. The person has *good title* to the instrument or is *authorized* to *obtain payment* by someone who has good title.
2. *All signatures* on the instrument are *genuine or authorized.*
3. The instrument has *not been materially altered.*
4. *No party* to the instrument has a *valid defense* against the person who is transferring it.

5. The person transferring the instrument has *no knowledge of any insolvency proceedings* against the maker, drawer, or acceptor [3–417(2)].

If the transfer is by indorsement, the warranties are made to any subsequent holder who takes the instrument in good faith.

Although contractual liability often furnishes a sufficient basis for suing a transferor when the party primarily liable does not pay, warranties are still important. First, they apply even when the transferor did not indorse. Second, unlike contractual liability, they do not depend on presentment, dishonor, and notice, but may be utilized before presentment has been made or after the time for giving notice has expired. Third, it may be easier to return the instrument to a transferor on the ground of breach of warranty than to prove one's status as a holder in due course against a maker or drawer.

CONCEPT REVIEW

TRANSFEROR'S WARRANTIES

The five transferor's warranties are:

1. The person transferring the instrument has *good title* or is authorized to obtain payment by someone who has good title.
2. All *signatures* are *genuine* or *authorized*.
3. The instrument has *not* been *materially altered*.
4. No *party* to the instrument has a *valid defense* against the person transferring it.
5. The person transferring it has *no knowledge* of any insolvency proceedings against the maker, drawer, or acceptor.

Who	What Warranties	To Whom
Nonindorsing Transferor	Makes all five transferor's warranties	To his immediate transferor only
Indorsing Transferor	Makes all five transferor's warranties	To all subsequent holders
Qualified Indorsing Transferor	Makes all five transferor's warranties, except the fourth one becomes, "The transferor has *no knowledge* of a valid defense against him."	To all subsequent holders

---

Rule of Finality of Payment

A person who presents a negotiable instrument for payment or a check to be certified makes a different set of warranties. Normally, the person to whom a negotiable instrument is presented for payment does not pay it unless he either is obligated to do so or is entitled to credit or payment from someone else if he does pay. For example, a drawee bank does not normally pay a check unless there are funds in the drawer's account. And it should know whether the signature on the check is that of its customer—the drawer of the check. If a drawee bank pays the check to a holder in due course, it cannot later get the money back from the holder in due course if it discovers that there are insufficient funds in the drawer's account. Payment is usually *final* in favor of a holder in due course or a person who in good faith changed his position in reliance on the payment [3–418] unless one of the three presentment warranties is broken.

Presentment Warranties

The three *warranties* that are made by a *person who is presenting an instrument for payment* are:

1. The presenter has *good title* to the instrument or is *authorized to obtain payment* by someone who has good title.
2. The presenter has *no knowledge that the signature of the maker or drawer is unauthorized*.
3. The instrument has *not been materially altered* [3–417(1)].

A holder in due course who presents a note to a maker does not warrant that the signature of the maker is valid or that the note has not been materially altered. The maker should recognize whether the signature on the note is her signature and whether the note has been altered. Similarly, a holder in due course does not warrant to the drawer of a check that the drawer's signature is valid or that the check has not been materially altered, because the drawer should recognize his signature and whether the check has been altered.

The *Garnac Grain Co. v. Boatmen's Bank & Trust Co. of Kansas City* case, which follows, illustrates the operation of presentment and transferor's warranties.

GARNAC GRAIN CO., INC. v. BOATMEN'S BANK & TRUST CO. OF KANSAS CITY
694 F. Supp 1389 (W.D. Mo. 1988)

Katherine Millison was employed by the Garnac Grain Company as a bookkeeper. She developed a scheme to embezzle money from Garnac whereby she would take home fully executed and valid checks payable to freight vendors and type "or L. R. Millison" (her husband's name) under the named payee with her manual typewriter. She would then indorse the check "L. R. Millison" on the back and deposit the check in a joint account she and her husband maintained at the State Bank of Oskaloosa. The altered checks were then forwarded through the Federal Reserve System (through First National Bank of Kansas City), presented for payment to the drawee bank, Boatmen's Bank & Trust Company of Kansas City, and paid. Millison would then intercept the monthly bank statements from Boatmen's Bank & Trust, remove the altered checks, and obliterate the "or L. R. Millison" on the face of the checks and the indorsement on the back.

The scheme was discovered and Millison was convicted of embezzlement. Garnac brought suit against Boatmen's Bank & Trust, alleging that the altered checks were wrongfully paid. It settled with Garnac and then brought suit against the State Bank of Oskaloosa, contending that it breached the UCC transfer warranties when it forwarded the altered checks for payment.

Hunter, Senior District Judge.   Boatmen's and First National contend that Oskaloosa is liable for the amount of their settlement with Garnac because it breached the UCC transfer warranties it made to them when it sent the checks altered by Millison to First National for payment by Boatmen's. Specifically it alleges that Oskaloosa breached the good title, material alterations, and genuine signature warranties.

Section 4–207 provides in pertinent part:

(1) Each customer or collecting bank who obtains payment or acceptance of an item and each prior customer and collecting bank warrants to the payor bank or other payor who in good faith pays or accepts the item that

  (a) he has good title to the item or is authorized to obtain payment or acceptance on behalf of one who has a good title; and

  (b) he has no knowledge that the signature of the maker or drawer is unauthorized . . . ; and

  (c) the item has not been materially altered . . .

(2) Each customer and collecting bank who transfers an item and receives a settlement or other consideration for it warrants to his transferee and to any subsequent collecting bank who takes the item in good faith that

  (a) he has a good title to the item or is authorized to obtain payment or acceptance on behalf of one who has a good title and the transfer is otherwise rightful; and

  (b) all signatures are genuine and authorized; and

  (c) the item has not been materially altered; . . .

Under this system, a payor bank in possession of a check containing, for example, a material alteration has the choice of bringing a warranty claim against the bank that transferred the check to it, or any other intermediate collecting bank or the depositary bank. If the payor bank brings the action against a bank other than the depositary bank, that bank can bring a claim against its transferor bank or any other previous collecting bank. As between the banks involved in the collection process, the liability for a materially altered check falls on the depositary bank. This is in accord with the loss allocation framework of Articles 3 and 4 of the U.C.C. which generally places the loss of a forged or altered item on the person or bank who dealt with the wrongdoer if the wrongdoer cannot be found or is judgment proof. Since there is no knowledge or notice requirement with respect to the material alteration warranties, the question of whether or not a party breached these warranties is simply a question of whether or not the checks were materially altered.

There seems to be no serious dispute among the parties but that the alterations made by Millison were material. Each check was drawn on Garnac's account at Boatmen's, was properly made out to barge freight vendors, and was properly signed by authorized representatives of Garnac. Millison altered the checks by typing "or L. R. Millison" underneath the payee's name. The court finds that, as a matter of law, an alteration which adds an alternative payee is a material alteration as that term is used in the U.C.C. *See* section 3–407. Thus, both Oskaloosa and First National breached their 3–207(1) warranties of no material alteration to Boatmen's; Oskaloosa breached its 4–207(2) warranty of no material alterations.

There is also no question that Oskaloosa breached its warranty of good title. Without the indorsement of the intended payees on the checks (i.e., the barge freight vendors) Oskaloosa could not obtain good title to the checks. The only indorsement on the back of the checks was "L. R. Millison." Neither Millison nor her husband was authorized to indorse the checks on behalf of the barge freight vendors shown as payees on the altered checks. Since Oskaloosa did not have good title when it transferred the checks to First National, it breached its section 4–207(1)(a) warranty to Boatmen's and its 4–207(2)(a) warranty to First National.

Summary judgment in favor of Boatmen's on its claims that the State Bank of Oskaloosa breached its warranties of good title and no material alterations.

Note: The court found that there were issues of material fact as to whether Garnac had exercised reasonable care and promptness in examining its bank statement to discover unauthorized signatures and alterations *and* whether Boatmen's had exercised ordinary care in paying the checks in question.

Operation of Warranties

Following are some examples that show how the transferor's and presentment warranties shift the liability back to a wrongdoer or to the person who dealt immediately with a wrongdoer and thus was in the best position to avert the wrongdoing.

Arthur makes a promissory note for $100 payable to the order of Betts. Carlson steals the note from Betts, indorses her name on the back, and gives it to Davidson in exchange for a television set. Davidson negotiates the note for value to Earle, who presents the note to Arthur for payment. Assume that Arthur refuses to pay the note because he has been advised by Betts that it has been stolen. Earle can then proceed to recover the face amount of the note from Davidson on the grounds that as a transferor Davidson has warranted that he had good title to the note and that all signatures were genuine. Davidson, in turn, can proceed against Carlson on the same basis—if he can find Carlson. If he cannot, then Davidson must bear the loss caused by Carlson's wrongdoing. Davidson was in the best position to ascertain whether Carlson was the owner of the note and whether the indorsement of Betts was genuine. Of course, even though Arthur does not have to pay the note to Earle, Arthur remains liable for his underlying obligation to Betts.

Anderson draws a check for $10 on her checking account at First Bank payable to the order of Brown. Brown cleverly raises the check to $110, indorses it, and negotiates it to Carroll. Carroll then presents the check for payment to First Bank, which pays her $110 and charges Anderson's account for $110. Anderson then asks the bank to recredit her account for the altered check, and it does so. The bank can proceed against Carroll for breach of the presentment warranty that the instrument had not been materially altered, which she implied to the bank when she presented the check for payment. Carroll in turn can proceed against Brown for breach of her transferor's warranty that the check had not been materially altered—if she can find her.

Bates steals Albers's checkbook and forges Albers's signature to a check for $100 payable to "cash," which he uses to buy $100 worth of groceries from a grocer. The grocer presents the check to Albers's bank, which pays the amount of the check to the grocer and charges Albers's account. Albers then demands that the bank recredit his account. The bank can recover against the grocer only if the grocer knew that Albers's signature had been forged. Otherwise, the bank must look for Bates. The bank had the responsibility to recognize the true signature of its drawer, Albers, and not to pay the check that contained an unauthorized signature. The bank, however, may be able to resist recrediting Albers's account if it can show he was negligent. The next section of this chapter discusses negligence.

OTHER LIABILITY RULES

Normally, a check that has a forged indorsement of the payee may not be charged to the drawer's checking account. Similarly, a maker does not have to pay a note to the person who currently possesses the note if the payee's signature has been forged. If a check or note has been materially altered—for example, by raising the amount—the drawer or maker is usually liable only for the instrument as it was originally written.

Negligence

A person can be so negligent in writing or signing a negotiable instrument that he in effect invites an alteration or an unauthorized signature on it. If a person has been negligent, he is not able to use the alteration or lack of authorization as a reason for not paying a holder in due course. A person is also not able to use the alteration or lack of authorization to claim that a payment was improperly made by a bank if the bank paid the item in good faith and in accordance with reasonable commercial standards [3–406].

For example, Diane Drawer makes out a check for $1 in such a way that someone could easily alter it to read $101. The check is so altered and is negotiated to Katherine Smith, who can qualify as a holder in due course. Smith can collect $101 from Drawer. Drawer cannot claim alteration as a defense to paying it, because of her negligence in making the alteration possible. Drawer then has to find the person who "raised" her check and try to collect the $100 from him.

The following case, *J. Gordon Neely Enterprises, Inc. v. National Bank of Huntsville*, illustrates the consequences to a drawer who is negligent in the way he draws a check.

J. GORDON NEELY ENTERPRISES, INC. v. NATIONAL BANK OF HUNTSVILLE

403 So.2d 887 (Ala. Sup. Ct. 1981)

Mr. and Mrs. Gordon Neely hired Louise Bradshaw as the bookkeeper for a Midas Muffler shop they owned and operated as a corporation, J. Gordon Neely Enterprises, Inc. (Neely). Bradshaw's duties included preparing company checks for Mrs. Neely's signature and reconciling the checking account when the bank statement and canceled checks were received each month. Bradshaw prepared several checks that were made payable to herself and contained a large space to the left of the amount written on the designated line. When the checks were signed by Mrs. Neely, she was aware of the large gaps. Subsequently, Bradshaw altered the checks by adding a digit or two to the left of the original amount and then cashed them at American National Bank, the drawee bank. Several months later, the Neelys hired a new accountant, who discovered the altered checks.

Neely brought suit against American National Bank to have its account recredited for the altered checks. The trial court held that the bank was not liable to Neely, and Neely appealed.

Adams, Justice.   Neely alleges that American is liable for paying out on altered instruments. Both parties rely upon Code section 3–406, stating:

> Any person who by his negligence substantially contributes to a material alteration of the instrument or to the making of an unauthorized signature is precluded from asserting the alteration or lack of authority against a holder in due course or against a drawee or other payor who pays the instrument in good faith and in accordance with the reasonable commercial standards of the drawee's or payor's business.

Neely argues that American National did not pay the instruments according to commercially reasonable standards because the checks allegedly bore visible marks of alteration. American National contends that Neely is precluded from asserting the material alterations as a basis for liability because Neely's negligence substantially contributed to the alterations by leaving large spaces to the left of the amount designation, and by entrusting the same employee with writing the checks and reconciling the bank statements without the protection of internal corporate controls.

We must first resolve whether American National acted in a commercially reasonable manner, because unless the bank acted reasonably, it cannot assert the defense that Neely's negligence substantially contributed to the alterations. American National produced expert witnesses testifying that although some of the words and numbers on the amount designation lines were slightly misaligned, and although a few checks visibly contained liquid erasure, the bank did not violate reasonable commercial standards when it paid out on these particular checks to Bradshaw. It was stated that the decision of whether to pay a particular check that may have appeared to be somewhat irregular on its face was based on a judgment call under the particular circumstances of that check. Based upon the judgment call surrounding the decision to pay each check, and after examining the checks exhibited, the trial court concluded that American National had acted in a commerically reasonable fashion under the circumstances.

We must next determine whether Neely, by its negligence, substantially contributed to the facilitation of the alterations. The Uniform Commercial Code does not define the negligence which will support the defense of section 3–406, and instructs that it is an issue strictly left to the factfinder. The official comment does advise, however, that "negligence usually has been found where spaces are left in the body of the instrument in which words or figures may be inserted." It is undisputed that Mrs. Neely signed the checks fully aware of the large gaps in front of the amount.

Similarly, two other examples of negligence are supported by the record: no inquiry was made into Bradshaw's veracity, although it was rumored that previously she had been in trouble with embezzlement in Tennessee; and Neely failed to maintain internal controls so that the employee writing the checks was not also the principal person reconciling the bank statements.

Based upon a thorough and sifting review of the record, we conclude that the accumulation of Mrs. Neely's negligent conduct set in motion an unfortunate chain of events which proximately culminated in the alterations, thus establishing Neely's substantial contribution.

Therefore, because American National acted in a commercially reasonable manner and Neely's negligence substantially contributed to the material alteration resulting in the bank's payment to Bradshaw, Neely cannot recover from American National.

Judgment for American National affirmed.

Impostor Rule

The Code establishes special rules for negotiable instruments made payable to *impostors* and *fictitious persons*. An **impostor** is a *person who poses as someone else and convinces a drawer to make a check payable to the person being impersonated*. When this happens, the Code makes any indorsement in the name of the impersonated person effective [3–405 (1)(a)]. For example, suppose that Arthur steals Paulsen's automobile. Arthur finds the certificate of title in the automobile and then, representing himself as Paulsen, sells the automobile to Berger Used Car Company. The car company draws its check payable to Paulsen for the agreed purchase price of the automobile and delivers the check to Arthur. Any person can negotiate the check by indorsing it in the name of Paulsen.

The rationale for the impostor rule is to put the responsibility for determining the true identity of the payee on the drawer of a check. The drawer is in a better position to do this than some later holder of the check who may be entirely innocent. The impostor rule allows that later holder to have good title to the check by making the payee's signature valid even though it is a forgery. It forces the drawer to go after the wrongdoer who tricked him into signing the check.

Fictitious Payee Rule

A **fictitious payee** commonly arises in the following situation: A dishonest employee draws checks payable to someone who does not exist, to a person who does not do business with his employer, or to a real person who does business with the employer but to whom the dishonest employee does not intend to send the check. If the employee has the authority to do so, he may sign the check himself. If he does not have such authority, he presents the check to his employer for signature and represents that the employer owes money to the person to whom the check is made payable. The dishonest employee then takes the check, indorses it in the name of the payee, presents it for payment, and pockets the money. The employee may be in a position to cover up the wrongdoing by intercepting the canceled checks and/or juggling the company's books.

The Code allows any indorsement in the name of the fictitious payee to be effective as the payee's indorsement [3–405(1)(b) and (c)]. For example, Anderson, who is employed by Moore Corporation as an accountant in charge of accounts payable, prepares a false invoice naming Parks, Inc., a supplier of Moore Corporation, as having supplied Moore Corporation with goods, and draws a check payable to Parks, Inc., for the amount of the invoice. Anderson then presents the check to Temple, treasurer of Moore Corporation, together with other checks with invoices attached, all of which Temple signs and returns to Anderson for mailing. Anderson then withdraws the check payable to Parks, Inc. Anyone, including Anderson, can negotiate the check by indorsing it in the name of Parks, Inc.

The rationale for the fictitious payee rule is similar to that for the impostor rule. If someone has a dishonest employee or agent who is responsible for the forgery of some checks, the immediate loss of those checks should rest on the employer of the wrongdoer rather than on some other innocent party. In turn, the employer must locate the unfaithful employee or agent and try to recover from him.

The *City of Phoenix v. Great Western Bank & Trust* case, which follows, illustrates the operation of the fictitious payee rule. As you read the case, determine what the city should have done to prevent the loss it suffered.

CITY OF PHOENIX v. GREAT WESTERN BANK & TRUST

42 UCC Rep. 1364 (Ariz. Ct. App. 1985)

Gary Hann opened a checking account at the Tucson branch of Great Western Bank & Trust in the name of Duncan Industries with a cash deposit of $200. He told the bank that Duncan Industries was a sole proprietorship involved in investments. Hann listed the mailing address of the business as a post office box and designated himself as the authorized signature on the account. Hann's confederate, Jay Maisel, worked for the City of Phoenix in a government-funded program to assist ex-convicts. Maisel had served nine years in prison for theft. City officials were aware of his background and initially placed him in a nonsensitive position. However, Maisel was promoted to a position in which he was responsible for preparing the documentation to pay the city's vendors. Six months after his promotion, Maisel prepared two claims packages for one vendor, Duncan Industries, causing the City to issue duplicate checks to the order of Duncan Industries, each in the amount of $514,320.40. The legitimate check was mailed to the vendor in Chicago; the fraudulent check was mailed to Hann in Tucson.

Hann deposited the check in the Duncan Industries account he had established where it was subject to a four-day hold. Once the hold expired, Hann withdrew over $441,000 from the account, much of it in cashier's checks made payable to coin, stamp, diamond, or bullion dealers. The city, on its own behalf and as assignee of the rights of the drawee bank, brought suit against the Great Western Bank to recover the amount of the check taken for deposit by it, contending, among other things, that the check contained a forged payee's indorsement. The trial court ruled in favor of the bank and the city appealed.

Corcoran, Judge.   Section 3–405 provides an exception to the general rule that forged indorsements are ineffective to pass title or to authorize a drawee to pay. Under section 4–401, a drawer can usually require the drawee bank to recredit the drawer account when the drawee pays a check on which a necessary indorsement is forged. The drawee bank can then shift the loss to previous indorsers on the ground of breach of warranty. The loss under the general rule will ultimately rest with the person who forged the instrument or the bank which took the instrument from the forger.

Section 3–405(1)(c), often referred to as the "fictitious payee rule," provides in pertinent part:

A. An indorsement by any person in the name of a named payee is effective if: . . .

3. An agent or employee of the maker or drawer has supplied him with the name of the payee intending the latter to have no such interest.

The exception places the loss from the activities of a faithless employee upon the employer rather than on the drawee bank. The loss is shifted by making the indorsement "effective" although it is unauthorized. Since the indorsement is "effective," the instrument passes as though there had been no forgery and as between a collecting bank and the drawer of the check, the loss must fall on the drawer employer. The rule, as applied, also eliminates any liability of a collecting bank for breach of warranty of the genuineness of the signatures because a signature that is "effective" is to be regarded as "genuine" for the purpose of warranty liability. Thus, in this case, the City, as assignee of its drawee bank, has no recourse against Great Western Bank based on the warranties contained in sections 3–417 and 4–207 owed by Great Western Bank to the drawee.

The basis of the fictitious payee rule is explained in section 3–405, Official Comment 4: The principle followed is that the loss should fall upon the employer as a risk of his business enterprise rather than upon the subsequent holder or drawee. The reasons are that the employer is normally in a better position to prevent such forgeries by reasonable care in the selection or supervision of his employees, or, if he is not, is at least in a better position to cover the loss by fidelity insurance: and that the cost of such insurance is properly an expense of his business rather than of the business of the holder or drawee.

The factual circumstances for application of the fictitious payee rule are met in this case. Maisel, an "employee" of the drawer, the City of Phoenix, supplied the City, as to the duplicate check, with the name of a "payee," Duncan Industries, with the intent of creating no interest in Duncan Industries.

Judgment for Great Western Bank affirmed.

Conversion

Conversion of an instrument is an *unauthorized assumption and exercise of ownership* over it. A negotiable instrument can be converted in a number of ways. For example, it might be presented for payment or acceptance, and the person to whom it is presented might refuse to pay, refuse to accept, or refuse to return it. An instrument is also converted if a person pays an instrument on a forged indorsement [3–419]. Thus, if a check that contains a forged indorsement is paid by a bank, the bank has converted the check by wrongfully paying it.

The bank then becomes liable for the face amount of the check to the person whose indorsement was forged [3–419].

For example, Arthur Able draws a check for $50 on his account at First Bank, payable to the order of Bernard Barker. Carol Collins steals the check, forges Barker's indorsement on it, and cashes it at First Bank. First Bank has converted Barker's property, because it had no right to pay the check without Barker's valid indorsement. First Bank must pay Barker $50, and then it can try to locate Collins to get the $50 back from her.

KELLY v. CENTRAL BANK & TRUST CO. OF DENVER

794 P.2d 1037 (Colo. Ct. App. 1990)

A number of investors, including Kelly, invested in a Cayman Islands entity, Tradecom, Ltd., a business involved in precious metals arbitrage. Their investments, in the form of cashier's checks, were payable to Tradecom and delivered to Arvey Down, Tradecom's agent. Down indorsed the checks and deposited them at the Central Bank & Trust Company of Denver into a checking account.

Most of the 934 checks worth $11,227,473 were indorsed:

Tradecom Limited
For deposit only
072 575

Other checks, totaling $576,850, were indorsed:

For deposit only
072 575

This included one check for $57,000, which apparently was deposited without indorsement and was indorsed by Central Bank's officer:

For deposit only
072 575
Tradecom by
Mark E. Thompson
Commercial Loan officer

The referenced account, No. 072 575, was not that of Tradecom (which had no accounts at Central Bank) but rather was that of Equity Trading Corporation, a company owned and managed by Down, also purportedly an agent of Tradecom.

The investors subsequently lost most of their investments in Tradecom and they sued Central Bank for, among other things, conversion. They alleged that neither Down nor Equity Trading was an agent of Tradecom and that the check indorsements were unauthorized and ineffective; that over the course of 13 months, the bank negligently or recklessly permitted Down to divert the checks payable to Tradecom into Equity Trading's checking acoount; and that Central Bank did not follow reasonable commercial standards. Central bank moved for summary judgment and in support of its motion submitted an executed power of attorney that indicated Down had the authority to indorse checks on behalf of Tradecom. The trial court awarded summary judgment to the Central Bank and the investors appealed.

Tursi, Judge.   Because there was no triable issue of fact concerning Down's agency and authority to indorse and deposit the cashier's checks, and because proof of a forged or unauthorized indorsement is a necessary predicate to Central Bank's liability, the investors could not prevail as to the 11 million dollars of checks that contained an indorsement which included the "Tradecom Limited" name. Consequently, with respect to the checks indorsed with Tradecom's name, we conclude that the trial court properly granted summary judgment for Central Bank.

The trial court erred, however, in granting Central Bank summary judgment on the $57,000 check indorsed by Central Bank's commercial loan officer. In order for Central Bank to have become a holder under this indorsement, and thus have obtained title, Central Bank would have had to have been authorized to provide Tradecom's indorsement under section 4–205(1). This, however, was impossible since Tradecom was not Central Bank's "customer." Consequently, this indorsement is unauthorized as a matter of law, and summary judgment should not have been ordered for Central Bank on this check.

The investors also contend that the trial court erred in granting summary judgment for Central Bank on the remaining $519,850 of cashier's checks lacking any signature and merely indorsed "For deposit only 072 575." We agree.

Under section 3–419(1)(c), a check is converted when it is paid on a forged indorsement. In this context, a collecting or paying bank "pays" a check when it credits its customer's account with the proceeds of a check collected from the drawee bank. If such a payment occurs on a check with no indorsement or a missing indorsement, it is the legal equivalent of payment on a forged indorsement.

The term "indorsement" is generally understood to mean the indorser's writing of his or her signature on the instrument or the affixing of the indorser's name or some designation identifying the indorser on the instrument. A check simply inscribed "For deposit only" to an account other than payee's account and without the payee's signature is not an effective "indorsement."

If the instrument is order paper and the depository bank does not, or cannot, supply the missing indorsement of its customer, the absence of the indorsement can be fatal to negotiation and transfer of title. One such situation is when the depository bank's customer and the payee are not the same person. In this case, the depository bank is unauthorized to, and cannot, supply the missing indorsement of the payee since the payee is not the bank's "customer" under section 4–205. In this situation, the depository bank does not become a holder of the checks and does not obtain good title to them. Payment of such proceeds to its depositor subjects the depository bank to liability for conversion.

In this case it was undisputed that Down, or someone in his employ, deposited $519,850 worth of cashier's checks at Central Bank bearing the simple inscription "For Deposit only 072 575." These checks, which bore no signature indorsement of the payee, Tradecom, or anyone else, were paid and credited to account 072 575. This was not an account of Tradecom, which was not a customer of Central Bank. Under these circumstances, Central Bank was not a holder of these checks by negotiation. It obtained no title to these checks. It is, consequently, subject to conversion liability under section 3–419(1)(c) for making payment on the equivalent of a forged indorsement.

Judgment for Central Bank reversed in part.

DISCHARGE OF NEGOTIABLE INSTRUMENTS

Discharge of Liability

Generally, all parties to a negotiable instrument are *discharged* or relieved from liability when the person who is primarily liable on it pays the amount in full to a holder of the instrument. Any person is discharged of his liability to the extent that the person pays the holder of the instrument [3–603]. For example, Anderson makes a note for $475 payable to the order of Bruce. Bruce indorses the note "Pay to the order of Carroll, Bruce" and negotiates it to Carroll. Carroll takes the note to Anderson, presents it for payment, and is paid $475 by Anderson. The payment to Carroll discharges Bruce's secondary liability as indorser and Anderson's primary liability as maker.

A person is not discharged of liability if he pays someone who acquired the instrument by theft or from someone who had stolen it [3–603(1)(a)]. Also, if a negotiable instrument has been restrictively indorsed, the person who pays must comply with the restrictive indorsement to be discharged [3–603(1)(b)]. For example, Arthur makes a note of $100 payable to the order of Bryan. Bryan indorses the note "Pay to the order of my account no. 16154 at First Bank, Bryan." Bryan then gives the note to his employee, Clark, to take to the bank. Clark takes the note to Arthur, who pays Clark the $100. Clark then runs off with the money. Arthur is not discharged of his primary liability on the note because he did not make his payment consistent with the restrictive indorsement. To be discharged, Arthur has to pay the $100 into Bryan's account at First Bank.

Discharge by Cancellation

The holder of a negotiable instrument may discharge the liability of the parties to the instrument by canceling it. If the holder mutilates or destroys a negotiable instrument with the intent that it no longer evidences an obligation to pay money, it has been canceled [3–605]. For example, a grandfather lends $1,000 to his grandson for college expenses. The grandson gives his grandfather a promissory note for $1,000. If the grandfather later tears up the note with the intent that the grandson no longer owes him $1,000, the note has been canceled.

An accidental destruction or mutilation of a negotiable instrument is not a cancellation and does not discharge the parties to it. If an instrument is lost, accidentally mutilated, or destroyed, the holder can still enforce it. In such a case, the holder must prove that the instrument existed and that she was its holder when it was lost, mutilated, or destroyed.

Discharge by Alteration

Generally, a *fraudulent and material change* in a negotiable instrument discharges any party whose contract is changed [3–407(2)]. An alteration of an instrument is material if it changes the contract of any of the parties to the instrument. For example, if the amount due on a note is raised from $10 to $10,000, the contract of the maker has been changed. The maker promised to pay $10, but after the change has been made, he would be promising to pay much more. A change that does not affect the contract of one of the parties, such as dotting an *i* or correcting the grammar, is not material.

Assume that Anderson signs a promissory note for $100 payable to Bond. Bond indorses the note "Pay to the order of Connolly, Bond" and negotiates it to Connolly. Connolly changes the $100 to read $100,000. Connolly's change is unauthorized, fraudulent, and material. As a result, Anderson is discharged from her primary liability as maker of the note and Bond is discharged from her secondary liability as indorser. Neither of them has to pay Connolly. The contracts of both Anderson and Bond were changed because the amount for which they agreed to be liable was altered.

There are exceptions to the general rule that a fraudulent and material alteration discharges parties whose contracts are changed. First, if in the preceding example Anderson was so negligent in writing the note that it could easily be altered, he cannot claim the alteration against a holder in due course of the note. Assume that Connolly indorsed the note "Connolly" and negotiated it to Davis, who qualifies as a holder in due course. If Davis was not aware of the alteration and it was not obvious, she could collect the $100,000 from Anderson. Anderson's only recourse would be to track down Connolly to try to get the difference between $100 and $100,000.

Second, a holder in due course who takes an instrument after it has been altered can enforce it for the original amount. When an incomplete instrument is completed after it leaves the drawer's or maker's hands, a holder in due course can enforce it as completed. For example, Swanson draws a check payable to Frank's Nursery, leaving the amount blank. He gives it to his gardener with instructions to purchase some fertilizer at

Frank's and to fill in the purchase price of the fertilizer when it is known. The gardener fills in the check for $100 and gives it to Frank's in exchange for the fertilizer ($7.25) and the difference in cash ($92.75). The gardener then leaves town with the cash. If Frank's had no knowledge of the unauthorized completion, it could enforce the check for $100 against Swanson.

Discharge by Impairment of Recourse

If a party to an instrument has posted collateral to secure his performance and a holder surrenders the collateral without the consent of the parties who would benefit from the collateral, such parties are discharged [3–606].

ETHICAL AND PUBLIC POLICY CONCERNS

1. Problem case 2 involves a situation where a sole shareholder of a corporation, Frederick J. Dowie, signed a corporate check without indicating he was signing in a representative capacity. If the state in which the activity took place follows the minority rule as set out in *Valley National Bank v. Cook*, should Dowie feel obligated by ethical considerations to personally make the check good? No!

2. Suppose you have taken a promissory note for $1,000 as payment for some carpentry work you did for a friend. You have some reason to believe that the maker is having some financial difficulty and may not be able to pay the note off when it is due. You discuss the possible sale of the note to an elderly neighbor as an investment and she agrees to buy it. Would it be ethical for you to indorse the note with a qualified indorsement ("without recourse")?

3. Problem case 11 involves a situation where a creditor made a mistake and returned a note marked "canceled" to the maker without collecting all of the interest due on it. Suppose that in that case, the maker/borrower realized that Crown Financial had made an error in not including in the subsequent note the interest due on the original note. Should the maker/borrower feel compelled by ethical considerations to pay the interest, even if not legally required to do so?

SUMMARY

Liability on a negotiable instrument may be based on (1) contract, (2) breach of warranty, (3) negligence, (4) improper payment, or (5) conversion. When a person signs a negotiable instrument, he generally becomes contractually liable on it. The terms of the contract of parties to a negotiable instrument are not written out on the instrument; they are supplied by Article 3 of the Code. Parties may be either primarily or secondarily liable. Makers of notes and acceptors of drafts and checks are primarily liable, while drawers of checks and drafts and indorsers of notes, checks, and drafts are secondarily liable. An accommodation party is liable in the capacity in which he signed the instrument.

Under the Code, a person cannot be held contractually liable on a negotiable instrument unless his signature appears on the instrument. A person may use any name or symbol as his signature. A person who signs in a representative capacity should make it clear that she is signing as an agent, so that the principal rather than the agent will be liable.

Presentment for payment is necessary to hold parties liable on an instrument. Failure to present the instrument in a timely fashion discharges the indorsers from their contractual liability to make the instrument good. An instrument has been dishonored when it has been duly presented and acceptance or payment cannot be obtained within the prescribed time. When an instrument has been dishonored and required notices have been timely given, the holder has a right of recourse against the drawers and prior indorsers.

The transferor of an instrument warrants to his transferee that he has good title, that the signatures are genuine or authorized, that the instrument has not been materially altered, that no defenses of any party are good against him (if he qualifies his warranty, he warrants that he has no knowledge of defenses to the instrument), and that he has no knowledge of any insolvency proceedings against the maker, acceptor, or drawer of the instrument.

Any person who obtains payment or acceptance of an instrument warrants to a person who in good faith accepts or pays the instrument that she has good title to the instrument or is authorized to act for a person who has good title and that the instrument has not been materially altered. A holder in due course acting in good faith does not warrant to a maker or drawer the genuineness of the maker's or drawer's signature or that the instrument has not been altered.

A person who is negligent in writing or signing a negotiable instrument may be precluded from asserting an unauthorized signature or alteration as a reason for not paying a holder in due course. If a negotiable instrument is made payable to an impostor or a fictitious payee, any signature in the name of the payee is effective as an indorsement. A person who converts an instrument—that is, exercises unauthorized ownership over it—may be held liable to the real owner.

Liability of a party on an instrument may be discharged by payment, cancellation, material alteration, or impairment of recourse.

PROBLEM CASES

1. Janota's signature appeared under the name of a corporation on a note acknowledging a $1,000 debt. No wording appeared other than Janota's name and the corporate name. The holder of the note sues Janota on the note. What will Janota argue, and what will the result be? *She will lose - can use parole evidence to bring CoLP*

2. Frederick Dowie was the president and sole stockholder of Fred Dowie Enterprises, Inc., a catering company. He obtained the opportunity to operate the concession stands at the Living History Farms during the pope's visit to Des Moines, Iowa. With high expectations, Dowie ordered 325,000 hot dog buns from Colonial Baking Company. Before the buns were delivered, he presented to Colonial Baking a postdated check in the amount of $28,640. The check showed the name of the corporation and its address in the upper left-hand corner. The signature on the check read "Frederick J. Dowie," and there were no other words of explanation. Unfortunately, only 300 buns were sold. Following a dispute over the ownership and responsibility for the remaining buns, Dowie stopped payment on the check. Colonial Baking then sued Dowie in his personal capacity as signer of the check. Is Dowie personally liable for the check? *No! Corporate name on check*

3. Phoenix Steel's board of directors adopted a resolution authorizing the Wilmington Bank to honor checks drawn on Phoenix's payroll account that bore facsimile signatures of designated officers. The resolution provided that the bank would be fully protected in acting on such authority. An employee of Phoenix later dishonestly and improperly affixed a facsimile signature of an officer to several blank payroll checks, and the bank unknowingly honored them. In an action by Phoenix against the bank for the alleged wrongful payment of the checks, will Phoenix prevail? *No!*

4. Wilson was presented with a check payable to Jones and Brown and drawn on Merchant's Bank. The check was indorsed by Brown alone. Wilson accepted the check, indorsed it, and submitted it to Merchant's Bank for payment. Merchant's Bank paid Wilson. Does

Merchant's Bank or Wilson bear the liability if Jones seeks payment on the check? *Merchant Bank*

5. First National Bank certified Smith's check in the amount of $29. After certification, Smith altered the check so that it read $2,900. He presented the check to a merchant in payment for goods. The merchant then submitted the check to the bank for payment. The bank refused, saying that it had only certified the instrument for $29. Can the merchant recover the $2,900 from the bank? *No!*

6. A check was drawn on First National Bank and made payable to Howard. It came into the possession of Carson, who forged Howard's indorsement and cashed it at Merchant's Bank. Merchant's Bank then indorsed it and collected from First National. Assuming that Carson is nowhere to be found, who bears the ultimate liability? *Merchant Bank!*

7. Doris Strahl was the payee on a $3,000 check drawn on Pacific First Federal Savings and Loan (drawee) by Puget Sound National Bank (drawer). Peter Miller, the owner of a service station, replaced the engine in a motor home owned by Strahl. His charge for the new engine was $2,500. Strahl gave him the $3,000 check without indorsing it, and he gave her $500 change. On March 22, 1979, Miller deposited the check in his business account at Southwestern Bank, which sent it for payment to Puget Sound National Bank. Puget Sound returned the check to Southwestern Bank on May 17, 1979, on the ground that the absence of an indorsement by the payee, Doris Strahl, constituted a breach by Southwestern Bank of the presentment warranty of good title. Southwestern in turn charged back Miller's account. Since Miller had written checks on his account in the interim, the charge-back resulted in his account being overdrawn. Miller brought suit against Southwestern Bank challenging the charge-back. Does Miller have a valid legal basis for challenging the charge-back? *No!*

8. On August 3, 1961, J. P. Leonard made out a check for $600, signed it as drawer, and indorsed his signature on the back of the check. He did not date the check, nor did he fill in the payee's name. Leonard claimed that he gave the check to a man named Santo, to whom he owed $600, and that he indorsed the check on the back so that Santo could cash it "at the track." When the check was returned to Leonard by the National Bank of West Virginia after it had charged the check to his account, "Thrity" [sic] had been written in front of "Six hundred," the name Martin Mattson had been entered as payee, and the indorsement of Martin Mattson appeared on the back of the check above Leonard's signature. Leonard then sued National Bank to have his account recredited for $3,600. Should Leonard be entitled to have his account recredited? 4/10

9. Mrs. Johnson mailed a loan application to First National Bank in her husband's name and without his knowledge. Having dealt with her husband before, the bank approved the application and mailed a check in the amount requested to Mr. Johnson. Mrs. Johnson then indorsed the check in her husband's name and cashed it at Merchant's Bank. Merchant's Bank indorsed the check and presented it for payment. First National, having discovered the deception, refused to pay. Is First National liable on the check? *Yes   H.J.C.*

10. Clarice Rich was employed by the New York City Board of Education as a clerk. It was her duty to prepare requisitions for checks to be issued by the board, to prepare the checks, to have them signed by the authorized personnel, and to send the checks to the recipients. In some instances, however, she retained them. Also, on a number of occasions, she prepared duplicate requisitions and checks, which, when signed, she likewise retained. She then forged the indorsement of the named payees on the checks she had retained and cashed the checks at Chemical Bank, where the Board of Education maintained its account. After the board discovered the forgeries, it demanded that Chemical Bank credit its account for the amount of the forged checks. Is Chemical Bank required to credit the board's account as requested? *No! Bad Employee Negligent*

11. Charles Peterson, a farmer and rancher, was indebted to Crown Financial Corporation on a $4,450,000 promissory note that was due on December 29, 1972. Shortly before the note was due, Crown sent Peterson a statement of interest due on the note ($499,658.850). Petersen paid the interest and executed a new note in the amount of $4,450,000 that was to mature in December 1975. The old note was then marked "canceled" and returned to Peterson. In 1975, Crown billed Peterson for $363,800 in interest that had been due on the first note but apparently not included in the statement. Peterson claimed that the interest had been forgiven and that he was not obligated to pay it. Was Peterson still obligated to pay interest on the note that had been returned to him marked "canceled"? *No!*

12. David Bluffestone lent money to Gary, Bert, and Lee Abrahams in connection with a car wash business that they operated together. When David died, his son-in-law, Alan Gilenko, came to help David's wife, Pearl, straighten out her financial affairs. He found a promissory note for $5,000 payable on demand signed by Gary, Bert, and Lee Abrahams among David's possessions. At the time, the note did not have any provision for monthly payments or for attorney's fees. Gilenko added provisions for monthly payments and attorney's fees to the note. Bert and Lee Abrahams then resigned the note with knowledge of the alterations. Gary did not sign the note again after the alterations had been made and did not have knowledge of them. When the Abrahams did not pay off the note, Pearl Bluffestone brought an action against Gary, Bert, and Lee to collect on the promissory note payable to her deceased husband. Gary Abrahams contended that he was not liable on the $5,000 note, because it had been materially altered without his consent or knowledge. Is the note enforceable against Gary Abrahams? *No! still liable for the amt that he originally created on the instrument*

CHAPTER 33

CHECKS AND DOCUMENTS OF TITLE

INTRODUCTION

For most people, a checking account provides the majority of their contact with negotiable instruments. This chapter focuses on the relationship between the drawer with a checking account and the drawee bank. It addresses such common questions as: What happens if a bank refuses to pay a check even though the depositor has sufficient funds in her account? Does the bank have the right to create an overdraft in a depositor's account by paying an otherwise properly payable check? What are the depositor's rights and the bank's obligation if the depositor stops payment on a check? What is the difference between a certified check and a cashier's check? What are the depositor's responsibilities when she receives her monthly statement and canceled checks? The second half of the chapter discusses the Code rules that apply to negotiable documents of title such as warehouse receipts and bills of lading.

THE DRAWER-DRAWEE RELATIONSHIP

There are always two sources that govern the relationship between the depositor and the drawee bank: the deposit agreement and Articles 3 and 4 of the Code. Article 4, which governs Bank Deposits and Collec-

tions, allows the depositor and drawee bank (which Article 4 calls the "payor bank") to vary Article 4's provisions with a few important exceptions. The deposit agreement cannot disclaim the bank's responsibility for its own lack of good faith or failure to exercise ordinary care or limit the measure of damages prescribed in Article 4 for such lack or failure [4–103(1)].[1]

The deposit agreement establishes many important relationships between the depositor and payor/drawee bank, one of which is their relationship as creditor and debtor, respectively. Thus, when a person deposits money in an account at the bank, he no longer is considered the owner of the money. Instead, he is a *creditor* of the bank to the extent of his deposits and the bank becomes his *debtor*. When the depositor deposits a check to a checking account, the bank also becomes his *agent* for collection of the check. The bank as the person's agent owes a *duty* to him to follow his *reasonable instructions* concerning payment of checks and other items from his account and a *duty of ordinary care* in collecting checks and other items deposited to the account.

---

[1] The numbers in brackets refer to the sections of the Uniform Commercial Code.

Bank's Duty to Pay

When a bank receives a properly drawn and payable check on a person's account and there are sufficient funds to cover the check, the bank is under a *duty* to pay it. If the person has sufficient funds in the account and the bank refuses to pay, or dishonors, the check, the bank is liable for the damages proximately caused by its wrongful dishonor. If the bank can show that it rejected the check by mistake, then the depositor can hold the bank liable only for any actual damages that the depositor can show that he suffered. These damages can include both direct and consequential damages [4–402]. Direct damages include charges imposed by retailers for returned checks; consequential damages include injury to the depositor's credit rating that results from the dishonor.

For example, Donald Dodson writes a check for $1,500 to Ames Auto Sales in payment for a used car. At the time that Ames Auto presents the check for payment at Dodson's bank, First National Bank, Dodson has $1,800 in his account. However, a teller mistakenly refuses to pay the check and stamps it NSF (not sufficient funds). Ames Auto then goes to the local prosecutor and signs a complaint against Dodson for writing a bad check. As a result, Dodson is arrested. Dodson can recover from First National the damages that he sustained because his check was wrongfully dishonored, including the damages involved in his arrest, such as his attorney's fees.

In the case that follows, *Buckley v. Trenton Savings Fund Society*, the bank is potentially liable for consequential damages sustained by the drawer if it cannot show that it dishonored checks by mistake.

LIABLE EVEN IF HONEST MISTAKE EVEN IF MISTAKE

BUCKLEY v. TRENTON SAVINGS FUND SOCIETY

524 A.2d 886 (N.J. Super. Ct. 1987)

*Misinformed Teller
Happens more
than once*

Buckley maintained a checking account at the Trenton Savings Fund Society. In 1981, he separated from his wife, Linda, and entered into a consent agreement with her in which he agreed to pay her $150 per week for food and support for herself and their children. On January 13, 1984, Buckley wrote a check for $150 and gave it to his wife. The next Saturday, she presented it for payment at one of Trenton Savings' branches but payment was refused even though Buckley had $900 in the account at the time. The following Monday, she took it to another branch where payment was again refused. The bank told Linda that it would not cash the check for her because Linda did not have an account at the bank. Subsequently, the bank agreed to cash checks for Linda, but on March 4, 1984, the bank again refused to pay one of Buckley's checks that she presented for payment. Linda was known to the bank because it held a mortgage on the home that she and Buckley jointly owned.

Shortly after Trenton Bank's failure to cash the two checks, Buckley received an irate call from Linda. He also received calls from his parents, his sister, and his best friend inquiring as to why he was not making the support payments. In addition, his children inquired "why daddy wouldn't give them food money." Buckley incurred severe emotional distress over the matter. He brought suit against Trenton Savings for wrongful dishonor and sought compensatory damages, as well as punitive damages, for the mental anguish he sustained. The trial court entered judgment for Buckley based on a jury verdict for $25,000, and the bank appealed.

Stern, Judge.   The bank contends that the jury should not have been permitted to award damages for emotional distress under the facts of this case.

A bank's liability for wrongful dishonor of a customer's check is defined in section 4–402 of the Uniform Commercial Code:

A payor bank is liable to its customer for damages proximately caused by the wrongful dishonor of an item. When the dishonor occurs through mistake, liability is limited to actual damages proved. If so proximately caused and proved, damages may include damages for an arrest or prosecution of the customer or other consequential damages. Whether any consequential damages are proximately caused by the wrongful dishonor is a question of fact to be determined in each case.

The UCC does not indicate the theory or basis for a bank's liability for wrongful dishonor. As explained in the UCC official comment to section 4–402, "The liability of the drawee for dishonor has sometimes been stated as one for breach of contract, sometimes as for negligence or other breach of a tort duty, and sometimes as for defamation. The drafters of the UCC did not intend to exclude the possibility of mental distress damages upon a wrongful dishonor by a bank. Since section 4–402 is silent on any restriction of damages when the dishonor is grounded on an action other than mistake, it implies that these damages are not precluded by the Code. Thus, out-of-state courts interpreting section 4–402 have concluded that mental suffering is compensable under this section.

The Legislature adopted section 4–402 as promulgated in the Uniform Commercial Code without substantive change. The section expressly limits recovery for "actual damages" when the dishonor results from "mistake" but otherwise expressly permits recovery of "consequential damages" proximately caused. As *White and Summer* explains:

When wrongful dishonors occur not "through mistake" but willfully, the court may impose damages greater than "actual damages."

* * * * *

Might one argue that "actual damages" excludes recovery for mental distress? We think not. In the first place, the drafters went to great efforts to assure that customers can recover for arrest and prosecution. It is inconsistent to allow recovery for embarrassment and mental distress deriving from arrest and prosecution and to deny similar recovery in other cases. Moreover, cases under the predecessor to 4–402, the American Association Statute, held that "actual damages" includes damages for mental distress. Thus we believe . . . that the Code drafter intended to allow recovery for mental distress and other intangible injury.

In this case the judge's instructions failed to delineate the distinction between mistake and intentional mistake and an intentional breach or wilful, wanton or reckless conduct. As a result, the matter must be remanded for a new trial and for a determination of damages based on appropriate instructions.

We preclude an award of punitive damages. Punitive damages are not generally recoverable for breach of contract, at least when the breach of contract does not also constitute a tort for which punitive damages are recoverable.

Reversed and remanded for new trial.

Bank's Right to Charge to Customer's Account

The drawee bank has the right to charge any *properly payable check* to the account of the customer or drawer. The bank has this right even though payment of the check creates an overdraft in the account [4–401]. If an account is overdrawn, the customer owes the bank the amount of the overdraft and the bank may take that amount out of the next deposit that the customer makes or from another account that the depositor maintains with the bank. Alternatively, the bank might seek to collect the amount directly from the customer. The *Pulaski State Bank v. Kalbe* case, which follows, illustrates this situation.

PULASKI STATE BANK v. KALBE

364 N.W.2d 162 (Wis. Ct. App. 1985)

Louise Kalbe signed a check drawn on her account at the Pulaski State Bank; later, that check was lost or stolen. The check was drafted for $7,260 payable to cash. The bank paid the check, which created an overdraft of $6,542.12 in Kalbe's account. The bank brought a lawsuit against Kalbe to recover the overdraft. The trial court awarded judgment to the bank and Kalbe appealed.

Dean, Judge.   The bank could properly pay the check even though it created an overdraft. Section 4–401 unambiguously states that a bank may charge a customer's account for an item otherwise properly payable even though the charge creates an overdraft. The bank's payment of an overdraft is treated as a loan to the depositor, which may be recovered.

Kalbe argues that checks creating unusually large overdrafts are not properly payable. She relies on the definition of properly payable that "includes the availability of funds for payment at the time of decision to pay or dishonor." Section 4–104(1)(i). Section 4–104(1)(i), however, is a source of bank discretion and does not limit the bank's power to pay overdrafts. The statute gives banks the option of dishonoring checks when sufficient funds are not available. The bank may consider the check to be not properly payable and refuse to pay without risk for wrongful dishonor. This does not prevent the bank from alternatively paying the overdraft check and, if it is otherwise properly payable, charging the customer's account. Section 4–401(1) places no limit on the size of the overdraft or the bank's reason for payment. Construing the statutes together, "otherwise properly payable" refers to those requirements other than availability of funds.

It is undisputed that in all other respects, the check was properly payable. Kalbe does not argue that the bank honored an altered check or a check bearing a forged or unauthorized maker's signature. The check was therefore properly payable and Kalbe's liability is complete. The check creating the overdraft carried Kalbe's implied promise to reimburse the bank.

Judgment for bank affirmed.

The bank does not owe a duty to its customer to pay any checks out of the account that are more than six months old. Such checks are called *stale checks*. However, the bank may in good faith pay a check that is more than six months old and charge it to the drawer-depositor's account [4–404].

If the bank in good faith pays a check drawn by the drawer-depositor but subsequently altered, it may charge the customer's account with the amount of the check as originally drawn. Also, if an incomplete check of a customer gets into circulation, is completed, and presented to the drawee bank for payment, and the bank pays the check, the bank can charge the amount as completed to the customer's account even though it knows that the check has been completed, unless it has notice that the completion was improper [4–401(2)]. The respective rights, obligations, and liabilities of drawee banks and their drawer-customers concerning forged and altered checks are discussed in more detail later in this chapter.

Article 4 recognizes that the bank's right or duty to pay a check or to charge the depositor's account for the check (including exercising its right to set off an amount due to it by the depositor) may be terminated, suspended, or modified by the depositor's order to stop payment (which is discussed in the next section of this chapter) or by events external to the relationship between the depositor and the bank. These external events include the filing of a bankruptcy petition by the depositor or by the depositor's creditors, and the garnishment of the account by a creditor of the depositor. The bank must receive the stop-payment order from its depositor or the notice of the bankruptcy filing or garnishment before the bank has certified the check, paid it in cash, settled with another bank for the amount of the item without a right to revoke the settlement, completed the process necessary to its decision to pay the check, or otherwise become accountable for the amount of the check under Article 4 [4–303]. These restrictions on the bank's right or duty to pay are discussed in later sections of this chapter.

Stop-Payment Order

A **stop-payment order** is a request made by the drawer of a check to the drawee bank instructing it not to pay or certify the check. As the drawer's agent in the payment of checks, the drawee bank must follow the reasonable orders of the drawer about payments made on the drawer's behalf. To be effective, a stop-payment order must be received in time to give the drawee bank a *reasonable opportunity to act* on it. This means that the stop-payment order must be given to the bank before it has paid or certified the check. The stop-payment order also must come soon enough to give the bank time to instruct its tellers and other employees that they should not pay or certify the check [4–403(1)]. The stop-payment order also must describe the check with sufficient detail for the bank's employees to recognize it as the check corresponding to the stop-payment order.

An *oral stop-payment order* can be given to the bank, but it is valid for only 14 days unless it is confirmed in writing during that time. A *written stop-payment order* is valid for six months and can be extended for an additional six months by giving the bank instructions in writing to continue the order [4–403(2)]. See Figure 1.

Sometimes the information given the bank by the customer concerning the check on which payment is to be stopped is incorrect. For example, there may be an error in the payee's name, the amount of the check, or the number of the check. The question then arises whether the customer has accorded the bank a reasonable opportunity to act on his request. The following *FJS Electronics v. Fidelity Bank* case involves such a problem.

FIGURE 1   Stop-Payment Order

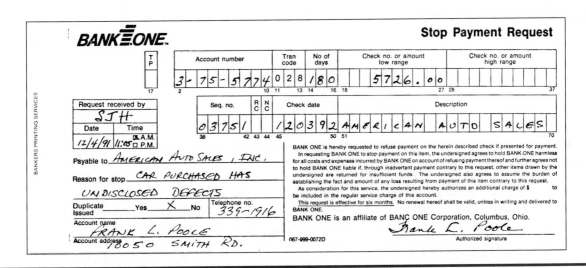

FJS ELECTRONICS, INC. v. FIDELITY BANK

28 UCC Rep. 1462 (Pa. Ct. C.P. 1980)

On February 27, 1976, Multi-Tek issued check number 896 in the face amount of $1,844.98, drawn on Multi-Tek's account at Fidelity and made payable to Multilayer Computer Circuits. However, on March 9, 1976, Frank J. Suttill, Multi-Tek's president, telephoned Fidelity and placed a stop-payment order on the check. The order was received and simultaneously recorded by Roanna M. Sanders, Fidelity's employee. This recordation contained the following information: the name of the account, the account number, the check number, the date of the check, the date and hour the stop-payment order was received, and the amount of the check as $1,844.48. This recordation was essentially correct in all respects, except for the amount of the check—there being a 50-cent difference between the face amount ($1,844.98) and the amount listed in the stop-payment order ($1,844.48).

Subsequently, a confirmation notice bearing the date "03/ 76" was mailed by Fidelity to Multi-Tek. It contained, among other things, the following information:

PAYEE: MULTILAYER COMPUTER CIRCUITS
AMOUNT: $1,844.48
CK. NO.: 896
DATE: 02/27/76

The instructions in this confirmation notice concluded with: PLEASE ENSURE AMOUNT IS CORRECT. This confirmation notice was signed by Suttill and returned to Fidelity.

Fidelity's computer was programmed to pull checks only if all of the digits on the stop-payment order agreed with those on the check. As a result, check number 896 was honored by Fidelity and charged to Multi-Tek's account. Multi-Tek then brought suit against Fidelity to recover $1,844.98 because the check was paid over the stop-payment order.

Marutani, Judge.   The Uniform Commercial Code, § 4–403(1), provides in pertinent part that: "A customer may by order to his bank stop payment of any item payable for his account but the order must be received at such time and in such manner as to afford the bank a reasonable opportunity to act on it prior to any action by the bank with respect to the item."

In this case, there is no question that the transmittal of the stop-payment order was made timely; this leaves for resolution only whether such order was given "in such *manner* as to afford the bank a reasonable opportunity to act on it": UCC § 4–403(1); emphasis added. While the parties "may by agreement determine the standards by which [the bank's] responsibility is to be measured if such standards are not manifestly unreasonable," at the same time "no agreement can disclaim a bank's responsibility for its failure to exercise ordinary care": UCC § 4–103(1).

The decisional law constituting § 4–403(1) appears to vary. Thus, in a recent decision of a trial court wherein the customer identified the check correctly as to the payee, the check number, and the date of issuance, but erred by 10 cents as to the amount of the check—$1,804.00 instead of the correct amount of $1,804.10—it was held that "the check was described with sufficient particularity and accuracy so that the bank should have known to give effect to the stop-payment order." However, where the customer provided the correct amount of the check but erred as to the date and name of the payee—one-day error in date, "Walter Morris Buick" instead of the correct name "Frank Morris Buick"—the Alabama Supreme Court held such to be insufficient notice.

In this case, as the parties by the stipulation agreed, "the Bank did not tell Mr. Suttill, nor did he request, information as to the procedure whereby the computer pulls checks on which stop payments have been issued." Under such circumstances, where the customer (Mr. Suttill) was called upon by the bank (Fidelity) to provide numerous data relating to the check in question, but the bank failed to emphasize to him that all such information may well be ineffective unless the amount of the check were absolutely accurate, we are constrained to be guided by the official comment to § 4–403 under "Purposes," which reads:

2. The position taken by this section is that stopping payment is a service which depositors expect and are entitled to receive from banks notwithstanding its difficulty, inconvenience and expense. The inevitable occasional losses through failure to stop should be borne by the banks as a cost of the business of banking.

Judgment for Multi-Tek.

Bank's Liability for Payment after Stop-Payment Order

While a stop-payment order is in effect, the drawee bank is liable to the drawer of a check that it pays for any loss that the drawer suffers by reason of such payment. However, the drawer has the burden of establishing the fact and amount of the loss. To show a loss, the drawer must establish that the drawee bank paid a person against whom the drawer had a valid defense to payment. To the extent that the drawer has such a defense, he has suffered a loss due to the drawee's failure to honor the stop-payment order.

For example, Brown buys what is represented to be a new car from Foster Ford and gives Foster Ford his check for $12,280 drawn on First Bank. Brown then discovers that the car is in fact a used demonstrator model and calls First Bank, ordering it to stop payment on the check. If Foster Ford presents the check for payment the following day and First Bank pays the check despite the stop-payment order, Brown can require the bank to recredit his account. (The depositor-drawer bases her claim to recredit on the fact that the bank did not follow her final instruction—the instruction not to pay the check.) Brown had a valid defense of misrepresentation that he could have asserted against Foster Ford if it had sued him on the check. Foster Ford would have been required to sue on the check or on Brown's contractual obligation to pay for the car.

Assume, instead, that Foster Ford negotiated the check to Smith and that Smith qualified as a holder in due course. Then, if the bank paid the check to Smith over the stop-payment order, Brown would not be able to have his account recredited, because Brown would not be able to show that he sustained any loss. If the bank had refused to pay the check, so that Smith came against Brown on his drawer's liability, Brown's personal defense of misrepresentation of the prior use of the car could not be used as a reason for not paying Smith. Brown's only recourse would be to go directly against Foster Ford on his misrepresentation claim.

The bank may ask the customer to sign a form in which the bank tries to disclaim or limit its liability for the stop-payment order. As explained at the beginning of this chapter, the bank is not permitted to disclaim its responsibility for its failure to act in good faith or to exercise ordinary care in paying a check over a stop-payment order [4–103].

If a bank pays a check after it has been given a stop-payment order, it acquires all the rights of the person to whom it makes payment, including rights arising from the transaction on which the check was based [4–407]. In the previous example involving Brown and Foster Ford, assume that Brown was able to have his account recredited because First Bank had paid the check to Foster Ford over his stop-payment order. Then, the bank would have any rights that Brown had against Foster Ford for the misrepresentation.

If a person stops payment on a check and the bank honors the stop-payment order, the person may still be liable to the holder of the check. Suppose Peters writes a check for $450 to Ace Auto Repair in payment for repairs to her automobile. While driving the car home, she concludes that the car was not properly repaired. She calls her bank and stops payment on the check. Ace Auto negotiated the check to Sam's Auto Parts, which took the check as a holder in due course. When Sam's takes the check to Peters's bank, payment is refused because of the stop-payment order. Sam's then comes after Peters on her drawer's liability. All Peters has is a personal defense against payment, which is not good against

FIGURE 2   Certified Check

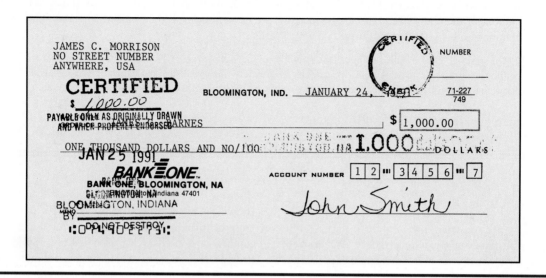

a holder in due course. So, Peters must pay Sam's the $450 and pursue her claim separately against Ace. If Ace were still the holder of the check, however, the situation would be different. Peters's personal defense concerning the faulty work could be used against Ace to reduce or possibly cancel her obligation to pay the check.

Certified Check

Normally, a drawee bank is not obligated to certify a check. When a drawee bank does *certify* a check, it substitutes its undertaking to pay the check and, as Article 3 provides, becomes *primarily liable for payment* of the check. At the time a check is certified, the bank usually debits the customer's account for the amount of the certified check and shifts the money to a special account at the bank. It also adds its signature to the check to show that it has accepted primary liability for paying it. The bank's signature is an essential part of the certification; the bank's signature must appear on the check [3–410(1)]. If the holder of a check chooses to have it certified, rather than seeking to have it paid at that time, the holder has made a conscious decision to look to the certifying bank for payment and is no longer relying on the drawer or the indorsers to pay it. See Figure 2 for an example of a certified check.

If a check is certified by the drawee bank at the request of the drawer, the drawer remains secondarily liable on the check. However, if the drawee bank certifies a check at the request of a holder of the check, then the drawer and any persons who have already indorsed the check are discharged of their liability on the check [3–411(1)].

Cashier's Check

A **cashier's check** differs from a **certified check.** A check on which a bank is both the drawer and the drawee is a cashier's check. The bank is primarily liable on the cashier's check. The question of whether a bank may refuse to honor a cashier's check has been the subject of considerable litigation. Some states consider the cashier's check to be a substitute for cash and do not allow banks to honor stop-payment requests against cashier's checks or to refuse to pay them. In other states, an issuing bank may raise appropriate defenses and may refuse to pay a cashier's check held by a party to the check with whom it has dealt. See Figure 3 for an example of a cashier's check. A **teller's check** is similar to a cashier's check in that it is a check on which one bank is the drawer and another bank is the drawee.

FIGURE 3   Cashier's Check

Death or Incompetence of Customer

Under the general principles of agency law, the death or incompetence of the principal terminates the agent's authority to act for the principal. However, slightly different rules apply to the authority of a bank to pay checks out of the account of a deceased or incompetent person. The bank has the right to pay the checks of an incompetent person until it has notice that a court has determined the person is incompetent. Once the bank learns of this fact, it loses its authority to pay that person's checks—because the depositor is not competent to issue instructions to pay.

Similarly, a bank has the right to pay the checks of a deceased customer until it has notice of the customer's death. Even if a bank knows of a customer's death, for a period of 10 days after the customer's death, it can pay checks written by the customer prior to his death. However, the deceased person's heirs or other persons claiming an interest in the account can order the bank to stop payment [4–405].

FORGED AND ALTERED CHECKS

Bank's Right to Charge Account

A check that bears a forged signature of the drawer or payee is generally not properly payable from the cus-

tomer's account because the bank is not following the instructions of the depositor precisely as he gave them. The bank is expected to be familiar with the authorized signature of its depositor. If it pays such a check, Article 4 will treat the transaction as one in which the bank paid out its own funds, rather than the depositor's funds.

Similarly, a check that was altered after the drawer made it out—for example, by increasing the amount of the check—generally is not properly payable from the customer's account. However, as noted earlier, if the drawer is *negligent* and contributes to the forgery or alteration, he may be barred from claiming it as the reason that a particular check should not be charged to his account.

For example, Barton makes a check for $1 in a way that makes it possible for someone to easily alter it to read $101, and it is so altered. If the drawee bank pays the check to a holder in good faith, it can charge the $101 to Barton's account if Barton's negligence contributed to the alteration. Similarly, if a company uses a mechanical checkwriter to write checks, it must use reasonable care to see that unauthorized persons do not have access to blank checks and to the checkwriter.

If the alteration is obvious, the bank should note that fact and refuse to pay the check when it is presented for payment. Occasionally, the alteration is so skillful that the bank cannot detect it. In that case, the bank is allowed to charge to the account the amount for which the check was originally written.

Customer's Duty to Report Forgeries and Alterations

Commonly, the bank will return the checks it has charged against the drawer's account, together with a statement of account, to the customer once a month. On receiving the checks and statement, the customer owes a duty to the bank to examine them promptly to discover whether any signatures on the checks are forgeries or unauthorized or whether any of the checks have been altered [4–406(1)].

A customer who fails to examine the checks and statement within a *reasonable time* cannot hold the bank responsible for the payment of checks on which there are forgeries, unauthorized signings, or alterations if the bank can show that it suffered a loss because of the customer's failure [4–406(2)(a)]. For example, the bank might show that the forger absconded during that time.

A different rule applies if a series of unauthorized drawer's signatures or alterations are made by the same wrongdoer. The customer generally cannot hold the bank responsible for paying any such checks if the bank can show (1) that it paid the check in good faith, (2) that it paid after the first check that had been signed on behalf of the drawer or altered without the drawer's authority was available to the customer for a reasonable period not exceeding 14 calendar days, and (3) before the bank received notification from the customer of any such unauthorized signature or alteration [4–406(2)(b)]. Unless the customer has notified the bank about the forgeries or alterations, then any subsequent forgeries or alterations by the same wrongdoer are the responsibility of the customer unless she can establish a lack of ordinary care on the part of the drawee bank [4–406(3)]. A lack of ordinary care includes, for example, payment of a check on which the

drawer's signature bears no resemblance to the depositor's signature on the deposit agreement, or of a check on which the alterations were very obvious.

Thus, checks forged or altered by the same person and presented to the bank more than 14 days after the first forged check was available to the customer are the customer's problem—not the bank's. The amount of checks forged or altered by the same person and presented to the bank before and during the 14-day period after the statement first revealing such forgeries or alterations has been sent to the customer are the bank's responsibility. The bank may not debit the customer's account in payment of such checks unless the bank can show that it suffered a loss because of the customer's failure to exercise reasonable care.

Suppose that Allen employs Farnum as an accountant and that over a period of three months, Farnum forges Allen's signature to 10 checks and cashes them. One of the forged checks is included in the checks returned to Allen at the end of the first month. Within 14 calendar days after the return of these checks, Farnum forges two more checks and cashes them. Allen does not examine the returned checks until three months after the checks that included the first forged check were returned to her. The bank would be responsible for the first forged check and for the two checks forged and cashed within the 14-day period after it sent the first statement and the canceled checks (unless the bank proves that it suffered a loss because of the customer's failure to examine the checks and notify it more promptly). It would not be liable for the seven forged checks cashed after the expiration of the 14-day period.

The case that follows, *Rhode Island Hospital Trust National Bank v. Zapata*, illustrates how the UCC applies to a series of a forgeries.

RHODE ISLAND HOSPITAL TRUST NATIONAL BANK v. ZAPATA CORP.

6 UCC Rep.2d 1 (1st Cir. 1988)

In early 1985, an employee of the Zapata Corporation stole some blank checks from the company. She wrote a large number of forged checks, almost all in amounts of $150 to $800 each, on Zapata's account at Rhode Island Hospital Trust National Bank. The bank, from March through July 1985, received and paid them. Bank statements that the bank regularly sent Zapata first began to reflect the forged checks in early 1985. Zapata failed to examine its statements closely until July 1985, when it found the forgeries. It immediately notified the bank, which then stopped clearing the checks. The bank had already processed and paid checks containing forged drawer's signatures totaling $109,247.16. Zapata then brought suit against the bank to have its account recredited for the checks. The district court held that the bank was liable to reimburse Zapata for the checks that it paid before April 25, 1985 (two weeks after Zapata received the first statement containing the forged checks), but held in favor of the bank as to the remaining checks. Zapata appealed.

Breyer, Circuit Judge.   The issue that this appeal presents is whether Zapata Corporation has shown that the system used by Rhode Island Hospital Trust National Bank for detecting forged checks—a system used by a majority of American banks—lacks the "ordinary care" that a bank must exercise under the Uniform Commercial Code section 4–406(3). The question arises out of the following district court determinations, all of which are adequately supported by the record and by Rhode Island law.

3. The Bank will (and legally must) reimburse Zapata in respect to all checks it cleared before April 25 (or for at least two weeks after Zapata received the statement that reflected the forgeries). See sections 3–401(1), 4–406(2).

4. In respect to checks cleared on and after April 25, the Bank need not reimburse Zapata because Zapata failed to "exercise reasonable care and promptness to examine the [bank] statements." Section 4–406(1).

The question before us is whether this last-mentioned conclusion is correct or whether Zapata can recover for the post–April 24 checks on the theory that, even if it was negligent, so was the Bank.

To understand this question, one must examine UCC section 4–406. Ordinarily a bank must reimburse an innocent customer for forgeries that it honors, section 3–401(1), but section 4–406 makes an important exception to the liability rule. The exception operates in respect to a series of forged checks, and it applies once a customer has had a chance to catch the forgeries by examining his bank statements and notifying the bank but has failed to do so.

The statute, in relevant part, reads as follows:

(1) *When a bank sends to its customer a statement of account* accompanied by items paid in good faith in support of the debit entries or holds the statement and items pursuant to a request or instructions of its customer or otherwise in a reasonable manner makes the statement and items available to the customer, *the customer must exercise reasonable care and promptness to examine the statement* and items *to discover his unauthorized signature* or any alteration on an item *and must notify the bank promptly* after discovery thereof.

(2) *If the bank establishes that the customer failed* with respect to an item *to comply with* the duties imposed on the customer by *subsection (1) the customer is precluded from asserting against the bank*

(a) *His unauthorized signature* or any alteration on the item if the bank also establishes that it suffered a loss by reason of such failure; *and*

(b) *An unauthorized signature or alteration by the same wrongdoer on any other item paid in good faith by the bank after the first item and statement was available to the customer for a reasonable period not exceeding fourteen (14) calendar days* and before the bank receives notification from the customer of any such unauthorized signature or alteration.

Section 4–406(1)–(2) (emphasis added).

The statute goes on to specify an important exception. It says:

(3) The preclusion under subsection (2) does not apply if the customer establishes lack of ordinary care on the part of the bank in paying the item(s).

Section 4–406(3). Zapata's specific claim on this appeal is that it falls within this "exception to the exception"—that the bank's treatment of the post–April 24 checks lacked "ordinary care."

The statute places the burden of proof on Zapata. It says that strict bank liability terminates fourteen days after the customer receives the bank's statement unless "the *customer establishes* lack of ordinary care."

The record convinces us that Zapata failed to carry its burden of establishing "lack of ordinary care" on the part of the Bank. First the Bank described its ordinary practices as follows: The Bank examines all signatures on checks for more than $1,000. It examines signatures on checks between $100 and $1,000 (those at issue here) if it has reason to suspect a problem, e.g. if a customer has warned it of a possible forgery or if the check was drawn on an account with insufficient funds. It examines the signatures of a randomly chosen one percent of all other checks between $100 and $1,000. But it does not examine the signatures on other checks between $100 and $1,000. Through expert testimony, the Bank also established that most other banks in the nation follow this practice and that banking industry experts recommend it. Indeed, the Bank's practices are conservative in this regard, as most banks set $2,500 or more, not $1,000, as the limit beneath which they will not examine each signature. This testimony made out a prima facie case of "ordinary care."

Second, both bank and industry experts pointed out that this industry practice, in general and in the particular case of the Bank, saved considerable expense, compared with the Bank's pre-1981 practice of examining each check by hand. To be specific, the change saved the Bank about $125,000 annually.

Third, both a Bank official and an industry expert testified that changing from an "individual signature examination" system to the new "bulk-filing" system led to *no* significant increase in the number of forgeries that were detected. Under the Bank's prior "individual signature examination" some forgeries still slipped through.

Fourth, even if one assumes, contrary to this uncontradicted evidence, that the new system meant *some* increase in the number of undetetected forged checks, Zapata still could not prevail, for it presented *no* evidence tending to show any such increased loss unreasonable in light of the costs that the new practice would save.

Judgment for Rhode Island Hospital Trust National Bank affirmed.

CONCEPT REVIEW

LIABILITY FOR MULTIPLE FORGERIES OR ALTERATIONS BY THE SAME PERSON

Date First Statement Disclosing an Altered or Forged Check Is Available to Customer	Date 14 Days Later	Date Customer Gives Notice of Alteration or Forgery
Customer is not liable for forged/altered checks paid during this period unless bank suffers a loss from customer's unreasonable delay in notifying bank of forgery or alteration.	Customer is liable for forged or altered checks paid during this period unless customer gives bank notice of forgery or alteration within a reasonable time after date the first statement containing a forged or altered check was available to customer.	Customer is not liable for forged or altered checks paid during this period.

In any event, a customer must discover and report to the bank any forgery of his signature or any alteration within one year from the time the checks are made available to him. If the customer does not do so, he cannot require the bank to recredit his account for such checks. Similarly, a customer has three years from the time his checks are made available to discover and report any unauthorized indorsement. The depositor's failure to discover and report these irregularities within the one- or three-year periods specified costs him the right to recredit the amount of the checks [4–406(4)].

CHECK COLLECTION AND FUNDS AVAILABILITY

Check Collection

As the Negotiable Instruments chapter describes, checks and other drafts collected through the banking system usually have at least three parties—the drawer, the drawee bank, and the payee. If the payee deposits the check at the same bank as the drawee bank, the latter will take a series of steps necessary to reflect the deposit as a credit to the payee's account and to decide whether to pay the check from the drawer's account. In connection with its handling of the deposit for the payee's benefit, it will make one ledger entry showing the deposit as a credit to the payee's account. In connection with its decision to pay, it will perform several steps commonly referred to as the *process of posting* [4–109]. These steps need not be taken in any particular order, but they customarily include comparing the drawer's signature on the check with that on the deposit agreement, determining whether there are sufficient funds to pay, debiting the drawer's account for the amount of the check, and placing the check into a folder for later return to the drawer (to satisfy its obligations under the "bank statement" rule [4–406(1)]).

If the payee deposits the check at a bank other than the drawee bank, the depositary bank, acting as the agent of the payee, will make the ledger entry showing the deposit as a credit to the payee's account. The next step of the collection process depends on where the depositary bank is located. If the drawee and depositary banks are in the same town or county, the depositary bank will indorse the check and deliver ("present") it to

the drawee bank for payment. It may deliver it by courier or through a local association of banks known as a "clearing house" [4–104(1)(d)]. The drawee-payor bank must settle for the check before midnight of the banking day of its receipt of the check, which means that it must give the depositary bank funds or a credit equal to the amount of the check. Once it settles for the check, the drawee-payor bank has until midnight of the banking day after the banking day of receipt to pay the check or to return the check or send notice of dishonor. This deadline for the drawee-payor bank's action on the check is known as the bank's "midnight deadline" [4–104(1)(h)]. The drawee-payor bank's failure to settle by midnight of the banking day of receipt, or its failure to pay or return the check, or send notice of dishonor, results in the drawee-payor bank becoming "accountable" for the amount of the check, which means it must pay the amount of the check [4–302(a)].

If the drawee and depositary banks are located in different counties, or in different states, the depositary bank will use an additional commercial bank, and one or more of the regional Federal Reserve Banks, in the collection of the check. In these cases, the depositary bank will send the check on to the drawee-payor bank through these "collecting banks." Each bank in the sequence must use ordinary care in presenting the check or sending it for presentment, and in sending notice of dishonor or returning the check after learning that the check has not been paid [4–202(1)]. The depositary and collecting banks have until their respective midnight deadlines—or, in some cases, a further reasonable time—to take the action required of them in the sequence of collection steps.

If the drawee-payor bank dishonors the check prior to its midnight deadline or shortly after the midnight deadline under circumstances specified in "Regulation CC" of the Federal Reserve (described in the next section of this chapter), it will send the check back to the depositary bank. Until September 1, 1988, the drawee-payor bank customarily sent the dishonored check back to the collecting bank from which it received the check, and the collecting bank sent it back to the bank from which it had received it, and through any other bank that handled the check in the "forward collection" process until the check again reached the depositary bank. The provisions of Article 4 still describe this sequence of the "return collection" process, although Regulation CC imposes new reponsibilities on the payor bank and on any other returning bank. Each bank in the return sequence adjusts its accounts to reflect the return and has until its midnight deadline to send the check on to the bank from which it originally had received the check. After September 1, 1988 (or in states that previously had adopted "direct return" (4–212(2)), the drawee-payor bank may return the check *directly* to the depositary bank—skipping all of the collecting banks and the delay represented by the midnight deadlines that each bank otherwise would have had.

Direct return also increases the likelihood that the depositary bank will know whether the check has been dishonored by the day on which Regulation CC requires the depositary bank to allow the payee to write checks or otherwise make withdrawals against the deposit. The next section of this chapter discusses this aspect of Regulation CC in more detail.

On receipt of the dishonored check, the depositary bank will return the check or otherwise notify the payee (its depositor) of the dishonor and will debit or charge back her account for the check it did not collect [4–212]. The depositary bank may charge back the deposit even if it previously had allowed the payee-depositor to withdraw against the credit given for the deposit.

When the depositor receives the notice of dishonor and returned check, it will take one of several steps depending on whether it received the check directly from the drawer, or took it by indorsement from another person. If the depositor was not the original payee of the check, it usually will prefer to return the check—giving notice of dishonor unless already given by the drawee bank or another collecting bank—to the person who negotiated the check to her, the prior indorser. Recall that indorsers agree that they will take up the check following dishonor and notice of dishonor [3–414(1)].

If the depositor received the check directly from the drawer, for example as payee, the depositor normally will demand payment from the drawer. Recall that the drawer has a contractual obligation to pay the check upon dishonor and notice of dishonor [3–413(2)]; alternatively, the payee may seek to enforce the underlying obligation for which the drawer originally issued the check, such as the purchase of groceries or an automobile.

Funds Availability

When a bank takes a check for deposit to a customer's account, it typically places a hold on the funds represented by the deposited check because it runs a number of risks in allowing a customer to withdraw deposits that have not been finally collected from the drawee bank. The risks that the check may be returned include: (1) there may be insufficient funds in the drawer's account or the account may have been closed; (2) the check may contain a forged drawer's or indorser's signature, or there may have been a material alteration of the check; (3) the possibility that the drawer is kiting checks or playing two accounts off against each other; or (4) a stop-payment order may have been placed against the check. These are real concerns to a depositary bank, and it has a significant interest in protecting itself against these possibilities.

Until recently, the risks run by a depositary bank were complicated by a very slow process used by drawee-payor banks in returning a dishonored check or notifying the bank of the dishonor. Moreover, depositary banks do not get direct notice from drawee-payor banks when they pay checks. Accordingly, banks often restricted the depositor's use of the deposit by placing relatively long holds on checks deposited with them for collection; these sometimes ran 15 to 20 days for items drawn on other than local banks.

The extensive use of holds, and a growing public sentiment that they were excessive and often unfair, led to the passage by Congress in 1987 of the *Expedited Funds Availability Act*. In the act, Congress set out mandatory schedules limiting check holds and specifying when funds are to be made available to customers by depositary institutions. The act also delegated to the Federal Reserve Board the authority to speed up the check processing system. The regulations adopted by the Board to speed up check processing supersede the provisions of Article 4 of the UCC (Bank Deposits and Collections) in a number of respects but will not be covered in this text.

The key elements of the mandatory funds availability schedules, which are set out in Federal Reserve Board Regulation CC and which are effective September 1, 1990, are:

1. Local checks (those drawn on banks in the same Federal Reserve check region as the depositary bank) must be made available for the depositor to draw against by the second business day following deposit.

2. Nonlocal checks (those drawn on banks located in the United States but outside the Federal Reserve check processing region in which the depositary bank is located) must be made available by the fifth business day following deposit.

3. Certain items must be made available by the next day after the day of deposit. These include:

a. Cash deposits where the deposit is banked in person to an employee of the depositary bank (i.e., not at an ATM).

b. Electronic payments.

c. Checks drawn on the U.S. Treasury.

d. U.S. Postal Service money orders.

e. Checks drawn on a Federal Reserve Bank or Federal Home Loan Bank.

f. Checks drawn by a state or a unit of local government (under certain conditions).

g. Cashier's, certified, or teller's checks.

h. Checks drawn on the depositary bank.

i. The lesser of $100 or the aggregate deposit on any one banking day.

4. If the next-day items are not deposited in person with an employee of the depositary institution but rather are deposited in an ATM machine or by mail, then the deposit does not have to be made available for withdrawal until the second business day after deposit.

5. Generally, the depositary bank must begin accruing interest to a depositor's interest-bearing account from the day it receives credit for cash and check deposits to an interest-bearing account.

Figure 4 shows graphically how the funds availability schedule works.

There are six major exceptions to the mandatory availability schedules set out above that are designed to safeguard depositary banks against higher risk situations. The exceptions are:

1. *The new account exception.* The depositary bank may suspend the availability rules for new accounts and can limit the next-day and second-day availability to the first $5,000 deposited.

2. *The large deposit exception.* The hold periods can be extended to the extent the aggregate deposit on any banking day exceeds $5,000.

3. *The redeposited check exception.* The hold period can be extended where a check has been returned one or more times.

4. *The repeated overdraft exception.* A longer hold period may be required for deposits to accounts that have been overdrawn repeatedly.

5. *The reasonable cause exception.* The scheduled availability may be extended where the bank has reasonable cause to believe the check is uncollectible.

6. *The emergency conditions exception.* The scheduled availability may be extended under certain emergency conditions such as a communications interruption or a computer failure.

Banks are required to disclose their funds availability policy to all of their customers; they may provide different policies to different classes or categories of customers.

ELECTRONIC BANKING

With the development of computer technology, many banks are encouraging their customers to transfer funds electronically by using computers rather than paper drafts and checks. A bank customer may use a specially coded card at terminals provided by the bank to make deposits to an account, to transfer money from one checking or savings account to another, to pay bills, or   to withdraw cash from an account.

These new forms of transferring money have raised questions about the legal rules that apply to them, and the questions are only beginning to be resolved. In at least one court decision, *State of Illinois v. Continental Illinois National Bank*, which follows, the court held that a customer's withdrawal from a checking account by using a bank card at an electronic terminal should be treated in the same way as cashing a check.

FIGURE 4   Funds Availablility Schedules (availability of different types of checks deposited the same day)

Monday (Day 0)	Tuesday (Day 1)	Wednesday (Day 2)	Thursday (Day 3)	Friday (Day 4)	Monday (Day 5)	Tuesday (Day 6)	Wednesday (Day 7)	Thursday (Day 8)

Local

$1,000 (Deposit)

1. $100 / 2. $900 (Check Writing)

1. $100 / 4. $400 / 5. $500 (Cash Withdrawals)

Nonlocal

$1,000 (Deposit)

1. $100 / 3. $900 (Check Writing)

1. $100 / 4. $400 / 5. $500 (Cash Withdrawals)

1. The first $100 of a day's deposit must be made available for either cash withdrawal or check-writing purposes at the start of the next business day § 229.10(c)(1)(vii).

2. Local checks must be made available for check-writing purposes by the second business day following deposit § 229.12(b).

3. Nonlocal checks must be made available for check-writing purposes by the fifth business day following deposit § 229.12(c).

4. $400 of the deposit must be made available for cash withdrawal no later than 5:00 P.M. on the day specified in the schedule. This is in addition to the $100 that must be made available on the business day following deposit § 229.12(d).

5. The remainder of the deposit must be made available for cash withdrawal at the start of business the following day § 229.12(d).

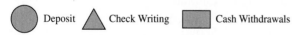

⬤ Deposit   △ Check Writing   ▢ Cash Withdrawals

Source: Chart Provided by Federal Reserve (53 Federal Register 19375, May 27, 1988).

〰〰〰〰〰〰〰〰〰〰〰〰〰〰〰〰〰〰〰〰〰〰〰〰〰〰〰〰〰〰〰〰〰〰

STATE OF ILLINOIS v. CONTINENTAL ILLINOIS NATIONAL BANK

536 F.2d 176 (7th Cir. 1976)

Continental Illinois National Bank operated several so-called Customer Bank Communication Terminals (CBCTs). These unstaffed terminals were connected directly with the main office computer of Continental Illinois. Customers of the bank inserted a specially coded card into the terminal, entered an identification number, and then pressed keys on the transaction keyboard to indicate the type and amounts of their transactions. The customer might:

1. Withdraw cash (in the amount of $25 or any multiple thereof, up to $100) from a savings, checking, or credit card account.

2. Deposit checks or currency in a checking or savings account. At the time of the transaction, the customer's receipt from the CBCT indicated the amount and date of the deposit. Until the deposit was received and verified at the main banking premises, it was not credited to his account and he could not draw on it.

3. Transfer funds between accounts: checking to savings, credit card to checking, or savings to checking.

4. Make payments on Continental Illinois installment loans or credit card charges.

When a transaction was completed, the customer received a receipt, and if she had withdrawn cash from her account, she received packets containing the cash. A copy of the receipt was retained in the machine, and the transaction was later verified by bank employees.

The Illinois banking commissioner brought an action against Continental Illinois to obtain a declaratory judgment that the unstaffed computer terminals that permitted customers using bank cards to withdraw cash, make deposits, transfer funds, or make payments constituted "branch banks." The U.S. district court held that the terminals amounted to branch banking, but it rejected the commissioner's contention that use of the machines to withdraw money from a customer's account constituted the "cashing of a check." The court of appeals reversed on this question, holding that this did constitute the cashing of a check.

Per Curiam.   The district court here based its conclusion on the functions of CBCT as to the withdrawing of cash and the payment of installments on loans upon the provisions of the Uniform Commercial Code (UCC), in particular § 3-104(2), which declares a check to be a negotiable instrument drawn on a bank and payable on demand; a writing signed by the maker or drawer and containing an unconditional promise or order to pay a sum certain in money; with negotiability being the essential characteristic of a check. From this the district court concluded that a card inserted into the CBCT machine to secure money was not the cashing of a check within the meaning of the UCC or in the common understanding of check cashing. We cannot agree. This is exalting form over substance. The check is merely the means used by the bank to attain the desired objective, i.e., the payment of money to its customer. The card serves the same purpose as the check. It is an order on the bank. Any order to pay which is properly executed by a customer, whether it be check, card, or electronic device, must be recognized as a routine banking function when used as here. The relationship between the bank and its customer is the same. Indeed, the trial court here recognized this when it characterized a CBCT withdrawal as the "functional equivalent" of a written check. And Continental Bank gives the card transaction the same significance:

The EFTS (Electronic Funds Transfer Systems) at issue in the present case are *extensions* of the principle of immediate access to customer accounts *in a manner dispensing with underlying paper such as checks*. *(Emphasis added.)*

Moreover, although the UCC defines a check as negotiable instrument, it also provides, § 3–104(3):

As used in other Articles of this Act, and as the context may require, the term "check" may refer to instruments which are not negotiable within this Article as well as instruments which are so negotiable.

Just as a transfer of funds by cable or telegraph is in law a check, despite the nonnegotiability of the cable, the card here for the purpose of withdrawing cash is a check. What must be remembered is that the foundation of the relationship between the bank and its customer is the former's agreement to pay out the customer's money according to the latter's order. There are many ways in which an order may be given, and one way of late is by computer record. And the Ninth Circuit accepts the same concept that computer impulses constitute sufficient writing to meet the order test.

Judgment for Continental Illinois.

Electronic Funds Transfer Act

The consumer who used electronic funds transfer systems (EFTs), the so-called cash machines or electronic tellers, in the early years often experienced problems in identifying and resolving mechanical errors resulting from malfunctioning EFTs. In response to these problems, Congress passed the Electronic Funds Transfer Act in 1978 to provide "a basic framework, establishing the rights, liabilities, and responsibilities of participants in electronic funds transfer systems" and especially to provide "individual consumer rights."[2]

The four basic EFT systems are automated teller machines, point-of-sale terminals, which allow consumers to use their EFT cards like checks; preauthorized payments, such as automatic paycheck deposits or mortgage or utility payments; and telephone transfers between accounts or to pay specific bills by phone.

Similar to the Truth in Lending Act and the Fair Credit Billing Act (FCBA) discussed in the Federal Trade Commission Act and Consumer Protection Laws chapter, the EFT Act requires disclosure of the terms and conditions of electronic fund transfers at the time the consumer contracts for the EFT service. Among the nine disclosures required are the following: the consumer's liability for unauthorized electronic fund transfers (those resulting from loss or theft), the nature of the EFT services under the consumer's account, any pertinent dollar or frequency limitations, any charges for the right to make EFTs, the consumer's right to stop payment of a preauthorized transfer, the financial institution's liability to the consumer for failure to make or stop payments, and the consumer's right to receive documentation of transfers both at the point or time of transfer and periodically. The act also requires 21 days' notice prior to the effective date of any change in the terms or conditions of the consumer's account that pertains to the required disclosures.

The EFT Act does differ from the Fair Credit Billing Act in a number of important respects. For example, under the EFT Act, the operators of EFT systems are given a maximum of 10 working days to investigate errors or provisionally recredit the consumer's account, whereas issuers of credit cards are given a maximum of 90 days under the FCBA. The liability of the consumer is different if an EFT card is lost or stolen than it is if a credit card is lost or stolen. Another important difference is that financial institutions cannot send consumers EFT cards that they did not request unless the cards are not valid for use; an unsolicited EFT card can be validated only at the consumer's request and only after the institution verifies that the consumer is the person whose name is on the card.

The case that follows, *Ognibene v. Citibank, N.A.*, illustrates the application of the EFT Act's provisions that limit a customer's liability for the unauthorized use of his card.

---

[2]Title 20 of the Financial Institutions Regulatory and Interest Rate Control Act of 1978, 15 U.S.C. § 1693 et seq.

OGNIBENE v. CITIBANK, N.A.

446 N.Y.S.2d 845 (N.Y.C. Civ. Ct. 1981)

On August 16, 1981, Frederick Ognibene went to the ATM area at a Citibank branch and activated one of the machines with his Citibank card, pressed in his personal identification code, and withdrew $20. When he approached the machine a person was using the customer service telephone located between two ATM machines and appeared to be telling customer service that one of the machines was malfunctioning. As Ognibene was making his withdrawal, the person said into the telephone, "I'll see if his card works in my machine." He then asked Ognibene if he could use his card to see if the other machine was working. Ognibene handed his card to him and saw him insert it into the adjoining machine at least two times while saying into the telephone, "Yes, it seems to be working." When Ognibene received his Citibank statement, it showed that two withdrawals of $200 each from his account were made at 5:42 P.M. and 5:43 P.M., respectively, on August 16. His own $20 withdrawal was made at 5:41 P.M. At the time Ognibene was unaware that any withdrawals from his account were being made from the adjoining machine. Ognibene sought to have his account recredited for $400, claiming that the withdrawals had been unauthorized. Citibank had been aware for some time of a scam being perpetrated against its customers by persons who observed the customer inserting his personal identification number into an ATM and then obtaining access to the customer's ATM card in the same manner as Ognibene's card was obtained. After learning about the scam, Citibank posted signs in ATM areas containing a red circle approximately 2 ½ inches in diameter in which was written "Do Not Let Your Citicard Be Used For Any Transaction But Your Own."

Thorpe, Judge.   The basic rights, liabilities and responsibilities of the banks which offer electronic money transfer services and the consumers who use them have been established by the federal legislation called the Electronic Funds Transfers Act (EFT). The EFT Act places various limits on a consumer's liability for electronic fund transfers from his account if they are "unauthorized." Insofar as is relevant here, a transfer is "unauthorized" if (1) it is initiated by a person other than the consumer and without actual authority to initiate such transfer, (2) the consumer receives no benefit from it, and (3) the consumer did not furnish such person "with the card, code or other means of access" to his account.

In an action involving a consumer's liability for an electronic fund transfer, such as the one at bar, the burden of going forward to show an "unauthorized" transfer from his account is on the consumer. The EFT Act places on the bank, however, the burden of proof for any consumer liability for the transfer. To establish full liability on the part of the consumer, the bank must prove that the transfer was authorized. To be entitled to even the limited liability imposed by the statute on the consumer, the bank must prove that certain conditions of consumer liability, set forth in 15 U.S.C.A. 1693g(a) have been met and that certain disclosures mandated by 15 U.S.C.A. 1693c(a)(1) and (2) have been met.

Ognibene met his burden of going forward. He did not initiate the withdrawals in question, did not authorize the person in the ATM area to make them, and did not benefit from them.

However, Citibank's position is, in essence, that although Ognibene was duped, the bank's burden of proof on the issue of authorization has been met by Ognibene's testimony that he permitted his card to be used in the adjoining machine by the other person. The court does not agree.

The EFT Act requires that the consumer have furnished to a person initiating the transfer the "code, card, or other means of access" to his account to be eligible for the limitations on liability afforded by the Act when transfers are "unauthorized." The evidence establishes that in order to obtain access to an account via an automatic teller machine both the card and the personal identification code must be used. Thus, by merely giving his card to the person initiating the transfer, a consumer does not furnish the "means of access" to his account. To do so, he would have to furnish the personal identification code as well.

The court finds that Ognibene did not furnish his personal identification code to the person initiating the $400.00 transfer within the meaning of the EFT Act. There is no evidence that he deliberately or even negligently did so. On the contrary, the unauthorized person was able to obtain the code because of Citibank's own negligence. Since the bank had knowledge of the scam and its operation details (including the central role of the customer service telephone), it was negligent in failing to provide Ognibene with information sufficient to alert him to the danger when he found himself in the position of potential victim. Although in June, 1981, after the scam came to Citibank's attention, it posted signs in its ATM areas containing a red circle approximately 2 ½ inches in diameter in which is written "Do Not Let Your Citicard Be Used For Any Transaction But Your Own," the court finds that this printed admonition is not a sufficient security measure since it fails to state the reason why one should not. Since a customer of Citibank's electronic fund transfer service must employ both the card and the personal identification code in order to withdraw money from his account, the danger of loaning the card briefly for the purpose of checking the functioning of an adjoining automated teller machine would not be immediately apparent to one who has not divulged his personal identification number and who is unaware that it has been revealed merely by virtue of his own transaction with the machine.

Judgment for Ognibene for $400.

DOCUMENTS OF TITLE

Introduction

Storing or shipping goods, giving a **warehouse receipt** or **bill of lading** representing the goods, and transferring such a receipt or bill of lading as representing the goods are practices of ancient origin. The warehouseman or the common carrier is a bailee of the goods who contracts to store or transport the goods and to deliver them to the owner or to act otherwise in accordance with the lawful directions of the owner. The warehouse receipt or the bill of lading may be either negotiable or nonnegotiable. To be *negotiable,* a warehouse receipt, bill of lading, or other document of title *must provide that the goods are to be delivered to the bearer or to the order of a named person* [7–104(1)]. The primary differences between the law of negotiable instruments and the law of negotiable documents of title are based on the differences between the obligation to pay money and the obligation to deliver specific goods.

The *Bishop v. Allied Van Lines, Inc.* case, which follows, illustrates the responsibility a warehouseman has to deliver the goods only as directed by the owner.

BISHOP v. ALLIED VAN LINES, INC.
399 N.E.2d 698 (Ill. Ct. App. 1980)

Estelle Smiley and her husband, R. V. Smiley, entered into an agreement with Allied Van Lines for the transfer and storage of household goods and were given a bill of lading. Afterward, the Smileys began divorce proceedings. Estelle Smiley then notified the agent for Allied not to deliver the household goods to either her or her husband without further instructions from her. The goods were delivered to R. V. Smiley after the notice had been given.

Estelle died, and Bishop, the executor of her estate, brought an action against Allied Van Lines, Inc., to recover damages for misdelivery of goods. The trial court dismissed the case for failure to state a cause of action, and Bishop appealed.

Craven, Judge.   The trial judge stated that a bailee is required to deliver the goods to a person entitled under the document upon payment of the bailee's lien. Person entitled under the document is defined in § 7–403 of the Code, subparagraph (4), as a holder in the case of a negotiable document or the person to whom delivery is to be made by the terms of or pursuant to written instructions under a nonnegotiable document. The bill of lading in question is conspicuously and expressly noted as nonnegotiable. Section 7–404 provides that a bailee in good faith and using reasonable commercial standards who delivers or otherwise disposes of the goods according to the terms of the document of title is not liable.

The Comments under that section state that delivery in the case of a nonnegotiable document is to the one to whom delivery is to be made under its terms or pursuant to written instructions under it. Such instructions would be a delivery order [§ 7–102(1)(d)]. Delivery order is a written order to deliver goods directed to a warehouseman, carrier, or other person who in the ordinary course of business issues warehouse receipts or bills of lading. No delivery orders were given at any time. Therefore, the person entitled under the document here, this being a nonnegotiable document, must be the person to whom delivery is made by the terms of the nonnegotiable document.

Ordinarily in a bill of lading where no delivery orders are given, there is a blank space for the consignee and his or her address. Section 7–102(1)(b) defines "consignee" as the person named in a bill to whom or to whose order the bill promises delivery. The bill of lading in this case is no different. There is a blank space for a consignee, delivery address, city, and state. Also, there is a blank space at the bottom of the nonnegotiable bill of lading where the consignee is supposed to sign. The bill of lading in question had only blank spaces for this information. In other words, there was neither a consignee named nor any address given, nor was there a signature of any consignee. There was, then, no consignee at all, nor were any delivery orders given. The bill of lading, issued by Allied Van Lines, states that the shipper was Mr. and Mrs. R. V. Smiley, signed by R. V. Smiley.

[The estate of] Mrs. Smiley alleges in the complaint that she was the owner of the stored property and she was named as a joint shipper in the bill of lading. Mrs. R. V. Smiley would, then, be a joint bailor. A bailment is merely the delivery of goods for some purpose upon a contract, express or implied, and after the purpose has been fulfilled the goods are to be redelivered to the bailor, or otherwise dealt with according to his directions, or kept until reclaimed. Joint delivery by Mrs. Smiley and her then husband carries with it a presumption of joint title and a concession of a joint right of action.

Section 7–404 states that a bailee who in good faith, including observance of reasonable commercial standards, has received goods and delivered or disposed of them according to the terms of the document is not liable. Here it is alleged that the bailee had knowledge of an adverse claim between the bailors. On these pleadings, we hold that it cannot be said that the bailee acted in good faith. It cannot be said that the bailee observed reasonable commercial standards when the bailee delivered the bailed goods with knowledge of adverse claims between the bailors. Indeed, § 7–603 excuses the bailee from delivery until he had a reasonable time to ascertain the validity of adverse claims.

Judgment reversed in favor of the Estelle Smiley estate.

Warehouse Receipts

A warehouse receipt, to be valid, need not be in any particular form, but if it does not embody within its written or printed form each of the following, the warehouseman is liable for damages caused by the omission to a person injured as a result of it: (a) the location of the warehouse where the goods are stored; (b) the date of issue; (c) the consecutive number of the receipt; (d) whether the goods are to be delivered to the bearer or to the order of a named person;[3] (e) the rate of storage and handling charges; (f) a description of the goods or of the packages containing them; (g) the signature of the warehouseman or his agent; (h) whether the warehouseman is the owner of the goods, solely, jointly, or in common with others; and (i) a statement of the amount of the advances made and of the liabilities incurred for which the warehouseman claims a lien or security interest. Other terms may be inserted [7–202].

A warehouseman is liable to a purchaser for value in good faith of a warehouse receipt for nonreceipt or misdescription of goods. The receipt may conspicuously qualify the description by a statement such as "contents, condition, and quantity unknown" [7–203].

Because a warehouseman is a bailee of the goods, he owes to the holder of the warehouse receipt the duties of a mutual benefit bailee and must exercise reasonable care [7–204]. The Personal Property and Bailments chapter discusses the duties of a bailee in detail. The warehouseman may terminate the relation by notification where, for example, the goods are about to deteriorate or where they constitute a threat to other goods in the warehouse [7–206]. Unless the warehouse receipt provides otherwise, the warehouseman must keep separate the goods covered by each receipt; however, different lots of fungible goods such as grain may be mingled [7–207].

---

[3]Where goods are stored under a field warehouse arrangement, a statement of that fact is sufficient on a nonnegotiable receipt.

A warehouseman has a lien against the bailor on the goods covered by his receipt for his storage and other charges incurred in handling the goods [7–209]. The Code sets out a detailed procedure for enforcing this lien [7–210].

Bills of Lading

In many respects, the rights and liabilities of the parties to a negotiable bill of lading are the same as the rights and liabilities of the parties to a negotiable warehouse receipt. The contract of the issuer of a bill of lading is to transport goods, whereas the contract of the issuer of a warehouse receipt is to store goods. Like the issuer of a warehouse receipt, the issuer of a bill of lading is liable for nonreceipt or misdescription of the goods, but he may protect himself from liability where he does not know the contents of packages by marking the bill of lading "contents or condition of packages unknown" or similar language. Such terms are ineffective when the goods are loaded by an issuer who is a common carrier unless the goods are concealed by packages [7–301].

Duty of Care

A carrier who issues a bill of lading, or a warehouse operator who issues a warehouse receipt, must exercise the same degree of care in relation to the goods as a reasonably careful person would exercise under similar circumstances. Liability for damages not caused by the negligence of the carrier may be imposed on him by a special law or rule of law. Under tariff rules, a common carrier may limit her liability to a shipper's declaration of value, provided that the rates are dependent on value [7–309]. In the case that follows, *Calvin Klein Ltd. v. Trylon Trucking Corp.,* a court enforced a $50 per shipment limitation that had been part of a long series of shipping contracts where the customer had the opportunity to declare a higher value and failed to do so.

CALVIN KLEIN LTD. v. TRYLON TRUCKING CORP.

892 F.2d 191 (2d Cir. 1989)

Trylon Trucking Corporation is a New Jersey trucking firm that engaged in the business of transporting goods from New York City's airports for delivery to its customers' facilities. For three years prior to 1986, Calvin Klein, a New York clothing company, used the services of Trylon involving hundreds of shipments. Calvin Klein, through its customs broker, would contact Trylon to pick up the shipment from the airport for delivery to Calvin Klein's facility. After completing the delivery carriage, Trylon would forward to Calvin Klein an invoice, which contained a limitation of liability provision as follows:

In consideration of the rate charged, the shipper agrees that the carrier shall not be liable for more than $50.00 on any shipment accepted for delivery to one consignee unless a greater value is declared, in writing, upon receipt at time of shipment and charge for such greater value paid, or agreed to be paid, by the shipper.

A shipment of 2,833 blouses from Hong Kong arrived at John F. Kennedy International Airport for Calvin Klein on March 27, 1986. Calvin Klein arranged for Trylon to pick up the shipment and deliver it to Calvin Klein's New Jersey warehouse. On April 2, Trylon dispatched its driver, J. Jefferson, to pick up this shipment. Jefferson signed a receipt for the shipment from Calvin Klein's broker. Later, on April 2, the parties discovered that Jefferson had stolen Trylon's truck and its shipment. The shipment was never recovered.

Calvin Klein sent a claim letter to Trylon for the full value of the lost blouses. When it did not receive a response from Trylon, Calvin Klein filed suit against Trylon, seeking to recover $150,000, the alleged value of the blouses. In the pleadings before the court, the parties agreed that Trylon was liable to Calvin Klein for the loss of the shipment and that it had been grossly negligent in the hiring and supervision of Jefferson. They also agreed that "the terms and conditions of Trylon's carriage were that liability for loss or damage to cargo is limited to $50 in accordance with the provision in Trylon's invoice forms." Calvin Klein conceded that it was aware of the limitation of liability and that it did not declare a value on the blouses at the time of shipment.

Trylon contended that its liability was limited to $50 in accordance with the provision in its invoice forms. Calvin Klein argued that the limitation clause was not enforceable for two reasons: (1) no agreement existed between it and Trylon as to the limitation of liability; and (2) even if an agreement existed, public policy would prevent its enforcement because of Trylon's gross negligence. The district court held that Calvin Klein had not assented to the limitation clause for this shipment and awarded damages to Calvin Klein of $101,542.62. Trylon appealed.

Miner, Circuit Judge.   A common carrier is strictly liable for the loss of goods in its custody. Where the loss is not due to excepted causes [that is, act of God or public enemy, inherent nature of goods, or shipper's fault], it is immaterial whether the carrier was negligent or not. Even in the case of loss from theft by third parties, liability may be imposed upon a negligent common carrier.

A shipper and a common carrier may contract to limit the carrier's liability in cases of loss to an amount agreed to by the parties, so long as the language of the limitation is clear, the shipper is aware of the terms of the limitation, and the shipper can change the terms by indicating the true value of the goods being shipped. Section 7–309(2). Such a limitation agreement is generally valid and enforceable despite carrier negligence. The limitation of liability provision involved here clearly provides that, at the time of delivery, the shipper may increase the limitation by written notice of the value of the goods to be delivered and by payment of a commensurately higher fee.

The parties stipulated to the fact that the $50 limitation of liability was a term and condition of carriage and that Calvin Klein was aware of that limitation. This stipulated fact removes the first issue, namely whether an agreement existed as to a liability limitation between the parties. Calvin Klein's argument that it never previously acknowledged this limitation by accepting only $50 in settlement of a larger loss does not alter this explicit stipulation. The district court erred in not accepting the limitation of liability as stipulated.

The remaining issue concerns the enforceability of the limitation clause in the light of Trylon's conceded gross negligence.

Since carriers are strictly liable for loss of shipments in their custody and are insurers of those goods, the degree of carrier negligence is immaterial. The common carrier must exercise reasonable care in relation to the shipment in its custody. Section 7–309(2). Carriers can contract with their shipping customers on the amount of liability each party will bear for the loss of a shipment, regardless of the amount of carrier negligence. Unlike a merchant acquiring a burglar alarm, the shipper can calculate the specific amount of its potential damages in advance, declare the value of the shipment based on that calculation, can pay a commensurately higher rate to carry the goods, in effect buying additional insurance from the common carrier.

In this case Calvin Klein and Trylon were business entities with an on-going commercial relationship involving numerous carriages of Calvin Klein goods by Trylon. Where such entities deal with each other in a commercial setting, and no special relationship exists between the parties, clear limitations between them will be enforced. Here, each carriage was under the same terms and conditions as the last, including a limitation of Trylon's liability. This is not a case in which the shipper was dealing with the common carrier for the first time or contracting under new or changed conditions. Calvin Klein was aware of the terms and was free to adjust the limitation upon a written declaration of the value of a given shipment, but failed to do so with the shipment at issue here. Since Calvin Klein failed to adjust the limitation, the limitation applies here, and no public policy that dictates otherwise can be identified.

Calvin Klein also argues that the limitation is so low as to be void. The amount is immaterial because Calvin Klein had the opportunity to negotiate the amount of coverage by declaring the value of the shipment. Commercial entities can easily negotiate the degree of risk each party will bear and which party will bear the cost of insurance. Calvin Klein had the opportunity to declare a higher value and we find all of its arguments relating to the unreasonableness of the limitation to be without merit.

District court judgment reversed with instructions to enter judgment for Calvin Klein for $50.

Negotiation of Document of Title

A negotiable document of title and a negotiable instrument are negotiated in substantially the same manner. If the document of title provides for the delivery of the goods to bearer, it may be negotiated by delivery. If it provides for delivery of the goods to the order of a named person, it must be indorsed by that person and delivered. If an order document of title is indorsed in blank, it may be negotiated by delivery unless it bears a special indorsement following the blank indorsement, in which event it must be indorsed by the special indorsee and delivered [7–501].

A person taking a negotiable document of title takes as a bona fide holder if she takes in good faith and in the regular course of business. The bona fide holder of a negotiable document of title has substantially the same advantages over a holder who is not a bona fide holder or over a holder of a nonnegotiable document of title as does a holder in due course of a negotiable instrument over a holder who is not a holder in due course or over a holder of a nonnegotiable instrument.

Rights Acquired by Negotiation

A person who acquires a negotiable document of title by due negotiation acquires (1) title to the document, (2) title to the goods, (3) the right to the goods delivered to the bailee after the issuance of the document, and (4) the direct obligation of the issuer to hold or deliver the goods according to the terms of the document [7–502(1)].

Under the broad general principle that a person cannot transfer title to goods he does not own, a thief—or the owner of goods subject to a perfected security interest—cannot, by warehousing or shipping the goods on a negotiable document of title and then negotiating the document of title, transfer to the purchaser of the document of title a better title than he has [7–503].

Warranties of Transferor of Document of Title

The transferor of a negotiable document of title warrants to his immediate transferee, in addition to any warranty of goods, only that the document is genuine, that he has no knowledge of any facts that would impair its validity or worth, and that his negotiation or transfer is rightful and fully effective with respect to the title to the document and the goods it represents [7–507].

ETHICAL AND PUBLIC POLICY CONCERNS

1. Suppose you take your car to a garage to have it repainted. When you go to pick it up, you are not happy with the quality of the work, but the garage owner refuses to release the car to you unless you pay him in full for the work. You give him a check in the amount requested, and on the way home stop at your bank and request that the bank stop payment on the check you have just written, an action you decided to take when you were writing out the check. Have you acted ethically?

2. Some banks take the position that because they process checks with the use of computers, a customer seeking to stop payment on a check must provide them with the amount of the check with every digit correct in order for the bank to be able to stop payment. What policy considerations are involved in deciding whether the bank's position should establish the minimum information required for a bank to have a "reasonable opportunity" to respond to the customer's request?

3. Suppose that you own and operate a warehouse. A local liquor store owner occasionally uses your facilities to store shipments of wine from France until he has room for the wine in his store. You are aware that from time to time your warehouse employees "borrow" a bottle from the crates of wine being stored in your warehouse. After a number of crates with a total of four bottles missing are delivered to the liquor store, the store owner queries you about the missing bottles and you tell him that they must have been broken in transit to your warehouse. Have you acted ethically?

SUMMARY

The relationship between a bank and a customer having a commercial account on which checks may be drawn is

that of debtor and creditor and principal and agent. In drawing a check, the customer authorizes the bank to honor the check. The bank is under an obligation to pay all properly drawn checks, provided that the funds in the account are sufficient to cover the checks. A bank may pay a check even if doing so creates an overdraft. A bank does not owe a duty to pay stale checks—those over six months old—but it may do so in good faith.

The customer has the right to order the bank to stop payment on a check that has not been certified, and if the order to stop payment is received by the bank at such a time and in such form as to give it a reasonable opportunity to do so, the bank owes a duty to refuse payment on the check. If the bank pays a check in disregard of a valid stop-payment order, it is liable to the drawer for any direct and consequential damages.

A bank is not obligated to certify a check, but on certification the bank becomes primarily liable on the check and, if the check has been certified at the request of the holder, the drawer and all prior indorsers are discharged. A bank may pay checks drawn during a customer's lifetime or while the customer is competent and for a period of 10 days after the customer's death or until the bank learns of an adjudication of incompetence.

Checks that have forged drawer's or payee's signatures and checks that have been materially altered are generally not properly chargeable to a customer's account. However, if the drawer is negligent and contributes to the forgery or alteration, she may be barred from claiming it as the reason that a particular item should not be charged to her account.

A customer owes a duty to report to the bank, within a reasonable time after a statement of account and canceled checks have been made available, any unauthorized signatures and alterations. Forged drawer's signatures and alterations must in any event be reported within one year, and unauthorized indorsements within three years, or the drawer cannot require that his account be recredited.

When a bank takes a check for deposit to a customer's account, it typically places a hold on the funds in the account represented by the deposited check because it runs a number of risks in allowing a customer to withdraw deposits that have not been finally collected from the drawee bank. The extensive use of holds, and a growing public sentiment that they were excessive and often unfair, led to the passage by Congress in 1987 of the Expedited Funds Availability Act. In the act, Congress set out mandatory schedules limiting check holds and specifying when funds are to be made available to customers by depositary institutions.

Increasingly, banks are encouraging their customers to transfer funds electronically and automated teller machines are now commonplace. The Electronic Funds Transfer Act, enacted by Congress in 1978, establishes the rights, liabilities, and reponsibilities of the participants in electronic funds transfer systems.

The warehouseman or common carrier is a bailee of goods, and he contracts to store or transport them. The warehouse receipt or bill of lading may be either negotiable or nonnegotiable. If the warehouse receipt issued by the warehouseman omits in its written or printed terms the information required under the provisions of the Code, the warehouseman is liable to a purchaser in good faith of a warehouse receipt for failure to describe the goods or for their misdescription. He owes to the holder of a warehouse receipt the duties of a mutual benefit bailee. The common carrier's liability on a negotiable bill of lading is the same in most respects as that of the issuer of a negotiable warehouse receipt. His liability may be increased by special law or rule.

The rules of law governing the negotiation of a negotiable document of title are the same in most respects as the rules of law governing the negotiation of negotiable commercial paper. In general, a holder by due negotiation of a negotiable document of title gets good title to the document and the goods and the contractual rights against the bailee. However, a thief or an owner of goods subject to a valid security interest cannot, by warehousing or shipping the goods on a negotiable document of title and negotiating it, pass to the transferee greater rights in the goods than she has. A holder who transfers a negotiable document of title warrants to his immediate transferee that the document is genuine, that he has no knowledge of any facts that would impair its validity or worth, and that his transfer is rightful and fully effective.

PROBLEM CASES

1. J. E. B. Stewart received a check in the amount of $185.48 in payment of a fee from a client. Stewart presented the check, properly indorsed, to the Citizen's & Southern Bank. The bank refused to cash the check even though there were sufficient funds in the drawer's account. Stewart then sued the bank for actual damages of

$185.48 and for punitive damages of $50,000 for its failure to cash a valid check drawn against a solvent account in the bank. Does Stewart have a good cause of action against the bank? *Yes!. bank has duty to pay*

2. Fitting wrote a check for $800 and gave it to the payee. She then had second thoughts about the check. She contacted the bank at which she had her checking account about the possibility of stopping payment on the check. A bank employee told her she could not file a stop-payment order until the bank opened the next morning. The next morning Fitting did not file a stop-payment order. Instead, she withdrew money from her account so that less than $800 remained in it. She believed the bank would not pay the $800 check if there were not sufficient funds in the account to cover it. However, the bank paid the check and created an overdraft in Fitting's account. The bank then sued Fitting to recover the amount of the overdraft. Can the bank pay Fitting's check even if doing so creates an overdraft in her checking account? *Yes. Bank can at its will pay a check even though it creates an overdraft*

3. On July 2, 1982, Staff Services Associates issued a check drawn on Midlantic National Bank payable to Lynn A. Gross for the sum of $4,117.12. On July 7, 1982, John Tracy, the president of Staff Services, executed a stop-payment order to Midlantic and incorrectly wrote the amount of the check as $4,117.72, an error of one digit. At the time, Tracy saw the statement at the bottom of the stop-payment order, which read:

IMPORTANT: The information on this Stop Payment Order must be correct, including the exact amount of the check to the penny, or the Bank will not be able to stop payment and this Stop Payment Order will be void.

As a result of the incorrect information provided by Tracy, the wrong amount was programmed in Midlantic's computer. When the check was presented for payment, it was paid, and the bank charged it to Staff Service's account. Staff Services then brought suit against Midlantic for wrongful payment of the check in violation of the stop-payment order. Was Midlantic justified in paying the check over the stop-payment order because of the one-digit error in the stop-payment order? *No! Error in amt can still make Bank Liable*

4. John Doe had a checking account at Highland National Bank in New York. Two days after John Doe died in Florida, but before Highland National knew of his death, John's sister appeared at the bank. She had a check signed by John Doe, but with the amount and the payee's name left blank. She told the bank her brother wanted to close his account. She asked how much was in the account, filled the check in for that amount, and made the check payable to herself. The bank checked her identification and verified the signature of John Doe. Then it paid the check to the sister. The executor of John Doe's estate later sued Highland National to recover the amount of money that was in John's account on the day that he died. The executor claimed that the bank had no authority to pay checks from John Doe's account after his death. Is the executor correct?

5. Winkie, Inc., maintained a checking account at the Heritage Bank of Whitefish Bay. Although several persons were authorized to sign Winkie checks, W. J. Winkie, Jr., the company's president, was the only person who ever signed checks drawn on the Winkie account. Doris Britton, a secretarial employee of Winkie, recorded invoices for supplies and services rendered to the company and presented the invoices and checks drawn on the account in payment of the invoices to W. J. Winkie, Jr., for review of the invoices and execution of the checks. In the years 1965 to 1973, Britton forged the signature of W. J. Winkie, Jr., to hundreds of checks totaling $148,171.30 drawn on the Winkie, Inc., account. In addition to forging the signature of W. J. Winkie, Jr., Britton forged the indorsements of the payee on many of the checks. None of the payees of the checks supplied the services or materials to Winkie, Inc., for which the forged checks were payment. Winkie, Inc., neither intended payment nor received benefit of any kind by reason of the issuance of the checks. Britton directly or indirectly received all the proceeds of the forged checks. In 1973, after approximately eight years of repeated forgeries, W. J. Winkie, Jr., discovered a forged check and immediately notified the bank. During the eight-year period, W. J. Winkie, Jr., did not personally examine the Winkie checks or reconcile the bank statements of the account. Another Winkie, Inc., employee, not alleged to be involved in the systematic forgeries, was assigned those duties. Winkie, Inc., utilized the services of a certified public accountant, but those services did not expressly include bank statement reconciliation or an audit. Thus, the bank account examination and reconciliation were left to a single, unsupervised Winkie employee. Winkie brought an action against the Heritage Bank to have its account recredited for the checks that had been forged by the Winkie employee and paid by the bank. Should the Heritage Bank be required to recredit the Winkie account for the amount of the checks that contained forged drawer's and payee's signatures?

6. Jensen opened a checking account at the Essexbank on January 7, 1981, with a deposit of $7,500 to facilitate payment of bills from the sale of his business. Although he signed a bank form in which he designated himself as the sole signatory of the account, he directed the bank to send all bank statements and bank checks to his attorney. From time to time, he would request his attorney to send him blank checks for his use. A check for $5,000 was drawn on Jensen's account on April 17, 1981, and a check for $500 was drawn on the account on July 1, 1981. Both checks were payable to the order of his attorney; neither had been signed by Jensen but someone else had signed his name. In August 1981, Jensen tried to cash a check drawn on the account and was told the account was overdrawn. He tried without success to reach his attorney to obtain copies of his statements. In 1982, Jensen's attorney was disbarred from the practice of law. On July 9, 1983, Jensen notified the Essexbank that his signature had been forged on the $5,000 and $500 checks. He sought to have his account recredited for $5,500. Is the Essexbank required to recredit his account for the amount of the checks containing a forged drawer's signature?

7. In 1982, Hirsch Food Company began storing cases of its pickles in a warehouse owned by Overmyer Company. Later that year, Overmyer began shutting down its warehouse operation and reduced its staff to one man who came to the warehouse only when Hirsch Company desired to remove some pickles. In 1983, when the last of the pickles were removed, 900 cases were missing. Where does the liability for the missing pickles lie? On what does it depend?

8. Griswold and Bateman Warehouse Company stored 337 cases of Chivas Regal Scotch Whiskey for Joseph H. Reinfeld, Inc., in its bonded warehouse. The warehouse receipt issued to Reinfeld limited Griswold and Bateman's liability for negligence to 250 times the monthly storage rate, a total of $1,925. When Reinfeld sent its truck to pick up the whiskey, 40 cases were missing. Reinfeld then brought suit seeking the wholesale market value of the whiskey, $6,417.60. Reinfeld presented evidence of the delivery of the whiskey, the demand for its return, and the failure of Griswold and Bateman to return it. Reinfeld claimed that the burden was on Griswold and Bateman to explain the disappearance of the whiskey. Griswold and Bateman admitted that it had been negligent, but sought to limit its liability to $1,925. Is Griswold and Bateman's liability limited to $1,925?

9. Everlens Mitchell entered into a written contract with All American Van & Storage to transport and store her household goods. She was to pay the storage charges on a monthly basis. As security, she granted All American a warehouseman's lien. All American had the right to sell the property if the charges remained unpaid for three months and if, in the opinion of the company, such action was necessary to protect the accrued charges. Mitchell fell eight months behind on her payments. On October 20, 1985, she received notice that if the unpaid charges, totaling $804.30, were not paid by October 31, her goods would be sold on November 7. Mitchell advised All American that she had a claim pending with the Social Security Administration and would soon receive a large sum of money. This was confirmed to All American by several government officials. However, All American sold Mitchell's property on November 7 for $925.50. At the end of the month, Mitchell received a $5,500 disability payment. She sued All American for improperly selling her goods. The trial court awarded judgment to All American. Should the decision be reversed on appeal?

10. On October 15, Young delivered 207 bags of rice to Atteberry's warehouse and received a nonnegotiable receipt. Young then transferred the receipt to Brock for a valuable consideration, and Brock notified Atteberry of the transfer on November 3. Prior to November 3, however, Young had procured a negotiable receipt for the rice along with some other rice he had deposited with Atteberry. Now Brock presents his nonnegotiable receipt to Atteberry and demands delivery of the rice. Atteberry contends that no rice is being held at the warehouse on Brock's account. Who is correct?

PART VIII

AGENCY LAW

CHAPTER 34

THE AGENCY RELATIONSHIP

INTRODUCTION

The Significance of Agency Law

In this text you encounter situations where businesses are legally bound by the actions of their employees or other representatives. For example, corporations frequently are liable on contracts their employees make or for torts those employees commit. We tend to take such liability for granted, but it is not immediately obvious why we should do so. A corporation is an artificial legal person distinct from the officers, employees, and other representatives who contract on its behalf and who may commit torts while performing their duties. Similarly, a sole proprietor is distinct from the people he may employ. How can corporations, sole proprietors, and other business actors be bound on contracts they did not make or for torts they did not commit? The reason is the law of **agency.**

Agency is a two-party relationship in which one party (the **agent**) is authorized to act on behalf of, and under the control of, the other party (the **principal**). Simple examples of the agency relation include hiring a salesperson to sell goods, retaining an attorney, and engaging a real estate broker to sell a house. Agency law's most important social function is to stimulate business and commercial activity. It does so by allowing people and businesses to increase the number of transactions that they can complete within a given time. Without agency, business and commercial life would proceed at a slow pace. A sole proprietor's ability to engage in trade would be limited by the need to make each of her purchase or sales contracts in person. As artificial persons, corporations can act *only* through their agents.

Topic Coverage and Organization

Agency law can be divided into two rough categories. The first involves the legal rules that control relations *between the principal and the agent*—including the rules governing formation of the agency relation, the duties the principal and the agent owe each other, and the ways that an agency can be terminated. Such topics and the principal's and the agent's liability on contracts made by the agent and for torts committed by the agent are this chapter's main concerns. The next chapter discusses the principal's and the agent's relations with *third parties.*

CREATION OF AN AGENCY AND RELATED MATTERS

Formation

An agency is created by the manifested agreement of two persons that one person (the agent) shall act for the benefit of the other (the principal) under the principal's direction.[1] As the term *manifested* suggests, the test for the existence of an agency is *objective*. If the parties' behavior and the surrounding facts and circumstances indicate an agreement that one person is to act for the benefit and under the control of another, courts hold that the relationship exists. If the facts establish an agency, it is immaterial whether either party knows of the agency's existence or subjectively desires that it exist. In fact, the agency relationship may be present even where the parties have expressly stated that they do not intend to create it, or intend to create some other legal relationship instead.

Often, parties create an agency by a written contract (sometimes called a *power of attorney*). But an agency contract may be oral unless state law provides otherwise.[2] Some states, for example, require written evidence of contracts to pay an agent a commission for the sale of real estate. More importantly, the agency relation need not be contractual at all. Thus, consideration is not necessary to form an agency. As the following *Warren v. United States* case illustrates, courts sometimes imply an agency from the parties' behavior and the surrounding

circumstances without discussing the need for a contract or for consideration.

Capacity

A principal or agent who lacks the necessary mental capacity at the time the agency is formed ordinarily can release himself from the agency at his option. Examples include those who are minors or who are insane when the agency is created. Of course, incapacity may occur or exist at other times as well; at various points in this and the next chapter, we discuss its effect in such cases.

As you have seen, business organizations such as corporations can and must appoint agents. In a partnership, each partner normally acts as the agent of the partnership in transacting partnership business, and partnerships can appoint nonpartner agents as well.[3] In addition, corporations, partnerships, and other business organizations themselves can act as agents.

Nondelegable Obligations

Certain duties or acts cannot be delegated by a principal to an agent. This means that the principal must perform such duties or acts personally. For example, making statements under oath, voting in public elections, and the signing of a will cannot be delegated to an agent. The same is true for service contracts in which the principal's personal performance is crucial. Examples include certain contracts by lawyers, doctors, artists, and entertainers.

---

[1]Sometimes it is said that an agency may also be created by ratification, estoppel, or operation of law. Usually, however, ratification and estoppel are regarded as ways of binding the principal to an agent's actions, not as ways of forming an agency in the first place. Ratification is discussed in the following chapter, and estoppel resembles the concept of apparent authority discussed later in this chapter and in the next. It is uncommon for an agency to be created by operation of law. An example might be a state statute designating the state's secretary of state as an out-of-state motorist's "agent" for purposes of receiving a summons and a complaint in a lawsuit against the motorist.

[2]Usually, the state law in question is the state's statute of frauds. On the statute of frauds, see the Writing chapter. Also, it is sometimes said that if the contract the agent is to form must be in writing, the agency agreement likewise must be written. However, it is doubtful whether this "equal dignity rule" enjoys widespread acceptance.

---

[3]See the Operation of Partnership and Related Forms chapter for a discussion of how agency law operates in the partnership context.

WARREN v. UNITED STATES

613 F.2d 591 (5th Cir. 1980)

Bobby and Modell Warren were cotton growers. For two years, they took their cotton crops to certain cotton gins that ginned and baled the cotton. Then, after being instructed to do so by the Warrens, the gins obtained bids for the cotton from prospective buyers and the Warrens told the gins which bids to accept. The gins sold the cotton to the designated buyers, collecting the proceeds. At the Warrens' instruction, the gins deferred payment of the proceeds to the Warrens until the year after the one in which each sale was made.

The Warrens did not report the proceeds as taxable income for the year when the gins received the proceeds, instead including the proceeds in the return for the following year. After an IRS audit, the Warrens were compelled to treat the proceeds as taxable income for the year when the proceeds were received, and to pay accordingly. The Warrens eventually won a refund action in federal district court. The government appealed. Its position was that: (1) the gins were agents of the Warrens; and (2) because of the established rule that receipt of proceeds by an agent is receipt by the principal, the proceeds were taxable income for the year in which they were received by the gins.

Johnson, Circuit Judge.   The relationship between the Warrens and the gins for the purpose of selling the cotton was indisputably that of principal and agent. The Warrens instructed the gins to solicit bids, the Warrens decided whether to accept the highest price offered, and the Warrens determined whether or not to instruct the gins to hold the proceeds from the sale until the following year. The gins' role in the sale of the cotton was to adhere to the Warrens' instructions. The Warrens were the owners of the cotton held for sale; the Warrens were in complete control of its disposition.

This case is distinguishable from those cases where it was recognized that proceeds from the sale of a crop by a farmer, pursuant to a bona fide arm's-length contract between the buyer and seller calling for payment in the taxable year following delivery, are includable in gross income for the taxable year in which payment is received. In the case at bar the bona fide arm's-length agreement was not between the buyer and seller but rather between the seller and his agent. The income was received by the Warrens' agents in the year of the sale. The fact that the Warrens restricted their access to the sales proceeds does not change the tax status of the money received.

Judgment reversed in favor of the government.

AGENCY CONCEPTS, DEFINITIONS, AND TYPES

In its development, agency law has come to include various concepts, definitions, and distinctions. As you will see in this chapter and the next chapter, these matters often determine the rights, duties, and liabilities of the principal, the agent, and third parties. In addition, they sometimes are important outside agency law. Because these basic topics are so crucial in so many different contexts, we outline them together here.

Authority

As you have seen, agency law allows principals to multiply their dealings by employing agents to represent them. Presumably, however, a principal should not be liable for *any* deal that his agent concludes. Thus, agency law generally allows the agent to bind the principal only when the agent has **authority** to do so.

The *Restatement (Second) of Agency* defines authority as the agent's ability to affect the principal's legal relations with third parties.[4] Authority comes in two general forms: **actual authority** and **apparent authority.** Each is based on the principal's manifested consent that the agent may act for and bind the principal. For actual authority this consent is communicated to the *agent*, while for apparent authority it is communicated to the *third party*.

The two kinds of actual authority are **express authority** and **implied authority.** Express authority is created by the principal's actual *words* (whether written or oral). Thus, an agent has express authority to bind a principal only when the principal has made a fairly precise statement to that effect. Often, however, it is impractical or impossible for a principal to specify the agent's authority fully and exactly. To avoid unnecessary

---

[4]See *Restatement (Second) of Agency* sections 7–8 (1959).

restrictions on an agent's ability to represent her principal, therefore, agency law also gives agents *implied authority* to bind their principals. In general, an agent has implied authority to do whatever it is reasonable to assume that the principal wanted him to do, given the principal's express statements and the surrounding circumstances. Courts seeking to determine an agent's implied authority typically examine matters such as the principal's express statements, the nature of the agency, the acts reasonably necessary to carry on the agency business, and the acts customarily done when conducting that business.

Sometimes, an agent who lacks express or implied authority may still *appear* to have such authority, and third parties may reasonably rely on this appearance of authority. To protect the third party in such situations, agency law allows agents to bind the principal on the basis of their *apparent authority.* Apparent authority arises when the principal's behavior causes a third party to form a reasonable belief that the agent is authorized to act for the principal. Note that apparent authority is based on what the *principal* communicates to the third party; this may occur either directly or through the agent. Thus, a principal might clothe an agent with apparent authority by making direct statements to the third party, telling the agent to do so, or allowing the agent to behave in a way that creates an appearance of authority. Communications to the agent generally are irrelevant unless they become known to the third party or affect the agent's behavior. Also, agents cannot give themselves apparent authority, and apparent authority does not exist where the agent creates an appearance of authority without the principal's consent. Finally, note that the third party must *reasonably* believe that the agent has authority. Trade customs and business practices can help courts determine whether there was reason to believe that the agent had authority.

Authority is important in a number of legal contexts, and we discuss its specific applications in those contexts. As you will see in the next chapter, for example, a principal's liability on contracts made by his agent usually depends on the agent's authority to make the contract in question. Moreover, a proper grant of authority is needed to create the relation of *subagency* described below. As discussed later in the chapter, the agent's authority also helps determine when the principal has a duty to reimburse or indemnify the agent. Finally, the concept of authority also assumes importance in various situations outside agency law. To take just one example, the chapter on the FTC Act and other consumer protection

laws discusses how the federal Truth in Lending Act limits a credit card holder's liability for unauthorized use of the card to $50. The act does so by effectively defining unauthorized use as use by someone who lacks express, implied, or apparent authority to use the card.

General and Special Agents

Although it may be falling out of favor with the courts, the blurred distinction between general and special agents still has some importance in agency law. A **general agent** is an agent *continuously* employed to conduct a series of transactions, while a **special agent** is an agent employed to conduct a single transaction or a small, simple group of transactions. Thus, a continuously employed general manager, construction project supervisor, or purchasing agent normally is a general agent; and a person employed to buy or sell a few objects on a one-shot basis usually is a special agent. In addition to being employed on a continuous basis, general agents often serve for longer periods, perform more acts, and deal with more parties than do special agents.

Gratuitous Agents

Earlier, you saw that consideration is not necessary for the creation of an agency. An agent who receives no compensation for his services is called a **gratuitous agent.** Gratuitous agents have the same power to bind their principals as do paid agents with the same authority. As discussed later in this chapter, however, the fact that the agent is gratuitous sometimes lowers the duties the principal and the agent owe each other, and also may increase the parties' ability to terminate the agency without incurring liability.

Subagents

A **subagent** basically is the agent of an agent. More precisely, a subagent is a person appointed by an agent to perform functions that the agent has undertaken to perform for his principal. For a subagency to exist, the agent must have the authority to make the subagent *his agent* for conducting the principal's business. If you retain an accounting firm as your agent, for example, the accountant actually handling your affairs is the firm's agent and your subagent. Sometimes, however, a party appointed by an agent is not a subagent because the appointing agent only had authority to appoint agents *for the principal*. For instance, sales agents appointed by a corporation's sales manager probably are agents of the corporation, not agents of the sales manager.

When an agent appoints a true subagent, the agent becomes a principal with respect to the subagent, his agent. Thus, the legal relations between agent and subagent closely parallel the legal relations between principal and agent. But the subagent is also the *original principal's* agent. Here, though, the normal rules governing principals and agents do not always apply. We occasionally refer to such situations in the pages ahead.

Employees and Independent Contractors

Many important legal questions hinge on a distinction between two relationships that overlap with the principal-agent relationship. These are an employer's (or master's) relationship with his **employee** (or servant), and a principal's relationship with an **independent contractor.** No sharp line separates these two relationships; the *VIP Tours* case that follows lists the factors often considered in making such determinations. By far the most important of these factors is the principal's *right to control the physical details of the work.* Employees typically are subject to such control. Independent contractors, on the other hand, generally contract with the principal to produce some result, and determine for themselves how that result will be accomplished.

Although many employees perform physical labor or are paid on an hourly basis, corporate officers also usually qualify as employees. Professionals such as brokers, accountants, and attorneys often are independent con-

tractors, although they may sometimes be employees. Consider the difference between a corporation represented by an attorney engaged in her own practice and a corporation that maintains a staff of salaried in-house attorneys. Franchisees, finally, usually are independent contractors.

When are employees and independent contractors agents? Although there is little consensus on this question, the *Restatement* position is clear, and we follow it in this text. According to the *Restatement*, employees are *always* agents, while independent contractors *may or may not* be agents.[5] An independent contractor qualifies as an agent when the basic tests for the existence of an agency—most importantly, sufficient control by the principal—are met. Figure 1 sketches the *Restatement's* position on the relationships among agents, employees, and independent contractors. In the *Warren* case, for example, the cotton gins probably were agent-independent contractors, while the cotton buyers discussed at the end of the opinion probably were nonagent-independent contractors.

As you will see in the next chapter, the employee-independent contractor distinction often is crucial in determining the principal's liability for an agent's torts. The distinction also can be important in defining the coverage of some of the employment regulations discussed in the Employment Law chapter. Unemployment compensation (the subject of *VIP Tours*) and workers' compensation are two clear examples.

[5]*Restatement (Second) of Agency* sections 2, 14N, 25, and the Introductory Note following section 218 (1959).

FIGURE 1   Agents, Employees, and Independent Contractors as the *Restatement* Sees Them

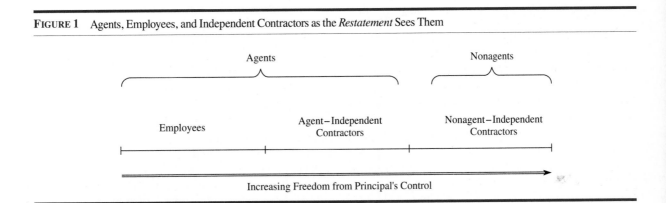

VIP TOURS, INC. v. FLORIDA

449 So. 2d 1307 (Fla. Ct. App. 1984)

VIP Tours, Inc., arranged tours of central Florida's attractions for visitors to the area. Cynthia Hoogland conducted 29 such tours for VIP between July 1980 and March 1981. Both Hoogland and VIP considered Hoogland an independent contractor. She worked for VIP only when it needed her services, and could reject particular assignments. She was also free to work for other tour services, and did so.

Once Hoogland accepted a job from VIP, she was told where to report and was given instructions about the job. She was also required to use a VIP-furnished vehicle and to wear a uniform with the VIP logo when conducting tours. Aside from ensuring that she departed on time, however, VIP did not tell her how long to stay or what kind of tour to conduct at each tourist attraction. Finally, Hoogland was paid on a per tour basis.

Hoogland later filed a claim for unemployment compensation benefits with the Florida Division of Labor and Employment Security. The division concluded that she was entitled to these benefits because she was VIP Tours' employee. VIP appealed the division's order to an intermediate appellate court.

Upchurch, Judge.   The [Florida] Supreme Court has approved the test set out in *Restatement (Second) of Agency* section 220 for determining whether one is an employee or an independent contractor:

In determining whether one acting for another is a servant or an independent contractor, the following matters of fact, among others, are considered:

(a) the extent of control which, by the agreement, the master may exercise over the details of the work;

(b) whether or not the one employed is engaged in a distinct occupation or business;

(c) the kind of occupation, with reference to whether, in the locality, the work is usually done under the direction of the employer or by a specialist without supervision;

(d) the skill required in the particular occupation;

(e) whether the employer or the workman supplies the instrumentalities, tools, and the place of work for the person doing the work;

(f) the length of time for which the person is employed;

(g) the method of payment, whether by the time or by the job;

(h) whether or not the work is part of the regular business of the employer;

(i) whether or not the parties believe that they are creating the relationship of master and servant; and

(j) whether the principal is or is not in business.

It has been said repeatedly that of all the factors, the right of control as to the mode of doing the work is the principal consideration.

VIP had no right of control over the tour guides other than to require them to show up at a particular place at a particular time wearing the VIP uniform and to travel in VIP transportation. These latter two factors appear to have been designed to facilitate identification of the guide and control insurance liability. VIP had little interest in the details of the guides' work, as is illustrated by the fact that the guides controlled the number of hours spent at a particular attraction and the nature of the tour at each exhibit. In addition, the guides were free to contract with other tour companies, as Hoogland did, and could accept or reject any assignment, factors further indicating a lack of control by VIP. Other factors set out in the *Restatement* also point toward independent contractor status here. The tour guides were engaged in a distinct occupation. They worked and were paid on a per-job basis. Both VIP and Hoogland considered the guides to be independent contractors.

Division order reversed.

DUTIES OF AGENT TO PRINCIPAL

Introduction

An agency normally is created by contract. Where this is so, the agent must perform according to the terms of the agreement and normal contract rules regarding interpretation, performance, and remedies apply. Also, regardless of whether the relationship is contractual, agency law establishes certain *fiduciary duties* owed by the agent to the principal. These duties exist because agency is a relationship of trust and confidence. They supplement the duties created by an agency contract. Often, however, the parties may eliminate or modify the fiduciary duties by agreement if they so desire.

Except for certain specific situations noted later, a *gratuitous agent* has the same fiduciary duties as a paid agent. But this is true only so long as a gratuitous agent continues to act as an agent. In other words, a gratuitous agent is not obligated to perform as promised, he normally can terminate the agency without incurring liability, and his fiduciary duties cease once the agency ends. However, a gratuitous agent *is* liable for his failure to perform as promised when his promise causes the principal to rely upon him to undertake certain acts, the principal thus refrains from performing those acts herself, and the principal suffers losses as a result. For example, suppose that the principal refrains from making a bid at an auction because her agent has gratuitously promised to make the bid for her, the agent attends the auction but fails to make the bid, and the bid would have been successful had it been made.

A *subagent* owes the agent (his principal) all the normal duties that agents owe their principals. A subagent who is aware of the original principal's existence also owes that principal all the usual duties agents owe their principals, except for those duties arising solely from the original principal's contract with the agent. Finally, the agent who appointed the subagent generally is responsible to the original principal for a subagent's conduct, and usually must compensate the principal when the principal is harmed by that conduct.

Agent's Duty of Loyalty

Because agency is a relationship of trust and confidence, an agent has a *duty of loyalty* to his principal. Thus, an agent must subordinate personal concerns by: (1) avoiding conflicts of interest with the principal, and (2) not disclosing confidential information received from the principal.

Conflicts of Interest   An agent whose interests conflict with the principal's interests may not be able to represent his principal effectively. When conducting the principal's business, therefore, an agent generally is forbidden to *deal with himself*. For example, an agent authorized to sell property cannot sell that property to himself. This rule often includes an agent's transactions with his relatives or business associates, or with business organizations in which he has an interest. However, an agent may enter into such transactions if the principal consents to his doing so. For this consent to be effective, the agent must disclose all of the relevant facts to the principal before dealing with the principal on his own behalf.

Unless the principal agrees otherwise, an agent also is forbidden to *compete with the principal* regarding the agency business so long as he remains an agent. Thus, an agent employed to purchase specific property may not buy it himself if the principal still desires it. Moreover, an agent may not solicit the principal's customers for a planned competing business while still employed by the principal.

Finally, an agent who is authorized to make a certain transaction cannot *act on behalf of the other party* to the transaction unless the principal knowingly consents to this. Thus, one ordinarily cannot act as agent for both parties to a transaction without first disclosing the double role to, and obtaining the consent of, both principals. Here, the agent has a duty to disclose to each principal all of the factors reasonably affecting each principal's decision. Occasionally, though, an agent who acts as a middleman may serve both parties to a transaction without notifying either. For instance, an agent may simultaneously be employed as a "finder" by a firm seeking suitable businesses to acquire and a firm looking for prospective buyers, so long as neither principal expects the agent to advise it or negotiate for it.

Confidential Information Another facet of the agent's duty of loyalty is the obligation to ensure that the agency relation is one of *confidentiality*. Unless otherwise agreed, an agent has a duty not to *use* or *disclose* confidential information acquired through the agency. Confidential information means facts that are valuable to the principal because they are not widely known, or that would harm the principal's business if they became widely known. Examples include the principal's business plans, financial condition, contract bids, technolog-

ical discoveries, manufacturing methods, customer files, and other trade secrets.[6] However, an agent is free to reveal confidential information that the principal is committing or is about to commit a crime.

Unless there is an agreement to the contrary,[7] an agent is free to compete with her principal after termination of the agency. But as the following *ABKCO* case illustrates, the duty not to use or disclose confidential information still remains.[8] The former agent may, however, utilize general knowledge and skills acquired during the agency.

---

[6] Trade secrets law is discussed in the Intellectual Property, Competitive Torts, and Unfair Competition chapter.

[7] Covenants not to compete are discussed in the contracts chapter on Illegality.

[8] For a discussion of the patent and trade secrets problems that arise when an employee or a former employee tries to utilize ideas, discoveries, or inventions found or created during the course of her employment, see the Intellectual Property, Competitive Torts, and Unfair Competition chapter.

ABKCO MUSIC, INC. v. HARRISONGS MUSIC, LTD.

722 F.2d 988 (2d Cir. 1983)

In 1963, a song called "He's So Fine" was a huge hit in the United States and Great Britain. In February of 1971, Bright Tunes Music Corporation, the copyright holder of "He's So Fine," sued ex-Beatle George Harrison and Harrisongs, Music, Ltd., in federal district court. Bright Tunes claimed that the Harrison composition "My Sweet Lord" infringed its copyright to "He's So Fine." At this time, Harrison's business affairs were handled by ABKCO Music, Inc., and Allen B. Klein, its president. Shortly after the suit began, Klein unsuccessfully tried to settle it by having ABKCO purchase Bright Tunes.

Shortly thereafter, Bright Tunes went into receivership, and it did not resume the suit until 1973. At this time, coincidentally, ABKCO's management contract with Harrison expired. In late 1975 and early 1976, however, Klein continued his efforts to have ABKCO purchase Bright Tunes. As part of these efforts, he gave Bright Tunes three schedules summarizing Harrison's royalty income from "My Sweet Lord," information he possessed because of his previous service to Harrison. Throughout the 1973–76 period, Harrison's attorneys had been trying to settle the copyright infringement suit with Bright Tunes. Because Klein's activities not only gave Bright Tunes information about the economic potential of its suit but also gave it an economic alternative to settling with Harrison, Klein may have impeded Harrison's efforts to settle.

When the copyright infringement suit finally came to trial in 1976, the court found that Harrison had infringed Bright Tunes' copyright. The issue of damages was scheduled for trial at a later date and this trial was delayed for some time. In 1978, ABKCO purchased the "He's So Fine" copyright and all rights to the infringement suit from Bright Tunes. This made ABKCO the plaintiff in the 1979 trial for damages on the infringement suit. At trial, Harrison counterclaimed for damages resulting from Klein's and ABKCO's alleged breaches of the duty of loyalty. Finding a breach of duty, the district judge issued a complex order reducing ABKCO's recovery. ABKCO appealed.

Pierce, Circuit Judge.   The relationship between Harrison and ABKCO prior to termination of the management agreement in 1973 was that of principal and agent. An agent has a duty not to use confidential knowledge acquired in his employment in competition with his principal. This duty exists as well after the employment as during its continuance. On the other hand, use of information based on general business knowledge is not covered by the rule, and the former agent is permitted to compete with his former principal in reliance on such publicly available information. The principal issue before us, then, is whether Klein (hence, ABKCO) improperly used confidential information, gained as Harrison's former agent, in negotiating for the purchase of Bright Tunes' stock in 1975–76.

One aspect of this inquiry concerns the nature of the schedules of "My Sweet Lord" earnings which Klein furnished to Bright Tunes in connection with the 1975–76 negotiations. It appears that at least some of [this] information was confidential. The evidence is not at all convincing that the information was publicly available.

Another aspect of the breach of duty issue concerns the timing and nature of Klein's entry into the negotiation picture and the manner in which he became a plaintiff in this action. We find this case analogous to those where an employee, with the use of information acquired through his former employment, completes for his own benefit a transaction originally undertaken on the former employer's behalf. Klein had commenced a purchase transaction with Bright Tunes in 1971 on behalf of Harrison, which he pursued on his own account after termination of his fiduciary relationship with Harrison. Klein pursued the later discussions armed with the intimate knowledge not only of Harrison's business affairs, but of the value of this lawsuit. Taking all of these circumstances together, we agree that Klein's conduct during the period 1975–78 did not meet the standard required of him as a former fiduciary.

ABKCO also contends that even if there was a breach of duty, such breach should not limit its recovery for copyright infringement because its conduct did not cause the Bright Tunes/Harrison settlement negotiations to fail. ABKCO urges, in essence, that a breach of duty by an agent, to be actionable, must have been the proximate cause of injury to the principal. We do not accept ABKCO's proffered causation standard. An action for breach of duty is a prophylactic rule intended to remove all incentive to breach—not simply to compensate for damages in the event of a breach.

District court decision in favor of Harrison on the breach of duty issue affirmed.

Agent's Duty to Obey Instructions

Because an agent acts under the principal's control and for the principal's benefit, she has a duty to *obey all reasonable instructions* given by the principal for carrying out the agency business. For the reasons suggested earlier, however, a gratuitous agent need not obey his principal's order to continue to act as an agent. Also, agents generally have no duty to obey orders to behave *illegally or unethically.* Thus, a sales agent need not follow directions to misrepresent the quality of the principal's goods and professionals such as attorneys and accountants are not obligated to obey directions that conflict with accepted ethical rules governing their professions.

Agent's Duty to Act with Care and Skill

A paid agent must possess and exercise the degree of *care and skill* that is standard in the locality for the kind of work that the agent is employed to perform. A gratuitous agent need only exercise the degree of care and skill required of nonagents who perform similar gratuitous undertakings for others. Paid agents who represent that they possess a higher-than-customary level of skill may be held to a correspondingly higher standard of performance. Similarly, an agent's duty may change if the principal and the agent agree that the agent must possess and exercise a greater- or lesser-than-customary degree of care and skill.

Agent's Duty to Notify the Principal

An agent has a duty to promptly communicate to the principal matters within his knowledge that are reasonably relevant to the agency business and that he knows or should know are of concern to the principal. As the following *Levin* case suggests, this *duty to notify* sometimes is treated as one facet of the duty to act with care and skill. The basis for the duty to notify is the principal's obvious interest in being informed of matters that are important to the agency business.

However, there is no duty to notify where the agent receives information that is privileged or confidential. For example, an attorney may acquire confidential information from a client and thus be obligated not to disclose it to a second client. If the attorney cannot properly represent the second client without revealing this information, he should refuse to represent that client.

LEVIN V. KASMIR WORLD TRAVEL, INC.

540 N.Y.S.2d 639 (N.Y. Civ. Ct. 1989)

In July of 1987, Marsha Levin bought her daughter a round-trip plane ticket from New York City to Paris from Kasmir World Travel, Inc. Upon arriving in Paris, Mrs. Levin's daughter was denied entry and was placed on the next return flight to the United States because she did not have a visa. The apparent reason for the visa requirement was the French government's effort to deal with terrorist activities directed at Americans abroad. Neither Mrs. Levin nor her daughter was aware of the requirement; indeed, a few years earlier Mrs. Levin had traveled to France without being required to present a visa.

Levin sued Kasmir for failing to notify her about the visa requirement. Kasmir moved to dismiss her complaint.

Saxe, Judge. The duty of a travel agent has been held to include such responsibilities as verifying or confirming reservations. In general terms, travel agents are required to have the degree of skill and knowledge requisite to the calling; to exercise good faith and reasonable skill, care, and diligence; and to possess reasonable knowledge of the types of carriers, lines, and accommodations that they select for their principals, and all significant attendant matters. Beyond the duty to confirm travel reservations, travel agents should be expected to provide information which is necessary and of importance to the traveler.

I conclude that Kasmir had a duty to notify the traveler about the need for a visa before entering France. This view is in accord with the expanding role of the travel agent to provide all relevant and necessary information to the consumer who reasonably relies on the agent's expertise. Here, it was reasonable to expect Kasmir to alert its [principal] to important changes in the visa requirements of foreign nations. It was also reasonable for Mrs. Levin to rely on Kasmir to supply this information. After all, the travel agency was clearly in a position to assemble and disseminate this basic and significant type of travel information.

I am aware of Kasmir's contention that its relationship to the claimant was merely that of a ticketing agent, and that consequently duties beyond the actual sale of the ticket could not implicate such an agent. [But] information concerning entry or visa requirements into foreign lands is so basic to the purchase or sale of the ticket that the seller must be obliged to furnish it to all affected consumers.

Kasmir's motion to dismiss denied.

OWE SOME DEGREE OF DUTY TO CUSTOMERS THEY BOOK!

Agent's Duties to Account

The agent's duties of loyalty and care require that the agent give the principal any money or property received in the course of the agency business. This obviously includes profits resulting from the agent's breach of the duty of loyalty, or other duties. It also includes incidental benefits received through the agency business. Examples include bribes, kickbacks, and gifts from third parties with whom the agent deals on the principal's behalf. However, the parties may agree that the agent can retain certain benefits received during the agency. Courts often conclude that such an agreement exists when it is customary for agents to retain tips from customers, or to accept entertainment provided by third parties with whom the agent does business.

Another type of *duty to account* concerns agents whose business involves collections, receipts, or expenditures. Here, the agent must keep accurate records and accounts of all transactions, and disclose these to the principal once the principal makes a reasonable demand for them. Also, an agent who obtains or holds property for the principal usually may not commingle that property with her own property. For example, an agent ordinarily cannot deposit the principal's funds in her own name or in her own bank account.

Remedies of the Principal

A principal has a wide choice of claims and remedies when her agent breaches a duty. The following examples are not an exhaustive list. If the agency relation was created by contract, the agent's wrongdoing may be a breach of that contract. If so, the principal should get the various kinds of contract damages where appropriate. Also, a principal may obtain injunctive relief where, for example, an agent discloses or threatens to disclose confidential information, or misappropriates or threatens to misappropriate the principal's property. In addition, a principal may rescind contracts entered into by an agent who has represented two principals without the knowl-

edge of one or both, has dealt with himself, or has failed to disclose relevant facts to his principal. Agents who retain money or property due the principal (including bribes or gifts), or who profit from the breach of duty, also may be liable for the amount of their unjust enrichment.

Tort claims also are possible when the agent has misbehaved. A principal may recover for losses caused by his agent's negligent failure to follow instructions, to notify, or to perform with appropriate skill and care. The tort of conversion is available where an agent has unjustifiably retained, stolen, transferred, destroyed, failed to separate, or otherwise misappropriated the principal's property.

DUTIES OF PRINCIPAL TO AGENT

Introduction

If an agency is formed by contract, the contract should set out the duties the principal owes the agent. In addition, the law implies certain duties from the existence of an agency relationship, however formed. The most important such duties are the principal's obligations to *compensate* the agent, to *reimburse* the agent for money spent in the principal's service, and to *indemnify* the agent for losses suffered in conducting the principal's business.[9] These duties generally can be eliminated or modified by agreement between the parties. Although there obviously is no duty to compensate a gratuitous agent, the principal still owes such an agent the other two duties absent an agreement to the contrary.

---

[9]A principal also may have other duties, including the duties to: provide the agent with an opportunity for service, not interfere with the agent's work, keep accounts, act in a manner not harmful to the agent's reputation or self-esteem, and (in the case of employees) maintain a safe workplace. The last duty has been greatly affected, if not superseded, by workers' compensation systems and the Occupational Safety and Health Act, which are discussed in the Employment Law chapter.

An agent's duties to a subagent are the same as a principal's duties to an agent. Absent an agreement to the contrary, however, the original principal has no contractual liability to a subagent. For example, such a principal normally is not obligated to compensate a subagent. But a principal is required to reimburse and indemnify subagents as he would agents generally.

Duty to Compensate Agent

Where the agency contract states the agent's compensation, disputes about that compensation are settled by applying the rules of contract interpretation. In other cases, the relationship of the parties and the surrounding circumstances determine whether and in what amount the agent is to be compensated. Absent a contract provision on compensation, for example, a principal generally is not required to pay for undertakings that she did not request, services to which she did not consent, and tasks that typically are undertaken without pay. Also, a principal usually is not obliged to compensate an agent who has materially breached the agency contract or has committed a serious breach of a fiduciary duty. Where compensation is due but its amount is not expressly stated, the amount is the market price or the customary price for the agent's services, or, if neither is available, their reasonable value.

Sometimes an agent's compensation is contingent on the accomplishment of a specific result. For instance, a plaintiff's attorney may be retained on a contingent fee basis (being paid a certain percentage of the recovery if the suit succeeds or is settled), or a real estate broker may be entitled to a fee only if a suitable buyer is found. In such cases, the agent is not entitled to compensation unless he achieves the result within the time stated or, if no time is stated, within a reasonable time. This is true regardless of how much effort or money the agent expends. However, the principal must cooperate with the agent in achieving the result and must not do anything to frustrate the agent's efforts. Otherwise, the agent is entitled to compensation despite the failure to perform as specified.

Duties of Reimbursement and Indemnity

If, while acting on the principal's behalf, an agent makes expenditures that were expressly or impliedly authorized by the principal, the agent is entitled to *reimbursement* for those expenditures absent an agreement to the contrary. Unless otherwise agreed, for example, an agent requested to make overnight trips as part of his agency duties can recover reasonable transportation and hotel expenses.

A principal's duty of reimbursement overlaps with her duty of *indemnity*. Agency law implies a promise by the principal to indemnify an agent for losses that result from the agent's authorized activities. These include authorized payments made on the principal's behalf and payments on contracts on which the agent was authorized to become liable. A principal may also be required to indemnify an agent if the agent's authorized acts constitute a breach of contract or a tort for which the agent is required to pay damages to a third party.

So long as the principal did not benefit from such behavior, however, he is *not* required to indemnify an agent for losses resulting (1) from unauthorized acts or (2) solely from the agent's negligence or other fault. Even where the principal directed the agent to commit a tortious act, moreover, there is no duty to indemnify if the agent knew that the act was tortious. But the principal must indemnify the agent for tort damages resulting from authorized conduct that the agent did not believe was tortious. For example, if a principal directs his agent to repossess goods located on another's property and the agent, believing her acts legal, becomes liable for conversion or trespass, the principal must indemnify the agent for the damages the agent pays.

Remedies of the Agent

An agent's claim for breach of the duties just discussed often is contractual, and normal contract remedies—except specific performance—are available. In some cases, the principal's failure to pay, indemnify, or reimburse the agent enables the agent to acquire a lien on property or funds of the principal that are in the agent's possession. This usually allows the agent to hold the property or funds until the principal's obligation has been paid. Also, an agent whose principal violates the duties to pay, indemnify, or reimburse can refuse to render further services to the principal.

Of course, an agent's *own* breach of duty—especially the duties of loyalty and obedience—may defeat his claim against the principal. Where the breach is not serious enough to give the principal a complete defense, the principal may still set off losses caused by the breach against the agent's recovery.

FIGURE 2   The Duties the Principal and the Agent Owe Each Other

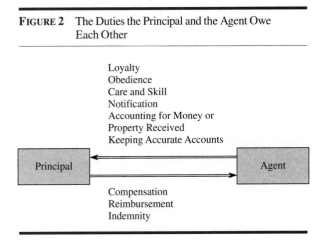

Loyalty
Obedience
Care and Skill
Notification
Accounting for Money or
Property Received
Keeping Accurate Accounts

Principal   Agent

Compensation
Reimbursement
Indemnity

TERMINATION OF THE AGENCY RELATIONSHIP

Agencies terminate in many ways.[10] These fall under two general headings: (1) termination by acts of the parties, and (2) termination by operation of law.

Termination by Acts of the Parties

The parties can control the termination of their agency through either the provisions they put in the agency agreement or their actions after concluding the agreement. Such *terminations by acts of the parties* occur in various ways.

1. An agency terminates at a time or upon the happening of an event *stated in the agreement*. If no such time or event is stipulated, the agency terminates after a *reasonable time.*

2. An agency created to accomplish a specified result terminates when *the specified result has been accomplished*. For example, if the only objective of an agency is to sell certain property, the agency terminates when the property is sold.

3. An agency may be terminated at any time by *mutual agreement of the parties.*

---

[10]The rules stated below generally apply to the termination of a subagency's authority as well. In general, a subagency terminates when relations between either the principal and the agent or the agent and the subagent are terminated in any of the ways to be described.

4. Finally, an agency can terminate at the *option of either party.* This is called *revocation* when done by the principal and *renunciation* when done by the agent. Generally, revocation or renunciation occurs when either party manifests to the other that he does not wish the agency to continue. Conduct inconsistent with the agency's continuance can constitute such a manifestation. For example, an agent may learn that his principal has hired another agent to perform the same job.

A party can revoke or renounce even if this violates the agency agreement. However, although either party has the *power* to terminate in such cases, there is no *right* to do so. This means that where one party terminates in violation of the agreement, she is not bound to perform any further but she may be liable for damages to the other party. As noted earlier, however, a gratuitous agency normally is terminable by either party without liability. Also, the terminating party is not liable where the revocation or renunciation is justified by the other party's serious breach of a fiduciary duty.

These principles are illustrated by the traditional termination rules governing agents who are paid *employees*. If the employment contract is for a *definite time period* and either party terminates before the period ends, the terminating party normally is liable to the other for breach of contract. Under the doctrine of **employment at will,** however, an employment contract for an *indefinite term* is not breached when either party terminates the employment. In such cases, both parties can end the employment at any time and for any reason without incurring contract liability. Nonetheless, terminated employees normally can recover for work actually done. Over the past 20 years, the courts of most states have recognized certain exceptions to the employment at will doctrine. These exceptions, which generally aim to protect employees against *wrongful discharge,* are discussed in detail in the Employment Law chapter.

Termination by Operation of Law

Numerous other events may terminate an agency. For the most part, these events do not involve the parties' willful choices. Instead, they normally involve situations where it is reasonable to believe that the principal would not wish the agent to act further, or where accomplishment of the agency objectives has become impossible or illegal. Although courts may recognize exceptions in certain cases, an agency relationship usually is terminated by:

1. *The death of the principal.* This is normally true even where the agent has no notice of the principal's death.

2. *The death of the agent.*

3. *The principal's permanent loss of capacity.* This is a *permanent* loss of capacity occurring *after* creation of the agency. The usual cause is the principal's insanity. Like the principal's death, the principal's permanent incapacity ends the agency even without notice to the agent. A brief period of insanity, on the other hand, may only cause a temporary suspension of the agency relation for the time that the principal is insane.

4. *The agent's loss of capacity to perform the agency business.* The scope of this basis for termination is unclear. As you will see in the next chapter, an agent who becomes insane or otherwise incapacitated after the agency is formed still can bind the principal to contracts with third parties. Thus, it probably makes little sense to treat the agency relationship as terminated in such cases. As a result, termination under this heading may be limited to such situations as the loss of a license needed to perform agency duties (for example, a license needed to sell certain goods).

5. *Changes in the value of the agency property or subject matter* (for example, a significant decline in the value of land to be sold by an agent).

6. *Changes in business conditions* (for example, a markedly lower supply and a greatly increased price for goods to be purchased by an agent).

7. *The loss or destruction of the agency property or subject matter or the termination of the principal's interest therein* (for example, a situation in which a house to be sold by a real estate broker burns down or is taken by a mortgage holder to satisfy a debt owed by the principal).

8. *Changes in the law that make the agency business illegal* (for example, a situation in which drugs to be sold by an agent are banned by the government).

9. *The bankruptcy of the principal*—as to transactions that the agent should realize are no longer desired by the principal. Consider, for example, the likely effect of the principal's bankruptcy on an agency to purchase antiques for the principal's home, as opposed to its likely effect on an agency to purchase necessities of life for the principal.

10. *The bankruptcy of the agent*—where the agent's financial condition affects his ability to serve the principal. This could occur where the agent is employed to purchase goods on his own credit for the principal.

11. *Impossibility of performance by the agent.* This covers a wide range of circumstances, some of which fall within the categories just stated. The *Restatement*, for example, includes within its definition of impossibility: (a) the destruction of the agency subject matter, (b) the termination of the principal's interest in the agency subject matter (as, for example, by the principal's bankruptcy), and (c) changes in the law or in other circumstances that make it impossible for the agent to accomplish the aims of the agency.[11]

12. *A serious breach of the agent's duty of loyalty.*

13. *The outbreak of war*—where this leads the agent to the reasonable belief that his services are no longer desired. One example might be the outbreak of war between the principal's country and the agent's country.

Termination of Agency Powers Given as Security

An agency power given as security for a duty owed by the principal, sometimes called an *agency coupled with an interest*, is an exception to some of the termination rules just discussed. Here, the agent has an interest in the subject matter of the agency that is distinct from the principal's interest and that is not exercised for the principal's benefit. This interest exists to benefit the agent or a third person by securing performance of an obligation owed by the principal. A common example is a secured loan agreement authorizing a lender (the agent) to sell property used as security if the debtor (the principal) defaults. For example, suppose that Allen lends Peters $100,000 and Peters gives Allen a lien or security interest on Peters's land to secure the loan. Such an agreement typically would authorize Allen to act as Peters's "agent" to sell the land if Peters fails to repay the loan.

Because the power given the "agent" in such cases is not for the principal's benefit, it is sometimes said that an agency coupled with an interest is not truly an agency. In any event, courts distinguish it from situations where the agent only has an interest in being compensated from the profits or proceeds of property held for the principal's benefit. For example, if an agent is promised a commission for selling the principal's property, the relationship is not an agency coupled with an interest. In this case, the power exercised by the agent (selling the principal's property) benefits the principal.

---

[11]*Restatement (Second) of Agency* section 124 (1959).

The main significance of the agency coupled with an interest is that the principal cannot revoke it. Also, it is not terminated by either the principal's or the agent's loss of capacity. In addition, the death of the agent does not terminate this relationship; the death of the principal does so only when the obligation owed by the principal ends with the principal's death. However, unless an agency coupled with an interest is held for the benefit of a third party, the agent can voluntarily surrender it. Of course, an agency coupled with an interest terminates when the principal performs her obligation as promised.

Effect of Termination on Agent's Authority

Sometimes agents continue to act on their principals' behalf even though the agency has ended. Do such ex-agents still have authority to bind their former principals? As Figure 3 states, once an agency has been terminated by any of the means just described, the agent's *express* authority and *implied* authority end along with the agency.

Third parties who are unaware of the termination, however, still may reasonably believe that the ex-agent has authority. To protect such parties when they rely on such a reasonable appearance of authority, an agent's *apparent authority* often persists after termination. This means that a former agent may be able to bind the principal under his apparent authority even though the agency has ended. But as Figure 3 also states, there are three important exceptions to this generalization. Apparent authority ends and an ex-agent cannot bind the principal where the termination was caused by: (1) the *principal's death*, (2) the *principal's loss of capacity*, or (3) *impossibility*.[12] Note from the previous discussion

---

[12]*Restatement (Second) of Agency* section 124A, comment a; and section 133 (1959). Subject to certain exceptions, moreover, section 132 of the *Restatement* says that the apparent authority of a *special agent* terminates along with termination of the agency.

that certain other bases for termination by operation of law may fit within the broad category of impossibility and also end the agent's apparent authority.

Notice to Third Parties   It follows from the nature of apparent authority that such authority ends when the third party receives appropriate *notice* of the termination. In general, any facts known to the third party that reasonably indicate the agency's termination constitute suitable notice. Some bases for termination by operation of law (for example, changed business conditions) may provide such notice.

To protect themselves against unwanted liability, however, prudent principals may want to notify third parties themselves. The type of notification required for this purpose varies with the third party in question.

1. *Third parties who have previously dealt with the agent or who have begun to deal with the agent.* Here, the principal must give *actual notification*. This can be accomplished by: (1) a direct personal statement to the third party; or (2) a writing delivered to the third party personally, to his place of business, or to some other place reasonably believed to be appropriate.

2. *All other third parties.* Usually, these are parties who are aware of the agency but did no business with the agent. For such parties, *constructive notification* is all that is required. This normally can be accomplished by advertising the agency's termination in a newspaper of general circulation in the place where the agency business regularly was carried on. Where no suitable publication exists, notification by other means reasonably likely to inform third parties of the termination —for example, posting a notice in public places— may suffice.

FIGURE 3   Termination of an Agent's Authority after Termination of the Agency

Type of Termination	Actual Authority	Apparent Authority
By Acts of the Parties	Ceases	Persists unless appropriate notice or notification to third party
By Operation of Law	Ceases	Ceases if termination by principal's death or loss of capacity, or by impossibility; persists in other cases unless appropriate notice or notification to third party

ETHICAL AND PUBLIC POLICY CONCERNS

1. Take another look at the doctrine of employment at will discussed in the section on termination of an agency. By now, the doctrine has various exceptions, which are discussed in the Employment Law chapter. In cases where the doctrine still applies, it allows employers to discharge employees for *any* reason, no matter how arbitrary, without suffering liability. Put more bluntly, it means that *you* might be fired from some future job for some arbitrary reason, even if your work performance was excellent. What can justify such a seemingly harsh rule?

2. Under one of the agent's duties to account, an agent might be required to return to the principal gifts from third parties with whom the agent deals on the principal's behalf. Where the gift is a genuine token of appreciation, the principal may be getting a windfall. What can justify this result?

3. A well-known ethical theory called *utilitarianism* generally asserts that the moral worth of actions should be judged by *their tendency to promote net aggregate satisfaction.* Some people regard the maximization of social wealth as a reasonable measuring rod for net aggregate satisfaction. Under a wealth-maximization criterion, does the rule forbidding an ex-agent from using or disclosing confidential information make sense? How might the rule promote wealth maximization? How might it hinder wealth maximization? In attempting to answer this question, you might consult the introduction to the section on trade secrets in the Intellectual Property, Competitive Torts, and Unfair Competition chapter.

What other ethical considerations might justify the rule against the disclosure of confidential information by an ex-agent? Are they utilitarian in the sense defined above?

SUMMARY

Because the agency relationship enables individuals and businesses to multiply their transactions, it is vital to a commercial economy. Courts hold that an agency exists if the facts indicate an agreement that one person will act for the benefit and under the control of another. However, certain duties cannot be delegated to an agent. Although the agency relationship is based on mutual consent, it need not be contractual. Thus, consideration is not essential and only rarely is a writing needed. The incapacity of either the principal or the agent at the time an agency is formed enables that party to avoid the agency at his option.

Agency law contains a number of basic definitions and concepts. An agent's *authority* is his ability to affect the principal's legal relations with third parties. Authority may be *express* (based on the principal's actual words), *implied* (created by operation of law from those words and the surrounding circumstances), or *apparent* (based on the third party's reasonable belief that the agent has authority). Agents may be classed as *general agents* (those authorized to perform a series of transactions involving continuity of service) or *special agents* (those authorized to conduct a few transactions or a single transaction not involving continuity of service). A *gratuitous agent* is an agent who receives no compensation or other consideration for his services. A *subagent* is an agent appointed to conduct the principal's business by an agent with authority to make the appointment. Parties who act for the principal, finally, may be classed as *employees* or *independent contractors*. The most important factor affecting the classification is the principal's right to control the physical details of the work.

Because the agency relationship is for the principal's benefit, agency law imposes a number of duties on the *agent*. These supplement the duties expressly created by an agency agreement. The agent's duties are: (1) loyalty to the principal; (2) obedience to the principal's reasonable, lawful, and ethical instructions; (3) care and skill in performing agency duties; (4) notification of matters affecting the principal's interest in the agency business; (5) the return of profits and other things of value received in the course of the agency business; and (6) an accounting of the agency's financial operations.

The agency relation also imposes certain duties on the *principal*. The most important such duties are: (1) to compensate the agent, (2) to reimburse the agent for expenditures connected with the agency business, and (3) to indemnify the agent for losses suffered in the course of the agency business.

An agency can be terminated by the acts of the parties or by operation of law. Termination by *acts of the parties* includes: (1) the occurrence of an event or the passage of a time period stated in the agency agreement, (2) the passage of a reasonable time (if no termination date has been set by agreement), (3) accomplishment of the results for which the agency was established, (4) mutual agreement of the parties, (5) the principal's revocation, and (6) the agent's renunciation. Termination *by operation of law* includes: (1) the death of the principal, (2) the death of the agent, (3) the principal's permanent loss of capacity, (4) the agent's loss of capacity to perform the agency business, (5) changes in the value of the agency property or subject matter, (6) changes in business conditions, (7) loss or destruction of the agency property or termination of the principal's interest therein, (8) changes in the law that make the agency business illegal, (9) the principal's or the agent's bankruptcy (in certain cases), (10) impossibility of performance (which includes various other grounds for termination by operation of law), (11) a serious breach of the agent's duty of loyalty, and (12) the outbreak of war (in certain cases). An agency coupled with an interest, however, cannot be terminated by the principal's revocation, the principal's or the agent's incapacity, the agent's death, or (sometimes) the principal's death.

Termination of the agency also terminates the agent's *express* and *implied* authority. Except where the termination is by the principal's death, the principal's loss of capacity, or impossibility, however, the agent's *apparent authority* continues until the third party receives proper *notice* of the termination. The type of notice required varies depending on the third party's previous dealings with the agent.

PROBLEM CASES

1. Joan Marie Ottensmeyer was a contestant for the title of Miss Hawaii–USA 1974. The pageant was run by Richard You as a franchisee of Miss Universe, Inc. After finishing as first runner-up, Ottensmeyer sued Miss Universe, Inc., arguing that as its agent, You had prevented her from winning a title to which she was rightfully entitled and from obtaining the benefits thereof. The franchise agreement between Miss Universe and You contained language explicitly stating that You was not Miss Universe's agent. By itself, is this language sufficient to prevent the formation of an agency relationship between Miss Universe and You?

2. Melabs of California manufactured a portable electric telephone that was designed to fit inside an attache case and to operate on the same airwaves as fixed telephone installations in vehicles. Melabs and Marlin American Corporation entered into a contract giving Marlin the right to distribute the phone. The contract gave Marlin the exclusive right to establish a sales and marketing program and to develop all brochures, sales aids, forms, advertising materials, and other marketing aids. On the other hand, it gave Melabs the right to approve all contract forms. It also established that uniform terms, conditions, and prices would be offered to the ultimate distributors of the phones. In addition, it transferred ownership of subsequent distributorships established by Marlin to Melabs in the event that Marlin went bankrupt. Finally, there was evidence that, in practice, Melabs exercised approval rights over the use of its trademark in advertising matters. On these facts, did Melabs possess sufficient control over Marlin to create an agency relationship between Melabs and Marlin?

3. Betty Jones established VISA and MasterCard accounts with a bank, and had credit cards for each account issued to herself and her husband in each of their names. In November of 1977, Jones informed the bank that she would no longer honor charges made by her husband on the two accounts. The bank immediately revoked both accounts and requested the return of the two cards. Jones, however, did not return the cards until March 9, 1978. During the interim, Jones's husband apparently had run up $2,685.70 in purchases on the cards. Jones refused to pay this amount, arguing that the federal Truth in Lending Act limits a cardholder's liability for unauthorized use of the card to $50. The provision in question basically defines unauthorized use as use without express, implied, or apparent authority. Was Jones's liability limited to $50?

4. New World Fashions, Inc., a firm in the business of assisting persons interested in entering the retail clothing business, employed Abbott Lieberman as a sales representative. While working for New World, Lieberman told one potential client that he would soon go into business himself in competition with New World and that he could offer her either New World's services or his own. Later, he contracted to set up a retail store for this person, a service that New World would otherwise have provided. There was nothing to indicate that New World knew about Lieberman's dealings with this potential client, or that it acquiesced in these dealings. Did Lieberman breach his duty of loyalty to New World?

5. Mark and Roberta Murray purchased a single-family home. Some time after they moved in, cracks appeared at various places in the house, and the Murrays eventually discovered that its foundation was defective. They sued the real estate broker who had represented them in the purchase, arguing that he breached his duty of care and skill by failing to conduct a reasonable investigation of the house. Did their broker owe the Murrays

[handwritten margin notes: "Buyers Broker Had to Ask Sellers Broker!"]

[handwritten margin notes: "Duty of Agent Not only what he knows, but also what he should know!!"]

such a duty? Assume that the *seller's* broker had a duty to make such an inspection and to disclose to the purchaser all facts materially affecting the value or desirability of the house. *[handwritten: Get an independent investigator]*

6. In February of 1989, Thomas Fix arranged for a Florida vacation package for himself and his sister with Travel Help, a travel agency. The travel agent selected an Eastern Airlines package that included Eastern vouchers for a rental car, Howard Johnson's Fountain Park, and Sea World. Aware of the labor and other problems Eastern was experiencing at that time, Fix's sister contacted the agent several times requesting that all the arrangements be made with another airline. The agent assured her that the flights could be changed and that the vouchers would be honored. After Eastern went into bankruptcy on March 9, 1989, the agent arranged for Fix and his sister to be transported to Florida on a different airline. After they arrived, however, the providers of the voucher bookings refused to honor Eastern's vouchers. Did the agent breach a duty to Fix (and his sister)? If so, which duty? You can assume that the travel agent was acting for both Fix and his sister, and that the communications to the agent by Fix's sister were communications to an agent by his principal. *[handwritten: Yes, care & skill in performance of duties]*

7. Southeastern Agri-Systems, Inc., was an agent for Otto Niederer. James Stanford was Agri-Systems' president and sole employee. Niederer instructed Stanford to accept payment for the sale of some equipment owned by Niederer, to deduct his commission from the payment, and to wire the remainder to Niederer. Instead, Stanford diverted the funds to his own purposes and refused to pay Niederer the amount due. When sued individually for breach of the agent's duty to obey, Stanford argued that Niederer had employed Agri-Systems as its agent, that he was merely an employee of Agri-Systems, and that he thus owed no duty to Niederer. Is Stanford correct? *[handwritten: No! Employee always considered an agent. Niederer is a subagent]*

8. Stanley Mazur owned an Oldsmobile Cutlass and a small Subaru pickup truck. He asked his insurance agent, Ken Curtis, to arrange "full coverage" on the truck similar to the coverage on his Cutlass. Although the policy on the Cutlass included personal injury protection, Curtis negligently failed to include such protection in the policy he obtained for the Subaru. Later, Mazur suffered personal injury from an accident in which he was involved while driving the Subaru. Because the policy did not cover such injury, he was unable to recover for it from the insurer, the Selected Risks Insurance Company.

Mazur recovered against Curtis for Curtis's failure to procure the requested coverage. Curtis then sued to have Selected indemnify him for this loss. Is Selected required to indemnify Curtis? Why or why not? You can assume that Curtis was acting as an agent for Selected as well as for Mazur. *[handwritten: No!]*

9. Ella Kelly died in January of 1982. She left the bulk of her estate to charity and to her niece and executrix, Mary McDonald. Kelly's grandchildren then undertook a lengthy legal challenge to the will, a challenge to which McDonald was effectively the opposing party. In January of 1986, the grandchildren made a demand of $50,000 on McDonald through her attorney, Malcolm McNeil. By this time, McDonald was hospitalized with a serious illness, and McNeil was communicating with her through her husband even though he had broad authority to settle the dispute. After McNeil made a $40,000 counteroffer, the grandchildren agreed in principle to this figure. Not wishing to settle the case without written authority from McDonald, McNeil then got the grandchildren to agree to a $40,000 settlement that was conditioned on his obtaining such authority. Before McNeil could obtain written authority from McDonald, however, she died on January 22, 1986. Nonetheless, McNeil went ahead and settled the case for $40,000 on January 30, 1986. Still later, the grandchildren petitioned the court to set aside the settlement.

Did McNeil have actual authority to settle on January 30, 1986? Did he have apparent authority to settle on that date? In each case, why or why not?

[handwritten: No! No Death cancel apparent auth]

CHAPTER 35

THIRD-PARTY RELATIONS OF THE PRINCIPAL AND THE AGENT

INTRODUCTION

As you saw in the previous chapter, the agency relation allows people to multiply their dealings with third parties, thereby stimulating business activity. But an agent's interactions with such parties create legal problems that agency law must resolve if it is to perform its functions effectively and fairly.

Agency law stimulates business activity by enabling principals to contract through their agents. Thus, rules for determining the principal's and the agent's liability on contracts completed by the agent are crucial to the successful functioning of the agency relation. Principals need some ability to predict and control their liability on contracts made by their agents. Also, third parties need some assurance that such contracts really bind the principal. In addition, both agents and third parties have an interest in knowing when the *agent* is bound on these contracts. The first half of this chapter discusses the principal's and the agent's contract liability.

Also, agents may harm third parties in various ways while acting on the principal's behalf. Normally, this makes the agent liable to the injured party in tort. Sometimes, moreover, a *principal* is liable for his agent's torts. For obvious monetary reasons, the rules for determining the principal's and the agent's tort liability are of great concern to principals, their agents, and third parties. Thus, we examine these subjects in the second half of this chapter. The chapter concludes with a brief treatment of the principal's and the agent's criminal liability.

CONTRACT LIABILITY OF THE PRINCIPAL

A principal's liability for contracts completed by his agent depends mainly on whether the agent had *express, implied, or apparent authority* to make the contract in question.[1] Occasionally, however, a principal's contract liability may be affected by other factors. The principal's incapacity, for example, may enable him to avoid a contract made by an agent. Even where the agent lacked authority to contract, moreover, a principal may bind herself by later *ratifying* the contract.

Express Authority

As previously discussed, **express authority** is created by a principal's *words* to his agent, whether written or oral. Thus, an agent has express authority to bind the principal to a particular contract if the principal

---

[1] In this connection, recall from the previous chapter that termination of the agency may or may not end the agent's authority.

has clearly told the agent that she could make that contract on the principal's behalf. For example, suppose that Payne instructs his agent, Andrews, to contract to sell a specific antique chair for $400 or more. If Andrews contracts to sell the chair to Tucker for $425, Payne is liable to Tucker on the basis of Andrews's express authority. However, Andrews would not have express authority to sell the chair for $375, or to sell a different chair.

Implied Authority

If express authority were the only way that agents could bind their principals, agency law's ability to stimulate business activity would be limited. In many cases, it is difficult or impossible for a principal to specify his agent's authority completely and precisely. Thus, an agent also can bind his principal on the basis of the agent's **implied authority.** As the *Adams* case later in this chapter states, implied authority is determined by inference from the circumstances, nature, and purposes of the agency. Courts attempting to determine an agent's implied authority often ask what the agent could reasonably assume that the principal wanted him to do in light of all the factors known or reasonably known to the agent. In making this determination, courts consider the principal's express statements to the agent, the nature of the agency business, the relations between principal and agent, and other relevant facts and circumstances.

A principal's express statements to her agent are an important source of implied authority. Implied authority, that is, often derives from a grant of express authority. For example, an agency expressly set up to conduct a certain business ordinarily gives the agent implied authority to make those contracts that are reasonably necessary for conducting the business or that are customarily made in conducting that business. Implied authority, however, cannot conflict with the principal's express statements. Thus, there is no implied authority to contract where a principal has limited her agent's authority by express statement or clear implication and the contract would conflict with that limitation.

On occasion, implied authority may exist even where there is no relevant grant of express authority. Here, courts generally derive implied authority from the nature of the agency business, the relations between principal and agent, customs in the trade, and other facts and circumstances. For example, there may be implied authority to make a certain contract if the agent has made similar past contracts with the principal's knowledge and without his objection.

Specific Examples of Implied Authority   The courts have created several general rules or presumptions for determining the implied authority of certain agents in certain situations. For example:

1. As just noted, an agent hired to *manage a business* normally has implied authority to make those contracts that are reasonably necessary for conducting the business or that are customary in the business. These include contracts for obtaining equipment and supplies, making repairs, employing employees, and selling goods or services. However, a manager generally has no power to borrow money or issue negotiable instruments in the principal's name unless the principal is a banking or financial concern regularly performing such activities.

2. An agent given *full control over real property* has implied authority to contract for repairs and insurance, and may rent the property for certain periods if this is customary. But such an agent may not sell the property or allow any third-party liens or other interests to be taken on it.

3. Agents appointed to *sell the principal's goods* may have implied authority to make customary warranties on those goods and to bind the principal to such warranties. In states that still recognize the distinction, the *general agent* described in the previous chapter is more likely to have such authority than the *special agent* described in that chapter.

Apparent Authority

Sometimes a principal's actions create a reasonable appearance of authority in an agent who may or may not have actual authority. In such cases, the principal may be bound to the agent's contracts on the basis of the agent's **apparent authority.** Apparent authority to contract arises when the principal's acts cause a third party to reasonably believe that the agent is authorized to deal on the principal's behalf. It is based on what the *principal* communicates to the *third party,* either directly or through the agent. Communications to the agent are irrelevant except as they become known to the third party or affect the agent's behavior. Also, agents cannot give themselves apparent authority without the principal's consent.

Examples of Apparent Authority   Principals can give their agents apparent authority through the statements they make, or tell their agents to make, to third parties; and through the actions they knowingly allow their agents to take. In all such cases, the principal's acts must cause the third party to form a reasonable belief that authority exists. As the *Adams* case suggests, background factors such as trade customs and established business practices often play a role in determining the reasonableness of the third party's belief. For instance, if a principal appoints his agent to a position such as general manager that customarily involves the power to make certain kinds of contracts, the agent normally has apparent authority to make those contracts. Here, the principal's behavior in appointing the agent to the position, as reasonably interpreted in light of business customs, creates apparent authority in the agent. This is true even if the principal expressly told the agent not to make such contracts, so long as this limitation remains unknown to the third party. Because agents cannot give themselves apparent authority, however, there would be no such authority if the agent falsely told third parties that he had been promoted to general manager without the principal's knowledge or permission.

Established business customs can help create apparent authority in other ways as well. For example, an agent often can bind his principal to forbidden promises that customarily accompany contracts the agent actually is authorized to complete, if the third party is unaware that the promises were forbidden. In states that continue to recognize the distinction, general agents are much more likely to have this kind of apparent authority than are special agents. Suppose that Perry employs Arthur as general sales agent for his manufacturing business. Certain warranties customarily accompany the products Perry sells, and agents like Arthur ordinarily are empowered to give these warranties. But Perry tells Arthur not to make any such warranties to buyers, thus cutting off Arthur's express and implied authority. Despite Perry's orders, however, Arthur makes the usual warranties in a sale to Thomas, who is familiar with customs in the trade. If Thomas did not know about the limitation on Arthur's authority, Perry is bound by Arthur's warranties.

Finally, apparent authority sometimes is found where the principal has, to the knowledge of a third person, permitted the agent to make contracts that the agent was expressly forbidden to make. Suppose Potter has told Abram, the manager of his business, to hire loaders for his trucks for no more than one day at a time. No one else knows about this limitation on Abram's actual authority. With Potter's knowledge and without his objection, however, Abram frequently has employed loaders by the week. Then Abram agrees to employ Trapp as a loader for a week. If Trapp knew about the earlier employment

by the week, Potter would be bound to the one-week employment contract on the basis of Abram's apparent authority.

Effect of Agent's Notification and Knowledge

In a few situations, the general agency rules regarding *notification* and *knowledge* can affect the principal's contract liability. If a third party gives proper notification to an agent having actual or apparent authority to receive it, the principal is bound as if the notification had been given directly to him. For example, where a contract between Phillips and Thomas made by Phillips's agent Anderson contains a clause allowing Thomas to cancel if she notifies Phillips, she can cancel by notifying Anderson if Anderson has actual or apparent authority to receive the notification. Similarly, notification to a third party by an agent with the necessary authority is considered notification by the principal.

In certain circumstances, an agent's knowledge of certain facts is imputed to the principal. This means that the principal's rights and liabilities are what they would have been if the principal had known what the agent knew. Generally, the agent's knowledge is imputed to the principal when it is relevant to activities that the agent is authorized to undertake, or when the agent is under a duty to disclose the knowledge to the principal. Suppose that Ames contracts with Timmons on Pike's behalf, knowing that Timmons is completely mistaken about a matter material to the contract. Even though Pike knew nothing about Timmons's unilateral mistake, Timmons probably can avoid his contract with Pike.[2]

Incapacity of Principal or Agent

As discussed in the last chapter, a principal who lacks capacity at the time the agency is formed usually may avoid the agency, and a principal's permanent loss of capacity after the agency's formation terminates the agency. Where the agency continues to exist, however, is a principal of limited mental capacity such as a minor or an insane person bound on contracts made by the agent? Subject to the exceptions discussed in the contracts chapter on Capacity to Contract, such contracts are voidable at the principal's option. These contracts normally would be voidable if made by the principal himself, and it is difficult to see why acting through an agent should increase the principal's capacity.

---

[2]On unilateral mistake in contract law, see the Reality of Consent chapter.

Like the principal, an agent can avoid the agency agreement if she lacks capacity at the time it is formed. Where the agency survives, however, the agent's incapacity usually does *not* affect the contract liability of a principal who has capacity. Just as an agent cannot increase the principal's capacity, neither can she diminish it. However, sometimes the principal may escape liability where an agent's incapacity is so extreme that the agent cannot receive or convey ideas, or cannot follow the principal's instructions.

Ratification

Ratification is a process whereby a principal binds himself to an unauthorized act done by an agent or by a person purporting to act as an agent. Ratification relates back to the time when the act was performed. For contracts, its effect is to bind the principal as if the agent had possessed authority at the time the contract was made.

Conduct Amounting to Ratification   For ratification to occur, the principal's words or other behavior must indicate an intent to treat the agent's unauthorized act as authorized. Ratification can be express or implied. An *express ratification* occurs when the principal communicates his intent to ratify by written or oral words to that effect. *Implied ratification* arises when the principal's behavior evidences an intent to ratify. Part performance of the agent's contract by a principal or a principal's acceptance of benefits under the contract may work an implied ratification. In some cases, even a principal's silence, acquiescence, or failure to repudiate the transaction may constitute ratification. This can occur in cases where the principal would be expected to object if he did not consent to the contract, the principal's silence leads the third party to believe that he does so consent, and the principal is aware of all the relevant facts.

Additional Requirements   Even if a principal's behavior indicates an intent to ratify, other requirements must be met before ratification occurs. These requirements have been variously stated; the following list is typical.

1. The act ratified must be one that would have been *valid* at the time it was performed. For example, an agent's illegal contract cannot be made binding by the principal's subsequent ratification. However, a contract that was voidable when made due to the principal's incapacity may be ratified by a principal who has later attained or regained capacity.

2. The principal must have been *in existence* at the time the agent acted. However, as discussed in the Organization, Financial Structure, and Dissolution of Corporations chapter, corporations may bind themselves to their promoters' preincorporation contracts by adopting such contracts.

3. At the time the act to be ratified occurred, the agent must have indicated to the third party that she was acting for *a* principal, and not for herself. But the agent need not have disclosed the principal's identity.

4. The principal must be *legally competent* at the time of ratification. For instance, an insane principal cannot ratify.

5. The principal must have *knowledge* of all the material facts regarding the prior act or contract at the time it is ratified. Here, the agent's knowledge is not imputed to the principal. In the *Adams* case that follows, the principal did not ratify because it lacked sufficient knowledge.

6. The principal must ratify the *entire* act or contract. He cannot ratify the beneficial parts of a contract and reject those that are detrimental.

7. In ratifying, the principal must use the *same formalities* that are required to give the agent authority to execute the transaction. As the preceding chapter related, few formalities normally are needed to give an agent authority. But where the original agency contract requires a writing, ratification likewise must be written.

Intervening Events   Certain events occurring after an agent's contract but before the principal's ratification may cut off the principal's power to ratify. These include:

1. The third party's *withdrawal* from the contract.

2. The third party's *death or loss of capacity.*

3. The principal's *failure to ratify within a reasonable time.* Of course, this assumes that the principal's silence did not already work a ratification.

4. *Changed circumstances.* Here, the power to ratify is especially likely to end where the change in circumstances places a greater burden on the third party than that party assumed when the contract was made.

In the following *Adams* case, a principal escaped liability because its agent lacked express, implied, or apparent authority, and because the principal did not ratify.

ADAMS v. LOUISIANA COCA-COLA BOTTLING CO.

531 So. 2d 501 (La. Ct. App. 1988)

Rosia Adams, an employee at a Jefferson Parish School Board warehouse, was injured when she slipped on a wet floor at the warehouse. The floor was wet because it had been mopped to clean a spill from a malfunctioning Coca-Cola vending machine leased to the school board by the Louisiana Coca-Cola Bottling Company (Coca-Cola). A warehouse inventory clerk had signed the lease on behalf of the school board.

Adams sued Coca-Cola for her injuries. Coca-Cola then filed a third-party action against the school board, alleging that under the terms of the lease, the school board was required to indemnify and insure Coca-Cola against injuries to employees like Adams. After trial, Adams obtained a jury verdict against Coca-Cola, and the trial judge dismissed Coca-Cola's claim against the school board. Coca-Cola then appealed the trial judge's decision dismissing its claim against the school board.

Ciaccio, Judge.   The question is whether the school board is obligated under the lease. The clerk who signed the lease did not have express authority to do so. Whether he had implied authority, the other component of actual authority, is determined by inference from the circumstances, purposes, and nature of the agency itself. An agent is invested with the implied authority to do all of those things necessary or incidental to the accomplishment of the purpose of the agency. Coca-Cola argues that the clerk was empowered with general authority to operate the warehouse. Such a mandate confers only a power of administration. The proof does not establish any particular circumstances, purposes, or nature of the agency beyond receiving and inventorying goods delivered to the warehouse. We do not find therein any implied authority to agree to indemnify and insure the lessor of a vending machine placed on the premises.

For apparent authority to apply, the principal must first act to manifest the agent's authority to [a] third party. Second, the third party must rely reasonably on the manifested authority of the agent. In support of its argument for the clerk's apparent authority to execute this lease on behalf of the board, Coca-Cola relies on the following facts. The clerk has worked for the school board for twenty years. During this time he has always handled soft drink vending machines on the premises. Either he or another school board employee initially contacted Coca-Cola to have a machine installed at the warehouse. The school board's representative admitted that employees all over the school board system were signing similar leases. He also admitted that some of the seven thousand school board employees have previously bound the school board without formal authorization.

There is no indication that the school board acted to manifest authority for the clerk to execute this lease. There is no evidence that the school board knew of the lease, much less its provisions. The board's role was passive; it apparently paid no attention to the vending machines on its premises. We do not find that this passiveness manifested authority in its employees to agree to indemnify and insure the lessor of these machines.

Further, we find unreasonable any reliance by Coca-Cola upon any perception of authority in the clerk. Coca-Cola did not inquire into the nature and extent of the clerk's authority. And agreeing to indemnify and insure Coca-Cola as lessor requires greater authority than one would reasonably perceive to be vested in an inventory clerk.

Coca-Cola finally argues that the school board ratified the lease by permitting the machine to remain at the warehouse, permitting another machine to be placed there, and [later] permitting over one hundred other machines to be placed at various other school board locations under similar lease conditions. There is no indication that the school board was aware that the machines were being leased, that the leases were being executed in its name, or that the leases contained onerous provisions that the board indemnify and insure Coca-Cola as lessor. We do not find the board's permitting the presence of the machine(s) to be a ratification of the lease provisions confected by Coca-Cola.

Judgment in favor of the school board on Coca-Cola's third-party claim affirmed.

Contracts Made by Subagents

The rules discussed in this section generally apply to contracts made by subagents. If an agent has authorized his subagent to make a certain contract and this authorization is within the authority granted the agent by his principal, the principal is bound to the subagent's contract. Suppose that Peters employs the Ajax Company to sell certain personal property while she is out of the country, with the understanding that one of Ajax's agents will handle the sale from start to finish. If Ajax authorizes its agent Sampson (Peters's subagent) to contract to sell the property and Sampson does so, Peters is bound to the contract.

Because the relationship between agent and subagent closely resembles the relationship between principal and agent, a subagent acting within the authority conferred by her principal (the agent) can bind the agent in contract. Finally, although it is difficult to find definitive statements on the subject, both the principal and the agent probably can ratify the contracts of subagents.

CONTRACT LIABILITY OF THE AGENT

Introduction

An *agent's* liability on contracts he makes for a principal usually depends on a different set of factors than those determining the principal's liability.[3] The most important of these variables is the *nature of the principal.* Thus, this section first examines the liability of agents who contract for several distinct kinds of principals. Then it discusses two ways that an agent can be bound

after contracting for almost any type of principal: by expressly agreeing to be liable, or by contracting without the necessary authority.

Disclosed Principal

A principal is *disclosed* if a third party knows or has reason to know two things: (1) that the agent is acting for a principal, and (2) the principal's identity. Unless he agrees to be bound, an agent who represents a disclosed principal is *not liable* on authorized contracts made for such a principal. Suppose that Adkins, a sales agent for Parker, calls on Thompson and presents a business card clearly identifying her as Parker's agent. If Adkins contracts to sell Parker's goods to Thompson with authority to do so, Parker is bound on the contract. Adkins, however, is not bound because Parker is a disclosed principal. This rule usually is consistent with the third party's intentions. Here, Thompson probably intended to contract only with Parker.

Partially Disclosed Principal

A principal is *partially disclosed* if the third party: (1) knows or has reason to know that the agent is acting for *a* principal, but (2) does *not* know or have reason to know the principal's identity. This can occur where an agent simply neglects to disclose his principal's identity. Also, a principal may direct that her agent keep her identity secret to preserve her bargaining position or for other reasons.

Among the factors affecting anyone's decision to contract are the integrity, reliability, and creditworthiness of the other party to the contract. Where the principal is partially disclosed, the third party ordinarily cannot make a judgment on these matters. As a result, he usually is depending on the agent's reliability to some degree. For this reason, and to give the third party additional legal protection, an agent generally is liable

---

[3]The rules stated here generally should govern the contract liability of subagents as well as agents. See *Restatement (Second) of Agency* § 361 (1959).

on contracts made for a partially disclosed principal unless the parties agree otherwise.

Undisclosed Principal

A principal is *undisclosed* where a third party lacks knowledge or reason to know *both* the principal's existence and the principal's identity. Such situations can arise where a principal judges that he will get a better deal if his existence and identity remain secret. As the following *Jensen* case reveals, a principal also may remain undisclosed because the agent simply neglected to make adequate disclosure.

Like a third party who deals with an agent for a partially disclosed principal, a third party who deals with an agent for an undisclosed principal cannot assess the principal's reliability, integrity, and creditworthiness. Indeed, here the third party reasonably believes that the *agent* is the other party to the contract. For these reasons, an agent is liable on contracts made for an undisclosed principal.

JENSEN V. ALASKA VALUATION SERVICE, INC.

688 P.2d 161 (Alaska Sup. Ct. 1984)

Arthur Jensen was president of Arthur Jensen, Inc., an Alaska corporation engaged in the housing construction business. Alaska Valuation Service, Inc. (AVS) conducted appraisals for Jensen from the early 1970s until 1979. AVS's president, Alfred Ferrara, later claimed that throughout most of this period, he was unaware that Jensen was doing business as a corporation. Ferrara also testified that almost all the builders with whom AVS contracted were sole proprietorships. However, during the period in question, Jensen had always paid AVS with checks bearing the Arthur Jensen, Inc., name.

On July 19, 1979, Jensen telephoned Ferrara to order appraisals on five homes. Ferrara recorded the order as being for "Art Jensen," and invoices for the appraisals were later sent to "Art Jensen, Jensen Builders." AVS appraised the five homes as requested, but Jensen never paid AVS its $823 fee. In 1980, Arthur Jensen, Inc., went into bankruptcy. AVS later sued Jensen personally for the $823 in small claims court. It was successful there and on subsequent appeals. Jensen finally appealed to the Alaska Supreme Court.

Compton, Justice.   Although officers of a corporation will not ordinarily be held personally liable for contracts they make as agents of the corporation, they must disclose their agency and the existence of the corporation before they will be absolved from liability. An agent who makes a contract for an undisclosed or partially disclosed principal will be liable as a party to the contract. Thus, Jensen can avoid liability only if his use of corporate checks disclosed the existence of Arthur Jensen, Inc. and Jensen's intention to contract on its behalf.

The question before us, then, is whether Jensen's continuing use of corporate checks gave AVS reason to know about the existence of Arthur Jensen, Inc. Courts in a number of jurisdictions have considered similar questions and have reached varying conclusions. The holdings have fallen into three categories: (1) that use of corporate checks is sufficient, as a matter of law, to provide notice; (2) that it is insufficient as a matter of law; and (3) that the question is one of fact which must be decided by the court.

We conclude that the third category of holdings is best supported by case law and by reason. It is neither possible nor desirable to announce a rigid rule of law identifying specific facts that constitute "full disclosure." An agent's use of corporate checks is one factor for consideration, but it is not necessarily determinative. The reasonableness of a third party's failure to deduce the existence of a corporate principal from its agent's use of corporate checks varies from case to case. In [one case], for example, where all meetings took place in the agent's house, and the transaction involved the printing of four issues of a new magazine, a court could reasonably conclude that the third party had insufficient notice of the corporation's existence. In [another case], where the transaction took place entirely in the corporation's offices, the corporation was a coal distributor, and $170,000 changed hands, the existence of the corporation was much more evident from the circumstances surrounding the use of corporate checks.

Since we have determined that the small claims court's finding that Jensen did not sufficiently disclose his agency is one of fact, we will not disturb it unless it is clearly erroneous. At trial, AVS's president testified that most builders he dealt with were not incorporated, and that he had done business with Jensen for many years without being aware that he represented a corporation. In light of this testimony we cannot say that the trial court clearly erred.

Judgment for AVS affirmed.

Nonexistent Principal

An agent who purports to act for a *legally nonexistent* principal such as an unincorporated association is personally liable. This is true even where the third party is aware that the principal is nonexistent.[4] However, this liability can be avoided if the parties so agree.

Principal Lacking Capacity

As stated earlier, a principal who lacks contractual capacity due to insanity or infancy can avoid contracts made by his agent. In this case, the *agent* also escapes liability unless: (1) she misrepresents the capacity of her principal, or (2) she has reason to believe that the third party is unaware of the principal's incapacity and she fails to disclose this. Also, unless the parties agree otherwise, an agent is liable on contracts made for a *wholly incompetent* principal such as a person who has been adjudicated insane.

Liability of Agent by Agreement

An agent may bind himself on contracts he makes for a principal by *expressly agreeing* that he is liable. This generally is true regardless of the principal's nature. An agent may render himself liable by: (1) making the contract in his own name rather than in the principal's name, (2) joining the principal as an obligor on the contract, or (3) acting as surety or guarantor for the principal.

Problems of contract interpretation can arise when it is claimed that an agent has expressly promised to be bound. In general, the two most important factors affecting the agent's liability are the wording of the contract and the way the agent has signed it. If you are an agent wishing to avoid liability, you should be careful that *you* make no express promises in the body of the agreement, and that the agreement clearly names *the principal* as the only party to be bound. In addition, you should use a signature form that clearly identifies the principal and indicates your representative capacity—for example, "Parker, by Adkins," or "Adkins, for Parker." Simply adding the word "agent" when signing your name ("Adkins, Agent") or signing without any indication of your status ("Adkins") could subject you to liability. Sometimes, as in the following *Wired Music* case, the body of the agreement suggests one result and the signature form another. Here, and generally, oral evidence or other extrinsic evidence of the parties' understanding may help resolve the uncertainty.[5]

---

[4]For a closely analogous situation, see the Organization, Financial Structure, and Dissolution of Corporations chapter's discussion of a promoter's liability on contracts made for a corporation before it comes into existence.

---

[5]However, the introduction of such evidence may be blocked by the parol evidence rule. See the contracts chapter entitled Writing.

WIRED MUSIC, INC. v. GREAT RIVER STEAMBOAT CO.

554 S.W.2d 466 (Mo. Ct. App. 1977)

A sales representative of Wired Music, Inc., sold Frank Pierson, president of the Great River Steamboat Company, a five-year Muzak Program Service for a riverboat and restaurant owned by Great River. Pierson signed a form contract drafted by Wired Music in the following manner:

By /s/ Frank C. Pierson, Pres.

Title

The Great River Steamboat Co.
~~Port of St. Louis Investments, Inc.~~

For the Corporation

In signing, Pierson crossed out "Port of St. Louis Investments, Inc.," which had been incorrectly listed as the name of the corporation, and inserted the proper name. The contract included the following clause arguably making Pierson a surety or guarantor for Great River: "The individual signing this agreement for the subscriber guarantees that all of the above provisions shall be complied with."

Great River made approximately four payments under the contract and then ceased to pay. Wired Music brought an action for contract damages against Pierson personally. The trial court ruled in Pierson's favor, and Wired Music appealed.

Gunn, Judge.   The general rule regarding liability incurred by an individual who signs an instrument on behalf of another party is: where the principal is disclosed and the capacity in which the individual signs is evident, e.g., president, secretary, agent, the liability is the principal's and not that of the individual signing for the principal. Of course, where the circumstances surrounding the transaction disclose a mutual intention to impose personal responsibility on the individual executing the agreement, the individual may be personally liable even though the form of the signature is that of the agent.

The determinative issue here is whether, in view of the form of the signature to the agreement, the language of the so-called guaranty clause is sufficient to manifest a clear and explicit intent by Pierson to assume a personal guaranty contract. We hold that standing alone it does not. The contract language imposing a personal obligation is inconsistent with the form of execution, which positively limited Pierson's participation to his official corporate capacity and not as an individual. Such inconsistency creates at least a latent ambiguity which permits the admission of parol evidence to explain the true intent of the parties.

Pierson has stressed that he neglected to read the contract prior to its signing. The law is settled that one who signs a contract is presumed to have known its contents and accepted its terms. Thus, Pierson's failure to examine the terms of the instrument would afford no defense to the corporation regarding its obligations under the contract, as his signature was sufficient to bind the corporation. Such neglect is a relevant circumstance, however, in ascertaining Pierson's intent to assume personal liability, as his personal signature appeared nowhere on the instrument. Without knowledge of the guaranty clause he could not have possessed the requisite intent to assume obligations under it. The record is destitute of any indication that Pierson was ever made aware of potential personal liability under the guaranty clause, and he steadfastly denied any such knowledge. Wired Music drafted the contract, and its agents procured Pierson's corporate signature without explanation of or bargaining over its terms. Under these circumstances we find that there was an absence of the meeting of the minds as to the nature and the extent of the personal obligations imposed, essential to the formation of a binding guaranty.

Judgment for Pierson affirmed.

Agent's Liability on Unauthorized Contracts

Regardless of whether he would otherwise be bound, an agent also may become liable to a third party if he *lacked authority* to make the contract in question. Here, the principal is not bound, and it arguably is unfair to leave the third party without any recovery. Thus, an agent generally is bound on the theory that he has made an implied warranty of his authority to contract.[6]

To illustrate, suppose that Allen is a traveling salesman for Prine, a seller of furs. Allen has actual authority to receive offers for the sale of Prine's furs, but not to make contracts of sale, which must be approved by Prine himself. Prine has long followed this practice, and it is customary in the markets where his agents work. Representing himself as Prine's agent but saying nothing about his authority, Allen contracts to sell Prine's furs to Thatcher on Prine's behalf. Thatcher, who should have known better, honestly believes that Allen has authority to contract to sell Prine's furs. Prine is not liable on Allen's contract because Allen lacked actual or apparent authority to bind him. But Allen is liable to Thatcher for breaching his implied warranty of authority.

However, an agent is *not* liable for making an unauthorized contract if:

1. The third party *actually knows* that the agent lacks authority. In such situations, of course, the principal is not liable either. However, note from the above example that an agent still is liable where the third party had *reason to know* that authority was lacking but honestly failed to realize this.

2. The principal subsequently *ratifies* the contract. Here, the principal is bound and the agent is discharged. Because ratification relates back to the time the contract was made, the relation of

the parties is the same as if the agent had possessed authority in the first place.

3. The agent adequately *notifies* the third party that he does not warrant his authority to contract.

CONTRACT SUITS AGAINST PRINCIPAL AND AGENT

Figure 1 sketches the most important situations where the principal, the agent, or both are liable as a result of the agent's contracts. As it suggests, a third party usually has *someone* to sue if neither the principal nor the agent performs on the agent's contract.

Absent ratification, of course, a principal is not liable on contracts made by an agent who lacked authority to contract. Here, though, the agent usually is bound under an implied warranty of authority. In addition, the agent is bound on the contract where the principal was partially disclosed, undisclosed, or legally nonexistent.[7] Authorized contracts for a disclosed principal do not bind an agent unless he has agreed to be liable. But here, the agent's actual or apparent authority binds the principal.

As Figure 1 further illustrates, in certain situations both the principal and the agent are liable on a contract made by the agent. This can occur where an agent with appropriate authority contracts on behalf of a partially disclosed or undisclosed principal. Also, an agent can bind himself by express agreement in situations where the principal also is bound. In such cases, which party is ultimately responsible to the third person? The complicated rules governing this question vary from situation to situation. Due to their complexity and variety, they are beyond the scope of this text. Sometimes, however, the principal or the agent is discharged once the third

---

[6]Also, an agent who intentionally misrepresents his authority may be liable to the third party in tort. In addition, some states may allow tort liability for negligent misrepresentations. Where the third party has a tort suit, he may often elect to recover damages or rescind the contract.

[7]Note, however, that it is impossible for an agent for an undisclosed principal to have apparent authority. Apparent authority exists when the principal's communications to the third party cause that party to reasonably believe that the agent has authority to contract for another. How can this occur when the principal is undisclosed?

FIGURE 1   Contract Liability of Principal and Agent:
The Major Possibilities

	Agent's Authority		
Principal	**Actual**	**Apparent**	**None**
Disclosed	P liable; A not liable unless agreement	P liable; A not liable unless agreement	P not liable; A usually liable
Partially Disclosed	P liable; A liable	P liable; A liable	P not liable; A liable
Undisclosed	P liable; A liable	Impossible	P not liable; A liable

party obtains or satisfies a judgment against the other. As discussed in the previous chapter, though, a principal sometimes is required to indemnify an agent who is contractually liable to a third party.

TORT LIABILITY OF THE PRINCIPAL

Introduction

A principal's liability for her agent's torts is a many-faceted subject.[8] First, under the doctrine of **respondeat superior**, an employer is liable for an employee's torts if those torts are committed within the scope of the employee's employment. Second, if the principal herself was at fault, she may be *directly* liable for an agent's tort. Third, although principals generally are not liable for torts committed by *independent contractors*, such liability does exist in a few cases. Continuing our discussion of the principal's tort liability is a separate subject that straddles tort and contract: a principal's liability for the agent's *misrepresentations*. We discuss each of these subjects in turn, before examining a principal's liability for torts committed by subagents.

Respondeat Superior Liability

Under the doctrine of **respondeat superior** (let the master answer), a principal who is an *employer* is liable for torts committed by agents who are *employees* and who commit the tort while acting within the *scope of their*

employment. This doctrine applies to an employee's negligence, recklessness, or intentional torts. The *VIP Tours* case in the last chapter outlined the main factors courts consider when determining whether an agent is an employee.[9] Recall that the most important of these factors is a principal's right to control the physical details of an agent's work.

Respondeat superior is a rule of *imputed* or *vicarious* liability because it bases an employer's liability on his relationship with the employee rather than his own fault. This imputation of liability to the employer reflects the following beliefs: (1) that the economic burdens of employee torts can best be borne by employers; (2) that employers often can protect themselves against such burdens by self-insuring or purchasing insurance; and (3) that the resulting costs frequently can be passed on to consumers, thus "socializing" the economic risk posed by employee torts. *Respondeat superior* also gives employers an incentive to ensure that their employees avoid tortious behavior. Because they typically control the physical details of the work, employers are fairly well positioned to reduce employee torts.

Scope of Employment   *Respondeat superior*'s scope of-employment requirement has been formulated in many ways and is notoriously flexible and ambiguous. In the past, for example, some courts considering this question asked whether the employee was on a "frolic" of his own, or merely made a "detour" from his assigned activity. According to the *Restatement*, an employee's conduct is within the scope of his employment if it meets each of the following four tests:[10]

* **1.**   *It was of the* **kind** *that the employee was employed to perform.* To meet this test, an employee's conduct need only be of the same general nature as work expressly authorized, or be incidental to its performance. For instance, the following *Gatzke* case treats on-the-job smoking as an act incidental to an employee's authorized work. But an employee hired only to care for his employer's horses probably is not within the scope of employment if he paints the employer's house without the employer's authorization.

---

[8]In addition to the various forms of tort liability discussed below, a principal can also *ratify* an agent's torts.

[9]Also, recall that this text follows the *Restatement (Second) of Agency* by treating *all* employees as agents (and their employers as principals). Independent contractors, on the other hand, may or may not be agents.

[10]*Restatement (Second) of Agency* § 228(1) (1959). This section adds that if an employee intentionally uses force on another, this must have been "not unexpectable" by the employer to be within the scope of employment.

Even criminal conduct occasionally may be within the scope of employment. Here, the test seems to be whether the employer could reasonably anticipate the criminal behavior in question. Thus, a delivery driver who exceeds the speed limit while on a rush job probably is covered, but a driver who shoots another driver after a traffic altercation almost certainly is not.

✳ **2.** *It occurred substantially within the* **time** *period authorized by the employer.* This is the time during which an employer has the right to control the details of an employee's work. Ordinarily, it is simply the employee's assigned time of work. Beyond this, there is an extra period of time during which the employment may continue. For instance, a security guard whose regular quitting time is 5:00 probably meets the time test if he unjustifiably injures an intruder at 5:15. Doing the same thing three hours later, however, would put the guard outside the scope of employment.

✳ **3.** *It occurred substantially within the* **location** *authorized by the employer.* This is the location authorized by the employer or a location not unreasonably distant from it. Determining whether the employee's conduct met this third test is generally a question of degree. For example, a saleswoman told to limit her activities to New York City probably would satisfy the location requirement while pursuing the employer's business in suburbs just outside the city limits, but not while pursuing the same business in Philadelphia. Generally, the smaller the authorized area of activity, the smaller the departure from that area needed to put the employee outside the scope of employment. For example, consider the different physical distance limitations that should apply to a factory worker and a traveling salesperson.

✳ **4.** *It was motivated* **at least in part** *by the* **purpose** *of serving the employer.* This test is met where the employee's conduct was motivated *to any appreciable extent* by the desire to serve the employer. Thus, an employee's tort may be within the scope of employment even if the motives for committing it were partly personal. For example, suppose than a delivery employee is behind schedule and for that reason has an accident while speeding to make a delivery in his employer's truck. The employee would be within the scope of employment even if another reason for his speeding was to impress a friend who was riding with him.

To repeat, the *Restatement* requires that an employee's tort meet *all four* of these tests to be within the scope of employment. This is exactly what happened in the *Edgewater Motels, Inc. v. Gatzke* case that follows.

EDGEWATER MOTELS, INC. v. GATZKE

277 N.W.2d 11 (Minn. Sup. Ct. 1979)

A. J. Gatzke, a district manager for the Walgreen Company, spent several weeks in Duluth, Minnesota, supervising the opening of a new Walgreen restaurant there. He remained at the restaurant approximately 17 hours a day, and he was on call 24 hours a day to handle problems arising in other Walgreen restaurants in the district. While in Duluth, he lived at the Edgewater Motel at Walgreen's expense. After some heavy drinking late one night, Gatzke returned to his motel room and spent some time at a desk filling out an expense account required by his employer. Gatzke was a heavy smoker, and he testified that he probably smoked a cigarette while completing the expense account. Shortly after Gatzke went to bed, a fire broke out in his motel room. Gatzke escaped, but fire damage to the motel totaled over $330,000. An expert witness testified that the fire was caused by a burning cigarette or a match and that it started in or near a wastebasket located beside the desk at which Gatzke worked.

Edgewater sued Walgreen for Gatzke's negligence. The jury found for Edgewater, in the process concluding that Gatzke acted within the scope of his employment when he filled out the form and disposed of the cigarette. The trial court, however, granted Walgreen's motion for judgment notwithstanding the verdict. Edgewater appealed. The question for the appellate court was whether the trial judge erred in setting aside the jury's finding that Gatzke's negligent conduct occurred within the scope of his employment.

Scott, Justice.   Gatzke's negligent smoking of a cigarette was a direct cause of the damages sustained by Edgewater. The question is whether the facts reasonably support the imposition of vicarious liability on Walgreen's for the conceded negligent act of its employee.

For an employer to be held vicariously liable for an employee's negligent conduct, the employee's wrongful act must be committed within the scope of his employment. To support [such] a finding, it must be shown that his conduct was, to some degree, in furtherance of the interests of his employer. This principle is recognized by *Restatement (Second) of Agency* section 235, which states: "An act of a servant is not within the scope of employment if it is done with no intention to perform it as part of or incident to a service on account of which he is employed." Other factors to be considered in the scope of employment determination are whether the conduct is of the kind that the employee is authorized to perform and whether the act occurs substantially within authorized time and space restrictions.

The initial question is whether an employee's smoking of a cigarette can constitute conduct within his scope of employment. The courts which have considered the question have not agreed on its resolution. A number of courts have ruled that the act of smoking, even when done simultaneously with work-related activity, is not within the employee's scope of employment because it is a matter personal to the employee which is not done in furtherance of the employer's interest. Other courts have reasoned that the smoking of a cigarette, if done while engaged in the business of the employer, is within an employee's scope of employment because it is a minor deviation from the employee's work-related activities, and thus merely incidental to employment. We agree with this analysis and hold that an employer can be vicariously liable for an employee's negligent smoking of a cigarette if he was otherwise acting in the scope of his employment at the time of the negligent act.

Thus, we must next determine whether Gatzke was otherwise in the scope of his employment at the time of his negligent act. Even assuming that Gatzke was outside the scope of his employment while he was at the bar, Gatzke resumed his employment activities after he returned to his motel room and filled out his expense account. The expense account was completed so that Gatzke could be reimbursed by Walgreen's for his work-related expenses. In this sense, Gatzke is performing an act for his own personal benefit. However, the completion of the expense account also furthers the employer's business in that it provides detailed documentation of business expenses so that they are properly deductible for tax purposes. In this light, the filling out of the expense form can be viewed as serving a dual purpose: that of furthering Gatzke's personal interests and promoting his employer's business purposes. Accordingly, the completion of the expense account is an act done in furtherance of the employer's business purposes.

Additionally, the record indicates that Gatzke was an executive type of employee who had no set working hours. He considered himself a 24-hour-a-day man; his room at the Edgewater Motel was his "office away from home." It [is] therefore reasonable to determine that the filling out of his expense account was done within authorized time and space limits of his employment.

Judgment reversed in favor of Edgewater.

Since he was working, the company would still be liable

Direct Liability

As the following *J. v. Victory Tabernacle Baptist Church* case should make clear, a principal's **direct liability** for an agent's torts differs greatly from *respondeat superior* liability. Here, the principal's liability is direct rather than imputed because the principal *himself* is at fault. There is no scope-of-employment requirement in direct liability cases, and the agent need not be an employee. Of course, a principal might incur both direct liability and *respondeat superior* liability in cases where, due to the principal's fault, an employee commits a tort within the scope of her employment.

A principal is directly liable to third parties for an agent's tortious conduct if the principal *directs* that conduct and *intends* that it occur. In such cases, the *agent's* behavior might be intentional, reckless, or negligent. For instance, if Petty tells his agent Able to beat up Tabler and Able does so, Petty is directly liable to Tabler. Petty also would be liable for harm to third parties that results from his intentionally telling Able to do construction work in a negligent, substandard fashion.

The typical direct liability case, however, involves harm caused by the principal's *negligence* regarding the agent. In such cases, the normal negligence rules discussed in the Negligence and Strict Liability chapter usually apply. Examples of direct liability for negligence include: (1) giving the agent improper or unclear instructions; (2) failing to make and enforce appropriate regulations to govern the agent's conduct; (3) hiring an unsuitable agent; (4) failing to discharge an unsuitable agent; (5) furnishing an agent with improper tools, instruments, or materials; and (6) carelessly supervising an agent. The complaint in the following *Victory Tabernacle* case alleged negligent hiring and negligent supervision, plus the defendant's negligent failure to warn.

J. v. VICTORY TABERNACLE BAPTIST CHURCH

372 S.E.2d 391 (Va. Sup. Ct. 1988)

A woman sued the Victory Tabernacle Baptist Church, alleging that due to its negligence, her 10-year-old daughter had been repeatedly raped and sexually assaulted by a church employee. The plaintiff's complaint claimed that when the church hired the employee, it knew or should have known that he had recently been convicted of aggravated sexual assault on a young girl, that he was on probation for this offense, and that a condition of his probation was that he not be involved with children. Despite all this, the complaint continued, the employee's duties allowed him freely to come into contact with children, including the plaintiff's daughter, and he was given keys enabling him to lock and unlock all the church's doors.

The complaint's three counts alleged negligent hiring, negligent supervision, and failure to warn the victim's parents of the employee's past criminal and sexual history. The church filed a demurrer to the entire complaint, and the trial court sustained the demurrer. The plaintiff appealed this decision, and the case reached the Virginia Supreme Court.

Thomas, Justice.   We decide only whether the allegations of negligent hiring state a cause of action in Virginia. This is so because the plaintiff failed to submit any authority concerning negligent supervision and failure to warn. Consequently, those issues have been abandoned.

Victory Baptist argues that the trial court properly sustained the demurrer on the question of negligent hiring because plaintiff failed to allege that the harm to the victim was caused by negligence on the part of the employee. According to this argument, the negligent hiring cause of action requires that the negligently hired individual negligently injured the plaintiff. We disagree. The very thing that allegedly should have been foreseen in this case is that the employee would commit a violent act upon a child. To say that a negligently hired employee who acts willfully or criminally thus relieves his employer of liability for negligent hiring when willful or criminal conduct is precisely what the employer should have foreseen would rob the tort of vitality.

Victory Baptist also argues that the [plaintiff's] allegations do not establish a sufficient nexus among the employer's breach of duty, the employee's conduct, and the employee's employment. In oral argument, counsel explained that there were no allegations that the employee was engaged in the church's business when the child was injured—no allegation, for example, that the employee was on duty for the church at the time the girl was raped. Counsel then made clear that what he was complaining about was that there were no allegations to bring the employee's conduct within the scope of his employment.

This argument demonstrates that Victory Baptist is confusing the doctrine of *respondeat superior* with the tort of negligent hiring. This distinction was succinctly stated in a recent law review article:

Under *respondeat superior*, an employer is vicariously liable for an employee's tortious acts committed within the scope of employment. In contrast, negligent hiring is a doctrine of primary liability; the employer is principally liable for negligently placing an unfit person in an employment situation involving an unreasonable risk of harm to others. Negligent hiring, therefore, enables plaintiffs to recover in situations where *respondeat superior*'s scope of employment limitation previously protected employers from liability.

Thus, Victory Baptist's contention is misplaced.

In our opinion, the [complaint] was fully sufficient to state a claim of negligent hiring, and thus it was error for the trial court to sustain the demurrer on that issue. The trial court's disposition of [the other two negligence] counts will be affirmed.

Judgment for the church affirmed in part and reversed in part. Case remanded for trial consistent with the Supreme Court's opinion.

Liability for Torts of Independent Contractors

Generally, a principal is *not* liable for torts committed by *independent contractors*. As compared with employees, independent contractors are more likely to have the size and resources to insure against tort liability and to pass on the resulting costs themselves. In at least some cases, therefore, the risk still can be socialized if the independent contractor is held responsible. Because the principal does not control the manner in which an independent contractor's work is performed, moreover, he has less ability to prevent a contractor's torts than an employer has to prevent an employee's torts. Thus, imposing liability on principals for the torts of independent contractors may be relatively ineffective in reducing the contractor's tortious behavior.

However, the general rule that principals are not liable for torts committed by independent contractors has exceptions. For example:

1. A principal can be *directly* liable for tortious behavior connected with the retention of an independent contractor. One example is the negligent hiring of a dangerously incompetent independent contractor.

2. A principal is liable for harm resulting from the independent contractor's failure to perform a *nondelegable duty*. A nondelegable duty is a duty whose proper performance is considered so important to the community that a principal cannot avoid liability by contracting it away to another party. Examples include a carrier's duty to transport its passengers safely, a municipality's duty to keep its streets in repair, a railroad's duty to

maintain safe crossings, and a landlord's duties to make repairs and to use care in doing so. Thus, a landlord who retains an independent contractor to repair the stairs in an apartment building is liable for injuries caused by the contractor's failure to repair the stairs properly.

3. A principal is liable for an independent contractor's negligent failure to take the special precautions needed to conduct certain *highly dangerous* or *inherently dangerous* activities.[11] Examples of such activities include excavations in publicly traveled areas, the clearing of land by fire, the construction of a dam, and the demolition of a building. For example, a contractor engaged in demolishing a building presumably has duties to warn pedestrians and to keep them at a safe distance. If injury results from the independent contractor's failure to meet these duties, the principal is liable.

Liability for Agent's Misrepresentations

A principal's liability for misrepresentations made by agents to third parties involves both contract and tort principles.[12] A principal is *directly* liable for misrepresentations made by her agent during authorized

---

[11]The range of activities considered "highly dangerous" or "inherently dangerous" is probably greater than the range of activities considered "ultrahazardous" or "abnormally dangerous" for strict liability purposes. On the latter activities, see the Negligence and Strict Liability chapter.

[12]On fraud and misrepresentation in the tort and contract contexts, see the Intentional Torts chapter and the Reality of Consent chapter.

transactions if she *intended* that the agent make the misrepresentations. In some states, a principal also may be directly liable if she *negligently* allows the agent to make misrepresentations.

Even where a principal is not directly at fault, she may be liable for an agent's misrepresentations if the agent had *actual or apparent authority to make true statements on the subject*. Suppose that an agent to sell farmland falsely states that a stream on the land has never flooded the property when in fact it does so almost every year, and that this statement induces a third party to buy the land. The principal is directly liable if she intended that the agent make this false statement. Even if the principal is personally blameless, she is liable if the agent had actual or apparent authority to make true statements about the spring.

If the agent intended to make the misrepresentation, or if the principal intended that the agent make it, the third party can recover in tort for the losses that result. In some states, a third party also may recover in tort for misrepresentations resulting from the principal's or the agent's negligence. In either case, the third party can elect to rescind the transaction instead of pursuing a tort suit.

Exculpatory Clauses   Both honest and dishonest principals may attempt to avoid liability for an agent's misrepresentations by including an exculpatory clause in contracts that the agent makes with third parties. Such clauses typically state that the agent only has authority to make the representations contained in the contract and that only those representations bind the principal. Exculpatory clauses do not protect a principal who intends or expects that an agent will make false statements. Otherwise, though, they insulate the principal from *tort* liability if the agent misrepresents. But the third party still may *rescind* the transaction, because it would be unjust to let the principal benefit from the transaction while disclaiming responsibility for it.

Torts of Subagents

The *Restatement* declares that the rules governing a principal's liability for an agent's torts generally control a principal's liability for the torts of *subagents*.[13] Thus, a principal might be directly liable for a subagent's tort where, for example, he orders the subagent to commit the tort. However, because an employer-employee relationship between principal and subagent is unlikely, a principal usually is not subject to *respondeat superior* liability for a subagent's torts. Occasionally, though, courts have found principals liable for their subagents' misrepresentations.

---

[13]*Restatement (Second) of Agency* § 255 (1959).

CONCEPT REVIEW

AN OUTLINE OF THE PRINCIPAL'S TORT LIABILITY

Respondeat Superior	1. Agent must be an employee, *and* 2. Employee must act within scope of employment while committing tort
Direct Liability	1. Principal intends and directs agent's intentional tort, recklessness, or negligence, *or* 2. Principal is negligent regarding agent
Torts of Independent Contractors	1. Principal generally is *not* liable 2. Exceptions for direct liability, highly dangerous activities, and nondelegable duties
Misrepresentation	1. Direct liability 2. Vicarious liability where agent had authority to make true statements on the subject of the misrepresentation 3. An exculpatory clause may eliminate the principal's tort liability, but the third party still can rescind
Torts of Subagents	The preceding rules govern the principal's liability, but their application varies

TORT LIABILITY OF THE AGENT

The rules stated in the previous section generally govern the liability of *agents* for torts committed by subagents whom they have appointed.[14] In addition, agents usually are liable for their *own* torts. The fact that an agent has acted at the principal's command normally does not absolve the agent from liability. As you might guess, however, there are certain exceptions to this generalization.

1. An agent can escape liability if she was *exercising a privilege of the principal.* Suppose that Tingle grants Parkham a valid right-of-way to transport his farm products over a private road crossing Tingle's land. If so, Parkham's agent, Adams, would not be liable in trespass for driving across Tingle's land to transport farm products if she did so at Parkam's command. However, an agent must not exceed the scope of the privilege and must act for the purpose for which the privilege was given. Thus, Adams would not be protected if she took her Jeep on a midnight joyride across Tingle's land. Also, the privilege given the agent must be delegable in the first place. If Tingle had given the easement to Parkham exclusively, Adams would not be privileged to drive across Tingle's land.

2. A principal who is *privileged to take certain actions in defense of his person or property* often may authorize an agent to do the same. In such cases, the agent escapes liability if the principal could have done so. For example, a properly authorized agent may use force to protect the life or property of his principal if the principal could have done the same.

3. An agent who makes *misrepresentations* while conducting the principal's business is not liable in tort unless he either *knew or had reason to know* of their falsity. Suppose Parker authorizes Arnold to sell his house, falsely telling Arnold that the house is fully insulated. Arnold does not know that the statement is false, and could not discover its falsity through an ordinary, reasonable inspection. If Arnold tells Thomas that the house is fully insulated and Thomas relies on this statement in purchasing the house, Parker is directly liable to Thomas, but Arnold is not liable.

4. An agent is not liable for injuries to third persons caused by defective tools or instrumentalities furnished by the principal unless the agent had actual knowledge or reason to know of the defect.

TORT SUITS AGAINST PRINCIPAL AND AGENT

In many cases, both principal and agent are liable for an agent's torts. Here, the principal and the agent are *jointly and severally* liable. This means that a third party may join the principal and the agent in one suit and get a judgment against each, or may sue either or both individually and get a judgment against either or both. However, the third party is entitled to only one satisfaction for his claim. Once the third party actually collects in full from either the principal or the agent, no further recovery is possible.

In some cases, therefore, either the principal or the agent has to satisfy the judgment alone despite the other party's liability. Here, the other party sometimes is required to *indemnify* the party who has satisfied the judgment. As discussed in the previous chapter, for example, there are situations where a principal may be required to indemnify an agent for tort liability the agent incurs. On the other hand, some torts committed by agents may involve the breach of a duty agents owe their principals, and a principal may be able to recover from an agent on this basis.

CRIMINAL LIABILITY

As a general proposition, principals are not liable for crimes committed by their agents or employees unless they directed, approved, or participated in the crime. Also, agents usually are liable for their own crimes, and their status as agents or the fact that they acted at the principal's direction has no effect on their criminal liability. Various state and federal criminal statutes, however, create exceptions to these generalizations. Perhaps more importantly, different criminal liability rules may apply where the principal is a corporation or other business entity. The Crimes chapter and the Management of Corporations chapter discuss the criminal liability of corporations, their directors, and their officers. The Operation of Partnership and Related Forms chapter examines the criminal liability of partnerships and their partners.

---

[14]*Restatement (Second) of Agency* § 362 (1959).

ETHICAL AND PUBLIC POLICY CONCERNS

1. As you have seen, one of the justifications for *respondeat superior* is that employers are in a relatively good position to absorb liability for employee torts, to insure against such liability, and to pass on the resulting costs. What are the advantages and disadvantages of applying this reasoning to make principals liable for all torts committed by *independent contractors* within the scope of their employment?

2. If the purposes underlying *respondeat superior* are sound ones, why limit the doctrine to employee torts committed within the scope of employment? In other words, why not make employers liable for *all* torts committed by their employees?

3. As you have seen, agents who make unauthorized contracts are not liable if the principal later ratifies the contract. The official justification for this rule is that, because ratification relates back to the time the unauthorized contract was made, the relations of the parties are the same as if the agent had originally had authority. However, there is another, much more down-to-earth, justification for this rule. What is it?

SUMMARY

A principal is liable on a contract made by his agent if the agent had *express, implied, or apparent authority* to make that contract. Even if the agent's contract was unauthorized, a principal may be bound to the contract by *ratifying* it. A principal who lacks capacity at the time of the contract may avoid it, but an agent's incapacity usually does not affect the liability of a principal who has capacity. Finally, a subagent with appropriate authority can bind the principal and the agent in contract.

An agent's contract liability usually depends on a different set of factors. Generally, an agent who contracts for a *disclosed principal* is not liable on contracts made for such a principal. However, an agent who contracts for a *partially disclosed* or an *undisclosed* principal typically is bound to the contract. Also, agents normally are liable on contracts they make on behalf of *legally nonexistent* principals. Moreover, agents may bind themselves to a contract by expressly so agreeing. And an agent who acts in excess of her authority may be liable to the third party under an implied warranty of authority, or for misrepresentation.

A principal's liability for his agent's torts comes in several forms. A principal is *vicariously* liable for the torts of an agent when the agent is an *employee* who has committed the tort within the *scope of his employment*. To be within the scope of employment, the employee's conduct usually must: (1) be of the kind that he was employed to perform, (2) occur substantially within the time limits of the employment, (3) occur substantially within the space limits of the employment, and (4) be motivated at least in part by the purpose of serving the employer. A principal is *directly* liable when he commands or authorizes the agent to engage in tortious behavior, or is negligent in hiring, retraining, instructing, directing, or equipping an agent. Subject to certain exceptions, a principal is not liable for the torts of *independent contractors*. Finally, a principal may be directly liable for her agent's *misrepresentations*, and also is liable for such misrepresentations when the agent had authority to make true statements on the subject of the misrepresentation. A principal who puts an *exculpatory clause* in contracts his agent makes with third parties, however, often escapes tort liability, although the third party usually may rescind the contract.

Agents generally are liable for their own torts, and, with a few exceptions, the fact that they acted for a principal does not relieve them of liability. Likewise, agents generally are liable for their own crimes. A principal usually is not liable for crimes committed by an agent unless he directed, approved, or participated in their commission. Under various statutes and the laws of corporations and partnership, however, different criminal liability rules sometimes obtain.

PROBLEM CASES

1. The Capital Dredge and Dock Corporation, a construction contractor, sued the city of Detroit for damages associated with certain construction work it had been performing for the city. One of the city's defenses was that Capital had released the city from liability on some of Capital's present claims during earlier, related litigation between Capital and the city. The releases were part of a settlement document signed by Capital Dredge's attorney, Alteri. Capital Dredge had held Alteri out as having authority to represent it in the relevant litigation, and this included authority to negotiate a settlement. However, unknown to the city, Capital Dredge also had specifically told Alteri not to compromise some of the claims he later actually settled. Under these circumstances, could Alteri have had implied authority to settle the claims in question? Could he have had apparent authority to do so?

2. Roma Funk, who co-owned a piece of land along with her seven brothers and sisters, contracted to sell the land to her neighbors. It was unclear whether Funk had authority to sell the land on behalf of her siblings. For certain, there was no writing giving her such authority. Funk's siblings eventually backed out of the deal, and the buyers sued for specific performance. They argued that Funk's siblings had ratified her contract by failing to come forward and repudiate it. Can a contract ever be ratified in this way? Regardless of your answer to this question, there is a dispositive reason why Funk's siblings could not have ratified this particular contract. What is it? Assume that in this state an agent who executes an agreement conveying an interest in land on behalf of his principal must be authorized in writing.

3. A certain law firm represented a man named Helric in a dispute over mining claims. The settlement reached in Helric's case permitted Helric to restake the disputed claims. The law firm assisted in having the claims restaked by retaining Free to do the job for Helric. When the firm first contacted Free, the partner in charge of the case told Free that the firm was representing Helric. Later correspondence between the firm and Free clearly stated that Helric was the owner of the claims Free was to restake. Free completed the job, and later sued the law firm for the amount due him. Is the firm liable to Free on the contract it made for Helric?

4. Seascape Restaurants, Inc., operated a restaurant called the Magic Moment. Jeff Rosenberg was one-third owner and president of Seascape. Van D. Costas, the president of Van D. Costas, Inc., contracted to construct a "magical entrance" to the Magic Moment. Jeff Rosenberg signed the contract on a line under which appeared the words "Jeff Rosenberg, the Magic Moment." The contract did not refer to Seascape, and Costas knew nothing of Seascape's existence. After a dispute over performance of the contract, Costas sued Rosenberg for breach of contract. Is Rosenberg personally liable to Costas?

5. Dale F. Everett did business as the Dale F. Everett Company, Inc. (the Company). He also formed a retail business known as The Clubhouse, which had no legal status aside from its registration as a trade name for the Company. Everett contracted with James Smith for $8,424 of advertising time. Everett signed his contract with Smith as follows: "THE CLUBHOUSE, Client, By Dale F. Everett." Smith later sent billing statements for the ads to "The Clubhouse, Inc." Everett never paid Smith the $8,424, and Smith sued Everett personally. Is Everett personally liable on the contract with Smith?

6. Twelve individuals agreed to sponsor and promote a group of Little League baseball teams called the Golden Spike Little League. The league was a loosely formed voluntary association without any legal identity. The 12 individuals arranged with Smith & Edwards to furnish the needed uniforms and equipment, signed for them, picked them up, and distributed them to the teams. No one ever paid Smith & Edwards the $3,900 bill for the uniforms and equipment. Smith & Edwards sued the 12 individuals in their personal capacities for the amount due. If they defend by saying that they acted as agents for a disclosed principal (the league), will the defense be successful? Why or why not?

7. Redford had been a backhoe operator for five years. Although he had worked for other sign companies, he had spent 90 percent of his time during the past three years working for Tube Art Display, Inc. Redford generally dug holes exactly as directed by the sign company employing him. He did, however, pay his own business taxes, and he did not participate in any of the fringe benefits available to Tube Art employees.

Tube Art obtained a permit to install a sign in the parking lot of a combination commercial and apartment building. Telling Redford how to proceed, Tube Art's service manager laid out the exact location of a 4 x 4 feet square on the asphalt surface with yellow paint and directed that the hole be six feet deep. After Redford began the job, he struck a small natural gas pipeline with the backhoe. He examined the pipe, and, finding no indication of a leak or break, concluded that the line was not in use and left the worksite. Later, an explosion and fire occurred in the building serviced by the line. As a result, a business owned by Massey was destroyed. Massey sued Tube Art for Redford's negligence under the doctrine of *respondeat superior.* Will Massey recover? You can assume that Redford was negligent.

8. John Hondzinski delivered newspapers in his own car for a newspaper called the *News Herald.* Under the contract between Hondzinski and the *News Herald,* Hondzinski was obligated to pick up and promptly deliver newspapers provided by the *News Herald,* but the means and the routes for doing so were within Hondzinski's control. While in the process of making deliveries for the *News Herald* one day, Hondzinski negligently allowed his car to collide with a car driven by Peter Janice. Janice sued the *News Herald* for Hondzinski's negligence. Can Janice recover against the *News Herald* under the doctrine of *respondeat superior?* Why or why not? *No. because your car i not an employee*

9. Kathy Kendall ordered some food at a Whataburger, Inc. restaurant. After becoming dissatisfied with the food or her service, she voiced her displeasure to Isaac Ervin, a young Whataburger employee working behind the service counter. In response, Ervin threw a metal french fry basket containing hot grease into her face. Kendall sued Whataburger for her resulting injuries. Under the four *Restatement* tests discussed in the text, was Ervin's action within the scope of his employment, thus making Whataburger liable under the doctrine of *respondeat superior?* Under what other theory might Kendall possibly recover against Whataburger? In answering the *first* question, assume that Whataburger had no reason to suspect that Ervin was capable of doing what he did. In answering the *second* question, leave this possibility open. *Most Company Not LIABLE for THE CRIMINAL ACT OF EMPLOYEE IN THIS CASE!*

you hear the agency practices

10. Susie Mae Woodson's husband was killed as the result of a cave-in at a construction site where he was

It's D&J's JOB, even though there not digging ditch. You could make a Case that they were overall negligence in their work of overseeing

laying sewer pipe in a trench dug by an independent contractor of Davidson & Jones, Inc. (D&J). The trench in which Mr. Woodson was working had not been braced or shored to prevent a cave-in, and this was a violation of federal occupational safety regulations. Mrs. Woodson sued D&J for the independent contractor's negligence. Will she recover? Assume that D&J was not in any way *directly* liable regarding the independent contractor.

11. Letbetter purchased merchandise from a salesperson representing United Laboratories. The contract of sale expressly provided that no representations of the salesperson would be binding upon the seller unless they were written into the order. The salesperson made representations about the suitability of the materials for certain uses, but the representations were not included in the sales orders. The materials were not suitable for the purposes represented. Is United Laboratories liable in tort for the salesperson's representations? Assume that United Laboratories did not intend that the salesperson make the representations and that it had no reason to think that they would be made.

Principal not liable in tort because of the disclaimer that was written above!!

Parole evidence
2 for the third party

IF AGENT HAS APPARENT AUTHORITY THEN THE PRINCIPAL IS going to BE LIABLE FOR THEIR AGENT!!

PARTNERSHIP LAW

CHAPTER 36

INTRODUCTION TO FORMS OF BUSINESS AND FORMATION OF PARTNERSHIPS

INTRODUCTION

In this chapter, you begin your study of business organizations. In the next eight chapters, you will study seven forms of business, including the four most important ones:

1. Sole proprietorship.
2. Partnership (sometimes called general partnership).
3. Limited partnership.
4. Corporation.

Early in this chapter, you will preview the basic characteristics of these most important forms of business and learn how to select an appropriate form for your business venture. Following that introduction, you will begin your in-depth study of partnerships, learning their characteristics and the formalities for their creation. You will study the operation of partnerships and their dissolution, limited partnerships, and corporations in the chapters that follow.

CHOOSING A FORM OF BUSINESS

One of the most important decisions made by a person beginning a business is choosing a **form of business.**

This decision is important because, among other reasons, the business owner's liability and control of the business vary greatly among the many forms of business. In addition, some business forms offer significant tax advantages to their owners.

Although other forms of business exist, usually a person starting a business will wish to organize the business as a sole proprietorship, partnership, limited partnership, or corporation.

Sole Proprietorship

A **sole proprietorship** has only one owner. The sole proprietorship is merely an extension of its owner: a *sole proprietor* owns his own business, and no one else owns any part of it.

As the only owner, the sole proprietor has the right to make all the management decisions of the business. In addition, all the profits of the business are his. In return for his complete managerial control and sole claim to profits, he assumes great liability: he is *personally liable* for all the obligations of the business. All the debts of the business, including debts on contracts signed only in the name of the business, are his debts. If the assets of the business are insufficient to pay the claims of its creditors, the creditors may require the sole proprietor to pay the claims using his individual, nonbusiness assets, such as money from his bank account and the proceeds from the sale of his house. A sole proprietor may lose everything if his business becomes insolvent. Hence, the sole proprietorship is a risky form of business for its owner.

In light of this risk, you may ask why any person would organize a business as a sole proprietorship. There are two reasons. First, the sole proprietorship is formed very easily and inexpensively. No formalities are necessary. Second, few people consider the business-form decision. They merely begin their businesses. Thus, by default, a person going into business by herself automatically creates a sole proprietorship when she fails to choose another business form. These two reasons explain why the sole proprietorship is the most common form of business in the United States.

Because the sole proprietorship is merely an extension of its owner, it has no life apart from its owner. Therefore, while the business of a sole proprietorship may be freely sold to someone else, legally the sole proprietorship as a form of business cannot be transferred to another person. The buyer of the business must create his own form of business to conduct the business.

A sole proprietorship is not a legal entity. It cannot sue or be sued. Instead, creditors must sue the owner. The sole proprietor, in his own name, must sue those who harm the business.

A sole proprietor may hire employees for the business, but they are employees of the sole proprietor. Under the law of agency, the sole proprietor is responsible for her employees' authorized contracts and for the torts they commit in the course of their employment. Also, a sole proprietorship is not an income tax-paying entity for federal income tax purposes. All of the income of a sole proprietorship is income to its owner and must be reported on the sole proprietor's individual federal income tax return. Likewise, any business losses are deductible without limit on the sole proprietor's individual tax return. This loss-deduction advantage explains why some wealthier taxpayers use the sole proprietorship for selected business investments—when losses are expected in the early years of the business, yet the risk of liability is low. Such an investor may form a sole proprietorship and hire a professional manager to operate the business.

Many sole proprietorships have trade names. For example, Caryl Stanley may operate her bagel shop under the name Caryl's Bagel Shop. Caryl would be required to file the trade name under a state statute requiring the registration of fictitious business names. If she were sued by a creditor, the creditor would address his complaint to "Caryl Stanley, doing business as Caryl's Bagel Shop."

Partnership

A **partnership** has two or more owners, called *partners*. The partners have the right to make all the management decisions for the business. In addition, all the profits of the business are shared by the partners.

In return for their complete managerial control and sole claim to profits, the partners assume personal liability for all the obligations of the business. All the debts of the business, including debts on authorized contracts signed only by one partner or by a partnership employee, are the debts of all the partners. Likewise, partners are liable for the torts committed in the course of business by their partners or by partnership employees. If the assets of the business are insufficient to pay the claims of its creditors, the creditors may require one or more of the partners to pay the claims using their individual, nonbusiness assets. Thus, a partner may have to pay more than his share of partnership liabilities. Hence, the partnership is a riskier form of business for its partners than is the sole proprietorship.

Like the sole proprietorship, the partnership is not a tax-paying entity for federal income tax purposes. All of the income of the partnership is income to its partners and must be reported on the individual partner's federal income tax return, even if the partnership did not distribute any profits to the partners. Likewise, any business losses are deductible without limit on the partner's individual tax return. This loss-deduction privilege gives the partnership an advantage over the limited partnership and corporation, which limit the owner's ability to deduct business losses.

The partnership has no life apart from its owners. When a partner dies or otherwise leaves the business, the partnership is dissolved. Therefore, while the business of a partnership may be freely sold to someone else by agreement of the partners, legally the partnership as a form of business cannot be transferred to another person.

Why would persons organize a business as a partnership? As with the sole proprietorship, formation of a partnership requires no formalities. Also, many partnerships are formed by default. A partnership is created automatically when persons own a business together without selecting another form. Also, the deductibility of partnership losses on individual tax returns is an attractive feature.

Limited Partnership

A **limited partnership** has one or more general partners and one or more limited partners. General partners have rights and liabilities similar to partners in a partnership. They manage the business of the limited partnership and have unlimited liability for the obligations of the limited partnership. Thus, a general partner may have to pay more than his share of a limited partnership's liabilities. Typically, however, the only general partner is a corporation, thereby protecting the human managers from unlimited liability.

Because the limited partnership is not a tax-paying entity for federal income tax purposes, general partners report their shares of the limited partnership's income and losses on their individual federal income tax returns. For general partners, losses of the business are deductible without limit.

Limited partners have no liability for the obligations of the limited partnership once they have paid their capital contributions to the limited partnership. Limited partners have no right to manage the business and may lose their limited liability for the business's obligations if they do manage the business.

A limited partner must pay federal income tax on his share of the profits of the business, but he may deduct his share of losses only to the extent of his investment in the business. In addition, a limited partner, as a passive investor, usually may use the losses only to offset income from other passive investments. The loss-deduction privilege gives the limited partnership an advantage over the corporation, but its limitation is a disadvantage compared to the partnership.

A limited partnership may have a life apart from its owners. When a limited partner dies or otherwise leaves the business, the limited partnership is not dissolved. When a general partner dies or withdraws, however, the limited partnership is dissolved absent a contrary agreement.

A general or limited partner's interest in a limited partnership may not be transferred to another person, absent a contrary agreement by the partners. Although in the late 1980s there was an attempt by some so-called **master limited partnerships** to create free transferability of limited partners' interests, the Internal Revenue Service snuffed out the effort by classifying such limited partnerships as associations, which are taxed like corporations, thus eliminating the ability of limited partners to deduct business losses on their individual federal income tax returns.

Unlike a sole proprietorship or partnership, a limited partnership may be created only by complying with a state statute permitting limited partnerships. Thus, no limited partnership may be created by default.

There are three main reasons why persons organize a business as a limited partnership. First, by using a corporate general partner, no human will have unlimited liability for the debts of the business. Second, losses of the business are deductible on individual owner's federal income tax returns. Third, because investors may contribute capital to the business and avoid unlimited liability and the obligation to manage the business, the limited partnership has the ability to attract large amounts of capital, much more than the sole proprietorship, which has only one owner, or the partnership, whose partners' fear of unlimited liability restricts the size of the business. Hence, for a business needing millions of dollars of capital and expecting to lose money in its early years, the limited partnership is a particularly good form of business.

Corporation

A **corporation** is owned by shareholders who elect a board of directors to manage the business. The board of directors often selects officers to run the day-to-day affairs of the business. Consequently, ownership and management of a corporation may be completely separate: no shareholder has the right to manage, and no officer or director needs to be a shareholder.

Like limited partners, shareholders have limited liability for the obligations of the corporation, even if a shareholder is elected as a director or selected as an officer. Directors and officers have no liability for the contracts they or the corporation's employees negotiate in the name of the corporation. The managers have no liability for corporate torts committed by corporate managers or employees other than themselves. Therefore, shareholders, officers, and directors have limited liability for the obligations of the business.

The usual corporation is a tax-paying entity for federal income tax purposes. The corporation pays taxes on its profits. Shareholders do not report their shares of corporation profits on their individual federal income tax returns. Instead, only when the corporation distributes its profits to the shareholders in the form of dividends or the shareholders sell their investments at a profit do the shareholders report income on their individual returns. This creates a *double-tax* possibility, as profits are taxed once at the corporation level and again at the shareholder level when dividends are paid.

Also, shareholders do not deduct corporate losses on their individual returns. They may, however, deduct their investment losses after they have sold their shares of the corporation.

There is one important exception to these corporate tax rules. The shareholders may elect to have the corporation and its shareholders taxed under Subchapter S of the Internal Revenue Code. By electing **S Corporation** status, the corporation and its shareholders are taxed nearly entirely like a partnership: income and losses of the business are reported on the shareholders' individual federal income tax returns. A corporation electing S Corporation status may have no more than 35 shareholders. Many of the shareholders of the typical S Corporation are involved in the management of the business.

A corporation has a life separate from its owners and its managers. When a shareholder or manager dies or otherwise leaves the business, the corporation is not dissolved. A shareholder may sell his shares of the corporation to other persons without limitation, absent a contrary agreement. The purchaser becomes a shareholder with all the rights of the selling shareholder. Like a limited partnership, a corporation may be created only by complying with a state statute permitting incorporation.

There are several reasons why persons organize a business as a corporation. First, no human has unlimited liability for the debts of the business. As a result, businesses in the riskiest industries—such as manufacturing—incorporate. Second, because investors may contribute capital to the business, avoid unlimited liability, escape the obligation to manage the business, and easily liquidate their investments by selling their shares, the corporation has the ability to attract large amounts of capital, even more than the limited partnership, whose partnership interests are not as freely transferable. Thus, the corporation has the capacity to raise the largest amount of capital.

The S Corporation has an additional advantage: losses of the business are deductible on individual federal income tax returns. However, because the S Corporation is limited to 35 shareholders, its ability to raise capital is severely limited. Also, while legally permitted to sell their shares, shareholders may be unable to find many investors willing to buy their shares and be re-

stricted from selling the shares pursuant to an agreement between the shareholders. See Figure 1 (next page) for a summary of business forms characteristics.

Franchising

Franchising is an agreement by which a **franchisee** has the right to sell goods or services under a marketing plan prescribed in substantial part by a **franchisor.** Thus, when a franchisee purchases a franchise, the franchisee buys a *business opportunity*, which the franchisee may choose to operate as any form of business. For example, if you obtain a McDonald's restaurant franchise for the south side of Minneapolis, you will probably choose to operate the business as a corporation.

Franchising has advantages for both the franchisee and the franchisor. The franchisee receives the franchisor's assistance in setting up the business and training employees. In addition, the franchisee may benefit from the franchisor's national advertising and strong trademark and goodwill. For example, a McDonald's franchisee obtains instant visibility and credibility from displaying the McDonald's golden arches. In return for this assistance, the franchisee usually pays a substantial purchase price plus a fee based on income, sales, or the purchase price of specified supplies. For example, an ice cream restaurant franchise may pay its franchisor 15 percent of the price it pays for its ice cream mix. The fee is collected for the franchisor by an authorized supplier of the mix.

The franchisor also benefits. Instead of making a high investment in several business locations, the franchisor shifts most of the investment risk to the franchisees. Yet the franchisor receives income from the franchisees' operation of their businesses. And while the franchisor's profits are tied to the franchisee's success, the franchisees typically have a sizable investment in the franchises and have a strong incentive to succeed. Also, the franchisor can adopt standards to ensure it selects high-quality franchisees with superior financial strength. Using franchising allows a franchisor to exploit its trademark and goodwill, yet also protect itself by requiring franchisees to adopt uniform image and marketing practices.

Nature of Franchisor/Franchisee Relationship Because a franchisor may exercise some control over parts of a franchisee's business, there is a risk that the franchisor may be liable for the torts and contracts of the franchisee. Most franchising agreements provide that

FIGURE 1   General Characteristics of Forms of Business

	Sole Proprietorship	Partnership	Limited Partnership	Corporation	S Corporation
Formation	When one person conducts business without forming a corporation	By agreement of owners *or* by default when two or more owners conduct business together without forming a limited partnership or a corporation	By agreement of owners; must comply with limited partnership statute	By agreement of owners; must comply with corporation statute	By agreement of owners; must comply with corporation statute; must elect S Corporation status under Subchapter S of Internal Revenue Code
Duration	Terminates on death or withdrawal of sole proprietor	Dissolves on death or withdrawal of general partner	Dissolves on death or withdrawal of general partner	Unaffected by death or withdrawal of shareholder	Unaffected by death or withdrawal of shareholder
Management	By sole proprietor	By partners	By general partners	By board of directors	By board of directors
Owner Liability	Unlimited	Unlimited	Unlimited for general partners; limited to capital contribution for limited partners	Limited to capital contribution	Limited to capital contribution
Transferability of Owners' Interest	None	None	None, unless partners agree otherwise	Freely transferable	Freely transferable unless shareholders agree otherwise
Federal Income Taxation	Only sole proprietor taxed	Only partners taxed	Only partners taxed	Corporation taxed; shareholders taxed on dividends (double tax)	Only shareholders taxed

the franchisee is not an agent or partner of the franchisor. Some courts refuse to accept this characterization of the relationship, especially when the degree and type of control by the franchisor suggest an agency relationship.

Today, most franchisors are careful not to assume such control. Nonetheless, when a franchisor has the right to control a specified portion of the franchisee's conduct, a court may hold the franchisor liable for torts or contracts arising from the controlled conduct. For example, when a franchisor has the right to control a franchisee's prices, the franchisee may be responsible for any resulting antitrust violation resulting from the franchisee's pricing decisions.

Franchisee Protection In response to abuses by franchisors, the courts, the Federal Trade Commission, and the states have created rules that protect franchisees. The typical franchising agreement gives a franchisor wide latitude to terminate a franchisee. Some courts have invalidated such termination power or required that terminations be made in good faith. In 1979, the Federal Trade Commission issued a franchise disclosure rule and guidelines requiring franchisors to disclose their financial fees and charges, the franchisees' obligations to purchase supplies, and territorial restrictions on the franchisees. In addition, most of the states require disclosure and termination protection for franchisees.

PARTNERSHIPS

History of Partnerships

The basic concept of partnership is as ancient as the history of collective human activity. Partnerships were known in ancient Babylonia, ancient Greece, and the Roman Empire. Hammurabi's Code, dating from 2300 B.C., regulated partnerships, and the definition of a partnership in the 6th-century Justinian Code of the Roman Empire does not differ materially from that in our laws today. The partnership was likewise known in Asian countries, including China. During the Middle Ages, much trade between nations was carried on by partnerships.

By the close of the 17th century, the partnership was recognized in the English common law. When the United States became an independent nation and adopted the English common law in 1776, the English law of partnerships became a part of American law. In the early part of the 19th century, the partnership became the most important form of association in the United States.

Modern American Partnership Law

Today, the American common law of partnership has been largely replaced by statutory law. Every state has a statute on partnership law. The Uniform Partnership Act (UPA) of 1914 has been adopted in 49 states (Louisiana is the exception) and the District of Columbia. The UPA is a model partnership statute that is the product of the National Conference of Commissioners on Uniform State Laws, a group of practicing lawyers, judges, and law professors. The aims of the UPA are to codify partnership law in one document, to make that law more nearly consistent with itself, and to attain uniformity throughout the country. Because of its nearly total adoption in the United States, the UPA is the framework of your study of partnerships. It is reproduced in an appendix to this book.

Entity and Aggregate Theories

Studying the list of partnership characteristics in Figure 2, you may perceive that in some respects the partnership is treated as an **entity,** that is, as a person separate and distinct from its partners. In other respects, the partnership is viewed as an **aggregate** of the partners, with no life or powers apart from them. The UPA recognizes the partnership primarily as an aggregate of the partners. In a few situations, however, the UPA confers entity status on a partnership, such as by permitting ownership of property in the firm name. In addition, the UPA gives creditors of the firm priority in partnership assets over creditors of the individual partners. It also permits the firm to continue its business in situations in which the aggregate theory would suggest immediate dissolution and liquidation.

CREATION OF PARTNERSHIP

Introduction

One of the most important issues in partnership law is whether two people who have associated in an enterprise have created a partnership. If they are partners, then the law of partnership applies to their disputes with each other and with persons with whom they have dealt.

No Formalities for Creation of Partnership

No formalities are necessary to create a partnership. Two persons may become partners in accordance with a written partnership contract (articles of partnership), they may agree orally to be partners, or they may become partners merely by arranging their affairs as if they were partners. If partners conduct business under a trade name, they must file the name with the secretary of state in compliance with state statutes requiring the registration of fictitious business names.

Articles of Partnership

When people decide to become partners, they should employ a lawyer to prepare a written partnership agreement. Although such **articles of partnership** are not required to form a partnership, they are highly desirable for the same reasons that written contracts are generally preferred. In addition, the statute of frauds requires a writing for a partnership having a term exceeding one year.

When there is no written partnership agreement, a dispute may arise over whether persons who are associated in some enterprise are partners. For example, someone may assert that she is a partner and, therefore, claim a share of the value of a successful enterprise. More frequently, an unpaid creditor may seek to hold a person liable for a debt incurred by another person in the same enterprise. To determine whether there is a partnership in the absence of an express agreement, the courts use the definition of partnership in the UPA.

FIGURE 2   Principal Characteristics of Partnerships under the UPA

1. A partnership may be created with no formalities. Two or more people merely need to agree to own and conduct a business together in order to create a partnership (aggregate theory).

2. Partners have unlimited liability for the obligations of the business (aggregate theory). However, a partner's personal creditors have first priority to that partner's assets, while partnership creditors have first priority to partnership assets (entity theory).

3. Each partner, merely by being an owner of the business, has a right to manage the business of the partnership (aggregate theory). He is an agent of the partnership and may make the partnership liable for contracts, torts, and crimes (entity theory). Because partners are liable for all obligations of the partnership, in effect each partner is an agent of the other partners. Each partner may hire agents, and every partner is liable for the agents' authorized contracts and for torts that the agents commit in the course of their employments (aggregate theory).

4. A partnership is not an employer of the partners, for most purposes. As a result, for example, a partner who leaves a partnership is not entitled to unemployment benefits (aggregate theory).

5. Partners are fiduciaries of the partnership. They must act in the best interests of the partnership, not in their individual best interests (entity theory).

6. The profits or losses of the business are shared by the partners, who report their shares of the profits or losses on their individual federal income tax returns, because the partnership does not pay federal income taxes (aggregate theory). Nonetheless, a partnership does keep its own financial records and must file an information return with the Internal Revenue Service (entity theory).*

7. A partnership may own property in its own name (entity theory).

8. A partnership may not sue or be sued in its own name. The partners must sue or be sued (aggregate theory).

9. A partner may not sue her partners. Her sole remedy is to seek an accounting between the partners (aggregate theory).

10. A partner's ownership interest in a partnership is not freely transferable A purchaser of a partner's interest does not become a partner, but is entitled to receive only the partner's share of the partnership's profits (aggregate theory).

11. Generally, a partnership has no life apart from its owners. If a partner dies, the partnership dissolves and may be terminated (aggregate theory). Under certain circumstances, however, the partnership may continue after the death of a partner (entity theory).

*The federal income tax return filed by a partnership is merely an information return in which the partnership indicates its gross income and deductions and the names and addresses of its partners (I.R.C. Sec. 6031). The information return allows the Internal Revenue Service to determine whether the partners accurately report partnership income on their individual returns.

UPA Definition of Partnership

UPA Section 6 defines a partnership as an "association of two or more persons to carry on as co-owners a business for profit." There are four distinct elements to the UPA definition:

1. An association of two or more persons.
2. Carrying on a business.
3. As co-owners of the business.
4. For profit.

If the definition is satisfied, then the courts will treat those involved as partners. A relationship may meet the UPA definition of partnership even when a person does not believe he is a partner, and occasionally, even if the parties agree that they are not partners.

Association of Two or More Persons

As an association, a partnership is a *voluntary and consensual relationship.* It cannot be imposed on a person; a person must agree expressly or impliedly to have a person associate with her. For example, a partner cannot force her partners to accept her daughter into the partnership.

No person can be a partner with herself: a partnership must have *at least two partners.* Nonetheless, a person may be a partner with his spouse.

Who Is a Person?   Not everyone or everything may be a partner. UPA Section 2 defines a person as an individual, partnership, corporation, or other association. A limited partnership may be a partner. Most states do not permit a trust to be a partner, but they allow the trustee of the trust to be a partner for the benefit of the trust.

Carrying On a Business

Any trade, occupation, or profession may qualify as a business. Carrying on a business usually requires a *series of transactions* conducted over a period of time. For example, a group of farmers that buys supplies in quantity to get lower prices is not carrying on a business, but only part of one. If the group buys harvesting equipment with which it intends to harvest crops for others for a fee for many years, it is carrying on a business.

Co-Ownership

Partners must *co-own the business* in which they associate. There is no requirement that the capital contributions or the assets of the business be co-owned.

Also, by itself, co-ownership of assets does not establish a partnership. For example, two persons who own a building as joint tenants are not necessarily partners. To be partners, they must co-own a business.

The two most important factors in establishing co-ownership of the business are the *sharing of profits* and the *sharing of management* of the business.

Sharing Profits   UPA Section 7(4) declares that the receipt by a person of a share of the profits of a business is *prima facie* evidence that she is a partner in the business. This means that persons sharing profits are partners, unless other evidence exists to disprove they are partners. The rationale for this rule is that a person would not be sharing the profits of a business unless she were a co-owner. This rule brings under partnership law many persons who fail to realize that they are partners. For example, two college students who purchase college basketball tickets, resell them, and split the profits are partners.

Sharing the gross revenues of a business does not create a presumption of partnership. The profits, not the gross receipts, must be shared. For example, brokers who split a commission on a sale of land are not partners.

Section 7(4) provides that *no* presumption of partnership may be made when a share of profits is received:

1. By a creditor as payment on a debt.
2. By an employee as wages.[1]
3. By a landlord as rent.[2]

4. By a widow, widower, or representative of a deceased partner for the value of that partner's share of the partnership.
5. By a creditor as interest on a loan.
6. As consideration to the transferor of a business or other property for his sale of the goodwill of the business or other property.

These exceptions reflect the normal expectations of the parties that no partnership exists in such situations.[3]

Sharing Management   Sharing management of a business is evidence tending to prove the existence of a partnership.[4] However, by itself, participation in management is not conclusive proof of the existence of a partnership. For example, a creditor may be granted considerable control in a business, such as a veto power over partnership decisions and the right of consultation, without becoming a partner. Also, a sole proprietor may hire someone to manage his business, yet the manager will not be a partner of the sole proprietor.

Although either sharing profits or sharing management is not, by itself, *conclusive* proof of a partnership, sharing both profits and management strongly implies the existence of a partnership.

Even if the parties claim that they share profits for one of the six reasons listed in UPA Section 7(4), the sharing of management may overcome the presumption that they are not partners. When the parties arrange their affairs in a manner that otherwise establishes an *objective intent* to create a partnership, the courts find that a partnership exists. For example, when a nonmanagerial employee initially shares profits as a form of employment compensation, the employee is not a partner of his employer. But when the employer and employee modify their relationship by having the employee exercise managerial control of the business, a partnership may exist. Nonetheless, when the employer and employee have agreed that the employee is a *managerial employee*, the managerial employee is not a partner of the employer, despite the employee's sharing profits and management.

Other persons sharing profits and control of a business may or may not be partners. For example, an owner of farmland and a farmer agree that the farmer will farm the land and that the owner and the farmer will share the

---

[1]See, e.g., *Montana Bank of Red Lodge v. Lightfield,* 771 P.2d 571 (Mont. Sup. Ct. 1989); *Associated Reforestation Contractors, Inc. v. State,* 650 P.2d 1068 (Ore. Ct. App. 1982).

[2]See, e.g., *Chariton Feed and Grain, Inc. v. Harder,* 369 N.W.2d 777 (Iowa Sup. Ct. 1985).

[3]*Peed v. Peed,* 325 S.E.2d 275 (N.C. Ct. App. 1985).

[4]*McCrary v. Butler,* 540 So.2d 736 (Ala. Sup. Ct. 1989).

FIGURE 3 Important Consequences of Being a Partner

1. You share ownership of the business. For example, you want to bring an employee into your business, which is worth $250,000. If you and the employee conduct your affairs like partners, your employee will own half of your business.
2. You share the profits of the business.
3. You share management of the business. Your partner must be allowed to participate in management decisions.
4. Your partner is your agent. You are liable for your partner's torts and contracts made in the ordinary course of business.
5. You owe fiduciary duties to your partnership and your partner, such as the duties to devote full time to the business, not to compete with the business, not to self-deal, and not to disclose confidential matters.

---

profits of the business. This is not a partnership, but merely a convenient way of paying rent to the owner for the value of the land to the farmer. Suppose, however, the owner and the farmer share not only the profits from the operation of the farm but also jointly determine which crops are to be planted or when livestock is to be sold. Courts often treat such an owner and a farmer as partners.

Creditors, however, occupy a privileged position. Many cases have permitted creditors to share profits and to exercise considerable control over a business without becoming partners. Creditor control is often justified on the grounds that it is merely reasonable protection for the creditor's risk.

For Profit

The owners of an enterprise must *intend to make a profit* to create a partnership. If the enterprise suffered losses, yet the owners intended to make a profit, a partnership may result. When an endeavor is carried on by several people for charitable or other nonprofit objectives, it is not a partnership. For example, Alex and Geri operate a restaurant booth at a county fair each year to raise money for a Boy Scout troop. Their relationship is not a partnership, but merely an association. (Nonetheless, like partners, they may be individually liable for the debts of the enterprise.)

Intent

Frequently, courts say that there must be *intent* to form a partnership. This rule is more correctly stated as follows: *the parties must intend to create a relationship that the*

law recognizes as a partnership. A partnership may exist even if the parties entered it inadvertently, without considering whether they had created a partnership. A written agreement to the effect that the parties do not intend to form a partnership is not conclusive if their *actions* provide evidence of their intent to form a relationship that meets the UPA partnership test. Intent is determined by the words and acts of the parties, interpreted in light of the circumstances.

There are several important consequences of being a partner. See Figure 3 for a summary of the most important consequences.

CREATION OF JOINT VENTURES AND MINING PARTNERSHIPS

Joint Ventures

Courts frequently distinguish **joint ventures** from partnerships. A joint venture may be found when a court is reluctant to call an arrangement a partnership because the purpose of the arrangement is not to establish an ongoing business involving many transactions; instead, it is limited to a single project. For example, an agreement to buy and resell for profit a particular piece of real estate, perhaps after development, is likely to be viewed as a joint venture rather than a partnership. In all other respects, joint ventures are created just as partnerships are created. The joint venturers may have a formal written agreement. In its absence, a court applies UPA Sections 6 and 7—modified so as not to require the carrying on of a business—to determine whether a joint venture has been created.

The legal implications of the distinction between a partnership and a joint venture are not entirely clear. Generally, partnership law applies to joint ventures. For example, all of the participants in a joint venture are personally liable for its debts, and joint venturers owe each other the fiduciary duties imposed on partners. Joint ventures are treated as partnerships for federal income tax purposes. The most significant difference between joint venturers and partners is that joint venturers are usually held to have *less implied and apparent authority* than partners, due to the limited scope of the enterprise.

The following cases illustrate the application of partnership law to the question of whether a joint venture has been created. In the first case, *Dority v. Driesel*, the court emphasized the importance of sharing profits and management.

DORITY v. DRIESEL

706 P.2d 995 (Ore. Ct. App. 1985)

Daon Corporation developed a housing subdivision near Portland, Oregon. It did not build any houses itself, but only improved the homesites for resale. To promote the sales of homesites, Daon created a marketing scheme, named Showcase of Homes, that involved Portland area builders. The builders, including Raymond Driesel, purchased homesites from Daon and built custom homes on the homesites. Daon advertised the Showcase of Homes, decorated and furnished model homes, and provided a landscaping plan to the builders. Both Driesel and Daon benefited from the Showcase program. Driesel benefited from Daon's advertising and the chance to show his home, leading to future home-building jobs. Daon benefited from having homes constructed in the subdivision, proving to prospective homesite buyers the feasibility and desirability of buying a homesite from Daon, leading to further homesite sales.

Theo Dority purchased the home built by Driesel. All negotiations and documents for the sale were between Dority, Driesel, and Driesel's real estate broker; Daon was not represented. Prior to the sale, Dority noticed obvious defects in the home. Driesel promised to correct the defects, but he failed to do so. Dority demanded that both Daon and Driesel correct the defects. When the defects were not remedied, Dority hired another contracter to make the corrections for $20,000. Dority sued Daon and Driesel for $20,000. The trial court found that a joint venture existed between Daon and Driesel; therefore, under the law of partnership, Daon was held liable to Dority for $20,000. Daon appealed to the Oregon Court of Appeals.

Gillette, Presiding Judge.   Simply stated, a joint venture is a partnership for a single transaction, and partnership law controls joint ventures. The essential test in determining the existence of partnership is whether the parties intended to establish such a relationship. However, the substance of legal intent rather than the actual intent may be controlling. Partnership status may be inferred from the conduct of the parties in relation to themselves and to third parties. The main earmarks of a partnership are the right of a party to share the profits and losses and the right to exert some control over the business.

Both Daon and Driesel denied any intention of creating a joint venture relationship when entering into the showcase project. In addition, the profits anticipated by Daon and Driesel to be derived from the Showcase were not to be shared jointly. Rather, each was hoping to enjoy a distinct form of gain independent of that of the other. Indeed, either one might profit from the Showcase while the other failed to receive any benefit at all. The fact that they acted in concert to achieve some economic objective, while relevant to the inquiry, is not enough to create a joint venture.

Also, any potential loss from the Showcase joint effort would also be unique to each party. Daon might fail to sell more lots, or Driesel might fail to obtain any future construction jobs, but the loss would not necessarily be a shared one.

Judgment reversed in favor of Daon.

In the following case, *In Re O. W. Limited Partnership*, a written agreement provided that the parties would share gross revenues. However, because the parties actually shared profits in their performance of the agreement, their relationship met the definition of partnership.

IN RE O.W. LIMITED PARTNERSHIP
668 P.2d 56 (Ha. Ct. App. 1983)

OWLP, a Hawaii limited partnership, owned the Outrigger West Hotel. In 1974, OWLP and Hawaii Hotels Operating Company (HHOC) agreed that OWLP and HHOC would jointly operate the hotel and share its revenues, allocating 73 percent to OWLP and 27 percent to HHOC. The agreement provided that revenues would be collected from the hotel and allocated daily according to the percentages above.

For the years 1974 through 1977, OWLP paid Hawaii's general excise taxes only on the gross hotel room revenues allocated to OWLP. The Hawaii Director of Taxes claimed that OWLP's gross revenues should have included the amount of revenues allocated to HHOC, unless OWLP and HHOC were partners. The Director of Taxes claimed that HHOC merely provided services to OWLP and that, therefore, OWLP and HHOC were not partners. Consequently, the Director of Taxes, assessed OWLP for additional taxes of $194,754. OWLP appealed the assessment to the tax appeal court, which ruled that OWLP and HHOC were partners or joint venturers. The Director of Taxes appealed.

Tanaka, Judge.   A joint venture is a mutual undertaking by two or more persons to carry out a single business enterprise for profit. A joint venture is closely akin to a partnership and the rules governing the creation and existence of partnerships are applicable to joint ventures.

The Director concedes that the revenue-sharing agreement provides for a joint operation by the parties. However, the Director argues that the agreement does not contemplate a partnership in that it does not deal with a sharing of profits and losses, but only in sharing gross receipts.

It is true that the sharing of gross receipts is not even prima facie evidence of a partnership. However, the evidence indicates that from 1974 to 1977, the allocation percentages were changed six times to permit each party to recover out-of-pocket expenses and to provide ultimately a return of 98 percent of the net income to OWLP and of 2 percent of the net income to HHOC. Thus, any amount recovered by each party according to the predetermined percentage in excess of its expenses would be its profit. Losses were shared pro rata like the profits.

The agreement was a minimum document to outline the joint venture's operations in case something happened to the people running it. Although the form selected by OWLP and HHOC did not precisely fit into the mold of partnership or joint venture, the substance of their business transactions was that of joint venture. The operation was and continued to be a joint venture.

Judgment for OWLP affirmed.

evidence that there was a partnership in fact

adjust revenues for expenses, essentially profits

Mining Partnerships

Although similar to an ordinary partnership or a joint venture, a mining partnership is recognized as a distinct relationship in a number of states. Persons who cooperate in the working of either a mine or an oil or gas well are treated as mining partners if there is (1) *joint ownership* of a mineral interest, (2) *joint operation* of the property, and (3) *sharing* of profits and losses. Joint operation requires more than merely financing the development of a mineral interest, but it does not require active physical participation in operations; it may be proved by furnishing labor, supplies, services, or advice. The delegation of sole operating responsibility to one of the participants does not bar treatment as a mining partnership.

PARTNERSHIP BY ESTOPPEL

Introduction

Two persons may not be partners, yet in the eyes of a third person, they may *appear* to be partners. If the third person deals with one of the apparent partners, he may be harmed and seek to recover damages from both of the apparent partners. The question, then, is whether the third person may collect damages from both of the apparent partners.

For example, Johnson thinks that Sanders, a wealthy person, is a partner of Dean, a poor person. Johnson decides to do business with Dean on the grounds that if Dean does not perform as agreed, he can recover damages from Sanders. If Johnson is wrong and Sanders is not Dean's partner, Johnson ordinarily has no recourse against Sanders. UPA Section 7(1) states that "persons who are not partners as to each other are not partners as to third persons." However, if Johnson can prove that Sanders led him to believe that she and Dean were partners, he may sue Sanders for Dean's failure to perform as agreed. This is an application of the doctrine of **partnership by estoppel.**

Partnership by estoppel is similar to two concepts that you have already studied: promissory estoppel[5] and apparent authority of agents.[6] It is based on a person's substantial, detrimental reliance on another person's representations.

---

[5] See the Introduction to Contracts chapter and the Consideration chapter.

[6] See the Third-Party Relations of the Principal and the Agent chapter.

Elements

UPA Section 16 defines partnership by estoppel. Essentially, Section 16 states that to recover against a party as if she were a partner, a person must prove that:

1. The party held herself out or consented to being held out as a partner of another person.
2. The person dealt with the party's purported partner in justifiable reliance on the holding out.
3. The person was injured as a result.

Holding Out   Few problems arise in determining whether a person holds himself out as a partner. For example, he might refer to himself as another person's partner. Or he might appear frequently in the office of a purported partner and confer with him. Perhaps he and another person share office space, have one door to an office with both of their names on it, have one telephone number, and share a secretary who answers the phone giving the names of both persons.

More difficult is determining when a person *consents* to being held out as another's partner. Mere knowledge that one is being held out as a partner is *not* consent. But a person's silence in response to a statement that the person is another's partner is consent. For example, suppose Chavez tells Eaton that Gold is a partner in Barb Birt's new retail shoe business. In fact, Gold is not Birt's partner. Later, Gold learns of the conversation between Chavez and Eaton. Gold does not have to seek out Chavez and Eaton to tell them that he is not Birt's partner in order to avoid being held liable as a partner for Birt's business debts. Had Chavez made the statement to Eaton in Gold's presence, however, Gold must deny the partnership relation, or he will be held liable for Eaton's subsequent reliance on Gold's silence.

Reasonable Reliance and Injury   A partner by estoppel is *not* liable to everyone who deals with the purported partnership. He is liable only to those persons who reasonably rely on the holding out and suffer injury thereby. This means that partnership by estoppel, like any estoppel concept, is determined on a case-by-case basis.

A person unaware of the holding out cannot prove partnership by estoppel.[7] For example, James tells Samuels that she is Timm's partner, but she does not tell this

---

[7] *Zehner v. MFA Ins.* Co., 451 N.E.2d 65 (Ind. Ct. App. 1983).

to Carlson. Samuels can prove partnership by estoppel, but Carlson cannot. If Samuels tells Carlson what James told him, then Carlson can prove partnership by estoppel.

A third person's reliance on the appearance of a partnership must be reasonable. When a person has information that would prevent a reasonable person from relying on the holding out, no partnership by estoppel may result. For example, Lindall knows that Frank and Stanton are employer and employee. Frank calls Stanton "my partner" in the presence of Stanton and Lindall. Frank and Stanton are not partners by estoppel. Because Lindall knows that Frank and Stanton are employer and employee, she may not rely on Frank's calling Stanton "my partner."

The injury suffered by the third person must be the result of his reliance. If the third person would have done business with another person whether or not that person was a partner of someone held out as a partner, there is no injury as a result of reliance. Hence, there is no partnership by estoppel.

Effect of Partnership by Estoppel

Once partnership by estoppel has been proved, the person who held himself out or who consented to being held out is liable as though he were a partner. He is liable on contracts entered into by third persons on their belief that he was a partner. He is liable for torts committed during the course of relationships entered by third persons who believed he was a partner.

Not a Partner in Fact   Although two parties are partners by estoppel to a person who knows of the holding out and who justifiably relies on it to his injury, the partners by estoppel are *not* partners in fact and do not share the profits, management, or value of the business of the purported partnership. Partnership by estoppel is merely a device to allow creditors to sue parties who mislead them into believing that a partnership exists.

In the following case, *Volkman v. DP Associates*, the appearance of partnership led the court to a finding of partnership by estoppel.

VOLKMAN v. DP ASSOCIATES

268 S.E.2d 265 (N.C. Ct. App. 1980)

Alvin and Carol Volkman decided to build a house. They contacted David McNamee for construction advice. McNamee informed the Volkmans that he was doing business with Phillip Carroll. Subsequently, the Volkmans received a letter from McNamee on DP Associates stationery. They assumed that the DP was derived from the first names of McNamee and Carroll: David and Phillip. Prior to the signing of the contract, McNamee introduced Carroll to Mr. Volkman at the DP Associates office, where Carroll said, "I hope we'll be working together." Carroll stated that McNamee would be the person at DP Associates primarily doing business with the Volkmans, but indicated that he also would be available for consultation.

The Volkmans reviewed the written contract in the DP Associates office with McNamee. McNamee suggested that they use a form to identify DP Associates as acting as a general contractor. He then left the room saying, "I will ask Phil." When he returned, he said that they would use the form.

After the contract was signed but before construction of the house began, Mr. Volkman visited the office of DP Associates. He again saw and spoke with Carroll, who said to him, "I am happy that we will be working with you." During construction, Mr. Volkman visited the office of DP Associates several times and saw Carroll there. During one visit, he expressed to Carroll his concern about construction delays, but Carroll told him not to worry, because McNamee would take care of it.

When DP Associates failed to perform the contract, the Volkmans sued DP Associates, McNamee, and Carroll. Carroll argued that he could not be liable to the Volkmans because he and McNamee were not partners. The trial court agreed and refused to let the jury decide the case. The Volkmans appealed to the North Carolina Court of Appeals.

Vaughn, Judge.   If the Volkmans are unable to prove a partnership in fact, they may be able to show that Carroll should be held as a partner by estoppel or under the agency theory of apparent authority.

Liability by estoppel may result either from Carroll's representation of himself as a partner "by words spoken or written" or "by conduct" or Carroll's "consent" to such a representation by another. The Volkmans indicated they may be able to show that Carroll by his oral statements to them and conduct in their presence and by his consent to the representations of McNamee to the Volkmans, some of which were in the presence of Carroll, represented himself as a partner and should be estopped to deny such association. They may be able to show further they relied upon these representations not knowing them to be false and that based upon the representations of Carroll and McNamee, the Volkmans changed their position and were thereby damaged.

In addition to an estoppel theory of liability, Carroll may be liable under apparent authority, a theory of agency law applicable to partnerships. There is virtually no difference between estoppel and apparent authority. Both depend on reliance by a third person on a communication from the principal. Despite the title, "Partner by Estoppel," the form of liability is more akin to that of apparent authority than to estoppel.

If this view is taken, the liability of the person seeking to deny partner status is not based on estoppel to deny agency or authority but on the objective theory of contract law, *i.e.,* a person should be bound by his words and conduct. Thus, when Carroll told Mr. Volkman, "I am happy that we will be working with you," and conducted himself as he did in the DP Associates office in the presence of Mr. Volkman, the jury may find that Carroll was indicating a willingness to be bound by the statements and acts of McNamee, that Carroll held himself out as a partner of McNamee in DP Associates, that McNamee had apparent authority to act for Carroll, and that the Volkmans reasonably relied upon this holding out. If so, Carroll is bound as if he directly dealt with the Volkmans.

Judgment reversed in favor of the Volkmans. Remanded to the trial court for jury trial.

PARTNERSHIP CAPITAL, PARTNERSHIP PROPERTY, AND PARTNERS' PROPERTY RIGHTS

Partnership Capital

When a partnership is formed, partners contribute cash or other property to the partnership. The partners' contribution is called **partnership capital.** To supplement beginning capital, other property may be contributed to the partnership as needed, such as by the partners permitting the partnership to retain some of its profits. Partnership capital is the equity of the business.

Loans made by partners to a partnership are not partnership capital, but instead are liabilities of the business. Partners who make loans to a partnership are both owners and creditors.

Partnership Property

The partnership may own all or only a part of the property it uses. For example, it may own the business and perhaps a small amount of working capital in the form of cash or a checking account, yet own no other assets. All other tangible and intangible property used by the partnership may be individually or jointly owned by one or more of the partners or rented by the partnership from third parties. A determination of what is partnership property becomes essential when the partnership is dissolved and the assets are being distributed and when creditors of either the partnership or one of the partners is seeking assets to satisfy a debt.

UPA Rule   Section 8 of the UPA provides that (1) all property originally brought into the partnership or subsequently acquired by purchase or otherwise, on account of the partnership, is partnership property, and (2) unless the contrary intention appears, property acquired with partnership funds is partnership property.

Intent   The *intent* of the partners controls. It is best to have a written record of the partners' intent as to ownership of all property used by the partnership, such as in the articles of partnership. Other writings—such as accounting records—show the partnership assets; assets appearing in the partnership's books are presumed to belong to the partnership. Also, the partnership's paying rent on property provides strong evidence that the property belongs to the partner receiving the rent.

Source of Purchase Funds   The presumption is very strong that property purchased with partnership funds and used in the partnership is partnership property.[8] No such presumption is accorded to a partner who purchases property with her own funds and then allows the partnership to use the property; other factors besides the partner's funding the purchase determine who owns the property.

Title to Partnership Property   If title is taken in the partnership name, it is presumed that the property is partnership property. However, the presumption is not as strong that real property held in the name of a partner is individual property.[9] Other indicia may prove that property held in a partner's name belongs to the partnership.

------

[8]*McCrary v. Butler*, 540 So.2d 736 (Ala. Sup. Ct. 1989).
[9]Id.

Other Indicia   The partnership's payment of property taxes or insurance premiums, the maintainance, repair, and improvement of property by the partnership, and the deduction of these expenses on the partnership income tax return are indications of the intent of the partners that property belongs to the partnership, despite title being held in the name of a partner.

Generally, the partnership's mere use of the property creates no presumption that it is partnership property. Nonetheless, it is presumed that money used by a partnership as working capital is partnership property in the absence of clear evidence that it was intended to be merely a loan.

Example   A tax accountant discovers that a partnership is using a building to which a partner, Jacob Smith, holds title. The partnership pays rent monthly to Smith, but the partnership pays for all maintenance and repairs on the building. The accountant wants to know whether the partnership or Smith should be paying real property taxes on the building. Smith is the owner and should be paying taxes on it because his partners' intent to allow Smith to retain ownership is evidenced by the partnership paying rent to Smith.

Suppose, however, that the partnership pays no rent to Smith, the partnership maintains and repairs the building, and the partnership pays real property taxes on the building, but the title is in Smith's name. The property belongs to the partnership, because all the objective criteria of ownership point toward partnership ownership. Therefore, when the partnership is liquidated, the building will be sold along with other partnership assets, and the proceeds of its sale will be distributed to partnership creditors and to all of the partners, not merely to Smith.

In the following case, the court held that a truck trailer held in the partnership's name was partnership property.

IN RE FULTON
43 B.R.273 (M.D.Tenn. 1984)

Padgett Carroll and Walter Fulton operated as a partnership a trucking business under the name of C & F Trucking. Carroll contributed a semi truck, which Fulton drove for the business. Carroll used $4,600 of his personal funds to purchase a used 42-foot trailer for C & F Trucking. The

[handwritten margin note: Evidence that Asset is part of partnership]

seller's invoice listed C & F Trucking as the purchaser of the trailer. The trailer's certificate of title listed C & F Trucking as the owner.

Fulton's personal financial problems forced him to file for bankruptcy. Fulton claimed ownership of the trailer among his assets. Carroll claimed that the trailer was his individual asset.

Paine, Bankruptcy Judge.   In determining whether property is partnership property or property owned by an individual, the court must focus primarily on the intentions of the partners at the time the property was acquired. Such intention of the partners must be determined from their apparent intention at the time the property was acquired and the conduct of the partners toward the property after the purchase.

Viewing evidence surrounding the purpose and use of the property, Tennessee courts have held that when property is titled in the name of the partnership, the party asserting that the property is not partnership property has the burden of proof.

The evidence establishes that the trailer is partnership property. Both a sales invoice and a certificate of title list the owner of the trailer as C & F Trucking. The trailer was purchased by Carroll for use in the C & F Trucking business and Fulton actually used the trailer in the business.

The claims of individual ownership asserted by both Fulton and Carroll lack substance. The property was indeed partnership property.

Judgment for Carroll.

[handwritten margin notes: Even if asset is titled in personal name, but its € upkeep paid by PARTNERSHIP — Evidence that could be a partnership asset; Jointly w/ right of survivorship → Partnership that owns the estate value of asset]

Partners' Property Rights

Under UPA Section 24, a partner has three property rights:

1. Her rights in specific partnership property.
2. Her partnership interest.
3. Her right to participate in the management of the business.

The first two rights are discussed here. The management right is discussed in the Operation of Partnership and Related Forms chapter.

Rights in Partnership Property

According to UPA Section 25, partnership property is owned by partners as **tenants in partnership.** This means that the partners as a group own partnership property as a whole; the partners as individuals do not own proportionate interests in separate items of partnership property.

As a tenant in partnership, each partner has the right to possess partnership property for partnership purposes. A partner has no individual right to use or possess partnership property for her own purposes, such as paying a personal debt, unless she has the consent of the other partners. Likewise, a partner's personal creditor may not make a claim against partnership assets.

On the death of a partner, his rights in partnership property pass to the surviving partners. This is called the **right of survivorship.**

The nature of a partner's rights in partnership property is explored in the following case, *State v. Birch.*

STATE v. BIRCH

675 P.2d 246 (Wash. Ct. App. 1984)

Richard DeLong and Ken Birch formed a partnership to build houses. They agreed that all sales proceeds would be deposited in a partnership bank checking account and that both of them must sign all checks. For two years, Birch and DeLong signed all checks, but then DeLong agreed that Birch could sign partnership checks by himself. Six years later, DeLong discovered that Birch paid some of his personal expenses with partnership checks. DeLong reported his discovery to the Prosecuting Attorney for the State of Washington, who prosecuted Birch for the crime of embezzlement. Embezzlement was defined in the Washington statute as exerting unauthorized control over the property of another. The trial judge ruled that a partner could not embezzle partnership funds because the partner would not be exerting unauthorized control over the property of another. The Prosecuting Attorney appealed to the Washington Court of Appeals.

Munson, Chief Judge.   In *State v. Eberhart (1919)*, the Supreme Court of Washington held that a partner cannot be prosecuted for use of partnership property because the theft statute requires the theft be of property of another. The title to partnership property cannot be in another because each partner is the ultimate owner of an undivided interest in all the partnership property, and none of such property can be said, with reference to any partner, to be the property of another.

Under both the common law and the Uniform Partnership Act, partnerships are treated both as aggregates of individuals and entities distinct from the people involved in the partnership. The common law indicated that each partner's interest in the property of a partnership was as a joint tenant. This is an aggregate theory because it does not recognize the partnership as a separate entity.

Although the Uniform Partnership Act speaks of the partnership as a separate entity, the issue is whether the title to property is in another. The title is not in another; the UPA retains the aggregate approach under which partners own partnership property as joint tenants.

The Prosecuting Attorney contends that the UPA imposes limitations upon partners' use of partnership property. Section 25 of the UPA states:

(1) A partner is a co-owner with his partners of specific partnership property holding as a tenant in partnership.

(2) The incidents of this tenancy are such that:

(a) A partner . . . has an equal right with his partners to possess specific partnership property for partnership purposes; but he has no right to possess such property for any other purpose without the consent of his partners.

Under the UPA, each partner's right in specific partnership property is subordinated to partnership use of the property for partnership purposes.

The Prosecuting Attorney correctly contends that the UPA Section 25 modifies the definition of property of another as it relates to partnership property. However, a statute relating to larceny by a partner was repealed by the Legislature in 1909. The statute construed in *Eberhart* remains substantially the same today. The Legislature is presumed to be aware of both *Eberhart* and the adoption of the UPA. The Legislature had the opportunity to make theft of partnership funds a crime. It did not do so.

Judgment for Birch affirmed.

Partnership Interest

As a co-owner of a partnership, a partner has an ownership interest in the partnership. A partner's ownership interest is called a **partnership interest** and is part of his personal property. Although a partner may not give his personal creditors any interest in separate items of partnership property, Section 27 of the UPA permits a partner to assign his partnership interest to a creditor. And although a partner's personal creditors may not obtain an execution of judgment against separate items of partnership property, a creditor may obtain execution against a partner's partnership interest by obtaining a charging order against that interest.

Assignment   The **assignment of a partnership interest** is a voluntary act of a partner. It entitles the assignee to receive the assigning partner's share of the partnership's profits, but it does not give the assignee the right to inspect the partnership's books and records or to manage the partnership.

A partner's assignment of his partnership interest does not dissolve the partnership; the assigning partner remains a partner. An assignee for value, including a creditor, may ask a court to dissolve a partnership at will.[10] Dissolution may be followed by liquidation of the partnership's assets and result in the creditor being paid from the proceeds of the sale of the partnership's assets.

The nonassigning partners may not exclude the assigning partner from the partnership. They may, however, rightfully dissolve the partnership by their *unanimous* agreement, even if the term or objective of the partnership has not been met.

Charging Order   Under UPA Section 28, a partner's personal creditor with a judgment against the partner may ask a court to issue a **charging order**; that is, an order charging the partner's partnership interest with payment of the unsatisfied amount of the judgment. Unlike assignment, a charging order is obtained without the partner's consent. As with assignment, however, the partner remains a partner, and the creditor is entitled to receive only the partner's share of the profits. If the profits are insufficient to pay the debt, the creditor may ask the court to order foreclosure and to sell the partner's interest to satisfy the charging order.

Neither the issuance of a charging order nor the purchase of a partnership interest at a foreclosure sale causes a dissolution. But the purchaser of a partnership interest, like the assignee for value, may ask a court to dissolve a partnership at will. Under UPA Section 28, the other partners may eliminate this potential threat to the continuation of the partnership by *redeeming* the charging order. The other partners redeem a charging order by paying the creditor the amount due on the judgment against the partner. If the other partners so choose, however, they may dissolve the partnership by their

unanimous agreement, just as nonassigning partners may do.

Joint Venturers   Transfers of interests in joint ventures are treated in the same way as transfers of partnership interests.

Mining Partners   A mining partner's interest is *freely transferable.* The transferee becomes a partner with all the rights of ownership and management, and the transferor loses all of his partnership rights. The other mining partners cannot object to the transfer, and their consent to a transfer is not required.

ETHICAL AND PUBLIC POLICY CONCERNS

1. A person who carefully considers which business form to use for his one-person business can achieve nearly any combination of results desirable to him. For example, by incorporating and electing S Corporation status, a person can limit his personal liability, deduct business losses on his individual federal income tax return, yet control the business by electing himself to the board of directors. Why should a careful planner obtain such advantages, while a person who merely begins his business has unlimited liability as a sole proprietor? Is the business of the careful planner more valuable to our society than the business of the person who does not choose a business form?

2. Why should all the partners in a partnership be individually liable for all the obligations of the partnership, while shareholders and managers of a corporation have no liability beyond their capital contributions? Is the corporate form of business or the business conducted by corporations more important to society than the partnership form or the business conducted by partnerships? Would benefits that businesses provide to society be reduced if limited liability were not extended to shareholders and managers of corporations?

3. What are the ethical underpinnings of partnership by estoppel? Why should a person be held liable for the business debts of another person when he does not benefit from the business? Could the person who relied on the appearance of partnership have protected himself by making inquiries? Should he be required to make such inquiries?

---

[10] A partnership at will is a partnership with no term, which may rightfully be dissolved by any partner at any time.

SUMMARY

The choice of business form is an important decision, for it affects the liability and taxation of the owners. The sole proprietorship imposes unlimited liability on its owner, and any income or loss of the business is income or loss of the owner. The partnership is like the sole proprietorship for liability and taxation purposes, but it has two or more partners. General partners of a limited partnership are treated like partners in an ordinary partnership, but limited partners have limited liability and limited ability to deduct business losses on their individual federal income tax returns. A corporation's shareholders enjoy limited liability, but there is a risk of double taxation, unless the shareholders elect S Corporation status.

Franchising provides significant advantages for both franchisees and franchisors. Franchisees may receive a virtual turnkey operation, while franchisors receive substantial income with small investment risk. Franchisors who control the activities of franchisees may have liability for the franchisees' torts and contracts. In addition, recent laws protect franchisees from franchisors' fraudulent disclosures and abusive terminations of franchising agreements.

The Uniform Partnership Act contains most of the law affecting partnerships. In some respects, the UPA treats the partnership as an entity separate from its members, but in other respects it adopts the aggregate theory.

No formalities are required to create a partnership. It is a voluntary association of two or more persons to carry on as co-owners a business for profit. Any person with legal capacity may become a partner, including partnerships and corporations. An association to conduct a single transaction is not a partnership but a joint venture, to which much of partnership law applies.

One who receives a share of the profits of a business is viewed as a partner unless it can be shown that the sharing was for certain specified purposes. The co-ownership requirement applies to the business; it is not necessary that all partners co-own the property used in the business. Generally, sharing the profits and the management of a business is sufficient evidence of the existence of a partnership.

People who hold themselves out or who permit others to hold them out as partners will be held liable as partners to persons who rely on these holdings out, under the doctrine of partnership by estoppel.

Whether property used by a partnership is partnership property is fundamentally a question of determining the intent of the parties. A written agreement is the best evidence, but title in the partnership's name and use of partnership funds to make the purchase are also important.

Each partner has the right to use partnership property for partnership purposes. The property is owned by the partners as tenants in partnership. A partner may not use partnership assets to pay his personal creditors, and a partner's personal creditor may not satisfy his claim against partnership property. A partner may assign his partnership interest to creditors, who then receive the assigning partner's share of the profits. Creditors may obtain charging orders against the interest of a partner; these orders entitle them to the debtor's share of the profits.

PROBLEM CASES

1. Gail Neild and Charles Wolfe were lovers who moved into an apartment in New York City. Only Charles signed the lease, but they agreed that Charles would pay two thirds of the rent and Gail would pay one third. Charles paid for all of the furnishings in the apartment. When their relationship deteriorated, Charles refused to let Gail into the apartment, and she found another place to live. Six months later, the landlord notified the tenants that the building would be converted to a cooperative. The conversion offered each tenant the opportunity to purchase his apartment at a bargain price below the fair market value of the apartment. Charles purchased the apartment he and Gail occupied. Gail sued Charles, seeking one third of the difference between Charles's purchase price of the apartment and its fair market value on the grounds that she and Charles had formed a partnership or joint venture, giving her a one-third interest in the apartment. Was there a partnership or joint venture?

2. Rusty Holler made an agreement with P & M Cattle Company, a partnership owned by Bill Poage and L. W. Maxfield, pursuant to which Rusty would pasture P & M's cattle on Rusty's land. The agreement provided that the cattle would be sold at a time agreeable to all the parties. Also, it provided that Rusty would receive 50 percent of the net proceeds from the sale of the cattle after deducting the cost of the cattle, freight charges, salt costs, and Rusty's $300 monthly salary. When the cattle

*From a
creditor point of view
could prove PARTNERSHIP BY
ESTOPPEL*

836   PART IX   PARTNERSHIP LAW

were sold at a loss, P & M argued that Rusty was a partner or joint venturer with P & M and must undertake his share of the loss. Was P & M correct?

3. Vearle Edwards owned and operated Edwards IGA grocery. Vearle advertised his grocery in the South Sioux City Star, but failed to pay for the advertising. When Vearle filed for bankruptcy, the Star sued Vearle's wife, Ila. The Star's managing editor believed that the grocery was a family-owned business, but he said that he spoke very few times with Ila about advertising since "she was not around." At one time, Ila had done some bookkeeping at the store, but for the last seven years she had no dealings with the grocery. She at no time dealt directly with any suppliers, made any management decisions, ordered any food or supplies, supervised any employees, or placed any advertisements. She contributed no resources to the store. She did not share in the profits or losses of the store, except as the wife of Vearle. Is Ila obligated to pay for the advertising in the Star? *No! But joint tenant could revew*

4. Dr. Woodward and Dr. Kaplan were the only shareholders and medical doctors in a professional corporation, Neurological Consultants, P.C. Dr. Woodward performed a spinal tap on Eugene Gibson. When the spinal tap was unsuccessful, he called Dr. Kaplan, who also performed unsuccessful taps. When requesting consent for the spinal taps from Gibson's wife, Dr. Woodward referred to Dr. Kaplan as "his partner." Subsequently, Gibson suffered permanent nerve damage from Dr. Kaplan's negligently performed spinal taps. Gibson sued Dr. Woodward claiming that Dr. Woodward was Dr. Kaplan's partner by estoppel. Was Dr. Woodward liable for Dr. Kaplan's negligence? *Yes! Because he permitted himself to be assumed a partner*

5. Coy Stephens did business as Audio Works. When he needed a bank loan for the business, Coy and his father, Vastine Stephens, executed a document stating that they were partners in the business and that Coy had the authority to sign for the business in all respects. In fact, Coy and Vastine were not partners, but they executed the document solely to induce a bank to loan the necessary funds to Coy. Relying on the document, Angelina National Bank loaned $33,000 to Audio Works. Angelina would not have loaned the money to Audio Works had it not believed that Vastine was Coy's partner. When Coy failed to repay the loan, Angelina sued Vastine. Was Vastine liable to Angelina? *Yes! because bank relied on statement & evidence in making the loan*

6. Joe Johnson, a logging contractor, hired Steve Olsen to log timber. Johnson advanced money to Olsen, totaling over $8,000 by July 1979. That same month, Bill Slusser worked for Olsen for three days. Johnson asked Olsen who was the stranger working with him, and he replied that it was his future father-in-law and that "they would probably go partners." Johnson paid Olsen and Slusser separately for their work. Slusser did not work again until late October, when he began to work full time. By that time, Johnson had advanced Olsen almost $10,000. In 1980, Olsen stopped working for Johnson. Olsen still had not repaid the $10,000 of advances. Slusser continued to work until Johnson refused to pay him for his work because Olsen had not repaid the $10,000 advance. Although Olsen and Slusser were not partners when the advances were made, Johnson argued that they were partners by estoppel and that, therefore, Slusser is obligated to repay the $10,000. Is Johnson correct? *No. they did nothing to act like a partner*

7. Barry Wilen owned a one-third interest in Bay Country Investments, a partnership. During the term of Barry's marriage to Loveta Wilen, Bay Country sold real property for $126,500. The partnership reinvested the proceeds in other real property. Subsequently, Loveta and Barry had marital problems. During a divorce proceeding, Loveta claimed that she was entitled to receive half of Barry's one-third share of the $126,500 proceeds. Was she correct? *Not by operation of Partnership But so* *marital*

8. Claude Gauldin and Joe Corn formed a partnership to raise cattle and hogs on land owned by Corn. Partnership funds were used to build two buildings on the land for use by the partnership. Gauldin and Corn did not discuss who owned the buildings. Gauldin knew when the buildings were constructed that they would be permanent improvements to the land and would become part of it. The partnership paid no rent for the land, and there was no agreement to consider the use of the land as a contribution by Corn. The taxes on the land were paid by Corn, as was the cost of upkeep. When Corn left the partnership, Gauldin claimed that the buildings were partnership assets and that he was entitled to half of their fair market value. Was Gauldin correct?

No! since Corn paid upkeep & paid taxes nor agreed to believe that it was Partnership asset

CHAPTER 37

OPERATION OF PARTNERSHIP AND RELATED FORMS

INTRODUCTION

This chapter discusses the rules concerning the operation of partnerships, joint ventures, and mining partnerships. Two relationships are important during the operation of a partnership business:

1. The relation of the partners to each other.
2. The relation of the partners to third parties who are affected by the business of the partnership.

These two relationships are like the relationships of agent and principal, principal and third party, and agent and third party. For example, a partner owes fiduciary duties to his partners, as does an agent to her principal. A partner may be liable for his partners' torts, just as a principal may be liable for his agent's torts. And like an agent, a partner may make contracts on behalf of her partners.

In this chapter, keep in mind these two partnership relations as you study partners' duties to each other, partners' management rights, and partners' liability for partnership contracts and torts. Let's begin with a brief look at these two relations.[1]

---

[1] Unless otherwise stated, all the law of partnership discussed in this chapter applies also to joint ventures and mining partnerships. Only the rules that uniquely affect joint ventures or mining partnerships will be pointed out.

Relations between Partners

A partnership relation is a fiduciary relation of the highest order. It is one of mutual trust, confidence, and honesty. The partners may, within certain limits, define the rights and duties owed to each other. In the absence of an agreement, the rights and duties of the parties are determined by the application of the rules of the Uniform Partnership Act (UPA).

Articles of Partnership Although not required, a written partnership agreement (usually a formal document known as the **articles of partnership**) is used by many partnerships. The major purpose of the partnership agreement is to state expressly the relations between the partners in carrying on and terminating the business. Generally, partners are free to make whatever contract they wish between themselves. They may not, however, remove the duty of trust that partners owe each other.

A partnership agreement may be modified by agreement of the partners. Unless another rule for amendment is provided in the agreement, a partnership agreement may be amended only by the unanimous consent of the partners. An inconsistent course of action followed by the partners may also cause a change in the agreement.

Relations of Partners to Third Persons

A partner is liable to third parties not only for her own contracts and torts but also for her partners' authorized contracts and for her partners' torts committed in the course of business. The partners and a third party may agree to alter this relationship between the partners and the third party. The modification is binding on only the third party and the partners who agree to it. The partners cannot, merely by agreement between themselves, diminish the duties and liabilities that they have to third persons with whom they deal on behalf of the partnership.

Now that you know the essence of these two relations, let us look at them in greater detail.

DUTIES OF PARTNERS TO THE PARTNERSHIP AND EACH OTHER

Duty of Loyalty and Good Faith

Because each partner is an agent of the partnership and the other partners, the partners' relation is one of trust and confidence. Therefore, partners owe to the partnership and each other the highest degree of *loyalty and good faith* in all partnership matters. Several duties are encompassed by the duty of loyalty and good faith:

1. Not to profit secretly from partnership transactions.

2. Not to compete with the partnership.

3. To serve the partnership.

4. To maintain the confidentiality of partnership information.

Secret Profits　Unless there is a contrary agreement, a partner's sole compensation from partnership affairs is a share of partnership profits. Therefore, a partner may not make a secret profit out of the transaction of partnership business. For example, a partner may not profit personally by receiving an undisclosed kickback from a partnership supplier. In addition, a partner may not profit secretly when she makes a contract with her partnership, such as selling a building she owns to her partnership without disclosing her ownership or her profit to her partners.

When a partner receives a secret profit, she has a conflict of interests, and there is a risk that she may prefer her own interests over those of the partnership. Therefore, the law permits a partner to profit personally from partnership transactions only if she deals in *good faith*, makes a *full disclosure* of all material facts affecting the transaction, and obtains *approval* from her partners. The remedy for a breach of this duty not to make a secret profit is a *return of the profit* that she made in the transaction with the partnership.

The following case imposed liability on a partner who profited secretly from the sale of a jet plane to the partnership.

LEVY v. DISHAROON
749 P.2d 84 (N. Mex. Sup. Ct. 1988)

Role of Appellate Court in Reviewing Punitive Damages
★ Was the law decided correct?
Damages awarded will not be touched normally unless clearly erroneous

Walter Levy and Henry Disharoon formed a partnership to purchase a jet airplane and to operate a charter airline business. Disharoon located a jet and informed Levy that the price was $963,000. After Levy approved the purchase, Disharoon contracted to buy the jet for $860,000. The partnership borrowed $975,000 to pay for the jet, which money was held by an escrow agent until the purchase was executed. When the purchase was executed, Disharoon directed the escrow agent to pay the seller $860,000 and to deposit in Disharoon's personal bank account the $103,000 difference between the actual purchase price and the purchase price represented to Levy.

After dissolution of the partnership, the trial court found that Disharoon misrepresented the purchase price of the jet with the intention of deceiving Levy. The trial court awarded Levy actual damages of $70,000 and punitive damages of $100,000. Disharoon appealed to the Supreme Court of New Mexico.

Sosa, Senior Justice.   Each partner has the right to have his co-partner exercise good faith in partnership matters. A partner is not allowed to gain any advantage over a co-partner by fraud, misrepresentation, or concealment. For any advantage so obtained he must account to the co-partner. The facts show that the jet was actually purchased for $860,000, but that Disharoon told Levy the sale price was $963,000. The difference was wired to Disharoon's personal banking account in Chicago. Thus, Disharoon defrauded the partnership in the amount of $103,000.

We conclude the trial court was correct in holding Disharoon accountable, but erred in awarding Levy $70,000 in actual damages. Levy's compensatory damages were one-half of the misappropriated funds or $51,500.

The trial court also awarded Levy $100,000 in punitive damages. The amount of punitive damages is left to the discretion of the fact finder and will not be disturbed on appeal unless it is so unrelated to the injury and actual damages proven as to plainly manifest passion and prejudice rather than reason and justice. The $100,000 punitive damage award is not so unrelated to the actual damages to be clearly erroneous. Disharoon's conduct in misrepresenting the jet's actual sale price and misappropriating the partnership's funds deserves punishment.

Judgment for Levy affirmed as modified.

Competing   A partner may not compete with his partnership unless he obtains consent from the other partners. For example, a partner of a retail clothing store may not open a clothing store nearby. However, he may open a grocery store and not breach his fiduciary duty. The partnership has the remedy of recovering the profits of the partner's competing venture.

In the following case, *Veale v. Rose,* a partner in an accounting partnership breached the duty not to compete by providing his own clients with the same types of accounting services that his accounting partnership could have provided.

VEALE v. ROSE

657 S.W.2d 834 (Tex. Ct. App. 1983)

Larry Rose, Paul G. Veale, Sr., Paul G. Veale, Jr., Gary Gibson, and James Parker offered professional accounting services as partners under the firm name Paul G. Veale and Co. Their written partnership agreement expressed the general duties of the partners, but recognized that Veale, Sr., and Rose had outside investments and a number of other business commitments. All of the partners were allowed to pursue other business activities, so long as the activities did not conflict with the partnership practice of public accounting or materially interfere with the partners' duties to the partnership. The partnership agreement provided, in part:

Except with the expressed approval of the other partners as to each specific instance, no partner shall perform any public accounting services or engage in the practice of public accounting other than for and on behalf of this partnership.

While a partner of Paul G. Veale and Co., Larry Rose performed accounting services for Right Away Foods and Ed Payne. He was paid personally by those clients. Rose was an officer and shareholder of Right Away. When the other partners discovered these actions, they claimed Rose owed them a share of his profits from the actions, which competed with the partnership. The jury found that Rose had not competed with the partnership. Rose's partners appealed.

Nye, Chief Justice.   Partners may be said to occupy a fiduciary relationship toward one another which requires of them the utmost degree of good faith and honesty in dealing with one another. Breaches of a partner's duty not to compete with the partnership are compensable at law by awarding to the injured partners their proportionate shares of the profits wrongfully acquired by the offending partner.

While a partner of Veale and Co., Rose rendered accounting services for Right Away Foods for which he billed and received payment personally. Rose admitted that he billed Right Away Foods for the services of a CPA. He also admitted that there was no reason why he could not have rendered the same services to Right Away Foods as a partner in the accounting firm. The preponderance of all of the evidence clearly establishes that Rose performed accounting services for Right Away Foods while a partner of Paul G. Veale and Co., in competition with the partnership.

Rose also admitted that he performed accounting services for various enterprises owned by Payne during his tenure as a partner at Veale, for which he billed and received payment personally. His later testimony that he performed these services, in effect, after hours, or in addition to his duties to the partnership, is of no value in light of the obligations imposed by the partnership agreement and by the common understanding of the term "competition."

Judgment reversed in favor of Rose's partners. Remanded for a new trial.

Duty to Serve   Each partner has a duty to serve the partnership unless the partners agree otherwise. The basis of this duty is the expectation that all partners will work. Sometimes, this duty is termed the duty to devote full time to the partnership. This duty requires a partner to undertake his share of responsibility for running the day-to-day operations of the partnership business.

Partners may agree to relieve a partner of the duty to serve. Often, so-called *silent partners* merely contribute capital to the partnership. They do not have the duty to serve; however, a silent partner has the same liability for partnership debts as any other partner.

The remedies for breach of the duty to serve include assessing the partner for the cost of hiring a person to do his work and paying the other partners additional compensation.

Other Duties   A partner must maintain the *confidentiality* of partnership information, such as a trade secret or a customer list. Also, a partner may not use partnership property for his individual purposes without the other partners' knowledge and consent.

Duty to Act within Actual Authority

A partner has the duty not to exceed the authority granted him by the partnership agreement or, if there is no agreement, the authority normally held by partners in his position. He is responsible to the partnership for losses resulting from unauthorized transactions negotiated in the name of the partnership. For example, suppose partners agree that no partner shall purchase supplies from Jasper Supply Company, which is unaware of the limitation on the partners' authority. When one partner purchases supplies from Jasper, and the partnership suffers a loss because the supplies are of low quality, the wrongdoing partner must bear the loss due to her breach of the partnership agreement.

Duty of Care

In transacting partnership business, each partner owes a duty to use *reasonable skill and care*. A partner is not liable to her partnership for losses resulting from honest errors in judgment, but a partner is liable for losses resulting from her negligence or lack of skill and care. She must make a *reasonable investigation* before making a decision, so that she has an adequate basis for making the decision. The decision she makes must be that of an *ordinarily prudent business manager* in her position.

For example, a grocery store has stocked avocados for three years and has always sold them. If one of the partners buys the same amount of avocados as usual, but they do not sell, the partner is not liable for the loss to the partnership. Her decision appears reasonable as of the time she made it. If prior to the time she made the decision, however, sales of avocados have fallen and trade magazines that she should have read published customer surveys showing lower expected sales of avocados, she would be liable.

Duties to Disclose and to Inform

Each partner owes a duty to disclose to the other partners all information material to the partnership business. She also owes a duty to inform the partners of notices she has received that affect the rights of the partnership.

For example, suppose Gordon Gekko, a partner of a stock brokerage firm, learns that National Motors Corporation is projecting a loss for the current year. The projection reduces the value of National stock, which the firm has been recommending that its customers buy. Gekko has a duty to disclose the projection to his partners to allow them to advise properly the customers of the brokerage.

Duty to Account

Like agents, partners have a duty *to account* for their use or disposal of partnership funds and partnership property, as well as their receipt of any benefit or profit without the consent of the other partners. Partnership property should be used for partnership purposes, not for a partner's personal use.

For example, when a partner of a firm that leases residential property to college students allows his daughter to live in a partnership-owned apartment, the partner must collect rent for the partnership from his daughter or risk breaching the duty to account, as well the duty not to use partnership property for individual purposes and the duty not to profit secretly, which were discussed above.

Each partner owes a duty to keep a reasonable record of all business transacted by him for the partnership and to make such records available to the person keeping the partnership books. The books must be kept at the partnership's principal place of business. Every partner must at all times have access to them and may inspect and copy them.

Right to an Accounting   In addition to a right to inspect the books of the partnership, a partner has a right to a formal **accounting** of the partnership affairs. It is generally by an accounting that a partner can recover from his partners for their breaches of their fiduciary duties.

An accounting is not merely a presentation of financial statements. It is a judicial review of all partnership and partners' transactions to determine whether partners have properly used partnership assets and to award each partner his rightful share of partnership assets. The court takes into consideration breaches of fiduciary duties and adjusts appropriately the amounts payable to the partners.

An accounting is an extreme action and is ordinarily taken only after dissolution of a partnership. UPA Section 22, however, specifically permits an accounting prior to dissolution—by court order, if necessary, such as when a partner is wrongfully excluded from management or a partner has not received his share of the profits.

Right of Indemnification   Closely related to the duty to account is the right of a partner to be *indemnified* for expenditures made from personal funds and for liabilities incurred during the ordinary conduct of the business. For example, a partner uses her own truck to pick up some partnership supplies, which she pays for with her personal check. The partner is entitled to be reimbursed for the cost of the supplies and for her cost of picking up the supplies, including fuel.

Joint Ventures and Mining Partnerships

The fiduciary duties of partners also exist in joint ventures and mining partnerships, although there are a few special rules regarding their enforcement. For example, a joint venturer may seek an accounting to settle claims between the joint venturers, or he may sue his joint venturers to recover joint property or to be indemnified for expenditures that he has made on behalf of the joint venture. A mining partner's remedy against his partners is an accounting; however, a mining partner has a lien against his partners' shares in the mining partnership for his expenditures on behalf of the mining partnership. The lien can be enforced against purchasers of his partners' shares.

CONCEPT REVIEW

PARTNER'S DUTIES

1. Duty not to make a secret profit while transacting for the partnership.
2. Duty not to compete with the partnership.
3. Duty to serve the partnership.
4. Duty to maintain the confidentiality of partnership information.
5. Duty not to use partnership property for personal purposes.
6. Duty to act within the actual authority possessed by the partner.
7. Duty to exercise the skill and care of the ordinarily prudent business manager.
8. Duty to disclose to the other partners information material to the partnership business.
9. Duty to inform partners of notices he has received.
10. Duty to account for the use and disposal of partnership funds and property.
11. Duty to indemnify other partners for expenditures they made from their personal funds and for liabilities they incurred on behalf of the partnership.

COMPENSATION OF PARTNERS

Partners' Compensation

A partner's compensation for working for the partnership is a share of the profits of the business. Ordinarily, a partner is not entitled to a salary or wages, even if he spends a disproportionate amount of time conducting the business of the partnership. A partner may enforce his right to receive his share of the profits and other compensation by seeking an accounting.

Profits and Losses

Pursuant to UPA Section 18(a), unless there is an agreement to the contrary, partners share partnership profits equally, according to the number of partners, and not according to their capital contributions or the amount of time that each devotes to the partnership. For example, a partnership has two partners, Juarez, who contributes $85,000 of capital to the partnership and does 35 percent of the work, and Easton, who contributes $15,000 and does 65 percent of the work. If they have made no agreement how to share profits, when the partnership makes a $50,000 profit in the first year, each partner receives $25,000, half of the profits.

Losses   When the partnership agreement is silent on how to share losses, losses are shared in the same proportions that profits are shared. The basis of this rule is

the presumption that partners want to share benefits and detriments in the same proportions. Nonetheless, the presumption does not work in reverse. If a partnership agreement specifies how losses are shared but does not specify how profits are shared, profits are shared equally by the partners, not as losses are shared.

Examples   For example, when there is no agreement regarding how profits or losses are shared, profits are shared equally, and because losses are shared like profits, losses are shared equally as well.

If two partners make no agreement how to share profits, but agree to share losses 60–40, losses are shared in that proportion, but profits are shared equally.

Partners may agree to split profits on one basis and losses on another basis for many reasons, including their making different capital and personal service contributions or a partner's having higher outside income than the other partners, which enables him better to use a partnership loss as a tax deduction.

Effect of Agreement on Creditors' Rights   Each partner has unlimited personal liability to partnership creditors. Loss-sharing agreements between partners *do not* bind partnership creditors, unless the creditors agree to be bound. For example, two partners agree to share losses 60–40, the same proportion in which they contributed capital to the partnership. After the partnership assets have been distributed to the creditors, $50,000 is still owed to them. The creditors may collect the entire

$50,000 from the partner who agreed to assume only 60 percent of the losses. That partner may, however, collect $20,000—40 percent of the amount—from the other partner.

In the following case, the court held that a partner who was the sole manager of several partnerships he owned with his brother was not entitled to compensation beyond his share of the business's profits.

ALTMAN v. ALTMAN

653 F.2d 755 (3d Cir. 1981)

From 1952 to 1973, two brothers, Sydney Altman and Ashley Altman, operated several partnerships. They shared equally in the management of the partnerships. They received identical salaries, and each brother was permitted to charge an equal amount of personal expenses to the partnerships.

In January 1973, Sydney moved to Florida to establish residency for the purpose of obtaining a divorce. The brothers agreed that Sydney would return to Pennsylvania after his divorce and resume full-time duties with the partnerships. For six months, Sydney commuted to Pennsylvania every week to work for two to three days. In July 1973, Ashley suggested that Sydney return to Pennsylvania once a month until his divorce became final.

Sydney told Ashley in November 1973 that he was considering retiring and remaining in Florida permanently. They tried to reach an agreement on Ashley's purchase of Sydney's partnership interests but were unable to do so. In September 1975, Sydney sued for a judicial dissolution of the partnerships. He alleged that Ashley had violated the partnership agreements and misappropriated partnership assets by paying himself compensation beyond his share of the profits of the businesses.

Ashley continued to manage the businesses by himself until June 1977. By that time, he had managed the partnerships by himself for nearly four years. The district court granted Sydney a judicial dissolution of the partnerships because it found that Ashley had breached the partnership agreements by unilaterally paying himself salaries and charging personal expenses in excess of what the brothers had agreed. Ashley was directed to pay Sydney $153,750.67. Ashley appealed.

Seitz, Chief Judge.   In the absence of an agreement to the contrary, a partner is not entitled to compensation beyond his share of the profits. A right to compensation arises only where the services rendered extend beyond normal partnership functions. Ashley, however, does not expressly contend that the services he performed went beyond normal partnership functions. Instead, he relies on *Greenan v. Ernst* (1962), in which the Pennsylvania Supreme Court concluded that it would be "highly inequitable" to deny compensation to an active partner who had assumed sole responsibility for the management of a partnership when the inactive partners either "could not or would not" assume any responsibility.

Ashley emphasizes that after August 1973, the entire management and supervision of the partnerships were left to him. He asserts that he not only preserved the partnerships' properties, but also maximized profits during this period. In addition, he points out the high caliber of his management of the partnerships.

Ashley apparently is contending that compensation is awarded under Pennsylvania law whenever it would be highly inequitable not to do so. However, *Greenan* does not support this contention. Ashley must show more than the fact that a failure to award compensation would be highly inequitable; he must also show that his services extended beyond normal partnership functions.

The district court found that the services performed by Ashley did not extend beyond normal partnership functions. The critical factor in *Greenan* was that the active partner had taken an existing partnership and expanded it substantially beyond its previous size and scope. In contrast, the services rendered by Ashley maintained the operation of existing businesses in the same manner as they had been operated before Sydney's departure. In addition, unlike the situation in *Greenan*, the lack of participation in the partnerships by Sydney was with the consent of Ashley.

Ashley is not entitled to compensation beyond his share of the partnership profits for managing the partnerships.

Judgment for Sydney Altman affirmed.

CONCEPT REVIEW

PARTNERS' SHARE OF PROFITS AND LOSSES

Profits	Partners share profits equally, unless the partners agree otherwise
Losses	Partners share losses in the same way they share profits, unless the partners agree to share losses in a different manner
Tax Effect	A partner's share of partnership losses may be deducted fully on the partner's individual federal income tax return
Right of Contribution	A partner who pays more than his share of a partnership loss may collect the excess paid from those partners whose shares he paid

MANAGEMENT POWERS OF PARTNERS

Individual Authority of Partners

Every partner is a *general manager* of the business of the partnership. This power is expressed in UPA Section 9(1), which states that a partnership is bound by the act of every partner for apparently carrying on *in the usual way* the business of the partnership. Such authority is implied from the nature of the business. It permits a partner to bind the partnership and his partners for acts within the *ordinary affairs* of the business. The scope of this **implied authority** is determined with reference to what is usual business for partnerships of the same general type in the locality.

Implied authority of a partner may not contradict a partner's **express authority,** which is created by agreement of the partners. An agreement among the partners can expand, restrict, or even completely eliminate the implied authority of a partner. For example, the partners in a newspaper publishing business may agree that one partner shall have the authority to purchase a magazine business for the partnership and that another partner shall not have the authority to sell advertising space in the newspaper. The partners' implied authority to be general managers is modified in accordance with these *express* agreements.

Express authority may be stated orally or in writing, or it may be obtained by acquiescence. For example, if one partner exceeds his implied authority and the other partners know of it and do not complain, that partner may have express authority to do such acts in the future. Regardless of the method of agreement, all of the partners must agree to the modification of implied authority. Together, a partner's express and implied authority constitute her *actual authority.*

Apparent Authority   When implied authority is restricted or eliminated, the partnership risks the possibility that **apparent authority** to do a denied act will remain. Apparent authority exists because it reasonably appears a partner has authority to do an act. To prevent apparent authority from arising when there is a limitation of a partner's actual authority, UPA Section 9(1) requires that third persons with whom the partner deals have *knowledge* of the limitation of his actual authority. Just as a principal must notify third persons of limitations of an agent's authority, so must a partnership notify its customers, suppliers, and others of express limitations of the actual authority of partners.

Suppose that Carroll, Melton, and Ramirez are partners and that they agree that Carroll will be the only purchasing agent for the partnership. This agreement must be communicated to third parties selling goods to the partnership, or Melton and Ramirez will have apparent authority to bind the partnership on purchase contracts. Melton and Ramirez do not have express authority to purchase goods, because they have agreed to such a restriction on their authority. They do not have implied authority to purchase, because implied authority may not contradict express authority.

Ratification   The agency rules of ratification apply with equal force to unauthorized acts of partners. Essentially, **ratification** occurs when the partners accept an act of a partner who had no actual or apparent authority to do the act when it was done.

For example, suppose Cabrillo and Boeglin are partners in an accounting firm. They agree that only Cabrillo has authority to make contracts to perform audits of clients, an agreement known by Mantron Company. Nonetheless, Boeglin and Mantron contract for the partnership to audit Mantron's financial statements. At this point, the partnership is not liable on the contract, because Boeglin has no express, implied, or apparent authority to make the contract. But suppose Boeglin takes the contract to Cabrillo, who reads it and says, "OK, we'll do this audit." Cabrillo, as the partner with express authority to make audit contracts, has ratified the contract and thereby bound the partnership to the contract.

CONCEPT REVIEW

AUTHORITY OF PARTNERS

Express Authority	1. Authority that the partners in writing, orally, or by acquiesence have conferred on a partner. 2. Example: Partners agree that one partner shall have the power to borrow large sums of money on behalf of the partnership. Thus, the partner has express authority to borrow large sums of money.
Implied Authority	1. Authority that is necessary to accomplish the objective of the partnership; gives a partner authority to do anything in the usual course of the partnership's business. 2. Implied authority may not contradict express authority. 3. Example: Because a retail hardware store buys and sells consumer tools in the usual course of business, a partner of a retail hardware store has the implied authority to purchase a dozen hammers.
Apparent Authority	1. Authority that a partner appears to have because of manifestations made by the partnership to third parties. 2. Example: All partners secretly agree that one partner will no have authority to buy tools for a retail hardware store. The partner retains apparent authority to buy tools because it appears that he, as a partner of a hardware store, has the authority to do anything within the usual course of business of a hardware store.
Ratification	1. Authority conferred on a partner after he acts. At the time the partner acts, the partner has no authority to do the act. Otherwise, the partner would have express, implied, or apparent authority to bind the partnership. 2. To ratify the partner's act, the partnership must accept the act or its benefits. 3. Example: A partner of a retail toy store purchases lumber in the name of the partnership. The partner wants to increase the storage area of the toy store. When the other partners tell the partner that the storage area is "a good idea" and to "go ahead and build it," they have ratified the partner's act of buying the lumber for the partnership.

Special Transactions

The validity of some partner's actions is affected by special partnership rules that reflect a concern for protecting important property and the credit standing of partners. This concern is especially evident in the rules for conveying the partnership's real property and for borrowing money in the name of the partnership.

Power to Convey Partnership Real Property

To bind the partnership, an individual partner's conveyance of a partnership's real property must be expressly, impliedly, or apparently authorized or be ratified by the partnership. For example, the partners may expressly agree that a partner may sell the partnership's real property.

The more difficult determination is whether a partner has *implied* and *apparent* authority to convey real property. A partner has implied and apparent authority to sell real property if a partnership sells real property in the usual course of the partnership business. Such would be the case with the partner of a real estate investment partnership that buys and sells land as its regular business. By contrast, a partner has no implied or apparent authority to sell the building in which the partnership's retail business is conducted. Here, unanimous agreement of the partners is required, since the sale of the building may affect the ability of the firm to continue. In addition, a partner has no implied or apparent authority to sell land held for investment not in the usual course of business. A sale of such land would be authorized only if the partners concurred.

Borrowing Money and Issuing Negotiable Instruments

One of the most significant powers that an agent may possess is the power to borrow money and to issue negotiable instruments in the name of her principal. You may remember from agency law that an agent ordinarily has no such implied authority. This rule is grounded in the fear that an agent might impose extensive liability on a principal. This rationale fails somewhat in the area of partnerships, because a partner binds herself when she binds the partnership on loans and negotiable instruments; therefore, some restraint exists on her willingness to borrow excessive amounts.

Nonetheless, partnership law restricts the ability of a partner to borrow and to issue negotiable instruments in the name of a partnership. Essentially, a partner must possess express, implied, or apparent authority. Express authority presents few problems. Finding implied and apparent authority to borrow is more difficult.

Trading and Nontrading Partnerships   Although the UPA does not explicitly recognize the distinction, a number of courts have distinguished between trading and nontrading partnerships. A **trading partnership** has an inventory; that is, its regular business is buying and selling merchandise, such as retailing, wholesaling, importing, or exporting. For example, a toy store and a clothing store are trading partnerships. Since there is a time lag between the date they pay for their inventory and the date they sell inventory to their customers, these firms need to borrow to avoid cash flow problems. Therefore, a partner of a trading partnership has implied and apparent authority to borrow money for the partnership.

A **nontrading partnership** has no substantial inventory but is engaged in providing services—for example, accounting services or real estate brokerage. Such partnerships have no normal borrowing needs. Therefore, a partner of a nontrading partnership has no implied or apparent authority to borrow money for the partnership.

The distinction between trading and nontrading partnerships is not always clear. Businesses such as general contracting, manufacturing, and dairy farming, although not exclusively devoted to buying and selling inventory, have been held to be trading partnerships. The rationale for their inclusion in this category is that borrowing is necessary in the ordinary course of business to augment their working capital.

This suggests why the distinction between trading partnerships and nontrading partnerships is useless or misleading. There is no necessary connection between borrowing money and buying and selling. The more important inquiry should be whether a partner's borrowing is in the ordinary course of business. When borrowing is in the ordinary course of business, a partner has implied and apparent authority to borrow money. If borrowing is not in the ordinary course of business, then no individual partner has implied or apparent authority to borrow money.

If a court finds that a partner has authority to borrow money, the partnership is liable for his borrowings on behalf of the partnership. There is a limit, however, to a partner's capacity to borrow. A partner may have authority to borrow, yet borrow beyond the *ordinary needs* of the business. A partnership will not be liable for any loan whose amount exceeds the ordinary needs of the business, unless otherwise agreed by the partners.

The power to borrow money on the firm's credit will ordinarily carry with it the power to grant the lender a *lien* or *security interest* in firm assets to secure the repayment of the borrowed money. Security interests are a normal part of business loan transactions.

Issuing Negotiable Instruments A partner who has the authority to borrow money also has authority to issue negotiable instruments such as promissory notes for that purpose. When a partnership has a checking account and a partner's name appears on the signature card filed with the bank, the partner has express authority to *draw checks*. A partner whose name is not on the signature card filed with the bank has apparent authority to issue checks, but only in respect to a third person who has no knowledge of the limitation on the partner's authority.

Negotiating Instruments A partnership receives many negotiable instruments during the course of its business. For example, an accounting firm's clients often pay fees by check. Even though borrowing money and issuing negotiable instruments may be beyond a partner's implied and apparent authority, a partner usually has implied and apparent authority to *negotiate* instruments on behalf of the partnership.

For example, when a partnership has a bank account, a partner has implied and apparent authority to *indorse and deposit* in the account checks drawn payable to the partnership. As a general rule, a partner also has implied and apparent authority to indorse and cash checks drawn payable to the order of the partnership. Likewise, partners have implied authority to indorse drafts and notes payable to the order of the partnership and to sell them at a discount.

In the following case, the court found that a partner had implied authority to indorse and deposit checks payable to the partnership.

GROSBERG v. MICHIGAN NATIONAL BANK

362 N.W.2d 715 (Mich. Sup. Ct. 1984)

Mervin Grosberg and Sheldon Goldman, as partners, constructed and operated the Chatham Fox Hills Shopping Center. Grosberg and Goldman had agreed that Goldman would receive rental checks from the shopping center's tenants and deposit them in an account in Grosberg's name at Manufacturers National Bank.

Without Grosberg's knowledge or permission, Goldman opened an account in both their names at Michigan National Bank. Goldman deposited in that account checks relating to the partnership business that were payable to the partnership or its partners. Goldman indorsed each check by signing the name of the partnership or the partners. Later, Goldman embezzled $112,000 of the deposited funds. At no time was Michigan National Bank aware that Grosberg and Goldman were partners.

When Grosberg discovered Goldman's embezzlement, Grosberg sued Michigan National Bank for conversion for accepting checks on which his or the partnership's indorsement was forged. The trial court found that Goldman had authority to indorse and to deposit partnership checks in the account. The court of appeals affirmed the trial court's decision, and Grosberg appealed.

Boyle, Justice. Goldman had *express* authority to indorse and deposit checks only in the account maintained by Grosberg at Manufacturers National Bank. We find, however, that Goldman's partner status invested him with *implied* authority to indorse and deposit each of the incoming checks in the account at Michigan National Bank.

Section 9 of the Uniform Partnership Act states:

The act of every partner, including the execution in the partnership name of any instrument, for apparently carrying on in the usual way the business of the partnership of which he is a member binds the partnership, unless the partner so acting has in fact no authority to act for the partnership in the particular matter, and the person with whom he is dealing has knowledge of the fact that he has no such authority.

The UPA phrase "for apparently carrying on in the usual way the business of the partnership," although it contains the word "apparent," need not be read to exclude the implied-authority notion of powers *that naturally flow from the partnership relationship.* Accordingly, we find that section 9 of the UPA applies *regardless* of the bank's lack of knowledge of the partnership relationship.

Grosberg entrusted Goldman with responsibility to receive and deposit incoming partnership checks. In light of the partnership relationship, we easily conclude that Goldman had *implied* authority to indorse all incoming checks on behalf of the partnership and the partners. The possibility that Goldman may have secretly intended at the time of indorsement to embezzle the funds cannot detract from his authority to affix indorsements, since at that time he was "apparently carrying on in the usual way the business of the partnership."

The question remains whether Goldman's subsequent conduct in depositing the checks in the account at Michigan National Bank invalidates that authority. This case involves a partner with general authority to indorse, a diversion to a joint account in which Grosberg had an equal ownership interest, and diverted checks in which Goldman had a partial ownership interest. The present circumstances are not so inconsistent with "carrying on in the usual way the business of the partnership" that Goldman's authority to make the deposits at issue cannot be implied. Goldman's inherent authority as a partner extended by implication to the deposit of partnership checks in an account ostensibly maintained in both partners' names.

Grosberg contends that the form of the account—joint tenancy with full right of survivorship—was inappropriate for the deposit of business checks and thus should have given the bank notice of Goldman's misconduct. We note that the form of the account is less significant to our analysis than the fact that the account was captioned in both partners' names. Moreover, since Goldman was expressly authorized to deposit checks payable to the shopping center entity into Grosberg's *individual* account at Manufacturers, we reject the argument that Goldman lacked authority to deposit such business checks to an individual account captioned in both their names.

Because of Goldman's implied authority both to indorse incoming checks and to deposit them in an account created in a manner consistent with "apparent partnership purposes," we conclude that no forgery occurred. Therefore, Michigan National Bank is free from liability in conversion.

Judgment for Michigan National Bank affirmed.

Admissions and Notice

Other rules governing the authority of partners are identical to those governing the authority of agents. Under UPA Section 11, a partnership is bound by *admissions* or *representations* made by a partner concerning partnership affairs that are within her express, implied, or apparent authority. Likewise, pursuant to UPA Section 12, *notice* to a partner is considered to be received by the partnership. Also, a partner's *knowledge* of material information relating to partnership affairs is **imputed** to the partnership. These rules reflect the reality that a partnership *speaks, sees, and hears* through its partners.

Disagreement among Partners

Usually, partners will discuss management decisions among themselves before taking action, even when doing so is not required by a partnership agreement and even when a partner has the implied authority to take the action by herself. When partners discuss a prospective action, they will usually vote on what action to take. Each partner has one vote, regardless of the relative sizes of their partnership interests or their shares of the profits. The vote of a majority of the partners controls ordinary business decisions and, thereby, limits the actual authority of the partners. Nonetheless, the apparent authority of the partners to bind the partnership on contracts in the ordinary course of business is unaffected by the majority vote of partners, unless the limitation on the partners' actual authority is communicated to third parties.

Effect of Partnership Agreement

The partners may modify the rules of management by their unanimous agreement. They may agree that a partner, such as a silent partner, will relinquish his management right, thus removing the partner's express and implied authority to manage the partnership. They may grant sole authority to manage the business to one or more partners. Such removals or delegations of management powers will not, however, eliminate a partner's apparent authority to bind the partnership for his acts within the usual course of business.

A partnership agreement may create classes of partners, some of which will have the power to veto certain actions. Some classes of partners may be given greater voting rights. Unequal voting rights are found often in very large partnerships, such as an accounting firm with several hundred partners. Such partnerships commonly have three classes of partners: junior partners, who have few management rights; senior partners, who have more management rights; and managing partners, to whom most management functions have been delegated.

Unanimous Partners' Agreement Required

Some partnership actions are so important that one partner should not be able to do them by himself. To make clear that no single partner has implied or apparent authority to do certain acts, in the absence of a contrary agreement, UPA Section 9(3) requires unanimity for five listed actions. These actions are:

1. Assignment of partnership property for the benefit of creditors.
2. Disposal of the goodwill of the business (such as selling the right to do business with a firm's customers to another business).
3. Action making it impossible to carry on the ordinary business of the partnership (such as the distress sale of the entire inventory of a retailing partnership).
4. Confession of judgment against the partnership.
5. Submission of a partnership claim or liability to arbitration.

In addition, Section 9(2) of the UPA requires unanimous approval of acts "not apparently for the carrying on of business of the partnership in the usual way." Such acts include an agreement for the partnership to pay or to assume an *individual debt of a partner* and to serve as a *surety or guarantor* of the debt of another (unless the partnership's ordinary business is suretyship and guaranty).

Also, other matters not in the usual course of business must be approved by all partners, unless there is a contrary agreement. For example, a decision to merge one accounting partnership with another partnership would have to be approved by all partners. Similarly, the decision of a grocery store partnership to move the business to another city would need unanimous partner approval. Nonetheless, the partners may agree in advance that such an unusual decision may be made by fewer than all the partners.

In the following case, the court applied UPA Section 9(3) and required unanimous partners' agreement for the sale of a motel building that housed the partnership's only business.

PATEL v. PATEL
260 Cal. Rptr. 255 (Cal. Ct. App. 1989)

L. G. and S. L. Patel, husband and wife, owned the City Center Motel in Eureka, California. On April 16, 1986, the Patels formed a partnership with their son, Raj. The purpose of the partnership was to own and operate the motel. The partnership agreement required Raj's approval of any sale of the motel building. Real estate records were not changed, however, and the motel remained recorded only in the names of L. G. and S. L. Patel.

On May 2, 1986, L. G. and S. L. contracted to sell the motel to P. V. and Kirit Patel, who were unaware of Raj's interest in the motel as a partner. When Raj was informed of the contract to sell the motel, he refused to give his approval. Three weeks later, P. V. and Kirit sued L. G., S. L., and Raj for specific performance to compel them to sell the motel. The trial court held the contract unenforceable; P. V. and Kirit appealed.

Channel, Associate Justice.   Generally, every partner is an agent of the partnership for the purpose of its business, and the act of every partner to carry on the business of the partnership binds the partnership. UPA Section 9(1). However, partners acting without the approval of the remaining partners may not do any act that would make it impossible to carry on the ordinary business of the partnership. UPA Section 9(3)(c).

Historically, partnerships were divided into two types: commercial or trading partnerships and noncommercial or nontrading partnerships. Although this distinction has been rejected in California, it remains a valuable tool in considering whether L. G. and S. L. exceeded their statutory authority by entering into the real estate contract, thus making it impossible to carry on the ordinary business of the partnership. In the case of a commercial or trading partnership in which the usual partnership business is to hold and sell real property, a contract such as that involved in this case—to sell the sole partnership asset—would be enforceable. By contrast, when—as in the present case—the usual partnership business is to run a business, rather than to hold it in anticipation of its eventual sale, the partnership is not bound by a contract selling that business without the approval of all the partners. Under these circumstances, the trial court properly denied specific performance of the unauthorized contract in order to prevent destruction of the partnership in compliance with UPA Section 9(3)(c).

Nevertheless, P. V. and Kirit contend that the trial court should have applied UPA Section 10(3). It states:

> Where title to real property is in the name of one or more of the partners, whether or not the record discloses the right of the partnership, the partners in whose name the title stands may convey title to such property, but the partnership may recover such property unless the property has been conveyed to a bona fide purchaser for value without knowledge that the partner executing the conveyance has exceeded his authority.

P. V. and Kirit contend that they are bona fide purchasers for value because they had no knowledge of Raj's unrecorded interest in the motel.

To enforce the contract of sale without Raj's approval would frustrate the purpose of UPA Section 9(3)(c) by making it impossible for the partnership to continue. As the purpose of the partnership is to operate a motel, rather than to hold it for eventual sale, we believe that the better result would be to preserve the partnership and hold the contract unenforceable.

Judgment for L. G., S. L., and Raj Patel affirmed.

Joint Ventures and Mining Partnerships

Most of the authority rules of partnerships apply to joint ventures and mining partnerships. These business organizations are in essence partnerships with limited purposes. Therefore, their members have less implied and apparent authority than do partners. Joint venturers have considerable apparent authority if third persons are unaware of the limited scope of the joint venture. A mining partner has no implied authority to borrow money or issue negotiable instruments. As with partners, joint venturers and mining partners may by agreement expand or restrict each other's agency powers.

LIABILITY FOR TORTS AND CRIMES

Torts

The standards and principles of agency law's **respondeat superior** are applied in determining the liability of the partnership and of the other partners for the torts of a partner. Under Sections 13 and 15 of the UPA, the partnership and the other partners are liable for torts of a partner committed within the ordinary course of partnership business or within the ordinary authority of that partner. In addition, if a partner commits a *breach of trust*, the partnership and all of the partners are liable under UPA Sections 14 and 15. For example, all of the partners in a stock brokerage firm are liable for a partner's embezzlement of a customer's securities and funds.

Intentional Torts   While the doctrine of respondeat superior usually imposes liability on all partners for their partner's *negligence,* the doctrine does not usually impose liability for their partner's *intentional* torts. The reason for this rule is that intentional torts are not usually within the ordinary scope of business or within the ordinary authority of a partner.

A few intentional torts may create liability for all partners. For example, a partner who repossesses consumer goods from debtors of the partnership may trespass on consumer property or batter a consumer. Such activities have been held to be in the ordinary course of business. Also, partners who authorize a partner to commit intentional torts are liable for such torts.

In the following case, *Vrabel v. Acri*, a partner was not held liable for the intentional tort of her partner.

VRABEL v. ACRI

103 N.E.2d 564 (Ohio Sup. Ct. 1952)

On February 17, 1947, Stephen Vrabel and a companion went into the Acri Cafe in Youngstown, Ohio, to drink a few beers. While Vrabel and his companion were sitting at the bar drinking, Michael Acri, without provocation, drew a .38-caliber gun, shot and killed Vrabel's companion, and shot and seriously injured Vrabel. Michael Acri was convicted of murder and sentenced to a life term in the state prison.

Since 1933, Florence and Michael Acri, as partners, had owned and operated the Acri Cafe. From the time of his marriage to Florence in 1931 until 1946, Michael had been in and out of hospitals, clinics, and sanitaria for the treatment of mental disorders and nervousness. Although Michael beat Florence when they had marital difficulties, he had not attacked, abused, or mistreated anyone else. Florence and Michael separated in September 1946, and Florence sued Michael for divorce soon afterward. Before their separation, Florence had operated and managed the cafe primarily only when Michael was ill. Following the marital separation and up until the time he shot Vrabel, Michael was in exclusive control of the management of the cafe.

Vrabel brought suit against Florence Acri to recover damages for his injuries on the ground that, as Michael's partner, she was liable for Michael's tort of battery of Vrabel. The trial court ordered Florence to pay Vrabel damages of $7,500. Florence appealed.

Zimmerman, Judge.   When a partnership is shown to exist, each member of the partnership project acts both as principal and agent of the others as to those things done within the apparent scope of the business of the project and for its benefit.

However, it is equally true that where one member of a partnership commits a wrongful and malicious tort not within the actual or apparent scope of the agency or the common business of the particular venture, to which the other members have not assented, and which has not been concurred in or ratified by them, they are not liable for the harm thereby caused.

Because at the time of Vrabel's injuries and for a long time prior thereto Florence had been excluded from the Acri Cafe and had no voice or control in its management, and because Florence did not know or have good reason to know that Michael was a dangerous individual prone to assault cafe patrons, the theory of negligence urged by Vrabel is hardly tenable. The willful and malicious attack by Michael Acri upon Vrabel in the Acri Cafe cannot reasonably be said to have come within the scope of the business of operating the cafe, so as to have rendered the absent Florence accountable.

Since the liability of a partner for the acts of his associates is founded upon the principles of agency, the statement is in point that an intentional and willful attack committed by an agent or employee, to vent his own spleen or malevolence against the injured person, is a clear departure from his employment, and his principal or employer is not reponsible therefor.

Judgment reversed in favor of Florence Acri.

Partners' Remedies   If the partnership and the other partners are held liable for a partner's tort, they may, during an accounting, recover the amount of their vicarious liability from the wrongdoing partner. This rule places ultimate liability on the wrongdoing partner without affecting the ability of tort victims to obtain recovery from the partnership or the other partners.

Crimes

When a partner commits a crime in the course and scope of transacting partnership business, his partners usually are *not* criminally liable. But when the partners have *participated* in the criminal act or *authorized* its commission, they are liable. They may also be liable when they know of a partner's criminal tendencies, yet place him in a position in which he may commit a crime.

Until recent times, a partnership could not be held liable for a crime in most states, because it was not viewed as a legal entity. However, modern criminal codes usually define a partnership as a "person" that may commit a crime when a partner, acting within the scope of his authority, engages in a criminal act.

LAWSUITS BY AND AGAINST PARTNERSHIPS AND PARTNERS

Suits by the Partnership and the Partners

Under the UPA, a partnership may not sue in its own name; instead, all of the partners must join in the suit.

This means that if the partnership wants to sue someone for breaching a contract or defaming the partnership business, *all* of the partners must agree to bring the suit. Especially for large partnerships, this requirement is cumbersome. Today, many state statutes differ from the UPA by permitting a partnership to sue in its own name.

Suits against the Partners

Section 15 of the UPA imposes on partners a different type of liability for torts than it does for contracts.

Joint and Several Liability for Torts   Partners are **jointly and severally** liable for partnership torts. This means that a tort victim may sue all of the partners (jointly) or sue fewer than all of the partners (severally). If a tort victim sues all of the partners jointly, the judgment may be satisfied against assets of the partnership and assets of the individual partners. If fewer than all of the partners are sued severally, the judgment may generally be satisfied from only the individual assets of the partners sued.

If fewer than all of the partners are sued and made to pay the entire amount of the tort victim's damages, those partners may seek **indemnification** or **contribution** from the other partners for their shares of the liability.

Joint Liability for Contracts   Partners are **jointly** liable for contractual obligations of the partnership. This means that all of the partners must be sued if the partnership has breached a contract. Otherwise, no individual partner may be required to pay a judgment and the assets of the partnership cannot be used to satisfy the contract creditor's judgment.

Courts and legislatures have fashioned many modifications to this requirement of joining all the partners in contract actions. Some states make partners jointly and severally liable for contracts. Others have *joint debtor* statutes that permit creditors—both contract and tort claimants—to sue fewer than all of the partners and yet collect from partnership property.

Other courts make it more difficult to hold individual partners liable for partnership contracts. Some courts, such as in the following case involving Donald Trump, refuse to permit partners to be sued on contract actions until partnership assets have been exhausted.

MEYER v. PARK SOUTH ASSOCIATES
552 N.Y.S.2d 614 (N.Y. App. Div. 1990)

Alvin Meyer was a resident of 100 Central Park South, an apartment building in Manhattan, New York, owned by a partnership, Park South Associates. Meyer sued the partnership and one of its partners, Donald Trump, for violation of the lease between Meyer and the partnership, for breach of the warranty of habitability, and for the tort of intentional infliction of emotional distress. Trump asked the trial court to dismiss the suit against him. The trial court refused to dismiss the suit against Trump, and he appealed to the Appellate Division.

Memorandum Decision.   No cause of action lies against an individual partner for violation of a lease by the partnership, absent an allegation that the partnership is insolvent or otherwise unable to pay its obligations. Here, the first cause of action seeks relief regarding a dispute concerning the lease and the second cause of action alleges a breach of the warranty of habitability by the landlord. Since both of these causes of action arise out of the lease and the business activities of the partnership-landlord, they cannot lie against a partner individually and they should be dismissed as to Trump.

In distinction, the third cause of action alleges tortious conduct by the partnership, reciting a litany of charges of abuse, and sufficiently pleads a cause of action in tort for intentional infliction of emotional distress. An individual partner is liable for a tortious action committed by the partnership, and an action may be brought against him in his individual capacity. Accordingly, the third cause of action should stand as against Trump.

Judgment for Meyer affirmed in part, and reversed in part in favor of Trump.

Suits against the Partnership

The UPA does not permit a partnership to be sued in its own name. This prohibition is especially cumbersome for a party suing for breach of contract. Since the UPA imposes joint liability on partners for partnership contracts, it is necessary to sue each of the joint obligors, which is especially difficult when the partners live in a number of states. As noted above, many states have responded to this difficulty by enacting statutes that make all joint obligations joint and several. In addition, *common-name statutes* permit suits against the partnership even if fewer than all of the partners are notified of the suit. Pursuant to such statutes, a judgment against the partnership is enforceable against the assets of the partnership and against the individual assets of those partners who have been served with process.

ETHICAL AND PUBLIC POLICY CONCERNS

1. Should the law require partners to owe each other fiduciary duties? Does a partner's breach of his fiduciary duty harm only the partners or is society at large also harmed? Should partners be allowed to agree that they do not owe fiduciary duties to each other?

2. Why should a partner have greater implied authority than an agent who is a general manager? Is there a greater risk that an agent will do something imprudent with a business that belongs entirely to someone else than that a partner will do something imprudent with a business that belongs in part to that partner?

3. Is it fair that a partner is liable for the contracts of his partners? Is it fair that a partner is liable for the torts of his partners? Should a partnership be entirely a beneficial relationship for the partners, by which the partners reap the benefits of their relationship with each other but suffer none of the detriments?

SUMMARY

Partners have great freedom to determine by agreement their relationships to each other. Partnership law provides rules that apply when no agreement is applicable. Partners may not by agreement eliminate their fiduciary duties to the partnership and to each other, and they may not, by agreement among themselves, diminish the duties they owe to third persons.

Partners are fiduciaries of each other, and they owe each other many of the same duties that agents owe their principals. Under partnership law, partners may not secretly profit from partnership transactions, they may not compete with the partnership, and they must devote full time to the partnership business, unless otherwise agreed. Partners owe a duty to exercise due care in making business decisions and to account for their business transactions.

All of the partners are entitled to free access to the records of the partnership, and under certain circumstances a partner may ask a court to order and supervise an accounting.

A partner's compensation is her share of the profits of the business, unless otherwise agreed. Usually, profits and losses are shared equally. If the partners agree to share profits on some other basis, then losses will also be shared on that basis, unless the partners agree to

share losses differently from the way in which they share profits.

Each partner has an equal voice in the management of the partnership. Each partner is ordinarily a general manager of the partnership. Therefore, a partner has broad implied and apparent authority to act for the partnership and may, despite a restrictive agreement among the partners, impose contractual liability on it. Partners in a trading partnership have authority to borrow money in the partnership name. When there are differences of opinion, a majority of the partners will rule, except that unanimity is required for major changes, as in the nature or location of the business.

The doctrine of *respondeat superior* applies in determining when a partner's tort imposes liability on the other partners and the partnership. Under modern criminal statutes, partnerships may be held liable for crimes committed by partners acting within the scope of their authority.

Partners are jointly liable on contracts of the partnership, and they are jointly and severally liable for torts. Although the UPA does not allow a partnership to sue or be sued in its own name, most states permit a partnership to sue and be sued in its own name.

PROBLEM CASES

1. Saul Birnbaum, Jay Birnbaum, and Ilene Flaum owned a partnership that developed and operated a shopping center. Due to a conflict between the partners, Saul was the sole manager of the partnership. Rather than develop the shopping center himself, Saul hired Victoria Tree, who later became his wife, to develop the shopping center for the partnership. Saul paid Victoria from partnership funds. Saul did not disclose his hiring of Victoria to Jay and Ilene. Did Saul violate a fiduciary duty?

2. Larry Rose, a partner of an accounting firm, used the firm's employees and computers to render services to his personal clients. The partnership received no compensation from Rose for the use of its employees and computers, and did not share in the profits Rose made serving those clients. Has Rose breached a fiduciary duty?

3. Russel Daub, Daniel Smith, and Frederick Stehlik formed a partnership. No formal partnership agreement was executed. During 1980, profits were distributed monthly, with Daub receiving $3,000 per month, Smith

How they actually divided profit

$1,500, and Stehlik $1,500. In the latter months of 1980, Stehlik received $1,700 per month, but the 1980 partnership tax return indicated that profits were divided 50 percent to Daub and 25 percent each to Smith and Stehlik. During 1981, profits were distributed 50 percent to Daub and 25 percent each to Smith and Stehlik. The 1981 partnership tax return showed the 50–25–25 profit ratio at the beginning of the year, but it showed a year-end ratio of one third to each partner. In 1982, profits were distributed 50–25–25. When the partnership was dissolved and liquidated, Smith and Stehlik argued that each was entitled to one third of the profits and one third of the value of the partnership. Are they correct? *Yes* *and to end*

Manner which Partner actually divided profit

4. Myron Greenleaf and Carolyn Ettinger were partners in a real estate investment firm. They agreed to make equal investments, to have equal liability, and to devote equal time to the partnership. Because Ettinger was inexperienced in real estate investment, Greenleaf devoted more time to the business than did Ettinger. Despite their many discussions that Ettinger should work more, Greenleaf continued to do more than 50 percent of the work. When the partnership dissolved, Greenleaf sought compensation for the value of services he performed in excess of the services rendered by Ettinger. Is Greenleaf entitled to compensation for his excess services? *No! did only what he expected to do. Recourse: dissolution*

5. Louis Covalt and William High were corporate officers and shareholders in Concrete Systems, Inc. (CSI). Covalt owned 25 percent of CSI, and High owned the remaining 75 percent. High and Covalt formed a partnership that bought land, constructed a building on it, and leased the building to CSI. Periodically, CSI and the partnership orally agreed to certain rental increases. When Covalt resigned his corporate position with CSI and was employed by a competitor, he remained a partner with High in the ownership of the land and the building. Covalt wrote to High demanding that the monthly rent for the building leased to CSI be increased from $1,850 to $2,850. High did not agree to the rent increase and took no action to renegotiate the amount of the monthly rent. Has High breached a fiduciary duty to Covalt by not agreeing to the rent increase? *No*

So creditor could not come in and take the land, building

6. Louise Garrett, Rex Voeller, and others owned Pay-Ont Drive-in Theatre, a partnership. Voeller, the managing partner of Pay-Ont, signed a contract to sell to Bill Hodge a small parcel of land belonging to the partnership. The contract stated that the title to the land was in the name of the partnership, and Voeller signed in the

name of the partnership. This land was adjacent to the theater. The contract reserved an easement for use as a driveway into the theater. When the partnership refused to deliver possession of the land to Hodge, he sued Garrett and the other partners. The partners argued that Voeller had no authority to sell the property. Did Voeller have such authority? *No! this requires Majority of Parties*

7. Roy Moyle and Kenneth McCue were the general partners of McCue-Moyle Development Company, a real estate investment partnership that bought, developed, and sold real estate. Robert Baker offered $1.1 million for one piece of partnership property. On behalf on the partnership, Moyle signed the offer. Subsequently, McCue objected to the sale price and argued that the contract was not binding on the partnership because McCue had not signed it. Was the partnership bound on the contract? *Could be Yes if it did not drastically affect biz run*

8. Samuel Bray, Michael Harrington, and Wayne Grimes were partners in Carolina Bonding Company, a business that loaned bond money to criminal defendants. Carolina Bonding loaned bond money to Chris Jones, who disappeared without repaying the loan. Late one evening, Juanita Gatlin, a friend of Jones, was awakened from her bed by Bray and two employees of Carolina Bonding, who pointed guns at her, forced her from her bed, and yelled, cursed, and threatened her, demanding to know where Jones was. They searched her apartment, overturned furniture, and rummaged through her personal effects. Gatlin sued Bray, Harrington, and Grimes for assault, trespass, and intentional infliction of emotional distress. Harrington and Grimes argued that they could not be liable to Gatlin because they were not participants in the actions. Are they correct? *No because tort was committed in scope of Biz*

9. Harold Schwartz, Gerald Dowell, and Lester Dowell formed a partnership to develop residential real estate. The Dowells gave Schwartz complete responsibility to sell the land. Although Schwartz and the Dowells knew that the land had not been surveyed, they conducted no survey because of the high cost of surveying. Instead, Schwartz relied on boundary information from a survey map, from land to the east that had been surveyed, and from boundary stakes placed by previous owners. In preparation for sale, Schwartz marked the boundaries with stakes and surveyor's ribbons. A prospective purchaser, Charles Nuttall, saw the stakes and flags placed by Schwartz and was told that they were "accurate within a couple of feet at the most." Nuttall bought land from the partnership relying on the representations made by Schwartz. Subsequent survey proved

[handwritten: Yes]
[handwritten: adversary counsel of Dowells]

the boundaries to be off by 130 feet, resulting in damages of $1,900 to Nuttall. Nuttall sued the Dowells. Are they liable for Schwartz's misrepresentations?

10. Ramada Inn West was a partnership operating a motel in Asheville, North Carolina. The partners were James Brandis, Ann Brandis, and Wallace Hyde. A Ramada Inn West waitress served four double shots of Tequila and four bottles of beer to Wayne Jordan, an underage drinker. On his way home, Jordan died in a one-car automobile accident. When Jordan's estate sued the partnership for causing his death, to whom did it address the complaint?

[handwritten: To Partnership if allowed & Also individual partners]

CHAPTER 38

DISSOLUTION, WINDING UP, AND TERMINATION OF PARTNERSHIPS

INTRODUCTION

This chapter is about the death of partnerships. Three terms are important in this connection: *dissolution, winding up,* and *termination.* Essentially, **dissolution** is a change in the relation of the partners, as when a partner dies. The partners' relations change because there is one fewer partner who can act for them and affect their liability. **Winding up,** which may follow dissolution, is the orderly liquidation of the partnership assets and the distribution of the proceeds to those having claims against the partnership. **Termination,** the end of the partnership's existence, automatically follows winding up.

DISSOLUTION

Dissolution Defined

Dissolution is defined in Section 29 of the Uniform Partnership Act (UPA) as "the change in the relation of the partners caused by any partner ceasing to be associated in the carrying on as distinguished from the winding up of the business." A dissolution may be caused by a partner's retirement, death, or bankruptcy, among other things. Whatever the cause of dissolution, however, it is characterized by a partner's *ceasing to take part in the carrying on of the partnership's business.*

Importance of Dissolution

Dissolution is the starting place for the winding up (liquidation) and termination of a partnership. Although winding up does not always follow dissolution, it often does. Winding up usually has a severe effect on a business: it usually ends the business, because the assets of the business are sold and the proceeds of the sale are distributed to creditors and partners. Hence, for a profitable business, winding up should be avoided. By preventing dissolution, winding up is avoided.

A dissolution and a winding up are followed by termination of the partnership. Although usually the case, termination of the *partnership* does not automatically result in a termination of the *business.* Instead, the business may be carried on without any interruption by the remaining partners, by one of the partners as a sole proprietorship, by a corporation formed by all or some of the partners, or by another purchaser.

Power and Right to Dissolve

Under UPA Section 31(2), a partner always has the *power* to dissolve the partnership *at any time,* such as by withdrawing from the partnership. A partner does not, however, always have the *right* to dissolve a partnership. For example, a partner has no right to withdraw from a partnership with a 20-year term before the term expires.

When a partner has the right to dissolve the partnership, the dissolution is nonwrongful. If a partner has the power—but not the right—to dissolve the partnership, the dissolution is wrongful. Because the consequences that follow a nonwrongful dissolution differ from those that follow a wrongful dissolution, it is necessary to distinguish a wrongful dissolution from a nonwrongful dissolution.

Nonwrongful Dissolution

A dissolution is nonwrongful when the dissolution does not violate the partnership agreement. UPA Section 31(1) lists the following actions as nonwrongful dissolutions:

1. Automatic dissolution at the end of the term stated in the partnership agreement. For example, a partnership with a 20-year term is automatically dissolved at the expiration of that term.

2. Automatic dissolution on the partnership's accomplishment of its objective. For example, a partnership organized to build 15 condominiums dissolves when it completes their construction.

3. Withdrawal of a partner at any time from a partnership at will. A partnership at will is a partnership whose partnership agreement does not specify any specific term or objective.

4. Unanimous agreement of the partners who have not assigned their partnership interests or suffered charging orders against their partnership interests.[1]

5. Expulsion of a partner in accordance with the partnership agreement. For example, the removal of a partner who has stolen partnership property dissolves the partnership if the partnership agreement allows removal on such grounds.

In addition, UPA Section 31 lists three other nonwrongful dissolutions:

6. The illegality of the partnership business.

7. The death of a partner.

8. The bankruptcy of a partner. The partner must be adjudicated a bankrupt. Mere insolvency does not effect a dissolution.

Finally, Section 32 of the UPA permits a partner or other person to go to court to request that the judge order a dissolution in several situations. Four of these grounds for **judicial dissolution** are nonwrongful:

9. The adjudicated insanity of a partner.

10. The inability of a partner to perform the partnership contract. For example, a two-person partnership that remodels kitchens is dissolved when one of the partners becomes paralyzed in an automobile accident.

11. The inability of the partnership to conduct business except at a loss. Often, a partnership is not making a profit because of irreconcilable differences among the partners that prevent the business from being conducted beneficially.

12. At the request of a purchaser of a partnership interest in a partnership at will. This allows the creditor to whom a partner has assigned his partnership interest to obtain a dissolution and then to seek a winding up. During winding up, the creditor is paid from the debtor/partner's share of the proceeds of the sale of partnership assets.

Consequences of Nonwrongful Dissolution When a dissolution is nonwrongful, each partner, including the dissolving partner, may demand that the business of the partnership be wound up;[2] also, each partner—unless deceased or bankrupt—may participate in the winding-up process. In addition, by their unanimous agreement, the partners—including the nonwrongfully dissolving partner—may decide to allow one or more of the partners to continue the business using the partnership's name. If unanimity to continue the business cannot be obtained, the business is wound up. Therefore, when dissolution is nonwrongful, any partner's demand to wind up will result in the partnership's liquidation.

Wrongful Dissolution

Under UPA Section 31(2), a partner wrongfully dissolves a partnership when she dissolves her partnership in violation of the partnership agreement. For example, a partner wrongfully dissolves a partnership by retiring before the partnership accomplishes its stated objective of inventing a process to make rubber from banana peels.

In addition, some judicial dissolutions may be wrongful with respect to some partners. Under UPA Section

---

[1] The Introduction to Forms of Business and Formation of Partnerships chapter covers the assignment of partnership interests and charging orders against partnership interests.

[2] In the case of a deceased partner, the deceased partner's legal representative shall have this right.

32, court-ordered dissolutions on the following grounds are wrongful dissolutions: (1) when a partner's conduct prejudicially affects the business, or (2) when a partner willfully and persistently breaches the partnership agreement or her fiduciary duties.

For example, a partner may continually insult customers, causing a loss of business; or a partner may persistently and substantially use partnership property for his own benefit; or three partners may refuse to allow a fourth partner to manage the partnership's business. In all of these situations, the aggrieved partners may seek judicial dissolution. As to the aggrieved partners, the dissolution would be nonwrongful. As to the wrongdoing partners, the dissolution would be wrongful.[3]

In the following case, the court found breaches of fiduciary duties by both partners and granted a dissolution. The court did not determine whether the dissolution was wrongful because both partners were wrongdoers.

---

[3]J. Crane and A. Bromberg, *Law of Partnership* Sec. 75(d) and 78(a) (1968).

SABALLUS v. TIMKE

460 N.E.2d 755 (Ill. Ct. App. 1983)

Ronald Saballus and Vernon Timke formed a partnership to acquire and improve Midwest Plaza North, an office building in Oak Brook, Illinois. Midwest Plaza North was one of two parcels of real estate owned by Saballus. Saballus transferred these two parcels to the partnership at what he represented to be his cost, $288,000. In fact, that was his purchase cost for four parcels of real estate, two of which he did not transfer to the partnership.

The partners executed a partnership agreement that obligated each partner to undertake 50 percent of the expense of operating the business. The agreement provided that if a partner failed to perform his obligations under the agreement, the other partner could terminate the interest of the breaching partner without terminating the business. The nonbreaching partner would be obligated to pay the breaching partner the value of his partnership interest as determined by a formula in the partnership agreement.

To finance the improvement of Midwest Plaza North, the partnership applied for a $1,825,000 loan. The lender required the partnership to deposit $275,000 with it as security for the loan. Because this amount exceeded the partnership's assets, it was necessary for each partner to contribute additional money to the partnership. It was not clear, however, by what amount the security deposit exceeded the assets of the partnership. Saballus attempted to find out from Timke what assets the partnership had, but Timke was evasive and refused to allow Saballus to see the partnership's books. Saballus then refused to pay his share of the $275,000 security deposit, so Timke deposited all of the required security with the lender. Within two months, Saballus withdrew $187,000 of the $275,000 and deposited it in a bank account over which he had exclusive control. From this account, Saballus paid his wife a $14,800 real estate commission, and he paid $25,195 to his own corporation for services rendered by it to the partnership.

Timke notified Saballus that he was terminating Saballus's partnership interest because Saballus had failed to pay his share of the security deposit. Saballus then sued Timke for an accounting and a dissolution. Timke counterclaimed, asking the court to order Saballus to surrender his partnership interest to Timke.

The trial court held that Saballus had breached the partnership agreement, and it ordered his partnership interest terminated in accordance with the partnership agreement. Timke was ordered to pay Saballus $53,682.66, the value of Saballus's partnership interest, less the payment to Saballus's wife and a payment to Saballus's corporation after his partnership interest was terminated by Timke. Both partners were displeased with the decision, and both appealed.

Lorenz, Justice.   While Timke persistently argues on appeal that Saballus breached their contractual agreement by failing to provide a pro rata share of the security requirement and must suffer the consequences of having his 50 percent partnership interest terminated, the circumstances surrounding the loan indicate that Timke himself breached his fiduciary duty by failing to render information on demand and to render an accounting to his partner.

Under UPA Section 22, any partner has the right to a formal accounting as to partnership affairs if he is wrongfully excluded from the partnership business or possession of its property by his co-partners, or "whenever other circumstances render it just and reasonable." Thus, a wrongful exclusion, or "freeze-out," of one partner by a co-partner from participation in the conduct of the business or from the management of the partnership business, will be grounds for judicial dissolution. Saballus, who repeatedly requested access to the partnership books kept by Timke in order to determine the accuracy or source of these figures on partnership funds available to be used as security for the loan, was both "put-off" and denied access to the partnership books by Timke prior to the loan closing.

It is also clear that Saballus did not disclose to Timke that four lots were included in the original purchase price of $288,000, and although he did pay partnership obligations out of the bank account, Saballus did not obtain Timke's consent in order to establish the account.

Thus, although it would be difficult to decide which of the parties is most in the wrong, we believe that equity demands a decree of dissolution in this case, where, as here, the relations existing between the partners render it impracticable for them to conduct business beneficially. We determine that a dissolution, and not a termination of Saballus's partnership interest, is proper.

Judgment reversed in favor of Saballus. Remanded to the trial court.

Consequences of Wrongful Dissolution   A partner who wrongfully dissolves a partnership (1) has no right to demand that the business be wound up; (2) has no right to participate in the winding up if the business is wound up; (3) has no right to have the goodwill of the business taken into account in valuing his interest; (4) may not use the firm's name in connection with any business he conducts after dissolution; and (5) is liable for damages for breach of the partnership agreement. Such damages may include the cost of seeking judicial dissolution, the expense of finding a substitute partner, and the legal fees for drafting new partnership agreements. Nonetheless, a wrongfully dissolving partner is entitled to his share of the value of the partnership, minus his share of the partnership goodwill and the damages he caused the partnership.

Right to Continue   In the event of a wrongful dissolution, UPA Section 38(2) gives the innocent partners the right to continue the business themselves or with new partners. They may continue to use the partnership's name. This right to continue the business prevents a wrongfully dissolving partner from forcing a liquidation of the partnership.

In addition, each of the innocent partners has all of the rights that are possessed by partners when there is a nonwrongful dissolution. This means that if there is a wrongful dissolution, any innocent partner may force a winding up. Usually, innocent partners choose to continue the business.

Acts Not Causing Dissolution

As you learned in a previous chapter, a partner's assignment of his partnership interest does not dissolve a partnership, and neither does a creditor's obtaining a charging order. In addition, many other acts appear to cause dissolution but in fact do not, including the following:

1. *Addition of a partner.* Because no one disassociates from the partnership when a partner is added, there is no dissolution.

2. *Disagreement among the partners.* Disagreements, even irreconcilable differences, are expectable, but they are not grounds for dissolution. If the disagreements threaten partnership assets or profitability, then a court may order dissolution.

3. *Death or withdrawal of a partner, but only when the partnership agreement states that death or withdrawal shall not cause a dissolution.* Although death or withdrawal clearly disassociates a partner from the carrying on of the business, several states permit the partners to vary the definition of dissolution by their agreement. Other states permit the partners to eliminate the right to demand a winding up after the death or withdrawal of a partner.

In the following case, *Great Hawaiian Financial Corp. v. Aiu,* the partnership agreement stated that withdrawal of the partners did not cause a dissolution.

GREAT HAWAIIAN FINANCIAL CORP. v. AIU
863 F.2d 617 (9th Cir. 1988)

Hilolani Acres Joint Venture was a partnership of 42 partners, including Benjamin Aiu. Four of the partners were designated managing partners. The partnership agreement stated that the purpose of the partnership was "dealing with" the Hilolani Acres, a housing development in Hawaii. The partnership agreement also provided for continuation of the business of the partnership in the event of a withdrawal of partners from the partnership.

In 1971, three of the managing partners withdrew from the partnership; in addition, title to Hilolani Acres was transferred to Great Hawaiian Mortgage Corporation, which would manage the development of Hilolani Acres for the partnership; Great Hawaiian received 35 percent of the profits from Hilolani Acres, the remainder going to the partnership. The nonmanaging partners claimed that these acts dissolved the partnership, and they sought to wind it up. Great Hawaiian sued the partners, claiming that there was no dissolution. The trial court held that both acts effected a dissolution, and Great Hawaiian appealed.

Per Curiam.   Evidence that three former managing partners withdrew from the partnership indicates that the original partnership including those partners was dissolved as to *those partners.* "The withdrawal of a partner from a partnership operates to dissolve the partnership as to the withdrawing partner. It does not effect a dissolution of the entire firm." *McKellar v. Bracewell* (1971).

The withdrawal of three partners does not necessarily affect the rights and obligations of the remaining partners. This is especially true where, as here, the agreement addressed the withdrawal of members of the partnership and contemplated continuation of the business in spite of such withdrawals. *Crane & Bromberg on Partnership*, sec. 73, at 417–19 (1968) (withdrawal of partner need not result in dissolution of entire firm where partnership agreement contemplates changes in membership).

The district court also found that the assignment of partnership assets to Great Hawaiian completed the sole undertaking for which the partnership was formed and thus caused its dissolution as a matter of law. The district court supported this determination by citing UPA Section 31(1)(a), which states that dissolution is caused "[b]y the termination of the definite term or particular undertaking specified in the agreement."

The joint venture agreement provided that the partnership was formed for the purpose of "dealing with," not merely holding title to, the property in question. The assignment of the property did not terminate this undertaking. Under the development agreement between the joint venture and Great Hawaiian Mortgage, the partnership retained the right to receive 65 percent of net profits from development of the property and the right to regain legal title to the property on demand and without cost. The agreement also prohibited Great Hawaiian from assigning or mortgaging developed lots without the prior written approval of the partnership. The development agreement thus clearly provided that the partnership, designated as the "owner" in the agreement, would continue to "deal with" and profit from the land in spite of the transfer of legal title to Great Hawaiian Mortgage. Moreover, the partners continued to reap tax benefits from their participation in the partnership subsequent to the transfer of title, indicating that the partners continued to benefit from their undertaking during the relevant period. The district court thus erred in concluding that the transfer of legal title to Great Hawaiian Mortgage necessarily terminated the particular undertaking of the partnership within the meaning of UPA Section 31(1)(a).

Judgment reversed in favor of Great Hawaiian. Remanded to the trial court.

CONCEPT REVIEW

CAUSES AND NONCAUSES OF DISSOLUTION

Causes of Dissolution	Wrongful dissolutions
	1. Any dissolution that violates the partnership agreement.
	2. Judicial dissolution due to a partner's prejudicially affecting the business.
	3. Judicial dissolution due to a partner's willful and persistent breach of the partnership agreement or her fiduciary duties.
	Nonwrongful dissolutions
	1. End of the term stated in the partnership agreement.
	2. The partnership's accomplishment of its objective.
	3. Withdrawal of a partner at any time from a partnership at will.
	4. Withdrawal of a partner in accordance with the partnership agreement.
	5. Expulsion of a partner in accordance with the partnership agreement.
	6. Unanimous agreement of the partners who have not assigned their partnership interests or suffered charging orders against their partnership interests.
	7. Illegality of the partnership business.
	8. Death of a partner.
	9. Bankruptcy of a partner.
	10. Judicial dissolution due to the adjudicated insanity of a partner.
	11. Judicial dissolution due to the inability of a partner to perform the partnership contract.
	12. Judicial dissolution due to the inability of the partnership to conduct business except at a loss.
	13. Judicial dissolution at the request of a purchaser of a partnership interest in a partnership at will.
Noncauses of Dissolution	1. Assignment of a partnership interest.
	2. Obtaining a charging order.
	3. Addition of a partner.
	4. Disagreement among the partners that does not threaten partnership assets or profitability.
	5. Death or withdrawal of a partner, when the partnership agreement states that death or withdrawal shall not cause a dissolution.

Joint Ventures and Mining Partnerships

Essentially, the partnership rules of dissolution apply to joint ventures. It is more likely in a joint venture than in a partnership that a member's death will not dissolve the joint venture or not permit a demand to wind up; courts often find that joint venturers made an implied agreement that the limited objective of the joint venture be completed.

Mining partnerships are more difficult to dissolve than general partnerships due to the free transferability of mining partnership interests. The death or bankruptcy of a mining partner does not effect a dissolution. In addition, a mining partner may sell his interest to another person and disassociate himself from the carrying on of the mining partnership's business without causing a dissolution. The other rules of partnership dissolution apply to mining partnerships.

WINDING UP THE PARTNERSHIP BUSINESS

The Process

When a partnership is to be terminated, the next step after the dissolution is **winding up** the partnership's affairs. This involves the orderly liquidation—or sale—of the assets of the business. Liquidation may be accomplished asset by asset; that is, each asset may be sold separately. It may also be accomplished by a sale of the business as a whole. Or it may be accomplished by a means somewhere between these two extremes.

Winding up does not always require the sale of the assets or the business. When a partnership has valuable assets, the partners may wish to receive the assets rather than the proceeds from their sale. Such *distributions-in-kind* are rarely permitted. They are allowed when there are no creditors' claims against the partnership, the value of the assets can be ascertained, and the assets can be distributed in a manner that is fair to each partner.

Fiduciary Duties

In winding up a partnership, the partners continue as fiduciaries to each other, especially in negotiating sales or making distributions of partnership assets to members of the partnership. Nonetheless, there is a termination of the fiduciary duties unrelated to winding up. For example, a partner who is not winding up the business may compete with his partnership during winding up.

Who May Demand Winding Up?

A partner who has not wrongfully dissolved the partnership may demand winding up. Thus, when a partnership has been dissolved nonwrongfully, any partner, even the dissolving partner, may demand winding up. If the partnership has been wrongfully dissolved, only the innocent partners may demand winding up.

Who May Wind Up?

Under UPA Section 37, any surviving, nonbankrupt partner who has not wrongfully dissolved the partnership may wind up. A partner who wrongfully dissolved the partnership has no right to wind up the business. When a dissolution is due to the death or bankruptcy of a partner, the surviving partners and the nonbankrupt partners have the right to wind up the business.

If the dissolution is by court decree, usually no partner winds up. Instead, a *receiver* is appointed by the court to wind up the business.

Compensation during Winding Up

Ordinarily, the compensation of a winding-up partner is only his share of the profits. Nonetheless, when the partners agree to give special compensation to the winding-up partner, he is entitled to the agreed-on compensation. In addition, when the winding-up partner provides extraordinary services or is the sole surviving partner after dissolution by death, he is entitled to the reasonable value of his winding-up services.

Partner's Authority during Winding Up

Dissolution terminates most of the express and implied authority of the partners because the purpose of winding up is liquidation, not continuation of the business. A large amount of *apparent authority* remains when proper notice of the dissolution is not given to creditors and other persons.

Express and Implied Authority   During winding up, a partner has the implied authority to do those acts *reasonably necessary to the winding up* of the partnership affairs. That is, he has the power to bind the partnership in any transaction necessary to the liquidation of the assets. He may collect money due, sue to enforce partnership rights, prepare assets for sale, sell partnership assets, pay partnership creditors, and do whatever else is appropriate to wind up the business. He may maintain and preserve assets or enhance them for sale, for example, by painting a building or by paying a debt to prevent foreclosure on partnership land.

Although these rules generally describe the authority of a partner during winding up, some transactions deserve separate attention. These transactions are completing executory contracts and borrowing money.

Completing Executory Contracts A partner has the implied authority to complete contracts made before dissolution. A partner may not enter into *new* contracts unless the contracts aid the liquidation of the partnership's assets.

For example, a partner may fulfill a contract to deliver coal, if the contract was made before dissolution. She may not make a new contract to deliver coal, unless doing so disposes of coal that the partnership owns or has contracted to purchase.

Borrowing Money As a general rule, a partner who is winding up a partnership business has no implied authority to borrow money in the name of the partnership. Nonetheless, when a partner can preserve the assets of the partnership or enhance them for sale by borrowing money, he has implied authority to engage in new borrowing. For example, a partnership may have a valuable machine repossessed and sold far below its value at a foreclosure sale unless it can refinance a loan. A partner may borrow the money needed to refinance the loan, thereby preserving the asset.

Apparent Authority When notice of dissolution is not given to nonpartners, persons who are aware of the partnership's existence but unaware of its dissolution may reasonably believe that each partner has the authority to conduct the business in the usual way. The failure to give nonpartners notice of dissolution, therefore, permits a third party to believe that a partner has *apparent authority* to transact for the partnership as if it were continuing its business. Such apparent authority of a partner makes the partnership liable for contracts made by the partner during winding up when the contracts would have been in the usual course of business prior to dissolution.

For example, a construction partnership dissolves and begins winding up, but does not notify anyone of its dissolution. After dissolution, a partner makes a contract with a customer to remodel the customer's building. The partner would have no implied authority to make the contract, because the contract is new business and does not help liquidate assets. Nonetheless, the contract may be within the partner's apparent authority, because to persons unaware of the dissolution, it appears that a partner may continue to make contracts that have been in the usual course of business.

Section 35 of the UPA specifies certain steps that the partnership may take to eliminate this apparent authority. Persons who have extended credit to the partnership must have actual—or personal—notice of the dissolution. **Actual notice** may be given by telephone or by a letter mailed or faxed to the creditor's place of business. Creditors may also receive actual notice by hearing of the dissolution by word of mouth or reading of it in a newspaper.

Persons who were not creditors but had merely done business with the partnership without extending credit or had merely been aware of the existence of the partnership must receive either actual notice or **constructive notice** of the dissolution. Constructive notice is notice published in a newspaper of general circulation in the places where the partnership did business. Such notice eliminates apparent authority of the partners even if the notice is not read by the noncreditors.

For persons who were previously unaware of the partnership's existence, no notice of any type need be given to eliminate apparent authority.

Disputes among Winding-Up Partners

When more than one partner has the right to wind up the partnership, the partners may disagree concerning which steps should be taken during winding up. For decisions in the ordinary course of winding up, the decision of a majority of the partners controls. When the decision is an extraordinary one, such as continuing the business for an extended period of time, unanimous partner approval is required.

In the following case, the court found that the decision concerning who should train and race a horse during winding up was not an ordinary decision that could be made by fewer than all the partners.

PACIARONI v. CRANE

408 A.2d 946 (Del. Ct. Ch. 1979)

Black Ace, a harness racehorse of exceptional speed, was the fourth best pacer in the United States in 1979. He was owned by a partnership: Richard Paciaroni owned 50 percent; James Cassidy, 25 percent; and James Crane, 25 percent. The partnership had no written agreement and had no term specified for its duration. Crane, a professional trainer, was in charge of the daily supervision of Black Ace, including training. It was understood that all of the partners would be consulted on the races in which Black Ace would be entered, the selection of drivers, and other major decisions; however, the recommendations of Crane were always followed by the other partners because of his superior knowledge of harness racing.

In 1978 as a two-year-old, Black Ace won three of his nine starts. In 1979, he raced primarily in three-year-old stakes races and won $96,969 through mid-August. Seven other races remained in 1979, including the prestigious Little Brown Jug and the Messenger at Roosevelt Raceway. The purse for these races was $600,000.

A disagreement among the partners arose when Black Ace developed a ringbone condition and Crane followed the advice of a veterinarian not selected by Paciaroni and Cassidy. The ringbone condition disappeared, but later Black Ace became uncontrollable by his driver, and in a subsequent race he fell and failed to finish the race. Soon thereafter, Paciaroni and Cassidy sent a telegram to Crane dissolving the partnership and directing him to deliver Black Ace to another trainer they had selected. Crane refused to relinquish control of Black Ace, so Paciaroni and Cassidy sued him in August 1979, asking the court to appoint a receiver who would race Black Ace in the remaining 1979 stakes races and then sell the horse. Crane objected to allowing anyone other than himself to enter the horse in races. Before the trial court issued the following decision, Black Ace had entered three additional races and won $40,000.

Brown, Vice Chancellor.   All three partners agree that the horse must be sold in order to wind up partnership affairs. The only dispute is as to when he must be sold and what is to be done with him in the meantime.

Paciaroni and Cassidy take the position that since the partnership relation continues until the time of termination and distribution of assets, then as a consequence the will of the majority of the partnership interests should control the manner of winding up. In particular, they rely on the first portion of Uniform Partnership Act Section 18(h) as giving them, as the majority, the right to have the horse finish the stakes racing season under the guidance of their new trainer and over the objection of Crane.

This argument I reject. I do so because Section 18(h) permits a majority vote to decide any "difference arising as to ordinary matters connected with the partnership business." Under the exceptional circumstances of this case, I do not view the difference between the partners to be one which has arisen in the ordinary course of partnership business. Quite the contrary. The partnership is dissolved. Crane is fearful that if the horse is allowed to continue racing with the changes made by the new trainer as authorized by Paciaroni and Cassidy, he may well suffer injury and decline from his present value before he can be sold, thus jeopardizing Crane's one-fourth interest. Paciaroni and Cassidy, on the other hand, say that the horse should be raced because his value may well be increased thereby. They say that they have the once-in-a-lifetime opportunity to be the owners of a champion caliber racehorse. They say that they also have the right to seek to obtain the highest possible price for him when he is sold, something that can only be done if he finishes out his stakes race season. This difference between the partners is hardly one that has arisen in the ordinary course of partnership business. Accordingly, I conclude that Paciaroni and Cassidy have no statutory right to wind up affairs simply because they can outvote Crane.

It is generally accepted that once dissolution occurs, the partnership continues only to the extent necessary to close out affairs and complete transactions begun but not then finished. It is not generally contemplated that new business will be generated or that new contractual commitments will be made. This, in principle, would work against permitting Black Ace to participate in the remaining few races for which he is eligible.

However, in Delaware, there have been exceptions to this. Where, because of the nature of the partnership business, a better price upon final liquidation is likely to be obtained by the temporary continuation of the business, it is permissible, during the winding up process, to have the business continue to the degree necessary to preserve or enhance its value upon liquidation, provided that such continuation is done in good faith with the intent to bring affairs to a conclusion as soon as reasonably possible. And one way to accomplish this is through an application to the Court for a winding up under UPA Section 37, which carries with it the power of the Court to appoint a receiver for that purpose.

The business purpose of the partnership was to own and race Black Ace for profit. The horse was bred to race. He has the ability to be competitive with the top pacers in the country. He is currently "racing fit" according to the evidence. He has at best only seven more races to go over a period of the next six weeks, after which time there are established horse sales at which he can be disposed of to the highest bidder. The purse for these remaining stake races is substantial. The fact that he could possibly sustain a disabling injury during this six-week period appears to be no greater than it was when the season commenced. Admittedly, an injury could occur at any time. But this is a fact of racing life which all owners and trainers are forced to accept. And the remaining stake races are races in which all three partners originally intended that he would compete, if able.

Under these circumstances, I conclude that the winding up of the partnership affairs should include the right to race Black Ace in some or all of the remaining 1979 stakes races for which he is now eligible. The final question, then, is who shall be in charge of racing him.

On this point, I rule in favor of Paciaroni and Cassidy. They may, on behalf of the partnership, continue to race the horse through their new trainer, subject, however, to the conditions hereafter set forth. Crane does have a monetary interest in the partnership assets that must be protected if Paciaroni and Cassidy are to be permitted to test the whims of providence in the name of the partnership during the next six weeks. Accordingly, I make the following ruling:

1. Paciaroni and Cassidy shall first post security in the sum of $100,000 so as to secure to Crane his share of the value of Black Ace.

2. If Paciaroni and Cassidy are unable or unwilling to meet this condition, then they shall forgo the right to act as liquidating partners. In that event, each party, within seven days, shall submit to the Court the names of two persons who they believe to be qualified, and who they know to be willing, to act as receiver for the winding up of partnership affairs.

3. In the event that no suitable person can be found to act as receiver, or in the event that the Court should deem it unwise to appoint any person from the names so submitted, then the Court reserves the power to terminate any further racing by Black Ace and to require that he simply be maintained and cared for until such time as he can be sold as a part of the final liquidation of the partnership.

Judgment for Paciaroni and Cassidy.

FIGURE 1   Partner's Authority during Winding Up

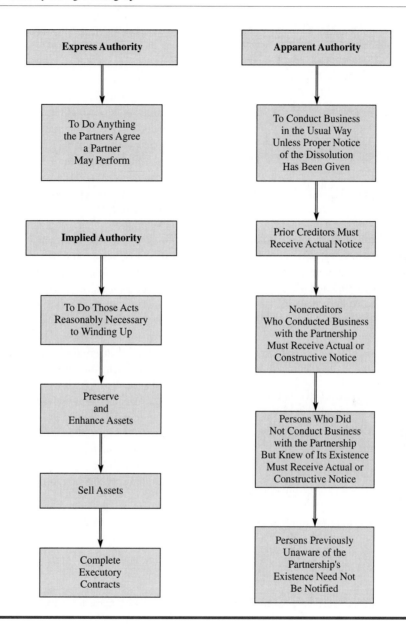

WHEN THE BUSINESS IS CONTINUED

Cessation of business need not follow dissolution of a partnership. The remaining partners could purchase the business during winding up, someone else could purchase the business, or the partnership agreement could provide that there will be no winding up and that the business may be carried on by the remaining partners.

And as stated earlier, partners who have not wrongfully dissolved the partnership may agree to continue the partnership and its business.

When there is no winding up and the business is continued, the claims of creditors may be affected, because old partners are no longer with the business and new partners may enter the business.

Successor's Liability for Prior Obligations

When the business of a partnership is continued after dissolution, creditors of the old partnership are creditors of the person or partnership continuing the business, giving these creditors equal status with the other creditors of such person or partnership. In addition, the original partners remain liable for obligations incurred prior to dissolution unless there is agreement with the creditors to the contrary. Thus, partners may not usually escape liability by forming a new partnership or a corporation to carry on the old business of the partnership.

Outgoing Partner's Liability for Prior Obligations

A partner who leaves a partnership is not automatically relieved of his liability for partnership obligations. Consequently, outgoing partners remain liable to their former partners and to partnership creditors for partnership losses and liabilities; however, **novation** will eliminate an outgoing partner's liability.

Novation   Novation occurs when two conditions are met:

1. The continuing partners release an outgoing partner from liability on a partnership debt.

2. A partnership creditor releases the outgoing partner from liability on the same obligation.

The consequence of novation is the elimination of the outgoing partner's liability on the partnership obligation.

Partners usually expressly release an outgoing partner from liability, but the release may be implied as well.

When a partner wrongfully dissolves a partnership and the remaining partners continue the business, the continuing partners *must* agree expressly to relieve the outgoing partner from liability for the obligations of the dissolved partnership. When a partner has dissolved a partnership nonwrongfully, the outgoing partner and the continuing partners *may* agree whether or not to release the outgoing partner from liability. If they fail to do so expressly, their release of the outgoing partner is usually presumed, especially when the continuing partners have purchased a retired partner's share of the partnership.[4]

To complete the requirements for novation, an outgoing partner must *also* secure his release by the partnership's creditors. A creditor's agreement to release an outgoing partner from liability may be express, but usually it is implied. *Implied* novation may be proved by a creditor's knowledge of a partner's withdrawal and his continued extension of credit to the partnership. In addition, a *material modification* of an obligation operates as a novation for an outgoing partner, when the creditor has knowledge that the continuing partners have released the outgoing partner from liability.

When former partners release an outgoing partner from liability but creditors do not, there is not a novation. As a result, creditors may enforce a partnership liability against an outgoing partner. However, the outgoing partner may recover from his former partners who have agreed to release him from liability.

In the following case, the court found both an implied novation and a material alteration operating as a novation. Consequently, the court relieved an outgoing partner from liability to a landlord.

_____

[4]J. Crane and A. Bromberg, *Law of Partnership* Sec. 78(c) (1968).

WESTER & CO. v. NESTLE

669 P.2d 1046 (Colo. Ct. App. 1983)

Junior Nestle and Eric Ellis were the owners of Red Rocks Meat and Deli, a partnership. They had no partnership agreement and no specified term for the partnership. They operated the partnership in a building that they leased from Wester & Company. In October 1978, Nestle left the business. John Herline purchased Nestle's partnership interest, including Nestle's entire interest in partnership equipment, leases, and other assets. In return, a new partnership of Ellis and Herline agreed to assume all the liabilities of the former partnership and to release Nestle from liability. A copy of the purchase and release agreement was mailed to Wester & Co., giving notice to Wester & Co. that Nestle was no longer a partner. Ellis introduced Herline to Wester & Co. as his new partner. Wester & Co. did not object to a change in partners or request that Nestle remain liable.

Soon after, Herline left the partnership, and Ellis operated the business as a sole proprietorship. In January 1980, Wester & Co. and Ellis modified the original lease to include adjacent space and to increase the rent. When the lease was modified, it was clear to Wester & Co. that Ellis was then operating the business as a sole proprietor. The president of Wester & Co. was told when the lease was modified that Nestle was no longer a partner.

In May 1980, when Ellis failed to pay the rent, Wester & Co. sued Nestle for the rent. The court found that due to Wester & Company's knowledge of the situation and the parties' course of dealings, it had consented to Nestle's release from liability. The court also concluded that the modified lease materially altered Nestle's liability on the underlying lease, thereby discharging Nestle from liability. Wester & Co. appealed.

Steinberg, Judge.   The dissolution of a partnership does not of itself discharge the existing liability of any partner. A partner is discharged from existing liability by an agreement to that effect between the withdrawing partner, the remaining partners, and the partnership creditor, and "such agreement may be inferred from the course of dealing between the creditor and the person or partnership continuing the business." A material alteration in an existing liability will discharge from liability a partner whose obligations have been assumed.

The trial court found that the conditions for discharge from liability under both of these subsections existed, and such factual findings, supported by the evidence, may not be disturbed upon appeal.

Judgment for Nestle affirmed.

Outgoing Partner's Liability for Obligations Incurred after Dissolution

Ordinarily, an outgoing partner has no liability on partnership obligations incurred after he leaves the partnership because he no longer controls the partnership or shares as a co-owner in its profits. Nonetheless, outgoing partners may be liable for obligations incurred by a person or partnership continuing the business after their departure, under the theory of *partnership by estoppel*. There is no such liability to creditors who are aware of the change in partners. Also, the risk of estoppel liability can be eliminated by giving the notice prescribed by Section 35 of the UPA.

Section 35 requires actual—or personal—notice to those persons who extended credit to the partnership prior to dissolution. Such notice may be either oral or written and must be actually delivered or received. Constructive notice—notice published several times in a newspaper of general circulation—is sufficient for those who knew of the partnership but were not prior creditors. No notice need be given to persons who were not previously aware of the partnership's existence or who knew of the dissolution.

Partnership by estoppel imposed liability on the partners in the *Royal Bank and Trust Co. v. Weintraub, Gold & Alper* case, which follows, because they failed to give timely notice of dissolution and appeared to be continuing their business as partners after dissolution.

ROYAL BANK AND TRUST CO. v. WEINTRAUB, GOLD & ALPER

497 N.E.2d 289 (N.Y. Ct. App. 1986)

Weintraub, Gold & Alper, a law firm partnership, was dissolved January 1, 1976. In 1977, during the winding up of the partnership's affairs, the firm's partners continued to occupy the same office space and to use the firm's name and letterhead as an aid in the partners' transition to individual law practices. In November 1977, Alper took office space elsewhere, formal notices of the dissolution were sent out, and use of the firm's name stopped.

Two months earlier, however, on September 27, 1977, Roger Allen sought a short-term $60,000 loan from Royal Bank and Trust Company. Allen told Royal Bank that for the entire term of the loan, the $60,000 would be kept in an escrow account of his lawyers, the firm of Weintraub, Gold & Alper. As proof that the money would be placed in the escrow account, Allen gave Royal Bank a letter on the law firm's stationery addressed to Allen and signed by Weintraub. The letter acknowledged that the money would be received by the firm as escrow agent, that it would be placed in a firm escrow account, and that the money would be returned to Royal Bank by October 5, 1977.

Royal Bank called its New York lawyers, who told Royal Bank that they had not heard of the firm of Weintraub, Gold & Alper, and that the three lawyers were listed separately in a lawyer directory as practicing law at the address given on the firm stationery. Royal Bank's credit officer found the firm listing in the current New York phone book at the address and phone number on the letterhead. When the officer dialed the number, the receptionist answered, "Weintraub, Gold and Alper." The officer spoke with Weintraub, who confirmed the escrow arrangement. That same day, Royal Bank made the loan to Allen, giving him a check payable to the law firm. The check was deposited in the firm's escrow account.

On October 5, when the loan was due, the escrowed check was not returned and the loan was not repaid. Royal Bank sued Gold, Alper, and the partnership, among others, to recover the $60,000. Gold and Alper argued that they and the partnership were not liable for Weintraub's actions in accepting the escrow money because the partnership had been dissolved at that time. Both the trial court and the appellate court held that Gold and Alper were liable. Gold and Alper appealed.

Kaye, Judge.   A partner who makes, and consents to, continued representations that a partnership in fact exists is estopped to deny that a partnership exists to defeat the claim of a creditor. Here, Gold and Alper are estopped to deny their relationship as against Royal Bank. Nearly two years after the alleged dissolution, the public indicia of the partnership remained undisturbed. Where the firm space, phone number, phone book listing, and stationery continued in use by the individuals, with no discernible sign of dissolution, we conclude that the partnership continued to be liable as such to a party reasonably relying to its detriment on the impression of an ongoing entity.

Gold and Alper contend that due to the separate listings in the lawyer directory, Royal Bank acted negligently in failing to investigate further. As Royal Bank correctly points out, individual listing in a lawyer directory, when measured against the uncontroverted proof of an apparently existing partnership, was insufficient to give rise to a genuine issue.

Judgment for Royal Bank affirmed.

Liability of Incoming Partners

A person joining an existing partnership has unlimited liability for all partnership obligations incurred *after* she becomes a partner. For partnership obligations incurred *before* she became a partner, she is liable as if she had been a partner when the obligations were incurred; however, her liability is limited to the partnership's assets. Once partnership assets are exhausted, she has no further liability for partnership obligations that were in-curred prior to her affiliation with the partnership. Nonetheless, if she has expressly or impliedly agreed to undertake unlimited liability for prior obligations, her liability will be unlimited. For example, she may agree with an outgoing partner to assume the outgoing part-ner's partnership obligations.

In the following case, incoming partners had no lia-bility beyond the assets of the partnership on a debt that arose prior to their joining the partnership.

KALICHMAN v. BEVERLY HOLDING CO.

520 N.Y.S.2d 255 (N.Y. App. Div. 1987)

Joseph Kalichman and Joseph Klein formed a partnership that owned and managed an apartment building in the Bronx, New York. The partnership borrowed $189,000 from National Savings Bank of Albany. Before the loan was repaid, Joseph Klein died, and his interest in the partnership passed to his sons, Jack and Frank, who received Joseph Klein's share of the partnership income. Jack and Frank did not, however, engage in management of the partnership business. When the partnership defaulted on the loans, National Savings Bank sued Kalichman. Kalichman settled the lawsuit by paying $100,000 to National Savings Bank and then sued Jack and Frank Klein to require them to pay their share of the liability. The trial court found Jack and Frank liable to Kalichman; Jack and Frank appealed.

Casey, Justice.   Jack and Frank assert that the existence of a partnership arrangement does not demonstrate or indicate their assumption of a preexisting obligation on the bonds, rendering them personally liable for such debt. We agree. UPA section 41(7) provides:

The liability of a third person becoming a partner in the partnership continuing the business under this section to the creditors of the dissolved partnership shall be satisfied out of partnership property only.

Although the primary purpose of UPA section 41 is the protection of creditors, it also limits incoming partners' liability to the partnership property unless personal liability is expressly as-sumed through the partnership agreement or otherwise. Here, Joseph Klein's death dissolved his partnership with Kalichman by operation of law. Kalichman then had the right to possess the property for a partnership purpose, as well as the duty to wind up the affairs of the partnership and to pay to Joseph Klein's legal representative Klein's proportionate share in partnership surplus. These events did not occur here, however, since Kalichman continued the partnership business with Jack and Frank's consent. Having continued to carry on the partnership business after Joseph Klein's death, Kalichman must bear all of the losses, while UPA section 41(7) limits Jack and Frank's liability to their interest in the Bronx property. Jack and Frank's only association with the partnership was to receive income from the same. While this fact might evidence the formation of a partnership between Jack, Frank, and Kalichman, it does not evidence that Jack and Frank ever assumed personal liability for preexisting loans incurred by Joseph Klein.

Judgment reversed in favor of Jack and Frank Klein.

Rights of Outgoing Partners

An outgoing partner is entitled to receive the value of his partnership interest. He becomes a creditor of the new partnership for the value of his partnership interest, but his claim is subordinate to the claims of other creditors of the partnership.

Valuation of the Outgoing Partner's Interest   The value of an outgoing partner's interest in the partnership is determined at the time of the dissolution. Often, the partnership agreement includes a method for calculating the value of a partnership interest. Usually, courts accept such an agreed-on valuation method. When, however, the agreed-on method results in an inequitable valuation, such as paying a partner 2 percent of the value of her interest, the partners' agreement may be disregarded as unconscionable.

The value of a partnership includes its goodwill. **Goodwill** is the well-founded expectation of continued public patronage of a business. It represents the difference between the going-concern value of a business and the liquidation value of its assets.

When a partnership business is continued after dissolution, it is frequently difficult to determine the value of the goodwill that is transferred to the continuing partners. In service partnerships, the goodwill may be so closely tied to the individual partners that no goodwill remains with the business when valuable partners withdraw from the partnership. These difficulties and uncertainties also make it advisable to have a partnership agreement on valuing the partnership, including the value of its goodwill.

Payment Options   In the absence of a contrary agreement, when dissolution results from death or retirement, UPA Section 42 permits the outgoing partner to choose between two payment options:

1. Taking the value of his partnership interest at the time of dissolution plus interest, or
2. Taking the value of his partnership interest at the time of dissolution plus a pro rata share of subsequent profits.

The latter option provides incentive for the continuing partners to settle promptly with an outgoing partner.

When there is no agreement and dissolution results from a cause other than death or retirement—as with dissolutions caused by bankruptcy or by willful, persistent breaches of the partnership agreement— the partner is entitled to receive the value of her interest at the time of dissolution. The outgoing partner may insist on immediate payment and receive interest for late payment.

Valuation of Interest of Wrongfully Dissolving Partner   A wrongfully dissolving partner must be paid the value of his partnership interest in cash by the continuing partners, or the partners must post a bond to have the privilege of continuing the business. In addition, they must agree to release him from all present and future partnership liabilities. However, goodwill is excluded from the valuation of the partnership interest of a partner who has wrongfully caused dissolution, and the valuation of that interest is further reduced by the damages that he has caused his partners due to his dissolution.

DISTRIBUTION OF ASSETS

After the partnership's assets have been sold during winding up, the proceeds are distributed to those persons who have claims against the partnership. Not only creditors but also partners have claims against the proceeds. As you might expect, the claims of creditors must be satisfied before the claims of partners may be paid.

Order of Distribution

Section 40 of the UPA states the order of distribution of the partnership assets:

1. Those owing to creditors other than partners.
2. Those owing to partners other than for capital and profits.
3. Those owing to partners in respect of capital.
4. Those owing to partners in respect of profits.

Note that item 2 places partners who are also creditors of the partnership subordinate to other creditors. This is done to prevent partners from underfunding a partnership to the detriment of creditors. The subordination of partner-creditors also emphasizes that the partners are liable for all the partnership's liabilities.

A partner who is also a creditor of the partnership, however, is paid his claim as a creditor before any partner receives any return of his capital contribution. Thus, for example, a partner's loan to the partnership is repaid before any partner has his capital returned.

If a partnership has not suffered losses that impair its capital, few problems are presented in the distribution of its assets. Everyone having an interest in the partnership is paid in full. If there is a disagreement about the amount due to a claimant, the dispute is usually resolved by an accounting ordered by the court. In the following case, the court calculated each partner's share of the assets of a solvent partnership.

LANGNESS v. O STREET CARPET SHOP

353 N.W.2d 709 (Neb. Sup. Ct. 1984)

NFL Associates was a partnership of three partners: Herbert Friedman, Strelsa Lee Langness, and The O Street Carpet Shop, Inc. At the partnership's creation in 1973, O Street Carpet contributed a contract worth $9,000, Langness contributed $14,000 in cash, and Friedman contributed his legal services, which were not valued. The partners used part of Langness's contribution to make an $8,000 payment to O Street Carpet. They used the remaining $6,000 to purchase investment property and for working capital. Later, O Street Carpet contributed an additional $4,005 in capital. The partners agreed that Friedman would receive 10 percent of the profits and that each of the other two partners would receive 45 percent of the profits. The partners agreed also that Langness would receive payments of $116.66 each month.

During the five-year term of the partnership, Langness received checks totaling $6,300.30. Langness did not pay income tax on these monthly payments. The partnership did not take expense deductions for those payments on its information return filed with the Internal Revenue Service. In 1978, the partnership dissolved and wound up its business, selling its investment property for $52,001.20. After paying partnership liabilities of $3,176.79, Friedman distributed the remaining $48,824.41 to the partners. Langness received $16,792.01, O Street Carpet received $26,808.58, and Friedman received $5,223.82. Langness was unhappy with the distribution and sued Friedman and O Street Carpet for a larger share. The trial court held that Langness was entitled to receive $24,082.43. The court imposed liability on Friedman and O Street Carpet for $7,290.42, the additional amount Langness should have received. Friedman appealed.

Per Curiam. Friedman's appeal is best analyzed by reviewing the capital contributions made by the partners, the nature of the payments made to Langness, and the distributions made to each of the three partners upon the winding up of the partnership. O Street Carpet made a contribution of property worth $9,000. However, $8,000 of the $14,000 contributed by Langness went to O Street Carpet, thereby reducing its capital contribution at that time to $1,000. O Street Carpet contributed an additional $4,005 in capital. Thus, O Street Carpet's total capital contribution is $5,005.

Friedman contributed no money or property. It is the general rule that a partner who contributes only services to a partnership is not deemed to have made a capital contribution to the partnership, unless the partners have agreed to the contrary. Friedman argues that since, by agreement, he was given 10 percent of the partnership, he was entitled to be credited with a like amount of the partnership capital upon dissolution. While the agreement specifically states that Friedman is entitled to 10 percent of the partnership profits, it mentions nothing concerning his rights to partnership capital upon dissolution. Therefore, Friedman made no capital contribution to the venture.

We next address the nature of the payments made to Langness. The partnership agreement called for the partnership to pay to Langness $116.66 per month for the life of the partnership.

While this provision of the articles is found under a section labeled "Distribution of Profits and Losses," the agreement does not state whether it is to be treated as an advance on profits or a capital withdrawal. Both accountants who testified at the trial stated that the payments were treated as capital withdrawals. Langness treated the payments as such when preparing her tax returns. The tax returns of the partnership did not treat them as expenses. We calculate her total capital withdrawals as $6,300.30, which reduced her capital in the partnership to $7,699.70.

We now reach the question of the appropriate amounts of the distribution to each of the partners. The partnership agreement provides: "Upon the dissolution of the partnership after settlement of all of its liabilities, the partners are entitled to all remaining assets of the partnership in equal proportions in liquidation of all of their respective interests in the partnership." Amounts owing to partners to reimburse them for capital contributions take priority over amounts owing to partners in respect to profits.

Of the $48,824.41 in assets remaining after payment of the partnership's debts, $7,699.70 is to be paid to Langness for her capital contribution and $5,005 to O Street Carpet for its capital contribution. The remaining $36,119.71 is to be divided according to the partners' share in the profits, which is on a 45–45–10 basis. This calculation requires $16,253.87 to be paid to Langness for profit, the same amount to O Street Carpet, and $3,611.97 to Friedman.

Therefore, Langness was entitled to a total distribution of $23,953.57. Since Langness was paid only $16,792.01, she is entitled to an additional $7,161.56.

Judgment for Langness affirmed as modified.

Distribution of Assets of Insolvent Partnership

When a partnership has suffered losses, distribution of the assets may be troublesome. For example, partnership creditors may compete with the creditors of individual partners to obtain payment from partnership assets and the assets of individual partners. Also, the partnership losses must be allocated among partners. In adjusting the rights of partnership creditors and the creditors of individual partners, the rule usually is that partnership creditors have first claim on partnership assets and that individual creditors have first claim on individual assets. This is an example of **marshaling of assets.**

Example   The distribution of assets and allocation of losses of an insolvent partnership can best be explained with an example. Suppose that Alden, Bass, and Casey form a partnership and that Alden contributes $25,000, Bass contributes $15,000, and Casey contributes $10,000. After operating for several years, the firm suffers losses and becomes insolvent. When the partnership is liquidated, its assets total $30,000 in cash. It owes $40,000 to partnership creditors. Therefore, the capital balance (net worth) of the partnership is a negative $10,000. This means that partnership losses totaled

$60,000 ($50,000 of capital already contributed and lost plus the $10,000 negative net worth). The situation could be represented by the following equation:

$$\text{Profit} = \text{Ending owner's capital} - \text{Beginning owner's capital}$$
$$-\$60,000 = -\$10,000 - \$50,000$$

Because the profit is negative, this is a loss of $60,000.

In the absence of a provision in the partnership agreement concerning the partner's shares of profits and losses, they are shared equally. Therefore, each partner's share of the loss is one third of the loss, $20,000. Their shares of the loss reduce the partners' capital claims against partnership assets, as shown in Figure 2.

Figure 2 shows that while each partner should have assumed $20,000 of the loss, Alden has taken $25,000

FIGURE 2

	Capital at Beginning		Share of Loss		Capital at Liquidation
Alden	$25,000	–	$20,000	=	$5,000
Bass	15,000	–	20,000	=	(5,000)
Casey	10,000	–	20,000	=	(10,000)
Totals	$50,000	–	$60,000	=	($10,000)

of the loss due to her $25,000 capital contribution. Therefore, unless she has $5,000 of her capital returned, she has assumed $5,000 of the loss she should not have assumed. Bass and Casey, on the other hand, have assumed too little of the loss, because their capital contributions were less than $20,000. Bass should undertake $5,000 more of the loss, and Casey should assume $10,000 more, amounts reflected in the last column of Figure 2.

Now we shall distribute partnership assets and pay the claims against the partnership. Following the order of distribution in UPA Section 40, the $30,000 in cash from the liquidation is distributed pro rata to pay the nonpartner creditors of the partnership. Because the creditors are owed $40,000, the $30,000 payment leaves $10,000 of partnership debts to outsiders unpaid. The partners are liable for the remaining $10,000. Because the partnership assets are gone, the partners must pay the debt from their individual assets.

To undertake their *shares* of the partnership liabilities, Bass is legally liable to contribute $5,000 and Casey $10,000 to the partnership, the negative amounts in the Capital at Liquidation column in Figure 2. This permits completion of the payment of the partnership creditors ($10,000) and the return of Alden's capital to the extent that it exceeded her share of the partnership loss—the $5,000 figure in the Capital at Liquidation column.

Unpaid partnership creditors have a right to collect from *any* solvent partner. Had they chosen to collect the entire amount from Alden, she would then have had to proceed against Bass and Casey for the amount she paid that Bass and Casey should have paid.

Termination

After the assets of a partnership have been distributed, the partnership automatically terminates.

ETHICAL AND PUBLIC POLICY CONCERNS

1. Why should a partner have the power to dissolve a partnership at any time, while in general a shareholder of a corporation has no such power? Is it important to your answer that a partner has liability for his partners' contracts and torts, while a shareholder generally has no liability for the contracts or the torts of the corporation? Why should a partner not have the right to dissolve a partnership at any time? Who should determine when a partner has the right to dissolve a partnership? Should only the partners determine the scope of this right or does society have the right to limit a partner's right to dissolve?

2. Why should a partnership give notice of the dissolution of a partnership? Why is the partnership liable to creditors who do not receive proper notice of the dissolution? Is fairness promoted by such a rule? Is economic efficiency promoted by such a rule?

3. Is it fair that a wrongfully dissolving partner is not entitled to receive a share of the value of the partnership's goodwill? What is goodwill? How much goodwill does the business lose when a dissolving partner leaves the partnership? Is more goodwill lost when a partner dissolves wrongfully than when he dissolves nonwrongfully? Do partners expect wrongful dissolutions? Do the expectations of the partners provide a rationale to deny goodwill to a wrongfully dissolving partner?

SUMMARY

A dissolution is a change in the relation of the partners caused by one or more partners disassociating herself from the carrying on of the business. Dissolution may be wrongful or nonwrongful. A wrongful dissolution is one in violation of the partnership agreement. Some judicial dissolutions may be wrongful, such as dissolution ordered due to a partner's willful, persistent breach of his fiduciary duties.

Nonwrongful dissolution is dissolution that is not in violation of the partnership agreement. Causes of nonwrongful dissolution include a partner's death or bankruptcy.

A wrongfully dissolving partner may not demand or perform winding up. In addition, she may not share in the goodwill of the business, and she must pay damages to the other partners for breaching the partnership agreement. After dissolution, partners who have not wrongfully dissolved the partnership may agree unanimously to continue its business.

Winding up is the orderly liquidation of the assets of the partnership. After dissolution, the surviving, nonbankrupt partners who have not wrongfully dissolved the partnership have the right to wind up the partnership business. The winding-up partners have the implied authority to do whatever is reasonably necessary to accomplish the winding up. They do not have actual authority to engage in new business. The partners still have apparent authority to bind the partnership to third parties who are unaware of the dissolution. This apparent authority may be cut off by actual notice to those who have extended credit to the partnership and by constructive notice to others.

If the partnership business is continued, the original partners remain liable on the debts of the former partnership unless there is a novation. Also, unless there is a contrary agreement, the creditors of the previous partnership remain creditors of the continuing business. A person joining an existing partnership assumes liability for its previous obligations, but usually only to the extent of the partnership assets.

In winding up a partnership, first, there is a marshaling of assets, whereby partnership creditors have first claim against partnership assets and creditors of individual partners have first claim on the individual assets of their debtors. After partnership creditors have been paid, partners are repaid their loans to the partnership. If assets remain, partners are entitled first to the return of their capital and then to their shares of any undistributed profits.

PROBLEM CASES

1. Jackson Wanlass and D. W. Ogden operated a title search business as partners at will. After Ogden and Wanlass died, the Ogden children excluded Mrs. Wanlass from the business and converted partnership funds. Mrs. Wanlass claimed that these actions amounted to a wrongful dissolution by the Ogden children. Was she correct? *Yes*

2. Vasso Corporation and Pav-Saver Corporation (PSC) were the only partners of Pav-Saver Manufacturing Company. The partnership agreement provided that the "partnership shall be permanent and shall not be terminated or dissolved by either partner except on mutual approval of both partners." The partnership was profitable until 1981, after which the partners disagreed on the direction the partnership should take. Subsequently, PSC wrote to Vasso dissolving the partnership. Vasso claimed that PSC wrongfully dissolved the business and that therefore Vasso was entitled to continue the business. Was Vasso correct? *No but can buy partner & continue*

3. Robert Cowan was a partner in a six-person law firm. The partnership agreement provided that the firm would not dissolve upon the withdrawal of a partner. Cowan initially indicated that he would withdraw from the partnership, but later changed his mind. By that time, however, the other partners had resolved to force Cowan from the partnership. The other partners transferred all partnership funds to accounts in their names only. However, a few days later, they set up an escrow account to protect the value of Cowan's partnership interest. Did the other partners' actions entitle Cowan to obtain a judicial dissolution of the partnership? *No because acting in his ...*

4. Kenneth Flynn and Rick Haddad were partners owning a beach-front lot with a small inn on it. Title to the lot was in both partners' names. Flynn gave Haddad a deed to Flynn's interest in the property, which was effective only upon Flynn's nonpayment of a loan. When the inn was destroyed by fire, the partners began construction of a new inn, but construction was stopped because it violated local zoning laws. The effect of the lawsuits halting construction was also to eliminate the market of potential buyers of the property. Haddad decided to sever his relationship with Flynn and, consequently, filed the deed to the property that had earlier been executed by Flynn, although Flynn had already repaid the loan. Has the partnership been dissolved? Should the property be sold during winding up or should Haddad receive title to it and be required to pay Flynn his share of the value of the property?

5. Roger Steeby and Charles Fial were the only partners of an auditing firm. They contracted to provide audit services for their clients, but instead of performing the audits themselves, they hired independent contractors to do the audits. Because Fial generated about 80 percent of the business of the firm, he became unhappy with their profit-sharing agreement and dissolved the partnership. Fial terminated the contracts with the firm's clients and signed the clients to contracts with Fial's corporation, Audit Consultants of Colorado, Inc. Fial's corporation used the same independent contractors to perform audits for the clients. Has Fial acted properly? *Yes*

6. By oral agreement, Kenneth Clark and Robert Feldman formed a partnership to raise Christmas trees. Clark, a forester with 30-years' experience, provided management and expertise to the partnership. Feldman provided labor and the land; he and his children did most of the planting of trees. Within two years, Feldman dissolved the partnership citing his dissatisfaction with Clark's management. During winding up, Feldman excluded Clark from the land. Consequently, Feldman provided all the labor and management during winding up. Is Feldman entitled to compensation for his labor and management provided during winding up?

No! not doing anything out of ordinary

7. Ralph Neitzert and his brother were the only partners of Jolly Jug Liquors, a retail liquor store. The partners signed a contract to lease refrigeration equipment from Colo-Tex Leasing, Inc. A month later, Ralph sold his interest in the partnership to his sister. Ralph did not notify Colo-Tex that he sold his interest to his sister. A year later, when the partnership breached the lease, Colo-Tex sued Ralph, his brother, and his sister. Is Ralph liable to Colo-Tex? *Yes! Because creditor wasn't*

8. In 1980, Southern Distilleries, a partnership, executed two promissory notes totaling $140,000 payable to Commercial State Bank. In 1981, the partnership admitted Julius Moselely as a partner. He contributed $100,000 to the partnership. Two months later, Southern Distilleries executed a new promissory note to replace the old notes. The old notes were marked paid. The new note was in the amount of $140,000 payable to Commercial State Bank. The note was not paid when it was due, and the bank sued Southern Distilleries and its partners. What is the amount of Moselely's liability to the bank on the $140,000 note?

made after he was already in Partnership
probably his investment in partnership

9. Thomas Bernabei, James Serra, and Howard Wenger formed a partnership, Fairway Development I. In 1981, Bernabei and Serra ceased their involvement with Fairway Development I and transferred all their rights in the partnership to Wenger and James Valentine. Wenger and Valentine continued the business as partners using the name Fairway Development II. Subsequently, Fairway II sought to enforce Fairway I's contract with Title Insurance Company of Minnesota (TICOM). TICOM argued that it was liable to Fairway I only and that Fairway I had been dissolved and terminated. Therefore, TICOM argued that Fairway II was a new partnership, was not a party to the contract, and could not sue TICOM. Was TICOM correct? *no!*

10. Mohammad Rasheed, his wife, and Asaad and Fayzah Mubarek formed a partnership. After the partnership was dissolved, Rasheed sued his partners and sought a final accounting of the partnership. The trial court appointed a CPA to perform the accounting. In valuing the partnership property, the CPA used book value instead of fair market value. Has the CPA valued partnership property correctly?

Yes!

for complete when in Dissolution & winding

CHAPTER 39

LIMITED PARTNERSHIPS

INTRODUCTION

The partnership form—with managerial control and un-limited liability for all partners—is not acceptable for all business arrangements. Often, business managers want an infusion of capital into a business, yet are reluctant to surrender managerial control to those contributing capital. Investors wish to contribute capital to a business, share in its profits, and yet limit their liability to the amount of their investment. A need, therefore, exists for a business form that has two types of owners: one type of owner who contributes capital to the business, manages it, shares in its profits, and possesses unlimited liability for its obligations; and a second type of owner who contributes capital and shares profits, but possesses no management powers and has liability limited to her investment in the business.

In 1822, New York and Connecticut were the first states to recognize this form—the **limited partnership.** Today, every state has a statute permitting the creation of limited partnerships, although Louisiana calls them partnerships *in commendam.*

The Uniform Limited Partnership Acts

The National Conference of Commissioners on Uniform State Laws—a body of lawyers, judges, and legal scholars—drafted the Uniform Limited Partnership Act (ULPA) in 1916. In 1976, the commissioners drafted the Revised Uniform Limited Partnership Act (RULPA), which more clearly and comprehensively states the law of limited partnership. The RULPA was amended in several significant ways in 1985. A majority of the states have adopted the RULPA; the remaining states, except for Louisiana, follow the ULPA. The RULPA as amended in 1985 forms the foundation of the discussion in this chapter. References are made to the Uniform Partnership Act (UPA), which applies to limited partnerships in the absence of an applicable provision in the RULPA. As shown in Figure 1, many characteristics of a limited partnership under the RULPA are similar to those of a partnership under the UPA. The RULPA and the UPA are reproduced in appendices to this book.

Use of Limited Partnerships

The limited partnership form is used primarily in tax shelter ventures and activities such as real estate investment, oil and gas drilling, and professional sports. Limited partnerships operate as tax shelters by allowing partners to reduce their personal federal income tax liability by deducting limited partnership losses on their individual income tax returns. General partners, however, receive a greater tax shelter advantage than do

---

FIGURE 1 Principal Characteristics of Limited Partnerships

1. A limited partnership may be *created only in accordance with a statute.*
2. A limited partnership has two types of partners: *general partners* and *limited partners.* It must have one or more of each type.
3. All partners, limited and general, *share the profits* of the business.
4. Each general partner has *unlimited liability* for the obligations of the business. Each limited partner has liability *limited to his capital contribution* to the business.
5. Each general partner has a *right to manage* the business, and she is an agent of the limited partnership. A limited partner has *no right to manage* the business or to act as its agent, but he does have the right to vote on fundamental matters. If a limited partner does manage the business, he may incur unlimited liability for partnership obligations.
6. General partners, as agents, are *fiduciaries* of the business. Limited partners are not fiduciaries.
7. A partner's interest in a limited partnership is *not freely transferable.* An assignee of a general or limited partnership interest is not a partner, but is entitled only to the assigning partner's share of capital and profits, absent a contrary agreement.
8. Withdrawal of a general partner *dissolves* a limited partnership, absent a contrary agreement of the partners. The withdrawal of a limited partner does not automatically dissolve a limited partnership.
9. A limited partnership *pays no federal income taxes.* Its partners report their shares of the profits and losses on their individual federal income tax returns. A limited partnership files an *information return* with the Internal Revenue Service, notifying the IRS of each partner's share of the year's profit or loss.

---

limited partners. Losses of the business allocated to a general partner offset his income from any other sources. Losses of the business allocated to limited partners may be used to offset only income from other *passive* investments. If a limited partner has sold her limited partnership interest or the limited partnership has terminated, her loss offsets any income.

CREATION OF LIMITED PARTNERSHIP

A limited partnership may be created only by complying with the applicable state statute. Yet the statutory requirements of the RULPA are minimal. RULPA Section 201 requires that a **certificate of limited partnership** must be executed and filed with the secretary of state. The certificate must be signed by *all general partners.* A limited partnership begins its existence at the time the certificate is filed with the office of the secretary of state or at any later time specified in the certificate. Figure 2 lists the contents of the certificate of limited partnership.

The certificate of limited partnership contains a minimal amount of information, reflecting the rationale for its use: to put third parties on notice that a limited partnership exists, and that the limited partnership has some partners with limited liability. The certificate constructively notifies third parties that only the general partners listed in the certificate have unlimited liability.

The certificate is required to contain little information that is important to the relationship between the partners. For example, the certificate is not required to state the names of the limited partners, the partners' capital contributions, the partners' shares of profits and other distributions, or the acts that cause a dissolution of the limited partnership. Nonetheless, the partners will usually include those and other matters in the certificate or in a separate **limited partnership agreement.**

Who May Be a Partner? Any *person* may be a general or limited partner. Persons include a natural person, partnership, limited partnership, trust, estate, association, or corporation. Hence, as commonly occurs, a corporation may be the sole general partner of a limited partnership.

FIGURE 2 Contents of Certificate of Limited Partnership

The following must be in the certificate:

1. The name of the limited partnership, which must contain the words *limited partnership.* The name may not include the surname of a limited partner, unless it is the same as the surname of a general partner or unless the business of the limited partnership has been carried on under that name prior to the admission of the limited partner.
2. The name and address of each general partner. Each general partner must sign the certificate.
3. The latest date the limited partnership will dissolve.
4. The name and address of an agent for service of process. Designating an agent for service of process in the certificate eases a creditor's obligation to notify a limited partnership that it is being sued by the creditor.

Types of Capital Contributions   The RULPA permits partners to make capital contributions of cash, property, services rendered, a promissory note, or a binding promise to contribute cash, property, or services.

Defective Compliance with Limited Partnership Statute

The RULPA requires at least *substantial compliance* with the previously listed requirements to create a limited partnership. Absent substantial compliance with the law, a limited partnership does not exist; therefore, a limited partner may lose her limited liability and become liable as a general partner. A lack of substantial compliance might result from failing to file a certificate of limited partnership or from filing a defective certificate. A defective certificate might, for example, misstate the name of the limited partnership.

Person Erroneously Believing She Is a Limited Partner   Infrequently, a person will believe that she is a limited partner but discover later that she has been designated a general partner in the limited partnership certificate and agreement. Or she may discover later that the general partners have not filed a certificate of limited partnership. In such circumstances and others, there is a risk that she will be liable as a general partner unless she takes action as required by the RULPA.

RULPA Section 304 permits a person who erroneously, but *in good faith,* believes that she is a limited partner to escape the liability of a general partner in either of two ways:

1. By causing a proper certificate of limited partnership (or an amendment thereto) to be filed with the secretary of state.
2. By withdrawing from future equity participation in the firm by filing a certificate declaring such withdrawal with the secretary of state.

However, such a person remains liable as a general partner to third parties who previously believed in good faith that such person was a general partner.

Generally, defects in compliance do not affect the *relations between the partners*. Even when a court finds that no limited partnership has been created, an ordinary partnership will be found if the relation of the partners satisfies the partnership definition that you studied in the Introduction to Forms of Business and Formation of Partnerships chapter. In such a situation, the rights of the partners between themselves are determined by their defective or defectively filed certificate of limited partnership or limited partnership agreement.

Amendments to Certificate

The RULPA requires that a limited partnership keep its filed certificate current. Current filings allow creditors to discover current facts, not merely those facts that existed when the original certificate was filed. For example, a certificate amendment must be filed when a new general partner is admitted or withdraws.

In the following case, the court considered the liability of new investors who believed they were limited partners even though the limited partnership had failed to file a new certificate.

---

8 BROOKWOOD FUND v. SLOATE

539 N.Y.S.2d 413 (N.Y. App. Div. 1989)

8 Brookwood Fund was a limited partnership formed to trade investment securities. The original certificate of limited partnership filed with the county clerk in April 1987 listed Kenneth Stein as the "General Partner" and Barbara Stein as the "Original Limited Partner." Between May and August 1987, additional limited partners were added to Brookwood. The new limited partners did not participate in the management of Brookwood. However, an amended certificate of limited partnership reflecting the new limited partners was not filed with the county clerk until October 23, 1987.

Brookwood had a securities margin account with the brokerage firm of Sloate, Weisman, Murray & Co. Brookwood's agreement with Sloate, Weisman provided for arbitration of any disputes between the parties. When the stock market crashed on October 19, 1987, Sloate, Weisman liquidated Brookwood's margin account. Brookwood sued Sloate, Weisman in a trial court, claiming that the liquidation of the account was improper. Sloate, Weisman sought to have the dispute resolved by arbitration. Brookwood asked the court to enjoin Sloate, Weisman from bringing any action or arbitration claim against the limited partners. Sloate, Weisman contested Brookwood's request for injunction on the grounds that the purported limited partners had the liability of general partners. The trial court held that the investors were limited partners and enjoined Sloate, Weisman. Sloate, Weisman appealed.

Memorandum by the Court. Sloate, Weisman argues that the certificate amending the original certificate of limited partnership, so as to reflect the newly added limited partners, had to be filed with the county clerk, and until October 23, 1987, when Brookwood complied with that statutory mandate, those investors who joined Brookwood after the filing of the original certificate of limited partnership were not limited partners, as they mistakenly believed, but rather were general partners, and therefore obligated to arbitrate any controversy arising out of the liquidation of Brookwood's margin account on October 19, 1987. However, even if we were to assume, arguendo, that there is merit to this argument, an affirmance would still be warranted. The record supports the finding of the trial court that the additional investors and purported limited partners in Brookwood, upon receiving a notice of intention to arbitrate from Sloate, Weisman dated October 26, 1987 "promptly renounced" their interests in the profits of the limited partnership, pursuant to New York Partnership Law Section 100. Partnership Law Section 100 provides as follows:

A person who has contributed to the capital of a business conducted by a person or partnership erroneously believing that he has become a limited partner in a limited partnership is not, by reason of his exercise of the rights of a limited partner, a general partner with the person or in the partnership carrying on the business, or bound by the obligations of such person or partnership; provided that on ascertaining the mistake he promptly renounces his interest in the profits of the business, or other compensation by way of income.

Accordingly, the trial court properly enjoined Sloate, Weisman from commencing any action or arbitration claim against Brookwood's limited partners.

Judgment for Brookwood affirmed.

False Statements in Filings Partners may be liable to persons suffering losses from their reliance on *false statements* in a certificate of limited partnership or a certificate of amendment. A general partner is liable if he *knows or should know* of a false statement in the certificate *when it was executed*. In addition, a general partner is liable if he knows or should know that a statement in a filed certificate *has become false* and he has not amended the certificate within a reasonable time. Each limited partner is liable only if she *knows* of a false statement in the certificate *when it was executed*. A limited partner is not liable when a statement becomes false subsequent to the execution of the certificate.

Foreign Limited Partnerships

A limited partnership is **domestic** in the state in which it is organized; it is **foreign** in every other state. The RULPA makes it clear that the laws of the domestic state apply to the internal affairs of the limited partnership, allowing a limited partner protection regardless of where business is conducted.

Nonetheless, to be privileged to do business in a foreign state, a limited partnership must *register* to do business in that state. To register, a limited partnership must file an **application for registration** with the secretary of state of the foreign state. The application must include the name and address of the limited partnership, the names and addresses of the general partners, the name and address of an agent for service of process, and the address of the office where the names, addresses, and capital contributions of the limited partners are kept. The application must be accompanied by the payment of a fee. The secretary of state reviews the application and, if all requirements are met, issues a **certificate of registration.**

Failure to Register as Foreign Limited Partnership

There are few penalties for failing to register as a foreign limited partnership. Although the RULPA does not impose fines for a failure to register, a few states have amended it to do so.

In addition, a foreign limited partnership may not use the foreign state's courts to sue to enforce any right or contract if it hasn't registered in the foreign state. Once it registers, a limited partnership may use the state courts, even if it sues to enforce a contract that was made before it registered.

Failure to register does not invalidate any contracts made in the foreign state or prevent a limited partnership from defending itself in a suit brought in the state's courts. The failure to register, by itself, does not make a limited partner liable as a general partner.

RIGHTS AND LIABILITIES OF PARTNERS IN LIMITED PARTNERSHIPS

The partners of a limited partnership have many rights and liabilities. Some are identical to those of partners in an ordinary partnership, but others are special to limited partnerships. Some are common to both general and limited partners, while others are not shared.

Rights and Liabilities Shared by General and Limited Partners

Capital Contributions   A partner is obligated to contribute as capital the cash, property, or other services that he promised to contribute. This obligation may be enforced by the limited partnership or by any of its creditors.

Share of Profits and Losses   Under the RULPA, profits and losses are shared on the basis of the *value of each partner's capital contribution* unless there is a written agreement to the contrary. For example, if 2 general partners contribute $1,000 each and 20 limited partners contribute $20,000 each, and the profit is $40,200, each

general partner's share of the profits is $100 and each limited partner's share is $2,000.

Because most limited partnerships are tax shelters, partnership agreements often provide for limited partners to take all the losses of the business, up to the limit of their capital contributions.

Share of Distributions   Under the RULPA, partners share distributions of a limited partnership's cash or other assets in relation to the amounts of their capital contributions, absent a written agreement to the contrary. If a partner is not paid a distribution to which he is entitled, he may sue the limited partnership as if he were a creditor.

However, a partner may not receive a distribution that impairs the limited partnership's ability to pay its creditors. Under the RULPA, after a distribution, the fair value of partnership assets must at least equal the limited partnership's liabilities to creditors.

Voting Rights   The RULPA permits the partners to establish the *voting rights* that partners have on partnership matters. The partnership agreement may require that certain transactions be approved by general partners, by limited partners, or by all the partners. The agreement may give each general partner more votes than it grants limited partners, or vice versa. The RULPA makes it clear that limited partners have *no inherent right* to vote on any matter *as a class*. They may receive such a right only by agreement of the partners.

Admission of New Partners   Similar to an ordinary partnership, a limited partnership is a *voluntary association*. Therefore, no new partner may be admitted unless each partner has consented to the admission. Under the RULPA, new partners may be admitted by unanimous written consent of the partners or in accordance with the limited partnership agreement.

Partnership Interest   Like a partner in an ordinary partnership, each partner in a limited partnership owns a **partnership interest.** It is his personal property. Under the RULPA, it may be sold or *assigned* to others such as creditors; a creditor may obtain a *charging order* against it. Generally, an assignee or a creditor with a charging order does *not* become a limited or general partner, but is entitled to receive only the partner's *share of distributions*.

Nonetheless, if the limited partnership agreement so provides or all the partners consent, an *assignee* of a *limited* or a *general* partner may become a *limited partner.* The new limited partner then assumes all the rights and liabilities of a limited partner, except for liabilities *unknown* to her at the time she became a partner.

A partner's assignment of his partnership interest *terminates* his status as a partner. The assignment does not, however, relieve him of liability for illegal distributions or for false filings with the secretary of state. When a court grants a charging order, the partner remains a partner.

A limited partnership agreement may *restrict*, but *not prohibit*, the assignment of a partnership interest. For example, a restriction may require limited partners to offer to sell their interests to the limited partnership before selling them to anyone else.

Right to Withdraw   Similar to partners in an ordinary partnership, partners in a limited partnership have the power to withdraw from the partnership and receive the fair value of their partnership interests. Fair value includes the going concern value of the partnership business, that is, its goodwill.

Under the RULPA, a general partner may withdraw from a limited partnership *at any time;* if a general partner's withdrawal breaches the limited partnership agreement, the value of her interest is reduced by the damages suffered by the limited partnership. The RULPA permits a limited partner to withdraw in accordance with a written limited partnership agreement. When there is no written agreement, a limited partner may withdraw after giving *six months' prior notice* to each general partner.

The RULPA limitation on the amount of assets that may be distributed to partners applies also to the payment of the value of a partner's interest. In addition, a partner who lawfully receives a return of capital is liable to the limited partnership *for one year* to the extent necessary to pay those who were creditors before the withdrawal.

Other Rights of General Partners

A general partner has the same *right to manage* and the same *agency powers* as a partner in an ordinary partnership. He has no right to compensation beyond his share of the profits, absent an agreement to the contrary. Since most limited partnerships are tax shelters that are designed to lose money during their early years of operation, most limited partnership agreements provide for the payment of salaries to general partners.

Other Liabilities of General Partners

The RULPA makes it clear that a general partner has the same *unlimited liability* for the obligations of a limited partnership as does a partner for the obligations of an ordinary partnership. In addition, a general partner is in a position of *trust* when he manages the business, and therefore owes *fiduciary duties* to the limited partnership (e.g., he may not profit secretly from limited partnership transactions or compete with the limited partnership). The following case imposed liability on a general partner for profiting from his sale of land to the limited partnership.

BAND v. LIVONIA ASSOCIATES
439 N.W.2d 285 (Mich. App. Ct. 1989)

Cornel Peleo was a general partner of Livonia Associates, a limited partnership. On December 3, 1971, Peleo and his wife purchased land for $9,000. On April 15, 1972, they sold the land to Livonia Associates for $18,000. In 1977, Livonia's limited partners, including Jerry Band, sued Peleo for breaching his fiduciary duty by making an undisclosed profit on the sale of land to the limited partnership. The trial court found Peleo liable for his $9,000 profit; Peleo appealed.

Per Curium.   Peleo admitted that he had not informed the limited partners that the lot was sold to the partnership for more than the Peleo's purchase price. Peleo told one limited partner that he had an interest in the property, but he did not tell him the amount. Peleo took the position that he had no duty to disclose.

The duty of the general partner is this case is based on sections 20 and 21 of the Uniform Partnership Act:

Section 20. Partners shall render on demand true and full information of all things affecting the partnership to any partner. . . .

Section 21(1). Every partner must account to the partnership for any benefit, and hold as trustee for it any profits derived by him without the consent of the other partners from any transaction connected with the formation, conduct, or liquidation of the partnership or from any use by him of its property;

Section 20 has been broadly interpreted as imposing a duty to disclose all known information that is significant and material to the affairs or property of the partnership.

The courts universally recognize the fiduciary relationship of partners and impose on them obligations of the utmost good faith and integrity in their dealings with one another in partnership affairs. Partners are held to a standard stricter than the morals of the marketplace and their fiduciary duties should be broadly construed, "connoting not mere honesty but the punctilio of honor most sensitive." The fiduciary duty among partners is generally one of the full and frank disclosure of all relevant information. Each partner has the right to know all that the others know, and each is required to make full disclosure of all material facts within his knowledge in any way relating to the partnership affairs.

Judgment for Band affirmed.

Other Rights of Limited Partners

Limited partners have the right to be *informed* about partnership affairs. The RULPA obligates the general partners to provide financial information and tax returns to the limited partners on demand. In addition, a limited partner may *inspect and copy* a list of the partners, information concerning contributions by partners, the certificate of limited partnership, tax returns, and partnership agreements.

Derivative Suits   RULPA Section 1001 permits a limited partner to sue to enforce a limited partnership right of action against a person who has harmed the limited partnership. This right of action is called a *derivative suit* or a derivative action because it derives from the limited partnership. Any recovery obtained by the limited partner goes to the limited partnership, since it is the entity that was harmed.

Ordinarily, the limited partner who initiates a derivative action must have been a partner at the time the wrong occurred and must have asked the general partners to sue, unless it is obvious that the general partners will not sue. Most derivative suits are brought against general partners who have breached the fiduciary duties that they owe to the limited partnership. In such cases, it is unnecessary to ask the general partners to sue themselves.

Because a limited partner incurs legal expenses if he brings a derivative suit, he may be paid for his expenses out of any judgment or settlement obtained for the limited partnership. When the limited partner loses the suit, however, he gets nothing.

In addition, when a limited partnership is sued and the limited partners fail to assert a defense, a limited partner may appear on behalf of the limited partnership and assert the defense.

Other Liabilities of Limited Partners

A limited partner's chief liability is for losses of the limited partnership, but *only to the extent of her contribution*. Once a limited partner has contributed all of her promised capital contribution, generally she has no further liability for partnership losses or obligations. In return for limited liability, however, a limited partner gives up the right to participate in the management of a limited partnership. Conversely, if a limited partner engages in management activities, she may *lose her limited liability*.

Limited Partner Engaged in Management A limited partner who participates in the *control* of the business is liable potentially to creditors of the limited partnership. Until the RULPA was amended in 1985, a limited partner who acted substantially like a general partner was liable to all creditors, even if the creditors did not believe that the limited partner was a general partner.

The 1985 amendments to RULPA substantially reduced a limited partner's risk of liability for managing the business. Limited partners who participate in control are liable only to those persons who transact with the limited partnership reasonably believing, based on the limited partner's conduct, that the limited partner is a general partner. Thus, three elements must be met in order for a limited partner to be liable as a general partner due to his participation in management:

1. The limited partner must participate in the control of the limited partnership.

2. That participation must lead a person to believe reasonably that the limited partner is a general partner.

3. That person must transact with the limited partnership while holding that belief.

Essentially, a creditor must prove **partnership by estoppel**; that is, a holding out that the limited partner was a general partner and detrimental reliance on the holding out.

For example, Larry Link, a limited partner who the general partners have allowed to make management decisions, is introduced to a limited partnership creditor has "a partner." Link does not correct the misimpression that he is a general partner, with the result that the creditor extends $10,000 credit to the limited partnership believing that Link is a general partner. Link is liable on the $10,000 debt to the creditor.

If Link is not participating in control, the introduction of Link as a partner and the creditor's reliance on the introduction are not sufficient to make Link liable on the debt, because all three requirements for liability must be met for Link to be liable.

Acts Constituting Control It is sometimes difficult to determine whether a limited partner's acts amount to control of the limited partnership. Control is best defined as participation in the firm's day-to-day management decisions as contrasted with isolated involvement with major decisions. For example, a limited partner of a real estate investment partnership would participate in control if she regularly decided which real estate the limited partnership should purchase. A limited partner who only once vetoed a loan agreement with a bank would not be participating in control.

The RULPA lists the kinds of management activities that limited partners may perform without becoming personally liable for partnership debts. Therefore, a limited partner may perform these acts and still retain his limited liability. The list of such activities appears in Figure 3.

Limited Partners as Managers of Corporate General Partners For most limited partnerships, the general partner is a corporation. Usually, the only shareholders, directors, and officers of the corporate general partner are the individuals who manage the limited partnership. Sometimes, these individuals are limited partners as well. The RULPA assures these individuals that they will not have the liability of a general partner, because they are officers, directors, or shareholders of a general partner, which is permitted under item 1 of Figure 3.

In the following case, *Alzado v. Blinder, Robinson & Co.,* the court held that a limited partner had not exercised sufficient control over the limited partnership to render the limited partner liable as a general partner.

FIGURE 3 Activities Not Constituting Control by a Limited Partner

1. Being *an agent, an employee, or a contractor* for the limited partnership or a general partner; or being an officer, director, or shareholder of a general partner that is a corporation.

2. Being a *consultant* or *adviser* to a general partner.

3. Acting as a *surety* for the limited partnership or guaranteeing or assuming specific obligations of the limited partnership. However, a limited partner who specifically assumes liability on a partnership obligation is liable on that obligation.

4. Pursuing a derivative suit on behalf of the limited partnership.

5. Requesting or attending a meeting of partners.

6. Proposing or voting on such partnership matters as dissolution, sale of substantially all the assets, changes in the nature of the business, admissions and removals of general or limited partners, and amendments to the partnership agreement.

7. Winding up the limited partnership as permitted by the RULPA.

ALZADO v. BLINDER, ROBINSON & CO.
752 P.2d 544 (Colo. Sup. Ct. 1988)

In 1979, Blinder, Robinson & Co. as limited partner and Combat Promotions, Inc., as general partner created Combat Associates to promote an eight-round exhibition boxing match between Muhammad Ali and Lyle Alzado, the pro football player. Combat Promotions was owned entirely by Alzado, his accountant, and his professional agent. Alzado was also vice president of Combat Promotions. Combat Associates agreed to pay Alzado $100,000 for his participation in the match.

Few tickets were sold, and the match proved to be a financial debacle. Alzado received no payments for participating in the boxing match. Alzado sued Blinder, Robinson, claiming that because of its conduct, Blinder, Robinson must be deemed a general partner of Combat Associates and, therefore, liable to Alzado under the agreement between Alzado and the limited partnership for Alzado's participation in the match. The trial court agreed with Alzado, but Blinder, Robinson appealed to the court of appeals, which held that Blinder, Robinson had no liability to Alzado. Alzado appealed to the Supreme Court of Colorado.

Kirshbaum, Justice.   A limited partner may become liable to partnership creditors as a general partner if the limited partner assumes control of partnership business. RULPA Section 303 provides that a limited partner does not participate in the control of partnership business solely by doing one or more of the following:

    (a) Being a contractor for or an agent or employee of the limited partnership or of a general partner;

    (b) Being an officer, director, or shareholder of a corporate general partner;

    (c) Consulting with and advising a general partner with respect to the business of the limited partnership . . . .

Any determination of whether a limited partner's conduct amounts to control over the business affairs of the partnership must be determined by consideration of several factors, including the purpose of the partnership, the administrative activities undertaken, the manner in which the entity actually functioned, and the nature and frequency of the limited partner's purported activities.

The record here reflects that Blinder, Robinson used its Denver office as a ticket outlet, gave two parties to promote the exhibition match and provided a meeting room for many of Combat Associates' meetings. Meyer Blinder, president of Blinder, Robinson, personally appeared on a television talk show and gave television interviews to promote the match. Blinder, Robinson made no investment, accounting or other financial decisions for the partnership; all such fiscal decisions were made by officers or employees of Combat Promotions, the general partner. The evidence established at most that Blinder, Robinson engaged in a few promotional activities. It does not establish that it took part in the management or control of the business affairs of the partnership. Accordingly, we agree with the Court of Appeals.

Alzado finally asserts that Blinder, Robinson fostered the appearance of being in control of Combat Associates, that such actions rendered Blinder, Robinson liable as a general partner and that this conduct allowed third parties to believe that Blinder, Robinson was in fact a general partner. The evidence does not support this argument. Certainly, as Vice President of Combat Promotions, Alzado had no misconception concerning the function and role of Blinder, Robinson as a limited partner only.

Judgment for Blinder, Robinson affirmed.

Limited Partner's Name in Firm Name   Including a limited partner's *surname* in the name of a limited partnership may mislead a creditor to believe that a limited partner is a general partner. Under the RULPA, a limited partner who *knowingly* permits her name to be included in the firm name is liable to creditors who have *no actual knowledge* that she is a limited partner, *unless* a general partner has the same surname as that of the limited partner or the business of the limited partnership was conducted under that name prior to the limited partner's admission to the limited partnership.

DISSOLUTION AND WINDING UP OF A LIMITED PARTNERSHIP

Dissolution

Similar to an ordinary partnership, a limited partnership may be dissolved and its affairs wound up. Because a limited partnership has limited partners—who are not involved in carrying on the business—some events that cause a dissolution of an ordinary partnership do not cause the dissolution of a limited partnership.

Causes of Dissolution   Under the RULPA, there are five causes of dissolution:

1. Expiration of the term specified in the certificate of limited partnership. For example, the certificate may provide that a limited partnership has a 20-year term.

2. Upon the happening of events specified *in writing* in the partnership agreement. For example, a written partnership agreement may provide for dissolution of a limited partnership after it has accomplished its objective of building a shopping mall.

3. By the written consent of all the partners.

4. Upon the withdrawal of a *general* partner, with few exceptions. Such a withdrawal includes retirement, death, bankruptcy, assignment of a general partnership interest, removal by the other partners, and adjudicated insanity. For a general partner that is not a natural person, such as a partnership or a corporation, its *own* dissolution is a withdrawal causing a dissolution of the limited partnership. The RULPA specifically permits a limited partnership to *avoid dissolution* after the withdrawal of a general partner if a written partnership agreement permits the business to be conducted by the remaining general partners or if all of the partners agree in writing to continue the business.

5. By court order, when it is *not reasonably practicable* to carry on the business in conformity with the limited partnership agreement. Judicial dissolution has frequently been granted when general partners continually violate their fiduciary duties, such as by secretly profiting from self-dealing with the limited partnership.

Events Not Causing Dissolution   The death, bankruptcy, insanity, or withdrawal of a *limited* partner does not result in dissolution unless the certificate of limited partnership compels dissolution. Also, the *addition* of a partner, general or limited, does not cause a dissolution.

Certificate of Cancellation   The RULPA requires a limited partnership to file a **certificate of cancellation** upon its dissolution and the commencement of winding up. The certificate of cancellation cancels the certificate of limited partnership. However, the failure to file a certificate of cancellation does not prevent a dissolution.

Winding Up

Nearly all of the winding-up rules that apply to ordinary partnerships also apply to limited partnerships.

When Winding Up Is Required   Under the RULPA, dissolution *requires* the winding up of a limited partnership's affairs. The only way to prevent winding up is to prevent dissolution, such as by an agreement of the partners that an event shall not cause a dissolution.

Who May Wind Up   The RULPA permits general partners who have *not wrongfully dissolved* a limited partnership to perform the winding up. Wrongful dissolution is defined by ordinary partnership law. It includes a dissolution in violation of the limited partnership agreement or wrongful conduct that leads to a judicial dissolution, such as a general partner's breach of his fiduciary duties.

Limited partners may wind up if there are no surviving general partners. In addition, any partner may *ask a court* to perform a winding up.

Powers during Winding Up   The winding-up partner has the same powers that a partner in an ordinary partnership has during winding up. He has the implied authority to do those acts that are reasonably necessary to liquidate the assets. He possesses the apparent authority to do all of the acts that he was able to do before dissolution, unless appropriate notice is given to persons who dealt with the partnership or knew of its existence.

Continuation of the Business   Usually, the assets of a limited partnership are sold individually during winding up. However, all the assets of the business of the limited partnership could be sold to someone who desires to continue the business. For example, some of the partners may wish to continue the business despite dissolution. The continuing partners are required to pay the outgoing partners the fair value of their partnership interests, including goodwill.

The RULPA, unlike the UPA, has no provision that permits an outgoing partner to choose between two payment options, a choice designed to provide some incentive for the continuing partners to settle promptly with an outgoing partner. Nonetheless, courts sometimes choose to apply the UPA rule, under which the outgoing partner chooses either (1) the value of his partnership interest at the time of dissolution plus interest or (2) the value of his partnership interest at the time of dissolution plus a share of subsequent profits. Other courts hold that an outgoing partner is a creditor entitled only to the value of his partnership interest plus interest.

Distribution of Assets

When the business is not continued by the partners and the assets have been sold during winding up, the pro-

---

FIGURE 4   Distribution of Limited Partnership Assets during Winding Up

1. To firm *creditors,* including partners who are creditors, except for unpaid distributions to partners.
2. To partners for *unpaid distributions,* including the return of capital to previously withdrawn partners.
3. To partners to the extent of their *capital contributions.*
4. To partners in the proportion in which they share distributions. Hence, the partners share the proceeds that remain after allother claimants have been paid.

Between partners, the order of distribution may be changed by a partnership agreement. For example, a limited partnership agreement may combine priorities (2) and (3) to provide that unpaid distributions to partners shall be paid at the same time capital contributions are returned. However, the priority of creditors may not be harmed by a partners' agreement, such as an agreement to pay creditors *after* partners have received the return of their capital.

---

ceeds of the sale of assets are distributed to those persons having claims against the limited partnership. Figure 4 states the RULPA rule for distribution of limited partnership assets.

In the following case, *Porter v. Barnhouse,* the court considered whether a limited partner's death caused dissolution of a limited partnership and whether an outgoing limited partner is a creditor entitled only to the value of his partnership interest plus interest.

PORTER v. BARNHOUSE

354 N.W.2d 227 (Iowa Sup. Ct. 1984)

The C. L. Barnhouse Company was founded in 1886 in Oskaloosa, Iowa. Beginning in 1956, the business was operated as a limited partnership. All the partners were descendants of C. L. Barnhouse, the founder of the company. The partners executed a partnership agreement that provided in Paragraph 6 that Charles L. Barnhouse III and Robert Barnhouse were the only general partners, each contributed capital of $4,500, and each received one eighth of the profits of the business. Irene Barnhouse was one of three limited partners, each of whom contributed capital of $9,000 and received one fourth of the profits. The other two limited partners were John Porter and Roy Kilpatrick, who were trustees of trusts established by their mothers (Irene Porter and Dorothy Kilpatrick, who were children of C. L. Barnhouse). John Porter and Roy Kilpatrick were limited partners on behalf of the trusts. The Kilpatrick trust agreement provided that upon Dorothy Kilpatrick's death, the trust terminated and all assets in the trust were required to be distributed to the trust beneficiaries.

Paragraphs 17 and 18 of the partnership agreement provided:

17. The partnership shall terminate upon the death of, or upon the sale or other disposition of any part of the interest of, any of the partners, either general or limited.

18. Upon the termination of the partnership, the capital contributions of the partners shall be returned and the remaining moneys, assets, and properties of the partnership shall be divided among the partners in the proportions provided in Paragraph 6.

The agreement also provided that the limited partnership would terminate on December 31, 1982.

On December 7, 1981, Dorothy Kilpatrick died, which triggered the termination of the Kilpatrick trust. Charles and Robert Barnhouse—the general partners—gave notice to the limited partners that Dorothy Kilpatrick's death dissolved the limited partnership. John Porter and Roy Kilpatrick—the trustees of the two trusts—claimed that no dissolution had occurred. When Charles and Robert continued the business as sole partners in a general partnership, the trustees sued Charles and Robert. The trial court found that the death of Dorothy Kilpatrick terminated the limited partnership and that the trustees—on behalf of the trusts—were entitled to the return of their capital contributions, their shares of the income earned before Kilpatrick's death, and their shares of the market value of all net partnership assets except goodwill. The trustees and Charles and Robert appealed the trial court's decision.

Carter, Judge.   The trustees contend that the trial court should have declared that the limited partnership was not dissolved until December 31, 1982, required Charles and Robert to account for profits generated by partnership assets after Dorothy Kilpatrick's death, and awarded the trustees a share of the goodwill of the partnership. Charles and Robert contend that the limited partners were entitled only to the return of their investment based upon book value of their interest at the time of Dorothy Kilpatrick's death.

Time of Dissolution. The first issue that we consider concerns the time at which the partnership was dissolved. The trustees urge that under Paragraph 17 of the partnership agreement, Dorothy Kilpatrick's death did not terminate the partnership because she was neither a general partner nor a limited partner. While this is correct, it appears without dispute that her death was an event that terminated the Kilpatrick trust requiring distribution of all trust assets (including the interest of the limited partner). Under Paragraph 17, disposition of any part of the interest of a limited partner is an act that triggers termination of a partnership.

The trustees urge that failure to file a certificate of cancellation with the county recorder cancelling the limited partnership certificate resulted in continuation of the partnership until its expiration on December 31, 1982. We conclude that the trustees are not aided as a result of such failure. The statutory requirement for filing a certificate of cancellation is a corollary to the requirement for filing a certificate of limited partnership. It is designed to protect third parties dealing with the partnership. Such filing requirements do not affect the rights of the limited partners and general partners between themselves. We find the trial court was correct in finding that dissolution occurred on December 7, 1981.

Distribution to Limited Partners. Paragraph 18 of the partnership agreement provides that in addition to return of all partners' capital contributions, both general and limited partners also have the right to a proportionate share of "remaining moneys, assets, and properties." That phrase is sufficiently broad to include all assets of the business, both tangible and intangible. The value of goodwill should be considered in determining the withdrawing limited partners' shares in the same manner as if the goodwill had been purchased by the continuing general partners for its reasonable present value at the date of dissolution. Accordingly, we find the trial court erred in not including goodwill among the assets to be valued in determining the extent of the trustees' distributions.

The trustees also urge that as noncontinuing partners, they are entitled to elect between receiving (1) interest on their distributions at the legal rate from the date of dissolution or (2) profits generated by the use of their assets in the business since that time. While this rule is applicable to general partnerships, it does not apply to the return of the interest of limited partners. The election to receive a share of the post-dissolution profits is to compensate the withdrawing partner for exposure to additional liability through the continuing partners' apparent authority and as compensation for the use of the outgoing partners' assets in the conduct of the business. Neither of these reasons apply to a limited partner. A limited partner has no continued exposure to additional liability except to the extent of the limited partner's capital contribution. In addition, the limited partner does not have a property interest in the assets used in the continuation of the business. The interest of a limited partner following dissolution is that of a creditor rather than an owner. The trustees are not entitled to share in post-dissolution profits. Instead, they are entitled to interest at the legal rate from the date of dissolution on the amount owed them.

Judgment affirmed in part and reversed in part. Remanded to the trial court.

ETHICAL AND PUBLIC POLICY CONCERNS

1. Is it fair that a limited partner has limited liability for the obligations of a limited partnership? Is it fair that a general partner has unlimited liability while a limited partner has limited liability?

2. Limited partners have a limited right to deduct limited partnership losses on their individual federal income tax returns, while general partners are not restricted. Is this fair? Are the general partners' investments or activities more socially desirable than the limited partners' investments or activities?

3. By having a corporation as the sole general partner of a limited partnership, no human will have unlimited liability for the obligations of the limited partnership. Is this fair? Does this produce a socially desirable result?

4. Do you think limited partners should be allowed to participate in the control of a limited partnership and retain their limited liability?

the tax consequences of partnership transactions directly through to the partners.

Generally, the rights and liabilities of general partners in limited partnerships are similar to the rights of partners in ordinary partnerships. A partner's right to withdraw funds or property is usually determined by the limited partnership agreement. However, this right is subject to the rights of creditors.

Limited partners are generally not liable for partnership debts in excess of their capital contributions. A limited partner who participates in control of the partnership may lose limited liability. The RULPA expressly permits certain types of management activities by limited partners.

Limited partnerships are dissolved and wound up in much the same way as ordinary partnerships, except that the death, bankruptcy, or withdrawal of a limited partner usually does not cause a dissolution. Also, partners who are creditors share the same priority during distribution as do the other creditors of the limited partnership.

SUMMARY

A limited partnership is a statutory form of business organization comprising one or more general partners and one or more limited partners. Statutory formalities must be followed to create a limited partnership, including the filing of a certificate of limited partnership. Limited partnerships are used mostly as tax shelters, by passing

PROBLEM CASES

1. In 1979, Jeffrey Shaughnessy organized a limited partnership, Capital City Investments. The partnership agreement listed Shaughnessy as the sole general partner. Shaughnessy signed the agreement. The limited partners were listed in the agreement, but none signed it. No certificate of limited partnership was filed in the

[handwritten: Must file]

county recorder's office, where recording was required. Has a limited partnership been created? *[handwritten: No!]*

2. Virginia Partners, Ltd., a limited partnership organized in Florida, was in the business of drilling oil wells. When Virginia Partners injected acid into an oil well in Kentucky, a bystander, Robert Day, was injured by acid that sprayed on him from a ruptured hose. Virginia Partners had failed to register as a foreign limited partnership in Kentucky. Are the limited partners of Virginia Partners liable to Day for his injuries? *[handwritten: No!]*

[handwritten in left margin: failure to register]

3. Palmetto Federal Savings & Loan Association made real estate loans to Beacon Reef Limited Partnership. When Beacon Reef defaulted on the loans, Palmetto Federal sued Beacon Reef. Beacon Reef's general partners decided not to raise the defense that Palmetto Federal charged a usurious rate on the loan. May Howard Wulsin, the only limited partner, on behalf of Beacon Reef, assert the defense of usury against Palmetto Federal? *[handwritten: derivative suit (Yes)]*

4. Paul Linnane was the sole general partner and Richard Stover was the sole limited partner of Linnane Magnavox Home Entertainment Center, a limited partnership. Stover possessed no power to manage daily partnership affairs and took no part in any partnership business. Linnane negotiated with General Electric Credit Corporation (GE Credit) to obtain financing for Linnane Magnavox. Two written contracts were executed and signed by GE Credit, Linnane, and Stover. Stover signed one contract, "by Richard Stover (Officer, Partner, Owner)." He signed the other contract, "by Richard Stover (V. Pres., Secy., Treas., Partner)." GE Credit would not have extended financing to Linnane Magnavox had Stover not signed the contracts. GE Credit was not aware of the limited partnership agreement between Linnane and Stover, although it was aware that Stover was a silent partner of Linnane. Stover signed the contracts at the request of Linnane, intended the signatures to be only in the capacity of limited partner, but did not communicate that intention to GE Credit. Is Stover liable on the contracts with GE Credit? *[handwritten: Liable! New RULPA; Not participating = not liable]*

5. The Securities Group 1980, a limited partnership, was created to provide tax deferral advantages for its limited partners. To offset a potential adverse tax consequence when the tax laws changed, the general partners arranged a sale of the limited partnership interests to a new partnership owned by the Securities Group's general partners. The limited partners received cash and promissory notes worth 105 percent of the net asset value of Securities Group. At that time, Securities

[handwritten at top: Yes. obvious trying to defraud creditors]

Group was indebted to various creditors. The new partnership subsequently became insolvent, with the result that the Securities Group creditors were unpaid. Are the Securities Group creditors able to collect from the former limited partners of Securities Group?

6. Leonard Mannon and Raleigh Baxter formed Union Properties, Inc., a corporation, to develop commercial real estate. When Union found a real estate opportunity, it formed a limited partnership to own and to develop the property, with Union as the sole general partner. Mannon and Baxter were the sole shareholders, directors, and officers of Union. Commercial Investors was one of the limited partnerships that Union created. Union was the sole general partner. Mannon and Baxter were the only limited partners. Mannon and Baxter, as president and secretary-treasurer of Union, signed a contract with Frigidaire Sales Corporation on behalf of Commercial. Frigidaire knew that Union was the only general partner in Commercial. When Commercial breached the contract with Frigidaire, Frigidaire sued Union, Mannon, and Baxter. Are Mannon and Baxter liable to Frigidaire?

7. Canal East Company was a limited partnership formed to operate a commercial real estate project known as Packett's Landing. John Flowers was the sole general partner. Scott Arrington, William May, and Robert Klimasewski were the only limited partners. Fishers Development Company was another partnership in which Arrington, May, and Klimasewski were the only limited partners. Fishers Development bought restaurant equipment and leased it to a restaurant-tenant at Packett's Landing. Flowers and Arrington were guarantors of the lease obligation to Fishers Development. When the restaurant-tenant became bankrupt, Flowers and Arrington obtained possession of the equipment pursuant to an assignment from the restaurant-tenant. They assigned the equipment lease to Canal East, which agreed to assume Flowers and Arrington's guaranty of the lease and to indemnify them from their liabilities under the lease or guaranty. Flowers and Arrington signed the agreement as assignors. In addition, Flowers signed the agreement as the general partner of Canal East, the assignee. May and Klimasewski sought judicial dissolution of the limited partnership claiming that Flowers and Arrington breached fiduciary duties. Will the court order dissolution?

8. Joseph Cox and F & S (a general partnership) were the only general partners of Second Montclair, a limited partnership. There were 11 limited partners.

During the term of the limited partnership, several actions occurred at Cox's direction and without notice to the limited partners: Second Montclair made monthly installment note payments for the purchase of a pickup truck owned by Cox Realty, a corporation of which Cox was the president. Also, Second Montclair paid the salary of Cox Realty's bookkeeper and attorney's fees to Cox's individual attorneys, although no benefit inured to Second Montclair. In addition, Cox Realty paid Second Montclair substantially less than market value for office space. F & S sought a judicial dissolution of the partnership. On what grounds will the court grant a dissolution?

9. Frontier Investment Associates, a limited partnership, was formed in 1976 to purchase, develop, lease, manage, and sell Park Place, a 56-story apartment building in Chicago. Sheldon Mandell, Howard Mandell, Jerome Mandell, and Norman Mandell were the limited partners. Centrum Frontier Corporation and William Thompson were the general partners. Thompson was the only shareholder of Centrum. The partnership agreement provided that unanimous consent of the partners was required to sell Park Place. In addition, Thompson could not convert the Park Place apartments to condominiums without the consent of a majority of the Mandells. For the first 17 months of operation, the partnership suffered an average *daily* cash loss of $4,100. In attempts to ease the cash flow problem, the Mandells and Thompson made separate efforts to sell Park Place. The Mandells rejected a sale negotiated by Thompson. Sheldon Mandell negotiated a profitable sale of Park Place, but Thompson refused to agree to that sale. The Mandells then sued Centrum and Thompson, asking the court to dissolve the limited partnership and order the sale of Park Place. Will the court order dissolution of the limited partnership?

PART X

CORPORATIONS

CHAPTER 40

HISTORY AND NATURE OF CORPORATIONS

INTRODUCTION

The modern corporation has facilitated the rapid economic development of the last 150 years by permitting businesses to attain economies of scale. Businesses organized as corporations can attain such economies because they have a greater capacity to raise **capital** than do other business forms. Corporation law allows persons to invest their money in a corporation and become owners without imposing unlimited liability or management responsibilities on themselves. Many people are willing to invest their savings in a large, risky business if they have limited liability and no management responsibilities. Far fewer are willing to invest in a partnership or other business form in which owners have unlimited liability and management duties.

The purpose of the next few chapters is to study the corporation as a business form. This chapter examines the history and nature of corporations and the history and nature of government regulation of corporations.

HISTORY OF CORPORATIONS

Although modern corporation law emerged only in the last 150 years, ancestors of the modern corporation existed in the times of Hammurabi, ancient Greece, and the Roman Empire. As early as 1248 in France, privileges of incorporation were given to mercantile ventures to encourage investment for the benefit of society. In England, the corporate form was used extensively before the 16th century.

British Trading Companies

The famous British trading companies, such as Russia Company and Massachusetts Bay Company, were the forerunners of the modern corporation. The British government gave these companies monopolies in trade and granted them powers to govern in the areas they colonized. They were permitted to operate as corporations due to the benefits they would confer on the British empire, such as the development of natural resources. Although these trading companies were among the few corporations of the time whose owners were granted limited liability, they sought corporate status ordinarily not because they wanted limited liability for their owners or perpetual life of the business form; instead, they sought corporate charters primarily because the government granted them *monopolies and governmental powers*.

Early American Corporation Law

Beginning in 1776, corporation law in the United States evolved independently of English corporation law. Early American corporations received *special charters* from state legislatures. These charters were granted one at a time by special action of the legislatures. Few special charters were granted.

Emergence of General Incorporation Statutes In the late 18th century, general incorporation statutes emerged in the United States. North Carolina in 1795 and Massachusetts in 1799 passed statutes permitting incorporation by any group of persons meeting the requirements of the statutes. Initially, these and other similar statutes permitted incorporation only for limited purposes beneficial to the public, such as operating toll bridges and water systems. Incorporation was still viewed as a privilege, and many restrictions were placed on corporations. Incorporation was permitted for only short periods of time. Maximum limits on capitalization were low. Ownership of real and personal property was often restricted.

During the last 150 years, such restrictive provisions have disappeared in most states. In 1837, Connecticut became the first state to permit the formation of corporations for "any lawful purpose." Today, modern incorporation statutes are mostly enabling, granting the persons who control a corporation great flexibility in establishing, financing, and operating it.

Emergence of Limited Liability of Owners

Limited liability for owners of *nontrading* companies—companies without inventory, such as those in service industries—was recognized in the 15th century. For *trading companies* government-granted charters in England were always accompanied by limited liability on the theory that the government had created a separate person. This limited liability of the owners of trading companies, however, was recognized mainly to prevent an owner's creditors from seizing corporate assets. In practice, many corporate charters expressly granted a corporation the power to assess its owners for money to pay its debts. In 1671, England's House of Lords held that this power could be asserted by creditors. In response, ingenious lawyers drafted corporate charters that eliminated such assessment power, thereby creating by contract limited liability for the owners. By the end of the 17th century, individual owners of a *trading* company were recognized as not being liable for its debts.

American Corporation Law The American incorporation statutes of the late 18th and early 19th centuries whittled away at the English development of limited liability. Some states provided for limited liability; others had double liability; and Massachusetts, for example, had unlimited liability for owners of manufacturing corporations. By 1830, when Massachusetts accepted limited liability, the general principle of limited liability of owners for corporate debts was well established. Today, modern statutes grant limited liability to the owners of corporations, with few exceptions.

See Figure 1 for a statement of the characteristics of corporations.

FIGURE 1 Principal Characteristics of Corporations

---

1. *Creation.* A corporation may be created only *by permission of a government.*

2. *Legal Status.* A corporation is a legal person and a legal *entity* independent of its owners (called *shareholders*) and its managers (called officers and the *board of directors*). Its life is unaffected by the retirement or death of its shareholders, officers, and directors. A corporation is a person under the Constitution of the United States.

3. *Powers.* A corporation may *acquire, hold, and convey property* in its own name. A corporation may *sue and be sued* in its own name. Harm to a corporation is not harm to the shareholders; therefore, with few exceptions, a shareholder may not sue to enforce a claim of the corporation.

4. *Management.* Shareholders elect a board of directors, which manages the corporation. The board of directors may delegate management duties to officers. A shareholder has *no right or duty to manage* the business of a corporation, unless he is elected to the board of directors or is appointed an officer. The directors and officers need not be shareholders.

5. *Owners' Liability.* The shareholders have *limited liability.* With few exceptions, they are not liable for the debts of a corporation after they have paid their promised capital contributions to the corporation.

6. *Transferability of Owners' Interest.* Generally, the ownership interest in a corporation is *freely transferable.* A shareholder may sell her shares to whomever she wants whenever she wants. The purchaser becomes a shareholder with the same rights that her seller had.

7. *Taxation.* A corporation *pays federal income taxes* on its income. Shareholders have personal income from the corporation only when the corporation makes a distribution of its assets to them. For example, a shareholder would have personal income from the corporation when the corporation paid him a dividend. This creates a *double-taxation* possibility: The corporation pays income tax on its profits, and when the corporation distributes the after-tax profits as dividends, the shareholders pay tax on the dividends.

CLASSIFICATIONS OF CORPORATIONS

Corporations may be divided into three classes: (1) corporations *for profit*, (2) corporations *not for profit*, and (3) *government-owned* corporations. State corporation statutes establish procedures for the incorporation of each of these classes and for their operation. In addition, a large body of common law applies to all corporations.

For-Profit Corporations

Most business corporations are for-profit corporations. For-profit corporations issue stock to their shareholders, who invest in the corporation with the expectation that they will earn a profit on their investment. That profit may take the form of dividends paid by the corporation or increased market value of their shares. Some shareholders of corporations with few shareholders obtain returns on their investments in an additional way: by receiving salaries for their managing the corporation.

Nearly all for-profit corporations are incorporated under the **general incorporation law** of a state. All of the states require professionals who wish to incorporate, such as physicians, dentists, lawyers, and accountants, to incorporate under **professional corporation acts.** In addition, for-profit corporations that especially affect the public interest, such as banks, insurance companies, and savings and loan associations, are usually required to incorporate under special statutes.

Close Corporations and Publicly Held Corporations

For-profit corporations range from huge international organizations such as General Motors Corporation to small, one-owner businesses. GM is an example of a **publicly held corporation** because its shares are generally available to public investors. Although its directors and officers may own shares of the corporation, the publicly held corporation tends to be managed by professional managers who own small percentages of the corporation. Nearly all the shareholders of the typical publicly held corporation are merely investors who are not concerned in the management of the corporation.

Corporations with very few shareholders whose shares are not available to the general public are called **close corporations.** In the typical close corporation, at least a majority of the shareholders are also managers of the business.

Usually, close corporations and publicly held corporations are subject to the same rules under state corporation law. Many states, however, allow close corporations greater latitude in the operation of their internal affairs than is granted to public corporations. For example, the shareholders of a close corporation may be permitted to dispense with the board of directors and manage the close corporation as if it were a partnership.

A Subchapter S corporation, or **S Corporation,** is a special type of close corporation. It is treated nearly like a partnership for federal tax purposes. Its shareholders report the earnings or losses of the business on their individual federal income tax returns. This means that an S Corporation's profits are taxed only once: at the shareholder level. Thus, electing S Corporation status eliminates the double-taxation penalty of incorporation. An S Corporation election is made by complying with Internal Revenue Code requirements, including the requirement that it have no more than 35 shareholders.

See Figure 2 for a summary of the types of nonprofit corporations.

FIGURE 2   Types of For-Profit Corporations

	Publicly Held Corporations	Close Corporations	
		Ordinary Close Corporations	S Corporations
Number of Shareholders	Unlimited	Usually 50 or fewer	No more than 35
Officers and Directors	Professional managers	Most of the shareholders	Most of the shareholders
Number of Classes of Shares	Unlimited	Unlimited	Only one
Income Taxation	Double tax possibility	Double tax possibility	Only shareholders pay taxes

Not-for-Profit Corporations

Unlike for-profit corporations, not-for-profit corporations do not issue stock and do not expect to make a profit. Instead, they provide services to their members under a plan that eliminates any profit motive. These corporations have *members* rather than shareholders, and none of the surplus revenue from their operations may be distributed to their members. Since they generally pay no income tax, nonprofit corporations can reinvest a larger share of their incomes in the business than can for-profit corporations. Examples of nonprofit corporations are charities, churches, fraternal organizations, community arts councils, cooperative grocery stores, and cooperative farmers' feed and supplies stores.

Government-Owned Corporations

Some corporations are owned by governments and perform governmental and business functions. A municipality (city) is one type of government-owned corporation. Other types are created to furnish more specific services: for example, school corporations, water companies, and irrigation districts. Still others, such as the Tennessee Valley Authority and the Federal Deposit Insurance Corporation, operate much like for-profit corporations except that at least some of their directors are appointed by governmental officials, and some or all of their financing frequently comes from government. The TVA and the FDIC are chartered by Congress, but government-owned corporations may also be authorized by states. Government-operated businesses seek corporate status to free themselves from governmental operating procedures, which are more cumbersome than business operating procedures.

REGULATION OF FOR-PROFIT CORPORATIONS

To become a corporation, a business must **incorporate** by complying with an incorporation statute. Incorporation is a fairly simple process usually requiring little more than paying a fee and filing a document with a designated government official—usually the secretary of state of the state of incorporation.

Incorporation of for-profit businesses has been entrusted primarily to the governments of the 50 states. Although the business conducted by for-profit corpora-

tions is regulated extensively by both the federal and state governments, the framers of the U.S. Constitution and the Congress have decided not to regulate the general business corporation as a form of business.

State Incorporation Statutes

State incorporation statutes set out the basic rules regarding the relationship between the corporation, its shareholders, and its managers. For example, an incorporation statute sets the requirements for a business to incorporate, the procedures for shareholders' election of directors, and the duties directors and officers owe to the corporation. A business incorporates in only one state. Although it may do business in many states, with rare exceptions the corporation law of only the state of incorporation applies to a corporation, at least in regard to the internal affairs of the corporation. That is, the relationship between the corporation, its shareholders, and its managers is regulated only by the state of incorporation.

Model Business Corporation Act   Although there is no need for a *uniform* state incorporation statute, the American Bar Association's Committee on Corporate Laws has prepared a *model* statute for adoption by state legislatures. The purpose of the model statute is to improve the rationality of corporation law. It is called the *Model Business Corporation Act* (MBCA). The MBCA has been amended many times, and it was completely revised in 1984.

The revised MBCA is the basis of corporation law in 11 states, including Virginia, Pennsylvania, and Indiana. Most of its provisions already represent the majority rule in the United States. Other revised MBCA provisions may become majority rules in the near future. Therefore, your study of statutory corporation law in this book concentrates on the revised MBCA. Most of the revised MBCA is reprinted in Appendix E.

Nonetheless, Delaware and several other major commercial and industrial states such as New York and California do not follow the MBCA. Therefore, selected provisions of the Delaware and other acts will be addressed.

Close Corporation Statutes   Several states have special provisions or statutes that are applicable only to close corporations. In 1982, the ABA's Committee on Corporate Laws adopted the *Statutory Close Corporation Supplement to the Model Business Corporation*

Act. The Supplement is designed to provide a rational, statutory solution to the special problems facing close corporations.

State Common Law of Corporations

Although nearly all of corporation law is statutory law, including the courts' interpretation of the statutes, there is a substantial body of common law of corporations (judge-made law). Most of this common law deals with creditor and shareholder rights. For example, the law of piercing the corporate veil, which you will study later in this chapter, is common law protecting creditors of corporations. Also, in recent years, the Delaware courts have created important new common law rights protecting shareholders.[1]

Criticisms of State Corporation Law

State corporation law places few restrictions on the managers of corporations. Most state law enables managers to conduct the business of the corporation with little interference by shareholders. Of course, shareholders can elect directors and remove them from office, but most shareholders tend to be passive investors who are only concerned that they receive a reasonable return on their investment in the corporation.

The freedom that the states give to businesses operating as corporations has been condemned by a few legal scholars and critics of business. The critics argue that leaving incorporation to the states has resulted in competition for incorporation fees and a "race for the bottom," which has been won by Delaware. Delaware owes its victory to the fact that historically its legislature and its courts have been attentive to business interests and have given corporate management much freedom from shareholder and creditor intervention.[2]

Several bills have been introduced in Congress that would require the largest corporations to incorporate under federal law instead of, or in addition to, state law. None of those bills have become law. Instead, proposals for federal incorporation have dropped from public view in favor of passage of federal regulatory statutes dealing with the primary concerns of those times. Such statutes apply to all forms of business, not just corporations. They include the Foreign Corrupt Practices Act of 1977, which was enacted to prevent American corporations from paying bribes to foreign government officials in exchange for the right to conduct business in the foreign country. A recent statute is the Federal Worker Notification and Retraining Act of 1989, which was passed to require business to take steps to soften the blow to employees whose jobs are lost when a plant is closed.

REGULATION OF FOREIGN CORPORATIONS

A corporation may be incorporated in one state, yet do business in many other states in which it is not incorporated. The corporation's contacts with those states may permit the state to regulate the corporation's transactions with their citizens, to subject the corporation to suits in their courts, or to tax the corporation. The circumstances under which a state may impose its laws on a business incorporated in another state is determined by the law of foreign corporations.

Definitions

A corporation is a **domestic corporation** in the state that has granted its charter; it is a **foreign corporation** in all the other states in which it does business. For example, a corporation organized in Delaware and doing business in Florida is domestic in Delaware and foreign in Florida. Note that a corporation domiciled in one country is an **alien corporation** in other countries in which it does business. Many of the rules that apply to foreign corporations apply as well to alien corporations.

State Jurisdiction over Foreign Corporations

Generally, a state may impose its laws on a foreign corporation if such imposition does not violate the Constitution of the United States, notably the Due Process Clause of the Fourteenth Amendment and the Commerce Clause.[3]

---

[1] See, for example, *Weinberger v. UOP,* 457 A.2d 701 (Del. Sup. Ct. 1983), discussed in the Management of Corporations chapter, and *Zapata Corp. v. Maldonado,* 430 A.2d 779 (Del. Sup. Ct. 1981), excerpted in the Shareholders' Rights and Liabilities chapter.

[2] As you will see in the Management of Corporations chapter and the Shareholders' Rights and Liabilities chapter, however, in recent years, the Delaware courts have pioneered in expanding the rights of shareholders. See, *supra,* n. 1.

[3] The Commerce Clause and the Due Process Clause are discussed in detail in the Business and the Constitution chapter.

Due Process Clause The Due Process Clause requires that a foreign corporation have sufficient contacts with a state before a state may exercise jurisdiction over the corporation. The leading case in this area is the *International Shoe* case.[4] In that case, the Supreme Court ruled that a foreign corporation must have "certain minimum contacts" with the state such that asserting jurisdiction over the corporation does not offend "traditional notions of fair play and substantial justice." The Supreme Court justified its holding with a "benefit theory": When a foreign corporation avails itself of the protection of a state's laws, it should suffer any reasonable burden that the state imposes as a consequence of such benefit. In other words, a foreign corporation should be required to "pay" for the benefits that it receives from the state.

Commerce Clause Under the Commerce Clause, the power to regulate interstate commerce is given to the federal government. The states have no power to exclude or to discriminate against foreign corporations that are engaged solely in *interstate* commerce. Nevertheless, a state may require a foreign corporation doing interstate business in the state to comply with its laws if the application of these laws does not unduly burden interstate commerce. When a foreign corporation enters interstate commerce to do *intrastate* business in a state, the state may regulate the corporation's activities, provided again that the regulation does not unduly burden interstate commerce.

A state statute does not unduly burden interstate commerce if (1) the statute serves a legitimate state interest, (2) the state has chosen the least burdensome means of promoting that interest, and (3) that legitimate state interest outweighs the statute's burden on interstate commerce. Because conducting intrastate business increases a corporation's contact with a state, it is easier to prove that the state has a legitimate interest and that there is no undue burden on interstate commerce when the corporation is conducting intrastate business.

Doing Business To aid their determination of whether a state may constitutionally impose its laws on a foreign corporation, courts have traditionally used the concept of *doing business*. Courts have generally held that a foreign corporation is subject to the laws of a state when it

is doing business in the state. The activities that constitute doing business differ, however, depending on the purpose of the determination. There are five such purposes: (1) to determine whether a corporation is *subject to a lawsuit* in a state's courts, (2) to determine whether the corporation's activities are *subject to taxation*, (3) to determine whether the corporation's activities are *subject to health and safety regulation* by the state, (4) to determine whether the corporation must *qualify* to carry on its activities in the state, and (5) to determine whether the state may *regulate the internal affairs* of the corporation.

Subjecting Foreign Corporations to Suit

The Supreme Court of the United States has held that a foreign corporation may be brought into a state's court in connection with its activities within the state, provided that the state does not violate the corporation's due process rights under the Fourteenth Amendment of the Constitution and its rights under the Commerce Clause.

Minimum Contacts Test The *International Shoe* minimum contacts test must be met. Subjecting the corporation to suit cannot offend "traditional notions of fair play and substantial justice." A court must weigh the corporation's contacts within the state against the inconvenience to the corporation of requiring it to defend a suit within the state. The burden on the corporation must be reasonable in relation to the benefit that it receives from conducting activities in the state.

Under the minimum contacts test, even an isolated event may be sufficient to confer jurisdiction on a state's courts. For example, driving a truck from Arizona through New Mexico toward a final destination in Florida provides sufficient contacts with New Mexico to permit a suit in New Mexico's courts against the foreign corporation for its driver's negligently causing an accident within New Mexico.

Long-Arm Statutes After the decision in the *International Shoe* case, most of the states passed **long-arm statutes** to permit their courts to exercise jurisdiction under that decision. These statutes frequently specify several kinds of corporate activities that make foreign corporations subject to suit within the state, such as the commission of a tort, the making of a contract, or the ownership of property. Most of the long-arm statutes grant jurisdiction over causes of action growing out of any transaction within the state.

---

[4] *International Shoe Co. v. State of Washington,* 326 U.S. 310 (1945).

A long-arm statute may not expand a state's jurisdictional limits beyond the limits of *International Shoe*. For example, in *Burger King Corp. v. Rudzewicz,* the Supreme Court stated that a contract with an out-of-state party cannot by itself establish the minimum contacts necessary to allow the other party's state to exercise jurisdiction.[5] Nonetheless, the Supreme Court held in that case that Florida's courts could exercise jurisdiction over a Michigan resident who had purchased a business franchise from a Florida franchisor. Although the Michigan resident had no physical ties with Florida and all negotiations to purchase the franchise occurred in Michigan, other facts established that the Michigan resident had a substantial and continuing relationship with Florida and had fair notice that he could be sued in Florida. Those other facts justifying jurisdiction were that the Michigan resident deliberately reached out to negotiate with a Florida corporation, the franchise contract provided for Florida law to apply to the franchise relation, the Florida corporation maintained supervisory control over the Michigan resident's operation of the franchise, the Michigan resident sent his franchise payments to the Florida corporation's headquarters in Miami, and the Michigan resident was a sophisticated and experienced businessman who did not act out of duress or disadvantage.

Some long-arm statutes give a state's courts jurisdiction in product liability cases if the foreign corporation should have expected use of the product in the state. The constitutionality of such a provision is doubtful, since the Supreme Court has held that the mere foreseeability of a product's use in a state does not permit a state's courts to exercise jurisdiction over the seller of the product.[6] In that case, New York residents bought a car in New York from a New York corporation. They were injured while driving the car in Oklahoma and sued the New York corporation in an Oklahoma court. The Supreme Court held that Oklahoma's courts had no jurisdiction over the New York corporation.

Stream-of-Commerce Test   While the mere use of a foreign corporation's product in a state is not sufficient contact with a state to justify a state's jurisdiction over a corporation, the *purchase* of a foreign corporation's product in a state may be enough. Taken together, *Burger King* and *World-Wide Volkswagen* indicate that a state may take jurisdiction over a foreign corporation that delivers its products into the *stream of commerce* with an expectation that they will be *purchased* by consumers in the state. A foreign corporation that delivers its products into the stream of commerce has fair warning that it will be subject to suits in those states where consumers purchase its products.

But the foreseeability that is critical to due process analysis is not the mere likelihood that a product will find its way into the State. Rather, it is that the corporation's conduct and connection with the State are such that it should reasonably anticipate being haled into court. [I]f the sale of a product of a manufacturer or distributor such as Audi or Volkswagen is not simply an isolated occurrence, but arises from the efforts of the manufacturer or distributor to serve directly or indirectly, the market for its product in other States, it is not unreasonable to subject it to suit in one of those States if its allegedly defective merchandise has been the source of injury to its owner or to others. The State does not exceed its powers under the Due Process Clause if it asserts jurisdiction over a corporation that delivers its products into the stream of commerce with the expection that they will be purchased by consumers in the State.[7]

In the following case, *Hervish v. Growables, Inc.,* the court applied the Louisiana long-arm statute.

---

[5] 471 U.S. 462 (1985).

[6] *World-Wide Volkswagen Corp. v. Woodson*, 444 U.S. 286 (1980).

[7] *Id.*, at 297–298.

HERVISH v. GROWABLES, INC.

449 So.2d 684 (La. Ct. App. 1984)

Growables, Inc., a manufacturer of furniture, was incorporated in St. Petersburg, Florida. In July 1982, Debra Hervish, a resident of Florida, obtained a brochure about Growables' line of children's furniture. She went to Growables' offices in Florida to place an order for 14 pieces of furniture. While at Growables' office, she deposited $2,000 toward the total purchase price of $2,662. She told Growables that she would soon be moving to Louisiana, and she asked that the furniture be shipped there. Growables agreed to do so.

In early August 1982, Mrs. Hervish moved to Kenner, Louisiana, and informed Growables of her new address. Thereafter, she contacted Growables three or four times to find out why shipment of the furniture had been delayed beyond the eight weeks estimated by Growables.

On November 2, 1982, the furniture was delivered to Mrs. Hervish by Ryder Truck Lines. At the time of delivery, she paid the Ryder driver the balance of the purchase price plus the shipping charges, a total of $877. Upon opening the cardboard cartons in which the furniture had been shipped, Mrs. Hervish discovered that every piece of furniture was damaged. After making futile demands for recovery from Ryder and Growables, she sued Growables in a Louisiana trial court.

Growables asked the trial court to dismiss the suit on the grounds that the Louisiana courts could not take long-arm jurisdiction over Growables. The trial court agreed with Growables and dismissed Hervish's suit. Hervish appealed.

Chehardy, Judge.   The Louisiana long-arm statute provides, in pertinent part,

A court may exercise personal jurisdiction over a nonresident, who acts directly or by an agent, as to a cause of action arising from the nonresident's:

   (a) transacting any business in this state;

   (b) contracting to supply services or things in this state;

   (c) causing injury or damage by an offense or quasi-offense committed through an act or omission in this state;

   (d) causing injury or damage in this state by an offense or quasi-offense committed through an act or omission outside of this state, if he regularly does or solicits business, or engages in any other persistent course of conduct, or derives substantial revenue from goods used or consumed or services rendered, in this state.

This statute was intended by the Legislature to extend the personal jurisdiction of Louisiana courts over nonresidents to the full limits of due process under the Fourteenth Amendment.

In order for the proper exercise of jurisdiction over a nonresident, there must be sufficient minimum contacts between the nonresident defendant and the forum state to satisfy due process and traditional notions of fair play and substantial justice. Whether or not a particular defendant has sufficient minimum contracts with a state is to be determined from the facts and circumstances peculiar to each case.

It is essential in each case that there be some act by which the defendant purposefully avails itself of the privilege of conducting activities within the state, thus invoking the benefits and protections of its law. It appears that knowledge alone or foreseeability that property will come to rest in a particular state is insufficient to subject a defendant to jurisdiction, unless the facts and circumstances lead to a conclusion that the defendant purposefully availed itself of the privilege of conducting activities within the forum state in such a manner that the defendant has clear notice that it would be subject to suit there.

Applying these standards to the case before us, we must examine the contacts between Growables, Inc., and Louisiana to determine whether the relationship is sufficient to satisfy due process requirements. At the time Mrs. Hervish ordered the furniture, she was a Florida resident. She obtained the brochure advertising the furniture in Florida; she went personally to the Growables office in Florida to place the order. The only incidents that took place in Louisiana are Mrs. Hervish's calls to Growables to question the delay in shipment, the delivery—through a third-party truck—of the furniture into this state, and Mrs. Hervish's payment of the balance of the purchase price to the truck driver upon delivery.

There is no evidence that Growables transacts any business in Louisiana, that its representatives or agents travel to Louisiana for business purposes, or that it advertises or otherwise solicits business in Louisiana or from Louisiana residents, either directly or by mail. There is no evidence that Growables derives any substantial revenue from business in Louisiana, or "engages in any persistent course of conduct" in this state.

In fact, the only classification of the long-arm statute Growables will fit into is subparagraph (b), "contracting to supply services or things in this state." We can, however, find no other case in which a Louisiana court has found an isolated incident of delivery, without other affiliating circumstances, sufficient to apply long-arm jurisdiction to a foreign corporation. This single transaction would not justify our concluding that Growables purposefully availed itself of the privilege of conducting activities within Louisiana in such a manner that it had clear notice it would be subject to suit here.

Accordingly, we conclude the district court properly found a lack of personal jurisdiction over Growables.

Judgment for Growables affirmed.

Taxation

A state may tax a foreign corporation if such taxation does not violate the Due Process Clause or the Commerce Clause. Generally, a state's imposition of a tax must serve a legitimate state interest and be reasonable in relation to a foreign corporation's contacts with the state. For example, a North Carolina corporation's *property* located in Pennsylvania is subject to property tax in Pennsylvania. The corporation enjoys Pennsylvania's protection of private property. It may be required to pay its share of the cost of such protection.

Greater contacts are needed to subject a corporation to state income and sales taxation in a state than are needed to subject it to property taxation. In *Complete Auto Transit, Inc. v. Brady*, the Supreme Court of the United States adopted a four-prong test to determine whether a state tax does not violate the Commerce Clause.[8] The tax must (1) be applied to an activity with a substantial connection with the taxing State, (2) be fairly apportioned, (3) not discriminate against interstate commerce, and (4) be fairly related to the services provided by the State. For example, in *Goldberg v. Sweet*,[9] the Supreme Court upheld Illinois's 5 percent tax on interstate telephone calls that were placed or received in Illinois and charged to an Illinois address, because (1) Illinois had a substantial connection with

interstate phone calls concerning and charged to Illinois addresses, (2) Illinois taxed only its fair share of interstate phone calls, (3) the tax fell entirely on Illinois telephone consumers, and (4) the tax was fairly related to the benefits received by Illinois telephone consumers, including police and fire protection.

In other cases, New Jersey may tax a portion of the entire net income of a corporation for the privilege of doing business, employing or owning capital or property, or maintaining an office in New Jersey when the portion of entire net income taxed is determined by an average of three ratios: in-state property to total property, in-state to total receipts, and in-state to total wages, salaries, and other employee compensation.[10] However, Pennsylvania could not assess a flat tax on the operation of all trucks on Pennsylvania highways. The flat tax imposed a disproportionate burden on interstate trucks as compared with intrastate trucks, because interstate trucks traveled fewer miles per year on Pennsylvania highways.[11]

Health and Safety Regulations

A state may subject foreign corporations to its health and safety regulations if the application of such regulations,

---

[8] 430 U.S. 274 (U.S. Sup. Ct. 1977).

[9] 109 S.Ct. 582 (U.S. S. Ct. 1989).

[10] *Amerada Hess Corp. v. Director of Taxation,* 109 S. Ct. 1617 (U.S. Sup. Ct. 1989).

[11] *American Trucking Assns., Inc. v. Scheiner,* 483 U.S. 266 (U.S. Sup. Ct. 1987).

as a reasonable exercise of the state's *police power*, does not violate the Constitution, principally the Commerce Clause and the Due Process Clause. The Tenth Amendment of the Constitution permits a state to regulate the health, safety, and welfare of its citizens. This police power allows a state to regulate highway speeds and the quality of merchandise sold in the state, among other things. For example, New York may require a Wisconsin dairy corporation that is selling in New York to comply with New York laws imposing sanitary standards for dairy products. Such laws protect state citizens from harmful food, a legitimate state interest that outweighs the small burden imposed on interstate commerce.

Qualifying to Do Business

A state may require that foreign corporations *qualify* to conduct *intrastate* business in the state. The level of doing business that constitutes intrastate business, and thereby justifies state jurisdiction, has been difficult to define. To help clarify the confusion in this area, MBCA Section 15.01 lists several activities that do *not* constitute doing intrastate business. For example, soliciting—by mail or through employees—orders that require acceptance outside the state is not doing intrastate business. Selling through independent contractors or owning real or personal property is not doing intrastate business.

Isolated Transaction   Also classified as not doing business is conducting an isolated transaction that is completed within 30 days and is not one in the course of repeated transactions of a like nature. This **isolated**

transaction safe harbor allows a tree grower to bring Christmas trees into a state in order to sell them to one retailer. However, a Christmas tree retailer who comes into a state for 29 days before Christmas and sells to consumers from a street corner is required to qualify. Although both merchants have consummated their transactions within 30 days, the grower has engaged in only one transaction, but the retailer has engaged in a series of transactions. In addition, other one-time transactions, such as the sale of a building or an entire stock of goods, are not doing business, coming within the isolated transaction exception.

Examples of Intrastate Business   The MBCA, in the comments to Section 15.01, indicates that maintaining an office to conduct intrastate business, selling personal property not in interstate commerce, entering into contracts relating to local business or sales, or owning or using real estate for general corporate purposes does constitute doing intrastate business. Passive ownership of real estate for investment, however, is not doing intrastate business.

Under the MBCA, maintaining a stock of goods within a state from which to fill orders, even if the orders are taken or accepted outside the state, is doing intrastate business. Performing service activities, such as machinery repair and construction work, may be doing intrastate business.

In the next case, the court applied the isolated transaction safe harbor and held that providing services for four days annually to an independent in-state business was not doing intrastate business requiring qualification.

COMMONWEALTH OF KENTUCKY v. NATIONAL STEEPLECHASE AND HUNT ASS'N.
612 S.W.2d 347 (Ky. Ct. App. 1981)

The National Steeplechase and Hunt Association (NSHA) is a New York corporation that sanctions, regulates, and supervises steeplechase races. Its first sanctioned race was the Oxmoor Steeplechase, near Louisville, Kentucky, in 1948. It has supervised the High Hope Steeplechase in Fayette County, Kentucky, since 1967 and the Hard Scuffle Steeplechase in Oldham County, near Louisville, since 1975. Each of the sanctioned events lasts no more than three to four days every year.

The NSHA has never obtained from the Kentucky secretary of state a certificate to do business in Kentucky as a foreign corporation. No annual reports have been filed, and no registration fees have been paid. The NSHA does not maintain a registered office or a registered agent in the state.

In 1975, the Commonwealth of Kentucky sued the NSHA to collect all of the fees and penalties due to the Commonwealth as a result of the failure of the NSHA to qualify to do business in Kentucky. The trial court held that the NSHA was not doing business in Kentucky and therefore did not need to qualify. The Commonwealth appealed.

Wintersheimer, Judge.   The sanctioning of steeplechase meetings does not constitute the transaction of business in Kentucky. The NSHA promulgates rules; approves the race courses, race officials, and the financial responsibility of the sponsoring organization; receives entries for each meeting by telephone or mail; assembles the information on the meetings; and prepares a booklet and identification badges for each meet. All of these functions are performed in the New York office. The NSHA maintains no offices or employees in Kentucky. All communications are conducted by mail or telephone. The NSHA provides a service and information to the local sponsoring organization. The attendance by NSHA employees at the meetings does not constitute the transaction of business in Kentucky.

The leasing of fences and jumps by the NSHA to the local organizations in Kentucky is within the exception provided for interstate commerce in the Kentucky statute. The NSHA driver transporting the jumps to Kentucky does not assist the local organization in setting up the equipment. The NSHA employee does not deal with the equipment after it is delivered.

The isolated transaction section applies to the activities of the NSHA employees in Kentucky. The statute makes an exception for isolated transactions completed within 30 days and not in the course of a number of repeated transactions of a like nature. Here, the meetings generally last no more than three to four days. Three different locations are now used annually. The presence of the NSHA's employees at these meetings and the occasional utilization of them as stewards falls within the isolated transaction section.

Judgment for the NSHA affirmed.

Qualification Requirements   A state's qualification (or admission) requirements must be reasonable in relation to the state's interests and the corporation's contacts with the state.

Constitutional problems are rare in this area, since all states permit foreign corporations to qualify to do business in their states by complying with a few simple statutory provisions. MBCA Sections 15.01 and 15.03 provide that a foreign corporation must apply for a **certificate of authority** from the secretary of state, pay an application fee, maintain a registered office and a registered agent in the state, file an annual report with the secretary of state, and pay an annual fee.

Penalties for Failure to Qualify   Doing intrastate business without qualifying usually subjects a foreign corporation to a fine, in some states as much as $10,000. The MBCA disables the corporation to use the state's courts to bring a lawsuit until it obtains a certificate of authority. The corporation may defend itself in the state's courts, however, even if it has no certificate of authority. A few states make void any contracts negotiated in the state by a foreign corporation that has failed to qualify.

In the following case, a foreign corporation that failed to qualify was precluded from using Missouri's courts to enforce a contract.

CAMPAIGN WORKS, LTD. v. HUGHES
779 S.W.2d 305 (Mo. Ct. App. 1989)

Campaign Works, Ltd., a business incorporated in Florida, was a consultant to candidates for political office. Campaign Works had offices in Florida and Washington, D.C. It had no office and no employees in Missouri and had not qualified to do business in Missouri. On January 18, 1988, Campaign Works contracted to provide political consulting services to Doug Hughes, a candidate to the U.S. Congress for Missouri. The contract was negotiated by telephone and concluded by mail between Campaign Works in Florida or Washington and Hughes in Missouri. The contract called for consultations with Hughes in Missouri and political research appropriate to his election campaign. Campaign Works actually performed election research for Hughes from its offices in Florida and Washington, and its president traveled to Missouri twice to consult with Hughes and his staff.

On May 1, 1988, the parties terminated the contract, with Hughes owing Campaign Works nearly $9,000. When Hughes failed to pay this amount, Campaign Works sued Hughes in a Missouri trial court. The trial court dismissed the action on the grounds that Campaign Works was doing intrastate business in Missouri, and since it had not qualified to do business in Missouri by obtaining a certificate of authority, it was barred from suing in Missouri's courts. Campaign Works appealed.

Clark, Judge.   No foreign corporation shall have the right to transact business in Missouri until it has procured a certificate of authority to do so. A foreign corporation shall not be considered to be transacting business in Missouri by reason of transacting any business in interstate commerce. No foreign corporation doing business in Missouri failing to procure a certificate of authority can maintain any suit in any of the courts of Missouri.

Campaign Works contends that its contract with Hughes amounted to interstate commerce, because the contract was negotiated from its offices outside Missouri, its product, consisting of services, was shipped into Missouri, and at no time did Campaign Works maintain any office or employees in Missouri.

If Campaign Works had merely given reports and the product of campaign research to Hughes from its offices in Florida and Washington, an arguable case of interstate commerce could have been made. Once Campaign Works sent its president to Missouri to consult with and give advice to Hughes regarding his campaign, however, it was doing business in the state and was required to register as a foreign corporation.

It is noted parenthetically that affirmance of the judgment in this case does not constitute a finding that the contract between Hughes and Campaign Works is void or that Hughes is entitled to a verdict on the merits of the suit. Failure by Campaign Works to qualify in Missouri as a foreign corporation merely renders the contract unenforceable until Campaign Works does qualify.

Judgment for Hughes affirmed.

Regulation of a Corporation's Internal Affairs

Regulation of the internal affairs of a corporation—that is, the relation between the corporation and its directors, officers, and shareholders—is usually only exercised by the state of incorporation. Nonetheless, a foreign corporation may conduct most of its business in a state other than the one in which it is incorporated. Such a corporation is called a **pseudo-foreign corporation** in the state in which it conducts most of its business.

A few states subject pseudo-foreign corporations to extensive regulation of their internal affairs, regulation similar to that imposed on their domestic corporations. California's statute requires corporations that have more than 50 percent of their business and ownership in California to elect directors by cumulative voting,[12] to hold annual directors' elections, and to comply with California's dividend payment restrictions, among other requirements. Foreign corporations raise many constitutional objections to the California statute, including violations of the Commerce Clause and the Due Process Clause.

The California statute's regulation of the internal affairs of pseudoforeign corporations is a positive development in corporate governance. As more states subject foreign corporations and domestic corporations to the same corporate governance provisions, the advantage of shopping for the state with the most lenient incorporation law may nearly disappear.

PIERCING THE CORPORATE VEIL

A corporation is a legal entity separate from its shareholders. Corporation law erects an imaginary wall between a corporation and its shareholders that protects shareholders from liability for a corporation's actions. Once shareholders have made their promised capital contributions to the corporation, they have no further financial liability. This means that contracts of a corporation are not contracts of its shareholders, and debts of a corporation are not debts of its shareholders.

Nonetheless, in order *to promote justice and to prevent inequity,* courts will sometimes ignore the separateness of a corporation and its shareholders by **piercing the corporate veil.** The primary consequence of piercing the corporate veil is that a corporation's shareholders may lose their limited liability.

Two requirements must exist for a court to pierce the corporate veil: (1) *domination* of a corporation by its shareholders; and (2) use of that domination for an *improper purpose.*

Domination

A court will disregard the fiction of a corporation's separate legal identity when a corporation is a mere instrumentality or agent of another corporation or of an individual owning all or most of its shares. As an entity separate from its shareholders, a corporation should act for itself, not for its shareholders. If the shareholders cause the corporation to act to its detriment and to the personal benefit of shareholders, **domination**—the first requirement for piercing the corporate veil—is proved. For example, shareholders' directing a corporation to pay a shareholder's personal expenses is domination. Domination is also proved if the shareholders cause the corporation to fail to observe corporate formalities (such as failing to hold shareholder and director meetings or to maintain separate accounting records). Some courts say that shareholder domination makes the corporation the **alter ego** (other self) of the shareholders. Other courts say that domination makes the corporation an *instrumentality* of the shareholders.

To prove domination, it is not sufficient, or even necessary, to show that there is only one shareholder. Many one-shareholder corporations will never have their veils pierced. However, nearly all corporations whose veils are pierced are close corporations, since domination is more easily accomplished in a close corporation than in a publicly held one.

Improper Use

In addition to domination, there must be an improper use of the corporation. The improper use may be any of three types: defrauding creditors, circumventing a statute, or evading an existing obligation.

Defrauding Creditors   Creditors reasonably expect that shareholder-managers will adequately finance their corporations and will not transfer corporate assets to themselves or to affiliated corporations other than for adequate consideration. If these expectations are not met, a court will find an improper use of the corporation.

---

[12] Cumulative voting is discussed in the Shareholders' Rights and Liabilities chapter.

Thin Capitalization   Shareholders must organize a corporation with sufficient capital to meet the initial capital needs of the business. Inadequate capitalization, called **thin capitalization,** is proved when capitalization is very small in relation to the nature of the business of the corporation and the risks the business necessarily entails.[13] Thin capitalization is measured at the time of formation: a corporation that is adequately capitalized when formed but which suffers losses reducing its capital is not usually considered to be undercapitalized.

Thin capitalization defrauds creditors of a corporation. An example of thin capitalization is forming a business with a high debt-to-equity ratio, such as a $10-million-asset business with only $1,000 of equity capital, with the shareholders sometimes contributing the remainder of the needed capital as secured creditors. By doing so, the shareholders elevate their bankruptcy repayment priority to a level above that of general creditors, thereby reducing the shareholders' risk. The high debt-to-equity ratio harms creditors by failing to provide an equity cushion sufficient to protect their claims. In such a situation, either the shareholders will be liable for the corporation's debts or the shareholders' loans to the corporation will be subordinated to the claims of other creditors. As a result, the nonshareholder-creditors are repaid all of their claims prior to the shareholder-creditors receiving payment from the corporation.

In the next case, the court held that $3,000 was inadequate initial capital for a business with assets of $430,000.

---

[13] *Southern Lumber & Coal Co. v. M. P. Olson Real Estate and Construct. Co.,* 426 N.W.2d 504, 509 (Nebr. 1988) ($1,000 cash, a promissory note for $7,500, and donation of equipment of unspecified value was adequate initial capital for a home construction business).

J. L. BROCK BUILDERS, INC. v. DAHLBECK

391 N.W.2d 110 (Neb. Sup. Ct. 1986)

In 1971, Eric Dahlbeck incorporated Viking Construction, Inc. Its initial capital was $3,000. In addition, Dahlbeck made a $7,000 loan to Viking. It had as assets 65 lots of land for development, which cost $430,000. For its entire existence, Viking's liabilities exceeded the book value of its assets. From 1972 through 1974, Dahlbeck and another officer received salaries totaling $53,750. Beginning in 1975, Viking's business steadily declined and creditors' claims became overdue. No salaries were paid thereafter. In 1978, Viking began liquidation and transferred assets to Dahlbeck to repay loans that Dahlbeck had made to Viking. Viking dissolved in 1980, having not paid several creditors, including J. L. Brock Builders, which was owed about $16,000. Brock sued Dahlbeck personally, claiming that Viking's corporate veil should be pierced. The trial court refused to pierce Viking's veil. Brock appealed to the Supreme Court of Nebraska.

Shanahan, Justice.   A creditor seeking to pierce the corporate veil and impose on a shareholder liability for a corporate debt has the burden to show that the corporate entity must be disregarded to prevent fraud or injustice to the creditor. One of the factors that is relevant in determining whether to disregard the corporate entity on the basis of fraud is grossly inadequate capitalization.

Viking was grossly inadequately capitalized at the time of its formation. Viking's capital was $3,000 at formation and it had as an asset 65 lots, 25 at $10,000 each and the remaining at $4,500 an acre. The scale of operations anticipated by both the number of lots and their value cannot be adequately capitalized by $3,000. The risk to creditors must be balanced by the availability of more capital should the corporation fail. In reaching our conclusion that Viking was inadequately capitalized, we note Dahlberg could have provided more capital to Viking at its formation, but chose instead to loan Viking $7,000.

Shareholders of an insolvent corporation cannot participate in the distribution of its assets until claims of creditors are paid. If the shareholders are allowed to withdraw assets leaving creditors unpaid, they may be compelled to repay what they have received.

Although he was aware of $78,000 in debts to Viking creditors, Dahlbeck, as Viking's sole shareholder, transferred all Viking's assets to himself. Dahlbeck's action constitutes an improper use of corporate funds, an injustice perpetrated by a shareholder.

Viking's corporate existence was used to commit a fraud upon Brock. Viking's corporate entity should be disregarded and liability imposed on Dahlbeck for the debt incurred by Viking.

Judgment reversed in favor of Brock.

Looting   Transfers of corporate assets to shareholders for less than fair market value (called **looting**) also defraud creditors. For example, shareholder-managers loot a corporation by paying themselves excessively high salaries or by having the corporation pay their personal credit card bills. When such payments leave insufficient assets in the corporation to pay creditors' claims, a court will hold the shareholders liable to the creditors.

Frequently, the same shareholders may own two corporations that transact with each other. The shareholders may cause one corporation to loot the other. When such looting occurs between corporations of common ownership, courts pierce the veils of these corporations. This makes each corporation liable to the creditors of the other corporation. For example, a shareholder-manager operates two corporations from the same office. Corporation 1 transfers inventory to Corporation 2, but it receives less than fair market value for the inventory. Also, both corporations employ the same workers, but all of the wages are paid by Corporation 1. In such a situation, the veils of the corporations will be pierced, allowing the creditors of Corporation 1 to satisfy their claims against the assets of Corporation 2.

In the next case, *Castleberry v. Branscum,* the shareholders' looting of a corporation was grounds to pierce the corporate veil.

CASTLEBERRY v. BRANSCUM

721 S.W.2d 270 (Tex. Sup. Ct. 1986)

In September 1980, Joe Castleberry, Byron Branscum, and Michael Byboth incorporated their furniture-moving business as Texan Transfer, Inc. Each owned one third of the shares of Texan Transfer. Byboth was president, Castleberry was vice president, and Branscum was secretary-treasurer. Soon thereafter, Branscum formed Elite Moving Company, a business that competed with Texan Transfer. Castleberry discovered the existence of Elite Moving and sued to claim that Texan Transfer owned the assets and revenues of Elite Moving. As a result, Branscum became very upset and threatened that Castleberry would not receive any return on his investment in Texan Transfer unless Castleberry abandoned his attempts to claim ownership of Elite Moving.

In July 1981, Castleberry sold his Texan Transfer shares back to Texan Transfer in exchange for a $42,000 promissory note payable by Texan Transfer. After the sale, Elite Moving took over more and more of Texan Transfer's business. Controlled by Branscum and Byboth, Texan Transfer allowed Elite Moving to use its employees and trucks. Elite Moving advertised for furniture moving, but Texan Transfer did not. While Texan Transfer's business declined, Elite Moving's prospered. For the 18 months prior to Castleberry's sale of his shares, Texan Transfer had a net income of $65,479. After the sale, its net income fell to $2,814 for the second half of 1981. In 1982, it lost more than $16,000. By contrast, Elite Moving had income in 1982 of $195,765.

In 1982, Branscum told his wife that Castleberry "would never get a dime, that he would file bankruptcy before Castleberry got any money out of the company and that he would open the company in another name so that Joe wouldn't get paid." In September 1982, Byboth and Branscum started Custom Carriers, Inc. At that time, Byboth and Branscum terminated Texan Transfer's contract with Freed Furniture, which contract comprised the majority of Texan Transfer's business. Byboth and Branscum obtained for Custom Carriers an identical contract with Freed Furniture, doing the same deliveries at the same rate. Byboth and Branscum then sold Texan Transfer's trucks to drivers hired to make deliveries for Custom Carriers. With the proceeds of the sales, Byboth and Branscum paid themselves back salaries.

Castleberry was paid only $1,000 of the $42,000 promissory note. He sued Branscum and Byboth, claiming that the corporate veil of Texan Transfer should be pierced to make them personally liable on the promissory note. The trial court found Branscum and Byboth liable to Castleberry. Branscum and Byboth appealed. The court of appeals reversed and held for Branscum and Byboth. Castleberry appealed to the Supreme Court of Texas.

Spears, Justice.   The corporate form normally insulates shareholders, officers, and directors from liability for corporate obligations; but when these individuals abuse the corporate privilege, courts will disregard the corporate fiction and hold them individually liable.

We disregard the corporate fiction when the corporate form has been used as part of a basically unfair device to achieve an inequitable result. Specifically, we disregard the corporate fiction:

1. When the fiction is used as a means of perpetrating fraud;
2. When the corporate fiction is resorted to as a means of evading an existing legal obligation;
3. When the corporate fiction is used to circumvent a statute.

We hold that there is some evidence of a sham to perpetrate a fraud. A jury could find that both Byboth and Branscum manipulated a closely held corporation—Texan Transfer—and formed competing businesses to ensure that Castleberry did not get paid.

The variety of shams is infinite, but many fit this case's pattern: a closely held corporation owes unwanted obligations; it siphons off corporate revenues, sells off much of the corporate assets, or does other acts to hinder the on-going business and its ability to pay off its debts; a new business then starts up that is basically a continuation of the old business with many of the same shareholders, officers, and directors.

Judgment reversed in favor of Castleberry.

Parent-Subsidiary Transactions Looting may occur also when one corporation (called the **parent corporation**) owns at least a majority of the shares of another corporation (called the **subsidiary corporation**). Ordinarily, the parent is liable for its own obligations and the subsidiary is liable for its own obligations, but the parent is not liable for its subsidiary's debts and the subsidiary is not liable for the parent's debts. Nonetheless, because a parent corporation is able to elect the directors of its subsidiary, and therefore can control the management of the subsidiary, the parent may cause its subsidiary to transact with the parent in a manner that benefits the parent but harms the subsidiary.

For example, a parent corporation may direct its subsidiary to sell its assets to the parent for less than fair market value. Because the subsidiary has given more assets to the parent than it has received from the parent, creditors of the subsidiary have been defrauded. Consequently, a court will pierce the veil between the parent and its subsidiary and hold the parent liable to the creditors of the subsidiary.

Circumventing a Statute corporation should not engage in a course of conduct that is prohibited by a statute. For example, a city ordinance prohibits retail businesses from being open on consecutive Sundays. To avoid the statute, a retail corporation forms a subsidiary owned entirely by the retail corporation; on alternate weeks, it leases its building and inventory to the subsidiary. A court will pierce the veil because the purpose of creating the subsidiary corporation is to circumvent the statutory prohibition.[14] Consequently, both the parent and the subsidiary will be liable for violating the statute.

Evading an Existing Obligation Sometimes, a corporation will attempt to escape liability on a contract by reincorporating or by forming a subsidiary corporation. The new corporation will claim that it is not bound by the contract, even though it is doing the same business as was done by the old corporation. In such a situation, courts pierce the corporate veil and hold the new corporation liable on the contract.

For example, to avoid an onerous labor union contract, a corporation creates a wholly owned subsidiary and sells its entire business to the subsidiary. The subsidiary will claim that it is not a party to the labor contract and may hire nonunion labor. A court will pierce the veil between the two corporations because the subsidiary was created only to avoid the union contract.

In *R. E. Pilkerton Elec., Inc. v. Westinghouse Elec. Supply Co., Inc.,*[15] the majority shareholder of a corporation caused the corporation to cease operations in order for the corporation to escape liability on a debt. Twelve days later, the shareholder organized a new corporation that conducted the business of the old corporation. The court held that the new corporation was liable for the debt of the old corporation. The court also held the majority shareholder liable for the debt on the grounds that the corporations were his alter egos.

For a summary of the law of Piercing the Corporate Veil, see Figure 3.

---

[14] *Sundaco, Inc. v. State of Texas,* 463 S.W.2d (Tex. Ct. Civ. App. 1970).

[15] 444 So. 2d 855 (Ala. 1984).

FIGURE 3   Examples of Piercing the Corporate Veil

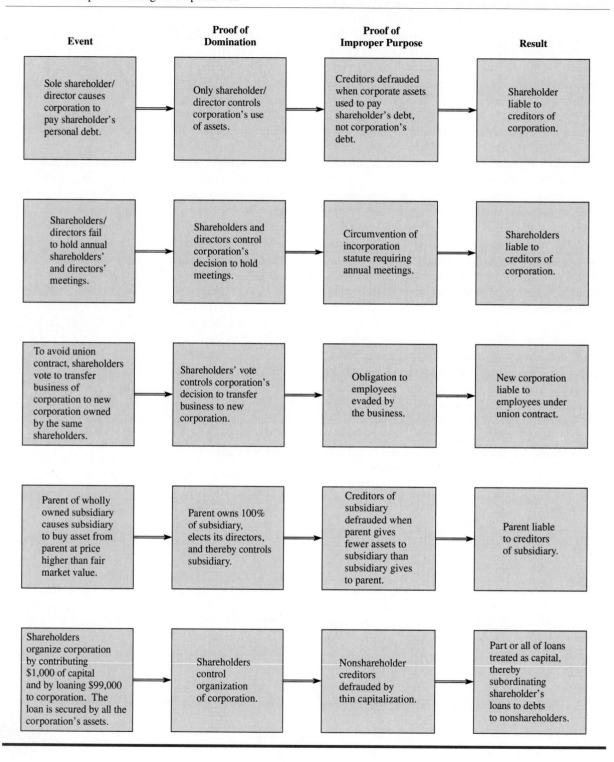

ETHICAL AND PUBLIC POLICY CONCERNS

1. Do you think it is right that shareholders of corporations have no liability for the obligations of their corporation once they have paid their promised capital contribution? What benefits does society receive from extending such a privilege to shareholders? What detriments does society suffer? Can those detriments be eliminated without changing corporation law, such as by prospective corporate creditors contracting for the unlimited liability of some or all shareholders of the corporations with whom they plan to transact? Why should shareholders have limited liability when sole proprietors and partners do not? Are the sole proprietorship and the partnership less socially desirable business forms than the corporation?

2. Should businesses be permitted to incorporate in a state that has a business incorporation law that extends the greatest freedom to managers of the business? Who benefits from businesses incorporating in such states? Who is harmed? Can the persons who are harmed protect themselves?

3. When a corporation engages in interstate business, should its managers attempt to reduce the risk that foreign states' courts will have jurisdiction over the corporation? Should the managers attempt to avoid taxation by foreign states? Should they try to avoid qualification requirements and health and safety regulations? Is it enough that the corporation complies exactly with the laws of the foreign states, or should the corporation attempt to return to the state—such as through taxes and qualification fees—an amount appropriate to the benefits it receives from customers in the foreign state? Is the corporation the only person benefiting from its doing business in a foreign state? What risk may arise if a state aggressively regulates foreign corporations?

4. Why should courts and corporation statutes require corporations to be adequately capitalized? Who is harmed by thin capitalization? Is it possible for creditors harmed by thin capitalization to protect themselves by examining the financial position of the corporation prior to extending credit to the corporation? Why should a court protect creditors who knowingly or carelessly extend credit to thinly capitalized corporations? Should a court treat a corporation's contract creditors differently from its tort creditors? Are a thinly capitalized corporation's contract creditors better able to protect themselves than are the corporation's tort victims?

SUMMARY

Corporations have existed for thousands of years. The modern corporation, characterized by limited liability for its shareholders, has emerged in only the last 150 years. The first modern corporate charters were special, restrictive grants of the Crown in England and of state legislatures in the United States. Today, general incorporation statutes impose few limitations on persons organizing, financing, operating, and dissolving corporations.

A corporation is a legal entity separate and distinct from its shareholders. A corporation can hold property and sue and be sued in its own name. The members of a corporation are not personally liable for its debts, and its existence is not affected by the death of its members. Corporations pay federal income taxes, unless the shareholders elect S Corporation status.

Corporations may be classified into several types. The principal ones are for-profit corporations, not-for-profit corporations, and governmental corporations. For-profit corporations include close and publicly held corporations.

A corporation is a domestic corporation in the state of its incorporation and a foreign corporation elsewhere. A state may impose its laws on a foreign corporation, provided that the application of its laws does not violate the federal Constitution, especially the Commerce Clause and the Due Process Clause.

The courts of a state may exercise jurisdiction over a foreign corporation if that corporation's contacts with the state and its citizens are sufficient to make it fair to subject the corporation to suit in the state. The taxing power of a state over business activities within the state is also very broad. A state may, within its police power, require a foreign corporation to comply with regulations that protect the health, safety, and welfare of its citizens. A corporation must be doing intrastate business in a state to be required to qualify to do business within the state. A pseudoforeign corporation may be required to comply with shareholder protection provisions that are applicable to domestic corporations.

Shareholders normally have no individual liability for the debts of the corporation, so their risk of loss is limited to their investment. However, courts may pierce the corporate veil when incorporation is for the purpose or effect of defrauding creditors, circumventing a law, or evading an obligation.

PROBLEM CASES

1. Nippon Electric Co., Ltd., a Japanese corporation with its principal place of business in Tokyo, manufactured telephone and computer equipment in Japan, which it sold to its wholly owned subsidiary, NEC America, a New York corporation authorized to do business in New Jersey. NEC America distributed Nippon equipment to its wholly owned subsidiary, NEC Telephone. NEC Telephone sold Nippon telephone equipment to Telecom Equipment Corporation, a New Jersey corporation. Telecom sold a portion of the equipment to Charles Gendler & Co. for installation at Gendler's place of business in New Jersey. The equipment failed to perform as promised, and Gendler sued Nippon in a New Jersey court. Nippon claimed that it could not be sued in a New Jersey court because it had not conducted any business in New Jersey, had no agents located there, had not advertised for or solicited business in New Jersey, did not have a telephone listing in the state, had not contracted with Gendler for the sale of the equipment, and had not received any direct income from Gendler or any other New Jersey resident. Nonetheless, Nippon acknowledged that the sale to Gendler was not an isolated transaction and that other Nippon equipment may have been sold in New Jersey. May Gendler sue Nippon in a New Jersey court?

2. A Hawaiian statute imposed a 20 percent wholesale excise tax on liquor sold in Hawaii. To encourage the development of Hawaiian liquor, the statute exempts from taxation Okolehao, a brandy distilled from the root of the ti plant, a native Hawaiian shrub. Bacchus Imports, a liquor wholesaler, claimed that the excise tax violates the Commerce Clause. Is Bacchus correct?

3. The City of Madison, Wisconsin, passed an ordinance that prohibited the sale of milk in Madison unless it was bottled within five miles of the center of Madison. The ordinance was passed to relieve its health inspectors of the burden of inspecting the plants of all milk producers who sold milk in Madison. Dean Milk Co., which bottled milk in plants in Illinois that were more than 65 miles from Madison, challenged the Madison ordinance. Was the ordinance held to be valid?

4. Duncan Construction Co., Inc., was hired as contractor to build a Holiday Inn motel in Alabama. On January 16, 1981, Sanjay, Inc., contracted to furnish work, labor, and materials to Duncan in connection with the construction of the motel. The materials were prefabricated outside of Alabama. In addition, Sanjay per-

formed accounting and engineering work for the construction project outside of Alabama. Sanjay was not incorporated in Alabama and had not qualified to do business in Alabama. Duncan knew that Sanjay was not qualified and offered assistance to Sanjay to make it legal for Sanjay to do the construction work. On September 18, 1981, Sanjay qualified to do business in Alabama. In February 1982, Sanjay completed its obligations under the contract. Duncan failed to pay Sanjay under the contract, and Sanjay sued in an Alabama court. Duncan argued that it owed Sanjay nothing, since Alabama law provided that a foreign corporation cannot enforce a contract to be performed in Alabama if the foreign corporation has failed to qualify to do business in Alabama on or before the date the contract is made. May Sanjay collect the money due under the contract?

5. Section 2115 of the California General Corporation Law requires that a foreign corporation doing a majority of its business in California (on the basis of its property, payroll, and sales) and having a majority of its outstanding voting securities owned by persons with addresses in California comply with certain internal governance provisions of the California corporation law, including section 708, which provides for the cumulative voting of shares for the election of directors. Louisiana-Pacific Resources, Inc. is a Utah corporation. The average of its property, payroll, and sales in California exceeded 50 percent, and more than 50 percent of its shareholders entitled to vote resided in California. Except for being domiciled in Utah and having a transfer agent there, Louisiana-Pacific had virtually no business connections with Utah. Its principal place of business had been in California since at least 1971; its meetings of shareholders and directors were held in California; and all of its employees and bank accounts were in California. Louisiana-Pacific argued that application of section 2115 to Louisiana-Pacific violated the Constitution of the United States. Is it correct?

6. Pacific Development, Inc., was incorporated in the District of Columbia in 1968 to engage in the business of international brokerage and consulting. Tongsun Park was Pacific's founder, president, and sole shareholder. It was doubtful whether Pacific had a board of directors prior to December 1974. The directors met infrequently after 1974. When they did meet, they approved without discussion or question corporate decisions made by Park. Park wrote checks on Pacific's bank accounts to cover his unrelated personal and business expenses. Pacific employees served as Park's household servants. Park made loans with Pacific funds to politically influential people and then forgave the loans. Pacific personnel provided administrative and managerial services for Park's other business ventures, and Pacific's profits were assigned to Park or to his other companies. In 1977, the Internal Revenue Service assessed $4.5 million in back income taxes against Park. To collect the taxes, the IRS seized some of Pacific's assets, claiming that the company was a mere alter ego of Park. Was the IRS correct?

7. Sea Pines Company owned 90 percent of the shares of Point South, Inc. The directors and officers of Point South were under the control of Sea Pines. Point South was organized with initial capital of $1,000. In February 1973, Point South had assets of $2.5 million and total net worth of $65,000, of which only $1,000 was capital contributions. By February 1974, Point South had become so unprofitable that it had a negative net worth of $177,000. During the period of unprofitability, Sea Pines paid the salary and expenses of Point South with the expectation that it would be reimbursed. In February 1974, when Point South was insolvent, its directors mortgaged a piece of property (worth $350,000) to secure a debt of Sea Pines. In exchange for the mortgage, Sea Pines reduced by $8,000 the amount it was owed by Point South. When Point South failed to repay a construction loan to American Bank & Trust Company, American sued Sea Pines. Was Sea Pines liable to American?

8. Vassilis Morfopolous was the sole shareholder of American Standards Testing Bureau (ASTB). ASTB was the sole shareholder of Architectural Research Corporation (ARC) and Ar-Lite Panelcraft, Inc. (API). ASTB, ARC, and API had the same officers, and Morfopolous ran all three businesses. ASTB made periodic loans to ARC that were secured by all of ARC's assets. When ARC defaulted on an obligation to Bodenhamer Building Corporation, Bodenhamer sued ARC and obtained a judgment for $50,000. To prevent Bodenhamer from collecting his judgment, ASTB foreclosed on its loan to ARC and obtained the auction sale of ARC's assets. At the auction, ASTB submitted the only bid, $115,000, which was considerably less than previous purchase offers ranging from $1 million to $2.2 million and earlier estimates that ARC's assets were worth from $345,000 to $600,000. ASTB took possession of the assets, leaving Bodenhamer and other ARC creditors unpaid. ARC ceased operations and ASTB leased the purchased assets to API, which had been incorporated solely to continue ARC's business had Bodenhamer been successful in obtaining a judgment against ARC. Bodenhamer sued ASTB and API to obtain payment of the judgment. Are they liable to Bodenhamer?

9. New York law required that every taxicab company carry $10,000 of accident liability insurance for each cab in its fleet. The purpose of the law was to ensure that passengers and pedestrians injured by cabs operated by these companies would be adequately compensated for their injuries. Carlton organized 10 corporations, each owning and operating two taxicabs in New York City. Each of these corporations carried $20,000 of liability insurance. Carlton was the principal shareholder of each corporation. The vehicles, the only freely transferable assets of these corporations, were collateral for claims of secured creditors. The 10 corporations were operated more or less as a unit with respect to supplies, repairs, and employees. Walkovszky was severely injured when he was run down by one of the taxicabs. He sued Carlton personally, alleging that the multiple corporate structure amounted to fraud upon those who might be injured by the taxicabs. Should the court pierce the corporate veil to reach Carlton individually?

10. Denzil and Stephanie Cooper obtained a court judgment for $31,800 against Seaside Pools, Inc. (SPI), a wholly owned subsidiary of Seaside Industries, Inc. (SI). SPI had sufficient funds to pay the judgment. Two weeks later, Bernard Leff, the sole owner of SI, incorporated Seaside Pools of Texas, Inc. (SPOT), and Seaside Enterprises, Inc. (SE). Leff transferred all his SI shares to SE, which as a result owned all the shares of SI, which still owned SPI. In addition, SE was the only shareholder of SPOT. Leff was president of all the corporations. Two months later, SPI ceased business, but SPOT began business using the same location, personnel, telephone, trade name, and advertising as SPI. When SPI failed to pay the Coopers, they sued Leff, SPOT, SE, and SI. Did the Coopers succeed?

CHAPTER 41

ORGANIZATION, FINANCIAL STRUCTURE, AND DISSOLUTION OF CORPORATIONS

INTRODUCTION

A person desiring to incorporate a business must comply with the applicable state corporation law. In this chapter, you will learn that failing to comply with these requirements can create various problems. For example, a person may make a contract on behalf of the corporation before it is incorporated. Is the corporation liable on this contract? Is the person who made the contract on behalf of the prospective corporation liable on the contract? Do the people who thought that they were shareholders of a corporation have limited liability, or do they have unlimited liability as partners of a partnership?

In addition, you will study the types of securities that a corporation may issue to finance its business and the rules that affect the issuance and transfer of corporate securities.

Finally, you will study the many ways a corporation may be dissolved. Dissolution ends the normal conduct of a corporation's business and precedes the winding up and the termination of the corporation.

PROMOTERS

A **promoter** of a corporation incorporates a business, organizes its initial management, and raises its initial capital. Typically, a promoter discovers a business or an idea to be developed, finds people who are willing to invest in the business, negotiates the contracts necessary for the initial operation of the proposed venture, incorporates the business, and helps management start the operation of the business. Consequently, a promoter may engage in many acts prior to the incorporation of the business. As a result, the promoter may have liability on the contracts he negotiates on behalf of the prospective corporation. In addition, the corporation may *not* be liable on the contracts the promoter makes on its behalf.

Relation of Promoter and Prospective Corporation

Because he is self-appointed and the corporation is not yet in existence, a promoter is not an agent of the prospective corporation, but nonetheless owes fiduciary duties to it. A promoter is not an agent of prospective investors in the business because they did not appoint him and they have no power to control him. By not being an agent of the prospective corporation or the prospective investors, the promoter will be unable to make them liable for contracts he purports to make on their behalf. For the prospective corporation and the prospective investors to become liable on the contracts he makes, the corporation or the investors must accept the contract or assume its benefits.

Although not an agent of the proposed corporation, a promoter owes a *fiduciary duty* to the corporation and to its prospective investors, including shareholders and possibly creditors. A promoter owes such parties a duty of full disclosure and honesty. For example, a promoter breaches this duty when she diverts money received from prospective shareholders to pay her expenses, unless the shareholders agree to such payment. The fiduciary duty also prevents a promoter from diverting a business opportunity from the corporation and giving it to himself instead.

Also, a promoter may not profit personally by transacting secretly with the corporation in his personal capacity. The promoter's failure to disclose her interest in the transaction and the material facts permits the corporation to rescind the transaction or to recover the promoter's secret profit. On the other hand, the promoter's full disclosure of her interest and the material facts of the transaction to an independent board of directors, which approves the transaction, prevents the corporation from recovering the promoter's profit. Note, however, that when a promoter is a director, approval of the transaction by the board of directors is not sufficient; the transaction must be intrinsically fair to the corporation.

In the following case, *Smith v. Bitter,* the court held that promoters are fiduciaries of the corporation they organize.

SMITH v. BITTER

319 N.W.2d 196 (Iowa Sup. Ct. 1982)

Joseph J. Smith, Steve J. Smith, and Joseph Bitter planned to open a tavern in the college town of Dubuque, Iowa. In the name of Gomer's, Inc., a corporation not yet formed, all three signed an offer to purchase a building in which to operate the tavern. After Gomer's, Inc., had been incorporated, the Smiths as corporate officers signed a contract to purchase the building in the name of the corporation. Soon after business began, differences arose between the Smiths and Bitter. When, despite Bitter's protests, the Smiths assumed control of the corporation, which included the building, Bitter sued the Smiths. Bitter asked the court to declare that Bitter and the Smiths as individuals owned the building and that Gomer's, Inc., had no interest in the building. The trial court held that Gomer's, Inc., owned the building. Bitter appealed to the Supreme Court of Iowa.

LeGrand, Justice.   This litigation culminates what started as a business venture among friends and terminated in acrimony and distrust.

In negotiating for the purchase of the real estate, Bitter and the Smiths were promoters acting for the corporation they were then in the process of organizing. A promoter stands in a fiduciary position toward both the corporation and its stockholders and is prohibited from acquiring a secret personal advantage from any action taken on behalf of the corporation.

The Smiths and Bitter owed a fiduciary duty to the corporation for which they were acting and to its shareholders. The fact that the promoters themselves were the stockholders does not alter that obligation. The record is clear that all negotiations for purchase of the real estate were made on behalf of Gomer's, Inc., which the Smiths and Bitter were then organizing. Bitter cannot profit personally from this transaction nor can he assert personal ownership of the real estate against those toward whom he was bound to exercise the utmost good faith.

Judgment for the Smiths affirmed.

Promoter's Preincorporation Contracts

A promoter may purport to make contracts for a corporation before it comes into existence. Such contracts are called **preincorporation contracts.** Three parties may have liability on such contracts: (1) the corporation, (2) the promoter, and (3) the third party with whom the promoter made the contract.

Corporation's Liability on Promoter's Contracts

When a corporation comes into existence, it does *not* automatically become liable on the *preincorporation* contracts made in its behalf by the promoter. It cannot be held liable as a principal whose agent made the contracts, since the promoter was not its agent and the corporation was not in existence when the contracts were made.

After incorporation, however, a corporation may become bound on a promoter's preincorporation contracts by its **adoption** of the promoter's contracts.

Adoption Adoption is based on the agency concept that permits a principal to ratify the unauthorized acts of an agent.[1] The basis of adoption is that the contract between the promoter and the other party contains an implied continuing offer to the corporation. The corporation accepts this offer when it accepts the contract as a binding obligation.

For the corporation to adopt a promoter's contract, the corporation must *accept* the contract *with knowledge of all its material facts.* In addition, the contract must be *within the powers* of the corporation.

Acceptance may be express or implied. Formal action is not required. The corporation's knowing receipt of the benefits of the contract is sufficient for acceptance. For example, a promoter makes a preincorporation contract with a genetic engineer, requiring the engineer to work for a prospective corporation for 10 years. After incorporation, the promoter presents the contract to the board of directors, but the board takes no formal action to accept the contract. Nonetheless, the board allows the engineer to work for the corporation for one year as the contract provides and

pays him the salary required by the contract. The board's actions constitute an acceptance of the contract, binding the corporation to the contract for its 10-year term.

Promoter's Liability on Preincorporation Contracts

Although the corporate form of business gives protection from liability to shareholders and managers, such protection is not normally given to promoters who transact on behalf of a corporation that has not yet come into existence. The Model Business Corporation Act (MBCA) imposes joint and several liability for all obligations incurred by persons who purport to act on behalf of a corporation knowing the corporation is not in existence. Therefore, a promoter and her copromoters are jointly and severally liable on preincorporation contracts the promoter negotiates in the name of the nonexistent corporation. This liability exists even when the promoters' names do not appear on the contract. Promoters are also jointly and severally liable for torts committed by their copromoters prior to incorporation.

If the corporation is *not formed*, a promoter remains liable on a preincorporation contract, unless the third party releases the promoter from liability. Also, the *mere formation* of the corporation does *not* release a promoter from liability. In addition, a promoter remains liable on a preincorporation contract even after the corporation's adoption of the contract, since *adoption* does not automatically release the promoter. The corporation cannot by itself relieve the promoter of liability to the third party; the third party must agree, expressly or impliedly, to release the promoter from liability by a process called *novation.*

Novation The promoter, the corporation, and the third party may agree to release the promoter from liability and to substitute the corporation for the promoter as the party liable on the contract. This is called a **novation.** Usually, novation will occur by express or implied agreement of all the parties.

Intent of Third Party and Promoter A few courts have held that a promoter is not liable on preincorporation contracts if the third party *knew of the nonexistence* of the corporation, yet insisted that the promoter sign the contract in behalf of the nonexistent corporation. Other courts have found that the

---

[1]Adoption is identical to ratification, except that it does not relate back to the time when the promoter made the contract and it does not automatically release the promoter from liability on the contract.

promoter is not liable if the third party clearly stated that he would *look only to the prospective corporation* for performance.

In the next case, the court held that a promoter failed to prove that the third party agreed to look only to the corporation for performance.

COOPERS & LYBRAND v. FOX

758 P.2d 683 (Colo. Ct. App. 1988)

On November 3, 1981, Garry Fox met with Coopers & Lybrand, a national accounting firm, to request a tax opinion and other accounting services. Fox told Coopers that he was acting on behalf of a corporation that he was in the process of forming, to be named G. Fox and Partners, Inc. Coopers accepted its engagement to provides services with the knowledge that the corporation was not yet in existence. Fox and Coopers had no agreement regarding Fox's personal liability for payment of the fee for the services.

G. Fox and Partners, Inc., was incorporated on December 4, 1981. Coopers completed its work on the contract by mid-December and billed "Mr. Garry Fox, Fox and Partners, Inc." in the amount of $10,827. When neither Fox nor the corporation paid the bill, Coopers sued Garry Fox individually based on the theory of promoter liability. The trial court held that Fox had no personal liability to Coopers. Coopers appealed to the Colorado Court of Appeals.

Kelly, Chief Judge. As a preliminary matter, we reject Fox's argument that he was acting only as an agent for the future corporation. One cannot act as the agent of a nonexistent principal.

On the contrary, the uncontroverted facts place Fox squarely within the definition of a promoter. A promoter is one who, alone or with others, undertakes to form a corporation and to procure for it the rights, instrumentalities, and capital to enable it to conduct business.

As a general rule, promoters are personally liable for the contracts they make, though made on behalf of a corporation to be formed. A well-recognized exception to the general rule of promoter liability is that if the contracting party knows the corporation is not in existence but nevertheless agrees to look solely to the corporation and not to the promoter for payment, then the promoter incurs no personal liability. In the absence of an express agreement, the existence of an agreement to release the promoter from liability may be shown by circumstances making it reasonably certain that the parties intended to and did enter into the agreement. Release of the promoter depends on the intent of the parties. The promoter has the burden of proving an alleged agreement to release the promoter from liability.

Fox seeks to bring himself within the exception to the general rule of promoter liability. However, as the proponent of the exception, he must bear the burden of proving the existence of the alleged agreement releasing him from liability. There was no agreement regarding Fox's liability. Thus, Fox failed to sustain his burden of proof, and the trial court erred in granting judgment in his favor.

Judgment reversed in favor of Coopers.

Liability of Third Party

While it may be desirable for the promoter to escape liability on a preincorporation contract, there is one disadvantage: Only when the promoter is liable on the preincorporation contract is the other party liable on the contract. This means that when the promoter is not liable on the contract, the other party to the contract may rescind the contract at any time prior to adoption by the corporation. Once the corporation has adopted the contract, the corporation and the third party are liable on it, and the contract cannot be rescinded without the consent of both parties.

To maintain the enforceability of a preincorporation contract prior to adoption, a promoter may want to be liable on a preincorporation contract at least until the corporation comes into existence and adopts the contract. To limit his liability, however, the promoter may wish to have his liability cease automatically upon adoption. Rather than rely on the whim of the corporation and the other party to release him from the contract, the promoter should ensure that the contract has an automatic novation clause. For example, a preincorporation contract may read that "the promoter's liability on this contract shall terminate upon the corporation's adoption of this contract." An automatic novation clause must be clear, however. If the preincorporation contract does not clearly state when the promoter's liability ceases, the promoter will retain liability after incorporation and adoption.[2]

Rather than rely on automatic novation clauses, today most well-advised promoters incorporate the business prior to making any contracts for the corporation. By doing so, only the corporation and the third party—and not the promoter—have liability on the contract.

Liability of Corporation to Promoter

Valuable as the services of a promoter may be to a prospective corporation and to society, a corporation generally is *not required* to compensate a promoter for her promotional services, or even her expenses, unless the corporation has agreed expressly to compensate the promoter. The justification for this rule is that the promoter is self-appointed and acts for a corporation that is not in existence.

Nonetheless, a corporation *may choose* to reimburse the promoter for her reasonable expenses and to pay her the value of her services to the corporation. Corporations often compensate their promoters with shares. The MBCA permits the issuance of shares for a promoter's preincorporation services.

Preincorporation Share Subscriptions

Promoters sometimes use **preincorporation share subscriptions** to ensure that the corporation will have adequate capital when it begins its business. Under the terms of a share subscription, a prospective shareholder offers to buy a specific number of the corporation's shares at a stated price. Generally, corporate acceptance of preincorporation subscriptions occurs by action of the board of directors after incorporation.

Under MBCA Section 6.20(a), a prospective shareholder may not revoke a preincorporation subscription for a six-month period, in the absence of a contrary provision in the subscription. However, unanimous agreement of the subscribers will effect a revocation.

Promoters have no liability on preincorporation share subscriptions. They have a duty, however, to make a good faith effort to bring the corporation into existence. When a corporation fails to accept a preincorporation subscription or becomes insolvent, the promoter is not liable to the disappointed subscriber, absent fraud or other wrongdoing by the promoter.

Today, most promoters incorporate the business and obtain promises to buy shares from prospective shareholders. These promises, which may take the form of postincorporation subscriptions or executory contracts to purchase shares, are discussed later in this chapter.

---

[2]*RKO–Stanley Warner Theatres, Inc. v. Graziano,* 355 A.2d 830 (PaSup. Ct. 1976).

CONCEPT REVIEW

PREINCORPORATION CONTRACTS

Promoter Liability	Promoter liable on preincorporation contract unless either:
	1. The third party knows of the nonexistence of the corporation and insists that the promoter sign in the name of the corporation.
	2. The third party knows of the nonexistence of corporation and agrees only to look to prospective corporation for performance.
	3. Novation occurs either:
	a. By agreement of the corporation and the third party.
	b. By use of an automatic novation clause.
Corporation Liability	Corporation *not* liable on preincorporation contract unless board of directors adopts contract
Third-Party Liability	Third party liable on preincorporation contract if either the promoter or the corporation is liable on the contract

---

INCORPORATION

Determining Where to Incorporate

Anyone seeking to incorporate a business must decide where to do so. If the business of a proposed corporation is to be primarily *intrastate*, it is usually cheaper to incorporate in the state where the corporation's business is to be conducted. For the business that is primarily *interstate*, however, the business may benefit by incorporating in a state different from the state in which it has its principal place of business.

Two factors affect the decision where to incorporate: (1) the cost of organizing and maintaining the corporation in the state and (2) the freedom from shareholder and creditor intervention that the state's corporation statute grants to the corporation's management.

Incorporation fees and taxes, annual fees, and other fees such as those on the transfer of shares or the dissolution of the corporation vary considerably from state to state. Delaware has been a popular state in which to incorporate because its fees tend to be low.

Promoters frequently choose to incorporate in a state whose corporation statute and court decisions grant managers broad management discretion. For example, it is easier to pay a large dividend and to effect a merger in Delaware than in many other states.

Steps in Incorporation

The steps prescribed by the incorporation statutes of the different states vary, but they generally include the following, which appear in the MBCA:

1. Preparation of articles of incorporation.
2. Signing and authenticating the articles by one or more incorporators.
3. Filing the articles with the secretary of state, accompanied by the payment of specified fees.
4. Return by the secretary of state of a copy of the articles of incorporation and a fee receipt. (Some states retain the old MBCA rule requiring issuance of a certificate of incorporation by the secretary of state.)
5. Holding an organization meeting for the purpose of adopting bylaws, electing officers, and transacting other business.

Because there are few requirements for incorporation, it is a fairly simple process and can be accomplished inexpensively in some cases.

Incorporators

The MBCA specifies that one or more persons, including corporations, partnerships, and unincorporated associations, may serve as the **incorporators**. Incorporators have no function beyond lending their names and signatures to the process of bringing the corporation into existence. No special liability attaches to a person merely because she serves as an incorporator.

Articles of Incorporation

The basic governing document of the corporation is the **articles of incorporation** (sometimes called the *charter*). The articles are similar to a constitution. They state many of the rights and responsibilities of the corporation, its management, and its shareholders. Figure 1 lists the contents of the articles.

Name   The incorporators must give the corporation a name that is distinguishable from the name of any other corporation incorporated or qualified to do business in the state. The name must include the word *corporation, incorporated, company,* or *limited,* or the abbreviation *corp., inc., co.,* or *ltd.*

Purpose   The MBCA does not require the inclusion of a statement of purpose in the articles. When a purpose is stated, it is sufficient to state, alone or together with specific purposes, that the corporation may engage in "any lawful activity."

Duration   The MBCA permits a corporation to have perpetual existence. If desired, the articles of incorporation may provide for a shorter duration.

Initial Capitalization   Most of the state corporation statutes require the articles to recite the initial capitalization of the business. Usually, the statutes require that there be a minimum amount of initial capital, such as $1,000. Since such a small amount of capital is rarely enough to protect creditors adequately, the MBCA dispenses with the need to recite a minimum amount of capital. Instead, the MBCA relies on the law of thin capitalization to protect creditors on a case-by-case basis.

Internal Governance Provisions   The articles may contain additional provisions not inconsistent with law for managing the corporation, regulating the internal affairs of the corporation, and establishing the powers of the corporation and its directors and shareholders. For example, these additional provisions may contain the procedures for electing directors, the quorum requirements for shareholders' and directors' meetings, and the dividend rights of shareholders.

Filing Articles of Incorporation

The articles of incorporation must be delivered to the office of the secretary of state, and a filing fee must be paid. The office of the secretary of state reviews the articles of incorporation that are delivered to it. If the articles contain everything that is required, the secretary of state stamps the articles "Filed" and returns a copy of

FIGURE 1   Contents of Articles of Incorporation (pursuant to MBCA)

The following *must* be in the articles:
1. The name of the corporation.
2. The number of shares that the corporation has authority to issue.
3. The address of the initial registered office of the corporation and the name of its registered agent.
4. The name and address of each incorporator.

The following *may* be included in the articles:
1. The names and addresses of the individuals who are to serve as the initial directors.
2. The purpose of the corporation.
3. The duration of the corporation.
4. The par value of shares of the corporation.
5. Additional provisions not inconsistent with law for managing the corporation, regulating the internal affairs of the corporation, and establishing the powers of the corporation and its directors and shareholders.

the stamped articles to the corporation along with a receipt for payment of incorporation fees.

The *existence* of the corporation begins when the articles are filed. Filing of the articles is conclusive proof of the existence of the corporation.

Some states require a *duplicate filing* of the articles with an office—usually the county recorder's office—in the county in which the corporation has its principal place of business. The purpose of a duplicate filing is to ease creditors' access to the articles.

The Organization Meeting

After the articles of incorporation have been approved by the secretary of state, an organization meeting is held. Usually, it is the first formal meeting of the directors, but some statutes allow the organization meeting to be held by the incorporators.

At the organizational meeting, frequently only bylaws are adopted and officers elected. If the meeting is the first meeting of the board of directors, the board may adopt a corporate seal, approve the form of share certificates, accept share subscriptions, authorize the issuance of shares, adopt preincorporation contracts, authorize reimbursement for promoters' expenses, and fix the salaries of officers. In addition, the board may transact any other business within its powers, such as ordering inventory and hiring employees.

Seal A corporation should adopt a *seal*, a design impressed on documents or affixed to them as proof of authenticity. Many states require that any corporate signing of documents pertaining to real estate (e.g., deeds and mortgages) be authenticated by a seal. If the corporation does not adopt a seal, it may be asked to certify that it has no seal when it executes such documents. Customarily, the seal is held by the corporate secretary and affixed to documents by him.

Bylaws of the Corporation

The function of the bylaws is to supplement the articles of incorporation by defining more precisely the powers, rights, and responsibilities of the corporation, its managers, and its shareholders and by stating other rules under which the corporation and its activities will be governed. Its common contents are listed in Figure 2.

Adoption and Amendment of Bylaws MBCA Section 2.06 gives the incorporators or the initial directors the *power to adopt* the initial bylaws. The board of directors holds the power *to repeal and to amend* the bylaws, unless the articles reserve this power to the shareholders. Under MBCA Section 10.20, the shareholders, as the ultimate owners of the corporation, always retain the power to amend the bylaws, even if the directors also have such power. To be valid, bylaws must be *consistent with the law and with the articles of incorporation*.

Filing Annual Report

To retain its status as a corporation in good standing, a corporation must file an annual report with the secretary of state of the state of incorporation and pay an annual franchise fee or tax. The amount of annual franchise tax varies greatly from state to state.

While the annual report includes very little information and repeats information already filed in the articles of incorporation, failure to file an annual report or pay the annual fee or tax may result in a dissolution of the corporation and an imposition of monetary penalties.

Close Corporation Elections

Close corporations face problems that normally do not affect publicly held corporations. In recognition of these problems, nearly half of the states have statutes that attend to the special needs of close corporations. For example, some corporation statutes allow a close corporation to be managed by its shareholders.

FIGURE 2 Contents of the Bylaws

1. The authority of the officers and the directors, specifying what they may and may not do.
2. The time and place at which the annual shareholders' meetings will be held.
3. The procedure for calling special meetings of shareholders.
4. The procedures for shareholders' and directors' meetings, including whether more than a majority is required for approval of specified actions.
5. Provisions for special committees of the board, defining their membership and the scope of their activities.
6. The procedures for the maintenance of share records.
7. The machinery for the transfer of shares.
8. The procedures and standards for the declaration and payment of dividends.

To take advantage of these close corporation statutes, most statutes require that a corporation make an *election* to be treated as a close corporation. Section 3 of the Statutory Close Corporation Supplement to the MBCA permits a corporation with *fewer than 50 shareholders* to elect to become a close corporation. The Close Corporation Supplement requires the articles of incorporation to state that the corporation is a statutory close corporation.

Since application of the close corporation statute is elective, there is no penalty for a corporation's failure to meet the election requirements. The only consequence of a failure to meet the requirements is that the close corporation statutory provisions are inapplicable. Instead, statutory corporation law will treat the corporation as it treats any other general corporation.

Note, however, that even when a corporation fails to meet the statutory requirements for treatment as a close corporation, a court may decide to apply special *common law* rules applicable only to close corporations.

DEFECTIVE ATTEMPTS TO INCORPORATE

Although business managers attempt to incorporate, sometimes they fail to comply with all the conditions for incorporation. For example, the incorporators may not have filed articles of incorporation or the directors may not have held an organization meeting. These are examples of *defective attempts to incorporate*, which may result in the business managers and investors having personal liability for the obligations of the defectively formed corporation.

Consequences

One possible consequence of defective incorporation is to make the managers and the purported shareholders *personally liable* for the obligations of the defectively formed corporation. This may include both *contract* and *tort* liability. For example, an employee of an insolvent corporation drives the corporation's truck over a pedestrian. If the pedestrian proves that the corporation was defectively formed, he may be able to recover damages for his injuries from the managers and the shareholders.

A second possible consequence of defective incorporation is that a party to a contract involving the purported corporation may claim nonexistence of the corporation in order to avoid a contract made in the name of the corporation. For example, a person makes an ill-advised contract with a corporation. If the person proves that the corporation was defectively formed, he may escape liability on the contract because he made a contract with a nonexistent person, the defectively formed corporation. As an alternative, the defectively formed corporation may escape liability on the contract on the grounds that its nonexistence makes it impossible for it to have liability.

The courts have tried to determine when these two consequences should arise by making a distinction between de jure corporations, de facto corporations corporations by estoppel, and corporations so defectively formed that they are treated as being nonexistent.

De Jure Corporation

A de jure corporation is formed when the promoters substantially comply with each of the *mandatory conditions precedent* to the incorporation of the business. They need not have complied with *directory provisions*.

Mandatory versus Directory Provisions *Mandatory* provisions are distinguished from *directory* provisions by statutory language and the purpose of the provision. Mandatory provisions are those that the corporation statute states "shall" or "must" be done or those that are necessary to protect the public interest. Directory provisions are those that "may" be done and that are unnecessary to protect the public interest.

For example, statutes provide that the incorporators shall file the articles of incorporation with the secretary of state. This is a mandatory provision, due not only to the use of the word *shall* but also to the importance of the filing in protecting the public interest. Other mandatory provisions include conducting an organization meeting. Directory provisions include minor matters such as the adoption of a seal and the inclusion of the incorporators' addresses in the articles of incorporation.

Effect of De Jure Status If a corporation has complied with each mandatory provision, it is a de jure corporation and is treated as a corporation for *all purposes*. The validity of a de jure corporation cannot be attacked, except in a few states in which the state, in a *quo warranto* proceeding, may attack the corporation for noncompliance *with a condition subsequent to incorporation,* such as a failure to file an annual report with the secretary of state.

De Facto Corporation

A de facto corporation exists when the incorporators fail in some material respect to comply with all of the mandatory provisions of the incorporation statute, yet comply with most such provisions. There are three requirements for a de facto corporation:

1. There is a *valid statute* under which the corporation could be organized.

2. The promoters or managers make an *honest attempt* to organize under the statute. This requires substantial compliance with the mandatory provisions taken as a whole.

3. The promoters or managers *exercise corporate powers*. That is, they act as if they were acting for a corporation.

Generally, failing to file the articles of incorporation with the secretary of state will prevent the creation of a de facto corporation. However, a de facto corporation will exist despite the lack of an organization meeting or the failure to make a *duplicate* filing of the articles with a county recorder.

Effect of De Facto Status A de facto corporation is treated as a corporation against either an attack by a third party or an attempt of the business itself to deny that it is a corporation. The state, however, may attack the claimed corporate status of the business in a *quo warranto* action.

Corporation by Estoppel

When people *hold themselves out* as representing a corporation or *believe themselves to be dealing with* a corporation, a court will *estop* those people from denying the existence of a corporation. This is called **corporation by estoppel.** For example, a manager states that a business has been incorporated and induces a third person to contract with the purported corporation. The manager will not be permitted to use a failure to incorporate as a defense to the contract because he has misled others to *believe reasonably* that a corporation exists.

Under the doctrine of estoppel, each contract must be considered individually to determine whether either party to the contract is estopped from denying the corporation's existence.

Liability for Defective Incorporation

If people attempt to organize a corporation, but their efforts are so defective that not even a corporation by estoppel is found to exist, the courts have generally held such persons to be partners with unlimited liability for the contracts and torts of the business. However, most courts impose the unlimited *contractual* liability of a partner only on those who are *actively engaged in the management* of the business or who are responsible for the defects in its organization. *Tort* liability, however, is generally imposed on everyone—the managers and the purported shareholders of the defectively formed corporation.

Modern Approaches to the Defective Incorporation Problem

As you can see, the law of defective incorporation is confusing. It becomes even more confusing when you consider that many of the defective incorporation cases look like promoter liability cases, and vice versa. A court may have difficulty deciding whether to apply the law of promoter liability or the law of defective incorporation to preincorporation contracts. It is not surprising, therefore, that modern corporation statutes have attempted to eliminate this confusion by adopting simple rules for determining the existence of a corporation and the liability of its promoters, managers, and shareholders.

Existence of Corporation under the MBCA   Most states have a provision similar to Section 56 of the MBCA of 1956. It states that the *issuance of a certificate of incorporation* by the secretary of state is *conclusive* proof of incorporation, except against the state, which is permitted to bring a *quo warranto* action challenging corporate status. Consequently, the incorporators may omit even a mandatory provision, yet create a corporation, provided that the secretary of state has issued a certificate of incorporation.[3] Some courts have held that a failure to obtain issuance of a certificate is conclusive proof of the *nonexistence* of the corporation. Some courts have held that the old MBCA eliminates the concepts of de facto corporation and corporation by estoppel.[4]

Revised MBCA Section 2.03 adopts essentially the same rule as old Section 56. It states that incorporation occurs when the articles are filed. The *filing* of the articles is *conclusive* proof of the existence of the corporation, except in a proceeding brought by the state.

Figure 3 summarizes the preceding discussion.

Liability for Defective Incorporation under the MBCA   Most of the state corporation statutes have sections similar to Section 146 of the MBCA of 1956. That section imposes joint and several liability on those persons "who assume to act as a corporation without authority to do so," such as when a certificate of incorporation has not been issued. Some courts have held that the *only* way for managers to escape personal liability is not to transact business until the secretary of state issues the certificate of incorporation. It is not clear in these cases, however, whether liability falls on shareholders who assume no role in the incorporation or management of the business.

Revised MBCA Section 2.04 clarifies the liability of shareholders when there is a defective attempt to incorporate. It imposes joint and several liability on those persons who purport to act on behalf of a corporation and know that there has been no incorporation. Section 2.04 would impose liability on managers and shareholders who both (1) *participate* in the operational decisions of the business and (2) *know* that the corporation does not exist.

Section 2.04 would, however, release from liability shareholders and others who either (1) take no part in the management of the defectively formed corporation

---

[3]*Hill v. Hill,* 318 S.E.2d 292 (Va. Sup. Ct. 1984).
[4]*Robertson v. Levy,* 197 A.2d 443 (D.C. Ct. App. 1964).

FIGURE 3   Defective Attempts to Incorporate

or (2) mistakenly believe that the corporation is in existence. Consequently, *passive* shareholders have no liability for the obligations of a defectively formed corporation even when they know that the corporation has not been formed. Likewise, managers of a defectively formed corporation have no liability when they believe that the corporation exists.

In the following case, *Bowers Bldg. Co. v. Altura Glass Co., Inc.*, the court held that no corporation could exist prior to issuance of the certificate of incorporation and held that the person acting on behalf of the nonexistent corporation could be held liable on a contract made for the nonexistent corporation.

BOWERS BLDG. CO. v. ALTURA GLASS CO., INC.

694 P. 2d 876 (Colo. Ct. App. 1984)

On April 9, 1980, Bowers Building Co. and Division 8, Inc., entered a contract for Division 8 to provide labor and materials to Bowers for a construction project. Division 8 was unable to complete the contract, which it assigned to Altura Glass Co., Inc., on January 9, 1981. On that date, Altura's president, Jack Crownover, wrote Bowers a letter requesting that Bowers issue future checks to "Altura Glass Co." Crownover signed the letter "Pres. Jack Crownover." On that same date, Crownover delivered to Altura's lawyer its articles of incorporation, which the lawyer mailed to the secretary of state of Colorado. The secretary of state issued a certificate of incorporation to Altura on January 12, 1981. The next day, Bowers issued a check payable to Altura Glass Company, which Altura accepted. When Altura breached the contract, Bowers sued Altura and its president, Crownover, arguing that Crownover had not taken all the necessary steps to incorporate Altura when the contract was assigned to Altura.

The trial court held that Altura was a de facto corporation at the time of the assignment. Therefore, it held Altura liable on the contract, but not Crownover. Bowers appealed to the Colorado Court of Appeals.

Tursi, Judge. In 1921, Colorado recognized that de facto corporate status exists. At that time, even though there were defects in compliance with the governing statute, the corporate status could not be attacked.

In 1958, the General Assembly adopted a new corporation code based on the Model Business Corporation Act. Under that act, a corporation comes into existence upon the issuance of the certificate of incorporation. Whether the Colorado Code abrogates the de facto corporation doctrine prior to issuance of the certificate of incorporation has not been addressed. However, the comment to the Model Business Corporation Act states, "any steps short of securing a certificate of incorporation would not constitute apparent compliance. Therefore, a de facto corporation cannot exist under the Model Act." Also, Fletcher's *Cyclopedia of the Law of Private Corporations* states that under the Model Act "a corporation comes into existence only when the certificate of incorporation has been issued and, until issuance of the certificate, there is no corporation de jure, de facto, or by estoppel." Further, the courts that have directly addressed the issue have concluded that there can be no de facto corporate existence prior to the issuance of the certificate of incorporation under statutes similar to ours.

Therefore, we conclude that prior to the issuance of a certificate of incorporation there is no de facto corporate status regardless of a substantial or colorable attempt to comply with the law effecting the creation of a corporation.

The case is remanded to the trial court to determine the respective liabilities of Altura and Crownover.

Judgment reversed in favor of Bowers; remanded to the trial court.

FINANCING THE CORPORATION

Sources of Funds

Any business needs money to operate and to grow. One advantage of incorporation is the large number of sources of funds that are available to businesses that incorporate. One such source is the sale of corporate **securities,** including shares, debentures, bonds, and long-term notes payable.

In addition to obtaining funds from the sale of securities, a corporation may be financed by other sources. A bank may lend money to the corporation in exchange for the corporation's short-term promissory notes, called *commercial paper.* Earnings provide a source of funds once the corporation is operating profitably. In addition, the corporation may use normal short-term financing, such as accounts receivable financing and inventory financing.

In this section, you will study only one source of corporate funds: a corporation's sale of securities. A corporate security may be either (1) a share in the corporation or (2) an obligation of the corporation. These two kinds of securities are called *equity securities* and *debt securities.*

Equity Securities

Every business corporation issues equity securities, which are commonly called stock or **shares.** The issuance of shares creates an ownership relationship: the holders of the shares—called stockholders or **shareholders**—are the owners of the corporation.

Modern statutes permit corporations to issue several classes of shares and to determine the rights of the various classes. Subject to minimum guarantees contained in the state business corporation law, the shareholders' rights are a matter of contract and appear in the articles of incorporation, in the bylaws, in a shareholder agreement, and on the share certificates.

There are two main types of equity securities: *common shares* and *preferred shares.*

Common Shares

Common shares (or common stock) are a type of equity security. Ordinarily, the owners of common shares—called *common shareholders*—have the exclusive right to elect the directors, who manage the corporation.

The common shareholders often occupy a position inferior to that of other investors, notably creditors and preferred shareholders. The claims of common shareholders are *subordinate* to the claims of creditors and other classes of shareholders when liabilities and dividends are paid and when assets are distributed upon liquidation.

In return for this subordination, however, the common shareholders have an exclusive claim to the corporate earnings and assets that exceed the claims of creditors and other shareholders. Therefore, the common shareholders bear the major risks of the corporate venture, yet stand to profit the most if it is successful.

Preferred Shares

Shares that have preferences with regard to assets or dividends over other classes of shares are called *preferred shares* (or *preferred stock*). Preferred shareholders are customarily given liquidation and dividend preferences over common shareholders. A corporation may have several classes of preferred shares. In such a situation, one class of preferred shares may be given preferences over another class of preferred shares. Under the MBCA, the preferences of preferred shareholders must be set out in the articles of incorporation.

The **liquidation preference** of preferred shares is usually a stated dollar amount. During a liquidation, this amount must be paid to each preferred shareholder before any common shareholder or other shareholder subordinated to the preferred class may receive his share of the corporation's assets.

Dividend preferences may vary greatly. For example, the dividends may be cumulative or noncumulative. Dividends on *cumulative* preferred shares, if not paid in any year, accumulate until paid. The entire accumulation must be paid before any dividends may be paid to common shareholders. Dividends on *noncumulative* preferred shares do not accumulate if unpaid. For such shares, only the current year's dividends must be paid to preferred shareholders prior to the payment of dividends to common shareholders.

Participating preferred shares have priority as to a stated amount or percentage of the dividends to be paid by the corporation. Then, the preferred shareholders participate with the common shareholders in additional dividends paid.

Some close corporations attempt to create preferred shares with a *mandatory dividend* right. These mandatory dividend provisions have generally been held illegal as unduly restricting the powers of the board of directors. Today, a few courts and some special close corporation statutes legitimize mandatory dividends.

A **redemption** provision in the articles allows a corporation at its option to repurchase preferred shareholders' shares at a price stated in the articles, despite the shareholders' unwillingness to sell. Some statutes permit the articles to give the shareholders the right to force the corporation to redeem preferred shares.[5]

Preferred shares may be **convertible** into another class of shares, usually common shares. A **conversion** right allows a preferred shareholder to exchange her preferred shares for another class of shares, usually common shares. The conversion rate or price is stated in the articles.

Preferred shares have **voting rights** unless the articles provide otherwise. Usually, most voting rights are taken from preferred shares, except for important matters such as voting for a merger or a change in preferred shareholders' dividend rights. Rarely are preferred shareholders given the right to vote for directors, except in the event of a corporation's default in the payment of dividends.

Authorized, Issued, and Outstanding Shares

Authorized shares are shares that a corporation is permitted to issue by its articles of incorporation. A corpo-

ration may not issue more shares than are authorized. **Issued** shares are shares that have been sold to shareholders. **Outstanding** shares are shares that are currently held by shareholders. The distinctions between these terms are important. For example, a corporation pays cash, property, and share dividends only on outstanding shares. Only outstanding shares may be voted at a shareholders' meeting.

Canceled Shares Sometimes, a corporation will purchase its own shares. A corporation may cancel repurchased shares. Canceled shares do not exist: They are neither authorized, issued, nor outstanding. Since canceled shares do not exist, they cannot be reissued.

Shares Restored to Unissued Status Repurchased shares may be *restored to unissued status* instead of being canceled. If this is done, the shares are merely authorized and they may be reissued at a later time.

Treasury Shares If repurchased shares are neither canceled nor restored to unissued status, they are called **treasury shares.** Such shares are authorized and issued, but not outstanding. They may be sold by the corporation at a later time. The corporation may not vote them at shareholders' meetings, and it may not pay a cash or property dividend on them.

The MBCA abolishes the concept of treasury shares. It provides that repurchased shares are restored to unissued status and may be reissued, unless the articles of incorporation require cancellation.

Options, Warrants, and Rights

Equity securities include options to purchase common shares and preferred shares. The MBCA expressly permits the board of directors to issue **options** for the purchase of the corporation's shares. Share options are often issued to top-level managers as an incentive to increase the profitability of the corporation. An increase in profitability should increase the market value of the corporation's shares, resulting in increased compensation to the employees who own and exercise share options.

Warrants are options evidenced by certificates. They are sometimes part of a package of securities sold as a unit. For example, they may be sold along with notes, bonds, or even shares. Underwriters may receive warrants as part of their compensation for aiding a corporation in selling its shares to the public.

Rights are short-term certificated options that are usually transferable. Rights are used to give present

[5]Redemption is discussed in greater detail in the Shareholders' Rights and Liabilities chapter.

security holders an option to subscribe to a proportional quantity of the same or a different security of the corporation. They are most often issued in connection with a **preemptive right** requirement, which obligates a corporation to offer each existing shareholder the opportunity to buy the corporation's newly issued shares in the same proportion as the shareholder's current ownership of the corporation's shares.[6]

Debt Securities

Corporations have power to borrow money necessary for their operations by issuing debt securities. The articles of incorporation do not have to authorize the corporation to issue debt securities. Debt securities include debentures, bonds, and notes payable.

Debt securities create a debtor-creditor relationship between the corporation and the security holder. With the typical debt security, the corporation is obligated to pay interest periodically and to pay the amount of the debt (the principal) on the maturity date.

Debentures are long-term, unsecured debt securities. Typically, a debenture has a term of 10 to 30 years. Debentures usually have indentures. An indenture is a contract that states the rights of the debenture holders. For example, an indenture defines what acts constitute default by the corporation and what rights the debenture holders have upon default. It may place restrictions on the corporation's right to issue other debt securities.

Bonds are long-term, secured debt securities that usually have indentures. They are identical to debentures except that bonds are secured by collateral. The collateral for bonds may be real property such as a building, or personal property such as an commercial airplane. If the debt is not paid, the bondholders may force the sale of the collateral and take the proceeds of the sale.

Generally, **notes** have a shorter duration than debentures or bonds. They seldom have terms exceeding five years. Notes may be secured or unsecured.

Convertible Debt Securities

It is not uncommon for notes or debentures to be *convertible* into other securities, usually preferred or common shares. The right to convert belongs to the *holder* of the convertible note or debenture. This conversion right

permits an investor to receive interest as a debt holder and, after conversion, to share in the increased value of the corporation as a shareholder.

CONSIDERATION FOR SHARES

The board of directors has the power to issue shares on behalf of the corporation. The board must decide at what *price* and for what *type of consideration* it will issue the shares. Corporation statutes restrict the discretion of the board in accepting specified kinds of consideration and in determining the value of the shares it issues.

Quality of Consideration for Shares

Not all kinds of consideration in contract law are acceptable as legal consideration for shares in corporation law. To protect creditors and other shareholders, the statutes require legal consideration to have *real value*. Many states' laws, such as in the *Kaiser v. Moulton* case that follows, permit shares to be issued only for cash, property, or services already performed for the corporation. Unperformed promises to pay money or to perform services for the corporation are improper types of consideration under these statutes.

Modern statutes, however, place few limits on the type of consideration that may be received for shares. The MBCA permits shares to be issued in return for any tangible or intangible property or *benefit to the corporation*, including cash, promissory notes, services performed for the corporation, contracts for services *to be performed* for the corporation, and securities of the corporation or another corporation. The rationale for the MBCA rule is a recognition that future services and promises of future services have value that is as real as that of tangible property. In addition, the MBCA permits corporations to issue shares to their promoters in consideration for their promoters' preincorporation services. This rule acknowledges that a corporation benefits from a promoter's preincorporation services.

Consequently, for example, a corporation may issue common shares to its president in exchange for the president's commitment to work for the corporation for three years or in exchange for bonds of the corporation or debentures issued by another corporation.

Quantity of Consideration for Shares

The board is required to issue shares for an adequate dollar amount of consideration. Whether shares have

---

[6] The preemptive right is discussed in greater detail in the Shareholders' Rights and Liabilities chapter.

been issued for an adequate amount of consideration depends in part on the *par value* of the shares. The more important concern, however, is whether the shares have been issued for *fair value.*

Par Value   Par value is an *arbitrary* dollar amount that may be assigned to the shares by the articles of incorporation. Par value does not reflect the fair market value of the shares, but par value is the *minimum* amount of consideration for which the shares may be issued.

Shares issued for less than par value are called **discount shares.** The board of directors is liable to the corporation for issuing shares for less than par value. A shareholder who purchases shares from the corporation for less than par value is liable to the corporation for the difference between the par value and the amount she paid.

Fair Value   It is not always enough, however, for the board to issue shares for their par value. Many times, shares are worth more than their par value. In addition, many shares today do not have a par value.[7] In such cases, the board must exercise care to ensure that the corporation receives the *fair value* of the shares it issues.

---

[7]In fact, the MBCA purports to eliminate the concept of par value as it affects the issuance of shares.

Absent par value problems, the board's judgment as to the amount of consideration that is received for the shares is *conclusive* when the board acts in good faith, exercises the care of ordinarily prudent directors, and acts in the best interests of the corporation.

Disputes may arise concerning the *value* of property that the corporation receives for its shares. For example, the value of a building may be difficult to determine. In all states, the board of directors has the authority to value the consideration received for shares. The board's valuation of the consideration is conclusive if it acts in good faith with the care of *prudent directors* and in a manner it reasonably believes to be in the *best interests of the corporation.* When the board impermissibly overvalues the consideration for shares, the shareholder receives **watered shares.** Both the board and the shareholder are liable to the corporation when there is a watered shares problem.

When a shareholder pays less than the amount of consideration determined by the board of directors, the corporation or its creditors may sue the shareholder to recover the deficit. When a shareholder has paid the proper amount of consideration, the shares are said to be *fully paid and nonassessable.*

The following case, *Kaiser v. Moulton,* illustrates the courts' deference to the board's judgment in valuing consideration. The court approved the issuance of shares for the finding of development land for the corporation, which was a service performed for the corporation.

KAISER v. MOULTON
631 S.W.2d 44 (Mo. Ct. App. 1981)

In April 1962, Arthur Kaiser and his cousin Jerry Kaiser incorporated Jerry Kaiser & Associates, Inc., a real estate development company. David Moulton entered the corporation in 1963. In June 1963, Arthur Kaiser told Jerry and David about the availability of some unimproved land. The land was subsequently acquired by Jerry Kaiser & Associates, Inc., and developed as Sherwood Manor Apartments.

On November 1, 1963, at a meeting of the directors, Jerry Kaiser, as the chairman of the board, announced that Arthur Kaiser had rendered services to the corporation. The board then approved the issuance to Arthur of 25 shares of $10 par value Class A common stock. The corporation issued to Arthur share certificate number 1 for 25 shares "of the $10 par value Class A nonvoting stock of Jerry Kaiser & Associates, Inc., fully paid and non-assessable."

In 1980, Arthur sued the corporation in an attempt to inspect the books of the corporation, but the corporation refused his request on the ground that he was not a shareholder because he had not paid for the shares with a proper type of consideration and had paid too little for the shares. The trial court held that Arthur was a shareholder; the corporation appealed.

Stewart, Judge.   The corporation contends that the issuance of 25 shares to Arthur Kaiser was void because it violated the Missouri Constitution, which states, "No corporation shall issue stock, except for money paid, labor done, or property actually received."

We are of the opinion that Arthur's shares were issued for "labor done." At the meeting of the board of directors, on November 1, 1963, Jerry Kaiser as chairman announced that Arthur had rendered services to the corporation, and the members of the board unanimously authorized the issuance of 25 shares of $10 par value Class A common stock. The stock as issued stated that it was fully paid and non-assessable. It is conceded that Arthur is the person who learned of the availability of the initial tract of land that was developed into Sherwood Manor. He brought the matter to the attention of Jerry Kaiser and David Moulton.

As set out in the Missouri corporation statute, "In the absence of actual fraud in the transaction, the judgment of the board of directors or the shareholders, as the case may be, as to the value of the consideration received for shares shall be conclusive." When we consider that the par value of the shares issued to Arthur Kaiser amounted to only $250, it would not be unreasonable for the trial court to conclude that Arthur's efforts in finding a major portion of the property used in developing Sherwood Manor were sufficient consideration for the issuance of the 25 shares. The trial court did not err in declaring Arthur the owner of the shares.

Judgment for Arthur Kaiser affirmed.

Treasury Shares and Par Value   The par value of shares is important *only when the shares are issued* by the corporation. Since treasury shares are issued but not outstanding, the corporation does not issue treasury shares when it resells them. Therefore, the board may sell treasury shares for less than par, provided that it sells the shares for an amount equal to their fair value.

Shareholder Resale of Shares   Since par value and fair value are designed to ensure only that the corporation receives adequate consideration for its shares, a shareholder may buy shares from another shareholder for less than par value or fair value and incur no liability. However, if the purchasing shareholder *knows* that the selling shareholder bought the shares from the corporation for less than par value, the purchasing shareholder *is* liable to the corporation for the difference between the par value and the amount paid by the selling shareholder.

Accounting for Consideration Received

The consideration received by a corporation for its equity securities appears in the equity or capital accounts in the shareholders' equity section of the corporation's balance sheet. The **stated capital** account records the product of the number of shares outstanding multiplied by the par value of each share. When the shares are sold for more than par value, the excess or surplus consideration received by the corporation is **capital surplus.**

Under the MBCA, the terms *stated capital* and *capital surplus* have been eliminated. All consideration received for shares is lumped under one accounting entry for that class of shares, such as common equity. Most states, however, recognize a distinction between stated capital and capital surplus.

SHARE SUBSCRIPTIONS

Nature of Share Subscriptions

Under the terms of a *share subscription*, a prospective shareholder promises to buy a specific number of shares of a corporation at a stated price. If the subscription is accepted by the corporation and the subscriber has paid for the shares, the *subscriber* is a *shareholder* of the corporation, even if the shares have not been issued.

Distinguished from Executory Contracts Subscriptions should not be confused with *executory contracts* to purchase shares. A prospective shareholder who merely has an executory contract to purchase shares is not a shareholder until the share certificate has been delivered. Subscriptions are distinguished from executory contracts by the *intent of the parties*. If a corporation and an investor intend that the investor have the rights of a shareholder immediately upon the creation of a contract, the contract is a subscription.

Writing Requirement Under the MBCA, subscriptions need not be in writing to be enforceable. Usually, however, subscriptions are written.

Under the Uniform Commercial Code (UCC) section 8–319, which has been adopted by all of the states, an executory contract to purchase shares must be in writing to be enforceable.

Uses of Subscriptions

Promoters use written share subscriptions in the course of selling shares of a proposed corporation to ensure that equity capital will be provided once the corporation comes into existence. These are called *preincorporation subscriptions*, which were covered in this chapter's discussion of promoters. Preincorporation subscriptions are not contracts binding on the corporation and the shareholders until the corporation comes into existence and its board of directors accepts the share subscriptions.

Close corporations may use share subscriptions when they seek to sell additional shares after incorporation. These are examples of *postincorporation subscriptions*, subscription agreements made *after* incorporation. A postincorporation subscription is a contract between the corporation and the subscriber at the time the subscription agreement is made.

Payment of Subscription Price

A subscription may provide for payment of the price of the shares on a specified day, in installments, or upon the demand of the board of directors. The board may not discriminate when it demands payment. It must demand payment from all the subscribers of a class of shares or from none of them.

A share certificate may not be issued to a share subscriber until the price of the shares has been fully paid. If the subscriber fails to pay as agreed, the corporation *may sue the subscriber* for the amount owed.

ISSUANCE OF SHARES

Function of Share Certificates

A *share certificate* is evidence that a person has been issued shares, owns the shares, and is a shareholder. The certificate states the corporation's name, the shareholder's name, and the number and class of shares. The certificate, however, is not the shares, which are intangible and cannot be possessed physically. A person can be a shareholder without receiving a share certificate, such as a holder of a share subscription. Under MBCA Section 6.25, share certificates are not required.

Liability for Overissuance under UCC

UCC Article 8 regulates, among other things, the issuance of securities. Under Article 8, a corporation has a duty to issue only the number of shares authorized by its articles. Overissued shares are void.

Even when a person is entitled to overissued shares, the corporation may not issue the shares. Under UCC section 8–104, however, the person has two remedies. The corporation must obtain identical shares—if such shares are reasonably available—and deliver them to the person entitled to issuance. If identical shares are unavailable, the corporation must reimburse the person for the value paid for the shares plus interest.

The directors may incur liability, including criminal liability, for an overissuance of shares. To prevent overissuance through error in the issuance or transfer of their shares, corporations often employ a bank or a trust company as a *registrar*.

TRANSFER OF SECURITIES

Function of Securities Certificates

Since securities certificates are evidence of the ownership of securities, their transfer is *evidence of the transfer* of the ownership of securities. UCC Article 8 covers the registration and transfer of investment securities, as represented by certificates.

Shares Share certificates are issued in *registered* form; that is, they are registered with the corporation in the name of a specific person. The indorsement of a share certificate on its back by its registered owner and the delivery of the certificate to another person transfers ownership of the shares to the other person. The transfer of a share certificate without naming a transferee creates a *street certificate*. A street certificate is similar to a bearer negotiable instrument. The transfer of a street certificate may be made by delivery without indorsement. Any holder of a street certificate is presumed to be the owner of the shares it represents. Therefore, a transferee should ask the corporation to reregister the shares in his name.

Debt Securities   Bonds, debentures, and notes, as investment securities, are also covered by Article 8. They may be *registered* (payable to a specified person in whose name the certificate is registered with the corporation) or *bearer* (payable to whoever holds the certificate). A registered debt security certificate is transferred in the same manner as a registered share certificate, while a bearer debt security certificate, like a street certificate, is transferred by delivery alone.

Corporation's Duty to Transfer Shares

Under UCC section 8–401, a corporation owes a duty to register the transfer of any registered shares presented to it for registration, provided that the shares have been properly indorsed. If the corporation refuses to make the transfer, it is liable to the transferee for either conversion or specific performance.

Bona Fide Purchaser

When an owner of shares claims that his shares have been lost, destroyed, or stolen, the corporation must issue new shares to the owner unless the corporation has notice that the shares have been acquired by a bona fide purchaser. A bona fide purchaser is a purchaser of the shares for value in good faith with no notice of any adverse claim against the shares. If, after the issuance of the new shares, a bona fide purchaser of the original shares presents them for registration, the corporation must register the transfer, unless overissuance would result.

Restrictions on Transferability of Shares

Historically, a shareholder has been free to sell her shares to whomever she wants whenever she wants. The courts have been reluctant to allow restrictions on the free transferability of shares, even if the shareholder agreed to a restriction on the transfer of her shares.

Gradually, the courts and the legislatures have recognized that there are good reasons to permit the use of some restrictions on the transfer of shares. Today, modern corporation statutes legitimize most transfer restrictions, especially when used by close corporations.

Uses of Transfer Restrictions

A corporation and its shareholders have a number of reasons to use transfer restrictions: (1) to maintain the balance of power, (2) to guarantee a market for the shares, (3) to prevent unwanted persons from becoming shareholders, (4) to preserve a close corporation or Subchapter S taxation election, and (5) to preserve an exemption from registration of a securities offering.

To Maintain the Balance of Power   For example, four persons may own 25 shares each in a corporation. No single person can control such a corporation. If one of the four can buy 26 additional shares from the other shareholders, he will acquire control. The shareholders may therefore agree that each shareholder is entitled to buy an equal amount of any shares sold by any selling shareholders.

To Guarantee a Market for the Shares   In a close corporation, there may be no ready market for the shares of the corporation. To ensure that a shareholder can obtain the value of her investment upon her retirement or death, the shareholders and the corporation may be required to buy a shareholder's shares upon the occurrence of a specific event such as death or retirement.

To Prevent Unwanted Persons from Becoming Shareholders   In a close corporation, the shareholders may want only themselves or other approved persons as shareholders. The shareholders may therefore agree that no shareholder will sell shares to someone who is not approved by the other shareholders.

To Preserve a Close Corporation or Subchapter S Election   Close corporation statutes and Subchapter S of the Internal Revenue Code limit the number of shareholders that a close corporation or S Corporation may have. A transfer restriction may prohibit the shareholders from selling shares such that there are too many shareholders to preserve a close corporation or S Corporation election.

To Preserve an Exemption from Registration of a Securities Offering   Under the Securities Act of 1933 and the state securities acts, an offering of securities is exempt from registration if the offering is to a limited number of investors, usually 35. A transfer restriction may require a selling shareholder to obtain permission from the corporation's legal counsel, which permission will be granted upon proof that the shareholder's sale of the shares does not cause the corporation to lose its registration exemption.

Types of Restrictions on Transfer

There are four types of restrictions on transfer that may be used to accomplish the objectives addressed above: (1) rights of first refusal and option agreements, (2) buy-and-sell agreements, (3) consent restraints, and (4) provisions disqualifying purchasers.

Rights of First Refusal and Option Agreements   A **right of first refusal** grants to the corporation and the other shareholders the right to match the offer that a selling shareholder receives for her shares. An **option agreement** grants the corporation and the other shareholders an option to buy the selling shareholder's shares at a price determined by the agreement. A right of first refusal or an option agreement is used primarily to maintain the corporate balance of power and to prevent unwanted persons from becoming shareholders.

An option agreement will usually state a formula used to calculate the price of the shares. Ordinarily, the courts will permit or require purchase of the shares at the agreement price even when the fair value of the shares is much lower or much higher than the agreement price.

Buy-and-Sell Agreements   A **buy-and-sell agreement** compels a shareholder to sell his shares to the corporation or to the other shareholders at the price stated in the agreement. It also obligates the corporation or the other shareholders to buy the selling shareholder's shares at that price. The agreement is called a *cross-purchase agreement* when the shareholders are obligated to buy and sell. It is called a *redemption agreement* when the corporation is the person that is obligated to buy. As with option agreements, the price of the shares is usually determined by a stated formula. This type of agreement is used primarily to ensure a market for the shares upon the death or retirement of a shareholder.

Consent Restraints   A **consent restraint** requires a selling shareholder to obtain the consent of the corporation or the other shareholders before she may sell her shares. Consent restraints may be used to preserve close corporation and S Corporation elections and to maintain securities registration exemptions.

Provisions Disqualifying Purchasers   A *provision disqualifying purchasers* may be used in rare situations to exclude unwanted persons from the corporation. For example, a transfer restriction may prohibit the shareholders from selling to a competitor of the business.

Legality of Transfer Restrictions

Corporation statutes permit the use of option agreements, rights of first refusal, and buy-and-sell agreements with virtually no restrictions. Consent restraints and provisions disqualifying purchasers may be used if they are not *manifestly unreasonable.*

MBCA Section 6.27(c) makes per se reasonable any restriction that maintains a corporation's status when that status is dependent on the number or identity of shareholders, as with close corporation or S Corporation status. The MBCA also makes per se reasonable any restriction that preserves registration exemptions under the Securities Act of 1933 and state securities laws. In addition, the MBCA has a catchall provision that authorizes transfer restrictions for any other reasonable purpose. The reasonableness of a restraint is judged in light of the character and needs of the corporation.

Enforceability

To be enforceable against a shareholder, a transfer restriction must be contained in the articles of incorporation, the bylaws, an agreement among the shareholders, or an agreement between the corporation and the shareholders. In addition, the shareholder must *agree* to the restriction or purchase the shares *with notice* of the restriction. Under MBCA Section 6.27(b), a purchaser of the shares has notice of a restriction if it is noted *conspicuously* on the face or the back of a share certificate or if it is a restriction of which he has *knowledge.* UCC section 8–204 requires that an enforceable restriction be noted *conspicuously* on the certificate or that the transferee have *actual knowledge* of the restriction. The next case addresses the issue of whether a restriction is reasonable and whether it is conspicuously noted on the certificate.

LING AND CO. v. TRINITY SAVINGS AND LOAN ASS'N.

482 S.W.2d 841 (Tex. Sup. Ct. 1972)

When Bruce Bowman borrowed some money from Trinity Savings and Loan Association, he pledged 1,500 shares of Ling and Company Class A common stock as collateral for the loan. Bowman failed to repay Trinity. Trinity sued Bowman on the loan and asked the court to order the sale of the shares pledged as collateral. Ling and Company objected to the sale of the shares on the grounds that Ling's articles of incorporation restricted transfer of its shares. Trinity sued Ling also, asking the court to invalidate the restrictions on transfer. The restrictions appeared in Article 4 of Ling's articles of incorporation. One restriction was an option agreement that granted to the corporation and the other shareholders a 10-day option to buy the shares before the shares could be sold to any other person.

On the front side of the share certificate, in small print, it was stated that the shares were subject to the provisions of the articles of incorporation, that a copy of the articles could be obtained from the secretary of the corporation or the secretary of state, and that specific references to provisions setting forth restrictions were on the back of the certificate. On the backside, also in small type, the reference to the articles was repeated and specific mention was made of Article 4. Here, the option agreement was referred to but not stated fully.

The trial court held that the restrictions were invalid and ordered the sale of the shares. After the court of appeals affirmed the trial court's decision, Ling appealed to the Supreme Court of Texas.

Reavley, Justice. The court of civil appeals struck down the restrictions for the lack of conspicuous notice on the share certificate and the unreasonableness of the restrictions.

The Texas Business Corporation Act provides that a corporation may impose restrictions on the transfer of its shares, if they are "expressly set forth in the articles of incorporation and copied at length or in summary form on the face or so copied on the back and referred to on the face of each certificate." The Legislature, at the same time, permitted an incorporation by reference on the face or back of a certificate of a provision in the articles of incorporation that restricts the transfer of the shares. In the present case, reference is made on the face of the certificate to the restrictions described on the reverse side; the notice on the reverse side refers to the particular article of the articles of incorporation as restricting the transfer or encumbrance of the shares and requiring "the holder thereof to grant options to purchase the shares represented hereby first to the Corporation and then pro rata to the other holders of the Class A Common Stock." We hold that the content of the certificate complies with the requirements of the Texas Business Corporation Act.

There remains the requirement that the restriction or reference on transferability be "noted conspicuously on the security." The UCC provides that a conspicuous term is so written as to be noticed by a reasonable person. Examples of conspicuous matter are given there as a "printed heading in capitals or larger or other contrasting type or color." This means that something must appear on the face of the certificate to attract the attention of a reasonable person when he looks at it. The line of print on the face of the Ling certificate does not stand out and cannot be considered conspicuous.

Our holding that the restriction is not noted conspicuously on the certificate does not entitle Trinity to a judgment under this record. The restriction is effective against a person with actual knowledge of it. The record does not establish conclusively that Trinity lacked knowledge of the restriction when Bowman executed an assignment of these shares to Trinity Savings and Loan.

A corporation may impose restrictions on the disposition of its shares, if the restrictions "do not unreasonably restrain or prohibit transferability." The court of appeals held that it is unreasonable to require a shareholder to notify all other record holders of Class A Common Stock of his intent to sell and give the other holders a 10-day option to buy. The record does not reveal the number of holders of this class of shares; we know only that there are more than 20. We find nothing unusual or oppressive in these first option provisions. Conceivably the number of shareholders might be so great as to make the burden too heavy upon the shareholder who wishes to sell and, at the same time, dispel any justification for contending that there exists a reasonable corporate purpose in restricting the ownership. There is, however, no proof of that.

Judgment reversed in favor of Ling. Case remanded to the trial court.

Corporation's Duty to Disclose Inside Information

Frequently, after a shareholder chooses or is compelled to sell his shares back to the corporation at a price determined by an option agreement or a buy-and-sell agreement, previously nonpublic information about the corporation may be disclosed. Such disclosure may reveal that the shares are worth far more than the price received by the shareholder. Courts hold that the corporation has a duty to disclose information that is material to the shareholder's exercise of his choice to sell his shares. However, if the shareholder has no choice whether or when to resell his shares to the corporation, the corporation has no disclosure obligation.[8]

---

[8] *Smith v. Duff and Phelps, Inc.* 891 F.2d 1567 (11th Cir. 1990).

Effect of Statutory Close Corporation Supplement

Although transfer restrictions are important to close corporations, many close corporation shareholders fail to address the share transferability problem. Therefore, a few states provide statutory resolution of the close corporation transferability problem. In these states, statutes offer solutions to the transferability problem that are similar to the solutions that the shareholders would have provided had they thought about the problem.

Not all transferability problems are settled by the Close Corporation Supplement. There is no statutory buy-and-sell provision, although under Section 14, the articles may require the corporation to purchase the shares of a deceased shareholder at the request of his estate, thereby guaranteeing a market for the deceased shareholder's shares. Section 14 was addressed in the following case.

GOODE v. RYAN

489 N.E.2d 1001 (Mass. Sup. Jud. Ct. 1986)

Alice Marr owned 800 of the 11,340 shares outstanding of Gloucester Ice & Storage Co., a closely held corporation with no ready market for its shares. When Marr died, Thomas Goode, the administrator of her will, demanded that Gloucester or its majority shareholder purchase Marr's shares. No provision restricting the transfer of shares or requiring the corporation or remaining shareholders to purchase shares on the death of a shareholder appeared in the corporation's articles of incorporation, bylaws, or agreement among shareholders. Therefore, the trial court held that neither Gloucester nor its majority shareholder was required to purchase Marr's shares. Goode appealed to the Supreme Judicial Court of Massachusetts.

Hennessey, Chief Justice.   One of the identifying characteristics of a close corporation is the absence of a ready market for corporate shares. A shareholder in a large, public-issue corporation can sell the shares on the financial markets at no price disadvantage relative to the other sellers of those shares. A member of a partnership can convert the investment to cash by exercising the right to dissolve the partnership. The shareholder who owns less than a majority interest in a close corporation does not have any of these options. In the absence of an agreement among shareholders or between the corporation and the shareholder, or a provision in the corporation's articles of incorporation or bylaws, neither the corporation nor a majority of shareholders is under any obligation to purchase the shares of minority shareholders when minority shareholders wish to dispose of their interest in the corporation.

Goode's argument that imposing a duty on a majority shareholder or a close corporation to purchase the shares of a deceased shareholder at the request of the administrator of the shareholder's estate would be consistent with the approach adopted in the Statutory Close Corporation Supplement to the Model Business Corporation Act is not correct. The provision requiring a corporation to purchase shares from the estate of a deceased shareholder applies only if the articles of incorporation of the close corporation contain the provision. Thus, the Close Corporation Supplement leaves share buy-out agreements to the agreement of the parties.

While Goode's predicament is unfortunate, the situation was not caused by the majority shareholder, but is merely one of the risks of ownership of shares in a close corporation. It is not the proper function of this court to reallocate the risks inherent in the ownership of corporate shares in the absence of corporate or majority shareholder misconduct.

Judgment for the majority shareholder affirmed.

DISSOLUTION AND TERMINATION OF CORPORATIONS

Just as there are requirements that must be met in order to create a corporation, certain requirements must be met in order to dissolve a corporation. A *dissolution* does not terminate a corporation. Instead, a dissolution requires a corporation to cease its business, to *wind up* its affairs, and to liquidate its assets. *Termination* occurs after the corporation's assets have been liquidated and the proceeds distributed to creditors and shareholders.

The MBCA permits voluntary and involuntary dissolutions. A voluntary dissolution may be accomplished only with the consent of the corporation. An involuntary dissolution may be accomplished without the corporation's consent and despite its opposition.

Voluntary Dissolution

Under MBCA Section 14.01, a corporation that has not issued shares or commenced business may be dissolved by the vote of a majority of its incorporators or initial directors.

MBCA Section 14.02 provides that a corporation doing business may be dissolved by action of its directors and shareholders. The directors must adopt a dissolution resolution, and a majority of the shares outstanding must be cast in favor of dissolution at a shareholders' meeting.

For a voluntary dissolution to be effective, the corporation must file articles of dissolution with the secretary of state. The dissolution is effective when the articles are filed.

Involuntary Dissolution

A corporation may be dissolved without its consent by *administrative action* of the secretary of state or by *judicial action* of a court.

Administrative Dissolution   MBCA Section 14.20 permits the secretary of state to commence an administrative proceeding to dissolve a corporation that has not filed its annual report, paid its annual franchise tax, appointed or maintained a registered office or agent in the state, or whose period of duration has expired.

Administrative dissolution requires that the secretary of state give written notice to the corporation of the grounds for dissolution. If, within 60 days, the corporation has not corrected the default or demonstrated that the default does not exist, the secretary dissolves the corporation by signing a certificate of dissolution.

Judicial Dissolution   Under the MBCA, the secretary of state, the shareholders, or the creditors may ask a court to order the involuntary dissolution of a corporation. The secretary of state may obtain judicial dissolution if it is proved that a corporation obtained its articles of incorporation by fraud or exceeded or abused its legal authority.

Any shareholder may obtain judicial dissolution when there is a deadlock of the directors that is harmful to the corporation, when the shareholders are deadlocked and cannot elect directors for two years, or when the directors are acting contrary to the best interests of the corporation. Creditors may request dissolution if the corporation is insolvent.

Dissolution of Close Corporations

Many close corporations are nothing more than incorporated partnerships, in which all the shareholders are managers and friends or relatives. Recently, corporation law has reflected the special needs of those shareholders of close corporations who want to arrange their affairs to make the close corporation more like a partnership.

The Close Corporation Supplement to the MBCA recognizes that a close corporation shareholder should have the same dissolution power as a partner. This section, like similar provisions in many states, permits the articles of incorporation to empower any shareholder to dissolve the corporation at will or upon the occurrence of a specified event such as the death of a shareholder.

Winding Up and Termination

A dissolved corporation continues its corporate existence, but may not carry on any business except that appropriate to winding up its affairs. Therefore, winding up (liquidation) must follow dissolution. Winding up is the orderly collection and disposal of the corporation's assets and the distribution of the proceeds of the sale of assets. From these proceeds, the claims of creditors will be paid first. Next, the liquidation preferences of preferred shareholders will be paid. Then, common shareholders receive any proceeds that remain.

After winding up has been completed, the corporation's existence terminates. A person who purports to act on behalf of a terminated corporation has the liability of a person acting for a corporation prior to its incorporation. Some courts, like the court in the next case, impose similar liability on a person acting on behalf of a dissolved corporation, especially when dissolution is obtained by the secretary of state, such as for the failure to file an annual report or to pay franchise taxes.

BODINE ALUMINUM CO., INC. V. MITAUER

776 S.W.2d 485 (Mo. Ct. App. 1989)

East Side Metals, Inc., a Missouri corporation, failed to file an annual registration statement required by the Missouri corporation statute. Consequently, in November 1984, its corporate charter was forfeited. On East Side's last annual registration statement, Harlin, Louis, and Bernice Mitauer were listed as its officers and directors. Although East Side's charter was forfeited, the Mitauers continued to operate the business. In 1985, the business purchased scrap aluminum from Bodine Aluminum Co., Inc. When the business failed to pay $17,064 of the purchase price, Bodine sued the Mitauers to recover the remainder. The trial court held that the Mitauers individually owed Bodine $17,064. The Mitauers appealed to the Missouri Court of Appeals.

Grimm, Judge.   The Missouri corporation statute provides:

If any corporation: (1) Fails to comply with the provisions of this chapter with respect to its annual registration the corporate rights and privileges of the corporation shall be forfeited, and the secretary of state shall notify the corporation that its corporate existence and rights in this state have been forfeited and canceled, and the corporation dissolved; and the directors and officers in office when the forfeiture occurs shall be the trustees of the corporation, who shall have full authority to wind up its business and affairs; and the trustees shall be jointly and severally responsible to the creditors and shareholders of the corporation to the extent of its property and effects that shall have come into their hands.

This statute places a limit on the liability of officers and directors as they wind up the affairs of a corporation after its corporate rights and privileges have been forfeited. When, however, the officers and directors continue to operate the business after forfeiture, individual liability may be imposed on them.

East Side's charter was forfeited on November 1, 1984. The Mitauers then became statutory trustees for the purpose of winding up the affairs of the corporation. When no effort was made to wind up, all post-forfeiture debts became the personal liability of the Mitauers.

Judgment affirmed for Bodine.

ETHICAL AND PUBLIC POLICY CONCERNS

1. Suppose that a promoter of a prospective business, Promoter 1, chooses to incorporate the business prior to making any contracts for the prospective business. Because incorporation is a fairly simple process, Promoter 1 has done little more than Promoter 2, who makes preincorporation contracts. Yet Promoter 1 will not ordinarily have liability on contracts signed in the name of the corporation, while Promoter 2 will have liability. Does this distinction seem fair to the promoters? Is it fair to the other parties to the contract? Would your answers change if Promoter 1 incorporated the business with the minimum amount of capital required by the incorporation statute and then negotiated contracts obligating the business in amounts exceeding $100,000?

2. Under the Model Business Corporation Act, investors who believe that they have contributed capital to a corporation have no personal liability for the debts of the corporation even if it has been defectively formed. Why should such investors not be held liable as partners? Is it fair that the defectively formed corporation's creditors cannot sue the investors? Should it matter whether the investors are involved in the operation of the defectively formed corporation? Should it matter whether the creditors believed there was no corporation and thought the investors were partners? Should it matter whether the creditors are contract creditors (who could have checked into the status of the corporation and its investors prior to contracting with the business) or tort creditors (who have no ability to investigate the corporation and its investors prior to being injured by the person acting on behalf of the defectively formed corporation)?

3. Why should the law impose limits on the use of share transfer restrictions? Who may be harmed if there are no such limits? Is it possible for those who would be harmed to be protected in ways other than by limiting the use of share transfer restrictions?

SUMMARY

The promoter brings the corporation into existence and begins its operation. Promoters are not agents, but they are fiduciaries of the corporation and its investors. The corporation is not liable on the promoter's preincorporation contracts until the board of directors accepts the contracts. The promoter normally remains liable on preincorporation contracts unless there is a novation.

The corporation law of the state of incorporation states what steps must be followed to incorporate. When a corporation is formed defectively, the promoter, the managers, and the shareholders may be liable for the debts of the business, unless the court finds that there is a corporation de jure, a corporation de facto, or a corporation by estoppel. Modern statutes establish that the return of a copy of the articles of incorporation stamped by the secretary of state is conclusive proof of the existence of the corporation.

Corporations are financed in part by the issuance of equity and debt securities. Corporations may issue two or more classes of shares with different preferences, limitations, and rights. If there is only one class of shares, these will be common shares. If both common and preferred shares are issued, common shareholders are generally given the right to elect directors, and preferred shareholders have priority over common shareholders on dividends and on the assets distributed upon liquidation. Corporations may issue debt securities, including notes, debentures, and bonds. The claims of the holders of such securities have a priority over the claims of shareholders.

A preincorporation share subscription is treated as an offer. A contract results when the offer is accepted by the corporation. Under the MBCA, acceptance occurs by act of the directors after incorporation. A postincorporation subscription is a contract when it is accepted by the corporation.

Article 8 of the UCC applies to investment securities and gives them characteristics of negotiable instruments. It establishes the duties and liabilities of corporations as issuers of shares and debt securities.

A corporation may restrict the transfer of its shares. To be enforceable against a shareholder, a restriction must be agreed to by the shareholder, noted conspicuously on the share certificate, or known to the shareholder prior to purchase. In addition, the restriction must be one authorized by statute, such as a buy-and-sell agreement, a right of first refusal, a consent restraint, or a provision disqualifying specified purchasers.

Dissolution ends the business of the corporation, except the business necessary to liquidate the assets. A corporation may be dissolved voluntarily or involuntarily. Involuntary dissolutions include administrative dissolutions by the secretary of state and judicial dissolutions at the request of the attorney general, a shareholder, or a creditor.

PROBLEM CASES

1. RKO–Stanley Warner Theatres, Inc., contracted to sell a theatre to Jack Jenofsky and Ralph Graziano, who were in the process of forming a corporation to be known as Kent Enterprises, Inc. The contract included the following, added by Jenofsky and Graziano's lawyer:

It is understood by the parties hereto that it is the intention of the Purchaser to incorporate. Upon condition that such incorporation be completed by the closing date, all agreements contained herein shall be construed to have been made between Seller and the resultant corporation.

Subsequently, Kent Enterprises, Inc., was incorporated. A final closing date was set, but the sale was never completed. RKO sued Jenofsky and Graziano on the contract. Jenofsky claimed that the quoted provision in the contract released him from any personal liability. Was he correct?

2. Max and Edward Gurwicz developed the Regency Towers Condominium (Towers), which sold condominium units to residents. The Gurwiczes also formed the Regency Towers Condominium Association (Association), which was to serve as an association of the condominium owners. Prior to the drafting of the Association's articles of incorporation, the Gurwiczes signed a lease in the name of the Association obligating the Association to make rental payment to the Towers. Three weeks later, the articles were filed by the secretary of state. After the filing, the Association's board of directors took no action in respect to the lease and made no rental payments to Towers. The condominium owners, who indirectly would be liable on the lease if the Association was bound by it, believed that the lease unreasonably burdened the Association. The condominium owners asked a court to rule that the Association was not liable on the lease. What did the court hold?

3. Stuart Lakes Club, Inc., a New York corporation, was a private game club owning 75 acres of land, two lakes, and a clubhouse. The board of directors adopted a bylaw provision that stated, "When any member ceases to be a member of the Club, either by death, resignation, or otherwise, his share shall be considered void and the certificate returned to the Treasurer for cancellation." The purpose of the bylaw provision was to make the last surviving member of the club its sole owner, and therefore the beneficial owner of the club's valuable land and clubhouse. Has the board of directors adopted an enforceable bylaw?

4. On October 11, 1978, Charles Goodwyne incorporated C & N Bottle Shop, Inc., for the purpose of operating a liquor store and doing any other lawful business. Since he was unable to obtain financing for a liquor store, Goodwyne decided to establish a salvage operation and to change the name of the corporation to

C & N Industries, Inc. On December 15, Goodwyne signed a promissory note as follows: "C & N Industries, Inc., by Charles Goodwyne." On February 26, 1979, the corporation filed articles of amendment with the secretary of state changing its name from C & N Bottle Shop to C & N Industries. Is Goodwyne personally obligated on the promissory note?

5. Eugene Levy agreed to buy a retail record business from Martin Robertson. Levy submitted for filing the articles of incorporation for Record Shack, Inc., but they were rejected by the secretary of state. Six days later, Robertson sold the assets of the business to the Record Shack and received a promissory note for the purchase price signed "Penn Ave. Record Shack, Inc., by Eugene M. Levy, President." Subsequently, Levy resubmitted the articles, and a certificate of incorporation of Penn Ave. Record Shack, Inc. was issued. Robertson accepted one payment on the promissory note from the corporation, but within six months, Record Shack ceased doing business; no assets remained. Robertson sued Levy for the balance of the promissory note. Was Levy liable on the promissory note?

6. John Gazda, Anthony Kolinski, and John Giamartino formed a corporation to operate Big Boy restaurants, with each owning one third of the shares. After a dispute resulted in the removal of Gazda as an officer, Kolinski and Giamartino, as controlling directors, voted to issue shares of the corporation for $100 per share. At the time, the book value of the corporation was $266 per share and the fair market value was between $497 and $572 per share. Gazda opposed the issuance of the shares. Was he successful at stopping the issuance?

7. Dale Frey intended to develop a 33-acre apartment complex, to be operated by Mt. Carmel Apartments, Inc., a corporation not yet formed. To promote and develop the complex, Frey contracted with Jess Burge. Their agreement provided that Burge would receive $70,000 payable in 12.5 percent of the shares of the corporation. Subsequently, Burge consulted with architects, calculated construction costs, executed a loan application, and consulted with prospective contractors on behalf of the complex. After incorporation of Mt. Carmel Apartments, Inc., the board of directors accepted the agreement between Frey and Burge, placed a $70,000 value on his services performed prior to incorporation, and issued 12.5 percent of the corporation's shares to Burge. After a dispute arose between Burge and the corporation, Frey claimed that the corporation acted wrongly by issuing the shares to Burge. Was Frey correct?

8. Kenneth Bitting was a shareholder of Merrill Lynch, a national securities brokerage. Under Merrill Lynch's original articles of incorporation, all common shares were restricted against transfer. Under the terms of the articles, Merrill Lynch was granted an option to purchase the holder's shares at an adjusted net book value price upon the death of the holder. This transfer restriction was conspicuously noted on each share certificate. On October 8, 1970, Bitting died. Pursuant to its articles, Merrill Lynch exercised its option to purchase Bitting's shares from his estate. The executors of Bitting's estate argued that the restriction on transfer was not permitted by state corporation law and that even if it were permitted, it was not binding on them as transferees of Bitting's shares. Are the executors correct?

9. The shareholders of KBM, Inc., a close corporation, executed a shareholders agreement that required a shareholder who resigned his employment with the corporation to first offer to sell all his shares to the corporation at book value. If the corporation did not buy all the shares, the shareholder was required to offer the unpurchased shares to the other shareholders. If there were any remaining unsold shares, the shareholder and the corporation were required to attempt to negotiate a "sale mutually satisfactory to all parties." If no mutually satisfactory agreement could be reached, the corporation was to be dissolved and liquidated, and its assets distributed to shareholders. Is this agreement legal?

10. On June 1, 1973, Isle of Eden, Inc., failed to file annual reports with the secretary of state of Virginia and was automatically dissolved under Virginia corporation law. On June 20, 1974, the president and secretary of Isle of Eden signed a promissory note on behalf of Isle of Eden. Subsequent to the execution of the note, Isle of Eden filed annual reports and consequently was reinstated as a corporation. When the note was not paid on its due date, the noteholder sued the shareholders, directors, and officers of Isle of Eden for the amount of the note. Are they liable on the note?

11. Albert Martin and Raymond Martin were brothers, each owning 50 percent of Martin's News Service, Inc., a retail store selling newspapers, lottery tickets, and cigarettes. Beginning in 1973, they had difficulty working together, eventually communicating only through their accountant. Directors' and shareholders' meetings ceased. In 1983, Albert fell ill and was unable to work in the store. In December 1983, Albert sued for a judicial dissolution of the corporation. Will the court order dissolution?

CHAPTER 42

MANAGEMENT OF CORPORATIONS

INTRODUCTION

Although shareholders own a corporation, they traditionally have possessed no right to manage the business of the corporation. Instead, shareholders elect individuals to a **board of directors,** to which management is entrusted. Often, the board delegates much of its management responsibilities to officers.

In publicly held corporations, shareholders have no power or right to interfere with the legitimate managerial discretion of the board or the officers. In close corporations, however, some courts have granted shareholders some management authority. Modern close corporation statutes have gone so far as to grant the shareholders of a close corporation the option of dispensing with a board of directors and managing the corporation as if it were a partnership.

This chapter explains the legal aspects of the board's and officers' management of the corporation. While the board and officers have management authority, they do not possess unlimited management discretion. Their management of the corporation must be consistent with the objectives and powers of the corporation, and they owe duties to the corporation to manage it prudently and in the best interests of the corporation and the shareholders as a whole. In addition, under tort and criminal law, management owes duties to the persons with whom it deals on behalf of the corporation.

CORPORATE OBJECTIVES AND POWERS

Profit Objective

Management of a corporation must be *consistent with the objectives* of business corporations as stated by the courts and the legislatures. The traditional objective of the business corporation has been to *enhance corporate profits and shareholder gain*. According to this objective, the managers of a corporation must seek the accomplishment of the profit objective to the exclusion of all inconsistent goals. Other interests such as employee and customer welfare must be subordinated to the interest of corporate profits. Interests other than profit maximization may be considered, provided that they do not hinder the ultimate profit objective.

Other Objectives

Nonetheless, some courts have permitted corporations to take *socially responsible actions* that were *beyond the profit-maximization requirement*.[1] In addition, every state recognizes corporate powers that are not economically inspired.[2] For example, corporations may make

---

[1] Mangrum, "In Search of a Paradigm of Corporate Social Responsibility," 17 *Creighton L. Rev.* 21, 55–65 (1983).

[2] Id. at 66.

947

contributions to colleges, political campaigns, child abuse prevention centers, literary associations, and employee benefit plans, regardless of economic benefit to the corporations. Also, every state expressly recognizes the right of shareholders to choose freely the extent to which profit maximization captures all of their interests and all of their sense of responsibility.[3]

Presently management can freely choose to act socially responsible, even if there exists no likelihood of resulting profits. At the same time the corporation may choose to be strictly profit oriented.[4]

In the following case, the court held that the board acted improperly by failing to act to maximize shareholder profit.

---

[3]Id. at 68.

[4]Id. at 65.

REVLON, INC. v. MACANDREWS & FORBES HOLDINGS, INC.
506 A.2d 173 (Del. Sup. Ct. 1986)

In 1985, Pantry Pride, Inc., informed Revlon, Inc., of its intent to acquire Revlon. Pantry Pride planned to "bust up" Revlon after the acquisition by selling its various lines of businesses individually. Revlon's board of directors rejected Pantry Pride's plan. Nonetheless, Pantry Pride made a hostile takeover bid for Revlon's shares at $47.50 per share.

In response to Pantry Pride's bid, Revlon's board sought to reduce the number of shares Pantry Pride could acquire by repurchasing some of it shares in exchange for new Senior Notes. The contract with the new Senior Noteholders protected the noteholders with covenants limiting Revlon's ability to incur more debt, sell assets, or pay dividends. The covenants, however, could be waived by the board's independent directors.

When this defense failed to deter Pantry Pride, the board recognized that a takeover was inevitable. Consequently, the board agreed to a friendly acquisition by Forstmann Little & Co. for $56 per share. Realizing the inevitability of a bust-up, Revlon's board agreed to break up its assets by selling its cosmetic division; Forstmann planned to sell two other divisions after the purchase.

In addition, Revlon's independent directors agreed to waive the Senior Note covenants. As a result, the value of the Senior Notes dropped 12 percent. Angry Senior Noteholders threatened to sue Revlon's directors. Concerned about their personal liability to the Senior Noteholders, the Revlon directors amended their agreement with Forstmann. Forstmann increased its offer to $57.25 per share and agreed to support the value of the Senior Notes. In return, Revlon gave Forstmann a lock-up option, promising to sell two valuable divisions to Forstmann at nearly $200 million below their market value if Pantry Pride was successful in taking over Revlon.

Pantry Pride sued Revlon to invalidate the lock-up option as beyond the objectives of the corporation. The trial court enjoined Revlon's directors from making concessions to Forstmann. Revlon appealed to the Supreme Court of Delaware.

Moore, Justice. The lock-up with Forstmann had as its emphasis shoring up the market value of the Senior Notes. The directors made support of the Senior Notes an integral part of the company's dealings with Forstmann, even though their primary responsibility at this stage was to the shareholders.

The original threat posed by Pantry Pride—the break-up of the company—had become a reality that even the directors embraced. Selective dealing to fend off a hostile bidder was no longer a proper objective. Instead, obtaining the highest price for the benefit of the shareholders should have been the central theme guiding director action.

The Revlon board argued that it acted in good faith in protecting the Senior Noteholders because Delaware law permits consideration of other corporate constituencies. Although such considerations may be permissible, there are fundamental limitations upon that prerogative. A board may have regard for various constituencies, provided there are rationally related benefits accruing to the shareholders. However, such concern for non-shareholder interests is inappropriate when an auction among active bidders is in progress, and the object no longer is to protect or maintain the corporate enterprise but to sell it to the highest bidder.

Revlon also contended that it had contractual obligations to the Senior Noteholders. However, any such duties are limited to the principle that one may not interfere with contractual relationships by improper actions. Here the rights of the Senior Noteholders were fixed by agreement, and there is nothing to suggest that any of those terms were violated. The Senior Notes covenants specifically contemplated a waiver.

In granting an asset option lock-up to Forstmann, the directors allowed considerations other than the maximization of shareholder profit to affect their judgment to the ultimate detriment of shareholders. No such defensive measure can be sustained.

Judgment for Pantry Pride affirmed.

Corporate Constituency Statutes

The decision in the *Revlon* case prodded most of the states to enact **corporate constituency statutes,** which broaden the legal objectives of corporations. Such statutes permit or require directors to take into account the interests of constituencies other than shareholders. These statutes direct the board to act in the best interests of the corporation, not just the interests of the shareholders, and to maximize corporate profits *over the long term.* The new laws recognize that a corporation is a collection of interests working together for the purpose of producing goods and services at a profit, and that the goal of corporate profit maximization over the long term is not necessarily the same as the goal of stock price maximization over the short term. For an example of the new statutes, see the excerpt from the Indiana statute in Figure 1.

Corporate Powers

The actions of management are limited not only by the objectives of business corporations but also by the *powers* granted to business corporations. Such limitations may appear in the state statute, the articles of incorporation, and the bylaws.

State Statutes   The primary source of a corporation's powers is the corporation statute of the state in which it is incorporated. Some state corporation statutes ex-

---

FIGURE 1   Indiana Code 23-1-35-1

(d) A director may, in considering the best interests of a corporation, consider the effects of any action on shareholders, employees, suppliers, and customers of the corporation, and the communities in which offices or other facilities of the corporation are located, and any other factors the director considers pertinent.

(f) [D]irectors are not required to consider the effects of a proposed corporate action on any particular corporate constituent group or interest as a dominant or controlling factor.

---

pressly specify the powers of corporations. These powers include making gifts for charitable and educational purposes, lending money to corporate officers and directors, and purchasing and disposing of the corporation's shares. Other state corporation statutes limit the powers of corporations, such as prohibiting the acquisition of agricultural land by corporations.

Modern statutes attempt to authorize corporations to engage in *any* activity. Model Business Corporation Act (MBCA) Section 3.02 contains an extensive list of corporate powers, but the preamble to that list makes it clear that a corporation has the power to do *anything that an individual may do.*

Articles of Incorporation   Most corporation statutes require a corporation to state its purpose in its articles of incorporation. The purpose is usually phrased in broad terms, even if the corporation has been formed with only one type of business in mind. For example, a corporation formed to mine gold may have a purpose clause stating that it has been formed "to mine gold and to engage in any other lawful business." Such a corporation would not be limited by its articles of incorporation. Most corporations have purpose clauses stating that they may engage in any lawful business.

Under the MBCA, the inclusion of a purpose clause in the articles is optional. Also, any corporation incorporated under the MBCA has the purpose of engaging in any lawful business, unless the articles state a narrower purpose. Hence, under the MBCA, a corporation with no purpose clause in its articles may engage in any lawful business, thereby being able to do what any individual may do.

Nonetheless, the promoters or the shareholders may desire to use the statement of purpose as a self-imposed limitation. In such instances, the purpose clause states the express powers of the corporation and becomes a promise of the corporation to its shareholders that it will confine its business to those express powers and the powers that may be implied therefrom.

The *Ultra Vires* Doctrine Historically, an act of a corporation beyond its powers was a nullity, as it was *ultra vires*, which is Latin for *beyond the powers*. Therefore, any act not permitted by the corporation statute or by the corporation's articles of incorporation was void due to lack of capacity.

This lack of capacity or power of the corporation was a *defense to a contract* assertable either by the corporation or by the other party that dealt with the corporation. Often, *ultra vires* was merely a convenient justification for reneging on an agreement that was no longer considered desirable. This misuse of the doctrine has led to its near abandonment.

Today, the *ultra vires* doctrine is of small importance for two reasons. First, the MBCA and other modern business corporation statutes grant corporations broad powers, and nearly all drafters of articles of incorporation use broad purpose clauses, thereby preventing any *ultra vires* problem. Second, the MBCA and most other statutes do not permit a corporation or the other party to an agreement to avoid an obligation on the ground that the corporate action is *ultra vires*.

Under MBCA Section 3.04, *ultra vires* may be asserted by only three types of persons: (1) by a shareholder seeking to enjoin a corporation from executing a proposed action that is *ultra vires*, (2) by the corporation suing its management for damages caused by exceeding the corporation's powers, and (3) by the state's attorney general, who may have the power to enjoin an *ultra vires* act or to dissolve a corporation that exceeds its powers.

THE BOARD OF DIRECTORS

Introduction

Traditionally, the board of directors has had the power and the duty to manage the corporation. Yet in a large publicly held corporation, it is impossible for the board to manage the corporation on a day-to-day basis, since many of the directors are high-level executives in other corporations and devote most of their time to their other business interests. Therefore, MBCA Section 8.01 permits a corporation to be managed *under the direction of* the board of directors. Consequently, the board of directors delegates major responsibility for management to committees of the board such as an executive committee, to individual board members such as the chairman of the board, and to the officers of the corporation, especially the chief executive officer (CEO). In theory, the board supervises the actions of its committees, the chairman, and the officers to ensure that the board's policies are being carried out and that the delegatees are managing the corporation prudently. Figure 2 lists the results of a survey of directors concerning their primary responsibilities.

FIGURE 2   Primary Responsibilities of Directors

	Percent*
1. Assure integrity of corporation's operations	60%
2. Counsel top management	58
3. Assure strategic plan for the future	55
4. Monitor performance of the CEO	47
5. Assure management succession	43
6. Serve the public interest	15
7. Monitor financial reporting	9

*Percent of directors surveyed citing each responsibility.

Source: Survey of directors, published by Arthur Young Executive Resource Consultants in *The New Director: Changing Views of the Board's Role* (1989).

Board Powers under Corporation Statutes

By statute, the board of directors may take several corporate actions *by itself*, that is, without obtaining shareholder approval of the action. These powers include not only the board's general power to manage or direct the corporation, but also the power to issue shares of stock and to set the price of shares. Among its other powers, the board may repurchase shares, declare dividends, adopt and amend bylaws, elect and remove officers, and fill vacancies on the board.

Some corporate actions require *board initiative*. That is, board approval is necessary to *propose such actions to the shareholders* who then must approve the action. Board initiative is required for important changes in the corporation, such as amendment of the articles of incorporation; merger of the corporation; the sale of all or substantially all of the corporation's assets; and voluntary dissolution.

Committees of the Board

Most publicly held corporations have committees of the board of directors. These committees, which have fewer members than the board has, can more efficiently handle management decisions and exercise board powers than can a large board. Only directors may serve on board committees.

Although many board powers may be delegated to committees of the board, some decisions are so important that corporation statutes require their *approval by the board as a whole.* Under MBCA Section 8.25(e), the powers that may not be delegated concern important corporate actions such as declaring dividends, filling vacancies on the board or its committees, adopting and amending bylaws, approving issuances of shares, and approving repurchases of the corporation's shares.

Executive Committee   The most common board committee is the executive committee. It is usually given authority to act for the board on most matters when the board is not in session. Generally, it consists of the inside directors and perhaps one or two outside directors who can attend a meeting on short notice.[5] Historically, the executive committee has been the most important committee of the board. Today, its importance has diminished. It is likely to be used only for routine matters.

Other Committees   Other common board committees include audit, nominating, compensation, and shareholder litigation committees. The membership of these committees usually includes only outside directors in order to eliminate potential conflicts of interests that may exist if inside directors were to make decisions affecting their personal interests.

Audit committees recommend independent public accountants and supervise the public accountants' audit of the corporate financial records. The Securities and Exchange Commission (SEC) strongly encourages all publicly held firms to have audit committees comprising independent directors.

Nominating committees choose management's slate of directors that is to be submitted to shareholders at the annual election of directors. Nominating committees also often plan generally for management succession. The SEC encourages corporations to form nominating committees that wholly or largely comprise outside directors.

Compensation committees review and approve the salaries, bonuses, stock options, and other benefits of high-level corporate executives. Although compensation committees usually comprise directors who have no affiliation with the executives or directors whose compensation is being approved, compensation committees may also set the compensation of their members. Outside directors of most large publicly held firms are compensated by an annual retainer fee plus an attendance fee for each board or committee meeting attended. Figure 3 lists the nine corporations that pay the highest director's fees.

FIGURE 3   Highest Average Total Director Compensation for 1988

ITT	$86,400
Sears	63,200
General Motors	58,917
Ford	57,750
Coastal	57,600
Dow Chemical	57,000
USX	55,833
Citicorp	53,759
RJR Nabisco	53,750

Source: Spencer Stuart.

---

[5]The term *inside director* is applied to one who is an officer of a corporation or its affiliated corporation and devotes substantially full time to it. The term is also often applied to controlling shareholders who are not officers and to former officers. *Outside directors* have no such affiliations with the corporation.

A shareholder litigation committee is given the task of determining whether a corporation should sue someone who has allegedly harmed the corporation. Usually, the committee of disinterested directors is formed when a shareholder asks the board of directors to cause the corporation to sue some or all of the directors for mismanaging the corporation. The use of shareholder litigation committees is discussed more fully in the Shareholders' Rights and Liabilities chapter.

Powers, Rights, and Liabilities of Directors as Individuals

A director is not an agent of the corporation *merely* by being a director. The directors may manage the corporation only when they act as a board, unless the board of directors grants agency powers to the directors individually.

A director has the *right to inspect* corporate books and records that contain corporate information essential to the director's performance of her duties. The director's right of inspection is denied when the director has an interest adverse to the corporation, as in the case of a director who plans to sell a corporation's trade secrets to a competitor.

Normally, a director does not have any personal liability for the contracts and torts of the corporation.

ELECTION AND REMOVAL OF DIRECTORS

Qualifications of Directors

MBCA Section 8.02 states no qualifications for directors. Generally, any individual may serve as a director of a corporation. A director need not even be a shareholder. Nonetheless, a corporation is permitted to specify qualifications for directors in the articles of incorporation.

Number of Directors

A board of directors may not act unless it has the number of directors required by the state corporation law. MBCA Section 8.03 and several state corporation statutes require a minimum of one director, recognizing that in close corporations with a single shareholder-manager, additional board members are superfluous. Several statutes, including the New York statute, require at least three directors, unless there are fewer than three shareholders, in which case the corporation may have no fewer directors than it has shareholders.

A corporation may have more than the minimum number of directors required by the corporation statute. The articles of incorporation or bylaws will state the number of directors of the corporation. Most large publicly held corporations have boards with more than 10 members. For example, General Motors has 25, IBM has 24, and ITT has 13.

Election of Directors

Directors are elected by the shareholders at the annual shareholder meeting. Usually, each shareholder is permitted to vote for as many nominees as there are directors to be elected. The shareholder may cast as many votes for each nominee as he has shares. The top vote-getters among the nominees are elected as directors. This voting process, called **straight voting,** permits a holder of more than 50 percent of the shares of a corporation to dominate the corporation by electing a board of directors that will manage the corporation as he wants it to be managed.

Class Voting and Cumulative Voting   To avoid domination by a large shareholder, among other reasons, some corporations allow class voting or cumulative voting. **Class voting** may give certain classes of shareholders the right to elect a specified number of directors. **Cumulative voting** permits shareholders to multiply the number of their shares by the number of directors to be elected and to cast the resulting total of votes for one or more directors. As a result, cumulative voting may permit minority shareholders to obtain representation on the board of directors. Class voting, cumulative voting, and other shareholder voting rights are discussed in detail in the Shareholders' Rights and Liabilities chapter.

The Proxy Solicitation Process

Most individual investors purchase corporate shares in the public market to increase their wealth, not to elect or to influence the directors of corporations. Nearly all institutional investors—such as pension funds, mutual funds, and bank trust departments—have the same profit motive. Generally, they are passive investors with little interest in exercising their shareholder right to elect directors by attending shareholder meetings.

Once public ownership of the corporation's shares exceeds 50 percent, the corporation cannot conduct any business at its shareholder meetings unless some of the shares of these passive investors are voted. This is because the corporation will have a shareholder *quorum* requirement, which may require that 50 percent or more of the shares be voted for a shareholder vote to be valid. Since passive investors rarely attend shareholder meetings, the management of the corporation must solicit **proxies,**[6] if it wishes to have a valid shareholder vote. Shareholders who will not attend a shareholder meeting must be asked to appoint someone else to vote their shares for them. This is done by furnishing each such shareholder with a proxy to sign. The proxy designates a person who may vote the shares for the shareholder.

Management Solicitation of Proxies   To ensure its *perpetuation in office* and the *approval of other matters* submitted for a shareholder vote, the corporation's management solicits proxies from shareholders for directors' elections and other important matters on which shareholders vote, such as mergers. The management designates an officer, a director, or some other person to vote the proxies received. The person who is designated to vote for the shareholder is also called a *proxy.* Typically, the chief executive officer (CEO) of the corporation, the president, or the chairman of the board of directors names the person who serves as the proxy.

Usually, the proxies are merely signed and returned by the public shareholders, including the institutional shareholders. Passive investors follow the **Wall Street rule:** either support management or sell the shares. As a result, management almost always receives enough votes from its proxy solicitation to ensure the reelection of directors and the approval of other matters submitted to the shareholders, even when other parties solicit proxies in opposition to management.

Effect on Corporate Governance   Management's solicitation of proxies produces a result that is quite different from the theory of corporate management that directors serve as representatives of the shareholders. The CEO usually nominates directors of his choice, and they are almost always elected. The directors appoint officers chosen by the CEO. The CEO's nominees for director are not unduly critical of his programs or of his methods for carrying them out. This is particularly true if a large proportion of the directors are officers of the company and thus are more likely to be dominated by the CEO.

In such situations, the CEO, not the shareholders, selects the directors, and the CEO, not the board of directors, manages the corporation. Furthermore, the board of directors does not even function effectively as a representative of the shareholders in supervising and evaluating the CEO and the other officers of the corporation. The board members and the other officers, who are generally chosen by the CEO, are, in effect, subordinates of the CEO, even though, as is true in most publicly held corporations, the CEO is not a major shareholder of the corporation.

Improving Corporate Governance   Proposals for improving corporate governance in public-issue corporations seek to develop a board that is capable of functioning independently of the CEO by changing the composition or the operation of the board of directors.

Independent Directors   Some corporate governance critics propose that a federal agency such as the Securities and Exchange Commission appoint one or more directors to serve as watchdogs of the public interest. Other critics would require that shareholders elect at least a majority of directors without prior ties to the corporation, thus excluding shareholders, suppliers, and customers from the board. The New York Stock Exchange requires a minimum of two directors independent of management for its listed companies.

Codetermination   Under codetermination, employee representatives constitute one third or more of the board. The corporation has two boards: a *supervisory board,* on which the employee representatives sit with the shareholder representatives, and a *managing board,* composed solely of corporate officers. Codetermination developed in post–World War II Germany, and it has spread through several countries of the European Economic Community. Recently, several American corporations, of which Chrysler is the best known, have put one or more *labor union representatives* on their boards.

Director Nominations   Other proposals recommend changing the method by which directors are nominated for election. One proposal would encourage shareholders to make nominations for directors. Supporters of this proposal argue that in addition to reducing the influence of the CEO, it would also broaden the range of backgrounds represented on the board. The SEC recommends that publicly held corporations establish a nominating committee composed of outside directors. This proposal has broad support, and many publicly held corporations have already adopted it.

Board Staff   The American Law Institute's Corporate Governance Project recommends that nonmanage-

---

[6]A proxy is usually a preprinted data processing form (computer card) with spaces for voting on matters submitted for a shareholder vote. See the Securities Regulation chapter for a discussion of the proxy requirements of the U.S. Securities and Exchange Commission.

ment directors be empowered to hire, at the corporation's expense, lawyers, accountants, and other experts to advise them on extraordinary problems arising in the exercise of their oversight function. By not relying on the CEO's staff, the board should be better able to exercise independent judgment.

Specialist Directors Ralph Nader and his associates propose that each board member be assigned to, if not especially chosen for, a special area of oversight responsibility, such as employee welfare, consumer protection, and environmental protection. Assignment of specific responsibilities to board committees would make the board of directors better informed and permit it to function more effectively.

Impact of Corporate Governance Proposals Mostly due to SEC and public pressures for changes in corporate governance, current boards of directors operate significantly differently from the boards of the 1960s and the early 1970s. Boards supervise officers more closely. More directors are outside rather than inside directors. Boards meet more frequently, and more important, they have working committees that assume specific responsibilities. In addition, today's directors *perceive* themselves as being more nearly independent of the CEO. As a consequence, they *are* more nearly independent of the CEO. See Figure 4.

FIGURE 4 Influence of Board on Key Management Decisions

	Strong*	Moderate*	None or Unknown*
Compensation of top management	71%	27%	2%
Mergers and acquisitions	62	33	5
Capital expenditures	32	60	8
Selection of senior executives	22	64	14
Long-range planning	21	70	9

*Percentage of directors surveyed citing the board's influence as strong, moderate, none, or unknown.

Source: Arthur Young Executive Resource Consultants survey of directors published in *The New Director: Changing Views of the Board's Role (1989).*

Term of Office

Directors usually hold office for only one year, but they may have longer terms. MBCA Section 8.06 permits *staggered terms* for directors. A corporation having a board of nine or more members may establish either two or three approximately equal classes of directors, with only one class of directors coming up for election at each annual shareholders' meeting. If there are two classes of directors, the directors serve two-year terms; if there are three classes, they serve three-year terms.

The original purpose of staggered terms was to permit continuity of management. Today, staggered terms are frequently used to make it difficult to remove existing directors. Someone who wants to replace management must mount successful proxy solicitation fights several years in a row. Staggered terms also frustrate the ability of minority shareholders to use cumulative voting to elect their representatives to the board of directors.

Vacancies on the Board

MBCA Section 8.10 permits the directors to fill vacancies on the board. A majority vote of the remaining directors is sufficient to select persons to serve out unexpired terms, even though the remaining directors are less than a quorum.[7]

Removal of Directors

Modern corporation statutes permit shareholders to remove directors *with or without cause*, unless the articles provide that directors may be removed only for cause. The rationale for the modern rule is that the shareholders should have the power to judge the fitness of directors at any time.

Most corporations have provisions in their articles authorizing the shareholders to remove directors *only for cause.* Cause for removal would include mismanagement or conflicts of interest. Before removal for cause, the director must be given notice and an opportunity for a hearing.

If a director has been elected by a class of shareholders or through cumulative voting, different rules apply.

---

[7]A quorum of directors is usually a majority of directors. Quorum requirements are discussed later in this chapter.

A director elected by a separate class of shareholders may be removed only by that class of shareholders, thereby protecting the voting rights of the class. A director elected by cumulative voting may not be removed if the votes cast against her removal would have been sufficient to elect her to the board, thereby protecting the voting rights of minority shareholders.

In the following case, a director—a minority shareholder—would not have been removed as a director had there been cumulative voting of shares.

LEHMAN v. PIONTKOWSKI

460 N.Y.S.2d 817 (N.Y. App. Div. 1983)

Jacob Lehman and Shlomo Piontkowski were surgeons who practiced together in a professional corporation. They were the directors and only shareholders, Lehman owning six shares and Piontkowski owning four shares. Each was an employee of the corporation. Piontkowski's employment contract granted to the board of directors of the corporation the power to terminate his employment for "personal misconduct of such a material nature as to be professionally detrimental to the corporation."

From 1977 to 1979, Lehman and Piontkowski disagreed on the distribution of the corporation's income. Dissatisfied with his share of the income, Piontkowski canceled surgery, informed his patients that he was on vacation, and planned to open his own office nearby.

Acting as president of the corporation, Lehman sent Piontkowski a letter stating that Piontkowski's actions violated his employment contract. As president, Lehman stated that he deemed these actions to be personal misconduct so material as to be professionally detrimental to the corporation.

At a special shareholder meeting, Lehman proposed that Piontkowski be removed as a director and voted his six shares to oust Piontkowski. Piontkowski did not vote his four shares. Lehman then nominated himself as sole director, voted his shares to elect himself sole director, and adjourned the shareholder meeting. Lehman then called the special directors' meeting to order and, as the sole director, dismissed Piontkowski as an employee.

Afterward, Lehman and the corporation sued Piontkowski, seeking to recover damages of $500,000 for Piontkowski's breach of contract by opening a competing medical practice. Piontkowski argued that his expulsion from the corporation was illegal and that therefore the corporation was not entitled to enforce the contract. The trial court denied Piontkowski's motion for summary judgment, and Piontkowski appealed.

Memorandum by the Court.   Piontkowski's expulsion as director and the termination of his employment were improper.

By letter, Piontkowski was informed that Lehman, as president, deemed Piontkowski's actions to be personal misconduct that was so material as to be professionally detrimental to the corporation. This opinion was not that of the board of directors, as was required by the employment contract, but rather was that of Lehman individually and as president of the corporation. The board had not formally met to make a determination that Piontkowski had committed detrimental misconduct as a material breach of the contract. Therefore, the letter was of no legal effect.

At the special shareholder meeting, Lehman's first order of business was to vote his majority of the shares to dismiss Piontkowski as a director. Such an act was of no effect in the present matter. The New York Business Corporation Law provides that "the number of directors . . . shall not be less than three, except that where all the shares of a corporation are owned . . . by less than three shareholders, the number of directors may be less than three but not less than the number of shareholders."

Here there were two shareholders at the commencement of the special shareholder meeting. Piontkowski's expulsion as a director and the election of Lehman as the sole director were therefore improper. The removal of Piontkowski as a director left the corporation with only one director and without a validly constituted board of directors. The New York statute prohibits such an occurrence. The subsequent act of an illegally constituted one-man board of directors in terminating Piontkowski's employment was invalid.

As Piontkowski's unilateral expulsion from the corporation was illegal, the corporation is not entitled to enforce Piontkowski's employment contract.

Judgment reversed in favor of Piontkowski.

DIRECTORS' MEETINGS

Traditionally, directors could act only when they were properly convened as a board. They could not vote by proxy or informally, as by telephone. This rule was based on a belief in the value of consultation and collective judgment.

Today, the corporation laws of a majority of the states and MBCA Section 8.21 specifically permit action by the directors without a meeting if all of the directors consent in writing to the action taken. Such authorization is useful for dealing with routine matters or for formally approving an action based on an earlier policy decision made after full discussion. Close corporations are more likely to take advantage of this method of action than are large public corporations that hold monthly meetings of the board.

MBCA Section 8.20 permits a board to meet by telephone or television hookup. This section permits a meeting of directors who may otherwise be unable to convene. The only requirement is that the directors be able to hear one another simultaneously.

Directors are entitled to reasonable notice of all *special* meetings, but not of regularly scheduled meetings. Most of the corporation statutes require that the notice for a special meeting state the purpose of the meeting, but the MBCA does not. A director's attendance at a meeting *waives* any required notice, unless at the beginning of the meeting the director objects to the lack of notice.

For the directors to act, a *quorum* of the directors must be present. The quorum requirement ensures that the decision of the board will represent the views of a substantial portion of the directors. MBCA Section 8.24 provides that a quorum shall be a *majority* of the number of directors, unless the articles or bylaws states a number that is no fewer than one third of the number of directors.

Each director has *one vote*. If a quorum is present, a vote of a majority of the directors present is an act of the board, unless the articles or the bylaws require the vote of a greater number of directors. Such *supermajority voting provisions* are common in close corporations but not in publicly held corporations. The use of supermajority voting provisions by close corporations is covered later in this chapter.

OFFICERS OF THE CORPORATION

Appointment of Officers

The board of directors has the authority to appoint the officers of the corporation. Most of the corporation statutes provide that the officers of a corporation shall be the *president*, one or more *vice presidents*, a *secretary*, and a *treasurer*. Some of the statutes permit fewer than four officers, and most allow more than four. Usually, any two or more offices may be held by the same person, except for the offices of president and secretary. Since some corporate documents must be signed by both the president and the secretary, the prohibition against having one person hold both offices provides a measure of safety by ensuring that no single individual can execute such documents.

MBCA Section 8.40 grants the corporation unusual flexibility in determining the number of its officers. The section requires only that there be an officer performing the duties normally granted to a corporate secretary. Under the MBCA, one person may hold several offices, including the offices of president and secretary.

Authority of Officers

The officers are agents of the corporation. As agents, officers have *express authority* conferred on them by the bylaws or the board of directors. In addition, officers have *implied authority* to do the things that are reasonably necessary to accomplish their express duties. Also, officers have *apparent authority* when the corporation leads third parties to believe reasonably that the officers have authority to act for the corporation. Like any principal, the corporation may *ratify* the unauthorized acts of its officers. This may be done expressly by a resolution of the board of directors or impliedly by the board's acceptance of the benefits of the officer's acts.

Inherent Authority   The most perplexing issue with regard to the authority of officers is whether an officer has *inherent authority* merely by virtue of the title of his office. Courts have held that certain *official titles confer authority* on officers, but such powers are much more restricted than you might expect.

Traditionally, a *president* possesses no power to bind the corporation by virtue of the office. Instead, she serves merely as the presiding officer at shareholder meetings and directors' meetings. Fewer problems arise in assessing the authority of a president with an additional title such as *general manager* or *chief executive officer*. Titles of this kind give the officer broad implied authority to make contracts and to do other acts in the ordinary business of the corporation.

A *vice president* has no authority by virtue of that office. An executive who is vice president of a specified department, however, such as a vice president of marketing, will have the authority to transact the normal corporate business falling within the function of the department.

The *secretary* usually keeps the minutes of directors' and shareholder meetings, maintains other corporate records, retains custody of the corporate seal, and certifies corporate records as being authentic. The secretary has no authority to make contracts for the corporation by virtue of that office. Nonetheless, the corporation is bound by documents certified by the secretary. For example, a corporation is bound by a board resolution certified by the secretary stating the president's authority to contract for the corporation even if the resolution was not properly adopted by the board.

The *treasurer* has custody of the corporation's funds. He is the proper officer to receive payments to the corporation and to disburse corporate funds for authorized purposes. The treasurer binds the corporation by his receipts, checks, and indorsements, but he does not by virtue of that office alone have authority to borrow money, to issue negotiable instruments, or to make other contracts on behalf of the corporation.

Officer Liability   Like any agent, a corporate officer ordinarily has *no liability on contracts* that she makes on behalf of her principal, the corporation. To avoid personal liability on corporate contracts, an officer should make clear that she signs for the corporation and not in her individual capacity. However, an officer who acts within her apparent authority, but beyond her actual authority, will be liable to the corporation for resulting losses for *exceeding her actual authority.*

Employees of the corporation who are not officers may also be empowered to act as agents for the corporation. The usual rules of agency apply to their relationships with the corporation and with third parties.

Termination of Officers   Officers serve the corporation at the pleasure of the board of directors, which may remove an officer at any time with or without cause. An officer who has been removed without cause has no recourse against the corporation, unless the removal violates an employment contract between the officer and the corporation.

MANAGING CLOSE CORPORATIONS

Many of the management formalities that you have studied in this chapter are appropriate for publicly held corporations, yet inappropriate for close corporations. Close corporations tend to be more loosely managed than public corporations. For example, they may have few board meetings. Frequently, each shareholder wants to be involved in management of the close corporation, or if he is not involved in management, he wants to protect his interests by placing *restrictions on the managerial discretion* of those who do manage the corporation.

Initially, courts struggled with the management problems of close corporations, attempting to solve those problems by applying traditional corporation law, which was designed with the publicly held corporation in mind. In recent years, however, courts and legislatures have adopted rules that respond to the special management problems of close corporations. These rules are designed to *reduce management formalities* and to *prevent the domination of minority shareholders*.

Reducing Management Formalities

Modern close corporation statutes permit close corporations to dispense with most, if not all, management formalities. Section 10 of the Statutory Close Corporation Supplement to the MBCA permits a close corporation to *dispense with a board of directors* and to be *managed by the shareholders*. California General Corporation Law Section 300 permits the close corporation to be managed *as if it were a partnership*.

Preventing Domination

A minority shareholder of a close corporation may be dominated by the shareholders who control the board of directors. These shareholders may dominate by dismissing the dominated shareholder as an employee or by paying her a lower salary than is paid to the dominating shareholder-employees. To prevent such domination, close corporation shareholders have resorted to two devices: *supermajority voting requirements* for board actions and *restrictions on the managerial discretion* of the board of directors.

Supermajority Director Voting Any corporation may require that board action be possible only with the approval of more than a majority of the directors, such as three fourths or unanimous approval. Supermajority voting requirements are uncommon in publicly held corporations, but their ability to protect valuable interests of minority shareholders makes their use in close corporations almost mandatory. A supermajority vote is often required to terminate the employment contract of an employee-shareholder, to reduce the level of dividends, and to change the corporation's line of business. Supermajority votes are rarely required for ordinary business matters, such as deciding with which suppliers the corporation should deal.

Restrictions on Board Discretion Traditionally, shareholders could not restrict the managerial discretion of directors. This rule recognized the traditional roles of the board as manager and of the shareholders as passive owners. Modern close corporation statutes permit shareholders to intrude into the sanctity of the boardroom. In Section 11, the Statutory Close Corporation Supplement grants the shareholders *unlimited* power to restrict the discretion of the board of directors. For example, the shareholders may agree that the directors may not fire or reduce the salaries of employee-shareholders and may not lower or eliminate dividends. And, as was stated above, close corporation statutes even permit the shareholders to dispense with a board of directors altogether and to manage the close corporation as if it were a partnership.

DIRECTORS' AND OFFICERS' DUTIES TO THE CORPORATION

Introduction

Directors and officers are in positions of trust and therefore owe *fiduciary duties* to the corporation. These duties are similar to the duties that an agent owes his principal. They are the duties to act within the authority of the position and within the objectives and powers of the corporation, to act with due care in conducting the affairs of the corporation, and to act with loyalty to the corporation.

Acting within Authority

Like any agent, an officer or director has a duty to act *within the authority* conferred on her by the articles of incorporation, the bylaws, and the board of directors. As discussed above in the section on corporate objectives, ordinarily the directors and officers must manage the corporation in the best interests of the corporation. In addition, as discussed in the section on the *ultra vires* doctrine, the directors and officers must act within the scope of the powers of the corporation. An officer or a director may be liable to the corporation if it is damaged by an act exceeding that person's or the corporation's authority.

Duty of Care

Directors and officers are liable for losses to the corporation resulting from their lack of *care or diligence*. MBCA Sections 8.30 and 8.42 are typical of modern statutes, which expressly state the standard of care that

---

FIGURE 5   MBCA Section 8.30

(a) A director shall discharge his duties as a director, including his duties as a member of a committee:
   (1) in good faith;
   (2) with the care an ordinarily prudent person in a like position would exercise under similar circumstances; and
   (3) in a manner he reasonably believes to be in the best interests of the corporation.

FIGURE 6   MBCA Section 2.02

(b) The articles of incorporation may set forth:
   (4) a provision eliminating or limiting the liability of a director to the corporation or its shareholders for money damages for any action taken or any failure to take any action, as a director, except liability for
    (A) the amount of financial benefit received by a director to which he is not entitled;
    (B) an intentional infliction of harm on the corporation or the shareholders;
    (C) a violation of Section 8.33 [illegal payment of dividends]; or
    (D) an intentional violation of criminal law.

---

must be exercised by directors and officers. Section 8.30 appears in Figure 5.

Prudent Person Standard   Managers need merely meet the standard of the ordinarily prudent *person* in the same circumstances, a standard focusing on the basic manager attributes of common sense, practical wisdom, and informed judgment. The duty of care does *not* hold directors and officers to the standard of a prudent businessperson, a person of some undefined level of business skill. A director's or officer's performance is evaluated at the time of the decision, thereby preventing the application of hindsight in judging her performance.

Good Faith and Reasonable Belief   The MBCA duty of care test requires that a director or officer make a *reasonable investigation* and *honestly believe* that her decision is in the best interests of the corporation. For example, the board of directors decides to purchase an existing manufacturing business for $15 million without inquiring into the value of the business or examining its past financial performance. Although the directors may believe that they made a prudent decision, they have no reasonable basis for that belief. Therefore, if the plant is worth only $5 million, the directors will be liable to the corporation for its damages—$10 million—for breaching the duty of care.

Recent Changes   In response to insurance companies' increasing unwillingness to insure directors and officers for breaches of their duty of care (and the resulting exodus of outside directors from corporate boards of directors), many state legislatures changed the wording of the duty of care, typically imposing liability only for willful or wanton misconduct or for gross negligence. While seemingly changing the duty of care, most of the changes are largely window dressing and nonsubstan-

tive, since courts—applying the business judgment rule—have imposed liability only for grossly negligent decisions. The business judgment rule is discussed in detail in the next section.

Changes in some statutes, however, are more substantial. For example, Ohio protects directors from monetary liability except when clear and convincing evidence demonstrates the directors' deliberate intent to injure the corporation or the directors' reckless disregard for its welfare. Delaware corporation law and MBCA Section 2.02(b)(4) allow corporations to amend their articles to reduce or eliminate directors' liability for monetary damages for breaches of the duty of care. Figure 6 contains the MBCA provision.

The Business Judgment Rule

Absent bad faith, fraud, or breach of fiduciary duty, the judgment of the board of directors is conclusive. This is the **business judgment rule.** When directors and officers have complied with the business judgment rule, they are protected from liability to the corporation for their unwise decisions. The business judgment rule precludes the courts from substituting their business judgment for that of the corporation's managers. The business judgment rule recognizes that the directors and officers—not the shareholders and the courts—are best able to make business judgments and should not ordinarily be vulnerable to second-guessing. Shareholders and the courts are ill-equipped to make better business decisions than those made by the officers and directors of a corporation, who have more business experience and are more familiar with the needs, strengths, and limitations of the corporation.

Purpose of Business Judgment Rule

The business judgment rule is designed to encourage persons to become corporate managers and to encourage them to make difficult business decisions. Boards of directors and officers continually make decisions involving the balancing of risks and benefits to the corporation. With the advantage of hindsight, some of these decisions may appear unwise. Such a result, however, should not by itself provide the basis for imposing personal liability on directors and officers.

Elements of the Business Judgment Rule

Three requirements must be met for the business judgment rule to protect a manager from liability:

1. The manager must make an informed decision.
2. The manager may have no conflicts of interest.
3. The manager must have a rational basis for his decision.

Managers must make an *informed decision.* They must take the steps necessary to become informed about the relevant facts before making a decision. These steps may include merely listening to a proposal, reviewing written materials, or making inquiries. Managers may rely on information collected and presented by other persons. In essence, the informed-decision component means that managers should do their homework if they want the protection of the business judgment rule.

Managers must be *free from conflicts of interest.* The managers may not benefit personally—other than as shareholders—when they transact on behalf of the corporation.

Managers must have a *rational basis* for believing that the decision is in the best interests of the corporation. This is the most difficult element to understand, for it seemingly contradicts the most fundamental aspect of the business judgment rule, namely, that the courts may not judge the correctness, wisdom, or reasonableness of the managers' decision.

Based on courts' statements of the business judgment rule, it appears that the rational basis element requires only that the managers' decision have a *logical connection to the facts* revealed by a reasonable investigation or that the decision *not be manifestly unreasonable.* Some courts have held that the directors' wrongdoing must amount to *gross negligence* for the directors to lose the protection of the business judgment rule.

When Business Judgment Rule Is Inapplicable

If the business judgment rule *does not apply* because one or more of its elements are missing, a court may *substitute its judgment* for that of the managers. If the court finds that the managers made an unwise decision that harmed the corporation, it may impose liability on the managers and order them to pay damages to the corporation. In addition, the court may award equitable relief, such as an injunction or rescission of the wrongful action.

Nonetheless, courts rarely refuse to apply the business judgment rule. As a result, the rule has been criticized frequently as providing too much protection for the managers of corporations. In one famous case, the court applied the business judgment rule to protect a 1965 decision made by the board of directors of the Chicago Cubs not to install lights and not to hold night baseball games at Wrigley Field.[8] Yet the business judgment rule is so flexible that it protected the decision of the Cubs' board of directors to install lights in 1988. The *Van Gorkom* case, noted in Figure 7, is one of the few cases that have held directors liable for failing to comply with the business judgment rule.

---

[8]*Shlensky v. Wrigley,* 237 N.E.2d 776 (Ill. Ct. App. 1968).

FIGURE 7 Note on *Smith v. Van Gorkom**

In *Smith v. Van Gorkom* (also referred to as the *Trans Union* case), the Supreme Court of Delaware seemingly limited the scope of protection of the business judgment rule. In that case, the court found that the business judgment rule did not apply to the board's approval of an acquisition of the corporation for $55 per share. The board approved the acquisition after only two hours' consideration. The board received no documentation to support the adequacy of the $55 price. Instead, it relied entirely on a 20-minute *oral* report of the chairman of the board. No written summary of the acquisition was presented to the board. The directors failed to obtain an investment banker's report, prepared after careful consideration, that the acquisition price was fair.

*488 A.2d 858 (Del. Sup. Ct. 1985).

FIGURE 7   *(concluded)*

In addition, the court held that the mere fact that the acquisition price exceeded the market price by $17 per share did not legitimize the board's decision. The board had frequently made statements prior to the acquisition that the market had undervalued the shares, yet the board took no steps to determine the intrinsic value of the shares. Consequently, the court found that at a minimum, the directors had been grossly negligent.

Van Gorkom has been heralded as restricting the application of the business judgment rule and imposing higher standards on directors. It is the only case in which the directors have been held personally liable for damages for selling the company at a large cash premium over market price. On the other hand, *Van Gorkom* has been described as "surely one of the worst decisions in the history of corporate law."[†] The increased unwillingness of insurance companies to insure directors and officers for breaches of the duty of care is in part due to the *Van Gorkom* decision. The decision is also at least partly responsible for recent state legislation limiting the liability of directors for violating the duty of care.

†Fischel, *The Business Judgment Rule and the Trans Union Case*, 40 Bus. Law. 1437, 1455 (1985).

Opposition to Acquisition of Control of a Corporation

In the last 25 years, many outsiders have attempted to acquire control of publicly held corporations. Typically, these outsiders (called **raiders**) will make a **tender offer** for the shares of a corporation (called the **target**). A tender offer is an offer to the shareholders to buy their shares at a price above the current market price. The raider hopes to acquire a majority of the shares, which will give it control of the target corporation.[9]

Most tender offers are opposed by the target corporation's management. The defenses to tender offers are many and varied, and they carry interesting names, such as the Pac-Man defense, the white knight, greenmail, the poison pill, and the lock-up option. See Figure 8 for definitions of these defenses.

When takeover defenses are successful, shareholders of the target may lose the opportunity to sell their shares at a price up to twice the market price of the shares prior to the announcement of the hostile bid. Frequently, the loss of this opportunity upsets shareholders, who then decide to sue the directors who have opposed the tender offer. Shareholders contend that the directors have opposed the tender offer only to preserve their corporate positions. Shareholders also argue that the target corporation's interests would have been better served if the tender offer had succeeded.

Generally, courts have refused to find directors liable for opposing a tender offer because the business judgment rule applies to a board's decision to oppose a tender offer, provided the board made an informed decision, had no conflicts of interest, and had a rational basis for its decision to oppose the tender offer. Many courts have held that directors are able to separate their interest in remaining directors from the best interests of the corporation. Therefore, a conflict of interest does not arise automatically when directors oppose a tender offer.

Nonetheless, the business judgment rule will not apply when the directors make a decision to oppose the tender offer before they have carefully studied it. In addition, if the directors' actions indicate that they opposed the tender offer in order to preserve their jobs, they will be liable to the corporation.

Recent court decisions have seemingly modified the business judgment rule as it is applied in the tender offer context. For example, a May 1985 decision of the Delaware Supreme Court, *Unocal Corp. v. Mesa Petroleum Co.*,[10] upheld the application of the business judgment rule to a board's decision to block a hostile tender offer by making a tender offer for its own shares that excluded the raider.[11] But in so ruling, the court held that the board does not have "unbridled discretion to defeat any perceived threat by any Draconian means available," but may use those defense tactics that are *reasonable* compared to the takeover threat. The board may consider a variety of concerns, including the "inadequacy of the price offered, nature and timing of the offer, questions of illegality, the

---

[9]Tender offer regulation is covered in the Securities Regulation chapter.

[10]493 A.2d 946 (Del. Sup. Ct. 1985).

[11]Discriminatory tender offers are now illegal pursuant to Securities Act Rule 13e-4. The rules regarding tender offers are addressed in the Securities Regulation chapter.

FIGURE 8   Tender Offer Defenses

Pac-Man

The target corporation turns the tables on the tender offeror or raider (which often is another publicly held corporation) by making a tender offer for the raider's shares. As a result, two tender offerors are trying to buy each other's shares. This is similar to the Pac-Man video game, in which Pac-Man and his enemies chase each other.

Greenmail

The target's repurchase of its shares from the raider at a substantial profit to the raider, upon the condition that the raider sign a standstill agreement in which it promises not to buy additional shares of the target for a stated period of time.

White Knight

A friendly tender offeror whom management prefers over the original tender offeror–called a black knight. The white knight rescues the corporation from the black knight (the raider) by offering more money for the corporation's shares. In the *Revlon* case that appeared earlier in the chapter, Forstmann was a white knight for Revlon.

Lock-Up Option

Used in conjunction with a white knight to ensure the success of the white knight's bid. The target and the white knight agree that the white knight will buy a highly valuable asset of the target at a very attractive price for the white knight (usually a below-market price) if the raider succeeds in taking over the target. For example, in the *Revlon* case, Revlon gave a lock-up option to Forstmann to reduce the amount of profit that Pantry Pride would make had it completed its takeover of Revlon.

Poison Pill

Also called a shareholders' rights plan. There are many types, but the typical poison pill involves the target's issuance of a new class of preferred shares to its common shareholders. The preferred shares have rights (share options) attached to them. These rights allow the target's shareholders to purchase shares of the raider or shares of the target at less than fair market value. The poison pill deters hostile takeover attempts by threatening the raider and its shareholders with severe dilutions in the value of the shares they hold.

impact on 'constituencies' other than shareholders (i.e., creditors, customers, employees, and perhaps even the community generally), the risk of nonconsummation, and the quality of securities being offered in the exchange."[12]

In *Unocal*, the threat was a two-tier, highly coercive tender offer. In the typical two-tier offer, the raider first offers cash for a majority of the shares. After acquiring a majority of the shares, the offeror initiates the second tier, in which the remaining shareholders are forced to sell their shares for a package of securities less attractive than the first tier. Because shareholders fear that they will be forced to take the less attractive second-tier securities if they fail to tender during the first tier, shareholders—including those who oppose the offer—are coerced in to tendering during the first tier. *Unocal* and later cases specifically authorize the use of defenses to defeat a coercive two-tier tender offer.

Since its decision in *Unocal*, the Supreme Court of Delaware has applied this modified business judgment rule to validate a poison pill tender offer defense tactic in *Moran v. Household Int'l, Inc.*[13] and to invalidate a lock-up option tender offer defense in the *Revlon* case, which appears earlier in this chapter. These cases confirmed the *Unocal* holding that the board of directors must show that:

1. It had reasonable grounds to believe that a danger to corporate policy and effectiveness was posed by the takeover attempt.

2. It acted primarily to protect the corporation and its shareholders from that danger.

3. The defense tactic was reasonable in relation to the threat posed to the corporation.

Such a standard appeared to impose a higher standard on directors than the rational basis requirement of

---

[12]493 A.2d at 955.

[13]500 A.2d 346 (Del. Sup. Ct. 1985).

the business judgment rule, which historically has been interpreted to require only that a decision of a board not be manifestly unreasonable. In addition, the *Revlon* case required the board to establish an auction market for the company and to sell it to the highest bidder when the directors have abandoned the long-term business objectives of the company by embracing a bust-up of the company.

In 1990, in the following case, the Supreme Court of Delaware expanded board discretion in fighting hostile takeovers, holding that a board may oppose a hostile takeover provided the board had a *pre-existing, deliberately conceived corporate plan* justifying its opposition. The existence of such a plan enabled Time's board to meet the rational-basis element of the business judgment rule.

PARAMOUNT COMMUNICATIONS, INC. v. TIME, INC.

571 A.2d 1140 (Del. Sup. Ct. 1989)

Since 1983, Time, Inc., had considered expanding its business beyond publishing magazines and books, owning Home Box Office and Cinemax, and operating television stations. In 1988, Time's board approved in principle a strategic plan for Time's acquisition of an entertainment company. The board gave management permission to negotiate a merger with Warner Communications, Inc. The board's consensus was that a merger of Time and Warner was feasible, but only if Time controlled the resulting corporation, preserving the editorial integrity of Time's magazines. The board concluded that Warner was the superior candidate because Warner could make movies and TV shows for HBO, Warner had an international distribution system, Warner was a giant in the music business, Time and Warner would control half of New York City's cable TV system, and the Time network could promote Warner's movies.

Negotiations with Warner broke down when Warner refused to agree to Time dominating the combined companies. Time continued to seek expansion, but informal discussions with other companies terminated when it was suggested the other companies purchase Time or control the resulting board. In January 1989, Warner and Time resumed negotiations, and on March 4, 1989, agreed to a combination by which Warner shareholders would own 62 percent of the resulting corporation, to be named Time-Warner. To retain the editorial integrity of Time, the merger agreement provided for a board committee dominated by Time representatives.

On June 7, 1989, Paramount Communications, Inc., announced a cash tender offer for all of Time's shares at $175 per share. (The day before, Time shares traded at $126 per share.) Time's financial advisers informed the outside directors that Time's auction value was materially higher than $175 per share. The board concluded that Paramount's $175 offer was inadequate. Also, the board viewed the Paramount offer as a threat to Time's control of its own destiny and retention of the Time editorial policy; the board found that a combination with Warner offered greater potential for Time.

In addition, concerned that shareholders would not comprehend the long-term benefits of the merger with Warner, on June 16, 1989, Time's board recast its acquisition with Warner into a two-tier acquisition, in which it would make a tender offer to buy 51 percent of Warner's shares for cash immediately and later buy the remaining 49 percent for cash and securities. The tender offer would eliminate the need for Time to obtain shareholder approval of the transaction.

On June 23, 1989, Paramount raised its offer to $200 per Time share. Three days later, Time's board rejected the offer as a threat to Time's survival and its editorial integrity; the board viewed the Warner acquisition as offering greater long-term value for the shareholders. Time shareholders and Paramount then sued Time and its board to enjoin Time's acquisition of Warner. The trial court held for Time. Paramount and Time shareholders appealed to the Supreme Court of Delaware.

Horsey, Justice.   Our decision does not require us to pass on the wisdom of the board's decision. That is not a court's task. Our task is simply to determine whether there is sufficient evidence to support the initial Time-Warner agreement as the product of a proper exercise of business judgment.

We have purposely detailed the evidence of the Time board's deliberative approach, beginning in 1983–84, to expand itself. Time's decision in 1988 to combine with Warner was made only after what could be fairly characterized as an exhaustive appraisal of Time's future as a corporation. Time's board was convinced that Warner would provide the best fit for Time to achieve its strategic objectives. The record attests to the zealousness of Time's executives, fully supported by their directors, in seeing to the preservation of Time's perceived editorial integrity in journalism. The Time board's decision to expand the business of the company through its March 4 merger with Warner was entitled to the protection of the business judgment rule.

The revised June 16 agreement was defense-motivated and designed to avoid the potentially disruptive effect that Paramount's offer would have had on consummation of the proposed merger were it put to a shareholder vote. Thus, we decline to apply the traditional business judgment rule to the revised transaction and instead analyze the Time board's June 16 decision under *Unocal*.

In *Unocal*, we held that before the business judgment rule is applied to a board's adoption of a defensive measure, the burden will lie with the board to prove (a) reasonable grounds for believing that a danger to corporate policy and effectiveness existed; and (b) that the defensive measure adopted was reasonable in relation to the threat posed.

Paramount argues a hostile tender offer can pose only two types of threats: the threat of coercion that results from a two-tier offer promising unequal treatment for nontendering shareholders; and the threat of inadequate value from an all-shares, all-cash offer at a price below what a target board in good faith deems to be the present value of its shares.

Paramount would have us hold that only if the value of Paramount's offer were determined to be clearly inferior to the value created by management's plan to merge with Warner could the offer be viewed—objectively—as a threat.

Paramount's position represents a fundamental misconception of our standard of review under *Unocal* principally because it would involve the court in substituting its judgment as to what is a "better" deal for that of a corporation's board of directors. The usefulness of *Unocal* as an analytical tool is precisely its flexibility in the face of a variety of fact scenarios. Thus, directors may consider, when evaluating the threat posed by a takeover bid, the inadequacy of the price offered, nature and timing of the offer, questions of illegality, the impact on constituencies other than shareholders, the risk of nonconsummation, and the quality of securities being offered in the exchange.

The Time board reasonably determined that inadequate value was not the only threat that Paramount's all-cash, all-shares offer could present. Time's board concluded that Paramount's offer posed other threats. One concern was that Time shareholders might elect to tender into Paramount's cash offer in ignorance or a mistaken belief of the strategic benefit which a business combination with Warner might produce.

Paramount also contends that Time's board had not duly investigated Paramount's offer. We find that Time explored the available entertainment companies, including Paramount, before determining that Warner provided the best strategic "fit." In addition, Time's board rejected Paramount's offer because Paramount did not serve Time's objectives or meet Time's needs. Time's board was adequately informed of the potential benefits of a transaction with Paramount. Time's failure to negotiate cannot be fairly found to have been uninformed. The evidence supporting this finding is materially enhanced by the fact that twelve of Time's sixteen board members were outside independent directors.

We turn to the second part of the *Unocal* analysis. The obvious requisite to determining the reasonableness of a defensive action is a clear identification of the nature of the threat. This requires an evaluation of the importance of the corporate objective threatened; alternative methods of protecting that objective; impacts of the defensive action, and other relevant factors.

The fiduciary duty to manage a corporate enterprise includes the selection of a time frame for achievement of corporate goals. Directors are not obliged to abandon a deliberately conceived corporate plan for a short-term shareholder profit unless there is clearly no basis to sustain the corporate strategy. Time's responsive action to Paramount's tender offer was not aimed at "cramming down" on its shareholders a management-sponsored alternative, but rather had as its goal the carrying forward of a pre-existing transaction in an altered form. Thus, the response was reasonably related to the threat. The revised agreement did not preclude Paramount from making an offer for the combined Time-Warner company or from changing the conditions of its offer so as not to make the offer dependent upon the nullification of the Time-Warner agreement. Thus, the response was proportionate.

Judgment for Time affirmed.

Shareholder Derivative Suits   A special application of the business judgment rule is made in the context of directors terminating a derivative suit by a shareholder of a corporation. Such a use of the business judgment rule is discussed in the shareholders' rights portion of the Shareholders' Rights and Liabilities chapter.

Duties of Loyalty

Directors and officers owe a duty of *utmost loyalty and fidelity* to the corporation. Judge Benjamin Cardozo stated this duty of trust. He declared that a director:

owes loyalty and allegiance to the corporation—a loyalty that is undivided and an allegiance that is influenced by no consideration other than the welfare of the corporation. Any adverse interest of a director will be subjected to a scrutiny rigid and uncompromising. He may not profit at the expense of his corporation and in conflict with its rights; he may not for personal gain divert unto himself the opportunities which in equity and fairness belong to his corporation.[14]

Directors and officers owe the corporation the same duties of loyalty that agents owe their principals, though many of these duties have special names in corporation law. The most important of these duties of loyalty are the duties not to *self-deal*, not to *usurp a corporate oppor-*

tunity, not to *oppress minority shareholders*, and not to *trade on inside information*.

Self-Dealing with the Corporation

When a director or officer *self-deals* with his corporation, the director or officer has a **conflict of interest** and may prefer his own interests over those of the corporation. The director's or officer's interest may be *direct*, such as his interest in selling his land to the corporation, or it may be *indirect*, such as his interest in having another business of which he is an owner, director, or officer supply goods to the corporation. When a director has a conflict of interest, the director's transaction with the corporation may be voided or rescinded.

Intrinsic Fairness Standard   Under MBCA Section 8.31, a self-dealing transaction will not be voided merely on the grounds of a director's conflict of interest when any one of the following is true:

1. The transaction has been approved by a majority of informed, disinterested directors,

2. The transaction has been approved by a majority of the shares held by informed, disinterested shareholders, or

3. The transaction is fair to the corporation.

Nonetheless, even when disinterested directors' or shareholders' approval has been obtained, courts will

---

[14]*Meinhard v. Salmon*, 164 N.E.2d 545, 546 (N.Y. Ct. App. 1928).

void a conflict-of-interest transaction that is unfair to the corporation. This is true even when the approval of the disinterested directors is accorded deference under the business judgment rule. Therefore, every corporate transaction in which a director has a conflict of interest must be fair to the corporation. If the transaction is fair, the self-dealing (interested) director is excused from liability to the corporation.[15]

A transaction is fair if reasonable persons in an *arm's-length bargain* would have bound the corporation to it. This standard is often called the **intrinsic fairness standard.**

Effect of Board or Shareholder Approval

The function of disinterested director or disinterested shareholder approval of a conflict-of-interest transaction is merely to shift the burden of proving unfairness. Under the MBCA, the burden of proving fairness lies initially on the interested director. The burden of proof shifts to the corporation that is suing the officer or director for self-dealing if the transaction was approved by the board of directors or the shareholders. Nonetheless, when disinterested directors approve a self-dealing transaction, substantial deference is given to the decision in accordance with the business judgment rule, especially when the disinterested directors compose a majority of the board.

Effect of Unanimous Shareholder Approval

Generally, *unanimous* approval of a self-dealing transaction by informed shareholders *conclusively* releases an interested director or officer from liability for self-dealing even if the transaction is unfair to the corporation. The rationale for this rule is that fully informed shareholders should know what is best for themselves and their corporation.

Loans to Directors

Under early corporation law, *loans* by the corporation *to directors or officers* were illegal, on the grounds that such loans might result in the looting of corporate assets. Modern corporation statutes, like MBCA 8.32, allow loans to directors only after certain procedures have been followed. Either the shareholders must approve the loan, or the directors, after finding that the loan benefits the corporation, must approve it.

---

[15]The MBCA conflict-of- interest rules do not apply to officers. Instead, general agency rules apply to an officer having a conflict of interest.

Parent-Subsidiary Transactions Self-dealing is a concern when a parent corporation *dominates* a subsidiary corporation. Often, the subsidiary's directors will be directors or officers of the parent also. When persons with dual directorships approve transactions between the parent and the subsidiary, the opportunity for *overreaching* arises. There may be *no arm's-length bargaining* between the two corporations. Hence, such transactions must meet the *intrinsic fairness* test.

Usurpation of a Corporate Opportunity

Directors and officers may steal not only assets of their corporations (such as computer hardware and software) but also *opportunities* that their corporations could have exploited. Both types of theft are equally wrongful. As fiduciaries, directors and officers are liable to their corporation for **usurping corporate opportunities.**

The opportunity must come to the director or officer *in her corporate capacity.* Clearly, opportunities received at the corporate offices are received by the manager in her corporate capacity. In addition, courts hold that CEOs and other high-level officers are nearly always acting in their corporate capacities, even when they are away from their corporate offices.

The opportunity must have a *relation or connection* to an *existing or prospective* corporate activity. Some courts apply the *line of business test*, considering how closely related the opportunity is to the lines of business in which the corporation is engaged. Other courts use the *interest or expectancy test*, requiring the opportunity to relate to property in which the corporation has an existing interest or in which it has an expectancy growing out of an existing right.

The corporation must be able *financially* to take advantage of the opportunity. Managers are required to make a good faith effort to obtain external financing for the corporation, but they are not required to use their personal funds to enable the corporation to take advantage of the opportunity.

A director or officer is free to exploit an opportunity that has been rejected by the corporation. Generally, an informed, disinterested majority of the directors may reject an opportunity unless rejection by the board is manifestly unreasonable. Informed, disinterested shareholders may also reject an opportunity.

In the following case, the court found that an opportunity to become the manufacturer of Pepsi-Cola syrup was usurped by the president of a corporation that manufactured beverage syrups and operated soda fountains.

GUTH v. LOFT, INC.

5 A.2d 503 (Del. Sup. Ct. 1939)

Loft, Inc., manufactured and sold candies, syrups, and beverages and operated 115 retail candy and soda fountain stores. Loft sold Coca-Cola at all of its stores, but it did not manufacture Coca-Cola syrup. Instead, it purchased its 30,000-gallon annual requirement of syrup and mixed it with carbonated water at its various soda fountains.

In May 1931, Charles Guth, the president and general manager of Loft, became dissatisfied with the price of Coca-Cola syrup and suggested to Loft's vice president that Loft buy Pepsi-Cola syrup from National Pepsi-Cola Company, the owner of the secret formula and trademark for Pepsi-Cola. The vice president said he was investigating the purchase of Pepsi syrup.

Before being employed by Loft, Guth had been asked by the controlling shareholder of National Pepsi, Megargel, to acquire the assets of National Pepsi. Guth refused at that time. However, a few months after Guth had suggested that Loft purchase Pepsi syrup, Megargel again contacted Guth about buying National Pepsi's secret formula and trademark for only $10,000. This time, Guth agreed to the purchase, and Guth and Megargel organized a new corporation, Pepsi-Cola Company, to acquire the Pepsi-Cola secret formula and trademark from National Pepsi. Eventually, Guth and his family's corporation owned a majority of the shares of Pepsi-Cola Company.

Very little of Megargel's or Guth's funds were used to develop the business of Pepsi-Cola. Instead, without the knowledge or consent of Loft's board of directors, Guth used Loft's working capital, its credit, its plant and equipment, and its executives and employees to produce Pepsi-Cola syrup. In addition, Guth's domination of Loft's board of directors ensured that Loft would become Pepsi-Cola's chief customer.

By 1935, the value of Pepsi-Cola's business was several million dollars. Loft sued Guth, asking the court to order Guth to transfer to Loft his shares of Pepsi-Cola Company and to pay Loft the dividends he had received from Pepsi-Cola Company. The trial court found that Guth had usurped a corporate opportunity and ordered Guth to transfer the shares and to pay Loft the dividends. Guth appealed.

Layton, Chief Justice.   Public policy demands of a corporate officer or director the most scrupulous observance of his duty to refrain from doing anything that would deprive the corporation of profit or advantage. The rule that requires an undivided and unselfish loyalty to the corporation demands that there shall be no conflict between duty and self-interest.

The real issue is whether the opportunity to secure a very substantial stock interest in a corporation to be formed for the purpose of exploiting a cola beverage on a wholesale scale was so closely associated with the existing business activities of Loft, and so essential thereto, as to bring the transaction within that class of cases where the acquisition of the property would throw the corporate officer purchasing it into competition with his company.

Guth suggests a doubt whether Loft would have been able to finance the project. The answer to this suggestion is two-fold. Loft's net asset position was amply sufficient to finance the enterprise, and its plant, equipment, executives, personnel and facilities were adequate. The second answer is that Loft's resources were found to be sufficient, for Guth made use of no other resources to any important extent.

Guth asserts that Loft's primary business was the manufacturing and selling of candy in its own chain of retail stores, and that it never had the idea of turning a subsidiary product into a highly advertised, nation-wide specialty. It is contended that the Pepsi-Cola opportunity was not in the line of Loft's activities, which essentially were of a retail nature.

Loft, however, had many wholesale activities. Its wholesale business in 1931 amounted to over $800,000. It was a large company by any standard, with assets exceeding $9 million, excluding goodwill. It had an enormous plant. It paid enormous rentals. Guth, himself, said that Loft's success depended upon the fullest utilization of its large plant facilities. Moreover, it was a manufacturer of syrups and, with the exception of cola syrup, it supplied its own extensive needs. Guth, president of Loft, was an able and experienced man in that field. Loft, then, through its own personnel, possessed the technical knowledge, the practical business experience, and the resources necessary for the development of the Pepsi-Cola enterprise. Conceding that the essential of an opportunity is reasonably within the scope of a corporation's activities, latitude should be allowed for development and expansion. To deny this would be to deny the history of industrial development.

We cannot agree that Loft had no concern or expectancy in the opportunity. Loft had a practical and essential concern with respect to some cola syrup with an established formula and trademark. A cola beverage has come to be a business necessity for soft drink establishments; and it was essential to the success of Loft to serve at its soda fountains an acceptable five-cent cola drink in order to attract into its stores the great multitude of people who have formed the habit of drinking cola beverages.

When Guth determined to discontinue the sale of Coca-Cola in the Loft stores, it became, by his own act, a matter of urgent necessity for Loft to acquire a constant supply of some satisfactory cola syrup, secure against probable attack, as a replacement; and when the Pepsi-Cola opportunity presented itself, Guth having already considered the availability of the syrup, it became impressed with a Loft interest and expectancy arising out of the circumstances and the urgent and practical need created by him as the directing head of Loft.

The fiduciary relation demands something more than the morals of the marketplace. Guth did not offer the Pepsi-Cola opportunity to Loft, but captured it for himself. He invested little or no money of his own in the venture, but commandeered for his own benefit and advantage the money, resources, and facilities of his corporation and the services of his officials. He thrust upon Loft the hazard, while he reaped the benefit. In such a manner he acquired for himself 91 percent of the capital stock of Pepsi-Cola, now worth many millions. A genius in his line he may be, but the law makes no distinction between the wrongdoing genius and the one less endowed.

Judgment for Loft affirmed.

Oppression of Minority Shareholders

Directors and officers owe a duty to manage a corporation in the best interests of the corporation and the shareholders as a whole. When, however, a group of shareholders has been isolated for beneficial treatment to the detriment of another isolated group of shareholders, the disadvantaged group may complain of **oppression.**

For example, oppression may occur when directors of a close corporation who are also the majority shareholders pay themselves high salaries yet refuse to pay dividends or to hire minority shareholders as employees of the corporation. Since there is no market for the shares of a close corporation (apart from selling to the other shareholders), these oppressed minority shareholders have investments that provide them no return. They receive no dividends or salaries, and they can sell their shares only to the other shareholders, who are usually unwilling to pay the true value of the shares.

Generally, courts treat oppression of minority shareholders the same way courts treat director self-dealing: The transaction must be intrinsically fair to the corporation and the minority shareholders.

Freeze-Outs   Since the late 1960s, a special form of oppression, the **freeze-out,** has proliferated. A freeze-out is usually accomplished by merging a corporation with a newly formed corporation under terms by which the minority shareholders do not receive shares of the new corporation, but instead receive only cash or other securities. The minority shareholders are thereby *frozen out as shareholders.*

Going private is a special term for a freeze-out of shareholders of *publicly owned corporations.* Some public corporations discover that the burdens of public ownership—such as the periodic disclosure requirements of the SEC—exceed the benefits of being public. Many of these publicly owned companies choose to freeze out their minority shareholders to avoid such burdens. Often, going private transactions appear abusive because the corporation goes public at a high price and goes private at a much lower price.

In 1977, the Supreme Court of Delaware, in *Singer v. Magnavox,*[16] adopted a *fairness* test and a *business purpose* test for freeze-outs. The court held that the use of corporate power *solely* to eliminate the minority shareholders violated the directors' fiduciary duty to the minority shareholders. Later in 1977, the same court, in *Tanzer v. Int'l Gen. Indus., Inc.,*[17] held that the interest of a majority shareholder could provide the proper business purpose justifying a freeze-out of minority shareholders.

In 1983, in *Weinberger v. UOP,*[18] the Delaware Supreme Court abandoned the business purpose test as un-

workable. The court held that a freeze-out between a parent corporation and a subsidiary that was dominated by the parent had to meet only the intrinsic fairness test applied to self-dealing transactions. The court held that in the freeze-out context, total fairness had two basic aspects: *fair dealing* and *fair price.* Fair dealing requires disclosing material information to directors and shareholders and providing an opportunity for negotiation. A determination of fair value requires the consideration of all *the factors relevant to the value* of the shares, except speculative projections.

Most states apply the total fairness test to freeze-outs. Some states apply the business purpose test as well. Other states place no restrictions on freeze-outs provided a shareholder has a **right of appraisal,** which is discussed in the Shareholders' Rights and Liabilities chapter. SEC Rules 13e-3 and 13e-4 under the Securities Exchange Act of 1934 require a *publicly held* company to make a statement on the fairness of its proposed going private transaction and to discuss in detail the material facts on which the statement is based.

In the next case, the court required that a freeze-out of minority shareholders of the New England Patriots football team meet both the business purpose and intrinsic fairness tests. The court held that freezing out the minority shareholders merely to allow the corporation to repay the majority shareholder's personal debts was not a proper business purpose.

---

[16]380 A.2d 969 (Del. Sup. Ct. 1977).
[17]379 A.2d 1121 (Del. Sup. Ct. 1977).
[18]457 A.2d 701 (Del. Sup. Ct. 1983).

COGGINS v. NEW ENGLAND PATRIOTS FOOTBALL CLUB, INC.

492 N.E.2d 1112 (Mass. Sup. Jud. Ct. 1986)

In 1959, the New England Patriots Football Club, Inc. (Old Patriots), was formed with one class of voting shares and one class of nonvoting shares. Each of the original 10 voting shareholders, including William H. Sullivan, purchased 10,000 voting shares for $2.50 per share. The 120,000 nonvoting shares were sold for $5 per share to the general public in order to generate loyalty to the Patriots football team. In 1974, Sullivan was ousted as president of Old Patriots. In November 1975, Sullivan succeeded in regaining control of Old Patriots by purchasing all 100,000 voting shares for $102 per share. He again became a director and president of Old Patriots.

To finance his purchase of the voting shares, Sullivan borrowed $5,350,000 from two banks. The banks insisted that Sullivan reorganize Old Patriots so that its income could be used to repay the loans made to Sullivan and its assets used to secure the loans. To make the use of Old Patriots' income and assets legal, it was necessary to freeze out the nonvoting shareholders. In November 1976, Sullivan organized a new corporation called the New Patriots Football Club, Inc. (New Patriots). Sullivan was the sole shareholder of New Patriots. In December 1976, the shareholders of Old Patriots approved a merger of Old Patriots and New Patriots. Under the terms of the merger, Old Patriots went out of business, New Patriots assumed the business of Old Patriots, Sullivan became the only owner of New Patriots, and the nonvoting shareholders of Old Patriots received $15 for each share they owned.

David A. Coggins, a Patriots fan from the time of their formation and owner of 10 Old Patriots nonvoting shares, objected to the merger and refused to accept the $15 per share payment for his shares. Coggins sued Sullivan and Old Patriots to obtain rescission of the merger. The trial judge found the merger to be illegal and ordered the payment of damages to Coggins and all other Old Patriots shareholders who voted against the merger and had not accepted the $15 per share merger payment. Sullivan and Old Patriots appealed to the Massachusetts Supreme Judicial Court.

Liacos, Justice.   When the director's duty of loyalty to the corporation is in conflict with his self-interest, the court will vigorously scrutinize the situation. The dangers of self-dealing and abuse of fiduciary duty are greatest in freeze-out situations like the Patriots merger, when a controlling shareholder and corporate director chooses to eliminate public ownership. Because the danger of abuse of fiduciary duty is especially great in a freeze-out merger, the court must be satisfied that the freeze-out was for the advancement of a legitimate corporate purpose. If satisfied that elimination of public ownership is in furtherance of a business purpose, the court should then proceed to determine if the transaction was fair by examining the totality of the circumstances. Consequently, Sullivan and Old Patriots bear the burden of proving, first, that the merger was for a legitimate business purpose, and second, that, considering the totality of circumstances, it was fair to the minority.

Sullivan and Old Patriots have failed to demonstrate that the merger served any valid corporate objective unrelated to the personal interests of Sullivan, the majority shareholder. The sole reason for the merger was to effectuate a restructuring of Old Patriots that would enable the repayment of the personal indebtedness incurred by Sullivan. Under the approach we set forth above, there is no need to consider further the elements of fairness of a transaction that is not related to a valid corporate purpose.

Judgment for Coggins affirmed as modified.

Trading on Inside Information

Officers and directors have *confidential access* to nonpublic information about the corporation. Sometimes, directors and officers purchase their corporation's securities with knowledge of inside information. Often, disclosure of previously nonpublic, **inside information** affects the value of the corporation's securities. Therefore, directors and officers may make a profit when the prices of the securities increase after the inside information has been disclosed publicly. Shareholders of the corporation claim that they have been harmed by such activity, either because the directors and officers misused confidential in-

formation that should have been used only for corporate purposes or because the directors and officers had an unfair informational advantage over the shareholders.

In this century, there has been a judicial trend toward finding a duty of directors and officers to disclose information that they have received confidentially from inside the corporation *before they buy or sell* the corporation's securities. As will be discussed fully in the Securities Regulation chapter, the illegality of insider trading is already federal law under the Securities Exchange Act; however, it remains only a minority rule under state corporation law.

Disclosure of Merger Negotiations

Sometimes, a shareholder will sell her shares, only to discover a few days later that at the time she sold her shares, her corporation was engaged in merger negotiations. Often those merger negotiations result in a merger agreement providing that a shareholder will be able to sell her shares at a price in excess of the previous market price. Not surprisingly, the shareholder who has already sold her shares at a lower price is upset that she has not been informed of the merger negotiations. Consequently, she sues the directors for failing to disclose the negotiations, arguing that had she known, she would have waited to sell her shares.

State corporation law has not imposed liability on the directors merely for failing to disclose secret merger negotiations. However, federal securities law—especially Securities Exchange Act Rule 10b-5—imposes disclosure duties on directors and officers. Among the most important of these duties is the obligation to disclose material corporate information, an obligation that is discussed in *Levinson v. Basic, Inc.,* which appears in the Securities Regulation chapter. The Supreme Court of the United States suggested that a corporation need not disclose secret merger negotiations that are material to a shareholder's investment decision absent special circumstances, such as when news of merger negotiations has leaked from the company into the market.[19] The Court hinted also that a board statement that "no corporate developments exist" when secret merger negotiations are ongoing imposes liability on the directors for making false statements.[20] The Court suggested, however, that silence or a response of "no comment" would not result in liability when the corporation has a business purpose to maintain the secrecy of merger negotiations.[21] The securities laws and their effect on the duties of directors, officers, and others who are considered insiders are discussed in detail in the Securities Regulation chapter.

Director's Right to Dissent

A director who *assents* to an action of the board of directors may be held liable for the board's exceeding its authority or its failing to meet its duty of due care or loyalty. A director who *attends a board meeting* is deemed to have assented to any action taken at the meeting, *unless he dissents.*

Under MBCA Section 8.24(d), to register his dissent to a board action, and thereby to protect himself from liability, the director must *not vote in favor* of the action and must *make his position clear* to the other board members. His position is made clear either by requesting that his dissent appear in the minutes or by giving written notice of his dissent to the chairman of the board at the meeting or to the secretary immediately after the meeting. These procedures ensure that the dissenting director will attempt to dissuade the board from approving an imprudent action.

Generally, directors are not liable for failing to attend meetings. However, a director is liable for *continually failing* to attend meetings, with the result that the director is unable to prevent the board from harming the corporation by its self-dealing.

CORPORATE AND MANAGEMENT LIABILITY FOR TORTS AND CRIMES

When directors, officers, and other employees of the corporation commit torts and crimes while conducting corporate affairs, the issue arises concerning who has liability. Should the individuals committing the torts and crimes be held liable, the corporation, or both?

Liability of the Corporation

Although courts struggled for many years to find a theory making a corporation liable for its agents' torts and crimes, today special statutes and the law of agency provide bases for imposing liability on corporations.

Torts   For torts, the vicarious liability rule of *respondeat superior* applies to corporations. The only issue is whether an employee acted within the scope of her employment, which encompasses not only acts the employee is authorized to commit, but may also include acts that the employee is expressly instructed to avoid.

Crimes   The traditional view was that a corporation could not be guilty of a crime, because criminal guilt required intent and a corporation, not having a mind, could form no intent. In addition, a corporation had

[19] 485 U.S. 224, 234 n. 17 (U.S. Sup. Ct. 1988).

[20] Id. at 235 and n. 20.

[21] Id. at 234 n. 17.

nobody that could be imprisoned.[22] In essence, courts refused to find corporate criminal liability for violations of statutes that set standards for persons by holding that a corporation was not a person for purposes of criminal liability.

Today, few courts have difficulty holding corporations liable for crimes. Modern criminal statutes either expressly provide that corporations may commit crimes or define the term *person* to include corporations.[23] In addition, some criminal statutes designed to protect the public welfare do not require intent as an element of some crimes, thereby removing the grounds used by early courts to justify relieving corporations of criminal liability.

Courts are especially likely to impose criminal liability on a corporation when the criminal act is requested, authorized, or performed by:

1. The board of directors.
2. An officer.
3. Another person having responsibility for formulating company policy.
4. A high-level administrator having supervisory responsibility over the subject matter of the offense and acting within the scope of his employment.

In addition, courts hold a corporation liable for crimes of its agent or employee committed within the scope of his authority, even if a higher corporate official has no knowledge of the act and has not ratified it.[24]

Directors' and Officers' Liability

A person is always *liable for his own torts and crimes*, even when committed on behalf of his principal. Every person in our society is expected to exercise independent judgment, not merely follow orders. Therefore, directors and officers are personally liable when they commit torts or crimes during the performance of their corporate duties.

A director or officer is usually not liable for the *torts* of employees of the corporation, since the corporation, not the director or the officer, is the principal. He will be liable, however, if he *authorizes* the tort or *participates* in its commission.

A director or officer has *criminal* liability if she *requests, authorizes, conspires*, or *aids and abets* the commission of a crime by an employee.

In the next case, *United States v. Cattle King Packing Co., Inc.,* the court considered the criminal liability of a corporation and its officers.

---

[22]*State v. Summers,* 692 S.W.2d 439 (Tenn. Ct. Crim. App. 1985) (since corporations cannot be incarcerated, it would seem necessary that fines be substantial for corporations to feel any sting from the punishment).

[23]*People v. General Dynamics Land Systems,* 438 N.E.2d 359 (Mich. Ct. App. 1989).

[24]*CGM Contractors v. Environmental Services, Inc.,* 383 S.E.2d 861 (W. Va. Sup. Ct. 1989).

UNITED STATES V. CATTLE KING PACKING CO., INC.

793 F.2d 232 (10th Cir. 1986)

On June 1, 1981, Butch Stanko started a meatpacking plant in Adams County, Colorado, under the name of Cattle King Packing Company, Inc. Stanko was an officer and shareholder of Cattle King. Gary Waderich was a general sales manager primarily responsible for commercial sales of meat food products and for the daily operation of Cattle King. Stanko set company policies and practices to circumvent the Federal Meat Inspection Act (FMIA), which policies and practices he instructed Waderich and other employees to follow. When Stanko returned to his home in Scottsbluff, Nebraska, he monitored operations by phone and visits to the plant to make certain that the policies and practices that he had established were being followed.

Among the violations of the Federal Meat Inspection Act were the following:

1. Stanko gave a Cattle King employee directions on how, when the government inspector was not around, to mix inedible scrap with edible meat and thereby increase the poundage of the meat.

2. When a shipment of meat was rejected by a grocer and returned to Cattle King, Waderich instructed an employee to rebox the meat and resell it, without government inspection. (The FMIA required all returned meat to be government inspected.) When a government veterinarian came on the reboxing scene and demanded to know what was going on, Waderich denied he knew of the reboxing. Later, Waderich told another employee, "Well, we tried, but we got caught."

3. Cattle King employees dated meat the date it was shipped rather than the date it was produced as required by the FMIA.

4. Spoiled meat rejected by a buyer and returned to Cattle King was in bags that were puffy with gas caused by the spoilage. On instructions by Waderich, an employee reworked the meat by poking the bags to release the gas, and the meat was reshipped to the same buyer.

The U.S. Attorney General prosecuted Waderich, Stanko, and Cattle King for criminal violations of the FMIA. The jury convicted them, and all three defendants appealed.

McWilliams, Circuit Judge.   There is little doubt that Cattle King's operation violated federal meat inspection law at about every turn. Cattle King employees adulterated the meat, misdated the meat, and evaded federal inspection when rejected meat was returned to the plant. Cattle King employees also reworked the returned meat and resold it. Because this activity directly involved Gary Waderich, his challenge of the sufficiency of the evidence must clearly fail.

Stanko would make much of the fact that he returned to Scottsbluff, Nebraska in February 1982, and points out that all of the crimes occurred after that date. He would have us believe that he was somehow insulated from transactions occurring in Colorado when he was in Nebraska. This is an overly simplistic view of the matter. The fact that Stanko was in Scottsbluff does not absolve him of the criminal acts, for example of Waderich, which were committed pursuant to instructions from Stanko himself.

As a variation on his "I-was-in-Scottsbluff" defense, Stanko charges that the trial court's reliance on *United States v. Park* (1975) was error. The rationale of the Supreme Court's decision in *Park* is based upon this premise: Companies that engage in the food business, and the people who manage them, have an affirmative duty to insure that the food they sell to the public is safe. Accordingly, a corporate officer, who is in a "responsible relationship" to some activity within a company that violates federal food laws, can be held criminally responsible even though that officer did not personally engage in that activity. The trial court gave the jury the opportunity to decide whether Butch Stanko was responsible for Cattle King's violations of federal meat inspection laws. The jury found that he was.

In any event, this is not an instance where Stanko was in Scottsbluff, Nebraska, *not* knowing what his employees were doing in Colorado. Rather, Stanko set in motion the very acts which were carried out, pursuant to his direction, by his employees. Scottsbluff is not a shield for Stanko.

The trial court instructed the jury that Cattle King could be found guilty only if one of its agents committed the crimes, and the other three elements were met:

1. The agent was acting within the scope of his or her employment.

2. The agent was authorized to do the act.

3. The agent was motivated, at least in part, to benefit the corporation.

Gary Waderich, an officer of Cattle King, was personally responsible for the commission of all the crimes. Given Waderich's position within Cattle King, there is no doubt that elements 1 and 2 are met. As for element 3, there is also no doubt that Cattle King benefited by the commission of these crimes. The principal effect of all the crimes committed was that Cattle King reaped great economic rewards. Selling meat which should be condemned, misdating boxes so that meat could be stockpiled and thus produced more cheaply, all directly benefited Cattle King economically. There is, therefore, sufficient evidence that Cattle King, as a company, is also guilty of all the crimes.

Judgment convicting Waderich, Stanko, and Cattle King affirmed.

INSURANCE AND INDEMNIFICATION

The extensive potential liability of directors deters many persons from becoming directors. They fear that their liability for their actions as directors may far exceed their fees as directors. To encourage persons to become directors, corporations *indemnify* them for their outlays associated with defending lawsuits brought against them and paying judgments and settlement amounts. In addition, or as an alternative, corporations purchase *insurance* that will make such payments for the directors. Indemnification and insurance are provided for officers also.

Indemnification of Directors

Today, all of the corporation statutes limit the ability of corporations to indemnify directors in order to preserve the deterrence function of tort and criminal law. For example, directors may not be indemnified if they personally benefited from a decision for which they were held liable. In addition, the corporation may indemnify directors only in regard to a legal proceeding in which the director is a party because he was a director of the corporation. If a director is sued because he is alleged to have harmed someone when he was not acting as a director, the corporation may not indemnify the director.

Mandatory Indemnification   Under MBCA Section 8.52, a director is entitled to *mandatory indemnification* of her reasonable litigation expenses when she is sued and *wins completely* (is *wholly successful*). The greatest part of such expenses is attorney's fees. Because indemnification is mandatory in this context, when the corporation refuses to indemnify a director who has won completely, she may ask a court to order the corporation to indemnify her.

Voluntary Indemnification   Under MBCA Section 8.51, a director who loses a lawsuit *may* be indemnified by the corporation. This is called *voluntary indemnification,* because the corporation may choose to indemnify the director, but is not required to do so.

The corporation must establish that the director acted in *good faith* and reasonably believed that she acted in the *best interests* of the corporation. When a director seeks indemnification for a *criminal* fine, the corporation must establish a third requirement: that the director had no reasonable cause to believe that her conduct was unlawful. Finally, any voluntary indemnification must be approved by someone independent of the director receiving indemnification: a disinterested board of directors, disinterested shareholders, or independent legal counsel. Voluntary indemnification may cover not only the director's reasonable expenses but also fines and damages that the director has been ordered to pay.

A corporation may not elect to indemnify a director who was held *liable to the corporation* or who was found to have received a *personal benefit*. Such a rule tends to prevent indemnification of directors who have wronged the corporation by failing to exercise due care or by breaching a fiduciary duty. However, if the director paid an amount to the corporation as part of a *settlement*, the director may be indemnified for his reasonable expenses, but not for the amount that he paid to the corporation. The purpose of these rules is to avoid the circularity of having the director pay damages to the corporation and then having the corporation indemnify the director for the same amount of money.

Court-Ordered Indemnification   A court may order a corporation to indemnify a director if it determines that the director meets the standard for *mandatory* indemnification or if the director is *fairly and reasonably* entitled to indemnification in view of all the relevant circumstances.

Advances A director may not be able to afford to make payments to her lawyer prior to the end of a lawsuit. More important, a lawyer may refuse to defend a director who cannot pay legal fees. Therefore, MBCA Section 8.53 permits a corporation to make advances to a director to allow the director to afford a lawyer.

Indemnification of Nondirectors

Under the MBCA, officers and employees who are not directors are entitled to the same mandatory indemnification rights as directors. The corporation may, however, expand nondirectors' indemnification rights beyond the limits imposed on directors' indemnification rights.

Insurance

The MBCA does not limit the ability of a corporation to purchase insurance on behalf of its directors, officers, and employees. Insurance companies, however, are unwilling to insure all risks. In addition, some risks are *legally uninsurable as against public policy.* Therefore, liability for misconduct such as self-dealing, usurpation, and securities fraud is uninsurable.

ETHICAL AND PUBLIC POLICY CONCERNS

1. Do you agree that the primary objective of a corporation should be to maximize profits for its shareholders? What other objectives should a corporation have in addition to or instead of maximizing profits? Should the board of directors engage in an activity that maximizes profits but harms the community in which the corporation is located? Is it possible for a board to maximize profits and to be socially responsible to the community in which the corporation is located?

2. Should corporation law absolutely prevent CEO domination of a corporation or merely allow shareholders to restrict CEO power if shareholders choose? Why do shareholders invest in a corporation in which the CEO dominates the corporation? Why don't shareholders elect directors who control the CEO?

3. Should corporation law allow a board of directors great discretion in fighting hostile takeovers of a corporation? Is your answer affected by whether the raider is able to manage the corporation better than current management? Is your answer affected by whether the raider intends to move the operations of the target to another community? What other factors might affect your view

of the law we have concerning takeover defenses? Suppose the raider plans to break up the corporation and to sell the divisible parts of the corporation's business to other corporations. Is board opposition to such a hostile bid more justifiable? Does society benefit from such a bust-up takeover?

SUMMARY

The objectives and powers of a corporation are determined by the state corporation statute, the articles of incorporation, and the bylaws. Corporate actions beyond the powers of the corporation are *ultra vires*. Modern statutes do not permit the corporation and the other party to a contract to use *ultra vires* as a defense. Shareholders may sue to enjoin an *ultra vires* act.

A corporation is managed under the direction of its board of directors. The board delegates many of its duties to committees of the board and to officers, but some board functions may not be delegated. Generally, directors may take action only at a properly convened meeting, yet many statutes permit action without a meeting if all of the directors consent in writing.

The directors are elected by the shareholders and may be removed by them. Some states require a minimum of three directors; the MBCA requires only one. In publicly held corporations, the proxy solicitation process frequently permits the chief executive officer to cause the election of his nominees and to dominate the board of directors. Recently, board members have assumed more independence. Directors normally hold office until the next annual meeting, but most of the corporation statutes also permit staggered terms.

Numerous proposals for changing the composition and functions of the board have been made. Audit, nominating, and compensation committees, when composed entirely or predominantly of outside directors, tend to strengthen the independence of the board.

Officers are agents of the corporation, and like all agents, they have express, implied, and apparent authority. Some officers, such as the treasurer, also have inherent authority, which arises from the titles of the offices they hold.

Special rules apply to the management of close corporations. Modern statutes permit a close corporation to dispense with a board of directors and to be managed like a partnership. Restrictions on the management discretion of the directors are permitted in close corporations.

Directors and officers must act within their authority and within the powers given to the corporation. They also have the duty to act with due care. Their duty of loyalty requires them to act in the best interests of the corporation as a whole. Most management actions are protected from judicial scrutiny by the business judgment rule.

The general agency rules concerning torts apply to corporations. Corporations may also be found guilty of crimes, including those requiring intent, if the offenses are authorized or performed by policymaking managers or high-level administrators acting within the scope and in the course of their employments.

Corporations are permitted to purchase insurance policies that will pay for a director's or officer's legal costs and judgments. Within constraints, a corporation may also indemnify a director or an officer.

PROBLEM CASES

1. A ballot in the San Francisco city election included Proposition T, which would prohibit the construction of any building more than 72 feet high unless plans for the proposed building were approved in advance by the voters. PG&E's management concluded that the proposition would raise its property taxes by an estimated $380,000 in the first year and by as much as $1,135,000 per year in 10 years and that the proposition would also require redesigning and obtaining additional land for an already planned electric power substation. Consequently, the executive committee approved a $10,000 political contribution to a group opposing Proposition T. Neither PG&E's articles of incorporation nor the laws of California expressly permitted PG&E to make political donations. Is the contribution *ultra vires?*

2. Concerned Citizens of the CVEC, Inc., is a nonprofit Alabama corporation. The Alabama Business Corporation Act provides that a director may be removed with or without cause. The bylaws of Concerned Citizens provides that a director may be removed only for cause. The members of concerned citizens wish to remove a director, J. P. Mitchell. Mitchell argues that the members must have cause to remove him. Is Mitchell correct?

3. Lillian Pritchard was a director of Pritchard & Baird Corporation, a business founded by her husband. After the death of her husband, her sons took control of the corporation. For two years, they looted the assets of

the corporation through theft and improper payments. The corporation's financial statements revealed the improper payments to the sons, but Mrs. Pritchard did not read the financial statements. She did not know what her sons were doing to the corporation or that what they were doing was unlawful. When Mrs. Pritchard was sued for failing to protect the assets of the corporation, she argued that she was a figurehead director, a simple housewife who served as a director as an accommodation to her husband and sons. Was Mrs. Pritchard held liable?

4. The Chicago National League Ball Club, Inc. (Chicago Cubs), operated Wrigley Field, the Cubs' homepark. Through the 1965 baseball season, the Cubs were the only major league baseball team that played no home games at night because Wrigley Field had no lights for nighttime baseball. Philip K. Wrigley, director and president of the corporation, refused to install lights because of his personal opinion that baseball was a daytime sport and that installing lights and scheduling night baseball games would result in the deterioration of the surrounding neighborhood. The other directors assented to this policy. From 1961 to 1965, the Cubs suffered losses from their baseball operations. The Chicago White Sox, whose weekday games were generally played at night, drew many more fans than did the Cubs. A shareholder sued the board of directors to force them to install lights at Wrigley Field and to schedule night games. What did the court rule?

5. The management of MacMillan Corporation recognized that it would not be able to prevent a takeover of the corporation. Therefore, management convinced the directors to authorize an auction of the company. Only two bidders emerged: Kohlberg Kravis Roberts & Co. (KKR) and Robert Maxwell. Management preferred KKR, and took steps to ensure than KKR would win the auction. Only hours before the deadline for bids, Mac-Millan's chairman and CEO tipped KKR that Maxwell's bid was lower than KKR's. Two hours before the deadline, MacMillan's auctioneer understood that Maxwell would top any KKR bid, yet allowed Maxwell to believe that he had made the higher bid. The board granted KKR a lock-up option of MacMillan's crown jewels— its most valuable assets. Has MacMillan's board acted properly? No! Must maximize value to shareholders!

6. Sinclair Oil Corporation (Sinclair), an oil explorer, producer, and marketer, owned about 97 percent of the shares of Sinclair Venezuelan Oil Company (Sinven). Nearly all of Sinven's directors were officers, directors, or employees of corporations owned by Sinclair. In 1961, Sinclair created Sinclair International Oil Company (International), a wholly owned subsidiary used for the purpose of coordinating all of Sinclair's foreign operations. Sinclair caused Sinven to make a contract with International that obligated Sinven to sell all of its crude oil and refined oil products to International. Sinclair caused International to breach this contract by allowing it to delay payments and to fail to comply with minimum purchase requirements under the contract. Francis Levien, a shareholder of Sinven, sued Sinclair on behalf of Sinven, alleging that Sinclair breached a fiduciary duty to Sinven. Is Levien correct?

Intrinsic Fairness Rule - Yes ✓

7. Arthur Modell owned 53 percent of the shares of the Cleveland Browns Football Company, Inc. (the Browns), a Delaware corporation. Robert Gries owned 43 percent of the shares. The directors of the Browns were Modell, Modell's wife, Gries, James Bailey, James Berick, Richard Cole, and Nate Wallack. Modell also owned 80 percent of the shares and was a director of Cleveland Stadium Corporation (CSC), which leased Cleveland Municipal Stadium from the city of Cleveland. Gries, Bailey, Berick, Cole, and Wallack were the other shareholders and directors of CSC. Modell proposed that the Browns purchase all the shares of CSC for $6 million. Gries believed the price to be inflated. The purchase was approved by the Browns' directors by a vote of 4 to 1, with Gries being the sole dissenter and the Modells not voting. Gries filed a shareholder suit challenging the action. He claimed that the intrinsic fairness standard should apply to the transaction. The Browns argued that the business judgment rule should apply. Who is correct? *Not enough to escape BJR - higher standard of Review*

8. Bryant, Phelps, and May were the majority shareholders, officers, and directors of Greene Group, a company that operated a greyhound racing track in Greene County, Alabama. When a new greyhound racing track was proposed in Macon County, Alabama, Bryant, Phelps, and May, on their own behalf, contracted with the owners of the new track for Bryant, Phelps, and May to operate the new track. The owners of the new track did not want Greene Group to be involved in the operation of the new track because of the bickering between the majority and minority shareholders of Greene Group. The owners of the new track specifically requested that Bryant, Phelps, and May alone operate the

new track. In the process of obtaining the contract to operate the new track, the three men used some property belonging to the Greene Group, including architectural plans and confidential marketing studies, and Greene Group employees and their expertise. Have Bryant, Phelps, and May done anything wrong?

9. Edwin Walhof and his family owned all the shares of Micom Holding Company, a corporation that owned 93 percent of Micom Corporation, a Minnesota corporation. To make Micom Corporation a closely held corporation owned only by the Walhof family, Micom Corporation merged into Micom Holding Company pursuant to the merger requirements of the Minnesota Corporation Law. Under the terms of the merger, Micom Holding Company, as the surviving corporation, carried on the prior business of Micom Corporation; the minority shareholders of Micom Corporation received $10 cash per share. James Sifferle, one of the minority shareholders of Micom Corporation, refused to accept the $10 per share and sued to set aside the merger. Was Sifferle successful?

10. A school bus was returning children to their homes in Livingston County, Kentucky. Phillip Kirkham, age 10, and his sister, Windy Kirkham, age 6, left the bus and attempted to cross the highway when a truck came on the scene. The truck was owned by Fortner LP Gas Company, Inc. The driver of the truck saw the bus, geared down, applied the brakes, but failed to stop the truck. The truck struck both children, injuring Phillip and killing Windy instantly. A subsequent inspection of the truck revealed grossly defective brakes. The Commonwealth of Kentucky prosecuted the corporation for manslaughter in the second degree for causing Windy's death. The corporation claimed that it could not commit the crime of manslaughter. Was it correct?

11. Shareholders collectively owning 80 percent of the shares of the Bank of New Mexico Holding Company made a shareholder's buy-sell agreement. Those shareholders included directors of the corporation. One of the agreeing shareholders sued the other shareholders, including the directors, to obtain a determination of the price of the shares under the agreement. The corporation reimbursed the legal expenses of the directors who, as shareholders, were defendants in the litigation. Did the corporation act properly in indemnifying the directors?

[left margin handwritten notes, partially legible: "keep price as low as possible" and "have directors have a conflict of interest"]

Business Judgment Rule - standard that courts will use to view conduct

CHAPTER 43

SHAREHOLDERS' RIGHTS AND LIABILITIES

INTRODUCTION

The **shareholders** are the ultimate owners of a corporation, but a shareholder has *no right to manage* the corporation. Instead, a corporation is managed by its board of directors and its officers for the benefit of its shareholders.

The shareholders' role in a corporation is limited to electing and removing directors, approving certain important matters, and ensuring that the actions of the corporation's managers are consistent with the applicable state corporation statute, the articles of incorporation, and the bylaws. For example, shareholders have the power and the right to vote on many corporate transactions such as a merger. Shareholders who oppose certain fundamental corporate actions may require the corporation to buy their shares. In addition, shareholders, on behalf of the corporation, may sue managers who breach their duties of care or loyalty.

Shareholders also assume a few responsibilities. For example, all shareholders are required to pay the promised consideration for shares. Shareholders are liable for receiving dividends beyond the lawful amount. In addition, controlling shareholders may owe special duties to minority shareholders.

Close corporation shareholders enjoy rights and owe duties beyond the rights and duties of shareholders of publicly owned corporations. As you learned in the Management of Corporations chapter, close corporation shareholders may agree to grant themselves the right of management. In addition, some courts have found close corporation shareholders to be fiduciaries of each other.

This chapter's study of the rights and responsibilities of shareholders begins with an examination of shareholders' meetings and voting rights.

SHAREHOLDERS' MEETINGS

Collective action of the shareholders is ordinarily taken at annual or special shareholders' meetings. Most of the states also permit shareholder action without a meeting.

Annual Meeting

The general corporation statutes of most states and Model Business Corporation Act (MBCA) Section 7.01 provide that an annual meeting of shareholders *shall* be held. The purpose of an annual shareholders' meeting is to elect new directors and to conduct other necessary business. Often, the shareholders are asked to approve the corporation's independent auditors, to ratify stock option plans for management, and to vote on shareholders' proposals.

Special Meetings

Special shareholders' meetings may be held whenever a corporate matter arises that requires immediate shareholders' action, such as the approval of a merger that cannot wait until the next annual shareholders' meeting. Under MBCA Section 7.02, a special shareholders' meeting may be called by the board of directors or by a person authorized to do so by the bylaws, usually the president or the chairman of the board. In addition, the holders of at least 10 percent of the shares entitled to vote at the meeting may call a special meeting.

Notice of Meetings

To permit shareholders to arrange their schedules for attendance at shareholders' meetings, MBCA Section 7.05 requires that an officer of the corporation give shareholders *notice* of annual and special meetings of shareholders. Notice need be given only to shareholders entitled to vote who are **shareholders of record** on a date fixed by the board of directors. Shareholders of record are those whose names appear on the share-transfer book of the corporation. Usually only shareholders of record—either in person or by proxy—are entitled to vote at shareholder meetings.

Notice of a *special meeting* must list the purpose of the meeting. Under the MBCA, notice of an *annual meeting* need not include the purpose of the meeting unless shareholders will be asked to approve extraordinary corporate changes, for example, amendments to the articles of incorporation and mergers.

Conduct of Meetings

The president or the chairman of the board usually presides at shareholders' meetings. Minutes of shareholders' meetings are usually kept by the secretary. To conduct business at a shareholders' meeting, a **quorum** of the outstanding shares must be represented in person or by proxy. If the approval of more than one class of shares is required, a quorum of each class of shares must be present. MBCA Sections 7.25 and 7.27 define a quorum as the majority of shares outstanding, yet permit a greater percentage to be established in the articles.

Ordinarily, a shareholder is entitled to cast as many votes as he has shares. A majority of the votes cast at the shareholders' meeting will decide issues that are put to a vote. If the approval of more than one class of shares is required, a majority of the votes cast by each class must favor the issue. MBCA Section 7.27 permits the articles to require a greater than majority vote. Such *supermajority voting requirements* are frequently used in close corporations to give minority shareholders veto power and, thereby, to prevent oppression of minority shareholders.

Action without a Meeting

Generally, shareholders can act only at a properly called meeting. However, MBCA Section 7.04 permits shareholders to act without a meeting if *all of the shareholders entitled to vote consent in writing* to the action.

In the following case, the court held that only the shareholders of record could vote shares at a special meeting of shareholders.

CAREY v. PENNSYLVANIA ENTERPRISES, INC.

876 F.2d 333 (3rd Cir. 1989)

Edward Carey owned 109,000 of the 2,700,341 outstanding shares of Pennsylvania Enterprises, Inc. (PEI). Concerned that Carey would attempt to take over PEI, its board of directors announced a proposal to widen the distribution of PEI shares. The proposal required shareholder approval. PEI announced that a special meeting of shareholders would be held on October 12, and its board of directors set the record date as September 2, 1988. Needing 1,350,171 votes to pass, the proposal received 1,373,968 votes in favor, passing with a margin of almost 24,000 votes. However, 79,118 of the shares voted in favor of the proposal were recorded in the names of Loriot & Co. and Cede & Co. but voted by other persons. Loriot and Cede were nominees for Manufacturer's Hanover Trust, which administered PEI's Dividend Reinvestment Plan (DRIP). Under the DRIP plan, PEI shareholders could opt to reinvest their cash dividends with PEI, which would issue new shares to the shareholders. Instead of registering the new shares in the names of the individual shareholders, however, PEI registered new shares to Loriot or Cede. A provision of the DRIP plan provided that the individual shareholders (beneficial shareholders), not Loriot and Cede, were able to vote the shares.

At the special shareholders' meeting, the election judges permitted the DRIP beneficial shareholders to vote the DRIP shares in favor of the proposal. Carey, however, claimed that only Loriot and Cede, as the shareholders of record, could vote the shares. Carey sued to invalidate the election. The district court found that the beneficial shareholders held the right to vote the shares. Carey appealed.

Greenberg, Circuit Judge.   Pennsylvania Business Corporation Law reads:

The board of directors may fix a time as a record date for the determination of the shareholders entitled to vote at any meeting of shareholders. Only such shareholders shall be entitled to vote at such meeting.

* * * * *

Save where otherwise indicated in the articles of incorporation, every shareholder of record shall have the right to one vote for every share standing in his name on the books of the corporation.

PEI's corporate bylaws provide:

Stockholders holding stock may vote the same at meetings. Each such stockholder shall be entitled to one vote for each such share of stock registered in his name on the books of the Company.

These provisions clearly indicate that the record rather than the beneficial owners of the DRIP shares were entitled to vote. Nothing can be construed to allow a beneficial owner in the situation of the DRIP shareholders to vote in place of the record owners absent a valid proxy. Thus, we reverse the judgment of the district court.

We recognize that the district court did not rely exclusively on the general policy favoring shareholder enfranchisement in upholding the determination of the election judges. It also relied on the provision in the DRIP plan that participants will be permitted to vote their shares.

We cannot permit the DRIP plan to substitute for a proxy because to do so would not be consistent with the interest of the corporation and the stockholders in determining stock ownership quickly by reference to the books showing record ownership. Moreover, the weight of authority establishes that the right to vote inheres in the record owner of the stock. Thus, if the record owner does not personally vote the shares, it follows that any person who attempts to do so must have a formal proxy from the record owner. Surely, a statement in a corporation's DRIP plan cannot be regarded as a proxy from the record owner.

Judgment reversed in favor of Carey.

ELECTION OF DIRECTORS AND SHAREHOLDER CONTROL DEVICES

For the most part, a corporation's management may manage the corporation free from interference by shareholders. Some matters, however, require shareholder approval because they involve fundamental changes in the corporation. Most important, shareholders possess the right to elect directors to the board.

Election of Directors

The most important shareholder voting right is the right to elect the directors.

Straight Voting   Normally, directors are elected by a single class of shareholders in **straight voting,** in which each share has one vote for each new director to be elected. With straight voting, a shareholder may vote for as many nominees as there are directors to be elected; a shareholder may cast for each such nominee as many votes as she has shares. For example, in a director election in which 15 people have been nominated for 5 director positions, a shareholder with 100 shares can vote for up to 5 nominees and can cast up to 100 votes for each of those 5 nominees.

Under straight voting, the nominees with the most votes are elected. Consequently, straight voting allows a majority shareholder to elect the entire board of directors. Thus, minority shareholders are unable to elect any representatives to the board without the cooperation of the majority shareholder.

Straight voting is also a problem in close corporations in which a few shareholders own equal numbers of shares. In such corporations, no shareholder controls the corporation, yet if the holders of a majority of the shares act together, those holders will elect all of the directors and control the corporation. Such control may be exercised to the detriment of the other shareholders.

Two alternatives to straight voting aid minority shareholders' attempts to gain representation on the board and prevent harmful coalitions in close corporations. These alternatives are **cumulative voting** and **class voting.**

Cumulative Voting   Many corporations allow a shareholder to *cumulate her votes* by multiplying the number of directors to be elected by the shareholder's number of shares. A shareholder may then allocate her votes among the nominees as she chooses. She may vote only for as many nominees as there are directors to be elected, but she may vote for fewer nominees. For example, she may choose to cast all of her votes for only one nominee. Cumulative voting is required by constitutions or statutes in almost half of the states. Most of the other states *permit* corporations to provide for cumulative voting in their articles.

Cumulative voting may permit minority shareholders to elect representatives to the board of directors. Sometimes, cumulative voting is used in close corporations to ensure a balance of power. For example, a close corporation has four directors and four shareholders, each of whom owns 25 shares. With straight voting, no shareholder is able to elect himself as a director. With cumulative voting, each shareholder is able to elect himself to the board.

See Figure 1 for a further explanation of the mechanics of cumulative voting.

Classes of Shares   A corporation may have several *classes of shares.* The two most common classes are

---

FIGURE 1   Cumulative Voting Formula

The formula for determining the minimum number of shares required to elect a desired number of directors under cumulative voting is:

$$X = \frac{S \times R}{D + 1} + 1$$

X = The number of shares needed to elect the desired number of directors

S = The total number of shares voting at the shareholders' meeting

R = The number of director representatives desired

D = The total number of directors to be elected at the meeting

Example: Sarah Smiles wants to elect two of the five directors of Oates Corporation. One thousand shares will be voted. In this case:

$$S = 1,000$$
$$R = 2$$
$$D = 5$$

Therefore:

$$X = 334.33$$

Fractions are ignored; thus, Sarah will need to hold at least 334 shares to be able to elect two directors.

---

common shares and *preferred shares*, but a corporation may have several classes of common shares and several classes of preferred shares.

MBCA Section 7.21 provides that *each share*, whether denoted common or preferred, is *entitled to one vote* on each of the matters voted on at a shareholders' meeting, including the election of directors, *unless* the articles provide otherwise. Usually, preferred shares do not have the right to vote for directors.

MBCA Section 6.01 permits a corporation to designate the voting rights of each class of shares. Many close corporations have two or more classes of common shares with *different voting rights.* Each class may be entitled to elect one or more directors, in order to balance power in a corporation.

For example, suppose a corporation has four directors and 100 shares held by four shareholders—each of whom owns 25 shares. With straight voting and no classes of shares, no shareholder owns enough shares to elect himself as a director, because 51 shares are necessary to elect a director. Suppose, however, that the corporation has four classes of shares, each with the right to elect one of the directors. Each class of shares is issued to only one shareholder. Now, as the sole owner of a class of shares entitling the class to elect one director, each shareholder can elect herself to the board.

Modern statutes also permit shares having more or less than one vote per share.

Other Shareholder Control Devices

While cumulative voting and class voting are two useful methods by which shareholders can allocate or acquire voting control of a corporation, there are three other devices that may also be used for these purposes: voting trusts; shareholder voting agreements; and proxies, especially irrevocable proxies. Until recently, such control devices were disfavored by courts on the grounds that they illegally separated the ownership of shares from the right to vote the shares. Today, however, modern courts and statutes place few restrictions on the use of shareholder control devices.

Voting Trusts   MBCA Section 7.30 permits shareholders to establish **voting trusts.** The shareholders transfer their shares to one or more voting trustees and receive voting trust certificates in exchange. The shareholders retain many of their rights, including the right to receive dividends, but the voting trustees vote for directors and other matters submitted to shareholders.

The purpose of a voting trust is to control the corporation through the concentration of shareholder voting power in the voting trustees, who often are participating shareholders. If several minority shareholders collectively own a majority of the shares of a corporation, they may create a voting trust and thereby control the corporation. You may ask why shareholders need a voting trust when they are in apparent agreement on how to vote their shares. The reason is that they may have disputes in the future that could prevent the shareholders from agreeing on how to vote. The voting trust ensures that the shareholder group will control the corporation despite the emergence of differences.

MBCA Section 7.30 limits the duration of voting trusts to *10 years*, though the participating shareholders may agree to extend the term for another 10 years. Also, a voting trust must be made public, with copies of the voting trust document available for inspection at the corporation's offices.

Shareholder Voting Agreements   As an alternative to a voting trust, shareholders may merely agree how they will vote their shares. A shareholder voting agreement must be written; only shareholders signing the agreement are bound by it. Shareholder voting agreements have two advantages over voting trusts. First, their duration may be *perpetual*. Second, they may be kept *secret* from the other shareholders; they usually do not have to be filed in the corporation's offices.

Until recently, these advantages have been offset by the courts' hostility toward voting agreements. Some court have invalidated voting agreements on the grounds that they were illegal attempts to circumvent restrictions on voting trusts. Other courts have refused to grant specific performance of voting agreements when a shareholder refused to vote as agreed, unless the agreement expressly provided for specific performance. Today, however, modern statutes validate shareholder voting agreements, exclude them from the requirements imposed on voting trusts, and make them specifically enforceable.

Proxies   As you learned in the Management of Corporations chapter, a shareholder may appoint a **proxy** to vote his shares. If several minority shareholders collectively own a majority of the shares of a corporation, they may appoint a proxy to vote their shares and thereby control the corporation.

There are several problems with using proxies to exercise control over a corporation. First, the ordinary proxy has only a limited duration—11 months under MBCA Section 7.22—unless a longer term is specified. Second, the ordinary proxy is *revocable* at any time.[1] As a result, unless there is careful planning, there is no guarantee that control agreements accomplished through the use of proxies will survive future shareholder disputes.

Modern corporation statutes, such as MBCA Section 7.22, allow proxies to be valid for longer than 11 months. Also proxies are *irrevocable* if they are coupled with an interest. MBCA Section 7.22 provides that a proxy is coupled with an interest when, among other things, the person holding the proxy is a party to a shareholder voting agreement or has agreed to purchase the shareholder's shares (as under a *buy-and-sell agreement*, which was discussed in the Organization, Financial Structure, and Dissolution of Corporations chapter). The principal use of irrevocable proxies is in conjunction with shareholder voting agreements.

In the next case, the court considered the legality of a shareholder voting agreement.

---

[1] *Concord Financial Group Inc. v. Tri-State Motor Transit Co.,* 567 A.2d 1 (Del. Ch. Ct. 1989) (first proxy automatically revoked by execution of second proxy postmarked after first proxy).

SCHREIBER v. CARNEY

447 A.2d 17 (Del. Ch. Ct. 1982)

Texas International Airlines, Inc. (TIA), proposed a new corporate structure in order to strengthen its financial position. To effect the restructuring, TIA would merge with Texas Air Company. The merger required approval of each of the four classes of TIA shareholders. Jet Capital Corporation owned all of the shares of Class C stock. Although Jet Capital believed that the merger would benefit TIA and the other shareholders, Jet Capital would suffer adverse tax consequences if the merger was effected. Thus, Jet Capital decided to vote against the merger. Jet Capital's adverse tax burden was due to its ownership of warrants to purchase TIA shares. Jet Capital could eliminate the merger's adverse tax impact by exercising the warrants prior to the merger, an alternative that Jet Capital was unwilling to choose since it would require a cash payment of over $3 million. Beyond its shares of TIA, Jet Capital had assets of only $200,000. To borrow the $3 million at market interest rates was too expensive.

Therefore, TIA and Jet Capital agreed that TIA would loan Jet Capital $3 million at a below-market interest rate. Since Jet Capital would give the cash from the loan immediately back to TIA when it exercised the warrants, the loan had virtually no impact on TIA's cash position. As a condition of the loan, Jet Capital agreed to vote in favor of the merger. The loan agreement was approved by a majority of the shares held by shareholders other than Jet Capital. Subsequently, the merger was approved by the TIA shareholders.

Leonard Schreiber, a TIA shareholder, brought a derivative suit on behalf of TIA against TIA's directors, including Robert Carney. Schreiber argued that the loan transaction constituted vote-buying and, therefore, was an illegal voting agreement.

Hartnett, Vice Chancellor. There are essentially two principles regarding vote-buying that appear in the Delaware caselaw. The first is that vote-buying is illegal *per se* if its object or purpose is to defraud or disenfranchise the other shareholders.

The second principle is that vote-buying is illegal *per se* as a matter of public policy, the reason being that each shareholder should be entitled to rely upon the independent judgment of his fellow shareholders.

The agreement in question was entered into primarily to further the interests of TIA's other shareholders. Indeed, the shareholders voted overwhelmingly in favor of the loan agreement. Thus, the underlying rationale for the argument that vote-buying is illegal *per se*, as a matter of public policy, ceases to exist when measured against the undisputed reason for the transaction.

Moreover, the rationale that vote-buying is, as a matter of public policy, illegal *per se* is founded upon considerations of policy that are now outmoded as a necessary result of an evolving corporate environment. According to 5 Fletcher *Cyclopedia Corporation* (Perm.Ed.) section 2066:

The theory that each shareholder is entitled to the personal judgment of each other shareholder expressed in his vote, and that any agreement among shareholders frustrating it was invalid, is obsolete because it is both impracticable and impossible of application to modern corporations with many widely scattered shareholders.

In *Ringling Bros.–Barnum & Bailey Combined Shows v. Ringling* (1947), the Delaware Supreme Court adopted a liberal approach to voting agreements. The court stated:

Generally speaking, a shareholder may exercise wide liberality of judgment in the matter of voting, and it is not objectionable that his motives may be for personal profit, or determined by whims or caprice, so long as he violates no duty owed his fellow shareholders.

It is clear that Delaware has discarded the presumption against voting agreements. Thus, an agreement involving the transfer of share voting rights without the transfer of ownership is not necessarily illegal and each arrangement must be examined in light of its object or purpose. To hold otherwise would be to exalt form over substance. Voting agreements in whatever form, therefore, should not be considered to be illegal *per se* unless the object or purpose is to defraud or in some way disenfranchise the other shareholders. This is not to say, however, that vote-buying accomplished for some laudible purpose is automatically free from challenge. Because vote-buying is so easily susceptible of abuse, it must be viewed as a voidable transaction subject to a test for intrinsic fairness.

Schreiber's motion for summary judgment is denied.

Other matters besides the election of directors require shareholder action, some because they make fundamental changes in the structure or business of the corporation.

Amendment of the Articles

Since the articles of incorporation embody the basic contract between a corporation and its shareholders, shareholders must approve most changes in the articles. For example, when the articles are amended to increase the number of outstanding shares or reduce the dividend rights of preferred shareholders, shareholder approval is needed.

Merger and Consolidation

A **merger** is a transaction in which one corporation merges into a second corporation. Usually, the first corporation dissolves; the second corporation takes all the business and assets of both corporations and becomes liable for the debts of both corporations. Usually, the shareholders of the dissolved corporation become shareholders of the surviving corporation. Ordinarily, both corporations' shareholders must approve a merger.

A **consolidation** is similar to a merger, except that both old corporations go out of existence and a new corporation takes the business, assets, and liabilities of the old corporations. Both corporations' shareholders must approve the consolidation. Modern corporate practice makes consolidations obsolete, since it is usually desirable to have one of the old corporations survive. The MBCA does not recognize consolidations. However, the effect of a consolidation can be achieved by creating a new corporation and merging the two old corporations into it.

Share Exchange

A **share exchange** is a transaction by which one corporation becomes the owner of all of the outstanding shares of a second corporation through a *compulsory* exchange of shares: The shareholders of the second corporation are compelled to exchange their shares for shares of the first corporation. The second corporation remains in existence and becomes a wholly owned subsidiary of the first corporation. Only the selling shareholders must approve the share exchange.

Sale of Assets

A sale of *all or substantially all* of the assets of the business other than in the regular course of business must be approved by the shareholders of the selling corporation, since it drastically changes the shareholders' investment. Thus, a corporation's sale of all its real property and equipment is a sale of substantially all its assets, even though the corporation continues its business by leasing the assets back from the purchaser. However, a corporation that sells its building, but retains its machinery with the intent of continuing operations at another location, has not sold all or substantially all of its assets.

Dissolution

A **dissolution** is the first step in the termination of the corporation's business. The usual dissolution requires shareholder approval. Dissolution was discussed in detail in the Organization, Financial Structure, and Dissolution of Corporations chapter.

Procedures Required

Most statutes establish similar procedures to effect all of the above fundamental changes. Under the MBCA, the procedure includes approval of the board of directors, notice to all of the shareholders whether or not they are entitled to vote, and majority approval of the votes held by shareholders entitled to vote under the statute, articles, or bylaws.[2] Majority approval will be insufficient if a corporation has a supermajority shareholder voting requirement, such as one requiring two-thirds approval.

If there are two or more classes of shares, the articles may provide that matters voted on by shareholders must be approved by each class substantially affected by the proposed transaction. For example, a merger may have to be approved by a majority of the preferred shareholders and a majority of the common shareholders. As an alternative, the articles may require only the approval of the shareholders as a whole.

Under MBCA Sections 10.04 and 11.03, voting by classes is required for mergers, share exchanges, and amendments of the articles if these would substantially affect the rights of the classes. For example, the approval of preferred shareholders is required if a merger would change the dividend rights of preferred shareholders.[3]

When Shareholder Approval Not Required

In many states, no approval of shareholders of the *surviving corporation* is required for a merger *if* the merger does not fundamentally alter the character of the business or substantially reduce the shareholders' voting or dividend rights.

Many statutes, including MBCA Section 11.04, permit a merger between a parent corporation and its subsidiary without the approval of the shareholders of either corporation. Instead, the board of directors of the parent approves the merger and sends a copy of the merger plan to the subsidiary's shareholders. This simplified merger is called a **short-form merger.** It is available only if the parent owns a high percentage of the subsidiary's shares—90 percent under the MBCA and the Delaware statute.

There are two reasons for this simpler procedure for effecting short-form mergers. One is that the parent's high ownership percentage makes obvious the outcome of any vote of the subsidiary's shareholders. The other is that the rights of the parent's shareholders are not materially changed, since the parent's ownership of the subsidiary's business has changed only from an indirect 90 percent ownership to a direct 100 percent ownership.

Other Matters Submitted to Shareholders

The articles of incorporation and the bylaws may require or permit other matters to be submitted for shareholder approval. For example, loans to officers, self-dealing transactions, and indemnifications of managers for litigation expenses may be approved by shareholders. Also, many of the states require shareholder approval of share option plans for high-level executive officers, but the MBCA does not.

Shareholder Proposals and Right to Speak

Among the rights of shareholders is *full participation* in shareholders' meetings. This includes the right to offer resolutions, to speak for and against proposed resolutions, and to ask questions of the officers of the corporation.

Typical shareholder resolutions are aimed at protecting or enhancing the interests of minority shareholders. The proposals have included amending the corporate articles to permit cumulative voting for directors, setting ceilings on executive pay, and limiting corporate charitable contributions. In addition, groups seek social or political changes by introducing resolutions that restrict the production of nuclear power, ban the manufacture of weapons, prohibit trade with South Africa, and require the protection of the environment.

None of these proposals has drawn more than a few percent of shareholders' votes.[4] As you learned in the

---

[2]Note that the shareholder control agreements that you studied above—voting trusts, shareholder voting agreements, and irrevocable proxies—may be used by a group of shareholders owning a majority of the shares to ensure that they will be able not only to elect directors but also to dictate the outcome of a shareholder vote on the above transactions.

[3] But see *Warner Communications, Inc. v. Chris-Craft Industries, Inc.*, 21 Sec.Reg.L.R. 1411 (Del. Ch. Ct. 1989) (preferred shareholders not entitled to vote as a class on proposed merger that adversely affected their interests).

[4] Six environmental proposals at Exxon Corporation's 1990 Annual Shareholders' Meeting were extraordinary in gathering at least 5.7 percent of the vote, with two exceeding 9 percent. Sullivan and Solomon, "Environmentalists Claim Gains at Exxon Meeting," *The Wall Street Journal*, p. B1, col. 5, April 26, 1990.

Management of Corporations chapter, most shareholders subscribe to the Wall Street Rule: sell the shares if you do not like what management is doing with the corporation. Nonetheless, such proposals do impose subtle pressure on corporate management and often sensitize directors and officers to important social issues of the times. Consequently, despite the failure of most proposals, frequently corporate management voluntarily adopts the proposals or complies with their spirit.

DISSENTERS' RIGHTS

Many times, shareholders will approve a corporate action by less than a unanimous vote, indicating that some shareholders opposed the action. For the most part, the dissenting shareholders have little recourse. Their choice is to remain shareholders or to sell their shares. For close corporation shareholders, there is no choice; the dissenting close corporation shareholder has no ready market for her shares, so she will remain a shareholder.

Some corporate transactions, however, so materially change a shareholder's investment in the corporation or have such an adverse effect on the value of a shareholder's shares that it has been deemed unfair to require the dissenting shareholder either to remain a shareholder merely because there is no fair market for the shares or to suffer a loss in value when he sells his shares on a market that has been adversely affected by the news of the corporate action. Corporate law has therefore responded by creating **dissenters' rights** (a right of appraisal) for shareholders who disagree with specified fundamental corporate transactions. Dissenters' rights require the corporation to pay dissenting shareholders the *fair value* of their shares.

Coverage

Under MBCA Section 13.02, the dissenters' rights cover mergers, short-form mergers, and sales of all or substantially all the assets other than in the ordinary course of business. In addition, the rights exist for share exchanges and significant amendments of the articles of incorporation. Some statutes cover consolidations also.

The MBCA requires that a dissenting shareholder seeking payment of the fair value of his shares have the *right to vote* on the action to which he objects; however,

a shareholder of a subsidiary in a short-form merger has dissenters' rights despite his lack of voting power. In addition, MBCA Section 13.21 requires that the shareholder *not vote in favor* of the transaction. The shareholder may either vote against the action or abstain from voting.

Most states' statutes exclude from dissenters' rights shares that are traded on a recognized securities exchange such as the New York Stock Exchange. Instead, these statutes expect a shareholder to sell his shares on the stock exchange if he dissents to the corporate action. The MBCA has no such exclusion, on the grounds that the market price may be *adversely affected by the news* of the proposed or consummated corporate action to which the shareholder objects.

Procedure

Generally, a shareholder must notify the corporation of his intent to seek payment before the shareholders have voted on the action. Next, the corporation informs dissenting shareholders how to demand payment. After the dissenting shareholders demand payment, the corporation and the shareholders negotiate a mutually acceptable price. If they cannot agree, a court will determine the fair value of the shares and order the corporation to pay that amount.

To determine fair value, most judges use the *Delaware Block Method*, a weighted average of several valuation techniques—such as market value,[5] comparisons with other similar companies, capitalization of earnings, and book value—to appraise the shares. However, the Supreme Court of Delaware recently abandoned the Delaware Block Method, recognizing the need for courts to value shares by methods generally considered acceptable in the financial community.[6]

In the following case, *Walters v. Double L, Inc.,* the court granted dissenters' rights to a shareholder of a corporation that sold substantially all its assets.

---

[5] *Hunter v. Mitek Industries Inc.,* 721 F. Supp. 1102 (E. Mo. D. Ct. 1989) (fair value of minority shares is not to be discounted by their lack of marketability).

[6] *Weinberger v. U.O.P., Inc.,* 457 A.2d 701 (Del. Sup. Ct. 1983). See also *In re Glosser Brothers, Inc.,* 555 A.2d 129 (Pa. Super. 1989).

WATERS v. DOUBLE L, INC.

755 P.2d 1294 (Idaho App. Ct. 1987)

Dale Waters was a minority shareholder of Double L, Inc., a business engaged in manufacturing agricultural machinery and related products. When Double L became financially distressed, the directors agreed to sell to Pioneer Astro all of Double L's real property and equipment and to issue sufficient shares to make Pioneer Astro an 80 percent shareholder of Double L. To improve Double L's financial position, Pioneer Astro agreed to pay cash for the assets and shares and to loan money to Double L. To allow Double L to continue its business, Pioneer Astro agreed to lease the purchased assets back to Double L.

At a shareholder meeting, shareholders approved the transaction with Pioneer Astro. Waters, however, abstained from voting and demanded that Double L pay him the fair value of his shares pursuant to dissenters' rights under Idaho law. Double L refused to buy Waters's shares, so Waters sued. The trial court ordered Double L to buy Waters's shares. Double L appealed.

Burnett, Judge.   Idaho Code section 30-1-80 lists the categories of corporate actions that trigger the right to dissent:

(a) Any shareholder of a corporation shall have the right to dissent from, and to obtain payment for his shares in the event of any of the following corporate actions:

* * * * *

(2) Any sale, lease, exchange, or other disposition of all or substantially all of the property and assets of the corporation not made in the usual or regular course of its business.

Double L points to the fact that it retained certain assets in the form of inventory, accounts receivable, and goodwill. However, in the deposition of Lynn Johnson, Double L's president, Johnson testified as follows:

Q: You made an agreement whereby Pioneer Astro invested heavily in Double L; is that right?

A: Yes.

Q: Pioneer Astro bought your land, your machinery, and the buildings owned by Double L?

A: Yes.

Q: Was that substantially all of your assets?

A: Yes.

Moreover, the corporation's own conduct—seeking and obtaining shareholder approval of the Pioneer Astro transaction—implicitly indicated that the transaction comprised a sale of substantially all of the corporation's assets. Had the transaction not embraced substantially all of the assets, or the transaction been in the ordinary course of business, it would not have required shareholder approval.

The corporation would have us hold that because its business continued to operate after the transaction was consummated, the transaction could not be regarded as a sale of all or substantially all of the corporation's assets. However, the mere fact that the corporation remained in business under the same name is not the critical criterion. The nature of the transaction takes precedence over its form. Our focus is upon the relationship between the assets transferred and those remaining. Here, the corporation sold all of its hard assets, retaining intangible assets of admittedly dubious value. Only by renting the hard assets back from Pioneer Astro was the corporation able to continue its operations. This is a classic "sale of assets" transaction.

The corporation after the Pioneer Astro transaction was not, in any real sense, the same entity that existed before the transaction.

Judgment for Waters affirmed.

SHAREHOLDERS' INSPECTION AND INFORMATION RIGHTS

Inspection Right

Inspecting a corporation's books and records is sometimes essential to the exercise of a shareholder's rights. For example, a shareholder may be able to decide how to vote in a director election only after examining corporate financial records that reveal whether the present directors are managing the corporation profitably. Also, a close corporation shareholder may need to look at the books to determine the value of his shares.

Many corporate managers are resistant to shareholders inspecting the corporation's books and records, charging that shareholders are nuisances or that shareholders often have improper purposes for making such an inspection. Sometimes, management objects solely on the ground that it desires secrecy.

Most of the state corporation statutes specifically grant shareholders inspection rights. The purpose of these statutes is to facilitate the shareholder's inspection of the books and records of corporations whose managements resist or delay proper requests by shareholders. A shareholder's lawyer or accountant may assist the shareholder's exercise of his inspection rights.

Absolute Right of Inspection MBCA Section 7.20 gives shareholders an *absolute right* of inspection of an alphabetical listing of the shareholders entitled to notice of a meeting, including the number of shares owned. Access to a *shareholder list* allows a shareholder to contact other shareholders about important matters such as shareholder proposals.

MBCA Section 16.02 also grants an absolute right of inspection of, among other things, the articles, bylaws, and minutes of shareholder meetings within the past three years.

Qualified Right of Inspection The shareholder's right to inspect other records, however, is *qualified* (restricted) by MBCA Section 16.02. To inspect accounting records, board and committee minutes, and shareholder minutes more than three years old, a shareholder must make the demand in *good faith* and have a *proper purpose.*

Proper purposes include inspecting the books of account to determine the value of shares or the propriety of dividends. On the other hand, learning business secrets and aiding a competitor are clearly improper purposes. In the next case, the court found that valuing shares and checking on allegations of corporate mismanagement were proper purposes.

CARTER v. WILSON CONSTRUCTION CO.

348 S.E.2d 830 (N.C. Ct. App. 1986)

William Carter owned 317 shares of Wilson Construction Company. He also owned 20 percent of the shares of Wilson Equipment Leasing, Inc., a company that leased equipment to and engaged in other transactions with Wilson Construction. Carter worked for Wilson Construction until he resigned his position in November 1983. Immediately, he organized and became a part owner and employee of C & L Contracting, Inc., a competitor of Wilson Construction. Carter offered to sell his shares to Wilson Construction, but his offer was rejected. In 1984, Carter demanded that Wilson Construction make available to him its books, records of account, minutes, and record of shareholders, on the grounds that he had been told and believed that the financial condition of Wilson Construction had deteriorated due to improper management. In addition, he requested the information to determine the value of his shares, the financial condition of the corporation, and whether it was efficiently managed in the best interests of the corporation. Wilson Construction refused the request on the grounds that Carter's stated purpose was a mask for improper purposes. Carter then sued Wilson Construction and its president, Ray Wilson, asking the court to order the corporation to make the records available to him. The trial court ordered the corporation to make the records available to Carter and allowed Carter to recover $500 in penalties from Wilson Construction and $500 in penalties from Ray Wilson. Wilson Construction and Ray Wilson appealed.

Johnson, Judge.　North Carolina law does not give a shareholder an absolute right of inspection and examination for a mere fishing expedition, or for a purpose not germane to the protection of his economic interest as a shareholder of the corporation. For a shareholder to have the right to visit a corporation's office and possibly disrupt its normal operation in order to inspect corporate books and records of account, our legislature has correctly decided that his motives must be "proper." Purposes that previously have been deemed proper are the shareholder's good faith desire to (1) determine the value of his shares; (2) investigate the conduct of management; and (3) determine the financial condition of the corporation. The burden of proof rests upon Wilson Construction, if it wishes to defeat Carter's demand, to allege and show by facts that Carter is motivated by some improper purpose.

Here, Carter stated a proper purpose. Carter tried to sell his shares in Wilson Construction back to Wilson Construction, which declined his offer to sell. Carter had personally guaranteed the debts of Wilson Equipment Leasing, a corporation that conducted related transactions with Wilson Construction, including indemnifying its debts and extending loans. Carter had reason to believe, based upon information from Wilson Construction's management consultant, that certain purchases had not been put on the corporate books and that funds were shuffled between Wilson Equipment Leasing and Wilson Construction, and that the net worth of Wilson Construction decreased from August 1983 to August 1984. This evidence supports Carter's allegation of a proper purpose.

The evidence produced by Wilson Construction showed that Carter is currently part owner and employee of C & L Contracting. According to Ray Wilson, "We are in direct competition on all work in the Piedmont, North Carolina, that is bridge work" and to allow Carter access to the books and records of Wilson Construction "would put us at a disadvantage."

This evidence is insufficient to override the presumption that Carter is acting in good faith. The mere possibility that a shareholder may abuse his right to gain access to corporate information will not be held to justify a denial of a legal right, if such right exists in the shareholder.

Judgment for Carter affirmed.

Information Rights

MBCA Section 16.20 requires a corporation to furnish its shareholders *financial statements*, including a balance sheet, an income statement, and a statement of changes in shareholders' equity. The Securities Exchange Act of 1934 also requires publicly held companies to furnish such statements, as well as other information, to their shareholders.[7]

---

[7] Financial reporting requirements of the Securities and Exchange Commission are discussed in the Securities Regulation chapter.

PREEMPTIVE RIGHT

Introduction

The market price of a shareholder's shares will be reduced if a corporation issues additional shares at a price less than the market price. In addition, a shareholder's proportionate voting, dividend, and liquidation rights may be adversely affected by the issuance of additional shares. For example, if a corporation's only four shareholders each own 100 shares worth $10 per share, then each shareholder has shares worth $1,000, a 25 percent interest in any dividends declared, 25 percent of the voting power, and a claim against 25 percent of the assets after creditors' claims have been satisfied. If the corporation subsequently issues 100 shares to another person for only $5 per share, the value of each shareholder's shares falls to $900 and his dividend, voting, and liquidation rights are reduced to 20 percent. In a worse scenario, the corporation issues 201 shares to one of the existing shareholders, giving that shareholder majority control of the corporation and reducing the other shareholders' interests to less than 17 percent each. As a result, the minority shareholders will be dominated by the majority shareholder and will receive a greatly reduced share of the corporation's dividends.

Such harmful effects of an issuance could have been prevented if the corporation had been required to offer each existing shareholder a percentage of the new shares equal to her current proportionate ownership. If, for example, in the situation described above, the corporation had offered 50 shares to each shareholder, each shareholder could have remained a 25 percent owner of the corporation; her interests in the corporation would not have been reduced, and her total wealth would not have been decreased.

Corporation law recognizes the importance of giving a shareholder the option of maintaining the value of his shares and retaining his proportionate interest in the corporation. This is the shareholder's **preemptive right**, an option to subscribe to a new issuance of shares in proportion to the shareholder's current interest in the corporation.

MBCA Section 6.30 is representative of modern statutory provisions that adopt a comprehensive scheme for determining preemptive rights. It provides that the preemptive right does not exist except to the extent provided by the articles. The MBCA permits the corporation to state expressly when the preemptive right arises.

When the preemptive right exists, the corporation must notify a shareholder of her option to buy shares, the number of shares that she is entitled to buy, the price of the shares, and when the option must be exercised. Usually, the shareholder is issued a **right,** a written option that she may exercise herself or sell to a person who wishes to buy the shares.

DISTRIBUTIONS TO SHAREHOLDERS

Introduction

During the life of a corporation, shareholders may receive distributions of the corporation's assets. Most people are familiar with one type of distribution, dividends, but there are other important types of distributions to shareholders, including payments to shareholders upon the corporation's repurchase of its shares.

There is one crucial similarity among all the types of distributions to shareholders: Corporate assets are transferred to shareholders. Consequently, an asset transfer to shareholders may harm the corporation's creditors and others with claims against the corporation's assets. For example, a distribution of assets may impair a corporation's ability to pay its creditors. In addition, a distribution to one class of shareholders may harm another class of shareholders who have a liquidation priority over the shareholders receiving the distribution. The existence of these potential harms compels corporation law to restrict the ability of corporations to make distributions to shareholders.

Dividends

One important objective of a business corporation is to make a profit. Shareholders invest in a corporation primarily to share in the expected profit either through appreciation of the value of their shares or through dividends. There are two types of dividends: *cash or property dividends* and *share dividends*. Only cash or property dividends are distributions of the corporation's assets. Share dividends are *not* distributions.

Cash or Property Dividends

Dividends are usually paid in cash. However, other assets of the corporation—such as airline discount coupons or shares of another corporation—may also be distributed as dividends. Cash or property dividends are declared by the board of directors and paid by the corporation on the date stated by the directors. Once declared, dividends are *debts* of the corporation and shareholders may sue to force payment of the dividends.[8]

The board's dividend declaration, including the amount of dividend and whether to declare a dividend, is protected by the business judgment rule. Nonetheless, there are limits to the board's discretion. For example, the board may not refuse to declare dividends when such refusal results in the oppression of minority shareholders, especially in a close corporation.

Preferred shares nearly always have a set dividend rate stated in the articles of incorporation. Even so, unless the preferred dividend is mandatory, which is rare, the board has discretion to determine whether to pay a preferred dividend and what amount to pay. Most preferred shares are *cumulative preferred shares*, on which unpaid dividends cumulate. The entire accumulation must be paid before common shareholders may receive any dividend. Even when preferred shares are noncumulative, the current dividend must be paid to preferred shareholders before any dividend may be paid to common shareholders.

The following is one of the few cases in which a court ordered the payment of a dividend. The court found that Henry Ford had the wrong motives for refusing to pay a dividend.

---

[8]*Anadarko Petroleum Corp. v. Panhandle Eastern Corp.*, 54 A.2d 1171 (Del. Sup. Ct. 1988).

DODGE v. FORD MOTOR CO.

170 N.W. 668 (Mich. Sup. Ct. 1919)

In 1916, brothers John and Horace Dodge owned 10 percent of the common shares of the Ford Motor Company. Henry Ford owned 58 percent of the outstanding common shares and controlled the corporation and its board of directors. Starting in 1911, the corporation paid a regular annual dividend of $1.2 million, which was 60 percent of its capital stock of $2 million but only about 1 percent of its total equity of $114 million. In addition, from 1911 to 1915, the corporation paid special dividends totaling $41 million.

The policy of the corporation was to reduce the selling price of its cars each year. In June 1915, the board and officers agreed to increase production by constructing new plants for $10 million, acquiring land for $3 million, and erecting an $11 million smelter. To finance the planned expansion, the board decided not to reduce the selling price of cars beginning in August 1915 and to accumulate a large surplus.

A year later, the board reduced the selling price of cars by $80 per car. The corporation was able to produce 600,000 cars annually, all of which, and more, could have been sold for $440 instead of the new $360 price, a forgone revenue of $48 million. At the same time, the corporation announced a new dividend policy of paying no special dividend. Instead, it would reinvest all earnings except the regular dividend of $1.2 million.

Henry Ford announced his justification for the new dividend policy in a press release: "My ambition is to employ still more men, to spread the benefits of this industrial system to the greatest possible number, to help them build up their lives and their homes." The corporation had a $112 million surplus, expected profits of $60 million, total liabilities of $18 million, $52.5 million in cash on hand, and municipal bonds worth $1.3 million.

The Dodge brothers sued the corporation and the directors to force them to declare a special dividend. The trial court ordered the board to declare a dividend of $19.3 million. Ford Motor Company appealed.

Ostrander, Chief Justice.   It is a well-recognized principle of law that the directors of a corporation, and they alone, have the power to declare a dividend of the earnings of the corporation, and to determine its amount. Courts will not interfere in the management of the directors unless it is clearly made to appear that they are guilty of fraud or misappropriation of the corporate funds, or they refuse to declare a dividend when the corporation has a surplus of net profits which it can, without detriment to the business, divide among its stockholders, and when a refusal to do so would amount to such an abuse of discretion as would constitute a fraud, or breach of that good faith that they are bound to exercise towards the shareholders.

The testimony of Mr. Ford convinces this court that he has to some extent the attitude towards shareholders of one who has dispensed and distributed to them large gains and that they should be content to take what he chooses to give. His testimony creates the impression that he thinks the Ford Motor Company has made too much money, has had too large profits, and that, although large profits might be still earned, a sharing of them with the public, by reducing the price of the output of the company, ought to be undertaken. We have no doubt that certain sentiments, philanthropic and altruistic, creditable to Mr. Ford, had large influence in determining the policy to be pursued by the Ford Motor Company.

There should be no confusion of the duties that Mr. Ford conceives that he and the shareholders owe to the general public and the duties that in law he and his co-directors owe to protesting, minority shareholders. A business corporation is organized and carried on primarily for the profit of the shareholders. The powers of the directors are to be employed for that end.

We are not, however, persuaded that we should interfere with the proposed expansion of the Ford Motor Company. In view of the fact that the selling price of products may be increased at any time, the ultimate results of the larger business cannot be certainly estimated. The judges are not business experts. It is recognized that plans must often be made for a long future, for expected competition, for a continuing as well as an immediately profitable venture. We are not satisfied that the alleged motives of the directors, in so far as they are reflected in the conduct of the business, menace the interests of shareholders.

Assuming the general plan and policy of expansion were for the best ultimate interest of the company and therefore of its shareholders, what does it amount to in justification of a refusal to declare and pay a special dividend? The Ford Motor Company was able to estimate with nicety its income and profit. It could sell more cars than it could make. The profit upon each car depended upon the selling price. That being fixed, the yearly income and profit was determinable, and, within slight variations, was certain.

There was appropriated for the smelter $11 million. Assuming that the plans required an expenditure sooner or later of $10 million for duplication of the plant, and for land $3 million, the total is $24 million. The company was a cash business. If the total cost of proposed expenditures had been withdrawn in cash from the cash surplus on hand August 1, 1916, there would have remained $30 million.

The directors of Ford Motor Company say, and it is true, that a considerable cash balance must be at all times carried by such a concern. But there was a large daily, weekly, monthly receipt of cash. The output was practically continuous and was continuously, and within a few days, turned into cash. Moreover, the contemplated expenditures were not to be immediately made. The large sum appropriated for the smelter plant was payable over a considerable period of time. So that, without going further, it would appear that, accepting and approving the plan of the directors, it was their duty to distribute on and near the 1st of August 1916, a very large sum of money to stockholders.

Judgment for the Dodge brothers affirmed.

Legal Capital Rules   To protect the claims of the corporation's creditors, all of the corporation statutes limit the extent to which dividends may be paid. Nearly all of the statutes make a dividend payment illegal if it would render the corporation **insolvent,** that is, unable to pay its currently maturing obligations. In addition, most of the statutes permit a dividend only to the extent of **earned surplus** (retained earnings). However, states such as Delaware permit a solvent corporation to pay a dividend to the extent of surplus, which includes retained earnings and capital surplus (additional paid-in capital).

While these limitations may seem restrictive, other provisions in most of the statutes permit the directors to increase the amount of dividends that may be paid by transferring amounts between the capital accounts of the corporation and by increasing the valuations of corporate assets. In addition, Delaware permits what is called a *nimble dividend*, allowing a corporation to pay a dividend out of current net profits even when the corporation has a negative surplus, but only if its capital equals the liquidation preferences of all shares.

MBCA Approach   The existence of the above statutes, which create the false impression that shareholder capital may not be distributed to shareholders, has led to simpler dividend payment rules. MBCA Section 6.40, for example, has two requirements: (1) the *solvency test* and (2) the *balance sheet test*, which appear in Figure 2.

To illustrate, Batt Company has $27,000 in excess liquidity that it does not need to pay its currently maturing obligations. It has assets of $200,000 and liabilities of $160,000. It has one class of common shareholders. Its one class of preferred shareholders has a liquidation preference of $15,000. Examining these facts, we find that Batt's excess solvency is $27,000, but its excess assets are only $25,000 ($200,000 − 160,000 − 15,000). Therefore, Batt's shareholders may receive a maximum cash or property dividend of $25,000, which will eliminate all of Batt's excess assets and leave Batt with $2,000 of excess solvency.

Share Dividends and Share Splits

Corporations sometimes distribute additional shares of the corporation to their shareholders. Often, this is done in order to give shareholders something instead of a cash dividend so that the cash can be retained and reinvested in the business. Another common objective

FIGURE 2   MBCA Legal Capital Rules for Dividends

Solvency Test
A dividend may not make a corporation insolvent, that is, unable to pay its debts as they come due in the usual course of business. This means that a corporation may pay a dividend to the extent it has *excess solvency;* that is, liquidity that it does not need to pay its currently maturing obligations. This requirement protects creditors, who are concerned primarily with the corporation's ability to pay debts as they mature.

Balance Sheet Test
After the dividend has been paid, the corporation's assets must be sufficient to cover its liabilities and the liquidation preference of shareholders having a priority in liquidation over the shareholders receiving the dividend. This means that a corporation may pay a dividend to the extent it has *excess assets;* that is, assets it does not need to cover its liabilities and the liquidation preferences of shareholders having a priority in liquidation over the shareholders receiving the dividends. This requirement protects not only creditors but also preferred shareholders. It prevents a corporation from paying to common shareholders a dividend that will impair the liquidation rights of preferred shareholders. In valuing the assets, directors are permitted to use any reasonable valuation method rather than merely historical cost.

is to adjust the market price of the shares so that it falls within the popular $20 to $40 per share range. Such an action may be called either a **share dividend** or a **share split.**

Traditional Rules   Traditionally, a **share dividend** of a *specified percentage of outstanding shares* is declared by the board of directors. For example, the board may declare a 10 percent share dividend. As a result, each shareholder will receive 10 percent more shares than she currently owns. A share dividend is paid on outstanding shares only. Unlike a cash or property dividend, a share dividend may be revoked by the board after it has been declared.[9]

When a corporation pays a share dividend, accounting rules require that a corporation transfer the par value of the shares from a surplus account (earned surplus or capital surplus) to a stated capital account.

Traditionally, a **share split** results in shareholders receiving a specified number of shares in exchange for each share that they currently own. For example, shares

---

[9]*Anadarko Petroleum Corp. v. Panhandle Eastern Corp.*, 54 A.2d 1171 (Del. Sup. Ct. 1988).

may be split two for one. Each shareholder will now have two shares for each share that he previously owned. A holder of 50 shares will now have 100 shares instead of 50. A share split affects all *authorized* shares, not merely outstanding shares.

For a share split, accounting rules require that the articles be amended by shareholder action to reduce the par value of the shares and to increase the number of authorized shares.

MBCA Approach The MBCA recognizes that a share split or a share dividend in the same class of shares does not affect the value of the corporation or the shareholders' wealth. The effect is like that produced by taking a pie with four pieces and dividing each piece in half. Each person may receive twice as many pieces of the pie, but each piece is worth only half as much. The total amount received by each person is unchanged. Therefore, MBCA Section 6.23 permits share splits and share dividends of the same class of shares to be made merely by action of the directors. The directors merely have the corporation issue to the shareholders the number of shares needed to effect the share dividend or split. The corporation must have a sufficient number of authorized, unissued shares to effect the share split or dividend; when it does not, its articles must be amended to create the required number of additional shares.

Usually, share dividends are paid in shares of the same class. However, a *share dividend of a different class* may be made. For example, common shareholders may receive a share dividend paid in preferred shares. Such a share distribution reduces the wealth of the shareholders of the class whose shares are issued, and it increases the wealth of the shareholders of the class that receives the shares. Therefore, when shares of one class are issued as share dividends to shareholders of another class, the share dividends must be authorized by the articles or approved by the shareholders of the class whose shares are issued.

The MBCA does not require any transfer between equity accounts when a share dividend or share split is effected. The MBCA recognizes, however, that some corporations may elect to have par value shares. In addition, some publicly held corporations are bound by accounting rules of exchanges on which their shares are traded, such as the New York Stock Exchange rules. In such situations, share dividends and share splits will be accounted for pursuant to the traditional rules discussed above.

Reverse Share Split

A *reverse share split* is a decrease in the number of shares of a class such that, for example, two shares become one share. For par value shares, a reverse share split increases the par value per share by the same factor by which the number of shares are reduced. Most of the state corporation statutes require shareholder action to amend the articles to effect a reverse share split because the number of authorized shares is reduced and the par value per share is increased. The purpose of a reverse share split is usually to increase the market price of the shares. Sometimes, it is used in a freeze-out transaction.[10]

Share Repurchases

Declaring a dividend is only one of the ways in which a corporation may distribute its assets. A corporation may also distribute its assets by repurchasing its shares from its shareholders. Like a dividend, such a repurchase may harm creditors and other shareholders.

All of the corporation statutes, including MBCA Section 6.31, permit a corporation to repurchase its shares. Such a repurchase may be either a *redemption* or an *open-market repurchase*.

The right of **redemption** (or a call) is usually a right of the corporation to force an *involuntary* sale by a shareholder at a fixed price. The shareholder must sell the shares to the corporation at the corporation's request; in most states, the shareholder cannot force the corporation to redeem the shares.

Under MBCA Section 6.01, the right of redemption must appear in the articles of incorporation. It is common for a corporation to issue preferred shares subject to redemption at the corporation's option. Usually, common shares are *not* redeemable.

In addition, a corporation may repurchase its shares *on the open market*. A corporation is empowered to purchase its shares from any shareholder who is willing to sell them. Such repurchases are *voluntary* on the shareholder's part, requiring the corporation to pay a current market price to entice the shareholder to sell.

Legal Capital Rules MBCA Section 6.40 requires a corporation repurchasing shares to meet tests that are the

---

[10] Freeze-outs are discussed in the Management of Corporations chapter.

same as its cash and property dividend rules, recognizing that financially, a repurchase of shares is no different from a dividend or any other distribution of assets to shareholders. See Figure 3.

SHAREHOLDERS' LAWSUITS

Shareholders' Individual Lawsuits

A shareholder has the right to sue in his own name to prevent or redress a breach of the shareholder's contract. For example, a shareholder may sue to recover dividends declared but not paid or dividends that should have been declared, to enjoin the corporation from committing an *ultra vires* act, to enforce the shareholder's right of inspection, and to enforce preemptive rights.

Shareholder Class Action Suits

When several people have been injured similarly by the same persons in similar situations, one of the injured people may sue for the benefit of all the people injured. Likewise, if several shareholders have been similarly affected by a wrongful act of another, one of these shareholders may bring a **class action** on behalf of all the affected shareholders.

An appropriate class action under state corporation law would be an action seeking a dividend payment that has been brought by a preferred shareholder for all of the preferred shareholders. Any recovery is prorated to all members of the class.

A shareholder who successfully brings a class action is entitled to be reimbursed from the award amount for his *reasonable expenses*, including attorney's fees. Otherwise, few rational shareholders would sue, since ordinarily the cost of the suit will far exceed the direct benefit to the shareholder. If the class action suit is unsuccessful and has no reasonable foundation, the court may order the suing shareholder to pay the defendants' reasonable litigation expenses, including attorney's fees.

Shareholders' Derivative Suits

When a corporation has been harmed by the actions of another person, the right to sue belongs to the corporation and any damages awarded by a court belong to the corporation. Hence, as a general rule, a shareholder has no right to sue in his own name when someone

FIGURE 3   MBCA Legal Capital Rules for Share Repurchase

Solvency Test
The repurchase may not make the corporation insolvent; that is, unable to pay its debts as they come due in the usual course of business. This means that a corporation may repurchase shares to the extent it has *excess solvency;* that is, liquidity that it does not need to pay its currently maturing obligations.

Balance Sheet Test
After the repurchase of shares, the corporation's assets must be sufficient to cover its liabilities and the liquidation preference of shareholders having a priority in liquidation over the shareholders whose shares were repurchased. This means that a corporation may repurchase shares to the extent it has *excess assets;* that is, assets it does not need to cover its liabilities and the liquidation preferences of shareholders having a priority in liquidation over the shareholders whose shares were repurchased.

has harmed the corporation, and he may not recover for himself damages from that person. This is the rule even when the tortfeasor's actions impair the value of the shareholder's investment in the corporation. If individual shareholders were permitted to sue for their proportionate shares of a wrong to the corporation, there might be a multiplicity of suits and the individual shareholders might benefit to the detriment of corporate creditors.

Nonetheless, one or more shareholders are permitted under certain circumstances to bring an action for the benefit of the corporation when the directors have failed to pursue a corporate cause of action. For example, if the corporation has a claim against its chief executive for wrongfully diverting corporate assets to her personal use, the corporation is unlikely to sue the chief executive because she controls the board of directors. Clearly, the CEO should not go unpunished. Consequently, corporation law authorizes a shareholder to bring a **derivative action** (or derivative suit) against the CEO on behalf of the corporation and for its benefit. Such a suit may also be used to bring a corporate claim against an outsider. If the derivative suit succeeds and damages are awarded, the damages ordinarily go to the corporate treasury for the benefit of the corporation. The suing shareholder is entitled only to reimbursement of his reasonable attorney's fees that he incurred in bringing the action. However, in a close corporation when the wrongdoing director or officer is a majority shareholder and thereby will benefit indirectly by a damage payment to the corporation, courts may award payment directly to the suing shareholders.[11]

Eligible Shareholders   Although allowing shareholders to bring derivative suits creates a viable procedure for suing wrongdoing officers and directors, this procedure is also susceptible to abuse. **Strike suits** (lawsuits brought to gain out-of-court settlements for the complaining shareholders personally or to earn large attorney's fees, rather than to obtain a recovery for the corporation) have not been uncommon. To discourage abuse, the Federal Rules of Civil Procedure and similar state rules and statutes require, with few exceptions, that the person bringing the action be a current shareholder who held his shares at the time the alleged wrong occurred. In addition, the shareholder must fairly and adequately represent the interests of shareholders similarly situated in enforcing the right of the corporation.

One exception to these rules is the **double derivative suit,** a suit brought by a shareholder of a parent corporation on behalf of a subsidiary corporation owned by the parent. Today, courts regularly permit double derivative suits.[12]

---

[11] For example, *Perlman v. Feldman,* 219 F.2d 173 (2d Cir. 1955). But see *Schacter v. Kulik,* 547 N.E.2d 71, 74 (N.Y. Ct. App. 1989) (awarding payment to shareholder might impair the rights of creditors whose claims are superior to that of an innocent shareholder).

[12] For example, *Brown v. Tenney,* 532 N.E.2d 230 (Ill. Sup. Ct. 1988) (both the subsidiary and the parent must have failed, refused, or been unable to redress the injury to the subsidiary).

Demand on Directors   Since a decision to sue someone is ordinarily made by corporate managers, the Federal Rules of Civil Procedure and state statutes or rules require that a shareholder first *demand* that the board of directors bring the suit. A demand informs the board that the corporation may have a right of action against a person that the board, in its business judgment, may decide to pursue. Therefore, if a demand is made and the board decides to bring the suit, the shareholder may not institute a derivative suit.

Problems arise, however, when a shareholder fails to make a demand or when a demand is made but the board refuses to sue.

Demand Excused   Ordinarily, a shareholder's failure to make a demand on the board prevents her from bringing a derivative suit. Nonetheless, the shareholder may initiate the suit if she proves that a demand on the board would have been useless or **futile.** Demand is futile, and therefore **excused,** if the board is unable to make a disinterested decision regarding whether to sue. Futility may be proved when all or a majority of the directors are interested in the challenged transaction, such as in a suit alleging that the directors issued shares to themselves at below-market prices.

Aronson v. Lewis, noted in Figure 4, presents the Delaware view of when demand is futile.

Demand Refused   If a shareholder makes a demand on the board and it **refuses** the shareholder's demand to bring a suit, the question arises whether the shareholder

---

FIGURE 4   Note on *Aronson v. Lewis,* 473 A.2d 805 (Del. Sup. Ct. 1984)

In *Aronson v. Lewis,* the Supreme Court of Delaware stated that futility would exist when there was a *reasonable doubt that the business judgment rule would apply.* This reasonable doubt may be due to many things, including the directors' interest in the challenged transaction, their lack of independence from the alleged wrongdoers, or their acting contrary to the best interests of the corporation.

The Delaware court refused to find futility in the case, however. The directors had approved an employment agreement between the corporation and one of the directors. That director owned 47 percent of the shares and nominated all of the directors. The court found that the suing shareholder had not proved that the directors lacked independence from the controlling director or that they were "beholden" to him. And the court found no proof that the agreement was a waste of corporate assets. The court ruled that approving the agreement was a valid exercise of business judgment.

should be permitted to bring the suit. Whether a corporation should bring a lawsuit is an ordinary business decision appropriate for a board of directors to make. The business judgment rule, therefore, is available to insulate from court review a board's decision not to bring a suit. The shareholders will not be able to bring a derivative suit after a board's refusal to sue.

Of course, if a shareholder derivative suit accuses the board of harming the corporation, such as by misappropriating the corporation's assets, the board's refusal will not be protected by the business judgment rule because the board has a conflict of interest in its decision to sue. In such a situation, the shareholder may sue the directors despite the board's refusal.

Shareholder Litigation Committees   In an attempt to ensure the application of the business judgment rule in demand refusal and demand futility situations, interested directors have tried to isolate themselves from the decision regarding whether to sue by creating a special committee of the board, called a *shareholder litigation committee* (SLC) (or independent investigation committee), whose purpose is to decide whether to sue. The SLC should consist of directors who are not defendants in the derivative suit, who are not interested in the challenged action, who are independent of the defendant directors, and if possible, who were not directors at the time the wrong occurred. Usually, the SLC has independent legal counsel that assists its determination regarding whether to sue.

Not surprisingly, SLCs rarely decide that the corporation should sue the directors, frequently stating that the litigation is not in the best interests of the corporation and is likely to disrupt management and harm employee morale, and that the cost of the litigation will outweigh the expected benefit to the corporation in light of the probable outcome of the lawsuit. Since the SLC is a committee of the board, its decision may be protected by the business judgment rule. Therefore, an SLC's decision not to sue may prevent a shareholder from suing.

Judicial Reaction to the Use of SLCs   Since 1976, however, several shareholder derivative suits have challenged the application of the business judgment rule to an SLC's decision to dismiss a shareholder derivative suit against some of the directors. The suing shareholders argue that it is improper for an SLC to dismiss a shareholder derivative suit because there is a *structural bias*. That is, the SLC members are motivated by a desire to avoid hurting their fellow directors and adversely affecting future working relationships within the board.

When demand is **not futile,** most of the courts that have been faced with this question have upheld the decisions of special litigation committees that comply with the business judgment rule. The courts require that the SLC members be *independent* of the defendant directors, be *disinterested* with regard to the subject matter of the suit, make a *reasonable investigation* into whether to dismiss the suit, and act in *good faith.*

When demand is futile or excused, most courts faced with the decision of an SLC have applied the rule of the *Zapata* case, which follows.

ZAPATA CORP. v. MALDONADO

430 A.2d 779 (Del. Sup. Ct. 1981)

Zapata Corporation had a share option plan that permitted its executives to purchase Zapata shares at a below-market price. Most of the directors participated in the share option plan. In 1974, the directors voted to advance the share option exercise date in order to reduce the federal income tax liability of the executives who exercised the share options, including the directors. An additional effect, however, was to increase the corporation's federal tax liability.

William Maldonado, a Zapata shareholder, believed that the board action was a breach of a fiduciary duty and that it harmed the corporation. In 1975, he instituted a derivative suit in a Delaware court on behalf of Zapata against all of the directors. He failed to make a demand on the directors to sue themselves, alleging that this would be futile since they were all defendants.

Not futile = because the board of directors are going to benefit from this action

The derivative suit was still pending in 1979, when four of the defendants were no longer directors. The remaining directors then appointed two new outside directors to the board and created an Independent Investigation Committee consisting solely of the two new directors. The board authorized the committee to make a final and binding decision regarding whether the derivative suit should be brought on behalf of the corporation. Following a three-month investigation, the committee concluded that Maldonado's derivative suit should be dismissed as against Zapata's best interests.

Zapata asked the Delaware court to dismiss the derivative suit. The court refused to dismiss the suit, holding that Maldonado possessed an individual right to maintain the derivative action and that the business judgment rule did not apply. Zapata appealed to the Supreme Court of Delaware.

Quillen, Justice.   We find that the trial court's determination that a shareholder, once demand is made and refused, possesses an independent, individual right to continue a derivative suit for breaches of fiduciary duty over objection by the corporation, as an absolute rule, is erroneous.

Derivative suits enforce corporate rights, and any recovery obtained goes to the corporation. We see no inherent reason why a derivative suit should automatically place in the hands of the litigating shareholder sole control of the corporate right throughout the litigation. Such an inflexible rule would recognize the interest of one person or group to the exclusion of all others within the corporate entity.

The question to be decided becomes: When, if at all, should an authorized board committee be permitted to cause litigation, properly initiated by a derivative stockholder in his own right, to be dismissed? The problem is relatively simple. If, on the one hand, corporations can consistently wrest bona fide derivative actions away from well-meaning derivative plaintiffs through the use of the committee mechanism, the derivative suit will lose much, if not all, of its effectiveness as an intracorporate means of policing boards of directors. If, on the other hand, corporations are unable to rid themselves of meritless or harmful litigation and strike suits, the derivative action, created to benefit the corporation, will produce the opposite, unintended result. It thus appears desirable to us to find a balancing point where bona fide shareholder power to bring corporate causes of action cannot be unfairly trampled on by the board of directors, but the corporation can rid itself of detrimental litigation.

We are not satisfied that acceptance of the business judgment rationale at this stage of derivative litigation is a proper balancing point. We must be mindful that directors are passing judgment on fellow directors in the same corporation and fellow directors, in this instance, who designated them to serve both as directors and committee members. The question naturally arises whether a "there but for the grace of God go I" empathy might not play a role. And the further question arises whether inquiry as to independence, good faith and reasonable investigation is sufficient safeguard against abuse, perhaps subconscious abuse.

We thus steer a middle course between those cases that yield to the independent business judgment of a board committee and this case as determined below, which would yield to unbridled shareholder control.

We recognize that the final substantive judgment whether a particular lawsuit should be maintained requires a balance of many factors—ethical, commercial, promotional, public relations, employee relations, fiscal, as well as legal. We recognize the danger of judicial overreaching but the alternatives seem to us to be outweighed by the fresh view of a judicial outsider.

After an objective and thorough investigation of a derivative suit, an independent committee may cause its corporation to file a motion to dismiss the derivative suit. The Court should apply a two-step test to the motion. First, the Court should inquire into the independence and good faith of the committee and the bases supporting its conclusions. The corporation should have the burden of proving independence, good faith, and reasonable investigation, rather than presuming independence, good faith, and reasonableness. If the Court determines either that the committee is not independent or has not shown reasonable bases for its conclusions, or if the Court is not satisfied for other reasons relating to the process, including but not limited to the good faith of the committee, the Court shall deny the corporation's motion to dismiss the derivative suit.

The second step provides the essential key in striking the balance between legitimate corporate claims as expressed in a derivative stockholder suit and a corporation's best interests as expressed by an independent investigating committee. The Court should determine, applying its own independent business judgment, whether the motion should be granted. The second step is intended to thwart instances where corporate actions meet the criteria of step one, but the result does not appear to satisfy its spirit, or where corporate actions would simply prematurely terminate a stockholder grievance deserving of further consideration in the corporation's interest. The Court of course must carefully consider and weigh how compelling the corporate interest in dismissal is when faced with a non-frivolous lawsuit. The Court should, when appropriate, give special consideration to matters of law and public policy in addition to the corporation's best interests.

The second step shares some of the same spirit and philosophy of the statement of the trial court: "Under our system of law, courts and not litigants should decide the merits of litigation."

Judgment reversed in favor of Zapata. Case remanded to the trial court.

Litigation Expenses   If a shareholder is *successful* in a derivative suit, she is entitled to a *reimbursement of her reasonable litigation expenses* out of the corporation's damage award.[13] On the other hand, if the suit is *unsuccessful* and has been brought *without reasonable cause*, most of the corporation statutes, including MBCA Section 7.45, authorize the court to require the shareholder to *pay the defendants' expenses*, including attorney's fees. The purpose of this rule is to deter strike suits by punishing shareholders who litigate in bad faith.

Defense of Corporation by Shareholder

Occasionally, the officers or managers will refuse to defend a suit brought against a corporation. If a shareholder shows that the corporation has a valid defense to the suit and that the refusal or failure of the directors to defend is a breach of their fiduciary duty to the corporation, the courts will permit the shareholder to *defend* for the benefit of the corporation, its shareholders, and its creditors.

---

[13] *Schacter v. Kulik*, 547 N.E.2d 71, 75 (N.Y. Ct. App. 1989) (the corporation that received the benefit of the shareholder suit must pay attorney fees).

SHAREHOLDER LIABILITY

Introduction

Shareholders have many responsibilities and liabilities in addition to their many rights. You have already studied shareholder liability when a shareholder pays too little consideration for shares, when a shareholder breaches a share subscription agreement, when a corporation is defectively formed, and when a corporation's veil is pierced. In this section, four other grounds for shareholder liability are discussed.

Shareholder Liability for Illegal Distributions

Dividends and other distributions of a corporation's assets received by a shareholder with *knowledge of their illegality* may be recovered on behalf of the corporation. Under MBCA Section 8.33(b), primary liability is placed on the directors who, failing to comply with the business judgment rule, authorized the unlawful distribution. However, the directors are entitled to contribution from shareholders who received an asset distribution knowing that it was illegally made. These liability rules enforce the asset-distribution legal capital rules that were discussed earlier in this chapter.

Shareholder Liability for Corporate Debts

One of the chief attributes of a shareholder is his *limited liability:* Ordinarily, he has no liability for corporate obligations beyond his capital contribution. As mentioned above, however, defective incorporation and piercing the corporate veil are grounds on which a shareholder may be held liable for corporate debts beyond his capital contribution. In addition, a few states impose personal liability on shareholders for *wages owed to corporate employees*, even if the shareholders have fully paid for their shares.

Sale of a Control Block of Shares

The per share value of the shares of a majority shareholder of a corporation is greater than the per share value of the shares of a minority shareholder. This difference in value is due to the majority shareholder's ability to control the corporation and to cause it to hire her as an employee at a high salary. Therefore, a majority shareholder can sell her shares for a *premium* over the fair market value of minority shares.

Majority ownership is not always required for control of a corporation. In a close corporation it is required, but in a publicly held corporation with a widely dispersed, hard-to-mobilize shareholder group, minority ownership of from 5 to 30 percent may be enough to obtain control. Therefore, a holder of minority control in such a corporation will also be able to receive a premium.

Noncontrolling shareholders often object when a controlling shareholder sells her shares for more money per share than the noncontrolling shareholders can obtain for their shares. Their objections may result in a suit against the controlling shareholder, asking the court to require her to share her premium with the other shareholders or to relinquish the premium to the corporation.

Current corporation law imposes no liability on any shareholder, whether or not the shareholder is a controlling shareholder, *merely* because she is able to sell her shares for a premium. Nonetheless, if the premium is accompanied by wrongdoing, controlling shareholders have been held liable either for the amount of the premium or for the damages suffered by the corporation. The two grounds that follow are the most common reasons courts find liability in sale-of-control cases.

Selling to Persons Who Will Harm the Corporation   A seller of control shares is liable for selling to a purchaser who harms the corporation if the seller had or should have had a *reasonable suspicion* that the purchaser would mismanage or loot the corporation. The seller is liable to the corporation for the harm caused.

In one case, for example, the sellers' knowledge of facts indicating the purchasers' *history of mismanagement and personal use of corporate assets* obligated them not to sell to the purchasers.[14] A seller may also be placed on notice of a purchaser's bad motives by other factors, such as the purchaser's *lack of interest in the physical facilities* of the corporation and the purchaser's great *interest in the liquid assets* of the corporation. These factors tend to indicate that the purchaser has a short-term interest in the corporation.

The mere payment of a premium is not enough to put the seller on notice. If the *premium is unduly high*, however, such as a $43.75 offer for shares traded in the $7 to $10 range, a seller must doubt whether the purchaser will be able to recoup his investment without looting the corporation.[15]

When a seller has, or should have, a reasonable suspicion that a purchaser will mismanage or loot the corporation, he must not sell to the purchaser unless a *reasonable investigation* shows there is no reasonable risk of wrongdoing. If the selling shareholder has no suspicion, and should have no suspicion, he has no duty to investigate the purchaser and may sell to the purchaser.

Sale of Corporate Asset   Applying the principles of usurpation of a corporate opportunity, a few courts find liability when a selling shareholder takes or sells a *corporate asset*. For example, if a purchaser wants to buy the corporation's assets and the controlling shareholder proposes that the purchaser buy her shares instead, the controlling shareholder is liable for usurping a corporate opportunity.

A more unusual situation existed in *Perlman v. Feldman*.[16] In that case, Newport Steel Corporation had excess demand for its steel production, due to the Korean War. Another corporation, in order to guarantee a steady supply of steel, bought at a premium a minority, yet controlling, block of shares of Newport from Feldman, its chairman and president. The court ruled that Feldman was required to share the premium with the other

---

[14]*DeBaun v. First Western Bank & Trust Co.,* 120 Cal. Rptr. 354 (Cal. Ct. App. 1975).

[15]*Clagett v. Hutchinson,* 583 F.2d 1259 (4th Cir. 1978).

[16]219 F.2d 173 (2d Cir. 1955).

shareholders because he had sold a corporate asset—the ability to exploit an excess demand for steel. The court reasoned that Newport could have exploited that asset to its advantage.

Oppression of Minority Shareholders

A few courts have recognized a fiduciary duty of controlling shareholders to use their ability to control the corporation in a fair, just, and equitable manner that benefits all of the shareholders proportionately. This is in part a duty to be impartial, that is, not to prefer themselves over the minority shareholders. For example, controlling shareholders have an fiduciary duty not to cause the corporation to repurchase their own shares or to pay themselves a dividend, unless the same offer is made to the minority shareholder.[17] When controlling shareholders purchase or causes the corporation to repurchase minority shares—such as pursuant to a buy-and-sell agreement—the controlling shareholders have a duty to disclose all the material facts and circumstances surrounding or affecting the minority shareholders' decision to sell,[18] including preliminary negotiations for the merger of the corporation and impending initiation of merger negotiations.[19]

A controlling shareholder breaches his fiduciary duty by causing another shareholder to breach a share transfer restriction.[20] However, a controlling shareholder breaches no fiduciary duty by enforcing an option agreement requiring a minority shareholder to sell his shares to the corporation, even when the corporation's right to buy the shares was triggered by the controlling shareholder's termination of the minority shareholder's employment with the corporation.[21]

One of the most common examples of oppression is the **freeze-out** of minority shareholders. It occurs in close corporations when controlling shareholders pay themselves high salaries while not employing or paying dividends to noncontrolling shareholders. Since there is usually no liquid market for the shares of the noncontrolling shareholders, they have an investment that provides them no return, while the controlling shareholders reap large gains. Such actions by the majority are especially wrongful when the controlling shareholders follow with an offer to buy the minority's shares at an unreasonably low price.

This duty of controlling shareholders is similar to the duty of managers not to oppress minority shareholders, which was discussed in the Management of Corporations chapter. Often, it is difficult to determine in a particular case whether the court is imposing a duty on the managers or on the controlling shareholders, since both are nearly always the same people. Some carefully written court opinions clearly indicate that the duty belongs to the controlling shareholders.[22]

In the following case, the court held that a majority shareholder violated a duty not to freeze-out minority shareholders.

---

[17]*McDonald v. U. S. Die Casting & Devel. Co.*, 541 So.2d 1064 (Ala. Sup. Ct. 1989).

[18]*Renberg v. Zarrow*, 667 P.2d 465, 471 (Okla. Sup. Ct. 1983); *Lynch v. Vickers Energy Corp.*, 383 A. 2d 278, 278–279 (Del. Sup. Ct. 1977).

[19]*Michaels v. Michaels*, 767 F.2d 751 (2d Cir. 1984). But see *Bershad v. Curtiss-Wright Corp.*, 535 A.2d 840, 847 (Del. Sup. Ct. 1987) (no duty to disclose preliminary negotiations when no offer to purchase corporation was made and sale was unlikely). The duty to disclose merger negotiations under the federal securities law is covered in detail in the Securities Regulation chapter.

[20]*Fought v. Morris*, 543 So.2d 167, 172 (Miss. Sup. Ct. 1989) (good faith standard).

[21]*Ingle v. Glamore Motor Sales Co.*, 535 N.E.2d 1311 (N.Y. Ct. App. 1989) (court specifically noted that the purchase price of the shares was not claimed to be unfair).

[22]See, for example, *Donahue v. Rodd Electrotype Co.*, 328 N.E.2d 505 (Mass. Sup. J. Ct. 1975); *Jones v. H. F. Ahmanson & Co.*, 460 P.2d 464 (Cal. Sup. Ct. 1969).

SUGARMAN v. SUGARMAN

797 F.2d 3 (1st Cir. 1986)

Three brothers—Joseph, Myer, and Samuel Sugarman—owned equal amounts each of the shares of Statler Tissue Corporation. Although ownership was initially balanced, a series of stock transactions resulted in Myer's son Leonard becoming the majority shareholder of the corporation. Samuel gave some of his stock to his son Hyman and to Hyman's children, James, Marjorie, and Jon Sugarman. Hyman sold his shares to Leonard. Joseph Sugarman's shares were repurchased by the corporation. By 1974, Leonard owned 61 percent of the shares and was president and chairman of the board. James, Marjorie, and Jon Sugarman owned 22 percent of the shares.

Marjorie had sought employment with the corporation but was not hired. Jon was employed from 1974 until his discharge in 1978. James never sought employment with the company. After 1975, Myer's value to the corporation was near zero because he had Alzheimer's disease; nonetheless, Myer was employed by the corporation and received a salary equal to Hyman's salary. In 1980, Leonard caused the company to double Myer's pre-1980 salary to $85,000 for 1980 and 1981, when Myer was 87 and 88 years of age. Hyman received no such increase. When Myer retired in 1982, Leonard caused the corporation to pay Myer a yearly pension of $75,000. When Hyman retired in 1980, he received no pension.

The corporation paid no dividends. In 1980, Leonard offered to buy Jon's and Marjorie's shares for $3.33 per share. At that time, Price Waterhouse had advised Leonard that the book value of the corporation's shares was $16.30 per share. Jon and Marjorie refused to sell their shares and instead sued Leonard alleging he had frozen them out of the corporation by depriving them of employment, paying himself and Myer excessive salaries, and refusing to pay dividends. The district court found Leonard liable to Jon and Marjorie for $538,000. Leonard appealed.

Coffin, Circuit Judge.   We first examine the legal standard that must be met to establish a freeze-out of minority shareholders. In *Donahue v. Rodd Electrotype Co.* (1975), the Massachusetts Supreme Judicial Court held that shareholders in a close corporation owe one another a fiduciary duty of "utmost good faith and loyalty." Stockholders in a close corporation "may not act out of avarice, expediency or self-interest in derogation of their duty of loyalty to the other stockholders and the corporation."

The court's decision in *Donahue* was premised on the rationale that the corporate form of a close corporation "supplies an opportunity for the majority stockholders to oppress or disadvantage minority stockholders."

Those who employ the freeze-out technique may refuse to declare dividends; they may drain off the corporation's earnings in the form of exorbitant salaries, and bonuses to the majority shareholder-officers and perhaps their relatives; they may deprive minority shareholders of corporate offices and of employment by the company; they may cause the corporation to sell its assets at an inadequate price to the majority shareholders. All of these devices are designed to ensure that the minority shareholders do not receive any financial benefits from the corporation. The minority stockholders must either suffer their losses or seek a buyer for their shares. This is often the capstone of the majority plan. Because minority shareholders cannot sell their stock on the open market, as can shareholders in public corporations, the minority shareholders may be compelled to deal with the majority and be vulnerable to low offers for their stock. When the minority stockholder agrees to sell out at less than fair value, the majority has won.

It is not sufficient to allege that the majority shareholder has offered to buy the stock of a minority shareholder at an inadequate price. In a close corporation, a minority shareholder who merely receives an offer from a majority shareholder to sell stock at an inadequate price, but does not accept that offer, can seek damages *if* the shareholder can prove that the offer was part of a plan to freeze the minority shareholder out of the corporation. That is, the minority shareholder must first establish that the majority shareholder employed various devices to ensure that the minority shareholder is frozen out of any financial benefits from the corporation through such means as the receipt of dividends or employment, and that the offer to buy stock at a low price is the capstone of the majority plan to freeze out the minority.

The necessary ingredients of a freeze-out of minority shareholders are present in this case. Leonard Sugarman took actions to ensure that Jon and Marjorie would not receive any financial benefits from the corporation. Leonard's overcompensation was designed to freeze out Jon and Marjorie from the company's benefits. Dividends had never been paid by the company. Marjorie had sought and been denied employment and Jon was improperly discharged from employment.

Leonard's offer to buy Jon and Marjorie's stock at an inadequate price was the capstone of a plan to freeze out Jon and Marjorie.

Judgment for Jon and Marjorie affirmed.

Close Corporation Statutes

Some statutes, such as Section 11 of the Statutory Close Corporation Supplement to the MBCA, permit close corporation shareholders to dispense with a board of directors or to arrange corporate affairs as if the corporation were a partnership. The effect of these statutes is to impose management responsibilities, including the fiduciary duties of directors, on the shareholders. In essence, the shareholders are partners and owe each other fiduciary duties similar to those owed between partners of a partnership.

CONCEPT REVIEW

ROLES OF SHAREHOLDERS AND THE BOARD OF DIRECTORS

Corporate Action	Board's Role	Shareholders' Role
Day-to-Day Management	Selects officers; supervises management	Elect and remove directors
Issuance of Shares	Issues shares	Protected by preemptive right
Merger and Share Exchange	Adopts articles of merger or share exchange	Vote to approve merger or share exchange; protected by dissenters' rights
Amendment of Articles of Incorporation	Proposes amendment	Vote to approve amendment
Dissolution	Proposes dissolution	Vote to approve dissolution
Dividends	Declares dividends	Receive dividends
Directors Harm Individual Shareholder Rights	None	Bring individual or class action against directors
Directors Harm Corporation	Sues wrongdoing directors	Bring derivative action against wrongdoing directors

ETHICAL AND PUBLIC POLICY CONCERNS

1. Why should shareholders in a close corporation be permitted to make a long-term voting agreement that permits them to control the corporation? Who benefits from shareholder voting agreements? Does the corporation benefit from such an agreement? Who is harmed by such an agreement? May such an agreement harm shareholders who are parties to the agreement? Is it possible for persons harmed by such agreements to protect themselves? Should there be a maximum legal time period for such agreements?

2. Are dissenters' rights to seek appraisal of their shares the only protection a shareholder needs when the corporation's board of directors proposes a merger harmful to the corporation? Should the shareholder be content with the fair value of his shares although he would rather stop the merger? How can shareholders use their dissenters' rights to deter the board of directors from effecting a merger harmful to the corporation?

3. Should a corporation be permitted to use a shareholder litigation committee (SLC) to decide the future of a shareholder derivative suit? Should the business judgment rule apply to the decision of a SLC, or should the *Zapata* two-step test apply? Do your answers depend on whether the shareholders are suing the directors or someone outside the corporation? How could it ever be in the best interests of a corporation not to sue directors who have personally profited by mismanaging the corporation?

4. Do you agree with the decision in the *Perlman v. Feldman* case, which is discussed in the last section of this chapter? Do you agree that Newport Steel lost its ability to exploit excess demand for steel merely by being acquired by another corporation? After the acquisition, Newport became a subsidiary of the acquiring corporation. Thinking back to the discussion of piercing the corporate veil (History and Nature of Corporations chapter) and the discussion of conflicts of interests (Management of Corporations chapter), what price must the parent corporation pay when it buys steel from Newport?

SUMMARY

Shareholders have a number of rights but few responsibilities. Shareholders have a right to attend annual and special shareholders' meetings. At meetings, all shareholders have the right to vote, unless the articles of incorporation remove that right. Shareholders elect and remove directors, amend the articles of incorporation, and vote on mergers, share exchanges, sales of all or substantially all the assets, and dissolutions. Shareholders have the right to offer resolutions and to comment and to ask questions at shareholders' meetings. A shareholder who dissents to certain matters approved by the shareholders may seek appraisal of her shares.

Cumulative voting and class voting are two means by which shareholders may allocate control of a corporation. In addition, shareholders may use voting trusts, shareholder voting agreements, and irrevocable proxies to obtain control of a corporation.

Shareholders have an absolute right to inspect the corporation's shareholder list and a conditional right to inspect other corporate records for a proper purpose. Shareholders may have a preemptive right to buy a proportionate share of additional shares that the corporation plans to sell, but many states permit corporations to avoid the preemptive right.

Corporation statutes specify the extent to which cash or property dividends may be paid to shareholders and the rules for share repurchases, share dividends, and share splits. The MBCA requires that a dividend payment not make the corporation insolvent or reduce the assets of a corporation below the corporation's liabilities and liquidation preferences. The declaration of dividends is the responsibility of the directors and is protected by the business judgment rule. The MBCA treats share repurchases the same as dividends. However, only director action is necessary to make a share dividend of the same class of shares or to effect a share split.

There are three types of shareholder lawsuits. Shareholders may bring actions in their own names to redress or to prevent a breach of their shareholder contract. They may bring a class action representing themselves and other shareholders who are similarly harmed as individual shareholders. They may also bring derivative suits on behalf of the corporation if the directors fail to sue. However, the board's decision not to sue may be protected by the business judgment rule. Any judgment awarded in a derivative suit goes to the corporation, not to the complaining shareholder.

A shareholder is liable for an illegal distribution if the shareholder knows of the illegality. Under certain circumstances, controlling shareholders will be liable to the corporation or to minority shareholders for selling their shares at a premium above the market price of the shares. Controlling shareholders may also be liable for oppressing minority shareholders.

PROBLEM CASES

1. Facing billions of dollars of creditors' claims, Manville Corporation sought a bankruptcy reorganization. In 1985, Manville's management and its creditors agreed to a reorganization plan, but a group of Manville shareholders objected to the plan's intent to eliminate 90 percent of the shareholders' equity in Manville. The shareholders sued to force Manville to have a shareholders' meeting at which shareholders would remove the current directors and replace them with directors who would negotiate a reorganization plan that would better preserve the shareholders' equity. Manville had not held a shareholders' meeting since 1982. Manville claimed that holding a shareholding meeting would obstruct its reorganization. Should the court grant the shareholders' request for a meeting?

2. Ringling Bros.–Barnum & Bailey Combined Shows had 1,000 common shares outstanding: 315 shares were held by Edith Conway Ringling, 315 by Aubrey Ringling Haley, and 370 by John Ringling North. The shares could be voted cumulatively in an election of directors. The corporation had seven directors. Mrs. Ringling and Mrs. Haley together had sufficient votes to elect five of the seven directors, regardless of how Mr. North voted. Mrs. Ringling and Mrs. Haley entered into a shareholder voting agreement to ensure that they would elect five directors. It provided that they would agree on how to vote their shares on any matter put to shareholders. In the event of their failure to agree, an arbitrator, Karl Loos, would determine how the shares would be voted. The term of the agreement was 10 years. Is this agreement legal?

3. Don Sanders owned 2 percent of the shares of Houston Sports Association (HSA). A group of minority shareholders, including Sanders, tried to enter a voting agreement with 51 percent of HSA shares. The purpose of the agreement was to oust from management John McMullen, the largest shareholder (34 percent) of HSA. However, McMullen promised Sanders that McMullen would vote his shares annually to elect Sanders to the HSA board of directors if Sanders agreed to withdraw his support from the minority shareholder group and to vote his shares to retain McMullen in management. Sanders agreed. Their agreement was only oral.

Subsequently, McMullen was able to acquire 63 percent ownership of HSA, and Sanders—at McMullen's request—increased his holdings to 13 percent. Two years later, Sanders was not reelected to the board despite McMullen's majority ownership of shares. Sanders sued McMullen for violating their voting agreement. Was McMullen held liable?

4. In July 1981, Amplica, Inc., made a public offering of its shares. David Steinberg bought 75 shares for $10 each. Three months later, Amplica announced that it planned to merge with another company. Under the terms of the merger, Amplica shareholders would receive $13.50 per share, which was $.50 more than the market price of Amplica shares on the day prior to the announcement of the merger. Amplica's shareholders approved the merger. Steinberg did not vote for or against the merger, but he turned in his shares and received $13.50 for each share. One month later, Steinberg discovered facts that he believed proved that Amplica's directors acted improperly in approving the merger. He also believed that the price he and other shareholders received was grossly inadequate. Is Steinberg able to enforce his dissenter's rights or to bring a derivative suit on behalf of Amplica against the directors?

5. Cox, the owner of 37.5 percent of Santee Oil Company, objected to a merger of Santee with another corporation. He sought to enforce his dissenter's rights. Three appraisers offered three different figures for the net value of Santee's assets: $1,304,000; $1,169,000; and $895,000. For its last three years, Santee's earnings averaged $53,748. At the time of the merger, oil stocks were selling at a price/earnings ratio of 12 to 1. About nine months prior to the merger, a willing purchaser had offered to buy 10 percent of Santee's shares for $93,160. For what amount should a court value Cox's shares?

6. In July 1969, Charles Pillsbury discovered that Honeywell, Inc., manufactured munitions used in the Vietnam war. Pillsbury had long opposed the Vietnam war, and he was upset to learn that bombs were produced in his own community. On July 14, Pillsbury's agent purchased 100 Honeywell shares in the name of a Pillsbury family nominee. The sole purpose of Pillsbury's purchase was to permit him to communicate with other Honeywell shareholders in the hope of persuading Honeywell's board of directors to cease producing munitions. Later in July, he learned that he was a contingent beneficiary of 242 shares of Honeywell under the terms of a trust formed for his benefit by his grandmother. On August 11, Pillsbury purchased one share of Honeywell in his own name. Pillsbury demanded to inspect Honeywell's shareholder list and all corporate records dealing with munitions manufacture. Must Honeywell make these records available to Pillsbury?

7. Historically, Liggett Group, Inc., had paid quarterly dividends to its shareholders in March, June, September, and December of each year. On May 14, 1980, the Liggett board of directors recommended that shareholders accept a tender offer by GM Sub Corporation at $69 per share. The tender offer provided that if GM Sub acquired more than 50 percent of the Liggett shares, GM Sub and Liggett would merge; the Liggett shareholders who did not tender during the tender offer would receive $69 per share under the merger. 87.4 percent of Liggett tendered their shares. The cash-out merger was effected on August 7. Because the Liggett board believed that it would have been unfair to the shareholders who accepted the tender offer, the board skipped the June 1980 dividend. The board believed that the shareholders who did not tender should not be rewarded for refusing to tender their shares to GM Sub knowing that they would receive the same price per share in the merger. Also, the board believed that $69 was a fair price for the shares. Gabelli & Co. surrendered its Liggett shares pursuant to the merger agreement, but then sued Liggett to force payment of the June 1980 dividend. Did Gabelli succeed?

8. Fred and Maxine Brandon and their four children owned all the shares of Brandon Construction Co., a family corporation. Fred and Maxine owned a majority of the shares. In 1987, the shareholders agreed that Fred and Maxine each would receive a monthly salary of least $12,500. Two months later, daughter Betty Brandon alleged that the salaries were excessive, and that Fred and Maxine were dismantling the corporation and distributing its assets to themselves, without regard for the children's rights as minority shareholders. She initiated a derivative action against her parents, but her siblings responded that Betty did not represent their interests as minority shareholders and that they were content with the salaries paid to their parents. Is Betty a proper person to bring a derivative suit?

9. Robert Orchard and Albert Covelli owned a majority of the shares of six corporations and all the shares of one corporation that operated McDonald's restaurant franchises. Covelli purchased the shares of the minority shareholders of the six corporations, making him the owner of 73 percent of the shares of the corporations and Orchard owner of 27 percent. Covelli owned 85 percent and Orchard 15 percent of the seventh corporation. Since Orchard and Covelli were by then dissatisfied with their relationship, Orchard asked Covelli to repurchase his shares at the same price Covelli paid for the minority shareholders' shares. Covelli agreed to pay Orchard for his shares of the six corporations, but wanted Orchard to give him the shares of the seventh corporation for no consideration. When Orchard refused to do so, Covelli made known his intent to force Orchard into bankruptcy and to remove him from any responsible positions in the corporations. Covelli terminated Orchard's employment with the corporations, removed him as a director, and replaced him with Covelli's son. Orchard remained a minority shareholder of the seven corporations, but the corporations paid no dividends. Does Orchard have any grounds upon which to sue Covelli?

10. H. F. Ahmanson & Co. was the controlling shareholder of United Savings and Loan Association. There was very little trading in the Association's shares, however. To create a public market for their shares, Ahmanson and a few other shareholders of the Association incorporated United Financial Corporation and exchanged each of their Association shares for United shares. United then owned more than 85 percent of the shares of the Association. The minority shareholders of the Association were not given an opportunity to exchange their shares. United made two public offerings of its shares. As a result, trading in United shares was very active, while sales of Association shares decreased to half of the formerly low level, with United as virtually the only purchaser. United offered to purchase Association shares from the minority shareholders for $1,100 per share. Some of the minority shareholders accepted this offer. At that time, the shares held by the majority shareholders were worth $3,700. United also caused the Association to decrease its dividend payments. Has Ahmanson done anything wrong?

CHAPTER 44

SECURITIES REGULATION

INTRODUCTION

Background

Modern securities regulation arose from the rubble of the great stock market crash of October 1929. After the crash, Congress studied its causes and discovered several common problems in securities transactions, the most important ones being:

1. Investors lacked the necessary information to make intelligent decisions whether to buy, sell, or hold securities.

2. Disreputable sellers of securities made outlandish claims about the expected performance of securities and sold securities in nonexistent companies.

Faced with these perceived problems, Congress chose to require securities sellers to **disclose** the information that investors need to make intelligent investment decisions. Congress found that investors are able to make intelligent investment decisions if they are given sufficient information about the company whose securities they are to buy. This **disclosure scheme** assumes that investors need assistance from government in acquiring information but that they need no help in evaluating information.

To implement its disclosure scheme, in the early 1930s Congress passed two major statutes, which remain essentially unchanged and are the hub of federal securities regulation in the United States today. These two statutes, the **Securities Act of 1933** and the **Securities Exchange Act of 1934**, have three basic purposes:

1. To require the disclosure of meaningful information about a security and its issuer to allow investors to make intelligent investment decisions.[1]

2. To impose liability on those persons who make inadequate and erroneous disclosures of information.

3. To require the registration of issuers, insiders, professional sellers of securities, securities exchanges, and other self-regulatory securities organizations.

The most important of these purposes is the first. The crux of the securities acts is to impose on issuers of securities, other sellers of securities, and selected buyers of securities the affirmative duty to disclose important

---

[1] An issuer of a security is the person in whom the security represents an ownership interest or of whom the security represents an obligation. For example, GM is the issuer of its common stock, which represents an ownership interest in GM. Also, GM is the issuer of its debentures, which represent debt obligations of GM.

information, even if they are not asked by investors to make the disclosures. This is a dramatic departure from the law of contracts and torts that was applied to securities transactions before 1933.

By requiring disclosure, Congress hoped to restore investor confidence in the securities markets. Congress wanted to bolster investor confidence in the honesty of the stock market and thus encourage more investors to invest in securities. Building investor confidence would increase capital formation and, it was hoped, help the American economy emerge from the Great Depression of the 1930s.

Securities Act of 1933

The Securities Act of 1933 (1933 Act) is concerned primarily with **public distributions** of securities. That is, the 1933 Act regulates the sale of securities while they are passing from the hands of the issuer into the hands of public investors. An issuer selling securities publicly must make necessary disclosures at the time the issuer sells the securities to the public. The 1933 Act is chiefly a **onetime disclosure** statute. Although some of the 1933 Act's liability provisions cover all fraudulent sales of securities, the mandatory disclosure provisions apply only during a public distribution of securities by the issuer and those assisting the issuer.

Securities Exchange Act of 1934

By contrast, the mandatory disclosure provisions of the Securities Exchange Act of 1934 (1934 Act) require **periodic disclosures** by issuers of securities. An issuer with publicly traded equity securities must report annually and quarterly to its shareholders. Any material information about the issuer must be disclosed as the issuer obtains it, unless the issuer has a valid business purpose for withholding disclosure.

Integrated Disclosure

Since the information required in the 1933 and 1934 acts' disclosure documents is duplicative in many respects, the SEC has taken steps to reduce the disclosure burdens of public issuers subject to the disclosure requirements of both acts. As a result, an issuer already making periodic disclosures of information under the 1934 Act may substantially reduce its 1933 Act disclosure burden by using 1934 Act documents when making an issuance under the 1933 Act. For example, the 1933

Act's Regulation D—which is discussed later in this chapter—permits an issuer to use the 1934 Act 10-K annual report to meet its disclosure obligations under Regulation D.

Securities and Exchange Commission

The Securities and Exchange Commission (SEC) was created by the 1934 Act. Its responsibility is to administer the 1933 and 1934 acts and other securities statutes. Like other federal administrative agencies, the SEC has legislative, executive, and judicial functions. Its legislative branch promulgates rules and regulations; its executive branch brings enforcement actions against alleged violators of the securities statutes and their rules and regulations; its judicial branch decides whether a person has violated the securities laws. For more information on the functions of administrative agencies like the SEC, see the Administrative Agencies chapter.

SEC Actions

The SEC is empowered to investigate violations of the 1933 and 1934 acts and to hold hearings to determine whether these acts have been violated. Such hearings are held before an administrative law judge, who is an employee of the SEC. The administrative law judge (ALJ) is a finder of both fact and law. Decisions of the ALJ are reviewed by the commissioners of the SEC. Decisions of the commissioners are appealed to the U.S. courts of appeals.

Most SEC actions are not litigated. Instead, the SEC issues consent orders, by which the defendant promises not to violate the securities laws in the future but does not admit to having violated them in the past.

In 1990, the SEC was granted new powers to impose civil penalties (fines) up to $500,000 and to issue **cease and desist orders**. A cease and desist order directs a defendant to stop violating the securities laws and to desist from future violations. Nonetheless, the SEC does not have the power to issue injunctions; only courts may issue injunctions. The 1933 Act and the 1934 Act empower the SEC only to ask federal district courts for injunctions against persons who have violated or are about to violate either Act. The SEC may also ask the courts to grant ancillary relief, a remedy in addition to an injunction. Ancillary relief may include, for example, the disgorgement of profits that a defendant has made in a fraudulent sale or in an illegal insider trading transaction.

CONCEPT REVIEW

THE SECURITIES AND EXCHANGE COMMISSION

Members of the Commission	☐ Five commissioners ☐ Appointed by the president of the United States with the advice and consent of the Senate ☐ Serve five-year terms ☐ No more than three commissioners may be members of the same political party
Statutes Administered by the SEC	☐ Securities Act of 1933; primarily regulates the sale of securities by issuers to public investors ☐ Securities Exchange Act of 1934; primarily regulates the trading of securities after issuers have sold the securities to the public ☐ Trust Indenture Act of 1939; requires the use of a trust indenture for debt securities issued under the 1933 Act ☐ Investment Company Act of 1940; regulates the operation of mutual funds and the marketing of their securities ☐ Investment Advisers Act of 1940; regulates all types of investment advisers, including those who provide individualized advice and those who publish investment newsletters ☐ Bankruptcy Reform Act of 1978; the SEC serves as an adviser to the bankruptcy courts in corporate reorganization proceedings in which there is a substantial public interest
Divisions and Offices of the SEC	☐ Division of Enforcement ☐ Division of Market Regulation ☐ Division of Corporate Finance ☐ Division of Investment Management ☐ The General Counsel ☐ Office of Economic Analysis ☐ Office of Chief Accountant ☐ Office of EDGAR Management (Electronic Data Gathering, Analysis, and Retrieval System) ☐ Office of Opinion and Review ☐ Office of Administrative Law Judges ☐ Office of Consumer Affairs and Information Services ☐ Office of International Affairs ☐ Office of Applications and Report Services
Powers of the SEC	☐ Investigate violations of the securities laws ☐ Subpoena witnesses with evidence relevant to its investigations ☐ Compel the production of books and records relevant to its investigations ☐ Promulgate rules and regulations ☐ Order and conduct administrative hearings ☐ Adjudicate civil liability for violations of the securities laws ☐ Issue cease and desist orders ☐ Impose monetary penalties on a defendant ☐ Issue consent orders in which the defendant promises not to violate the securities laws in the future ☐ Suspend brokers and accountants from practicing before the SEC ☐ Suspend the sale of securities
Powers the SEC Does *Not* Have	☐ Bring criminal actions against violators of the securities laws; but the SEC may refer a criminal matter to the U.S. Department of Justice (attorney general), which brings criminal actions ☐ Issue injunctions; but the SEC may ask a court to issue an injunction; the SEC may also ask a court to award ancillary relief, which may include disgorgement of profits made in a transaction violating the securities laws

WHAT IS A SECURITY?

The first issue in securities regulation is the definition of a security. If a transaction involves no security, then the law of securities regulation does not apply. The 1933 Act defines the term *security* broadly:

Unless the context otherwise requires the term "security" means any note, stock, bond, debenture, evidence of indebtedness, certificate of interest of participation in any profit-sharing agreement, . . . preorganization certificate or subscription, . . . investment contract, voting trust certificate, . . . fractional undivided interest in oil, gas, or mineral rights, . . . or, in general, any interest or instrument commonly known as a "security."

The 1934 Act definition of security is similar, but excludes notes and drafts that mature not more than nine months from the date of issuance.

Investment Contract

While typical securities like common shares, preferred shares, bonds, and debentures are defined as securities, the definition of a security also includes many contracts that the general public may believe are not securities. This is because the term **investment contract** is broadly defined by the courts. The Supreme Court's three-part test for an investment contract, called the *Howey* test, has been the guiding beacon in the area for the past 45 years.[2] The *Howey* test states that an investment contract is an investment of money in a common enterprise with an expectation of profits solely from the efforts of others.

------
[2] *SEC v. W. J. Howey Co.*, 328 U.S. 293 (U.S. Sup. Ct. 1946).

1. An investment of money. The purchaser must have an investment motive, not a consumption motive (as with a golfer purchasing a membership in a country club) or a commercial motive (as with a bank lending money to a corporate creditor).

2. A common enterprise. The fortunes of the investors must be similarly affected by the efforts of the investment promoters or managers.

3. An expectation of profits from the efforts of others. The undeniably significant efforts that determine the success or failure of the venture must be those of the investment promoters or managers, not those of the investors.[3]

Examples   In the *Howey* case, the sales of plots in an orange grove along with a management contract were held to be sales of securities. The purchasers had investment motives (they did not consume the oranges produced by the trees). They were similarly affected by the efforts of the sellers who grew and sold the oranges for all investors. The sellers, not the buyers, did all of the work needed to make the plots profitable.

In other cases, sales of limited partnership interests, Scotch whisky receipts, and restaurant franchises have been held to constitute investment contracts and, therefore, securities. In the following case, *Long v. Shultz Cattle Co., Inc.*, the court applied the *Howey* test to cattle feeding consulting agreements.

------
[3] *SEC v. Glenn W. Turner Enterprises, Inc.*, 474 F.2d 476, 482 (9th Cir.), cert. denied, 414 U.S. 821 (1973).

LONG v. SHULTZ CATTLE CO., INC.
881 F.2d 129 (5th Cir. 1989)

Jim Long, Jerome Atchley, and Jon and Linda Coleman invested in a cattle-feeding program offered by Shultz Cattle Company, Inc. (SCCI). They first intended to be limited partners in SCCI's cattle-feeding limited partnership, but when SCCI failed to obtain regulatory approval of the sale of limited partnership interests, they switched to SCCI's individual feeding program, under which investors would purchase and raise their own cattle. However, each investor was required to sign a consulting agreement by which SCCI agreed to provide advice regarding the purchase, feeding, and sale of the investor's cattle. SCCI received only a flat-rate consulting fee of $20 per head of cattle for these services and received no share of the investors' profits.

To receive tax benefits from the investment, the tax laws required investors to participate actively in farming. Therefore, SCCI required each investor to represent that "he will exert substantial and significant control over, and will, exercising independent judgment, make all principal and significant management decisions concerning his cattle feeding operations."

Investors could limit any real risk of loss of investment by hedging their cattle: By buying or selling commodities futures they could lock in a price and minimize their potential losses. SCCI arranged for hedging transactions to be conducted through financial institutions, feedyards, and a brokerage firm of which SCCI was a branch office.

Long, Atchley, and the Colemans' cattle were fed, along with those of many other SCCI clients, in a feedyard in which the cattle were commingled. The cattle were tagged by pen number and not by individual investor. Each investor therefore owned a percentage of the total pounds of cattle in the pen. If any cattle died, the loss was not attributed to a single investor, but was distributed pro rata among the investors.

During the first year, Long, Atchley, and the Colemans hedged all their cattle and lost half of the money they had invested. In the second year, they decided to hedge only half of their 1,450 head of cattle. When beef prices declined drastically, they lost over $100,000. They sued SCCI for selling unregistered securities. The jury found that the consulting agreements were not investment contracts or otherwise securities. Long, Atchley, and the Colemans appealed.

King, Circuit Judge. In *S.E.C. v. W. J. Howey Co.* (1946), the Supreme Court held that to determine whether a scheme is an investment contract, the test is whether the scheme involves (1) an investment of money (2) in a common enterprise (3) with profits to come solely from the efforts of others. The parties do not dispute that the first prong of the *Howey* test is satisfied in this case. Only the latter two elements—whether the cattle-feeding scheme was a common enterprise and whether the investors expected profits solely from the efforts of others—are contested. Because the controversy centers primarily on the third prong, we will discuss that issue first.

To ensure that the securities laws are not easily circumvented by agreements requiring a "modicum of effort" by investors, the word "solely" in the third prong of the *Howey* test has not been construed literally. The critical inquiry is instead whether the efforts made by those other than the investor are the undeniably significant ones, those essential managerial efforts which affect the failure or success of the enterprise. Even where an investor formally possesses substantial powers, the third prong of the *Howey* test may be met if the investor demonstrates that he is so inexperienced and unknowledgeable in the field of business at issue that he is incapable of intelligently exercising the rights he formally possesses.

Long, Atchley, and the Colemans had a substantial degree of theoretical control over their investments. They could, theoretically, move their cattle to a different feedyard, decide what to feed them, provide their own veterinary care, or seek buyers on their own. Moreover, the investors were *required* to authorize every management decision involving their cattle. However, at each juncture, the investors relied solely on the advice of SCCI: they followed SCCI's recommendations regarding the purchase of cattle, the choice of a feedyard, the choice of financial institution to provide financing, the choice of commodities brokers, the decision when to sell, and the decision to whom to sell.

Long, Atchley, and the Colemans, who lived in places far removed from their cattle, lacked the experience necessary to care for, feed, and market their cattle. SCCI relies on the theory that the cattle-feeding business does not require a great deal of specialized knowledge but rather depends upon a finite number of macroeconomic or big picture decisions. There is one crucial flaw in SCCI's theory: its clients acquire *from* SCCI all of the knowledge necessary to "actively manage" their "individual" cattle-feeding businesses. SCCI contends, in other words, that investors may become knowledgeable through the educative efforts of the promoters. We do not believe that the securities laws may be avoided so easily.

SCCI hopes to avoid the securities laws by simply attaching the label "consulting agreement" to a package of services which otherwise would clearly be an investment contract. The label "consulting agreement" cannot bear the meaning SCCI has given it. Indeed, SCCI's "individual" cattle-feeding program differs only in form from its limited partnerships. Although clients in the individual program technically were required to make their own decisions, SCCI performed for them—*at a higher cost*—all the services it performed for the limited partners in the other program.

Although Long, Atchley, and the Colemans's decision to hedge only half of their cattle was "undeniably significant" in terms of the risks to which the investors were exposed, it does not alter the essential character of the SCCI scheme. An investor may authorize the assumption of particular risks that would create the possibility of greater profits or losses but still depend on a third party for all of the essential managerial efforts without which the risk could not pay off. The fact that Long, Atchley, and the Colemans chose the riskier course cannot, by itself, transform the essential nature of the underlying contract any more than the fact that an individual investor chooses to buy high-risk junk bonds rather than low-risk AAA bonds causes one bond and not the other to be a security.

We conclude that the third prong of the *Howey* test was established as a matter of law. The jury's verdict would nevertheless stand if the evidence could support the conclusion that the second prong of the *Howey* test—the existence of a common enterprise—was not met. The Third, Sixth, and Seventh Circuits hold that a showing of "horizontal commonality"—a pooling of investors—is necessary to meet the common enterprise requirement. Under this standard, investors' fortunes must be tied to one another in order to constitute a common enterprise.

This court, together with the Ninth and Eleventh Circuits, has explicitly rejected the view that horizontal commonality is a prerequisite to establishing a common enterprise and has focused instead on the "vertical commonality" between the investors and the promoter. The critical factor is not the similitude or coincidence of investor input, but rather the uniformity of impact of the promoter's decisions.

While our standard requires interdependence between the investors and the promoter, it does not define that interdependence narrowly in terms of shared profits and losses. Rather, the necessary interdependence may be demonstrated by the investors' collective reliance on the promoter's expertise even where the promoter receives only a flat fee or commission rather than a share in the profits of the venture.

We recognize that under our standard the second and third prongs of the *Howey* test may in some cases overlap and that our standard has been criticized for that reason. We are not convinced that it would be desirable to adopt a rigid requirement that profits and losses be shared on a *pro rata* basis among investors, or that the promoter's fortunes correlate directly to the profits and losses of investors.

Here, all of SCCI's clients were dependent on SCCI's expertise to manage their investments. Moreover, SCCI's fortunes clearly were interwoven with those of their clients. SCCI received substantial "consulting fees" from its clients in exchange for its services in constructing and administering effective tax shelters through the cattle-feeding business. Through the inexorable force of the market, SCCI's success would correspond to that of its clients.

Judgment reversed in favor of Long, Atchley, and the Colemans.

Economic Realities Test

In recent years, the courts have used the *Howey* test to hold that some contracts with typical security names are not securities. Using an economic realities test, the courts point out that some of these contracts possess few of the typical characteristics of a security. For example, in *United Housing Foundation, Inc. v. Forman*,[4] the Supreme Court held that although tenants in a cooperative apartment building purchased contracts labeled as stock, the contracts were not securities. The "stock" possessed few of the typical characteristics of stock and the economic realities of the transaction bore few similarities to those of the typical stock sale: The stock gave tenants no dividend rights or voting rights in proportion to the number of shares owned, it was not negotiable, and it could not appreciate in value. More important, tenants bought the stock not for the purpose of investment but to acquire suitable living space.

However, the Supreme Court has made it clear that when investors are misled to believe that the securities laws apply because a seller sold a contract bearing both the name of a typical security and significant characteristics of that security, the securities laws do apply to the sale of the security.[5] The application of this doctrine led, in 1985, to the Supreme Court's rejection of the sale-of-business doctrine, which had held that the sale of 100 percent of the shares of a corporation to a single purchaser who would manage the corporation was not a security.[6] The rationale for the sale-of-business doctrine was that the purchaser failed to meet element 3 of the *Howey* test because he expected to make a profit from his own efforts in managing the business. Today, when a business sale is effected by the sale of stock, the transaction is covered by the securities acts if the stock possesses the characteristics of stock.

Family Resemblance Test

In 1990, the Supreme Court further extended this rationale in *Reves v. Ernst & Young*,[7] adopting the **family**

resemblance test to determine whether promissory notes were securities. The Supreme Court held that it is inappropriate to apply the *Howey* test to notes. Instead, applying the family resemblance test, the Court held that notes are presumed to be securities unless they bear a "strong family resemblance" to a type of note that is not a security. Types of notes that are not securities include consumer notes, mortgage notes, short-term notes secured by a lien on a small business, short-term notes secured by accounts receivable, and notes evidencing loans by commercial banks for current operations.

In addition, the Court listed four factors relevant to a determination of whether a note is a security. The four factors are:

1. The motivations that would prompt a reasonable buyer and seller to enter into the transaction. For example, when the seller's purpose is to raise money for the general use of the business and the buyer is primarily interested in the profit the note is expected to generate, the note is likely to be a security.

2. The plan of distribution of the note to determine whether there was common trading for speculation or investment.

3. The reasonable expectations of the investing public concerning whether the notes are securities.

4. Whether some factor, such as the existence of another regulatory scheme, reduces the risk of the notes, thereby rendering application of the securities statutes unnecessary.

SECURITIES ACT OF 1933

Introduction

The 1933 Act has two principal regulatory components: (1) registration provisions and (2) antifraud provisions. The registration requirements of the 1933 Act are designed to give investors the information they need to make intelligent decisions whether to purchase securities when an issuer sells its securities to the public. The issuer of the securities is required to file a **registration statement** with the Securities and Exchange Commission and to make a **prospectus** available to prospective purchasers. The various antifraud provisions in the 1933 Act impose liability on sellers of securities for misstating or omitting facts of material significance to investors.

---

[4] *United Housing Foundation, Inc. v. Forman*, 421 U.S. 837 (U.S. Sup. Ct. 1975).

[5] *Id.*

[6] *Landreth Timber Co. v. Landreth*, 471 U.S. 681 (U.S. Sup. Ct. 1985). *Accord, Gould v. Ruefenacht*, 471 U.S. 701 (U.S. Sup. Ct. 1985) (privately negotiated sale of 50 percent of shares of corporation is a sale of securities).

[7] 110 S.Ct. 945 (U.S. Sup. Ct. 1990).

Registration of Securities under the 1933 Act

The 1933 Act usually requires the issuer of securities to register the securities with the SEC prior to the issuer's offer or sale of the securities.

Registration Statement   Historical and current data about the issuer and its business, full details about the securities to be offered, and the use of the proceeds of the issuance, among other information, must be included in a **registration statement** prepared by the issuer of the securities. Generally, the registration statement must include audited balance sheets as of the end of each of the two most recent fiscal years, in addition to audited income statements and audited statements of changes in financial position for each of the last three fiscal years. The issuer must file the registration statement with the SEC.

The registration statement must be signed by the issuer, its chief executive officer, its chief financial officer, its chief accounting officer, and at least a majority of its board of directors. Signing a registration statement is an important event, for it makes a person potentially liable for errors in the statement.

The registration statement becomes **effective** after it has been reviewed by the SEC. The SEC reviews only whether a registration statement is complete and whether it contains *per se fraudulent* statements. Examples of per se fraudulent statements are statements that tout the securities ("These are the best securities you can buy") and forecasts that are not reasonably based (a start-up company promising a 35 percent annual return on investment on its common stock).

The 1933 Act provides that the registration statement becomes effective on the 20th day after its filing. However, the SEC may advance the date or it may require an amendment that will restart the 20-day period; because the SEC usually requires an amendment, the effective date is usually later than 20 days after the original filing date.

Prospectus   The prospectus is the basic selling document of an offering registered under the 1933 Act. Most of the information in the registration statement must be included in the prospectus. It must be furnished to every purchaser of the registered security prior to or concurrently with the delivery of the security to the purchaser. The prospectus enables an investor to base his investment decision on all of the relevant data concerning the issuer, not merely on the favorable information that the issuer may be inclined to disclose voluntarily.

Section 5: Timing, Manner, and Content of Offers and Sales

The 1933 Act restricts the issuer's ability to communicate with prospective purchasers of the securities. Section 5 of the 1933 Act states the basic rules regarding the timing, manner, and content of offers and sales. It creates three important periods of time in the life of a security offering: (1) the pre-filing period, (2) the waiting period, and (3) the post-effective period.

The Pre-filing Period

Prior to the filing of the registration statement (the **pre-filing period**), the issuer and any other person may **not offer or sell** the securities to be registered. A prospective issuer, its directors and officers, and its underwriters must avoid publicity about the issuer and the prospective issuance of securities during the prefiling period. Press releases, advertisements, speeches, and press conferences may be deemed offers if their intent or effect is to *condition the market* to receive the securities.

SEC Rule 135 permits the issuer to publish a notice about a prospective offering during the pre-filing period. The notice may contain only the name of the issuer and a basic description of the securities and the offering. It may not name the underwriters or state the price at which the securities will be offered.[8]

The Waiting Period

The **waiting period** is the time between the filing date and the effective date of the registration statement, when the issuer is waiting for the SEC to declare the registration statement effective. During the waiting period, Section 5 permits the securities to be **offered but not sold.** However, not all kinds of offers are permitted. Face-to-face oral offers (including personal phone calls) are allowed during the waiting period. However, written offers may be made only by a statutory prospectus, usually a **preliminary prospectus** that often omits the price of the securities. (A final prospectus will be available after the registration statement becomes effective. It will contain the price of the securities.)

---

[8] In this context, underwriters are professional sellers of securities whom the issuer hires to assist the issuer's sale of the securities to the public. The definition of underwriter in this context should not be confused with the broader definition of underwriter in the Rule 144 context discussed later in this chapter.

FIGURE 1   Example of Tombstone Ad

This announcement is neither an offer to sell nor a solicitation of an offer to buy any of these Securities.
The offer is made only by the Prospectus.

April 27, 1990

2,250,000 Shares

Common Stock

Price $8 Per Share

Copies of the Prospectus may be obtained in any State from only such of the
undersigned as may legally offer these Securities in compliance with
the securities laws of such State.

Robertson, Stephens & Company   **Bateman Eichler, Hill Richards**
Incorporated

Donaldson, Lufkin & Jenrette   **Hambrecht & Quist**
Securities Corporation   Incorporated

Merrill Lynch Capital Markets   **Prudential–Bache Capital Funding**

Blunt Ellis & Loewi   **Crowell, Weedon & Co.**   **Gordon, Haskett Capital Corporation**
Incorporated

Interstate/Johnson Lane   **Needham & Company, Inc.**   **Ragen MacKenzie**
Corporation   Incorporated

Seidler Amdec Securities Inc.   **Sutro & Co.**   **Tucker Anthony**
Incorporated   Incorporated

Wedbush Morgan Securities   **Wessels, Arnold & Henderson**

As during the pre-filing period, general publicity during the waiting period may be construed as an illegal offer because it conditions the market to receive the securities. One type of general advertisement, called the **tombstone ad** (see Figure 1), is permitted during the waiting period and thereafter. The tombstone ad, which appears in financial publications, is permitted by SEC Rule 134, which allows disclosure of the same informa-

tion as is allowed by Rule 135 plus the general business of the issuer, the price of the securities, and the names of the underwriters who are helping the issuer to sell the securities. In addition, Rule 134 requires the tombstone ad to state that it is not an offer.

The waiting period is an important part of the regulatory scheme of the 1933 Act. It provides an investor with adequate time (at least 20 days) to judge the wisdom of buying the security during a period when he cannot be pressured to buy it. Not even a contract to buy the security may be made during the waiting period.

The Post-effective Period

After the effective date (the date on which the SEC declares the registration effective), Section 5 permits the security not only to be offered but also to be sold, provided that the buyer has received a **final prospectus** (a preliminary prospectus is not acceptable for this purpose). Written offers not previously allowed are permitted during the post-effective period, if each offeree has received a final prospectus.

CONCEPT REVIEW

COMMUNICATIONS WITH INVESTORS BY OR ON BEHALF OF ISSUER PERMITTED BY SECTION 5 DURING A 1933 ACT REGISTRATION

Type of Communication	Pre-filing Period	Filing Date of Registration Statement — Waiting Period	Effective Date of Registration Statement — Post-effective Period
Annual Reports, Press Releases, and Quarterly Reports	Yes; unless designed to assist the placement of securities or arouse interest in a prospective sale of securities	Yes; unless designed to assist the placement of securities or arouse interest in a prospective sale of securities	Yes; without restriction if used contemporaneously with or after delivery of final prospectus
Notice of Proposed Offering (Rule 135)	Yes	Yes	Yes
Tombstone Ad (Rule 134)	No	Yes	Yes
Offer by Preliminary Prospectus	No	Yes	No
Offer by Final Prospectus	No	No	Yes
Oral-Face-to-Face Offers (including telephone calls)	No	Yes	Yes
Oral Offers at Sales Meeting	No	Yes, if each investor has an opportunity to ask unlimited questions	Yes, if each investor has an opportunity to ask unlimited questions, or if each investor has received a final prospectus
Offer by Free-Writing	No	No	Yes, contemporaneously with or after delivery of final prospectus
Sale	No	No	Yes, contemporaneously with or after delivery of final prospectus

EXEMPTIONS FROM THE REGISTRATION REQUIREMENTS OF THE 1933 ACT

Complying with the registration requirements of the 1933 Act is a burdensome, time-consuming, and expensive process. Planning and executing an issuer's first public offering may consume six months and cost in excess of $1 million. Consequently, some issuers prefer to avoid registration when they sell securities. Fortunately for them, several exemptions from registration are available to issuers.

There are two types of exemptions from the registration requirements of the 1933 Act: securities exemptions and transaction exemptions.

Exempt Securities

Exempt securities never need to be registered, regardless of who sells the securities, how they are sold, or to whom they are sold. The following are the most important securities exemptions.[9]

1. *Securities issued or guaranteed by any government in the United States and its territories.* For example, municipal bonds (issued by city governments) are exempt securities. A debenture issued by a corporation and guaranteed by the federal government is also exempt.

2. A *note or draft that has a maturity date not more than nine months after its date of issuance.* For example, commercial paper issued by General Motors Corporation and due in three months is exempt. The reasons for the exemption are that such commercial paper is used primarily in lending transactions, not investment transactions, and that the lender and the borrower have nearly equal bargaining power. The lender should be able to protect itself without the benefit of a securities registration.

3. A *security issued by a nonprofit religious, charitable, educational, benevolent, or fraternal organization.* For example, bonds issued by a nonprofit university

or by a nonprofit church would be exempt from registration under the 1933 Act.

4. *Securities issued by banks and by savings and loan associations.* The issuance of these securities is subject to regulation by other administrative agencies.

5. *Securities issued by railroads and trucking companies regulated by the Interstate Commerce Commission.* The ICC regulates the issuance of such securities.

6. *An insurance policy or an annuity contract.* For example, a life insurance contract is exempt from 1933 Act registration. Such contracts are regulated by the various state insurance departments.

Not Antifraud Exemptions

Although the types of securities listed above are exempt from the registration provisions of the 1933 Act, they are not exempt from the antifraud provisions of the act. Therefore, any fraud committed in the course of selling such securities can be attacked by the SEC and by the persons who were defrauded.

Transaction Exemptions

The most important 1933 Act exemptions are the transaction exemptions. If a security is sold pursuant to a transaction exemption, that sale is exempt. Subsequent sales, however, are not automatically exempt. Future sales must be made pursuant to a registration or another exemption.

As with the securities exemptions, the transaction exemptions are exemptions from the registration provisions only. The antifraud provisions of the 1933 Act apply equally to exempted and nonexempted transactions.

Transaction Exemptions for Issuers

The most important transaction exemptions are those available to issuers of securities. These exemptions are the intrastate offering exemption, the private offering exemption, and the small offering exemptions.

Intrastate Offering Exemption

Under section 3(a)(11), an offering of securities solely to investors in one state by an issuer resident and doing business in that state is exempt from the 1933 Act's registration requirements. The reason for the exemption is that there is little federal government interest in

---

[9] Excluded from the list of securities exemptions are the intrastate offering and small offering exemptions. Although the 1933 Act denotes them (except for the section 4(6) exemption) as securities exemptions, they are in practice transaction exemptions. An exempt security is exempt from registration forever. But when securities originally sold pursuant to an intrastate or small offering exemption are resold at a later date, the subsequent sales may have to be registered. The exemption of the earlier offering does not exempt a future offering. The SEC treats these two exemptions as transaction exemptions. Consequently, this chapter also treats them as transaction exemptions.

an offering that occurs in only one state. Although the offering may be exempt from SEC regulation, state securities law may require a registration.[10] The expectation is that state securities regulation will adequately protect investors.

---

[10] State securities law is covered at the end of this chapter.

The SEC has defined the intrastate offering exemption more precisely in Rule 147. An issuer must have 80 percent of its gross revenues and 80 percent of its assets in the state and use 80 percent of the proceeds of the offering in the state. Resale of the securities is limited to persons within the state for nine months.

Rule 147, however, is not an exclusive rule. In the following case, the court applied only the standard in Securities Act section 3(a)(11).

BUSCH v. CARPENTER

827 F.2d 653 (10th Cir. 1987)

Sonic Petroleum, Inc., was incorporated in Utah for the purpose of acquiring, extracting, and marketing natural resources such as oil, gas, and coal. Its corporate office, books, and records were in Utah. During October and November 1980, Sonic publicly offered and sold 25 million shares entirely to residents of Utah. The proceeds were $500,000. Sonic did not file a Securities Act registration statement with the SEC, instead relying on the exemption from registration for intrastate offerings. At the time of the offering, Sonic had not undertaken any business activities in Utah or anywhere else.

Craig Carpenter, Sonic's president, negotiated Sonic's acquisition of an Illinois drilling corporation owned by William Mason. On May 25, 1981, Sonic issued a controlling block of its shares to Mason in exchange for Mason's corporation. Shortly thereafter, Sonic deposited in Illinois $350,000 of the proceeds from the sale of shares to Utah residents. At about the same time, Mason and Carpenter helped create a public market for Sonic shares. As a result, Paul and Linda Busch, who were California residents, purchased Sonic shares from Utah residents who had purchased shares in October and November 1980. When the shares' value dropped, the Busches sued Carpenter for selling unregistered securities. The trial court held that Sonic sold the shares pursuant to the intrastate offering exemption and, therefore, did not need to register the shares. The Busches appealed.

Seymour, Circuit Judge. Section 5 of the Securities Act of 1933 prohibits the offer or sale of any security unless a proper registration statement has first been filed with the SEC. However, Congress also recognized that the protections of the 1933 Act were not essential for those securities that could be supervised effectively by the states. Section 3(a)(11) therefore exempts from the Act's registration requirements

Any security which is part of an issue offered and sold only to persons resident within a single State or Territory, where the issuer of such security is a person resident and doing business within or, if a corporation, incorporated by and doing business within, such State or Territory.

In order to fall within the intrastate exemption, initial sales to state residents must be bona fide. The intrastate exemption becomes unavailable whenever sales or purchases by a subsequent purchaser circumvent the federal securities laws. The SEC has consistently maintained that a distribution of securities must have actually come to rest in the hands of the resident investors—persons purchasing for investment intent and not for purpose of resale.

The Busches contend that Sonic had the burden to prove that the original buyers bought with investment intent. We reject this argument. The intrastate offering exemption requires that the issue be "offered and sold only to persons resident within a single state." In face of Sonic's undisputed showing that all of the original buyers were Utah residents, the Busches were therefore required to produce evidence that the stock had not come to rest but had been sold to people who intended to resell it out of state. The interstate purchases of freely trading shares several months after the completion of the intrastate offering do not, without more, impugn the investment intent of the original buyers.

The Busches alternatively contend that Sonic was not entitled to the intrastate exemption because the corporate issuer was not doing business in Utah as required by section 3(a)(11). There is no dispute that the newly formed company, not yet operational, maintained its offices, books, and records in Salt Lake City. The decisive issue concerns whether Sonic's failure to invest a portion of the proceeds from its initial public offering in Utah could defeat the intrastate exemption.

An issuer cannot claim the exemption simply by opening an office in a particular state. Conducting substantially all income-producing operations elsewhere defeats the exemption, as do the plans of recently organized companies to invest the net proceeds of initial public offerings only in other states.

Here Sonic never did more than maintain its office, books, and records in Utah. This was not sufficient to make a showing of compliance with the intrastate offering exemption. Sonic transferred essentially all of its assets to Illinois and made no prior efforts whatever at locating investment opportunities within Utah. Sonic may have been intending all along to invest its assets outside the state. A newly formed company may not claim the exemption while planning covertly to invest the proceeds of a local offering in other states.

Judgment reversed in favor of the Busches; remanded for trial.

Private Offering Exemption

Section 4(2) of the 1933 Act provides that the registration requirements of the 1933 Act "shall not apply to transactions by an issuer not involving any public offering." The rationale for the private offering exemption is that the purchasers in a private placement of securities do not need the registration protections of the 1933 Act. Such purchasers can protect themselves because they are wealthy or because they are sophisticated in investment matters and have access to the information that they need to make intelligent investment decisions.

Courts have struggled to define the private offering exemption, leading to a great deal of subjectivity in court decisions. To create greater objectivity—and also greater certainty for issuers—the SEC adopted Rule 506. Although an issuers may exempt a private offering under either the courts' interpretation of section 4(2) or Rule 506, the SEC tends to treat Rule 506 as the exclusive way to obtain the exemption.

Rule 506 Under Rule 506, which is part of Securities Act Regulation D,[11] the issuer must reasonably believe that each purchaser is either (a) an accredited investor or (b) an unaccredited investor who "has such knowledge and experience in financial and business matters that he is capable of evaluating the merits and risks of the prospective investment." Accredited investors include institutional investors (such as banks and mutual funds), wealthy investors, and high-level insiders of the issuer (such as executive officers, directors, and partners).

An issuer may sell to no more than 35 unaccredited purchasers who have sufficient investment knowledge and experience, but it may sell to an unlimited number

---

[11] SEC Regulation D was promulgated in 1982 to make the private offering and small offering exemptions more easily available for small issuers. The purpose of Regulation D is to promote capital formation for small issuers. Regulation D includes the small offering exemption Rules 504 and 505, which are discussed later in this chapter in addition to Rule 506.

of accredited purchasers, regardless of their investment sophistication.

Each purchaser must be given or have access to the information she needs to make an informed investment decision. For an issuer required to make periodic disclosure under the 1934 Act, purchasers must receive information in a form required by the 1934 Act, such as a 10-K or annual report.[12] For an issuer that is not a 1934 Act reporting company, the issuer must provide much of the same information required in a registered offering. If the amount of the issuance is $2 million or less, only one

year's balance sheet need be audited. If the amount issued is $7.5 million or less, only one year's financial statements need be audited. If the amount issued exceeds $7.5 million, financial statements must be audited as required in a registration statement. In any offering of any amount under Rule 506, when auditing would involve unreasonable effort or expense, only an audited balance sheet is needed. However, whenever a limited partnership issuer finds that auditing involves unreasonable effort or expense, the limited partnership may use financial statements prepared by an independent accountant in conformance with the requirements of federal tax law. Figure 2 summarizes the disclosure requirements of Regulation D.

---

[12] Issuers required to disclose under the 1934 Act and the disclosure requirements of the 1934 Act are covered late r in this chapter.

FIGURE 2   Disclosure under Regulation D

Type of Issuer \ Size of Offering	$2 Million or Less	More Than $2 Million But Not More Than $7.5 Million	More Than $7.5 Million	Any Amount When Auditing Involves Unreasonable Effort or Expense
Issuer Required to Disclose under 1934 Act	Same nonaccounting information as disclosed under the 1934 Act. The following financial statements must be audited: Balance sheet for last 2 years. Income statement for last 3 years. Statement of changes in financial position for last 3 years.			
Issuer Not Required to Disclose under 1934 Act	Same nonaccounting information as required for 1933 Act registration statement.			
Non-1934 Act Issuer Is Not a Limited Partnership ——— Non-1934 Act Issuer Is a Limited Partnership	Only balance sheet for last year must be audited.	Balance sheet, income statement, and statement of changes in financial position for last year must be audited.	The following financial statements must be audited: Balance sheet for 2 years. Income statement for 3 years. Statement of changes in financial position for 3 years.	Only balance sheet for last year must be audited. ——— Issuer may use financial statements prepared for tax purposes.

Rule 506 prohibits the issuer from making any general public selling effort. This prevents the issuer from using the radio, newspapers, and television. In addition, the issuer must take reasonable steps to ensure that the purchasers do not resell the securities in a manner that makes the issuance a public distribution rather than a private one. Usually, an **investment letter** is used to provide this information. In such a letter, the investor states that she is purchasing the securities for investment and not for resale within two years.

In the following case, *Mark v. FSC Securities Corp.*, the issuer failed to prove it was entitled to a private offering exemption under section 4(2) or Rule 506.

MARK v. FSC SECURITIES CORP.

870 F.2d 331 (6th Cir. 1989)

FSC Securities Corp., a securities brokerage, sold limited partnership interests in Malaga Arabian Limited Partnership to James Mark and his wife. A total of 28 investors purchased limited partnership interests in Malaga. All investors were asked to execute subscription documents, including a suitability letter in which the purchaser stated his income level, that he had an opportunity to obtain relevant information, and that he had sufficient knowledge and experience in business affairs to evaluate the risks of the investment.

When the value of the limited partnership interests fell, the Marks sued FSC to rescind their purchase on the grounds that FSC sold unregistered securities in violation of the Securities Act of 1933. The jury held that the offering was exempt as an offering not involving a public offering. The Marks appealed.

Simpson, Judge.   Section 4(2) of the Securities Act exempts from registration with the SEC "transactions by an issuer not involving any public offering." There are no hard and fast rules for determining whether a securities offering is exempt from registration under the general language of section 4(2). However, several factors are significant: (a) the number of offerees; (b) the manner of the offering; (c) the number of units offered; (d) the relationship of the offerees to each other and to the issuer; and (e) the size of the offering.

Based on consideration of those factors, only one conclusion is, in this case, reasonable: The Malaga limited-partnership offering was not exempt under section 4(2). FSC offered no evidence as to the actual *number* of offerees, let alone their individual characteristics. Moreover, numerous broker-dealers undertook to sell interests in the Malaga offering, somewhere between ten and twenty. As for the number of units offered, the copy numbers on the Marks' "Receipt for Private Placement Offering Memorandum" were 135, 274, and 477, suggesting the broker-dealers distributed the offering memorandum for the Malaga offering to many more than the ultimate 28 purchasers.

These factors, taken together, indicate a wide-ranging sales effort and suggest a public, rather than a private, offering. Once such a wide-ranging distribution scheme is undertaken, evidence that each and every offeree had access to enough relevant information so as to make registration unnecessary is required to rebut the public offering inference. For example, if there is some special, close relationship between the offerees and issuer, then there may be access to the sort of information that registration would disclose. But in this case, there was no evidence that any of the offerees had any relationship to the issuer. Instead, the list of 28 purchasers shows they were a diverse, unrelated group who resided in many different communities in twelve different states. That the purchasers are so diverse suggests the offerees were likewise diverse and unrelated, militating against a private offering. Without evidence that *all* those offerees had information enabling them to fend for themselves, there is no section 4(2) exemption.

Even if FSC failed to prove an exemption under the subjective test of section 4(2), the "safe harbor" provision of Regulation D, Rule 506, deems certain transactions to be not involving any public offering within the meaning of section 4(2). However, FSC had to prove that certain objective tests were met. These conditions include the general conditions not in dispute here, and the following specific conditions:

(i) *Limitation on number of purchasers*. The issuer shall reasonably believe that there are no more than thirty-five purchasers of securities in any offering under this Section.

(ii) *Nature of purchasers*. The issuer shall reasonably believe immediately prior to making any sale that each purchaser who is not an accredited investor either alone or with his purchaser representative(s) has such knowledge and experience in financial and business matters that he is capable of evaluating the merits and risks of the propective investment.

In this case, we take the issuer to be the general partners of Malaga. FSC is required to offer evidence of the issuer's reasonable belief as to the nature of *each* purchaser. The only testimony at trial competent to establish the issuer's belief as to the nature of the purchasers was that of Laurence Leafer, a general partner in Malaga. By his own admission, he had no knowledge about any purchaser, much less any belief, reasonable or not, as to the purchasers' knowledge and experience in financial and business matters.

> Q: What was done to determine if investors were, in fact, reasonably sophisticated?
>
> A: Well, there were two things. Number one, we had investor suitability standards that had to be met. You had to have a certain income, be in a certain tax bracket, this kind of thing. Then in the subscription documents themselves, they, when they sign it, supposedly represented that they had received information necessary to make an informed investment decision, and that they were sophisticated. And if they were not, they relied on an offering representative who was.
>
> Q: Did you review the subscription documents that came in for the Malaga offering?
>
> A: No.
>
> Q: So do you know whether all of the investors in the Malaga offering met the suitability and sophistication requirements?
>
> A: I don't.

FSC also offered as evidence the Marks' executed subscription documents, as well as a set of documents in blank, to establish the procedure it followed in the Malaga sales offering. Although the Marks' executed documents may have been sufficient to establish the reasonableness of any belief the issuer may have had as to the Marks' particular qualifications, that does not satisfy Rule 506. The documents offered no evidence from which a jury could conclude the issuer reasonably believed *each* purchaser was suitable. Instead, all that was proved was the sale of 28 limited partnership interests, and the circumstances under which those sales were *intended* to have been made. The blank subscriptions documents simply do not amount to probative evidence, when it is the answers and information received *from* purchasers that determine whether the conditions of Rule 506 have been met.

Having concluded that the Malaga limited-partnership offering did not meet the registration exemption requirement of either section 4(2) or Rule 506 of Regulation D, we conclude that the Marks are entitled to the remedy of rescission.

Judgment reversed in favor of the Marks; remanded to the trial court.

Small Offering Exemptions

Sections 3(b) and 4(6) of the 1933 Act permit the SEC to exempt from registration any offering by an issuer not exceeding $5 million. Several SEC rules and regulations permit an issuer to sell small amounts of securities and avoid registration. The rationale for these exemptions is that the dollar amount of the securities or the number of purchasers is too small for the federal government to be concerned with registration. State securities law may require registration, however.

Rule 504   SEC Rule 504 of Regulation D allows the issuer to sell up to $1 million of securities in a 12-month period and avoid registration. However, any amount of a securities offering under Rule 504 exceeding $500,000 must be registered under state securities law. For example, an issuer planning to sell $800,000 of securities under Rule 504 may sell $500,000 of securities without any federal or state registration, but $300,000 of the securities must be registered under state law.

As with Rule 506, no general selling efforts are permitted and resale is restricted. Rule 504 sets no limits on the number of offerees or purchasers. The purchasers need not be sophisticated in investment matters, and the issuer need disclose information only as required by state securities law.

Rule 505   Rule 505 of Regulation D allows the issuer to sell up to $5 million of securities in a 12-month period and avoid registration. As with Rules 504 and 506, no general selling efforts are allowed and resale is restricted. As with Rule 506, there may be no more than 35 unaccredited purchasers, but there is no limit on the

number of accredited investors. Rule 505 has the same disclosure requirements as Rule 506. As with Rule 504, the purchasers need not be sophisticated in investment matters.

Regulation A   Regulation A permits an issuer to sell up to $1.5 million of securities in a one-year period. There is no limit on the number of purchasers, no purchaser sophistication requirement, and no resale restriction.

For offerings that exceed $100,000, Regulation A requires disclosure and regulates the manner and timing of offers and sales much as a registered offering is regulated. In fact, Regulation A is more nearly a low-level registration than an exemption from registration. The Regulation A disclosure document is the offering circular, which must be filed with the SEC. Financial statements in the offering circular must be audited if the issuer is a 1934 Act reporting company. There is a 10-day waiting period after the filing of the offering circular, during which no offers or sales may be made. Ten days after the filing date, oral offers are permitted, as are written offers accompanied or preceded by an offering circular. Sales are permitted after the waiting period.

Integration of Offerings

It might seem possible to avoid a registration by separating one offering into several smaller offerings and finding an exemption for each of the smaller offerings. Not surprisingly, the SEC has acted to stop such a circumvention of the registration provisions of the 1933 Act by requiring the integration of offerings that are essentially only one offering.

CONCEPT REVIEW

COMPARISON OF RULES 504, 505, AND 506 OF REGULATION D

	Issuers Covered	Amount Sold	Number of Purchasers	Must Purchasers Be Sophisticated?	Disclosure Required	General Solicitations Permitted	Resale Restricted	File Form D
Rule 504	Only nonpublic issuers	$1 million; but any amount exceeding $500,000 must be unregistered under state law	No limit	No	No	No	Yes	Yes
Rule 505	All	$5 million	35 unaccredited purchasers; unlimited number of accredited purchasers	No	Yes, unless sold to accredited purchasers only	No	Yes	Yes
Rule 506	All	No limit	35 unaccredited purchasers; unlimited number of accredited purchasers	Yes, unless accredited investors	Yes, unless sold to accredited purchasers only	No	Yes	Yes

Transaction Exemptions for Nonissuers

Although it is true that the registration provisions apply primarily to issuers and those who help issuers sell their securities publicly, the 1933 Act states that every person who sells a security is potentially subject to Section 5's restrictions on the timing of offers and sales. You must learn the most important rule of the 1933 Act: **Every transaction in securities must be registered with the SEC or be exempt from registration.**

This rule applies to every person, including the small investor who, through the New York Stock Exchange, sells securities that may have been registered by the issuer 15 years earlier. That small investor must either have the issuer register her sale of securities or find an exemption from registration that applies to her situation. Fortunately, most small investors who resell securities will have an exemption from the registration requirements of the 1933 Act. The transaction exemption ordinarily used by these resellers is Section 4(1) of the 1933

Act. It provides an exemption for "transactions by any person other than an issuer, underwriter, or dealer."

For example, if you buy GM common shares on the New York Stock Exchange, you may freely resell them without a registration. You are not an issuer (GM is). You are not a dealer (because you are not in the business of selling securities). And you are not an underwriter (because you are not helping GM distribute the shares to the public).

Application of this exemption when an investor sells shares that are already publicly traded is easy; however, it is more difficult to determine whether an investor can use this exemption when the investor sells **restricted securities.**

Sale of Restricted Securities

Restricted securities are securities issued pursuant to a private or small offering exemption, including

Scheme of coverage &
what they are designed to
do.

FIGURE 3   Securities and Transaction Exemptions from the Registration Requirements of the Securities Act of 1933

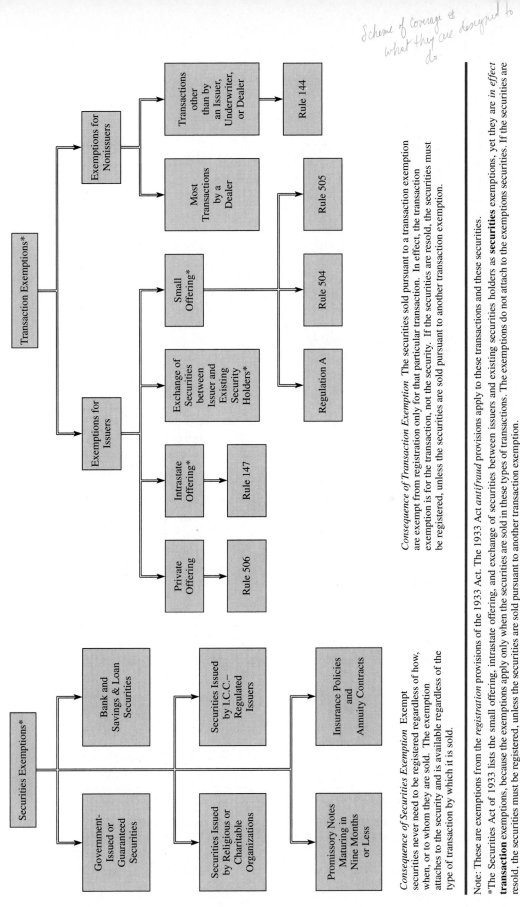

Consequence of Securities Exemption Exempt securities never need to be registered regardless of how, when, or to whom they are sold. The exemption attaches to the security and is available regardless of the type of transaction by which it is sold.

Consequence of Transaction Exemption The securities sold pursuant to a transaction exemption are exempt from registration only for that particular transaction. In effect, the transaction exemption is for the transaction, not the security. If the securities are resold, the securities must be registered, unless the securities are sold pursuant to another transaction exemption.

Note: These are exemptions from the *registration* provisions of the 1933 Act. The 1933 Act *antifraud* provisions apply to these transactions and these securities.

*The Securities Act of 1933 lists the small offering, intrastate offering, and exchange of securities between issuers and existing securities holders as **securities** exemptions, yet they are *in effect* **transaction** exemptions, because the exemptions apply only when the securities are sold in these types of transactions. The exemptions do not attach to the exemptions securities. If the securities are resold, the securities must be registered, unless the securities are sold pursuant to another transaction exemption.

Rules 504, 505, and 506. Restricted securities are supposed to be held by the purchaser for two years. If they are sold earlier, the investor may be deemed an underwriter.

For example, an investor buys 10,000 common shares issued by Arcom Corporation pursuant to a Rule 506 private offering exemption. One month later, the investor sells the securities to 40 other investors. The original investor is an *underwriter* because he has helped Arcom distribute the shares to the public. The original investor may not use the issuer's private offering exemption because it exempted only the issuer's sale to him. This example illustrates the importance of heeding the rule discussed earlier: every transaction in securities must be registered with the SEC or be exempt from registration.

SEC Rule 144 SEC Rule 144 allows purchasers of restricted securities to resell the securities and not be deemed underwriters. The resellers must hold the securities for at least two years. Investment information concerning the issuer of the securities must be publicly available. In any three-month period, the reseller may sell only a limited amount of securities: the greater of 1 percent of the outstanding securities or the average weekly volume of trading. And the reseller must file a notice (Form 144) with the SEC.

If a purchaser who is not an insider of the issuer has held the restricted securities for at least three years, Rule 144 permits her to sell unlimited amounts of the securities. In addition, investment information concerning the issuer need not be publicly available.

Figure 3 summarizes the 1933 Act exemptions from registration.

LIABILITY PROVISIONS OF THE 1933 ACT

Introduction

To deter fraud, deception, and manipulation and to provide remedies to the victims of such practices, Congress included a number of liability provisions in the Securities Act of 1933.

Liability for Improper Offers and Sales

Section 12(1) of the 1933 Act imposes liability on any person who violates the provisions of Section 5. As you learned above, Section 5 states when sales may be made and what types of offers may be made at what times during the registration process. Liability extends to any purchaser to whom an illegal offer or sale was made. The purchaser's remedy is rescission or damages.

Liability for Defective Registration Statements

Section 11 of the 1933 Act provides civil liabilities for damages when a 1933 Act registration statement on its effective date misstates or omits a material fact. A purchaser of securities issued pursuant to the defective registration statement may sue certain classes of persons that are listed in Section 11: the issuer, its chief executive officer, its chief accounting officer, its chief financial officer, the directors, other signers of the registration statement, the underwriter, and experts who contributed to the registration statement (such as auditors who certified the financial statements or lawyers who issued an opinion concerning the tax aspects of a limited partnership). The purchaser's remedy under Section 11 is for damages caused by the misstatement or omission.

Section 11 was a radical liability section when it was enacted, and it remains so today. It is radical for three reasons. First, reliance is usually not required; that is, the purchaser need not show that she relied on the misstatement or omission in the registration statement. In fact, the purchaser need not have read the registration statement or have seen it. Second, privity is not required; that is, the purchaser need not prove that she purchased the securities from the defendant. All she has to prove is that the defendant is in one of the classes of persons liable under Section 11. Third, the purchaser need not prove that the defendant negligently or intentionally misstated or omitted a material fact. Instead, the defendant has the burden of proving that he exercised due diligence.

Section 11 Defenses A defendant can escape liability under Section 11 by proving that the purchaser knew of the misstatement or omission when she purchased the security. The defendant's other defense is the **due diligence defense.** It is the more important of the two defenses.

The Due Diligence Defense Any defendant except the issuer may escape liability under Section 11 by proving that he acted with due diligence in determining the accuracy of the registration statement. The due diligence defense basically requires the defendant to prove that he was not negligent. The exact defense varies, however, according to the class of defendant and the portion of the registration statement that is defective. Most defendants must prove that after a *reasonable investigation* they had *reasonable grounds to believe and did believe* that the registration statement was true and contained no omission of material fact.

Experts need to prove due diligence only in respect to the parts that they have contributed. For example, independent auditors must prove due diligence in ascertaining the accuracy of financial statements they certify. Due diligence requires that an auditor at least comply with generally accepted auditing standards (GAAS).

Nonexperts (the directors, officers, partners, and underwriters) are liable for the entire registration statement. However, they generally have no duty of investigation in respect to the parts of the registration statement contributed by experts (*expertised portions*). The nonexperts need merely show that they had *no reason to believe and did not believe* that the expertised portions of the registration statement contained any misstatement or omission of material fact. For the *non-expertised* portions of the registration statement, non-experts must make a *reasonable investigation and reasonably believe* that those portions contain no mis-statements or omissions of material fact.

Other Liability Provisions

Section 12(2) prohibits misstatements or omissions of material fact in any written or oral communication in connection with the offer or sale of any security (except government-issued or -guaranteed securities). Section 17(a) prohibits the use of any device or artifice to de-fraud, or the use of any untrue or misleading statement, in connection with the offer or sale of any security. Two of the subsections of Section 17(a) require that the defendant merely act negligently, while the third subsection requires proof of scienter. Scienter is the intent to deceive, manipulate, or defraud the purchaser. Some courts have held that scienter also includes recklessness. The Supreme Court has not decided whether a buyer has a private right of action for damages under Section 17(a), and the courts of appeals are split on the issue.

Jurisdictional Requirement

Since these liability sections are part of federal law, there must be some connection between the illegal activity and interstate commerce for liability to exist. Section 11 merely requires the filing of a registration statement with the SEC. Sections 12(1), 12(2), and 17(a) require the use of the mails or other instrumentality or means of interstate communication or transportation.

Criminal Liability

Section 24 of the 1933 Act provides for criminal liability for any person who willfully violates the Act or its rules and regulations. The maximum penalty is a $10,000 fine and five years' imprisonment. Criminal actions under the 1933 Act are brought by the attorney general of the United States, not by the SEC.

In the following case, the court construed the due diligence defense of Section 11.

ESCOTT v. BARCHRIS CONSTRUCTION CORP.

283 F. Supp. 643 (S.D.N.Y. 1968)

BarChris Construction Corporation was in the business of constructing bowling centers. With the introduction of automatic pinsetters in 1952, there was a rapid growth in the popularity of bowling, and BarChris's sales increased from $800,000 in 1956 to over $9 million in 1960. By 1960, it was building about 3 percent of the lanes constructed, while Brunswick Corporation and AMF were building 97 percent. BarChris contracted with its customers to construct and equip bowling alleys for them. Under the contracts, a customer was required to make a small down payment in cash. After the alleys were constructed, customers gave BarChris promissory notes for the balance of the purchase price. BarChris discounted the notes with a factor. The factor kept part of the face value of the notes as a reserve until the customer paid the notes. BarChris was obligated to repurchase the notes if the customer defaulted.

In 1960, BarChris offered its customers an alternative financing method in which BarChris sold the interior of a bowling alley to a factor, James Talcott, Inc. Talcott then leased the alley either to a BarChris customer (Type A financing) or to a BarChris subsidiary that then subleased to the customer (Type B financing). Under Type A financing, BarChris guaranteed 25 percent of the customer's obligation under the lease. With Type B financing, BarChris was liable for 100 percent of its subsidiaries' lease obligations. Under either financing method, BarChris made substantial expenditures before receiving payment from customers and, therefore, experienced a constant need of cash.

In early 1961, BarChris decided to issue debentures and to use part of the proceeds to help its cash position. In March 1961, BarChris filed with the SEC a registration statement covering the debentures. The statement became effective on May 16. The proceeds of the offering were received by BarChris on May 24, 1961. By that time, BarChris had difficulty collecting from some of its customers, and other customers were in arrears on their payments to the factors of the discounted notes. Due to overexpansion in the bowling alley industry, many BarChris customers failed. On October 29, 1962, BarChris filed a petition for bankruptcy. On November 1, it defaulted on the payment of interest on the debentures.

Escott and other purchasers of the debentures sued BarChris and its officers, directors, and auditors, among others, under Section 11 of the Securities Act of 1933. BarChris's registration statement contained material misstatements and omitted material facts. It misstated current assets by $609,689 (15.6 percent) in the 1960 balance sheet certified by its auditors, Peat, Marwick, Mitchell & Co. Sales for 1960 were overstated by $653,900 (7.7 percent) and earnings per share by 10 cents (15.4 percent). The registration statement understated BarChris's contingent liabilities by $618,853 (42.8 percent) as of April 30, 1961. It overstated gross profit for the first quarter of 1961 by $230,755 (92 percent), and sales for the first quarter of 1961 by $519,810 (32.1 percent). The March 31, 1961, backlog was overstated by $4,490,000 (186 percent). The 1961 figures were not audited by Peat, Marwick.

In addition, the registration statement reported that prior loans from officers had been repaid, but failed to disclose that officers had made new loans to BarChris totaling $386,615. BarChris had used $1,160,000 of the proceeds of the debentures to pay old debts, a use not disclosed in the registration statement. BarChris's potential liability of $1,350,000 to factors due to customer delinquencies on factored notes was not disclosed. The registration statement represented BarChris's contingent liability on Type B financings as 25 percent instead of 100 percent. It misrepresented the nature of BarChris's business by failing to disclose that BarChris was already engaged and was about to become more heavily engaged in the operation of bowling alleys, including one called Capitol Lanes, as a way of minimizing its losses from customer defaults.

Trilling, BarChris's controller, signed the registration statement. Auslander, a director, signed the registration statement. Peat, Marwick consented to being named as an expert in the registration statement. All three, therefore, would be liable to Escott unless they could meet the due diligence defense of Section 11.

McLean, District Judge.   The question is whether Trilling, Auslander, and Peat, Marwick have proved their due diligence defenses. The position of each defendant will be separately considered.

TRILLING

Trilling was BarChris's controller. He signed the registration statement in that capacity, although he was not a director. Trilling entered BarChris's employ in October 1960. He was Kircher's [BarChris's treasurer] subordinate. When Kircher asked him for information, he furnished it.

Trilling was not a member of the executive committee. He was a comparatively minor figure in BarChris. The description of BarChris's management in the prospectus does not mention him. He was not considered to be an executive officer.

Trilling may well have been unaware of several of the inaccuracies in the prospectus. But he must have known of some of them. As a financial officer, he was familiar with Bar Chris's finances and with its books of account. He knew that part of the cash on deposit on December 31, 1960, had been procured temporarily by Russo [BarChris's executive vice president] for window-dressing purposes. He knew that BarChris was operating Capitol Lanes in 1960. He should have known, although perhaps through carelessness he did not know at the time, that BarChris's contingent liability on Type B lease transactions was greater than the prospectus stated. In the light of these facts, I cannot find that Trilling believed the entire prospectus to be true.

But even if he did, he still did not establish his due diligence defenses. He did not prove that as to the parts of the prospectus expertised by Peat, Marwick he had no reasonable ground to believe that it was untrue. He also failed to prove, as to the parts of the prospectus not expertised by Peat, Marwick, that he made a reasonable investigation which afforded him a reasonable ground to believe that it was true. As far as appears, he made no investigation. He did what was asked of him and assumed that others would properly take care of supplying accurate data as to the other aspects of the company's business. This would have been well enough but for the fact that he signed the registration statement. As a signer, he could not avoid responsibility by leaving it up to others to make it accurate. Trilling did not sustain the burden of proving his due diligence defenses.

AUSLANDER

Auslander was an outside director, i.e., one who was not an officer of BarChris. He was chairman of the board of Valley Stream National Bank in Valley Stream, Long Island. In February 1961, Vitolo [BarChris's president] asked him to become a director of BarChris. In February and early March 1961, before accepting Vitolo's invitation, Auslander made some investigation of Bar-Chris. He obtained Dun & Bradstreet reports that contained sales and earnings figures for periods earlier than December 31, 1960. He caused inquiry to be made of certain of BarChris's banks and was advised that they regarded BarChris favorably. He was informed that inquiry of Talcott had also produced a favorable response.

On March 3, 1961, Auslander indicated his willingness to accept a place on the board. Shortly thereafter, on March 14, Kircher sent him a copy of BarChris's annual report for 1960. Auslander observed that BarChris's auditors were Peat, Marwick. They were also the auditors for the Valley Stream National Bank. He thought well of them.

Auslander was elected a director on April 17, 1961. The registration statement in its original form had already been filed, of course without his signature. On May 10, 1961, he signed a signature page for the first amendment to the registration statement which was filed on May 11, 1961. This was a separate sheet without any document attached. Auslander did not know that it was a signature page for a registration statement. He vaguely understood that it was something "for the SEC."

At the May 15 directors' meeting, however, Auslander did realize that what he was signing was a signature sheet to a registration statement. This was the first time that he had appreciated the fact. A copy of the registration statement in its earlier form as amended on May 11, 1961, was passed around at the meeting. Auslander glanced at it briefly. He did not read it thoroughly. At the May 15 meeting, Russo and Vitolo stated that everything was in order and that the prospectus was correct. Auslander believed this statement.

In considering Auslander's due diligence defenses, a distinction must be drawn between the expertised and nonexpertised portions of the prospectus. As to the former, Auslander knew that

Peat, Marwick had audited the 1960 figures. He believed them to be correct because he had confidence in Peat, Marwick. He had no reasonable ground to believe otherwise.

As to the nonexpertised portions, however, Auslander is in a different position. He seems to have been under the impression that Peat, Marwick was responsible for all the figures. This impression was not correct, as he would have realized if he had read the prospectus carefully. Auslander made no investigation of the accuracy of the prospectus. He relied on the assurance of Vitolo and Russo, and upon the information he had received in answer to his inquiries back in February and early March. These inquiries were general ones, in the nature of a credit check. The information which he received in answer to them was also general, without specific reference to the statements in the prospectus, which was not prepared until some time thereafter.

It is true that Auslander became a director on the eve of the financing. He had little opportunity to familiarize himself with the company's affairs. The question is whether, under such circumstances, Auslander did enough to establish his due diligence.

Section 11 imposes liability upon a director, no matter how new he is. He is presumed to know his responsibility when he becomes a director. He can escape liability only by using that reasonable care to investigate the facts that a prudent man would employ in the management of his own property. In my opinion, a prudent man would not act in an important matter without any knowledge of the relevant facts, in sole reliance upon general information which does not purport to cover the particular case. To say that such minimal conduct measures up to the statutory standard would, to all intents and purposes, absolve new directors from responsibility merely because they are new. This is not a sensible construction of Section 11, when one bears in mind its fundamental purpose of requiring full and truthful disclosure for the protection of investors.

Auslander has not established his due diligence defense with respect to the misstatements and omissions in those portions of the prospectus other than the audited 1960 figures.

PEAT, MARWICK

The part of the registration statement purporting to be made upon the authority of Peat, Marwick as an expert was the 1960 figures. But because the statute requires the court to determine Peat, Marwick's belief, and the grounds thereof, "at the time such part of the registration statement became effective," for the purposes of this affirmative defense, the matter must be viewed as of May 16, 1961, and the question is whether at that time Peat, Marwick, after reasonable investigation, had reasonable ground to believe and did believe that the 1960 figures were true and that no material fact had been omitted from the registration statement which should have been included in order to make the 1960 figures not misleading. In deciding this issue, the court must consider not only what Peat, Marwick did in its 1960 audit, but also what it did in its subsequent S–1 review. The proper scope of that review must also be determined.

THE 1960 AUDIT

Peat, Marwick's work was in general charge of a member of the firm, Cummings, and more immediately in charge of Peat, Marwick's manager, Logan. Most of the actual work was performed by a senior accountant, Berardi, who had junior assistants, one of whom was Kennedy.

Berardi was then about 30 years old. He was not yet a CPA. He had had no previous experience with the bowling industry. This was his first job as a senior accountant. He could hardly have been given a more difficult assignment.

It is unnecessary to recount everything that Berardi did in the course of the audit. We are concerned only with the evidence relating to what Berardi did or did not do with respect to those items which I have found to have been incorrectly reported in the 1960 figures in the prospectus. More narrowly, we are directly concerned only with such of those items as I have found to be material.

First and foremost is Berardi's failure to discover that Capitol Lanes had not been sold. This error affected both the sales figure and the liability side of the balance sheet. Fundamentally, the error stemmed from the fact that Berardi never realized that Heavenly Lanes and Capitol were two different names for the same alley. Berardi assumed that Heavenly was to be treated like any other completed job.

Berardi read the minutes of the board of directors meeting of November 22, 1960, which recited that "the Chairman recommended that the Corporation operate Capitol Lanes." Berardi knew from various BarChris records that Capitol Lanes, Inc., was paying rentals to Talcott. Also, a Peat, Marwick work paper bearing Kennedy's initials recorded that Capitol Lanes, Inc., held certain insurance policies.

Berardi testified that he inquired of Russo about Capitol Lanes and that Russo told him that Capitol Lanes, Inc., was going to operate an alley someday but as yet it had no alley. Berardi testified that he understood that the alley had not been built and that he believed that the rental payments were on vacant land.

I am not satisfied with this testimony. If Berardi did hold this belief, he should not have held it. The entries as to insurance and as to "operation of alley" should have alerted him to the fact that an alley existed. He should have made further inquiry on the subject. It is apparent that Berardi did not understand this transaction.

He never identified this mysterious Capitol with the Heavenly Lanes which he had included in his sales and profit figures. The vital question is whether he failed to make a reasonable investigation which, if he had made it, would have revealed the truth.

Certain accounting records of BarChris, which Berardi testified he did not see, would have put him on inquiry. One was a job cost ledger card for job no. 6036, the job number which Berardi put on his own sheet for Heavenly Lanes. This card read "Capitol Theatre (Heavenly)." In addition, two accounts receivable cards each showed both names on the same card, Capitol and Heavenly. Berardi testified that he looked at the accounts receivable records but that he did not see these particular cards. He testified that he did not look on the job cost ledger cards because he took the costs from another record, the costs register.

The burden of proof on this issue is on Peat, Marwick. Although the question is a rather close one, I find that Peat, Marwick has not sustained that burden. Peat, Marwick has not proved that Berardi made a reasonable investigation as far as Capitol Lanes was concerned and that his ignorance of the true facts was justified.

I turn now to the errors in the current assets. As to cash, Berardi properly obtained a confirmation from the bank as to BarChris's cash balance on December 31, 1960. He did not know that part of this balance had been temporarily increased by the deposit of reserves returned by Talcott to BarChris conditionally for a limited time. I do not believe that Berardi reasonably should have known this. It would not be reasonable to require Berardi to examine all of BarChris's correspondence files [which contained correspondence indicating that BarChris was to return the cash to Talcott] when he had no reason to suspect any irregularity.

THE S–1 REVIEW

The purpose of reviewing events subsequent to the date of a certified balance sheet (referred to as an S–1 review when made with reference to a registration statement) is to ascertain whether any material change has occurred in the company's financial position which should be disclosed in order to prevent the balance sheet figures from being misleading. The scope of such a review, under generally accepted auditing standards, is limited. It does not amount to a complete audit.

Berardi made the S–1 review in May 1961. He devoted a little over two days to it, a total of $20\frac{1}{2}$ hours. He did not discover any of the errors or omissions pertaining to the state of affairs in 1961, all of which were material. The question is whether, despite his failure to find out anything, his investigation was reasonable within the meaning of the statute.

What Berardi did was to look at a consolidating trial balance as of March 31, 1961, which had been prepared by BarChris, compare it with the audited December 31, 1960 figures, discuss with Trilling certain unfavorable developments which the comparison disclosed, and read certain minutes. He did not examine any important financial records other than the trial balance.

In substance, Berardi asked questions, he got answers which he considered satisfactory, and he did nothing to verify them. Since he never read the prospectus, he was not even aware that there had ever been any problem about loans from officers. He made no inquiry of factors about delinquent notes in his S–1 review. Since he knew nothing about Kircher's notes of the executive committee meetings, he did not learn that the delinquency situation had grown worse. He was content with Trilling's assurance that no liability theretofore contingent had become direct. Apparently the only BarChris officer with whom Berardi communicated was Trilling. He could not recall making any inquiries of Russo, Vitolo, or Pugliese [a BarChris vice-president].

There had been a material change for the worse in BarChris's financial position. That change was sufficiently serious so that the failure to disclose it made the 1960 figures misleading. Berardi did not discover it. As far as results were concerned, his S–1 review was useless.

Accountants should not be held to a standard higher than that recognized in their profession. I do not do so here. Berardi's review did not come up to that standard. He did not take some of the steps which Peat, Marwick's written program prescribed. He did not spend an adequate amount of time on a task of this magnitude. Most important of all, he was too easily satisfied with glib answers to his inquiries.

This is not to say that he should have made a complete audit. But there were enough danger signals in the materials which he did examine to require some further investigation on his part. Generally accepted auditing standards require such further investigation under these circumstances. It is not always sufficient merely to ask questions.

Here again, the burden of proof is on Peat, Marwick. I find that burden has not been satisfied. I conclude that Peat, Marwick has not established its due diligence defense.

Judgment for Escott and the other purchasers.

SECURITIES EXCHANGE ACT OF 1934

Introduction

The Securities Exchange Act of 1934 is chiefly concerned with requiring the disclosure of material information to investors. Unlike the 1933 Act, which is primarily a one-time disclosure statute, the 1934 Act requires *periodic disclosure* by issuers with publicly held equity securities. In addition, the 1934 Act regulates insiders' transactions in securities, proxy solicitations, tender offers, brokers and dealers, and securities exchanges. The 1934 Act also has several sections prohibiting fraud and manipulation in securities transactions. The ultimate purpose of the 1934 Act is to keep investors fully informed to allow them to make intelligent investment decisions.

Registration of Securities under the 1934 Act

Under the 1934 Act, issuers must register *classes* of securities. This is different from the 1933 Act, which requires issuers to register *issuances* of securities. Under the 1933 Act, securities are registered only for the term of an issuance. Under the 1934 Act, registered classes of securities remain registered until the issuer takes steps to deregister the securities.

Issuers with securities registered under the 1934 Act become subject to certain further requirements that will be discussed later in this chapter, such as the rules pertaining to the solicitation of proxies and the filing of certain periodic reports. In addition, **insiders** of issuers with registered securities may be required to report their transactions in the shares of the company and may be subject to the recapture of profits they make on company shares.

Securities Covered   Two types of securities must be *registered* under the 1934 Act.

1. An issuer whose total assets exceed $5 million must register a class of equity securities with at least 500 shareholders, if the securities are traded in interstate commerce.
2. An issuer must register any security traded on a national security exchange, such as common shares traded on the American Stock Exchange.

The information required in the 1934 Act registration statement is similar to that required under the 1933 Act, except that offering information is omitted.

Termination of Registration   An issuer may avoid the expense and burden of complying with the periodic disclosure and other requirements of the 1934 Act if the issuer terminates its registration. A 1934 Act registration may be terminated if the issuer has fewer than 300 shareholders. In addition, such a registration may be terminated if the issuer has fewer than 500 shareholders of any class of equity securities and assets of no more than $5 million. However, an issuer with securities listed on a national securities exchange would not be able to terminate a registration of the listed securities.

Periodic Reports

To maintain a steady flow of material information to investors, the 1934 Act requires public issuers to *file periodic reports* with the SEC. Three types of issuers must file such reports:

1. An issuer with assets of more than $5 million and at least 500 holders of any class of equity securities traded in interstate commerce.
2. An issuer whose equity securities are traded on a national securities exchange.
3. An issuer who has made a registered offering under the 1933 Act.

The first two types of issuers—which are issuers that must also register securities under the 1934 Act—must file several periodic reports, including an annual report (Form 10-K) and a quarterly report (Form 10-Q). They must file a monthly report (Form 8-K) when material events occur. Comparable reports must also be sent to their shareholders. The third type of issuer— an issuer who must disclose only because it has made a public offering under the 1933 Act—must file the same reports as the other issuers, except that it need not provide an annual report to its shareholders. Despite its significance as part of the federal securities disclosure system, the annual report to shareholders is not a part of the requirement to file periodic reports with the SEC, but rather is required by the proxy rules in connection with the annual shareholders' meeting. Since the proxy rules apply only to issuers with securities registered under the 1934 Act, the third type of issuer does not have to distribute an annual report to shareholders.

The *10-K* annual report must include audited financial statements plus current information about the conduct of the business, its management, and the status of its securities. The 10-K financial-statement auditing requirements are the same as for a 1933 Act registration statement: two years' audited balance sheets and three years' audited income statements and audited changes in financial position. The 10-K report is intended to update the information required in the 1934 Act registration statement.

The quarterly report, the *10-Q*, requires only a summarized, unaudited operating statement and unaudited figures on capitalization and shareholders' equity. The *8-K* monthly report must be filed within 10 days of the end of any month in which any specified event occurs, such as a change in the amount of securities, a default under the terms of an issue of securities, an acquisition or disposition of assets, a change in control of the company, a revaluation of assets, or "any materially important event."

Most securities issuers file paper reports with the SEC. Since September 1984, however, a few issuers have filed computerized reports, transmitting them by telephone or by sending computer tapes or disks to the SEC. These computerized filings are made with the SEC's Electronic Data Gathering, Analysis, and Retrieval system: EDGAR. The purpose of EDGAR is to ease the issuer's burden of filing reports and to facilitate access to filed reports.

Suspension of Duty to File Reports   An issuer's duty to file periodic reports is suspended if the issuer has fewer than 300 shareholders. In addition, a suspension occurs if the issuer has fewer than 500 shareholders of any class of equity securities and assets of no more than $5 million. However, an issuer with securities traded on a national securities exchange would remain obligated to file periodic reports.

Holdings and Trading by Insiders

Section 16(a) of the 1934 Act requires that statutory insiders individually file a statement disclosing their holdings of any class of the issuer's equity securities. A **statutory insider** is a person who falls into any of the following categories:

1. An *officer* of a corporation with equity securities registered under the 1934 Act.

2. A *director* of such a corporation.

3. An *owner of more than 10 percent* of a class of equity securities registered under the 1934 Act.

In addition, statutory insiders must report any transaction in such securities within 10 days following the end of the month in which the transaction occurs. They must also report purchases and sales made up to six months before and up to six months after becoming an officer, director, or a 10 percent holder.

Short-Swing Trading by Insiders Section 16(b) of the 1934 Act provides that any profit made by a statutory insider is recoverable by the issuer if the profit resulted from the purchase and sale (or the sale and purchase) of any class of the issuer's equity securities within less than a six-month period. This provision was designed to stop speculative insider trading on the basis of information that "may have been obtained by such owner, director, or officer by reason of his relationship to the issuer." The application of the provision is without regard to intent to use or actual use of inside information. However, a few cases, such as the following, have held that sales made by a statutory insider without actual access to inside information do not violate Section 16(b).

C.R.A. REALTY CORP. v. CROTTY
878 F.2d 562 (2d Cir. 1989)

Joseph Crotty was a vice president of United Artists Communications, Inc. (UA), a corporation with equity securities registered under the Securities Exchange Act of 1934. Crotty was the head film buyer of UA's western division, supervising a staff of 30 people. He had virtually complete and autonomous control of film buying for the 351 UA theaters in the western United States, including negotiating and signing movie acquisition agreements, supervising movie distribution, and settling contracts after the movies had been shown. Consequently, Crotty knew how many contracts were being negotiated at any one time and the price UA was paying for the rental of each movie.

Crotty was required to consult with higher officers only if he wanted to exceed a certain limit on the amount of the cash advance paid to a distributor for a movie. This occurred no more than two or three times a year. The gross revenue from Crotty's division was about 35–36 percent of UA's gross revenue from movie exhibitions and around 15–18 percent of its total gross revenue.

During a six-month period, Crotty purchased 7,500 shares of UA and sold 3,500 shares, realizing a large profit. C.R.A. Reality Corp., a UA shareholder, sued Crotty on behalf of UA to recover Crotty's profit, on the grounds that Crotty's trading violated Section 16(b) of the 1934 Act. The trial court held that Crotty was not an officer for purposes of Section 16(b), and C.R.A. appealed.

Timbers, Circuit Judge. Section 16(b) imposes a strict prophylactic rule with respect to insider, short-swing trading. Any corporate official within the statutory meaning of an officer who engages in short-swing trading automatically will be required to surrender any profit from the trading, without proof of actual abuse of insider information, and without proof of intent to profit on the basis of such information. This objective test was chosen by Congress because of the difficulty of proving whether a corporate insider actually abused confidential information to which he had access or purchased or sold an issuer's stock with the intention of profiting from such information.

In Securities Exchange Act Rule 3b-2, the SEC defined the term officer as including a vice-president of an issuer. C.R.A. asserts that, since Crotty is a vice-president of UA, this rule places him within the purview of Section 16(b). It is significant, however, that the SEC itself does not believe that this rule should be rigidly applied in determining who is an officer within the meaning of Section 16. For example, two SEC releases show that the SEC does not consider an employee's title as an officer to bring the employee automatically under Section 16.

Moreover, the trial court's holding is consistent with the law of this Circuit. In *Colby v. Klune* (1949), we held that a corporate employee who did not hold the title of a corporate officer nevertheless could be an officer within the meaning of Section 16(b) if he performed important executive duties of such character that he would be likely, in discharging these duties, to obtain confidential information about the company's affairs that would aid him if he engaged in personal market transactions. We believe that the reasoning of *Colby* applies here. It is an employee's duties and responsibilities—rather than his actual title—that determine whether he is an officer within the purview of Section 16(b).

The Supreme Court of the United States has emphasized that potential access to inside information is the key to finding liability, rather than rigid application of statutory designations. In *Kern County Land Co. v. Occidental Petroleum Corp.* (1973), the Court held that, even if a hostile bidder held 10 percent or more of the stock of a target company when it exchanged the issuer's stock for stock issued as part of a merger designed to fend off the bidder, the bidder didnot come within the ambit of Section 16(b), since its hostile status precluded it from having any inside information about the target issuer. These cases reflect an interpretation of Section 16(b) that best serves the congressional purpose of curbing short-swing speculation by corporate insiders.

All that is required by *Colby* is that the plaintiff establish that it is more likely than not that the employee's duties gave him access to inside information. A plaintiff need not show that the employee actually obtained inside information or used it to his advantage.

Viewing his responsibilities, Crotty had no access to inside information such as the financial or operational plans of UA. He was not a director of the company, never attended a directors' meeting, and never received any information from the Board of Directors that was not available to the general public.

The only information that Crotty had that arguably might be said to be inside information was concerning daily revenue receipts or film grosses from UA's movie exhibition. Entertainment Data, Inc., an independent contractor, collected the daily film grosses from the western division theaters and gave them to Crotty on an overnight basis. Entertainment Data, however, also gave daily film gross information to most of the major movie exhibitors and distributors in Los Angeles and San Francisco. This information also was distributed to daily trade publications. Accordingly, the film gross information was not inside information and gave Crotty no advantage over other investors.

Judgment for Crotty affirmed.

PROXY SOLICITATION REGULATION

Introduction

Section 14 of the 1934 Act regulates the *solicitation of proxies*. In a public corporation, shareholders rarely attend and vote at shareholder meetings. Many shareholders are able to vote at shareholder meetings only by **proxy,** a document by which shareholders direct other persons to vote their shares. Just as investors need information to be able to make intelligent investment decisions, shareholders need information to make intelligent voting and proxy decisions.

Proxy Statement

SEC Regulation 14A requires any person soliciting proxies from holders of securities registered under the 1934 Act to furnish each holder with a **proxy statement** containing voting information. Usually, the only party soliciting proxies is the corporation's management, which is seeking proxies from common shareholders to enable it to reelect itself to the board of directors.

If the management of the corporation does not solicit proxies, it must nevertheless inform the shareholders of material information affecting matters that are to be put to a vote of the shareholders. This **information statement,** which contains about the same information as a proxy statement, must be sent to all shareholders that are entitled to vote at the meeting. The proxy statement or information statement must be filed with the SEC at least 10 days before it is mailed to the shareholders. If the proxy or information statement is issued in connection with an annual meeting of shareholders at which directors are to be elected, the shareholders must also receive a current annual report of the corporation.

The primary purpose of the SEC rules concerning information that must be included in the proxy or information statement is to permit shareholders to make informed decisions while voting for directors and considering any resolutions proposed by the management or shareholders. Information on each director nominee must include the candidate's principal occupation, his shareholdings in the corporation, his previous service as a director of the corporation, his material transactions with the corporation (such as goods or services pro-

vided), and his directorships in other corporations. The total remuneration of the five directors or officers who are highest paid, including bonuses, grants under stock option plans, fringe benefits, and other perquisites, must also be included in the proxy statement.

Proxies

The rules regarding the content of proxies ensure that the shareholder understands how his proxy will be voted. The proxy form must indicate in boldface type on whose behalf it is being solicited—for example, the corporation's management. Generally, the proxy must permit the shareholder to vote for or against the proposal or to abstain from voting on any resolutions on the meeting's agenda. The proxy form may ask for discretionary voting authority if the proxy indicates in bold print how the shares will be voted. For directors' elections, the shareholders must be provided with a means for withholding approval for each nominee.

False Statements

Rule 14a-9 prohibits misstatements or omissions of material fact in the course of a proxy solicitation. If a violation is proved, a court may enjoin the holding of the shareholders' meeting, void the proxies that were illegally obtained, or rescind the action taken at the shareholders' meeting. In the following case, the court held that management did not violate Rule 14a-9 by failing to disclose its motives for seeking amendment of the company's articles of incorporation.

LEWIS v. POTLATCH CORP.
716 F. Supp. 807 (S.D.N.Y. 1989)

Potlatch Corporation was in the forests products industry, an industry that had experienced a wave of takeovers in the 1980s. In 1985, the Potlatch board of directors approved a voting rights amendment to the articles of incorporation. The amendment granted four votes per share to current shareholders and other specified shareholders. New shareholders would have only one vote per share until they held the shares for four years. The effect of the amendment, if it were approved by shareholders, would be to deter and frustrate a hostile takeover of Potlatch. To obtain shareholder approval of the voting rights amendment, on October 22, 1985, the board issued a proxy statement in connection with its solicitation of proxies from the shareholders. The voting rights amendment was approved by shareholders on December 12, 1985.

Harry Lewis and other Potlatch shareholders sued the company under Section 14(a) of the 1934 Act, seeking to void the shareholders' approval of the voting rights amendment. Lewis claimed that the shareholders' votes were procured by fraud because the board's proxy statement was materially false and misleading.

Sprizzo, Judge. A letter issued along with the proxy statement stated that the intent of the voting rights amendment was to give longterm shareholders a greater voice in the affairs of Potlatch. Lewis alleges that this statement was false because management's real purpose was entrenchment.

However, where all of the relevant facts which a reasonable shareholder would need to make a decision on a proposed corporate action are disclosed, the proxy material need not disclose management motive. In this case, the proxy statement fully described the proposed voting rights amendment and the effect it would have on stockholders. Indeed, it specifically disclosed that directors and officers of the company could have an increasingly higher percentage of the voting power of the company if the amendment were adopted. Moreover, it stated that "the Amendment could increase the likelihood that incumbent Directors and officers will retain their positions." Any shareholder voting for the proposal, therfore, was informed that passage of the amendment could concentrate control in hands of present management and that entrenchment of the present board could result.

The proxy statement disclosed that under current New York Stock Exchange rules, adoption of the voting rights amendment could lead to the delisting of Potlatch stock on the exchange, that the NYSE rules were being reviewed, and that "stockholders should assume that if [the] Amendment is adopted the Common Stock may not be permitted to continue to be listed on the NYSE." Lewis alleges that the proxy statement failed to disclose that the possible delisting of Potlatch stock on the NYSE was a disadvantage.

The disclosure here was clearly adequate. A proxy statement need not state what would be apparent to a reasonable shareholder. Moreover, a proxy statement need not characterize the obvious effect of disclosed information.

Judgment for Potlatch.

Proxy Contests

A shareholder may decide to solicit proxies in competition with management. Such a competition is called a **proxy contest,** and a solicitation of this kind is also subject to SEC rules. To facilitate proxy contests, the SEC requires the corporation either to furnish a shareholder list to shareholders who desire to wage a proxy contest or to mail the competing proxy material for them.

Shareholder Proposals

In a large public corporation, it is very expensive for a shareholder to solicit proxies in support of a proposal for corporate action that she will offer at a shareholders' meeting. Therefore, she usually asks the management to include her proposal in its proxy statement. SEC Rule 14a-8 covers proposals by shareholders.

Under Rule 14a-8, the corporation must include a shareholder's proposal in its proxy statement if, among other things, the shareholder owns at least 1 percent or $1,000 of the securities to be voted at the shareholders' meeting. A shareholder may submit only one proposal per meeting. The proposal and its supporting statement may not exceed 500 words.

Excludable Proposals Under Rule 14a-8, a corporation's management may exclude many types of shareholder proposals from its proxy statement. For example, the following are excludable:

1. The proposal deals with the ordinary business operations of the corporation. Few well-drafted proposals are excluded on this basis. For example, TRW, Inc., was required to include in its proxy statement a proposal that it establish a shareholder advisory committee that would advise the board of directors on the interests of shareholders. However, Pacific Telesis Group was permitted on this ground to omit a proposal that the board consider adding an environmentalist director and designate a vice president for environmental matters for each subsidiary.

2. The proposal relates to operations that account for less than 5 percent of a corporation's total assets and is not otherwise significantly related to the company's business. For example, Harsco Corp. could not omit a proposal that it sell its 50 percent interest in a South African firm even though the investment was arguably economically insignificant—only 4.5 percent of net earnings, because the issues raised by the proposal were significantly related to Harsco's business.

3. A proposal that would require the issuer to violate a state or federal law. For example, one shareholder asked North American Bank to put a lesbian on the board of directors. The SEC staff advised North American Bank that the proposal was excludable because it may have required the corporation to violate antidiscrimination laws.

4. The proposal relates to a personal claim or grievance. A proposal that the corporation pay the shareholder $1 million for damages that she suffered from using one of the corporation's products would be excludable.

In addition, one part of Rule 14a-8 prevents a shareholder from submitting a proposal similar to recent proposals that have been overwhelmingly rejected by shareholders in recent years.

LIABILITY PROVISIONS OF THE 1934 ACT

To prevent fraud, deception, or manipulation and to provide remedies to the victims of such practices, Congress included a number of liability provisions in the 1934 Act.

Manipulation of a Security's Price

Section 9 specifically prohibits a number of deceptive practices that may be used to cause security prices to rise or fall by stimulating market activity. The prohibited practices include simultaneous purchases and sales of securities (called wash sales).

Liability for False Statements in Filed Documents

Section 18 is the 1934 Act counterpart to Section 11 of the 1933 Act. Section 18 imposes liability on any person responsible for a false or misleading statement of material fact in any document filed with the SEC under the 1934 Act. (Filed documents include the 10-K report, 8-K report, and proxy statements, but not the 10-Q report.) Any person who relies on a false or misleading statement in such a filed document may sue for damages. As with Section 11, the purchaser need not prove that the defendant was negligent or acted with scienter. Instead, the defendant has a defense that he acted in good faith and had no knowledge that the statement was false or misleading. This defense is easier to meet than the Section 11 due diligence defense, requiring only that the defendant prove that he did not act with scienter.

Section 10(b) and Rule 10b-5

The most important liability section in the 1934 Act is Section 10(b), an extremely broad provision prohibiting the use of any manipulative or deceptive device in contravention of any rules that the SEC prescribes as "necessary or appropriate in the public interest or for the protection of investors." Rule 10b-5 was adopted by the SEC under Section 10(b). The rule states:

It shall be unlawful for any person, directly or indirectly, by use of any means or instrumentality of interstate commerce or of the mails, or of any facility of any national securities exchange,

   (a) to employ any device, scheme, or artifice to defraud,
   (b) to make any untrue statement of a material fact or to omit to state a material fact necessary in order to make the statements made, in the light of the circumstances under which they were made, not misleading, or
   (c) to engage in any act, practice, or course of business which operates or would operate as a fraud or deceit upon any person,

in connection with the purchase or sale of any security.

Rule 10b-5 applies to all transactions in all securities. Securities need not be registered under the 1933 Act or the 1934 Act for Rule 10b-5 to apply.

Elements of a Rule 10b-5 Violation

The most important elements of a Rule 10b-5 violation are a misstatement or omission of material fact, scienter, and reliance. In addition, private persons suing under the rule must be purchasers or sellers.

Misstatement or Omission of Material Fact   The essence of fraud, deception, and manipulation is *falsity* or *nondisclosure when there is a duty to speak*. Liability for falsity occurs when a person *misstates* material facts. For example, if a manager of an unprofitable business induces shareholders to sell their stock to him by stating that the business will fail, although he knows that the business has become potentially profitable, he violates Rule 10b-5.

Liability for nondisclosure arises when a person *omits* material facts when he has a *duty to disclose*. For a person to be liable for an omission, there must be a duty of trust or confidence breached either by a nondisclosure or by the incomplete disclosure of information. For example, a securities broker is liable to his customer for not disclosing that he owns the shares that he recommends to the customer. As an agent of the customer, he owes a fiduciary duty to his customer to disclose his conflict of interest. In addition, a person is liable for omitting to tell all of the material facts after he has chosen to disclose some of them. His incomplete disclosure created the duty to disclose all of the material facts.

However, in *Santa Fe Industries, Inc. v. Green*,[13] the Supreme Court held that a mere breach of a fiduciary duty, such as mismanagement of the company by the directors, creates no Rule 10b-5 liability. In addition to a breach of a fiduciary duty, there must be deception or manipulation. Deception may be proved when the fiduciary duty breached is a duty of confidentiality or a duty of disclosure.

Materiality   The misstated or omitted fact must be material. In essence, material information is any information that is likely to have an impact on the price of a security in the market. In *TSC Industries, Inc. v. Northway*,[14] a Rule 14a-9 case, the Supreme Court stated:

An omitted fact is material if there is a substantial likelihood that a reasonable shareholder would consider it important to his decision. The standard contemplates a showing of a substantial likelihood that the omitted fact would have assumed actual significance in the deliberations of the reasonable shareholder. There must be a substantial likelihood that the disclosure of the omitted fact would have been viewed by the reasonable investor as having significantly altered the total mix of information made available.

It is generally believed that the *Northway* materiality standard applies to all of the liability sections of the securities acts. Such matters as proposed mergers, tender offers for the corporation's shares, plans to introduce an important new product, or indications of an abrupt change in the expectations of the company are examples of what would be considered material facts. The Supreme Court expressly adopted the *Northway* test for the Rule 10b-5 context.

In some situations, there is doubt whether an important event will occur. In the *Texas Gulf Sulphur* case,[15] the court held that materiality of the doubtful event can be determined by "a balancing of both the indicated probability that the event will occur and the anticipated magnitude of the event in light of the totality of the company activity." The Supreme Court has approved this definition of materiality.

Scienter   For fraud, deception, or manipulation to exist, the defendant must have acted with scienter. **Scienter** is an intent to deceive, manipulate, or defraud. The Supreme Court has not decided whether recklessness is sufficient for the scienter requirement, though many lower courts have held that reckless conduct violates Rule 10b-5. Mere negligence is *not* enough under Rule 10b-5.[16]

Other Elements   The Supreme Court has held that Rule 10b-5 requires that private plaintiffs seeking damages be *actual purchasers or sellers* of securities.[17] Persons who were deterred from purchasing securities by fraudulent statements may not recover lost profits under Rule 10b-5.

Under Rule 10b-5, private plaintiffs alleging misstatements must prove that they *relied* on the misstatement of material fact. The SEC as plaintiff need not prove reliance. For private plaintiffs, reliance is not usually required in omission cases; the investor need merely prove that the omitted fact was material.

---

[13] 430 U.S. 462 (U.S. Sup. Ct. 1977).
[14] 426 U.S. 438 (U.S. Sup. Ct. 1976).

[15] *SEC v. Texas Gulf Sulphur Co.*, 401 F.2d 833 (2d Cir. 1968).
[16] *Ernst & Ernst v. Hochfelder*, 425 U.S. 185 (1976).
[17] *Blue Chip Stamps v. Manor Drug Stores*, 421 U.S. 723 (1975).

In *Shores v. Sklar*,[18] the court held that an investor's reliance on the availability of the securities on the market satisfied the reliance requirement of Rule 10b-5 because the securities market had been defrauded as to the value of the securities. Due to the fraud on the securities market, this market reliance existed even though the sellers had never communicated with the purchaser. In *Levinson v. Basic, Inc.*,[19] the Supreme Court held that the fraud-on-the-market theory permits a court to presume an investor's reliance merely from the public availability of material misrepresentations. That presumption, however, is rebuttable, such as by evidence that an investor knew the market price was incorrect.

For Rule 10b-5 to apply, the wrongful action must be accomplished by the mails, with an instrumentality of interstate commerce, or on a national securities exchange. This element satisfies the federal jurisdiction requirement. Use of the mails or a telephone within one state has been held to meet this element.

Conduct Covered by Rule 10b-5

The scope of activities proscribed by Rule 10b-5 is not immediately obvious. While it is easy to understand that actual fraud and price manipulation are covered by the rule, two other areas are less easily mastered: the corporation's continuous disclosure obligation and insider trading.

Continuous Disclosure of Material Information

The purpose of the securities acts is to ensure that investors have the information they need in order to make intelligent investment decisions *at all times*. The periodic reporting requirements of the 1934 Act are designed to accomplish this result. If important developments arise between the disclosure dates of reports, however, investors will not have all of the information they need to make intelligent decisions unless the corporation discloses the material information immediately. Rule 10b-5, as interpreted in the *Texas Gulf Sulphur* case,[20] may be read to require a corporation to disclose material information immediately, unless the corporation has a valid business purpose for withholding disclosure. In addition, *Texas Gulf Sulphur* held that when the corporation does choose to disclose information or comment on information that it has no duty to disclose, it must do so accurately.

Until 1988, courts had disagreed on whether Rule 10b-5 requires disclosure of merger and other acquisition negotiations prior to an agreement in principle. In the close corporation context especially, courts have been willing to find materiality of preliminary acquisition negotiations. For example, in *Michaels v. Michaels*, the court held that a shareholder in a closely held company purchasing another shareholder's shares had a duty to disclose that acquisition negotiations were going to be initiated.[21]

In the following case, decided in 1988, the Supreme Court of the United States held that materiality of merger negotiations is to be determined on a case-by-case basis. The Court held that materiality depends on the probability that the transaction will be consummated and its significance to the issuer of the securities. In addition, the Court stated that a corporation that chooses to comment on acquisition negotiations must do so truthfully.

---

[18]647 F.2d 462 (5th Cir. 1982).
[19]485 U.S. 224 (U.S. Sup. Ct. 1988).

[20]401 F.2d 833 (2d Cir. 1968).
[21]767 F.2d 751 (2d Cir. 1984).

LEVINSON v. BASIC, INC.

485 U.S. 224 (U.S. Sup. Ct. 1988)

For over a decade, Combustion Engineering, Inc. (CEI) had been interested in acquiring Basic, Inc. When antitrust barriers to such an acquisition were eliminated in 1976, CEI's secret strategic plan listed the acquisition of Basic as an objective. Between September 1976 and October 1977, the managements of Basic and CEI privately discussed several times a possible acquisition of Basic by CEI. Throughout 1977 and 1978, despite the secrecy of merger negotiations, there were repeated instances of abnormal trading in Basic's shares on the New York Stock Exchange. On October 19 and 20, 1977, the trading volume in Basic's shares rose from an average of 7,000 shares per day to 29,000 shares. On October 21, 1977, Max Muller, the president of Basic, made a public announcement, reported in a major newspaper, that "the company knew no reason for the stock's activity and that no negotiations were under way with any company for a merger."

Secret contacts between Basic and CEI continued, however. On June 7, 1978, CEI offered $28 per share for Basic, which Basic rejected as too low. CEI stated it would make a better offer, but Muller told CEI to "hold off until we tell you," because Muller wanted to see an investment banker's valuation of Basic before evaluating any CEI offer. Muller and other Basic officials decided to ask CEI for its "best offer." On July 10, 1978, Muller and CEI agreed that CEI would make an informal offer to Basic. CEI advised Muller to make no public disclosures about the negotiations.

On July 14, 1978, the price of Basic shares rose more than 12 percent to $27 per share on trading of 18,200 shares. The New York Stock Exchange called Basic and asked it to explain the trading in its shares. Basic denied that any undisclosed merger or acquisition plans or any other significant corporate development existed. On September 24, 1978, the price of Basic shares rose more than 2 points to $30 per share on volume of 31,900 shares. The next day, the price rose almost 3 points to $33 per share on volume of 28,500 shares, even though the Dow Jones Industrial Average fell more than 3 points. Again the Exchange asked Basic whether there were any undisclosed acquisition plans or any other significant corporate developments. Basic flatly denied that there were any corporate developments and issued a press release that stated:

management is unaware of any present or pending corporate development that would result in the abnormally heavy trading activity and price fluctuation in company shares that have been experienced in the past few days.

Secret contacts between Basic and CEI continued. In early November, Basic sent a quarterly report to its shareholders in which it stated:

With regard to the stock market activity in the Company's shares we remain unaware of any present or pending developments that would account for the high volume of trading and price fluctuations in recent months.

On November 27, 1978, CEI secretly offered to buy Basic's outstanding shares for $35 per share. Basic rejected the offer. On December 14, 1978, CEI offered $46 per share. The next day, Friday, December 15, the price of Basic's shares soared. Again Basic answered the Exchange's inquiry with a denial of corporate developments. On Monday, December 18, 1978, Basic asked the Exchange to suspend trading in Basic shares, because it had been "approached" concerning a possible merger. The next day, Basic accepted CEI's offer. On the following day, December 19, Basic announced its acceptance of CEI's offer to buy Basic's outstanding shares for $46 per share.

Max Levinson and several other Basic shareholders sold their Basic shares between October 21, 1977 and December 15, 1978, at a price lower than CEI's offer. They claimed that Basic's statements denying that any merger discussions were occurring violated Section 10(b) and Rule 10b-5 of the Securities Exchange Act of 1934. The district court held that the statements were not material as a matter of law. Levinson appealed to the Sixth Circuit Court of Appeals, which held that although possessing no general duty to disclose the merger negotiations, Basic released statements that were so incomplete as to be misleading. Basic appealed to the Supreme Court.

Blackmun, Justice.   Underlying the adoption of extensive disclosure requirements of the 1934 Act was a legislative philosophy: There cannot be honest markets without honest publicity. Manipulation and dishonest practices of the market place thrive upon mystery and secrecy.

The Court previously has explicitly defined a standard of materiality under the securities laws, concluding in the proxy-solicitation context that "[a]n omitted fact is material if there is a substantial likelihood that a reasonable shareholder would consider it important in deciding how to vote." *TSC Industries, Inc. v. Northway, Inc.* (1976). Acknowledging that certain information concerning corporate developments could well be of "dubious significance," the Court was careful not to set too low a standard of materiality; it was concerned that a minimal standard might bring an overabundance of information within its reach, and lead management "simply to bury the shareholders in an avalanche of trivial information—a result that is hardly conducive to informed decisionmaking." It further explained that to fulfill the materiality requirement "there must be a substantial likelihood that the disclosure of the omitted fact would have been viewed by the reasonable investor as having significantly altered the 'total mix' of information made available." We now expressly adopt the *TSC Industries* standard of materiality for the Section 10(b) and Rule 10b-5 context.

The application of this materiality standard to preliminary merger discussions is not self-evident. Where the event is contingent or speculative in nature, it is difficult to ascertain whether the "reasonable investor" would have considered the omitted information significant at the time. Merger negotiations, because of the ever-present possibility that the contemplated transaction will not be effectuated, fall into this category.

Basic urges upon us the Third Circuit test for resolving this difficulty. Under this approach, preliminary merger discussions do not become material until "agreement-in-principle" as to the price and structure of the transaction has been reached between the would-be merger partners. See *Greenfield v. Heublein, Inc.* (3d Cir. 1984). By definition, then, information concerning any negotiations not yet at the agreement-in-principle stage could be withheld or even misrepresented without a violation of Rule 10b-5.

Three rationales have been offered in support of the "agreement-in-principle" test. The first derives from the concern expressed in *TSC Industries* that an investor not be overwhelmed by excessively detailed and trivial information and focuses on the substantial risk that preliminary merger discussions may collapse: because such discussions are inherently tentative, disclosure of their existence itself could mislead investors and foster false optimism. The other two justifications for the agreement-in-principle standard are based on management concerns: because the requirement of "agreement-in-principle" limits the scope of disclosure obligations, it helps preserve the confidentiality of merger discussions where earlier disclosure might prejudice the negotiations; and the test also provides a usable, bright-line rule for determining when disclosure must be made.

None of these policy-based rationales, however, purports to explain why drawing the line at agreement-in-principle reflects the significance of the information upon the investor's decision. The first rationale "assumes that investors are nitwits, unable to appreciate—even when told—that mergers are risky propositions up until the closing." *Flamm v. Eberstadt* (7th Cir. 1987).

The second rationale, the importance of secrecy during the early stages of merger discussions, also seems irrelevant to an assessment whether their existence is significant to the trading decision of a reasonable investor. To avoid a "bidding war" over its target, an acquiring firm often will insist that negotiations remain confidential and at least one Court of Appeals has stated that "silence pending settlement of the price and structure of a deal is beneficial to most investors, most of the time." *Flamm v. Eberstadt.*

We need not ascertain, however, whether secrecy necessarily maximizes shareholder wealth—although we note that the proposition is at least disputed as a matter of theory and empirical research—for this case does not concern the timing of a disclosure; it concerns only its accuracy and completeness. We face here the narrow question whether information concerning the existence and status of preliminary merger discussions is significant to the reasonable investor's trading decision. Arguments based on the premise that some disclosure would be "premature" in a sense are more properly considered under the rubric of an issuer's duty to disclose. The "secrecy" rationale is simple inapposite to the definition of materiality.

The final justification offered in support of the agreement-in-principle test seems to be directed solely at the comfort of corporate managers. A bright-line rule indeed is easier to follow than a standard that requires the exercise of judgment in light of all the circumstances. But ease of application alone is not an excuse for ignoring the purposes of the securities acts and Congress' policy decisions.

We therefore find no valid justification for artificially excluding from the definition of materiality information concerning merger discussions, which would otherwise be considered significant to the trading decision of a reasonable investor, merely because agreement-in-principle as to price and structure has not yet been reached by the parties or their representatives.

Even before this Court's decision in *TSC Industries*, the Second Circuit had explained the role of the materiality requirement of Rule 10b-5, with respect to contingent or speculative information or events. Under such circumstances, materiality "will depend at any given time upon a balancing of both the indicated probability that the event will occur and the anticipated magnitude of the event in light of the totality of the company activity." *SEC v. Texas Gulf Sulphur Co.* (2d Cir. 1968).

The late Judge Friendly applied the *Texas Gulf Sulphur* probability/magnitude approach in the specific context of preliminary merger negotiations. He stated:

Since a merger in which it is bought out is the most important event that can occur in a small corporation's life, to wit, its death, we think that inside information, as regards a merger of this sort, can become material at an earlier stage than would be the case as regards lesser transactions—and this even though the mortality rate of mergers in such formative stages is doubtless high. *SEC v. Geon Industries, Inc.* (2d Cir. 1976).

We agree with that analysis.

Whether merger discussions in any particular case are material therefore depends on the facts. Generally, in order to assess the probability that the event will occur, a factfinder will need to look to indicia of interest in the transaction at the highest corporate levels. Board resolutions, instructions to investment bankers, and actual negotiations between principals or their intermediaries may serve as indicia of interest. To assess the magnitude of the transaction to the issuer of the securities allegedly manipulated, a factfinder will need to consider such facts as the size of the two corporate entities and of the potential premiums over market value. No particular event or factor short of closing the transaction need be either necessary or sufficient by itself to render merger discussions material.

As we clarify today, materiality depends on the significance the reasonable investor would place on the withheld or misrepresented information. Because the standard of materiality we have adopted differs from that used by both courts below, we remand the case for reconsideration.

We turn to the question of reliance and the fraud-on-the market theory. Succinctly put:

The fraud on the market theory is based on the hypothesis that, in an open and developed securities market, the price of a company's stock is determined by the available material information regarding the company and its business. . . . Misleading statements will therefore defraud purchasers of stock even if the purchasers do not directly rely on the misstatements. . . . The causal connection between the defendants' fraud and the plaintiffs' purchase of stock in such a case is no less significant than in a case of direct reliance on misrepresentations. *Peil v. Speiser* (3d Cir. 1986).

Our task is to consider whether it was proper for the courts below to apply a rebuttable presumption of reliance, supported in part by the fraud-on-the-market theory.

Reliance is an element of a Rule 10b-5 cause of action. Reliance provides the requisite causal connection between a defendant's misrepresentation and a plaintiff's injury. There is, however, more than one way to demonstrate the causal connection.

In face-to-face transactions, the inquiry into an investor's reliance upon information is into the subjective pricing of that information by that investor. With the presence of a market, the market is interposed between seller and buyer and, ideally, transmits information to the investor in the processed form of a market price.

Thus the market is performing a substantial part of the valuation process performed by the investor in a face-to-face transaction. The market is acting as the unpaid agent of the investor, informing him that given all the information available to it, the value of the stock is worth the market price. *In re LTV Securities Litigation* (N.D. Tex. 1980).

The presumption of reliance employed in this case supports the congressional policy embodied in the 1934 Act. In drafting that Act, Congress expressly relied on the premise that securities markets are affected by information, and enacted legislation to facilitate an investor's reliance on the integrity of those markets:

No investor, no speculator, can safely buy and sell securities upon the exchanges without having an intelligent basis for forming his judgment as to the value of the securities he buys or sells. The idea of a free and open public market is built upon the theory that competing judgments of buyers and sellers as to the fair price of a security bring about a situation where the market price reflects as nearly as possible a just price. Just as an artificial manipulation tends to upset the true function of an open market, so the hiding and secreting of important information obstructs the operation of the markets as indices of real value. H.R. Rep. No. 1383, 73 Cong., 2d Session 11 (1934).

The presumption is also supported by common sense and probability. Recent empirical studies have tended to confirm Congress' premise that the market price of shares traded on well-developed markets reflects all publicly available information, and hence, any material misrepresentations. Because most publicly available information is reflected in market price, an investor's reliance on any public material misrepresentations, therefore, may be presumed for purposes of a Rule 10b-5 action.

The Court of Appeals found that Basic "made public, material misrepresentations and Levinson sold Basic stock in an impersonal, efficient market. Thus Levinson and the other shareholders have established the threshold facts for proving their loss." The court acknowledged that Basic may rebut proof of the elements giving rise to the presumption, or show that the misrepresentation in fact did not lead to a distortion of price or that a shareholder traded or would have traded despite his knowing the statement was false.

Any showing that severs the link between the alleged misrepresentation and either the price received (or paid) by the plaintiff, or his decision to trade at a fair market price, will be sufficient to rebut the presumption of reliance.

Judgment vacated and remanded to the Court of Appeals.

In response to the *Basic* decision, in 1989 the SEC released guidelines to help public companies decide whether they must disclose merger negotiations. A company is not required to disclose merger negotiations if

1. The company did not make any prior disclosures about the merger negotiations,

2. Disclosure is not compelled by other SEC rules, and

3. Management determines that disclosure would jeopardize completion of the merger transaction.

Trading on Inside Information

Many interesting Rule 10b-5 cases involve securities trading by a corporate insider possessing nonpublic, corporate information. Some of these cases involve face-to-face transactions between an insider who has corporate information and another shareholder who does not possess similar information. In other cases, the buyer and seller have not met face-to-face. Instead, the transaction has been executed on a stock exchange. Even though the buyer and the seller never meet, trading on an exchange by a person in possession of confidential corporate information has been held to violate Rule 10b-5.

In **insider trading** cases, a person with nonpublic, confidential, inside information may not use that information when trading with a person who does not possess that information. He must either *disclose the information before trading or refrain from trading.* The difficult task in the insider trading area is determining when a person is subject to this *disclose-or-refrain rule.*

Insider Liability   In *United States v. Chiarella,*[22] the Supreme Court laid down the test for determining an insider's liability for trading on nonpublic, corporate information:

The duty to disclose arises when one party has information that the other party is entitled to know because of a fiduciary or similar relation of trust and confidence between them. A relationship of trust and confidence exists between the shareholders of a corporation and those insiders who have obtained confidential information by reason of their position with that corporation. This relationship gives rise to a duty to disclose because of the necessity of preventing a corporate insider from taking unfair advantage of the uninformed stockholders.

_____

[22] 445 U.S. 222 (U.S. Sup. Ct. 1980).

Under this test, insiders include not only officers and directors of the corporation, but also anyone who is *entrusted with corporate information for a corporate purpose.* Insiders include outside consultants, lawyers, independent auditors, engineers, investment bankers, public relations advisers, news reporters, and personnel of government agencies who are given confidential corporate information for a corporate purpose.

Tippee Liability   **Tippees** are recipients of inside information (tips) from insiders. Tippees of insiders, such as relatives and friends of insiders, stockbrokers, and security analysts, are forbidden to trade on inside information and are subject to recovery of their profits if they do.

In the following case, the Supreme Court stated the applicability of Rule 10b-5 to tippees. The Court held that a tippee has liability if (1) an insider has breached a fiduciary duty of trust and confidence to the shareholders by disclosing to the tippee and (2) the tippee knows or should know of the insider's breach. In addition, the court held that an insider has not breached her fiduciary duty to the shareholders unless she has received a personal benefit by disclosing to the tippee.

SEC v. DIRKS

463 U.S. 646 (U.S. Sup. Ct. 1983)

On March 6, 1973, Raymond Dirks, a security analyst in a New York brokerage firm, received nonpublic information from Ronald Secrist, a former officer of Equity Funding of America, a seller of life insurance and mutual funds. Secrist alleged that the assets of Equity Funding were vastly overstated as the result of fraudulent corporate practices. He also stated that the SEC and state insurance departments had failed to act on similar charges of fraud made by Equity Funding employees. Secrist urged Dirks to verify the fraud and to disclose it publicly.

Dirks visited Equity Funding's headquarters in Los Angeles and interviewed several officers and employees of the corporation. The senior management denied any wrongdoing, but certain employees corroborated the charges of fraud. Dirks openly discussed the information he had obtained with a number of his clients and investors. Some of these persons sold their holdings of Equity Funding securities.

Dirks urged a *Wall Street Journal* reporter to write a story on the fraud allegations. The reporter, fearing libel, declined to write the story.

During the two-week period in which Dirks investigated the fraud and spread the word of Secrist's charges, the price of Equity Funding stock fell from $26 per share to less than $15 per share. The New York Stock Exchange halted trading in Equity Funding stock on March 27. On that date, Dirks voluntarily presented his information on the fraud to the SEC. Only then did the

SEC institute an action for fraud against Equity Funding. Shortly thereafter, California insurance authorities impounded Equity Funding's records and uncovered evidence of the fraud. On April 2, *The Wall Street Journal* published a front-page story based largely on information assembled by Dirks. Equity Funding immediately went into receivership.

The SEC brought an administrative proceeding against Dirks for violating Rule 10b-5 by passing along confidential inside information to his clients. The SEC found that he had violated Rule 10b-5, but it merely censured him, since he had played an important role in bringing the fraud to light. Dirks appealed to the Court of Appeals for the District of Columbia Circuit. The court of appeals affirmed the judgment. Dirks then appealed to the Supreme Court.

Powell, Justice. In *U.S. v. Chiarella* (1980), we accepted the two elements set out in *In re Cady, Roberts* (1961) for establishing a Rule 10b-5 violation: (i) the existence of a relationship affording access to inside information intended to be available only for a corporate purpose, and (ii) the unfairness of allowing a corporate insider to take advantage of that information by trading without disclosure. The Court found that there is no general duty to disclose before trading on material nonpublic information, and held that a duty to disclose under Section 10(b) does not arise from the mere possession of nonpublic market information. Such a duty arises from the existence of a fiduciary relationship.

There can be no duty to disclose when the person who has traded on inside information was not the corporation's agent, was not a fiduciary, or was not a person in whom the sellers of the securities had placed their trust and confidence. Not to require such a fiduciary relationship would depart radically from the established doctrine that duty arises from a specific relationship between two parties and would amount to recognizing a general duty between all participants in market transactions to forgo actions based on material, nonpublic information.

This requirement of a specific relationship between the shareholders and the individual trading on inside information has created analytical difficulties for the SEC and courts in policing tippees who trade on inside information. Unlike insiders who have independent fiduciary duties to both the corporation and its shareholders, the typical tippee has no such relationship.[23] In view of this absence, it has been unclear how a tippee acquires the *Cady, Roberts* duty to refrain from trading on inside information.

We affirm today that a duty to disclose arises from the relationship between the parties and not merely from one's ability to acquire information because of his position in the market.

The conclusion that recipients of inside information do not invariably acquire a duty to disclose or abstain does not mean that such tippees always are free to trade on the information. Not only are insiders forbidden by their fiduciary relationship from personally using undisclosed corporate information to their advantage, but also they may not give such information to an outsider for the same improper purpose of exploiting the information for their personal gain. The transactions of those who knowingly participate with the fiduciary in such a breach are as forbidden as transactions on behalf on the trustee himself. A contrary rule would open up opportunities for devious dealings in the name of the others that the trustee could not conduct in his own. Thus, the tippee's duty to disclose or abstain is derivative from that of the insider's duty. As we noted in *Chiarella*,

---

[23] [Footnote 14 by the Court.] Under certain circumstances, such as where corporate information is revealed legitimately to an underwriter, accountant, lawyer, or consultant working for the corporation, these outsiders may become fiduciaries of the shareholders. The basis for recognizing this fiduciary duty is not simply that such persons acquired nonpublic corporate information, but rather that they have entered into a special confidential relationship in the conduct of the business of the enterprise and are given access to information solely for corporate purposes. When such a person breaches his fiduciary relationship, he may be treated more properly as a tipper than a tippee. For such a duty to be imposed, however, the corporation must expect the outsider to keep the disclosed nonpublic information confidential, and the relationship at least must imply such a duty.

the tippee's obligation has been viewed as arising from his role as a participant after the fact in the insider's breach of a fiduciary duty.

Thus, a tippee assumes a fiduciary duty to the shareholders of a corporation not to trade on material nonpublic information only when the insider has breached his fiduciary duty to the shareholders by disclosing the information to the tippee and the tippee knows or should know that there has been a breach.

In determining whether a tippee is under an obligation to disclose or abstain, it thus is necessary to determine whether the insider's tip constituted a breach of the insider's fiduciary duty. Whether disclosure is a breach of duty therefore depends in large part on the purpose of the disclosure. Thus, the test is whether the insider personally will benefit, directly or indirectly, from his disclosure. Absent some personal gain, there has been no breach of duty to stockholders. And absent a breach by the insider, there is no derivative breach.

This requires courts to focus on objective criteria, *i.e.*, whether the insider receives a direct or indirect personal benefit from the disclosure, such as a pecuniary gain or a reputational benefit that will translate into future earnings. For example, there may be a relationship between the insider and the recipient that suggests a *quid pro quo* from the latter, or an intention to benefit the particular recipient. The elements of fiduciary duty and exploitation of nonpublic information also exist when an insider makes a gift of confidential information to a relative or friend who trades. The tip and trade resemble trading by the insider himself followed by a gift of the profits to the recipient.

Under the inside-trading and tipping rules set forth above, we find that there was no violation by Dirks. Dirks was a stranger to Equity Funding, with no pre-existing fiduciary duty to its shareholders. He took no action, directly or indirectly, that induced the shareholders or officers of Equity Funding to repose trust or confidence in him. There was no expectation by Dirks' sources that he would keep their information in confidence. Nor did Dirks misappropriate or illegally obtain the information about Equity Funding. Unless the insiders breached their *Cady, Roberts* duty to shareholders in disclosing the nonpublic information to Dirks, he breached no duty when he passed it on to investors as well as to *The Wall Street Journal*.

It is clear that neither Secrist nor the other Equity Funding employees violated their *Cady, Roberts* duty to the corporation's shareholders by providing information to Dirks. Secrist intended to convey relevant information that management was unlawfully concealing, and he believed that persuading Dirks to investigate was the best way to disclose the fraud. The tippers received no monetary or personal benefit for revealing Equity Funding's secrets, nor was their purpose to make a gift of valuable information to Dirks. The tippers were motivated by a desire to expose the fraud. In the absence of a breach of duty to shareholders by the insiders, there was no derivative breach by Dirks. Dirks therefore could not have been a participant after the fact in an insider's breach of a fiduciary duty.

Judgment reversed in favor of Dirks.

Misappropriation of Nonpublic Information In *Chiarella* and *Dirks*, the Supreme Court held that liability for inside trading is premised on an insider's breach of a fiduciary duty owed to the shareholders of the corporation whose shares are traded. Some federal courts of appeals have held that a misappropriation of confidential information from someone other than the corporation whose shares are traded or a breach of a fiduciary duty owed to someone other than the shareholders of the corporation whose shares are traded can create Rule 10b-5 liability.

Relying on Justice Burger's dissent in *Chiarella*,[24] the Second Circuit held in *United States v. Newman*[25] that criminal liability might attach to a person who had breached a duty of confidentiality owed to his employer by misappropriating nonpublic information, even though no duty was owed to the shareholders of the corporation whose shares were purchased. In *Moss v. Morgan Stanley*,[26] a case with the same facts as *Newman*, the same court held that the shareholders could *not* bring a suit for damages against the person who breached a fiduciary duty to his employer but breached no duty owed to the shareholders of the corporation whose shares he traded. The court refused to expand the holding of *Newman* to create a duty of disclosure to the general public.

In 1987, the Supreme Court declined an opportunity to clarify its position concerning the misappropriation theory when the justices upheld the conviction of R. Foster Winans on mail fraud grounds, but could not agree whether he had violated Rule 10b-5.[27] Winans, the "Heard on the Street" columnist for *The Wall Street Journal*, had been charged with violating Rule 10b-5 because he had tipped his lover about which companies he planned to feature in upcoming columns. The justices' disagreement left standing the Second Circuit's holding that Winans's misappropriation of the *Journal*'s confidential information operated as a fraud or deceit.

Extent of Liability for Insider Trading   Section 20A of the 1934 Act allows persons who traded in the securities at about the same time as the insider or tippee to recover damages from the insider or tippee. However, as there may be several persons trading at about the same time, the insider or tippee's total liability cannot exceed the profit she has made or the loss she has avoided by trading on inside information.

This limitation, which merely requires disgorgement of profits, has been assailed as not adequately deterring insider trading, because the defendant may realize an enormous profit if her trading is not discovered, but lose nothing beyond her profits if it is. In response to this issue of liability, in 1984 Congress passed an amendment to the 1934 Act permitting the SEC to seek a civil penalty of three times the profit gained or the loss avoided by trading on inside information. This treble penalty is paid to the Treasury of the United States. The penalty applies only to SEC actions; it does not affect the amount of damages that may be recovered by private plaintiffs. The 1988 Insider Trading and Securities Fraud Enforcement Act amended the 1934 Act and granted the SEC power to award up to 10 percent of any triple-damage penalty as a bounty to informants who helped the SEC uncover insider trading.

Criminal Liability

Like the 1933 Act, the 1934 Act provides for liability for criminal violations of the Act. Section 32 provides for a fine of up to $2.5 million and imprisonment of up to five years for willful violations of the 1934 Act or the related SEC rules.

TENDER OFFER REGULATION

History

Until the early 1960s, the predominant procedure by which one corporation acquired another was the merger, a transaction requiring the cooperation of the acquired corporation's management. Since the 1960s, the **tender offer** has become an often used acquisition device. A tender offer is a public offer by a **bidder** to purchase a **subject company's** equity securities directly from its shareholders at a specified price for a fixed period of time. The offering price is usually well above the market price of the shares. Such offers are often made even though there is opposition from the subject company's management. Opposed offers are called hostile tender offers.[28]

---

[24]"There is some language in the Court's opinion to suggest that only 'a relationship between the defendant and the sellers . . . could give rise to a duty [to disclose].' The Court's holding, however, is much more limited, namely, that mere possession of material, nonpublic information is insufficient to create a duty to disclose or to refrain from trading. Accordingly, it is my understanding that the Court has not rejected the view that an absolute duty to disclose or refrain arises from the very act of misappropriating nonpublic information." 445 U.S. at 245, n. 4 (Burger, C. J., dissenting).

[25]664 F.2d 12 (2d Cir. 1981).

[26]719 F.2d 5 (2d Cir. 1983).

[27]*United States v. Carpenter*, 484 U.S. 19 (U.S. Sup. Ct.1987).

---

[28] Defenses to hostile tender offers are addressed in detail in the Management of Corporations chapter.

In 1968, the Williams Act amendments to the 1934 Act were passed to provide shareholders with more information on which to base their decision whether to sell their shares to a bidder. The aim of the amendments is to give the bidder and the subject company equal opportunities to present their cases to the shareholders. Strict disclosure and procedural requirements are established for both parties. The Williams Act applies only when the subject company's equity securities are registered under the 1934 Act.

Definition of Tender Offer

The Williams Act does not define a tender offer, but the courts have compiled a list of factors to determine whether a person has made a tender offer. The greater the number of people solicited and the lower their investment sophistication, the more likely it is that the bidder will be held to have made a tender offer. Also, the shorter the offering period, the more rigid the price, and the greater the publicity concerning the offer, the more likely it is that the purchase efforts of the bidder will be treated as a tender offer. Given these factors, a person who purchases shares directly from several shareholders risks having a court treat the purchases like a tender offer. The Williams Act clearly states, however, that there is no tender offer unless the bidder intends to become a holder of at least 5 percent of the subject company's shares.

Regulation of Tender Offers

A bidder making a tender offer must file a tender offer statement, Schedule 14D-1, with the SEC when the offer commences. The information in this schedule includes the terms of the offer (for example, the price), the background of the bidder, and the purpose of the tender offer (including whether the bidder intends to control the subject company).

SEC Rule 14e-1 requires the bidder to keep the tender offer open for at least 20 business days and prohibits any purchase of shares during that time. The purpose of this rule is to give shareholders adequate time to make informed decisions regarding whether to tender their shares. Rule 14d-7 permits tendering shareholders to withdraw their tendered shares during the entire term of the offer. These rules allow the highest bidder to buy the shares, as in an auction.

All tender offers, whether made by the issuer or by a third-party bidder, must be made to all holders of the targeted class of shares.[29] When a bidder increases the offering price during the term of the tender offer, all of the shareholders must be paid the higher price even if they tendered their shares at a lower price.[30] If more shares are tendered than the bidder offered to buy, the bidder must prorate its purchases among all of the shares tendered.[31] This proration rule is designed to foster careful shareholder decisions about whether to sell shares. Shareholders might rush to tender their shares if the bidder could accept shares on a first-come, first-served basis.

Subject Company's Response   The management of the subject company is required to inform the shareholders of its position on the tender offer, with its reasons, within 10 days after the offer has been made.[32] It must also provide the bidder with a list of the holders of the equity securities that the bidder seeks to acquire.

Private Acquisitions of Shares

The Williams Act regulates private acquisitions of shares differently from tender offers. When the bidder privately seeks a controlling block of the subject company's shares on a stock exchange or in face-to-face negotiations with only a few shareholders, no advance notice to the SEC or disclosure to shareholders is required. However, a person making a private acquisition is required to file a *Schedule 13D* with the SEC and to send a copy to the subject company within 10 days after he becomes a *holder of 5 percent* of its shares. A *Schedule 13G* (which requires less disclosure than a 13D) must be filed when a 5 percent holder has purchased no more than 2 percent of the shares within the past 12 months.

In the following case, the Belzbergs violated the 1934 Act by filing a Schedule 13D 12 days after the 10-day deadline.

---

[29] SEA Rule 14d-10(a)(1).
[30] SEA Rule 14d-10(a)(2).
[31] SEA Rule 14d-8.
[32] SEA Rule 14e-2.

SEC v. First City Financial Corp., Ltd.
890 F.2d 1215 (D.C. Cir. 1989)

First City Financial Corp., a Canadian company controlled by the Belzberg familty, was engaged in the business of investing in publicly held American corporations, often by hostile acquisition. Marc Belzberg identified Ashland Oil Company as a potential target and on February 11, 1986, secretly purchased 61,000 shares of Ashland stock for First City. By February 26, additional secret purchases of Ashland shares pushed First City's holdings to just over 4.9 percent of Ashland's stock. These last two purchases were effected for First City by Alan "Ace" Greenberg, the chief executive officer of Bear Stearns, a large Wall Street brokerage. On March 4, Belzberg called Greenberg and told him, "It wouldn't be a bad idea if you bought Ashland Oil here." Immediately after the phone call, Greenberg purchased 20,500 Ashland shares for about $44 per share. If purchased for First City, those shares would have increased First City's Ashland holdings above 5 percent. Greenberg believed he was buying the shares for First City under a put and call agreement, under which First City had the right to buy the shares from Bear Stearns and Bear Stearns had the right to require First City to buy the shares from it. Between March 4 and 14, Greenberg purchased an additional 330,700 shares. On March 17, First City and Bear Stearns signed a formal put and call agreement covering all the shares Greenberg purchased.

On March 25, First City announced publicly for the first time that it intended to make a tender offer for all of Ashland's shares. First City filed a Schedule 13D on March 26. First City's 13D stated its intent to make a tender offer for all of Ashland's shares at $60 per share. Almost immediately, the market price of Ashland's shares rose to $55. Ashland convinced the Kentucky legislature to pass legislation hampering First City's takeover, with the result that First City abandoned its takeover attempt. To eliminate First City as a shareholder, Ashland purchased First City's holdings for $51 per share.

The SEC brought an action against First City, claiming that Greenberg's March 4 purchase of Ashland shares triggered First City's obligation to file a Schedule 13D within 10 days. The SEC asked the district court to enjoin First City from violating section 13(d) and to order First City to disgorge the profit it made on shares purchased between March 14 and 25. The district court ordered an injuction and disgorgement of $2.7 million. First City appealed on the grounds that its intent and belief was that Greenberg bought the shares for Bear Stearns's account.

Silberman, Circuit Judge.   A shareholder must comply with the section 13(d) disclosure law if he beneficially owns 5 percent of a public company's equity securities. Under Securities Exchange Act Rule 13d-3(a), whenever a person possesses investment or voting power through any agreement or understanding, he enjoys beneficial ownership. Rule 13d-3 is crafted broadly enough to sweep within its purview informal, oral arrangements that confer upon a person voting or investment power. A put and call agreement, even if informal, constitutes beneficial ownership to the investor of the stock subject to the agreement.

The case turns on the question whether the put and call agreement between First City and Bear Stearns was entered into on March 4 or not until March 17. We think the SEC presented a powerful case that Belzberg did intend to enter into a put-call agreement with Greenberg on March 4 and therefore purposely sought to circumvent section 13(d)'s disclosure requirements.

First, on February 26, Belzberg asked Greenberg to buy directly approximately 53,000 shares of Ashland *for First City*. It certainly seems more than a little strange that after having directed Bear Stearns to buy for First City's account, Belzberg, only a week later, would call Greenberg only to suggest that Bear Stearns buy Ashland stock for itself.

Perhaps the most important piece of circumstantial evidence tending to show that Belzberg had asked Greenberg on March 4 to buy stock for First City under a put-call agreement is the price First City paid Bear Stearns for the stock. The price was $450,000 below market on March 17, but reflected the market price on the dates that Bear Stearns purchased the stock.

At the threshold of Belzberg's version of the events is his claim that on March 4 he had "recommended" to Greenberg that Bear Stearns buy Ashland stock for Bear Stearns's own account, because *if* it subsequently turned out that First City wished to acquire Ashland, the takeover would be more easily accomplished if Ashland stock were held by arbitrageurs (short-term speculators more inclined to cash in on a quick profit) rather than remain in what First City refers to as forgotten safe deposit boxes. This explanation is unconvincing. Although it may well be true that *after* a tender offer is launched the acquiring company would wish as much stock as possible to be gathered by arbitrageurs, who typically buy for the very purpose of tendering, we had not previously heard the theory that it would be helpful for arbitrageurs to start their buying *before* the acquiring company publicly signals its intention.

During the period before it unveiled its takeover plan, First City took pains to keep its interest in Ashland secret. The very last thing Belzberg would do in light of those efforts would be to tout Ashland to a prospective speculator as a good investment. Indeed, if his purpose was to induce arbitrageurs to buy Ashland, he presumably would have contacted more than just Bear Stearns; he would have openly disclosed his interest to all of Wall Street.

Moving on to other elements in Belzberg's story, we are struck by his reaction to the $450,000 discount off the market price that Greenberg offered him on March 17 if there had been no put-call agreement on March 4. Belzberg said he was not surprised by the price since he thought Bear Stearns was acting like "Santa Claus" by offering "a bit of a break" to gain more First City business. Bit of a break indeed! And unsolicited at that. We thought that Wall Street Santa Clauses were confined to the sidewalk during Christmas time. Greenberg testified that if he gave clients a half million dollar break on stock for which Bear Stearns bore the market risk, he would "go broke within a week." Greenberg added, quite convincingly we might add, that he "does not run that risk for anybody."

We conclude that the district court's finding that First City deliberately violated section 13(d) should be affirmed.

The district court directed disgorgement of profits. This presents an issue of first impression—whether federal courts have the authority to employ that remedy with respect to section 13(d) violations and whether it is appropriate in this sort of case.

Disgorgement is an equitable remedy designed to deprive a wrongdoer of his unjust enrichment and to deter others from violating the securities laws. Disgorgement is rather routinely ordered for insider trading violations despite a lack of specific authorizations for that remedy under the securities laws. We see no relevant distinction between disgorgement of inside trading profits and disgorgement of section 13(d) violation profits.

There remains the question of how the court measures those illegal profits. First City vigorously disputes the $2.7 million figure that the district court arrived at by calculating all of the profits First City realized on the 890,000 shares First City purchased between March 14 and 25. This disgorgment figure is predicated on the assumption that had First City made its section 13(d) disclosure on March 14, at the end of the statutory 10-day period, the stock it purchased during the March 14–25 period would have been purchased in a quite different and presumably more expensive market. That market would have been affected by the disclosure that the Belzbergs had taken a greater than 5 percent stake in Ashland and would soon propose a tender offer.

First City asserts that the hypothetical market the district court accepted was simplistic and quite unrealistic. It did not take into account other variables—besides the section 13(d) disclosure—which caused the price of the stock to rise. If exact information were obtainable at negligible cost, we would not hesitate to impose upon the government a strict burden to produce data to measure the precise amount of the ill-gotten gains. Despite sophisticated econometric modeling, predicting stock market responses to alternative variables is at best speculative. Rules for calculating disgorgement must recognize that separating legal from illegal profits exactly may at times be a near-impossible task. Accordingly, disgorgement need only be a reasonable approximation of profits causally connected to the violation. The line between restitution and penalty is unfortunately blurred, but the risk of uncertainty should fall on the wrongdoer whose illegal conduct created that uncertainty.

We uphold the permanent injunction and disgorgement orders.

Judgment for the SEC affirmed.

State Regulation of Tender Offers

Statutes that apply to tender offers have been enacted by about two thirds of the states. Until the mid-1980s, many state statutes were held unconstitutional as being preempted by the Williams Act or as violating the Commerce Clause of the U.S. Constitution.[33] In recent years, however, state statutes like Indiana's control share law, which is highly protective of subject companies, have been held constitutional by the Supreme Court of the United States.[34] The Indiana statute gives shareholders other than the bidder the right to determine whether the shares acquired by the bidder may be voted in directors' elections and other matters. The statute, which essentially gives a subject company the power to require shareholder approval of a hostile tender offer, has been copied by several states.

Other states, like Delaware, have adopted business-combination moratorium statutes. These statutes delay the effectuation of a merger of the corporation with a shareholder owning a large percentage of shares (such as 15 percent), unless the board of director's approval is obtained. Because the typical large shareholder in a public company is a bidder who has made a tender offer, these state statutes primarily affect the ability of a bidder to effectuate a merger after a tender offer, and therefore, may have the effect of deterring hostile acquisitions.

THE FOREIGN CORRUPT PRACTICES ACT

Background

The Foreign Corrupt Practices Act (FCPA) was passed by Congress in 1977 as an amendment to the Securities Exchange Act of 1934. Its passage followed discoveries that more than 400 American corporations had given bribes or made other improper or questionable payments in connection with business abroad and within the United States. Many of these payments were bribes to high-level officials of foreign governments for the purpose of obtaining contracts for the sale of goods or services. Officers of the companies that had made the payments, even when admitting that the payments were bribes, argued that such payments were customary and necessary in business transactions in many countries. This argument was pressed forcefully with regard to *facilitating payments*. Such payments were said to be essential to get lower-level government officials in a number of countries to perform their nondiscretionary or ministerial tasks, such as preparing or approving necessary import or export documents.

In a significant number of cases, bribes had been accounted for as commission payments, as normal transactions with foreign subsidiaries, or as payments for services rendered by professionals or other firms, or had in other ways been made to appear as normal business expenses. These bribes were then illegally deducted as normal business expenses in income tax returns filed with the Internal Revenue Service.

The FCPA makes it a crime for any American firm—whether or not it has securities registered under the 1934 Act—to offer, promise, or make payments or gifts of anything of value to foreign officials and certain others. The FCPA also establishes recordkeeping and internal control requirements for firms subject to the periodic disclosure provisions of the Securities Exchange Act of 1934.

The Payments Prohibition

Payments are prohibited if the person making the payment knows or should know that some or all of it will be

---

[33] For example, *Edgar v. MITE Corp.*, 457 U.S. 624 (U.S. Sup. Ct. 1982).

[34] *CTS Corp. v. Dynamics Corp.*, 481 U.S. 69 (1987).

used for the purpose of influencing a governmental decision. An offer to make a prohibited payment or a promise to do so is a violation even if the offer is not accepted or the promise is not carried out. The FCPA prohibits offers or payments to foreign political parties and candidates for office as well as offers and payments to government officials. Payments of kickbacks to foreign businesses and their officials are not prohibited unless it is known or should be known that these payments will be passed on to government officials or other illegal recipients.

Facilitating or grease payments are not prohibited by the FCPA. Payments are not illegal so long as the recipient has no discretion in carrying out a governmental function. For example, suppose a corporation applies for a radio license in Italy and makes a payment to the government official who issues the licenses. If the official grants licenses to every applicant and the payment merely speeds up the processing of the application, the FCPA is not violated. On the other hand, if only a few applicants are granted licenses and the payment is made to ensure that the corporation will obtain a license, the payment is illegal.

Substantial penalties for violations may be imposed. A company may be fined up to $2 million. Directors, officers, employees, or agents participating in violations are liable for fines of up to $100,000 and prison terms of up to five years.

Recordkeeping and Internal Controls Requirements

The FCPA added Section 13(b)(2) to the 1934 Act. It imposes recordkeeping and internal controls requirements on firms that are subject to the 1934 Act. The purpose of such controls is to prevent unauthorized payments and transactions and unauthorized access to company assets that may result in illegal payments.

The new section requires the making and keeping of records and accounts "which, in reasonable detail, accurately, and fairly reflect the transactions and dispositions of the assets of the issuer" of securities. It also requires the establishment and maintenance of a system of internal accounting controls. This system must provide "reasonable assurances" that the firm's transactions are executed in accordance with management's authorization and that the firm's assets are used or disposed of only as authorized by management. In addition, the recording of transactions must permit the preparation of financial statements that conform to generally accepted accounting principles. Furthermore, at reasonable intervals,

management must see that the records are compared with the actual assets available, and if they do not agree, it must determine the reason for the discrepancy.

These requirements apply not only to transactions and records relating to business with foreign governments or conducted in foreign countries but also to purely domestic business activities. The payment of a bribe is not essential to a violation of this part of the act. No specific penalties are provided; the general penalties of the 1934 Act apply.

STATE SECURITIES LEGISLATION

Purpose and History

State securities laws are frequently referred to as **blue-sky laws,** since the early state securities statutes were designed to protect investors from promoters and security salespersons who would "sell building lots in the blue sky." The first state to enact a securities law was Kansas, in 1911. All of the states now have such legislation.

Uniform Securities Act

The National Conference of Commissioners on Uniform State Laws has adopted the Uniform Securities Act of 1956. The act contains antifraud provisions, requires the registration of securities, and demands broker-dealer registration. About two thirds of the states have adopted the act, but many states have made significant changes in it.

Securities Fraud

All of the state securities statutes provide penalties for fraudulent sales and permit the issuance of injunctions to protect investors from additional or anticipated fraudulent acts. Most of the statutes grant broad power to investigate fraud to some state official—usually the attorney general or his appointee as securities administrator. All of the statutes provide criminal penalties for selling fraudulent securities and conducting fraudulent transactions.

Registration of Securities

Most of the state securities statutes adopt the philosophy of the 1933 Act that informed investors can make intelligent investment decisions. The states with such statutes have a registration scheme much like the 1933 Act, with required disclosures for public offerings and exemptions from registration for small and private offerings. Other states reject the contention that investors with full information can make intelligent investment decisions. The securities statutes in these states have a *merit registration* requirement, giving a securities administrator power to deny registration on the merits of the security and its issuer. Only securities that are not unduly risky and promise an adequate return to investors may receive administrator approval.

All state statutes have a limited number of exemptions from registration. Most statutes have private offering exemptions that are similar to Securities Act Rule 506 of Regulation D. In addition, a person may avoid the registration requirements of state securities laws by not offering or selling securities. However, as illustrated by the *Capital General* case, which follows, state courts broadly define the term *sale* in order to prevent abusive attempts to circumvent the registration requirements.

Registration by Coordination   The Uniform Securities Act permits an issuer to register its securities by coordination. Instead of filing a registration statement under the Securities Act of 1933 and a different one as required by state law, registration by coordination allows an issuer to file the 1933 Act registration statement with the state securities administrator. Registration by coordination decreases an issuer's expense of complying with state law when making an interstate offering of its securities.

CAPITAL GENERAL CORP. v. UTAH DEPARTMENT OF BUSINESS REGULATION, SECURITIES DIVISION
777 P. 2d 494 (Utah Ct. App. 1989)

On January 7, 1986, Amenity, Inc., was incorporated with capitalization of 100 million shares. On January 8, 1986, 1 million shares of Amenity, Inc., stock were issued to Capital General Corporation (CGC), a financial consulting firm, for $2,000. CGC distributed a total of 90,000 of those shares to approximately 900 of its clients, business associates, and other contacts to create and maintain goodwill among its clients and contacts. CGC did not receive any monetary or other direct financial consideration from those receiving the stock.

Amenity, Inc., had no actual business function at this time and its sole asset was the $2,000 CGC had paid for the 1 million shares. Through CGC efforts, Amenity, Inc., was acquired by another company, which paid CGC $25,000 for its efforts.

On June 5, 1986, the Utah Securities Division sought to suspend trading in Amenity, Inc., stock on the grounds that CGC distributed the Amenity, Inc., stock in violation of the Utah Securities Act.

A hearing was held before an administrative law judge, who held that the Act's registration requirements did not apply to CGC's distribution of the Amenity, Inc., stock. The Securities Division obtained a hearing by the Utah Securities Advisory Board. The Board concluded that CGC's distribution of the 90,000 shares was covered by the Act. The Board issued an order of suspension. CGC filed a petition in the district court seeking reversal of the Board's order. The district court affirmed the Board's decision, and CGC appealed.

Orme, Judge.   The Utah Securities Act provides, "It is unlawful for any person to *offer or sell* any security in this state unless it is registered . . . or the security or transaction is exempted." Thus, we must determine if CGC's disposition of the 90,000 shares was an "offer or sale" of Amenity, Inc., securities.

The Act provides that an "offer or sale" includes the "disposition of . . . a security for value." Value is gained by the creation of a public market. Such value includes: 1) an enhanced ability to borrow; 2) an enhanced ability to raise equity; 3) the availability of a method of valuing assets; 4) an enhanced liquidity of assets; and 5) the prestige associated with publicly held companies.

The Board's determination that CGC's disposition of the Amenity, Inc. stock was "for value" is reasonable and rational. By "giving away" 90,000 shares (or 9 percent of its total holdings), CGC essentially transformed Amenity, Inc., into a publicly held company, ripe for acquisition, in which it held most of the stock. "Value" can include enhanced abilities to borrow, raise capital, and other general benefits associated with publicly held companies, all of which CGC received through the disposition. These economic benefits render the disposition "for value" even though those benefits flowed indirectly from the marketplace rather than directly from the transferees.

CGC additionally argues the disposition was a "good faith gift" under the Act. CGC bears the burden to prove its entitlement to the "good faith gift" exception to the definition of "offer or sale." CGC fails to meet this burden. CGC's veiled but fairly obvious purpose was to advance its own economic objectives rather than to make a gift for reasons of simple generosity.

CGC's actual purpose in making the distribution included an intent to convert a private company into a public company without registration. The effect of this transformation, in addition to circumventing the Act's registration requirements, was to greatly enhance the value of the significant block of Amenity, Inc.'s outstanding stock which CGC continued to hold. CGC similarly converted at least thirty other private companies into public companies using the same method employed here. At least three of these companies were then acquired by other companies, resulting in substantial profits for CGC.

Judgment for the Securities Division affirmed.

ETHICAL AND PUBLIC POLICY CONCERNS

1. Should the federal and state governments require disclosure by issuers of securities? Are investors able to protect themselves by insisting that issuers provide relevant information prior to the investors' purchasing securities from issuers? How can current securities owners ensure that they will continue to receive relevant investment information?

2. Who are the primary beneficiaries of the securities laws; that is, who primarily buys and sells securities? Nearly all securities are owned by persons whose wealth places them in the top 10 percent of the population. Is securities regulation merely welfare for the wealthy? Does anyone else benefit from securities regulation? Does the benefit to those persons justify the costs of securities regulation?

3. Should insider trading be illegal? Is insider trading unfair? To whom is it unfair? What are the social and economic costs of insider trading? What are the social and economic benefits of insider trading? Does insider trading improve the efficiency of the securities markets? Should shareholders be given the power to authorize in-

siders to trade on inside information? Why might shareholders want insiders to trade on inside information?

4. Should the payments prohibition part of the Foreign Corrupt Practices Act be repealed? What is unethical about an American corporation making bribes to foreign government officials and political parties? What benefits does the United States receive from the making of such payments? What detriments does the United States suffer from the making of such payments? Does the analysis change if bribery is a standard way of business life in a foreign country?

SUMMARY

The federal securities acts passed in 1933 and 1934 require that investors be given accurate and adequate information concerning securities. They also prohibit fraudulent, deceptive, and manipulative practices. A security is broadly defined to include any investment in a common enterprise with an expectation of profits from the efforts of others.

The Securities Act of 1933 requires issuers of securities to file a registration statement with the SEC. There are two categories of exemptions from this requirement: securities exemptions, such as government-guaranteed securities; and transaction exemptions, such as the small offering exemptions, the private offering exemption, and the intrastate offering exemption.

The most important liability provision of the 1933 Act is Section 11, which imposes liability on certain defendants for material defects in the registration statement, unless they can prove their due diligence defenses.

Issuers register classes of securities under the 1934 Act, rather than issuances of securities. Companies of a certain size must register, whether or not their securities are traded on a stock exchange. The 1934 Act also imposes periodic reporting requirements on issuers and regulates proxy solicitations.

Directors, officers, and 10 percent holders of registered shares must file reports of their shareholdings and transactions in the shares of an issuer with securities registered under the 1934 Act. Insiders' profits from transactions in the issuer's shares may be recovered by the corporation.

The most often used liability provision of the 1934 Act is Section 10(b), under which SEC Rule 10b-5 has been issued. The rule has been used extensively to impose liabilities for failure to provide an investor with adequate information, for deceptive practices, and for insider trading.

The 1934 Act regulates tender offers, requiring bidders to disclose material information concerning the acquisition. SEC rules give shareholders procedural protections to allow them to make careful, intelligent decisions.

The Foreign Corrupt Practices Act was passed in 1977. It prohibits payments or gifts to officials and political parties in foreign governments. Grease payments, however, are not prohibited. The FCPA also requires all issuers of registered securities to maintain accurate accounting records.

All of the states have enacted blue-sky laws in order to protect investors. Some of these laws are quite similar in approach to the federal securities statutes. Others give a state administrator authority to bar the sale of unduly risky securities.

PROBLEM CASES

1. In 1980, Continental Minerals Corporation (CMC), a gold-mining company, devised a means of raising capital by selling its gold in the form of coins. Purchasers could buy 12 one-ounce coins either by paying for each coin separately 30 days in advance of delivery or by prepaying for the entire set of coins. If purchasers prepaid for the entire set, the price was $375 per coin, about 48 percent below the prevailing market price for gold. CMC promised to begin delivery on November 15, 1980, and to deliver an additional coin every two months. To provide purchasers protection against a decrease in the price of gold below $375 per ounce, CMC promised to pay purchasers the difference between the prepayment price and the world price of gold on the delivery date. CMC informed the purchasers that "the gold offered for future delivery has not yet been extracted. Obviously, if sufficient quantities of gold were being mined currently, these would be sold at world market prices and not offered at substantial discount." Subsequently, CMC failed to make any deliveries of gold coins. CMC had spent all $3.5 million it received from the sale of coins. The SEC sued 24 salesmen of CMC gold coins on the grounds that they had sold unregistered securities in violation of Section 5 of the Securities Act. Were any securities involved in the sale of the gold coins?

2. Attempting to reach as wide an audience as possible, a mutual fund company inserts prospectuses for the issuance of its shares in local newspapers and magazines. In subsequent editions of the newspapers and issues of the magazines, the company distributes additional sales materials. Is the company violating the requirements of Section 5 of the Securities Act of 1933?

3. King's College is a private college organized under the not-for-profit corporation law of New York. The Internal Revenue Service has issued King's College an exemption from federal income taxation. The college proposes to sell $500,000 of bonds to raise funds for equipment purchases and other capital improvements. The college will sell the bonds in the minimum amount of $500 and will offer them to no more than 1,000 individuals. Only individuals having shown a prior interest in King's College will be solicited. Is the bond offering exempt from the registration requirements of the 1933 Act?

4. Western-Realco Limited Partnership sold $800,000 of its limited partnership interests through the services of securities brokers. Western-Realco did not supervise the brokers and was unaware of whether the brokers solicited their clients in a newsletter or to the public in general. Will Western-Realco be able to use the private offering exemption or Rule 504 to avoid a 1933 Act registration?

5. Capital Sunbelt Securities, Inc. (Sunbelt) and Phoenix Financial Corp. were two brokerages that sold limited partnership interests in Capital: Maple Leaf Estates, Ltd. (Capital) and Maple Leaf Estates, Ltd. (Maple Leaf). Capital was to purchase a mobile home park that would be operated by Maple Leaf. Sunbelt and Phoenix kept logs reflecting the persons to whom they distributed copies of the limited offering circulars for Capital and Maple Leaf. Ninety-six persons received copies of the Capital offering circular and 34 received the Maple Leaf circular. The circulars contained the same information as a 1933 Act registration statement. In addition, Capital and Maple Leaf promised to make available any additional information requested by investors. All offerees had a prior relationship with Phoenix or Sunbelt, and there were no seminars or meetings attended by the general public. There was no advertising, and each offering circular was addressed to a specific person. All investors were required to state that they were acquiring the limited partnership interests for investment. Proceeds of the offerings were $2,677,000 for Capital and $950,000 for Maple Leaf. Phoenix offered to sell Capital limited partnership interests to 228 persons and sold to 33 investors, 16 of which had a net worth in excess of $1 million. There were 187 offerees of the Maple Leaf limited partnership interests and 13 purchasers, 9 of whom had a net worth over $1 million. At the conclusion of the offerings, no Form D was filed with the SEC. Were the offerings exempt from registration under Section 4(2) or Rule 506 of the Securities Act?

6. Commonwealth Edison Co. registered 3 million common shares with the SEC and sold the shares for about $28 per share. The price of the purchasers' stock dropped to $21 when the Atomic Safety and Licensing Board denied ComEd's application to license one of its reactors. It was the first and only time the Board had denied a license application. ComEd assumed that the license would be granted; therefore its registration statement failed to disclose the pendency of the license application. Did ComEd violate Section 11 of the Securities Act?

7. Two limited partnerships created a partnership for the purpose of attempting a takeover of Goodyear Tire and Rubber Co. One limited partnership acquired 8.17 percent and the other 2.37 percent of Goodyear's shares. Although combined the two limited partnerships owned

11.5 percent of the shares, their partnership held no Goodyear shares for its own account. The limited partnerships sold their Goodyear shares at a profit in fewer than six months after the purchases. Have the limited partnerships violated Section 16(b) of the 1934 Act?

8. J. C. Harrelson, the president and chief shareholder of Alabama Supply and Equipment Company (ASECo), and Clarence Hamilton conspired to defraud investors. They induced Frisco City, Alabama, to create the Industrial Development Board of Frisco City to issue tax-exempt bonds to investors. The Board offered and sold bonds pursuant to an offering circular, which misstated or omitted several material facts, due to misrepresentations made by Harrelson and Hamilton. The Board used the proceeds of the bond issuance to build a manufacturing plant for ASECo. After the ASECo plant was constructed, ASECo ceased all operations and defaulted on its rental payments to the Board, causing the value of the bonds to drop precipitously. The building was sold in an attempt to pay the principal on the bonds. After the sale of the industrial facility, the bondholders received only $373.33 for each $1,000 bond. Clarence Bishop had purchased four of the bonds for $4,096. He never saw the offering circular or knew that one existed. He bought the bonds solely on his broker's oral representations that they were a good investment and that others in the community had purchased them. Can Bishop sue Harrelson and Hamilton under Rule 10b-5 even though he failed to read or even to seek to read the offering circular?

9. James Jordan was a shareholder of Duff & Phelps, Inc., a closely held corporation, and one of its employees in its Chicago office. The transferability of his shares was restricted, such that if he terminated his employment with Duff & Phelps, he was required to resell his shares to the corporation. Between May and August 1983, Duff & Phelps and Security Pacific Corporation negotiated a merger of the two corporations. The negotiators reached an agreement, but it was vetoed by a high official within Security Pacific on August 11, 1983. During this same time, Jordan was looking for a new job. On November 16, 1983, Jordan told Duff & Phelps that he was going to resign effective at the end of the year in order to accept a job in Houston. Jordan did not ask about any potential merger and Duff & Phelps did not volunteer any information, even though two days earlier its board of directors had decided to seek offers to acquire the company. In December 1983, Duff & Phelps and Security Pacific had serious merger discussions after the high official who vetoed the deal on August 11 changed his mind. On December 30, 1983, Jordan delivered his shares to Duff & Phelps and received a check for $23,225. On January 6, 1984, Duff & Phelps and Security Pacific reached an agreement in principle to merge. The agreement was announced on January 10, at which point Jordan realized that he would have received at least $452,000 for his shares had he not resigned from Duff & Phelps. Does Jordan have any recourse against Duff & Phelps under Rule 10b-5?

10. In May 1983, Phil Gutter read a report in *The Wall Street Journal* that listed certain corporate bonds as trading with interest. Relying on the report, Gutter purchased $36,000 of the bonds. In reality, the bonds were trading without interest. When *The Wall Street Journal* corrected its error, the price of the bonds fell, resulting in Gutter suffering a loss of $1,692. Is *The Wall Street Journal* liable to Gutter for his loss under Rule 10b-5?

11. When he was the Oklahoma Sooner football coach, Barry Switzer attended a track meet, where he met and spoke with friends and acquaintances, including G. Platt, a director of Phoenix Corporation and chief executive officer of Texas International Company (TIC), a business that sponsored Switzer's coach's television show. TIC owned more than 50 percent of Phoenix's shares. Switzer moved around the bleachers at the track meet in order to talk to various people. After speaking with Platt and his wife Linda for the last of five times, Switzer lay down to sunbathe on a row of bleachers behind the Platts. G. Platt, unaware that Switzer was behind him, carelessly spoke too loud while talking with his wife about his desire to sell or liquidate Phoenix. He also talked about several companies making bids to buy Phoenix. Switzer also overheard that an announcement of a possible liquidation of Phoenix might be made within a week. Switzer used the information he obtained in deciding to purchase Phoenix shares. Did Switzer trade illegally on inside information?

12. Edper, Inc., identified Brascan, Inc., as a potential takeover target. On behalf of Edper, a securities broker contacted 40 institutional investors and 12 substantial individual holders of Brascan shares who were his clients. The broker told the investors that Edper was interested in buying 3 to 4 million shares. Eventually, Edper bought 6.3 million shares—nearly 25 percent of Brascan's outstanding shares—from these investors at a price that the broker and each individual investor agreed upon. Did Edper make a tender offer for Brascan's shares that required it to file a Schedule 14D-1 prior to the making the offers to the investors?

CHAPTER 45

LEGAL RESPONSIBILITIES OF ACCOUNTANTS

INTRODUCTION

This chapter covers the legal responsibilities of accountants. It considers the professional relationships of accountants with their clients and others who rely on their work. This chapter also covers the criminal and administrative sanctions for wrongful professional conduct by accountants.

General Standard of Performance

The general duty that accountants owe to their clients and to other persons who are affected by their actions is *to exercise the skill and care of the ordinarily prudent accountant* in the same circumstances. Hence, accountants must act carefully and diligently, but they are not guarantors of the accuracy of their work. For example, an accountant who is performing an audit of a client's financial records has a duty to discover whatever an ordinarily prudent auditor would find, but has no duty to discover incorrect accounting treatments or to detect embezzlements that an ordinarily prudent accountant would not find. The accountant's duty to exercise reasonable care is a subset of the *negligence* standard of tort law.

Two elements compose the general duty of performance: skill and care. An accountant must have the *skill*

of the ordinarily prudent accountant. This element focuses on the education or knowledge of the accountant, whether acquired formally at school or by self-instruction. For example, to prepare tax returns, an accountant must *know* the tax laws as well as the ordinarily prudent accountant does. To audit financial records, an accountant must *know* generally accepted auditing standards (GAAS) and generally accepted accounting principles (GAAP). GAAS and GAAP are standards and principles embodied in the rules, releases, and pronouncements of the Securities and Exchange Commission, the American Institute of Certified Public Accountants (AICPA), and the Financial Accounting Standards Board (FASB).

The *care* element requires an accountant to *act* as carefully or diligently as the ordinarily prudent accountant. For example, in preparing a tax return, he must discover the income exclusions, the deductions, and the tax credits that the reasonably careful accountant would find are available to the client. When auditing financial statements, he must follow the rules of GAAS and GAAP.

Deference to Professional Standards

Courts and legislatures usually defer to the members of each profession in determining what the ordinarily prudent professional would do. Such deference recognizes the lawmakers' lack of understanding of the nuances of each profession's practices. This lack of understanding means that courts must rely on members of a profession to give expert testimony as to the professional standards of conduct. For example, in a trial against an accountant for malpractice, other accountants will appear as witnesses to aid the court's determination of what the ordinarily prudent accountant would have done in the same circumstances.

Courts will not always defer to the standards of conduct set by a profession. A profession will not be permitted to establish a standard of conduct that is harmful to the interests of clients or other members of society. For example, a court would not defer to an FASB pronouncement that states that the cost of a building with a 40-year life may be expensed entirely in the year of acquisition; such a pronouncement would be so unreasonable as to be undeserving of judicial deference.

Until the late 1970s, some courts found accountants liable despite their claims that they had followed professional standards embodied in GAAS and GAAP.[1] These courts insisted that attention be focused on substance rather than form: The financial statements must as a whole fairly present the financial condition of a client company and the results of its operations. These decisions are contradictory, because GAAP requires that financial statements fairly present the financial condition of the company and the results of its operations.[2] In recent decisions, informed courts have regularly held that compliance with GAAP and GAAS in good faith discharges an auditor's professional obligations.

Local versus National Standard

Originally, professionals were held to the standard of the ordinarily prudent person in his locality. This local standard has given way to a national standard in recent years. Due to improved means of communication in the modern world, few professionals today can argue that they are unaware of modern professional techniques. Consequently, accountants are held to the standard of the ordinarily prudent accountant in the United States.

ACCOUNTANTS' LIABILITY TO CLIENTS

Although the greatest increase in litigation against accountants in the last 20 years has been in third-party suits—that is, suits by nonclients—accountants are frequently sued by their **clients.** For example, an accountant may wrongfully claim deductions on an individual's tax return. When the IRS discovers the wrongful deduction, the individual will have to pay the extra tax, interest, and perhaps a penalty. The individual may sue his accountant to recover the amount of the penalty. For another example, consider an accountant who prepares an income statement that understates a client's income. The client uses the income statement to apply for a loan, but is denied the loan because her stated net income is inadequate. The client may sue her accountant for damages caused by the erroneous income statement.

There are three principal bases of liability of an accountant to his client: contract, tort, and trust. We will consider each of these separately.

Contractual Liability

As a party to a contract with her client, an accountant owes a duty to the client to perform as he has agreed to perform. This includes an implied duty to perform the contract as the ordinarily prudent accountant would perform it. If the accountant fails to perform as agreed, ordinarily an accountant is liable only for those damages that are reasonably contemplated by the client and the accountant. For example, an accountant is liable for a client's tax penalties if she completely fails to prepare the client's tax return.

An accountant is not liable for breach of contract if the client obstructs the accountant's performance of the contract. For example, an accounting firm would not be liable for failing to complete an audit on time if the client refused to give the firm access to needed records and property.

An accountant may not delegate his duty to perform a contract without the consent of the client. Delegation is not permitted because the performance of a contract for accounting services depends on the skill, training, and character of the accountant. As a result, for example, Price Waterhouse & Co., a public accounting firm, may not delegate to Ernst & Young, another public accounting firm, the contractual duty to audit the financial statements of GM, even though both firms are nearly equally skillful and careful.

---

[1]Compare *United States v. Simon*, 425 F.2d 796 (2d Cir. 1969) with *SEC v. Arthur Young & Co.*, 590 F.2d 785 (9th Cir. 1979).

[2] AICPA *SAS No. 5* sec. 3.

Tort Liability

Accountants' tort liability to their clients may be based on the common law concepts of negligence and fraud or on the violation of a statute, principally the federal and state securities laws.

Negligence   As stated earlier, the duty of an accountant to exercise the skill and care of the ordinarily prudent accountant is grounded in *negligence.* Hence, a client who suffers a loss that is proximately caused by an accountant's failure to exercise the skill and care of the ordinarily prudent accountant may sue the accountant to recover his damages under the tort theory of negligence. For example, a client may recover excess taxes that he paid because of his accountant's lack of due care in claiming allowable deductions on a tax return. In addition, an accountant is liable for negligently giving tax advice, such as telling a client that she can reduce her tax liability by establishing a certain type of trust fund for her children. When the Internal Revenue Service rules that the trust's income is income to the client, not her children, the accountant may be liable to the client.

Sometimes, an accountant will audit a company, yet fail to uncover an embezzlement or other intentional wrongdoing or fraud by an employee of the company. Ordinarily, an accountant has no specific duty to uncover employee embezzlement or fraud. Nonetheless, an accountant must uncover employee fraud or embezzlement if an ordinarily prudent accountant would have discovered it. In addition, an accountant owes a duty to investigate suspicious circumstances that tend to indicate fraud, regardless of how he became aware of those circumstances. Also, an accountant has a duty to inform a proper party of his suspicions. It is not enough to inform or confront the person suspected of fraud.

When an accountant is hired to perform a fraud audit to investigate suspected fraud or embezzlement, she has a greater duty to investigate. She must be as skillful and careful as the ordinarily prudent auditor performing a fraud audit.

When an accountant negligently fails to discover embezzlement, generally he is liable to his client only for an amount equal to the embezzlement that occurred *after* he should have discovered the embezzlement. The accountant is usually not liable for any part of the embezzlement that occurred *prior* to the time he should have uncovered the embezzlement, unless his tardy discovery prevented the client from recovering embezzled funds.

In the following case, an accounting firm was held liable to its client for failing to meet the standard of the profession.

DIVERSIFIED GRAPHICS, LTD. v. GROVES
868 F.2d 293 (8th Cir. 1989)

Diversified Graphics, Ltd. (D.G.), hired Ernst & Whinney (E & W) to assist it in obtaining a computer system to fit its data processing needs. D.G. had a longstanding relationship with E & W during which D.G. developed great trust and reliance upon E & W's services. Because D.G. lacked computer expertise, it decided to entrust E & W with the selection and implementation of an in-house computer data processing system. E & W had promised to locate a "turnkey" system, which would be fully operational without the need for extensive employee training. D.G. instead received a system that was difficult to operate and failed to meet its needs. D.G. sued E & W and its partners, including Ray Groves, for negligence. The jury found in favor of D.G.; E & W and its partners appealed.

Lay, Chief Judge.   D.G.'s theory for recovery based on negligence encompasses the notion of a consultant-client relationship and therefore the existence of a professional standard of care.

The degree of skill and care that may be required of a professional is a question of fact for the jury. We find that there was substantial evidence regarding the applicable standard of a professional consultant.

E & W's Guidelines to Practice incorporates the Management Advisory Services Practice Standards which were adopted by the American Institute of Certified Public Accountants, Inc. (AICPA Standards). The AICPA Standards require that "due professional care" is to be exercised in providing management advisory services. These standards in part generally provide:

> In performing management advisory services, a practitioner must act with integrity and objectivity and be independent in mental attitude.
>
> Engagements are to be performed by practitioners having competence in the analytical approach and process, and in the technical subject matter under consideration.
>
> Due professional care is to be exercised in the performance of a management advisory services engagement.
>
> Before accepting an engagement, a practitioner is to notify the client of any reservations he has regarding anticipated benefits.
>
> Before undertaking an engagement, a practitioner is to inform his client of all significant matters related to the engagement.
>
> Engagements are to be adequately planned, supervised, and controlled.
>
> Sufficient relevant data is to be obtained, documented, and evaluated in developing conclusions and recommendations.
>
> All significant matters relating to the results of the engagement are to be communicated to the client.

AICPA Standards Nos. 1–8.

D.G. had determined that it required a "turnkey" computer system that would fully perform all of its data processing in-house. The term "turnkey" is intended to describe a self-sufficient system which the purchaser need only "turn the key" to commence operation. The purchaser should not have to hire programmers, and current employees should not have to undergo extensive training to be able to operate the system. To procure this type of customized and fully operational system, great care must be taken to carefully detail a business's needs and to properly develop specifications for the computer system. Potential vendors must be carefully scrutinized to discover all of the inadequacies of their data processing systems. Once a vendor is chosen, proper implementation is imperative to ensure that the purchaser truly need only "turn the key" to commence full operation of the system. A fundamental part of implementation involves testing the system through parallel data processing operation. Finally, the existence of adequate documentation regarding the operation of the system is crucial once the system is up and running. As previously stated, employees will have had only minimal training and will depend heavily on the instructions for operation. Moreover, documentation is particularly important because this type of system is highly customized and standard instruction sources will have only limited value.

Thus, the jury could conclude that E & W's conduct fell short of adhering to the applicable professional standard of care.

Judgment for Diversified Graphics affirmed.

Contributory Negligence of Client Courts are reluctant to permit an accountant to escape liability to a client merely because the client was **contributorily negligent.** Since the accountant has skills superior to those of the client, courts generally allow clients to rely on the accountant's duty to discover employee fraud, available tax deductions, and other matters for which the accountant is hired. The client is not required to exercise reasonable care to discover these things himself.

Nonetheless, some courts allow the defense of contributory negligence or the defense of comparative negligence, such as when clients negligently fail to follow an accountant's advice or when clients possess information that makes their reliance on the accountant unwarranted.

In the following case, *Halla Nursery, Inc. v. Baumann-Furrie & Co.,* the court permitted an accountant to raise the client's negligence as a defense.

HALLA NURSERY, INC. v. BAUMANN-FURRIE & CO.

454 N.W.2d 905 (Minn. Sup. Ct. 1990)

From 1983 to 1985, Baumann-Furrie & Co. provided accounting services to Halla Nursery, Inc. During this time, Halla's bookkeeper embezzled $135,000. In 1986, Halla sued Baumann-Furrie alleging it negligently failed to detect the embezzlement. Baumann-Furrie raised the defense of Halla's contributory negligence for failing to put in place internal financial controls to protect the company from embezzlement.

The jury found Halla 80 percent at fault and Baumann-Furrie 20 percent at fault. The trial court ordered a judgment of no recovery for Halla. Halla appealed to the court of appeals, which held that Halla's contributory negligence could be raised as a defense only if that negligence directly interfered with Baumann-Furrie's ability to perform the contract in accordance with generally accepted accounting practices. Baumann-Furrie appealed to the Supreme Court of Minnesota.

Wahl, Justice.   The issue is whether, in the context of an accountant malpractice action, the scope of the principles of comparative fault should be limited in their application. The court of appeals adopted the rule of *Lincoln Grain, Inc. v. Coopers & Lybrand* (1984), which held that the contributory negligence of a client in an accountant malpractice case is a defense only where it had contributed to the accountant's failure to perform the contract and report the truth.

Halla argues that without the *Lincoln Grain* rule, accountants are rendered immune from the consequences of their own negligence simply because those who employ them may have conducted their own businesses negligently. Baumann-Furrie, on the other hand, argues that the contributory negligence exception adopted by the court of appeals is inappropriate in the context of our broad, expansive doctrine of comparative fault. They argue further that the exception was adopted initially to mitigate the harsh consequences of the common law rule of contributory negligence, an exception not necessary in a comparative fault state like Minnesota. Finally, they argue that the rule imposes a heavy evidentiary burden on the accountant: applying *Lincoln Grain* to a malpractice case would require that the defendant-accountant must prove not only that the plaintiff's negligence caused or contributed to the plaintiff's loss, but also that the plaintiff's negligence caused defendant's negligence.

We recognize, however, that professional malpractice actions pose peculiar problems and that the comparison of fault between a layperson and a professional should be approached with caution. Accountants, like other professionals, are held to a standard of care which requires that they "exercise the average ability and skill of those engaged in that profession." By the same token, the persons who hire accountants, usually businesspersons, should also be required to conduct their business activities in a reasonable and prudent manner.

We hold that the trial court did not err in applying the principles of comparative fault in this action by a client against an accountant for negligent failure to discover embezzlements. The application of the broad definition of fault as set forth in the comparative fault statute can be particularly appropriate in such actions. This is not to say that there would never be a case where a limiting exception might be necessary, for example, where the scope of employment is such that discovery of defalcation is clearly emcompassed. This is not such a case.

Judgment reversed in favor of Baumann-Furrie.

Fraud

An accountant is liable to his client for fraud when he misstates or omits facts in communications with his client and acts with **scienter.** An accountant acts with scienter when he knows of the falsity of a statement or he recklessly disregards the truth. Thus, accountants are liable in fraud for their intentional or reckless disregard for accuracy in their work.

Recklessness has been defined as "the pretense of knowledge when knowledge there is none."[3] For example, an accountant chooses not to examine the current figures in a client's books of account, but relies on last year's figures because he is behind in his work for other clients. As a result, the accountant understates the client's income on an income statement that the client uses to apply for a loan. The client obtains a loan, but he has to pay a higher interest rate because his low stated income makes the loan a higher risk for the bank. Such misconduct by the accountant proves scienter and, therefore, amounts to fraud.

Scienter also includes recklessly ignoring facts, such as an auditor's finding obvious evidence of embezzlement, yet failing to notify a client of the embezzlement.

The chief advantage of establishing fraud is that the client may get a higher damage award than when the accountant is merely negligent. Usually, a client may receive only compensatory damages for a breach of contract or negligence. By proving fraud, a client may be awarded punitive damages as well.

Breach of Trust

The accountant-client relation is a confidential, fiduciary relation. Information and assets that are entrusted to an accountant may be used only to benefit the client. Therefore, an accountant may not disclose sensitive matters such as a client's income and wealth. In addition, an accountant may not use the assets of his client for his own benefit.

Increasingly in recent years, accounting firms have provided nonaudit services to their clients. For example, an accounting firm may provide management consulting advice to a client. An accounting firm acting as a management consultant must maintain the confidentiality of the client's information entrusted to the accounting firm.

Securities Law

As the Securities Regulation chapter indicates, federal and state securities law creates several rights of action for persons harmed in connection with the purchase or sale of securities. These rights of action are based in tort, usually fraud. Although available to clients of an accountant, they are rarely used for that purpose. Usually, third parties (nonclients) sue under the securities law. Therefore, the securities law sections that apply to accountants are discussed later in this chapter.

[3]*Ultramares Corp. v. Touche,* 174 N.E. 441, 444 (N.Y. Ct. App. 1931).

CONCEPT REVIEW

COMMON LAW BASES OF LIABILITY OF ACCOUNTANT TO CLIENTS

Breach of Contract	Tort	Breach of Trust
Account fails to perform as contract requires; includes implied duty to perform the contract skillfully and carefully	Negligence: Accountant fails to exercise the skill and care of the ordinarily prudent accountant Fraud: Accountant knowingly or recklessly misrepresents facts to his client	Accountant fails to maintain confidentiality of information entrusted to accountant by client

ACCOUNTANTS' LIABILITY TO THIRD PERSONS: COMMON LAW

Introduction

Other persons besides an accountant's clients may use her work product. Banks may use financial statements prepared by a loan applicant's accountant in deciding whether to make a loan to the applicant. Investors may use financial statements certified by a company's auditors in deciding whether to buy or sell the company's securities. These documents prepared by an accountant may prove incorrect, resulting in damages to the nonclients who relied on them. For example, banks may lend money to a corporation only because an income statement prepared by an accountant overstated the corporation's income. When the corporation fails to repay the loan, the bank may sue the accountant to recover the damages it suffered.

As with clients, nonclients may sue accountants for common law negligence, common law fraud, and violations of the securities laws. In this section, common law negligence and fraud are discussed.

Negligence

As you have already learned, when an accountant fails to perform as the ordinarily prudent accountant would perform, she risks having liability for negligence. Although courts freely make accountants liable to their *clients* for negligence, many courts have restricted the ability of *nonclients* to sue an accountant for negligence. These courts limit nonclient suits on the grounds that nonclient users of an accountant's work product have not contracted with the accountant and, therefore, are not in *privity of contract* with the accountant. As a result, these courts prevent most creditors and shareholders from obtaining damages caused by the accountant's negligence. Essentially, these courts hold that an accountant owes no duty to nonclients to exercise ordinary skill and care.

This judicial stance conflicts with the usual principles of negligence law under which a negligent person is liable to all persons who are reasonably foreseeably damaged by his negligence. The rationale for the restrictive judicial stance was expressed in the *Ultramares* case,[4] a

decision of the highest court in New York. In that case, Judge Benjamin Cardozo refused to hold an auditor liable to third parties for mere negligence. His rationale was stated as follows:

> If liability for negligence exists, a thoughtless slip or blunder, the failure to detect a theft or forgery beneath the cover of deceptive entries, may expose accountants to a liability in an indeterminate amount for an indeterminate time to an indeterminate class.

Ultramares dominated the thinking of judges for many years, and its impact is still felt today. In fact, New York's highest court recently reaffirmed the holding of *Ultramares*.[5] However, many courts understand that many nonclients use and reasonably rely on the work product of accountants. To varying degrees, these courts have relaxed the privity requirement and expanded the class of persons who may sue an accountant for negligence.

Today, most courts adopt one of the following three tests to determine whether a nonclient may sue an accountant for negligence.

Primary Benefit Test   The *Ultramares* court adopted a **primary benefit** test for imposing liability for negligence. Under this test, an accountant has liability for negligence only to those persons for whose primary benefit the accountant prepares financial reports and other documents. It is not enough that the accountant be able to foresee use by a nonclient. The accountant must actually foresee the nonclient's use and prepare the document primarily for use by a specified nonclient. The accountant must know two things: (1) the name of the person who will use the accountant's work product and (2) the particular purpose for which that person will use the work product. Courts applying this test have been reluctant to find that nonclients are primary beneficiaries of reports prepared by an accountant.

In the following case, *William Iselin & Co. v. Landau,* the court refused to hold an accountant liable to an unknown user of the accountant's reports.

---

[4]*Ultramares Corp. v. Touche,* 174 N.E. 441, 444 (N.Y. Ct. App. 1931).

[5]*William Iselin & Co. v. Landau,* 522 N.E.2d 21 (N.Y. Ct. App. 1988); *Credit Alliance Corp. v. Arthur Andersen & Co.,* 483 N.E. 2d 110 (N.Y. Ct. App. 1985).

~~~~~~

WILLIAM ISELIN & CO. v. LANDAU
522 N.E.2d 21 (N.Y. Ct. App. 1988)

William Iselin & Co. is a corporation engaged in commercial finance. Between 1976 and 1981, Iselin made unsecured overadvances of up to $1 million annually to Suits Galore, Inc. The overadvances consistently were repaid in the same year in which they were made.

Mann Judd Landau is a national accounting firm that was initially engaged by Suits in 1979 to review and report annually on Suits's financial statements. At some point following completion by Mann of its Review Report for Suits's fiscal year ended May 31, 1982, Iselin came into possession of a copy of the Report. Thereafter, Iselin increased Suits's overadvance line to $2 million. By June 1983, Mann issued its Review Report for Suits's fiscal year ended May 31, 1983. Following Iselin's receipt of the Report in mid-September 1983, Iselin informed Suits that the over-advance level must be substantially reduced. In December 1983, Suits was unable to meet its financial obligations and filed for protection under the bankruptcy laws. Much of its outstanding debt to Iselin remained unpaid.

Iselin sued Mann for negligence, alleging that the 1982 Review Report overstated inventory, understated liabilities, and failed to disclose the looting of Suits's assets. The trial court held that Mann could be liable to Iselin for negligence. Mann appealed to the appellate division, which held that Iselin failed to satisfy the test established in *Credit Alliance Corp. v. Andersen & Co.* (1985), for holding an accountant liable to a nonclient for negligence. Mann appealed to the highest court in New York.

Dillon, Judge. Preliminarily, we note that a Review Report is not to be equated with the traditional certified audit. The latter requires the auditor's certification that the audit was performed under generally accepted auditing standards (GAAS) and that the statements were prepared according to generally accepted accounting principles (GAAP). The accountant's review is not performed under GAAS; no physical inventory is taken; the review consists principally of inquiries of the client's management and analysis of financial information supplied by the client. The report offers only the limited assurance that the accountant is not aware of any material modifications that should be made to the client's financial statements in order for them to conform with GAAP.

While the essential character of a Review Report thus differs from that of the traditional audit, the accountant nevertheless has a duty to exercise due care in performance of its engagement. That duty runs primarily, of course, to the party contracting for the accountant's services. In the absence of a contractual relationship between the accountant and the party claiming injury, the potential for accountant liability is carefully circumscribed. In *Credit Alliance Corp. v. Andersen & Co.*, we said that the accountants may be held liable to noncontractual parties who rely to their detriment on negligently prepared financial reports only when certain prerequisites are satisfied: "(1) the accountants must have been aware that the financial reports were to be used for a particular purpose or purposes; (2) in the furtherance of which a known party or parties was intended to rely; and (3) there must have been some conduct on the part of the accountants linking them to that party or parties, which evinces the accountants' understanding of that party or parties' reliance." In sum, the noncontractual party must demonstrate a relationship with the accountants "sufficiently approaching privity."

Mann demonstrated the absence of either a contract or a relationship approaching privity with Iselin. Thus, Iselin was obligated to submit evidence of Mann's awareness that Suits, intending that Iselin would rely on the Reports, would use them for the purpose of procuring credit from Iselin.

Beyond that, Iselin was required to show a nexus with Mann from which Mann's understanding of Iselin's reliance could be drawn.

Iselin offered the 1979 engagement letter from Mann to Suits. That part of the engagement letter from Mann to Suits which is relied upon by Iselin recites: "During the period of our engagement we will undoubtedly receive credit inquiries and requests for current financial information from banks, factors, converters, or any other source from whom you would expect to receive credit. It is understood that we have your permission to use our judgment in disclosing whatever information we believe necessary under the circumstances." While that language may be evidence of an incidental or collateral purpose of the contractual relationship between Mann and Suits, it is no evidence of the purpose to be served by the Review Reports. Indeed, Iselin makes no showing that Mann was employed by Suits for the purpose of inducing Iselin to extend credit, and no proof is submitted showing an intention that Iselin should rely on the Reports in doing so. Nor is it shown that the Review Reports were prepared for Iselin's use or according to Iselin's requirements. Even if it were properly shown that a Review Report was sent by Mann to Iselin at Suits's request, the single act of sending the Report at an undetermined time for an unknown purpose would not satisfy the burden of coming forth with evidence evincing Mann's understanding of Iselin's reliance.

We find nothing in relation to the contacts between Mann and Iselin which would establish a nexus between them sufficiently approaching privity.

Judgment for Mann affirmed.

Foreseen Users and Foreseen Class of Users Test   By 1965, a draft of the *Restatement (Second) of Torts* proposed that the law of professional negligence expand the class of protected persons beyond merely primary beneficiaries to *foreseen users* and *users within a foreseen class of users* of reports. Under this test, the accountant must know either the user of the work product or the use to be made of the work product. The protected persons are (1) those persons who an accountant knows will use the accountant's work product and (2) those persons who use an accountant's work product in a way the accountant knew the work product would be used.

For example, an accountant prepares an income statement that he knows his client will use to obtain a loan at Bank X. Any bank to which the client supplies the statement to obtain a loan, including Bank Y, may sue the accountant for damages caused by a negligently prepared income statement. Bank X is a foreseen user, and Bank Y is in a class of foreseen users. On the other hand, if an accountant prepares an income statement for a tax return and the client, without the accountant's knowledge, uses the income statement to apply for a loan from a bank, the bank is not among the protected class of persons: The accountant did not know that the tax return would be used for that purpose.

Foreseeable Users Test   In the last 25 years, a few courts have applied traditional negligence causation principles to accountants' negligence. They have extended liability to *foreseeable users* of an accountant's reports who suffered damages that were proximately caused by the accountant's negligence. To be liable to a nonclient, an accountant need merely be able to expect or foresee the nonclient's use of the accountant's work product. It is not necessary for the nonclient to prove that the accountant actually expected or foresaw the nonclient's use.

Some courts have adopted a modified foreseeable users test by extending liability to reasonably foreseeable users who request and receive an accountant's work product from the accountant's client for a *proper business purpose.*[6] Such a test protects parties who request, receive, and rely on an accountant's work product, yet it also protects the accountant from having liability to an unlimited number of potential users.[7]

---

[6]For example, *H. Rosenblum, Inc. v. Adler,* 461 A.2d 138 (N.J. Sup. Ct. 1983).

[7]*Touche Ross & Co. v. Commercial Union Insurance Co.,* 514 So.2d 315, 322-323 (Miss. Sup. Ct. 1987).

Although few courts have adopted the foreseeable users test, there is a clear judicial trend toward expanding the class of persons to whom accountants owe a duty of ordinary skill and care. The *Timm,* *Schmidt* case, which follows, expresses some of the reasons for this trend, including the desire of courts to deter accountants' negligence and to reduce the cost of credit.

CITIZENS STATE BANK v. TIMM, SCHMIDT & CO.

335 N.W.2d 361 (Wis. Sup. Ct. 1983)

Timm, Schmidt & Co. was an accounting firm in Stevens Point, Wisconsin. For the years 1973–76, Timm prepared financial statements for Clintonville Fire Apparatus, Inc. (CFA). For every year except 1973, Timm sent an opinion letter to CFA stating that the financial statements fairly presented the financial condition of CFA and that the statements were prepared in accordance with generally accepted accounting principles.

In November 1975, CFA obtained a $300,000 loan from Citizens State Bank. Citizens made the loan to CFA after reviewing the financial statements that Timm had prepared. Citizens made additional loans to CFA in 1976. By the end of 1976, CFA owed Citizens $380,000.

In early 1977, Timm employees discovered that the 1974 and 1975 financial statements contained a number of material errors totaling over $400,000. When Timm informed Citizens of the errors, Citizens called all of CFA's loans due. As a result, CFA was liquidated. CFA's assets were insufficient to pay the loans from Citizens. Citizens sued Timm seeking to recover $152,000, the amount due on its loans to CFA. Timm failed to comply with generally accepted auditing standards (GAAS) when it first audited the 1974 and 1975 financial statements.

The trial court held that Citizens was not within the class of persons to whom Timm could be held liable for its negligent acts. Citizens appealed to the court of appeals, which affirmed the trial court's decision. Citizens next appealed to the Supreme Court of Wisconsin.

Day, Justice. Accountants have long been held not liable for their negligence to relying third parties not in privity under an application of Judge Cardozo's decision in *Ultramares v. Touche* (1931). In recent years, *Ultramares* has received new attention and courts have started to find accountants liable to third parties.

Unless liability is imposed, third parties who rely upon the accuracy of the financial statements will not be protected. Unless an accountant can be held liable to a relying third party, this negligence will go undeterred.

There are additional policy reasons to allow the imposition of liability. If relying third parties, such as creditors, are not allowed to recover, the cost of credit to the general public will increase because creditors will either have to absorb the costs of bad loans made in reliance on faulty information or hire independent accountants to verify the information received. Accountants may spread the risk through the use of liability insurance.

We conclude that the absence of privity alone should not bar negligence actions by relying third parties against accountants. Although the absence of privity does not bar this action, the question remains as to the extent of an accountant's liability to injured third parties.

The fundamental principle of Wisconsin negligence law is that a tortfeasor is fully liable for all foreseeable consequences of his act except as those consequences are limited by policy factors. We conclude that accountants' liability to third parties should be determined under the accepted principles of Wisconsin negligence law. According to these principles, liability will be imposed on Timm for the foreseeable injuries resulting from its negligent acts unless recovery is denied on grounds of public policy.

Timm's affidavits do not dispute that Citizens' reliance upon the financial statements led to the making of the loans and ultimately to the losses that were incurred. Each affidavit recites that Timm employees had no knowledge that the financial statements would actually be used by CFA to apply for a new bank loan or to increase existing loan indebtedness. However, the affidavit of Elmer Timm stated that "as a certified public accountant, I know that audited statements are used for many purposes and that it is common for them to be supplied to lenders and creditors, and other persons."

Therefore, we conclude that the trial judge erred in granting judgment for Timm.

Judgment reversed in favor of Citizens State Bank. Remanded for trial.

Fraud

Fraud is such reprehensible conduct that the courts have extended an accountant's liability for fraud to all *foreseeable users* of his work product who suffered damages that were proximately caused by the accountant's fraud. Privity of contract, therefore, is not required when a person sues an accountant for fraud. To prove fraud, a nonclient must establish that an accountant acted with scienter.

Correcting Erroneous Reports

An accountant's duty to nonclients includes the duty to correct his report when he subsequently discovers that the report is false or misleading. In such a situation, the accountant has a duty to disclose the new information to anyone who he knows is relying on the earlier report.[8] Liability for a failure to correct erroneous reports may be based on negligence or fraud. Of course, disclosure of the correct facts *after* a person's reliance will not relieve an accountant from liability for damages caused by the earlier reliance.

---

[8] *Fisher v. Kletz,* 266 F. Supp. 180 (S.D.N.Y. 1967).

CONCEPT REVIEW

COMMON LAW BASES OF LIABILITY OF ACCOUNTANT TO NONCLIENTS

Privity Test Adopted by State	Basis of Liability	
	Negligence	**Fraud**
Primary Benefit Test	Accountant liable only to foreseen users (accountant knew name of user and purpose of the user's use)	Regardless of test adopted, accountant liable to all persons whose damages were caused by their reliance on accountant's fraud
Restatement of Torts Test	Accountant liable to foreseen users and users in a class of foreseen users (accountant knew at least the purpose of the user's use)	
Foreseeable Users Test	Accountant liable to all foreseeable users (accountant can expect or foresee the purpose of the user's use)	

ACCOUNTANTS' LIABILITY TO THIRD PARTIES: SECURITIES LAW

The slow reaction of the common law in creating a negligence remedy for third parties led to an increased use of securities law, especially the federal securities acts, by nonclients—persons who were not in privity with an accountant. Many liability sections in these statutes either eliminate the privity requirement or expansively define privity.

Securities Act of 1933

There are several liability sections under the Securities Act of 1933 (1933 Act). The 1933 Act is discussed in detail in the Securities Regulation chapter. The most important liability section of the Securities Act of 1933 is Section 11, which imposes liability for errors in 1933 Act registration statements. The 1933 Act registration statement must be filed with the Securities and Exchange Commission by an issuer making a public distribution of securities. The following is a summary of liability sections that are discussed more fully in the Securities Regulation chapter.

Section 11 Liability

Section 11 specifically imposes on auditors and other experts liability for misstatements or omissions of material fact in information (usually certified financial statements) that they provide for Securities Act registration statements filed with and declared effective by the Securities and Exchange Commission. An auditor is liable to *any purchaser* of securities issued pursuant to a defective registration statement. The purchaser need *not* establish privity of contract with the auditor; he need merely prove that the auditor is a person who furnished the certified financial statements for inclusion in the registration statement. Usually, the purchaser need *not* prove he relied on the misstated or omitted material fact; he need not even have read or seen the defective financial statement.

For example, an auditor certifies a client's income statement that overstates net income by 85 percent. The defective income statement is included in the client's registration statement pursuant to which the client sells its preferred shares. Without reading the registration statement or the income statement, a person buys from the client 100 preferred shares for $105 per share. After the correct income figure is released, the price of the shares drops to $25 per share. The auditor will most likely be liable to the purchaser for $8,000.

Under Section 11, an auditor is potentially liable to a purchaser of registered securities for the purchaser's entire loss. However, if an auditor proves that a purchaser's loss was caused in full or in part by another person's misstatements or omissions or by a general decline in the price of all securities, the auditor's liability is reduced accordingly.

Due Diligence Defense   Under Section 11, as interpreted by *Escott v. BarChris*, which appears in the Securities Regulation chapter, auditors may escape liability by proving that they exercised due diligence. This due diligence defense requires that an auditor of certified financial statements prove that she made a *reasonable investigation* and that she *reasonably believed* that the certified financial statements were accurate *at the time the registration statement became effective*. Since the effective date is often several months after an audit has been completed, an auditor must perform an additional review of the audited statements to ensure that the statements are accurate as of the effective date. In essence, due diligence means that an auditor was not negligent, which is proved usually by showing that she complied with GAAS and GAAP.

Statute of Limitations

Under Section 11, an auditor has liability for only a limited period of time, pursuant to the **statute of limitations** in Section 13. A purchaser must sue the auditor within one year after the misstatement or omission was or should have been discovered. In addition, a purchaser may sue the auditor no more than three years after the securities were offered to the public. Although the word *offered* is used, this three-year period usually does not begin until after the registered securities are first delivered to a purchaser.

Other 1933 Act Liability Sections

Sections 12(2) and 17(a) of the 1933 Act have also been used against accountants. Both sections require that the wrongful act have a connection with interstate commerce or the mails.

Section 12(2) requires that a purchaser rely on a material misstatement or omission by an accountant in connection with the offer or sale of a security. In addition, the purchaser must prove privity between the purchaser and the accountant being sued; few courts, however, require that the accountant actually sell the security to the purchaser. Instead, well-reasoned opinions hold that privity exists when the accountant's acts were a substantial factor in bringing about the sale, such as an accountant's certifying financial statements that had the effect of encouraging an investor to buy the security.

The accountant may escape liability by proving that she did not know and could not reasonably have known of the untruth or omission; that is, she must prove that she was not negligent. Section 12 has a one-year/three-year statute of limitations similar to the one for Section 11. However, the three-year period begins when the security is sold to the purchaser.

Under Section 17(a), a purchaser of a security must prove his reliance on a misstatement or omission of material fact for which an accountant is responsible. Under two of the subsections of Section 17(a), the investor need prove only negligence. Under the third, the investor must prove scienter. The Supreme Court has not decided whether a private right of action exists under Section 17(a), and the courts of appeals are divided on the issue.

Securities Exchange Act of 1934

Two sections of the 1934 Act—Section 18(a) and Section 10(b)—especially affect the liability of accountants to nonclients. The following is a summary of these sections. A fuller discussion appears in the Securities Regulation chapter.

Section 18(a)

Section 18(a) of the 1934 Act imposes liability on accountants who furnish misleading and false statements of material fact in any report or document filed with the Securities and Exchange Commission under the 1934 Act. Such reports or documents include the annual 10-K report, which includes certified financial statements; the monthly 8-K report; and proxy statements.[9]

Under Section 18(a), a purchaser or seller of a security must have actually known of and relied on the defective statement in the filed document. Usually, this means that a plaintiff must have *read and relied*

on the defective statement in the filed document. This is sometimes called **eyeball reliance.** In addition, he must prove that the misleading and false information caused his damages. Lastly, he must show that the security's price was affected by the false and misleading statement.

An accountant may escape Section 18(a) liability by proving that she acted in *good faith* and had *no knowledge* that the information was misleading. That is, she must show that she acted *without scienter.* Being negligent is not enough to incur liability under Section 18(a).

In addition, Section 18 has a statute of limitations. An auditor must be sued within one year after discovery of the facts constituting a violation and within three years after the violation occurred.

Section 10(b) and Rule 10b-5

Securities Exchange Act Rule 10b-5, pursuant to Section 10(b), has been the basis for most of the recent suits investors have brought against accountants. Rule 10b-5 prohibits any person from making a misstatement or omission of material fact in connection with the purchase or sale of any security. The wrongful act must have a connection with interstate commerce, the mails, or a national securities exchange. Rule 10b-5 applies to misstatements or omissions in any communications with investors, covering any use of documents prepared by accountants that results in a purchase or sale of a security. It is, therefore, the broadest and most dangerous liability provision from the accountant's viewpoint.

A purchaser or seller of a security may sue an accountant who has misstated or omitted a material fact. Privity is *not* required. The purchaser or seller must rely on the misstatement or omission. In omission cases, reliance may be inferred from materiality.

In addition, the accountant must act with *scienter.* In this context, scienter is an intent to deceive, manipulate, or defraud. Negligence is not enough. Although the Supreme Court of the United States has not ruled whether scienter encompasses gross recklessness or recklessness, some courts have held that it does, especially when a fiduciary duty is owed by the accountant to the plaintiff. Generally, gross negligence does not satisfy the scienter requirement, but a few courts have held gross negligence to be sufficient when a fiduciary duty is present. Ordinarily, however, only a client, not a third party, will be able to prove the existence of a fiduciary duty.

---

[9]The quarterly 10-Q report, which includes unaudited financial statements, is excluded from Section 18(a) coverage by SEC Rule 15d-13(d). Annual reports sent to shareholders are not covered by Section 18(a), since they are filed with the SEC only for information purposes.

No 1934 Act section expressly places a statute of limitations on suits brought under Rule 10b-5. However, the Supreme Court ruled that the Section 18 statute of limitations should apply to Rule 10b-5.[10] Consequently, an action under Rule 10b-5 must be commenced within one year after discovery of the facts constituting a violation and within three years of the violation.

[10] *Lampf, Pleva, Lipkind, Prupis & Petigrow v. Gilbertson*, 59 U.S.L.W. 4688 (June 20, 1991).

CONCEPT REVIEW

COMPARISON OF 1933 ACT AND 1934 ACT LIABILITY

	Wrongful Conduct	Covered Communications	Reliance Required?	Privity Required?	Defendant's Mental State	Mental State Defense
Securities Act of 1933 Section 11	Misstatement or omission of material fact	1933 Act registration statement only	No	No	Negligence	Reasonable investigation and reasonable belief that no misstatement or omission exists
Securities Exchange Act of 1934 Section 18(a)	False or misleading statement of material fact	1934 Act 10-K; 1934 Act 8-K; 1934 Act registration statement; 1934 Act proxy statement; 1934 Act tender offer statement	Yes	No	Scienter	Good faith and no knowledge that the statement was false or misleading
Securities Exchange Act of 1934 Section 10(b) and Rule 10b-5	Misstatement or omission of material fact	Any communication	Yes	No	Scienter	Plaintiff has burden of proving scienter

Aiding and Abetting

Accountants may also be held liable for aiding and abetting violations of the securities acts by others. Aiding and abetting is proved when a person (1) has a general awareness that his role is part of an overall activity that is improper and (2) knowingly and substantially assists the overall activity. For example, accountants who wrongfully overlook misrepresentations by others or encourage the dissemination of misleading information prepared by others may be held liable as aiders and abettors. Proof of aiding and abetting also allows a purchaser to overcome the privity requirement of Securities Act Section 12(2).

In the following case, the court held that Arthur Andersen's alleged failure to disclose to investors that it was aware of John DeLorean's misuse of investors' funds could meet the requirements for aiding and abetting liability under Rule 10b-5.

RUDOLPH v. ARTHUR ANDERSEN & CO.

800 F.2d 1040 (11th Cir. 1986)

John DeLorean needed capital to fund the research and development of his vision of the ultramodern sports car. DeLorean set up a limited partnership, DeLorean Research Limited Partnership (DRLP), to raise the necessary capital. The limited partnership made a private placement of limited partnership interests pursuant to a private placement memorandum dated March 23, 1978. The placement memorandum contained audit reports and other financial statements that were prepared by Arthur Andersen & Co. and were included in the placement memorandum with Andersen's permission. The placement memorandum, in parts not contributed by Andersen, stated that capital obtained from limited partners would be used for research and development of a sports car to be manufactured in Puerto Rico. In July 1978, DeLorean and officials of Northern Ireland signed an agreement under which DeLorean would locate his factory in Northern Ireland in return for substantial financial benefits. The financial benefits offered by Northern Ireland made it unnecessary to obtain research and development funds through DRLP. Nonetheless, on September 22, 1978, DRLP completed its sale of limited partnership interests. However, DeLorean did not use the funds for research and development, but instead diverted them to other uses. At no time were the DRLP limited partners told of the change in plans to use the funds. Subsequently, DeLorean's venture lost substantial amounts of money, with the result that the limited partners lost their investments in DRLP.

One of the limited partners, Sidney Rudolph, sued Arthur Andersen under Securities Exchange Act Rule 10b-5 for fraud and for aiding and abetting DeLorean's fraud. Rudolph alleged that due to its business relationship with DeLorean, Andersen knew or recklessly failed to learn of DeLorean's intention to divert the partnership funds, and that Andersen willfully or recklessly failed to disclose the alleged fraud. The district court dismissed Rudolph's lawsuit on the grounds that the facts alleged by Rudolph did not establish a violation of Rule 10b-5. Rudolph appealed.

Vance, Circuit Judge.   It is clear that if read literally, Rule 10b-5 would reach the alleged conduct of Andersen. The rule prohibits omitting to state a material fact necessary to make the statements made not misleading.

Rule 10b-5, however, is not read literally. Instead, a defendant's omission to state a material fact is proscribed only when the defendant has a duty to disclose. Such a duty may exist when the law imposes special obligations depending on the circumstances of the case. In evaluating the circumstances, we consider the relationship between the plaintiff and the defendant, the parties' relative access to the information to be disclosed, the benefit derived by the defendant's awareness of plaintiff's reliance on defendant in making its investment decision, and defendant's role in initiating the purchase or sale. A duty to disclose may also be created by a defendant's previous decision to speak voluntarily. When a defendant's failure to speak would render the defendant's own prior speech misleading or deceptive, a duty to disclose arises.

Other courts have held that accountants have a duty to take reasonable steps to correct misstatements they have discovered in previous financial statements on which they know the public is relying. This duty arises from the fact that investors are likely to rely on an accountant's work. On the other hand, courts have refused to hold accountants liable for not disclosing ordinary business information discovered after the completion of a report, when the information did not indicate that the report was inaccurate as of the date it was issued.

The rule that an accountant is under no duty to disclose ordinary business information, unless it shows a previous report to have been misleading or incorrect when issued, is a sensible one. It would be asking too much to expect accountants to make difficult and time-consuming judgment calls about the nature of routine facts and figures turned up after a report has been completed. The situation is quite different, however, when the issue is disclosure of actual knowledge of fraud. Standing idly by while knowing one's good name is being used to perpetrate a fraud is inherently misleading. An investor might reasonably assume that an accounting firm would not permit inclusion of an audit report it prepared in a placement memo for an offering the firm knew to be fraudulent, and that such a firm would let it be known if it discovered to be fraudulent an offering with which it was associated. It is not unreasonable to expect an accountant, who stands in a "special relationship of trust vis-à-vis the public," and whose "duty it is to safeguard the public interest," to disclose fraud in this type of circumstance, when the accountant's information is obviously superior to that of the investor, the cost to the accountant of revealing the information is minimal, and the cost to investors of the information remaining secret is potentially enormous.

The complaint alleges that Andersen performed nonauditing business services for DeLorean. Rudolph possibly could prove at trial that through these services Andersen had spoken previously with respect to the DRLP offering—through its audit reports and statements included in the placement memo—and that Andersen knew investors would rely to some extent on those reports and statements. Rudolph might also prove that Andersen failed to disclose DeLorean's fraud even though it had actual knowledge of that fraud, and that Andersen's access to information concerning the fraud was far greater than Rudolph's. Proof of these circumstances would be sufficient to establish that Andersen had a duty to disclose.

Rudolph's complaint also states a valid claim against Andersen for aiding and abetting securities violations by DeLorean. Liability for aiding and abetting under Rule 10b-5 attaches if some other party has committed a securities law violation, if the accused party has general awareness that his role was part of an overall activity that is improper, and if the accused aider-abettor knowingly and substantially assisted the violation.

When the act alleged to constitute aiding and abetting is mere silence—failure to disclose fraud—the requirement of "knowing" assistance does not require a conscious intent to aid the fraud if the aider and abettor was under a duty to disclose. Whether the assistance was "substantial" depends on the totality of the circumstances.

As we discussed above, Rudolph could, consistently with his allegations, prove at trial that DeLorean committed securities violations, that Andersen knew about DeLorean's fraudulent scheme, that Andersen did not disclose the scheme, and that in doing so Andersen violated a duty to disclose. Proof of such facts, sufficient to establish primary liability on the part of Andersen, could also suffice to prove aiding and abetting.

Judgment reversed in favor of Rudolph. Remanded to the trial court.

State Securities Law

All states have securities statutes with liability sections. Most of the states have a liability section similar to Section 12(2) of the Securities Act. Nonetheless, accountants are rarely sued under state securities statutes.

QUALIFIED OPINIONS, DISCLAIMERS OF OPINION, AND AUDITED REPORTS

After performing an audit of financial statements, an independent auditor **certifies** the financial statements by issuing an **opinion letter.** The opinion letter expresses whether the audit has been performed in compliance with GAAS and whether, in the auditor's opinion, the financial statements fairly present the client's financial position and results of operations in conformity with GAAP. Usually, an auditor issues an **unqualified opinion;** that is, an opinion that there has been compliance with GAAS and GAAP. Sometimes, an auditor issues a qualified opinion, a disclaimer of opinion, or an adverse opinion. Up to this point, you have studied the liability of an auditor who has issued unqualified opinions, yet has not complied with GAAS and GAAP.

What liability should be imposed on an auditor who discloses that he has not complied with GAAS and GAAP? An auditor is relieved of responsibility only to the extent that a qualification or disclaimer is *specifically expressed* in the opinion letter. Therefore, letters that purport to totally disclaim liability for false and misleading financial statements are too general to excuse an accountant from exercising ordinary skill and care.

For example, an auditor qualifies his opinion of the ability of financial statements to present the financial position of a company by indicating that there is uncertainty about how a antitrust suit against the company may be decided. He would not be held liable for damages resulting from an unfavorable verdict in the antitrust suit. He would remain liable, however, for failing to make an examination in compliance with GAAS that would have revealed other serious problems.

For another example, consider an auditor who, due to the limited scope of the audit, disclaims any opinion on the ability of the financial statements to present the financial position of the company. She would nonetheless be liable for the nondiscovery of problems that the limited audit should have revealed.

Likewise, an accountant who issued an adverse opinion that depreciation had not been calculated according to GAAP would not be liable for damages resulting from the wrongful accounting treatment of depreciation, but he would be liable for damages resulting from the wrongful treatment of receivables.

Merely issuing unaudited statements does not create a disclaimer as to their accuracy. The mere fact that the statements are unaudited only permits an accountant to exercise a lower level of inquiry. Even so, an accountant must act as the ordinarily prudent accountant would act under the same circumstances in preparing unaudited financial statements. *William Iselin & Co. v. Landau*, which appears earlier in this chapter, illustrates this rule.

CRIMINAL, INJUNCTIVE, AND ADMINISTRATIVE PROCEEDINGS

In addition to being held liable for damages to clients and third parties, an accountant may be found criminally liable for his violations of securities, tax, and other laws. For criminal violations, he may be fined and imprisoned. His wrongful conduct may also result in the issuance of an injunction, which bars him from doing the same acts in the future. In addition, his wrongful conduct may be the subject of administrative proceedings by the Securities and Exchange Commission and state licensing boards. An administrative proceeding may result in the revocation of an accountant's license to practice or the suspension from practice. Finally, disciplinary proceedings may be brought against an accountant by professional societies such as the AICPA.

Criminal Liability under the Securities Laws

Both the Securities Act of 1933 and the Securities Exchange Act of 1934 have criminal provisions that can be applied to accountants. Section 24 of the 1933 Act imposes criminal liability for willful violations of any section of the 1933 Act, including Sections 11, 12(2), and 17(a), or any SEC rule or regulation. Also, willfully making an untrue statement or omitting any material fact in a 1933 Act registration statement imposes criminal liability on an accountant. An accountant who knows that financial statements are false and misleading, yet certifies them for inclusion in a registration statement, will be criminally liable under Section 24. The maximum penalty for a criminal violation of the 1933 Act is a $10,000 fine and five years' imprisonment.

Section 32(a) of the 1934 Act imposes criminal penalties for willful violations of any section of the 1934 Act, such as Sections 10(b) and 18(a), and any SEC rule or regulation, such as Rule 10b-5. In addition, willfully making false or misleading statements in reports that are required to be filed under the 1934 Act incurs criminal liability. Such filings include 10-Ks, 8-Ks, and proxy statements. An accountant may be fined up to $1 million and imprisoned for up to 10 years for a criminal violation of the 1934 Act. An accounting firm may be fined up to $2.5 million. An accountant who proves that he had no knowledge of an SEC rule or regulation may not be imprisoned for violating that rule or regulation.

Most of the states have statutes imposing criminal penalties on accountants who willfully falsify financial statements or other reports in filings under the state securities laws and who willfully violate the state securities laws or aid and abet criminal violations of these laws by others.

In the following case, accountants permitting a client to book unbilled sales after the close of the fiscal period subjected the accountants to the criminal penalties of the 1934 Act.

UNITED STATES v. NATELLI
527 F.2d 311 (2d Cir. 1975)

Anthony Natelli was the partner in charge of the Washington, D.C., office of Peat, Marwick, Mitchell & Co., a large CPA firm. In August 1968, Peat, Marwick became the independent public auditor of National Student Marketing Corporation. Natelli was the engagement partner for the audit of Student Marketing. Joseph Scansaroli was Peat, Marwick's audit supervisor on that engagement.

Student Marketing provided its corporate clients with a wide range of marketing services to help them reach the lucrative youth market. In its financial statements for the nine months ended May 31, 1968, Student Marketing had counted as income the entire amount of oral customer commitments to pay fees in Student Marketing's "fixed-fee marketing programs," even though those fees had not yet been paid. They were to be paid for services that Student Marketing would provide over a period of several years. Standard accounting practice required that part of the unpaid fees be considered income in the present year but that part be deferred as income until the years when Student Marketing actually performed the services for which the fees were paid. Therefore, in making the year-end audit, Natelli concluded that he would use a percentage-of-completion approach on these commitments, taking as income in the present year only those fees that were to be paid for services in that year.

However, the customer fee commitments were oral only, making it difficult to verify whether they really existed. In addition, Student Marketing had not even recorded the fee commitments in its financial records during the 1968 fiscal year. The decision regarding whether to include the fee commitments as income was critical. Excluding them would result in showing a large loss—$232,000—for the fiscal year at a time when Student Marketing's stock was selling for $80, an increase of $74 in the five months since Student Marketing had first sold its shares publicly.

Natelli directed Scansaroli to try to verify the fee commitments by telephoning the customers, but not by seeking written verification. However, Scansaroli never called Student Marketing's clients. Instead, Scansaroli accepted a schedule prepared by Student Marketing showing estimates of the percentage of completion of services for each corporate client and the amount of the fee commitment from each client. This resulted in an adjustment of $1.7 million for "unbilled accounts receivable." The adjustment turned a loss for the year into a profit twice that of the year before.

By May 1969, a total of $1 million of the customer fee commitments had been written off as uncollectible. The effect of the write-off was to reduce 1968 income by $209,750. However, Scansaroli, with Natelli's approval, offset this by reversing a deferred tax item of approximately the same amount.

Student Marketing issued a proxy statement in September 1969, in connection with a shareholders' meeting to consider merging six companies into Student Marketing. The proxy statement was filed with the Securities and Exchange Commission. It contained several financial statements, some of which had been audited by Peat, Marwick. Others had not been audited, but Peat, Marwick had aided in their preparation. In the proxy statement, a footnote to the financial statements failed to show that the write-off of customer fee commitments had affected Student Marketing's fiscal 1968 income.

The proxy statement required an unaudited statement of nine months' earnings through May 31, 1969. This statement was prepared by Student Marketing with Peat, Marwick's assistance Student Marketing produced a $1.2 million commitment from the Pontiac Division of General Motors Corporation two months after the end of May, but it was dated April 28, 1969. At 3 A.M. on the day the proxy statement was to be printed, Natelli informed Randall, the chief executive officer and founder of Student Marketing, that this commitment could not be included, because it was not a legally binding contract. Randall responded at once that he had "a commitment from Eastern Airlines" for a somewhat comparable amount attributable to the same period. Such a letter was produced at the printing plant a few hours later, and the Eastern commitment was substituted for the Pontiac sale in the proxy. Shortly thereafter, another Peat, Marwick accountant, Oberlander, discovered $177,547 in "bad" commitments from 1968. These were known to Scansaroli in May 1969 as being doubtful, but they had not been written off. Oberlander suggested to the company that these commitments plus others, for a total of $320,000, be written off, but Scansaroli, after consulting with Natelli, decided against the suggested write-off.

There was no disclosure in the proxy statement that Student Marketing had written off $1 million (20 percent) of its 1968 sales and over $2 million of the $3.3 million of unbilled sales booked in 1968 and 1969. A true disclosure would have shown that Student Marketing had made no profit for the first nine months of 1969.

Subsequently, it was revealed that many of Student Marketing's fee commitments were fictitious. The attorney general of the United States brought a criminal action against Natelli and Scansaroli for violating the Securities Exchange Act of 1934 by willfully and knowingly making false and misleading statements in a proxy statement. The district court jury convicted both Natelli and Scansaroli, and they appealed.

Gurfein, Circuit Judge.   Natelli argues that there is insufficient evidence to establish that he knowingly assisted in filing a proxy statement that was materially false. We are constrained to find that there was sufficient evidence for his conviction.

The original action of Natelli in permitting the booking of unbilled sales after the close of the fiscal period in an amount sufficient to convert a loss into a profit was contrary to sound accounting practice. When the uncollectibility, and indeed, the nonexistence of these large receivables was established in 1969, the revelation stood to cause Natelli severe criticism and possible liability. He had a motive, therefore, intentionally to conceal the write-offs that had to be made.

With this background of motive, the jury could assess what Natelli did with regard to (1) the footnote and (2) the Eastern commitment and the Oberlander "bad" contracts. Honesty should have impelled Natelli and Scansaroli to disclose in the footnote that annotated their own audited statement for fiscal 1968 that substantial write-offs had been taken, after year-end, to reflect a loss for the year. A simple desire to right the wrong that had been perpetrated on the stockholders and others by the false audited financial statement should have dictated that course.

The accountant owes a duty to the public not to assert a privilege of silence until the next audited annual statement comes around in due time. Since companies were being acquired by Student Marketing for its shares in this period, Natelli had to know that the 1968 audited statement was being used continuously.

Natelli contends that he had no duty to verify the Eastern commitment because the earnings statement within which it was included was unaudited.

This raises the issue of the duty of the CPA in relation to an unaudited financial statement contained within a proxy statement where the figures are reviewed and to some extent supplied by the auditors. The auditors were associated with the statement and were required to object to anything they actually knew to be materially false. In the ordinary case involving an unaudited statement, the auditor would not be chargeable simply because he failed to discover the invalidity of booked accounts receivable, inasmuch as he had not undertaken an audit with verification. In this case, however, Natelli knew the history of post-period bookings and the dismal consequences later discovered.

We do not think this means, in terms of professional standards, that the accountant may shut his eyes in reckless disregard of his knowledge that highly suspicious figures, known to him to be suspicious, were being included in the unaudited earnings figures in the proxy statement with which he was associated.

There is some merit to Scansaroli's point that he was simply carrying out the judgments of his superior, Natelli. The defense of obedience to higher authority has always been troublesome. There is no sure yardstick to measure criminal responsibility except by measurement of the degree of awareness on the part of a defendant that he is participating in a criminal act, in the absence of physical coercion such as a soldier might face. Here the motivation to conceal undermines Scansaroli's argument that he was merely implementing Natelli's instructions, at least with respect to concealment of matters that were within his own ken. We think the jury could properly have found him guilty on the specification relating to the footnote.

With respect to the Eastern commitment, we think Scansaroli stands in a position different from that of Natelli. Natelli was his superior. He was the man to make the judgment whether or not to object to the last-minute inclusion of a new commitment in the nine-months statement. There is insufficient evidence that Scansaroli engaged in any conversations about the Eastern commitment or that he was a participant with Natelli in any check on its authenticity. Since in the hierarchy of the accounting firm it was not his responsibility to decide whether to book the Eastern contract, his mere adjustment of the figures to reflect it under orders was not a matter for his discretion.

Conviction of Natelli affirmed. Conviction of Scansaroli affirmed in part and reversed in part.

Criminal Violations of Tax Law

Federal tax law imposes on accountants a wide range of penalties for a wide range of wrongful conduct. At one end of the penalty spectrum is a $25 fine for failing to furnish a client with a copy of his income tax return or failing to sign a client's return. At the other end is a fine of $100,000 and imprisonment of three years for tax fraud. In between is the penalty for promoting abusive tax shelters. The fine is $1,000, or 10 percent of the accountant's income from her participation in the tax shelter, whichever is greater. In addition, all of the states impose criminal penalties for specified violations of their tax laws.

Other Crimes

Several other federal statutes also impose criminal liability on accountants. The most notable of these statutes is the general *mail fraud* statute, which prohibits the use of the mails to commit fraud. To be held liable, an accountant must know or foresee that the mails will be used to transmit materials containing fraudulent statements provided by her.

In addition, the general false-statement-to-government-personnel statute prohibits fraudulent statements to government personnel. The false-statement-to-bank statute proscribes fraudulent statements on a loan application to a bank or other financial institution.

Injunctions

Adminstrative agencies such as the SEC and the Internal Revenue Service may bring injunctive actions against an accountant in a federal district court. The purpose of such an injunction is to prevent an accountant from committing a future violation of the securities or tax laws. Hence, the mere existence of a past violation will not be sufficient grounds for the SEC or the IRS to obtain an injunction. There must be proof of the likelihood of a future violation.

After an injunction has been issued, violating the injunction may result in serious sanctions. Not only may penalties be imposed for contempt, but a criminal violation may also be more easily proven.

Administrative Proceedings

The SEC has the authority to bring administrative proceedings against persons who violate the provisions of the securities acts. In recent years, the SEC has stepped up enforcement of SEC Rule of Practice 2(e). Rule 2(e) permits the SEC to bar temporarily or permanently from practicing before the SEC an accountant who does not possess the qualifications required to practice before it. Rule 2(e) also permits the SEC to take action against an accountant who has willfully violated or aided and abetted another's violation of the securities acts. An SEC administrative law judge hears the case and makes an initial determination. The SEC commissioners then issue a final order, which may be appealed to a federal court of appeals.

Rule 2(e) administrative proceedings can impose severe penalties on an accountant. By suspending an accountant from practicing before it, the SEC may take away a substantial part of an accountant's practice. Also, the SEC may impose civil penalties up to $500,000.

In addition, state licensing boards may suspend or revoke an accountant's license to practice if she engages in illegal or unethical conduct. If such action is taken, an accountant may lose her entire ability to practice accounting.

OWNERSHIP OF WORKING PAPERS AND ACCOUNTANT–CLIENT PRIVILEGE

Working Papers

The personal records that a client entrusts to an accountant remain the property of the client. An accountant must return these records to his client. Nonetheless, the working papers produced by independent auditors belong to the accountant, not the client. Working papers are the records made during an audit. They include such items as work programs or plans for the audit, evidence of the testing of accounts, explanations of the handling of unusual matters, data reconciling the accountant's report with the client's records, and comments about the client's internal controls. The client has a right of access to the working papers. The accountant must obtain the client's permission before the working papers can be transferred to another accountant.

Accountant-Client Privilege

A lawyer-client privilege has long been recognized by the common law. This privilege protects most of the communications between lawyers and their clients. In addition, it protects a lawyer's working papers from the discovery procedures available in a lawsuit.

The common law does *not* recognize such a privilege between accountants and their clients. However, a large minority of the states have granted such a privilege by statute. The provisions of the statutes vary, but usually the privilege belongs to the client, and an accountant may not refuse to disclose the privileged material in a courtroom if the client consents to its disclosure.

Generally, the state-granted privileges are recognized in both state and federal courts deciding questions of state law. Nonetheless, federal courts do not recognize the privilege in matters involving federal questions, including antitrust and criminal matters.

In federal tax matters, for example, no privilege of confidentiality is recognized on the grounds that an accountant has a duty as a public watchdog to ensure that his client correctly reports his income tax liability. Consequently, an accountant can be required to bring his working papers into court and to testify as to matters involving the client's tax records and discussions with the client regarding tax matters. In addition, an accountant may be required by subpoena to make available his working papers involving a client who is being investigated by the IRS or who has been charged with tax irregularities. The same holds true for SEC investigations.

In the next case, *Gatewood v. U.S. Cellular Corp.,* the court held that Pennsylvania's accountant-client privilege did not cover a business appraisal or the communications concerning the appraisal.

GATEWOOD v. U.S. CELLULAR CORP.

124 F.R.D. 504 (D.D.C. 1989)

Robert Gatewood and two other limited partners entered a limited partnership agreement with United States Cellular Corporation (USCC), the sole general partner. The agreement provided that in the event the partners were unable to agree on the value of a cellular phone system in which they had an interest, each would select an appraiser, and the two appraisers would select a third. An impasse arose concerning the selection of this third appraiser, and a federal district court was asked to resolve the dispute.

During litigation, USCC took the deposition of Terry Korn, a Pennsylvania certified public accountant and appraiser selected by the limited partners. USCC sought to inquire about the conduct and results of Korn's appraisal as well as any communications between Korn and the limited partners. The limited partners directed Korn not to respond to any of these questions, asserting that the communications were covered by the Pennsylvania statutory accountant-client privilege.

Attridge, Magistrate. The Pennsylvania accountant-client privilege protects from disclosure ". . . information of which he may have come possessed relative to and in connection with any professional services as a certified public accountant, (or) public accountant. . . ." This statute being in derogation of common law is to be strictly construed. Thus, in order for the statute to be at lease prima facially applicable, there must be a showing that an accountant's services were sought in an accounting capacity. In these proceedings, there is nothing to show that Korn was acting in his capacity as an accountant in making his appraisal. Appraisals may be rendered by experts with varying backgrounds who may be otherwise qualified. The appraisal process is not unique to the accounting field. Moreover, the records used to evaluate the financial value of the cellular phone system were not private documents of the limited partners, but rather, records of the system to be evaluated. The purpose of the statute, to foster the free flow of financial data to an accountant by a client in order to obtain financial advice, would not be advanced nor promoted by applying the statute to the events that took place in these proceedings.

The appraisal performed by Korn was not an accounting function and the communications he had with the limited partners were not communications protected by the accountant-client privilege. The fact that Korn is an accountant is merely an accidental circumstance rather than a controlling event.

Judgment for United States Cellular Corporation.

ETHICAL AND PUBLIC POLICY CONCERNS

1. Is it enough that an accountant acts in accordance with the standards of the accounting profession? What risk arises if society entrusts the accounting profession with regulating itself? How great is the risk? Can clients collectively or individually reduce this risk? Is it fair that some clients cannot protect themselves from this risk and yet may have no legal recourse?

2. Should accountants have liability for negligence to persons who are not their clients? What are the social and economic costs of making accountants liable to all users of their work product? What are the social and economic costs of relieving accountants from liability to persons who are not their clients? Is it fair to allow an accountant to be negligent and not have liability to those who relied on the accountant's work product?

3. Should an accountant-client privilege exist? What are the social benefits and costs? In the tax context, why should an accountant be burdened with the public watchdog function when lawyers are not; that is, why must accountants ensure that their clients comply with the tax laws, when a lawyer is permitted to serve the best interests of his client? When a tax accountant is working for a client who also has a lawyer, how can the accountant's work product become privileged? Does the answer to that question suggest a logical or ethical inconsistency in the law?

SUMMARY

Recently, accountants have been frequent targets of lawsuits. These suits may be brought by clients under the common law for breach of contract, for negligence, for fraud, and for breach of trust. In addition, clients may sue under state and federal securities laws.

An accountant is generally held to the standard of the ordinarily prudent accountant. If she meets this standard, few courts will hold her liable. If the standard is breached, clients may sue the accountant for damages caused thereby. Courts have different rules on whether a nonclient may sue an accountant for negligence. Some require the nonclient to be the primary beneficiary of the accountant's work. Others require that the nonclient be a foreseen user or within a foreseen class of users. A few courts impose liability for negligence if the use of the accountant's work by a nonclient is foreseeable. If an accountant has committed fraud, she is liable to foreseeable third parties.

Nonclients may sue accountants under the federal securities laws. Accountants may be held liable for incomplete and incorrect information that they furnish for use in a Securities Act registration statement, unless they can prove that they have exercised due diligence. Under Section 10(b) and Rule 10b-5 of the Securities Exchange Act, accountants are liable for misstatements or omissions of material fact in connection with the purchase or sale of a security. The accountant must have acted with scienter to be found liable. In addition, an accountant may be held liable for aiding and abetting violations of the securities acts by others.

Accountants have been found criminally liable under the federal securities acts, tax laws, and mail fraud laws. The SEC and the IRS may obtain injunctions against accountants to prevent future violations. The SEC may suspend from practicing before it an accountant who has violated the securities laws.

The working papers of accountants belong to them rather than to their clients, but the client has a right of access to the papers. Accountants may be required to produce in court their records concerning a client. Some states recognize a privilege of confidentiality in such records, but this privilege is not recognized by federal courts for federal questions.

PROBLEM CASES

1. The 1136 Tenants' Corporation, a cooperative apartment house, hired Max Rothenberg & Co., a firm of certified public accountants, to perform accounting services for it. Rothenberg discovered that several invoices were missing from the financial records of the apartment house. These invoices were needed to prove that payments of $44,000 had been made to creditors of the apartment house and were not embezzled by someone with authority to make payments for the apartment house. Rothenberg noted the missing invoices on his worksheet, but failed to notify the apartment house that there were missing invoices. In fact, there were no invoices. Jerome Riker, the apartment house manager, had embezzled the $44,000 from the apartment house by ordering it to make unauthorized payments to him. Riker embezzled more money after the audit was completed. Is Rothenberg liable to its client for failing to inform it of Riker's embezzlement?

2. O'Connor, Brooks & Co., an accounting firm, negligently failed to discover embezzlements by an officer of its client, American Trust & Savings Bank. O'Connor, Brooks claimed that certain bank directors breached their duty of care to the bank, thereby permitting the embezzlement to occur. Does O'Connor, Brooks have a defense to liability?

3. When Robert Hicks offered to sell his shares in Intermountain Merchandising, Inc. (IMI), to Montana Merchanding (MM), IMI hired Alan Bloomgren, a CPA, to audit IMI. Based on Bloomgren's clean opinion on IMI's balance sheet, MM purchased Hicks's shares, advanced funds to IMI, and signed financial guarantees for IMI. Bloomgren knew that MM would rely on the audit and that the audit would be used to aid MM in buying out IMI, including making loans and guarantees. Bloomgren's audit was materially defective, failing to represent that IMI had a negative net worth. MM sued Bloomgren for negligence. Is Bloomgren liable to MM?

4. Max Mitchell & Co., a public accounting firm, performed an audit of the financial statements of C.M.

Systems, Inc. At the time Mitchell performed the audit, it was not known that the audited financial statements would be used to obtain a loan from First Florida Bank. However, subsequent to preparing the audited financial statements, Mitchell negotiated a loan with First Florida Bank on behalf of C.M. Mitchell personally delivered the financial statements to the bank. Relying on the financial statements, First Florida loaned $500,000 to C.M. After C.M. defaulted on the loan, First Florida discovered that the financial statements materially understated C.M.'s liabilities and materially overstated its assets and net income. Is Mitchell liable to First Florida under the theory of negligence?

5. To aid its decision whether to purchase all the shares of Gillespie Furniture Company, DMI Furniture, Inc., hired Arthur Young & Co. to review an audit of Gillespie's financial statements that had been performed by Brown, Kraft & Company. Arthur Young wrote a letter stating that Brown, Kraft had "performed a quality audit." Based on this letter, DMI decided to buy all of Gillespie's shares. When Gillespie became less profitable than DMI expected, DMI sued Arthur Young under Rule 10b-5. DMI alleged that Arthur Young acted recklessly in failing to detect and to disclose that Brown, Kraft's audit report was inaccurate and misleading because it grossly overstated inventory and showed a profit when there was a loss. Do DMI's allegations establish that Arthur Young has violated Rule 10b-5?

6. In early 1984, Arthur Andersen & Co. advised Financial Corporation of America (FCA) that FCA could account for Government National Mortgage Association (Ginny Mae) repurchase transactions as it accounted for financing transactions, thereby recording the purchase liability without recognizing any loss or gain. Following this advice, FCA bought $2 billion of Ginny Maes and resold them to the original holders subject to reverse repurchase agreements. In mid-1984, the Securities and Exchange Commission announced that repurchase transactions must be accounted for as forward commitments with profits or losses recognized as they accrue. As a result, FCA was obliged to report a net loss of $107 million for the quarter ended June 30, 1984, resulting in a drop in the price of FCA's shares. FCA alleged that it would not have purchased the Ginny Maes had not Arthur Andersen knowingly or recklessly disregarded the fact that accounting for the repurchases as financing transactions was wholly inappropriate. Do FCA's allegations establish a Rule 10b-5 violation?

7. In March 1971, Lawrence and Theodore Oleck sold their shares in Blue Circle Telephone Answering Service to Sherwood Diversified Services, Inc., in exchange for cash and promissory notes of Sherwood. The Olecks were given and relied on Sherwood's 1970 financial statements that had been audited and certified by Arthur Andersen & Co. Before the notes were paid in full, Sherwood became insolvent. The Olecks alleged that Andersen failed to disclose adequately (1) the high probability that Sherwood would not be able to collect on $2.5 million of notes issued by New Media International Corporation and (2) that Sherwood would have to pay an additional $2 million as a guarantor of New Media's bank loan. Sherwood's risk in these transactions depended on New Media's ability to collect its accounts receivable. Accordingly, Andersen devised a 10-step program to evaluate New Media's receivables problem. Based on figures and projections furnished primarily by New Media, Andersen concluded that New Media had growing sales proceeding for the current year at a rate exceeding $17.8 million, with booked orders totaling $5.9 million for the next four months. It observed that New Media's accounts were "mostly major firms." A summary prepared by Andersen concluded that New Media's "cash projections were reasonable and attainable and that the cash flow shows the ability to pay principal and interest on the Sherwood notes without any detriment to its cash position." Andersen interviewed New Media's bankers and found "no plans to request payment against their $2 million loan." The New Media receivables were found to be more than adequate security to cover the bank debt and the Sherwood notes. Andersen also obtained and relied on an opinion of Sherwood's counsel to the effect that Sherwood's lien on the Media receivables was enforceable. Based on these investigations, Andersen concluded that "a reserve for collectibility of $500,000 would be sufficient." Has Andersen violated Rule 10b-5?

8. John Schulzetenberg was the engagement partner for Touche Ross & Co.'s audit of the financial statements of Inter-Regional Financial Group, Inc. (IRF). The audited financial statements were filed with the Securities and Exchange Commission. From 1981 through 1983, IRF's management misrepresented the delinquency status of its receivables, which accounted for more than 90 percent of its assets. Schulzetenberg's 1981 audit of the receivables was insufficiently planned, supervised, and executed, and did not meet the requirements of GAAS. As a result, he failed to detect that IRF's allowance for uncollectable receivables was materially understated. In 1982, Schulzetenberg failed to correct the 1981 errors, even though it should have been clear to him that the 1981 allowance was materially understated. Is Schulzetenberg subject to penalties under SEC Rule of Practice 2(e)?

9. Bill Thomas, a CPA, was a member of Lawhon, Thomas, Holmes & Co. (LTH), a public accounting firm. When LTH performed accounting services for Xenerex Corp., LTH received 144,000 Xenerex shares instead of cash. LTH continued to hold the Xenerex shares when the three LTH members joined the accounting firm Oppenheim, Appel, Dixon & Co. (OAD). LTH ceased operations and sold all its assets except the Xenerex shares to OAD. The three former LTH members, including Thomas, retained ownership of LTH. After he joined OAD, Thomas immediately solicited Xenerex as a client for OAD. Thomas, on behalf of OAD, signed a new client acceptance form for Xenerex, giving a negative response to the question, "Are there any known independence problems?" Thomas prepared and signed OAD's report on Xenerex's financial statements and annual report filed on Form 10-K with the SEC. Has Thomas violated SEC Rule of Practice 2(e)?

10. While performing a routine audit of the tax returns of Amerada Hess Corporation, the Internal Revenue Service discovered questionable payments of $7,830. The IRS issued a summons to Arthur Young & Co., the accounting firm that had prepared the tax accrual working papers that might reveal the nature of the payments. The working papers had been prepared in the process of Arthur Young's review of Amerada Hess's financial statements, as required by federal securities law. In the summons, the IRS ordered Arthur Young to make available to the IRS all of its Amerada Hess files, including its tax accrual working papers. Amerada Hess directed Arthur Young not to comply with the summons on the grounds that they were protected by an accountant-client privilege. Is Amerada Hess correct?

PART XI

REGULATION OF BUSINESS

CHAPTER 46

ADMINISTRATIVE AGENCIES

INTRODUCTION

One of the basic themes of this part of this textbook is that businesses today operate in a highly regulated environment. The fundamental vehicle for the creation and enforcement of modern regulation has been the **administrative agency.** Administrative agencies are governmental bodies other than courts or legislatures that have the legal power to take actions affecting the rights of private individuals and organizations. In *FTC v. Ruberoid Co.*,[1] Supreme Court Justice Robert H. Jackson said:

> The rise of administrative bodies probably has been the most significant legal trend of the last century and perhaps more values today are affected by their decisions than by those of all of the courts, review of administrative decisions apart. They also have begun to have important consequences on personal rights. . . . They have become a veritable fourth branch of the Government, which has deranged our three-branch legal theories as much as the concept of a fourth dimension unsettles our three-dimensional thinking.

Although this chapter focuses on federal administrative agencies, you should understand that the great growth in *federal* regulation we have experienced in this century has been accompanied by a comparable growth in *state and local* regulation and state and local regulatory agencies.

It is difficult to think of an area of modern individual life that is not somehow touched by the action of administrative agencies. The energy that heats and lights your home and workplace, the clothes you wear, the food you eat, the medicines you take, the design of the car you drive, the programs you watch on television, and the contents of (and label on) the pillow on which you lay your head at night are all shaped in some way by regulation.

If anything, this observation is even more appropriate to corporations than to individuals. Virtually every significant aspect of contemporary corporate operations is regulated to the point that the *legal* consequences of a corporation's actions are nearly as important to its future success as the *business* consequences of its decisions.

Because administrative agencies have enormous power and some novel characteristics, they have always been objects of controversy. Are they protectors of the public or impediments to business efficiency? Are they guardians of competitive market structures or a shield behind which noncompetitive firms have sought refuge

---

[1]343 U.S. 470 (U.S. Sup. Ct. 1952).

from more vigorous competitors? Have they been impartial, efficient agents of the public interest or are they more often overzealous, or inept, or "captives" of the industries they supposedly regulate? At various times, and where various agencies are concerned, each of the above allegations has probably been true. Why, then, did we resort to such controversial entities to perform the regulatory function?

The Origins of Administrative Agencies

In the latter decades of the 19th century, the United States was in the midst of a dramatic transformation from an agrarian nation to a major industrial power. Improved means of transportation and communication facilitated a dramatic market expansion. Large business organizations acquired unheard of economic power, and new technologies promised additional social transformations.

The tremendous growth that resulted from these developments, however, was not attained without some cost. Large organizations sometimes abused their power at the expense of their customers, distributors, and competitors. New technologies often posed risks of harm to large numbers of citizens. Yet traditional institutions of legal control, such as courts and legislatures, were not particularly well suited to the regulatory needs of an increasingly complex, interdependent society in the throes of rapid change.

Courts, after all, are passive institutions that must await a genuine "case or controversy" before they can act.[2] Courts also may lack the technical expertise necessary to address many regulatory issues intelligently. In addition, they are constrained by the formalistic rules of procedure and evidence that make litigation a time-consuming and expensive process.

Legislatures, on the other hand, are theoretically able to anticipate social problems and to act in a comprehensive fashion to minimize or avoid social harm. In reality, however, legislatures rarely act until a problem has become severe enough to generate strong political support for a regulatory solution. And like courts, legislatures may lack the expertise necessary to make rational policy regarding highly technical activities.

What was needed, therefore, appeared to be a new type of governmental entity: one exclusively devoted to monitoring a particular area of activity; one that could,

by its exclusive focus and specialized hiring practices, develop a reservoir of expertise about the object of its efforts; and one that could provide the continuous attention and constant policy development demanded by a rapidly changing environment. Such new entities, it was thought, could best perform their regulatory tasks if they were given considerable latitude in the procedures they followed and the approaches they took to achieve regulatory goals.

In 1887, the modern regulatory era was born when Congress, in response to complaints about discriminatory ratemaking practices by railroads, passed the Interstate Commerce Act. This statute created the Interstate Commerce Commission and gave it the power to regulate transportation industry ratemaking practices. Thereafter, new administrative agencies have been added whenever pressing social problems (such as the threat to competition that led to the creation of the Federal Trade Commission) or new technologies, such as aviation (Federal Aviation Administration), communications (Federal Communications Commission), and nuclear power (Nuclear Regulatory Commission), have generated a political consensus in favor of regulation. More recently, developing scientific knowledge about the dangers that modern technologies and industrial processes pose to the environment and to industrial workers has led to the creation of new federal agencies empowered to regulate environmental pollution (Environmental Protection Agency) and to promote workplace safety (Occupational Safety and Health Administration). The following sections examine the legal dimensions of the process by which such administrative agencies are created.

AGENCY CREATION

Enabling Legislation

Administrative agencies are statutorily created when Congress passes **enabling legislation** specifying the name, composition, and powers of the agency. For example, consider the following language from section 1 of the Federal Trade Commission Act:

> A commission is created and established, to be known as the Federal Trade Commission, which shall be composed of five commissioners, who shall be appointed by the President, by and with the advice and consent of the Senate.

This section creates the Federal Trade Commission (FTC). Section 5 of the FTC Act prohibits "unfair

---

[2]The "case or controversy" requirement is discussed in the Resolution of Private Disputes chapter.

methods of competition" and "unfair or deceptive acts or practices in commerce" and empowers the FTC to prevent such practices.[3] Section 5 also describes the procedures the Commission must follow to charge persons or organizations with violations of the act and provides for judicial review of agency orders. Subsequent portions of the statute give the FTC the power "to make rules and regulations for the purpose of carrying out the provisions of the Act," to conduct investigations of business practices, to require reports from interstate corporations concerning their practices and operations, to investigate possible violations of the antitrust laws,[4] to publish reports concerning its findings and activities, and to recommend new legislation to Congress.

Thus, Congress has given the FTC powers typically associated with the three traditional branches of government. Like the courts, it can *adjudicate* disputes concerning alleged violations of the statute; like the executive branch, it can *investigate* and *prosecute* alleged violations; and like the legislative branch, it can *promulgate rules* that have binding legal effect on future behavior. The broad mix of governmental powers typically possessed by modern administrative agencies such as the FTC makes these agencies potentially powerful agents of social control.

But great power to do good can also be great power to do evil. Regulatory bias, zeal, insensitivity, or corruption, if left unchecked, can infringe on the basic freedoms that are the essence of our system of government. Accordingly, the fundamental problem in administrative law, a problem that will surface repeatedly throughout the remainder of this chapter, is how to design a system of control over agency action that minimizes the potential for arbitrariness and harm yet preserves the power and flexibility that make administrative agencies uniquely valuable instruments of public policy.

Administrative Agencies and the Constitution

Because administrative agencies are governmental bodies, administrative action is *governmental action* and, as such, is subject to the basic constitutional checks discussed in the Business and the Constitution Chapter. As the *Mallen* case, which follows, demonstrates, this "fourth branch of government" is bound by basic constitutional guarantees such as *due process, equal protection*, and *freedom of speech*, just like the three traditional branches. However, one basic constitutional principle is uniquely important when the creation of administrative agencies is at issue: the principle of **separation of powers.**

One of the fundamental attributes of our Constitution is its dispersion of governmental power among the three branches of government. Lawmaking power is given to the legislative branch, law-enforcing power to the executive branch, and law-interpreting power to the judicial branch. By limiting the powers of each branch, and by giving each branch some checks on the exercise of power by the other branches, the Constitution seeks to assure that governmental power remains accountable to the public will. In reality, of course, this separation is never perfectly complete. As you learned in the chapter The Nature of Law, courts often "make" law when developing common law doctrines or interpreting broadly worded statutes. Likewise, the Merger Guidelines[5] of the Department of Justice (part of the executive branch) do not technically have the force of law, but nonetheless may play a major role in shaping behavior.

Administrative agencies, exercising powers resembling those of each of the three branches of government, create obvious concerns about separation of powers. In particular, the congressional delegation of legislative power to an agency in its enabling legislation may be challenged as violating the separation of powers principle if such legislation is so broadly worded as to indicate that Congress has abdicated its lawmaking responsibilities. Early judicial decisions exploring the manner in which Congress could delegate its power tended to require enabling legislation to contain fairly specific guidelines and standards limiting the exercise of agency discretion.

More recently, the courts have tended to sustain quite broad delegations of power to administrative agencies. For example, section 5 of the FTC Act is a broad delegation of power. A great range of unspecified behavior falls within the statute's prohibition of "unfair methods of competition" and "unfair or deceptive acts or practices." Modern courts tend to approve broad delegations of power when Congress has expressed an "intelligible principle" to guide the agency's actions.[6]

---

[3]Section 5 of the FTC Act is discussed in detail in the Federal Trade Commission Act and Consumer Protection Laws chapter.

[4]The antitrust laws are discussed in detail in the Sherman Act chapter and the Clayton Act chapter.

[5] The Justice Department's Merger Guidelines are discussed in the Clayton Act chapter.

[6]*J. W. Hampton, Jr. & Co. v. United States*, 276 U.S. 394 (U.S. Sup. Ct. 1928).

FEDERAL DEPOSIT INSURANCE CORP. v. MALLEN

486 U.S. 230 (U.S. Sup. Ct. 1988)

On December 10, 1986, James Mallen was indicted by a federal grand jury in Iowa for making false statements to the Federal Deposit Insurance Corporation (FDIC) and for making false statements to Farmers State Bank for the purpose of influencing the actions of the FDIC. At the time of the indictment, Mallen was the president and a director of a federally insured bank. On January 20, 1987, the FDIC issued an *ex parte* order finding that Mallen's continued service might "pose a threat to the interests of the bank's depositors or threaten to impair public confidence in the bank," suspending him as president and as a director of the bank, and prohibiting him "from further participation in any manner in the conduct of the affairs of the Bank, or any other bank insured by the FDIC."

In issuing the suspension order without first holding a hearing on the matter, the FDIC was acting pursuant to a section of the Financial Institutions Supervisory Act of 1966 [12 U.S.C. section 1818(g)]. A copy of the order was served on Mallen on January 26, 1987, and four days later Mallen's attorney filed a written request for an "immediate administrative hearing" to commence no later than February 9, 1987. The FDIC set a hearing date for February 18, 1987, but on February 6, 1987, Mallen filed suit against the FDIC in the Federal District Court for the Northern District of Iowa. When the District Court ruled in Mallen's favor, entering a preliminary injunction against the suspension order, the FDIC appealed.

Stevens, Justice.   The District Court expressed no opinion on the merits of the suspension; its decision rested entirely on the perceived procedural shortcomings in the post-suspension process. It is undisputed that Mallen's interest in the right to continue to serve as president of the bank and to participate in the conduct of its affairs is a property right protected by the Fifth Amendment Due Process Clause. The FDIC cannot arbitrarily interfere with Mallen's employment relationship with the bank, nor with his interest as a substantial stockholder in the bank's holding company. It is also undisputed that the FDIC's order affected a deprivation of this property interest.

Once it is determined that due process applies, the question remains what process is due. Mallen does not contend that he was entitled to an opportunity to be heard prior to the order of suspension. An important governmental interest, accompanied by a substantial assurance that the deprivation is not baseless or unwarranted, may in limited cases demanding prompt action justify postponing the opportunity to be heard until after the initial deprivation. In this case, the postponement of the hearing is supported by such an interest. The legislation under scrutiny is premised on the congressional finding that prompt suspension of indicted bank officers may be necessary to protect the interests of depositors and to maintain public confidence in our banking institutions.

Moreover, Mallen's suspension was supported by findings that assure that the suspension was not baseless. A grand jury had determined that there was probable cause to believe that he had committed a felony. Such an *ex parte* finding of probable cause provides sufficient basis for an arrest, which of course consitutes a temporary deprivation of liberty. It should certainly be sufficient to support the order entered in this case even though the FDIC did not provide Mallen with a separate pre-suspension hearing.

We cannot agree with the District Court that Mallen was denied a sufficiently prompt post-deprivation hearing. The District Court was properly concerned about the importance of providing prompt post-deprivation procedures in situations in which an agency's discretionary impairment of an individual's property is not preceded by an opportunity for a pre-deprivation hearing. However, the District Court seems to have been improperly concerned with the danger of an interminable delay by the agency, rather than by what would have happened in this case if the proceedings had not been interrupted, or indeed, if the FDIC had been as dilatory as the statute permits. For even though there is a point at which an unjustified delay in completing a post-deprivation proceeding would become a constitutional violation, the significance of such a delay cannot be evaluated in a vacuum.

Section 1818(g)(3) requires the FDIC to hold a hearing within 30 days of a written request for an opportunity to appear before the agency to contest a suspension and requires that it notify the suspended officer of its decision within 60 days of the hearing. Thus, at a maximum, the suspended officer receives a decision with 90 days of his or her request for a hearing. In this case, the agency reported that it would have been able to issue a written decision within 30 days after the hearing. In addition, the initial hearing was scheduled to take place 19 days after it was formally requested.

Mallen's interest in continued employment is without doubt an important interest that ought not be interrupted without substantial justification. Yet, even assuming that the FDIC required the complete 90 days to hear the case and reach its decision, we are not persuaded that this exceeds permissible limits. In fact, a suspended bank officer has an interest in seeing that a decision concerning his or her continued suspension is not made with excessive haste. The statute imposes a permissive standard for continuing a suspension, and presumably, when in doubt, the agency may give greater weight to the public interest and leave the suspension in place, particularly when the suspension does not impose the additional harm of a significant, incremental injury to reputation. Through the return of an indictment, the Government has already accused Mallen of serious wrongdoing. The incidental suspension is not likely to augment this injury to his reputation. We thus conclude that the 90 day period is not so long that it will always violate due process.

In many cases, perhaps most, it will be justified by an important government interest coupled with factors minimizing the risk of an erroneous deprivation. The magnitude of the public interest in a correct decision counsels strongly against any constitutional imperative that might require overly hasty decisionmaking. Congress has determined that the integrity of the banking industry requires that indicted bank officers be suspended until it is determined that they do not pose a threat to the interests of the bank's depositors or threaten to undermine public confidence in the bank. To return these officers to a position of influence in the conduct of the bank's affairs prior to an opportunity to weigh the evidence carefully would threaten these interests in the same way as allowing them to remain in office from the start.

Moreover, there is little likelihood that the deprivation is without basis. The returning of the indictment establishes that an independent body has determined that there is probable cause to believe that the officer has committed a crime. This finding is relevant in at least two important ways. First, the finding of probable cause by an independent body demonstrates that the suspension is not arbitrary. Second, the indictment itself is an objective fact that will in most cases raise serious public concern that the bank is not being managed in a responsible manner.

The post-suspension procedure authorized by section 1818(g)(3) is not unconstitutional on its face; nor do we find any unfairness in the FDIC's use of that procedure in this case.

District Court preliminary injunction reversed.

AGENCY TYPES AND ORGANIZATION

Agency Types

Administrative agencies may be found under a variety of labels. They may be called "administration," "agency," "authority," "board," "bureau," "commission," "department," "division," or "service." They sometimes have a governing body, which may be appointed or elected. They almost inevitably have an administrative head (variously called "Chairman," "Commissioner," "Director," etc.), and a staff. Since our focus is on federal administrative agencies, it is important for us to distinguish between the two basic types of federal administrative agencies: executive agencies and "independent" agencies.

Executive Agencies   Administrative agencies that reside within the Executive Office of the President or within the executive departments of the president's cabinet are called **executive agencies.** Examples of such executive agencies and their cabinet homes are: the Food and Drug Administration (Department of Health and Human Services); the Nuclear Regulatory Agency and the Federal Energy Regulatory Agency (Department of Energy); the Occupational Safety and Health Administration (Department of Labor); and the Internal Revenue Service (Treasury Department). In addition to their executive home, such agencies share one other important attribute: Their administrative heads serve "at the pleasure of the President"—they are appointed and removable at his will.

Independent Agencies   The Interstate Commerce Commission was the first independent administrative agency created by Congress. Much of the most significant regulation businesses face emanates from independent agencies such as the FTC, the National Labor Relations Board, the Consumer Product Safety Commission, the Equal Employment Opportunity Commission, the Environmental Protection Agency, and the Securities and Exchange Commission. Independent agencies are usually headed by a board or a commission (e.g., the FTC has five commissioners) whose members are appointed by the president "with the advice and consent of the Senate." Commissioners or board members are usually appointed for fixed terms (e.g., FTC commissioners serve seven-year, staggered terms) and are removable only for cause (e.g., FTC commissioners may be removed only for "inefficiency, neglect of duty, or

malfeasance in office"). Finally, it is quite common for enabling legislation to require political balance in agency appointments (e.g., the FTC Act provides that "Not more than three of the commissioners shall be members of the same political party").

Agency Organization

As the organizational chart of the FTC reproduced in Figure 1 indicates, an agency's organizational structure is largely a function of its regulatory mission. Thus, the operational side of the FTC is divided into three bureaus: the Bureau of Competition, which enforces the antitrust laws and unfair competitive practices; the Bureau of Consumer Protection, which focuses on unfair or deceptive trade practices; and the Bureau of Economics, which gathers data, compiles statistics, and furnishes technical assistance to the other bureaus. The Commission is headquartered in Washington, D.C., but it also maintains regional offices in Atlanta, Boston, Chicago, Cleveland, Dallas, Denver, Los Angeles, New York, San Francisco, and Seattle. This regional office system enhances the Commission's enforcement, investigative, and educational missions by locating Commission staff closer to the public it serves.

AGENCY POWERS AND PROCEDURES

Introduction

The powers administrative agencies possess may be classified in a variety of ways. Some agencies' powers are largely *ministerial* in nature, concerned primarily with the routine performance of duties imposed by law. The most important administrative agencies, however, have broad *discretionary* powers that necessitate the exercise of significant discretion and judgment when they are employed. The most important formal discretionary powers agencies can possess are **investigative power, rulemaking power,** and **adjudicatory power.**

The formal powers an agency possesses are those granted by its enabling legislation. Important federal agencies like the FTC normally enjoy significant levels of each of the formal discretionary powers. But, as the following sections illustrate, even such powerful agencies face significant limitations on the exercise of their powers. In addition to explicit limits on agency proceedings contained in enabling legislation, basic constitutional provisions restrict agency action.

FIGURE 1   Federal Trade Commission

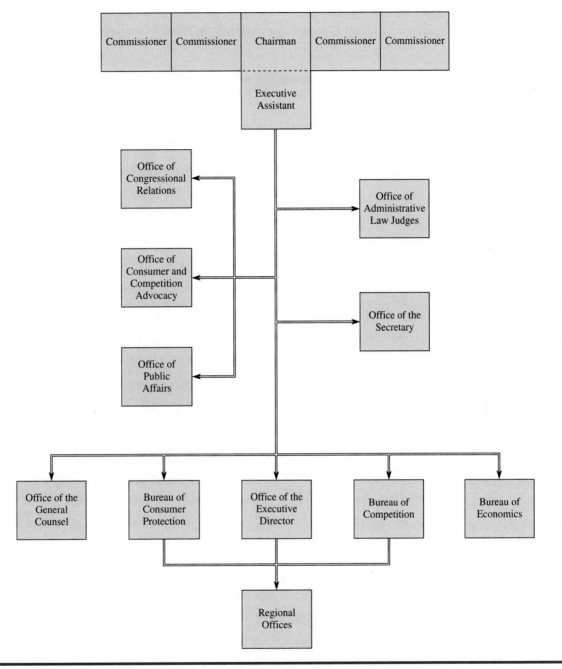

Source: *U.S. Government Manual 1989–90* (Washington, D.C.: U.S. Government Printing Office, 1989), p. 603.

A federal agency's exercise of its rulemaking and adjudicatory powers is also constrained by the **Administrative Procedure Act** (APA). The APA was enacted by Congress in 1946 in an attempt to standardize federal agency procedures and to respond to critics who said that administrative power was out of control. The APA applies to all federal agencies, although it will not displace stricter procedural requirements contained in a particular agency's enabling legislation. In addition to specifying agency procedures, the APA plays a major role in shaping the conditions under which courts will review agency actions and the standards courts will use when conducting such a review. Most states have adopted "baby APAs" to govern the activities of state administrative agencies.

Finally, as later parts of this chapter will confirm, each of the three traditional branches of government possesses substantial powers to mold and constrain the powers of the "fourth branch." That being said, one final point needs to be made before we turn to a detailed examination of formal agency powers and procedures. An agency's formal powers also confer on it significant *informal* power. Agency "advice," "suggestions," or "guidelines," which technically lack the legal force of formal agency regulations or rulings, may nonetheless play a major role in shaping the behavior of regulated industries because they carry with them the implicit or explicit threat of formal agency action in the event that they are ignored. Such gentle persuasion can be a highly effective regulatory tool, and one that is subject to far fewer constraints than formal agency action.

Investigative Power

Effective regulation is impossible without accurate information. Administrative agencies need information about business practices and activities not only so that they can detect and prosecute regulatory violations, but also to enable them to identify areas in which new rules are needed or existing rules are in need of modification. Much of the information agencies require to do their jobs is readily available. "Public interest" groups, complaints from customers or competitors, and other regulatory agencies are all important sources of information.

However, much of the information necessary to effective agency enforcement can come only from sources that may be strongly disinclined to provide it: the individuals and business organizations who are subject to regulation. This reluctance may be due to the desire to avoid or delay the regulation or regulatory action that

disclosure would generate. It might also, however, be the product of more legitimate concerns, such as a desire to protect personal privacy, a desire to prevent competitors from acquiring trade secrets and other sensitive information from agency files, or a reluctance to incur the costs that sometimes can accompany compliance with substantial information demands. Agencies, therefore, need the means to compel unwilling possessors of information to comply with legitimate demands for information. The two most important (and most intrusive) investigative tools employed by administrative agencies are *subpoenas* and *searches and seizures*.

Subpoenas There are two basic types of subpoena: the subpoena *ad testificandum* and the subpoena *duces tecum*. Subpoenas *ad testificandum* can be used by an agency to compel unwilling witnesses to appear and testify at agency hearings. Subpoenas *duces tecum* can be used by an agency to compel the production of most types of documentary evidence, such as accounting records and office memoranda.

It should be obvious that unlimited agency subpoena power would sacrifice individual liberty and privacy in the name of regulatory efficiency. Accordingly, the courts have formulated a number of limitations that seek to balance an agency's legitimate need to know against an investigated target's legitimate privacy interests.

Agency investigations must be *authorized by law* and *conducted for a legitimate purpose*. The former requirement means that the agency's enabling legislation must have granted the agency the investigative power that it is seeking to assert. The latter requirement prohibits bad faith investigations pursued for improper motives (e.g., Internal Revenue Service investigations undertaken solely to harass political opponents of an incumbent administration).

Even when the investigation is legally authorized and is undertaken for a legitimate purpose, the information sought must be *relevant to that lawful purpose*, as is illustrated in the *Larouche* case, which follows. The Fourth Amendment to the Constitution is the source of this limitation on agency powers. However, an agency seeking the issuance of an administrative subpoena need not demonstrate the "probable cause" that the Fourth Amendment requires for the issuance of regular search warrants.[7] In the words of the Supreme Court, an

---

[7]The Fourth Amendment "warrant clause" is discussed in detail in the Crimes chapter.

agency "can investigate merely on the suspicion that the law is being violated, or even just because it wants assurance that it is not."[8] This lesser standard makes sense in the agency context, since the only evidence of many regulatory violations is documentary and, therefore, "probable cause" might be demonstrable only after inspection of the target's records. In such cases, a probable cause requirement would effectively negate agency enforcement power.

Similarly, agency information demands must be *sufficiently specific* and *not unreasonably burdensome.* This requirement also derives from the Fourth Amendment's prohibition against "unreasonable searches and seizures,"[9] and it means that agency subpoenas must describe adequately the information the agency seeks. It also means that the cost to the target of complying with the agency's demand (e.g., the cost of assembling and reproducing the data, of disruption of business operations, or the risk that proprietary information will be indirectly disclosed to competitors) must not be unreasonably disproportionate to the agency's interest in obtaining the information.

Finally, the information sought *must not be privileged.* Various statutory and common law privileges can, at times, limit an agency's power to compel the production of information. However, by far the most important privilege in this respect is the Fifth Amendment *privilege against compulsory testimonial self-incrimination,* or "the right to silence." As you learned in the Crimes chapter, however, this privilege is subject to serious limitations in the business context. The "right to silence" in the administrative context is further limited by the fact that it is only available in *criminal* proceedings. In some regulatory contexts, the potential sanctions for violation may be labeled "civil penalties" or "forfeitures." Only when such sanctions are essentially punitive in their intent or effect will they be considered "criminal" for the purpose of allowing the invocation of the privilege.

---

[8]*United States v. Morton Salt*, 338 U.S. 632 (U.S. Sup. Ct. 1950).

[9]The Fourth Amendment guarantee against unreasonable searches and seizures is discussed in detail in the Crimes chapter.

FEDERAL ELECTION COMMISSION v. LAROUCHE CAMPAIGN, INC.

817 F.2d 233 (2d Cir. 1987)

In November 1984, the Federal Election Commission (FEC) began an investigation of the activities of the Lyndon Larouche Campaign for the Democratic Party's presidential nomination. The investigation centered on allegations that the campaign had falsified its records and obtained federal election matching funds by claiming that donations via credit cards had been made by individuals who denied making the donations. In December 1984, the FEC issued a subpoena requiring the campaign to produce records regarding the solicitation of contributions (including the names of solicitors and those solicited), contributions actually received, and all telephone records regarding the solicitation of funds. When the Larouche campaign failed to comply with the subpoena, the FEC brought an action in a federal district court to obtain enforcement. The district court ordered the campaign to comply with the subpoena. The Larouche campaign appealed.

Per Curiam.   In ordinary circumstances, the district court's analysis of this case would be entirely unobjectionable. As is nearly always appropriate, the court accorded substantial deference to the administrative subpoena and applied the familiar test that enforces such a subpoena so long as it is for a proper purpose, the information sought is relevant to that purpose, and the statutory procedures are observed. However, different considerations come into play when a case implicates First Amendment concerns. In that circumstance, the usual deference to the administrative agency is not appropriate, and the protection of the constitutional liberties of the target of the subpoena calls for a more exacting scrutiny of the justification offered by the agency.

The district court erred in holding essentially that because the campaign had not made a showing that disclosure of those associated with it was likely to result in reprisals, harrassment, or threats, the FEC needed only to show the information sought was relevant to the FEC's investigation. In an area rife with First Amendment associational concerns, an admininstrative agency is not automatically entitled to obtain all material that may in some way be relevant to a proper investigation. Rather, when the disclosure sought will compromise the privacy of individual political associations, and hence risks a chilling of unencumbered associational choices, the agency must make some showing of need for the material sought beyond its mere relevance to a proper investigation.

Here, the FEC has failed to make such a showing with regard to the identities of the campaign's solicitors. The focus of the instant investigation is the campaign's suspected use of credit card fraud to obtain contributions that may not have been authorized at all. Investigating such charges surely requires access to the list of contributors, who presumably can tell the FEC whether they did or did not make the claimed donations. But the FEC has not established that once it has access to the list of contributors, it also would have a need to identify the campaign's solicitors that would outweigh the solicitors' First Amendment interests. Absent such a showing, the FEC has failed to demonstrate that there are governmental interests sufficiently important to outweigh the possibility of infringement of the exercise of First Amendment rights.

Thus, the order enforcing compliance with the FEC's subpoena is modified by striking from the subpoena the requirement for disclosure of the names of the campaign's solicitors.

Judgment in favor of the Federal Election Commission affirmed as modified.

Searches and Seizures Sometimes the evidence necessary to prove a regulatory violation can be obtained only by entering private property such as a home, an office, or a factory. When administrative agencies seek to gather information by such an entry, the Fourth Amendment's prohibition against unreasonable searches and seizures and its warrant requirement come into play. As the *Dow Chemical* case in the Crimes chapter indicates, the owners of commercial property, although afforded less Fourth Amendment protection than the owners of private dwellings, do have some legitimate expectations of privacy in their business premises.

Dow also illustrates, however, that not all agency information-gathering efforts will be considered so intrusive as to amount to a prohibited "search and seizure." In *Dow*, the Environmental Protection Agency's warrantless aerial photography of one of Dow's plants was upheld. Finally, in its most definitive statement on the subject to date, in *State of New York v. Burger*, the Supreme Court upheld the constitutionality of warrantless administrative inspections of the premises of "closely regulated" businesses so long as three criteria are satis-

fied.[10] There must be a substantial government interest in the regulatory scheme in question, the warrantless inspections must be necessary to further the scheme, and the inspection program must provide a constitutionally adequate substitute for a warrant by giving owners of commercial property adequate notice that their property is subject to inspection and by limiting the discretion of inspecting officers.

Rulemaking Power

An agency's rulemaking power derives from its enabling legislation. For example, the FTC Act gives the FTC the power "to make rules and regulations for the purpose of carrying out the provisions of this Act." The Administrative Procedure Act (APA) defines a rule as "an agency statement of general or particular applicability and future effect designed to complement, interpret or prescribe law or policy." All agency rules are compiled and published in the *Code of Federal Regulations*.

---

[10]482 U.S. 691 (U.S. Sup. Ct. 1987).

FIGURE 2   FTC Procedural Rule

---

§ 1.10 Advance notice of proposed rulemaking.

(a) Prior to the commencement of any trade regulation rule proceeding, the Commission shall publish in the FEDERAL REGISTER an advance notice of such proposed proceeding.

(b) The advance notice shall: (1) Contain a brief description of the area of inquiry under consideration, the objectives which the Commission seeks to achieve, and possible regulatory alternatives under consideration by the Commission; and (2) invite the response of interested persons with respect to such proposed rulemaking, including any suggestions or alternative methods for achieving such objectives.

(c) The advance notice shall be submitted to the Committee on Commerce, Science, and Transportation of the Senate and to the Committee on Interstate and Foreign Commerce of the House of Representatives.

(d) The Commission may, in addition to the publication of the advance notice, use such additional mechanisms as it considers useful to obtain suggestions regarding the content of the area of inquiry before publication of an initial notice of proposed rulemaking pursuant to § 1.11.

Source: 16 Code of Federal Regulations § 1.10 (1990).

Types of Rules   Administrative agencies create three types of rules: procedural rules, interpretive rules, and legislative rules. *Procedural rules* specify how the agency will conduct itself. Figure 2 provides an example of such a rule, which the FTC adopted to determine the manner in which notice of Commission rulemaking proceedings will be disseminated.

Interpretive rules are designed to advise regulated individuals and entities of the manner in which an agency interprets the statutes it enforces. Interpretive rules technically do not have the force of law and, therefore, are not binding on businesses or on the courts. However, courts engaged in interpreting regulatory statutes often give agency interpretations substantial weight in deference to the agency's familiarity with the statutes it administers and its presumed expertise in the general area being regulated. Business is also likely to pay attention to agency interpretive rules because such rules indicate the circumstances in which an agency is likely to take formal enforcement action. Figure 3 provides an example of an interpretive rule; in this case, an FTC rule interpreting the meaning of the term *consumer product* as used in the Magnuson-Moss Consumer Warranty Act.

Legislative rules, if they are consistent with an agency's enabling legislation and the Constitution, and if they are created in accordance with the procedures dictated by the APA, have the full force and effect of law and are binding on the courts, the public, and the agency. Figure 4 provides an example of an FTC legislative rule.

Given their greater relative importance, you should not be surprised to learn that the process by which legislative rules are promulgated, unlike the process by which procedural and interpretive rules are created, is highly regulated by the APA and closely scrutinized by the courts. At present, there are three basic types of agency rulemaking: informal rulemaking, formal rulemaking, and hybrid rulemaking.

Informal Rulemaking   Informal, or "notice and comment," rulemaking is the rulemaking method most commonly employed by administrative agencies that are not forced by their enabling legislation to follow the more stringent procedures of formal rulemaking. The informal rulemaking process commences with the publication in the *Federal Register* of a *"Notice of Proposed Rulemaking."* The APA requires that such notices contain: a statement of the time and place at which the proceedings will be held; a statement of the nature of the proceedings; a statement of the legal authority for the proceedings (usually the agency's enabling legislation); and either a statement of the terms of the proposed rule or a description of the subjects or issues to be addressed by the rule.

Publication of notice must then be followed by a *comment period* during which interested parties can submit to the agency written comments detailing their views about the proposed rule. After comments have been received and considered, the agency must publish the regulation in its final form in the *Federal Register*. As a general rule, the rule cannot become effective until at least 30 days after its final publication in the *Federal Register*. The APA, however, recognizes a "good cause" exception to the 30-day-waiting-period requirement, and to the notice-of-rulemaking requirement as well, when notice would be impractical, unnecessary, or contrary to the public interest.

From the above discussion, it should be apparent why agencies tend to favor the informal rulemaking process—it allows quick and efficient regulatory action. Such quickness and efficiency, however, are purchased at

---

FIGURE 3 FTC Interpretive Rule

---

§ 700.1 Products covered.

(a) The Act applies to written warranties on tangible personal property which is normally used for personal, family, or household purposes. This definition includes property which is intended to be attached to or installed in any real property without regard to whether it is so attached or installed. This means that a product is a "consumer product" if the use of that type of product is not uncommon. The percentage of sales or the use to which a product is put by any individual buyer is not determinative. For example, products such as automobiles and typewriters which are used for both personal and commercial purposes come within the definition of consumer product. Where it is unclear whether a particular product is covered under the definition of consumer product, any ambiguity will be resolved in favor of coverage.

Source: 16 Code of Federal Regulations § 700.1 (1990).

FIGURE 4 FTC Legislative Rule

---

§ 417.6 The rule.

The Commission hereby promulgates, as a Trade Regulation Rule, its conclusion and determination that in connection with the sale or offering for sale in commerce, as "commerce" is defined in the Federal Trade Commission Act, of quick-freeze aerosol spray products containing Fluorocarbon 12 (Dichlorodifluoromethane) designed for the frosting of beverage glasses it is an unfair or deceptive act or practice to fail to provide a clear and conspicuous warning on the labels of such products, that the contents thereof should not be inhaled in concentrated form and that injury or death may result from such inhalation. Examples of proper warning statements include:

(1) "WARNING: Use only as directed—inhalation of the concentrated vapors of this product is harmful and may cause death."

(2) "WARNING: Use only as directed—misuse of this product by inhaling its concentrated vapors is harmful and may cause death."

Source: 16 Code of Federal Regulations § 417.6 (1990).

---

a significant cost: a relatively minimal opportunity for interested parties to participate in the rule-formation process. Giving interested parties the opportunity to be heard may, in some cases, ultimately further regulatory goals. For example, the vigorous debate about a proposed rule that a public hearing can provide may contribute to the creation of more effective rules. Also, providing interested parties with what they perceive to be an adequate opportunity to participate in the rulemaking process helps to legitimatize that process and the rules it produces, thereby enhancing the chances of voluntary compliance by the regulated industry.

Formal Rulemaking Formal, or "on the record," rulemaking is designed to afford interested parties with a far greater opportunity to make their views heard than that afforded by informal rulemaking. Formal rulemaking, like informal rulemaking, begins with publication in the *Federal Register* of a "Notice of Proposed Rulemaking." Unlike the notice employed to announce informal rulemaking procedures, however, this notice must include notice of a time and place at which a public hearing concerning the proposed rule will be held.

Such hearings resemble trials in that the agency must produce evidence justifying the proposed regulation, and interested parties are likewise allowed to present evidence in opposition to it. Both sides are entitled to examine each other's exhibits and to cross-examine each other's witnesses. At the conclusion of the proceedings, the agency must prepare a formal, written document detailing its findings based on the evidence presented in the hearing.

While the formal rulemaking process affords interested parties greatly enhanced opportunities to be heard, this greater access is purchased at significant expense and at the risk that some parties will abuse their access rights to impede the regulatory process. By tireless cross-examination of government witnesses and lengthy presentations of their own, opponents seeking to derail or delay regulation may consume months, or even years, of agency time. The classic example of such behavior is the Food and Drug Administration's hearings on a proposed rule requiring that the minimum peanut content of peanut butter be set at 90 percent. Industry forces favored an 87 percent minimum and were able to delay regulation almost 10 years.

Hybrid Rulemaking   Frustration over the lack of access afforded by informal rulemaking and the potential for paralyzing the regulatory process that is inherent in formal rulemaking have led some courts and legislators to attempt the creation of a rulemaking process embodying some of the elements of informal and formal procedures. Although hybrid rulemaking procedures are insufficiently established and standardized at this point to permit a detailed discussion of them, some general tendencies are evident. Hybrid procedures, like formal rulemaking, involve some sort of hearing, but, unlike formal rulemaking procedures, hybrid procedures tend to limit the right of interested parties to cross-examine agency witnesses.

Adjudicatory Power

Most major federal agencies possess substantial adjudicatory powers. They not only have the power to investigate alleged violations and to produce regulations that have legal effect, they can also instigate and hold proceedings to determine whether regulatory or statutory violations have occurred. The administrative adjudication process is at once similar to, but substantially different from, the judicial process you studied in the Resolution of Private Disputes chapter.

The administrative adjudication process normally begins with a complaint filed by the agency. The party charged in the complaint (called the *respondent*) files an answer. Respondents are normally entitled to a hearing before the agency, at which they may be represented by legal counsel, confront and cross-examine agency witnesses, and present evidence of their own. No juries are present in administrative adjudications, however, and the cases are heard by an agency employee usually called an **administrative law judge** (ALJ). Also, unlike normal criminal prosecutions, the burden of proof in administrative proceedings is normally the civil *preponderance of the evidence* standard, and constitutional procedural safeguards such as the exclusionary rule do not protect the respondent.[11]

The agency, in effect, functions as police officer, prosecutor, judge, and jury. The APA attempts to deal with the obvious potential for abuse inherent in this combination in a number of ways. First, the APA attempts to assure that ALJs are as independent as possible by requiring internal separation between an agency's judges and its investigative and prosecutorial functions. Note, for example, the organizational separation of the FTC's Office of Administrative Law Judges illustrated in Figure 1. The APA also prohibits ALJs from having private (*ex parte*) consultations with anyone who is a party to an agency proceeding and shields them from agency disciplinary action other than for "good cause." Finally, insufficient separation between an agency's adjudication function and its other functions can be contrary to basic due process requirements.

After each party to the proceeding has been heard, the ALJ renders a decision stating her findings of fact and conclusions of law and imposing whatever penalty she deems appropriate within the parameters established by the agency's enabling legislation (e.g., a fine or a cease and desist order). If neither party challenges the ALJ's decision, it becomes final.

The losing party, however, may appeal an ALJ's decision, in which case it will be subjected to a **de novo review** by the governing body of the agency (e.g., appeals from FTC ALJ decisions are heard by the five FTC commissioners).[12] *De novo* review means that the agency can treat the proceedings as if they were occurring for the first time and may totally ignore the ALJ's findings. Often, however, an agency will adopt the ALJ's findings, and, in any event, such findings will be part of the record if a disappointed respondent seeks judicial review of an agency's decision.

Finally, when considering agency adjudicatory powers, it is important to note that many agency proceedings are settled by a **consent order** before completion of the adjudication process. Consent orders are similar to the nolo contendere pleas discussed in the Crimes chapter. Respondents who sign consent orders do not admit guilt, but they waive all rights to judicial review, agree to accept a specific sanction imposed by the agency, and commonly agree to discontinue the business practice that triggered the agency action. Figure 5 graphically depicts the major powers of the "fourth branch" of government.

[11]*INS v. Lopez-Mendoza*, 468 U.S. 1032 (U.S. Sup. Ct. 1984). The exclusionary rule and the "beyond a reasonable doubt" standard employed in criminal cases are discussed in the Crimes chapter. The "preponderance of the evidence" standard is discussed in the Intentional Torts chapter.

[12]For an example of a decision by the full Federal Trade Commission, see the *International Harvester* case in the Federal Trade Commission Act and Consumer Protection Laws chapter.

FIGURE 5   Administrative Agencies and Separation of Powers

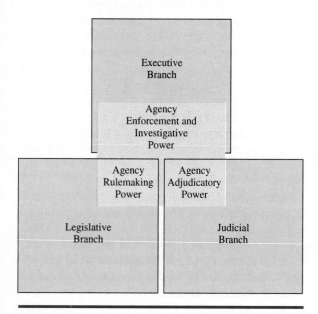

CONTROLLING ADMINISTRATIVE AGENCIES

Introduction

At this point in our discussion of administrative agencies, we have already encountered several legal controls on agency action, such as the terms of an agency's enabling legislation, the procedural requirements imposed by the APA, and the basic constraints that the Constitution places on all governmental action. The following sections continue to focus on the important theme of agency control by examining the various devices, both formal and informal, by which the three traditional branches of government influence and control the actions of the "fourth branch."

Presidential Controls

The executive branch has at its disposal a number of tools that can be employed to shape agency action. The most obvious among them is the president's power to appoint and remove agency administrators. For example you will learn in later chapters that President Reagan's appointees to the Department of Justice and the FTC made major changes in governmental antitrust enforcement policies because of their commitment to "Chicago School" antitrust ideas. This presidential power is obvi-

ously more limited in the case of "independent" agencies than it is where executive agencies are concerned, but the president generally has the power to appoint the chairmen of independent agencies, demoting the prior chairman without cause. Skillful use of the new chair's managerial powers, the most important of which is probably the power to influence agency hiring policies, can eventually effect substantial changes in agency policy. Also, significant and sustained policy differences between an independent agency and the executive branch often eventually trigger resignations by agency commissioners, thus providing the president with the opportunity to appoint new members whose philosophies are more congruent with his own.

The executive branch also exercises significant control over agency action through the Office of Management and Budget (OMB). The OMB plays a major role in the creation of the annual executive budget the president presents to Congress. In the process, the OMB reviews, and sometimes modifies, the budgetary requests of executive agencies. In addition, by Executive Order 12291,[13] President Reagan directed all executive agencies to prepare cost-benefit and least-cost analyses for all major proposed rules and to submit such proposals to the OMB for review prior to seeking public comments. This and a subsequent executive order requiring agencies to give the OMB "early warning" as soon as the agency begins to contemplate a possible rule change have made the OMB a powerful player in the rulemaking process.

Finally, the president's power to *veto* legislation concerning administrative agencies represents another point of executive influence over agency operations.

Congressional Controls

Like the executive branch, the legislative branch possesses a number of devices, both formal and informal, by which it can influence agency action. Obvious avenues of congressional control include the Senate's "advice and consent" role in agency appointments, the power to amend an agency's enabling legislation (what Congress has given, Congress can take away), and the power to pass legislation that mandates changes in agency practices or procedures. Examples of the latter include the National Environmental Policy Act (NEPA), which dictated that administrative agencies file *environmental*

---

[13]46 *Federal Register* 13193 (1981).

impact statements for every agency action that might significantly affect the quality of the environment,[14] and the Regulatory Flexibility Act of 1980, which ordered changes in agency rulemaking procedures designed to give small businesses improved notice of agency rule-making activities that may have a substantial impact on them. Congress can also pass *sunset legislation* providing for the automatic expiration of an agency's authority unless Congress expressly extends it by a specified date. Such legislation ensures periodic congressional review of the initial decision to delegate legislative authority to an administrative agency.

Congress also enjoys several other less obvious, but no less important, points of influence over agency action. For example, Congress must authorize agency budgetary appropriations. Thus, Congress may limit or deny funding for agency programs with which it disagrees. Also, the Governmental Operations Committees of both houses of Congress exercise significant oversight over agency activities, reviewing agency programs, and conducting hearings concerning proposed agency appointments and appropriations. Finally, individual members of Congress may seek to influence agency action through "casework"—informal contacts with an agency on behalf of constituents who are involved with the agency.

Judicial Review

As important as the roles of the executive and legislative branches are in controlling agency action, the courts exercise the greatest amount of control over agency behavior. This may be due, in part, to the fact that they are the branch of government most accessible to members of the public aggrieved by agency action. The APA provides for judicial review of most agency action, which takes place either in one of the U.S. courts of appeals or a U.S. district court, depending on the nature of the agency action at issue. The Supreme Court, if it chooses to grant certiorari, is the court of last resort for review of agency action.[15]

The Right to Judicial Review   Not all agency actions are subject to judicial review and only certain individuals may challenge those that are reviewable. Individuals or organizations seeking judicial review must satisfy a number of threshold requirements. First, plaintiffs must demonstrate the **reviewability** of the challenged action. Ordinarily, this is not very difficult because the APA creates a strong presumption in favor of reviewability. As indicated by the *Webster* case, which follows, this presumption may be overcome only by a showing that "statutes preclude review" or that the decision in question is "committed to agency discretion by law." These limitations on reviewability come from Congress's power to dictate the jurisdiction of the federal courts and from judicial deference to the proper functions of the other branches of government (e.g., a decision relating to matters of foreign policy is likely to be seen as outside the proper province of the judiciary).

Once reviewability has been established, plaintiffs need to demonstrate that they have **standing to sue,** that is, that they are "an aggrieved party" whose interests have been substantially affected by the challenged action. Initially, the courts took a relatively restrictive view of this basic requirement, requiring plaintiffs to show harm to a legally protected interest. More recently, however, the courts have liberalized the standing requirement somewhat, requiring plaintiffs to demonstrate that they have suffered an "injury" to an interest that lies within the "zone of interests" protected by the statute or constitutional provision that serves as the basis of their challenge. Demonstrating an economic loss remains the surest way to satisfy the "injury" requirement, but emotional, aesthetic, and environmental injuries have been found sufficient on occasion.

Once standing has been established, two further obstacles confront the aspiring plaintiff: **exhaustion** and **ripeness.** Courts do not want to allow regulated parties to short-circuit the regulatory process. They also want to give agencies the chance to correct their own mistakes and to develop fully their positions in disputed matters. Accordingly, they normally insist that aggrieved parties *exhaust available administrative remedies* before they will grant judicial review. The requirement that a dispute be *ripe* for judicial review is a general requirement emanating from the Constitution's insistence that only "cases or controversies" are judicially resolvable.[16] In determining ripeness, the courts weigh the hardship to the parties of withholding judicial review against the degree of refinement of the issues still possible (e.g., might further administrative action alter the nature of the issues or eliminate the need for judicial review?).

---

[14]NEPA and environmental impact statements are discussed in detail in the Environmental Regulation chapter.

[15]The Supreme Court's certiorari jurisdiction is discussed in the Resolution of Private Disputes chapter.

[16]Ripeness and the "case or controversy" requirement are discussed in the Resolution of Private Disputes chapter.

WEBSTER v. DOE

486 U.S. 592 (U.S. Sup. Ct. 1988)

John Doe began work at the Central Intelligence Agency (CIA or Agency) in 1973 as a clerk-typist. Periodic fitness reports consistently rated him as an excellent or outstanding employee, and by 1977 he had been promoted to covert electronics technician. In January 1982, Doe voluntarily told a CIA security officer that he was a homosexual. Almost immediately, the Agency placed Doe on paid administrative leave and began an investigation of his sexual orientation and conduct. Doe submitted to an extensive polygraph examination during which he denied having sexual relations with foreign nationals and maintained that he had not disclosed classified information to any of his sexual partners. The polygraph officer told Doe that the test results indicated that his responses had been truthful.

Nonetheless, a month later Doe was told that the Agency's Office of Security had determined that his homosexuality posed a threat to security, but declined to explain the nature of the danger. Doe was asked to resign, and when he refused to do so he was dismissed by CIA Director William Webster, who "deemed it necessary and advisable in the interests of the United States to terminate [Doe's] employment with this Agency pursuant to section 102(c) of the National Security Act." Doe filed suit against the CIA, arguing that his discharge was unconstitutional and violated the Administrative Procedure Act. The CIA moved to dismiss Doe's complaint, arguing that the director's decision was not subject to judicial review. After a federal district court and the Court of Appeals for the District of Columbia held that the decision was judicially reviewable, the Supreme Court granted certiorari.

Rehnquist, Chief Justice.   The APA's provisions allow any person "adversely affected or aggrieved" by an agency action to obtain judicial review, so long as the decision challenged represents a "final agency action for which there is no other adequate remedy in a court." Typically, a litigant will contest an action (or failure to act) by an agency on the ground that the agency has neglected to follow the statutory directives of Congress. Section 701(a), however, limits the application of the entire APA to situations in which judicial review is not precluded by statute [701(a)(1)], and the agency action is not committed to agency discretion by law [701(a)(2)].

In *Citizens to Preserve Overton Park v. Volpe* (1971), we explained the distinction between subsections 701(a)(1) and 701(a)(2). Subsection (a)(1) is concerned with whether Congress expressed an intent to prohibit judicial review; subsection (a)(2) applies in those rare instances where statutes are drawn in such broad terms that in a given case there is no law to apply. Under subsection 701(a)(2), even when Congress has not affirmatively precluded judicial oversight, review is not to be had if the statute is drawn so that a court would have no meaningful standard against which to judge the agency's exercise of discretion.

Subsection 701(a)(2) requires careful examination of the statute on which the claim of agency illegality is based. In the present case, Doe's claims against the CIA arise from the Director's asserted violation of section 102(c) of the National Security Act, which allows termination of an Agency employee whenever the Director "shall *deem* such termination necessary or advisable in the interests of the United States" (emphasis added), not simply when the dismissal *is* necessary or advisable to those interests. This standard fairly exudes deference to the Director, and appears to us to foreclose the application of any meaningful judicial standard of review. Short of permitting cross-examination of the Director concerning his views of the Nation's security and whether the discharged employee was inimical to those interests, we see no basis on which a reviewing court could properly assess an Agency termination decision. The language of section 102(c) thus strongly suggests that its implementation was "committed to agency discretion by law."

So too does the overall structure of the National Security Act. Passed shortly after the close of the Second World War, the NSA created the CIA and gave its Director the responsibility "for protecting intelligence sources and methods from unauthorized disclosure." Section 102(c) is an integral part of that statute, because the Agency's efficacy, and the Nation's security, depend in large measure on the reliability and trustworthiness of the Agency's employees. Employment with the CIA entails a high degree of trust that is perhaps unmatched in government service. We thus find that the language and structure of section 102(c) indicate that Congress meant to commit individual employee discharges to the Director's discretion, and that section 701(a)(2) accordingly precluded judicial review of these decisions under the APA.

In addition to his claim that the Director failed to abide by the statutory dictates of section 102(c), Doe also alleged that the Director's termination of his employment deprived him of property and liberty interests under the Due Process Clause, denied him equal protection of the laws, and unjustifiably burdened his right to privacy. We share the confusion of the Court of Appeals as to the precise nature of Doe's constitutional claims. It is difficult, if not impossible, to ascertain from the complaint whether Doe contends that his termination, based on *his* homosexuality, is constitutionally impermissible, or whether he asserts that a more pervasive discrimination policy exists in the CIA's employment practices regarding *all* homosexuals.

Webster maintains that, no matter what the nature of Doe's constitutional claim, judicial review is precluded by the language and intent of section 102(c). We do not think section 102(c) may be read to exclude review of constitutional claims. Where Congress intends to preclude judicial review of constitutional claims its intent to do so must be clear. Nothing in the language of section 102(c) persuades us that Congress meant to preclude consideration of colorable constitutional claims arising out of the actions of the Director pursuant to that section; we believe that a constitutional claim based on an individual discharge may be reviewed by the District Court.

Judgment of the Court of Appeals affirmed in part and reversed in part; case remanded for further proceedings.

The Bases for Judicial Review There are several legal theories on which agency action may be attacked. It may be alleged that the agency's action was *ultra vires* (exceeded its authority as granted by its enabling legislation) or that the agency substantially *deviated from procedural requirements* contained in the APA or in its enabling legislation. Agency action may also be challengeable as *unconstitutional* or, as illustrated by the following *Bowen* case, it may be attacked as the product of an *erroneous interpretation of statutes*. Finally, agency action may be reversible because it is *unsubstantiated by the facts* before the agency when it acted.

The Standards for Review The degree of scrutiny that courts will apply to agency action depends on the nature of issues under dispute and the type of agency proceedings that produced the challenged action. Courts are least likely to defer to agency action when *questions of law* are at issue. Although courts afford substantial consideration to an agency's interpretations of the statutes it enforces, the courts are still the ultimate arbiters of the meaning of statutes and constitutional provisions.

When *questions of fact* or *policy* are at issue, however, courts are more likely to defer to the agency because presumably it has superior expertise and because the agency fact finders who heard and viewed the evidence were better situated to judge its merit. When agency factual judgments are at stake, the APA provides for three standards of review, the most rigorous of which is *de novo* review.

When conducting a *de novo* review, courts make an independent finding of the facts after conducting a new hearing. Efficiency considerations plainly favor limited judicial review of the facts. Accordingly, *de novo* review is employed only when required by statute, when inadequate fact-finding proceedings were used in an agency adjudicatory proceeding, or when new factual issues that were not before the agency are raised in a proceeding to enforce a nonadjudicatory agency action.

When courts are reviewing formal agency adjudications or formal rulemaking, the APA calls for the application of a *substantial evidence* test. Only agency findings that are "unsupported by substantial evidence" will be overturned. In conducting "substantial evidence" reviews, courts look at the reasonableness of an agency's actions in relation to the facts before it rather than conducting an independent fact-finding hearing, such as that which is done in *de novo* reviews. For an example of an agency order that was set aside for failure to meet the "substantial evidence" test, see the *Tenneco* case in the

Clayton Act chapter. The substantial evidence test also tends to be employed in hybrid rulemaking cases.

The judicial standard of review used in cases involving informal agency adjudications or rulemaking is the *arbitrary and capricious* test. This is the least rigorous standard of judicial review, due to the great degree of deference it accords agency decisions. In deciding whether an agency's action was "arbitrary and capricious," a reviewing court theoretically should not substitute its judgment for that of the agency. Instead, it should ask whether there was an adequate factual basis for the agency's action, and should sustain actions that do not amount to a "clear error of judgment." While, in theory, the substantial evidence and arbitrary and capricious tests are separate and distinct, in practice, such distinctions often tend to blur.

BOWEN v. AMERICAN HOSPITAL ASSOCIATION
476 U.S. 610 (U.S. Sup. Ct. 1986)

In April 1982, the parents of an infant with Down's syndrome and other handicaps refused consent to surgery to remove an obstruction in the infant's esophagus that prevented oral feeding. In May 1982, after the child's death, the Secretary of Health and Human Services promulgated rules that, among other things, required hospitals and other health care providers to post notices that health care should not be withheld from infants on the basis of mental or physical handicap. The rules were adopted pursuant to section 504 of the Rehabilitation Act of 1973, which permits the head of any executive branch agency to promulgate rules prohibiting discrimination against an "otherwise qualified handicapped individual . . . solely by reason of his handicap." The American Hospital Association challenged the validity of the rules. The District Court found the rules invalid, and the Second Circuit Court of Appeals affirmed. The secretary appealed to the Supreme Court of the United States.

Stevens, Justice. It is an axiom of administrative law that an agency's explanation of the basis for its decision must include a rational connection between the facts found and the choice made. Agency deference has not come so far that we will uphold regulations whenever it is possible to conceive a basis for administrative action. The mere fact that there is some rational basis within the knowledge and experience of the agency under which it might have concluded that the regulation was necessary to discharge its statutorily authorized mission will not suffice to validate agency decisionmaking. Our recognition of Congress's need to vest administrative agencies with ample power to assist in the difficult task of governing a vast and complex Nation carries with it the correlative responsibility of the agency to explain the rationale and factual basis for its decision, even though we show respect for the agency's judgment in both.

Before examining the Secretary's reasons for issuing the Rules, it is essential to understand the pre-existing state-law framework governing the provision of medical care to handicapped infants. In broad outline, state law vests decisional responsibility in the parents, subject to review in exceptional cases by the State acting as *parens patriae*. Prior to the regulatory activity culminating in the Rules, the federal government was not a participant in the process of making treatment decisions for newborn infants. We presume that this general framework was familiar to Congress when it enacted section 504 of the Rehabilitation Act.

The Secretary contends that a hospital's refusal to furnish a handicapped infant with medically beneficial treatment solely by reason of its handicap constitutes unlawful discrimination. Yet the preamble to the Rules correctly states that when "a non-treatment decision, no matter how discriminatory, is made by parents, rather than by the hospital," section 504 does not mandate that the hospital unilaterally overrule the parental decision and provide treatment notwithstanding the lack of consent by the parents. A hospital's withholding of treatment when no parental consent has been given cannot violate section 504, for without the consent of the parents or a surrogate decisionmaker, the infant is neither "otherwise qualified" for treatment nor has he been denied care "solely by reason of his handicap." Indeed, it would almost certainly be a tort as a matter of state law to operate on an infant without parental consent. This analysis makes clear that the Secretary's heavy reliance on the analogy to race-based refusals is misplaced. If a hospital refused to operate on a black child whose parents had withheld their consent to treatment, the hospital's refusal would not be based on the race of the child even if it were assumed that the parents based *their decision* entirely on a mistaken assumption that the race of the child made the operation inappropriate.

The Rules are not needed to prevent hospitals from denying treatment to handicapped infants. The record contains no evidence that hospitals have ever refused treatment authorized either by the infant's parents or by a court order. In promulgating the Rules, the Secretary relied upon 49 cases that the Department of Health and Human Services had processed prior to December 1, 1983. Curiously, however, *none* of the 49 cases resulted in a finding of discriminatory withholding of medical care. In fact, in the entire list of 49 cases, there is no finding that a hospital failed or refused to provide treatment to a handicapped infant for which parental consent had been given.

The Secretary has substantial leeway to explore areas in which discrimination against the handicapped poses particularly significant problems and to devise regulations to prohibit such discrimination. Even according the greatest respect to the Secretary's action, however, deference cannot fill the lack of an evidentiary foundation on which the Rules must rest. The history of these Rules exposes the inappropriateness of the extraordinary deference—virtually a *carte blanche*—requested by the Secretary. The Secretary regards the mission of the Department of Health and Human Services as one principally concerned with the quality of medical care for handicapped infants rather than with the implementation of section 504. But nothing in the Rehabilitation Act authorizes the Secretary to dispense with the law's focus on discrimination and instead to employ federal resources to save the lives of handicapped newborns, without regard to whether they are victims of discrimination. Section 504 does not authorize the Secretary to give unsolicited advice either to parents or to hospitals who are faced with difficult treatment decisions concerning handicapped children.

Judgment for the American Hospital Association affirmed.

Information Controls

Over the last two decades, Congress has enacted three major statutes aimed at controlling administrative agencies through the regulation of information. Each of these statutes represents a compromise between competing social interests of significant importance. On one hand, we have a strong democratic preference for public disclosure of governmental operations, believing that "government in the dark" is less likely to be consistent with the public interest than is "government in the sunshine."

On the other hand, we also recognize that some sensitive governmental activities must be shielded from the scrutiny of unfriendly parties, and also that disclosure of some information can unjustifiably invade personal privacy, hinder government law enforcement efforts, and provide the competitors of a company about which information is being disclosed with proprietary information that could be used unfairly to the competitors' advantage.

The Freedom of Information Act   Congress passed the **Freedom of Information Act** (FOIA) in 1966 and later amended it in 1974. The FOIA was designed to enable private citizens to have access to documents in the government's possession. Agencies must respond to public requests for documents within 10 days after such a request has been received. An agency bears the burden of justifying any denial of any FOIA request, and denials are appealable to an appropriate federal district court. Successful plaintiffs may recover their costs and attorney's fees.

Not all government-held documents are obtainable under the FOIA, however. The FOIA exempts from disclosure documents that:

1. Must be kept secret in the interest of national security.

2. Concern an agency's internal personnel practices.

3. Are specifically exempted from disclosures by statute.

4. Contain trade secrets or other confidential or privileged commercial or financial information.

5. Reflect internal agency deliberations on matters of policy or proceedings.

6. Contain individual personnel or medical information if disclosure would constitute an invasion of privacy.

7. Would threaten the integrity of a law enforcement agency's investigations or jeopardize an individual's right to a fair trial.

8. Relate to the supervision or regulation of financial institutions.

9. Contain geological or geophysical data.

Frequent users of the FOIA include the media, industry trade associations, "public interest" groups, and companies seeking to obtain useful information about their competitors. It is important to note that although the FOIA allows agencies to refuse to disclose exempted documents, it does not impose on them the affirmative duty to do so. The Supreme Court has held that individuals cannot compel an agency to deny an FOIA request for allegedly exempt documents that contain sensitive information about them.[17]

The FOIA recently has been the focus of considerable controversy on two points. First, governmental budgetary cutbacks have combined with growing numbers of requests for information to produce agency delays as long as two years in responding to information requests. Courts tend to tolerate agency delays if the agency can show that it is making a "due-diligence" effort to respond. Second, the dramatic increase in computerized information storage that has occurred since the passage of the FOIA has created problems unanticipated by the statute, which focuses on information stored in documentary form. Do interested parties have the same rights of access to data stored in agency computers that they have to government documents? May the government destroy electronic mail messages, or must it save them? Future legislative or judicial action will be necessary to resolve such questions.

The Privacy Act of 1974   This federal statute allows individuals to inspect files that agencies maintain on them and to request that erroneous or incomplete records be corrected. It also attempts to prevent agencies from gathering unnecessary information about individuals and forbids the disclosure of an individual's records without his written permission, except in certain specifically exempted circumstances. For example, records may be disclosed to employees of the collecting agency who need them to perform their duties (the "need to know" exception), to law enforcement agencies, to other agencies' personnel for "routine use" (uses for purposes compatible with the purpose for which the record was collected), to persons filing legitimate FOIA requests, and pursuant to court order.

The Government in the Sunshine Act   The Government in the Sunshine Act of 1976 was designed to insure that "Every portion of every meeting of an agency shall be open to public observation." However, complete public access to all agency meetings could have the same negative consequences that unrestrained public access to agency records can sometimes produce. Accordingly, the Sunshine Act exempts certain agency meetings from public scrutiny under circumstances similar to those

---

[17]*Chrysler Corp. v. Brown*, 441 U.S. 281 (U.S. Sup. Ct. 1980).

under which documents are exempt from disclosure under the FOIA.

ISSUES IN REGULATION

"Old" Regulation versus "New" Regulation

Some interested observers of regulatory developments over the last 25 years have noted significant differences between the regulations that originated during the Progressive (1902 to 1914) and New Deal (1933 to 1938) eras and many more recent regulations.[18] They argue not only that the number and scope of regulatory controls have increased substantially in recent years, but also that the focus and the impact of regulation have changed significantly.

Whereas earlier regulation often focused on business practices that harmed the economic interests of specific segments of society (e.g., workers, small-business people, investors), many modern regulations focus on the health and safety of all citizens. Similarly, whereas earlier regulations often focused on a particular industry or group of industries (e.g., the railroads or the securities industry), many modern regulations affect large segments of industry (e.g., Title VII of the Civil Rights Act of 1964 and regulations governing environmental pollution and workplace safety). Finally, whereas earlier congressional delegations of regulatory power tended to be quite broad (e.g., the FTC Act's prohibition of "unfair methods of competition" and "unfair or deceptive acts or practices"), many more recent regulatory statutes (e.g., the Clean Air Acts of 1970 and 1977) have been extremely detailed.

What are the consequences of these changes in the nature of regulation? Far more businesses than ever before feel the impact of federal regulation, and far more areas of internal corporate decision making are affected by regulation. These changes tend to erode the historic distinction between "regulated" and other industries, and to heighten the importance of business-government relations. Detailed regulatory statutes also increase Congress's role in shaping regulatory policy at the expense of administrative discretion, making regulatory policy arguably more vulnerable to legislative lobbying efforts.

---

[18]See, for example, David Vogel, "The 'New' Social Regulation in Historical and Comparative Perspective," in *Regulation in Perspective,* ed. T. McGraw (Cambridge, Mass.: Harvard University Press, 1981), p. 155.

Agency "Capture" versus Agency "Shadows"

Proponents of regulation have traditionally feared that regulatory agencies would become "captives" of the industries they were charged with regulating. Through "revolving door" appointments by which key figures moved back and forth between government and the private sector, and by excessive reliance on "experts" beholden to industry, the independence of administrative agencies may be compromised and their effectiveness as regulators may be destroyed.

More recently, commentators sympathetic to business have argued that similar dangers to agency independence exist in the form of the nonindustry "shadow" groups that "public interest" organizations maintain to monitor agency actions (e.g., the Center for Auto Safety, which monitors the work of the Highway Transportation Safety Administration). Agencies may develop dependency relationships with their "shadows" or at least make decisions based in part on their "shadows'" anticipated reactions. Such informal means of shaping regulatory policy, when combined with the ability to challenge agency actions in court due to liberalized standing rules, have made "public interest" organizations important players in the contemporary regulatory process.

Deregulation versus Reregulation

A useful axiom for understanding the process of social and legal evolution is that *the cost of the status quo is easier to perceive than the cost of change.* Few things are more illustrative of the operation of this axiom than the history of regulation in the United States.

In the latter years of the 19th century, the social costs of living in an unregulated environment were readily apparent. Large business organizations often abused their power at the expense of their customers, suppliers, employees, and distributors, and sought to increase their power by acquiring their competitors or driving them out of business. Market forces, standing alone, were apparently unable to protect the public from defective, and in some cases dangerous, products. As a result of these and numerous other social and historical factors, this century has witnessed a tremendous growth in government and in government regulation of business.

But regulation, too, has its costs. Regulatory bureaucracies generate their own internal momentum and have their own interests to protect. They may become insensitive to the legitimate concerns of the industries they regulate and the public they supposedly serve. They may continue to seek higher and higher levels of safety, heedless of the fact that life necessarily involves some elements of risk and that the total elimination of risk in a modern technological society may be impossible, or, if possible, obtainable at a cost that we cannot afford to pay. At a time when many Americans are legitimately concerned about economic efficiency, as well as the ability of U.S. companies to compete effectively in world markets against competitors who operate in less-regulated environments, these and other costs of regulation are readily apparent.

As a result, in the last decade, we witnessed substantial "deregulation" in a number of industries such as the airline, banking, railroad, and trucking industries. The results of these efforts are, at best, mixed. The case of airline regulation should suffice to make the point. Proponents of deregulation cite the generally lower fares that deregulation has produced. Opponents tend to point to increased airline "overbooking" practices, reduced or eliminated services to smaller communities, and increased safety problems, all of which, they argue, are products of deregulation. The costs of deregulation have generated predictable calls for reregulating the airline industry. The ultimate outcome of the deregulation versus reregulation debate will depend upon which costs we as a society decide we would prefer to pay.

ETHICAL AND PUBLIC POLICY CONCERNS

1. Earlier in the chapter you learned that agency formal rulemaking procedures are vulnerable to industry tactics aimed at delaying regulation (e.g., the example concerning the minimum peanut content of peanut butter). Are such industry tactics ethically justifiable?

2. In our discussion of the Freedom of Information Act you learned that companies seeking to obtain useful information about their competitors frequently seek access to documents covered by the Act. Is this an ethical way to gain access to information?

3. Although the first question above focuses on delaying tactics practiced by industry, it is important to note that agencies also have been known to engage in delay and other tactics designed to frustrate citizens and organizations with whom they interact. For example, an agency may delay its response to an FOIA request, untruthfully arguing that staff shortages prevent a timely response, or it may refuse to turn over documents that it knows are not exempt from disclosure, forcing those seeking disclosure to engage in expensive and time-

consuming litigation to attain their ends. Are such agency tactics ethically justifiable?

SUMMARY

Administrative agencies arose because courts and legislatures were incapable of handling all of the regulatory tasks that were necessary in a high-speed, interdependent, technological society. Agencies have a pervasive influence on modern individual and business life, and are sometimes called the *fourth branch of government*.

An agency is created by a statute called *enabling legislation*, which dictates its structure, powers, and procedures. Agencies perform investigative, legislative, and judicial functions normally reserved to the three traditional branches of government. The fundamental problem of administrative law is how to limit agencies' ability to abuse their powers while preserving their ability to achieve regulatory goals.

One of the major checks on agency power is the Constitution. In addition to the basic constitutional safeguards that limit all governmental action, the constitutional principle of separation of powers serves as an important limit on the power that can be delegated to administrative agencies. Enabling legislation that is so broad that it fails to provide an "intelligible principle" to guide agency action is an unconstitutional violation of separation of powers.

There are two basic federal agency types: executive agencies and "independent" agencies. Executive agencies are housed in the executive branch of government, and their heads serve at the will of the president. "Independent" agencies are headed by boards or commissions whose members are presidentially appointed with the "advice and consent" of the Senate for fixed terms and are removable only for cause.

Most major agencies possess both *ministerial* and *discretionary* powers. Ministerial powers involve the routine performance of duties imposed by law. Discretionary powers, such as investigation, rulemaking, and adjudicatory power, involve the exercise of significant discretion and judgment by an agency. The Administrative Procedure Act (APA) places procedural limits on an agency's exercise of rulemaking power and also shapes the standards courts will use to review agency actions. Also, agencies possess important informal powers to influence the behavior of regulated entities.

Major agencies possess substantial investigative powers, the most important of which are the power to subpoena documents and testimony and the power to conduct searches to seize evidence of regulatory violations. The Fourth and Fifth Amendments to the Constitution place important limits on these investigative powers.

Agencies create *procedural* rules to govern their internal operations, *interpretive* rules to inform interested parties of the agencies' interpretation of the statutes they administer, and *legislative* rules that have binding legal effect on regulated entities. The APA dictates the procedures agencies must follow to exercise their rulemaking power.

There are three basic types of agency rulemaking: formal rulemaking, informal rulemaking, and hybrid rulemaking. With formal rulemaking, interested parties appear at a trial-like hearing to examine the agency's evidence, cross-examine its witnesses, and present evidence of their own. With informal rulemaking, interested parties submit written comments about a proposed rule, but they are not entitled to a hearing. Hybrid rulemaking provides a hearing, but limits interested parties' ability to cross-examine agency witnesses.

Agency adjudicatory hearings differ from judicial trials in a number of ways. They are instigated by a complaint filed by the agency and heard by an agency employee called an administrative law judge (ALJ). The APA attempts to insure that ALJs are independent from intra-agency or outside influences, and ALJ decisions are appealable to the governing body of the agency.

Each of the three traditional branches of government enjoys significant control over agency action. The president, through his appointment power, his power to issue executive orders, his veto power, and his ability, through the Office of Management and Budget, to affect executive agency budget requests, has a variety of tools at his disposal to shape agency policy.

Congress also can influence agency action in a variety of ways. It can amend enabling legislation, pass statutes that order changes in agency practice or procedures, deny or limit agency budgetary appropriations, and exercise less-formal influence through congressional "oversight" committees and "casework" on behalf of individual constituents.

The power of the courts to review agency adjudications and rulemaking is probably the most important check on agency action. Not all agency actions are judicially reviewable, however, and plaintiffs who can prove reviewability also must demonstrate that they have standing to sue and that the issues are ripe for judicial review. There are three standards of review of agency factual judgments under the APA: *de novo* review, the "substantial evidence" test, and the "arbitrary and capricious" test.

Finally, Congress has passed several statutes designed to control the information agencies collect and the uses to which that information is put. The Freedom of Information Act requires government agencies to allow interested parties access to documents in their possession. The Privacy Act of 1974 limits the data agencies can collect on individuals and the entities to whom collected data may be disseminated without individual permission. It also allows individuals to obtain access to their records. The Government in the Sunshine Act of 1976 requires that agency meetings be open to public observation.

PROBLEM CASES

1. In 1985, without recourse to notice-and-comment procedures, the Department of Transportation (DOT) issued an "Order Granting Exemption" from an earlier regulation dealing with deceptive practices in airfare advertising. The exemption allowed advertisers to separate a $3 international departure tax adopted by Congress in 1978 from the total advertised price. In 1988, the DOT issued an "Order Amending Exemption," which included all government-imposed surcharges within the exemption. The effect of this order was to allow foreign departure taxes, immigration fees, customs fees, security fees, and any other charges that might be imposed by various governments to be excluded from the total advertised ticket price so long as such charges were clearly identified and stated somewhere else in the ad. The attorneys general of 25 states filed a petition seeking review of the order, arguing that it was contrary to their interpretations of their own states' consumer protection statutes and that the DOT's failure to employ notice-and-comment rulemaking rendered the order invalid. The DOT argued that the states lacked standing to challenge the order and that the order was merely a rule interpreting the 1985 exemption order and therefore was not subject to APA notice-and-comment requirements. Should the order stand?

2. In the late 1960s, the Federal Aviation Administration (FAA), in an attempt to reduce takeoff and landing delays at five major airports, adopted a regulation limiting the number of takeoff and landing slots at those airports. At Washington National Airport, 40 slots per hour were assigned to commercial aircraft. Prior to 1980, the airlines voluntarily allocated these slots among themselves. In 1980, however, a new airline wanted some of the National Airport slots, but none of the existing airlines would voluntarily give up any slots. The airlines' existing slot allocation agreement was due to expire on November 30, 1980. If the slot allocations changed, some lead time was necessary to enable the airlines to make schedule adjustments, notify passengers, and rearrange ticket reservations taken under the existing schedules. To avoid chaos in the skies during the 1980 Thanksgiving–Christmas holiday season, the Secretary of Transportation proposed a regulation allocating the National Airport slots. Notice of the proposed regulation was published in the *Federal Register* on October 20, 1980. The comment period was set for a seven-day period starting on October 16, 1980, the date the proposed regulation was issued by the Secretary. Thirty-seven comments were received from airlines and others. Northwest Airlines, however, filed suit, arguing that the Administrative Procedure Act required at least a 30-day comment period for proposed regulations. Should Northwest win?

3. The Occupational Safety and Health Act was passed "to assure so far as possible every working man and woman in the Nation safe and healthful working conditions." The Act authorized the secretary of labor to promulgate regulatory standards governing workplace health and safety. The Act also provided that the secretary should set standards that, "to the extent possible," assure that no employee will suffer material health consequences even from a lifetime of exposure to an occupational hazard. In 1978, the secretary, acting through the Occupational Safety and Health Administration (OSHA), promulgated a strict standard limiting occupational exposure to cotton dust. The American Textile Manufacturers Institute, an organization representing the cotton industry, challenged the validity of the cotton dust standard, arguing that the Act required the secretary to demonstrate a reasonable relationship between the costs and the benefits associated with the standard. Should the standard be overturned?

4. Fenster, president and part owner of Utica Packing Company, was convicted of bribing a federal meat inspector, an employee of the United States Department of Agriculture (USDA). In a hearing before an administrative law judge (ALJ), the USDA sought a withdrawal of meat inspection services from Utica unless Fenster sold his ownership of Utica and withdrew from its management. The ALJ ruled in the USDA's favor, effectively eliminating Utica's ability to conduct its business. Utica appealed the decision to the USDA judicial officer, Donald Campbell, who had the power to make final adjudicative orders for the USDA. Campbell affirmed the ALJ's decision, and so did a federal district court. The Sixth Circuit Court of Appeals, however, held that Campbell erred by not considering mitigating circumstances in the case. Upon reconsideration, Campbell reluctantly held that the mitigating circumstances prevented him from finding that Utica was unfit to receive inspection services. USDA executive officials strongly disagreed with Campbell's decision. They got the secretary of agriculture to replace Campbell with Deputy Assistant Secretary John Franke, who was not a lawyer and had no adjudicatory experience. Franke then reconsidered Campbell's decision at the USDA's request, finding that the mitigating circumstances were insufficient to justify Fenster's bribing the meat inspector. Utica appealed, arguing that its due process rights had been violated. Is Utica right?

5. The Medicare Act established a health insurance program to be administered by the secretary of health and human services. Judicial review of a denial of a medicare claim is available only after the secretary renders a final decision. A final decision is made only after a medicare claimant has had four opportunities to have his claim considered, including consideration by an administrative law judge (ALJ) and the Appeals Council of the Department of Health and Human Services. In January 1979, the secretary issued an administrative instruction that no medicare payments should be made for a surgical procedure known as bilateral carotid body resection (BCBR) when performed to relieve respiratory distress, on the grounds that BCBR surgery was not reasonable or necessary, the standard required by the Medicare Act. Many claimants whose BCBR claims were initially denied sought review before ALJs, who consistently ruled in favor of BCBR claimants, as did the Appeals Council. In response to these rulings, the secretary issued a formal administrative ruling prohibiting ALJs and the Appeals Council in all cases from ordering medicare payments for BCBR operations performed after October 28, 1980. Sanford Holmes had BCBR surgery before October 28, 1980. His claim for medicare benefits was rejected. Holmes did not seek a hearing on his claim before an ALJ or a review in the Appeals Council. Instead, he sued the secretary in a federal district court, challenging her decision that BCBR surgery was not necessary or reasonable. Will the district court review the secretary's decision?

6. Chaney and other prison inmates were sentenced to death under the laws of Oklahoma and Texas. They were to be executed by lethal injection of drugs. The drugs were approved by the Food and Drug Administration for medical purposes stated on their labels. The FDA had not, however, approved their use for human executions. Chaney claimed that use of the drugs for human executions violated the Food, Drug, and Cosmetic Act (FDCA) as an unapproved use of an approved drug. He argued that, under the FDCA, the FDA was required to approve the drugs as "safe and effective" for human execution before they could be distributed. Chaney asked the FDA to investigate these perceived violations of the FDCA and to take enforcement actions, including seizing the drugs from state prisons and recommending the prosecution of those who knowingly distribute or purchase the drugs with the intent to use them for human executions. The FDA refused to take any action on the grounds that it had no power to interfere with the use of lethal injections in a state criminal justice system. Chaney sought judicial review of the FDA's refusal to act, and the district court held that the FDA's refusal to take enforcement action was not subject to judicial review. Was the district court's decision correct?

7. On August 1, 1982, Larry Morrison, a pilot for Northwest Airlines, piloted a passenger airliner while he was intoxicated. Four days later, Northwest Airlines discharged him as an employee. The next day, Morrison began four weeks of voluntary alcoholism treatment. He attended weekly counseling sessions thereafter. On January 20, 1983, the Federal Aviation Administration (FAA) temporarily suspended his pilot certificate. Without a pilot certificate, Morrison could not pilot airplanes within the United States. On September 2, 1983, Morrison requested recertification, which the FAA granted subject to a few restrictions. Northwest Airlines sought judicial review of the FAA's recertification on the grounds that (1) recertifying Morrison would make the skies unsafe for Northwest airplanes, its crews, and its passengers and (2) the FAA's lenient recertification policy would make it more difficult for Northwest to deter drinking among its pilots and other employees. Are these injuries sufficient to give Northwest standing to seek judicial review of the FAA's decision to recertify Morrison?

8. The Federal Land Policy and Management Act (FLPMA) empowers the secretary of the interior to "dispose of a tract of public land by exchange when the public interest is well served." In 1982, the secretary approved a three-way exchange of land by which the National Park Service received previously privately owned land within the boundaries of Grand Teton National Park and the federal government gave up federal coal lands in the Corral Canyon, Wyoming, area. The Corral Canyon lands were alternate sections of a checkerboard. The recipient of the Corral Canyon lands was Rocky Mountain Energy Company, a coal mining company that already owned land in the Corral Canyon area. The exchange yielded Rocky Mountain a contiguous tract of land more suitable to coal mining. In addition, the lands were close to lines of the Union Pacific Railroad, a company owned by the same corporation that owned Rocky Mountain. The exchange was overwhelmingly supported by all groups, including environmental groups, except the National Coal Association (NCA) and the Mining and Reclamation Council of America (MRCA), trade associations whose members produced most of the nation's coal. The NCA and MRCA claimed that the secretary erred in approving the land exchange, since the Mineral Leasing Act (MLA) prohibited the secretary from leasing federal coal lands to a railroad that is in the business of mining coal. The MLA was enacted out of the fear "that if railroads were allowed to own coal mines they would discriminate in transportation against competing coal mines that depended on rail transportation." The NCA and the MRCA contended that the exchange, by allowing Rocky Mountain Energy to mine a large tract of previously unminable land, threatened their members with more rigorous competition. Is this threat of injury sufficient to give the NCA and the MRCA standing to challenge the secretary's approval of the exchange?

9. An agent of the Pennsylvania Department of Environmental Resources saw Disposal Service's loaded trash truck backing into a building that was used to compact waste to be loaded onto tractor-trailers for transportation and final disposal. Knowing the building's purpose and that Disposal Service did not have the permit to operate it as a transfer station required by the state Solid Waste Management Act (SWMA), the agent entered the property, went into the building, and observed the operation. Disposal Service was later prosecuted for operating a transfer station without a permit. Disposal Service moved to suppress the agent's evidence, arguing that his warrantless entry onto the property violated the Fourth Amendment. The state argued that the SWMA's provisions allowing such warrantless inspections were constitutional. Should the evidence be suppressed?

10. *The New York Times* (the *Times*) filed a Freedom of Information Act (FOIA) request with the National Aeronautics and Space Administration (NASA) asking for "transcripts of all voice and data communications recorded aboard the space shuttle Challenger" on the day when the shuttle self-destructed, killing all seven astronauts on board. The *Times* also requested copies of voice communication tapes. NASA provided a written transcript of the only voice recording made, but refused to turn over a copy of the tape itself, arguing that to do so would violate the privacy of the astronauts' families by exposing them to replays of their loved ones' voices. NASA argued that the tape was exempt from disclosure under Exemption 6 to the FOIA because the human voice, being unique to each individual, "clearly is infor-mation about the individual and identifiable as such." Should NASA turn over the tape?

11. Britt, a major in the Marine Corps Reserve, was investigated by the Naval Investigative Service (NIS) in connection with allegations that one of his Reserve sub-ordinates had improperly stored ordnance in his home. While the investigation was in progress, the NIS con-tacted Britt's regular employer, the Immigration and Naturalization Service (INS), and provided his INS su-pervisor with reports and other material from the inves-tigation. After Britt was later cleared of all charges by the Marines, he filed suit against the NIS arguing that it had violated the Privacy Act by releasing information about the investigation to the INS. Were the NIS's ac-tions proper?

THE FEDERAL TRADE COMMISSION ACT AND CONSUMER PROTECTION LAWS

INTRODUCTION

At various points in this text, we note how the emergence of large corporations has created a perceived need for government intervention to protect people from the superior power such firms often possess. In few areas of the law is this more true than in the area sometimes called consumer law. As the Product Liability chapter demonstrated, consumers' ability to recover civil damages for defective products increased dramatically during the 1960s and 1970s. But *direct government regulation* of consumer matters also grew tremendously during those decades.

This chapter examines the many kinds of federal consumer protection regulation. It begins with a general discussion of America's main consumer watchdog: the Federal Trade Commission (FTC). After describing how the FTC operates, the chapter examines the FTC's regulation of anticompetitive private behavior. After this, the chapter discusses how the Commission regulates deceptive and unfair business practices. Then, following a brief look at selected provisions of the Magnuson-Moss Warranty Act, the chapter turns to a series of laws that regulate consumer credit arrangements. The chapter concludes with a brief survey of federal product safety regulation.

THE FEDERAL TRADE COMMISSION

The Commission

The Federal Trade Commission was formed shortly after passage of the Federal Trade Commission Act (FTC Act) in 1914.[1] The FTC is an independent federal agency, which means that it is outside the executive branch of the federal government and is less subject to political control than agencies that are executive departments. The FTC is headed by five commissioners appointed by the president and confirmed by the Senate for staggered seven-year terms. The president also designates one of the commissioners as chairman of the FTC. As Figure 1 indicates, in 1990 the FTC had headquarters in Washington, D.C., and 10 regional offices located in large cities throughout the United States. The Administrative Agencies chapter sets out the Commission's internal organization.

---

[1] See the Administrative Agencies chapter for further discussion of the FTC's creation, organization, powers, and status as an independent agency.

FIGURE 1   The Offices of the Federal Trade Commission

Headquarters	Address	
Washington, D.C.	Pennsylvania Avenue at Sixth St., N.W. Washington, D.C. 20580	

Regional Offices	Address	States Included
Atlanta	1718 Peachtree St. NW, Atlanta, GA 30367	Alabama, Florida, Georgia, Mississippi, North Carolina, South Carolina, Tennessee, Virginia
Boston	10 Causeway St., Boston, MA 02222–1073	Connecticut, Maine, Massachusetts, New Hampshire, Rhode Island, Vermont
Chicago	55 E. Monroe St., Chicago, IL 60603	Illinois, Indiana, Iowa, Kentucky, Minnesota, Missouri, Wisconsin
Cleveland	668 Euclid Ave., Cleveland, OH 44114	Delaware, Maryland, Michigan, Ohio, Pennsylvania, West Virginia
Dallas	100 N. Central Expressway, Dallas, TX 75201	Arkansas, Louisiana, New Mexico, Oklahoma, Texas
Denver	1405 Curtis St., Denver, CO 80202–2393	Colorado, Kansas, Montana, Nebraska, North Dakota, South Dakota, Utah, Wyoming
Los Angeles	11000 Wilshire Blvd., Los Angeles, CA 90024	Arizona, Southern California
New York	26 Federal Plaza, New York, NY 10278	New Jersey, New York
San Francisco	901 Market St., San Francisco, CA 94103	Northern California, Hawaii, Nevada
Seattle	915 2nd Avenue, Seattle, WA 98174	Alaska, Idaho, Oregon, Washington

Source: *1989–90 United States Government Manual.*

The FTC's Powers

The FTC's principal missions are to keep the U.S. economy both *free* and *fair*. The Commission promotes free competition by attacking business practices that restrict such competition. It also regulates unfair and deceptive practices in the marketing and advertising of goods and services.

As Figure 2 suggests, Congress has given the FTC many tools for accomplishing these missions. By far the most important of these tools is section 5 of the FTC Act, which empowers the Commission to prevent (1) unfair methods of competition and (2) unfair or deceptive acts or practices. Each of these bases of FTC authority is examined later in this chapter. The Commission also enforces the consumer protection and consumer credit measures discussed in the last half of this chapter. Finally, the FTC enforces various other federal acts, some of which are listed in Figure 2. To assist in the performance of all these functions, the

FTC has broad powers to investigate and engage in economic fact finding.

FTC Enforcement Procedures

The FTC has many legal tools for ensuring compliance with the statutes it administers. Here, we discuss only the three most important FTC enforcement devices: its procedures for facilitating voluntary compliance, its issuance of trade regulation rules, and its adjudicative proceedings.

Voluntary Compliance   The FTC promotes voluntary, cooperative business behavior by giving advisory opinions and issuing industry guides. An **advisory opinion** is the Commission's response to a private party's query about the legality of proposed business conduct. The FTC is not obligated to furnish advisory opinions. Even where it does furnish such an opinion, the Commission

---

FIGURE 2   Some of the Major Acts Enforced by the FTC

Regulation of Economic Competition

FTC Act Section 5 (including Sherman Act standards)—discussed in this chapter and in the Antitrust chapter on the Sherman Act

Clayton Act—discussed in the chapter entitled The Clayton Act, the Robinson-Patman Act, and Antitrust Exemptions and Immunities

Robinson-Patman Act—discussed in the same chapter as the Clayton Act

Hart-Scott-Rodino Antitrust Improvements Act of 1976—requires that certain companies planning mergers notify and provide information to the FTC and the Justice Department

Consumer Protection Measures Discussed in This Chapter

FTC Act Section 5

Magnuson-Moss Warranty Act

Truth in Lending Act (including 1988 Fair Credit and Charge Card Disclosure Act and Home Equity Loan Consumer Protection Act)

Consumer Leasing Act

Fair Credit Reporting Act

Equal Credit Opportunity Act

Fair Credit Billing Act

Fair Debt Collection Practices Act

Other Measures

Export Trade Act—empowers FTC to supervise registration and operation of associations of American exporters engaged in export trade

Fair Packaging and Labeling Act—regulates packaging and labeling of consumer products to ensure accurate quality and value comparisons

Flammable Fabrics Act—FTC has some enforcement powers under act regulating manufacture, sale, and importation of flammable fabrics

Fur Products Labeling Act—regulates labeling, other identification, and advertising of fur products

Hobby Protection Act—regulates certain imitations of political campaign materials and certain imitation coins and paper money

Lanham Act—empowers FTC to petition for the cancellation of certain trademarks

Smokeless Tobacco Act—empowers FTC to approve manufacturers' plans for rotation and display of statements on smokeless tobacco packages and ads

Textile Fiber Products Identification Act—regulates labeling and other identification of textile fiber products

Wool Products Labeling Act—regulates labeling and other identification of wool products

---

Sources: *1989–90 United States Government Manual* and various statutes.

---

may rescind it when the public interest requires. But when the FTC does so, it cannot proceed against the opinion's recipient for actions taken in good faith reliance on the opinion without giving the recipient notice of the rescission and an opportunity to discontinue those actions.

Industry guides are FTC interpretations of the laws it administers.[2] Their purpose is to encourage the members of an industry to voluntarily abandon certain un-

lawful practices. To further this end, industry guides are written in lay language. Industry guides do not have the force of law. Often, however, behavior that violates an industry guide also violates one of the statutes or other rules that the Commission enforces.

Trade Regulation Rules   Unlike industry guides, FTC **trade regulation rules** are written in legalistic language and have the force of law.[3] Thus, the FTC can

---

[2]Industry guides exemplify the *interpretive rules* discussed in the Administrative Agencies chapter.

[3]Trade regulation rules exemplify the *legislative rules* discussed in the Administrative Agencies chapter.

proceed directly against practices forbidden by a trade regulation rule. This can occur through the *adjudicative proceedings* discussed immediately below. In addition, the Commission can obtain a federal district court *civil penalty* of up to $10,000 for each knowing violation of a rule. It may also institute court proceedings to obtain various forms of *consumer redress*, including the payment of damages, the refund of money, the return of property, and the reformation or rescission of contracts.

FTC Adjudicative Proceedings   Often, the FTC proceeds against violations of its statutes or trade regulation rules by administrative action within the Commission itself. The FTC gets evidence of possible violations from private parties, government bodies, and its own investigations. If, after further investigation and discussion, it decides to proceed against the alleged offender (the *respondent*), it enters a formal complaint. The case itself is heard in a public administrative hearing called an *adjudicative proceeding* before an FTC administrative law judge.[4] The judge's decision can be appealed to the FTC's five commissioners, and then to the federal courts of appeals and the U.S. Supreme Court.

The usual penalty resulting from a final decision against the respondent is an FTC **cease and desist order.** As its name suggests, this is basically a command to the respondent ordering it to stop its illegal behavior. As you will see later in this chapter, however, the courts have upheld FTC orders going beyond the mere command to cease and desist. The civil penalty for failing to comply with a cease and desist order is up to $10,000 per violation. Where there is a continuing failure to obey a final order, each day that the violation continues is considered a separate violation.

Many alleged violations are never adjudicated by the FTC, but instead are settled through a **consent order.** This is an order approving a negotiated agreement in which the respondent promises to cease and desist from certain activities. Consent orders normally provide that the respondent does not admit any violation of the law. The failure to observe a consent order is punishable by civil penalties.

ANTICOMPETITIVE BEHAVIOR

As noted earlier, one of the FTC's most important functions is to attack anticompetitive behavior. To that end,

section 5 of the FTC Act empowers the Commission to prevent "unfair methods of competition" in or affecting interstate commerce. This language allows the FTC to regulate anticompetitive practices made illegal by the Sherman Act.[5] The Commission also has specific statutory authority to enforce the Clayton and Robinson-Patman Acts.[6]

For the most part, section 5's application to anticompetitive behavior has been limited to the orthodox antitrust violations discussed in this text's antitrust chapters. But section 5 also reaches anticompetitive behavior *not covered* by other antitrust statutes. As the Supreme Court declared in 1986, "[t]he standard of 'unfairness' under the FTC Act is, by necessity, an elusive one, encompassing not only practices that violate the Sherman Act and the other antitrust laws, . . . but also practices that the Commission determines are against public policy for other reasons."[7] In an earlier case,[8] for example, the Court held that the Sperry and Hutchinson Company's attempt to suppress trading stamp exchanges dealing in its Green Stamps was illegal under section 5, even though that attempt violated neither the letter nor the spirit of the antitrust laws. Section 5 also enables the FTC to proceed against *potential* or *incipient* antitrust violations. Finally, a 1976 statute requires that companies planning certain kinds of mergers give notice to the FTC and to the Justice Department's Antitrust Division, and supply certain data to those bodies.

The following *SCTLA* case demonstrates how section 5 incorporates the Sherman Act's standards. It discusses two basic forms of Sherman Act antitrust analysis: *per se rules* and the *rule of reason*. Per se rules identify certain kinds of anticompetitive behavior that are *conclusively presumed* to be illegal under section 1 of the Sherman Act. In rule of reason cases, on the other hand, courts examine the actual anticompetitive effects of the respondent's conduct, any procompetitive effects it might have, and any other positive social benefits it might produce. Here, section 1 liability exists only when the respondent's behavior had a significant anticompetitive effect that was not offset by any positive effect on competition or any other social benefit. Per se rules and the rule of reason are discussed in more detail in the chapter entitled Antitrust: The Sherman Act.

---

[4]The Administrative Agencies chapter describes federal administrative proceedings.

[5]See the chapter on the Sherman Act.

[6]See the chapter on the Clayton and Robinson-Patman Acts.

[7]*FTC v. Indiana Federation of Dentists,* 476 U.S. 447 (1986).

[8]*FTC v. Sperry & Hutchinson Co.*, 405 U.S. 233 (1972).

FTC v. SUPERIOR COURT TRIAL LAWYERS ASSOCIATION

110 S. Ct. 768 (U.S. Sup. Ct. 1990)

In the District of Columbia, indigent defendants in the less serious criminal cases usually are represented by private attorneys appointed and compensated under a D.C. statute. This legal work basically is voluntary, and during the early 1980s most of it was performed by approximately 100 "regulars" who derived most of their income from representing indigents. At that time, local law capped the regulars' fees at $30 per hour for court time and $20 per hour for out-of-court time. These rates had long been opposed by various D.C. bar organizations.

On August 11, 1983, the regulars agreed not to accept any new cases after September 6 of that year unless legislation increasing their fees to $55 per hour for in-court work and $45 per hour for out-of-court work was passed by that date. The legislation was not forthcoming, and on September 6 about 90 percent of the regulars refused to take any new assignments. Thereafter, new criminal cases continued to flood the D.C. criminal courts, other members of the D.C. bar generally refused to handle them, and the district's public defender system soon was overwhelmed. Shortly thereafter, the mayor met with the regulars' strike committee and offered to support an immediate temporary increase to $35 per hour, as well as a subsequent permanent increase to $45 for out-of-court work and $55 for in-court work. By September 21, the city council had enacted an increase to $35 and the regulars went back to work.

Later, the FTC filed a complaint against the Superior Court Trial Lawyers Association (SCTLA), the organization through which the regulars had acted. The complaint alleged that the SCTLA had engaged in unfair methods of competition under section 5 of the FTC Act. The FTC administrative law judge dismissed the complaint, but the full Commission reversed, entering a cease-and-desist order prohibiting the SCTLA from initiating another boycott. The Court of Appeals for the D.C. Circuit vacated the Commission's order, returning the case to the FTC for a determination whether the regulars had significant market power. Both the FTC and the SCTLA appealed to the U.S. Supreme Court.

Stevens, Justice.   Reasonable lawyers may differ about the wisdom of this enforcement proceeding. We may assume that the preboycott rates were unreasonably low, and that the increase has produced better legal representation for indigent defendants. We may also assume that without the boycott there would have been no increase in fees. These assumptions do not control the case, for it is not our task to pass upon the social utility or political wisdom of price-fixing agreements.

The boycott constituted a classic restraint of trade within the meaning of section 1 of the Sherman Act. As such, it also violated the prohibition against unfair methods of competition in section 5 of the FTC Act. Prior to the boycott, the regulars were in competition with one another, each deciding independently whether and how often to provide services at established rates. The agreement among the regulars was designed to obtain higher prices for their services and was implemented by a concerted refusal to serve an important customer in the market for legal services and, indeed, the only customer for the particular services the regulars offered. This constriction of supply is the essence of price-fixing, whether it be accomplished by agreeing upon a price or an output. It is no excuse that the prices fixed are themselves reasonable.

The court of appeals assumed that the antitrust laws permit, but do not require, the condemnation of price-fixing and boycotts without proof of market power. The [court of appeals'] opinion further assumed that the *per se* rule prohibiting such activity is only a rule of administrative convenience and efficiency. [But] *per se* rules also reflect a longstanding judgment that the prohibited practices have a substantial potential for impact on competition. Antitrust law generates two complementary categories of analysis. In the first category are agreements [that] are so plainly anticompetitive that no elaborate study of the industry is needed to establish their illegality—they are illegal *per se*. In the second are agreements whose competitive effect can only be evaluated by analyzing the facts peculiar to the business, the history of the restraint, and the reasons why it was imposed. Once experience with a particular kind of restraint enables the Court to predict with confidence that the rule of reason will condemn it, it has applied a conclusive presumption that the restraint is unreasonable.

So it is with boycotts and price-fixing. Every such horizontal arrangement among competitors poses some threat to the free market. A small participant in the market is less likely to cause persistent damage than a large participant. Other participants may act quickly and effectively to take the small participant's place. For reasons including market inertia and information failures, however, a small conspirator may be able to impede competition over some period of time. Given an appropriate set of circumstances and some luck, the period can be long enough to inflict real injury upon particular consumers or competitors. Conspirators need not achieve the dimensions of a monopoly, or even a degree of market power any greater than that disclosed by this record, to warrant condemnation under the antitrust laws.

Court of appeals decision reversed insofar as it held the *per se* rule inapplicable to this boycott. Case remanded to the court of appeals for further proceedings consistent with the Supreme Court's opinion.

DECEPTION AND UNFAIRNESS

Section 5 of the FTC Act also prohibits "unfair or deceptive acts or practices." This language enables the FTC to regulate a wide range of activities that disadvantage consumers. In doing so, the Commission may proceed under the theory that the activity is *deceptive*, or that it is *unfair*.

Here we set out the general standards that the FTC now uses to define each of these section 5 violations. Much of this discussion involves FTC regulation of advertising,[9] but the standards we outline apply to a wide range of misrepresentations, omissions, and practices. Although their details are beyond the scope of this text, the Commission has also enacted numerous trade regulation rules defining specific deceptive and unfair practices.

Deception

The FTC determines the deceptiveness of advertising and other business practices on a case-by-case basis. Courts usually defer to the Commission's decisions in this area. To be considered deceptive under the FTC's 1983 Policy Statement on Deception, an activity must: (1) involve a *material* misrepresentation, omission, or practice; (2) that is *likely to mislead* a consumer; (3) who acts *reasonably* under the circumstances.

Representation, Omission, or Practice Likely to Mislead Often, sellers expressly make false or misleading claims in their advertisements or other representations. But false or misleading statements also can be *implied* from the surrounding circumstances. In one case, for instance, the conclusion that Listerine mouthwash could prevent and cure colds and sore throats was implied from the close conjunction of the following two advertising claims: (1) that Listerine "Kills Germs by Millions on Contact" and (2) that Listerine should be used "For General Oral Hygiene, Bad Breath, Colds, and Resultant Sore Throats." Also, as the *International Harvester* case at the end of the section makes clear, a seller's *omissions* may be deceptive. Finally, certain deceptive *marketing practices* can violate section 5. In one

---

[9]Deceptive advertising may give rise to civil liability as well. Buyers, for example, may have a fraud or express warranty claim against a seller whose ads were untruthful. And a seller's competitors sometimes may have claims for defamation or injurious falsehood, or for palming off or unfair competition under section 43(a) of the Lanham Act. These various theories of recovery are discussed in the chapters entitled Intentional Torts; Intellectual Property, Competitive Torts, and Unfair Competition; Reality of Consent; and Product Liability.

such case, encyclopedia salesmen gained entry to the homes of potential customers by posing as surveyors engaged in advertising research.

In all of these situations, the statement, omission, or practice must be *likely to mislead* a consumer. *Actual* deception is not required. Of course, determining whether an ad or practice is likely to mislead requires that the FTC evaluate the accuracy of the seller's claims. In some cases, moreover, the Commission requires that sellers *substantiate* objective claims about their products by showing that they have a reasonable basis for making such claims.

The "Reasonable Consumer" Test To be deceptive, the representation, omission, or practice also must be likely to mislead *reasonable consumers under the circumstances*. The purpose behind this requirement is to protect sellers from liability for every foolish, ignorant, or outlandish misconception that some consumer might entertain. As the Commission noted some years ago, advertising an American-made pastry as "Danish Pastry" does not violate section 5 just because "a few misguided souls believe . . . that all Danish Pastry is made in Denmark."[10] Also, section 5 usually is not violated by statements of opinion, sales talk, or "puffing"; statements about matters that consumers can easily evaluate for themselves; and statements regarding subjective matters such as taste or smell. This is because such statements are unlikely to deceive reasonable consumers.

Materiality Finally, the representation, omission, or practice must be *material*. Material information is information that is important to reasonable consumers and that is likely to affect their choice of a product or service. Examples include statements or omissions regarding a product's cost, safety, effectiveness, performance, durability, quality, and warranty protection. In addition, the Commission presumes that express statements are material.

Unfairness

Section 5's prohibition of *unfair* acts or practices enables the FTC to attack behavior that, while not necessarily deceptive, is objectionable for other reasons. In the 1960s and 1970s, the FTC often interpreted its un-

fairness jurisdiction broadly; one well-known example was its late-1970s attempt to promulgate rules governing television advertising aimed at children. Apparently underlying this and other such efforts was the perception that modern mass advertising can be manipulative even when it is not deceptive. In 1980, however, Congress took away the FTC's authority to issue a children's advertising rule based on the concept of unfairness. In that year, Congress also put a moratorium on the FTC's power to make new trade regulation rules governing unfair advertising. The moratorium has continued through 1990, but it has not prevented the FTC from using its adjudicative procedures to attack *individual instances* of unfair advertising, or from enacting trade regulation rules aimed at *deceptive* advertising.

As the *International Harvester* case demonstrates, the FTC now focuses on *consumer injury* when it attacks unfair acts or practices in its own proceedings. To violate section 5, this injury must be:

1. *Substantial.* Monetary loss and unwarranted health and safety risks usually constitute substantial harm, but emotional distress or the perceived offensiveness of certain advertisements generally do not.

2. *Not outweighed by any offsetting consumer or competitive benefits produced by the challenged practice.* This element requires the Commission to balance the harm caused by the act or practice against its benefits to consumers and to competition generally. A seller's failure to give a consumer complex technical data about a product, for example, may disadvantage the consumer in certain ways, but it may also reduce the product's price. Only when such an act or practice is injurious in its *net effects* can it be unfair under section 5.

3. *One that consumers could not reasonably have avoided.* An injury is considered reasonably unavoidable when a seller's actions significantly interfere with a consumer's ability to make informed decisions that would have prevented the injury. For example, this may occur if a seller withholds otherwise-unavailable information about important product features, or uses high-pressure sales tactics on vulnerable consumers.

Remedies

Several types of orders can result from a successful FTC adjudicative proceeding attacking deceptive or unfair behavior. One possibility discussed earlier is an order telling the respondent to cease engaging in the deceptive or unfair conduct. Another is the *affirmative disclosure*

---

[10]*Heinz v. W. Kirchner,* 63 F.T.C. 1282, 1290 (1963).

of information whose absence made the advertisement deceptive or unfair. Yet another is *corrective advertising*. This requires the seller's future advertisements to correct false impressions created by its past advertisements. In certain cases, moreover, the FTC may issue an *all-products order* extending beyond the product or service whose advertisements violated section 5, and including future advertisements for *other* products or services marketed by the seller. Finally, the FTC sometimes may go to court to seek the civil penalties or consumer redress noted earlier, or to seek injunctive relief.

First Amendment Considerations

As discussed in the chapter entitled Business and the Constitution, the Supreme Court has given commercial speech such as advertising a degree of First Amendment protection. Because the various FTC orders just discussed often restrict commercial speech, they are potentially vulnerable to a First Amendment challenge. However, the constitutional protection given commercial speech does not extend to utterances that are false or misleading. Thus, FTC regulation of *deceptive* advertising usually poses few constitutional problems. A few courts, however, have read the First Amendment as requiring a fairly close relationship between the FTC order and the transgressions it seeks to correct, and have occasionally narrowed the scope of a Commission order on that basis. FTC regulation of *unfair* advertising that is not false or misleading also may pose constitutional problems.

The following *International Harvester* case considers behavior that allegedly was both deceptive and unfair under FTC Act section 5.

IN THE MATTER OF INTERNATIONAL HARVESTER COMPANY
104 F.T.C. 949 (1984)

Since at least the early 1950s, gasoline-powered tractors manufactured by the International Harvester Company had been subject to "fuel geysering." This was a phenomenon in which hot liquid gasoline would shoot from the tractor's gas tank when the filler cap was opened. The hot gasoline could cause severe burns and, more importantly, could ignite and cause a fire. Over the years, at least 90 fuel geysering incidents involving International Harvester tractors occurred, at least 12 of these involved significant burn injuries, and at least one caused a death.

International Harvester first discovered the full dimensions of the fuel geysering problem in 1963. In that year, it revised its owner's manuals to warn buyers of new gas-powered tractors not to remove the gas cap from a hot or running tractor. In 1976, it produced a new fuel tank decal with a similar warning. Due to an industrywide shift to diesel-powered tractors, however, this warning had a very limited distribution to buyers of new tractors, and it rarely reached former buyers. International Harvester never specifically warned either new or old buyers about the geysering problem until 1980, when on its own volition it made a mass mailing to 630,000 customers.

In 1980, the FTC issued a complaint against International Harvester, alleging that its failure to warn buyers of the fuel geysering problem for 17 years was both deceptive and unfair under FTC Act section 5. The administrative law judge agreed with the Commission on each charge. Due to International Harvester's notification program, however, he concluded that a cease-and-desist order was unnecessary. Both International Harvester and the FTC's complaint counsel appealed to the full Commission.

Douglas, Commissioner. The basic law of this case is section 5 of the FTC Act. That section states that "unfair or deceptive acts or practices . . . are declared unlawful."

Deception. A deception case requires a showing of three elements: (1) there must be a representation, practice, or omission likely to mislead consumers; (2) consumers must be interpreting the message reasonably under the circumstances; and (3) the misleading effects must be material. Our deception analysis focuses on risk of consumer harm, and actual injury need not be shown. Deception is harmful to consumers, undermines the rational functioning of the marketplace, and never offers increased efficiency or other countervailing benefits.

Deception theory is not limited to false or misleading statements. Under two general circumstances it can also reach omissions. First, it can be deceptive to tell only half the truth, and to omit the rest. This may occur where a seller fails to disclose qualifying information necessary to prevent his affirmative statements from creating a misleading impression. The Commission has challenged the advertising of baldness cures for failing to disclose that most baldness results from male heredity and cannot be treated. It can also be deceptive for a seller to simply remain silent, if he does so under circumstances that constitute an implied but false representation. Such implied representations may arise from the physical appearance of the product, or from the circumstances of a transaction, or they may be based on ordinary consumer expectations. The Commission has upheld charges against sellers who failed to disclose that an apparently new product was actually used, that land sold for investment purposes was poorly suited to that use due to its remote location, and that a book was an abridged rather than a complete edition. One generalization that emerges from these cases is that by offering goods for sale the seller impliedly represents that they are reasonably fit for their intended uses. The concept of reasonable fitness includes a further implied representation that the products are free of gross safety hazards.

However, the implied warranty of fitness is not violated by all undisclosed safety problems. Where the risk of mishap is very small, it cannot be said that the product is unfit for normal use. Such a case could therefore not satisfy the first element of the deception test, a misleading representation. Harvester manufactured approximately 1.3 million gasoline-powered tractors in the period after 1939. Of this number, twelve are known to have been involved in geysering incidents involving bodily injury. This is an accident rate of less than .001 percent, over a period of more than 40 years.

Unfairness. The unfairness theory is the Commission's general law of consumer protection, of which deception is one specific application. Unfairness analysis focuses on three criteria: (1) whether the practice creates a serious consumer injury; (2) whether this injury exceeds any offsetting consumer benefits; and (3) whether the injury was one that consumers could not reasonably have avoided. We find that all three criteria are satisfied in the present case.

There clearly has been serious consumer injury. At least one person has been killed and eleven others burned. Many of the burn injuries have been major ones. It is true that [these injuries] involve only limited numbers of people, but conduct causing a very severe harm to a small number will be covered.

The second criterion states that the consumer injury must not be outweighed by any countervailing benefits to consumers or to competition that the practice also brings about. The principal tradeoff to be considered in this analysis is that involving compliance costs. More information may be helpful to consumers, but such information can be produced only by incurring costs that are ultimately borne as higher prices by those same consumers. Harvester's program which finally led to an effective warning cost the company approximately $2.8 million. Here, however, Harvester's expenses were not large in relation to the injuries that could have been avoided. We therefore conclude that the costs and benefits in this case satisfy the second unfairness criterion.

Finally, the injury must be one that consumers could not reasonably have avoided. Here, tractor operators could have avoided their injuries if they had refrained from removing the cap from a hot or running tractor—something that both the owner's manuals and common knowledge suggested was a dangerous practice. However, whether some consequence is reasonably avoidable depends, not just on whether people know the steps to take to prevent it, but also on whether they understand the necessity of taking those steps. Farmers may have known that loosening the fuel cap was generally a poor practice, but they did not know the full consequences that might follow. Since fuel geysering was a risk that they were not aware of, they could not reasonably have avoided it. This is so even though they had been informed of measures to prevent it. Such information was not the same thing as an effective warning.

Remedy. Having found that Harvester was engaged in unfair practices, we must now determine what corrective measures the public interest will require. Under the particular circumstances of this case, we will issue no order at all. First, Harvester's voluntary notification program has already provided all the relief that could be expected from a Commission order. Second, Harvester has not made a gasoline tractor since 1978 and does not appear likely to do so again in the future.

Decision of the administrative law judge affirmed in part and reversed in part.

THE MAGNUSON–MOSS WARRANTY ACT

Introduction

After authorizing several studies concluding that product warranties are often confusing, misleading, and frustrating to consumers, Congress passed the Magnuson-Moss Warranty Act in 1975. One of the act's aims is to provide minimum warranty protection for consumers; some of its provisions on that subject are discussed in the Product Liability chapter. Here, we focus on Magnuson-Moss's rules requiring that consumer warranties contain certain information and that this information be made available to buyers before the sale.

The Magnuson-Moss Act mainly applies to *written warranties* for *consumer products*. Nothing in the act requires sellers to give a written warranty, and sellers who decline to give such a warranty generally are not covered. A consumer product is personal property that is ordinarily used for personal, family, or household purposes. In addition, many Magnuson-Moss provisions apply only when a written warranty is given in connection with the sale of a consumer product to a *consumer*. A consumer is a buyer or transferee of a consumer product who does not use it either for resale or in his own business. Retailers purchasing inventory, for example, generally do not qualify as Magnuson-Moss consumers.

Required Warranty Information

The Magnuson-Moss Act and its regulations require the simple, clear, and conspicuous presentation of certain information in written warranties to consumers for con-

sumer products costing more than \$15.[11] The most important kinds of information that must be included are: (1) the persons who are protected by the warranty when coverage is limited to the original purchaser or is otherwise limited; (2) the products, parts, characteristics, components, or properties covered by the warranty; (3) what the warrantor will do in case of a product defect or other failure to conform to the warranty, including the items or services that the warrantor will pay for or provide; (4) the time the warranty begins (if different from the purchase date) and its duration; and (5) a step-by-step explanation of the procedure that the consumer should follow to obtain the performance of warranty obligations, including detailed information on those authorized to perform such obligations.

The act also requires that a warrantor disclose (1) any limitations on the duration of implied warranties and (2) any attempt to limit consequential damages or other consumer remedies.[12] If a seller limits the duration of an implied warranty, the seller must also include the following language: "Some states do not allow limitations on how long an implied warranty lasts, so the above limitation may not apply to you." If a seller attempts to limit the consumer's remedies, the following language must be included: "Some states do not allow the exclusion or limitation of incidental or consequential damages, so the above limitation or exclusion may not apply

---

[11]For the rules in this section and the following section, the act itself states a \$5 figure. However, the regulations implementing the act state a \$15 figure. Note also that the dollar figure for triggering the Magnuson-Moss full and limited warranty provisions discussed in the Product Liability chapter is \$10.

[12]The Product Liability chapter discusses limitations on an implied warranty's duration and on a consumer's remedies.

FIGURE 3   The FTC's Door-to-Door Sales Rule: 16 C.F.R. section 702.3(d) (1990)

(d) *Door-to-door sales.* (1) For purposes of this paragraph:

(i) "Door-to-Door sale" means a sale of consumer products in which the seller or his representative personally solicits the sale, including those in response to or following an invitation by a buyer, and the buyer's agreement to offer to purchase is made at a place other than the place of business of the seller.

(ii) "Prospective buyer" means an individual solicited by a door-to-door seller to buy a consumer product who indicates sufficient interest in that consumer product or maintains sufficient contact with the seller for the seller reasonably to conclude that the person solicited is considering purchasing the product.

(2) Any seller who offers for sale to consumers consumer products with written warranties by means of door-to-door sales shall, prior to the consummation of the sale, disclose the fact that the sales representative has copies of the warranties for the warranted products being offered for sale, which may be inspected by the prospective buyer at any time during the sales presentation. Such disclosure shall be made orally and shall be included in any written materials shown to prospective buyers.

---

to you." Finally, all covered warranties must include the following statement: "This warranty gives you specific legal rights, and you may also have other rights which vary from state to state."

Presale Availability of Warranty Information

The regulations accompanying the Magnuson-Moss Act also contain detailed rules requiring that warranty terms be made available to a buyer before the sale. These rules generally govern sales of consumer products costing more than $15 to consumers. They set out certain duties that must be met by sellers (usually retailers) and by warrantors (usually manufacturers) of such products. Very briefly, these regulations require that:

1. *Sellers* must make the text of the warranty available for the prospective buyer's review prior to the sale, either by displaying the warranty in close proximity to the product, or by furnishing the warranty upon request after posting signs informing buyers of its availability.

2. *Catalog or mail-order sellers* must clearly and conspicuously disclose in their catalog or solicitation either the full text of the warranty or the address from which a free copy of the warranty can be obtained.

3. *Door-to-door sales.* To provide you with a concrete illustration of an FTC trade regulation rule governing a fairly common occurrence, we include the full text of its door-to-door sales rule in Figure 3. As FTC rules go, this one is fairly short and straightforward.

4. *Warrantors* must provide sellers with the warranty materials necessary for them to comply with the duties stated above in paragraph 1; and must provide catalog, mail-order, and door-to-door sellers with copies of the warranties that they need to meet their duties.

Enforcement

Any failure to comply with the above rules violates section 5 of the FTC Act and can trigger Commission action against the violator. In addition, either the FTC or the attorney general may sue in federal district court to obtain injunctive relief against such violations, and against certain deceptive warranties covering consumer products. The Magnuson-Moss Act also creates various civil actions for private parties; some of these are discussed in the Product Liability chapter.

CONSUMER CREDIT LAWS

In addition to being harmed by defective products, deceptive or unfair advertising, and inadequate disclosure of warranty terms, consumers may be victimized in the process of obtaining credit. Because many consumer purchases are credit sales, Congress has enacted several statutes designed to protect consumers from unfair treatment throughout the course of their credit transactions.

Truth in Lending Act

In the past, creditors often failed to state credit information important to consumer borrowers, or stated it in ways that did not allow consumers to compare creditors. Interest rate or finance charge formulas, for example, often can be stated in several ways—many of them confusing to the average consumer either in isolation or when compared with other statements. In response to such problems, Congress passed the Truth in Lending Act (TILA) in 1968. The TILA's basic aims are to increase consumer knowledge and understanding of credit terms by compelling their *disclosure*, and to help consumers better shop for credit by commanding *uniform* disclosures. But the act protects consumers in other ways as well.

Coverage The TILA generally applies to: (1) creditors, (2) that extend consumer credit, (3) to a debtor, (4) in an amount no greater than $25,000. A *creditor* is a party that regularly extends consumer credit; examples include banks, credit card issuers, and savings and loan associations. Extending credit need not be the creditor's primary business. Auto dealers and retail stores, for instance, are creditors if they regularly arrange or extend credit financing. To qualify as a creditor, the party in question also must either impose a finance charge, or by agreement require payment in more than four installments.

Consumer credit is credit enabling the purchase of goods, services, or real estate used primarily for personal, family, or household purposes. Commercial, business, or agricultural purposes are not covered. The TILA *debtor* must be a natural person; the act does not protect business organizations. Finally, except for the real property situations discussed later, the amount financed must be *$25,000 or less* for the TILA to apply.

Disclosure Provisions The TILA's disclosure provisions and the Federal Reserve Board regulations implementing them are long, detailed, and complex. The most important such provisions break down into three categories.

1. *Open-end credit.* The TILA defines an open-end credit plan as one that contemplates repeated transactions and that involves a finance charge that may be computed from time to time on the unpaid balance. Such plans normally allow consumers the option of paying in variable installments or in full; examples include credit card plans and revolving charge accounts offered by retail stores. Open-end credit plans require two general forms of disclosure: (a) an initial statement made before the first transaction under the plan, and (b) a series of periodic statements (usually, one for each billing cycle). In each case, the required disclosures must be made clearly, conspicuously, and in meaningful sequence.

Among the disclosures required in the *initial statement* are: (a) when a finance charge is imposed and how it is determined (including the annual percentage rate or APR, and the method for establishing the balance on which the finance charge is computed), (b) the amount of any additional charges and the method for computing them, (c) the fact that the creditor has taken or will acquire a security interest in the debtor's property, and (d) the debtor's billing rights. *Periodic statements* require an even lengthier list of disclosures. Much of the information contained in a monthly credit card statement, for example, is compelled by the TILA.

2. *Closed-end credit.* The TILA requires a different set of disclosures for other credit plans, which generally involve *closed-end* credit. Closed-end credit such as a car loan or a consumer loan from a finance company is extended for a specific time period; and the total amount financed, number of payments, and due dates are all agreed on at the time of the transaction. Examples of the disclosures necessary before the completion of a closed-end credit transaction include: (a) the total finance charge; (b) the APR; (c) the amount financed; (d) the total number of payments, their due dates, and the amount of each payment; (e) the total dollar value of all payments; (f) any late charges imposed for past-due payments; and (g) any security interest taken by the creditor and the property that it covers.

3. *Credit card applications and solicitations.* In 1988, Congress amended the TILA to impose disclosure requirements on credit card *applications and solicitations*. These elaborate requirements differ depending on whether the application or solicitation is made by direct mail, telephone, or other means such as catalogs and magazines. For example, *direct mail* applications and solicitations must include information about matters such as the APR, annual fees, the grace period for paying without incurring a finance charge, and the method for computing the balance on which the finance charge is based. The amendment also includes a section imposing disclosure requirements on applications or solicitations for *charge cards*—cards involving an extension of credit that is not subject to a finance charge.

Real Estate-Related Transactions *Disclosure* As noted previously, credit transactions involving the sale of real estate—for example, the purchase of a home—are subject to the TILA. Here, the disclosure requirements differ slightly from those applied to other closed-end credit transactions. More importantly, the usual $25,000 maximum does not apply where a creditor takes a security interest in a debtor's real property or in personal property used as the debtor's principal dwelling (e.g., a mobile home).

The Three-Day Rescission Right In certain con-sumer credit transactions involving a creditor's retention of a security interest on a debtor's principal dwelling, the debtor may also have a *three-day rescission right*. This means that the debtor can cancel the transaction within three business days of either (1) its completion or (2) the time the creditor has made all the material disclosures required by the TILA. Except for the $25,000 maxi-mum, most of the TILA coverage requirements dis-cussed earlier must be met for the rescission right to exist. More importantly, this right does not apply to mortgages and other security interests taken to finance the *acquisition or initial construction* of the debtor's principal dwelling. Thus, the ordinary home buyer does not have this rescission right. Instead, it applies to such things as a major home repair whose financing is secured by a lien on the debtor's home.

Home Equity Loans In 1988, the TILA was amended to regulate open-end consumer credit plans in-volving an extension of credit that is secured by a con-sumer's principal dwelling—basically, the popular home equity loans. The act now controls the content of *adver-tisements* for such plans, requiring certain information in specified situations and forbidding such misleading terms as "free money." It also imposes elaborate disclo-sure requirements in *applications* for such plans. These include matters such as interest rates, fees, repayment options, minimum payments, repayment periods, and many more.

Finally, the act also controls the *terms* of such a plan and the *actions* a creditor can take pursuant to it. For example: (1) if the plan involves a variable interest rate, the index rate to which changes in the APR are pegged must be based on some publicly available rate and must not be under the creditor's control; (2) a creditor cannot unilaterally terminate the plan and require immediate repayment of the outstanding balance unless a consumer has made material misrepresentations, has failed to re-pay the balance as agreed, or has done something to adversely affect the creditor's security; and (3) the plan cannot contain a provision allowing a creditor to unilat-erally alter important terms of the plan.

Other TILA Provisions Along with the home equity loan advertising regulations just discussed, the Truth in Lending Act also has general provisions dealing with *consumer credit advertising*. For example, the act pre-vents a creditor from "baiting" customers by advertising loan or down payment amounts that it does not usually

make available. In addition, the TILA requires that if advertisements for open-end consumer credit plans state any of the plan's specific terms, they must state various other terms as well. For instance, an advertisement using such terms as "$100 down payment," "8 percent inter-est," or "$99 per month" also must state various other relevant terms such as the APR. The aim of this all-or-nothing provision is to help consumers put the advertised term in proper perspective.

Finally, the TILA has a few other rules relating to credit cards. The most important of these rules limits a cardholder's liability for unauthorized use of the card to a maximum of $50. Unauthorized use is use of the card by a person other than the cardholder, where this person lacks express, implied, or apparent authority for such use.[13]

Enforcement Various federal agencies enforce the TILA. Except in areas specifically committed to a par-ticular agency, however, overall enforcement authority rests in the FTC. In addition, those who willfully and knowingly violate the act may face criminal prosecu-tion. Civil actions by private parties, including class ac-tions, also are possible.

Consumer Leasing Act

People often lease rather than purchase consumer prod-ucts such as cars, appliances, and televisions. As origi-nally drafted, the Truth in Lending Act applied to only some of these consumer leases. In order to regulate such leases more effectively, Congress passed the Consumer Leasing Act in 1976. The act covers leases of personal property: (1) to natural persons (not organizations), (2) for consumer purposes, (3) for an amount not exceeding $25,000, and (4) for a period exceeding four months.

The act requires that a lessor make numerous written *disclosures* to a lessee before the consummation of the lease transaction. Examples include: a description or identification of the leased property; the number, amount, and due dates of the lease payments; their total amount; any express warranties made by the lessor; and any security interest taken by the lessor. Like the TILA's all-or-nothing provision, the act also requires that lease *advertisements* include certain additional information if they already state the amount of any payment, the

---

[13]Express, implied, and apparent authority are discussed in the part on agency law.

number of required payments, the amount of the down payment, or that no down payment is required.

The Consumer Leasing Act subjects creditors violating its disclosure requirements to the same civil suits that are permitted under the TILA. Also, the FTC enforces the act.

Fair Credit Reporting Act

Credit bureaus and the reports they provide to various users can significantly affect a person's ability to obtain credit, insurance, employment, and many of life's other goods. Often, affected individuals are unaware of the influence that credit reports had on such decisions. The Fair Credit Reporting Act (FCRA) was enacted in 1970 to give people some protection against abuses in the process of disseminating information about their creditworthiness.

Duties of Consumer Reporting Agencies The FCRA imposes a number of duties on consumer reporting agencies—agencies that regularly compile credit-related information on individuals for the purpose of furnishing consumer credit reports to users. A consumer reporting agency must adopt *reasonable procedures* to:

1. Assure that users employ the information only for the following purposes: consumer credit sales, employment evaluations, the underwriting of insurance, the granting of a government license or other benefit, or any other business transaction where the user has a legitimate business need for the information.

2. Avoid including in a report obsolete information predating the report by more than a stated period. This period is usually 7 years; for a prior bankruptcy, it is 10 years. This duty does not apply to credit reports used in connection with certain large credit transactions, certain life insurance policies, and certain applications for employment.

3. Assure the maximum possible accuracy regarding the information contained in credit reports.

However, the act does little to limit the *types* of data that can be included in credit reports. In fact, all kinds of information regarding a person's character, reputation, personal traits, and mode of life seemingly are permitted.

Disclosure Duties on Users The Fair Credit Reporting Act also imposes certain disclosure duties on *users*

of credit reports—mainly credit sellers, lenders, employers, and insurers. One of these duties applies to users that order an *investigative consumer report*. This is a credit report that includes information on a person's character, reputation, personal traits, or mode of living and that is based on interviews with neighbors, friends, associates, and the like. If a user procures such a report, it must disclose to the person affected that the report has been requested, that the report may contain information of the sort just described, and that the person has a right to obtain further disclosures about the user's investigation. If the person requests such disclosures within a reasonable time, the user must reveal the nature and scope of the investigation.

Another disclosure duty arises when, because of information contained in any credit report, a user (1) rejects an applicant for consumer credit, insurance, or employment; or (2) charges a higher rate for credit or insurance. In these situations, the user must maintain *reasonable procedures* for advising the affected individual that it relied on the credit report in making its decision, and for stating the name and address of the consumer reporting agency that supplied the report.

Finally, the FCRA also imposes a disclosure duty on users who deny consumer credit to a consumer, or increase the charge for such credit, because of information obtained from *a person other than a consumer reporting agency*. If a consumer makes a written request for such information within 60 days after learning about the denial or the increased charge, the user must disclose the information to the consumer within a reasonable time. Also, the user must inform the consumer of her right to make such a request at the time its unfavorable credit decision is communicated to her.

Disclosure and Correction of Credit Report Information After a request from a properly identified individual, a *consumer reporting agency* must disclose to that individual: (1) the nature and substance of all its information about the individual (except medical information), (2) the sources of this information (except for information used solely for investigative reports), and (3) the recipients of any credit reports that it has furnished within certain defined time periods. Then, a person disputing the completeness or accuracy of the agency's information can compel it to reinvestigate. If, after this investigation, the credit bureau finds the information to be inaccurate or unverifiable, it must delete the information from the person's file. An individual who is not satisfied with the agency's investigation may file a brief statement setting forth the nature of her dispute with the agency. If this is done, any subsequent credit report containing the disputed information must note that it is disputed and must provide either the individual's statement or a clear and accurate summary of it. Also, an agency may be required to notify certain prior recipients of deleted, unverifiable, or disputed information if the individual requests this. However, there is no duty to investigate or to include the consumer's version of the facts if the credit bureau has reason to believe that the individual's request is frivolous or irrelevant.

Enforcement   Violations of the Fair Credit Reporting Act are violations of section 5 of the FTC Act, and the Commission may use its normal enforcement procedures in such cases. Other federal agencies may also enforce the FCRA in certain situations. The FCRA establishes criminal penalties for (1) persons who knowingly and willfully obtain consumer information from a credit bureau under false pretenses and (2) credit bureau officers or employees who knowingly or willfully provide information to unauthorized persons. Violations of the FCRA may also trigger private civil suits against consumer reporting agencies and users. If the violation is willful, punitive damages are possible.

Equal Credit Opportunity Act

Responding to studies showing sex discrimination in the granting or denial of credit, Congress passed the Equal Credit Opportunity Act (ECOA) in 1974. Originally, the act only prohibited credit discrimination on the bases of sex or marital status. In 1976, however, it was amended to include age, race, color, national origin, religion, and the obtaining of income from public assistance as additional forbidden grounds for credit decisions. The ECOA covers all entities that regularly arrange, extend, renew, or continue credit. Examples of covered entities include banks; savings and loan associations; credit card issuers; and many retailers, auto dealers, and realtors. Finally, the act is not limited to consumer credit, and also covers business and commercial loans.

ECOA Provisions   The ECOA governs all phases of a credit transaction. As authorized by the act, the Federal Reserve Board has promulgated detailed regulations covering, among other things, the information that creditors may require in credit applications, the ways in which creditors can evaluate applications, and the permissible reasons for deciding whether to extend credit. These regulations cover matters such as requests for information about a loan applicant's spouse; requests for the applicant's gender, race, color, religion, or national origin; and credit decisions based on assumptions about the likelihood that the applicant will bear a child and thus lose future income. Even where the regulations do not specifically prohibit certain creditor behavior, moreover, that behavior still may violate the act itself. Finally, even credit practices that are perfectly neutral on their face may sometimes result in ECOA violations. In such cases, some courts have required the plaintiff to demonstrate that the practice has an adverse statistical impact on one of the ECOA's protected classes.[14]

The ECOA also requires that creditors notify applicants of the action taken on a credit application within 30 days of its receipt, or any longer reasonable time stated in the regulations. If the action is unfavorable, an applicant is entitled to a statement of reasons from the creditor. The ECOA and the regulations go into great detail when describing what a creditor must do to meet this requirement.

Enforcement   The ECOA is enforced by several federal agencies, with overall enforcement resting in the hands of the FTC. Which agency enforces the act depends on the type of creditor or credit involved. Civil actions by aggrieved private parties, including class actions, also are possible.

The following case, *Miller v. Elegant Junk,* shows how the ECOA and the Fair Credit Reporting Act can interact.

---

[14] This resembles the adverse impact or disparate impact method of proof used in employment discrimination cases under Title VII of the 1964 Civil Rights Act. See the Employment Law chapter.

MILLER v. ELEGANT JUNK

616 F. Supp. 551 (S.D. W.Va. 1985).

Sylvia Miller, a married woman, visited a retail furniture store called Elegant Junk, and saw a pair of loveseats that she wanted to purchase. The store offered to arrange financing for Miller through the Public Industrial Loan Company (Public Finance). After Miller filled out a loan application, Public Finance informed her that it would deny the application unless her husband cosigned it. The claimed reason for this decision was an unfavorable credit report on Miller.

Still wanting to buy the loveseats, Miller arranged for her husband to sign the application. After taking possession of the goods, she paid off the loan in a timely fashion. In the meantime, she sued Elegant Junk and Public Finance under the ECOA for credit discrimination on the bases of sex and marital status. Because Elegant Junk had gone into bankruptcy, the proceedings against it were stayed. Public Finance moved for summary judgment.

Haden, District Judge.   If Public Finance denied Miller's credit application on the basis of creditworthiness instead of her marital status or sex, it would have an absolute defense to this action. The basis for the defense of creditworthiness can be found in the regulations issued by the Federal Reserve Board pursuant to the ECOA. "[A] creditor shall not require the signature of an applicant's spouse or other person, other than a joint applicant, on any credit instrument if the applicant qualifies under the creditor's standards of creditworthiness for the amount in terms of the credit requested." This defense is also reflected in the congressional intent of making "credit equally available to all creditworthy customers without regard to sex or marital status" [quoting the original ECOA].

To controvert the claimed reliance of Public Finance on the credit reporting agency, Miller has submitted an affidavit detailing her income and obligations. However, Miller must do more than show her good financial state. She must make some showing that the credit reporting agency accurately reported her [good] financial state to Public Finance. The record now reflects an uncontroverted fact presented by Public Finance—a fact which provides it an absolute defense to a claim of discrimination. If the fact is not controverted, summary judgment is appropriate.

Congress has explicitly recognized the reliance which credit institutions place on credit reporting agencies. Inaccurate credit reports directly impair the efficiency of the banking system and unfair credit reporting methods undermine the public confidence which is essential to the continued functioning of the banking system. Consequently, Congress has dictated that the preparers of consumer reports must follow reasonable procedures to assure maximum possible accuracy of the information reported. Upon request the consumer can obtain the nature and substance of all information in the files of the reporting agency. These references to the Fair Credit Reporting Act are relevant on three points. First, the act reinforces the propriety exhibited by Public Finance in relying upon information supplied by a credit reporting agency. Second, under the act Miller is provided with access to information which could put Public Finance's reliance on the reporting agency in issue. Third, the act suggests what may be the appropriate remedy for Miller: an [FCRA] action against the reporting agency for supplying inaccurate information.

When a motion for summary judgment is made and supported, an adverse party may not rest upon the allegations of his pleading, but must set forth specific facts showing that there is a genuine issue for trial. Miller not having controverted Public Finance's reliance upon the credit reporting agency, the court holds summary judgment to be appropriate.

Public Finance's motion for summary judgment granted.

Fair Credit Billing Act

The Fair Credit Billing Act, effective in 1975, is mainly aimed at credit card issuers. Although it regulates the credit card business in other ways, its most important provisions involve billing disputes.[15] In order to trigger these provisions, a cardholder must give the issuer written notice of an alleged error in a billing statement within 60 days of the time that the statement is sent to the cardholder. Then, within two complete billing cycles or 90 days (whichever is less), the issuer must either (1) correct the cardholder's account, or (2) send the cardholder a written statement justifying the statement's accuracy. Until the issuer takes either of these steps, it may not (1) restrict or close the cardholder's account because of her failure to pay the disputed amount, (2) try to collect the disputed amount, or (3) report or threaten to report the cardholder's failure to pay the disputed amount to a third party such as a consumer reporting agency.

Once an issuer has met the act's requirements, it must also give a cardholder at least 10 days to pay the disputed amount before making an unfavorable report to a third party. If the cardholder disputes the issuer's justification within the 10-day period allowed for payment, the issuer can make such a report only if it also tells the third party that the debt is disputed and gives the cardholder the third party's name and address. In addition, the issuer must report the final resolution of the dispute to the third party.

Finally, an issuer that fails to comply with any of these rules forfeits its right to collect $50 of the disputed amount from the cardholder. Because the issuer still may be able to collect the balance on large disputed debts, it is doubtful whether this provision does much to deter violations of the act.

Fair Debt Collection Practices Act

Public concern over various abusive, deceptive, and unfair practices by debt collectors led Congress to pass the Fair Debt Collection Practices Act (FDCPA) in 1977. The act applies to debts that involve money, property, insurance, or services obtained by a *consumer* for *consumer purposes*. Normally, the act only covers those who are in the business of collecting debts owed to *others*. However, creditors who collect their own

debts are covered when, by using a name other than their own name, they indicate that a third party is collecting the debt.

Communication Rules   Except where necessary to *locate* a debtor, the FDCPA generally prevents debt collectors from contacting third parties such as the debtor's employer, relatives, or friends. The act also limits a collector's contacts with the debtor himself. Unless the debtor consents, for instance, a collector cannot contact him at unusual or inconvenient times or places, or at his place of employment if the employer forbids such contacts. Also, a collector cannot contact a debtor if it knows that the debtor is represented by an attorney, unless the attorney consents to such contact or fails to respond to the collector's communications. In addition, a collector must cease most communications with a debtor if the debtor gives the creditor written notification that he refuses to pay the debt or that he does not desire further communications from the collector.

The FDCPA also requires a collector to give a debtor certain information about the debt (including its amount and the creditor's name) within five days of the collector's first communication with the debtor. If the debtor disputes the debt in writing within 30 days after receiving this information, the collector must cease its collection efforts until it sends verification of the debt to the debtor.

Specific Forbidden Practices   The FDCPA sets out categories of forbidden collector practices and lists many specific examples of each category. The listed examples, however, do not exhaust the ways that debt collectors can violate the act. The categories are:

1. *Harassment, oppression, or abuse.* Examples of such behavior include threats of violence, obscene or abusive language, and repeated phone calls.

2. *False or misleading misrepresentations.* Among the FDCPA's listed examples are statements that a debtor will be imprisoned for failure to pay, that a collector is affiliated with the government, or that misstate the amount of the debt.

3. *Unfair practices.* These include: collecting from a debtor an amount exceeding the amount legally due, getting a debtor to accept a collect call before revealing the call's true purpose, and falsely or unjustifiably threatening to take a debtor's property.

Enforcement   The FTC is the principal enforcement agency for the FDCPA, although other agencies enforce it in certain cases. However, the FTC cannot

---

[15]The Federal Reserve Board has promulgated regulations regarding the resolution of billing errors, and the FTC has some enforcement authority under the act as well.

promulgate trade regulation rules to enforce the act. The FDCPA also permits individual civil actions and class actions by the affected debtor or debtors.[16]

However, such suits fail if the violation was an *unintentional bona fide error.*

The following *Rutyna* case discusses examples of harassment, oppression, or abuse; false or misleading misrepresentations; and unfair practices other than those listed earlier.

[16]Also, some debt collection practices might lead to tort liability for invasion of privacy, or perhaps even for intentional infliction of emotional distress. The Intentional Torts chapter discusses these torts.

RUTYNA v. COLLECTION ACCOUNTS TERMINAL, INC.

478 F. Supp. 980 (N.D. Ill. 1979)

Josephine Rutyna was a 60-year-old widow who suffered from high blood pressure and epilepsy. In late 1976 and early 1977, she incurred a debt for medical services. At the time, she believed that this debt had been paid by medicare or private health insurance. According to Rutyna, an agent of Collection Accounts Terminal, Inc. telephoned her in July 1978, informing her that she still owed $56 in medical expenses. When she denied the existence of the debt, the voice on the telephone responded: "You owe it, you don't want to pay, so we're going to have to do something about it."

On August 10, 1978, Rutyna received a letter from Collection, which stated:

You have shown that you are unwilling to work out a friendly settlement with us to clear the above debt. Our field investigator has now been instructed to make an investigation in your neighborhood and to personally call on your employer. The immediate payment of the full amount, or a personal visit to this office, will spare you this embarrassment.

The top of the letter stated the creditor's name and the amount of the alleged debt. The envelope containing the letter stated Collection's full name and its return address.

Rutyna claimed that she became very nervous, upset, and worried after receiving this letter. She was particularly concerned that Collection would embarrass her by informing her neighbors about the debt and about her medical problems. She sued Collection under the FDCPA in federal district court. Later, she moved for summary judgment.

McMillen, District Judge. *Harassment or Abuse.* The FDCPA provides [that] a debt collector may not engage in any conduct the natural consequence of which is to harass, oppress, or abuse any person in connection with the collection of a debt. This section then lists six specifically prohibited types of conduct, without limiting the general application of the foregoing [provision]. Mrs. Rutyna does not allege conduct which falls within the specific prohibitions, but Collection's letter to her does violate this general standard. Without doubt Collection's letter has the natural (and intended) consequence of harassing, oppressing, and abusing the recipient. The tone of the letter is one of intimidation, and was intended as such in order to effect a collection. The threat of an investigation and resulting embarrassment to the alleged debtor is clear.

Deception and Improper Threats. The FDCPA [also] bars a debt collector from using any false, deceptive, or misleading representation or means in connection with the collection of any debt. Sixteen specific practices are listed in this provision, without limiting the application of this general standard. [This section of the act specifically] bars a threat to take any action that cannot legally be taken or that is not intended to be taken. Collection's letter threatened embarrassing contacts with Mrs. Rutyna's employer and neighbors. [Because the FDCPA] prohibits communication by the debt collector with third parties (with certain limited exceptions not here relevant),

Mrs. Rutyna's neighbors and employer could not legally be contacted by defendant in connection with this debt. The letter falsely represents to the contrary.

Unfair Practice/Return Address. The envelope received by Mrs. Rutyna bore a return address, which began "COLLECTION ACCOUNTS TERMINAL, INC." The FDCPA also bars unfair or unconscionable means to collect or attempt to collect any debt. It specifically bars:

Using any language or symbol, other than the debt collector's address, on any envelope when communicating with a consumer by use of the mails or by telegram, except that a debt collector may use his business name if such name does not indicate that he is in the debt collection business.

Collection's return address violated this provision, because its business name does indicate that it is in the debt collection business. The purpose of this provision is apparently to prevent embarrassment resulting from a conspicuous name on the envelope, indicating that the contents pertain to debt collection.

Rutyna's motion for summary judgment granted.

REGULATION OF PRODUCT SAFETY

Yet another facet of consumer protection law is federal regulation aimed at increasing product safety. As discussed in the Product Liability chapter, sellers and manufacturers of dangerously defective products are often civilly liable to those injured by such products. Damage recoveries, however, are at best an after-the-fact remedy for injuries caused by hazardous consumer products. Thus, federal law also seeks to promote product safety by *direct regulation* of dangerously defective products.

The most important federal product safety measure is the Consumer Product Safety Act of 1972 (CPSA). The CPSA established the Consumer Product Safety Commission (CPSC), an independent regulatory agency that is the main federal body concerned with product safety. The CPSC's authority is basically limited to *consumer products*. Not within the Commission's domain, however, are certain consumer products regulated by other agencies, including motor vehicles and equipment, firearms, aircraft, pesticides, boats, drugs, cosmetics, food products, and tobacco products. Figure 4 lists several other federal product safety measures, some of which regulate the products just noted and some of which are enforced by the CPSC.

Among the CPSC's activities are the following:

1. *Issuing consumer product safety standards.* These standards may: (a) involve the performance of consumer products or (b) require product warnings or instructions. A product safety standard should be issued only when the product in question presents an *unreasonable* risk of injury and the standard is *reasonably necessary* to prevent or reduce that risk.

2. *Issuing rules banning certain hazardous products.* Such rules are permissible when, in addition to presenting an unreasonable risk of injury, the product is so dangerous that no feasible product safety standard would protect the public from the risks it poses.

3. *Bringing suit in federal district court to eliminate the dangers presented by imminently hazardous consumer products.* Imminently hazardous consumer products are those that pose an immediate and unreasonable risk of death, serious illness, or severe personal injury.

4. *Receiving and acting on notification of substantial product hazards.* The CPSA requires that manufacturers, distributors, and retailers notify the CPSC if they have reason to know that their products present a substantial product hazard. Such a hazard exists when the product creates a substantial risk of injury to the public, either because it violates a Commission safety rule or for other reasons. In such cases, the CPSC may, among other things, order the private party to give notice of the problem to those affected by it, repair or replace the product, or submit its own corrective action plan.

The CPSA provides a host of other remedies and enforcement devices in addition to those already discussed. The Commission and the U.S. attorney general may sue for *injunctive relief* or the *seizure* of products to enforce various provisions of the act. *Civil penalties* against those who knowingly violate various CPSA provisions and CPSC rules also are possible. *Criminal penalties* may be imposed on those who knowingly and willfully violate such provisions and rules after CPSC notification of their failure to comply. Upon compliance with certain notice requirements, moreover, a private party may sue

FIGURE 4   Some Other Federal Product Safety-Related Statutes

Child Protection and Toy Safety Act	Regulates hazardous toys and imposes labeling requirements on certain toys
Cigarette Labeling and Advertising Act	Requires warning labels on cigarette packages
Egg Products Inspection Act	Regulates marketing of egg products and requires inspections of egg products and plants for their manufacture
Federal Meat Inspection Act	Regulates labeling and packaging and requires inspection of meat and meat products
Flammable Fabrics Act	Regulates manufacture, sale and importation of flammable fabrics
Food, Drug, and Cosmetics Act	Comprehensively regulates marketing of food, drugs, and cosmetics
Hazardous Substances Act	As part of comprehensive regulation of hazardous substances, imposes certain restrictions on marketing of such substances
Insecticide, Fungicide, and Rodenticide Act	Requires registration and inspection of pesticides broadly defined and of establishments of their manufacture; regulates sales of pesticides
National Highway Traffic and Motor Vehicle Safety Act	Establishes motor vehicle safety standards
Poison Prevention Packaging Act	Regulates packaging of household substances for protection of children
Poultry Products Inspection Act	Requires inspections of establishments producing poultry products; regulates slaughtering of poultry and marketing, labeling, and containers for poultry products
Smokeless Tobacco Act	Bans television and radio advertisements for smokeless tobacco; requires warnings on packages and other advertisements

for an *injunction* to enforce any CPSC rule or order—so long as the Commission or the attorney general has not begun a civil or criminal action against the alleged violation. Finally, those injured due to a knowing and willful violation of a CPSC rule or order may sue for *damages* if the amount in controversy exceeds $10,000.

ETHICAL AND PUBLIC POLICY CONCERNS

1. In the *International Harvester* case earlier in the chapter, the FTC weighed the consumer injury caused by fuel geysering against the costs of providing effective warnings about it. In this case, 12 people had been seriously burned by fuel geysering over a period of about 40 years, and one of these people died. The Commission concluded that the injuries that could have been avoided by a warning outweighed the $2.8 million apparently required for an effective warning. However, its method clearly left open the possibility that in some cases, a practice's benefits to consumers or to competition might outweigh the harm it causes.

Is it morally right to balance personal injury and human life against economic gain? Doesn't this amount to putting a dollar value on human life? Isn't each human life infinitely precious? How can decisionmaking processes like the FTC's ever be justified?

On the other hand, if you think that the Commission's balancing exercise *is* justifiable, how is one to strike the balance? How would you have struck the balance in the *International Harvester* case?

2. Over the years, some people have argued that modern mass advertising for consumer products and services is much more *manipulative* than *informative*. The idea is that by playing on unconscious or semiconscious consumer impulses of all kinds, such advertising motivates consumers to buy products for reasons other than those products' innate attributes. Generally speaking, do you think that this charge is accurate or inaccurate? In answering, consider: (a) whether advertisers often try such ploys, and (b) whether they are generally effective when tried. If you think that the charge is accurate, what does it do to the idea that free competition maximizes consumer welfare by rewarding those who sell superior products and services and weeding out their inferior competitors?

Assuming for the sake of argument that the charge is generally accurate, does FTC Act section 5's ban on *deceptive* advertising do much to address the problem? What body of law discussed in this chapter might conceivably do so?

3. Review the various FTC enforcement devices discussed earlier in this chapter. Taken as a whole, how often do they provide injured consumers with a dollar recovery against those who violate the laws the Commission enforces? How much incentive do consumers have to complain to the FTC? What set of private parties *do* have such an incentive? What specific FTC remedy does give consumers some monetary incentive to complain to the FTC?

4. In the *SCTLA* case earlier in this chapter, the Supreme Court decided that the regulars' behavior was per se illegal under Sherman Act section 1 and FTC Act section 5. Thus, it did not consider the reasons for the regulars' conduct, its real or imagined social benefits, or its actual anticompetitive effects. Presumably, the Court would have been better able to weigh and consider all relevant factors and values had it done so. But what disadvantages would such a rule of reason approach involve?

SUMMARY

America's primary consumer protection agency, the Federal Trade Commission, performs a number of functions. It attacks anticompetitive practices made illegal by the Sherman, Clayton, and Robinson-Patman Acts. In addition, section 5 of the Federal Trade Commission Act gives the FTC the ability to attack anticompetitive behavior that cannot be reached under other antitrust statutes. Perhaps the most important power granted the FTC by section 5, however, is its authority to regulate *deceptive* and *unfair* acts or practices. The most important such acts or practices involve advertising. The FTC also enforces many other federal consumer protection statutes.

The Commission uses a variety of means to enforce the various laws it administers. It tries to assure voluntary compliance with these statutes by issuing *advisory opinions* and *industry guides*. It also formulates *trade regulation rules* that describe specific illegal practices and have the force of law. Violations of these rules, or of many statutes that the FTC enforces, may be attacked in an FTC *adjudicative proceeding*. In deception and unfairness cases under section 5, the proceeding is governed by substantive standards that the FTC has articulated. If the administrative law judge concludes that there has been a violation, he usually issues an order that the offending party *cease and desist* from its illegal

behavior. In some situations, however, the FTC may avoid an adjudicative proceeding by settling the case through a *consent order*.

The federal consumer protection mission is also furthered by a number of specific consumer protection measures that are enforced by the FTC and other regulatory bodies. One of these is the *Magnuson-Moss Warranty Act*, which contains provisions requiring that written warranties for consumer products costing more than $15 and sold to a consumer must contain certain information that is made available to the buyer before the sale.

Most of the other federal consumer protection measures discussed in this chapter involve consumer credit transactions. Under the *Truth in Lending Act*, creditors are required to make a number of disclosures to consumer debtors where the amount financed is $25,000 or less. The act also regulates certain real estate-related transactions, certain credit card-related matters, and credit advertising. The *Consumer Leasing Act* applies disclosure and advertising requirements to *consumer leases*. The *Fair Credit Reporting Act* places a number of duties on consumer reporting agencies such as credit bureaus, and on users of information received from such agencies. In addition, it establishes procedures for affected individuals to dispute and correct erroneous information contained in an agency's files. The *Equal Credit Opportunity Act* forbids credit decisions made on the bases of sex, marital status, age, race, color, national origin, religion, and the obtaining of income from public assistance. The *Fair Credit Billing Act* establishes a number of requirements to which credit card issuers must conform. The most important of these requirements involves disputes over credit card billing. Finally, the *Fair Debt Collection Practices Act* regulates the behavior of debt collection agencies. The act limits the ability of collectors to contact both the debtor and third parties. It also contains lengthy lists of forbidden collector actions that amount to harassment or abuse, false or misleading misrepresentations, and unfair practices.

In addition to providing civil recoveries for those injured by defective products, the law promotes product safety by direct regulation. The most important federal agency seeking to advance this goal is the Consumer Product Safety Commission, which was established by the Consumer Product Safety Act. Among other things, the CPSC issues product safety standards for consumer products that pose an unreasonable risk of injury, may ban products that are especially hazardous, and may sue to eliminate the dangers posed by imminently hazardous consumer products. In addition to the Consumer Product Safety Act, a number of other federal statutes regulate the safety of specific products.

PROBLEM CASES

1. For a long time, advertisements for Listerine Antiseptic Mouthwash had claimed that Listerine was beneficial in the treatment of colds, cold symptoms, and sore throats. An FTC adjudicative proceeding concluded that these claims were false. Thus, the Commission ordered Warner-Lambert Company, the manufacturer of Listerine, to include the following statement in future Listerine advertisements: "Contrary to prior advertising, Listerine will not help prevent colds or sore throats or lessen their severity." Warner-Lambert argued that this order was invalid because it went beyond a command to simply cease and desist from illegal behavior. Is Warner-Lambert correct?

2. Figgie International, Inc., sold its own heat detectors for alerting homeowners to fires, and also sold smoke detectors manufactured by other firms. Figgie's promotional literature claimed that its heat detectors provided sufficient warning to allow the occupants of a home to escape a fire, and that the combination of heat and smoke detectors provided significantly greater fire warning protection than smoke detectors alone. Were these statements *material* under the FTC's policy statement on deceptive advertising? Why or why not?

3. World Travel Vacation Brokers, Inc., advertised Hawaii vacations by offering $29 certificates that could be redeemed for round-trip airfare to Hawaii. To get these certificates, consumers had to book hotel reservations through World Travel for a minimum of eight days and seven nights at World Travel's "hotel cost." The ads stated that World Travel could offer this $29 price because it had purchased excess frequent flyer coupons, its huge purchasing volume had enabled it to obtain big discounts from airlines, and the package was part of a promotional "deregulation special" offered by the airlines.

World Travel sold between 600,000 and 700,000 of the $29 Hawaii vacation certificates. Unfortunately for their purchasers, World Travel had effectively charged them full airfare by jacking up the "hotel cost." Language on the certificates, however, stated that "prices do not reflect actual hotel rates." Under the FTC's section 5 policy statement on deceptive advertising, did the con-

sumers who purchased the certificates act *reasonably under the circumstances*?

4. Between 1966 and 1975, the Orkin Exterminating Company, the world's largest termite and pest control firm, offered its customers a "lifetime" guarantee that could be renewed each year by paying a definite amount specified in its contracts with the customers. The contracts gave no indication that the fees could be raised for any but narrowly specified reasons. Beginning in 1980, Orkin unilaterally breached these contracts by imposing higher-than-agreed-upon annual renewal fees. About 200,000 contracts were breached in this way, and Orkin realized about $7 million in additional revenues from customers who renewed at the higher fees. The additional fees did not purchase a higher level of service than that originally provided for in the contracts. Also, while some of Orkin's competitors may have been willing to assume Orkin's pre-1975 contracts at the fees stated therein, they would not have offered a fixed, locked-in "lifetime" renewal fee like that Orkin originally provided. Under the three-part test stated in the text, did Orkin's behavior violate FTC Act section 5's prohibition against *unfair* acts or practices?

5. Patron Aviation, Inc., an aviation company, bought an airplane engine from L&M Aircraft. The engine was assembled and shipped to L&M by Teledyne Industries, Inc. L&M installed the engine in one of Patron's airplanes. The engine turned out to be defective, and Patron sued L&M and Teledyne. One of the issues presented by the case was whether the Magnuson-Moss Act was applicable. Does the Magnuson-Moss Act apply to this transaction?

6. John and Marilyn Olson ran their farming business through a corporation. They obtained a number of loans from a local bank. Give *two* reasons why the Truth in Lending Act does *not* apply to these loans.

7. Gardner and North were in the business of renovating, remodeling, and repairing homes. They extended credit to homeowners for whom they performed services. Although their company did not take a mortgage or other lien on a homeowner's property, state law gave home improvement contractors a contractor's or mechanic's lien on the customer's home at the time the work was performed. Would a homeowner be able to rescind an agreement with Gardner and North after completion of the agreement? If so, how quickly would the homeowner have to act? (Hint: the regulations accompanying the Truth in Lending Act define the term *security interest* to include "liens created by operation of law such as mechanic's, materialman's, artisan's, and similar liens.")

8. Smith rented a television set from ABC Rental Systems. The rental agreement stated that the lease was a week-to-week arrangement and that it was terminable by either party at any time. The agreement stated the figures "$16.00/55.00" in a space provided for the rental rate. The $16 figure was the weekly rate, and the $55 figure was a reduced monthly rate available to a consumer who wished to pay monthly. Smith was never provided with any of the disclosures required by the Consumer Leasing Act. Does the Consumer Leasing Act apply to this transaction?

9. The Credit Bureau, Inc. (CBI) maintains credit records on consumers, among them a Mr. and Mrs. Rush. The Rushes obtained a CBI report on themselves, and found an "R-9" credit rating (the lowest possible) next to the entry for their Macy's account. This poor credit rating caused the Rushes to be denied credit on several occasions. The Rushes sued Macy's under the Fair Credit Reporting Act. Will they win under the FCRA? You can assume for purposes of argument that the entry was erroneous and was the fault of Macy's.

10. Maurice Miller received an American Express credit card, and later arranged for his wife Virginia to receive a supplementary card. After Maurice died, American Express canceled Virginia's account. The termination had nothing to do with Virginia's creditworthiness. Instead, American Express acted pursuant to its general policy of automatically terminating the accounts of supplementary cardholders upon the death of the basic cardholder. American Express argued that Virginia's termination cannot violate the Equal Credit Opportunity Act, because the policy was perfectly neutral with respect to marital status, applying equally to widows or widowers. Is there any way that American Express might be subject to ECOA liability here?

11. John E. Koerner & Co., Inc. applied for a credit card account with the American Express Company. The application was for a company account designed for business customers. Koerner asked American Express to issue cards bearing the company's name to Louis Koerner and four other officers of the corporation. Mr. Koerner was required to sign a company account form, agreeing that he would be jointly and severally liable with the company for all charges incurred through use of the company card. American Express issued the cards requested by the company. Thereafter, the cards were used almost totally for business purposes, although Mr. Koerner occasionally used his card for personal expenses. Later, a dispute regarding charges appearing on the company account arose. Does the Fair Credit Billing Act apply to this dispute?

CHAPTER 48

ANTITRUST: THE SHERMAN ACT

INTRODUCTION

After the Civil War, an important economic phenomenon emerged on the American scene: the growth of large industrial combines and trusts. Many of these large business entities acquired dominant positions in their industries by buying up smaller competitors or engaging in practices aimed at driving smaller competitors out of business. This behavior produced a public outcry for legislation to preserve competitive market structures and prevent the accumulation of great economic power in the hands of a few firms. The common law had long held that contracts unreasonably restraining trade were contrary to public policy, but all that the courts could do to police this rule was refuse to enforce such a contract if one of the parties objected to it. Legislation was therefore necessary to give the courts greater power to deal with this new social problem.

Congress responded by passing the Sherman Act in 1890 and later supplementing it with the Clayton Act in 1914 and the Robinson-Patman Act in 1936. In doing so, Congress adopted a public policy in favor of preserving and promoting free competition as the most efficient means of allocating social resources. The Supreme Court summarized the rationale for this faith in the positive effects of competition when it said:

Basic to faith that a free economy best promotes the public weal is that goods must stand the cold test of competition; that the public, acting through the market's impersonal judgment, shall allocate the nation's resources and thus direct the course its economic development will take.[1]

The passage of the antitrust laws reflected a congressional assumption that competition was more likely to exist in an industrial structure characterized by a large number of competing firms than in concentrated industries dominated by a few large competitors. As Judge Learned Hand put it in the famous case of *United States v. Aluminum Company of America, Inc.*:

Many people believe that possession of an unchallenged economic power deadens initiative, discourages thrift, and depresses energy; that immunity from competition is a narcotic, and rivalry is a stimulant, to industrial progress; that the spur of constant stress is necessary to counteract an inevitable disposition to let well enough alone.[2]

Despite this long-standing policy in favor of competitive market structures, the antitrust laws have not been very successful in halting the trend toward concentration

---

[1] *Times-Picayune Co. v. United States*, 345 U.S. 594 (U.S. Sup. Ct. 1953).

[2] 148 F.2d 416 (2d Cir. 1945).

in U.S. industry. The market structure in many important industries today is highly *oligopolistic* with the bulk of production accounted for by the output of a few dominant firms. Traditional antitrust concepts are often quite difficult to apply to the behavior of firms in such highly concentrated markets. Recent years have witnessed the emergence of new ideas that challenge many of the long-standing assumptions of traditional antitrust policy.

THE ANTITRUST POLICY DEBATE

Antitrust enforcement necessarily reflects fundamental public policy judgments about the economic activities that should be allowed and about the industrial structure that is best suited to foster desirable economic activity. Because such judgments are vitally important to the future of the U.S. economy, it is not surprising that antitrust policy is often the subject of vigorous public debate. In recent years, traditional antitrust values have faced a highly effective challenge from commentators and courts advocating the application of microeconomic theory to antitrust enforcement. As many of these new ideas originated among scholars associated with the University of Chicago, these new methods of antitrust analysis are commonly called *Chicago School theories.*

Chicago School advocates tend to view *economic efficiency* as the primary, if not the sole, goal of antitrust enforcement. They are far less concerned with the supposed effects of industrial concentration than are traditional antitrust thinkers. Even highly concentrated industries, they argue, may engage in significant forms of nonprice competition, such as competition in advertising, styling, and warranties. They also point out that concentration in a particular industry does not necessarily preclude *interindustry competition* among related industries. For example, a highly concentrated glass container industry may still face significant competition from the makers of metal, plastic, and fiberboard containers. Chicago School advocates are also quick to point out that many markets today are international in scope, so that highly concentrated domestic industries such as automobiles, steel, and electronics may nonetheless face effective foreign competition. In fact, they argue that the technological developments necessary for U.S. industry to compete more effectively in international markets may require the great concentrations of capital that result from concentration in domestic industry.

From the Chicago School viewpoint, the traditional antitrust focus on the structure of industry has improperly emphasized protecting *competitors* rather than protecting *competition*. Chicago School theorists argue that the primary thrust of antitrust policy should involve *anticonspiracy* efforts rather than *anticoncentration* efforts. In addition, most of these theorists take a rather lenient view toward various vertically imposed restrictions on price and distribution that have been traditionally seen as undesirable, because they believe that such restrictions can promote efficiencies in distribution. Thus, they tend to be more tolerant of attempts by manufacturers to control the prices at which their products are resold and to establish exclusive distribution systems for those products.

Traditional antitrust thinkers, however, contend that although economic efficiency is *an* important goal of antitrust enforcement, antitrust policy has historically embraced *political* as well as economic values. Concentrated economic power, they argue, is undesirable for a variety of noneconomic reasons. It can lead to antidemocratic concentrations of political power, and it can stimulate greater governmental intrusions into the economy in the same way that the activities of the trusts after the Civil War led to the passage of the antitrust laws. Lessening concentration, in their view, enhances individual freedom by reducing the barriers to entry that confront would-be competitors and by assuring a broader input into economic decisions that may have important social consequences. Judge Learned Hand summed up this way of looking at antitrust policy when he said in the *Alcoa* case:

Great industrial consolidations are inherently undesirable, regardless of their economic results. Throughout the history of these statutes [sections 1 and 2 of the Sherman Act] it has been constantly assumed that one of their purposes was to perpetuate and preserve, for its own sake and in spite of possible cost, an organization of industry in small units which can effectively compete with each other.[3]

Chicago School ideas, however, have had a significant impact on the course of antitrust enforcement in recent years. The Supreme Court and many of President Reagan's appointees to the lower federal courts have given credence to Chicago School economic arguments in many cases. Also, many of President Reagan's

---

[3]*United States v. Aluminum Co. of America, Inc.*, 148 F.2d 416 (2d Cir. 1945).

appointees to the Justice Department and the Federal Trade Commission were sympathetic to Chicago School policy views. The Bush administration's agency appointees appear to be more inclined toward vigorous enforcement of the antitrust laws, but the presence on the federal bench of so many judges embracing Chicago School ideas means that those views are likely to continue to have an impact on the shape of antitrust law for the foreseeable future.

JURISDICTION, PENALTIES, AND STANDING

Jurisdiction

The Sherman Act makes monopolization and agreements in restraint of trade illegal. However, since the federal government's power to regulate business originates in the Commerce Clause of the U.S. Constitution, the federal antitrust laws apply only to behavior that has some significant impact on our *interstate* or *foreign* commerce.[4] Given the interdependent nature of our national economy, it is generally fairly easy to demonstrate

---

[4]The Business and the Constitution chapter discusses the Commerce Clause in detail.

that a challenged activity either involves interstate commerce (the "in commerce" jurisdiction test) or has a substantial effect on interstate commerce (the "effect on commerce" jurisdiction test). As the following *McClain* case indicates, this may well be true even though the activity in question occurs solely within the borders of one state. Activities that are purely *intrastate* in their effects, however, are outside the scope of federal antitrust jurisdiction and must be challenged under state law.

The federal antitrust laws have also been extensively applied to activities affecting the international commerce of the United States. The activities of U.S. firms operating outside our borders may be attacked under our antitrust laws if they have an intended effect on our foreign commerce. Likewise, foreign firms that are "continuously engaged" in our domestic commerce are subject to federal antitrust jurisdiction. Determining the full extent of the extraterritorial reach of our antitrust laws often involves courts in difficult questions of antitrust exemptions and immunities.[5] It also presents the troubling prospect that aggressive attempts to expand the reach of antitrust beyond our borders may produce a conflict between our antitrust policy and our foreign policy in general.

---

[5] The next chapter discusses these issues in detail.

McCLAIN v. REAL ESTATE BOARD OF NEW ORLEANS, INC.

444 U.S. 232 (U.S. Sup. Ct. 1980)

McClain and others brought a private antitrust action under the Sherman Act against the Real Estate Board of New Orleans. They alleged price-fixing by means of fixed commission rates, fee splitting, and the suppression of market information useful to buyers. The trial court granted the board's motion for dismissal on the ground that real estate brokerage activities were wholly local in nature and, therefore, lacked the effect on interstate commerce necessary to invoke the Sherman Act. McClain appealed.

Burger, Chief Justice. To establish the jurisdictional element of a Sherman Act violation it would be sufficient for McClain to demonstrate a substantial effect on interstate commerce generated by the Board's brokerage activity. McClain need not make a more particularized showing of an effect on interstate commerce caused by the alleged conspiracy to fix commission rates or by those other aspects of defendants' activity that are alleged to be unlawful.

It is clear that an appreciable amount of commerce is involved in the financing of residential property in the Greater New Orleans area and in the insuring of titles to such property. The presidents of two of the many lending institutions in the area stated in their deposition testimony that those institutions committed hundreds of millions of dollars to residential financing during the period covered by the complaint. The testimony further demonstrates that this appreciable commercial activity has occurred in interstate commerce. Funds were raised from out-of-state investors and from interbank loans obtained from interstate financial institutions. Multistate lending institutions took mortgages insured under federal programs which entailed interstate transfers of premiums and settlements. Mortgage obligations physically and constructively were traded as financial instruments in the interstate secondary mortgage market. Before making a mortgage loan in the Greater New Orleans area, lending institutions usually, if not always, required title insurance which was furnished by interstate corporations.

Brokerage activities necessarily affect both the frequency and the terms of residential sales transactions. Ultimately, whatever stimulates or retards the volume of residential sales, or has an impact on the purchase price, affects the demand for financing and title insurance, those two commercial activities that on this record are shown to have occurred in interstate commerce.

Judgment reversed in favor of McClain. Case remanded for trial.

Penalties

Violations of the Sherman Act may give rise to both criminal and civil liability. Individuals convicted of Sherman Act violations may receive a fine of up to $350,000 per violation and/or a term of imprisonment of up to three years. Corporations convicted of violating the Sherman Act may be fined up to $10 million per violation. Before an individual may be found criminally responsible under the Sherman Act, however, the government must prove both an *anticompetitive effect* flowing from the challenged activities and *criminal intent* on the part of the defendant. The level of criminal intent required for a violation is a "knowledge of [the act's] probable consequences" rather than a specific intent to violate the antitrust laws.[6] Civil violations of the antitrust laws, on the other hand, may be proven by evidence of either an unlawful purpose or an anticompetitive effect.

The federal courts have broad injunctive powers to remedy civil antitrust violations. They can order convicted defendants to *divest* themselves of the stock or assets of acquired companies, to *divorce* themselves from a functional level of their operations (e.g., they can order a manufacturer to sell its captive retail outlets), to refrain from particular conduct in the future, and to cancel existing contracts. In extreme cases, they can also enter a *dissolution* decree ordering a defendant to liquidate its assets and go out of business. Private individuals, as well as the Department of Justice—the arm of the federal government charged with enforcing the Sherman Act—may seek such injunctive relief from antitrust violations.

A significant percentage of the antitrust cases filed by the Department of Justice are settled out of court by the use of *nolo contendere* pleas in criminal cases and *consent* decrees in civil cases. Technically, a defendant who pleads nolo contendere has not admitted guilt, although a sentencing court may elect to impose the same penalty that would be appropriate in the case of a guilty plea or a conviction. Consent decrees involve a defendant's consent to remedial measures aimed at remedying the competitive harm resulting from his actions. Both of these devices are often attractive to antitrust defendants, because neither a nolo plea nor a consent decree is admissible as proof of a violation of the Sherman Act in a later civil suit filed by a private plaintiff.

Section 4 of the Clayton Act gives private individuals a significant incentive to enforce the antitrust laws by providing that persons injured by violations of the Sherman Act or the Clayton Act may recover *treble damages* plus costs and attorney's fees from the defendant. This means that once antitrust plaintiffs have proved the amount of their actual losses, such as lost profits or increased costs of doing business resulting from the challenged violation, this amount is tripled to compute the amount of their recovery. The potential for treble

---

[6]*United States v. U.S. Gypsum Co.,* 438 U.S. 422 (U.S. Sup. Ct. 1978).

damage liability plainly presents a significant deterrent threat to potential antitrust violators. For example, a famous antitrust case against General Electric Company and several other electrical equipment manufacturers resulted in treble damage awards in excess of $200 million. Some Chicago School critics of antitrust have argued that treble damages should be available only for per se violations of the antitrust laws, with plaintiffs who prove "rule of reason" violations being restricted to a recovery of their actual damages. (We discuss both per se and rule of reason violations later in this chapter.)

Standing

Private plaintiffs seeking to enforce the antitrust laws must first demonstrate that they have *standing* to sue. This means that they must show a *direct antitrust injury* as a result of the challenged behavior. An *antitrust injury* results from the unlawful aspects of the challenged behavior and is the type that Congress sought to prevent by enacting the antitrust laws. For example, in *Brunswick Corp. v. Pueblo Bowl-o-Mat, Inc.*, the operator of a chain of bowling centers (Pueblo) challenged a bowling equipment manufacturer's (Brunswick) acquisition of a number of competing bowling centers that had defaulted on payments owed to the manufacturer for equipment purchases.[7] The gist of Pueblo's complaint was that, had Brunswick not acquired the failing businesses, they would have gone out of business and Pueblo's profits would have increased. The Supreme Court rejected Pueblo's claim, however, because Pueblo's claimed losses flowed from the fact that Brunswick had preserved competition by acquiring the failing centers. Allowing recovery for such losses would be contrary to the antitrust purpose of promoting competition. The antitrust injury requirement also played a major role in the *Atlantic Richfield* case later in the chapter.

Proof that an antitrust injury is *direct* is important because the Supreme Court, in *Illinois Brick Co. v. State of Illinois,* held that *indirect purchasers* lack standing to sue for antitrust violations.[8] In that case, the state of Illinois and several other governmental entities could not recover treble damages from concrete block suppliers who, they alleged, were guilty of illegally fixing the price of the block used in the construction of public buildings. The plaintiffs acknowledged that the builders hired to construct the buildings in question had actually paid the inflated prices for the blocks, but argued that these illegal costs had probably been passed on to them in the form of higher prices for building construction. The Supreme Court refused to allow recovery, however, on the ground that granting standing to indirect purchasers would create a risk of "duplicative recoveries" by purchasers at various levels in a product's chain of distribution. The Court also said that affording standing to indirect purchasers would cause difficult problems of tracing competitive injuries through several levels of distribution and assessing the extent of an indirect purchaser's actual losses.

A number of state legislatures responded to *Illinois Brick* by passing statutes allowing indirect purchasers to sue under state antitrust statutes. The Supreme Court recently unanimously held that such statutes are not preempted by its *Illinois Brick* holding.[9]

Section 1—Restraints of Trade

Concerted Action

Section 1 of the Sherman Act provides: "Every contract, combination in the form of trust or otherwise, or conspiracy, in restraint of trade or commerce among the several states, or with foreign nations is declared to be illegal."

A *contract* is any agreement, express or implied, between two or more persons or business entities to restrain competition; a *combination* is a continuing partnership in restraint of trade; and a *conspiracy* occurs when two or more persons or business entities join for the purpose of restraining trade. From the language of the statute, it is apparent that Section 1 of the Sherman Act is *aimed at joint* or *concerted action* in restraint of trade. The statute expresses a basic public policy that requires persons or business entities to make important competitive decisions on their own, rather than in conjunction with competitors. Thus, *purely unilateral action* by a competitor is never a violation of Section 1. Adam Smith, in his famous book *The Wealth of Nations* (1776), acknowledged the danger to competition

---

[7] 429 U.S. 477 (U.S. Sup. Ct. 1977).

[8] 431 U.S. 720 (U.S. Sup. Ct. 1977).

[9]*California v. ARC America Corp.*, 490 U.S. 93 (U.S. Sup. Ct. 1989).

inherent in concerted action and the tendency for competitors to engage in it when he said: "People of the same trade seldom meet together, even for merriment and diversion, but the conversation ends in a conspiracy against the public, or in some contrivance to raise prices."

The concerted action requirement of Section 1 presents two major problems to antitrust enforcers. First, how separate must two business entities be before their joint activities are subject to the act's prohibitions? For example, it has long been held that a corporation cannot conspire with itself or its employees and that a corporation's employees cannot be guilty of a conspiracy in the absence of some independent party. But what about conspiracies among related corporate entities? In two earlier cases, the Supreme Court appeared to hold that a corporation could violate the Sherman Act by conspiring with a wholly owned subsidiary.[10] More recently, however, in *Copperweld Corporation v. Independence Tube Corporation*, the Court repudiated the "intra-enterprise conspiracy doctrine" by holding, as a matter of law, that a parent company is incapable of conspiring with a wholly owned subsidiary in violation of the Sherman Act because an agreement between a parent and its subsidiary does not result in the risk to competition that results when two independent entities begin to act in concert.[11] Whether this new approach extends to corporate subsidiaries and affiliates that are not wholly owned remains to be seen. The logic of *Copperweld* would appear to cover any subsidiary in which the parent firm has a controlling interest, however.

A second more difficult problem that constantly occurs in the enforcement of Section 1 concerns the circumstances in which a court *infers* that an agreement or conspiracy to restrain trade exists in the absence of any *overt* agreement by the parties. Should parallel pricing behavior by several firms be enough, for example, to justify the inference that a price-fixing conspiracy exists? To date, the courts have consistently held that proof of pure "conscious parallelism," standing alone, is *not* enough to establish a violation of Section 1.[12] Instead, some other evidence must be presented to show that the defendants' actions were the product of an *agreement*, express or implied, rather than the results of independent business decisions. This makes it quite difficult to attack *oligopolies* (a few large firms that share one market) under Section 1, because such firms may independently elect to follow the pricing policies of the industry "price leader," rather than risk their large market shares by engaging in vigorous price competition.

Rule of Reason versus Per Se Analysis

The statutory language of Section 1 condemns *every* contract, combination, and conspiracy in restraint of trade, but the Supreme Court has long held that the Sherman Act applies only to behavior that *unreasonably* restrains competition.[13] The Court has developed two fundamentally different approaches to analyzing behavior challenged under the act. It has concluded that some forms of behavior always have a negative effect on competition that can never be excused or justified. Such behavior is classed as *per se illegal* conclusively presumed to violate the act. Per se rules provide sure guidance to business and simplify otherwise lengthy antitrust litigation: Once per se illegal behavior is proven, there are no justifications that a defendant may assert to avoid liability. Per se rules, however, are frequently criticized on the ground that they tend to oversimplify complex economic realities. Recent decisions indicate that the Court is moving away from per se rules in favor of rule of reason analysis for some economic activities. This trend is consistent with the Court's increased inclination to consider new economic theories that seek to justify behavior previously held to be illegal per se.

Behavior that is not classed as per se illegal is judged under the *rule of reason*. This requires a detailed inquiry into the actual competitive effects of the defendant's actions and includes consideration of any justifications that the defendant may advance. If the court concludes that the challenged activity had a significant anticompetitive effect that was not offset by any positive effect on competition or other social benefit, such as enhanced economic efficiency, the activity is found to be in violation of Section 1. The following are some of the kinds of behavior that have been held to violate the Sherman Act.

---

[10]*Kiefer-Stewart Co. v. Joseph E. Seagram & Sons, Inc.*, 340 U.S. 211 (U.S. Sup. Ct. 1951); *United States v. Yellow Cab Co.*, 332 U.S. 218 (U.S Sup. Ct. 1947).

[11]467 U.S. 752 (U.S. Sup. Ct. 1984).

[12]*Theatre Enterprises v. Paramount Film Distributing Corp.*, 346 U.S 537 (U.S. Sup. Ct. 1954).

[13]*Standard Oil Co. of New Jersey v. United States*, 221 U.S. 1 (U.S. Sup. Ct. 1911).

Price-Fixing

An essential attribute of a free market is that the price of goods and services is determined by the free play of the impersonal forces of the marketplace. Attempts by competitors to interfere with market forces and control prices, called **horizontal price-fixing,** have long been held per se illegal under Section 1.[14] Price-fixing may take the form of direct agreements among competitors about the price at which they sell or buy a particular product or service. It may also be accomplished by agreements on the quantity of goods that will be produced, offered for sale, or bought. In one famous case, an agreement by major oil refiners to purchase and store the excess production of small independent refiners was held to amount to price-fixing because the purpose of the agreement was to affect the market price for gasoline by artificially limiting the available supply.[15] Recently, some commentators have suggested that agreements among competitors to fix *maximum* prices should be treated under a rule of reason approach rather than under the harsher per se standard because, in some instances, such agreements may result in savings to consumers. However, the *Maricopa County* case, which follows, indicates that the Supreme Court has yet to deviate from its long-standing rule of per se illegality for any form of horizontal price-fixing.

---

[14]*United States v. Trenton Potteries Co.,* 273 U.S. 392 (U.S. Sup. Ct. 1927).

[15]*United States v. Socony-Vacuum Oil Co.,* 310 U.S. 150 (U.S. Sup. Ct. 1940).

ARIZONA v. MARICOPA COUNTY MEDICAL SOCIETY
457 U.S. 332 (U.S. Sup. Ct. 1982)

The Maricopa Foundation for Medical Care was a nonprofit organization established by the Maricopa County Medical Society to promote fee-for-service medicine. About 70 percent of the physicians in Maricopa County belonged to the foundation. The foundation's trustees set maximum fees that members could charge for medical services provided to policyholders of approved medical insurance plans. To obtain the foundation's approval, insurers had to agree to pay the fees of member physicians up to the prescribed maximum. Member physicians were free to charge less than the prescribed maximum, but had to agree not to seek additional payments in excess of the maximum from insured patients.

The Arizona attorney general filed suit for injunctive relief against the Maricopa County Medical Society and the foundation, arguing that the fee agreement constituted per se illegal horizontal price-fixing. The district court denied the state's motion for a partial summary judgment, and the Ninth Circuit Court of Appeals affirmed on the ground that the per se rule was not applicable to the case.

Stevens, Justice.   By 1927, the Court was able to state that "it has often been decided and always assumed that uniform price-fixing by those controlling in any substantial manner a trade or business in interstate commerce is prohibited by the Sherman Law." Thirteen years later, the Court could report that:

[F]or over 40 years this Court has consistently and without deviation adhered to the principle that price-fixing agreements are unlawful *per se* under the Sherman Act and that no showing of so-called competitive abuses or evils which those agreements were designed to eliminate or alleviate may be interposed as a defense. *United States v. Socony-Vacuum Oil Co.* (1940).

In that case a glut in the spot market for gasoline had prompted the major oil refiners to engage in a concerted effort to purchase and store surplus gasoline in order to maintain stable prices. Absent the agreement, the companies argued, competition was cutthroat and self-defeating. The argument did not carry the day. The application of the *per se* rule to maximum price-fixing agreements in *Kiefer-Stewart Co. v. Seagram & Sons* (1951), followed ineluctably from *Socony-Vacuum.* Over the objection that maximum price-fixing agreements were not the "economic equivalent" of minimum price-fixing agreements, *Kiefer-Stewart* was reaffirmed in *Albrecht v. Herald Co.* (1968). *Kiefer-Stewart* and *Albrecht* place horizontal agreements to fix maximum prices on the same legal—even if not economic—footing as agreements to fix minimum or uniform prices. The *per se* rule is grounded on faith in price competition as a market force and not on a policy of low selling prices at the price of eliminating competition. In this case the rule is violated by a price restraint that tends to provide the same economic rewards to all practitioners regardless of their skill, experience, training, or willingness to employ innovative and difficult procedures in individual cases. Such a restraint also may discourage entry into the market and may deter experimentation and new developments by individual entrepreneurs. It may be a masquerade for an agreement to fix uniform prices, or it may in the future take on that character.

Nor does the fact that doctors—rather than nonprofessionals—are the parties to the price-fixing agreements support Maricopa's position. In *Goldfarb v. Virginia State Bar* (1975), we stated that the "public service aspect, and other features of the professions, may require that a particular practice, which could properly be viewed as a violation of the Sherman Act in another context, be treated differently." The price-fixing agreements in this case, however, are not premised on public service or ethical norms. Maricopa's claim for relief from the *per se* rule is simply that the doctors' agreement not to charge certain insureds more than a fixed price facilitates the successful marketing of an attractive insurance plan. But the claim that the price restraint will make it easier for customers to pay does not distinguish the medical profession from any other provider of goods or services.

Maricopa's principal argument is that the *per se* rule is inapplicable because its agreements are alleged to have procompetitive justifications. The argument indicates a misunderstanding of the *per se* concept. The anticompetitive potential inherent in all price-fixing agreements justifies their facial invalidation even if procompetitive justifications are offered for some. Those claims of enhanced competition are so unlikely to prove significant in any particular case that we adhere to the rule of law that is justified in its general application.

Judgment reversed in favor of Arizona.

Attempts by manufacturers to control the resale price of their products can also fall within the scope of Section 1. This behavior, called **vertical price-fixing** or **resale price maintenance,** has long been held to be per se illegal.[16] Manufacturers can lawfully state a suggested retail price for their products, because such an action is purely unilateral in nature and does not involve the concerted action necessary for a violation of Section 1. However, any *agreement*, express or implied, between a manufacturer and its customers obligating the customers to resell at a price dictated by the manufacturer is sufficient to trigger per se illegality.

The Section 1 emphasis on concerted action provides the basis for two indirect methods that some manufacturers may lawfully be able to use to control resale prices: *consignment sales* and *unilateral refusal to deal*. Consignments are agreements in which an owner of goods (the consignor) delivers them to another who is to act as the owner's agent in selling them (the consignee). Because the consignee is, in effect, the consignor's agent in selling the goods, and because the owners of goods generally have the right to determine the price at which

[16] *Dr. Miles Medical Co. v. John D. Park & Sons, Co.*, 220 U.S. 373 (U.S. Sup. Ct. 1911).

their goods are sold, one early Supreme Court case held that consignment sales were not covered by Section 1.[17] However, more recent cases have cast some doubt on the legality of resale price maintenance achieved by consignment dealing.[18] Consignment selling systems whose primary purpose is resale price maintenance may be held unlawful if they result in restraining price competition among a large number of consignees who would otherwise be in competition with one another. This is especially likely to be true in cases where the consignor has sufficient economic power over his consignees to permit him to refuse to deal with them on any basis other than a consignment. Finally, to have any hope of avoiding liability, the arrangement in question must be a true consignment: The consignor must retain title to the goods and bear the risk of loss of the goods while they are in the consignee's hands, and the consignee must have the right to return unsold goods.

In *United States v. Colgate & Co.*, the Supreme Court held that a manufacturer could *unilaterally refuse to deal* with dealers who failed to follow its suggested resale prices.[19] The idea behind this exception is that a single firm can deal or not deal with whomever it chooses without violating Section 1, because unilateral action, by definition, is not the concerted action prohibited by the Sherman Act. Subsequent cases, however, have narrowly construed the *Colgate* doctrine. Manufacturers enlisting the aid of wholesalers or other dealers who are not price-cutting to help enforce their pricing policies, or engaging in other joint action to further their policies, probably will be held to have violated Section 1.

Recent events have cast doubt on the long-term future of the rule of per se illegality for resale price maintenance agreements. Chicago School theorists argue that many of the same reasons that led the Supreme Court in the *Sylvania* case to declare that vertically imposed nonprice restraints on distribution should be judged under the rule of reason are equally applicable to vertical price-fixing agreements.[20] In particular, they argue that vertical restrictions limiting the maximum price at which a dealer can resell may prevent dealers with dominant market positions from exploiting consumers by price-gouging. The following *Atlantic Richfield* case, contains hints that the Court may be inclined to reconsider the per se rule for vertically imposed maximum price restraints.

---

[17] *United States v. General Electric Co.*, 272 U.S. 476 (U.S. Sup. Ct.1926).

[18] *Simpson v. Union Oil Co. of California*, 377 U.S. 13 (U.S. Sup. Ct.1964).

[19] 250 U.S. 300 (U.S. Sup. Ct. 1919).

[20] This case appears later in the chapter.

ATLANTIC RICHFIELD CO. v. USA PETROLEUM CO.

110 S. Ct. 1884 (U.S. Sup. Ct. 1990)

Atlantic Richfield (ARCO) is an integrated oil company that sells gasoline to consumers both directly through its own stations and indirectly through ARCO-brand dealers. USA is an independent retail marketer of gasoline which, like other independents, buys gasoline from major petroleum companies for resale under its own brand name. USA competes directly with ARCO dealers at the retail level. Its outlets typically are low-overhead, high-volume "discount" stations that charge less than stations selling equivalent quality gasoline under major brand names.

In early 1982, ARCO adopted a new marketing strategy in order to compete more effectively with independents such as USA. ARCO encouraged its dealers to match the retail gasoline prices offered by independents in various ways, making available to its dealers and distributors short-term discounts and reducing its dealers' costs by, for example, eliminating credit card sales. ARCO's strategy increased its sales and market share. When USA's sales dropped, it sued ARCO charging that ARCO and its dealers were engaged in a per se illegal vertical price-fixing scheme.

The district court granted ARCO a summary judgment, holding that USA had not shown an antitrust injury resulting from ARCO's actions. When the Ninth Circuit Court of Appeals reversed, ARCO appealed.

Brennan, Justice.   A private plaintiff may not recover damages under section 4 of the Clayton Act merely by showing injury causally linked to an illegal presence in the market. Instead, a plaintiff must prove the existence of *antitrust* injury, injury of the type the antitrust laws were intended to prevent that flows from that which makes defendants' acts unlawful. Injury, although causally related to an antitrust violation, nevertheless will not qualify as "antitrust injury" unless it is attributable to an anticompetitive aspect of the practice under scrutiny, since it is inimical to the antitrust laws to award damages for losses stemming from continued competition.

In *Albrecht v. Herald Co.* (1968) we found that a vertical, maximum price-fixing scheme was unlawful *per se* under section 1 of the Sherman Act. We assume, *arguendo*, that *Albrecht* correctly held that vertical, maximum price-fixing is subject to the *per se* rule.

In holding such a vertical agreement illegal, we analyzed the manner in which it might restrain competition by dealers. First, we noted that such a scheme, by substituting the perhaps erroneous judgment of a seller for the forces of the competitive market, may severely intrude upon the ability of buyers to compete and survive in that market. We further explained that maximum prices may be fixed too low for the dealer to furnish services essential to the value which goods have for the consumer or to furnish services and conveniences which consumers desire and for which they are willing to pay. By limiting the ability of small dealers to engage in nonprice competition, a maximum price-fixing agreement might channel distribution through a few large or specifically advantaged dealers. Finally, we observed that if the actual price charged under a maximum price scheme is nearly always the fixed maximum price, which is increasingly likely as the maximum price approaches the actual cost of the dealer, the scheme tends to acquire all the attributes of an arrangement fixing minimum prices.

USA alleges that it has suffered losses as a result of competition with firms following a vertical, maximum price-fixing agreement. But in *Albrecht* we held such an agreement *per se* unlawful because of its potential effects on dealers and consumers, not because of its effect on *competitors*. USA's asserted injury does not resemble any of the potential dangers described in *Albrecht*. For example, if a vertical agreement fixes maximum prices too low for the dealer to furnish services desired by consumers, or in such a way as to channel business to large distributors, then a firm dealing in a competing brand would not be harmed. USA was *benefitted* rather than harmed if ARCO's pricing policies restricted ARCO sales to a few large dealers or prevented ARCO's dealers from offering services desired by consumers such as credit card sales. Even if the maximum price agreement ultimately had acquired all of the attributes of a minimum price-fixing scheme, USA still would not have suffered antitrust injury because higher ARCO prices would have worked to USA's advantage.

USA argues that even if it was not harmed by any of the anticompetitive effects identified in *Albrecht*, it nonetheless suffered antitrust injury because of the low prices produced by the vertical restraint. We disagree. When a firm, or even a group of firms adhering to a vertical agreement, lowers prices but maintains them above predatory levels, the business lost by rivals cannot be viewed as an "anticompetitive" consequence of the claimed violation. A firm complaining about the harm it suffers from nonpredatory price competition "is really claiming that it [is] unable to raise prices." Blair & Harrison, Rethinking Antitrust Injury, 42 Vand. L. Rev. 1539, 1554 (1989). This is not *antitrust* injury; indeed, cutting prices in order to increase business often is the very essence of competition. The antitrust laws were enacted for the protection of *competition*, not *competitors*. To hold that the antitrust laws protect competitors from the loss of profits due to nonpredatory price competition would, in effect, render illegal any decision by a firm to cut prices in order to increase market share.

We also reject USA's suggestion that no antitrust injury need be shown where a *per se* violation is involved. The *per se* rule is a method of determining whether section 1 of the Sherman Act has been violated, but it does not indicate whether a private plaintiff has suffered antitrust injury and thus whether he may recover damages under section 4 of the Clayton Act. *Per se* and rule-of-reason analysis are but two methods of determining whether a restraint is "unreasonable," *i.e.*, whether its anticompetitive effects outweigh its procompetitive effects. The *per se* rule is a presumption of unreasonableness based on business certainty and litigation efficiency. It represents a long-standing judgment that the prohibited practices by their nature have a substantial potential for impact on competition.

The purpose of the antitrust injury requirement is different. It ensures that the harm claimed by the plaintiff corresponds to the rationale for finding a violation in the first place, and it prevents losses that stem from competition from supporting suits by private plaintiffs for either damages or equitable relief. Actions *per se* unlawful under the antitrust laws may nonetheless have *some* procompetitive effects, and private parties might suffer losses therefrom.

When a manufacturer provides a dealer an exclusive area within which to distribute a product, the manufacturer's decision to fix a maximum resale price may actually protect consumers against exploitation by the dealer acting as a local monopolist. The manufacturer acts not out of altruism, of course, but out of a desire to increase its own sales—whereas the dealer's incentive, like that of any monopolist, is to reduce output and increase price. Vertical, maximum price-fixing thus may have procompetitive interbrand effects even if it is *per se* illegal because of its potential effects on dealers and consumers. The procompetitive potential of a vertical maximum price restraint is more evident now than it was when *Albrecht* was decided, because exclusive territorial arrangements and other nonprice restrictions were unlawful *per se* in 1968. These agreements are currently subject only to rule-of-reason scrutiny, making monopolistic behavior by dealers more likely.

Insofar as the *per se* rule permits the prohibition of efficient practices in the name of simplicity, the need for the antitrust injury requirement is underscored. "[P]rocompetitive or efficiency-enhancing aspects of practices that nominally violate the antitrust laws may cause serious harm to individuals, but this kind of harm is the essence of competition and should play no role in the definition of antitrust damages." Page, The Scope of Liability for Antitrust Violations, 37 Stan. L. Rev. 1445, 1460 (1985). We decline to dilute the antitrust injury requirement here because we find that there is no need to encourage private enforcement by competitors of the rule against vertical, maximum price-fixing. If such a scheme causes the anticompetitive consequences detailed in *Albrecht*, consumers and the manufacturer's own dealers may bring suit.

Judgment reversed in favor of ARCO.

Division of Markets

It has traditionally been said that **horizontal division of markets** agreements, those agreements among competing firms to divide up the available market by assigning one another certain exclusive territories or certain customers, are illegal per se. Such agreements plainly represent agreements not to compete and result in each firm being isolated from competition in the affected market. In 1972 the Supreme Court reaffirmed this long-standing principle when it struck down a horizontal divison of

markets agreement among the members of a cooperative association of local and regional supermarket chains in *United States v. Topco Associates, Inc.*[21] The Court's decision in *Topco* was widely criticized, however, on the ground that its per se approach ignored the fact that the defendants' joint activities in promoting Topco brand products were aimed at enabling them to compete more

_____

[21] 405 U.S. 596 (U.S. Sup. Ct. 1972).

effectively with national supermarket chains. When such horizontal restraints were ancillary to procompetitive behavior, critics argued, they should be judged under the rule of reason.

Such criticism has had an impact, for several recent opinions by lower federal courts have distinguished between "naked" horizontal restraints, which can have no other purpose or effect except restraining competition, and "ancillary" horizontal restraints, which are a necessary part of a larger joint undertaking serving procompetitive ends.[22] These courts continue to apply the per se rule to "naked" horizontal restraints while applying a rule of reason approach to "ancillary" restraints. In determining whether ancillary restraints are lawful under the rule of reason, courts weigh the harm to competition resulting from such restraints against the alleged offsetting benefits to competition. One factor likely to be of substantial importance in this weighing process is the market strength of the defendants. The idea here is that an agreement restraining competition among firms that lack market power because they face strong competition from other firms not party to the agreement is unlikely to harm consumers. This is because the existence of competition limits the ability of the agreeing firms to exploit their agreement by raising prices. Whether the Supreme Court ultimately will endorse such departures from *Topco* remains to be seen. However, the Court's post-*Topco* tendency to discard per se rules in favor of a rule of reason approach in other areas, and the greater tolerance the Court has shown for some other horizontal activities in recent cases, such as the following *Northwest Wholesale Stationers* case, suggest that *Topco's* critics may ultimately win their case.

Vertically imposed restraints on distribution also fall within the scope of the Sherman Act. A manufacturer has always had the power to *unilaterally* assign exclusive territories to its dealers or to limit the dealerships it grants in a particular geographic area. However, manufacturers may run afoul of Section 1 by requiring their dealers to *agree* not to sell outside their dealership territories or by placing other restrictions on their dealers' right to resell their products (e.g., a prohibition against sales to unfranchised dealers inside the dealer's assigned territory). In 1967 in *United States v. Arnold, Schwinn & Co.*, the Warren Court held that such **vertical restraints on distribution** were per se illegal when applied to goods that the manufacturer had sold to its dealers (consignment sales being treated under the rule of reason).[23] The Burger Court disagreed, however; in the *Sylvania* case, which follows, the Court abandoned the per se rule in favor of a rule of reason approach to most vertical restraints on distribution. In doing so, the Court accepted many Chicago School arguments concerning the potential economic efficiencies that could result from such restraints. These were alleged to offer a chance for increased *interbrand* competition among the product lines of competing manufacturers at the admitted cost of restraining *intrabrand* competition among dealers in a particular manufacturer's product.

Subsequent decisions in this area have emphasized the importance of the market share of the manufacturer imposing vertical restraints on distribution in determining the legality of the restraints. Restraints imposed by manufacturers with large market shares are more likely to be found unlawful under the rule of reason because the resultant harm to intrabrand competition is unlikely to be offset by significant positive effects on interbrand competition.

---

[22] See, for example, *Polk Bros., Inc. v. Forest City Enterprises, Inc.*, 776 F.2d 185 (7th Cir. 1985). In this case an agreement between two retailers who were erecting and sharing a new building that they would not compete in the sale of certain product lines was upheld as ancillary to the agreement to develop the joint facility.

---

[23] 338 U.S. 365 (U.S. Sup. Ct. 1967).

CONTINENTAL T.V., INC. v. GTE SYLVANIA, INC.

433 U.S. 36 (U.S. Sup. Ct. 1977)

In the early 1950s, Sylvania's share of the national TV market had declined to about 1 percent. In an attempt to remedy this situation, Sylvania phased out all wholesalers and limited the retail franchises that it granted for a given area. Sylvania also required that each franchisee sell Sylvania products only from the sales location described in its franchise agreement. This strategy apparently contributed to increasing sales by Sylvania, but it led to friction with some dealers when Sylvania shuffled sales location areas and refused to grant requests for expansion of some sales areas.

Continental, a Sylvania dealer, became unhappy when Sylvania franchised another dealer in part of Continental's market and then refused Continental's request for permission to expand into another market area. As the dispute developed, Sylvania reduced Continental's credit line. In response, Continental withheld all payments owed to the finance company that handled all credit arrangements between Sylvania and its retailers. Shortly thereafter, Sylvania terminated Continental's franchise and the finance company filed suit to recover payments due on merchandise purchased by Continental. Continental cross-claimed against Sylvania, arguing that Sylvania's location restriction was a per se violation of Section 1 of the Sherman Act. The trial jury agreed and awarded Continental $1.7 million in treble damages. The Ninth Circuit Court of Appeals reversed, holding that Sylvania's location restriction should be judged under the rule of reason because it presented less of a threat to competition than did the restrictions held per se illegal in the *Schwinn* case. Continental appealed.

Powell, Justice.   Vertical restrictions reduce intrabrand competition by limiting the number of sellers of a particular product competing for the business of a given group of buyers. Location restrictions have this effect because of practical constraints on the effective marketing area of retail outlets. Although intrabrand competition may be reduced, the ability of retailers to exploit the resulting market may be limited both by the ability of consumers to travel to other franchised locations and, perhaps more importantly, to purchase the competing products of other manufacturers. None of these key variables, however, is affected by the form of the transaction by which a manufacturer conveys his products to the retailers.

Vertical restrictions promote interbrand competition by allowing the manufacturer to achieve certain efficiencies in the distribution of his products. New manufacturers and manufacturers entering new markets can use the restrictions in order to induce competent and aggressive retailers to make the kind of investment of capital and labor that is often required in the distribution of products unknown to the consumer. Established manufacturers can use them to induce retailers to engage in promotional activities or to provide service and repair facilities necessary to the efficient marketing of their products. Service and repair are vital for many products, such as automobiles and major household appliances. The availability and quality of such services affect a manufacturer's goodwill and the competitiveness of his product. Because of market imperfections such as the so-called free rider effect, these services might not be provided by retailers in a purely competitive situation, despite the fact that each retailer's benefit would be greater if all provided services than if none did.

Economists also have argued that manufacturers have an economic interest in maintaining as much intrabrand competition as is consistent with the efficient distribution of their products. Although the view that the manufacturer's interest necessarily corresponds with that of the public is not universally shared, even the leading critic of vertical restrictions concedes that *Schwinn's* distinction between sale and nonsale transactions is essentially unrelated to any relevant economic impact.

We revert to the standard articulated in *Northern Pac. R. Co.*, for determining whether vertical restrictions must be "conclusively presumed to be unreasonable and therefore illegal without elaborate inquiry as to the precise harm they have caused or the business excuse for their use." Such restrictions, in varying forms, are widely used in our free market economy. There is substantial scholarly and judicial authority supporting their economic utility. There is relatively no showing in this case, either generally or with respect to Sylvania's agreements, that vertical restrictions have or are likely to have a "pernicious effect on competition" or that they "lack any redeeming virtue." Accordingly, the *per se* rule stated in *Schwinn* must be overruled. In so holding we do not foreclose the possibility that particular applications of vertical restrictions might justify *per se* prohibition under *Northern Pac. R. Co.* But we do make clear that departure from the rule of reason standard must be based upon demonstrable economic effect rather than—as in *Schwinn*—upon formalistic line drawing.

Judgment for Sylvania affirmed.

Group Boycotts and Concerted Refusals to Deal

Under the "Colgate doctrine," a single firm can lawfully refuse to deal with certain firms. However, agreements by two or more business entities to refuse to deal with others, or to deal with others only on certain terms and conditions, or to coerce suppliers or customers not to deal with one of their competitors are *joint* restraints on trade, which historically have been per se illegal under Section 1. For example, when a trade association of garment manufacturers agreed not to sell to retailers that sold clothing or fabrics with designs pirated from legitimate manufacturers, the agreement was held to be a per se violation of the Sherman Act.[24]

Recent antitrust developments, however, indicate that not all concerted refusals to deal will be subjected to per se analysis. A manufacturer that terminates a distributor in response to complaints from other distributors that the terminated distributor was selling to customers outside its prescribed sales territory violates Section 1 only if the termination results in a significant harm to competition. This result follows logically from the *Sylvania* case; if vertical restraints on distribution are judged under the rule of reason, the same standard should apply to a vertical boycott designed to enforce such restraints.

However, even distributors who argue that they were terminated as part of a per se illegal vertical price-fixing scheme have found recovery increasingly difficult to obtain in recent years. In *Monsanto v. Spray-Rite Service Corp.*, the Supreme Court held that the fact that a manufacturer had terminated a discounting distributor after receiving complaints from its other distributors was not enough to trigger per se liability for vertical price-fixing absent additional evidence "that tends to exclude the possibility that the manufacturer and nonterminated distributors were acting independently."[25] More recently, in *Business Electronics Corp. v. Sharp Electronics Corp.*, the Court held that even proof of a conspiracy between a manufacturer and its nonterminated distributors to terminate a price-cutter would not trigger per se liability unless it was accompanied by proof that the manufacturer and nonterminated dealers were also engaged in a vertical price-fixing conspiracy.[26] *Monsanto* and *Sharp* have generated a substantial controversy, and, as this book went to press, Congress was considering legislation aimed at overruling them and also at codifying the per se rule for vertical price-fixing. Whether or not such legislation ultimately becomes law, the *Northwest Wholesale Stationers* case, which follows, indicates that the Court is now even willing to relax the per se rule for some *horizontal* boycotts.

---

[24] *Fashion Originators' Guild v. FTC*, 312 U.S. 457 (U.S. Sup. Ct. 1941).

[25] 465 U.S. 752 (U.S. Sup. Ct. 1984).
[26] 485 U.S. 108 (U.S. Sup. Ct. 1988).

NORTHWEST WHOLESALE STATIONERS, INC. v. PACIFIC STATIONERY & PRINTING CO.
472 U.S. 284 (U.S. Sup. Ct. 1985)

Northwest Wholesale Stationers is a purchasing cooperative made up of approximately 100 office-supply retailers in the Pacific Northwest states. Northwest acts as the primary wholesaler for its member retailers. Although nonmember retailers can buy supplies from Northwest at the same price as members, Northwest's practice of distributing year-end profits to its members in the form of a percentage rebate on purchases means that members effectively buy supplies at substantially lower prices than nonmembers. In fiscal 1978, Northwest had $5.8 million in sales.

Pacific Stationery, Inc., sells office supplies at both the wholesale and retail levels, with total combined sales in fiscal 1978 of $7.6 million. Pacific had been a member of Northwest since 1958; when Northwest amended its bylaws in 1974 to prohibit members from engaging in both wholesale and retail selling, a grandfather clause preserved Pacific's membership rights. In 1977, ownership of a controlling share of Pacific's stock changed hands, but the new owners failed to officially bring the change to the attention of Northwest's directors, a violation of the bylaws.

In 1978, Northwest's membership voted to expel Pacific from the cooperative. No explanation for the expulsion was given at the time [Northwest later justified the expulsion by pointing to Pacific's bylaw violation], and Pacific was given neither notice, a hearing, nor any other opportunity to challenge the decision. Pacific later filed suit against Northwest alleging that its expulsion was a result of its wholesale operations and amounted to a per se illegal group boycott. The trial court refused to apply the per se rule and granted summary judgment for Northwest under the rule of reason because it found no anticompetitive effect. On appeal, the Ninth Circuit Court of Appeals reversed, finding per se liability appropriate. Northwest then appealed to the Supreme Court.

Brennan, Justice.   This case turns on whether the decision to expel Pacific is properly viewed as a group boycott or concerted refusal to deal mandating per se invalidation. "Group boycotts" are often listed among the classes of economic activity that merit per se invalidation under Section 1. Exactly what types of activity fall within the forbidden category is, however, far from certain. "[T]here is more confusion about the scope and operation of the per se rule against group boycotts than in reference to any other aspect of the per se doctrine." L. Sullivan, *Law of Antitrust* 229–230 (1977). Some care is therefore necessary in defining the category of concerted refusals to deal that mandate per se condemnation.

Cases to which this Court has applied the per se approach have generally involved joint efforts by a firm or firms to disadvantage competitors by either directly denying or persuading or coercing suppliers or customers to deny relationships the competitors need in the competitive struggle. In these cases, the boycott often cut off access to a supply, facility, or market necessary to enable the boycotted firm to compete, and frequently the boycotting firms possessed a dominant position in the relevant market. In addition, the practices were generally not justified by plausible arguments that they were intended to enhance overall efficiency and make markets more competitive. Under such circumstances the likelihood of anticompetitive effects is clear and the possibility of countervailing procompetitive effects is remote.

Although a concerted refusal to deal need not necessarily possess all of these traits to merit per se treatment, not every cooperative activity involving a restraint or exclusion will share with the per se forbidden boycotts the likelihood of predominantly anticompetitive consequences.

Wholesale purchasing cooperatives such as Northwest are not a form of concerted activity characteristically likely to result in predominantly anticompetitive effects. Rather, such cooperative arrangements seem designed to increase economic efficiency and render markets more, rather than less, competitive. The arrangement permits the participating retailers to achieve economies of scale in both the purchase and warehousing of wholesale supplies, and also ensures ready access to a stock of goods that might otherwise be unavailable on short notice. The cost savings and order-filling guarantees enable smaller retailers to reduce prices and maintain their retail stock so as to compete more effectively with larger retailers.

The act of expulsion from a wholesale cooperative does not necessarily imply anticompetitive animus and thereby raise a probability of anticompetitive effect. Wholesale purchasing cooperatives must establish and enforce reasonable rules in order to function effectively. Disclosure rules, such as the one on which Northwest relies, may well provide the cooperative with a needed means for monitoring the creditworthiness of its members. Nor would the expulsion characteristically be likely to result in predominantly anticompetitive effects, unless the cooperative possesses market power or exclusive access to an element essential to effective competition. Absent such a showing with respect to a cooperative buying arrangement, courts should apply a rule of reason analysis. At no time has Pacific made a threshold showing that these structural characteristics are present in this case.

Judgment reversed in favor of Northwest; case remanded to Court of Appeals for review of trial court's rule of reason analysis.

Tying Agreements

Tying agreements occur when a seller refuses to sell a buyer one product (the *tying product*) unless the buyer also agrees to purchase a different product (the *tied product*) from the seller. For example, a fertilizer manufacturer refuses to sell its dealers fertilizer (the tying product) unless they also agree to buy its line of pesticides (the tied product). The potential anticompetitive effect of a tying agreement is that the seller's competitors in the sale of the tied product may be foreclosed from competing with the seller for sales to customers that have entered into tying agreements with the seller. To the extent that tying agreements are coercively imposed, they also deprive buyers of the freedom to make independent decisions concerning their purchases of the tied product. The legality of tying agreements may be challenged under both Section 1 of the Sherman Act and Section 3 of the Clayton Act.[27]

Tying agreements are often said to be per se illegal under Section 1, but, because a tying agreement must meet certain criteria before it is subjected to per se analysis and because evidence of certain justifications is sometimes considered in tying cases, the rule against tying agreements is, at best, a soft per se rule. Before a challenged agreement is held to be an illegal tying agreement in violation of Section 1, several things must be proved: (1) The agreement involves *two* separate and distinct items rather than integrated components of a larger product, service, or system of doing business. (2) The tying product cannot be purchased unless the tied product is also purchased. (3) The seller has sufficient economic power in the market for the tying product to appreciably restrain competition in the tied product market, such as a patent or a large market share. (4) A "not insubstantial" amount of commerce in the tied product is affected by the seller's tying agreements.[28]

The first two of these elements have been particularly relevant in some recent cases involving alleged tying agreements among franchisors and their franchised dealers. For example, a suit by a McDonald's franchisee alleged that McDonald's violated Section 1 by requiring franchisees to lease their stores from McDonald's to acquire a McDonald's franchise. The Eighth Circuit Court of Appeals rejected the franchisee's claim, however, on the ground that no tying agreement was involved, because the franchise and the lease were integral components of a well-thought-out system of doing business.[29]

The lower federal courts have recognized two other possible justifications for true tying agreements. First, tying arrangements that are instrumental in launching a new competitor with an uncertain future may be lawful until the new business has established itself in the marketplace. The logic of this new business exception is obvious: If a tying agreement enables a fledgling firm to become a viable competitor, the ultimate net effect of the agreement on competition is a positive one. Also, some courts have recognized that, in some cases, tying agreements may be necessary to protect the reputation of the seller's product line. For example, one of the seller's products functions properly only if used in conjunction with another of its products. To successfully utilize this exception, however, the seller must convince the court that no viable means to protect its goodwill exists other than a tying arrangement.

---

[27]Section 3 of the Clayton Act applies, however, only when both the tying and the tied products are commodities. The next chapter discusses Clayton Act standards for tying agreement legality.

[28]*U.S. Steel Corp. v. Fortner Enterprises, Inc.*, 429 U.S. 610 (U.S. Sup Ct. 1977).

[29]*Principe v. McDonald's Corp.*, 631 F.2d 303 (4th Cir. 1980).

Chicago School thinkers have long criticized the courts' approach to tying agreements because they do not believe that most tie-ins result in any significant economic harm. They argue that sellers that try to impose a tie-in in competitive markets gain no increased profits from the tie-in. This is so because, instead of participating in a tying agreement, buyers may turn to substitutes for the tying product or may purchase the tying product from competing sellers. The net effect of a tie-in may therefore be that any increase in the seller's sales in the tied product is offset by a loss in sales of the tying product. Only when the seller has substantial power in the tying product market does the potential arise that a tie-in may be used to increase the seller's power in the tied product market. However, even where the seller has such market power in the tying product, Chicago School thinkers argue that no harm to competition is likely to result if the seller faces strong competition in the tied product market. For these and other reasons, Chicago School thinkers favor a rule of reason approach to all tying agreements. As the following *Jefferson Parish Hospital Dist. No. 2 v. Hyde* case indicates, a majority of the Supreme Court has yet to accept these arguments. Several current members of the Court, however, appear to have done so. If other members of the Court are similarly persuaded in the future, a substantial change in the legal criteria applied to tying agreements will be the likely result.

JEFFERSON PARISH HOSPITAL DIST. NO. 2 v. HYDE

466 U.S. 2 (U.S. Sup. Ct. 1984)

In July 1977 Edwin G. Hyde, an anesthesiologist, applied for admission to the medical staff of East Jefferson Hospital in New Orleans. The credentials committee and the medical staff executive committee recommended approval, but the hospital board denied the application because the hospital was a party to a contract providing that all anesthesiological services required by the hospital's patients would be performed by Roux & Associates, a professional medical corporation. Hyde filed suit against the board, arguing that the contract violated Section 1 of the Sherman Act.

The district court ruled in favor of the board, finding that the anticompetitive effects of the contract were minimal and outweighed by the benefits of improved patient care. It noted that there were at least 20 hospitals in the New Orleans metropolitan area and that about 70 percent of the patients residing in Jefferson Parish went to hospitals other than East Jefferson. It therefore concluded that East Jefferson lacked any significant market power and could not use the contract for anticompetitive ends. The Fifth Circuit Court of Appeals reversed, holding that the relevant market was the East Bank Jefferson Parish rather than the New Orleans metropolitan area. The Court therefore concluded that because 30 percent of the parish residents used East Jefferson and "patients tend to choose hospitals by location rather than price or quality," East Jefferson possessed sufficient market power to make the contract a per se illegal tying contract. The board appealed.

Stevens, Justice.   It is far too late in the history of antitrust jurisprudence to question the proposition that certain tying arrangements pose an unacceptable risk of stifling competition and therefore are unreasonable per se. The rule was first enunciated in *International Salt Co. v. United States* (1947), and has been endorsed by this Court many times since. The rule also reflects congressional policies underlying the antitrust laws. In enacting Section 3 of the Clayton Act, Congress expressed great concern about the anticompetitive character of tying arrangements. While this case does not arise under the Clayton Act, the congressional finding made therein concerning the competitive consequences of tying is illuminating, and must be respected.

It is clear, however, that every refusal to sell two products separately cannot be said to restrain competition. If each of the products may be purchased separately in a competitive market, one seller's decision to sell the two in a single package imposes no unreasonable restraint on either market, particularly if competing suppliers are free to sell either the entire package or its several parts. For example, we have written that "if one of a dozen food stores in a community were to refuse to sell flour unless the buyer also took sugar it would hardly tend to restrain competition if its competitors were ready and able to sell flour by itself."

The essential characteristic of an invalid tying arrangement lies in the seller's exploitation of its control over the tying product to force the buyer into the purchase of a tied product that the buyer either did not want at all, or might have preferred to purchase elsewhere on different terms. When such "forcing" is present, competition on the merits in the market for the tied item is restrained and the Sherman Act is violated. Accordingly, we have condemned tying arrangements when the seller has some special ability—usually called "market power"—to force a purchaser to do something that he would not do in a competitive market.

Per se condemnation—condemnation without inquiry into actual market conditions—is only appropriate if the existence of forcing is probable. As a threshold matter there must be a substantial potential for impact on competition in order to justify *per se* condemnation. If only a single purchaser were "forced" with respect to the purchase of a tied item, the resultant impact on competition would not be sufficient to warrant the concern of antitrust law. For this reason we have refused to condemn tying arrangements unless a substantial volume of commerce is foreclosed thereby. Similarly, when a purchaser is "forced" to buy a product he would not have otherwise bought even from another seller in the tied product market, there can be no adverse impact on competition because no portion of the market which would otherwise have been available to other sellers has been foreclosed.

Once this threshold is surmounted, *per se* prohibition is appropriate if anticompetitive forcing is likely. For example, if the government has granted the seller a patent or similar monopoly over a product, it is fair to presume that the inability to buy the product elsewhere gives the seller market power. Thus, the sale or lease of a patented item on condition that the buyer make all his purchases of a separate tied product from the patentee is unlawful.

The same strict rule is appropriate in other situations in which the existence of market power is probable. When the seller's share of the market is high, or when the seller offers a unique product that competitors are not able to offer, the Court has held that the likelihood that market power exists and is being used to restrain competition in a separate market is sufficient to make *per se* condemnation appropriate.

When, however, the seller does not have either the degree or kind of market power that enables him to force customers to purchase a second, unwanted product in order to obtain the tying product, an antitrust violation can be established only by evidence of an unreasonable restraint on competition in the relevant market. Thus, in this case our analysis must focus on the hospital's sale of services to its patients, rather than its contractual arrangements with the providers of anesthesiological services. We must consider whether the hospital is selling two separate products that may be tied together, and, if so, whether it has used its market power to force its patients to accept the tying arrangement.

Unquestionably, the anesthesiological component of the package offered by the hospital could be provided separately and could be selected either by the individual patient or by the patient's doctors if the hospital did not insist on including anesthesiological services in the package it offers to its customers. As a matter of actual practice, anesthesiological services are billed separately from hospital services. Patients or surgeons often request specific anesthesiologists to come to a hospital and provide anesthesia, and the choice of an individual anesthesiologist separate from the choice of a hospital is particularly frequent in Hyde's specialty, obstetric anesthesiology.

Thus, the hospital's requirement that its patients obtain necessary anesthesiological services from Roux combined the purchase of two distinguishable services in a single transaction. Nevertheless, only if patients are forced to purchase Roux's services as a result of the hospital's market power would the arrangement have anticompetitive consequences. Hyde's only basis for invoking the *per se* rule against tying is by relying on the preference of persons residing in Jefferson Parish to go to East Jefferson, the closest hospital. A preference of this kind, however, is not necessarily probative of significant market power. Seventy percent of the patients residing in Jefferson Parish enter hospitals other than East Jefferson. Thus, East Jefferson's "dominance" over persons residing in Jefferson Parish is far from overwhelming. The geographic data does not establish the kind of dominant market position that obviates the need for further inquiry into actual competitive conditions.

In order to prevail in the absence of *per se* liability, Hyde has the burden of proving that the Roux contract violated the Sherman Act because it unreasonably restrained competition. That necessarily involves an inquiry into the actual effect of the exclusive contract on competition among anesthesiologists. This competition takes place in a market that has not been defined. The market is not necessarily the same as the market in which hospitals compete in offering services to patients; it may encompass competition among anesthesiologists for exclusive contracts such as the Roux contract and might be statewide or merely local. There is, however, insufficient evidence in this record to provide a basis for finding that the Roux contract, as it actually operates in the market, has unreasonably restrained competition.

Judgment reversed in favor of Jefferson Parish.

Reciprocal Dealing Agreements

A **reciprocal dealing agreement** is one in which a buyer attempts to exploit its purchasing power by conditioning its purchases from its suppliers on reciprocal purchases of some product or service offered for sale by the buyer. For example, an oil company with a chain of wholly owned gas stations refuses to purchase the tires it sells in those stations from a tire manufacturer unless the tire manufacturer agrees to purchase from the oil company the petrochemicals used in the tire manufacturing process. Reciprocal dealing agreements are otherwise quite similar in motivation and effect to tying agreements, and the courts tend to treat them in a similar fashion. In seeking to impose the reciprocal dealing agreement on the tire manufacturer, the oil company is trying to gain a competitive advantage over its competitors in the petrochemical market. A court judging the legality of such an agreement would look at the dollar amount of petrochemical sales involved and at the oil company's economic power as a purchaser of tires.

Exclusive Dealing Agreements

Exclusive dealing agreements require the buyers of a particular product or service to purchase that product or service exclusively from a particular seller. For example, Standard Lawnmower Corporation requires its retail dealers to sell only Standard brand mowers. A common variation of an exclusive dealing agreement is the **requirements contract,** in which the buyer of a particular product agrees to purchase all of its requirements for that product from a particular supplier. For example, a candy manufacturer agrees to buy all of its sugar requirements from one sugar refiner. Exclusive dealing contracts present a threat to competition similar to that involved in tying contracts: They can reduce interbrand competition by foreclosing a seller's competitors from the opportunity to compete for sales to its customers. Unlike tying contracts, however, exclusive dealing agreements can sometimes enhance efficiencies in distribution and stimulate interbrand competition. Exclusive dealing agreements reduce a manufacturer's sales costs and provide dealers with a secure source of supply. They may also encourage dealer efforts to more effectively market the manufacturer's products, because a dealer that sells only one product line has a greater stake in the success of that line than does a dealer that sells the products of several competing manufacturers.

Because many exclusive dealing agreements involve commodities, they may also be challenged under Section 3 of the Clayton Act. The legal tests applicable to exclusive dealing agreements under both Acts are identical. Therefore, we defer discussing them until the following chapter.

Joint Ventures by Competitors

A **joint venture** is a combined effort by two or more business entities for a limited purpose such as a joint research venture. Because joint ventures may yield enhanced efficiencies by integrating the resources of more than one firm, they are commonly judged under the rule of reason. Under this approach, the courts tend to ask whether any restraints on competition that are incidental to the venture are necessary to accomplish its lawful objectives and, if so, whether these restraints are offset by the positive effects of the venture. Joint ventures whose primary purpose is illegal per se, however, have often been treated as per se illegal; for example, two competing firms form a joint sales agency that is empowered to fix the price of their products.

Antitrust critics have long argued that the threat of antitrust prosecution seriously inhibits the formation of joint research and development ventures, with the result that U.S. firms are placed at a competitive disadvantage in world markets. Such arguments have recently enjoyed more acceptance, given existing concerns about the performance of the U.S. economy. Congress passed the National Cooperative Research Act in 1984. The act applies to "joint research and development ventures" (JRDVs), which are broadly defined to include basic and applied research and joint activities in the licensing of technologies developed by such research. The act requires the application of a reasonableness standard, instead of a per se rule, in judging a JRDV's legality. It also requires firms contemplating a JRDV to provide the Justice Department and the Federal Trade Commission with advance notice of their intent to do so, and it provides that only single (not treble) damages may be recovered for losses flowing from a JRDV that is ultimately found to be in violation of Section 1. In addition, the act contains a novel provision that allows the parties to a challenged JRDV to recover attorney's fees from an unsuccessful challenger if the suit is shown to be "frivolous, unreasonable, without foundation, or in bad faith." Legislation has since been introduced before Congress to amend the act's provisions to extend its application to joint *production* ventures. See Figure 1 for a summary of the ways in which various business practices are treated under Section 1.

FIGURE 1   Potentially Illegal Practices and Their Treatment under Sherman Act Section 1

Potentially Illegal Practice	Judicial Treatment	
	Per Se	**Rule of Reason**
Horizontal price-fixing	*	
Vertical price-fixing	* ?	
Horizontal division of markets	* ?	* ?
Vertical division of markets		*
Horizontal boycotts	*	*
Vertical boycotts	*	*
Tying agreements	* ?	*
Reciprocal dealing agreements	* ?	*
Exclusive dealing agreements		*
Joint ventures	*	*

Note: an entry with an * in both columns means the facts of the individual case determine the treatment. A ? indicates the future treatment is in question.

SECTION 2—MONOPOLIZATION

Introduction

Firms that acquire **monopoly power** in a given market have defeated the antitrust laws' objective of promoting competitive market structures. Monopolists, by definition, have the power to fix prices unilaterally because they have no effective competition. Section 2 of the Sherman Act was designed to prevent the formation of monopoly power. It provides: "Every person who shall monopolize, or attempt to monopolize, or combine or conspire with any other person to monopolize any part of trade or commerce among the several states, or with foreign nations shall be deemed guilty of a felony." The language of Section 2 does not, however, outlaw monopolies: It outlaws the act of "monopolizing." Under Section 2, a *single firm* can be guilty of "monopolizing" or "attempting to monopolize" a part of trade or commerce. The proof of joint action required for violations of Section 1 is required only when two or more firms are charged with a conspiracy to monopolize under Section 2.

Monopolization

As the following *Grinnell* case indicates, **monopolization** is currently defined as "the willful acquisition or maintenance of monopoly power in a relevant market as opposed to growth as a consequence of superior product, business acumen, or historical accident." This means that to be guilty of monopolization a defendant must not only possess monopoly power but must also have demonstrated an **intent to monopolize.**

Monopoly Power   Monopoly power is usually defined for antitrust purposes as the power to *fix prices* or *exclude competitors* in a given market. Monopoly power is generally inferred from the fact that a firm has captured a predominant share of the relevant market. Although the exact percentage share necessary to support an inference of monopoly power remains unclear and courts often look at other economic factors, such as the existence in the industry of barriers to the entry of new competitors, market shares in excess of 70 percent have historically justified an inference of monopoly power.

Before a court can determine a defendant's market share, it must first define the **relevant market.** This is a crucial part of Section 2 proceedings because a broad definition of the relevant market normally results in a smaller market share for the defendant and a resulting reduction in the likelihood that the defendant is found to possess monopoly power. The two components to a relevant market determination are the relevant *geographic market* and the relevant *product market.*

The economic realities prevailing in the industry determine the relevant geographic market. In which parts of the country can the defendant effectively compete with other firms in the sale of the product in question? To whom may buyers turn for alternative sources of supply? Factors such as transportation costs may also play a critical role in relevant market determinations. Thus, the relevant market for coal may be regional in nature, but the relevant market for transistors may be national in scope.

The relevant product market is composed of those products "reasonably interchangeable by consumers for the same purposes," those meeting the *functional interchangeability* test. This test recognizes that a firm's ability to fix the price for its products is limited by the availability of competing products that buyers view as acceptable substitutes. In a famous antitrust case, for example, Du Pont was charged with monopolizing the national market for cellophane because it had a 75 percent share. The Supreme Court concluded, however, that the relevant market was all "flexible wrapping materials," including aluminum foil, waxed paper, and polyethylene, and that Du Pont's 20 percent share of that product market was far too small to amount to monopoly power.[30]

Intent to Monopolize

Proof of monopoly power standing alone, however, is never sufficient to prove a violation of Section 2. The defendant's intent to monopolize must also be shown. Early cases under Section 2 required evidence that the defendant either acquired monopoly power by predatory or coercive means that violated antitrust rules (e.g., price-fixing or discriminatory pricing) or abused monopoly power in some way after acquiring it, such as price-gouging.[31] Contemporary courts look at how the defendant acquired monopoly power: If the defendant *intentionally acquired it* or *attempted to maintain it* after having acquired it, this is sufficient evidence of an intent to monopolize. Defendants that have monopoly power thrust on them due to the superiority of their products or business decisions, or that hold monopoly power by virtue of a historical accident (e.g., the owner of a professional sports franchise in an area too small to support a competing franchise), are not in violation of Section 2.

Purposeful acquisition or maintenance of monopoly power may be demonstrated in a variety of ways. A famous monopolization case involved Alcoa, which had a 90 percent market share of the U.S. market for virgin aluminum ingot. Alcoa was found guilty of purposefully maintaining its monopoly power by acquiring every new opportunity relating to the production or marketing of aluminum, thereby excluding potential competitors.[32] As the following *Grinnell* case indicates, firms that develop monopoly power by acquiring ownership or control of their competitors are very likely to be held to have demonstrated an intent to monopolize.

---

[30] *United States v. E. I. du Pont de Nemours & Co.,* 351 U.S. 377 (U.S. Sup. Ct. 1956).

[31] *Standard Oil Co. of New Jersey v. United States,* 221 U.S. 1 (U.S. Sup. Ct. 1911).

[32] *United States v. Aluminum Co. of America, Inc.,* 148 F.2d 416 (2d Cir. 1945).

UNITED STATES v. GRINNELL CORP.
384 U.S. 563 (U.S. Sup. Ct. 1966)

Grinnell manufactured plumbing supplies and fire sprinkler systems. It also owned 76 percent of the stock of ADT, 89 percent of the stock of AFA, and 100 percent of the stock of Holmes. ADT provided both burglary and fire protection services; Holmes provided burglary services alone; AFA supplied only fire protection service. Each offered a central station service under which hazard-detecting devices installed on the protected premises automatically transmitted an electrical signal to a central station. There were other forms of protective services. But the record indicated that subscribers to an accredited central station service (i.e., one approved by the insurance underwriters) received reductions in their insurance premiums substantially greater than the reductions received by the users of other protection services. In 1961 ADT, Holmes, and AFA were the three largest central station service companies in terms of revenue, with about 87 percent of the business.

In 1907 Grinnell entered into a series of agreements with the other defendants that allocated the major cities and markets for central station alarm services in the United States. Each defendant agreed not to compete outside the market areas allocated. Over the years, the defendants bought 30 other companies providing burglar or fire alarm services. After Grinnell acquired control of the other defendants, the latter continued in their attempts to acquire central station companies—offers being made to at least eight companies between 1955 and 1961, including four of the five largest remaining companies in the business. When the present suit was filed, each of those defendants had outstanding an offer to purchase one of the four largest nondefendant companies.

Over the years ADT reduced its minimum basic rates to meet competition and renewed contracts at substantially increased rates in cities where it had a monopoly of accredited central station service. ADT threatened retaliation against firms that contemplated inaugurating central station service.

The government filed suit against Grinnell under Section 2 of the Sherman Act, asking that Grinnell be forced to divest itself of ADT, Holmes, and AFA and for other injunctive relief. The district court ruled in favor of the government, and Grinnell appealed.

Douglas, Justice.   The offense of monopoly under Section 2 of the Sherman Act has two elements: (1) the possession of monopoly power in the relevant market and (2) the willful acquisition or maintenance of that power as distinguished from growth or development as a consequence of a superior product, business acumen, or historic accident. This second ingredient presents no major problem here, as what was done in building the empire was done plainly and explicitly for a single purpose. In *United States v. E. I. du Pont de Nemours & Co.*, we defined monopoly power as "the power to control prices or exclude competition." The existence of such power ordinarily may be inferred from the predominant share of the market. In *American Tobacco Co. v. United States*, we said that "over two thirds of the entire domestic field of cigarettes, and over 80 percent of the field of comparable cigarettes" constituted "a substantial monopoly." In *United States v. Aluminum Co. of America*, 90 percent of the market constituted monopoly power. In the present case, 87 percent of the accredited central station service business leaves no doubt that these defendants have monopoly power—power which they did not hesitate to wield—if that business is the relevant market. The only remaining question therefore is, what is the relevant market?

A product may be of such a character that substitute products must also be considered, as customers may turn to them if there is a slight increase in the price of the main product. That is the teaching of the *Du Pont* case, that commodities reasonably interchangeable make up that "part" of trade or commerce which Section 2 protects against monopoly power. The District Court treated the entire accredited central station service business as a single market and it was justified in so doing. Grinnell argues that the different central station services offered are so diverse that they cannot under *Du Pont* be lumped together to make up the relevant market. For example, burglar alarm services are not interchangeable with fire alarm services. It further urges that *Du Pont* requires that protective services other than those of the central station variety be included in the market definition.

We see no barrier to combining in a single market a number of different products or services where that combination reflects commercial realities. There is here a single basic service—the protection of property through use of a central service station—that must be compared with all other forms of property protection. There are, to be sure, substitutes for the accredited central station service. But none of them appears to operate on the same level as the central station service so as to meet the interchangeability test. What Grinnell overlooks is that the high degree of differentiation between central station protection and the other forms means that for many customers, only central station protection will do.

As the District Court found, the relevant market for determining whether the defendants have monopoly power is not the several local areas which the individual stations serve, but the broader national market that reflects the reality of the way in which they built and conduct their business. We have said enough about the great hold that the defendants have on this market. The percentage is so high as to justify the finding of monopoly. And this monopoly was achieved in large part by unlawful and exclusionary practices. The agreements that pre-empted for each company a segment of the market where it was free of competition of the others were one device. Pricing practices that contained competitors were another. The acquisition by Grinnell of ADT, AFA, and Holmes were still another. Its control of the three other defendants eliminated any possibility of an outbreak of competition that might have occurred when the 1907 agreements terminated. By those acquisitions it perfected the monopoly power to exclude competitors and fix prices.

Judgment for the government affirmed.

Attempted Monopolization

As the following *Indiana Grocery* case indicates, firms that have not yet attained monopoly power may nonetheless be guilty of an *attempt to monopolize* in violation of Section 2 if they are dangerously close to acquiring monopoly power and are employing methods likely to result in monopoly power if left unchecked. In addition to proof of the probability that monopoly power will be acquired, attempt to monopolize cases—similar to monopolization cases—normally require proof of the relevant market. Unlike monopolization cases, attempt cases also require proof that the defendant possessed a specific intent to acquire monopoly power by anticompetitive means.

One controversial Section 2 issue that surfaces in many attempted monopolization cases concerns the role

that *predatory pricing* can play in proving an intent to monopolize. The Supreme Court has recently defined predatory pricing as "pricing below an appropriate measure of cost for the purpose of eliminating competitors in the short run and reducing competition in the long run."[33] What constitutes "an appropriate measure of cost" in predatory pricing cases has long been a subject of debate among antitrust scholars, a debate which the Court has declined to resolve definitively. What the Court's recent opinions do tell us is that it is likely to take a skeptical view of predatory pricing claims in the future. In another recent case the Court described preda-

---

[33]*Cargill, Inc. & Excel Corp. v. Monfort of Colorado, Inc.,* 479 U.S. 484 (U.S. Sup. Ct. 1986).

tory pricing schemes as "rarely tried, and even more rarely successful."[34] In doing so, the Court indicated that it agrees with those economists who have argued that predatory pricing schemes are often economically irrational because, to be successful, the predator must maintain monopoly power long enough after it has driven its competitors out of business to recoup the lost profits it gave up by predatory pricing. The predator would be able to sustain monopoly power only if high barriers to entry prevented new competitors from being drawn into the market by the supra-competitive prices the predator would have to charge to recoup its losses.

Conspiracy to Monopolize

When two or more business entities *conspire to monopolize* a relevant market, this can amount to a violation of Section 2. This part of Section 2, however, largely overlaps Section 1, because it is difficult to conceive of a conspiracy to monopolize that would not also amount to a conspiracy in restraint of trade. The lower federal courts differ on the elements necessary to prove a con-

---

[34]*Matsushita Electric Industrial Co., Ltd. v. Zenith Radio Corp.,* 475 U.S. 574 (U.S. Sup. Ct. 1986).

FIGURE 2   Elements of Section 2 Offenses

Offense	Monopoly Power	Intent to Monopolize	Concerted Action
Monopolization	Required	Required	Not required
Attempted monopolization	"Dangerously close"	Specific intent required	Not required
Conspiracy to monopolize	Not required	Specific intent required	Required

spiracy to monopolize. Some courts require proof of the relevant market, a specific intent to acquire monopoly power, and overt action in furtherance of the conspiracy in addition to proof of the existence of a conspiracy. Other courts do not require extensive proof of the relevant market, holding that proof that the defendants conspired to acquire control over prices in, or exclude competitors from, some significant area of commerce is sufficient to establish a violation. Figure 2 summarizes the elements of Section 2 offenses.

INDIANA GROCERY, INC. v. SUPER VALU STORES, INC.

864 F.2d 1409 (7th Cir. 1989)

In mid-1982 Indiana Grocery (Indiana) owned 28 supermarkets in the Indianapolis area and sold about 13 percent of the area's groceries. In 1985 Indiana bought Preston-Safeway, and since 1986 all of Indiana's Indianapolis stores have operated under the Preston-Safeway name.

The Kroger Company (Kroger) operates over 1,400 supermarkets throughout the United States. In 1983, Kroger operated 32 stores in the Indianapolis area and sold about 28 percent of the area's groceries. Super Valu Stores, Inc., is primarily a grocery wholesaler, but since 1980 it has owned and franchised Cub retail food stores in various states. Cub stores are substantially larger than conventional supermarkets and offer a low level of services to customers in exchange for prices that normally are 6 percent to 10 percent lower than those of conventional stores.

Between 1983 and 1986 four Cub stores were opened in the Indianapolis area. This ushered in a period of intense price competition as Kroger and others, realizing that gains by Cub would come at their expense, sought to compete. By early 1985 Cub had captured a 15 percent share of

Indianapolis retail grocery sales. Nevertheless, in 1987 Kroger (with 33 stores), Marsh (with 30), Indiana (with 24), O'Malia (with 9), Mr. D's (with 5), Aldi (with 5), and Seven-Eleven (with 4), all remained in the Indianapolis market along with other firms operating approximately 38 more supermarkets.

In 1985 Indiana filed suit against Kroger and Super Valu, charging, among other things, that by predatory pricing they had attempted to monopolize the Indianapolis retail grocery market. Indiana later voluntarily dismissed its monopolization claim against Super Valu. When the district court granted Kroger a summary judgment, Indiana appealed.

Bauer, Chief Judge.   To prove attempted monopolization under section 2 of the Sherman Act, a plaintiff must show (1) specific intent to achieve monopoly power, (2) predatory or anticompetitive conduct directed to accomplishing this unlawful purpose, and most important for purposes of this case, (3) a dangerous probability that the attempt to monopolize will be successful. The "dangerous probability" element of attempted monopolization reflects the well-established notion that section 2 governs single-firm conduct only when it threatens actual monopolization. The Sherman Act protects competition, not competitors, and does not reach conduct that is only unfair, impolite, or unethical.

Monopoly power has long been defined as the power to exclude competition or to control price, a definition we have alternatively stated in this circuit as "power over price" or "the ability to cut back the market's total output and so raise price." It is with this definition that Indiana runs into trouble. The output of the Indianapolis retail grocery market is, of course, groceries, *and Indiana conceded that Kroger could never control the supply of groceries to the Indianapolis retail market.* If so, it is very difficult to see how Kroger could ever restrict total market output and thereby raise prices.

As if this is an unimportant concession, Indiana argues that Kroger's alleged predatory pricing scheme nevertheless created a dangerous probability of monopoly power because Kroger's market share of grocery sales during the alleged predation period rose to 35 percent in the Indianapolis area as a whole and to nearly 50 percent in two submarkets. But while market share may indicate market power in certain cases, the two are not necessarily the same. Market share indicates market power only when sales reflect control of the productive assets in the business, for only then does it reflect an ability to curtail total market output. If a firm's share of market sales does not reflect control of a significant percentage of the market's productive assets, it does not indicate market power. The ultimate inquiry in any attempted monopolization case remains whether the defendant has or reasonably might come close to having the ability to control total market output and prices, something Indiana has conceded Kroger never will be able to do.

An interesting twist on all this, however, is Indiana's assertion and Kroger's concession—for purposes of its summary judgment motion—that the retail grocery market is characterized by high barriers to entry. The existence of such barriers may make an otherwise implausible predatory pricing scheme more plausible. Since the success of any predatory scheme depends on *maintaining* monopoly power for long enough both to recoup the predator's losses and to harvest some additional gain, high barriers to entry might convince a competitor that a predatory scheme could some day pay off. But Indiana has conceded that Kroger could never obtain monopoly power. If a firm can never gain monopoly power it matters little that high barriers to entry might exist to help that firm maintain power it could never achieve.

Judgment for Kroger affirmed.

ETHICAL AND PUBLIC POLICY CONCERNS

1. Early in this chapter you read a quote from Judge Learned Hand's famous *Alcoa* decision that said that "[g]reat industrial consolidations are inherently undesirable, regardless of their economic results." Yet you also learned that Chicago School antitrust thinkers, who have very different notions about the effects of industrial concentration, have had an important influence on antitrust policy in recent years. Identify two aspects of the current global business environment that might make today's American policymakers less willing than Judge Hand to "perpetuate and preserve, for its own sake and in spite of possible cost, an organization of industry in small units which can effectively compete with each other."

2. Several of the cases in this chapter recite the statement that antitrust was designed to protect competition, not competitors. How is this statement consistent with the ethical justification of markets as the most efficient form of economic organization? Consider the case of a competitor who is driven out of business by another competitor's ultimately unsuccessful predatory pricing efforts (new competitors are quickly drawn into the relevant market by the predator's supracompetitive prices). Although competition may not suffer in such a case, does such a competitor have any *ethical* claim to compensation? What public policy argument could be made in favor of compensation?

3. Tying arrangements that fail to satisfy the criteria for per se illegality enumerated in the *Jefferson Parish* case are judged under the rule of reason, where they will be judged lawful unless the evidence demonstrates that they unreasonably restrain competition. Is there an ethical basis for arguing that any involuntarily imposed tie-ins are wrong, regardless of their effect on competition?

SUMMARY

The antitrust laws represent a congressional attempt to preserve competition as the most efficient means of allocating scarce social resources. Traditional antitrust policy placed significant emphasis on the structure of industry, believing that a fragmented market structure would foster competition. This and other long-standing premises of antitrust policy have been challenged by critics espousing Chicago School economic ideas. Chicago School thinkers tend to see economic efficiency as the primary goal of antitrust laws and are less concerned about industrial structure than are traditional antitrust thinkers.

The Sherman Act, passed in 1890, was the first of the federal antitrust laws. The Sherman Act is aimed at restraints of trade and monopolization of our interstate and foreign commerce. Economic activity that is solely intrastate in impact is outside the scope of the Sherman Act and must be regulated by state antitrust statutes. In today's interdependent economy, however, even economic activity carried on solely within the borders of one state is often found to have a significant enough impact on interstate commerce to justify federal antitrust jurisdiction.

The Sherman Act made restraints of trade and monopolization illegal and also gave the federal courts broad injunctive powers to remedy antitrust violations. Individuals who violate the Sherman Act may be fined up to $250,000 per violation and imprisoned for up to three years. Corporate offenders may be fined up to $1 million per violation. Among the injunctive remedies that the federal courts may order in civil antitrust cases are divorcement, divestiture, and dissolution. The Clayton Act provides that private plaintiffs injured by antitrust violations may recover treble damages plus costs and attorney's fees from defendants that violated the antitrust laws. To recover treble damages, private plaintiffs must prove they have suffered a direct antitrust injury.

Section 1 of the Sherman Act is aimed at joint or concerted action in restraint of trade. It outlaws contracts, combinations, and conspiracies in restraint of trade. Thus, a single firm cannot violate Section 1. This presents major enforcement problems because it raises difficult issues about how separate two business entities must be before they are capable of violating the act and about the nature of the proof required to infer that parallel business behavior is the product of an illegal agreement to restrain trade rather than lawful unilateral action.

Two main methods of analysis are employed under Section 1. Activities that always have a negative effect on competition and that can never be justified are classed as per se illegal and conclusively presumed to violate the act. All other activities are analyzed under the rule of reason, which means that the actual economic effects of the challenged activity must be examined to determine whether any negative effects on competition are offset by any positive effect on competition or by any other social benefit. In recent years, the Supreme Court has tended to move away from per se analysis in favor of affording rule of reason treatment to an increasing variety of economic activities.

Horizontal price-fixing and horizontal division of market schemes have long been held to be per se illegal, and the former are likely to remain so. Some recent lower federal court opinions indicate a willingness to judge some horizontal division of market agreements under the rule of reason if such agreements are ancillary to joint activities that are procompetitive in nature. Vertical price-fixing, also called resale price maintenance, remains per se illegal, but Chicago School antitrust critics have argued that it should be treated under the rule of reason. Vertically imposed customer and market restrictions, once per se illegal, are now treated under the rule of reason, and many of the arguments used to justify this change in treatment have also been made on behalf of resale price maintenance.

Boycotts, or concerted refusals to deal, have historically been said to be per se illegal. Recent cases, however, indicate that not all boycotts are treated in this fashion. The rule of reason standard has been applied to vertical boycotts involving vertical restraints on distribution, and the Supreme Court has imposed burdensome proof requirements on distributors arguing that they were terminated pursuant to a resale price maintenance conspiracy. The Court has also recently applied a rule of reason standard to certain horizontal boycotts.

Tying agreements are often said to be per se illegal under Section 1, but because a tying arrangement must satisfy several tests to violate the act and because certain justifications may be advanced to legitimize some tying agreements, this is, at best, a soft per se rule.

Reciprocal dealing agreements are similar in many respects to tying agreements and tend to be treated in a similar fashion by the courts. Exclusive dealing agreements can violate the Sherman Act. Tying agreements, reciprocal dealing agreements, and exclusive dealing agreements can also be challenged under Section 3 of the Clayton Act if they involve commodities.

Joint ventures by competitors can violate Section 1. Joint ventures tend to be scrutinized under the rule of reason unless their primary purpose is per se illegal. Some antitrust critics have charged that this potential illegality discourages joint venture activity and places U.S. firms at a competitive disadvantage in the world marketplace. Congress has passed legislation to reduce the antitrust threat to joint ventures.

Section 2 of the Sherman Act prohibits monopolization, attempts to monopolize, and conspiracies to mo-

nopolize. A single firm can be guilty of monopolization or attempting to monopolize. To be guilty of monopolization, a firm must have monopoly power and an intent to monopolize. Monopoly power is normally inferred if the defendant has captured a predominant share of a relevant market. The relevant market determination, involving both the relevant product market and the relevant geographic market, is therefore a crucial part of any monopolization case. Intent to monopolize may be proved if it can be shown that a firm purposefully acquired or maintained monopoly power.

To be convicted of attempted monopolization, a defendant must be dangerously close to acquiring monopoly power and employ methods that, if left unchecked, are likely to result in monopoly power. Attempt cases also require proof that the defendant has a specific intent to acquire monopoly power by anticompetitive means.

The conspiracy to monopolize portion of Section 2 is largely an overlap of the Section 1 prohibition of conspiracies in restraint of trade. The courts differ, however, on the elements required to prove a conspiracy to monopolize.

PROBLEM CASES

1. In 1981 Syufy Enterprises, a motion picture exhibitor operating theaters in four states, entered the Las Vegas first-run movie exhibition market by opening a six-screen cinema complex. Before Syufy's entry there were 17 first-run theaters in Las Vegas, a situation that produced intensive bidding among theater owners for first-run film exhibition rights because there often were not enough such films to fill all 17 screens. This meant owners paid substantially more for the right to exhibit such films than they paid in other comparable markets. To reduce this competition, Syufy bought out the owners of six Las Vegas theaters. In late July 1984 Syufy submitted successful bids for the right to show the movie *The Cotton Club* during the Christmas season in Las Vegas and several other locations. On October 18, 1984, Syufy bought out Cragin, the owner of the remaining first-run theaters in Las Vegas. On October 23, 1984, after seeing the first trade screening of *The Cotton Club*, Syufy cancelled the guarantees included in its bids for *The Cotton Club* on the grounds that the movie was not as good as represented by its distributor Orion Pictures and that, contrary to Orion's representations, a viewable version of the film had been available when the blind bids for exhibition rights were solicited. Orion filed suit against Syufy for breach of contract and for monopolizing and attempting to monopolize the Las Vegas market. Orion sought to recover the difference between the amount guaranteed in its contracts with Syufy and the amount it actually earned renting the film to other theaters. Was it proper for the district court to direct a verdict in Syufy's favor on the Sherman Act claims on the ground that Orion had failed to show an antitrust injury?

2. Co-Operative Theatres (Co-op), a Cleveland-area movie theater booking agent, began seeking customers in southern Ohio. Shortly thereafter, Tri-State Theatre Services (Tri-State), a Cincinnati booking agent, began to solicit business in the Cleveland area. Later, however, they allegedly entered into an agreement not to actively solicit each other's customers. The Justice Department prosecuted them for agreeing to restrain trade in violation of Section 1 of the Sherman Act. Under a government grant of immunity, Tri-State's vice president testified that Co-op's vice president had approached him at a trade convention and threatened to start taking Tri-State's accounts if Tri-State did not stop calling on Co-op's accounts. He also testified that at a luncheon meeting he attended with officials from both firms the presidents of each company said that it would be in the interests of both firms to stop calling on each other's accounts. Several Co-op customers testified that Tri-State had refused to accept their business because of the agreement with Co-op. The trial court found both firms guilty of a per se violation of the Sherman Act, rejecting their argument that the rule of reason should have been applied and refusing to allow them to introduce evidence that the agreement did not have a significant anti-competitive effect. Should the rule of reason have been applied?

3. Advanced Health-Care Services (ACHS), a supplier of durable medical equipment (DME) such as wheelchairs, hospital beds, walkers, crutches, and other equipment used by persons convalescing at home after hospitalization, filed a Sherman Act suit against Radford Community Hospital and Radford's holding company owner, Southwest Virginia Health Services Corp. (Southwest). ACHS's complaint alleged, among other things, that Radford, which provided acute health care services to approximately 75 percent of the residents of the greater Radford, Virginia, region, and another wholly owned subsidiary of Southwest's had conspired together to prevent Radford patients from dealing with ACHS, instead inducing them to purchase DME from

the Southwest subsidiary. ACHS argued that Radford and Southwest were guilty of conspiring to restrain trade in violation of Section 1 of the Sherman Act and were also guilty of monopolization and conspiracy to monopolize under Section 2. Was the district court's summary dismissal of all of ACHS's claims proper?

4. Hobart International, Inc., manufactures high-quality commercial kitchen equipment. In January of 1976 Hobart had eight distributors in the highly competitive Denver, Colorado, market; the most successful was Nobel. In 1973 Westman Commission Company, a Denver-area wholesale grocer, entered the restaurant equipment supply business by purchasing a division of Wilscam Enterprises. Wilscam had previously enjoyed an informal arrangement with Hobart allowing it to distribute Hobart products. For about 14 months after Westman's purchase of the Wilscam division, Hobart continued to make sales to Westman on a casual basis, but failed to offer Westman a formal distributorship agreement. Hobart subsequently refused to grant Westman a distributorship and, in January 1976, refused to make further sales to Westman on a casual basis. Westman filed suit against Hobart, arguing that Hobart had declined to grant the distributorship in response to pressure from Nobel, which feared competition from Westman. The trial court found that Hobart's refusal to deal amounted to a per se illegal vertical boycott. Should this decision stand on appeal?

5. In 1986 Market Force, Inc. (MFI) began operating in the Milwaukee real estate market as a buyer's broker. MFI signed exclusive contracts with prospective home buyers providing that it would receive a fee equal to 40 percent of the sales commission if it located a house that the buyer ultimately purchased. This 40 percent commission was the same commission that selling brokers (those who ultimately produced a buyer, but whose duty of loyalty was to the seller) earned when they sold property placed on the local multiple listing service (MLS) by other brokers. MFI's contracts anticipated that the buyer would ask the listing broker (the one who had listed the property for sale on behalf of its owners and who received 60 percent of the commission when the property sold) to pay MFI the commission at the time of the sale. If the listing broker agreed to do so, the buyer had no further obligation to MFI. For some time after MFI began operations other real estate firms treated it inconsistently; some paid the full 40 percent commission while others paid nothing. In the fall of 1987, Wauwatosa Realty Co. and Coldwell Banker, the top two firms listing high-quality homes in Milwaukee, issued formal policies on splitting commissions with buyer's brokers. Wauwatosa said it would pay 20 percent of the selling agent's 40 percent commission, while Coldwell Banker said it would pay 20 percent of the total sales commission. Several other real estate firms followed suit, setting their rates at 10 percent or 20 percent of the total sales commission, with the result that firms accounting for 31 percent of the annual listings of the MLS adopted policies and disseminated them to other MLS members. MFI filed suit against the brokers who had announced policies, arguing that they had conspired to restrain trade in violation of Section 1 of the Sherman Act. At trial, the defendants introduced evidence of numerous business justifications for their policies and argued that the fact that they had all knowingly adopted similar policies was not enough, standing alone, to justify finding a violation of the Sherman Act. Is this argument correct?

6. When Triple-A Baseball Club Associates was in the process of building the Old Orchard Beach Ballpark, both Gemini Concerts, Inc., and Don Law Co., Inc., expressed interest in promoting concerts at the ballpark. Triple-A, however, had neither the time nor money to make the facility suitable for concerts, and Gemini eventually ceased its efforts to use the facility. Law, however, persisted, and after several years of discussions Law and Triple-A signed an agreement giving Law the exclusive right to promote concerts at the ballpark for two years, with an option to renew for another five years. In return, Law paid for many of the capital improvements necessary to equip the ballpark for concerts and shared with Triple-A the cost of others. Gemini filed suit against Triple-A and Law, arguing that their exclusive dealing contract violated Section 1 of the Sherman Act. Should the trial court grant the restraining order requested by Gemini?

7. In 1973 Subaru of America (SOA), concerned that its dealers might not have sufficient spare parts to make repairs on recently purchased Subaru cars, decided to require them to keep certain spare parts kits on hand. Grappone, Inc., was a New Hampshire Subaru dealer that also had AMC, Pontiac, Jeep, Toyota, and Peugot franchises. Grappone acquired its cars from Subaru of New England, Inc. (SNE), a regional Subaru distributor. Grappone objected when told by SNE that it needed to purchase two "dealer's kits" containing 88 parts for 1974 cars and two "supplemental kits" containing 44 parts each (there are between 4,000 and 5,000 different Su-

baru parts). SNE refused to give Grappone its 1974 car allotment until Grappone bought the kits. Grappone went 10 months without cars; then it agreed to take the kits. Later, Grappone sued SNE, arguing that SNE violated Section 1 of the Sherman Act by tying the sale of the parts kits to the sale of cars. The evidence introduced at trial indicated that Subaru's national market share was under 1 percent and its share of the New Hampshire market was 3.4 percent. Was the trial court judgment in Grappone's behalf proper?

8. Kentucky Fried Chicken Corporation (KFC) required its franchisees to buy the seasoning to make its Original Recipe Kentucky Fried Chicken from Stange Company. To protect the secrecy of its seasoning recipe KFC had two companies, Stange and John W. Sexton Co., each prepare a portion of the recipe. The portions were then blended by Stange. Neither Stange nor Sexton knew the complete formula and both had entered secrecy agreements with KFC. KFC filed a tortious interference with contract suit against Marion-Kay Company for selling seasoning to KFC franchisees for use in preparing Original Recipe Kentucky Fried Chicken. Marion-Kay counterclaimed against KFC, arguing that KFC had unlawfully tied the sale of KFC seasoning to the sale of KFC franchises in violation of Section 1 of the Sherman Act. Should Marion-Kay win its counterclaim?

9. In 1972 Eastman Kodak Company introduced its new 110 pocket instamatic camera and its supporting photographic system. That system included a new generation of film (Kodacolor II), photographic paper, and photographic film processing and printing chemicals, all of which were incompatible with the existing products of Kodak's competitors. Foremost Pro Color, an authorized Kodak dealer and an independent photo-finisher, filed suit against Kodak, alleging, among other things, that Kodak's introduction of the 110 system violated Section 2 of the Sherman Act. Foremost argued that by "continually researching and developing new products" Kodak was trying to "render obsolete existing competitive products" and thereby monopolize the amateur photographic market. Was the trial court correct in dismissing Foremost's monopolization claim?

10. When Foremost Pro Color sued Eastman Kodak over its introduction of the 110 photographic system (see Problem Case 9 above), Foremost also argued that Kodak's marketing of the integrated 110 system constituted a per se illegal tying contract under Section 1 of the Sherman Act. The trial court also dismissed this claim. Was it correct in doing so?

11. Häagen-Dazs was the first "super premium" ice cream manufacturer to achieve national distribution. Häagen-Dazs refused to sell its products to any distributor who also sold a comparable, competing ice cream brand. Two Count had been a Häagen-Dazs distributor in the San Francisco area since 1976. In 1985 Two Count agreed to also become a distributor for Double Rainbow, another "super premium" ice cream manufacturer. When informed of this agreement, Häagen-Dazs terminated Two Count's distributorship. Two Count and Double Rainbow subsequently sued Häagen-Dazs, arguing, among other things, that Häagen-Dazs was guilty of monopolizing, or attempting to monopolize, the "super premium" ice cream market. At trial, Häagen-Dazs introduced uncontroverted evidence indicating that all grades of ice cream compete with one another for customer preference and space in retailers' freezers. Häagen-Dazs's share of the San Francisco ice cream market was 4 percent to 5 percent, and its national market share was in the same range. Should the trial court grant Häagen-Dazs's motion for summary judgment on the Section 2 claims?

CHAPTER 49

THE CLAYTON ACT, THE ROBINSON–PATMAN ACT, AND ANTITRUST EXEMPTIONS AND IMMUNITIES

INTRODUCTION

Despite the passage of the Sherman Act, the trend toward concentration in the U.S. economy continued. Early restrictive judicial interpretations of Section 2 of the act made it difficult to attack many monopolists; critics argued for legislation to "nip monopolies in the bud" before they achieved full-blown restraint of trade or monopoly power. In 1914 Congress responded by passing the Clayton Act, which was designed to attack some of the specific practices that monopolists had historically employed to acquire monopoly power. Such practices included tying and exclusive dealing arrangements designed to squeeze competitors out of the market, mergers and acquisitions aimed at reducing competition through the removal of competitors from the market, interlocking corporate directorates designed to reduce competition among competitors by placing them under common leadership, and predatory or discriminatory pricing designed to force competitors out of business. Each of these practices will be discussed in the following pages.

Congress intended the Clayton Act to be a *preventive* measure. As a result, only a *probability* of a significant anticompetitive effect must be shown for most Clayton Act violations.

Because the Clayton Act deals only with probable harms to competition, there are no criminal penalties for violating its provisions. Private plaintiffs, however, can sue for treble damages or injunctive relief if they are injured, or threatened with injury, by a violation of the act's provisions. The Justice Department and the Federal Trade Commission (FTC) share the responsibility for enforcing the Clayton Act; both agencies have the power to seek injunctive relief to prevent or remedy violations of the act. In addition, the FTC has the power to enforce the act through the use of cease and desist orders, which were discussed in the Federal Trade Commission Act and Consumer Protection Laws chapter.

CLAYTON ACT SECTION 3

Section 3 of the Clayton Act makes it unlawful for any person engaged in interstate commerce to *lease or sell commodities*, or to *fix a price* for commodities, on the *condition, agreement, or understanding* that the lessee or buyer of the commodities will not use or deal in the commodities of the lessor's or seller's competitors, where the effect of doing so *may be to substantially lessen competition* or *tend to create a monopoly* in any line of commerce. Section 3 is aimed primarily at two potentially anticompetitive behaviors: *tying contracts* and *exclusive dealing contracts*. As you learned in the preceding chapter, both tying contracts and exclusive dealing contracts may also amount to restraints of trade in violation of Section 1 of the Sherman Act. The language of Section 3, however, imposes several limitations on its application to such agreements.

First, Section 3 applies only to those tying contracts and exclusive dealing contracts that involve *commodities*. Therefore, when such agreements involve services, real estate, or intangibles, they must be attacked under the Sherman Act. Also, Section 3 applies only when there has been a *lease or sale* of commodities, so it does not apply to true consignment agreements, because no sale or lease occurs in a consignment. Finally, although Section 3 speaks of sales on the "condition, agreement, or understanding" that the buyer or lessee not deal in the commodities of the seller's or lessor's competitors, no formal agreement is required. Whenever a seller or lessor uses its economic power to prevent its customers from dealing with its competitors, this is sufficient to satisfy the Clayton Act.

Tying Agreements

Tying agreements can plainly fall within the statutory language of Section 3. Any agreement that requires a buyer to purchase one product (the tied product) from a seller as a condition of purchasing another product from the same seller (the tying product) necessarily prevents the buyer from purchasing the tied product from the seller's competitors.

Only tying agreements that may "substantially lessen competition or tend to create a monopoly," however, vio-late Section 3. The nature of the proof necessary to demonstrate such a probable anticompetitive effect is currently the subject of some disagreement among the lower federal courts. Over 30 years ago, the Supreme Court appeared to indicate that a tying agreement would violate the Clayton Act if the seller either had monopoly power over the tying product or restrained a substantial volume of commerce in the tied product.[1]

As the following *Mozart* case indicates, many lower federal courts today require essentially the same elements of proof for a Clayton Act violation that they require for a violation of the Sherman Act: proof that the challenged agreement involves two separate products, that sale of the tying product is conditioned on an accompanying sale of the tied product, that the seller has sufficient economic power in the market for the tying product to appreciably restrain competition in the tied product market, and that the seller's tying arrangements restrain a "not insubstantial" amount of commerce in the tied product market. However, a few courts continue to apply a less demanding standard for Clayton Act tying liability, dispensing with proof of the seller's economic power in the market for the tying product as long as the seller's tying arrangements involve a "not insubstantial" amount of commerce in the tied product. The *Mozart* case also demonstrates the fact that defenses to tying liability that are effective under the Sherman Act are also applicable to tying claims brought under the Clayton Act.[2]

---

[1] *Times-Picayune Publ. Co. v. United States,* 345 U.S. 594 (U.S. Sup. Ct. 1953).

[2] Defenses to tying liability were discussed in the preceding chapter.

MOZART CO. v. MERCEDES-BENZ OF NORTH AMERICA, INC.

833 F.2d 1342 (9th Cir. 1987)

Mercedes-Benz of North America (MBNA) is the exclusive U.S. distributor of Mercedes-Benz (MB) automobiles and is a wholly owned subsidiary of Daimler-Benz Aktiengesellschaft, the manufacturer of MB automobiles. MBNA required the approximately 400 franchised Mercedes-Benz dealers to agree not to sell, or to use any parts in the repair or servicing of MB automobiles, other than genuine MB parts. Mozart, a wholesale automotive parts distributor, filed an antitrust suit against MBNA alleging, among other things, that MBNA had violated both Section 1 of the Sherman Act and Section 3 of the Clayton Act by tying the sale of MB parts to the sale of Mercedes-Benz automobiles. When the trial court ruled in favor of MBNA on all counts, Mozart appealed.

Sneed, Circuit Judge.   In *Jefferson Parish Hospital v. Hyde* (1984), a bare majority reaffirmed the per se rule against tying. The majority opinion concluded that it was "far too late in the history of our antitrust jurisprudence to question the proposition that certain tying arrangements pose an unacceptable risk of stifling competition." Three elements are necessary to establish a per se illegal tying arrangement: (1) a tie-in between two distinct products or services; (2) sufficient economic power in the tying product to impose significant restrictions in the tied product market; and (3) an effect on a non-insubstantial volume of commerce in the tied product market.

The district court determined as a matter of law that the Mercedes passenger car and its replacement parts were separate products tied together by the terms of the MBNA dealer agreement, and that the tying arrangement affected a substantial amount of interstate commerce. The market power issue was submitted to the jury, which found that MBNA possessed the requisite power in the tying product, the Mercedes passenger car.

The instructions employed in submitting this issue to the jury were flawed, however. That flaw pertained to the "market power" that the defendant must possess in the tying product to justify the invocation of the per se standard. The required market power must be sufficient to "force a purchaser to do something he would not do in a competitive market." Such "forcing" is the equivalent of increasing the price of the tying product to increase profits.

In *Hyde*, the Court identified three sources of market power. First, when the government has granted the seller a patent or similar monopoly over a product, it is fair to presume that the inability to buy the product elsewhere gives the seller market power. The second is when the seller's share of the market is high. The third is when the seller offers a unique product that competitors are not able to offer. Mozart's theory of this case is that the Mercedes automobile is sufficiently unique to confer economic power on MBNA in the tying product.

The jury was instructed that "[a] prestigious and desirable trademark can be persuasive evidence of economic power." First, a prestigious trademark is not itself persuasive evidence of economic power. It is true that we have previously held that *copyright* protection may be evidence of market power because it creates barriers to entry for competitors in the tying market. *Digidyne Corp. v. Data General Corp.* (1984). However, unlike a patent or copyright, which is designed to protect the uniqueness of the product itself, a trademark protects only the name or symbol of the product. Market power, if any, is derived from the product, not from the name or symbol as such.

Second, the court's instructions indicate that somehow market power can be proven from the uniqueness of the Mercedes automobile. The difficulty with this is that while many individual purchasers undoubtedly regard a Mercedes as unique, it is by no means clear that dealers view the Mercedes in the same manner. The critical issue is whether MBNA possesses the market power to force dealers to purchase the tied product rather than acquire the franchise to sell a different automobile. Obviously there are costs of surrendering one franchise and acquiring another, but these are costs unrelated to the market power of a unique automobile. These costs will enable the car maker to extract concessions from the dealer, but this power is related to the franchise method of doing business, not to the possible uniqueness of the car.

However, we do not find that the flawed instructions necessitate a reversal of the judgment. The instructions were more favorable to Mozart than would be a proper recasting. This brings us to the heart of this case, whether the tying arrangement was justified by business necessity. A tie-in does not violate the antitrust laws if implemented for a legitimate purpose and if no less restrictive alternative is available. The defendant bears the burden of showing that the case falls within the contours of this affirmative defense.

The justification asserted by MBNA is that the tying arrangement is necessary to assure quality control and to protect its goodwill. The difficulty confronting MBNA is the problem of "free-riding" by Mercedes dealers. To MBNA it is crucial that a dealer offer standardized products. Only then can customers confidently rely on the Mercedes name. Franchisees, on the other hand, experience a conflict of interest. True, they wish to maintain the goodwill of MBNA, but some will yield to avarice and increase their profits by supplying inferior products while continuing to attract customers at the expense of dealers who conform to quality standards. The cost of these transgressions will be borne by all franchisees in the form of decreased future demand. Although a consumer may realize that a particular franchisee "cut a corner," the adverse reaction of consumers as a group is not confined to that particular franchisee because they are apppropriately reacting to the poor job of policing done by the franchisor.

Substantial evidence exists to support MBNA's claim that the tie-in was used to assure quality control. MBNA purchases approximately 80 percent of its replacement parts from DBAG. Of those parts half are manufactured by DBAG itself, and half are acquired from other original equipment manufacturers (OEMs). These OEMs produce the parts according to DBAG specifications. A selection of each shipment of OEM parts, which has already passed through one round of inspection, is tested a second time by DBAG. If any of the test parts is deficient, the whole lot is rejected. The remaining 20 percent of the replacement parts purchased by MBNA come directly from OEMs that have met DBAG's standards. Mozart purchased most of the parts it sold from OEMs in the United States.

MBNA introduced evidence showing that DBAG's strict testing standards helped to assure the high quality of replacement parts. MBNA maintains an excellent reputation in the automobile industry for reliable service and quality replacement parts. In fact, 75 percent of Mercedes automobile owners are repeat purchasers, and over one-third of the owners return to the dealer for service and repairs. There was considerable testimony by dealers and employees of MBNA about the inferiority of parts supplied by independent jobbers. Although Mozart introduced evidence to the contrary, the jury was entitled to make credibility determinations in favor of MBNA.

Mozart insists that MBNA could have furnished manufacturing specifications for replacement parts, and that such specifications would eliminate the need for a tie-in. The jury rejected this contention. Mozart is right, of course, when it insists that MBNA could have furnished design specifications for Mercedes replacement parts. That alone, however, does not eliminate the business justification defense. MBNA offered evidence that DBAG's vigorous testing programs could not be replicated by individual dealerships. The evidence further indicates the impracticality of Mozart's suggestion that MBNA could have inspected all replacement products furnished to independents. There was evidence from which the jury could find that the cost of such an undertaking would be prohibitive. We do not believe MBNA was required to make extreme steps to protect its legitimate interest in assuring public confidence in the quality of its trademarked product.

The elements for establishing a Sherman Act Section 1 claim and a Clayton Act Section 3 claim are virtually the same. There is no reason for allowing a business justification for a Section 1 claim and not for a Section 3 claim. Courts permit a business justification defense to tying claims because of a frank recognition that a package transaction with substantial justifications and few harmful effects should not be condemned. That recognition applies with equal force to the Sherman Act and the Clayton Act. The Section 3 claim falls with the Section 1 claim.

Judgment for MBNA affirmed.

Exclusive Dealing Arrangements

In the last chapter, we discussed the nature of **exclusive dealing arrangements.** Such arrangements plainly fall under the language of Section 3 because buyers who agree to handle one seller's product exclusively, or to purchase all of their requirements for a particular commodity from one seller, are by definition agreeing not to purchase similar items from the seller's competitors. Once again, however, not all exclusive dealing agreements are illegal. Section 3 outlaws only those agreements that may "substantially lessen competition or tend to create a monopoly."

Exclusive dealing agreements were initially treated in much the same way as tying agreements. The courts looked at the dollar amount of commerce involved and declared agreements involving a "not insubstantial" amount of commerce illegal. For example, this quantitative substantiality test was employed by the U.S. Supreme Court in *Standard Oil Co. of California v. United States*.[3] Standard Oil of California was the largest refiner and supplier of gasoline in several western states, with roughly 14 percent of the retail market. Roughly half of these sales were made by retail outlets owned by Standard, and the other half were made by independent dealers who had entered into exclusive dealing contracts with Standard. Standard's six major competitors had entered into similar contracts with their own independent dealers. The Court recognized that exclusive dealing contracts, unlike tying agreements, could benefit both buyers and sellers, but declared Standard's contracts illegal on the ground that nearly $58 million in commerce was involved.[4]

The Court's decision in the *Standard Oil* case provoked considerable criticism, and, in *Tampa Electric Co. v. Nashville Coal Co.*, the Court applied a broader, qualitative substantiality test to gauge the legality of a long-term requirements contract for the sale of coal to an electric utility.[5] In *Tampa*, the Court looked at the "area of effective competition," that is, the total market for coal in the geographic region from which the utility could reasonably purchase its coal needs. The Court then determined the percentage of total coal sales in this region that the challenged contract represented and, finding that percentage share to amount to less than 1 percent of total sales, upheld the agreement, although it represented more than $100 million in coal sales.

Tampa, however, is distinguishable from *Standard Oil*, and the Court did not expressly overrule its earlier decision in the case against Standard. *Tampa*, unlike *Standard Oil*, involved parties with relatively equal bargaining power and an individual agreement rather than an industrywide practice. In addition, there were obvious reasons why an electric utility such as Tampa Electric might want to lock in its coal costs by using a long-term requirements contract. Although lower court opinions can be found employing both tests, as the following *Dresser Industries* case indicates, the qualitative approach employed in *Tampa* is the one most likely to be employed by the current Court.

---

[3]337 U.S. 293 (U.S. Sup. Ct. 1949).

[4]See the discussion of this point in the preceding chapter.
[5]365 U.S. 320 (1961).

ROLAND MACHINERY CO. v. DRESSER INDUSTRIES, INC.

749 F.2d 380 (7th Cir. 1984)

Roland Machinery Company, a substantial dealer in construction equipment and related items serving a 45-county area in central Illinois, was for many years the area's exclusive distributor of International Harvester's construction equipment. International Harvester got into serious financial trouble in 1982 and sold its construction-equipment division to Dresser Industries. Dresser promptly signed a dealership agreement with Roland. The agreement provided that it could be terminated by either party, without cause, on 90 days' notice. It did not contain an exclusive-dealing clause, that is, a clause forbidding the dealer to sell any competing manufacturer's construction equipment. Eight months after signing the agreement, Roland signed a similar agreement with Komatsu, a Japanese manufacturer of construction equipment. Several months after discovering that Roland had done this, Dresser gave notice that it would exercise its contract right to terminate its dealership agreement with Roland without cause. Roland filed suit shortly before the end of the 90-day notice period, charging that Dresser had violated Section 3 of the Clayton Act. The district judge granted Roland a preliminary injunction, and Dresser appealed.

Posner, Circuit Judge.   Roland must show that it is more likely than not to win. Only then would the error of denying Roland a preliminary injunction should it later win on the merits be more costly than the error of granting it the injunction should it later lose on the merits.

In order to prevail on its Section 3 claim, Roland will have to show both that there was an agreement, though not necessarily an explicit agreement, between it and Dresser that it not carry a line of construction equipment competitive with Dresser's, and that the agreement was likely to have a substantial though not necessarily an immediate anticompetitive effect. Nothing in the dealership agreement even hints at a requirement of exclusive dealing and the fact that after signing the agreement with Dresser, Roland applied for a Komatsu dealership is evidence that Roland itself did not think it had made an implied commitment to exclusive dealing. The fact that Dresser was hostile to dealers who would not live and die by its product (as the district judge put it), and acted on its hostility by canceling a dealer who did the thing to which it was hostile, does not establish an agreement, but if anything the opposite: a failure to agree on a point critical to one of the parties.

But even if Roland can prove at trial that there was an exclusive-dealing agreement, it will have grave difficulty—we infer from this record—in proving that the agreement is anticompetitive. The objection to exclusive- dealing agreements is that they deny outlets to a competitor during the term of the agreement. At one time it was thought that this effect alone would condemn exclusive-dealing agreements under Section 3 of the Clayton Act, provided that the agreements covered a large fraction of the market. *Standard Oil Co. v. United States* (1949) (*Standard Stations*). Although the Supreme Court has not decided an exclusive-dealing case in many years, it now appears most unlikely that such agreements, whether challenged under Section 3 of the Clayton Act or Section 1 of the Sherman Act, will be judged by the simple and strict test of *Standard Stations*. They will be judged under the Rule of Reason, and thus condemned only if found to restrain trade unreasonably. *Tampa Elec. Co. v. Nashville Coal Co.* (1961).

A plaintiff must prove two things to show that an exclusive-dealing agreement is unreasonable. First, he must prove that it is likely to keep at least one significant competitor of the defendant from doing business in a relevant market. If there is no exclusion of a significant competitor, the agreement cannot possibly harm competition. Second, he must prove that the probable (not certain) effect of the exclusion will be to raise prices above (and therefore reduce output below) the competitive level, or otherwise injure competition; he must show in other words that the anticompetitive effects (if any) of the exclusion outweigh any benefits to competition from it.

On the present record it appears that Komatsu cannot be kept out of the central Illinois market even if every manufacturer of construction equipment prefers exclusive dealers and will cancel any dealer who switches to the Komatsu line. Komatsu is the second largest manufacturer of construction equipment in the world. Its total sales of such equipment are four times as great as Dresser's. Already it is a major factor in the U.S. construction-equipment market; in some items it outsells Dresser. The nationwide practice of exclusive dealing has not kept Komatsu from becoming a major factor in the U.S. market, apparently in a short period of time. The reason is evident. Since dealership agreements in this industry are terminable by either party on short notice, Komatsu, to obtain its own exclusive dealer in some area, has only to offer a better deal to some other manufacturer's dealer in the area.

The calculus of competitive effect must also include some consideration of the possible competitive benefits of exclusive dealing in this industry. A dealer who expresses his willingness to carry only one manufacturer's brand of a particular product indicates his commitment to pushing that brand; he doesn't have divided loyalties. If the dealer carries several brands, his stake in the success of each is reduced. Exclusive dealing may also enable a manufacturer to prevent dealers from taking a free ride on his efforts (for example, national advertising) to promote his brand. The dealer who carried competing brands as well might switch customers to a lower-priced substitute on which he got a higher margin, thus defeating the manufacturer's effort to recover the costs of his promotional expenditures by charging the dealer a higher price.

Therefore, even if, in signing on with Komatsu, Roland did not intend to discontinue its sales of the Dresser line eventually and in the meantime to begin phasing Dresser out, Dresser still has a plausible argument that an exclusive dealer would promote its line more effectively than a nonexclusive dealer, and by doing so would increase competition in the market for construction equipment. The argument is no more than plausible; it is supported by very little evidence; it may be wrong. But when we consider how tenuous is the evidence that exclusive dealing in this market will exclude or even significantly retard Komatsu—how tenuous even is the inference that there was an exclusive-dealing agreement—even weak evidence of competitive gains from exclusive dealing must reinforce our conclusion that Roland has failed to show that it is more likely than not to prevail at the trial on the merits.

Judgment reversed in favor of Dresser.

CLAYTON ACT SECTION 7

Introduction

Section 7 of the Clayton Act was designed to attack **mergers**—a term broadly used in this chapter to refer to the acquisition of one company by another. Our historical experience indicates that one of the ways in which monopolists acquired monopoly power was by acquiring control of their competitors. Section 7 prohibits any person engaged in commerce or in any activity affecting commerce from *acquiring* the *stock* or *assets* of any other such person where in *any line of commerce* or in any activity affecting commerce in *any section of the country* the effect *may be* to *substantially lessen competition* or *tend to create a monopoly*. The difference between Section 7 and Section 2 of the Sherman Act is obvious: Rather than waiting until a would-be monopolist has acquired monopoly power or has come dangerously close to doing so, Section 7 attempts to "nip monopolies in the bud" by barring mergers that may have an anticompetitive effect.

Section 7 is plainly an anticoncentration device, although, as the following text indicates, Section 7 has also been used to attack mergers that have had no direct effect on concentration in a particular industry. As such, its future evolution is in doubt, given the influence of Chicago School economic theories on the development of contemporary antitrust law and the more tolerant stance that those theories take toward merger activity. The Justice Department's merger guidelines, which were first announced in 1982 and amended in 1984, indicate a significant shift in the government's views about the proper role of Section 7 and, it is probably fair to say, signal a more permissive approach to merger activity. Of course, the guidelines only indicate the criteria that the department employs in deciding whether to challenge particular mergers, and private enforcement of Section 7 is still possible.

Predictions concerning the ultimate judicial treatment that Section 7 will receive are complicated considerably by the fact that many of the important merger cases in recent years have been settled out of court. This leaves interested observers of antitrust policy with no definitive recent judicial statements about the Supreme Court's current thinking on many merger issues. Most of the available indications, however, point to significant revisions of merger policy in the years to come.

Relevant Market Determination

Regardless of the treatment that Section 7 ultimately receives in the courts, the determination of the *relevant market* affected by a merger is likely to remain a crucial component of any Section 7 case. Before a court can determine whether a particular merger will have the *probable* anticompetitive effect required by the Clayton Act, it must first determine the *line of commerce*, or relevant product market, and the *section of the country*, or relevant geographic market, that will probably be affected by the merger. In most cases, a broad relevant market definition adopted by the court means that the government or a private plaintiff has greater difficulty in demonstrating a probable anticompetitive effect flowing from a challenged merger.

Relevant Product Market "Line of commerce" determinations under the Clayton Act have traditionally employed *functional interchangeability* tests similar to those employed in relevant product market determinations under Section 2 of the Sherman Act. Which products do the acquired and acquiring firms manufacture (assuming a merger between competitors), and which products are reasonably interchangeable by consumers to serve the same purposes? The Justice Department merger guidelines indicate that the department includes in its relevant market determination those products that consumers view as "good substitutes at prevailing prices." The department also indicates that it includes any products that a significant percentage of current customers would shift to in the event of a "small, but significant and nontransitory increase in [the] price" of the products of the merged firms. Initially, the department stated that this meant a 5 percent increase in price sustained over a one-year period. More recently, recognizing that the 5 percent figure might not be appropriate to all cases, given the wide disparity among the prevailing profit margins in many industries, the department has indicated that varying percentage figures may be employed, depending on the industry in question. By expanding the interchangeability standard in this fashion, the Justice Department has recognized that any price increases that result from a merger may be only temporarily sustainable because they may provoke further product substitution choices by consumers.

Relevant Geographic Market To determine the probable anticompetitive effect of a particular merger on a section of the country, the courts have traditionally asked where the effects of the merger will be "direct and immediate."[6] This means that the relevant geographic market may not be as broad as the markets in which the acquiring and acquired firms actually operate or, in the case of a merger between competitors, the markets in

which they actually compete. The focus of the relevant market inquiry is on those sections of the country in which competition is most likely to be injured by the merger. As a result, in a given case the relevant geographic market could be drawn as narrowly as one metropolitan area or as broadly as the nation as a whole. All that is necessary to satisfy this aspect of Section 7 is proof that the challenged merger might have a significant negative effect on competition in any economically significant geographic market.

The Justice Department's merger guidelines adopt a somewhat different approach to determining the relevant geographic market. They define the relevant geographic market as the geographic area in which a sole supplier of the product in question could profitably raise its price without causing outside suppliers to begin selling in the area. The department begins with the existing markets in which the parties to a merger compete, and then adds the markets of those suppliers that would enter the market in response to a "small, but significant and nontransitory increase in price." In most cases, this means a 5 percent price increase sustained over a one-year period, but different percentages may be employed to reflect the economic realities of particular industries.

Horizontal Mergers

The analytical approach employed to gauge a merger's probable effect on competition varies according to the nature of the merger in question. **Horizontal mergers,** mergers among firms competing in the same product and geographic markets, have traditionally been subjected to the most rigorous scrutiny because they clearly result in an increase in concentration in the relevant market. To determine the legality of such a merger, the courts look at the *market share of the resulting firm.* In *United States v. Philadelphia National Bank*, the Supreme Court indicated that a horizontal merger producing a firm with an "undue percentage share" of the relevant market (33 percent in this case) and resulting in a "significant increase in concentration" of the firms in that market would be presumed illegal absent convincing evidence that the merger would not have an anticompetitive effect.[7]

In the past, mergers involving firms with smaller market shares than those involved in the *Philadelphia National Bank* case were also frequently enjoined if

---

[6] *United States v. Phillipsburg National Bank,* 399 U.S. 350 (U.S. Sup. Ct. 1970).

[7] 374 U.S. 321 (1963).

other economic or historical factors pointed toward a probable anticompetitive effect. Some of the factors traditionally considered relevant by the courts have been:

1. A trend toward concentration in the relevant market—Has the number of competing firms decreased over time?

2. The competitive position of the merging firms— Are the defendants dominant firms despite their relatively small market shares?

3. A past history of acquisitions by the acquiring firm—Are we dealing with a would-be empire builder?

4. The nature of the acquired firm—Is it an aggressive, innovative competitor despite its small market share?

Recent developments, however, indicate that the courts and federal antitrust enforcement agencies have become increasingly less willing to presume that anticompetitive effects will necessarily result from a merger that produces a firm with a relatively large market share. Instead, a more detailed inquiry is made into the nature of the relevant market and of the merging firms to ascertain the likelihood of a probable harm to competition as a result of a challenged merger. The Justice Department merger guidelines indicate that, in assessing the probable effect of a merger, the department focuses on the existing concentration in the relevant market, the increase in concentration as a result of the proposed merger, and other nonmarket share factors. The more concentrated the existing market, and the greater the increase in concentration that would result from the proposed merger, the more likely the merger is to be challenged by the department.

The nonmarket share factors that the department considers are more traditional. They include the existence of barriers to the entry of new competitors into the relevant market, the prior conduct of the merging firms, and the probable future competitive strength of the acquired firm. The last factor is particularly important because both the courts and the Justice Department have acknowledged that a firm's current market share may not reflect its ability to compete in the future. For example, the courts have long recognized a "failing company" justification for some mergers. If the acquired firm is a failing company and no other purchasers are interested in acquiring it, its acquisition by a competitor may be lawful under Section 7. Similarly, if an acquired firm has financial problems that reflect some underlying structural weakness, or if it lacks new technologies that are necessary to compete effectively in the future, its current market share may overstate its future competitive importance.

Finally, given the greater weight that is currently being assigned to economic arguments in antitrust cases, two other merger justifications may be granted greater credence in the future. Some lower federal courts have recognized the idea that a merger between two small companies may be justifiable, despite the resulting statistical increase in concentration, if as a result of the merger they are able to compete more effectively with larger competitors. In a somewhat similar vein, some commentators have argued that mergers that result in enhanced economic efficiencies should sometimes be allowed despite the fact that they may have some anticompetitive impact. The courts have not been very receptive to efficiency arguments in the past, and the 1982 Justice Department guidelines rejected efficiency arguments on the ground that they were very difficult to prove. The 1984 amended guidelines, however, indicate that the department considers efficiency claims supported by clear and convincing evidence in deciding whether to challenge a merger.

UNITED STATES v. WASTE MANAGEMENT, INC.

743 F.2d 976 (2d Cir. 1984)

Waste Management, Inc. (WMI), a company in the solid waste disposal business, acquired the stock of EMW Ventures, Inc. EMW was a diversified holding company, one of whose subsidiaries was Waste Resources. WMI and Waste Resources each had subsidiaries operating in or near

Dallas, Texas. The government challenged the merger, arguing that it violated Section 7 of the Clayton Act. The trial court (Judge Griesa) agreed, defining the relevant market as including all forms of trash collection, except at single-family or multiple-family residences or small apartment complexes, in Dallas County plus a small fringe area. The combined WMI and Waste Resources subsidiaries had 48.8 percent of the market so defined, a market share which the trial court found presumptively illegal. WMI appealed.

Winter, Circuit Judge.   A post-merger market share of 48.8 percent is sufficient to establish prima facie illegality under *United States v. Philadelphia National Bank.* That decision held that large market shares are a convenient proxy for appraising the danger of monopoly power resulting from a horizontal merger. Under its rationale, a merger resulting in a large market share is presumptively illegal, rebuttable only by a demonstration that the merger will not have anticompetitive effects. Thus in *United States v. General Dynamics Corp.* (1974) the Court upheld a merger of two leading coal producers because substantially all of the production of one firm was tied up in long-term contracts and its reserves were insubstantial. Since that firm's future ability to compete was negligible, the Court reasoned that its disappearance as an independent competitor could not affect the market.

WMI does not claim that 48.8 percent is too small a share to trigger the *Philadelphia National Bank* presumption. Rather, it argues that the presumption is rebutted by the fact that competitors can enter the Dallas waste hauling market with such ease that the finding of a 48.8 percent market share does not accurately reflect market power. WMI argues that it is unable to raise prices over the competitive level because new firms would quickly enter the market and undercut them.

The Supreme Court has never directly held that ease of entry may rebut a showing of *prima facie* illegality under *Philadelphia National Bank.* However, on several occasions it has held that appraisal of the impact of a proposed merger upon competition must take into account potential competition from firms not presently active in the relevant product and geographic markets. Moreover, under *General Dynamics*, a substantial existing market share is insufficient to void a merger where that share is misleading as to actual future competitive effect. In that case, long-term contracts and declining reserves negated the inference of market power drawn from the existing market share. In the present case, a market definition artificially restricted to existing firms competing at one moment may yield market share statistics that are not an accurate proxy for market power when substantial potential competition able to respond quickly to price increases exists.

Finally, the *Merger Guidelines* issued by the government itself not only recognize the economic principle that ease of entry is relevant to appraising the impact upon competition of a merger but also state that it may override all other factors. Where entry is "so easy that existing competitors could not succeed in raising prices for any significant period of time," the government has announced that it will usually not challenge a merger.

Turning to the evidence in this case, we believe that entry into the relevant product and geographic market by new firms or by existing firms in the Fort Worth area is so easy that any anticompetitive impact of the merger before us would be eliminated more quickly by such competition than by litigation. Judge Griesa specifically found that individuals operating out of their homes can acquire trucks and some containers and compete successfully "with any other company." His conclusion that "there is no showing of any circumstances, related to ease of entry or the trend of the business, which promises in and of itself to materially erode the [defendants'] competitive strength" is consistent with our decision. They may well retain their present market share. However, in view of the findings as to ease of entry, that share can be retained only by competitive pricing. Ease of entry constrains not only WMI, but every firm in the market. Should WMI attempt to exercise market power by raising prices, none of its small competitors would be able to follow the price increases because of the ease with which new competitors would appear.

WMI would then face lower prices charged by all existing competitors as well as entry by new ones, a condition fatal to its economic prospects if not rectified.

Judgment reversed in favor of Waste Management, Inc.

Vertical Mergers

A **vertical merger** is a merger between firms that previously had, or could have had, a supplier-customer relationship. For example, a manufacturer may seek to vertically integrate its operations by acquiring a company that controls retail outlets that could sell the manufacturer's product line. Or it could vertically merge by acquiring a company that makes a product that the manufacturer regularly uses in its production processes. Vertical mergers, unlike horizontal mergers, do not directly result in an increase in concentration. Nonetheless, they traditionally have been thought to threaten competition in a variety of ways.

First, vertical mergers may *foreclose competitors* from a share of the relevant market. For example, if a major customer for a particular product acquires a captive supplier of that product, the competitors of the acquired firm are thereafter foreclosed from competing with it for sales to the acquiring firm. Similarly, if a manufacturer acquires a captive retail outlet for its products, the manufacturer's competitors are foreclosed from competing for sales to that retail outlet. In the latter case, a vertical merger may also result in reduced competition at the retail level. For example, a shoe manufacturer acquires a chain of retail shoe stores that has a dominant share of the retail market in certain geographic areas and that has previously carried the brands of several competing manufacturers. If after the merger the retailer carries only the acquiring manufacturer's brands, competition among the acquiring manufacturer and its competitors is reduced in the retail market for shoes.

Second, vertical mergers may also result in *increased barriers to entry* confronting new competitors. For example, if a major purchaser of a particular product acquires a captive supplier of that product, potential producers of the product may be discouraged from commencing production due to the contraction of the market for the product resulting from the merger.

Third, some vertical mergers may *eliminate potential competition* in one of two ways. First, an acquiring firm may be perceived by existing competitors in the acquired firm's market as a likely potential entrant into that market. The threat of such a potential entrant "waiting in the wings" may moderate the behavior of existing competitors because they fear that pursuing pricing policies that exploit their current market position might induce the potential entrant to enter the market. The acquiring firm's entry into the market by the acquisition of an existing competitor means the end of its moderating influence as a potential entrant. Second, a vertical merger may deprive the market of the potential benefits that would have resulted had the acquiring firm entered the market in a more competitive manner, by creating its own entrant into the market through a process of internal expansion or by making a toehold acquisition of a small existing competitor and subsequently building it into a more significant competitor.

Historically, courts seeking to determine the legality of vertical mergers have tended to look at the *share of the relevant market foreclosed to competition*. If a more than insignificant market share is foreclosed to competition, they consider other economic and historical factors. Factors viewed as aggravating the anticompetitive potential of a vertical merger include a trend toward concentration or vertical integration in the industry, a past history of vertical integration in the industry, a past history of vertical acquisitions by the acquiring company, and significant barriers to entry resulting from the merger. This approach to determining the legality of vertical mergers has been criticized by some commentators who argue that vertical integration can yield certain efficiencies of distribution and that vertical integration by merger may be more economically efficient than vertical integration by internal expansion. The Justice Department's 1984 amended merger guidelines indicate that the department affords greater weight to efficiency arguments in cases involving vertical mergers than in cases involving horizontal mergers. The guidelines also indicate that the department applies the same criteria to all nonhorizontal mergers. We discuss these criteria in the following section.

Conglomerate Mergers

A **conglomerate merger** is a merger between two firms that are not in competition with each other because they compete in different product or geographic markets, and that do not have a supplier-customer relationship. Conglomerate mergers come in two varieties: *market extension* mergers and *product extension* mergers. In a market extension merger, the acquiring firm expands into a new geographic market by purchasing an existing competitor in that market. For example, a conglomerate that owns an East Coast grocery chain buys a West Coast grocery chain. In a product extension merger, the acquiring firm diversifies its operations by purchasing a company in a new product market. For example, a conglomerate with interests in the aerospace and electronics industries purchases a chain of department stores. Considerable disagreement exists over the economic effects of conglomerate acquisitions. Although some conglomerate mergers have been attacked successfully under Section 7, there is general agreement that the Clayton Act is not well suited to dealing with conglomerate mergers. This realization has produced calls for specific legislation on the subject. Such legislation is probably desirable in the event that we ultimately conclude that conglomerate merger activity is a proper subject for regulation.

Three kinds of conglomerate mergers have been challenged with some degree of success under Section 7: mergers that involve *potential reciprocity*, mergers that *eliminate potential competition*, and mergers that give an acquired firm an *unfair advantage* over its competitors. A conglomerate merger may create a risk of potential reciprocity if the acquired firm produces a product that the acquiring firm's suppliers regularly purchase. Such suppliers, eager to continue their relationship with the acquiring firm, may thereafter purchase the acquired firm's products rather than those of its competitors.

A conglomerate merger, similar to some vertical mergers, may also result in the elimination of potential competition. If existing competitors perceive the acquiring company as a potential entrant in the acquired company's market, the acquiring company's entry by a conglomerate acquisition may result in the loss of the moderating influence that it had while waiting in the wings. Also, when the acquiring company actually enters the new market by acquiring a well-established competitor rather than by starting a new competitor through internal expansion (a *de novo* entry) or by making a toehold acquisition, the market is deprived of the potential for increased competition flowing from the reduction in concentration that would have resulted from

either of the latter strategies. The most recent Supreme Court cases on this point suggest, however, that a high degree of proof is required before either potential competition argument is accepted. Arguments that a conglomerate merger eliminated a *perceived potential entrant* must be accompanied by proof that existing competitors actually perceived the acquiring firm as a potential entrant.[8] Arguments that a conglomerate acquisition eliminated an *actual* potential entrant, depriving the market of the benefits of reduced concentration, must be accompanied by evidence that the acquiring firm had the ability to enter the market by internal expansion or a toehold acquisition and that doing so would have ultimately yielded a substantial reduction in concentration.[9]

Finally, when a large firm acquires a firm that already enjoys a significant position in its market, the acquired firm may gain an unfair advantage over its competitors through its ability to draw on the greater resources and expertise of its new owner. This may entrench the acquired firm in its market by deterring existing competitors from actively competing with it for market share and by producing barriers to entry to new competitors reluctant to enter the market after the acquisition. Virtually all of the important recent conglomerate merger cases have been settled out of court. As a result, we do not have a clear indication of the Supreme Court's current thinking on conglomerate merger issues. The Justice Department merger guidelines indicate that the department may decline to employ many of the theories that have been used to challenge conglomerate mergers in the past. The guidelines indicate that the primary theories that the department uses to attack all nonhorizontal mergers are the elimination of perceived and actual potential competition theories. In employing these analytical tools, the department also considers certain other economic factors. These include: (1) the degree of concentration in the acquired firm's market; (2) the existence of barriers to entry into the market and the presence or absence of other firms with a comparable ability to enter; and (3) the market share of the acquired firm—challenges are unlikely where this is 5 percent or less and likely where it is 20 percent or more. Whether or not the Supreme Court will accept this more restrictive view of the scope of Section 7 remains to be seen. Figure 1, which follows, summarizes the types of mergers covered by Section 7.

---

[8]*United States v. Falstaff Brewing Corp.*, 410 U.S. 526 (U.S. Sup. Ct. 1973).

[9] *United States v. Marine Bancorporation, Inc.*, 418 U.S. 602 (U.S. Sup. Ct. 1974).

FIGURE 1	Types of Mergers Covered by Section 7	
Category	**Description**	**Example**
Horizontal	Between competitors	One automobile manufacturer merges with another automobile manufacturer
Vertical	Between a supplier and its customer	An oil producer merges with an oil refiner
Conglomerate	Between two largely unrelated businesses	A candy company merges with a greeting card company

TENNECO, INC. v. FTC

689 F.2d 346 (2d Cir. 1982)

In 1975 Tenneco, Inc. was the 15th largest industrial corporation in America. Tenneco's Walker Manufacturing Division produced and distributed a wide variety of automotive parts, the most important of which were exhaust system parts. In 1975 and 1976 Walker was the nation's leading seller of exhaust system parts. Tenneco acquired control of Monroe Auto Equipment Company, a leading manufacturer of automotive shock absorbers. Monroe was the number two firm in the national market for replacement shock absorbers. Monroe and Gabriel, the industry leader, accounted for over 77 percent of replacement shock absorber sales in 1976. General Motors and Questor Corporation, the third and fourth largest firms, controlled another 15 percent of the market.

The replacement shock absorber market exhibited significant barriers to the entry of new competitors. Economies of scale in the industry dictated manufacturing plants of substantial size, and the nature of the industry required would-be entrants to acquire significant new technologies and marketing skills unique to the industry. The Federal Trade Commission (FTC) ordered Tenneco to divest itself of Monroe on the grounds that Tenneco's acquisition of Monroe violated Section 7 of the Clayton Act by eliminating both perceived and actual potential competition in the replacement shock absorber market. Tenneco appealed.

Meskill, Circuit Judge.   The Supreme Court has described the theory of perceived potential competition, which it has approved for application to cases brought under Section 7 of the Clayton Act, as the principal focus of the potential competition doctrine. The Court has recognized that:

A market extension merger may be unlawful if the target market is substantially concentrated, if the acquiring firm has the characteristics, capabilities, and economic incentive to render it a perceived potential *de novo* entrant, and if the acquiring firm's presence on the fringe of the target market in fact tempered oligopolistic behavior on the part of existing participants in that market. *United States v. Marine Bancorporation, Inc.* (1974).

The actual potential competition theory, which has yet to receive sanction from the Supreme Court, would

proscribe a market extension merger solely on the ground that such a merger eliminates the prospect for long-term deconcentration of an oligopolistic market that in theory might result if the acquiring firm were forbidden to enter except through a *de novo* undertaking or through the acquisition of a small existing entrant.

We reject the Commission's finding that Tenneco was an actual potential entrant likely to increase competition in the market for replacement shock absorbers. Tenneco was actively considering entry into the market and was pursuing all leads to that end at least since the late 1960s or early 1970s. Moreover, Tenneco clearly possessed adequate financial resources to make the large initial investment needed to attempt to penetrate the market. The record, however, is deficient in evidence that there were viable toehold options available to Tenneco or that Tenneco would have entered the market *de novo*.

The Commission conceded that Tenneco never expressed any interest in entering the market for replacement shock absorbers "on a completely *de novo* basis." However, the Commission found that Tenneco had expressed interest in entering the market essentially *de novo*, building the required production facilities from scratch and acquiring the necessary technology via a license from an established foreign shock absorber producer. The Commission concluded that Tenneco would likely have done so absent its acquisition of Monroe.

The Commission's reasoning is flawed. It ignores Tenneco's decision not to enter the market during the 1960s and early 1970s, a period of high profitability for shock absorber manufacturers, because of anticipated inadequate earnings during early years. The record is devoid of evidentiary support for the Commission's assertion that in the period relevant to this case, when industry earnings were in decline, Tenneco would have been willing to suffer the "cost disadvantage" inherent in the building of an efficient scale plant that would remain underutilized "for a number of years."

The Commission's conclusion that Tenneco would likely have entered the replacement shock absorber market through toehold acquisition is similarly flawed. The Commission identified Armstrong Patents, Ltd. ("Armstrong"), a British shock absorber manufacturer, DeCarbon Shock Absorber Co. ("DeCarbon"), a French company, and Blackstone Manufacturing Corp. ("Blackstone"), a small United States producer of shock absorbers, as potential toeholds. However, Tenneco in fact negotiated unsuccessfully with Armstrong and DeCarbon. Armstrong management indicated that Tenneco would have to offer a 100 percent premium over the market price of its stock to generate its interest. Tenneco's negotiations with DeCarbon, which were conducted through an independent broker, were equally fruitless. DeCarbon had asked a selling price of 100 times its earnings.

As for Blackstone, the Commission itself described that company as "a small, struggling domestic firm burdened with aged equipment, a less than complete product line, declining market share and a mediocre reputation." Since 1974 Blackstone had unsuccessfully sought a buyer for its business, soliciting, among others, Midas International Corp., which operates a chain of muffler installation shops, and Questor. Nevertheless, the Commission remarkably concluded that Blackstone "would have served as a viable method of toehold entry."

We also conclude that the record contains inadequate evidence to support the Commission's conclusion that Tenneco's acquisition of Monroe violated Section 7 by eliminating Tenneco as a perceived potential competitor in the market for replacement shock absorbers. There is abundant evidence that the oligopolists in the market for replacement shock absorbers perceived Tenneco as a potential entrant. Industry executives testified that they considered Tenneco one of very few manufacturers with both the incentive and the capability to enter the market. This perception was based on Tenneco's financial strength and on the compatibility of shock absorbers with exhaust system parts produced by Tenneco's Walker Division.

However, the Commission's conclusion that the perception of Tenneco as a potential entrant actually tempered the conduct of oligopolists in the market must also be supported by substantial evidence. It is not. Tenneco argued that in the years immediately preceding its acquisition of Monroe the market for replacement shock absorbers had become highly competitive. The Commission apparently agrees with this assessment. The rate of increase in advertised retail prices for shock absorbers fell significantly behind inflation, and mass merchandisers such as Sears, Roebuck replaced traditional wholesale distributors as the leading purchasers of replacement shock absorbers from manufacturers. Sears's retail prices for shock absorbers were frequently below the prices that manufacturers charged wholesale distributors, who were several levels above the retail customer in the traditional chain of distribution.

The advent of increased sales by mass merchandisers coincided with aggressive competition among shock absorber manufacturers. Manufacturers offered substantial discounts off their circulated price sheets to traditional wholesalers and implemented "stocklifting," a practice in which a manufacturer buys a wholesaler's inventory of a competing manufacturer's product and replaces it with his own product.

While agreeing that competitive activity increased dramatically in the mid-1970s, the Commission stated:

> We disagree with [Tenneco] over the cause of that new competitive vigor. In brief, we find that the source of the improved economic performance lay in industry fears that Tenneco was likely to attempt entry—an actual "edge effect"—rather than in the buyer power supposedly asserted by mass merchants against their suppliers.

The Commission's hypothesis depends almost entirely on inferences drawn from the activity of Maremont [Gabriel's owner]. We have no doubt that direct evidence of an "edge effect" is not required to support a Commission finding of a Section 7 violation. In this case, however, direct evidence concerning Tenneco's "edge effect" on Maremont was elicited by the Commission, though it does not support the Commission's conclusion. During the testimony of Byron Pond, Senior Vice-President and Director of Maremont, the following colloquy occurred:

> Q [By Commission Counsel]: Did the presence of Walker, IPC or Midas and/or TRW as likely potential entrants into the shock absorber market, have any effect on Maremont's decisions, business decisions?

> A [By Mr. Pond]: I don't think that we looked specifically at competitors on a periodic basis or potential competitors in developing our strategy. I think we developed our strategy and approach to the business based on how we perceive it and how we perceived the opportunities.

Mr. Pond's testimony constitutes direct evidence that Tenneco had no direct effect on Maremont's business decisions or competitive activity. In the face of this contrary and unchallenged direct evidence, the substantiality of circumstantial evidence arguably suggesting an "edge effect" vanishes. Accordingly, we hold that the Commission's finding that Maremont's actions were probably taken in response to its desire to dissuade Tenneco from entering the market is unsupported by substantial evidence in the record.

FTC order set aside in favor of Tenneco.

CLAYTON ACT SECTION 8

If the same people control theoretically competing corporations, an obvious potential exists for collusive anticompetitive conduct such as price-fixing or division of markets. Section 8 of the Clayton Act was intended to minimize the risks posed by such interlocks. Section 8 initially prohibited any person from serving as a director of two or more corporations (other than banks or common carriers) if either had "capital, surplus, and undivided profits aggregating more than $1,000,000" and the corporations were, or had been, competitors, "so that

elimination of competition by agreement between them" would violate any of the antitrust laws. The Antitrust Amendments Act of 1990 amended Section 8's original language to increase the amount required to trigger the statute from $1,000,000 to $10,000,000 (a figure that will be adjusted annually by an amount equal to the percentage increase or decrease in the gross national product).

Section 8 establishes a per se standard of liability in the sense that no harm to competition need be shown for an interlock to violate the statute. However, the statute's prohibition against interlocks was until recently quite limited in scope: it prohibits only interlocking directorates. Nothing in the language of the statute prohibited one person from serving as an officer of two competing corporations, or as an officer of one competitor and a director of another. The Antitrust Amendments Act of 1990 expanded the scope of the statute by including senior "officers" (defined as an officer elected or chosen by the Board of Directors) within its reach.

Historically, government enforcement of Section 8 has been quite lax, though recent years have seen some signs of growing government interest in the statute. The most recent Supreme Court case involving Section 8, however, resulted in a denial of the government's bid for a more expansive interpretation of the statute. *BankAmerica Corp. v. United States* [10] grew out of a 1975 Justice Department attempt to police interlocking directorates between banks and insurance companies. Never before had an interlock involving a bank been challenged under Section 8 because of the specific statutory language prohibiting interlocks between corporations "other than banks." Concerned about the increasing areas in which banks and a variety of other businesses were competing in rapidly changing financial markets, the Justice Department argued that the statutory exception should apply only when both of the companies at issue were banks. Had the department been successful, the consequences for the banking industry could have been significant, given the long history of interlocking directorates between banks and other business corporations. The Supreme Court, however, rejected the government's broad reading of the statute, holding that the "most natural reading" of the statute was that the interlocking corporations must all be corporations "other than banks." The Antitrust Amendments Act of 1990 retains the statutory language exempting banks.

Signs of renewed government interest in Section 8 produced significant concern in an era of conglomerate merger activity. Given the wide diversification that characterizes many large corporations, it would be increasingly easy to demonstrate some degree of competitive overlap among a substantial number of large, diversified corporations. Critics alleged that Section 8 has operated to discourage qualified persons from serving as directors when no potential for actual competitive harm exists. In response to such criticism, the Antitrust Amendments Act of 1990 permits individuals to serve as officers or directors of competing corporations where the "competitive overlap" between them is an insignificant part of either company's total sales.

THE ROBINSON-PATMAN ACT

Background

Section 2 of the Clayton Act originally prohibited *local and territorial price discrimination* by sellers, a practice monopolists frequently used to destroy smaller competitors. A large company operating in a number of geographic markets would sell at or below cost in markets where it faced local competitors, making up its losses by selling at higher prices in areas where it faced no competition. Faced with such tactics, the smaller local competitors might eventually be driven out of business. Section 2 was aimed at such *primary level* (or first line) price discrimination.

In the 1930s Congress was confronted with complaints that large chain stores were using their buying power to induce manufacturers to sell to them at lower prices than those offered to their smaller, independent competitors. Chain stores were also able to receive other payments and services not available to their smaller competitors. Being able to purchase at lower prices and to obtain discriminatory payments and services arguably gave large firms a competitive advantage over their smaller competitors. Such price discrimination in sales to the competing customers of a particular seller is known as *secondary level* (or second line) price discrimination.

In addition, the customers of a manufacturer's favored customer (such as a wholesaler receiving a functional discount) may gain a competitive advantage over *their* competitors (for example, other retailers purchasing directly from the manufacturer at a higher price) if the favored customer passes on all or a portion of its discount to them. This form of price discrimination is known as *tertiary level* (or third line) price discrimination.

Congress responded to these problems by passing the Robinson-Patman Act in 1936. The act amended Section 2 of the Clayton Act to outlaw secondary and tertiary level direct price discrimination and to prohibit indirect price discrimination in the form of discriminatory payments and services to a seller's customers. Since its enactment, the Robinson-Patman Act has been the subject of widespread dissatisfaction and criticism. Critics have long charged that in many cases the act protects competitors at the expense of promoting competition.

---

[10]462 U.S. 122 (U.S. Sup. Ct. 1983).

FIGURE 2   Levels of Price Discrimination

Type of Discrimination	Type of Harm	Example
First Line	Injury to the seller's competitors	A seller subsidizes its low prices in an area of high competition by raising its prices in areas where it has little competition.
Second Line	Injury to the competitors of the favored buyer	A high-volume, chain store induces its suppliers to give it discriminatorily low prices, enabling it to undersell its competitors.
Third Line	Injury to the competitors of the favored buyer's buyers	A wholesaler receiving discriminatorily low prices from its manufacturer passes the savings on to its retailers, enabling them to undersell their competitors.

Governmental enforcement of the act has been somewhat haphazard over the years, and current top officials in the Justice Department and the Federal Trade Commission have voiced significant disagreement with many of the act's underlying policies and assumptions. This governmental stance, when combined with recent Supreme Court decisions making private enforcement of the act more difficult, raises serious questions concerning the act's future importance as a component of our antitrust laws. Figure 2, above, summarizes the three levels of price discrimination.

Jurisdiction

The Robinson-Patman Act applies only to discriminatory acts that occur "in commerce." This test is narrower than the "affecting commerce" test employed under the Sherman Act. At least one of the discriminatory acts complained of must take place in interstate commerce. Thus, the act probably would not apply if a Texas manufacturer discriminated in price in sales to two Texas customers. Some lower federal courts have indicated, however, that even wholly intrastate sales may be deemed "in the flow of commerce" if the nonfavored buyer bought the goods for resale to out-of-state customers.[11]

Section 2(a)

Section 2(a) of the Robinson-Patman Act prohibits sellers from *discriminating in price* "between different purchasers of commodities of like grade or quality" where

the effect of such discrimination may be "substantially to lessen competition or tend to create a monopoly in any line of commerce" or "to injure, destroy, or prevent competition with any person who either grants [primary level] or knowingly receives [secondary level] the benefit of such discrimination, or with the customers of either of them [tertiary level]."

Price Discrimination   To violate Section 2(a), a seller must have made two or more sales to different purchasers at different prices. Merely quoting a discriminatory price or refusing to sell except at a discriminatory price is not a violation of the statute, because no actual purchase is involved. For the same reason, price discrimination in lease or consignment transactions is also not covered by Section 2(a). Nor will actual sales at different prices to different purchasers necessarily be treated as discriminatory unless the sales were fairly close in time.

For purposes of deciding whether discriminatory prices have been charged to two or more purchasers, the degree of control that a parent corporation exercises over its subsidiaries can sometimes assume major importance. For example, a parent that sells a product directly to one customer at a low price may be found guilty of price discrimination if a wholesaler actively controlled by the parent contemporaneously sells the same product at a higher price to a competitor of the parent's customer. On the other hand, contemporaneous sales by a parent to a wholly owned subsidiary and to an independent competitor at different prices are not treated as price discrimination because no true sale has been made to the subsidiary.

Finally, Section 2(a) does not directly address the legality of functional discounts, those discounts granted to buyers at various levels in a product's chain of distribution because of differences in the functions that those

---

[11]*L & L Oil Co. v. Murphy Oil Corp.*, 674 F.2d 1113 (5th Cir. 1982).

buyers perform in the distribution system. As the following *Texaco* case indicates, the legality of such discounts depends on their competitive effect. Charging wholesale customers lower prices than retail customers does not violate the act unless the lower wholesale prices are somehow passed on to retailers in competition with the seller's other retail customers.

Commodities of Like Grade and Quality Section 2(a) applies only to price discrimination in the sale of *commodities*. Price discrimination involving intangibles, real estate, or services must be challenged under the Sherman Act (as a restraint of trade or an attempt to monopolize) or under the FTC Act (as an unfair method of competition).[12] The essence of price discrimination is that two or more buyers are charged differing prices for the *same* commodity. Sales of commodities of varying grades or quality at varying prices, therefore, do not violate Section 2(a) so long as uniform prices are charged for commodities of equal quality. Some *physical difference* in the grade or quality of two products must be shown to justify a price differential between them. Differences solely in the brand name or label under which a product is sold, such as the seller's standard brand and a house brand sold to a large customer for resale under the customer's label, do not justify discriminatory pricing.

Competitive Effect Only price discrimination that has a *probable* anticompetitive effect is prohibited by Section 2(a). Traditionally, the courts have required a higher degree of proof of likely competitive injury in cases involving primary level price discrimination that may damage the seller's competitors than in cases involving secondary or tertiary level discrimination that threatens competition among the seller's customers or its customers' customers. To prove a primary level violation, a market analysis must show that actual competitive injury has occurred or that the seller engaged in significant and sustained local price discrimination with the intent of punishing or disciplining a local competitor. Proof of predatory pricing is often offered as evidence of a seller's anticompetitive intent. As is the case with similar claims under Section 2 of the Sherman Act, however, the courts disagree on the proper test for predatory pricing.

In secondary or tertiary level cases, the courts tend to infer the existence of competitive injury from evidence of substantial price discrimination between competing purchasers over time. Several qualifications on this point are in order, however. Price discrimination for a short period of time ordinarily does not support an inference of competitive injury. Likewise, if the evidence indicates that nonfavored buyers could have purchased the same goods from other sellers at prices identical to those that the defendant seller charged its favored customers, no competitive injury is inferred. Finally, buyers seeking treble damages for secondary or tertiary level harm must still prove that they suffered some actual damages as a result of a violation of the act.

---

[12]The FTC Act was discussed in the chapter The Federal Trade Commission Act and Consumer Protection Laws.

TEXACO, INC. v. HASBROUCK
110 S.Ct. 2535 (U.S. Sup. Ct. 1990)

Ricky Hasbrouck and 11 other plaintiffs were Texaco retail service station dealers in the Spokane area; they purchased gasoline directly from Texaco and resold it at retail under the Texaco trademark. Throughout the relevant time period (1972–81) Texaco also supplied gasoline to two gasoline distributors, Dompier Oil Company and Gull Oil Company, at a price that was at various times between 2.5 cents and 5.75 cents per gallon lower than the price Hasbrouck paid. Dompier and Gull sold the gasoline they purchased from Texaco to independent retail service stations. Dompier sold the gasoline to retailers under the Texaco trademark; Gull marketed it under private brand names. Gull's customers either sold their gasoline on consignment (in which case they set their own prices) or on commission (in which case Gull set their resale prices). Gull retained title until the gas was sold to a retail customer in either case. Some of the retail stations supplied by Dompier were owned and operated by Dompier's salaried employees. Both Dompier and Gull picked up gas at the Texaco bulk plant and delivered it to their retail customers, a service for which Dompier was compensated by Texaco at the common carrier rate.

Hasbrouck and the other dealers filed a price discrimination suit against Texaco under Section 2(a) of the Robinson-Patman Act. At trial, Texaco argued that its lower prices to Gull and Dompier were lawful "functional discounts." The jury awarded the plaintiffs $1,349,700 in treble damages. When the Ninth Circuit Court of Appeals affirmed the jury award, Texaco appealed.

Stevens, Justice.   Section 2(a) contains no express reference to functional discounts. It does contain two affirmative defenses that provide protection for two categories of discounts—those that are justified by savings in the seller's cost of manufacture, delivery, or sale, and those that represent a good faith response to the equally low prices of a competitor. In order to establish a violation of the Act, plaintiffs had the burden of proving four facts: (1) that Texaco's sales to Gull and Dompier were made in interstate commerce; (2) that the gasoline sold to them was of the same grade and quality as that sold to plaintiffs; (3) that Texaco discriminated in price as between Gull and Dompier on the one hand and plaintiffs on the other; and (4) that the discrimination had a prohibited effect on competition.

The first two elements of plaintiffs' case are not disputed in this Court. Texaco does argue, however, that although it charged different prices, it did not "discriminate in price" within the meaning of the Act, and that, at least to the extent that Gull and Dompier acted as wholesalers, the price differentials did not injure competition. Texaco's first argument would create a blanket exception for all functional discounts. Indeed, carried to its logical conclusion, it would exempt all price differentials except those given to competing purchasers. The primary basis for Texaco's argument is the following comment by Congressman Utterback, an active sponsor of the Act:

In its meaning as simple English, a discrimination is more than a mere difference. Underlying the meaning of the word is the idea that some relationship exists between the parties to the discrimination which entitles them to equal treatment, whereby the difference granted to one casts some burden or disadvantage upon the other. . . . [W]here no such relationship exists, where the goods are sold in different markets and the conditions affecting those markets set different price levels for them, the sale to different customers at . . . different prices would not constitute discrimination within the meaning of this bill.

We have previously considered this excerpt from the legislative history, and have refused to draw from it the conclusion Texaco proposes. Although the excerpt does support Texaco's argument, we remain persuaded that the argument is foreclosed by the text of the Act itself. In a statute that plainly reveals a concern with competitive consequences at different levels of distribution, and carefully defines specific affirmative defenses, it would be anomalous to assume that Congress intended the term "discriminate" to have such a limited meaning. Since we have already decided that a price discrimination within the meaning of section 2(a) "is merely a price difference," we must reject Texaco's first argument.

In *FTC v. Morton Salt Co.*, 334 U.S. 37 (1948), we held that an injury to competition may be inferred from evidence that some purchasers had to pay their supplier "substantially more for their goods than their competitors had to pay." Texaco, supported by the United States and the Federal Trade Commission as *amici curiae*, argues that this presumption should not apply to differences between prices charged to wholesalers and those charged to retailers. Moreover, they argue that it would be inconsistent with fundamental antitrust policies to construe the Act as requiring a seller to control his customers' resale prices. The seller should not be held liable for the independent pricing decisions of his customers. As the Government correctly notes, this argument endorses the position advocated 35 years ago in the Report of the Attorney General's Nation Committee to Study the Antitrust Laws (1955).

After observing that suppliers ought not to be held liable for the independent pricing decisions of their buyers, and that without functional discounts distributors might go uncompensated for the services they performed, the Committee wrote:

On the other hand, the law should tolerate no subterfuge. For instance, where a wholesaler-retailer *buys* only part of his goods as a wholesaler, he must not claim a functional discount on all. Only to the extent that a buyer *actually* performs certain functions, assuming all the risk, investment, and costs involved, should he legally qualify for a functional discount.

We generally agree with this description of the legal status of functional discounts. A supplier need not satisfy the rigorous requirements of the cost justification defense in order to prove that a particular functional discount is reasonable and accordingly did not cause any substantial lessening of competition between a wholesaler's customers and the supplier's direct customers. The record in this case, however, adequately supports the finding that Texaco violated the Act.

The hypothetical predicate for the Committee's entire discussion of functional discounts is a price differential "that merely accords due recognition and reimbursement for actual marketing functions." Such a discount is not illegal. In this case, however, both the District Court and the Court of Appeals concluded that there was no substantial evidence indicating that the discounts to Gull and Dompier constituted a reasonable reimbursement for the value to Texaco of their actual marketing functions. Indeed, Dompier was separately compensated for its hauling function, and neither Gull nor Dompier maintained any significant storage facilities.

Both Gull and Dompier received the full discount on all their purchases even though most of their volume was resold directly to consumers. The extra margin on those sales obviously enabled them to price aggressively in both their retail and their wholesale marketing. To the extent that Dompier and Gull competed with plaintiffs in the retail market, the presumption of adverse effect on competition recognized in the *Morton Salt* case becomes all the more appropriate. The evidence indicates, moreover, that Texaco affirmatively encouraged Dompier to expand its retail business and was fully informed about the persistent and marketwide consequences of its own pricing policies. Indeed, its own executives recognized that the dramatic impact on the market was almost entirely attributable to the magnitude of the distributor discount and the hauling allowance. The special facts of this case thus make it peculiarly difficult for Texaco to claim that it is being held liable for the independent pricing decisions of Gull or Dompier.

The competitive injury component of a Robinson-Patman Act violation is not limited to the injury to competition between the favored and disfavored purchaser; it also encompasses the injury to competition between their customers. This conclusion is compelled by the statutory language, which specifically encompasses not only the adverse effect of price discrimination on persons who either grant or knowingly receive the benefit of such discrimination, but also to the "customers of either of them." Such indirect competitive effects surely may not be presumed automatically in every functional discount setting, and, indeed, one would expect that most functional discounts will be legitimate discounts that do not harm competition. At the least, a functional discount that constitutes a reasonable reimbursement for the purchasers' actual marketing functions will not violate the Act. Yet it is also true that not every functional discount is entitled to a judgment of legitimacy, and that it will sometimes be possible to produce evidence showing that a particular discount caused a price discrimination of the sort that the Act prohibits. When such anticompetitive effects are proved—as we believe they were in this case—they are covered by the Act.

Judgment for Hasbrouck affirmed.

Defenses to Section 2(a) Liability

The three major statutory defenses to liability under Section 2(a) are *cost justification, changing conditions*, and *meeting competition in good faith.*

Cost Justification   Section 2(a) specifically legalizes price differentials that make only a due allowance for differences in the "cost of manufacture, sale, or delivery resulting from the differing methods or quantities" in which goods are sold or delivered to buyers. This defense recognizes the simple fact that it may be less costly for a seller to service some buyers than others. Sales to buyers purchasing large quantities may in some cases be more cost effective than small-quantity sales to their competitors. Sellers are allowed to pass on such cost savings to their customers.

Utilizing this *cost justification* defense is quite difficult and expensive for sellers, however, because quantity discounts must be supported by *actual evidence* of cost savings. Sellers are allowed to average their costs and classify their customers into categories based on their average sales costs, but the customers included in any particular classification must be sufficiently similar to justify similar treatment.

Changing Conditions   Section 2(a) also specifically exempts price discriminations that reflect "changing conditions in the market for or the marketability of the goods." This defense has been narrowly confined to temporary situations caused by the physical nature of the goods. Examples include the deterioration of perishable goods or a declining market for seasonal goods. It also applies to forced judicial sales of the goods, such as during bankruptcy proceedings involving the seller, and to good-faith sales by sellers that have decided to cease selling the goods in question.

Meeting Competition   Section 2(b) of the Robinson-Patman Act specifically states that price discrimination may be lawful if the discriminatory lower price was charged "in good faith to meet an equally low price of a competitor." Such an exception is necessary to prevent the act from stifling the very competition it was designed to preserve. For example, suppose Sony Corporation has been selling a particular model of video recorder to its customers for $350 per unit. Sony then learns that Sharp Electronics is offering a comparable recorder to Acme Appliance Stores for $300 per unit. Acme, however, competes with Best Buy Video Stores, a Sony customer that has recently been charged the $350 price. Should Sony be forced to refrain from offering the lower competitive price to Acme for fear that, if it does so, Best Buy will charge Sony with price discrimination? If so, competition between Sony and Sharp will plainly suffer.

Section 2(b) avoids this undesirable result by allowing sellers to charge a lower price to some customers if they have reasonable grounds for believing that the lower price is necessary to meet an equally low price offered by a competitor. Sellers may also meet competition offensively to gain a new customer, as well as defensively to keep an existing customer. However, this defense is subject to several significant qualifications. First, the lower price must be necessary to meet a lower price charged by a competitor of the *seller*, not to enable a customer of the seller to compete more effectively with that customer's competitors. Second, the seller may lawfully seek only to *meet, not beat*, its competitor's price. A seller may not, however, be held in violation of the act for beating a competitor's price if it did so unknowingly in a good-faith attempt to meet competition. Third, the seller may reduce its price only to meet competitors' prices for products of *similar quality.*

In addition, the courts have held that the discriminatory price must be a response to an individual competitive situation rather than the product of a seller's wholesale adoption of a competitor's discriminatory pricing system. However, a seller's competitive response need not be on a customer-by-customer basis, so long as the lower price is offered only to those customers that the seller reasonably believes are being offered a lower price by its competitors.

Indirect Price Discrimination

When Congress passed the Robinson-Patman Act, it recognized that a seller could also discriminate among competing buyers by making discriminatory payments to them or by furnishing them with services not available to their competitors. Three sections of the act are designed to prevent such practices.

False Brokerage   Section 2(c) prohibits sellers from granting, and buyers from receiving, any "commission, brokerage, or other compensation, or any allowance or discount in lieu thereof, except for services rendered in connection with the sale or purchase of goods." This provision prevents large buyers, either directly or through subsidiary brokerage agents, from receiving phony commissions or brokerage payments from their suppliers. The courts and the FTC originally interpreted Section 2(c) as prohibiting any brokerage payments to a buyer or its agent, regardless of whether the buyer or agent had in fact provided services in connection with the sale that would otherwise have been performed by the seller or an independent broker. This narrow interpretation drew heavy criticism, however, because it operated to create a closed shop for independent brokers by denying large buyers any incentive to create their own brokerage services. This interpretation also made it difficult for small, independent retailers to create cooperative buying organizations and thereby to match more closely the buying power of their large competitors. More recent decisions have responded to these criticisms to allow payments for services actually performed by buyers and representing actual cost savings to sellers.

Section 2(c), unlike Section 2(a), establishes a per se standard of liability. No demonstration of probable anticompetitive effect is required for a violation, and neither the cost justification nor meeting competition defense is available in 2(c) cases. However, the following *Metrix* case reminds us that individual plaintiffs still must prove that they have suffered some injury as a result of a 2(c) violation before they are entitled to recover damages.

Discriminatory Payments and Services   Sellers and their customers both benefit from merchandising activities that customers employ to promote the sellers' products. Section 2(d) prohibits sellers from making *discriminatory payments* to competing customers for such services as advertising and promotional activities, or such facilities as shelf space, that customers furnish in connection with the sale of the goods. Section 2(e) prohibits sellers from discriminating in the *services* that they provide to competing customers, for example, providing favored customers with a display case or a demonstration kit.

A seller may lawfully provide such payments or services only if they are made available to all competing customers on *proportionately equal terms*. This means informing all customers of the availability of the payments or services and distributing them on some rational basis, such as the quantity of goods bought by the customer. The seller must also devise a flexible plan that enables its various classes of customers to participate in the program in an appropriate way.

Sections 2(d) and 2(e), like Section 2(c), create a per se liability standard. No proof of probable harm to competition is required for a violation, and no cost justification defense is available. However, the meeting competition defense provided by Section 2(b) is applicable to 2(d) and 2(e) actions.

Buyer Inducement of Discrimination   Section 2(f) of the Robinson-Patman Act makes it illegal for a buyer *knowingly to induce or receive* a discriminatory price in violation of Section 2(a). The logic of the section is that buyers who are successful in demanding discriminatory prices should be punished along with the sellers that acceded to their demands. To violate Section 2(f), the buyer must know that the price it received was unjustifiably discriminatory, that is, probably not cost justified or not made in response to changing conditions. Section 2(f) does not apply to buyer inducements of discriminatory payments or services prohibited by Sections 2(d) and 2(e). Such buyer actions may, however, be attacked as unfair methods of competition under Section 5 of the FTC Act.

In *Great Atlantic and Pacific Tea Co. v. FTC*, the Supreme Court further narrowed the effective reach of Section 2(f) by holding that buyers that knowingly receive a discriminatory price do not violate the act if their seller has a valid defense to the charge of violating Section 2(a).[13] In that case, the seller had a "meeting competition in good faith" defense under Section 2(b). This fact was held to insulate the buyer from liability even though the buyer knew that the seller had beaten, rather than merely met, its competitors' price.

---

[13]440 U.S. 69 (U.S. Sup. Ct. 1979).

METRIX WAREHOUSE v. DAIMLER-BENZ AKTIENGESELLSCHAFT
828 F.2d 1033 (4th Cir. 1987)

Metrix Warehouse, Inc. (Metrix), an independent parts distributor, filed suit against Daimler-Benz Aktiengesellschaft (DBAG), the manufacturer of Mercedes-Benz automobiles, and Mercedes-Benz of North America (MBNA), the exclusive importer of such automobiles, arguing that MBNA's practice of requiring franchised Mercedes-Benz dealers to use and sell only genuine Mercedes-Benz parts was an illegal tying arrangement in violation of Section 1 of the Sherman Act. MBNA counterclaimed, arguing that Metrix's practice of offering "incentive" payments to parts managers who ordered parts from Metrix violated Section 2(c) of the Robinson-Patman Act. The trial jury denied MBNA any recovery on the ground that it had not been injured by the incentive program. The trial judge granted judgment notwithstanding the verdict to MBNA, and Metrix appealed.

Sprouse, Circuit Judge.   We held in a prior interlocutory appeal that Metrix's incentive program violated Section 2(c) of the Robinson-Patman Act. We described the salient facts of Metrix's program as follows:

Metrix['s] . . . incentive program involves the awarding of points redeemable for either merchandise or cash or the payment of cash directly to the parts managers of Mercedes-Benz dealers. These payments are based on a percentage of total parts purchased from Metrix. As consideration for the payments, the payees perform no services other than placing their employers' purchase orders with Metrix.

Between February 1974 and June 1980, Metrix paid at least $119,980.80 in cash and $394,551.53 in cash and/or merchandise to parts managers of Mercedes-Benz dealers for the placement of approximately $13,000,000 in spare parts orders with Metrix. Payments are mailed monthly by Metrix to the parts managers at their home address. The value of the points is approximately 3.5 percent of the purchase price.

In granting the judgment notwithstanding the verdict, the district court reasoned that "Metrix, acting rationally, would not have persisted in such a program unless it took sales from competitors," and that it was "simply irrational [for the jury] to find that Mercedes-Benz would not have made any extra sales but for the illegal incentive program." On appeal, Metrix contends that the jury's finding of no antitrust injury was clearly supported by the evidence. We agree. While injury usually results from per se violations of the antitrust laws, this is not always true. The discrete characteristics of the replacement parts market simply do not lead inevitably to such a conclusion.

At trial, MBNA attempted to show that absent the unlawful "incentives," some of Metrix's sales would have gone to it and that Metrix's program caused it to suffer approximately $2.3 million in lost profits. Metrix's evidence showed that "incentive" programs were standard among independent warehouse distributors and that if it had abolished its program, dealership personnel simply would have turned to other warehouse distributors for parts they otherwise would have brought from Metrix. According to the testimony of Metrix's witnesses, the dealerships that purchased parts from warehouse distributors were motivated by a combination of lower prices, quicker deliveries, and the availability of "incentives;" since MBNA offered none of these amenities, it lost no sales as a result of Metrix's program.

Metrix presented evidence that even without "incentive" payments, dealership personnel would have continued to purchase from warehouse distributors because their prices were lower than MBNA's prices. Virtually every dealer who testified at trial stated that lower prices were the primary reason he or she purchased parts from warehouse distributors. The lower prices translated into a higher profit margin for the dealerships.

MBNA would have had the jury believe that any sales Metrix gained by virtue of the "incentive" program necessarily caused it to lose sales. This argument assumes that MBNA and Metrix were the only participants in the affected market and ignores the seven other independent warehouse distributors. Any sales increases attributable to Metrix's program may well have come from sales previously enjoyed by the warehouse distributors only. For that matter, benign factors, including generally lower prices and quicker deliveries, could have determined whether a dealer made a particular purchase from an independent distributor or from MBNA. These were questions for the jury and it was MBNA's burden to demonstrate a causal connection between Metrix's unlawful program and its lost profits.

In our view, MBNA's evidence failed to sustain that burden. Metrix's evidence was easily sufficient to support the jury's finding that MBNA suffered no lost sales from the "incentive program."

Judgment notwithstanding the verdict reversed in favor of Metrix.

ANTITRUST EXCEPTIONS AND EXEMPTIONS

Introduction

A wide variety of economic activities occur outside the reach of the antitrust laws, either because these activities have been specifically exempted by statute or because the courts have carved out nonstatutory exceptions designed to balance our antitrust policy in favor of competition against other, competing social policies. Critics have charged that a number of existing exemptions are no longer justifiable, and recent years have witnessed a judicial tendency to narrow the scope of many exemptions.

Statutory Exemptions

Sections 6 and 20 of the Clayton Act and the Norris-LaGuardia Act of 1932 provide that *labor unions* are not combinations or conspiracies in restraint of trade and exempt certain union activities, including boycotts and secondary picketing, from antitrust scrutiny. This statutory exemption does not, however, exempt union combinations with nonlabor groups aimed at restraining trade or creating a monopoly; for example, a union agrees with Employer A to call a strike at Employer B's plants. In an attempt to accommodate the strong public policy in favor of collective bargaining, the courts have also created a limited nonstatutory exemption for legitimate agreements between unions and employers arising out of the collective bargaining context.

Section 6 of the Clayton Act and the Capper-Volstead Act exempt the formation and collective marketing activities of *agricultural cooperatives* from antitrust liability. This exemption, like many statutory antitrust exemptions, has been narrowly construed by the courts. Cooperatives including members not engaged in the production of agricultural commodities have been denied exempt status. One example would be a cooperative including retailers or wholesalers who do not also produce the commodity in question. Also, the exemption extends only to legitimate collective marketing activities; it does not legitimize coercive or predatory practices that are unnecessary to accomplish lawful cooperative goals, such as a boycott to force nonmembers to adhere to prices established by the cooperative.

The Webb-Pomerene Act exempts the *joint export activities* of U.S. companies, so long as those activities do not "artificially or intentionally enhance or depress prices within the United States." The purpose of the act is to encourage export activity by domestic firms by allowing them to form combinations to compete more effectively with foreign cartels. Some critics have charged, however, that this exemption is no longer needed, because today there are far fewer foreign cartels and U.S. firms often play a dominant role in foreign trade. Others question whether any group of U.S. firms enjoying significant domestic market shares in the sale of a particular product could agree on an international marketing strategy, such as the amounts that they will export, without indirectly affecting domestic supplies and prices.

The McCarran-Ferguson Act exempts from federal antitrust scrutiny those aspects of the *business of insurance* that are subject to state regulation. The act provides, however, that state law cannot legitimize any agreement to boycott, coerce, or intimidate others. Because the insurance industry is extensively regulated by the states, many practices in the industry are outside the reach of the federal antitrust laws. In recent years, however, the courts have tended to decrease the scope of this exemption by narrowly construing the meaning of the "business of insurance." For example, in *Union Labor Life Insurance Co. v. Pireno*, the Supreme Court held that a peer review system in which an insurance company used a committee established by a state chiropractic association to review the reasonableness of particular chiropractors' charges was outside the scope of the insurance exemption.[14] To qualify for exemption, the Court said that the challenged practice must have the effect of transferring or spreading policyholders' risk and be an integral part of the policy relationship between the insured and the insurer. Thus, only practices related to traditional functions of the insurance business such as underwriting and risk-spreading are likely to be exempt. More recently, legislation has been introduced in Congress to repeal McCarran-Ferguson while allowing insurers to continue to participate in specific joint activities such as collecting and exchanging information on fraudulent claims, pooling historical loss data, and developing standardized policy forms.

Many other *regulated industries* enjoy various degrees of antitrust immunity. The airline, banking, utility, railroad, shipping, and securities industries traditionally have been regulated in the public interest. The regulatory agencies supervising such industries have frequently been given the power to approve industry practices such as rate-setting and mergers that would otherwise violate antitrust laws. In recent years, there has been a distinct tendency to deregulate many regulated industries. If this trend continues, a greater portion of the economic activity in these industries will be subjected to antitrust scrutiny.

State Action Exemption

In *Parker v. Brown*, the Supreme Court held that a California state agency's regulation of the production and price of raisins was a *state action* exempt from the federal antitrust laws.[15] The state action exemption recognizes the states' right to regulate economic activity in the interest of their citizens. It also, however, may tempt state economic interests to seek "friendly" state regulation as a way of shielding anticompetitive activity from antitrust supervision. Recognizing this fact, the courts have placed several important limitations on the scope of the exemption.

First, the exemption extends only to governmental actions by a state or to actions compelled by a state acting in its sovereign capacity. Second, as the following *Patrick* case indicates, to qualify for immunity under this exemption the challenged activity must be "clearly articulated and affirmatively expressed as state policy" and "actively supervised" by the state. In other words, the price of antitrust immunity is real regulation by the state. Finally, the Supreme Court has held that the state action exemption does not automatically confer immunity on the actions of municipalities.[16] Municipal conduct is only immune if it was authorized by the state legislature and if its anticompetitive effects were a foreseeable result of the authorization. This caused considerable concern that the threat of treble damage liability might inhibit legitimate regulatory action by municipal authorities. As a result, Congress passed the Local Government Antitrust Act of 1984. The act eliminates damage actions against municipalities and their officers, agents, and employees for antitrust violations and makes injunctive relief the sole remedy in such cases. It does not, however, bar damage suits against private individuals who engage in anticompetitive conduct with local government agencies.

---

[14]458 U.S. 119 (U.S. Sup. Ct. 1982).

[15]317 U.S. 341 (U.S. Sup. Ct. 1943).

[16]*Community Communications Co., Inc. v. City of Boulder,* 455 U.S. 40 (U.S. Sup. Ct. 1982).

PATRICK v. BURGET

486 U.S. 94 (U.S. Sup. Ct. 1988)

Timothy Patrick is a general and vascular surgeon practicing in Astoria, Oregon. The only hospital in Astoria is Columbia Memorial Hospital (CMH). Patrick became an employee of the Astoria Clinic, a private group medical practice, in 1972. The majority of the staff members at CMH were also employees or partners of the Clinic. One year later, Patrick was invited to become a partner of the Clinic. He declined this offer, instead beginning an independent practice in competition with the Clinic's surgical practice, although he continued to serve on the staff of CMH.

After Patrick started his independent practice, the physicians associated with the Clinic refused to have professional dealings with him. They referred patients needing surgery to surgeons as far as 50 miles from Astoria and refused to assist Patrick with his own patients by giving consultations or providing back-up coverage (although they repeatedly criticized him for failing to obtain outside consultations and back-up coverage). In 1979 Boelling, a Clinic partner, complained to CMH's medical staff executive committee about an incident in which Patrick had left a patient in the care of a recently hired associate, who then left the patient unattended. The executive committee referred the complaint, along with information about other cases handled by Patrick, to the state Board of Medical Examiners (BOME). Franklin Russell, another partner at the Clinic, chaired the BOME committee investigating such complaints. The BOME ultimately issued to Patrick a letter of reprimand that had been drafted by Russell. When Patrick sought judicial review of the BOME proceedings, the BOME retracted the letter in its entirety.

Two years later, at the request of Richard Harris, a Clinic surgeon, the CMH medical staff executive committee initiated a review of Patrick's hospital privileges that ultimately resulted in those privileges being revoked on the ground that his care of patients was below hospital standards. Patrick filed suit against the Clinic partners under Sections 1 and 2 of the Sherman Act, arguing that they had initiated and participated in the hospital peer-review proceedings to reduce competition from him rather than to improve patient care. A jury awarded Patrick $1.95 million in treble damages. When the Ninth Circuit Court of Appeals reversed on the ground that the hospital's peer-review procedures were immune to antitrust scrutiny, Patrick appealed.

Marshall, Justice.   In *Parker v. Brown* (1943), this Court considered whether the Sherman Act prohibits anticompetitive actions of a State. Petitioner in that case was a raisin producer who brought suit against the California Director of Agriculture to enjoin the enforcement of a marketing plan adopted under the State's Agricultural Prorate Act. That statute restricted competition among food producers in the State in order to stabilize prices and prevent economic waste. Relying on principles of federalism and state sovereignty, this Court refused to find in the Sherman Act "an expressed purpose to nullify a state's control over its officers and agents." The Sherman Act was not intended to restrain state action or official action directed by a state.

Although *Parker* involved a suit against a state official, the Court subsequently recognized that *Parker's* federalism rationale demanded that the state action exemption also apply in certain suits against private parties. If the Federal Government or a private litigant always could enforce the Sherman Act against private parties, then a State could not effectively implement a program restraining competition among them. The Court, however, also sought to ensure that private parties could claim state action immunity only when their anticompetitive acts were truly the product of state regulation. We accordingly established a rigorous two-pronged test to determine whether anticompetitive conduct engaged in by private parties should be deemed state action and thus shielded from the antitrust laws.

First, the challenged restraint must be one clearly articulated and affirmatively expressed as state policy. Second, the anticompetitive conduct must be actively supervised by the State itself. *California Retail Liquor Dealers Assn. v. Midcal Aluminum, Inc.* (1980). Only if an anticompetitive act of a private party meets both of these requirements is it fairly attributable to the State. In this case, we need not consider the "clear articulation" prong of the *Midcal* test, because the "active supervision" requirement is not satisfied. The active supervision requirement stems from the recognition that where a private party is engaging in the anticompetitive activity, there is a real danger that he is acting to further his own interests, rather than the governmental interests of the State. The requirement is designed to ensure that the state action doctrine will shelter only the particular anticompetitive acts of private parties that, in the judgment of the State, actually further state regulatory policies.

Respondents in this case contend that the State of Oregon actively supervises the peer-review process through the state Health Division, the BOME, and the state judicial system. The Court of Appeals also relied primarily on the powers and responsibilities of these state actors. Neither the Court of Appeals nor respondents, however, have succeeded in showing that any of these actors reviews—or even could review—private decisions regarding hospital privileges to determine whether such decisions comport with state regulatory policy and to correct abuses.

Hospitals in Oregon are under a statutory obligation to establish peer-review procedures and to review those procedures on a regular basis. The Health Division may initiate judicial proceedings against any hospital violating this law. In addition, the Division may deny, suspend, or revoke a hospital's license for failure to comply with the statutory requirement. Oregon law specifies no other ways in which the Division may supervise the peer-review process.

Similarly, the BOME does not engage in active supervision over private peer-review decisions. The principal function of the BOME is to regulate the licensing of physicians in the State. Oregon hospitals are required by statute to notify the BOME promptly of a decision to terminate or restrict privileges. Neither this statutory provision nor any other, however, indicates that the BOME has the power to disapprove private privilege decisions. The apparent purpose of the reporting requirement is to give the BOME an opportunity to determine whether additional action on its part, such as revocation of a physician's license, is warranted.

The only remaining alleged supervisory authority is the state judiciary. This Court has not previously considered whether state courts, acting in their judicial capacity, can adequately supervise private conduct for purposes of the state action doctrine. This case, however, does not require us to decide the broad question whether judicial review of private conduct ever can constitute active supervision, because judicial review of privilege-termination decisions in Oregon, if such review exists at all, falls far short of satisfying the active supervision requirement.

It is not clear that Oregon law affords any direct judicial review of private peer-review decisions. Oregon has no statute expressly providing for judicial review of privilege terminations. Moreover, we are aware of no case in which an Oregon court has held that judicial review of peer-review decisions is available. Moreover, the Oregon courts have indicated that even if they were to provide judicial review of hospital peer-review proceedings, the review would be of a very limited nature. The Oregon Supreme Court, in its most recent decision addressing this matter, stated that a court "should [not] decide the merits of plaintiff's dismissal" and that "[i]t would be unwise for a court to do more than to make sure that some sort of reasonable procedure was afforded and that there was evidence from which it could be found that plaintiff's conduct posed a threat to patient care." Under this standard, a state court would not review the merits of a termination decision to determine whether it accorded with state regulatory policy. Such constricted review does not convert the action of a private party in terminating a physician's privileges into the action of the State for purposes of the state action doctrine.

Judgment reversed in favor of Patrick.

The *Noerr-Pennington* Doctrine

In the *Noerr* and *Pennington* cases, the Supreme Court held that "the Sherman Act does not prohibit two or more persons from associating together in an attempt to persuade the legislature or the executive to take particular action with respect to a law that would produce a restraint or a monopoly."[17] This exemption recognizes that the right to petition government provided by the Bill of Rights takes precedence over the antitrust policy in

[17]*Eastern R.R. President's Conference v. Noerr Motor Freight, Inc.*, 365 U.S. 127 (U.S. Sup. Ct. 1961); *United Mine Workers v. Pennington*, 381 U.S. 657 (U.S. Sup. Ct. 1965).

favor of competition. The exemption does not, however, extend to sham activities that are attempts to interfere with the business activities of competitors rather than legitimate attempts to influence governmental action.[18]

Patent Licensing

There is a basic tension between the antitrust objective of promoting competition and the patent laws, which seek to promote innovation by granting a limited monopoly to those who develop new products or processes.[19] In the early case of *United States v. General Electric Company*, the Supreme Court allowed General Electric to control the price at which other manufacturers sold light bulbs that they had manufactured under patent licensing agreements with General Electric.[20] The Court recognized that an important part of holding a patent was the right to license others to manufacture the patented item. This right would be effectively negated if licensees were allowed to undercut the prices that patent holders charged for their own sales of patented products.

Patent holders cannot, however, lawfully control the price at which patented items are resold by distributors that purchase them from the patent holder. Nor can patent holders use their patents to impose tying agreements on their customers by conditioning the sale of patented items on the purchase of nonpatented items unless such agreements are otherwise lawful under the Sherman and Clayton Acts. Finally, firms that seek to monopolize an area by acquiring most, or all, of the patents related to that area of commerce may be guilty of violating Section 2 of the Sherman Act or Section 7 of the Clayton Act because a patent has been held to be an asset within the meaning of Section 7.

Foreign Commerce

When foreign governments are involved in commercial activities affecting the domestic or international commerce of the United States, our antitrust policy may be at odds with our foreign policy. Congress and the courts have created a variety of antitrust exemptions aimed at reconciling this potential conflict. The Foreign Sovereign Immunities Act of 1976 (FSIA) provides that the

governmental actions of foreign sovereigns and their agents are exempt from antitrust liability. The commercial activities of foreign sovereigns, however, are not included within this **sovereign immunity** exemption. Significant international controversy exists over the proper criteria for determining whether a particular governmental act is commercial in nature. Under the FSIA, the courts employ a *nature of the act* test, holding that a commercial activity is one that an individual might customarily carry on for a profit.

The **act of state doctrine** provides that a U.S. court cannot adjudicate a politically sensitive dispute that would require the court to judge the legality of a sovereign act by a foreign state. This doctrine reflects judicial deference to the primary role of the executive and legislative branches in the adoption and execution of our foreign policy. Similar to the doctrine of sovereign immunity, the act of state doctrine recognizes the importance of respecting the sovereignty of other nations. Unlike the doctrine of sovereign immunity, however, the act of state doctrine also reflects a fundamental attribute of our system of government: the principle of separation of powers.

Finally, the **sovereign compulsion doctrine** provides a defense to private parties that have been compelled by a foreign sovereign to commit acts within that sovereign's territory that would otherwise violate the antitrust laws due to their negative impact on our international commerce. To employ this defense successfully, a defendant must show that the challenged actions were the product of actual compulsion by a foreign sovereign, not mere encouragement or approval. See Figure 3 for a summary of the various antitrust exceptions and exemptions.

ETHICAL AND PUBLIC POLICY CONCERNS

1. Refer to the facts of the *Mozart* and *Metrix* cases in this chapter. Assume that some Mercedes dealers sold their customers nonauthorized parts at the same price that they charged for genuine Mercedes parts and without telling customers that the parts installed were not genuine Mercedes parts. Is such a practice ethically justifiable? Would your answer change if you were convinced that the nonauthorized parts were equal in quality to genuine Mercedes replacement parts?

2. Refer to the facts of the *Patrick* case in this chapter. Assume that Patrick's factual allegations concerning

---

[18]*California Motor Transport v. Trucking Unlimited,* 404 U.S. 508 (U.S. Sup Ct. 1982).

[19]Chapter 8 discusses the patent laws in detail.

[20] 272 U.S. 476 (U.S. Sup. Ct. 1926).

FIGURE 3   Antitrust Exceptions and Exemptions

Exception/Exemption	Activities Covered	Source
Statutory Labor	Legitimate union activities	Clayton Act, Norris-LaGuardia Act
Nonstatutory Labor	Collective bargaining agreements	Judicial decision (policy favoring collective bargaining)
Agricultural Cooperatives	Legitimate cooperative activities	Clayton Act, Capper-Volstead Act
Export Trade Associations	Joint export activities	Webb-Pomerene Act
Insurance	Business of insurance	McCarran-Ferguson Act
Regulated Industries	Anticompetitive activities shielded by federal regulation	Regulatory statutes
State Action	State authorized and supervised anticompetitive activities	Judicial decision (federalism)
***Noerr-Pennington* Doctrine**	Attempts to induce anticompetitive governmental action	Judicial decision (First Amendment)
Patent Licensing	Legitimate activities of patent holders	Judicial decision (patent laws)
Sovereign Immunity	Governmental acts of foreign sovereigns	Foreign Sovereign Immunities Act
Act of State Doctrine	Sovereign acts of foreign sovereigns	Judicial decision (separation of powers)
Sovereign Compulsion Doctrine	Private acts compelled by foreign sovereigns	Judicial decision

the behavior and motivations of the defendants were true. Were the defendant physicians ethically justified in refusing to refer patients to Patrick, refusing to provide consultations for Patrick's patients, criticizing Patrick for failing to secure consultations, and using the peer-review process to discipline a competitor?

3. Refer to the facts of Problem Case 9 at the end of this chapter. Is paying a disguised bribe to win a contract ethically justifiable under such circumstances? Would your answer change if such bribes were a customary means of doing business in Nigeria rather than a violation of Nigerian law?

SUMMARY

The Clayton Act was passed as a result of congressional disappointment at the Sherman Act's failure to halt the trend toward concentration in the U.S. economy. The Clayton Act attempts to "nip monopolies in the bud" by outlawing specific practices that monopolists use to gain monopoly power.

Section 3 of the Clayton Act prohibits tying and exclusive dealing agreements involving commodities if those agreements represent a probable threat to competition. Section 3 does not apply to tying or exclusive dealing agreements involving real estate, intangibles, or services. Such agreements must be challenged under the Sherman Act. Moreover, since Section 3 applies only if a sale or lease has occurred, refusals to deal and consignment dealing are also outside the scope of the act. Some courts require the same level of proof for tying illegality under the Clayton Act as they do under the Sherman Act. That is, it must be shown that: the challenged agreement involves two separate products; the sale of the tying product is conditioned on an accompanying sale of the tied product; the seller has sufficient economic power in the market for the tying product to appreciably restrain competition in the tied product market; and the seller's tying agreements foreclose competitors from a "not insubstantial" amount of commerce in the tied product market. Other courts do not require proof of the seller's market power in the tying product as long as the other three elements of tying liability are present.

There is similar confusion over the proper standard for judging the legality of exclusive dealing agreements. Courts tend to apply the same standards of legality to exclusive dealing agreements challenged under the Clayton Act as they do to those attacked under the Sherman Act. Two distinct approaches, however, have been used in exclusive dealing cases. Early Supreme Court cases employed a "quantitative substantiality" test, focusing on the annual dollar volume of the commerce foreclosed to the seller's competitors as a result of the challenged agreement. The most recent Supreme Court case, however, employed a "qualitative substantiality" approach, stressing the percentage share of the market foreclosed to competition and a variety of other economic factors.

Section 7 of the Clayton Act prohibits mergers and acquisitions that may substantially lessen competition or tend to create a monopoly in any line of commerce in any section of the country. The future of Section 7 is somewhat in doubt, as current merger guidelines announced by federal antitrust enforcers indicate a much more tolerant attitude toward merger activity and most important recent merger cases have been settled out of court. Legal analysis of mergers under Section 7 has traditionally varied depending on the nature of the challenged merger.

Horizontal mergers between competitors involve the most immediate risk of harm to competition and consequently have been subjected to the most stringent standards. Traditional analysis looks at the market share of the merged firm, together with other economic and historical factors. Recent Justice Department merger guidelines indicate that the department focuses on the current degree of concentration in the relevant market and the increase in concentration that would result from the challenged merger.

Vertical merger (supplier-customer) analysis traditionally focused on the share of the relevant market foreclosed to competitors as a result of the challenged merger, although vertical mergers may also result in barriers to entry and an elimination of potential competition. Conglomerate mergers (those that are neither horizontal nor vertical) have traditionally been challenged on one or more of three theories: potential reciprocity, unfair advantage, or elimination of potential competition. The most recent Justice Department merger guidelines indicate, however, that the department employs the same criteria to judge all nonhorizontal mergers and that these criteria emphasize an elimination of potential competition analysis.

Section 8 of the Clayton Act prohibits interlocking directorates between competing companies if either

company has capital, surplus, or undivided profits in excess of $1 million. The enforcement of this section has historically been rather lax, but there are recent indications of renewed governmental interest in enforcing this part of the act.

Section 2 of the original Clayton Act attacks primary level price discrimination: localized price cuts by sellers designed to drive smaller rivals out of business. In 1936 Congress amended Section 2 by enacting the Robinson-Patman Act to attack price discrimination that resulted in secondary or tertiary level harms: price discrimination in sales to competing customers that results in a competitive advantage to a favored customer or to the customers of a favored customer. Section 2(a) of the Robinson-Patman Act prohibits direct price discrimination that results in a probability of competitive injury at any of these three levels. Price discrimination occurs when a seller makes relatively contemporaneous sales of products of like grade or quality at different prices to two or more customers. Price discrimination may in some cases be cost justified or justified by changing conditions affecting the marketability of the product in question. Section 2(b) of the act also provides a "meeting competition in good faith" defense that may excuse some discriminations in price. Section 2(f) makes it unlawful for a buyer knowingly to induce or receive a discriminatory price in violation of Section 2(a).

The Robinson-Patman Act also prohibits indirect price discrimination. Section 2(c) of the act prohibits false brokerage payments, and Sections 2(d) and 2(e) prohibit sellers from discriminating in promotional payments or services made to their customers unless such payments are made available to all customers on a proportionately equal basis.

A wide variety of economic activities occur outside the reach of the antitrust laws. Labor unions, agricultural cooperatives, exporters, insurance companies, and other regulated industries enjoy partial statutory exemptions from antitrust liability. The courts have also created antitrust exemptions designed to balance our antitrust policy in favor of competition against other important social policies. The state action exemption confers antitrust immunity to bona fide state regulatory activities and to private behavior pursuant to such activities. The *Noerr-Pennington* doctrine immunizes legitimate political action by competitors from antitrust scrutiny, even though such action may be aimed at anticompetitive ends. The patent licensing doctrine grants patent holders limited rights to exploit their patents by practices that would otherwise violate the antitrust laws. Finally, some activities by U.S. firms in foreign countries and certain actions by foreign sovereigns may lie outside the reach of our antitrust laws due to three doctrines: sovereign immunity, act of state, and sovereign compulsion.

PROBLEM CASES

1. Crossland started his own vending machine business in the early 1960s. In 1973 he bid successfully for the vending business at Fort Bliss, Texas, an expansion that exacerbated his company's existing financial problems. In 1974, after months of negotiations, Crossland signed a contract agreeing to become a franchisee of Canteen Corporation. The agreement called for Canteen to provide the business with badly needed capital by buying all of Crossland's vending equipment for $350,000 and leasing it back to him. Crossland continued to have financial problems, reaching the point where his company owed Canteen $420,000. Crossland ultimately sued Canteen, arguing that Canteen had tied the lease-back of the equipment to the sale of the Canteen franchise in violation of both the Sherman and Clayton Acts. Was Canteen correct in arguing that both claims should be dismissed?

2. Sterling Electric manufactured electric motors and replacement parts for them. No one else made parts compatible with Sterling motors. Sterling was acquired by A. O. Smith Corporation and under its new management instituted new distribution programs. Its new agreement with distributors who stocked its parts required that such "stocking" distributors buy and promote aggressively minimum quantities of Sterling motors in return for being able to buy parts for less than "referral" distributors who merely passed on orders for Sterling parts. On October 1, 1982, Sterling terminated Parts and Electric Motors, Inc. (P&E), a stocking distributor, for insufficient motor purchases. P&E then filed suit against Sterling, arguing that the motor purchase requirement was an illegal tying arrangement under the Sherman and Clayton Acts. At trial, P&E introduced evidence that the purchase requirement forced dealers to increase their motor purchases by more than $250,000. Was the jury verdict in P&E's favor proper?

3. In 1961 Ford Motor Company bought Autolite, a manufacturer of spark plugs, to enter the profitable aftermarket for spark plugs sold as replacement parts. Ford and the other major automobile manufacturers had previously purchased original equipment spark plugs (those installed in new cars when they leave the factory) from independent producers such as Autolite and Champion at or below the producer's cost. The independents were willing to sell original equipment plugs so cheaply because aftermarket mechanics often replace original equipment plugs with the same brand of spark plug. General Motors (GM) had previously moved into the spark plug market by developing its own AC division. Ford decided to do so by a vertical merger and acquired Autolite. Prior to acquiring Autolite, Ford bought 10 percent of the total spark plug output. The merger left Champion as the only major independent spark plug producer, and Champion's market share declined thereafter because Chrysler was the only major original equipment spark plug purchaser remaining in the market. The government filed a divestiture suit against Ford, arguing that Ford's acquisition of Autolite violated Section 7 of the Clayton Act. Should Ford be ordered to divest itself of Autolite?

4. In 1979 Siemens, a diversified firm with interests in the medical equipment field, notified the Justice Department that it intended to acquire control of Searle Diagnostics (SD), a manufacturer of nuclear medical equipment. In 1969 Siemens failed in an attempt to start its own nuclear medical equipment division, and in 1972 it considered trying to reenter the field but concluded that it would not be able to recoup the investment reentry required. The top four firms in the nuclear medical equipment market accounted for 77 percent of total sales in 1979. This figure, however, was down from 1975, when they accounted for 92 percent of total sales. SD, although still first in 1979, had seen its market share fall from 50 percent to 22 percent during the same five-year period. These facts, together with the fact that SD had lost money in 1978 and 1979, led SD's parent firm to agree to the sale to Siemens. The Justice Department sought a preliminary injunction against the merger, arguing that it would violate Section 7 by eliminating both perceived and actual potential competition. The department, however, presented no evidence that any attractive toehold purchase was available to Siemens or that Siemens, as an acknowledged likely entrant, had had any actual impact on the conduct of existing firms in the market. Should the preliminary injunction be granted?

5. In 1983 Warner Communications, Inc., the second largest distributor of prerecorded music in the United States (18.9 percent market share) with its Warner, Atlantic, and Elektra/Asylum labels, agreed to merge part of their record operations and form a joint venture company with Polygram Records, Inc., the sixth largest distributor (7.1 percent market share). The Federal Trade Commission applied for a preliminary injunction to block the joint venture. The FTC presented evidence that the top four distributors commanded 67 percent of the domestic market and that, if the joint venture were completed, their market share would increase to 75 percent. Evidence was also presented showing a trend toward concentration in the industry and high barriers to entry confronting new competitors. Should the trial court's ruling that the FTC had failed to demonstrate the likelihood of ultimate success necessary to justify a preliminary injunction be affirmed on appeal?

6. First Comics, Inc., wanted to enter the comic-book publishing business. First hired World Color Press to print its comics because World had a less expensive method of printing than other comic-book printers. World allegedly promised to charge First the same price it charged its larger customers such as Marvel Comics Group and DC Comics. When First discovered it was being charged 4.3 cents per copy more than Marvel, it demanded reimbursement or a future credit. When World refused, First filed a price discrimination suit against World under the Robinson-Patman Act. Does the Robinson-Patman Act apply to this case?

7. Indian Coffee Company, a coffee roaster in Pittsburgh, Pennsylvania, sold its Breakfast Cheer coffee in the Pittsburgh area, where it had an 18 percent market share, and in Cleveland, Ohio, where it had a significant, but smaller, market share. Late in 1971 Folger Coffee Company, then the leading seller of branded coffee west of the Mississippi, entered the Pittsburgh market for the first time. In its effort to gain market share in Pittsburgh, Folger granted retailers high promotional allowances in the form of coupons that retail customers could use to obtain price cuts and that redeeming retailers could use as credits against invoices. For a time, Indian tried to retain its market share by matching Folger's price concessions, but because Indian only operated in two areas, it could not subsidize such sales with profits from other areas. Indian was finally forced out of business in 1974, later filing a Robinson-Patman suit against Folger. At trial, Indian introduced evidence that Folger's Pittsburgh promotional allowances were far higher than its allowances in other geographic areas, and that Folger's Pittsburgh prices were below green (unroasted) coffee cost, below material and manufacturing costs, below total cost, and below marginal cost or average variable cost. Was the trial court's directed verdict in favor of Folger proper?

8. Peugeot Motors of America, Inc. (PMA), the exclusive domestic importer of Peugeot products, controlled all U.S. Peugeot distributors except EAD, the exclusive distributor for Peugeot cars in the southeastern United States. EAD filed suit against PMA, arguing that PMA had violated Sections 2(d) and 2(e) of the Robinson-Patman Act by providing cash incentives, training facilities, and parts repurchase programs (allowing dealers to return for credit a part of their obsolete parts inventory) to PMA's dealers that were not made available to EAD's dealers. The evidence at trial indicated that Memphis, Tennessee, was the only place in the United States where an EAD dealer was within 50 miles of a PMA dealer and that less than 1 percent of national Peugeot sales were cross-border sales between PMA and EAD territories. EAD's president also testified that he did not know the reason for any of the cross-border sales and admitted that some such sales occurred for reasons other than competition between the two sets of dealers. Should the trial court's directed verdict in favor of PMA be affirmed on appeal?

9. In 1982 a subsidiary of W. S. Kirkpatrick & Co. won a Nigerian defense ministry contract for the construction and equipment of an aeromedical center at a Nigerian Air Force base. Environmental Tectonics Corporation (Environmental), an unsuccessful bidder for the same contract, filed RICO and Robinson-Patman claims against Kirkpatrick. Environmental alleged that Kirkpatrick had won the contract by paying a 20 percent "commission" to bribe certain Nigerian officials. The parties agreed that the bribes, if paid, were in violation of Nigerian law. Was the trial court correct in holding that the act of state doctrine barred Environmental's claim?

10. Pocahontas Coal Company filed suit against a number of other companies engaged in the mining and production of coal in West Virginia, alleging that the defendant companies were involved in a conspiracy to control the production and pricing of coal. One of Pocahontas's claims was that the defendants had violated Section 8 of the Clayton Act by "deputizing" various persons to sit on the boards of competing subsidiaries. The defendants moved for summary judgment on the Section 8 claim, noting that Pocahontas's complaint contained no factual allegations showing that any of the defendants were competitors, failed to name any of the alleged "deputies," and was ambiguous because it alleged that certain persons were "officers and/or directors" of competing companies. The trial court offered Pocahontas the opportunity to clarify the complaint by bringing forth additional information on these points. Did the court properly grant the defendants summary judgment when Pocahontas declined to do so?

CHAPTER 50

EMPLOYMENT LAW

INTRODUCTION

Years ago, it was unusual to see a separate employment law chapter in a business law text. Traditionally, the rights, duties, and liabilities accompanying employment mainly have been governed by such basic legal institutions as contract, tort, and agency. These common law principles continue to control relations between employers and their employees unless displaced by state or federal regulation, or by new judge-made rules applying specifically to employment. By now, however, such rules and regulations have become so numerous that they touch almost every facet of the employment relationship. This chapter discusses the most important of these legal controls on employment. To see how and why these regulations emerged, and to get some perspective on them, the chapter opens with an historical overview of American employment law.

THE EVOLUTION OF AMERICAN EMPLOYMENT LAW

Early American Employment Law

From colonial times through the mid-19th century, much of the American population was self-employed. For many Americans, therefore, the problems created by the employment relation did not exist. For those who *were* employed during this period, the relation sometimes was authoritarian and paternalistic.

In the apprenticeship relations that were common in early America, for example, a master's duties were frequently compared to those of a parent and an apprentice's to those of a son. Among other things, a master often was obligated to train his apprentices and to see to their religious and secular education. Moreover, many states limited a master's power to discharge his apprentices without good cause. Also common during this period were indentured servants, who basically sold themselves to a master for a period of time and thus resembled temporary slaves. Although the law imposed certain duties of fair and humane treatment on a master, often an indentured servant could not marry without his master's consent and was denied the rights to vote and to engage in trade. In the southern states, moreover, the law regulated and enforced the oppressive system of black slavery. Further reinforcing the employer's power during this period was the courts' tendency to declare that labor unions were illegal criminal conspiracies.

The Period of Industrialization and Laissez-Faire

By the end of the Civil War, self-employment was less prevalent than formerly. In addition, the employment relation had lost much of its earlier authoritarian and paternalistic character. Increasingly, employer and employee came to be regarded as free and equal parties whose relations were governed by the highly individualistic principles of 19th-century contract law,[1] and whose other duties to each other were few.

This change, however, did not markedly improve the employee's position, and may have worsened it in some respects. For one thing, employees frequently bargained from a position of inferior power. Among the reasons were the existence of a large labor pool increasingly composed of immigrants, and the eventual emergence of large corporate employers. For another thing, this changed view of the employment relation helped insulate employers from liability to employees who were injured on the job. This was consistent with one of 19th-century America's main public policy goals: promoting the nation's industrialization by protecting infant industries against potentially crippling damage recoveries. Two important 19th-century legal developments—the employment-at-will rule and the rules governing negligence suits by injured employees—illustrate the individualism and prodevelopment thrust of 19th-century employment law.

Employment at Will Employment at will first clearly appeared after 1870. The rule states that either party can terminate an employment contract that is not for a definite time period, and can do so for any reason. This includes contracts for "steady," "regular," or "permanent" employment. The termination can occur at any time and can be for good, bad, or no cause. However, employees may recover for work actually done.

The rise of employment at will illustrates how the employment relation was influenced by 19th-century contract law and the economic laissez-faire on which it was based. The rule expresses the 19th-century view that parties should be bound only to contract terms on which they have clearly agreed, and that courts should not imply contract terms. Thus, where a contract left the employment's duration uncertain, courts usually would not impose a definite time term. Without such a term, either party could terminate at any time and for any reason. Employment at will also reflects laissez-faire values in a more general way, because it maximizes the freedom of both employer and employee.

In addition, employment at will has given employers the flexibility to meet changing business conditions by discharging employees whose services are no longer needed. As a result, it has promoted economic efficiency and the development of the American economy. Where labor was mobile and job opportunities were abundant, employment at will probably worked to the employee's advantage as well. In other situations, however, the doctrine's benefits were obtained at the cost of exposing discharged employees to the mercies of an uncertain economy.

Because it lets employers fire employees for any reason, employment at will contrasts with the earlier tendency to permit masters to discharge their apprentices only for good cause. As you will see at the end of this chapter, however, modern courts have moved back toward this earlier view. They have done so by creating exceptions to the employment-at-will rule. These exceptions effectively make employers liable for **unjust dismissal** or **wrongful discharge**.

On-the-Job Injuries As noted, one of 19th-century America's main public policy goals was to promote industrialization by protecting infant industries from potentially crippling lawsuits. In part for this reason, 19th-century law made it difficult for employees to recover when they sued their employers in negligence[2] for injuries suffered in on-the-job accidents. At that time, employers had an *implied assumption of risk* defense under which an employee was regarded as having assumed all the normal and customary risks of his employment simply by taking the job. Because these risks included the possibility of being injured by a coemployee's negligence, employers had another defense called the *fellow servant rule*, which stated that where an employee's injury resulted from the negligence of a coemployee (or fellow servant), his employer would not be liable. If an employee's own carelessness played some role in his injury, finally, employers often could avoid liability under the traditional rule that even a slight degree of *contributory negligence* is a complete defense to a negligence suit.

The Rise of Organized Labor

By the 1860s, most courts had removed one obstacle to unionization by abandoning the old doctrine that trade

---

[1] See the Introduction to Contracts chapter for a discussion of 19th-century contract law.

[2] See the Negligence and Strict Liability chapter for a discussion of negligence law and the defenses of assumption of risk and contributory negligence.

unions are criminal conspiracies. But the main forces behind organized labor's rise in the late 19th century were the increasing size and power of corporate employers and the workplace hazards accompanying industrialization. Underlying the trade union movement was the belief that the power of corporate groups could only be countered by creating new groups representing the interests of workers. The rise of these new groups triggered various legal responses.

Over time, organized labor's increasing political power and the growing numbers of wage earners in the electorate influenced the state legislatures. As a result, many laws protecting workers were passed in the late 19th and early 20th centuries. These included statutes outlawing "yellow dog" contracts (under which an employee would agree not to join or remain a member of a union), minimum wage and maximum hours legislation, laws regulating the employment of women and children, all sorts of factory safety measures, and the workers' compensation systems to be discussed shortly.

The courts, however, tended to represent business interests during this period. Thus, some of the measures just mentioned were struck down on constitutional grounds. Also, some courts were quick to issue temporary and permanent injunctions to restrain union picketing and boycotts and to help quell strikes. As the remainder of this chapter demonstrates, however, business's efforts to stem the rising tide of legislation protecting workers obviously were unsuccessful in the long run.

Employment Law Today

Throughout the 20th century, both employers and (until recently) unions have grown in size and social power. Today, relatively few people are self-employed, and many work for large public and private organizations with which they cannot deal on an equal footing. Although labor market conditions influence the terms and conditions employers offer, individual job applicants usually have little power to bargain over those terms and conditions. Once employed, they occupy positions and perform functions whose nature is largely determined by the institution for which they work. A person's employer and his position within that organization also affect his nonworking life in various ways. Much sociological writing testifies to the way organizational affiliations determine a person's economic prospects, social position, lifestyle, and even values. For union members, however, employer power is somewhat blunted by the union's own power. But here, employees gain protection from their employers only by submitting to another organized group.

The importance of the employment relation to most people, their dependence on their employers, and employer power over them have inspired numerous efforts to protect employees against abuses of that power during the 20th century. Thus, despite becoming increasingly subservient to organized groups, the tangible position of employees has improved for most of this century. Employers themselves have come to assume paternalistic duties toward their employees—for example, by providing fringe benefits such as pensions, health insurance, and life insurance. More importantly, legislatures, administrative agencies, and courts have attempted to protect employees by regulating more and more aspects of the employment relation. As Figure 1 illustrates, they have pursued certain general goals in the process. The many employment regulations listed in Figure 1 and discussed in this chapter are basically a series of exceptions to the 19th-century's contract-based model of the employment relation. That is, they are yet another example of government intervention prompted by perceived disparities in power between contracting parties.

SOME BASIC EMPLOYMENT STATUTES

Modern American employment law is so vast and complex a subject that texts designed for lawyers seldom address it in its entirety. Indeed, specialized subjects like labor law and employment discrimination often get book-length treatment in their own right. This chapter's overview of employment law focuses most heavily on three topics that have attracted much attention in recent years—employment discrimination, employee privacy, and the demise of employment at will. But no discussion of employment law is complete without outlining certain basic regulations that significantly affect the conditions of employment for many Americans.

Workers' Compensation

Despite safety advances within most industries, employees continue to face dangerous workplace conditions. As you have seen, 19th-century law made it difficult for workers to sue their employers for on-the-job injuries. Making an injured employee's suit even more difficult was the need to *prove* negligent behavior

FIGURE 1   The Ends and Means of Modern Employment Law

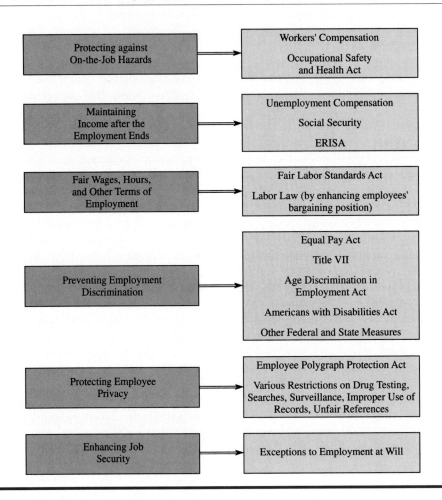

on the employer's part. State workers' compensation statutes, which first began to appear at the beginning of the 20th century, were a response to this situation. Today, all 50 states have such systems.[3]

Basic Features The coverage of workers' compensation statutes varies from state to state. States usually exempt certain *employers* from the system. One common

exemption is for firms employing fewer than a stated number of employees (often three). Also, workers' compensation only protects *employees* and not independent contractors.[4] In addition, many states specifically exempt casual, agricultural, and domestic employees, among others. State and local government employees may be covered by the state's workers' compensation system, or by some alternative state system.

---

[3] In addition, various federal statutes regulate on-the-job injuries suffered by employees of the federal government and other employees such as railroad workers, seamen, longshoremen, and harbor workers.

[4] The chapter entitled The Agency Relationship discusses the employee-independent contractor distinction.

Where they apply, however, all workers' compensation systems share certain basic features. They allow injured employees to recover on the basis of *strict liability*,[5] thus removing any need to prove employer negligence. They also *eliminate the employer's traditional defenses* of contributory negligence, assumption of risk, and the fellow-servant rule. In addition, they make workers' compensation an employee's *exclusive remedy* against her employer for covered injuries. Usually, however, employees who are injured by their employer's *intentional torts* may sue the employer outside workers' compensation.

Workers' compensation is basically a social compromise. Because it is based on strict liability and eliminates the three traditional employer defenses, workers' compensation greatly increases the *probability* that an injured employee will recover. Such recoveries may usually include: (1) hospital and medical expenses (including vocational rehabilitation), (2) disability benefits, (3) specified recoveries for the loss of certain body parts, and (4) death benefits to survivors and/or dependents. But each category of damages usually is limited in various ways, so that the *amount* recoverable under workers' compensation often is lower than the amount obtainable in a successful tort suit. Thus, as the following *Tolbert* case illustrates, injured employees sometimes deny that they are covered by workers' compensation so that they can pursue a tort suit against their employer instead.

Even though workers' compensation is an injured employee's sole remedy against her *employer*, she may be able to sue *other parties* whose behavior helped cause her injury. One example is a product liability suit against a third-party manufacturer who supplies an employer with defective machinery or raw materials that cause an on-the-job injury. However, a majority of the states give co-employees whose tortious behavior harmed the plaintiff much the same immunity they give an employer. Complicated questions of contribution, indemnity, and subrogation can arise where an injured employee is able to recover, or actually recovers, against both an employer and a third party.

The Work-Related Injury Requirement Another basic feature of workers' compensation is that an employee can recover only for *work-related* injuries. The general test for work-relatedness is that the injury must (1) arise out of the employment and (2) happen in the course of the employment. These tests have been variously interpreted, and they have generated much case law.

The arising-out-of-the-employment test usually requires a sufficiently close relationship between the injury and the *nature* of the employment. As the *Tolbert* case illustrates, there is considerable disagreement about the standards to be used in applying this test. A factory worker assaulted by a trespasser, for example, probably would be denied a workers' compensation recovery under the "increased risk" analysis discussed in *Tolbert*, but probably would recover under the "positional risk" doctrine also described there. If the same trespasser assaulted an on-duty security guard, however, the guard should recover under either approach.

The in-the-course-of-the-employment test requires courts to determine whether the injury occurred within the *time, place, and circumstances* of the employment. Employees injured off the employer's premises generally are outside the course of the employment. For example, injuries suffered while traveling to or from work usually are not compensable under workers' compensation. But an employee may be covered where the off-the-premises injury occurred while she was performing employment-related duties. Injuries suffered during business trips or while running employment-related errands are examples.

Other work-related injury problems on which the courts have disagreed include mental injuries allegedly arising from the employment and injuries resulting from employee horseplay. Virtually all the states, however, regard intentionally self-inflicted injuries as outside the scope of workers' compensation. Recovery for occupational diseases, on the other hand, is usually allowed today. And employees who can prove that a preexisting disease has been aggravated by their employment sometimes recover workers' compensation benefits.

Administration and Funding Workers' compensation systems usually are administered by a state agency that adjudicates workers' claims and administers the system's overall operation. Its decisions on such claims can generally be appealed to the state courts.

---

[5] Strict liability is discussed in the Negligence and Strict Liability chapter.

The states assure funding for workers' compensation recoveries by compelling covered employers to: (1) purchase private insurance, (2) self-insure (e.g., by maintaining a contingency fund), or (3) make payments into a state insurance fund. Because employers generally pass on the costs of insurance to their customers, workers' compensation systems tend to spread the economic risk of workplace injuries throughout society.

TOLBERT v. MARTIN MARIETTA CORPORATION
621 F. Supp. 1099 (D. Colo. 1985)

Deborah Tolbert, a secretary employed by the Martin Marietta Corporation, was raped by a Martin Marietta janitor while on her way to lunch within the secured defense facility where she worked. She sued Martin Marietta, alleging that it had negligently hired the janitor and had negligently failed to make its premises safe for employees. Martin Marietta moved for summary judgment, alleging that Tolbert could not sue in negligence because workers' compensation was her sole remedy.

Carrigan, District Judge.   The sole issue is whether the Colorado Workmen's Compensation Act covers Tolbert's injury. If it does, workers' compensation is her exclusive remedy and this tort action is barred. Tolbert asserts that her injury is not covered by workers' compensation, presumably because she expects that a tort action would yield a larger recovery. Martin Marietta, on the other hand, apparently is willing to pay the workers' compensation award to avoid risking a large tort verdict.

Workers' compensation applies where the injury or death is proximately caused by an injury or occupational disease arising out of and in the course of the employee's employment and is not intentionally self-inflicted. Although her injury did arise in the course of her employment, Tolbert contends that it did not "arise out of" the employment. The "arising out of" condition creates a prerequisite that there be some causal relationship between the employment and the injury. Courts have interpreted the "arising out of" language in a number of different ways. Unfortunately, Colorado courts have not consistently applied any single test. Martin Marietta argues that positional-risk analysis applies to categorize the case as one covered by compensation. The positional-risk doctrine has been defined thus by a leading authority:

> An injury arises out of the employment if it would not have occurred but for the fact that the conditions and obligations of the employment placed claimant in the position where he was injured. . . . This theory supports compensation in cases of stray bullets, roving lunatics and other situations in which the only connection of the employment with the injury is that its obligations placed the employee in the particular place at the particular time when he was injured by some neutral force, meaning by "neutral" neither personal to the claimant nor distinctly associated with the employment.

Invoking this rule, Martin Marietta asserts that Tolbert's injury is covered by workers' compensation because: (1) her employment placed her within the building where she was injured, and (2) the assault was a neutral force.

[However,] *Industrial Commission v. Ernest Irvine, Inc.* (1923) . . . applied the "increased-risk" test of causality. Under the increased-risk test, compensation is awarded only if the employment increases the worker's risk of injury above that to which the general public is exposed. If Colorado presently applies the increased-risk analysis, Tolbert would not be covered by workers' compensation. Certainly her employment as a secretary within a secured defense facility would not be expected to increase her risk of sexual assault above that to which women in the general public are exposed.

Colorado first applied positional risk analysis four years after *Ernest Irvine, Inc.* was decided. [In this later case,] the court upheld an award to a farmhand who was struck by lightning. It can readily been seen that the positional-risk test provides substantially broader coverage than does the increased-risk test. Unfortunately, the Colorado courts on several more recent occasions have departed from the positional-risk test to impose a higher standard of causal relationship to the employment.

It is clear that the rape was a nonemployment-motivated act directed at the plaintiff because she was a woman. There is nothing to indicate that any other woman—whether or not a Martin employee—who happened to be in the same area at the time of the attack would not have become the victim. It is clear that Tolbert was not raped because of the nature of her duties or the nature of her workplace environment, or because of any incident or quarrel growing out of the work.

Both applicable Colorado precedent and sound rationale support holding that the workers' compensation statute has not abolished Tolbert's tort claim. Adopting this position has the additional advantage of providing employers an incentive to make reasonable efforts to screen prospective employees so as to avoid hiring rapists or those having the identifiable characteristics of potential rapists. Tort law does not impose strict liability; Tolbert still has the burden of showing negligence, causation, and damages.

Martin Marietta's motion for summary judgment denied; case proceeds to trial on Tolbert's negligence theories.

The Occupational Safety and Health Act

Although it may stimulate employers to remedy hazardous working conditions, workers' compensation does not directly forbid such conditions. However, some states have created various workplace safety regulations, and Congress has enacted health and safety legislation for certain hazardous industries. The most important measure for promoting workplace safety, however, is the federal Occupational Safety and Health Act of 1970.

The Occupational Safety and Health Act generally applies to all employers engaged in a business affecting interstate commerce. Exempted, however, are the U.S. government, the states and their political subdivisions, and certain industries regulated by other federal safety legislation. The Occupational Safety and Health Act is mainly administered by the Occupational Safety and Health Administration (OSHA) of the Department of Labor. It is not intended to preempt state regulation of workplace safety, and the states can regulate areas subject to federal standards, albeit under federal supervision and control.

General Standards The act requires that employers provide their employees with employment and a place of employment free from recognized hazards that are likely to cause death or serious physical harm. It also requires employers to comply with specific regulations promulgated by OSHA. These regulations are voluminous and often quite detailed.

Enforcement and Penalties OSHA can inspect places of employment for violations of the act and its regulations, although employers can require the agency to obtain a search warrant before doing so. (Workers who notify OSHA of possible violations are protected against employer retaliation.) If an employer is found to violate the act's general duty provision or any specific standard, OSHA issues a written citation. It must do so with reasonable promptness, and in no event more than six months after the violation. The citation becomes final after 15 workdays following its service on the employer, unless it is contested. Contested citations are reviewed by the Occupational Safety and Health Review Commission, a three-member body composed of presidential appointees. Further review by the federal courts of appeals is possible.

The main sanctions for violations of the act and the regulations are civil penalties imposed by OSHA. Such penalties are mandatory when an employer receives a citation for a serious violation of the act or its regulations, and discretionary when the violation is nonserious. Other civil penalties are possible for willful or repeated violations and for the failure to correct a violation after a citation. In addition, any employer who commits a willful violation resulting in death to an employee may suffer a fine, imprisonment, or both. Finally, the secretary of labor may seek injunctive relief when an employment hazard presents an imminent danger of death or physical harm that cannot be promptly eliminated by normal citation procedures.

Recordkeeping, Reporting, and Notice Under the act, employers must maintain accurate records of, and make periodic reports on, work-related deaths, illnesses, and injuries other than minor injuries. Employers also must maintain accurate records of employee exposures to certain toxic and harmful materials. Employees exposed to specified concentrations of such materials must receive prompt notification from their employer.

Social Security

Under a system of complete laissez-faire, an employer's financial obligations to its employees would cease once the employment ends, unless the parties had contracted otherwise. Today, however, the law requires employers to assist in ensuring that their employees receive financial protection after termination of the employment. One example is the federal social security system, which began in 1935. Social security is mainly financed by the Federal Insurance Contributions Act (FICA), which applies to a wide range of employers. FICA operates by imposing a flat percentage tax on all employee income below a certain base figure and by requiring employers to pay a similar tax.

Today, FICA revenues finance various forms of financial assistance in addition to the old-age benefits that people usually call social security. These include survi-

vors' benefits to family members of deceased workers, disability benefits, and medical and hospitalization benefits for the elderly (the medicare system).

Unemployment Compensation

Another way that the law protects employees after their employment ends is by providing unemployment compensation for discharged workers. Since 1935, various federal statutes have authorized joint federal-state efforts in this area. Today, each of the states administers its own unemployment compensation system under general federal guidelines; the costs of the system are met by subjecting employers to federal and state unemployment compensation taxes.

Unemployment insurance plans vary somewhat from state to state, but usually are similar in certain general respects. To prevent payments to those who have not recently been employed, states often condition the receipt of benefits on the recipient's having earned a certain minimum income during a specified prior time period. Generally, those who have voluntarily quit work without good cause, have been fired for bad conduct, fail to actively seek suitable new work, or refuse such work are ineligible for benefits. Benefit levels vary from state to state, as does the length of time that benefits can be received. Under federal law and the laws of a few states, the benefit period may be extended under certain circumstances.

ERISA

In addition to making compulsory payments to unemployment compensation systems and to the social security system, many employers voluntarily contribute to their employees' postemployment income by maintaining pension plans. For years, the main federal law regulating private pension plans was the Internal Revenue Code, which did not concern itself with the details of pension plan operation. Partly for this reason, abuses and injustices such as arbitrary plan terminations, arbitrary benefit reductions, and mismanagement of fund assets were not uncommon.

The Employee Retirement Income Security Act of 1974 (ERISA) was a response to these problems. In many ways, ERISA is a cautious regulatory response to the problems it addresses, for Congress did not wish to discourage the creation of pension plans by enacting overly strict controls. Thus, the act does not require employers to establish or fund benefit plans and does not set benefit levels. Instead, it attempts to prevent abuses in the operation of private pension plans and to protect an employee's expectation that promised pension benefits will be paid.

ERISA is a very long, complex, and detailed statute whose main concern is to set certain standards that pension plans must meet. Thus, the act imposes various *fiduciary duties* on pension fund managers. To take just one example, it requires that managers diversify the plan's investments to minimize the risk of large losses, unless this is clearly imprudent under the circumstances. ERISA also imposes *recordkeeping, reporting, and disclosure* requirements. For instance, it requires that covered plans provide annual reports to their participants, and specifies the contents of those reports. In addition, the act has a provision restricting an employer's ability to *delay an employee's participation* in the plan. In some situations, for example, an employee who completes one year of service with an employer cannot be denied participation in a plan. Furthermore, ERISA contains *funding* and *plan termination insurance* requirements designed to help protect plan participants against loss of pension income. The Labor Department's Pension Benefit Guaranty Corporation is the insurance agency established by the act. Finally, ERISA contains complex *vesting* requirements that determine when an employee's right to receive particular pension benefits becomes nonforfeitable. These requirements are important because they help prevent employers from using a late vesting date to avoid pension obligations to employees who change jobs or are fired before that date.

ERISA allows plan participants and beneficiaries to enforce their benefit rights and other rights under the plan. Along with the secretary of labor, they also may obtain equitable relief against violations of the act, and both legal and equitable relief against plan managers who breach their fiduciary duties. In addition, those who willfully violate the act's provisions can suffer criminal penalties.

Labor Law

American labor law is a complex topic whose many details are beyond the scope of this text. However, no discussion of employment law is complete without outlining federal regulation of labor-management relations in the 20th century. The following brief survey of labor law illustrates many of the general themes discussed at the beginning of this chapter.

Introduction   During the late 19th and early 20th centuries, the legal system often helped employers check the growing power of organized labor. Employment at will enabled them to fire prounion employees, and employers sometimes blacklisted such employees. Judicial injunctions and restraining orders, and the contempt citations that courts would issue upon their violation, continued to be useful in suppressing strikes and other union activities. Some union tactics were held to violate the antitrust laws. Yellow-dog contracts continued to be used, and state legislation forbidding such contracts sometimes was declared unconstitutional. Despite all these measures, however, the power of organized labor continued to grow. That power was cemented in the 1930s, when Congress explicitly recognized labor's rights to organize and to bargain collectively by passing the National Labor Relations Act. Later federal regulation of labor-management relations mainly has addressed certain perceived abuses by unions. Although such regulations may have limited organized labor's power somewhat, they have not seriously disturbed the position that it achieved in the 1930s.

The rise of organized labor is a clear example of what has been called *countervailing power:* the checking of organized group power by the creation of competing groups. By organizing to counter the influence of corporate groups over their working lives, workers have been able to achieve wages and working conditions that they probably would have been unable to obtain otherwise. In the process, however, they have become subordinate to another organized group—the union.

This section also illustrates a theme that pervades this text: the activist role played by government in the 20th century. In particular, the section emphasizes government's contemporary role as mediator between competing group interests.

The National Labor Relations Act   In 1926, Congress passed the Railway Labor Act, which regulates labor relations in the railroad industry, and which later was amended to include airlines. This was followed by the Norris-LaGuardia Act of 1932, which limited the circumstances in which federal courts could enjoin strikes and picketing in labor disputes. The act also prohibited federal court enforcement of yellow-dog contracts.

These two statutes, however, were only a prelude to the most important 20th-century American labor statute, the National Labor Relations Act of 1935 (the NLRA or Wagner Act). The act gave employees the *right to organize* by enabling them to form, join, and assist labor organizations. It also allowed them to *bargain collectively* through representatives of their own choosing and to engage in other activities that would promote collective bargaining. In addition, the Wagner Act prohibited certain employer practices that were believed to discourage collective bargaining, and declared these to be *unfair labor practices*. Included in its list of unfair labor practices are:

1. Interfering with employees in the exercise of their rights to form, join, and assist labor unions.

2. Dominating or interfering with the formation or administration of any labor union, or giving financial or other support to a union.

3. Discriminating against employees in hiring, tenure, or any term of employment because of their union membership.

4. Discriminating against employees because they have filed charges or given testimony under the act.

5. Refusing to bargain collectively with any duly designated representative of the employees.

The NLRA also established the National Labor Relations Board (NLRB). The NLRB's main functions are: (1) to handle representation cases (which involve the process by which a union becomes the certified representative of the employees within a particular bargaining unit), and (2) to decide whether challenged employer or union activity constitutes an unfair labor practice.

The Labor Management Relations Act   In 1947, Congress amended the NLRA by passing the Labor Management Relations Act (LMRA or Taft-Hartley Act). In part, the changes made by the Taft-Hartley Act reflected the more conservative political climate and the revival of business power that emerged after World War II. Perhaps more importantly, they reflected public concern over frequent strikes, the perceived excessive power of union bosses, and various unfair practices by unions. Thus, the Taft-Hartley Act declared that certain acts by *unions* were unfair labor practices. These include:

1. Restraining or coercing employees in the exercise of their guaranteed bargaining rights—in particular, their rights to refrain from joining a union or to engage in collective bargaining.

2. Causing an employer to discriminate against an employee who is not a union member, unless the employee is not a member because of a failure to pay union dues.

3. Refusing to bargain collectively with an employer.

4. Conducting a secondary strike or a secondary boycott for a specified illegal purpose. These are strikes or boycotts aimed at a third party with which the union has no real dispute. Their purpose is to coerce that party not to deal with an employer with which the union does have a dispute, and thus to gain some leverage over the employer.

5. Requiring employees covered by union-shop contracts to pay excessive or discriminatory initiation fees or dues.

6. Featherbedding—forcing an employer to pay for work not actually performed.

The LMRA also established an 80-day cooling off period for strikes that the president finds likely to endanger national safety or health. In addition, it created a Federal Mediation and Conciliation Service to assist employers and unions in settling labor disputes.

The Labor Management Reporting and Disclosure Act   Congressional investigations during the 1950s uncovered much corruption in internal union affairs, and also revealed that the internal procedures of many unions were undemocratic. In response to these findings, Congress enacted the Labor Management Reporting and Disclosure Act (or Landrum-Griffin Act) in 1959. The act established a "bill of rights" for union members and attempted to make internal union affairs more democratic. It also amended the NLRA by adding to the LMRA's list of unfair labor practices by unions.

The Fair Labor Standards Act

Federal labor law is a significant departure from the individualistic model of the employment relation that prevailed during the 19th century. Still, it does permit many terms of employment to be determined by private bargaining. Since the 1930s, however, the law sometimes has directly regulated such key terms of employment as wages and hours worked. The most important example is the Fair Labor Standards Act (FLSA) of 1938.

The FLSA's most important provisions concern the regulation of *wages and hours*. Employees covered by the act are entitled to: (1) a specified minimum wage whose amount has changed over time, and (2) a time-

and-a-half rate for work in excess of 40 hours per week. The FLSA's wages and hours provisions basically apply to employees who are engaged in interstate commerce or the production of goods for such commerce, or who are employed by an enterprise that does the same and that has annual gross sales of sufficient size. State and local employees are also covered. Among the classes of employees exempted from the FLSA's wages-and-hours provisions are executive, administrative, professional, and outside sales personnel.

The FLSA also prohibits certain kinds of *child labor.* It forbids the use of "oppressive child labor" by any employer engaged in interstate commerce or in the production of goods for such commerce, and also forbids the interstate shipment of goods produced in an establishment where oppressive child labor takes place. Oppressive child labor includes: (1) most employment of children below the age of 14; (2) employment of children aged 14–15, unless they work in one of a list of approved occupations set out by the Department of Labor; and (3) employment of children aged 16–17 who work in occupations such as mining that have been declared particularly hazardous by the Labor Department. Subject to conditions that vary with the age of the child, these provisions do not apply to agricultural employment. Also exempt from these provisions are children who work as actors or performers in radio, television, movie, and theatrical productions.

Both injured employees and the Labor Department can sue for violations of the FLSA's wages and hours provisions. They can recover the amount of the unpaid minimum wages or overtime, plus an additional equal amount as liquidated damages. A suit by the Labor Department terminates an employee's right to sue, but the department pays the amounts it recovers to the injured party. In addition, violations of both the act's wages and hours provisions and its child labor provisions may result in civil penalties. Finally, the Labor Department may sue for injunctive relief to enforce the FLSA's various provisions, and willful violations of those provisions subject employers to criminal liability.

The Equal Pay Act

The Equal Pay Act (EPA), which forbids *sex* discrimination regarding *pay*, was passed as an amendment to the FLSA in 1963. Its coverage is very similar to the coverage of the FLSA's minimum wage provisions. Unlike the FLSA, however, the EPA covers executive, administrative, and professional employees.

The Equal Pay Act forbids gender-based pay discrimination against men. But the typical EPA case involves an aggrieved woman who claims that she has received lower pay than a male employee performing substantially equal work for the same employer. The substantially-equal-work requirement is met if the plaintiff's job and the higher-paid male employee's job involve *each* of the following: (1) equal effort, (2) equal skill, (3) equal responsibility, and (4) similar working conditions.

Effort basically means physical or mental exertion. *Skill* refers to the experience, training, education, and ability required for the positions being compared. Here, the question is not whether the two employees actually possess equal skills, but whether the *jobs require or utilize* substantially the same skills. *Responsibility* (or accountability) involves such factors as the degree of supervision each job requires and the importance of each job to the employer. For instance, a retail sales position in which an employee is allowed to approve customer checks without higher-level review probably is not equal to a sales position in which an employee lacks this authority. *Working conditions* refers to such factors as temperature, weather, fumes, ventilation, toxic conditions, and risk of injury. Note that these need only be *similar,* not equal.

Once it has been shown that the two jobs are substantially equal and that they are compensated unequally, an employer must prove one of the EPA's four defenses or it will lose the case. That is, the employer must show that the pay disparity is based on: (1) seniority, (2) merit, (3) quality or quantity of production (e.g., a piecework system), or (4) any factor other than sex. As the following *Grove* case emphasizes in the case of merit, the first three defenses usually require an employer to show some organized, systematic, communicated rating system with predetermined criteria that apply equally to employees of each sex. Highly discretionary, subjective systems capable of serving as a cover for gender discrimination ordinarily do not suffice. The any-factor-other-than-sex defense is a catchall category that may include shift differentials, bonuses paid because the job is part of a training program, and differences in the profitability of the products or services on which the employees work.

The EPA's remedial scheme is very similar to the FLSA scheme described earlier. Under the EPA, however, employee suits are for the amount of *back pay* lost because of an employer's discrimination, not for unpaid minimum wages or overtime. As before, an employee also may recover an equal sum as liquidated damages. In addition, the EPA is enforced by the Equal Employment Opportunity Commission (EEOC), not the Labor Department.[6] Unlike some of the employment discrimina-

tion statutes described later, however, the EPA does not require that private plaintiffs submit their complaints to the EEOC or a state agency for evaluation and attempted conciliation before mounting suit.

The following case, *Grove v. Frostburg National Bank,* considers both the EPA's equal work requirement and some of its defenses. Like many other cases, it does not examine effort, skill, and responsibility individually. Instead, it discusses how they are affected by the male employee's extra tasks.

---

[6] The EEOC, established by the Civil Rights Act of 1964, is an independent federal agency with a sizable staff and many regional offices. The EEOC's functions include: (1) enforcement of most of the employment discrimination laws discussed in this chapter through lawsuits that it initiates or in which it intervenes, (2) conciliation of employment discrimination charges (e.g., by encouraging their negotiated settlement), (3) investigation of a wide range of discrimination-related matters, and (4) interpretation of the statutes it enforces through regulations and guidelines.

GROVE v. FROSTBURG NATIONAL BANK

549 F. Supp. 922 (D. Md. 1982)

Sheila Grove and David Klink were hired as loan tellers by the Frostburg National Bank in 1967. Both were high school graduates at the time, and neither had prior work experience. Each was paid the same yearly starting salary in 1967. Klink was drafted into the army late in 1967, and he returned to the bank in 1969. From that time until 1976, he basically performed a loan teller's duties, although he also took on a variety of miscellaneous tasks. Grove also basically performed loan teller duties during the period 1969–76. Throughout that period, Klink's yearly salary exceeded Grove's. Salary and raise determinations were made by David P. Willetts, the bank's vice president, who based these determinations primarily on his own observations of employees. Grove sued the bank in federal district court under the Equal Pay Act.

Jones, District Judge.   The burden is on the plaintiff to make a prima facie showing that the employer pays different wages to males and females for equal work requiring equal skill, effort, and responsibility under similar working conditions. Once that showing is made, the employer has the burden of showing that the pay differential is justified under one of the four statutory exceptions. Only substantial equality of work need be proved; the jobs need not be identical. A wage differential is justified by extra tasks only if they create significant variations in skill, effort, and responsibility. If the purported extra tasks are not done; if females also have extra tasks of equal skill, effort, and responsibility; if females are not given the opportunity to do the extra tasks; or if the extra tasks only involve minimal time and are of peripheral importance, they do not justify a wage differential.

Sheila Grove performed work substantially equal to that of David Klink from 1969 through September, 1976. As loan tellers, [each] had basically the same duties. Klink had some extra tasks from time to time. He set up the drive-in branch in 1970. He reviewed the safe deposit box rent records and noted some delinquencies and increases in 1971. After 1971, he arranged for drilling the boxes. Some time in the 1970s, he began shredding paper.

Setting up the drive-in branch was a one-time task, involving taking supplies and equipment to the drive-in installation. To the extent that it involved any different skills or effort than the normal work of the loan tellers, they were largely physical. Moreover, no female loan teller had an opportunity to perform this task, because it was done at the request of Willetts. Although Klink's initiative in bringing the box rents up to date is commendable, the work did not consume a significant amount of time, as compared with his other duties. It was a one-time project. To the extent that he performed extra tasks thereafter in arranging for the drilling, no significant amount of time was involved. Shredding paper is a task involving less skill, effort, and responsibility than the regular work of loan tellers. It did not involve a significant amount of time, only occasional afternoons or Saturdays.

Grove has sustained her burden of demonstrating that her work as loan teller was substantially equal to that of Klink. The bank tried to justify Klink's higher salary on two grounds. It stated that Klink was paid a higher salary when he returned to the bank in 1969, which was perpetuated through yearly increases, as a reward for his patriotism in serving in the Army. The bank also claimed that Klink received higher pay because he was more responsible, conscientious, and harder-working: that is, on merit.

The bank has failed to show that Klink's 1969 salary was based on a factor other than sex. Even assuming that military service could be a proper reason for a wage differential, Klink was drafted into the service. No female worker could have been.

The bank has also failed to show that the wage differential was based on a legitimate merit system. A merit system need not be in writing to be recognized; it must, however, be an organized and structured procedure with systematic evaluations under predetermined criteria. If it is not in writing, employees must be aware of it. The system used by Willetts does not meet this test. It was not organized or structured; Willetts did not recall, for example, whether he had consulted with department supervisors at the end of each year concerning individual employees. A systematic evaluation, using predetermined criteria, was not made. Although Willetts cited a number of factors that influenced his pay decisions, these were not applied uniformly, and he eventually admitted that the primary criterion was his "gut feeling" about the employee. Finally, employees were not aware of the existence of any merit system.

Judgment for Grove.

Title VII

Introduction

As you may have noticed, there is a significant difference between the Equal Pay Act and the other laws discussed in the previous section. Because it forbids unequal pay on the basis of gender, the EPA is an *employment discrimination* provision. Employment discrimination might be defined as employer behavior that penalizes certain individuals because of personal traits that they cannot control and that bear no relation to effective job performance. Such discrimination was common before the 1960s. In part, this was because traditional social values differed from those that prevail today. The view that women belong in the home and not in the workplace, for example, was much more prevalent

50 or 100 years ago than it is now. But the highly individualistic 19th-century model of the employment relation also helps explain why employment discrimination was so common for so long. To the maximum extent possible, it was felt, no party to an employment contract should be bound to terms not of his choosing. Therefore, employers generally could hire, fire, promote, and compensate on any basis they desired, no matter how arbitrary.

As our earlier discussion has suggested, this traditional thinking has become progressively less influential over the course of the 20th century. But it was not until the 1960s and 1970s that the law began to attack employment discrimination. When the tide finally turned, though, it did so with a vengeance. Today, employers are confronted with a maze of legal rules forbidding employment discrimination on the basis of certain personal traits. Changed social values—mainly, America's greater commitment to equal opportunity and its decreased reverence for freedom of contract—are the most important explanation for this new legal picture.

Of the many employment discrimination laws in force today, the most important is Title VII of the 1964 Civil Rights Act. Unlike the Equal Pay Act, Title VII is a comprehensive employment discrimination provision. It prohibits discrimination based on *race, color, religion, sex, and national origin*. It forbids such discrimination not just when it affects an employee's pay,[7] but also when it occurs in hiring, firing, job assignments, access to training and apprenticeship programs, and most other employment decisions.

Basic Features of Title VII

In discussing Title VII, we first examine some general rules that apply to all the kinds of discrimination it forbids.[8] Then we examine each forbidden basis of discrimination in detail.

Covered Entities   Title VII covers all employers employing 15 or more employees and engaging in an industry affecting interstate commerce. The term *employer* includes individuals, partnerships, corporations, colleges and universities, labor unions (with respect to their own employees), and state and local governments.[9] Also, *referrals* by employment agencies are covered no matter what the size of the agency, if an *employer serviced by the agency* has 15 or more employees. In addition, Title VII covers certain unions—mainly those with 15 or more members—in their capacity as *employee representative*. Among those specifically exempted from Title VII's coverage are religious educational institutions and religious organizations (but only for discrimination based on religion), bona fide tax-exempt private clubs, and Indian tribes.

Procedures   Although the EEOC can sue to enforce Title VII in certain circumstances, the usual Title VII suit is a private action. The complicated procedures that must be followed in private Title VII suits are beyond

the scope of this text, but a few points should be kept in mind. Private parties with a Title VII claim have no automatic right to sue. Instead, they first must file a *charge* with the EEOC, or with a state agency in states having suitable fair employment laws and enforcement schemes. The point of this requirement is to allow the EEOC or the state agency to investigate the claim, attempt conciliation if the claim has substance, or sue the employer itself. If a plaintiff files with a state agency and the state fails to act, the plaintiff can still file a charge with the EEOC. Even if the EEOC fails to act on the claim, a plaintiff may still mount his or her own suit. In such situations, the EEOC issues a "right to sue letter" enabling the plaintiff to file suit.

Proving Discrimination   The permissible methods for *proving* a Title VII violation are critical to its effectiveness against employment discrimination. Proof of discrimination is easy in cases such as the *Johnson Controls* case later in this chapter, where the employer had an *express policy* disfavoring one of Title VII's protected classes. *Direct evidence* of a discriminatory motive such as testimony or written evidence obviously is useful to plaintiffs as well. As the following discussion should indicate, however, employers can discriminate without leaving such obvious tracks. If Title VII were unable to prohibit such behavior, it would be a toothless tiger in the fight against employment discrimination.

The methods for proving a Title VII claim mainly have been devised by the courts, and have undergone some change over time. At this chapter's completion in mid-1991, two methods predominated.

The Disparate Treatment Method   Title VII disparate treatment suits usually involve an individual plaintiff who alleges some specific instance or instances of discriminatory treatment. Such cases generally follow a three-step sequence.

1. First, a plaintiff must show a **prima facie case:** a case strong enough to require a counterargument from the defendant. The proof needed for a prima facie case varies with the type of employment decision at issue. In many *hiring* cases, for instance, it must be shown that: (a) the plaintiff is within one of Title VII's five protected classes; (b) she applied for, and was qualified to perform, a job for which the employer was seeking applicants; (c) she was denied the job; and (d) the employer continued to seek applications from people with the plaintiff's qualifications after the rejection.

---

[7] Thus, suits attacking sex-based pay discrimination can proceed under both the EPA and Title VII. As discussed later in this chapter, the EPA's defenses—but not its equal work requirement—apply in Title VII suits of this kind.

[8] This discussion reflects the state of the law as of mid-1991.

[9] Employment discrimination within the federal government is beyond the scope of this text.

2. Once the plaintiff establishes a prima facie case, the defendant must allege *legitimate, nondiscriminatory reasons* for its treatment of the plaintiff or it will lose the lawsuit. In a hiring case, for example, an employer might allege that it refused to hire the plaintiff because she did not meet its criteria for the position in question.

3. If the defendant alleges satisfactory reasons, it will win unless the plaintiff shows that the reasons are merely a *pretext* for a decision made with a discriminatory purpose. For example, a rejected female job applicant might try to show that the employer's allegedly legitimate, nondiscriminatory criteria were not applied to similarly situated men.

The Adverse Impact Method Title VII's adverse impact (or disparate impact) method of proof most often is used when a group of plaintiffs mount a class action. Its details have been controversial, and some of those details may have changed by the time you read this text. For this reason, we merely outline the method in general terms.

1. First, the plaintiffs must identify the *specific employment practice* of which they complain. Often, this is an employer rule that is neutral on its face but has a disproportionate adverse effect on one of Title VII's protected groups—for example, a height, weight, or high school diploma requirement for hiring, or a written test for hiring or promotion. But other practices qualify as well, including such subjective practices as interviews and qualitative promotion evaluations.

2. The plaintiffs must then show that the practice in question had a *substantial adverse impact* on a group protected by Title VII. For example, blacks alleging racial discrimination might show that a high school diploma requirement for a manufacturing job caused substantially fewer blacks than whites to be hired for that job.

3. If the plaintiffs make the showing just described, the employer must produce evidence that the practice is justified by *business necessity* because it is sufficiently *job-related*. If the employer fails to do so, it will lose the case. In our previous example, this should require the employer to show some significant relationship between its high school diploma requirement and effective job performance.

4. Even if the employer provides satisfactory evidence that the practice is job-related, the plaintiffs still can win if they show that the employer's legitimate business needs can be advanced by *other, less discriminatory* practices. For example, our black plaintiffs might show that the employer's legitimate needs can be met by a test that directly measures the skills needed for the manufacturing job.

Other Methods of Proof In some Title VII cases (usually suits by the government), it is alleged that the employer has engaged in a pervasive *pattern or practice* of discrimination. Here, the plaintiff's proof is usually statistical, but the statistics can be supplemented with specific evidence of discrimination. Of course, a defendant may be able to rebut the plaintiff's evidence in various ways.

Finally, plaintiffs may argue that the employer has adopted a *neutral rule that perpetuates the effects of past discrimination*. For example, suppose a labor union that has long excluded blacks finally abandons this discrimination, but retains a rule that new members must be related to, or recommended by, current members. In such cases, a defendant may try to justify its rule by business necessity and a plaintiff may allege a less discriminatory alternative means in much the fashion described above.

Defenses Even if a plaintiff proves a violation of Title VII, the employer still prevails if it can establish one of Title VII's various defenses. The most important such defenses are:

1. *Seniority*. Title VII is not violated if the employer treats different employees differently pursuant to a *bona fide seniority system*. To be bona fide, such a system at least must treat all employees equally on its face, not have been created for discriminatory reasons, and not operate in a discriminatory fashion.

2. *The various "merit" defenses*. An employer also escapes Title VII liability if it acts pursuant to a *bona fide merit system*, a system basing earnings on *quantity or quality of production*, or the results of a *professionally developed ability test*. Presumably, such systems and tests at least must meet the general standards for seniority systems stated above. Also, the EEOC has promulgated lengthy *Uniform Guidelines on Employee Selection Procedures* that speak to these and other matters.

3. *The BFOQ defense*. Finally, Title VII allows employers to discriminate on the bases of sex, religion, or national origin where one of those traits is a *bona fide occupational qualification* (BFOQ) that is reasonably necessary to the business in question. Note that this BFOQ defense does not protect *race or color* discrimination. As the following *Johnson Controls* case makes clear, moreover, the defense is a narrow one even where it does apply. Generally, it is available only where a certain gender, religion, or national origin is necessary for effective job performance. For example, a BFOQ probably would exist where a female is employed to model women's clothing or to fit women's undergarments, or a French restaurant hires a French chef. But the BFOQ defense usually is unavailable where the discrimination is based on stereotypes (e.g., that women are less aggressive than men) or on the preferences of co-workers or customers (e.g., the preference of airline travelers for female rather than male flight attendants). As *Johnson Controls* also suggests, the defense apparently is unavailable where the employer's discriminatory practice promotes goals, such as fetal protection, that do not concern effective job performance.

AUTO WORKERS v. JOHNSON CONTROLS, INC.

111 S. Ct. 1196 (U.S. Sup. Ct. 1991)

Johnson Controls, Inc. manufactures batteries. Lead is a primary ingredient in that manufacturing process. A female employee's occupational exposure to lead involves a risk of harm to any fetus she carries. For this reason, Johnson Controls excluded women who are pregnant or who are capable of bearing children from jobs that involve exposure to lead. Numerous plaintiffs, including a woman who had chosen to be sterilized to avoid losing her job, entered a federal district court class action alleging that Johnson Controls' policy constituted illegal sex discrimination under Title VII. The district court entered a summary judgment for Johnson Controls and the court of appeals affirmed. The plaintiffs appealed to the U.S. Supreme Court.

Blackmun, Justice. Johnson Controls' fetal-protection policy explicitly discriminates against women on the basis of their sex. The policy excludes women with childbearing capacity from lead-exposed jobs and so creates a facial classification based on gender. [But] an employer may discriminate on the basis of "religion, sex, or national origin in those certain instances where religion, sex, or national origin is a bona fide occupational qualification reasonably necessary to the normal operation of that particular business or enterprise." The BFOQ defense is written narrowly, and this Court has read it narrowly.

Johnson Controls argues that its fetal-protection policy falls within the so-called safety exception [of] the BFOQ. Discrimination on the basis of sex because of safety concerns is allowed only in narrow circumstances. In *Dothard v. Rawlinson* (1977), we allowed the employer to hire only male guards in contact areas of maximum-security male penitentiaries only because more was at stake than the individual woman's decision to weigh and accept the risks of employment. We found sex to be a BFOQ inasmuch as the employment of a female guard would create real risks of safety to others if [rape-related] violence broke out because the guard was a woman. Sex discrimination was tolerated because sex was related to the guard's ability to do the job—maintaining prison security. Similarly, some courts have approved airlines' layoffs of pregnant flight attendants on the ground that the employer's policy was necessary to ensure the safety of passengers. In two of these cases, the courts pointedly indicated that fetal, as opposed to passenger, safety was best left to the mother.

Therefore, the safety exception is limited to instances in which sex or pregnancy actually interferes with the employee's ability to perform the job. . . . [Thus,] Johnson Controls cannot establish a BFOQ. Fertile women, as far as appears in the record, manufacture batteries as efficiently as anyone else. Johnson Controls' professed moral and ethical concerns about the next generation do not suffice to establish a BFOQ of female sterility. Decisions about the welfare of future children must be left to the parents who conceive, bear, support, and raise them rather than to the employers who hire those parents.

Judgment in favor of Johnson Controls reversed; case returned to the lower courts for further proceedings consistent with the Supreme Court's opinion.

White, Justice, Concurring in Part. For the fetal protection policy in this case to be a BFOQ, the policy must be "reasonably necessary" to the "normal operation" of making batteries, which is Johnson Controls' "particular business." Although that is a difficult standard to satisfy, nothing in the statute's language indicates that it could *never* support a sex-specific fetal protection policy.

A fetal protection policy would be justified if, for example, an employer could show that exclusion of women from certain jobs was reasonably necessary to avoid substantial tort liability. It is part of the normal operation of business to avoid causing injury to third parties, if for no other reason than to avoid tort liability. Every state currently allows children born alive to recover in tort for prenatal injuries caused by third parties, and an increasing number of courts have recognized a right to recover even for prenatal injuries caused by torts committed prior to conception.

The Court dismisses the possibility of tort liability by speculating that if Title VII bans sex-specific fetal protection policies, the employer fully informs the woman of the risk, and the employer has not acted negligently, the basis for holding an employer liable seems remote. Such speculation will be small comfort to employers. First, it is far from clear that compliance with Title VII will preempt state tort liability. Second, although warnings may preclude claims by injured *employees*, they will not preclude claims by injured children. Finally, although state tort liability for prenatal injuries generally requires negligence, it will be difficult for employers to determine in advance what will constitute negligence. Compliance with OSHA standards, for example, has been held not to be a defense to state tort liability. Moreover, it is possible that employers will be held strictly liable if, for example, their manufacturing process is considered "abnormally dangerous."

Remedies   Various remedies are possible once private plaintiffs or the EEOC win a Title VII suit. If the discrimination has caused lost wages, employees can obtain back pay accruing from a date two years before the filing of the charge. A successful private plaintiff is also likely to recover attorney's fees. However, consequential damage recoveries for such things as emotional distress or loss of credit are unlikely, and punitive damage recoveries are very unlikely. As this text was completed in mid-1991, however, Congress was considering legislation that would allow some consequential and punitive damage recoveries.

Title VII also gives courts broad powers to fashion equitable remedies tailored to the case. These can include awards of retroactive seniority and orders compelling a plaintiff's hiring or reinstatement. Various affirmative action orders—for example, injunctions compelling the active recruitment of minorities—are also possible. On occasion, moreover, the courts have ordered quotalike minority preferences in Title VII cases.[10] After determining that an employer has engaged in a pattern or practice of hiring discrimination against racial minorities, for example, a court might order that whites and minorities be hired on a 50-50 basis until minority representation in the employer's work force reaches some specified percentage. Generally speaking, such orders are permissible if: (1) an employer has engaged in severe, widespread, or long-standing discrimination; (2) the order does not unduly restrict the employment interests of white people; and (3) it does not force an employer to hire unqualified workers. This is true even where the beneficiaries of the order did not

---

[10] Occasionally, such preferential relief may be ordered in *sex* discrimination cases as well.

themselves suffer discrimination. Minority preferences may also appear in the *consent decrees* courts issue when approving the terms on which the parties have settled a Title VII case. Such decrees sometimes may provide minorities with broader relief than a court could order on its own after finding the defendant liable under Title VII.

Race or Color Discrimination

At this point in our discussion of Title VII, we consider each of its prohibited bases of discrimination in more detail. *Race or color* discrimination includes discrimination against blacks, other racial minorities, and American Indians.

Title VII also prohibits racial discrimination against whites. In *United Steelworkers v. Weber*,[11] however, the Supreme Court upheld a voluntary employment preference that favored minorities. To survive a Title VII attack under *Weber*, such preferences must: (1) be intended to correct a "manifest imbalance" reflecting underrepresentation of minorities in "traditionally segregated job categories," (2) not "unnecessarily trammel" the rights of white employees or create an absolute bar to their advancement, and (3) be only temporary. Unlike the other examples of reverse discrimination discussed previously, *Weber* does not involve the use of minority preferences as a *remedy* for a Title VII violation. Instead, it considers whether such preferences *themselves violate* Title VII when established by an employer on a voluntary basis.

National Origin Discrimination

National origin discrimination is discrimination based on: (1) the country of one's or one's ancestors' origin; or (2) one's possession of physical, cultural, or linguistic characteristics identified with people of a particular nation. Thus, plaintiffs in national origin discrimination cases need not have been born in the country at issue. In fact, if the discrimination is based on physical, cultural, or linguistic traits identified with a particular nation, even the plaintiff's ancestors need not have been born there. Thus, a person of pure French ancestry may have a Title VII case if she suffers discrimination because she looks like, acts like, or talks like a German.

---

[11] *Weber* appears in the chapter entitled the Nature of Law. The version of the case excerpted there, however, does not include the language quoted here.

Certain formally neutral employment practices can also constitute national origin discrimination. Employers who hire only U.S. citizens may violate Title VII if their policy has the purpose or effect of discriminating against one or more national origin groups. This could happen where the employer is located in an area where aliens of a particular nationality are heavily concentrated. Also, employment criteria such as height, weight, and fluency in English may violate Title VII if they have an adverse impact on a national origin group and are not job-related.

Religious Discrimination

For Title VII purposes, the term *religion* is broadly defined. Although not all courts agree, the EEOC's position is that it includes almost any set of moral beliefs that are sincerely held with the same strength as traditional religious views. In fact, Title VII forbids religious discrimination against atheists. It also forbids discrimination based on religious *observances or practices*—for example, grooming, clothing, or the refusal to work on the Sabbath. But such discrimination is permissible if an employer cannot reasonably accommodate the religious practice without undue hardship. Undue hardship exists when the accommodation imposes more than a minimal cost on an employer.

Sex Discrimination

Title VII's ban on sex discrimination was added as a late amendment to the 1964 Civil Rights Act. As a result, there is little legislative history on this provision of Title VII and some disagreement about its scope. Clearly, though, the provision is aimed at *gender* discrimination and does not forbid discrimination on the basis of homosexuality or transsexuality. Just as clearly, Title VII's prohibition of sex discrimination applies to gender-based discrimination against both men and women. Still, certain voluntary employer programs favoring women in hiring or promotion may survive a Title VII attack. To do so, such programs must meet the *Weber* tests for voluntary *racial* preferences that were discussed above. Here, of course, these tests are reformulated to reflect gender rather than race. Finally, a 1978 amendment to Title VII forbids discrimination on the basis of pregnancy or childbirth. This amendment generally requires employers to treat pregnancy like any other condition similarly affecting working ability in their sick leave programs, medical benefit and disability plans, and other fringe benefits.

Although the following *Price Waterhouse* case does not fit neatly within the Title VII proof rules discussed earlier, it demonstrates how another kind of sex discrimination—sexual stereotyping—violates Title VII. The decision also demonstrates the problems created by so-called mixed motive cases. By the time you read the case, however, the causation rules set out below may have been changed by Congress.

PRICE WATERHOUSE v. HOPKINS

Ann Hopkins was a senior manager at Price Waterhouse, a major national accounting partnership. During Hopkins's five years with Price Waterhouse, her intelligence, competence, integrity, and money-making ability were almost universally praised. Nevertheless, when Hopkins was proposed for admission to the partnership in 1982, she was neither granted nor denied admission to the firm. Later, the firm refused to repropose her for partnership, and eventually she resigned.

At the time in question, Price Waterhouse's system for selecting new partners relied heavily on written comments by the firm's existing partners. From the written comments on Hopkins and other evidence, it was clear that two general factors underlay her failure to make partner. The first was her excessive abrasiveness, especially in her relations with the firm's staff. The second was the apparent feeling among some partners that Hopkins behaved in ways that were inappropriate for a woman. For example, one partner described her as "macho," another wrote that she "overcompensated for being a woman," yet another advised that she take "a course at charm school," and still others objected to her use of profanity. Also, a partner who explained to Hopkins why her partnership application was being placed on hold told her that to improve her chances of making partner, she should walk more femininely, dress more femininely, wear makeup, have her hair styled, and wear jewelry.

Hopkins sued Price Waterhouse in federal district court for sex discrimination under Title VII. The district court held for Hopkins, and the court of appeals affirmed. Price Waterhouse appealed to the U.S. Supreme Court.

Brennan, Justice.   In passing Title VII, Congress made the simple yet momentous announcement that sex, race, religion, and national origin are not relevant to the selection, evaluation, or compensation of employees. Yet the statute does not limit the other qualities and characteristics that employers *may* take into account in making employment decisions. Therefore, Title VII eliminates certain bases for distinguishing among employees while otherwise preserving employers' freedom of choice.

The statute forbids an employer to [discriminate in certain ways against an individual] "*because of* such individual's sex." These words mean that gender must be irrelevant to employment decisions. When, therefore, an employer considers both gender and legitimate factors at the time of making a decision, that decision was "because of" sex and the other, legitimate considerations. [In such cases,] an employer shall not be liable if it can prove that, even if it had not taken gender into account, it would have come to the same decision.

An employer who acts on the basis of a belief that a woman cannot be aggressive, or that she must not be, has acted on the basis of gender. A number of the partners' comments showed sex stereotyping at work. We are beyond the day when an employer could evaluate employees by assuming or insisting that they match the stereotype associated with their group. An employer who objects to aggression in women but whose positions require this trait places women in an intolerable and impermissible Catch-22: out of a job if they behave aggressively and out of a job if they don't.

The courts below held that an employer who has allowed a discriminatory impulse to play a motivating part in an employment decision must prove by clear and convincing evidence that it would have made the same decision in the absence of discrimination. The better rule is that the employer must make this showing by a preponderance of the evidence. The lower courts did not determine whether Price Waterhouse had proved by a preponderance of the evidence that it would have placed Hopkins's candidacy on hold even if it had not permitted sex-linked evaluations to play a part in the decision making process. Thus, we remand the case so that determination can be made.

Court of appeals decision for Hopkins reversed and case remanded to that court for further proceedings consistent with the Supreme Court's opinion.

Comparable Worth   The sex discrimination theory known as *comparable worth* asserts that certain jobs largely held by women, such as secretarial and nursing positions, are systematically underpaid relative to their true worth, and should get the same compensation as jobs of comparable real worth. The usual criterion for determining worth is the job's value to the organization or to society, and *not* the value set by labor markets. This value often is determined by studies that give different jobs point ratings under factors resembling the Equal Pay Act criteria, add the ratings together, and compare the totals. Various jobs, for example, might be given a numerical score reflecting the skill, responsibility, effort, and working conditions they involve. The total number of points received would indicate the worth of the position, thus providing a basis for determining which positions are underpaid.

For reasons too numerous to discuss here, comparable worth is a very controversial sex discrimination theory. Thus, it has not made significant inroads under federal employment discrimination law. Comparable worth suits cannot be brought under the Equal Pay Act because of the EPA's *equal* work requirement. In 1981, however, the Supreme Court opened the door to possible comparable worth suits under Title VII by holding that only the EPA's *defenses*, and not its equal work limitation, apply to Title VII cases alleging sex discrimination regarding pay. However, the Court emphasized that it was not deciding whether Title VII embraces comparable worth claims. Since then, it is probably safe to say that comparable worth has not been received with great enthusiasm by the few courts considering its status under Title VII. As noted later in this chapter, however, some states and localities have adopted loosely worded "pay equity" laws that could be regarded as comparable worth provisions.

Sexual Harassment   Unwelcome sexual advances, requests for sexual favors, and other verbal or physical conduct of a sexual nature can violate Title VII under two different theories.[12] The first, called **quid pro quo** sexual harassment, involves some express or implied linkage between an employee's submission to sexually oriented behavior and tangible job consequences. Such cases usually arise when an employee who refuses to submit suffers a tangible job detriment as a result. An easy example is the situation where a male supervisor fires a female secretary because of her refusal to have sexual relations with him or her refusal to submit to other sex-related behavior. Such conduct by a supervisor would violate Title VII whether or not he expressly told the secretary that she would be fired for refusing to submit. Title VII also is violated if a supervisor denies a female subordinate a deserved promotion or other job benefit for refusing to submit. Most courts require that the plaintiff show some *tangible job detriment* of an economic nature in order to recover for quid pro quo sexual harassment. Thus, an employee who rejects a supervisor's advances but suffers no unfavorable job consequences may not have a case.

---

[12] Where they are relevant, the principles stated here also apply to race, color, religious, and national origin harassment. In addition, men can sue for sexual harassment by women. A few courts have allowed recoveries for homosexually oriented sexual harassment. Suits by employees who were denied deserved job benefits because another employee benefited by submitting to sex-related behavior may also be possible.

But no quid pro quo and no tangible job detriment are required when an employee is subjected to **work environment** sexual harassment. This is unwelcome sexual behavior that has the purpose or effect of unreasonably interfering with an individual's work performance or of creating an intimidating, hostile, or offensive work environment. Work environment sexual harassment can be inflicted by both supervisors and co-workers; the following *Gus* case is an example of the latter. Because such behavior must be *unwelcome*, however, an employee may have trouble recovering if she instigated or contributed to the sex-related behavior. Also, the offending behavior must be *severe or pervasive* before an employee can recover under Title VII.

When is an *employer* liable for sexual harassment committed by its employees? In *Meritor Savings Bank v. Vinson* (1986), the Supreme Court said that courts should consult the common law of agency when determining an employer's liability. After *Meritor*, the courts have settled into the following pattern on the question: (1) employers are strictly liable for quid pro quo harassment, and (2) employers are liable for work environment harassment if they knew or should have known of the harassment and failed to take appropriate corrective action. In *Gus*, the court used agency principles of *direct liability* to justify the second standard and to find the employer liable for its employees' work environment sexual harassment.[13]

---

[13] Direct liability and various other agency principles employed by the courts in sexual harassment cases are discussed in the chapter entitled Third Party Relations of the Principal and the Agent. But while *Gus* is an exception, it is doubtful whether many of the courts' employer liability decisions really can be justified under agency law.

HALL v. GUS CONSTRUCTION COMPANY

842 F.2d 1010 (8th Cir. 1988)

Three women were hired as "flag persons" (traffic controllers) by the Gus Construction Company, an Iowa firm engaged in road construction. No other women worked on the construction crew to which they were assigned. Immediately after the women began work, male members of the crew began to inflict various kinds of sex-related abuse on them. For example, male crew members repeatedly asked one of the women if she wanted to have sexual intercourse and oral sex with them. Male crew members also frequently mooned the women. In addition, male crew members sometimes rubbed their hands down the women's thighs and also grabbed one woman's breasts. Furthermore, the men also used surveying equipment to observe the women urinating into a ditch after refusing to give them a truck to take to town for a bathroom break.

Male crew members also subjected the three women to abuse that was not so obviously of a sexual nature. For example, the men named one of the women "Herpes" after she developed a skin reaction from an allergy to the sun. In addition, several men urinated into the gas tank of another woman's car, causing it to malfunction.

One of Gus's foremen observed all or most of these incidents—and many others—but did little to stop their occurrence. The women eventually quit their jobs about seven months after their hiring. Then they sued Gus for sexual harassment under Title VII. A trial before a federal district court magistrate resulted in a judgment for the women, and Gus appealed.

Wollman, Circuit Judge.   Sexual discrimination that creates a hostile or abusive work environment is a violation of Title VII. Unlike quid pro quo sexual harassment, which occurs when submission to sexual conduct is made a condition of concrete employment benefits, hostile work environment harassment arises when sexual conduct has the purpose or effect of unreasonably interfering with an individual's work performance or creating an intimidating, hostile, or offensive working environment.

Gus contends that the district court erred in not distinguishing between conduct of a sexual nature and other forms of harassment. It points to various incidents that it contends were not sexual and should not have been considered. For example, Gus argues that calling one of the women "Herpes" might have been cruel, but was not conduct of a sexual nature. The incident in which the male crew members urinated in the car's gas tank was a practical joke, Gus argues, not conduct of a sexual nature. [But] the acts underlying a sexual harassment claim need not be clearly sexual in nature. Intimidation and hostility toward women because they are women can obviously result from conduct other than explicit sexual advances.

We are convinced that the harassment directed toward each woman was sufficiently severe or pervasive to alter the conditions of her employment and create an abusive working environment. Gus's final challenge to the district court's finding of sexual harassment is that it erred in imposing employer liability. A company will be liable if management-level employees knew or should have known about a barrage of offensive conduct. This principle is sometimes incorrectly described as an application of *respondeat superior*, [which] makes an employer liable only for wrongs of its employees that are committed in furtherance of the employment. The tortfeasing employee must think (however misguidedly) that he is doing the employer's business in committing the wrong. It would be the rare case where harassment against a co-worker could be thought by the author of the harassment to help the employer's business.

But an employer is *directly* liable independently of *respondeat superior* for torts committed against one employee by another that the employer could have prevented by reasonable care in hiring, supervising, or (if necessary) firing the tortfeasor. Consistent with this principle, an employer who has reason to know that one of his employees is being harassed, and does nothing about it, is blameworthy. He is unlikely to know or have reason to know of casual, isolated, and infrequent slurs; it is only when they are egregious, numerous, and concentrated that the employer will be culpable for failing to discover what is going on and to take remedial steps. In this case, the foreman, as the agent of Gus, had actual and constructive notice of the harassment. Even if he did not know everything that went on, the incidents were so numerous that Gus is liable for failing to discover what was going on and to take steps to end it.

District court judgment in favor of the three women affirmed.

OTHER IMPORTANT EMPLOYMENT DISCRIMINATION PROVISIONS

Section 1981

In cases where it applies, a post–Civil War civil rights statute called section 1981 sets employment discrimination standards resembling those of Title VII. Section 1981 has been applied to public and private employment discrimination against blacks, people of certain racially characterized national origins such as Hispanics, and occasionally aliens. In such cases, courts have applied Title VII's methods of proof and its defenses.

Section 1981's coverage currently is unclear. In a controversial 1989 decision denying a racial harassment claim, the Supreme Court limited section 1981 to discrimination regarding the making and enforcement of private contracts—mainly, to discrimination surrounding the hiring process. Some lower courts, however, have tried to circumvent this limitation on the section's scope. This question is important because section 1981 gives plaintiffs certain advantages that Title VII does not provide them. For example, Title VII's limitations on covered employers and its complex procedural requirements do not apply in section 1981 cases, and recoverable damages are apt to be greater under section 1981. For these reasons, Congressional foes of the Supreme Court decision have attempted to pass legislation that effectively would overrule the Court's limitation on section 1981's scope. As of mid-1991, however, such efforts had not succeeded.

The Age Discrimination in Employment Act

The 1967 Age Discrimination in Employment Act (ADEA) prohibits employment-related age discrimination against employees who are *at least 40 years of age*. People within this age group are protected against age discrimination in favor of both younger and older individuals, including favored individuals inside the protected age group.

Coverage   The entities covered by the ADEA include individuals, partnerships, labor organizations (as to their employees), and corporations. Each of these entities must: (1) be engaged in an industry affecting interstate commerce and (2) employ at least 20 persons. In addition, the act applies to state and local governments.[14] Referrals by an employment agency to a covered employer are within the ADEA's scope regardless of the agency's size. Moreover, the ADEA covers labor union practices affecting *union members*; usually, unions with 25 or more members are subject to the act. Like Title VII, the ADEA protects covered individuals against discrimination in a wide range of employment contexts, including hiring, firing, pay, job assignment, and fringe benefits.

In 1986, the ADEA was amended to include certain exemptions from coverage that apply through 1993. The amendment allows state and local governments to discharge or refuse to hire *firefighters* and *law enforcement officers* (including prison guards) due to their age. Also, institutions of higher education may retire *tenured instructors* who have reached the age of 70. In the interim, the EEOC must propose guidelines on the use of physical and mental fitness tests for police officers and firefighters, and must study the consequences of eliminating mandatory retirement in higher education.

Procedural Requirements   The complex procedural requirements for an ADEA suit are beyond the scope of this text. Like Title VII, the ADEA requires that a private plaintiff file a charge with the EEOC or an appropriate state agency (if one exists) before she can sue in her own right. The EEOC also may sue to enforce the ADEA; such a suit precludes private suits arising from the same alleged violation. For both government and private suits, the statute of limitations is three years

---

[14]Age discrimination in the federal government is beyond the scope of this text.

from the date of an alleged *willful* violation and two years from the date of an alleged *nonwillful* violation.

Proving Age Discrimination   Proof of age discrimination is no problem where an employer uses an explicit age classification, and may be easy where there is direct evidence of discrimination such as testimony or incriminating documents. Most ADEA cases, however, are brought under the Title VII disparate treatment theory discussed earlier. In addition, a few courts have used Title VII's adverse impact theory in ADEA cases.

Defenses   The ADEA allows employers to discharge or otherwise penalize an employee for *good cause*, and to use *reasonable factors other than age* in their employment decisions. It also allows employers to observe the terms of a *bona fide seniority system*, except where such a system is used to require or permit the involuntary retirement of anyone 40 or over.

In addition, the ADEA has a *bona fide occupational qualification* defense. In general, an employer seeking to use this defense must show that its age classification is reasonably necessary to the proper performance of the job in question. In most cases raising this defense, the employer argues that age is reasonably necessary to safe performance of the job. To succeed, the employer must show *either:* (1) that it had reasonable grounds for believing that all or substantially all employees of a certain age cannot perform the job safely, or (2) that it is impossible or highly impractical to test employees on an individualized basis. For example, an employer that refuses to hire anyone over 60 as a helicopter pilot should have a BFOQ defense if it somehow shows a reasonable basis for concluding that 60-and-over helicopter pilots pose significant safety risks, or that it is not feasible to test older pilots individually. Usually, however, courts construe the ADEA's BFOQ defense narrowly.

Remedies   Remedies available after a successful ADEA suit include unpaid back wages and other benefits resulting from the discrimination; an additional equal award of liquidated damages where the employer acted willfully; attorney's fees; and equitable relief, including hiring, reinstatement, and promotion. Most courts do not allow punitive damages and recoveries for pain, suffering, mental distress, and so forth.

The following *Guthrie* case shows the disparate impact theory at work in a suit involving an age-based firing.

GUTHRIE v. J. C. PENNEY CO.

803 F.2d 202 (5th Cir. 1986)

William Guthrie began managing a J. C. Penney Company store in Meridian, Mississippi in 1973. At that time, J. C. Penney had a written policy that all store managers retire at age 60, but Penney later sent its employees a letter announcing a change in this policy to comply with the ADEA. In the spring of 1979, just before Guthrie's 60th birthday, various Penney employees made a series of inquiries about his retirement plans—some of which amounted to not-so-subtle hints that he ought to resign. From 1979 through 1981, however, Guthrie remained as manager of the Meridian store. During this period, he received satisfactory performance ratings and annual merit pay increases, and the store did well in sales and profits. Early in 1982, though, a Penney reorganization placed Guthrie under a new district manager, James Moore. In February of that year, Moore visited the store and reprimanded Guthrie before store employees over a relatively minor matter. During a June 1982 visit to the store, Moore again criticized Guthrie before store employees, and overrode Guthrie's decisions on a number of matters normally reserved to the store manager. After the visit, Moore lowered Guthrie's performance rating and assigned him a number of difficult future performance objectives.

Feeling that his discharge was inevitable, Guthrie resigned in August of 1982. Even though the store's sales and profits declined under the younger manager who succeeded him, this manager received satisfactory performance ratings and was allowed to run the store without interference. Later, Guthrie sued J. C. Penney in federal district court under the ADEA. After a jury found that Penney had constructively discharged Guthrie in violation of the act, Penney appealed.

Johnson, Circuit Judge.   When a plaintiff in an ADEA case cannot present direct evidence of discrimination, the courts have developed a three-part test modeled on the one used by Title VII plaintiffs. First, the plaintiff must make a prima facie case by proving that he was in the age group protected by the act, he was qualified for the position, he was discharged, and he was replaced by a younger employee. In the second stage, the burden shifts to the employer to produce evidence that dismissal was due to a business reason other than age. At the third stage, the plaintiff can prevail by showing that the articulated reason was a pretext. Penney attacks the sufficiency of the evidence supporting the jury's verdict at two points: constructive discharge and the pretextual nature of Penney's business reasons. The court will not overturn the jury verdict unless it is not supported by substantial evidence.

An employee can prove constructive discharge by showing that his employer created conditions so intolerable that a reasonable person in the employee's shoes would have felt compelled to resign. The jury had substantial evidence to find [Guthrie's decision] reasonable.

Secondly, Penney asserts that it acted as it did for business reasons, and that Guthrie did not prove these reasons to be pretextual. Specifically, Penney says that its repeated inquiries about Guthrie's retirement plans were due to the need to anticipate staff vacancies; that Moore's decision to criticize and downgrade Guthrie formed part of a general "get tough" attitude on his part; and that it had the right to assign little weight to the sales and profit performance of Guthrie's store. Penney is correct that the ADEA is not a license to second-guess legitimate business judgments. Thus, the courts would not interfere if Penney in fact decided to ignore sales and profit performance in evaluating store managers. However, the question is what Penney's motive actually was, not what it could have been. In reaching this determination, the jury is entitled to weigh the credibility of witnesses and to disbelieve self-serving testimony.

In this case, the jury could have believed that Penney's repeated inquiries [about Guthrie's retirement plans] constituted intentional harassment. Moreover, the jury heard considerable evidence tending to show that Moore singled out Guthrie for criticism and applied tougher standards to him than to his younger colleagues. For example, Guthrie's younger successor experienced the same problems and received a [higher] rating. While Penney may choose to downplay sales and profit performance in evaluating a manager, its own company manual lists them as key factors.

In sum, the jury heard substantial evidence from which to conclude that Guthrie met his burden of showing that he was constructively discharged and that Penney's stated reasons for doing so were pretextual.

Judgment for Guthrie affirmed so far as ADEA liability is concerned.

The Americans with Disabilities Act

Until recently, federal regulation of employment discrimination against handicapped people mainly was limited to certain federal contractors and recipients of federal financial assistance. By passing Title I of the Americans with Disabilities Act of 1990 (ADA), however, Congress addressed this problem comprehensively. This portion of the ADA becomes effective during the summer of 1992. It is primarily enforced by the EEOC, and its procedures and remedies are the same as for Title VII.

Covered Entities For two years following its effective date, Title I of the ADA covers employers who have 25 or more employees and who are engaged in an industry affecting interstate commerce. After that, the limit is 15 or more employees. The term *employer* includes individuals, partnerships, corporations, colleges and universities, labor unions (regarding their own employees), and state and local governments. Not included, however, are the U.S. government and its wholly owned corporations, Indian tribes, and certain tax-exempt private clubs. The act also covers certain labor unions in their capacity as employee representative, as well as employment agencies' treatment of their clients.

Substantive Protections The ADA forbids covered entities from discriminating against *qualified individuals with a disability* because of that disability. It covers discrimination regarding hiring, firing, promotion, pay, and innumerable other employment decisions. The act defines a *disability* as: (1) a physical or mental impairment that substantially limits one or more of an individual's major life activities, (2) a record of such an impairment, or (3) one's being regarded as having such an impairment. (The last two categories protect, among others, those who have previously been misdiagnosed or who have recovered from earlier impairments.) Not protected, however, are those who are discriminated against for currently engaging in the illegal use of drugs. Also, employers may prohibit workplace alcohol use, require that employees not be under the influence of alcohol at the workplace, and hold alcoholics to the same standards as other employees. Furthermore, homosexuality, bisexuality, transvestism, and various other sex-related traits or conditions are not considered disabilities.

A *qualified individual* with a disability is a person who can perform the essential functions of the relevant job either *without or without reasonable accommodation*. Thus, the ADA protects both individuals who can perform their jobs despite their handicap, and handicapped individuals who could perform their jobs if reasonable accommodation is provided. *Reasonable accommodation* includes acts such as making existing facilities readily accessible and usable, acquiring new equipment, restructuring jobs, modifying work schedules, and making reassignments to vacant positions, among others. But employers need not make reasonable accommodation—and thus can discriminate against people whose impairments prevent them from properly performing their jobs—where doing so would cause them to suffer *undue hardship*. The act defines undue hardship as significant difficulty or expense, and lists various factors by which it should be determined. These factors include the cost of the accommodation, the covered entity's overall financial resources, and the accommodation's effect on the covered entity's activities.

Defenses The ADA protects employers whose allegedly discriminatory decisions are based on *job-related criteria and business necessity*, so long as proper job performance cannot be accomplished by reasonable accommodation. This includes situations where the affected individual poses a direct threat to the health or safety of other workers that cannot be eliminated through a reasonable accommodation. Also, employers can refuse to employ as food handlers those with diseases that have been determined by the secretary of health and human services to be transmitted by the handling of food, unless reasonable accommodation can be made.

Executive Order 11246

Executive Order 11246, issued in 1965 and later amended, forbids race, color, national origin, religion, and sex discrimination by certain federal contractors. The order is enforced by the Office of Federal Contract Compliance Programs (OFCCP) of the Labor Department. Under the order and its accompanying OFCCP regulations, each federal agency must insert an "equal opportunity clause" in most of its private-sector contracts for $10,000 or more. Among other things, this clause requires that the contractor not discriminate on the grounds mentioned above and that it undertake affirmative action to prevent such discrimination.

State Antidiscrimination Laws

Most of the states have statutes that parallel Title VII and the ADEA. Many have laws protecting the handicapped. Some of these statutes provide more extensive protection than their federal counterparts. In addition, some states prohibit forms of discrimination not barred by federal law. Examples include discrimination on the bases of marital status, physical appearance, sexual orientation, and political affiliation. Also, many states prohibit discrimination against AIDS victims or people who carry the AIDS virus. Finally, some states and localities have adopted "pay equity" laws that could be read as comparable worth provisions. Many of these laws apply only to public employment.

CONCEPT REVIEW

THE EMPLOYMENT DISCRIMINATION LAWS COMPARED

	Protected Traits	Covered Employer Decisions	Need to File Charge in Private Suit?
Equal Pay Act	Sex only	Pay only	No
Title VII	Race, color, national origin, religion, sex	Wide range	Yes
Section 1981	Race, racially characterized national origin, perhaps alienage	Currently unclear	No
Age Discrimination in Employment Act	Age, if victim 40 or over	Wide range	Yes
Americans with Disabilities Act	Existence of disability, if person qualified to perform job with or without reasonable accommodation	Wide range	Yes
Executive Order 11246	Race, color, religion, national origin, sex	Wide range	Not applicable; enforced by OFCCP

EMPLOYEE PRIVACY

Modern technology has given employers various means for monitoring their employees' reliability and work performance. While doing so, however, employers may violate those employees' sense of selfhood or their personal dignity. Also, an employer's compilation of information regarding an employee may be used in ways that harm her. The term *employee privacy* is often used to describe both this group of personal interests and the legal issues their violation can present. Here, we outline the most important problems that have arisen in this recently emergent and swiftly developing area.

Polygraph Testing

During the 1970s and 1980s, employers made increasing use of polygraph and other lie detector tests—most often, to screen job applicants and to investigate employee thefts. This led to greater concern about the accuracy of such tests; the personal questions sometimes asked by examiners; and the tests' resulting impact on job prospects, job security, and personal privacy. Such worries have led many states to require that people administrating lie detector tests be licensed, to wholly or partially ban those tests in employment, or to restrict the dissemination of their results. In 1988, Congress significantly limited employers' use of lie detector tests by passing the Employee Polygraph Protection Act.

The Employee Polygraph Protection Act mainly regulates lie detector tests, which include polygraph tests and certain other specific mechanical and electrical devices for assessing a person's honesty. Most of its prohibitions apply to employers engaged in, producing goods for, or affecting interstate commerce. Such employers may not: (1) require, suggest, request, or cause employees or prospective employees to take any lie detector test; (2) use, accept, refer to, or inquire about the results of any lie detector test administered to employees or prospective employees; and (3) take or threaten to take almost any unfavorable employment-related action against employees or prospective employees because of the results of any lie detector test, or because such parties failed or refused to take such a test.

However, certain employers and tests are exempt from these provisions. They include: (1) federal, state, and local government employers; (2) certain national defense and security-related tests by the federal government; (3) certain tests by security service firms whose business involves the public health and safety; and (4) certain tests by firms manufacturing and distributing controlled substances. The act also contains a limited exemption for private employers that use polygraph tests when investigating economic losses caused by theft, embezzlement, industrial espionage, and so forth. Finally, the act restricts the disclosure of test results by examiners and by most employers.

The Polygraph Protection Act is enforced by the Labor Department, which has issued regulations in furtherance of that mission. It does not preempt state laws that prohibit lie detector tests or that set standards stricter than those imposed by federal law. Violations of the act or its regulations can result in civil penalties, suits for equitable relief by the Labor Department, and private suits for damages and equitable relief. Under these provisions, workers and job applicants can obtain employment, reinstatement, promotion, and payment of lost wages and benefits.

Drug and Alcohol Testing

Due to their impact on employees' safe and effective job performance, employers have become increasingly concerned about both on-the-job and off-the-job drug and alcohol use. Thus, employers increasingly require employees and job applicants to undergo urine tests for drugs and/or alcohol. Because those who test positive may be either disciplined or induced to undergo treatment, and because the tests themselves can raise privacy concerns, some legal checks on their use have emerged.

Drug and alcohol testing by *public* employers can be attacked under the Fourth Amendment's search-and-seizure provisions. However, such tests generally are constitutional where there is a reasonable basis for suspecting that an employee is illegally using drugs or alcohol, or such use in a particular job could threaten the public interest or public safety. In 1989, for example, the Supreme Court upheld an internal Customs Service drug-testing program requiring urinalysis before employees can be transferred or promoted to jobs involving matters such as drug interdiction and the carrying of firearms.

Due to the government action requirement discussed in the Business and the Constitution chapter, employees generally have no federal constitutional protection against drug and alcohol testing by *private* employers. Some *state* constitutions, however, lack a government action requirement. In addition, a number of states now regulate private drug and/or alcohol testing by statute. Moreover, such testing sometimes is challenged by unionized employees under their collective bargaining agreements. Finally, tort suits for invasion of privacy or infliction of emotional distress may be possible in some cases.[15]

Despite these protections, however, federal law *requires* private-sector drug testing in certain situations. Under a 1988 Defense Department rule, for example, employers who contract with the department must agree to establish a drug-testing program under which employees who work in sensitive positions sometimes may be tested. Also, 1988 Transportation Department regulations require random testing of public and private employees occupying safety-sensitive or security-related positions in industries such as aviation, trucking, railroads, mass transit, and others. Other regulations of this kind may follow.[16] Such rules could be challenged on constitutional grounds. In 1989, however, the Supreme Court upheld a Federal Railroad Administration program mandating drug and urine tests for railroad employees involved in major train accidents.

Employer Searches

Employers concerned about thefts, drug use, and other misbehavior by their employees sometimes conduct searches of those employees' offices, desks, lockers, files, briefcases, packages, vehicles, and even bodies in an effort to confirm their suspicions. In 1987, the Supreme Court held that public employees sometimes may have a reasonable expectation of privacy in areas such as their offices, desks, or files. But it also held that searches of those areas are constitutional under the Fourth Amendment when they are reasonable under the circumstances. In the process, the Court said that neither probable cause nor a warrant is necessary for such searches to proceed.

As noted above, the U.S. Constitution ordinarily does not apply to private employment. Nonetheless, both private and public employees can mount common law invasion of privacy suits against employers who conduct searches. In such cases, courts usually weigh the intrusiveness of the search against the purposes justifying it, and consider the availability of less intrusive alternatives

that still would satisfy the employer's legitimate needs. Such suits tend not to succeed where there is some reasonable justification for the search and it was no more intrusive than necessary under the circumstances.

Employer Monitoring

Although employers always have monitored their employees' work, recent technological advances enable such monitoring to occur without those employees' knowledge. Examples include closed-circuit television, telephone monitoring, the monitoring of computer workstations (e.g., by counting keystrokes), and metal detectors at plant entrances. Such monitoring has encountered objections because employees are often unaware that it exists, or may suffer stress when they do know or suspect its existence. Employers counter these objections by stressing that monitoring is highly useful in evaluating employee performance, improving efficiency, and reducing theft.

Telephone monitoring may be illegal under federal wiretapping law, but the relevant provision has many exceptions. Although such claims have been uncommon, invasion of privacy suits may succeed in situations where an employer's need for surveillance is slight and it is conducted in areas such as restrooms and lounges in which employees have a reasonable expectation of privacy. Despite various state and federal bills proposing legislation regulating various forms of monitoring, very few such laws had been passed as of mid-1991.

Records and References

Many states allow both public and private employees access to personnel files maintained by their employers, although some limit the types of documents that can be examined. Also, some states limit third-party access to such records. In addition, employers who transmit such data to third parties may be civilly liable for defamation or invasion of privacy.[17] However, truth is a defense in defamation cases, and in both defamation and invasion of privacy suits the employer's actions may be privileged. These defenses often protect employers who are sued for truthful, good faith statements made in references for former employees.

---

[15]Invasion of privacy and intentional infliction of emotional distress are discussed in the Intentional Torts chapter, and negligent infliction of emotional distress is discussed in the Negligence and Strict Liability chapter.

[16]However, one recent antidrug measure, the Drug-Free Workplace Act of 1988, does not require testing.

---

[17]Defamation and invasion of privacy are discussed in the Intentional Torts chapter, which examines defamation suits against employers by their ex-employees in greater detail than does this chapter.

THE EROSION OF EMPLOYMENT AT WILL

As discussed earlier in this chapter, the traditional employment-at-will doctrine allows either party to an employment contract for an indefinite term to terminate the contract at any time and for any reason. Helping to explain the doctrine's emergence were the individualism of 19th-century society and 19th-century contract law and its tendency to promote economic efficiency by allowing employers to terminate unneeded employees. Although employment at will remains important, it has been eroded by many of the developments described in this chapter. For example, the NLRA forbids dismissal for union affiliation, and labor contracts frequently bar termination without just cause. Also, Title VII prohibits terminations based on certain personal traits, the ADEA blocks firings on the basis of age, and the ADA forbids discharges for covered personal disabilities.

The Common Law Exceptions

In recent years, courts have been carving out further exceptions to employment at will. The three most important such exceptions are discussed immediately below. Although a few courts have flatly refused to do so, most states recognize one or more of these exceptions. In such states, a terminated employee can sue her employer for **unjust dismissal** or **wrongful discharge.** The remedies in successful unjust dismissal cases vary, and depend heavily on whether the plaintiff's claim is regarded as sounding in contract or in tort. Tort remedies, of course, usually are more advantageous for plaintiffs.

The Public Policy Exception   The *public policy* exception to the employment-at-will doctrine, which has been recognized by over three-fourths of the states, is the most common basis for a wrongful discharge suit. It is usually regarded as a tort claim. In such cases, the terminated employee argues that his discharge was unlawful because it violated public policy. Many courts limit "public policy" to the policies furthered by *existing laws* such as constitutional provisions and statutes—and perhaps administrative regulations and common law rules as well. In such states, the ex-employee must show that his termination violated public policy because he was fired for acts, or refusals to act, which were in harmony with the policies expressed in existing legal rules. For example, an employee who is fired for filing a workers' compensation claim normally recovers against her employer, because the act that provoked the firing (filing the claim) obviously is consistent with the policies furthered by the state's workers' compensation statute.

Other examples of successful public policy exception claims include firings based on employees' performing jury duty, refusing to participate in illegal price-fixing, refusing to commit perjury at a state hearing, whistle-blowing,[18] refusing to date a foreman, insisting that the employer comply with state law, and refusing to take a polygraph test where such tests were forbidden by state law. Situations where the exception was *not* recognized include discharges caused by an employee's objection to the marketing of an allegedly defective product, and by an employee's refusal to work on drug research that she felt to be medically unethical. In the following *Foley* case, the court refused to decide whether public policy should be based only on constitutional or statutory provisions, and decided for the employer because the policy it allegedly violated was not *public.*

The Implied Covenant of Good Faith and Fair Dealing   A wrongful discharge suit based on the *implied covenant of good faith and fair dealing* usually is a contract claim. Here, the employee argues that her discharge was unlawful because it was not made in good faith or did not amount to fair dealing, thus violating the implied contract term. Only about 20 percent of the states have recognized this exception to employment at will, and some of these give it a narrow scope. The apparent reasons are this theory's open-ended nature and its resulting potential for restricting business freedom.

The Implied-in-Fact Contract Exception   Courts sometimes imply additional terms in contracts. One example involves *implied-in-fact* contract terms, which often arise from statements or conduct by the parties at or after the formation of their contract. As *Foley* relates, implied-in-fact contract terms giving employees additional job security come from many sources. By far the most common of these, however, are oral statements made by employers during hiring or employee orientation, or written statements in company employee manuals and handbooks. If such sources expressly state the reasons for which employees will be fired or the procedures accompanying employee terminations and if an employer fails to follow those express promises, it may be liable for breach of contract. As *Foley* suggests, such liability also may stem from other employer behavior in

---

[18] Whistle blowers are employees who publicly disclose dangerous, illegal, or improper employer behavior. A few states have passed statutes protecting the employment rights of certain whistle blowers.

addition to its express promises. At least two-thirds of the states recognize the implied-in-fact contract exception to employment at will.

Recent Developments

Due to the increasing number and size of plaintiffs' recoveries, courts and other lawmakers apparently are having second thoughts about employer liability for wrongful discharge. The *Foley* case is a possible example. In addition, a few courts have enforced express disclaimers of wrongful discharge liability in employment contracts. Others have held that where the cause of the unjust dismissal is employment discrimination or some other wrong dealt with by existing regulations, the case should be decided under those regulations and not under the law of wrongful discharge. Still other emergent or proposed moves to reduce employers' legal exposure include arbitration and limitations on damages. As of mid-1991, work on a uniform employment termination act was underway, and at least one state already had comprehensively regulated and limited unjust dismissal claims by statute.

As our previous discussion suggests, the following *Foley* case involves all three exceptions to the employment-at-will doctrine.

FOLEY v. INTERACTIVE DATA CORPORATION
254 Cal. Rptr. 211 (Cal. Sup. Ct. 1988)

Daniel Foley was hired by the Interactive Data Corporation in 1976. His employment contract did not expressly state the time period of his employment, and also did not expressly limit Interactive Data's ability to fire him. Over the next six years and nine months, Foley received a steady series of salary increases, promotions, bonuses, awards, and superior performance evaluations. During this period, Foley claimed, Interactive Data's officers gave him repeated assurances of job security so long as his work performance remained adequate. Over this time, moreover, the firm maintained written "Termination Guidelines" that set forth express grounds for discharge and a mandatory seven-step pretermination procedure.

In 1982, Interactive Data hired Robert Kuhne, who was ultimately intended to replace Richard Earnest as Foley's immediate supervisor. After learning that Kuhne was under FBI investigation for embezzling funds from his former employer, Foley reported this to Earnest early in 1983, while Earnest was still his supervisor. Approximately two months later, Foley was fired.

Alleging that the firing was due to his statements about Kuhne (who eventually pleaded guilty to embezzlement), Foley sued Interactive Data for wrongful discharge in a California trial court. He had three claims: (1) a tort claim alleging a discharge in violation of public policy, (2) a contract claim for breach of an implied-in-fact promise to discharge only for good cause, and (3) a claim for tortious breach of the implied covenant of good faith and fair dealing. The trial court granted Interactive Data's motion to dismiss each claim, and an intermediate appellate court affirmed. Foley appealed to the California Supreme Court.

Lucas, Chief Justice.   *Public Policy.* The employer's right to discharge an at-will employee is subject to limits imposed by public policy. We do not decide in this case whether a tort action alleging a breach of public policy may be based only on policies derived from a statute or constitutional provision, or whether nonlegislative sources may provide the basis for such a claim. Even where a statutory touchstone has been asserted, we must still inquire whether the discharge is against public policy and affects a duty which inures to the benefit of the *public at large* rather than to a particular employer or employee.

Foley alleges that Interactive Data discharged him in derogation of a public policy that imposes a legal duty on employees to report relevant business information to management. An employee is an agent, and [under common law agency rules] is required to disclose to his principal all information relevant to the subject matter of the agency. It is unclear whether the alleged duty [also] is one founded in statute. Whether or not there is a statutory duty, we do not find a substantial public policy prohibiting an employer from discharging an employee for performing that duty. Past decisions recognizing a tort action for discharge in violation of public policy seek to protect the public—by protecting the employee who refuses to commit a crime; who reports criminal activity to proper authorities; or who discloses other illegal, unethical, or unsafe practices. No equivalent *public* interest bars the discharge of Foley.

Breach of Employment Contract. Foley's second cause of action alleged that over the course of his employment, the company's own conduct and personnel policies gave rise to [a contract] not to fire him without good cause. He alleges that a course of conduct, including various oral representations, created a reasonable expectation to that effect. His cause of action is properly described as one for breach of an implied-in-fact contract. [The presumption of at-will employment] may be overcome by evidence that the parties agreed that the employer's power to terminate would be limited in some way. Courts seek to enforce the actual understanding of the parties to a contract, and in so doing may inquire into the parties' conduct to determine if it demonstrates an implied contract.

In the employment context, factors used to ascertain the existence and content of an [implied] agreement include the personnel policies or practices of the employer, the employee's longevity of service, [and] actions or communications by the employer reflecting assurances of continued employment. Six years and nine months is sufficient time for an implied contract. Foley alleged repeated assurances of job security and consistent promotions, salary increases, and bonuses—contributing to his reasonable expectation that he would not be discharged except for good cause. Breach of the written "Termination Guidelines" [also] may be sufficient for breach of an employment contract. The trier of fact can infer an agreement to limit the grounds for termination based on the employee's reasonable reliance on the company's personnel manual or policies. In sum, Foley has pleaded facts which, if proved, may be sufficient for a jury to find an implied-in-fact contract limiting Interactive Data's right to discharge him arbitrarily.

Implied Covenant of Good Faith and Fair Dealing. Foley asserts that we should recognize *tort* remedies for breach [of the implied covenant of good faith and fair dealing] in the employment context. Every contract imposes upon each party a duty of good faith and fair dealing in its performance and its enforcement. The courts employ the good faith doctrine to effectuate the intentions of parties, or to protect their reasonable expectations. The covenant is read into contracts in order to protect the express promises of the contract, not to protect some general public policy not directly tied to the contract's purposes.

Several factors combine to persuade us that contractual remedies should remain the sole available relief for breaches of the implied covenant of good faith and fair dealing in the employment context. It is important that employers not be unduly deprived of discretion to dismiss an employee by the fear that doing so will give rise to potential tort liability in every case. Moreover, it would be difficult to formulate a rule that would assure that only "deserving" cases give rise to tort relief. In a tort action based on an employee's discharge, it is likely that each case would involve a dispute as to the subjective intentions of the employer [his bad faith]. Finally, the expansion of tort remedies in the employment context has potentially enormous consequences for the stability of the business community.

Dismissal of Foley's public policy claim and his claim for tortious breach of the implied covenant of good faith and fair dealing affirmed; dismissal of Foley's implied-in-fact contract claim reversed. Case returned to the lower courts for action consistent with the Supreme Court's opinion.

ETHICAL AND PUBLIC POLICY CONCERNS

1. Over the past 150 years, a moral theory known as *utilitarianism* has been very influential. Although it comes in many forms, utilitarianism basically asserts that the test for determining the rightness or wrongness of actions (including laws) is their ability to produce the greatest net balance of satisfactions over dissatisfactions throughout society as a whole. Give a utilitarian justification for the *traditional* employment-at-will rule described at the beginning of this chapter. You can assume that economic well-being counts as a "satisfaction" for utilitarian purposes. You can also assume that the people fired under the traditional employment-at-will rule suffer from their firing.

2. Suppose someone argues that almost all the 20th-century employment law rules discussed in this chapter demonstrate how this country has abandoned the traditional principles that made it great. In particular, this person asserts, these rules show that America has abandoned the idea that people are—and should be—rugged, self-reliant *individuals* who are capable of making their own contracts in free and equal labor markets. Instead, he continues, Americans have become pathetic weaklings who need government protection throughout the employment relationship. Based on the materials presented in this chapter, what is wrong with this argument? In answering, assume that ruggedness, self-reliance, and so forth are morally desirable traits.

3. The *comparable worth* theory discussed in the chapter is very controversial. Consider the following questions about, and criticisms of, comparable worth.

   a. What are the most likely causes of the wage disparities that comparable worth plans would rectify? Do these disparities really result from *discrimination* in any meaningful sense of the word?

   b. Are the methods for determining the inherent worth of jobs really "objective" and "scientific," or do they necessarily depend on subjective factors?

   c. What would be the likely economic consequences if comparable worth were widely adopted throughout American society?

   d. Which women would and would not benefit if comparable worth were widely adopted?

SUMMARY

Nineteenth-century employment law was heavily influenced by the individualistic principles of that century's contract law, and it usually favored the stronger party—the employer—as a result. In the 20th century, employer power probably has increased, and the employment relationship is even more important to employees. Perhaps for these reasons, employment law has become far more protective of employees. In fact, modern employment law can be seen as a series of exceptions to the contract-based 19th-century model of the employment relation.

Legal protection against on-the-job injuries is a major concern of modern employment law. Thus, state *workers' compensation* systems provide injured employees with a strict liability recovery for work-related injuries. In such cases, the employer's traditional defenses of assumption of risk, contributory negligence, and the fellow-servant rule do not apply; but an injured employee's recovery often is less than would have been obtained in a successful negligence suit. The law also seeks to protect workers through direct regulation of workplace safety. The most important example is the federal *Occupational Safety and Health Act*.

Modern employment law also seeks to maintain the income of those who involuntarily lose their jobs through no fault of their own or who retire. State *unemployment compensation* systems protect the former group for limited time periods. The *Federal Insurance Contributions Act* finances a system of old-age, survivors, disability, and medical and hospital insurance. The *Employee Retirement Income Security Act* protects individuals from abuses in the operation of private pension plans.

Today, the law also protects employees by regulating the terms and conditions of their employment. By recognizing the right of employees to bargain collectively through unions, *federal labor law* has powerfully (if indirectly) affected the terms and conditions of employment. Federal labor law also protects employees by prohibiting certain unfair labor practices by both employers and unions. The *Fair Labor Standards Act* regulates wages and hours worked, and also forbids certain kinds of child labor.

Perhaps the best-known and most discussed aspect of employment law today is its protection against employment discrimination. The *Equal Pay Act* prohibits sex discrimination with respect to pay. *Title VII* of the 1964 Civil Rights Act, the single most important employment discrimination provision, forbids such discrimination on the bases of race, color, national origin, sex, and religion. *Section 1981*, a post–Civil War antidiscrimination measure, affords some protection against discrimination based on an employee's ancestry or ethnic characteristics. The *Age Discrimination in Employment Act* protects those aged 40 or over against employer age discrimination. The new *Americans with Disabilities Act* protects qualified individuals with a disability against discrimination based on their disability. Under *Executive Order 11246*, certain federal contractors are forbidden from discriminating on the bases of race, national origin, religion, and sex; and may be required to undertake affirmative action to prevent such discrimination. Finally, the states usually prohibit these and other forms of employment discrimination.

In recent years, the law has begun to protect *employee privacy* in a variety of different contexts. These include lie detector tests, drug and alcohol testing, searches of the employee's work area, electronic surveillance of employees, and misuse of information about employees and ex-employees. In this emerging and rapidly changing area of legal concern, employees may be able to utilize constitutional search-and-seizure protections, state statutes, and civil suits for defamation or invasion of privacy, depending on the circumstances.

For about a century, the doctrine of *employment at will* has been a centerpiece of American employment law. The doctrine states that either party to an employment contract for an indefinite term can terminate the contract at any time for any reason. The doctrine has been eroded by many of the legal rules described in this chapter. In recent years, courts have further eroded the doctrine by recognizing employee suits for *unjust dismissal* or *wrongful discharge*. They have done so under three theories: (1) that the dismissal is wrongful because it violates public policy (usually, a policy expressed in existing law), (2) that the dismissal is wrongful because it violates an implied term of good faith and fair dealing that courts read into the employment contract, or (3) that the dismissal violates implied-in-fact terms of the employment contract.

PROBLEM CASES

1. Beverly Waters worked as a customer service representative for an insurance agency. Although she occasionally filled in for one of the agency's sales agents, her duties were not the same as those of the firm's male agents. She also was paid less than those male agents. For this reason, she sued her employer under the Equal Pay Act. The employer argued that Waters had no EPA claim because her job was different from the male agents' jobs. However, Waters asserted that the reason for this unequal work was that her employer had discriminated against her on the basis of her gender by not allowing her to work as an agent even though she was qualified for the job. Thus, she argued, her Equal Pay Act claim should succeed. Does the *Grove* case in the text contain any language supporting Waters's argument? If Waters's argument fails under the Equal Pay Act, under what other law could she pursue such a claim, and why?

2. For a long time, T.I.M.E.–D.C., a nationwide trucking concern, and the International Brotherhood of Teamsters had discriminated against blacks and other racial minorities regarding access to the firm's intercity, over-the-road driver positions. Such positions were in a different union bargaining unit than the city driver and service jobs in which blacks and minorities had been concentrated. After the passage of Title VII in 1964, the company significantly reduced this sort of discrimination, but it retained a seniority system that based the ability to get choice jobs and to avoid layoffs on length of service in a particular bargaining unit. This meant that minorities who now could move up to intercity driver positions would have to forfeit all the seniority that they had earned in their previous bargaining unit. This tended to deter minorities from taking such positions. What method of proving a Title VII violation could black or minority plaintiffs use in this case? What defense might the company and the union have?

3. Dianne Rawlinson, a rejected female applicant for employment as a prison guard in the Alabama prison system, challenged certain state rules restricting her employment prospects under Title VII. They were: (1) requirements that all prison employees be at least 5 feet 2 inches tall and weigh at least 120 pounds, and (2) a rule expressly prohibiting women from assuming close-contact prison guard positions in maximum-security prisons (most of which were all male). What method of proving a Title VII case should Rawlinson use in attacking the height and weight requirements? Does she need to use one of these methods to attack the second rule? What argument should the state use if Rawlinson establishes a prima facie case against the height and weight requirements? What Title VII defense might the state have for the second rule? With regard to the second rule, assume that at this time Alabama's maximum security prisons housed their male prisoners dormitory-style rather than putting them in cells, and that they did not separate sex offenders from other prisoners.

4. Farah Manufacturing Company had a long-standing policy against employing aliens. Cecilia Espinoza, a lawfully admitted alien married to an American citizen, applied for employment as a seamstress at Farah. She was rejected, and sued Farah for discrimination on the basis of national origin in violation of Title VII. Did Farah's decision violate Title VII? Assume that Espinoza's suit is based on the policy just described and that she is not making either a disparate treatment or an adverse impact argument.

5. Manjit Bhatia, a machinist for Chevron U.S.A., Inc., was a devout Sikh whose religion forbade the cutting or shaving of any body hair. In compliance with standards promulgated by California's Occupational Safety and Health Administration, Chevron required all machinists whose duties involved potential exposure to toxic gases to shave any facial hair that prevented them from achieving a gas-tight face seal when wearing a respirator. Bhatia was one of these machinists, and he told Chevron that his religious beliefs made it impossible for him to comply with the new policy. Chevron then suspended Bhatia from his machinist position, unsuccessfully tried to find him an equal-paying position that did not require a respirator, and finally offered him various lower-paying jobs. Bhatia accepted one of these jobs, but then sued Chevron under Title VII, arguing that his discharge from the machinist position was due to religious discrimination. Will Chevron succeed if it simply argues that it is not discriminating on the basis of religion, but instead merely is penalizing Bhatia for his refusal to shave his facial hair? Will Chevron have a defense if it claims that it could not retain Bhatia in a machinist position without incurring undue hardship?

6. When the Westinghouse Corporation established a formal wage structure late in the 1930s, all job classifications were segregated by sex. At that time, the "female" jobs were generally lower paid than the "male" jobs. Later, men were employed in what had been women's jobs, and vice versa. In such cases, the pay scales for each job were the same no matter what the gender of the jobholder. In 1965, Westinghouse consolidated all of its job classifications, eliminating the former sex segregation. But the formerly female jobs still generally were lower paid than the formerly male jobs. Moreover, the

vast majority of women were still employed in the formerly female jobs.

The International Union of Electrical Workers sued Westinghouse for sex discrimination under Title VII, arguing that Westinghouse's new system did not provide comparable pay for jobs of comparable worth. Westinghouse defended by arguing that the reach of Title VII is no greater than the reach of the Equal Pay Act. As a result, Westinghouse claimed, Title VII only forbade unequal pay for *equal* work. Will Westinghouse's argument succeed?

7. Mechelle Vinson alleged that during her four years with the Meritor Savings Bank, her supervisor Sidney Taylor repeatedly demanded sexual favors from her, and that she had sexual intercourse with him on 40 to 50 separate occasions. She also contended that Taylor fondled her in front of other employees, followed her into the women's restroom, exposed himself to her, and forcibly raped her on several occasions. Despite these allegations, however, Vinson apparently was well treated by her employer in other respects. In fact, she received three promotions during her time with the bank, and it was undisputed that her advancement was based solely on merit. Assuming that Vinson's allegations are true and that Taylor's behavior was unwelcome to her, can she recover against the bank for quid pro quo sexual harassment? Can she recover for work environment sexual harassment? Assume that the bank would be liable for Taylor's behavior.

8. William Massarsky was hired by General Motors in 1963 at the age of 40. Due to a divisionwide force reduction caused by economic conditions, he was laid off in 1971. The layoff was pursuant to a company policy stating that, where ability, merit, and capacity are equal, those with the least time of service in a particular job classification would be the first to be released. When GM released Massarsky, it retained Joseph Biondo, age 25, an employee with over two years less service than Massarsky. Biondo was a student in the General Motors Institute (GMI), a five-year work-study program allowing its 2,350 tuition-paying students to earn a college degree in engineering or management while working for GM. Because GM felt that it had a considerable investment in GMI students, it had an unpublicized company policy exempting GMI students from layoffs.

Can Massarsky successfully argue that the layoff violated the Age Discrimination in Employment Act because the policy exempting GMI students *expressly* discriminated on the basis of age? If Massarsky mounts a *disparate treatment* suit against GM, what would you argue on GM's behalf to show that it had a legitimate nondiscriminatory reason for favoring Biondo? Finally, if Massarsky sued under a *disparate impact* theory, what would he have to show?

9. At the age of 66, Fleming Tullis was discharged from his job as a school bus driver with a private school. He sued the school under the Age Discrimination in Employment Act. Did the school have a BFOQ defense here? Assume for purposes of this question that tests for determining the driving ability of individual people are available and reliable. Also, assume that the school failed to produce any evidence showing that people in their 60s cannot safely operate school buses.

10. Paul Luedtke was an at-will "driller" with Nabors Alaska Drilling, Inc. His job was to oversee a drilling crew on an oil rig on Alaska's North Slope. After a urinalysis suggested that Luedtke was using marijuana, he was suspended from his job. Then, he was told that he would have to pass two new, scheduled urinalysis tests before he would be allowed to return to work. Luedtke refused to take the first test, claiming that it violated his privacy, and was fired as a result. Can he recover for wrongful discharge under the implied covenant of good faith and fair dealing on the theory that the test violated his privacy rights? Assume that Alaska has adopted this exception to the employment-at-will doctrine, that violation of a public policy can constitute a breach of the covenant, and that the public policy need not be expressed in existing law.

11. Catherine Sue Wagenseller was fired from her job as paramedic coordinator in the Scottsdale Memorial Hospital's emergency department. She sued the hospital for wrongful discharge under the public policy exception to the employment-at-will doctrine, alleging that she was fired because of animosity resulting from her refusal to participate in an off-the-job group parody of the song *Moon River* in which group members mooned the audience. A state statute provided that: "A person commits indecent exposure if he or she exposes his or her genitals or anus . . . and another person is present, and the defendant is reckless about whether such other person, as a reasonable person, would be offended or alarmed by the act." Assuming that the audience to the parody enjoyed watching the mooning, would Wagenseller have been criminally liable if she had participated? Does this necessarily defeat her civil claim for wrongful discharge under the public policy exception?

CHAPTER 51

ENVIRONMENTAL REGULATION

INTRODUCTION

Today's businessperson must be concerned with not only competing effectively against competitors but also complying with a myriad of regulatory requirements. For many businesses, particularly those that manufacture goods or that generate wastes, the environmental laws and regulations loom large in terms of the requirements and costs they impose. They can have a significant effect on the way businesses have to be conducted as well as on their profitability. This area of the law has expanded dramatically over the last two decades and environmental issues are a major concern of people and governments around the world. This chapter will briefly discuss the development of environmental law and will outline the major federal statutes that have been enacted to control pollution of air, water, and land.

Historical Perspective

Historically, people assumed that the air, water, and land around them would absorb their waste products. In recent times, however, it has become clear that nature's capacity to assimilate people's wastes is not infinite. Burgeoning population, economic growth, affluence, and the products of our industrial society can pose risks to human health and the environment.

Concern about the environment is not a recent phenomenon. In medieval England, Parliament passed smoke control acts making it illegal to burn soft coal at certain times of the year. Where the owner or operator of a piece of property is using it in such a manner as to unreasonably interfere with another owner's (or the public's) health or enjoyment of his property, the courts have long entertained suits to abate the nuisance. Nuisance actions, which are discussed in the Real Property and Insurance chapter, are frequently not ideal vehicles for dealing with widespread pollution problems. Rather than a hit-or-miss approach, a comprehensive across-the-board approach may be required.

Realizing this, the federal government, as well as many state and local governments, had passed laws to abate air and water pollution by the late 1950s and 1960s. As the 1970s began, concern over the quality and future of the environment produced new laws and fresh public demands for action. During the 1980s, these laws were refined and, in some cases, their coverage was extended. As the 1990s begin, it is readily apparent that environmental concerns are prominent around the globe and many countries, both individually and collectively, are taking steps to address these concerns. Accordingly, it is increasingly important that the businessperson be cognizant of the legal requirements and the public's environmental concerns in operating a business.

The Environmental Protection Agency

In 1970, the Environmental Protection Agency was created to consolidate the federal government's environmental responsibilities. This was an explicit recognition that the problems of air and water pollution, solid waste disposal, water supply, and pesticide and radiation control were interrelated and required a consolidated approach. Congress subsequently passed comprehensive new legislation covering, among other things, air and water pollution, pesticides, ocean dumping, and waste disposal. Among the factors prompting these laws were protection of human health, aesthetics, economic costs of continued pollution, and protection of natural systems.

The initial efforts were aimed at problems that could largely be seen, smelled, or tasted. As control requirements have been put in place, implemented by industry and government, and progress has been noted in the form of cleaner air and water, attention has focused increasingly on problems that are somewhat less visible but potentially more threatening—the problems posed by toxic substances. These problems have come into more prominence as scientific research has disclosed the risks posed by some substances, as detection technology has enabled us to find the suspect substances in ever more minute quantities in the world around us, and as we do increased monitoring and testing.

The National Environmental Policy Act

The National Environmental Policy Act (NEPA) was signed into law on January 1, 1970. In addition to creating the Council of Environmental Quality in the Executive Office of the President, the act required that an **environmental impact statement** be prepared for every recommendation or report on legislation and for every *major federal action significantly affecting the quality of the environment.* The environmental impact statement must: (1) describe the environmental impact of the proposed action, (2) discuss impacts that cannot be avoided, (3) discuss the alternatives to the proposed action, (4) indicate differences between short- and long-term impacts, and (5) detail any irreversible commitments of resources.

NEPA requires a federal agency to consider the environmental impact of a project before the project is undertaken. Other federal, state, and local agencies, as well as interested citizens, have an opportunity to comment on the environmental impact of a project before

the agency can proceed. Where the process is not followed, citizens can and have gone to court to force compliance with NEPA. A number of states and local governments have passed their own environmental impact laws requiring NEPA-type statements for major public and private developments.

While the federal and state laws requiring the preparation of environmental impact statements appear directed at government actions, it is important to note that the government actions covered often include the granting of permits to private parties. Thus, businesspeople may readily find themselves involved in the preparation of an environmental impact statement—for example, in connection with a marina to be built in a navigable waterway or a resort development that will impact wetlands, both of which require permits from the U.S. Army Corps of Engineers. Similarly, a developer seeking a local zoning change so she can build a major commercial or residential development may find that she is asked to finance a study of the potential environmental impact of her proposed project.

AIR POLLUTION

Background

Fuel combustion, industrial processes, and solid waste disposal are the major contributors to air pollution. People's initial concern with air pollution related to that which they could see—visible or smoke pollution. For instance, in the 1880s, Chicago and Cincinnati enacted smoke control ordinances. As the technology became available to deal with smoke and particulate emissions, attention focused on other, less visible gases that could adversely affect human health and vegetation, or that could increase the acidity of lakes, thus making them unsuitable for fish.

Clean Air Act

The first federal legislation came in 1955, when Congress authorized $5 million each year for air pollution research. While the federal role was modestly increased through intervening enactments, the comprehensive legislation enacted in 1970 and known as the Clean Air Act provides the basis for our present approach to air pollution control. In 1977 Congress modified the 1970 act and enacted provisions designed to prevent deterioration of the air in areas where its quality currently exceeds that required by federal law. Thirteen years then passed before Congress, in 1990, enacted a major revision to the act to deal with acid rain, air toxics, and urban smog problems that were not satisfactorily dealt with under the existing legislation.

Ambient Air Control Standards

The Clean Air Act established a comprehensive approach for dealing with air pollution. EPA is required to set **national ambient air quality standards** for the major pollutants that have an adverse impact on human health—that is, to regulate the amount of a given pollutant that may be present in the air around us. The ambient air quality standards are set at two levels: (1) primary standards are designed to protect the public's health from harm; and (2) secondary standards are designed to protect vegetation, materials, climate, visibility, and economic values. Pursuant to this statutory mandate, EPA has set national ambient air quality standards for carbon monoxide, nitrogen oxide, sulfur oxide, ozone, lead, and particulate matter.

The country is divided into air quality regions; each region is required to have a **state implementation plan** for meeting national ambient air quality standards. This necessitates an inventory of the various sources of air pollution and their contribution to the total air pollution in the air quality region. The major emitters of pollutants are then required to reduce their emissions to a level that ensures that overall air quality meets the national standards. For example, a factory may be required to limit its emissions of volatile organic compounds (a contributor to ozone or smog) to a certain amount per unit of production or hour of operation; similarly, a power plant might have its emissions of sulfur oxides and nitrogen oxides limited to so many pounds per Btu of energy produced. The states have the responsibility for selecting which activities must be regulated or curtailed so that overall emissions at any point in the state or area do not exceed the national standards.

Because by the late 1980s many of the nation's major urban areas were still not in compliance with the health-based standards for ozone and carbon monoxide, Congress, in its 1990 amendments, imposed an additional set of requirements on the areas that were not in compliance. Thus, citizens living in the areas and existing businesses, as well as prospective businesses seeking to locate in the designated areas, face increasingly stringent control measures designed to bring the areas into

attainment with the national standards. These new requirements will mean that businesses such as bakeries that are generally not thought of as major polluters of the air will have to further control their emissions, and that paints and other products that contain solvents may have to be reformulated.

Acid Rain Controls

Responding to the 1970 Clean Air Act, which sought to protect the air in the area near sources of air pollution, many electric generating facilities built tall smokestacks so that the emissions were dispersed over a broader area. Unwittingly, this contributed to long-range transport of some of the pollutants, which changed chemically enroute and fell to earth many miles away in the form of acid rain, snow, fog, or dry deposition. For a number of years, a considerable debate ensued over acid rain, in particular as to whether it was a problem, what kind of damage it caused, whether anything should be done about it, and who should pay for the cost of limiting it. The 1990 amendments address acid deposition by among other things placing a cap on the overall emissions of the contributors to it (the oxides of sulfur and nitrogen) and requiring electric utilities to reduce their emissions to specified levels in two steps over the next decade. This will require most electric generating facilities in the country to install large control devices known as scrubbers, to switch to lower sulfur coal, or to install so-called clean coal technologies. The 1990 amendments also provide an innovative system whereby companies whose emissions are cleaner than required by law can sell their rights to emit more sulfur oxide to other companies that may be finding it more difficult to meet the standards.

Control of Air Toxics

The 1970 Clean Air Act also required EPA to regulate the emission of toxic air pollutants. Under this authority, EPA has only set standards for asbestos, beryllium, mercury, vinyl chloride, benzene, and radionuclides. Unhappy with the slow pace of regulation of toxic air pollutants, Congress in 1990 specified a list of chemicals for which EPA is required to issue regulations requiring the installation of the *maximum available control technology*. The regulations are to be developed and the control technology installed by industry in phases over the next decade. Thus, while many toxic emissions have largely gone unregulated, that situation will change in the next few years. In addition, a number of companies have announced they are voluntarily reducing their emissions of toxic chemicals to levels below those they are required to meet by law.

The case that follows, *United States v. Tzavah Urban Renewal Corporation*, involves the enforcement of an existing EPA regulation that controls the removal and disposal of asbestos and asbestos-containing material from buildings.

UNITED STATES v. TZAVAH URBAN RENEWAL CORP.

696 F. Supp. 1013 (D. N.J. 1988)

In August 1986, Tzavah Urban Renewal Corporation purchased from the city of Newark a building at 16 Park Place formerly known as the Old Military Park Hotel. While the buyer was given an opportunity to inspect the building, it was not informed by the city that the building was permeated with asbestos-containing material. At the time of the purchase, the building was in great disrepair and had been uninhabited for many years. Its proposed renovation was to be a major urban renewal project.

In June 1987, Tzavah contracted with Greer Industrial Corporation to "gut" the building. While the work was going on, an EPA inspector visited the site and concluded that the hotel was contaminated with asbestos. He observed Greer employees throwing asbestos-laced objects out of the windows of the building and noted an uncovered refuse pile next to the hotel that contained asbestos. The workers were not wetting the debris before heaving it out the windows and the refuse pile was also dry. As a result, asbestos dust was being released into the air. Although the hotel was located in a commercial district, there were private homes nearby.

Renovation of buildings contaminated with asbestos is regulated under the Clean Air Act. The EPA regulations require building owners or operators to notify EPA before commencing renovation or demolition and prescribe various procedures for storage and removal of the asbestos. Tzavah failed to provide the required notice or to comply with the procedures required. After being notified by EPA of the violation of the law, Tzavah stopped the demolition work, left the building unsecured, and left the waste piles dry and uncovered. EPA tried informally to get Tzavah to complete the work in accordance with the asbestos regulations; when Tzavah did not take action, EPA brought a lawsuit against Tzavah to do so.

Lechner, District Judge.   As the facts reveal, the EPA has attempted to remedy the hazardous conditions at 16 Park Place for almost a year. Thus far, the Agency's efforts to assure full compliance with the National Emission Standard for Hazardous Air Pollutants (NESHAP) regulations have proved ineffective. Asbestos is still present at the facility and continues to pose a significant danger to the health of the community. In order to ensure that this danger is abated, the Government brought this action for injunctive relief pursuant to the Clean Air Act.

Defendants assert that an injunction is unnecessary because there is "no current renovation operation being conducted at 16 Park Place." This argument is based on a fundamental misinterpretation of the asbestos NESHAP. As the Government correctly points out, the NESHAP regulations are activated when demolition or renovation begins and remain in effect until the facility has been rid of the dangers posed by asbestos dust. To permit a building owner to commence renovation and when asbestos is discovered, simply discontinue work with impunity, defies the purpose and logic of the statute. The procedures for asbestos emissions control and the waste disposal provisions of the regulations anticipate that once asbestos is identified, it will be rendered non-hazardous by proper disposal. Defendants cannot circumvent the affirmative obligation imposed upon them by federal law and simply walk away from the Park Place project. Indeed, the defendants' numerous efforts at compliance underscore their awareness of this responsibility.

Motion granted enjoining the defendants to secure the facility, properly dispose of the asbestos containing material, and to comply with the EPA's orders.

New Source Controls

The Clean Air Act requires that new stationary sources such as factories and power plants install the *best available technology* for reducing air pollution. EPA is required to establish the standards to be met by new stationary sources and has done so for the major stationary sources of air pollution. This means that a new facility covered by the regulations must install state of the art control technology, even if it is locating in area where the air quality is much better than that required by law.

Enforcement

The primary responsibility for enforcing air quality standards lies with the states, but the federal government has the right to enforce the standards where the states fail to do so. The Clean Air Act also provides for suits by citizens to force industry or the government to fully comply with the act's provisions.

Automobile Pollution

The Clean Air Act provides specifically for air pollution controls on transportation sources such as automobiles. The major pollutants from automobiles are carbon monoxide, hydrocarbons, and nitrogen oxides. Carbon monoxide is a colorless, odorless gas that can dull mental performance and even cause death when inhaled in large quantities. Hydrocarbons, in the form of unburned fuel, are part of a category of air pollutants known as volatile organic compounds (VOCs). VOCs combine with nitrogen oxides under the influence of sunlight to become ozone—we know it as smog.

The 1970 Clean Air Act required a reduction of 90 percent of the carbon monoxide and hydrocarbons emitted by automobiles by 1975 and a 90 percent reduction in the nitrogen oxides emitted by 1976. At the time, these requirements were "technology forcing"; that is,

the manufacturers could not rely on already existing technology to meet the standards but rather had to develop new technology. Ultimately, most manufacturers had to go beyond simply making changes in engine design and utilize pollution control devices known as catalytic converters.

Subsequently, Congress addressed the question of setting even more stringent limits on automobile emissions while at the same time requiring that the new automobiles get better gas mileage. The 1990 amendments require further limitations on emissions from tailpipes, the development of so-called clean-fueled vehicles for use in cities with dirty air, and the availability of oxygenated fuels (which are cleaner) in specified areas of the country that are having difficulty meeting the air quality limits at least part of the year. These new requirements have significant ramifications for the oil and automobile industries.

Under the Clean Air Act, no manufacturer may sell vehicles subject to emission standards without prior certification from EPA that the vehicles meet the required standards. The tests are performed on prototype vehicles and if they pass, a certificate of conformity covering that type of engine and vehicle is issued. EPA subsequently can test vehicles on the assembly line to make sure that the production vehicles covered by the certificate are meeting the standards. The manufacturers are required to warrant that the vehicle, if properly maintained, will comply with the emission standards for its useful life. If EPA discovers that vehicles in actual use exceed the emission standards, it may order the manufacturer to recall and repair the defective models; this is a power that EPA has exercised on a number of occasions.

The act also provides for the regulation and registration of fuel additives such as lead. In the 1980s, lead was largely phased out of use as an octane enhancer in gasoline. As indicated previously, the 1990 amendments provide for the availability of alternative fuels based on ethanol and methanol.

International Air Problems

During the late 1970s and 1980s, concern developed that the release of chlorine-containing substances such as chlorofluorocarbons (CFCs) used in air conditioning, refrigeration, and certain foam products was depleting the stratospheric ozone layer. This could lead to more ultraviolet radiation reaching the earth and, in turn, more skin cancer. Subsequently, a number of nations, acting under the aegis of the United Nations, signed a treaty agreeing first to limit any increases in production of chlorine-containing substances and ultimately to significantly phase out their use. The 1990 amendments to the Clean Air Act implement the obligations of the United States under the treaty and provide for the phasedown and phaseout of a number of chlorofluorcarbons; accordingly, many businesses are trying to develop or to locate substitutes for those chemicals that will be available only in reduced quantities, if at all.

Other air pollution issues with international dimensions that may result in multinational control efforts are acid rain and global warming/climate change resulting, in part, from increased emissions of carbon dioxide to the atmosphere.

Indoor Air Pollution

As we increased the insulation and made our buildings airtight to conserve energy, we generally reduced the air exchange and increased the concentrations of pollutants in our homes and workplaces. In recent years, attention has focused on a range of indoor air problems, sometimes known under the term *sick building syndrome*, including radon gas, asbestos, the products of combustion from fireplaces and stoves, molds and pollens, formaldehyde, cigarette smoke, pesticides, and cleaning products. Some of these problems are being dealt with on a problem-by-problem, or product-by-product, basis under various laws. Others are being addressed by providing information to consumers so that they can take appropriate actions to protect themselves. In some cases, Congress and other legislative bodies have required that steps be taken to minimize the risks, such as the federal requirement for schools to inspect for asbestos and to remove it where certain unsafe conditions are found.

Radiation Control

In recent years, people have been concerned about radioactivity, particularly radioactivity from nuclear-fueled power plants. Some of these concerns were accentuated by the accident at Chernobyl in the USSR and the one at Three Mile Island in the United States. Citizens are specifically concerned about the release of radioactivity into the environment during normal operation of the nuclear reactors, accidents through human error or mechanical failure, and disposal of the radioactive wastes generated by the reactors. They are also concerned that the discharge of heated water used to cool the reactor—thermal pollution—may cause damage to the environment.

Currently, the problems of reactor safety are under the jurisdiction of the Nuclear Regulatory Commission, which exercises licensing authority over nuclear power plants. EPA is responsible for setting standards for radioactivity in the overall environment and for dealing with the problem of disposal of some radioactive waste. EPA also handles the thermal pollution problem pursuant to its water pollution control authority. In addition, EPA is responsible for regulating emissions from a variety of other sources, such as uranium mill tailing piles and uranium mines.

WATER POLLUTION

Background

History is replete with plagues and epidemics brought on by poor sanitation and polluted water. Indeed, preventing waterborne disease has always been the major reason for combating water pollution. In the early 1970s, fishing and swimming were prohibited in many bodies of water, and game fish could no longer survive in some waters where they had formerly thrived. Lake Erie was becoming choked with algae and considered to be dying. The nation recognized that water pollution could affect public health, recreation, commercial fishing, agriculture, water supplies, and aesthetics. During the 1970s, Congress enacted three major statutes to protect our water resources: the Clean Water Act; the Marine Protection, Research, and Sanctuaries Act; and the Safe Drinking Water Act.

Early Federal Legislation

Federal water pollution legislation dates back to the 19th century when Congress enacted the River and Harbor Act of 1886. In fact, this statute, recodified in the River and Harbor Act of 1899, furnished the legal basis for

EPA's initial enforcement actions against polluters. The act provided that people had to obtain a discharge permit from the Army Corps of Engineers to deposit or discharge refuse into a navigable waterway. Under some contemporary court decisions, even hot water discharged from nuclear power plants was considered refuse. The permit system established pursuant to the "Refuse Act" was replaced in 1972 by a more comprehensive permit system now administered by EPA.

Congress passed the initial Federal Water Pollution Control Act (FWPCA) in 1948. Amendments to the FWPCA in 1956, 1965, 1966, and 1970 increased the federal government's role in water pollution abatement and strengthened its enforcement powers.

Clean Water Act   The 1972 amendments to the FWPCA—known as the Clean Water Act—were as comprehensive in the water pollution field as the 1970 Clean Air Act was in the air pollution field. They proclaimed two general goals for this country: (1) to achieve wherever possible by July 1, 1983, water clean enough for swimming and other recreational uses and clean enough for the protection and propagation of fish, shellfish, and wildlife; and (2) to have no discharges of pollutants into the nation's waters by 1985. These goals reflected a national frustration with the lack of progress in dealing with water pollution and a commitment to end such pollution. The new law set out a series of specific actions that federal, state, and local governments and industry were to take by certain dates and also provided strong enforcement provisions to back up the deadlines. In 1977 and again in 1987, Congress modified the 1972 act by adjusting some of the deadlines and otherwise fine-tuning the act.

State Role

Under the Clean Water Act, the states have the primary responsibility for preventing, reducing, and eliminating water pollution. The states have to do this within a national framework and EPA is empowered to move in if the states do not fulfill their responsibilities.

Controls on Industrial Wastes

The act set a number of deadlines to control water pollution from industrial sources. It required industries discharging wastes into the nation's waterways to install the *best available* water pollution control technology; new sources of industrial pollution must use the *best avail-*

able demonstrated control technology. In each instance, EPA is responsible for issuing guidelines as to the best available technologies. Industries that discharge their wastes into municipal systems are required to *pretreat* the wastes so that they do not interfere with the biological operation of the plant or pass through the plant without treatment.

Water Quality Standards

The act continued and expanded the previously established system of setting *water quality standards* by designating the uses of specific bodies of water for recreation, public water supply, propagation of fish and wildlife, and agricultural and industrial water supply. Then, the maximum daily loads of various pollutants are set so that the water is suitable for the designated use.

Discharge Permits

The act requires all municipal and industrial dischargers to obtain *permits* that spell out the amounts and specific pollutants that permit holders are allowed to discharge and any steps that they must take to reduce their present or anticipated discharge. Dischargers are also required to keep records, install and maintain monitoring equipment, and sample their discharges.

Enforcement

Both civil and criminal sanctions are included in the act. Criminal penalties for violating the law range from a minimum of $2,500 for a first offense up to $50,000 per day and two years in prison for subsequent violations. The act is enforced by federal and state governments. In addition, any citizen or group of citizens whose interests are adversely affected has the right to bring a court action against anyone violating an effluent standard, limitation, or order issued by EPA or a state. Citizens also have the right to take court action against EPA if it fails to carry out mandatory provisions of the law.

Wetlands

Another aspect of the Clean Water Act having the potential to affect businesses as well as individual property owners is the wetlands provision. Commonly, wetlands are transition zones between land and open water. Under Section 404 of the act, any dredging or filling activity in a wetland that is connected to the waters of the United States requires a permit before any activity begins. The permit program is administered by the Army Corps of Engineers, with the involvement of the Environmental Protection Agency.

As can be seen in the *Bersani v. U.S. Environmental Protection Agency* case, which follows, the permit requirement can limit a landowner's use of his property where the fill activity is viewed as injurious to the values protected by the act.

BERSANI v. U.S. ENVIRONMENTAL PROTECTION AGENCY
674 F. Supp. 405 (N.D.N.Y. 1987) aff'd 395 F.2d 36 (2d Cir. 1988)

Pyramid Companies was an association of partnerships that was in the business of developing, constructing, and operating shopping centers; John Bersani was a principal in one of the partnerships. In 1983, Pyramid became interested in developing a shopping mall in the Attleboro, Massachusetts, area and focused its attention on an 82-acre site known as Sweeden's Swamp along an interstate highway in South Attleboro. The project contemplated altering or filling some 32 acres of the 49.6 acres of wetlands on the property. At the same time, Pyramid planned to excavate 9 acres of uplands (nonwetlands) to create new wetlands and to alter some 13 acres of existing wetlands to enhance their value for fish and wildlife.

In 1984, Pyramid applied to the U.S. Army Corps of Engineers for a permit under Section 404 of the Clean Water Act to do the dredge and fill work in the wetlands. As part of its application, it was required to submit information on practicable alternative sites for its shopping mall. One site subsequently focused on by the Corps and the Environmental Protection Agency was about three miles north in North Attleboro. Pyramid relied on several factors in claiming that the site was not a practicable alternative to its proposed site: namely, the site lacked sufficient traffic volume and access from local roads, potential department store tenants had expressed doubts about the feasibility of the site, and previous attempts to develop the site had met with strong resistance from the surrounding community. However, after Pyramid examined the site, another major developer of shopping centers had taken an option to acquire the property.

The New England Division Engineer of the Corps recommended that the permit be denied because a practicable alternative with a less adverse effect on the environment existed. The Chief of Engineers directed that the permit be issued, noting that the alternative site was not available to Pyramid because it was owned by a competitor. He also believed that even if it was considered available, Pyramid had made a convincing case that the site would not fulfill its objectives for a successful project. EPA then exercised its prerogative under the Clean Water Act to veto the permit on the grounds that filling Sweeden's Swamp to build the shopping mall would have an unacceptable adverse effect on the environment. In its view, another less environmentally damaging site had been available to Pyramid at the time it made its site selection; thus, any adverse effects on Sweeden's Swamp were avoidable. Bersani and Pyramid then brought suit challenging the denial of its permit application.

McAvo, Judge.   Section 404(a) authorizes the Secretary of the Army, acting through the Corps, to issue permits for the discharge of dredged or fill material at specified disposal sites. Criteria developed by the EPA in conjunction with the Corps govern these permitting decisions. Generally, the Corps must employ a "practicable alternative" analysis in determining whether to allow a proposed discharge. Section 230.10 of the regulations provides:

> (a) . . . no discharge of dredged or fill material shall be permitted if there is a practicable alternative to the proposed discharge which would have less adverse impact on the aquatic ecosystem, so long as the alternative does not have other significant adverse environmental consequences.

(2) An alternative is practicable if it is available and capable of being done, after taking into account cost, existing technology, and logistics in light of overall project purposes. If it is otherwise a practicable alternative, an area not presently owned by the applicant which could reasonably be obtained, utilized, expanded or managed in order to fulfill the basic purpose of the proposed activity may be considered.

(3) Where the activity associated with a discharge which is proposed for a special aquatic site (including a wetland) does not require access or proximity to or siting within the special aquatic site in question to fulfill its basic purpose (i.e., is not "water dependent"), practicable alternatives that do not involve special aquatic sites are presumed to be available unless clearly demonstrated otherwise. In addition, where a discharge is proposed for a special aquatic site, all practicable alternatives to the proposed discharge which do not involve a discharge into a special aquatic site are presumed to have less adverse impact on the aquatic ecosystem, unless clearly demonstrated otherwise.

Where the proposed discharge involves a special aquatic site such as wetlands, a more stringent standard is imposed. Indeed Section 230.10(a)(3) creates a presumption that a practicable alternative exists when the discharge involves wetlands and the activity, here a shopping mall, is not "water dependent." Then the applicant must "clearly demonstrate" that no such alternative does in fact exist.

Pyramid argues that EPA's determination of feasibility was based on its erroneous conclusion that the marketplace considered the North Attleboro site suitable for a virtually identical regional shopping mall. Pyramid notes that six other shopping center developers over the past fifteen years have tried and failed to develop the North Attleboro site as a shopping center. It contends that EPA has substituted its own judgment for that of the marketplace in an area in which it cannot claim expertise.

The EPA, however, contends that it did not simply substitute its judgment for that of the developer. Instead, the EPA argues that the evidence on the record demonstrates that the North Attleboro site is suitable in fact for a regional shopping center mall virtually identical to that proposed by Pyramid. In this respect, the fact that a competing developer, the New England Development Company, had found the site suitable for a similar shopping mall, and its own marketing analysis weighed in reaching this decision. The EPA also engaged in a review of the specific features that Pyramid found objectionable; namely, the distance from the primary trade area, lack of visibility from nearby highways, zoning, past failures of prior attempts to develop a shopping mall at the site, and various considerations. Consequently, the court finds that EPA's feasibility determination was not arbitrary.

Summary judgment granted for EPA.

Ocean Dumping

The Marine Protection, Research, and Sanctuaries Act of 1972 set up a permit system regulating the dumping of all types of materials into ocean waters. EPA has the responsibility for designating disposal sites and for establishing the rules governing ocean disposal. The Ocean Dumping Ban Act of 1987 requires that all ocean dumping of municipal sewage sludge and industrial wastes be terminated by December 31, 1991. Thus, the major remaining questions of ocean dumping concern the disposal of dredge spoils from dredging to keep harbors open.

Drinking Water

In 1974, Congress passed, and in 1986 amended, the Safe Drinking Water Act that is designed to protect and enhance the quality of our drinking water. Under the act, EPA sets *primary drinking water standards*, minimum levels of quality for water consumed by humans. The act also establishes a program governing the injection of wastes into wells. The primary responsibility for complying with the federally established standards lies with the states. Where the states fail to enforce the drinking water standards, the federal government has the right to enforce them.

WASTE DISPOSAL

Background

Historically, concern about the environment focused on decreasing air and water pollution as well as protecting natural resources and wildlife. People paid relatively little attention to the disposal of wastes on land. Until the early 1970s, much of the solid and hazardous waste generated was disposed of in open dumps and landfills. Although some of the waste we produce can be disposed of without presenting significant health or environmental problems, some industrial, agricultural, and mining wastes—and even some household wastes—are hazardous and can present serious problems. Unless wastes are properly disposed of, they can cause air, water, and land pollution as well as contamination of the underground aquifers from which much of our drinking water is drawn. Once aquifers have been contaminated, they can take a very long time to cleanse themselves of pollutants.

In the 1970s, the discovery of abandoned dump sites such as Love Canal in New York and the Valley of the Drums in Kentucky heightened public concern about the disposal of toxic and hazardous wastes. Congress has enacted several laws regulating the generation and disposal of hazardous waste: The Resource Conservation and Recovery Act mandates proper management and disposal of wastes currently generated; and the Comprehensive Environmental Response, Compensation, and Liability Act focuses on cleaning up past disposal sites threatening public health and the environment.

The Resource Conservation and Recovery Act

Congress originally enacted the Resource Conservation and Recovery Act (RCRA) in 1976 and significantly amended it in 1984. RCRA provides the federal government and the states with the authority to regulate facilities that generate, treat, store, and dispose of hazardous waste. Most of the wastes defined as hazardous are subject to a cradle-to-the-grave tracking system and must be handled and disposed of in defined ways.

RCRA requires persons who *generate, treat, store, or transport* specified quantities of hazardous waste to obtain permits, to meet certain standards and follow specified procedures in the handling of the wastes, and to keep records. In addition, operators of land waste disposal facilities must meet financial responsibility requirements and monitor groundwater quality. EPA determines whether certain wastes should be banned entirely from land disposal; a significant number of wastes must be treated before they can be disposed of in land disposal units.

Underground Storage Tanks

In 1984, Congress directed that EPA also regulate underground product storage tanks such as gasoline tanks to prevent and respond to leaks that might contaminate underground water. The regulations that EPA issued to implement these requirements impose significant costs on many businesses such as gasoline stations that utilize such storage tanks.

State Responsibilities

EPA sets minimum requirements for state RCRA programs and then delegates the responsibility for conducting programs to the states when they have the legal ability and interest to administer them. Until a state assumes partial or complete responsibility for a RCRA program, the federal government administers the program.

Enforcement

Failure to comply with the hazardous waste regulations promulgated under RCRA can subject violators to civil and criminal penalties. In the *Johnson & Towers* case, which follows, employees of a company that disposed of hazardous waste without a RCRA permit were held criminally liable.

UNITED STATES v. JOHNSON & TOWERS, INC.

21 E.R.C. 1433 (3d Cir. 1984)

Johnson & Towers, Inc. is in the business of overhauling large motor vehicles. It uses degreasers and other industrial chemicals such as methylene chloride and trichloroethylene that are classified as hazardous wastes under the Resource Conservation and Recovery Act (RCRA). For some period of time, employees drained waste chemicals from cleaning operations into a holding tank and, when the tank was full, pumped them into a trench. The trench flowed from the plant property into Parker's Creek, a tributary of the Delaware River. Under RCRA, generators of such wastes must obtain a permit for disposal from the Environmental Protection Agency (EPA). EPA had neither issued, nor received an application for, a permit for the Johnson & Towers's operations.

Over a three-day period, federal agents saw workers pump waste from the tank into the trench, and on the third day toxic chemicals flowed into the creek. The company and two of its employees, foreman Jack Hopkins and service manager Peter Angel, were indicted for unlawfully disposing of hazardous wastes. The company pleaded guilty. The federal district court dismissed the criminal charges against the two individuals, holding that RCRA's criminal penalty provisions imposing fines and imprisonment did not apply to employees. The government appealed.

Sloviter, Circuit Judge.   The single issue in this appeal is whether the individual defendants are subject to prosecution under RCRA's criminal provision (Section 6928 [d]) which applies to:

any person who . . .
   (2) knowingly treats, stores, or disposes of any hazardous waste identified or listed under this subchapter either
   (A) without having obtained a permit under section 6925 of this title . . . or
   (B) in knowing violation of any material condition or requirement of such permit.

The permit provision in section 6925 requires "each person owning or operating a facility for the treatment, storage, or disposal of hazardous waste identified or listed under this subchapter to have a permit" from the EPA.

The parties offer contrary interpretations of section 6928(d). Defendants consider it an administrative enforcement mechanism, applying only to those who come within section 6925 and fail to comply; the government reads it as penalizing anyone who handles hazardous waste without a permit or in violation of a permit. Neither party has cited another case, nor have we found one, considering the application of this criminal provision to an individual other than an owner or operator.

Though the result may appear harsh, it is well established that criminal penalties attached to regulatory statutes intended to protect public health, in contrast to statutes based on common law crimes, are to be construed to effectuate the regulatory purpose.

Congress enacted RCRA in 1976 as a "cradle-to-grave" regulatory scheme for toxic materials, providing "nationwide protection against the dangers of improper hazardous waste disposal." RCRA was enacted to provide "a multifaceted approach toward solving the problems associated with the 3–4 billion tons of discarded materials generated each year, and the problems resulting from the anticipated 8 percent annual increase in the volume of such waste." The committee reports accompanying legislative consideration of RCRA contain numerous statements evincing the congressional view that improper disposal of toxic materials was a serious national problem.

The original statute made knowing disposal (but not treatment or storage) of such waste without a permit a misdemeanor. Amendments in 1978 and 1980 expanded the criminal provision to cover treatment and storage and made violation of section 6928 a felony. The fact that Congress amended the statute twice to broaden the scope of its substantive provisions and enhance the penalty is a strong indication of Congress' increasing concern about the seriousness of the prohibited conduct.

Although Congress' concern may have been directed primarily at owners and operators of generating facilities, since it imposed upon them in section 6925 the obligation to secure the necessary permit, Congress did not explicitly limit criminal liability for impermissible treatment, storage, or disposal to owners and operators. The House Committee's discussion of enforcement contains several references relevant only to owners and operators, but it says, in addition: "This section also provides for criminal penalties for the person who disposes of any hazardous waste without a permit under this title." The "also" demonstrates that the reach of section 6928(d) is broader than that of the rest of the statute, particularly the administrative enforcement remedies. The acts that were made the subject of the criminal provision were distinguished in the House Report from the other conduct subject to administrative regulation because they were viewed as more serious offenses. As the Report explained, "the justification for the penalties section is to permit a broad variety of mechanisms so as to stop the illegal disposal of hazardous wastes."

We conclude that in RCRA, Congress endeavored to control hazards that, "in the circumstances of modern industrialism, are largely beyond self-protection." It would undercut the purposes of the legislation to limit the class of potential defendants to owners and operators when others also bear responsibility for handling regulated materials. The phrase, "without having obtained a permit under section 6925" (emphasis added) merely references the section under which the permit is required and exempts from prosecution under section 6928(d)(2)(A) anyone who has obtained a permit; we conclude that it has no other limiting effect. Therefore we reject the district court's construction limiting the substantive criminal provision by confining "any person" in section 6928 to owners or operators of facilities that store, treat, or dispose of hazardous waste, as an unduly narrow view of both the statutory language and the congressional intent.

Case remanded to district court for trial.

Solid Waste

Mining, commercial, and household activities generate a large volume of waste material that can present problems if not properly disposed. As population density has increased, causing a corresponding increase in the total volume of waste, it has become more difficult to find land or incinerators where the waste material can be disposed of properly. RCRA authorizes EPA to set minimum standards for such disposal, but states and local governments bear the primary responsibility for the siting and regulation of such activity.

As the cost and difficulty of disposing of waste increases, public attention focuses on reducing the waste to be disposed, on looking for opportunities to recycle some of the waste material, and on changing the characteristics of the material that must ultimately be disposed of so that it poses fewer environmental problems. One of the significant challenges faced by tomorrow's businessperson will be in designing products, packaging, and production processes so as to minimize the waste products that result.

A significant problem for both government and industry is the difficulty in trying to site new waste facilities. The NIMBY, or not-in-my-backyard syndrome, is pervasive as people almost universally desire to have the wastes from their everyday lives and from the economic activity in their community disposed of in someone else's neighborhood—anyplace but their own. As governments try to cope with the reality of finding places to dispose of wastes in an environmentally safe manner and at the same time cope with public opposition to siting new facilities, the temptation is strong to try to bar wastes from other areas from being disposed of in local facilities. In the landmark case that follows, *City of Philadelphia v. New Jersey*, the U.S. Supreme Court struck down an attempt by the state of New Jersey to prohibit the importation of most solid waste originating outside the state. An ironic twist is that more than a decade later, we find a number of other eastern and midwestern states trying to find ways to block the importation of wastes from New Jersey into their states.

CITY OF PHILADELPHIA v. NEW JERSEY
437 U.S. 617 (1978)

New Jersey passed a state law (ch. 363 of 1973 N.J. Laws) that took effect early in 1974 and provided as follows:

> No person shall bring into this State any solid or liquid waste which originated or was collected outside the territorial limits of the State, except garbage to be fed to swine in the State of New Jersey, until the commissioner [of the State Department of Environmental Protection] shall determine that such action can be permitted without endangering the public health, safety and welfare and has promulgated regulations permitting and regulating the treatment and disposal of such waste in this State.

As authorized by the law, the Commissioner promulgated four categories of waste to enter the State. Apart from these narrow exceptions, however, New Jersey closed its borders to all waste from other states.

Immediately affected by these developments were the operators of private landfills in New Jersey, and several cities in other states that had agreements with these operators for waste disposal. They brought suit against New Jersey claiming, among other things, that the statute violated the Commerce Clause of the U.S. Constitution. The trial court found the statute to be unconstitutional because it discriminated against interstate commerce. The New Jersey Supreme Court reversed the trial court, finding that the statute advanced vital health and environmental objectives with no economic discrimination against, and with little burden on, interstate commerce. That decision was appealed to the U.S. Supreme Court.

Stewart, Justice.   The opinions of the Court through the years have reflected an alertness to the evils of "economic isolation" and protectionism, while at the same time recognizing that incidental burdens on interstate commerce may be unavoidable when a state wishes to safeguard the health and safety of its people. Thus, where simple economic protectionism is effected by state legislation, a virtual *per se* rule of invalidity has been errected. But where other legislative objectives are credibly advanced and there is no patent discrimination against interstate trade, the Court has adopted a much more flexible approach, the general contours of which were outlined in *Pike v. Bruce Church, Inc.*

> Where the statute regulates evenhandedly to effectuate a legitimate local interest, and its effects on interstate commerce are only incidental, it will be upheld unless the burden imposed on such commerce is clearly excessive in relation to the putative local benefits.

The purpose of ch. 363 is set out in the statute itself as follows:

> The legislature finds and determines that . . . the volume of solid and liquid waste continues to rapidly increase, that the treatment and disposal of these wastes continues to pose an even greater threat to the quality of the environment of New Jersey, that the available and appropriate land fill sites within the State are being diminished, that the environment continues to be threatened by the treatment and disposal of waste which originated or was collected outside the State, and that the public safety and welfare require the treatment and disposal within this State of all wastes generated outside of this State be prohibited.

It does not matter whether the ultimate aim of ch. 363 is to reduce the waste disposal costs of New Jersey residents or to save remaining open lands from pollution, for we assume New Jersey has every right to protect its residents' pocketbooks as well as their environment. And it may be assumed as well that New Jersey may pursue those ends by slowing the flow of *all* waste into the State's remaining landfills, even though interstate commerce may incidentally be affected. But whatever New Jersey's ultimate purpose, it may not be accomplished by discriminating against articles of commerce coming from outside the State unless there is some reason, apart from their origin, to treat them differently. Both on its face, and in its plain effect, ch. 363 violates this principle of nondiscrimination.

The New Jersey law at issue in this case falls squarely within the area that the Commerce Clause puts off limits to state regulation. On its face, it imposes on out-of-state commercial interests the full burden of conserving the State's remaining landfill space. It is true that in our previous cases the scarce natural resource was itself the article of commerce, whereas here the scarce resource and the article of commerce are distinct. But that difference is without consequence. In both instances, the State has overtly moved to slow or freeze the flow of commerce for protectionist reasons. It does not matter that the State has shut the article of commerce inside the State in one case and outside the State in the other. What is crucial is the attempt by one State to isolate itself from a problem common to many by erecting a barrier against the movement of interstate trade.

Today, cities in Pennsylvania and New York find it expedient or necessary to send their waste into New Jersey for disposal, and New Jersey claims the right to close its borders to such traffic. Tomorrow, cities in New Jersey may find it expedient or necessary to send their waste into Pennsylvania or New York for disposal, and those States might then claim the right to close their borders. The Commerce Clause will protect New Jersey in the future, just as it protects her neighbors now, from effects by one State to isolate itself in the stream of interstate commerce from a problem shared by all.

Judgment reversed in favor of Philadelphia and the other plaintiffs.

Superfund

In 1980, Congress passed the Comprehensive Environmental Response Compensation and Liability Act (CERCLA), commonly known as *Superfund,* to deal with the problem of uncontrolled or abandoned hazardous waste sites. In 1986, it strengthened and expanded the law. Under the Superfund law, EPA identified and assessed the sites in the United States where hazardous wastes had been spilled, stored, or abandoned.

Eventually, EPA expects to identify 30,000 such sites. The sites are ranked on the basis of the type, quantity, and toxicity of the wastes; the number of people potentially exposed to the wastes; the different ways (e.g., in the air or drinking water) in which they might be exposed; the risks to contamination of aquifers; and other factors. The sites with the highest ranking are put on the National Priority List to receive priority federal and/or state attention for cleanup. At these sites, EPA makes careful scientific and engineering studies to determine the most appropriate cleanup plans. Once a site has been cleaned up, the state is responsible for managing it to prevent future environmental problems. EPA also has the authority to quickly initiate actions at hazardous waste sites—whether or not the site is on the priority list—to address *imminent hazards* such as the risk of fire, explosion, or contamination of drinking water.

The cleanup activity is financed by a tax on chemicals and feedstocks. However, EPA is authorized to require that a site be cleaned up by those persons responsible for contaminating it, either as the owner or operator of the site, a transporter of wastes to the site, or the owner of wastes deposited at the site. Where EPA expends money to clean up a site, it has the legal authority to recover its costs from those who were responsible for the problem. The courts have held that such persons are "jointly and severally responsible for the cost of cleanup." The Negligence and Strict Liability chapter discusses the concept of joint liability. The *Chem-Dyne* case, which follows, involves a challenge to the concept of joint and several liability by the contributors to a major hazardous waste site. Of concern to many businesspeople is the fact that this stringent and potentially very expensive liability can in some instances be imposed on a current owner of a site who had nothing to do with the contamination, such as a subsequent purchaser of the land or even a bank that financed the purchase of the property and subsequently took it over when the purchaser defaulted on its obligation to the bank.

UNITED STATES v. CHEM-DYNE CORP.

572 F. Supp. 802 (S.D. Ohio 1983)

The United States brought a lawsuit under the Comprehensive Environmental Response, Compensation, and Liability Act (CERCLA) against 24 defendants who had allegedly generated or transported some of the hazardous substances located at the Chem-Dyne treatment facility in Ohio. The government sought to be reimbursed for money that it had spent in cleaning up hazardous wastes at the facility and asserted that each defendant was jointly and severally liable for the entire cost of the cleanup. The defendants contested the claim that they were jointly and severally liable and moved for summary judgment in their favor on this issue.

Rubin, Chief Judge.   CERCLA was enacted both to provide rapid responses to the nationwide threats posed by the 30,000–50,000 improperly managed hazardous waste sites in this country as well as to induce voluntary responses to those sites. The legislation established a $1.6 billion trust fund ("Superfund"), drawn from industry and federal appropriations, to finance the clean-up and containment efforts. The state or federal government may then pursue rapid recovery of the costs incurred from persons liable to reimburse the Superfund money expended. This recovery task may prove difficult when several companies used a site, when dumped chemicals react with others to form new or more toxic substances, or when records are unavailable. Nevertheless, those responsible for the problems caused by the hazardous wastes were intended to bear the costs and responsibilities for remedying the condition. The House sponsor, Representative Florio, commented at length:

> The liability provisions of this bill do not refer to the terms strict, joint and several liability, terms which were contained in the version of H.R. 7020 passed earlier by this body. The standard of liability in these amendments is intended to be strict liability. . . . I have concluded that despite the absence of these specific terms, the strict liability standard already approved by this body is preserved. Issues of joint and several liability not resolved by this bill shall be governed by traditional and evolving principles of common law. The terms "joint and several" have been deleted with the intent that the liability of joint tortfeasors be determined under common or previous statutory law.

Typically, as in this case, there will be numerous hazardous substance generators or transporters who disposed of wastes at a particular site. The term joint and several liability was deleted from the express language of the statute in order to avoid its universal application to inappropriate circumstances. An examination of the common law reveals that when two or more persons acting independently cause a distinct or single harm for which there is a reasonable basis for division according to the contribution of each, each is subject to liability only for the portion of the total harm that he has himself caused. But where two or more persons cause a single and indivisible harm, each is subject to liability for the entire harm. *Restatement (Second) of Torts*, § 875. Furthermore, where the conduct of two or more persons liable under CERCLA has combined to violate the statute, and one or more of the defendants seek to limit their liability on the ground that the entire harm is capable of apportionment, the burden of proof as to apportionment is upon each defendant.

The question of whether the defendants are jointly or severally liable for the clean-up costs turns on a fairly complex factual determination. Read in the light most favorable to the United States, the following facts illustrate the nature of the problem. The Chem-Dyne facility contains a variety of hazardous waste from 289 generators or transporters, consisting of about 608,000 pounds of material. Some of the wastes have been commingled, but the identities of the sources of these wastes remain unascertained. The fact of the mixing of the wastes raises an issue as to the divisibility of the harm. Further, a dispute exists over which of the wastes have contaminated the groundwater, the degree of their migration, and the concomitant health hazard. Finally, the volume of waste of a particular generator is not an accurate predictor of the risk associated with the waste because the toxicity or migratory potential of a particular hazardous substance generally varies independently with the volume of the waste.

This case, as do most pollution cases, turns on the issue of whether the harm caused at Chem-Dyne is "divisible" or "indivisible." If the harm is divisible and if there is a reasonable basis for apportionment of damages, each defendant is liable only for the portion of harm he himself caused. In this situation, the burden of proof as to apportionment is upon each defendant. On the other hand, if the defendants caused an indivisible harm, each is subject to liability for the entire harm. The defendants have not carried their burden of demonstrating the divisibility of the harm and the degrees to which each defendant is responsible.

Defendants' motion for summary judgment is denied.

Community Right to Know and Emergency Cleanup

As part of its 1986 amendments to Superfund, Congress enacted a series of requirements for emergency planning, notification of spills and accidents involving hazardous materials, disclosure by industry to the community of the presence of certain listed chemicals, and notification of the amounts of various chemicals being routinely released into the environment in the area of a facility. This legislation was in response to the industrial accident at Bhopal, India, in 1984 and to several similar incidents in the United States. Firms subject to the requirements have to carefully plan how they will communicate with the surrounding community what chemicals are being regularly released and what precautions the facility has taken to protect the community from regular or accidental releases. Mindful of the difficulty of explaining to a community why large emissions of hazardous substances are taking place, a significant number of companies have undertaken to reduce those emissions below levels they are currently required to meet by law.

REGULATION OF CHEMICALS

Background

More than 60,000 chemical substances are manufactured in the United States and used in a variety of products. Although these chemicals contribute much to the standard of living we enjoy, some of them are toxic or have the potential to cause cancer, birth defects, reproductive failures, and other health-related problems. These risks may be posed in the manufacturing process, during the use of a product, or as a result of the manner of disposal of the chemical or product.

EPA has two statutory authorities that give it the ability to prevent or restrict the manufacture and use of new and existing chemicals to remove unreasonable risks to human health or the environment. These authorities are the Federal Insecticide, Fungicide, and Rodenticide Act and the Toxic Substances Control Act.

Regulation of Agricultural Chemicals

The vast increase in the American farmer's productivity over the past few decades has been in large measure attributable to the farmer's use of chemicals to kill the insects, pests, and weeds that have historically competed with the farmer for crops. Some of these chemicals, such as pesticides and herbicides, were a mixed blessing. They enabled people to dramatically increase productivity and to conquer disease. On the other hand, dead fish and birds provided evidence that chemicals were not only building up in the food chain but also proving fatal to some species. Unless such chemicals are carefully used and disposed of, they can present a danger to the applier and to the consumer of food and water. Gradually, people realized the need to focus on the effects of using such chemicals.

EPA enforces the Federal Insecticide, Fungicide, and Rodenticide Act (FIFRA). This act gives EPA the authority to *register* pesticides before they can be sold, to provide for the certification of appliers of pesticides designated for restrictive use, to set limits on the pesticide residue permitted on crops that provide food for people or animals, and to register and inspect pesticide manufacturing establishments.

When the EPA administrator has reason to believe that continued use of a particular pesticide poses an "imminent hazard," he may *suspend* its registration and remove the product from the market. When the administrator believes that there is a less than imminent hazard but that the environmental risks of continuing to use a pesticide outweigh its benefits, the administrator may initiate a *cancellation of registration* proceeding. This proceeding affords all interested persons—manufacturers, distributors, users, environmentalists, and scientists—an opportunity to present evidence on the proposed cancellation. Cancellation of the registration occurs when the administrator finds that the product causes unreasonable adverse effects on the environment.

Those involved in the food production and distribution process must keep a close watch on regulatory developments at EPA concerning the registration, cancellation, and suspension of products as well as actions it takes concerning permissible residues of pesticides on food products. During the 1980s, the agency took highly publicized actions concerning the use of ethylene dibromide (EDB), a fumigant, on citrus and grain products, the use of sulfites on table grapes, the use of alar on apples, and the use of chlordane as a treatment against termite infestation. In each instance, the economic well-being of many businesses was at risk if they did not adequately anticipate and/or deal with the EPA's actions and the publicity that resulted from these actions.

The following is an excerpt of the EPA administrator's decision to cancel the use of DDT. It was a landmark decision when it was made in 1972, and it illustrates the consideration of costs and benefits that the agency must weigh in making decisions today concerning the use of pesticides.

CONSOLIDATED DDT HEARINGS OPINION AND ORDER OF THE ADMINISTRATOR

37 Fed. Reg. 13,369 (1972)

On January 15, 1971, the Environmental Protection Agency commenced a formal administrative review of all registrations for DDT products and uses pursuant to Section 4(c) of the Federal Insecticide, Fungicide, and Rodenticide Act. Thirty-one companies holding DDT registrations challenged EPA's cancellation of DDT use registrations. The U.S. Department of Agriculture intervened on the side of the registrants, and the Environmental Defense Fund intervened along with EPA to help present the case for cancellation.

After a lengthy public hearing, on April 25, 1972, the hearing examiner issued an opinion recommending to the EPA administrator that all essential uses of DDT be retained and that cancellation be lifted. The administrator took the opinion under advisement and received oral and written briefs both supporting and taking exception to the hearing officer's findings of fact and conclusions of law. The administrator then issued his opinion and order canceling virtually all uses of DDT as of December 31, 1972, except for its use on several minor crops and for disease control and other health-related uses.

Ruckelshaus, Administrator. This hearing represents the culmination of approximately three years of intensive administrative inquiry into the uses of DDT.

Background. DDT is the familiar abbreviation for the chemical (1,1,1,trichlorophenyl ethane), which was for many years the most widely used chemical pesticide in this country. DDT's insecticidal properties were originally discovered, apparently by accident, in 1939, and during World War II it was used extensively for typhus control. Since 1945, DDT has been used for general control of mosquitoes, boll-weevil infestation in cotton-growing areas, and a variety of other uses. Peak use of DDT occurred at the end of the 1950s, and present domestic use of DDT in various formulations has been estimated at 6,000 tons per year. According to Admission 7 of the record, approximately 86 percent or 10,277,258 pounds of domestically used DDT is applied to cotton crops. The same admission indicates that 603,053 pounds and 937,901 pounds, or approximately 5 percent and 9 percent of the total formulated by 27 of the petitioners in these hearings, are used respectively on soybean and peanut crops. All other uses of the 11,996,196 pounds amount to 158,833 pounds of the total, or a little over 1 percent.

For the above uses it appears that DDT is sold in four different formulations: emulsifiable sprays; dust; wettable powder; and granular form.

Public concern over the widespread use of pesticides was stirred by Rachel Carson's book *Silent Spring*, and a natural outgrowth was the investigation of this popular and widely sprayed chemical. DDT, which for many years has been used with apparent safety, was, the critics alleged, a highly dangerous substance which killed beneficial insects, upset the natural ecological balance, and collected in the food chain, thus posing a hazard to man, and other forms of advanced aquatic and avian life.

Application of Risk-Benefit to Crop Uses of DDT. The Agency and the Environmental Defense Fund (EDF) have established that DDT is toxic to nontarget insects and animals, persistent, mobile, and transferable and that it builds up in the food chain. No label directions for use can completely prevent these hazards. In short, they have established at the very least the risk of the unknown. That risk is compounded where, as is the case with DDT, man and animals tend to accumulate and store the chemical. These facts alone constitute risks that are unjustified where apparently safer alternatives exist to achieve the same benefit. Where, however, there is a demonstrated laboratory relationship between the chemical and toxic effects in man or animals, this risk is, generally speaking, rendered even more unacceptable, if alternatives exist. In the case before us the risk to human health from using DDT cannot be discounted. While these risks might be acceptable were we forced to use DDT, they are not so trivial that we can be indifferent to assuming them unnecessarily.

The evidence of record showing storage in man and magnification in the food chain is a warning to the prudent that man may be exposing himself to a substance that may ultimately have a serious effect on his health.

As Judge Leventhal recently pointed out, cancer is a "sensitive and fright-laden" matter and as he noted earlier in his opinion, carcinogenic effects are "generally cumulative and irreversible when discovered." The possibility that DDT is a carcinogen is at present remote and unquantifiable; but if it is not a siren to panic, it is a semaphore which suggests that an identifiable public benefit is required to justify continued use of DDT. Where one chemical tests tumorigenic in a laboratory and one does not, and both accomplish the same risk, the latter is to be preferred, absent some extenuating circumstances.

The risks to the environment from continued use of DDT are more clearly established. There is no doubt that DDT runoff can cause contamination of waters, and given its propensity to volatilize and disperse during application, there is no assurance that curtailed usage on the order of 12 million pounds per year will not continue to affect widespread areas beyond the location of application. The agency staff established as well, the existence of acceptable substitutes for all crop uses of DDT except on onions and sweet potatoes in storage and green peppers.

Registrants attempted but failed to surmount the evidence of established risks and the existence of substitutes by arguing that the buildup of DDT in the environment and its migration to remote areas have resulted from past uses and misuses. There is, however, no persuasive evidence of record to show that the aggregate volume of use of DDT for all uses in question, given the method of application, will not result in continuing dispersal and buildup in the environment and thus add to or maintain the stress on the environment resulting from past use.

The Department of Agriculture has, for its part, emphasized DDT's low acute toxicity in comparison to that of alternative chemicals and thus tried to make the risk and benefit equation balance out favorably for the continued use of DDT. While the acute toxicity of methyl parathion must, in the short run, be taken into account, it does not justify continued use of DDT on a long-term basis. Where a chemical can be safely used if label directions are followed, a producer cannot avoid the risk of his own negligence by exposing third parties and the environment to a long-term hazard.

All crop uses of DDT are canceled except for application to onions for control of cutworms, weevils on stored sweet potatoes, and sweet peppers.

Toxic Substances Control Act

The other major statute regulating chemical use focuses on toxic substances—such as asbestos and PCBs—and on the new chemical compounds that are developed each year. The Toxic Substances Control Act, enacted in 1976, requires that chemicals be tested by manufacturers or processors to determine their effect on human health or the environment before the chemicals are introduced into commerce. The act also gives EPA the authority to regulate chemical substances or mixtures that present an *unreasonable risk of injury to health or the environment* and to take action against any such substances or mixtures that pose an *imminent hazard*.

This legislation was enacted in response to the concern that thousands of new substances were being released into the environment each year, sometimes without adequate consideration of their potential for harm, and that it was not until damage from a substance occurs that its manufacture or use was properly regulated. At the same time, a goal of the act is not to unduly impede, or create unnecessary economic barriers to, technological innovation.

Biotechnology

The development of techniques to genetically manipulate organisms—often referred to generally as biotechnology—offers considerable promise to aid our ability to provide food and health care and to generate a range of new products and production processes. At the same time, they raise concerns about their potential to adversely affect human health or the environment. Responsiblity for regulating research and use of biotechnology is shared in the federal government between the Food and Drug Administration, the Department of Agriculture, the Environmental Protection Agency, and the National Institutes of Health. Generally, a review is required of such activity before it takes place. This process is of considerable import to companies that are developing genetically engineered organisms for commercial purposes; it can affect both the speed at which they are able to get the products to market and the public's confidence that release of the organisms does not pose an unreasonable risk.

CONCEPT REVIEW

MAJOR ENVIRONMENTAL LAWS

Act	Focus
Clean Air Act	Protects quality of ambient (outdoor) air through national ambient air quality standards, state implementation plans, control of air toxics, new source performance standards, and controls on automobiles and fuels
Clean Water Act	Protects and enhances quality of surface waters by setting water quality standards and limiting discharges by industry and municipalities to those waters through permit system; also regulates dredging and filling of wetlands
Marine Protection, Research, and Sanctuaries Act	Regulates dumping of all types of material into ocean waters
Resource Conservation and Recovery Act (RCRA)	Establishes a cradle-to-the-grave regulatory system for handling and disposal of hazardous wastes; also deals with solid waste
Comprehensive Environmental Response Compensation and Liability Act (Superfund)	Provides a program to deal with hazardous waste that was inadequately disposed of in the past; financed in part by tax on chemicals and feedstocks
Federal Insecticide, Fungicide, and Rodenticide Act (FIFRA)	Regulates the sale and use of chemicals to be used as pesticides and herbicides, including residues permitted on crops intended for use as food
Toxic Substances Control Act (TSCA)	Requires preclearance of new chemicals and provides for regulation of existing chemicals that pose an unreasonable risk to health or the environment

ETHICAL AND PUBLIC POLICY CONCERNS

1. Suppose that a multinational chemical company with its primary manufacturing facilities in the United States plans to build a manufacturing facility in a developing country where there are few, if any, real state-imposed environmental regulations. Is it sufficient for the company to simply meet the environmental requirements of the host country? Is there any ethical obligation to do more—for example, to build the facility to meet the requirements it would have to meet in this country?

2. Suppose a manufacturing facility emits a chemical into the air that it has reason to believe is inadequately regulated by EPA and that poses a significant threat to nearby residents even at levels lower than permitted by EPA. As manager of the facility, would you be satisfied to meet the EPA required level or would you install the additional controls you believe necessary to achieve a reasonably safe level?

3. Suppose that you own some valuable seashore property that contains some marshland and wetlands that are critical to the local ecology. In evaluating whether or not to develop your property, what weight would you give to the value that the marshland and wetlands have as a part of the local ecological system?

SUMMARY

In the 1970s, Congress passed many new environmental laws. Older tools for protecting human health and welfare—such as the action to abate a nuisance—have, to a large extent, been supplanted by comprehensive legislation prescribing across-the-board measures to deal with the major kinds and sources of pollution. Most of these laws were then refined and strengthened when they were reauthorized in the 1980s. The National Environmental Policy Act requires the federal government to take into account the environmental effects of the actions that it proposes to take.

The Clean Air Act of 1970, as amended in 1977 and 1990, provides a comprehensive scheme for dealing with air pollution from mobile and stationary sources. The act sets out time schedules by which certain control measures must be instituted to reduce air pollution.

Water pollution has posed potential health problems for many years. Federal water pollution control legislation was first passed in 1948 and has been amended several times. The Clean Water Act of 1972 established a comprehensive framework for controlling water pollution. It provides for setting standards, issuing permits, and constructing municipal wastewater treatment systems with federal assistance.

The Resource Conservation and Recovery Act of 1976 regulates disposal of hazardous waste. The Superfund law, passed initially in 1980, provides a mechanism for identifying and cleaning up the most hazardous uncontrolled waste sites.

Use of agricultural chemicals in the last few decades has led to vast increases in productivity and at the same time posed increased risks to the environment. The Federal Insecticide, Fungicide, and Rodenticide Act gives EPA the responsibility to register pesticides before they can be sold, restrict their use, set limits on residues on food products, and provide for the certification of appliers. Pesticides whose risks outweigh their benefits may have their registration canceled or suspended.

The Toxic Substances Control Act regulates the development, use, storage, transportation, and disposal of toxic and other hazardous substances.

PROBLEM CASES

1. The Interstate Commerce Commission (ICC) has the power to approve or set the tariff rates that railroads charge shippers. As a result of past ICC approvals, the railroad tariffs call for higher shipping charges to carry scrap metals and paper than to carry virgin materials. This disparity operates as an economic discrimination against recycled goods. A group of law students has formed an organization known as SCRAP (Students Challenging Regulatory Agency Procedures). SCRAP is concerned that the ICC-approved rate structure discourages the environmentally desirable use of recycled goods. The ICC approved a 2.5 percent across-the-board surcharge in railroad shipping rates and indicated that no environmental impact statement was necessary because there was no environmental impact. SCRAP is concerned that the increase will further the discrimination against used materials and filed suit against the ICC to require that an environmental impact statement be prepared. Should the court decide that an environmental impact statement is required?

2. In July 1984, Vanguard Corporation began operating a metal furniture manufacturing plant in Brooklyn, New York. The plant is located in an area that has not attained the national ambient air quality standards for ozone. The plant is a major stationary source (i.e., has the potential to emit more than 100 tons a year) of volatile organic compounds that contribute to the production of ozone in the atmosphere. The New York state implementation plan (SIP) requires that metal-coating facilities use paint that contains less than three pounds of organic solvent (minus water) per gallon at the time of coating. On August 24, 1984, EPA notified Vanguard that it was not in compliance with the SIP provision concerning coatings and issued it a notice of violation. Vanguard sought to defend against the notice of violation on the grounds that it had used its best faith efforts to comply but that full compliance was technologically and economically infeasible. It indicated that it wanted 18 more months to come into compliance. Should Vanguard be held to be in violation of the Clean Air Act?

3. As part of its iron ore processing operations at Silver Bay, Minnesota, Reserve Mining discharges asbestos fibers into the air. Minnesota air pollution control regulations prohibit the operation of an emission source unless it has filtration equipment that collects 99 percent, by weight, of the particulate matter discharged by the plant. The Reserve filtration equipment did not comply with this standard, thus resulting in levels of asbestos in the air that were potentially harmful to public health. The state of Minnesota brought suit to enjoin the asbestos discharges as a public nuisance. Should an injunction be granted?

4. Charles Hanson owned land abutting on Keith Lake, a freshwater lake that was subject to some tidal flooding as a result of its connection with tidal waters. In order to minimize the detrimental effects from the tidal activities and consequent flooding, Hanson deposited a large quantity of dirt, rock, bricks, sheet metal, and other debris along the shoreline of his property. He did so without obtaining a permit from the U.S. Army Corps of Engineers under section 404 of the Clean Water Act, which controls dumping and filling activities in navigable waters of the United States. Under the law, discharges of pollutants into navigable waters without a permit are forbidden. The term *pollutant* is defined to include "dredged spoil, solid waste, incinerator residue, sewage, garbage, sewage sludge, munitions, chemical wastes, biological materials, radioactive materials, heat, wrecked or discarded equipment, rock, sand, cellar dirt, and industrial, municipal and agricultural waste discharged into water." EPA brought an enforcement action against Hanson claiming he had violated the Clean Water Act. Should the court find that Hanson violated the act?

5. In 1979, Anne Arundel County, Maryland, enacted two related ordinances. One absolutely prohibited the disposal in and the transportation through Anne Arundel County of various hazardous wastes not originating in that county. Another ordinance required a license to dispose of hazardous waste in Anne Arundel County; it also requires a license to transport hazardous wastes through the county. Browning-Ferris, Inc. (BFI), is the owner and operator of a landfill located in Anne Arundel County that is licensed by the state of Maryland to receive hazardous wastes. BFI is also a hauler of hazardous wastes within the county. The county notified BFI that it expected BFI to comply with the new regulations, and BFI filed a lawsuit challenging the ordinances and seeking to have them enjoined. How should the court rule?

6. The Royal McBee Corporation manufactured typewriters at a factory in Springfield, Missouri. As a part of the manufacturing process, Royal McBee generated cyanide-based electroplating wastes, sludge from the bottom of electroplating tanks, and spent plating bath solution. As part of their duties, Royal McBee employees dumped the wastes onto the surface of the soil on a vacant lot adjoining the factory. This took place between 1959 and 1962. Over time, the waste materials migrated outward and downward from the original dumping site, contaminating a large area. In 1970, the manufacturing facility and lot were sold to General Electric, which operated the plant but did not engage in the dumping of wastes on the vacant lot. In the mid-1980s, General Electric was required by EPA and the state of Missouri, under the authority of the federal Superfund law, to clean up the contamination at the site. General Electric then brought a lawsuit against the successor corporation of Royal McBee's typewriter business, Litton Business Systems, to recover for the costs incurred in cleaning up the site. Under the Superfund

law, "any person who at the time of disposal of any hazardous substance owned or operated any facilities at which such hazardous substances were disposed of, shall be liable for any other necessary costs of response incurred by any other person" consistent with the Superfund law and regulations. Is General Electric entitled to recover its cleanup costs from Litton?

7. Chemlawn sells pesticide products for use on residential lawns. The active ingredients in Chemlawn's products are registered with the Environmental Protection Agency pursuant to the Federal Insecticide, Fungicide, and Rodenticide Act (FIFRA). Deborah Ryan brought a lawsuit against Chemlawn seeking damages in tort for injuries she claimed that she and her son Kevin sustained from the use of Chemlawn products. Ryan claims that the products are unsafe for commercial use and that they have been inadequately tested by the EPA. Chemlawn contends that Ryan should take her complaints to EPA, which has the responsibility for determining whether the products are safe to be sold. How should the court decide?

8. Wilson owned a farm in Jefferson County, Virginia, on which cotton was grown. Three quarters of a mile away, the Elm Company owned land on which it grew rice. On a day when no wind was blowing, the Elm Company had its rice crop carefully dusted by an aviator who was a professional crop duster. He used 2-4-D, a powerful chemical manufactured by Chapman Chemical Company. The chemical is very damaging to any broad-leaved plant with which it has contact, but does no damage to grasses and plants that are not broad-leaved. The 2-4-D drifted and settled on the cotton on the Wilson farm, greatly reducing the yield of cotton. Wilson brought suit against Elm Company and Chapman Chemical Company to recover compensation for the damage. While Chapman warned users of the damage that the product would cause to broad-leaved plants, it had not done any tests to determine what dangers were posed by dusting 2-4-D by airplane, which it knew was a common way of applying agricultural chemicals. In fact, it recommended this method for applying 2-4-D. Users of agricultural chemicals, such as Elm Company, knew that these chemicals normally did not float more than 50–100 feet beyond the area where they were applied and were given no reason by Chapman to suspect otherwise as to 2-4-D. Should Elm and/or Chapman be liable for the damage caused to Wilson's cotton crop?

SPECIAL TOPICS

CHAPTER 52

THE LEGAL ENVIRONMENT FOR INTERNATIONAL BUSINESS

INTRODUCTION

Since 1945, American businesses have steadily increased the number and size of transactions with people in foreign markets. American businesses export their goods to other countries, import foreign goods into the United States, establish manufacturing, drilling, and other operations on foreign soil, and license their patents and other technology to foreign businesses. With the remarkable economic changes that have swept eastern Europe after the December 1989 revolutions, foreign trade by American firms in the 1990s should accelerate.

Each international business transaction is attended by dozens of legal and practical problems. For example, U.S. law forbids the export of some goods and technology. American law also prohibits or restricts trade with businesses in specified foreign countries such as Cuba. Many foreign nations require that any firm doing business within their boundaries be owned by their government or by their citizens. Several socialist countries have confiscated or expropriated the business assets of U.S. firms doing business in those countries. In addition, American firms doing business abroad must comply with other domestic laws of the host country, such as antitrust, securities, and employment law. For example, many Arabic countries prohibit alcohol consumption and forbid women to operate motor vehicles.

Practical problems abound as well. There are language and cultural differences. Contract negotiations may be either more or less formal than in America. There are different currencies, some of which—like the Russian ruble—may be nearly worthless on the world market. Other currencies' values may quickly depreciate, increasing the risk that a buyer of goods will underpay for goods, unless the parties designate a stable currency in their sales contract.

In addition, the parties to international transactions are much less likely to know each other well because they are separated by great distances, thereby increasing a seller's risk of nonpayment by the buyer and a buyer's risk of nondelivery by the seller. The resolution of disputes is especially troublesome, as each party may seek to have a dispute resolved in his home court, applying law favorable to his side, even though their sales contract may provide for arbitration.

Sources of International Business Law

The answers to legal questions raised by international business transactions come from a mix of the laws of our own country, those of the other country or countries involved, and doctrines of international law. For example, American exporters must comply with American laws concerning the export of goods and foreign laws that restrict the importation of goods. While many nations have signed agreements designed to remove importation restrictions, such international law is not binding on a signatory nation unless its legislature has passed a statute to implement the agreement.

When an American business enters a contract to sell goods to a foreign buyer, the buyer and seller may choose to follow American contract law or foreign contract law. They may use international law embodied in the United Nations Convention on Contracts for the International Sale of Goods (CISG). Usually, the CISG will not apply unless the seller's or buyer's nation has adopted the CISG. The United States has adopted the CISG.

When an American firm makes a direct foreign investment such as by establishing a manufacturing plant abroad, the firm must comply with all of the foreign nation's laws applicable to its operations, such as employee safety and dismissal laws, antitrust laws, and toxic waste disposal regulations. In addition, the foreign nation's laws may restrict the American firm's ability to take its profits back to the United States: Reinvestment of profits in the foreign nation may be required.

Disputes between an American seller and a foreign buyer may be resolved in the courts of either nation or in an international arbitration tribunal. The court or tribunal may apply American law, foreign law, or international law. For example, some foreign nations have seized or expropriated the foreign operations of American firms. When that occurs, the American firm may seek a remedy in an American court applying international law requiring the payment of adequate compensation. However, the American court may apply the **act of state** doctrine or the doctrine of **sovereign immunity** to deny a recovery to the American firm. The act of state doctrine, while not international law, is a matter of comity or courtesy between nations. It holds that no nation is permitted to question the act of another nation committed within its own boundaries. The doctrine of sovereign immunity is international law; it holds that a nation can do no wrong. It is founded in the ancient principle that "The King can do no wrong" and, therefore, a king could not be sued by his subjects. Nonetheless, the United States has breached the doctrine of sovereign immunity by allowing limited actions against foreign governments under the Foreign Sovereign Immunity Act.[1]

Scope of This Chapter

Only some of the complexities of international business transactions can be explored within the limited scope of this chapter. The intent of this chapter, therefore, is to give you a sense of the legal environment of international business by examining the most important legal questions that arise in connection with international sales, licensing, and investment. Because most international business transactions entered into by an American business must comply with trade restrictions imposed by the United States and other governments, this chapter begins with a consideration of trade limitations.

LIMITATIONS ON TRADE

Many governmentally imposed barriers to trade affect international business transactions. The most important are export and import controls, including tariffs.

Export Controls

For political or economic purposes, most nations place export controls on certain goods and technology leaving their countries. For example, in 1990, most of the nations placed an embargo on Iraqi exports in response to its invasion of Kuwait. Another example is the restriction on the sale of militarily sensitive technology by western nations so that it is not obtained by countries whose governments are considered unfriendly. The restrictions are agreed on unanimously by western countries who are members of the Paris-based Coordinating Committee for Multilateral Export Controls (COCOM).[2] The restrictions are then enforced through laws passed in each country. Failure to abide by the restrictions can lead to imprisonment of the sellers of the restricted goods.

The Export Administration Act of 1985   The Export Administration Act of 1985 is the main law controlling **exports** from the United States. The Act is enforced by the Office of Export Administration (OEA) of the Department of Commerce. The Act is designed to accomplish three purposes:

1. To enhance national security.
2. To aid in the accomplishment of the objective of American foreign policy.

---

[1]For example, *Wolf v. Banco Nacional de Mexico, S.A.,* 739 F.2d 1458 (9th Cir. 1984) (bank's sale of certificate of deposit is commercial activity).

[2]Members of COCOM are Japan, Australia, and the countries in the North Atlantic Treaty Organization (NATO), except for Iceland.

3. To preserve commodities and technology essential to the protection of the American economy.

Commodity Control List   The OEA implements the Act by administering a licensing procedure and maintaining a **commodity control list** of goods and technical data subject to the Act. The OEA generally requires an exporter to obtain a **license** prior to exportation of the good or technology.

Before applying for a license, an exporter must consult the commodity control list to determine whether exports to the country of destination are restricted. For example, exports to Cuba, Vietnam, Cambodia, and North Korea are almost totally prohibited. Libya's role in international terrorism has resulted in heavy restrictions on exports to Libya. Exports to communistic countries are restricted as well. Exports to most western hemisphere nations are not restricted.

When the commodity control list indicates that exportation of the good or technology to the destination country is prohibited, the exporter must abandon its attempt to export. When the exportation is legal, the exporter must consult the commodity control list to determine whether it needs a general or a validated license issued by the OEA.

A **general license** is a blanket authorization to export the covered goods or technology without obtaining permission for a specific export. A general license appears in the form of an administrative regulation and authorizes every exporter to export the covered goods or technology. Thus, an exporter need not obtain specific OEA approval when the OEA has issued a general license to export beer to Canada.

A **validated license** authorizes a specific exporter to export a specific good or technology to a specific country. A validated license may validate one export or a series of exports. The OEA's refusal to grant a validated license may be appealed to the assistant secretary of commerce for trade administration. However, his decision is final; there is no judicial review of his administrative decision.

The commodity control list applies not merely to the exportation by an American firm to a foreign country. It also controls the **reexportation** of American goods and technology by the foreign buyer to a second foreign nation. As a result, when American goods are exported to Germany and reexported to Iraq, the OEA would regulate both the America-to-Germany and Germany-to-Iraq transactions.

The OEA does not have authority to issue licenses for all goods and technology. For example, weapons export is usually controlled by the State Department; the export of nuclear materials is licensed by the Nuclear Regulatory Commission.

In the following case, the court found that the Department of Commerce's commodity control list restricted the export of tires for F-14 fighter aircraft.

UNITED STATES v. GEISSLER
731 F. Supp. 93 (E.D.N.Y. 1990)

Roger Geissler was an exporter of military arms and parts. He exported tires for F-14 fighter jets to Iran for use by the Iranian Air Force. Because Geissler did not obtain a validated license to export the F-14 tires, the U.S. attorney general obtained an indictment against Geissler on the grounds that Geissler committed a criminal violation of the Export Administration Act and regulations thereunder. Geissler moved to dismiss his indictment on the grounds that F-14 tires were not commodities covered by the Department of Commerce's commodity control list (CCL).

Spatt, Judge.   The general export proscription contained in the Export Administration Regulations (EAR) is as follows:

the export from the United States of all commodities . . . is hereby prohibited unless and until a general license authorizing such export shall have been established or a validated license or other authorization for such export shall have been granted by the Office of Export Licensing.

The term "commodities" is defined broadly, as "[a]ny article, material or supply except technical data." All commodities under the export licensing jurisdiction of the Department of Commerce are contained on the CCL. The CCL is broken down into ten general groups. Contained within each group are commodity entries identified by a four digit number plus a letter—the Export Control Commodity Number (ECCN).

The instant indictment concerns CCL Commodity Group Four, entitled "Transportation Equipment." Group Four contains twenty-four ECCNs. The Government contended that an export license was required for the F-14 military tires (allegedly destined for Iran) by reason of Commodity Group Four, ECCN 6498F, which contains the following description: "Other aircraft parts and components, n.e.s. [not elsewhere specified]." ECCN 6498F also specifically states that a validated license is required for 6498F commodities exported to Iran.

The EAR delineates the categories of commodities outside of Commerce Department jurisdiction. The EAR provides that "Regulations administered by the Office of Munitions Control, U.S. Department of State, . . . govern the export of defense articles and defense services on the U.S. Munitions List." By the terms of Category VIII(g) of the U.S. Munitions List, export of F-14 aircraft tires are clearly excluded from State Department licensing jurisdiction.

The Court finds that F-14 aircraft tires are contained in the Commodity Control List and therefore are covered by the EAR. The term "commodities" certainly encompasses F-14 aircraft tires. The EAR does not explicitly exclude coverage of F-14 aircraft tires from its jurisdiction and no other government agency controls the export of F-14 tires. Moreover, the only other agency which presumably would regulate the export of F-14 tires—the State Department—explicitly excludes F-14 aircraft tires from its jurisdiction. It is reasonable to conclude, therefore, that F-14 tires are within Commerce Department jurisdiction.

The specific EAR provision governing F-14 aircraft tires is Group 4, ECCN 6498F: "Other aircraft parts and components, n.e.s." A plain reading of this language indicates that F-14 aircraft tires come within the terms of 6498F. A reasonably prudent person, no less a sophisticated businessman and arms exporter, would read and understand ECCN 6498F as including F-14 aircraft tires.

Motion by Geissler to dismiss the indictment is denied.

Import Controls

Countries restrict the importation of goods and technology primarily to protect domestic industry. These restrictions commonly take the form of quotas, licensing requirements, or tariffs. By setting a quota on the importation of Japanese automobiles, the United States has forced Japan to limit the number of automobiles it sells in the United States as a way of opening up markets for American products in the United States and reducing the unfavorable balance of trade with Japan.

By requiring the licensing of foreign technology, Japan has improved the ability of its manufacturers to obtain more favorable bargaining terms. Instead of having different Japanese manufacturers compete with one another to get a desirable piece of technology from an American licensor, with the licensor awarding the

license to the highest bidder, the Japanese licensing agency in effect tells the licensor that it will be excluded from the Japanese market unless it agrees to accept considerably less favorable terms than would have resulted without the regulation.

In developing nations, licensing regulations may ensure a country's scarce resources are not being used unless the imported technology fits into the country's basic development plans. To protect domestic employees, technical training of local personnel may be required in return for import approval.

Most countries also maintain a list of prohibited imports. In addition, some sellers dump goods in foreign markets at lower prices than they sell in the domestic market, and some governments subsidize the manufacture of domestic goods exported to other countries.

The United States protects its industry from dumping and subsidies with antidumping and countervailing duty laws. In addition, U.S. laws protect American firms from the importation of counterfeit goods and grey market goods. Each of these laws is considered separately below.

Prohibited Imports

There are a large number of goods that may not be imported into the United States. For example, the American fur industry is protected by a prohibition on the import of furs from the Soviet Union. Public morals are protected by the exclusion of obscene materials and lottery tickets. The fishing industry is served by prohibiting the importation of fish from nations that seize American fishing boats.

Tariffs

A **tariff** is a tax or duty assessed on goods, generally when they are imported into a country. The duty is *ad valorem;* that is, a percentage of the value of the goods, such as 10 percent. Through the use of tariffs, governments can restrict imports and protect domestic industry from foreign competition. A sufficiently high ad valo-

rem duty makes the product so expensive that most consumers will refuse to buy it; consequently, consumers do without the good or buy a domestically produced equivalent.

In the United States, import duties are assessed and collected by the U.S. Customs Service. Imported goods are unloaded under the supervision of the Customs Service and taken to a warehouse, where they are kept until a formal entry into the United States is made. **Entry** is the presentation of documentation necessary to classify the goods and assess the duty. After a bond is posted to ensure payment of the duty, the goods are examined. If importation of the goods is prohibited or the goods are not listed on the invoices, the goods may be seized and criminal charges brought against the importer. If the goods pass examination, a tentative duty is assessed and the goods are released to the importer. The Customs Service has the right to charge an additional duty at a later time. The importer may protest or ask for review of the duty before an appraisal specialist at the Customs Headquarters. Further reviews are heard by the Court of International Trade and the Court of Appeals for the Federal Circuit in Washington, D.C.

In the next case, the Federal Circuit affirmed the decision of the Court of International Trade that imported G.I. Joe toys were dutiable as dolls.

HASBRO INDUSTRIES, INC. v. U.S.

879 F.2d 838 (Fed. Cir. 1989)

Hasbro Industries, Inc., imported G.I. Joe Action Figures from Hong Kong. G.I. Joe figures are made of plastic, are approximately 3½ inches tall, and have the appearance of humans dressed and equipped in a manner associated with actual or fictional warfare. They are noticeably lifelike and constructed in a manner that permits a range of movements. The head turns and the arms are jointed at the shoulder and elbow. They can turn at the waist and also bend slightly in all directions from the waist. The legs have a wide range of movement.

Each figure is packaged singly in a large plastic blister mounted on a large card that contains specific biographical information for each figure. For example, First Sergeant, Code Name: Duke, has the following personnel card:

File Name: Hauser, Conrad S.

Primary Military Specialty: Airborn Infantryman

Birthplace: St. Louis, MO   Grade: E-8 (Master Sergeant)

Duke was fluent in French, German, and English when he enlisted in 1967. Graduated top of his class at airborne school, Fort Benning. Went Special Forces in 1979. Ran four different Special Forces schools.

Turned down a commission in 1971. Statement after declining commission: "They tell me that an officer's job is to impel others to take the risks—so that the officer survives to take the blame in the event of total catastrophe. With all due respect, sir . . . if that's what an officer does, I don't want any part of it."

In addition, each figure comes with its own specialized accessories. For example, First Sergeant comes with plastic pieces representing binoculars, a helmet, an assault pack, and an M-32 submachine gun.

In 1982 and 1983, the U.S. Customs Service classified G.I. Joe figures as "other dolls" under the Tariff Schedule of the United States (TSUS) and assessed a duty on the figures. Hasbro claimed that G.I. Joe was not a doll and should be importable free of duty. Hasbro appealed the Custom Service's decision to the Court of International Trade, which affirmed the decision. Hasbro next appealed to the Federal Circuit Court of Appeals.

Michel, Judge.   Hasbro argues that these toy figures are excepted from duty because they are properly classifiable as "Toy figures of animate objects (except dolls): Not having a spring mechanism: Not stuffed: Other" under the TSUS. Hasbro contends that G.I. Joe is nothing more than a modern version of a traditional toy soldier.

To determine the common meaning of a tariff term like "doll," the court may consult dictionaries, scientific authorities, and other reliable information sources to ascertain that common meaning. The Court of International Trade referred to a general dictionary defining the word "doll" as a representation of a human being used as a child's plaything. While we conclude that this summary definition is not an all-inclusive definition for the term "doll," we determine that it is suitable for this case.

Given this broad common meaning of the term "doll," we next review whether the Court of International Trade clearly erred when it found that the G.I. Joe action figure fit within that term. We determine it did not. The evidence includes testimony (including expert testimony), magazine articles referring to G.I. Joe as a doll, letters from purchasers to Hasbro also referring to G.I. Joe as a doll, doll collector books, and the imported articles themselves.

Finally, we turn to Hasbro's argument that the long established practice of the Customs Service is to exclude traditional toy soldiers from the tariff provision for dolls. As the Court of International Trade explained, the individual personality of each of these figures, as evidenced by his biographical file cards and physical characteristics inviting "intimate and manipulative" play, indicates that these figures are not comparable to the identical, immobile faceless soldiers of yesteryear that were sold in groups of a dozen or so in bags.

Although Hasbro has fought valiantly that these figures are not dolls, we are unable to agree. Even though G.I. Joe has lost this battle, hopefully he will not lose his courage for combat, despite being officially designated by the United States Customs Service as a "doll."

Judgment for the United States affirmed.

GATT   Tariffs have been the most common barrier to free trade, and as a result, many governments are cooperating to control or eliminate tariffs. One of the most comprehensive efforts at cooperation has been the rounds of negotiations under the **General Agreement on Tariffs and Trade (GATT),** a treaty subscribed to by more than 80 nations.

Negotiations under GATT have resulted in significant tariff reductions. The focus of GATT is much broader than tariff reduction, however; its purpose is to reduce all trade barriers and promote a stable world trade environment. Among other ways, it attempts to do this through a **most favored nation** clause, which requires a signatory nation such as the United States to offer all other signatory nations treatment as favorable as that granted by the United States to any individual signatory country. Thus, with some exceptions, this eliminates discrimination among countries on the basis of tariffs and duties.

The EEC   Another way that tariffs and trade barriers have been reduced is through the formation of regional associations fostering free trade within the association, and often requiring most favored nation treatment by a nonassociation country dealing with any of the countries in the association. There are many such economic unions, but the best known is the **European Economic Community (EEC),** also known as the Common Market.

Formed in 1957, the European Common Market comprises most of the western European countries.[3] The purpose of the EEC is to establish an economic community by promoting free trade within its boundaries. It does this by eliminating tariffs among its members and establishing common tariffs for outside countries, promoting the free movement of workers, goods, and capital among its members, establishing a common monetary policy with the eventual goal of establishing a single monetary unit, and generally promoting the welfare of individuals within the union through economic development. Through this union, the member countries have created an economic force that is far greater than any individual member could have generated on its own.

In the Single European Act, the EEC has committed to completion of the Common Market by 1992. The year 1992 should mark the end of barriers to the passage of goods, services, capital, and people across the boundaries between EEC nations.

Dumping and Subsidized Goods

One of the most common reasons the EEC and other countries impose tariffs today is to counteract dumping and subsidizing goods. **Dumping** is the selling of goods at unfairly low prices. The selling of imported goods at these low prices means that domestic manufacturers cannot effectively compete with them. Thus, duties are imposed on the goods to offset the difference between the import price and the fair price as determined by the nation of import.

In the United States, dumping is regulated by an **antidumping** law, the Trade Agreement Act of 1979. When dumping is alleged, the allegation is investigated by the International Trade Commission (ITC) of the Department of Commerce to determine if the goods are being sold at less than fair value. If the allegation is proved and the ITC determines that the dumping has harmed a domestic industry, an antidumping duty can be assessed.

Subsidized goods are goods that in some way have been economically supported by the government of their country of origin. For example, Spain has subsidized exported goods by rebating domestic taxes to exporters.[4] Because of this support, subsidized goods can then be sold for less than goods not receiving subsidies. Governments impose **countervailing duties** against subsidized imported goods to protect competing domestic goods. Both the United States and the EEC have imposed duties against Japanese goods because of government subsidies. The Trade Agreement Act of 1979 applies to subsidized goods imported into the United States.

Counterfeit and Grey Market Goods

Piracy and other unauthorized uses of American goods or technology protected by U.S. patent, copyright, and trademark law have become a major problem of American businesses. For example, foreign jeans manufacturers may without authorization place the Levi's label on their jeans, thereby damaging the business of Levi Strauss & Co. by depriving it of some of the jeans' market and damaging the value of the Levi trademark, especially if the imported jeans are of inferior quality. This is an example of **counterfeit goods,** goods unlawfully bearing a trademark. Counterfeit goods may also unlawfully appropriate patented technology or copyrighted material. For example, a foreign musical recording company may pirate the latest M.C. Hammer album and import thousands of copies of it into the United States.

American firms harmed by the importation of counterfeit goods may obtain injunctions[5] and damages under the Tariff Act of 1930, the Lanham Trademark Act

---

[3]Belgium, Denmark, France, Greece, Ireland, Italy, Luxembourg, The Netherlands, Portugal, Spain, the United Kingdom, and Germany are members of the EEC.

[4]*Industrial Quimica del Nalon, S.A. v. United States,* 729 F. Supp. 103 (Ct. Int'l. Trade 1989).

[5]*Bally/Midway Mfg. Co. v. U.S. Int'l. Trade Comm.,* 714 F. 2d 1117 (Fed. Cir. 1983) (excluded import of video games infringing Pac-Man copyrights and trademarks).

of 1946, the Copyright Act, and federal patent law.[6] In addition, the Trademark Counterfeiting Act of 1984 establishes criminal penalties for counterfeiting goods. It also allows an American firm to recover from a counterfeiter three times its damages or three times the counterfeiter's profits (whichever is greater).

Patent, copyright, and trademark piracy is increasing in many parts of the world, especially developing nations. Some developing nations believe that technology should be transferred freely to foster their economic growth. Consequently, they either encourage piracy or choose not to oppose it. This trend could be reversed if the proposed GATT Code on Discouraging Trade in Counterfeit Goods becomes international law.

Grey market goods are goods lawfully bearing trademarks or using patents and copyrighted material, but they enter the American market without authorization. For example, Parker Pen Co. may authorize a Japanese manufacturer to make and sell Parker pens only in Japan. When an American firm imports the Japanese-made Parker pens into the United States, the goods become grey market goods.

While importing grey market goods may violate the contract between American firm and its foreign licensee, it is not clear in what contexts it violates U.S. importation, trademark, patent, or copyright law.[7] The Trademark Counterfeiting Act of 1984 specifically excludes grey market goods from its coverage.

FOREIGN SALES OF DOMESTICALLY MANUFACTURED PRODUCTS

The export of a product manufactured at home is the most common form of international transaction engaged in by American firms. Once an American exporter has determined that the sale of its product to a buyer in a foreign nation is permitted by American export law and the foreign nation's import law, the exporter may enter a contract with the foreign buyer. In addition to the

---

[6]The American trademark, copyright, and patent laws are discussed more fully in the chapter Intellectual Property, Competitive Torts, and Unfair Competition.

[7]Compare *Coalition to Preserve the Integrity of American Trademarks v. United States*, 790 F.2d 903 (D.C. Cir. 1986) (importation of grey market goods manufactured by trademark owner's foreign subsidiary or licensee and imported by unrelated persons without authorization of trademark owners violates the Tariff Act) with *Weil Ceramics & Glass, Inc. v. Dash*, 878 F.2d 659 (3d Cir. 1989) (neither Tariff Act nor Lanham Act violated by importation of grey market goods by importer who purchased trademarked goods from parent company of the American trademark owner).

logistical problems of negotiation at long distance perhaps in two languages, the primary legal questions are what contract law applies to the transaction and what terms the contract should include.

Regulation of International Sales Contract

Countries have attempted to address some of the problems raised by international transactions through their agreement to codes that apply across national boundaries. Typically, countries agree to be bound by them, then adjust their internal laws, if necessary, so they are in compliance with the laws laid out in the code. Although such codes have existed since the early part of this century, it has only been in the last half of this century that they have gained many signatories. As the pace of international trade has increased, so has support for such agreements.

An example of such an agreement is the United Nations Convention on Contracts for the International Sale of Goods (CISG), which became effective in 1988. Although fewer than 20 nations, including the United States, have adopted the CISG, it is certain to become the dominant source of sales law for international business transactions.

The CISG is designed to provide a uniform code for international contracts much the same way that the Uniform Commercial Code (UCC) provides uniformity and certainty for transactions among contracting parties from different states in the United States. The Convention provides rules governing the formation of international contracts and regulates the transfer of goods under those contracts. For example, a contract between an American exporter and a French importer is ruled by the CISG unless the contract states otherwise. If the contract is between an American exporter and an importer in a nation that has not adopted the CISG, the CISG applies only if the contract states that American law applies. Thus, the CISG gives clear preference to itself over the purely domestic law of the nation such as the UCC, which applies to domestic sales contracts.

There are substantial differences between the CISG and the UCC. The CISG does not require any sales contract to be written. Offers easily become irrevocable. The offeree need reasonably believe that it is irrevocable; even oral promises to keep an offer open are irrevocable. An attempted acceptance that changes the terms of the offer is not an acceptance.

Even when the CISG applies to an international sales contract, the parties should not rely exclusively on its protections. Instead, they should draft a comprehensive contract that carefully addresses the major legal and practical problems that may arise in the performance of the contract. The content of the contract varies according to the manner of relationship between the buyer and the seller: (1) A firm may make direct sales to customers abroad, or (2) it may appoint one or more distributors for a particular country or region, which distributors purchase the product from the American firm and resell it to customers in their territories. These two methods of exploiting the world market can involve different legal problems. The following discussion is based on the typical way these transactions are structured to deal with the international climate.

DIRECT SALE TO A FOREIGN BUYER

The Sales Contract

Although a writing is not required by the CISG, the seller and buyer in an international transaction should execute a written contract to ensure their complete understanding of the basic terms and conditions of the contract. The interpretation and enforcement of most of these terms and conditions—such as price, method of payment, currency of payment, and product warranties—primarily involve contract law. To the extent that the CISG does not apply and there is a difference between the contract law of the seller's jurisdiction and that of the buyer, courts typically respect the choice of the parties as to which law applies if the parties, as is usual, have included a **choice of law clause** in the agreement. In addition, the following other terms and conditions should be included in the written contract.

Force Majeure **Clause** International sales contracts should include a *force majeure* clause, which excuses performance due to conditions beyond the parties' control. For example, a *force majeure* clause may excuse a seller of oil from performing when the outbreak of war threatens shipping lanes in the Persian Gulf. *Force majeure* clauses are often drafted by trade associations for use by their members; such clauses reflect the risks known to have occurred in the past.

As an alternative or in addition to a *force majeure* clause, the CISG has a frustration defense that is similar to the commercial impracticability defense of the UCC.[8] CISG Article 79 excuses nonperformance due to an im-

pediment beyond a party's control that the party could not reasonably have been expected to take into account at the time the contract was made or to avoid or overcome at the time of performance.

Currency of Payment An international sales contract should specify the currency in which payment is to be made. American dollars are usually selected because their value is relatively stable, while the currencies of other nations—for example, Brazil—continually fall in value due to high inflation. For example, suppose an American firm contracts to sell five trucks worth $100,000 to a Brazilian firm for 150,000 cruzados. If payment is delayed for three months, Brazilian inflation may cause the 150,000-cruzado payment to be worth only $90,000.

Assuring Payment of the Sales Price

Perhaps the most important provisions in the international sales contract cover the manner by which the buyer pays the seller. Frequently, a foreign buyer's contractual promise to pay when the goods arrive does not provide the seller with sufficient assurance of payment. The seller may not know the overseas buyer well enough to determine the buyer's financial condition or inclination to refuse payment if the buyer no longer wants the goods when they arrive. When the buyer fails to make payment, the seller will find it difficult and expensive to pursue its legal rights under the contract. Even if the seller is assured that the buyer will pay for the goods on arrival, the time required for shipping the goods often means that payment is not received until months after shipment.

To solve these problems, the seller often insists on receiving an **irrevocable letter of credit.** The buyer obtains from a bank in the buyer's country a letter of credit, under which the bank promises to pay the amount of the sales contract to the seller if the seller produces a **negotiable bill of lading** and other documents proving that it shipped the goods required by the sales contract in conformity with the terms of the letter of credit.[9] A letter of credit is irrevocable when it cannot be revoked by the buyer's bank without the consent of the seller and the buyer.

---

[8]The doctrine of commercial impracticability is covered in the Illegality chapter.

[9]A bill of lading is a document issued by a carrier acknowledging that the seller has delivered particular goods to it and entitling the holder of the bill of lading to receive these goods at the place of destination.

Letters of credit may be confirmed or advised. On a *confirmed* letter of credit, the seller's bank agrees to assume liability on the letter of credit. On an *advised* letter of credit, the seller's bank merely acts as an agent for collection of the amount owed to the seller.

Typically, under a confirmed letter of credit, the buyer's bank issues a letter of credit to the seller; the seller's bank confirms the letter of credit; the seller delivers the goods to a carrier; the carrier issues a negotiable bill of lading to the seller; the seller delivers the bill of lading to the seller's bank and presents a draft[10] drawn on the

buyer demanding payment for the goods; the seller's bank pays the seller for the goods; the buyer's bank reimburses the seller's bank; and the buyer reimburses its bank. Figure 1 summarizes the confirmed letter of credit transaction.

Under an advised letter of credit, the seller's bank acts as agent for the seller by collecting from the buyer's bank and giving the payment to the seller. The buyer's bank is reimbursed by the buyer.

The confirmed letter of credit is the least risky payment method for sellers. The confirmation is needed because the seller, unlike the confirming bank, may not know any more about the financial integrity of the issuing bank than it knows about that of the buyer. The seller has a promise of immediate payment from an entity it

---

[10]A draft is a negotiable instrument by which the drawer (in this case, the seller) orders the drawee (the buyer) to pay the payee (the seller). Drafts are explained more fully in the part on Commercial Paper.

FIGURE 1 Confirmed Letter of Credit Transaction

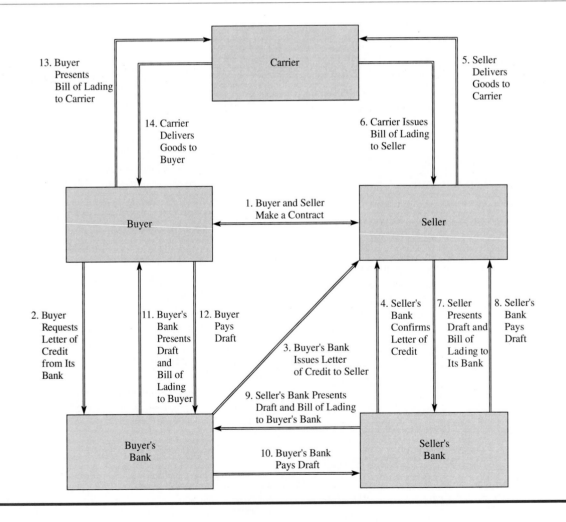

knows to be financially solvent—the confirming bank. If the draft drawn pursuant to the letter of credit is not paid, the seller may sue the confirming bank, which is a bank in his home country.

Under the confirmed letter of credit, payment is made to the seller well before the goods arrive. Thus, the buyer cannot claim that the goods are defective and refuse to pay for them. When the goods are truly defective on arrival, however, the customer can commence an action for damages against the seller based on their original sales contract.

Conforming and Nonconforming Documents   In a letter of credit transaction, the promises made by the buyer's and seller's banks are independent of the underlying sales contract between the seller and the buyer. Therefore, when the seller presents a bill of lading and other documents that *conform* to the terms of the letter

of credit, the issuing bank and the confirming bank are required to pay, even if the buyer refuses to pay its bank or even, generally, if the buyer claims to know that the goods are defective. However, if the bill of lading or other required documents *do not conform* to the terms of the letter of credit, a bank may properly refuse to pay. A bill of lading is *nonconforming* when, for example, it indicates the wrong goods were shipped, states the wrong person to receive the goods, or states a buyer's address differently than the letter of credit.[11]

The following case demonstrates that a bank that issues (or confirms) a letter of credit must pay when documents conforming to the letter of credit are presented by the seller, even though the *goods are nonconforming*.

---

[11]*Texpor Traders, Inc. v. Trust Co. Bank*, 720 F. Supp. 1100 (S.D.N.Y. 1989).

BENETTON SERVICES v. BENEDOT, INC.
551 So.2d 295 (Ala. Sup. Ct. 1989)

Benetton Services Corporation was an Italian clothing manufacturer. Benedot, Inc., was formed for the purpose of selling Benetton clothing at retail outlets in Dothan and Auburn, Alabama. Benedot placed several orders with Benetton over a period of approximately 36 months. All of the orders were delivered late, and all contained some nonconforming merchandise. Benetton told Benedot that Benetton had made changes in personnel, and that future orders would be conforming and would be delivered on time. Relying on this representation, Benedot placed an order with Benetton for spring and summer 1988 clothing.

As a condition to shipping Benedot's order, Benetton required Benedot to pay $20,000, and to have issued to Benetton an irrevocable letter of credit in the amount of $61,000. On behalf of Benedot, Southland Bank of Dothan, Alabama, issued an irrevocable letter of credit for $61,000 to Benetton.

The spring/summer 1988 order was delivered late and it contained nonconforming goods. Benedot accepted the shipment, because it was very difficult and expensive to return the goods to Italy. Nonetheless, to prevent Benetton from collecting for the goods, Benedot obtained a temporary restraining order directing Southland Bank not to pay Benetton. At a hearing, the trial court issued a preliminary injunction enjoining Southland Bank from paying Benetton. Benetton appealed to the Supreme Court of Alabama.

Shores, Justice.   Payment under a irrevocable letter of credit, upon compliance with its terms, is independent of the underlying contract. The issuer of a letter of credit must honor a draft drawn thereunder that complies with the terms of the letter of credit, regardless of whether the goods conform to the underlying contract.

Because the letter of credit represents an independent obligation of the issuer to the beneficiary, payment under an irrevocable letter of credit may not be enjoined absent evidence of forgery or fraud in the issuance of the letter or fraud in the underlying transaction for which the letter of credit was issued.

Benedot has failed to prove fraud. Benetton promised that, upon receipt of the $20,000 and a letter of credit, it would ship conforming goods and that delivery would be timely. This is clearly a promise to do an act in the future; to base a fraud claim on that promise, Benedot had to prove that Benetton, when it made the agreement, did not intend to comply with its terms. Also, Benedot had to prove that, at the time that promise was made, Benetton had an intent to deceive. The record is devoid of any such evidence. The evidence would support, at most, a finding that the promise was recklessly made. A reckless misrepresentation cannot support a fraud action where that misrepresentation relates to a future act. Furthermore, the failure to perform a promised act is not in itself evidence that the defendant, at the time the promise was made, intended to deceive.

The trial court's order granting the preliminary injuctions is reversed and the case is remanded with instructions to release the funds due and owing to Benetton pursuant to the letter of credit issued by Southland.

Judgment reversed in favor of Benetton; remanded to the trial court.

Standby Letters of Credit

Although an ordinary letter of credit protects the seller, it leaves a buyer at risk if the seller ships defective goods. Therefore, the buyer may insist that the seller obtain a letter of credit from the seller's bank, under which the sellers' bank promises to pay the buyer if the seller defaults on the sales contract. Such a **standby letter of credit** operates as a guarantee or insurance for the buyer. The buyer pays the seller, expecting the seller to perform; if the seller defaults on the contract, such as by shipping defective goods, the buyer exercises its rights under the standby letter of credit and obtains payment from the seller's bank. (If the standby letter of credit is confirmed, the buyer would collect from the buyer's confirming bank, which would then collect from the seller's bank.) The seller's bank collects the amount of the payment from the seller, if it has not done so already. Because the seller's bank is in the same city as the seller, it can more easily than the buyer obtain collection from the seller.

Dispute Resolution

The contract should include a **choice of forum clause,** which designates which court or arbitration tribunal will resolve disputes between the parties. Of course, each party wants to have the dispute resolved in its national courts applying national or local law. As a compromise, an arbitration panel is often the forum of choice.

Arbitration, the settlement of disputes by a non-judicial third party, is often called for in international contracts because it may be cheaper, quicker, and more private than resolving disputes through litigation. Equally important, however, is the fact that it can take place in a neutral location. The increase in trade with countries such as China, Japan, and Korea, where mediation rather than litigation of disputes is traditional, has given impetus to this trend. The growing attractiveness of arbitration has resulted in the establishment of arbitration centers in world capitals such as London, Paris, Cairo, Hong Kong, and Stockholm, and major cities such as Geneva and New York.

After an American firm successfully litigates an action against a foreign firm, another problem may arise: enforcement of the judgment or decision. For example, an American firm may obtain a judgment in a U.S. court awarding it $50,000 against a Iranian firm. However, the firm may not have any assets in the United States. When the American firm seeks enforcement of the judgment it Iran, an Iranian court may refuse to recognize the judgment or to enforce it. Thus, the firm may find it necessary to relitigate in Iran the issues decided by the American court.

Recognition and enforcement of international arbitration agreements and awards are generally controlled through multilateral treaties including the Foreign Arbitral Awards Convention.

Sales to Nonmarket Economies

The international sales transaction is complicated when an American buyer sells to a buyer in a nation that has a **nonmarket economy (NME).** NMEs exist in socialist nations, in which a central government owns and controls all significant means of production. This means that a sale by an American seller to a NME will usually be to a buyer that is authorized by its government to enter international sales contracts. Yugoslavia, Cuba, and the Soviet Union are among the nations having NMEs.

The typical NME buyer is a **foreign trade corporation.** A socialist economy usually has several foreign trade corporations, each empowered to conduct the whole business of exporting or importing a particular good. Contract negotiations with a foreign trade corporation may be slow and costly, due to the unusually high but necessary precision with which the contract is written. Once agreement has been reached, however, foreign trade corporations have an excellent performance record.

Most foreign trade corporations insist that all disputes be resolved by arbitration in their country. This is normally not a great risk for an American seller because most socialist arbitration tribunals have a good record for efficiency and impartiality. When a foreign trade corporation is sued in a court outside its boundaries, it may raise the doctrine of sovereign immunity. However, most nations deny immunity to the commercial activities of governments, including the international business transactions of foreign trade corporations.

Countertrade

Often, a socialist nation will condition its agreement to buy goods from an American seller on the seller's agreement to purchase NME goods. This is known as a countertrade, of which two kinds are most common. In a **counterpurchase,** an American firm sells its goods to a NME nation and purchases from the NME nation goods *unrelated* to the goods it sells. For example, in a countertrade agreement with the Soviet Union, Pepsico sold bottling rights to Pepsi-Cola and purchased Stolychnaya vodka produced by the Soviet Union. A counterpurchase is not to be confused with a **barter** transaction, which is a nonmoney transaction in which goods are exchanged. Countertrade involves two reciprocal sales in which

each party is paid in money, usually the currency of the NME.

In a **compensation** or buy-back **transaction,** an American firm sells equipment or technology to the NME nation and agrees to purchase some of the goods produced with the equipment or technology. For example, Occidental Petroleum sold to the Soviet Union technology for the construction and operation of ammonia plants and purchased ammonia produced by the plants.

Accepting countertrade may benefit an American seller. It may be the only way an American firm can obtain access to a NME, and it does provide a greater assurance of payment. However, payment is in the NME currency, which either cannot be taken out of the NME nation or has little value on world monetary markets. Also, the goods obtained from the NME nation may not fit into an American firm's normal distribution network and may be of inferior quality. Therefore, an American firm may have difficulty disposing of countertraded goods.

SALES ABROAD THROUGH A DISTRIBUTOR

If a U.S. firm believes that there is a substantial market for its product in some area abroad, it may find that appointing a distributor located in that area (the territory of the distributorship) is a more effective and efficient way to exploit the market than selling directly to buyers. If so, it signs a distribution agreement, a contract between the seller and the distributor that sets forth a wide range of terms and conditions of the distributorship. This contract should be written and should contain provisions similar to those in a direct sales contract. However, a distributorship agreement may have additional provisions that cause violations of American and foreign antitrust laws. The following is a general discussion of antitrust law. A more complete explanation of antitrust law appears in the chapter Antitrust: The Sherman Act and the chapter The Clayton Act, the Robinson-Patman Act, and Antitrust Exemptions and Immunities.

Antitrust Issues

Two possible provisions in an international distribution agreement can raise antitrust problems. The first is an exclusive dealing or requirements contract provision, whereby the distributor promises not to distribute competing products of any other manufacturer. A seller often wants such a provision because it encourages the distributor to devote its full efforts to sales of the seller's product and not to sales of a competing product. Such an agreement may be illegal under American antitrust laws because it limits the ability of competing firms to export into that territory. The second provision, an exclusive distributorship whereby the seller promises that it will not appoint another distributor in the same territory, is more likely to be challenged under foreign antitrust laws. Distributors frequently want such a provision in order to protect their efforts to build up a base of customers.

Extraterritorial Application of American Antitrust Laws The Sherman Act states, "every contract, combination . . . or conspiracy in restraint of trade or commerce among the several states or with foreign nations is declared illegal." This language has been interpreted to mean that the actions of foreign entities having an anticompetitive effect in the United States can be challenged, as can acts limiting American access to markets abroad. The extent to which the United States can control activities outside its borders has been a matter of considerable litigation.

In general, before American courts exert antitrust jurisdiction over acts that have an extraterritorial effect, the acts must be shown to have had a *substantial effect* on American commerce. This standard was codified in the Foreign Trade Antitrust Improvements Act of 1982. The Act requires a showing that the challenged activity has a direct, substantial, and reasonably foreseeable effect on domestic commerce or exports. In addition, courts will not apply American antitrust law unless American interests outweigh those of the foreign country in regulating the activity. Finally, American antitrust law will not be applied to contracts between American firms and foreign governments, on the grounds that the act of state doctrine protects the actions of foreign governments from challenge.

As the trade balance of the United States worsened and its imports began to exceed its exports, Congress recognized the importance of facilitating exports. One response to this was its passage of the Export Trading Company Act of 1982. This act allows exporters whose goods or services are not resold in the United States to apply to the Department of Commerce for a *certificate of review*. If the Commerce Department finds that the exporter's activities do not unduly restrain trade or affect domestic prices, and the exporter's activities meet certain other statutory requirements, the Department issues the certificate with the approval of the Justice Department. The certificate protects the exporter from antitrust liability, thereby providing exporters with a more certain trading environment.

Antitrust Laws of the EEC Articles 85 and 86 of the Treaty of Rome contain the EEC's antitrust laws. Article 85 states: "all agreements which . . . may affect trade between member states and which have as their object or effect the prevention, restriction or distortion of competition within the common market" are void, and fines may be imposed on parties entering into such agreements. Article 86 prohibits entities with a dominant market position in a substantial portion of the EEC from taking improper advantage of that position. Exclusive distributorship agreements have been especially susceptible to challenge under Article 85. If a firm is uncertain whether its activities will be challenged under Article 85 or 86, it can apply for negative clearance, which is, in effect, a finding that the commercial activity is not violative of the articles.

LIABILITY OF CARRIERS OF GOODS

When an American firm ships goods to a foreign buyer, the goods may be shipped by ground, air, or water carrier. The duties and extent of liability of these various carriers is largely determined by domestic statutes and international law.

Ground Carriers

American trucking and railroad companies are regulated by the Interstate Commerce Commission pursuant to the Interstate Commerce Act. American carriers are liable for any loss or damage to the goods with few exceptions: for example, damage caused by act of God and acts of the shipper (usually the seller of the goods), such as poorly packaging the goods. An American carrier may limit its liability by contract, provided it allows the shipper to obtain full liability by paying a higher shipping charge.

Most European trucking companies are covered by the Convention on the Contract for International Carriage of Goods by Road (CMR); most European railroads are governed by the International Convention Concerning Carriage of Goods by Rail (CIM). These international agreements place liability on carriers for damages to goods they carry with few exceptions: for example, defective packaging by the shipper and circumstances beyond the carrier's control. Each also limits a carrier's liability to an amount stated in the CMR or CIM, unless the shipper agrees to pay for greater liability.

Air Carriers

The Warsaw Convention governs the liability of international air carriers. Most nations have ratified the Warsaw Convention in its original or amended form. Under the Convention, an air carrier is liable to the shipper for damages to goods with few exceptions, including that it was impossible for the carrier to prevent the loss or that the damage was caused by the negligence of the shipper. The Warsaw Convention limits a carrier's liability to a stated amount per pound, unless the shipper pays for greater liability.

Water Carriers

The Hague Rules govern the liability of international water carriers. The Hague Rules were amended in Visby, Sweden, in 1968. The United States codified the Hague Rules in the Carriage of Goods by Sea Act (COGSA), but unlike many other nations, has not ratified the Visby amendments, which do not substantially change the liability of international water carriers.

The Hague-Visby Rules and the COGSA impose on international water carriers the duties to (1) furnish a seaworthy ship and (2) stow the cargo carefully to prevent it from breaking loose during storms at sea. When these duties are met, a water carrier will not usually be liable for damages to cargo. Water carriers have no liability for damages due to circumstances beyond their control—poor packaging, piracy, or acts of war, among others. Under COGSA, liability is limited to $500 per package, unless the shipper agrees to pay a higher shipping fee. Under the Hague-Visby Rules, liability will be the value of the goods declared by the shipper.

Under COGSA or the Hague-Visby Rules, the owner of cargo will be liable for damage his cargo does to other cargo. Also, under the ancient maritime doctrine of **general average,** when a carrier sacrifices an owner's cargo, such as throwing it overboard in order to save the ship and the other cargo, the other owners have liability to the owner whose cargo was sacrificed; liability is pro rated to each owner according to the value of each owner's goods in relation to the value of the voyage (the value of the ship plus the value of the other owners' goods plus the carrier's total shipping fees).

The doctrine of general average is commonly expanded by the contract between the carrier and cargo owners in **New Jason clauses.**[12] Typically, a New Jason clause provides that in *all* cases when goods are damaged and the carrier is not liable under COGSA, the goods owner is entitled to general average contributions from all other cargo owners.[13]

LICENSING FOREIGN MANUFACTURERS

An American firm can also enter the world market by licensing its product or service to a foreign manufacturer. In exchange for granting a license to the foreign licensee, the American licensor will receive royalties from the sale of the licensed product or service. Usually, the licensed product or service or the name under which it is sold will be protected by American intellectual property law, such as patent, trade secret, copyright, or trademark law. Because American intellectual property law does not protect the property outside the boundaries of the United States, a licensor needs to take steps to ensure that its intellectual property will acquire protection in the foreign nation. Otherwise, the licensor risks that a competitor may appropriate the intellectual property without penalty.

Patents and Trade Secrets

A patent filing must be made in each nation in which protection is desired. It is not difficult for a firm to acquire parallel patents in each of the major countries maintaining a patent system. Many countries are parties to the Paris Convention for the Protection of Industrial Property. This results in a certain degree of uniformity in their patent laws and in a recognition of the date of the first filing in any nation as the filing date for all, but only if subsequent filings are in fact made within a year of the first filing.

When technology is not patented, either because it is not patentable or because a firm makes a business decision not to patent it, a licensor may control its foreign use abroad under **trade secret** law. For example, an American firm can license its manufacturing know-how to a foreign manufacturer for use in a defined territory in

---

[12]*New Jason,* 225 U.S. 32 (U.S. Sup. Ct. 1912) (upheld the validity of general average clauses in bills of lading).

[13]*Holsatia Shipping Corp. v. Fidelity & Cas. Co. of N.Y.,* 535 F. Supp. 139 (S.D.N.Y. 1982).

return for promises to pay royalties and to keep the trade secret confidential.

Copyright

An American firm may license a foreign manufacturer to produce literary, artistic, or musical materials for which the firm holds an American copyright. For example, a computer software development firm may grant a license to a foreign manufacturer of software. Also, the American owner of copyrights protecting "The Simpsons" cartoon characters may license a Taiwanese firm to manufacture Simpsons dolls.

International copyright protection is governed by the Berne Convention, which states that a copyright registration in one signatory nation grants the copyright owner rights in all signatory nations. The United States is a signatory of the Berne Convention.

Trademarks

The holder of an American trademark may license the use of its trademark in a foreign nation. For example, McDonald's may license a French firm to use the McDonald's name and golden arches at a restaurant on the Champs-Elysees. Or the holder of the Calvin Klein trademark may license a South Korean firm to manufacture Calvin Klein jeans. In addition to the grey market goods problem discussed earlier in this chapter, the holder of an American trademark who licenses his product or services abroad runs the risk of losing trademark protection in the foreign market.

Trademark registrations must be made in each nation in which protection is desired. As with patent filings, parallel trademark registrations may be made in compliance with the Paris Convention for the Protection of Industrial Property. Under the Paris Convention, the date of the first filing in any nation is the filing date for all nations, if the subsequent filings are made within six months of the first filing.

The Madrid Agreement permits a firm to register a trademark in all its signatory nations simultaneously by filing an application for registration with the World Intellectual Property Organization in Geneva. The United States is not a signatory of the Madrid Agreement.

Antitrust Problems

International licensing of intellectual property, if done on an exclusive basis, can give rise to the same kinds of antitrust questions under the laws of a foreign nation as

do exclusive distributorships. An exclusive license of a product innovation means that no one other than the licensee, not even the licensor, can manufacture or sell the product or service in the designated territory. Competition among products using the same technology is limited and, therefore, may be illegal.

DIRECT FOREIGN INVESTMENT

The easiest way for an American firm to enter the world market is to continue to manufacture at home and sell to buyers abroad. However, an American firm may earn greater profits by directly investing in a foreign economy, such as building a manufacturing plant and making its goods near foreign customers. Foreign production may give access to lower-priced labor and raw materials as well as avoid the tariff and other trade barriers erected by foreign nations.

Before an American firm decides to establish a manufacturing operation abroad, its officers must examine a wide variety of legal issues. Some of the issues are ones we have already discussed, such as protection of patents and trademarks. These and many other legal issues may be peculiar to the particular country being considered as the location of the facility. Foreign labor laws may be very different from American law and may impose long-term obligations on the employer. For example, Japanese custom is to hire an employee for life, and in The Netherlands, an employer must obtain governmental approval to dismiss an employee. Import license requirements and high tariffs may force the firm to use local sources of supplies and raw materials and to manufacture locally a certain percentage of the parts used in assembling the final product. Some countries, such as Mexico and India, prohibit foreigners from having a majority equity interest in any operation within their borders. In socialist nations, direct foreign investment is usually prohibited, although some NME nations—such as Yugoslavia and China—allow an American firm to co-own a business with a government-owned entity.

When these legal problems are surmounted, and the American firm establishes a successful operation in a foreign nation, two additional problems may arise: (1) restrictions on investment repatriation and (2) expropriation.

Repatriation of Earnings and Investment

Repatriation is bringing back to the United States earnings from a direct foreign investment. Many countries, particularly those in the developing world, have regulations concerning the conversion of their currency into a foreign currency such as dollars, and the removal of the converted currency to another country such as the United States. When an American firm wishes to repatriate some of the earnings from an operation in a country with such regulations, it must obtain permission from the host nation's currency exchange authorities. These authorities operate under rules intended to encourage foreign firms to reinvest their earnings in the country rather than send them home. Some countries place an absolute limit, stated in terms of a set percentage of the amount that a firm has invested, on the amount of earnings that may be repatriated each year. Other countries place a substantial *income withholding tax* on repatriated earnings, which increases in percentage with the amount repatriated.

When an American firm wants to sell or liquidate its operations, all proceeds in excess of the original investment are usually considered dividends, and their repatriation may be either prohibited or taxed at a very high rate. The existence of such regulations in a country means that an American firm should normally not consider a major investment in that country unless it is prepared to make a long-term commitment.

Expropriation

One of the biggest fears of an American firm investing in a politically unstable country is **expropriation,** the taking of its facilities by the host government without adequate compensation. Since 1945, expropriations have been common, including the expropriation of oil fields and refineries in Iran, Saudi Arabia, Libya, and other Arab countries.

Few firms have been fairly compensated by the expropriating nation. Even in foreign nations that have a constitutional provision like the Fifth Amendment to the U.S. Constitution, fair compensation will be unlikely when the government is socialist or the judiciary is dominated by the political rulers.[14] Even when a fair compensation is paid, an American firm may have difficulty repatriating the proceeds.

When an American firm's foreign investment is expropriated for less than adequate compensation, and legal and political remedies within the foreign nation have been exhausted, the only legal option is to try to find property located outside the country that belongs to the host government and to seek compensation from the proceeds of the sale of that property. This requires finding a court of another nation or an international arbitration tribunal that is willing to listen, establishing that the taking without compensation has damaged the firm in violation of international law, and convincing the authority having jurisdiction over the host government's property that the property should be used to satisfy the claim. This is a very difficult course of action, and there is a high probability that the firm will be frustrated at some step and be left without compensation.

Law of Expropriation The first problem is that there is no consensus as to what compensation international law requires. The United States takes the position that international law requires adequate, effective, and prompt compensation whenever a foreign government takes property belonging to someone who is not a citizen of that country. Although this position, which is consistent with our Constitution, is shared by most of the developed western nations, it is rejected by many of the developing countries and by the Communist countries. Some of these countries contend that international law requires only nondiscriminatory treatment of their citizens and noncitizens. Others recognize the principle that compensation is required, but assert that it may be delayed if immediate payment would frustrate what they view as vital state programs, as would almost always be the case where there is a social revolution that includes a program of massive expropriation.

Finding a Forum The next problem is the difficulty of persuading a court to take and listen to such a claim. American courts will usually not interfere on the grounds that the foreign government's action is entitled to deference as an act of state. In addition, the court may refuse to allow a foreign government to be sued by an American firm under the doctrine of sovereign immunity. A foreign court is an even less likely forum because it is not anxious to put itself in the middle of a dispute between a citizen of one foreign country and the government of another.

No arbitration tribunal is available unless both parties consented at some point to use one. And even in a case

---

[14] The Fifth Amendment's Takings Clause provides that the federal government shall not take private property without just compensation. The Takings Clause is addressed fully in the Business and the Constitution chapter.

where there was such a consent, though able to hear the case and render a decision, the tribunal would not have the power to order the use of the host government's property to satisfy any claim that it might feel the American firm established. That order must be sought from a court having jurisdiction over the property after a favorable decision of the tribunal.

As the following case shows, however, some courts are willing to find a duty to compensate fairly an American firm for the expropriation of its property, at least when a treaty between the United States and the expropriating nation provides for such a remedy. Note, also, that the American court had jurisdiction over funds of the expropriating nation.

KALAMAZOO SPICE EXTRACTION CO. v. PROVISIONAL MILITARY GOVERNMENT OF SOCIALIST ETHIOPIA

729 F.2d 422 (6th Cir. 1984)

In 1966, Kalamazoo Spice Extraction Co. (Kal-Spice), an American corporation, entered a joint venture with Ethiopian citizens. They created the Ethiopian Spice Extraction Co. (ESESCO), an Ethiopian-based corporation that was to engage in the production of spices. Kal-Spice owned approximately 80 percent of the shares of ESESCO, contributed capital, built a production facility, and trained ESESCO's staff, which consisted of Ethiopian citizens. After four years of preparation, construction, and training, production began in 1970.

In 1974, the Provisional Military Government of Socialist Ethiopia (PMGSE) came to power. In February 1975, as part of its program to assure that Ethiopian industries would "be operated according to the philosophy of Ethiopian socialism," the PMGSE announced the seizure of several businesses, including ESESCO. As a result of the expropriation, Kal-Spice's ownership interest in ESESCO was reduced to 39 percent. In December 1975, the PMGSE established a Compensation Commission, which in October 1981 offered Kal-Spice the equivalent of $450,000 in Ethiopian currency. Believing it was entitled to compensation of $11 million, Kal-Spice rejected the offer and, in retaliation, refused to pay for $1.9 million of spices that ESESCO had shipped to Kal-Spice in Michigan. When ESESCO (controlled by the PMGSE) sued Kal-Spice for payment, Kal-Spice counterclaimed against the PMGSE for damages for expropriating part of its interest in ESESCO. The trial court decided that the act of state doctrine precluded adjudication of the claims against the PMGSE. Kal-Spice appealed to the Sixth Circuit Court of Appeals.

Keith, Judge. The Act of State doctrine is an exception to the general rule that a court of the United States will decide cases by choosing the rules from among various sources of law, including international law. The roots of the doctrine can be traced to *Underhill v. Hernandez* (1987), where the Supreme Court held:

Every sovereign state is bound to respect the independence of every other sovereign state, and the courts of one country will not sit in judgment on the acts of the government of another done within its own territory.

Kal-Spice requests that this Court recognize a "treaty exception" to the Act of State doctrine. *Banco Nacional de Cuba v. Sabbatino* (1964) provides the basis for a treaty exception:

[T]he Judicial Branch will not examine the validity of a taking of property within its own territory by a foreign sovereign government, extant and recognized by this country at the time of suit, *in the absence of a treaty or other unambiguous agreement regarding controlling legal principles*, even if the complaint alleges that the taking violates customary international law.

This language and the existence of a treaty between the United States and Ethiopia, asserts Kal-Spice, requires a "treaty" exception to the rule that a United States court will not exercise jurisdiction over a foreign sovereign for an act done by that sovereign within its borders. The treaty in existence between the United States and Ethiopia is the 1953 Treaty of Amity and Economic Relations. That treaty provides:

Property of nationals and companies of either High Contracting Party, including interests in property, shall receive the most constant protection and security within the territories of the other High Contracting Party. *Such property shall not be taken except for a public purpose, nor shall it be taken without prompt payment of just and effective compensation* (emphasis added).

The standard of compensation provided for in the Treaty of Amity between Ethiopia and the United States can provide a basis for determining the extent of compensation to which Kal-Spice may be entitled. Numerous treaties employ the standard of compensation used in the 1953 Treaty of Amity between Ethiopia and the United States. Undoubtedly, the widespread use of this compensation standard is evidence that it is an agreed upon principle in international law.

There is a great national interest to be served in this case, i.e., the recognition and execution of treaties that we enter into with foreign nations. The failure of this court to recognize a properly executed treaty would indeed be an egregious error because of the position that treaties occupy in our body of law.

Judgment reversed in favor of Kal-Spice; remanded to the trial court.

Insurance   The best protection against the risk of expropriation is insurance. To encourage American investment in developing countries, the U.S. government established the Overseas Private Investment Corporation (OPIC). OPIC offers low-cost expropriation insurance for certain investment projects in designated countries.

If an expropriation of an insured project occurs, the American firm receives compensation from OPIC in return for assigning to OPIC the firm's claim against the host government. The program is available only for investments in countries that have signed executive agreements with the United States recognizing in advance the legitimacy of such assignments and providing for arbitration if any dispute does arise.

In the case of an uninsured expropriation, the U.S. government has a general policy of using measured diplomatic pressure to aid the American firm involved, but the amount of pressure varies from administration to administration and from case to case. In many cases, this remedy, unlike the purely legal remedies described earlier, results in at least partial satisfaction of the firm's claim.

OFF-SHORE BANKING AND OTHER USES OF TAX HAVENS

Because differences in the business taxation rates of developed nations are minimal, tax shopping among developed nations provides little benefit to an international business. However, small countries in North America and Europe provide significant tax advantages to American firms. These **tax havens,** including the Bahamas, the Cayman Islands, and Bermuda, have no income tax. In addition, some tax havens, such as Switzerland, the Bahamas, and the Cayman Islands not only have low or no income taxes but also protect the secrecy of banking accounts. Consequently, many American firms have established insurance, banking, and investment company subsidiaries in these tax havens.

Not surprisingly, many persons using tax havens have done so to mask illegal activities, especially drug dealing and insider trading in securities.[15] During the 1980s, the U.S. government pressured the Swiss government to

---

[15] Insider trading of securities is covered in detail in the Securities Regulation chapter.

remove its bank secrecy protections to help the United States prosecute drug dealers, tax defrauders, and inside traders. The United States has not, however, exerted similar pressure against other tax havens that have strong bank secrecy laws.

THE FOREIGN CORRUPT PRACTICES ACT

As discussed in the Securities Regulation chapter, in 1977 the Congress of the United States passed the Foreign Corrupt Practices Act (FCPA) in response to discoveries that over 400 American firms had made bribes to foreign businesses and government officials in connection with international business transactions. The FCPA makes it a crime for any American firm to offer, promise, or make payments or gifts of anything of value to a foreign official or any other person if the firm knows or should know that it will be used to influence a *discretionary* governmental decision. An American firm may be fined up to $2 million. Any officer or director who violates the payments prohibition may be fined up to $100,000 and imprisoned up to five years.

ETHICAL AND PUBLIC POLICY CONCERNS

1. Do you think it is right for nations to use export controls for political ends? Consider the 1990 and 1991 world embargo of Iraqi exports in response to its invasion of Kuwait. Did the benefits of such an embargo outweigh its costs? Does it matter that Iraqi citizens were harmed by an embargo that was aimed at Iraq's political leaders?

2. Do you think that foreign governments should restrict the repatriation of earnings and investment? Why do foreign governments restrict repatriation? What are the long-term costs and benefits of restricting repatriation? Would you make a direct foreign investment in a country that has a history of expropriating American investments without adequate compensation? Do you think American firms have given as much to the economies of developing nations as they have taken out of the economies?

3. Do you think it is right for an American firm to establish a banking or other subsidiary in the Cayman Islands? Who benefits from such a decision? Who suffers by such a decision? Would you invest in an American firm that has a banking subsidiary in a tax haven?

SUMMARY

International sales of goods greatly increase a firm's potential market for its goods and services. They can also greatly increase the complexity and risks of business transactions. A wide variety of treaties, agreements, statutes, and regulations can apply to a particular international transaction. These can range from conventions like the Convention on the International Sale of Goods to regulations like the commodity control list of the Department of Commerce. To some extent, the parties can protect themselves by anticipating problems arising from the type of transaction chosen and making arrangements to minimize the risks.

Countries imposes export and import controls on goods and technical data leaving and entering their countries. The United States heavily restricts exportations to socialist countries and other hostile nations. The United States imposes tariffs on goods coming into the United States, usually to protect domestic industry. Because tariffs are barriers to trade, there have been many international efforts to reduce tariffs, including the GATT and the formation of regional trade associations such as the European Economic Community.

Countries also restrict imports by imposing duties on foreign goods that are dumped in their markets or that are subsidized by the government of origin. Protection of patents, copyrights, and trademarks is provided by laws against the importation of counterfeit and grey market goods.

When American firms sell to foreign buyers, they reduce their nonpayment risk by using irrevocable letters of credit. When confirmed by the seller's bank, the seller has little to fear. The buyer can reduce his risk of receiving nonconforming goods by using a standby letter of credit.

An international sales or distribution agreement providing for sales through a foreign distributor should contain provisions spelling out where and under whose laws a dispute will be resolved should one arise. Often parties choose arbitration rather than litigation to settle disputes.

Direct sales to buyers in nonmarket economies are usually made to a foreign trade corporation. Sometimes, to sell to a buyer in a NME, an American buyer must agree to countertrade. International sales through distributors frequently involve an exclusive dealing arrangement that may lead to antitrust challenges. Licensing foreign manufacturers to use an American firm's patents, trade secrets, copyrights, and trademarks requires the firm to take steps to ensure international protection of its intellectual property.

American firms making direct foreign investments must comply with a larger number of laws of the host nation. In addition, an American firm may be compelled to accept local citizens or the host government as a partner. Many nations restrict the repatriation of earnings, and socialist governments have a history of expropriating the assets of American firms without paying adequate compensation.

High domestic business tax rates have encouraged some American firms to establish some operations, especially banking, in nations with no or low business taxes. Popular tax havens include the Cayman Islands and the Bahamas. The U.S. government believes that some tax havens are used to conceal illegal activities, such as drug dealing and insider trading, and has taken steps with other nations to detect illegal activity.

PROBLEM CASES

1. Edward Elkins, an American businessman, was approached about selling Lockheed aircraft to a buyer in Libya. The aircraft had potential military uses. The U.S. Department of State told Elkins the sale would not be approved because of a presidential order prohibiting trade to Libya. Elkins conceived of a plan to obtain validated licenses to sell the aircraft to a German company owned and operated by Libyans and to route the aircraft through Bordeaux, France, to Benin (a small African country), and then to Libya. Is the export of the aircraft in this manner a violation of the Export Administration Act?

2. Holly Stores, Inc. imported into the United States clothing hung on wire or plastic hangers. The Tariff Schedules provided that reusable hangers for clothing were dutiable at a lower rate than nonreusable hangers, which were dutiable at the higher rate for clothing. The hangers were of fairly durable construction and it was physically possible to reuse them. Retailers discarded 99 percent of the hangers; the other 1 percent were given to customers with the clothes on them, used to replace broken hangers, or used to return clothes to a warehouse. Should the hangers be dutied as clothing?

3. To encourage investment and development, the governments of Canada, Alberta, Ontario, and Saskatchewan gave investment tax credits and monetary grants to Canadian producers of tubular steel, including Ipsco Steel, Inc. Ipsco exported tubular steel to the United States. American producers claimed to be harmed by Ipsco's exports. What remedy is available to the American producers?

4. Olympus Corporation (Olympus) was the exclusive American licensee and distributor of the camera products of Olympus Optical Co. (Optical). Olympus owned the American rights to Optical's trademark. A discount retailer in New York City, 47th Street Photo, Inc., purchased Optical's cameras from Optical's authorized dealers abroad and imported them into the United States. Will Olympus be able to enjoin 47th Street Photo's importations of Optical's cameras on the grounds that it has violated the Tariff Act and the Lanham Act?

5. Dessaleng Beyene, an American resident, agreed to sell two prefabricated houses to Mohammed Sofan, a resident of Yemen. Sofan obtained a letter of credit from a Yemen bank. The letter of credit was confirmed by Irving Trust Company in New York. Beyene shipped the houses to Sofan and received a bill of lading addressed to "Mohammed Soran." When Beyene presented the bill of lading to Irving Trust, it refused to pay Beyene's draft drawn against the letter of credit. Has Irving Trust acted properly?

6. In 1980, National Oil Corporation (NOC), a company owned by the Libyan government, and Libyan Sun Oil Co., a Delaware corporation, entered an agreement to drill for oil in Libya. Their contract contained a *force majeure* clause and provided for arbitration of any dispute by the International Chamber of Commerce (ICC) in Paris. When the United States banned the importation into the United States of Libyan oil, Sun Oil notified NOC that the *force majeure* clause excused its future performance. NOC requested and obtained arbitration before the ICC, which held that the *force majeure* clause did not excuse Sun Oil and found Sun Oil liable to NOC for $20 million. NOC sought to enforce the award of the ICC in a U.S. federal district court. Did the American court enforce the ICC award?

7. China National Light Industrial Products Import and Export Corp. purchased 25,000 tons of wood pulp from Celulosa Arauco y Constitucion, S.A., a Chilean corporation. Celulosa shipped the wood pulp on the *Damodar Tanaba* from Chile to China. The bill of lading contained a New Jason clause, as did the other bills of lading for goods shipped on the vessel. The wood pulp caught fire; after 75 hours, the fire was extinguished. However, all the wood pulp was ruined, either due to the fire or to water damage from the firefighting efforts. Will China National Light be able to recover a portion of its damages from the owners of the other cargo on the vessel?

8. Soon after the Fidel Castro regime came to power in Cuba, the Cuban socialist government expropriated four Cuban branches of the Chase Manhattan Bank. The Cuban government made no payment to Chase. At the same time, Chase sold for $17 million collateral it held securing $10 million of loans Chase made to two government-owned Cuban banks. Chase kept the $7 million excess proceeds. Banco Nacional de Cuba, a government-owned Cuban bank and the successor of the two banks, sued Chase in a U.S. court to recover the $7 million. Will the recovery of Banco Nacional be reduced by the value of the Chase bank branches expropriated by the government?

CHAPTER 53

COMPUTER LAW

INTRODUCTION

Our society has exploded into the computer age. Computers have become almost indispensable to businesses of all sizes, governments at all levels, and health, educational, religious, and charitable organizations of all kinds. Whereas the size and expense of early computers precluded their use by most segments of the population, technological advances that dramatically reduced the size and cost of computers have put them within the reach of even small businesses and ordinary consumers. They manage an almost limitless array of functions affecting our daily lives, from managing urban transportation to transferring funds and corporate shares electronically to planning household budgets. The capability of computers to process, store, and retrieve vast quantities of information makes possible greater organization, planning, conservation of human and material resources, and overall efficiency.

The benefits of this new technology are not gained without cost, however. In many instances, computer technology creates new risks of harm to which the law must respond. For example, as an increasing amount of information about people is collected, stored, and integrated, individual privacy is threatened. Unquestioning reliance on computer output that may be based on faulty or misleading data may result in a variety of wrongs, such as the reporting of derogatory credit information or the wrongful repossession of goods or the termination of utility services. Furthermore, the widespread use of computers creates a climate in which knowledgeable but dishonest individuals have the opportunity to use computer technology to accomplish criminal objectives or to vandalize computer systems belonging to others.

The acquisition of computer systems and the marketing of computer products and services are also fraught with uncertainty and risk. Lawsuits seeking compensation from computer suppliers for losses caused by defective systems are now almost commonplace. In such cases, courts must adapt contract and product liability doctrines to computer transactions to determine who will bear the cost of malfunctions or defects in computer systems. Moreover, those who invest massive resources in the development and production of computer products are placed at risk by technology that makes it easy to copy computer equipment and programs. To respond to their need for legal protection against infringement and misappropriation, modifications in traditional law regarding the protection of intellectual property have been necessary.

Courts and legislatures are now engaged in adapting law to computer technology. Although this developing body of law may be termed **computer law**, it is really not a distinct area of law. Rather, it is an integration of a host of traditional areas of law as they apply to the use of computers. Issues concerning computers cut across almost every area of law. Because of limitations of space and scope, this chapter will focus on a selection of some of the more prevalent legal issues relating to the use of computers: contract and product liability issues, computer crime, invasion of privacy, and protection of producers' rights in computer software.

CONTRACTING FOR THE ACQUISITION OF COMPUTERS

The Applicability of the Uniform Commercial Code

In resolving contracts problems that arise regarding computers, one of the first issues encountered is whether the contract is governed by the Uniform Commercial Code or the common law of contracts. This determination has considerable significance. If the UCC applies, the Code's warranties, rules regarding disclaimers, statute of limitations, and other provisions apply.[1] If the common law of contracts applies, no implied warranties of quality will be applied, general disclaimers and exculpatory clauses[2] are more likely to be enforced, and other common law provisions such as non-UCC statutes of limitation will be applied. As you learned in the Introduction to Contracts chapter, Article 2 of the UCC applies to "transactions in goods." Because computer-related products and services differ in nature and are supplied in different ways, it can be difficult to determine whether there has been a transaction in goods.

A person may acquire computer **hardware** (the physical machinery components of the computer, such as the central processing unit, keyboard, and printer) and **software** (the programs or set of instructions used with the hardware to accomplish a certain result). Software may be packaged for general uses (such as household accounting or word processing) or custom-designed by a software manufacturer or an independent consultant for a particular application. Software is often "licensed" rather than sold. The purpose of such licenses is to permit the producer to retain title to the software while giving the customer the right to use it with strict restrictions on his ability to make copies of the program. (Software licenses will be discussed later in this chapter.) Hardware and software can be acquired together from the same source or separately from different suppliers. Some systems, marketed as "turnkey" systems, contain both hardware and software ready for use. Computer systems may be either purchased or leased from a manufacturer or other seller or a leasing company. In some transactions, a person may contract with a *consultant* or *programmer* for the provision of expert advice or design services.

Obviously, some of the transactions described above are more readily characterized as the sale of goods than are others that are more service-oriented. It is clear that the sale of hardware is a sale of goods, just like the sale of any other manufactured product. The UCC has been held to apply to leases of hardware (and combinations of hardware and software), under the reasoning that such leases are analogous to sales and that they, too, constitute a transaction in goods.

The classification of software and the services of consultants or programmers are more difficult because these involve a blend of tangible goods and services. Computer programs are largely conceptual in nature, except for their tangible manifestation in tapes, disks, or punched cards. Custom-designed software is often the end result of the services of an independent consultant, and thus may be less readily characterized as a sale of goods.

In determining the applicability of the UCC to these situations, a number of courts have asked whether the customer was bargaining primarily for goods or services. If the goods were the primary factor in the contract and the services provided were incidental to the sale of goods, the Code will apply. If the reverse is true and the tangible goods supplied were merely incidental to the services provided, the common law of contracts will apply. In determining the primary objective of the parties, a court might compare the relative cost of the goods and services aspects of the contract. You will see these principles applied in the *RRX Industries, Inc. v. Lab-Con, Inc.* case, which follows.

When software (even custom-designed software) is acquired along with hardware, the transaction normally is considered a sale of goods. When packaged software is purchased, it, too, is likely to be considered a sale of goods. The classification of sales of customized programs provided as the end product of a consultant's services is not as clear, but there is some authority to the effect that such transactions are also sales of goods.

---

[1]Specific provisions of Article 2 of the UCC are discussed in the Formation and Terms of Sales Contracts chapter, the Product Liability chapter, and Performance of Sales Contracts chapter.

[2]The Illegality chapter and the Product Liability chapter discuss such clauses.

RRX Industries, Inc. v. Lab-Con, Inc.

772 F.2d 543 (9th Cir. 1985)

Thomas E. Kelly Associates (TEKA) entered into a contract with RRX Industries in which TEKA agreed to supply RRX with a software system for use in its medical laboratories. The contract obligated TEKA to correct any malfunctions or "bugs" that arose in the system, but limited TEKA's liability to the contract price. TEKA then formed Lab-Con to market its software system and assigned the RRX contract to Lab-Con.

Bugs appeared in the software system soon after TEKA finished installing it. TEKA attempted to repair the bugs by telephone patching. Later, it upgraded the system to make it compatible with more sophisticated hardware. The system remained unreliable, however, because defects continued to exist.

RRX then filed suit against TEKA, Lab-Con, and other defendants for breach of contract. It sought to recover the amount paid under the contract and consequential damages. The trial court awarded damages to RRX, and the defendants appealed.

Wright, Circuit Judge.   The district court relied on the Uniform Commercial Code to award RRX consequential damages. Such reliance was proper only if the computer software system may be characterized as a "good" rather than a service. The Code defines a good as "all things (including specially manufactured goods) which are movable at the time of identification to the contract for sale other than the money in which the price is to be paid, investment securities, and things in action."

In determining whether a contract is one of sale or to provide services, we look to the essence of the agreement. When a sale predominates, incidental services provided do not alter the basic transaction. Because software packages vary depending on the needs of the individual consumer, we apply a case-by-case analysis. Here, the sales aspect of the transaction predominates. The employee training, repair services, and system upgrading were incidental to the sale of the software package and did not defeat characterization of the system as a good.

Under the Code, a plaintiff may pursue all of the remedies available for breach of contract if its exclusive or limited remedy fails of its essential purposes. TEKA and Lab-Con argue that the award of consequential damages was nevertheless improper because the contract limited damages to the amount paid.

The district court concluded that since TEKA and Lab-Con were either unwilling or unable to provide a system that worked as represented or to fix the "bugs" in the software, these limited remedies failed of their essential purpose. The district court properly found the default of the seller so total and fundamental that its consequential damages limitation was expunged from the contract. The facts here justify the result. Neither bad faith nor procedural unconscionability is necessary under section 2–719(2). It provides an independent limit when circumstances render a damages limitation clause oppressive and invalid. The award of consequential damages was proper.

Judgment for RRX affirmed.

Contract Problems in Computer Transactions

Almost any contract issue that arises in other transactions may arise in a transaction involving computers. Thus, the general principles that you have learned in earlier chapters regarding formation, performance, and third-party rights in contract law will be used to resolve contract problems involving computers.

Given the large investment involved in acquiring a computer system and the technical nature of the contract, people entering into contracts for the purchase or lease of computer products or services must take special care to define their needs and, if possible, to bargain for contractual protection. Unfortunately, it is not always possible for a buyer or a lessee to negotiate favorable terms. Because of the relatively new and rapidly expanding nature of computer technology, computer-related products often do not have the same degree of reliability as other marketed products. Recognizing the potential for tremendous loss that can result from a computer system's failure, sellers of computer-related products attempt to place the risk of malfunction on the buyer through contract provisions that effectively limit or exclude seller liability. A buyer's ability to bargain for favorable terms is likely to be limited, particularly in the purchase of microcomputers and packaged software, which are usually accompanied by printed disclaimers about which the buyer (who is often a first-time user) has no opportunity to bargain. Thus, questions regarding the enforceability of contract clauses that limit or exclude liability are heightened in computer transactions. In some cases, buyers have successfully challenged harsh terms in computer contracts under the doctrine of unconscionability.[3]

Box Top Licenses   For various purposes, including attempting to prevent buyers of software from copying programs[4] and attempting to avoid liability under product liability doctrines, producers of software often market their products through licenses rather than outright sales. This device is intended to preserve the producer's title to the software and to limit the customer's right to make and sell copies of the program. Mass-marketed packaged software is often accompanied by a license agreement placed on the box inside a shrink-wrapped

covering. Thus, such licenses have come to be called "box top licenses." They frequently state that the buyer's act of breaking the wrapping constitutes acceptance of the terms of the license. Licenses of this kind include such terms as restrictions on the user's ability to make copies of the program or to use the program on more than one computer. They also commonly contain nondisclosure agreements and restrictions on the use of the program by third parties. Furthermore, most of these licenses contain provisions that disclaim warranty protection and limit the remedies available to the buyer.

The enforceability of box top licenses has been debated for some time. Software producers argue that the licenses are necessary to protect their interests in the sale of mass-produced software. Opponents contend that the licenses are contracts of adhesion, which deprive unsuspecting purchasers of rights they would normally have. The unilateral way in which the terms are imposed and the licensee's total inability to negotiate raise contract questions such as whether there was a "meeting of the minds" on the terms and whether the terms were unconscionable. Since many purchasers of packaged software accompanied by box top licenses are consumers and often first-time users, concern about unconscion-ability is increased. The enforceability of such clauses in box top licenses is still unsettled.[5]

PRODUCT LIABILITY AND THE COMPUTER

Warranties of Quality

If the computer transaction is deemed to be a sale of goods within the definition of the Uniform Commercial Code, UCC warranties of quality may apply. As you learned in the Product Liability chapter, there are three such warranties: express warranties, implied warranties of merchantability, and implied warranties of fitness for a particular purpose.

Computer contracts sometimes contain formal, **express warranties** for a limited time. Representations about the capacity, function, or nature of the system also can be express warranties because affirmations of fact

---

[3]The Illegality chapter covers the factors that indicate unconscionability.

[4]We discuss the protection of proprietary rights in software later in this chapter. The Intellectual Property, Competitive Torts, and Unfair Competition chapter describes copyright, patent, and trade secrets.

[5]Two states, Louisiana and Illinois, enacted legislation that set the parameters for enforcement of box top licenses. The Illinois statute was later repealed, however, and crucial parts of the Louisiana law were struck down by a federal court as being in conflict with federal copyright law. *Vault v. Quaid Software Ltd.*, 847 F.2d 255 (5th Cir. 1988).

and descriptions of goods, promises, and displays of samples or models that become part of the basis of the bargain create express warranties, too. A product demonstration may be considered a sample or model of goods and might also constitute an express warranty. If the contract contains specifications or representations about the quality of the product, the seller's attempt to disclaim the express warranty will probably be ineffective.[6]

The **implied warranty of merchantability** will exist in any sale or lease of computer products deemed to be goods if the products are sold by a merchant, unless the warranty has been effectively disclaimed. This would mean that such a warranty would exist in a sale or lease by a manufacturer, retailer, leasing company, or other commercial enterprise engaged in the sale or lease of computer products. The **implied warranty of fitness for a particular purpose** applies when the seller has reason to know of the buyer's particular purpose and the sale is made under circumstances in which the seller has reason to know that the buyer is relying on him to select suitable goods. This warranty seems particularly appropriate in situations in which the seller sells a computer system specially manufactured or customized for a buyer's particular uses.

Disclaimers of Warranty   As a practical matter, a buyer's warranty protection is likely to be fairly limited. Almost all of the manufacturers that give express warranties limit the duration of the warranty, sometimes to as short a period as 90 days. This may not be an adequate time for the user to determine whether the computer system works. While it is difficult to disclaim an express warranty, it is relatively easy to disclaim the implied warranties, provided that the seller follows the guidelines described in the Product Liability chapter.

Limitation of Remedies   A common clause included in contracts for the sale of computer products is one that excludes liability for consequential and incidental damages[7] and limits the remedies available to the buyer in case of the breach of a warranty.[8] In addition, such

clauses usually provide that the buyer's *exclusive* remedy for breach of warranty is the repair or replacement of the system. The **limitation of remedies clause** is a highly effective means of limiting the seller's potential exposure to liability. Suppose Dillman buys a computer system for $20,000 under a contract that excludes consequential and incidental damages and contains a provision limiting remedies to repair or replacement. The system never works properly, causing losses of $10,000 for lost productivity and overtime pay for his employees. The application of the consequential damage exclusion and limited remedy clause would mean that Dillman could not recover for the losses resulting from the system's failure and that he could not procure a substitute system and recover for the difference in cost. Instead, his compensation is limited to having the system repaired or replaced by the seller. Given the delay that this is likely to entail, the remedy is not very satisfactory from Dillman's point of view.

Under section 2–719 of the UCC, contract clauses limiting remedies to one or more exclusive remedies will not be enforced if the exclusive remedy proves to be totally inadequate, or "fails of its essential purpose."[9] You saw an example of this in the *RRX Industries* case. Some courts take a different approach and hold that even if the exclusive remedy "fails of its essential purpose," a contract clause excluding consequential damages will be enforced unless it is unconscionable.

Merger Clauses   Before investing in a computer system, a prospective buyer or lessee will seek information about the system from the seller. In the negotiation or marketing phase of the transaction, the seller is likely to make a number of representations to the buyer that could be considered warranties. The parol evidence rule would operate to exclude from the contract evidence of prior statements if the contract is considered to be *fully integrated* (that is, if the written contract states the totality of the parties' agreement).[10] Most written computer contracts contain **merger** or **integration** clauses that expressly state that the written contract is fully integrated. Because the effect of these clauses is to exclude from the contract any presale representations or statements, a buyer must be sure that all of the important promises and representations that have been made to him are contained in the written contract.

---

[6]See the Product Liability chapter for a discussion of disclaimer of express and implied warranties.

[7]Consequential and incidental damages are discussed in the Performance and Remedies chapter and the Remedies for Breach of Sales Contracts chapter.

[8]See the Product Liability chapter for further discussion of the validity of contract provisions limiting the remedies available to the buyer.

---

[9]The Product Liability chapter discusses this concept further.

[10]The Writing chapter discusses the operation of the parol evidence rule.

Tort Liability in the Sale of Computers

Because of the obstacles to recovery for breach of contract or warranty, a number of frustrated computer buyers have turned to tort causes of action. Pursuing a tort remedy—if one is available—may hold more promise for the buyer because the warranty disclaimers and limitations of remedy that are so prevalent in computer contracts are, as a general rule, not effective to exclude tort liability.

Fraud and Misrepresentation   A buyer who has been induced to enter the contract by the seller's misrepresentations of material fact may bring suit based on **fraud.** This may be difficult to establish, because fraud and the tort of deceit require proof of an intent to deceive.[11] There are, however, two related causes of action involving misrepresentation that do not require intent to deceive. These may be applicable to a computer transaction. The first is **negligent misrepresentation,** which is stated in section 552b of the *Restatement (Second) of Torts.* The buyer may establish negligent misrepresentation when he has been injured by his justifiable reliance on false information negligently supplied by one who supplies that information in the course of his business or employment. In addition, the buyer may bring an action for **innocent misrepresentation** (section 552c of the *Restatement (Second) of Torts*) if his injury results from justifiable reliance on a misstatement of material fact made by the seller in a sale, rental, or exchange transaction. The remedies for negligent misrepresentation and innocent misrepresentation are more limited than those available for fraud, however.

Negligence   A buyer injured by a defective computer system may have a cause of action in negligence. Establishing negligence may be difficult, however, particularly when the alleged negligence involves the design of a computer program. One problematic issue is that it is difficult to define the standard of care expected of computer designers and programmers. Some plaintiffs have attempted to press **malpractice** claims against computer designers and programmers who develop custom application software, arguing that such individuals are professionals who should be held to a standard of care higher than that of the reasonable person[12] or to an implied promise that he has the skill to do the job he has undertaken. The few courts that have considered this issue are in disagreement. There are no particular industry standards or licensing requirements for computer programmers, and some courts have declined to characterize designers and programmers as professionals. As computer technology becomes increasingly well established, designers and programmers may be subject to governmental regulation and better-defined standards of care. It remains to be seen whether the tort of computer malpractice will be widely recognized.

A further problem with the use of a negligence cause of action is that plaintiffs in computer product liability suits are likely to have suffered only economic harm (direct and consequential economic loss), and such losses have been held not to be compensable in a negligence suit.

Strict Liability in Tort   At present, the bulk of the product liability litigation concerning defective computers involves *economic loss* rather than *personal injury* or *property damage.* Because strict liability is generally limited to cases in which a person has suffered personal injury or property damage, warranty claims have been much more common in computer cases than strict liability claims. In fact, several cases have held that strict liability is inapplicable to computer cases involving only direct and consequential economic loss.

Presumably, the strict liability analysis that you learned in the Product Liability chapter would apply to a case in which a buyer or user suffered personal injury or property damage as a result of a defect in a computer or computer system that made it unreasonably dangerous.

The increasing use of computers raises the potential for defective software to cause personal injury, although actual cases have not yet been reported. For example, a faulty "expert system" (a computer program that uses artificial intelligence to resolve a particular problem) relied upon for medical diagnosis could cause personal injury. In such a case, a court still might find that the tort liability of the software supplier would be governed by negligence principles rather than strict liability, because the software might well be characterized as a service rather than as a product.

---

[11]The Intentional Torts chapter and the Reality of Consent chapter discuss other elements of fraud and the tort of deceit.

[12]See the Legal Responsibilities of Accountants chapter for a discussion of the standard of care applied to accountants and other professionals.

CONCEPT REVIEW

POSSIBLE CAUSES OF ACTION FOR DEFECTIVE COMPUTER SYSTEMS

I. Contract Theories	Seller makes promise, description, or statement of fact about the
A. Express Warranty	computer and/or software or displays a sample or model of the goods that becomes part of the basis of the bargain
B. Implied Warranty of Merchantability	Merchant seller sells computer and/or software and does not disclaim the warranty
C. Implied Warranty of Fitness for a Particular Purpose	Seller has reason to know the buyer's purpose for the computer and/or software and the buyer is relying on the seller to select appropriate computer and/or software

But Watch Out for:
- ☐ Disclaimers of warranty
- ☐ Limitations of remedy clauses
- ☐ Possible privity requirements under state law
- ☐ UCC and its warranties will be inapplicable if the computer system is considered primarily a service rather than a sale of goods

II. Tort Theories	Buyer reasonably relies on seller's knowing and intentionally false
A. Fraud (deceit)	assertion of fact
B. Negligent Misrepresentation	Buyer injured by justifiable reliance on false information negligently supplied by one who supplies such information in the course of his business
C. Innocent Misrepresentation	Buyer's injury results from justifiable reliance on misstatement of material fact made by seller in a sale, rental, or exchange transaction
D. Negligence	Seller breaches duty of care, proximately causing injuries to buyer
E. Strict Liability in Tort	Seller in the business of selling computer products sells computer and/or software in a defective and unreasonably dangerous condition, causing personal injuries or property damage

But Watch Out for:
- ☐ In cases in which buyer has suffered only economic injury, negligence and strict liability may not be applicable
- ☐ Standard of care for computer programmers is not well-settled
- ☐ Strict liability will not be applicable if the defective computer system is considered primarily a service rather than a sale of goods

COMPUTER CRIME

The use of computers to accomplish criminal objectives has become a growing problem. As our society becomes increasingly dependent on computers to manage such functions as the transfer of funds and other valuables and the storage of personal records, new opportunities for crime have been created. Some of these "computer crimes" are crimes such as vandalism or theft of computer hardware and software in which the computer system itself is the target of the crime. Others involve the use of the computer as the instrumentality of crimes.

Common examples are theft, embezzlement, espionage, blackmail, and fraud.

The law's response to computer crimes involving unauthorized access has grown more severe as the devastating losses resulting from computer viruses or stolen files become apparent. Computer hacking—once tolerated as a mischievous but clever activity—has recently led to significant prison sentences and fines for some individuals.

Because of its technical nature, computer crime can be difficult to detect and to prosecute, however. One major problem in punishing and deterring computer crime has been that traditional criminal statutes often do not address the types of crime that can be committed through the use of computers. If the state statute regarding theft or larceny defined the crime as the theft of "property," for example, a court might find it difficult to construe data stored in a computer as property, and dismiss the prosecution. Some courts have interpreted the elements of existing criminal laws narrowly so as to exclude instances of computer abuse, while others have interpreted them broadly. In light of the uncertainties that attend judicial interpretation of existing statutes, legislatures on both the state and federal level have become increasingly aware of the need to revise their criminal codes to be sure that they encompass the types of crimes that can be accomplished through the use of computers.

State Computer Crime Laws

Approximately 48 states have enacted criminal statutes specifically outlawing certain abuses of computers. Most of these statutes focus on unauthorized accessing of a computer system, tampering with files or causing damage to a system (e.g., by spreading a virus or deleting files), invading the privacy of others, use of a computer to commit fraud or theft, or trafficking in passwords or access codes. Under Maine's recently enacted computer crime statute,[13] for example, "criminal invasion of computer privacy" is prohibited. This crime is committed when one intentionally accesses a computer resource knowing that one is unauthorized to do so. An aggravated form of the crime, for which a stronger penalty is imposed, occurs when a person who has knowingly gained unauthorized access then intentionally makes an unauthorized copy of computer software, a program, or information, damages any computer resource of another person, or allows the introduction of a computer virus into any computer resource.

---

[13]*Maine Advance Legislative Service*, Ch. 620, sections 432 and 433 (1990).

Federal Computer Crime Legislation

Computer-assisted crime on the federal level has been prosecuted with some success under existing federal statutes, primarily the statutes forbidding mail fraud, wire fraud, transportation of stolen property, and various theft of property offenses. As has been true of prosecutions on the state level, successful prosecution of such cases often depends on broad interpretation of the statutory prerequisites.

The Computer Fraud and Abuse Act, first enacted in 1984 and then amended in 1986, is the federal criminal statute that specifically outlaws certain abuses of computers. The act focuses on the use of computers to gain certain information or the unauthorized access to computers it calls "federal interest computers." These are computers used by or for the federal government and financial institutions, and those that operate in interstate commerce (in two or more states).

The act prohibits the unauthorized use of a computer to obtain specified information, such as restricted government information, information contained in a financial record of a financial institution, and information about a consumer contained in a file of a consumer reporting agency.

The act also prohibits accessing a computer of a department or agency of the United States if this affects the government's use of the computer. The act also forbids accessing a federal interest computer knowingly or with intent to defraud and obtaining anything of value (other than the use of the computer itself). Unauthorized accessing of a federal interest computer in a way that alters or destroys information is a crime if it causes $1,000 or more in losses or potentially or actually modifies or impairs the medical diagnosis, treatment, or care of another.

Finally, the act forbids trafficking in passwords and other access information if such trafficking affects interstate or foreign commerce, or the computer is used by or for the U.S. government.

The following case, *U.S. v. Riggs*, illustrates the use of two of these federal statutes to prosecute an incident of unauthorized invasion of another's computer system.

U.S. v. RIGGS

739 F. Supp. 414 (N.D. Ill. 1990)

In the fall of 1988, Robert Riggs and Craig Neidorf allegedly devised and began implementing a scheme to defraud Bell South Telephone Company. The objective of the scheme was to steal Bell South's computer text file that contained information regarding its enhanced 911 (E911) system for handling emergency calls to police, fire, ambulance, and other emergency services in municipalities. The text file that they planned to steal specifically detailed the procedures for installation, operation, and maintenance of E911 systems. Bell South considered this file to contain valuable proprietary information and closely guarded it. Riggs and Neidorf wanted to obtain this text file so it could be printed in a newsletter known as "PHRACK," which Neidorf edited and published.

Riggs used his home computer to gain unlawful access to Bell South's computer system located at its corporate headquarters. After gaining access, Riggs downloaded the text file. He then transferred the stolen data file by way of an interstate computer data network to a Lockport, Illinois, computer bulletin board system. This system is used by computer "hackers" as a location for exchanging and developing software tools and other information that could be used for unauthorized intrusion into computer systems. Neidorf, a student at the University of Missouri in Columbia, used a computer located at his school to access the bulletin board and retrieve the E911 text file. Neidorf revised the file to conceal the fact that it had been stolen from Bell South, then uploaded his revised version back into the bulletin board. In November, Neidorf published his edited version of the E911 text file in his PHRACK newsletter.

Riggs and Neidorf were indicted on a variety of counts, including wire fraud, interstate transportation of stolen property, and violation of the Computer Fraud and Abuse Act. Neidorf filed a motion to dismiss several counts of the indictment dealing with interstate transportation of stolen property, and this is the judge's opinion.

Bua, District Judge.   Counts III and IV charge Riggs and Neidorf with violating 18 U.S.C. section 2314, which provides:

Whoever transports, transmits, or transfers in interstate or foreign commerce any goods, wares, merchandise, securities or money, of the value of $5,000 or more, knowing the same to have been stolen, converted, or taken by fraud . . . shall be fined not more than $10,000, or imprisoned not more than ten years, or both.

Surprisingly, despite the prevalence of computer-related crime, this is a case of first impression. The government argues that reading section 2314 as covering Neidorf's conduct in this case is a natural adaptation of the statute to modern society. Conversely, Neidorf contends that his conduct does not fall within the purview of section 2314 and that the government is seeking an unreasonable expansion of the statute. He urges the court to dismiss the charge on two grounds.

Neidorf's first argument is that the only thing which he allegedly caused to be transferred across state lines was "electronic impulses." Neidorf maintains that this conduct does not come within the scope of section 2314 since electronic impulses do not constitute "goods, wares, or merchandise." The court is unpersuaded by Neidorf's disingenuous argument that he merely transferred electronic impulses across state lines. Several courts have upheld section 2314 charges based on the wire transfer of fraudulently obtained money, rejecting the arguments of the defendants in those cases that only electronic impulses, not actual money, crossed state lines. Similarly, Neidorf's conduct is not properly characterized as the mere transmission of electronic impulses.

Through the use of his computer, Neidorf allegedly transferred proprietary business information. The information was accessible at Neidorf's computer terminal in Missouri before he transferred it, and the information was also accessible at the Lockport, Illinois computer bulletin board after Neidorf transferred it. Therefore, the mere fact that the information actually crossed state lines via computer-generated electronic impulses does not defeat a charge under section 2314.

The question this case presents is whether the proprietary information contained in Bell South's E911 text file constitutes a "good, ware, or merchandise" within the purview of the statute. This court answers that question affirmatively. It is well-settled that when proprietary business information is affixed to some tangible medium, such as a piece of paper, it constitutes "goods, wares, or merchandise" within the meaning of section 2314. This court sees no reason to hold differently simply because Neidorf stored the information inside computers instead of printing it out on paper. In either case, the information is in a transferable, accessible, even salable form.

Neidorf argues that a section 2314 charge cannot survive when the "thing" actually transferred never takes tangible form. This court is reluctant to believe that any court would construe section 2314 so narrowly. Even if tangibility is a requirement under section 2314, the computer-stored business information in this case satisfies that requirement. Although not printed out on paper, a more conventional form of tangibility, the information in Bell South's E911 file was allegedly stored on computer. Thus, by simply pressing a few buttons, Neidorf could recall that information from computer storage and view it on his computer terminal. The information was also accessible to others in the same fashion if they simply pressed the right buttons on their computers. This ability to access the information in viewable form from a reliable storage place differentiates this case from the mere memorization of a formula and makes this case more similar to cases where proprietary information was also stored, but in a more traditional manner—on paper.

In order to sustain a charge against Neidorf under section 2314, the government must allege that Neidorf executed the transfer knowing the goods were "stolen, converted, or taken by fraud." Neidorf maintains that the charges should be dismissed because the "things" he allegedly transferred are not the type of property which is capable of being "stolen, converted, or taken by fraud." This case involves the transfer of confidential, proprietary business information. The owner of confidential, proprietary business information possesses something which has clearly been recognized as an item of property. As such, it is certainly capable of being misappropriated, which, according to the indictment, is exactly what happened to the information in Bell South's E911 file.

In his final gasp, Neidorf notes that Congress has enacted a statute—the Computer Fraud and Abuse Act (CFAA)—which is specifically designed to address computer-related crimes, such as unauthorized computer access. Neidorf claims that the enactment of the CFAA precludes a finding that section 2314 reaches his alleged conduct in this case. This court is unable to find anything in the legislative history of the CFAA which suggests that the statute was intended to be the exclusive law governing computer-related crimes, or that its enactment precludes the application of other criminal statutes to computer-related conduct. Therefore, the court rejects Neidorf's claim that applying section 2314 to the instant case would undermine the Congressional intent behind the CFAA.

Neidorf's motion to dismiss denied.

CONCEPT REVIEW

COMPUTER FRAUD AND ABUSE ACT

Application	☐ Computers exclusively for the use of a financial institution or the U.S. government
	☐ Computers used by or for a financial institution or the U.S. government, when the defendant's conduct affects the operation of such a computer
	☐ Computers used in interstate commerce (between two or more states)
Prohibitions	☐ Knowingly accessing a computer without authorization to obtain government information that is protected from disclosure (e.g., national defense information)
	☐ Intentionally accessing a computer without authorization to obtain information from a financial institution or consumer reporting agency
	☐ Intentionally and without authorization accessing a computer used by or for the U.S. government
	☐ Knowingly and with intent to defraud accessing a federal interest computer without authorization and obtaining anything of value
	☐ Intentionally accessing a federal interest computer without authorization and altering, damaging, or destroying information, or preventing an authorized person from using the computer if this causes losses to another of $1,000 or more or threatens another's medical treatment or diagnosis
	☐ Knowingly and with intent to defraud traffics in any password or other device through which a computer can be accessed without authorization if this affects interstate or foreign commerce or the computer is used by or for the U.S. government
	☐ Attempting to commit any of the above offenses

PRIVACY AND THE COMPUTER

An increasing amount of information about each of us is constantly being entered and stored in computers. Every time you write a check, register for college courses, apply for a credit card or a student loan, donate money to a charitable organization, order a magazine subscription, claim benefits under a medical insurance or property insurance policy, or file a tax return, information about you is entered into a computer, where it can be stored and easily retrieved. Advances in computer technology make it possible to link separate databases and unify files so as to aggregate large quantities of information about an individual. It may thus be possible for unknown observers to trace an individual's activities and associations and glean a "profile" of his character. While the efficient collection and retrieval of information helps to facilitate effective social and business planning, it also presents a threat to an individual's right of privacy, one aspect of which is the right of an individual to control the disclosure of *information* about himself. Individuals are also concerned that they may lose the ability to control the *accuracy* of the information that is disclosed.

Common Law Privacy Doctrines

The tort of invasion of privacy, which you learned about in the Intentional Torts chapter, may be applied to some invasions of privacy accomplished by the use of computers. The two categories of this tort that are most likely to be applied to computer-assisted invasions of privacy are the *intrusion* theory and the *public disclosure of private facts* theory. Unauthorized intrusion into such private records as personal records kept on a home computer, medical records, or bank accounts might constitute an invasion of privacy under the intrusion theory, for example.

Although the tort cause of action for invasion of privacy might permit a person to obtain compensation for a given invasion, the existence of that remedy is not adequate to deter the problem created by the widespread collection of private information. Many such privacy invasions may be undetected or difficult to prove. Moreover, as was true in the criminal law context, it may be difficult for a plaintiff to satisfy the traditional elements of the tort. For example, one element of the public disclosure theory of invasion of privacy is that the private fact must be disclosed to the public, or a large number of people. When information is transferred from one agency or business to another, a potential plaintiff may be unable to establish that the information was disclosed to a sufficiently large number of people to satisfy this element.

Statutory Protection of Privacy

Mindful of the growing threat to individual privacy posed by the "information explosion," legislatures on both the federal and state level have enacted a number of statutes that serve to limit the circumstances under which certain types of private information can be obtained and used and, in some cases, to provide ways of challenging the accuracy of such information and remedies for the use of inaccurate information. While these state and federal privacy laws usually are not uniquely applicable to computer-assisted invasions of privacy, computers are generally used to collect, store, and transmit the private information involved.

Numerous federal statutes deal with protection of privacy in differing situations. For example, the Family Educational Rights and Privacy Act of 1974 limits access to educational records held by institutions of higher education. The Fair Credit Reporting Act provides procedural safeguards that ensure that consumer reporting agencies exercise care in providing accurate information and in respecting consumers' privacy.[14] Another significant piece of federal legislation affecting privacy is the Right to Financial Privacy Act of 1978, which forbids financial institutions to give the *government* access to a customer's financial records or to any information contained in them unless the customer authorizes such disclosure or the government properly requests it.

In addition, the Computer Matching and Privacy Protection Act of 1988, which became effective in 1989, regulates computer matching programs operated by federal and nonfederal agencies for the purpose of checking eligibility for and compliance with federal benefit programs. A matching program is a computerized comparison of two or more automated systems of records. The focus of the act is to impose procedures likely to protect due process and privacy interests of those whose records are matched.

A number of states have passed laws that protect different aspects of individual privacy, but these laws are by no means uniform. Some states have enacted statutes modeled on the Fair Credit Reporting Act and the Financial Privacy Act. A number of states have specifically declared that it is a crime to use a computer to gain access to private records.

PROTECTION OF COMPUTER SOFTWARE

The mechanisms set up by our legal system to encourage creativity and protect the competitive advantage that creativity affords are of special concern to companies engaged in the development and production of computer software. The development of computer software is a time-consuming and expensive endeavor. Yet the profits that a software supplier hopes to gain are imperiled by the relative ease with which software can be copied and distributed by users and improved upon by competitors. As a result, the life cycle of computer software is short. To protect their enormous investment, software developers and distributors justifiably seek legal protection against infringement and misappropriation of their products through patent, copyright, and trade secrets law.[15]

Patent Protection of Software

A patent on software would give the software producer the exclusive right to make, use, and sell the software for 17 years. This is very valuable protection, because it extends to the concept embodied in the software, and not merely to the form in which it is expressed. For some years a number of courts took the position that computer programs could not be patented. The 1981 Supreme Court case of *Diamond v. Diehr*[16] opened the door to the patenting of computer software by holding that an invention that included a computer program was patentable. Still, to be patented, software must meet the tests for patentability discussed in the Intellectual Property, Competitive Torts, and Unfair Competition chapter.

Copyright Protection of Computer Software

In 1980, Congress amended the Copyright Act to include computer programs in the list of creative works that are the subject of copyright protection. Another 1980 amendment to the Copyright Act permits persons

---

[14]You can read more about the FCRA in the Federal Trade Commission Act and Consumer Protection Laws chapter.

[15]See the Intellectual Property, Competitive Torts, and Unfair Competition chapter for a more detailed discussion of patent, copyright, and trade secret protection.

[16]450 U.S. 175 (U.S. Sup. Ct. 1981)

who buy copyrighted software to make copies and adaptations of the software for their own use and for archival purposes. Under some circumstances, these copies can be transferred by the owner of the software. To avoid the application of this section, most software producers market software through **licenses** rather than sales.

The scope of copyright protection of computer software is still controversial. It is fairly well settled now that copyright law protects the "object code" (program instructions written in a form that is machine-readable only and not intelligible to humans) as well as the "source code" of a program (instructions intelligible to humans). An important issue in recent years has been whether copyright protection is available for more than the literal elements of a program. A copyright protects

the *expression* of an idea, but not the idea or concept of the software itself. It can be difficult to distinguish an idea from an expression of an idea in the context of computer programs, however. Does copyright protection *only* prevent the duplication of the object code or source code of a program, or does it also prevent a competitor from using the structure, organization, and "user interface" (screens and commands that the user uses to interact with the program) of the program? This issue is not yet resolved, but some courts have substantially increased the copyright protection of software producers by holding that such "nonliteral" elements can be copyrightable. The *Lotus Development Corp. v. Paperback Software International* case presents a good example of such a case.

LOTUS DEVELOPMENT CORP. v. PAPERBACK SOFTWARE INTERNATIONAL AND STEPHENSON SOFTWARE, LTD.
740 F. Supp. 37 (D. Mass. 1990)

Lotus produced and marketed Lotus 1-2-3, a highly successful spreadsheet program. Stephenson Software and Paperback Software produced VP-Planner, also a spreadsheet program. To make VP-Planner a commercial success, Paperback and Stephenson made it compatible with 1-2-3. This was accomplished by conforming the arrangement and names of commands and menus in VP-Planner to 1-2-3. This compatibility allowed users to transfer spreadsheets created in 1-2-3 to VP-Planner without loss of functionality for any macros in the spreadsheet. Also, it allowed users to switch from 1-2-3 to VP-Planner without any retraining.

Lotus brought suit against Stephenson and Paperback alleging copyright infringement of these "nonliteral" elements of the 1-2-3 program. The case was tried without a jury, and the judge rendered this opinion on the issue of the copyrightability of the nonliteral elements of 1-2-3.

Keeton, District Judge. The expression of an idea is copyrightable. The idea itself is not. When applying these two settled rules of law, how can a decisionmaker distinguish between an idea and its expression?

This case concerns two competing application programs—Lotus 1-2-3 and VP-Planner—which are primarily spreadsheet programs, but which also support other tasks. The parties agree, as a general proposition, that literal manifestations of a computer program—including both source code and object code—if original, are copyrightable. Paperback and Stephenson vigorously dispute, however, the copyrightability of any nonliteral elements of computer programs. That is, they assert that only literal manifestations of computer programs are copyrightable. Lotus, on the other hand, maintains that copyright protection extends to all elements of computer programs that embody original expression, whether literal or non-literal, including any original expression embodied in a program's "user interface."

One difficulty with Lotus's argument is the amorphous nature of "nonliteral" elements of computer programs. Unlike the written code of a computer or a flowchart that can be printed on paper, nonliteral elements—including such elements as the overall organization of a program, the structure of a program's command system, and the presentation of information on the screen—

may be less tangibly represented. Whether these elements are copyrightable, and if so, how the nonliteral elements that are copyrightable may be identified, are central to deciding this case.

With respect to such things as musical, dramatic, and motion picture works, and works of literature, it is crystal clear that, to the extent original, the literal manifestation of such works are protected by copyright. Thus, during the period of copyright protection, one cannot copy an author's book, score, or script without authorization. It is also well settled that a copyright in a musical, dramatic, or motion picture work, or a work of literature, may be infringed even if the infringer has not copied the literal aspects of the work. That is, even if an infringer does not copy the words or dialogue of a book or play, infringement may be found if there is copying of the work's expression of setting, characters or plot with a resulting substantial similarity. This type of copying of nonliteral expression, if sufficiently extensive, has never been upheld as permissible copying; rather it has always been viewed as copying of elements of an expression of creative originality.

Copyright monopolies are not granted for the purpose of rewarding authors. Rather, Congress has granted copyright monopolies to serve the public welfare by encouraging authors to generate new ideas and disclose them to the public, being free to do so in any uniquely expressed way they may choose. In construing the relevant statutory mandates the court must be faithful to the statutory language and mindful of both the ultimate goal of copyright law—the advancement of public welfare—and Congress' chosen method of achieving this goal—private reward to the individual author. Courts should not draw the line between copyrightable and non-copyrightable elements of computer programs in such a way as to harm the public welfare, nor should courts ignore the accommodation struck by Congress in choosing to advance the public welfare by rewarding authors.

Congress manifested an intention to use the idea-expression distinction as part of the test of copyrightability for computer programs. That is, rather than adopting some other test of copyrightability that made the idea expression irrelevant (such as defendants' proposed literal-nonliteral distinction), Congress chose to extend copyright protection to original expression embodied in computer programs, but not to any idea, method, or process described by that expression.

Even if the "idea" cannot be completely disentangled from its expression, to determine what is copyrightable a decisionmaker must understand the meaning of "idea" within the idea-expression distinction. First, in making the determination of "copyrightability," the decisionmaker must focus on alternatives along the scale from the most generalized conception to the most particularized, and choose some formulation for the purpose of distinguishing between the idea and its expression. Second, the decisionmaker must focus upon whether an alleged expression of the idea is limited to elements essential to expression of that idea (or is one of only a few ways of expressing the idea) or instead includes identifiable elements of expression not essential to every expression of that idea. Third, having identified elements of expression not essential to every expression of the idea, the decisionmaker must focus on whether those elements are a substantial part of the allegedly copyrightable work.

I conclude that a menu command structure is capable of being expressed in many if not an unlimited number of ways, and that the command structure of 1-2-3 is an original and nonobvious way of expressing a command structure. Accordingly, the menu structure taken as a whole—including the choice of command terms, the structure and order of those terms, their presentation on the screen, and the long prompts—is an aspect of 1-2-3 that is not present in every expression of an electronic spreadsheet.

Finally, I consider whether the structure, sequence, and organization of the menu command system is a substantial part of the alleged copyrighted work—here Lotus 1-2-3. That the answer to this question is "yes" is incontrovertible. The user interface of 1-2-3 is its most unique element, and is the aspect that has made 1-2-3 so popular. Taking into account all three elements of the legal test, I determine that copyrightability of the user interface of 1-2-3 is established.

The court's comparison of the 1-2-3 menu command hierarchy and the VP-Planner hierarchy confirms that VP-Planner "has the same command tree" as 1-2-3—that is, that defendants copied the expression embodied in the 1-2-3. Accordingly, I conclude that it is indisputable that defendants have copied substantial copyrightable elements of Lotus's copyrighted work. I therefore conclude that liability has been established.

Order in favor of Lotus.

Trade Secret Protection of Software

In contrast to copyright protection, trade secret protection covers not only the expression of an idea but the idea itself. Furthermore, in contrast to both patent and copyright protection, trade secret protection requires no registration, expensive and lengthy procedures, notice, or disclosure of the secret. Thus, computer software is an ideal subject for trade secret protection if the proper precautions are taken to preserve secrecy.[17]

Since the essence of trade secret protection is to afford a business protection of secret information that gives it a competitive advantage, trade secret protection can be lost if the formula, information, or other secret is not closely guarded. While the information may be disclosed to some people (such as customers and employees), it must be clear that the business took steps to keep the information a secret. This can be shown by the fact that only a few people were allowed access to the secret, that the information was disclosed on a confidential basis, or that the persons to whom the secret was disclosed signed a nondisclosure agreement. Information that is disclosed to a large number of people without proper precautions or that becomes generally known in the trade cannot constitute a trade secret.

The preservation of secrecy is the most difficult aspect of maintaining trade secret protection for software. To preserve secrecy, it is necessary for a software producer to use great care in maintaining internal security and in disclosing secret information to customers only under confidential circumstances. It is common for a software producer to execute secrecy agreements with employees and to restrict access to the secret.

Furthermore, software licensing agreements are designed to preserve secrecy by restricting the licensee's disclosure of the program. They typically forbid the licensee to copy the program except for backup and archival purposes, require that the licensee and its employees sign confidentiality agreements, require that such employees use the program only in the scope of their jobs, and specify that the licensee use the program only in a single central processing unit.

Courts have also considered whether federal copyright law preempts (forecloses) state trade secret protection. Most of the courts that have dealt with this question have held that it does not and that trade secret protection and copyright protection can exist at the same time. A related issue is whether the placing of a copyright notice on a program forecloses the program's status as a trade secret, since it indicates the intent to disclose the secret. Again, the weight of authority is that copyright notice does not prevent trade secret protection for the program.

ETHICAL AND PUBLIC POLICY CONCERNS

1. Do you believe that it is good public policy for a court to interpret a criminal statute broadly to encompass computer-assisted crime, as the court in *U.S. v. Riggs* did? Would it be preferable for the court to give the statutory language its plain English meaning, thus creating pressure on legislatures to revise the statute to specifically address computer crime?

2. What privacy problems do you foresee with the increasing use of computers and computerized databases? How should the law respond?

SUMMARY

The rapid proliferation of computers has produced a host of legal problems, some of which are not easily resolved

---

[17]For a discussion of the features of trade secrets law, see the Intellectual Property, Competitive Torts, and Unfair Competition chapter.

by traditional legal doctrines. Courts and legislatures are engaged in adapting law to computer technology.

One question that arises at the outset of any contract case involving computer products is whether the Uniform Commercial Code applies to the contract. This requires the court to characterize the transaction as being primarily a contract for the sale of goods rather than a contract for services. Transactions in which the parties primarily bargained for the sale of goods are governed by the UCC, even though services incidental to the sale of goods may be provided. The trend appears to be in the direction of treating sales of software, even custom-designed software, as sales of goods under the UCC.

With regard to contracts for the sale of computer products, it is often difficult for a buyer to negotiate favorable terms that protect his right to compensation in case of defects or malfunction of the system. Terms that are unreasonably advantageous to the seller and are presented under circumstances in which the buyer has no meaningful choice but to agree may be attacked on the ground of *unconscionability*.

When a computer system proves to be defective, a buyer may seek a remedy under warranty law. There are three possible warranties that may apply: express warranty, implied warranty of merchantability, and implied warranty of fitness for a particular purpose. Warranty protection is likely to be strictly limited in the contract for sale of a computer, however. Sellers of computers often provide formal, express warranties for a very limited period of time in lieu of all implied warranties. In addition, such contracts usually contain disclaimers of implied warranties, provisions excluding consequential and incidental damages and limiting the remedies available for breach of warranty, and merger clauses to prevent the inclusion of precontract representations. So long as such contract provisions meet the requirements for disclaimers and limitations of remedies specified in the UCC, and so long as they are not unconscionable, they will be enforced.

An injured buyer may also attempt to proceed against the seller in a tort action, such as one based on fraud or misrepresentation. He may bring an action grounded in negligence. Courts are not in agreement about the standard of care to be applied to computer programmers. In addition, strict liability may be applied when defective computer products cause personal injury. It is unlikely that either negligence law or strict liability can be used in a case in which the plaintiff has suffered only economic injury and no personal injury or property damages.

The increasing use of computers to accomplish the transfer of funds and the storage and analysis of important information has created new opportunities for highly lucrative criminal activity. The statutory elements of traditional crimes are often ill-suited to the types of activities involved in computer crimes, although many courts have interpreted their criminal statutes broadly to encompass criminal activity accomplished through the use of computers. A strong trend now exists for legislatures to amend their criminal codes to outlaw specifically certain types of computer crimes. Forty-eight states have passed statutes specifically outlawing computer crime, and the federal Computer Fraud and Abuse Act outlaws specific abuses of computers.

The widespread use of computers to collect, store, and integrate information about people has led to well-founded concern about the loss of individual privacy. The common law tort of invasion of privacy may provide a remedy to a person injured by such an invasion. In addition, a host of statutes exists on both the state and federal level that guard against different types of invasion of privacy by the government and others. The Computer Matching and Privacy Protection Act of 1988 regulates computerized comparison of two or more automated systems of records by federal and nonfederal agencies done for the purpose of checking eligibility for and compliance with federal benefit programs.

Another very important issue in computer law relates to the means by which a producer of computer products may obtain protection against infringement and misappropriation of its inventions, expressions, and trade secrets. This is a particular problem for producers of computer software. A producer of computer software may be able to obtain protection through patents, copyrights, and trade secret law.

PROBLEM CASES

1. Apple Computer, Inc. is one of the leading manufacturers of microcomputers, related equipment, and computer programs. Franklin Computer Corporation is a much smaller manufacturer of computers. It manufactures and sells the ACE 100 personal computer, which was designed to be "Apple compatible," so that peripheral equipment and software developed for use with the Apple II could be used with the ACE 100. In manufacturing the ACE 100, Franklin used 14 Apple operating programs. Apple brought suit against Franklin, claiming infringement of the copyrights it held in the 14 programs. Franklin's principal defense is that the Apple operating system programs are not capable of copyright protection because they are written in "object code," which is readable only by machines. Is this defense likely to be successful?

2. Chatlos Systems contacted NCR about purchasing a computer system. NCR represented that its 399/656 system would provide six functions for Chatlos: accounts receivable, payroll, order entry, inventory deletion, state income tax, and cash receipts. NCR also stated that the system would be programmed by capable NCR personnel and be "up and running" within six months. Chatlos signed a contract for the system. It provided that the equipment was warranted for 12 months after delivery and that NCR's obligation was limited to correcting any error in the program that appeared within 60 days after the program was furnished. The hardware was delivered in December 1974. By March 1975, only one of the functions was in operation. One year later, the remaining functions were still not operative, despite repeated efforts by NCR to solve the problems. In August of 1976, Chatlos experienced problems with the payroll function, the only function that the computer had been performing properly. Chatlos eventually brought suit against NCR for breach of warranty. Will the UCC be applied? Will the limited remedy clause be enforced?

3. Parrish worked for J & K Computer Systems as a computer programmer. J & K required Parrish to sign an employment contract, one of the terms of which provided as follows:

Disclosure of Information: The Employee recognizes and acknowledges that a list of the Employer's customers and the methods and programs used in conducting the Employer's business are valuable, special and unique assets of the Employer's business. The Employee will not, during or after the terms of employment, disclose methods or programs used in conducting the Employer's business or any part thereof to any person, firm, corporation, association, or other entity for any reason or purpose whatever.

Parrish developed an open-item/balance forward accounts receivable program and installed it on behalf of J & K at the Arnold Machinery Company. He also contacted E. A. Miller and Sons Meat Packing Company about the possibility of installing the program. Parrish later quit J & K and went into business with his brother-in-law, Chlarson, another former J & K employee who had also signed the nondisclosure agreement. Parrish

contracted to provide Arnold Machinery with programming services and also contracted with E. A. Miller for the installation of the accounts receivable program. In addition, he made an electronic copy of the accounts receivable program that J & K had installed at Arnold Machinery. J & K learned of this and filed suit against Parrish and Chlarson for misappropriation of a trade secret. Parrish and Chlarson claim that the accounts receivable programs were not trade secrets. Were they?

4. Wilson purchased a computer-assisted electrocardiographic system called MUSE from Marquette. Before the sale, Marquette orally represented that the system had a throughput capacity of 10,000 EKGs per month, that the system would not have "downtime" of more than 24 hours over two times per year, that the service given would be priority service, and that the equipment would operate in the environment of the Wilson office facility with the existing power facilities and temperature range. The system was accompanied by a written manual that did not contain any provisions relating to warranties. When the system was put into operation, a number of significant problems became evident. It would not operate in Wilson's office building environment, and it was capable of only 5,000 throughputs per month. Furthermore, the system was unreliable and experienced a number of breakdowns, many for more than 24 hours in duration. Wilson brought suit for breach of warranty. What warranties were created in this transaction?

5. McGraw was employed as a computer operator by the City of Indianapolis. The city leased computer services on a flat rate basis, so the cost of the services was not varied by the extent to which they were used. McGraw was provided with a terminal at his desk and assigned a portion of the computer's information storage capacity, called a "private library," for his use in performing his duties. No other employees were authorized to use his terminal or his library. At the time McGraw was hired, he had received the handbook given to all new employees, which stated that the unauthorized use of city property was prohibited. McGraw became involved in a private sales venture for a product known as NaturSlim. He began soliciting his co-workers and using part of his assigned library to maintain his personal business records, such as client lists, inventory control, birthdates of clients, and copies of letters. He was reprimanded several times for selling his products on office time, and he was eventually discharged for unsatisfactory job performance and for continuing his personal business activities during office hours. McGraw's activities were discovered after his discharge, and he was charged with theft. The theft statute provides:

A person who knowingly or intentionally exerts unauthorized control over property of another person with intent to deprive the other of any part of its value or use, commits theft . . .

Using a narrow interpretation of the statutory language, was McGraw properly charged with the crime of theft?

6. Honeywell approached Triangle Underwriters to sell or lease Honeywell's H–110 computer system to Triangle. The H–110 is a package consisting of both hardware and software. Honeywell supplies both standard programming aids of general application and custom application software designed specifically for the customer's individual needs. Honeywell submitted a formal proposal to Triangle regarding the installation of the H–110 system. It was to be a turnkey system, with the software pre-prepared and the system ready for immediate functioning. Honeywell submitted a proposal providing that the system was to be fully operational within 105 days. Honeywell employees were to install the system and train Triangle employees in its use, whereupon Triangle would take over immediate supervision. The proposal contained no provision requiring Honeywell to update or amend the software after the Triangle employees assumed supervision. The parties entered into a lease, and Honeywell began preparation of the custom application software. The system was installed in January 1971. The system failed to function effectively from the beginning. Various programs did not function as had been represented, and there were numerous errors in the system. Honeywell attempted to correct the defects until some time in 1972. In August 1975, Triangle brought suit against Honeywell on a variety of theories, including breach of express and implied warranties. Honeywell defends on the ground that the UCC's four-year statute of limitations had elapsed. Triangle counters that the six-year statute of limitations applicable to non-UCC contracts applies. Does the UCC apply to this case?

7. Someone using a computer repeatedly attempted to enter the Yavapai Telephone Exchange long-distance system using unauthorized personal identification numbers. An investigation conducted by the exchange revealed that these attempts originated from a telephone located in Johnston's apartment. Johnston's apartment was searched pursuant to a warrant, and the computer that was used to gain access to the long-distance system was found in the bedroom used by Johnston's son and seized. The state filed a petition for forfeiture of the computer. The petition cited the Arizona computer fraud statute as the statutory authority for the forfeiture. That statute makes it a crime to intentionally and without authorization access any computer system. The statute provides a criminal penalty, but does not provide for forfeiture of a computer. The state racketeering statute would allow forfeiture, but it must be shown that property or services stolen had a value of $250 or more. At trial, an exchange employee testified that the exchange had suffered at least $20,000 in losses from computer hacking, but there was no evidence as to the amount of losses caused by Johnston's son's hacking. Should the judgment of forfeiture be reversed?

Appendixes

THE CONSTITUTION OF THE UNITED STATES

PREAMBLE

We the People of the United States, in Order to form a more perfect Union, establish Justice, insure domestic Tranquility, provide for the common defence, promote the general Welfare, and secure the Blessings of Liberty to ourselves and our Posterity, do ordain and establish this Constitution for the United States of America.

ARTICLE I

Section 1.   All legislative Powers herein granted shall be vested in a Congress of the United States, which shall consist of a Senate and House of Representatives.

Section 2.   [1] The House of Representatives shall be composed of Members chosen every second Year by the People of the several States, and the Electors in each State shall have the qualifications requisite for Electors of the most numerous Branch of the State Legislature.

[2] No Person shall be a Representative who shall not have attained to the Age of twenty five Years, and been seven Years a citizen of the United States, and who shall not, when elected, be an Inhabitant of that State in which he shall be chosen.

[3] Representatives and direct Taxes shall be apportioned among the several States which may be included within this Union, according to their respective Numbers, which shall be determined by adding to the whole Number of free Persons, including those bound to service for a Term of Years, and excluding Indians not taxed, three fifths of all other Persons. The actual Enumeration shall be made within three Years after the first meeting of the Congress of the United States, and within every subsequent Term of ten Years, in such Manner as they shall by Law direct. The Number of Representatives shall not exceed one for every thirty Thousand, but each state shall have at Least one Representative; and until such enumeration shall be made, the State of New Hampshire shall be entitled to chuse three, Massachusetts eight, Rhode Island and Providence Plantations one, Connecticut five, New York six, New Jersey four, Pennsylvania eight, Delaware one, Maryland six, Virginia ten, North Carolina five, South Carolina five, and Georgia three.

[4] When vacancies happen in the Representation from any State, the Executive authority thereof shall issue Writs of Election to fill such Vacancies.

[5] The House of Representatives shall chuse their Speaker and other Officers; and shall have the sole Power of Impeachment.

Section 3.   [1] The Senate of the United States shall be composed of two Senators from each State, chosen by the Legislature thereof, for six Years; and each Senator shall have one Vote.

[2] Immediately after they shall be assembled in Consequence of the first Election, they shall be divided as equally as may be into three Classes. The Seats of the Senators of the first Class shall be vacated at the Expiration of the second Year, of the second Class at the Expiration of the fourth Year, and of the third Class at the Expiration of the sixth Year, so that one third may be chosen every second Year; and if Vacancies happen by Resignation, or otherwise, during the Recess of the Legislature of any State, the Executive thereof may make temporary

Appointments until the next Meeting of the Legislature, which shall then fill such Vacancies.

[3] No Person shall be a Senator who shall not have attained to the Age of thirty Years, and been nine Years a Citizen of the United States, and who shall not when elected, be an Inhabitant of that State for which he shall be chosen.

[4] The Vice President of the United States shall be President of the Senate, but shall have no Vote, unless they be equally divided.

[5] The Senate shall chuse their other Officers, and also a President pro tempore, in the Absence of the Vice President, or when he shall exercise the Office of President of the United States.

[6] The Senate shall have the sole Power to try all Impeachments. When sitting for that Purpose, they shall be on Oath of Affirmation. When the President of the United States is tried, the Chief Justice shall preside: And no Person shall be convicted without the Concurrence of two thirds of the Members present.

[7] Judgment in Cases of Impeachment shall not extend further than to removal from Office, and disqualification to hold and enjoy any Office of honor, Trust, or Profit under the United States: but the Party convicted shall nevertheless be liable and subject to Indictment, Trial, Judgment, and Punishment, according to Law.

Section 4. [1] The Times, Places and Manner of holding election for Senators and Representatives, shall be prescribed in each State by the Legislature thereof; but the Congress may at any time by Law make or alter such Regulations, except as to the Places of chusing Senators.

[2] The Congress shall assemble at least once in every Year, and such Meeting shall be on the first Monday in December, unless they shall by Law appoint a different Day.

Section 5. [1] Each House shall be the Judge of the Elections, Returns, and Qualifications of its own Members, and a Majority of each shall constitute a Quorum to do Business; but a smaller Number may adjourn from day to day, and may be authorized to compel the Attendance of absent Members, in such Manner, and under such Penalties as each House may provide.

[2] Each House may determine the Rules of its Proceedings, punish its Members for disorderly Behaviour, and with the Concurrence of two thirds, expel a Member.

[3] Each House shall keep a Journal of its Proceedings, and from time to time publish the same, excepting such Parts as may in their Judgment require Secrecy; and the Yeas and Nays of the Members of either House on any question shall, at the Desire of one fifth of those Present, be entered on the Journal.

[4] Neither House, during the Session of Congress, shall, without the consent of the other, adjourn for more than three days, nor to any other Place than that in which the two Houses shall be sitting.

Section 6. [1] The Senators and Representatives shall receive a Compensation for their Services, to be ascertained by Law, and paid out of the Treasury of the United States. They shall in all Cases, except Treason, Felony and Breach of the Peace, be privileged from Arrest during their Attendance at the Session of their respective Houses, and in going to and returning from the same; and for any Speech or Debate in either House, they shall not be questioned in any other Place.

[2] No Senator or Representative shall, during the time for which he was elected, be appointed to any civil Office under the Authority of the United States, which shall have been created, or the Emoluments whereof shall have been increased during such time; and no Person holding any Office under the United States, shall be a Member of either House during his Continuance in Office.

Section 7. [1] All Bills for raising Revenue shall originate in the House of Representatives; but the Senate may propose or concur with Amendments as on other Bills.

[2] Every Bill which shall have passed the House of Representatives and the Senate, shall, before it become a Law, be presented to the President of the United States; If he approve he shall sign it, but if not he shall return it, with his Objections to that House in which it shall have originated, who shall enter the Objections at large on their Journal, and proceed to reconsider it. If after such Reconsideration two thirds of that House shall agree to pass the Bill, it shall be sent together with the Objections, to the other House, by which it shall likewise be reconsidered, and if approved by two thirds of that House, it shall become a Law. But in all such Cases the Votes of both Houses shall be determined by Yeas and Nays, and the Names of the Persons voting for and against the Bill shall be entered on the Journal of each House respectively. If any Bill shall not be returned by the President within ten Days (Sundays excepted) after it shall have been presented to him, the Same shall be a Law, in like Manner as if he had signed it, unless the Congress by their Adjournment prevent its return in which Case it shall not be a Law.

[3] Every Order, Resolution, or Vote, to Which the Concurrence of the Senate and House of Representatives may be necessary (except on a question of Adjournment) shall be presented to the President of the United States; and before the Same shall take Effect, shall be approved by him, or being disapproved by him, shall be repassed by two thirds of the Senate and House of Representatives, according to the Rules and Limitations prescribed in the Case of a Bill.

Section 8. [1] The Congress shall have Power To lay and collect Taxes, Duties, Imposts and Excises, to pay the Debts and provide for the common Defence and general Welfare of the United States; but all Duties, Imposts and Excises shall be uniform throughout the United States;

[2] To borrow money on the credit of the United States;

[3] To regulate Commerce with foreign Nations, and among the several States, and with the Indian Tribes;

[4] To establish an uniform Rule of Naturalization, and uniform Laws on the subject of Bankruptcies throughout the United States;

[5] To coin Money, regulate the Value thereof, and of foreign Coin, and fix the Standard of Weights and Measures;

[6] To Provide for the Punishment of counterfeiting the Securities and current Coin of the United States;

[7] To Establish Post Offices and Post Roads;

[8] To promote the Progress of Science and useful Arts, by securing for limited Times to Authors and Inventors the exclusive Right to their respective Writings and Discoveries;

[9] To constitute Tribunals inferior to the supreme Court;

[10] To define and punish Piracies and Felonies committed on the high Seas, and Offences against the Law of Nations;

[11] To declare War, grant Letters of Marque and Reprisal, and make Rules concerning Captures on Land and Water;

[12] To raise and support Armies, but no Appropriation of Money to that Use shall be for a longer term than two Years;

[13] To provide and maintain a Navy;

[14] To make Rules for the Government and Regulation of the land and naval Forces;

[15] To provide for calling forth the Militia to execute the Laws of the Union, suppress Insurrections and repel Invasions;

[16] To provide for organizing, arming, and disciplining, the Militia, and for governing such Part of them as may be employed in the Service of the United States, reserving to the States respectively, the Appointment of the Officers, and the Authority of training the Militia according to the discipline prescribed by Congress;

[17] To exercise exclusive Legislation in all Cases whatsoever, over such District (not exceeding ten Miles square) as may, by Cession of particular States, and the Acceptance of Congress, become the Seat of the Government of the United States, and to exercise like Authority over all Places purchased by the Consent of the Legislature of the State in which the Same shall be, for the Erection of Forts, Magazines, Arsenals, dock-Yards, and other needful Buildings;—And

[18] To make all Laws which shall be necessary and proper for carrying into Execution the foregoing Powers, and all other Powers vested by this Constitution in the Government of the United States, or in any Department or Officer Thereof.

Section 9.   [1] The Migration or Importation of Such Persons as any of the States now existing shall think proper to admit, shall not be prohibited by the Congress prior to the Year one thousand eight hundred and eight, but a Tax or duty may be imposed on such Importation, not exceeding ten dollars for each Person.

[2] The Privilege of the Writ of Habeas Corpus shall not be suspended, unless when in Cases of Rebellion or Invasion, the public Safety may require it.

[3] No Bill of Attainder or ex post facto Law shall be passed.

[4] No Capitation, or other direct, Tax shall be laid, unless in Proportion to the Census or Enumeration herein before directed to be taken.

[5] No Tax or Duty shall be laid on Articles exported from any State.

[6] No Preference shall be given by any Regulation of Commerce or Revenue to the Ports of one State over those of another: nor shall Vessels bound to, or from, one State be obliged to enter, clear, or pay Duties in another.

[7] No money shall be drawn from the Treasury, but in consequence of Appropriations made by Law; and a regular Statement and Account of the Receipts and Expenditures of all public Money shall be published from time to time.

[8] No Title of Nobility shall be granted by the United States: And No Person holding any Office of Profit or Trust under them, shall, without the consent of the Congress, accept of any present, Emolument, Office, or Title, of any kind whatever, from any King, Prince, or foreign State.

Section 10.   [1] No State shall enter into any Treaty, Alliance, or Confederation; grant Letters of Marque and Reprisal; coin Money; emit Bills of Credit; make any Thing but gold and silver Coin a Tender in Payment of Debts; pass any Bill of Attainder, ex post facto Law, or Law impairing the Obligation of Contracts, or grant any Title of Nobility.

[2] No State shall, without the consent of the Congress, lay any Imposts or Duties on Imports or Exports, except what may be absolutely necessary for executing its inspection Laws: and the net Produce of all Duties and Imposts, laid by any State on Imports or Exports, shall be for the Use of the Treasury of the United States; and all such Laws shall be subject to the Revision and Control of the Congress.

[3] No State shall, without the consent of the Congress, lay any Duty of Tonnage, keep Troops, or Ships of War in time of Peace, enter into any Agree-ment or compact with another State, or with a foreign Power or engage in War, unless actually invaded, or in such imminent Danger as will not admit of delay.

ARTICLE II

Section 1.   [1] The executive Power shall be vested in a President of the United States of America. He shall hold his Office during the term of four Years, and together with the Vice President, chosen for the same Term, be elected, as follows:

[2] Each State shall appoint, in such Manner as the Legislature thereof may direct, a Number of Electors, equal to the whole Number of Senators and Representatives to which the State may be entitled in the Congress; but no Senator or Representative, or Person holding an Office of Trust or Profit under the United States, shall be appointed an Elector.

[3] The Electors shall meet in their respective States, and vote by Ballot for two Persons, of whom one at least shall not be an Inhabitant of the same State with themselves. And they shall make a List of all the Persons voted for, and of the Number of Votes for each; which List they shall sign and certify, and transmit sealed to the Seat of the Government of the United States, directed to the President of the Senate. The President of the Senate shall, in the Presence of the Senate and House of Representatives, open all the Certificates, and

the Votes shall then be counted. The Person having the greatest Number of Votes shall be the President, if such Number be a Majority of the whole Number of Electors appointed; and if there be more than one who have such Majority, and have an equal Number of Votes, then the House of Representatives shall immediately chuse by Ballot one of them for President; and if no Person have a Majority, then from the five highest on the List the said House shall in like Manner chuse the President. But in chusing the President, the Votes shall be taken by States, the Representation from each State having one Vote; a quorum for this Purpose shall consist of a Member or Members from two thirds of the States, and a Majority of all the States shall be necessary to a Choice. In every Case, after the Choice of the President, the Person having the greater number of Votes of the Electors shall be the Vice President. But if there should remain two or more who have equal Votes, the Senate shall chuse from them by Ballot the Vice President.

[4] The Congress may determine the Time of chusing the Electors, and the Day on which they shall give their Votes; which Day shall be the same throughout the United States.

[5] No person except a natural born citizen, or a citizen of the United States, at the time of the Adoption of this Constitution, shall be eligible to the Office of President; neither shall any Person be eligible to that Office who shall not have attained to the Age of thirty-five Years, and been fourteen Years a Resident within the United States.

[6] In case of the removal of the President from Office, or of his Death, Resignation or Inability to discharge the Powers and Duties of the said Office, the Same shall devolve on the Vice President, and the Congress may by Law provide for the Case of Removal, Death, Resignation or Inability, both of the President and Vice President, declaring what Officer shall then act as President, and such Officer shall act accordingly, until the Disability be removed, or a President shall be elected.

[7] The President shall, at stated Times, receive for his Services, a Compensation, which shall neither be increased nor diminished during the Period for which he shall have been elected, and he shall not receive within that Period any other Emolument from the United States, or any of them.

[8] Before he enter on the Execution of his Office, he shall take the following Oath or Affirmation: "I do solemnly swear (or affirm) that I will faithfully execute the Office of President of the United States, and will to the best of my Ability, preserve, protect and defend the Constitution of the United States."

Section 2.   [1] The President shall be Commander in Chief of the Army and Navy of the United States, and of the militia of the several States, when called into the actual Service of the United States; he may require the Opinion, in writing, of the principal Officer in each of the Executive departments, upon any Subject relating to the duties of their respective Offices, and he shall have Power to grant Reprieves and Pardons for Offenses against the United States, except in Cases of Impeachment.

[2] He shall have Power, by and with the Advice and Consent of the Senate to make Treaties, provided two thirds of the Senators present concur; and he shall nominate, and by and with the Advice and Consent of the Senate, shall appoint Ambassadors, other public Ministers and Consuls, Judges of the supreme Court, and all other Officers of the United States, whose Appointments are not herein otherwise provided for, and which shall be established by Law; but the Congress may by Law vest the Appointment of such inferior Officers, as they think proper, in the Heads of Departments.

[3] The President shall have Power to fill up all Vacancies that may happen during the Recess of the Senate, by granting Commissions which shall expire at the End of their next Session.

Section 3.   He shall from time to time give to the Congress Information of the State of the Union, and recommend to their Consideration such Measures as he shall judge necessary and expedient; he may, on extraordinary Occasions, convene both Houses, or either of them, and in Case of Disagreement between them, with Respect to the Time of Adjournment, he may adjourn them to such Time as he shall think proper; he shall receive Ambassadors and other public Ministers; he shall take Care that the Laws be faithfully executed, and shall Commission all the Officers of the United States.

Section 4.   The President, Vice President and all civil Officers of the United States, shall be removed from Office on Impeachment for, and Conviction of, Treason, Bribery, or other high Crimes and Misdemeanors.

ARTICLE III

Section 1.   The judicial Power of the United States, shall be vested in one supreme Court, and in such inferior Courts as the Congress may from time to time ordain and establish. The Judges, both of the supreme and inferior Courts, shall hold their Offices during good Behaviour, and shall, at stated Times, receive for their Services a Compensation, which shall not be diminished during their Continuance in Office,

Section 2.   [1] The judicial Power shall extend to all Cases, in Law and Equity, arising under this Constitution, the Laws of the United States, and Treaties made or which shall be made, under their Authority;—to all Cases affecting Ambassadors, other public Ministers and Consuls;—to all Cases of admiralty and maritime Jurisdiction;—to Controversies to which the United States shall be a Party;—to Controversies between two or more States;—between a State and Citizens of another State;—between Citizens of different States;—between Citizens of the same State claiming Lands under the Grants of different States, and between a State, or the Citizens thereof, and foreign States, Citizens or Subjects.

[2] In all Cases affecting Ambassadors, other public Ministers and Consuls, and those in which a State shall be a Party, the supreme Court shall have original Jurisdiction. In all the other Cases before mentioned, the supreme Court shall have

appellate Jurisdiction, both as to Law and Fact, with such Exceptions, and under such Regulations as the Congress shall make.

[3] The trial of all Crimes, except in Cases of Impeachment, shall be by Jury; and such Trial shall be held in the State where the said Crimes shall have been committed; but when not committed within any State, the Trial shall be at such Place or Places as the Congress may by Law have directed.

Section 3.   [1] Treason against the United States, shall consist only in levying War against them, or, in adhering to their Enemies, giving them Aid and Comfort. No Person shall be convicted of Treason unless on the Testimony of two Witnesses to the same overt Act, or on Confession in open Court.

[2] The Congress shall have Power to declare the Punishment of Treason, but no Attainder of Treason shall work Corruption of Blood, or Forfeiture except during the Life of the Person attainted.

ARTICLE IV

Section 1.   Full Faith and Credit shall be given in each State to the Public Acts, Records, and judicial Proceedings of every other State. And the Congress may by general Laws prescribe the Manner in which such Acts, Records and Proceedings shall be proved, and the Effect thereof.

Section 2.   [1] The Citizens of each State shall be entitled to all Privileges and Immunities of Citizens in the several States.

[2] A Person charged in any State with Treason, Felony, or other Crime, who shall flee from Justice, and be found in another State, shall on demand of the executive Authority of the State from which he fled, be delivered up, to be removed to the State having Jurisdiction of the Crime.

[3] No Person held to Service or Labour in one State, under the Laws thereof, escaping into another, shall, in Consequence of any Law or Regulation therein, be discharged from such Service or Labour, but shall be delivered up on Claim of the Party to whom such Service or Labour may be due.

Section 3.   [1] New States may be admitted by the Congress into this Union; but no new State shall be formed or erected within the Jurisdiction of any other State; nor any State be formed by the Junction of two or more States, or Parts of States, without the Consent of the Legislatures of the States concerned as well as of the Congress.

[2] The Congress shall have Power to dispose of and make all needful Rules and Regulations respecting the Territory or other Property belonging to the United States; and nothing in this Constitution shall be so construed as to Prejudice any Claims of the United States, or of any particular State.

Section 4.   The United States shall guarantee to every State in this Union a Republican Form of Government, and shall protect each of them against Invasion; and on Application of the Legislature, or of the Executive (when the Legislature cannot be convened) against domestic Violence.

ARTICLE V

The Congress, whenever two thirds of both Houses shall deem it necessary, shall propose Amendments to this Constitution, or, on the Application of the Legislatures of two thirds of the several States, shall call a convention for proposing Amendments, which in either case, shall be valid to all Intents and Purposes, as part of this Constitution, when ratified by the Legislatures of three fourths of the several States, or by Conventions in three fourths thereof, as the one or the other Mode of Ratification may be proposed by the Congress; Provided that no Amendment which may be made prior to the Year One thousand eight hundred and eight shall in any Manner affect the first and fourth clauses in the Ninth Section of the first Article; and that no State, without its Consent, shall be deprived of its equal Suffrage in the Senate.

ARTICLE VI

[1] All Debts contracted and Engagements entered into, before the Adoption of this Constitution, shall be as valid against the United States under this Constitution, as under the Confederation.

[2] This Constitution, and the Laws of the United States which shall be made in Pursuance thereof; and all Treaties made, or which shall be made, under the Authority of the United States, shall be the supreme Law of the Land; and the Judges in every State shall be bound thereby, any Thing in the Constitution or Laws of any State to the Contrary notwithstanding.

[3] The Senators and Representatives before mentioned, and the Members of the several State Legislatures, and all executive and judicial Officers, both of the United States and of the several States, shall be bound by Oath or Affirmation, to support this Constitution; but no religious Test shall ever be required as a Qualification to any Office or public Trust under the United States.

ARTICLE VII

The Ratification of the Conventions of nine States shall be sufficient for the Establishment of this Constitution between the States so ratifying the Same.

AMENDMENTS

Articles in addition to, and amendment of, the Constitution of the United States of America, proposed by Congress, and ratified by the Legislatures of the several States pursuant to the Fifth Article of the original Constitution.

Amendment I [1791]

Congress shall make no law respecting an establishment of religion, or prohibiting the free exercise thereof; or abridging the freedom of speech, or of the right of the people peaceably to assemble, and to petition the Government for a redress of grievances.

Amendment II [1791]

A well regulated Militia, being necessary to the security of a free State, the right of the people to keep and bear Arms, shall not be infringed.

Amendment III [1791]

No Soldier shall, in time of peace be quartered in any house, without the consent of the Owner, or in time of war, but in a manner to be prescribed by law.

Amendment IV [1791]

The right of the people to be secure in their persons, houses, papers, and effects, against unreasonable searches and seizures, shall not be violated, and no Warrants shall issue, but upon probable cause, supported by Oath or affirmation, and particularly describing the place to be searched, and the persons or things to be seized.

Amendment V [1791]

No person shall be held to answer for a capital, or otherwise infamous crime, unless on a presentment or indictment of a Grand Jury, except in cases arising in the land or naval forces, or in the Militia, when in actual service in time of War or public danger; nor shall any person be subject for the same offence to be twice put in jeopardy of life or limb; nor shall be compelled in any criminal case to be a witness against himself, nor be deprived of life, liberty, or property, without due process of law; nor shall private property be taken for public use, without just compensation.

Amendment VI [1791]

In all criminal prosecutions, the accused shall enjoy the right to a speedy and public trial, by an impartial jury of the State and district wherein the crime shall have been committed, which district shall have been previously ascertained by law, and to be informed of the nature and cause of the accusation; to be confronted with the witnesses against him; to have compulsory process for obtaining witnesses in his favor, and to have the Assistance of Counsel for his defence.

Amendment VII [1791]

In Suits at common law, where the value in controversy shall exceed twenty dollars, the right of trial by jury shall be preserved, and no fact tried by jury, shall be otherwise re-examined in any Court of the United States, than according to the rules of common law.

Amendment VIII [1791]

Excessive bail shall not be required, nor excessive fines imposed, nor cruel and unusual punishments inflicted.

Amendment IX [1791]

The enumeration in the Constitution, of certain rights, shall not be construed to deny or disparage others retained by the people.

Amendment X [1791]

The powers not delegated to the United States by the Constitution, nor prohibited by it to the States, are reserved to the States respectively, or to the people.

Amendment XI [1798]

The Judicial power of the United States shall not be construed to extend to any suit in law or equity, commenced or prosecuted against one of the United States by Citizens of another State, or by Citizens or Subjects of any Foreign State.

Amendment XII [1804]

The Electors shall meet in their respective states and vote by ballot for President and Vice-President, one of whom, at least, shall not be an inhabitant of the same state with themselves; they shall name in their ballots the person voted for as President, and in distinct ballots the person voted for as Vice-President, and they shall make distinct lists of all persons voted for as President, and of all persons voted for as Vice-President, and of the number of votes for each, which lists they shall sign and certify, and transmit sealed to the seat of the government of the United States, directed to the President of the Senate;— The President of the Senate shall, in the presence of the Senate and House of Representatives, open all the certificates and the votes shall then be counted;—The person having the greatest number of votes for President, shall be the President, if such number be a majority of the whole number of Electors appointed; and if no person have such majority, then from the persons having the highest numbers not exceeding three on the list of those voted for as President, the House of Representatives shall choose immediately, by ballot, the President. But in choosing the President, the votes shall be taken by states, the representation from each state having one vote; a quorum for this purpose shall consist of a member or members from two-thirds of the states, and a majority of all the states shall be necessary to a choice. And if the House of Representatives shall not choose a President whenever the right of choice shall devolve upon them before the fourth day of March next following, then the Vice-President shall act as President, as in the case of the death or other constitutional disability of the President.—The person having the greatest number of votes as Vice-President, shall be the Vice-President, if such number be a majority of the whole number of Electors appointed, and if no person have a majority, then from the two highest numbers on the list, the Senate shall choose the Vice-President; a quorum for the purpose shall consist of two-thirds of the whole number of Senators, and a majority of the whole number shall be necessary to a choice. But no person constitutionally ineligible to the office of President shall be eligible to that of Vice-President of the United States.

Amendment XIII [1865]

Section 1.   Neither slavery nor involuntary servitude, except as punishment for crime whereof the party shall have been duly convicted, shall exist within the United States, or any place subject to their jurisdiction.

Section 2.   Congress shall have power to enforce this article by appropriate legislation.

Amendment XIV [1868]

Section 1.   All persons born or naturalized in the United States, and subject to the jurisdiction thereof, are citizens of the United States and of the State wherein they reside. No State shall make or enforce any law which shall abridge the privileges or immunities of citizens of the United States; nor shall any State deprive any person of life, liberty, or property, without due process of law; nor deny to any person within its jurisdiction the equal protection of the laws.

Section 2.   Representatives shall be apportioned among the several States according to their respective numbers, counting the whole number of persons in each State, excluding Indians not taxed. But when the right to vote at any election for the choice of electors for President and Vice President of the United States, Representatives in Congress, the Executive and Judicial officers of a State, or the members of the Legislature thereof, is denied to any of the male inhabitants of such State, being twenty-one years of age, and citizens of the United States, or in any way abridged, except for participation in rebellion, or other crime, the basis of representation therein shall be reduced in the proportion which the number of such male citizens shall bear to the whole number of male citizens twenty-one years of age in such State.

Section 3.   No person shall be a Senator or Representative in Congress, or elector of President and Vice President, or hold any office, civil or military, under the United States, or under any State, who having previously taken an oath, as a member of Congress, or as an officer of the United States, or as a member of any State legislature, or as an executive or judicial officer of any State, to support the Constitution of the United States, shall have engaged in insurrection or rebellion against the same, or given aid or comfort to the enemies thereof. But Congress may by a vote of two-thirds of each House, remove such disability.

Section 4.   The validity of the public debt of the United States, authorized by law, including debts incurred for payment of pensions and bounties for services in suppressing insurrection or rebellion, shall not be questioned. But neither the United States nor any State shall assume or pay any debt or obligation incurred in aid of insurrection or rebellion against the United States, or any claim for the loss or emancipation of any slave; but all such debts, obligations and claims shall be held illegal and void.

Section 5.   The Congress shall have power to enforce, by appropriate legislation, the provisions of this article.

Amendment XV [1870]

Section 1.   The right of citizens of the United States to vote shall not be denied or abridged by the United States or by any State on account of race, color, or previous condition of servitude.

Section 2.   The Congress shall have power to enforce this article by appropriate legislation.

Amendment XVI [1913]

The Congress shall have power to lay and collect taxes on incomes, from whatever source derived, without apportionment among the several States, and without regard to any census or enumeration.

Amendment XVII [1913]

[1] The Senate of the United States shall be composed of two Senators from each State, elected by the people thereof, for six years; and each Senator shall have one vote. The electors in each State shall have the qualifications requisite for electors of the most numerous branch of the State legislatures.

[2] When vacancies happen in the representation of any State in the Senate, the executive authority of such State shall issue writs of election to fill such vacancies: *Provided,* That the legislature of any State may empower the executive thereof to make temporary appointments until the people fill the vacancies by election as the legislature may direct.

[3] The amendment shall not be so construed as to affect the election or term of any Senator chosen before it becomes valid as part of the Constitution.

Amendment XVIII [1919]

Section 1.   After one year from the ratification of this article the manufacture, sale, or transportation of intoxicating liquors within, the importation thereof into, or the exportation thereof from the United States and all territory subject to the jurisdiction thereof for beverage purposes is hereby prohibited.

Section 2.   The Congress and the several States shall have concurrent power to enforce this article by appropriate legislation.

Section 3.   This article shall be inoperative unless it shall have been ratified as an amendment to the Constitution by the legislatures of the several States, as provided in the Constitution, within seven years from the date of the submission hereof to the States by the Congress.

Amendment XIX [1920]

[1] The right of citizens of the United States to vote shall not be denied or abridged by the United States or by any State on account of sex.

[2] Congress shall have power to enforce this article by appropriate legislation.

Amendment XX [1933]

Section 1.   The terms of the President and Vice President shall end at noon on the 20th day of January, and the terms of Senators and Representatives at noon on the 3d day of January, of the years in which such terms would have ended if this article had not been ratified; and the terms of their successors shall then begin.

Section 2.   The Congress shall assemble at least once in every year, and such meeting shall begin at noon on the 3d day of January, unless they shall by law appoint a different day.

Section 3.   If, at the time fixed for the beginning of the term of the President, the President elect shall have died, the Vice President elect shall become President. If the President shall not have been chosen before the time fixed for the beginning of his term, or if the President elect shall have failed to qualify, then the Vice President elect shall act as President until a President shall have qualified; and the Congress may by law provide for the case wherein neither a President elect nor a Vice President elect shall have qualified, declaring who shall then act as President, or the manner in which one who is to act shall be selected, and such person shall act accordingly until a President or Vice President shall have qualified.

Section 4.   The Congress may by law provide for the case of the death of any of the persons from whom the House of Representatives may choose a President whenever the right of choice shall have devolved upon them, and for the case of the death of any of the persons from whom the Senate may choose a Vice President whenever the right of choice shall have devolved upon them.

Section 5.   Sections 1 and 2 shall take effect on the 15th day of October following the ratification of this article.

Section 6.   This article shall be inoperative unless it shall have been ratified as an amendment to the Constitution by the legislatures of three-fourths of the several States within seven years from the date of its submission.

Amendment XXI [1933]

Section 1.   The eighteenth article of amendment to the Constitution of the United States is hereby repealed.

Section 2.   The transportation or importation into any State, Territory, or possession of the United States for delivery or use therein of intoxicating liquors, in violation of the laws thereof, is hereby prohibited.

Section 3.   This article shall be inoperative unless it shall have been ratified as an amendment to the Constitution by conventions in the several States, as provided in the Constitution, within seven years from the date of the submission hereof to the States by the Congress.

Amendment XXII [1951]

Section 1.   No person shall be elected to the office of the President more than twice, and no person who has held the office of President, or acted as President for more than two years of a term to which some other person was elected President shall be elected to the office of President more than once. But this Article shall not apply to any person holding the office of President when this Article was proposed by the Congress, and shall not prevent any person who may be holding the office of President, or acting as President, during the term within which this Article becomes operative from holding the office of President or acting as President during the remainder of such term.

Section 2.   This article shall be inoperative unless it shall have been ratified as an amendment to the Constitution by the legislatures of three-fourths of the several States within seven years from the date of its submission to the States by the Congress.

Amendment XXIII [1961]

Section 1.   The District constituting the seat of Government of the United States shall appoint in such manner as the Congress may direct:

A number of electors of President and Vice President equal to the whole number of Senators and Representatives in Congress to which the District would be entitled if it were a State, but in no event more than the least populous state; they shall be in addition to those appointed by the states, but they shall be considered, for the purposes of the election of President and Vice President, to be electors appointed by a state; and they shall meet in the District and perform such duties as provided by the twelfth article of amendment.

Section 2.   The Congress shall have power to enforce this article by appropriate legislation.

Amendment XXIV [1964]

Section 1.   The right of citizens of the United States to vote in any primary or other election for President or Vice President, for electors for President or Vice President, or for Senator or Representative in Congress, shall not be denied or abridged by the United States, or any State by reason of failure to pay any poll tax or other tax.

Section 2.   The Congress shall have power to enforce this article by appropriate legislation.

Amendment XXV [1967]

Section 1.   In case of the removal of the President from office or of his death or resignation, the Vice President shall become President.

Section 2.   Whenever there is a vacancy in the office of the Vice President, the President shall nominate a Vice President who shall take office upon confirmation by a majority vote of both Houses of Congress.

Section 3.   Whenever the President transmits to the President pro tempore of the Senate and the Speaker of the House of Representatives his written declaration that he is unable to discharge the powers and duties of his office, and until he transmits to them a written declaration to the contrary, such powers and duties shall be discharged by the Vice President as Acting President.

Section 4.   Whenever the Vice President and a majority of either the principal officers of the executive departments or of such other body as Congress may by law provide, transmit to the President pro tempore of the Senate and the Speaker of the House of Representatives their written declaration that the President is unable to discharge the powers and duties of his office, the Vice President shall immediately assume the powers of the office as Acting President.

Thereafter, when the President transmits to the President pro tempore of the Senate and the Speaker of the House of Representatives his written declaration that no inability exists, he shall resume the powers and duties of his office unless the Vice President and a majority of either the principal officers of the executive department or of such other body as Congress may by law provide, transmit within four days to the President pro tempore of the Senate and the Speaker of the House of Representatives their written declaration that the President is unable to discharge the powers and duties of his office. Thereupon Congress shall decide the issue, assembling within forty-eight hours for that purpose if not in session. If the Congress, within twenty-one days after receipt of the latter written declaration, or, if Congress is not in session, within twenty-one days after Congress is required to assemble, determines by two-thirds vote of both Houses that the President is unable to discharge the powers and duties of his office, the Vice President shall continue to discharge the same as Acting President; otherwise, the President shall resume the powers and duties of his office.

Amendment XXVI [1971]

Section 1.   The right of citizens of the United States, who are eighteen years of age or older, to vote shall not be denied or abridged by the United States or by any State on account of age.

Section 2.   The Congress shall have power to enforce this article by appropriate legislation.

UNIFORM COMMERCIAL CODE (1978 TEXT)*

Title

An Act

To be known as the Uniform Commercial Code, Relating to Certain Commercial Transactions in or regarding Personal Property and Contracts and other Documents concerning them, including Sales, Commercial Paper, Bank Deposits and Collections, Letters of Credit, Bulk Transfers, Warehouse Receipts, Bills of Lading, other Documents of Title, Investment Securities, and Secured Transactions, including certain Sales of Accounts, Chattel Paper, and Contract Rights; Providing for Public Notice to Third Parties in Certain Circumstances; Regulating Procedure, Evidence and Damages in Certain Court Actions Involving such Transactions, Contracts or Documents; to Make Uniform the Law with Respect Thereto; and Repealing Inconsistent Legislation.

ARTICLE 1   GENERAL PROVISIONS

Part 1   Short Title, Construction, Application and Subject Matter of the Act

§ 1–101.   Short Title

This Act shall be known and may be cited as Uniform Commercial Code.

§ 1–102.   Purposes; Rules of Construction; Variation by Agreement

(1) This Act shall be liberally construed and applied to promote its underlying purposes and policies.

(2) Underlying purposes and policies of this Act are

(a) to simplify, clarify and modernize the law governing commercial transactions;

(b) to permit the continued expansion of commercial practices through custom, usage and agreement of the parties;

(c) to make uniform the law among the various jurisdictions.

(3) The effect of provisions of this Act may be varied by agreement, except as otherwise provided in this Act and

except that the obligations of good faith, diligence, reasonableness and care prescribed by this Act may not be disclaimed by agreement but the parties may by agreement determine the standards by which the performance of such obligations is to be measured if such standards are not manifestly unreasonable.

(4) The presence in certain provisions of this Act of the words "unless otherwise agreed" or words of similar import does not imply that the effect of other provisions may not be varied by agreement under subsection (3).

(5) In this Act unless the context otherwise requires

(a) words in the singular number include the plural, and in the plural include the singular;

(b) words of the masculine gender include the feminine and the neuter, and when the sense so indicates words of the neuter gender may refer to any gender.

§ 1–103. Supplementary General Principles of Law Applicable

Unless displaced by the particular provisions of this Act, the principles of law and equity, including the law merchant and the law relative to capacity to contract, principal and agent, estoppel, fraud, misrepresentation, duress, coercion, mistake, bankruptcy, or other validating or invalidating cause shall supplement its provisions.

§ 1–104. Construction Against Implicit Repeal

This Act being a general act intended as a unified coverage of its subject matter, no part of it shall be deemed to be impliedly repealed by subsequent legislation if such construction can reasonably be avoided.

§ 1–105. Territorial Application of the Act; Parties' Power to Choose Applicable Law

(1) Except as provided hereafter in this section, when a transaction bears a reasonable relation to this state and also to another state or nation the parties may agree that the law either of this state or of such other state or nation shall govern their rights and duties. Failing such agreement this Act applies to transactions bearing an appropriate relation to this state.

(2) Where one of the following provisions of this Act specifies the applicable law, that provision governs and a contrary agreement is effective only to the extent permitted by law (including the conflict of laws rules) so specified:

Rights of creditors against sold goods. Section 2–402.

Applicability of the Article on Bank Deposits and Collections. Section 4–102.

Bulk transfers subject to the Article on Bulk Transfers. Section 6–102.

Applicability of the Article on Investment Securities. Section 8–106.

Perfection provisions of the Article on Secured Transactions. Section 9–103.

§ 1–106. Remedies to Be Liberally Administered

(1) The remedies provided by this Act shall be liberally administered to the end that the aggrieved party may be put in as good a position as if the other party had fully performed but neither consequential or special nor penal damages may be had except as specifically provided in this Act or by other rule of law.

(2) Any right or obligation declared by this Act is enforceable by action unless the provision declaring it specifies a different and limited effect.

§ 1–107. Waiver or Renunciation of Claim or Right After Breach

Any claim or right arising out of an alleged breach can be discharged in whole or in part without consideration by a written waiver or renunciation signed and delivered by the aggrieved party.

§ 1–108. Severability

If any provision or clause of this Act or application thereof to any person or circumstances is held invalid, such invalidity shall not affect other provisions or applications of the Act which can be given effect without the invalid provision or application, and to this end the provisions of this Act are declared to be severable.

§ 1–109. Section Captions

Section captions are parts of this Act.

Part 2 General Definitions and Principles of Interpretation

§ 1–201. General Definitions

Subject to additional definitions contained in the subsequent Articles of this Act which are applicable to specific Articles or Parts thereof, and unless the context otherwise requires, in this Act:

(1) "Action" in the sense of a judicial proceeding includes recoupment, counterclaim, set-off, suit in equity and any other proceedings in which rights are determined.

(2) "Aggrieved party" means a party entitled to resort to a remedy.

(3) "Agreement" means the bargain of the parties in fact as found in their language or by implication from other circumstances including course of dealing or usage of trade or course of performance as provided in this Act (Sections 1–205 and 2–208). Whether an agreement has legal consequences is determined by the provisions of this Act, if applicable; otherwise by the law of contracts (Section 1–103). (Compare "Contract.")

(4) "Bank" means any person engaged in the business of banking.

(5) "Bearer" means the person in possession of an instrument, document of title, or certificated security payable to bearer or indorsed in blank.

(6) "Bill of lading" means a document evidencing the receipt of goods for shipment issued by a person engaged in the business of transporting or forwarding goods, and includes an airbill. "Airbill" means a document serving for air transportation as a bill of lading does for marine or rail transportation, and includes an air consignment note or air waybill.

(7) "Branch" includes a separately incorporated foreign branch of a bank.

(8) "Burden of establishing" a fact means the burden of persuading the triers of fact that the existence of the fact is more probable than its nonexistence.

(9) "Buyer in ordinary course of business" means a person who in good faith and without knowledge that the sale to him is in violation of the ownership rights or security interest of a third party in the goods buys in ordinary course from a person in the business of selling goods of that kind but does not include a pawnbroker. All persons who sell minerals or the like (including oil and gas) at wellhead or minehead shall be deemed to be persons in the business of selling goods of that kind. "Buying" may be for cash or by exchange of other property or on secured or unsecured credit and includes receiving goods or documents of title under a pre-existing contract for sale but does not include a transfer in bulk or as security for or in total or partial satisfaction of a money debt.

(10) "Conspicuous": A term or clause is conspicuous when it is so written that a reasonable person against whom it is to operate ought to have noticed it. A printed heading in capitals (as: NON-NEGOTIABLE BILL OF LADING) is conspicuous. Language in the body of a form is "conspicuous" if it is in larger or other contrasting type or color. But in a telegram any stated term is "conspicuous." Whether a term or clause is "conspicuous" or not is for decision by the court.

(11) "Contract" means the total legal obligation which results from the parties' agreement as affected by this Act and any other applicable rules of law. (Compare "Agreement.")

(12) "Creditor" includes a general creditor, a secured creditor, a lien creditor and any representative of creditors, including an assignee for the benefit of creditors, a trustee in bankruptcy, a receiver in equity and an executor or administrator of an insolvent debtor's or assignor's estate.

(13) "Defendant" includes a person in the position of defendant in a cross-action or counterclaim.

(14) "Delivery" with respect to instruments, documents of title, chattel paper, or certificated securities means voluntary transfer of possession.

(15) "Document of title" includes bill of lading, dock warrant, dock receipt, warehouse receipt or order for the delivery of goods, and also any other document which in the regular course of business or financing is treated as adequately evidencing that the person in possession of it is entitled to receive, hold and dispose of the document and the goods it covers.

To be a document of title a document must purport to be issued by or addressed to a bailee and purport to cover goods in the bailee's possession which are either identified or are fungible portions of an identified mass.

(16) "Fault" means wrongful act, omission or breach.

(17) "Fungible" with respect to goods or securities means goods or securities of which any unit is, by nature or usage of trade, the equivalent of any other like unit. Goods which are not fungible shall be deemed fungible for the purposes of this Act to the extent that under a particular agreement or document unlike units are treated as equivalents.

(18) "Genuine" means free of forgery or counterfeiting.

(19) "Good faith" means honesty in fact in the conduct or transaction concerned.

(20) "Holder" means a person who is in possession of a document of title or an instrument or a certificated investment security drawn, issued, or indorsed to him or his order or to bearer or in blank.

(21) To "honor" is to pay or to accept and pay, or where a credit so engages to purchase or discount a draft complying with the terms of credit.

(22) "Insolvency proceedings" includes any assignment for the benefit of creditors or other proceedings intended to liquidate or rehabilitate the estate of the person involved.

(23) A person is "insolvent" who either has ceased to pay his debts in the ordinary course of business or cannot pay his debts as they become due or is insolvent within the meaning of the federal bankruptcy law.

(24) "Money" means a medium of exchange authorized or adopted by a domestic or foreign government as a part of its currency.

(25) A person has "notice" of a fact when

(a) he has actual knowledge of it; or

(b) he has received a notice or notification of it; or

(c) from all the facts and circumstances known to him at the time in question he has reason to know that it exists.

A person "knows" or has "knowledge" of a fact when he has actual knowledge of it. "Discover" or "learn" or a word or phrase of similar import refers to knowledge rather than to reason to know. The time and circumstances under which a notice or notification may cease to be effective are not determined by this Act.

(26) A person "notifies" or "gives" a notice or notification to another by taking such steps as may be reasonably required to inform the other in ordinary course whether or not such other actually comes to know of it. A person "receives" a notice or notification when

(a) it come to his attention; or

(b) it is duly delivered at the place of business through which the contract was made or at any other place held out by him as the place for receipt of such communications.

(27) Notice, knowledge or a notice or notification received by an organization is effective for a particular transaction from the time when it is brought to the attention of the individual con-

ducting that transaction, and in any event from the time when it would have been brought to his attention if the organization had exercised due diligence. An organization exercises due diligence if it maintains reasonable routines for communicating significant information to the person conducting the transaction and there is reasonable compliance with the routines. Due diligence does not require an individual acting for the organization to communicate information unless such communication is part of his regular duties or unless he has reason to know of the transaction and that the transaction would be materially affected by the information.

(28) "Organization" includes a corporation, government or governmental subdivision or agency, business trust, estate, trust, partnership or association, two or more persons having a joint or common interest, or any other legal or commercial entity.

(29) "Party," as distinct from "third party," means a person who has engaged in a transaction or made an agreement within this Act.

(30) "Person" includes an individual or an organization (See Section 1–102).

(31) "Presumption" or "presumed" means that the trier of fact must find the existence of the fact presumed unless and until evidence is introduced which would support a finding of its nonexistence.

(32) "Purchase" includes taking by sale, discount, negotiation, mortgage, pledge, lien, issue or reissue, gift or any other voluntary transaction creating an interest in property.

(33) "Purchaser" means a person who takes by purchase.

(34) "Remedy" means any remedial right to which an aggrieved party is entitled with or without resort to a tribunal.

(35) "Representative" includes an agent, an officer of a corporation or association, and a trustee, executor or administrator of an estate, or any other person empowered to act for another.

(36) "Rights" includes remedies.

(37) "Security interest" means an interest in personal property or fixtures which secures payment or performance of an obligation. The retention or reservation of title by a seller of goods notwithstanding shipment or delivery to the buyer (Section 2–401) is limited in effect to a reservation of a "security interest." The term also includes any interest of a buyer of accounts or chattel paper which is subject to Article 9. The special property interest of a buyer of goods on identification of such goods to a contract for sale under Section 2–401 is not a "security interest" but a buyer may also acquire a "security interest" by complying with Article 9. Unless a lease or consignment is intended as security, reservation of title thereunder is not a "security interest" but a consignment is in any event subject to the provisions on consignment sales (Section 2–326). Whether a lease is intended as security is to be determined by the facts of each case; however, (a) the inclusion of an option to purchase does not of itself make the lease one intended for security, and (b) an agreement that upon compliance with the terms of the lease the lessee shall become or

has the option to become the owner of the property for no additional consideration or for a nominal consideration does make the lease one intended for security.

(38) "Send" in connection with any writing or notice means to deposit in the mail or deliver for transmission by any other usual means of communication with postage or cost of transmission provided for and properly addressed and in the case of an instrument to an address specified thereon or otherwise agreed, or if there be none to any address reasonable under the circumstances. The receipt of any writing or notice within the time at which it would have arrived if properly sent has the effect of a proper sending.

(39) "Signed" includes any symbol executed or adopted by a party with present intention to authenticate a writing.

(40) "Surety" includes guarantor.

(41) "Telegram" includes a message transmitted by radio, teletype, cable, any mechanical method of transmission, or the like.

(42) "Term" means that portion of an agreement which relates to a particular matter.

(43) "Unauthorized" signature or indorsement means one made without actual, implied or apparent authority and includes a forgery.

(44) "Value." Except as otherwise provided with respect to negotiable instruments and bank collections (Sections 3–303, 4–208 and 4–209) a person gives "value" for rights if he acquires them

(a) in return for a binding commitment to extend credit or for the extension of immediately available credit whether or not drawn upon and whether or not a chargeback is provided for in the event of difficulties in collection; or

(b) as security for or in total or partial satisfaction of a preexisting claim; or

(c) by accepting delivery pursuant to a preexisting contract for purchase; or

(d) generally, in return for any consideration sufficient to support a simple contract.

(45) "Warehouse receipt" means a receipt issued by a person engaged in the business of storing goods for hire.

(46) "Written" or "writing" includes printing, typewriting or any other intentional reduction to tangible form.

§ 1–202. Prima Facie Evidence by Third Party Documents

A document in due form purporting to be a bill of lading, policy or certificate of insurance, official weigher's or inspector's certificate, consular invoice, or any other document authorized or required by the contract to be issued by a third party shall be prima facie evidence of its own authenticity and genuineness and of the facts stated in the document by the third party.

§ 1–203. Obligation of Good Faith

Every contract or duty within this Act imposes an obligation of good faith in its performance or enforcement.

§ 1–204.   Time; Reasonable Time; "Seasonably"

(1) Whenever this Act requires any action to be taken within a reasonable time, any time which is not manifestly unreasonable may be fixed by agreement.

(2) What is a reasonable time for taking any action depends on the nature, purpose and circumstances of such action.

(3) An action is taken "seasonably" when it is taken at or within the time agreed or if no time is agreed at or within a reasonable time.

§ 1–205.   Course of Dealing and Usage of Trade

(1) A course of dealing is a sequence of previous conduct between the parties to a particular transaction which is fairly to be regarded as establishing a common basis of understanding for interpreting their expressions and other conduct.

(2) A usage of trade is any practice or method of dealing having such regularity of observance in a place, vocation or trade as to justify an expectation that it will be observed with respect to the transaction in question. The existence and scope of such a usage are to be proved as facts. If it is established that such a usage is embodied in a written trade code or similar writing the interpretation of the writing is for the court.

(3) A course of dealing between parties and any usage of trade in the vocation or trade in which they are engaged or of which they are or should be aware give particular meaning to and supplement or qualify terms of an agreement.

(4) The express terms of an agreement and an applicable course of dealing or usage of trade shall be construed wherever reasonable as consistent with each other; but when such construction is unreasonable express terms control both course of dealing and usage of trade and course of dealing controls usage of trade.

(5) An applicable usage of trade in the place where any part of performance is to occur shall be used in interpreting the agreement as to that part of the performance.

(6) Evidence of a relevant usage of trade offered by one party is not admissible unless and until he has given the other party such notice as the court finds sufficient to prevent unfair surprise to the latter.

§ 1–206.   Statute of Frauds for Kinds of Personal Property Not Otherwise Covered

(1) Except in the cases described in subsection (2) of this section a contract for the sale of personal property is not enforceable by way of action or defense beyond five thousand dollars in amount or value of remedy unless there is some writing which indicates that a contract for sale has been made between the parties at a defined or stated price, reasonably identifies the subject matter, and is signed by the party against whom enforcement is sought or by his authorized agent.

(2) Subsection (1) of this section does not apply to contracts for the sale of goods (Section 2–201) nor of securities (Section 8–319) nor to security agreements (Section 9–203).

§ 1–207.   Performance or Acceptance Under Reservation of Rights

A party who with explicit reservation of rights performs or promises performance or assents to performance in a manner demanded or offered by the other party does not thereby prejudice the rights reserved. Such words as "without prejudice," "under protest" or the like are sufficient.

§ 1–208.   Option to Accelerate at Will

A term providing that one party or his successor in interest may accelerate payment or performance or require collateral or additional collateral "at will" or "when he deems himself insecure" or in words of similar import shall be construed to mean that he shall have power to do so only if he in good faith believes that the prospect of payment or performance is impaired. The burden of establishing lack of good faith is on the party against whom the power has been exercised.

§ 1–209.   Subordinated Obligations

An obligation may be issued as subordinated to payment of another obligation of the person obligated, or a creditor may subordinate his right to payment of an obligation by agreement with either the person obligated or another creditor of the person obligated. Such a subordination does not create a security interest as against either the common debtor or a subordinated creditor. This section shall be construed as declaring the law as it existed prior to the enactment of this section and not as modifying it.

Note: This new section is proposed as an optional provision to make it clear that a subordination agreement does not create a security interest unless so intended.

ARTICLE 2   SALES

Part 1   Short Title, General Construction and Subject Matter

§ 2–101.   Short Title

This Article shall be known and may be cited as Uniform Commercial Code—Sales.

§ 2–102.   Scope; Certain Security and Other Transactions Excluded From This Article

Unless the context otherwise requires, this Article applies to transactions in goods; it does not apply to any transaction which although in the form of an unconditional contract to sell or present sale is intended to operate only as a security transaction nor does this Article impair or repeal any statute regulating sales to consumers, farmers or other specified classes of buyers.

§ 2–103. Definitions and Index of Definitions

(1) In this Article unless the context otherwise requires

(a) "Buyer" means a person who buys or contracts to buy goods.

(b) "Good faith" in the case of a merchant means honesty in fact and the observance of reasonable commercial standards of fair dealing in the trade.

(c) "Receipt" of goods means taking physical possession of them.

(d) "Seller" means a person who sells or contracts to sell goods.

(2) Other definitions applying to this Article or to specified Parts thereof, and the sections in which they appear are:

"Acceptance." Section 2–606.

"Banker's credit." Section 2–325.

"Between merchants." Section 2–104.

"Cancellation." Section 2–106(4).

"Commercial unit." Section 2–105.

"Confirmed credit." Section 2–325.

"Conforming to contract." Section 2–106.

"Contract for sale." Section 2–106.

"Cover." Section 2–712.

"Entrusting." Section 2–403.

"Financing agency." Section 2–104.

"Future goods." Section 2–105.

"Goods." Section 2–105.

"Identification." Section 2–501.

"Installment contract." Section 2–612.

"Letter of Credit." Section 2–325.

"Lot." Section 2–105.

"Merchant." Section 2–104.

"Overseas." Section 2–323.

"Person in position of seller." Section 2–707.

"Present sale." Section 2–106.

"Sale." Section 2–106.

"Sale on approval." Section 2–326.

"Sale or return." Section 2–326.

"Termination." Section 2–106.

(3) The following definitions in other Articles apply to this Article:

"Check." Section 3–104.

"Consignee." Section 7–102.

"Consignor." Section 7–102.

"Consumer goods." Section 9–109.

"Dishonor." Section 3–507.

"Draft." Section 3–104.

(4) In addition Article 1 contains general definitions and principles of construction and interpretation applicable throughout this Article.

§ 2–104. Definitions: "Merchant"; "Between Merchants"; "Financing Agency"

(1) "Merchant" means a person who deals in goods of the kind or otherwise by his occupation holds himself out as having knowledge or skill peculiar to the practices or goods involved in the transaction or to whom such knowledge or skill may be attributed by his employment of an agent or broker or other intermediary who by his occupation holds himself out as having such knowledge or skill.

(2) "Financing agency" means a bank, finance company or other person who in the ordinary course of business makes advances against goods or documents of title or who by arrangement with either the seller or the buyer intervenes in ordinary course to make or collect payment due or claimed under the contract for sale, as by purchasing or paying the seller's draft or making advances against it or by merely taking it for collection whether or not documents of title accompany the draft. "Financing agency" includes also a bank or other person who similarly intervenes between persons who are in the position of seller and buyer in respect to the goods (Section 2–707).

(3) "Between merchants" means in any transaction with respect to which both parties are chargeable with the knowledge or skill of merchants.

§ 2–105. Definitions: Transferability; "Goods"; "Future Goods"; "Lot"; "Commercial Unit"

(1) "Goods" means all things (including specially manufactured goods) which are moveable at the time of identification to the contract for sale other than the money in which the price is to be paid, investment securities (Article 8) and things in action. "Goods" also includes the unborn young of animals and growing crops and other identified things attached to realty as described in the section on goods to be severed from realty (Section 2–107).

(2) Goods must be both existing and identified before any interest in them can pass. Goods which are not both existing and identified are "future" goods. A purported present sale of future goods or of any interest therein operates as a contract to sell.

(3) There may be a sale of a part interest in existing identified goods.

(4) An undivided share in an identified bulk of fungible goods is sufficiently identified to be sold although the quantity of the bulk is not determined. Any agreed proportion of such a bulk or any quantity thereof agreed upon by number, weight or other measure may to the extent of the seller's interest in the bulk be sold to the buyer who then becomes an owner in common.

(5) "Lot" means a parcel or a single article which is the subject matter of a separate sale or delivery, whether or not it is sufficient to perform the contract.

(6) "Commercial unit" means such a unit of goods as by commercial usage is a single whole for purposes of sale and division of which materially impairs its character or value on the market or in use. A commercial unit may be a single article (as a machine) or a set of articles (as a suite of furniture or an assortment of sizes) or a quantity (as a bale, gross, or carload) or any other unit treated in use or in the relevant market as a single whole.

§ 2–106.   Definitions: "Contract"; "Agreement"; "Contract for Sale"; "Sale"; "Present Sale"; "Conforming to Contract"; "Termination"; "Cancellation"

(1) In this Article unless the context otherwise requires "contract" and "agreement" are limited to those relating to the present or future sale of goods. "Contract for sale" includes both a present sale of goods and a contract to sell goods at a future time. A "sale" consists in the passing of title from the seller to the buyer for a price (Section 2–401). A "present sale" means a sale which is accomplished by the making of the contract.

(2) Goods or conduct including any part of a performance are "conforming" or conform to the contract when they are in accordance with the obligations under the contract.

(3) "Termination" occurs when either party pursuant to a power created by agreement or law puts an end to the contract otherwise than for its breach. On "termination" all obligations which are still executory on both sides are discharged but any right based on prior breach or performance survives.

(4) "Cancellation" occurs when either party puts an end to the contract for breach by the other and its effect is the same as that of "termination" except that the cancelling party also retains any remedy for breach of the whole contract or any unperformed balance.

§ 2–107.   Goods to Be Severed From Realty: Recording

(1) A contract for the sale of minerals or the like (including oil and gas) or a structure or its materials to be removed from realty is a contract for the sale of goods within this Article if they are to be severed by the seller but until severance a purported present sale thereof which is not effective as a transfer of an interest in land is effective only as a contract to sell.

(2) A contract for the sale apart from the land of growing crops or other things attached to realty and capable of severance without material harm thereto but not described in subsection (1) or of timber to be cut is a contract for the sale of goods within this Article whether the subject matter is to be severed by the buyer or by the seller even though it forms part of the realty at the time of contracting, and the parties can by identification effect a present sale before severance.

(3) The provisions of this section are subject to any third party rights provided by the law relating to realty records, and the contract for sale may be executed and recorded as a document transferring an interest in land and shall then constitute notice to third parties of the buyer's rights under the contract for sale.

Part 2   Form, Formation and Readjustment of Contract

§ 2–201.   Formal Requirements; Statute of Frauds

(1) Except as otherwise provided in this section a contract for the sale of goods for the price of $500 or more is not enforceable by way of action or defense unless there is some writing sufficient to indicate that a contract for sale has been made between the parties and signed by the party against whom enforcement is sought or by his authorized agent or broker. A writing is not insufficient because it omits or incorrectly states a term agreed upon but the contract is not enforceable under this paragraph beyond the quantity of goods shown in such writing.

(2) Between merchants if within a reasonable time a writing in confirmation of the contract and sufficient against the sender is received and the party receiving it has reason to know its contents, it satisfies the requirements of subsection (1) against such party unless written notice of objection to its contents is given within 10 days after it is received.

(3) A contract which does not satisfy the requirements of subsection (1) but which is valid in other respects is enforceable

(a) if the goods are to be specially manufactured for the buyer and are not suitable for sale to others in the ordinary course of the seller's business and the seller, before notice of repudiation is received and under circumstances which reasonably indicate that the goods are for the buyer, has made either a substantial beginning of their manufacture or commitments for their procurement; or

(b) if the party against whom enforcement is sought admits in his pleading, testimony or otherwise in court that a contract for sale was made, but the contract is not enforceable under this provision beyond the quantity of goods admitted; or

(c) with respect to goods for which payment has been made and accepted or which have been received and accepted (Section 2–606).

§ 2–202.   Final Written Expression: Parol or Extrinsic Evidence

Terms with respect to which the confirmatory memoranda of the parties agree or which are otherwise set forth in a writing intended by the parties as a final expression of their agreement with respect to such terms as are included therein may not be contradicted by evidence of any prior agreement or of a contemporaneous oral agreement but may be explained or supplemented

(a) by course of dealing or usage of trade (Section 1–205) or by course of performance (Section 2–208); and

(b) by evidence of consistent additional terms unless the court finds the writing to have been intended also as a complete and exclusive statement of the terms of the agreement.

§ 2–203.   Seals Inoperative

The affixing of a seal to a writing evidencing a contract for sale or an offer to buy or sell goods does not constitute the writing a sealed instrument and the law with respect to sealed instruments does not apply to such a contract or offer.

§ 2–204.   Formation in General

(1) A contract for sale of goods may be made in any manner sufficient to show agreement, including conduct by both parties which recognizes the existence of such a contract.

(2) An agreement sufficient to constitute a contract for sale may be found even though the moment of its making is undetermined.

(3) Even though one or more terms are left open a contract for sale does not fail for indefiniteness if the parties have intended to made a contract and there is a reasonably certain basis for giving an appropriate remedy.

§ 2–205. Firm Offers

An offer by a merchant to buy or sell goods in a signed writing which by its terms gives assurance that it will be held open is not revocable, for lack of consideration, during the time stated or if no time is stated for a reasonable time, but in no event may such period of irrevocability exceed three months; but any such term of assurance on a form supplied by the offeree must be separately signed by the offeror.

§ 2–206. Offer and Acceptance in Formation of Contract

(1) Unless otherwise unambiguously indicated by the language or circumstances

(a) an offer to make a contract shall be construed as inviting acceptance in any manner and by any medium reasonable in the circumstances;

(b) an order or other offer to buy goods for prompt or current shipment shall be construed as inviting acceptance either by a prompt promise to ship or by the prompt or current shipment of conforming or nonconforming goods, but such a shipment of nonconforming goods does not constitute an acceptance if the seller seasonably notifies the buyer that the shipment is offered only as an accommodation to the buyer.

(2) Where the beginning of a requested performance is a reasonable mode of acceptance an offeror who is not notified of acceptance within a reasonable time may treat the offer as having lapsed before acceptance.

§ 2–207. Additional Terms in Acceptance or Confirmation

(1) A definite and seasonable expression of acceptance or a written confirmation which is sent within a reasonable time operates as an acceptance even though it states terms additional to or different from those offered or agreed upon, unless acceptance is expressly made conditional on assent to the additional or different terms.

(2) The additional terms are to be construed as proposals for addition to the contract. Between merchants such terms become part of the contract unless:

(a) the offer expressly limits acceptance to the terms of the offer;

(b) they materially alter it; or

(c) notification of objection to them has already been given or is given within a reasonable time after notice of them is received.

(3) Conduct by both parties which recognizes the existence of a contract is sufficient to establish a contract for sale although the writings of the parties do not otherwise establish a contract. In such case the terms of the particular contract consist of those terms on which the writings of the parties agree, together with any supplementary terms incorporated under any other provisions of this Act.

§ 2–208. Course of Performance or Practical Construction

(1) Where the contract for sale involves repeated occasions for performance by either party with knowledge of the nature of the performance and opportunity for objection to it by the other, any course of performance accepted or acquiesced in without objection shall be relevant to determine the meaning of the agreement.

(2) The express terms of the agreement and any such course of performance, as well as any course of dealing and usage of trade, shall be construed whenever reasonable as consistent with each other; but when such construction is unreasonable, express terms shall control course of performance and course of performance shall control both course of dealing and usage of trade (Section 1–205).

(3) Subject to the provisions of the next section on modification and waiver, such course of performance shall be relevant to show a waiver or modification of any term inconsistent with such course of performance.

§ 2–209. Modification, Rescission and Waiver

(1) An agreement modifying a contract within this Article needs no consideration to be binding.

(2) A signed agreement which excludes modification or rescission except by a signed writing cannot be otherwise modified or rescinded, but except as between merchants such a requirement on a form supplied by the merchant must be separately signed by the other party.

(3) The requirements of the statute of frauds section of this Article (Section 2–201) must be satisfied if the contract as modified is within its provisions.

(4) Although an attempt at modification or rescission does not satisfy the requirements of subsection (2) or (3) it can operate as a waiver.

(5) A party who has made a waiver affecting an executory portion of the contract may retract the waiver by reasonable notification received by the other party that strict performance will be required of any term waived, unless the retraction would be unjust in view of a material change of position in reliance on the waiver.

§ 2–210. Delegation of Performance; Assignment of Rights

(1) A party may perform his duty through a delegate unless otherwise agreed or unless the other party has a substantial interest in having his original promisor perform or control the

acts required by the contract. No delegation of performance relieves the party delegating of any duty to perform or any liability for breach.

(2) Unless otherwise agreed all rights of either seller or buyer can be assigned except where the assignment would materially change the duty of the other party, or increase materially the burden or risk imposed on him by his contract, or impair materially his chance of obtaining return performance. A right to damages for breach of the whole contract or a right arising out of the assignor's due performance of his entire obligation can be assigned despite agreement otherwise.

(3) Unless the circumstances indicate the contrary a prohibition of assignment of "the contract" is to be construed as barring only the delegation to the assignee of the assignor's performance.

(4) An assignment of "the contract" or of "all my rights under the contract" or an assignment in similar general terms is an assignment of rights and unless the language or the circumstances (as in an assignment for security) indicate the contrary, it is a delegation of performance of the duties of the assignor and its acceptance by the assignee constitutes a promise by him to perform those duties. This promise is enforceable by either the assignor or the other party to the original contract.

(5) The other party may treat any assignment which delegates performance as creating reasonable grounds for insecurity and may without prejudice to his rights against the assignor demand assurances from the assignee (Section 2–609).

Part 3 General Obligation and Construction of Contract

§ 2–301. General Obligations of Parties

The obligation of the seller is to transfer and deliver and that of the buyer is to accept and pay in accordance with the contract.

§ 2–302. Unconscionable Contract or Clause

(1) If the court as a matter of law finds the contract or any clause of the contract to have been unconscionable at the time it was made the court may refuse to enforce the contract, or it may enforce the remainder of the contract without the unconscionable clause, or it may so limit the application of any unconscionable clause as to avoid any unconscionable result.

(2) When it is claimed or appears to the court that the contract or any clause thereof may be unconscionable the parties shall be afforded a reasonable opportunity to present evidence as to its commercial setting, purpose and effect to aid the court in making the determination.

§ 2–303. Allocation or Division of Risks

Where this Article allocates a risk or a burden as between the parties "unless otherwise agreed," the agreement may not only shift the allocation but may also divide the risk or burden.

§ 2–304. Price Payable in Money, Goods, Realty, or Otherwise

(1) The price can be made payable in money or otherwise. If it is payable in whole or in part in goods each party is a seller of the goods which he is to transfer.

(2) Even though all or part of the price is payable in an interest in realty the transfer of the goods and the seller's obligations with reference to them are subject to this Article, but not the transfer of the interest in realty or the transferor's obligations in connection therewith.

§ 2–305. Open Price Term

(1) The parties if they so intend can conclude a contract for sale even though the price is not settled. In such case the price is a reasonable price at the time for delivery if

(a) nothing is said as to price; or

(b) the price is left to be agreed by the parties and they fail to agree; or

(c) the price is to be fixed in terms of some agreed market or other standard as set or recorded by a third person or agency and it is not so set or recorded.

(2) A price to be fixed by the seller or by the buyer means a price for him to fix in good faith.

(3) When a price left to be fixed otherwise than by agreement of the parties fails to be fixed through fault of one party the other may at his option treat the contract as cancelled or himself fix a reasonable price.

(4) Where, however, the parties intend not to be bound unless the price be fixed or agreed and it is not fixed or agreed there is no contract. In such a case the buyer must return any goods already received or if unable so to do must pay their reasonable value at the time of delivery and the seller must return any portion of the price paid on account.

§ 2–306. Output, Requirements and Exclusive Dealings

(1) A term which measures the quantity by the output of the seller or the requirements of the buyer means such actual output or requirements as may occur in good faith, except that no quantity unreasonably disproportionate to any stated estimate or in the absence of a stated estimate to any normal or otherwise comparable prior output or requirements may be tendered or demanded.

(2) A lawful agreement by either the seller or the buyer for exclusive dealing in the kind of goods concerned imposes unless otherwise agreed an obligation by the seller to use best efforts to supply the goods and by the buyer to use best efforts to promote their sale.

§ 2–307. Delivery in Single Lot or Several Lots

Unless otherwise agreed all goods called for by a contract for sale must be tendered in a single delivery and payment is due only on such tender but where the circumstances give either party the right to make or demand delivery in lots the price if it can be apportioned may be demanded for each lot.

§ 2–308. Absence of Specified Place for Delivery

Unless otherwise agreed

(a) the place for delivery of goods is the seller's place of business or if he has none his residence; but

(b) in a contract for sale of identified goods which to the knowledge of the parties at the time of contracting are in some other place, that place is the place for their delivery; and

(c) documents of title may be delivered through customary banking channels.

§ 2–309. Absence of Specific Time Provisions; Notice of Termination

(1) The time for shipment or delivery or any other action under a contract if not provided in this Article or agreed upon shall be a reasonable time.

(2) Where the contract provides for successive performances but is indefinite in duration it is valid for a reasonable time but unless otherwise agreed may be terminated at any time by either party.

(3) Termination of a contract by one party except on the happening of an agreed event requires that reasonable notification be received by the other party and an agreement dispensing with notification is invalid if its operation would be unconscionable.

§ 2–310. Open Time for Payment or Running of Credit: Authority to Ship Under Reservation

Unless otherwise agreed

(a) payment is due at the time and place at which the buyer is to receive the goods even though the place of shipment is the place of delivery; and

(b) if the seller is authorized to send the goods he may ship them under reservation, and may tender the documents of title, but the buyer may inspect the goods after their arrival before payment is due unless such inspection is inconsistent with the terms of the contract (Section 2–513); and

(c) if delivery is authorized and made by way of documents of title otherwise than by subsection (b) then payment is due at the time and place at which the buyer is to receive the documents regardless of where the goods are to be received; and

(d) where the seller is required or authorized to ship the goods on credit the credit period runs from the time of shipment but post-dating the invoice or delaying its dispatch will correspondingly delay the starting of the credit period.

§ 2–311. Options and Cooperation Respecting Performance

(1) An agreement for sale which is otherwise sufficiently definite (subsection (3) of Section 2–204) to be a contract is not made invalid by the fact that it leaves particulars of performance to be specified by one of the parties. Any such specification must be made in good faith and within limits set by commercial reasonableness.

(2) Unless otherwise agreed specifications relating to assortment of the goods are at the buyer's option and except as otherwise provided in subsection (1)(c) and (3) of Section 2–319 specifications or arrangements relating to shipment are at the seller's option.

(3) Where such specification would materially affect the other party's performance but is not seasonably made or where one party's cooperation is necessary to the agreed performance of the other but is not seasonably forthcoming, the other party in addition to all other remedies

(a) is excused for any resulting delay in his own performance; and

(b) may also either proceed to perform in any reasonable manner or after the time for a material part of his own performance treat the failure to specify or to cooperate as a breach by failure to deliver or accept the goods.

§ 2–312. Warranty of Title and Against Infringement; Buyer's Obligation Against Infringement

(1) Subject to subsection (2) there is in a contract for sale a warranty by the seller that

(a) the title conveyed shall be good, and its transfer rightful; and

(b) the goods shall be delivered free from any security interest or other lien or encumbrance of which the buyer at the time of contracting has no knowledge.

(2) A warranty under subsection (1) will be excluded or modified only by specific language or by circumstances which give the buyer reason to know that the person selling does not claim title in himself or that he is purporting to sell only such right or title as he or a third person may have.

(3) Unless otherwise agreed a seller who is a merchant regularly dealing in goods of the kind warrants that the goods shall be delivered free of the rightful claim of any third person by way of infringement or the like but a buyer who furnishes specifications to the seller must hold the seller harmless against any such claim which arises out of compliance with the specifications.

§ 2–313. Express Warranties by Affirmation, Promise, Description, Sample

(1) Express warranties by the seller are created as follows:

(a) Any affirmation of fact or promise made by the seller to the buyer which relates to the goods and becomes part of the basis of the bargain creates an express warranty that the goods shall conform to the affirmation or promise.

(b) Any description of the goods which is made part of the basis of the bargain creates an express warranty that the goods shall conform to the description.

(c) Any sample or model which is made part of the basis of the bargain creates an express warranty that the whole of the goods shall conform to the sample or model.

(2) It is not necessary to the creation of an express warranty that the seller use formal words such as "warrant" or "guarantee" or that he have a specific intention to make a warranty, but an affirmation merely of the value of the goods or a statement purporting to be merely the seller's opinion or commendation of the goods does not create a warranty.

§ 2–314.   Implied Warranty: Merchantability; Usage of Trade

(1) Unless excluded or modified (Section 2–316), a warranty that the goods shall be merchantable is implied in a contract for their sale if the seller is a merchant with respect to goods of that kind. Under this section the serving for value of food or drink to be consumed either on the premises or elsewhere is a sale.

(2) Goods to be merchantable must be at least such as

(a) pass without objection in the trade under the contract description; and

(b) in the case of fungible goods, are of fair average quality within the description; and

(c) are fit for the ordinary purposes for which such goods are used; and

(d) run, within the variations permitted by the agreement, of even kind, quality and quantity within each unit and among all units involved; and

(e) are adequately contained, packaged, and labeled as the agreement may require; and

(f) conform to the promises or affirmations of fact made on the container or label if any.

(3) Unless excluded or modified (Section 2–316) other implied warranties may arise from course of dealing or usage of trade.

§ 2–315.   Implied Warranty: Fitness for Particular Purpose

Where the seller at the time of contracting has reason to know any particular purpose for which the goods are required and that the buyer is relying on the seller's skill or judgment to select or furnish suitable goods, there is unless excluded or modified under the next section an implied warranty that the goods shall be fit for such purpose.

§ 2–316.   Exclusion or Modification of Warranties

(1) Words or conduct relevant to the creation of an express warranty and words or conduct tending to negate or limit warranty shall be construed wherever reasonable as consistent with each other; but subject to the provisions of this Article on parol or extrinsic evidence (Section 2–202) negation or limitation is inoperative to the extent that such construction is unreasonable.

(2) Subject to subsection (3), to exclude or modify the implied warranty of merchantability or any part of it the language must mention merchantability and in case of a writing must be conspicuous, and to exclude or modify any implied warranty of fitness the exclusion must be by a writing and conspicuous. Language to exclude all implied warranties of fitness is

sufficient if it states, for example, that "There are no warranties which extend beyond the description on the face hereof."

(3) Notwithstanding subsection (2)

(a) unless the circumstances indicate otherwise, all implied warranties are excluded by expressions like "as is," "with all faults" or other languages which in common understanding calls the buyer's attention to the exclusion of warranties and makes plain that there is no implied warranty; and

(b) when the buyer before entering into the contract has examined the goods or the sample or model as fully as he desired or has refused to examine the goods there is no implied warranty with regard to defects which an examination ought in the circumstances to have revealed to him; and

(c) an implied warranty can also be excluded or modified by course of dealing or course of performance or usage of trade.

(4) Remedies for breach of warranty can be limited in accordance with the provisions of this Article on liquidation or limitation of damages and on contractual modification of remedy (Section 2–718 and 2–719).

§ 2–317.   Cumulation and Conflict of Warranties Express or Implied

Warranties whether express or implied shall be construed as consistent with each other and as cumulative, but if such construction is unreasonable the intention of the parties shall determine which warranty is dominant. In ascertaining that intention the following rules apply:

(a) Exact or technical specifications displace an inconsistent sample or model or general language of description.

(b) A sample from an existing bulk displaces inconsistent general language of description.

(c) Express warranties displace inconsistent implied warranties other than an implied warranty of fitness for a particular purpose.

§ 2–318.   Third Party Beneficiaries of Warranties Express or Implied

Note: If this Act is introduced in the Congress of the United States this Section should be omitted. (States to select one alternative.)

Alternative A

A seller's warranty whether express or implied extends to any natural person who is in the family or household of his buyer or who is a guest in his home if it is reasonable to expect that such person may use, consume or be affected by the goods and who is injured in person by breach of the warranty. A seller may not exclude or limit the operation of this section.

Alternative B

A seller's warranty whether express or implied extends to any natural person who may reasonably be expected to use, consume or be affected by the goods and who is injured in person by breach of the warranty. A seller may not exclude or limit the operation of this section.

Alternative C

A seller's warranty whether express or implied extends to any person who may reasonably be expected to use, consume or be affected by the goods and who is injured by breach of the warranty. A seller may not exclude or limit the operation of this section with respect to injury to the person of an individual to whom the warranty extends.

§ 2–319.   F.O.B. and F.A.S. Terms

(1) Unless otherwise agreed the term F.O.B. (which means "free on board") at a named place, even though used only in connection with the stated price, is a delivery term under which

(a) when the term is F.O.B. the place of shipment, the seller must at that place ship the goods in the manner provided in this Article (Section 2–504) and bear the expense and risk of putting them into the possession of the carrier; or

(b) when the term is F.O.B. the place of destination, the seller must at his own expense and risk transport the goods to that place and there tender delivery of them in the manner provided in this Article (Section 2–503);

(c) when under either (a) or (b) the term is also F.O.B. vessel, car or other vehicle, the seller must in addition at his own expense and risk load the goods on board. If the term is F.O.B. vessel the buyer must name the vessel and in an appropriate case the seller must comply with the provisions of this Article on the form of bill of lading (Section 2–323).

(2) Unless otherwise agreed the term F.A.S. vessel (which means "free alongside") at a named port, even though used only in connection with the stated price, is a delivery term under which the seller must

(a) at his own expense and risk deliver the goods alongside the vessel in the manner usual in that port or on a dock designated and provided by the buyer; and

(b) obtain and tender a receipt for the goods in exchange for which the carrier is under a duty to issue a bill of lading.

(3) Unless otherwise agreed in any case falling within subsection (1)(a) or (c) or subsection (2) the buyer must seasonably give any needed instructions for making delivery, including when the term is F.A.S. or F.O.B. the loading berth of the vessel and in an appropriate case its name and sailing date. The seller may treat the failure of needed instructions as a failure of cooperation under this Article (Section 2–311). He may also at his option move the goods in any reasonable manner preparatory to delivery or shipment.

(4) Under the term F.O.B. vessel or F.A.S. unless otherwise agreed the buyer must make payment against tender of the required documents and the seller may not tender nor the buyer demand delivery of the goods in substitution for the documents.

§ 2–320.   C.I.F. and C. & F. Terms

(1) The term C.I.F. means that the price includes in a lump sum the cost of the goods and the insurance and freight to the named destination. The term C. & F. or C.F. means that the price so includes cost and freight to the named destination.

(2) Unless otherwise agreed and even though used only in connection with the stated price and destination, the term C.I.F. destination or its equivalent requires the seller at his own expense and risk to

(a) put the goods into the possession of a carrier at the port for shipment and obtain a negotiable bill or bills of lading covering the entire transportation to the named destination; and

(b) load the goods and obtain a receipt from the carrier (which may be contained in the bill of lading) showing that the freight has been paid or provided for; and

(c) obtain a policy or certificate of insurance, including any war risk insurance, of a kind and on terms then current at the port of shipment in the usual amount, in the currency of the contract, shown to cover the same goods covered by the bill of lading and providing for payment of loss to the order of the buyer or for the account of whom it may concern; but the seller may add to the price the amount of the premium for any such war risk insurance; and

(d) prepare an invoice of the goods and procure any other documents required to effect shipment or to comply with the contract; and

(e) forward and tender with commercial promptness all the documents in due form and with any indorsement necessary to perfect the buyer's rights.

(3) Unless otherwise agreed the term C. & F. or its equivalent has the same effect and imposes upon the seller the same obligations and risks as a C.I.F. term except the obligation as to insurance.

(4) Under the term C.I.F. & C. & F. unless otherwise agreed the buyer must make payment against tender of the required documents and the seller may not tender nor the buyer demand delivery of the goods in substitution for the documents.

§ 2–321.   C.I.F. or C. & F.: "Net Landed Weights"; "Payment on Arrival"; Warranty of Condition on Arrival

Under a contract containing a term C.I.F. or C. & F.

(1) Where the price is based on or is to be adjusted according to "net landed weights," "delivered weights," "out turn" quantity or quality or the like, unless otherwise agreed the seller must reasonably estimate the price. The payment due on tender of the documents called for by the contract is the amount so estimated, but after final adjustment of the price a settlement must be made with commercial promptness.

(2) An agreement described in subsection (1) or any warranty of quality or condition of the goods on arrival places upon the seller the risk of ordinary deterioration, shrinkage and the like in transportation but has no effect on the place or time of

identification to the contract for sale or delivery or on the passing of the risk of loss.

(3) Unless otherwise agreed where the contract provides for payment on or after arrival of the goods the seller must before payment allow such preliminary inspection as is feasible; but if the goods are lost delivery of the documents and payment are due when the goods should have arrived.

§ 2–322.   Delivery "Ex- Ship"

(1) Unless otherwise agreed a term for delivery of goods "ex-ship" (which means from the carrying vessel) or in equivalent language is not restricted to a particular ship and requires delivery from a ship which has reached a place at the named port of destination where goods of the kind are usually discharged.

(2) Under such a term unless otherwise agreed

(a) the seller must discharge all liens arising out of the carriage and furnish the buyer with a direction which puts the carrier under a duty to deliver the goods; and

(b) the risk of loss does not pass to the buyer until the goods leave the ship's tackle or are otherwise properly unloaded.

§ 2–323.   Form of Bill of Lading Required in Overseas Shipment; "Overseas"

(1) Where the contract contemplates overseas shipment and contains a term C.I.F. or C. & F. or F.O.B. vessel, the seller unless otherwise agreed must obtain a negotiable bill of lading stating that the goods have been loaded on board or, in the case of a term C.I.F. or C. & F., received for shipment.

(2) Where in a case within subsection (1) a bill of lading has been issued in a set of parts, unless otherwise agreed if the documents are not to be sent from abroad the buyer may demand tender of the full set; otherwise only one part of the bill of lading need be tendered. Even if the agreement expressly requires a full set

(a) due tender of a single part is acceptable within the provisions of this Article on cure of improper delivery (subsection (1) of Section 2–508); and

(b) even though the full set is demanded, if the documents are sent from abroad the person tendering an incomplete set may nevertheless require payment upon furnishing an indemnity which the buyer in good faith deems adequate.

(3) A shipment by water or by air or a contract contemplating such shipment is "overseas" insofar as by usage of trade or agreement it is subject to the commercial, financing or shipping practices characteristic of international deep water commerce.

§ 2–324.   "No Arrival, No Sale" Term

Under a term "no arrival, no sale" or terms of like meaning, unless otherwise agreed,

(a) the seller must properly ship conforming goods and if they arrive by any means he must tender them on arrival but he assumes no obligation that the goods will arrive unless he has caused the nonarrival; and

(b) where without fault of the seller the goods are in part lost or have so deteriorated as no longer to conform to the contract or arrive after the contract time, the buyer may proceed as if there had been casualty to identified goods (Section 2–613).

§ 2–325.   "Letter of Credit" Term; "Confirmed Credit"

(1) Failure of the buyer seasonably to furnish an agreed letter of credit is a breach of the contract for sale.

(2) The delivery to seller of a proper letter of credit suspends the buyer's obligation to pay. If the letter of credit is dishonored, the seller may on seasonable notification to the buyer require payment directly from him.

(3) Unless otherwise agreed the term "letter of credit" or "banker's credit" in a contract for sale means an irrevocable credit issued by a financing agency of good repute and, where the shipment is overseas, of good international repute. The term "confirmed credit" means that the credit must also carry the direct obligation of such an agency which does business in the seller's financial market.

§ 2–326.   Sale on Approval and Sale or Return; Consignment Sales and Rights of Creditors

(1) Unless otherwise agreed, if delivered goods may be returned by the buyer even though they conform to the contract, the transaction is

(a) a "sale on approval" if the goods are delivered primarily for use, and

(b) a "sale or return" if the goods are delivered primarily for resale.

(2) Except as provided in subsection (3), goods held on approval are not subject to the claims of the buyer's creditors until acceptance; goods held on sale or return are subject to such claims while in the buyer's possession.

(3) Where goods are delivered to a person for sale and such person maintains a place of business at which he deals in goods of the kind involved, under a name other than the name of the person making delivery, then with respect to claims of creditors of the person conducting the business the goods are deemed to be on sale or return. The provisions of this subsection are applicable even though an agreement purports to reserve title to the person making delivery until payment or resale or uses such words as "on consignment" or "on memorandum." However, this subsection is not applicable if the person making delivery

(a) complies with an applicable law providing for a consignor's interest or the like to be evidenced by a sign, or

(b) establishes that the person conducting the business is generally known by his creditors to be substantially engaged in selling the goods of others, or

(c) complies with the filing provisions of the Article on Secured Transactions (Article 9).

(4) Any "or return" term of a contract for sale is to be treated as a separate contract for sale within the statute of frauds section of this Article (Section 2–201) and as contradicting the sale aspect of the contract within the provisions of this Article on parol or extrinsic evidence (Section 2–202).

§ 2–327. Special Incidents of Sale on Approval and Sale or Return

(1) Under a sale on approval unless otherwise agreed

(a) although the goods are identified to the contract the risk of loss and the title do not pass to the buyer until acceptance; and

(b) use of the goods consistent with the purpose of trial is not acceptance but failure seasonably to notify the seller of election to return the goods is acceptance, and if the goods conform to the contract acceptance of any part is acceptance of the whole; and

(c) after due notification of election to return, the return is at the seller's risk and expense but a merchant buyer must follow any reasonable instructions.

(2) Under a sale or return unless otherwise agreed

(a) the option to return extends to the whole or any commercial unit of the goods while in substantially their original condition, but must be exercised seasonably; and

(b) the return is at the buyer's risk and expense.

§ 2–328. Sale by Auction

(1) In a sale by auction if goods are put up in lots each lot is the subject of a separate sale.

(2) A sale by auction is complete when the auctioneer so announces by the fall of the hammer or in other customary manner. Where a bid is made while the hammer is falling in acceptance of a prior bid the auctioneer may in his discretion reopen the bidding or declare the goods sold under the bid on which the hammer was falling.

(3) Such a sale is with reserve unless the goods are in explicit terms put up without reserve. In an auction with reserve the auctioneer may withdraw the goods at any time until he announces completion of the sale. In an auction without reserve, after the auctioneer calls for bids on an article or lot, that article or lot cannot be withdrawn unless no bid is made within a reasonable time. In either case a bidder may retract his bid until the auctioneer's announcement of completion of sale, but a bidder's retraction does not revive any previous bid.

(4) If the auctioneer knowingly receives a bid on the seller's behalf or the seller makes or procures such a bid, and notice has not been given that liberty for such bidding is reserved, the buyer may at his option avoid the sale or take the goods at the price of the last good faith bid prior to the completion of the sale. This subsection shall not apply to any bid at a forced sale.

Part 4   Title, Creditors and Good Faith Purchasers

§ 2–401. Passing of Title; Reservation for Security; Limited Application of This Section

Each provision of this Article with regard to the rights, obligations and remedies of the seller, the buyer, purchasers or other third parties applies irrespective of title to the goods except where the provision refers to such title. Insofar as situations are not covered by the other provisions of this Article and matters concerning title become material the following rules apply:

(1) Title to goods cannot pass under a contract for sale prior to their identification to the contract (Section 2–501), and unless otherwise explicitly agreed the buyer acquires by their identification a special property as limited by this Act. Any retention or reservation by the seller of the title (property) in goods shipped or delivered to the buyer is limited in effect to a reservation of a security interest. Subject to these provisions and to the provisions of the Article on Secured Transactions (Article 9), title to goods passes from the seller to the buyer in any manner and on any conditions explicitly agreed on by the parties.

(2) Unless otherwise explicitly agreed title passes to the buyer at the time and place at which the seller completes his performance with reference to the physical delivery of the goods, despite any reservation of a security interest and even though a document of title is to be delivered at a different time or place; and in particular and despite any reservation of a security interest by the bill of lading

(a) if the contract requires or authorizes the seller to send the goods to the buyer but does not require him to deliver them at destination, title passes to the buyer at the time and place of shipment; but

(b) if the contract requires delivery at destination, title passes on tender there.

(3) Unless otherwise explicitly agreed where delivery is to be made without moving the goods,

(a) if the seller is to deliver a document of title, title passes at the time when and the place where he delivers such documents; or

(b) if the good are at the time of contracting already identified and no documents are to be delivered, title passes at the time and place of contracting.

(4) A rejection or other refusal by the buyer to receive or retain the goods, whether or not justified, or a justified revocation of acceptance revests title to the goods in the seller. Such revesting occurs by operation of law and is not a "sale."

§ 2–402. Rights of Seller's Creditors Against Sold Goods

(1) Except as provided in subsections (2) and (3), rights of unsecured creditors of the seller with respect to goods which

have been identified to a contract for sale are subject to the buyer's rights to recover the goods under this Article (Section 2–502 and 2–716).

(2) A creditor of the seller may treat a sale or an identification of goods to a contract for sale as void if as against him a retention of possession by the seller is fraudulent under any rule of law of the state where the goods are situated, except that retention of possession in good faith and current course of trade by a merchant-seller for a commercially reasonable time after a sale or identification is not fraudulent.

(3) Nothing in this Article shall be deemed to impair the rights of creditors of the seller

   (a) under the provisions of the Article on Secured Transactions (Article 9); or

   (b) where identification to the contract or delivery is made not in current course of trade but in satisfaction of or as security for a pre-existing claim for money, security or the like and is made under circumstances which under any rule of law of the state where the goods are situated would apart from this Article constitute the transaction a fraudulent transfer or voidable preference.

§ 2–403.   Power to Transfer; Good Faith Purchase of Goods; "Entrusting"

(1) A purchaser of goods acquires all title which his transferor had or had power to transfer except that a purchaser of a limited interest acquires rights only to the extent of the interest purchased. A person with voidable title has power to transfer a good title to a good faith purchaser for value. When goods have been delivered under a transaction of purchase the purchaser has such power even though

   (a) the transferor was deceived as to the identity of the purchaser, or

   (b) the delivery was in exchange for a check which is later dishonored, or

   (c) it was agreed that the transaction was to be a "cash sale," or

   (d) the delivery was procured through fraud punishable as larcenous under the criminal law.

(2) Any entrusting of possession of goods to a merchant who deals in goods of that kind gives him power to transfer all rights of the entruster to a buyer in ordinary course of business.

(3) "Entrusting" includes any delivery and any acquiescence in retention of possession regardless of any condition expressed between the parties to the delivery or acquiescence and regardless of whether the procurement of the entrusting or the possessor's disposition of the goods have been such as to be larcenous under the criminal law.

(4) The rights of other purchasers of goods and of lien creditors are governed by the Articles on Secured Transactions (Article 9), Bulk Transfers (Article 6) and Documents of Title (Article 7).

Part 5   Performance

§ 2–501.   Insurable Interest in Goods; Manner of Identification of Goods

(1) The buyer obtains a special property and an insurable interest in goods by identification of existing goods as goods to which the contract refers even though the goods so identified are nonconforming and he has an option to return or reject them. Such identification can be made at any time and in any manner explicitly agreed to by the parties. In the absence of explicit agreement identification occurs

   (a) when the contract is made if it is for the sale of goods already existing and identified;

   (b) if the contract is for the sale of future goods other than those described in paragraph (c), when goods are shipped, marked or otherwise designated by the seller as goods to which the contract refers;

   (c) when the crops are planted or otherwise become growing crops or the young are conceived if the contract is for the sale of unborn young to be born within twelve months after contracting or for the sale of crops to be harvested within twelve months or the next normal harvest season after contracting whichever is longer.

(2) The seller retains an insurable interest in goods so long as title to or any security interest in the goods remains in him and where the identification is by the seller alone he may until default or insolvency or notification to the buyer that the identification is final substitute other goods for those identified.

(3) Nothing in this section impairs any insurable interest recognized under any other statute or rule of law.

§ 2–502.   Buyer's Right to Goods on Seller's Insolvency

(1) Subject to subsection (2) and even though the goods have not been shipped a buyer who has paid a part or all of the price of goods in which he has a special property under the provisions of the immediately preceding section may on making and keeping good a tender of any unpaid portion of their price recover them from the seller if the seller becomes insolvent within ten days after receipt of the first installment on their price.

(2) If the identification creating his special property has been made by the buyer he acquires the right to recover the goods only if they conform to the contract for sale.

§ 2–503.   Manner of Seller's Tender of Delivery

(1) Tender of delivery requires that the seller put and hold conforming goods at the buyer's disposition and give the buyer any notification reasonably necessary to enable him to take delivery. The manner, time and place for tender are determined by the agreement and this Article, and in particular

   (a) tender must be at a reasonable hour, and if it is of goods they must be kept available for the period reasonably necessary to enable the buyer to take possession; but

(b) unless otherwise agreed the buyer must furnish facilities reasonably suited to the receipt of the goods.

(2) Where the case is within the next section respecting shipment tender requires that the seller comply with its provisions.

(3) Where the seller is required to deliver at a particular destination tender requires that he comply with subsection (1) and also in any appropriate case tender documents as described in subsections (4) and (5) of this section.

(4) Where goods are in the possession of a bailee and are to be delivered without being moved

(a) tender requires that the seller either tender a negotiable document of title covering such goods or procure acknowledgment by the bailee of the buyer's right to possession of the goods; but

(b) tender to the buyer of a non-negotiable document of title or of a written direction to the bailee to deliver is sufficient tender unless the buyer seasonably objects, and receipt by the bailee of notification of the buyer's rights fixes those rights as against the bailee and all third persons; but risk of loss of the goods and of any failure by the bailee to honor the nonnegotiable document of title or to obey the direction remains on the seller until the buyer has had a reasonable time to present the document or direction, and a refusal by the bailee to honor the document or to obey the direction defeats the tender.

(5) Where the contract requires the seller to deliver documents

(a) he must tender all such documents in correct form, except as provided in this Article with respect to bills of lading in a set (subsection (2) of Section 2–323); and

(b) tender through customary banking channels is sufficient and dishonor of a draft accompanying the documents constitutes non-acceptance or rejection.

§ 2–504.   Shipment by Seller

Where the seller is required or authorized to send the goods to the buyer and the contract does not require him to deliver them at a particular destination, then unless otherwise agreed he must

(a) put the goods in the possession of such a carrier and make such a contract for their transportation as may be reasonable having regard to the nature of the goods and other circumstances of the case; and

(b) obtain and promptly deliver or tender in due form any document necessary to enable the buyer to obtain possession of the goods or otherwise required by the agreement or by usage of trade; and

(c) promptly notify the buyer of the shipment. Failure to notify the buyer under paragraph (c) or to make a proper contract under paragraph (a) is a ground for rejection only if material delay or loss ensues.

§ 2–505.   Seller's Shipment Under Reservation

(1) Where the seller has identified goods to the contract by or before shipment:

(a) his procurement of a negotiable bill of lading to his own order or otherwise reserves in him a security interest in the goods. His procurement of the bill to the order of a financing agency or of the buyer indicates in addition only the seller's expectation of transferring that interest to the person named.

(b) a non-negotiable bill of lading to himself or his nominee reserves possession of the goods as security but except in a case of conditional delivery (subsection (2) of Section 2–507) a non-negotiable bill of lading naming the buyer as consignee reserves no security interest even though the seller retains possession of the bill of lading.

(2) When shipment by the seller with reservation of a security interest is in violation of the contract for sale it constitutes an improper contract for transportation within the preceding section but impairs neither the rights given to the buyer by shipment and identification of the goods to the contract nor the seller's powers as a holder of a negotiable document.

§ 2–506.   Rights of Financing Agency

(1) A financing agency by paying or purchasing for value a draft which relates to a shipment of goods acquires to the extent of the payment or purchase and in addition to its own rights under the draft and any document of title securing it any rights of the shipper in the goods including the right to stop delivery and the shipper's right to have the draft honored by the buyer.

(2) The right to reimbursement of a financing agency which has in good faith honored or purchased the draft under commitment to or authority from the buyer is not impaired by subsequent discovery of defects with reference to any relevant document which was apparently regular on its face.

§ 2–507.   Effect of Seller's Tender; Delivery on Condition

(1) Tender of delivery is a condition to the buyer's duty to accept the goods and, unless otherwise agreed, to his duty to pay for them. Tender entitles the seller to acceptance of the goods and to payment according to the contract.

(2) Where payment is due and demanded on the delivery to the buyer of goods or documents of title, his right as against the seller to retain or dispose of them is conditional upon his making the payment due.

§ 2–508.   Cure by Seller of Improper Tender or Delivery; Replacement

(1) Where any tender or delivery by the seller is rejected because non-conforming and the time for performance has not yet expired, the seller may seasonably notify the buyer of his intention to cure and may then within the contract time make a conforming delivery.

(2) Where the buyer rejects a non-conforming tender which the seller had reasonable grounds to believe would be accept-

able with or without money allowance the seller may if he seasonably notifies the buyer have a further reasonable time to substitute a conforming tender.

§ 2–509.   Risk of Loss in the Absence of Breach

(1) Where the contract requires or authorizes the seller to ship the goods by carrier

(a) if it does not require him to deliver them at a particular destination, the risk of loss passes to the buyer when the goods are duly delivered to the carrier even though the shipment is under reservation (Section 2–505); but

(b) if it does require him to deliver them at a particular destination and the goods are there duly tendered while in the possession of the carrier, the risk of loss passes to the buyer when the goods are there duly so tendered as to enable the buyer to take delivery.

(2) Where the goods are held by a bailee to be delivered without being moved, the risk of loss passes to the buyer.

(a) on his receipt of a negotiable document of title covering the goods; or

(b) on acknowledgment by the bailee of the buyer's right to possession of the goods; or

(c) after his receipt of a non-negotiable document of title or other written direction to deliver, as provided in subsection (4)(b) of Section 2–503.

(3) In any case not within subsection (1) or (2), the risk of loss passes to the buyer on his receipt of the goods if the seller is a merchant; otherwise the risk passes to the buyer on tender of delivery.

(4) The provisions of this section are subject to contrary agreement of the parties and to the provisions of this Article on sale on approval (Section 2–327) and on effect of breach on risk of loss (Section 2–510).

§ 2–510.   Effect of Breach on Risk of Loss

(1) Where a tender or delivery of goods so fails to conform to the contract as to give a right of rejection the risk of their loss remains on the seller until cure or acceptance.

(2) Where the buyer rightfully revokes acceptance he may to the extent of any deficiency in his effective insurance coverage treat the risk of loss as having rested on the seller from the beginning.

(3) Where the buyer as to conforming goods already identified to the contract for sale repudiates or is otherwise in breach before risk of their loss has passed to him, the seller may to the extent of any deficiency in his effective insurance coverage treat the risk of loss as resting on the buyer for a commercially reasonable time.

§ 2–511.   Tender of Payment by Buyer; Payment by Check

(1) Unless otherwise agreed tender of payment is a condition to the seller's duty to tender and complete any delivery.

(2) Tender of payment is sufficient when made by any means

or in any manner current in the ordinary course of business unless the seller demands payment in legal tender and gives any extension of time reasonably necessary to procure it.

(3) Subject to the provisions of this Act on the effect of an instrument on an obligation (Section 3–802), payment by check is conditional and is defeated as between the parties by dishonor of the check on due presentment.

§ 2–512.   Payment by Buyer Before Inspection

(1) Where the contract requires payment before inspection non-conformity of the goods does not excuse the buyer from so making payment unless

(a) the non-conformity appears without inspection; or

(b) despite tender of the required documents the circumstances would justify injunction against honor under the provisions of this Act (Section 5–114).

(2) Payment pursuant to subsection (1) does not constitute an acceptance of goods or impair the buyer's right to inspect or any of his remedies.

§ 2–513.   Buyer's Right to Inspection of Goods

(1) Unless otherwise agreed and subject to subsection (3), where goods are tendered or delivered or identified to the contract for sale, the buyer has a right before payment or acceptance to inspect them at any reasonable place and time and in any reasonable manner. When the seller is required and authorized to send the goods to the buyer, the inspection may be after their arrival.

(2) Expenses of inspection must be borne by the buyer but may be recovered from the seller if the goods do not conform and are rejected.

(3) Unless otherwise agreed and subject to the provisions of this Article on C.I.F. contracts (subsection (3) of Section 2–321), the buyer is not entitled to inspect the goods before payment of the price when the contract provides

(a) for delivery "C.O.D." or on other like terms; or

(b) for payment against documents of title, except where such payment is due only after the goods are to become available for inspection.

(4) A place or method of inspection fixed by the parties is presumed to be exclusive but unless otherwise expressly agreed it does not postpone identification or shift the place for delivery or for passing the risk of loss. If compliance becomes impossible, inspection shall be as provided in this section unless the place or method fixed was clearly intended as an indispensable condition failure of which avoids the contract.

§ 2–514.   When Documents Deliverable on Acceptance; When on Payment

Unless otherwise agreed documents against which a draft is drawn are to be delivered to the drawee on acceptance of the draft if it is payable more than three days after presentment; otherwise, only on payment.

§ 2–515.   Preserving Evidence of Goods in Dispute

In furtherance of the adjustment of any claim or dispute

(a) either party on reasonable notification to the other and for the purpose of ascertaining the facts and preserving evidence has the right to inspect, test and sample the goods including such of them as may be in the possession or control of the other; and

(b) the parties may agree to a third party inspection or survey to determine the conformity or condition of the goods and may agree that the findings shall be binding upon them in any subsequent litigation or adjustment.

Part 6   Breach, Repudiation and Excuse

§ 2–601.   Buyer's Rights on Improper Delivery

Subject to the provisions of this Article on breach in installment contracts (Section 2–612) and unless otherwise agreed under the sections on contractual limitations of remedy (Sections 2–718 and 2–719), if the goods or the tender of delivery fail in any respect to conform to the contract, the buyer may

(a) reject the whole; or

(b) accept the whole; or

(c) accept any commercial unit or units and reject the rest.

§ 2–602.   Manner and Effect of Rightful Rejection

(1) Rejection of goods must be within a reasonable time after their delivery or tender. It is ineffective unless the buyer seasonably notifies the seller.

(2) Subject to the provisions of the two following sections on rejected goods (Sections 2–603 and 2–604),

(a) after rejection any exercise of ownership by the buyer with respect to any commercial unit is wrongful as against the seller; and

(b) if the buyer has before rejection taken physical possession of goods in which he does not have a security interest under the provisions of this Article (subsection (3) of Section 2–711), he is under a duty after rejection to hold them with reasonable care at the seller's disposition for a time sufficient to permit the seller to remove them; but

(c) the buyer has no further obligations with regard to goods rightfully rejected.

(3) The seller's rights with respect to goods wrongfully rejected are governed by the provisions of this Article on Seller's remedies in general (Section 2–703).

§ 2–603.   Merchant Buyer's Duties as to Rightfully Rejected Goods

(1) Subject to any security interest in the buyer (subsection (3) of Section 2–711), when the seller has no agent or place of business at the market of rejection a merchant buyer is under a duty after rejection of goods in his possession or control to follow any reasonable instructions received from the seller

with respect to the goods and in the absence of such instructions to make reasonable efforts to sell them for the seller's account if they are perishable or threaten to decline in value speedily. Instructions are not reasonable if on demand indemnity for expense is not forthcoming.

(2) When the buyer sells goods under subsection (1), he is entitled to reimbursement from the seller or out of the proceeds for reasonable expenses of caring for and selling them, and if the expenses include no selling commission then to such commission as is usual in the trade or if there is none to a reasonable sum not exceeding ten per cent on the gross proceeds.

(3) In complying with this section the buyer is held only to good faith and good faith conduct hereunder is neither acceptance nor conversion nor the basis of an action for damages.

§ 2–604.   Buyer's Options as to Salvage of Rightfully Rejected Goods

Subject to the provisions of the immediately preceding section on perishables if the seller gives no instructions within a reasonable time after notification of rejection the buyer may store the rejected goods for the seller's account or reship them to him or resell them for the seller's account with reimbursement as provided in the preceding section. Such action is not acceptance or conversion.

§ 2–605.   Waiver of Buyer's Objections by Failure to Particularize

(1) The buyer's failure to state in connection with rejection a particular defect which is ascertainable by reasonable inspection precludes him from relying on the unstated defect to justify rejection or to establish breach

(a) where the seller could have cured it if stated seasonably; or

(b) between merchants when the seller has after rejection made a request in writing for a full and final written statement of all defects on which the buyer proposes to rely.

(2) Payment against documents made without reservation of rights precludes recovery of the payment for defects apparent on the face of the documents.

§ 2–606.   What Constitutes Acceptance of Goods

(1) Acceptance of goods occurs when the buyer

(a) after a reasonable opportunity to inspect the goods signifies to the seller that the goods are conforming or that he will take or retain them in spite of their non-conformity; or

(b) fails to make an effective rejection (subsection (1) of Section 2–602), but such acceptance does not occur until the buyer has had a reasonable opportunity to inspect them; or

(c) does any act inconsistent with the seller's ownership; but if such act is wrongful as against the seller it is an acceptance only if ratified by him.

(2) Acceptance of a part of any commercial unit is acceptance of that entire unit.

§ 2–607.   Effect of Acceptance; Notice of Breach; Burden of Establishing Breach After Acceptance; Notice of Claim or Litigation to Person Answerable Over

(1) The buyer must pay at the contract rate for any goods accepted.

(2) Acceptance of goods by the buyer precludes rejection of the goods accepted and if made with knowledge of a non-conformity cannot be revoked because of it unless the acceptance was on the reasonable assumption that the non-conformity would be seasonably cured but acceptance does not of itself impair any other remedy provided by this Article for non-conformity.

(3) Where a tender has been accepted

(a) the buyer must within a reasonable time after he discovers or should have discovered any breach notify the seller of breach or be barred from any remedy; and

(b) if the claim is one for infringement or the like (subsection (3) of Section 2–312) and the buyer is sued as a result of such a breach he must so notify the seller within a reasonable time after he receives notice of the litigation or be barred from any remedy over for liability established by the litigation.

(4) The burden is on the buyer to establish any breach with respect to the goods accepted.

(5) Where the buyer is sued for breach of a warranty or other obligation for which his seller is answerable over

(a) he may give his seller written notice of the litigation. If the notice states that the seller may come in and defend and that if the seller does not do so he will be bound in any action against him by his buyer by any determination of fact common to the two litigations, then unless the seller after seasonable receipt of the notice does come in and defend he is so bound.

(b) if the claim is one for infringement or the like (subsection (3) of Section 2–312) the original seller may demand in writing that his buyer turn over to him control of the litigation including settlement or else be barred from any remedy over and if he also agrees to bear all expense and to satisfy any adverse judgment, then unless the buyer after seasonable receipt of the demand does turn over control the buyer is so barred.

(6) The provisions of subsections (3), (4) and (5) apply to any obligation of a buyer to hold the seller harmless against infringement or the like (subsection (3) of Section 2–312).

§ 2–608.   Revocation of Acceptance in Whole or in Part

(1) The buyer may revoke his acceptance of a lot or commercial unit whose non-conformity substantially impairs its value to him if he has accepted it

(a) on the reasonable assumption that its non-conformity would be cured and it has not been seasonably cured; or

(b) without discovery of such non-conformity if his acceptance was reasonably induced either by the difficulty of discovery before acceptance or by the seller's assurances.

(2) Revocation of acceptance must occur within a reasonable time after the buyer discovers or should have discovered the ground for it and before any substantial change in condition of the goods which is not caused by their own defects. It is not effective until the buyer notifies the seller of it.

(3) A buyer who so revokes has the same rights and duties with regard to the goods involved as if he had rejected them.

§ 2–609.   Right to Adequate Assurance of Performance

(1) A contract for sale imposes an obligation on each party that the other's expectation of receiving due performance will not be impaired. When reasonable grounds for insecurity arise with respect to the performance of either party the other may in writing demand adequate assurance of due performance and until he receives such assurance may if commercially reasonable suspend any performance for which he has not already received the agreed return.

(2) Between merchants the reasonableness of grounds for insecurity and the adequacy of any assurance offered shall be determined according to commercial standards.

(3) Acceptance of any improper delivery or payment does not prejudice the aggrieved party's right to demand adequate assurance of future performance.

(4) After receipt of a justified demand failure to provide within a reasonable time not exceeding thirty days such assurance of due performance as is adequate under the circumstances of the particular case is a repudiation of the contract.

§ 2–610.   Anticipatory Repudiation

When either party repudiates the contract with respect to a performance not yet due the loss of which will substantially impair the value of the contract to the other, the aggrieved party may

(a) for a commercially reasonable time await performance by the repudiating party; or

(b) resort to any remedy for breach (Section 2–703 or Section 2–711), even though he has notified the repudiating party that he would await the latter's performance and has urged retraction; and

(c) in either case suspended his own performance or proceed in accordance with the provisions of this Article on the seller's right to identify goods to the contract notwithstanding breach or to salvage unfinished goods (Section 2–704).

§ 2–611.   Retraction of Anticipatory Repudiation

(1) Until the repudiating party's next performance is due he can retract his repudiation unless the aggrieved party has since the repudiation cancelled or materially changed his position or otherwise indicated that he considers the repudiation final.

(2) Retraction may be by any method which clearly indicates to the aggrieved party that the repudiating party intends to perform, but must include any assurance justifiably demanded under the provisions of this Article (Section 2–609).

(3) Retraction reinstates the repudiating party's right under the contract with due excuse and allowance to the aggrieved party for any delay occasioned by the repudiation.

§ 2–612. "Installment Contract"; Breach

(1) An "installment contract" is one which requires or authorizes the delivery of goods in separate lots to be separately accepted, even though the contract contains a clause "each delivery is a separate contract" or its equivalent.

(2) The buyer may reject any installment which is non-conforming if the non-conformity substantially impairs the value of that installment and cannot be cured or if the non-conformity is a defect in the required documents; but if the non-conformity does not fall within subsection (3) and the seller gives adequate assurance of its cure the buyer must accept that installment.

(3) Whenever non-conformity or default with respect to one or more installments substantially impairs the value of the whole contract there is a breach of the whole. But the aggrieved party reinstates the contract if he accepts a non-conforming installment without seasonably notifying of cancellation or if he brings an action with respect only to past installments or demands performance as to future installments.

§ 2–613. Casualty to Identified Goods

Where the contract requires for its performance goods identified when the contract is made, and the goods suffer casualty without fault of either party before the risk of loss passes to the buyer, or in a proper case under a "no arrival, no sale" term (Section 2–324) then

(a) if the loss is total the contract is avoided; and

(b) if the loss is partial or the goods have so deteriorated as no longer to conform to the contract the buyer may nevertheless demand inspection and at his option either treat the contract as avoided or accept the goods with due allowance from the contract price for the deterioration or the deficiency in quantity but without further right against the seller.

§ 2–614. Substituted Performance

(1) Where without fault of either party the agreed berthing, loading, or unloading facilities fail or an agreed type of carrier becomes unavailable or the agreed manner of delivery otherwise becomes commercially impracticable but a commercially reasonable substitute is available, such substitute performance must be tendered and accepted.

(2) If the agreed means or manner of payment fails because of domestic or foreign governmental regulation, the seller may withhold or stop delivery unless the buyer provides a means or manner of payment which is commercially a substantial equivalent. If delivery has already been taken, payment by the means or in the manner provided by the regulation discharges the buyer's obligation unless the regulation is discriminatory, oppressive or predatory.

§ 2–615. Excuse by Failure of Presupposed Conditions

Except so far as a seller may have assumed a greater obligation and subject to the preceding section on substituted performance:

(a) Delay in delivery or non-delivery in whole or in part by a seller who complies with paragraphs (b) and (c) is not a breach of his duty under a contract for sale if performance as agreed has been made impracticable by the occurrence of a contingency the nonoccurrence of which was a basic assumption on which the contract was made or by compliance in good faith with any applicable foreign or domestic governmental regulation or order whether or not it later proves to be invalid.

(b) Where the causes mentioned in paragraph (a) affect only a part of the seller's capacity to perform, he must allocate production and deliveries among his customers but may at his option include regular customers not then under contract as well as his own requirements for further manufacture. He may so allocate in any manner which is fair and reasonable.

(c) The seller must notify the buyer seasonably that there will be delay or non-delivery and, when allocation is required under paragraph (b), of the estimated quota thus made available for the buyer.

§ 2–616. Procedure on Notice Claiming Excuse

(1) Where the buyer receives notification of a material or indefinite delay or an allocation justified under the preceding section he may by written notification to the seller as to any delivery concerned, and where the prospective deficiency substantially impairs the value of the whole contract under the provisions of this Article relating to breach of installment contracts (Section 2–612), then also as to the whole,

(a) terminate and thereby discharge any unexecuted portion of the contract; or

(b) modify the contract by agreeing to take his available quota in substitution.

(2) If after receipt of such notification from the seller the buyer fails so to modify the contract within a reasonable time not exceeding thirty days the contract lapses with respect to any deliveries affected.

(3) The provisions of this section may not be negated by agreement except in so far as the seller has assumed a greater obligation under the preceding section.

Part 7 Remedies

§ 2–701. Remedies for Breach of Collateral Contracts Not Impaired

Remedies for breach of any obligation or promise collateral or ancillary to a contract for sale are not impaired by the provisions of this Article.

§ 2–702. Seller's Remedies on Discovery of Buyer's Insolvency

(1) Where the seller discovers the buyer to be insolvent he may refuse delivery except for cash including payment for all goods theretofore delivered under the contract, and stop delivery under this Article (Section 2–705).

(2) Where the seller discovers that the buyer has received goods on credit while insolvent he may reclaim the goods upon demand made within ten days after the receipt, but if misrepresentation of solvency has been made to the particular seller in writing within three months before delivery the ten day limitation does not apply. Except as provided in this subsection the seller may not base a right to reclaim goods on the buyer's fraudulent or innocent misrepresentation of solvency or of intent to pay.

(3) The seller's right to reclaim under subsection (2) is subject to the rights of a buyer in ordinary course or other good faith purchaser under this Article (Section 2–403). Successful reclamation of goods excludes all other remedies with respect to them.

§ 2–703. Seller's Remedies in General

Where the buyer wrongfully rejects or revokes acceptance of goods or fails to make a payment due on or before delivery or repudiates with respect to a part or the whole, then with respect to any goods directly affected and, if the breach is of the whole contract (Section 2–612), then also with respect to the whole undelivered balance, the aggrieved seller may

(a) withhold delivery of such goods;

(b) stop delivery by any bailee as hereafter provided (Section 2–705);

(c) proceed under the next section respecting goods still unidentified to the contract;

(d) resell and recover damages as hereafter provided (Section 2–706);

(e) recover damages for non-acceptance (Section 2–708) or in a proper case the price (Section 2–709);

(f) cancel.

§ 2–704. Seller's Right to Identify Goods to the Contract Notwithstanding Breach or to Salvage Unfinished Goods

(1) An aggrevieted seller under the preceding section may

(a) identify to the contract conforming goods not already identified if at the time he learned of the breach they are in his possession or control;

(b) treat as the subject of resale goods which have demonstrably been intended for the particular contract even though those goods are unfinished.

(2) Where the goods are unfinished an aggrieved seller may in the exercise of reasonable commercial judgment for the purposes of avoiding loss and of effective realization either complete the manufacture and wholly identify the goods to the contract or cease manufacture and resell for scrap or salvage value or proceed in any other reasonable manner.

§ 2–705. Seller's Stoppage of Delivery in Transit or Otherwise

(1) The seller may stop delivery of goods in the possession of a carrier or other bailee when he discovers the buyer to be insolvent (Section 2–702) and may stop delivery of carload, truckload, planeload or larger shipments of express or freight when the buyer repudiates or fails to make a payment due before delivery or if for any other reason the seller has a right to withhold or reclaim the goods.

(2) As against such buyer the seller may stop delivery until

(a) receipt of the goods by the buyer; or

(b) acknowledgment to the buyer by any bailee of the goods except a carrier that the bailee holds the goods for the buyer; or

(c) such acknowledgment to the buyer by a carrier by re-shipment or as warehouseman; or

(d) negotiation to the buyer of any negotiable document of title covering the goods.

(3)(a) To stop delivery the seller must so notify as to enable the bailee by reasonable diligence to prevent delivery of the goods.

(b) After such notification the bailee must hold and deliver the goods according to the directions of the seller but the seller is liable to the bailee for any ensuing charges or damages.

(c) If a negotiable document of title has been issued for goods the bailee is not obliged to obey a notification to stop until surrender of the document.

(d) A carrier who has issued a non-negotiable bill of lading is not obliged to obey a notification to stop received from a person other than the consignor.

§ 2–706. Seller's Resale Including Contract for Resale

(1) Under the conditions stated in Section 2–703 on seller's remedies, the seller may resell the goods concerned or the undelivered balance thereof. Where the resale is made in good faith and in a commercially reasonable manner the seller may recover the difference between the resale price and the contract price together with any incidental damages allowed under the provisions of this Article (Section 2–710), but less expenses saved in consequence of the buyer's breach.

(2) Except as otherwise provided in subsection (3) or unless otherwise agreed resale may be at public or private sale including sale by way of one or more contracts to sell or of identification to an existing contract of the seller. Sale may be as a unit or in parcels and at any time and place and on any terms but every aspect of the sale including the method, manner, time, place and terms must be commercially reasonable. The resale must be reasonably identified as referring to the broken contract, but it is not necessary that the goods be in existence or that any

or all of them have been identified to the contract before the breach.

(3) Where the resale is at private sale the seller must give the buyer reasonable notification of his intention to resell.

(4) Where the resale is at public sale

(a) only identified goods can be sold except where there is a recognized market for a public sale of futures in goods of the kind; and

(b) it must be made at a usual place or market for public sale if one is reasonably available and except in the case of goods which are perishable or threaten to decline in value speedily the seller must give the buyer reasonable notice of the time and place of the resale; and

(c) if the goods are not to be within the view of those attending the sale the notification of sale must state the place where the goods are located and provide for their reasonable inspection by prospective bidders; and

(d) the seller may buy.

(5) A purchaser who buys in good faith at a resale takes the goods free of any rights of the original buyer even though the seller fails to comply with one or more of the requirements of this section.

(6) The seller is not accountable to the buyer for any profit made on any resale. A person in the position of a seller (Section 2–707) or a buyer who has rightfully rejected or justifiably revoked acceptance must account for any excess over the amount of his security interest, as hereinafter defined (subsection (3) of Section 2–711).

§ 2–707. "Person in the Position of a Seller"

(1) A "person in the position of a seller" includes as against a principal an agent who has paid or become responsible for the price of goods on behalf of his principal or anyone who otherwise holds a security interest or other right in goods similar to that of a seller.

(2) A person in the position of a seller may as provided in this Article withhold or stop delivery (Section 2–706) and recover incidental damages (Section 2–710).

§ 2–708. Seller's Damages for Non-Acceptance or Repudiation

(1) Subject to subsection (2) and to the provisions of this Article with respect to proof of market price (Section 2–723), the measure of damages for non-acceptance or repudiation by the buyer is the difference between the market price at the time and place for tender and the unpaid contract price together with any incidental damages provided in this Article (Section 2–710), but less expenses saved in consequence of the buyer's breach.

(2) If the measure of damages provided in subsection (1) is inadequate to put the seller in as good a position as performance would have done then the measure of damages is the profit (including reasonable overhead) which the seller would have made from full performance by the buyer, together with any incidental damages provided in this Article (Section 2–710), due allowance for costs reasonably incurred and due credit for payments or proceeds of resale.

§ 2–709. Action for the Price

(1) When the buyer fails to pay the price as it becomes due the seller may recover, together with any incidental damages under the next section, the price

(a) of goods accepted or of conforming goods lost or damaged within a commercially reasonable time after risk of their loss has passed to the buyer; and

(b) of goods identified to the contract if the seller is unable after reasonable effort to resell them at a reasonable price or the circumstances reasonably indicate that such effort will be unavailing.

(2) Where the seller sues for the price he must hold for the buyer any goods which have been identified to the contract and are still in his control except that if resale becomes possible he may resell them at any time prior to the collection of the judgment. The net proceeds of any such resale must be credited to the buyer and payment of the judgment entitles him to any goods not resold.

(3) After the buyer has wrongfully rejected or revoked acceptance of the goods or has failed to make a payment due or has repudiated (Section 2–610), a seller who is held not entitled to the price under this section shall nevertheless be awarded damages for non-acceptance under the preceding section.

§ 2–710. Seller's Incidental Damages

Incidental damages to an aggrieved seller include any commercially reasonable charges, expenses or commissions incurred in stopping delivery, in the transportation, care and custody of goods after the buyer's breach, in connection with return or resale of the goods or otherwise resulting from the breach.

§ 2–711. Buyer's Remedies in General; Buyer's Security Interest in Rejected Goods

(1) Where the seller fails to make delivery or repudiates or the buyer rightfully rejects or justifiably revokes acceptance then with respect to any goods involved, and with respect to the whole if the breach goes to the whole contract (Section 2–612), the buyer may cancel and whether or not he has done so may in addition to recovering so much of the price as has been paid

(a) "cover" and have damages under the next section as to all the goods affected whether or not they have been identified to the contract; or

(b) recover damages for non-delivery as provided in this Article (Section 2–713).

(2) Where the seller fails to deliver or repudiates the buyer may also

(a) if the goods have been identified recover them as provided in this Article (Section 2–502); or

(b) in a proper case obtain specific performance or replevy the goods as provided in this Article (Section 2–716).

(3) On rightful rejection or justifiable revocation of acceptance a buyer has a security interest in goods in his possession or control for any payments made on their price and any expenses reasonably incurred in their inspection, receipt, transportation, care and custody and may hold such goods and resell them in like manner as an aggrieved seller (Section 2–706).

§ 2–712.   "Cover"; Buyer's Procurement of Substitute Goods

(1) After a breach within the preceding section the buyer may "cover" by making in good faith and without unreasonable delay any reasonable purchase of or contract to purchase goods in substitution for those due from the seller.

(2) The buyer may recover from the seller as damages the difference between the cost of cover and the contract price together with any incidental or consequential damages as hereinafter defined (Section 2–715), but less expenses saved in consequence of the seller's breach.

(3) Failure of the buyer to effect cover within this section does not bar him from any other remedy.

§ 2–713.   Buyer's Damages for Non-Delivery or Repudiation

(1) Subject to the provisions of this Article with respect to proof of market price (Section 2–723), the measure of damages for non-delivery or repudiation by the seller is the difference between the market price at the time when the buyer learned of the breach and the contract price together with any incidental and consequential damages provided in this Article (Section 2–715), but less expenses saved in consequence of the seller's breach.

(2) Market price is to be determined as of the place for tender or, in cases of rejection after arrival or revocation of acceptance, as of the place of arrival.

§ 2–714.   Buyer's Damages for Breach in Regard to Accepted Goods

(1) Where the buyer has accepted goods and given notification (subsection (3) of Section 2–607) he may recover as damages for any non-conformity of tender the loss resulting in the ordinary course of events from the seller's breach as determined in any manner which is reasonable.

(2) The measure of damages for breach of warranty is the difference at the time and place of acceptance between the value of the goods accepted and the value they would have had if they had been as warranted, unless special circumstances show proximate damages of a different amount.

(3) In a proper case any incidental and consequential damages under the next section may also be recovered.

§ 2–715.   Buyer's Incidental and Consequential Damages

(1) Incidental damages resulting from the seller's breach include expenses reasonably incurred in inspection, receipt, transportation and care and custody of goods rightfully rejected, any commercially reasonable charges, expenses or commissions in connection with effecting over and any other reasonable expense incident to the delay or other breach.

(2) Consequential damages resulting from the seller's breach include

(a) any loss resulting from general or particular requirements and needs of which the seller at the time of contracting had reason to know and which could not reasonably be prevented by cover or otherwise; and

(b) injury to person or property proximately resulting from any breach of warranty.

§ 2–716.   Buyer's Right to Specific Performance or Replevin

(1) Specific performance may be decreed where the goods are unique or in other proper circumstances.

(2) The decree for specific performance may include such terms and conditions as to payment of the price, damages, or other relief as the court may deem just.

(3) The buyer has a right of replevin for goods identified to the contract if after reasonable effort he is unable to effect cover for such goods or the circumstances reasonably indicate that such effort will be unavailing or if the goods have been shipped under reservation and satisfaction of the security interest in them has been made or tendered.

§ 2–717.   Deduction of Damages From the Price

The buyer on notifying the seller of his intention to do so may deduct all or any part of the damages resulting from any breach of the contract from any part of the price still due under the same contract.

§ 2–718.   Liquidation or Limitation of Damages; Deposits

(1) Damages for breach by either party may be liquidated in the agreement but only at an amount which is reasonable in the light of the anticipated or actual harm caused by the breach, the difficulties of proof of loss, and the inconvenience or nonfeasibility of otherwise obtaining an adequate remedy. A term fixing unreasonably large liquidated damages is void as a penalty.

(2) Where the seller justifiably withholds delivery of goods because of the buyer's breach, the buyer is entitled to restitution of any amount by which the sum of his payments exceeds

(a) the amount to which the seller is entitled by virtue of terms liquidating the seller's damages in accordance with subsection (1), or

(b) in the absence of such terms, twenty percent of the value of the total performance for which the buyer is obligated under the contract or $500, whichever is smaller.

(3) The buyer's right to restitution under subsection (2) is subject to offset to the extent that the seller establishes

(a) a right to recover damages under the provisions of this Article other than subsection (1), and

(b) the amount or value of any benefits received by the buyer directly or indirectly by reason of the contract.

(4) Where a seller has received payment in goods their reasonable value or the proceeds of their resale shall be treated as payments for the purposes of subsection (2); but if the seller has notice of the buyer's breach before reselling goods received in part performance, his resale is subject to the conditions laid down in this Article on resale by an aggrieved seller (Section 2–706).

§ 2–719.   Contractual Modification or Limitation of Remedy

(1) Subject to the provisions of subsections (2) and (3) of this section and of the preceding section on liquidation and limitation of damages,

(a) the agreement may provide for remedies in addition to or in substitution for those provided in this Article and may limit or alter the measure of damages recoverable under this Article, as by limiting the buyer's remedies to return of the goods and repayment of the price or to repair and replacement of non-conforming goods or parts; and

(b) resort to a remedy as provided is optional unless the remedy is expressly agreed to be exclusive, in which case it is the sole remedy.

(2) Where circumstances cause an exclusive or limited remedy to fail of its essential purpose, remedy may be had as provided in this Act.

(3) Consequential damages may be limited or excluded unless the limitation or exclusion is unconscionable. Limitation of consequential damages for injury to the person in the case of consumer goods is prima facie unconscionable but limitation of damages where the loss is commercial is not.

§ 2–720.   Effect of "Cancellation" or "Rescission" on Claims for Antecedent Breach

Unless the contrary intention clearly appears, expressions of "cancellation" or "rescission" of the contract or the like shall not be construed as a renunciation or discharge of any claim in damages for an antecedent breach.

§ 2–721.   Remedies for Fraud

Remedies for material misrepresentation or fraud include all remedies available under this Article for nonfraudulent breach. Neither rescission or a claim for rescission of the contract for sale nor rejection or return of the goods shall bar or be deemed inconsistent with a claim for damages or other remedy.

§ 2–722.   Who Can Sue Third Parties for Injury to Goods

Where a third party so deals with goods which have been identified to a contract for sale as to cause actionable injury to a party to that contract

(a) a right of action against the third party is in either party to the contract for sale who has title to or a security interest or a special property or an insurable interest in the goods; and if the goods have been destroyed or converted a right of action is also in the party who either bore the risk of loss under the contract for sale or has since the injury assumed that risk as against the other;

(b) if at the time of the injury the party plaintiff did not bear the risk of loss as against the other party to the contract for sale and there is no arrangement between them for disposition of the recovery, his suit or settlement is, subject to his own interest, as a fiduciary for the other party to the contract;

(c) either party may with the consent of the other sue for the benefit of whom it may concern.

§ 2–723.   Proof of Market Price: Time and Place

(1) If an action based on anticipatory repudiation comes to trial before the time for performance with respect to some or all of the goods, any damages based on market price (Section 2–708 or Section 2–713) shall be determined according to the price of such goods prevailing at the time when the aggrieved party learned of the repudiation.

(2) If evidence of a price prevailing at the times or places described in this Article is not readily available the price prevailing within any reasonable time before or after the time described or at any other place which in commercial judgment or under usage of trade would serve as a reasonable substitute for the one described may be used, making any proper allowance for the cost of transporting the goods to or from such other place.

(3) Evidence of a relevant price prevailing at a time or place other than the one described in this Article offered by one party is not admissible unless and until he has given the other party such notice as the court finds sufficient to prevent unfair surprise.

§ 2–724.   Admissibility of Market Quotations

Whenever the prevailing price or value of any goods regularly bought and sold in any established commodity market is in issue, reports in official publications or trade journals or in newspapers or periodicals of general circulation published as the reports of such market shall be admissible in evidence. The circumstances of the preparation of such a report may be shown to affect its weight but not its admissibility.

2–725.   Statute of Limitations in Contracts for Sale

(1) An action for breach of any contract for sale must be commenced within four years after the cause of action has accrued. By the original agreement the parties may reduce

the period of limitation to not less than one year but may not extend it.

(2) A cause of action accrues when the breach occurs, regardless of the aggrieved party's lack of knowledge of the breach. A breach of warranty occurs when tender of delivery is made, except that where a warranty explicitly extends to future performance of the goods and discovery of the breach must await the time of such performance the cause of action accrues when the breach is or should have been discovered.

(3) Where an action commenced within the time limited by subsection (1) is so terminated as to leave available a remedy by another action for the same breach such other action may be commenced after the expiration of the time limited and within six months after the termination of the first action unless the termination resulted from voluntary discontinuance or from dismissal for failure or neglect to prosecute.

(4) This section does not alter the law on tolling of the statute of limitations nor does it apply to causes of action which have accrued before this Act becomes effective.

ARTICLE 3   COMMERCIAL PAPER

Part 1   Short Title, Form and Interpretation

§ 3–101.   Short Title

This Article shall be known and may be cited as Uniform Commercial Code—Commercial Paper.

§ 3–102.   Definitions and Index of Definitions

(1) In this Article unless the context otherwise requires

    (a) "Issue" means the first delivery of an instrument to a holder or a remitter.

    (b) An "order" is a direction to pay and must be more than an authorization or request. It must identify the person to pay with reasonable certainty. It may be addressed to one or more such persons jointly or in the alternative but not in succession.

    (c) A "promise" is an undertaking to pay and must be more than an acknowledgment of an obligation.

    (d) "Secondary party" means a drawer or endorser.

    (e) "Instrument" means a negotiable instrument.

(2) Other definitions applying to this Article and the sections in which they appear are:

    "Acceptance." Section 3–410.
    "Accommodation party." Section 3–415.
    "Alteration." Section 3–407.
    "Certificate of deposit." Section 3–104.
    "Certification." Section 3–411.
    "Check." Section 3–104.
    "Definite time." Section 3–109.
    "Dishonor." Section 3–507.
    "Draft." Section 3–104.

    "Holder in due course." Section 3–302.
    "Negotiation." Section 3–202.
    "Note." Section 3–104.
    "Notice of dishonor." Section 3–508.
    "On demand." Section 3–108.
    "Presentment." Section 3–504.
    "Protest." Section 3–509.
    "Restrictive Indorsement." Section 3–205.
    "Signature." Section 3–401.

(3) The following definitions in other Articles apply to this Article:

    "Account." Section 4–104.
    "Banking Day." Section 4–104.
    "Clearing house." Section 4–104.
    "Collecting bank." Section 4–105.
    "Customer." Section 4–104.
    "Depositary Bank." Section 4–105.
    "Documentary Draft." Section 4–104.
    "Intermediary Bank." Section 4–105.
    "Item." Section 4–104.
    "Midnight deadline." Section 4–104.
    "Payor bank." Section 4–105.

(4) In addition Article 1 contains general definitions and principles of construction and interpretation applicable throughout this Article.

§ 3–103.   Limitations on Scope of Article

(1) This Article does not apply to money, documents of title or investment securities.

(2) The provisions of this Article are subject to the provisions of the Article on Bank Deposits and Collections (Article 4) and Secured Transactions (Article 9).

§ 3–104.   Form of Negotiable Instruments; "Draft"; "Check "; "Certificate of Deposit"; "Note"

(1) Any writing to be a negotiable instrument within this Article must

    (a) be signed by the maker or drawer; and

    (b) contain an unconditional promise or order to pay a sum certain in money and no other promise, order, obligation or power given by the maker or drawer except as authorized by this Article; and

    (c) be payable on demand or at a definite time; and

    (d) be payable to order or to bearer.

(2) A writing which complies with the requirements of this section is

    (a) a "draft" ("bill of exchange") if it is an order;

    (b) a "check" if it is a draft drawn on a bank and payable on demand;

    (c) a "certificate of deposit" if it is an acknowledgment by a bank of receipt of money with an engagement to repay it;

    (d) a "note" if it is a promise other than a certificate of deposit.

(3) As used in other Articles of this Act, and as the context may require, the terms "draft," "check," "certificate of de-

posit" and "note" may refer to instruments which are not negotiable within this Article as well as to instruments which are so negotiable.

§ 3–105.   When Promise or Order Unconditional

(1) A promise or order otherwise unconditional is not made conditional by the fact that the instrument

(a) is subject to implied or constructive conditions; or

(b) states its consideration, whether performed or promised, or the transaction which gave rise to the instrument, or that the promise or order is made or the instrument matures in accordance with or "as per" such transaction; or

(c) refers to or states that it arises out of a separate agreement or refers to a separate agreement for rights as to repayment or acceleration; or

(d) states that it is drawn under a letter of credit; or

(e) states that it is secured, whether by mortgage, reservation of title or otherwise; or

(f) indicates a particular account to be debited or any other fund or source from which reimbursement is expected; or

(g) is limited to payment out of a particular fund or the proceeds of a particular source, if the instrument is issued by a government or governmental agency or unit; or

(h) is limited to payment out of the entire assets of a partnership, unincorporated association, trust or estate by or on behalf of which the instrument is issued.

(2) A promise or order is not unconditional if the instrument

(a) states that it is subject to or governed by any other agreement; or

(b) states that it is to be paid only out of a particular fund or source except as provided in this section.

§ 3–106.   Sum Certain

(1) The sum payable is a sum certain even though it is to be paid

(a) with stated interest or by stated installments; or

(b) with stated different rates of interest before and after default or a specified date; or

(c) with a stated discount or addition if paid before or after the date fixed for payment; or

(d) with exchange or less exchange, whether at a fixed rate or at the current rate; or

(e) with costs of collection or an attorney's fee or both upon default.

(2) Nothing in this section shall validate any term which is otherwise illegal.

§ 3–107.   Money

(1) An instrument is payable in money if the medium of exchange in which it is payable is money at the time the instrument is made. An instrument payable in "currency" or "current funds" is payable in money.

(2) A promise or order to pay a sum stated in a foreign currency is for a sum certain in money and, unless a different medium of payment is specified in the instrument, may be satisfied by payment of that number of dollars which the stated foreign currency will purchase at the buying sight rate for that currency on the day on which the instrument is payable or, if payable on demand, on the day of demand. If such an instrument specifies a foreign currency as the medium of payment the instrument is payable in that currency.

§ 3–108.   Payable on Demand

Instruments payable on demand include those payable at sight or on presentation and those in which no time for payment is stated.

§ 3–109.   Definite Time

(1) An instrument is payable at a definite time if by its terms it is payable

(a) on or before a stated date or at a fixed period after a stated date; or

(b) at a fixed period after sight; or

(c) at a definite time subject to any acceleration; or

(d) at a definite time subject to extension at the option of the holder, or to extension to a further definite time at the option of the maker or acceptor or automatically upon or after a specified act or event.

(2) An instrument which by its terms is otherwise payable only upon an act or event uncertain as to time of occurrence is not payable at a definite time even though the act or event has occurred.

§ 3–110.   Payable to Order

(1) An instrument is payable to order when by its terms it is payable to the order or assigns of any person therein specified with reasonable certainty, or to him or his order, or when it is conspicuously designated on its face as "exchange" or the like and names a payee. It may be payable to the order of

(a) the maker or drawer; or

(b) the drawee; or

(c) a payee who is not maker, drawer or drawee; or

(d) two or more payees together or in the alternative; or

(e) an estate, trust or fund, in which case it is payable to the order of the representative of such estate, trust or fund or his successors; or

(f) an office, or an officer by his title as such in which case it is payable to the principal but the incumbent of the office or his successors may act as if he or they were the holder; or

(g) a partnership or unincorporated association, in which case it is payable to the partnership or association and may be indorsed or transferred by any person thereto authorized.

(2) An instrument not payable to order is not made so payable by such words as "payable upon return of this instrument properly indorsed."

(3) An instrument made payable both to order and to bearer is payable to order unless the bearer words are handwritten or typewritten.

§ 3–111.   Payable to Bearer

An instrument is payable to bearer when by its terms it is payable to

(a) a bearer or the order of bearer; or

(b) a specified person or bearer; or

(c) "cash" or the order of "cash" or any other indication which does not purport to designate a specific payee.

§ 3–112.   Terms and Omissions Not Affecting Negotiability

(1) The negotiability of an instrument is not affected by

(a) the omission of a statement of any consideration or of the place where the instrument is drawn or payable; or

(b) a statement that collateral has been given to secure obligations either on the instrument or otherwise of an obligor on the instrument or that in case of default on those obligations the holder may realize on or dispose of the collateral; or

(c) a promise or power to maintain or protect collateral or to give additional collateral; or

(d) a term authorizing a confession of judgment on the instrument if it is not paid when due; or

(e) a term purporting to waive the benefit of any law intended for the advantage or protection of any obligor; or

(f) a term in a draft providing that the payee by indorsing or cashing it acknowledges full satisfaction of an obligation of the drawer; or

(g) a statement in a draft drawn in a set of parts (Section 3–801) to the effect that the order is effective only if no other part has been honored.

(2) Nothing in this section shall validate any term which is otherwise illegal.

§ 3–113.   Seal

An instrument otherwise negotiable is within this Article even though it is under a seal.

§ 3–114.   Date, Antedating, Postdating

(1) The negotiability of an instrument is not affected by the fact that it is undated, antedated or postdated.

(2) Where an instrument is antedated or postdated the time when it is payable is determined by the stated date if the instrument is payable on demand or at a fixed period after date.

(3) Where the instrument or any signature thereon is dated, the date is presumed to be correct.

§ 3–115.   Incomplete Instruments

(1) When a paper whose contents at the time of signing show that it is intended to become an instrument is signed while still incomplete in any necessary respect it cannot be enforced until completed, but when it is completed in accordance with authority given it is effective as completed.

(2) If the completion is unauthorized the rules as to material alteration apply (Section 3–407), even though the paper was not delivered by the maker or drawer; but the burden of establishing that any completion is unauthorized is on the party so asserting.

§ 3–116.   Instruments Payable to Two or More Persons

An instrument payable to the order of two or more persons

(a) if in the alternative is payable to any one of them and may be negotiated, discharged or enforced by any of them who has possession of it;

(b) if not in the alternative is payable to all of them and may be negotiated, discharged or enforced only by all of them.

§ 3–117.   Instruments Payable With Words of Description

An instrument made payable to a named person with the addition of words describing him

(a) as agent or officer of a specified person is payable to his principal but the agent or officer may act as if he were the holder;

(b) as any other fiduciary for a specified person or purpose is payable to the payee and may be negotiated, discharged or enforced by him;

(c) in any other manner is payable to the payee unconditionally and the additional words are without effect on subsequent parties.

§ 3–118.   Ambiguous Terms and Rules of Construction

The following rules apply to every instrument:

(a) Where there is doubt whether the instrument is a draft or a note the holder may treat it as either. A draft drawn on the drawer is effective as a note.

(b) Handwritten terms control typewritten and printed terms, and typewritten control printed.

(c) Words control figures except that if the words are ambiguous figures control.

(d) Unless otherwise specified a provision for interest means interest at the judgment rate at the place of payment from the date of the instrument, or if it is undated from the date of issue.

(e) Unless the instrument otherwise specifies two or more persons who sign as maker, acceptor or drawer or indorser and as a part of the same transaction are jointly and severally liable even though the instrument contains such words as "I promise to pay."

(f) Unless otherwise specified consent to extension authorizes a single extension for not longer than the original period. A consent to extension, expressed in the instrument, is binding on secondary parties and accommodation makers. A holder may not exercise his option to extend an instrument over the objection of a maker or acceptor or other party who in accordance with Section 3–604 tenders full payment when the instrument is due.

§ 3–119. Other Writings Affecting Instrument

(1) As between the obligor and his immediate obligee or any transferee the terms of an instrument may be modified or affected by any other written agreement executed as a part of the same transaction, except that a holder in due course is not affected by any limitation of his rights arising out of the separate written agreement if he had no notice of the limitation when he took the instrument.

(2) A separate agreement does not affect the negotiability of an instrument.

§ 3–120. Instruments "Payable Through" Bank

An instrument which states that it is "payable through" a bank or the like designates that bank as collecting bank to make presentment but does not of itself authorize the bank to pay the instrument.

§ 3–121. Instruments Payable at Bank

Note: If this Act is introduced in the Congress of the United States this section should be omitted. (States to select either alternative.)

Alternative A

A note or acceptance which states that it is payable at a bank is the equivalent of a draft drawn on the bank payable when it falls due out of any funds of the maker or acceptor in current account or otherwise available for such payment.

Alternative B

A note or acceptance which states that it is payable at a bank is not of itself an order or authorization to the bank to pay it.

§ 3–122. Accrual of Cause of Action

(1) A cause of action against a maker or an acceptor accrues
    (a) in the case of a time instrument on the day after maturity;
    (b) in the case of a demand instrument upon its date or, if no date is stated, on the date of issue.

(2) A cause of action against the obligor of a demand or time certificate of deposit accrues upon demand, but demand on a time certificate may not be made until on or after the date of maturity.

(3) A cause of action against a drawer of a draft or an indorser of any instrument accrues upon demand following dishonor of the instrument. Notice of dishonor is a demand.

(4) Unless an instrument provides otherwise, interest runs at the rate provided by law for a judgment
    (a) in the case of a maker, acceptor or other primary obligor of a demand instrument, from the date of demand;
    (b) in all other cases from the date of accrual of the cause of action.

Part 2 Transfer and Negotiation

§ 3–201. Transfer: Right to Indorsement

(1) Transfer of an instrument vests in the transferee such rights as the transferor has therein, except that a transferee who has himself been a party to any fraud or illegality affecting the instrument or who as a prior holder had notice of a defense or claim against it cannot improve his position by taking from a later holder in due course.

(2) A transfer of a security interest in an instrument vests the foregoing rights in the transferee to the extent of the interest transferred.

(3) Unless otherwise agreed any transfer for value of an instrument not then payable to bearer gives the transferee the specifically enforceable right to have the unqualified indorsement of the transferor. Negotiation takes effect only when the indorsement is made and until that time there is no presumption that the transferee is the owner.

§ 3–202. Negotiation

(1) Negotiation is the transfer of an instrument in such form that the transferee becomes a holder. If the instrument is payable to order it is negotiated by delivery with any necessary indorsement; if payable to bearer it is negotiated by delivery.

(2) An indorsement must be written by or on behalf of the holder and on the instrument or on a paper so firmly affixed thereto as to become a part thereof.

(3) An indorsement is effective for negotiation only when it conveys the entire instrument or any unpaid residue. If it purports to be of less it operates only as a partial assignment.

(4) Words of assignment, condition, waiver, guaranty, limitation or disclaimer of liability and the like accompanying an indorsement do not affect its character as an indorsement.

§ 3–203. Wrong or Misspelled Name

Where an instrument is made payable to a person under a misspelled name or one other than his own he may indorse in that name or his own or both; but signature in both names may be required by a person paying or giving value for the instrument.

§ 3–204. Special Indorsement; Blank Indorsement

(1) A special indorsement specifies the person to whom or to whose order it makes the instrument payable. Any instrument specially indorsed becomes payable to the order of the special indorsee and may be further negotiated by his indorsement.

(2) An indorsement in blank specifies no particular indorsee and may consist of a mere signature. An instrument payable to order and indorsed in blank becomes payable to bearer and may be negotiated by delivery alone until specially indorsed.

(3) The holder may convert a blank indorsement into a special indorsement by writing over the signature of the indorser in blank any contract consistent with the character of the indorsement.

§ 3–205.   Restrictive Indorsements

An indorsement is restrictive which either

(a) is conditional; or

(b) purports to prohibit further transfer of the instrument; or

(c) includes the words "for collection," "for deposit," "pay any bank," or like terms signifying a purpose of deposit or collection; or

(d) otherwise states that it is for the benefit or use of the indorser or of another person.

§ 3–206.   Effect of Restrictive Indorsement

(1) No restrictive indorsement prevents further transfer or negotiation of the instrument.

(2) An intermediary bank, or a payor bank which is not the depositary bank, is neither given notice nor otherwise affected by a restrictive indorsement of any person except the bank's immediate transferor or the person presenting for payment.

(3) Except for an intermediary bank, any transferee under an indorsement which is conditional or includes the words "for collection," "for deposit," "pay any bank," or like terms (subparagraphs (a) and (c) of Section 3–205) must pay or apply any value given by him for or on security of the instrument consistently with the indorsement and to the extent that he does so he becomes a holder for value. In addition such transferee is a holder in due course if he otherwise complies with the requirements of Section 3–302 on what constitutes a holder in due course.

(4) The first taker under an indorsement for the benefit of the indorser or another person (subparagraph (d) of Section 3–205) must pay or apply any value given by him for or on the security of the instrument consistently with the indorsement and to the extent that he does so he becomes a holder for value. In addition such taker is a holder in due course if he otherwise complies with the requirements of Section 3–302 on what constitutes a holder in due course. A later holder for value is neither given notice nor otherwise affected by such restrictive indorsement unless he has knowledge that a fiduciary or other person has negotiated the instrument in any transaction for his own benefit or otherwise in breach of duty (subsection (2) of Section 3–304).

§ 3–207.   Negotiation Effective Although It May Be Rescinded

(1) Negotiation is effective to transfer the instrument although the negotiation is

(a) made by an infant, a corporation exceeding its powers, or any other person without capacity; or

(b) obtained by fraud, duress or mistake of any kind; or

(c) part of an illegal transaction; or

(d) made in breach of duty.

(2) Except as against a subsequent holder in due course such negotiation is in an appropriate case subject to rescission, the declaration of a constructive trust or any other remedy permitted by law.

§ 3–208.   Reacquisition

Where an instrument is returned to or reacquired by a prior party he may cancel any indorsement which is not necessary to his title and reissue or further negotiate the instrument, but any intervening party is discharged as against the reacquiring party and subsequent holders not n due course and if his indorsement has been cancelled is discharged as against subsequent holders in due course as well.

Part 3   Rights of a Holder

§ 3–301.   Rights of a Holder

The holder of an instrument whether or not he is the owner may transfer or negotiate it and, except as otherwise provided in Section 3–603 on payment or satisfaction, discharge it or enforce payment in his own name.

§ 3–302.   Holder in Due Course

(1) A holder in due course is a holder who takes the instrument

(a) for value, and

(b) in good faith; and

(c) without notice that it is overdue or has been dishonored or of any defense against or claim to it on the part of any person.

(2) A payee may be a holder in due course.

(3) A holder does not become a holder in due course of an instrument:

(a) by purchase of it at judicial sale or by taking it under legal process; or

(b) by acquiring it in taking over an estate; or

(c) by purchasing it as part of a bulk transaction not in regular course of business of the transferor.

(4) A purchaser of a limited interest can be a holder in due course only to the extent of the interest purchased.

§ 3–303.   Taking for Value

A holder takes the instrument for value

(a) to the extent that the agreed consideration has been performed or that he acquires a security interest in or a lien on the instrument otherwise than by legal process; or

(b) when he takes the instrument in payment of or as security for an antecedent claim against any person whether or not the claim is due; or

(c) when he gives a negotiable instrument for it or makes an irrevocable commitment to a third person.

§ 3–304.   Notice to Purchaser

(1) The purchaser has notice of a claim or defense if

(a) the instrument is so incomplete, bears such visible evidence of forgery or alteration, or is otherwise so irregular as to call into question its validity, terms or ownership or to create an ambiguity as to the party to pay; or

(b) the purchaser has notice that the obligation of any party is voidable in whole or in part, or that all parties have been discharged.

(2) The purchaser has notice of a claim against the instrument when he has knowledge that a fiduciary has negotiated the instrument in payment of or as security for his own debt or in any transaction for his own benefit or otherwise in breach of duty.

(3) The purchaser has notice that an instrument is overdue if he has reason to know

(a) that any part of the principal amount is overdue or that there is an uncured default in payment of another instrument of the same series; or

(b) that acceleration of the instrument has been made; or

(c) that he is taking a demand instrument after demand has been made or more than a reasonable length of time after its issue. A reasonable time for a check drawn and payable within the states and territories of the United States and the District of Columbia is presumed to be thirty days.

(4) Knowledge of the following facts does not of itself give the purchaser notice of a defense or claim

(a) that the instrument is antedated or postdated;

(b) that it was issued or negotiated in return for an executory promise or accompanied by a separate agreement, unless the purchaser has notice that a defense or claim has arisen from the terms thereof;

(c) that any party has signed for accommodation;

(d) that an incomplete instrument has been completed, unless the purchaser has notice of any improper completion;

(e) that any person negotiating the instrument is or was a fiduciary;

(f) that there has been default in payment of interest on the instrument or in payment of any other instrument, except one of the same series.

(5) The filing or recording of a document does not of itself constitute notice within the provisions of this Article to a person who would otherwise be a holder in due course.

(6) To be effective notice must be received at such time and in such manner as to give a reasonable opportunity to act on it.

§ 3–305. Rights of a Holder in Due Course

To the extent that a holder is a holder in due course he takes the instrument free from

(1) all claims to it on the part of any person; and

(2) all defenses of any party to the instrument with whom the holder has not dealt except

(a) infancy, to the extent that it is a defense to a simple contract; and

(b) such other incapacity, or duress, or illegality of the transaction, as renders the obligation of the party a nullity; and

(c) such misrepresentation as has induced the party to sign the instrument with neither knowledge nor reasonable opportunity to obtain knowledge of its character or its essential terms; and

(d) discharge in insolvency proceedings; and

(e) any other discharge of which the holder has notice when he takes the instrument.

§ 3–306. Rights of One Not Holder in Due Course

Unless he has the rights of a holder in due course any person takes the instrument subject to

(a) all valid claims to it on the part of any person; and

(b) all defenses of any party which would be available in an action on a simple contract; and

(c) the defenses of want or failure of consideration, non-performance of any condition precedent, non-delivery, or delivery for a special purpose (Section 3–408); and

(d) the defense that he or a person through whom he holds the instrument acquired it by theft, or that payment or satisfaction to such holder would be inconsistent with the terms of a restrictive indorsement. The claim of any third person to the instrument is not otherwise available as a defense to any party liable thereon unless the third person himself defends the action for such party.

§ 3–307. Burden of Establishing Signatures, Defenses and Due Course

(1) Unless specifically denied in the pleadings each signature on an instrument is admitted. When the effectiveness of a signature is put in issue

(a) the burden of establishing it is on the party claiming under the signature; but

(b) the signature is presumed to be genuine or authorized except where the action is to enforce the obligation of a purported signer who has died or become incompetent before proof is required.

(2) When signatures are admitted or established, production of the instrument entitles a holder to recover on it unless the defendant establishes a defense.

(3) After it is shown that a defense exists a person claiming the rights of a holder in due course has the burden of establishing that he or some person under whom he claims is in all respects a holder in due course.

Part 4 Liability of Parties

§ 3–401. Signature

(1) No person is liable on an instrument unless his signature appears thereon.

(2) A signature is made by use of any name, including any trade or assumed name, upon an instrument, or by any word or mark used in lieu of a written signature.

§ 3–402.   Signature in Ambiguous Capacity

Unless the instrument clearly indicates that a signature is made in some other capacity it is an indorsement.

§ 3–403.   Signature by Authorized Representative

(1) A signature may be made by an agent or other representative, and his authority to make it may be established as in other cases of representation. No particular form of appointment is necessary to establish such authority.

(2) An authorized representative who signs his own name to an instrument

(a) is personally obligated if the instrument neither names the person represented nor shows that the representative signed in a representative capacity;

(b) except as otherwise established between the immediate parties, is personally obligated if the instrument names the person represented but does not show that the representative signed in a representative capacity.

(3) Except as otherwise established the name of an organization preceded or followed by the name and office of an authorized individual is a signature made in a representative capacity.

§ 3–404.   Unauthorized Signatures

(1) Any unauthorized signature is wholly inoperative as that of the person whose name is signed unless he ratifies it or is precluded from denying it; but it operates as the signature of the unauthorized signer in favor of any person who in good faith pays the instrument or takes it for value.

(2) Any unauthorized signature may be ratified for all purposes of this Article. Such ratification does not of itself affect any rights of the person ratifying against the actual signer.

§ 3–405.   Imposters; Signature in Name of Payee

(1) An indorsement by any person in the name of a named payee is effective if

(a) an imposter by use of the mails or otherwise has induced the maker or drawer to issue the instrument to him or his confederate in the name of the payee; or

(b) a person signing as or on behalf of a maker or drawer intends the payee to have no interest in the instrument; or

(c) an agent or employee of the maker or drawer has supplied him with the name of the payee intending the latter to have no such interest.

(2) Nothing in this section shall affect the criminal or civil liability of the person so indorsing.

§ 3–406.   Negligence Contributing to Alteration or Unauthorized Signature

Any person who by his negligence substantially contributes to a material alteration of the instrument or to the making of an unauthorized signature is precluded from asserting the alteration or lack of authority against a holder in due course or against a drawee or other payor who pays the instrument in good faith and in accordance with the reasonable commercial standards of the drawee's or payor's business.

§ 3–407.   Alteration

(1) Any alteration of an instrument is material which changes the contract of any party thereto in any respect, including any such change in

(a) the number or relations of the parties; or

(b) an incomplete instrument, by completing it otherwise than as authorized; or

(c) the writing as signed, by adding to it or by removing any part of it.

(2) As against any person other than a subsequent holder in due course.

(a) alteration by the holder which is both fraudulent and material discharges any party whose contract is thereby changed unless that party assents or is precluded from asserting the defense.

(b) no other alteration discharges any party and the instrument may be enforced according to its original tenor, or as to incomplete instruments according to the authority given.

(3) A subsequent holder in due course may in all cases enforce the instrument according to its original tenor, and when an incomplete instrument has been completed, he may enforce it as completed.

§ 3–408.   Consideration

Want or failure of consideration is a defense as against any person not having the rights of a holder in due course (Section 3–305), except that no consideration is necessary for an instrument or obligation thereon given in payment of or as security for an antecedent obligation of any kind. Nothing in this section shall be taken to displace any statute outside this Act under which a promise is enforceable notwithstanding lack or failure of consideration. Partial failure of consideration is a defense pro tanto whether or not the failure is in an ascertained or liquidated amount.

§ 3–409.   Draft Not an Assignment

(1) A check or other draft does not of itself operate as an assignment of any funds in the hands of the drawee available for its payment, and the drawee is not liable on the instrument until he accepts it.

(2) Nothing in this section shall affect any liability in contract, tort or otherwise arising from any letter of credit or other obligation or representation which is not an acceptance.

§ 3–410.   Definition and Operation of Acceptance

(1) Acceptance is the drawee's signed engagement to honor the draft as presented. It must be written on the draft, and may consist of his signature alone. It becomes operative when completed by delivery or notification.

(2) A draft may be accepted although it has not been signed by the drawer or is otherwise incomplete or is overdue or has been dishonored.

(3) Where the draft is payable at a fixed period after sight and the acceptor fails to date his acceptance the holder may complete it by supplying a date in good faith.

§ 3–411. Certification of a Check

(1) Certification of a check is acceptance. Where a holder procures certification the drawer and all prior indorsers are discharged.

(2) Unless otherwise agreed a bank has no obligation to certify a check.

(3) A bank may certify a check before returning it for lack of proper indorsement. If it does so the drawer is discharged.

§ 3–412. Acceptance Varying Draft

(1) Where the drawee's proffered acceptance in any manner varies the draft as presented the holder may refuse the acceptance and treat the draft as dishonored in which case the drawee is entitled to have his acceptance cancelled.

(2) The terms of the draft are not varied by an acceptance to pay at any particular bank or place in the United States, unless the acceptance states that the draft is to be paid only at such bank or place.

(3) Where the holder assents to an acceptance varying the terms of the draft each drawer and indorser who does not affirmatively assent is discharged.

§ 3–413. Contract of Maker, Drawer and Acceptor

(1) The maker or acceptor engages that he will pay the instrument according to its tenor at the time of his engagement or as completed pursuant to Section 3–115 on incomplete instruments.

(2) The drawer engages that upon dishonor of the draft and any necessary notice of dishonor or protest he will pay the amount of the draft to the holder or to any indorser who takes it up. The drawer may disclaim this liability by drawing without recourse.

(3) By making, drawing or accepting the party admits as against all subsequent parties including the drawee the existence of the payee and his then capacity to indorse.

§ 3–414. Contract of Indorser; Order of Liability

(1) Unless the indorsement otherwise specifies (as by such words as "without recourse") every indorser engages that upon dishonor and any necessary notice of dishonor and protest he will pay the instrument according to its tenor at the time of his indorsement to the holder or to any subsequent indorser who takes it up, even though the indorser who takes it up was not obligated to do so.

(2) Unless they otherwise agree indorsers are liable to one another in the order in which they indorse, which is presumed to be the order in which their signatures appear on the instrument.

§ 3–415. Contract of Accommodation Party

(1) An accommodation party is one who signs the instrument in any capacity for the purpose of lending his name to another party to it.

(2) When the instrument has been taken for value before it is due the accommodation party is liable in the capacity in which he has signed even though the taker knows of the accommodation.

(3) As against a holder in due course and without notice of the accommodation oral proof of the accommodation is not admissible to give the accommodation party the benefit of discharges dependent on his character as such. In other cases the accommodation character may be shown by oral proof.

(4) An indorsement which shows that it is not in the chain of title is notice of its accommodation character.

(5) An accommodation party is not liable to the party accommodated, and if he pays the instrument has a right of recourse on the instrument against such party.

§ 3–416. Contract of Guarantor

(1) "Payment guaranteed" or equivalent words added to a signature mean that the signer engages that if the instrument is not paid when due he will pay it according to its tenor without resort by the holder to any other party.

(2) "Collection guaranteed" or equivalent words added to a signature mean that the signer engages that if the instrument is not paid when due he will pay it according to its tenor, but only after the holder has reduced his claim against the maker or acceptor to judgment and execution has been returned unsatisfied, or after the maker or acceptor has become insolvent or it is otherwise apparent that it is useless to proceed against him.

(3) Words of guaranty which do not otherwise specify guarantee payment.

(4) No words of guaranty added to the signature of a sole maker or acceptor affect his liability on the instrument. Such words added to the signature of one of two or more makers or acceptors create a presumption that the signature is for the accommodation of the others.

(5) When words of guaranty are used presentment, notice of dishonor and protest are not necessary to charge the user.

(6) Any guaranty written on the instrument is enforcible notwithstanding any statute of frauds.

§ 3–417. Warranties on Presentment and Transfer

(1) Any person who obtains payment or acceptance and any prior transferor warrants to a person who in good faith pays or accepts that

    (a) he has a good title to the instrument or is authorized to obtain payment or acceptance on behalf of one who has a good title; and

(b) he has no knowledge that the signature of the maker or drawer is unauthorized, except that this warranty is not given by a holder in due course acting in good faith

(i) to a maker with respect to the maker's own signature; or

(ii) to a drawer with respect to the drawer's own signature, whether or not the drawer is also the drawee; or

(iii) to an acceptor of a draft if the holder in due course took the draft after the acceptance or obtained the acceptance without knowledge that the drawer's signature was unauthorized; and

(c) the instrument has not been materially altered, except that this warranty is not given by a holder in due course acting in good faith

(i) to the maker of a note; or

(ii) to the drawer of a draft whether or not the drawer is also the drawee; or

(iii) to the acceptor of a draft with respect to an alteration made prior to the acceptance if the holder in due course took the draft after the acceptance, even though the acceptance provided "payable as originally drawn" or equivalent terms; or

(iv) to the acceptor of a draft with respect to an alteration made after the acceptance.

(2) Any person who transfers an instrument and receives consideration warrants to his transferee and if the transfer is by indorsement to any subsequent holder who takes the instrument in good faith that

(a) he has a good title to the instrument or is authorized to obtain payment or acceptance on behalf of one who has a good title and the transfer is otherwise rightful; and

(b) all signatures are genuine or authorized; and

(c) the instrument has not been materially altered; and

(d) no defense of any part is good against him; and

(e) he has no knowledge of any insolvency proceeding instituted with respect to the maker or acceptor or the drawer of an unaccepted instrument.

(3) By transferring "without recourse" the transferor limits the obligation stated in subsection (2)(d) to a warranty that he has no knowledge of such a defense.

(4) A selling agent or broker who does not disclose the fact that he is acting only as such gives the warranties provided in this section, but if he makes such disclosure warrants only his good faith and authority.

§ 3–418.   Finality of Payment or Acceptance

Except for recovery of bank payments as provided in the Article on Bank Deposits and Collections (Article 4) and except for liability for breach of warranty on presentment under the preceding section, payment or acceptance of any instrument is final in favor of a holder in due course, or a person who has in good faith changed his position in reliance on the payment.

§ 3–419.   Conversion of Instrument; Innocent Representative

(1) An instrument is converted when

(a) a drawee to whom it is delivered for acceptance refuses to return it on demand; or

(b) any person to whom it is delivered for payment refuses on demand either to pay or to return it; or

(c) it is paid on a forged indorsement.

(2) In an action against a drawee under subsection (1) the measure of the drawee's liability is the face amount of the instrument. In any other action under subsection (1) the measure of liability is presumed to be the face amount of the instrument.

(3) Subject to the provisions of this Act concerning restrictive indorsements a representative, including a deposit ary or collecting bank, who has in good faith and in accordance with the reasonable commercial standards applicable to the business of such representative dealt with an instrument or its proceeds on behalf of one who was not the true owner is not liable in conversion or otherwise to the true owner beyond the amount of any proceeds remaining in his hands.

(4) An intermediary bank or payor bank which is not a depositary bank is not liable in conversion solely by reason of the fact that proceeds of an item indorsed restrictively (Sections 3–205 and 3–206) are not paid or applied consistently with the restrictive indorsement of an indorser other than its immediate transferor.

Part 5   Presentment, Notice of Dishonor and Protest

§ 3–501.   When Presentment, Notice of Dishonor, and Protest Necessary or Permissible

(1) Unless excused (Section 3–511) presentment is necessary to charge secondary parties as follows:

(a) presentment for acceptance is necessary to charge the drawer and indorsers of a draft where the draft so provides, or is payable elsewhere than at the residence or place of business of the drawee, or its date of payment depends upon such presentment. The holder may at his option present for acceptance any other draft payable at a stated date:

(b) presentment for payment is necessary to charge any indorser;

(c) in the case of any drawer, the acceptor of a draft payable at a bank or the maker of a note payable at a bank, presentment for payment is necessary, but failure to make presentment discharges such drawer, acceptor or maker only as stated in Section 3–502(1)(b).

(2) Unless excused (Section 3–511)

(a) notice of any dishonor is necessary to charge any indorser;

(b) in the case of any drawer, the acceptor of a draft payable at a bank or the maker of a note payable at a bank, notice of any dishonor is necessary, but failure to give such notice discharges such drawer, acceptor or maker only as stated in Section 3–502(1)(b).

(3) Unless excused (Section 3–511) protest of any dishonor is necessary to charge the drawer and indorsers of any draft which on its face appears to be drawn or payable outside of the states, territories, dependencies and possessions of the United States, the District of Columbia and the Commonwealth of Puerto Rico. The holder may at his option make protest of any dishonor of any other instrument and in the case of a foreign draft may on insolvency of the acceptor before maturity make protest for better security.

(4) Notwithstanding any provision of this section, neither presentment nor notice of dishonor nor protest is necessary to charge an indorser who has indorsed an instrument after maturity.

§ 3–502.   Unexcused Delay; Discharge

(1) Where without excuse any necessary presentment or notice of dishonor is delayed beyond the time when it is due

(a) any indorser is discharged; and

(b) any drawer or the acceptor of a draft payable at a bank or the maker of a note payable at a bank who because the drawee or payor bank becomes insolvent during the delay is deprived of funds maintained with the drawee or payor bank to cover the instrument may discharge his liability by written assignment to the holder of his rights against the drawee or payor bank in respect of such funds, but such drawer, acceptor or maker is not otherwise discharged.

(2) Where without excuse a necessary protest is delayed beyond the time when it is due any drawer or indorser is discharged.

§ 3–503.   Time of Presentment

(1) Unless a different time is expressed in the instrument the time for any presentment is determined as follows:

(a) where an instrument is payable at or a fixed period after a stated date any presentment for acceptance must be made on or before the date it is payable;

(b) where an instrument is payable after sight it must either be presented for acceptance or negotiated within a reasonable time after date or issue whichever is later;

(c) where an instrument shows the date on which it is payable presentment for payment is due on that date;

(d) where an instrument is accelerated presentment for payment is due within a reasonable time after the acceleration;

(e) with respect to the liability of any secondary party presentment for acceptance or payment of any other instrument is due within a reasonable time after such party becomes liable thereon.

(2) A reasonable time for presentment is determined by the nature of the instrument, any usage of banking or trade and the facts of the particular case. In the case of an uncertified check which is drawn and payable within the United States and which is not a draft drawn by a bank the following are presumed to be reasonable periods within which to present for payment or to initiate bank collection:

(a) with respect to the liability of the drawer, thirty days after date or issue whichever is later; and

(b) with respect to the liability of an indorser, seven days after his indorsement.

(3) Where any presentment is due on a day which is not a full business day for either the person making presentment or the party to pay or accept, presentment is due on the next following day which is a full business day for both parties.

(4) Presentment to be sufficient must be made at a reasonable hour, and if at a bank during its banking day.

§ 3–504.   How Presentment Made

(1) Presentment is a demand for acceptance or payment made upon the maker, acceptor, drawee or other payor by or on behalf of the holder.

(2) Presentment may be made

(a) by mail, in which event the time of presentment is determined by the time of receipt of the mail; or

(b) through a clearing house; or

(c) at the place of acceptance or payment specified in the instrument or if there be none at the place of business or residence of the party to accept or pay. If neither the party to accept or pay nor anyone authorized to act for him is present or accessible at such place presentment is excused.

(3) It may be made

(a) to any one of two or more makers, acceptors, drawees or other payors; or

(b) to any person who has authority to make or refuse the acceptance or payment.

(4) A draft accepted or a note made payable at a bank in the United States must be presented at such bank.

(5) In the cases described in Section 4–210 presentment may be made in the manner and with the result stated in that section.

§ 3–505.   Rights of Party to Whom Presentment Is Made

(1) The party to whom presentment is made may without dishonor require

(a) exhibition of the instrument; and

(b) reasonable identification of the person making presentment and evidence of his authority to make it if made for another; and

(c) that the instrument be produced for acceptance or payment at a place specified in it, or if there be none at any place reasonable in the circumstances; and

(d) a signed receipt on the instrument for any partial or full payment and its surrender upon full payment.

(2) Failure to comply with any such requirement invalidates the presentment but the person presenting has a reasonable

time in which to comply and the time for acceptance or payment runs from the time of compliance.

§ 3–506. Time Allowed for Acceptance or Payment

(1) Acceptance may be deferred without dishonor until the close of the next business day following presentment. The holder may also in a good faith effort to obtain acceptance and without either dishonor of the instrument or discharge of secondary parties allow postponement of acceptance for an additional business day.

(2) Except as a long time is allowed in the case of documentary drafts drawn under a letter of credit, and unless an earlier time is agreed to by the party to pay, payment of an instrument may be deferred without dishonor pending reasonable examination to determine whether it is properly payable, but payment must be made in any event before the close of business on the day of presentment.

§ 3–507. Dishonor; Holder's Right of Recourse; Term Allowing Re–Presentment

(1) An instrument is dishonored when

(a) a necessary or optional presentment is duly made and due acceptance or payment is refused or cannot be obtained within the prescribed time or in case of bank collections the instrument is seasonably returned by the midnight deadline (Section 4–301); or

(b) presentment is excused and the instrument is not duly accepted or paid.

(2) Subject to any necessary notice of dishonor and protest, the holder has upon dishonor an immediate right of recourse against the drawers and indorsers.

(3) Return of an instrument for lack of proper indorsement is not dishonor.

(4) A term in a draft or an indorsement thereof allowing a stated time for representment in the event of any dishonor of the draft by nonacceptance if a time draft or by nonpayment if a sight draft gives the holder as against any secondary party bound by the term an option to waive the dishonor without affecting liability of the secondary party and he may present again up to the end of the stated time.

§ 3–508. Notice of Dishonor

(1) Notice of dishonor may be given to any person who may be liable on the instrument by or on behalf of the holder or any party who has himself received notice, or any other party who can be compelled to pay the instrument. In addition an agent or bank in whose hands the instrument is dishonored may give notice to his principal or customer or to another agent or bank from which the instrument was received.

(2) Any necessary notice must be given by a bank before its midnight deadline and by any other person before midnight of the third business day after dishonor or receipt of notice of dishonor.

(3) Notice may be given in any reasonable manner. It may be oral or written and in any terms which identify the instrument and state that it has been dishonored. A misdescription which does not mislead the party notified does not vitiate the notice. Sending the instrument bearing a stamp, ticket or writing stating that acceptance or payment has been refused or sending a notice of debit with respect to the instrument is sufficient.

(4) Written notice is given when sent although it is not received.

(5) Notice to one partner is notice to each although the firm has been dissolved.

(6) When any party is in insolvency proceedings instituted after the issue of the instrument notice may be given either to the party or to the representative of his estate.

(7) When any party is dead or incompetent notice may be sent to his last known address or given to his personal representative.

(8) Notice operates for the benefit of all parties who have rights on the instrument against the party notified.

§ 3–509. Protest; Noting for Protest

(1) A protest is a certificate of dishonor made under the hand and seal of a United States consul or vice consul or a notary public or other person authorized to certify dishonor by the law of the place where dishonor occurs. It may be made upon information satisfactory to such person.

(2) The protest must identify the instrument and certify either that due presentment has been made or the reason why it is excused and that the instrument has been dishonored by nonacceptance or nonpayment.

(3) The protest may also certify that notice of dishonor has been given to all parties or to specified parties.

(4) Subject to subsection (5) any necessary protest is due by the time that notice of dishonor is due.

(5) If, before protest is due, an instrument has been noted for protest by the officer to make protest, the protest may be made at any time thereafter as of the date of the noting.

§ 3–510. Evidence of Dishonor and Notice of Dishonor

The following are admissible as evidence and create a presumption of dishonor and of any notice of dishonor therein shown:

(a) a document regular in form as provided in the preceding section which purports to be a protest;

(b) the purported stamp or writing of the drawee, payor bank or presenting bank on the instrument or accompanying it stating that acceptance or payment has been refused for reasons consistent with dishonor;

(c) any book or record of the drawee, payor bank, or any collecting bank kept in the usual course of business which shows dishonor, even though there is no evidence of who made the entry.

§ 3–511. Waived or Excused Presentment, Protest or Notice of Dishonor or Delay Therein

(1) Delay in presentment, protest or notice of dishonor is excused when the party is without notice that it is due or when the delay is caused by circumstances beyond his control and he exercises reasonable diligence after the cause of the delay ceases to operate.

(2) Presentment or notice or protest as the case may be is entirely excused when

(a) the party to be charged has waived it expressly or by implication either before or after it is due; or

(b) such party has himself dishonored the instrument or has countermanded payment or otherwise has no reason to expect or right to require that the instrument be accepted or paid; or

(c) by reasonable diligence the presentment or protest cannot be made or the notice given.

(3) Presentment is also entirely excused when

(a) the maker, acceptor, or drawee of any instrument except a documentary draft is dead or in insolvency proceedings instituted after the issue of the instrument; or

(b) acceptance or payment is refused but not for want of proper presentment.

(4) Where a draft has been dishonored by nonacceptance a later presentment for payment and any notice of dishonor and protest for nonpayment are excused unless in the meantime the instrument has been accepted.

(5) A waiver of protest is also a waiver of presentment and of notice of dishonor even though protest is not required.

(6) Where a waiver of presentment or notice or protest is embodied in the instrument itself it is binding upon all parties; but where it is written above the signature of an indorser it binds him only.

Part 6 Discharge

§ 3–601. Discharge of Parties

(1) The extent of the discharge of any party from liability on an instrument is governed by the sections on

(a) payment or satisfaction (Section 3–603); or

(b) tender of payment (Section 3–604); or

(c) cancellation or renunciation (Section 3–605); or

(d) impairment of right of recourse or of collateral (Section 3–606); or

(e) reacquisition of the instrument by a prior party (Section 3–208); or

(f) fraudulent and material alteration (Section 3–407); or

(g) certification of a check (Section 3–411); or

(h) acceptance varying a draft (Section 3–412); or

(i) unexcused delay in presentment or notice of dishonor or protest (Section 3–502).

(2) Any party is also discharged from his liability on an instrument to another party by any other act or agreement with such party which would discharge his simple contract for the payment of money.

(3) The liability of all parties is discharged when any party who has himself no right of action or recourse on the instrument

(a) reacquires the instrument in his own right; or

(b) is discharged under any provision of this Article, except as otherwise provided with respect to discharge for impairment of recourse or of collateral (Section 3–606).

§ 3–602. Effect of Discharge Against Holder in Due Course

No discharge of any party provided by this Article is effective against a subsequent holder in due course unless he has notice thereof when he takes the instrument.

§ 3–603. Payment or Satisfaction

(1) The liability of any party is discharged to the extent of his payment or satisfaction to the holder even though it is made with knowledge of a claim of another person to the instrument unless prior to such payment or satisfaction the person making the claim either supplies indemnity deemed adequate by the party seeking the discharge or enjoins payment or satisfaction by order of a court of competent jurisdiction in an action in which the adverse claimant and the holder are parties. This subsection does not, however, result in the discharge of the liability.

(a) of a party who in bad faith pays or satisfies a holder who acquired the instrument by theft or who (unless having the rights of a holder in due course) holds through one who so acquired it; or

(b) of a party (other than an intermediary bank or a payor bank which is not a depositary bank) who pays or satisfies the holder of an instrument which has been restrictively indorsed in a manner not consistent with the terms of such restrictive indorsement.

(2) Payment or satisfaction may be made with the consent of the holder by any person including a stranger to the instrument. Surrender of the instrument to such a person gives him the rights of a transferee (Section 3–201).

§ 3–604. Tender of Payment

(1) Any party making tender of full payment to a holder when or after it is due is discharged to the extent of all subsequent liability for interest, costs and attorney's fees.

(2) The holder's refusal of such tender wholly discharges any party who has a right of recourse against the party making the tender.

(3) Where the maker or acceptor of an instrument payable otherwise than on demand is able and ready to pay at every place of payment specified in the instrument when it is due, it is equivalent to tender.

§ 3–605.   Cancellation and Renunciation

(1) The holder of an instrument may even without consideration discharge any party

(a) in any manner apparent on the face of the instrument or the indorsement, as by intentionally cancelling the instrument or the party's signature by destruction or mutilation, or by striking out the party's signature; or

(b) by renouncing his rights by a writing signed and delivered or by surrender of the instrument to the party to be discharged.

(2) Neither cancellation nor renunciation without surrender of the instrument affects the title thereto.

§ 3–606.   Impairment of Recourse or of Collateral

(1) The holder discharges any party to the instrument to the extent that without such party's consent the holder

(a) without express reservation of rights releases or agrees not to sue any person against whom the party has to the knowledge of the holder a right of recourse or agrees to suspend the right to enforce against such person the instrument or collateral or otherwise discharges such person, except that failure or delay in effecting any required presentment, protest or notice of dishonor with respect to any such person does not discharge any party as to whom presentment, protest or notice of dishonor is effective or unnecessary; or

(b) unjustifiably impairs any collateral for the instrument given by or on behalf of the party or any person against whom he has a right of recourse.

(2) By express reservation of rights against a party with a right of recourse the holder preserves

(a) all his rights against such party as of the time when the instrument was originally due; and

(b) the right of the party to pay the instrument as of that time; and

(c) all rights of such party to recourse against others.

Part 7   Advice of International Sight Draft

§ 3–701.   Letter of Advice of International Sight Draft

(1) A "letter of advice" is a drawer's communication to the drawee that a described draft has been drawn.

(2) Unless otherwise agreed when a bank receives from another bank a letter of advice of an international sight draft the drawee bank may immediately debit the drawer's account and stop the running of interest pro tanto. Such a debit and any resulting credit to any account covering outstanding drafts leaves in the drawer full power to stop payment or otherwise dispose of the amount and creates no trust or interest in favor of the holder.

(3) Unless otherwise agreed and except where a draft is drawn under a credit issued by the drawee, the drawee of an international sight owes the drawer no duty to pay an unadvised draft but if it does so and the draft is genuine, may appropriately debit the drawer's account.

Part 8   Miscellaneous

§ 3–801.   Drafts in a Set

(1) Where a draft is drawn in a set of parts, each of which is numbered and expressed to be an order only if no other part has been honored, the whole of the parts constitutes one draft but a taker of any part may become a holder in due course of the draft.

(2) Any person who negotiates, indorses or accepts a single part of a draft drawn in a set thereby becomes liable to any holder in due course of that part as if it were the whole set, but as between different holders in due course to whom different parts have been negotiated the holder whose title first accrues has all rights to the draft and its proceeds.

(3) As against the drawee the first presented part of a draft drawn in a set is the part entitled to payment, or if a time draft to acceptance and payment. Acceptance of any subsequently presented part renders the drawee liable thereon under subsection (2). With respect both to a holder and to the drawer payment of a subsequently presented part of a draft payable at sight has the same effect as payment of a check notwithstanding an effective stop order (Section 4–407).

(4) Except as otherwise provided in this section, where any part of a draft in a set is discharged by payment or otherwise the whole draft is discharged.

§ 3–802.   Effect of Instrument on Obligation for Which It Is Given

(1) Unless otherwise agreed where an instrument is taken for an underlying obligation

(a) the obligation is pro tanto discharged if a bank is drawer, maker or acceptor of the instrument and there is no recourse on the instrument against the underlying obligor; and

(b) in any other case the obligation is suspended pro tanto until the instrument is due or if it is payable on demand until its presentment. If the instrument is dishonored action may be maintained on either the instrument or the obligation; discharge of the underlying obligor on the instrument also discharges him on the obligation.

(2) The taking in good faith of a check which is not postdated does not of itself so extend the time on the original obligation as to discharge a surety.

§ 3–803.   Notice to Third Party

Where a defendant is sued for breach of an obligation for which a third person is answerable over under this Article he may give the third person written notice of the litigation, and the person notified may then give similar notice to any other person who is answerable over to him under this Article. If the notice states that the person notified may come in and defend and that if the person notified does not do so he will in any action against him by the person giving the notice be bound by any determination of fact common to the two litigations, then unless after seasonable receipt of the notice the person notified does come in and defend he is so bound.

§ 3–804.   Lost, Destroyed or Stolen Instruments

The owner of an instrument which is lost, whether by destruction, theft or otherwise, may maintain an action in his own name and recover from any party liable thereon upon due proof of his ownership, the facts which prevent his production of the instrument and its terms. The court may require security indemnifying the defendant against loss by reason of further claims on the instrument.

§ 3–805.   Instruments Not Payable to Order or to Bearer

This Article applies to any instrument whose terms do not preclude transfer and which is otherwise negotiable within this Article but which is not payable to order or to bearer, except that there can be no holder in due course of such an instrument.

ARTICLE 4   BANK DEPOSITS AND COLLECTIONS

Part 1   General Provisions and Definitions

§ 4–101.   Short Title

This Article shall be known and may be cited as Uniform Commercial Code—Bank Deposits and Collections.

§ 4–102.   Applicability

(1) To the extent that items within this Article are also within the scope of Articles 3 and 8, they are subject to the provisions of those Articles. In the event of conflict the provisions of this Article govern those of Article 3 but the provisions of Article 8 govern those of this Article.

(2) The liability of a bank for action or non-action with respect to any item handled by it for purposes of presentment, payment or collection is governed by the law of the place where the bank is located. In the case of action or non-action by or at a branch or separate office of a bank, its liability is governed by the law of the place where the branch or separate office is located.

§ 4–103.   Variation by Agreement; Measure of Damages; Certain Action Constituting Ordinary Care

(1) The effect of the provisions of this Article may be varied by agreement except that no agreement can disclaim a bank's responsibility for its own lack of good faith or failure to exercise ordinary care or can limit the measure of damages for such lack of failure; but the parties may by agreement determine the standards by which such responsibility is to be measured if such standards are not manifestly unreasonable.

(2) Federal Reserve regulations and operating letters, clearing house rules, and the like, have the effect of agreements under subsection (1), whether or not specifically assented to by all parties interested in items handled.

(3) Action or non-action approved by this Article or pursuant to Federal Reserve regulations or operating letters constitutes the exercise of ordinary care and, in the absence of special instructions, action or non-action consistent with clearing house rules and the like or with a general banking usage not disapproved by this Article, prima facie constitutes the exercise of ordinary care.

(4) The specification or approval of certain procedures by this Article does not constitute disapproval of other procedures which may be reasonable under the circumstances.

(5) The measure of damages for failure to exercise ordinary care in handling an item is the amount of the item reduced by an amount which could not have been realized by the use of ordinary care, and where there is bad faith it includes other damages, if any, suffered by the party as a proximate consequence.

§ 4–104.   Definitions and Index of Definitions

(1) In this Article unless the context otherwise requires

(a) "Account" means any account with a bank and includes a checking, time, interest or savings account;

(b) "Afternoon" means the period of a day between noon and midnight;

(c) "Banking day" means that part of any day on which a bank is open to the public for carrying on substantially all of its banking functions;

(d) "Clearing house" means any association of banks or other payor regularly clearing items;

(e) "Customer" means any person having an account with a bank or for whom a bank has agreed to collect items and includes a bank carrying an account with another bank;

(f) "Documentary draft" means any negotiable or non-negotiable draft with accompanying documents, securities or other papers to be delivered against honor of the draft;

(g) "Item" means any instrument for the payment of money even though it is not negotiable but does not include money;

(h) "Midnight deadline" with respect to a bank is midnight on its next banking day following the banking day on which it receives the relevant item or notice or from which the time for taking action commences to run, whichever is later;

(i) "Properly payable" includes the availability of funds for payment at the time of decision to pay or dishonor;

(j) "Settle" means to pay in cash, by clearing house settlement, in a charge or credit or by remittance, or otherwise as instructed. A settlement may be either provisional or final;

(k) "Suspends payments" with respect to a bank means that it has been closed by order of the supervisory authorities, that a public officer has been appointed to take it over or that it ceases or refuses to make payments in the ordinary course of business.

(2) Other definitions applying to this Article and the sections in which they appear are:

"Collecting bank." Section 4–105.
"Depositary bank." Section 4–105.
"Intermediary bank." Section 4–105.
"Payor bank." Section 4–105.
"Presenting bank." Section 4–105.
"Remitting bank." Section 4–105.

(3) The following definitions in other Articles apply to this Article:

"Acceptance." Section 3–410.
"Certificate of deposit." Section 3–104.
"Certification." Section 3–411.
"Check." Section 3–104.
"Draft." Section 3–104.
"Holder in due course." Section 3–302.
"Notice of dishonor." Section 3–508.
"Presentment." Section 3–504.
"Protest." Section 3–509.
"Secondary party." Section 3–102.

(4) In addition Article 1 contains general definitions and principles of construction and interpretation applicable throughout this Article.

§ 4–105.   "Depositary Bank "; "Intermediary Bank "; "Collecting Bank "; "Payor Bank "; "Presenting Bank "; "Remitting Bank "

In this Article unless the context otherwise requires:

(a) "Depositary bank" means the first bank to which an item is transferred for collection even though it is also the payor bank;

(b) "Payor bank" means a bank by which an item is payable as drawn or accepted;

(c) "Intermediary bank" means any bank to which an item is transferred in course of collection except the depositary or payor bank;

(d) "Collecting bank" means any bank handling the item for collection except the payor bank;

(e) "Presenting bank" means any bank presenting an item except a payor bank;

(f) "Remitting bank" means any payor or intermediary bank remitting for an item.

§ 4–106.   Separate Office of a Bank

A branch or separate office of a bank [maintaining its own deposit ledgers] is a separate bank for the purpose of computing the time within which and determining the place at or to which action may be taken or notices or orders shall be given under this Article and under Article 3.

Note: The brackets are to make it optional with the several states whether to require a branch to maintain its own deposit ledgers in order to be considered to be a separate bank for certain purposes under Article 4. In some states "maintaining its own deposit ledgers" is a satisfactory test. In others branch banking practices are such that this test would not be suitable.

§ 4–107.   Time of Receipt of Items

(1) For the purpose of allowing time to process items, prove balances and make the necessary entries on its books to determine its position for the day, a bank may fix an afternoon hour of 2 P.M. or later as a cut-off hour for the handling of money and items and the making of entries on its books.

(2) Any item or deposit of money received on any day after a cut-off hour so fixed or after the close of the banking day may be treated as being received at the opening of the next banking day.

§ 4–108.   Delays

(1) Unless otherwise instructed, a collecting bank in a good faith effort to secure payment may, in the case of specific items and with or without the approval of any person involved, waive, modify or extend time limits imposed or permitted by this Act for a period not in excess of an additional banking day without discharge of secondary parties and without liability to its transferor or any prior party.

(2) Delay by a collecting bank or payor bank beyond time limits prescribed or permitted by this Act or by instructions is excused if caused by interruption of communication facilities, suspension of payments by another bank, war, emergency conditions or other circumstances beyond the control of the bank provided it exercises such diligence as the circumstances require.

§ 4–109.   Process of Posting

The "process of posting" means the usual procedure followed by a payor bank in determining to pay an item and in recording the payment including one or more of the following or other steps as determined by the bank:

(a) verification of any signature;

(b) ascertaining that sufficient funds are available;

(c) affixing a "paid" or other stamp;

(d) entering a charge or entry to a customer's account;

(e) correcting or reversing an entry or erroneous action with respect to the item.

Part 2 Collection of Items: Depositary and Collecting Banks

§ 4–201. Presumption and Duration of Agency Status of Collecting Banks and Provisional Status of Credits; Applicability of Article; Item Indorsed "Pay Any Bank"

(1) Unless a contrary intent clearly appears and prior to the time that a settlement given by a collecting bank for an item is or becomes final (subsection (3) of Section 4–211 and Sections 4–212 and 4–213) the bank is an agent or sub-agent of the owner of the item and any settlement given for the item is provisional. This provision applies regardless of the form of indorsement or lack of indorsement and even though credit given for the item is subject to immediate withdrawal as of right or is in fact withdrawn; but the continuance of ownership of an item by its owner and any rights of the owner to proceeds of the item are subject to rights of a collecting bank such as those resulting from outstanding advances on the item and valid rights of set-off. When an item is handled by banks for purposes of presentment, payment and collection, the relevant provisions of this Article apply even though action of parties clearly establishes that a particular bank has purchased the item and is the owner of it.

(2) After an item has been indorsed with the words "pay any bank" or the like, only a bank may acquire the rights of a holder

(a) until the item has been returned to the customer initiating collection; or

(b) until the item has been specially indorsed by a bank to a person who is not a bank.

§ 4–202. Responsibility for Collection; When Action Seasonable

(1) A collecting bank must use ordinary care in

(a) presenting an item or sending it for presentment; and

(b) sending notice of dishonor or non-payment or returning an item other than a documentary draft to the bank's transferor [or directly to the depositary bank under subsection (2) of Section 4–212] (*See note to Section 4–212*) after learning that the item has not been paid or accepted, as the case may be; and

(c) settling for an item when the bank receives final settlement; and

(d) making or providing for any necessary protest; and

(e) notifying its transferor of any loss or delay in transit within a reasonable time after discovery thereof.

(2) A collecting bank taking proper action before its midnight deadline following receipt of an item, notice or payment acts seasonably; taking proper action within a reasonably longer time may be seasonable but the bank has the burden of so establishing.

(3) Subject to subsection (1)(a), a bank is not liable for the insolvency, neglect, misconduct, mistake or default of another bank or person or for loss or destruction of an item in transit or in the possession of others.

§ 4–203. Effect of Instructions

Subject to the provisions of Article 3 concerning conversion of instruments (Section 3–419) and the provisions of both Article 3 and this Article concerning restrictive indorsements only a collecting bank's transferor can give instructions which affect the bank or constitute notice to it and a collecting bank is not liable to prior parties for any action taken pursuant to such instructions or in accordance with any agreement with its transferor.

§ 4–204. Methods of Sending and Presenting; Sending Direct to Payor Bank

(1) A collecting bank must send items by reasonably prompt method taking into consideration any relevant instructions, the nature of the item, the number of such items on hand, and the cost of collection involved and the method generally used by it or others to present such items.

(2) A collecting bank may send

(a) any item direct to the payor bank;

(b) any item to any non-bank payor if authorized by its transferor; and

(c) any item other than documentary drafts to any non-bank payor, if authorized by Federal Reserve regulation or operating letter, clearing house rule or the like.

(3) Presentment may be made by a presenting bank at a place where the payor bank has requested that presentment be made.

§ 4–205. Supplying Missing Indorsement; No Notice from Prior Indorsement

(1) A depositary bank which has taken an item for collection may supply any indorsement of the customer which is necessary to title unless the item contains the words "payee's indorsement required" or the like. In the absence of such a requirement a statement placed on the item by the depositary bank to the effect that the item was deposited by a customer or credited to his account is effective as the customer's indorsement.

(2) An intermediary bank, or payor bank which is not a depositary bank, is neither given notice nor otherwise affected by a restrictive indorsement of any person except the bank's immediate transferor.

§ 4–206. Transfer Between Banks

Any agreed method which identifies the transferor bank is sufficient for the item's further transfer to another bank.

§ 4–207.   Warranties of Customer and Collecting Bank on Transfer or Presentment of Items; Time for Claims

(1) Each customer or collecting bank who obtains payment or acceptance of an item and each prior customer and collecting bank warrants to the payor bank or other payor who in good faith pays or accepts the item that

(a) he has a good title to the item or is authorized to obtain payment or acceptance on behalf of one who has a good title; and

(b) he had no knowledge that the signature of the maker or drawer is unauthorized, except that this warranty is not given by any customer or collecting bank that is a holder in due course and acts in good faith

(i) to a maker with respect to the maker's own signature; or

(ii) to a drawer with respect to the drawer's own signature, whether or not the drawer is also the drawee; or

(iii) to an acceptor of an item if the holder in due course took the item after the acceptance or obtained the acceptance without knowledge that the drawer's signature was unauthorized; and

(c) the item has not been materially altered, except that this warranty is not given by any customer or collecting bank that is a holder in due course and acts in good faith

(i) to the maker of a note; or

(ii) to the drawer of a draft whether or not the drawer is also the drawee; or

(iii) to the acceptor of an item with respect to an alteration made prior to the acceptance if the holder in due course took the item after the acceptance, even though the acceptance provided "payable as originally drawn" or equivalent terms; or

(iv) to the acceptor of an item with respect to an alteration made after the acceptance.

(2) Each customer and collecting bank who transfers an item and receives a settlement or other consideration for it warrants to his transferee and to any subsequent collecting bank who takes the item in good faith that

(a) he has a good title to the item or is authorized to obtain payment or acceptance on behalf of one who has a good title and the transfer is otherwise rightful; and

(b) all signatures are genuine or authorized; and

(c) the item has not been materially altered; and

(d) no defense of any party is good against him; and

(e) he has no knowledge of any insolvency proceeding instituted with respect to the maker or acceptor or the drawer of an unaccepted item.

In addition each customer and collecting bank so transferring an item and receiving a settlement or other consideration engages that upon dishonor and any necessary notice of dishonor and protest he will take up the item.

(3) The warranties and the engagement to honor set forth in the two preceding subsections arise notwithstanding the absence of indorsement or words of guaranty or warranty in the transfer or presentment and a collecting bank remains liable for their breach despite remittance to its transferor. Damages for breach of such warranties or engagement to honor shall not exceed the consideration received by the customer or collecting bank responsible plus finance charges and expenses related to the item, if any.

(4) Unless a claim for breach of warranty under this section is made within a reasonable time after the person claiming learns of the breach, the person liable is discharged to the extent of any loss caused by the delay in making claim.

§ 4–208.   Security Interest of Collecting Bank in Items, Accompanying Documents and Proceeds

(1) A bank has a security interest in an item and any accompanying documents or the proceeds of either

(a) in case of an item deposited in an account to the extent to which credit given for the item has been withdrawn or applied;

(b) in case of an item for which it has given credit available for withdrawal as of right, to the extent of the credit given whether or not the credit is drawn upon and whether or not there is a right of charge-back; or

(c) if it makes an advance on or against the item.

(2) When credit which has been given for several items received at one time or pursuant to a single agreement is withdrawn or applied in part the security interest remains upon all the items, any accompanying documents or the proceeds of either. For the purpose of this section, credits first given are first withdrawn.

(3) Receipt by a collecting bank of a final settlement for an item is a realization on its security interest in the item, accompanying documents and proceeds. To the extent and so long as the bank does not receive final settlement for the item or give up possession of the item or accompanying documents for purposes other than collection, the security interest continues and is subject to the provisions of Article 9 except that

(a) no security agreement is necessary to make the security interest enforceable (subsection (1)(a) of Section 9–203); and

(b) no filing is required to perfect the security interest; and

(c) the security interest has priority over conflicting perfected security interests in the item, accompanying documents or proceeds.

§ 4–209.   When Bank Gives Value for Purposes of Holder in Due Course

For purposes of determining its status as a holder in due course, the bank has given value to the extent that it has a security interest in an item provided that the bank otherwise complies with the requirements of Section 3–302 on what constitutes a holder in due course.

§ 4–210. Presentment by Notice of Item Not Payable by, through or at a Bank; Liability of Secondary Parties

(1) Unless otherwise instructed, a collecting bank may present an item not payable by, through or at a bank by sending to the party to accept or pay a written notice that the bank holds the item for acceptance or payment. The notice must be sent in time to be received on or before the day when presentment is due and the bank must meet any requirement of the party to accept or pay under Section 3–505 by the close of the bank's next banking day after it knows of the requirement

(2) Where presentment is made by notice and neither honor nor request for compliance with a requirement under Section 3–505 is received by the close of business on the day after maturity or in the case of demand items by the close of business on the third banking day after notice was sent, the presenting bank may treat the item as dishonored and charge any secondary party by sending him notice of the facts.

§ 4–211. Media of Remittance; Provisional and Final Settlement in Remittance Cases

(1) A collecting bank may take in settlement of an item

(a) a check of the remitting bank or of another bank on any bank except the remitting bank; or

(b) a cashier's check or similar primary obligation of a remitting bank which is a member of or clears through a member of the same clearing house or group as the collecting bank; or

(c) appropriate authority to charge an account of the remitting bank or of another bank with the collecting bank; or

(d) if the item is drawn upon or payable by a person other than a bank, a cashier's check, certified check or other bank check or obligation.

(2) If before its midnight deadline the collecting bank properly dishonors a remittance check or authorization to charge on itself or presents or forwards for collection a remittance instrument of or on another bank which is of a kind approved by subsection (1) or has not been authorized by it, the collecting bank is not liable to prior parties in the event of the dishonor of such check, instrument or authorization.

(3) A settlement for an item by means of a remittance instrument or authorization to charge is or becomes a final settlement as to both the person making and the person receiving the settlement

(a) if the remittance instrument or authorization to charge is of a kind approved by subsection (1) or has not been authorized by the person receiving the settlement and in either case the person receiving the settlement acts seasonably before its midnight deadline in presenting, forwarding for collection or paying the instrument or authorization,—at the time the remittance instrument or authorization is finally paid by the payor by which it is payable.

(b) if the person receiving the settlement has authorized remittance by a non-bank check or obligation or by a cashier's

check or similar primary obligation of or a check upon the payor or other remitting bank which is not of a kind approved by subsection (1)(b),—at the time of the receipt of such remittance check or obligation; or

(c) if in a case not covered by sub-paragraphs (a) or (b) the person receiving the settlement fails to seasonably present, forward for collection, pay or return a remittance instrument or authorization to it to charge before its midnight deadline,—at such midnight deadline.

§ 4–212. Right of Charge-Back or Refund

(1) If a collecting bank has made provisional settlement with its customer for an item and itself fails by reason of dishonor, suspension of payments by a bank or otherwise to receive a settlement for the item which is or becomes final, the bank may revoke the settlement given by it, charge back the amount of any credit given for the item to its customers' account or obtain refund from its customer whether or not it is able to return the items if by its midnight deadline or within a longer reasonable time after it learns the facts it returns the item or sends notification of the facts. These rights to revoke, charge-back and obtain refund terminate if and when a settlement for the item received by the bank is or becomes final (subsection (3) of Section 4–211 and subsection (2) and (3) of Section 4–213).

[(2) Within the time and manner prescribed by this section and Section 4–301, an intermediary or payor bank, as the case may be, may return an unpaid item directly to the depositary bank and may send for collection a draft on the depositary bank and obtain reimbursement. In such case, if the depositary bank has received provisional settlement for the item, it must reimburse the bank drawing the draft and any provisional credits for the item between banks shall become and remain final.]

Note: Direct returns is recognized as an innovation that is not yet established bank practice, and therefore, Paragraph 2 has been bracketed. Some lawyers have doubts whether it should be included in legislation or left to development by agreement.

(3) A depositary bank which is also the payor may charge-back the amount of an item to its customer's account or obtain refund in accordance with the section governing return of an item received by a payor bank for credit on its books (Section 4–301).

(4) The right to charge-back is not affected by

(a) prior use of the credit given for the item; or

(b) failure by any bank to exercise ordinary care with respect to the item but any bank so failing remains liable.

(5) A failure to charge-back or claim refund does not affect other rights of the bank against the customer or any other party.

(6) If credit is given in dollars as the equivalent of the value of an item payable in a foreign currency the dollar amount of any

charge-back or refund shall be calculated on the basis of the buying sight rate for the foreign currency prevailing on the day when the person entitled to the charge-back or refund learns that it will not receive payment in ordinary course.

§ 4–213.   Final Payment of Item by Payor Bank;
When Provisional Debits and Credits Become Final;
When Certain Credits Become Available for Withdrawal

(1) An item is finally paid by a payor bank when the bank has done any of the following, whichever happens first:

(a) paid the item in cash; or

(b) settled for the item without reserving a right to revoke the settlement and without having such right under statute, clearing house rule or agreement; or

(c) completed the process of posting the item to the indicated account of the drawer, maker or other person to be charged therewith; or

(d) made a provisional settlement for the item and failed to revoke the settlement in the time and manner permitted by statute, clearing house rule or agreement.

Upon a final payment under subparagraphs (b), (c) or (d) the payor bank shall be accountable for the amount of the item.

(2) If provisional settlement for an item between the presenting and payor banks is made through a clearing house or by debits or credits in an account between them, then to the extent that provisional debits or credits for the item are entered in accounts between the presenting and payor banks or between the presenting and successive prior collecting banks seriatim, they become final upon final payment of the item by the payor bank.

(3) If a collecting bank receives a settlement for an item which is or becomes final (subsection (3) of Section 4–211, subsection (2) of Section 4–213) the bank is accountable to its customer for the amount of the item and any provisional credit given for the item in an account with its customer becomes final.

(4) Subject to any right of the bank to apply the credit to an obligation of the customer, credit given by a bank for an item in an account with its customer becomes available for withdrawal as of right

(a) in any case where the bank has received a provisional settlement for the item,—when such settlement becomes final and the bank has had a reasonable time to learn that the settlement is final.

(b) in any case where the bank is both a depositary bank and a payor bank and the item is finally paid,—at the opening of the bank's second banking day following receipt of the item.

(5) A deposit of money in a bank is final when made but, subject to any right of the bank to apply the deposit to an obligation of the customer, the deposit becomes available for withdrawal as of right at the opening of the bank's next banking day following receipt of the deposit.

§ 4–214.   Insolvency and Preference

(1) Any item in or coming into the possession of a payor or collecting bank which suspends payment and which item is not finally paid shall be returned by the receiver, trustee or agent in charge of the closed bank to the presenting bank or the closed bank's customer.

(2) If a payor bank finally pays an item and suspends payments without making a settlement for the item with its customer or the presenting bank which settlement is or becomes final, the owner of the item has a preferred claim against the payor bank.

(3) If a payor bank gives or a collecting bank gives or receives a provisional settlement for an item and thereafter suspends payments, the suspension does not prevent or interfere with the settlement becoming final if such finality occurs automatically upon the lapse of certain time or the happening of certain events (subsection (3) of Section 4–211, subsections (1)(d), (2) and (3) of Section 4–213).

(4) If a collecting bank receives from subsequent parties settlement for an item which settlement is or becomes final and suspends payments without making a settlement for the item with its customer which is or becomes final, the owner of the item has a preferred claim against such collecting bank.

Part 3   Collection of Items; Payor Banks

§ 4–301.   Deferred Posting; Recovery of Payment
by Return of Items; Time of Dishonor

(1) Where an authorized settlement for a demand item (other than a documentary draft) received by a payor bank otherwise than for immediate payment over the counter has been made before midnight of the banking day of receipt the payor bank may revoke the settlement and recover any payment if before it has made final payment (subsection (1) of Section 4–213) and before its midnight deadline it

(a) returns the item; or

(b) sends written notice of dishonor or nonpayment if the item is held for protest or is otherwise unavailable for return.

(2) If a demand item is received by a payor bank for credit on its books it may return such item or send notice of dishonor and may revoke any credit given or recover the amount thereof withdrawn by its customer, if it acts within the time limit and in the manner specified in the preceding subsection.

(3) Unless previous notice of dishonor has been sent an item is dishonored at the time when for purposes of dishonor it is returned or notice sent in accordance with this section.

(4) An item is returned:

(a) as to an item received through a clearing house, when it is delivered to the presenting or last collecting bank or to the clearing house or is sent or delivered in accordance with its rules; or

(b) in all other cases, when it is sent or delivered to the bank's customer or transferor or pursuant to his instructions.

§ 4–302. Payor Banks' Responsibility for Late Return of Item

In the absence of a valid defense such as breach of a presentment warranty (subsection (1) of Section 4–207), settlement effected or the like, if an item is presented on and received by a payor bank the bank is accountable for the amount of

(a) a demand item other than a documentary draft whether properly payable or not if the bank, in any case where it is not also the depositary bank, retains the item beyond midnight of the banking day of receipt without settling for it or, regardless of whether it is also the depositary bank, does not pay or return the item or send notice of dishonor until after its midnight deadline, or

(b) any other properly payable item unless within the time allowed for acceptance or payment of that item the bank either accepts or pays the item or returns it and accompanying documents.

§ 4–303. When Items Subject to Notice, Stop-Order, Legal Process or Setoff; Order in Which Items May Be Charged or Certified

(1) Any knowledge, notice or stop-order received by, legal process served upon or setoff exercised by a payor bank, whether or not effective under other rules of law to terminate, suspend or modify the bank's right or duty to pay an item or to charge its customer's account for the item, comes too late to so terminate, suspend or modify such right or duty if the knowledge, notice, stop-order or legal process is received or served and a reasonable time for the bank to act thereon expires or the setoff is exercised after the bank has done any of the following:

(a) accepted or certified the item;

(b) paid the item in cash;

(c) settled for the item without reserving a right to revoke the settlement and without having such right under statute, clearing house rule or agreement;

(d) completed the process of posting the item to the indicated account of the drawer, maker or other person to be charged therewith or otherwise has evidenced by examination of such indicated account and by action its decision to pay the item; or

(e) become accountable for the amount of the item under subsection (1)(d) of Section 4–213 and Section 4–302 dealing with the payor bank's responsibility for late return of items.

(2) Subject to the provisions of subsection (1) items may be accepted, paid, certified or charged to the indicated account of its customer in any order convenient to the bank.

Part 4   Relationship Between Payor Bank and Its Customer

§ 4–401. When Bank May Charge Customer's Account

(1) As against its customer, a bank may charge against his account any item which is otherwise properly payable from that account even though the charge creates an over draft.

(2) A bank which in good faith makes payment to a holder may charge the indicated account of its customer according to

(a) the original tenor of his altered item; or

(b) the tenor of his completed item, even though the bank knows the item has been completed unless the bank has notice that the completion was improper.

§ 4–402. Bank's Liability to Customer for Wrongful Dishonor

A payor bank is liable to its customer for damages proximately caused by the wrongful dishonor of an item. When the dishonor occurs through mistake liability is limited to actual damages proved. If so proximately caused and proved damages may include damages for an arrest or prosecution of the customer or other consequential damages. Whether any consequential damages are proximately caused by the wrongful dishonor is a question of fact to be determined in each case.

§ 4–403. Customer's Right to Stop Payment; Burden of Proof of Loss

(1) A customer may by order to his bank stop payment of any item payable for his account but the order must be received at such time and in such manner as to afford the bank a reasonable opportunity to act on it prior to any action by the bank with respect to the item described in Section 4–303.

(2) An oral order is binding upon the bank only for fourteen calendar days unless confirmed in writing within that period. A written order is effective for only six months unless renewed in writing.

(3) The burden of establishing the fact and amount of loss resulting from the payment of an item contrary to a binding stop payment order is on the customer.

§ 4–404. Bank Not Obligated to Pay Check More Than Six Months Old

A bank is under no obligation to a customer having a checking account to pay a check, other than a certified check, which is presented more than six months after its date, but it may charge its customer's account for a payment made thereafter in good faith.

§ 4–405. Death or Incompetence of Customer

(1) A payor or collecting bank's authority to accept pay or collect an item or to account for proceeds of its collection if otherwise effective is not rendered ineffective by incompetence of a customer of either bank existing at the time the item is issued or its collection is undertaken if the bank does not know of an adjudication of incompetence. Neither death nor incompetence of a customer revokes such authority to accept, pay, collect or account until the bank knows of the fact of death or of an adjudication of incompetence and has reasonable opportunity to act on it.

(2) Even with knowledge a bank may for 10 days after the date of death pay or certify checks drawn on or prior to that date unless ordered to stop payment by a person claiming an interest in the account.

§ 4–406.   Customer's Duty to Discover and Report Unauthorized Signature or Alteration

(1) When a bank sends to its customer a statement of account accompanied by items paid in good faith in support of the debit entries or holds the statement and items pursuant to a request or instructions of its customer or otherwise in a reasonable manner makes the statement and items available to the customer, the customer must exercise reasonable care and promptness to examine the statement and items to discover his unauthorized signature or any alteration on an item and must notify the bank promptly after discovery thereof.

(2) If the bank establishes that the customer failed with respect to an item to comply with the duties imposed on the customer by subsection (1) the customer is precluded from asserting against the bank

(a) his unauthorized signature or any alteration on the item if the bank also establishes that it suffered a loss by reason of such failure; and

(b) an unauthorized signature or alteration by the same wrongdoer on any other item paid in good faith by the bank after the first item and statement was available to the customer for a reasonable period not exceeding fourteen calendar days and before the bank receives notification from the customer of any such unauthorized signature or alteration.

(3) The preclusion under subsection (2) does not apply if the customer establishes lack of ordinary care on the part of the bank in paying the item(s).

(4) Without regard to care or lack of care of either the customer or the bank a customer who does not within one year from the time the statement and items are made available to the customer (subsection (1)) discover and report his unauthorized signature or any alteration on the face or back of the item or does not within 3 years from that time discover and report any unauthorized indorsement is precluded from asserting against the bank such unauthorized signature or indorsement or such alteration.

(5) If under this section a payor bank has a valid defense against a claim of a customer upon or resulting from payment of an item and waives or fails upon request to assert the defense the bank may not assert against any collecting bank or other prior party presenting or transferring the item a claim based upon the unauthorized signature or alteration giving rise to the customer's claim.

§ 4–407.   Payor Bank's Right to Subrogation on Improper Payment

If a payor bank has paid an item over the stop payment order of the drawer or maker or otherwise under circumstances giving a basis for objection by the drawer or maker, to prevent unjust enrichment and only to the extent necessary to prevent loss to the bank by reason of its payment of the item, the payor bank shall be subrogated to the rights

(a) of any holder in due course on the item against the drawer or maker; and

(b) of the payee or any other holder of the item against the drawer or maker either on the item or under the transaction out of which the item arose; and

(c) of the drawer or maker against the payee or any other holder of the item with respect to the transaction out of which the item arose.

Part 5   Collection of Documentary Drafts

§ 4–501.   Handling of Documentary Drafts; Duty to Send for Presentment and to Notify Customer of Dishonor

A bank which takes a documentary draft for collection must present or send the draft and accompanying documents for presentment and upon learning that the draft has not been paid or accepted in due course must seasonably notify its customer of such fact even though it may have discounted or bought the draft or extended credit available for withdrawal as of right.

§ 4–502.   Presentment of "On Arrival" Drafts

When a draft or the relevant instructions require presentment "on arrival," "when goods arrive" or the like, the collecting bank need not present until in its judgment a reasonable time for arrival of the goods has expired. Refusal to pay or accept because the goods have not arrived is not dishonor; the bank must notify its transferor of such refusal but need not present the draft again until it is instructed to do so or learns of the arrival of the goods.

§ 4–503.   Responsibility of Presenting Bank for Documents and Goods; Report of Reasons for Dishonor; Referee in Case of Need

Unless otherwise instructed and except as provided in Article 5 a bank presenting a documentary draft

(a) must deliver the documents to the drawee on acceptance of the draft if it is payable more than three days after presentment; otherwise, only on payment; and

(b) upon dishonor, either in the case of presentment for acceptance or presentment for payment, may seek and follow instructions from any referee in case of need designated in the draft or if the presenting bank does not choose to utilize his services it must use diligence and good faith to ascertain the reason for dishonor, must notify its transferor of the dishonor and of the results of its effort to ascertain the reasons therefor and must request instructions.

But the presenting bank is under no obligation with respect to goods represented by the documents except to follow any reasonable instructions seasonably received; it has a right to reimbursement for any expense incurred in following instructions and to prepayment of or indemnity for such expenses.

§ 4–504. Privilege of Presenting Bank to Deal With Goods; Security Interest for Expenses

(1) A presenting bank which, following the dishonor of a documentary draft, has seasonably requested instructions but does not receive them within a reasonable time may store, sell, or otherwise deal with the goods in any reasonable manner.

(2) For its reasonable expenses incurred by action under subsection (1) the presenting bank has a lien upon the goods or their proceeds, which may be foreclosed in the same manner as an unpaid seller's lien.

ARTICLE 5 LETTERS OF CREDIT

§ 5–101. Short Title

This Article shall be known and may be cited as Uniform Commercial Code—Letters of Credit.

§ 5–102. Scope

(1) This Article applies

(a) to a credit issued by a bank if the credit requires a documentary draft or a documentary demand for payment; and

(b) to a credit issued by a person other than a bank if the credit requires that the draft or demand for payment be accompanied by a document of title; and

(c) to a credit issued by a bank or other person if the credit is not within subparagraphs (a) or (b) but conspicuously states that it is a letter of credit or is conspicuously so entitled.

(2) Unless the engagement meets the requirements of subsection (1), this Article does not apply to engagements to make advances or to honor drafts or demands for payment, to authorities to pay or purchase, to guarantees or to general agreements.

(3) This Article deals with some but not all of the rules and concepts of letters of credit as such rules or concepts have developed prior to this act or may hereafter develop. The fact that this Article states a rule does not by itself require, imply or negate application of the same or a converse rule to a situation not provided for or to a person not specified by this Article.

§ 5–103. Definitions

(1) In this Article unless the context otherwise requires

(a) "Credit" or "letter of credit" means an engagement by a bank or other person made at the request of a customer and of a kind within the scope of this Article (Section 5–102) that the issuer will honor drafts or other demands for payment upon compliance with the conditions specified in the credit. A credit may be either revocable or irrevocable. The engagement may be either an agreement to honor or a statement that the bank or other person is authorized to honor.

(b) A "documentary draft" or a "documentary demand for payment" is one honor of which is conditioned upon the presentation of a document or documents. "Document" means any paper including document of title, security, invoice, certificate, notice of default and the like.

(c) An "issuer" is a bank or other person issuing a credit.

(d) A "beneficiary" of a credit is a person who is entitled under its terms to draw or demand payment.

(e) An "advising bank" is a bank which gives notification of the issuance of a credit by another bank.

(f) A "confirming bank" is a bank which engages either that it will itself honor a credit already issued by another bank or that such a credit will be honored by the issuer or a third bank.

(g) A "customer" is a buyer or other person who causes an issuer to issue a credit. The term also includes a bank which procures issuance or confirmation on behalf of that bank's customer.

(2) Other definitions applying to this Article and the sections in which they appear are:

"Notation of Credit." Section 5–108.

"Presenter." Section 5–112(3).

(3) Definitions in other Articles applying to this Article and the sections in which they appear are:

"Accept" or "Acceptance." Section 3–410.

"Contract for sale." Section 2–106.

"Draft." Section 3–104.

"Holder in due course." Section 3–302.

"Midnight deadline." Section 4–104.

"Security." Section 8–102.

(4) In addition, Article 1 contains general definitions and principles of construction and interpretation applicable throughout this Article.

§ 5–104. Formal Requirements; Signing

(1) Except as otherwise required in subsection (1)(c) of Section 5–102 on scope, no particular form of phrasing is required for a credit. A credit must be in writing and signed by the issuer and a confirmation must be in writing and signed by the confirming bank. A modification of the terms of a credit or confirmation must be signed by the issuer or confirming bank.

(2) A telegram may be a sufficient signed writing if it identifies its sender by an authorized authentication. The authentication may be in code and the authorized naming of the issuer in an advance of credit is a sufficient signing.

§ 5–105. Consideration

No consideration is necessary to establish a credit or to enlarge or otherwise modify its terms.

§ 5–106. Time and Effect of Establishment of Credit

(1) Unless otherwise agreed a credit is established

(a) as regards the customer as soon as a letter of credit is sent to him or the letter of credit or an authorized written advice of its issuance is sent to the beneficiary; and

(b) as regards the beneficiary when he receives a letter of credit or an authorized written advice of its issuance.

(2) Unless otherwise agreed once an irrevocable credit is established as regards the customer it can be modified or revoked only with the consent of the customer and once it is established as regards the beneficiary it can be modified or revoked only with his consent.

(3) Unless otherwise agreed after a revocable credit is established it may be modified or revoked by the issuer without notice to or consent from the customer or beneficiary.

(4) Notwithstanding any modification or revocation of a revocable credit any person authorized to honor or negotiate under the terms of the original credit is entitled to reimbursement for or honor of any draft or demand for payment duly honored or negotiated before receipt of notice of the modification or revocation and the issuer in turn is entitled to reimbursement from its customer.

§ 5–107. Advice of Credit; Confirmation; Error in Statement of Terms

(1) Unless otherwise specified an advising bank by advising a credit issued by another bank does not assume any obligation to honor drafts drawn or demands for payment made under the credit but it does assume obligation for the accuracy of its own statement.

(2) A confirming bank by confirming a credit becomes directly obligated on the credit to the extent of its confirmation as though it were its issuer and acquires the rights of an issuer.

(3) Even though an advising bank incorrectly advises the terms of a credit it has been authorized to advise the credit is established as against the issuer to the extent of its original terms.

(4) Unless otherwise specified the customer bears as against the issuer all risks of transmissions and reasonable translation or interpretation of any message relating to a credit.

§ 5–108. "Notation Credit"; Exhaustion of Credit

(1) A credit which specifies that any person purchasing or paying drafts drawn or demands for payment made under it must note the amount of the draft or demand on the letter or advice of credit is a "notation credit."

(2) Under a notation credit

(a) a person paying the beneficiary or purchasing a draft or demand for payment from him acquires a right to honor only if the appropriate notation is made and by transferring or forwarding for honor the documents under the credit such a person warrants to the issuer that the notation has been made; and

(b) unless the credit or a signed statement that an appropriate notation has been made accompanies the draft or demand for payment the issuer may delay honor until evidence of notation has been procured which is satisfactory to it but its obligation and that of its customer continue for a reasonable time not exceeding thirty days to obtain such evidence.

(3) If the credit is not a notation credit

(a) the issuer may honor complying drafts or demands for payment presented to it in the order in which they are presented and is discharged pro tanto by honor of any such draft or demand;

(b) as between competing good faith purchasers of complying drafts or demands the person first purchasing has priority over a subsequent purchaser even though the later purchased draft or demand has been first honored.

§ 5–109. Issuer's Obligation to Its Customer

(1) An issuer's obligation to its customer includes good faith and observance of any general banking usage but unless otherwise agreed does not include liability or responsibility

(a) for performance of the underlying contract for sale or other transaction between the customer and the beneficiary; or

(b) for any act or omission of any person other than itself or its own branch or for loss or destruction of a draft, demand or document in transit or in the possession of others; or

(c) based on knowledge or lack of knowledge of any usage of any particular trade.

(2) An issuer must examine documents with care so as to ascertain that on their face they appear to comply with the terms of the credit but unless otherwise agreed assumes no liability or responsibility for the genuineness, falsification or effect of any document which appears on such examination to be regular on its face.

(3) A non-bank issuer is not bound by any banking usage of which it has no knowledge.

§ 5–110. Availability of Credit in Portions; Presenter's Reservation of Lien or Claim

(1) Unless otherwise specified a credit may be used in portions in the discretion of the beneficiary.

(2) Unless otherwise specified a person by presenting a documentary draft or demand for payment under a credit relinquishes upon its honor all claims to the documents and a person by transferring such draft or demand or causing such presentment authorizes such relinquishment. An explicit reservation of claim makes the draft or demand noncomplying.

§ 5–111. Warranties on Transfer and Presentment

(1) Unless otherwise agreed the beneficiary by transferring or presenting a documentary draft or demand for payment warrants to all interested parties that the necessary conditions of the credit have been complied with. This is in addition to any warranties arising under Articles 3, 4, 7 and 8.

(2) Unless otherwise agreed a negotiating, advising, confirming, collecting or issuing bank presenting or transferring a draft or demand for payment under a credit warrants only the matters warranted by a collecting bank under Article 4 and any such bank transferring a document warrants only the matters warranted by an intermediary under Articles 7 and 8.

§ 5–112.   Time Allowed for Honor or Rejection; Withholding Honor or Rejection by Consent; "Presenter"

(1) A bank to which a documentary draft or demand for payment is presented under a credit may without dishonor of the draft, demand or credit

(a) defer honor until the close of the third banking day following receipt of the documents; and

(b) further defer honor if the presenter has expressly or impliedly consented thereto.

Failure to honor within the time here specified constitutes dishonor of the draft or demand and of the credit [except as otherwise provided in subsection (4) of Section 5–114 on conditional payment].

Note: The bracketed language in the last sentence of subsection (1) should be included only if the optional provisions of Section 5–114(4) and (5) are included.

(2) Upon dishonor the bank may unless otherwise instructed fulfill its duty to return the draft or demand and the documents by holding them at the disposal of the presenter and sending him an advice to that effect.

(3) "Presenter" means any person presenting a draft or demand for payment for honor under a credit even though that person is a confirming bank or other correspondent which is acting under an issuer's authorization.

§ 5–113.   Indemnities

(1) A bank seeking to obtain (whether for itself or another) honor, negotiation or reimbursement under a credit may give an indemnity to induce such honor, negotiation or reimbursement.

(2) An indemnity agreement inducing honor, negotiation or reimbursement

(a) unless otherwise explicitly agreed applies to defects in the documents but not in the goods; and

(b) unless a longer time is explicitly agreed expires at the end of ten business days following receipt of the documents by the ultimate customer unless notice of objection is sent before such expiration date. The ultimate customer may send notice of objection to the person from whom he received the documents and any bank receiving such notice is under a duty to send notice to its transferor before its midnight deadline.

§ 5–114.   Issuer's Duty and Privilege to Honor; Right to Reimbursement

(1) An issuer must honor a draft or demand for payment which complies with the terms of the relevant credit regardless of whether the goods or documents conform to the underlying contract for sale or other contract between the customer and the beneficiary. The issuer is not excused from honor of such a draft or demand by reason of an additional general term that all documents must be satisfactory to the issuer, but an issuer may require that specified documents must be satisfactory to it.

(2) Unless otherwise agreed when documents appear on their face to comply with the terms of a credit but a required document does not in fact conform to the warranties made on negotiations or transfer of a document of title (Section 7–507) or of a certified security (Section 8–306) or is forged or fraudulent or there is fraud in the transaction:

(a) the issuer must honor the draft or demand for payment if honor is demanded by a negotiating bank or other holder of the draft or demand which has taken the draft or demand under the credit and under circumstances which would make it a holder in due course (Section 3–302) and in an appropriate case would make it a person to whom a document of title has been duly negotiated (Section 7–502) or a bona fide purchaser of a certificated security (Section 8–302); and

(b) in all other cases as against its customer, an issuer acting in good faith may honor the draft or demand for payment despite notification from the customer of fraud, forgery or other defect not apparent on the face of the document but a court of appropriate jurisdiction may enjoin such honor.

(3) Unless otherwise agreed an issuer which has duly honored a draft or demand for payment is entitled to immediate reimbursement of any payment made under the credit and to be put in effectively available funds not later than the day before maturity of any acceptance made under the credit.

[(4) When a credit provides for payment by the issuer on receipt of notice that the required documents are in the possession of a correspondent or other agent of the issuer

(a) any payment made on receipt of such notice is conditional; and

(b) the issuer may reject documents which do not comply with the credit if it does so within three banking days following its receipt of the documents; and

(c) in the event of such rejection, the issuer is entitled by charge back or otherwise to return of the payment made.]

[(5) In the case covered by subsection (4) failure to reject documents within the time specified in subparagraph (b) constitutes acceptance of the documents and makes the payment final in favor of the beneficiary.]

Note: Subsections (4) and (5) are bracketed as optional. If they are included the bracketed language in that last sentence of Section 5–112(1) should also be inlcuded.

§ 5–115.   Remedy for Improper Dishonor or Anticipatory Repudiation

(1) When an issuer wrongfully dishonors a draft or demand for payment presented under a credit the person entitled to honor has with respect to any documents the rights of a person in the position of a seller (Section 2–707) and may recover from the issuer the face amount of the draft or demand together with incidental damages under Section 7–710 on seller's incidental damages and interest but less any amount realized by resale or other use or disposition of the subject matter of the transaction. In the event no resale or other utilization is made the documents, goods or other subject matter

involved in the transaction must be turned over to the issuer on payment of judgment.

(2) When an issuer wrongfully cancels or otherwise repudiates a credit before presentment of a draft or demands for payment drawn under it the beneficiary has the rights of a seller after anticipatory repudiation by the buyer under Section 2–610 if he learns of the repudiation in time reasonably to avoid procurement of the required documents. Otherwise the beneficiary has an immediate right of action for wrongful dishonor.

§ 5–116. Transfer and Assignment

(1) The right to draw under a credit can be transferred or assigned only when the credit is expressly designated as transferable or assignable.

(2) Even though the credit specifically states that it is nontransferable or nonassignable the beneficiary may before performance of the conditions of the credit assign his right to proceeds. Such an assignment is an assignment of an account under Article 9 on Secured Transactions and is governed by that Article except that

(a) the assignment is ineffective until the letter of credit or advice of credit is delivered to the assignee which delivery constitutes perfection of the security interest under Article 9; and

(b) the issuer may honor drafts or demands for payment drawn under the credit until it receives a notification of the assignment signed by the beneficiary which reasonably identifies the credit involved in the assignment and contains a request to pay the assignee; and

(c) after what reasonably appears to be such a notification has been received the issuer may without dishonor refuse to accept or pay even to a person otherwise entitled to honor until the letter of credit or advice of credit is exhibited to the issuer.

(3) Except where the beneficiary has effectively assigned his right to draw or his right to proceeds, nothing in this section limits his right to transfer or negotiate drafts or demands drawn under the credit.

§ 5–117. Insolvency of Bank Holding Funds for Documentary Credit

(1) Where an issuer or an advising or confirming bank or a bank which has for a customer procured issuance of a credit by another bank becomes insolvent before final payment under the credit and the credit is one to which this Article is made applicable by paragraphs (a) or (b) of Section 5–102(1) on scope, the receipt or allocation of funds or collateral to secure or meet obligations under the credit shall have the following results:

(a) to the extent of any funds or collateral turned over after or before the insolvency as indemnity against or specifically for the purpose of payment of drafts or demands for payment drawn under the designated credit, the drafts or demands are entitled to payment in preference over depositors or other general creditors of the issuer or bank; and

(b) on expiration of the credit or surrender of the beneficiary's rights under it unused any person who has given such funds or collateral is similarly entitled to return thereof; and

(c) a charge to a general or current account with a bank if specifically consented to for the purpose of indemnity against or payment of drafts or demands for payment drawn under the designated credit falls under the same rules as if the funds had been drawn out in cash and then turned over with specific instructions.

(2) After honor or reimbursement under this section the customer or other person for whose account the insolvent bank has acted is entitled to receive the documents involved.

ARTICLE 6   BULK TRANSFERS

§ 6–101. Short Title

This Article shall be known and may be cited as Uniform Commercial Code—Bulk Transfers.

§ 6–102. "Bulk Transfers"; Transfers of Equipment; Enterprises Subject to This Article; Bulk Transfers Subject to This Article

(1) A "bulk transfer" is any transfer in bulk and not in the ordinary course of the transferor's business of a major part of the materials, supplies, merchandise or other inventory (Section 9–109) of an enterprise subject to this Article.

(2) A transfer of a substantial part of the equipment (Section 9–109) of such an enterprise is a bulk transfer if it is made in connection with a bulk transfer of inventory, but not otherwise.

(3) The enterprises subject to this Article are all those whose principal business is the sale of merchandise from stock, including those who manufacture what they sell.

(4) Except as limited by the following section all bulk transfers of goods located within this state are subject to this Article.

§ 6–103. Transfers Excepted from This Article

The following transfers are not subject to this Article:

(1) Those made to give security for the performance of an obligation;

(2) General assignments for the benefit of all the creditors of the transferor, and subsequent transfers by the assignee thereunder;

(3) Transfers in settlement or realization of a lien or other security interests;

(4) Sales by executors, administrators, receivers, trustees in bankruptcy, or any public officer under judicial process;

(5) Sales made in the course of judicial or administrative proceedings for the dissolution or reorganization of a corporation and of which notice is sent to the creditors of the corporation pursuant to order of the court or administrative agency;

(6) Transfers to a person maintaining a known place of business in this State who becomes bound to pay the debts of the

transferor in full and gives public notice of that fact, and who is solvent after becoming so bound;

(7) A transfer to a new business enterprise organized to take over and continue the business, if public notice of the transaction is given and the new enterprise assumes the debts of the transferor and he receives nothing from the transaction except an interest in the new enterprise junior to the claims of creditors;

(8) Transfers of property which is exempt from execution.

Public notice under subsection (6) or subsection (7) may be given by publishing once a week for two consecutive weeks in a newspaper of general circulation where the transferor had its principal place of business in this state an advertisement including the names and addresses of the transferor and transferee and the effective date of the transfer.

§ 6–104.   Schedule of Property, List of Creditors

(1) Except as provided with respect to auction sales (Section 6–108), a bulk transfer subject to this Article is ineffective against any creditor of the transferor unless:

(a) The transferee requires the transferor to furnish a list of his existing creditors prepared as stated in this section; and

(b) The parties prepare a schedule of the property transferred sufficient to identify it; and

(c) The transferee preserves the list and schedule for six months next following the transfer and permits inspection of either or both and copying therefrom at all reasonable hours by any creditor of the transferor, or files the list and schedule in (a public office to be here identified).

(2) The list of creditors must be signed and sworn to or affirmed by the transferor or his agent. It must contain the names and business addresses of all creditors of the transferor, with the amounts when known, and also the names of all persons who are known to the transferor to assert claims against him even though such claims are disputed. If the transferor is the obligor of an outstanding issue of bonds, debentures or the like as to which there is an indenture trustee, the list of creditors need include only the name and address of the indenture trustee and the aggregate outstanding principal amount of the issue.

(3) Responsibility for the completeness and accuracy of the list of creditors rests on the transferor, and the transfer is not rendered ineffective by errors or omissions therein unless the transferee is shown to have had knowledge.

§ 6–105.   Notice to Creditors

In addition to the requirements of the preceding section, any bulk transfer subject to this Article except one made by auction sale (Section 6–108) is ineffective against any creditor of the transferor unless at least ten days before he takes possession of the goods or pays for them, whichever happens first, the transferee gives notice of the transfer in the manner and to the persons hereafter provided (Section 6–107).

§ 6–106.   Application of the Proceeds

In addition to the requirements of the two preceding sections:

(1) Upon every bulk transfer subject to this Article for which new consideration becomes payable except those made by sale at auction it is the duty of the transferee to assure that such consideration is applied so far as necessary to pay those debts of the transferor which are either shown on the list furnished by the transferor (Section 6–104) or filed in writing in the place stated in the notice (Section 6–107) within thirty days after the mailing of such notice. This duty of the transferee runs to all the holders of such debts, and may be enforced by any of them for the benefit of all.

(2) If any of said debts are in dispute the necessary sum may be withheld from distribution until the dispute is settled or adjudicated.

[(3) If the consideration payable is not enough to pay all of the said debts in full distribution shall be made pro rata.]

Note: This section is bracketed to indicate division of opinion as to whether or not it is a wise provision, and to suggest that this is a point on which State enactments may differ without serious damage to the principle of uniformity.

In any State where this section is omitted, the following parts of sections, also bracketed in the text, should also be omitted, namely:

Section 6–107(2)(e).
6–108(3)(c).
6–109(2).

In any State where this section is enacted, these other provisions should be also.

Optional Subsection (4)

[(4) The transferee may within ten days after he takes possession of the goods pay the consideration into the (specify court) in the county where the transferor had its principal place of business in this state and thereafter may discharge his duty under this section by giving notice by registered or certified mail to all the persons to whom the duty runs that the consideration has been paid into that court and that they should file their claims there. On motion of any interested party, the court may order the distribution of the consideration to the persons entitled to it.]

Note: Optional subsection (4) is recommended for those states which do not have a general statute providing for payment of money into court.

§ 6–107.   The Notice

(1) The notice to creditors (Section 6–105) shall state:

(a) that a bulk transfer is about to be made; and

(b) the names and business addresses of the transferor and transferee, and all other business names and addresses used by the transferor within three years last past so far as known to the transferee; and

(c) whether or not all the debts of the transferor are to be paid in full as they fall due as a result of the transaction, and if so, the address to which creditors should send their bills.

(2) If the debts of the transferor are not to be paid in full as they fall due or if the transferee is in doubt on that point then the notice shall state further:

(a) the location and general description of the property to be transferred and the estimated total of the transferor's debts;

(b) the address where the schedule of property and list of creditors (Section 6–104) may be inspected;

(c) whether the transfer is to pay existing debts and if so the amount of such debts and to whom owing;

(d) whether the transfer is for new consideration and if so the amount of such consideration and the time and place of payment; [and]

[(e) if for new consideration the time and place where creditors of the transferor are to file their claims.]

(3) The notice in any case shall be delivered personally or sent by registered or certified mail to all the persons shown on the list of creditors furnished by the transferor (Section 6–104) and to all other persons who are known to the transferee to hold or assert claims against the transferor.

Note: The words in brackets are optional. See Note under Section 6–106.

§ 6–108.   Auction Sales; "Auctioneer"

(1) A bulk transfer is subject to this Article even though it is by sale at auction, but only in the manner and with the results stated in this section.

(2) The transferor shall furnish a list of his creditors and assist in the preparation of a schedule of the property to be sold, both prepared as before stated (Section 6–104).

(3) The person or persons other than the transferor who direct, control or are responsible for the auction are collectively called the "auctioneer." The auctioneer shall:

(a) receive and retain the list of creditors and prepare and retain the schedule of property for the period stated in this Article (Section 6–104);

(b) give notice of the auction personally or by registered or certified mail at least ten days before it occurs to all persons shown on the list of creditors and to all other persons who are known to him to hold or assert claims against the transferor; [and]

[(c) assure that the net proceeds of the auction are applied as provided in this Article (Section 6–106).]

(4) Failure of the auctioneer to perform any of these duties does not affect the validity of the sale or the title of the purchasers, but if the auctioneer knows that the auction constitutes a bulk transfer such failure renders the auctioneer liable to the creditors of the transferor as a class for the sums owing to them from the transferor up to but not exceeding the net proceeds of the auction. If the auctioneer consists of several persons their liability is joint and several.

Note: The words in brackets are optional. See Note under Section 6–106.

§ 6–109.   What Creditors Protected; [Credit for Payment to Particular Creditors]

(1) The creditors of the transferor mentioned in this Article are those holding claims based on transactions or events occurring before the bulk transfer, but creditors who become such after notice to creditors is given (Sections 6–105 and 6–107) are not entitled to notice.

[(2) Against the aggregate obligation imposed by the provisions of this Article concerning the application of the proceeds (Section 6–106 and subsection (3)(c) of 6–108) the transferee or auctioneer is entitled to credit for sums paid to particular creditors of the transferor, not exceeding the sums believed in good faith at the time of the payment to be properly payable to such creditors.]

Note: The words in brackets are optional. See Note under Section 6–106.

§ 6–110.   Subsequent Transfers

When the title of a transferee to property is subject to a defect by reason of his non-compliance with the requirements of this Article, then:

(1) A purchaser of any of such property from such transferee who pays no value or who takes with notice of such noncompliance takes subject to such defect, but

(2) A purchaser for value in good faith and without such notice takes free of such defect.

§ 6–111.   Limitation of Actions and Levies

No action under this Article shall be brought nor levy made more than six months after the date on which the transferee took possession of the goods unless the transfer has been concealed. If the transfer has been concealed, actions may be brought or levies made within six months after its discovery.

Article 7   Warehouse Receipts, Bills of Lading and Other Documents of Title

Part 1   General

§ 7–101.   Short Title

This Article shall be known and may be cited as Uniform Commercial Code—Documents of Title.

§ 7–102.   Definitions and Index of Definitions

(1) In this Article, unless the context otherwise requires:

(a) "Bailee" means the person who by a warehouse receipt, bill of lading or other document of title acknowledges possession of goods and contracts to deliver them.

(b) "Consignee" means the person named in a bill to whom or to whose order the bill promises delivery.

(c) "Consignor" means the person named in a bill as the person from whom the goods have been received for shipment.

(d) "Delivery order" means a written order to deliver goods directed to a warehouseman, carrier or other person who in the ordinary course of business issues warehouse receipts or bills of lading.

(e) "Document" means document of title as defined in the general definitions in Article 1 (Section 1–201).

(f) "Goods" means all things which are treated as movable for the purposes of a contract of storage or transportation.

(g) "Issuer" means a bailee who issues a document except that in relation to an unaccepted delivery order it means the person who orders the possessor of goods to deliver. Issuer includes any person for whom an agent or employee purports to act in issuing a document if the agent or employee has real or apparent authority to issue documents, notwithstanding that the issuer received no goods or that the goods were misdescribed or that in any other respect the agent or employee violated his instructions.

(h) "Warehouseman" is a person engaged in the business of storing goods for hire.

(2) Other definitions applying to this Article or to specified Parts thereof, and the sections in which they appear are:

"Duly negotiate." Section 7–501.

"Person entitled under the document." Section 7–403(4).

(3) Definitions in other Articles applying to this Article and the sections in which they appear are:

"Contract for sale." Section 2–106.

"Overseas." Section 2–323.

"Receipt" of goods. Section 2–103.

(4) In addition Article 1 contains general definitions and principles of construction and interpretation applicable throughout this Article.

§ 7–103.   Relation of Article to Treaty, Statute, Tariff, Classification or Regulation

To the extent that any treaty or statute of the United States, regulatory statute of this State or tariff, classification or regulation filed or issued pursuant thereto is applicable, the provisions of this Article are subject thereto.

§ 7–104.   Negotiable and Non-Negotiable Warehouse Receipt, Bill of Lading or Other Document of Title

(1) A warehouse receipt, bill of lading or other document of title is negotiable

(a) if by its terms the goods are to be delivered to bearer or to the order of a named person; or

(b) where recognized in overseas trade, if it runs to a named person or assigns.

(2) Any other documents is non-negotiable. A bill of lading in which it is stated that the goods are consigned to a named person is not made negotiable by a provision that the goods are to be delivered only against a written order signed by the same or another named person.

§ 7–105.   Construction Against Negative Implication

The omission from either Part 2 or Part 3 of this Article of a provision corresponding to a provision made in the other Part does not imply that a corresponding rule of law is not applicable.

Part 2   Warehouse Receipts: Special Provisions

§ 7–201.   Who May Issue a Warehouse Receipt; Storage Under Government Bond

(1) A warehouse receipt may be issued by any warehouseman.

(2) Where goods including distilled spirits and agricultural commodities are stored under a statute requiring a bond against withdrawal or a license for the issuance of receipts in the nature of warehouse receipt, a receipt issued for the goods has like effect as a warehouse receipt even though issued by a person who is the owner of the goods and is not a warehouseman.

§ 7–202.   Forms of Warehouse Receipt; Essential Terms; Optional Terms

(1)   A warehouse receipt need not be in any particular form.

(2) Unless a warehouse receipt embodies within its written or printed terms each of the following, the warehouseman is liable for damages caused by the omission to a person injured thereby:

(a) the location of the warehouse where the goods are stored;

(b) the date of issue of the receipt;

(c) the consecutive number of the receipt;

(d) a statement whether the goods received will be delivered to the bearer, to a specified person, or to a specified person or his order;

(e) the rate of storage and handling charges, except that where goods are stored under a field warehousing arrangement a statement of that fact is sufficient on a non-negotiable receipt;

(f) a description of the goods or of the packages containing them;

(g) the signature of the warehouseman, which may be made by his authorized agent;

(h) if the receipt is issued for goods of which the warehouseman is owner, either solely or jointly or in common with others, the fact of such ownership; and

(i) a statement of the amount of advances made and of liabilities incurred for which the warehouseman claims a lien or security interest (Section 7–209). If the precise amount of such advances made or of such liabilities incurred is, at the time of the issue of the receipt, unknown to the warehouseman or to his agent who issues it, a statement of the fact that advances have been made or liabilities incurred and the purpose thereof is sufficient.

(3) A warehouseman may insert in his receipt any other terms which are not contrary to the provisions of this Act and

do not impair his obligation of delivery (Section 7–403) or his duty of care (Section 7–204). Any contrary provisions shall be ineffective.

§ 7–203.   Liability for Non-Receipt or Misdescription

A party to or purchaser for value in good faith of a document of title other than a bill of lading relying in either case upon the description therein of the goods may recover from the issuer damages caused by the non-receipt or misdescription of the goods, except to the extent that the document conspicuously indicates that the issuer does not know whether any part or all of the goods in fact were received or conform to the description, as where the description is in terms of marks or labels or kind, quantity or condition, or the receipt or description is qualified by "contents, condition and quality unknown," "said to contain" or the like, if such indication be true, or the party or purchaser otherwise has notice.

§ 7–204.   Duty of Care; Contractual Limitation of Warehouseman's Liability

(1) A warehouseman is liable for damages for loss of or injury to the goods caused by his failure to exercise such care in regard to them as a reasonably careful man would exercise under like circumstances but unless otherwise agreed he is not liable for damages which could not have been avoided by the exercise of such care.

(2) Damages may be limited by a term in the warehouse receipt or storage agreement limiting the amount of liability in case of loss or damage, and setting forth a specific liability per article or item, or value per unit of weight, beyond which the warehouseman shall not be liable; provided, however, that such liability may on written request of the bailor at the time of signing such storage agreement or within a reasonable time after receipt of the warehouse receipt be increased on part or all of the goods thereunder, in which event increased rates may be charged based on such increased valuation, but that no such increase shall be permitted contrary to a lawful limitation of liability contained in the warehouseman's tariff, if any. No such limitation is effective with respect to the warehouseman's liability for conversion to his own use.

(3) Reasonable provisions as to the time and manner of presenting claims and instituting actions based on the bailment may be included in the warehouse receipt or tariff.

(4) This section does not impair or repeal . . .

Note: Insert in subsection (4) a reference to any statute which imposes a higher responsibility upon the warehouseman or invalidates contractural limitations which would be permissible under this Article.

§ 7–205.   Title under Warehouse Receipt Defeated in Certain Cases

A buyer in the ordinary course of business of fungible goods sold and delivered by a warehouseman who is also in the business of buying and selling such goods takes free of any claim under a warehouse receipt even though it has been duly negotiated.

§ 7–206.   Termination of Storage at Warehouseman's Option

(1) A warehouseman may on notifying the person on whose account the goods are held and any other person known to claim an interest in the goods require payment of any charges and removal of the goods from the warehouse at the termination of the period of storage fixed by the document, or, if no period is fixed, within a stated period not less than thirty days after the notification. If the goods are not removed before the date specified in the notification, the warehouseman may sell them in accordance with the provisions of the section on enforcement of a warehouseman's lien (Section 7–210).

(2) If a warehouseman in good faith believes that the goods are about to deteriorate or decline in value to less than the amount of his lien within the time prescribed in subsection (1) for notification, advertisement and sale, the warehouseman may specify in the notification any reasonable shorter time for removal of the goods and in case the goods are not removed, may sell them at public sale held not less than one week after a single advertisement or posting.

(3) If as a result of a quality or condition of the goods of which the warehouseman had no notice at the time of deposit the goods are a hazard to other property or to the warehouse or to persons, the warehouseman may sell the goods at public or private sale without advertisement on reasonable notification to all persons known to claim an interest in the goods. If the warehouseman after a reasonable effort is unable to sell the goods he may dispose of them in any lawful manner and shall incur no liability by reason of such disposition.

(4) The warehouseman must deliver the goods to any person entitled to them under this Article upon due demand made at any time prior to sale or other disposition under this section.

(5) The warehouseman may satisfy his lien from the proceeds of any sale or disposition under this section but must hold the balance for delivery on the demand of any person to whom he would have been bound to deliver the goods.

§ 7–207.   Goods Must Be Kept Separate; Fungible Goods

(1) Unless the warehouse receipt otherwise provides, a warehouseman must keep separate the goods covered by each receipt so as to permit at all times identification and delivery of those goods except that different lots of fungible goods may be commingled.

(2) Fungible goods so commingled are owned in common by the persons entitled thereto and the warehouseman is severally liable to each owner for that owner's share. Where because of overissue a mass of fungible goods is insufficient to meet all the receipts which the warehouseman has issued against it, the

persons entitled include all holders to whom overissued receipts have been duly negotiated.

§ 7–208. Altered Warehouse Receipts

Where a blank in a negotiable warehouse receipt has been filled in without authority, a purchaser for value and without notice of the want of authority may treat the insertion as authorized. Any other unauthorized alteration leaves any receipt enforceable against the issuer according to its original tenor.

§ 7–209. Lien of Warehouseman

(1) A warehouseman has a lien against the bailor on the goods covered by a warehouse receipt or on the proceeds thereof in his possession for charges for storage or transportation (including demurrage and terminal charges), insurance, labor, or charges present or future in relation to the goods, and for expenses necessary for preservation of the goods or reasonably incurred in their sale pursuant to law. If the person on whose account the goods are held is liable for like charges or expenses in relation to other goods whenever deposited and it is stated in the receipt that a lien is claimed for charges and expenses in relation to other goods, the warehouseman also has a lien against him for such charges and expenses whether or not the other goods have been delivered by the warehouseman. But against a person to whom a negotiable warehouse receipt is duly negotiated a warehouseman's lien is limited to charges in an amount or at a rate specified on the receipt or if no charges are so specified then to a reasonable charge for storage of the goods covered by the receipt subsequent to the date of receipt.

(2) The warehouseman may also reserve a security interest against the bailor for a maximum amount specified on the receipt for charges other than those specified in subsection (1), such as for money advanced and interest. Such a security interest is governed by the Article on Secured Transactions (Article 9).

(3)(a) A warehouseman's lien for charges and expenses under subsection (1) or a security interest under subsection (2) is also effective against any person who so entrusted the bailor with possession of the goods that a pledge of them by him to a good faith purchaser for value would have been valid but is not effective against a person as to whom the document confers no right in the goods covered by it under Section 7–503.

(b) A warehouseman's lien on household goods for charges and expenses in relation to the goods under subsection (1) is also effective against all persons if the depositor was the legal possessor of the goods at the time of deposit. "Household goods" means furniture, furnishings, and personal effects used by the depositor in a dwelling.

(4) A warehouseman loses his lien on any goods which he voluntarily delivers or which he unjustifiably refuses to deliver.

§ 7–210. Enforcement of Warehouseman's Lien

(1) Except as provided in subsection (2), a warehouseman's lien may be enforced by public or private sale of the goods in block or in parcels, at any time or place and on any terms which are commercially reasonable, after notifying all persons known to claim an interest in the goods. Such notification must include a statement of the amount due, the nature of the proposed sale and the time and place of any public sale. The fact that a better price could have been obtained by a sale at a different time or in a different method from that selected by the warehouseman is not of itself sufficient to establish that the sale was not made in a commercially reasonable manner. If the warehouseman either sells the goods in the usual manner in any recognized market therefor, or if he sells at the price current in such market at the time of his sale, of if he has otherwise sold in conformity with commercially reasonable practices among dealers in the type of goods sold, he has sold in a commercially reasonable manner. A sale of more goods than apparently necessary to be offered to insure satisfaction of the obligation is not commercially reasonable except in cases covered by the preceding sentence.

(2) A warehouseman's lien on goods other than goods stored by a merchant in the course of his business may be enforced only as follows:

(a) All persons known to claim an interest in the goods must be notified.

(b) The notification must be delivered in person or sent by registered or certified letter to the last known address of any person to be notified.

(c) The notification must include an itemized statement of the claim, a description of the goods subject to the lien, a demand for payment within a specified time not less than ten days after receipt of the notification, and a conspicuous statement that unless the claim is paid within that time the goods will be advertised for sale and sold by auction at a specified time and place.

(d) The sale must conform to the terms of the notification.

(e) The sale must be held at the nearest suitable place to that where the goods are held or stored.

(f) After the expiration of the time given in the notification, an advertisement of the sale must be published once a week for two weeks consecutively in a newspaper of general circulation where the sale is to be held. The advertisement must include a description of the goods, the name of the person on whose account they are being held, and the time and place of the sale. The sale must take place at least fifteen days after the first publication. If there is no newspaper of general circulation where the sale is to be held, the advertisement must be posted at least ten days before the sale in not less than six conspicuous places in the neighborhood of the proposed sale.

(3) Before any sale pursuant to this section any person claiming a right in the goods may pay the amount necessary to satisfy the lien and the reasonable expenses incurred under this section. In that event the goods must not be sold, but must be retained by the warehouseman subject to the terms of the receipt and this Article.

(4) The warehouseman may buy at any public sale pursuant to this section.

(5) A purchaser in good faith of goods sold to enforce a warehouseman's lien takes the goods free of any rights of persons against whom the lien was valid, despite noncompliance by the warehouseman with the requirements of this section.

(6) The warehouseman may satisfy his lien from the proceeds of any sale pursuant to this section but must hold the balance, if any, for delivery on demand to any person to whom he would have been bound to deliver the goods.

(7) The rights provided by this section shall be in addition to all other rights allowed by law to a creditor against his debtor.

(8) Where a lien is on goods stored by a merchant in the course of his business the lien may be enforced in accordance with either subsection (1) or (2).

(9) The warehouseman is liable for damages caused by failure to comply with the requirements for sale under this section and in case of willful violation is liable for conversion.

Part 3   Bills of Lading: Special Provisions

§ 7–301.   Liability for Non-Receipt or Misdescription; "Said to Contain"; "Shipper's Load and Count"; Improper Handling

(1) A consignee of a non-negotiable bill who has given value in good faith or a holder to whom a negotiable bill has been duly negotiated relying in either case upon the description therein of the goods, or upon the date therein shown, may recover from the issuer damages caused by the misdating of the bill or the non-receipt or misdescription of the goods, except to the extent that the document indicates that the issuer does not know whether any part or all of the goods in fact were received or conform to the description, as where the description is in terms of marks or labels or kind, quantity, or condition or the receipt or description is qualified by "contents or condition of contents of packages unknown," "said to contain," "shipper's weight, load and count" or the like, if such indication be true.

(2) When goods are loaded by an issuer who is a common carrier, the issuer must count the packages of goods if package freight and ascertain the kind and quantity if bulk freight. In such cases "shipper's weight, load and count" or other words indicating that the description was made by the shipper are ineffective except as to freight concealed by packages.

(3) When bulk freight is loaded by a shipper who makes available to the issuer adequate facilities for weighing such freight, an issuer who is a common carrier must ascertain the kind and quantity within a reasonable time after receiving the written request of the shipper to do so. In such cases "shipper's weight" or other words of like purport are ineffective.

(4) The issuer may by inserting in the bill the words "shipper's weight, load and count" or other words of like purport indicate that the goods were loaded by the shipper; and if such statement be true the issuer shall not be liable for damages caused by the improper loading. But their omission does not imply liability for such damages.

(5) The shipper shall be deemed to have guaranteed to the issuer the accuracy at the time of shipment of the description, marks, labels, number, kind, quantity, condition and weight, as furnished by him; and the shipper shall indemnify the issuer against damage caused by inaccuracies in such particulars. The right of the issuer to such indemnity shall in no way limit his responsibility and liability under the contract of carriage to any person other than the shipper.

§ 7–302.   Through Bills of Lading and Similar Documents

(1) The issuer of a through bill of lading or other document embodying an undertaking to be performed in part by persons acting as its agents or by connecting carriers is liable to anyone entitled to recover on the document for any breach by such other persons or by a connecting carrier of its obligation under the document but to the extent that the bill covers an undertaking to be performed overseas or in territory not contiguous to the continental United States or an undertaking including matters other than transportation this liability may be varied by agreement of the parties.

(2) Where goods covered by a through bill of lading or other document embodying an undertaking to be performed in part by persons other than the issuer are received by any such person, he is subject with respect to his own performance while the goods are in his possession to the obligation of the issuer. His obligation is discharged by delivery of the goods to another such person pursuant to the document, and does not include liability for breach by any other such persons or by the issuer.

(3) The issuer of such through bill of lading or other document shall be entitled to recover from the connecting carrier or such other person in possession of the goods when the breach of the obligation under the document occurred, the amount it may be required to pay to anyone entitled to recover on the document therefor, as may be evidenced by any receipt, judgment, or transcript thereof, and the amount of any expense reasonably incurred by it in defending any action brought by anyone entitled to recover on the document therefor.

§ 7–303.   Diversion; Reconsignment; Change of Instructions

(1) Unless the bill of lading otherwise provides, the carrier may deliver the goods to a person or destination other than that stated in the bill or may otherwise dispose of the goods on instructions from

   (a) the holder of a negotiable bill; or

   (b) the consignor on a non-negotiable bill notwithstanding contrary instructions from the consignee; or

   (c) the consignee on a non-negotiable bill in the absence of contrary instructions from the consignor, if the goods have arrived at the billed destination or if the consignee is in possession of the bill; or

   (d) the consignee on a non-negotiable bill if he is entitled as against the consignor to dispose of them.

(2) Unless such instructions are noted on a negotiable bill of lading, a person to whom the bill is duly negotiated can hold the bailee according to the original terms.

§ 7–304.   Bills of Lading in a Set

(1) Except where customary in overseas transportation, a bill of lading must not be issued in a set of parts. The issuer is liable for damages caused by violation of this subsection.

(2) Where a bill of lading is lawfully drawn in a set of parts, each of which is numbered and expressed to be valid only if the goods have not been delivered against any other part, the whole of the parts constitute one bill.

(3) Where a bill of lading is lawfully issued in a set of parts and different parts are negotiated to different persons, the title of the holder to whom the first due negotiation is made prevails as to both the document and the goods even though any later holder may have received the goods from the carrier in good faith and discharged the carrier's obligation by surrender of his part.

(4) Any person who negotiates or transfers a single part of a bill of lading drawn in a set is liable to holders of that part as if it were the whole set.

(5) The bailee is obliged to deliver in accordance with Part 4 of this Article against the first presented part of a bill of lading lawfully drawn in a set. Such delivery discharges the bailee's obligation on the whole bill.

§ 7–305.   Destination Bills

(1) Instead of issuing a bill of lading to the consignor at the place of shipment a carrier may at the request of the consignor procure the bill to be issued at destination or at any other place designated in the request.

(2) Upon request of anyone entitled as against the carrier to control the goods while in transit and on surrender of any outstanding bill of lading or other receipt covering such goods, the issuer may procure a substitute bill to be issued at any place designated in the request.

§ 7–306.   Altered Bills of Lading

An unauthorized alteration or filling in of a blank in a bill of lading leaves the bill enforceable according to its original tenor.

§ 7–307.   Lien of Carrier

(1) A carrier has a lien on the goods covered by a bill of lading for charges subsequent to the date of its receipt of the goods for storage or transportation (including demurrage and terminal charges) and for expenses necessary for preservation of the goods incident to their transportation or reasonably incurred in their sale pursuant to law. But against a purchaser for value of a negotiable bill of lading a carrier's lien is limited to charges stated in the bill or the applicable tariffs, or if no charges are stated then to a reasonable charge.

(2) A lien for charges and expenses under subsection (1) on goods which the carrier was required by law to receive for transportation is effective against the consignor or any person entitled to the goods unless the carrier had notice that the consignor lacked authority to subject the goods to such charges and expenses. Any other lien under subsection (1) is effective against the consignor and any person who permitted the bailor to have control or possession of the goods unless the carrier had notice that the bailor lacked such authority.

(3) A carrier loses his lien on any goods which he voluntarily delivers or which he unjustifiably refuses to deliver.

§ 7–308.   Enforcement of Carrier's Lien

(1) A carrier's lien may be enforced by public or private sale of the goods, in block or in parcels, at any time or place and on any terms which are commercially reasonable, after notifying all persons known to claim an interest in the goods. Such notification must include a statement of the amount due, the nature of the proposed sale and the time and place of any public sale. The fact that a better price could have been obtained by a sale at a different time or in a different method from that selected by the carrier is not of itself sufficient to establish that the sale was not made in a commercially reasonable manner. If the carrier either sells the goods in the usual manner in any recognized market therefor or if he sells at the price current in such market at the time of his sale or if he has otherwise sold in conformity with commercially reasonable practices among dealers in the type of goods sold he has sold in a commercially reasonable manner. A sale of more goods than apparently necessary to be offered to ensure satisfaction of the obligation is not commercially reasonable except in cases covered by the preceding sentence.

(2) Before any sale pursuant to this section any person claiming a right in the goods may pay the amount necessary to satisfy the lien and the reasonable expenses incurred under this section. In that event the goods must not be sold, but must be retained by the carrier subject to the terms of the bill and this Article.

(3) The carrier may buy at any public sale pursuant to this section.

(4) A purchaser in good faith of goods sold to enforce a carrier's lien takes the goods free of any rights of persons against whom the lien was valid, despite noncompliance by the carrier with the requirements of this section.

(5) The carrier may satisfy his lien from the proceeds of any sale pursuant to this section but must hold the balance, if any, for delivery on demand to any person to whom he would have been bound to deliver the goods.

(6) The rights provided by this section shall be in addition to all other rights allowed by law to a creditor against his debtor.

(7) A carrier's lien may be enforced in accordance with either subsection (1) or the procedure set forth in subsection (2) of Section 7–210.

(8) The carrier is liable for damages caused by failure to comply with the requirements for sale under this section and in case of willful violation is liable for conversion.

§ 7–309.   Duty of Care; Contractual Limitation of Carrier's Liability

(1) A carrier who issues a bill of lading whether negotiable or non-negotiable must exercise the degree of care in relation to the goods which a reasonably careful man would exercise under like circumstances. This subsection does not repeal or change any law or rule of law which imposes liability upon a common carrier for damages not caused by its negligence.

(2) Damages may be limited by a provision that the carrier's liability shall not exceed a value stated in the document if the carrier's rates are dependent upon value and the consignor by the carrier's tariff is afforded an opportunity to declare a higher value or a value as lawfully provided in the tariff, or where no tariff is filed he is otherwise advised of such opportunity; but no such limitation is effective with respect to the carrier's liability for conversion to its own use.

(3) Reasonable provisions as to the time and manner of presenting claims and instituting actions based on the shipment may be included in a bill of lading or tariff.

Part 4   Warehouse Receipts and Bills of Lading: General Obligations

§ 7–401.   Irregularities in Issue of Receipt or Bill or Conduct of Issuer

The obligations imposed by this Article on an issuer apply to a document of title regardless of the fact that

(a) the document may not comply with the requirements of this Article or of any other law or regulation regarding its issue, form or content; or

(b) the issuer may have violated laws regulating the conduct of his business; or

(c) the goods covered by the document were owned by the bailee at the time the document was issued; or

(d) the person issuing the document does not come within the definition of warehouseman if it purports to be a warehouse receipt.

§ 7–402.   Duplicate Receipt or Bill; Overissue

Neither a duplicate nor any other document of title purporting to cover goods already represented by an outstanding document of the same issuer confers any right in the goods, except as provided in the case of bills in a set, overissue of documents for fungible goods and substitutes for lost, stolen or destroyed documents. But the issuer is liable for damages caused by his overissue or failure to identify a duplicate document as such by conspicuous notation on its face.

§ 7–403.   Obligation of Warehouseman or Carrier to Deliver; Excuse

(1) The bailee must deliver the goods to a person entitled under the document who complies with subsections (2) and (3), unless and to the extent that the bailee establishes any of the following:

(a) delivery of the goods to a person whose receipt was rightful as against the claimant;

(b) damage to or delay, loss or destruction of the goods for which the bailee is not liable [, but the burden of establishing negligence in such cases is on the person entitled under the document];

Note: The brackets in (1)(b) indicate that State enactments may differ on this point without serious damage to the principle of uniformity.

(c) previous sale or other disposition of the goods in lawful enforcement of a lien or on warehouseman's lawful termination of storage;

(d) the exercise by a seller of his right to stop delivery pursuant to the provisions of the Article on Sales (Section 2–705);

(e) a diversion, reconsignment or other disposition pursuant to the provisions of this Article (Section 7–303) or tariff regulating such right;

(f) release, satisfaction or any other fact affording a personal defense against the claimant;

(g) any other lawful excuse.

(2) A person claiming goods covered by a document of title must satisfy the bailee's lien where the bailee so requests or where the bailee is prohibited by law from delivering the goods until the charges are paid.

(3) Unless the person claiming is one against whom the document confers no right under Sec. 7–503(1), he must surrender for cancellation or notation of partial deliveries any outstanding negotiable document covering the goods, and the bailee must cancel the document or conspicuously note the partial delivery thereon or be liable to any person to whom the document is duly negotiated.

(4) "Person entitled under the document" means holder in the case of a negotiable document, or the person to whom delivery is to be made by the terms of or pursuant to written instructions under a non-negotiable document.

§ 7–404.   No Liability for Good Faith Delivery Pursuant to Receipt or Bill

A bailee who in good faith including observance of reasonable commercial standards has received goods and delivered or otherwise disposed of them according to the terms of the document of title or pursuant to this Article is not liable therefor. This rule applies even though the person from whom he received the goods has no authority to procure the document or to dispose of the goods and even though the person to whom he delivered the goods had no authority to receive them.

Part 5　Warehouse Receipts and Bills of Lading:
Negotiation and Transfer

§ 7–501.　Form of Negotiation and Requirements of "Due Negotiation"

(1) A negotiable document of title running to the order of a named person is negotiated by his indorsement and delivery. After his indorsement in blank or to bearer any person can negotiate it by delivery alone.

(2)(a) A negotiable document of title is also negotiated by delivery alone when by its original terms it runs to bearer.

(b) When a document running to the order of a named person is delivered to him the effect is the same as if the document had been negotiated.

(3) Negotiation of a negotiable document of title after it has been indorsed to a specified person requires indorsement by the special indorsee as well as delivery.

(4) A negotiable document of title is "duly negotiated" when it is negotiated in the manner stated in this section to a holder who purchases it in good faith without notice of any defense against or claim to it on the part of any person and for value, unless it is established that the negotiation is not in the regular course of business or financing or involves receiving the document in settlement or payment of a money obligation.

(5) Indorsement of a non-negotiable document neither makes it negotiable nor adds to the transferee's rights.

(6) The naming in a negotiable bill of a person to be notified of the arrival of the goods does not limit the negotiability of the bill nor constitute notice to a purchaser thereof of any interest of such person in the goods.

§ 7–502.　Rights Acquired by Due Negotiation

(1) Subject to the following section and to the provisions of Section 7–205 on fungible goods, a holder to whom a negotiable document of title has been duly negotiated acquires thereby:

(a) title to the document;

(b) title to the goods;

(c) all rights accruing under the law of agency or estoppel, including rights to goods delivered to the bailee after the document was issued; and

(d) the direct obligation of the issuer to hold or deliver the goods according to the terms of the document free of any defense or claim by him except those arising under the terms of the document or under this Article. In the case of a delivery order the bailee's obligation accrues only upon acceptance and the obligation acquired by the holder is that the issuer and any indorser will procure the acceptance of the bailee.

(2) Subject to the following section, title and rights so acquired are not defeated by any stoppage of the goods represented by the document or by surrender of such goods by the bailee, and are not impaired even though the negotiation or any prior negotiation constituted a breach of duty or even though any person has been deprived of possession of the document by misrepresentation, fraud, accident, mistake, duress, loss, theft or conversion, or even though a previous sale or other transfer of the goods or document has been made to a third person.

§ 7–503.　Document of Title to Goods Defeated in Certain Cases

(1) A document of title confers no right in goods against a person who before issuance of the document had a legal interest or a perfected security interest in them and who neither

(a) delivered or entrusted them or any document of title covering them to the bailor or his nominee with actual or apparent authority to ship, store or sell or with power to obtain delivery under this Article (Section 7–403) or with power of disposition under this Act (Section 2–403 and 9–307) or other statute or rule of law; nor

(b) acquiesced in the procurement by the bailor or his nominee of any document of title.

(2) Title to goods based upon an unaccepted delivery order is subject to the rights of anyone to whom a negotiable warehouse receipt or bill of lading covering the goods has been duly negotiated. Such a title may be defeated under the next section to the same extent as the rights of the issuer or a transferee from the issuer.

(3) Title to goods based upon a bill of lading issued to a freight forwarder is subject to the rights of anyone to whom a bill issued by the freight forwarder is duly negotiated; but delivery by the carrier in accordance with Part 4 of this Article pursuant to its own bill of lading discharges the carrier's obligation to deliver.

§ 7–504.　Rights Acquired in the Absence of Due Negotiation; Effect of Diversion; Seller's Stoppage of Delivery

(1) A transferee of a document, whether negotiable or non-negotiable, to whom the document has been delivered but not duly negotiated, acquires the title and rights which his transferor had or had actual authority to convey.

(2) In the case of a non-negotiable document, until but not after the bailee receives notification of the transfer, the rights of the transferee may be defeated

(a) by those creditors of the transferor who could treat the sale as void under Section 2–402; or

(b) by a buyer from the transferor in ordinary course of business if the bailee has delivered the goods to the buyer or received notification of his rights; or

(c) as against the bailee by good faith dealings of the bailee with the transferor.

(3) A diversion or other change of shipping instructions by the consignor in a non-negotiable bill of lading which causes the

bailee not to deliver to the consignee defeats the consignee's title to the goods if they have been delivered to a buyer in ordinary course of business and in any event defeats the consignee's rights against the bailee.

(4) Delivery pursuant to a non-negotiable document may be stopped by a seller under Section 2–705, and subject to the requirement of due notification there provided. A bailee honoring the seller's instructions is entitled to be indemnified by the seller against any resulting loss or expense.

§ 7–505. Indorser Not a Guarantor for Other Parites

The indorsement of a document of title issued by a bailee does not make the indorser liable for any default by the bailee or by previous indorsers.

§ 7–506. Delivery without Indorsement: Right to Compel Indorsement

The transferee of a negotiable document of title has a specifically enforceable right to have his transferor supply any necessary indorsement but the transfer becomes a negotiation only as of the time the indorsement is supplied.

§ 7–507. Warranties on Negotiation or Transfer of Receipt or Bill

Where a person negotiates or transfers a document of title for value otherwise than as a mere intermediary under the next following section, then unless otherwise agreed he warrants to his immediate purchaser only in addition to any warranty made in selling the goods

(a) that the document is genuine; and

(b) that he has no knowledge of any fact which would impair its validity or worth; and

(c) that his negotiation or transfer is rightful and fully effective with respect to the title to the document and the goods it represents.

§ 7–508. Warranties of Collecting Bank as to Documents

A collecting bank or other intermediary known to be entrusted with documents on behalf of another or with collection of a draft or other claim against delivery of documents warrants by such delivery of the documents only its own good faith and authority. This rule applies even though the intermediary has purchased or made advances against the claim or draft to be collected.

§ 7–509. Receipt or Bill: When Adequate Compliance with Commercial Contract

The question whether a document is adequate to fulfill the obligations of a contract for sale or the conditions of a credit is governed by the Articles on Sales (Article 2) and on Letters of Credit (Article 5).

Part 6 Warehouse Receipts and Bills of Lading: Miscellaneous Provisions

§ 7–601. Lost and Missing Documents

(1) If a document has been lost, stolen or destroyed, a court may order delivery of the goods or issuance of a substitute document and the bailee may without liability to any person comply with such order. If the document was negotiable the claimant must post security approved by the court to idemnify any person who may suffer loss as a result of non-surrender of the document. If the document was not negotiable, such security may be required at the discretion of the court. The court may also in its discretion order payment of the bailee's reasonable costs and counsel fees.

(2) A bailee who without court order delivers goods to a person claiming under a missing negotiable document is liable to any person injured thereby, and if the delivery is not in good faith becomes liable for conversion. Delivery in good faith is not conversion if made in accordance with a filed classification or tariff or, where no classification or tariff is filed, if the claimant posts security with the bailee in an amount at least double the value of the goods at the time of posting to indemnify any person injured by the delivery who files a notice of claim within one year after the delivery.

§ 7–602. Attachment of Goods Covered by a Negotiable Document

Except where the document was originally issued upon delivery of the goods by a person who had no power to dispose of them, no lien attaches by virtue of any judicial process to goods in the possession of a bailee for which a negotiable document of title is outstanding unless the document be first surrendered to the bailee or its negotiation enjoined, and the bailee shall not be compelled to deliver the goods pursuant to process until the document is surrendered to him or impounded by the court. One who purchases the document for value without notice of the process or injunction takes free of the lien imposed by judicial process.

§ 7–603. Conflicting Claims; Interpleader

If more than one person claims title or possession of the goods, the bailee is excused from delivery until he has had a reasonable time to ascertain the validity of the adverse claims or to bring an action to compel all claimants to interplead and may compel such interpleader, either in defending an action for non-delivery of the goods, or by original action, whichever is appropriate.

ARTICLE 8 INVESTMENT SECURITIES

Part 1 *Short Title and General Matters*

§ 8–101. Short Title

This Article shall be known and may be cited as Uniform Commercial Code—Investment Securities.

§ 8–102. Definitions and Index of Definitions

(1) In this Article, unless the context otherwise requires:

(a) A "certified security" is a share, participation, or other interest in property of or an enterprise of the issuer or an obligation of the issuer which is

(i) represented by an instrument issued in bearer or registered form;

(ii) of a type commonly dealt in on securities exchanges or markets or commonly recognized in any area in which it is issued or dealt in as a medium for investment; and

(iii) either one of a class or series or by its terms divisible into a class or series of shares, participations, interests, or obligations.

(b) An "uncertificated security" is a share, participation, or other interest in property or an enterprise of the issuer or an obligation of the issuer which is

(i) not represented by an instrument and the transfer of which is registered upon books maintained for that purpose by or on behalf of the issuer;

(ii) of a type commonly dealt in on securities exchanges or markets; and

(iii) either one of a class or series or by its terms divisible into a class or series of shares, participations, interests, or obligations.

(c) A "security" is either a certificated or an uncertificated security. If a security is certificated, the terms "security" and "certificated security" may mean either the intangible interest, the instrument representing that interest, or both, as the context requires. A writing that is a certificated security is governed by this Article and not by Article 3, even though it also meets the requirements of that Article. This Article does not apply to money. If a certificated security has been retained by or surrendered to the issuer or its transfer agent for reasons other than registration of transfer, other temporary purpose, payment, exchange, or acquisition by the issuer, that security shall be treated as an uncertificated security for purposes of this Article.

(d) A certificated security is in "registered form" if

(i) it specifies a person entitled to the security or the rights it represents; and

(ii) its transfer may be registered upon books maintained for that purpose by or on behalf of the issuer, or the security so states.

(e) A certificated security is in "bearer form" if it runs to bearer according to its terms and not by reason of any indorsement.

(2) A "subsequent purchaser" is a person who takes other than by original issue.

(3) A "clearing corporation" is a corporation registered as a "clearing agency" under the federal securities laws or a corporation:

(a) at least 90 percent of whose capital stock is held by or for one or more organizations, none of which, other than a national securities exchange or association, holds in excess of 20 percent of the capital stock of the corporation, and each of which is

(i) subject to supervision or regulation pursuant to the provisions of federal or state banking laws or state insurance laws,

(ii) a broker or dealer or investment company registered under the federal securities laws, or

(iii) a national securities exchange or association registered under the federal securities laws; and

(b) any remaining capital stock of which is held by individuals who have purchased it at or prior to the time of their taking office as directors of the corporation and who have purchased only so much of the capital stock as is necessary to permit them to qualify as directors.

(4) A "custodian bank" is a bank or trust company that is supervised and examined by state or federal authority having supervision over banks and is acting as custodian for a clearing corporation.

(5) Other definitions applying to this Article or to specified Parts thereof and the sections in which they appear are:

"Adverse claim." Section 8–302.
"Bona fide purchaser." Section 8–302.
"Broker." Section 8–303.
"Debtor." Section 9–105.
"Financial intermediary." Section 8–313.
"Guarantee of the signature." Section 8–402.
"Initial transaction statement." Section 8–408.
"Instruction." Section 8–308.
"Intermediary bank." Section 4–105.
"Issuer." Section 8–201.
"Overissue." Section 8–104.
"Secured Party." Section 9–105.
"Security Agreement." Section 9–105.

(6) In addition, Article 1 contains general definitions and principles of construction and interpretation applicable throughout this Article.

§ 8–103. Issuer's Lien

A lien upon a security in favor of an issuer thereof is valid against a purchaser only if:

(a) the security is certificated and the right of the issuer to the lien is noted conspicuously thereon; or

(b) the security is uncertificated and a notation of the right of the issuer to the lien is contained in the initial transaction statement sent to the purchaser or, if his interest is transferred to him other than by registration of transfer, pledge, or release, the initial transaction statement sent to the registered owner or the registered pledgee.

§ 8–104. Effect of Overissue; "Overissue"

(1) The provisions of this Article which validate a security or compel its issue or reissue do not apply to the extent that validation, issue, or reissue would result in overissue; but if:

(a) an identical security which does not constitute an overissue is reasonably available for purchase, the person entitled to issue or validation may compel the issuer to purchase the security for him and either to deliver a certificated security or to register the transfer of an uncertificated security to him, against surrender of any certificated security he holds; or

(b) a security is not so available for purchase, the person entitled to issue or validation may recover from the issuer the price he or the last purchaser for value paid for it with interest from the date of his demand.

(2) "Overissue" means the issue of securities in excess of the amount the issuer has corporate power to issue.

§ 8–105. Certificated Securities Negotiable; Statements and Instructions Not Negotiable; Presumptions

(1) Certificated securities governed by this Article are negotiable instruments.

(2) Statements (Section 8–408), notices, or the like, sent by the issuer of uncertificated securities and instructions (section 8–308) are neither negotiable instruments nor certificated securities.

(3) In any action on a security:

(a) unless specifically denied in the pleadings, each signature on a certificated security, in a necessary indorsement, on an initial transaction statement, or on an instruction, is admitted;

(b) if the effectiveness of a signature is put in issue, the burden of establishing it is on the party claiming under the signature, but the signature is presumed to be genuine or authorized.

(c) if signatures on a certificated security are admitted or established, production of the security entitles a holder to recover on it unless the defendant establishes a defense or a defect going to the validity of the security;

(d) if signatures on an initial transaction statement are admitted or established, the facts stated in the statement are presumed to be true as of the time of its issuance; and

(e) after it is shown that a defense or defect exists, the plaintiff has the burden of establishing that he or some person under whom he claims is a person against whom the defense or defect is ineffective (Section 8–202).

§ 8–106. Applicability

The law (including the conflict of laws rules) of the jurisdiction of organization of the issuer governs the validity of a security, the effectiveness of registration by the issuer, and the rights and duties of the issuer with respect to:

(a) registration of transfer of a certificated security;

(b) registration of transfer, pledge, or release of an uncertificated security; and

(c) sending of statements of uncertificated securities.

§ 8–107. Securities Transferable; Action for Price

(1) Unless otherwise agreed and subject to any applicable law or regulation respecting short sales, a person obligated to transfer securities may transfer any certificated security of the specified issue in bearer form or registered in the name of the transferee, or indorsed to him or in blank, or he may transfer an equivalent uncertificated security to the transferee or a person designated by the transferee.

(2) If the buyer fails to pay the price as it comes due under a contract of sale, the seller may recover the price of:

(a) certificated securities accepted by the buyer;

(b) uncertificated securities that have been transferred to the buyer or a person designated by the buyer; and

(c) other securities if efforts at their resale would be unduly burdensome or if there is no readily available market for their resale.

§ 8–108. Registration of Pledge and Release of Uncertificated Securities

A security interest in an uncertificated security may be evidenced by the registration of pledge to the secured party or a person designated by him. There can be no more than one registered pledge of an uncertificated security at any time. The registered owner of an uncertified security is the person in whose name the security is registered, even if the security is subject to a registered pledge. The rights of a registered pledgee of an uncertified security under this Article are terminated by the registration of release.

Part 2   Issue—Issuer

§ 8–201. "Issuer"

(1) With respect to obligations on or defenses to a security, "issuer" includes a person who:

(a) places or authorizes the placing of his name on a certificated security (otherwise than as authenticating trustee, registrar, transfer agent, or the like) to evidence that it represents a share, participation, or other interest in his property or in an enterprise, or to evidence his duty to perform an obligation represented by the certificated security;

(b) creates shares, participations, or other interests in his property or in an enterprise or undertakes obligations, which shares, participations, interests, or obligations are uncertificated securities;

(c) directly or indirectly creates fractional interests in his rights or property, which fractional interests are represented by certificated securities; or

(d) becomes responsible for or in place of any other person described as an issuer in this section.

(2) With respect to obligations on or defenses to a security, a guarantor is an issuer to the extent of his guaranty, whether or not his obligation is noted on a certificated security or on statements of uncertificated securities sent pursuant to Section 8–408.

(3) With respect to registration of transfer, pledge, or release (Part 4 of this Article), "issuer" means a person on whose behalf transfer books are maintained.

§ 8–202. Issuer's Responsibility and Defenses; Notice of Defect or Defense

(1) Even against a purchaser for value and without notice, the terms of a security include:

(a) if the security is certificated, those stated on the security;

(b) if the security is uncertificated, those contained in the initial transaction statement sent to such purchaser, or, if his interest is transferred to him other than by registration of transfer, pledge, or release, the initial transaction statement sent to the registered owner or registered pledgee; and

(c) those made part of the security by reference, on the certificated security or in the initial transaction statement, to another instrument, indenture, or document or to a constitution, statute, ordinance, rule, regulation, order or the like, to the extent that the terms referred to do not conflict with the terms stated on the certificated security or contained in the statement. A reference under this paragraph does not of itself charge a purchaser for value with notice of a defect going to the validity of the security, even though the certificated security or statement expressly states that a person accepting it admits notice.

(2) A certificated security in the hands of a purchaser for value or an uncertificated security as to which an initial transaction statement has been sent to a purchaser for value, other than a security issued by a government or governmental agency or unit, even though issued with a defect going to its validity, is valid with respect to the purchaser if he is without notice of the particular defect unless the defect involves a violation of constitutional provisions, in which case the security is valid with respect to a subsequent purchaser for value and without notice of the defect. This subsection applies to an issuer that is a government or governmental agency or unit only if either there has been substantial compliance with the legal requirements governing the issue or the issuer has received a substantial consideration for the issue as a whole or for the particular security and a stated purpose of the issue is one for which the issuer has power to borrow money or issue the security.

(3) Except as provided in the case of certain unauthorized signatures (Section 8–205), lack of genuineness of a certificated security or an initial transaction statement is a complete defense, even against a purchaser for value and without notice.

(4) All other defenses of the issuer of a certificated or uncertificated security, including nondelivery and conditional delivery of a certificated security, are ineffective against a purchaser for value who has taken without notice of the particular defense.

(5) Nothing in this section shall be construed to affect the right of a party to a "when, as and if issued" or a "when distributed" contract to cancel the contract in the event of a material change in the character of the security that is the subject of the contract or in the plan or arrangement pursuant to which the security is to be issued or distributed.

§ 8–203. Staleness as Notice of Defects or Defenses

(1) After an act or event creating a right to immediate performance of the principal obligation represented by a certificated security or that sets a date on or after which the security is to be presented or surrendered for redemption or exchange, a purchaser is charged with notice of any defect in its issue or defense of the issuer if:

(a) the act or event is one requiring the payment of money, the delivery of certificated securities, the registration of transfer of uncertificated securities, or any of these on presentation or surrender of the certificated security, the funds or securities are available on the date set for payment or exchange, and he takes the security more than one year after that date; and

(b) the act or event is not covered by paragraph (a) and he takes the security more than 2 years after the date set for surrender or presentation or the date on which performance became due.

(2) A call that has been revoked is not within subsection (1).

§ 8–204. Effect of Issuer's Restrictions on Transfer

A restriction on transfer of a security imposed by the issuer, even if otherwise lawful, is ineffective against any person without actual knowledge of it unless:

(a) the security is certificated and the restriction is noted conspicuously thereon; or

(b) the security is uncertificated and a notation of the restriction is contained in the initial transaction statement sent to the person or, if his interest is transferred to him other than by registration of transfer, pledge, or release, the initial transaction statement sent to the registered owner or the registered pledgee.

§ 8–205. Effect of Unauthorized Signature on Certificated Security or Initial Transaction Statement

An unauthorized signature placed on a certificated security prior to or in the course of issue or placed on an initial transaction statement is ineffective, but the signature is effective in favor of a purchaser for value of the certificated security or a purchaser for value of an uncertificated security to whom the initial transaction statement has been sent, if the purchaser is without notice of the lack of authority and the signing has been done by:

(a) an authenticating trustee, registrar, transfer agent, or other person entrusted by the issuer with the signing of the security, of similar securities, or of initial transaction statements or the immediate preparation of signing of any of them; or

(b) an employee of the issuer, or of any of the foregoing, entrusted with responsible handling of the security or initial transaction statement.

§ 8–206. Completion or Alteration of Certificated Security or Initial Transaction Statement

(1) If a certificated security contains the signatures necessary to its issue or transfer but is incomplete in any other respect:

(a) any person may complete it by filling in the blanks as authorized; and

(b) even though the blanks are incorrectly filled in, the security as completed is enforceable by a purchaser who took it for value and without notice of the incorrectness.

(2) A complete certificated security that has been improperly altered, even though fraudulently, remains enforceable, but only according to its original terms.

(3) If an initial transaction statement contains the signatures necessary to its validity, but is incomplete in any other respect:

(a) any person may complete it by filling in the blanks as authorized; and

(b) even though the blanks are incorrectly filled in, the statement as completed is effective in favor of the person to whom it is sent if he purchased the security referred to therein for value and without notice of the incorrectness.

(4) A complete initial transaction statement that has been improperly altered, even though fraudulently, is effective in favor of a purchaser to whom it has been sent, but only according to its original terms.

§ 8–207. Rights and Duties of Issuer With Respect to Registered Owners and Registered Pledges

(1) Prior to due presentment for registration of transfer of a certificated security in registered form, the issuer or indenture trustee may treat the registered owner as the person exclusively entitled to vote, to receive notifications, and otherwise to exercise all rights and powers of an owner.

(2) Subject to the provisions of subsections (3), (4), and (6), the issuer or indenture trustee may treat the registered owner of an uncertificated security as the person exclusively entitled to vote, to receive notifications, and otherwise to exercise all the rights and powers of an owner.

(3) The registered owner of an uncertificated security that is subject to a registered pledge is not entitled to registration of transfer prior to the due presentment to the issuer of a release instruction. The exercise of conversion rights with respect to a convertible uncertificated security is a transfer within the meaning of this section.

(4) Upon due presentment of a transfer instruction from the registered pledgee of an uncertificated security, the issuer shall:

(a) register the transfer of the security to the new owner free of pledge, if the instruction specifies a new owner (who may be the registered pledgee) and does not specify a pledgee;

(b) register the transfer of the security to the new owner subject to the interest of the existing pledgee, if the instruction specifies new owner and the existing pledgee; or

(c) register the release of the security from the existing pledge and register the pledge of the security to the other pledgee, if the instruction specifies the existing owner and another pledgee.

(5) Continuity of perfection of a security interest is not broken by registration of transfer under subsection (4)(b) or by registration of release and pledge under subsection (4)(c), if the security interest is assigned.

(6) If an uncertificated security is subject to a registered pledge:

(a) any uncertificated securities issued in exchange for or distributed with respect to the pledged security shall be registered subject to the pledge;

(b) any certificated securities issued in exchange for or distributed with respect to the pledged security shall be delivered to the registered pledgee; and

(c) any money paid in exchange for or in redemption of part or all of the security shall be paid to the registered pledgee.

(7) Nothing in this Article shall be construed to affect the liability of the registered owner of a security for calls, assessments, or the like.

§ 8–208. Effect of Signature of Authenticating Trustee, Registrar, or Transfer Agent

(1) A person placing his signature upon a certificated security or an initial transaction statement as authenticating trustee, registrar, transfer agent, or the like, warrants to a purchaser for value of the certificated security or a purchaser for value of an uncertificated security to whom the initial transaction statement has been sent, if the purchaser is without notice of the particular defect, that:

(a) the certificated security or initial transaction statement is genuine;

(b) his own participation in the issue or registration of the transfer, pledge, or release of the security is within his capacity and within the scope of the authority received by him from the issuer; and

(c) he has reasonable grounds to believe the security is in the form and within the amount the issuer is authorized to issue.

(2) Unless otherwise agreed, a person by so placing his signature does not assume responsibility for the validity of the security in other respects.

Part 3 Transfer

§ 8–301. Rights Acquired by Purchaser

(1) Upon transfer of a security to a purchaser (Section 8–313), the purchaser acquires the rights in the security which his transferor had or had actual authority to convey unless the purchaser's rights are limited by Section 8–302(4).

(2) A transferee of a limited interest acquires rights only to the extent of the interest transferred. The creation or release of a security interest in a security is the transfer of a limited interest in that security.

§ 8–302. "Bona Fide Purchaser"; "Adverse Claim"; Title Acquired by Bona Fide Purchaser

(1) A "bona fide purchaser" is a purchaser for value in good faith and without notice of any adverse claim:

(a) who takes delivery of a certificated security in bearer form or in registered form, issued or indorsed to him or in blank;

(b) to whom the transfer, pledge, or release of an uncertificated security is registered on the books of the issuer; or

(c) to whom a security is transferred under the provisions of paragraph (c), (d)(i), or (g) of Section 8–313(1).

(2) "Adverse claim" includes a claim that a transfer was or would be wrongful or that a particular adverse person is the owner of or has an interest in the security.

(3) A bona fide purchaser in addition to acquiring the rights of a purchaser (Section 8–301) also acquires his interest in the security free of any adverse claim.

(4) Notwithstanding Section 8–301(1), the transferee of a particular certificated security who has been a party to any fraud or illegality affecting the security, or who as a prior holder of that certificated security had notice of an adverse claim, cannot improve his position by taking from a bona fide purchaser.

§ 8–303. "Broker"

"Broker" means a person engaged for all or part of his time in the business of buying and selling securities, who in the transaction concerned acts for, buys a security from, or sells a security to, a customer. Nothing in this Article determines the capacity in which a person acts for purposes of any other statute or rule to which the person is subject.

§ 8–304. Notice to Purchaser of Adverse Claims

(1) A purchaser (including a broker for the seller or buyer, but excluding an intermediary bank) of a certificated security is charged with notice of adverse claims if:

(a) the security, whether in bearer or registered form, has been indorsed "for collection" or "for surrender" or for some other purpose not involving transfer; or

(b) the security is in bearer form and has on it an unambiguous statement that it is the property of a person other than the transferor. The mere writing of a name on a security is not such a statement.

(2) A purchaser (including a broker for the seller or buyer, but excluding an intermediary bank) to whom the transfer, pledge, or release of an uncertificated security is registered is charged with notice of adverse claims as to which the issuer has a duty under Section 8–403(4) at the time of registration and which are noted in the initial transaction statement sent to the purchaser or, if his interest is transferred to him other than by registration of transfer, pledge, or release, the initial transaction statement sent to the registered owner or the registered pledgee.

(3) The fact that the purchaser (including a broker for the seller or buyer) of a certificated or uncertificated security has notice that the security is held for a third person or is registered in the name of or indorsed by a fiduciary does not create a duty of inquiry into the rightfulness of the transfer or constitute constructive notice of adverse claims. However, if the purchaser (excluding an intermediary bank) has knowledge that the proceeds are being used or that the transaction is for the individual benefit of the fiduciary or otherwise in breach of duty, the purchaser is charged with notice of adverse claims.

§ 8–305. Staleness as Notice of Adverse Claims

An act or event that creates a right to immediate performance of the principal obligation represented by a certificated security or sets a date on or after which a certificated security is to be presented or surrendered for redemption or exchange does not itself constitute any notice of adverse claims except in the case of a transfer:

(a) after one year from any date set for presentment or surrender for redemption or exchange; or

(b) after 6 months from any date set for payment of money against presentation or surrender of the security if funds are available for payment on that date.

§ 8–306. Warranties on Presentment and Transfer of Certificated Securities; Warranties of Originators of Instructions

(1) A person who presents a certificated security for registration of transfer or for payment or exchange warrants to the issuer that he is entitled to the registration, payment, or exchange. But, a purchaser for value and without notice of adverse claims who receives a new, reissued, or reregistered certificated security on registration of transfer or receives an initial transaction statement confirming the registration of transfer of an equivalent uncertificated security to him warrants only that he has no knowledge of any unauthorized signature (Section 8–311) in a necessary indorsement.

(2) A person by transferring a certificated security to a purchaser for value warrants only that:

(a) his transfer is effective and rightful;

(b) the security is genuine and has not been materially altered; and

(c) he knows of no fact which might impair the validity of the security.

(3) If a certificated security is delivered by an intermediary known to be entrusted with delivery of the security on behalf of another or with collection of a draft or other claim against delivery, the intermediary by delivery warrants only his own good faith and authority, even though he has purchased or made advances against the claim to be collected against the delivery.

(4) A pledgee or other holder for security who redelivers a certificated security received, or after payment and on order of the debtor delivers that security to a third person, makes only the warranties of an intermediary under subsection (3).

(5) A person who originates an instruction warrants to the issuer that:

(a) he is an appropriate person to originate the instruction; and

(b) at the time the instruction is presented to the issuer he will be entitled to the registration of transfer, pledge, or release.

(6) A person who originates an instruction warrants to any person specially guaranteeing his signature (subsection 8–312(3)) that:

(a) he is an appropriate person to originate the instruction; and

(b) at the time the instruction is presented to the issuer

(i) he will be entitled to the registration of transfer, pledge, or release; and

(ii) the transfer, pledge, or release requested in the instruction will be registered by the issuer free from all liens, security interests, restrictions, and claims other than those specified in the instruction.

(7) A person who originates an instruction warrants to a purchaser for value and to any person guaranteeing the instruction (Section 8–312(6)) that:

(a) he is an appropriate person to originate the instruction;

(b) the uncertificated security referred to therein is valid; and

(c) at the time the instruction is presented to the issuer

(i) the transferor will be entitled to the registration of transfer, pledge, or release;

(ii) the transfer, pledge, or release requested in the instruction will be registered by the issuer free from all liens, security interests, restrictions, and claims other than those specified in the instruction; and

(iii) the requested transfer, pledge, or release will be rightful.

(8) If a secured party is the registered pledgee or the registered owner of an uncertificated security, a person who originates an instruction of release or transfer to the debtor or, after payment and on order of the debtor, a transfer instruction to a third person, warrants to the debtor or the third person only that he is an appropriate person to originate the instruction and, at the time the instruction is presented to the issuer, the transferor will be entitled to the registration of release or transfer. If a transfer instruction to a third person who is a purchaser for value is originated on order of the debtor, the debtor makes to the purchaser the warranties of paragraphs (b), (c)(ii) and (c)(iii) of subsection (7).

(9) A person who transfers an uncertificated security to a purchaser for value and does not originate an instruction in connection with the transfer warrants only that:

(a) his transfer is effective and rightful; and

(b) the uncertificated security is valid.

(10) A broker gives to his customer and to the issuer and a purchaser the applicable warranties provided in this section and has the rights and privileges of a purchaser under this section. The warranties of and in favor of the broker, acting as an agent are in addition to applicable warranties given by and in favor of his customer.

§ 8–307. Effect of Delivery Without Indorsement; Right to Compel Indorsement

If a certificated security in registered form has been delivered to a purchaser without a necessary indorsement he may become a bona fide purchaser only as of the time the indorsement is supplied; but against the transferor, the transfer is complete upon delivery and the purchaser has a specifically enforceable right to have any necessary indorsement supplied.

§ 8–308. Indorsements; Instructions

(1) An indorsement of a certificated security in registered form is made when an appropriate person signs on it or on a separate document an assignment or transfer of the security or a power to assign or transfer it or his signature is written without more upon the back of the security.

(2) An indorsement may be in blank or special. An indorsement in blank includes an indorsement to bearer. A special indorsement specifies to whom the security is to be transferred, or who has power to transfer it. A holder may convert a blank indorsement into a special indorsement.

(3) An indorsement purporting to be only of part of a certificated security representing units intended by the issuer to be separately transferable is effective to the extent of the indorsement.

(4) An "instruction" is an order to the issuer of an uncertificated security requesting that the transfer, pledge, or release from pledge of the uncertificated security specified therein be registered.

(5) An instruction originated by an appropriate person is:

(a) a writing signed by an appropriate person; or

(b) a communication to the issuer in any form agreed upon in a writing signed by the issuer and an appropriate person.

If an instruction has been originated by an appropriate person but is incomplete in any other respect, any person may complete it as authorized and the issuer may rely on it as completed even though it has been completed incorrectly.

(6) "An appropriate person" in subsection (1) means the person specified by the certificated security or by special indorsement to be entitled to the security.

(7) "An appropriate person" in subsection (5) means:

(a) for an instruction to transfer or pledge an uncertificated security which is then not subject to a registered pledge, the registered owner; or

(b) for an instruction to transfer or release an uncertificated security which is then subject to a registered pledge, the registered pledgee.

(8) In addition to the persons designated in subsections (6) and (7), "an appropriate person" in subsections (1) and (5) includes:

(a) if the person designated is described as a fiduciary but is no longer serving in the described capacity, either that person or his successor;

(b) if the persons designated are described as more than one person as fiduciaries and one or more are no longer serving in the described capacity, the remaining fiduciary or fiduciaries, whether or not a successor has been appointed or qualified.

(c) if the person designated is an individual and is without capacity to act by virtue of death, incompetence, infancy, or otherwise, his executor, administrator, guardian, or like fiduciary;

(d) if the persons designated are described as more than one person as tenants by the entirety or with right of survivorship and by reason of death all cannot sign, the survivor or survivors;

(e) a person having power to sign under applicable law or controlling instrument; and

(f) to the extent that the person designated or any of the foregoing persons may act through an agent, his authorized agent.

(9) Unless otherwise agreed, the indorser of a certificated security by his indorsement or the originator of an instruction by his origination assumes no obligation that the security will be honored by the issuer but only the obligations provided in Section 8–306.

(10) Whether the person signing is appropriate is determined as of the date of signing and an indorsement made by or an instruction originated by him does not become unauthorized for the purposes of this Article by virtue of any subsequent change of circumstances.

(11) Failure of a fiduciary to comply with a controlling instrument or with the law of the state having jurisdiction of the fiduciary relationship, including any law requiring the fiduciary to obtain court approval of the transfer, pledge, or release, does not render his indorsement or an instruction originated by him unauthorized for the purposes of this Article.

§ 8–309.   Effect of Indorsement Without Delivery

An indorsement of a certificated security, whether special or in blank, does not constitute a transfer until delivery of the certificated security on which it appears or, if the indorsement is on a separate document, until delivery of both the document and the certificated security.

§ 8–310.   Indorsement of Certificated Security in Bearer Form

An indorsement of a certificated security in bearer form may give notice of adverse claims (Section 8–304) but does not otherwise affect any right to registration the holder possesses.

§ 8–311.   Effect of Unauthorized Indorsement or Instruction

Unless the owner or pledgee has ratified an unauthorized indorsement or instruction or is otherwise precluded from asserting its ineffectiveness:

(a) he may assert its ineffectiveness against the issuer or any purchaser, other than a purchaser for value and without notice of adverse claims, who has in good faith received a new, reissued, or reregistered certificated security on registration of transfer or received an initial transaction statement confirming the registration of transfer, pledge, or release of an equivalent uncertificated security to him; and

(b) an issuer who registers the transfer of a certificated security upon the unauthorized indorsement or who registers the transfer, pledge, or release of an uncertificated security upon the unauthorized instruction is subject to liability for improper registration (Section 8–404).

§ 8–312.   Effect of Guaranteeing Signature, Indorsement or Instruction

(1) Any person guaranteeing a signature of an indorser of a certificated security warrants that at the time of signing:

(a) the signature was genuine;

(b) the signer was an appropriate person to indorse (Section 8–308); and

(c) the signer had legal capacity to sign.

(2) Any person guaranteeing a signature of the originator of an instruction warrants that at the time of signing:

(a) the signature was genuine;

(b) the signer was an appropriate person to originate the instruction (Section 8–308) if the person specified in the instruction as the registered owner or registered pledgee of the uncertificated security was, in fact, the registered owner or registered pledgee of the security, as to which fact the signature guarantor makes no warranty;

(c) the signer had legal capacity to sign; and

(d) the taxpayer identification number, if any, appearing on the instruction as that of the registered owner or registered pledgee was the taxpayer identification number of the signer or of the owner or pledgee for whom the signer was acting.

(3) Any person specially guaranteeing the signature of the originator of an instruction makes not only the warranties of a signature guarantor (subsection (2)) but also warrants that at the time the instruction is presented to the issuer:

(a) the person specified in the instruction as the registered owner or registered pledgee of the uncertificated security will be the registered owner or registered pledgee; and

(b) the transfer, pledge, or release of the uncertificated security requested in the instruction will be registered by the issuer free from all liens, security interests, restrictions, and claims other than those specified in the instruction.

(4) The guarantor under subsections (1) and (2) or the special guarantor under subsection (3) does not otherwise warrant the rightfulness of the particular transfer, pledge, or release.

(5) Any person guaranteeing an indorsement of a certificated security makes not only the warranties of a signature guarantor under subsection (1) but also warrants the rightfulness of the particular transfer in all respects.

(6) Any person guaranteeing an instruction requesting the transfer, pledge, or release of an uncertificated security makes not only the warranties of a special signature guarantor under subsection (3) but also warrants the rightfulness of the particular transfer, pledge, or release in all respects.

(7) No issuer may require a special guarantee of signature (subsection (3)), a guarantee of indorsement (subsection (5)), or a guarantee of instruction (subsection (6)) as a condition to registration of transfer, pledge, or release.

(8) The foregoing warranties are made to any person taking or dealing with the security in reliance on the guarantee, and the guarantor is liable to the person for any loss resulting from breach of the warranties.

§ 8–313.   When Transfer to Purchaser Occurs; Financial Intermediary as Bona Fide Purchaser; "Financial Intermediary"

(1) Transfer of a security or a limited interest (including a security interest) therein to a purchaser occurs only:

(a) at the time he or a person designated by him acquires possession of a certificated security;

(b) at the time the transfer, pledge, or release of an uncertificated security is registered to him or a person designated by him;

(c) at the time his financial intermediary acquires possession of a certificated security specially indorsed to or issued in the name of the purchaser;

(d) at the time a financial intermediary, not a clearing corporation, sends him confirmation of the purchase and also by book entry or otherwise identifies as belonging to the purchaser

(i) a specific certificated security in the financial intermediary's possession;

(ii) a quantity of securities that constitute or are part of a fungible bulk of certificated securities in the financial intermediary's possession or of uncertificated securities registered in the name of the financial intermediary; or

(iii) a quantity of securities that constitute or are part of a fungible bulk of securities shown on the account of the financial intermediary on the books of another financial intermediary;

(e) with respect to an identified certificated security to be delivered while still in the possession of a third person, not a financial intermediary, at the time that person acknowledges that he holds for the purchaser;

(f) with respect to a specific uncertificated security the pledge or transfer of which has been registered to a third person, not a financial intermediary, at the time that person acknowledges that he holds for the purchaser;

(g) at the time appropriate entries to the account of the purchaser or a person designated by him on the books of a clearing corporation are made under Section 8–320;

(h) with respect to the transfer of a security interest where the debtor has signed a security agreement containing a description of the security, at the time a written notification, which, in the case of the creation of the security interest, is signed by the debtor (which may be a copy of the security agreement) or which, in the case of the release or assignment of the security interest created pursuant to this paragraph, is signed by the secured party, is received by

(i) a financial intermediary on whose books the interest of the transferor in the security appears;

(ii) a third person, not a financial intermediary, in possession of the security, if it is certificated;

(iii) a third person, not a financial intermediary, who is the registered owner of the security, if it is uncertificated and not subject to a registered pledge; or

(iv) a third person, not a financial intermediary, who is the registered pledgee of the security, if it is uncertificated and subject to a registered pledge;

(i) with respect to the transfer of a security interest where the transferor has signed a security agreement containing a description of the security, at the time new value is given by the secured party; or

(j) with respect to the transfer of a security interest where the secured party is a financial intermediary and the security has already been transferred to the financial intermediary under paragraphs (a), (b), (c), (d), or (g), at the time the transferor has signed a security agreement containing a description of the security and value is given by the secured party.

(2) The purchaser is the owner of a security held for him by a financial intermediary, but cannot be a bona fide purchaser of a security so held except in the circumstances specified in paragraphs (c), (d)(i), and (g) of subsection (1). If a security so held is part of a fungible bulk, as in the circumstances specified in paragraphs (d)(ii) and (d)(iii) of subsection (1), the purchaser is the owner of a proportionate property interest in the fungible bulk.

(3) Notice of an adverse claim received by the financial intermediary or by the purchaser after the financial intermediary takes delivery of a certificated security as a holder for value or after the transfer, pledge, or release of an uncertificated security has been registered free of the claim to a financial intermediary who has given value is not effective either as to the financial intermediary or as to the purchaser. However, as between the financial intermediary and the purchaser the purchaser may demand transfer of an equivalent security as to which no notice of adverse claim has been received.

(4) A "financial intermediary" is a bank, broker, clearing corporation, or other person (or the nominee of any of them) which in the ordinary course of its business maintains security

accounts for its customers and is acting in that capacity. A financial intermediary may have a security interest in securities held in account for its customer.

§ 8–314. Duty to Transfer, When Completed

(1) Unless otherwise agreed, if a sale of a security is made on an exchange or otherwise through brokers:

(a) the selling customer fulfills his duty to transfer at the time he:

(i) places a certificated security in the possession of the selling broker or a person designated by the broker;

(ii) causes an uncertificated security to be registered in the name of the selling broker or a person designated by the broker;

(iii) if requested, causes an acknowledgment to be made to the selling broker that a certificated or uncertificated security is held for the broker; or

(iv) places in the possession of the selling broker or of a person designated by the broker a transfer instruction for an uncertificated security, providing the issuer does not refuse to register the requested transfer if the instruction is presented to the issuer for registration within 30 days thereafter; and

(b) the selling broker, including a correspondent broker acting for a selling customer, fulfills his duty to transfer at the time he:

(i) places a certificated security in the possession of the buying broker or a person designated by the buying broker;

(ii) causes an uncertificated security to be registered in the name of the buying broker or a person designated by the buying broker;

(iii) places in the possession of the buying broker or of a person designated by the buying broker a transfer instruction for an uncertificated security, providing the issuer does not refuse to register the requested transfer if the instruction is presented to the issuer for registration within 30 days thereafter; or

(iv) effects clearance of the sale in accordance with the rules of the exchange on which the transaction took place.

(2) Except as provided in this section or unless otherwise agreed, a transferor's duty to transfer a security under a contract of purchase is not fulfilled until he:

(a) places a certificated security in form to be negotiated by the purchaser in the possession of the purchaser or of a person designated by the purchaser;

(b) causes an uncertificated security to be registered in the name of the purchaser or a person designated by the purchaser; or

(c) if the purchaser requests, causes an acknowledgment to be made to the purchaser that a certificated or uncertificated security is held for the purchaser.

(3) Unless made on an exchange, a sale to a broker purchasing for his own account is within subsection (2) and not within subsection (1).

§ 8–315. Action Against Transferee Based upon Wrongful Transfer

(1) Any person against whom the transfer of a security is wrongful for any reason, including his incapacity, as against anyone except a bona fide purchaser, may:

(a) reclaim possession of the certificated security wrongfully transferred;

(b) obtain possession of any new certificated security representing all or part of the same rights;

(c) compel the origination of an instruction to transfer to him or a person designated by him an uncertificated security constituting all or part of the same rights; or

(d) have damages.

(2) If the transfer is wrongful because of an unauthorized indorsement of a certificated security, the owner may also reclaim or obtain possession of the security or a new certificated security, even from a bona fide purchaser, if the ineffectiveness of the purported indorsement can be asserted against him under the provisions of this Article on unauthorized indorsements (Section 8–311).

(3) The right to obtain or reclaim possession of a certificated security or to compel the origination of a transfer instruction may be specifically enforced and the transfer of a certificated or uncertificated security enjoined and a certificated security impounded pending the litigation.

§ 8–316. Purchaser's Right to Requisites for Registration of Transfer, Pledge, or Release on Books

Unless otherwise agreed, the transferor of a certificated security or the transferor, pledgor, or pledgee of an uncertificated security on due demand must supply his purchaser with any proof of his authority to transfer, pledge, or release or with any other requisite necessary to obtain registration of the transfer, pledge, or release of the security; but if the transfer, pledge, or release is not for value, a transferor, pledgor, or pledgee need not do so unless the purchaser furnishes the necessary expenses. Failure within a reasonable time to comply with a demand made gives the purchaser the right to reject or rescind the transfer, pledge, or release.

§ 8–317. Creditor's Rights

(1) Subject to the exceptions in subsections (3) and (4), no attachment or levy upon a certificated security or any share or other interest represented thereby which is outstanding is valid until the security is actually seized by the officer making the attachment or levy, but a certificated security which has been surrendered to the issuer may be reached by a creditor by legal process at the issuer's chief executive office in the United States.

(2) An uncertificated security registered in the name of the debtor may not be reached by a creditor except by legal process at the issuer's chief executive office in the United States.

(3) The interest of a debtor in a certificated security that is in the possession of a secured party not a financial intermediary or in an uncertificated security registered in the name of a secured party not a financial intermediary (or in the name of a nominee of the secured party) may be reached by a creditor by legal process upon the secured party.

(4) The interest of a debtor in a certificated security that is in the possession of or registered in the name of a financial intermediary or in an uncertificated security registered in the name of a financial intermediary may be reached by a creditor by legal process upon the financial intermediary on whose books the interest of the debtor appears.

(5) Unless otherwise provided by law, a creditor's lien upon the interest of a debtor in a security obtained pursuant to subsection (3) or (4) is not a restraint on the transfer of the security, free of the lien, to a third party for new value; but in the event of a transfer, the lien applies to the proceeds of the transfer in the hands of the secured party or financial intermediary, subject to any claims having priority.

(6) A creditor whose debtor is the owner of a security is entitled to aid from courts of appropriate jurisdiction, by injunction or otherwise, in reaching the security or in satisfying the claim by means allowed at law or in equity in regard to property that cannot readily be reached by ordinary legal process.

§ 8–318.   No Conversion by Good Faith Conduct

An agent or bailee who in good faith (including observance of reasonable commercial standards if he is in the business of buying, selling, or otherwise dealing with securities) has received certificated securities and sold, pledged, or delivered them or has sold or caused the transfer or pledge of uncertificated securities over which he had control according to the instructions of his principal, is not liable for conversion or for participation in breach of fiduciary duty although the principal had no right so to deal with the securities.

§ 8–319.   Statute of Frauds

A contract for the sale of securities is not enforceable by way of action or defense unless:

(a) there is some writing signed by the party against whom enforcement is sought or by his authorized agent or broker, sufficient to indicate that a contract has been made for sale of a stated quantity of described securities at a defined or stated price;

(b) delivery of a certificated security or transfer instruction has been accepted, or transfer of an uncertificated security has been registered and the transferee has failed to send written objection to the issuer within 10 days after receipt of the initial transaction statement confirming the registration, or payment has been made, but the contract is enforceable under this provision only to the extent of the delivery, registration, or payment;

(c) within a reasonable time a writing in confirmation of the sale or purchase and sufficient against the sender under paragraph (a) has been received by the party against whom enforcement is sought and he has failed to send written objection to its contents within 10 days after its receipt; or

(d) the party against whom enforcement is sought admits in his pleading, testimony, or otherwise in court that a contract was made for the sale of a stated quantity of described securities at a defined or stated price.

§ 8–320.   Transfer or Pledge Within Central Depositary System

(1) In addition to other methods, a transfer, pledge, or release of a security or any interest therein may be effected by the making of appropriate entries on the books of a clearing corporation reducing the account of the transferor, pledgor, or pledgee and increasing the account of the transferee, pledgee, or pledgor by the amount of the obligation or the number of shares or rights transferred, pledged, or released, if the security is shown on the account of a transferor, pledgor, or pledgee on the books of the clearing corporation; is subject to the control of the clearing corporation; and

(a) if certificated,

(i) is in the custody of the clearing corporation, another clearing corporation, a custodian bank, or a nominee of any of them; and

(ii) is in bearer form or indorsed in blank by an appropriate person or registered in the name of the clearing corporation, a custodian bank, or a nominee of any of them; or

(b) if uncertificated, is registered in the name of the clearing corporation, another clearing corporation, a custodian bank, or a nominee of any of them.

(2) Under this section entries may be made with respect to like securities or interests therein as a part of a fungible bulk and may refer merely to a quantity of a particular security without reference to the name of the registered owner, certificate or bond number, or the like, and, in appropriate cases, may be on a net basis taking into account other transfers, pledges, or releases of the same security.

(3) A transfer under this section is effective (Section 8–313) and the purchaser acquires the rights of the transferor (Section 8–301). A pledge or release under this section is the transfer of a limited interest. If a pledge or the creation of a security interest is intended, the security interest is perfected at the time when both value is given by the pledgee and the appropriate entries are made (Section 8–321). A transferee or pledgee under this section may be a bona fide purchaser (Section 8–302).

(4) A transfer or pledge under this section is not a registration of transfer under Part 4.

(5) That entries made on the books of the clearing corporation as provided in subsection (1) are not appropriate does not affect the validity or effect of the entries or the liabilities or obligations of the clearing corporation to any person adversely affected thereby.

§ 8–321. Enforceability, Attachment, Perfection and Termination of Security Interests

(1) A security interest in a security is enforceable and can attach only if it is transferred to the secured party or a person designated by him pursuant to a provision of Section 8–313(1).

(2) A security interest so transferred pursuant to agreement by a transferor who has rights in the security to a transferee who has given value is a perfected security interest, but a security interest that has been transferred solely under paragraph (i) of Section 8–313(1) becomes unperfected after 21 days unless within that time, the requirements for transfer under any other provision of Section 8–313(1) are satisfied.

(3) A security interest in a security is subject to the provisions of Article 9, but:

(a) no filing is required to perfect the security interest; and

(b) no written security agreement signed by the debtor is necessary to make the security interest enforceable, except as provided in paragraph (h), (i), or (j) of Section 8–313(1). The secured party has the rights and duties provided under Section 9–207, to the extent they are applicable, whether or not the security is certificated, and, if certificated, whether or not it is in his possession.

(4) Unless otherwise agreed, a security interest in a security is terminated by transfer to the debtor or a person designated by him pursuant to a provision of Section 8–313(1). If a security is thus transferred, the security interest, if not terminated, becomes unperfected unless the security is certificated and is delivered to the debtor for the purpose of ultimate sale or exchange or presentation, collection, renewal, or registration of transfer. In that case, the security interest becomes unperfected after 21 days unless, within that time the security (or securities for which it has been exchanged) is transferred to the secured party or a person designated by him pursuant to a provision of Section 8–313(1).

Part 4   Registration

§ 8–401.   Duty of Issuer to Register Transfer, Pledge, or Release

(1) If a certificated security in registered form is presented to the issuer with a request to register transfer or an instruction is presented to the issuer with a request to register transfer, pledge, or release, the issuer shall register the transfer, pledge, or release as requested if:

(a) the security is indorsed or the instruction was originated by the appropriate person or persons (Section 8–308);

(b) reasonable assurance is given that those indorsements or instructions are genuine and effective (Section 8–402);

(c) the issuer has no duty as to adverse claims or has discharged the duty (Section 8–403);

(d) any applicable law relating to the collection of taxes has been complied with; and

(e) the transfer, pledge, or release is in fact rightful or is to a bona fide purchaser.

(2) If an issuer is under a duty to register a transfer, pledge, or release of a security, the issuer is also liable to the person presenting a certificated security or an instruction for registration or his principal for loss resulting from any unreasonable delay in registration or from failure or refusal to register the transfer, pledge, or release.

§ 8–402.   Assurance that Indorsements and Instructions Are Effective

(1) The issuer may require the following assurance that each necessary indorsement of a certificated security or each instruction (Section 8–308) is genuine and effective:

(a) in all cases, a guarantee of the signature (Section 8–312(1) or (2)) of the person indorsing a certificated security or originating an instruction including, in the case of an instruction, a warranty of the taxpayer identification number or, in the absence thereof, other reasonable assurance of identity;

(b) if the indorsement is made or the instruction is originated by an agent, appropriate assurance of authority to sign;

(c) if the indorsement is made or the instruction is originated by a fiduciary, appropriate evidence of appointment or incumbency;

(d) if there is more than one fiduciary, reasonable assurance that all who are required to sign have done so; and

(e) if the indorsement is made or the instruction is originated by a person not covered by any of the foregoing, assurance appropriate to the case corresponding as nearly as may be to the foregoing.

(2) A "guarantee of the signature" in subsection (1) means a guarantee signed by or on behalf of a person reasonably believed by the issuer to be responsible. The issuer may adopt standards with respect to responsibility if they are not manifestly unreasonable.

(3) "Appropriate evidence of appointment or incumbency" in subsection (1) means:

(a) in the case of a fiduciary appointed or qualified by a court, a certificate issued by or under the direction or supervision of that court or an officer thereof and dated within 60 days before the date of presentation for transfer, pledge, or release; or

(b) in any other case, a copy of a document showing the appointment or a certificate issued by or on behalf of a person reasonably believed by the issuer to be responsible or, in the absence of that document or certificate, other evidence reasonably deemed by the issuer to be appropriate. The issuer may adopt standards with respect to the evidence if they are not manifestly unreasonable. The issuer is not charged with notice of the contents of any document obtained pursuant to this paragraph (b) except to the extent that the contents relate directly to the appointment or incumbency.

(4) The issuer may elect to require reasonable assurance

beyond that specified in this section, but if it does so and, for a purpose other than that specified in subsection (3)(b), both requires and obtains a copy of a will, trust, in denture, articles of co-partnership, by-laws, or other controlling instrument, it is charged with notice of all matters contained therein affecting the transfer, pledge, or release.

§ 8–403.   Issuer's Duty as to Adverse Claims

(1) An issuer to whom a certificated security is presented for registration shall inquire into adverse claims if:

(a) a written notification of an adverse claim is received at a time and in a manner affording the issuer a reasonable opportunity to act on it prior to the issuance of a new, reissued, or re-registered certificated security, and the notification identifies the claimant, the registered owner, and the issue of which the security is a part, and provides an address for communications directed to the claimant; or

(b) the issuer is charged with notice of an adverse claim from a controlling instrument it has elected to require under Section 8–402(4).

(2) The issuer may discharge any duty of inquiry by any reasonable means, including notifying an adverse claimant by registered or certified mail at the address furnished by him or, if there be no such address, at his residence or regular place of business that the certificated security has been presented for registration of transfer by a named person, and that the transfer will be registered unless within 30 days from the date of mailing the notification, either:

(a) an appropriate restraining order, injunction, or other process issues from a court of competent jurisdiction; or

(b) there is filed with the issuer an indemnity bond, sufficient in the issuer's judgment to protect the issuer and any transfer agent, registrar, or other agent of the issuer involved from any loss it or they may suffer by complying with the adverse claim.

(3) Unless an issuer is charged with notice of an adverse claim from a controlling instrument which it has elected to require under Section 8–402(4) or receives notification of an adverse claim under subsection (1), if a certificated security presented for registration is indorsed by the appropriate person or persons the issuer is under no duty to inquire into adverse claims. In particular:

(a) an issuer registering a certificated security in the name of a person who is a fiduciary or who is described as a fiduciary is not bound to inquire into the existence, extent, or correct description of the fiduciary relationship; and thereafter the issuer may assume without inquiry that the newly registered owner continues to be the fiduciary until the issuer receives written notice that the fiduciary is no longer acting as such with respect to the particular security;

(b) an issuer registering transfer on an indorsement by a fiduciary is not bound to inquire whether the transfer is made in compliance with a controlling instrument or with the law of the state having jurisdiction of the fiduciary relationship, in-

cluding any law requiring the fiduciary to obtain court approval of the transfer; and

(c) the issuer is not charged with notice of the contents of any court record or file or other recorded or unrecorded document even though the document is in its possession and even though the transfer is made on the indorsement of a fiduciary to the fiduciary himself or to his nominee.

(4) An issuer is under no duty as to adverse claims with respect to an uncertificated security except:

(a) claims embodied in a restraining order, injunction, or other legal process served upon the issuer if the process was served at a time and in a manner affording the issuer a reasonable opportunity to act on it in accordance with the requirements of subsection (5);

(b) claims of which the issuer has received a written notification from the registered owner or the registered pledgee if the notification was received at a time and in a manner affording the issuer a reasonable opportunity to act on it in accordance with the requirements of subsection (5);

(c) claims (including restrictions on transfer not imposed by the issuer) to which the registration of transfer to the present registered owner was subject and were so noted in the initial transaction statement sent to him; and

(d) claims as to which an issuer is charged with notice from a controlling instrument it has elected to require under Section 8–402(4).

(5) If the issuer of an uncertificated security is under a duty to an adverse claim, he discharges that duty by:

(a) including a notation of the claim in any statements sent with respect to the security under Sections 8–408(3), (6), and (7); and

(b) refusing to register the transfer or pledge of the security unless the nature of the claim does not preclude transfer or pledge subject thereto.

(6) If the transfer of pledge of the security is registered subject to an adverse claim, a notation of the claim must be included in the initial transaction statement and all subsequent statements sent to the transferee and pledgee under Section 8–408.

(7) Notwithstanding subsections (4) and (5), if an uncertificated security was subject to a registered pledge at the time the issuer first came under a duty as to a particular adverse claim, the issuer has no duty as to that claim if transfer of the security is requested by the registered pledgee or an appropriate person acting for the registered pledgee unless:

(a) the claim was embodied in legal process which expressly provides otherwise;

(b) the claim was asserted in a written notification from the registered pledgee;

(c) the claim was one as to which the issuer was charged with notice from a controlling instrument it required under Section 8–402(4) in connection with the pledgee's request for transfer; or

(d) the transfer requested is to the registered owner.

§ 8–404. Liability and Non-Liability for Registration

(1) Except as provided in any law relating to the collection of taxes, the issuer is not liable to the owner, pledgee, or any other person suffering loss as a result of the registration of a transfer, pledge, or release of a security if:

(a) there were on or with a certificated security the necessary indorsements or the issuer had received an instruction originated by an appropriate person (Section 8–308); and

(b) the issuer had no duty as to adverse claims or has discharged the duty (Section 8–403).

(2) If an issuer has registered a transfer of a certificated security to a person not entitled to it, the issuer on demand shall deliver a like security to the true owner unless:

(a) the registration was pursuant to subsection (1);

(b) the owner is precluded from asserting any claim for registering the transfer under Section 8–405(1); or

(c) the delivery would result in overissue, in which case the issuer's liability is governed by Section 8–104.

(3) If an issuer has improperly registered a transfer, pledge, or release of an uncertificated security, the issuer on demand from the injured party shall restore the records as to the injured party to the condition that would have obtained if the improper registration had not been made unless:

(a) the registration was pursuant to subsection (1); or

(b) the registration would result in overissue, in which case the issuer's liability is governed by Section 8–104.

§ 8–405. Lost, Destroyed, and Stolen Certificated Securities

(1) If a certificated security has been lost, apparently destroyed, or wrongfully taken, and the owner fails to notify the issuer of that fact within a reasonable time after he has notice of it and the issuer registers a transfer of the security before receiving notification, the owner is precluded from asserting against the issuer any claim for registering the transfer under Section 8–404 or any claim to a new security under this section.

(2) If the owner of a certificated security claims that the security has been lost, destroyed, or wrongfully taken, the issuer shall issue a new certificated security or, at the option of the issuer, an equivalent uncertificated security in place of the original security if the owner:

(a) so requests before the issuer has notice that the security has been acquired by a bona fide purchaser;

(b) files with the issuer a sufficient indemnity bond; and

(c) satisfies any other reasonable requirements imposed by the issuer.

(3) If, after the issue of a new certificated or uncertificated security, a bona fide purchaser of the original certificated security presents it for registration of transfer, the issuer shall register the transfer unless registration would result in overissue, in which event the issuer's liability is governed by Section 8–104. In addition to any rights on the indemnity bond, the issuer may recover the new certificated security from the person to whom it was issued or any person taking under him except a bona fide purchaser or may cancel the uncertificated security unless a bona fide purchaser or any person taking under a bona fide purchaser is then the registered owner or registered pledgee thereof.

§ 8–406. Duty of Authenticating Trustee, Transfer Agent, or Registrar

(1) If a person acts as authenticating trustee, transfer agent, registrar, or other agent for an issuer in the registration of transfers of its certificated securities or in the registration of transfers, pledges, and releases of its uncertificated securities, in the issue of new securities, or in the cancellation of surrendered securities:

(a) he is under a duty to the issuer to exercise good faith and due diligence in performing his functions; and

(b) with regard to the particular functions he performs, he has the same obligation to the holder or owner of a certificated security or to the owner or pledgee of an uncertificated security and has the same rights and privileges as the issuer has in regard to those functions.

(2) Notice to an authenticating trustee, transfer agent, registrar or other agent is notice to the issuer with respect to the functions performed by the agent.

§ 8–407. Exchangeability of Securities

(1) No issuer is subject to the requirements of this section unless it regularly maintains a system for issuing the class of securities involved under which both certificated and uncertificated securities are regularly issued to the category of owners, which includes the person in whose name the new security is to be registered.

(2) Upon surrender of a certificated security with all necessary indorsements and presentation of a written request by the person surrendering the security, the issuer, if he has no duty as to adverse claims or has discharged the duty (Section 8–403), shall issue to the person or a person designated by him an equivalent uncertificated security subject to all liens, restrictions, and claims that were noted on the certificated security.

(3) Upon receipt of a transfer instruction originated by an appropriate person who so requests, the issuer of an uncertificated security shall cancel the uncertificated security and issue an equivalent certificated security on which must be noted conspicuously any liens and restrictions of the issuer and any adverse claims (as to which the issuer has a duty under Section 8–403(4)) to which the uncertificated security was subject. The certificated security shall be registered in the name of and delivered to:

(a) the registered owner, if the uncertificated security was not subject to a registered pledge; or

(b) the registered pledgee, if the uncertificated security was subject to a registered pledge.

§ 8–408.   Statements of Uncertificated Securities

(1) Within 2 business days after the transfer of an uncertificated security has been registered, the issuer shall send to the new registered owner and, if the security has been transferred subject to a registered pledge, to the registered pledgee a written statement containing:

(a) a description of the issue of which the uncertificated security is a part;

(b) the number of shares or units transferred;

(c) the name and address and any taxpayer identification number of the new registered owner and, if the security has been transferred subject to a registered pledge, the name and address and any taxpayer identification number of the registered pledgee;

(d) a notation of any liens and restrictions of the issuer and any adverse claims (as to which the issuer has a duty under Section 8–403(4)) to which the uncertificated security is or may be subject at the time of registration or a statement that there are none of those liens, restrictions, or adverse claims; and

(e) the date the transfer was registered.

(2) Within 2 business days after the pledge of an uncertificated security has been registered, the issuer shall send to the registered owner and the registered pledgee a written statement containing:

(a) a description of the issue of which the uncertificated security is a part;

(b) the number of shares or units pledged;

(c) the name and address and any taxpayer identification number of the registered owner and the registered pledgee;

(d) a notation of any liens and restrictions of the issuer and any adverse claims (as to which the issuer has a duty under Section 8–403(4)) to which the uncertificated security is or may be subject at the time of registration or a statement that there are none of those liens, restrictions, or adverse claims; and

(e) the date the pledge was registered.

(3) Within 2 business days after the release from pledge of an uncertificated security has been registered, the issuer shall send to the registered owner and the pledgee whose interest was released a written statement containing:

(a) a description of the issue of which the uncertificated security is a part;

(b) the number of shares or units released from pledge;

(c) the name and address and any taxpayer identification number of the registered owner and the pledgee whose interest was released;

(d) a notation of any liens and restrictions of the issuer and any adverse claims (as to which the issuer has a duty under Section 8–403(4)) to which the uncertificated security is or may be subject at the time of registration or a statement that there are none of those liens, restrictions, or adverse claims; and

(e) the date the release was registered.

(4) An "initial transaction statement" is the statement sent to:

(a) the new registered owner and, if applicable, to the registered pledgee pursuant to subsection (1);

(b) the registered pledgee pursuant to subsection (2); or

(c) the registered owner pursuant to subsection (3).

Each initial transaction statement shall be signed by or on behalf of the issuer and must be identified as "Initial Transaction Statement."

(5) Within 2 business days after the transfer of an uncertificated security has been registered, the issuer shall send to the former registered owner and the former registered pledgee, if any, a written statement containing:

(a) a description of the issue of which the uncertificated security is a part;

(b) the number of shares or units transferred;

(c) the name and address and any taxpayer identification number of the former registered owner and of any former registered pledgee; and

(d) the date the transfer was registered.

(6) At periodic intervals no less frequent than annually and at any time upon the reasonable written request of the registered owner, the issuer shall send to the registered owner of each uncertificated security a dated written statement containing:

(a) a description of the issue of which the uncertificated security is a part;

(b) the name and address and any taxpayer identification number of the registered owner;

(c) the number of shares or units of the uncertificated security registered in the name of the registered owner on the date of the statement;

(d) the name and address and any taxpayer identification number of any registered pledgee and the number of shares of units subject to the pledge; and

(e) a notation of any liens and restrictions of the issuer and any adverse claims (as to which the issuer has a duty under Section 8–403(4)) to which the uncertificated security is or may be subject or a statement that there are none of those liens, restrictions, or adverse claims.

(7) At periodic intervals no less frequent than annually and at any time upon the reasonable written request of the registered pledgee, the issuer shall send to the registered pledgee of each uncertificated security a dated written statement containing:

(a) a description of the issue of which the uncertificated security is a part;

(b) the name and address and any taxpayer identification number of the registered owner;

(c) the name and address and any taxpayer identification number of the registered pledgee;

(d) the number of shares or units subject to the pledge; and

(e) a notation of any liens and restrictions of the issuer and any adverse claims (as to which the issuer has a duty under Section 8–403(4)) to which the uncertificated security is or may be subject or a statement that there are none of those liens, restrictions, or adverse claims.

(8) If the issuer sends the statements described in subsections (6) and (7) at periodic intervals no less frequent than quarterly, the issuer is not obliged to send additional statements upon request unless the owner or pledgee requesting them pays to the issuer the reasonable cost of furnishing them.

(9) Each statement sent pursuant to this section must bear a conspicuous legend reading substantially as follows: "This statement is merely a record of the rights of the addressee as of the time of its issuance. Delivery of this statement, of itself, confers no rights on the recipient. This statement is neither a negotiable instrument nor a security."

ARTICLE 9   SECURED TRANSACTIONS; SALES OF ACCOUNTS AND CHATTEL PAPER

Part 1   Short Title, Applicability and Definitions

§ 9–101.   Short Title
This Article shall be known and may be cited as Uniform Commercial Code—Secured Transactions.

§ 9–102.   Policy and Subject Matter of Article
(1) Except as otherwise provided in Section 9–104 on excluded transactions, this Article applies

(a) to any transaction (regardless of its form) which is intended to create a security interest in personal property or fixtures including goods, documents, instruments, general intangibles, chattel paper or accounts; and also

(b) to any sale of accounts or chattel paper.

(2) This Article applies to security interests created by contract including pledge, assignment, chattel mortgage, chattel trust, trust deed, factor's lien, equipment trust, conditional sale, trust receipt, other lien or title retention contract and lease or consignment intended as security. This Article does not apply to statutory liens except as provided in Section 9–310.

(3) The application of this Article to a security interest in a secured obligation is not affected by the fact that the obligation is itself secured by a transaction or interest to which this Article does not apply.

§ 9–103.   Perfection of Security Interest in Multiple State Transactions
(1) Documents, instruments and ordinary goods.

(a) This subsection applies to documents and instruments and to goods other than those covered by a certificate of title described in subsection (2), mobile goods described in subsection (3), and minerals described in subsection (5).

(b) Except as otherwise provided in this subsection, perfection and the effect of perfection or non-perfection of a security interest in collateral are governed by the law of the jurisdiction where the collateral is when the last event occurs on which is based the assertion that the security interest is perfected or unperfected.

(c) If the parties to a transaction creating a purchase money security interest in goods in one jurisdiction understand at the time that the security interest attaches that the goods will be kept in another jurisdiction, then the law of the other jurisdiction governs the perfection and the effect of perfection or non-perfection of the security interest from the time it attaches until thirty days after the debtor receives possession of the goods and thereafter if the goods are taken to the other jurisdiction before the end of the thirty-day period.

(d) When collateral is brought into and kept in this state while subject to a security interest perfected under the law of the jurisdiction from which the collateral was removed, the security interest remains perfected, but if action is required by Part 3 of this Article to perfect the security interest,

(i) if the action is not taken before the expiration of the period of perfection in the other jurisdiction or the end of four months after the collateral is brought into this state, whichever period first expires, the security interest becomes unperfected at the end of that period and is thereafter deemed to have been unperfected as against a person who became a purchaser after removal;

(ii) if the action is taken before the expiration of the period specified in subparagraph (i), the security interest continues perfected thereafter;

(iii) for the purpose of priority over a buyer of consumer goods (subsection (2) of Section 9–307), the period of the effectiveness of a filing in the jurisdiction from which the collateral is removed is governed by the rules with respect to perfection in subparagraphs (i) and (ii).

(2) Certificate of title.

(a) This subsection applies to goods covered by a certificate of title issued under a statute of this state or of another jurisdiction under the law of which indication of a security interest on the certificate is required as a condition of perfection.

(b) Except as otherwise provided in this subsection, perfection and the effect of perfection or non-perfection of the security interest are governed by the law (including the conflict of law rules) of the jurisdiction issuing the certificate until four months after the goods are removed from that jurisdiction and thereafter until the goods are registered in another jurisdiction, but in any event not beyond surrender of the certificate. After the expiration of that period, the goods are not covered by the certificate of title within the meaning of this section.

(c) Except with respect to the rights of a buyer described in the next paragraph, a security interest, perfected in another jurisdiction otherwise than by notation on a certificate of title, in goods brought into this state and thereafter covered by a certificate of title issued by this state is subject to the rules stated in paragraph (d) of subsection (1).

(d) If goods are brought into this state while a security interest therein is perfected in any manner under the law of the jurisdiction from which the goods are removed and a certificate of title is issued by this state and the certificate does not show that the goods are subject to the security interest or that they may be subject to security interests not shown on the certificate, the security interest is subordinate to the rights of a buyer of the goods who is not in the business of selling goods of that kind to the extent that he gives value and receives delivery of the goods after issuance of the certificate and without knowledge of the security interest

(3) Accounts, general intangibles and mobile goods.

(a) This subsection applies to accounts (other than an account described in subsection (5) on minerals) and general intangibles (other than uncertificated securities) and to goods which are mobile and which are of a type normally used in more than one jurisdiction, such as motor vehicles, trailers, rolling stock, airplanes, shipping containers, road building and construction machinery and commercial harvesting machinery and the like, if the goods are equipment or are inventory leased or held for lease by the debtor to others, and are not covered by a certificate of title described in subsection (2).

(b) The law (including the conflict of laws rules) of the jurisdiction in which the debtor is located governs the perfection and the effect of perfection or non-perfection of the security interest.

(c) If, however, the debtor is located in a jurisdiction which is not a part of the United States, and which does not provide for perfection of the security interest by filing or recording in that jurisdiction, the law of the jurisdiction in the United States in which the debtor has its major executive office governs the perfection and the effect of perfection or non-perfection of the security interest through filing. In the alternative, if the debtor is located in a jurisdiction which is not a part of the United States or Canada and the collateral is accounts or general intangibles for money due or to become due, the security interest may be perfected by notification to the account debtor. As used in this paragraph, "United States" includes its territories and possessions and the Commonwealth of Puerto Rico.

(d) A debtor shall be deemed located at his place of business if he has one, at his chief executive office if he has more than one place of business, otherwise at his residence. If, however, the debtor is a foreign air carrier under the Federal Aviation Act of 1958, as amended, it shall be deemed located at the designated office of the agent upon whom service of process may be made on behalf of the foreign air carrier.

(e) A security interest perfected under the law of the jurisdiction of the location of the debtor is perfected until the expiration of four months after a change of the debtor's location to another jurisdiction, or until perfection would have ceased by the law of the first jurisdiction, whichever period first expires. Unless perfected in the new jurisdiction before the end of that period, it becomes unperfected thereafter and is deemed to have been unperfected as against a person who became a purchaser after the change.

(4) Chattel paper. The rules stated for goods in subsection (1) apply to a possessory security interest in chattel paper.

The rules stated for accounts in subsection (3) apply to a non-possessory security interest in chattel paper, but the security interest may not be perfected by notification to the account debtor.

(5) Minerals. Perfection and the effect of perfection or non-perfection of a security interest which is created by a debtor who has an interest in minerals or the like (including oil and gas) before extraction and which attaches thereto as extracted, or which attaches to an account resulting from the sale thereof at the wellhead or minehead are governed by the law (including the conflict of laws rules) of the jurisdiction wherein the wellhead or minehead is located.

(6) Uncertificated securities. The law (including the conflict of laws rules) of the jurisdiction or organization of the issuer governs the perfection and the effect of perfection or nonperfection of a security interest in uncertificated securities.

§ 9–104.   Transactions Excluded From Article

This Article does not apply

(a) to a security interest subject to any statute of the United States, to the extent that such statute governs the rights of parties to and third parties affected by transactions in particular types of property; or

(b) to a landlord's lien; or

(c) to a lien given by statute or other rule of law for services or materials except as provided in Section 9–310 on priority of such liens; or

(d) to a transfer of a claim for wages, salary or other compensation of an employee; or

(e) to a transfer by a government or governmental subdivision or agency; or

(f) to a sale of accounts or chattel paper as part of a sale of the business out of which they arose, or an assignment of accounts or chattel paper which is for the purpose of collection only, or a transfer of a right to payment under a contract to an assignee who is also to do the performance under the contract or a transfer of a single account to an assignee in whole or partial satisfaction of a preexisting indebtedness; or

(g) to a transfer of an interest in or claim in or under any policy of insurance, except as provided with respect to proceeds (Section 9–306) and priorities in proceeds (Section 9–312); or

(h) to a right represented by a judgment (other than a judgment taken on a right to payment which was collateral); or

(i) to any right of set-off; or

(j) except to the extent that provision is made for fixtures in Section 9–313, to the creation or transfer of an interest in or lien on real estate, including a lease or rents thereunder; or

(k) to a transfer in whole or in part of any claim arising out of tort; or

(l) to a transfer of an interest in any deposit account (subsection (1) of Section 9–105), except as provided with respect to proceeds (Section 9–306) and priorities in proceeds (Section 9–312).

§ 9–105. Definitions and Index of Definitions

(1) In this Article unless the context otherwise requires:

(a) "Account debtor" means the person who is obligated on an account, chattel paper or general intangible;

(b) "Chattel paper" means a writing or writings which evidence both a monetary obligation and a security interest in or a lease of specific goods, but a charter or other contract involving the use or hire of a vessel is not chattel paper. When a transaction is evidenced both by such a security agreement or a lease and by an instrument or a series of instruments, the group of writings taken together constitutes chattel paper;

(c) "Collateral" means the property subject to a security interest, and includes accounts and chattel paper which have been sold;

(d) "Debtor" means the person who owes payment or other performance of the obligation secured, whether or not he owns or has rights in the collateral, and includes the seller of accounts or chattel paper. Where the debtor and the owner of the collateral are not the same person, the term "debtor" means the owner of the collateral in any provision of the Article dealing with the collateral, the obligor in any provision dealing with the obligation, and may include both where the context so requires;

(e) "Deposit account" means a demand, time, savings, passbook or like account maintained with a bank, savings and loan association, credit union or like organization, other than an account evidenced by a certificate of deposit;

(f) "Document" means document of title as defined in the general definitions of Article 1 (Section 1–201), and a receipt of the kind described in subsection (2) of Section 7–201;

(g) "Encumbrance" includes real estate mortgages and other liens on real estate and all other rights in real estate that are not ownership interests;

(h) "Goods" includes all things which are movable at the time the security interest attaches or which are fixtures (Section 9–313), but does not include money, documents, instruments, accounts, chattel paper, general intangibles, or minerals or the like (including oil and gas) before extraction. "Goods" also includes standing timber which is to be cut and removed under a conveyance or contract for sale, the unborn young of animals, and growing crops;

(i) "Instrument" means a negotiable instrument (defined in Section 3–104), or a certificated security (defined in Section 8–102) or any other writing which evidences a right to the payment of money and is not itself a security agreement or lease and is of a type which is in ordinary course of business transferred by delivery with any necessary indorsement or assignment;

(j) "Mortgage" means a consensual interest created by a real estate mortgage, a trust deed on real estate, or the like;

(k) An advance is made "pursuant to commitment" if the secured party has bound himself to make it, whether or not a subsequent event of default or other event not within his control has relieved or may relieve him from his obligation;

(l) "Security agreement" means an agreement which creates or provides for a security interest;

(m) "Secured party" means a lender, seller or other person in whose favor there is a security interest, including a person to whom accounts or chattel paper have been sold. When the holders of obligations issued under an indenture of trust, equipment trust agreement or the like are represented by a trustee or other person, the representative is the secured party;

(n) "Transmitting utility" means any person primarily engaged in the railroad, street railway or trolley bus business, the electric or electronics communications transmission business, the transmission of goods by pipeline, or the transmission or the production and transmission of electricity, steam, gas or water, or the provision of sewer service.

(2) Other definitions applying to this Article and the sections in which they appear are:

"Account." Section 9–106.
"Attach." Section 9–203.
"Construction mortgage." Section 9–313(1).
"Consumer goods." Section 9–109(1).
"Equipment." Section 9–109(2).
"Farm products." Section 9–109(3).
"Fixture." Section 9–313(1).
"Fixture filing." Section 9–313(1).
"General intangibles." Section 9–106.
"Inventory." Section 9–109(4).
"Lien creditor." Section 9–301(3).
"Proceeds." Section 9–306(1).
"Purchase money security interest." Section 9–107.
"United States." Section 9–103.

(3) The following definitions in other Articles apply to this Article:

"Check." Section 3–104.
"Contract for sale." Section 2–106.
"Holder in due course." Section 3–302.
"Note." Section 3–104.
"Sale." Section 2–106.

(4) In addition Article 1 contains general definitions and principles of construction and interpretation applicable throughout this Article.

§ 9–106. Definitions: "Account"; "General Intangibles"

"Account" means any right to payment for goods sold or leased or for services rendered which is not evidenced by an instrument or chattel paper, whether or not it has been earned by performance. "General intangibles" means any personal property (including things in action) other than goods, accounts, chattel paper, documents, instruments, and money. All rights to payment earned or unearned under a charter or other contract involving the use or hire of a vessel and all rights incident to the charter or contract are accounts.

§ 9–107.   Definitions: "Purchase Money Security Interest"

A security interest is a "purchase money security interest" to the extent that it is

(a) taken or retained by the seller of the collateral to secure all or part of its price; or

(b) taken by a person who by making advances or incurring an obligation gives value to enable the debtor to acquire rights in or the use of collateral if such value is in fact so used.

§ 9–108.   When After-Acquired Collateral Not Security for Antecedent Debt

Where a secured party makes an advance, incurs an obligation, releases a perfected security interest, or otherwise gives new value which is to be secured in whole or in part by after-acquired property his security interest in the after-acquired collateral shall be deemed to be taken for new value and not as security for an antecedent debt if the debtor acquires his rights in such collateral either in the ordinary course of his business or under a contract of purchase made pursuant to the security agreement within a reasonable time after new value is given.

§ 9–109.   Classification of Goods; "Consumer Goods"; "Equipment"; "Farm Products"; "Inventory"

Goods are

(1) "consumer goods" if they are used or bought for use primarily for personal, family or household purposes;

(2) "equipment" if they are used or bought for use primarily in business (including farming or a profession) or by a debtor who is a non-profit organization or a governmental subdivision or agency of if the goods are not included in the definitions of inventory, farm products or consumer goods;

(3) "farm products" if they are crops or livestock or supplies used or produced in farming operations or if they are products of crops or livestock in their unmanufactured states (such as ginned cotton, wool-clip, maple syrup, milk and eggs), and if they are in the possession of a debtor engaged in raising, fattening, grazing or other farming operations. If goods are farm products they are neither equipment nor inventory;

(4) "inventory" if they are held by a person who holds them for sale or lease or to be furnished under contracts of service or if he has so furnished them, or if they are raw materials, work in process or materials used or consumed in a business. Inventory of a person is not to be classified as his equipment.

§ 9–110.   Sufficiency of Description

For the purposes of this Article any description of personal property or real estate is sufficient whether or not it is specific if it reasonably identifies what is described.

§ 9–111.   Applicability of Bulk Transfer Laws

The creation of a security interest is not a bulk transfer under Article 6 (see Section 6–103).

§ 9–112.   Where Collateral Is Not Owned by Debtor

Unless otherwise agreed, when a secured party knows that collateral is owned by a person who is not the debtor, the owner of the collateral is entitled to receive from the secured party any surplus under Section 9–502(2) or under Section 9–504(1), and is not liable for the debt or for any deficiency after resale, and he has the same right as the debtor

(a) to receive statements under Section 9–208;

(b) to receive notice of and to object to a secured party's proposal to retain the collateral in satisfaction of the indebtedness under Section 9–505;

(c) to redeem the collateral under Section 9–506;

(d) to obtain injunctive or other relief under Section 9–507(1); and

(e) to recover losses caused to him under Section 9–208(2).

§ 9–113.   Security Interests Arising under Article on Sales

A security interest arising solely under the Article on Sales (Article 2) is subject to the provisions of this Article except that to the extent that and so long as the debtor does not have or does not lawfully obtain possession of the goods

(a) no security agreement is necessary to make the security interest enforceable; and

(b) no filing is required to perfect the security interest; and

(c) the rights of the secured party on default by the debtor are governed by the Article on Sales (Article 2).

§ 9–114.   Consignment

(1) A person who delivers goods under a consignment which is not a security interest and who would be required to file under this Article by paragraph (3)(c) of Section 2–326 has priority over a secured party who is or becomes a creditor of the consignee and who would have a perfected security interest in the goods if they were the property of the consignee, and also has priority with respect to identifiable cash proceeds received on or before delivery of the goods to a buyer, if

(a) the consignor complies with the filng provision of the Article on Sales with respect to consignments (paragraph (3)(c) of Section 2–326) before the consignee receives possession of the goods; and

(b) the consignor gives notification in writing to the holder of the security interest if the holder has filed a financing statement covering the same types of goods before the date of the filing made by the consignor; and

(c) the holder of the security interest receives the notification within five years before the consignee receives possession of the goods; and

(d) the notification states that the consignor expects to deliver goods on consignment to the consignee, describing the goods by item or type.

(2) In the case of a consignment which is not a security interest and in which the requirements of the preceding subsection have not been met, a person who delivers goods to another is

subordinate to a person who would have a perfected security interest in the goods if they were the property of the debtor.

Part 2   *Validity of Security Agreement and Rights of Parties Thereto*

§ 9–201.   General Validity of Security Agreement

Except as otherwise provided by this Act a security agreement is effective according to its terms between the parties, against purchasers of the collateral and against creditors. Nothing in this Article validates any charge or practice illegal under any statute or regulation thereunder governing usury, small loans, retail installment sales, or the like, or extends the application of any such statute or regulation to any transaction not otherwise subject thereto.

§ 9–202.   Title to Collateral Immaterial

Each provision of this Article with regard to rights, obligations and remedies applies whether title to collateral is in the secured party or in the debtor.

§ 9–203.   Attachment and Enforceability of Security Interest; Proceeds; Formal Requisites

(1) Subject to the provisions of Section 4–208 on the security interest of a collecting bank, Section 8–321 on security interests in securities and Section 9–113 on a security interest arising under the Article on Sales, a security interest is not enforceable against the debtor or third parties with respect to the collateral and does not attach unless:

  (a) the collateral is in the possession of the secured party pursuant to agreement, or the debtor has signed a security agreement which contains a description of the collateral and in addition, when the security interest covers crops growing or to be grown or timber to be cut, a description of the land concerned;

  (b) value has been given; and

  (c) the debtor has rights in the collateral.

(2) A security interest attaches when it becomes enforceable against the debtor with respect to the collateral. Attachment occurs as soon as all of the events specified in subsection (1) have taken place unless explicit agreement postpones the time of attaching.

(3) Unless otherwise agreed a security agreement gives the secured party the rights to proceeds provided by Section 9–306.

(4) A transaction, although subject to this Article, is also subject to . . . . *, and in the case of conflict between the provisions of this Article and any such statute, the provisions of such statute control. Failure to comply with any applicable statute has only the effect which is specified therein.

Note: At * in subsection (4) insert reference to any local statute regulating small loans, retail installment sales and the like.

The foregoing subsection (4) is designed to make it clear that certain transactions, although subject to this Article, must also comply with other applicable legislation.

This Article is designed to regulate all the "security" aspects of transactions within its scope. There is, however, much regulatory legislation, particularly in the consumer field, which supplements this Article and should not be repealed by its enactment. Examples are small loan acts, retail installment selling acts and the like. Such acts may provide for licensing and rate regulation and may prescribe particular forms of contract. Such provisions should remain in force despite the enactment of this Article. On the other hand if a retail installment selling act contains provisions on filing, rights on default, etc., such provisions should be repealed as inconsistent with this Article except that inconsistent provisions as to deficiencies, penalties, etc., in the Uniform Consumer Credit Code and other recent related legislation should remain because those statutes were drafted after the substantial enactment of the Article and with the intention of modifying certain provisions of this Article as to consumer credit.

§ 9–204.   After-Acquired Property; Future Advances

(1) Except as provided in subsection (2), a security agreement may provide that any or all obligations covered by the security agreement are to be secured by after-acquired collateral.

(2) No security interest attaches under an after-acquired property clause to consumer goods other than accessions (Section 9–314) when given as additional security unless the debtor acquires rights in them within ten days after the secured party gives value.

(3) Obligations covered by a security agreement may include future advances or other value whether or not the advances or value are given pursuant to commitment (subsection (1) of Section 9–105).

§ 9–205.   Use or Disposition of Collateral without Accounting Permissible

A security interest is not invalid or fraudulent against creditors by reason of liberty in the debtor to use, commingle or dispose of all or part of the collateral (including returned or repossessed goods) or to collect or compromise accounts or chattel paper, or to accept the return of goods or make repossessions, or to use, commingle or dispose of proceeds, or by reason of the failure of the secured party to require the debtor to account for proceeds or replace collateral. This section does not relax the requirements of possession where perfection of a security interest depends upon possession of the collateral by the secured party or by a bailee.

§ 9–206.   Agreement Not to Assert Defenses against Assignee; Modification of Sales Warranties Where Security Agreement Exists

(1) Subject to any statute or decision which establishes a different rule for buyers or lessees of consumer goods, an agreement by a buyer or lessee that he will not assert against an assignee any claim or defense which he may have against the seller or lessor is enforceable by an assignee who takes his assignment for value, in good faith and without notice of a claim or defense, except as to defenses of a type which may be

asserted against a holder in due course of a negotiable instrument under the Article on Commercial Paper (Article 3). A buyer who as part of one transaction signs both a negotiable instrument and a security agreement makes such an agreement.

(2) When a seller retains a purchase money security interest in goods the Article on Sales (Article 2) governs the sale and any disclaimer, limitation or modification of the seller's warranties.

§ 9–207.   Rights and Duties When Collateral Is in Secured Party's Possession

(1) A secured party must use reasonable care in the custody and preservation of collateral in his possession. In the case of an instrument or chattel paper reasonable care includes taking necessary steps to preserve rights against prior parties unless otherwise agreed.

(2) Unless otherwise agreed, when collateral is in the secured party's possession

   (a) reasonable expenses (including the cost of any insurance and payment of taxes or other charges) incurred in the custody, preservation, use or operation of the collateral are chargeable to the debtor and are secured by the collateral;

   (b) the risk of accidental loss or damage is on the debtor to the extent of any deficiency in any effective insurance coverage;

   (c) the secured party may hold as additional security any increase or profits (except money) received from the collateral, but money so received, unless remitted to the debtor, shall be applied in reduction of the secured obligation;

   (d) the secured party must keep the collateral identifiable but fungible collateral may be commingled;

   (e) the secured party may repledge the collateral upon terms which do not impair the debtor's right to redeem it.

(3) a secured party is liable for any loss caused by his failure to meet any obligation imposed by the preceding subsections but does not lose his security interest.

(4) A secured party may use or operate the collateral for the purpose of preserving the collateral or its value or pursuant to the order of a court of appropriate jurisdiction or, except in the case of consumer goods, in the manner and to the extent provided in the security agreement.

§ 9–208.   Request for Statement of Account or List of Collateral

(1) A debtor may sign a statement indicating what he believes to be the aggregate amount of unpaid indebtedness as of a specified date and may send it to the secured party with a request that the statement be approved or corrected and returned to the debtor. When the security agreement or any other record kept by the secured party identifies the collateral a debtor may similarly request the secured party to approve or correct a list of the collateral.

(2) The secured party must comply with such a request within two weeks after receipt by sending a written correction or approval. If the secured party claims a security interest in all of a particular type of collateral owned by the debtor he may indicate that fact in his reply and need not approve or correct an itemized list of such collateral. If the secured party without reasonable excuse fails to comply he is liable for any loss caused to the debtor thereby; and if the debtor has properly included in his request a good faith statement of the obligation or a list of the collateral or both the secured party may claim a security interest only as shown in the statement against persons misled by his failure to comply. If he no longer has an interest in the obligation or collateral at the time the request is received he must disclose the name and address of any successor in interest known to him and he is liable for any loss caused to the debtor as a result of failure to disclose. A successor in interest is not subject to this section until a request is received by him.

(3) A debtor is entitled to such a statement once every six months without charge. The secured party may require payment of a charge not exceeding $10 for each additional statement furnished.

Part 3   Rights of Third Parties; Perfected and Unperfected Security Interests; Rules of Priority

§ 9–301.   Persons Who Take Priority over Unperfected Security Interests; Rights of "Lien Creditor"

(1) Except as otherwise provided in subsection (2), an unperfected security interest is subordinate to the rights of

   (a) persons entitled to priority under Section 9–312;

   (b) a person who becomes a lien creditor before the security interest is perfected;

   (c) in the case of goods, instruments, documents, and chattel paper, a person who is not a secured party and who is a transferee in bulk or other buyer not in ordinary course of business or is a buyer of farm products in ordinary course of business, to the extent that he gives value and receives delivery of the collateral without knowledge of the security interest and before it is perfected;

   (d) in the case of accounts and general intangibles, a person who is not a secured party and who is a transferee to the extent that he gives value without knowledge of the security interest and before it is perfected.

(2) If the secured party files with respect to a purchase money security interest before or within ten days after the debtor receives possession of the collateral, he takes priority over the rights of a transferee in bulk or of a lien creditor which arise between the time the security interest attaches and the time of filing.

(3) A "lien creditor" means a creditor who has acquired a lien on the property involved by attachment, levy or the like and includes an assignee for benefit of creditors from the time of assignment, and a trustee in bankruptcy from the date of the filing of the petition or a receiver in equity from the time of appointment.

(4) A person who becomes a lien creditor while a security interest is perfected takes subject to the security interest only to the extent that it secures advances made before he becomes a lien creditor or within 45 days thereafter or made without knowledge of the lien or pursuant to a commitment entered into without knowledge of the lien.

§ 9–302. When Filing Is Required to Perfect Security Interest; Security Interests to Which Filing Provisions of This Article Do Not Apply

(1) A financing statement must be filed to perfect all security interests except the following:

(a) a security interest in collateral in possession of the secured party under Section 9–305;

(b) a security interest temporarily perfected in instruments or documents without delivery under Section 9–304 or in proceeds for a 10 day period under Section 9–306;

(c) a security interest created by an assignment of a beneficial interest in a trust or a decedent's estate;

(d) a purchase money security interest in consumer goods; but filing is required for a motor vehicle required to be registered; and fixture filing is required for priority over conflicting interests in fixtures to the extent provided in Section 9–313;

(e) an assignment of accounts which does not alone or in conjunction with other assignments to the same assignee transfer a significant part of the outstanding accounts of the assignor;

(f) a security interest of a collecting bank (Section 4–208) or in securities (Section 8–321) or arising under the Article on Sales (see Section 9–113) or covered in subsection (3) of this section;

(g) an assignment for the benefit of all the creditors of the transferor, and subsequent transfers by the assignee thereunder.

(2) If a secured party assigns a perfected security interest, no filing under this Article is required in order to continue the perfected status of the security interest against creditors of the transferees from the original debtor.

(3) The filing of a financing statement otherwise required by this Article is not necessary or effective to perfect a security interest in property subject to

(a) a statute or treaty of the United States which provides for a national or international registration or a national or international certificate of title or which specifies a place of filing different from that specified in this Article for filing of the security interest; or

(b) the following statutes of this state; [list any certificate of title statute covering automobiles, trailers, mobile homes, boats, farm tractors, or the like, and any central filing statute.*]; but during any period in which collateral is inventory held for sale by a person who is in the business of selling goods of that kind, the filing provisions of this Article (Part 4) apply to a security interest in that collateral created by him as debtor; or

(c) a certificate of title statute of another jurisdiction under the law of which indication of a security interest on the certificate is required as a condition of perfection (subsection (2) of Section 9–103).

(4) Compliance with a statute or treaty described in subsection (3) is equivalent to the filing of a financing statement under this Article, and a security interest in property subject to the statute or treaty can be perfected only by compliance therewith except as provided in Section 9–103 on multiple state transactions. Duration and renewal of perfection of a security interest perfected by compliance with the statute or treaty are governed by the provisions of the statute or treaty; in other respects the security interest is subject to this Article.

Note: *It is recommended that the provisions of certificate of title acts for perfection of security interests by notation on the certificates should be amended to exclude coverage of inventory held for sale.

§ 9–303. When Security Interest Is Perfected; Continuity of Perfection

(1) A security interest is perfected when it has attached and when all of the applicable steps required for perfection have been taken. Such steps are specified in Sections 9–302, 9–304, 9–305 and 9–306. If such steps are taken before the security interest attaches, it is perfected at the time when it attaches.

(2) If a security interest is originally perfected in any way permitted under this Article and is subsequently perfected in some other way under this Article, without an intermediate period when it was unperfected, the security interest shall be deemed to be perfected continuously for the purposes of this Article.

§ 9–304. Perfection of Security Interest in Instruments, Documents, and Goods Covered by Documents; Perfection by Permissive Filing; Temporary Perfection Without Filing or Transfer of Possession

(1) A security interest in chattel paper or negotiable documents may be perfected by filing. A security interest in money or instruments (other than certificated securities or instruments which constitute part of chattel paper) can be perfected only by the secured party's taking possession, except as provided in subsections (4) and (5) of this section and subsections (2) and (3) of Section 9–306 on proceeds.

(2) During the period that goods are in the possession of the issuer of a negotiable document therefor, a security interest in the goods is perfected by perfecting a security interest in the document, and any security interest in the goods otherwise perfected during such period is subject thereto.

(3) A security interest in goods in the possession of a bailee other than one who has issued a negotiable document therefor is perfected by issuance of a document in the name of the secured party or by the bailee's receipt of notification of the secured party's interest or by filing as to the goods.

(4) A security interest in instruments (other than certificated securities) or negotiable documents is perfected without filing or the taking of possession for a period of 21 days from the time it attaches to the extent that it arises from new value given under a written security agreement.

(5) A security interest remains perfected for a period of 21 days without filing where a secured party having a perfected security interest in an instrument (other than a certificated security), a negotiable document or goods in possession of a bailee other than one who has issued a negotiable document therefor

(a) makes available to the debtor the goods or documents representing the goods for the purpose of ultimate sale or exchange or for the purpose of loading, unloading, storing, shipping, transshipping, manufacturing, processing or otherwise dealing with them in a manner preliminary to their sale or exchange, but priority between conflicting security interests in the goods is subject to subsection (3) of Section 9–312; or

(b) delivers the instrument to the debtor for the purpose of ultimate sale or exchange or of presentation, collection, renewal or registration of transfer.

(6) After the 21 day period in subsections (4) and (5) perfection depends upon compliance with applicable provisions of this Article.

§ 9–305.   When Possession by Secured Party Perfects Security Interest Without Filing

A security interest in letters of credit and advices of credit (subsection (2)(a) of Section 5–116), goods, instruments (other than certificated securities), money, negotiable documents, or chattel paper may be perfected by the secured party's taking possession of the collateral. If such collateral other than goods covered by a negotiable document is held by a bailee, the secured party is deemed to have possession from the time the bailee receives notification of the secured party's interest. A security interest is perfected by possession from the time possession is taken without a relation back and continues only so long as possession is retained, unless otherwise specified in this Article. The security interest may be otherwise perfected as provided in this Article before or after the period of possession by the secured party.

§ 9–306.   "Proceeds"; Secured Party's Rights on Disposition of Collateral

(1) "Proceeds" includes whatever is received upon the sale, exchange, collection or other disposition of collateral or proceeds. Insurance payable by reason of loss or damage to the collateral is proceeds, except to the extent that it is payable to a person other than a party to the security agreement. Money, checks, deposit accounts, and the like are "cash proceeds." All other proceeds are "non-cash proceeds."

(2) Except where this Article otherwise provides, a security interest continues in collateral notwithstanding sale, exchange or other disposition thereof unless the disposition was authorized by the secured party in the security agreement or otherwise, and also continues in any identifiable proceeds including collections received by the debtor.

(3) The security interest in proceeds is a continuously perfected security interest if the interest in the original collateral was perfected but it ceases to be a perfected security interest and becomes unperfected ten days after receipt of the proceeds by the debtor unless

(a) a filed financing statement covers the original collateral and the proceeds are collateral in which a security interest may be perfected by filing in the office or offices where the financing statement has been filed and, if the proceeds are acquired with cash proceeds, the description of collateral in the financing statement indicates the types of property constituting the proceeds; or

(b) a filed financing statement covers the original collateral and the proceeds are identifiable cash proceeds; or

(c) the security interest in the proceeds is perfected before the expiration of the ten day period. Except as provided in this section, a security interest in proceeds can be perfected only by the methods or under the circumstances permitted in this Article for original collateral of the same type.

(4) In the event of insolvency proceedings instituted by or against a debtor, a secured party with a perfected security interest in proceeds has a perfected security interest only in the following proceeds:

(a) in identifiable non-cash proceeds and in separate deposit accounts containing only proceeds;

(b) in identifiable cash proceeds in the form of money which is neither commingled with other money nor deposited in a deposit account prior to the insolvency proceedings;

(c) in identifiable cash proceeds in the form of checks and the like which are not deposited in a deposit account prior to the insolvency proceedings; and

(d) in all cash and deposit accounts of the debtor in which proceeds have been commingled with other funds, but the perfected security interest under this paragraph (d) is

(i) subject to any right to setoff; and

(ii) limited to an amount not greater than the amount of any cash proceeds received by the debtor within ten days before the institution of the insolvency proceedings less the sum of (I) the payments to the secured party on account of cash proceeds received by the debtor during such period and (II) the cash proceeds received by the debtor during such period to which the secured party is entitled under paragraph (a) through (c) of this subsection (4).

(5) If a sale of goods results in an account or chattel paper which is transferred by the seller to a secured party, and if the goods are returned to or are repossessed by the seller or the secured party, the following rules determine priorities:

(a) If the goods were collateral at the time of sale, for an indebtedness of the seller which is still unpaid, the original security interest attaches again to the goods and continues as a perfected security interest if it was perfected at the time when the goods were sold. If the security interest was originally perfected by a filing which is still effective, nothing further is required to continue the perfected status; in any other case, the secured party must take possession of the returned or repossessed goods or must file.

(b) An unpaid transferee of the chattel paper has a security interest in the goods against the transferor. Such security interest is prior to a security interest asserted under paragraph (a) to the extent that the transferee of the chattel paper was entitled to priority under Section 9–308.

(c) An unpaid transferee of the account has a security interest in the goods against the transferor. Such security interest is subordinate to a security interest asserted under paragraph (a).

(d) A security interest of an unpaid transferee asserted under paragraph (b) or (c) must be perfected for protection against creditors of the transferor and purchasers of the returned or repossessed goods.

§ 9–307. Protection of Buyers of Goods

(1) A buyer in ordinary course of business (subsection (9) of Section 1–201) other than a person buying farm products from a person engaged in farming operations takes free of a security interest created by his seller even though the security interest is perfected and even though the buyer knows of its existence.

(2) In the case of consumer goods, a buyer takes free of a security interest even though perfected if he buys without knowledge of the security interest, for value and for his own personal, family or household purposes unless prior to the purchase the secured party has filed a financing statement covering such goods.

(3) A buyer other than a buyer in ordinary course of business (subsection (1) of this section) takes free of a security interest to the extent that it secures future advances made after the secured party acquires knowledge of the purchase, or more than 45 days after the purchase, whichever first occurs, unless made pursuant to a commitment entered into without knowledge of the purchase and before the expiration of the 45 day period.

§ 9–308. Purchase of Chattel Paper and Instruments

A purchaser of chattel paper or an instrument who gives new value and takes possession of it in the ordinary course of his business has priority over a security interest in the chattel paper or instrument

(a) which is perfected under Section 9–304 (permissive filing and temporary perfection) or under Section 9–306 (perfection as to proceeds) if he acts without knowledge that the specific paper or instrument is subject to a security interest; or

(b) which is claimed merely as proceeds of inventory subject to a security interest (Section 9–306) even though he knows that the specific paper or instrument is subject to the security interest.

§ 9–309. Protection of Purchasers of Instruments, Documents and Securities

Nothing in this Article limits the rights of a holder in due course of a negotiable instrument (Section 3–302) or a holder to whom a negotiable document of title has been duly negotiated (Section 7–501) or a bona fide purchaser of a security (Section 8–302) and the holders or purchasers take priority over an earlier security interest even though perfected. Filing under this Article does not constitute notice of the security interest to such holders or purchasers.

§ 9–310. Priority of Certain Liens Arising by Operation of Law

When a person in the ordinary course of his business furnishes services or materials with respect to goods subject to a security interest, a lien upon goods in the possession of such person given by statute or rule of law for such materials or services takes priority over a perfected security interest unless the lien is statutory and the statute expressly provides otherwise.

§ 9–311. Alienability of Debtor's Rights: Judicial Process

The debtor's rights in collateral may be voluntarily or involuntarily transferred (by way of sale, creation of a security interest, attachment, levy, garnishment or other judicial process) notwithstanding a provision in the security agreement prohibiting any transfer or making the transfer constitute a default.

§ 9–312. Priorities among Conflicting Security Interests in the Same Collateral

(1) The rules of priority stated in other sections of this Part and in the following sections shall govern when applicable: Section 4–208 with respect to the security interests of collecting banks in items being collected, accompanying documents and proceeds; Section 9–103 on security interests related to other jurisdictions; Section 9–114 on consignments.

(2) A perfected security interest in crops for new value given to enable the debtor to produce the crops during the production season and given not more than three months before the crops become growing crops by planting or otherwise takes priority over an earlier perfected security interest to the extent that such earlier interest secures obligations due more than six months before the crops become growing crops by planting or otherwise, even though the person giving new value had knowledge of the earlier security interest.

(3) A perfected purchase money security interest in inventory has priority over a conflicting security interest in the same inventory and also has priority in identifiable cash proceeds received on or before the delivery of the inventory to a buyer if

(a) the purchase money security interest is perfected at the time the debtor receives possession of the inventory; and

(b) the purchase money secured party gives notification in writing to the holder of the conflicting security interest if the holder had filed a financing statement covering the same types of inventory (i) before the date of filing made by the purchase money secured party, or (ii) before the beginning of the 21 day period where the purchase money security interest is temporarily perfected without filing or possession (subsection (5) of Section 9–304); and

(c) the holder of the conflicting security interest receives the notification within five years before the debtor receives possession of the inventory; and

(d) the notification states that the person giving the notice has or expects to acquire a purchase money security interest in inventory of the debtor, describing such inventory by item or type.

(4) A purchase money security interest in collateral other than inventory has priority over a conflicting security interest in the same collateral or its proceeds if the purchase money security interest is perfected at the time the debtor receives possession of the collateral or within ten days thereafter.

(5) In all cases not governed by other rules stated in this section (including cases of purchase money security interests which do not qualify for the special priorities set forth in subsections (3) and (4) of this section), priority between conflicting security interests in the same collateral shall be determined according to the following rules:

(a) Conflicting security interests rank according to priority in time of filing or perfection. Priority dates from the time a filing is first made covering the collateral or the time the security interest is first perfected, whichever is earlier, provided that there is no period thereafter when there is neither filing nor perfection.

(b) So long as conflicting security interests are unperfected, the first to attach has priority.

(6) For the purposes of subsection (5) a date of filing or perfection as to collateral is also a date of filing or perfection as to proceeds.

(7) If future advances are made while a security interest is perfected by filing, the taking of possession, or under Section 8–321 on securities, the security interest has the same priority for the purposes of subsection (5) with respect to the future advances as it does with respect to the first advance. If a commitment is made before or while the security interest is so perfected, the security interest has the same priority with respect to advances made pursuant thereto. In other cases a perfected security interest has priority from the date the advance is made.

§ 9–313.   Priority of Security Interests in Fixtures

(1) In this section and in the provisions of Part 4 of this Article referring to fixture filing, unless the context otherwise requires

(a) goods are "fixtures" when they become so related to particular real estate that an interest in them arises under real estate law

(b) a "fixture filing" is the filing in the office where a mortgage on the real estate would be filed or recorded of a financing statement covering goods which are or are to become fixtures

and conforming to the requirements of subsection (5) of Section 9–402

(c) a mortgage is a "construction mortgage" to the extent that it secures an obligation incurred for the construction of an improvement on land including the acquisition cost of the land, if the recorded writing so indicates.

(2) A security interest under this Article may be created in goods which are fixtures or may continue in goods which become fixtures, but no security interest exists under this Article in ordinary building materials incorporated into an improvement on land.

(3) This Article does not prevent creation of an encumbrance upon fixtures pursuant to real estate law.

(4) A perfected security interest in fixtures has priority over the conflicting interest of an encumbrancer or owner of the real estate where

(a) the security interest is a purchase money security interest, the interest of the encumbrancer or owner arises before the goods become fixtures, the security interest is perfected by a fixture filing before the goods become fixtures or within ten days thereafter, and the debtor has an interest of record in the real estate or is in possession of the real estate; or

(b) the security interest is perfected by a fixture filing before the interest of the encumbrancer or owner is of record, the security interest has priority over any conflicting interest of a predecessor in title of the encumbrancer or owner, and the debtor has an interest of record in the real estate or is in possession of the real estate; or

(c) the fixtures are readily removable factory or office machines or readily removable replacements of domestic appliances which are consumer goods, and before the goods become fixtures the security interest is perfected by any method permitted by this Article; or

(d) the conflicting interest is a lien on the real estate obtained by legal or equitable proceedings after the security interest was perfected by any method permitted by this Article.

(5) A security interest in fixtures, whether or not perfected, has priority over the conflicting interest of an encumbrancer or owner of the real estate where

(a) the encumbrancer or owner has consented in writing to the security interest or has disclaimed an interest in the goods as fixtures; or

(b) the debtor has a right to remove the goods as against the encumbrancer or owner. If the debtor's right terminates, the priority of the security interest continues for a reasonable time.

(6) Notwithstanding paragraph (a) of subsection (4) but otherwise subject to subsections (4) and (5), a security interest in fixtures is subordinate to a construction mortgage recorded before the goods become fixtures if the goods become fixtures before the completion of the construction. To the extent that it is given to refinance a construction mortgage, a mortgage has this priority to the same extent as the construction mortgage.

(7) In cases not within the preceding subsections, a security interest in fixtures is subordinate to the conflicting interest of

an encumbrancer or owner of the related real estate who is not the debtor.

(8) When the secured party has priority over all owners and encumbrancers of the real estate, he may, on default, subject to the provisions of Part 5, remove his collateral from the real estate but he must reimburse any encumbrancer or owner of the real estate who is not the debtor and who has not otherwise agreed for the cost of repair of any physical injury, but not for any diminution in value of the real estate caused by the absence of the goods removed or by any necessity of replacing them. A person entitled to reimbursement may refuse permission to remove until the secured party gives adequate security for the performance of this obligation.

§ 9–314. Accessions

(1) A security interest in goods which attaches before they are installed in or affixed to other goods takes priority as to the goods installed or affixed (called in this section "accessions") over the claims of all persons to the whole except as stated in subsection (3) and subject to Section 9–315(1).

(2) A security interest which attaches to goods after they become part of a whole is valid against all persons subsequently acquiring interests in the whole except as stated in subsection (3) but is invalid against any person with an interest in the whole at the time the security interests attaches to the goods who has not in writing consented to the security interest or disclaimed an interest in the goods as part of the whole.

(3) The security interests described in subsections (1) and (2) do not take priority over

(a) a subsequent purchaser for value of any interest in the whole; or

(b) a creditor with a lien on the whole subsequently obtained by judicial proceedings; or

(c) a creditor with a prior perfected security interest in the whole to the extent that he makes subsequent advances if the subsequent purchase is made, the lien by judicial proceedings obtained or the subsequent advance under the prior perfected security interest is made or contracted for without knowledge of the security interest and before it is perfected. A purchaser of the whole at a foreclosure sale other than the holder of a perfected security interest purchasing at his own foreclosure sale is a subsequent purchaser within this section.

(4) When under subsections (1) and (2) and (3) a secured party has an interest in accessions which has priority over the claims of all persons who have interests in the whole, he may on default subject to the provisions of Part 5 remove his collateral from the whole but he must reimburse any encumbrancer or owner of the whole who is not the debtor and who has not otherwise agreed for the cost of repair of any physical injury but not for any diminution in value of the whole caused by the absence of the goods removed or by any necessity for replacing them. A person entitled to reimbursement may refuse permission to remove until the secured party gives adequate security for the performance of this obligation.

§ 9–315. Priority When Goods Are Commingled or Processed

(1) If a security interest in goods was perfected and subsequently the goods or a part thereof have become part of a product or mass, the security interest continues in the product or mass if

(a) the goods are so manufactured, processed, assembled or commingled that their identity is lost in the product or mass; or

(b) a financing statement covering the original goods also covers the product into which the goods have been manufactured, processed or assembled. In a case to which paragraph (b) applies, no separate security interest in that part of the original goods which have been manufactured, processed or assembled into the product may be claimed under Section 9–314.

(2) When under subsection (1) more than one security interest attaches to the product or mass, they rank equally according to the ratio that the cost of the goods to which each interest originally attached bears to the cost of the total product or mass.

§ 9–316. Priority Subject to Subordination

Nothing in this Article prevents subordination by agreement by any person entitled to priority.

§ 9–317. Secured Party Not Obligated on Contract of Debtor

The mere existence of a security interest or authority given to the debtor to dispose of or use collateral does not impose contract or tort liability upon the secured party for the debtor's acts or omissions.

§ 9–318. Defenses against Assignee; Modification of Contract after Notification of Assignment; Term Prohibiting Assignment Ineffective; Identification and Proof of Assignment

(1) Unless an account debtor has made an enforceable agreement not to assert defenses or claims arising out of a sale as provided in Section 9–206 the rights of an assignee are subject to

(a) all the terms of the contract between the account debtor and assignor and any defense or claim arising therefrom; and

(b) any other defense or claim of the account debtor against the assignor which accrues before the account debtor receives notification of the assignment.

(2) So far as the right to payment or a part thereof under an assigned contract has not been fully earned by performance, and notwithstanding notification of the assignment, any modification of or substitution for the contract made in good faith and in accordance with reasonable commercial standards is effective against an assignee unless the account debtor has otherwise agreed but the assignee acquires corresponding rights

under the modified or substituted contract. The assignment may provide that such modification or substitution is a breach by the assignor.

(3) The account debtor is authorized to pay the assignor until the account debtor receives notification that the amount due or to become due has been assigned and that payment is to be made to the assignee. A notification which does not reasonably identify the rights assigned is ineffective. If requested by the account debtor, the assignee must seasonably furnish reasonable proof that the assignment has been made and unless he does so the account debtor may pay the assignor.

(4) A term in any contract between an account debtor and an assignor is ineffective if it prohibits assignment of an account or prohibits creation of a security interest in a general intangible for money due or to become due or requires the account debtor's consent to such assignment or security interest.

Part 4   Filing

§ 9–401.   Place of Filing; Erroneous Filing; Removal of Collateral

First Alternative Subsection (1)

(1) The proper place to file in order to perfect a security interest is as follows:

(a) when the collateral is timber to be cut or is minerals or the like (including oil and gas) or accounts subject to subsection (5) of Section 9–103, or when the financing statement is filed as a fixture filing (Section 9–313) and the collateral is goods which are or are to become fixtures, then in the office where a mortgage on the real estate would be filed or recorded;

(b) in all other cases, in the office of the [Secretary of State].

Second Alternative Subsection (1)

(1) The proper place to file in order to perfect a security interest is as follows:

(a) when the collateral is equipment used in farming operations, or farm products, or accounts or general intangibles arising from or relating to the sale of farm products by a farmer, or consumer goods, then in the office of the . . . . in the county of the debtor's residence or if the debtor is not a resident of this state then in the office of the . . . . in the county where the goods are kept, and in addition when the collateral is crops growing or to be grown in the office of the . . . . in the county where the land is located;

(b) when the collateral is timber to be cut or is minerals or the like (including oil and gas) or accounts subject to subsection (5) of Section 9–103, or when the financing statement is filed as a fixture filing (Section 9–313) and the collateral is goods which are or are to become fixtures, then in the office where a mortgage on the real estate would be filed or recorded;

(c) in all other cases, in the office of the [Secretary of State].

Third Alternative Subsection (1)

(1) The proper place to file in order to perfect a security interest is as follows:

(a) when the collateral is equipment used in farming operations, or farm products, or accounts or general intangibles arising from or relating to the sale of farm products by a farmer, or consumer goods, then in the office of the . . . . in the county of the debtor's residence or if the debtor is not a resident of this state then in office of the . . . . in the county where the goods are kept, and in addition when the collateral is crops growing or to be grown in the office of the . . . . in the county where the land is located;

(b) when the collateral is timber to be cut or is minerals or the like (including oil and gas) or accounts subject to subsection (5) of Section 9–103, or when the financing statement is filed as a fixture filing (Section 9–313) and the collateral is goods which are or are to become fixtures, then in the office where a mortgage on the real estate would be filed or recorded;

(c) in all other cases, in the office of the [Secretary of State] and in addition, if the debtor has a place of business in only one county of this state, also in the office of . . . . of such county, or, if the debtor has no place of business in this state, but resides in the state, also in the office of . . . . of the county in which he resides.

Note: One of the three alternatives should be selected as subsection (1).

(2) A filing which is made in good faith in an improper place or not in all of the places required by this section is nevertheless effective with regard to any collateral as to which the filing complied with the requirements of this Article and is also effective with regard to collateral covered by the financing statement against any person who has knowledge of the contents of such financing statement.

(3) A filing which is made in the proper place in this state continues effective even though the debtor's residence or place of business or the location of the collateral or its use, whichever controlled the original filing, is thereafter changed.

Alternative to Subsection (3)

[(3) A filing which is made in the proper county continues effective for four months after a change to another county of the debtor's residence or place of business or the location of the collateral, whichever controlled the original filing. It becomes ineffective thereafter unless a copy of the financing statement signed by the secured party is filed in the new county within said period. The security interest may also be perfected in the new county after the expiration of the four-month period; in such case perfection dates from the time of perfection in the new county. A change in the use of the collateral does not impair the effectiveness of the original filing.]

(4) The rules stated in Section 9–103 determine whether filing is necessary in this state.

(5) Notwithstanding the preceding subsections, and subject to subsection (3) of Section 9–302, the proper place to file in order to perfect a security interest in collateral, including fixtures, of a transmitting utility is the office of the [Secretary of State]. This filing constitutes a fixture filing (Section 9–313) as to the collateral described therein which is or is to become fixtures.

(6) For the purposes of this section, the residence of an organization is its place of business if it has one or its chief executive office if it has more than one place of business.

Note: Subsection (6) should be used only if the state chooses the Second or Third Alternative Subsection (1).

§ 9–402. Formal Requisites of Financing Statement; Amendments; Mortgage as Financing Statement

(1) A financing statement is sufficient if it gives the names of the debtor and the secured party, is signed by the debtor, gives an address of the secured party from which information concerning the security interest may be obtained, gives a mailing address of the debtor and contains a statement indicating the types, or describing the items, of collateral. A financing statement may be filed before a security agreement is made or a security interest otherwise attaches. When the financing statement covers crops growing or to be grown, the statement must also contain a description of the real estate concerned. When the financing statement covers timber to be cut or covers minerals or the like (including oil and gas) or accounts subject to subsection (5) of Section 9–103, or when the financing statement is filed as a fixture filing (Section 9–313) and the collateral is goods which are or are to become fixtures, the statement must also comply with subsection (5). A copy of the security agreement is sufficient as a financing statement if it contains the above information and is signed by the debtor. A carbon, photographic or other reproduction of a security agreement or a financing statement is sufficient as a financing statement if the security agreement so provides or if the original has been filed in this state.

(2) A financing statement which otherwise complies with subsection (1) is sufficient when it is signed by the secured party instead of the debtor if it is filed to perfect a security interest in

   (a) collateral already subject to a security interest in another jurisdiction when it is brought into this state, or when the debtor's location is changed to this state. Such a financing statement must state that the collateral was brought into this state or that the debtor's location was changed to this state under such circumstances; or

   (b) proceeds under Section 9–306 if the security interest in the original collateral was perfected. Such a financing statement must describe the original collateral; or

   (c) collateral as to which the filing has lapsed; or

   (d) collateral acquired after a change of name, identity or corporate structure of the debtor (subsection (7)).

(3) A form substantially as follows is sufficient to comply with subsection (1):

Name of debtor (or assignor) . . . .

Address . . . .

Name of secured party (or assignee). . . . .

Address . . . .

1. This financing statement covers the following types (or items) of property:

(Describe): . . . .

2. (If collateral is crops) The above described crops are growing or are to be grown on:

(Describe Real Estate) . . . .

3. (If applicable) The above goods are to become fixtures on:*

(Describe Real Estate). . . . .

and this financing statement is to be filed [for record] in the real estate records. (If the debtor does not have an interest of record) The name of a record owner is

. . . .

4. (If products of collateral are claimed) Products of the collateral are also covered.

(Use whichever is applicable)

. . . .

Signature of Debtor (or Assignor)

. . . .

Signature of Secured Party (or Assignee)

*Where appropriate substitute either "The above timber is standing on . . ." or "The above minerals or the like (including oil and gas) or accounts will be financed at the wellhead or minehead of the well or mine located on . . ."

(4) A financing statement may be amended by filing a writing signed by both the debtor and the secured party. An amendment does not extend the period of effectiveness of a financing statement. If any amendment adds collateral, it is effective as to the added collateral only from the filing date of the amendment. In this Article, unless the context otherwise requires, the term "financing statement" means the original financing statement and any amendments.

(5) A financing statement covering timber to be cut or covering minerals or the like (including oil and gas) or accounts subject to subsection (5) of Section 9–103, or a financing statement filed as a fixture filing (Section 9–313) where the debtor is not a transmitting utility, must show that it covers this type of collateral, must recite that it is to be filed [for record] in the real estate records, and the financing statement must contain a description of the real estate [sufficient if it were contained in a mortgage of the real estate to give constructive notice of the mortgage under the law of this state]. If the debtor does not have an interest of record in the real estate, the financing statement must show the name of a record owner.

(6) A mortgage is effective as a financing statement filed as a fixture filing from the date of its recording if

(a) the goods are described in the mortgage by item or type; and

(b) the goods are or are to become fixtures related to the real estate described in the mortgage; and

(c) the mortgage complies with the requirements for a financing statement in this section other than a recital that it is to be filed in the real estate records; and

(d) the mortgage is duly recorded.

No fee with reference to the financing statement is required other than the regular recording and satisfaction fees with respect to the mortgage.

(7) A financing statement sufficiently shows the name of the debtor if it gives the individual, partnership or corporate name of the debtor, whether or not it adds other trade names or names of partners. Where the debtor so changes his name or in the case of an organization its name, identity or corporate structure that a filed financing statement becomes seriously misleading, the filing is not effective to perfect a security interest in collateral acquired by the debtor more than four months after the change, unless a new appropriate financing statement is filed before the expiration of that time. A filed financing statement remains effective with respect to collateral transferred by the debtor even though the secured party knows of or consents to the transfer.

(8) A financing statement substantially complying with the requirements of this section is effective even though it contains minor errors which are not seriously misleading.

Note: Language in brackets is optional.

Note: Where the state has any special recording system for real estate other than the usual grantor-grantee index (as, for instance, a tract system or a title registration or Torrens system) local adaptations of subsection (5) and Section 9–403(7) may be necessary. See Mass. Gen. Laws Chapter 106, Section 9–409.

§ 9–403. What Constitutes Filing; Duration of Filing; Effect of Lapsed Filing; Duties of Filing Officer

(1) Presentation for filing of a financing statement and tender of the filing fee or acceptance of the statement by the filing officer constitutes filing under this Article.

(2) Except as provided in subsection (6) a filed financing statement is effective for a period of five years from the date of filing. The effectiveness of a filed financing statement lapses on the expiration of the five year period unless a continuation statement is filed prior to the lapse. If a security interest perfected by filing exists at the time insolvency proceedings are commenced by or against the debtor, the security interest remains perfected until termination of the insolvency proceedings and thereafter for a period of sixty days or until expiration of the five year period, whichever occurs later. Upon lapse the security interest becomes unperfected, unless it is perfected without filing. If the security interest becomes unperfected upon lapse, it is deemed to have been unperfected as against a person who became a purchaser or lien creditor before lapse.

(3) A continuation statement may be filed by the secured party within six months prior to the expiration of the five year period specified in subsection (2). Any such continuation statement must be signed by the secured party, identify the original statement by file number and state that the original statement is still effective. A continuation statement signed by a person other than the secured party of record must be accompanied by a separate written statement of assignment signed by the secured party of record and complying with subsection (2) of Section 9–405, including payment of the required fee. Upon timely filing of the continuation statement, the effectiveness of the original statement is continued for five years after the last date to which the filing was effective whereupon it lapses in the same manner as provided in subsection (2) unless another continuation statement is filed prior to such lapse. Succeeding continuation statements may be filed in the same manner to continue the effectiveness of the original statement. Unless a statute on disposition of public records provides otherwise, the filing officer may remove a lapsed statement from the files and destroy it immediately if he has retained a microfilm or other photographic record, or in other cases after one year after the lapse. The filing officer shall so arrange matters by physical annexation of financing statements to continuation statements or other related filings, or by other means, that if he physically destroys the financing statements of a period more than five years past, those which have been continued by a continuation statement or which are still effective under subsection (6) shall be retained.

(4) Except as provided in subsection (7) a filing officer shall mark each statement with a file number and with the date and hour of filing and shall hold the statement or a microfilm or other photographic copy thereof for public inspection. In addition the filing officer shall index the statement according to the name of the debtor and shall note in the index the file number and the address of the debtor given in the statement.

(5) The uniform fee for filing and indexing and for stamping a copy furnished by the secured party to show the date and place of filing for an original financing statement or for a continuation statement shall be $ . . . . . . if the statement is in the standard form prescribed by the [Secretary of State] and otherwise shall be $ . . . . . . , plus in each case, if the financing statement is subject to subsection (5) of Section 9–402, $ . . . . . . The uniform fee for each name more than one required to be indexed shall be $ . . . . . . The secured party may at his option show a trade name for any person and an extra uniform indexing fee of $ . . . . . . shall be paid with respect thereto.

(6) If the debtor is a transmitting utility (subsection (5) of Section 9–401) and a filed financing statement so states, it is effective until a termination statement is filed. A real estate mortgage which is effective as a fixture filing under subsection (6) of Section 9–402 remains effective as a fixture filing until the mortgage is released or satisfied of record or its effectiveness otherwise terminates as to the real estate.

(7) When a financing statement covers timber to be cut or covers minerals or the like (including oil and gas) or accounts subject to subsection (5) of Section 9–103, or is filed as a fixture filing, [it shall be filed for record and] the filing officer shall index it under the names of the debtor and any owner of record shown on the financing statement in the same fashion as if they were the mortgagors in a mortgage of the real estate described, and, to the extent that the law of this state provides for the indexing of mortgages under the name of the mortgagee, under the name of the secured party as if he were the mortgagee thereunder, or where indexing is by description in the same fashion as if the financing statement were a mortgage of the real estate described.

Note: In states in which writings will not appear in the real estate records and indices unless actually recorded the bracketed language in subsection (7) should be used.

§ 9–404.   Termination Statement
(1) If a financing statement covering consumer goods is filed on or after . . . . . . , then within one month or within ten days following written demand by the debtor after there is no outstanding secured obligation and no commitment to make advances, incur obligations or otherwise give value, the secured party must file with each filing officer with whom the financing statement was filed, a termination statement to the effect that he no longer claims a security interest under the financing statement, which shall be identified by file number. In other cases whenever there is no outstanding secured obligation and no commitment to make advances, incur obligations or otherwise give value, the secured party must on written demand by the debtor send the debtor, for each filing officer with whom the financing statement was filed, a termination statement to the effect that he no longer claims a security interest under the financing statement, which shall be identified by file number. A termination statement signed by a person other than the secured party of record must be accompanied by a separate written statement of assignment signed by the secured party of record complying with subsection (2) of Section 9–405, including payment of the required fee. If the affected secured party fails to file such a termination statement as required by this subsection, or to send such a termination statement within ten days after proper demand therefor, he shall be liable to the debtor for one hundred dollars, and in addition for any loss caused to the debtor by such failure.
(2) On presentation to the filing officer of such a termination statement he must note it in the index. If he has received the termination statement in duplicate, he shall return one copy of the termination statement to the secured party stamped to show the time of receipt thereof. If the filing officer has a microfilm or other photographic record of the financing statement, and of any related continuation statement, statement of assignment and statement of release, he may remove the originals from the files at any time after receipt of the termination

statement, or if he has no such record, he may remove them from the files at any time after one year after receipt of the termination statement.
(3) If the termination statement is in the standard form prescribed by the [Secretary of State], the uniform fee for filing and indexing the termination statement shall be $. . . . . . , and otherwise shall be $. . . . . . , plus in each case an additional fee of $. . . . . for each name more than one against which the termination statement is required to be indexed.

Note: The date to be inserted should be the effective date of the revised Article 9.

§ 9–405.   Assignment of Security Interest; Duties of Filing Officer; Fees
(1) A financing statement may disclose an assignment of a security interest in the collateral described in the financing statement by indication in the financing statement of the name and address of the assignee or by an assignment itself or a copy thereof on the face or back of the statement. On presentation to the filing officer of such a financing statement the filing officer shall mark the same as provided in Section 9–403(4). The uniform fee for filing, indexing and furnishing filing data for a financing statement so indicating an assignment shall be $. . . . . if the statement is in the standard form prescribed by the [Secretary of State] and otherwise shall be $. . . . . . , plus in each case an additional fee of $. . . . . for each name more than one against which the financing statement is required to be indexed.
(2) A secured party may assign of record all or part of his rights under a financing statement by the filing in the place where the original financing statement was filed of a separate written statement of assignment signed by the secured party of record and setting forth the name of the secured party of record and the debtor, the file number and the date of filing of the financing statement and the name and address of the assignee and containing a description of the collateral assigned. A copy of the assignment is sufficient as a separate statement if it complies with the preceding sentence. On presentation to the filing officer of such a separate statement, the filing officer shall mark such separate statement with the date and hour of the filing. He shall note the assignment on the index of the financing statement, or in the case of a fixture filing, or a filing covering timber to be cut, or covering minerals or the like (including oil and gas) or accounts subject to subsection (5) of Section 9–103, he shall index the assignment under the name of the assignor as grantor and, to the extent that the law of this state provides for indexing the assignment of a mortgage under the name of the assignee, he shall index the assignment of the financing statement under the name of the assignee. The uniform fee for filing, indexing and furnishing filing data about such a separate statement of assignment shall be $. . . . . . if the statement is in the standard form prescribed by the [Secretary of State] and otherwise shall be $. . . . . . , plus in each case an additional fee of $. . . . . for each name more than one against

which the statement of assignment is required to be indexed. Notwithstanding the provisions of this subsection, an assignment of record of a security interest in a fixture contained in a mortgage effective as a fixture filing (subsection (6) of Section 9–402) may be made only by an assignment of the mortgage in the manner provided by the law of this state other than this Act.

(3) After the disclosure or filing of an assignment under this section, the assignee is the secured party of record.

§ 9–406.   Release of Collateral; Duties of Filing Officer; Fees

A secured party of record may by his signed statement release all or a part of any collateral described in a filed financing statement. The statement of release is sufficient if it contains a description of the collateral being released, the name and address of the debtor, the name and address of the secured party, and the file number of the financing statement. A statement of release signed by a person other than the secured party of record must be accompanied by a separate written statement of assignment signed by the secured party of record and complying with subsection (2) of Section 9–405, including payment of the required fee. Upon presentation of such a statement of release to the filing officer he shall mark the statement with the hour and date of filing and shall note the same upon the margin of the index of the filing of the financing statement. The uniform fee for filing and noting such a statement of release shall be $. . . . . if the statement is in the standard form prescribed by the [Secretary of State] and otherwise shall be $. . . . . ., plus in each case an additional fee of $. . . . . . for each name more than one against which the statement of release is required to be indexed.

[§ 9–407.   Information from Filing Officer]

[(1) If the person filing any financing statement, termination statement, statement of assignment, or statement of release, furnishes the filing officer a copy thereof, the filing officer shall upon request note upon the copy the file number and date and hour of the filing of the original and deliver or send the copy to such person.]

[(2) Upon request of any person, the filing officer shall issue his certificate showing whether there is on file on the date and hour stated therein, any presently effective financing statement naming a particular debtor and any statement of assignment thereof and if there is, giving the date and hour of filing of each such statement and the names and addresses of each secured party therein. The uniform fee for such a certificate shall be $. . . . . if the request for the certificate is in the standard form prescribed by the [Secretary of State] and otherwise shall be $. . . . . Upon request the filing officer shall furnish a copy of any filed financing statement or statement of assignment for a uniform fee of $. . . . . per page.]

Note: This section is proposed as an optional provision to require filing officers to furnish certificates. Local law and practices should be consulted with regard to the advisability of adoption.

§ 9–408.   Financing Statements Covering Consigned or Leased Goods

A consignor or lessor of goods may file a financing statement using the terms "consignor," "consignee," "lessor," "lessee" or the like instead of the terms specified in Section 9–402. The provisions of this Part shall apply as appropriate to such a financing statement but its filing shall not of itself be a factor in determining whether or not the consignment or lease is intended as security (Section 1–201(37)). However, if it is determined for other reasons that the consignment or lease is so intended, a security interest of the consignor or lessor which attaches to the consigned or leased goods is perfected by such filing.

Part 5   Default

§ 9–501.   Default; Procedure When Security Agreement Covers Both Real and Personal Property

(1) When a debtor is in default under a security agreement, a secured party has the rights and remedies provided in this Part and except as limited by subsection (3) those provided in the security agreement. He may reduce his claim to judgment, foreclose or otherwise enforce the security interest by an available judicial procedure. If the collateral is documents the secured party may proceed either as to the documents or as to the goods covered thereby. A secured party in possession has the rights, remedies and duties provided in Section 9–207. The rights and remedies referred to in this subsection are cumulative.

(2) After default, the debtor has the rights and remedies provided in this Part, those provided in the security agreement and those provided in Section 9–207.

(3) To the extent that they give rights to the debtor and impose duties on the secured party, the rules stated in the subsections referred to below may not be waived or varied except as provided with respect to compulsory disposition of collateral (subsection (3) of Section 9–504 and Section 9–505) and with respect to redemption of collateral (Section 9–506) but the parties may by agreement determine the standards by which the fulfillment of these rights and duties is to be measured if such standards are not manifestly unreasonable:

(a) subsection (2) of Section 9–502 and subsection (2) of Section 9–504 insofar as they require accounting for surplus proceeds of collateral;

(b) subsection (3) of Section 9–504 and subsection (1) of Section 9–505 which deal with disposition of collateral;

(c) subsection (2) of Section 9–505 which deals with acceptance of collateral as discharge of obligation;

(d) section 9–506 which deals with redemption of collateral; and

(e) subsection (1) of Section 9–507 which deals with the secured party's liability for failure to comply with this Part.

(4) If the security agreement covers both real and personal property, the secured party may proceed under this Part as to

the personal property or he may proceed as to both the real and the personal property in accordance with his rights and remedies in respect of the real property in which case the provisions of this Part do not apply.

(5) When a secured party has reduced his claim to judgment the lien of any levy which may be made upon his collateral by virtue of any execution based upon the judgment shall relate back to the date of the perfection of the security interest in such collateral. A judicial sale, pursuant to such execution, is a foreclosure of the security interest by judicial procedure within the meaning of this section, and the secured party may purchase at the sale and thereafter hold the collateral free of any other requirements of this Article.

§ 9–502. Collection Rights of Secured Party

(1) When so agreed and in any event on default the secured party is entitled to notify an account debtor or the obligor on an instrument to make payment to him whether or not the assignor was theretofore making collections on the collateral, and also to take control of any proceeds to which he is entitled under Section 9–306.

(2) A secured party who by agreement is entitled to charge back uncollected collateral or otherwise to full or limited recourse against the debtor and who undertakes to collect from the account debtors or obligors must proceed in a commercially reasonable manner and may deduct his reasonable expenses of realization from the collections. If the security agreement secures an indebtedness, the secured party must account to the debtor for any surplus, and unless otherwise agreed, the debtor is liable for any deficiency. But, if the underlying transaction was a sale of accounts or chattel paper, the debtor is entitled to any surplus or is liable for any deficiency only if the security agreement so provides.

§ 9–503. Secured Party's Rights to Take Possession after Default

Unless otherwise agreed a secured party has on default the right to take possession of the collateral. In taking possession a secured party may proceed without judicial process if this can be done without breach of the peace or may proceed by action. If the security agreement so provides the secured party may require the debtor to assemble the collateral and make it available to the secured party at a place to be designated by the secured party which is reasonably convenient to both parties. Without removal a secured party may render equipment unusable, and may dispose of collateral on the debtor's premises under Section 9–504.

§ 9–504. Secured Party's Right to Dispose of Collateral After Default; Effect of Disposition

(1) A secured party after default may sell, lease or otherwise dispose of any or all of the collateral in its then condition or following any commercialy reasonable preparation or processing. Any sale of goods is subject to the Article on Sales (Article

2). The proceeds of disposition shall be applied in the order following to

(a) the reasonable expenses of retaking, holding, preparing for sale or lease, selling, leasing and the like and, to the extent provided for in the agreement and not prohibited by law, the reasonable attorney's fees and legal expenses incurred by the secured party;

(b) the satisfaction of indebtedness secured by the security interest under which the disposition is made;

(c) the satisfaction of indebtedness secured by any subordinate security interest in the collateral if written notification of demand therefor is received before distribution of the proceeds is completed. If requested by the secured party, the holder of a subordinate security interest must reasonably furnish reasonable proof of his interest, and unless he does so, the secured party need not comply with his demand.

(2) If the security interest secures an indebtedness, the secured party must account to the debtor for any surplus, and, unless otherwise agreed, the debtor is liable for any deficiency. But if the underlying transaction was a sale of accounts or chattel paper, the debtor is entitled to any surplus or is liable for any deficiency only if the security agreement so provides.

(3) Disposition of the collateral may be by public or private proceedings and may be made by way of one or more contracts. Sale or other disposition may be as a unit or in parcels and at any time and place and on any terms but every aspect of the disposition including the method, manner, time, place and terms must be commercially reasonable. Unless collateral is perishable or threatens to decline speedily in value or is of a type customarily sold on a recognized market, reasonable notification of the time and place of any public sale or reasonable notification of the time after which any private sale or other intended disposition is to be made shall be sent by the secured party to the debtor, if he has not signed after default a statement renouncing or modifying his right to notification of sale. In the case of consumer goods no other notification need be sent. In other cases notification shall be sent to any other secured party from whom the secured party has received (before sending his notification to the debtor or before the debtor's renunciation of his rights) written notice of a claim of an interest in the collateral. The secured party may buy at any public sale and if the collateral is of a type customarily sold in a recognized market or is of a type which is the subject of widely distributed standard price quotations he may buy at private sale.

(4) When collateral is disposed of by a secured party after default, the disposition transfers to a purchaser for value all of the debtor's rights therein, discharges the security interest under which it is made and any security interest or lien subordinate thereto. The purchaser takes free of all such rights and interests even though the secured party fails to comply with the requirements of this Part or of any judicial proceedings

(a) in the case of a public sale, if the purchaser has no knowledge of any defects in the sale and if he does not buy in collusion with the secured party, other bidders or the person conducting the sale; or

(b) in any other case, if the purchaser acts in good faith.

(5) A person who is liable to a secured party under a guaranty, indorsement, repurchase agreement or the like and who receives a transfer of collateral from the secured party or is subrogated to his rights has thereafter the rights and duties of the secured party. Such a transfer of collateral is not a sale or disposition of the collateral under this Article.

§ 9–505.   Compulsory Disposition of Collateral; Acceptance of the Collateral as Discharge of Obligation

(1) If the debtor has paid sixty per cent of the cash price in the case of a purchase money security interest in consumer goods or sixty per cent of the loan in the case of another security interest in consumer goods, and has not signed after default a statement renouncing or modifying his rights under this Part a secured party who has taken possession of collateral must dispose of it under Section 9–504 and if he fails to do so within ninety days after he takes possession the debtor at his option may recover in conversion or under Section 9–507(1) on secured party's liability.

(2) In any other case involving consumer goods or any other collateral a secured party in possession may, after default, propose to retain the collateral in satisfaction of the obligation. Written notice of such proposal shall be sent to the debtor if he has not signed after default a statement renouncing or modifying his rights under this subsection. In the case of consumer goods no other notice need be given. In other cases notice shall be sent to any other secured party from whom the secured party has received (before sending his notice to the debtor or before the debtor's renunciation of his rights) written notice of a claim of an interest in the collateral. If the secured party receives objection in writing from a person entitled to receive notification within twenty-one days after the notice was sent, the secured party must dispose of the collateral under Section 9–504. In the absence of such written objection the secured party may retain the collateral in satisfaction of the debtor's obligation.

§ 9–506.   Debtor's Right to Redeem Collateral

At any time before the secured party has disposed of collateral or entered into a contract for its disposition under Section 9–504 or before the obligation has been discharged under Section 9–505(2) the debtor or any other secured party may unless otherwise agreed in writing after default redeem the collateral by tendering fulfillment of all obligations secured by the collateral as well as the expenses reasonably incurred by the secured party in retaking, holding and preparing the collateral for disposition, in arranging for the sale, and to the extent provided in the agreement and not prohibited by law, his reasonable attorney's fees and legal expenses.

§ 9–507.   Secured Party's Liability for Failure to Comply with This Part

(1) If it is established that the secured party is not proceeding in accordance with the provisions of this Part disposition may be ordered or restrained on appropriate terms and conditions. If the disposition has occurred the debtor or any person entitled to notification or whose security interest has been made known to the secured party prior to the disposition has a right to recover from the secured party any loss caused by a failure to comply with the provisions of this Part. If the collateral is consumer goods, the debtor has a right to recover in any event an amount not less than the credit service charge plus ten per cent of the principal amount of the debt or the time price differential plus 10 per cent of the cash price.

(2) The fact that a better price could have been obtained by a sale at a different time or in a different method from that selected by the secured party is not of itself sufficient to establish that the sale was not made in a commercially reasonable manner. If the secured party either sells the collateral in the usual manner in any recognized market therefor or if he sells at the price current in such market at the time of his sale or if he has otherwise sold in conformity with reasonable commercial practices among dealers in the type of property sold he has sold in a commercially reasonable manner. The principles stated in the two preceding sentences with respect to sales also apply as may be appropriate to other types of disposition. A disposition which has been approved in any judicial proceeding or by any bona fide creditors' committee or representative of creditors shall conclusively be deemed to be commercially reasonable, but this sentence does not indicate that any such approval must be obtained in any case nor does it indicate that any disposition not so approved is not commercially reasonable.

Author's note: Articles 10 and 11 have been omitted as unnecessary for the purposes of this text.

UNIFORM PARTNERSHIP ACT (1914)*

Part I Preliminary Provisions

§ 1. Name of Act

This act may be cited as Uniform Partnership Act.

§ 2. Definition of Terms

In this act, "Court" includes every court and judge having jurisdiction in the case.

"Business" includes every trade, occupation, or profession.

"Person" includes individuals, partnerships, corporations, and other associations.

"Bankrupt" includes bankrupt under the Federal Bankruptcy Act or insolvent under any state insolvent act.

"Conveyance" includes every assignment, lease, mortgage, or encumbrance.

"Real property" includes land and any interest or estate in land.

§ 3. Interpretation of Knowledge and Notice

(1) A person has "knowledge" of a fact within the meaning of this act not only when he has actual knowledge thereof, but also when he has knowledge of such other facts as in the circumstances shows bad faith.

(2) A person has "notice" of a fact within the meaning of this act when the person who claims the benefit of the notice:

(a) States the fact to such person, or

(b) Delivers through the mail, or by other means of communication, a written statement of the fact to such person or to a proper person at his place of business or residence.

§ 4. Rules of Construction

(1) The rule that statutes in derogation of the common law are to be strictly construed shall have no application to this act.

(2) The law of estoppel shall apply under this act.

(3) The law of agency shall apply under this act.

(4) This act shall be so interpreted and construed as to effect its general purpose to make uniform the law of those states which enact it.

(5) This act shall not be construed so as to impair the obligations of any contract existing when the act goes into effect, nor to affect any action or proceedings begun or right accrued before this act takes effect.

§ 5. Rules for Cases Not Provided for in This Act

In any case not provided for in this act the rules of law and equity, including the law merchant, shall govern.

Part II Nature of Partnership

§ 6. Partnership Defined

(1) A partnership is an association of two or more persons to carry on as co-owners a business for profit.

*Source: National Conference of Commissioners on Uniform State Laws. Copies may be obtained at a nominal cost by writing to the conference's office at 676 N. St. Clair Street, Suite 1700, Chicago, Illinois, 60611, or by calling (312) 915-0195.

(2) But any association formed under any other statute of this state, or any statute adopted by authority, other than the authority of this state, is not a partnership under this act, unless such association would have been a partnership in this state prior to the adoption of this act; but this act shall apply to limited partnerships except in so far as the statutes relating to such partnerships are inconsistent herewith.

§ 7. Rules for Determining the Existence of a Partnership

In determining whether a partnership exists, these rules shall apply:

(1) Except as provided by section 16 persons who are not partners as to each other are not partners as to third persons.

(2) Joint tenancy, tenancy in common, tenancy by the entireties, joint property, common property, or part ownership does not of itself establish a partnership, whether such co-owners do or do not share any profits made by the use of the property.

(3) The sharing of gross returns does not of itself establish a partnership, whether or not the persons sharing them have a joint or common right or interest in any property from which the returns are derived.

(4) The receipt by a person of a share of the profits of a business is prima facie evidence that he is a partner in the business, but no such inference shall be drawn if such profits were received in payment:

  (a) As a debt by installments or otherwise,

  (b) As wages of an employee or rent to a landlord,

  (c) As an annuity to a widow or representative of a deceased partner,

  (d) As interest on a loan, though the amount of payment vary with the profits of the business,

  (e) As the consideration for the sale of a goodwill of a business or other property by installments or otherwise.

§ 8. Partnership Property

(1) All property originally brought into the partnership stock or subsequently acquired by purchase or otherwise, on account of the partnership, is partnership property.

(2) Unless the contrary intention appears, property acquired with partnership funds is partnership property.

(3) Any estate in real property may be acquired in the partnership name. Title so acquired can be conveyed only in the partnership name.

(4) A conveyance to a partnership in the partnership name, though without words of inheritance, passes the entire estate of the grantor unless a contrary intent appears.

Part III Relations of Partners to Persons Dealing with the Partnership

§ 9. Partner Agent of Partnership as to Partnership Business

(1) Every partner is an agent of the partnership for the purpose of its business, and the act of every partner, including the execution in the partnership name of any instrument, for apparently carrying on in the usual way the business of the partnership of which he is a member binds the partnership, unless the partner so acting has in fact no authority to act for the partnership in the particular matter, and the person with whom he is dealing has knowledge of the fact that he has no such authority.

(2) An act of a partner which is not apparently for the carrying on of the business of the partnership in the usual way does not bind the partnership unless authorized by the other partners.

(3) Unless authorized by the other partners or unless they have abandoned the business, one or more but less than all the partners have no authority to:

  (a) Assign the partnership property in trust for creditors or on the assignee's promise to pay the debts of the partnership,

  (b) Dispose of the good-will of the business,

  (c) Do any other act which would make it impossible to carry on the ordinary business of a partnership,

  (d) Confess a judgment,

  (e) Submit a partnership claim or liability to arbitration or reference.

(4) No act of a partner in contravention of a restriction on authority shall bind the partnership to persons having knowledge of the restriction.

§ 10. Conveyance of Real Property of the Partnership

(1) Where title to real property is in the partnership name, any partner may convey title to such property by a conveyance executed in the partnership name; but the partnership may recover such property unless the partner's act binds the partnership under the provisions of paragraph (1) of section 9, or unless such property has been conveyed by the grantee or a person claiming through such grantee to a holder for value without knowledge that the partner, in making the conveyance, has exceeded his authority.

(2) Where title to real property is in the name of the partnership, a conveyance executed by a partner, in his own name, passes the equitable interest of the partnership, provided the act is one within the authority of the partner under the provisions of paragraph (1) of section 9.

(3) Where title to real property is in the name of one or more but not all the partners, and the record does not disclose the right of partnership, the partners in whose name the title stands may convey title to such property, but the partnership may recover such property if the partners' act does not bind the partnership under the provisions of paragraph (1) of section 9, unless the purchaser or his assignee, is a holder for value, without knowledge.

(4) Where the title to real property is in the name of one or more or all the partners, or in a third person in trust for the partnership, a conveyance executed by a partner in the partnership name, or in his own name, passes the equitable interest of the partnership, provided the act is one within

the authority of the partner under the provisions of paragraph (1) of section 9.

(5)   Where the title to real property is in the names of all the partners a conveyance executed by all the partners passes all their rights in such property.

§ 11.   Partnership Bound by Admission of Partner

An admission or representation made by any partner concerning partnership affairs within the scope of his authority as conferred by this act is evidence against the partnership.

§ 12.   Partnership Charged with Knowledge of or Notice to Partner

Notice to any partner of any matter relating to partnership affairs, and the knowledge of the partner acting in the particular matter, acquired while a partner or then present to his mind, and the knowledge of any other partner who reasonably could and should have communicated it to the acting partner, operate as notice to or knowledge of the partnership, except in the case of a fraud on the partnership committed by or with the consent of that partner.

§ 13.   Partnership Bound by Partner's Wrongful Act

Where, by any wrongful act or omission of any partner acting in the ordinary course of the business of the partnership or with the authority of his co-partners, loss or injury is caused to any person, not being a partner in the partnership, or any penalty is incurred, the partnership is liable therefor to the same extent as the partner so acting or omitting to act.

§ 14.   Partnership Bound by Partner's Breach of Trust

The partnership is bound to make good the loss:

(a)   Where one partner acting within the scope of his apparent authority receives money or property of a third person and misapplies it; and

(b)   Where the partnership in the course of its business receives money or property of a third person and the money or property so received is misapplied by any partner while it is in the custody of the partnership.

§ 15.   Nature of Partner's Liability

All partners are liable

(a)   Jointly and severally for everything chargeable to the partnership under sections 13 and 14.

(b)   Jointly for all other debts and obligations of the partnership; but any partner may enter into a separate obligation to perform a partnership contract.

§ 16.   Partner by Estoppel

(1)   When a person, by words spoken or written or by conduct, represents himself, or consents to another representing him to any one, as a partner in an existing partnership or with one or more persons not actual partners, he is liable to any such person to whom such representation has been made, who has, on the faith of such representation, given credit to the actual or apparent partnership, and if he has made such representation or consented to its being made in a public manner he is liable to such person, whether the re presentation has or has not been made or communicated to such person so giving credit by or with the knowledge of the apparent partner making the representation or consenting to its being made.

(a)   When a partnership liability results, he is liable as though he were an actual member of the partnership.

(b)   When no partnership liability results, he is liable jointly with the other persons, if any, so consenting to the contract or representation as to incur liability, otherwise separately.

(2)   When a person has been thus represented to be a partner in an existing partnership, or with one or more persons not actual partners, he is an agent of the persons consenting to such representation to bind them to the same extent and in the same manner as though he were a partner in fact, with respect to persons who rely upon the representation. Where all the members of the existing partnership consent to the representation, a partnership act or obligation results; but in all other cases it is the joint act or obligation of the person acting and the persons consenting to the representation.

§ 17.   Liability of Incoming Partner

A person admitted as a partner into an existing partnership is liable for all the obligations of the partnership arising before his admission as though he had been a partner when such obligations were incurred, except that this liability shall be satisfied only out of partnership property.

Part IV   Relations of Partners to One Another

§ 18.   Rules Determining Rights and Duties of Partners

The rights and duties of the partners in relation to the partnership shall be determined, subject to any agreement between them, by the following rules:

(a)   Each partner shall be repaid his contributions, whether by way of capital or advances to the partnership property and share equally in the profits and surplus remaining after all liabilities, including those to partners, are satisfied; and must contribute towards the losses, whether of capital or otherwise, sustained by the partnership according to his share in the profits.

(b)   The partnership must indemnify every partner in respect of payments made and personal liabilities reasonably incurred by him in the ordinary and proper conduct of its business, or for the preservation of its business or property.

(c)   A partner, who in aid of the partnership makes any payment or advance beyond the amount of capital which he agreed to contribute, shall be paid interest from the date of the payment or advance.

(d) A partner shall receive interest on the capital contributed by him only from the date when repayment should be made.

(e) All partners have equal rights in the management and conduct of the partnership business.

(f) No partner is entitled to remuneration for acting in the partnership business, except that a surviving partner is entitled to reasonable compensation for his services in winding up the partnership affairs.

(g) No person can become a member of a partnership without the consent of all the partners.

(h) Any difference arising as to ordinary matters connected with the partnership business may be decided by a majority of the partners; but no act in contravention of any agreement between the partners may be done rightfully without the consent of all the partners.

§ 19. Partnership Books

The partnership books shall be kept, subject to any agree ment between the partners, at the principal place of business of the partnership, and every partner shall at all times have access to and may inspect and copy any of them.

§ 20. Duty of Partners to Render Information

Partners shall render on demand true and full information of all things affecting the partnership to any partner or the legal representative of any deceased partner or partner under legal disability.

§ 21. Partner Accountable as a Fiduciary

(1) Every partner must account to the partnership for any benefit, and hold as trustee for it any profits derived by him without the consent of the other partners from any transaction connected with the formation, conduct, or liq ui dation of the partnership or from any use by him of its property.

(2) This section applies also to the representatives of a deceased partner engaged in the liquidation of the affairs of the partnership as the personal representatives of the last surviving partner.

§ 22. Right to an Account

Any partner shall have the right to a formal account as to partnership affairs:

(a) If he is wrongfully excluded from the partnership business or possession of its property by his co-partners,

(b) If the right exists under the terms of any agreement,

(c) As provided by section 21,

(d) Whenever other circumstances render it just and reasonable.

§ 23. Continuation of Partnership Beyond Fixed Term

(1) When a partnership for a fixed term or particular undertaking is continued after the termination of such term or particular undertaking without any express agreement, the rights and duties of the partners remain the same as they were at such termination, so far as is consistent with a partnership at will.

(2) A continuation of the business by the partners or such of them as habitually acted therein during the term, without any settlement or liquidation of the partnership affairs, is prima facie evidence of a continuation of the partnership.

Part V   Property Rights of a Partner

§ 24. Extent of Property Rights of a Partner

The property rights of a partner are (1) his rights in specific partnership property, (2) his interest in the partnership, and (3) his right to participate in the management.

§ 25. Nature of a Partner's Right in Specific Partnership Property

(1) A partner is co-owner with his partners of specific partnership property holding as a tenant in partnership.

(2) The incidents of this tenancy are such that:

(a) A partner, subject to the provisions of this act and to any agreement between the partners, has an equal right with his partners to possess specific partnership property for partnership purposes; but he has no right to possess such property for any other purpose without the consent of his partners.

(b) A partner's right in specific partnership property is not assignable except in connection with the assignment of rights of all the partners in the same property.

(c) A partner's right in specific partnership property is not subject to attachment or execution, except on a claim against the partnership. When partnership property is attached for a partnership debt the partners, or any of them, or the representatives of a deceased partner, cannot claim any right under the homestead or exemption laws.

(d) On the death of a partner his right in specific partnership property vests in the surviving partner or partners, except where the deceased was the last surviving partner, when his right in such property vests in his legal representative. Such surviving partner or partners, or the legal representative of the last surviving partner, has no right to possess the partnership property for any but a partnership purpose.

(e) A partner's right in specific partnership property is not subject to dower, curtesy, or allowances to widows, heirs, or next of kin.

§ 26. Nature of Partner's Interest in the Partnership

A partner's interest in the partnership is his share of the profits and surplus, and the same is personal property.

§ 27.   Assignment of Partner's Interest

(1) A conveyance by a partner of his interest in the partnership does not of itself dissolve the partnership, nor, as against the other partners in the absence of agreement, entitle the assignee, during the continuance of the partnership, to interfere in the management or administration of the partnership business or affairs, or to require any information or account of partnership transactions, or to inspect the partnership books; but it merely entitles the assignee to receive in accordance with his contract the profits to which the assigning partner would otherwise be entitled.

(2) In case of a dissolution of the partnership, the assignee is entitled to receive his assignor's interest and may require an account from the date only of the last account agreed to by all the partners.

§ 28.   Partner's Interest Subject to Charging Order

(1) On due application to a competent court by any judgment creditor of a partner, the court which entered the judgment, order, or decree, or any other court, may charge the interest of the debtor partner with payment of the unsatisfied amount of such judgment debt with interest thereon; and may then or later appoint a receiver of his share of the profits, and of any other money due or to fall due to him in respect of the partnership, and make all other orders, directions, accounts and inquiries which the debtor partner might have made, or which the circumstances of the case may require.

(2) The interest charged may be redeemed at any time before foreclosure, or in case of a sale being directed by the court may be purchased without thereby causing a dissolution:

(a) With separate property, by any one or more of the partners, or

(b) With partnership property, by any one or more of the partners with the consent of all the partners whose interests are not so charged or sold.

(3) Nothing in this act shall be held to deprive a partner of his right, if any, under the exemption laws, as regards his interest in the partnership.

Part VI   Dissolution and Winding Up

§ 29.   Dissolution Defined

The dissolution of a partnership is the change in the relation of the partners caused by any partner ceasing to be associated in the carrying on as distinguished from the winding up of the business.

§ 30.   Partnership Not Terminated by Dissolution

On dissolution the partnership is not terminated, but continues until the winding up of partnership affairs is completed.

§ 31.   Causes of Dissolution

Dissolution is caused:

(1) Without violation of the agreement between the partners,

(a) By the termination of the definite term or particular undertaking specified in the agreement,

(b) By the express will of any partner when no definite term or particular undertaking is specified,

(c) By the express will of all the partners who have not assigned their interests or suffered them to be charged for their separate debts, either before or after the termination of any specified term or particular undertaking,

(d) By the expulsion of any partner from the business bona fide in accordance with such power conferred by the agreement between the partners.

(2) In contravention of the agreement between the partners, where the circumstances do not permit a dissolution under any other provision of this section, by the express will of any partner at any time;

(3) By any event which makes it unlawful for the business of the partnership to be carried on or for the members to carry it on in partnership;

(4) By the death of any partner;

(5) By the bankruptcy of any partner or the partnership;

(6) By decree of court under section 32.

§ 32.   Dissolution by Decree of Court

(1) On application by or for a partner the court shall decree a dissolution whenever;

(a) A partner has been declared a lunatic in any judicial proceeding or is shown to be of unsound mind,

(b) A partner becomes in any other way incapable of performing his part of the partnership contract,

(c) A partner has been guilty of such conduct as tends to affect prejudicially the carrying on of the business,

(d) A partner wilfully or persistently commits a breach of the partnership agreement, or otherwise so conducts himself in matters relating to the partnership business that it is not reasonably practicable to carry on the business in partnership with him,

(e) The business of the partnership can only be carried on at a loss,

(f) Other circumstances render a dissolution equitable.

(2) On the application of the purchaser of a partner's interest under sections 27 and 28:

(a) After the termination of the specified term or particular undertaking,

(b) At any time if the partnership was a partnership at will when the interest was assigned or when the charging order was issued.

§ 33.   General Effect of Dissolution on Authority of Partner

Except so far as may be necessary to wind up partnership affairs or to complete transactions begun but not then finished, dissolution terminates all authority of any partner to act for the partnership,

(1) With respect to the partners,

(a) When the dissolution is not by the act, bankruptcy or death of a partner; or

(b) When the dissolution is by such act, bankruptcy or death of a partner, in cases where section 34 so requires.

(2) With respect to persons not partners, as declared in section 35.

§ 34.   Right of Partner to Contribution from Co-Partners after Dissolution

Where the dissolution is caused by the act, death or bankruptcy of a partner, each partner is liable to his co-partners for his share of any liability created by any partner acting for the partnership as if the partnership had not been dissolved unless

(a) The dissolution being by act of any partner, the partner acting for the partnership had knowledge of the dissolution, or

(b) The dissolution being by the death or bankruptcy of a partner, the partner acting for the partnership had knowledge or notice of the death or bankruptcy.

§ 35.   Power of Partner to Bind Partnership to Third Persons after Dissolution

(1) After dissolution a partner can bind the partnership except as provided in Paragraph (3).

(a) By any act appropriate for winding up partnership affairs or completing transactions unfinished at dissolution;

(b) By any transaction which would bind the partnership if dissolution had not taken place, provided the other party to the transaction

I. Had extended credit to the partnership prior to dissolution and had no knowledge or notice of the dissolution; or

II. Though he had not so extended credit, had nevertheless known of the partnership prior to dissolution, and, having no knowledge or notice of dissolution, the fact of dissolution had not been advertised in a newspaper of general circulation in the place (or in each place if more than one) at which the partnership business was regularly carried on.

(2) The liability of a partner under Paragraph (1b) shall be satisfied out of partnership assets alone when such partner had been prior to dissolution

(a) Unknown as a partner to the person with whom the contract is made; and

(b) So far unknown and inactive in partnership affairs that the business reputation of the partnership could not be said to have been in any degree due to his connection with it.

(3) The partnership is in no case bound by any act of a partner after dissolution.

(a) Where the partnership is dissolved because it is unlawful to carry on the business, unless the act is appropriate for winding up partnership affairs; or

(b) Where the partner has become bankrupt; or

(c) Where the partner has no authority to wind up partnership affairs; except by a transaction with one who

I. Had extended credit to the partnership prior to dissolution and had no knowledge or notice of his want of authority; or

II. Had not extended credit to the partnership prior to dissolution, and having no knowledge or notice of his want of authority, the fact of his want of authority has not been advertised in the manner provided for advertising the fact of dissolution in Paragraph (1b II).

(4) Nothing in this section shall affect the liability under Section 16 of any person who after dissolution represents himself or consents to another representing him as a partner in a partnership engaged in carrying on business.

§ 36.   Effect of Dissolution on Partner's Existing Liability

(1) The dissolution of the partnership does not of itself discharge the existing liability of any partner.

(2) A partner is discharged from any existing liability upon dissolution of the partnership by an agreement to that effect between himself, the partnership creditor and the person or partnership continuing the business; and such agreement may be inferred from the course of dealing between the creditor having knowledge of the dissolution and the person or partnership continuing the business.

(3) Where a person agrees to assume the existing obligations of a dissolved partnership, the partners whose obligations have been assumed shall be discharged from any liability to any creditor of the partnership who, knowing of the agreement, consents to a material alteration in the nature or time of payment of such obligations.

(4) The individual property of a deceased partner shall be liable for all obligations of the partnership incurred while he was a partner but subject to the prior payment of his separate debts.

§ 37.   Right to Wind Up

Unless otherwise agreed the partners who have not wrongfully dissolved the partnership or the legal representative of the last surviving partner, not bankrupt, has the right to wind up the partnership affairs; provided, however, that any partner, his legal representative or his assignee, upon cause shown, may obtain winding up by the court.

§ 38.   Rights of Partners to Application of Partnership Property

(1) When dissolution is caused in any way, except in contravention of the partnership agreement, each partner, as against his co-partners and all persons claiming through them in respect of their interests in the partnership, unless otherwise agreed, may have the partnership property applied to discharge its liabilities, and the surplus applied to pay in cash the net amount owing to the respective partners. But if dissolution is caused by expulsion of a partner, bona fide under the partnership agreement and if the expelled partner is discharged from

all partnership liabilities, either by payment or agreement under section 36(2), he shall receive in cash only the net amount due him from the partnership.

(2) When dissolution is caused in contravention of the partnership agreement the rights of the partners shall be as follows:

(a) Each partner who has not caused dissolution wrongfully shall have,

I. All the rights specified in paragraph (1) of this section, and

II. The right, as against each partner who has caused the dissolution wrongfully, to damages for breach of the agreement.

(b) The partners who have not caused the dissolution wrongfully, if they all desire to continue the business in the same name, either by themselves or jointly with others, may do so, during the agreed term for the partnership and for that purpose may possess the partnership property, provided they secure the payment by bond approved by the court, or pay to any partner who has caused the dissolution wrongfully, the value of his interest in the partnership at the dissolution, less any damages recoverable under clause (2a II) of this section, and in like manner indemnify him against all present or future partnership liabilities.

(c) A partner who has caused the dissolution wrongfully shall have:

I. If the business is not continued under the provisions of paragraph (2b) all the rights of a partner under paragraph (1), subject to clause (2a II), of this section,

II. If the business is continued under paragraph (2b) of this section the right as against his co-partners and all claiming through them in respect of their interests in the partnership, to have the value of his interest in the partnership, less any damages caused to his co-partners by the dissolution, ascertained and paid to him in cash, or the payment secured by bond approved by the court, and to be released from all existing liabilities of the partnership; but in ascertaining the value of the partner's interest the value of the good-will of the business shall not be considered.

§ 39.   Rights Where Partnership Is Dissolved for Fraud or Misrepresentation

Where a partnership contract is rescinded on the ground of the fraud or misrepresentation of one of the parties thereto, the party entitled to rescind is, without prejudice to any other right, entitled:

(a) To a lien on, or a right of retention of, the surplus of the partnership property after satisfying the partnership liabilities to third persons for any sum of money paid by him for the purchase of an interest in the partnership and for any capital or advances contributed by him; and

(b) To stand, after all liabilities to third persons have been satisfied, in the place of the creditors of the partnership for any

payments made by him in respect of the partnership liabilities; and

(c) To be indemnified by the person guilty of the fraud or making the representation against all debts and liabilities of the partnership.

§ 40.   Rules for Distribution

In setting accounts between the partners after dissolution, the following rules shall be observed, subject to any agreement to the contrary:

(a) The assets of the partnership are:

I. The partnership property,

II. The contributions of the partners necessary for the payment of all the liabilities specified in clause (b) of this paragraph.

(b) The liabilities of the partnership shall rank in order of payment, as follows:

I. Those owing to creditors other than partners,

II. Those owing to partners other than for capital and profits,

III. Those owing to partners in respect of capital,

IV. Those owing to partners in respect of profits.

(c) The assets shall be applied in the order of their declaration in clause (a) of this paragraph to the satisfaction of the liabilities.

(d) The partners shall contribute, as provided by section 18 (a) the amount necessary to satisfy the liabilities; but if any, but not all, of the partners are insolvent, or, not being subject to process, refuse to contribute, the other partners shall contribute their share of the liabilities, and, in the relative proportions in which they share the profits, the additional amount necessary to pay the liabilities.

(e) An assignee for the benefit of creditors or any person appointed by the court shall have the right to enforce the contributions specified in clause (d) of this paragraph.

(f) Any partner or his legal representative shall have the right to enforce the contributions specified in clause (d) of this paragraph, to the extent of the amount which he has paid in excess of his share of the liability.

(g) The individual property of a deceased partner shall be liable for the contributions specified in clause (d) of this paragraph.

(h) When partnership property and the individual properties of the partners are in possession of a court for distribution, partnership creditors shall have priority on partnership property and separate creditors on individual property, saving the rights of lien or secured creditors as heretofore.

(i) Where a partner has become bankrupt or his estate is insolvent the claims against his separate property shall rank in the following order:

I. Those owing to separate creditors,

II. Those owing to partnership creditors,

III. Those owing to partners by way of contribution.

§ 41.   Liability of Persons Continuing the Business in Certain Cases

(1) When any new partner is admitted into an existing partnership, or when any partner retires and assigns (or the representative of the deceased partner assigns) his rights in partnership property to two or more of the partners, or to one or more of the partners and one or more third persons, if the business is continued without liquidation of the partnership affairs, creditors of the first or dissolved partnership are also creditors of the partnership so continuing the business.

(2) When all but one partner retire and assign (or the representative of a deceased partner assigns) their rights in partnership property to the remaining partner, who continues the business without liquidation of partnership affairs, either alone or with others, creditors of the dissolved partnership are also creditors of the person or partnership so continuing the business.

(3) When any partner retires or dies and the business of the dissolved partnership is continued as set forth in paragraphs (1) and (2) of this section, with the consent of the retired partners or the representative of the deceased partner, but without any assignment of his right in partnership property, rights of creditors of the dissolved partnership and of the creditors of the person or partnership continuing the business shall be as if such assignment has been made.

(4) When all the partners or their representatives assign their rights in partnership property to one or more third persons who promise to pay the debts and who continue the business of the dissolved partnership, creditors of the dissolved partnership are also creditors of the person or partnership continuing the business.

(5) When any partner wrongfully causes a dissolution and the remaining partners continue the business under the provisions of section 38(2b), either alone or with others, and without liquidation of the partnership affairs, creditors of the dissolved partnership are also creditors of the person or partnership continuing the business.

(6) When a partner is expelled and the remaining partners continue the business either alone or with others, without liquidation of the partnership affairs, creditors of the dissolved partnership are also creditors of the person or partnership continuing the business.

(7) The liability of a third person becoming a partner in the partnership continuing the business, under this section, to the creditors of the dissolved partnership shall be satisfied out of partnership property only.

(8) When the business of a partnership after dissolution is continued under any conditions set forth in this section the creditors of the dissolved partnership, as against the separate creditors of the retiring or deceased partner or the representative of the deceased partner, have a prior right to any claim of the retired partner or the representative of the deceased partner against the person or partnership continuing the business, on account of the retired or deceased partner's interest in the dissolved partnership or on account of any consideration promised for such interest or for his right in partnership property.

(9) Nothing in this section shall be held to modify any right of creditors to set aside any assignment on the ground of fraud.

(10) The use by the person or partnership continuing the business of the partnership name, or the name of a deceased partner as part thereof, shall not of itself make the individual property of the deceased partner liable for any debts contracted by such person or partnership.

§ 42.   Rights of Retiring or Estate of Deceased Partner When the Business Is Continued

When any partner retires or dies, and the business is continued under any of the conditions set forth in section 41(1, 2, 3, 5, 6), or section 38(2b) without any settlement of accounts as between him or his estate and the person or partnership continuing the business, unless otherwise agreed, he or his legal representative as against such persons or partnership may have the value of his interest at the date of dissolution ascertained, and shall receive as an ordinary creditor an amount equal to the value of his interest in the dissolved partnership with interest, or, at his option or at the option of his legal representative, in lieu of interest, the profits attributable to the use of his right in the property of the dissolved partnership; provided that the creditors of the dissolved partnership as against the separate creditors, or the representative of the retired or deceased partner, shall have priority on any claim arising under this section, as provided by section 41(8) of this act.

§ 43.   Accrual of Actions

The right to an account of his interest shall accrue to any partner, or his legal representative, as against the winding up partners or the surviving partners or the person or partnership continuing the business, at the date of dissolution, in the absence of any agreement to the contrary.

Part VII   Miscellaneous Provisions

§ 44.   When Act Takes Effect

This act shall take effect on the . . . . day of
. . . . one thousand nine hundred and
. . . .

§ 45.   Legislation Repealed

All acts or parts of acts inconsistent with this act are hereby repealed.

REVISED UNIFORM LIMITED PARTNERSHIP ACT (1976) WITH THE 1985 AMENDMENTS*

ARTICLE 1. GENERAL PROVISIONS

§ 101. Definitions

As used in this [Act], unless the context otherwise requires:

(1) "Certificate of limited partnership" means the certificate referred to in Section 201, and the certificate as amended or restated.

(2) "Contribution" means any cash, property, services rendered, or a promissory note or other binding obligation to contribute cash or property or to perform services, which a partner contributes to a limited partnership in his capacity as a partner.

(3) "Event of withdrawal of a general partner" means an event that causes a person to cease to be a general partner as provided in Section 402.

(4) "Foreign limited partnership" means a partnership formed under the laws of any state other than this State and having as partners one or more general partners and one or more limited partners.

(5) "General partner" means a person who has been admitted to a limited partnership as a general partner in accordance with the partnership agreement and named in the certificate of limited partnership as a general partner.

(6) "Limited partner" means a person who has been admitted to a limited partnership as a limited partner in accordance with the partnership agreement.

(7) "Limited partnership" and "domestic limited partnership" mean a partnership formed by two or more persons under the laws of this State and having one or more general partners and one or more limited partners.

(8) "Partner" means a limited or general partner.

(9) "Partnership agreement" means any valid agreement, written or oral, of the partners as to the affairs of a limited partnership and the conduct of its business.

(10) "Partnership interest" means a partner's share of the profits and losses of a limited partnership and the right to receive distribution of partnership assets.

(11) "Person" means a natural person, partnership, limited partnership (domestic or foreign), trust, estate, association, or corporation.

(12) "State" means a state, territory, or possession of the United States, the District of Columbia, or the Commonwealth of Puerto Rico.

§ 102. Name

The name of each limited partnership as set forth in its certificate of limited partnership:

(1) shall contain without abbreviation the words "limited partnership";

(2) may not contain the name of a limited partner unless (i) it is also the name of a general partner or the corporation name of a corporate general partner, or (ii) the business of the limited

---

*Source : National Conference of Commissioners on Uniform State Laws. Copies may be obtained at a nominal cost by writing to the conference's office at 676 N. St. Clair Street, Suite 1700, Chicago, Illinois, 60611, or by calling (312) 915-0195.

partnership had been carried on under that name before the admission of that limited partner;

(3) may not be the same as, or deceptively similar to, the name of any corporation or limited partnership organized under the laws of this State or licensed or registered as a foreign corporation or limited partnership in this State; and

(4) may not contain the following words [here insert prohibited words].

§ 103.　Reservation of Name

(a) The exclusive right to the use of a name may be reserved by:

(1) any person intending to organize a limited partnership under this [Act] and to adopt that name;

(2) any domestic limited partnership or any foreign limited partnership registered in this State which, in either case, intends to adopt that name;

(3) any foreign limited partnership intending to register in this State and adopt that name; and

(4) any person intending to organize a foreign limited partnership and intending to have it register in this State and adopt that name.

(b) The reservation shall be made by filing with the Secretary of State an application, executed by the applicant, to reserve a specified name. If the Secretary of State finds that the name is available for use by a domestic or foreign limited partnership, he [or she] shall reserve the name for the exclusive use of the applicant for a period of 120 days. Once having so reserved a name, the same applicant may not again reserve that same name until more than 60 days after the expiration of the last 120-day period for which that applicant reserved that name. The right to the exclusive use of a reserved name may be transferred to any other person by filing in the office of the Secretary of State a notice of the transfer, executed by the applicant for whom the name was reserved and specifying the name and address of the transferee.

§ 104.　Specified Office and Agent

Each limited partnership shall continuously maintain in this State:

(1) an office, which may but need not be a place of its business in this State, at which shall be kept the records required by Section 105 to be maintained; and

(2) an agent for service of process on the limited partnership, which agent must be an individual resident of this State, a domestic corporation, or a foreign corporation authorized to do business in this State.

§ 105.　Records to be Kept

(a) Each limited partnership shall keep at the office referred to in Section 104(1) the following:

(1) a current list of the full name and last known business address of each partner, separately identifying the general partners (in alphabetical order) and the limited partners (in alphabetical order);

(2) a copy of the certificate of limited partnership and all certificates of amendment thereto, together with executed copies of any powers of attorney pursuant to which any certificate has been executed;

(3) copies of the limited partnership's federal, state and local income tax returns and reports, if any, for the three most recent years;

(4) copies of any then effective written partnership agreements and of any financial statements of the limited partnership for the three most recent years; and

(5) unless contained in a written partnership agreement, a writing setting out:

(i) the amount of cash and a description and statement of the agreed value of the other property or services contributed by each partner and which each partner has agreed to contribute;

(ii) the times at which or events on the happening of which any additional contributions agreed to be made by each partner are to be made;

(iii) any right of a partner to receive, or of a general partner to make, distributions to a partner which include a return of all or any part of the partner's contribution; and

(iv) any events upon the happening of which the limited partnership is to be dissolved and its affairs wound up.

(b) Records kept under this section are subject to inspection and copying at the reasonable request and at the expense of any partner during ordinary business hours.

§ 106.　Nature of Business

A limited partnership may carry on any business that a partnership without limited partners may carry on except [here designate prohibited activities].

§ 107.　Business Transactions of Partner with Partnership

Except as provided in the partnership agreement, a partner may lend money to and transact other business with the limited partnership and, subject to other applicable law, has the same rights and obligations with respect thereto as a person who is not a partner.

ARTICLE 2.　FORMATION; CERTIFICATE OF LIMITED PARTNERSHIP

§ 201.　Certificate of Limited Partnership

(a) In order to form a limited partnership, a certificate of limited partnership must be executed and filed in the office of the Secretary of State. The certificate shall set forth:

(1) the name of the limited partnership;

(2) the address of the office and the name and address of the agent for service of process required to be maintained by Section 104;

(3) the name and the business address of each general partner;

(4) the latest date upon which the limited partnership is to dissolve; and

(5) any other matters the general partners determine to include therein.

(b) A limited partnership is formed at the time of the filing of the certificate of limited partnership in the office of the Secretary of State or at any later time specified in the certificate of limited partnership if, in either case, there has been substantial compliance with the requirements of this section.

§ 202. Amendments to Certificate

(a) A certificate of limited partnership is amended by filing a certificate of amendment thereto in the office of the Secretary of State. The certificate shall set forth:

(1) the name of the limited partnership;

(2) the date of filing the certificate; and

(3) the amendment to the certificate.

(b) Within 30 days after the happening of any of the following events, an amendment to a certificate of limited partnership reflecting the occurrence of the event or events shall be filed:

(1) the admission of a new general partner;

(2) the withdrawal of a general partner; or

(3) the continuation of the business under Section 801 after an event of withdrawal of a general partner.

(c) A general partner who becomes aware that any statement in a certificate of limited partnership was false when made or that any arrangements or other facts described have changed, making the certificate inaccurate in any respect, shall promptly amend the certificate.

(d) A certificate of limited partnership may be amended at any time for any other proper purpose the general partners determine.

(e) No person has any liability because an amendment to a certificate of limited partnership has not been filed to reflect the occurrence of any event referred to in subsection (b) of this section if the amendment is filed within the 30-day period specified in subsection (b).

(f) A restated certificate of limited partnership may be executed and filed in the same manner as a certificate of amendment.

§ 203. Cancellation of Certificate

A certificate of limited partnership shall be cancelled upon the dissolution and the commencement of the winding up of the partnership or at any time there are no limited partners. A certificate of cancellation shall be filed in the office of the Secretary of State and set forth:

(1) the name of the limited partnership;

(2) the date of filing of its certificate of limited partnership;

(3) the reason for filing the certificate of cancellation;

(4) the effective date (which shall be a date certain) of cancellation if it is not to be effective upon the filing of the certificate; and

(5) any other information the general partners filing the certificate determine.

§ 204. Execution of Certificates

(a) Each certificate required by this Article to be filed in the office of the Secretary of State shall be executed in the following manner:

(1) an original certificate of limited partnership must be signed by all general partners;

(2) a certificate of amendment must be signed by at least one general partner and by each other general partner designated in the certificate as a new general partner; and

(3) a certificate of cancellation must be signed by all general partners.

(b) Any person may sign a certificate by an attorney-in-fact, but power of attorney to sign a certificate relating to the admission of a general partner must specifically describe the admission.

(c) The execution of a certificate by a general partner constitutes an affirmation under the penalties of perjury that the facts stated therein are true.

§ 205. Execution by Judicial Act

If a person required by Section 204 to execute any certificate fails or refuses to do so, any other person who is adversely affected by the failure or refusal may petition the [designate the appropriate court] to direct the execution of the certificate. If the court finds that it is proper for the certificate to be executed and that any person so designated has failed or refused to execute the certificate, it shall order the Secretary of State to record an appropriate certificate.

§ 206. Filing in Office of Secretary of State

(a) Two signed copies of the certificate of limited partnership and of any certificates of amendment or cancellation (or of any judicial decree of amendment or cancellation) shall be delivered to the Secretary of State. A person who executes a certificate as an agent or fiduciary need not exhibit evidence of his [or her] authority as a prerequisite to filing. Unless the Secretary of State finds that any certificate does not conform to law, upon receipt of all filing fees required by law he [or she] shall:

(1) endorse on each duplicate original the word "Filed" and the day, month and year of the filing thereof;

(2) file one duplicate original in his [or her] office; and

(3) return the other duplicate original to the person who filed it or his [or her] representative.

(b) Upon the filing of a certificate of amendment (or judicial decree of amendment) in the office of the Secretary of State, the certificate of limited partnership shall be amended as set forth therein, and upon the effective date of a certificate of cancellation (or a judicial decree thereof), the certificate of limited partnership is cancelled.

§ 207. Liability for False Statement in Certificate

If any certificate of limited partnership or certificate of amendment or cancellation contains a false statement, one who suffers loss by reliance on the statement may recover damages for the loss from:

(1) any person who executes the certificate, or causes another to execute it on his behalf, and knew, and any general partner who knew or should have known, the statement to be false at the time the certificate was executed; and

(2) any general partner who thereafter knows or should have known that any arrangement or other fact described in the certificate has changed, making the statement inaccurate in any respect within a sufficient time before the statement was relied upon reasonably to have enabled that general partner to cancel or amend the certificate, or to file a petition for its cancellation or amendment under Section 205.

§ 208. Scope of Notice

The fact that a certificate of limited partnership is on file in the office of the Secretary of State is notice that the partnership is a limited partnership and the persons designated therein as general partners are general partners, but it is not notice of any other fact.

§ 209. Delivery of Certificates to Limited Partners

Upon the return by the Secretary of State pursuant to Section 206 of a certificate marked "Filed," the general partners shall promptly deliver or mail a copy of the certificate of limited partnership and each certificate of amendment or cancellation to each limited partner unless the partnership agreement provides otherwise.

ARTICLE 3. LIMITED PARTNERS

§ 301. Admission of Limited Partners

(a) A person becomes a limited partner:

(1) at the time the limited partnership is formed;

or

(2) at any later time specified in the records of the limited partnership for becoming a limited partner.

(b) After the filing of a limited partnership's original certificate of limited partnership, a person may be admitted as an additional limited partner:

(1) in the case of a person acquiring a partnership interest directly from the limited partnership, upon compliance with the partnership agreement or, if the partnership agreement does not so provide, upon the written consent of all partners; and

(2) in the case of an assignee of a partnership interest of a partner who has the power, as provided in Section 704, to grant the assignee the right to become a limited partner, upon

the exercise of that power and compliance with any conditions limiting the grant or exercise of the power.

§ 302. Voting

Subject to Section 303, the partnership agreement may grant to all or a specified group of the limited partners the right to vote (on a per capita or other basis) upon any matter.

§ 303. Liability to Third Parties

(a) Except as provided in section (d), a limited partner is not liable for the obligations of a limited partnership unless he [or she] is also a general partner or, in addition to the exercise of his [or her] rights and powers as a limited partner, he [or she] participates in the control of the business. However, if the limited partner participates in the control of the business, he [or she] is liable only to persons who transact business with the limited partnership reasonably believing, based upon the limited partner's conduct, that the limited partner is a general partner.

(b) A limited partner does not participate in the control of the business within the meaning of subsection (a) solely by doing one or more of the following:

(1) being a contractor for or an agent or employee of the limited partnership or of a general partner or being an officer, director, or shareholder of a general partner that is a corporation;

(2) consulting with and advising a general partner with respect to the business of the limited partnership;

(3) acting as surety for the limited partnership or guaranteeing or assuming one or more specific obligations of the limited partnership;

(4) taking any action required or permitted by law to bring or pursue a derivative action in the right of the limited partnership;

(5) requesting or attending a meeting of partners;

(6) proposing, approving, or disapproving, by voting or otherwise, one or more of the following matters:

(i) the dissolution and winding up of the limited partnership;

(ii) the sale, exchange, lease, mortgage, pledge, or other transfer of all or substantially all of the assets of the limited partnership;

(iii) the incurrence of indebtedness by the limited partnership other than in the ordinary course of its business;

(iv) a change in the nature of the business;

(v) the admission or removal of a general partner;

(vi) the admission or removal of a limited partner;

(vii) a transaction involving an actual or potential conflict of interest between a general partner and the limited partnership or the limited partners;

(viii) an amendment to the partnership agreement or certificate of limited partnership; or

(ix) matters related to the business of the limited partnership not otherwise enumerated in this subsection (b), which the partnership agreement states in writing may be subject to the approval or disapproval of limited partners;

(7) winding up the limited partnership pursuant to Section 803; or

(8) exercising any right or power permitted to limited partners under this [Act] and not specifically enumerated in this subsection (b).

(c) The enumeration in subsection (b) does not mean that the possession or exercise of any other powers by a limited partner constitutes participation by him [or her] in the business of the limited partnership.

(d) A limited partner who knowingly permits his [or her] name to be used in the name of the limited partnership, except under circumstances permitted by Section 102(2), is liable to creditors who extend credit to the limited partnership without actual knowledge that the limited partner is not a general partner.

§ 304. Person Erroneously Believing Himself [or Herself] Limited Partner

(a) Except as provided in subsection (b), a person who makes a contribution to a business enterprise and erroneously but in good faith believes that he [or she] has become a limited partner in the enterprise is not a general partner in the enterprise and is not bound by its obligations by reason of making the contribution, receiving distributions from the enterprise, or exercising any rights of a limited partner, if, on ascertaining the mistake, he [or she]:

(1) causes an appropriate certificate of limited partnership or certificate of amendment to be executed and filed; or

(2) withdraws from future equity participation in the enterprise by executing and filing in the office of the Secretary of State a certificate declaring withdrawal under this section.

(b) A person who makes a contribution of the kind described in subsection (a) is liable as a general partner to any third party who transacts business with the enterprise (i) before the person withdraws and an appropriate certificate is filed to show withdrawal, or (ii) before an appropriate certificate is filed to show that he [or she] is not a general partner, but in either case only if the third party actually believed in good faith that the person was a general partner at the time of the transaction.

§ 305. Information

Each limited partner has the right to:

(1) inspect and copy any of the partnership records required to be maintained by Section 105; and

(2) obtain from the general partners from time to time upon reasonable demand (i) true and full information regarding the state of the business and financial condition of the limited partnership, (ii) promptly after becoming available, a copy of the limited partnership's federal, state and local income tax returns for each year, and (iii) other information regarding the affairs of the limited partnership as is just and reasonable.

Article 4.   General Partners

§ 401. Admission of Additional General Partners

After the filing of a limited partnership's original certificate of limited partnership, additional general partners may be admitted as provided in writing in the partnership agreement or, if the partnership agreement does not provide in writing for the admission of additional general partners, with the written consent of all partners.

§ 402. Events of Withdrawal

Except as approved by the specific written consent of all partners at the time, a person ceases to be a general partner of a limited partnership upon the happening of any of the following events:

(1) the general partner withdraws from the limited partnership as provided in Section 602;

(2) the general partner ceases to be a member of the limited partnership as provided in Section 702;

(3) the general partner is removed as a general partner in accordance with the partnership agreement;

(4) unless otherwise provided in writing in the partnership agreement, the general partner: (i) makes an assignment for the benefit of creditors; (ii) files a voluntary petition in bankruptcy; (iii) is adjudicated a bankrupt or insolvent; (iv) files a petition or answer seeking for himself [or herself] any reorganization, arrangement, composition, readjustment, liquidation, dissolution or similar relief under any statute, law, or regulation; (v) files an answer or other pleading admitting or failing to contest the material allegations of a petition filed against him [or her] in any proceeding of this nature; or (vi) seeks, consents to, or acquiesces in the appointment of a trustee, receiver, or liquidator of the general partner or of all or any substantial part of his [or her] properties;

(5) unless otherwise provided in writing in the partnership agreement, [120] days after the commencement of any proceeding against the general partner seeking reorganization, arrangement, composition, readjustment, liquidation, dissolution or similar relief under any statute, law, or regulation, the proceeding has not been dismissed, or if within [90] days after the appointment without his [or her] consent or acquiescence of a trustee, receiver, or liquidator of the general partner or of all or any substantial part of his [or her] properties, the appointment is not vacated or stayed or within [90] days after the expiration of any such stay, the appointment is not vacated;

(6) in the case of a general partner who is a natural person,

(i) his [or her] death; or

(ii) the entry of an order by a court of competent jurisdiction adjudicating him [or her] incompetent to manage his [or her] person or his [or her] estate;

(7) in the case of a general partner who is acting as a general partner by virtue of being a trustee of a trust, the termination of the trust (but not merely the substitution of a new trustee);

(8) in the case of a general partner that is a separate partnership, the dissolution and commencement of winding up of the separate partnership;

(9) in the case of a general partner that is a corporation, the filing of a certificate of dissolution, or its equivalent, for the corporation or the revocation of its charter; or

(10) in the case of an estate, the distribution by the fiduciary of the estate's entire interest in the partnership.

§ 403. General Powers and Liabilities

(a) Except as provided in this [Act] or in the partnership agreement, a general partner of a limited partnership has the rights and powers and is subject to the restrictions of a partner in a partnership without limited partners.

(b) Except as provided in this [Act], a general partner of a limited partnership has the liabilities of a partner in a partnership without limited partners to persons other than the partnership and the other partners. Except as provided in this [Act] or in the partnership agreement, a general partner of a limited partnership has the liabilities of a partner in a partnership without limited partners to the partnership and to the other partners.

§ 404. Contributions by General Partner

A general partner of a limited partnership may make contributions to the partnership and share in the profits and losses of, and in distributions from, the limited partnership as a general partner. A general partner also may make contributions to and share in profits, losses, and distributions as a limited partner. A person who is both a general partner and a limited partner has the rights and powers, and is subject to the restrictions and liabilities, of a general partner and except as provided in the partnership agreement, also has the powers, and is subject to the restrictions, of a limited partner to the extent of his [or her] participation in the partnership as a limited partner.

§ 405. Voting

The partnership agreement may grant to all or certain identified general partners the right to vote (on a per capita or any other basis), separately or with all or any class of the limited partners, on any matter.

ARTICLE 5. FINANCE

§ 501. Form of Contribution

The contribution of a partner may be in cash, property, or services rendered, or a promissory note or other obligation to contribute cash or property or to perform services.

§ 502. Liability for Contribution

(a) A promise by a limited partner to contribute to the limited partnership is not enforceable unless set out in writing signed by the limited partner.

(b) Except as provided in the partnership agreement, a partner is obligated to the limited partnership to perform any enforceable promise to contribute cash or property or to perform services, even if he [or she] is unable to perform because of death, disability, or any other reason. If a partner does not make the required contribution of property or services, he [or she] is obligated at the option of the limited partnership to contribute cash equal to that portion of the value, as stated in the partnership records required to be kept pursuant to Section 105, of the stated contribution which has not been made.

(c) Unless otherwise provided in the partnership agreement, the obligation of a partner to make a contribution or return money or other property paid or distributed in violation of this [Act] may be compromised only by consent of all partners. Notwithstanding the compromise, a creditor of a limited partnership who extends credit or otherwise acts in reliance on that obligation after the partner signs a writing which reflects the obligation and before the amendment or cancellation thereof to reflect the compromise may enforce the original obligation.

§ 503. Sharing of Profits and Losses

The profits and losses of a limited partnership shall be allocated among the partners, and among classes of partners, in the manner provided in writing in the partnership agreement. If the partnership agreement does not so provide in writing, profits and losses shall be allocated on the basis of the value, as stated in the partnership records required to be kept pursuant to Section 105, of the contributions made by each partner to the extent they have been received by the partnership and have not been returned.

§ 504. Sharing of Distributions

Distributions of cash or other assets of a limited partnership shall be allocated among the partners and among classes of partners in the manner provided in writing in the partnership agreement. If the partnership agreement does not so provide in writing, distribution shall be made on the basis of the value, as stated in the partnership records required to be kept pursuant to Section 105, of the contributions made by each partner to the extent they have been received by the partnership and have not been returned.

ARTICLE 6. DISTRIBUTIONS AND WITHDRAWAL

§ 601. Interim Distributions

Except as provided in this Article, a partner is entitled to receive distributions from a limited partnership before his [or her] withdrawal from the limited partnership and before the dissolution and winding up thereof to the extent and at the times or upon the happening of the events specified in the partnership agreement.

§ 602.   Withdrawal of General Partner

A general partner may withdraw from a limited partnership at any time by giving written notice to the other partners, but if the withdrawal violated the partnership agreement, the limited partnership may recover from the withdrawing general partner damages for breach of the partnership agreement and offset the damages against the amount otherwise distributable to him [or her].

§ 603.   Withdrawal of Limited Partner

A limited partner may withdraw from a limited partnership at the time or upon the happening of events specified in writing in the partnership agreement. If the agreement does not specify in writing the time or the events upon the happening of which a limited partner may withdraw or a definite time for the dissolution and winding up of the limited partnership, a limited partner may withdraw upon not less that six months' prior written notice to each general partner at his [or her] address on the books of the limited partnership at its office in this State.

§ 604.   Distribution upon Withdrawal

Except as provided in this Article, upon withdrawal any withdrawing partner is entitled to receive any distribution to which he [or she] is entitled under the partnership agreement and, if not otherwise provided in the agreement, he [or she] is entitled to receive, within a reasonable time after withdrawal, the fair value of his [or her] interest in the limited partnership as of the date of withdrawal based upon his [or her] right to share in distributions from the limited partnership.

§ 605.   Distribution in Kind

Except as provided in writing in the partnership agreement, a partner, regardless of the nature of his [or her] contribution, has no right to demand and receive any distribution from a limited partnership in any form other than cash. Except as provided in writing in the partnership agreement, a partner may not be compelled to accept a distribution of any asset in kind from a limited partnership to the extent that the percentage of the asset distributed to him [or her] exceeds a percentage of that asset which is equal to the percentage in which he [or she] shares in distributions from the limited partnership.

§ 606.   Right to Distribution

At the time a partner becomes entitled to receive a distribution, he [or she] has the status of, and is entitled to all remedies available to, a creditor of the limited partnership with respect to the distribution.

§ 607.   Limitations on Distribution

A partner may not receive a distribution from a limited partnership to the extent that, after giving effect to the distribution, all liabilities of the limited partnership, other than liabilities to partners on account of their partnership interests, exceed the fair value of the partnership assets.

§ 608.   Liability upon Return of Contributions

(a) If a partner has received the return of any part of his [or her] contribution without violation of the partnership agreement or this [Act], he [or she] is liable to the limited partnership for a period of one year thereafter for the amount of the returned contribution, but only to the extent necessary to discharge the limited partnership's liabilities to creditors who extended credit to the limited partnership during the period the contribution was held by the partnership.

(b) If a partner has received the return of any part of his [or her] contribution in violation of the partnership agreement or this [Act], he [or she] is liable to the limited partnership for a period of six years thereafter for the amount of the contribution wrongfully returned.

(c) A partner receives a return of his [or her] contribution to the extent that a distribution to him [or her] reduces his [or her] share of the fair value of the net assets of the limited partnership below the value, as set forth in the partnership records required to be kept pursuant to Section 105, of his contribution which has not been distributed to him [to her].

ARTICLE 7.   ASSIGNMENT OF PARTNERSHIP INTERESTS

§ 701.   Nature of Partnership Interest

A partnership interest is personal property.

§ 702.   Assignment of Partnership Interest

Except as provided in the partnership agreement, a partnership interest is assignable in whole or in part. An assignment of partnership interest does not dissolve a limited partnership or entitle the assignee to become or to exercise any rights of a partner. An assignment entitles the assignee to receive, to the extent assigned, only the distribution to which the assignor would be entitled. Except as provided in the partnership agreement, a partner ceases to be a partner upon assignment of all his [or her] partnership interest.

§ 703.   Rights of Creditor

On application to a court of competent jurisdiction by any judgment creditor of a partner, the court may charge the partnership interest of the partner with payment of the unsatisfied amount of the judgment with interest. To the extent so charged, the judgment creditor has only the rights of an assignee of the partnership interest. This [Act] does not deprive any partner of the benefit of any exemption laws applicable to his [or her] partnership interest.

§ 704.   Right of Assignee to Become Limited Partner

(a) An assignee of a partnership interest, including an assignee of a general partner, may become a limited partner if and to the extent that (i) the assignor gives the assignee that right in accordance with authority described in the partnership agreement, or (ii) all other partners consent.

(b) An assignee who has become a limited partner has, to the extent assigned, the rights and powers, and is subject to the restrictions and liabilities, of a limited partner under the partnership agreement and this [Act]. An assignee who becomes a limited partner also is liable for the obligations of his [or her] assignor to make and return contributions as provided in Articles 5 and 6. However, the assignee is not obligated for liabilities unknown to the assignee at the time he [or she] became a limited partner.

(c) If an assignee of a partnership interest becomes a limited partner, the assignor is not released from his [or her] liability to the limited partnership under Sections 207 and 502.

§ 705. Power of Estate of Deceased or Incompetent Partner

If a partner who is an individual dies or a court of competent jurisdiction adjudges him [or her] to be incompetent to manage his [or her] person or his [or her] property, the partner's executor, administrator, guardian, conservator, or other legal representative may exercise all the partner's rights for the purpose of settling his [or her] estate or administering his [or her] property, including any power the partner had to give an assignee the right to become a limited partner. If a partner is a corporation, trust, or other entity and is dissolved or terminated, the powers of that partner may be exercised by its legal representative or successor.

ARTICLE 8.   DISSOLUTION

§ 801. Nonjudicial Dissolution

A limited partnership is dissolved and its affairs shall be wound up upon the happening of the first to occur of the following:

(1) at the time specified in the certificate of limited partnership;

(2) upon the happening of events specified in writing in the partnership agreement;

(3) written consent of all partners;

(4) an event of withdrawal of a general partner unless at the time there is at least one other general partner and the written provisions of the partnership agreement permit the business of the limited partnership to be carried on by the remaining general partner and that partner does so, but the limited partnership is not dissolved and is not required to be wound up by reason of any event of withdrawal if, within 90 days after the withdrawal, all partners agree in writing to continue the business of the limited partnership and to the appointment of one or more additional general partners if necessary or desired; or

(5) entry of a decree of judicial dissolution under Section 802.

§ 802. Judicial Dissolution

On application by or for a partner the [designate the appropriate court] court may decree dissolution of a limited partnership whenever it is not reasonably practicable to carry on the business in conformity with the partnership agreement.

§ 803. Winding Up

Except as provided in the partnership agreement, the general partners who have not wrongfully dissolved a limited partnership or, if none, the limited partners, may wind up the limited partnership's affairs; but the [designate the appropriate court] court may wind up the limited partnership's affairs upon application of any partner, his [or her] legal representative, or assignee.

§ 804. Distribution of Assets

Upon the winding up of a limited partnership, the assets shall be distributed as follows:

(1) to creditors, including partners who are creditors, to the extent permitted by law, in satisfaction of liabilities of the limited partnership other than liabilities for distributions to partners under Section 601 or 604;

(2) except as provided in the partnership agreement to partners and former partners in satisfaction of liabilities for distributions under Section 601 or 604; and

(3) except as provided in the partnership agreement, to partners first for the return of their contributions and secondly respecting their partnership interests, in the proportions in which the partners share in distributions.

ARTICLE 9.   FOREIGN LIMITED PARTNERSHIPS

§ 901. Law Governing

Subject to the Constitution of this State, (i) the laws of the state under which a foreign limited partnership is organized govern its organization and internal affairs and the liability of its limited partners, and (ii) a foreign limited partnership may not be denied registration by reason of any difference between those laws and the laws of this State.

§ 902. Registration

Before transacting business in this State, a foreign limited partnership shall register with the Secretary of State. In order to register, a foreign limited partnership shall submit to the Secretary of State, in duplicate, an application for registration as a foreign limited partnership, signed and sworn to by a general partner and setting forth:

(1) the name of the foreign limited partnership and, if different, the name under which it proposes to register and transact business in this State;

(2) the State and date of its formation;

(3) the name and address of any agent for service of process on the foreign limited partnership whom the foreign limited partnership elects to appoint; the agent must be an individual resident of this State, a domestic corporation, or foreign corporation having a place of business in, and authorized to do business in, this State;

(4) a statement that the Secretary of State is appointed the agent of the foreign limited partnership for service of process if no agent has been appointed under paragraph (3) or, if appointed, the agent's authority has been revoked or if the agent cannot be found or served with the exercise of reasonable diligence;

(5) the address of the office required to be maintained in the state of its organization by the laws of that state or, if not so required, of the principal office of the foreign limited partnership;

(6) the name and business address of each general partner; and

(7) the address of the office at which is kept a list of the names and addresses of the limited partners and their capital contributions, together with an undertaking by the foreign limited partnership to keep those records until the foreign limited partnership's registration in this State is cancelled or withdrawn.

§ 903. Issuance of Registration

(a) If the Secretary of State finds that an application for registration conforms to law and all requisite fees have been paid, he [or she] shall:

(1) endorse on the application the word "Filed," and the month, day and year of the filing thereof;

(2) file in his [or her] office a duplicate original of the application; and

(3) issue a certificate of registration to transact business in this State.

(b) The certificate of registration, together with a duplicate original of the application, shall be returned to the person who filed the application or his [or her] representative.

§ 904. Name

A foreign limited partnership may register with the Secretary of State under any name, whether or not it is the name under which it is registered in its state of organization, that includes without abbreviation the words "limited partnership" and that could be registered by a domestic limited partnership.

§ 905. Changes and Amendments

If any statement in the application for registration of a foreign limited partnership was false when made or any arrangements or other facts described have changed, making the application inaccurate in any respect, the foreign limited partnership shall promptly file in the office of the Secretary of State a certificate, signed and sworn to by a general partner, correcting such statement.

§ 906. Cancellation of Registration

A foreign limited partnership may cancel its registration by filing with the Secretary of State a certificate of cancellation signed and sworn to by a general partner. A cancellation does not terminate the authority of the Secretary of State to accept service of process on the foreign limited partnership with respect to [claims for relief] [causes of action] arising out of the transactions of business in this State.

§ 907. Transaction of Business
Without Registration

(a) A foreign limited partnership transacting business in this State may not maintain any action, suit, or proceeding in any court of this State until it has registered in this State.

(b) The failure of a foreign limited partnership to register in this State does not impair the validity of any contract or act of the foreign limited partnership or prevent the foreign limited partnership from defending any action, suit, or proceeding in any court of this State.

(c) A limited partner of a foreign limited partnership is not liable as a general partner of the foreign limited partnership solely by reason of having transacted business in this State without registration.

(d) A foreign limited partnership, by transacting business in this State without registration, appoints the Secretary of State as its agent for service of process with respect to [claims for relief] [causes of action] arising out of the transaction of business in this State.

§ 908. Action by [Appropriate Official]

The [designate the appropriate official] may bring an action to restrain a foreign limited partnership from transacting business in this State in violation of this Article.

ARTICLE 10.   DERIVATIVE ACTIONS

§ 1001. Right of Action

A limited partner may bring an action in the right of a limited partnership to recover a judgment in its favor if general partners with authority to do so have refused to bring the action or if an effort to cause those general partners to bring the action is not likely to succeed.

§ 1002. Proper Plaintiff

In derivative action, the plaintiff must be a partner at the time of bringing the action and (i) must have been a partner at the time of the transaction of which he [or she] complains or (ii) his [or her] status as a partner must have devolved upon him [or her] by operation of law or pursuant to the terms of the partnership agreement from a person who was a partner at the time of the transaction.

§ 1003. Pleading

In a derivative action the complaint shall set forth with particularity the effort of the plaintiff to secure initiation of the action by a general partner or the reasons for not making the effort.

§ 1004. Expenses

If a derivative action is successful, in whole or in part, or if anything is received by the plaintiff as a result of a judgment, compromise or settlement of an action or claim, the court may award the plaintiff reasonable expenses, including reasonable attorney's fees, and shall direct him [or her] to remit the limited partnership the remainder of those proceeds received by him [or her].

ARTICLE 11. MISCELLANEOUS

§ 1101. Construction and Application

This [Act] shall be so applied and construed to effectuate its general purpose to make uniform the law with respect to the subject of this [Act] among states enacting it.

§ 1102. Short Title

This [Act] may be cited as the Uniform Limited Partnership Act.

§ 1103. Severability

If any provision of the [Act] or its application to any person or circumstance is held invalid, the invalidity does not affect other provisions or applications of the [Act] which can be given effect without the invalid provision or application, and to this end the provisions of this Act are severable.

§ 1104. Effective Date, Extended Effective Date, and Repeal

Except as set forth below, the effective date of this [Act] is _____ and the following acts [list existing limited partnership acts] are hereby repealed:

(1) The existing provisions for execution and filing of certificates of limited partnerships and amendments thereunder and cancellations thereof continue in effect until [specify time required to create central filing system], the extended effective date, and Sections 102, 103, 104, 105, 201, 202, 203, 204, and 206 are not effective until the extended effective date.

(2) Section 402, specifying the conditions under which a general partner ceases to be a member of a limited partnership, is not effective until the extended effective date.

(3) Sections 501, 502, and 608 apply only to contributions and distributions made after the effective date of this [Act].

(4) Section 704 applies only to assignments made after the effective date of this [Act].

(5) Article 9, dealing with registration of foreign limited partnerships, is not effective until the extended effective date.

(6) Unless otherwise agreed by the partners, the applicable provisions of existing law governing allocation of profits and losses (rather than the provisions of Section 503), distributions to a withdrawing partner (rather than the provisions of Section 604), and distribution of assets upon the winding up of a limited partnership (rather than the provisions of Section 804) govern limited partnerships formed before the effective date of this [Act].

§ 1105. Rules for Cases Not Provided for in this [Act]

In any case not provided for in this [Act] the provisions of the Uniform Partnership Act govern.

§ 1106. Savings Clause

The repeal of any statutory provision by this Act does not impair, or otherwise affect, the organization or the continued existence of a limited partnership existing at the effective date of this Act, nor does the repeal of any existing statutory provision by this Act impair any contract or affect any right accrued before the effective date of this Act.

REVISED MODEL BUSINESS CORPORATION ACT (1984) (AS AMENDED THROUGH 1987)*

CHAPTER 1.   GENERAL PROVISIONS

Subchapter A.   Short Title and Reservation of Power

§ 1.01.   Short Title
This Act shall be known and may be cited as the "[name of state] Business Corporation Act."

§ 1.02.   Reservation of Power to Amend or Repeal
The [name of state legislature] has power to amend or repeal all or part of this Act at any time and all domestic and foreign corporations subject to this Act are governed by the amendment or repeal.

Subchapter B.   Filing Documents

§ 1.20.   Filing Requirements
(a) A document must satisfy the requirements of this section, and of any other section that adds to or varies these requirements, to be entitled to filing by the secretary of state.

(b) This Act must require or permit filing the document in the office of the secretary of state.

(c) The document must contain the information required by this Act. It may contain other information as well.

(d) The document must be typewritten or printed.

(e) The document must be in the English language. A corporate name need not be in English if written in English letters or Arabic or Roman numerals, and the certificate of existence required of foreign corporations need not be in English if accompanied by a reasonably authenticated English translation.

(f) The document must be executed:

   (1) by the chairman of the board of directors of a domestic or foreign corporation, by its president, or by another of its officers;

   (2) if directors have not been selected or the corporation has not been formed, by an incorporator; or

   (3) if the corporation is in the hands of a receiver, trustee, or other court-appointed fiduciary, by that fiduciary.

(g) The person executing the document shall sign it and state beneath or opposite his signature his name and the capacity in which he signs. The document may but need not contain: (1) the corporate seal, (2) an attestation by the secretary or assistant secretary, (3) an acknowledgment, verification, or proof.

(h) If the secretary of state has prescribed a mandatory form for the document under Section 1.21, the document must be in or on the prescribed form.

(i) The document must be delivered to the office of the secretary of state for filing and must be accompanied by one exact or conformed copy (except as provided in Sections 5.03 and 15.09), the correct filing fee, and any franchise tax, license fee, or penalty required by this Act or other law.

---

*Reprinted with permission of the American Bar Foundation and Law & Business, Inc.

§ 1.21. Forms

(a) The secretary of state may prescribe and furnish on request forms for: (1) an application for a cerificate of existence, (2) a foreign corporation's application for a certificate of authority to transact business in this state, (3) a foreign corporation's application for a certificate of withdrawal, and (4) the annual report. If the secretary of state so requires, use of these forms is mandatory.

(b) The secretary of state may prescribe and furnish on request forms for other documents required or permitted to be filed by this Act but their use is not mandatory.

§ 1.22. Filing, Service, and Copying Fees

(*Text omitted.*)

§ 1.23. Effective Time and Date of Document

(a) Except as provided in subsection (b) and section 1.24(c), a document accepted for filing is effective:

(1) at the time of filing on the date it is filed, as evidenced by the secretary of state's date and time endorsement on the original document; or

(2) at the time specified in the document as its effective time on the date it is filed.

(b) A document may specify a delayed effective time and date, and if it does so the document becomes effective and at the time and date specified. If a delayed effective date but no time is specified, the document is effect at the close of business on that date. A delayed effective date for a document may not be later than the 90th day after the date it is filed.

§ 1.24. Correcting Filed Document

(a) A domestic or foreign corporation may correct a document filed by the secretary of state if the document (1) contains an incorrect statement or (2) was defectively executed, attested, sealed, verified, or acknowledged.

(b) A document is corrected:

(1) by preparing articles of correction that (i) describe the document (including its filing date) or attach a copy of it to the articles, (ii) specify the incorrect statement and the reason it is incorrect or the manner in which the execution was defective, and (iii) correct the incorrect statement or defective execution; and

(2) by delivering the articles to the secretary of state for filing.

(c) Articles of correction are effective on the effective date of the document they correct except as to person relying on the uncorrected document and adversely affected by the correction. As to those persons, articles of correction are effective when filed.

§ 1.25. Filing Duty of Secretary of State

(a) If a document delivered to the office of the secretary of state for filing satisfies the requirements of section 1.20, the secretary of state shall file it.

(b) The secretary of state files a document by stamping or otherwise endorsing "Filed," together with his name and official title and the date and time of receipt, on both the original and the document copy and on the receipt for the filing fee. After filing a document, except as provided in sections 5.03 and 15.10, the secretary of state shall deliver the document copy, with the filing fee receipt (or acknowledgement of receipt if no fee is required) attached, to the domestic or foreign corporation or its representative.

(c) If the secretary of state refuses to file a document, he shall return it to the domestic or foreign corporation or its representative within five days after the document was delivered, together with a brief, written explanation of the reason for his refusal.

(d) The secretary of state's duty to file documents under this section is ministerial. His filing or refusing to file a document does not:

(1) affect the validity or invalidity of the document in whole or part;

(2) relate to the correctness or incorrectness of information contained in the document;

(3) create a presumption that the document is valid or invalid or that information contained in the document is correct or incorrect.

§ 1.26. Appeal from Secretary of State's Refusal to File Document

(a) If the secretary of state refuses to file a document delivered to his office for filing, the domestic or foreign corporation may appeal the refusal to the [name or describe] court [of the county where the corporation's principal office (or, if none in this state, its registered office) is or will be located] [of _____ county]. The appeal is commenced by petitioning the court to compel filing the document and by attaching to the petition the document and the secretary of state's explanation of his refusal to file.

(b) The court may summarily order the secretary of state to file the document or take other action the court considers appropriate.

(c) The court's final decision may be appealed as in other civil proceedings.

§ 1.27. Evidentiary Effect of Copy of Filed Document

A certificate attached to a copy of a document filed by the secretary of state, bearing his signature (which may be in facsimile) and the sale of this state, is conclusive evidence that the original document is on file with the secretary of state.

§ 1.28. Certificate of Existence

(a) Anyone may apply to the secretary of state to furnish a certificate of existence for a domestic corporation or a certificate of authorization for a foreign corporation.

(b) A certificate of existence or authorization sets forth:

(1) the domestic corporation's corporate name or the foreign corporation's corporate name used in this state;

(2) that (i) the domestic corporation is duly incorporated under the law of this state, the date of its incorporation, and the period of its duration if less than perpetual; or (ii) that the foreign corporation is authorized to transact business in this state;

(3) that all fees, taxes, and penalties, owed to this state have been paid, if (i) payment is reflected in the records of the secretary of state and (ii) nonpayment affects the existence or authorization of the domestic or foreign corporation;

(4) that its most recent annual report required by section 16.22 has been delivered to the secretary of state;

(5) that articles of dissolution have not been filed; and

(6) other facts of record in the office of the secretary of state that may be requested by the applicant.

(c) Subject to any qualification stated in the certificate, a certificate of existence or authorization issued by the secretary of state may be relied upon as conclusive evidence that the domestic or foreign corporation is in existence or is authorized to transact business in this state.

§ 1.29.   Penalty for Signing False Document

(a) A person commits an offense if he signs a document he knows is false in any material respect with intent that the document be delivered to the secretary of state for filing.

(b) An offense under this section is a [_____] misdemeanor [punishable by a fine of not to exceed $_____].

Subchapter C.   Secretary of State

§ 1.30.   Powers

The secretary of state has the power reasonably necessary to perform the duties required of him by this Act.

Subchapter D.   Definitions

§ 1.40.   Act Definitions

In this Act:

(1) "Articles of incorporation" include amended and restated articles of incorporation and articles of merger.

(2) "Authorized shares" means the shares of all classes a domestic or foreign corporation is authorized to issue.

(3) "Conspicuous" means so written that a reasonable person against whom the writing is to operate should have noticed it. For example, printing in italics or boldface or contrasting color, or typing in capitals or underlined, is conspicuous.

(4) "Corporation" or "domestic corporation" means a corporation for profit, which is not a foreign corporation, incorporated under or subject to the provisions of this Act.

(5) "Deliver" includes mail.

(6) "Distribution" means a direct or indirect transfer of money or other property (except its own shares) or incurrence of indebtedness by a corporation to or for the benefit of its shareholders in respect of any of its shares. A distribution may be in the form of a declaration or payment of a dividend; a purchase, redemption, or other acquisition of shares; a distribution of indebtedness; or otherwise.

(7) "Effective date of notice" is defined in section 1.41.

(8) "Employee" includes an officer but not a director. A director may accept duties that make him also an employee.

(9) "Entity" includes corporation and foreign corporation; not-for-profit corporation; profit and not-for-profit unincorporated association; business trust, estate, partnership, trust, and two or more persons having a joint or common economic interest; and state, United States, and foreign government.

(10) "Foreign corporation" means a corporation for profit incorporated under a law other than the law of this state.

(11) "Governmental subdivision" includes authority, county, district, and municipality.

(12) "Includes" denotes a partial definition.

(13) "Individual" includes the estate of an incompetent or deceased individual.

(14) "Means" denotes an exhaustive definition.

(15) "Notice" is defined in section 1.41.

(16) "Person" includes individual and entity.

(17) "Principal office" means the office (in or out of this state) so designated in the annual report where the principal executive offices of a domestic or foreign corporation are located.

(18) "Proceeding" includes civil suit and criminal, administrative, and investigatory action.

(19) "Record date" means the date established under chapter 6 or 7 on which a corporation determines the identity of its shareholders and their shareholdings for purposes of this Act. The determinations shall be made as of the close of business on the record date unless another time for doing so is specified when the record date is fixed.

(20) "Secretary" means the corporate officer to whom the board of directors has delegated responsibility under section 8.40(c) for custody of the minutes of the meetings of the board of directors and of the shareholders and for authenticating records of the corporation.

(21) "Share" means the unit into which the proprietary interests in a corporation are divided.

(22) "Shareholder" means the person in whose name shares are registered in the records of a corporation or the beneficial owner of shares to the extent of the rights granted by a nominee certificate on file with a corporation.

(23) "State," when referring to a part of the United States, includes a state and commonwealth (and their agencies and governmental subdivisions) and a territory, and insular possession (and their agencies and governmental subdivisions) of the United States.

(24) "Subscriber" means a person who subscribes for shares in a corporation, whether before or after incorporation.

(25) "United States" includes district, authority, bureau, commission, department, and any other agency of the United States.

(26) "Voting group" means all shares of one or more classes or series that under the articles of incorporation or this Act are entitled to vote and be counted together collectively on a matter at a meeting of shareholders. All shares entitled by the articles of incorporation or this Act to vote generally on the matter are for that purpose a single voting group.

§1.41. Notice

(a) Notice under this Act shall be in writing unless oral notice is reasonable under the circumstances.

(b) Notice may be communicated in person; by telephone, telegraph, teletype, or other form of wire or wireless communication; or by mail or private carrier. If these forms of personal notice are impracticable, notice may be communicated by a newspaper of general circulation in the area where published; or by radio, television, or other form of public broadcast communication.

(c) Written notice by a domestic or foreign corporation to its shareholder, if in a comprehensible form, is effective when mailed, if mailed postpaid and correctly addressed to the shareholder's address shown in the corporation's current record of shareholders.

(d) Written notice to a domestic or foreign corporation (authorized to transact business in this state) may be addressed to its registered agent at its registered office or to the corporation or its secretary at its principal office shown in its most recent annual report or, in the case of a foreign corporation that has not yet delivered an annual report, in its application for a certificate of authority.

(e) Except as provided in subjections (c) and (d), written notice, if in a comprehensible form, is effective at the earliest of the following:

(1) when received;

(2) five days after its deposit in the United States Mail, as evidenced by the postmark, if mailed postpaid and correctly addressed;

(3) on the date shown on the return receipt, if sent by registered or certified mail, return receipt requested, and the receipt is signed by or on behalf of the addressee.

(f) Oral notice is effective when communicated if communicated in a comprehensible manner.

(g) If this Act prescribes notice requirements for particular circumstances, those requirements govern. If articles of incorporation or bylaws prescribe notice requirements, not inconsistent with this section or other provisions of this Act, those requirements govern.

§1.42. Number of Shareholders

(a) For purposes of this Act, the following identified as a shareholder in a corporation's current record of shareholders constitutes one shareholder:

(1) three or fewer co-owners;

(2) a corporation, partnership, trust, estate, or other entity;

(3) the trustees, guardians, custodians, or other fiduciaries of a single trust, estate, or account.

(b) For purposes of this Act, shareholdings registered in substantially similar names constitute one shareholder if it is reasonable to believe that the names represent the same person.

CHAPTER 2.   INCORPORATION

§2.01. Incorporators

One or more persons may act as the incorporator or incorporators of a corporation by delivering articles of incorporation to the secretary of state for filing.

§2.02.   Articles of Incorporation

(a) The articles of incorporation must set forth:

(1) a corporate name for the corporation that satisfies the requirements of section 4.01;

(2) the number of shares the corporation is authorized to issue;

(3) the street address of the corporation's initial registered office and the name of its initial registered agent at that office; and

(4) the name and address of each incorporator.

(b) The articles of incorporation may set forth:

(1) the names and addresses of the individuals who are to serve as the initial directors;

(2) provisions not inconsistent with law regarding;

(i) the purpose or purposes for which the corporation is organized;

(ii) managing the business and regulating the affairs of the corporation;

(iii) defining, limiting, and regulating the powers of the corporation, its board of directors, and shareholders;

(iv) a par value for authorized shares or classes of shares;

(v) the imposition of personal liability on shareholders for the debts of the corporation to a specified extent and upon specified conditions; and

(3) any provision that under this Act is required or permitted to be set forth in the bylaws.

(c) The articles of incorporation need not set forth any of the corporate powers enumerated in this Act.

§2.03.   Incorporation

(a) Unless a delayed effective date is specified, the corporate existence begins when the articles of incorporation are filed.

(b) The secretary of state's filing of the articles of incorporation is conclusive proof that the incorporators satisfied all conditions precedent to incorporation except in a proceeding by the state to cancel or revoke the incorporation or involuntarily dissolve the corporation.

§2.04.   Liability for Preincorporation Transactions

All persons purporting to act as or on behalf of a corporation, knowing there was no incorporation under this Act, are jointly and severally liable for all liabilities created while so acting.

§ 2.05. Organization of Corporation

(a) After incorporation:

(1) If initial directors are named in the articles of incorporation, the initial directors shall hold an organizational meeting at the call of a majority of the directors, to complete the organization of the corporation by appointing officers, adopting bylaws, and carrying on any other business brought before the meeting;

(2) If initial directors are not named in the articles, the incorporator or incorporators shall hold an organizational meeting at the call of a majority of the incorporators.

(i) to elect directors and complete the organization of the corporation; or

(ii) to elect a board of directors who shall complete the organization of the corporation.

(b) Action required or permitted by this Act to be taken by incorporators at an organizational meeting may be taken without a meeting if the action taken is evidenced by one or more written consents describing the action taken and signed by each incorporator.

(c) An organizational meeting may be held in or out of this state.

§ 2.06. Bylaws

(a) The incorporators or board of directors of a corporation shall adopt initial bylaws for the corporation.

(b) The bylaws of a corporation may contain any provision for managing the business and regulating the affairs of the corporation that is not inconsistent with law or the articles of incorporation.

§ 2.07. Emergency Bylaws

(a) Unless the articles of incorporation provide otherwise, the board of directors of a corporation may adopt bylaws to be effective only in an emergency defined in subsection (d). The emergency bylaws, which are subject to amendment or repeal by the shareholders, may make all provisions necessary for managing the corporation during the emergency, including:

(1) procedures for calling a meeting of the board of directors;

(2) quorum requirements for the meeting; and

(3) designation of additional or substitute directors.

(b) All provisions of the regular bylaws consistent with the emergency bylaws remain effective during the emergency. The emergency bylaws are not effective after the emergency ends.

(c) Corporate action taken in good faith in accordance with the emergency bylaws:

(1) binds the corporation; and

(2) may not be used to impose liability on a corporate director, officer, employee, or agent.

(d) An emergency exists for purposes of this section if a quorum of the corporation's directors cannot readily be assembled because of some catastrophic event.

CHAPTER 3. PURPOSES AND POWERS

§ 3.01. Purposes

(a) Every corporation incorporated under this Act has the purpose of engaging in any lawful business unless a more limited purpose is set forth in the articles of incorporation.

(b) A corporation engaging in a business that is subject to regulation under another statute of this state may incorporate under this Act only if permitted by, and subject to all limitations of, the other statute.

§ 3.02. General Powers

Unless its articles of incorporation provide otherwise, every corporation has perpetual duration and succession in its corporate name and has the same powers as an individual to do all things necessary or convenient to carry out its business and affairs, including without limitation power:

(1) to sue and be sued, complain and defend in its corporate name;

(2) to have a corporate seal, which may be altered at will, and to use it, or a facsimile of it, by impressing or affixing it or in any other manner reproducing it;

(3) to make and amend bylaws, not inconsistent with its articles of incorporation or with the laws of this state, for managing the business and regulating the affairs of the corporation;

(4) to purchase, receive, lease, or otherwise acquire, and own, hold, improve, use, and otherwise deal with, real or personal property, or any legal or equitable interest in property, wherever located;

(5) to sell, convey, mortgage, pledge, lease, exchange, and otherwise dispose of all or any part of its property;

(6) to purchase, receive, subscribe for, or otherwise acquire; own, hold, vote, use, sell, mortgage, lend, pledge, or otherwise dispose of; and deal in and with shares or other interests in, or obligations of, any other entity;

(7) to make contracts and guarantees, incur liabilities, borrow money, issue its notes, bonds, and other obligations, (which may be convertible into or include the option to purchase other securities of the corporation), and secure any of its obligations by mortgage or pledge of any of its property, franchises, or income;

(8) to lend money, invest and reinvest its funds, and receive and hold real and personal property as security for repayment;

(9) to be a promoter, partner, member, associate, or manager of any partnership, joint venture, trust, or other entity;

(10) to conduct its business, locate offices, and exercise the powers granted by this Act within or without this state;

(11) to elect directors and appoint officers, employees, and agents of the corporation, define their duties, fix their compensation, and lend them money and credit;

(12) to pay pensions and establish pension plans, pension trusts, profit sharing plans, share bonus plans, share option plans, and benefit or incentive plans for any or all of its current or former directors, officers, employees, and agents;

(13) to make donations for the public welfare or for charitable, scientific, or educational purposes;

(14) to transact any lawful business that will aid governmental policy;

(15) to make payments or donations, or do any other act, not inconsistent with law, that furthers the business and affairs of the corporation.

§ 3.03. Emergency Powers

(a) In anticipation of or during an emergency defined in subsection (d), the board of directors of a corporation may:

(1) modify lines of succession to accommodate the incapacity of any director, officer, employee, or agent; and

(2) relocate the principal office, designate alternative principal offices or regional offices, or authorize the officers to do so.

(b) During an emergency defined in subsection (d), unless emergency bylaws provide otherwise:

(1) notice of a meeting of the board of directors need be given only to those directors whom it is practicable to reach and may be given in any practicable manner, including by publication and radio; and

(2) one or more officers of the corporation present at a meeting of the board of directors may be deemed to be directors for the meeting, in order of rank and within the same rank in order of seniority, as necessary to achieve a quorum.

(c) Corporate action taken in good faith during an emergency under this section to further the ordinary business affairs of the corporation:

(1) binds the corporation; and

(2) may not be used to impose liability on a corporate director, officer, employee, or agent.

(d) An emergency exists for purposes of this section if a quorum of the corporation's directors cannot readily be assembled because of some catastrophic event.

§ 3.04. Ultra Vires

(a) Except as provided in subsection (b), the validity of corporate action may not be challenged on the ground that the corporation lacks or lacked power to act.

(b) A corporation's power to act may be challenged:

(1) in a proceeding by a shareholder against the corporation to enjoin the act;

(2) in a proceeding by the corporation, directly, derivatively, or through a receiver, trustee, or other legal representative, against an incumbent or former director, officer, employee, or agent of the corporation; or

(3) in a proceeding by the Attorney General under section 14.30.

(c) In a shareholder's proceeding under subsection (b)(1) to enjoin an unauthorized corporate act, the court may enjoin or set aside the act, if equitable and if all affected persons are parties to the proceeding, and may award damages for loss (other than anticipated profits) suffered by the corporation or another party because of enjoining the unauthorized act.

CHAPTER 4.   NAME

§ 4.01.   Corporate Name

(a) A corporate name:

(1) must contain the word "corporation," "incorporated," "company," or "limited," or the abbreviation "corp.," "inc.," "co.," or "ltd.", or words or abbreviations of like import in another language; and

(2) may not contain language stating or implying that the corporation is organized for a purpose other than that permitted by section 3.01 and its articles of incorporation.

(b) Except as authorized by subsections (c) and (d), a corporate name must be distinguishable upon the records of the secretary of state from:

(1) the corporate name of a corporation incorporated or authorized to transact business in this state;

(2) a corporate name reserved or registered under section 4.02 or 4.03;

(3) the fictitious name adopted by a foreign corporation authorized to transact business in this state because its real name is unavailable; and

(4) the corporate name of a not-for-profit corporation incorporated or authorized to transact business in this state.

(c) A corporation may apply to the secretary of state for authorization to use a name that is not distinguishable upon his records from one or more of the names described in subsection (b). The secretary of state shall authorize use of the name applied for if:

(1) the other corporation consents to the use in writing and submits an undertaking in form satisfactory to the secretary of state to change its name to a name that is distinguishable upon the records of the secretary of state from the name of the applying corporation; or

(2) the applicant delivers to the secretary of state a certified copy of the final judgment of a court of competent jurisdiction establishing the applicant's right to use the name applied for in this state.

(d) A corporation may use the name (including the fictitious name) of another domestic or foreign corporation that is used in this state if the other corporation is incorporated or authorized to transact business in this state and the proposed user corporation:

(1) has merged with the other corporation;

(2) has been formed by reorganization of the other corporation; or

(3) has acquired all or substantially all of the assets, including the corporate name, of the other corporation.

(e) This Act does not control the use of fictitious names.

§ 4.02.   Reserved Name

(a) A person may reserve the exclusive use of a corporate name, including a fictitious name for a foreign corporation whose corporate name is not available, by delivering an application to the secretary of state for filing. The application must set forth the name and address of the applicant and the name proposed to be reserved. If the secretary of state finds that the corporate name applied for is available, he shall reserve the name for the applicant's exclusive use for a nonrenewable 120-day period.

(b) The owner of a reserved corporate name may transfer the reservation to another person by delivering to the secretary of state a signed notice of the transfer that states the name and address of the transferee.

§ 4.03.   Registered Name

(a) A foreign corporation may register its corporate name, or its corporate name with any addition required by section 15.06, if the name is distinguishable upon the records of the secretary of state from the corporate names that are not available under section 4.01(b)(3).

(b) A foreign corporation registers its corporate name, or its corporate name with any addition required by section 15.06, by delivering to the secretary of state for filing an application:

(1) setting forth its corporate name, or its corporate name with any addition required by section 15.06, the state or country and date of its incorporation, and a brief description of the nature of the business in which it is engaged; and

(2) accompanied by a certificate of existence (or a document of similar import) from the state or country of incorporation.

(c) The name is registered for the applicant's exclusive use upon the effective date of the application.

(d) A foreign corporation whose registration is effective may renew it for successive years by delivering to the secretary of state for filing a renewal applicaton, which complies with the requirements of subsection (b), between October 1 and December 31 of the preceeding year. The renewal application renews the registration for the following calendar year.

(e) A foreign corporation whose registration is effective may thereafter qualify as a foreign corporation under that name or consent in writing to the use of that name by a corporation thereafter incorporated under this Act or by another foreign corporation thereafter authorized to transact business in this state. The registration terminates when the domestic corporation is incorporated or the foreign corporation qualifies or consents to the qualification of another foreign corporation under the registered name.

Chapter 5.   Office and Agent

§ 5.01.   Registered Office and Registered Agent

Each corporation must continuously maintain in this state:

(1) a registered office that may be the same as any of its places of business; and

(2) a registered agent, who may be:

(i) an individual who resides in this state and whose business office is identical with the registered office;

(ii) a domestic corporation or not-for-profit domestic corporation whose business office is identical with the registered office; or

(iii) a foreign corporation or not-for-profit foreign corporation authorized to transact business in this state whose business office is identical with the registered office.

§ 5.02.   Change of Registered Office or Registered Agent

(a) A corporation may change its registered office or registered agent by delivering to the secretary of state for filing a statement of change that sets forth:

(1) the name of the corporation;

(2) the street address of its current registered office;

(3) if the current registered office is to be changed, the street address of the new registered office;

(4) the name of its current registered agent;

(5) if the current registered agent is to be changed, the name of the new registered agent and the new agent's written consent (either on the statement or attached to it) to the appointment; and

(6) that after the change or changes are made, the street addresses of its registered office and the business office of its registered agent will be identical.

(b) If a registered agent changes the street address of his business office, he may change the street address of the registered office of any corporation for which he is the registered agent by notifying the corporation in writing of the change and signing (either manually or in facsimile) and delivering to the secretary of state for filing a statement that complies with the requirements of subsection (a) and recites that the corporation has been notified of the change.

§ 5.03.   Resignation of Registered Agent

(a) A registered agent may resign his agency appointment by signing and delivering to the secretary of state for filing the signed original and two exact or conformed copies of a statement of resignation. The statement may include a statement that the registered office is also discontinued.

(b) After filing the statement the secretary of state shall mail one copy to the registered office (if not discontinued) and the other copy to the corporation at its principal office.

(c) The agency appointment is terminated, and the registered office discontinued if so provided, on the 31st day after the date on which the statement was filed.

§ 5.04.   Service on Corporation

(a) A corporation's registered agent is the corporation's agent for service of process, notice, or demand required or permitted by law to be served on the corporation.

(b) If the corporation has no registered agent, or the agent cannot with reasonable diligence be served, the corporation may be served by registered or certified mail, return receipt requested, addressed to the secretary of the corporation at its principal office. Service is perfected under this subsection at the earliest of:

(1) the date the corporation receives the mail;

(2) the date shown on the return receipt, if signed on behalf of the corporation; or

(3) five days after its deposit in the United States Mail, if mailed postpaid and correctly addressed.

(c) This section does not prescribe the only means, or necessarily the required means, of serving a corporation.

CHAPTER 6. SHARES AND DISTRIBUTIONS

Subchapter A. Shares

§ 6.01. Authorized Shares

(a) The articles of incorporation must prescribe the classes of shares and the number of shares of each class that the corporation is authorized to issue. If more than one class of shares is authorized, the articles of incorporation must prescribe a distinguishing designation for each class, and prior to the issuance of shares of a class the preferences, limitations, and relative rights of that class must be described in the articles of incorporation. All shares of a class must have preferences, limitations, and relative rights identical with those of other shares of the same class except to the extent otherwise permitted by section 6.02.

(b) The articles of incorporation must authorize (1) one or more classes of shares that together have unlimited voting rights, and (2) one or more classes of shares (which may be the same class or classes as those with voting rights) that together are entitled to receive the net assets of the corporation upon dissolution.

(c) The articles of incorporation may authorize one or more classes of shares that:

(1) have special, conditional, or limited voting rights, or no right to vote, except to the extent prohibited by this Act;

(2) are redeemable or convertible as specified in the articles of incorporation (i) at the option of the corporation, the shareholder, or another person or upon the occurrence of a designated event; (ii) for cash, indebtedness, securities, or other property; (iii) in a designated amount or in an amount determined in accordance with a designated formula or by reference to extrinsic data or events;

(3) entitle the holder to distributions calculated in any manner, including dividends that may be cumulative, noncumulative, or partially cumulative;

(4) have preference over any other class of shares with respect to distributions, including dividends and distributions upon the dissolution of the corporation.

(d) The description of the designations, preferences, limitations, and relative rights of share classes in subsection (c) is not exhaustive.

§ 6.02. Terms of Class or Series Determined by Board of Directors

(a) If the articles of incorporation so provide, the board of directors may determine, in whole or part, the preferences, limitations, and relative rights (within the limits set forth in section 6.01) or (1) any class of shares before the issuance of any shares of that class or (2) one or more series within a class before the issuance of any shares of that series.

(b) Each series of a class must be given a distinguishing designation.

(c) All shares of a series must have preferences, limitations, and relative rights identical with those of other shares of the same series and, except to the extent otherwise provided in the description of the series, of those of other series of the same class.

(d) Before issuing any shares of a class or series created under this section, the corporation must deliver to the secretary of state for filing articles of amendment, which are effective without shareholder action, that set forth:

(1) the name of the corporation;

(2) the text of the amendment determining the terms of the class or series of shares;

(3) the date it was adopted; and

(4) a statement that the amendment was duly adopted by the board of directors.

§ 6.03. Issued and Outstanding Shares

(a) A corporation may issue the number of shares of each class or series authorized by the articles of incorporation. Shares that are issued are outstanding shares until they are reacquired, redeemed, converted, or cancelled.

(b) The reacquisition, redemption, or conversion of outstanding shares is subject to the limitations of subsection (c) of this section and to section 6.40.

(c) At all times that shares of the corporation are outstanding, one or more shares that together have unlimited voting rights and one or more shares that together are entitled to receive the net assets of the corporation upon dissolution must be outstanding.

§ 6.04. Fractional Shares

(a) A corporation may:

(1) issue fractions of a share or pay in money the value of fractions of a share;

(2) arrange for disposition of fractional shares by the shareholders;

(3) issue scrip in registered or bearer form entitling the holder to receive a full share upon surrendering enough scrip to equal a full share.

(b) Each certificate representing scrip must be conspicuously labeled "scrip" and must contain the information required by section 6.25(b).

(c) The holder of a fractional share is entitled to exercise the rights of a shareholder, including the right to vote, to receive dividends, and to participate in the assets of the corporation upon liquidation. The holder of scrip is not entitled to any of these rights unless the scrip provides for them.

(d) The board of directors may authorize the issuance of scrip subject to any condition considered desirable, including:

(1) that the scrip will become void if not exchanged for full shares before a specified date; and

(2) that the shares for which the scrip is exchangeable may be sold and the proceeds paid to the scripholders.

Subchapter B. *Issuance of Shares*

§ 6.20. **Subscription for Shares Before Incorporation**

(a) A subscription for shares entered into before incorporation is irrevocable for six months unless the subscription agreement provides a longer or shorter period or all the subscribers agree to revocation.

(b) The board of directors may determine the payment terms of subscriptions for shares that were entered into before incorporation, unless the subscription agreement specifies them. A call for payment by the board of directors must be uniform so far as practicable as to all shares of the same class or series, unless the subscription agreement specifies otherwise.

(c) Shares issued pursuant to subscriptions entered into before incorporation are fully paid and nonassessable when the corporation receives the consideraton specified in the subscription agreement.

(d) If a subscriber defaults in payment of money or property under a subscription agreement entered into before incorporation, the corporation may collect the amount owed as any other debt. Alternatively, unless the subscription agreement provides otherwise, the corporation may rescind the agreement and may sell the shares if the debt remains unpaid more than 20 days after the corporation sends written demand for payment to the subscriber.

(e) A subscription agreement entered into after incorporation is a contract between the subscriber and the corporation subject to section 6.21.

§ 6.21. **Issuance of Shares**

(a) The powers granted in this section to the board of directors may be reserved to the shareholders by the articles of incorporation.

(b) The board of directors may authorize shares to be issued for consideration consisting of any tangible or intangible property or benefit to the corporation, including cash, promissory notes, services performed, contracts for services to be performed, or other securities of the corporation.

(c) Before the corporation issues shares, the board of directors must determine that the consideration received or to be received for shares to be issued is adequate. That determination by the board of directors is conclusive insofar as the adequacy of consideration for the issuance of shares relates to whether the shares are validly issued, fully paid, and nonassessable.

(d) When the corporation receives the consideration for which the board of directors authorized the issuance of shares, the shares issued therefor are fully paid and nonassessable.

(e) The corporation may place in escrow shares issued for a contract for future services or benefits or a promissory note, or make other arrangements to restrict the transfer of the shares, and may credit distributions in respect of the shares against their purchase price, until the services are performed, the note is paid, or the benefits received. If the services are not performed, the note is not paid, or the benefits are not received, the shares escrowed or restricted and the distributions credited may be cancelled in whole or part.

§ 6.22. **Liability of Shareholders**

(a) A purchaser from a corporation of its own shares is not liable to the corporation or its creditors with respect to the shares except to pay the consideration for which the shares were authorized to be issued (section 6.21) or specified in the subscription agreement (section 6.20).

(b) Unless otherwise provided in the articles of incorporation, a shareholder of a corporation is not personally liable for the acts or debts of the corporation except that he may become personally liable by reason of his own acts or conduct.

§ 6.23. **Share Dividends**

(a) Unless the articles of incorporation provide otherwise, shares may be used pro rata and without consideration to the corporation's shareholders or to the shareholders of one or more classes or series. An issuance of shares under this subsection is a share dividend.

(b) Shares of one class or series may not be issued as a share dividend in respect of shares of another class or series unless (1) the articles of incorporation so authorize, (2) a majority of the votes entitled to be cast by the class or series to be issued approve the issue, or (3) there are no outstanding shares of the class or series to be issued.

(c) If the board of directors does not fix the record date for determining shareholders entitled to a share dividend, it is the date the board of directors authorizes the share dividend.

§ 6.24. **Share Options**

A corporation may issue rights, options, or warrants for the purchase of shares of the corporation. The board of directors shall determine the terms upon which the rights, options, or warrants are issued, their form and content, and the consideration for which the shares are to be issued.

§ 6.25. **Form and Content of Certificates**

(a) Shares may but need not be represented by certificates. Unless this Act or another statute expressly provides otherwise, the rights and obligations of shareholders are identical whether or not their shares are represented by certificates.

(b) At a minimum each share certificate must state on its face:

(1) the name of the issuing corporation and that it is organized under the law of this state;

(2) the name of the person to whom issued; and

(3) the number and class of shares and the designation of the series, if any, the certificate represents.

(c) If the issuing corporation is authorized to issue different classes of shares or different series within a class, the designations, relative rights, preferences, and limitations applicable to each class and the variations in rights, preferences, and limitations determined for each series (and the authority of the board of directors to determine variations for future series) must be summarized on the front or back of each certificate. Alternatively, each certificate may state conspicuously on its front or back that the corporation will furnish the shareholder this information on request in writing and without charge.

(d) Each share certificate (1) must be signed (either manually or in facsimile) by two officers designated in the bylaws or by the board of directors and (2) may bear the corporate seal or its facsimile.

(e) If the person who signed (either manually or in facsimile) a share certificate no longer holds office when the certificate is issued, the certificate is nevertheless valid.

§ 6.26. Shares Without Certificates

(a) Unless the articles of incorporation or bylaws provide otherwise, the board of directors of a corporation may authorize the issue of some or all of the shares of any or all of its classes or series without certificates. The authorization does not affect shares already represented by certificates until they are surrendered to the corporation.

(b) Within a reasonable time after the issue or transfer of shares without certificates, the corporation shall send the shareholder a written statement of the information required on certificates by section 6.25(b) and (c), and, if applicable, section 6.27.

§ 6.27. Restriction on Transfer of Shares and Other Securities

(a) The articles of incorporation, bylaws, an agreement among shareholders, or an agreement between shareholders and the corporation may impose restrictions on the transfer or registration of transfer of shares of the corporation. A restriction does not affect shares issued before the restriction was adopted unless the holders of the shares are parties to the restriction agreement or voted in favor of the restriction.

(b) A restriction on the transfer or registration of transfer of shares is valid and enforceable against the holder or a transferee of the holder if the restriction is authorized by this section and its existence is noted conspicuously on the front or back of the certificate or is contained in the information

statement required by section 6.26(b). Unless so noted, a restriction is not enforceable against a person without knowledge of the restriction.

(c) A restriction on the transfer or registration of transfer of shares is authorized:

(1) to maintain the corporation's status when it is dependent on the number or identity of its shareholders;

(2) to preserve exemptions under federal or state securities law;

(3) for any other reasonable purpose.

(d) A restriction on the transfer or registration of transfer of shares may:

(1) obligate the shareholder first to offer the corporation or other persons (separately, consecutively, or simultaneously) an opportunity to acquire the restricted shares;

(2) obligate the corporation or other persons (separately, consecutively, or simultaneously) to acquire the restricted shares;

(3) require the corporation, the holders of any class of its shares, or another person to approve the transfer of the restricted shares, if the requirement is not manifestly unreasonable;

(4) prohibit the transfer of the restricted shares to designated persons or classes of persons, if the prohibition is not manifestly unreasonable.

(e) For purposes of this section, "shares" includes a security convertible into or carrying a right to subscribe for or acquire shares.

§ 6.28. Expense of Issue

A corporation may pay the expenses of selling or underwriting its shares, and of organizing or reorganizing the corporation, from the consideration received for shares.

Subchapter C. Subsequent Acquisition of Shares by Shareholders and Corporation

§ 6.30. Shareholders' Preemptive Rights

(a) The shareholders of a corporation do not have a preemptive right to acquire the corporation's unissued shares except to the extent the articles of incorporation so provide.

(b) A statement included in the articles of incorporation that "the corporation elects to have preemptive rights" (or words of similar import) means that the following principles apply except to the extent the articles of incorporation expressly provide otherwise:

(1) The shareholders of the corporation have a preemptive right, granted on uniform terms and conditions prescribed by the board of directors to provide a fair and reasonable opportunity to exercise the right, to acquire proportional amounts of the corporation's unissued shares upon the decision of the board of directors to issue them.

(2) A shareholder may waive his preemptive right. A waiver evidenced by a writing is irrevocable even though it is not supported by consideration.

(3) There is no preemptive right with respect to:

(i) shares issued as compensation to directors, officers, agents, or employees of the corporation, its subsidiaries or affiliates;

(ii) shares issued to satisfy conversion or option rights created to provide compensation to directors, officers, agents, or employees of the corporation, its subsidiaries or affiliates;

(iii) shares authorized in articles of incorporation that are issued within six months from the effective date of incorporation;

(iv) shares sold otherwise than for money.

(4) Holders of shares of any class without general voting rights but with preferential rights to distributions or assets have no preemptive rights with respect to shares of any class.

(5) Holders of shares of any class with general voting rights but without preferential rights to distributions or assets have no preemptive rights with respect to shares of any class with preferential rights to distributions or assets unless the shares with preferential rights are convertible into or carry a right to subscribe for or acquire shares without preferential rights.

(6) Shares subject to preemptive rights that are not acquired by shareholders may be issued to any person for a period of one year after being offered to shareholders at a consideration set by the board of directors that is not lower than the consideration set for the exercise of preemptive rights. An offer at a lower consideration or after the expiration of one year is subject to the shareholders' preemptive rights.

(c) For purposes of this section, "shares" includes a security convertible into or carrying a right to subscribe for or acquire shares.

§ 6.31. Corporation's Acquisition of Its Own Shares

(a) A corporation may acquire its own shares and shares so acquired constitute authorized but unissued shares.

(b) If the articles of incorporation prohibit the reissue of acquired shares, the number of authorized shares is reduced by the number of shares acquired, effective upon amendment of the articles of incorporation.

(c) Articles of amendment may be adopted by the board of directors without shareholder action, shall be delivered to the secretary of state for filing and shall set forth:

(1) the name of the corporation;

(2) the reduction in the number of authorized shares, itemized by class and series; and

(3) the total number of authorized shares, itemized by class and series, remaining after reduction of the shares.

Subchapter D.   Distributions

§ 6.40.   Distributions to Shareholders

(a) A board of directors may authorize and the corporation may make distributions to its shareholders subject to restriction by the articles of incorporation and the limitation in subsection (c).

(b) If the board of directors does not fix the record date for determining shareholders entitled to a distribution (other than one involving a purchase, redemption, or other acquisition of the corporation's shares) it is the date the board of directors authorizes the distribution.

(c) No distribution may be made if, after giving it effect:

(1) the corporation would not be able to pay its debts as they become due in the usual course of business; or

(2) the corporation's total assets would be less than the sum of its total liabilities plus (unless the articles of incorporation permit otherwise) the amount that would be needed, if the corporation were to be dissolved at the time of the distribution, to satisfy the preferential rights upon dissolution of shareholders whose preferential rights are superior to those receiving the distribution.

(d) The board of directors may base a determination that a distribution is not prohibited under subsection (c) either on financial statements prepared on the basis of accounting practices and principles that are reasonable in the circumstances or on a fair valuation or other method that is reasonable in the circumstances.

(e) Except as provided in subsection (g), the effect of a distribution under subsection (c) is measured:

(1) in the case of distribution by purchase, redemption, or other acquisition of the corporation's shares, as of the earlier of (i) the date money or other property is transferred or debt incurred by the corporation or (ii) the date the shareholder ceases to be a shareholder with respect to the acquired shares;

(2) in the case of any other distribution of indebtedness, as of the date the indebtedness is distributed; and

(3) in all other cases, as of (i) the date the distribution is authorized if the payment occurs within 120 days after the date of authorization or (ii) the date the payment is made if it occurs more than 120 days after the date of authorization.

(f) A corporation's indebtedness to a shareholder incurred by reason of a distribution made in accordance with this section is at parity with the corporation's indebtedness to its general, unsecured creditors except to the extent subordinated by agreement.

(g) Indebtedness of a corporation, including indebtedness issued as a distribution, is not considered a liability for purposes of determinations under subsection (c) if its terms provide that payment of principal and interest are made only if and to the extent that payment of a distribution to shareholders could then be made under this section. If the indebtedness is issued as a distribution, each payment of principal or interest is treated as a distribution, the effect of which is measured on the date the payment is actually made.

Chapter 7.   Shareholders

Subchapter A.   Meetings

§ 7.01.   Annual Meeting

(a) A corporation shall hold annually at a time stated in or fixed in accordance with the bylaws a meeting of shareholders.

(b) Annual shareholders' meetings may be held in or out of this state at the place stated in or fixed in accordance with the bylaws. If no place is stated in or fixed in accordance with the bylaws, annual meetings shall be held at the corporation's principal office.

(c) The failure to hold an annual meeting at the time stated in or fixed in accordance with a corporation's bylaws does not affect the validity of any corporate action.

§ 7.02.   Special Meeting

(a) A corporation shall hold a special meeting of shareholders:

(1) on call of its board of directors or the person or persons authorized to do so by the articles of incorporation or bylaws; or

(2) if the holders of at least 10 percent of all the votes entitled to be cast on any issue proposed to be considered at the proposed special meeting sign, date, and deliver to the corporation's secretary one or more written demands for the meeting describing the purpose or purposes for which it is to be held.

(b) If not otherwise fixed under sections 7.03 or 7.07, the record date for determining shareholders entitled to demand a special meeting is the date the first shareholder signs the demand.

(c) Special shareholders' meetings may be held in or out of this state at the place stated in or fixed in accordance with the bylaws. If no place is stated or fixed in accordance with the bylaws, special meetings shall be held at the corporation's principal office.

(d) Only business within the purpose or purposes described in the meeting notice required by section 7.05(c) may be conducted at a special shareholders' meeting.

§ 7.03.   Court-Ordered Meeting

(a) The [name or describe] court of the county where a corporation's principal office (or, if none in this state, its registered office) is located may summarily order a meeting to be held:

(1) on application of any shareholder of the corporation entitled to participate in an annual meeting if an annual meeting was not held within the earlier of 6 months after the end of the corporation's fiscal year or 15 months after its last annual meeting; or

(2) on application of a shareholder who signed a demand for a special meeting valid under section 7.02 if:

(i) notice of the special meeting was not given within 30 days after the date the demand was delivered to the corporation's secretary; or

(ii) the special meeting was not held in accordance with the notice.

(b) The court may fix the time and place of the meeting, determine the shares entitled to participate in the meeting, specify a record date for determining shareholders entitled to notice of and to vote at the meeting, prescribe the form and content of the meeting notice, fix the quorum required for specific matters to be considered at the meeting (or direct that the votes represented at the meeting constitute a quorum for action on those matters), and enter other orders necessary to accomplish the purpose or purposes of the meeting.

§ 7.04.   Action Without Meeting

(a) Action required or permitted by this Act to be taken at a shareholders' meeting may be taken without a meeting if the action is taken by all the shareholders entitled to vote on the action. The action must be evidenced by one or more written consents describing the action taken, signed by all the shareholders entitled to vote on the action, and delivered to the corporation for inclusion in the minutes or filing with the corporate records.

(b) If not otherwise determined under sections 7.03 or 7.07, the record date for determining shareholders entitled to take action without a meeting is the date the first shareholder signs the consent under subsection (a).

(c) A consent signed under this section has the effect of a meeting vote and may be described as such in any document.

(d) If this Act requires that notice of proposed action be given to nonvoting shareholders and the action is to be taken by unanimous consent of the voting shareholders, the corporation must give its nonvoting shareholders written notice of the proposed action at least 10 days before the action is taken. The notice must contain or be accompanied by the same material that, under this Act, would have been required to be sent to nonvoting shareholders in a notice of meeting at which the proposed action would have been submitted to the shareholders for action.

§ 7.05.   Notice of Meeting

(a) A corporation shall notify shareholders of the date, time, and place of each annual and special shareholders' meeting no fewer than 10 nor more than 60 days before the meeting date. Unless this Act or the articles of incorporation require otherwise, the corporation is required to give notice only to shareholders entitled to vote at the meeting.

(b) Unless this Act or the articles of incorporation require otherwise, notice of an annual meeting need not include a description of the purpose or purposes for which the meeting is called.

(c) Notice of a special meeting must include a description of the purpose or purposes for which the meeting is called.

(d) If not otherwise fixed under sections 7.03 or 7.07, the record date for determining shareholders entitled to notice of and to vote at an annual or special shareholders' meeting is the day before the first notice is delivered to shareholders.

(e) Unless the bylaws require otherwise, if an annual or special shareholders' meeting is adjourned to a different date, time, or place, notice need not be given of the new date, time, or place if the new date, time, or place is announced at the meeting before adjournment. If a new record date for the adjourned meeting is or must be fixed under section 7.07, however, notice of the adjourned meeting must be given under this section to persons who are shareholders as of the new record date.

§ 7.06.   Waiver of Notice

(a) A shareholder may waive any notice required by this Act, the articles of incorporation, or bylaws before or after the date and time stated in the notice. The waiver must be in writing, be signed by the shareholder entitled to the notice, and be delivered to the corporation for inclusion in the minutes or filing with the corporate records.

(b) A shareholders' attendance at a meeting.

(1) waives objection to lack of notice or defective notice of the meeting, unless the shareholder at the beginning of the meeting objects to holding the meeting or transacting business at the meeting.

(2) waives objection to consideration of a particular matter at the meeting that is not within the purpose or purposes described in the meeting notice, unless the shareholder objects to considering the matter when it is presented.

§ 7.07.   Record Date

(a) The bylaws may fix or provide the manner of fixing the record date for one or more voting groups in order to determine the shareholders entitled to notice of a shareholders' meeting, to demand a special meeting, to vote, or to take any other action. If the bylaws do not fix or provide for fixing a record date, the board of directors of the corporation may fix a future date as the record date.

(b) A record date fixed under this section may not be more than 70 days before the meeting or action requiring a determination of shareholders.

(c) A determination of shareholders entitled to notice of or to vote at a shareholders' meeting is effective for any adjournment of the meeting unless the board of directors fixes a new record date, which it must do if the meeting is adjourned to a date more than 120 days after the date fixed for the original meeting.

(d) If a court orders a meeting adjourned to a date more than 120 days after the date fixed for the original meeting, it may provide that the original record date continues in effect or it may fix a new record date.

Subchapter B.   Voting

§ 7.20.   Shareholders' List for Meeting

(a) After fixing a record date for a meeting, a corporation shall prepare an alphabetical list of the names of all its shareholders who are entitled to notice of a shareholders' meeting. The list must be arranged by voting group (and within each voting group by class or series of shares) and show the address of and number of shares held by each shareholder.

(b) The shareholders' list must be available for inspection by any shareholder, beginning two business days after notice of the meeting is given for which the list was prepared and continuing through the meeting, at the corporation's principal office or at a place identified in the meeting notice in the city where the meeting will be held. A shareholder, his agent, or attorney is entitled on written demand to inspect and, subject to the requirements of section 16.02(c), to copy the list, during regular business hours and at his expense, during the period it is available for inspection.

(c) The corporation shall make the shareholders' list available at the meeting, and any shareholder, his agent, or attorney is entitled to inspect the list at any time during the meeting or any adjournment.

(d) If the corporation refuses to allow a shareholder, his agent, or attorney to inspect the shareholders' list before or at the meeting (or copy the list as permitted by subsection (b)), the [name or describe] court of the county where a corporation's principal office (or, if none in this state, its registered office) is located, on application of the shareholder, may summarily order the inspection or copying at the corporation's expense and may postpone the meeting for which the list was prepared until the inspection or copying is complete.

(e) Refusal or failure to prepare or make available the shareholders' list does not affect the validity of action taken at the meeting.

§ 7.21.   Voting Entitlement of Shares

(a) Except as provided in subsections (b) and (c) or unless the articles of incorporation provide otherwise, each outstanding share, regardless of class, is entitled to one vote on each matter voted on at a shareholders' meeting. Only shares are entitled to vote.

(b) Absent special circumstances, the shares of a corporation are not entitled to vote if they are owned, directly or indirectly, by a second corporation, domestic or foreign, and the first corporation owns, directly or indirectly, a majority of the shares entitled to vote for directors of the second corporation.

(c) Subsection (b) does not limit the power of a corporation to vote any shares, including its own shares, held by it in a fiduciary capacity.

(d) Redeemable shares are not entitled to vote after notice of redemption is mailed to the holders and a sum sufficient to redeem the shares has been deposited with a bank, trust company, or other financial institution under an irrevocable obligation to pay the holders the redemption price on surrender of the shares.

§ 7.22. Proxies

(a) A shareholder may vote his shares in person or by proxy.

(b) A shareholder may appoint a proxy to vote or otherwise act for him by signing an appointment form, either personally or by his attorney-in-fact.

(c) An appointment of a proxy is effective when received by the secretary or other officer or agent authorized to tabulate votes. An appointment is valid for 11 months unless a longer period is expressly provided in the appointment form.

(d) An appointment of a proxy is revocable by the shareholder unless the appointment form conspicuously states that it is irrevocable and the appointment is coupled with an interest. Appointments coupled with an interest include the appointment of:

(1) a pledgee;

(2) a person who purchased or agreed to purchase the shares;

(3) a creditor of the corporation who extended it credit under terms requiring the appointment;

(4) an employee of the corporation whose employment contract requires the appointment; or

(5) a party to a voting agreement created under section 7.31.

(e) The death or incapacity of the shareholder appointing a proxy does not affect the right of the corporation to accept the proxy's authority unless notice of the death or incapacity is received by the secretary or other office or agent authorized to tabulate votes before the proxy exercises his authority under the appointment.

(f) An appointment made irrevocable under subsection (d) is revoked when the interest with which it is coupled is extinguished.

(g) A transferee for value of shares subject to an irrevocable appointment may revoke the appointment if he did not know of its existence when he acquired the shares and the existence of the irrevocable appointment was not noted conspicuously on the certificate representing the shares or on the information statement for shares without certificates.

(h) Subject to section 7.24 and to any express limitation on the proxy's authority appearing on the face of the appointment form, a corporation is entitled to accept the proxy's vote or other action as that of the shareholder making the appointment.

§ 7.23. Shares Held by Nominees

(a) A corporation may establish a procedure by which the beneficial owner of shares that are registered in the name of a nominee is recognized by the corporation as the shareholder. The extent of this recognition may be determined in the procedure.

(b) The procedure may set forth:

(1) the types of nominees to which it applies;

(2) the rights or privileges that the corporation recognizes in a beneficial owner;

(3) the manner in which the procedure is selected by the nominee;

(4) the information that must be provided when the procedure is selected;

(5) the period for which selection of the procedure is effective; and

(6) other aspects of the rights and duties created.

§ 7.24. Corporation's Acceptance of Votes

(a) If the name signed on a vote, consent, waiver, or proxy appointment corresponds to the name of a shareholder, the corporation if acting in good faith is entitled to accept the vote, consent, waiver, or proxy appointment and give it effect as the act of the shareholder.

(b) If the name signed on a vote, consent, waiver, or proxy appointment does not correspond to the name of its shareholder, the corporation if acting in good faith is nevertheless entitled to accept the vote, consent, waiver, or proxy appointment and give it effect as the act of the shareholder if:

(1) the shareholder is an entity and the name signed purports to be that of an officer or agent of the entity;

(2) the name signed purports to be that of an administrator, executor, guardian, or conservator representing the shareholder and, if the corporation requests, evidence of fiduciary status acceptable to the corporation has been presented with respect to the vote, consent, waiver, or proxy appointment.

(3) the name signed purports to be that of a receiver or trustee in bankruptcy of the shareholder and, if the corporation requests, evidence of this status acceptable to the corporation has been presented with respect to the vote, consent, waiver, or proxy appointment;

(4) the name signed purports to be that of a pledgee, beneficial owner, or attorney-in-fact of the shareholder and, if the corporation requests, evidence acceptable to the corporation of the signatory's authority to sign for the shareholder has been presented with respect to the vote, consent, waiver, or proxy appointment;

(5) two or more persons are the shareholder as cotenants or fiduciaries and the name signed purports to be the name of at least one of the coowners and the person signing appears to be acting on behalf of all the coowners.

(c) The corporation is entitled to reject a vote, consent, waiver, or proxy appointment if the secretary or other officer or agent authorized to tabulate votes, acting in good faith, has reasonable basis for doubt about the validity of the signature on it or about the signatory's authority to sign for the shareholder.

(d) The corporation and its officer or agent who accepts or rejects a vote, consent, waiver, or proxy appointment in good faith and in accordance with the standards of this section are not liable in damages to the shareholder for the consequences of the acceptance or rejection.

(e) Corporate action based on the acceptance or rejection of a vote, consent, waiver, or proxy appointment under this section is valid unless a court of competent jurisdiction determines otherwise.

§ 7.25.   Quorum and Voting Requirements for Voting Groups

(a) Shares entitled to vote as a separate voting group may take action on a matter at a meeting only if a quorum of those shares exists with respect to that matter. Unless the articles of incorporation or this Act provide otherwise, a majority of the votes entitled to be cast on the matter by the voting group constitutes a quorum of that voting group for action on that matter.

(b) Once a share is represented for any purpose at a meeting, it is deemed present for quorum purposes for the remainder of the meeting and for any adjournment of that meeting unless a new record date is or must be set for that adjourned meeting.

(c) If a quorum exists, action on a matter (other than the election of directors) by a voting group is approved if the votes cast within the voting group favoring the action exceed the votes cast opposing the action, unless the articles of incorporation or this Act require a greater number of affirmative votes.

(d) An amendment of articles of incorporation adding, changing, or deleting a quorum or voting requirement for a voting group greater than specified in subsection (b) or (c) is governed by section 7.27.

(e) The election of directors is governed by section 7.28.

§ 7.26.   Action by Single and Multiple Voting Groups

(a) If the articles of incorporation or this Act provide for voting by a single voting group on a matter, action on that matter is taken when voted upon by that voting group as provided in section 7.25.

(b) If the articles of incorporation or this Act provide for voting by two or more voting groups on a matter, action on that matter is taken only when voted upon by each of those voting groups counted separately as provided in section 7.25. Action may be taken by one voting group on a matter even though no action is taken by another voting group entitled to vote on the matter.

§ 7.27.   Greater Quorum or Voting Requirements

(a) The articles of incorporation may provide for a greater quorum or voting requirement for shareholders (or voting groups of shareholders) than is provided for by this Act.

(b) An amendment to the articles of incorporation that adds, changes, or deletes a greater quorum or voting requirement must meet the same quorum requirement and be adopted by the same vote and voting groups required to take action under the quorum and voting requirements then in effect or proposed to be adopted, whichever is greater.

§ 7.28.   Voting for Directors; Cumulative Voting

(a) Unless otherwise provided in the articles of incorporation, directors are elected by a plurality of the votes cast by the shares entitled to vote in the election at a meeting at which a quorum is present.

(b) Shareholders do not have a right to cumulate their votes for directors unless the articles of incorporation so provide.

(c) A statement included in the articles of incorporation that "[all] [a designated voting group of] shareholders are entitled to cumulate their votes for directors" (or words of similar import) means that the shareholders designated are entitled to multiply the number of votes they are entitled to cast by the number of directors for whom they are entitled to vote and cast the product for a single candidate or distribute the product among two or more candidates.

(d) Shares otherwise entitled to vote cumulatively may not be voted cumulatively at a particular meeting unless:

(1) the meeting notice or proxy statement accompanying the notice states conspicuously that cumulative voting is authorized; or

(2) a shareholder who has the right to cumulate his votes gives notice to the corporation not less than 48 hours before the time set for the meeting of his intent to cumulate his votes during the meeting, and if one shareholder gives this notice all other shareholders in the same voting group participating in the election are entitled to cumulate their votes without giving further notice.

Subchapter C.   Voting Trusts and Agreements

§ 7.30.   Voting Trusts

(a) One or more shareholders may create a voting trust, conferring on a trustee the right to vote or otherwise act for them, by signing an agreement setting out the provisions of the trust (which may include anything consistent with its purpose) and transferring their shares to the trustee. When a voting trust agreement is signed, the trustee shall prepare a list of the names and addresses of all owners of beneficial interests in the trust, together with the number and class of shares each transferred to the trust, and deliver copies of the list and agreement to the corporation's principal office.

(b) A voting trust becomes effective on the date the first shares subject to the trust are registered in the trustee's name. A voting trust is valid for not more than 10 years after its effective date unless extended under subsection (c).

(c) All or some of the parties to a voting trust may extend it for additional terms of not more than 10 years each by signing an extension agreement and obtaining the voting trustee's written consent to the extension. An extension is valid for 10 years from the date the first shareholder signs the extension agreement. The voting trustee must deliver copies of the extension agreement and list of beneficial owners to the corporation's principal office. An extension agreement binds only those parties signing it.

§ 7.31. Voting Agreements

(a) Two or more shareholders may provide for the manner in which they will vote their shares by signing an agreement for that purpose. A voting agreement created under this section is not subject to the provisions of section 7.30.

(b) A voting agreement created under this section is specifically enforceable.

Subchapter D.   Derivative Proceedings

§ 7.40. Subchapter Definitions

In this subchapter:

(1) "Derivative proceeding" means a civil suit in the right of a domestic corporation or, to the extent provided in section 7.47, in the right of a foreign corporation.

(2) "Shareholder" includes a beneficial owner whose shares are held in a voting trust or held by a nominee on the beneficial owner's behalf.

§ 7.41. Standing

A shareholder may not commence or maintain a derivative proceeding unless the shareholder:

(1) was a shareholder of the corporation at the time of the act or omission complained of or became a shareholder through transfer by operation of law from one who was a shareholder at that time; and

(2) fairly and adequately represents the interests of the corporation in enforcing the right of the corporation.

§ 7.42. Demand

No shareholder may commence a derivative proceeding until:

(1) a written demand has been made upon the corporation to take suitable action; and

(2) 90 days have expired from the date the demand was made unless the shareholder has earlier been notified that the demand has been rejected by the corporation or unless irreparable injury to the corporation would result by waiting for the expiration of the 90 day period.

§ 7.43. Stay of Proceedings

If the corporation commences an inquiry into the allegations made in the demand or complaint, the court may stay any derivative proceeding for such period as the court deems appropriate.

§7.44. Dismissal

(a) A derivative proceeding shall be dismissed by the court on motion by the corporation if one of the groups specified in subsections (b) or (f) has determined in good faith after conducting a reasonable inquiry upon which its conclusions are based that the maintenance of the derivative proceeding is not in the best interests of the corporation.

(b) Unless a panel is appointed pursuant to subsection (f), the determination in subsection (a) shall be made by:

(1) a majority vote of independent directors present at a meeting of the board of directors if the independent directors constitute a quorum; or

(2) a majority vote of a committee consisting of two or more independent directors appointed by majority vote of independent directors present at a meeting of the board of directors, whether or not such independent directors constituted a quorum.

(c) None of the following shall by itself cause a director to be considered not independent for purposes of this section:

(1) the nomination or election of the director by persons who are defendants in the derivative proceeding or against whom action is demanded;

(2) the naming of the director as a defendant in the derivative proceeding or as a person against whom action is demanded; or

(3) the approval by the director of the act being challenged in the derivative proceeding or demand if the act resulted in no personal benefit to the director.

(d) If a derivative proceeding is commenced after a determination has been made rejecting a demand by a shareholder, the complaint shall allege with particularity facts establishing either (1) that a majority of the board of directors did not consist of independent directors at the time the determination was made or (2) that the requirements of subsection (a) have not been met.

(e) If a majority of the board of directors does not consist of independent directors at the time the determination is made, the corporation shall have the burden of proving that the requirements of subsection (a) have been met. If a majority of the board of directors consists of independent directors at the time the determination is made, the plaintiff shall have the burden of proving that the requirements of subsection (1) have not been met.

(f) The court may appoint a panel of one or more independent persons upon motion by the corporation to make a determination whether the maintenance of the derivative proceeding is in the best interests of the corporation. In such case, the plaintiff shall have the burden of proving that the requirements of subsection (a) have not been met.

§ 7.45 Discontinuance or Settlement

A derivative proceeding may not be discontinued or settled without the court's approval. If the court determines that a proposed discontinuance or settlement will substantially affect the interests of the corporation's shareholders or a class of shareholders, the court shall direct that notice be given to the shareholders affected.

§ 7.46 Payment of Expenses

On termination of the derivative proceeding the court may:

(1) order the corporation to pay the plaintiff's reasonable expenses (including counsel fees) incurred in the proceeding if it finds that the proceeding has resulted in a substantial benefit to the corporation;

(2) order the plaintiff to pay any defendant's reasonable expenses (including counsel fees) incurred in defending the proceeding if it finds that the proceeding was commenced or maintained without reasonable cause or for an improper purpose; or

(3) order a party to pay an opposing party's reasonable expenses (including counsel fees) incurred because of the filing of a pledging, motion or other paper, if it finds that the pleading, motion or other paper was not well grounded in fact, after reasonable inquiry, or warranted by existing law or a good faith argument for the extension, modification or reversal of existing law and was interposed for an improper purpose, such as to harass or to cause unnecessary delay or needless increase in the cost of litigation.

§ 7.47 Applicability to Foreign Corporations

In any derivative proceeding in the right of a foreign corporation, the matters covered by this subchapter shall be governed by the laws of the jurisdiction of incorporation of the foreign corporation except for sections 7.43, 7.45 and 7.46.

Chapter 8. Directors and Officers

Subchapter A. Board of Directors

§ 8.01. Requirement for and Duties of Board of Directors

(a) Except as provided in subsection (c), each corporation must have a board of directors.

(b) All corporate powers shall be exercised by or under the authority of, and the business and affairs of the corporation managed under the direction of, its board of directors, subject to any limitation set forth in the articles of incorporation.

(c) A corporation having 50 or fewer shareholders may dispense with or limit the authority of a board of directors by describing in its articles of incorporation who will perform some or all of the duties of a board of directors.

§ 8.02. Qualifications of Directors

The articles of incorporation or bylaws may prescribe qualifications for directors. A director need not be a resident of this state or a shareholder of the corporation unless the articles of incorporation or bylaws so prescribe.

§ 8.03. Number and Election of Directors

(a) A board of directors must consist of one or more individuals, with the number specified in or fixed in accordance with the articles of incorporation or bylaws.

(b) If a board of directors has power to fix or change the number of directors, the board may increase or decrease by 30 percent or less the number of directors last approved by the shareholders, but only the shareholders may increase or decrease by more than 30 percent the number of directors last approved by the shareholders.

(c) The articles of incorporation or bylaws may establish a variable range for the size of the board of directors by fixing a minimum and maximum number of directors. If a variable range is established, the number of directors may be fixed or changed from time to time, within the minimum and maximum, by the shareholders or the board of directors. After shares are issued, only the shareholders may change the range for the size of the board or change from a fixed to a variable-range size board or vice versa.

(d) Directors are elected at the first annual shareholders' meeting and at each annual meeting thereafter unless their terms are staggered under section 8.06.

§ 8.04. Election of Directors by Certain Classes of Shareholders

If the articles of incorporation authorize dividing the shares into classes, the articles may also authorize the election of all or a specified number of directors by the holders of one or more authorized classes of shares. Each class (or classes) of shares entitled to elect one or more directors is a separate voting group for purposes of the election of directors.

§ 8.05. Terms of Directors Generally

(a) The terms of the initial directors of a corporation expire at the first shareholders' meeting at which directors are elected.

(b) The terms of all other directors expire at the next annual shareholders' meeting following their election unless their terms are staggered under section 8.06.

(c) A decrease in the number of directors does not shorten an incumbent director's term.

(d) The term of a director elected to fill a vacancy expires at the next shareholders' meeting at which directors are elected.

(e) Despite the expiration of a director's term, he continues to serve until his successor is elected and qualifies or until there is a decrease in the number of directors.

§ 8.06. Staggered Terms for Directors

If there are nine or more directors, the articles of incorporation may provide for staggering their terms by dividing the total number of directors into two or three groups, with each group containing one half or one-third of the total, as near as may be. In that event, the terms of directors in the first group expire at the first annual shareholders' meeting after their election, the terms of the second group expire at the second annual shareholders' meeting after their election, and the terms of the third group, if any, expire at the third annual shareholders' meeting after their election. At each annual shareholders' meeting held thereafter, directors shall be chosen for a term of two years or three years, as the case may be, to succeed those whose terms expire.

§ 8.07. Resignation of Directors

(a) A director may resign at any time by delivering written notice to the board of directors, its chairman, or to the corporation.

(b) A resignation is effective when the notice is delivered unless the notice specifies a later effective date.

§ 8.08.   Removal of Directors by Shareholders

(a) The shareholders may remove one or more directors with or without cause unless the articles of incorporation provide that directors may be removed only for cause.

(b) If a director is elected by a voting group of shareholders, only the shareholders of that voting group may participate in the vote to remove him.

(c) If cumulative voting is authorized, a director may not be removed if the number of votes sufficient to elect him under cumulative voting is voted against his removal. If cumulative voting is not authorized, a director may be removed only if the number of votes cast to remove him exceeds the number of votes cast not to remove him.

(d) A director may be removed by the shareholders only at a meeting called for the purpose of removing him and the meeting notice must state that the purpose, or one of the purposes, of the meeting is removal of the director.

§ 8.09.   Removal of Directors by Judicial Proceeding

(a) The [name or describe] court of the county where a corporation's principal office (or, if none in this state, its registered office) is located may remove a director of the corporation from office in a proceeding commenced either by the corporation or by its shareholders holding at least 10 percent of the outstanding shares of any class if the court finds that (1) the director engaged in fraudulent or dishonest conduct, or gross abuse of authority or discretion, with respect to the corporation and (2) removal is in the best interest of the corporation.

(b) The court that removes a director may bar the director from reelection for a period prescribed by the court.

(c) If shareholders commence a proceeding under subsection (a), they shall make the corporation a party defendant.

§ 8.10.   Vacancy on Board

(a) Unless the articles of incorporation provide otherwise, if a vacancy occurs on a board of directors, including a vacancy resulting from an increase in the number of directors:

  (1) the shareholders may fill the vacancy;

  (2) the board of directors may fill the vacancy; or

  (3) if the directors remaining in office constitute fewer than a quorum of the board, they may fill the vacancy by the affirmative vote of a majority of all the directors remaining in office.

(b) If the vacant office was held by a director elected by a voting group of shareholders, only the holders of shares of that voting group are entitled to vote to fill the vacancy if it is filled by the shareholders.

(c) A vacancy that will occur at a specific later date (by reason of a resignation effective at a later date under section 8.07(b) or otherwise) may be filled before the vacancy occurs but the new director may not take office until the vacancy occurs.

§ 8.11.   Compensation of Directors

Unless the articles of incorporation or bylaws provide otherwise, the board of directors may fix the compensation of directors.

Subchapter B.   Meetings and Action of the Board

§ 8.20.   Meetings

(a) The board of directors may hold regular or special meetings in or out of this state.

(b) Unless the articles of incorporation or bylaws provide otherwise, the board of directors may permit any or all directors to participate in a regular or special meeting by, or conduct the meeting through the use of, any means of communication by which all directors participating may simultaneously hear each other during the meeting. A director participating in a meeting by this means is deemed to be present in person at the meeting.

§ 8.21.   Action Without Meeting

(a) Unless the articles of incorporation or bylaws provide otherwise, action required or permitted by this Act to be taken at a board of directors' meeting may be taken without a meeting if the action is taken by all members of the board. The action must be evidenced by one or more written consents describing the action taken, signed by each director, and included in the minutes or filed with the corporate records reflecting the action taken.

(b) Action taken under this section is effective when the last director signs the consent, unless the consent specifies a different effective date.

(c) A consent signed under this section has the effect of a meeting vote and may be described as such in any document.

§ 8.22.   Notice of Meeting

(a) Unless the articles of incorporation or bylaws provide otherwise, regular meetings of the board of directors may be held without notice of the date, time, place, or purpose of the meeting.

(b) Unless the articles of incorporation or bylaws provide for a longer or shorter period, special meetings of the board of directors must be preceded by at least two days' notice of the date, time, and place of the meeting. The notice need not describe the purpose of the special meeting unless required by the articles of incorporation or bylaws.

§ 8.23.   Waiver of Notice

(a) A director may waive any notice required by this Act, the articles of incorporation, or bylaws before or after the date and time stated in the notice. Except as provided by subsection (b), the waiver must be in writing, signed by the director entitled to the notice, and filed with the minutes or corporate records.

(b) A director's attendance at or participation in a meeting waives any required notice to him of the meeting unless the director at the beginning of the meeting (or promptly upon his arrival) objects to holding the meeting or transacting business at the meeting and does not thereafter vote for or assent to action taken at the meeting.

§ 8.24.   Quorum and Voting

(a) Unless the articles of incorporation or bylaws require a greater number, a quorum of a board of directors consists of:

(1) a majority of the fixed number of directors if the corporation has a fixed board size; or

(2) a majority of the number of directors prescribed, or if no number is prescribed the number in office immediately before the meeting begins, if the corporation has a variable-range size board.

(b) The articles of incorporation or bylaws may authorize a quorum of a board of directors to consist of no fewer than one-third of the fixed or prescribed number of directors determined under subsection (a).

(c) If a quorum is present when a vote is taken, the affirmative vote of a majority of directors present is the act of the board of directors unless the articles of incorporation or bylaws require the vote of a greater number of directors.

(d) A director who is present at a meeting of the board of directors or a committee of the board of directors when corporate action is taken is deemed to have assented to the action taken unless: (1) he objects at the beginning of the meeting (or promptly upon his arrival) to hold it or transacting business at the meeting; (2) his dissent or abstention from the action taken is entered in the minutes of the meeting; or (3) he delivers written notice of his dissent or abstention to the presiding officer of the meeting before its adjournment or to the corporation immediately after adjournment of the meeting. The right of dissent or abstention is not available to a director who votes in favor of the action taken.

§ 8.25.   Committees

(a) Unless the articles of incorporation or bylaws provide otherwise, a board of directors may create one or more committees and appoint members of the board of directors to serve on them. Each committee may have two or more members, who serve at the pleasure of the board of directors.

(b) The creation of a committee and appointment of members to it must be approved by the greater of (1) a majority of all the directors in office when the action is taken or (2) the number of directors required by the articles of incorporation or bylaws to take action under section 8.24.

(c) Sections 8.20 through 8.24, which govern meetings, action without meetings, notice and waiver of notice, and quorum and voting requirements of the board of directors, apply to committees and their members as well.

(d) To the extent specified by the board of directors or in the articles of incorporation or bylaws, each committee may exercise the authority of the board of directors under section 8.01.

(e) A committee may not, however:

(1) authorize distributions;

(2) approve or propose to shareholders action that this Act requires to be approved by shareholders;

(3) fill vacancies on the board of directors or on any of its committees;

(4) amend articles of incorporation pursuant to section 10.02;

(5) adopt, amend, or repeal bylaws;

(6) approve a plan of merger not requiring shareholder approval;

(7) authorize or approve reacquisition of shares, except according to a formula or method prescribed by the board of directors; or

(8) authorize or approve the issuance or sale or contract for sale of shares, or determine the designation and relative rights, preferences, and limitations of a class or series of shares, except that the board of directors may authorize a committee (or a senior executive officer of the corporation) to do so within limits specifically prescribed by the board of directors.

(f) The creation of, delegation of authority to, or action by a committee does not alone constitute compliance by a director with the standards of conduct described in section 8.30.

Subchapter C.   Standards of Conduct

§ 8.30.   General Standards for Directors

(a) A director shall discharge his duties as a director, including his duties as a member of a committee:

(1) in good faith;

(2) with the care an ordinarily prudent person in a like position would exercise under similar circumstances; and

(3) in a manner he reasonably believes to be in the best interests of the corporation.

(b) In discharging his duties a director is entitled to rely on information, opinions, reports, or statements, including financial statements and other financial data, if prepared or presented by:

(1) one or more officers or employees of the corporation whom the director reasonably believes to be reliable and competent in the matters presented;

(2) legal counsel, public accountants, or other persons as to matters the director reasonably believes are within the person's professional or expert competence; or

(3) a committee of the board of directors of which he is not a member if the director reasonably believes the committee merits confidence.

(c) A director is not acting in good faith if he has knowledge concerning the matter in question that makes reliance otherwise permitted by subsection (b) unwarranted.

(d) A director is not liable for any action taken as a director, or any failure to take any action, if he performed the duties of his office in compliance with this section.

§ 8.31. Director Conflict of Interest

(a) A conflict of interest transaction is a transaction with the corporation in which a director of the corporation has a direct or indirect interest. A conflict of interest transaction is not voidable by the corporation solely because of the director's interest in the transaction if any one of the following is true:

(1) the material facts of the transaction and the director's interest were disclosed or known to the board of directors or a committee of the board of directors and the board of directors or committee authorized, approved, or ratified the transaction;

(2) the material facts of the transaction and the director's interest were disclosed or known to the shareholders entitled to vote and they authorized, approved, or ratified the transaction; or

(3) the transaction was fair to the corporation.

(b) For purposes of this section, a director of the corporation has an indirect interest in a transaction if (1) another entity in which he has a material financial interest or in which he is a general partner is a party to the transaction or (2) another entity of which he is a director, officer, or trustee is a party to the transaction and the transaction is or should be considered by the board of directors of the corporation.

(c) For purposes of subsection (a)(1), a conflict of interest transaction is authorized, approved, or ratified if it receives the affirmative vote of a majority of the directors on the board of directors (or on the committee) who have no direct or indirect interest in the transaction, but a transaction may not be authorized, approved, or ratified under this section by a single director. If a majority of the directors who have no direct or indirect interest in the transaction vote to authorize, approve, or ratify the transaction, a quorum is present for the purpose of taking action under this section. The presence of, or a vote cast by, a director with a direct or indirect interest in the transaction does not affect the validity of any action taken under subsection (a)(1) if the transaction is otherwise authorized, approved, or ratified as provided in that subsection.

(d) For purposes of subsection (a)(2), a conflict of interest transaction is authorized, approved, or ratified if it receives the vote of a majority of the shares entitled to be counted under this subsection. Shares owned by or voted under the control of a director who has a direct or indirect interest in the transaction, and shares owned by or voted under the control of an entity described in subsection (b)(1), may not be counted in a vote of shareholders to determine whether to authorize, approve, or ratify a conflict of interest transaction under subsection (a)(2). The vote of those shares, however, shall be counted in determining whether the transaction is approved under other sections of this Act. A majority of the shares, whether or not present, that are entitled to be counted in a vote on

the transaction under this subsection constitutes a quorum for the purpose of taking action under this section.

[The drafters of the Revised Model Business Corporation Act have proposed deleting § 8.31 and substituting for it proposed §§ 8.60, 8.61, 8.62, and 8.63, which appear later in this appendix.]

§ 8.32. Loans to Directors

(a) Except as provided by subsection (c), a corporation may not lend money to or guarantee the obligation of a director of the corporation unless:

(1) the particular loan or guarantee is approved by a majority of the votes represented by the outstanding voting shares of all classes, voting as a single voting group, except the votes of shares owned by or voted under the control of the benefited director; or

(2) the corporation's board of directors determines that the loan or guarantee benefits the corporation and either approves the specific loan or guarantee or a general plan authorizing loans and guarantees.

(b) The fact that a loan or guarantee is made in violation of this section does not affect the borrower's liability on the loan.

(c) This section does not apply to loans and guarantees authorized by statute regulating any special class of corporations.

§ 8.33. Liability for Unlawful Distributions

(a) A director who votes for or assents to a distribution made in violation of section 6.40 or the articles of incorporation is personally liable to the corporation for the amount of the distribution that exceeds what could have been distributed without violating section 6.40 or the articles of incorporation if it is established that he did not perform his duties in compliance with section 8.30. In any proceeding commenced under this section, a director has all of the defenses ordinarily available to a director.

(b) A director held liable under subsection (a) for an unlawful distribution is entitled to contribution:

(1) from every other director who could be held liable under subsection (a) for the unlawful distribution; or

(2) from each shareholder for the amount the shareholder accepted knowing the distribution was made in violation of section 6.40 or the articles of incorporation.

(c) A proceeding under this section is barred unless it is commenced within two years after the date on which the effect of the distribution was measured under section 6.40(e) or (g).

Subchapter D. Officers

§ 8.40. Required Officers

(a) A corporation has the officers described in its bylaws or appointed by the board of directors in accordance with the bylaws.

(b) A duly appointed officer may appoint one or more officers or assistant officers if authorized by the bylaws or the board of directors.

(c) The bylaws or the board of directors shall delegate to one of the officers responsibility for preparing minutes of the directors' and shareholders' meetings and for authenticating records of the corporation.

(d) The same individual may simultaneously hold more than one office in a corporation.

§ 8.41.   Duties of Officers

Each officer has the authority and shall perform the duties set forth in the bylaws or, to the extent consistent with the bylaws, the duties prescribed by the board of directors or by direction of an officer authorized by the board of directors to prescribe the duties of other officers.

§ 8.42.   Standards of Conduct for Officers

(a) An officer with discretionary authority shall discharge his duties under that authority:

(1) in good faith;

(2) with the care an ordinarily prudent person in a like position would exercise under similar circumstances; and

(3) in a manner he reasonably believes to be in the best interests of the corporation.

(b) In discharging his duties an officer is entitled to rely on information, opinions, reports, or statements, including financial statements and other financial data, if prepared or presented by:

(1) one or more officers or employees of the corporation whom the officer reasonably believes to be reliable and competent in the matters presented; or

(2) legal counsel, public accountants, or other persons as to matters the officer reasonably believes are within the person's professional or expert competence.

(c) An officer is not acting in good faith if he has knowledge concerning the matter in question that makes reliance otherwise permitted by subsection (b) unwarranted.

(d) An officer is not liable for any action taken as an officer, or any failure to take any action, if he performed the duties of his office in compliance with this section.

§ 8.43.   Resignation and Removal of Officers

(a) An officer may resign at any time by delivering notice to the corporation. A resignation is effective when the notice is delivered unless the notice specifies a later effective date. If a resignation is made effective at a later date and the corporation accepts the future effective date, its board of directors may fill the pending vacancy before the effective date if the board of directors provides that the successor does not take office until the effective date.

(b) A board of directors may remove any officer at any time with or without cause.

§ 8.44.   Contract Rights of Officers

(a) The appointment of an officer does not itself create contract rights.

(b) An officer's removal does not affect the officer's contract rights, if any, with the corporation. An officer's resignation does not affect the corporation's contract rights, if any, with the officer.

Subchapter E.   Indemnification

§ 8.50.   Subchapter Definitions

In this subchapter:

(1) "Corporation" includes any domestic or foreign predecessor entity of a corporation in a merger or other transaction in which the predecessor's existence ceased upon consummation of the transaction.

(2) "Director" means an individual who is or was a director of a corporation or an individual who, while a director of a corporation, is or was serving at the corporation's request as a director, officer, partner, trustee, employee, or agent of another foreign or domestic corporation, partnership, joint venture, trust, employee benefit plan, or other enterprise. A director is considered to be serving an employee benefit plan at the corporation's request if his duties to the corporation also impose duties on, or otherwise involve services by, him to the plan or to participants in or beneficiaries of the plan. "Director" includes, unless the context requires otherwise, the estate or personal representative of a director.

(3) "Expenses" include counsel fees.

(4) "Liability" means the obligation to pay a judgment, settlement, penalty, fine (including an excise tax assessed with respect to an employee benefit plan), or reasonable expenses incurred with respect to a proceeding.

(5) "Official capacity" means: (i) when used with respect to a director, the office of director in a corporation; and (ii) when used with respect to an individual other than a director, as contemplated in section 8.56, the office in a corporation held by the officer or the employment or agency relationship undertaken by the employee or agent on behalf of the corporation. "Official capacity" does not include service for any other foreign or domestic corporation or any partnership, joint venture, trust, employee benefit plan, or other enterprise.

(6) "Party" includes an individual who was, is, or is threatened to be made a named defendant or respondent in a proceeding.

(7) "Proceeding" means any threatened, pending, or completed action, suit, or proceeding, whether civil, criminal, administrative, or investigative and whether formal or informal.

§ 8.51.   Authority to Indemnify

(a) Except as provided in subsection (d), a corporation may indemnify an individual made a party to a proceeding because he is or was a director against liability incurred in the proceeding if:

  (1) he conducted himself in good faith; and

  (2) he reasonably believed:

    (i) in the case of conduct in his official capacity with the corporation, that his conduct was in its best interest; and

    (ii) in all other cases, that his conduct was at least not opposed to its best interests; and

  (3) in the case of any criminal proceeding, he had no reasonable cause to believe his conduct was unlawful.

(b) A director's conduct with respect to an employee benefit plan for a purpose he reasonably believed to be in the interests of the participants in and beneficiaries of the plan is conduct that satisfies the requirement of subsection (a)(2)(ii).

(c) The termination of a proceeding by judgment, order, settlement, conviction, or upon a plea of nolo contendere or its equivalent is not, of itself, determinative that the director did not meet the standard of conduct described in this section.

(d) A corporation may not indemnify a director under this section:

  (1) in connection with a proceeding by or in the right of the corporation in which the director was adjudged liable to the corporation; or

  (2) in connection with any other proceeding charging improper personal benefit to him, whether or not involving action in his official capacity, in which he was adjudged liable on the basis that personal benefit was improperly received by him.

(e) Indemnification permitted under this section in connection with a proceeding by or in the right of the corporation is limited to reasonable expenses incurred in connection with the proceeding.

§ 8.52. Mandatory Indemnification

Unless limited by its articles of incorporation, a corporation shall indemnify a director who was wholly successful, on the merits or otherwise, in the defense of any proceeding to which he was a party because he is or was a director of the corporation against reasonable expenses incurred by him in connection with the proceeding.

§ 8.53. Advance for Expenses

(a) A corporation may pay for or reimburse the reasonable expenses incurred by a director who is a party to a proceeding in advance of final disposition of the proceeding if:

  (1) the director furnishes the corporation a written affirmation of his good faith belief that he has met the standard of conduct described in section 8.51;

  (2) the director furnishes the corporation a written undertaking, executed personally or on his behalf, to repay the advance if it is ultimately determined that he did not meet the standard of conduct; and

  (3) a determination is made that the facts then known to those making the determination would not preclude indemnification under this subchapter.

(b) The undertaking required by subsection (a)(2) must be an unlimited general obligation of the director but need not be secured and may be accepted without reference to financial ability to make repayment.

(c) Determinations and authorizations of payments under this section shall be made in the manner specified in section 8.55.

§ 8.54. Court-Ordered Indemnification

Unless a corporation's articles of incorporation provide otherwise, a director of the corporation who is a party to a proceeding may apply for indemnification to the court conducting the proceeding or to another court of competent jurisdiction. On receipt of an application, the court after giving any notice the court considers necessary may order indemnification if it determines:

  (1) the director is entitled to mandatory indemnification under section 8.52, in which case the court shall also order the corporation to pay the director's reasonable expenses incurred to obtain court-ordered indemnification; or

  (2) the director is fairly and reasonably entitled to indemnification in view of all the relevant circumstances, whether or not he met the standard of conduct set forth in section 8.51 or was adjudged liable as described in section 8.51(d), but if he was adjudged so liable his indemnification is limited to reasonable expenses incurred.

§ 8.55. Determination and Authorization of Indemnification

(a) A corporation may not indemnify a director under section 8.51 unless authorized in the specific case after a determination has been made that indemnification of the director is permissible in the circumstances because he has met the standard of conduct set forth in section 8.51.

(b) The determination shall be made:

  (1) by the board of directors by majority vote of a quorum consisting of directors not at the time parties to the proceeding;

  (2) if a quorum cannot be obtained under subdivision (1), by majority vote of a committee duly designated by the board of directors (in which designation directors who are parties may participate), consisting solely of two or more directors not at the time parties to the proceeding;

  (3) by special legal counsel:

    (i) selected by the board of directors or its committee in the manner prescribed in subdivision (1) or (2); or

    (ii) if a quorum of the board of directors cannot be obtained under subdivision (1) and a committee cannot be designated under subdivision (2), selected by majority vote of the full board of directors (in which selection directors who are parties may participate); or

  (4) by the shareholders, but shares owned by or voted under the control of directors who are at the time parties to the proceeding may not be voted on the determination.

(c) Authorization of indemnification and evaluation as to reasonableness of expenses shall be made in the same manner as the determination that indemnification is permissible, except that if the determination is made by special legal counsel, authorization of indemnification and evaluation as to reasonableness of expenses shall be made by those entitled under subsection (b)(3) to select counsel.

§ 8.56. Indemnification of Officers, Employees, and Agents

Unless a corporation's articles of incorporation provide otherwise:

(1) an officer of the corporation who is not a director is entitled to mandatory indemnification under section 8.52, and is entitled to apply for court-ordered indemnification under section 8.54, in each case to the same extent as a director;

(2) the corporation may indemnify and advance expenses under this subchapter to an officer, employee, or agent of the corporation who is not a director to the same extent as to a director; and

(3) a corporation may also indemnify and advance expenses to an officer, employee, or agent who is not a director to the extent, consistent with public policy, that may be provided by its articles of incorporation, bylaws, general or specific action of its board of directors, or contract.

§ 8.57. Insurance

A corporation may purchase and maintain insurance on behalf of an individual who is or was a director, officer, employee, or agent of the corporation, or who, while a director, officer, employee, or agent of the corporation, is or was serving at the request of the corporation as a director, officer, partner, trustee, employee, or agent of another foreign or domestic corporation, partnership, joint venture, trustee, employee benefit plan, or other enterprise, against liability asserted against or incurred by him in that capacity or arising from his status as a director, officer, employee, or agent, whether or not the corporation would have power to indemnify him against the same liability under section 8.51 or 8.52.

§ 8.58. Application of Subchapter

(a) A provision treating a corporation's indemnification of or advance for expenses to directors that is contained in its articles of incorporation, bylaws, a resolution of its shareholders or board of directors, or in a contract or otherwise, is valid only if and to the extent the provision is consistent with this subchapter. If articles of incorporation limit indemnification or advance for expenses, indemnification and advance for expenses are valid only to the extent consistent with the articles.

(b) This subchapter does not limit a corporation's power to pay or reimburse expenses incurred by a director in connection with his appearance as a witness in a proceeding at a time when he has not been made a named defendant or respondent to the proceeding.

[The drafters of the MBCA have proposed the following Subchapter F (§§ 8.60, 8.61, 8.62, and 8.63) as a substitution for § 8.31.]

Proposed Subchapter F. Director's Conflicting Interest Transactions

Proposed § 8.60. Subchapter Definitions

In this subchapter:

(1) "Conflicting interest" with respect to a corporation means the interest a director of the corporation has respecting a transaction effected or proposed to be effected by the corporation (or by a subsidiary of the corporation or any other entity in which the corporation has a controlling interest) if:

(i) whether or not the transaction is brought before the board of directors of the corporation for action, the director knows at the time of commitment that he or a related person is a party to the transaction or has a beneficial financial interest in or so closely linked to the transaction and of such financial significance to the director or a related person that the interest would reasonably be expected to exert an influence on the director's judgment if he were called upon to vote on the transaction; or

(ii) the transaction is brought (or is of such character and significance to the corporation that it would in the normal course be brought) before the board of directors of the corporation for action, and the director knows at the time of commitment that any of the following persons is either a party to the transaction or has a beneficial financial interest in or so closely linked to the transaction and of such financial significance to the person that the interest would reasonably be expected to exert an influence on the director's judgment if he were called upon to vote on the transaction: (A) an entity (other than the corporation) of which the director is a director, general partner, agent, or employee; (B) an entity that controls, is controlled by, or is under common control with one or more of the entities specified in subclause (A); or (C) an individual who is a general partner, principal, or employer of the director.

(2) "Director's conflicting interest transaction" with respect to a corporation means a transaction effected or proposed to be effected by the corporation (or by a subsidiary of the corporation or any other entity in which the corporation has a controlling interest) respecting which a director of the corporation has a conflicting interest.

(3) "Related person" of a director means (i) a child, grandchild, sibling, parent, or spouse of, or an individual occupying the same household as, the director, or a trust or estate of which an individual specified in this clause (i) is a substantial beneficiary; or (ii) a trust, estate, incompetent, conservatee, or minor of which the director is a fiduciary.

(4) "Required disclosure" means disclosure by the director who has a conflicting interest of (i) the existence and nature of his conflicting interest, and (ii) all facts known to him respecting the subject matter of the transaction that an ordinarily

prudent person would reasonably believe to be material to a judgment about whether or not to proceed with the transaction.

(5) "Time of commitment" respecting a transaction means the time when the transaction is consummated or, if made pursuant to contract, the time when the corporation (or its subsidiary or the entity in which it has a controlling interest) becomes contractually obligated so that its unilateral withdrawal from the transaction would entail significant loss, liability, or other damage.

Proposed § 8.61. Judicial Action

(a) A transaction effected or proposed to be effected by a corporation (or by a subsidiary of the corporation or any other entity in which the corporation has a controlling interest) that is not a director's conflicting interest transaction may not be enjoined, set aside, or give rise to an award of damages or other sanctions, in a proceeding by a shareholder or by or in the right of the corporation, because a director of the corporation, or any person with whom or which he has a personal, economic, or other association, has an interest in the transaction.

(b) A director's conflicting interest transaction may not be enjoined, set aside, or give rise to an award of damages or other sanctions, in a proceeding by a shareholder or by or in the right of the corporation, because the director, or any person with whom or which he has a personal, economic, or other association, has an interest in the transaction, if:

(1) directors' action respecting the transaction was at any time taken in compliance with section 8.62;

(2) shareholders' action respecting the transaction was at any time taken in compliance with section 8.63;

(3) the transaction, judged according to the circumstances at the time of commitment, is established to have been fair to the corporation; or

(4) the transaction pertained to the compensation, or the reimbursement of expenses, of one or more directors unless the transaction, judged according to the circumstances at the time of commitment, is established to have been unfair to the corporation.

Proposed § 8.62. Directors' Action

(a) Directors' action respecting a transaction is effective for purposes of section 8.61(b)(1) if the transaction received the affirmative vote of a majority (but no fewer than two) of those qualified directors on the board of directors or on a duly empowered committee of the board who voted on the transaction after either required disclosure to them (to the extent the information was not known by them) or compliance with subsection (b).

(b) If a director has a conflicting interest respecting a transaction, but neither he nor a related person of the director specified in section 8.60(3)(i) is a party to the transaction, and if the director has a duty under law or professional canon,

or a duty of confidentiality to another person, respecting information relating to the transaction such that the director may not make the disclosure described in section 8.60(4)(ii), then disclosure is sufficient for purposes of subsection (a) if the director (1) discloses to the directors voting on the transaction the existence and nature of his conflicting interest and informs them of the character and limitations imposed by that duty before their vote on the transaction, and (2) plays no part, directly or indirectly, in their deliberations or vote.

(c) A majority (but no fewer than two) of all the qualified directors on the board of directors, or on the committee, constitutes a quorum for purposes of action that complies with this section. Directors' action that otherwise complies with this section is not affected by the presence or vote of a director who is not a qualified director.

(d) For purposes of this section, "qualified director" means, with respect to a director's conflicting interest transaction, any director who does not have either (1) a conflicting interest respecting the transaction, or (2) a familial, financial, professional, or employment relationship with a second director who does have a conflicting interest respecting the transaction, which relationship would, in the circumstances, reasonably be expected to exert an influence on the first director's judgment when voting on the transaction.

Proposed § 8.63. Shareholders' Action

(a) Shareholders' action respecting a transaction is effective for purposes of section 8.61(b)(2) if a majority of the votes entitled to be cast by the holders of all qualified shares were cast in favor of the transaction after (1) notice to shareholders describing the director's conflicting interest transaction, (2) provision of the information referred to in subsection (d), and (3) required disclosure to the shareholders who voted on the transaction (to the extent the information was not known by them).

(b) For purposes of this section, "qualified shares" means any shares entitled to vote with respect to the director's conflicting interest transaction except shares that, to the knowledge, before the vote, of the secretary (or other officer or agent of the corporation authorized to tabulate votes), are beneficially owned (or the voting of which is controlled) by a director who has a conflicting interest respecting the transaction or by a related person of the director, or both.

(c) A majority of the votes entitled to be cast by the holders of all qualified shares constitutes a quorum for purposes of action that complies with this section. Subject to the provisions of subsections (d) and (e), shareholders' action that otherwise complies with this section is not affected by the presence of holders, or the voting, of shares that are not qualified shares.

(d) For purposes of compliance with subsection (a), a director who has a conflicting interest respecting the transaction shall, before the shareholders' vote, inform the secretary (or other officer or agent of the corporation authorized to tabulate votes) of the number, and the identity of persons holding or controlling the vote, of all shares that the director knows are beneficially owned (or the voting of which is controlled) by the director or by a related person of the director, or both.

(e) If a shareholders' vote does not comply with subsection (a) solely because of a failure of a director to comply with subsection (d), and if the director establishes that his failure did not determine and was not intended by him to influence the outcome of the vote, the court may, with or without further proceedings respecting section 8.61(b)(3), take such action respecting the transaction and the director, and give such effect, if any, to the shareholders' vote, as it considers appropriate in the circumstances.

CHAPTER 9.   [Reserved]

CHAPTER 10.   AMENDMENT OF ARTICLES OF INCORPORATION AND BYLAWS

Subchapter A.   Amendment of Articles of Incorporation

§ 10.01.   Authority to Amend

(a) A corporation may amend its articles of incorporation at any time to add or change a provision that is required or permitted in the articles of incorporation or to delete a provision not required in the articles of incorporation. Whether a provision is required or permitted in the articles of incorporation is determined as of the effective date of the amendment.

(b) A shareholder of the corporation does not have a vested property right resulting from any provision in the articles of incorporation, including provisions relating to management, control, capital structure, dividend entitlement, or purpose or duration of the corporation.

§ 10.02.   Amendment by Board of Directors

Unless the articles of incorporation provide otherwise, a corporation's board of directors may adopt one or more amendments to the corporation's articles of incorporation without shareholder action:

(1) to extend the duration of the corporation if it was incorporated at a time when limited duration was required by law;

(2) to delete the names and addresses of the initial directors;

(3) to delete the name and address of the initial registered agent or registered office, if a statement of change is on file with the secretary of state.

(4) to change each issued and unissued authorized share of an outstanding class into a greater number of whole shares if the corporation has only shares of that class outstanding.

(5) to change the corporate name by substituting the word "corporation," "incorporated," "company," "limited," or the abbreviation "corp.," "inc.," "co.," or "ltd.," for a similar word or abbreviation in the name, or by adding, deleting, or changing a geographical attribution for the name; or

(6) to make any other change expressly permitted by this Act to be made without shareholder action.

§ 10.03.   Amendment by Board of Directors and Shareholders

(a) A corporation's board of directors may propose one or more amendments to the articles of incorporation for submission to the shareholders.

(b) For the amendment to be adopted:

(1) the board of directors must recommend the amendment to the shareholders unless the board of directors determines that because of conflict of interest or other special circumstances it should make no recommendation and communicates the basis for its determination to the shareholders with the amendment; and

(2) the shareholders entitled to vote on the amendment must approve the amendment as provided in subsection (e).

(c) The board of directors may condition its submission of the proposed amendment on any basis.

(d) The corporation shall notify each shareholder, whether or not entitled to vote, of the proposed shareholders' meeting in accordance with section 7.05. The notice of meeting must also state that the purpose, or one of the purposes, of the meeting is to consider the proposed amendment and contain or be accompanied by a copy of summary of the amendment.

(e) Unless this Act, the articles of incorporation, or the board of directors (acting pursuant to subsection (c)) requires a greater vote or a vote by voting groups, the amendment to be adopted must be approved by:

(1) a majority of the votes entitled to be cast on the amendment by any voting group with respect to which the amendment would create dissenters' rights; and

(2) the votes required by sections 7.25 and 7.26 by every other voting group entitled to vote on the amendment.

§ 10.04.   Voting on Amendments by Voting Groups

(a) The holders of the outstanding shares of a class are entitled to vote as a separate voting group (if shareholder voting is otherwise required by this Act) on a proposed amendment if the amendment would:

(1) increase or decrease the aggregate number of authorized shares of the class;

(2) effect an exchange or reclassification of all or part of the shares of the class into shares of another class;

(3) effect an exchange or reclassification, or create the right of exchange, of all or part of the shares of another class into shares of the class;

(4) change the designation, rights, preferences, or limitations of all or part of the shares of the class;

(5) change the shares of all or part of the class into a different number of shares of the same class;

(6) create a new class of shares having rights or preferences with respect to distributions or to dissolution that are prior, superior, or substantially equal to the shares of the class;

(7) increase the rights, preferences, or number of authorized shares of any class that, after giving effect to the amendment, have rights or preferences with respect to distributions or to dissolution that are prior, superior, or substantially equal to the shares of the class;

(8) limit or deny an existing preemptive right of all or part of the shares of the class; or

(9) cancel or otherwise affect rights to distributions or dividends that have accumulated but not yet been declared on all or part of the shares of the class.

(b) If a proposed amendment would affect a series of a class of shares in one or more of the ways described in subsection (a), the shares of that series are entitled to vote as a separate voting group on the proposed amendment.

(c) If a proposed amendment that entitles two or more series of shares to vote as separate voting groups under this section would affect those two or more series in the same or a substantially similar way, the shares of all the series so affected must vote together as a single voting group on the proposed amendment.

(d) A class or series of shares is entitled to the voting rights granted by this section although the articles of incorporation provide that the shares are nonvoting shares.

§ 10.05. Amendment Before Issuance of Shares

If a corporation has not yet issued shares, its incorporators or board of directors may adopt one or more amendments to the corporation's articles of incorporation.

§ 10.06. Articles of Amendment

A corporation amending its articles of incorporation shall deliver to the secretary of state for filing articles of amendment setting forth:

(1) the name of the corporation;

(2) the text of each amendment adopted;

(3) if an amendment provides for an exchange, reclassification, or cancellation of issued shares, provisions for implementing the amendment if not contained in the amendment itself;

(4) the date of each amendment's adoption;

(5) if an amendment was adopted by the incorporators or board of directors without shareholder action, a statement to that effect and that shareholder action was not required;

(6) if an amendment was approved by the shareholders:

(i) the designation, number of outstanding shares, number of votes entitled to be cast by each voting group entitled to vote separately on the amendment, and number of votes of each voting group indisputably represented at the meeting;

(ii) either the total number of votes cast for and against the amendment by each voting group entitled to vote separately on the amendment or the total number of undisputed votes cast for the amendment by each voting group and a statement that the number cast for the amendment by each voting group was sufficient for approval by that voting group.

§ 10.07. Restated Articles of Incorporation

(a) A corporation's board of directors may restate its articles of incorporation at any time with or without shareholder action.

(b) The restatement may include one or more amendments to the articles. If the restatement includes an amendment requiring shareholder approval, it must be adopted as provided in section 10.03.

(c) If the board of directors submits a restatement for shareholder action, the corporation shall notify each shareholder, whether or not entitled to vote, of the proposed shareholders' meeting in accordance with section 7.05. The notice must also state that the purpose, or one of the purposes, of the meeting is to consider the proposed restatement that identifies any amendment or other change it would make in the articles.

(d) A corporation restating its articles of incorporation shall deliver to the secretary of state for filing articles for restatement setting forth the name of the corporation and the text of the restated articles of incorporation together with a certificate setting forth:

(1) whether the restatement contains an amendment to the articles requiring shareholder approval and, if it does not, that the board of directors adopted the restatement; or

(2) if the restatement contains an amendment to the articles requiring shareholder approval, the information required by section 10.06.

(e) Duly adopted restated articles of incorporation supersede the original articles of incorporation and all amendments to them.

(f) The secretary of state may certify restated articles of incorporation, as the articles of incorporation currently in effect, without including the certificate information required by subsection (d).

§ 10.08. Amendment Pursuant To Reorganization

(a) A corporation's articles of incorporation may be amended without action by the board of directors or shareholders to carry out a plan of reorganization ordered or decreed by a court of competent jurisdiction under federal statute if the articles of incorporation after amendment contain only provisions required or permitted by section 2.02.

(b) The individual or individuals designated by the court shall deliver to the secretary of state for filing articles of amendment setting forth:

(1) the name of the corporation;

(2) the text of each amendment approved by the court;

(3) the date of the court's order or decree approving the articles of amendment;

(4) the title of the reorganization proceeding in which the order or decree was entered; and

(5) a statement that the court had jurisdiction of the proceeding under federal statute.

(c) Shareholders of a corporation undergoing reorganization do not have dissenters' rights except as and to the extent provided in the reorganization plan.

(d) This section does not apply after entry of a final decree in the reorganization proceeding even though the court retains jurisdiction of the proceeding for limited purposes unrelated to consummation of the reorganization plan.

§ 10.09.   Effect of Amendment

An amendment to articles of incorporation does not affect a cause of action existing against or in favor of the corporation, a proceeding to which the corporation is a party, or the existing rights of persons other than shareholders of the corporation. An amendment changing a corporation's name does not abate a proceeding brought by or against the corporation in its former name.

Subchapter B.   Amendment of Bylaws

§ 10.20.   Amendment by Board of Directors or Shareholders

(a) A corporation's board of directors may amend or repeal the corporation's bylaws unless:

(1) the articles of incorporation or this Act reserve this power exclusively to the shareholders in whole or part; or

(2) the shareholders in amending or repealing a particular bylaw provide expressly that the board of directors may not amend or repeal that bylaw.

(b) A corporation's shareholders may amend or repeal the corporation's bylaws even though the bylaws may also be amended or repealed by its board of directors.

§ 10.21.   Bylaw Increasing Quorum or Voting Requirements For Shareholders

(a) If expressly authorized by the articles of incorporation, the shareholders may adopt or amend a bylaw that fixes a greater quorum or voting requirement for shareholders (or voting groups of shareholders) than is required by this Act. The adoption or amendment of a bylaw that adds, changes, or deletes a greater quorum or voting requirement for shareholders must meet the same quorum requirement and be adopted by the same vote and voting groups required to take action under the quorum and voting requirement then in effect or proposed to be adopted whichever is greater.

(b) A bylaw that fixes a greater quorum or voting requirement for shareholders under subsection (a) may not be adopted, amended, or repealed by the board of directors.

§ 10.22.   Bylaw Increasing Quorum or Voting Requirement for Directors

(a) A bylaw that fixes a greater quorum or voting requirement for the board of directors may be amended or repealed:

(1) if originally adopted by the shareholders, only by the shareholders;

(2) if originally adopted by the board of directors, either by the shareholders or by the board of directors.

(b) A bylaw adopted or amended by the shareholders that fixes a greater quorum or voting requirement for the board of directors may provide that it may be amended or repealed only by a specific vote of either the shareholders or the board of directors.

(c) Action by the board of directors under subsection (a)(2) to adopt or amend a bylaw that changes the quorum or voting requirement for the board of directors must meet the same quorum requirement and be adopted by the same vote required to take action under the quorum and voting requirement then in effect or proposed to be adopted, whichever is greater.

CHAPTER 11.   MERGER AND SHARE EXCHANGE

§ 11.01.   Merger

(a) One or more corporations may merge into another corporation if the board of directors of each corporation adopts and its shareholders (if required by section 11.03) approve a plan of merger.

(b) The plan of merger must set forth:

(1) the name of each corporation planning to merge and the name of the surviving corporation into which each other corporation plans to merge;

(2) the terms and conditions of the merger; and

(3) the manner and basis of converting the shares of each corporation into shares, obligations, or other securities of the surviving or any other corporation or into cash or other property in whole or part.

(c) The plan of merger may set forth:

(1) amendments to the articles of incorporation of the surviving corporation; and

(2) other provisions relating to the merger.

§ 11.02.   Share Exchange

(a) A corporation may acquire all of the outstanding shares of one or more classes or series of another corporation if the board of directors of each corporation adopts and its shareholders (if required by section 11.03) approve the exchange.

(b) The plan of exchange must set forth:

(1) the name of the corporation whose shares will be acquired and the name of the acquiring corporation;

(2) the terms and conditions of the exchange;

(3) the manner and basis of exchanging the shares to be acquired for shares, obligations, or other securities of the acquiring or any other corporation or for cash or other property in whole or part.

(c) The plan of exchange may set forth other provisions relating to the exchange.

(d) This section does not limit the power of a corporation to acquire all or part of the shares of one or more classes or series of another corporation through a voluntary exchange or otherwise.

§ 11.03. Action on Plan

(a) After adopting a plan of merger or share exchange, the board of directors of each corporation party to the merger, and the board of directors of the corporation whose shares will be acquired in the share exchange, shall submit the plan of merger (except as provided in subsection (g)) or share exchange for approval by its shareholders.

(b) For a plan of merger or share exchange to be approved:

(1) the board of directors must recommend the plan of merger or share exchange to the shareholders, unless the board of directors determines that because of conflict of interest or other special circumstances it should make no recommendation and communicates the basis for its determination to the shareholders with the plan; and

(2) the shareholders entitled to vote must approve the plan.

(c) The board of directors may condition its submission of the proposed merger or share exchange on any basis.

(d) The corporation shall notify each shareholder, whether or not entitled to vote, of the proposed shareholders' meeting in accordance with section 7.05. The notice must also state that the purpose, or one of the purposes, of the meeting is to consider the plan of merger or share exchange and contain or be accompanied by a copy or summary of the plan.

(e) Unless this Act, the articles of incorporation, or the board of directors (acting pursuant to subsection (c)) requires a greater vote or a vote by voting groups, the plan of merger or share exchange to be authorized must be approved by each voting group entitled to vote separately on the plan by a majority of all the votes entitled to be cast on the plan by that voting group.

(f) Separate voting by voting groups is required.

(1) on a plan of merger if the plan contains a provision that, if contained in a proposed amendment to articles of incorporation, would require action by one or more separate voting groups on the proposed amendment under section 10.04;

(2) on a plan of share exchange by each class or series of shares included in the exchange, with each class or series constituting a separate voting group.

(g) Action by the shareholders of the surviving corporation on a plan of merger is not required if:

(1) the articles of incorporation of the surviving corporation will not differ (except for amendments enumerated in section 10.02) from its articles before the merger;

(2) each shareholder of the surviving corporation whose shares were outstanding immediately before the effective date of the merger will hold the same number of shares, with identical designations, preferences, limitations, and relative rights, immediately after;

(3) the number of voting shares outstanding immediately after the merger, plus the number of voting shares issuable as a result of the merger (either by the conversion of securities issued pursuant to the merger or the exercise of rights and war-

rants issued pursuant to the merger), will not exceed by more than 20 percent the total number of voting shares of the surviving corporation outstanding immediately before the merger; and

(4) the number of participating shares outstanding immediately after the merger, plus the number of participating shares issuable as a result of the merger (either by the conversion of securities issued pursuant to the merger or the exercise of rights and warrants issued pursuant to the merger), will not exceed by more than 20 percent the total number of participating shares outstanding immediately before the merger.

(h) As used in subsection (g):

(1) "Participating shares" means shares that entitle their holders to participate without limitation in distributions.

(2) "Voting shares" means shares that entitle their holders to vote unconditionally in elections of directors.

(i) After a merger or share exchange is authorized, and at any time before articles of merger or share exchange are filed, the planned merger or share exchange may be abandoned (subject to any contractual rights), without further shareholder action, in accordance with the procedure set forth in the plan of merger or share exchange or, if none is set forth, in the manner determined by the board of directors.

§ 11.04. Merger of Subsidiary

(a) A parent corporation owning at least 90 percent of the outstanding shares of each class of a subsidiary corporation may merge the subsidiary into itself without approval of the shareholders of the parent or subsidiary.

(b) The board of directors of the parent shall adopt a plan of merger that sets forth:

(1) the names of the parent and subsidiary; and

(2) the manner and basis of converting the shares of the subsidiary into shares, obligations, or other securities of the parent or any other corporation or into cash or other property in whole or part.

(c) The parent shall mail a copy or summary of the plan of merger to each shareholder of the subsidiary who does not waive the mailing requirement in writing.

(d) The parent may not deliver articles of merger to the secretary of state for filing until at least 30 days after the date it mailed a copy of the plan of merger to each shareholder of the subsidiary who did not waive the mailing requirement.

(e) Articles of merger under this section may not contain amendments to the articles of incorporation of the parent corporation (except for amendments enumerated in section 10.02).

§ 11.05. Articles of Merger or Share Exchange

(a) After a plan of merger or share exchange is approved by the shareholders, or adopted by the board of directors if shareholder approval is not required, the surviving or acquiring corporation shall deliver to the secretary of state for filing articles of merger or share exchange setting forth:

(1) the plan of merger or share exchange;

(2) if shareholder approval was not required, a statement to that effect;

(3) if approval of the shareholders of one or more corporations party to the merger or share exchange was required:

(i) the designation, number of outstanding shares, and number of votes entitled to be cast by each voting group entitled to vote separately on the plan as to each corporation; and

(ii) either the total number of votes cast for and against the plan by each voting group entitled to vote separately on the plan or the total number of undisputed votes cast for the plan separately by each voting group and a statement that the number cast for the plan by each voting group was sufficient for approval by that voting group.

(b) Unless a delayed effective date is specified, a merger or share exchange takes effect when the articles of merger or share exchange are filed.

§ 11.06.   Effect of Merger or Share Exchange

(a) When a merger takes effect:

(1) every other corporation party to the merger merges into the surviving corporation and the separate existence of every corporation except the surviving corporation ceases;

(2) the title to all real estate and other property owned by each corporation party to the merger is vested in the surviving corporation without reversion or impairment;

(3) the surviving corporation has all liabilities of each corporation party to the merger;

(4) a proceeding pending against any corporation party to the merger may be continued as if the merger did not occur or the surviving corporation may be substituted in the proceeding for the corporation whose existence ceased;

(5) the articles of incorporation of the surviving corporation are amended to the extent provided in the plan of merger; and

(6) the shares of each corporation party to the merger that are to be converted into shares, obligations, or other securities of the surviving or any other corporation or into cash or other property are converted and the former holders of the shares are entitled only to the rights provided in the articles of merger or to their rights under chapter 13.

(b) When a share exchange takes effect, the shares of each acquired corporation are exchanged as provided in the plan, and the former holders of the shares are entitled only to the exchange rights provided in the articles of share exchange or to their rights under chapter 13.

§ 11.07.   Merger or Share Exchange With Foreign Corporation

(a) One or more foreign corporations may merge or enter into a share exchange with one or more domestic corporations if:

(1) in a merger, the merger is permitted by the law of the state or country under whose law each foreign corporation is

incorporated and each foreign corporation complies with that law in effecting the merger;

(2) in a share exchange, the corporation whose shares will be acquired is a domestic corporation, whether or not a share exchange is permitted by the law of the state or country under whose law the acquiring corporation is incorporated;

(3) the foreign corporation complies with section 11.05 if it is the surviving corporation of the merger or acquiring corporation of the share exchange; and

(4) each domestic corporation complies with the applicable provisions of sections 11.01 through 11.04 and, if it is the surviving corporation of the merger or acquiring corporation of the share exchange, with section 11.05.

(b) Upon the merger or share exchange taking effect, the surviving foreign corporation of a merger and the acquiring foreign corporation of a share exchange is deemed:

(1) to appoint the secretary of state as its agent for service of process in a proceeding to enforce any obligation or the rights of dissenting shareholders of each domestic corporation party to the merger or share exchange; and

(2) to agree that it will promptly pay to the dissenting shareholders of each domestic corporation party to the merger or share exchange the amount, if any, to which they are entitled under chapter 13.

(c) This section does not limit the power of a foreign corporation to acquire all or part of the shares of one or more classes or series of a domestic corporation through a voluntary exchange or otherwise.

CHAPTER 12.   SALE OF ASSETS

§ 12.01.   Sale of Assets in Regular Course of Business and Mortgage of Assets

(a) A corporation may, on the terms and conditions and for the consideration determined by the board of directors:

(1) sell, lease, exchange, or otherwise dispose of all, or substantially all, of its property in the usual and regular course of business,

(2) mortgage, pledge, dedicate to the repayment of indebtedness (whether with or without recourse), or otherwise encumber any or all of its property whether or not in the usual and regular course of business, or

(3) transfer any or all of its property to a corporation all the shares of which are owned by the corporation.

(b) Unless the articles of incorporation require it, approval by the shareholders of a transaction described in subsection (a) is not required.

§ 12.02.   Sale of Assets Other Than in Regular Course of Business

(a) A corporation may sell, lease, exchange, or otherwise dispose of all, or substantially all, of its property (with or without the good will), otherwise than in the usual and regular course of business, on the terms and conditions and for the consideration determined by the corporation's board of directors, if the board of directors proposes and its shareholders approve the proposed transaction.

(b) For a transaction to be authorized:

(1) the board of directors must recommend the proposed transaction to the shareholders unless the board of directors determines that because of conflict of interest or other special circumstances it should make no recommendation and communicates the basis for its determination to the shareholders with the submission of the proposed transaction; and

(2) the shareholders entitled to vote must approve the transaction.

(c) The board of directors may condition its submission of the proposed transaction on any basis.

(d) The corporation shall notify each shareholder, whether or not entitled to vote, of the proposed shareholders' meeting in accordance with section 7.05. The notice must also state that the purpose, or one of the purposes, of the meeting is to consider the sale, lease, exchange, or other disposition of all, or substantially all, the property of the corporation and contain or be accompanied by a description of the transaction.

(e) Unless the articles of incorporation or the board of directors (acting pursuant to subsection (c)) require a greater vote or a vote by voting groups, the transaction to be authorized must be approved by a majority of all the votes entitled to be cast on the transaction.

(f) After a sale, lease, exchange, or other disposition of property is authorized, the transaction may be abandoned (subject to any contractual rights) without further shareholder action.

(g) A transaction that constitutes a distribution is governed by section 6.40 and not by this section.

CHAPTER 13. DISSENTERS' RIGHTS

Subchapter A. Right to Dissent and Obtain Payment for Shares

§ 13.01. Definitions

In this chapter:

(1) "Corporation" means the issuer of the shares held by a dissenter before the corporate action, or the surviving or acquiring corporation by merger or share exchange of that issuer.

(2) "Dissenter" means a shareholder who is entitled to dissent from corporate action under section 13.02 and who exercises that right when and in the manner required by sections 13.20 through 13.28.

(3) "Fair value," with respect to a dissenter's shares, means the value of the shares immediately before the effectuation of the corporate action to which the dissenter objects, excluding any appreciation or depreciation in anticipation of the corporate action unless exclusion would be inequitable.

(4) "Interest" means interest from the effective date of the corporate action until the date of payment, at the average rate currently paid by the corporation on its principal bank loans or, if none, at a rate that is fair and equitable under all the circumstances.

(5) "Record shareholder" means the person in whose name shares are registered in the records of a corporation or the beneficial owner of shares to the extent of the rights granted by a nominee certificate on file with a corporation.

(6) "Beneficial shareholder" means the person who is a beneficial owner of shares held in a voting trust or by a nominee as the record shareholder.

(7) "Shareholder" means the record shareholder or the beneficial shareholder.

§ 13.02. Right to Dissent

(a) A shareholder is entitled to dissent from, and obtain payment of the fair value of his shares in the event of, any of the following corporate actions:

(1) consummation of a plan of merger to which the corporation is a party (i) if shareholder approval is required for the merger by section 11.03 or the articles of incorporation and the shareholder is entitled to vote on the merger or (ii) if the corporation is a subsidiary that is merged with its parent under section 11.04;

(2) consummation of a plan of share exchange to which the corporation is a party as the corporation whose shares will be acquired, if the shareholder is entitled to vote on the plan;

(3) consummation of a sale or exchange of all, or substantially all, of the property of the corporation other than in the usual and regular course of business, if the shareholder is entitled to vote on the sale or exchange, including a sale in dissolution, but not including a sale pursuant to court order or a sale for cash pursuant to a plan by which all or substantially all of the net proceeds of the sale will be distributed to the shareholders within one year after the date of sale;

(4) an amendment of the articles of incorporation that materially and adversely affects rights in respect of a dissenter's shares because it:

(i) alters or abolishes a preferential right of the shares;

(ii) creates, alters, or abolishes a right in respect of redemption, including a provision respecting a sinking fund for the redemption or repurchase, of the shares;

(iii) alters or abolishes a preemptive right of the holder of the shares to acquire shares or other securities;

(iv) excludes or limits the right of the shares to vote on any matter, or to cumulate votes, other than a limitation by dilution through issuance of shares or other securities with similar voting rights; or

(v) reduces the number of shares owned by the shareholder to a fraction of a share if the fractional share so created is to be acquired for cash under section 6.04; or

(5) any corporate action taken pursuant to a shareholder vote to the extent the articles of incorporation, bylaws, or a resolution of the board of directors provides that voting or non-

voting shareholders are entitled to dissent and obtain payment for their shares.

(b) A shareholder entitled to dissent and obtain payment for his shares under this chapter may not challenge the corporate action creating his entitlement unless the action is unlawful or fraudulent with respect to the shareholder or the corporation.

§ 13.03. Dissent by Nominees and Beneficial Owners

(a) A record shareholder may assert dissenters' rights as to fewer than all the shares registered in his name only if he dissents with respect to all shares beneficially owned by any one person and notifies the corporation in writing of the name and address of each person on whose behalf he asserts dissenters' rights. The rights of a partial dissenter under this subsection are determined as if the shares as to which he dissents and his other shares were registered in the names of different shareholders.

(b) A beneficial shareholder may assert dissenters' rights as to shares held on his behalf only if:

(1) he submits to the corporation the record shareholder's written consent to the dissent not later than the time the beneficial shareholder asserts dissenters' rights; and

(2) he does so with respect to all shares of which he is the beneficial shareholder or over which he has power to direct the vote.

Subchapter B. Procedure for Exercise of Dissenters' Rights

§ 13.20. Notice of Dissenters' Rights

(a) If proposed corporate action creating dissenters' rights under section 13.02 is submitted to a vote at a shareholders' meeting, the meeting notice must state that shareholders are or may be entitled to assert dissenters' rights under this chapter and be accompanied by a copy of this chapter.

(b) If corporate action creating dissenters' rights under section 13.02 is taken without a vote of shareholders, the corporation shall notify in writing all shareholders entitled to assert dissenters' rights that the action was taken and send them the dissenters' notice described in section 13.22.

§ 13.21. Notice of Intent to Demand Payment

(a) If proposed corporate action creating dissenters' rights under section 13.02 is submitted to a vote at a shareholders' meeting, a shareholder who wishes to assert dissenters' rights (1) must deliver to the corporation before the vote is taken written notice of his intent to demand payment for his shares if the proposed action is effectuated and (2) must not vote his shares in favor of the proposed action.

(b) A shareholder who does not satisfy the requirements of subsection (a) is not entitled to payment for his shares under this chapter.

§ 13.22. Dissenters' Notice

(a) If proposed corporate action creating dissenters' rights under section 13.02 is authorized at a shareholders' meeting, the corporation shall deliver a written dissenters' notice to all shareholders who satisfied the requirements of section 13.21.

(b) The dissenters' notice must be sent no later than 10 days after the corporate action was taken, and must:

(1) state where the payment demand must be sent and where and when certificates for certificated shares must be deposited;

(2) inform holders of uncertified shares to what extent transfer of the shares will be restricted after the payment demand is received;

(3) supply a form for demanding payment that includes the date of the first announcement to news media or to shareholders of the terms of the proposed corporate action and requires that the person asserting dissenters' rights certify whether or not he acquired beneficial ownership of the shares before that date;

(4) set a date by which the corporation must receive the payment demand, which date may not be fewer than 30 nor more than 60 days after the date the subsection (a) notice is delivered; and

(5) be accompanied by a copy of this chapter.

§ 13.23. Duty to Demand Payment

(a) A shareholder sent a dissenters' notice described in section 13.22 must demand payment, certify whether he acquired beneficial ownership of the shares before the date required to be set forth in the dissenter's notice pursuant to section 13.22(b)(3), and deposit his certificates in accordance with the terms of the notice.

(b) The shareholder who demands payment and deposits his shares under section (a) retains all other rights of a shareholder until these rights are cancelled or modified by the taking of the proposed corporate action.

(c) A shareholder who does not demand payment or deposit his share certificates where required, each by the date set in the dissenters' notice, is not entitled to payment for his shares under this chapter.

§ 13.24. Share Restrictions

(a) The corporation may restrict the transfer of uncertificated shares from the date the demand for their payment is received until the proposed corporate action is taken or the restrictions released under section 13.26.

(b) The person for whom dissenters' rights are asserted as to uncertificated shares retains all other rights of a shareholder until these rights are cancelled or modified by the taking of the proposed corporate action.

§ 13.25. Payment

(a) Except as provided in section 13.27, as soon as the proposed corporate action is taken, or upon receipt of a payment demand, the corporation shall pay each dissenter who complied with section 13.23 the amount the corporation estimates to be the fair value of his shares, plus accrued interest.

(b) The payment must be accompanied by:

(1) the corporation's balance sheet as of the end of a fiscal year ending not more than 16 months before the date of payment, an income statement for that year, a statement of changes in shareholders' equity for that year, and the latest available interim financial statements, if any;

(2) a statement of the corporation's estimate of the fair value of the shares;

(3) an explanation of how the interest was calculated;

(4) a statement of the dissenter's right to demand payment under section 13.28; and

(5) a copy of this chapter.

§ 13.26. Failure to Take Action

(a) If the corporation does not take the proposed action within 60 days after the date set for demanding payment and depositing share certificates, the corporation shall return the deposited certificates and release the transfer restrictions imposed on uncertificated shares.

(b) If after returning deposited certificates and releasing transfer restrictions, the corporation takes the proposed action, it must send a new dissenters' notice under section 13.22 and repeat the payment demand procedure.

§ 13.27. After-Acquired Shares

(a) A corporation may elect to withhold payment required by section 13.25 from a dissenter unless he was the beneficial owner of the shares before the date set forth in the dissenters' notice as the date of the first announcement to news media or to shareholders of the terms of the proposed corporate action.

(b) To the extent the corporation elects to withhold payment under subsection (a), after taking the proposed corporate action, it shall estimate the fair value of the shares, plus accrued interest, and shall pay this amount to each dissenter who agrees to accept it in full satisfaction of his demand. The corporation shall send with its offer a statement of its estimate of the fair value of the shares, an explanation of how the interest was calculated, and a statement of the dissenter's right to demand payment under section 13.28.

§ 13.28. Procedure if Shareholder Dissatisfied with Payment or Offer

(a) A dissenter may notify the corporation in writing of his own estimate of the fair value of his shares and amount of interest due, and demand payment of his estimate (less any payment under section 13.25), or reject the corporation's offer under section 13.27 and demand payment of the fair value of his shares and interest due, if:

(1) the dissenter believes that the amount paid under section 13.25 or offered under section 13.27 is less than the fair value of his shares or that the interest due is incorrectly calculated;

(2) the corporation fails to make payment under section 13.25 within 60 days after the date set for demanding payment; or

(3) the corporation, having failed to take the proposed action, does not return the deposited certificates or release the transfer restrictions imposed on uncertificated shares within 60 days after the date set for demanding payment.

(b) A dissenter waives his right to demand payment under this section unless he notifies the corporation of his demand in writing under subsection (a) within 30 days after the corporation made or offered payment for his shares.

Subchapter C.   *Judicial Appraisal of Shares*

§ 13.30.   Court Action

(a) If a demand for payment under section 13.28 remains unsettled, the corporation shall commence a proceeding within 60 days after receiving the payment demand and petition the court to determine the fair value of the shares and accrued interest. If the corporation does not commence the proceeding within the 60-day period, it shall pay each dissenter whose demand remains unsettled the amount demanded.

(b) The corporation shall commence the proceeding in the [name or describe] court of the county where a corporation's principal office (or, if none in this state, its registered office) is located. If the corporation is a foreign corporation without a registered office in this state, it shall commence the proceeding in the county in this state where the registered office of the domestic corporation merged with or whose shares were acquired by the foreign corporation was located.

(c) The corporation shall make all dissenters (whether or not residents of this state) whose demands remain unsettled parties to the proceeding as in an action against their shares and all parties must be served with a copy of the petition. Nonresidents may be served by registered or certified mail or by publication as provided by law.

(d) The jurisdiction of the court in which the proceeding is commenced under subsection (b) is plenary and exclusive. The court may appoint one or more persons as appraisers to receive evidence and recommend decision on the question of fair value. The appraisers have the powers described in the order appointing them, or in any amendment to it. The dissenters are entitled to the same discovery rights as parties in other civil proceedings.

(e) Each dissenter made a party to the proceeding is entitled to judgment (1) for the amount, if any, by which the court finds the fair value of his shares, plus interest, exceeds the amount paid by the corporation or (2) for the fair value, plus accrued interest, of his after-acquired shares for which the corporation elected to withhold payment under section 13.27.

§ 13.31.   Court Costs and Counsel Fees

(a) The court in an appraisal proceeding commenced under section 13.30 shall determine all costs of the proceeding, including the reasonable compensation and expenses of appraisers appointed by the court. The court shall assess the costs against the corporation, except that the court may assess costs against all or some of the dissenters, in amounts the court finds equitable to the extent the court finds the dissenters acted arbitrarily, vexatiously, or not in good faith in demanding payment under section 13.28.

(b) The court may also assess the fees and expenses of counsel and experts for the respective parties, in amounts the court finds equitable:

(1) against the corporation and in favor of any or all dissenters if the court finds the corporation did not substantially comply with the requirements of sections 13.20 through 13.28; or

(2) against either the corporation or a dissenter, in favor of any other party, if the court finds that the party against whom the fees and expenses are assessed acted arbitrarily, vexatiously, or not in good faith with respect to the rights provided by this chapter.

(c) If the court finds that the services of counsel for any dissenter were of substantial benefit to other dissenters similarly situated, and that the fees for those services should not be assessed against the corporation, the court may award to these counsel reasonable fees to be paid out of the amounts awarded the dissenters who were benefited.

CHAPTER 14.   DISSOLUTION

Subchapter A.   Voluntary Dissolution

§ 14.01.   Dissolution by Incorporators or Initial Directors

A majority of the incorporators or initial directors of a corporation that has not issued shares or has not commenced business may dissolve the corporation by delivering to the secretary of state for filing articles of dissolution that set forth:

(1) the name of the corporation;

(2) the date of its incorporation;

(3) either (i) that none of the corporation's shares has been issued or (ii) that the corporation has not commenced business;

(4) that no debt of the corporation remains unpaid;

(5) that the net assets of the corporation remaining after winding up have been distributed to the shareholders, if shares were issued; and

(6) that a majority of the incorporators or initial directors authorized the dissolution.

§ 14.02.   Dissolution by Board of Directors and Shareholders

(a) A corporation's board of directors may propose dissolution for submission to the shareholders.

(b) For a proposal to dissolve to be adopted:

(1) the board of directors must recommend dissolution to the shareholders unless the board of directors determines that

because of conflict of interest or other special circumstances it should make no recommendation and communicates the basis for its determination to the shareholders; and

(2) the shareholders entitled to vote must approve the proposal to dissolve as provided in subsection (e).

(c) The board of directors may condition its submission of the proposal for dissolution on any basis.

(d) The corporation shall notify each shareholder, whether or not entitled to vote, of the proposed shareholders' meeting in accordance with section 7.05. The notice must also state that the purpose, or one of the purposes, of the meeting is to consider dissolving the corporation.

(e) Unless the articles of incorporation or the board of directors (acting pursuant to subsection (c)) require a greater vote or a vote by voting groups, the proposal to dissolve to be adopted must be approved by a majority of all the votes entitled to be cast on that proposal.

§ 14.03.   Articles of Dissolution

(a) At any time after dissolution is authorized, the corporation may dissolve by delivering to the secretary of state for filing articles of dissolution setting forth:

(1) the name of the corporation;

(2) the date dissolution was authorized;

(3) if dissolution was approved by the shareholders:

(i) the number of votes entitled to be cast on the proposal to dissolve; and

(ii) either the total number of votes cast for and against dissolution or the total number of undisputed votes cast for dissolution or the total number of undisputed votes cast for dissolution and a statement that the number cast for dissolution was sufficient for approval.

(4) If voting by voting groups is required, the information required by subparagraph (3) shall be separately provided for each voting group entitled to vote separately on the plan to dissolve.

(b) A corporation is dissolved upon the effective date of its articles of dissolution.

§ 14.04.   Revocation of Dissolution

(a) A corporation may revoke its dissolution within 120 days of its effective date.

(b) Revocation of dissolution must be authorized in the same manner as the dissolution was authorized unless that authorization permitted revocation by action by the board of directors alone, in which event the board of directors may revoke the dissolution without shareholder action.

(c) After the revocation of dissolution is authorized, the corporation may revoke the dissolution by delivering to the secretary of state for filing articles of revocation of dissolution, together with a copy of its articles of dissolution, that set forth:

(1) the name of the corporation;

(2) the effective date of the dissolution that was revoked;

(3) the date that the revocation of dissolution was authorized;

(4) if the corporation's board of directors (or incorporators) revoked the dissolution, a statement to that effect;

(5) if the corporation's board of directors revoked a dissolution authorized by the shareholders, a statement that revocation was permitted by action by the board of directors alone pursuant to that authorization; and

(6) if shareholder action was required to revoke the dissolution, the information required by section 14.03(3) or (4).

(d) Unless a delayed effective date is specified, revocation of dissolution is effective when articles of revocation of dissolution are filed.

(e) When the revocation of dissolution is effective, it relates back to and take effect as of the effective date of the dissolution and the corporation resumes carrying on its business as if dissolution had never occurred.

§ 14.05.   Effect of Dissolution

(a) A dissolved corporation continues its corporate existence but may not carry on any business except that appropriate to wind up and liquidate its business and affairs, including:

(1) collecting its assets;

(2) disposing of its properties that will not be distributed in kind to its shareholders;

(3) discharging or making provision for discharging its liabilities;

(4) distributing its remaining property among its shareholders according to their interests; and

(5) doing every other act necessary to wind up and liquidate its business and affairs.

(b) Dissolution of a corporation does not:

(1) transfer title to the corporation's property;

(2) prevent transfer of its shares or securities, although the authorization to dissolve may provide for closing the corporation's share transfer records;

(3) subject its directors or officers to standards of conduct different from those prescribed in chapter 8;

(4) change quorum or voting requirements for its board of directors or shareholders; change provisions for selection, resignation, or removal of its directors or officers or both; or change provisions for amending its bylaws;

(5) prevent commencement of a proceeding by or against the corporation in its corporate name;

(6) abate or suspend a proceeding pending by or against the corporation on the effective date of disolution; or

(7) terminate the authority of the registered agent of the corporation.

§ 14.06.   Known Claims Against Dissolved Corporation

(a) A dissolved corporation may dispose of the known claims against it by following the procedure described in this section.

(b) The dissolved corporation shall notify its known claimants in writing of the dissolution at any time after its effective date. The written notice must:

(1) describe information that must be included in a claim;

(2) provide a mailing address where a claim may be sent;

(3) state the deadline, which may not be fewer than 120 days from the effective date of the written notice, by which the dissolved corporation must receive the claim; and

(4) state that the claim will be barred if not received by the deadline.

(c) A claim against the dissolved corporation is barred:

(1) if a claimant who was given written notice under subsection (b) does not deliver the claim to the dissolved corporation by the deadline;

(2) if a claimant whose claim was rejected by the dissolved corporation does not commence a proceeding to enforce the claim within 90 days from the effective date of the rejection notice.

(d) For purposes of this section, "claim" does not include a contingent liability or a claim based on an event occurring after the effective date of dissolution.

§ 14.07.   Unknown Claims Against Dissolved Corporation

(a) A dissolved corporation may also publish notice of its dissolution and request that persons with claims against the corporation present them in accordance with the notice.

(b) The notice must:

(1) be published one time in a newspaper of general circulation in the county where the dissolved corporation's principal office (or, if none in this state, its registered office) is or was last located;

(2) describe the information that must be included in a claim and provide a mailing address where the claim may be sent; and

(3) state that a claim against the corporation will be barred unless a proceeding to enforce the claim is commenced within five years after the publication of the notice.

(c) If the dissolved corporation publishes a newspaper notice in accordance with the subsection (b), the claim of each of the following claimants is barred unless the claimant commences a proceeding to enforce the claim against the dissolved corporation within five years after the publication date of the newspaper notice:

(1) a claimant who did not receive written notice under section 14.06;

(2) a claimant whose claim was timely sent to the dissolved corporation but not acted on;

(3) a claimant whose claim is contingent or based on an event occurring after the effective date of dissolution.

(d) A claim may be enforced under this section:

(1) against the dissolved corporation, to the extent of its undistributed assets; or

(2) if the assets have been distributed in liquidation, against a shareholder of the dissolved corporation to the extent of his pro rata share of the claim or the corporate assets distributed to him in liquidation, whichever is less, but a shareholder's total liability for all claims under this section may not exceed the total amount of assets distributed to him.

Subchapter B.   Administrative Dissolution

§ 14.20.   Grounds for Administrative Dissolution

The secretary of state may commence a proceeding under section 14.21 to administratively dissolve a corporation if:

(1) the corporation does not pay within 60 days after they are due any franchise taxes or penalties imposed by this Act or other law;

(2) the corporation does not deliver its annual report to the secretary of state within 60 days after it is due;

(3) the corporation is without a registered agent or registered office in this state for 60 days or more;

(4) the corporation does not notify the secretary of state within 60 days that its registered agent or registered office has been changed, that its registered agent has resigned, or that its registered office has been discontinued; or

(5) the corporation's period of duration stated in its articles of incorporation expires.

§ 14.21.   Procedure for and Effect of Administrative Dissolution

(a) If the secretary of state determines that one or more grounds exist under section 14.20 for dissolving a corporation, he shall serve the corporation with written notice of his determination under section 5.04.

(b) If the corporation does not correct each ground for dissolution or demonstrate to the reasonable satisfaction of the secretary of state that each ground determined by the secretary of state does not exist within 60 days after service of the notice is perfected under section 5.04, the secretary of state shall administratively dissolve the corporation by signing a certificate of dissolution that recites the ground or grounds for dissolution and its effective date. The secretary of state shall file the original of the certificate and serve a copy on the corporation under section 5.04.

(c) A corporation administratively dissolved continues its corporate existence but may not carry on any business except that necessary to wind up and liquidate its business and affairs under section 14.05 and notify claimants under sections 14.06 and 14.07.

(d) The administrative dissolution of a corporation does not terminate the authority of its registered agent.

§ 14.22.   Reinstatement Following Administrative Dissolution

(a) A corporation administratively dissolved under section 14.21 may apply to the secretary of state for reinstatement within two years after the effective date of dissolution. The application must:

(1) recite the name of the corporation and the effective date of its administrative dissolution;

(2) state that the ground or grounds for dissolution either did not exist or have been eliminated;

(3) state that the corporation's name satisfies the requirements of section 4.01; and

(4) contain a certificate from the [taxing authority] reciting that all taxes owed by the corporation have been paid.

(b) If the secretary of state determines that the application contains the information required by subsection (a) and that the information is correct, he shall cancel the certificate of dissolution and prepare a certificate of reinstatement that recites his determination and the effective date of reinstatement, file the original of the certificate, and serve a copy on the corporation under section 5.04.

(c) When the reinstatement is effective, it relates back to and takes effect as of the effective date of the administrative dissolution and the corporation resumes carrying on its business as if the administrative dissolution had never occurred.

§ 14.23.   Appeal from Denial of Reinstatement

(a) If the secretary of state denies a corporation's application for reinstatement following administrative dissolution, he shall serve the corporation under section 5.04 with a written notice that explains the reason or reasons for denial.

(b) The corporation may appeal the denial of reinstatement to the [name or describe] court within 30 days after service of the notice of denial is perfected. The corporation appeals by petitioning the court to set aside the dissolution and attaching to the petition copies of the secretary of state's certificate of dissolution, the corporation's application for reinstatement, and the secretary of state's notice of denial.

(c) The court may summarily order the secretary of state to reinstate the dissolved corporation or may take other action the court considers appropriate.

(d) The court's final decision may be appealed as in other civil proceedings.

Subchapter C.   Judicial Dissolution

§ 14.30.   Grounds for Judicial Dissolution

The [name or describe court or courts] may dissolve a corporation:

(1) in a proceeding by the attorney general if it is established that:

(i) the corporation obtained its articles of incorporation through fraud; or

(ii) the corporation has continued to exceed or abuse the authority conferred upon it by law;

(2) in a proceeding by a shareholder if it is established that:

(i) the directors are deadlocked in the management of the corporate affairs, the shareholders are unable to break the deadlock, and irreparable injury to the corporation is threatened or being suffered, or the business and affairs of the corporation can no longer be conducted to the advantage of the shareholders generally, because of the deadlock;

(ii) the directors or those in control of the corporation have acted, are acting, or will act in a manner that is illegal, oppressive, or fraudulent;

(iii) the shareholders are deadlocked in voting power and have failed, for a period that includes at least two consecutive annual meeting dates, to elect successors to directors whose terms have expired; or

(iv) the corporate assets are being misapplied or wasted;

(3) in a proceeding by a creditor if it is established that:

(i) the creditor's claim has been reduced to judgment, the execution on the judgment returned unsatisfied, and the corporation is insolvent; or

(ii) the corporation has admitted in writing that the creditor's claim is due and owing and the corporation is insolvent; or

(4) in a proceeding by the corporation to have its voluntary dissolution continued under court supervision.

§ 14.31.   Procedure for Judicial Dissolution

(a) Venue for a proceeding by the attorney general to dissolve a corporation lies in [name the county or counties]. Venue for a proceeding brought by any other party named in section 14.30 lies in the county where a corporation's principal office (or, if none in this state, its registered office) is or was last located.

(b) It is not necessary to make shareholders parties to a proceeding to dissolve a corporation unless relief is sought against them individually.

(c) A court in a proceeding brought to dissolve a corporation may issue injunctions, appoint a receiver or custodian pendente lite with all powers and duties the court directs, take other action required to preserve the corporate assets wherever located, and carry on the business of the corporation until a full hearing can be held.

§ 14.32.   Receivership or Custodianship

(a) A court in a judicial proceeding brought to dissolve a corporation may appoint one or more receivers to wind up and liquidate, or one or more custodians to manage, the business and affairs of the corporation. The court shall hold a hearing, after notifying all parties to the proceeding and any interested persons designated by the court, before appointing a receiver or custodian. The court appointing a receiver or custodian has exclusive jurisdiction over the corporation and all its property wherever located.

(b) The court may appoint an individual or a domestic or foreign corporation (authorized to transact business in this state) as a receiver or custodian. The court may require the receiver or custodian to post bond, with or without sureties, in an amount the court directs.

(c) The court shall describe the powers and duties of the receiver or custodian in its appointing order, which may be amended from time to time. Among other powers:

(1) the receiver (i) may dispose of all or any part of the assets of the corporation wherever located, at a public or private sale, if authorized by the court; and (ii) may sue and defend in his own name as receiver of the corporation in all courts of this state;

(2) the custodian may exercise all of the powers of the corporation, through or in place of its board of directors or officers, to the extent necessary to manage the affairs of the corporation in the best interests of its shareholders and creditors.

(d) The court during a receivership may redesignate the receiver a custodian, and during a custodianship may redesignate the custodian a receiver, if doing so is in the best interests of the corporation, its shareholders, and creditors.

(e) The court from time to time during the receivership or custodianship may order compensation paid and expense disbursements or reimbursements made to the receiver or custodian and his counsel from the assets of the corporation or proceeds from the sale of the assets.

§ 14.33.   Decree of Dissolution

(a) If after a hearing the court determines that one or more grounds for judicial dissolution described in section 14.30 exist, it may enter a decree dissolving the corporation and specifying the effective date of the dissolution, and the clerk of the court shall deliver a certified copy of the decree to the secretary of state, who shall file it.

(b) After entering the decree of dissolution, the court shall direct the winding up and liquidation of the corporation's business and affairs in accordance with section 14.05 and the notification of claimants in accordance with sections 14.06 and 14.07.

Subchapter D.   Miscellaneous

§ 14.40.   Deposit with State Treasurer

Assets of a dissolved corporation that should be transferred to a creditor, claimant, or shareholder of the corporation who cannot be found or who is not competent to receive them shall be reduced to cash and deposited with the state treasurer or other appropriate state official for safekeeping. When the creditor, claimant, or shareholder furnishes satisfactory proof of entitlement to the amount deposited, the state treasurer or other appropriate state official shall pay him or his representative that amount.

CHAPTER 15.   FOREIGN CORPORATIONS

Subchapter A.   Certificate of Authority

§ 15.01.   Authority to Transact Business Required

(a) A foreign corporation may not transact business in this state until it obtains a certificate of authority from the secretary of state.

(b) The following activities, among others, do not constitute transaction business within the meaning of subsection (a):

(1) maintaining, defending, or settling any proceeding;

(2) holding meetings of the board of directors or shareholders or carrying on other activities concerning internal corporate affairs;

(3) maintaining bank accounts;

(4) maintaining offices or agencies for the transfer, exchange, and registration of the corporation's own securities or maintaining trustees or depositaries with respect to those securities;

(5) selling through independent contractors;

(6) soliciting or obtaining orders, whether by mail or through employees or agents or otherwise, if the orders require acceptance outside this state before they become contracts;

(7) creating or acquiring indebtedness, mortgages, and security interests in real or personal property;

(8) securing or collecting debts or enforcing mortgages and security interests in property securing the debts;

(9) owning, without more, real or personal property;

(10) conducting an isolated transaction that is completed within 30 days and that is not one in the course of repeated transactions of a like nature;

(11) transacting business in interstate commerce.

(c) The list of activities in subsection (b) is not exhaustive.

§ 15.02. Consequences of Transacting Business Without Authority

(a) A foreign corporation transacting business in this state without a certificate of authority may not maintain a proceeding in any court in this state until it obtains a certificate of authority.

(b) The successor to a foreign corporation that transacted business in this state without a certificate of authority and the assignee of a cause of action arising out of that business may not maintain a proceeding based on that cause of action in any court in this state until the foreign corporation or its successor obtains a certificate of authority.

(c) A court may stay a proceeding commenced by a foreign corporation, its successor, or assignee until it determines whether the foreign corporation or its successor requires a certificate of authority. If it so determines, the court may further stay the proceeding until the foreign corporation or its successor obtains the certificate.

(d) A foreign corporation is liable for a civil penalty of $_____ for each day, but not to exceed a total of $_____ for each year, it transacts business in this state without a certificate of authority. The attorney general may collect all penalties due under this subsection.

(e) Notwithstanding subsections (a) and (b), the failure of a foreign corporation to obtain a certificate of authority does not impair the validity of its corporate acts or prevent it from defending any proceeding in this state.

§ 15.03. Application for Certificate of Authority

(a) A foreign corporation may apply for a certificate of authority to transact business in this state by delivering an application

to the secretary of state for filing. The application must set forth:

(1) the name of the foreign corporation or, if its name is unavailable for use in this state, a corporate name that satisfies the requirements of section 15.06;

(2) the name of the state or country under whose law it is incorporated;

(3) its date of incorporation and period of duration;

(4) the street address of its principal office;

(5) the address of its registered office in this state and the name of its registered agent at that office; and

(6) the names and usual business addresses of its current directors and officers.

(b) The foreign corporation shall deliver with the completed application a certificate of existence (or a document of similar import) duly authenticated by the secretary of state or other official having custody of corporate records in the state or country under whose law it is incorporated.

§ 15.04. Amended Certificate of Authority

(a) A foreign corporation authorized to transact business in this state must obtain an amended certificate of authority from the secretary of state if it changes:

(1) its corporate name;

(2) the period of its duration; or

(3) the state or country of its incorporation.

(b) The requirements of section 15.03 for obtaining an original certificate of authority apply to obtaining an amended certificate under this section.

§ 15.05. Effect of Certificate of Authority

(a) A certificate of authority authorizes the foreign corporation to which it is issued to transact business in this state subject, however, to the right of the state to revoke the certificate as provided in this Act.

(b) A foreign corporation with a valid certificate of authority has the same but no greater rights and has the same but no greater privileges as, and except as otherwise provided by this Act is subject to the same duties, restrictions, penalties, and liabilities now or later imposed on, a domestic corporation of like character.

(c) This Act does not authorize this state to regulate the organization or internal affairs of a foreign corporation authorized to transact business in this state.

§ 15.06. Corporate Name of Foreign Corporation

(a) If the corporate name of a foreign corporation does not satisfy the requirements of section 4.01, the foreign corporation to obtain or maintain a certificate of authority to transact business in this state:

(1) may add the word "corporation," "incorporated," "company," or "limited," or the abbreviation "corp.," "inc.," "co.," or "ltd.," to its corporate name for use in this state; or

(2) may use a fictitious name to transact business in this state if its real name is unavailable and it delivers to the secre-

tary of state for filing a copy of the resolution of its board of directors, certified by its secretary, adopting the fictitious name.

(b) Except as authorized by subsections (c) and (d), the corporate name (including a fictitious name) of a foreign corporation must be distinguishable upon the records of the secretary of state from:

(1) the corporate name of a corporation incorporated or authorized to transact business in this state;

(2) a corporate name reserved or registered under section 4.02 or 4.03;

(3) the fictitious name of another foreign corporation authorized to transact business in this state; and

(4) the corporate name of a not-for-profit corporation incorporated or authorized to transact business in this state.

(c) A foreign corporation may apply to the secretary of state for authorization to use in this state the name of another corporation (incorporated or authorized to transact business in this state) that is not distinguishable upon his records from the name applied for. The secretary of state shall authorize use of the name applied for if:

(1) the other corporation consents to the use in writing and submits an undertaking in form satisfactory to the secretary of state to change its name to a name that is distinguishable upon the records of the secretary of state from the name of the applying corporation; or

(2) the applicant delivers to the secretary of state a certified copy of a final judgment of a court of competent jurisdiction establishing the applicant's right to use the name applied for in this state.

(d) A foreign corporation may use in this state the name (including the fictitious name) of another domestic or foreign corporation that is used in this state if the other corporation is incorporated or authorized to transact business in this state and the foreign corporation:

(1) has merged with the other corporation;

(2) has been formed by reorganization of the other corporation; or

(3) has acquired all or substantially all of the assets, including the corporate name, of the other corporation.

(e) If a foreign corporation authorized to transact business in this state changes its corporate name to one that does not satisfy the requirements of section 4.01, it may not transact business in this state under the changed name until it adopts a name satisfying the requirements of section 4.01 and obtains an amended certificate of authority under section 15.04.

§ 15.07. Registered Office and Registered Agent of Foreign Corporation

Each foreign corporation authorized to transact business in this state must continuously maintain in this state:

(1) a registered office that may be the same as any of its places of business; and

(2) a registered agent, who may be:

(i) an individual who resides in this state and whose business office is identical with the registered office;

(ii) a domestic corporation or not-for-profit domestic corporation whose business office is identical with the registered office; or

(iii) a foreign corporation or foreign not-for-profit corporation authorized to transact business in this state whose business office is identical with the registered office.

§ 15.08. Change of Registered Office or Registered Agent of Foreign Corporation

(a) A foreign corporation authorized to transact business in this state may change its registered office or registered agent by delivering to the secretary of state for filing a statement of change that sets forth:

(1) its name;

(2) the street address of its current registered office;

(3) if the current registered office is to be changed, the street address of its new registered office;

(4) the name of its current registered agent;

(5) if the current registered agent is to be changed, the name of its new registered agent and the new agent's written consent (either on the statement or attached to it) to the appointment; and

(6) that after the change or changes are made, the street addresses of its registered office and the business office of its registered agent will be identical.

(b) If a registered agent changes the street address of his business office, he may change the street address of the registered office of any foreign corporation for which he is the registered agent by notifying the corporation in writing of the change and signing (either manually or in facsimile) and delivering to the secretary of state for filing a statement of change that complies with the requirements of subsection (a) and recites that the corporation has been notified of the change.

§ 15.09. Resignation of Registered Agent of Foreign Corporation

(a) The registered agent of a foreign corporation may resign his agency appointment by signing and delivering to the secretary of state for filing the original and two exact or conformed copies of a statement of resignation. The statement of resignation may include a statement that the registered office is also discontinued.

(b) After filing the statement, the secretary of state shall attach the filing receipt to one copy and mail the copy and receipt to the registered office if not discontinued. The secretary of state shall mail the other copy to the foreign corporation at its principal office address shown in its most recent annual report.

(c) The agency appointment is terminated, and the registered office discontinued if so provided, on the 31st day after the date on which the statement was filed.

§ 15.10.   Service on Foreign Corporation

(a) The registered agent of a foreign corporation authorized to transact business in this state is the corporation's agent for service of process, notice, or demand required or permitted by law to be served on the foreign corporation.

(b) A foreign corporation may be served by registered or certified mail, return receipt requested, addressed to the secretary of the foreign corporation at its principal office shown in its application for a certificate of authority or in its most recent annual report if the foreign corporation:

(1) has no registered agent or its registered agent cannot with reasonable diligence be served.

(2) has withdrawn from transacting business in this state under section 15.20; or

(3) has had its certificate of authority revoked under section 15.31.

(c) Service is perfected under subsection (b) at the earliest of:

(1) the date the foreign corporation receives the mail;

(2) the date shown on the return receipt, if signed on behalf of the foreign corporation; or

(3) five days after its deposit in the United States Mail, as evidenced by the postmark, if mailed postpaid and correctly addressed.

(d) This section does not prescribe the only means, or necessarily the required means, of serving a foreign corporation.

Subchapter B.   Withdrawal

§ 15.20.   Withdrawal of Foreign Corporation

(a) A foreign corporation authorized to transact business in this state may not withdraw from this state until it obtains a certificate of withdrawal from the secretary of state.

(b) A foreign corporation authorized to transact business in this state may apply for a certificate of withdrawal by delivering an application to the secretary of state for filing. The application must set forth:

(1) the name of the foreign corporation and the name of the state or country under whose law it is incorporated;

(2) that it is not transacting business in this state and that it surrenders its authority to transact business in this state;

(3) that it revokes the authority of its registered agent to accept service on its behalf and appoints the secretary of state as its agent for service of process in any proceeding based on a cause of action arising during the time it was authorized to transact business in this state;

(4) a mailing address to which the secretary of state may mail a copy of any process served on him under subdivision (3); and

(5) a commitment to notify the secretary of state in the future of any change in its mailing address.

(c) After the withdrawal of the corporation is effective, service of process on the secretary of state under this section is service on the foreign corporation. Upon receipt of process, the secretary of state shall mail a copy of the process to the foreign corporation at the mailing address set forth under subsection (b).

Subchapter C.   Revocation of Certificate of Authority

§ 15.30.   Grounds for Revocation

The secretary of state may commence a proceeding under section 15.31 to revoke the certificate of authority of a foreign corporation authorized to transact business in this state if:

(1) the foreign corporation does not deliver its annual report to the secretary of state within 60 days after it is due;

(2) the foreign corporation does not pay within 60 days after they are due any franchise taxes or penalties imposed by this Act or other law;

(3) the foreign corporation is without a registered agent or registered office in this state for 60 days or more;

(4) the foreign corporation does not inform the secretary of state under section 15.08 or 15.09 that its registered agent or registered office has changed, that its registered agent has resigned, or that its registered office has been discontinued within 60 days of the change, resignation, or discontinuance;

(5) an incorporator, director, officer, or agent of the foreign corporation signed a document he knew was false in any material respect with intent that the document be delivered to the secretary of state for filing;

(6) the secretary of state receives a duly authenticated certificate from the secretary of state or other official having custody of corporate records in the state or country under whose law the foreign corporation is incorporated stating that it has been dissolved or disappeared as the result of a merger.

§ 15.31.   Procedure for and Effect of Revocation

(a) If the secretary of state determines that one or more grounds exist under section 15.30 for revocation of a certificate of authority, he shall serve the foreign corporation with written notice of his determination under section 15.10.

(b) If the foreign corporation does not correct each ground for revocation or demonstrate to the reasonable satisfaction of the secretary of state that each ground determined by the secretary of state does not exist within 60 days after service of the notice is perfected under section 15.10, the secretary of state may revoke the foreign corporation's certificate of authority by signing a certificate of revocation that recites the ground or grounds for revocation and effective date. The secretary of state shall file the original of the certificate and serve a copy on the foreign corporation under section 15.10.

(c) The authority of a foreign corporation to transact business in this state ceases on the date shown on the certificate revoking its certificate of authority.

(d) The secretary of state's revocation of a foreign corporation's certificate of authority appoints the secretary of state the foreign corporation's agent for service of process in any proceeding based on a cause of action which arose during the time the foreign corporation was authorized to transact business in this state. Service of process on the secretary of state under this subsection is service on the foreign corporation. Upon receipt of process, the secretary of state shall mail a copy of the process to the secretary of the foreign corporation at its principal office shown in its most recent annual report or in any subsequent communication received from the corporation stating the current mailing address of its principal office, or, if none are on file, in its application for a certificate of authority.

(e) Revocation of a foreign corporation's certificate of authority does not terminate the authority of the registered agent of the corporation.

§ 15.32.   Appeal from Revocation

(a) A foreign corporation may appeal the secretary of state's revocation of its certificate of authority to the [name or describe] court within 30 days after service of the certificate of revocation is perfected under section 15.10. The foreign corporation appeals by petitioning the court to set aside the revocation and attaching to the petition copies of its certificate of authority and the secretary of state's certificate of revocation.

(b) The court may summarily order the secretary of state to reinstate the certificate of authority or may take any other action the court considers appropriate.

(c) The court's final decision may be appealed as in other civil proceedings.

CHAPTER 16.   RECORDS AND REPORTS

Subchapter A.   Records

§ 16.01.   Corporate Records

(a) A corporation shall keep as permanent records minutes of all meetings of its shareholders and board of directors, a record of all actions taken by the shareholders or board of directors without a meeting, and a record of all actions taken by a committee of the board of directors in place of the board of directors on behalf of the corporation.

(b) A corporation shall maintain appropriate accounting records.

(c) A corporation or its agent shall maintain a record of its shareholders, in a form that permits preparation of a list of the names and addresses of all shareholders, in alphabetical order by class of shares showing the number and class of shares held by each.

(d) A corporation shall maintain its records in written form or in another form capable of conversion into written form within a reasonable time.

(e) A corporation shall keep a copy of the following records at its principal office:

(1) its articles or restated articles of incorporation and all amendments to them currently in effect;

(2) its bylaws or restated bylaws and all amendments to them currently in effect;

(3) resolutions adopted by its board of directors creating one or more classes or series of shares, and fixing their relative rights, preferences, and limitations, if shares issued pursuant to those resolutions are outstanding;

(4) the minutes of all shareholders' meetings, and records of all action taken by shareholders without a meeting, for the past three years;

(5) all written communications to shareholders generally within the past three years, including the financial statements furnished for the past three years under section 16.20;

(6) a list of the names and business addresses of its current directors and officers; and

(7) its most recent annual report delivered to the secretary of state under section 16.22.

§ 16.02.   Inspection of Records by Shareholders

(a) Subject to section 16.03(c), a shareholder of a corporation is entitled to inspect and copy, during regular business hours at the corporation's principal office, any of the records of the corporation described in section 16.01(e) if he gives the corporation written notice of his demand at least five business days before the date on which he wishes to inspect and copy.

(b) A shareholder of a corporation is entitled to inspect and copy, during regular business hours at a reasonable location specified by the corporation, any of the following records of the corporation if the shareholder meets the requirements of subsection (c) and gives the corporation written notice of his demand at least five business days before the date on which he wishes to inspect and copy:

(1) excerpts from minutes of any meeting of the board of directors, records of any action of a committee of the board of directors while acting in place of the board of directors on behalf of the corporation, minutes of any meeting of the shareholders, and records of action taken by the shareholders or board of directors without a meeting, to the extent not subject to inspection under section 16.02(a);

(2) accounting records of the corporation; and

(3) the record of shareholders.

(c) A shareholder may inspect and copy the records identified in subsection (b) only if:

(1) his demand is made in good faith and for a proper purpose;

(2) he describes with reasonable particularity his purpose and the records he desires to inspect; and

(3) the records are directly connected with his purpose.

(d) The right of inspection granted by this section may not be abolished or limited by a corporation's articles of incorporation or bylaws.

(e) This section does not affect:

(1) the right of a shareholder to inspect records under section 7.20 or, if the shareholder is in litigation with the corporation, to the same extent as any other litigant;

(2) the power of a court, independently of this Act, to compel the production of corporate records for examination.

(f) For purposes of this section, "shareholder" includes a beneficial owner whose shares are held in a voting trust or by a nominee on his behalf.

§ 16.03.   Scope of Inspection Right

(a) A shareholder's agent or attorney has the same inspection and copying rights as the shareholder he represents.

(b) The right to copy records under section 16.02 includes, if reasonable, the right to receive copies made by photographic, xerographic, or other means.

(c) The corporation may impose a reasonable charge, covering the costs of labor and material, for copies of any documents provided to the shareholder. The charge may not exceed the estimated cost of production or reproduction of the records.

(d) The corporation may comply with a shareholder's demand to inspect the record of shareholder's under section 16.02(b)(3) by providing him with a list of its shareholders that was compiled no earlier than the date of the shareholder's demand.

§ 16.04.   Court-Ordered Inspection

(a) If a corporation does not allow a shareholder who complies with section 16.02(a) to inspect and copy any records required by that subsection to be available for inspection, the [name or describe court] of the county where the corporation's principal office (or, if none in this state, its registered office) is located may summarily order inspection and copying of the records demanded at the corporation's expense upon application of the shareholder.

(b) If a corporation does not within a reasonable time allow a shareholder to inspect and copy any other record, the shareholder who complies with section 16.02(b) and (c) may apply to the [name or describe court] in the county where the corporation's principal office (or, if none in this state, its registered office) is located for an order to permit inspection and copying of the records demanded. The court shall dispose of an application under this subsection on an expedited basis.

(c) If the court orders inspection and copying of the records demanded, it shall also order the corporation to pay the shareholders' costs (including reasonable counsel fees) incurred to obtain the order unless the corporation proves that it refused inspection in good faith because it had a reasonable basis for doubt about the right of the shareholder to inspect the records demanded.

(d) If the court orders inspection and copying of the records demanded, it may impose reasonable restrictions on the use or distribution of the records by the demanding shareholder.

Subchapter B.   Reports

§ 16.20.   Financial Statements for Shareholders

(a) A corporation shall furnish its shareholders annual financial statements, which may be consolidated or combined statements of the corporation and one or more of its subsidiaries, as appropriate, that include a balance sheet as of the end of the fiscal year, an income statement for that year, and a statement of changes in shareholders' equity for the year unless that information appears elsewhere in the financial statements. If financial statements are prepared for the corporation on the basis of generally accepted accounting principles, the annual financial statements must also be prepared on that basis.

(b) If the annual financial statements are reported upon by a public accountant, his report must accompany them. If not, the statements must be accompanied by a statement of the president or the person responsible for the corporation's accounting records:

(1) stating his reasonable belief whether the statements were prepared on the basis of generally accepted accounting principles and, if not, describing the basis of preparation; and

(2) describing any respects in which the statements were not prepared on a basis of accounting consistent with the statements prepared for the preceding year.

(c) A corporation shall mail the annual financial statements to each shareholder within 120 days after the close of each fiscal year. Thereafter, on written request from a shareholder who was not mailed the statements, the corporation shall mail him the latest financial statements.

§ 16.21.   Other Reports to Shareholders

(a) If a corporation indemnifies or advances expenses to a director under section 8.51, 8.52, 8.53, or 8.54 in connection with a proceeding by or in the right of the corporation, the corporation shall report the indemnification or advance in writing to the shareholders with or before the notice of the next shareholders' meeting.

(b) If a corporation issues or authorizes the issuance of shares for promissory notes or for promises to render services in the future, the corporation shall report in writing to the shareholders the number of shares authorized or issued, and the consideration received by the corporation, with or before the notice of the next shareholders' meeting.

§ 16.22.   Annual Report for Secretary of State

(a) Each domestic corporation, and each foreign corporation authorized to transact business in this state, shall deliver to the secretary of state for filing an annual report that sets forth:

(1) the name of the corporation and the state or country under whose law it is incorporated;

(2) the address of its registered office and the name of its registered agent at that office in this state;

(3) the address of its principal office;

(4) the names and business addresses of its directors and principal officers;

(5) a brief description of the nature of its business;

(6) the total number of authorized shares, itemized by class and series, if any, within each class; and

(7) the total number of issued and outstanding shares, itemized by class and series, if any, within each class.

(b) Information in the annual report must be current as of the date the annual report is executed on behalf of the corporation.

(c) The first annual report must be delivered to the secretary of state between January 1 and April 1 of the year following the calendar year in which a domestic corporation was incorporated or a foreign corporation was authorized to transact business. Subsequent annual reports must be delivered to the secretary of state between January 1 and April 1 of the following calendar years.

(d) If an annual report does not contain the information required by this section, the secretary of state shall promptly notify the reporting domestic or foreign corporation in writing and return the report to it for correction. If the report is corrected to contain the information required by this section and delivered to the secretary of state within 30 days after the effective date of notice, it is deemed to be timely filed.

CHAPTER 17.   TRANSITION PROVISIONS

§ 17.01.   Application to Existing Domestic Corporations (*Text omitted.*)

§ 17.02.   Application to Qualified Foreign Corporations (*Text omitted.*)

§ 17.03.   Saving Provisions (*Text omitted.*)

§ 17.04.   Severability (*Text omitted.*)

§ 17.05.   Repeal (*Text omitted.*)

§ 17.06.   Effective Date (*Text omitted.*)

Abatement An action of stopping or removing.

Ab Initio From the beginning. A contract that is void ab initio is void from its inception.

Abstract of Title A summary of the conveyances, transfers, and other facts relied on as evidence of title, together with all such facts appearing of record that may impair its validity. It should contain a brief but complete history of the title.

Abuse of Process An intentional tort designed to protect against the initiation of legal proceedings for a primary purpose other than the one for which such proceedings were designed.

Acceleration The shortening of the time for the performance of a contract or the payment of a note by the operation of some provision in the contract or note itself.

Acceptance The actual or implied receipt and retention of that which is tendered or offered.

Accession The acquisition of property by its incorporation or union with other property.

Accommodation Paper A negotiable instrument signed without consideration by a party as acceptor, drawer, or indorser for the purpose of enabling the payee to obtain credit.

Accommodation Party A person who signs a negotiable instrument for the purpose of adding his name and liability to another party to the instrument.

Accord and Satisfaction A legally binding agreement to settle a disputed claim for a definite amount.

Account Stated An account that has been rendered by one to another and which purports to state the true balance due and that balance is either expressly or impliedly admitted to be due by the debtor.

Acknowledgment A form for authenticating instruments conveying property or otherwise conferring rights. It is a public declaration by the grantor that the act evidenced by the instrument is his act and deed. Also, an admission or confirmation.

Acquit To set free or judicially to discharge from an accusation; to release from a debt, duty, obligation, charge, or suspicion of guilt.

Actionable Capable of being remedied by a legal action or claim.

Action ex Contractu An action arising out of the breach of a contract.

Action ex Delicto An action arising out of the violation of a duty or obligation created by positive law independent of contract. An action in tort.

Act of God An occurrence resulting exclusively from natural forces that could not have been prevented or whose effect could not have been avoided by care or foresight.

Act of State Doctrine A doctrine of international law that no nation is permitted to judge the act of another nation committed within its own boundaries.

Adjudge To give judgment; to decide; to sentence.

Adjudicate To adjudge; to settle by judicial decree, as a court.

Ad Litem During the pendency of the action or proceeding.

Administrator The personal representative appointed by a probate court to settle the estate of a deceased person who died intestate (without leaving a valid will).

Adoption In corporation law, a corporation's acceptance of a preincorporation contract by action of its board of directors, by which the corporation becomes liable on the contract.

Adverse Possession Open and notorious possession of real property over a given length of time that denies ownership in any other claimant.

Advised Letter of Credit See **Letter of Credit, Advised.**

Advisement A court's delaying its decision until it has examined and considered the questions involved.

Affidavit A signed writing containing statements of fact to whose accuracy the signing party has sworn. Used in a variety of judicial proceedings, including the motion for summary judgment.

Affirm To confirm or uphold a former judgment or order of a court. Appellate courts, for instance, may affirm the decisions of lower courts.

After-Acquired Property Property of the debtor that is obtained after a security interest in the debtor's property has been created.

Agency   A legal relationship in which an agent acts under the direction of a principal for the principal's benefit. Also used to refer to government regulatory bodies of all kinds.

Agent   One who acts under the direction of a principal for the principal's benefit in a legal relationship known as agency. See **Principal.**

Aggregate Theory   In partnership law, the view that there is no distinction between a partnership and the partners who own it. See **Entity Theory.**

Aggrieved   One whose legal rights have been invaded by the act of another is said to be aggrieved. Also, one whose pecuniary interest is directly affected by a judgment, or whose right of property may be divested thereby, is to be considered a party aggrieved.

Alienation   The voluntary act or acts by which one person transfers his or her own property to another.

Alien Corporation   A corporation incorporated in one country that is doing business in another country. See **Foreign Corporation.**

Allegation   A statement of a party to an action in a declaration or pleading of what the party intends to prove.

Allege   To make a statement of fact; to plead.

Alter Ego   Latin for "other self." In corporation law, a doctrine that permits a court to pierce a corporation's veil and to hold a shareholder liable for the actions of a corporation dominated by the shareholder.

Amortize   To provide for the payment of a debt by creating a sinking fund or paying in installments.

Ancillary   Auxiliary to. An ancillary receiver is a receiver who has been appointed in aid of, and in subordination to, the primary receiver.

Ancillary Covenant Not to Compete   A promise that is ancillary to (part of) a valid contract whereby one party to a contract agrees not to compete with the other party for a specified time and within a specified location. Also called *non-competition clause.*

Answer   The pleading of a defendant in which he or she may deny any or all the facts set out in the plaintiff's declaration or complaint.

Anticipatory Breach   A contracting party's indication before the time for performance that he cannot or will not perform the contract.

Appearance   The first act of the defendant in court.

Appellant   The party making an appeal.

Appellate Jurisdiction   Jurisdiction to revise or correct the work of a subordinate court.

Appellee   A party against whom a favorable court decision is appealed. May be called the *respondent* in some jurisdictions.

Applicant   A petitioner; one who files a petition or application.

Appraisal, Right of   A shareholder's right to receive the fair value of her shares from her corporation when she objects to a corporate transaction that significantly alters her rights in the corporation.

Appurtenance   An accessory; something that belongs to another thing.

Arbitrate   To submit some disputed matter to selected persons and to accept their decision or award as a substitute for the decision of a judicial tribunal.

Argument   The discussion by counsel for the respective parties of their contentions on the law and the facts of the case being tried in order to aid the jury in arriving at a correct and just conclusion.

Articles of Incorporation   A document that must be filed with a secretary of state to create a corporation. Usually, it includes the basic rights and responsibilities of the corporation and the shareholders.

Articles of Partnership   A formal written contract between the partners of a partnership that states the rights and the responsibilities of the partners.

Artisan's Lien   A common law possessory security interest arising out of the improvement of property by one skilled in some mechanical art or craft; the lien entitles the improver of the property to retain possession in order to secure the agreed-upon price or the value of the work performed.

Assault   An intentional tort that prohibits any attempt or offer to cause harmful or offensive contact with another if it results in a well-grounded apprehension of imminent battery in the mind of the threatened person.

Assent   To give or express one's concurrence or approval of something done.

Assignable   Capable of being lawfully assigned or transferred; transferable; negotiable. Also, capable of being specified or pointed out as an assignable error.

Assignee   A person to whom an assignment is made.

Assignment   A transfer or setting over of property or some right or interest therein, from one person to another.

Assignment of Partnership Interest   A partner's voluntary transfer of her partnership interest to the partner's personal creditor, giving the creditor the right to receive the partner's share of partnership profits.

Assignor   The maker of an assignment.

Assumpsit   An action at common law to recover damages for breach of contract.

Assumption of Risk   A traditional defense to negligence liability based on the argument that the plaintiff voluntarily exposed himself to a known danger created by the defendant's negligence.

Assurance   To provide confidence or to inform positively.

Attachment   In general, the process of taking a person's property under an appropriate judicial order by an appropriate officer of the court. Used for a variety of purposes, including the acquisition of jurisdiction over the property seized and the securing of property that may be used to satisfy a debt.

Attest To bear witness to; to affirm; to be true or genuine.

Attorney-in-Fact An agent who is given express, written authorization by his principal to do a particular act or series of acts on behalf of the principal.

Audit Committee In corporation law, a committee of the board that recommends and supervises the public accountant who audits the corporation's financial records.

Authentication Such official attestation of a written instrument as will render it legally admissible in evidence.

Authority In agency law, an agent's ability to affect his principal's legal relations with third parties. Also used to refer to an actor's legal power or ability to do something. In addition, sometimes used to refer to a statute, case, or other legal source that justifies a particular result.

Authorized Shares Shares that a corporation is empowered to issue by its articles of incorporation.

Automatic Stay Under the Bankruptcy Act, the suspension of all litigation against the debtor and his property, which is triggered by the filing of a bankruptcy petition.

Averment A positive statement of fact made in a pleading.

Avoid To nullify a contractual obligation.

Bad Faith A person's actual intent to mislead or deceive another; an intent to take an unfair and unethical advantage of another.

Bailee The person to whom a bailment is made.

Bailment The transfer of personal property by its owner to another person with the understanding that the property will be returned to the owner in the future.

Bailor The owner of bailed property; the one who delivers personal property to another to be held in bailment.

Bankruptcy The state of a person who is unable to pay his or her debts without respect to time; one whose liabilities exceed his or her assets.

Bar As a collective noun, it is used to include those persons who are admitted to practice law, members of the bar. The court itself. A plea or peremptory exception of a defendant sufficient to destroy the plaintiff's action.

Battery An intentional tort that prohibits the harmful or offensive touching of another without his consent.

Bearer The designation of the bearer as the payee of a negotiable instrument signifies that the instrument is payable to the person who seems to be the holder.

Bench Generally used as a synonym for the term *court* or the judges of a court.

Beneficiary The person for whose benefit an insurance policy, trust, will, or contract is established. In the case of a contract, the beneficiary is called a *third party beneficiary.*

Bequeath In a will, a gift of particular property.

Bid To make an offer at an auction or at a judicial sale. As a noun, it means an offer.

Bilateral Contract A contract in which the promise of one of the parties forms the consideration for the promise of the other; a contract formed by an offer requiring a reciprocal promise.

Bill of Exchange An unconditional order in writing by one person to another, signed by the person giving it, requiring the person to whom it is addressed to pay on demand or at a fixed or determinable future time a sum certain in money to order or to bearer.

Bill of Lading A written acknowledgment of the receipt of goods to be transported to a designated place and delivery to a named person or to his or her order.

Bill of Sale A written agreement by which one person assigns or transfers interests or rights in personal property to another.

Binder Also called a *binding slip*—a brief memorandum or agreement issued by an insurer as a temporary policy for the convenience of all the parties, constituting a present insurance in the amount specified, to continue in force until the execution of a formal policy.

"Blue Sky" Laws The popular name for state statutes that regulate securities transactions.

Bona Fide Made honestly and in good faith; genuine.

Bona Fide Purchaser An innocent buyer for valuable consideration who purchases goods without notice of any defects in the title of the goods acquired.

Bond A long-term debt security that is secured by collateral.

Bonus Shares Also called *bonus stock*. Shares issued for no lawful consideration. See **Discount Shares** and **Watered Shares.**

Breaking Bulk The division or separation of the contents of a package or container.

Brief A statement of a party's case or legal arguments, usually prepared by an attorney. Often used to support some of the motions described in The Resolution of Private Disputes chapter, and also used to make legal arguments before appellate courts. Also, an abridgment of a reported case.

Broker An agent who bargains or carries on negotiations in behalf of the principal as an intermediary between the latter and third persons in transacting business relative to the acquisition of contractual rights, or to the sale or purchase of property the custody of which is not intrusted to him or her for the purpose of discharging the agency.

Bulk Transfer The sale or transfer of a major part of the stock of goods of a merchant at one time and not in the ordinary course of business.

Burden of Proof Used to refer both to the necessity or obligation of proving the facts needed to support a party's claim, and the persuasiveness of the evidence used to do so. Regarding the second sense of the term, the usual burden of proof in a civil case is a preponderance of the evidence, and in a criminal case it is proof beyond a reasonable doubt.

Business Judgment Rule A rule protecting business managers from liability for making bad decisions when they have acted prudently and in good faith.

Buy-and-Sell Agreement A share transfer restriction compelling a shareholder to sell his shares to the other shareholders or the corporation and obligating the other shareholders or the corporation to buy the shareholder's shares.

Buyer in Ordinary Course of Business A person who, in good faith and without knowledge that the sale to him is in violation of a third party's ownership rights or security interest in the goods, buys in ordinary course from a person who is in the business of selling goods of that kind.

Bylaws In corporation law, a document that supplements the articles of incorporation and contains less important rights, powers, and responsibilities of a corporation and its shareholders, officers, and directors.

C & F The price of the goods includes the cost of the goods plus the freight to the named destination.

Call See **Redemption**. Also, a type of option permitting a person to buy a fixed number of securities at a fixed price at a specified time. See **Put**.

Canceled Shares Previously outstanding shares repurchased by a corporation and canceled by it; such shares no longer exist.

Cancellation The act of crossing out a writing. The operation of destroying a written instrument.

Capacity The ability to incur legal obligations and acquire legal rights.

Capital Contributions of money and other property to a business made by the owners of the business.

Capital Stock See **Stated Capital.**

Capital Surplus Also called *additional paid capital*. A balance sheet account; the portion of shareholders' contributions exceeding the par or stated value of shares.

Case Law The law extracted from decided cases.

Cashier's Check A draft (including a check) drawn by a bank on itself and accepted by the act of issuance.

Causa Mortis In contemplation of approaching death.

Cause of Action A legal rule giving the plaintiff the right to obtain some legal relief once certain factual elements are proven. Often used synonymously with the terms *claim* or *theory of recovery.*

Caveat Emptor "Let the buyer beware."

Caveat Venditor "Let the seller beware."

Certificate of Deposit An acknowledgment by a bank of the receipt of money with an engagement to pay it back.

Certificate of Limited Partnership A document that must be filed with a secretary of state to create a limited partnership.

Certification The return of a writ; a formal attestation of a matter of fact; the appropriate marking of a certified check.

Certified Check A check that has been "accepted" by the drawee bank and has been so marked or certified that it indicates such acceptance.

Chancellor A judge of a court of chancery.

Chancery Equity or a court of equity.

Charge The legal instructions that a judge gives a jury before the jury begins its deliberations. In the prosecution of a crime, to formally accuse the offender or charge him with the crime.

Charging Order A court's order granting rights in a partner's partnership interest to a personal creditor of the partner; a creditor with a charging order is entitled to the partner's share of partnership profits.

Charter An instrument or authority from the sovereign power bestowing the right or power to do business under the corporate form of organization. Also, the organic law of a city or town, and representing a portion of the statute law of the state.

Chattel An article of tangible property other than land.

Chattel Mortgage An instrument whereby the owner of chattels transfers the title to such property to another as security for the performance of an obligation subject to be defeated on the performance of the obligation. Under the UCC, called merely a *security interest.*

Check A written order on a bank or banker payable on demand to the person named or his order or bearer and drawn by virtue of credits due the drawer from the bank created by money deposited with the bank.

Chose in Action A personal right not reduced to possession but recoverable by a suit at law.

CIF An abbreviation for cost, freight, and insurance, used in mercantile transactions, especially in import transactions.

Citation A writ issued out of a court of competent jurisdiction, commanding the person therein named to appear on a day named to do something therein mentioned.

Citation of Authorities The reference to legal authorities such as reported cases or treatises to support propositions advanced.

Civil Action An action brought to enforce a civil right; in contrast to a criminal action.

Class Action An action brought on behalf of the plaintiff and others similarly situated.

Close Corporation A corporation with few shareholders generally having a close personal relationship to each other and participating in the management of the business.

COD "Cash on delivery." When goods are delivered to a

carrier for a cash on delivery shipment the carrier must not deliver without receiving payment of the amount due.

Code A system of law; a systematic and complete body of law.

Codicil Some addition to or qualification of one's last will and testament.

Collateral Property put up to secure the performance of a promise, so that if the promisor fails to perform as promised, the creditor may look to the property to make him whole.

Collateral Attack An attempt to impeach a decree, a judgment, or other official act in a proceeding that has not been instituted for the express purpose of correcting or annulling or modifying the decree, judgment, or official act.

Collateral Contract A contract in which one person agrees to pay the debt of another if the principal debtor fails to pay. See **Guaranty.**

Comaker A person who with another or others signs a negotiable instrument on its face and thereby becomes primarily liable for its payment.

Commercial Impracticability The standards used by the UCC, replacing the common law doctrine of impossibility, to define when a party is relieved of his or her contract obligations because of the occurrence of unforeseeable, external events beyond his or her control.

Commercial Law The law that relates to the rights of property and persons engaged in trade or commerce.

Commercial Paper Negotiable paper such as promissory notes, drafts, and checks that provides for the payment of money and can readily be transferred to other parties.

Commercial Unit Under the UCC, any unit of goods that is treated by commercial usage as a single whole. It may, for example, be a single article or a set of articles such as a dozen, bale, gross, or carload.

Common Area In landlord-tenant law, an area over which the landlord retains control but which is often used by or for the benefit of tenants. For example, hallways in an apartment building.

Common Carrier One who undertakes, for hire or reward, to transport the goods of such of the public as choose to employ him.

Common Law That law made and applied by judges in cases not governed by other forms of positive law.

Common Shareholders Shareholders who claim the residual profits and assets of a corporation, and usually have the exclusive power and right to elect the directors of the corporation.

Comparative Fault Often used synonymously with comparative negligence. But also sometimes used to refer to a defense that operates like comparative negligence but considers the plaintiff's and the defendant's overall fault rather than either's negligence alone.

Comparative Negligence The contemporary replacement for the traditional doctrine of contributory negligence. The basic idea is that damages are apportioned between the parties to a negligence action in proportion to their relative fault. The details vary from state to state.

Compensatory Damages See **Damages, Compensatory.**

Complaint The pleading in a civil case in which the plaintiff states his claim and requests relief.

Composition with Creditors An agreement between creditors and their common debtor and between themselves whereby the creditors agree to accept the sum or security stipulated in full payment of their claims.

Concealment In contract law, taking active steps to prevent another from learning the truth.

Concurrent Running with; simultaneously with. The word is used in different senses. In contracts, concurrent conditions are conditions that must be performed simultaneously by the mutual acts required by each of the parties.

Condemn To appropriate land for public use. To adjudge a person guilty; to pass sentence upon a person convicted of a crime.

Condition In contract law, a future, uncertain event that creates or extinguishes a duty of performance; a provision or clause in a contract that operates to suspend or rescind a party's duty to perform. In property law, a qualification or restriction annexed to a conveyance of lands, whereby it is provided that in case a particular event does or does not happen, or in case the grantor or grantees do or omit to do a particular act, an estate shall commence, be enlarged, or be defeated.

Conditional Acceptance An acceptance of a bill of exchange containing some qualification limiting or altering the acceptor's liability on the bill.

Conditional Sale The term is most frequently applied to a sale wherein the seller reserves the title to the goods, though the possession is delivered to the buyer, until the purchase price is paid in full.

Condition Precedent A condition that operates to give rise to a contracting party's duty to perform.

Condition Subsequent A condition that operates to relieve or discharge one from his obligation under a contract.

Confession of Judgment An entry of judgment upon the admission or confession of the debtor without the formality, time, or expense involved in an ordinary proceeding.

Confirmed Letter of Credit See **Letter of Credit, Confirmed.**

Confusion The inseparable intermixture of property belonging to different owners.

Consent Decree or Consent Order Used to refer to the order courts or administrative agencies issue when approving the settlement of a lawsuit or administrative action against some party.

Consent Restraint   A security transfer restriction requiring a shareholder to obtain the consent of the corporation or its shareholders prior to the shareholder's sale of her shares.

Consequential Damages   See **Damages, Consequential**.

Conservator (of an incompetent person)   A person appointed by a court to take care of and oversee the person and estate of an incompetent person.

Consideration   In contract law, a basic requirement for an enforceable agreement under traditional contract principles, defined in this text as legal value, bargained for and given in exchange for an act or promise. In corporation law, cash or property contributed to a corporation in exchange for shares, or a promise to contribute such cash or property.

Consignee   A person to whom goods are consigned, shipped, or otherwise transmitted, either for sale or for safekeeping.

Consignment   A bailment for sale. The consignee does not undertake the absolute obligation to sell or pay for the goods.

Consignor   One who sends goods to another on consignment. A shipper or transmitter of goods.

Conspicuous   Noticeable by a reasonable person, such as a term or clause in a contract that is in bold print, in capitals, or a contrasting color or type style.

Constructive Eviction   In landlord-tenant law, a breach of duty by the landlord that makes the premises uninhabitable or otherwise deprives the tenant of the benefit of the lease and gives rise to the tenant's right to vacate the property and terminate the lease.

Construe   To read a statute or document for the purpose of ascertaining its meaning and effect, but in doing so the law must be regarded.

Contempt   Conduct in the presence of a legislative or judicial body tending to disturb its proceedings or impair the respect due to its authority, or a disobedience to the rules or orders of such a body, which interferes with the due administration of law.

Contra   Otherwise; disagreeing with; contrary to.

Contract   A legally enforceable promise or set of promises.

Contract of Adhesion   A contract in which a stronger party is able to dictate terms to a weaker party, leaving the weaker party no practical choice but to "adhere" to the terms. If the stronger party has exploited its bargaining power to achieve unfair terms, the contract is against public policy.

Contribution   In business organization law, the cash or property contributed to a business by its owners.

Contributory Negligence   A traditional defense to negligence liability based on the plaintiff's failure to exercise reasonable care for his own safety.

Conversion   Any distinct act of dominion wrongfully exerted over another's personal property in denial of or inconsistent with his rights therein. That tort committed by a person who deals with chattels not belonging to him in a manner that is inconsistent with the ownership of the lawful owner.

Convertible Securities   Securities giving their holders the power to exchange those securities for other securities without paying any additional consideration.

Conveyance   A written instrument transferring the title to land or some interest therein from one person to another.

Copartnership   A partnership.

Corporation   A form of business organization that is owned by owners, called *shareholders*, who have no inherent right to manage the business, and is managed by a board of directors that is elected by the shareholders.

Corporation by Estoppel   A doctrine that prevents persons from denying that a corporation exists when the persons hold themselves out as representing a corporation or believe themselves to be dealing with a corporation.

Corporeal   Possessing physical substance; tangible; perceptible to the senses.

Counterclaim   A legal claim made in response to the plaintiff's initial claim in a civil suit. Unlike a defense, the counterclaim is the defendant's affirmative attempt to obtain legal relief; in effect, it states a cause of action entitling the defendant to such relief. Often, the counterclaim must arise out of the occurrence that forms the basis for the plaintiff's claim.

Counteroffer   A cross-offer made by the offeree to the offeror.

Countertrade   A buyer's purchase of the seller's goods in exchange for the seller's agreement to purchase goods of the buyer or other person; usually required as a condition to selling goods to a foreign trade corporation.

Course of Dealing   A sequence of previous conduct between the parties to a transaction that is fairly to be regarded as establishing a common basis for interpreting their contract.

Covenant   A contract; a promise.

Cover   To obtain substitute or equivalent goods.

Credible   As applied to a witness, competent.

Creditor   A person to whom a debt or legal obligation is owed, and who has the right to enforce payment of that debt or obligation.

Crime   An act prohibited by the state; a public wrong.

Cross-Action   Cross-complaint; an independent action brought by a defendant against the plaintiff.

Culpable   Blameworthy; denotes breach of legal duty but not necessarily criminal conduct.

Cumulative Voting   A procedure for voting for directors that permits a shareholder to multiply the number of shares he owns by the number of directors to be elected and to cast the resulting total of votes for one or more directors. See **Straight Voting.**

Curtesy   At common law, a husband's right in property owned by his wife during her life.

Custody   The bare control or care of a thing as distinguished from the possession of it.

Cy Pres   "As near as possible." In the law of trusts, a doctrine applied to prevent a charitable trust from failing when the application of trust property to the charitable beneficiary designated by the settlor becomes illegal or impossible to carry out; in such a case, cy pres allows the court to redirect the distribution of trust property for some purpose that is "as near as possible" to the settlor's general charitable intent.

Damages   The sum of money recoverable by a plaintiff who has received a judgment in a civil case.

Compensatory   Damages that will compensate a party for direct losses due to an injury suffered.

Consequential   Damages that do not flow directly and immediately from an act but rather flow from the results of the act; damages that are indirect consequences of a breach of contract or certain other legal wrongs. Examples include personal injury, damage to property, and lost profits.

Incidental   Collateral damages that result from a breach of contract, including all reasonable expenses that are incurred because of the breach; damages that compensate a person injured by a breach of contract for reasonable costs he incurs in an attempt to avoid further loss.

Liquidated   Damages made certain by the prior agreement of the parties.

Nominal   Damages that are recoverable when a legal right is to be vindicated against an invasion that has produced no actual present loss.

Punitive   Damages designed to punish flagrant wrongdoers and to deter them and others from engaging in similar conduct in the future.

Special   Actual damages that would not necessarily but because of special circumstances do in fact flow from an injury.

Treble   Three times provable damages, as may be granted to private parties bringing an action under the antitrust laws.

Date of Issue   As applied to notes, bonds, etc., of a series, the arbitrary date fixed as the beginning of the term for which they run, without reference to the precise time when convenience or the state of the market may permit their sale or delivery.

D/B/A   Doing business as; indicates the use of a trade name.

Deal   To engage in transactions of any kind, to do business with.

Debenture   A long-term, unsecured debt security.

Debtor   A person who is under a legal obligation to pay a sum of money to another (the creditor).

Decedent   A person who has died.

Deceit   A tort involving intentional misrepresentation or cheating by means of some device.

Decision   The judgment of a court; the opinion merely represents the reasons for that judgment.

Declaration   The pleadings by which a plaintiff in an action at law sets out his cause of action. An admission or statement subsequently used as evidence in the trial of an action.

Declaratory Judgment   One that expresses the opinion of a court on a question of law without ordering anything to be done.

Decree   An order or sentence of a court of equity determining some right or adjudicating some matter affecting the merits of the cause.

Deed   A writing, sealed and delivered by the parties; an instrument conveying real property.

Deed of Trust   A three-party instrument used to create a security interest in real property in which the legal title to the real property is placed in one or more trustees to secure the repayment of a sum of money or the performance of other conditions.

De Facto   In fact, actual. Often used in contrast to *de jure* to refer to a real state of affairs.

De Facto Corporation   A corporation that has complied substantially with the mandatory conditions precedent to incorporation, taken as a whole.

Defalcation   The word includes both embezzlement and misappropriation and is a broader term than either.

Defamation   An intentional tort that prohibits the publication of false and defamatory statements concerning another.

Default   Fault; neglect; omission; the failure of a party to an action to appear when properly served with process; the failure to perform a duty or obligation; the failure of a person to pay money when due or when lawfully demanded.

Defeasible   Regarding title to property, capable of being defeated. A title to property that is open to attack or that may be defeated by the performance of some act.

Defend   To oppose a claim or action; to plead in defense of an action; to contest an action suit or proceeding.

Defendant   The party who is sued in a civil case, or the party who is prosecuted in a criminal case.

Defendant in Error   Any of the parties in whose favor a judgment was rendered that the losing party seeks to have reversed or modified by writ of error and whom he names as adverse parties.

Defense   A rule of law entitling the defendant to a judgment in his favor even if the plaintiff proves all elements of his claim or cause of action.

Deficiency   That part of a debt that a mortgage was made to secure, not realized by the liquidation of the mortgaged property. Something which is lacking.

Defraud   To deprive another of a right by deception or artifice.

De Jure   According to the law; legitimate; by legal right.

De Jure Corporation   A corporation that has complied

substantially with each of the mandatory conditions precedent to incorporation.

Delegation   In constitutional law and administrative law, a process whereby a legislature effectively hands over some of its legislative power to an administrative agency that it has created, thus giving the agency power to make law within the limits set by the legislature. In contract law, a transaction whereby a person who owes a legal duty to perform under a contract appoints someone else to carry out his performance.

Deliver   To surrender property to another person.

Demand   A claim; a legal obligation; a request to perform an alleged obligation; a written statement of a claim. In corporation law, a request that the board of directors sue a person who has harmed the corporation; a prerequisite to a shareholder derivative suit.

De Minimis Non Curat Lex   The law is not concerned with trifles. The maxim has been applied to exclude the recovery of nominal damages where no unlawful intent or disturbance of a right of possession is shown, and where all possible damage is expressly disproved.

Demurrer   A civil motion that attacks the plaintiff's complaint by assuming the truth of the facts stated in the complaint for purposes of the motion, and by arguing that even if these facts are true, there is no rule of law entitling the plaintiff to recovery. Roughly similar to the motion to dismiss for failure to state a claim upon which relief can be granted.

De Novo   Anew; over again; a second time. A trial de novo, for example, is a new trial in which the entire case is retried.

Deposition   A form of discovery consisting of the oral examination of a party or a party's witness by the other party's attorney.

Deputy   A person subordinate to a public officer whose business and object is to perform the duties of the principal.

Derivative Suit   Also called *derivative action*. A suit to enforce a corporate right of action brought on behalf of a corporation by one or more of its shareholders.

Descent   Hereditary succession. It is the title whereby upon the death of an ancestor, acquiring the ancestor's estate as an heir under state law.

Detinue   A common law action, now seldom used, which lies where a party claims the specific recovery of goods unlawfully detained from him.

Detriment   Any act or forbearance by a promisee. A loss or harm suffered in person or property.

Devise   In a will, a gift of real property.

Dictum   Language in a judicial opinion that is not necessary for the decision of the case and that, while perhaps persuasive, does not bind subsequent courts. Distinguished from *holding*.

Directed Verdict   A verdict issued by a judge who has, in effect, taken the case away from the jury by directing a verdict for one party. Usually, the motion for a directed verdict is made at trial by one party after the other party has finished presenting his evidence.

Disaffirm   In contract law, a party's exercise of his power to avoid a contract entered before the party reached the age of majority; a minor's cancellation of his contract.

Discharge   Release from liability.

Discharge in Bankruptcy   An order or decree rendered by a court in bankruptcy proceedings, the effect of which is to satisfy all debts provable against the estate of the bankrupt as of the time when the bankruptcy proceedings were initiated.

Disclaimer   A term in a contract whereby a party attempts to relieve itself of some potential liability associated with the contract. The most common example is the seller's attempt to disclaim liability for defects in goods that it sells.

Discount   A loan upon an evidence of debt, where the compensation for the use of the money until the maturity of the debt is deducted from the principal and retained by the lender at the time of making the loan.

Discount Shares   Also called *discount stock*. Shares issued for less than their par value or stated value. See **Bonus Shares** and **Watered Shares.**

Discovery   A process of information-gathering that takes place before a civil trial. See **Deposition** and **Interrogatory.**

Dishonor   The failure to pay or accept a negotiable instrument that has been properly presented.

Dismiss   To order a cause, motion, or prosecution to be discontinued or quashed.

Dissolution   In partnership law, the change in the relation of the partners caused by any partner ceasing to be associated with the carrying on of the business.

Distribution   In business organization law, a business's gratuitous transfer of its assets to the owners of the business. Includes cash and property dividends and redemptions.

Divided Court   A court is so described when there has been a division of opinion between its members on a matter that has been submitted to it for decision.

Dividends, Cash or Property   A corporation's distribution of a portion of its assets to its shareholders, usually corresponding to current or historical corporate profits; unlike a redemption, it is not accompanied by a repurchase of shares.

Dividends, Share   Also called *stock dividends*. A corporation's pro rata issuance of shares to existing shareholders for no consideration.

Domain   The ownership of land; immediate or absolute ownership. The public lands of a state are frequently termed the *public domain*.

Domicile   A place where a person lives or has his home; in a strict legal sense, the place where he has his true, fixed, permanent home and principal establishment, and to which place he has, whenever he is absent, the intention of returning.

Donee   A person to whom a gift is made.

Donor   A person who makes a gift.

Double Jeopardy Clause   A constitutional provision designed to protect criminal defendants from multiple prosecutions for the same offense.

Dower   The legal right or interest that a wife has in her husband's real estate by virtue of their marriage.

Draft   A written order drawn upon one person by another, requesting him to pay money to a designated third person. A bill of exchange payable on demand.

Drawee   A person upon whom a draft or bill of exchange is drawn by the drawer.

Drawer   The maker of a draft or bill of exchange.

Due Bill   An acknowledgment of a debt in writing, not made payable to order.

Dummy   One posing or represented as acting for himself, but in reality acting for another. A tool or "straw man" for the real parties in interest.

Dumping   The selling of goods by a seller in a foreign nation at unfairly low prices.

Durable Power of Attorney   A power of attorney that is not affected by the principal's incapacity. See **Power of Attorney** and **Attorney-in-Fact.**

Duress   Overpowering of the will of a person by force or fear.

Earned Surplus   Also called *retained earnings*. A balance sheet account; a corporation's profits that have not been distributed to shareholders.

Earnest Money   Something given as part of the purchase price to bind the bargain.

Easement   The right to make certain uses of another person's property or to prevent another person from making certain uses of his own property.

Edict   A command or prohibition promulgated by a sovereign and having the effect of law.

Effects   As used in wills, personal property. It denotes property in a more extensive sense than goods and includes all kinds of personal property but will be held not to include real property, unless the context discloses an intention on the part of the testator to dispose of his realty by the use of the word.

E.g.   For example.

Ejectment   By statute in some states, an action to recover the immediate possession of real property.

Eleemosynary Corporation   A corporation created for a charitable purpose or for charitable purposes.

Emancipate   To release; to set free. In contract law, a parent's waiver of his rights to control and receive the services of his minor child.

Embezzlement   A statutory offense consisting of the fraudulent conversion of another's personal property by one to whom it has been intrusted, with the intention of depriving the owner thereof, the gist of the offense being usually the violation of relations of a fiduciary character.

Eminent Domain   A governmental power whereby the government can take or condemn private property for a public purpose upon the payment of just compensation.

Enabling Legislation   The statute by which a legislative body creates an administrative agency.

En Banc (in Banc)   By all the judges of a court, with all the judges of a court sitting.

Encumbrance   A right in a third person which diminishes the value of the land, but is consistent with the passing of ownership of the land by deed.

Endorsement   See **Indorsement.**

Entity Theory   In partnership law, the view that a partnership is a legal entity distinct from the partners who own it. See **Aggregate Theory.**

Entry   Recordation; noting in a record; going on land; taking actual possession of land.

Environmental Impact Statement   A document that the National Environmental Policy Act requires federal agencies to prepare in connection with any legislative proposals or proposed actions that will significantly affect the environment.

Equity   A system of justice that developed in England separate from the common law courts. Few states in the United States still maintain separate equity courts, though most apply equity principles and procedures when remedies derived from the equity courts are sought. A broader meaning denotes fairness and justice. In business organization law, the capital contributions of owners plus profits that have not been distributed to the owners; stated capital plus capital surplus plus earned surplus.

Error   A mistake of law or fact; a mistake of the court in the trial of an action.

Escheat   The reversion of land to the state in the event that a decedent dies leaving no heirs.

Estate   1. An interest in land. 2. Property owned by a decedent at the time of his death.

Estop   To bar or stop.

Estoppel   That state of affairs that arises when one is forbidden by law from alleging or denying a fact because of his previous action or inaction.

Et Al.   "And another" or "and others." An abbreviation for the Latin *et alius* meaning "and another"; also of *et alii* meaning "and others."

Et Ux.   An abbreviation for the Latin *et uxor* meaning "and his wife."

Eviction   Depriving the tenant of the possession of leased premises.

Evidence   That which makes clear or ascertains the truth of the fact or point in issue either on the one side or the other;

those rules of law whereby we determine what testimony is to be admitted and what rejected in each case and what is the weight to be given to the testimony admitted.

Exception An objection; a reservation; a contradiction.

Exclusionary Rule The rule that bars the admissibility in criminal proceedings of evidence seized in violation of the Fourth Amendment's prohibition against unreasonable searches and seizures.

Ex Contractu From or out of a contract.

Exculpatory Clause A clause in a contract or trust instrument that excuses a party from some duty.

Ex Delicto From or out of a wrongful act; tortious; tortiously.

Executed When applied to written instruments, synonymous with the word "signed;" more frequently, it imports that everything has been done to complete the transaction; that is, the instrument has been signed, sealed, and delivered. An executed contract is one in which the object of the contract is performed.

Execution 1. A process of enforcing a judgment, usually by having an appropriate officer seize property of the defendant and sell it at a judicial sale. 2. The final consummation of a contract or other instrument, including completion of all the formalities needed to make it binding.

Executor The personal representative appointed to administer the estate of a person who died leaving a valid will.

Executory Not yet executed; not yet fully performed, completed, fulfilled, or carried out; to be performed wholly or in part.

Executrix Feminine of executor.

Exemption A release from some burden, duty, or obligation; a grace; a favor; an immunity; taken out from under the general rule, not to be like others who are not exempt.

Exhibit A copy of a written instrument on which a pleading is founded, annexed to the pleading and by reference made a part of it. Any paper or thing offered in evidence and marked for identification.

Ex Post Facto After the fact. The U.S. Constitution prohibits *ex post facto* criminal laws, meaning those that criminalize behavior that was legal when committed.

Express Warranty A warranty made in words, either oral or written.

Expropriation A government's taking of a business's assets, such as a manufacturing facility, usually without just compensation.

Face Value The nominal or par value of an instrument as expressed on its face; in the case of a bond, this is the amount really due, including interest.

Factor An agent who is employed to sell goods for a principal, usually in his own name, and who is given possession of the goods.

False Imprisonment An intentional tort that prohibits the unlawful confinement of another for an appreciable time without his consent.

FAS An abbreviation for the expression "free alongside steamer."

Federal Supremacy The ability of federal laws to defeat inconsistent state laws in case they conflict.

Fee Simple Absolute The highest form of land ownership, which gives the owner the right to possess and use the land for an unlimited period of time, subject only to governmental or private restrictions, and unconditional power to dispose of the property during his lifetime or upon his death.

Felony As a general rule, all crimes punishable by death or by imprisonment in a state prison.

Fiction An assumption made by the law that something is true that is or may be false.

Fiduciary One who holds goods in trust for another or one who holds a position of trust and confidence.

Field Warehousing A method of protecting a security interest in the inventory of a debtor whereby the creditor or his agent retains the physical custody of the debtor's inventory, which is released to the debtor as he complies with the underlying security agreement.

Firm Offer Under the Uniform Commercial Code, a signed, written offer by a merchant containing assurances that it will be held open, and which is not revocable for the time stated in the offer, or for a reasonable time if no such time is stated.

Fixture A thing that was originally personal property and that has been actually or constructively affixed to the soil itself or to some structure legally a part of the land.

FOB An abbreviation of "free on board."

Force Majeure Clause A contract provision, commonly encountered in international agreements for the sale of goods, that excuses nonperformance that results from conditions beyond the parties' control.

Foreclosure To terminate the rights of the mortgagor/owner of property.

Foreign Corporation A corporation incorporated in one state doing business in another state. See **Alien Corporation.**

Foreign Trade Corporation A corporation in a NME nation that is empowered by the government to conduct the whole business of exporting or importing a particular product.

Forwarder A person who, having no interest in goods and no ownership or interest in the means of their carriage, undertakes, for hire, to forward them by a safe carrier to their destination.

Franchise A special privilege conferred by government upon individuals, and which does not belong to the citizens of a country generally, of common right. Also a contractual relationship establishing a means of marketing goods or services giving certain elements of control to the supplier (franchisor) in return for the right of the franchisee to use the supplier's tradename or trademark, usually in a specific marketing area.

Fraud Misrepresentation made with knowledge of its falsity and intent to deceive. See **Misrepresentation.**

Freeze-Out In corporation law, a type of oppression by which only minority shareholders are forced to sell their shares.

Fungible Goods Goods any unit of which is from its nature or by mercantile custom treated as the equivalent of any other unit.

Future Advances Money or other value provided to a debtor by a creditor subsequent to the time a security interest in the debtor's collateral is taken by that creditor.

Futures Contracts for the sale and future delivery of stocks or commodities, wherein either party may waive delivery, and receive or pay, as the case may be, the difference in market price at the time set for delivery.

Garnishee Used as a noun, the third party who is subjected to the process of garnishment. Used as a verb, to institute garnishment proceedings; to cause a garnishment to be levied on the garnishee.

Garnishment A statutory proceeding whereby money, property, wages, or credits of the defendant that are in the hands of a third party are seized to satisfy a judgment or legally valid claim that the plaintiff has against the defendant.

General Partnership See **Partnership.**

Good Faith Honesty in fact; an honest intention to abstain from taking an unfair advantage of another.

Goodwill The value of a business due to expected continued public patronage of the business.

Grantee A person to whom a grant is made.

Grantor A person who makes a grant.

Gravamen The gist, essence, or central point of a legal claim or argument.

Grey Market Goods Goods lawfully bearing trademarks or using patented or copyrighted material, but imported into a foreign market without the authorization of the owner of the trademark, patent, or copyright.

Guarantor A person who promises to perform the same obligation as another person (called the *principal*), upon the principal's default.

Guaranty An undertaking by one person to be answerable for the payment of some debt, or the due performance of some contract or duty by another person, who remains liable to pay or perform the same.

Guardian A person (in some rare cases, a corporation) to whom the law has entrusted the custody and control of the person, or estate, or both, of an incompetent person.

Habeas Corpus Any of several common law writs having as their object to bring a party before the court or judge. The only issue it presents is whether the prisoner is restrained of his liberty by due process.

Hearing The supporting of one's contentions by argument and if need be, by proof.

Hedging A market transaction in which a party buys a certain quantity of a given commodity at the price current on the date of the purchase and sells an equal quantity of the same commodity for future delivery for the purpose of getting protection against loss due to fluctuation in the market.

Heirs Those persons appointed by law to succeed to the real estate of a decedent who has died without leaving a valid will.

Holder A person in possession of a document of title or an instrument payable or indorsed to him, his order, or to bearer.

Holder in Due Course A holder who has taken a negotiable instrument under the following conditions: (1) that it is complete and regular on its face; (2) that he became the holder of it before it was overdue, and without notice that it had been previously dishonored, if such was the fact; (3) that he took it in good faith and for value; and (4) that at the time it was negotiated to him he had no notice of any infirmity in the instrument or defect in the title of the person negotiating it.

Holding Language in a judicial opinion that is necessary for the decision the court reached and that is said to be binding on subsequent courts. Distinguished from *dictum.*

Holding Company A corporation whose purpose or function is to own or otherwise hold the shares of other corporations either for investment or control.

Holographic Will A will written in the handwriting of the testator.

Homestead In a legal sense, the real estate occupied as a home and also the right to have it exempt from levy and forced sale. It is the land, not exceeding the prescribed amount, upon which the dwelling house, or residence, or habitation, or abode of the owner thereof and his family resides, and includes the dwelling house as an indispensable part.

I.e. That is.

Illusory Deceiving or intending to deceive, as by false appearances; fallacious. An illusory promise is a promise that appears to be binding but that in fact does not bind the promisor.

Immunity A personal favor granted by law, contrary to the general rule.

Impanel To place the names of the jurors on a panel; to make a list of the names of those persons who have been selected for jury duty; to go through the process of selecting a jury that is to try a cause.

Implied Warranty   A warranty created by operation of law.

Implied Warranty of Habitability   Implied warranty arising in lease or sale of residential real estate that the property will be fit for human habitation.

Impossibility   A doctrine under which a party to a contract is relieved of his or her duty to perform when that performance has become impossible because of the occurrence of an event unforeseen at the time of contracting.

Inalienable   Incapable of being alienated, transferred, or conveyed; nontransferrable.

In Camera   In the judge's chambers; in private.

Incapacity   A legal disability, such as infancy or want of authority.

Inception   Initial stage. The word does not refer to a state of actual existence but to a condition of things or circumstances from which the thing may develop.

Inchoate   Imperfect; incipient; not completely formed.

Incidental Damages   See **Damages, Incidental.**

Independent Contractor   A person who contracts with a principal to perform some task according to his own methods, and who is not under the principal's control regarding the physical details of the work. Under the *Restatement (Second) of Agency*, an independent contractor may or may not be an agent.

Indictment   A finding by a grand jury that there is probable cause to believe an accused committed a crime.

Indorsement   Writing on the back of an instrument; the contract whereby the holder of an instrument (such as a draft, check, or note) or a document (such as a warehouse receipt or bill of lading) transfers to another person his right to such instrument and incurs the liabilities incident to the transfer.

Infant   See **Minor**.

Information   A written accusation of crime brought by a public prosecuting officer to a court without the intervention of a grand jury.

Injunction   An equitable remedy whereby the defendant is ordered to perform certain acts or to desist from certain acts.

In Pari Delicto   Equally at fault in tort or crime; in equal fault or guilt.

In Personam   Against a person. For example, in personam jurisdiction.

In Re   In the matter of.

In Rem   Against a thing and not against a person; concerning the condition or status of a thing; for example, in rem jurisdiction.

Inside Information   Confidential information possessed by a person due to his relationship with a business.

Insolvency   In corporation law, the inability of a business to pay its currently maturing obligations.

In Status Quo   In the existing state of things. In contract law, the existing state of things at time the contract was made.

Instrument   Formal or legal documents in writing, such as contracts, deeds, wills, bonds, leases, and mortgages.

Insurable Interest   Any interest in property such that the owner would experience a benefit from the continued existence of the property or a loss from its destruction.

Inter Alia   Among other things.

Interlocutory   Something not final but deciding only some subsidiary matter raised while a lawsuit is pending.

Interpleader   An equitable remedy applicable where one fears injury from conflicting claims. Where a person does not know which of two or more persons claiming certain property held by him has a right to it, filing a bill of interpleader forces the claimants to litigate the title between themselves.

Interrogatory   Written questions directed to a party, answered in writing, and signed under oath.

Inter Se   Between or among themselves.

Intervening Cause   An intervening force that plays so substantial a role in causing a particular plaintiff's injury that it relieves a negligent defendant of any responsibility for that injury. Also called *superseding cause.*

Intervention   A proceeding by which one not originally made a party to an action or suit is permitted, on his own application, to appear therein and join one of the original parties in maintaining his cause of action or defense, or to assert some cause of action against some or all of the parties to the proceeding as originally instituted.

Inter Vivos   A transaction between living persons.

Intestate   Having died without leaving a valid will.

In Toto   Wholly, completely.

In Transitu   On the journey. Goods are as a rule considered as in transitu while they are in the possession of a carrier, whether by land or water, until they arrive at the ultimate place of their destination and are delivered into the actual possession of the buyer, whether or not the carrier has been named or designated by the buyer.

Investment Contract   In securities law, a type of security encompassing any contract by which an investor invests in a common enterprise with an expectation of profits solely from the efforts of persons other than the investor.

Invitee   A person who is on private premises for a purpose connected with the business interests of the possessor of those premises, or a member of the public who is lawfully on land open to the public.

Ipso Facto   By the fact itself; by the very fact.

Irrevocable Letter of Credit   See **Letter of Credit, Irrevocable.**

Issued Shares   A corporation's shares that a corporation has sold to its shareholders. Includes shares repurchased by the corporation and retained as treasury shares, but not shares canceled or returned to unissued status.

Issuer   In securities law, a person who issues or proposes to issue a security; the person whose obligation is represented by a security.

Joint and Several Liability   Liability of a group of persons in which the plaintiff may sue any member of the group individually and get a judgment against that person, or may sue all members of the group collectively.

Joint Bank Account   A bank account of two persons so fixed that they shall be joint owners thereof during their mutual lives, and the survivor shall take the whole on the death of other.

Joint Liability   Liability of a group of persons in which, if one of these persons is sued, he can insist that the other liable parties be joined to the suit as codefendants, so that all must be sued collectively.

Jointly   Acting together or in concert or cooperating; holding in common or interdependently, not separately. Persons are "jointly bound" in a bond or note when both or all must be sued in one action for its enforcement, not either one at the election of the creditor.

Joint Tenancy   An estate held by two or more jointly, with an equal right in all to share in the enjoyments of the land during their lives. An incident of joint tenancy is the right of survivorship.

Joint Venture   A form of business organization identical to a partnership, except that it is engaged in a single project, not carrying on a business.

Judgment   A court's final resolution of a lawsuit or other proceeding submitted to it for decision.

Judgment Lien   The statutory lien on the real property of a judgment debtor that is created by the judgment itself. At common law, a judgment imposes no lien upon the real property of the judgment debtor, and to subject the property of the debtor to the judgment, it was necessary to take out a writ called an *elegit*.

Judgment notwithstanding the Verdict   A judgment made by a judge contrary to a prior jury verdict whereby the judge effectively overrules the jury's verdict. Also called the *judgment n.o.v.* or the judgment *non obstante veredicto*. Similar to the directed verdict, except that it occurs after the jury has issued its verdict.

Judicial Review   The courts' power to declare the actions of the other branches of government unconstitutional.

Jurisdiction   The power of a court to hear and decide a case.

Jurisprudence   The philosophy of law. Also sometimes used to refer to the collected positive law of some jurisdiction.

Jury   A body of lay persons, selected by lot, or by some other fair and impartial means, to ascertain, under the guidance of the judge, the truth in questions of fact arising either in civil litigation or a criminal process.

Kite   To secure the temporary use of money by issuing or negotiating worthless paper and then redeeming such paper with the proceeds of similar paper. The word is also used as a noun, meaning the worthless paper thus employed.

Laches   The established doctrine of equity that, apart from any question of statutory limitation, its courts will discourage delay and sloth in the enforcement of rights. Equity demands conscience, good faith, and reasonable diligence.

Land Contract   A conditional agreement for the sale and purchase of real estate in which the legal title to the property is retained by the seller until the purchaser has fulfilled the agreement, usually by completing the payment of the agreed-upon purchase price.

Larceny   The unlawful taking and carrying away of personal property with the intent to deprive the owner of his property permanently.

Last Clear Chance   Under traditional tort principles, a doctrine that allowed a contributorily negligent plaintiff to recover despite his failure to exercise reasonable care for his own safety by arguing that the defendant had the superior opportunity ("last clear chance") to avoid the harm.

Law Merchant   The custom of merchants, or lex mercatorio, which grew out of the necessity and convenience of business, and which, although different from the general rules of the common law, was engrafted into it and became a part of it. It was founded on the custom and usage of merchants.

Leading Case   The most significant and authoritative case regarded as having settled and determined a point of law. Often, the first case to have done so in a definitive and complete fashion.

Leading Questions   Those questions that suggest to the witness the answer desired, those that assume a fact to be proved that is not proved, or that, embodying a material fact, admit of an answer by a simple negative or affirmative.

Lease   A contract for the possession and use of land on one side, and a recompense of rent or other income on the other; a conveyance to a person for life, or years, or at will in consideration of a return of rent or other recompense.

Legacy   A bequest; a testamentary gift of personal property. Sometimes incorrectly applied to a testamentary gift of real property.

Legal   According to the principles of law; according to the method required by statute; by means of judicial proceedings; not equitable.

Letter of Credit   An instrument containing a request (general or special) to pay to the bearer or person named money, or sell him or her some commodity on credit or give something of value and look to the drawer of the letter for recompense.

Advised The seller's bank acts as the seller's agent to collect against the letter of credit issued by the buyer's bank.

Confirmed The seller's bank agrees to assume liability on the letter of credit issued by the buyer's bank.

Irrevocable The issuing bank may not revoke the letter of credit issued by the buyer's bank.

Standby The seller's bank promises to pay the buyer if the seller defaults on his contract to deliver conforming goods.

Levy At common law, a levy on goods consisted of an officer's entering the premises where they were and either leaving an assistant in charge of them or removing them after taking an inventory. Today, courts differ as to what is a valid levy, but by the weight of authority there must be an actual or constructive seizure of the goods. In most states, a levy on land must be made by some unequivocal act of the officer indicating the intention of singling out certain real estate for the satisfaction of the debt.

Libel The defamation action appropriate to printed or written defamations, or to those that have a physical form.

License A personal privilege to do some act or series of acts on the land of another, without possessing any estate therein. A permit or authorization to do what, without a license, would be unlawful.

Licensee A person lawfully upon land in possession of another for purposes unconnected with the business interests of the possessor.

Lien In its most extensive meaning, it is a charge on property for the payment or discharge of a debt or duty; a qualified right; a proprietary interest that, in a given case, may be exercised over the property of another.

Life Estate A property interest that gives a person the right to possess and use property for a time that is measured by his lifetime or that of another person.

Limited Partner An owner of a limited partnership who has no right to manage the business, but who possesses liability limited to his capital contribution to the business.

Limited Partnership A form of business organization that has one or more general partners who manage the business and have unlimited liability for the obligations of the business and one or more limited partners who do not manage and have limited liability.

Liquidated Damages The stipulation by the parties to a contract of the sum of money to be recovered by the aggrieved party in the event of a breach of the contract by the other party.

Liquidated Debt A debt that is "due and certain." That is, one that is not the subject of a bona fide dispute either as to its existence or the amount that is owed.

Lis Pendens A pending suit. As applied to the doctrine of lis pendens, it is the jurisdiction, power, or control that courts acquire over property involved in a suit, pending the continuance of the action, and until its final judgment therein.

Listing Contract A so-called contract whereby an owner of real property employs a broker to procure a purchaser without giving the broker an exclusive right to sell. Under such an agreement, it is generally held that the employment may be terminated by the owner at will, and that a sale of the property by the owner terminates the employment.

Litigant A party to a lawsuit.

Living Will A document executed with specific legal formalities stating a person's preference that heroic life support measures should not be used if there is no hope of the person's recovery.

Long-Arm Statute A state statute that grants to a state's courts broad authority to exercise jurisdiction over out-of-state persons who have contacts with the state.

Looting In corporation law, the transfer of a corporation's assets to its managers or controlling shareholders at less than fair value.

Magistrate A word commonly applied to the lower judicial officers such as justices of the peace, police judges, town recorders, and other local judicial functionaries. In a broader sense, a magistrate is a public civil officer invested with some part of the legislative, executive, or judicial power given by the Constitution. The president of the United States is the chief magistrate of the nation.

Maker A person who makes or executes an instrument, the signer of an instrument.

Malfeasance The doing of an act that a person ought not to do at all. It is to be distinguished from misfeasance, that is the improper doing of an act which a person might lawfully do.

Malicious Prosecution An intentional tort designed to protect against the wrongful initiation of criminal proceedings.

Mandamus "We command." It is a command issuing from a competent jurisdiction, in the name of the state or sovereign, directed to some inferior court, officer, corporation, or person, requiring the performance of a particular duty therein specified, which duty results from the official station of the party to whom it is directed, or from operation of law.

Margin A deposit by a buyer in stocks with a seller or a stockbroker, as security to cover fluctuations in the market in reference to stocks that the buyer has purchased, but for which he has not paid. Commodities are also traded on margin.

Marshals Ministerial officers belonging to the executive department of the federal government, who with their deputies have the same powers of executing the laws of the United States in each state as the sheriffs and their deputies in such state may have in executing the laws of that state.

Material Important. In securities law, a fact is material if a reasonable person would consider it important in his decision to purchase shares or to vote shares.

Materialman's Lien A claim created by law for the purpose of securing a priority of payment of the price or value of materials furnished in erecting or repairing a building or other structure.

Mechanic's Lien A claim created by law for the purpose of securing a priority of payment of the price or value of work performed and materials furnished in erecting or repairing a building or other structure; as such, it attaches to the land as well as to the buildings erected therein.

Memorandum A writing.

Mens Rea A guilty mind; criminal intent.

Merchant Under the Uniform Commercial Code, one who regularly deals in goods of the kind sold in the contract at issue, or holds himself out as having special knowledge or skill relevant to such goods, or who makes the sale through an agent who regularly deals in such goods or claims such knowledge or skill.

Merchantable Of good quality and salable, but not necessarily the best. As applied to articles sold, the word requires that the article shall be such as is usually sold in the market, of medium quality, and bringing the average price.

Merger In corporation law, traditionally, a transaction by which one corporation acquires another corporation, with the acquiring corporation being owned by the shareholders of both corporations and the acquired corporation going out of existence. Today, loosely applied to any negotiated acquisition of one corporation by another.

Merger Clause A contract clause providing that the written contract is the complete expression of the parties' agreement. Also called *integration clause*.

Mining Partnership A form of business organization used for mining and drilling mineral resources that is identical to a partnership, except that mining partnership interests are freely transferable and the death or bankruptcy of a mining partner does not cause a dissolution.

Minor A person who has not reached the age at which the law recognizes a general contractual capacity (called *majority*), which is 18 in most states.

Misdemeanor Any crime that is punishable neither by death nor by imprisonment in a state prison.

Misrepresentation The assertion of a fact that is not in accord with the truth. A contract can be rescinded on the ground of misrepresentation when the assertion relates to a material fact or is made fraudulently and the other party actually and justifiably relies on the assertion.

Mistrial An invalid trial due to lack of jurisdiction, error in selection of jurors, or some other fundamental requirement.

Mitigation of Damages A reduction in the amount of damages due to extenuating circumstances.

Mortgage A conveyance of property to secure the performance of some obligation, the conveyance to be void on the due performance thereof.

Mortgagee The creditor to whom property has been mortgaged to secure the performance of an obligation.

Mortgagor The owner of the property that has been mortgaged or pledged as security for a debt.

Motion to Dismiss A motion made by the defendant in a civil case to defeat the plaintiff's case, usually after the complaint or all the pleadings have been completed. The most common form of motion to dismiss is the motion to dismiss for failure to state a claim upon which relief can be granted, which attacks the legal sufficiency of the plaintiff's complaint. See **Demurrer.**

Motive The cause or reason that induced a person to commit a crime.

Mutuality Reciprocal obligations of the parties required to make a contract binding on either party.

National Ambient Air Quality Standards Federally established air pollution standards designed to protect the public health and welfare.

Necessaries That which is reasonably necessary for a minor's proper and suitable maintenance, in view of the income level and social position of the minor's family.

Negligence The omission to do something that a reasonable person, guided by those considerations that ordinarily regulate human affairs, would do, or doing something that a prudent and reasonable person would not do.

Negligence Per Se The doctrine that provides that a conclusive presumption of breach of duty arises when a defendant has violated a statute and thereby caused a harm the statute was designed to prevent to a person the statute was designed to protect.

Negotiable Capable of being transferred by indorsement or delivery so as to give the holder a right to sue in his or her own name and to avoid certain defenses against the payee.

Negotiable Instrument An instrument that may be transferred or negotiated, so that the holder may maintain an action thereon in his own name.

NME A nonmarket economy; a socialist economy in which a central government owns and controls all significant means of production, thereby setting prices and the levels of production.

Nolo Contendere A "no contest" plea by the defendant in a criminal case that has much the same effect as a guilty plea, but that cannot be used as an admission of guilt in other legal proceedings.

Nominal Damages See **Damages, Nominal.**

Non Compos Mentis Mentally incompetent. The term denotes a person entirely destitute or bereft of his memory or understanding.

Nonfeasance In the law of agency, it is the total omission or failure of an agent to enter on the performance of some distinct duty or undertaking that he or she has agreed with the principal to do.

Non Obstante Veredicto Notwithstanding the verdict. J.N.O.V. See **Judgment notwithstanding the Verdict.**

Nonsuit A judgment given against a plaintiff who is unable to prove a case, or when the plaintiff refuses or neglects to proceed to trial.

No-Par Value Stock Stock of a corporation having no face or par value.

Novation A mutual agreement, between all parties concerned, for the discharge of a valid existing obligation by the substitution of a new valid obligation on the part of the debtor or another, or a like agreement for the discharge of a debtor to his creditor by the substitution of a new creditor.

Nudum Pactum A naked promise, a promise for which there is no consideration.

Nuisance That which endangers life or health, gives offense to the senses, violates the laws of decency, or obstructs the reasonable and comfortable use of property.

Nuncupative Will An oral will. Such wills are valid in some states, but only under limited circumstances and to a limited extent.

Oath Any form of attestation by which a person signifies that he is bound in conscience to perform an act faithfully and truthfully. It involves the idea of calling on God to witness what is averred as truth, and it is supposed to be accompanied with an invocation of His vengeance, or a renunciation of His favor, in the event of falsehood.

Obiter Dictum That which is said in passing; a rule of law set forth in a court's opinion, but not necessary to decide the case. See **Dictum.**

Objection In the trial of a cases the formal remonstrance made by counsel to something that has been said or done, in order to obtain the court's ruling thereon.

Obligee A person to whom another is bound by a promise or other obligation; a promisee.

Obligor A person who is bound by a promise or other obligation; a promisor.

Offer A proposal by one person to another that is intended of itself to create legal relations on acceptance by the person to whom it is made.

Offeree A person to whom an offer is made.

Offeror A person who makes an offer.

Opinion The opinion of the court represents merely the reasons for its judgment, while the decision of the court is the judgment itself.

Oppression The officers, directors, or controlling shareholder's isolation of one group of shareholders for disadvantageous treatment to the benefit of another group of shareholders.

Option A separate contract in which an offeror agrees not to revoke her offer for a stated period of time in exchange for some valuable consideration.

Option Agreement A share transfer restriction granting a corporation or its shareholders an option to buy a selling shareholder's shares at a price determined by the agreement.

Ordinance A legislative enactment of a county or an incorporated city or town.

Original Jurisdiction The power to decide a case as a trial court.

Outstanding Shares A corporation's shares currently held by shareholders.

Overdraft The withdrawal from a bank by a depositor of money in excess of the amount of money he or she has on deposit there.

Overdue When an instrument is not paid when due or at maturity.

Overplus That which remains; a balance left over.

Owner's Risk A term employed by common carriers in bills of lading and shipping receipts to signify that the carrier does not assume responsibility for the safety of the goods.

Par Par means equal, and par value means a value equal to the face of a bond or a stock certificate.

Parent Corporation A corporation that owns a controlling interest of another corporation, called a *subsidiary corporation.*

Parol Oral; verbal; by word of mouth.

Parol Evidence Where a written contract exists, evidence about promises or statements made prior to or during the execution of the writing that are not contained in the written contract.

Parties All persons who are interested in the subject matter of an action and who have a right to make defense, control the proceedings, examine and cross-examine witnesses, and appeal from the judgment.

Partition A proceeding the object of which is to enable those who own property as joint tenants or tenants in common to put an end to the tenancy so as to vest in each a sole estate in specific property or an allotment of the lands and tenements. If a division of the estate is impracticable, the estate ought to be sold and the proceeds divided.

Partners The owners of a partnership.

Partnership A form of business organization; specifically, an association of two or more persons to carry on as co-owners of a business for profit.

Partnership by Estoppel The appearance of partnership when there is no partnership; it arises when a person misleads a second person into believing that the first person is a partner of a third person; a theory that allows the second person to recover from the first person all reasonable damages the second person has suffered due to his reliance on the appearance of partnership.

Partnership Interest A partner's ownership interest in a partnership.

Party to Be Charged   The person against whom enforcement of a contract is sought; the person who is asserting the statute of frauds as a defense.

Par Value   An arbitrary dollar amount assigned to shares by the articles of incorporation, representing the minimum amount of consideration for which the corporation may issue the shares and the portion of consideration that must be allocated to the stated capital amount.

Patent   A patent for land is a conveyance of title to government lands by the government; a patent of an invention is the right of monopoly secured by statute to those who invent or discover new and useful devices and processes.

Patentee   The holder of a patent.

Pawn   A pledge; a bailment of personal property as security for some debt or engagement, redeemable on certain terms, and with an implied power of sale on default.

Payee   A person to whom a payment is made or is made payable.

Pecuniary   Financial; pertaining or relating to money.

Pendente Lite   During the litigation.

Per Curiam   By the court as a whole, without an opinion signed by a particular judge.

Peremptory Challenge   A challenge to a proposed juror that a defendant may make as an absolute right, and that cannot be questioned by either opposing counsel or the court.

Perfection   The process or method by which a secured party obtains a priority in certain collateral belonging to a debtor against creditors or claimants of a debtor; it usually entails giving notice of the security interest, such as by taking possession or filing a financial statement.

Performance   The fulfillment of a contractual duty.

Periodic Tenancy   The tenancy that exists when the landlord and tenant agree that rent will be paid in regular successive intervals until notice to terminate is given, but do not agree on a specific duration of the lease. A typical periodic tenancy is a tenancy from month-to-month.

Perjury   The willful and corrupt false swearing or affirming, after an oath lawfully administered, in the course of a judicial or quasi-judicial proceeding as to some matter material to the issue or point in question.

Per Se   In itself or as such.

Petition   In equity pleading, a petition is in the nature of a pleading (at least when filed by a stranger to the suit) and forms a basis for independent action.

Piercing the Corporate Veil   Holding a shareholder responsible for acts of a corporation due to a shareholder's domination and improper use of the corporation.

Plaintiff   The party who sues in a civil case.

Plaintiff in Error   The unsuccessful party to the action who prosecutes a writ of error in a higher court.

Plea   A plea is an answer to a declaration or complaint or any material allegation of fact therein that, if untrue, would defeat the action. In criminal procedure, a plea is the matter that the accused, on his arraignment, alleges in answer to the charge against him.

Pleadings   The documents the parties file with the court when they state their claims and counterarguments early in a civil case. Examples include the complaint and the answer.

Pledge   A pawn; a bailment of personal property as security for some debt or engagement, redeemable on certain terms, and with an implied power of sale on default.

Pledgee   A person to whom personal property is pledged by a pledgor.

Pledgor   A person who makes a pledge of personal property to a pledgee.

Police Power   The states' power to regulate to promote the public health, safety, morals, and welfare.

Positive Law   Laws actually and specifically enacted or adopted by proper authority for the government of a jural society as distinguished from principles of morality or laws of honor.

Possession   Respecting real property, exclusive dominion and control such as owners of like property usually exercise over it. Manual control of personal property either as owner or as one having a qualified right in it.

Power of Attorney   A written authorization by a principal to an agent to perform specified acts on behalf of the principal. See **Attorney-in-Fact.**

Precedent   A past judicial decision relied upon as authority in a present case.

Preemptive Right   A shareholder's option to purchase new issuances of shares in proportion to the shareholder's current ownership of the corporation.

Preference   The act of a debtor in paying or securing one or more of his creditors in a manner more favorable to them than to other creditors or to the exclusion of such other creditors. In the absence of statute, a preference is perfectly good, but to be legal it must be bona fide, and not a mere subterfuge of the debtor to secure a future benefit to himself or to prevent the application of his property to his debts.

Preferential   Having priority.

Preferred Shareholders   Shareholders who have dividend and liquidation preferences over other classes of shareholders, usually common shareholders.

Prenuptial Contract   A contract between prospective marriage partners respecting matters such as property ownership and division.

Preponderance   Most; majority; more probable than not.

Prerogative   A special power, privilege, or immunity, usually used in reference to an official or his office.

Presentment   A demand for acceptance or payment of a negotiable instrument made upon the maker, acceptor, drawee, or other payor by or on behalf of the holder.

Presumption   A term used to signify that which may be assumed without proof, or taken for granted. It is asserted as a self-evident result of human reason and experience.

Pretermitted   In the law of wills, an heir born after the execution of the testator's will.

Prima Facie   At first sight; a fact that is presumed to be true unless disproved by contrary evidence.

Prima Facie Case   A case sufficiently strong that, unless rebutted by the defendant in some fashion, it entitles the plaintiff to recover against the defendant.

Principal   In agency law, one under whose direction an agent acts and for whose benefit that agent acts.

Priority   Having precedence or the better right.

Privilege   Generally, a legal right to engage in conduct that would otherwise result in legal liability. Privileges are commonly classified as *absolute* (unqualified) or *conditional* (qualified). Occasionally, *privilege* is also used to denote a legal right to refrain from particular behavior (e.g., the constitutional privilege against self-incrimination).

Privity of Contract   The existence of a direct contractual relation between two parties.

Probate   A term used to include all matters of which probate courts have jurisdiction, which in many states are the estates of deceased persons and of persons under guardianship.

Process   Generally, the summons or notice of beginning of suit.

Proceeds   Whatever is received on the sale, exchange, collection, or other disposition of collateral.

Proffer   To offer for acceptance or to make a tender of.

Profit   An interest in land giving a person the right to enter land owned by another and remove natural resources (e.g., timber) from the land. Also called *profit à prendre*.

Promisee   The person to whom a promise is made.

Promisor   A person who makes a promise to another; a person who promises.

Promissory Estoppel   An equitable doctrine that protects those who foreseeably and reasonably rely on the promises of others by enforcing such promises when enforcement is necessary to avoid injustice, even though one or more of the elements normally required for an enforceable agreement is absent.

Promissory Note   Commercial paper or instrument in which the maker promises to pay a specific sum of money to another person, to his order, or to bearer.

Promoter   A person who incorporates a business, organizes its initial management, and raises its initial capital.

Pro Rata   Proportionate; in proportion.

Prospectus   In securities law, a document given to prospective purchasers of a security that contains information about an issuer of securities and the securities being issued.

Pro Tanto   For so much; to such an extent.

Proximate Cause   A legal limitation on a negligent wrongdoer's liability for the actual consequences of his actions. Such wrongdoers are said to be relieved of responsibility for consequences that are too remote, or not the proximate result of their actions. Various tests for proximate cause are employed by the courts.

Proxy   A person who is authorized to vote the shares of another person. Also, the written authorization empowering a person to vote the shares of another person.

Pseudoforeign Corporation   A corporation incorporated under the laws of a state but doing most of its business in one other state.

Publicly Held Corporation   A corporation owned by a large number of widely dispersed shareholders.

Punitive Damages   See **Damages, Punitive.**

Purchase Money Security Interest   A security interest that is (1) taken or retained by the seller of collateral to secure all or part of its purchase price or (2) taken by a debtor to acquire rights in or the use of the collateral if the value is so used.

Put   A type of option permitting a person to sell a fixed number of securities at a fixed price at a specified time. See **Call.**

Qualified Acceptance   A conditional or modified acceptance. In order to create a contract, an acceptance must accept the offer substantially as made; hence, a qualified acceptance is no acceptance at all, is treated by the courts as a rejection of the offer made, and is in effect an offer by the offeree, which the offeror may, if he chooses, accept and thus create a contract.

Quantum Meruit   As much as is deserved. A part of a common law action in assumpsit for the value of services rendered.

Quash   To vacate or make void.

Quasi-Contract   The doctrine by which courts imply, as a matter of law, a promise to pay the reasonable value of goods or services when the party receiving such goods or services has knowingly done so under circumstances that make it unfair to retain them without paying for them.

Quasi-Judicial   Acts of public officers involving investigation of facts and drawing conclusions from them as a basis of official action.

Quiet Title, Action to   An action to establish a claimant's title in land by requiring adverse claimants to come into court to prove their claim or to be barred from asserting it later.

Quitclaim Deed   A deed conveying only the right, title, and interest of the grantor in the property described, as distinguished from a deed conveying the property itself.

Quorum   That number of persons, shares represented, or officers who may lawfully transact the business of a meeting called for that purpose.

Quo Warranto "By what authority." The name of a writ (and also of the whole pleading) by which the government commences an action to recover an office or franchise from the person or corporation in possession of it.

Ratification The adoption or affirmance by a person of a prior act that did not bind him.

Rebuttal Testimony addressed to evidence produced by the opposite party; rebutting evidence.

Receiver One appointed by a court to take charge of a business or the property of another during litigation to preserve it and/or to dispose of it as directed by the court.

Recklessness Behavior that indicates a conscious disregard for a known high risk of probable harm to others.

Recognizance At common law, an obligation entered into before some court of record or magistrate duly authorized, with a condition to do some particular act, usually to appear and answer to a criminal accusation. Being taken in open court and entered upon the order book, it was valid without the signature or seal of any of the obligors.

Recorder A public officer of a town or county charged with the duty of keeping the record books required by law to be kept in his or her office and of receiving and causing to be copied in such books such instruments as by law are entitled to be recorded.

Redemption The buying back of one's property after it has been sold. The right to redeem property sold under an order or decree of court is purely a privilege conferred by, and does not exist independently of, statute.

Redemption Right Also called a *call*. In corporation law, the right of a corporation to repurchase shares held by existing shareholders.

Redress Remedy; indemnity; reparation.

Reformation An equitable remedy in which a court effectively rewrites the terms of a contract.

Rejection In contract law, an express or implied manifestation of an offeree's unwillingness to contract on the terms of an offer. In sales law, a buyer's refusal to accept goods because they are defective or nonconforming.

Release The giving up or abandoning of a claim or right to a person against whom the claim exists or the right is to be enforced or exercised. It is the discharge of a debt by the act of the party, in distinction from an extinguishment that is a discharge by operation of law.

Remainderman One who is entitled to the remainder of the estate after a particular estate carved out of it has expired.

Remand A process whereby an appellate court returns the case to a lower court (usually a trial court) for proceedings not inconsistent with the appellate court's decision.

Remedy The appropriate legal form of relief by which a remediable right may be enforced.

Remittitur The certificate of reversal issued by an appellate court upon reversing the order or judgment appealed from.

Repatriation An investor's removal to the investor's nation of profits from his investment in a foreign nation.

Replevin A common law action by which the owner recovers possession of his own goods.

Res The thing; the subject matter of a suit; the property involved in the litigation; a matter; property; the business; the affair; the transaction.

Rescind As the word is applied to contracts, to terminate the contract as to future transactions or to annul the contract from the beginning.

Rescission The rescinding or cancellation of a contract or transaction. In general, its effect is to restore the parties to their original precontractual position.

Residue Residuary; all that portion of the estate of a testator of which no effectual disposition has been made by his will otherwise than in the residuary clause.

Res Ipsa Loquitur Literally, "the thing speaks for itself." A doctrine that, in some circumstances, gives rise to an inference that a defendant was negligent and that his negligence was the cause of the plaintiff's injury.

Res Judicata A matter that has been adjudicated; that which is definitely settled by a judicial decision.

Respondeat Superior A legal doctrine making an employer (or master) liable for the torts of an employee (servant) that are committed within the scope of the employee's employment.

Respondent A term often used to describe the party charged in an administrative proceeding. The party adverse to the appellant in a case appealed to a higher court. In this sense, often synonymous with *appellee*.

Restatement(s) Collections of legal rules produced by the American Law Institute, covering certain subject matter areas. Although *Restatements* are often persuasive to courts, they are not legally binding unless adopted by the highest court of a particular state.

Restitution A remedy whereby one is able to obtain the return of that which he has given the other party, or an amount of money equivalent to that which he has given the other party.

Restrictive Covenant An agreement restricting the use of real property.

Revocation In general, the recalling or voiding of a prior action. In contract law, the withdrawal of an offer by the offeror prior to effective acceptance by the offeree.

Right An interest given and protected by law. In corporation law, an option to purchase shares given to existing shareholders, permitting them to buy quantities of newly issued securities in proportion to their current ownership.

Right of Appraisal See **Appraisal, Right of.**

Right of First Refusal In corporation law, a share transfer restriction granting a corporation or its shareholders an option to match the offer that a selling shareholder receives for her shares. See also **Option Agreement.**

Right of Survivorship A feature of some types of co-ownership of property causing a co-owner's interest in property to be transferred on his death immediately and by operation of law to his surviving co-owner(s). See **Tenancy by the Entireties, Tenant in Partnership,** and **Joint Tenancy.**

Riparian Pertaining to or situated on the bank of a river.

Sale of Goods The transfer of ownership to tangible personal property in exchange for money, other goods, or the performance of service.

Sale on Approval A conditional sale that is to become final only in case the buyer, after a trial, approves or is satisfied with the article sold.

Sale or Return A contract in which the seller delivers a quantity of goods to the buyer on the understanding that if the buyer desires to retain, use, or sell any portion of the goods, he will consider such part as having been sold to him, and that he will return the balance or hold it as bailee for the seller.

Sanction The penalty that will be incurred by a wrongdoer for the violation of a law.

Satisfaction A performance of the terms of an accord. If such terms require a payment of a sum of money, then satisfaction means that such payment has been made.

Scienter In cases of fraud and deceit, the word means knowledge on the part of the person making the representations, at the time when they are made, that they are false. In an action for deceit, scienter must be proved.

S Corporation Also called *Subchapter S corporation.* A close corporation whose shareholders have elected to be taxed essentially like partners are taxed under federal income tax law.

Seal At common law, a seal is an impression on wax or some other tenacious material, but in modern practice the letters *l.s.* (locus sigilli) or the word *seal* enclosed in a scroll, either written, or printed, and acknowledged in the body of the instrument to be a seal, are often used as substitutes.

Security An instrument commonly dealt with in the securities markets or commonly recognized as a medium of investment and evidencing an obligation of an issuer or a share, participation, or other interest in an enterprise.

Security Agreement An agreement that creates or provides a security interest or lien on personal property. A term used in the UCC including a wide range of transactions in the nature of chattel mortgages, conditional sales, and so on.

Security Interest A lien given by a debtor to his creditor to secure payment or performance of a debt or obligation.

Seizin In a legal sense, the word means possession of premises with the intention of asserting a claim to a freehold estate therein; it is practically the same thing as ownership; it is a possession of a freehold estate, such as by the common law is created by livery of seizin.

Service As applied to a process of courts, the word ordinarily implies something in the nature of an act or proceeding adverse to the party served, or of a notice to him.

Set off That right that exists between two parties, each of whom, under an independent contract, owes an ascertained amount to the other, to calculate their respective debts by way of mutual deduction, so that, in any action brought for the larger debt, the residue only, after such deduction, shall be recovered.

Settlor A person who creates a trust. Also called *trustor.*

Severable Contract A contract that is not entire or indivisible. If the consideration is single, the contract is entire; but if it is expressly or by necessary implication apportioned, the contract is severable. The question is ordinarily determined by inquiring whether the contract embraces one or more subject matters, whether the obligation is due at the same time to the same person, and whether the consideration is entire or apportioned.

Share An equity security, representing a shareholder's ownership of a corporation.

Share Dividend See **Dividends, Share.**

Shareholder Also called *stockholder.* An owner of a corporation, who has no inherent right to manage the corporation, but has liability limited to his capital contribution.

Share Split Also called *stock split.* Traditionally, a corporation's dividing existing shares into two or more shares, thereby increasing the number of authorized, issued, and outstanding shares and reducing their par value. In modern corporation law, treated like a share dividend.

Sight A term signifying the date of the acceptance or that of protest for the nonacceptance of a bill of exchange; for example, 10 days after sight.

Sinking Fund A fund established by an issuer of securities to accumulate funds to repurchase the issuer's securities.

Situs Location; local position; the place where a person or thing is, is his situs. Intangible property has no actual situs, but it may have a legal situs, and for the purpose of taxation, its legal situs is at the place where it is owned and not at the place where it is owed.

Slander The defamation action appropriate to oral defamation.

Sole Proprietor The owner of a sole proprietorship.

Sole Proprietorship A form of business under which one person owns and controls the business.

Sovereign Immunity Generally, the idea that the sovereign (or state) may not be sued unless it consents to be sued. In antitrust law, the statutory immunity from antitrust liability for governmental actions that foreign governments enjoy under the Foreign Sovereign Immunities Act of 1976.

Special Damages See **Damages, Special.**

Specific Performance   A contract remedy whereby the defendant is ordered to perform according to the terms of his contract.

Stale Check   A check more than six months past its date of issue.

Standing   The legal requirement that anyone seeking to challenge a particular action in court must demonstrate that such action substantially affects his legitimate interests before he will be entitled to bring suit.

Standby Letter of Credit   See **Letter of Credit, Standby.**

Stare Decisis   A doctrine whereby a court is said to be bound to follow past cases that are "like" the present case on the facts and on the legal issues it presents, and that are issued by an authoritative court.

Stated Capital   Also called *capital stock*. A balance sheet account; shareholders' capital contributions representing the par value of par shares or stated value of no-par shares.

Stated Value   An arbitrary dollar amount assigned to shares by the board of directors, representing the minimum amount of consideration for which the corporation may issue the shares and the portion of consideration that must be allocated to the stated capital account.

State Implementation Plan   A document prepared by states in which the emissions to the air from individual sources are limited legally so that the area will meet the national ambient air quality standards.

Status Quo   The existing state of things. In contract law, returning a party to status quo or "status quo ante" means putting him in the position he was in before entering the contract.

Statute of Frauds   A statute that provides that no lawsuit may be brought to enforce certain classes of contracts unless there is a written note or memorandum signed by the party against whom enforcement is sought or by his agent.

Statute of Limitations   A statute that requires that certain classes of lawsuits must be brought within defined limits of time after the right to begin them accrued or the right to bring the lawsuit is lost.

Stipulation   An agreement between opposing counsel in a pending action, usually required to be made in open court and entered on the minutes of the court, or else to be in writing and filed in the action, ordinarily entered into for the purpose of avoiding delay, trouble, or expense in the conduct of the action.

Stock   A business's inventory. Also, as used in corporation and securities law, see **Share**.

Stock Dividend   See **Dividends, Share.**

Stockholder   See **Shareholder.**

Stock Split   See **Share Split.**

Stoppage in Transitu   A right that the vendor of goods on credit has to recall them, or retake them, on the discovery of the insolvency of the vendee. It continues so long as the carrier remains in the possession and control of the goods or until there has been an actual or constructive delivery to the

vendee, or some third person has acquired a bona fide right in them.

Stop Payment Order   A request made by the drawer of a check to the drawee asking that the order to pay not be followed.

Straight Voting   A form of voting for directors that ordinarily permits a shareholder to cast a number of votes equal to the number of shares he owns for as many nominees as there are directors to be elected. See **Cumulative Voting.**

Strict Liability   Legal responsibility placed on an individual for the results of his actions irrespective of whether he was culpable or at fault.

Strike Suit   In corporation law, a derivative suit motivated primarily by an intent to gain an out-of-court settlement for the suing shareholder personally or to earn large attorney's fees for lawyers, rather than to obtain a recovery for the corporation.

Subchapter S Corporation   See **S Corporation.**

Sub Judice   Before a court.

Sublease   A transfer of some but not all of a tenant's remaining right to possess property under a lease.

Sub Nom.   Under the name of.

Subpoena   A process for compelling a witness to appear before a court and give testimony.

Subrogation   The substitution of one person in the place of another with reference to a lawful claim or right, frequently referred to as the doctrine of substitution. It is a device adopted or invented by equity to compel the ultimate discharge of a debt or obligation by the person who in good conscience ought to pay it.

Subscription   In corporation law, a promise by a person to purchase from a corporation a specified number of shares at a specified price.

Subsidiary Corporation   A corporation owned and controlled by another corporation, called a *parent corporation*.

Sui Generis   Of its own kind, unique, peculiar to itself.

Summary Judgment   A method of reaching a judgment in a civil case before trial. The standard for granting a motion for summary judgment is that there be no significant issue of material fact and that the moving party be entitled to judgment as a matter of law.

Summary Proceedings   Proceedings, usually statutory, in the course of which many formalities are dispensed with. But such proceedings are not concluded without proper investigation of the facts, or without notice, or an opportunity to be heard by the person alleged to have committed the act, or whose property is sought to be affected.

Summons   A writ or process issued and served upon a defendant in a civil action for the purpose of securing his appearance in the action.

Superseding Cause   See **Intervening Cause.**

Supra   Above; above mentioned; in addition to.

Surety   A person who promises to perform the same obligation as another person (the principal) and who is jointly liable along with the principal for that obligation's performance. See **Guarantor.**

T/A   Trading as, indicating the use of a trade name.

Tacking   The adding together of successive periods of adverse possession of persons in privity with each other, in order to constitute one continuous adverse possession for the time required by the statute, to establish title.

Takeover   A tender offer; also applied generally to any acquisition of one business by another business.

Tangible   Having a physical existence; real; substantial; evident.

Tariff   A tax or duty imposed on goods by a nation when the goods are imported into that nation.

Tax Haven   A nation that has no or minimal taxation of personal, business, and investment income.

Tenancy   General term indicating a possessory interest in property. In landlord-tenant law, a property owner's conveyance to another person of the right to possess the property exclusively for a period of time.

Tenancy at Sufferance   The leasehold interest that occurs when a tenant remains in possession of property after the expiration of a lease.

Tenancy at Will   A leasehold interest that occurs when property is leased for an indefinite period of time and is terminable at the will of either landlord or tenant.

Tenancy by the Entireties   A form of co-ownership of property by a married couple that gives the owners a right of survivorship and cannot be severed during life by the act of only one of the parties.

Tenancy for a Term   A leasehold interest that results when the landlord and tenant agree on a specific duration for a lease and fix the date on which the tenancy will terminate.

Tenancy in Common   A form of co-ownership of property that is freely disposable both during life and at death, and in which the co-owners have undivided interests in the property and equal rights to possess the property.

Tenant in Partnership   The manner in which partners co-own partnership property, much like a tenancy in common, except that partners have a right of survivorship.

Tender   An unconditional offer of payment, consisting in the actual production in money or legal tender of a sum not less than the amount due.

Tender Offer   A public offer by a bidder to purchase a subject company's shares directly from its shareholders at a specified price for a fixed period of time.

Tenure   The manner of holding or occupying lands or offices. The most common estate in land is tenure in fee simple. With respect to offices, tenure imports time; for example, tenure for life or during good behavior.

Testament   A will; the disposition of one's property to take effect after death.

Testator   A deceased person who died leaving a will.

Testatrix   Feminine of testator.

Testimony   In some contexts, the word bears the same import as the word *evidence*, but in most connections it has a much narrower meaning. Testimony is the words heard from the witness in court, and evidence is what the jury considers it worth.

Thin Capitalization   In corporation law, a ground for piercing the corporate veil due to the shareholders' contributing too little capital to the corporation in relation to its needs.

Third Party Beneficiary   A person who is not a party to a contract but who has the right to enforce it because the parties to the contract made the contract with the intent to benefit him.

Title   Legal ownership; also, a document evidencing legal rights to real or personal property.

Tombstone Advertisement   A brief newspaper advertisement alerting prospective shareholders that an issuer is offering to sell the securities described in the advertisement.

Tort   A private (civil) wrong against a person or his property.

Tortfeasor   A person who commits a tort; a wrongdoer.

Tortious   Partaking of the nature of a tort; wrongful; injurious.

Trade Fixtures   Articles of personal property that have been annexed to real property leased by a tenant during the term of the lease and that are necessary to the carrying on of a trade.

Transcript   A copy of a writing.

Transferee   A person to whom a transfer is made.

Transferor   A person who makes a transfer.

Treasury Shares   Previously outstanding shares repurchased by a corporation that are not canceled or restored to unissued status.

Treble Damages   See **Damages, Treble.**

Trespass   An unauthorized entry on another's property.

Trial   An examination before a competent tribunal, according to the law of the land, of the facts or law put in issue in a cause, for the purpose of determining such issue. When the court hears and determines any issue of fact or law for the purpose of determining the rights of the parties, it may be considered a trial.

Trover   A common law action for damages due to a conversion of personal property.

Trust   A legal relationship in which a person who has legal title to property has the duty to hold it for the use or benefit of another person. The term is also used in a general sense to mean confidence reposed in one person by another.

Trustee   A person in whom property is vested in trust for another.

Trustee in Bankruptcy   The federal bankruptcy act defines the term as an officer, and he is an officer of the courts in a certain restricted sense, but not in any such sense as a receiver. He takes the legal title to the property of the bankrupt and in respect to suits stands in the same general position as a trustee of an express trust or an executor. His duties are fixed by statute. He is to collect and reduce to money the property of the estate of the bankrupt.

Ultra Vires   Latin for "beyond the powers." In administrative law, it describes an act that is beyond the authority granted to an administrative agency by its enabling legislation. In corporation law, it describes a corporation's performing an act beyond the limits of its purposes as stated in its articles of incorporation.

Unconscionable   In contract law, a contract that is grossly unfair or one-sided; one that "shocks the conscience of the court." The Uniform Commercial Code expressly gives courts the broad discretionary powers to deal with such contracts.

Unilateral Contract   A contract formed by an offer or a promise on one side for an act to be done on the other, and a doing of the act by the other by way of acceptance of the offer or promise; that is, a contract wherein the only acceptance of the offer that is necessary is the performance of the act.

Unliquidated   Undetermined in amount.

Usage of Trade   Customs and practices generally known by people in the business and usually assumed by parties to a contract for goods of that type.

Usurpation   In corporation law, an officer, director, or shareholder's taking to himself a business opportunity that belongs to his corporation.

Usury   The taking of more than the law allows on a loan or for forbearance of a debt. Illegal interest; interest in excess of the rate allowed by law.

Utter   As applied to counterfeiting, to utter and publish is to declare or assert, directly or indirectly, by words or action, that the money or note is good. Thus, to offer it in payment is an uttering or publishing.

Valid   Effective; operative; not void; subsisting; sufficient in law.

Value   Under the Code (except for negotiable instruments and bank collections), generally any consideration sufficient to support a simple contract. Sec. 1–201(44).

Vendee   A purchaser of property. The word is more commonly applied to a purchaser of real property, the word buyer being more commonly applied to the purchaser of personal property.

Vendor   A person who sells property to a vendee. The words *vendor* and *vendee* are more commonly applied to the seller

and purchaser of real estate, and the words *seller* and *buyer* are more commonly applied to the seller and purchaser of personal property.

Venire   The name of a writ by which a jury is summoned.

Venue   A requirement distinct from jurisdiction that the court be geographically situated so that it is the most appropriate and convenient court to try the case.

Verdict   Usually, the decision made by a jury and reported to the judge on the matters or questions submitted to it at trial. In some situations, however, the judge may be the party issuing a verdict, as, for example, in the motion for a directed verdict. See **Directed Verdict.**

Versus   Against.

Vest   To give an immediate fixed right of present or future enjoyment.

Vicarious Liability   The imposition of liability on one party for the wrongs of another. Also called *imputed liability*. For example, the civil liability of a principal for the wrongs his agent commits when acting within the scope of his employment. See **Respondeat Superior.** Such liability is also occasionally encountered in the criminal context (e.g., the criminal liability that some regulatory statutes impose on managers for the actions of employees under their supervision).

Void   That which is entirely null. A void act is one that is not binding on either party, and that is not susceptible of ratification.

Voidable   Capable of being made void; not utterly null, but annullable, and hence that may be either voided or confirmed. See **Avoid.**

Voidable Title   A title that is capable of, or subject to, being judged invalid or void.

Voting Trust   A type of shareholder voting arrangement by which shareholders transfer their voting rights to a voting trustee.

Waive   To throw away; to relinquish voluntarily, as a right that one may enforce, if he chooses.

Waiver   The intentional relinquishment of a known right. It is a voluntary act and implies an election by the party to dispense with something of value, or to forgo some advantage that he or she might have demanded and insisted on.

Warehouse Receipt   A receipt issued by a person engaged in the business of storing goods for hire.

Warrant   An order authorizing a payment of money by another person to a third person. Also, an option to purchase a security. As a verb, the word means to defend; to guarantee; to enter into an obligation of warranty.

Warrant of Arrest   A legal process issued by competent authority, usually directed to regular officers of the law, but occasionally issued to private persons named in it, directing the arrest of a person or persons on grounds stated therein.

Warranty An undertaking relating to characteristics of a thing being sold; a guarantee.

Waste The material alteration, abuse, or destructive use of property by one in rightful possession of it that results in injury to one having an underlying interest in it.

Watered Shares Also called *watered stock*. Shares issued in exchange for property that has been overvalued. See **Bonus Shares** and **Discount Shares.**

Will A document executed with specific legal formalities that contains a person's instructions about the disposition of his property at his death.

Winding Up In partnership and corporation law, the orderly liquidation of the business's assets.

Writ A commandment of a court given for the purpose of compelling certain action from the defendant, and usually executed by a sheriff or other judicial officer.

Writ of Certiorari An order of a court to an inferior court to forward the record of a case for reexamination by the superior court.

Wrongful Use of Civil Proceedings An intentional tort designed to protect against the wrongful initiation of civil proceedings.

CASE INDEX

SUBJECT INDEX